NEW)

WITHDRAWN

WITHDRAWN

ENCYCLOPEDIA OF
WORLD BIOGRAPHY

17

ENCYCLOPEDIA OF
WORLD BIOGRAPHY

SECOND EDITION

Index 17

GALE

DETROIT · NEW YORK · TORONTO · LONDON

Staff

Senior Editor: Paula K. Byers
Project Editor: Suzanne M. Bourgoin
Managing Editor: Neil E. Walker

Editorial Staff: Luann Brennan, Frank V. Castronova, Laura S. Hightower, Karen E. Lemerand, Stacy A. McConnell, Jennifer Mossman, Maria L. Munoz, Katherine H. Nemeh, Terrie M. Rooney, Geri Speace

Permissions Manager: Susan M. Trosky
Permissions Specialist: Maria L. Franklin
Permissions Associate: Michele M. Lonoconus
Image Cataloger: Mary K. Grimes

Production Director: Mary Beth Trimper
Production Manager: Evi Seoud
Production Associate: Shanna Heilveil
Product Design Manager: Cynthia Baldwin
Senior Art Director: Mary Claire Krzewinski

Research Manager: Victoria B. Cariappa
Research Specialists: Michele P. LaMeau, Andrew Guy Malonis, Barbara McNeil, Gary J. Oudersluys
Research Associates: Julia C. Daniel, Tamara C. Nott, Norma Sawaya, Cheryl L. Warnock
Research Assistant: Talitha A. Jean

Graphic Services Manager: Barbara Yarrow
Image Database Supervisor: Randy Bassett
Imaging Specialist: Mike Logusz

Manager of Data Entry Services: Eleanor M. Allison
Data Entry Coordinator: Kenneth D. Benson

Manager of Technology Support Services: Theresa A. Rocklin
Programmers/Analysts: Mira Bossowska, Jeffrey Muhr, Christopher Ward

Copyright © 1998
Gale Research
835 Penobscot Bldg.
Detroit, MI 48226-4094

ISBN 0-7876-2221-4 (Set)
ISBN 0-7876-2557-4 (Volume 17)

Library of Congress Cataloging-in-Publication Data

Encyclopedia of world biography / [edited by Suzanne Michele Bourgoin and Paula Kay Byers].
     p. cm.
    Includes bibliographical references and index.
    Summary: Presents brief biographical sketches which provide vital statistics as well as information on the importance of the person listed.
    ISBN 0-7876-2221-4 (set : alk. paper)
    1. Biography—Dictionaries—Juvenile literature. [1. Biography.]
I. Bourgoin, Suzanne Michele, 1968- . II. Byers, Paula K. (Paula Kay), 1954- .
CT 103.E56   1997
920' .003—dc21
                                97-42327
                                CIP
                                AC

Printed in the United States of America
10 9 8 7 6 5 4 3 2

CONTENTS

ACKNOWLEDGMENTS

Photographs and illustrations in *Encyclopedia of World Biography* have been used with the permission of the following sources:

American Automobile Manufacturers Association: Walter P. Chrysler, Alfred P. Sloan Jr.

American Museum of Natural History: Henry Hudson

AP/Wide World Photos, Inc.: Abbas I, Berenice Abbott, Bella Stavisky Abzug, Chinua Achebe, Ansel Adams, Hank Adams, Giovanni Agnelli, Madeleine Korbel Albright, Horatio Alger, Paula Gunn Allen, Salvador Allende Gossens, Giulio Andreotti, Iuri Vladimirovich Andropov, Maya Angelou, Jean Anouilh, Michel Aoun, Corazon Cojoangco Aquino, Jean-Bertrand Aristide, Louis Daniel Armstrong, Matthew Arnold, Arthur Robert Ashe Jr., Hanan Mikhail Ashrawi, Hafiz Assad, Fred Astaire, Aung San Suu Kyi, Patricio Aylwin Azocar, Jose Azcona Hoyo, Bruce Babbitt, Polly Baca-Barragan, James Baker, Dennis J. Banks, John Bardeen, Luis Barragan, Marion Barry, Mikhail Baryshnikov, Kathleen Battle, Etienne-Emile Baulieu, The Beatles, Stephen Davison Bechtel, Clyde Bellecourt, Joseph Bernardin, Nabih Berri, Mary Frances Berry, Joseph Beuys, Benazir Bhutto, Steve Biko, Larry Bird, Mel Blanc, Judy Blume, William E. Boeing, Dietrich Bonhoeffer, Norman Borlaug, Robert Bourassa, Boutros Boutros-Ghali, Barbara Boxer, Ed R. Bradley, Benjamin Britten, Earl Russell Browder, Carol Browner, Susan Brownmiller, Dennis Brutus, Pat(rick) Buchanan, Warren Buffett, Anthony Burgess, William S. Burroughs, George Bush, Ben Nighthorse Campbell, Joseph Campbell, Jennifer Capriati, George Carey, William J. Casey, Wilt Chamberlain, Charles (Prince of Wales), Linda Chavez, Benjamin Chavis, Richard Cheney, Judy Chicago, Julia Child, May Edward Chinn, Jacques Chirac, Shirley Chisholm, Joaquin Chissano, Connie Chung, Henry Cisneros, Sandra Cisneros, Tom Clancy, James Cleveland, William Jefferson Clinton, Hillary Rodham Clinton, Johnnie Cochran, Johnnetta Cole, Eileen Collins, Marva Delores Collins, Fernando Collor de Mello, Padraic Colum, Barry Commoner, Bert Corona, Corrigan and Williams, Charles E. Coughlin, Noel Coward, Seymour Cray, Edith Cresson, (John) Michael Crichton, Alfredo Cristiani, Walter Cronkite, Countee Cullen, Merce Cunningham, Dalai Lama, Henry Dale, Mahmud Darwish, Angela Davis, Simone De Beauvoir, Edward DeBartolo Jr., Ada E. Deer, Fredrik Willem de Klerk, Doi Takako, Rita Dove, Charles Richard Drew, William E. Dubois, Jean Dubuffet, Albrecht Durer, Sylvia A. Earle, Marian Wright Edelman, Joycelyn Elders, Gertrude B. Elion, Ralph Waldo Ellison, Akihito, Julius Erving, Myrlie Evers-Williams, Louis Farrakhan, Federico Fellini, W.C. Fields, Paul Flory, Dian Fossey, Helen Frankenthaler, Aretha Franklin, Karl von Frisch, Athol Fugard, Alberto Fujimori, J. W.Fulbright, Muammar al-Gaddafi, Gabriel Garcia Marquez, William (Bill) Gates, Helene Gayle, Clifford Geertz, Murray Gell-Mann, Lillian Gilbreth, Newt Gingrich, Philip Glass, Kurt Godel, Whoopi Goldberg, James Goldsmith, Felipe Gonzalez Marquez, Ellen Goodman, Raisa Maximovna Gorbachev, Berry Gordy, Al Gore, Stephen J. Gould, Cary Grant, Nancy Graves, Robert Graves, William H. Gray, III, Andrew Greeley, Graham Greene, Wayne Gretzky, Nicolas Guillen, Alec Guinness, Woody (Woodrow Wilson) Guthrie, George Amman Habash, Fritz Haber, Alex Haley, Barbara Harris, Patricia Roberts Harris, Francis Brett Harte, Hassan II, Stephen Hawking, Coleman Hawkins, Roland Hayes, Rita Hayworth, Bernadine Healy, Seamus Heaney, Joseph Heller, Walter Heller, Lillian Hellman, Ernest Hemingway, Jimi Hendrix, O. Henry (William Sydney Porter), Matthew Alexander Henson, Katharine Hepburn, Anita Hill, Gregory Hines, Soichiro Honda, Frederick Gowland Hopkins, Edward Hopper, Godfrey Hounsfield, Gordie Howe, Aldous Huxley, Lee Iacocca, Patricia Ireland, Kareem Abdul Jabbar, Jesse Jackson, Maynard Jackson, Michael Jackson, Reggie Jackson, Shirley Ann Jackson, John E. Jacob, Mick Jagger, Helmut Jahn, Daniel James, Jr., P. D. James, Mae

C. Jemison, Jiang Zemin, Juan Ramon Jimenez, Robert Joffrey, John Paul II, Betsey Johnson, Earvin "Magic" Johnson, Philip Johnson, Virginia Johnson, James Earl Jones, Quincy Jones, June Jordan, Franz Kafka, Louis Kahn, Radovan Karadzic, Isabella L. Karle, George Kaufman, Gerald Kaufman, Kenneth Kaunda, Yasunari Kawabata, Helen Keller, Gene Kelly, Jomo Kenyatta, J. Robert Kerrey, Sayyed Ali Khamenei, Har Gobind Khorana, Kim Il Sung, Kim Young-sam, B. B. King, Coretta Scott King, Calvin Klein, Helmut Kohl, Ray(mond Albert) Kroc, Elizabeth Kubler-Ross, Hans Kung, Madeline Kunin, Akira Kurosawa, Estee Lauder, Mary Leakey, Richard Leakey, John Le Carre, Spike Lee, Annie Leibovitz, Jean-Marie Le Pen, Rita Levi-Montalcini, James Levine, David Levy, Carl Lewis, Roy Lichtenstein, Maya Lin, Little Richard, David Lodge, Henry Wadsworth Longfellow, Kathleen Lonsdale, Konrad Lorenz, Susan Love, Robert Lowell, Gerardo Machado y Morales, Samora Machel, Hugh MacLennan, Malcolm X, Andre Malraux, David Mamet, Nelson Rolihlahla Mandela, Winnie Mandela, Wilma Mankiller, Ferdinand Edralin Marcos, Paule Marshall, Lynn Martin, Quett Masire, William Masters, (Ian) Robert Maxwell, Robert Maynard, Ernst Mayr, Hattie McDaniel, John McEnroe, Floyd B. McKissick, Terry McMillan, Robert Strange McNamara, Aimee Semple McPherson, Margaret Mead, Russell Means, Golda Meir, Rigoberta Menchu, Carlos Menem, James Meredith, James Merrill, Kweisi Mfume, Ludwig Mies Van Der Rohe, Harvey Milk, Arthur Miller, C. Wright Mills, Yukio Mishima, Isaac Mizrahi, Mobutu Sese Seko, N. Scott Momaday, Thelonious Monk, Joe Montana, Marianne Craig Moore, Garrett A. Morgan, Robin Morgan, Akio Morita, Mark Morris, Toni Morrison, John Mortimer, Carol Moseley-Braun, Grandma Moses (Anna Mary Robertson), Mother Teresa, Shirley "Cha Cha" Muldowney, (Martin) Brian Mulroney, Rupert Murdoch, Ralph Nader, Irene Natividad, Martina Navratilova, Gloria Naylor, Benjamin Netanyahu, Louise Nevelson, S. I. Newhouse, Jr., Huey Newton, Anais Nin, Joshua Nkomo, Isamu Noguchi, Jessye Norman, Robert Noyce, Sam (Shafihuna) Nujoma, Sam Nunn, Julius K. Nyerere, Sandra Day O'Connor, Joyce Carol Oates, Clifford Odets, Oginga Odinga, Jose Ortega y Gasset, John Kingsley Orton, George Orwell, John Osborne, Ruth Bryan Owen, Jesse Owens, Turgut Ozal, David Packard, Leon Panetta, Dorothy Parker, Rosa Parks, Ruth Patrick, Luciano Pavarotti, Norman Vincent Peale, Robert Edwin Peary, Ieoh Ming Pei, Leonard Peltier, Carlos Andres Perez, Javier Perez de Cuellar, Harold Robert Perry, Saint John Perse, Paloma Picasso, Edith Piaf, Pickney Benton Stewart Pinchback, Augusto Pinochet, Harold Pinter, Luigi Pirandello, Sylvia Plath, Sidney Poitier, Cole Albert Porter, Katherine Anne Porter, Ezra Pound, Adam Clayton Powell, Jr., Colin L. Powell, Elvis Presley, Marcel Proust, Yitzhak Rabin, Cyril Ramaphosa, Fidel Ramos, Charles Rangel, Jeannette Rankin, Simon Rattle, Dixie Lee Ray, Ronald Reagan,

Vanessa Redgrave, Walter Reed, Erich Maria Remarque, Rembrandt, Janet Reno, Anne Rice, Elmer Rice, Adrienne Rich, Charles Richter, Leni Riefenstahl, Richard Riordan, Edwin Arlington Robinson, Jackie Robinson, Mary Robinson, Max Robinson, Theodore Roethke, Rolling Stones, Julius and Ethel Rosenberg, Diana Ross, Philip Roth, Mark Rothko, Carl T. Rowan, Maude Royden, Wilma Rudolph, Elizabeth S. Russell, Bayard Rustin, Ernesto Sabato, Antoine de St. Exupery, J. D. Salinger, Frederick Sanger, Margaret Sanger, Jean Paul Sartre, Jonas Savimbi, Edward Schillebeeckx, Phyllis Schlafly, Charles Schulz, Norman Schwarzkopf, Albert Schweitzer, Walter Scott, Bobby Seale, Pete Seeger, Anne Sexton, William Shakespeare, John Shalikashvili, Anatoly Shcharansky, Percy Shelley, Robert E. Sherwood, John R. Silber, Karen Silkwood, Georges Simenon, Louis Simpson, Frank Sinatra, Upton Sinclair, Margaret Chase Smith, Charles Percy Snow, Aleksandr Solzhenitsyn, Stephen Sondheim, Susan Sontag, John Philip Sousa, Benjamin Spock, Danielle Steele, John Steinbeck, Gloria Steinem, Frank Stella, Robert Louis Stevenson, Bram Stoker, Carl B. Stokes, Oliver Stone, Robert Stone, Tom Stoppard, Richard Strauss, Alfredo Stroessner, Wes Studi, William Styron, Leon Howard Sullivan, Helen Suzman, Oliver Tambo, Ida Minerva Tarbell, Helen Brooke Taussig, Kiri Te Kanawa, Studs Terkel, William Thackeray, Twyla Tharp, Margaret Thatcher, Clarence Thomas, Dylan Marlais Thomas, Hunter S.Thompson, George Paget Thomson, James Thurber, Jacobo Timerman, Jan Tinbergen, J.R.R. Tolkein, Mildred Trotter, Franjo Tudjman, Tina Turner, Desmond Tutu, Peter Ueberroth, Sigrid Undset, John Updike, George Vancouver, Victor Vasarely, Sarah Vaughan, Nydia Velazquez, Robert Venturi, John Von Neumann, Kurt Vonnegut, Marilyn vos Savant, Hugo de Vries, Lech Walesa, Alice Walker, Margaret Abigail Walker, Ernest T. S. Walton, Sam Walton, An Wang, Andy Warhol, Maxine Waters, Thomas J. Watson, Robert Weaver, Andrew Lloyd Webber, Kurt Julian Weill, Herbert George Wells, Eudora Welty, William Westmoreland, Patrick Victor Martindale White, Theodore H. White, Walter Francis White, Alfred North Whitehead, Christine Todd Whitman, Kathryn J. Whitmire, Sheila Widnall, Elie Wiesel, Richard Wilbur, Lawrence Douglas Wilder, Tennessee Williams, August Wilson, Edward O. Wilson, Oprah Winfrey, Carter Goodwin Woodson, Yevgeni Yevtushenko, Andrew Young, Coleman A.Young, Marguerite Yourcenar, Babe (Mildred Ella) Didriksen Zaharias, Ernesto Zedillo, Zhao Ziyang, Vladimir Zhirinovsky, Emile Zola

Archive Photos, Inc.: Abdul-Hamid II, Peter Abelard, Dean Gooderham Acheson, Theodore Weisengrund Adorno, Georgius Agricola (Georg Bauer), Ahmadou Ahidjo, Anna Akhmatova, Edward Albee, Albertus Magnus, Sholom Aleichem, Miguel Aleman Valdes, Alexander II, ibn Abi Talib Ali, Ramiz Alia, Isabel Allende,

Jorge Allessandri Rodriguez, Saint Ambrose, American Horse, Idi Amin Dada, Roald Amundsen, Hans Christian Andersen, Mario Andretti, Edmund Andros, Saint Anslem, Moshe Arens, Oscar Arias Sanchez, Aristophanes, Giorgio Armani, Thomas Augustine Arne, Raymond Aron, Jean Arp, Les Aspin, Atahuallpa, Clement Richard Attlee, John James Audubon, Saint Augustine, Richard Avedon, Johann Christian Bach, Johann Sebastian Bach, Phillip Emanuel Bach, Francis Bacon, Roger Bacon, Nathaniel Bacon, Russell Baker, Samuel White Baker, Mikhail Bakunin, George Balanchine, Stanley Baldwin, George Ball, Hubert Howe Bancroft, Joseph Banks, Hugo Banzer Suarez, Bao-Dai, Ehud Barak, Samuel Barber, Klaus Barbie, Daniel Barenboim, P(hineas) T(aylor) Barnum, Paul Jean Francois Nicolas De Barras, Raymond Barre, Rene Ortuno Barrientos, Justo Rufino Barrios, Bela Bartok, William Bartram, Johann Bernhard Basedow, Basil I, Ferdinand Christian Baur, Beatrix Wilhelmina von Amsburg, Samuel Beckett, Saint Bede, Henry Ward Beecher, Vincenzo Bellini, Saul Bellow, James Gordon Bennett, Jr., William Bennett, Jack Benny, Thomas Hart Benton, Lloyd Millard Bentsen, Alban Berg, Saint Bernard, (Ernst) Ingmar Bergman, Lavrenti Pavlovich Beria, Sali Berisha, William Berkeley, Georges Bernanos, Romulo Betancourt, John Betjeman, James Luther Bevel, Zulfikar Ali Bhutto, Patrick M. S. Blackett, Harry A. Blackmun, Ernst Bloch, Charles (Chip) Bohlen, Heinrich Boll, Louis Bonaparte, Bonaventure, Boniface, Aleksandr P. Borodin, Hieronymus Bosch, William Joseph Brennan, Jr., Andre Breton, Kingman Brewster, Jr., Stephen Breyer, Harry A. R. Bridges, John Bright, Benjamin Helm Bristow, Joseph Brodsky, Charlotte Bronte, Joyce Diane Brothers, Joseph Emerson Brown, Elizabeth Barrett Browning, Alois Brunner, John Bruton, Paul "Bear" Bryant, 1st Duke of Buckingham, William F. Buckley, Jr., Guillaume Bude, James Buel, Buffalo Bill, Nikolai Ivanovich Bukharin, Nikolai Bulganin, Rudolf Karl Bultmann, Luis Bunuel, Robert O'Hara Burke, Frank M. Burnet, Fanny Burney, Arthur F. Burns, Richard Burton, Kofi Busia, William Byrd, Jane Margaret Byrne, James Francis Byrnes, Calamity Jane, Alexander Calder, Rafael Caldera Rodriquez, (Leonard) James Callaghan, Alexander Campbell, Albert Camus, Joseph G. Cannon, Eddie Cantor, Robert Capa, Al Capone, Al(fred Gerald) Capp, Frank Capra, Andrew Carnegie, Venustiano Carranza, Peter Carrington, Johnny Carson, Elliott Carter, Jacques Cartier, Giovanni Giacomo Casanova De Seingalt, Mary Cassatt, Humberto de Castelo Branco, Louis Ferdinand Celine, Chadli Benjedid, James Chadwick, Joseph Chamberlain, Whitaker Chambers, Coco Chanel, Sydney Chapman, J. B. Simeon Chardin, Erwin Chargaff, Charles IV, Charles IV, Charles The Bold, Charles VIII, Chiang Kai-shek, Roberto Chiari, Noam Chomsky, Frederic Chopin, Joseph-Jacques-Jean Chretien, Warren Christopher, Chun Doo-hwan, Tansu Ciller, Liz Claiborne, Margaret Clapp, Samuel Clarke, John M. Clayton, Clement of Alexandria, Patsy Cline, Henry Clinton, Ty(rus Raymond)Cobb, George Michael Cohan, Daniel Cohn-Bendit, Edward Coke, John Colet, Gasperd de Coligny, Henry Steele Commager, Roscoe Conkling, John Bowden Connally, Jr., Joseph Conrad, Constantine XI, Jay Cooke, Erza Cornell, Victor Cousin, Norman Cousins, Henry Cowell, Archibald Cox, Tench Coxe, Hart Crane, Bettino Craxi, Francesco Crispi, Bing (Harry Lillis) Crosby, Oswaldo Cruz, Glenn Hammond Curtiss, Albert Cuyp, Thascius Caecilianus Cyprianus, Edouard Daladier, David, Arthur Vining Davis, John Davis, Willem De Kooning, Miguel De La Madrid Hurtado, Agnes De Mille, James Dean, Claude Debussy, Daniel Defoe, (Ferdinand Victor) Eugen Delacroix, Martin Robinson Delany, David Dellinger, Cecil B. DeMille, Andre Derain, Jacques Derrida, Pierre Jean DeSmet, Bernadette Devlin, Thomas Edmund Dewey, Diana (Princess of Wales), Bartholomeu Dias de Novais, Richard Diebenkorn, John George Diefenbaker, Joe DiMaggio, Karen Dinesen Blixen-Finecke, David Dinkins, Otto Dix, Elizabeth Dole, Josef Ignaz Von Dollinger, Domitian, Do Muoi, Jose E. Dos Santos, Fyodor Dostoevsky, Thomas Clement Douglas, William Orville Douglas, John William Draper, Daniel Drew, John Dryden, David Dubinsky, Alexander Duff, Isadora Duncan, Saint Dunstan, Asher Brown Durand, Thomas Clark Durant, Thomas Eakins, Amelia Earhart, Charles Eastman, Abba Solomon Eban, John Carew Eccles, Bulet Ecevit, Luis Alvarez Echeverria, Edward III, Edward IV, Mamie Dodd Eisenhower, Sergei Mikhailovich Eisenstein, Eleanor of Aquitaine, Daniel Ellsberg, John England, Epicurus, Ludwig Erhard, Leif Ericson, Erik Erikson, Max Ernst, Erte, Sam J. Ervin, Jr., Leonhard Euler, Euripides, Oliver Evans, William Maxwell Evarts, Edward Everett, Hubert Van Eyck, Jan van Eyck, Ezekiel, Laurent Fabius, William G. Fargo, Suzanne Farrell, Father Divine, Brian Faulkner, Jules Feiffer, Lyonel Feininger, Ferdinand II, Ferdinand VII, Geraldine Ferraro, Jules Ferry, Marshall Field, Henry Fielding, Jose Figueres, Louis Finkelstein, Bobby Fischer, Garret Fitzgerald, Robert Flaherty, Titus Q. Flamininus, Abraham Flexner, Thomas Foley, Jane Fonda, Michael Foot, Malcolm Forbes, John Ford, E(dward) M(organ) Forster, Abe Fortas, Bob Fosse, Joseph Fouche, John Fowles, Francis II, Saint Francis de Sales, John Franklin, Antonia Fraser, Malcolm Fraser, Simon Fraser, Frederick William, Frederick William III, Frederick William IV, Gilberto Freyre, Milton Friedman, Jean Froissart, Erich Fromm, James A. Froude, William H. Fry, Carlos Fuentes, Richard Buckminster Fuller, Clark Gable, Naum Gabo, Dennis Gabor, Marius Gaius, George Gallup, Rajiv Gandhi, Federico Garcia Lorca, John Gardner, Judy Garland, Jean P. Gaultier, Ernesto Geisel, Hans Dietrich Genscher, Richard Gephardt, J. Paul Getty, Sr., Alberto Giacometti, Vo Nguyen Giap, William Gibson, Humphrey Gilbert,

Allen Ginsberg, Valery Giscard D'Estaing, Rudolf Giuliani, Kiro Gligorov, John Glubb, Godfrey of Bouillon, Manuel de Godoy, Johann Goethe, Arthur Goldberg, Harry Golden, George Peabody Gooch, Benny Goodman, Andrew Goodpaster, Mikhail Gorbachev, Klement Gottwald, Jean Goujon, Joao Goulart, Jay Gould, William Russell Grace, Ramon Grau San Martin, Asa Gray, Robert Gray, Graham Greene, Alan Greenspan, Germaine Greer, David Lewelyn Wark Griffith, Juan Gris, John Grisham, Jennie Grossinger, George Grosz, Jerzy Grotowski, Lamine Gueye, Gustavus I, Gustavus III, Philip Guston, Tyrone Guthrie, Alexander Haig, George Ellery Hale, Hamilcar Barca, Armand Hammer, George Frederic Handel, Hannibal Barca, Thomas Hardy, Keith Haring, Harold II, Michael Harrington, William Henry Harrison, Gary W. Hart, George Haussmann, Robert James Lee Hawke, Victor-Raul Haya de la Torre, Helen Hayes, Robert Y. Hayne, Henry I, King of England, Henry I, King of Germany, Henry II, Henry III, Holy Roman Emperor, Henry III, King of England, Henry VI, Audrey Hepburn, Barbara Hepworth, Johann Friedrich Herbart, Edward Herbert, George Herbert, Felipe Herrera, Chaim Herzog, Roman Herzog, Theodore Martin Hesburgh, Abram Stevens Hewitt, Herbert Hill, Edmund Hillary, Sidney Hillman, Hipparchus, Alger Hiss, Alfred Hitchcock, Thomas Hobbes, David Hockney, Dorothy Hodgkin, Jimmy Hoffa, Abbie Hoffman, August Wihelm von Hofmann, Hanya Holm, Keith Holyoake, Homer, Sidney Hook, Thomas Hooker, J. Edgar Hoover, Horace, Lena Horne, Harry Houdini, A(lfred) E(dward) Housman, Elias Howe, Geoffrey Howe, Enver Hoxha, Howard Hughes, John Hughes, William Hull, Friedensreich Hundertwasser, H.L. Hunt, William Hunter, Douglas Hurd, Gustav Husak, Thomas Hutchinson, Dolores Ibarruri, Ignatius of Loyola, Ion Iliescu, Eugene Ionesco, Isaiah, Alija Izetbegovic, Vladimir Jabotinsky, Henry M. Jackson, Robert Jackson, James I, King of Scotland, Wojciech Witold Jaruzelski, Karl Jaspers, Jean Jaures, John Rushworth Jellicoe, Roy Jenkins, Jeremiah, George Jessel, Steven Jobs, Isaac Jogues, John III, John Maurice, Count of Nassau-Siegen, John of Gaunt, John the Baptist, John Johnson, John H. Johnson, Samuel Johnson, Jean Sire de Joinville, Al Jolson, Ernest Jones, Louis Jordan, Joseph II, Holy Roman Emperor, Flavius Josephus, Julian, Julius II, Kamal Jumblatt, Carl Jung, Ernst Junger, Justinian I, Dimitry Kabalevsky, Janos Kadar, Donna Karan, Theodore Karman, Abeid A. Karume, Joseph Kasavubu, Nancy Landon Kassebaum, Rashidi Kawawa, Paul Keating, Estes Kefauver, Modibo Keita, Ellsworth Kelly, Petra Kelly, Fanny Kemble, Anthony Kennedy, James Kent, Rockwell Kent, Jack Kerouac, Clark Kerr, Francis Scott Key, Valdimer Orlando Key, Jr., John Maynard Keynes, Seretse M. Khama, Ed Kienholz, Kim Dae-Jung, Billie Jean King, Charles Kingsley, Neil Kinnock, Samuel Kirkland, Jeane Kirkpatrick, Nobusuki Kishi, Benedicto

Kiwanuka, Abraham Klein, Friedrich Gottlieb Klopstock, Philander Chase Knox, Ed Koch, Ivan Stefanovich Konev, Lavr Georgyevich Kornilov, Andrey Vladimirovich Kozyrev, Bruno Kreisky, Ernst Krenek, Juanita Kreps, Krishna Menon, Paul Kruger, Juscelino Kubitschek de Oliveira, Milan Kundera, William Kunstler, Kuo Mo-Jo, Spiros Kyprianou, Jean de La Bruyere, Oskar Lafontaine, Karl Lagerfeld, Melvin Laird, Lucius Quintus Cincinnatus Lamar, Charles Lamb, Joseph Lancaster, Hugh Latimer, Ralph Lauren, Henri Laurens, Wilfred Laurier, Francois Laval, Pierre Laval, John Law, Abbott Lawrence, T.E. Lawrence, Thomas Lawrence, Henry Charles Lea, Edward Lear, Timothy Leary, William Edward Hartpole Lecky, Jacques LeClerc, Le Corbusier, Le Duan, Arthur Lee, Anton Van Leeuwenhoek, Herbert H.Lehman, Earl of Leicester, Peter Lely, Lyman Louis Lemnitzer, John Lennon, Leo I, Leo III, Leo IX, Leo X, Leo XIII, Leopold I, Leopold II, Mikhail Yurievich Lermontov, Alain Rene Le Sage, Vicomte de Lesseps, Carlo Levi, Cecil Day Lewis, Matthew Gregory Lewis, Trydve Halvdan Lie, John Lilburne, Lydia Kamakaeha Liliuokalani, John Lindsay, Jacques Lipchitz, Fritz Abert Lipmann, Walter Lippmann, Edward Livingston, Robert R. Livingston, Livy, James Logan, Peter Lombard, Vince Lombardi, Huey Long, Carlos Lopez, Pierre Loti, Rudolf Herman Lotze, Louis I, Louis XI, Louis XII, Louis XIII, Louis XV, Louis XVIII, Louis Phillipe, Seth Low, James Russell Lowell, Ernst Lubitsch, Lucas van Leyden, Henry Robinson Luce, Lucian, Robert Ludlum, Saint Luke, Jean Lully, Joseph Luns, Rosa Luxemburg, John Lydgate, Diosdado P. Macapagal, Edward Alexander MacDowell, John William Mackay, Alexander MacKenzie, Harold Macmillian, Rene Magritte, Mahmud II, William Mahone, John Major, Makarios, Bernard Malamud, Thomas Robert Malthus, Horace Mann, Mickey Mantle, Alessandro Manzoni, Gabriel Marcel, Rocky Marciano, Imelda Marcos, William Learned Marcy, Margaret of Anjou, Francis Marion, Saint Mark, 1st Duke of Marlborough, Othniel Charles Marsh, Agnes Martin, Luther Martin, William McChesney Martin, Jr., Harriet Martineau, Andrew Marvell, Harpo, Groucho, and Chico Marx, Karl Marx, Mary I, Mary II, Masaccio, George Mason, James Murray Mason, Lowell Mason, Philip Massinger, Quentin Massys, Increase Mather, Enrico Mattei, Saint Matthew, William H. Mauldin, Maurice of Nassau, John Frederick Denison Maurice, Willie Mays, Jules Mazarin, Giuseppe Mazzini, Amadou M'Bow, William Gibbs McAdoo, John McCloskey, John W. McCormack, James McCosh, Hugh McCulloch, George McDuffie, Ralph Emerson McGill, George Stanley McGovern, John McLean, Marshall McLuhan, Andrew George Latta McNaughton, Butterfly McQueen, Joseph Medill, Richard Meier, Henry Meiggs, Arthur Meighen, Philip Melanchthon, 2nd Viscount Melbourne, Andrew W. Mellon, Herman Melville, Gregor Mendel, Moses

Mendelssohn, Pierre Mendes-France, Anton Raphael Mengs, Menno Simons, (Philip) Metacom, Robert Gordon Menzies, Robert K. Merton, Olivier Messiaen, Michelangelo, Thomas Middleton, Barbara Mikulski, John Everett Millais, Joaquin Miller, Samuel Freeman Miller, William Miller, Slobodan Milosevic, Miltiades, Comte de Mirabeau, George John Mitchell, Francois Mitterrand, Ratko Mladic, Amedeo Modigliani, Mehmed the Conqueror, Daniel Arap Moi, Count Helmuth Karl Bernhard von Moltke, Theodor Mommsen, Geroge Monck, Duke of Monmouth and Buccleugh, Jean-Omer-Marie-Gabriel Monnet, Marilyn Monroe, Eugenio Montale, Claudio Monteverdi, Montezuma II, Richard Montgomery, Dwight Lyman Moody, Daniel Morgan, J(ohn) P(ierpont) Morgan, John Morgan, Samuel Eliot Morison, John Morley, Aldo Moro, Justin Smith Morrill, Gouverneur Morris, Lewis Morris, Robert Morris, William Morris, Oliver Perry Morton, Robert Moses, Rudolf Mossbauer, Robert Motherwell, John Lothrop Motley, Bill Moyers, Daniel Patrick Moynihan, Hosni Mubarak, Elijah Muhammad, William Augustus Muhlenberg, Lewis Mumford, Thomas Munzer, Joachim Murat, Bartolome Esteban Murillo, James Murray, Edward R. Murrow, Edmund Sixtus Muskie, Louis Charles Alfred de Musset, Abraham J. Muste, Karl Gunnar Myrdal, Jayaprkash Narayan, Thomas Nast, Carrie Nation, Jacques Necker, Jawaharlal Nehru, Alexander Sutherland Neill, Horatio Nelson, Saint Philip Neri, Pier Luigi Nervi, Agostinho Neto, Richard Neutra, Allan Nevins, Michel Ney, Ronald Ngala, Nicholas I, Jack Nicklaus, Friedrich Nietzsche, Vaslav Fomich Nijinsky, Umberto Nobile, Amalie Emmy Noether, Manuel Noriega, Federick North, John Humphrey Noyes, U Nu, Rudolph Nureyev, Annie Oakley, Titus Oates, Adolph Simon Ochs, Jacques Offenbach, David Ogilvy, Claes Oldenburg, Sylvanos Olympio, Terrence O'Neill, Lars Onsager, Charles d'Orleans, Bobby Orr, John Boyd Orr, Daniel Ortega, William Osler, Elisha Graves Otis, Philip William Otterbein, Otto III, Leroy "Satchel" Paige, Ian Paisley, William Paley, William S. Paley, Andrea Palladio, Arnold Palmer, Vijaya Lakshmi Pandit, Emmeline Pankhurst, Andreas Papandreou, Philippus Aureolus Theophrastus Paracelsus, Jacques Parizeau, Chung Hee Park, Charlie Parker, Boris Pasternak, Kenneth Patchen, William Paterson, Alan (Stewart) Paton, Saint Patrick, Saint Paul, Paul I, Paul IV, Octavio Paz, Victor Paz Estenssoro, Robert Peel, Pele, J. C. Penney, William Pepperell, Pericles, Frances Perkins, Isabel Peron, Ross Perot, William Perry, Saint Peter, Francesco Petrarch, Philip II, King of France, Philip II, King of Macedon, Philip III, Philip IV, Philip IV, Philip V, Philip VI, Wendell Phillips, Renzo Piano, Francis Picabia, Charles Alfred Pillsbury, Pindar, Allen Pinkerton, William Pitt the Younger, Pius II, Pius IX, Pius V, Pius VI, Pius X, Pius XI, Plutarch, Jacopo Da Pontormo, Alexander Pope, Francis Poulenc, Nicholas Poussin, Terence Vincent Powderly,

John Wesley Powell, Lewis Powell, Powhatan, Michael Praetorius, Ranasinghe Premadasa, Sergei Prokofiev, Pierre Joseph Proudhon, William Proxmire, Ptolemy I, Ptolemy II, Joseph Pulitzer, Henry Purcell, Ernie Pyle, Qianlong, Dan Quayle, Francois Rabelais, Jean Baptise Racine, Thomas Stamford Raffles, Bhagwan Shree Rajneesh, Jean Phillipe Rameau, David Ramsay, Edmund Randolph, John Randolph, Leopold von Ranke, Raphael Rasputin, Johannes Rau, Robert Rauschenberg, John Ray, Man Ray, Satyajit Ray, Red Jacket, Donald Regan, William Hubbs Rehnquist, Thomas Reid, Max Reinhardt, Guido Reni, James Renwick, Ottorino Respighi, Albert Reynolds, Jusepe de Ribera, Richard I, Richard III, Richelieu, Germaine Richier, Wesley Branch Rickey, Matthew B. Ridgeway, George Ripley, Larry Rivers, Marion G. (Pat) Robertson, Frank Robinson, Michel Rocard, David Rockefeller, John D. Rockefeller, Jr., Nelson Rockefeller, 2nd Marquess of Rockingham, Norman Rockwell, Richard Charles Rodgers, Auguste Rodin, George Brydges Rodney, John Rogers, Roh Tae Woo, George Romney, Pierre de Ronsard, Ned Rorem, Salvator Rosa, Harold Ross, James Clark Ross, Georges Rouault, Jerry Rubin, Margaret Rudkin, Jacob van Ruisdale, Salman Rushdie, John Russell, Albert B. Sabin, Hans Sachs, Saddam Hussein, Ruth St. Denis, Louis Antoine Saint-Just, Duc de Saint-Simon, Charles Augustine Sainte-Beuve, Carlos Salinas, Harrison Salisbury, George Sand, Edwin Sandys, Satanta, Erik Satie, Girolamo Savonarola, Comte de Saxe, Oscar Luigi Scalfaro, Antonin Scalia, Philip Schaff, Rudolf Scharping, Fredrich Wilhelm Joseph Von Schelling, Karl Friedrich Schinkel, Friedrich Ernst Daniel Schleiermacher, James R. Schlesinger, Heinrich Schliemann, Arthur Schnitzler, Arnold Schoenberg, Henry Rowe Schoolcraft, Robert Schumann, Heinrich Schutz, Philip Schuyler, Publius Cornelius Scipio Africanus, Martin Scorsese, Robert Scott, Alexander Nikolayevich Scriabin, George Segal, Andres Segovia, Peter Sellers, Mack Sennett, Elizabeth Ann Seton, Georges-Pierre Seurat, Lucius Septimus Severus, Samuel Sewall, Ernest Shackleton, 1st Earl of Shaftesbury, 7th Earl of Shaftesbury, Yitzhak Shamir, Albert Shanker, Ariel Sharon, Al Sharpton, Fulton Sheen, Alan Shepard, Sam Shepard, John Sherman, Roger Sherman, Edward Shevardnadze, Edward Shippen, William Shirer, George Shultz, Philip Sidney, Benjamin Silliman, John J.Sirica, Sixtus V, John Smeaton, Alfred E. Smith, Gerrit Smith, William Smith, Olympia Snowe, John Soane, Mario Soares, Solomon, Solon, Thomas Octave Murdoch Sopwith, Wole Soyinka, Steven Spielberg, Squanto, Matthew Stanley Quay, David Steel, Edward Steichen, Alexander Hamilton Stephens, Robert Stephenson, Baron Von Steuben, John Paul Stevens, Alexander Turney Stewart, William Still, William Grant Still, Henry L. Stimson, Robert Field Stockton, Theodor Storm, Joseph Story, 1st Earl of Strafford, Lee Strasberg, Igor Stravinsky, Charles Edward

Louis Philip Casimir Stuart, Gilbert Charles Stuart, James Ewell Brown Stuart, Lucius Cornelius Sulla, Arthur Seymour Sullivan, John L. Sullivan, Arthur Ochs Sulzberger, Algernon Charles Swinburne, Amy Ruth Tan, Lewis Tappan, Brook Taylor, Elizabeth Taylor, Pierre Teilhard de Chardin, Sylvanus Thayer, Theodoric The Great, Saint Theresa, Nguyen Van Thieu, James Thomson, James Francis Thorpe, Thucydides, Strom Thurmond, Laurence Alan and Preston Robert Tisch, Leonid Tolstoy, Robert Augustus Toombs, Omar Torrijos Herrera, Arturo Toscanini, Henri de Toulouse-Lautrec, Albion Winegar Tourgee, Heinrich Von Treitschke, Lyman Trumbull, Donald Trump, Joseph Mallord William Turner, Ted Turner, Tutankhamen, Valerian, Paul Valery, Clement Laird Vallandigham, Giuseppe Verdi, Giovanni Verrazano, Andreas Vesalius, Vespasian, Victor Amadeus II, Victor Emmanuel II, Queen Victoria, Vincent de Paul, John Heyl Vincent, Virgil, Antonio Vivaldi, Walther von der Vogelweide, Benjamin Franklin Wade, Morrison Remick Waite, Lillian Wald, Peter Waldo, DeWitt Wallace, Henry Wallace, Henry Agard Wallace, Lewis Wallace, William Wallace, Albrecht Wenzel Eusebius Von Wallenstein, Robert Walpole, Barbara Walters, Izaac Walton, Artemus Ward, Mercy Otis Warren, Jacob Wassermann, Muddy Waters, John Watson, Thomas Edward Watson, Antoine Watteau, Francis Wayland, Anthony Wayne, John Wayne, Karl Maria Von Weber, Max Weber, Noah Webster, Thurlow Weed, Casper Weinberger, August Friedrich Leopold Weismann, Gideon Welles, Richard Wellesley, Horace Wells, Abraham Werner, Charles Wesley, Benjamin West, Vivienne Westwood, Rogier van der Weyden, James Abbott McNeill Whistler, Edward Douglas White, Stanford White, George Whitefield, Charles Wilkes, John Wilkes, Emma Willard, Frances Elizabeth Willard, William I, The Prince of Orange, William I, Emperor of Germany, William II, King of England, William II, Emperor of Germany, William III, William IV, Roger Williams, Henry Wilson, James P. Wilson, Pete Wilson, Johann Winckelmann, Edward Winslow, John Winthrop, James Wolfe, Thomas Kennerly Wolfe, Thomas Wolsey, Fernando Wood, Leonard Wood, Robert Woodward and Carl Bernstein, Christopher Wren, Carroll Davidson Wright, Frances Wright, Ahmed Yamani, William Lowndes Yancey, Chen Ning Yang, Mary Alexander (Molly) Yard, William Butler Yeats, Boris Yeltsin, Lester Young, Whitney Young, Jr., Zeno of Citium, Florenz Ziegfeld, Nicholas Ludwig Zinzendorf

Arte Público Press: Juana Ines de la Cruz, Jaime Escalante, Miguel de Hidalgo y Costilla, Rolando Hinojosa, Lope de Vega, Francisco de Miranda, Jose Celestino Mutis, Tito Puente, Luis Munoz Rivera, Oscar Romero, Luis Valdez.

Kathleen Barry: Shirley Caesar.

Jerry Bauer: Kobo Abe, Sherman Alexie, Julia Alvarez, Jorge Amado, Aharon Appelfeld, Anita Brookner, Edward Morley Callaghan, Peter Carey, Camilo Jose Cela y Trulock, Alice Childress, Jean Cocteau, J.M. Coetzee, Jill Ker Conway, Jose Donoso, Lawrence Durrell, Max Frisch, Jean Genet, Natalia Ginzburg, Nadine Gordimer, Peter Handke, Christopher Isherwood, Elia Kazan, Yashar Kemal, Jacques Lacan, Doris Lessing, Primo Levi, Claude Levi-Strauss, Jakov Lind, Francois Mauriac, Katherine Murray Millet, Czeslaw Milosz, Alberto Moravia, Jean Iris Murdoch, Vladimir Nabokov, V.S. Naipaul, R.K. Narayan, Pablo Neruda, Amos Oz, Elena Poniatowska, Anthony Powell, J.B. Priestley, V.S. Pritchett, E. Annie Proulx, Alain Robbe-Grillet, Nathalie Sarraute, Peter Levin Shaffer, Muriel Spark, Stephen Spender, Paul Theroux, William Trevor, Mario Vargas Llosa, Derek Walcott, Robert Penn Warren, Fay Weldon, Cornel West.

Boston Symphony Orchestra: Seiji Ozawa.

Octavia E. Butler: Octavia E. Butler.

Cambridge University Press: Osip Mandelstam.

James Collinson, from a portrait by: Christina Rossetti

Corbis Images: Gerald Adams, Alexander III, Alexander the Great, Muhammad Ali, Judith Anderson, Sherwood Anderson, Anthony, Attila, Wystan Hugh Auden, Djuna Barnes, Catherine Beecher, Ruth Fulton Benedict, Owen Bieber, Ambrose Bierce, Joseph Black, Humphrey Bogart, James Bradley, Tom Bradley, Constantin Brancusi, Bertolt Brecht, Helen Gurley Brown, Edmund Burke, Samuel Butler, Alvar Nunez Cabeza De Vaca, John Cabot, Juan Rodriguez Cabrillo, Frances Xavier Cabrini, John Cage, John Caldwell Calhoun, Annie Jump Cannon, Lazaro Cardenas, Benjamin N. Cardozo, Rod Carew, Anna Ella Carroll, Paul Cezanne, Thomas Chatterton, Chief Joseph, Paul Ching-Wu Chu, Bessie Coleman, Elizabeth Cotten, William Cowper, Walt(er)Disney, John Donne, Marcel Duchamp, George Eastman, Clint Eastwood, Mary Baker Eddy, Ralph Waldo Emerson, Pierre de Fermat, Jean-Bernard-Leon Foucault, Francis Ferdinand, Francis of Assisi, Frederick the Great, Vivian Fuchs, Yuri Gagarin, Paul Gauguin, Hans Wilhelm Geiger, Theodor S. Geisel (Dr. Suess), Genghis Khan, Kahlil Gibran, Andre Gide, Charlotte P. Gilman, Ruth Ginsburg, Sheldon L. Glashow, Emma Goldman, Barry Goldwater, El Greco, William R. Green, Augusta Gregory, Walter Adolph Gropius, Hadrian, Dag Hammarskjold, William Christopher Handy, Lorraine Hansberry, Duane Hanson, Vaclav Havel, Joseph Henry, Herod the Great, Alexander Herzen, Michael Heseltine, Hermann Hesse, Bob Hope, Charles H.Houston, William Dean Howells, Jan Hus, Anne Hutchinson, Hypatia of Alexandria, Irene of Athens, Ivan IV, Jiang Qing, John, King of England, John XXIII, Jasper Johns,

Mary Harris Jones, Scott Joplin, Barbara Jordan, Michael Jordan, James Joyce, Kamehameha III, Wassily Kandinsky, Nicolai Mikhailovich Karamzin, John Keats, Baron Kelvin of Largs, Thomas a Kempis, Edward Kennedy, William Lyon Mackenzie King, Gustav Robert Kirchhoff, Lincoln Kirstein, Paul Klee, Alfred A. Knopf, Oscar Kokoschka, Alexander Kolchack, Aleksandra Mikhailovna Kollontai, Kathe Kollwitz, Fumimaro Konoe, Tadeusz Kosciuszko, Leonid Kravchuk, Jiddu Krishnamurti, Peter Kropotkin, Kuang Hsu, Mikhail Kutuzov, Simon Kuznets, Fiorello Henry La Guardia, Par Fabian Lagerkvist, Selma Ottiliana Lovisa Lagerlof, Otto Graf Lambsdorff, Julien Offray de La Mettrie, Fritz Lang, Lao-Tzu, Nella Larsen, Karl Spencer Lashley, Harold Joseph Laski, Roland De Lassus, Archille Lauro, Charles Martel Allemand Lavigerie, Charles Le Brun, Gilbert Newton Lewis, Lee Hesien Loong, Lee Kuan Yew, Lee Teng-Hui, Sardar Farooq Amed Khan Leghari, Augusto Bernardino Leguia y Salcedo, Jacob Leisler, Georges-Henri LeMaitre, Antoine Le Nain, Andre Le Notre, Giacomo Leopardi, John Letcher, Urbain Jean Joseph Leverrier, Kurt Lewin, Clive Staples Lewis, Li Peng, Li Po, Max Liebermann, Yegor Kuzmich Ligachev, Gyorgy Ligeti, Benjamin Lincoln, (Nicholas) Vachel Lindsay, Filippo Lippi, Richard Lippold, Georg Friederich List, Royal Little, Maxim Maximovich Litvinov, Robert A. Livingston, Nicolai Lobachevski, Marcus Loew, William Edmund Logan, Alfred-Firmin Loisy, Cesare Lombroso, Mikhail Lomonosov, Crawford Williamson Long, Francisco Solano Lopez, Louis VI, Louis VII, Elijah Parish Lovejoy, Richard Lovelace, Bernard Lovell, Amy Lowell, Francis Cabot Lowell, Erich Friedrich Wilhelm von Ludendorff, Gyorgy Lukacs, Raymond Lull, Benjamin Lundy, Albert Luthuli, Witold Lutoslawski, Lysander, Jean Mabillon, Dwight MacDonald, Ramsay MacDonald, Guillaume de Machaut, Donald Baxter MacMillan, Francisco Indalecio Madero, Mahathir Mohamad, Mahdi, Aristide Maillol, Joseph Maistre, Francis Makemie, Daniel F. Malan, Nicholas Malebranche, Bronislaw Malinowski, Marcello Malpighi, Edouard Manet, Michael Manley, Henry Edward Manning, Katherine Mansfield, Giacomo Manzu, Franz Marc, Marcus Aurelius, Herbert Marcuse, John Marin, Christopher Marlowe, Reginald Marsh, Bohuslav Martinu, Tomas Garrigue Masaryk, Charles Maurras, Douglas Mawson, Jean Mayer, Barbara McClintock, William Holmes McGuffey, Samuel McIntire, Cosimo de'Medici, Zubin Mehta, Christopher Memminger, Menander, Mengzi Mencius, H(enry) L(ouis)Mencken, Menelik II, Mariam Mengistu Haile, Gian Carlo Menotti, Dmitri Sergeyevich Merezhkovsky, Charles E. Merrill, Franz A. Mesmer, Darius Milhaud, Henry Miller, Jean-Francois Millet, Robert Mills, Alfred Milner, Margaret Mitchell, Mohammad Reza Pahlavi, Lazlo Moholy-Nagy, Vyacheslav Mikhailovich Molotov, John Monash, Walter Mondale, Simon de Montfort, Manuel Montt, Henry Spencer Moore, Francisco

Morazan, John Pierpont Morgan, Jr., Junius Spencer Morgan, Dwight W. Morrow, Wayne Morse, Heinrich Melchior Muhlenberg, Mujibur Rahman, Johannes Peter Muller, Edvard Munch, George William Mundelein, Roderick Impey Murchison, Philip Murray, Modest Petrovich Mussorgsky, Carl Mydans, Mohammad Najibullah, Yasuhiro Nakasone, Lewis Bernstein Namier, Fridthof Nansen, Panfilo De Narvez, Ne Win, Motilal Nehru, Howard Nemerov, Nero Claudius Caesar, Karl Robert Nesselrode, Simon Newcomb, John Henry Newman, Barthold Georg Niebuhr, Reihold Niebuhr, Carl August Nielsen, Oscar Niemeyer Soares Filho, Luigi Nono, Nils Adolf Erik Nordenskjold, George W. Norris, Michel Nostradamus, Novalis, Odoacer, Howard Washington Odum, John O'Hara, Omar Khayyam, Abraham Ortelius, Toshimichi Okubo, Olaf II, Johan Van Oldenbarnevelt, James Oliver, Frederick Law Olmsted, Omar ibn al-Khattab, Juan de Onate, Thomas Philip O'Neill, Jan Oort, Origen, Vittorio Emanuele Orlando, Thomas Mott Osborne, Sergio Osmena, Harrison Gray Otis, David Owen, Robert Dale Owen, Richard Owen, Axel Gustafsson Oxenstierna, Jose Antonio Paez, John Knowles Paine, Giovanni Pierluigi Da Palestrina, A(lexander) Mitchell Palmer, Nathaniel B. Palmer, Franz von Papen, Louis Joseph Papineau, William Hallock Park, Horatio W. Parker, Charles Stewart Parnell, Vallabhbhai Patel, Walter Pater, Simon Patino, Jaime Paz Zamora, Peter Pazmany, Elizabeth Peabody, George Peabody, Rembrandt Peale, Patrick Henry Pearse, Lester Pearson, Pedro I, Charles S. Peirce, Krzysztof Penderecki, Edmund Pendleton, George Pendleton, Boies Penrose, Samuel Pepys, Adolfo Perez, Giovanni Battista Pergolesi, Charles Perrault, Pietro de Perugino, Carl Peters, Phidias, Philip II, King of Spain, Philip the Good, Arthur Phillip, Duncan Phyfe, Jean Piaget, Auguste Piccard, Giovanni Pico Della Mirandola, Philippe Pinel, Horace Pippin, Giovanni B. Piranesi, Antonio Pisanello, Walter Piston, Pius IV, Pius VII, Titus Maccius Plautus, Galo Plaza, Pliny the Elder, Pliny the Younger, Plotinus, Jules-Henri Poincare, (M.) Raymond Poincare, John Polanyi, Jackson Pollock, Marco Polo, Juan Ponce de Leon, John Russell Pope, Giambattista della Porta, Grigori Potemkin, Dennis Potter, Hiram Powers, Manuel Prado, Rajendra Prasad, Praxiteles, Raul Prebisch, Fritz Pregl, William H. Prescott, Abbe Prevost, Richard Price, Ivy Baker Priest, Procopius, Pierre Prudhon, Nikolai Mikhailovich Przhevalski, Samuel von Pufendorf, Emelyan Ivanovich Pugachev, Edward Bouverie Pusey, Pierre Puvis de Chavannes, Francis Pym, John Pym, Thomas R. Pynchon, Qaboos Ibn Sa'id, Salvatore Quasimodo, Edith H. Quimby, Marcus Fabius Quintilian, Elpidio Quirino, Karl Bernardovich Radek, Sarvepalli Radhakrishnan, Karl Rahner, Chakravarti Rajagopal-achari, Petrus Ramus, Arthur Michael Ramsey, Eleanor Florence Rathbone, 1st Marquess of Reading, Thomas Reed, Tadeus Reichstein, Karl Renner, Auguste Renoir, James B. Reston, Walter

Philip Reuther, Alfonso Reyes, Syngman Rhee, Robert Barnwell Rhett, David Ricardo, Matteo Ricci, Henry Hobson Richardson, Samuel Richardson, Louis Riel, Cola di Rienzi, Nikolai Andreevich Rimsky-Korsakov, Albrecht Ritschl, Karl Ritter, Jerome Robbins, Maximilien Robespierre, George Rochberg, Peter Wallace Rodino, Jr., Jose Enrique Rodo, Washington Augustus Roebling, Carl Ransom Rogers, Edith Nourse Rogers, Richard Rogers, Robert Rogers, Richard Rolle of Hampole, Carlos Romero Barcelo, Juan Manuel De Rosas, Antonio Rosmini-Serbati, Dante G. Rossetti, Walt Whitman Rostow, Henry A. Rowland, Manuel Roxas, Josiah Royce, Mike Royko, Peter Paul Rubens, Helena Rubenstein, Edmund Ruffin, Count Rumford, Karl Rudolf Gerd von Rundstedt, Ernst August Friedrich Ruska, Charles Marion Russell, Nolan Ryan, Gilbert Ryle, Eero Saarinen, Sacajawea, Nelly Sachs, Anwar Sadat, Sa'di, Comte De Sade, William Safire, Comte de Saint Simon, Ali Abdallah Salih, Sallust, Paul Anthony Samuelson, Jose Francisco De San Martin, Pedro Santana, Sappho, Domingo Faustino Sarmiento, David Sarnoff, Paola Sarpi, Siegfried Sassoon, Augusta Savage, Frederick Karl Von Savigny, Alessandro Scarlatti, Domenico Scarlatti, Hjalmar Horace Greeley Schacht, Frederich Von Schlegel, Arthur Schlesinger, Jr., Helmut Schmidt, Gustav Von Schmoller, Rose Schneiderman, Kurt Schumacher, Kurt Von Schuschnigg, Caspar Schwenckfeldt, Publius Cornelius Scipio Africanus Minor, Edward Wyllis Scripps, Samuel Seabury, Adam Sedgwick, Selim I, Selim III, Lucius Annaeus Seneca, Ludwig Senfl, Michael Servetus, Roger Huntington Sessions, John Sevier, Betty Shabazz, 3rd Earl of Shaftesbury, Ben Shahn, Anna Howard Shaw, Lemeul Shaw, Richard Norman Shaw, Mary Wollstonecraft Shelley, Henry Miller Shreve, Jacob and Lee Shubert, Jacob J. Shubert, Walter Richard Sickert, Henryk Sienkiewiez, Emmanuel Sieyes, Luca Signorelli, Norodom Sihanouk, Paul Simon, Jaime Sin, Isaac Bashevis Singer, Maxine Singer, Ranjit Singh, David A.Siqueiros, Albertina Sisulu, Walter Sisulu, Edith Sitwell, John Skelton, John Sloan, Eleanor Smeal, Charles Edward K. Smith, Edgar P. Snow, Robert Mangaliso Sobukwe, Socrates, Nathan Soerderblom, Sophocles, Pierre Soule, Lazzarro Spallanzani, Spartacus, John Hanning Speke, Francis Joseph Spellman, Philipp Jakob Spener, Oswald Spengler, Alexander Spotswood, Georg Ernst Stahl, Leland Stanford, Konstantin Stanislavsky, Richard Steele, Vilhjalmur Steffansson, Stendhal, Nicolaus Steno, Stephen, King of England, Uriah Smith Stephens, George Stephenson, Aloysius Stepinac, John Stevens, Adlai Stevenson, Dugald Stewart, Alfred Stieglitz, Joseph Warren Stilwell, Karl Heinz Stockhausen, Petr Arkadevich Stolypin, Edward Durell Stone, Strabo, John Strachan, Lytton Strachey, Franz Josef Strauss, Robert S. Strauss, Gustav Stresemann, August Strindberg, Roberto Suazo Cordova, John Suckling, Antonio Jose de Sucre, Hermann Sudermann, Gaius

Tranquillus Suetonius, Sukarno, Suleiman I, William Graham Sumner, Graham Sutherland, Aleksandr Vasilievich Suvorov, Gerard Swope, Thomas Sydenham, William Sylvis, Karol Syzmanowski, Henrietta Szold, Horace Tabor, Tacitus, Robert Alphonso Taft, King Taharqa, Thomas Tallis, Kakuei Tanaka, Henry O. Tanner, Banastre Tarleton, Guiseppe Tartini, Abel J. Tasman, Allen Tate, Maxwell Davenport Taylor, Alexander Nikolayevich Tcherepnin, Georg Philipp Telemann, William Temple, Terence, Tertullian, Themistocles, Theocritus, Theodora, (Christian Friedrich) Theodore Thomas, George Henry Thomas, Martha Carey Thomas, Dorothy Thompson, Joseph John Thomson, Virgil Garnett Thomson, Maurice Thorez, Gaston Thorn, Edward L. Thorndike, (Johann) Ludwig Tieck, Samuel Jones Tilden, Benjamin R.Tillman, Tintoretto, Tipu Sultan, Nicolae Titulescu, Alexis de Tocqueville, Palmiro Togliatti, Evangelista Torricelli, Sekou Toure, Charles Townes, Francis Everitt Townsend, (Arnold) Joseph Toynbee, Spencer Tracy, Juan T. Trippe, Anthony Trollope, Garretson Beekman Trudeau, Francois Truffaut, Rafael Trujillo Molina, Rexford Guy Tugwell, Ivan Turgenev, Anne Robert Jacques Turgot, Frederick J. Turner, Nat(haniel) Turner, William M.Tweed, William Tyndale, Walter Ulbricht, Ulfilas, Domitius Ulpian, Miguel de Unamuno, Urban II, Urban VI, Justo Jose Urquiza, Jack Valenti, Vincent Van Gogh, Jacobus Hendricus Van't Hoff, John Vanbrugh, Cyrus Vance, Zebulon Baird Vance, Edgard Varese, Getulio Vargas, Harold Varmus, Marcus Terentius Varro, Lodocvico di Varthema, Giorgio Vasari, Ralph Vaughan Williams, Nikolai Ivanovich Vavilov, Thorstein B. Veblen, Jose M. Velasco, Diego Rodriguez de Silva Velazquez, Paolo Veronese, Andrea del Verrocchio, Hendrik Frensch Verwoerd, Giambattista Vico, Victor Emmanuel III, Gore Vidal, Jorge Rafael Videla, Giacomo da Vignola, Comte de Vigny, Heitor Villa-Lobos, Oswald G. Villard, Francois Villon, Frederick Vinson, Eugene Emmanuel Viollett-le-Duc, Gian Galcazzo Visconti, Vladimir I, Hans Vogel, Paul Volcker, Joost Van den Vondel, Diane von Furstenberg, B(althazar) J(ohann)Vorster, Andrei Vyshinsky, Robert Ferdinand Wagner, Jonathan Wainwright, Terry Waite, William Walker, Raoul Wallenberg, Thomas "Fats" Waller, Thomas J. Walsh, William Walton, Wang Ching-wei, Paul Moritz Warburg, Lester Frank Ward, Elkanah Watson, Robert A. Watson-Watt, Archibald Percival Wavell, Beatrice Potter Webb, Max Weber, Anton Webern, Frank Wedekind, Josiah Wedgwood, Alfred Wegener, Ezer Weizman, Chaim Weizmann, William Henry Welch, Sumner Welles, Franz Werfel, Max Wertheimer, Eleazar Wheelock, Andrew Dickson White, E.B. White, Kevin Hogan White, Edward Gough Whitlam, Marcus Whitman, Frank Whittle, Christoph Martin Wieland, Simon Wiesenthal, Mary Wigman, William Wilberforce, Wihelmina, George Hubert Wilkins, James Wilkinson, George F. Will, Daniel Hale Williams, David Wilmot, Alexander Wilson,

Charles Erwin Wilson, Charles T.R. Wilson, Harold Wilson, Richard Wilson, Isaac Mayer Wise, Stephen S. Wise, John Witherspoon, Johan de Witt, Friedrich August Wolf, Thomas C.Wolfe, Wolfram von Eschenbach, Grant Wood, Robert E. Wood, Robert Woodruff, Comer van Woodward, Frank Winfield Woolworth, Frank Lloyd Wright, Wilbur and Orville Wright, Wu Pei-fu, Wilhelm Wundt, Alexander Helwig Wyant, William Wycherley, Andrew Wyeth, Iannis Xenakis, Xenophon, Aritomo Yamagata, Tomoyuki Yamashita, Chuck Yeager, Yen Hsi-shan, Shigeru Takeuchi Yoshida, Owen D. Young, Yuan Shih Kai, Ossip Joselyn Zadkine, Peterson Zah, Israel Zangwill, Jose Santos Zelaya, (John) Peter Zenger, Zenobia, Todor Zhivkov, Mohammad Zia-ul-Haq, Grigori Evseevich Zinoviev, Zoe, Zoroaster, Elmo Zumwalt, Ellen Taaffe Zwilich

Nancy Crampton: Simon J. Ortiz

EMI Classics: Mstislav Rostropovich

Mary Evans Picture Library: Nikolaas Tinbergen

Fisk University Library: Charlotte Hawkins Brown

FPG International Corp.: Nefertiti

Gale Research: Goh Chok Tong

Mark Gerson Photography: Ted Hughes, Evelyn Waugh

Fay Goodwin's Photo Files: Philip Larkin

The Granger Collection Ltd.: Amos Bad Heart Bull, Pierre Paul Brazza, Etienne Brule, Francis Xavier, Vasco da Gama, Ricarda Huch, Ernest Everett Just, Joaquim Maria Machado de Assis, Jean-Baptiste Marchand, Claude McKay, Lucretia Coffin Mott, Mutsuhito, Pierre-E(sprit) Radisson, Burrhus Frederic Skinner, Tobias George Smollett, Nikola Tesla, C.J. Walker, Maggie L. Walker, Sarah Winnemucca, Zhao Kuang-yin, Vladimir Kosma Zworykin

Hulton Deutsch Collection Limited: Obafemi Awolowo

Hulton-Getty/Tony Stone Images: Jozsef Mindszenty

Institute of Islamic Culture: Muhammad Jalal-ud-Din Rumi

Randall Jarrell, the Estate of: Randall Jarrell

Maulana Karenga: Maulana Karenga

Kenyon College: John Crowe Ransom

The Library of Congress: Hugo Aalto, Ferhat Abbas, Lyman Abbott, Ibrahim Abboud, Iowith Wilber Abel, Ralph Abernathy, Israel Abrahams, Charles Francis Adams, Alfred Adler, Felix Adler, Edgar Douglas Adrian, Aeschylus, Aga Khan, Jean Louis Rodolphe Agassiz, James Agee, Agha Mohammed Khan, Spiro T. Agnew, Shmuel Yoseph Agnon, Conrad Aiken, Alvin Ailey, Lucas

Alaman, Alaric, Duke of Alba, Afonso de Albuquerque, Alcibiades, James Lusk Alcorn, Jean le Rond d'Alembert, Arturo Alessandri Palma, Alexander of Yugoslavia, Alexander I, Alexander of Tunis, Alexis Romanov, Alexius I, Vittoria Alfieri, Alfonso X, Alfonso XIII, Alfred the Great, Nelson Algren, Saul David Alinsky, Florence Allen, Woody Allen, Edmund Henry Hynman Allenby, Washington Allston, Diego De Almagro, Albrecht Altdorfer, John Altgeld, Thomas J.J. Altizer, Luis W. Alvarez, B(himrao) R(amji) Ambedkar, Eric Ambler, Amenemhet I, Amenhotep III, Adelbert Ames, Jeffery Amherst, Jose De Anchieta, Carl David Anderson, Carl David Anderson, Maxwell Anderson, Jose Bonifacio De Andrada e Silva, Julius Andrassy, Andrea del Sarto, Salomon August Andree, Roy C. Andrews, Fra Angelico, James Rowland Angell, Anna Ivanovna, Susan B. Anthony, Antiochus III, Antonello da Messina, Mark Antony, Nathan Appleton, Edward Victor Appleton, Yasir Arafat, Louis Aragon, Osvaldo Aranha, Jacobo Arbenz Guzman, Archimedes, Alexander Archipenko, Elizabeth Arden, Hannah Arendt, Juan Jose Arevalo, Arnulfo Arias, Aristotle, Arius, Jacobus Arminius, Edwin Howard Armstrong, Benedict Arnold, Thomas Arnold, Svante August Arrhenius, Chester Alan Arthur, Francis Asbury, Shalom Asch, Harry Scott Ashmore, Jehudi Ashmun, Isaac Asimov, Herbert Henry Asqith, Francis William Aston, John Jacob Astor, Athanasius, Margaret Eleanor Atwood, Augustine, Augustus, Aurangzeb, Stephen Fuller Austin, Oswald Theodore Avery, Mohammed Ayub Khan, Manuel Azana Diaz, Sayyid Ismail al-Azhari, Nnamdi Azikiwe, Babar the Conqueror, Charles Babbage, Alexander Bache, Isaac Backus, Pietro Badoglio, Leo Baeck, Karl Ernst von Baer, Buenaventura Baez, Joan Baez, William Chandler Bagley, Egon Bahr, F. Lee Bailey, Josephine Baker, Newton Diehl Baker, Ray Stannard Baker, Joaquin Balaguer (y Ricardo), Vasco Nunez de Balboa, Emily Greene Balch, James Baldwin, Robert Baldwin, Lucille Ball, Hastings Kamuzu Banda, Sirimavo Bandaranaike, Frederick Grant Banting, Aleksandr Andreievich Baranov, Joel Barlow, Christiaan N.Barnard, Edward Emerson Barnard, Frederick Augustus Barnard, Henry Barnard, Pio Baroja y Nessi, Salo Wittmayer Baron, James Matthew Barrie, John Barry, Ethel Barrymore, Heinrich Barth, Karl Barth, Bruce Barton, Edmund Barton, Bernard M.Baruch, Count Basie, Basil II,Daisy Mae Bates, Henry Walter Bates, Katharine Lee Bates, Charles Baudelaire, L. Frank Baum, Richard Baxter, Pierre Bayle, Augustinus Bea, Moses Yale Beach, George W.Beadle, Charles Austin Beard, Mary Ritter Beard, Romare Bearden, Francis Beaumont, Ludwig August Beck, James (Jim) P. Beckwourth, Antoine Henri Becquerel, Lyman Beecher, Ludwig Van Beethoven, Emil Adolph von Behring, David Belasco, Terry Fernando Belaunde, Manuel Belgrano, Belisarius, Andrew Bell, Daniel Bell, Edward Bellamy, Robert Bellarmine, Giovanni Bellini, Ahmadu Bello, (Joseph) Hilaire (Pierre Rene) Belloc, Henry Whit-

ney Bellows, Pietro Bembo, Ahmed Ben Bella, Jacinto Benavente (y Martinez), Robert C. Benchley, Benedict XV, Edward Benes, Stephen Vincent Benet, Tony Benn, James Gordon Bennett, Richard Bedford Bennett, Paul Berg, Henri Bergson, George Berkeley, Adolf Berle, Irving Berlin, Isaiah Berlin, Claude Bernard, Edward L. Bernays, Gian Lorenzo Bernini, Leonard Bernstein, Daniel Berrigan, Chuck Berry, Alphonse Bertillon, Jons Jacob Berzelius, Friedrich Wilhelm Bessel, Henry Bessemer, Charles Herbert Best, Hans Albrecht Bethe, Theobald Von Bethmann Hollweg, Mary McLeod Bethune, Bruno Bettelheim, Aneurin Bevan, Ernest Bevin, Homi Jehangir Bhabha, Hayyim Nahman Bialik, Marie Francois Xavier Bichat, Nicholas Biddle, Sieur de Bienville , Albert Bierstadt, John Bigelow, James Billington, James Gillespie Birney, Elizabeth Bishop, Georges Bizet, Bjornstjerne Bjornson, Hugo Lafayette Black, William Blackstone, Elizabeth Blackwell, James Gillespie Blaine, Francis Preston Blair, James Blair, Louis Blanc, Sarah Gibson Blanding, Felix Bloch, Konrad E.Bloch, Herbert Block, Amelia Jenks Bloomer, Ella Reeve (Mother) Bloor, Gebhard Leberecht von Blucher, Leon Blum, Franz Boas, Giovanni Boccaccio, Hermann Boerhaave, Niels Henrik David Bohr, Ludwig Boltzmann, Julian Bond, Margaret Grace Bondfield, Boniface VIII, Richard Parkes Bonington, George Boole, Daniel Boone, Daniel J. Boorstin, Edwin Booth, Evangeline Booth, John Wilkes Booth, William Booth, Betty Boothroyd, William Edgar Borah, Jorge Luis Borges, Lucrezia Borgia, Max Born, Juan Bosch, Jagadis Chandra Bose, Subhas Chandra Bose, Jacques Bossuet, Louis Botha, Walther Wihelm George Franz Bothe, Sandro Botticelli, Francois Boucher, Dion Boucicault, Leon Bourgeois, Margaret Bourke-White, Henry Bowditch, James Bowdoin, Elizabeth Bowen, Claude Gernade Bowers, Isaiah Bowman, Robert Boyle, Edward Braddock, Charles Bradlaugh, Mathew B.Brady, William Henry Bragg, Tycho Brahe, Johannes Brahms, Louis Dembitz Brandeis, Marlon Brando, Sebastian Brant, George Braque, Walter H.Brattain, Ferdinand Braun, James Henry Breasted, Clemens Brentano, Marcel Lajos Breuer, William. Brewster, Fanny Brice, James Bridger, Percy Williams Bridgman, Richard Bright, Charlie Dunbar Broad, Isaac Brock, Peter Brook, James Brooke, Gwendolyn Brooks, Adriaen Brouwer, Benjamin G.Brown, George Brown, James Brown, Moses Brown, Thomas Browne, William Brownlow, Dave Brubeck, David Bruce, James Bruce, Joseph Anton Bruckner, Isambard Kingdom Brunel, Giordano Bruno, Marcus Junius Brutus, William Jennings Bryan, William Cullen Bryant, Zbigniew Brzezinski, Martin Buber, James Buchanan, Frederick Buech ner, Charles Bulfinch, Philippe J.Bunau-Varilla, Ralph J.Bunche, McGeorge Bundy, Robert Wilhelm Bunsen, Gordon Bunshaft, John Bunyan, Luther Burbank, Charles Burchfield, Warren E.Burger, Kenneth Burke, Selma Burke, Anson

Burlingame, Edward Coley Burne-Jones, Gilbert Burnet, Daniel Hudson Burnham, (Linden) Forbes Burnham, George Burns, Aaron Burr, Elihu Burritt, John Burroughs, Richard Burton, Robert Burton, Vannevar Bush, Horace Bushnell, Ferruccio Benvenuto Busoni, William Bustamante, Sr., 3d Earl of Bute , (Mangosuthu) Gatsha Buthelezi, Nicholas Murray Butler, John Butterfield, Richard Evelyn Byrd, George Gordon Noel Byron, James Branch Cabell, Richard Clarke Cabot, Sebastian Cabot, Pedro Alvares Cabral, Gaius Julius Caesar, Abraham Cahan, Erskine Caldwell, Sarah Caldwell, Daniel J.Callahan, Plutarco Elias Calles, Cab Calloway, John Calvin, Melvin Calvin, Italo Calvino, Simon Cameron, George Canning, Antonio Canova, Georg Ferdinand Ludwig Philipp Cantor, Karel Capek, Truman Capote, Caravaggio, Hattie W.Caraway, Guy Carelton, Henry Carey, Tiburcio Carias Andino, George Carlin, Thomas Carlyle, Stokely Carmichael, Hattie Carnegie, Lazare Nicolas Marguerite Carnot, Nicolas Leonard Sadi Carnot, Jean Baptiste Carpeaux, Agostino Carracci, Annibale Carracci, Ludovico Carracci, Alexis Carrel, Jose Miguel Carrera, John Carroll, Christopher (Kit) Carson, Rachel Louise Carson, James Earl Carter, Peter Cartwright, George Washington Carver, Jonathan Carver, Pablo Casals, Johnny Cash, Lewis Cass, Baldassare Castiglione, Vernon and Irene Castle, Viscount Castlereagh, Fidel Castro Ruz, Willa Cather, Catherine de Medici, Catherine the Great, Catiline, Cato the Younger, Carrie Chapman Catt, Augustin Louis Cauchy, Henry Cavendish, Conte Di Cavour, Cecil of Chelwood , Carlos Manuel de Cespedes, Edwin Chadwick, Marc Chagall, Ernst Boris Chain, Thomas Chalmers, (Joseph) Austen Chamberlain, (Arthur) Neville Chamberlain, Jean Francois Champollion, Raymond Chandler, Zachariah Chandler, Chang Chein, Tso-lin Chang, William Ellery Channing, Charles (Charlie) Chaplin, Jean Martin Charcot, Charlemagne, Charles II, Charles III, Charles V, Charles VI, Charles X, Ray Charles, Philander Chase, Salmon Portland Chase, William Merritt Chase, Vicomte de Chateaubriand, Charles Chauncy, Carlos Chavez, Cesar Chavez, Dennis Chavez, John Cheever, Anton Chekov, Pavel Alekseevich Cherenkov, Nikolai Chernyshevsky, Luigi Carlo Cherubini, Chiang Ching-kuo, Lydia Maria Child, Thomas Chippendale, Chou En-lai, Agatha Christie, Edwin Pearce Christy, Chu Teh, Frederick Edwin Church, Winston Churchill, Winston Leonard Spencer Churchill, Andre-Gustave Citroen, Hugh Clapperton, 1st Earl of Clarendon, John Clark, John Maurice Clark, Kenneth Clark, Tom Campbell Clark, William Clark, Claude Lorrain , Paul Claudel, Rudolf Julius Emanuel Clausius, Henry Clay, Georges Clemenceau, Cleopatra, (Stephen) Grover Cleveland, George Clinton, Robert Clive, Jean Clouet, William Cobbett, John Douglas Cockcroft, William Sloane Coffin, Jr., Jean-Baptiste Colbert, Cadwallader Colden, George Douglas Cole, Nat King Cole, John Collier, Edward K.Collins, Michael Collins, William Wilkie

Collins, John Coltrane, Christopher Columbus, Anna Comnena, Arthur Holly Compton, Anthony Comstock, Auguste Comte, Barber B. Conable, Jr., James Byrant Conant, Etienne Bonnot de Condillac, William Congreve, John Constable, (John)Calvin Coolidge, Peter Cooper, Thomas Cooper, Nicolaus Copernicus, John Singleton Copley, Gerty T.Cori, Erastus Corning, Correggio, Michael Corrigan, William Henry Cosby , Jr., Liam Cosgrave, John Cotton, George Sylvester Counts, Jean Desire Gustave Courbet, Jacques-Yves Cousteau, Miles Coverdale, Abraham Cowell, George Crabbe, Lucas Cranach the Elder, Prudence Crandall, Stephen Crane, William Harris Crawford, Crazy Horse, George Creel, Thomas Crerar, Francis Harry Crompton Crick, 1st Earl of Cromer, Thomas Cromwell, George Crook, William Crookes, Paul Cuffe, Marie Sklodowska Curie, Pierre Curie, James Curley, Arthur William Currie, Jabez Lamar Monroe Curry, Andrew Gregg Curtin, George N.Curzon, Harvey Williams Cushing, Charlotte Cushman, George Armstrong Custer, Mannaseh Cutler, Georges Leopold Cuvier, Cyril, Gabriele D'Annunzio, Louis Jacques Mande Daguerre, Roald Dahl, Gottlieb Daimler, Richard J.Daley, Salvador Dali,_ 1st Marquess of Dalhousie , Luigi Dallapiccola, John Dalton, Father Damien, William Dampier, Richard Henry Dana, Jr., Enrico Dandolo, Darius I, Clarence Seward Darrow, Charles Robert Darwin, Alphonse Daudet, Honore Daumier, John Davenport, Jacques Louis David, Henry Winter Davis, Miles Davis, Ossie Davis, Richard Harding Davis, Sammy Davis , Jr., Humphry Davy, Moshe Dayan, Silas Deane, James D(unwoody) B(rownson) DeBow, Eugene V. Debs, Peter Debye, Ruby Dee, Lee DeForest, Alcide DeGasperi, Charles De Gaulle, Max Delbruck, Theophile Delcasse, Daniel DeLeon, Vine Deloria, Jr., Suleyman Demirel, Democritus, Jack Dempsey, Rauf Denktash, Rene Descartes, Hernando deSoto, Jean Jacques Dessalines, Eamon DeValera, George Dewey, Melvil Dewey, Jose de la Cruz Porfirio Diaz, Charles John Huffam Dickens, Emily Dickinson, John Dickinson, Dennis Diderot, Ngo Dinh Diem, Rudolf Diesel, John Dillinger, Georgi Dimitrov, Robert Dinwiddie, Diocletian, Diogenes, Christian Dior, Paul Dirac, Everett McKinley Dirksen, Theodosius Dobzhansky, Robert Dole, Sanford Ballard Dole, Engelbert Dollfuss, Gerhard Domagk, Placido Domingo, Donatello, Pham Van Dong, Gaetano Donizetti, Ignatius Donnelly, Hilda Doolittle, James H.Doolittle, Rheta Childe Dorr, John Dos Passos, Stephen A. Douglas, Frederick Douglass, Neal Dow, Andrew Jackson Downing, Luis Maria Drago, Daniel Drake, Francis Drake, Michael Drayton, (Herman) Theodore Dreiser, George Russell Drysdale, Jose Napoleon Duarte, Alan Dugan, Michael Dukakis, Jean Henri Dunant, Paul Laurence Dunbar, William Dunbar, Katherine Dunham, Finley Peter Dunne, John Duns Scotus, Marquis Dupleix, Eleuthere Irenee duPont, Pierre Samuel duPont de Nemours, William Crapo Durant,

James Buchanan Eads, Edward Murray East, Max Forrester Eastman, Dorman Bridgman Eaton, Friedrich Ebert, Anthony Eden, Maria Edgeworth, Thomas Alva Edison, Edward I, Edward II, Edward Eggleston, Paul Ehrlich, Albert Einstein, Dwight D.Eisenhower, Milton Eisenhower, Cyprian Ekwensi, Edward Elgar, 8th Earl of Elgin, Charles William Eliot, Ge orge Eliot, T(homas) S(tearns) Eliot, Elizabeth I, Elizabeth II, Edward Kennedy ("Duke") Ellington, Lincoln Ellsworth, Empedocles, John F.Enders, Epaminondas, Jacob Epstein, Olaudah Equiano, John Ericsson, Joseph Erlanger, Matthias Erzberger, Richard Estes, Manuel Estrada Cabrera, Tomas Estrada Palma, Euclid, Eugene of Savoy, Edith Mary Evans, George Henry Evans, Herbert Vere Evatt, John Evelyn, Philip Evergood, Medgar W.Evers, Louis Leon Cesar Faidherbe, Ellen Louks Fairclough, Faisal I, Jerry Falwell, Amintore Fanfani, James Aloysius Farley, James Farmer, Moses Gerrish Farmer, D(avid) G(lasgow) Farragut, James T. Farrell, William Faulkner, Millicent Fawcett, Gustav Theodor Fechner, John G. Fee, Diogo Antonio Feijo, Feng Yu-hsiang, Edna Ferber, Ferdinand III, Ferdinand V, Adam Ferguson, Richard P. Feynman, Johann Gottlieb Fichte, Marsilio Ficino, Arthur Fiedler, David D. Field, Millard Fillmore, Charles Grandison Finney, Harvey Samuel Firestone, Emil Fischer, Hans Fischer, Johann Bernhard Fischer von Erlach, Hamilton Fish, Ronald A. Fisher, James Fisk, John Fiske, Minnie M. Fiske, John Fitch, John Flamsteed, Gustave Flaubert, Alexander Fleming, John Fletcher, Matthew Flinders, Howard Walter Florey, Carlisle Floyd, Elizabeth Flynn, Ferdinand Foch, John Forbes, Robert Bennet Forbes, Ford Madox Ford, Gerald R.Ford, Henry Ford, II, Paul Leicester Ford, James Forman, Harry Emerson Fosdick, Stephen Collins Foster, William Zebulon Foster, Francois C.M. Fourier, Jean-Baptiste Joseph Fourier, Anatole France, Francis I, James Franck, Anne Frank, Felix Frankfurter, Benjamin Franklin, John Hope Franklin, Peter Fraser, Joseph von Fraunhofer, Frederick III, Douglas S. Freeman, Eduardo Frei Montalvi, John Charles Fremont, Daniel C. French, Henry Bartle Edward Frere, Girolamo Frescobaldi, Augustin Jean Fresnel, Sigmund Freud, Gustav Freytag, Henry Clay Frick, Betty Friedan, Carl Joachim Friedrich, Friedrich II, Arturo Frondizi, Compte de Frontenac, Robert Frost, Elizabeth Gurney Fry, (Sarah) Margaret Fuller, Robert Fulton, Joseph Furphy, Henry Fuseli, Johann Joseph Fux, Ange Jacques Gabriel, Matilda J.Gage, Thomas Gainsborough, Jorge Eliecer Gaitan, Hugh Gaitskell, John Kenneth Galbraith, Benito Perez Galdos, Galileo Galilei, Albert Gallatin, Thomas Hopkins Gallaudet, Romulo Gallegos Freire, Joseph Galloway, Alexander Galt, Francis Galton, Luigi Galvani, Bernardo De Galvez, Leon Gambetta, George Gamow, Indira Priyadarshi Nehru Gandhi, Mohandas K.Gandhi, Greta Garbo, Carlos P.Garcia, Gabriel Garcia Moreno, Inca Garcilaso De La Vega, James Abram Garfield, Francois X. Garneau, Francis Garnier, Jean-Louis Charles

Garnier, John Work Garrett, Thomas Garrett, William Lloyd Garrison, Elbert H.Gary, Pedro de la Gasca, Elizabeth Cleghorn Gaskell, Richard Jordan Gatling, Antonio Gaudi i Cornet, Giovanni-Battista Gaulli, Karl Friedrich Gauss, John Gay, Joseph Gay-Lussac, Patrick Geddes, Edmund Charles Genet, George I, George II, George IV, George V, George VI, James Zachariah George, Jean Louis Andre Theodore Gericault, Geronimo, George Gershwin, Jean de Gerson, Lorenzo Ghiberti, Domenico Ghirlandaio, Amadeo Peter Giannini, James Gibbons, James Gibbs, Josiah Willard Gibbs, Althea Gibson, John Gielgud, William Gilbert, Ernest Giles, Dizzy Gillespie, Daniel Coit Gilman, Alberto Ginastera, Giovanni Giolitti, Giotto, Stephen Girard, Francois Girardon, Washington Gladden, William Ewart Gladstone, Ellen Glasgow, Mikhail Ivanovich Glinka, Duke of Gloucester, Christoph Willibald Gluck, Robert H.Goddard, William Godwin, Maria Goeppert-Mayer, Nikolai Gogol, George (Dashwood) Taubman Goldie, William Golding, Oliver Goldsmith, Laureano E. Gomez Castro, Juan Vicente Gomez, Samuel Gompers, Vadislav Gomulka, Edmond de Goncourt, Jane Goodall, John Inkster Goodlad, Charles Goodyear, Charles G. Gordon, John Brown Gordon, Josiah Gorgas, Hermann Goring, Maxim Gorky, Gottfried von Strassburg, Glenn Herbert Gould, Francisco Goya y Lucientes, Jan Van Goyen, Billy Graham, Katherine Graham, Martha Graham, Sylvester Graham, Ulysses S.Grant, Gunter Grass, Thomas Gray, Horace Greeley, A(dolphus) W(ashington) Greely, Constance M. Green, Edith Starrett Green, Nathanael Greene, Gregory I, Gregory XIII, Charles Grey, Edvard Hagerup Grieg, Franz Grillparzer, Sarah (Moore) Grimke, Wilhelm and Jakob Grimm, Red Grooms, Baron Gros, Hugo Grotius, Matthias Grunewald, Guercino, Otto von Guericke, Johann Gutenberg, Ernst Haeckel, Frank Hague, Otto Hahn, Douglas Haig, Haile Selassie, John Burdon Sanderson Haldane, Stephen Hales, Margaret A. Haley, Earl of Halifax, Asaph Hall, Donald Hall, Granville Stanley Hall, Albrecht von Haller, Edmund Halley, William Frederick Halsey, Jr., Johann George Hamann, Fannie Lou Hamer, Alice Hamilton, Oscar Hammerstein, II, Samuel Dashiell Hammett, James Henry Hammond, Hammurabi, John Hampden, Wade Hampton, Knut Hamsun, Oscar Handlin, Alvin H.Hansen, Julia Butler Hansen, Howard Hanson, Norman Hapgood, Kei Hara, (James) Keir Hardie, Warren G.Harding, Robert Hare, Robert Harley, Edward Henry Harriman, William Averell Harriman, James Harrington, Joel Chandler Harris, Roy Harris, Townsend Harris, William Torrey Harris, Benjamin Harrison, David Hartley, William Harvey, Warren Hastings, William Henry Hatch, Mohammad Hatta, Gerhart Hauptmann, John Milton Hay, Thomas Emmet Hayden, (Franz) Joseph Haydn, Patrick Joseph Hayes, Rutherford B.Hayes, Samuel Hearne, William Randolph Hearst, Ben Hecht, Isaac Thomas Hecker, Margaret O'Shaughnessy Heckler, Hugh M. Hefner, Georg Wilhelm Friedrich Hegel, Werner Karl Heisenberg, Hermann von Helmholtz, Jesse A. Helms, Claude-Adrien Helvetius, Arthur Henderson, Richard Henderson, Henry IV, King of France, Henry IV, King of England, Henry V, Henry VII, King of England, Henry VIII, Herodotus, Edouard Herriot, John Frederick Herschel, William Herschel, Alfred Day Hershey, Heinrich Hertz, James Barry Munnik Hertzog, Theodor Herzl, Victor F. Hess, Paul Johann Ludwig von Heyse, Marguerite Higgins, Archibald V. Hill, Benjamin H. Hill, Nicholas Hilliard, Carla Anderson Hills, Heinrich Himmler, Paul Von Hindenburg, Cyril N. Hinshelwood, Hippocrates, Ando Hiroshige, Adolf Hitler, John Henry Hobart, William E. Hocking, Alan Lloyd Hodgkin, Ferdinand Hodler, Richard Hofstadter, Hokusai, Johann Christian Friedrich Holderin, Billie Holiday, John Philip Holland, John Haynes Holmes, Oliver Wendell Holmes, Oliver Wendell Holmes, Jr., Gustav Holst, Richard Hooker, Benjamin Lawson Hooks, Herbert Hoover, Esek Hopkins, Harry L.Hopkins, Francis Hopkinson, Grace Hopper, Herman Harrell Horne, Matina Souretis Horner, Vladimir Horowitz, Nicholas Horthy de Nagybanya, (Jean) Antoine Houdon, Edward Mandell House, Bernardo Houssay, Samuel Houston, Joseph Howe, Julia Ward Howe, Richard Howe, William Howe, Hu Shih , Edwin Powell Hubble, Langston Hughes, David Hume, Hubert Horatio Humphrey, William Holman Hunt, Zora Neale Hurston, King Hussein, Robert Maynard Hutchins, Ulrich von Hutton, James Hutton, Julian Huxley, Christiaan Huygens, Douglas Hyde, Libbie Henrietta Hyman, Abd al-Aziz ibn Saud, Henrik Ibsen, Daisaku Ikeda, Ivan Illich, Imhotep, William Ralph Inge, Jan Ingen-Housz, Robert Green Ingersoll, Jean Auguste Dominique Ingres, George Inness, Innocent III, Ismet Inonu, John Ireland, Hopolito Irigoyen, Washington Irving, Isabella I, Isabella II, Hirobumi Ito, Agustin de Iturbide, Charles Ives, Tomomi Iwakura, Andrew Jackson, Helen Maria Fiske Hunt Jackson, Abraham Jacobi, Friedrich Heinrich Jacobi, James II, James III, Henry James, Leon Jaworski, William Jay, Jean de Meun, (John) Robinson Jeffers, Thomas Jefferson, Harold Jeffreys, Edward Jenner, Saint Jerome, William Stanley Jevons, Mohammed Ali Jinnah, Joan of Arc, Joseph J.C. Joffre, Saint John, John Chrysostom , Augustus Edwin John, Andrew Johnson, Charles S(purgeon) Johnson, Hiram Johnson, Jack Johnson, James Weldon Johnson, William H. Johnson, Joseph Johnston, Frederick Joliot-Curie, Irene Joliot-Curie, Inigo Jones, Robert E. Jones, Robert Tyre Jones, Ben(jamin) Jonson, Jacob Jordaens, David S. Jordan, Vernon Jordan, James Prescott Joule, Juan Carlos I , Adoniram Judson, Justin , Augustine Justo, Frida Kahlo , Albert Kahn, Henry John Kaiser, David Kalakaua, Kumaraswami Kamaraj, Kamehameha I, K'ang Yu-wei, Immanuel Kant, Peter Kapista, Mordecai M. Kaplan, Stephen W. Kearny, Frances Kellor, Jack French Kemp, Jr., Amos Kendall, Edward C. Kendall, John Kendrew, John F. Kennedy, John Pendleton

Kennedy, Elizabeth Kenny, Johannes Kepler, Aleksandr F. Kerensky, Charles Franklin Kettering, Nikita Khrushchev, William H.Kilpatrick, Rufus King, Charles Kingsford Smith, Alfred Kinsey, Joseph Lane Kirkland, Henry Kissinger, Heinrich von Kleist, Seaman Knapp, John Knox, William S. Knudsen, (Heinrich Hermann) Robert Koch, Zoltan Kodaly, Kojong, Arthur Kornberg, Otto Von Kotzebue, Hans Adolf Krebs, (Schack) August (Steenberg) Krogh, Alfred Krupp, Kublai Khan, John La Farge, Francis LaFlesche, Louis Hippolyte LaFontaine, Joseph Louis Lagrange, Chevalier de Lamarck, Edwin H. Land, Lev Davidovich Landau, Karl Landsteiner, Dorothea Lange, Samuel (Pierpont) Langley, Irving Langmuir, John Mercer Langston, Sidney Lanier, Robert Lansing, Marquis de Laplace, Ring(gold Wilmer) Lardner, Francois-Alexandre-Frederic de La Rochefoucauld-Liancourt, Sieur de La Salle , Bartolome de Las Casas, Benjamin Henry Latrobe, William Laud, Juan Antonio Lavallega, Ernest Lavisse, Antoine Lavoisier, Ernest Orlando Lawrence, Jacob Lawrence, Henry Lawson, Thomas William Lawson, Louis Leakey, Mary Elizabeth Clyens Lease, Joshua Lederberg, Gottfried Leibniz, Curtis E. Lemay, Daniel Leonard, Leonardo da Vinci, Rene Levesque, John L. Lewis, Meriwether Lewis, (Harry) Sinclair Lewis, Li Hung-chan, Willard F. Libby, Francis Lieber, Justus von Liebig, David E. Lilienthal, Abraham Lincoln, Anne Morrow Lindbergh, Charles A(ugustus) Lindbergh, Benjamin Barr Lindsey, Carl Linnaeus, Joseph Lister, Franz Liszt, 2nd Earl of Liverpool, Livia, David Livingstone, Henry Demarest Lloyd, David Lloyd George, John Locke, Henry Cabot Lodge, Jr., Otto Loewi, Jack London, Adolfo Lopez Mateos, Audre Lorde, Hendrik Antoon Lorentz, Louis IX, Joe Louis, Pierre Charles Alexandre Louis, Abbott Lawrence Lowell, Josephine Lowell, Clare Boothe Luce, George Benjamin Luks, Edward (Landseer) Lutyens, Andre Lwoff, Charles Lyell, Mary Lyon, Antonio Maceo, Ernst Mach, Archibald MacLeish, Nathaniel Macon, Lachlan MacQuarie, Maurice Maeterlinck, Alfred Thayer Mahan, Mahendra, Norman Mailer, Stephane Mallarme, Manco Capac, (Luiz) Heinrich Mann, Thomas Mann, Carl Gustaf Emil von Mannerheim, Marcel Marceau, Guglielmo Marconi, Margaret of Denmark, Margaret of Scotland, Juan de Mariana, Marie Antoinette, Constance Markievicz, Jacques Marquette, Thurgood Marshall, Jose Marti, Mary Martin, Simone Martini, Mary Queen of Scots , Massasoit, William Ferguson Massey, Cotton Mather, Matilda of Tuscany, Henri Matisse, W(illiam) Somerset Maugham, Matthew Fontaine Maury, Hiram Stevens Maxim, Maxmilian II, James Clerk Maxwell, Mary McCarthy, George B. McClellan, Cyrus H. McCormick, Robert Rutherford McCormick, William McKinley, John McLoughlin, George Herbert Mead, Lise Meitner, George Wallace Melville, Dmitrii Ivanovich Mendeleev, Felix Mendelssohn(-Bartholdy), Pedro Menendez de Aviles, Mario Garcia Menocal, George Meredith, Ottmar Mer-

genthaler, Prosper Merimee, Elic Metchnikoff, Otto Meyerhof, Albert (Abraham) Michelson, P(avel) N(ikolayevich) Miliukov, John Stuart Mill, Edna St. Vincent Millay, Robert A. Millikan, John Milton, Peter Minuit, Joan Miro, Gabriela Mistral, John Mitchell, Maria Mitchell, Bartolome Mitre, Mohammed, Mohammed V, Mohammed Ali , Moliere, Claude Monet, Jacques Lucien Monod, James Monroe, Michel Eyquem de Montaigne, Juan Montalvo, Baron de Montesquieu, Maria Montessori, Jacques and Joseph Montgolfier, Thomas Moran, Thomas More, C(onway) Lloyd Morgan, (Lewis) Henry Morgan, Thomas Hunt Morgan, Hans J. Morgenthau, Henry Morgenthau, Samuel Finley Breese Morse, William T.G. Morton, Mohammad Mossadegh, William Sidney Mount, Wolfgang Amadeus Mozart, Hermann Joseph Muller, (Jose) Luis (Alberto) Munoz Marin, Frank Andrew Munsey, Charles F. Murphy, Frank Murphy, Benito Mussolini, John Napier, James Nasmyth, George (Jean) Nathan, Walther Hermann Nernst, Gerard de Nerval, Isaac Newton, Marshall Warren Nirenberg, Richard M. Nixon, Alfred Nobel, Nils Otto Nordenskjold, John Howard Northrop, Severo Ochoa, Hans Christian Oersted, James Oglethorpe, Bernardo O'Higgins, Georg Simon Ohm, Georgia O'Keeffe, Adriano Olivetti, Laurence Olivier, J(ulius) Robert Oppenheimer, Jose Clemente Orozco, Herbert Levi Osgood, Ignace Jan Paderewski, Niccolo Paganini, Walter Page, Ambroise Pare, Theodore Parker, Francis Parkman, Charles A. Parsons, Blaise Pascal, Louis Pasteur, George S. Patton, Paul III, Paul VI , Wolfgang Pauli, Linus Pauling, Ivan Petrovich Pavlov, Anna Pavlova, John H. Payne, Thomas Love Peacock, Charles Willson Peale, Wilder G. Penfield, Claude Pepper, William Perkins, Eva Peron, Jean Baptiste Perrin, Matthew Calbraith Perry, Ralph Barton Perry, John J(oseph) Pershing, Max Perutz, Johann H(einrich) Pestalozzi, Peter I, William Matthew Flinders Petrie, Photius, Pablo Picasso, Franklin Pierce, Joseph Pilsudski, Henri Pirenne, Camille Pissaro, Solomon Tshekisho Plaatje, Max Planck, Plato, Thomas C. Platt, Angelo Poliziano, James Knox Polk, Leonidas Polk, Albert Frederick Pollard, Marques de Pombal, Pompey, Candido Portinari, Charles (William) Post, Emily Post, Luiz Carlos Prestes, (Mary) Leontyne Price, Joseph Priestley, Miguel Primo De Rivera Y Orbaneja, Augustus Welby Northmore Pugin, George Pullman, Michael Idvorsky Pupin, Robert Purvis, Aleksandr Pushkin, Israel Putnam, I(sidor) I(saac) Rabi, C(handrasekhar) V(enkata) Raman, William Ramsay, Norman Foster Ramsey, Walther Rathenau, 3d Baron Rayleigh, Claro Mayo Recto, Robert Redfield, John (Silas) Reed, Bernard Dov Revel, Richard II, Ellen H. Richards, Theodore William Richards, Charles Robert Richet, Conrad Richter, Edward (Vernon) Rickenbacker, Hyman G(eorge) Rickover, David Riesman, Arthur Rimbaud, Bernardino Rivadavia, Diego Rivera, Jose Eustasio Rivera, Jose Fructuoso Rivera, Jose Protasio Rizal, Paul Robeson, Harriet H. Robinson, James Harvey Robinson,

Julio Argentino Roca, John D. Rockefeller, John Augustus Roebling, Wilhelm Konrad Rontgen, Will Rogers, Ruth Bryant Owen Rohde, Gustavo Rojas-Pinilla, Erwin Rommel, Carlos Pena Romulo, (Anna) Eleanor Roosevelt, Theodore Roosevelt, Ileana Ros-Lehtinen, Julius Rosenwald, (Francis) Peyton Rous, Lucille Roybal-Allard, Paul Marvin Rudolph, Abraham Ruef, Harold Ordway Rugg, Bertrand Russell, Charles Taze Russell, James Earl Russell, John Brown Russwurm, George Herman Ruth, Jr., Ernest Rutherford, John Rutledge, Albert Pinkham Ryder, Paul Sabatier, Florence Rena Sabin, Nicola Sacco and Bartolomeo Vanzetti, Carl Sagan, Augustus Saint-Gaudens, Charles Camille Saint-Saens, Kimmochi Saionji, Andrei Sakharov, Antonio de Oliveira Salazar, Robert Arthur Talbot Salisbury, Jonas Salk, Carl Sandburg, Augusto Cesar Sandino, Giuliano da Sangallo, Antonio Lopez de Santa Ana, George Santayana, Alberto Santos-Dumont, William Saroyan, Eisaku Sato, Saw Maung, Gerhard David von Scharnhorst, Solomon Schechter, Carl Wilhelm Scheele, Jacob H. Schiff, Martin Schongauer, Erwin Schrodinger, Patricia Schroeder, Franz Schubert, Gunther Schuller, Carl Schurz, Charles Michael Schwab, Theodor Ambrose Schwann, Rosika Schwimmer, Dred Scott, Winfield Scott, Glenn T. Seaborg, Chief Seattle, Richard John Seddon, Florence B.Seibert, Seleucus I, Nikolai Semenov, Ignaz Philipp Semmelweis, Leopold Senghor, Sequoyah, Junipero de Serra, Jean-Jacques Servan-Schreiber, Ernest Thompson Seton, Horatio Seymour, Shah Jahan, Ralph Shapey, Harlow Shapley, George Bernard Shaw, Charles (Monroe) Sheldon, Richard Brinsley Sheridan, Charles Scott Sherrington, Sivaji, William Shockley, Mikhail Aleksandrovich Sholokhov, Jean Julius Christian (Johann) Sibelius, Henry Sidgwick, Clifford Sifton, Igor Ivan Sikorsky, Beverly Sills, Ignazio Silone, Abba Hillel Silver, William Gilmore Simms, Jules (Francois) Simon, Konstantin Mikhailovich Simonov, George Gaylord Simpson, Ndabaningi Sithole, Samuel Slater, John Slidell, Robert Smalls, John Smibert, Adam Smith, Ian Douglas Smith, Joseph Smith, Lillian Smith, Smohalla, Jan Christian Smuts, Sturluson Snorri, Frederick Soddy, Werner Sombart, Duke of Somerset , Georges Sorel, Jacques Germain Soufflot, Martim Affonso de Sousa, Phouma Souvanna, Paul Henri Spaak, Mikhail Mikhailovich Speransky, Elmer Sperry, Frank Julian Sprague, Myles Standish, Henry Morton Stanley, Wendell Meredith Stanley, Gertrude Stein, Heinrich Friedrich Karl vom und zu Stein, Charles Proteus Steinmetz, James Stephens, Edward R.Stettinius, Thaddeus Stevens, Wallace Stevens, Harlan Fiske Stone, Lucy Stone, Samuel A. Stouffer, Mark Strand, Isidor Straus, Charles Sturt, Peter Stuyvesant, (El P.) Francisco Suarez, Harry Stack Sullivan, William A. (Billy) Sunday, John Augustus Sutter, Daisetz Teitaro Suzuki, Jan Pieterszoon Sweelinck, Jonathan Swift, Mary Elizabeth Switzer, Charles Edward Sydenham, Albert (von) Szent-Gyorgyi, Leo Szilard,

Lorado Taft, William Howard Taft, Maria Tallchief, Charles Maurice de Talleyrand(-Perigord), Tamerlane, Kenzo Tange, (Newton) Booth Tarkington, Niccolo Fontana Tartaglia, Edward Plunket Taylor, Zachary Taylor, Peter Ilyich Tchaikovsky, Bernardino Telesio, Edward Teller, Alfred Tennyson, Gerard Ter Borch, Valentina Tereshkova, Gabriel Terra, Tewfik Pasha, Eli Thayer, Max Theiler, Hugh Theorell, Christian Thomasius, Henry David Thoreau, Thutmose III, Giovanni Battista Tiepolo, Samuel Leonard Tilley, Jean Tinguely, Tirso de Molina, Arne Tiselius, Titian, Alexander Robertus Todd, Hideki Tojo, Vincente Lombardo Toledano, Sin-Itiro Tomonaga, George Macauley Trevelyan, Pierre Elliott Trudeau, Harry S. Truman, Moise K.Tshombe, Konstantin (Eduardovich) Tsiolkovsky, Harriet Tubman, Charles Tupper, John Henry Twachtman, Mark Twain, John Tyler, Ralph Winfred Tyler, Edward Burnett Tylor, John Tyndall, Jorge Ubico, Jose Hipolito Unanue, Harold Urey, Martin Van Buren, William Van Horne, Kiliaen Van Rensselaer, III, Cornelius Vanderbilt, Henry Vane, Jose Vasconcelos, Eleutherios Venizelos, Amerigo Vespucci, Jean(-Baptiste-Marie) Vianney, Giovanni Villani, Rudolf (Ludwig) Carl Virchow, Wernher Von Braun, Max Von Laue, (Wilhelm) Richard Wagner, Edward Gibbon Wakefield, Selman A. Waksman, George Wald, Alfred Russel Wallace, George Wallace, Otto Warburg, Earl Warren, Booker Taliaferro Washington, Benjamin Waterhouse, James Dewey Watson, James Watt, Daniel Webster, Steven Weinberg, Robert W. Welch, Roy Welensky, Mary Wells, Wenceslaus IV, John Wesley, George Westinghouse, Nancy Wexler, Edith Wharton, Phillis Wheatley, George Hoyt Whipple, Byron R. White, William Allen White, Walt(er) Whitman, Eli Whitney, Josiah Dwight Whitney, John Greenleaf Whittier, Norbert Wiener, Eugene Paul Wigner, Oscar Wilde, Thornton Wilder, Harvey Washington Wiley, Roy Wilkins, Adrian Willaert, William I, William the Silent, Richard Willstatter, (Thomas) Woodrow Wilson, John Winthrop, Sergey Yulyevich Witte, Christian Von Wolff, Harry A. Wolfson, Stefan Wolpe, Anna May Wong, Victoria Woodhull, Ellen Sullivan Woodward, Richard Wright, Thomas Wyatt, John Wyclif, Rosalyn S.Yalow, Isoroku Yamamoto, Robert Mearns Yerkes, Brigham Young, Stark Young, Thomas Young, Hideki Yukawa, Samuel Zemurray, Juan Zorrilla De San Martin, Francisco De Zurbaran

Lutfe Ozkak: Ezekiel Mphalele

Hilary Masters: Edgar Lee Masters, Leslie Marmon Silko

Peter Menzel: Jaron Lanier

Ministry of Internal Relations, Caracas, Venezuela: Simón Bolívar, Charles Bukowski

National Archives and Records Administration: Henry (Hank) Aaron, John Adams, Samuel Adams, Richmond Barthe, Clara Barton, Joseph Brant, John Brown, Sitting

Bull, Charles Cornwallis, Jefferson Davis, George III, Rudolf Hess, Alexander Hamilton, John Hancock, James Butler "Wild Bill" Hickok, Tsuyosi Inukai, John Jay, John Paul Jones, Martin Luther King, Jr., Henry Knox, Pierre Charles L'Enfant, Marquis de Lafayette, Robert E.Lee, Leopold III, Irene D. Long, Douglas MacArthur, Dolly Madison, James Madison, Manuelito, Osceola, Thomas Paine, Quanah Parker, Timothy Pickering, Red Cloud, Paul Revere, Count de Rochambeau, Betsy Ross, William Henry Seward, Elizabeth Cady Stanton, Harriet Beecher Stowe, Charles Sumner, Washakie

The National Portrait Gallery: Fisher Ames, Elbridge Gerry, Patrick Henry, Oliver Hazard Perry, A(sa) Philip Randolph, Daniel Shays, John Smith

New Directions Publishing Corporation: Thomas Merton

The New Republic: Herbert David Croly

The New York Public Library: Nellie Bly

New York Public Library Picture Collection: Averroes, Toyotomi Hideyoshi, Handsome Lake, Martin Luther

The Nobel Foundation: Bertha von Suttner

Oklahoma Historical Society: John Ross

Frederick D. Patterson Research Institute: Frederick D. Patterson

PGA Tour: Vijay Singh

Photo Researchers Inc.: William Huggins

Photographers/Aspen Inc.: Elaine Pagels

Pinderhughes Photography Inc.: bell hooks

Pontiac, Michigan, City of: Pontiac.

The Public Archives of Canada: Sandford Fleming

Public Domain: Creighton W. Abrams, Jalal-ud-din Muhammed Akbar, Jane Addams, John Quincy Adams, Joseph Addison, Konrad Adenauer, Albert, Leon Battista Alberti, Louisa May Alcott, Alexander VI, Ethan Allen, Richard Allen, Andre Marie Ampere, Queen Anne, Lodovico Ariosto, Richard Arkwright, Samuel Chapman Armstrong, Jane Austen, Avicenna, Arthur James Balfour, Honore de Balzac, George Bancroft, Benjamin Banneker, Fulgencio Batista y Zaldivar, Aubrey Beardsley, Pierre Augustin Caron De Beaumarchais, Pierre Gustave Toutant Beauregard, Thomas Becket, Judah Philip Benjamin, Enoch Arnold Bennett, Jeremy Bentham, Annie Wood Besant, Otto Eduard Leopold von Bismarck, William Blake, Nicolas Boileau-Despreaux, Robert Borden, Ceasare Borgia, William Bradford, Louis Braille, Donato Bramante, Aristide Briand, Emily Bronte, Charles Brockden Brown, Robert Browning, Blanche Kelso Bruce, Pearl S. Buck, Buddha, Georges Louis Leclerc Buffon, John Burgoyne, Robert Burns, George Washington Cable, George Calvert, Canute I the Great, Caracalla, Lewis Carroll, Catherine of Siena, William Caxton, Nicolae Ceausescu, Miguel de Cervantes, Samuel de Champlain, George Chapman, Charles I, Charles V, Charles VII, Charles XII, Samuel Chase, Geoffrey Chaucer, Gilbert Keith Chesterton, Katherine (Kate) Chopin, Marcus Tullius Cicero, 1st Earl of Clarendon, Georges Rogers Clark, Dewitt Clinton, Samuel Taylor Coleridge, Sidonie-Gabrielle Colette, William Collins, Samuel Colt, Confucius, Constantine I, James Fenimore Cooper, Aaron Copland, Arcangelo Corelli, Pierr Corneille, Jean Baptiste Camille Corot, Hernan Cortes, Benedetto Croce, David (Davy) Crockett, Oliver Cromwell, Cyrus the Great, Giorgione, Charles Anderson Dana, Georges Jacques Danton, Ruben Dario, Benjamin O. Davis, Sr., Dorothy Day, Stephen Decatur, (Hilaire Germain) Edgar Degas, Deng Xiaoping, John Dewey, Benjamin Disraeli, Arthur Conan Doyle, John Foster Dulles, Alexandre Dumas, Jean Baptiste Andre Dumas, Edward, The Black Prince, Edward The Confessor, Edward VII, El Cid, John Eliot, Robert Emmet, Friedrich Engels, Desiderius Erasmus, Francois Fenelon, Enrico Fermi, Cyrus Field, Stephen Johnson Field, F. Scott Fitzgerald, Henry Ford, Charles James Fox, George Fox, Jean-Honore Fragonard, Francis Joseph I, Francisco Franco, William Franklin, Frederick II, the Great, Martin Frobisher, Charles Frohman, Thomas Gage, John Galsworthy, Giuseppe Garibaldi, Marcus Garvey, Henry George, Edward Gibbon, William Glackens, Carlo Goldoni, William Crawford Gorgas, Charles Gounod, Henry Woodfin Grady, Dick Gregory, Ernesto "Che" Guevara, Francois Pierre Guizot, Sarah Josepha Hale, Frans Hals, Marcus Alonzo Hanna, John Marshall Harlan, Hatshepsut, Nathaniel Hawthorne, J(oseph) E. Casely Hayford, Edward (Richard George) Heath, Sven Hedin, Heinrich Heine, Jan Van Helmont, Henry V, Josiah Henson, Johann Gottfried Von Herder, Robert Herrick, Morris Hillquit, Hirohito, Ho Chi Minh, Oveta Culp Hobby, Hugo von Hofmannsthal, William Hogarth, Gerard Manley Hopkins, Oliver Otis Howard, Charles Evans Hughes, Victor Hugo, Cordell Hull, Collis Potter Huntington, Thomas Henry Huxley, Joris Karl Huysmans, Ivan III, T(homas) J(onathan) "Stonewall" Jackson, Henry James, William James, Jesse James, Joseph Jefferson, Jesus of Nazareth, Sarah Jewett, Lyndon B. Johnson, Benito Juarez, Gottfried Keller, William Kelly, Robert Kennedy, Ayatollah Khomeini, Soren Kierkegaard, Ernest Joseph King, Rudyard Kipling, Louis Kossuth, Jean De La Fontaine, Comtesse de LaFayette, Jules Laforgue, Bert Lahr, Alphonse Marie de Lamartine, Walter Savage Landor, Henry Laurens, Antoine Laurent Lavoisier, David Herbert Lawrence, James Lawrence, Richard Henry Lee, Tsung Dao Lee, Fernand Leger, Valdimir (Ilich Ulyanv) Lenin, Leopold II, Gotthold Ephraim Lessing, Louis XIV,

Nat Love, Patrice Lumumba, Louis Hubert Gonzalve Lyautey, Thomas Babington Macaulay, Macbeth, John Alexander MacDonald, Niccolo Machiavelli, Ferdinand Magellan, Gustav Mahler, Maimonides, Mao Tse-tung, Jean Paul Marat, Edwin Markham, George Marshall, John Marshall, Henri Rene Albert Guy de Maupassant, Maximilian I, Vladimir Mayakovsky, Charles Horace Mayo, Benjamin E.Mays, Thomas Joseph Mboya, Joseph McCarthy, John Bach McMaster, George Gordon Meade, Lorenzo de Medici, Gerhardus Mercator, Klemens von Metternich, Giacomo Meyerbeer, Jules Michelet, Nelson Appleton Miles, Comte De Montalembert, Marquis de Montcalm De Saint-Veran, Bernard Law Montgomery, Susanna Strickland Moodie, Napoleon I, Napoleon III, Nebuchadnezzar, Florence Nightingale, Chester W. Nimitz, Kwame Nkrumah, Daniel O'Connell, Flannery O'Connor, Jacqueline Kennedy Onassis, Osman I, James Otis, Otto I, Ovid, 3d Viscount Palmerston, Robert Newton Peck, Pedro II, William Penn, Henri Philippe Petain, Peter I, Zebulon M. Pike, Charles C. Pinckney, William Pitt the Elder, Pius XII, Francisco Pizarro, Pocahontas, Edgar Allan Poe, Georges Pompidou, Giacomo Puccini, Casimir Pulaski, Manuel Luis Quezon, Horacio Quiroga, Walter Raleigh, Sri Ramakrishna, Ramses II, Knud Rasmussen, Maurice Ravel, Sam(uel Taliaferro) Rayburn, Ernest Renan, Hiram R. Revels, Joshua Reynolds, Johann Paul Friedrich Richter, Jacob August Riis, James Whitcomb Riley, David Rittenhouse, Robert I, Frederick Sleigh Roberts, Franklin D(elano) Roosevelt, Elihu Root, Jean-Jacques Rousseau, Benjamin Rush, Saladin, John Singer Sargent, (Johann Christoph) Friedrich von Schiller, William Tecumseh Sherman, Taishi Shotoku, Bedrich Smetana, Bessie Smith, Anastasio Somoza, Jared Sparks, Edmund Spenser, Baruch Spinoza, Joseph Stalin, Edwin M. Stanton, (Joseph) Lincoln Steffens, Potter Stewart, Suharto, Louis Henri Sullivan, Sun Yat-sen, (Edmund) John Millington Synge, Roger Brooke Taney, Louis Adolphe Thiers, Thomas Aquinas, Norman Thomas, Paul Tillich, Marshal Tito, Tokugawa Ieyasu, François Toussaint L'Ouverture, Trajan, Leon Trotsky, Sojourner Truth, Henry McNeal Turner, Anthony Van Dyck, Jules Verne, Pancho Villa, Alessandro Volta, Voltaire, Ida B. Wells-Barnett, Virginia Woolf, William Wordsworth, Xerxes, Emiliano Zapata

Faith Ringgold: Faith Ringgold

The Saturday Evening Post: Orson Welles

Schomburg Center for Research in Black Culture: Susie King Taylor

State Historical Society of Wisconsin: Robert M. La Follette, Sr.

Stock Montage: Vilfredo Pareto

The Supreme Court Historical Society Collection: David H. Souter.

Sandra S. Swans: Toni Cade Bambara

Anne Tyler: Anne Tyler

Marty Umans: Ming Cho Lee

United Nations: Andrei Andreevich Gromyko, Alexei Kosygin, Ramon Magsaysay, Gamal Abdel Nasser, Dean Rusk, Kurt Waldheim

U.S. Army: Philip Sheridan

U.S. National Aeronautics and Space Administration: Neil A. Armstrong, Alexander Graham Bell, Guion S. Bluford, John Glenn, Ellen Ochoa, Sally Ride

Thomas Victor: Susan Eloise Hinton

True Yasui: Minoru Yazui

HOW TO USE THE INDEX

The *Encyclopedia of World Biography (EWB)* Index is designed to serve two purposes. First, it locates information on thousands of specific topics mentioned in the encyclopedia—persons, places, events, organizations, institutions, ideas, titles of works, inventions, and schools, styles, and movements in an art or a field of knowledge. Second, it classifies the subjects of *EWB* articles according to shared characteristics. Vocational categories are the most numerous—for example, Artists, Authors, Military leaders, Philosophers, Scientists, Statesmen. But there are other groupings, besides the vocational, bringing together disparate people who share a common characteristic—for example, Assassinations, Child prodigies, Immigrants.

The structure of the Index is quite simple. The biographical entries often provide enough information to meet immediate reference needs. Thus people mentioned in the Index are identified and their life dates, when known, are given. Because this is an index to a *biographical* encyclopedia, every reference includes the *name* of the article to which the reader is directed as well as the volume and page numbers. Below are a few points that will make the Index easy to use.

Typography. All main entries are set in boldface type. Entries that are also the titles of articles in EWB are set entirely in capitals; other main entries are set in initial capitals and lowercase letters. Where a main entry is followed by a great many references, these are organized by subentries in alphabetical sequence. In certain cases—for example, the names of countries for which there are many references—a special class of subentries, set in small capitals and preceded by boldface dots, is used to mark significant divisions.

Alphabetization. The Index is alphabetized word by word. For example, all entries beginning with *New* as a separate word (*New Jersey, New York*) come before *Newark*. Commas in inverted entries are treated as full stops (*Berlin; Berlin, congress of; Berlin, University of; Berlin Academy of Sciences*). Other commas are ignored in filing. When file words are identical, persons come first and subsequent entries are alphabetized by their parenthetical qualifiers (such as *book, city, painting*).

Titled persons may be alphabetized by family name or by title. The more familiar form is used—for example, *Disraeli, Benjamin* rather than *Wellesley, Arthur*. Cross-references are provided from alternative forms and spellings of names. Identical names of the same nationality are filed chronologically.

Titles of books, plays, and poems, and of paintings and other works of art beginning with an article are filed on the following word (*Bard, The*). Titles beginning with a preposition are filed on the preposition (*In Autumn*). In subentries, however, prepositions are ignored; thus *influenced by* would precede the subentry *in literature*.

Literary characters are filed on the last name. Acronyms, such as UNESCO, are treated as single words. Abbreviations, such as *Mr., Mrs.,* and *St.,* are alphabetized as though they were spelled out.

Cross-references. Both *see* and *see also* references are used throughout the Index. The *see* references appear both as main entries and as subentries. The *see also* references appear as subentries. These provide access to information related to the subject of original interest. Cross-references to occupational categories omit the national qualifier. Thus, the reader interested in Spanish poets will be directed by the main entry *Poets* to *Authors—poets,* where she will find the subentry *poets* under *Authors, Spanish.*

This introduction to the Index is necessarily brief. The reader will soon find, however, that the Index provides ready reference to both highly specific subjects and broad areas of information. For quick reference or for conscientious study, the Index should be consulted first to make best use of *EWB*.

INDEX

INDEX

A

"A"
see Arnold, Matthew

"A.B."
see Pinto, Isaac

A.B. Dick Co.
Edison, Thomas Alva **5** 206-208

A cappella (music)
Schütz, Heinrich **14** 48-49

A ceux de mon pays (poem)
Morin, Paul **11** 174

A la altura de las circunstancias (book)
Guillén, Nicolás **7** 34-35

À la Malibran (poem)
Musset, Louis Charles Alfred de
11 271-272

À la recherche du temps perdu (novel)
Proust, Marcel **12** 465-467

À l'échelle humaine (book)
Blum, Léon **2** 343-344

À l'ombre des jeunes filles en fleur (novel)
Proust, Marcel **12** 465-467

A priori (philosophy)
Kant, Immanuel **8** 430-432
Lewis, Clarence Irving **9** 381
Mill, John Stuart **11** 21-23

À quoi rêvent les jeunes filles (verse)
Musset, Louis Charles Alfred de
11 271-272

À rebours (novel; Huysmans)
Huysmans, Joris Karl **8** 81-82
Mallarmé, Stéphane **10** 172-173

A secreto agravio, secreta venganza (play)
Calderón, Pedro **3** 221-222

À vau-l'eau (novel)
Huysmans, Joris Karl **8** 81-82

Aachen (Aix-la-Chapelle, Germany)
Charlemagne **3** 445-447
see also Aix-la-Chapelle, Congress of;
Aix-la-Chapelle, Treaty of

Aachen, Councils of (816; 817)
Louis I **9** 522-523

AALTO, HUGO ALVAR HENRIK (born
1898), Finnish architect, designer, and
town planner **1** 1-2

Aaron (14th-13th century B.C.), Hebrew
priest
Moses **11** 200-201

AARON, HENRY LOUIS (Hank; born
1934), American baseball player **1** 2-3

Aaron's Rod (novel)
Lawrence, David Herbert **9** 247-248

Ab urbe condita (book)
Livy **9** 465-467

ABAKO (Bakongo association)
Kasavubu, Joseph **8** 453-455
Lumumba, Patrice Emery **10** 43-45

Abancay, battle of (1537)
Almagro, Diego de **1** 177-178

Abandon, L' (poem)
Crémazie, Octave **4** 305-306

Abandoned Ones (sculpture)
Barlach, Ernst **2** 5-6

Abarbanel
see Abravanel

ABBA ARIKA (circa 175-circa 247), Babylonian rabbi **1** 3-4
Judah I **8** 372-373

Abbas, Abd al- (566?-652), uncle of
Mohammed
Mansur, Abu Jafar ibn Muhammad al-
10 214-215

ABBAS, FERHAT (born 1899), Algerian
statesman **1** 6-7
Ben Bella, Ahmed **2** 148-149

ABBAS I (1571-1629), Safavid shah of Persia 1588-1629 **1** 4-6

Abbas II (1874-1944), khedive of Egypt
Abduh ibn Hasan Khayr Allah, Muham-
mad **1** 16-17
Fuad I **6** 139

Abbas II (book)
Cromer, 1st Earl of **4** 317

Abbas al Saffah, Abu al- (721?-754),
Abbasid caliph 750-754
Mansur, Abu Jafar ibn Muhammad al-
10 214-215

Abbas the Great
see Abbas I

Abbasids (Islamic dynasty; ruled 750-1258)
caliphs
Harun al-Rashid **7** 188
Mamun, Abdallah al- **10** 183
Mansur, Abu Jafar ibn Muhammad
al- **10** 214-215
caliphs as figureheads
Ghazali, Abu Hamid Muhammad
al- **6** 290-291
Mongols defeat
Hulagu Khan **8** 27-28
Mutazilites supported
Ashari, Abu al- Hasan Ali al-
1 327-328
poets
Abu Nuwas **1** 33-34
Umayyad rivalry
Abd al-Rahman I **1** 13-14
Abd al-Rahman III **1** 14

Abbatini, Antonio Maria (1595-1680), Italian musician
Cesti, Pietro **3** 399-400

Abbé Sieyès
see Sieyès, Comte Emmanuel Joseph

Abbey Theatre (Dublin, Ireland)
Colum, Padraic **4** 174-175
Gregory, Augusta **6** 535-536
O'Casey, Sean **11** 459-460
Synge, Edmund John Millington **15** 61-62
Yeats, William Butler **16** 445-447, 482

Abbot, The (novel)
Scott, Walter **14** 68-70

Abbotsford (estate, near Melrose, Scotland)
Scott, Walter **14** 68-70

ABBOTT, BERENICE (1898-1991), American artist and photographer **1** 7-9

ABBOTT, GRACE (1878-1939), American
social worker and agency administrator
1 9-10

Abbott, Jacob (1803-1879), American Congregationalist clergyman
Abbott, Lyman **1** 10-11

ABBOTT, LYMAN (1835-1922), American Congregationalist clergyman, author, and editor **1** 10-11
    Gladden, Washington **6** 356-357
    Holmes, John Haynes **7** 456-457

ABBOUD, EL FERIK IBRAHIM (1900-1983), Sudanese general, prime minister, 1958-1964 **1** 11-12
    Azhari, Sayyid Ismail al- **1** 399-401
    Khalil, Sayyid Abdullah **8** 531-532

Abby (literary character)
    O'Neill, Eugene **11** 514-516

ABC mediation (1914)
    Wilson, Thomas Woodrow **16** 330-332

ABC of Color, An (literary collection)
    Du Bois, William Edward Burghardt **5** 116-118

ABC's of Observation (book)
    Herbart, Johann Friedrich **7** 321-322

Abd Allah (ruled 888-912), Umayyad emir in Spain
    Abd al-Rahman III **1** 14

ABD AL-MALIK (646-705), Umayyad caliph 685-705 **1** 12-13

ABD AL-MUMIN (circa 1094-1163), Almohad caliph 1133-63 **1** 13
    ibn Tumart, Muhammad **8** 96-97

ABD AL-RAHMAN I (731-788), Umayyad emir in Spain 756-88 **1** 13-14

ABD AL-RAHMAN III (891-961), Umayyad caliph of Spain **1** 14

Abd al-Rahman ibn Khaldun
    see Ibn Khaldun, Abd al-Rahman ibn Muhammad

ABD EL-KADIR (1807-1883), Algerian political and religious leader **1** 15
    Bugeaud de la Piconnerie, Thomas Robert **3** 111

ABD EL-KRIM EL-KHATABI, MOHAMED BEN (circa 1882-1963), Moroccan Berber leader **1** 15-16
    Lyautey, Louis Hubert Gonzalve **10** 60-61
    Primo de Rivera y Orbaneja, Miguel **12** 454-455

Abdala (poem)
    Martí, José **10** 285-286

Abdallah ben Yassin
    see Abdullah ibn Yasin

Abdications (politics)
    Belgium
        Leopold III **9** 347-348
    Brazil
        Pedro I **12** 179-180
    Cambodia
        Sihanouk, Norodom **14** 222-223
    China
        Hsüan-tsung, T'ang **8** 7-8
    Egypt
        Farouk I **5** 387-388
    Ethiopia
        Lalibela **9** 170

    France
        Napoleon I **11** 306-310
    Germany
        William II **16** 294-295
    Great Britain
        Edward VIII **5** 215-217
        Richard II **13** 130-131
    Hejaz
        Husein ibn Ali **8** 63
    Holy Roman Empire
        Charles V **3** 457-459
    Iran
        Reza Shah Pahlavi **13** 116-117
    Italy
        Victor Emmanuel III **15** 484-485
    Korea
        Sejo **14** 90-91
    Libya
        Idris I **8** 102
    Netherlands
        William I **16** 291-292
    Norway
        Harold I **7** 161-162
    Portugal
        Pedro I **12** 179-180
    Russia
        Nicholas II **11** 378-380
    Sardinia
        Charles Albert, King of Sardinia **3** 466
        Victor Amadeus II **15** 482-483
    Spain
        Alfonso XIII **1** 151
        Charles IV **3** 456-457
        Ferdinand VII **5** 418-420
        Isabella II **8** 145-146
        Philip V **12** 276-277
    Vietnam
        Bao Dai **1** 496-497

Abduction from the Seraglio (opera)
    Mozart, Wolfgang Amadeus **11** 218-221

Abduction of Helen of Troy (lithograph)
    Daumier, Honoré Victorin **4** 403-405

ABDUH IBN HASAN KHAYR ALLAH, MUHAMMAD (1849-1905), Egyptian nationalist and theologian **1** 16-17
    Zaghlul Pasha, Saad **16** 485-486

Abdu-I-Malik
    see Abd al-Malik

Abdul Hamid I (1725-1789), Ottoman sultan 1774-1789
    Selim III **14** 95-96

Abdul the Damned
    see Abdul-Hamid II

ABDUL-HAMID II (1842-1918), Ottoman sultan 1876-1909 **1** 17-18
    Enver Pasha **5** 290-291
    Gökalp, Mehmet Ziya **6** 395-396
    Herzl, Theodor **7** 352-354

'ABDULLAH AL-SALIM AL-SABAH, SHAYKH (1895-1965), Amir of Kuwait (1950-1965) **1** 18-19

ABDULLAH IBN HUSEIN (1882-1951), king of Jordan 1949-1951, of Transjordan 1946-49 **1** 19-20
    Husein ibn Ali **8** 63
    Lawrence, Thomas Edward **9** 253-254

ABDULLAH IBN YASIN (died 1059), North African founder of the Almoravid movement **1** 20
    ibn Tashufin, Yusuf **8** 95-96

Abdullahi (ruled 1885-1898), caliph of Mahdist state
    Mahdi **10** 137-138

Abdul-Medjid I (1823-1861), Ottoman sultan 1839-1861
    Abdul-Hamid II **1** 17-18
    Mahmud II **10** 145-147

Abe, Iso (1865-1949), Japanese politician
    Katayama, Sen **8** 457

ABE, KOBO (born Kimifusa Abe; also transliterated as Abe Kobo; 1924-1993), Japanese writer, theater director, photographer **1** 20-22

Abe Lincoln in Illinois (play)
    Sherwood, Robert Emmet **14** 189-190

Abeille canadienne, L' (journal)
    Garneau, François-Xavier **6** 219-220

Abel (play)
    Alfieri, Vittoria **1** 145-146

Abel, Christian Ferdinand (flourished 1715-1737), German cellist
    Bach, Johann Sebastian **1** 416-419

Abel, Sir Frederick Augustus (1827-1902), English chemist
    Hofmann, August Wilhelm von **7** 441-442

Abel, Friedrich (1725-1787), German composer and violist
    Bach, Johann Christian **1** 415-416

ABEL, IORWITH WILBER (1908-1987), United States labor organizer **1** 22-23

Abel, Niels Henrik (1802-1829), Norwegian mathematician
    Cauchy, Augustin Louis **3** 378-380
    Gauss, Karl Friedrich **6** 240-242

ABELARD, PETER (1079-1142), French philosopher and theologian **1** 23-25
    Arnold of Brescia **1** 314-315
    Bernard of Clairvaux **2** 207-208
    John of Salisbury **8** 284-285
    Lombard, Peter **9** 490-491
    Pope, Alexander **12** 395-397

Abend musiken (musicals)
    Buxtehude, Dietrich **3** 185-186

Abenteuerliche Simplicissimus Teutsch, Der
    see Simplicissimus

ABERDEEN, 4TH EARL OF (George Hamilton Gordon; 1784-1860), British statesman, prime minister 1852-55 **1** 25-26
    Gladstone, William Ewart **6** 357-360
    Palmerston, 3d Viscount **12** 81-83
    Russell, John **13** 380-381

Victoria **15** 485-487

Aberdeen, University of (Scotland)
established (1858)
  Maxwell, James Clerk **10** 361-364
faculty
  Gilson, Étienne Henry **6** 327-328
  MacIver, Robert Morrison
    10 100-101
  Marcel, Gabriel **10** 233-234
  Soddy, Frederick **14** 321-323
  Thomson, George Paget **15** 198-199

Aberdeen Act (1845)
Pedro II **12** 180-181

ABERHART, WILLIAM (1878-1943), Canadian statesman and educator **1** 26-27
Crerar, Thomas Alexander **4** 306

ABERNATHY, RALPH DAVID (born 1926), United States minister and civil rights leader **1** 27-28
King, Martin Luther Jr. **9** 20-22, 207

Abhandlungen über die Fabel (book)
Lessing, Gotthold Ephraim **9** 357-359

Abhandlungen über die mechanische Wármetheorie (book)
Clausius, Rudolf Julius Emanuel
  4 92-94

Abhijnanasakuntalam (play)
Kalidasa **8** 414-415

Abijah (Old Testament character)
Samuel **13** 457-458

Abilene, (town, Kansas)
Hickok, James Butler **7** 374-375
McCoy, Joseph Geiting **10** 403-404

Abinger Harvest (essays)
Forster, Edward Morgan **6** 14-16

Abituriententag, Der (novel)
Werfel, Franz **16** 204-205

Abner (Old Testament character)
David, Jacques Louis **4** 407-409

Abnormal Children (book)
Binet, Alfred **2** 277-278

Abo (Finland)
see Turku

Abolition, Act of (England, 1833)
Wilberforce, William **16** 269-270

Abolitionism (book)
Nabuco de Araujo, Joaquim Aurelio
  11 288-289

Abolitionists, African
Crowther, Samuel Adjai **4** 326
Cugoano, Ottobah **4** 332-333

Abolitionists, American
African Americans
  Banneker, Benjamin **1** 490-491
  Brown, William Wells **3** 48-49
  Burns, Anthony **3** 151
  Cinque, Joseph **4** 62
  Douglass, Frederick **5** 85-86
  Forten, James **6** 17-18
  Jacobs, Harriet A. **8** 190-193

Henson, Josiah **7** 311-312
Prosser, Gabriel **12** 460-461
Purvis, Robert **12** 485-486
Remond, Charles Lennox **13** 95
Scott, Dred **14** 65-66
Still, William **14** 454-455
Truth, Sojourner **15** 320-321
Tubman, Harriet Ross **15** 330-331
Turner, Nathaniel **15** 354
Vesey, Denmark **15** 475
Walker, David **16** 62-63
colonizationists
  Ashmun, Jehudi **1** 335-336
  Birney, James Gillespie **2** 283-284
  Clay, Henry **4** 94-96
  Cuffe, Paul **4** 331-332
  Delany, Martin Robinson **4** 473-474
  Dew, Thomas Roderick **4** 519
  Drake, Daniel **5** 93-94
  Forten, James **6** 17-18
  Hopkins, Samuel **7** 496
  Lundy, Benjamin **10** 45-46
critics
  Dunning, William Archibald
    5 148-149
  Weed, Thurlow **16** 169-170
  see also Slavery—United States supporters
gradualists
  Bailey, Gamaliel **1** 444-445
  Jay, William **8** 232-233
moral suasion
  Anthony, Susan Brownell **1** 246-248
  Cartwright, Peter **3** 344-345
  Channing, William Ellery **3** 435-436
  Child, Lydia Maria Francis
    3 520-521
  Coxe, Tench **4** 285-286
  Crandall, Prudence **4** 291
  Dow, Neal **5** 89-90
  Franklin, Benjamin **6** 60-64
  Grimké, Sarah Moore and Angelina Emily **7** 2-3
  Lovejoy, Elijah Parish **10** 6-7
  Parker, Theodore **12** 112-113
  Phillips, Wendell **12** 281-282
  Stone, Lucy **14** 471-472
  Tappan brothers **15** 105-106
  Thoreau, Henry David **15** 203-205
  Weld, Theodore Dwight **16** 186
  Woolman, John **16** 382-383
  Wright, Elizur **16** 396-397
radical action
  Bowditch, Henry Ingersoll
    2 459-460
  Brown, John **3** 39-41
  Cinque, Joseph **4** 62
  Foster, Abigail Kelley **6** 25
  Garrett, Thomas **6** 225-226
  Garrison, William Lloyd **6** 226-228
  Higginson, Thomas Wentworth
    7 380
  Howe, Samuel Gridley **7** 537
  Mott, Lucretia Coffin **11** 212-213
  Phillips, Wendell **12** 281-282
  Pinkerton, Allan **12** 314-315

Smith, Gerrit **14** 290-291
Southern opponents of slavery
  Coffin, Levi **4** 135
  Fee, John Gregg **5** 402-403
  Helper, Hinton Rowan **7** 272-273
  Johnson, Andrew **8** 294-295
  see also Antislavery movement (United States)

Abolitionists, Arab
Abu Bakr **1** 31-32

Abolitionists, Brazilian
Barbosa, Ruy **1** 503-504
Castro Alves, Antônio de **3** 364-365
Nabuco de Araujo, Joaquim Aurelio
  11 288-289
Pedro II **12** 180-181

Abolitionists, Cuban
Gómez, Máximo **6** 418-419

Abolitionists, English
Dickens, Charles John Huffam
  4 538-541
Equiano, Olaudah **5** 296-297
Martineau, Harriet **10** 296-297
see also Antislavery movement (British)

Abolitionists, French
Condorcet, Marquis de **4** 195-196
Lavigerie, Charles Martel Allemand
  9 240
Montalembert, Comte de **11** 118-119

Abominations, Tariff of
see Tariff of Abominations (1828)

Aborigines, Australian
Bates, Daisy Mae **2** 52-53
Drysdale, George Russell **5** 107-109
Namatjira, Albert **11** 300-301

Abortion of the Young Steam Engineer's Guide, The (book)
Evans, Oliver **5** 338

Aboth de Rabbi Nathan (book)
Schechter, Solomon **13** 524

Aboukir Bay, battle of (1798)
Napoleon I **11** 306-310
Nelson, Horatio **11** 336-338

About Nature (book)
Anaxagoras **1** 208-209

About Paris (book)
Davis, Richard Harding **4** 422-423

Above the Battle (essays)
Rolland, Romain **13** 260

Abraham, Karl (1877-1925), German psychoanalyst
Bleuler, Eugen **2** 325

Abraham and Isaac (musical composition)
Stravinsky, Igor Fedorovich **14** 502-506

Abraham Lincoln (book; Hay-Nicolay)
Hay, John **7** 215-216

Abraham Lincoln (film)
Griffith, David Wark **6** 544-545

Abraham Lincoln (symphony)
Harris, Roy **7** 175-176

Abraham, Plains of
see Quebec, Battle of (1759)

ABRAHAMS, ISRAEL (1858-1925), British scholar **1** 29

Abramovitch, Sholem Jacob
see Mendele Mocher Sefarim

ABRAMS, CREIGHTON W. (1914-1974), United States Army commander in World War II and Vietnam **1** 29-31

Abrams v. United States (legal case)
Holmes, Oliver Wendell Jr. **7** 458-459

ABRAVANEL, ISAAC BEN JUDAH (1437-1508), Jewish philosopher and statesman **1** 31

Abrechnung folgt (lithographs)
Grosz, George **7** 17-18

Abreha
see Ezana

Abridged Catechism, An (book)
Canisius, Peter **3** 258

Abridgement of the History of England, The (book)
Burke, Edmund **3** 138-141

Abridgement of the Public Laws of Virginia, An (book)
Beverley, Robert **2** 252

Abridgement of the Talmud (book; Tschernowitz)
Kaufmann, Ezekiel **8** 460

Abridgement of the Vedanta (book)
Roy, Ram Mohun **13** 18

Absalom (Old Testament character)
David, Jacques Louis **4** 407-409

Absalom, Absalom! (novel)
Faulkner, William **5** 395-397

Absalom and Achitophel (satire)
Dryden, John **5** 106-107

Absentee, The (play)
Edgeworth, Maria **5** 205-206

Absentee Ownership (book)
Veblen, Thorstein Bunde **15** 449-450

Absents, Les (play)
Daudet, Alphonse **4** 402-403

Absinthe (painting)
Degas, Hilaire Germain Edgar **4** 461-462

Absinthe Drinker (painting)
Manet, Édouard **10** 193-194

Absolute (philosophy)
Royce, Josiah **13** 334-335

Absolute certitude (philosophy)
Chrysippus **4** 35-36

Absolute Ego (philosophy)
Schelling, Friedrich Wilhelm Joseph von **13** 526-527

Absolute idealism (philosophy)
Bradley, Francis Herbert **2** 481-482

Absolute monarchy
see Monarchy, absolute

Absolute reality (philosophy)
Bradley, Francis Herbert **2** 481-482

Absolute Spirit (philosophy)
Hegel, Georg Wilhelm Friedrich **7** 254-256

Absolute Spirit (theology)
Krochmal, Nachman Kohen **9** 104-105

Absolutism (government)
Asia and Africa
  Abbas I **1** 4-6
  Mohammed V **11** 79-81
  Seleucus I **14** 92-93
Europe
  Alexander III **1** 133-134
  Frederick William **6** 85-86
  Louis XIV **9** 531-533
  Mirabeau, Comte de **11** 51-52
Latin America
  Carrera, José Rafael **3** 324-325
  Reyes, Rafael **13** 113
opponents
  Lafayette, Marquis de **9** 151-152
  Orléans, Philippe II D' **11** 530-531
  Palmerston, 3d Viscount **12** 81-83
  Stein, Heinrich Friedrich Karl vom und zum **14** 415-416
supporters
  Filmer, Robert **5** 448
  Hobbes, Thomas **7** 421-423
  Laud, William **9** 224-225
  Mansart, Jules Hardouin **10** 212
  see also Autocracy; Monarchy, absolute

Absolutism, ethical (philosophy)
Cudworth, Ralph **4** 331

Abstract art
basis established
  Picasso, Pablo **12** 292-295
development
  Cézanne, Paul **3** 400-402
  Delaunay, Robert **4** 475-476
  see also individual schools, styles, and movements

Abstract expressionism (art)
Bussotti, Sylvano **3** 174-175
de Kooning, Willem **4** 468-469
Diebenkorn, Richard **5** 2-4
Gottlieb, Adolph **6** 462-463
Guston, Philip **7** 47-48
Hesse, Eva **7** 365-367
Johns, Jasper **8** 291-293
Kline, Franz **9** 55
Krasner, Lee **9** 93-94
Lippold, Richard **9** 440-442
Louis, Morris **9** 538-539
Motherwell, Robert **11** 210-211
Newman, Barnett **11** 365
Pollock, Jackson **12** 379-380
Rothko, Mark **13** 320-321
Still, Clyfford **14** 453-454

Abstraction (art)
Cézanne, Paul **3** 400-402
Dove, Arthur Garfield **5** 86-87

Kupka, Frantisek **9** 134-135
Manet, Édouard **10** 193-194
Noguchi, Isamu **11** 416-418
Rodchenko, Alexander Mikhailovich **13** 233-234
Sheeler, Charles **14** 170-171
Tobey, Mark **15** 249-250
Vasarely, Victor **15** 440-442

Abstraction (philosophy)
Locke, John **9** 478-480

Abstraction (sculpture)
Duchamp-Villon, Raymond **5** 123
González, Julio **6** 428-429
Rodchenko, Alexander Mikhailovich **13** 233-234

Abstraction-Création group (art)
Arp, Jean **1** 317-318
Gabo, Naum **6** 158-159
González, Julio **6** 428-429
Hepworth, Barbara **7** 318-319
Nicholson, Ben **11** 380-381
Pevsner, Antoine **12** 263-264
Taeuber-Arp, Sophie **15** 73-74
van Doesburg, Theo **15** 421

Absurd (literature)
Beckett, Samuel **2** 102-104
Camus, Albert **3** 255-257
Frisch, Max **6** 118-119
Grass, Günter **6** 496-497
Ionesco, Eugène **8** 131-132

ABU BAKR (circa 573-634), Moslem leader, first caliph of Islam **1** 31-32
Ali **1** 155-156
ibn Tashufin, Yusuf **8** 95-96
Muawiya ibn Abu Sufyan **11** 223-224
Omar ibn al-Khattab **11** 508-509

Abu Bakr II (died 1312), ruler of Mali empire
Musa Mansa **11** 266

Abu Dhabi, Emirate of
Zayid bin Sultan Al-Nahyan **16** 491-492

Abu Hanifa (699-767), Moslem legal scholar
Anan ben David **1** 207-208
Suleiman I **15** 20-21

ABU MUSA (born Said Musa Maragha circa 1930), a leader of the Palestinian Liberation Organization **1** 32-33

ABU NUWAS (al-Hasan ibn-Hani; circa 756-813), Arab poet **1** 33-34

Abu Simbel temple (Ipsambul, Egypt)
Ramses II **13** 22-23

Abu Yaqub Yusuf
see Yusuf, Abu Yaqub

Abubacer
see Ibn Tufayl, Abu Bakr Muhammad

Abuelo, El (play)
Galdós, Benito Pérez **6** 177-178

Abul Fazl (Abu'l-Fadl; 1551-1602), Indo-Persian historian
Akbar, Jalal-ud-din Mohammed **1** 96

Abulafia, Abraham (1240-1290), Jewish philosopher
Leon, Moses de **9** 336

ABU-L-ALA AL-MAARRI (973-1058), Arab poet and philosopher **1** 32

Abydos (ancient city, Egypt)
Petrie, William Matthew Flinders **12** 261-262
Ramses II **13** 22-23

Abysmal Brute, The (book)
London, Jack **9** 494-495

Abyssinia
see Ethiopia

ABZUG, BELLA STAVISKY (born 1920), lawyer, politician, and congresswoman **1** 34-35

Academia Mexicana de la Lengua (Mexico)
Reyes, Alfonso **13** 112-113

Academic Discourse at Havana (poem)
Stevens, Wallace **14** 443-445

Academic Festival Overture (musical composition)
Brahms, Johannes **2** 490-492

Academic freedom (education)
Chinese supporters
Ts'ai Yüan-p'ei **15** 322
concept rejected
Heidegger, Martin **7** 257-258
Egyptian supporters
Husayn, Taha **8** 61-62
German restrictions
Kotzebue, Otto von **9** 91-92
United States defenders
Beard, Charles Austin **2** 84
Cohen, Morris Raphael **4** 139-140
Harper, William Rainey **7** 163-164
Johnson, Alvin Saunders **8** 293-294
Lowell, Abbott Lawrence **10** 12-13
MacIver, Robert Morrison **10** 100-101
Mills, C. Wright **11** 35-36
Stone, Harlan Fiske **14** 468-470
Sumner, William Graham **15** 32
Tolman, Edward Chace **15** 261-262
see also Scopes trial; Student protest

Academic Freedom in Our Time (book)
MacIver, Robert Morrison **10** 100-101

Académie Nationale de Musique
see Opéra (Paris)

Academy (Athens)
Aristotle **1** 295-296
Chrysippus **4** 35-36
Heraclides of Pontus **7** 319-320
Plato **12** 345-347
Proclus Diadochus **12** 457

Academy of Arts and Sciences (Russia; established 1921)
Kandinsky, Wassily **8** 420-422

Acadia (region, Canada)
Champlain, Samuel de **3** 419-421
Charnisay, Charles de Menou **3** 470-471

Acão Integralista (Brazil)
Vargas, Getulio Dornelles **15** 433-434

Accademia degli Incamminati
see Carracci Academy

Accademia Olimpica (Vicenza; established 1555)
Palladio, Andrea **12** 75-77

Accasa, Ambro (flourished 1770), Fanti chief
Cugoano, Ottobah **4** 332-333

Acceptance World, The (novel)
Powell, Anthony **12** 422-423

Accessory Transit Company (Nicaragua)
Walker, William **16** 68-69

Acción Democrática (political party; Venezuela)
Betancourt, Rómulo **2** 237-238
Gallegos Freire, Rómulo **6** 185-186
Pérez, Carlos Andrés **12** 212-214

Acción Republicana (political party; Spain)
Azaña Diaz, Manuel **1** 396-397

Accommodation method (missiology)
Ricci, Matteo **13** 124-125

Accord of Forms (sculpture)
Nadelman, Elie **11** 289-290

Accordée de village (painting)
Watteau, Antoine **16** 143-144

Account of ... the Mississippi (book)
Pike, Zebulon **12** 302-304

Account of Corsica ... (book)
Boswell, James **2** 432-434

Account of the European Settlement in America, An (book)
Burke, Edmund **3** 138-141

Acetate (biochemistry)
Krebs, Hans Adolf **9** 95-97

Acetone (chemistry)
Northrop, John Howard **11** 430-431

Acetylcholine (chemistry)
Dale, Henry Hallett **4** 371-373
Loewi, Otto **9** 486-487

Achad Haam
see Ahad Haam

Achaea (ancient Greek province)
Cleomenes III **4** 103-104
Constantine XI **4** 211-212
Epaminondas **5** 291-292
Michael VIII **11** 1-2

Achaean League (Greek federation)
Aratus **1** 273-274
Polybios **12** 384-385

Achaemenid dynasty (Persia; reigned 550-330 B.C.)
Cyrus the Great **4** 363-364
Darius I **4** 394-395
Xerxes **16** 420

Achaeus (died 214 B.C.), Syrian governor in Asia Minor
Antiochus III **1** 249-250

Acharnians, The (play)
Aristophanes **1** 293-294

Achdut Ha'Avodah (labor organization, Israel)
Meir, Golda **10** 462-463

ACHEBE, CHINUA (born 1930), Nigerian novelist **1** 35-37

ACHESON, DEAN GOODERHAM (1893-1971), American statesman **1** 37-38
Marshall, George Catlett **10** 278-279
McCarthy, Joseph Raymond **10** 388-389
Truman, Harry S. **15** 314-316

Acheson-Lilienthal plan (atomic energy)
Bohr, Niels Henrik David **2** 366-368

Achiasaph (publishing house, Palestine)
Ahad Haam **1** 88-89

Achievement tests (psychology)
Terman, Lewis Madison **15** 153-154

Achievements of Liberty, The (book)
McClure, Samuel Sidney **10** 398-399

Achilleis (literary work)
Goethe, Johann Wolfgang von **6** 388-391

Achilles (Greek mythology)
Alexander the Great **1** 137-141
Homer **7** 465-467
Polykleitos **12** 385-386
Sophocles **14** 343-345

Achimoto College (Ghana)
Busia, Kofi Abrefa **3** 172-173
Hayford, J. E. Casely **7** 228-230

Achitophel (literary character; J. Dryden)
Milton, John **11** 43-46

Achorripsis (musical composition)
Xenakis, Iannis **16** 416-418

Acid (chemistry)
Boyle, Robert **2** 469-471
Lewis, Gilbert Newton **9** 384-385

Acis (mythologic character)
Góngora y Argote, Luis de **6** 427-428

Acis and Galatea (opera; Handel)
Gay, John **6** 243-244
Handel, George Frederick **7** 116-119
Mozart, Wolfgang Amadeus **11** 218-221

ACLU
see American Civil Liberties Union

Acmeist movement (Russian literature)
Akhmatova, Anna **1** 96-97
Mandelstam, Osip Emilyevich **10** 191

Acoma Pueblo Indians (North American)
Ortiz, Simon J. **12** 9-12

Aconcagua Indians (Chile)
Valdivia, Pedro de **15** 400-401

Acosta-Ñú, battle of (1869)
Morínigo, Higinio **11** 174-175

Acoustics (physics)
Euler, Leonard **5** 331-332

Rayleigh, 3d Baron **13** 62

Acquainted with the Night (narrative)
Frost, Robert Lee **6** 130-133

Acquaviva, Giulio (1546-1574), Italian cardinal
Cervantes, Miguel de Saavedra **3** 395-398

Acquaviva, Trojano (1695-1747), Italian cardinal
Casanova de Seinglat, Giacomo Jacopo Girolamo **3** 350-351

Acque e terre (poems)
Quasimodo, Salvatore **12** 506

Acquired immune deficiency syndrome (AIDS)
Gayle, Helene Doris **6** 244-245
Montagnier, Luc **11** 114-116

Acquisitive Society, The (pamphlet)
Tawney, Richard Henry **15** 120-121

Acre (city, Palestine)
Edward I **5** 208-210
Judas Maccabeus **8** 374-375
Napoleon I **11** 306-310
Philip II **12** 268-269
Saladin **13** 441-442

Acre (territory, Western Brazil)
Rio Branco, Barão do **13** 177

Acropolis (Athens)
Myron **11** 285
Pericles **12** 219-221
Phidias **12** 265-267

Acropolis (film)
Sherwood, Robert Emmet **14** 189-190

Across Arctic America (book)
Rasmussen, Knud Johan Victor **13** 44

Across Spoon River (autobiography)
Masters, Edgar Lee **10** 326-327

Across the River and into the Trees (novel)
Hemingway, Ernest Miller **7** 274-277

ACS
see American Colonization Society

Act and Being (book)
Bonhoeffer, Dietrich **2** 389-391

Act in Restraint of Appeals (England)
Henry VIII **7** 302-305

Act of
see under latter part of the term

Acta (book)
Mabillon, Jean **10** 72

Acta eruditorum (journal)
Leibniz, Gottfried Wilhelm von **9** 307-310

Actin (protein)
Hill, Archibald Vivian **7** 385-386
Szent—Györgyi, Albert von **15** 62-64

Acting (drama)
Stanislavsky, Constantin **14** 398-399
Strasberg, Lee **14** 494-495
see also Actors and entertainers

Actinium-B (element—chemistry)
Soddy, Frederick **14** 321-323

ACTION, JOHN EMERICH EDWARD DAL-BERG (1834-1902), English historian and philosopher **1** 38
Clapham, John Harold **4** 71
Döllinger, Josef Ignaz von **5** 47-48
Gooch, George Peabody **6** 432-433

Action Committee for the United States of Europe (established 1955)
Monnet, Jean **11** 109-110

Action Française (French political league)
Maurras, Charles Marie Photius **10** 350-351
Pius X **12** 336-337

Action Française (newspaper)
Bernanos, Georges **2** 206-207

Action Group (political party; Nigeria)
Awolowo, Obafemi **1** 389-390

Action painting
see Abstract expressionism

Actions and Reactions (stories)
Kipling, Joseph Rudyard **9** 32-33

Actions of Probabilities (musical composition)
Xenakis, Iannis **16** 416-418

Actium, battle of (31 B.C.)
Antony, Mark **1** 253-254
Cleopatra **4** 105-106
Virgil **15** 507-510

Active powers (philosophy)
Cudworth, Ralph **4** 331

Active Service (novel)
Crane, Stephen **4** 293-295

Activists
American
see Activists, American
Argentine
Pérez Esquivel, Adolfo **12** 215-217
Australian
Singer, Peter Albert David **14** 253-254
Austrian
Harand, Irene **7** 139-145
Suttner, Bertha von **15** 42-44
British
Bondfield, Margaret Grace **2** 388-389
Diana, Princess of Wales **4** 529-533
Fawcett, Millicent Garrett **5** 398-400
Fry, Elizabeth **6** 134-136
Garrett (Anderson), Elizabeth **6** 222-225
Hodgkin, Dorothy Crowfoot **7** 432-434
Redgrave, Vanessa **13** 74-75
Royden, Agnes Maude **13** 335-337
Waite, Terry **16** 47-48
Burmese
Aung San Suu Kyi **1** 375-376
Canadian
Atwood, Margaret Eleanor **1** 362-364

Chinese
Song Sisters **14** 338-341
Xiang Jingyu **16** 421-422
Egyptian
Sadat, Jihan **13** 414-415
French
Perrin, Jean Baptiste **12** 233-236
German
Baum, Herbert **2** 66-73
Böll, Heinrich **2** 377-378
Kelly, Petra **8** 486-487
Soelle, Dorothee **14** 324-325
Zetkin, Clara **16** 504-505
Guatemalan
Menchú, Rigoberta **10** 479-480
Hungarian
Elizabeth of Hungary **5** 271-272
Schwimmer, Rosika **14** 57-60
Irish
Corrigan and Williams **4** 251-253
Lonsdale, Kathleen **9** 501-502
Markievicz, Constance **10** 267-271
Japanese
Niwano, Nikkyo **11** 400-401
Mexican
Fuentes, Carlos **6** 141-142
New Zealander
Hillary, Edmund **7** 389-390
Palestinian
Ashrawi, Hanan Mikhail **1** 336-338
Romanian
Blandiana, Ana **2** 321-322
Russian
Breshkovsky, Catherine **2** 517-519
Sakharov, Andrei **13** 439-441
South African
Boesak, Allan Aubrey **2** 359-360
First, Ruth **5** 453-454
Sobukwe, Robert Mangaliso **14** 318-319
South Korean
Kim Dae-jung **9** 3-4
Spanish
Casals, Pablo **3** 348-350
Swiss
Dunant, Jean Henri **5** 139-141
Hepburn, Audrey **7** 314-316

Activists, American
AIDS
Ashe, Arthur Robert Jr. **1** 328-330
anti-nuclear
Bernardin, Joseph Cardinal **2** 210-211
Franck, James **6** 49-52
Silkwood, Karen **14** 227-229
anti-Vietnam War
Baez, Joan **1** 433-435
Coffin, William Sloane Jr. **4** 135-137
Dellinger, David **4** 480-481
Ellsberg, Daniel **5** 275-277
Fonda, Jane **5** 501-502
Gregory, Dick **6** 536-537
Hayden, Thomas Emmet **7** 217-219
Hoffman, Abbie **7** 437-439
King, Coretta Scott **9** 16-17

Lynd, Staughton **10** 65-66
Rubin, Jerry **13** 344-346
Spock, Benjamin **14** 383-385
Asian American issues
　Yasui, Minoru **16** 440-444
children's issues
　Edelman, Marian Wright **5** 202-204
　McEnroe, John Patrick Jr.
　　10 408-411
　Mendenhall, Dorothy Reed
　　10 491-492
citizen reform groups
　Alinsky, Saul David **1** 161-162
civil rights
　Barry, Marion Shepilov Jr. **2** 25-28
　Berry, Mary Frances **2** 226-229
　Bond, Horace Mann **2** 384-386
　Chávez, Dennis **3** 488-489
　Chavez, Linda **3** 489-491
　Chavis, Benjamin **3** 491-493
　Cochran, Johnnie **4** 128-131
　Collier, John **4** 160-162
　Dee, Ruby **4** 449-452
　Deer, Ada E. **4** 452-454
　Deloria, Vine Jr. **4** 481-484
　Dees, Morris S. Jr. **4** 456-457
　Divine, Father **5** 29-32
　Dudley, Barbara **5** 123-124
　Dunham, Katherine **5** 145-146
　Edelman, Marian Wright **5** 202-204
　Evers, Medgar **5** 345-348
　Evers-Williams, Myrlie **5** 348-350
　Flory, Paul **5** 492-494
　Fortune, Timothy Thomas **6** 18-21
　Goldberg, Whoopi **6** 398-402
　Gregory, Dick **6** 536-537
　Hamer, Fannie Lou **7** 93-94
　Harris, Barbara Clementine
　　7 171-172
　Henry, Aaron **7** 306-307
　Houston, Charles Hamilton
　　7 523-526
　Jacob, John Edward **8** 185-188
　Kunstler, William M. **9** 131-133
　McKissick, Floyd B. **10** 420-422
　Meredith, James H. **10** 514-515
　Mfume, Kweisi **10** 539-542
　Morton, Nelle Katherine
　　11 195-197
　Parks, Rosa Lee McCauley
　　12 115-116
　Poitier, Sidney **12** 368-370
　Savage, Augusta Christine
　　13 499-501
　Seeger, Pete **14** 83-84
　Shabazz, Betty **14** 130-132
　Sharpton, Al **14** 159-162
　Smith, James McCune **14** 293-294
　Sullivan, Leon Howard **15** 25-27
　Waters, Maxine **16** 132-134
　Yasui, Minoru **16** 440-444
education
　Beecher, Catharine **2** 110-112
　Perot, Henry Ross **12** 230-231
　Rice, Joseph Mayer **13** 127-128
environmental

Allen, Paula Gunn **1** 165-167
Browner, Carol M. **3** 50-52
Chavis, Benjamin **3** 491-493
Dudley, Barbara **5** 123-124
Earle, Sylvia A. **5** 180-181
Patrick, Ruth **12** 137-138
Seeger, Pete **14** 83-84
gay rights
　Ireland, Patricia **8** 134-135
　Milk, Harvey Bernard **11** 19-21
health care issues
　Love, Susan M. **10** 2-3
Hispanic American issues
　Baca-Barragán, Polly **1** 412-414
　Chavez, Linda **3** 489-491
　Corona, Bert **4** 243-247
　Prichard, Diana García **12** 448-449
　Ros-Lehtinen, Ileana **13** 294-296
　Valdez, Luis **15** 399-400
　Velázquez, Nydia Margarita
　　15 456-459
labor organizers
　Bieber, Owen **2** 266-268
　Bloor, Ella Reeve **2** 338-340
　Corona, Bert **4** 243-247
　Haley, Margaret A. **7** 78-79
　Hoffa, James R. **7** 436-437
　Jones, Mary Harris **8** 338-339
　Pesotta, Rose **12** 248-249
media portrayal
　McQueen, Butterfly **10** 434-437
Native American rights
　Adams, Hank **1** 45
　Banks, Dennis J. **1** 488-489
　Bellecourt, Clyde **2** 136-137
　Collier, John **4** 160-162
　Deer, Ada E. **4** 452-454
　Deloria, Vine Jr. **4** 481-484
　La Flesche (Tibbles), Susette
　　9 154-155
　Mankiller, Wilma **10** 198-199
　Manuelito **10** 220-222
　McNickle, D'Arcy **10** 433
　Means, Russell **10** 441-444
　Montezuma, Carlos **11** 129-132
　Ortiz, Simon J. **12** 9-12
　Peltier, Leonard **12** 193-195
　Plenty Coups **12** 352-355
　Satanta **13** 493-494
　Winnemucca, Sarah **16** 336-338
　Zah, Peterson **16** 486-487
occupational health and safety
　Hardy, Harriet **7** 150
peace
　Abzug, Bella Stavisky **1** 34-35
　Andrews, Fannie Fern Phillips
　　1 231-232
　Balch, Emily Greene **1** 463-464
　Berrigan, Daniel J. **2** 222-223
　Rankin, Jeannette Pickering
　　13 35-37
　Rustin, Bayard **13** 382-383
　Waters, Maxine **16** 132-134
　Zinn, Howard **16** 520-521
relief aid
　Booth, Evangeline Cory **2** 402-403

right-wing
　Buckley, William F. Jr. **3** 96-97
　Falwell, Jerry **5** 375-376
　Schlafly, Phyllis **14** 9-10
　Welch, Robert **16** 184-185
scientific responsibility
　Singer, Maxine **14** 251-252
social reform
　Ashe, Arthur Robert Jr. **1** 328-330
　Beard, Mary Ritter **2** 85-86
　Harris, Barbara Clementine
　　7 171-172
　hooks, bell **7** 477-481
　Houston, Charles Hamilton
　　7 523-526
　Kellor, Frances **8** 481-482
　Lee, Ann **9** 285-288
　Milk, Harvey Bernard **11** 19-21
　Owen, Ruth Bryan **12** 41-43
　Sheen, Fulton J. **14** 171-172
　Strong, Josiah **14** 512-513
socio-economic change
　Bernardin, Joseph Cardinal
　　2 210-211
　Bloor, Ella Reeve **2** 338-340
　Bly, Nellie **2** 346-348
　Dee, Ruby **4** 449-452
　Divine, Father **5** 29-32
　Goldberg, Whoopi **6** 398-402
　Harrington, Michael **7** 167-169
　Jacob, John Edward **8** 185-188
　McKissick, Floyd B. **10** 420-422
　Sullivan, Leon Howard **15** 25-27
women's rights
　Abzug, Bella Stavisky **1** 34-35
　Allen, Florence Ellinwood
　　1 164-165
　Allen, Paula Gunn **1** 165-167
　Baker, Sara Josephine **1** 455-456
　Berry, Mary Frances **2** 226-229
　Brownmiller, Susan **3** 56-57
　Dodge, Grace Hoadley **5** 37-38
　Friedan, Betty **6** 109-111
　Harris, Barbara Clementine
　　7 171-172
　Hill, Anita **7** 382-385
　hooks, bell **7** 477-481
　Ireland, Patricia **8** 134-135
　King, Coretta Scott **9** 16-17
　Lyon, Mary **10** 67-69
　Morgan, Robin **11** 168-170
　Natividad, Irene **11** 322-324
　Owen, Ruth Bryan **12** 41-43
　Park, Maud Wood **12** 102
　Pesotta, Rose **12** 248-249
　Rohde, Ruth Bryan Owen
　　13 252-253
　Roybal-Allard, Lucille **13** 332-334
　Sabin, Florence Rena **13** 402-405
　Waters, Maxine **16** 132-134
　Yard, Mary Alexander **16** 438-439
women's suffrage
　Beard, Mary Ritter **2** 85-86
　Bloor, Ella Reeve **2** 338-340
　Gage, Matilda Joslyn **6** 167-169
　Park, Maud Wood **12** 102

Robinson, Harriet Hanson **13** 203-207

Actomyosin (protein)
Hill, Archibald Vivian **7** 385-386
Szent-Györgyi, Albert von **15** 62-64

Actors and entertainers, African
filmmakers/directors
Cissé, Souleymane **4** 65-66
Faye, Safi **5** 400-401
Kawawa, Rashidi Mfaume **8** 464-465
Ousmane, Sembene **12** 32-33

Actors and entertainers, American
cartoon voices
Blanc, Mel **2** 319-320
choreographers
Ailey, Alvin **1** 91-94
Astaire, Fred **1** 348-350
Balanchine, George **1** 461-462
Cunningham, Merce **4** 337-338
de Mille, Agnes **4** 486-488
Dunham, Katherine **5** 145-146
Fosse, Bob **6** 22-23
Graham, Martha **6** 485-486
Joffrey, Robert **8** 268-270
Kelly, Gene **8** 484-486
Morris, Mark **11** 184-185
Robbins, Jerome **13** 190-192
Smuin, Michael **14** 307-309
St. Denis, Ruth **13** 430-431
Tharp, Twyla **15** 164-165
circuses
Barnum, Phineas Taylor **2** 13-15
comedians
Allen, Woody **1** 169-171
Ball, Lucille **1** 472-473
Benchley, Robert **2** 150-151
Benny, Jack **2** 174-176
Brice, Fanny **3** 1-2
Burns, George **3** 153-155
Cantor, Eddie **3** 264-265
Carlin, George **3** 301-303
Carson, Johnny **3** 335-337
Cosby, William Henry Jr. **4** 257-258
Fields, W. C. **5** 444
Goldberg, Whoopi **6** 398-402
Gregory, Dick **6** 536-537
Hope, Bob **7** 487-489
Jefferson, Joseph **8** 237
Jessel, George **8** 249-251
Lahr, Bert **9** 167-168
Marx brothers **10** 303-304
Sennett, Mack **14** 108-109
dancers
Ailey, Alvin **1** 91-94
Astaire, Fred **1** 348-350
Baker, Josephine **1** 448-451
Baryshnikov, Mikhail **2** 43-44
Castle, Vernon and Irene **3** 361-363
Davis, Sammy Jr. **4** 423-424
de Mille, Agnes **4** 486-488
Duncan, Isadora **5** 144-145
Dunham, Katherine **5** 145-146
Farrell, Suzanne **5** 391-393

Fonteyn, Dame Margot **5** 504-505
Fosse, Bob **6** 22-23
Hayworth, Rita **7** 233-235
Hines, Gregory Oliver **7** 401-403
Holm, Hanya **7** 454-455
Joffrey, Robert **8** 268-270
Kelly, Gene **8** 484-486
Madonna **10** 123-125
Martin, Mary **10** 292-293
Smuin, Michael **14** 307-309
Tallchief, Maria **15** 88-89
Tharp, Twyla **15** 164-165
Turner, Tina **15** 357-359
filmmakers/directors
Allen, Woody **1** 169-171
Capra, Frank **3** 276-278
Crichton, John Michael **4** 308-310
DeMille, Cecil Blount **4** 488-490
Disney, Walter Elias **5** 26-27
Eastwood, Clint **5** 188-190
Flaherty, Robert **5** 476-477
Ford, John **6** 7-8
Fosse, Bob **6** 22-23
Goldwyn, Samuel **6** 416
Griffith, David Wark **6** 544-545
Hitchcock, Alfred **7** 415-416
Jessel, George **8** 249-251
Jones, Quincy Delight Jr. **8** 339-341
Kazan, Elia **8** 465-466
Lang, Fritz **9** 190-192
Lee, Spike **9** 295-299
Mailer, Norman Kingsley **10** 148-150
Odets, Clifford **11** 470-471
Poitier, Sidney **12** 368-370
Scorsese, Martin **14** 63-65
Smithson, Robert **14** 301-303
Sontag, Susan **14** 342-343
Spielberg, Steven **14** 379-381
Stone, Oliver **14** 472-475
Valdez, Luis **15** 399-400
Welles, Orson **16** 190-191
Wiseman, Frederick **16** 345-346
film stars
Allen, Woody **1** 169-171
Anderson, Judith **1** 215-216
Astaire, Fred **1** 348-350
Barrymores **2** 28-30
Black, Shirley Temple **2** 303-305
Bogart, Humphrey **2** 363-364
Brando, Marlon **2** 497-499
Burns, George **3** 153-155
Cantor, Eddie **3** 264-265
Cosby, William Henry Jr. **4** 257-258
Crosby, Harry Lillis **4** 324-326
Davis, Ossie **4** 421-422
Davis, Sammy Jr. **4** 423-424
Dean, James **4** 433-434
Dee, Ruby **4** 449-452
Eastwood, Clint **5** 188-190
Fonda, Jane **5** 501-502
Gable, William Clark **6** 157-158
Garbo, Greta **6** 205-207
Garland, Judy **6** 218-219
Goldberg, Whoopi **6** 398-402

Hayworth, Rita **7** 233-235
Hepburn, Katharine **7** 316-317
Hope, Bob **7** 487-489
Horne, Lena **7** 504-506
Houdini, Harry **7** 514-516
Jessel, George **8** 249-251
Jolson, Al **8** 329-330
Jones, James Earl **8** 334-337
Kelly, Gene **8** 484-486
Lahr, Bert **9** 167-168
Lee, Spike **9** 295-299
Madonna **10** 123-125
Martin, Mary **10** 292-293
McDaniel, Hattie **10** 405-408
McQueen, Butterfly **10** 434-437
Monroe, Marilyn **11** 113-114
Poitier, Sidney **12** 368-370
Presley, Elvis Aron **12** 441-442
Ross, Diana **13** 298-300
Shepard, Sam **14** 180-181
Sinatra, Francis Albert **14** 246-248
Strasberg, Lee **14** 494-495
Studi, Wes **15** 1-2
Taylor, Elizabeth Rosemond **15** 124-125
Tracy, Spencer Bonaventure **15** 289-290
Wayne, John **16** 150-151
Welles, Orson **16** 190-191
Winfrey, Oprah Gail **16** 333-336
Wong, Anna May **16** 366-367
film writers
Hecht, Ben **7** 248-250
King, Stephen **9** 23-25
Miller, Arthur **11** 25-26
Odets, Clifford **11** 470-471
magicians and illusionists
Houdini, Harry **7** 514-516
news broadcasters
Bradley, Ed **2** 478-481
Chung, Connie **4** 47-48
Cronkite, Walter Leland Jr. **4** 321-322
Huntley and Brinkley **8** 49-51
opera singers
Battle, Kathleen **2** 59-60
radio
Benny, Jack **2** 174-176
Brice, Fanny **3** 1-2
Burns, George **3** 153-155
Cantor, Eddie **3** 264-265
McDaniel, Hattie **10** 405-408
Terkel, Louis **15** 152-153
singers
Baez, Joan **1** 433-435
Baker, Josephine **1** 448-451
Battle, Kathleen **2** 59-60
Brice, Fanny **3** 1-2
Brown, James **3** 37-39
Caesar, Shirley **3** 210-211
Calloway, Cab **3** 236-238
Cantor, Eddie **3** 264-265
Cline, Patsy **4** 110-112
Crosby, Harry Lillis **4** 324-326
Davis, Sammy Jr. **4** 423-424

Dylan, Bob **5** 170-171
Fitzgerald, Ella **5** 468-469
Franklin, Aretha **6** 58-60
Garland, Judy **6** 218-219
Hayes, Roland **7** 225-227
Holiday, Billie **7** 452-453
Horne, Lena **7** 504-506
Jackson, Michael Joe **8** 178-180
Jessel, George **8** 249-251
Jolson, Al **8** 329-330
Jordan, Louis **8** 353-355
King, B. B. **9** 11-14
Little Richard **9** 447-449
Madonna **10** 123-125
Martin, Mary **10** 292-293
Norman, Jessye **11** 425-427
Presley, Elvis Aron **12** 441-442
Robeson, Paul Leroy **13** 198-199
Ross, Diana **13** 298-300
Seeger, Pete **14** 83-84
Sills, Beverly **14** 230-231
Sinatra, Francis Albert **14** 246-248
Turner, Tina **15** 357-359
Vaughan, Sarah Lois **15** 445-446
Waller, Thomas Wright **16** 81-82
see also Musicians
stage directors
    Belasco, David **2** 124-125
    Flanagan, Hallie **5** 478-479
    Hammerstein, Oscar Clendenning II
        7 104-106
    Holm, Hanya **7** 454-455
    Jones, Robert Edmond **8** 341-342
    Kazan, Elia **8** 465-466
    Robbins, Jerome **13** 190-192
    Smuin, Michael **14** 307-309
    Strasberg, Lee **14** 494-495
    Ziegfeld, Florenz **16** 516-517
stage performers
    Anderson, Judith **1** 215-216
    Angelou, Maya **1** 238-239
    Ball, Lucille **1** 472-473
    Barrymores **2** 28-30
    Bogart, Humphrey **2** 363-364
    Booth, Edwin **2** 401-402
    Booth, John Wilkes **2** 404
    Boucicault, Dion **2** 442-443
    Brando, Marlon **2** 497-499
    Cushman, Charlotte **4** 354-355
    Davis, Ossie **4** 421-422
    Dee, Ruby **4** 449-452
    Fiske, Minnie Maddern **5** 466-467
    Forrest, Edwin **6** 11-12
    Goldberg, Whoopi **6** 398-402
    Hayes, Helen **7** 223-224
    Hepburn, Katharine **7** 316-317
    Jessel, George **8** 249-251
    Jolson, Al **8** 329-330
    Jones, James Earl **8** 334-337
    Kemble, Frances Anne **8** 491
    Ludlum, Robert **10** 28-29
    Martin, Mary **10** 292-293
    McQueen, Butterfly **10** 434-437
    Payne, John Howard **12** 159
    Robeson, Paul Leroy **13** 198-199

Wong, Anna May **16** 366-367
story tellers
    Ortiz, Simon J. **12** 9-12
television
    Angelou, Maya **1** 238-239
    Astaire, Fred **1** 348-350
    Ball, Lucille **1** 472-473
    Benny, Jack **2** 174-176
    Carlin, George **3** 301-303
    Carson, Johnny **3** 335-337
    Cosby, William Henry Jr. **4** 257-258
    Crosby, Harry Lillis **4** 324-326
    Davis, Ossie **4** 421-422
    Fonda, Jane **5** 501-502
    Hope, Bob **7** 487-489
    Jessel, George **8** 249-251
    Jones, James Earl **8** 334-337
    Jones, Quincy Delight Jr. **8** 339-341
    Lahr, Bert **9** 167-168
    Martin, Mary **10** 292-293
    Presley, Elvis Aron **12** 441-442
    Rivers, Larry **13** 186-187
    Ross, Diana **13** 298-300
    Walters, Barbara **16** 86-88
    Winfrey, Oprah Gail **16** 333-336
vaudeville
    Benny, Jack **2** 174-176
    Brice, Fanny **3** 1-2
    Burns, George **3** 153-155
    Cantor, Eddie **3** 264-265
    Christy, Edwin P. **4** 34-35
    Cohan, George Michael **4** 137-138
    Davis, Sammy Jr. **4** 423-424
    Hope, Bob **7** 487-489
    Jolson, Al **8** 329-330
    Lahr, Bert **9** 167-168
    McDaniel, Hattie **10** 405-408
    Rogers, Will **13** 251-252
videocassettes
    Fonda, Jane **5** 501-502
    Jackson, Michael Joe **8** 178-180
    Madonna **10** 123-125
western shows
    Buffalo Bill **3** 105-106
    Oakley, Annie **11** 453-454

Actors and entertainers, Arabic
Fairuz **5** 368-369

Actors and entertainers, Canadian
actors
    Greene, Graham (born circa 1952)
        6 523-524
filmmakers/directors
    Grierson, John **6** 542-543

Actors and entertainers, European
Great Britain
    comedians
        Sellers, Peter Richard Henry
            14 98-99
    filmmakers/directors
        Grierson, John **6** 542-543
    film stars
        Burton, Richard **3** 163-164
        Chaplin, Charles Spencer
            3 438-440
        Evans, Edith **5** 336-337

Grant, Cary **6** 490-492
Guinness, Alec **7** 37-38
Olivier, Laurence **11** 502-503
Redgrave, Vanessa **13** 74-75
Sellers, Peter Richard Henry
    14 98-99
radio
    Sellers, Peter Richard Henry
        14 98-99
stage directors
    Appia, Adolphe **1** 263-264
    Brook, Peter **3** 19-21
    Guthrie, Tyrone **7** 50-51
    Olivier, Laurence **11** 502-503
stage performers
    Burton, Richard **3** 163-164
    Coward, Noel **4** 279-280
    Craig, Edward Gordon
        4 288-289
    Evans, Edith **5** 336-337
    Gielgud, John **6** 310-311
    Guinness, Alec **7** 37-38
    Kemble, Frances Anne **8** 491
    Olivier, Laurence **11** 502-503
the Continent
    actors
        Hepburn, Audrey **7** 314-316
    choreographers
        Bausch, Pina **2** 75-76
    dancers
        Baker, Josephine **1** 448-451
        Bausch, Pina **2** 75-76
        Taeuber-Arp, Sophie **15** 73-74
        Wigman, Mary **16** 267-268
    filmmakers/directors
        Antonioni, Michelangelo
            1 252-253
        Bergman, Ernst Ingmar
            2 190-191
        Buñuel, Luis **3** 127-128
        Cocteau, Jean **4** 132-133
        Eisenstein, Sergei Mikhailovich
            5 240-242
        Fellini, Federico **5** 408-409
        Lang, Fritz **9** 190-192
        Lubitsch, Ernst **10** 18-19
        Meyerhold, Vsevolod Emilievich
            10 539
        Richter, Hans **13** 149-150
        Riefenstahl, Leni **13** 161-163
        Truffaut, François **15** 311-313
    guitarists
        Segovia, Andrés **14** 87-88
    mime
        Marceau, Marcel **10** 231-233
    singers
        Baker, Josephine **1** 448-451
        Behrens, Hildegard **2** 120-121
        Pavarotti, Luciano **12** 152-154
        Piaf, Edith **12** 285-287
    stage directors
        Copeau, Jacques **4** 225
        Reinhardt, Max **13** 89-90
        Stanislavsky, Constantin
            14 398-399
    stage performers

Artaud, Antonin **1** 320-321
Bernhardt, Sarah **2** 212-214
Stanislavsky, Constantin
14 398-399
theater directors
Grotowski, Jerzy **7** 19-20

Actors and entertainers, Indian (Asia)
Ray, Satyajit **13** 60-61

Actors and entertainers, Japanese
Kurosawa, Akira **9** 135-137
Zarlino, Gioseffo **16** 490-491

Actors and entertainers, Russian
dancers
Baryshnikov, Mikhail **2** 43-44
Diaghilev, Sergei **4** 525-527
Nijinsky, Vaslav **11** 393-395
Nureyev, Rudolph **11** 445-446
Pavlova, Anna **12** 157-159
Plisetskaya, Maya Mikhailovna
12 356-358
Ulanova, Galina **15** 382-383

Actors and entertainers, South African
Fugard, Athol **6** 142-143

Actor's Equity (labor union, United States)
Cantor, Eddie **3** 264-265

Actors Studio (New York City)
Strasberg, Lee **14** 494-495

Acts of the Apostles (New Testament)
John **8** 273-274
Luke **10** 38
Mark **10** 266-267
Paul **12** 141-143
Peter **12** 252-253

Actualités Africaines (newspaper)
Mobutu Sese Seko **11** 69-71

Acushnet (ship)
Melville, Herman **10** 472-476

Ad Atticum (letters)
Cicero, Marcus Tullius **4** 55-58

Ad familares (letters)
Cicero, Marcus Tullius **4** 55-58

Ad M. Brutum (letters)
Cicero, Marcus Tullius **4** 55-58

Ad Pauca Respicientes (tract)
Nicholas of Oresme **11** 380

Ad Quintum fratrem (letters)
Cicero, Marcus Tullius **4** 55-58

Ad se ipsum (letter)
Petrarch **12** 259-261

Ada (novel)
Nabokov, Vladimir **11** 287-288

Adagia (book)
Erasmus, Desiderius **5** 298-300

Adagio for Strings (musical composition)
Barber, Samuel **1** 500-501

Adam (Old Testament character)
Edwards, Jonathan **5** 220-222

Adam Bede (novel)
Eliot, George **5** 254-256

ADAM, JAMES (1730-1794), British architect **1** 38-40
McIntire, Samuel **10** 415

Adam, Lambert Sigisbert (1700-1759), French sculptor
Clodion **4** 121

ADAM, ROBERT (1728-1792), British architect **1** 38-40
associates
Piranesi, Giovanni Battista
12 321-322
influence of
Bulfinch, Charles **3** 116-117
Hepplewhite, George **7** 317-318
McIntire, Samuel **10** 415
Sheraton, Thomas **14** 181-182
neoclassic designs
Chippendale, Thomas **4** 1-2

Adam, William (1689-1748), Scottish architect
Adam, Robert and James **1** 38-40

Adam in Ballingschap (play)
Vondel, Joost van den **16** 19-20

Adam in Exile (play)
Vondel, Joost van den **16** 19-20

Adam Smith and Modern Sociology (book)
Small, Albion Woodbury **14** 277

Adamkiewicz color test
see Glyoxylic test (biochemistry)

Adams, Abigail Smith (1744-1818), wife of John Adams
Adams, John **1** 48-51
Adams, John Quincy **1** 52-54

Adams, Abraham (literary character)
Fielding, Henry **5** 442-444

ADAMS, ANSEL (1902-1984), landscape photographer and conservationist
1 40-41

Adams, Brooks
see Adams, Peter Chardon Brooks

ADAMS, CHARLES FRANCIS (1807-1886), American diplomat and politician
1 41-42
Adams, Peter Chardon Brooks **1** 54
Adams, Henry Brooks **1** 45-47
Burlingame, Anson **3** 144-145

Adams, Franklin Pierce (1881-1960), American journalist
Kaufman, George S. **8** 457-458

ADAMS, GERALD (born 1948), president of the Sinn Fein Irish political party
1 42-44

ADAMS, HANK (born 1944), Native American activist **1** 45

ADAMS, HENRY BROOKS (1838-1918), American historian and author **1** 45-47
associates
La Farge, John **9** 149-150
influence of
Channing, Edward **3** 435
quoted
Parkman, Francis **12** 113-115

Swinburne, Algernon Charles
15 54-55
relatives
Adams, Charles Francis **1** 41-42
Treaty of Ghent
Gallatin, Albert **6** 183-184
wife's memorial
Saint-Gaudens, Augustus **13** 432
White, Stanford **16** 235-236

ADAMS, HERBERT BAXTER (1850-1901), American historian and teacher **1** 47
Andrews, Charles McLean **1** 231
Haskins, Charles Homer **7** 191-192

ADAMS, JAMES LUTHER (1901-1994), American social ethicist, theologian, and defender of religious and political liberalism **1** 47-48

ADAMS, JOHN (1735-1826), American statesman and diplomat, president 1797-1801 **1** 48-51
church attendance
Priestley, Joseph **12** 452-453
election campaigns
Chase, Samuel **3** 475-476
Clinton, George **4** 113-114
Jefferson, Thomas **8** 238-241
historical treatment
Warren, Mercy Otis **16** 120-121
independence movement
Jefferson, Thomas **8** 238-241
Lee, Richard Henry **9** 291-292
Otis, James Jr. **12** 25-27
law office
Tyler, Royall **15** 371-372
military appointees
Barry, John **2** 24-25
Washington, George **16** 126-129
"Olive Branch" petition
Dickinson, John **4** 543-544
opponents
Coxe, Tench **4** 285-286
Duane, William **5** 109
Hamilton, Alexander **7** 95-98
Leonard, Daniel **9** 336-337
political appointees
Gerry, Elbridge **6** 282-283
Harrison, William Henry **7** 180-181
Otis, Harrison Gray **12** 25
Pickering, Timothy **12** 298-299
portraits of
Stuart, Gilbert **14** 513-515
quoted
Chase, Samuel **3** 475-476
Henry, Patrick **7** 309-311
relatives
Adams, Henry Brooks **1** 45-47
Adams, John Quincy **1** 52-54
Adams, Samuel **1** 55-56
scandalized
Jones, John Paul **8** 337-338
Treaty of Paris (1783)
Franklin, Benjamin **6** 60-64
XYZ affair
Jefferson, Thomas **8** 238-241
Madison, James **10** 121-123

Marshall, John **10** 279-281
Pinckney, Charles Cotesworth **12** 310

ADAMS, JOHN COUCH (1819-1892),
English mathematical astronomer **1** 51-52
Leverrier, Urbain Jean Joseph **9** 361-362

ADAMS, JOHN QUINCY (1767-1848),
American statesman and diplomat, president 1825-29 **1** 52-54
diplomatic appointments
Harrison, William Henry **7** 180-181
King, Rufus **9** 22-23
election campaigns
Clay, Henry **4** 94-96
Crawford, William Harris **4** 299-300
Jackson, Andrew **8** 168-172
McLean, John **10** 422-423
Monroe Cabinet
Monroe, James **11** 111-113
quoted
Clay, Henry **4** 94-96
Lovejoy, Elijah Parish **10** 6-7
relatives
Adams, Charles Francis **1** 41-42
Adams, Henry Brooks **1** 45-47
Adams, John **1** 48-51
Downing, Andrew Jackson **5** 90-91
slavery issue
Cinque, Joseph **4** 62
Lundy, Benjamin **10** 45-46
Weld, Theodore Dwight **16** 186
supporters
Webster, Daniel **16** 162-164
Treaty of Ghent
Gallatin, Albert **6** 183-184
vice president
Calhoun, John Caldwell **3** 226-228

Adams, Nick (literary character)
Hemingway, Ernest Miller **7** 274-277

ADAMS, PETER CHARDON BROOKS
(1848-1927), American historian **1** 54
Adams, Charles Francis **1** 41-42
Mather, Cotton **10** 330-332

ADAMS, SAMUEL (1722-1803), American
colonial leader and propagandist **1** 55-56
anti-British agitation
Gage, Thomas **6** 169-170
Gerry, Elbridge **6** 282-283
Hancock, John **7** 114-116
Otis, James Jr. **12** 25-27
Revere, Paul **13** 110-111
artistic interests
Billings, William **2** 274-275
Bulfinch, Charles **3** 116-117
Copley, John Singleton **4** 228-230
ostracizes Paine
Paine, Thomas **12** 66-67
political opponents
Ames, Fisher **1** 199-200
Hutchinson, Thomas **8** 71-72
praised
Warren, Mercy Otis **16** 120-121

Adams, Sherman (1899-1986), American
politician
Eisenhower, Dwight David **5** 233-236

Adams, W.S. (1876-1956), American
astronomer
Eddington, Arthur Stanley **5** 201-202

Adana (city, Turkey)
Ibrahim Pasha **8** 97-98

Adaptation (biology)
Adrian, Edgar Douglas **1** 67-69

Adaptation (law)
Montesquieu **11** 123-125

Adassa, battle of (161 B.C.)
Judas Maccabeus **8** 374-375

ADDAMS, JANE (1860-1935), American
social worker, reformer, and pacifist
1 56-57
Hamilton, Alice **7** 98-99
Kelley, F. **8** 483-484
King, William Lyon Mackenzie **9** 25-26
Lloyd, Henry Demarest **9** 468-469
influence of
Abbott, Grace **1** 9-10

Adding Machine, The (play)
Rice, Elmer **13** 126-127

Addington, Henry (1st Viscount Sidmouth;
1757-1844), English statesman
Liverpool, 2nd Earl of **9** 456-457
Pitt, William the Younger **12** 329-331

Addis Ababa (city, Ethiopia)
Heruy Wäldä-Sellasé **7** 348-349
Menelik II **10** 495-497

Addis Ababa, Duke of
see Badoglio, Pietro

Addis Ababa, University College of
Haile Selassie **7** 68-70

ADDISON, JOSEPH (1672-1719), English
essayist and politician **1** 57-58
associates
Berkeley, George **2** 197-198
Congreve, William **4** 200-201
Pope, Alexander **12** 395-397
Steele, Richard **14** 407-409
Swift, Jonathan **15** 51-54
drama
Arne, Thomas Augustine **1** 307-308
Hallam, Lewis Sr. and Jr. **7** 87
influence of
Franklin, Benjamin **6** 60-64
Irving, Washington **8** 141-143
Milton, John **11** 43-46

Addison, Lancelot (1632-1703), English
clergyman and author
Addison, Joseph **1** 57-58

ADDISON, THOMAS (1793-1860), English
physician **1** 58-59
Bright, Richard **3** 7-8

Addisonian anemia
see Pernicious anemia

Addison's disease (medical)
Addison, Thomas **1** 58-59
Reichstein, Tadeus **13** 85-87
Szent-Györgyi, Albert von **15** 62-64

Additional Act (1834; Brazil)
Feijó, Diogo Antônio **5** 405-406

Additional Notes ... about Building ...
(book)
Downing, Andrew Jackson **5** 90-91

Additions (book)
Saint-Simon, Duc de **13** 436

Addled Parliament (1614)
James I **8** 204-206

Address on Church Music (book)
Mason, Lowell **10** 321-322

Address tae the Deil (poem)
Burns, Robert **3** 155-156
Dickinson, John **4** 543-544
Lee, Richard Henry **9** 291-292

Address to the Inhabitants of Quebec
(1774)
Dickinson, John **4** 543-544

Address to the King (1774)
Lee, Richard Henry **9** 291-292

Address to the Nations of the World
(essay)
Du Bois, William Edward Burghardt
5 116-118

Address to the People of Great Britain
(1774)
Lee, Richard Henry **9** 291-292

Address to the People of New York, An
(tract)
Jay, John **8** 230-232

Address to the Public ..., An (petition)
Willard, Emma Hart **16** 288-289

Address to the Unco Guid (poem)
Burns, Robert **3** 155-156

Addresses to the German Nation (book)
Fichte, Johann Gottlieb **5** 435-436

Adela (1062?-1137), countess of Blois
William I **16** 290-291

Adelaide, St. (931?-999), queen mother of
Germany 973-983
Otto III **12** 29-30

Adelaide, University of (Australia)
Bragg, William Henry **2** 488-489
Mawson, Douglas **10** 354-355

Adelaide of Savona (died 1118), countess
of Sicily
Roger II **13** 244-245

Adelard of Bath (early 12th century), English scholastic philosopher
Khwarizmi, Muhammad ibn Musa al-
8 541

Adelchi (play)
Manzoni, Alessandro **10** 222-224

Adelphoe (play)
Terence **15** 146-148

Adelson e Salvini (opera)
Bellini, Vincenzo **2** 138-139

Adena (house, Chillicothe, Ohio)
Latrobe, Benjamin Henry **9** 222-224

ADENAUER, KONRAD (1876-1967), German statesman, chancellor of the Federal Republic 1949-63 **1** 59-61
Ben-Gurion, David **2** 160-161
Erhard, Ludwig **5** 302-304

Adenosine diphosphate (biochemistry)
Meyerhof, Otto Fritz **10** 537-539

Adenosine-triphosphatase (biochemistry)
Hill, Archibald Vivian **7** 385-386
Meyerhof, Otto Fritz **10** 537-539
Szent-Györgyi, Albert von **15** 62-64

Adenylic compounds (biochemistry)
Meyerhof, Otto Fritz **10** 537-539

Adi Granth (Sikh book)
Nanak **11** 303

Adieu ces bon vins de Lannoys (song)
Dufay, Guillaume **5** 125-126

Adieu mes amours (song)
Josquin des Prez **8** 361-363

Adkins v. Children's Hospital (legal case)
Taft, William Howard **15** 78-81

ADLER, ALFRED (1870-1937), Austrian psychiatrist **1** 61-63
Freud, Sigmund **6** 103-106
Horney, Karen Danielsen **7** 508-509
Jung, Carl Gustav **8** 388-389

Adler, Cyrus (1863-1940), American Jewish educator and author
Szold, Henrietta **15** 66-67

Adler, D., and Co. (architecture firm; Chicago)
Sullivan, Louis Henri **15** 27-28

Adler, Dankmar (1844-1900), American architect
Sullivan, Louis Henri **15** 27-28
Wright, Frank Lloyd **16** 398-401

ADLER, FELIX (1851-1933), American educator and Ethical Culture leader **1** 63-64
Eddy, Mary Baker **5** 202

Adler, Guido (1855-1941), Moravian musicologist
Webern, Anton **16** 160-162

Admeto (opera)
Handel, George Frederick **7** 116-119

Admetus (literary character)
Euripides **5** 332-334

Admetus and Other Poems (literary collection)
Laye, Camara **9** 257-259

Administration of Justice Act (1774)
see Intolerable Acts

Admirable Bashville (play)
Shaw, George Bernard **14** 163-164

Admirable Crichton, The (play)
Barrie, James Matthew **2** 21-22

Admiral of the Ocean Sea (book)
Morison, Samuel Eliot **11** 175-176

Admiralty House (London)
Adam, Robert and James **1** 38-40

Admiralty law (United States)
Story, Joseph **14** 480-481

Admonitions of the Instructress to the Ladies of the Court (painting)
Ku K'ai-chih **9** 125-126

Adolescence (book)
Hall, Granville Stanley **7** 85-86

Adolescence (psychology)
Erikson, Erik Homburger **5** 309-310

Adolf of Nassau (1250?-1298), Holy Roman emperor 1292-1298
Henry VII **7** 299-300

Adolphe (novel; Constant)
Staël, Germaine de **14** 391-392

Adolphe I
see Thiers, Adolphe

Adolphus Frederick (1710-1771), king of Sweden 1751-1771
Gustavus III **7** 45-46

Adonais (poem; Shelley)
Arnold, Matthew **1** 311-313
Shelley, Percy Bysshe **14** 176-178

ADONIS ('Ali Ahmad Said; born 1930), Lebanese poet **1** 64-65

Adonis (poem)
La Fontaine, Jean de **9** 156-157

Adoptionism (heresy)
Alcuin of York **1** 122-123

Adorable Clio (book)
Giraudoux, Jean **6** 349-350

Adoration of the Golden Calf (painting)
Tintoretto **15** 232-234

Adoration of the Kings (painting)
Giorgione **6** 340-341
Titian **15** 242-244

Adoration of the Magi (altarpiece)
Gentile da Fabriano **6** 266-267
Leonardo da Vinci **9** 337-340
Lochner, Stephan **9** 475
Rubens, Peter Paul **13** 339-342

Adoration of the Magi (painting)
Botticelli, S.
Geertgen tot Sint Jans **6** 248
Ghirlandaio, Domenico **6** 292-293
Lucas van Leyden **10** 20-21
Perugino **12** 245-246
Poussin, Nicolas **12** 418-420
Sassetta **13** 492

Adoration of the Magi (panel)
van der Goes, Hugo **15** 416-417

Adoration of the Magi (sculpture)
Pisano, Nicola **12** 325

Adoration of the Magi (tondo)
Lippi, Filippo **9** 439
Veneziano, Domenico **15** 459-460

Adoration of the Moon (painting)
Weber, Max **16** 160

Adoration of the Shepherds (altarpiece)
Correggio **4** 249-251
Stoss, Veit **14** 481-482

Adoration of the Shepherds (painting)
Ghirlandaio, Domenico **6** 292-293
Giorgione **6** 340-341
Greco **6** 511-514
Jordaens, Jacob **8** 347-349

Adoration of the Trinity (altarpiece)
Dürer, Albrecht **5** 159-161

Adornment of Spiritual Marriage, The (book)
Ruysbroeck, Jan van **13** 388-389

ADORNO, THEODOR W. (1903-1969), German philosopher and leader of the Frankfurt School **1** 65-67

Adoula, Cyrille (1921-1978), Congolese statesman
Kasavubu, Joseph **8** 453-455
Mobutu Sese Seko **11** 69-71
Tshombe, Moïse Kapenda **15** 325-326

ADP
see Adenosine diphosphate

Adrenal cortex (anatomy)
Reichstein, Tadeus **13** 85-87

Adrenal glands (anatomy)
Addison, Thomas **1** 58-59
Kendall, Edward Calvin **8** 495

Adrenaline (biochemistry)
Dale, Henry Hallett **4** 371-373
Houssay, Bernardo Alberto **7** 522-523
Loewi, Otto **9** 486-487

Adrenocorticotropic hormone (corticosteroid)
Reichstein, Tadeus **13** 85-87

Adrian (died 1700), Russian Orthodox patriarch of Moscow
Peter I **12** 253-256

ADRIAN, EDGAR DOUGLAS (1st Baron Adrian of Cambridge; 1889-1977), English neurophysiologist **1** 67-69
Eccles, John Carew **5** 195-196
Hodgkin, Alan Lloyd **7** 431-432
Sherrington, Charles Scott **14** 187-189

Adrian I (ruled 772-795), pope
Alcuin of York **1** 122-123
Charlemagne **3** 445-447

Adrian IV (Nicholas Breakspear; 1100?-1159), pope 1154-1159
Arnold of Brescia **1** 314-315
Frederick I **6** 78-79

Adrian V (Ottoboni Fieschi; died 1276), pope 1276
Arnolfo di Cambio **1** 315-316
Boniface VIII **2** 392-393

Adrian VI (1459-1523), pope 1522-1523
Bembo, Pietro **2** 144-145

Adrianople, Treaty of (1829)
Mahmud II **10** 145-147

Adsorption analysis (biochemistry)
Tiselius, Arne Wilhelm Kaurin
15 240-241

Adulateur, The (pamphlet)
Warren, Mercy Otis **16** 120-121

Adultery (as capital crime)
Calvin, John **3** 239-242
Cranmer, Thomas **4** 295-296

Aduwa, Battle of (1896)
Menelik II **10** 495-497

Advaita (philosophy)
Shankara **14** 150-151

Advaita Vedanta (Indian religion)
Maharishi Mahesh Yogi **10** 132-133

Advancement of Learning, The (book)
Bacon, Francis **1** 422-424

Advantages of Vegetarianism, The (book)
Hidayat, Sadiq **7** 377-378

Advent (poems)
Rilke, Rainer Maria **13** 171-172

Adventist movement (religion; United States)
Miller, William **11** 30-31
Russell, Charles Taze **13** 376-377

Adventure (book)
Ferrero, Guglielmo **5** 429-430

Adventure (ship)
Cook, James **4** 214-215

Adventurer, The (essays)
Johnson, Samuel **8** 315-317

Adventurers
Casanova de Seinglat, Giacomo Jacopo Girolamo **3** 350-351
Walker, William **16** 68-69
see also Explorers; Frontiersmen

Adventures in Contentment (book)
Baker, Ray Stannard **1** 451-452

Adventures in the Skin Trade ... (stories)
Thomas, Dylan Marlais **15** 188-190

Adventures in Value (book; Cummings-Morehouse)
Cummings, Edward Estlin **4** 334-336

Adventures of a White-collar Man (autobiography)
Sloan, Alfred Pritchard Jr. **14** 274

Adventures of a Young Man (novel)
Dos Passos, John Roderigo **5** 69-71

Adventures of an Atom, The (satire)
Smollett, Tobias George **14** 305-307

Adventures of Augie March, The (novel)
Bellow, Saul **2** 141-143

Adventures of Caleb Williams, The (novel)
Godwin, William **6** 383-384

Adventures of Captain Bonneville, U.S.A. (book)
Irving, Washington **8** 141-143

Adventures of Captain Hatteras, The (novel)
Verne, Jules **15** 467-469

Adventures of David Simple, The (novel)
Fielding, Henry **5** 442-444

Adventures of Dollie, The (film)
Griffith, David Wark **6** 544-545

Adventures of Ferdinand Count Fathom, The (novel)
Smollett, Tobias George **14** 305-307

Adventures of Harry Richmond, The (novel)
Meredith, George **10** 512-513

Adventures of Huckleberry Finn, The (novel)
Twain, Mark **15** 363-366

Adventures of Ideas (book)
Whitehead, Alfred North **16** 242-244

Adventures of Philip, The (novel)
Thackeray, William Makepeace **15** 159-161

Adventures of Robinson Crusoe, The (film)
Buñuel, Luis **3** 127-128
see also Robinson Crusoe (novel)

Adventures of Roderick Random, The (book)
Smollett, Tobias George **14** 305-307

Adventures of Sherlock Holmes (series)
Doyle, Arthur Conan **5** 91-92

Adventures of Sir Launcelot Greaves, The (book)
Smollett, Tobias George **14** 305-307

Adventures of the Dialectic, The (essays)
Merleau-Ponty, Maurice **10** 518

Adventures of Tom Sawyer, The (novel)
Twain, Mark **15** 363-366

Adventures of Ulysses, The (book)
Lamb, Charles **9** 176-177

Adventures while Preaching the Gospel of Beauty (book)
Lindsay, Vachel **9** 424-425

Adversaria anatomica (essays)
Morgagni, Giovanni Battista **11** 158-159

Advertisement to the Jurymen ... (book)
Filmer, Robert **5** 448

Advertisements for Myself (literary collection)
Mailer, Norman Kingsley **10** 148-150

Advertisements for the Unexperienced Planters ... (pamphlet)
Smith, John **14** 295-297

Advertising industry
Ogilvy, David MacKenzie **11** 481-482
Post, Charles William **12** 408-409
Wells, Mary Georgene Berg **16** 197-198

Advice (poems)
Smollett, Tobias George **14** 305-307

Advice to the Privileged Orders (book)
Barlow, Joel **2** 6-7

Advocate (magazine)
Evans, George Henry **5** 337-338

Advocate of Peace ... (book)
Burritt, Elihu **3** 160

Advocate, The (romance)
Heavysege, Charles **7** 246

Adzhubei, Alexei Ivanovich (1924-1993), Russian journalist
John, XXIII **8** 277-280

AE
see Russell, George William

Aedes aegypti (mosquito)
Finlay, Carlos Juan **5** 450
Reed, Walter **13** 78

Aedile (Roman office)
Caesar, Gaius Julius **3** 207-210
Drusus, Marcus Livius **5** 105-106

Aedui (ancient European tribe)
Caesar, Gaius Julius **3** 207-210

AEG
see Allgemeine Elektrizitätsgesellschaft

Aegates (modern Egadi Islands; Mediterranean Sea)
Hamilcar Barca **7** 94-95

Aegean Islands (Greece)
Homer **7** 465-467

Aegina (city-state, Greece)
Cleomenes I **4** 103
Pindar **12** 312-313

Aegineticus (speech)
Isocrates **8** 151

Aegisthus (mythology)
Euripides **5** 332-334
Sophocles **14** 343-345

Aegospotami, Battle of (405 B.C.)
Lysander **10** 70

Aegyptus (literary character)
Aeschylus **1** 70-72

Aelbert (died 781/782), archbishop of York from 767
Alcuin of York **1** 122-123

Aelfgyfu (Emma; flourished 1002-1018), wife of Ethelred II and of Canute I
Canute I, the Great **3** 266-269
Edward the Confessor **5** 218-219

AELFRIC (955-circa 1012), Anglo-Saxon monk, scholar, and writer **1** 69-70

Aelst, Pieter Coecke van
see Coecke van Aelst, Pieter

Aemilianus (206?-253), Roman emperor 253
Valerian **15** 404-405

Aeneas (mythology)
Cortona, Pietro da **4** 256
Geoffrey of Monmouth **6** 268
Ovid **12** 34-36
Virgil **15** 507-510
Vondel, Joost van den **16** 19-20

Aeneid (epic; Virgil)
Cato, Marcus Porcius the Elder **3** 375
Douglas, Gavin **5** 77-78

Gibbon, Edward **6** 299-300
Virgil **15** 507-510
Vondel, Joost van den **16** 19-20

Aeneids, The (book)
Morris, William **11** 187-188

Aengus (ancient Irish hero)
Yeats, William Butler **16** 445-447

Aerial Construction (sculpture)
Smith, David **14** 287-288

Aerial Experiment Association (Hammond-sport, New York State)
Bell, Alexander Graham **2** 129-131
Curtiss, Glenn Hammond **4** 350-351

Aerial Ways (publication)
Pasternak, Boris Leonidovich
12 124-125

Aerodrome (airplane)
Langley, Samuel Pierpont **9** 195-196

Aerodynamics (physics)
Kármán, Theodore von **8** 451-452

Aerograph (art composition)
Ray, Man **13** 59-60

Aeronautics (science)
balloons
Curtiss, Glenn Hammond
4 350-351
Montgolfier, Joseph and Jacques
Michel Étienne **11** 133-134
Santos-Dumont, Alberto **13** 477-478
engineers
Widnall, Sheila E. **16** 258-259
pioneers
Curtiss, Glenn Hammond
4 350-351
Douglas, Donald Wills **5** 77
Langley, Samuel Pierpont **9** 195-196
Sikorsky, Igor **14** 223-224
Tsiolkovsky, Konstantin Eduardovich
15 326-328
Wright brothers **16** 394-396
turbojet propulsion
Whittle, Frank **16** 257-258

Aeronautics, Bureau of (United States Navy)
Byrd, Richard Evelyn **3** 186-187
King, Ernest Joseph **9** 17-18

Aerostatica (ship)
Canot, Theodore **3** 262-263

Aertsen, Pieter (circa 1508-circa 1575), Flemish painter
Clouet, Jean and François **4** 122-123

Aeschines (389-314 B.C.), Athenian orator and politician
Demosthenes **4** 495-496

AESCHYLUS (524-456 B.C.), Greek playwright **1** 70-72
adapted and translated
Leconte de Lisle, Charles Marie
René **9** 273-274
Lowell, Robert Trail Spence Jr.
10 16-17
The Persae

Pericles **12** 219-221
in comedy
Aristophanes **1** 293-294
influence of
Euripides **5** 332-334, 33
O'Neill, Eugene **11** 514-516
Sophocles **14** 343-345

Aesop (circa 620-560 B.C.), Greek fabulist
Edward VI **5** 213-214
Marie de France **10** 259

Aesop's Fables (book)
Calder, Alexander **3** 216-218
Jordaens, Jacob **8** 347-349

Aesthetic Papers (journal)
Peabody, Elizabeth Palmer **12** 167-168

Aesthetics (book)
Croce, Benedetto **4** 313-314

Aesthetics in a Nutshell (essay)
Hamann, Johann Georg **7** 92

Aetius (flourished 500), Greek physician
Celsus, Aulus Cornelius **3** 393

Aëtius, Flavius (396?-454), Roman general
Attila **1** 360

Aetolian League (Greek federation)
Agis IV **1** 81-82
Aratus **1** 273-274

A-fang Palace
see O-pang Palace

Afar in the Forest (book)
Traill, Catharine Parr **15** 291

Afäwärq Gäbrä Iyasus (novel)
Heruy Wäldä-Sellasé **7** 348-349

Affair, The (novel)
Snow, Charles Percy **14** 311-312

Affinity, chemical
Berthollet, Claude Louis **2** 229-230
Berzelius, Jöns Jacob **2** 231-233

Affirmation Bill (1888; England)
Bradlaugh, Charles **2** 478

Affluent Society, The (book)
Galbraith, John Kenneth **6** 174-177

AFFONSO I (1460?-1545), king of Kongo
1 72
Nzinga Nkuwu **11** 451-452

Affrico (literary character)
Boccaccio, Giovanni **2** 351-353

Afghan wars
First (1839-1842)
Aga Khan **1** 74-76
Second (1878-1890)
Lugard, Frederick John Dealtry
10 31-32
Roberts, Frederick Sleigh
13 195-196
Third (1919)
Chelmsford, Frederic John Napier
Thesiger **3** 497

Afghani, Jamal al-Din al-
see Jamal ud-Din al-Afghani

Afghanistan (nation, Central Asia)
British and
Frere, Henry Bartle Edward
6 100-101
Roberts, Frederick Sleigh
13 195-196
Chinese and
Chou En-lai **4** 20-22
French exploration
Bonvalot, Pierre Gabriel Édouard
2 396
Ghaznavids
Mahmud of Ghazni **10** 147
India and
Chandragupta Maurya **3** 426
Curzon, George Nathaniel
4 351-352
Ranjit Singh **13** 32-33
Persia attacked
Nader, Ralph **11** 290-291
see also Afghan wars
Union of Soviet Socialist Republics and
Karmal, Babrak **8** 449-451
Najibullah, Mohammad **11** 296-298

AFINOGENOV, ALEKSANDR NIKOLAE-VICH (1904-1941), Russian dramatist
1 72-73

AFL
see American Federation of Labor

'AFLAQ, MICHEL (born 1910), Syrian founder and spiritual leader of the Ba'th party **1** 73-74

AFL-CIO
see American Federation of Labor and Congress of Industrial Organizations

Afloat and Ashore (novel)
Cooper, James Fenimore **4** 220-223

Africa (book)
Padmore, George **12** 57-58

Africa (continent)
African empires
Affonso I **1** 72
Ali, Sunni **1** 158-159
Anokye, Okomfo **1** 242-243
Cetshwayo **3** 400
Dingane **5** 14-15
Ja Ja of Opobo **8** 201-204
Maherero, Samuel **10** 139-142
Menelik II **10** 495-497
Moshweshwe **11** 203-205
Muhammad Ture, Askia **11** 231-232
Musa Mansa **11** 266
Mutesa I **11** 277
Mutesa II **11** 277-278
Mwanga **11** 282-283
Nzinga Nkuwu **11** 451-452
Sundiata Keita **15** 33-34
Uthman don Fodio **15** 397-398
see also Ethiopia—rulers
archeology
Leakey, Louis Seymour Bazett **9** 262
see also Egyptology
Chinese exploration
Cheng Ho **3** 500

colonialism
 Crispi, Francesco **4** 310-311
 Faidherbe, Louis Léon César
  5 366-367
 see also Imperialism, British; Imperialism, French
Communist policy
 Chou En-lai **4** 20-22
 Touré, Sékou **15** 275-277
culture
 Dinesen Blixen-Finecke, Karen
  5 13-14
 Diop, Cheikh Anta **5** 21-22
 Du Bois, William Edward Burghardt
  5 116-118
 Gluckman, Max **6** 374-375
 Herskovits, Melville Jean **7** 345
 see also African art; African literature
European exploration
 Baikie, William Balfour **1** 440
 Barth, Heinrich **2** 30-31
 Bruce, James **3** 63-64
 Burckhardt, Johann Ludwig **3** 133
 Cadamosto, Alvise da **3** 206-207
 Clapperton, Hugh **4** 72-73
 Livingstone, David **9** 463-465
 Marchand, Jean-Baptiste
  10 234-237
 Peters, Carl **12** 257-258
 see also Explorers, English—of Africa;
  Explorers, French—of Africa;
  Explorers, Portuguese—of Africa
independent states (1945-1770)
 see individual countries
nationalism
 see Nationalism, African;
  Pan-Africanism
North (Islamic Empire)
 Abd al-Mumin **1** 13
 ibn Tashufin, Yusuf **8** 95-96
 ibn Tumart, Muhammad **8** 96-97
 Muawiya ibn Abu Sufyan
  11 223-224
 Yakub al-Mansur, Abu Yusuf **16** 426
 see also Islamic Empire
North (Roman and Byzantine)
 Belisarius **2** 128-129
 Caesar, Gaius Julius **3** 207-210
 Catiline **3** 372-373
 Diocletian **5** 19-20
 Donatus **5** 56-57
 Gaiseric **6** 172
 Gracchus, Tiberius and Gaius Sempronius **6** 479-480
 Masinissa **10** 315-317
 Zenobia **16** 500-503
trade (East Africa)
 Lugard, Frederick John Dealtry
  10 31-32
 Said, Seyyid **13** 428-429
 Tippu Tip **15** 235-236
trade (West Africa)
 Ja Ja of Opobo **8** 201-204

Africa (poem)
 Petrarch **12** 259-261

Africa (symphony)
 Still, William Grant **14** 455-456
Africa and the World (newspaper)
 Wallace-Johnson, Isaac Theophilus
  Akunna **16** 76-77
Africa and World Peace (book)
 Padmore, George **12** 57-58
Africa Dances (painter series)
 Ewonwu, Benedict Chuka **5** 351-352
Africa for the Africans (book)
 Booth, Joseph **2** 404-405
Africa Squadron (United States Navy)
 Perry, Matthew Calbraith **12** 237-239
Africaine, L' (opera)
 Meyerbeer, Giacomo **10** 536-537
African American art
 see African American history (United
  States)
African American history (United States)
 • CIVIL RIGHTS MOVEMENT (United
  States)
  Nationalism
   Farrakhan, Louis **5** 389-390
 • MILITARY LEADERS
  Army generals
   Davis, Benjamin O. Sr.
    4 414-415
   James, Daniel Jr. **8** 209-211
   Powell, Colin Luther **12** 424-425
 • POLITICIANS
  cabinet officials
   Brown, Ronald H. **3** 44-47
   Dinkins, David **5** 15-18
   Weaver, Robert C. **16** 152-153
  governors
   Pinchback, Pinckney Benton
    Stewart **12** 306-308
   Wilder, Lawrence Douglas
    16 274-276
  mayors
   Barry, Marion Shepilov Jr.
    2 25-28
   Bradley, Tom **2** 484-485
   Jackson, Maynard Holbrook Jr.
    8 176-178
   Young, Andrew Jackson Jr.
    16 467-469
   Young, Coleman Alexander
    16 470-471
  members of Congress
   Chisholm, Shirley Anita St. Hill
    4 7-9
   Gray, William H. III **6** 510-511
   Lewis, John Robert **9** 388-390
   Mfume, Kweisi **10** 539-542
   Mosely-Braun, Carol **11** 199-200
   Powell, Adam Clayton Jr.
    12 421-422
   Rangel, Charles B. **13** 31-32
   Waters, Maxine **16** 132-134
   Young, Andrew Jackson Jr.
    16 467-469
  presidential candidates

    Chisholm, Shirley Anita St. Hill
     4 7-9
    Jackson, Jesse Louis **8** 174-176
   state
    Bond, Julian **2** 386-387
 • RECONSTRUCTION-1896
  Atlanta Compromise (1895)
   Washington, Booker Taliaferro
    16 125-126
  Civil Rights Act (1866)
   Bristow, Benjamin Helm **3** 9-10
   Brown, Benjamin Gratz **3** 32-33
   Johnson, Andrew **8** 294-295
   Stevens, Thaddeus **14** 442-443
  equal protection denied
   Field, Stephen Johnson
    5 441-442
   Harlan, John Marshall **7** 156-157
   Miller, Samuel Freeman
    11 29-30
   Turner, Henry McNeal
    15 351-352
   Waite, Morrison Remick **16** 46
   Wells-Barnett, Ida. B.
    16 198-199
   see also Constitution of the United States—Amendments (14th)
  jury service upheld (1880)
   Waite, Morrison Remick **16** 46
  nationalism
   Delany, Martin Robinson
    4 473-474
  Reconstruction officials
   Bruce, Blanche Kelso **3** 62-63
   Delany, Martin Robinson
    4 473-474
   Douglass, Frederick **5** 85-86
   Revels, Hiram Rhoades
    13 109-110
   Smalls, Robert **14** 277-278
   see also Reconstruction (United
    States)
  voting rights
   Coffin, Levi **4** 135
   Lodge, Henry Cabot **9** 482-483
   Miller, Samuel Freeman
    11 29-30
   see also Constitution of the United States—Amendments
    (15th); Suffrage
 • "SEPARATE BUT EQUAL" (1896-1954)
  baseball test case
   Rickey, Wesley Branch
    13 153-155
   Robinson, Jack Roosevelt
    13 207-208
  civil rights activist
   Bond, Horace Mann **2** 384-386
  civil rights leaders
   Du Bois, William Edward
    Burghardt **5** 116-118
   Grimké, Archibald Henry **7** 1-2
   Houston, Charles Hamilton
    7 523-526
   Johnson, James Weldon
    8 304-305

Powell, Adam Clayton Jr.
12 421-422
Talbert, Mary Morris Burnett
15 86-88
Trotter, William Monroe
15 306-307
Washington, Booker Taliaferro
16 125-126
Wells-Barnett, Ida. B.
16 198-199
White, Walter Francis
16 238-239
see also National Association for
the Advancement of Colored
People; Niagara movement
discrimination bans (Federal)
Randolph, A. Philip **13** 28-29
Truman, Harry S. **15** 314-316
educators
Brown, Charlotte Eugenia
Hawkins **3** 34
nationalism
Du Bois, William Edward
Burghardt **5** 116-118
Garvey, Marcus Mosiah
6 228-229
Turner, Henry McNeal
15 351-352
see also Nationalism, African;
Pan-Africanism
other rights cases
Black, Hugo Lafayette **2** 301-303
Hughes, Charles Evans **8** 15-16
segregation constitutional (*Plessy v.
Ferguson*; 1896)
Harlan, John Marshall **7** 156-157
Tourgée, Albion Winegar
15 277-278
segregation unconstitutional (*Brown
v. Board of Education of Topeka*;
1954)
Eisenhower, Dwight David
5 233-236
Marshall, Thurgood **10** 282-284
Warren, Earl **16** 117-120
"separate but equal" precedent
(1849)
Shaw, Lemuel **14** 164-165
• 'SIXTIES and 'SEVENTIES
African American Muslims
Cleaver, Leroy Eldridge **4** 97-98
Malcolm X **10** 165-166
Black Panthers
Carmichael, Stokely **3** 305-308
Cleaver, Leroy Eldridge **4** 97-98
Davis, Angela **4** 412-413
Fonda, Jane **5** 501-502
Forman, James **6** 10-11
Newton, Huey P. **11** 367-369
Seale, Robert George **14** 77-78
Black Power movement
Cone, James Hall **4** 196-197
Civil Rights Act (1957)
Eisenhower, Dwight David
5 233-236
Johnson, Lyndon Baines
8 308-312

Civil Rights Act (1964)
Johnson, Lyndon Baines
8 308-312
King, Martin Luther Jr. **9** 20-22
Wallace, George Corley
16 71-72
civil rights leaders
Abernathy, Ralph David **1** 27-28
Baldwin, James Arthur
1 465-466
Bambara, Toni Cade **1** 482-483
Bevel, James Luther **2** 250-251
Bond, Julian **2** 386-387
Bunche, Ralph Johnson
3 121-122
Cleaver, Leroy Eldridge **4** 97-98
Evers, Medgar **5** 345-348
Gregory, Dick **6** 536-537
Henry, Aaron **7** 306-307
Jackson, Jesse Louis **8** 174-176
Jacob, John Edward **8** 185-188
Jordan, Vernon **8** 357-358
King, Coretta Scott **9** 16-17
King, Martin Luther Jr. **9** 20-22
Malcolm X **10** 165-166
Marshall, Thurgood **10** 282-284
Meredith, James H. **10** 514-515
Randolph, A. Philip **13** 28-29
Robeson, Paul Leroy **13** 198-199
Rustin, Bayard **13** 382-383
Wilkins, Roy **16** 282-283
Young, Whitney Moore Jr.
16 476-477
see also National Urban League
CORE, SCLC, and SNCC
Bevel, James Luther **2** 250-251
Carmichael, Stokely **3** 305-308
Farmer, James **5** 383-385
Forman, James **6** 10-11
Hamer, Fannie Lou **7** 93-94
Hooks, Benjamin Lawson
7 481-483
Jackson, Jesse Louis **8** 174-176
King, Martin Luther Jr. **9** 20-22
Lewis, John Robert **9** 388-390
McKissick, Floyd B. **10** 420-422
Parks, Rosa Lee McCauley
12 115-116
Rustin, Bayard **13** 382-383
Young, Andrew Jackson Jr.
16 467-469
crises and protests
Bunche, Ralph Johnson
3 121-122
Eisenhower, Dwight David
5 233-236
Evers-Williams, Myrlie
5 348-350
Kennedy, John Fitzgerald
8 502-506
King, Martin Luther Jr. **9** 20-22
see also March on Washington
for Jobs and Freedom; Nonvio-
lent protest movement; Poor
People's March

desegregation resistance Federal
offense (1960)
Eisenhower, Dwight David
5 233-236
nationalism
Baraka, Imamu Amiri **1** 498-499
Cleaver, Leroy Eldridge **4** 97-98
Malcolm X **10** 165-166
Robeson, Paul Leroy **13** 198-199
Stokes, Carl B. **14** 464-465
see also Nationalism, African;
Pan-Africanism
photographic record
Freeman, Roland L. **6** 92-93
Soledad Brothers
Davis, Angela **4** 412-413
• SOCIETY and CULTURE
art
Bannister, Edward Mitchell
1 491-493
Barthé, Richmond **2** 33-34
Bearden, Romare Howard
2 86-88
Burke, Selma **3** 143-144
Edwards, Melvin **5** 222-223
Johnson, William H. **8** 320-322
Johnston, Joshua **8** 323-325
Lawrence, Jacob **9** 250-251
Pippin, Horace **12** 318-319
Poitier, Sidney **12** 368-370
Puryear, Martin **12** 486-487
Ringgold, Faith **13** 175-177
Savage, Augusta Christine
13 499-501
Tanner, Henry Ossawa
15 102-103
aviators
Coleman, Bessie **4** 152-154
business leaders
Gordy, Berry Jr. **6** 450-451
Johnson, John Harold **8** 306-308
Morgan, Garrett A. **11** 161-162
Spaulding, Charles Clinton
14 364-365
Sullivan, Leon Howard **15** 25-27
Walker, C. J. **16** 61-62
Walker, Maggie Lena **16** 65-66
cowboys
Love, Nat **10** 1-2
cultural influence
Frazier, Edward Franklin **6** 77
Herskovits, Melville Jean **7** 345
Karenga, Maulana **8** 444-447
Myrdal, Karl Gunnar **11** 284
dance
Ailey, Alvin **1** 91-94
Davis, Sammy Jr. **4** 423-424
Dunham, Katherine **5** 145-146
diplomacy
Anderson, Marian **1** 218-219
Bunche, Ralph Johnson
3 121-122
Grimké, Archibald Henry **7** 1-2
Johnson, James Weldon
8 304-305
Langston, John Mercer **9** 197

economic analysis/development
    Harris, Abram Lincoln Jr.
       7 169-171
    Sullivan, Leon Howard **15** 25-27
education
    Benezet, Anthony **2** 159-160
    Bethune, Mary McLeod
       2 241-242
    Bond, Horace Mann **2** 384-386
    Cole, Johnnetta **4** 147-149
    Collins, Marva **4** 165-167
    Franklin, John Hope **6** 65-67
    Granville, Evelyn Boyd
       6 494-496
    Hope, John **7** 489-490
    Johnson, Charles Spurgeon
       8 296-297
    Johnson, James Weldon
       8 304-305
    Langston, John Mercer **9** 197
    Locke, Alain **9** 475-478
    Mays, Benjamin E. **10** 374-376
    Patterson, Frederick Douglas
       12 139-140
    Revels, Hiram Rhoades
       13 109-110
    Washington, Booker Taliaferro
       16 125-126
educational aid (white)
    Armstrong, Samuel Chapman
       1 306-307
    Crandall, Prudence **4** 291
    Howard, Oliver Otis **7** 528-529
    Rockefeller, John D. Jr.
       13 225-226
    Rosenwald, Julius **13** 293
exploration
    Henson, Matthew A. **7** 312-314
inventors
    Morgan, Garrett A. **11** 161-162
journalism
    Bradley, Ed **2** 478-481
    Fortune, Timothy Thomas
       6 18-21
    Rowan, Carl T. **13** 329-330
Kwanzaa celebrations
    Karenga, Maulana **8** 444-447
law
    Cochran, Johnnie **4** 128-131
    Delany, Martin Robinson
       4 473-474
    Johnson, James Weldon
       8 304-305
    Marshall, Thurgood **10** 282-284
    Thomas, Clarence **15** 186-188
literature (18th century)
    Wheatley, Phillis **16** 221-222
literature (19th century)
    Brown, William Wells **3** 48-49
    Delany, Martin Robinson
       4 473-474
    Dunbar, Paul Laurence
       5 141-142
    Henson, Josiah **7** 311-312
    Russwurm, John Brown
       13 381-382

Smith, James McCune
    14 293-294
    Wilson, Harriet E. **16** 320-322
literature (20th century)
    Angelou, Maya **1** 238-239
    Baldwin, James Arthur
       1 465-466
    Baraka, Imamu Amiri **1** 498-499
    Bearden, Romare Howard
       2 86-88
    Brooks, Gwendolyn **3** 24-26
    Childress, Alice **3** 522-524
    Cullen, Countee **4** 333-334
    Davis, Ossie **4** 421-422
    Ellison, Ralph Waldo **5** 274-275
    Giovanni, Yolande Cornelia Jr.
       6 346-347
    Haley, Alex **7** 76-78
    Hansberry, Lorraine Vivian
       7 130-131
    hooks, bell **7** 477-481
    Hughes, Langston **8** 18-19
    Hurston, Zora Neale **8** 55-56
    Johnson, James Weldon
       8 304-305
    Jordan, June **8** 351-353
    Larsen, Nella **9** 209-210
    Lorde, Audre **9** 513-515
    Marshall, Paule Burke
       10 281-282
    McKay, Claude **10** 416
    McMillan, Terry **10** 427-428
    Morrison, Toni **11** 188-190
    Naylor, Gloria **11** 328-329
    Walker, Alice Malsenior
       16 59-61
    Walker, Margaret **16** 67
    Wilson, August **16** 314-316
    Wright, Richard **16** 401-402
medicine
    Delany, Martin Robinson
       4 473-474
    Drew, Charles Richard
       5 100-101
    Taylor, Susie King **15** 127-128
    Williams, Daniel Hale
       16 302-303
music
    Anderson, Marian **1** 218-219
    Armstrong, Louis Daniel
       1 303-304
    Brown, James **3** 37-39
    Caesar, Shirley **3** 210-211
    Cleveland, James **4** 106-108
    Coltrane, John **4** 173-174
    Cotten, Elizabeth **4** 261-263
    Davis, Miles **4** 419-421
    Davis, Sammy Jr. **4** 423-424
    Dawson, William Levi
       4 427-428
    Dett, Robert Nathaniel **4** 512
    Ellington, Edward Kennedy
       5 273-274
    Franklin, Aretha **6** 58-60
    Gillespie, Dizzy **6** 320-322
    Gordy, Berry Jr. **6** 450-451

Handy, William Christopher
    7 123-124
    Hayes, Roland **7** 225-227
    Hendrix, Jimi **7** 279-283
    Jackson, Michael Joe **8** 178-180
    Jones, Quincy Delight Jr.
       8 339-341
    Joplin, Scott **8** 345-347
    Jordan, Louis **8** 353-355
    King, B. B. **9** 11-14
    Monk, Thelonious **11** 104-108
    Parker, Charles Christopher Jr.
       12 105-106
    Ross, Diana **13** 298-300
    Smith, Bessie **14** 285-287
    Still, William Grant **14** 455-456
    Waters, Muddy **16** 134-136
philosophy
    West, Cornel **16** 212-213
photography
    Freeman, Roland L. **6** 92-93
    VanDer Zee, James **15** 418-419
poetry
    Dove, Rita Frances **5** 87-89
politics
    Bruce, Blanche Kelso **3** 62-63
    Langston, John Mercer **9** 197
    Revels, Hiram Rhoades
       13 109-110
    Smalls, Robert **14** 277-278
    Stokes, Carl B. **14** 464-465
publishing
    Johnson, John Harold **8** 306-308
    Maynard, Robert Clyve
       10 366-367
    Work, Monroe **16** 388-389
recorders of
    Johnson, Guy Benton **8** 299-300
    Woodson, Carter Godwin
       16 374-376
religion
    Allen, Richard **1** 168
    Divine, Father **5** 29-32
    Farrakhan, Louis **5** 389-390
    Hope, John **7** 489-490
    King, Martin Luther Jr. **9** 20-22
    Muhammad, Elijah **11** 230-231
    Perry, Harold Robert **12** 236-237
    Sharpton, Al **14** 159-162
    Turner, Henry McNeal
       15 351-352
science
    Banneker, Benjamin **1** 490-491
    Carver, George Washington
       3 346-347
    Chinn, May Edward **3** 525-526
    Forten, James **6** 17-18
    Gayle, Helene Doris **6** 244-245
    Jackson, Shirley Ann **8** 183-184
    Jemison, Mae C. **8** 243-244
    Just, Ernest **8** 392-393
    Long, Irene D. **9** 497-498
    Patrick, Jennie R. **12** 136-137
sociology
    Clark, Kenneth B. **4** 78-79
    Frazier, Edward Franklin **6** 77

Johnson, Charles Spurgeon
8 296-297
sports
Aaron, Henry Louis (Hank) **1** 2-3
Ali, Muhammad **1** 156-158
Ashe, Arthur Robert Jr.
1 328-330
Chamberlain, Wilt **3** 413-415
Erving, Julius Winfield
5 317-319
Gibson, Althea **6** 305-306
Jabbar, Kareem Abdul **8** 164-165
Jackson, Reginald Martinez
8 180-182
Johnson, Jack **8** 301-304
Johnson, Marietta Louise Pierce
8 312-313
Jordan, Michael **8** 355-357
Lewis, Carl **9** 377-380
Louis, Joe **9** 537-538
Mays, Willie **10** 376-379
Owens, Jesse **12** 43-44
Paige, Satchel **12** 62-65
Rickey, Wesley Branch
13 153-155
Robinson, Frank Jr. **13** 202-203
Robinson, Jack Roosevelt
13 207-208
Rudolph, Wilma **13** 350-352
Walker, LeRoy Tashreau
16 64-65
television
Cosby, William Henry Jr.
4 257-258
Winfrey, Oprah Gail **16** 333-336
theater
Baraka, Imamu Amiri **1** 498-499
Davis, Ossie **4** 421-422
Dee, Ruby **4** 449-452
Hansberry, Lorraine Vivian
7 130-131
Jones, James Earl **8** 334-337
Robeson, Paul Leroy **13** 198-199
• THROUGH CIVIL WAR
abolitionists
Brown, William Wells **3** 48-49
Burns, Anthony **3** 151
Douglass, Frederick **5** 85-86
Forten, James **6** 17-18
Purvis, Robert **12** 485-486
Remond, Charles Lennox **13** 95
Still, William **14** 454-455
Truth, Sojourner **15** 320-321
Walker, David **16** 62-63
see also Abolitionists; Antislavery
movement; Slave trade,
African; Slavery
African colonization
Ashmun, Jehudi **1** 335-336
Cuffe, Paul **4** 331-332
Delany, Martin Robinson
4 473-474
Hopkins, Samuel **7** 496
Russwurm, John Brown
13 381-382
Brown v. Bd. of Educ; 1954

Eisenhower, Dwight David
5 233-236
Marshall, Thurgood **10** 282-284
Warren, Earl **16** 117-120
citizenship denied
see Dred Scott decision
civil rights granted (Mass; 1783)
Cuffe, Paul **4** 331-332
Civil War service
Douglass, Frederick **5** 85-86
Forrest, Nathan Bedford **6** 13-14
Grant, Ulysses Simpson
6 492-494
Higginson, Thomas Wentworth
7 380
see also Civil War, United States
offense (1960)
Eisenhower, Dwight David
5 233-236
segregation cases
Shaw, Lemuel **14** 164-165
Truth, Sojourner **15** 320-321
"separate but equal" precedent
(1849)
Shaw, Lemuel **14** 164-165
slaves
Allen, Richard **1** 168
Brown, William Wells **3** 48-49
Bruce, Blanche Kelso **3** 62-63
Burns, Anthony **3** 151
Carver, George Washington
3 346-347
Christophe, Henri **4** 32
Cinque, Joseph **4** 62
Douglass, Frederick **5** 85-86
Henson, Josiah **7** 311-312
Jacobs, Harriet A. **8** 190-193
Langston, John Mercer **9** 197
Prosser, Gabriel **12** 460-461
Scott, Dred **14** 65-66
Smalls, Robert **14** 277-278
Truth, Sojourner **15** 320-321
Tubman, Harriet Ross
15 330-331
Turner, Nathaniel **15** 354
Vesey, Denmark **15** 475
Wheatley, Phillis **16** 221-222
slaves' revolts
Dew, Thomas Roderick **4** 519
Garrison, William Lloyd
6 226-228
Monroe, James **11** 111-113
Prosser, Gabriel **12** 460-461
Turner, Nathaniel **15** 354
Vesey, Denmark **15** 475
see also Brown, John—Harper's
Ferry
Underground Railroad (African
Americans)
Allen, Richard **1** 168
Brown, William Wells **3** 48-49
Henson, Josiah **7** 311-312
Purvis, Robert **12** 485-486
Smith, James McCune
14 293-294
Still, William **14** 454-455

Tubman, Harriet Ross
15 330-331
Underground Railroad (whites)
Coffin, Levi **4** 135
Gage, Matilda Joslyn **6** 167-169
Garrett, Thomas **6** 225-226
Mott, Lucretia Coffin **11** 212-213
Pinkerton, Allan **12** 314-315
Voting Rights Act (1965)
Johnson, Lyndon Baines
8 308-312
King, Martin Luther Jr. **9** 20-22
white support for rights
Chase, Salmon Portland
3 473-475
Conkling, Roscoe **4** 201-202
Coxe, Tench **4** 285-286
Davis, Henry Winter **4** 415-416
Hampton, Wade III **7** 112
McLean, John **10** 422-423
see also Abolitionists; Antislavery
movement; Civil liberties; Civil
rights movement; Minority
rights; Supreme Court (United
States)—civil liberties cases

African American Life Insurance Co. (Jacksonville, Florida)
Bethune, Mary McLeod **2** 241-242

African American Symphony (musical
composition)
Still, William Grant **14** 455-456

African Americans
see African American history (United
States)

African art
Ewonwu, Benedict Chuka **5** 351-352
Kirchner, Ernst Ludwig **9** 34-35
Picasso, Pablo **12** 292-295
Williams, Henry Sylvester **16** 303-304

African Association (established 1897)
Williams, Henry Sylvester **16** 303-304

African Colonization Society
Canot, Theodore **3** 262-263

African Committee
see Committee of Merchants Trading to
Africa

African Communities League (established
1914)
Garvey, Marcus Mosiah **6** 228-229

African Continental Bank (established
1944)
Azikiwe, Nnamdi **1** 401-402

African independence movements
see Nationalism, African

African Intelligencer (newspaper)
Ashmun, Jehudi **1** 335-336

African Lakes Co.
Livingstone, David **9** 463-465

African Life and Customs (book)
Blyden, Edward Wilmot **2** 348-349

African literature, modern
in Amharic

Heruy Wäldä-Sellasé **7** 348-349
Mäkonnen Endalkačäw **10** 161-162
in Arabic
Husayn, Taha **8** 61-62
in English
Achebe, Chinua **1** 35-37
Ekwensi, Cyprian **5** 242-243
Equiano, Olaudah **5** 296-297
Imam, Alhadji Abubakar **8** 114-115
Laurence, Margaret **9** 229-230
Mphahlele, Ezekiel **11** 221-223
Ngugi wa Thiong'o **11** 375-376
Nkosi, Lewis **11** 407-408
Paton, Alan Stewart **12** 134-135
Plaatje, Solomon Tshekisho
12 341-342
Soyinka, Wole **14** 358-359
Tutuola, Amos **15** 361-362
in French
Beti, Mongo **2** 242-243
Laye, Camara **9** 257-259
Ousmane, Sembene **12** 32-33
Rabearivelo, Jean Joseph
12 523-524
Senghor, Léopold Sédar **14** 106-107
in Gikuyu
Ngugi wa Thiong'o **11** 375-376
in Hausa
Imam, Alhadji Abubakar **8** 114-115
in Swahili
Shaaban Robert **14** 128-129
in Xhosa
Mqhayi, Samuel Edward Krune
11 223
in Zulu
Dube, John Langalibalele **5** 113
Mofolo, Thomas **11** 74

African Methodist Episcopal Church (United States)
Allen, Richard **1** 168
Turner, Henry McNeal **15** 351-352

African Morning Post (newspaper)
Azikiwe, Nnamdi **1** 401-402
Wallace-Johnson, Isaac Theophilus
Akunna **16** 76-77

African National Congress (ANC)
Kaunda, Kenneth David **8** 460-461
Lembede, Anton **9** 318-319
Luthuli, Albert John **10** 51-52
Mandela, Nelson Rolihlahla
10 185-186
Sisulu, Nontsikelelo Albertina
14 259-261
Sisulu, Walter Max Ulyate **14** 261-262
Tambo, Oliver Reginald **15** 92-94
Verwoerd, Hendrik Frensch **15** 472-473
Vorster, Balthazar Johannes **16** 30-32

African nationalism
see Nationalism, African

African Nationalism (book)
Sithole, Ndabaningi **14** 262-264

African Orthodox Church (United States)
Garvey, Marcus Mosiah **6** 228-229

African Protestant Episcopal Church (United States)
Allen, Richard **1** 168

African Queen, The (film)
Bogart, Humphrey **2** 363-364

African Sentinel (newspaper)
Wallace-Johnson, Isaac Theophilus
Akunna **16** 76-77

African Studies Association (United States)
Herskovits, Melville Jean **7** 345

African Trading Company (Prussia)
Frederick William **6** 85-86

African Workers' Union (Nigeria)
Wallace-Johnson, Isaac Theophilus
Akunna **16** 76-77

Afrikakorps (German military)
Rommel, Erwin **13** 268-269

Afrikaner party (South Africa)
Hertzog, James Barry Munnik
7 347-348
Vorster, Balthazar Johannes **16** 30-32

Afro-American League (civil rights organization)
Fortune, Timothy Thomas **6** 18-21

Afro-Asian Conference (Bandung; 1955)
Wright, Richard **16** 401-402

Afro-Asian Solidarity Conference (1965)
Wallace-Johnson, Isaac Theophilus
Akunna **16** 76-77

Afro-Shirazi Party (Zanzibar)
Karume, Abeid Amani **8** 452-453

After Apple-picking (poem)
Frost, Robert Lee **6** 130-133

After Bread (story)
Sienkiewicz, Henryk **14** 216-217

After Dinner at Ornans (painting)
Courbet, Jean Desiré Gustave
4 271-273

After Nihilism (book)
Benn, Gottfried **2** 164

After Strange Gods (book)
Eliot, Thomas Stearns **5** 258-261

After Such Pleasures (stories)
Parker, Dorothy Rothschild **12** 106

After the Ball (song; Harris)
Sousa, John Philip **14** 353-354

After the Fall (play)
Miller, Arthur **11** 25-26

After the Hunt (painting)
Harnett, William Michael **7** 160-161

After the Whirlwind (book)
Russell, Charles Edward **13** 374-375

Aftergrowth (autobiography)
Bialik, Hayyim Nahman **2** 262-263

Afternoon Meal of the Workers (painting)
Amorsolo, Fernando **1** 204

Afternoon Men (novel)
Powell, Anthony **12** 422-423

Afternoon of a Faun (musical composition)
Debussy, Achille Claude **4** 445-447

Afterthoughts on the U.S.S.R. (book)
Gide, André **6** 308-309

Afzal Khan (died 1659), Bijapur general
Shivaji **14** 199-200

Against Our Will (book)
Brownmiller, Susan **3** 56-57

AGA KHAN (title), chief commander of
Moslem Nizari Ismailis **1** 74-76
Aga Khan I (Hasan Ali Shah;
1800-1881) **1** 74-76
Aga Khan II (Ali Shah; died 1885)
1 74-76
Aga Khan III (Sultan Sir Muhammad
Shah; 1877-1957) **1** 74-76
Aga Khan IV (Prince Karim; born 1936)
1 74-76
Jinnah, Mohammad Ali **8** 262-263

Agade
see Akkad

Agag (flourished 11th century B.C.), king of
the Amalekites
Saul **13** 498

Against ... (speeches)
Demosthenes **4** 495-496

Against an Ignorant Bookbuyer (satire)
Lucian **10** 25-26

Against Apion (book)
Josephus Flavius **8** 360-361

Against Euthynus (speech)
Isocrates **8** 151

Against Lochites (speech)
Isocrates **8** 151

Against Praxeas (book)
Tertullian **15** 155-156

Against the Grain (novel; Huysmans)
Huysmans, Joris Karl **8** 81-82
Redon, Odilon **13** 75-76

Against the Sophists (book)
Isocrates **8** 151

Against the Stream (book)
Barth, Karl **2** 31-32

Agamemnon (musical composition; Milhaud-Claudel)
Milhaud, Darius **11** 17-18

Agamemnon (mythology)
Aeschylus **1** 70-72
Euripides **5** 332-334
Sophocles **14** 343-345

Agamemnon (play)
Aeschylus **1** 70-72
Seneca the Younger, Lucius Annaeus
14 103-105
Thomson, James **15** 199-200

Agamemnon (ship)
Nelson, Horatio **11** 336-338

Agassiz, Alexander (1835-1910), American
naturalist
Agassiz, Jean Louis Rodolphe **1** 76-78

Agassiz, Elizabeth Cabot Cary
(1822-1907), American author
Agassiz, Jean Louis Rodolphe **1** 76-78

AGASSIZ, JEAN LOUIS RODOLPHE
(1807-1873), Swiss-American naturalist
and anatomist **1** 76-78
James, William **8** 215-217
Jordan, David Starr **8** 350-351

Agathe (literary character)
Musil, Robert Edler Von **11** 268-269

Agathius (flourished 6th century) Greek
writer
Zoroaster **16** 528-530

Agathocles (6th-5th century B.C.), Greek
poet
Pindar **12** 312-313

Agathon (flourished 5th century B.C.),
Athenian tragic poet
Plato **12** 345-347
Socrates **14** 320-321

Agathon (novel)
Wieland, Christoph Martin **16** 260-261

Agave (literary character)
Euripides **5** 332-334

Âge d'or, L' (film)
Buñuel, Luis **3** 127-128

Age of Anxiety, The (symphony)
Bernstein, Leonard **2** 218-219

Age of Bronze (sculpture)
Rodin, Auguste **13** 236-238

Age of Constantine the Great (book)
Burckhardt, Jacob Christoph **3** 132-133

Age of Innocence (novel)
Wharton, Edith **16** 221

Age of Innocence (painting)
Reynolds, Joshua **13** 115-116

Age of Jackson, The (book)
Schlesinger, Arthur Meier Jr. **14** 13-15

Age of Provincial Wars (Japan; 1477-1573)
Nobunaga, Oda **11** 413-414

Age of Reason, The (pamphlet)
Paine, Thomas **12** 66-67

Age of Roosevelt (book series)
Schlesinger, Arthur Meier Jr. **14** 13-15

Age of Sesostris, The (book)
Gibbon, Edward **6** 299-300

Age of the Chartists, The (book)
Hammond, Lawrence and Lucy **7** 109

AGEE, JAMES (1909-1955), American poet,
journalist, novelist, and screenwriter
1 78-79
Barber, Samuel **1** 500-501
Bogart, Humphrey **2** 363-364
Chaplin, Charles Spencer **3** 438-440

Agency for International Development
(AID; U.S.)
Duvalier, François **5** 165-166
Gayle, Helene Doris **6** 244-245
Stroessner, Alfredo **14** 511-512

Agent in the Proper Sense ... (book)
Kindi, Abu-Yusuf Yaqub ibn-Ishaq al-
9 10-11

Agent Intellect (philosophy)
Averroës **1** 382-383

Agents and Patients (novel)
Powell, Anthony **12** 422-423

Ages of Man (Greek literature)
Hesiod **7** 361-362

Ages, The (poem)
Bryant, William Cullen **3** 83-85

Agesilaus (3rd century B.C.), Spartan noble
Agis IV **1** 81-82

Agesilaus (book)
Xenophon **16** 418-420

AGESILAUS II (circa 444-360 B.C.), king of
Sparta circa 399-360 B.C. **1** 79-80
Lysander **10** 70
Xenophon **16** 418-420

Aggiornamento (Roman Catholic Church)
Bea, Augustinus **2** 79
John, XXIII **8** 277-280

Agglutinins
see Antibodies

Agglutinogens
see Antigens

Agha (title)
Agha Mohammad Khan **1** 80-81

AGHA MOHAMMAD KHAN (circa
1742-1797), shah of Persia **1** 80-81

Aghlabid dynasty (North Africa; ruled
800-909)
Harun al-Rashid **7** 188

Agincourt, battle of (1415)
English forces
Gloucester, Duke of **6** 370-371
Henry V **7** 296-297
Marlborough, 1st Duke of
10 271-272
French forces
Charles VI **3** 460-461
Joan of Arc **8** 264-265
Orléans, Charles D' **11** 530

Aging (biology)
Metchnikoff, Élie **10** 532-533

Agis II (398 B.C.), king of Sparta circa
426-399 B.C.
Agesilaus II **1** 79-80
Alcibiades **1** 119-120
Lysander **10** 70

AGIS IV (circa 262-241 B.C.), king of Spar-
ta **1** 81-82
Aratus **1** 273-274
Cleomenes III **4** 103-104

Aglaura (play)
Suckling, John **15** 10-11

Aglavaine et Sélysette (play)
Maeterlinck, Maurice **10** 125-126

AGNELLI, GIOVANNI (born 1920), Italian
industrialist **1** 82-83

Agnes Bernauer (play)
Hebbel, Friedrich **7** 247

AGNEW, SPIRO THEODORE (1918-1996),
Republican United States vice president
under Richard Nixon **1** 83-85
Nixon, Richard Milhous **11** 401-404

Agnew Clinic (painting)
Eakins, Thomas **5** 176-177

Agnolo, Baccio d' (1460?-1543), Italian
architect
Sangallo family **13** 464-466

AGNON, SHMUEL YOSEPH (1888-1970),
author **1** 85-86

Agnostic (theology)
Huxley, Thomas Henry **8** 77-79
Ingersoll, Robert Green **8** 120-121

Agnus Dei (musical composition)
Machaut, Guillaume de **10** 93-94
see also Mass (music)

Agon (ballet)
Stravinsky, Igor Fedorovich **14** 502-506

Agon (rhetoric)
Euripides **5** 332-334

Agony (painting)
Gorky, Arshile **6** 458

Agony in the Garden (painting)
Bellini, Giovanni **2** 137-138
Mantegna, Andrea **10** 215-216
Titian **15** 242-244

Agony of Christianity, The (book)
Unamuno y Jugo, Miguel de
15 386-387

Agora (Athens)
Phidias **12** 265-267

AGOSTINO (1557-1602) **1** 86
Bernini, Gian Lorenzo **2** 214-216

Agostino (novel)
Moravia, Alberto **11** 153-155

AGOSTINO DI DUCCIO (1418-1481?),
Italian sculptor **1** 86

Agramonte, Ignacio (1841-1873), Cuban
revolutionist
Céspedes, Carlos Manuel de **3** 398-399

Agrarian Labor party (Chile)
Ibáñez del Campo, Carlos **8** 88

Agrarian Problem ... (book)
Tawney, Richard Henry **15** 120-121

Agrarian Question ... (pamphlet)
Lenin, Vladimir Ilich **9** 323-326

Agrarian reform
see Land reform

Agreement of the People, An (pamphlet)
Lilburne, John **9** 409-410

Agricola
see Crèvecoeur, St. J.

Agricola (book)
Tacitus **15** 70-72

Agricola (sculpture series)
Smith, David **14** 287-288

AGRICOLA, GEORGIUS (1494-1555),
German mineralogist and writer **1** 86-87
Biringuccio, Vannoccio **2** 283

Agricola, Gnaeus Julius (40-93), Roman
general
Domitian **5** 52-53
Tacitus **15** 70-72
Titus Flavius Vespasianus **15** 247-248

Agricultural Adjustment Act (1933; United
States)
Cardozo, Benjamin Nathan **3** 288-290
Stone, Harlan Fiske **14** 468-470

Agricultural Commodities Agreement
(1957)
Magsaysay, Ramon **10** 130-131

Agricultural Origins and Dispersals (book)
Sauer, Carl Ortwin **13** 496-497

Agricultural Recovery Act of 1935 (United
States)
Hughes, Charles Evans **8** 15-16

Agricultural Society (New York State)
Buel, Jesse **3** 105

Agriculturalists
see Agriculturists

Agriculture (Australia)
Deakin, Alfred **4** 432-433

Agriculture (Canada)
Saunders, Charles Edward **13** 498-499
Sifton, Clifford **14** 219-220

Agriculture (China)
Fan Chung-yen **5** 376-377
Ts'ao Ts'ao **15** 322-323

Agriculture (developing countries)
Borlaug, Norman Ernest **2** 418-420

Agriculture (Roman Empire)
Trajan **15** 291-292

Agriculture (Russia)
Lysenko, Trofim Denisovich **10** 71
Mendeleev, Dmitrii Ivanovich
10 486-488
Stalin, Joseph **14** 393-396

Agriculture (United States)
dairy industry
Babcock, Stephen Moulton
1 410-411
fairs
Watson, Elkanah **16** 136
Federal programs
Harding, Warren Gamaliel
7 148-149
Hoover, Herbert Clark **7** 483-485
Knapp, Seaman Asahel **9** 58
machinery
Deere, John **4** 455
Deering, William **4** 455-456
McCormick, Cyrus Hall **10** 400-401
Oliver, James **11** 500-501
see also Business and industrial
leaders—agricultural machinery
industry

organizations
Kelley, Oliver Hudson **8** 480-481
Watson, Elkanah **16** 136
publicists
Wallace, Henry **16** 73
scientific
Buel, Jesse **3** 105
Carver, George Washington
3 346-347
Couper, James Hamilton **4** 270
Dunbar, William **5** 143-144
Ruffin, Edmund **13** 354-355
surpluses (1920s)
Coolidge, John Calvin **4** 217-219
training
Cornell, Ezra **4** 236-237
unions
Chavez, Cesar **3** 486-487

Agriculture, United States Department of
Carver, George Washington **3** 346-347
Hatch, William Henry **7** 196
Kelley, Oliver Hudson **8** 480-481
Knapp, Seaman Asahel **9** 58
Knipling, Edward Fred **9** 59-60
Pinchot, Gifford **12** 308-309
Wiley, Harvey Washington **16** 277-278

Agriculturists, American
colonial planters
Byrd, William **3** 188-189
Hampton, Wade **7** 111-112
19th century
Applegate, Jesse **1** 264-265
Bidwell, John **2** 265
Buel, Jesse **3** 105
Couper, James Hamilton **4** 270
Kelley, Oliver Hudson **8** 480-481
Knapp, Seaman Asahel **9** 58
Polk, Leonidas Lafayette **12** 376-377
Ruffin, Edmund **13** 354-355
Watson, Elkanah **16** 136
20th century
Babcock, Stephen Moulton
1 410-411
Carver, George Washington
3 346-347
see also Scientists, American—horti-
culturists

Agriculturists, Canadian
Saunders, Charles Edward **13** 498-499

Agriculturists, English
Booth, Joseph **2** 404-405

Agriculturists, Scottish
Hutton, James **8** 73-74

Agrigento (painting)
Hofmann, Hans **7** 442-443

Agrippina (opera)
Handel, George Frederick **7** 116-119

Agrippina, Julia (15-59), Roman empress
Claudius Germanicus, Tiberius **4** 91-92
Nero Claudius Caesar **11** 342-344
Seneca the Younger, Lucius Annaeus
14 103-105

Agrippina, Vipsania (14 B.C.?-33 A.D.),
Roman noblewoman
Caligula **3** 228-229

Agrippina with the Ashes of Germanicus
(painting)
West, Benjamin **16** 210-212

Agrupacio Courbet (art organization)
Miró, Joan **11** 53-54

Agua Prieta, Plan of (1920)
Calles, Plutarco Elías **3** 234-235
Cárdenas, Lázaro **3** 286-287
Carranza, Venustiano **3** 321-322
Obregón, Álvaro **11** 458-459
Villa, Pancho **15** 495-496

Aguascalientes, Convention of (1914)
Cárdenas, Lázaro **3** 286-287

Agudeza y arte de ingenio (book)
Gracián y Morales, Baltasar Jerónimo
6 481-482

Aguesseau, Henri François d' (1668-1751),
French chancellor
Diderot, Denis **5** 1-2

Aguila de blasón (play)
Valle Inclán, Ramón Maria del
15 407-408

AGUINALDO, EMILIO (1869-1964),
Philippine revolutionary leader **1** 88
opponents
Bonifacio, Andres **2** 393-394
Root, Elihu **13** 283-284
supporters
Mabini, Apolinario **10** 72-73
Quezon, Manuel Luis **12** 511-513
Rómulo, Carlos P. **13** 270-271

Aguirre Cerda, Pedro (1879-1941), Chilean
statesman, president 1938-1941
Alessandri Palma, Arturo **1** 128-129

Aguja de navegar cultos (book)
Quevedo Y Villegas, Francisco Gómez
de **12** 511

Agulhas (cape; South Africa)
Dias de Novais, Bartolomeu **4** 533-534

Agustin I
see Iturbide, Augustin de

Ah Q cheng-chuan (story)
Lu Hsün **10** 35-37

Ah Sin (literary character)
Harte, Francis Brett **7** 184-185

Ah Wilderness! (play; O'Neill)
Cohan, George Michael **4** 137-138
O'Neill, Eugene **11** 514-516

Ahab, Captain (literary character)
Melville, Herman **10** 472-476

AHAD HAAM (pseudonym of Asher T.
Ginsberg, 1856-1927), Russian-born
author **1** 88-89
Bialik, Hayyim Nahman **2** 262-263
Gordon, Aaron David **6** 447-448
Kaufmann, Ezekiel **8** 460

Ahaz (died 715 B.C.?), king of Judah circa
735-715 B.C.
Isaiah **8** 146-147
Tiglath-pileser III **15** 221-222

AHIDJO, AHMADOU (1924-1989), first
president of the Federal Republic of
Cameroon **1** 89-90
Beti, Mongo **2** 242-243

Ahijah (Old Testament prophet)
Jeroboam I **8** 248-249

Ahimsa (Buddhism)
Buddha **3** 97-101
Mahavira, Vardhamana **10** 135-137

Ahle, Johann Georg (1651-1706), German
organist and composer
Bach, Johann Sebastian **1** 416-419

Ahle, Johann Rudolf (1625-1673), German
organist and composer
Bach, Johann Sebastian **1** 416-419

Ahmad ibn-Abi-Duad (flourished 9th century), Mutazilite theologian
Mamun, Abdallah al- **10** 183

Ahmad Shah (1898-1930), shah of Iran
1909-1925
Reza Shah Pahlavi **13** 116-117

Ahmadabad
see Ahmedabad

Ahmed Mirza
see Ahmad Shah

Ahmedabad (city, India)
Calder, Alexander **3** 216-218
Gandhi, Mohandas Karamchand
6 201-204

Ahmedabad Congress (India)
Das, Chitta Ranjan **4** 401-402

Ahnen, Die (book)
Freytag, Gustav **6** 107-108

Ahnfrau, Die (play)
Grillparzer, Franz **6** 546-547

Ahomadegbe, Justin Tometin (born 1917),
Dahomean politician
Apithy, Sourou Migan **1** 259-260

Ahriman (Angra Mainyu; Zoroastrian)
Augustine **1** 367-370
Zoroaster **16** 528-530

Ahuitzótl (died 1502), Aztec king
1486-1502
Cuauhtemoc **4** 329
Montezuma, II **11** 128-129

Ahura Mazda (Zoroas, god)
Darius I **4** 394-395
Zoroaster **16** 528-530

Aiace (play)
Foscolo, Ugo **6** 21

Ai-ch'ing ti san-pu-ch'u (novel)
Pa Chin **12** 53-54

AID
see Agency for International Development

Aida, I (opera; Verdi)
Caruso, Enrico **3** 345
Toscanini, Arturo **15** 270-271
Verdi, Giuseppe Fortunino Francesco
15 463-465

Aids to Reflection (book)
Coleridge, Samuel Taylor **4** 154-156

AIKEN, CONRAD (1889-1973), American
poet, essayist, novelist, and critic **1** 90-91
Eliot, Thomas Stearns **5** 258-261

Aileron (aeronautics)
Curtiss, Glenn Hammond **4** 350-351

AILEY, ALVIN (1931-1989), African American dancer and choreographer **1** 91-94

AILLY, PIERRE D' (1350-1420), French
scholar and cardinal **1** 94
Columbus, Christopher **4** 176-179
Dufay, Guillaume **5** 125-126
Gerson, John **6** 285-286
Martin V **10** 287-288

Ailred, St. (1109?-1166), English abbot and
author
Jean de Meun **8** 234-235

Aims of the Philosophers, The (book)
Ghazali, Abu Hamid Muhammad al-
6 290-291

Ain Jalut (site, Egypt)
Hulagu Khan **8** 27-28

Ain Shams University (Egypt)
Farouk I **5** 387-388

Ain-i-Akbari (book, Abul Fazl)
Akbar, Jalal-ud-din Mohammed **1** 96

Ain't Misbehavin' (musical revue)
Waller, Thomas Wright **16** 81-82

Ainu (religious sect)
Kammu **8** 420

Aiolos (literary character)
Homer **7** 465-467

Air (gas)
Boyle, Robert **2** 469-471
Hess, Victor Francis **7** 362-363

Air (philosophy)
Anaximenes **1** 210

Air brake (railroad)
Westinghouse, George **16** 215

Air conditioning
Carrier, Wills **3** 325-326

Air Pioneering in the Arctic (book)
Ellsworth, Lincoln **5** 277

Air pioneers
see Aviators

Air pressure (physics)
Hooke, Robert **7** 475

Air research (Great Britain)
Cockcroft, John Douglas **4** 131-132
Lovell, Alfred Charles Bernard **10** 8-9

Air-conditioned Nightmare, The (book)
Miller, Henry **11** 26-27

Aircraft (aeronautics)
development
Langley, Samuel Pierpont **9** 195-196
Wright brothers **16** 394-396
helicopter
Sikorsky, Igor **14** 223-224
instrumentation
Compton, Arthur Holly **4** 186-188
jet-propelled
Douglas, Donald Wills **5** 77
Tupolev, Andrei Nikolaevich
15 341-342
manufacturers
Boeing, William Edward **2** 357-358
Sopwith, Thomas Octave Murdoch
14 345-346
military
Arnold, Henry Harley **1** 310-311
De Gaulle, Charles André Joseph
Marie **4** 463-465
Kármán, Theodore von **8** 451-452
pilots
Coleman, Bessie **4** 152-154
Earhart, Amelia Mary **5** 177-179
rocket-propelled
Tsiolkovsky, Konstantin Eduardovich
15 326-328
see also Aeronautics; Business and
industrial leaders—aircraft industry

Aircraft, Battle Force (United States)
Halsey, William Frederick **7** 91-92
King, Ernest Joseph **9** 17-18

Airplane-crash victims
Barrientos Ortuño, René **2** 22-23
Bhabha, Homi Jehangir **2** 253-254
Bose, Subhas Chandra **2** 430-431
Castelo Branco, Humberto **3** 359-360
Hammarskjöld, Dag **7** 100-101
Leclerc, Jacques Philippe **9** 272-273
Reuther, Walter Philip **13** 107-108
Zia ul-Haq, Mohammad **16** 513-515

Airport design
Saarinen, Eliel and Eero **13** 396-398

Aisha (611-678), wife of Mohammed
Abu Bakr **1** 31-32
Ali **1** 155-156

Aitia (book)
Callimachus **3** 235-236

AITKEN, WILLIAM MAXWELL (Lord
Beaverbrook; 1879-1964), Canadian
businessman and politician **1** 94-96

Aix-la-Chapelle, Congress of (1818)
Castlereagh, Viscount **3** 363-364
Metternich, Klemens von **10** 533-536

Aix-la-Chapelle, Treaty of (1748)
Charles Edward Louis Philip Casimir
Stuart **3** 466-467
Clive, Robert **4** 119-120
Dupleix **5** 153
Pepperell, William **12** 206-207

Ajax (play)
Sophocles **14** 343-345

Ajax Burned by Lightning (painting)
Apollodorus **1** 261

Ajayi and His Inherited Property (book)
Tutuola, Amos **15** 361-362

Ajnadain, battle of (634)
Abu Bakr **1** 31-32

Akan (African people)
Anokye, Okomfo **1** 242-243

Akan Doctrine of God, The (book)
Danquah, Joseph B. **4** 388-389

AKBAR, JALAL-UD-DIN MOHAMMED
(1542-1605), Mogul emperor of India
1556-1605 **1** 96
Jahangir **8** 196-199
Shah Jahan **14** 138-139

Akbar Nama (book; Abul Fazl)
Akbar, Jalal-ud-din Mohammed **1** 96

Akechi Mitsuhide (1526-1582), Japanese
general
Ieyasu, Tokugawa **8** 103-106
Nobunaga, Oda **11** 413-414
Toyotomi Hideyoshi **15** 286-289

AKHMATOVA, ANNA (pseudonym of Anna
A. Gorenko, 1889-1966), Russian poet
1 96-97
Ehrenburg, Ilya Grigorievich **5** 224-225

AKIBA BEN JOSEPH (circa 50-circa 135),
Palestinian founder of rabbinic Judaism
1 97-98
Johanan ben Zakkai **8** 271-272
Judah I **8** 372-373

AKIHITO (born 1933), 125th emperor of
Japan **1** 98-99
Hirohito **7** 410-412

Akiko (flourished 1007-1010), Japanese
empress
Fujiwara Michinaga **6** 145-146
Murasaki Shikibu **11** 252-253

Akil (flourished 1470-1480), African Tuareg
chief
Ali, Sunni **1** 158-159

Akintola, S.L. (died 1966), Nigerian politician
Awolowo, Obafemi **1** 389-390

Akkad (ancient city, Mesopotamia)
Sargon of Agade **13** 483

Akkadian dynasty (Mesopotamia; ruled
circa 2340-2189 B.C.)
Sargon of Agade **13** 483

Akroinon, Battle of (740)
Leo III **9** 330-332

Aksakov, Konstantin Sergeevich
(1817-1860), Russian playwright and
poet
Lermontov, Mikhail Yurievich
9 352-353

Al Araaf, Tamerlane and Minor Poems
(book)
Poe, Edgar Allan **12** 363-365

Al cor gentil rempaira sempre amore (canzone)
Guinizzelli, Guido **7** 36-37

Al márgen de los clásicos (book)
Ruíz, José Martínez **13** 358

Al Que Quiere (poems)
Williams, William Carlos **16** 308-309

Al Smith and His America (book)
Handlin, Oscar **7** 121-122

Ala and Lolli (ballet)
Prokofiev, Sergei Sergeevich
12 458-460

Ala Hamish al-Sirah (novel)
Husayn, Taha **8** 61-62

Ala ibn Mughith, al- (died 763), Arab revolutionary in Spain
Abd al-Rahman I **1** 13-14

Alabama (ship)
see Alabama claims

Alabama (state, United States)
Curry, Jabez Lamar Monroe **4** 346-347
de Soto, Hernando **4** 510-511
Dix, Dorothea Lynde **5** 32-33
Wallace, George Corley **16** 71-72
Yancey, William Lowndes **16** 436-437

Alabama Claims (1872)
Alabama cruise
Semmes, Raphael **14** 102-103
arbitration tribunal
Evarts, William Maxwell **5** 340-341
Waite, Morrison Remick **16** 46
United States diplomacy
Adams, Charles Francis **1** 41-42
Fish, Hamilton **5** 461-462
Seward, William Henry **14** 124-125

Alabama Council on Human Relations
(civic group)
King, Martin Luther Jr. **9** 20-22

Alabama, University of (University)
Barnard, Frederick Augustus Porter
2 9-10
Bryant, Paul **3** 82-83
Gorgas, Josiah **6** 453-454

al-Ahram (newspaper)
Haykal, Muhammad Husain **7** 230-231

Alam Halfa, battle of (1942)
Alexander of Tunis, 1st Earl **1** 135-136

Aläm warätäñña (book)
Mäkonnen Endalkačäw **10** 161-162

ALAMÁN, LUCAS (1792-1853), Mexican
statesman **1** 99-100
Juárez, Benito **8** 369-372
Santa Ana, Antonio López de
13 471-472

Alamanni (Germanic tribe)
Caracalla **3** 281-282
Clovis I **4** 124

Alamein, 1st Viscount Montgomery of
see Montgomery, Bernard Law

Alamein, El, battle of (1942)
Alexander of Tunis, 1st Earl **1** 135-136
Montgomery, Bernard Law **11** 135-136

Alamo, battle of the (1836)
Crockett, David **4** 314-316
Travis, William Barret **15** 292-293

ALARCÓN, PEDRO ANTONIO DE
(1833-1891), Spanish writer and politician **1** 100-101

Alarcón, Pedro de (16th century), Spanish
explorer
Solís, Juan Díaz de **14** 326

ALARCÓN Y MENDOZA, JUAN RUIZ DE
(1581?-1639), Spanish playwright **1** 101
Alemán, Mateo **1** 126

Alarcos, battle of (1195)
Yakub al-Mansur, Abu Yusuf **16** 426

ALARIC (circa 370-410), Visigothic leader
1 101-102
Leo I **9** 329-330
Pelagius **12** 189-190
Stilicho, Flavius **14** 452-453

Alarm Clock (magazine)
Chekhov, Anton Pavlovich **3** 494-497

Alaska (state, United States)
Baranov, Aleksandr Andreievich
1 499-500
Hay, John **7** 215-216
Lansing, Robert **9** 200
Lodge, Henry Cabot **9** 482-483
Seward, William Henry **14** 124-125

Alastor (poem; Shelley)
Keats, John **8** 470-472
Shelley, Percy Bysshe **14** 176-178

Alau
see Hulagu Khan

ALA-UD-DIN (died 1316), Khalji sultan of
Delhi **1** 102-103

ALAUNGPAYA (1715-1760), king of Burma
1752-1760 **1** 103

Alawid dynasty (Egypt; ruled 1805-1953)
Farouk I **5** 387-388

Al-Ayyam (autobiography)
Husayn, Taha **8** 61-62

Al-Azar (Mosque University, Cairo)
Abduh ibn Hasan Khayr Allah, Muham-
mad **1** 16-17
Goya y Lucientes, Francisco de Paula
José de **6** 476-478
Marāghī, Mustafā al- **10** 228-229

Alba, Duchess of (died 1802), Spanish art
patron
Goya y Lucientes, Francisco de Paula
José de **6** 476-478

ALBA, DUKE OF (Fernando Álvarez de
Toledo; 1507-1582), Spanish general and
statesman **1** 103-104
Encina, Juan del **5** 283
William the Silent **16** 300-302

Alban, St. (died circa 304), first British martyr
Matthew Paris **10** 341-342

Albani, Alessandro (1692-1779), Italian
cardinal
West, Benjamin **16** 210-212
Winckelmann, Johann Joachim
16 332-333

Albania (nation, Southeastern Europe)
Alia, Ramiz **1** 159
Berisha, Sali **2** 195-197
Hoxha, Enver **8** 1-3
Mahmud II **10** 145-147
Mehmed the Conqueror **10** 452-454
Mohammed Ali **11** 81-82
Zog I **16** 525-526

AL-BANNA, HASSAN (1906-1949), Egyptian religious leader and founder of the
Muslim Brotherhood **1** 104-106

Albany (city, New York State)
Burgoyne, John **3** 137-138
Corning, Erastus **4** 238-239
McCloskey, John **10** 395

Albany, 1st Duke of (Robert Stewart;
1340?-1420), Scottish statesman
Henry IV **7** 292-293
James I **8** 206-207
Robert III **13** 194-195

Albany Congress (1754)
Hutchinson, Thomas **8** 71-72
see also Plan of Union

Albany, Countess of (Louise de Stolberg
Stuart; 1753-1824), German wife of
Charles Edward Stuart
Alfieri, Vittoria **1** 145-146

Albany, Duke of (Alexander Stewart;
1454?-1485), Scottish statesman
James III **8** 208-209

Albany Evening Journal (newspaper)
Weed, Thurlow **16** 169-170

Albany Nursery (experimental farm)
Buel, Jesse **3** 105

Albany Plan (1754)
see Plan of Union (1754)

Albany race riots (Georgia; 1961)
King, Martin Luther Jr. **9** 20-22

Albany Regency (Northern Democratic pol-
itics)
Corning, Erastus **4** 238-239
Tilden, Samuel Jones **15** 222-223

Albategnius
see Battani, al-

ALBEE, EDWARD FRANKLIN, III (born
1928), American playwright **1** 106-108

Albemarle, 2d Earl of (William A. Keppel;
1702-1754), British general
Gage, Thomas **6** 169-170

Albemarle, Dukes of
see Monck

ALBÉNIZ, ISAAC (1860-1909), Spanish
composer and pianist **1** 108-109

ALBERDI, JUAN BAUTISTA (1810-1884),
Argentine political theorist **1** 109-110
Mármol, José **10** 274

Albergati, Niccolò, Bl. (1375-1443), Italian
cardinal
Alberti, Leon Battista **1** 113-115

Albergo sul porto, Un (play)
Betti, Ugo **2** 246

Alberic of Rheims (12th century), French
philosopher
Abelard, Peter **1** 23-25

Alberoni, Giulio (1664-1752), Spanish cardinal and statesman
Philip V **12** 276-277

ALBERS, JOSEPH (1888-1976), American
artist and art and design teacher **1** 110
Gorky, Arshile **6** 458
Rauschenberg, Robert **13** 52-53

Albert (1559-1621), archduke of Austria
Rubens, Peter Paul **13** 339-342

ALBERT (1819-1861), Prince Consort of
Great Britain **1** 110-112
Edward VII **5** 214-215
Leopold I **9** 345-346
Tennyson, Alfred **15** 144-146
Victoria **15** 485-487

Albert (story)
Tolstoy, Leo **15** 262-265

Albert, Charles d' (1578-1621), duc de
Luynes
Louis XIII **9** 529-531

Albert, Eugen d' (1864-1932),
Scottish-born German composer and
pianist
Liszt, Franz **9** 445-447

Albert I (1250?-1308), king of Germany
1298-1308
Rudolf I **13** 347-348

ALBERT I (1875-1934), king of the Belgians
1909-1934 **1** 112
Leopold II **9** 346-347
Leopold III **9** 347-348

Albert II (1397-1439), king of Germany
1438-1439
Frederick III **6** 84-85

ALBERT II (born 1934), sixth king of the
Belgians **1** 112-113

Albert Herring (opera)
Britten, Benjamin **3** 10-11

Albert, Lake (Africa)
Baker, Samuel White **1** 454-455

Albert of Brandenberg
see Albrecht of Brandenberg

Albert Schweitzer Hospital (Haiti)
Schweitzer, Albert **14** 55-56

Albert Schweitzer Hospital (Lambaréné,
Gabon)
Schweitzer, Albert **14** 55-56

Albert the Great
see Albertus Magnus, St.

Alberta (province, Canada)
Aberhart, William **1** 26-27
Bennett, Richard Bedford **2** 171-172

Laurier, Wilfrid **9** 232-234

Alberti, Giuseppe (1640-1716), Haitian
painter
Troger, Paul **15** 300

ALBERTI, LEON BATTISTA (1404-1472),
Italian writer, humanist, and architect
1 113-115
Agostino di Duccio **1** 86
Ghiberti, Lorenzo **6** 291-292
Luca della Robbia **10** 19-20
Masaccio **10** 312-313

Alberti, Rafael (born 1902), Spanish poet
Lorca, Federico García **9** 511-513

Albertine disparue (novel)
Proust, Marcel **12** 465-467

ALBERTUS MAGNUS, ST. (circa
1193-1280), German philosopher and
theologian **1** 115-116
as thinker
Bonaventure **2** 383-384
influence of
Eckhart, Johann **5** 200-201
Rabelais, François **12** 524-526
Thomas Aquinas **15** 183-186
influenced by
ibn Gabirol, Solomon ben Judah
8 92
Maimonides **10** 151-152
Paul **12** 141-143

Albigensians (religious sect)
Dominic **5** 51-52
Frederick II **6** 79
Innocent III **8** 125-127
Thibaut IV **15** 180-181
Wolfram von Eschenbach **16** 360-361

Albinus, Decimus Clodius Septimus (died
197), Roman general
Caracalla **3** 281-282
Septimius Severus, Lucius **14** 109-110

Alborada del gracioso (musical composition)
Ravel, Maurice Joseph **13** 54-55

Albornoz
see Carillo de Albornoz

Albrecht of Brandenburg (1490-1545),
German cardinal
Grünewald, Matthias **7** 23-24

Albrechtsberger, Johann Georg
(1736-1809), Austrian composer and theorist
Beethoven, Ludwig van **2** 114-117

Albret, Charlotte d' (married 1499), sister
of Jean d'Albret, king of Navarre
Borgia, Cesare **2** 412-413

Albret, Henri d'
see Henry II, king of Navarre

ALBRIGHT, MADELEINE KORBEL (born
1937), United States secretary of state
1 116-118

Album for the Young (musical composition)
Schumann, Robert Alexander **14** 41-43

Albuminuria (medicine)
Bright, Richard **3** 7-8

ALBUQUERQUE, AFONSO DE (circa 1460-1515), Portuguese viceroy to India **1** 118-119
Manuel I **10** 219-220

Albury Platform (painting)
Drysdale, George Russell **5** 107-109

Alcaeus (born circa 620 B.C.), Greek lyric poet
Horace **7** 500-503
Sappho **13** 479-480

Alcalá Zamora y Torres, Niceto
see Zamora y Torres, Niceto Alcalá

Alcalde de Zalamea, El (play; Calderón)
Calderón, Pedro **3** 221-222
Cervantes, Miguel de Saavedra **3** 395-398

Alcántara, Pedro de
see Pedro II

Alcarria (region, Spain)
Cela y Trulock, Camilo José **3** 389-390

Alcázar (Toledo)
Herrera, Juan de **7** 335

Alcestas, rebellion of (320 B.C.)
Antigonus I **1** 248-249

Alceste (literary character)
Molière **11** 86-88

Alceste (opera)
Gluck, Christoph Willibald **6** 372-374

Alceste (play)
Smollett, Tobias George **14** 305-307

Alcestiad, The (play)
Wilder, Thornton Niven **16** 276-277

Alcestis (play)
Euripides **5** 332-334

Alchemist, The (play)
Jonson, Ben **8** 343-345

Alchemists
see Scientists, Arab

Alchemy
Jabir ibn Hayyan **8** 167
Jung, Carl Gustav **8** 388-389
Paracelsus, Philippus Aureolus **12** 91-93

ALCIBIADES (circa 450-404 B.C.), Athenian general and politician **1** 119-120
Agesilaus II **1** 79-80
Lysander **10** 70
Socrates **14** 320-321

Alcibiades (book)
Antisthenes **1** 250-251

Alcibiades (dialogue; Plato)
Alcibiades **1** 119-120
Zoroaster **16** 528-530

Alcimus (died 159 B.C.), Judean high priest 164-159 B.C.
Judas Maccabeus **8** 374-375

Alcina (opera)
Handel, George Frederick **7** 116-119

Alciphron (dialogue)
Berkeley, George **2** 197-198

Alcmena and the Daughters of Herakles ... (painting)
Apollodorus **1** 261

Alcmeonidae (ancient Greek clan)
Cleisthenes **4** 98-99
Pericles **12** 219-221

Alcools (poems)
Apollinaire, Guillaume **1** 260

ALCORN, JAMES LUSK (1816-1894), American lawyer and politician **1** 120-121

Alcorn College (Mississippi)
Revels, Hiram Rhoades **13** 109-110

ALCOTT, AMOS BRONSON (1799-1888), American educator **1** 121
associates
Hawthorne, Nathaniel **7** 212-215
Peabody, Elizabeth Palmer **12** 167-168
quoted
Brown, John **3** 39-41
relatives
Alcott, Louisa May **1** 122
transcendentalism
Emerson, Ralph Waldo **5** 278-280
Fuller, Sarah Margaret **6** 150-151

ALCOTT, LOUISA MAY (1832-1888), American author and reformer **1** 122
Alcott, Amos Bronson **1** 121
French, Daniel Chester **6** 98-99

Alcotts, The (musical composition)
Ives, Charles Edward **8** 159-160

Alcuin (novel)
Brown, Charles Brockden **3** 33

ALCUIN OF YORK (730?-804), English educator, statesman, and liturgist **1** 122-123
Charlemagne **3** 445-447

Alcyone (literary collection)
Lampman, Archibald **9** 180-181

Aldehydes (chemistry)
Baeyer, Johann Friedrich Adolf von **1** 432
Carothers, Wallace Hume **3** 317-318

Alder, Kurt (1902-1958), German chemist
Diels, Otto Paul Hermann **5** 5-6

Aldie, battle of (1863)
Custer, George Armstrong **4** 355-356

Aldington, Richard (1892-1962), English poet and novelist
Doolittle, Hilda **5** 65-66

Aldobrandini, Pietro (1571-1621), Italian cardinal
Porta, Giacomo della **12** 402-403

Aldobrandini Villa (Frascati)
Porta, Giacomo della **12** 402-403

Aldosterone (hormone)
Reichstein, Tadeus **13** 85-87

ALDRICH, NELSON WILMARTH (1841-1915), American statesman and financier **1** 123-124
Penrose, Boies **12** 203-204
Warburg, Paul Moritz **16** 111-112

Aldrich Plan (United States; 1911)
Aldrich, Nelson Wilmarth **1** 123-124

Aldrich-Vreeland emergency banking bill (1908)
Aldrich, Nelson Wilmarth **1** 123-124

Aldrin, Edwin (born 1930), American astronaut
Armstrong, Neil Alden **1** 304-306
Gagarin, Yuri Alexeivich **6** 166-167

Aleatory music
Boulez, Pierre **2** 444-445
Bussotti, Sylvano **3** 174-175
Byrd, William **3** 187-188
Ginastera, Alberto Evaristo **6** 328-329
Halffter, Christóbal **7** 79-80
Lutoslawski, Witold **10** 52-53
Stockhausen, Karlheinz **14** 460-461

ALEICHEM, SHOLOM (Sholom Rabinowitz; 1859-1916), writer of literature relating to Russian Jews **1** 124-125

ALEIJADINHO, O (Antônio Francisco Lisbôa; 1738-1814), Brazilian architect and sculptor **1** 125-126

Aleko (opera)
Rachmaninov, Sergei Vasilievich **12** 531-532

Alem, Leandro (1842?-1896), Argentine politician
Irigoyen, Hipólito **8** 139-140

ALEMÁN, MATEO (1547-after 1615), Spanish novelist **1** 126

ALEMÁN VALDÉS, MIGUEL (1902-1983), Mexican statesman, president 1946-1952 **1** 126-127
Ávila Camacho, Manuel **1** 387-388

Alemani (religious group)
Columban **4** 176

ALEMBERT, JEAN LE ROND D' (1717-1783), French mathematician and physicist **1** 127-128
as mathematician
Bougainville, Louis Antoine de **2** 443-444
Diderot, Denis **5** 1-2
Lagrange, Joseph Louis **9** 164-166
Laplace, Marquis de **9** 202-204
as music theorist
Euler, Leonard **5** 331-332

Alençon, François, Duc d' (1554-1584), French nobleman
Bodin, Jean **2** 356-357
Henry IV **7** 293-295
Hilliard, Nicholas **7** 391-392
Spenser, Edmund **14** 373-376

Alençon, John II, Duc d' (flourished 1429-1440), French noble
Joan of Arc **8** 264-265

Alenu (Jewish prayer)
Abba Arika **1** 3-4

Aleph, The (stories)
Borges, Jorge Luis **2** 411-412

Aleppo (ancient city, Syria)
Alp Arslan **1** 178-179

Alès, edict of (1629)
Louis XIII **9** 529-531

Alesia, battle of (52 B.C.)
Caesar, Gaius Julius **3** 207-210

ALESSANDRI PALMA, ARTURO
(1868-1950), Chilean statesman, president 1920-1925 and 1932-1938
1 128-129
Alessandri Rodriguez, Jorge **1** 129-130
Ibáñez del Campo, Carlos **8** 88

ALESSANDRI RODRIGUEZ, JORGE (born 1896), Chilean statesman, president 1958-1964 **1** 129-130
Alessandri Palma, Arturo **1** 128-129
Ibáñez del Campo, Carlos **8** 88

Alessandro (opera)
Handel, George Frederick **7** 116-119

Alessandro nell'Indie (opera)
Bach, Johann Christian **1** 415-416

Aleutian Islands (Bering Sea)
Baranov, Aleksandr Andreievich
1 499-500

Alexander (died 1661), American Wampanoag Indian chief
Philip **12** 267-268

Alexander (died 220 B.C.), satrap of Persia
Antiochus III **1** 249-250

Alexander (book)
Aristotle **1** 295-296

Alexander (letter)
Isocrates **8** 151

ALEXANDER I (1777-1825), czar of Russia 1801-1825 **1** 130-132
and Napoleonic Wars
Kutuzov, Mikhail Ilarionovich
9 137-138
Napoleon I **11** 306-310
Nesselrode, Karl Robert **11** 348-349
Stein, Heinrich Friedrich Karl vom und zum **14** 415-416
Talleyrand, Charles Maurice de
15 89-90
as baptismal sponsor
Victoria **15** 485-487
Congress of Vienna
Castlereagh, Viscount **3** 363-364
Metternich, Klemens von
10 533-536
reforms
Speranski, Mikhail Mikhailovich
14 376-377
relatives
Catherine the Great **3** 370-372
Nicholas I **11** 377-378
Paul I **12** 143-144
United States relations

Adams, John Quincy **1** 52-54

Alexander I (died 1124), king of Scotland
David I **4** 407

Alexander I (Obrenovic; 1876-1903), king of Serbia 1889-1903
Peter I **12** 256

Alexander I (ruled 342-330 B.C.), king of Epirus
Philip II **12** 269-271

Alexander I (ruled 495-450 B.C.), king of Macedon
Pindar **12** 312-313

Alexander I, king of Yugoslavia
see Alexander of Yugoslavia

ALEXANDER II (1818-1881), czar of Russia 1855-1881 **1** 132-133
Alexander III **1** 133-134
Cahan, Abraham **3** 214
Chernyshevsky, Nikolai Gavrilovich
3 504-505
Kropotkin, Peter Alekseevich **9** 107-108

Alexander II (died 1073), pope 1061-1073
Henry III **7** 290-292

Alexander II (ruled 272-circa 240 B.C.), king of Epirus
Asoka **1** 341-342

Alexander III (1241-1286), king of Scotland 1249-1286
Robert I **13** 192-194

ALEXANDER III (1845-1894), emperor of Russia 1881-1894 **1** 133-134
Nicholas II **11** 378-380
Pilsudski, Joseph **12** 305-306
Pobedonostsev, Konstantin Petrovich
12 360-361
Witte, Sergei Yulyevich **16** 349-350

Alexander III (Orlando Bandinelli; circa 1105-1181), pope 1159-1181
Alfonso I **1** 148
Becket, Thomas **2** 101-102
Frederick I **6** 78-79
Henry II **7** 287-289
Manuel I **10** 218-219
Waldo, Peter **16** 55-56

Alexander III, king of Macedon
see Alexander the Great

Alexander IV (323-310 B.C.), king of Macedon
Antigonus I **1** 248-249

Alexander IV (Rinaldo Conti; died 1261), pope 1254-1261
Albertus Magnus **1** 115-116
Joachim of Fiore **8** 263-264

Alexander V (Pietro di Candia; 1340?-1410), antipope 1409-1410
Ailly, Pierre d' **1** 94
Martin V **10** 287-288

Alexander VI, pope
Borgia,, Lucrezia Duchess of Ferrara
2 413-416

ALEXANDER VI (Rodrigo Borgia; 1431-1503), pope 1492-1503 **1** 134-135
cardinals created
Paul III **12** 144-145
family
Borgia, Cesare **2** 412-413, 80
opponents
Julius II **8** 384-386
Leo X **9** 332-334
Savonarola, Girolamo **13** 505-506
Sforza, Lodovico **14** 127-128
Treaty of Tordesillas
Columbus, Christopher **4** 176-179

Alexander VIII (Pietro Ottoboni; 1610-1691), pope 1689-1691
Corelli, Arcangelo **4** 230-231

Alexander, Cosmo (circa 1724-1772), Scottish-American painter
Stuart, Gilbert **14** 513-515

Alexander, James (1691-1756), Scottish-American lawyer and statesman
Zenger, John Peter **16** 497-498

Alexander Karageorgevic (1806-1885), prince of Serbia 1842-1858
Peter I **12** 256

Alexander, Prince (literary character)
Chrestien de Troyes **4** 23-24

Alexander, Robert E. (born 1907), American architect
Neutra, Richard Joseph **11** 355-356

Alexander, St. (died 328), bishop of Alexandria 313-328
Arius **1** 297-298
Athanasius **1** 358-359

ALEXANDER, SAMUEL (1859-1938), British philosopher **1** 141

Alexander, William (1726-1783), American Revolutionary officer
Monroe, James **11** 111-113

Alexander Balus (musical composition)
Handel, George Frederick **7** 116-119

Alexander Brown and Sons (export firm)
Brown, Alexander **3** 31-32

Alexander Karageorgevich (1888-1934)
see Alexander of Yugoslavia

Alexander Keraunophoros (painter)
Apelles **1** 257

Alexander Nevsky
see Nevsky, Alexander

Alexander Nevsky (film)
Eisenstein, Sergei Mikhailovich
5 240-242
Prokofiev, Sergei Sergeevich
12 458-460

Alexander of Aphrodisias (flourished circa 200), Greek philosopher
Boethius, Anicius Manlius Severinus
2 360-361

ALEXANDER OF TUNIS, 1ST EARL (Harold Rupert Leofric George Alexander; born 1891), British field marshal **1** 135-136
Montgomery, Bernard Law **11** 135-136

ALEXANDER OF YUGOSLAVIA
(1888-1934), king of the Serbs, Croats, and Slovenes 1921-1929 and of Yugoslavia, 1929-1934 **1** 136-137
Peter I **12** 256

Alexander Severus, Marcus Aurelius
(208?-235), Roman emperor 222-235
Ulpian, Domitius **15** 385-386

ALEXANDER THE GREAT (356-323 B.C.),
king of Macedon **1** 137-141
court
Apelles **1** 257
Aristotle **1** 295-296
Demosthenes **4** 495-496
family
Philip II **12** 269-271
influence of
Caracalla **3** 281-282
Chandragupta Maurya **3** 426
military affairs
Antigonus I **1** 248-249
Kautilya **8** 462
Ptolemy I **12** 470-472
Seleucus I **14** 92-93

Alexander the Great (literary work)
Kazantzakis, Nikos **8** 466-468

Alexander von Humboldt Foundation
Heisenberg, Werner Karl **7** 261-263

Alexander's Bridge (novel)
Cather, Willa Sibert **3** 368-369

Alexander's Feast (cantata; Handel)
Handel, George Frederick **7** 116-119
Mozart, Wolfgang Amadeus **11** 218-221

Alexander's Ragtime Band (song)
Berlin, Irving **2** 200-201

Alexandra (1844-1925), queen consort of Edward VII
George V **6** 273-275
Victoria **15** 485-487

Alexandra Feodorovna (1872-1918),
empress of Russia
Rasputin, Grigori Efimovich **13** 44-45

Alexandre (play)
Racine, Jean Baptiste **12** 532-535

Alexandria (book)
Forster, Edward Morgan **6** 14-16

Alexandria (city, Egypt)
and Sparta
Cleomenes III **4** 103-104
Early Christian period
Arius **1** 297-298
Clement of Alexandria **4** 102-103
Leo I **9** 329-330
Nestorius **11** 349-350
founding and growth
Alexander the Great **1** 137-141
Ptolemy I **12** 470-472
Ptolemy II **12** 472-473
French capture (1798)
Napoleon I **11** 306-310
museum library

Eratosthenes of Cyrene **5** 301-302
Roman period
Caesar, Gaius Julius **3** 207-210
Cleopatra **4** 105-106
Ptolemy, Claudius **12** 473-474
university founded
Farouk I **5** 387-388
Husayn, Taha **8** 61-62

Alexandria Quartet, The (book series)
Durrell, Lawrence **5** 163-164

Alexandrian poetry (Greek literature)
Callimachus **3** 235-236

Alexandrians (philosophy)
Pomponazzi, Pietro **12** 390-391

Alexandros of Abonuteichos (biography)
Lucian **10** 25-26

Alexeyev, Constantin Sergeyevich
see Stanislavsky, Constantin

Alexiad (book)
Comnena, Anna **4** 185-186

ALEXIE, SHERMAN (born 1966), Native American writer, poet, and translator **1** 141-142

Alexis (flourished 4th-3rd century B.C.),
Greek dramatist
Menander **10** 477-478

ALEXIS MIKHAILOVICH ROMANOV
(1629-1676), czar of Russia 1645-1676 **1** 142-143
Chmielnicki, Bogdan **4** 12-13
Nikon, Nikita Minov **11** 395
Peter I **12** 253-256

Alexis Nikolaevich (1904-1918), czarevitch of Russia
Nicholas II **11** 378-380
Rasputin, Grigori Efimovich **13** 44-45

Alexis Petrovich (1690-1718), czarevitch of Russia
Peter I **12** 253-256

Alexis und Dora (ballad)
Goethe, Johann Wolfgang von **6** 388-391

ALEXIUS I (circa 1048-1118), Byzantine emperor 1081-1118 **1** 143-144
Bohemund I **2** 364
Comnena, Anna **4** 185-186
Guiscard, Robert **7** 39-40

Alexius III Angelus (died 1210), Byzantine emperor 1195-1203
Dandolo, Enrico **4** 386-387
Villehardouin, Geffroi de **15** 499

Alexius IV Angelus (died 1204), Byzantine emperor 1203-1204
Villehardouin, Geffroi de **15** 499

Alfano, Franco (1877-1957), Italian composer
Puccini, Giacomo **12** 474-476

ALFARO, JOSÉ ELOY (1842-1912),
Ecuadorian revolutionary, president 1895-1901 and 1906-1911 **1** 144-145
Montalvo, Juan María **11** 119-120

Alfaro y Gomez, Juan de (1640-1680),
Spanish painter
Velázquez, Diego Rodríguez de Silva y **15** 454-456

Alfasi, Isaac (flourished 12th century), Jewish rabbi and scholar
Judah Halevi **8** 373

ALFIERI, CONTE VITTORIA (1749-1803),
Italian playwright **1** 145-146

ALFONSÍN, RAUL RICARDO (born 1927),
politician and president of Argentina (1983-) **1** 146-148

Alfonsine Tables (astronomy)
Alfonso X **1** 150-151

Alfonso (died 1491), Portuguese prince
Manuel I **10** 219-220

ALFONSO I (Henriques; 1109?-1185), king of Portugal 1139-1185 **1** 148

Alfonso I, king of Castile
see Alfonso VI, king of León

Alfonso I, king of Naples
see Alfonso V, king of Aragon

Alfonso I, king of Sicily
see Alfonso V, king of Aragon

Alfonso II (1185-1223), king of Portugal 1211-1223
Alfonso III **1** 148-149

Alfonso II (1448-1495), king of Naples
Sforza, Lodovico **14** 127-128

ALFONSO III (1210-1279), king of Portugal 1248-1279 **1** 148-149
Alfonso X **1** 150-151

Alfonso V (1385-1458), king of Aragon and of Naples and Sicily
Pisanello **12** 323-324
Valla, Lorenzo **15** 406

Alfonso V (Alfonso the African; 1432-1481), king of Portugal 1438-1481
Abravanel, Isaac ben Judah **1** 31
Isabella I **8** 144-145

ALFONSO VI (1040-1109), king of León, 1065-1109, and of Castile, 1072-1109 **1** 149
Alfonso I **1** 148
Cid **4** 58-59
ibn Tashufin, Yusuf **8** 95-96

Alfonso VIII (died 1214), king of Castile 1158-1214
Yakub al-Mansur, Abu Yusuf **16** 426

ALFONSO X (1221-1284), king of Castile and León 1252-1284 **1** 150-151
Alfonso III **1** 148-149
Herrera, Juan de **7** 335
Rudolf I **13** 347-348

Alfonso XII (1857-1885), king of Spain 1874-1885
Isabella II **8** 145-146

ALFONSO XIII (1886-1941), king of Spain 1886-1931 **1** 151
Franco Bahamonde, Francisco **6** 52-54

Primo de Rivera y Orbaneja, Miguel
12 454-455

Alfonso the African
see Alfonso V, king of Portugal

Alfonso the Wise
see Alfonso X, king of Castile and León

Alfonso und Estrella (opera)
Schubert, Franz Peter **14** 35-37

ALFRED (849-899), Anglo-Saxon king of
Wessex 871-899 **1** 151-153
Aelfric **1** 69-70
Bede **2** 109-110
Edward the Elder **5** 219-220
Ethelred the Unready **5** 327
Marie de France **10** 259

Alfred (masque)
Thomson, James **15** 199-200

Alfred Sisley and His Wife (painting)
Renoir, Pierre Auguste **13** 101-102

Alfred the Great
see Alfred, king of Wessex

Algabal (poems)
George, Stefan **6** 277-278

Algazel
see Ghazali, Abu Hamid Muhammad
al-

Algebra (mathematics)
abstract
Noether, Emmy **11** 414-416
algebraic geometry
Riemann, Georg Friedrich Bernard
13 164-165
Boolean algebra
Boole, George **2** 396-397
development (9th-16th century)
Cardano, Geronimo **3** 285-286
Fibonacci, Leonardo **5** 434-435
Gauss, Karl Friedrich **6** 240-242
Hasan ibn al-Haytham **7** 190-191
Khwarizmi, Muhammad ibn Musa
al- **8** 541
Lagrange, Joseph Louis **9** 164-166
Recorde, Robert **13** 68-69
equations
Euler, Leonard **5** 331-332
Fourier, Jean Baptiste Joseph **6** 32-33
Gauss, Karl Friedrich **6** 240-242
noncommutative principles
Hamilton, William Rowan **7** 99-100
theory of invariance
Lagrange, Joseph Louis **9** 164-166
Noether, Emmy **11** 414-416

ALGER, HORATIO (1832-1899), American
author **1** 153-154
Ford, Paul Leicester **6** 9-10

**Algeria, Democratic and Popular Republic
of** (nation, North Africa)
Almohads and Almoravids
Abd al-Mumin **1** 13
ibn Tashufin, Yusuf **8** 95-96
as Barbary State
Jones, John Paul **8** 337-338

French in
Abd el-Kadir **1** 15
Bugeaud de la Piconnerie, Thomas
Robert **3** 111
De Gaulle, Charles André Joseph
Marie **4** 463-465
Faidherbe, Louis Léon César
5 366-367
Lavigerie, Charles Martel Allemand
9 240
Ly, Abdoulaye **10** 60
Lyautey, Louis Hubert Gonzalve
10 60-61
Mahmud II **10** 145-147
international role
Chadli Benjedid **3** 402-404
Islamic Reform Movement
Ben Badis, 'Abd al-Hamid
2 147-148
nationalist movement
Messali Hadj **10** 527-528
revolt and independence
Abbas, Ferhat **1** 6-7
Ben Bella, Ahmed **2** 148-149
Boumediene, Houari **2** 445-446
Fanon, Frantz **5** 379-380
Houphouët-Boigny, Felix **7** 519-520
John XXIII **8** 277-280

Algerine Captive, The (novel)
Tyler, Royall **15** 371-372

Algerine War (1815)
Decatur, Stephen **4** 448-449

Algic Researches (book)
Schoolcraft, Henry Rowe **14** 29

Algoa Bay (South Africa)
Dias de Novais, Bartolomeu **4** 533-534

Algonquian Indians (North America)
Brûlé, Étienne **3** 67-68
Eliot, John **5** 256-258
Pocahontas **12** 361-362
Powhatan **12** 429-430

Algonquin Club (Boston)
McKim, Charles Follen **10** 417-418

Algonquin Round Table (literary group)
Benchley, Robert **2** 150-151
Parker, Dorothy Rothschild **12** 106
Ross, Harold **13** 300-302

Algorism (mathematics)
Khwarizmi, Muhammad ibn Musa al-
8 541

ALGREN, NELSON (Abraham; 1909-1981),
American author **1** 154-155

Alhambra, The (stories)
Irving, Washington **8** 141-143

Alhazen
see Hassan ibn al-Haytham

Al-Hudaybiya, Treaty of (628)
Mohammed **11** 76-78

ALI (circa 600-661), fourth caliph of the
Islamic Empire **1** 155-156
Muawiya ibn Abu Sufyan **11** 223-224

Ali, Haidar
see Haidar Ali

ALI, MUHAMMAD (Cassius Clay; born
1942), American boxer **1** 156-158

ALI, SUNNI (died 1492), king of Gao,
founder of the Songhay empire
1 158-159
Muhammad Ture, Askia **11** 231-232

Ali al-Reza (Rida, or Riza; died 818), eighth
imam of the Shii Moslems
Abbas I **1** 4-6
Mamun, Abdallah al- **10** 183

Ali Ber
see Ali, Sunni

Ali Shah (died 1885)
see Aga Khan II

Ali the Great
see Ali, Sunni

ALIA, RAMIZ (born 1925), president of
Albania (1985-) **1** 159

Alianca Nacional Libertadora (Brazil)
Prestes, Luiz Carlos **12** 442-444
Vargas, Getulio Dornelles **15** 433-434

Alianza Popular Revolucionaria Americana
(APRA; Peru)
Mariátegui, José Carlos **10** 255-256
Prado Ugarteche, Manuel **12** 430-431
Vallejo, César Abraham **15** 408-409

Alianza Republicana Nacionalista (ARENA;
political party, El Salvador)
Cristiani, Alfredo **4** 311-313
Daly, Mary **4** 380-381

Alice Adams (novel)
Tarkington, Newton Booth **15** 109

Alice Fell (poem)
Wordsworth, William **16** 385-388

Alice in Wonderland
see Alice's Adventures in Wonderland

Alice Seligsberg Trade School for Girls
(Jerusalem)
Szold, Henrietta **15** 66-67

Alice's Adventures in Wonderland (book;
Carroll)
Carroll, Lewis **3** 332-333
Nabokov, Vladimir **11** 287-288

Alice's Adventures under Ground (book)
Carroll, Lewis **3** 332-333

Alice-Sit-by-the-Fire (play)
Barrymores **2** 28-30

Alide (book)
Lazarus, Emma **9** 260-261

Alien Act (Great Britain)
Fox, Charles James **6** 35-37

Alien and Sedition Acts (United States;
1798)
enforcement
Chase, Samuel **3** 475-476
Pickering, Timothy **12** 298-299
Federalist goals
Adams, John **1** 48-51

opposed
  Cooper, Thomas **4** 224
  Gallatin, Albert **6** 183-184
  Jefferson, Thomas **8** 238-241
  Livingston, Edward **9** 460-461
  Macon, Nathaniel **10** 114-115
  Madison, James **10** 121-123
  Taylor, John **15** 126victims

Alien Land Law (California, 1913)
  Johnson, Hiram Warren **8** 300-301

Alienation (literature)
  Brecht, Bertolt **2** 512-514
  Hawthorne, Nathaniel **7** 212-215
  Moravia, Alberto **11** 153-155
  Rimbaud, Jean Nicolas Arthur
    13 172-174

Alienation (psychology)
  Horney, Karen Danielsen **7** 508-509

Aligarh Moslem University (India)
  Aga Khan **1** 74-76
  Nizami, Khaliq Ahmad **11** 405

Aligny, Théodore Caruelle d' (1798-1871),
  French painter
  Corot, Jean Baptiste Camille **4** 247-249

Alimardan Khan (flourished 1747-1750),
  Persian Bakhtyari leader
  Karim Khan Zand **8** 447

ALINSKY, SAUL DAVID (1909-1972), U.S.
  organizer of neighborhood citizen reform
  groups **1** 161-162

Alipur bomb conspiracy (1908)
  Das, Chitta Ranjan **4** 401-402

Alissa (literary character)
  Gide, André **6** 308-309

Alive, Son of Awake (book)
  ibn Tufayl, Abu Bakr Muhammad **8** 96

Alizarin (dye)
  Baeyer, Johann Friedrich Adolf von
    1 432

Aljubarrota, rout of (1385)
  López de Ayala, Pedro **9** 508-509

Alkaios
  see Alcaeus

Alkali (chemistry)
  Black, Joseph **2** 303
  Gay-Lussac, Joseph Louis **6** 245-246
  Hinshelwood, Cyril Norman **7** 405-406

Alkali spectra (physics)
  Pauli, Wolfgang Ernst **12** 149

Alkaloid (chemistry)
  Diels, Otto Paul Hermann **5** 5-6
  Liebig, Justus von **9** 403-404

Alkastiel, Joseph (flourished 15th century),
  Spanish mystic
  Luria, Isaac ben Solomon Ashkenazi
    10 47-48

Al-kimiya (Arabian science)
  Jabir ibn Hayyan **8** 167

All for Love (play)
  Dryden, John **5** 106-107

All God's Chillun Got Wings (play; O'Neill)
  O'Neill, Eugene **11** 514-516
  Robeson, Paul Leroy **13** 198-199

All in the Day's Work (autobiography)
  Tarbell, Ida Minerva **15** 107-108

All Is Shattered (poem)
  Tschernichowsky, Saul **15** 323

All Men Are Brothers (novel)
  Hu Shih **8** 63-65

All My Sons (play)
  Miller, Arthur **11** 25-26

All Night Long (book)
  Caldwell, Erskine **3** 223-224

All Out on the Road to Smolensk (book)
  Caldwell, Erskine **3** 223-224

All Quiet on the Western Front (novel)
  Remarque, Erich Maria **13** 91

All Russian Extraordinary Commission
  see Cheka

All Souls College (Oxford University)
  Cole, George Douglas Howard
    4 146-147

All That Swagger (novel)
  Franklin, Stella Maraia Sarah Miles
    6 68-69

All the King's Men (novel)
  Warren, Robert Penn **16** 121-122

All the King's Men (opera)
  Bennett, Richard Rodney **2** 172

All the President's Men (book)
  Woodward and Bernstein **16** 376-378

All the Sad Young Men (stories)
  Fitzgerald, Francis Scott Key **5** 470-472

All the Way (autobiography)
  Cecil, of Chelwood Viscount **3** 388-389

All the Year Round (magazine)
  Collins, William Wilkie **4** 169-170
  Dickens, Charles John Huffam
    4 538-541, 370

Alladine et Palomides (play)
  Maeterlinck, Maurice **10** 125-126

All-African National Action Council (established 1961)
  Mandela, Nelson Rolihlahla
    10 185-186

All-African Peoples' Conference (Accra;
  1958)
  Lumumba, Patrice Emery **10** 43-45

Allahabad Pioneer (newspaper)
  Kipling, Joseph Rudyard **9** 32-33

ALLAL AL-FASSI, MOHAMED
  (1910-1974), Moroccan nationalist leader
  1 162

Allan, Sir Hugh (1810-1882), Canadian financier
  Cartier, George-Étienne **3** 342-343

All-Burma Peasants League
  Aung San **1** 374-375

All-Burma Students' Union
  Aung San **1** 374-375

All-China Federation of Labor
  Liu Shao-Ch'i **9** 453-455

All-China Federation of Women
  Chou En-lai **4** 20-22

Allegheny County Jail (Pittsburgh, Pennsylvania)
  Richardson, Henry Hobson **13** 139-141

Allegheny River (river, Pennsylvania-New
  York State)
  Roebling, John Augustus **13** 241-242

Allegorical Portrait of Charles V (painting)
  Parmigianino **12** 117

Allegory (art)
  Bosch, Hieronymus **2** 426-428
  Peale, Rembrandt **12** 172-173
  Tiepolo, Giovanni Battista **15** 219-220

Allegory (literature)
  poetry
    Chaucer, Geoffrey **3** 482-485
    Dante Alighieri **4** 389-391
    Jean de Meun **8** 234-235
    Orléans, Charles D' **11** 530
  prose
    Bunyan, John **3** 128-129
    Gracián y Morales, Baltasar Jeróni-
      mo **6** 481-482
    Juana Inés de la Cruz **8** 367-368
    Lewis, Clive Staples **9** 381-382

Allegory (painting)
  Bellini, Giovanni **2** 137-138

Allegory of History and Time (fresco)
  Mengs, Anton Raphael **10** 505

Allegory of Hunting (sculpture)
  Falconet, Étienne Maurice **5** 372

Allegory of Imperial France (sculpture)
  Carpeaux, Jean Baptiste **3** 318-319

Allegory of Justice (fresco; Titian)
  Giorgione **6** 340-341

Allegory of Music (sculpture)
  Falconet, Étienne Maurice **5** 372

Allegory of Riches and Poverty (painting)
  Altdorfer, Albrecht **1** 179-180

Allegory of the Art of Painting (painting)
  Vermeer, Jan **15** 466-467

Allegory of the Catholic Faith (painting)
  Vermeer, Jan **15** 466-467

Allegory of the Destiny of Art (painting)
  Maulbertsch, Franz Anton **10** 345

Allegory of the Holy League (painting)
  Greco **6** 511-514

Allegory of Tolerance (etching)
  Maulbertsch, Franz Anton **10** 345

**Allegory with Venus, Cupid, Folly, and
  Time** (painting)
  Bronzino **3** 19

Allegri, Antonio
  see Correggio

Allegria di naufragi (poems)
Ungaretti, Giuseppe **15** 389-390

Allegro, L' (poem; Milton)
Blake, William **2** 316-318
Handel, George Frederick **7** 116-119
Milton, John **11** 43-46

Allemande (music)
Corelli, Arcangelo **4** 230-231
Froberger, Johann Jakob **6** 120-121

ALLEN, ETHAN (1738-1789), American Revolutionary War soldier **1** 163-164
Arnold, Benedict **1** 309-310

ALLEN, FLORENCE ELLINWOOD (1884-1966), American lawyer, judge, and women's rights activist **1** 164-165

Allen, Ira (1751-1814), American Revolutionary politician
Allen, Ethan **1** 163-164

ALLEN, PAULA GUNN (born 1939), Native American writer, poet, literary critic; women's rights, environmental, and anti-war activist **1** 165-167

ALLEN, RICHARD (1760-1831), African American bishop **1** 168

Allen, William Francis (1830-1889), American classical scholar
Turner, Frederick Jackson **15** 350-351

ALLEN, WOODY (born Allen Stewart Konigsberg; b. 1935), American actor, director, filmmaker, author, comedian **1** 169-171

ALLENBY, EDMUND HENRY HYNMAN (1861-1936), English field marshal **1** 171-172
Lawrence, Thomas Edward **9** 253-254
Wavell, Archibald Percival **16** 147-148

Allende, Ignacio José (1779-1811), Mexican army officer
Hidalgo y Costilla, Miguel **7** 375-377

ALLENDE, ISABEL (born 1942), Chilean novelist, journalist, dramatist **1** 172-174

ALLENDE GOSSENS, SALVADOR (1908-1973), socialist president of Chile (1970-1973) **1** 174-176
Alessandri Rodriguez, Jorge **1** 129-130
Frei Montalva, Eduardo **6** 94-95
Herrera, Juan de **7** 335
Pinochet Ugarte, Augusto **12** 315-317

Allerton, Isaac (1586-1658/59), Pilgrim father
Winslow, Edward **16** 338-339

Alleu et le domaine rural ... (book)
Fustel de Coulanges, Numa Denis **6** 155

Alley, Alphonse (born 1930), Dahomean statesman
Apithy, Sourou Migan **1** 259-260

Alleyne, Ellen
see Rossetti, Christina Georgina

Allgemeine Elektrizitätsgesellschaft (AEG)
Behrens, Peter **2** 121-122
Rathenau, Walther **13** 48-49

Allgemeine Krankenhaus (hospital; Vienna)
Freud, Sigmund **6** 103-106

Allgemeine Zeitung (newspaper)
Herzl, Theodor **7** 352-354

Alliance (ship)
Barry, John **2** 24-25

Alliance for Labor Action (United States)
Reuther, Walter Philip **13** 107-108

Alliance for National Unity (German politics)
Kapp, Wolfgang **8** 436

Alliance for Progress (United States-Latin America)
Kennedy, John Fitzgerald **8** 502-506
Kubitschek de Oliveira, Juscelino **9** 113-115

Alliance Movement
see National Alliance Movement

Alligator (ship)
Stockton, Robert Field **14** 461-462

All-India Moslem Educational Conference (Delhi, 1904)
Aga Khan **1** 74-76

All-India Moslem League
Aga Khan **1** 74-76

All-India Trades Union Congress
Nehru, Jawaharlal **11** 332-334

Alliteration (literature)
Ennius, Quintus **5** 289
Hopkins, Gerard Manley **7** 492-494
Langland, William **9** 194-195

Allon, Yigal (1918-1980), Israeli general
Meir, Golda **10** 462-463

Allport, Gordon (1897-1967), American psychologist
Kluckhohn, Clyde **9** 56-57
Le Bon, Gustave **9** 268-269

All's Well That Ends Well (play)
Shakespeare, William **14** 142-145

All-Souls Unitarian Church (New York City)
Bellows, Henry Whitney **2** 143-144

ALLSTON, WASHINGTON (1779-1843), American painter **1** 176-177
influence of
La Farge, John **9** 149-150
Moran, Thomas **11** 151-152
Morse, Samuel Finley Breese **11** 192-193
Rimmer, William **13** 174
style compared
Vanderlyn, John **15** 417
tribute to
Peabody, Elizabeth Palmer **12** 167-168

Allworthy, Squire (literary character)
Fielding, Henry **5** 442-444

Alma castellana, El (book)
Ruiz, Juan **13** 358-359

Alma Mater (sculpture)
French, Daniel Chester **6** 98-99

Taft, Lorado **15** 75-76

Almagest (book; Ptolemy)
Apollonius of Perga **1** 261-262
Bitruji, Nur al-Din Abu Ishaq al **2** 296
Hipparchus **7** 407-408
Ptolemy, Claudius **12** 473-474
Regiomontanus **13** 81-82

ALMAGRO, DIEGO DE (circa 1474-1538), Spanish conquistador and explorer **1** 177-178
in Central America
Pedrarias **12** 179
in literature
Tirso de Molina **15** 237-238
Las Salinas war
Orellana, Francisco de **11** 527-528
Pizarro, Francisco **12** 340-341
Valdivia, Pedro de **15** 400-401
Peruvian conquests
Benalcázar, Sebastián de **2** 145-146
Manco Capac **10** 184-185
Pizarro, Francisco **12** 340-341

Almagro the Lad (died 1542), Panamanian explorer
Almagro, Diego de **1** 177-178

Almas de violeta (poems)
Jiménez, Juan Ramón **8** 261-262

Almaviva (opera)
Rossini, Gioacchino **13** 311-312

Almayer's Folly (novel)
Conrad, Joseph **4** 205-207

Almazán, Juan Andreu (1891-1965), Mexican army officer
Ávila Camacho, Manuel **1** 387-388

Almeida, Francisco de (1450?-1510), Portuguese viceroy to India
Albuquerque, Afonso de **1** 118-119
Manuel I **10** 219-220
Varthema, Ludovico di **15** 439-440

Almira (opera)
Handel, George Frederick **7** 116-119

Almohads (ruled 1147-1269), Islamic sect and dynasty
in Spain and Portugal
Abd al-Mumin **1** 13
Alfonso I **1** 148
Maimonides **10** 151-152
Yakub al-Mansur, Abu Yusuf **16** 426
sect founded
ibn Tumart, Muhammad **8** 96-97

Almonte, Juan (1804?-1869), Mexican general and statesman
Maximilian of Hapsburg **10** 358-360

Almoravids (ruled 1062-1147), Islamic sect and dynasty
Almohad rivalry
Abd al-Mumin **1** 13
ibn Tumart, Muhammad **8** 96-97
in Portugal
Alfonso I **1** 148
in Spain
Alfonso VI **1** 149

Cid **4** 58-59
ibn Tashufin, Yusuf **8** 95-96
sect founded
Abdullah ibn Yasin **1** 20

Almy, Brown and Slater (textile firm)
Brown, Moses **3** 42-43
Slater, Samuel **14** 272-273

ALN
see Armée Nationale de Libération
(ALN; Algeria)

Aloha Oe (song)
Liliuokalani, Lydia Kamakaeha
9 411-412

Alompra
see Alaungpaya

Alone (book)
Byrd, Richard Evelyn **3** 186-187
Strindberg, August **14** 509-511

Along This Way (autobiography)
Johnson, James Weldon **8** 304-305

Alonso (Araucanian chief)
see Lautaro

Alonso, Dámaso (1898-1990), Spanish
poet
Góngora y Argote, Luis de **6** 427-428

Alouette, L' (play)
Anouilh, Jean **1** 243-244

ALP ARSLAN (1026/32-1072), Seljuk sultan
of Persia and Iraq **1** 178-179

Alpetragius
see Bitruji, Nur al-Din Abu Ishaq al-

Alpha and Omega (lithograph)
Munch, Edvard **11** 247-248

Alpha helix (chemistry)
Pauling, Linus Carl **12** 150-152

Alpha radiation (physics)
bombardment
Bothe, Walther **2** 438-439
Chadwick, James **3** 405-406
decay
Fermi, Enrico **5** 422-424
Soddy, Frederick **14** 321-323
discovered
Rutherford, Ernest **13** 384-387
ionization of gases
Bragg, William Henry **2** 488-489
scattering
Rutherford, Ernest **13** 384-387
spinthariscope
Crookes, William **4** 323-324
tracks photographed
Kapitsa, Pyotr Leonidovich
8 433-435

Alphabet, development of
Braille, Louis **2** 492-493
Champollion, Jean François **3** 421
Cyril and Methodius, Saints **4** 362-363
Sejong **14** 91-92
Sequoyah **14** 110-111
Ulfilas **15** 384

"Alphabet of thoughts" (logic)
Leibniz, Gottfried Wilhelm von
9 307-310

Alphonse, Jean (died 1549), French pirate
Menéndez de Avilés, Pedro **10** 499-500

Alphonse the Wise
see Alfonso X, king of Castile

Alphonsine tables (astronomy)
Alfonso X **1** 150-151

Al-Qanun al-Masudi (book)
Biruni, Abu Rayhan al- **2** 284-285

Al-Qanun fi al Tibb
see Canon (book)

Alsace (former province, France)
Charles the Bold **3** 467-469
Charles V **3** 457-459

Alsace-Lorraine (region, France)
Bethmann Hollweg, Theobald von
2 239-240
Bismarck, Otto Eduard Leopold von
2 294-296
Gambetta, Léon **6** 198-199

Also sprach Zarathustra (musical composition; Strauss)
Bartók, Béla **2** 35-36

Alston, Theodosia Burr
see Burr, Theodosia

Alta California (Upper California)
Portolá, Gaspar de **12** 408

Alta Luisiana
see Missouri

Altamira cave paintings (Spain)
Breuil, Henri Edouard Prosper
2 521-522

ALTAMIRA Y CREVEA, RAFAEL
(1866-1951), Spanish critic, historian,
and jurist **1** 179

Altan Khan (died 1584), Mongol prince of
the Ordos
Dalai Lama **4** 369-371

Altarpiece (art)
Dürer, Albrecht **5** 159-161
Orcagna **11** 526-527
see also specific titles

Altarpiece of St. Peter (painting)
Witz, Konrad **16** 351-352

Altarpiece of St. Wolfgang (panels)
Pacher, Michael **12** 53

Altdeutsche Wälder (book)
Grimm, Jakob and Wilhelm Karl **7** 3-4

ALTDORFER, ALBRECHT (circa
1480-1538), German painter, printmaker,
and architect **1** 179-180
Claude Lorrain **4** 89-90
Cranach, Lucas the Elder **4** 289-290
Dürer, Albrecht **5** 159-161

Alte Post (Berlin)
Schlüter, Andreas **14** 18-19

Alternating current (electronic)
Tesla, Nikola **15** 156-157

Alternating current (motor)
Westinghouse, George **16** 215

Alternation, principle of (music)
Vivaldi, Antonio **16** 3-4

Altes Museum (Berlin)
Schinkel, Karl Friedrich **14** 8

ALTGELD, JOHN PETER (1847-1902),
American jurist and politician **1** 180-182
Darrow, Clarence Seward **4** 396-397
Lindsay, Vachel **9** 424-425

Althan Palace (Frain, Moravia)
Fischer von Erlach, Johann Bernhard
5 459-461

Al-Thulathia (book trilogy)
Mahfuz, Najib **10** 142-144

ALTHUSSER, LOUIS (1918-1990), French
Communist philosopher **1** 182-183

ALTIZER, THOMAS J. J. (born 1927), American theologian **1** 183-184

Altman, Benjamin (1840-1913), American
merchant
Davies, Arthur Bowen **4** 409-410

Altmark, Treaty of (1629)
Oxenstierna, Axel Gustafsson **12** 44-45

Alto Rhapsody (musical composition)
Brahms, Johannes **2** 490-492

Alton (town, Illinois)
Lovejoy, Elijah Parish **10** 6-7

Alton Locke (novel; Kingsley)
Kingsley, Charles **9** 28
Trollope, Anthony **15** 300-302

Alton Towers (Staffordshire)
Pugin, Augustus Welby Northmore
12 479-480

Altranstädt, Treaty of (1706)
Augustus II **1** 373-374

Altruist in Politics, The (speech)
Cardozo, Benjamin Nathan **3** 288-290

Altruistic Love (book)
Sorokin, Pitirim A. **14** 348-349

Alumbrados (religious group)
Molinos, Miguel de **11** 88-89

Aluminum (element; chemistry)
Davy, Humphry **4** 426-427

Aluminum Company of America
Davis, Arthur Vining **4** 413-414
Mellon, Andrew William **10** 469-470
Parbo, Arvi **12** 93-94
Stone, Harlan Fiske **14** 468-470

Aluminum industry (Ghana)
Nkrumah, Kwame **11** 408-410

Alva, Duke of
see Alba, Duke of

Alvarado, Pedro de (1495?-1541), Spanish
statesman
Almagro, Diego de **1** 177-178
Cabrillo, Juan Rodríguez **3** 204-205

Alvarez, Jorge Guillén y
see Guillén y Alvarez, Jorge

ÁLVAREZ, JUAN (1780-1867), Mexican soldier and statesman, president 1855 **1** 184-185
    Juárez, Benito **8** 369-372
    Maximilian of Hapsburg **10** 358-360
    Santa Ana, Antonio López de **13** 471-472

ÁLVAREZ, JULIA (born 1950), Hispanic American novelist, poet **1** 185-187

ÁLVAREZ, LUIS W. (1911-1988), American physicist **1** 187-189

Alvear, Marcelo Torcuato de (1868-1942), Argentine president 1922-1928
    Irigoyen, Hipólito **8** 139-140
    Justo, Agustin Pedro **8** 396

Alvin Ailey American Dance Theater
    Ailey, Alvin **1** 91-94

Alving, Mrs. (literary character)
    Ibsen, Henrik **8** 98-100

Alvsborg (province, Sweden)
    Gustavus II **7** 43-45

Always Young and Fair (novella)
    Richter, Conrad Michael **13** 148-149

Aly Khan (Ali Shah Ikbal; born 1911-1960), Moslem prince
    Aga Khan **1** 74-76

Alyosha (literary character)
    Dostoevsky, Fyodor **5** 74-77

Al-zij al-Malikshahi (astronomical tables)
    Omar Khayyam **11** 510-511

Alzire (play)
    Voltaire **16** 14-16

Am Leben hin (tales)
    Rilke, Rainer Maria **13** 171-172

Amadigi (musical composition)
    Handel, George Frederick **7** 116-119

Amadigi (poem; B. Tasso)
    Tasso, Torquato **15** 114-116

Amadis de Gaula (poem)
    Tasso, Torquato **15** 114-116

AMADO, JORGE (born 1912), Brazilian novelist **1** 189-190

Amahl and the Night Visitors (opera)
    Menotti, Gian Carlo **10** 509-510

AMAL (Shi'ite movement)
    Berri, Nabih **2** 220-222
    Sadr, Musa al- **13** 420-422

Amalasuntha (498-535?), Ostrogothic queen, regent 526-535?
    Theodoric the Great **15** 175-176

Amalekites (Old Testament people)
    Saul **13** 498

Amalgamated Clothing Workers of America (established 1914)
    Hillman, Sidney **7** 392-393

Amalgamated Copper Co. (United States)
    Lawson, Thomas William **9** 255-256

Amalgamated Iron and Steel Workers Union (United States)
    Carnegie, Andrew **3** 309-312
    Frick, Henry Clay **6** 108-109

Amalgamated Textile Workers of America (union)
    Muste, Abraham Johannes **11** 276-277

Amalia (novel)
    Mármol, José **10** 274

Amalienburg (Munich)
    Cuvilliés, François **4** 359-360

Amalric I (1135-1174), king of Jerusalem 1162-1174
    Saladin **13** 441-442
    William of Tyre **16** 299-300

Ama-no-hashidate (painting)
    Sesshu, Toya **14** 116-117

Amantes del Pais (Peru)
    Unánue, José Hipólito **15** 387-388

Amarilis (literary character)
    Lope Félix de Vega Carpio **9** 503-506

Amarna Letters (Egyptian archeology)
    Ikhnaton **8** 110-111

Amata (literary character)
    Virgil **15** 507-510

Amaurotes (literary characters)
    Rabelais, François **12** 524-526

Amauta (magazine)
    Mariátegui, José Carlos **10** 255-256

Amaziah (flourished 8th century B.C.), Israelite priest
    Amos **1** 205

Amazon (sculpture)
    Phidias **12** 265-267
    Polykleitos **12** 385-386

Amazon River (South America)
    Azara, Félix de **1** 397-398
    Bates, Henry Walter **2** 53-54
    Ludwig, Daniel Keith **10** 29-31
    Quesada, Gonzalo Jiménez de **12** 509-510
    Orellana, Francisco de **11** 527-528
    Rondon, Candido Mariano da Silva **13** 271

Amazons in the New World (play)
    Tirso de Molina **15** 237-238

Ambarvalia (literary collection)
    Clough, Arthur Hugh **4** 123-124

Ambassadors, The (novel)
    James, Henry **8** 211-212

Ambassadors, The (painting)
    Holbein, Hans the Younger **7** 449-450

AMBEDKAR, BHIMRAO RAMJI (1891-1956), Indian social reformer and politician **1** 190-191
    Gandhi, Mohandas Karamchand **6** 201-204

Amber (resin)
    Baekeland, Leo Hendrik **1** 430-431

Ambizioni sbagliate, Le (novel)
    Moravia, Alberto **11** 153-155

AMBLER, ERIC (born 1909), English novelist **1** 191-192

Amboise, Georges d' (1460-1510), French cardinal and statesman
    Francis I **6** 40-43
    Louis XII **9** 528-529

Amboise, château of (France)
    Clouet, Jean and François **4** 122-123

Ambrogini, Angelo
    see Poliziano, Angelo

AMBROSE, ST. (339-397), Italian bishop **1** 192-193
    Augustine **1** 367-370
    Erasmus, Desiderius **5** 298-300
    Origen **11** 528-529
    Theodosius **15** 176

Ambrosio (novel)
    Lewis, Matthew Gregory **9** 390-391

Amda Sion (ruled 1314-1344), Ethiopian king
    Yekuno Amlak **16** 449

Amdo (Asian people)
    Dalai Lama **4** 369-371

Amdrup, Georg Karl (1866-1947), Danish naval officer
    Nordenskold, Nils Otto Gustaf **11** 422-423

Ame enchantée, L' (novel)
    Rolland, Romain **13** 260

Amélia (1812-1873), empress of Brazil
    Pedro I **12** 179-180

Amelia (novel)
    Fielding, Henry **5** 442-444

Amelia Goes to the Ball (opera)
    Menotti, Gian Carlo **10** 509-510

Amen Corner, The (play)
    Baldwin, James Arthur **1** 465-466

AMENEMHET I (ruled 1991-1962 B.C.), pharaoh of Egypt **1** 193-194

AMENHOTEP III (ruled 1417-1379 B.C.) pharaoh of Egypt **1** 194-195
    Ikhnaton **8** 110-111

Amenhotep IV
    see Ikhnaton

Amenophis IV
    see Ikhnaton

America (book)
    Blake, William **2** 316-318
    Schaff, Philip **13** 519-520

America (continent; named)
    Vespucci, Amerigo **15** 476-478-138
    Waldseemüller, Martin **16** 56
    see also Latin America; North America; and individual countries

America (musical composition)
    Bloch, Ernest **2** 326-327
    Gottschalk, Louis Moreau **6** 463-464

America (sculpture)
Powers, Hiram **12** 428-429

America First Committee (United States organization)
Lindbergh, Charles Augustus **9** 421-423
Morgenthau, Henry Jr. **11** 172-173
Wood, Robert Elkington **16** 370-371

América poetica (anthology; J.D. Cortés)
González Prada, Manuel **6** 431

America the Beautiful (poem)
Bates, Katharine Lee **2** 54-55

American Academy (Rome)
McKim, Charles Follen **10** 417-418

American Academy for Jewish Research (New York City)
Baron, Salo Wittmayer **2** 16-17
Ginzberg, Louis **6** 337-338

American Academy of Fine Arts (New York City)
Peale, Rembrandt **12** 172-173
Trumbull, John **15** 316-317

American and British Claims Arbitration (1912-1914)
Lansing, Robert **9** 200

American Antislavery Society
founded
Garrison, William Lloyd **6** 226-228
Purvis, Robert **12** 485-486
Tappan brothers **15** 105-106
Illinois auxiliary
Lovejoy, Elijah Parish **10** 6-7
officers and agents
Birney, James Gillespie **2** 283-284
Remond, Charles Lennox **13** 95
Smith, Gerrit **14** 290-291
Weld, Theodore Dwight **16** 186
women in
Foster, Abigail Kelley **6** 25
Grimké, Sarah Moore and Angelina Emily **7** 2-3
Mott, Lucretia Coffin **11** 212-213
see also Antislavery Society (United States)

American architecture
Adam style
McIntire, Samuel **10** 415
airports
Saarinen, Eliel and Eero **13** 396-398
city planning
Saarinen, Eliel and Eero **13** 396-398
classical
L'Enfant, Pierre Charles **9** 322-323
McKim, Charles Follen **10** 417-418
Pope, John Russell **12** 397-399
colonial
Benjamin, Asher **2** 162-163
Bulfinch, Charles **3** 116-117
Harrison, Peter **7** 179-180
corporate headquarters
Roche, Kevin **13** 222-224
eclectic style
Hunt, Richard Morris **8** 44
Gothic revival

Davis, Alexander Jackson **4** 411
Latrobe, Benjamin Henry **9** 222-224
Renwick, James **13** 102-103
Richardson, Henry Hobson **13** 139-141
Sullivan, Louis Henri **15** 27-28
Upjohn, Richard **15** 392
Greek revival
Latrobe, Benjamin Henry **9** 222-224
Mills, Robert **11** 36-37
historic buildings
Moore, Charles Willard **11** 143-145
innovations (19th century)
Burnham, Daniel Hudson **3** 148-149
Richardson, Henry Hobson **13** 139-141
International Style
Bunshaft, Gordon **3** 125-127
Meier, Richard **10** 456-458
Mies van der Rohe, Ludwig **11** 10-12
Neutra, Richard Joseph **11** 355-356
Pei, I. M. **12** 184-187
Stone, Edward Durrell **14** 466-468
landscape architecture
Downing, Andrew Jackson **5** 90-91
Olmsted, Frederick Law **11** 503-504
late 20th century
Pelli, Cesar **12** 191-192
memorials
Lin, Maya Ying **9** 413-415
modern
Breuer, Marcel **2** 520-521
Bunshaft, Gordon **3** 125-127
Eisenman, Peter D. **5** 239-240
Freed, James Ingo **6** 88-90
Fuller, Richard Buckminster **6** 149-150
Gehry, Frank O. **6** 250-251
Jahn, Helmut **8** 199-201
Johnson, Philip **8** 313-314
Kahn, Albert **8** 407-408
Kahn, Louis I. **8** 408-410
Rudolph, Paul Marvin **13** 348-350
Sullivan, Louis Henri **15** 27-28
Wright, Frank Lloyd **16** 398-401
museums
Meier, Richard **10** 456-458
neoclassicism
Benjamin, Asher **2** 162-163
post-modern
Graves, Michael **6** 500-502
Venturi, Robert **15** 461-463
private homes
Morgan, Julia **11** 165-166
religious structures
Jones, Fay **8** 332-333
Renaissance
McKim, Charles Follen **10** 417-418
White, Stanford **16** 235-236
Romanesque
Richardson, Henry Hobson **13** 139-141
see also American art
skyscrapers

Bunshaft, Gordon **3** 125-127

American Argument (essay; Buck-Robeson)
Buck, Pearl Sydenstricker **3** 91-93

American art
abstract
Dove, Arthur Garfield **5** 86-87
Marin, John III **10** 259-260
Nevelson, Louise **11** 356-357
Stella, Frank **14** 420-422
abstract expressionism
see Abstract expressionism
action painting
Rivers, Larry **13** 186-187
African American
Johnson, William H. **8** 320-322
Savage, Augusta Christine **13** 499-501
American scene painting
Burchfield, Charles **3** 131-132
Homer, Winslow **7** 468-469
Rockwell, Norman Percevel **13** 231-233
art for art's sake
Whistler, James Abbott McNeill **16** 225-226
Art Nouveau
Tiffany, Louis Comfort **15** 220-221
Ashcan school
see Ashcan school
assemblage
Nevelson, Louise **11** 356-357
Bauhaus ideas
Moholy-Nagy, László **11** 82-83
bird paintings
Audubon, John James **1** 366-367
cartoons
Block, Herbert **2** 333-334
Capp, Al **3** 275-276
Disney, Walter Elias **5** 26-27
Feiffer, Jules Ralph **5** 403-404
Grosz, George **7** 17-18
Mauldin, Bill **10** 345-346
Nast, Thomas **11** 318-319
Oliphant, Patrick Bruce **11** 498-500
Perelman, S. J. **12** 209-210
Schulz, Charles M. **14** 38-39
Thurber, James Grove **15** 213-214
Trudeau, Garretson Beekman **15** 308-309
collaborative
Chicago, Judy **3** 515-516
collage
Cornell, Joseph **4** 237-238
Krasner, Lee **9** 93-94
color-field abstraction
Frankenthaler, Helen **6** 56-57
Newman, Barnett **11** 365
Noland, Kenneth **11** 418-419
"combines"
Rauschenberg, Robert **13** 52-53
Conceptualist
LeWitt, Sol **9** 393-395
concrete art
Richter, Hans **13** 149-150
constructivist sculpture

Lippold, Richard **9** 440-442
criticism
Mumford, Lewis **11** 246-247
critics
Kirstein, Lincoln **9** 39-41
cubism
see Cubism
Dada
Koons, Jeff **9** 83-84
Ray, Man **13** 59-60
eclecticism
Rauschenberg, Robert **13** 52-53
environmental artworks
Christo Vladimiroff Javacheff
4 30-31
Grooms, Red **7** 11-12
Smithson, Robert **14** 301-303
experimental films
Cornell, Joseph **4** 237-238
expressionism
Hartley, Marsden **7** 186
Lipchitz, Jacques **9** 432-433
Weber, Max **16** 160
Fauvism
Hofmann, Hans **7** 442-443
federal support for
Hanks, Nancy **7** 126-127
feminist
Chicago, Judy **3** 515-516
Ringgold, Faith **13** 175-177
figurative tradition
Guston, Philip **7** 47-48
Shahn, Ben **14** 139-140
filmmaking
Flaherty, Robert **5** 476-477
Warhol, Andy **16** 114-115
furniture
Phyfe, Duncan **12** 284-285
Stovall, Luther (Lou) McKinley
14 483-484
futurism
Stella, Joseph **14** 422
genre painting
Bingham, George Caleb **2** 278-279
Johnson, Earvin Jr. **8** 297-299
Mount, William Sidney **11** 213-214
Peale, Charles Willson **12** 169-171
glass
La Farge, John **9** 149-150
Stiegel, Henry William **14** 451
Tiffany, Louis Comfort **15** 220-221
graffiti art
Haring, Keith **7** 154-155
happenings
Oldenburg, Claes **11** 496-498
hard-edge
Kelly, Ellsworth **8** 482-483
history painting
Trumbull, John **15** 316-317
Vanderlyn, John **15** 417
Hudson River School
Church, Frederick Edwin **4** 49-50
Cole, Thomas **4** 151-152
Durand, Asher Brown **5** 156-157
impressionism

see Impressionism (art)
kinetic
Calder, Alexander **3** 216-218
Ray, Man **13** 59-60
landscapes
Bannister, Edward Mitchell
1 491-493
Chase, William Merritt **3** 476-477
Earl, Ralph **5** 179
Moran, Thomas **11** 151-152
Wyant, Alexander Helwig
16 409-410
lithography
Currier and Ives **4** 345-346
luminism
Heade, Martin Johnson **7** 236
Lane, Fitz Hugh **9** 189
metalwork
Revere, Paul **13** 110-111
Tiffany, Louis Comfort **15** 220-221
Minimalist
Judd, Donald **8** 376-377
LeWitt, Sol **9** 393-395
Louis, Morris **9** 538-539
Martin, Agnes **10** 288-289
murals
La Farge, John **9** 149-150
narrative painting
Lawrence, Jacob **9** 250-251
National Academy of Design
Morse, Samuel Finley Breese
11 192-193
Native American
Bad Heart Bull, Amos **1** 427-428
Native American in
Catlin, George **3** 373-374
naturalism
Eakins, Thomas **5** 176-177
Homer, Winslow **7** 468-469
neoclassic
Powers, Hiram **12** 428-429
Revere, Paul **13** 110-111
Vanderlyn, John **15** 417
West, Benjamin **16** 210-212
Neo-Conceptualist
Holzer, Jenny **7** 462-463
neo-folk
Johnson, William H. **8** 320-322
New Journalism
Capote, Truman **3** 273-275
patrons
Luhan, Mabel Dodge **10** 32-34
Pattern and Decoration Movement
(1974)
Schapiro, Miriam **13** 520-521
photography
Adams, Ansel **1** 40-41
Arbus, Diane Nemerov **1** 276-277
Avedon, Richard **1** 381-382
Bourke-White, Margaret **2** 455-456
Capa, Robert **3** 269-271
Evans, Walker **5** 339
Freeman, Roland L. **6** 92-93
Lange, Dorothea **9** 193-194
Leibovitz, Annie **9** 310-312
Mapplethorpe, Robert **10** 227-228

Mydans, Carl **11** 283-284
Ray, Man **13** 59-60
Steichen, Edward **14** 411-412
Stieglitz, Alfred **14** 451-452
VanDer Zee, James **15** 418-419
pop art
Haring, Keith **7** 154-155
Johns, Jasper **8** 291-293
Kienholz, Edward **8** 546-547
Koons, Jeff **9** 83-84
Lichtenstein, Roy **9** 398-399
Oldenburg, Claes **11** 496-498
Warhol, Andy **16** 114-115
populist
Chicago, Judy **3** 515-516
portraiture (18th-19th century)
Copley, John Singleton **4** 228-230
Johnston, Joshua **8** 323-325
Peale, Charles Willson **12** 169-171
Smibert, John **14** 282
Stuart, Gilbert **14** 513-515
portraiture (19th century)
Chase, William Merritt **3** 476-477
Eakins, Thomas **5** 176-177
Johnson, Earvin Jr. **8** 297-299
Mount, William Sidney **11** 213-214
Peale, Rembrandt **12** 172-173
Sargent, John Singer **13** 481-482
postimpressionism
Prendergast, Maurice Brazil **12** 440
Post-Modern
Salle, David **13** 452-453
precisionism
Demuth, Charles **4** 497-498
O'Keeffe, Georgia **11** 487-489
Sheeler, Charles **14** 170-171
primitivism
Hicks, Edward **7** 375
Kane, John **8** 422
Moses, Grandma **11** 201-202
Pippin, Horace **12** 318-319
psychological novels
Capote, Truman **3** 273-275
ready-mades
Ray, Man **13** 59-60
realism
Estes, Richard **5** 322-323
Hopper, Edward **7** 497-498
Kent, Rockwell **8** 511
Luks, George Benjamin **10** 38-39
Oldenburg, Claes **11** 496-498
Sloan, John **14** 274-275
Wyeth, Andrew Newell **16** 413-415
regionalism
Benton, Thomas Hart **2** 178-179
Rembrandt Harmensz van Rijn
13 91-95
Russell, Charles Marion **13** 375-376
Wood, Grant **16** 368-369
romantic classicism
Rimmer, William **13** 174
romanticism
Allston, Washington **1** 176-177
Bierstadt, Albert **2** 270-271
Cole, Thomas **4** 151-152

Ryder, Albert Pinkham **13** 391-392
scene painting
  Burchfield, Charles **3** 131-132
  Homer, Winslow **7** 468-469
sculpture (19th century)
  Powers, Hiram **12** 428-429
  Rogers, John **13** 248
  Saint-Gaudens, Augustus **13** 432
sculpture (20th century)
  Barthé, Richmond **2** 33-34
  Borglum, John Gutzon de la Mothe **2** 416-417
  Bourgeois, Louise **2** 451-452
  Burke, Selma **3** 143-144
  Christo Vladimiroff Javacheff **4** 30-31
  Edwards, Melvin **5** 222-223
  Flannagan, John Bernard **5** 480
  Graves, Nancy Stevenson **6** 502-504
  Hanson, Duane **7** 133-135
  Hesse, Eva **7** 365-367
  Lachaise, Gaston **9** 147
  Lippold, Richard **9** 440-442
  Nadelman, Elie **11** 289-290
  Noguchi, Isamu **11** 416-418
  Oldenburg, Claes **11** 496-498
  Puryear, Martin **12** 486-487
  Savage, Augusta Christine **13** 499-501
  Segal, George **14** 85-87
  Smith, David **14** 287-288
  Taft, Lorado **15** 75-76
  Zorach, William **16** 528
silkscreen
  Begay, Harrison **2** 117-118
  Stovall, Luther (Lou) McKinley **14** 483-484
social realism
  Evergood, Philip **5** 345
  Grosz, George **7** 17-18
super-realist
  Hanson, Duane **7** 133-135
surrealism
  Gorky, Arshile **6** 458
  Ray, Man **13** 59-60
The Eight
  see Eight, The
Ten, The
  Hassam, Frederick Childe **7** 192
traditionalism
  Kent, Rockwell **8** 511
tromp l'oeil
  Harnett, William Michael **7** 160-161
  Peto, John Frederick **12** 259
watercolors
  Begay, Harrison **2** 117-118
white writing
  Tobey, Mark **15** 249-250
woodcarving
  Rush, William **13** 365-366
  see also American architecture;
    African American history—society
    and culture

American Association for the Advancement of Science
  Barnard, Frederick Augustus Porter **2** 9-10
  Bell, Alexander Graham **2** 129-131
  Henry, Joseph **7** 307-308

American Association of University Professors
  Cohen, Morris Raphael **4** 139-140
  Dewey, John **4** 520-523
  Seligman, Edwin Robert Anderson **14** 93-94

American Association of University Women
  Richards, Ellen H. **13** 134-136

American Astronomical Society
  Pickering, Edward Charles **12** 298

American at Home, The (anthology)
  Haliburton, Thomas Chandler **7** 80

American Atheist Radio (program series)
  O'Hair, Madalyn Murray **11** 484-485

American Ballet (dance company)
  Balanchine, George **1** 461-462
  Baryshnikov, Mikhail **2** 43-44

American Ballet Theater
  de Mille, Agnes **4** 486-488
  Joffrey, Robert **8** 268-270

American Beauty (novel)
  Ferber, Edna **5** 413

American Bible Society (established 1810)
  Jay, William **8** 232-233

American Board of Commissioners for Foreign Missions (established 1810)
  Judson, Adoniram **8** 377-378

American Builder's Companion, The (book)
  Benjamin, Asher **2** 162-163

American Caravan, The (publication)
  Mumford, Lewis **11** 246-247

American Chants (poems)
  Anderson, Sherwood **1** 220-221

American Chronicle (autobiography)
  Baker, Ray Stannard **1** 451-452

American Civil Liberties Union (ACLU)
  founders
    Dewey, John **4** 520-523
    Flynn, Elizabeth Gurley **5** 496-497
    Frankfurter, Felix **6** 57
    Holmes, John Haynes **7** 456-457
    Thomas, Norman Mattoon **15** 191-192
  officers
    Ashmore, Harry Scott **1** 334-335
    Cabot, Richard Clarke **3** 200
    Ross, Edward Alsworth **13** 300
  predecessors
    Wald, Lillian **16** 53-54
  Women's Rights Project
    Ginsburg, Ruth Bader **6** 333-336

American Claimant, The (book)
  Twain, Mark **15** 363-366

American Colonies ... (book)
  Osgood, Herbert Levi **12** 18-19

American Colonization Society (ACS)
  African American opposition
    Allen, Richard **1** 168
    Cuffe, Paul **4** 331-332
    Delany, Martin Robinson **4** 473-474
    Russwurm, John Brown **13** 381-382
  buys African land
    Stockton, Robert Field **14** 461-462
  founded
    Clay, Henry **4** 94-96
  supporters
    Ashmun, Jehudi **1** 335-336
    Birney, James Gillespie **2** 283-284
    Dew, Thomas Roderick **4** 519
    Smith, Gerrit **14** 290-291

American Commonwealth, The (book)
  Bryce, James **3** 85

American Council of Learned Societies
  Haskins, Charles Homer **7** 191-192

American Crisis Biographies series (books)
  Du Bois, William Edward Burghardt **5** 116-118

American Democracy, The (book)
  Laski, Harold J. **9** 215-216

American Democrat, The (book)
  Cooper, James Fenimore **4** 220-223

American Dictionary of the English Language, An (book)
  Webster, Noah **16** 164-166

American Dilemma, An (book; Myrdal)
  Bunche, Ralph Johnson **3** 121-122
  Myrdal, Karl Gunnar **11** 284

American Dream, An (novel)
  Mailer, Norman Kingsley **10** 148-150

American Earth (novel)
  Caldwell, Erskine **3** 223-224

American Economic Association
  Mayo-Smith, Richmond **10** 371-372
  Seligman, Edwin Robert Anderson **14** 93-94

American Ephemeris and Nautical Almanac Office
  Mitchell, Maria **11** 61
  Newcomb, Simon **11** 361-362

American Ethnological Society
  Boas, Franz **2** 349-351
  Gallatin, Albert **6** 183-184

American Express Co.
  Butterfield, John **3** 184-185
  Fargo, William George **5** 380-381

American Federation of Labor (AFL)
  CIO and
    Green, William R. **6** 521
    Reuther, Walter Philip **13** 107-108
    see also American Federation of
      Labor and Congress of Industrial
      Organizations
  founded
    Gompers, Samuel **6** 420-422

Homestead strike (1892)
    Carnegie, Andrew **3** 309-312-378
    Frick, Henry Clay **6** 108-109
officials
    Dubinsky, David **5** 114-115
    Green, William R. **6** 521
    Kirkland, Joseph Lane **9** 35-37
    Mitchell, John **11** 58-59
    Randolph, A. Philip **13** 28-29
other unions and
    Haywood, William Dudley
      7 232-233
    Hillman, Sidney **7** 392-393
    Lewis, John Llewellyn **9** 387-388
police strike (1919)
    Coolidge, John Calvin **4** 217-219
political policies
    La Follette, Robert Marion
      9 155-156
    Perkins, Frances **12** 221-222

American Federation of Labor and Congress of Industrial Organizations
(AFL-CIO)
    Chavez, Cesar **3** 486-487
    Kirkland, Joseph Lane **9** 35-37
    Meany, George **10** 444
    Perkins, Frances **12** 221-222
    Randolph, A. Philip **13** 28-29
    Reuther, Walter Philip **13** 107-108

American Federation of Teachers
    Shanker, Albert **14** 151-153

American Film Institute
    Valenti, Jack Joseph **15** 401-403

American Foundation of Religion and Psychiatry
    Peale, Norman Vincent **12** 171-172

American Fur Co.
    Astor, John Jacob **1** 351-352
    Comstock, Henry Tompkins Paige **4** 189
    Fitzpatrick, Thomas **5** 474-475
    Ogden, Peter Skene **11** 480-481
    Thompson, David **15** 194-195

American Gazetteer, The (book)
    Morse, Jedidiah **11** 191-192

American Geography (book)
    Morse, Jedidiah **11** 191-192

American Gothic (painting)
    Wood, Grant **16** 368-369

American High School Today, The (book)
    Conant, James Bryant **4** 192-193

American Historical Association
founders
    Adams, Herbert Baxter **1** 47
    Channing, Edward **3** 435
    Dunning, William Archibald
      5 148-149
    Tyler, Moses Coit **15** 369-370
presidents
    Becker, Carl Lotus **2** 100-101
    Eggleston, Edward **5** 223-224
    Roosevelt, Theodore **13** 280-283

American Home Economics Association
    Richards, Ellen H. **13** 134-136

AMERICAN HORSE (aka Iron Shield; 1840?-1876), Sioux leader **1** 195-198

American in Paris, An (ballet)
    Gershwin, George **6** 284-285

American Independence (poem)
    Freneau, Philip Morin **6** 99-100

American Indian Defense Association
(U.S.)
    Collier, John **4** 160-162

American Indian Movement (AIM; U.S.)
    Means, Russell **10** 441-444
    Peltier, Leonard **12** 193-195

American Indians
    see Indians (North America); Indians (South America)

American Institute for Psychoanalysis
    Horney, Karen Danielsen **7** 508-509

American Institute of Architects
    Hunt, Richard Morris **8** 44
    Upjohn, Richard **15** 392

American Iron and Steel Institute
    Gary, Elbert Henry **6** 229-230

American Jewish Congress
    Wise, Stephen Samuel **16** 344-345

American Jitters (book)
    Wilson, Edmund **16** 318-319

American Journal of Education
    Barnard, Henry **2** 10

American Journal of Obstetrics
    Jacobi, Abraham and Mary Putnam **8** 188-189

American Journal of Psychoanalysis
    Horney, Karen Danielsen **7** 508-509

American Journal of Psychology
    Hall, Granville Stanley **7** 85-86

American Journal of Science and Arts
    Silliman, Benjamin **14** 229-230

American Labor party (United States politics)
    Du Bois, William Edward Burghardt **5** 116-118
    Dubinsky, David **5** 114-115
    Hillman, Sidney **7** 392-393

American Landscape (play)
    Rice, Elmer **13** 126-127

American Language, The (book)
    Mencken, Henry Louis **10** 481-483

American League (baseball)
    Ruth, George Herman Jr. **13** 384

American Letters (book)
    Sienkiewicz, Henryk **14** 216-217

American Liberty League
    du Pont, Pierre Samuel **5** 154-155

American Library Association
    Dewey, Melvil **4** 523-524

American literature
    abolitionist

    Smith, James McCune **14** 293-294
African American fiction and drama
    Angelou, Maya **1** 238-239
    Bambara, Toni Cade **1** 482-483
    Baldwin, James Arthur **1** 465-466
    Childress, Alice **3** 522-524
    Ellison, Ralph Waldo **5** 274-275
    Haley, Alex **7** 76-78
    Hurston, Zora Neale **8** 55-56
    Marshall, Paule Burke **10** 281-282
    McMillan, Terry **10** 427-428
    Morrison, Toni **11** 188-190
    Naylor, Gloria **11** 328-329
    Walker, Alice Malsenior **16** 59-61
    Walker, Margaret **16** 67
    Wilson, August **16** 314-316
    Wilson, Harriet E. **16** 320-322
    Wright, Richard **16** 401-402
    see also Harlem Renaissance
African American poetry
    Jordan, June **8** 351-353
agrarianism (20th century)
    Ransom, John Crowe **13** 39-40
American scene poetry
    Sandburg, Carl **13** 461-462
art criticism
    Kirstein, Lincoln **9** 39-41
Asian American
    Tan, Amy **15** 95-96
autobiographical novels
    Roth, Philip **13** 318-320
autobiographical poetry
    Plath, Sylvia **12** 344-345
    Sexton, Anne **14** 125-126
autobiography
    Angelou, Maya **1** 238-239
    Banks, Dennis J. **1** 488-489
    Bukowski, Charles **3** 113-115
    Davis, Angela **4** 412-413
    Eastman, Charles A. **5** 183-185
    Hearst, Patricia **7** 242-243
    Ryan, Nolan **13** 389-391
    Turner, Tina **15** 357-359
    Wilson, Harriet E. **16** 320-322
automatic writing
    Stein, Gertrude **14** 414-415
Beat generation
    Burroughs, William S. **3** 162-163
    Ginsberg, Allen **6** 332-333
    Kerouac, Jean-Louis Lebris de **8** 518-519
biography
    Clapp, Margaret Antoinette **4** 71-72
    Ford, Paul Leicester **6** 9-10
    Forman, James **6** 10-11
    Harris, Frank **7** 172-173
    Irving, Washington **8** 141-143
    Nevins, Allan **11** 357-359
    Weems, Mason Locke **16** 170
Chicago group
    Anderson, Sherwood **1** 220-221
children's literature
    Asimov, Isaac **1** 338-341
    Bambara, Toni Cade **1** 482-483
    Baum, L. Frank **2** 73-74

Blume, Judy **2** 344-345
Bradbury, Ray **2** 473-474
Geisel, Theodor (Dr. Seuss)
   6 255-256
Jarrell, Randall **8** 222-223
Peck, Robert Newton **12** 177-178
Steel, Danielle **14** 404-406
Tan, Amy **15** 95-96
Tyler, Anne **15** 367-368
White, E. B. **16** 228-230
colonial diaries
   Byrd, William II **3** 189-190
   Sewall, Samuel **14** 123-124
comparative mythology
   Campbell, Joseph **3** 253-255
complex novels
   Pynchon, Thomas **12** 496-498
   Welty, Eudora **16** 199-201
confessional poetry
   Sexton, Anne **14** 125-126
Connecticut Wits
   Barlow, Joel **2** 6-7
   Dwight, Timothy **5** 169
copyright reform (19th century)
   Webster, Noah **16** 164-166
crime stories
   Chandler, Raymond Jr. **3** 423-425
criticism
   Burke, Kenneth **3** 141-142
   Eliot, Thomas Stearns **5** 258-261
   Greenberg, Clement **6** 521-523
   Howells, William Dean **7** 539-541
   Jarrell, Randall **8** 222-223
   Macdonald, Dwight **10** 81-83
   McCarthy, Mary T. **10** 389-391
   Mencken, Henry Louis **10** 481-483
   Poe, Edgar Allan **12** 363-365
   Wilder, Amos Niven **16** 273-274
   Wilson, Edmund **16** 318-319
cultural independence
   Channing, William Ellery **3** 435-436
detective stories
   Hammett, Dashiell **7** 106-108
developers of writers of
   Perkins, William Maxwell Evarts
      12 222-223
dialect
   Dunbar, Paul Laurence **5** 141-142
   Harris, Joel Chandler **7** 173-174
   Riley, James Whitcomb **13** 170-171
diaries
   Chesnut, Mary Boykin **3** 506-508
   Lindbergh, Anne Morrow **9** 420-421
   Nin, Anais **11** 397-398
   Rorem, Ned **13** 284-286
drama criticism
   Nathan, George Jean **11** 319-321
   Young, Stark **16** 474-475
epic poetry
   Merrill, James **10** 521-522
erotica
   Nin, Anais **11** 397-398
   Rice, Anne **13** 125-126
essays
   Agee, James **1** 78-79

Ames, Fisher **1** 199-200
Baldwin, James Arthur **1** 465-466
Bourne, Randolph Silliman
   2 456-457
Buckley, William F. Jr. **3** 96-97
Holmes, Oliver Wendell **7** 457-458
Lovecraft, H. P. **10** 3-6
Macdonald, Dwight **10** 81-83
McCarthy, Mary T. **10** 389-391
Rorem, Ned **13** 284-286
Sontag, Susan **14** 342-343
Updike, John **15** 390-392
Vidal, Eugene Luther Gore
   15 488-490
Vonnegut, Kurt Jr. **16** 25-27
White, E. B. **16** 228-230
experimental verse
   Cummings, Edward Estlin **4** 334-336
   Patchen, Kenneth **12** 128-129
   Robinson, Edwin Arlington
      13 201-202
expressionism
   Rice, Elmer **13** 126-127
fairy tales
   Owen, Ruth Bryan **12** 41-43
fantasy
   Bradbury, Ray **2** 473-474
feminist poetry
   Jordan, June **8** 351-353
   Rich, Adrienne **13** 128-130
feminist writings
   Gilman, Charlotte Anna Perkins
      6 323-325
   Millett, Kate **11** 31-33
   Starhawk **14** 403-404
   Steinem, Gloria **14** 418-419
   Walker, Alice Malsenior **16** 59-61
folk themes
   Benét, Stephen Vincent **2** 157-158
   Hurston, Zora Neale **8** 55-56
   Irving, Washington **8** 141-143
   Lindsay, Vachel **9** 424-425
   Silko, Leslie **14** 226-227
formalist poetry
   Wilbur, Richard Purdy **16** 271-272
free verse
   Masters, Edgar Lee **10** 326-327
   Whitman, Walt **16** 249-251
"Fugitive" poets
   Ransom, John Crowe **13** 39-40
gothic novel (18th century)
   Brown, Charles Brockden **3** 33
Harlem Renaissance
   see Harlem Renaissance
Hispanic
   Alvarez, Julia **1** 185-187
   Cisneros, Sandra **4** 64-65
   Hinojosa, Rolando **7** 403-405
historical fiction
   Churchill, Winston **4** 50-51
   Eggleston, Edward **5** 223-224
   Ford, Paul Leicester **6** 9-10
   Gilman, Charlotte Anna Perkins
      6 323-325
   Glasgow, Ellen **6** 360-361
   Mitchell, Margaret **11** 59-60

Rice, Anne **13** 125-126
Simms, William Gilmore
   14 235-236
Wallace, Lewis **16** 74-75
histories
   Asimov, Isaac **1** 338-341
   Bad Heart Bull, Amos **1** 427-428
   Billington, James Hadley **2** 275-276
   Mattingly, Garrett **10** 342-344
   Tuchman, Barbara **15** 331-332
horror
   King, Stephen **9** 23-25
   Lovecraft, H. P. **10** 3-6
how-to books
   Palmer, Arnold Daniel **12** 78-80
humor
   Irving, Washington **8** 141-143
   Lardner, Ringgold Wilmer
      9 204-205
   Parker, Dorothy Rothschild **12** 106
   Perelman, S. J. **12** 209-210
   Rogers, Will **13** 251-252
   Thurber, James Grove **15** 213-214
   Twain, Mark **15** 363-366
   Ward, Artemus **16** 112-113
   Welty, Eudora **16** 199-201
idealism
   Longfellow, Henry Wadsworth
      9 499-500
imagist poetry
   see Imagism (literature)
impressionism
   Crane, Stephen **4** 293-295
intellectual histories
   Conway, Jill Kathryn Ker **4** 213-214
Irish literary revival
   Colum, Padraic **4** 174-175
juvenile
   see Literature for children—United
      States
kinetic poetry (20th century)
   Olson, Charles **11** 505-506
legal thrillers
   Grisham, John **7** 6-8
lexicography
   Webster, Noah **16** 164-166
local color
   see Regionalism and local color
lyric poetry
   Dickinson, Emily **4** 541-543
   Millay, Edna St. Vincent **11** 24-25
metaphysical poetry
   Roethke, Theodore **13** 243-244
modern (drama)
   Shaffer, Peter Levin **14** 133-135
modern novel development
   James, Henry **8** 211-212
modernist fiction
   Barnes, Djuna **2** 11-13
moral tales
   O'Connor, Flannery **11** 467-468
   Weems, Mason Locke **16** 170
mysteries
   Vidal, Eugene Luther Gore
      15 488-490
mythic themes

West, Nathanael **16** 213-214
Native American
   Alexie, Sherman **1** 141-142
   Allen, Paula Gunn **1** 165-167
   Banks, Dennis J. **1** 488-489
   Deloria, Vine Jr. **4** 481-484
   Eastman, Charles A. **5** 183-185
   McNickle, D'Arcy **10** 433
   Momaday, N. Scott **11** 92-94
   Ortiz, Simon J. **12** 9-12
   Silko, Leslie **14** 226-227
naturalism
   Farrell, James Thomas **5** 390-391
   Norris, Benjamin Franklin Jr.
    11 427-428
   O'Neill, Eugene **11** 514-516
New Criticism
   see New Criticism
New England stories
   Proulx, E. Annie **12** 463-465
novels of violence
   Stone, Robert Anthony **14** 475-476
oral histories
   Terkel, Louis **15** 152-153
parables
   Gibran, Kahlil **6** 303-305
   Malamud, Bernard **10** 162-163
parody
   Perelman, S. J. **12** 209-210
patriotic poetry
   Bates, Katharine Lee **2** 54-55
patrons
   Luhan, Mabel Dodge **10** 32-34
personal-political essays
   Baker, Russell **1** 452-454
   Goodman, Ellen Holtz **6** 438-439
picaresque novel (18th-19th century)
   Brackenridge, Hugh Henry
    2 472-473
poetic portraits
   Brooks, Gwendolyn **3** 24-26
poetic renaissance
   Lowell, Amy **10** 13
poetry
   Bishop, Elizabeth **2** 290-292
   Cisneros, Sandra **4** 64-65
   Dove, Rita Frances **5** 87-89
   Dugan, Alan **5** 127-128
   Ginsburg, Ruth Bader **6** 333-336
   Giovanni, Yolande Cornelia Jr.
    6 346-347
   Hall, Donald **7** 84-85
   Key, Francis Scott **8** 525-527
   Lorde, Audre **9** 513-515
   Merrill, James **10** 521-522
   Momaday, N. Scott **11** 92-94
   Nemerov, Howard **11** 338-340
   Sexton, Anne **14** 125-126
   Simpson, Louis Aston Marantz
    14 243-244
   Strand, Mark **14** 491-493
   Updike, John **15** 390-392
   Van Duyn, Mona **15** 422-423
political commentary
   Chavez, Linda **3** 489-491
   Feiffer, Jules Ralph **5** 403-404

FitzGerald, Frances **5** 469-470
   Jacobs, Harriet A. **8** 190-193
   Reston, James Barrett **13** 104-105
   Royko, Mike **13** 337-339
   Safire, William **13** 422-424
   Thompson, Hunter Stockton
    15 196-198
   Updike, John **15** 390-392
   Vidal, Eugene Luther Gore
    15 488-490
   Will, George Frederick **16** 286-287
popular poetry (19th century)
   Holmes, Oliver Wendell **7** 457-458
   Lazarus, Emma **9** 260-261
   Whittier, John Greenleaf
    16 256-257
popular poetry (20th century)
   White, E. B. **16** 228-230
popular science
   Gamow, George **6** 199-200
   Sagan, Carl E. **13** 424-425
proletarian novels
   Steinbeck, John Ernst **14** 416-417
protest poetry
   Lowell, Robert Trail Spence Jr.
    10 16-17
   Markham, Edwin **10** 267
psychological novels
   Bellow, Saul **2** 141-143
   Chopin, Katherine **4** 18-20
   Heller, Joseph **7** 263-265
   Larsen, Nella **9** 209-210
   Rice, Anne **13** 125-126
   Salinger, J. D. **13** 447-448
   Tyler, Anne **15** 367-368
Puritan poetry
   Taylor, Edward **15** 122-123
   Wigglesworth, Michael **16** 266-267
realism
   see Realism (literature)
regionalism
   see Regionalism and local color
religious literature
   Merton, Thomas **10** 523-525
   Sheldon, Charles M. **14** 172-174
Revolutionary era poetry
   Freneau, Philip Morin **6** 99-100
   Wheatley, Phillis **16** 221-222
romantic literature
   Cabell, James Branch **3** 195-196
   Hawthorne, Nathaniel **7** 212-215
   Steel, Danielle **14** 404-406
satire
   Capp, Al **3** 275-276
   Heller, Joseph **7** 263-265
   Hopkinson, Francis **7** 496-497
   Kaufman, George S. **8** 457-458
   Lewis, Harry Sinclair **9** 385-387
   Parker, Dorothy Rothschild **12** 106
   Perelman, S. J. **12** 209-210
   Vonnegut, Kurt Jr. **16** 25-27
science fiction
   Asimov, Isaac **1** 338-341
   Bradbury, Ray **2** 473-474
   Butler, Octavia E. **3** 182-183
   Donnelly, Ignatius **5** 62

self-help
   vos Savant, Marilyn **16** 32-33
social commentary
   Algren, Nelson **1** 154-155
   Baldwin, James Arthur **1** 465-466
   Bambara, Toni Cade **1** 482-483
   Bukowski, Charles **3** 113-115
   Cheever, John **3** 493-494
   Childress, Alice **3** 522-524
   Crèvecoeur, John de **4** 307-308
   Hansberry, Lorraine Vivian
    7 130-131
   hooks, bell **7** 477-481
   Irving, Washington **8** 141-143
   Lowell, James Russell **10** 14-15
   Riesman, David **13** 167-168
   Rogers, Will **13** 251-252
   Rowan, Carl T. **13** 329-330
   Royko, Mike **13** 337-339
   Thompson, Hunter Stockton
    15 196-198
   Tourgée, Albion Winegar
    15 277-278
   Updike, John **15** 390-392
   Vidal, Eugene Luther Gore
    15 488-490
   Vonnegut, Kurt Jr. **16** 25-27
   Wharton, Edith **16** 221
   Wolfe, Thomas Kennerly Jr.
    16 356-357
sociohistorical fiction
   Lewis, Harry Sinclair **9** 385-387
sociological novels
   Phillips, David Graham **12** 280-281
southern
   Smith, Lillian Eugenia **14** 298-299
   Styron, William **15** 6-8
   Welty, Eudora **16** 199-201
sports fiction
   Lardner, Ringgold Wilmer
    9 204-205
subjective realism
   Stein, Gertrude **14** 414-415
supernatural themes
   Rice, Anne **13** 125-126
suspense
   Grisham, John **7** 6-8
   Ludlum, Robert **10** 28-29
techno-thrillers
   Clancy, Tom **4** 70-71
   Crichton, John Michael **4** 308-310
Theater of the Absurd
   Albee, Edward Franklin III
    1 106-108
theory
   Burke, Kenneth **3** 141-142
traditionalist poetry
   Frost, Robert Lee **6** 130-133
   Moore, Marianne **11** 148-149
travel literature
   Carver, Jonathan **3** 347-348
   Irving, Washington **8** 141-143
   Owen, Ruth Bryan **12** 41-43
   Theroux, Paul **15** 179-180
verse drama (20th century)
   Anderson, Maxwell **1** 219-220

Eliot, Thomas Stearns **5** 258-261
MacLeish, Archibald **10** 109-110
women's issues
Beecher, Catharine **2** 110-112
young adult
Hinton, Susan Eloise **7** 406-407
see also Authors, American; Journalism, American

American Locomotive Co. (Pittsburgh)
Chrysler, Walter Percy **4** 36-37

American Loneliness, The (lecture)
Wilder, Thornton Niven **16** 276-277

American Magazine (1757-1758)
Bradford, William **2** 477

American Magazine (1787-1788)
Webster, Noah **16** 164-166

American Magazine (1906-1956)
Baker, Ray Stannard **1** 451-452
Dunne, Finley Peter **5** 147-148
Reed, John Silas **13** 76-77
Tarbell, Ida Minerva **15** 107-108

American Marconi Co.
Sarnoff, David **13** 485-486

American Merchants' Union Express Co. Building (Chicago)
Richardson, Henry Hobson **13** 139-141
Sullivan, Louis Henri **15** 27-28

American Mercury (magazine)
Frankfurter, Felix **6** 57
Mencken, Henry Louis **10** 481-483

American Michelangelo
see Rimmer, William

American Mind, The (book)
Commager, Henry Steele **4** 181-183

American Missionary Association
Armstrong, Samuel Chapman **1** 306-307
Tappan brothers **15** 105-106

American Museum of Natural History (New York City)
Andrews, Roy Chapman **1** 232-233
Boas, Franz **2** 349-351
Mead, Margaret **10** 438-440
Simpson, George Gaylord **14** 240-242
Weidenreich, Franz **16** 171-172

American music
19th century
Gottschalk, Louis Moreau **6** 463-464
MacDowell, Edward Alexander **10** 87-88
Paine, John Knowles **12** 65
Thomas, Theodore **15** 192-193
20th century
art songs
Rorem, Ned **13** 284-286
ballet
Griffes, Charles Tomlinson **6** 543-544
Stravinsky, Igor Fedorovich **14** 502-506
bebop

Gillespie, Dizzy **6** 320-322
chamber music
Diamond, David **4** 527-529
Tower, Joan **15** 279-281
Zwilich, Ellen Taaffe **16** 536-537
chromaticism
Sessions, Roger Huntington **14** 117-118
classical
Diamond, David **4** 527-529
Hayes, Roland **7** 225-227
Wolpe, Stefan **16** 362-364
contemporary
Cage, John **3** 211-214
Carter, Elliott Cook Jr. **3** 338-339
Copland, Aaron **4** 227-228
Ives, Charles Edward **8** 159-160
Schuller, Gunther **14** 37-38
Shapey, Ralph **14** 154-155
Varèse, Edgard **15** 432-433
country and western
Cash, Johnny **3** 353-355
Cline, Patsy **4** 110-112
critics
Thomson, Virgil **15** 202-203
electronic music
Babbitt, Milton **1** 410
Cage, John **3** 211-214
federal support for
Hanks, Nancy **7** 126-127
folk and national themes
Cotten, Elizabeth **4** 261-263
Dett, Robert Nathaniel **4** 512
Dylan, Bob **5** 170-171
Foster, Stephen Collins **6** 25-27
Guthrie, Woodrow Wilson **7** 51-52
Handy, William Christopher **7** 123-124
Harris, Roy **7** 175-176
Heinrich, Anthony Philip **7** 261
Seeger, Pete **14** 83-84
Still, William Grant **14** 455-456
gospel
Caesar, Shirley **3** 210-211
Cleveland, James **4** 106-108
Franklin, Aretha **6** 58-60
Hayes, Roland **7** 225-227
grand virtuoso tradition
Horowitz, Vladimir **7** 509-510
jazz and blues
Armstrong, Louis Daniel **1** 303-304
Basie, Count **2** 48-49
Calloway, Cab **3** 236-238
Charles, Ray **3** 469-470
Cole, Nat **4** 149-151
Coltrane, John **4** 173-174
Ellington, Edward Kennedy **5** 273-274
Fitzgerald, Ella **5** 468-469
Gillespie, Dizzy **6** 320-322
Goodman, Benny **6** 436-438
Handy, William Christopher **7** 123-124
Hawkins, Coleman **7** 208-210

Holiday, Billie **7** 452-453
Jordan, Louis **8** 353-355
King, B. B. **9** 11-14
Monk, Thelonious **11** 104-108
Parker, Charles Christopher Jr. **12** 105-106
Smith, Bessie **14** 285-287
Waller, Thomas Wright **16** 81-82
Waters, Muddy **16** 134-136
Young, Lester Willis **16** 471-473
latin jazz and salsa
Puente, Tito **12** 476-477
magazines about
Guccione, Bob Jr. **7** 26
marches and band
Sousa, John Philip **14** 353-354
minimalism
Glass, Philip **6** 362-364
Reich, Steve **13** 84-85
Motown
Gordy, Berry Jr. **6** 450-451
Jackson, Michael Joe **8** 178-180
Jones, Quincy Delight Jr. **8** 339-341
Ross, Diana **13** 298-300
neoclassic
Griffes, Charles Tomlinson **6** 543-544
Piston, Walter **12** 327-328
Stravinsky, Igor Fedorovich **14** 502-506
neoromanticism
Hanson, Howard **7** 135-136
opera and oratorio
Anderson, June **1** 216-218
Caldwell, Sarah **3** 224-226
Fry, William Henry **6** 136-137
Hopkinson, Francis **7** 496-497
Joplin, Scott **8** 345-347
Levine, James **9** 369-371
Menotti, Gian Carlo **10** 509-510
Parker, Horatio William **12** 109
Price, Leontyne **12** 446-447
Sills, Beverly **14** 230-231
Thomson, Virgil **15** 202-203
Weill, Kurt **16** 174-175
orchestral music
Diamond, David **4** 527-529
Falletta, JoAnn **5** 373-375
Fiedler, Arthur **5** 437-438
Rostropovich, Mstislav Leopoldovich **13** 317-318
Tower, Joan **15** 279-281
Wolff, Hugh **16** 358-360
Zwilich, Ellen Taaffe **16** 536-537
percussion, use of
Tower, Joan **15** 279-281
"phase" music
Reich, Steve **13** 84-85
popular and show music
Cohan, George Michael **4** 137-138
Fiedler, Arthur **5** 437-438
Hammerstein, Oscar Clendenning II **7** 104-106
Jackson, Michael Joe **8** 178-180

Kern, Jerome David **8** 517-518
Madonna **10** 123-125
Payne, John Howard **12** 159
Porter, Cole Albert **12** 405-406
Rodgers, Richard Charles
13 234-236
Sinatra, Francis Albert
14 246-248
Sondheim, Stephen **14** 337-338
"pulse" music
Reich, Steve **13** 84-85
quotation
Rochberg, George **13** 221-222
ragtime
Castle, Vernon and Irene
3 361-363
Joplin, Scott **8** 345-347
recording industry
Gordy, Berry Jr. **6** 450-451
Jones, Quincy Delight Jr.
8 339-341
rock and roll
Cash, Johnny **3** 353-355
Hendrix, Jimi **7** 279-283
Little Richard **9** 447-449
Presley, Elvis Aron **12** 441-442
Shepard, Sam **14** 180-181
sacred music
Billings, William **2** 274-275
Mason, Lowell **10** 321-322
soul
Franklin, Aretha **6** 58-60
Ross, Diana **13** 298-300
traditionalist
Piston, Walter **12** 327-328
twelve-tone and serial music
Babbitt, Milton **1** 410
Perle, George **12** 223-224
Rochberg, George **13** 221-222
Shapey, Ralph **14** 154-155
Wuorinen, Charles **16** 404
see also Musicians, American

American Music Festival
Hanson, Howard **7** 135-136

American Negro Academy
Grimké, Archibald Henry **7** 1-2

**American Negro Leadership Conference
on Africa** (1962)
Mondlane, Eduardo Chivambo
11 100-101

American Negro Theater (Harlem, New
York City)
Davis, Ossie **4** 421-422

**American Orchestra and Theodore
Thomas, The** (book)
Russell, Charles Edward **13** 374-375

American Ornithology (book)
Wilson, Alexander **16** 313-314

American party (United States politics)
see Know-Nothing movement

American Peace League
Andrews, Fannie Fern Phillips
1 231-232

American Peace Society (established 1828)
Brown, William Wells **3** 48-49
Ladd, William **9** 149

American Personalism (philosophy)
Brightman, Edgar Sheffield **3** 8-9

American Pharos, The (book)
Mills, Robert **11** 36-37

American Philosophical Society
Bartram, John **2** 40-41

American Physical Society
Bridgman, Percy Williams **3** 5-6
Rowland, Henry Augustus **13** 330-331

American Place, An (art gallery)
Dove, Arthur Garfield **5** 86-87
Stieglitz, Alfred **14** 451-452

American Plan (economics)
see American System

American Popular Revolutionary Alliance
see Alianza Popular Revolucionaria
Americana

American Psychoanalytic Association
(established 1911)
Jones, Ernest Alfred **8** 331-332
White, William Alanson **16** 239-240

American Psychological Association
Cattell, James McKeen **3** 376-377
Hall, Granville Stanley **7** 85-86

American Railway Union (ARU)
Altgeld, John Peter **1** 180-182
Cleveland, Stephen Grover **4** 108-110
Debs, Eugene Victor **4** 444-445
Olney, Richard **11** 504-505

American Red Cross (established 1881)
Barton, Clara **2** 37-39
Drew, Charles Richard **5** 100-101

American Rembrandt
see Johnson, Jonathan Eastman

American Revolution (1775-1783)
American army
Allen, Ethan **1** 163-164
Arnold, Benedict **1** 309-310
Clark, George Rogers **4** 75-76
Dunbar, William (scientist)
5 143-144
Greene, Nathanael **6** 525-526
Hull, William **8** 29-30
Knox, Henry **9** 64
Kościuszko, Tadeusz Andrzej
Bonawentura **9** 88
Lincoln, Benjamin **9** 418-419
Marion, Francis **10** 262-263
Montgomery, Richard **11** 138-139
Morgan, Daniel **11** 160-161
Morgan, John **11** 162-163
Pickering, Timothy **12** 298-299
Putnam, Israel **12** 491-492
Revere, Paul **13** 110-111
Schuyler, Philip John **14** 49-50
Shays, Daniel **14** 168
St. Clair, Arthur **13** 429-430
Washington, George **16** 126-129
Wayne, Anthony **16** 149-150

Wilkinson, James **16** 284-286
American diplomacy
Adams, John **1** 48-51
Deane, Silas **4** 435-437
Franklin, Benjamin **6** 60-64
Gerry, Elbridge **6** 282-283
Jay, John **8** 230-232
Lee, Arthur **9** 288-289
Morris, Gouverneur **11** 182-183
American finances and supply
Fitch, John **5** 467-468
Hancock, John **7** 114-116
Morris, Robert **11** 185-187
American navy
Barry, John **2** 24-25
Forten, James **6** 17-18
Hopkins, Esek **7** 490-491
Jones, John Paul **8** 337-338
American neutralists
Coxe, Tench **4** 285-286
American politics
Adams, John **1** 48-51
Adams, Samuel **1** 55-56
Bowdoin, James **2** 461-462
Clinton, George **4** 113-114
Deane, Silas **4** 435-437
Dickinson, John **4** 543-544
Hamilton, Alexander **7** 95-98
Hancock, John **7** 114-116
Henry, Patrick **7** 309-311
Jay, John **8** 230-232
Jefferson, Thomas **8** 238-241
Laurens, Henry **9** 232
Lee, Richard Henry **9** 291-292
Livingston, Robert R. **9** 462-463
Madison, James **10** 121-123
Marshall, John **10** 279-281
Martin, Luther **10** 289-290
Mason, George **10** 319-320
Morris, Gouverneur **11** 182-183
Paterson, William **12** 132-133
Pendleton, Edmund **12** 197-198
Pinckney, Charles Cotesworth
12 310
Rush, Benjamin **13** 364-365
Rutledge, John **13** 387-388
Sherman, Roger **14** 185-186
Washington, George **16** 126-129
Wilson, James **16** 323-324
Winthrop, John **16** 341-342
Wythe, George **16** 415
American publicists
Adams, Samuel **1** 55-56
Bradford, William **2** 477
Freneau, Philip Morin **6** 99-100
Otis, James Jr. **12** 25-27
Paine, Thomas **12** 66-67
Pinto, Isaac **12** 318
British army
Burgoyne, John **3** 137-138
Carleton, Guy **3** 300-301
Clinton, Henry **4** 114-115
Cornwallis, Charles **4** 241-243
Gage, Thomas **6** 169-170
Howe, William **7** 538-539

Tarleton, Banastre **15** 110
Tryon, William **15** 321
British navy
Howe, Richard **7** 536-537
Phillip, Arthur **12** 279-280
Rodney, George Brydges
13 239-240
British politics
Fox, Charles James **6** 35-37
George III **6** 270-272
North, Frederick **11** 429-430
Pitt, William the Elder **12** 328-329
Rockingham, 2d Marquess of
13 230-231
British sympathy with
Pitt, William the Elder **12** 328-329
Price, Richard **12** 447-448
Priestley, Joseph **12** 452-453
Wilkes, John **16** 280-281
doctors and chaplains (American)
Brackenridge, Hugh Henry
2 472-473
Morgan, John **11** 162-163
Rush, Benjamin **13** 364-365
flag
Ross, Betsy **13** 297-298
foreign allies (American)
Bougainville, Louis Antoine de
2 443-444
Kościuszko, Tadeusz Andrzej
Bonawentura **9** 88
Lafayette, Marquis de **9** 151-152
L'Enfant, Pierre Charles **9** 322-323
Pulaski, Casimir **12** 480-481
Rochambeau, Comte de **13** 220-221
Saint-Simon, Comte de **13** 436-437
Steuben, Frederick William Augustus
von **14** 438-439
historians of
Channing, Edward **3** 435
Osgood, Herbert Levi **12** 18-19
Ramsay, David **13** 21
Sparks, Jared **14** 363
Tyler, Moses Coit **15** 369-370
Warren, Mercy Otis **16** 120-121
in art
Trumbull, John **15** 316-317
in literature
Condorcet, Marquis de **4** 195-196
Cooper, James Fenimore **4** 220-223
Simms, William Gilmore
14 235-236
influence of
Emmet, Robert **5** 281-282
Grattan, Henry **6** 499
Miranda, Francisco de **11** 52-53
Loyalists
Butler, John **3** 180
Carleton, Guy **3** 300-301
Franklin, William **6** 69-70
Fraser, Simon **6** 74-75
Galloway, Joseph **6** 186-187
Howe, William **7** 538-539
Johnson, John **8** 305-306
Leonard, Daniel **9** 336-337
Paine, Thomas **12** 66-67

Rumford **13** 360-362
Seabury, Samuel **14** 76
Shippen, Edward **14** 197-198
Smith, William **14** 301
Tilley, Samuel Leonard **15** 223-224
Native American allies (American)
Kirkland, Samuel **9** 37
Native American allies (British)
Brant, Joseph **2** 500-501
Brant, Mary (Molly) **2** 501-503
Cornplanter **4** 239-241
Girty, Simon **6** 350
Lewis, Andrew **9** 376-377
Red Jacket **13** 71-73
philosophy
Jefferson, Thomas **8** 238-241
Spain in
Charles III **3** 454-455
Gálvez, Bernardo de **6** 195-196
American Slavery as It Is (book)
Weld, Theodore Dwight **16** 186
American Smelting and Refining Co.
Guggenheim, Meyer **7** 31-32
American Society of Church History
(established 1888)
Schaff, Philip **13** 519-520
American Society of Human Genetics
Muller, Hermann Joseph **11** 238-239
American Society of International Law
Lansing, Robert **9** 200
American Sociological Society
Small, Albion Woodbury **14** 277
American Soldier, The (book)
Stouffer, Samuel A. **14** 482-483
American Songbook, The (songs)
Sandburg, Carl **13** 461-462
American State Politics (book)
Key, Vladimir Orlando Jr. **8** 527-528
American Statistical Association
Mayo-Smith, Richmond **10** 371-372
American Steel and Wire Co.
Gary, Elbert Henry **6** 229-230
American Sunday School movement
Vincent, John Heyl **15** 502-503
American System (economics)
Blair, Francis Preston **2** 313-315
Clay, Henry **4** 94-96
Lawrence, Abbott **9** 246
American Telegraph Co.
Cooper, Peter **4** 223-224
American Telephone and Telegraph Co.
Bell, Alexander Graham **2** 129-131
American, The (novel and play)
James, Henry **8** 211-212
American Thought (book)
Cohen, Morris Raphael **4** 139-140
American Tobacco Co.
Duke, James Buchanan **5** 133-134
American Tragedy, An (novel)
Dreiser, Herman Theodore **5** 98-100

Eisenstein, Sergei Mikhailovich
5 240-242
American Unitarian Association
Channing, William Ellery **3** 435-436
American Universal Geography, The (book)
Morse, Jedidiah **11** 191-192
American Woman Suffrage Association
(established 1869)
Howe, Julia Ward **7** 535-536
Stanton, Elizabeth Cady **14** 402-403
Stone, Lucy **14** 471-472
American Woodsman
see Audubon, John James
American Workers party (United States)
McKay, Claude **10** 416
Muste, Abraham Johannes **11** 276-277
American Wright Co.
Wright brothers **16** 394-396
Americanism (heresy)
Hecker, Isaac Thomas **7** 250-251
Ireland, John **8** 133-134
American-Jewish Committee
Straus, Isidor **14** 496
Americans for Democratic Action
Niebuhr, Reinhold **11** 387-388
Americans in Process (book)
Woods, Robert Archey **16** 374
Americans, The (trilogy)
Boorstin, Daniel J. **2** 398-400
Amerika (novel fragment)
Kafka, Franz **8** 403-406
Amerika-Breve (novel)
Rölvaag, Ole Edvart **13** 265
Amerinds
see Indians (North America); Indians
(South America)
Amériques (musical composition)
Varèse, Edgard **15** 432-433
Amers (poem)
Perse, Saint-John **12** 242-243
AMES, ADELBERT (1835-1933), American
politician **1** 198
Bruce, Blanche Kelso **3** 62-63
Ames, Ezra (1768-1836), American painter
Stuart, Gilbert **14** 513-515
AMES, FISHER (1758-1808), American
statesman **1** 199-200
Washington, George **16** 126-129
Ameto, L' (book)
Boccaccio, Giovanni **2** 351-353
Amfitriões (poem)
Camoëns, Luis Vaz de **3** 247-249
Amharic (Ethiopian language)
Heruy Wäldä-Sellasé **7** 348-349
Mäkonnen Endalkačäw **10** 161-162
Yekuno Amlak **16** 449
Amherst (city, Massachusetts)
Dickinson, Emily **4** 541-543

AMHERST, JEFFERY (1717-1797), English general and statesman **1** 200-201
  Louisbourg
    Carleton, Guy **3** 300-301
    Wolfe, James **16** 354-355
  Montreal
    Gage, Thomas **6** 169-170
    Johnson, William **8** 319-320
    Vaudreuil-Cavagnal, Marquis de **15** 444

Amherst College (Massachusetts)
  Clark, John Bates **4** 76-77
  Clark, John Maurice **4** 77-78
  Drew, Charles Richard **5** 100-101
  Frost, Robert Lee **6** 130-133

Amica America (book)
  Giraudoux, Jean **6** 349-350

Amicaliste movement (Congo)
  Eboué, Adolphe Felix Sylvestre **5** 194

Amiche, Le (film)
  Antonioni, Michelangelo **1** 252-253

Amico Francesco, L' (opera; Morelli)
  Caruso, Enrico **3** 345

Amida Buddhism (religion)
  Honen **7** 473
  Shinran **14** 197

Amiens, battle of (1918)
  Currie, Arthur William **4** 345

Amiens, Mise of (1264)
  Henry III **7** 290-292
  Montfort, Simon de **11** 132-133

Amiens, Peter of
  see Peter the Hermit

Amiens, Treaty of (1802)
  Bonaparte, Joseph **2** 381-382
  Cornwallis, Charles **4** 241-243
  Liverpool, 2nd Earl of **9** 456-457
  Napoleon I **11** 306-310
  Nelson, Horatio **11** 336-338

AMIET, CUNO (1868-1961), Swiss Postimpressionist painter **1** 201-202
  Kirchner, Ernst Ludwig **9** 34-35

Amin, al- (785?-813), Abbasid caliph 809-813
  Mamun, Abdallah al- **10** 183

AMIN DADA, IDI (born circa 1926), president of Uganda (1971-1979) **1** 202-204
  Obote, Apolo Milton **11** 457

Amino acids (chemistry)
  Fischer, Emil **5** 456-457
  Khorana, Har Gobind **8** 537-538
  Krebs, Hans Adolf **9** 95-97
  Liebig, Justus von **9** 403-404
  Sanger, Frederick **13** 466-467

Aminta (play)
  Tasso, Torquato **15** 114-116

Amistad (ship)
  Cinque, Joseph **4** 62

Amitabha Buddha
  see Buddha

Amitié du Prince (poems)
  Perse, Saint-John **12** 242-243

Ammanati, Bartolommeo (1511-1592), Italian sculptor and architect
  Cellini, Benvenuto **3** 391-392
  Vignola, Giacomo da **15** 493-494

Ammonia (chemistry)
  Diesel, Rudolf **5** 7
  Haber, Fritz **7** 56-58
  Hofmann, August Wilhelm von **7** 441-442
  Krebs, Hans Adolf **9** 95-97

Ammonites (Biblical tribe)
  Saul **13** 498

Ammonius Saccas (circa 175-242), Alexandrian philosopher
  Origen **11** 528-529

Amnesty International (human rights organization)
  Peltier, Leonard **12** 193-195

Amoenitates (book)
  Baudelaire, Charles Pierre **2** 61-63

Amoenitates academicae (periodical)
  Linnaeus, Carl **9** 427-429

Amon (Egyptian god)
  Amenemhet I **1** 193-194
  Ikhnaton **8** 110-111
  Tutankhamen **15** 359-360

Amon, Temple of (Karnak)
  Thutmose III **15** 216-217

Among My Books (book)
  Lowell, James Russell **10** 14-15

Among School Children (poem)
  Yeats, William Butler **16** 445-447

Among the Millet (poems)
  Lampman, Archibald **9** 180-181

Among the Ruins There He Lingered (painting)
  Moran, Thomas **11** 151-152

Amontons, Guillaume (1663-1705), French physicist
  Fahrenheit, Gabriel Daniel **5** 366

Amor, honor y poder (play)
  Calderón, Pedro **3** 221-222

Amor and Psyche (art work)
  Kokoschka, Oskar **9** 75-76

Amor brujo, El (ballet)
  Falla, Manuel de **5** 372-373

Amor médico, El (play)
  Tirso de Molina **15** 237-238

Amoraim (Jewish scholars)
  Abba Arika **1** 3-4
  Judah I **8** 372-373

Amore Coniugale, L' (novel)
  Moravia, Alberto **11** 153-155

Amores (poems)
  Lawrence, David Herbert **9** 247-248
  Ovid **12** 34-36

Amoretti (sonnets)
  Spenser, Edmund **14** 373-376

Amorite dynasty (Babylonia; established 19th century B.C.)
  Hammurabi **7** 109-110

Amorosa visione, L' (poems)
  Boccaccio, Giovanni **2** 351-353

AMORSOLO, FERNANDO (1892-1972), Philippine painter **1** 204

Amorum libri tres (poems)
  Boiardo, Matteo Maria **2** 369

AMOS (flourished 8th century B.C.), Biblical prophet **1** 205

Amos Barton (story)
  Eliot, George **5** 254-256

Amour courtois movement (French literature)
  Marie de France **10** 259

Amour et la vérité, L' (play)
  Marivaux, Pierre Carlet de Chamblain de **10** 265-266

Amour fou, L' (book)
  Breton, André **2** 519-520

Amoureuses, Les (poems)
  Daudet, Alphonse **4** 402-403

Amours (poems)
  Ronsard, Pierre de **13** 271-273

Amours de Psyché et de Cupidon, Les (book)
  La Fontaine, Jean de **9** 156-157

Amours de Voyage (poem)
  Clough, Arthur Hugh **4** 123-124

Amoy (city, China)
  Chu Hsi **4** 40-43

Ampere (electrical unit)
  Rayleigh, 3d Baron **13** 62

AMPÈRE, ANDRÉ MARIE (1775-1836), French physicist **1** 205-206
  Avogadro, Lorenzo Romano Amedeo Carlo **1** 388-389
  Cauchy, Augustin Louis **3** 378-380
  Oersted, Hans Christian **11** 476-478

Ampère, Jean Jacques (1800-1864), French essayist
  Ampère, André Marie **1** 205-206

Ampère's law (physics)
  Ampère, André Marie **1** 205-206

Amphictyonic League (ancient Greece)
  Demosthenes **4** 495-496

Amphilochia (religious work)
  Photius **12** 283-284

Amphipolis (ancient city, Greece)
  Cleon **4** 104-105

Amphitruo (play; Plautus)
  Camoëns, Luis Vaz de **3** 247-249
  Plautus **12** 348-350

Amphitryon (play)
  Dryden, John **5** 106-107
  Kleist, Heinrich von **9** 52-53

Plautus **12** 348-350

Amphitryon 38 (play)
Giraudoux, Jean **6** 349-350

Amphore, L' (sculpture)
Richier, Germaine **13** 145-146

Amritsar massacre (India; 1919)
Bose, Subhas Chandra **2** 430-431
Gandhi, Mohandas Karamchand
6 201-204
Nehru, Jawaharlal **11** 332-334
Reading, 1st Marquess of **13** 64

Amsterdam, University of (Netherlands)
van der Waals, Johannes Diderik
15 417-418
Van't Hoff, Jacobus Hendricus
15 431-432
Vries, Hugo de **16** 33-36

Amu Darya (river; Central Asia)
Bonvalot, Pierre Gabriel Édouard **2** 396

Amun
see Amon

AMUNDSEN, ROALD (1872-1928), Norwegian explorer **1** 206-207
Ellsworth, Lincoln **5** 277
Nobile, Umberto **11** 411-412
Scott, Robert Falcon **14** 67-68

Amymone, The (play)
Aeschylus **1** 70-72

Amyntas II (ruled 394-370 B.C.), king of Macedon
Philip II **12** 269-271

Amyntas III (died 336 B.C.), king of Macedon 360-359 B.C.
Philip II **12** 269-271

Amyntor (biography)
Toland, John **15** 256

An Belinden (poems)
Goethe, Johann Wolfgang von
6 388-391

An den Mond (lyrics)
Goethe, Johann Wolfgang von
6 388-391

An die Freude (poems; Schiller)
Beethoven, Ludwig van **2** 114-117
Schiller, Johann Christoph Friedrich von
14 4-7

An die Musik (hymn)
Schubert, Franz Peter **14** 35-37

AN LU-SHAN (703-757), Chinese rebel leader **1** 239-240
Wang Wei **16** 106-108
see also An Lu-shan Rebellion

An Lu-shan Rebellion (755-763)
An Lu-shan **1** 239-240
Hsüan-tsung, T'ang **8** 7-8
Li Po **9** 437-439
Tu Fu **15** 335-336
Wu Tao-tzu **16** 405-406
Zhao Kuang-yin **16** 505-508

An Schwager Kronos (poems)
Goethe, Johann Wolfgang von
6 388-391

An Wasserflüssen Babylon (musical composition)
Bach, Johann Sebastian **1** 416-419

Ana (literary character)
Alarcón, Pedro Antonio de **1** 100-101

Anabaptists (religious sect)
America
Beissel, Johann Conrad **2** 123-124
Europe
John of Leiden **8** 283
Menno Simons **10** 505-506
Münzer, Thomas **11** 251-252
opposed
Calvin, John **3** 239-242
Vondel, Joost van den **16** 19-20

Anabase (poems)
Perse, Saint-John **12** 242-243

Anabasis (book)
Xenophon **16** 418-420

Anabasis (book; Arrian)
Ptolemy I **12** 470-472

Anacletus II (died 1138), antipope 1130-1138
Bernard of Clairvaux **2** 207-208
Roger II **13** 244-245

Anaconda Copper Mining Co.
Clark, William Andrews **4** 83-85
Daly, Marcus **4** 379-380
Hearst, George **7** 242

Anacreon (572?-488? B.C.), Greek lyric poet
Tschernichowsky, Saul **15** 323

Anacreontic verses (literature)
Goethe, Johann Wolfgang von
6 388-391

Anactoria (poem)
Swinburne, Algernon Charles **15** 54-55

Anahuac (book)
Tylor, Edward Burnett **15** 372-373

Anaideia (philosophy)
Diogenes **5** 20-21

Anaklasis (musical composition)
Penderecki, Krzysztof **12** 195-197

Analects (book; Confucius)
Confucius **4** 197-200
Shotoku Taishi **14** 205-207
Wang Pi **16** 104-105
Yi Hwang **16** 457

Analogue computer
Bush, Vannevar **3** 169-171

Analogy, The (book)
Butler, Joseph **3** 180-181

Analysis (mathematics)
Cauchy, Augustin Louis **3** 378-380
Gauss, Karl Friedrich **6** 240-242
Ramanujan Aiyangar, Srinivasa
13 14-15

Analysis of Knowledge and Valuation
(book)
Lewis, Clarence Irving **9** 381

Analysis of Law (book; Hale)
Blackstone, William **2** 310-311

Analysis of Mind (book)
Russell, Bertrand Arthur William
13 373-374

Analysis of the Phenomena of the Human Mind (book)
Mill, James **11** 21

Analytic cubism (art)
Braque, Georges **2** 504-505

Analytic geometry
see Geometry—analytic

Analytic judgment (philosophy)
Kant, Immanuel **8** 430-432

Analytic philosophy
Moore, George Edward **11** 146
Nagel, Ernest **11** 291-292
Russell, Bertrand Arthur William
13 373-374
Ryle, Gilbert **13** 393-394
Wittgenstein, Ludwig **16** 350-351

Anamnesis (philosophy)
Plato **12** 345-347

ANAN BEN DAVID (flourished 8th century), Jewish Karaite leader in Babylonia
1 207-208

Ananda Mahidol (1925-1946), king of Thailand 1935-1946
Phibun Songkhram, Luang **12** 264-265
Pridi Phanomyong **12** 449

Anandamath (novel)
Chatterji, Bankimchandra **3** 480-481

Ananites
see Karaite sect

Anaphylaxis (physiology)
Dale, Henry Hallett **4** 371-373
Richet, Charles Robert **13** 144-145

ANAPO (political party; Colombia)
Rojas Pinilla, Gustavo **13** 255-256

Anarchiad (papers)
Barlow, Joel **2** 6-7

Anarchism (political philosophy)
civil liberties and
Goldman, Emma **6** 406-407
Sacco and Vanzetti **13** 408-410
Fourierism
Fourier, François Charles Marie
6 31-32
Haymarket Riot
Altgeld, John Peter **1** 180-182
Howells, William Dean **7** 539-541
libertarian
Godwin, William **6** 383-384
opponents
Marx, Karl **10** 304-308
theorists
Bakunin, Mikhail Aleksandrovich
1 458-460

Kropotkin, Peter Alekseevich
9 107-108
Proudhon, Pierre Joseph **12** 461-463
Stirner, Max **14** 459-460

Anarchy, State, and Utopia (book)
Nozick, Robert **11** 438-439

Anastasius (mid-5th century), bishop of
Thessalonica
Leo I **9** 329-330

Anastasius I (circa 430-518), Byzantine
emperor 491-518
Justinian I **8** 393-395

Anastasius II (died 721), Byzantine emper-
or 713-715
Leo III **9** 330-332

Anastomosis (medicine)
Carrel, Alexis **3** 322-323

Anathomia (treatise)
Luzzi, Mondino de' **10** 58

Anatman (Buddhism)
Buddha **3** 97-101

Anatol (play)
Schnitzler, Arthur **14** 23-24

Anatolikon Theme (Byzantine province;
Asia Minor)
Leo III **9** 330-332

Anatomy (book)
Paré, Ambroise **12** 94-95

Anatomy (science)
comparative
  see Comparative anatomy
founders
  Bichat, Marie François Xavier
  2 263-264
  Erasistratus **5** 297-298
  Vesalius, Andreas **15** 473-475
histology
  Ehrlich, Paul **5** 225-226
  Malpighi, Marcello **10** 176-178
  Schwann, Theodor **14** 51-52
mammalian
  Buffon, Comte de **3** 109-111
osteology
  Trotter, Mildred **15** 305-306
pathological
  Bright, Richard **3** 7-8
  Morgagni, Giovanni Battista
  11 158-159
  Sabin, Florence Rena **13** 402-405
  Virchow, Rudolf Ludwig Carl
  15 506-507
uterine
  Hunter, William **8** 48-49
  Luzzi, Mondino de' **10** 58
  see also Scientists—anatomists

Anatomy Lesson of Dr. Joan Deyman
(painting)
Rembrandt Harmensz van Rijn
13 91-95

Anatomy of Melancholy, The (treatise)
Burton, Robert **3** 166-167

ANAXAGORAS (circa 500-circa 428 B.C.),
Greek philosopher **1** 208-209
Lucretius **10** 26-27
Thucydides **15** 211-212

Anaxandridas (died circa 520 B.C.), king of
Sparta
Cleomenes I **4** 103

ANAXIMANDER (circa 610-circa 546
B.C.), Greek philosopher and astronomer
1 209-210
Anaximenes **1** 210

ANAXIMENES (flourished 546 B.C.), Greek
philosopher **1** 210

ANC
see African National Congress (ANC)

Ancestors, The (book)
Freytag, Gustav **6** 107-108

Ancestral Footstep, The (book)
Hawthorne, Nathaniel **7** 212-215

Ancestress, The (play)
Grillparzer, Franz **6** 546-547

ANCHIETA, JOSÉ DE (1534-1597), Portuguese Jesuit missionary **1** 210-211

Anchises (mythology)
Virgil **15** 507-510

Anciens Canadiens, Les (novel)
Aubert de Gaspé, Philippe **1** 364

Ancient History (lithography series)
Daumier, Honoré Victorin **4** 403-405

Ancient Judaism (book)
Weber, Max **16** 157-160

Ancient Lament (poem)
Carducci, Giosuè **3** 290-291

Ancient Law (book)
Maine, Henry James Sumner **10** 152

Ancient Mariner, The (play)
O'Neill, Eugene **11** 514-516

Ancient Mariner, The (poem; Coleridge)
Bartram, William **2** 41-42
Coleridge, Samuel Taylor **4** 154-156

Ancient Records of Egypt (books)
Breasted, James Henry **2** 510-511

Ancient Religion of the Gentiles (book)
Herbert, Edward **7** 324

Ancient Society (book)
Morgan, Lewis Henry **11** 167-168

Ancient Times (book)
Breasted, James Henry **2** 510-511

Ancient Voices of Children (musical composition)
Crumb, George **4** 326-328

Ancients (French literature)
Boileau-Despréaux, Nicholas
2 369-371

Ancillon, J.P.F. (1767-1837), Prussian
preacher-statesman
Frederick William IV **6** 87-88

Ancon Hospital (Panama Canal Zone)
Whipple, George Hoyt **16** 224-225

Ancona (region, Italy)
Manuel I **10** 218-219

Ancre, Concino Concini, Marquis de (died
1617), Italian adventurer
Louis XIII **9** 529-531

And It Came to Pass (poem)
Bialik, Hayyim Nahman **2** 262-263

And No One Knows Where to Go (poems)
Sachs, Nelly **13** 411-412

And Other Stories (book)
O'Hara, John **11** 485

And Quiet Flows the Don (novel)
Sholokhov, Mikhail Aleksandrovich
14 203-204

And Then (novel)
Natsume, Soseki **11** 324-325

And Then There Were None (play)
Christie, Agatha **4** 25-26

Andalusia (region, Spain)
Alfonso X **1** 150-151
Falla, Manuel de **5** 372-373

Andante (musical composition)
Franck, César **6** 48-49
Harris, Roy **7** 175-176

Andechs, church of (Germany)
Zimmermann, Johann Baptist and
Domenikus **16** 518

ANDERSEN, DOROTHY (1901-1963),
American physician and pathologist
1 212

ANDERSEN, HANS CHRISTIAN
(1805-1875), Danish author **1** 212-214
Dinesen Blixen-Finecke, Karen **5** 13-14

ANDERSON, CARL DAVID (1905-1991),
American physicist **1** 214-215
Dirac, Paul Adrien Maurice **5** 23-24
Hess, Victor Francis **7** 362-363
Yukawa, Hideki **16** 481-482

Anderson, Charley (literary character)
Dos Passos, John Roderigo **5** 69-71

Anderson, Herbert L. (1914-1988), American physicist
Fermi, Enrico **5** 422-424

ANDERSON, JUDITH (1898-1992), American stage and film actress **1** 215-216

ANDERSON, JUNE (born 1953), American
opera singer **1** 216-218

Anderson, Karl (1874-1956), American
painter and illustrator
Anderson, Sherwood **1** 220-221

ANDERSON, MARIAN (1902-1993),
African American singer **1** 218-219

ANDERSON, MAXWELL (1888-1959),
American playwright **1** 219-220
Bogart, Humphrey **2** 363-364
Sacco and Vanzetti **13** 408-410
Weill, Kurt **16** 174-175

ANDERSON, SHERWOOD (1876-1941),
American writer **1** 220-221
Burchfield, Charles **3** 131-132

Caldwell, Erskine **3** 223-224
Hemingway, Ernest Miller **7** 274-277
Lewis, Harry Sinclair **9** 385-387
Stein, Gertrude **14** 414-415
Twain, Mark **15** 363-366

Andersonville Prison (Georgia)
Barton, Clara **2** 37-39

Andes Mountains (Peru)
Meiggs, Henry **10** 458-459
Nordenskold, Nils Otto Gustaf
11 422-423

Andes of Southern Peru, The (book)
Bowman, Isaiah **2** 464-465

Andorra (play)
Frisch, Max **6** 118-119

Andover House (Boston)
see South End House

ANDRADA E SILVA, JOSÉ BONIFÁCIO DE
(1763-1838), Brazilian-born statesman
and scientist **1** 221-222
Pedro I **12** 179-180

Andragogy
Knowles, Malcolm Shepherd **9** 62-64

ANDRÁSSY, COUNT JULIUS (1823-1890),
Hungarian statesman, prime minister
1867-1871 **1** 222-223
Deák, Francis **4** 431-432

Andrássy, Count Julius (1860-1929), Hungarian statesman and Austrian foreign
minister
Andrássy, Julius **1** 222-223

André, John (1751-1780), British soldier
Arnold, Benedict **1** 309-310

André del Sarto (play)
Musset, Louis Charles Alfred de
11 271-272

Andrea (born 1929), Yugoslavian prince
Alexander of Yugoslavia **1** 136-137

Andrea (play; Belasco-Long)
Belasco, David **2** 124-125

Andrea da Pontedera
see Andrea Pisano

ANDREA DEL CASTAGNO (1421-1457),
Italian painter **1** 223-224
Donatello **5** 55-56
Mantegna, Andrea **10** 215-216
Veneziano, Domenico **15** 459-460

ANDREA DEL SARTO (1486-1530), Italian
painter **1** 224-225
influenced by
Leonardo da Vinci **9** 337-340
Michelangelo Buonarroti **11** 2-5
students
Pontormo **12** 394-395
Rosso, Il **13** 312-313
Vasari, Giorgio **15** 442-443

ANDREA PISANO (circa 1290/95-1348),
Italian sculptor and architect **1** 225-226
Brunelleschi, Filippo **3** 70-72
Ghiberti, Lorenzo **6** 291-292
Giotto **6** 342-345

Orcagna **11** 526-527

ANDRÉE, SALOMON AUGUST
(1854-1897), Swedish engineer and Arctic balloonist **1** 226

Andrei (ruled 1246-1252), grand prince of
Vladimir
Nevsky, Alexander **11** 359

Andreino
see Andrea del Sarto

Andrenio (literary character)
Gracián y Morales, Baltasar Jerónimo
6 481-482

ANDREOTTI, GIULIO (born 1919), leader
of Italy's Christian Democratic party
1 226-228

Andrés Pérez, maderista (novel)
Azuela, Mariano **1** 402

ANDRETTI, MARIO (born 1940),
Italian/American race car driver
1 228-230

ANDREW, JOHN ALBION (1818-1867),
American politician **1** 230-231

Andrew, St. (1st century), Apostle of Jesus
Peter **12** 252-253

Andrewes, Lancelot (1555-1626), English
bishop
Spenser, Edmund **14** 373-376

ANDREWS, CHARLES McLEAN
(1863-1943), American historian **1** 231

ANDREWS, FANNIE FERN PHILLIPS
(1867-1950), American educator,
reformer, pacifist **1** 231-232

ANDREWS, ROY CHAPMAN (1884-1960),
American naturalist and explorer
1 232-233

Andrews (F.W.) House (Newport, Rhode
Island)
Richardson, Henry Hobson **13** 139-141

Andreyev, Leonid Nikolayevich
(1871-1919), Russian author
Chekhov, Anton Pavlovich **3** 494-497
Stanislavsky, Constantin **14** 398-399

Andri (literary character)
Frisch, Max **6** 118-119

Andria (play)
Machiavelli, Niccolò **10** 97-99

Andria (play; Terence)
Terence **15** 146-148
Wilder, Thornton Niven **16** 276-277

Andrians (painting)
Titian **15** 242-244

Androcles and the Lion (play)
Shaw, George Bernard **14** 163-164

Andromache (play)
Euripides **5** 332-334

Andromache by the Body of Hector (painting)
David, Jacques Louis **4** 407-409

Andromaque (play)
Racine, Jean Baptiste **12** 532-535

Andromeda (poems)
Kingsley, Charles **9** 28

Andromeda Fountain (Vienna)
Donner, Georg Raphael **5** 63

Andromeda Nebula (astronomy)
Hubble, Edwin Powell **8** 10-11

Andronicus II Palaeologus (1260-1332),
Byzantine emperor
Michael VIII **11** 1-2

Andronicus of Rhodes (flourished 1st century B.C.), Greek philosopher
Aristotle **1** 295-296

ANDROPOV, IURY VLADIMIROVICH
(1914-1984), head of the Soviet secret
police and ruler of the Soviet Union
(1982-1984) **1** 233-234

ANDROS, SIR EDMUND (1637-1714),
English colonial governor in America
1 234-235
Leisler, Jacob **9** 313-314
Mather, Cotton **10** 330-332
Phips, William **12** 283
Taylor, Edward **15** 122-123
Winthrop, John **16** 341
Wise, John **16** 343-344

Andrusovo, Treaty of (1667)
Alexis Mikhailovich Romanov
1 142-143
Chmielnicki, Bogdan **4** 12-13

Anecdota (documentary collection)
Muratori, Lodovico Antonio
11 254-255

Anecdotal method (psychology)
Morgan, Conway Lloyd **11** 159-160

Anecdotes (book; J. Spence)
Pope, Alexander **12** 395-397

Anecdotes of Destiny (book)
Dinesen Blixen-Finecke, Karen **5** 13-14

Anemia (medicine)
dietary factors
Whipple, George Hoyt **16** 224-225
pernicious
Addison, Thomas **1** 58-59
Whipple, George Hoyt **16** 224-225
sickle cell
Pauling, Linus Carl **12** 150-152

Anesthesia (medicine)
Apgar, Virginia **1** 257-259
Cushing, Harvey Williams **4** 353-354
Long, Crawford Williamson **9** 495-496
Morton, William Thomas Green
11 198-199
Pauling, Linus Carl **12** 150-152
Wells, Horace **16** 196

Anet (château, France)
l'Orme, Philibert de **9** 519

Aneurysms (medicine)
DeBakey, Michael Ellis **4** 437-438

Anfa, Conference of (1943)
Mohammed V **11** 79-81

Anfu Clique (Chinese politics)
Chang Tso-lin **3** 434-435
Wu P'ei-fu **16** 404-405

Angel and Demon (poem)
Eminescu, Mihail **5** 280-281

Angel Appearing to the Shepherds (etching)
Rembrandt Harmensz van Rijn
13 91-95

Angel Goes to Babylon, An (play)
Dürrenmatt, Friedrich **5** 164-165

Angel of Bethesda, The (book)
Mather, Cotton **10** 330-332

Angel of Death and the Young Sculptor (sculpture)
French, Daniel Chester **6** 98-99

Angel of the Crimea
see Nightingale, Florence

Angel Releasing St. Peter from Prison (painting)
Allston, Washington **1** 176-177

Angel That Troubled the Waters, The (literary collection)
Wilder, Thornton Niven **16** 276-277

Angel, The (poem)
Lermontov, Mikhail Yurievich
9 352-353

Angel with Crown of Thorns (sculpture)
Bernini, Gian Lorenzo **2** 214-216

Angelic Doctor, The (book)
Maritain, Jacques **10** 263

Angelica (literary character)
Ariosto, Ludovico **1** 289-290
Boiardo, Matteo Maria **2** 369

ANGELICO, FRA (circa 1400-1455), Italian
painter **1** 235-236
Botticelli, Sandro **2** 439-440
Fouquet, Jean **6** 31
Ruskin, John **13** 371-372
Signorelli, Luca **14** 221-222
Veneziano, Domenico **15** 459-460

ANGELL, JAMES ROWLAND (1869-1949),
American psychologist and leader in
higher education **1** 236-237
Watson, John Broadus **16** 138-139

Angelo (literary character)
Shakespeare, William **14** 142-145

Angelo de Cosimo
see Bronzino

ANGELOU, MAYA (Marguerite Johnson;
born 1928), American author, poet, playwright, stage and screen performer, and
director **1** 238-239

Angels Bring What Is Longed For (painting)
Klee, Paul **9** 47-49

Angels with Dirty Faces (film)
Bogart, Humphrey **2** 363-364

Angelus (painting)
Millet, Jean François **11** 31

Angelus Temple (Los Angeles, California)
McPherson, Aimee Semple **10** 434

Anger (play)
Menander **10** 477-478

Anger of Achilles, The (book)
Graves, Robert Ranke **6** 504-506

Angers, David d'
see David d'Angers

Angevin dynasty
see Plantagenet dynasty

Angina victims
Seurat, Georges Pierre **14** 120-122
Shackleton, Ernest Henry **14** 132-133

Angkor (ancient city, Indochina)
Rama Khamhaeng **13** 11

Anglais mangeur d'opium, L' (book)
Musset, Louis Charles Alfred de
11 271-272

Anglais Mort à Florence (poem)
Stevens, Wallace **14** 443-445

Angles (English people)
Augustine of Canterbury **1** 370-371

Anglican King's College
see Toronto, University of (Canada)

Anglican Mission (Nigeria)
Crowther, Samuel Adjai **4** 326

Anglicanism (religion)
and women
Harris, Barbara Clementine
7 171-172
Anglican Orders
Pusey, Edward Bouverie **12** 488-489
defenders
Clarendon, 1st Earl of **4** 73-75
Gladstone, William Ewart
6 357-360
Inge, William Ralph **8** 118-119
ecumenism
Paul VI **12** 146-148
Ramsey, Arthur Michael **13** 23-25
education of poor
Lancaster, Joseph **9** 182-183
established
Henry VIII **7** 302-305
evangelical
Carey, George Leonard **3** 293-294
heresy trials
Jowett, Benjamin **8** 364-365
opposed
Crashaw, Richard **4** 296
Gorges, Ferdinando **6** 455-456
Makemie, Francis **10** 158-159
Ryerson, Adolphus Egerton
13 392-393
reform attempts
Cromwell, Oliver **4** 317-320

see also England, Church of; Protestant Episcopal Church
theologians
Macquarrie, John **10** 116-117

Anglo-American Telegraph Co.
Field, Cyrus West **5** 438-439

Anglo-Boer War
see Boer War (1899-1902)

Anglo-Burmese Wars
First (1824-1826)
Brooke, James **3** 21-22
Judson, Adoniram **8** 377-378
Mindon Min **11** 47
Second (1852)
Mindon Min **11** 47
Third (1885)
Mindon Min **11** 47

Anglo-Catholic revival (19th century)
Froude, James Anthony **6** 133-134

Anglo-Dutch Wars
see Dutch Wars
Chulalongkorn **4** 43-45
Mannix, Daniel **10** 210

Anglo-French Declaration (Thailand; 1896)
Chulalongkorn **4** 43-45

Anglo-Irish Treaty (1922)
Mannix, Daniel **10** 210

Anglo-Japanese Alliance (1905)
Balfour, Arthur James **1** 469-470

Anglo-Japanese Treaty (1902)
Salisbury, 3d Marquess of **13** 448-449

Anglo-Mysore Wars
see Mysore Wars (1767-1799)

Anglo-Persian Oil Co.
Reza Shah Pahlavi **13** 116-117

Anglo-Russian treaty (1805)
Alexander I **1** 130-132

Anglo-Saxon Chronicle (book)
Alfred **1** 151-153

Anglo-Saxon literature
Alfred **1** 151-153
Pound, Ezra Loomis **12** 415-417

Anglo-Saxons (British Saxons)
see England—5th century-1066
(Anglo-Saxon)

Angola (West Africa)
Kasavubu, Joseph **8** 453-455
Nzinga Nkuwu **11** 451-452
Salazar, António de Oliveira
13 442-443
independence movement
de Andrade, Mario **4** 434-435
Neto, António Agostinho
11 351-352
Savimbi, Jonas Malheiros
13 503-505
post-independence
Neto, António Agostinho
11 351-352
Savimbi, Jonas Malheiros
13 503-505

Angra Mainyu
  see Ahriman

Angriff, Der (newspaper)
  Goebbels, Joseph Paul **6** 384-385

Angry Black, The (book; editor J.A. Williams)
  Ellison, Ralph Waldo **5** 274-275

Angry Young Men (literary group)
  Osborne, John **12** 16-17

Anguish (poems)
  Lagerkvist, Pär Fabian **9** 162-163

Anhwei Army (China)
  Yüan Shih-k'ai **16** 480-481

Anhwei Clique (China)
  Ch'en Tu-hsiu **3** 501-502

Aniline (chemistry)
  Hofmann, August Wilhelm von **7** 441-442

Animal behavior
  Frisch, Karl von **6** 117-118
  Lorenz, Konrad Z. **9** 516-517
  Morgan, Conway Lloyd **11** 159-160
  Thorndike, Edward Lee **15** 208-209
  Tinbergen, Nikolaas **15** 229-230

Animal Caricature scrolls (Choju Giga)
  Toba Sojo **15** 248-249

Animal Crackers (musical)
  Marx brothers **10** 303-304

Animal Destinies (painting)
  Marc, Franz **10** 231

Animal electricity (physiology)
  Volta, Alessandro **16** 12-14

Animal Farm (novel)
  Orwell, George **12** 14-15, 222

Animal husbandry
  Buel, Jesse **3** 105

Animal Intelligence (book; Romanes)
  Morgan, Conway Lloyd **11** 159-160

Animal Intelligence (thesis)
  Thorndike, Edward Lee **15** 208-209

Animal Kingdom, The (book)
  Cuvier, Georges Léopold **4** 357-359

Animal Liberation (book)
  Singer, Peter Albert David **14** 253-254

Animal Life and Intelligence (book)
  Morgan, Conway Lloyd **11** 159-160

Animal Magnetism (book)
  Binet, Alfred **2** 277-278

Animal systematics (zoology)
  Cuvier, Georges Léopold **4** 357-359
  Darwin, Charles Robert **4** 397-399
  Huxley, Thomas Henry **8** 77-79
  Ray, John **13** 57-59

Animism (philosophy)
  Sherrington, Charles Scott **14** 187-189
  Stahl, Georg Ernst **14** 392-393
  Tylor, Edward Burnett **15** 372-373

Anitya (Buddhism)
  Buddha **3** 97-101

Anjou (French fief)
  Henry II **7** 287-289

Anjou, Duc d' (1554-1584)
  see Alençon, François, Duc d'

Anjou, House of
  see Plantagenet dynasty

Ankara, battle of (1402)
  Tamerlane **15** 94-95

Ankor Wat (book)
  Ginsberg, Allen **6** 332-333

ANL
  see Aliança National Libertadora

Ann Vickers (novel)
  Lewis, Harry Sinclair **9** 385-387

Anna Christie (film)
  Garbo, Greta **6** 205-207

Anna Christie (play)
  O'Neill, Eugene **11** 514-516

Anna Comnena
  see Comnena, Anna

ANNA IVANOVNA (1693-1740), empress of Russia 1730-1740 **1** 240-241
  Elizabeth, the Queen Mother **5** 261-263

Anna Karenina (film)
  Garbo, Greta **6** 205-207

Anna Karenina (novel)
  Tolstoy, Leo **15** 262-265

Anna Leopoldovna (1718-1746), Russian grand duchess, regent 1740-1741
  Anna Ivanovna **1** 240-241
  Elizabeth, the Queen Mother **5** 261-263

Anna of the Five Towns (novel)
  Bennett, Arnold **2** 167-168

Annalen der Chemie und Pharmacie (journal)
  Liebig, Justus von **9** 403-404

Annalen der Physik und Chemie (periodical)
  Carnot, Nicolas Léonard Sadi **3** 315

Annales (poem)
  Ennius, Quintus **5** 289

Annales de géographie (publication)
  Vidal de la Blache, Paul **15** 490

Annales des mines (journal)
  Le Play, Guillaume Frédéric **9** 350-351

Annales d'histoire économique et social (journal)
  Bloch, Marc **2** 332-333

Annales ecclesiastici (book; Baronius)
  Canisius, Peter **3** 258

Annales politiques (book)
  Saint-Pierre, Abbé de **13** 434-435

Annales revolutionnaires (journal)
  Mathiez, Albert **10** 333-334

Annali d'Italia (book)
  Muratori, Lodovico Antonio **11** 254-255

Annals (book)
  Tacitus **15** 70-72

Annam (former kingdom; Indochina)
  see Vietnam

Annapolis Convention (1786)
  Coxe, Tench **4** 285-286
  Dickinson, John **4** 543-544
  Hamilton, Alexander **7** 95-98
  Madison, James **10** 121-123
  Randolph, Edmund **13** 29-30

Annapolis Royal (Nova Scotia)
  Charnisay, Charles de Menou **3** 470-471
  Phips, William **12** 283

Annates (papal tax)
  Clement V **4** 101-102

ANNE (1665-1714), queen of England 1702-1714 and of Great Britain 1707-1714 **1** 241-242
  Anglicanism
    Burnet, Gilbert **3** 147
    Mary II **10** 309-310
    Swift, Jonathan **15** 51-54
  Blenheim Palace
    Churchill, Winston Leonard Spencer **4** 51-53
    Vanbrugh, John **15** 409-410
  in literature
    Pope, Alexander **12** 395-397
  policymakers
    Bolingbroke, Viscount **2** 374-375
    Godolphin, Sidney **6** 380-381
    Marlborough, 1st Duke of **10** 271-272

Anne (born 1950), English princess
  Elizabeth II **5** 266-269

Anne de Beaujeu (1460-1522), queen regent of France 1483-1491
  Charles VIII **3** 462-463

Anne Frank House
  Frank, Anne **6** 54-56

Anne of a Thousand Days (play)
  Anderson, Maxwell **1** 219-220

Anne of Austria (1601-1666), Spanish princess, queen regent of France 1643-1661
  art patronage
    Le Brun, Charles **9** 269-270
    Mansart, François **10** 211
  as regent
    Louis XIV **9** 531-533
    Mazarin, Jules **10** 379-380
  funeral oration
    Bossuet, Jacques Bénigne **2** 431-432
  marriage
    Louis XIII **9** 529-531
    Philip III **12** 273-274
  plot against Richelieu
    Richelieu, Armand Jean du Plessis de **13** 142-144

Anne of Brittany (1477-1514), queen of
France 1491-1498 and 1499-1514
Charles VIII **3** 462-463
Louis XII **9** 528-529

Anne of Cleves (1515-1557), fourth wife of
Henry VIII
Cromwell, Thomas **4** 320-321
Henry VIII **7** 302-305
Holbein, Hans the Younger **7** 449-450
Mary I **10** 308-309
Northumberland, Duke of **11** 431-432

Anne of Denmark (1574-1619), queen of
James I of England
Charles I **3** 450-452
James I **8** 204-206
Jones, Inigo **8** 333-334

Anne of Geierstein (novel)
Scott, Walter **14** 68-70

Anne of Green Gables (book)
Montgomery, Lucy Maud **11** 136-138

Année sociologique (journal)
Durkheim, Émile **5** 162-163

Annette (literary character)
Goethe, Johann Wolfgang von
6 388-391

Annibal (play)
Marivaux, Pierre Carlet de Chamblain
de **10** 265-266

Annibale
see Padovano, Annibale

Annie Get Your Gun (musical)
Berlin, Irving **2** 200-201

Anniversaries, The (poems)
Donne, John **5** 60-61

Anno Domini MCMXXI (book)
Akhmatova, Anna **1** 96-97

Annonce faite à Marie, L' (play)
Claudel, Paul Louis Charles **4** 90-91

Annotationes in XXIV Pandectarum libros
(book)
Budé, Guillaume **3** 102-103

Annuities on Lives (book)
Demoivre, Abraham **4** 494-495

Annunciation (altarpiece)
Martini, Simone **10** 298-299

Annunciation (diptych)
Martini, Simone **10** 298-299

Annunciation (engraving)
Schongauer, Martin **14** 26-28

Annunciation (fresco)
Botticelli, Sandro **2** 439-440
Giotto **6** 342-345
Pisanello **12** 323-324

Annunciation (miniature)
Limbourg brothers, The **9** 412-413

Annunciation (painting)
Angelico **1** 235-236
Eyck, Hubert and Jan van **5** 352-354
Greco **6** 511-514
Leonardo da Vinci **9** 337-340

Lippi, Filippo **9** 439
Lorenzetti, Pietro and Ambrogio
9 517-518
Tanner, Henry Ossawa **15** 102-103
Titian **15** 242-244
Tura, Cosimo **15** 343-344
van der Goes, Hugo **15** 416-417
Weyden, Rogier van der **16** 219-221

Annunciation (sculpture)
Donatello **5** 55-56
Günther, Ignaz **7** 41-42
Quercia, Jacopo della **12** 509

Annunzio, Gabriele d'
see D'Annunzio, Gabriel

Annus Domini (book)
Rossetti, Christina Georgina
13 307-308

Annus mirabilis (poem)
Dryden, John **5** 106-107

ANOKYE, OKOMFO (Kwame Frimpon
Anokye; flourished late 17th century),
Ashanti priest and statesman **1** 242-243

Anomie (sociology)
Durkheim, Émile **5** 162-163

Another Country (novel)
Baldwin, James Arthur **1** 465-466

Another Part of the Forest (play)
Hellman, Lillian Florence **7** 267-268

Another Philosophy of History... (book)
Herder, Johann Gottfried von **7** 327-328

Another's Nest (play)
Benavente y Martinez, Jacinto
2 146-147

ANOUILH, JEAN (1910-1987), French
playwright **1** 243-244
Hellman, Lillian Florence **7** 267-268

Anp'yong (1418-1453), Korean prince
Sejo **14** 90-91
Sejong **14** 91-92

Ansar movement (Sudan)
Mahdi **10** 137-138

Anschluss (1938)
Chamberlain, Arthur Neville **3** 409-411
Hitler, Adolf **7** 417-420
Horthy de Nagybánya, Nicholas
7 510-512
Schuschnigg, Kurt von **14** 45-46

Anschütz, Richard (1852-1937), German
chemist
Couper, Archibald Scott **4** 269-270

Ansco Co.
Eastman, George **5** 186

Anselm (book)
Barth, Karl **2** 31-32

ANSELM OF CANTERBURY, ST.
(1033-1109), Italian archbishop and the-
ologian **1** 244-245
Abelard, Peter **1** 23-25
Henry I **7** 286-287
Lombard, Peter **9** 490-491
William II **16** 293-294

William of Ockham **16** 298-299

Anselm of Laon (died 1117), French the-
ologian
Abelard, Peter **1** 23-25
Lombard, Peter **9** 490-491

Ansermet, Ernest (1883-1969), Swiss
orchestral conductor
Bloch, Ernest **2** 326-327

Anshutz, Thomas (1815-1912), American
painter
Demuth, Charles **4** 497-498
Glackens, William **6** 355-356
Sloan, John **14** 274-275

Anson, Charles Edward
see Markham, Edwin

Answering Magistrate Chang (poem)
Wang Wei **16** 106-108

Antalcidas, Peace of
see King's Peace (386 B.C.)

Antar Symphony (musical composition)
Rimsky-Korsakov, Nikolai Andreevich
13 174-175

Antarctic exploration
Australian
Mawson, Douglas **10** 354-355
Wilkins, George Hubert **16** 281-282
British
Cook, James **4** 214-215
Franklin, John **6** 64-65
Fuchs, Vivian **6** 140
Ross, James Clark **13** 302-303
Scott, Robert Falcon **14** 67-68
Shackleton, Ernest Henry
14 132-133
Norwegian
Amundsen, Roald **1** 206-207
South Pole
Amundsen, Roald **1** 206-207
Scott, Robert Falcon **14** 67-68
Swedish
Nordenskold, Nils Otto Gustaf
11 422-423
United States
Byrd, Richard Evelyn **3** 186-187
Ellsworth, Lincoln **5** 277
Palmer, Nathaniel Brown **12** 80-81
Wilkes, Charles **16** 279-280

Antaryami (book)
Das, Chitta Ranjan **4** 401-402

Anteriority of Black Civilizations (book)
Diop, Cheikh Anta **5** 21-22

Anthemius (died 472), Roman emperor
467-472
Ricimer, Flavius **13** 151-152

Anthology of Another Town, The (book)
Howe, Edgar Watson **7** 529

Anthoniszoon, Jeroen
see Bosch, Hieronymus

Anthony, Mark
see Antony, Mark

Anthony, Peter
see Shaffer, Peter Levin

ANTHONY, ST. (circa 250-356), Egyptian hermit and monastic founder **1** 246-248
Athanasius **1** 358-359
Benedict, Ruth Fulton **2** 154-155
Donatello **5** 55-56

ANTHONY, SUSAN BROWNELL (1820-1906), American leader of suffrage movement **1** 246-248
dress
Bloomer, Amelia Jenks **2** 337
in opera
Thomson, Virgil **15** 202-203
women's suffrage
Catt, Carrie Chapman **3** 375-376
Gage, Matilda Joslyn **6** 167-169
Howe, Julia Ward **7** 535-536
Shaw, Anna Howard **14** 162-163
Stanton, Elizabeth Cady **14** 402-403
Stone, Lucy **14** 471-472

Anthony Abbott, St.
see Anthony, St.

Anthony Burns (book)
Burns, Anthony **3** 151

Anthony of Egypt, St.
see Anthony, St.

Anthrax bacillus (bacteriology)
Koch, Heinrich Hermann Robert **9** 69-70
Pasteur, Louis **12** 125-127

Anthropocentrism (philosophy)
Chrysippus **4** 35-36

Anthropological linguistics
see Linguistics

Anthropology (social science)
Australian aborigines
Bates, Daisy Mae **2** 52-53
Radcliffe-Brown, A. R. **12** 535-536
Boasian school
Boas, Franz **2** 349-351
Kroeber, Alfred Louis **9** 105-106
cultural
see Cultural anthropology
culture of poverty
Lewis, Oscar **9** 392-393
development
Fletcher, Alice Cunningham **5** 486-487
Hrdlička, Aleš **8** 3-4
ethnology
Freyre, Gilberto **6** 106-107
Mauss, Marcel **10** 352-353
fossil man
Howells, William White **7** 541-542
Hrdlička, Aleš **8** 3-4
Leakey, Louis Seymour Bazett **9** 262
Leakey, Mary Douglas **9** 263-264
Leakey, Richard Erskine Frere **9** 264-265
Weidenreich, Franz **16** 171-172
functional school

Malinowski, Kaspar Bronislaw **10** 170-171
historical perspective
Evans-Pritchard, Edward Evan **5** 340
Sauer, Carl Ortwin **13** 496-497
interdisciplinary approach
Freud, Sigmund **6** 103-106
Fries, Jakob Friedrich **6** 116-117
Kluckhohn, Clyde **9** 56-57
Kulturkreis school
Kluckhohn, Clyde **9** 56-57
Native Americans
Hrdlička, Aleš **8** 3-4
Lowie, Robert Harry **10** 18
Radin, Paul **12** 538-539
White, Leslie A. **16** 232-233
Oceania
Howells, William White **7** 541-542
professionalized
Boas, Franz **2** 349-351
Fletcher, Alice Cunningham **5** 486-487
religion and mythology
Frazer, James George **6** 76
Radin, Paul **12** 538-539
Tylor, Edward Burnett **15** 372-373
social
Douglas, Mary Tew **5** 79-80
Gluckman, Max **6** 374-375
Lévi-Strauss, Claude Gustave **9** 371-372
Radcliffe-Brown, A. R. **12** 535-536
Redfield, Robert **13** 73-74
see also Social scientists—anthropologists
South African societies
Radcliffe-Brown, A. R. **12** 535-536

Anthropometry (science)
Bertillon, Alphonse **2** 230-231
Boas, Franz **2** 349-351
Galton, Francis **6** 193-194
Lombroso, Cesare **9** 493

Antibiotics (medicine)
Brown, Rachel Fuller **3** 43-44
Chain, Ernst Boris **3** 407-408
Domagk, Gerhard Johannes Paul **5** 48-50
Dubos, René Jules **5** 119
Fleming, Alexander **5** 483-485
Florey, Howard Walter **5** 491-492
Waksman, Selman Abraham **16** 49-50

Antibodies (biochemistry)
Landsteiner, Karl **9** 188-189
Pauling, Linus Carl **12** 150-152
Richet, Charles Robert **13** 144-145

Antic Hay (novel)
Huxley, Aldous Leonard **8** 74-75

Antichita di Roma, Le (book)
Palladio, Andrea **12** 75-77

Anti-Christ (book)
Merezhkovsky, Dmitry Sergeyevich **10** 515-516
Nietzsche, Friedrich **11** 390-392

Anti-Christ, The (play)
Alarcón, Pedro Antonio de **1** 100-101

Anticipations (book)
Wells, Herbert George **16** 195-196

Anticlericalism (liberal movement)
France
Dreyfus, Alfred **5** 103-105
Leo XIII **9** 334-336
Poincaré, Raymond **12** 366-368
Holy Roman Empire
Leopold II **9** 346
Low Countries
Leo XIII **9** 334-336
Mexico
Calles, Plutarco Elías **3** 234-235
Díaz, José de la Cruz Porfirio **4** 534-536
Lerdo de Tejada, Miguel **9** 351-352
papal opposition
Pius IX **12** 335-336
Pius VI **12** 333-334
Spain
Azaña Diaz, Manuel **1** 396-397

Anticolonialism
see Nationalism

Anti-Communist Labour party (Australia)
see Democratic Labour party

Anti-Conscription League (Australia)
Curtin, John Joseph **4** 348-349

Anticosti Island (Gulf of St. Lawrence)
Cartier, Jacques **3** 343-344
Jolliet, Louis **8** 328-329

Anticristo, El (play)
Alarcón, Pedro Antonio de **1** 100-101

Anticyclone theory (meteorology)
Galton, Francis **6** 193-194

Antidosis (book)
Isocrates **8** 151

Anti-Dühring (book)
Engels, Friedrich **5** 286-288

Antietam, battle of (1862)
Jackson, Shirley Ann **8** 183-184
Lee, Robert Edward **9** 292-294
Lincoln, Abraham **9** 415-418
McClellan, George Brinton **10** 391-392
Meade, George Gordon **10** 440-441

Antifascist Congress (Brussels; 1935)
Sábato, Ernesto **13** 399-400

Antifascist National Committee (Romania)
Ceausescu, Nicolae **3** 387-388

Anti-Fascist People's Freedom League (Burma)
Aung San **1** 374-375
Thant, U **15** 161-162

Antifederalists (United States politics)
Clinton, DeWitt **4** 112-113
Clinton, George **4** 113-114
Gerry, Elbridge **6** 282-283
Lee, Richard Henry **9** 291-292
Livingston, Edward **9** 460-461
Macon, Nathaniel **10** 114-115

see also Democratic-Republican party
(United States); Federalists

Antigens (biochemistry)
Landsteiner, Karl **9** 188-189
Medawar, Peter Brian **10** 444-445
Richet, Charles Robert **13** 144-145

Anti-Goeze (book)
Lessing, Gotthold Ephraim **9** 357-359

Antigone (opera)
Honegger, Arthur **7** 472-473

Antigone (play)
Alfieri, Vittoria **1** 145-146
Anouilh, Jean **1** 243-244
Cocteau, Jean **4** 132-133
Sophocles **14** 343-345

ANTIGONUS I (382-301 B.C.), king of
Macedon 306-301 B.C. **1** 248-249
Ptolemy I **12** 470-472
Seleucus I **14** 92-93

Antigonus II (80?-37 B.C.), king of Judea
40-37 B.C.
Herod the Great **7** 333-334

Antigonus II Gonatus (319?-239 B.C.), king
of Macedon 283-239 B.C.
Aratus **1** 273-274
Asoka **1** 341-342
Zeno of Citium **16** 499-500

Antigonus III Doson (died 221 B.C.), king
of Macedon 229-221 B.C.
Aratus **1** 273-274
Cleomenes III **4** 103-104

Antigua, Penny, Puce (novel)
Graves, Robert Ranke **6** 504-506

Antihistamines (pharmacology)
Dale, Henry Hallett **4** 371-373

Anti-Imperialist League (Berlin)
Ho Chi Minh **7** 426-428

Anti-Jesus (play)
Eisenstein, Sergei Mikhailovich
5 240-242

Anti-Machiavel (book)
Frederick II **6** 81-84

Anti-Masonic party (United States)
Fillmore, Millard **5** 447-448
Harrison, William Henry **7** 180-181
Seward, William Henry **14** 124-125
Stevens, Thaddeus **14** 442-443
Weed, Thurlow **16** 169-170

Antimatter (physics)
Anderson, Carl David **1** 214-215
Dirac, Paul Adrien Maurice **5** 23-24

Antimémoires (essays)
Malraux, André **10** 178-180

Antimony (chemistry)
Hofmann, August Wilhelm von
7 441-442

Antinomianism (religion)
Davenport, John **4** 405-406
Hutchinson, Anne Marbury **8** 69-71
Junayd, Abu al-Qasim ibn Muhammad
al **8** 388

Winthrop, John (1588-1649) **11** 409

Antinomy (philosophy)
Kant, Immanuel **8** 430-432
Poincaré, Jules Henri **12** 365-366

Antioch (ancient city, Syria)
Ignatius of Antioch **8** 107-108
Justinian I **8** 393-395
Nestorius **11** 349-350
Seleucus I **14** 92-93

Antioch College (Yellow Springs, Ohio)
Bellows, Henry Whitney **2** 143-144
Hall, Granville Stanley **7** 85-86
Mann, Horace **10** 202-204

Antioch, siege of (1097-1098)
Alexius I **1** 143-144
Bohemund, I **2** 364

Antiochus I (324-261 B.C.), king of Syria
280-261 B.C.
Ptolemy II **12** 472-473
Seleucus I **14** 92-93

Antiochus II (286-247 B.C.), king of Syria
261-247 B.C.
Asoka **1** 341-342
Ptolemy II **12** 472-473

ANTIOCHUS III (241-187 B.C.), king of
Syria 223-187 B.C. **1** 249-250
Cato, Marcus Porcius the Elder **3** 375
Flamininus, Titus Quinctius **5** 477
Hannibal Barca **7** 128-130
Polybios **12** 384-385
Scipio Africanus Major, Publius Cor-
nelius **14** 61-62

ANTIOCHUS IV (circa 215-163 B.C.), king
of Syria 175-163 B.C. **1** 250
Judas Maccabeus **8** 374-375

Antiochus Dying ... (painting)
David, Jacques Louis **4** 407-409

Antiochus the Great
see Antiochus III

Anti-Ovid (poem)
Wieland, Christoph Martin **16** 260-261

Antiparticle (physics)
Anderson, Carl David **1** 214-215
Dirac, Paul Adrien Maurice **5** 23-24

Antipater (398?-319 B.C.), Macedonian
general
Alexander the Great **1** 137-141
Antigonus I **1** 248-249
Aristotle **1** 295-296
Seleucus I **14** 92-93

Antipater (died 43 B.C.), Judean procurator
47-43 B.C.
Herod the Great **7** 333-334

Antipater (letter)
Isocrates **8** 151

Antiphon (circa 480-411 B.C.), Greek orator
Thucydides **15** 211-212

Antiquarian's Family, The (play)
Goldoni, Carlo **6** 408-409

Antiquary, The (novel)
Scott, Walter **14** 68-70

Antique Vision (mural)
Puvis de Chavannes, Pierre **12** 492-493

Antiquitates italicae medii aevi (dissertation)
Muratori, Lodovico Antonio
11 254-255

Antiquités de Rome (book; Du Bellay)
Castiglione, Baldassare **3** 360-361

Antiquités troyennes (book)
Schliemann, Heinrich **14** 17-18

Antiquities of the Jews (book; Josephus)
John the Baptist **8** 290
Josephus Flavius **8** 360-361
Judas Maccabeus **8** 374-375

Antiquities of Things Human and Divine
(book)
Varro, Marcus Terentius **15** 438-439

Antirealistic revolution (French literature)
Giraudoux, Jean **6** 349-350

Anti-Regency party (United States)
Clinton, DeWitt **4** 112-113

Anti-Semitism
ancient
Philo Judaeus **12** 282-283
Justin Martyr **8** 395-396
Moses **11** 200-201
Austria
Harand, Irene **7** 139-145
Czechoslovakia
Fleischmann, Gisi **5** 482-483
Masaryk, Tomáš Garrigue
10 314-315
France
Barbie, Klaus **1** 501-503
Bloch, Marc **2** 332-333
Philip IV **12** 274
see also Dreyfus Affair
Germany (19th century)
Cohen, Hermann **4** 138-139
Lazarus, Emma **9** 260-261
Treitschke, Heinrich von
15 293-294
Wagner, Richard **16** 40-43
Germany (20th century)
Brunner, Alois **3** 73-74
Buber, Martin **3** 87-89
Cassirer, Ernst **3** 358-359
Chamberlain, Houston Stewart
3 411
Dubnov, Simon **5** 115-116
Eichmann, Adolf **5** 226-227
Frank, Anne **6** 54-56
Goebbels, Joseph Paul **6** 384-385
Himmler, Heinrich **7** 398-399
Hitler, Adolf **7** 417-420-293
Sachs, Nelly **13** 411-412
Holland
Frank, Anne **6** 54-56
Italy
Mussolini, Benito **11** 272-274
Pius XI **12** 337-339

Pius XII **12** 339-340
opponents
Harand, Irene **7** 139-145
Poland
Luxemburg, Rosa **10** 55-56
Penderecki, Krzysztof **12** 195-197
Russia
Alexander III **1** 133-134
Bialik, Hayyim Nahman **2** 262-263
Dubnov, Simon **5** 115-116
Ehrenburg, Ilya Grigorievich
5 224-225
Lazarus, Emma **9** 260-261
Nicholas II **11** 378-380
Yevtushenko, Yevgeny Alexan-
drovich **16** 455-456
Spain and Portugal
Abravanel, Isaac ben Judah **1** 31
Ferdinand V **5** 417-418
Isabella I **8** 144-145
Judah Halevi **8** 373
Manuel I **10** 219-220
Vieira, Antônio **15** 492
United States
Baruch, Bernard Mannes **2** 42-43
Brandeis, Louis Dembitz **2** 496-497
Cohen, Morris Raphael **4** 139-140
Coughlin, Charles Edward
4 265-266
Dewey, Melvil **4** 523-524
Ford, Henry **6** 5-6
writers against
Appelfeld, Aharon **1** 262-263

Antiseptics (medicine)
Fleming, Alexander **5** 483-485
Lister, Joseph **9** 444-445
Semmelweis, Ignaz Philipp **14** 101-102

Antislavery and Aborigines Protection Society (Lagos, Nigeria)
Macaulay, Herbert **10** 78-79

Anti-Slavery Harp, The (poems)
Brown, William Wells **3** 48-49

Antislavery movement (Great Britain)
Baker, Samuel White **1** 454-455
Fox, Charles James **6** 35-37
Livingstone, David **9** 463-465
Oglethorpe, James Edward **11** 482-483
Palmerston, 3d Viscount **12** 81-83
Priestley, Joseph **12** 452-453
Wilberforce, William **16** 269-270

Antislavery movement (United States)
Africa squadron (USN)
Perry, Matthew Calbraith
12 237-239
authors and editors
Emerson, Ralph Waldo **5** 278-280
Hildreth, Richard **7** 382
Howe, Julia Ward **7** 535-536
Lea, Henry Charles **9** 261-262
Lovejoy, Elijah Parish **10** 6-7
Medill, Joseph **10** 451-452
Melville, Herman **10** 472-476
Paine, Thomas **12** 66-67
Weld, Theodore Dwight **16** 186

Whittier, John Greenleaf
16 256-257
emancipationists
Beecher, Lyman **2** 113
Bristow, Benjamin Helm **3** 9-10
Brown, Moses **3** 42-43
Miller, Samuel Freeman **11** 29-30
Sewall, Samuel **14** 123-124
Free Soil party
Andrew, John Albion **1** 230-231
Blair, Francis Preston **2** 313-315
Bryant, William Cullen **3** 83-85
Burlingame, Anson **3** 144-145
Field, David Dudley **5** 439-440
Sumner, Charles **15** 30-31
legal aspects
Chase, Salmon Portland **3** 473-475
Curtis, Benjamin Robbins **4** 349
Dana, Richard Henry Jr. **4** 385-386
Dawes, Henry Laurens **4** 427
Shaw, Lemuel **14** 164-165
Stevens, Thaddeus **14** 442-443
Tyler, Royall **15** 371-372
other supporters
Adams, John Quincy **1** 52-54
Benezet, Anthony **2** 159-160
Burritt, Elihu **3** 160
Chandler, Zachariah **3** 425-426
Ladd, William **9** 149
Lee, Richard Henry **9** 291-292
Woolman, John **16** 382-383
see also Abolitionists, American;
Antislavery Society (United States);
Slavery—United States supporters

Antislavery Society (United States)
Bailey, Gamaliel **1** 444-445
Brown, William Wells **3** 48-49
Phillips, Wendell **12** 281-282
Remond, Charles Lennox **13** 95
Stone, Lucy **14** 471-472
see also American Antislavery Society

ANTISTHENES (circa 450-360 B.C.), Greek
philosopher **1** 250-251
Diogenes **5** 20-21
Zeno of Citium **16** 499-500

Antistrophe (ode)
Pindar **12** 312-313

Antisubversion Law (Philippines)
Magsaysay, Ramon **10** 130-131

Antisymbol (French literature)
Robbe-Grillet, Alain **13** 189-190

Antitheses (literature)
Gracián y Morales, Baltasar Jerónimo
6 481-482

Antithesis (philosophy)
Marx, Karl **10** 304-308

Antitoxic immunity (physiology)
Richet, Charles Robert **13** 144-145

Antitoxins (medicine)
Behring, Emil Adolph von **2** 122-123

Antitrust laws (United States)
businesses exempted

Harding, Warren Gamaliel
7 148-149
cases
Gary, Elbert Henry **6** 229-230
Hand, Billings Learned **7** 116
Morgan, John Pierpont **11** 163-165
Watson, Thomas J. **16** 140
White, Edward Douglass
16 230-231
Federal Trade Commission Act
see Federal Trade Commission
prosecutions initiated
Arnold, Thurman Wesley **1** 314
Knox, Philander Chase **9** 66-67
Roosevelt, Theodore **13** 280-283
Sherman Act
see Sherman Antitrust Act
see also Capitalism; Monopoly

Antoine de Bourbon (1518-1562), king of
Navarre 1555-1562
Henry IV **7** 293-295

ANTONELLO DA MESSINA (circa
1430-1479), Italian painter **1** 251-252
Bellini, Giovanni **2** 137-138

Antonina (novel)
Collins, William Wilkie **4** 169-170

Antoninus, Marcus Aurelius
see Caracalla

Antoninus Pius (86-161), Roman emperor
138-161
Hadrian **7** 60-61
Marcus Aurelius Antoninus **10** 243-245
Zeno of Citium **16** 499-500

Antônio, Dom (1531-1594), Portuguese
noble, claimant to the throne
Essex, 2d Earl of **5** 321-322

Antonio, Donato di Pascuccio d'
see Bramante, Donato

Antonio Azorin (novel)
Ruíz, José Martínez **13** 358

Antonio Broccardo (portrait)
Giorgione **6** 340-341

Antonio da Sangallo the Elder
Giorgione **6** 340-341
Sanmicheli, Michele **13** 469-470

Antonio da Sangallo the Younger
Sanmicheli, Michele **13** 469-470
Lescot, Pierre **9** 354
Michelangelo Buonarroti **11** 2-5
Sanmicheli, Michele **13** 469-470
Vignola, Giacomo da **15** 493-494

Antonio de Covarrubias (painting)
Greco **6** 511-514

ANTONIONI, MICHELANGELO (born
1912), Italian film director **1** 252-253
Bergman, Ernst Ingmar **2** 190-191

Antonius, Marcus
see Antony, Mark

Antonov Apples (story)
Bunin, Ivan Alekseevich **3** 124

ANTONY, MARK (circa 82-30 B.C.),
Roman politician and general **1** 253-254
Egypt and Judea
Cleopatra **4** 105-106
Herod the Great **7** 333-334
opponents
Brutus, Marcus Junius **3** 79-80
Cato, the Younger **3** 374-375
Horace **7** 500-503
Varro, Marcus Terentius **15** 438-439
Triumvirate
Augustus **1** 371-373
Cicero, Marcus Tullius **4** 55-58

Antony and Cleopatra (opera)
Barber, Samuel **1** 500-501

Antony and Cleopatra (play; Shakespeare)
Dryden, John **5** 106-107
Shakespeare, William **14** 142-145

Antwerp Cathedral (Belgium)
Rubens, Peter Paul **13** 339-342

Antwerp Ferry (painting)
Jordaens, Jacob **8** 347-349

Antwerp school (Flemish art)
Jordaens, Jacob **8** 347-349

Anual, battle of (1921)
Abd el-Krim el-Khatabi, Mohamed ben **1** 15-16

Anushervan the Just
see Khosrow I

Anxious Bench, The (book)
Nevin, John Williamson **11** 357

Any Old Place with You (song)
Rodgers, Richard Charles **13** 234-236

Anything Goes (musical)
Porter, Cole Albert **12** 405-406

Anytus (flourished 5th-4th century B.C.),
Athenian politician
Socrates **14** 320-321

ANZA, JUAN BAUTISTA DE (1735-1788),
Spanish explorer **1** 254-255
Curtin, John Joseph **4** 348-349
Evatt, Herbert Vere **5** 341-343

Anzac pact (1944)
Curtin, John Joseph **4** 348-349
Evatt, Herbert Vere **5** 341-343

Anzio, battle of (1944)
Alexander of Tunis, 1st Earl **1** 135-136

Anzus Security Treaty (1951)
Evatt, Herbert Vere **5** 341-343
Menzies, Robert Gordon **10** 510-511

AOUN, MICHEL (born 1935), Christian
Lebanese military leader and prime minister **1** 255-257

Apache Indians (North America)
Anza, Juan Bautista de **1** 254-255
Carson, Christopher **3** 334-335
Cochise **4** 128
Crook, George **4** 322-323
Geronimo **6** 281-282

Mangas Coloradas **10** 194-196

Apache Napoleon
see Cochise

Aparajito (film)
Ray, Satyajit **13** 60-61

Apartheid (South Africa)
critics
Paton, Alan Stewart **12** 134-135
Bok, Derek Curtis **2** 371-372
de Klerk, Fredrik Willem **4** 466-468
First, Ruth **5** 453-454
Fugard, Athol **6** 142-143
Suzman, Helen **15** 45-46
opponents
Berry, Mary Frances **2** 226-229
Biko, Steve **2** 273-274
Boesak, Allan Aubrey **2** 359-360
Brutus, Dennis **3** 77-78
Buthelezi, Mangosuthu Gatsha **3** 178-179
Luthuli, Albert John **10** 51-52
Mandela, Nelson Rolihlahla **10** 185-186
Mandela, Winnie **10** 187-189
Masire, Quett Ketumile **10** 318-319
Ramaphosa, Matemela Cyril **13** 15-16
Sisulu, Nontsikelelo Albertina **14** 259-261
Sisulu, Walter Max Ulyate **14** 261-262
Sithole, Ndabaningi **14** 262-264
Sobukwe, Robert Mangaliso **14** 318-319
Sullivan, Leon Howard **15** 25-27
Tambo, Oliver Reginald **15** 92-94
Tutu, Desmond **15** 360-361
supporters
Botha, Louis **2** 434-436
Botha, Pieter Willem **2** 436-438
Hertzog, James Barry Munnik **7** 347-348
Malan, Daniel Francois **10** 163-164
Retief, Pieter **13** 105-106
Verwoerd, Hendrik Frensch **15** 472-473
Vorster, Balthazar Johannes **16** 30-32

Apathia (philosophy)
Zeno of Citium **16** 499-500

Apatzingán constitution (1814)
Morelos, José María **11** 157-158

Apeiron (philosophy)
Anaximander **1** 209-210

APELLES (flourished after 350 B.C.), Greek
painter **1** 257

Apelles' Figure (story)
Pasternak, Boris Leonidovich **12** 124-125

Apemea, Peace of (188 B.C.)
Antiochus III **1** 249-250

APGAR, VIRGINIA (1909-1974), American
medical educator, researcher **1** 257-259

Apgar Newborn Scoring System
Apgar, Virginia **1** 257-259

Aphasia (psychology)
Freud, Sigmund **6** 103-106

Aphid (insect)
Leeuwenhoek, Anton van **9** 300-301

Aphorism (literature)
Dickinson, Emily **4** 541-543
Howe, Edgar Watson **7** 529

Aphrodite Anadyomene (painting)
Apelles **1** 257

Aphrodite of Knidos (sculpture)
Praxiteles **12** 433-434

Aphrodite Ourania (sculpture)
Phidias **12** 265-267

Apiculture (science)
Mendel, Johann Gregor **10** 483-486

Apion (flourished 1st century), Greek grammarian
Josephus Flavius **8** 360-361

APITHY, SOUROU MIGAN (1913-1989),
Dahomean political leader **1** 259-260

Apocalypse (New Testament)
see Revelation, Book of (New Testament)

Apocalypse (woodcuts)
Dürer, Albrecht **5** 159-161

Apocalypsis explicata (book)
Swedenborg, Emanuel **15** 49-50

Apocolocyntosis (satire)
Seneca the Younger, Lucius Annaeus **14** 103-105

Apocrypha (Protestant, Old Testament)
Jesus ben Sira **8** 251

Apocryphal Gospels
Jesus of Nazareth **8** 251-255

Apocryphal Texts (Confucianism)
Kuang-wu-ti **9** 112-113
Wang Mang **16** 101-103

APOLLINAIRE, GUILLAUME (1880-1918),
French lyric poet **1** 260
associates
Breton, André **2** 519-520
Chagall, Marc **3** 406-407
Cocteau, Jean **4** 132-133
Duchamp, Marcel **5** 122-123
Ungaretti, Giuseppe **15** 389-390
Bateau Lavoir group
Picasso, Pablo **12** 292-295
eulogies
Rousseau, Henri **13** 323-324
musical settings
Poulenc, Francis **12** 414-415

Apollo (ballet)
Balanchine, George **1** 461-462
Stravinsky, Igor Fedorovich **14** 502-506

Apollo (mythology)
Aeschylus **1** 70-72
Bernini, Gian Lorenzo **2** 214-216
Callimachus **3** 235-236
Polykleitos **12** 385-386

Apollo (sculpture)
Giovanni da Bologna **6** 345-346

Apollo and Daphne (painting)
Pollaiuolo, Antonio **12** 377-378
Poussin, Nicolas **12** 418-420

Apollo and Daphne (sculpture)
Bernini, Gian Lorenzo **2** 214-216

Apollo and Marsyas (painting)
Tintoretto **15** 232-234

Apollo and Orpheus (ballet)
Stravinsky, Igor Fedorovich **14** 502-506

Apollo and the Nymphs of Thetis (sculpture)
Girardon, François **6** 348-349

Apollo Belvedere (sculpture)
French, Daniel Chester **6** 98-99
Reynolds, Joshua **13** 115-116

Apollo Bringing Barbarossa His Bride (painting)
Tiepolo, Giovanni Battista **15** 219-220

Apollo e Daphne and Aci (musical composition)
Handel, George Frederick **7** 116-119

Apollo Guarding the Herds of Admetus (painting)
Claude Lorrain **4** 89-90

Apollo Parnopios (sculpture)
Phidias **12** 265-267

Apollo program (United States)
Armstrong, Neil Alden **1** 304-306
von Braun, Wernher **16** 17-18

Apollo Sauroktonos (sculpture)
Praxiteles **12** 433-434

APOLLODORUS (flourished circa 408 B.C.), Greek painter **1** 261

Apollodorus of Carystus (300-260 B.C.), Greek playwright
Terence **15** 146-148

APOLLONIUS OF PERGA (flourished 210 B.C.), Greek mathematician **1** 261-262
Euclid **5** 327-329
Fermat, Pierre de **5** 421-422
Pascal, Blaise **12** 122-124

Apollonius of Rhodes (flourished 240 B.C.), Greek poet
Callimachus **3** 235-236
Eratosthenes of Cyrene **5** 301-302

Apologética historia de las Indias (book)
Las Casas, Bartolomé de **9** 211-212

Apologia (book)
Pomponazzi, Pietro **12** 390-391

Apologia pro Galileo (book)
Campanella, Tommaso **3** 249

Apologia pro vita sua (autobiography; Newman)
Kingsley, Charles **9** 28
Newman, John Henry **11** 365-367

Apologies (book)
Justin Martyr **8** 395-396

Apologies to the Iroquois (book)
Wilson, Edmund **16** 318-319

Apology (book)
Tertullian **15** 155-156

Apology (dialogue; Plato)
Plato **12** 345-347
Socrates **14** 320-321

Apology and Voyages, The (book)
Paré, Ambroise **12** 94-95

Apology for a Wrong Greeting (dialogue)
Lucian **10** 25-26

Apology for Actors (pamphlet)
Heywood, Thomas **7** 373-374

Apology for Bad Dreams (poem)
Jeffers, John Robinson **8** 236-237

Apology for Poetry (book)
Sidney, Philip **14** 214-215

Apology for Raymond Sebond, The (essay)
Montaigne, Michel Eyquem de **11** 116-117

Apology for the Life of Mrs. Shamela Andrews, An (pamphlet)
Fielding, Henry **5** 442-444

Apology of the Commons (tract)
James I **8** 204-206

Apologye (polemic)
More, Thomas **11** 156-157

Apophoreta (book)
Martialis, Marcus Valerius **10** 286-287

Apoplexy victims
Cabet, Étienne **3** 196
Daudet, Alphonse **4** 402-403
La Bruyère, Jean de **9** 145
Philip V **12** 276-277
Prévost, Abbé **12** 445-446
Velázquez de Cuéllar, Diego **15** 459
Wilson, Henry **16** 322-323

Apostate (Jewish law)
Gershom ben Judah **6** 283-284

Apostate, the
see Julian

Apostle of
California
see Serra, Junipero
Democracy
see Madero, Francisco Indalecio
East Indies
see Francis Xavier, St.
England
see Augustine of Canterbury, St.
Germany
see Boniface, St.
Indians
see Eliot, John
Rome
see Neri, St. Philip
Slavs
see Cyril and Methodius, Sts.
West Indies
see Claver, St. Peter

Apostle, The (trilogy)
Asch, Shalom **1** 325-326

Apostles
see Bible—New Testament

Apostles (Cambridge University)
Strachey, Giles Lytton **14** 487-488
Tennyson, Alfred **15** 144-146

Apotelesmatica (book)
Ptolemy, Claudius **12** 473-474

Apotheosis of Charles VI as Apollo (painting)
Troger, Paul **15** 300

Apotheosis of Francesco Barbaro (painting)
Tiepolo, Giovanni Battista **15** 219-220

Apotheosis of Homer (mural)
Ingres, Jean Auguste Dominique **8** 121-123

Apotheosis of St. Eusebius (fresco)
Mengs, Anton Raphael **10** 505

Appalachen
see Tallahassee

Appalachian Spring (ballet)
Copland, Aaron **4** 227-228
Cunningham, Merce **4** 337-338
Graham, Martha **6** 485-486

Apparition (painting)
Hofmann, Hans **7** 442-443

Apparition (poem)
Mallarmé, Stéphane **10** 172-173

Appassionata Sonata (musical composition)
Beethoven, Ludwig van **2** 114-117

Appeal ... of Americans Called Africans (tract)
Child, Lydia Maria Francis **3** 520-521

Appeal of the Caravan, The (novella)
Husayn, Taha **8** 61-62

Appeal to Honour and Justice (book)
Defoe, Daniel **4** 457-459

Appeal to Reason, An (book)
Mann, Thomas **10** 204-207

Appeal to the Christian Women of the South, An (pamphlet; A. Grimké)
Grimké, Sarah Moore and Angelina Emily **7** 2-3

Appeal to the World, An (essay)
Du Bois, William Edward Burghardt **5** 116-118

Appearance and Reality (book)
Bradley, Francis Herbert **2** 481-482

Appearance of Man, The (book)
Teilhard de Chardin, Marie Joseph Pierre **15** 134-136

Appeasement policy (English politics)
Chamberlain, Arthur Neville **3** 409-411
Eden, Anthony **5** 204-205
Hitler, Adolf **7** 417-420
Macmillan, Harold **10** 112-113

Appel au soldat, L' (novel)
Barrès, Auguste Maurice **2** 20-21

APPELFELD, AHARON (born 1932), Israeli who wrote about anti-Semitism and the Holocaust **1** 262-263

Appell an die Vernunft (book)
Mann, Thomas **10** 204-207

Appelles (pseudonym)
see Scheiner, Christopher

Appendix Vergiliana (poems)
Virgil **15** 507-510

Apperceptive masses (psychology)
Herbart, Johann Friedrich **7** 321-322

APPIA, ADOLPHE (1862-1928), Swiss stage director **1** 263-264

Appian Law (Rome)
Cato, Marcus Porcius the Elder **3** 375

Appius Claudius Pulcher
see Claudius Pulcher, Appius

Apple, The (poems)
Yevtushenko, Yevgeny Alexandrovich **16** 455-456

Apple Computer Company
Jobs, Steven **8** 265-267

APPLEGATE, JESSE (1811-1888), American surveyor, pioneer, and rancher **1** 264-265

Apples (painting)
Hofmann, Hans **7** 442-443

APPLETON, EDWARD VICTOR (1892-1965), British pioneer in radio physics **1** 265-266

APPLETON, NATHAN (1779-1861), American merchant and manufacturer **1** 266-267

Appleton, Samuel (1766-1853), American merchant and manufacturer
Appleton, Nathan **1** 266-267

Appleton Collegiate Institute (Wisconsin)
Jordan, David Starr **8** 350-351

Appointment in Samarra (novel)
O'Hara, John **11** 485

Appolonian culture (North America)
Benedict, Ruth Fulton **2** 154-155

Appomattox, battle of (1865)
Gordon, John Brown **6** 449-450
Grant, Ulysses Simpson **6** 492-494
Lee, Robert Edward **9** 292-294

Apportionment (United States; law)
Black, Hugo Lafayette **2** 301-303
Warren, Earl **16** 117-120

Appreciations (literary criticism)
Pater, Walter Horatio **12** 130-131

Apprentice's Vade Mecum, The (book)
Richardson, Samuel **13** 141-142

APRA
see Alianza Popular Revolucionaria Americana

Après-midi d'un faune, L' (poem)
Mallarmé, Stéphane **10** 172-173

Après-midi d'un faune, Prélude à l' (musical composition; ballet)
Debussy, Achille Claude **4** 445-447

April and May Mornings (play)
Calderón, Pedro **3** 221-222

April in Paris (song)
Basie **2** 48-49

April Twilights (poems)
Cather, Willa Sibert **3** 368-369

Aprismo (ideology)
Haya de la Torre, Victor Raul **7** 216-217

Aprista party (Latin America)
Haya de la Torre, Victor Raul **7** 216-217
Leguía y Salcedo, Augusto Bernardino **9** 305-306

Apropos of Delores (book)
Wells, Herbert George **16** 195-196

Apsley House (London)
Adam, Robert and James **1** 38-40

Apthorpe Houses (Cambridge; New York State)
Harrison, Peter **7** 179-180

Aptitude testing (psychology)
Hull, Clark Leonard **8** 28

Apuleius, Lucius (2d century), philosopher and rhetorician
La Fontaine, Jean de **9** 156-157

Apulia (region, Italy)
Guiscard, Robert **7** 39-40
Julius II **8** 384-386

Apulia, Robert Guiscard, Count and Duke of
see Guiscard, Robert

Apuntes carpetovetónicos (book)
Cela y Trulock, Camilo José **3** 389-390

Aqaba, Gulf of (Red Sea)
Burckhardt, Johann Ludwig **3** 133

Aquae Sextiae, battle of (102 B.C.)
Marius, Gaius **10** 264-265

Aqueducts, Roman
Frontinus, Sextus Julius **6** 130

Aquileia (city, Italy)
Attila **1** 360
Marcus Aurelius Antoninus **10** 243-245
Mark **10** 266-267

Aquileia, council of (381)
Ambrose **1** 192-193

Aquinas, St. Thomas
see Thomas Aquinas, St.

AQUINO, BENIGNO ("Nino"; 1933-1983), Filipino activist murdered upon his return from exile **1** 267-268

AQUINO, CORAZON COJOANGCO (born 1933), first woman president of the Republic of the Philippines **1** 268-270
Marcos, Ferdinand **10** 240-242

Aquis Submersus (novella)
Storm, Theodor **14** 479-480

Aquitaine (duchy, France)
Charlemagne **3** 445-447
Edward III **5** 211-212
Edward the Black Prince **5** 217-218
Henry II **7** 287-289

Arab Empire
see Islamic Empire
Abdullah ibn Husein **1** 19-20
Faisal I **5** 370-371

Arab National Congress (Damascus, 1920)
Abdullah ibn Husein **1** 19-20
Faisal I **5** 370-371

Arab Nationalists' Movement (1952)
Habash, George **7** 55-56

Arab Revolt (Syria; 1916)
Abdullah ibn Husein **1** 19-20
Faisal I **5** 370-371
Husein ibn Ali **8** 63
Lawrence, Thomas Edward **9** 253-254

Arab Socialist Resurrection party (Syria)
'Aflaq, Michel **1** 73-74

Arab Socialist Union (Egypt)
Sadat, Anwar **13** 412-414

Arab States, League of
Fādil al-Jamālī, Muhammad **5** 361-362
Fahd ibn Abdul Aziz Al-Saud **5** 364-366
Farouk I **5** 387-388
Husayn, Taha **8** 61-62
Tito, Marshal **15** 244-246

Arab Village (musical composition)
Schuller, Gunther **14** 37-38

Arabella (opera)
Strauss, Richard **14** 500-501

Arabesque (art form)
Gorky, Arshile **6** 458
Hilliard, Nicholas **7** 391-392
Ingres, Jean Auguste Dominique **8** 121-123

Arabesques (literary collection)
Gogol, Nikolai **6** 391-393

Arabi Pasha (Colonel Ahmed Arabi; 1841?-1911), Egyptian revolutionist
Mahdi **10** 137-138
Tewfik Pasha **15** 157-158
Zaghlul Pasha, Saad **16** 485-486

Arabia
see Islamic Empire; Saudi Arabia

Arabian American Oil Co. (ARAMCO)
Yamani, Ahmed Zaki **16** 433-435

Arabian Nights (lithograph)
Chagall, Marc **3** 406-407

Arabic (language)
Abd al-Malik **1** 12-13
Atatürk, Ghazi Mustapha Kemal
1 356-357

Arabic literature
medieval
Abu Nuwas **1** 33-34
Ibn al-Arabi, Muhyi al-Din **8** 91
ibn Battuta, Muhammad **8** 91-92
ibn Tufayl, Abu Bakr Muhammad
8 96
Masudi, Ali ibn al- Husayn al-
10 328-329
Saadia ben Joseph al-Fayumi **13** 396
modern
Adonis **1** 64-65
Darwish, Mahmud **4** 399-401
Gibran, Kahlil **6** 303-305
renaissance (20th century)
Abduh ibn Hasan Khayr Allah,
Muhammad **1** 16-17
Husayn, Taha **8** 61-62
Mahfuz, Najib **10** 142-144

Arabic music
Fairuz **5** 368-369

Arabic numerals (mathematics)
Asoka **1** 341-342
Fibonacci, Leonardo **5** 434-435
Khwarizmi, Muhammad ibn Musa al-
8 541

Arab-Israeli wars
1948
Abdullah ibn Husein **1** 19-20
Arafat, Yasser **1** 270-271
Begin, Menachem **2** 118-120
Ben-Gurion, David **2** 160-161
Bunche, Ralph Johnson **3** 121-122
Dayan, Moshe **4** 429-431
Glubb, John Bagot **6** 371-372
Hussein ibn Talal **8** 65-67
Nasser, Gamal Abdel **11** 317-318
Peres, Shimon **12** 210-211
Rabin, Yitzchak **12** 527-529
Sharon, Ariel **14** 157-159
Weizman, Ezer **16** 181-182
1955
Nasser, Gamal Abdel **11** 317-318
1956 (Sinai Peninsula)
Eban, Abba **5** 191-192
Peres, Shimon **12** 210-211
Sharon, Ariel **14** 157-159
1967 (Six Day War)
Arafat, Yasser **1** 270-271
Assad, Hafiz **1** 346-348
Begin, Menachem **2** 118-120
Dayan, Moshe **4** 429-431
Eban, Abba **5** 191-192
Habash, George **7** 55-56
Hussein ibn Talal **8** 65-67
Mubarak, Hosni **11** 225-226
Nasser, Gamal Abdel **11** 317-318
Rabin, Yitzchak **12** 527-529
Sadat, Anwar **13** 412-414
Sharon, Ariel **14** 157-159

Thant, U **15** 161-162
Tito, Marshal **15** 244-246
Weizman, Ezer **16** 181-182
1973 (Yom Kippur War)
Assad, Hafiz **1** 346-348
Eban, Abba **5** 191-192
Mubarak, Hosni **11** 225-226
Peres, Shimon **12** 210-211
Sadat, Anwar **13** 412-414
Sharon, Ariel **14** 157-159
Waldheim, Kurt **16** 54-55
1982 (invasion of Lebanon)
Abu Musa **1** 32-33
Arafat, Yasser **1** 270-271
Assad, Hafiz **1** 346-348
Begin, Menachem **2** 118-120
Gemayel, Amin **6** 258-259
Peres, Shimon **12** 210-211
Sharon, Ariel **14** 157-159

Arachne (literary character)
Ovid **12** 34-36

ARAFAT, YASSER (also spelled Yasir; born
1929), chairman of the Palestinian Liberation Organization **1** 270-271
Abu Musa **1** 32-33

Arago, Dominique François John
(1786-1853), French physicist
Fizeau, Hippolyte Armand Louis **5** 475
Foucault, Jean Bernard Léon **6** 28-29
Laplace, Marquis de **9** 202-204

Aragon (region, Spain)
Cid **4** 58-59
Ferdinand V **5** 417-418
Innocent III **8** 125-127
Isabella I **8** 144-145
Peter III **12** 256-257

ARAGON, LOUIS (1897-1982), French sur-
realist author **1** 271-272
Barrès, Auguste Maurice **2** 20-21
Breton, André **2** 519-520

Arahat (Buddhism)
Buddha **3** 97-101

Arakcheev, Aleksei Andreevich
(1769-1834), Russian soldier and statesman
Alexander I **1** 130-132

Arakida Moritake (1473-1549), Japanese
poet
Basho, Matsuo **2** 45-48

Arámburu, Pedro Eugenio (1903-1970),
Argentine politician
Sábato, Ernesto **13** 399-400

ARAMCO (oil co.)
ibn Saud, Abd al-Aziz **8** 94-95

Arameans (ancient Syrian people)
Ashurbanipal **1** 338
Saul **13** 498

Arango, Doroteo
see Villa, Francisco "Pancho"

ARANHA, OSVALDO (1894-1960), Brazilian political leader **1** 272-273

Aranjuez Palace (Spain)
Charles IV **3** 456-457
Herrera, Juan de **7** 335

Arano (anthology; Kakei)
Basho, Matsuo **2** 45-48

Arapaho Indians (North America)
Fitzpatrick, Thomas **5** 474-475
Kroeber, Alfred Louis **9** 105-106

Araros (flourished 387-375 B.C.), Greek
dramatist
Aristophanes **1** 293-294

Aratea (poem; Aratus)
Cicero, Marcus Tullius **4** 55-58

ARATUS (271-213 B.C.), Greek statesman
and general **1** 273-274
Agis IV **1** 81-82
Cicero, Marcus Tullius **4** 55-58
Cleomenes III **4** 103-104
Hipparchus **7** 407-408

Araucana, La (epic; Ercilla)
Camoëns, Luis Vaz de **3** 247-249
Lautaro **9** 235

Araucanian Indians (South America)
Ercilla y Zúñiga, Alonso de **5** 302
Lautaro **9** 235
Montt Torres, Manuel **11** 139-140
Valdivia, Pedro de **15** 400-401

Araucano, El (newspaper)
Bello, Ahmadu **2** 139-140

Arawak Indians (America)
Columbus, Christopher **4** 176-179

Arba Turim (Jewish code)
Caro, Joseph ben Ephraim **3** 316-317

Arbeiter, Der (book)
Jünger, Ernst **8** 391-392

Arbeiter Zeitung (newspaper)
Hillquit, Morris **7** 393-394

Arbela (modern Erbil province, Iraq)
Alexander the Great **1** 137-141

Arbella (ship)
Bradstreet, Anne Dudley **2** 486-487
Winthrop, John **16** 339-341

ARBENZ GUZMÁN, JACOBO
(1913-1971), president of Guatemala
(1951-1954) **1** 274-276
Arévalo, Juan José **1** 285-286
Guevara, Ernesto **7** 30-31

Arbitrants (play)
Menander **10** 477-478

Arbitration, industrial
see Labor unions

Arblay, Madame d'
see Burney, Fanny

Arbogast (died circa 394), Frankish general
Theodosius **15** 176

Arbol de la ciencia, El (novel)
Baroja y Nessi, Pío **2** 15-16

ARBUS, DIANE NEMEROV (1923-1971),
American photographer **1** 276-277

Arbuthnot, John (1667-1735), Scottish
physician
Pope, Alexander **12** 395-397
Swift, Jonathan **15** 51-54

Arbuthnot, John (1841-1920)
see Fisher of Kilverstone, 1st Baron

Arc de Triomphe (novel)
Remarque, Erich Maria **13** 91

Arc du Carrousel (Paris)
Clodion **4** 121

Arcades (play)
Milton, John **11** 43-46

Arcadia (novel)
Lope Félix de Vega Carpio **9** 503-506
Sidney, Philip **14** 214-215

Arcadia (poem; J. Sannazzaro)
Giorgione **6** 340-341

Arcadia (region, Greece)
Cleomenes I **4** 103

Arcadian League (Greek federation)
Epaminondas **5** 291-292

Arcadian Shepherds (painting)
Poussin, Nicolas **12** 418-420

Arcadius (377?-408), Byzantine emperor
395-408
Stilicho, Flavius **14** 452-453
Theodosius **15** 176

Arcana (musical composition)
Varèse, Edgard **15** 432-433

Arcana coelestia (book)
Swedenborg, Emanuel **15** 49-50

Arc-de-Senans (France)
Ledoux, Claude Nicolas **9** 277-278

Arcesilaus (316-241 B.C.), Greek philoso-
pher
Carneades **3** 309
Chrysippus **4** 35-36
Eratosthenes of Cyrene **5** 301-302

Arch Street Theater (Philadelphia, Pennsyl-
vania)
Barrymores **2** 28-30
Jefferson, Joseph **8** 237

Archaeology
see Archeology

Archaeology, Institute of (London)
Childe, Vere Gordon **3** 521-522

Archaism (art)
Earl, Ralph **5** 179
Hartley, Marsden **7** 186

Archaism (literature)
Malherbe, François de **10** 169-170

Archangel (city, Russia)
Cabot, Sebastian **3** 200-201
Chancellor, Richard **3** 422

Archangels (painting)
Klee, Paul **9** 47-49

Arche (ode)
Pindar **12** 312-313

Archelaus (died 399 B.C.), king of Macedon 413-399 B.C.
Euripides **5** 332-334

Archelaus (book)
Antisthenes **1** 250-251

Archeologist king
see Ashurbanipal

Archeologists
see Scientists—archeologists

Archeology
East Africa
Leakey, Mary Douglas **9** 263-264
Leakey, Richard Erskine Frere
9 264-265
Europe
Breuil, Henri Edouard Prosper
2 521-522
Childe, Vere Gordon **3** 521-522
Greece
Evans, Arthur John **5** 335-336
Schliemann, Heinrich **14** 17-18
Middle America
Kidder, Alfred Vincent **8** 541-542
Near East
Petrie, William Matthew Flinders
12 261-262
Renan, Ernest **13** 95-96
scientific approach
Kidder, Alfred Vincent **8** 541-542
Petrie, William Matthew Flinders
12 261-262
Winckelmann, Johann Joachim
16 332-333
United States
Kidder, Alfred Vincent **8** 541-542
Kroeber, Alfred Louis **9** 105-106
Linton, Ralph **9** 431

Archetype (psychology)
Jung, Carl Gustav **8** 388-389

Archeus (medicine)
Paracelsus, Philippus Aureolus **12** 91-93

Archidamus (treatise)
Isocrates **8** 151

Archidamus II (ruled 476-427 B.C.), king of
Sparta
Agesilaus II **1** 79-80

Archidamus III (ruled 360-338 B.C.), king
of Sparta
Isocrates **8** 151

Archidamus V (died circa 227 B.C.), king of
Sparta
Cleomenes III **4** 103-104

Archilochus (flourished 7th century B.C.),
Greek poet
Horace **7** 500-503

ARCHIMEDES (circa 287-212 B.C.), Greek
mathematician **1** 277-280
editions
Tartaglia, Niccolo **15** 111-112
influence of

Galileo Galilei **6** 180-183
Omar Khayyam **11** 510-511
influenced by
Democritus **4** 493-494
mathematics
Apollonius of Perga **1** 261-262
Euclid **5** 327-329
Eudoxus of Cnidus **5** 329-330
Thales **15** 161

Archimedes' principle (physics)
Archimedes **1** 277-280

ARCHIPENKO, ALEXANDER (1887-1964),
Russian-American sculptor and teacher
1 280-281

Architects
see Artists—architects

Architects' Collaborative, The (TAC)
Gropius, Walter **7** 13-14

Architectural Record (magazine)
Croly, Herbert David **4** 316-317

Architectural Review (magazine)
Asplund, Eric Gunnar **1** 344

Architectural Sketches... (book)
Shaw, Richard Norman **14** 167-168

Architecture
Barragán, Luis **2** 17-19
Bofill, Ricardo **2** 362-363
Eisenman, Peter D. **5** 239-240
Erickson, Arthur Charles **5** 304-306
Freed, James Ingo **6** 88-90
Fuller, Richard Buckminster **6** 149-150
Gehry, Frank O. **6** 250-251
Isozaki, Arata **8** 152-153
Jahn, Helmut **8** 199-201
Jones, Fay **8** 332-333
Lin, Maya Ying **9** 413-415
Loos, Adolf **9** 502-503
Lutyens, Edwin Landseer **10** 54-55
Maki, Fumihiko **10** 159-161
Melnikov, Konstantin Stepanovich
10 470-471
Mies van der Rohe, Ludwig **11** 10-12
Moore, Charles Willard **11** 143-145
Morgan, Julia **11** 165-166
Nervi, Pier Luigi **11** 346-348
Piano, Renzo **12** 289-291
Pope, John Russell **12** 397-399
Roche, Kevin **13** 222-224
Rossi, Aldo **13** 309-310
Venturi, Robert **15** 461-463
see also American architecture; English
architecture; etc., and separate styles
and movements

Architecture of Country Houses (book)
Downing, Andrew Jackson **5** 90-91

Archiv für Physiologie (journal)
Du Bois-Reymond, Emil **5** 118-119

Archives for Pathological Anatomy... (journal)
Virchow, Rudolf Ludwig Carl
15 506-507

Archives for Social Science... (journal)
Weber, Max **16** 157-160

Archytas of Tarentum (flourished 400-365 B.C.), Greek philosopher
Plato **12** 345-347

Arcot (city; India)
Clive, Robert **4** 119-120

Arctic exploration
adaptation theories
Stefansson, Vilhjalmur **14** 409-410
aircraft in
Andrée, Salomon August **1** 226
Byrd, Richard Evelyn **3** 186-187
Ellsworth, Lincoln **5** 277
Nobile, Umberto **11** 411-412
Australian
Wilkins, George Hubert **16** 281-282
Danish
Rasmussen, Knud Johan Victor **13** 44
Dutch
Barents, Willem **2** 4-5
English
Baffin, William **1** 435-436
Franklin, John **6** 64-65
Hearne, Samuel **7** 241-242
McClintock, Francis Leopold **10** 394-395
Ross, James Clark **13** 302-303
German
Wegener, Alfred Lothar **16** 170-171
Norwegian
Amundsen, Roald **1** 206-207
Nansen, Fridtjof **11** 304-305
Russian
Kolchak, Aleksandr Vasilievich **9** 77-78
Swedish
Nordenskjöld, Nils Adolf Erik **11** 421-422
Nordenskold, Nils Otto Gustaf **11** 422-423
United States
Byrd, Richard Evelyn **3** 186-187
Ellsworth, Lincoln **5** 277
Greely, Adolphus Washington **6** 517-518
Henson, Matthew A. **7** 312-314
MacMillan, Donald Baxter **10** 111-112
Melville, George Wallace **10** 472
Peary, Robert Edwin **12** 175-176

Arctic Highlanders
see Greenland Eskimos

Ardashir I (ruled circa 226-241), king of Persia
Mani **10** 196-197
Kesselring, Albert Field Marshal **8** 522-523

Ardeatine Caves massacre (1944)
Kafka, Franz **8** 403-406

ARDEN, ELIZABETH (Florence Nightingale Graham; 1878?-1966), American businesswoman **1** 281-282

Ardennes counteroffensive
see Bulge, battle of the (1944)

Ardres, Treaty of (1546)
Northumberland, Duke of **11** 431-432

Are We Civilized? (book)
Lowie, Robert Harry **10** 18

ARENA (Salvadoran political party)
Cristiani, Alfredo **4** 311-313

Arena Chapel (Padua)
Giotto **6** 342-345-409
Pisano, Giovanni **12** 324-325

ARENDT, HANNAH (1906-1975), Jewish philosopher **1** 282-284

ARENS, MOSHE (born 1925), aeronautical engineer who became a leading Israeli statesman **1** 284-285

Arensky, Anton Stephanovich (1861-1906), Russian composer
Rachmaninov, Sergei Vasilievich **12** 531-532

Areopagitica (pamphlet)
Milton, John **11** 43-46

Areopagiticus (treatise)
Isocrates **8** 151

Areopagus Council (ancient Greece)
Pericles **12** 219-221
Solon **14** 327-328

Arequipa (city; Peru)
Meiggs, Henry **10** 458-459

Aretas IV (9 B.C.-A.D. 40), Nabataean king
John the Baptist **8** 290

Arete (philosophy))
Plato **12** 345-347

Aretino, Pietro (1492-1556), Italian satirist
Rosso, Il **13** 312-313
Sansovino, Jacopo **13** 470-471
Tintoretto **15** 232-234

ARÉVALO, JUAN JOSÉ (1904-1951), Guatemalan statesman, president 1944-1951 **1** 285-286

Argall, Samuel (flourished early 17th century), English mariner
Pocahontas **12** 361-362
Powhatan **12** 429-430

Argenteuil (region, France)
Abelard, Peter **1** 23-25
Monet, Claude **11** 102-104

Argentina (Argentine Republic; nation, South America)
Bolivia and
Rosas, Juan Manuel de **13** 290-291
Santa Cruz, Andrés de **13** 472-473
Brazil and
Pedro II **12** 180-181
Rio Branco, Barão do **13** 177
economic nationalism
Frondizi, Arturo **6** 127-128
Falkland Islands War (1982)

Galtieri, Leopoldo Fortunato **6** 191-193
human rights
Pérez Esquivel, Adolfo **12** 215-217
independence wars
Belgrano, Manuel **2** 126-127
Güemes, Martín **7** 26-27
Rivadavia, Bernardino **13** 182-183
San Martín, José de **13** 468-469
oligarchy
Roca, Julio Argentino **13** 218
Paraguayan war (1865-1870)
López, Francisco Solano **9** 507-508
Mitre, Bartolomé **11** 62-63
Roca, Julio Argentino **13** 218
Sarmiento, Domingo Faustino **13** 484-485
republic (1853)
Alberdi, Juan Bautista **1** 109-110
Mitre, Bartolomé **11** 62-63
Rosas regime (1829-1852)
Rosas, Juan Manuel de **13** 290-291
Sarmiento, Domingo Faustino **13** 484-485
Urquiza, Justo José **15** 396-397
20th century
Alfonsín, Raúl Ricardo **1** 146-148
Drago, Luis María **5** 92-93
Galtieri, Leopoldo Fortunato **6** 191-193
Justo, Agustin Pedro **8** 396
Lamas, Carlos Saavedra **9** 175-176
Menem, Carlos Sául **10** 497-499
Perón, Eva Duarte de **12** 225-226
Perón, Isabel Martinez de **12** 226-228
Perón, Juan Domingo **12** 228-230
Videla, Jorge Rafaél **15** 490-492
Uruguay and
Lavalleja, Juan Antonio **9** 238-239
Rosas, Juan Manuel de **13** 290-291
see also Argentine literature; Argentine music

Argentine art
Pérez Esquivel, Adolfo **12** 215-217

Argentine literature
fiction
Güiráldez, Ricardo **7** 38-39
Mármol, José **10** 274
Sábato, Ernesto **13** 399-400
nonfiction
Sarmiento, Domingo Faustino **13** 484-485
poetry
Borges, Jorge Luis **2** 411-412
Echeverría, José Estéban **5** 197-198
Hernández, José **7** 328-329

Argentine music
Ginastera, Alberto Evaristo **6** 328-329

Argia, L' (opera)
Cesti, Pietro **3** 399-400

Arginase (enzyme)
Krebs, Hans Adolf **9** 95-97

Arginine (amino acid)
Krebs, Hans Adolf **9** 95-97

Arginusae, battle of (406 B.C.)
Lysander **10** 70

Argive school (Greek art)
Polykleitos **12** 385-386

Argon (element—chemistry)
Mendeleev, Dmitrii Ivanovich **10** 486-488
Ramsay, William **13** 21-22
Rayleigh, 3d Baron **13** 62

Argonauten, Die (opera)
Mahler, Gustav **10** 144-145

Argos (flourished circa 500 B.C.), Greek tyrant
Cleomenes I **4** 103

Argos (Greek city-state)
Alcibiades **1** 119-120
Cleomenes III **4** 103-104

Argos (hound)
Homer **7** 465-467

Argument to Prove That the Abolishing of Christianity in England... (book)
Swift, Jonathan **15** 51-54

Argus Corporation (Canada)
Black, Conrad Moffat **2** 300-301
Taylor, Edward Plunket **15** 123-124

Argus of Western America (newspaper)
Blair, Francis Preston **2** 313-315
Kendall, Amos **8** 494

Ari Ha-qodesh
see Luria, Isaac ben Solomon

Aria da Capo (play)
Millay, Edna St. Vincent **11** 24-25

Ariadne (painting; Vanderlyn)
Durand, Asher Brown **5** 156-157
Vanderlyn, John **15** 417

Ariadne auf Naxos (opera; Strauss)
Hofmannsthal, Hugo von **7** 443-444
Strauss, Richard **14** 500-501

Ariamazes (fortress, Iran)
Alexander the Great **1** 137-141

Ariane et Barbe Bleu (play)
Maeterlinck, Maurice **10** 125-126

Arianism (Christian heresy)
doctrine condemned
Arius **1** 297-298
Constantine I **4** 209-211
opponents
Ambrose **1** 192-193
Anthony, Susan Brownell **1** 246-248
Athanasius **1** 358-359
Basil the Great **2** 51-52
Isidore of Seville **8** 149-150
Justinian I **8** 393-395
supporters
Gaiseric **6** 172
Theodoric the Great **15** 175-176
Ulfilas **15** 384

Arianna (opera)
Handel, George Frederick **7** 116-119
Monteverdi, Claudio Giovanni Antonio **11** 126-128

Ariano, Assizes of (1140)
Roger II **13** 244-245

ARIAS, ARNULFO (1901-1988), thrice elected president of Panama **1** 286-287

ARIAS SANCHEZ, OSCAR (born 1941), Costa Rican politician, social activist, president, and Nobel Peace Laureate (1987) **1** 287-289

Arias tristes (poems)
Jiménez, Juan Ramón **8** 261-262

Ariel (pamphlet)
Rodó, José Enrique **13** 240-241

Ariettes oubliées (musical composition)
Debussy, Achille Claude **4** 445-447

Arikara War (United States; 1823)
Fitzpatrick, Thomas **5** 474-475
Smith, Jedediah S. **14** 294-295

Ariosti, Attilio (1660?-1740?), Italian composer
Handel, George Frederick **7** 116-119

ARIOSTO, LUDOVICO (1474-1533), Italian poet and playwright **1** 289-290
Boiardo, Matteo Maria **2** 369
Camoëns, Luis Vaz de **3** 247-249
Plautus **12** 348-350

Ariovistus (flourished 71?-58 B.C.), Germanic Suevi chief
Caesar, Gaius Julius **3** 207-210

Ariq Böge (died 1266), Mongol leader
Kublai Khan **9** 115-118

Aristaenetus (flourished 5th or 6th century), Greek author
Sheridan, Richard Brinsley **14** 183-184

Aristagoras (died 497 B.C.), Ionian tyrant of Miletus
Cleomenes I **4** 103

ARISTARCHUS OF SAMOS (circa 310-230 B.C.), Greek astronomer **1** 290-291
Archimedes **1** 277-280
Hipparchus **7** 407-408

ARISTIDE, JEAN-BERTRAND (born 1953), president of Haiti (1990-91 and 1994-95); deposed by a military coup in 1991; restored to power in 1994 **1** 291-293

Aristio
see Unánue, José Hipólito

Aristipp und einige seiner Zeitgenossen (novel)
Wieland, Christoph Martin **16** 260-261

Aristocrat, The (novel)
Richter, Conrad Michael **13** 148-149

Aristogeiton (died 514 B.C.), Athenian hero
Horace **7** 500-503

Ariston of Chios (flourished 250 B.C.), Greek philosopher
Eratosthenes of Cyrene **5** 301-302

ARISTOPHANES (450/445-after 385 B.C.), Greek playwright **1** 293-294
Cleon **4** 104-105
Euripides **5** 332-334
Gorgias **6** 456
Menander **10** 477-478
Protagoras **12** 461
Socrates **14** 320-321

Aristophanes of Byzantium (257?-180 B.C.), Greek scholar and critic
Callimachus **3** 235-236
Menander **10** 477-478

Aristotelianism (philosophy)
Christian philosophy
Bonaventure **2** 383-384
Duns Scotus, John **5** 149-150
Eckhart, Johann **5** 200-201
Ficino, Marsilio **5** 436-437
Otto of Freising **12** 30
Thomas Aquinas **15** 183-186, 421-422
see also Scholasticism
critics
Bacon, Francis **1** 422-424
Bruno, Giordano **3** 75-76
Campanella, Tommaso **3** 249
Ramus, Petrus **13** 27-28
Valla, Lorenzo **15** 406
epistemology
Bonaventure **2** 383-384
William of Ockham **16** 298-299
experimentation
Heron of Alexandria **7** 334-335
Islamic philosophy
Ashari, Abu al- Hasan Ali al- **1** 327-328
Avicenna **1** 386-387
ibn Hazm, Abu Muhammad Ali **8** 93
Kindi, Abu-Yusuf Yaqub ibn-Ishaq al- **9** 10-11
Jewish philosophy
Levi ben Gershon **9** 363-364
Maimonides **10** 151-152
logic
Kant, Immanuel **8** 430-432
Zeno of Citium **16** 499-500
metaphysics
Plotinus **12** 358-359
Suárez, Francisco **15** 8
Neoplatonism
Proclus Diadochus **12** 457
Platonism
Aristotle **1** 295-296
Pico della Mirandola, Giovanni **12** 299-300
Plato **12** 345-347
Renaissance philosophy
Descartes, René **4** 505-508
Pomponazzi, Pietro **12** 390-391
Spenser, Edmund **14** 373-376
Telesio, Bernardino **15** 138-139
see also Aristotle

Aristotelicae animadversiones (book)
Ramus, Petrus **13** 27-28

ARISTOTLE (384-322 B.C.), Greek philosopher and scientist **1** 295-296
 animal classification
  Gesner, Konrad von **6** 287
  Linnaeus, Carl **9** 427-429
  Ray, John **13** 57-59
  Schwann, Theodor **14** 51-52
 astronomy
  Aristarchus of Samos **1** 290-291
  Bitruji, Nur al-Din Abu Ishaq al **2** 296
  Bruno, Giordano **3** 75-76
  Copernicus, Nicolaus **4** 226-227
  Hasan ibn al-Haytham **7** 190-191
  Heraclides of Pontus **7** 319-320
 commentaries on
  Abelard, Peter **1** 23-25
  Averroës **1** 382-383
  Boethius, Anicius Manlius Severinus **2** 360-361
  Brentano, Franz Clemens **2** 516-517
  Galileo Galilei **6** 180-183
 drama and poetry
  Corneille, Pierre **4** 234-236
  Euripides **5** 332-334
  Lessing, Gotthold Ephraim **9** 357-359
  Molière **11** 86-88
  Sophocles **14** 343-345
  Tasso, Torquato **15** 114-116
 education and
  John of Salisbury **8** 284-285
 elements
  Albertus Magnus **1** 115-116
  Boyle, Robert **2** 469-471
  Helmont, Jan Baptista van **7** 269-271
 in art
  Raphael **13** 40-42
  Rembrandt Harmensz van Rijn **13** 91-95
 on philosophers
  Anaximenes **1** 210
  Archimedes **1** 277-280
  Democritus **4** 493-494
  Empedocles **5** 282
  Eudoxus of Cnidus **5** 329-330
  Thales **15** 161
  Zeno of Elea **16** 500
 philosophy
  see Aristotelianism
 political theory
  Filmer, Robert **5** 448
  Las Casas, Bartolomé de **9** 211-212
 students
  Alexander the Great **1** 137-141
  Heraclides of Pontus **7** 319-320
  Ptolemy I **12** 470-472
 translations
  Jowett, Benjamin **8** 364-365
  Nicholas of Oresme **11** 380
  Simon, Jules François **14** 237-238
  Thomas Aquinas **15** 183-186

Aristotle Contemplating a Bust of Homer (painting)
 Rembrandt Harmensz van Rijn **13** 91-95

Arithmetica universalis (book; I. Newton)
 Hamilton, William Rowan **7** 99-100

ARIUS (died circa 336), Libyan theologian and heresiarch **1** 297-298
 see also Arianism

Arizona (state, United States)
 Chisum, John Simpson **4** 11
 Cochise **4** 128
 Coronado, Francisco Vásquez de **4** 247
 Crook, George **4** 322-323
 Kino, Eusebio Francisco **9** 30-31
 Santa Ana, Antonio López de **13** 471-472
 governors
  Babbitt, Bruce Edward **1** 408-410

Ark of the Covenant (Judaism)
 David, Jacques Louis **4** 407-409
 Saul **13** 498

Arkansas (ship)
 Farragut, David Glasgow **5** 388-389

Arkansas (state, United States)
 Clinton, William Jefferson **4** 117-119
 Fulbright, James William **6** 147-149
 Jackson, Andrew **8** 168-172

Arkansas River (United States)
 Jolliet, Louis **8** 328-329

Arkansas Share Cropper's Family (photography)
 Shahn, Ben **14** 139-140

Arkansas, University of
 Fulbright, James William **6** 147-149
 Smith, David **14** 287-288

Arkhitectonics (sculpture)
 Malevich, Kasimir **10** 168-169

ARKWRIGHT, SIR RICHARD (1732-1792), English inventor and industrialist **1** 298
 Brown, Moses **3** 42-43
 Coxe, Tench **4** 285-286
 Slater, Samuel **14** 272-273

Arlequin poli par l'amour (play)
 Marivaux, Pierre Carlet de Chamblain de **10** 265-266

Arles, Council of (314)
 Donatus **5** 56-57

Arlésienne, L' (play)
 Bizet, Georges **2** 296-297
 Daudet, Alphonse **4** 402-403

Arlington, 1st Earl of (1618-1685), English statesman
 Buckingham, 2d Duke of **3** 94-95

Arm Yrself or Harm Yrself (play)
 Baraka, Imamu Amiri **1** 498-499

Armada, Spanish (1588)
 English commanders
  Davis, John **4** 419
  Drake, Francis **5** 94-96
  Frobisher, Martin **6** 121-122
  Hawkins, John **7** 210-211
 English mobilization
  Elizabeth I **5** 263-266
  Leicester, Earl of **9** 312-313
  Raleigh, Walter **13** 9-11
 papal support
  Sixtus V **14** 267-268
 Spanish mobilization
  Menéndez de Avilés, Pedro **10** 499-500
  Philip II **12** 271-273

Armada, The (book)
 Mattingly, Garrett **10** 342-344

Armadale (novel)
 Collins, William Wilkie **4** 169-170

Armagnacs (French politics)
 Charles VI **3** 460-461

Armaments industry
 see Business and industrial leaders—armament industry

Armance (novel)
 Stendhal **14** 422-425

ARMANI, GIORGIO (1935-1997), Italian fashion designer **1** 299-301

Armant (town, Egypt)
 Thutmose III **15** 216-217

Arme Heinrich, Der (play)
 Hauptmann, Gerhart Johann Robert **7** 199-201

Armée Nationale de Libération (Algeria)
 Ben Bella, Ahmed **2** 148-149

Armen, Die (novel)
 Mann, Heinrich **10** 201-202

Armenia (ancient nation, Western Asia)
 Abbasid rule
  Mansur, Abu Jafar ibn Muhammad al- **10** 214-215
 Byzantine rule
  Basil II **2** 50-51
 Persian rule
  Abbas I **1** 4-6
  Shahpur II **14** 140-141
 Roman rule
  Hadrian **7** 60-61
  Marcus Aurelius Antoninus **10** 243-245
  Nero Claudius Caesar **11** 342-344
  Stilicho, Flavius **14** 452-453
  Trajan **15** 291-292
 Seleucid rule
  Antiochus III **1** 249-250
 Turkish rule
  Abdul-Hamid II **1** 17-18
  Alp Arslan **1** 178-179
  Barton, Clara **2** 37-39
  Enver Pasha **5** 290-291

Armenian music
 Khachaturian, Aram Ilich **8** 530-531

Armida (literary character)
 Tasso, Torquato **15** 114-116

Armide (play; Quinault)
 Gluck, Christoph Willibald **6** 372-374

Armies of the Night, The (book)
  Mailer, Norman Kingsley **10** 148-150

Arminianism (religion)
  Arminius, Jacobus **1** 301-302
  Grotius, Hugo **7** 18-19
  Laud, William **9** 224-225
  Oldenbarnevelt, Johan van **11** 495-496
  Vondel, Joost van den **16** 19-20

ARMINIUS, JACOBUS (1560-1609), Dutch theologian **1** 301-302
  see also Arminianism

Armory Show (1913; New York City)
  American exhibitors
    Bellows, George Wesley **2** 143
    Davis, Stuart **4** 424-425
    Kent, Rockwell **8** 511
    Lachaise, Gaston **9** 147
    Marin, John III **10** 259-260
    Prendergast, Maurice Brazil **12** 440
    Sheeler, Charles **14** 170-171
    Sloan, John **14** 274-275
    Weber, Max **16** 160
    Zorach, William **16** 528
  Canadian exhibitors
    Milne, David Brown **11** 37-38
  French exhibitors
    Duchamp, Marcel **5** 122-123
    Redon, Odilon **13** 75-76
  organizers
    Davies, Arthur Bowen **4** 409-410
    Glackens, William **6** 355-356
    Luks, George Benjamin **10** 38-39
    Stieglitz, Alfred **14** 451-452

Armour, Jean (1767-1834), Scottish wife of R. Burns
  Burns, Robert **3** 155-156

ARMOUR, PHILIP DANFORTH (1832-1901), American industrialist **1** 302

Armour Institute of Technology
  Armour, Philip Danforth **1** 302

Arms and the Man (play)
  Shaw, George Bernard **14** 163-164

Arms control
  see Nuclear arms control

ARMSTRONG, EDWIN HOWARD (1890-1954), American electrical engineer and radio inventor **1** 302-303
  De Forest, Lee **4** 459-460

Armstrong, John (1758-1843), American diplomat
  Biddle, Nicholas **2** 264-265
  Madison, James **10** 121-123
  Monroe, James **11** 111-113

ARMSTRONG, LOUIS DANIEL (1900-1971), African American jazz musician **1** 303-304

ARMSTRONG, NEIL ALDEN (born 1930), American astronaut **1** 304-306
  Gagarin, Yuri Alexeivich **6** 166-167

ARMSTRONG, SAMUEL CHAPMAN (1839-1893), American educator **1** 306-307

Armstrong engineering works (Newcastle-upon-Tyne)
  Parsons, Charles Algernon **12** 120-121

Army Air Corps
  see United States Air Force

Army Life in a Black Regiment (book)
  Higginson, Thomas Wentworth **7** 380

Army Mental Tests (book)
  Yerkes, Robert Mearns **16** 454-455

Army, United States
  see United States Army
  McCarthy, Joseph Raymond **10** 388-389

Army-McCarthy hearings (United States; 1954)
  McCarthy, Joseph Raymond **10** 388-389

Arnauld, Antoine (1612-1694), French philosopher and theologian
  Pascal, Blaise **12** 122-124
  Simon, Jules François **14** 237-238

Arnauld, Henri (1597-1692), French theologian
  Jansen, Cornelis **8** 220-221

Arne (story)
  Bjørnson, Bjørnstjerne **2** 299-300

ARNE, THOMAS AUGUSTINE (1710-1778), English composer **1** 307-308
  Handel, George Frederick **7** 116-119
  Thomson, James **15** 199-200

Arnhem, battle of (1591)
  Maurice of Nassau **10** 348-349

ARNIM, ACHIM VON (Ludwig Joachim von Achim; 1781-1831), German writer **1** 308-309
  Brentano, Clemens **2** 515-516
  Grimm, Jakob and Wilhelm Karl **7** 3-4

Arnim, Bettina (Elisabeth) von (1785-1859), German author
  Arnim, Achim von **1** 308-309
  Brentano, Franz Clemens **2** 516-517
  Goethe, Johann Wolfgang von **6** 388-391

ARNOLD, GEN. BENEDICT (1741-1801), American general and traitor **1** 309-310
  Quebec campaign
    Carleton, Guy **3** 300-301
    Montgomery, Richard **11** 138-139
    Morgan, Daniel **11** 160-161
  relatives
    Shippen, Edward **14** 197-198
  Ticonderoga
    Allen, Ethan **1** 163-164

Arnold, Franz
  see Lieber, Francis

ARNOLD, HENRY HARLEY (Hap; 1886-1950), American general **1** 310-311
  Kármán, Theodore von **8** 451-452

ARNOLD, MATTHEW (1822-1888), English poet and critic **1** 311-313
  friends
    Clough, Arthur Hugh **4** 123-124
    Hardy, Thomas **7** 150-152
  musical settings
    Barber, Samuel **1** 500-501
  poetic values
    Bryant, William Cullen **3** 83-85
    Lampman, Archibald **9** 180-181
  relatives
    Arnold, Thomas **1** 313-314

ARNOLD, THOMAS (1795-1842), English educator **1** 313-314
  Arnold, Matthew **1** 311-313

ARNOLD, THURMAN WESLEY (1891-1969), American statesman **1** 314

ARNOLD OF BRESCIA (circa 1100-1155), Italian religious reformer **1** 314-315
  Abelard, Peter **1** 23-25
  Frederick I **6** 78-79

Arnolfini Wedding
  see Giovanni Arnolfini and His Wife

ARNOLFO DI CAMBIO (1245?-1302), Italian sculptor and architect **1** 315-316
  Giotto **6** 342-345
  Vasari, Giorgio **15** 442-443

Aromas de leyenda (poem)
  Valle Inclán, Ramón Maria del **15** 407-408

Aromatic compounds (chemistry)
  Baeyer, Johann Friedrich Adolf von **1** 432
  Couper, Archibald Scott **4** 269-270
  Hofmann, August Wilhelm von **7** 441-442

ARON, RAYMOND (1905-1983), academic scholar, teacher, and journalist **1** 316-317

Arosemena Monroy, Carlos Julio (born 1920), Ecuadorean politician, president 1961-1963
  Velasco Ibarra, José María **15** 452-454

Arouet, François Marie
  see Voltaire

Around about America (book)
  Caldwell, Erskine **3** 223-224

Around the World in Eighty Days (novel)
  Verne, Jules **15** 467-469

Arouser of the German Nation (book)
  Hutten, Ulrich von **8** 72-73

ARP, JEAN (Hans Arp; 1887-1966), French sculptor and painter **1** 317-318
  associates
    Duchamp, Marcel **5** 122-123
    Kandinsky, Wassily **8** 420-422
    Miró, Joan **11** 53-54
    van Doesburg, Theo **15** 421
  biomorphic form

Brancusi, Constantin **2** 494-496
Moore, Henry **11** 146-148

Arpino, Giuseppe Cavaliere d'
(1568?-1640), Italian painter
Caravaggio **3** 282-284

Arrabbiata, L' (novel)
Heyse, Paul Johann Ludwig **7** 372-373

Arrah-na-Pogue (play)
Boucicault, Dion **2** 442-443
James I **8** 204-206

Arran, Earl of (James Stewart; died 1596),
Scottish statesman
James I **8** 204-206

**Arrangement in Grey and Black, the
Artist's Mother** (painting)
Currie, Arthur William **4** 345
Whistler, James Abbott McNeill
16 225-226

Arras, battle of (1917)
Currie, Arthur William **4** 345

Arras Sketchbook
Bosch, Hieronymus **2** 426-428

Arras, Treaty of (1435)
Philip the Good **12** 278-279

ARRHENIUS, SVANTE AUGUST
(1859-1927), Swedish chemist and physi-
cist **1** 318-320
Haber, Fritz **7** 56-58
Túpac Amaru, José Gabriel **15** 341
Vries, Hugo de **16** 33-36

Arriaga, Antonio de (died 1780), Spanish
colonial governor
Túpac Amaru, José Gabriel **15** 341

Arrian (Flavius Arrianus; flourished 2d cen-
tury), Greek historian
Butler, Joseph **3** 180-181
Epictetus **5** 292

Arrogance of Power (book)
Fulbright, James William **6** 147-149

Arrow and the Song, The (poem)
Longfellow, Henry Wadsworth
9 499-500

Arrow of God (novel)
Achebe, Chinua **1** 35-37

Arrow War (1856-1860)
Feng Kuei-fen **5** 411-412
Wo-jen **16** 352

Arrowhead Farm (Pittsfield, Massachusetts)
Hawthorne, Nathaniel **7** 212-215

Arrowsmith (film)
Goldwyn, Samuel **6** 416

Arrowsmith (novel)
Lewis, Harry Sinclair **9** 385-387

Arroyo del Rio, Carlos Alberto
(1893-1969), Ecuadorean statesman,
president 1940-1944
Velasco Ibarra, José María **15** 452-454

Arroyo Grande, battle of (1842)
Rivera, Fructuoso **13** 184-185

Ars, Curé of
see Vianney, St. Jean Baptiste

Ars amatoria (poem; Ovid)
Titian **15** 242-244

Ars cantus mensurabilis (treatise)
Franco of Cologne **6** 52

Ars magna (book)
Cardano, Geronimo **3** 285-286

Ars nova (music)
Machaut, Guillaume de **10** 93-94
Vitry, Philippe de **16** 2

Ars Poetica (poem)
MacLeish, Archibald **10** 109-110

Ars poetica (treatise)
Horace **7** 500-503
Gustavus II **7** 43-45

Ars Regeringsform (1634)
Gustavus II **7** 43-45

Arsenal at Springfield, The (poem)
Longfellow, Henry Wadsworth
9 499-500

Arsenal for Creation (painting)
Marc, Franz **10** 231

Arsenic (element—chemistry)
Bunsen, Robert Wilhelm **3** 124-125
Domagk, Gerhard Johannes Paul
5 48-50

Arseniyev's Life (novel)
Bunin, Ivan Alekseevich **3** 124

Arsuf, battle of (1191)
Richard I **13** 130
Saladin **13** 441-442

Art
and society
Kiefer, Anselm **8** 544-546
Melnikov, Konstantin Stepanovich
10 470-471
Rodchenko, Alexander Mikhailovich
13 233-234
Tatlin, Vladimir Evgrafovich
15 117-118
collections
Hearst, William Randolph
7 243-244
collectors
Hammer, Armand **7** 103-104
criticism
Greenberg, Clement **6** 521-523
history
Burckhardt, Jacob Christoph
3 132-133
Pater, Walter Horatio **12** 130-131
history of
Brookner, Anita **3** 23-24
philosophy of
Freud, Sigmund **6** 103-106
Gabo, Naum **6** 158-159
Pater, Walter Horatio **12** 130-131
Rodchenko, Alexander Mikhailovich
13 233-234
Vasarely, Victor **15** 440-442

see also American art; English art;
etc., and separate styles and
movements

Art Anatomy (book)
Rimmer, William **13** 174

Art and the Reformation (book)
Coulton, George Gordon **4** 267

Art as Experience (book)
Dewey, John **4** 520-523

Art brut, L' (naïve art)
Dubuffet, Jean Philippe Arthur
5 119-120

Art critics
see Artists—critics

Art de toucher le clavecin, L' (music)
Couperin, François **4** 270-271

Art et critique (periodical)
Bonnard, Pierre **2** 395-396

Art Institute of Chicago (Illinois)
Field, Marshall **5** 440-441

Art moderne, L' (book)
Huysmans, Joris Karl **8** 81-82

Art music
Copland, Aaron **4** 227-228
Landini, Francesco **9** 185-186

Art Nouveau (Jugendstil)
architecture
Gaudí i Cornet, Antoni **6** 235-236
Olbrich, Joseph Maria **11** 494-495
Saarinen, Eliel and Eero **13** 396-398
Sullivan, Louis Henri **15** 27-28
glass design
Lachaise, Gaston **9** 147
Tiffany, Louis Comfort **15** 220-221
illustration
Beardsley, Aubrey Vincent **2** 88-89
influence of
Kandinsky, Wassily **8** 420-422
Klee, Paul **9** 47-49
Léger, Fernand **9** 302-303
Marc, Franz **10** 231
Nadelman, Elie **11** 289-290
Thomson, Tom **15** 202
neobaroque
Garnier, Jean Louis Charles
6 221-222
painting
Behrens, Peter **2** 121-122
Klimt, Gustav **9** 53-55
theory
Van de Velde, Henry **15** 419-420

Art of Fiction, The (book)
Maugham, William Somerset
10 344-345

Art of Finding Curves... (book)
Euler, Leonard **5** 331-332

Art of Judging Music, The (book)
Thomson, Virgil **15** 202-203

Art of Law Giving, The (book)
Harrington, James **7** 166-167

Art of Love (poem; Ovid)
  Chrestien de Troyes **4** 23-24
  Ovid **12** 34-36

Art of Measurable Music, The (treatise)
  Franco of Cologne **6** 52

Art of Speech Is a Capital Investment, The (literary collection)
  Imam, Alhadji Abubakar **8** 114-115

Art of the Fugue (musical collection)
  Bach, Johann Sebastian **1** 416-419

Art of This Century Gallery (New York City)
  Motherwell, Robert **11** 210-211
  Pollock, Jackson **12** 379-380
  Rothko, Mark **13** 320-321

Art of War (book; Sun Wu)
  Yo Fei **16** 462

Art of Worldly Wisdom, The (literary collection)
  Gracián y Morales, Baltasar Jerónimo **6** 481-482

Art poétique (book)
  Boileau-Despréaux, Nicholas **2** 369-371

Art poétique (poem)
  Verlaine, Paul Marie **15** 465-466

Art romantique, L' (book)
  Baudelaire, Charles Pierre **2** 61-63

Art Students League (New York City)
  established
    Robinson, Theodore **13** 217
  faculty
    Bellows, George Wesley **2** 143
    Chase, William Merritt **3** 476-477
    Davis, Stuart **4** 424-425
    Grosz, George **7** 17-18
    Hofmann, Hans **7** 442-443
    Lawrence, Jacob **9** 250-251
    Luks, George Benjamin **10** 38-39
    Sloan, John **14** 274-275
    Twachtman, John Henry **15** 362-363
    Zadkine, Ossip Joselyn **16** 484
    Zorach, William **16** 528

Art Students' League (Philadelphia)
  Eakins, Thomas **5** 176-177

Art, The (literary collection)
  Lull, Raymond **10** 39-40

Artamonov Business, The (novel)
  Gorky, Maxim **6** 458-460

Artang (book)
  Mani **10** 196-197

Artaserse (opera)
  Gluck, Christoph Willibald **6** 372-374

ARTAUD, ANTONIN (1896-1948), developed the theory of the Theater of Cruelty **1** 320-321
  Balthus **1** 476-477

Artavasdes I (ruled circa 52-34 B.C.), king of Armenia
  Cleopatra **4** 105-106

Artaxerxes (opera)
  Arne, Thomas Augustine **1** 307-308

Artaxerxes I (died 424 B.C.), king of Persia 464-424 B.C.
  Ezra **5** 356-357

Artaxerxes II (circa 436-359 B.C.), king of Persia 404-359 B.C.
  Xenophon **16** 418-420

Art-Deco (1930s)
  Erté **5** 314-316
  Lichtenstein, Roy **9** 398-399

Arte e scienza (essay)
  Pirandello, Luigi **12** 319-321

Arte nuevo de hacer comedias (book)
  Lope Félix de Vega Carpio **9** 503-506

Artemis (mythology)
  Callimachus **3** 235-236
  Euripides **5** 332-334

Artemis Bruaronia (sculpture)
  Praxiteles **12** 433-434

Artemus Ward in London (book)
  Ward, Artemus **16** 112-113

Artevelde, James van (1290?-1345), Flemish statesman
  Edward III **5** 211-212

Art-for-art's sake
  literature
    Kuo Mo-jo **9** 133-134
    Morin, Paul **11** 174
    Pater, Walter Horatio **12** 130-131
    Wilde, Oscar Fingall O'Flahertie Wills **16** 272-273
  painting
    Whistler, James Abbott McNeill **16** 225-226

Arthasastra (book; Kautilya)
  Chandragupta Maurya **3** 426
  Kautilya **8** 462

ARTHUR, CHESTER ALAN (1830-1886), American statesman, president 1881-1885 **1** 321-323
  Conkling, Roscoe **4** 201-202
  Eaton, Dorman Bridgman **5** 190-191
  Garfield, James Abram **6** 213-214
  McCulloch, Hugh **10** 404-405
  Wright, Carroll Davidson **16** 396

Arthur, Duke of Brittany (1187-1203), nephew of John of England
  Eleanor of Aquitaine **5** 246-247

Arthur, King
  see Arthurian legend

Arthur Merwyn (novel)
  Brown, Charles Brockden **3** 33

Arthurdale (town, West Virginia)
  Roosevelt, Eleanor **13** 275-277

Arthurian legend
  development
    Layamon **9** 256-257
  history
    Geoffrey of Monmouth **6** 268
  in literature

    Chrestien de Troyes **4** 23-24
    Froissart, Jean **6** 124-125
    Malory, Thomas **10** 175-176
    Marie de France **10** 259
    Peacock, Thomas Love **12** 169
    Tennyson, Alfred **15** 144-146
    Wolfram von Eschenbach **16** 360-361

Arthus, Nicolas Maurice (1862-1945), French physiologist
  Richet, Charles Robert **13** 144-145

Articles of Confederation (United States; 1781)
  central government
    Clinton, George **4** 113-114
    Hamilton, Alexander **7** 95-98
    Marshall, John **10** 279-281
  Congress
    Monroe, James **11** 111-113
    Sherman, Roger **14** 185-186
  debates
    Lee, Richard Henry **9** 291-292
    Paine, Thomas **12** 66-67
    Witherspoon, John **16** 346-348
  drafted
    Dickinson, John **4** 543-544
    Franklin, Benjamin **6** 60-64
  history of
    Fitch, John **5** 467-468
  officials under
    Jay, John **8** 230-232
    Lincoln, Benjamin **9** 418-419
    Livingston, Robert R. **9** 462-463
    Morris, Robert **11** 185-187
  signers
    Gerry, Elbridge **6** 282-283
    Sherman, Roger **14** 185-186
  weaknesses
    Shays, Daniel **14** 168

Articulata (zoology)
  Cuvier, Georges Léopold **4** 357-359

ARTIGAS, JOSÉ GERVASIO (1764-1850), Uruguayan patriot **1** 323
  Lavalleja, Juan Antonio **9** 238-239
  Rivera, Fructuoso **13** 184-185
  Zorrilla de San Martin, Juan **16** 530-531

Artis magnae sive de regulis algebraicis (book)
  Cardano, Geronimo **3** 285-286

Artist and His Mother (painting)
  Gorky, Arshile **6** 458

Artist and the Connoisseur, The (drawing)
  Bruegel, Pieter the Elder **3** 65-67

Artist in His Museum, The (painting)
  Peale, Charles Willson **12** 169-171

Artist, The (book)
  Rank, Otto **13** 33

Artist, The (play)
  Mencken, Henry Louis **10** 481-483

Artists, American
  architects (18th century)
    Harrison, Peter **7** 179-180

architects (18th-19th century)
    Latrobe, Benjamin Henry **9** 222-224
    L'Enfant, Pierre Charles **9** 322-323
    McIntire, Samuel **10** 415
architects (19th century)
    Benjamin, Asher **2** 162-163
    Bulfinch, Charles **3** 116-117
    Burnham, Daniel Hudson
      3 148-149
    Davis, Alexander Jackson **4** 411
    Hunt, Richard Morris **8** 44
    McKim, Charles Follen **10** 417-418
    Mills, Robert **11** 36-37
    Renwick, James **13** 102-103
    Richardson, Henry Hobson
      13 139-141
    Upjohn, Richard **15** 392
architects (19th-20th century)
    Sullivan, Louis Henri **15** 27-28
    White, Stanford **16** 235-236
    Wright, Frank Lloyd **16** 398-401
architects (20th century)
    Breuer, Marcel **2** 520-521
    Bunshaft, Gordon **3** 125-127
    Eisenman, Peter D. **5** 239-240
    Freed, James Ingo **6** 88-90
    Fuller, Richard Buckminster
      6 149-150
    Gehry, Frank O. **6** 250-251
    Graves, Michael **6** 500-502
    Jahn, Helmut **8** 199-201
    Johnson, Philip **8** 313-314
    Jones, Fay **8** 332-333
    Kahn, Albert **8** 407-408
    Kahn, Louis I. **8** 408-410
    Lin, Maya Ying **9** 413-415
    Meier, Richard **10** 456-458
    Mies van der Rohe, Ludwig
      11 10-12
    Moore, Charles Willard **11** 143-145
    Morgan, Julia **11** 165-166
    Neutra, Richard Joseph **11** 355-356
    Pei, I. M. **12** 184-187
    Pelli, Cesar **12** 191-192
    Pope, John Russell **12** 397-399
    Roche, Kevin **13** 222-224
    Rudolph, Paul Marvin **13** 348-350
    Saarinen, Eliel and Eero **13** 396-398
    Stone, Edward Durrell **14** 466-468
    Venturi, Robert **15** 461-463
cartoonists
    Block, Herbert **2** 333-334
    Capp, Al **3** 275-276
    Disney, Walter Elias **5** 26-27
    Feiffer, Jules Ralph **5** 403-404
    Grosz, George **7** 17-18
    Mauldin, Bill **10** 345-346
    Nast, Thomas **11** 318-319
    Oliphant, Patrick Bruce **11** 498-500
    Schulz, Charles M. **14** 38-39
    Thurber, James Grove **15** 213-214
    Trudeau, Garretson Beekman
      15 308-309
collagists
    Cornell, Joseph **4** 237-238
    Krasner, Lee **9** 93-94

critics
    Mumford, Lewis **11** 246-247
draftsmen
    LeWitt, Sol **9** 393-395
    Stovall, Luther (Lou) McKinley
      14 483-484
electronic communicators
    Holzer, Jenny **7** 462-463
engravers
    Durand, Asher Brown **5** 156-157
    Revere, Paul **13** 110-111
fashion designers
    Carnegie, Hattie **3** 313
    Claiborne, Liz **4** 68-69
    Johnson, Betsey **8** 295-296
    Karan, Donna **8** 442-444
    Klein, Calvin **9** 50-52
    Lauren, Ralph **9** 228-229
    Mizrahi, Isaac **11** 66-67
    von Furstenberg, Diane **16** 20-21
filmmakers
    Allen, Woody **1** 169-171
    Cornell, Joseph **4** 237-238
furniture designers
    Albers, Josef **1** 110
    Breuer, Marcel **2** 520-521
    McIntire, Samuel **10** 415
    Phyfe, Duncan **12** 284-285
    Saarinen, Eliel and Eero **13** 396-398
    Stovall, Luther (Lou) McKinley
      14 483-484
glass designers
    Stiegel, Henry William **14** 451
    Tiffany, Louis Comfort **15** 220-221
illustrators (19th century)
    Davies, Arthur Bowen **4** 409-410
    Davis, Alexander Jackson **4** 411
    Moran, Thomas **11** 151-152
    Nast, Thomas **11** 318-319
    Rembrandt Harmensz van Rijn
      13 91-95
illustrators (20th century)
    Demuth, Charles **4** 497-498
    Feininger, Lyonel **5** 406-407
    Kent, Rockwell **8** 511
    Rockwell, Norman Percevel
      13 231-233
    Wyeth, Andrew Newell **16** 413-415
jewelry
    Campbell, Ben Nighthorse
      3 252-253
landscape architects
    Downing, Andrew Jackson **5** 90-91
    Olmsted, Frederick Law **11** 503-504
lithographers
    Bellows, George Wesley **2** 143
    Currier and Ives **4** 345-346
    Oliphant, Patrick Bruce **11** 498-500
    Whistler, James Abbott McNeill
      16 225-226
object makers (20th century)
    Ray, Man **13** 59-60
painters (18th century)
    Copley, John Singleton **4** 228-230
    Earl, Ralph **5** 179
    Smibert, John **14** 282

painters (18th-19th century)
    Fulton, Robert **6** 151-152
    Johnston, Joshua **8** 323-325
    Peale, Charles Willson **12** 169-171
    Stuart, Gilbert **14** 513-515
    Trumbull, John **15** 316-317
    West, Benjamin **16** 210-212
painters (19th century)
    Allston, Washington **1** 176-177
    Audubon, John James **1** 366-367
    Bannister, Edward Mitchell
      1 491-493
    Bierstadt, Albert **2** 270-271
    Bingham, George Caleb **2** 278-279
    Blakelock, Ralph Albert **2** 318
    Catlin, George **3** 373-374
    Chase, William Merritt **3** 476-477
    Church, Frederick Edwin **4** 49-50
    Cole, Thomas **4** 151-152
    Davies, Arthur Bowen **4** 409-410
    Durand, Asher Brown **5** 156-157
    Eakins, Thomas **5** 176-177
    Harnett, William Michael **7** 160-161
    Heade, Martin Johnson **7** 236
    Hicks, Edward **7** 375
    Inness, George **8** 123-124
    Johnson, Earvin Jr. **8** 297-299
    La Farge, John **9** 149-150
    Lane, Fitz Hugh **9** 189
    Morse, Samuel Finley Breese
      11 192-193
    Mount, William Sidney **11** 213-214
    Nast, Thomas **11** 318-319
    Peale, Rembrandt **12** 172-173
    Peto, John Frederick **12** 259
    Rembrandt Harmensz van Rijn
      13 91-95
    Rimmer, William **13** 174
    Robinson, Theodore **13** 217
    Ryder, Albert Pinkham **13** 391-392
    Twachtman, John Henry **15** 362-363
    Wood, Grant **16** 368-369
    Wyant, Alexander Helwig
      16 409-410
painters (19th-20th century)
    Cassatt, Mary **3** 356-357
    Hassam, Frederick Childe **7** 192
    Homer, Winslow **7** 468-469
    Kane, John **8** 422
    Moran, Thomas **11** 151-152
    Prendergast, Maurice Brazil **12** 440
    Russell, Charles Marion **13** 375-376
    Sargent, John Singer **13** 481-482
    Tanner, Henry Ossawa **15** 102-103
    Tiffany, Louis Comfort **15** 220-221
    Vanderlyn, John **15** 417
    Whistler, James Abbott McNeill
      16 225-226
painters (20th century)
    Albers, Josef **1** 110
    Bearden, Romare Howard **2** 86-88
    Begay, Harrison **2** 117-118
    Bellows, George Wesley **2** 143
    Benton, Thomas Hart **2** 178-179
    Burchfield, Charles **3** 131-132
    Davis, Stuart **4** 424-425

de Kooning, Willem **4** 468-469
Demuth, Charles **4** 497-498
Diebenkorn, Richard **5** 2-4
Dove, Arthur Garfield **5** 86-87
Estes, Richard **5** 322-323
Evergood, Philip **5** 345
Feininger, Lyonel **5** 406-407
Frankenthaler, Helen **6** 56-57
Gilliam, Sam **6** 322-323
Glackens, William **6** 355-356
Gorky, Arshile **6** 458
Gottlieb, Adolph **6** 462-463
Grosz, George **7** 17-18
Guston, Philip **7** 47-48
Haring, Keith **7** 154-155
Hartley, Marsden **7** 186
Hesse, Eva **7** 365-367
Hofmann, Hans **7** 442-443
Hopper, Edward **7** 497-498
Johns, Jasper **8** 291-293
Johnson, William H. **8** 320-322
Kelly, Ellsworth **8** 482-483
Kent, Rockwell **8** 511
Kline, Franz **9** 55
Krasner, Lee **9** 93-94
Lawrence, Jacob **9** 250-251
Lichtenstein, Roy **9** 398-399
Louis, Morris **9** 538-539
Luks, George Benjamin **10** 38-39
Marin, John III **10** 259-260
Marsh, Reginald **10** 276-277
Martin, Agnes **10** 288-289
Moses, Grandma **11** 201-202
Motherwell, Robert **11** 210-211
Newman, Barnett **11** 365
Noland, Kenneth **11** 418-419
O'Keeffe, Georgia **11** 487-489
Oldenburg, Claes **11** 496-498
Pippin, Horace **12** 318-319
Pollock, Jackson **12** 379-380
Rauschenberg, Robert **13** 52-53
Ray, Man **13** 59-60
Richter, Hans **13** 149-150
Ringgold, Faith **13** 175-177
Rivers, Larry **13** 186-187
Rockwell, Norman Percevel
    13 231-233
Rothko, Mark **13** 320-321
Salle, David **13** 452-453
Schapiro, Miriam **13** 520-521
Shahn, Ben **14** 139-140
Sheeler, Charles **14** 170-171
Sloan, John **14** 274-275
Steichen, Edward **14** 411-412
Stella, Frank **14** 420-422
Stella, Joseph **14** 422
Still, Clyfford **14** 453-454
Tobey, Mark **15** 249-250
Warhol, Andy **16** 114-115
Weber, Max **16** 160
Wyeth, Andrew Newell **16** 413-415
Zorach, William **16** 528
photographers
    Abbott, Berenice **1** 7-9
    Adams, Ansel **1** 40-41

Arbus, Diane Nemerov **1** 276-277
Avedon, Richard **1** 381-382
Bourke-White, Margaret **2** 455-456
Brady, Mathew B. **2** 487-488
Capa, Robert **3** 269-271
Evans, Walker **5** 339
Freeman, Roland L. **6** 92-93
Gilpin, Laura **6** 326-327
Lange, Dorothea **9** 193-194
Leibovitz, Annie **9** 310-312
Mapplethorpe, Robert **10** 227-228
Mydans, Carl **11** 283-284
Ray, Man **13** 59-60
Shahn, Ben **14** 139-140
Smithson, Robert **14** 301-303
Steichen, Edward **14** 411-412
Stieglitz, Alfred **14** 451-452
VanDer Zee, James **15** 418-419
pictographers
    Bad Heart Bull, Amos **1** 427-428
printmakers
    Albers, Josef **1** 110
    Marsh, Reginald **10** 276-277
    Rauschenberg, Robert **13** 52-53
sculptors (18th-19th century)
    Rush, William **13** 365-366
sculptors (19th century)
    Powers, Hiram **12** 428-429
    Rembrandt Harmensz van Rijn
        13 91-95
    Rimmer, William **13** 174
    Rogers, John **13** 248
    Saint-Gaudens, Augustus **13** 432
sculptors (19th-20th century)
    French, Daniel Chester **6** 98-99
    Russell, Charles Marion **13** 375-376
    Taft, Lorado **15** 75-76
sculptors (20th century)
    Barthé, Richmond **2** 33-34
    Borglum, John Gutzon de la Mothe
        2 416-417
    Bourgeois, Louise **2** 451-452
    Burke, Selma **3** 143-144
    Calder, Alexander **3** 216-218
    Chicago, Judy **3** 515-516
    Christo Vladimiroff Javacheff
        4 30-31
    Edwards, Melvin **5** 222-223
    Flannagan, John Bernard **5** 480
    Graves, Nancy Stevenson **6** 502-504
    Grooms, Red **7** 11-12
    Hanson, Duane **7** 133-135
    Hesse, Eva **7** 365-367
    Johns, Jasper **8** 291-293
    Judd, Donald **8** 376-377
    Kienholz, Edward **8** 546-547
    Koons, Jeff **9** 83-84
    Lachaise, Gaston **9** 147
    LeWitt, Sol **9** 393-395
    Lichtenstein, Roy **9** 398-399
    Lipchitz, Jacques **9** 432-433
    Lippold, Richard **9** 440-442
    Millett, Kate **11** 31-33
    Nadelman, Elie **11** 289-290
    Nevelson, Louise **11** 356-357

Noguchi, Isamu **11** 416-418
Oldenburg, Claes **11** 496-498
Oliphant, Patrick Bruce **11** 498-500
Puryear, Martin **12** 486-487
Ringgold, Faith **13** 175-177
Savage, Augusta Christine
    13 499-501
Segal, George **14** 85-87
Smith, David **14** 287-288
Smithson, Robert **14** 301-303
Zorach, William **16** 528
silkscreeners
    Begay, Harrison **2** 117-118
    Stovall, Luther (Lou) McKinley
        14 483-484
silversmiths
    Revere, Paul **13** 110-111
stage set designers
    Lee, Ming Cho **9** 289-290
tableaux creators
    Kienholz, Edward **8** 546-547
town planners
    Burnham, Daniel Hudson
        3 148-149

Artists, Argentine
    Pérez Esquivel, Adolfo **12** 215-217

Artists, Australian
    Dobell, William **5** 34-35
    Drysdale, George Russell **5** 107-109
    Namatjira, Albert **11** 300-301
    Nolan, Sidney Robert **11** 418
    Rees, Lloyd Frederic **13** 78-79
    Streeton, Arthur Ernest **14** 507-508
architects
    Fischer von Erlach, Johann Bernhard
        5 459-461
    Hildebrandt, Johann Lucas von
        7 380-381
    Prandtauer, Jakob **12** 432
painters
    Kokoschka, Oskar **9** 75-76
    Maulbertsch, Franz Anton **10** 345
    Rottmayr, Johann Michael **13** 321
    Troger, Paul **15** 300
sculptors
    Donner, Georg Raphael **5** 63

Artists, Austrian
architects
    Hoffmann, Josef **7** 440-441
    Loos, Adolf **9** 502-503
    Olbrich, Joseph Maria **11** 494-495
    Wagner, Otto **16** 39-40
draftsmen
    Schiele, Egon **14** 1-2
painters
    Hundertwasser, Friedensreich
        8 36-37
    Klimt, Gustav **9** 53-55
    Schiele, Egon **14** 1-2

Artist's Bedroom at Arles (painting)
    Van Gogh, Vincent **15** 427-429

Artists, Belgian
    Ensor, James **5** 289-290
    Magritte, René **10** 128-130

Van de Velde, Henry **15** 419-420

Artists, Brazilian
Aleijadinho, O **1** 125-126
Niemeyer Soares Filho, Oscar **11** 389-390
Portinari, Cândido **12** 407-408

Artists, Bulgarian
sculptors
Christo Vladimiroff Javacheff **4** 30-31

Artists, Canadian
architects
Erickson, Arthur Charles **5** 304-306
etchers
Milne, David Brown **11** 37-38
goldsmiths
Reid, William Ronald **13** 88-89
landscape architects
Erickson, Arthur Charles **5** 304-306
painters (19th century)
Cullen, Maurice Galbraith **4** 334
Kane, Paul **8** 422-423
Krieghoff, Cornelius **9** 101
painters (19th-20th century)
Seton, Ernest Thompson **14** 119-120
painters (20th century)
Carr, Emily **3** 319
Cullen, Maurice Galbraith **4** 334
Milne, David Brown **11** 37-38
Morrice, James Wilson **11** 181-182
Thomson, Tom **15** 202

Artists, Catalan
Gaudí i Cornet, Antoni **6** 235-236

Artists, Chinese
Lee, Ming Cho **9** 289-290
calligraphers
Chao Meng-fu **3** 436-437
Hui-Tsung **8** 25
Mi Fei **11** 12-13
Su Shih **15** 39-40
Tung Ch'i-ch'ang **15** 339-340
painters (4th century)
Ku K'ai-chih **9** 125-126
painters (7th-8th century)
Wang Wei **16** 106-108
Wu Tao-tzu **16** 405-406
Yen Li-pen **16** 453-454
painters (11th-12th century)
Hui-Tsung **8** 25
Mi Fei **11** 12-13
Su Shih **15** 39-40
painters (13th-14th century)
Chao Meng-fu **3** 436-437
Hsia Kuei **8** 4-5
Ma Yüan **10** 379
Ni Tsan **11** 400
painters (16th-17th century)
Tung Ch'i-ch'ang **15** 339-340
painters (20th century)
Ch'i Pai-shih **3** 526-527

Artists, Czech
Kupka, Frantisek **9** 134-135

Artists, Dutch
van Dongen, Kees **15** 421-422
architects
Oud, Jacobus Johannes Pieter **12** 32
Rietveld, Gerrit Thomas **13** 169
furniture designers
Rietveld, Gerrit Thomas **13** 169
painters (15th century)
Bouts, Dirk **2** 458-459
painters (16th century)
Lucas van Leyden **10** 20-21
painters (17th century)
Cuyp, Aelbert **4** 360-361
Goyen, Jan van **6** 478-479
Hals, Frans **7** 89-91
Hooch, Pieter de **7** 473-474
Rembrandt Harmensz van Rijn **13** 91-95
Ruisdael, Jacob van **13** 357-358
Ter Borch, Gerard **15** 146
Vermeer, Jan **15** 466-467
painters (19th century)
Van Gogh, Vincent **15** 427-429
painters (20th century)
Dole, Sanford Ballard **5** 46
Mondrian, Piet **11** 101-102
sculptors
Sluter, Claus **14** 275-276
see also Artists, Netherlandish

Artists, Egyptian
Imhotep **8** 116-117

Artists, English
architects (17th century)
Jones, Inigo **8** 333-334
architects (17th-18th century)
Hawksmoor, Nicholas **7** 211-212
Vanbrugh, John **15** 409-410
Wren, Christopher **16** 393-394
architects (18th-19th century)
Nash, John **11** 316
Pugin, Augustus Welby Northmore **12** 479-480
Soane, John **14** 314-315
architects (20th century)
Lutyens, Edwin Landseer **10** 54-55
Rogers, Richard **13** 248-250
Stirling, James **14** 458-459
critics
Pater, Walter Horatio **12** 130-131
Ruskin, John **13** 371-372
engravers
Blake, William **2** 316-318
Hogarth, William **7** 446-447
fashion designers
Westwood, Vivienne **16** 217-218
furniture designers
Ashley, Laura **1** 332-333
Chippendale, Thomas **4** 1-2
Hepplewhite, George **7** 317-318
Morris, William **11** 187-188
Sheraton, Thomas **14** 181-182
illustrators
Beardsley, Aubrey Vincent **2** 88-89
Burne-Jones, Edward Coley **3** 145-146

Lear, Edward **9** 265-266
landscape architects
Le Nôtre, André **9** 328-329
lithographers
Lear, Edward **9** 265-266
painters (16th century)
Hilliard, Nicholas **7** 391-392
painters (17th century)
Lely, Peter **9** 315
painters (18th century)
Gainsborough, Thomas **6** 170-172
Hogarth, William **7** 446-447
Reynolds, Joshua **13** 115-116
Romney, George **13** 269-270
Wilson, Richard **16** 329-330
painters (18th-19th century)
Blake, William **2** 316-318
Lawrence, Thomas **9** 252-253
West, Benjamin **16** 210-212
painters (19th century)
Bonington, Richard Parkes **2** 394-395
Burne-Jones, Edward Coley **3** 145-146
Constable, John **4** 208-209
Hunt, William Holman **8** 44-45
Johnston, Henry Hamilton **8** 322-323
Lear, Edward **9** 265-266
Millais, John Everett **11** 23-24
Morris, William **11** 187-188
Rossetti, Dante Gabriel **13** 308-309
Turner, Joseph Mallord William **15** 352-354
painters (20th century)
Bacon, Francis **1** 421-422
Hockney, David **7** 429-431
John, Augustus Edwin **8** 291
Nicholson, Ben **11** 380-381
Sickert, Walter Richard **14** 212-213
Sutherland, Graham **15** 40-41
photographers
Carroll, Lewis **3** 332-333
Hockney, David **7** 429-431
potters
Wedgwood, Josiah **16** 168-169
printers
Caxton, William **3** 386-387
sculptors
Caro, Anthony **3** 316
Epstein, Jacob **5** 295-296
Hepworth, Barbara **7** 318-319
Moore, Henry **11** 146-148
set designers
Hockney, David **7** 429-431
town planners
Nash, John **11** 316

Artist's Family (portrait)
Holbein, Hans the Younger **7** 449-450

Artists, Finnish
Aalto, Hugo Alvar Henrik **1** 1-2
Saarinen, Eliel and Eero **13** 396-398

Artists, Flemish
architects
Cuvilliés, François **4** 359-360

painters (15th century)
   Campin, Robert **3** 255
   Christus, Petrus **4** 33-34
   Eyck, Hubert and Jan van **5** 352-354
   van der Goes, Hugo **15** 416-417
   Weyden, Rogier van der **16** 219-221
painters (15th-16th century)
   Massys, Quentin **10** 325-326
painters (17th century)
   Brouwer, Adriaen **3** 29-30
   Jordaens, Jacob **8** 347-349
   Rubens, Peter Paul **13** 339-342
   Van Dyck, Anthony **15** 423-425

Artists, French
architects (13th-17th century)
   l'Orme, Philibert de **9** 519
   Le Vau, Louis **9** 360-361
   Lescot, Pierre **9** 354
   Mansart, François **10** 211
   Mansart, Jules Hardouin **10** 212
   Montreuil, Pierre de **11** 139
   Perrault, Claude **12** 232-233
architects (18th-20th century)
   Boffrand, Gabriel Germain **2** 361
   Gabriel, Ange Jacques **6** 160-161
   Garnier, Jean Louis Charles
    6 221-222
   Labrouste, Pierre François Henri
    9 144
   Ledoux, Claude Nicolas **9** 277-278
   Perret, Auguste **12** 233
   Soufflot, Jacques Germain
    14 349-350
   Viollet-le-Duc, Eugène Emmanuel
    15 505-506
critics
   Baudelaire, Charles Pierre **2** 61-63
draftsmen
   Boucher, François **2** 440-442
   Le Brun, Charles **9** 269-270
   Rousseau, Théodore **13** 328
fashion designers
   Chanel, Coco **3** 429
   Dior, Christian **5** 22
   Gaultier, Jean Paul **6** 239-240
   Lagerfeld, Karl **9** 161-162
illuminators
   Fouquet, Jean **6** 31
lithographers
   Daubigny, Charles François **4** 402
   Daumier, Honoré Victorin
    4 403-405
   Redon, Odilon **13** 75-76
   Rouault, Georges **13** 321-322
painters (15th-18th century)
   Boucher, François **2** 440-442
   Chardin, Jean Baptiste Siméon
    3 442-443
   Charonton, Enguerrand **3** 471
   Claude Lorrain **4** 89-90
   Clouet, Jean and François **4** 122-123
   David, Jacques Louis **4** 407-409
   Fouquet, Jean **6** 31
   Fragonard, Jean Honoré **6** 38-39
   Greuze, Jean Baptiste **6** 539

La Tour, George de **9** 222
Le Brun, Charles **9** 269-270
Le Nain, Antoine, Louis and Math-
   ieu **9** 321-322
Poussin, Nicolas **12** 418-420
Prud'hon, Pierre Paul **12** 469
Watteau, Antoine **16** 143-144
painters (19th century)
   Carpeaux, Jean Baptiste **3** 318-319
   Cézanne, Paul **3** 400-402
   Corot, Jean Baptiste Camille
    4 247-249
   Courbet, Jean Desiré Gustave
    4 271-273
   Daguerre, Louis Jacques Mandé
    4 365-366
   Daubigny, Charles François **4** 402
   Daumier, Honoré Victorin
    4 403-405
   Degas, Hilaire Germain Edgar
    4 461-462
   Delacroix, Ferdinand Victor Eugène
    4 469-471
   Gauguin, Paul **6** 236-238
   Géricault, Jean Louis André
    Théodore **6** 280-281
   Gros **7** 14-15
   Ingres, Jean Auguste Dominique
    8 121-123
   Manet, Édouard **10** 193-194
   Millet, Jean François **11** 31
   Pissaro, Camille **12** 326-327
   Prud'hon, Pierre Paul **12** 469
   Puvis de Chavannes, Pierre
    12 492-493
   Renoir, Pierre Auguste **13** 101-102
   Rousseau, Théodore **13** 328
   Seurat, Georges Pierre **14** 120-122
   Toulouse-Lautrec, Henri de
    15 273-274
painters (19th-20th century)
   Matisse, Henri **10** 336-337
   Monet, Claude **11** 102-104
   Redon, Odilon **13** 75-76
   Rousseau, Henri **13** 323-324
   van Dongen, Kees **15** 421-422
   Vuillard, Jean Édouard **16** 36
painters (20th century)
   Arp, Jean **1** 317-318
   Balthus **1** 476-477
   Bonnard, Pierre **2** 395-396
   Braque, Georges **2** 504-505
   Delaunay, Robert **4** 475-476
   Derain, André **4** 503
   Dubuffet, Jean Philippe Arthur
    5 119-120
   Duchamp, Marcel **5** 122-123
   Léger, Fernand **9** 302-303
   Picabia, Francis **12** 291-292
   Rouault, Georges **13** 321-322
   Soulages, Pierre **14** 350-351
   Soutine, Chaim **14** 356-357
   Staël, Nicolas de **14** 392
   Tanguy, Yves **15** 101
   Vasarely, Victor **15** 440-442
   Vlaminck, Maurice **16** 6

sculptors (16th-18th century)
   Clodion **4** 121
   Coysevox, Antoine **4** 287-288
   Falconet, Étienne Maurice **5** 372
   Girardon, François **6** 348-349
   Goujon, Jean **6** 466-467
   Houdon, Antoine **7** 516-517
   Pilon, Germain **12** 305
sculptors (19th-20th century)
   Arp, Jean **1** 317-318
   Bourdelle, Emile-Antoine **2** 449-450
   Carpeaux, Jean Baptiste **3** 318-319
   Daumier, Honoré Victorin
    4 403-405
   Degas, Hilaire Germain Edgar
    4 461-462
   Duchamp-Villon, Raymond **5** 123
   Gauguin, Paul **6** 236-238
   Houdon, Antoine **7** 516-517
   Laurens, Henri **9** 230-231
   Maillol, Aristide **10** 150-151
   Matisse, Henri **10** 336-337
   Richier, Germaine **13** 145-146
   Rodin, Auguste **13** 236-238
stage designers
   Balthus **1** 476-477

Artists, German
architects (16th-18th century)
   Altdorfer, Albrecht **1** 179-180
   Asam, Cosmas Damian and Egid
    Quirin **1** 323-324
   Neumann, Balthasar **11** 354-355
   Schlüter, Andreas **14** 18-19
   Zimmermann, Johann Baptist and
    Domenikus **16** 518
architects (19th-20th century)
   Behrens, Peter **2** 121-122
   Gropius, Walter **7** 13-14
   Mendelsohn, Erich **10** 488
   Schinkel, Karl Friedrich **14** 8
architects (20th century)
   Jahn, Helmut **8** 199-201
art actions
   Beuys, Joseph **2** 246-248
cartoonists
   Grosz, George **7** 17-18
collagists
   Schwitters, Kurt **14** 60-61
engravers
   Altdorfer, Albrecht **1** 179-180
   Cranach, Lucas the Elder **4** 289-290
   Kollwitz, Käthe **9** 79-81
   Schongauer, Martin **14** 26-28
fashion designers
   Lagerfeld, Karl **9** 161-162
graphic artists
   Kollwitz, Käthe **9** 79-81
   Pechstein, Hermann Max
    12 176-177
painters (15th-18th century)
   Altdorfer, Albrecht **1** 179-180
   Asam, Cosmas Damian and Egid
    Quirin **1** 323-324
   Cranach, Lucas the Elder **4** 289-290
   Dürer, Albrecht **5** 159-161

Grünewald, Matthias **7** 23-24
Holbein, Hans the Younger
7 449-450
Lochner, Stephan **9** 475
Mengs, Anton Raphael **10** 505
Pacher, Michael **12** 53
Schongauer, Martin **14** 26-28
Witz, Konrad **16** 351-352
Zimmermann, Johann Baptist and
Domenikus **16** 518
painters (19th-20th century)
Beckmann, Max **2** 104-105
Behrens, Peter **2** 121-122
Corinth, Lovis **4** 234
Ernst, Max **5** 311-312
Friedrich, Caspar David **6** 114-115
Grosz, George **7** 17-18
Hoffmann, Ernst Theodor Amadeus
7 439-440
Kirchner, Ernst Ludwig **9** 34-35
Liebermann, Max **9** 402-403
Marc, Franz **10** 231
Modersohn-Becker, Paula **11** 71-72
Mueller, Otto **11** 226-227
Nolde, Emil **11** 419-420
Salomon, Charlotte **13** 454-455
Schinkel, Karl Friedrich **14** 8
Schlemmer, Oskar **14** 12-13
Schwitters, Kurt **14** 60-61
painters (20th century)
Dix, Otto **5** 33-34
Macke, August **10** 102-103
Pechstein, Hermann Max
12 176-177
Richter, Hans **13** 149-150
painters (20th century)
Kiefer, Anselm **8** 544-546
photographers
Riefenstahl, Leni **13** 161-163
printers
Gutenberg, Johann **7** 48-49
sculptors (15th-17th century)
Riemenschneider, Tilman **13** 166
Schlüter, Andreas **14** 18-19
Stoss, Veit **14** 481-482
sculptors (18th-20th century)
Asam, Cosmas Damian and Egid
Quirin **1** 323-324
Barlach, Ernst **2** 5-6
Günther, Ignaz **7** 41-42
Lehmbruck, Wilhelm **9** 307
Schlüter, Andreas **14** 18-19
sculptors (20th century)
Beuys, Joseph **2** 246-248
Kollwitz, Käthe **9** 79-81
Schlemmer, Oskar **14** 12-13
stage designers
Schlemmer, Oskar **14** 12-13
typographers
Schwitters, Kurt **14** 60-61
wood carvers
Pacher, Michael **12** 53
woodcutters
Holbein, Hans the Younger
7 449-450

Pechstein, Hermann Max
12 176-177
Artists, Greek
architects
Ictinus **8** 101
painters
Apelles **1** 257
Apollodorus **1** 261
sculptors
Myron **11** 285
Phidias **12** 265-267
Polykleitos **12** 385-386
Praxiteles **12** 433-434
Artists, Hungarian
Moholy-Nagy, László **11** 82-83
Vasarely, Victor **15** 440-442
Artists, Italian
architects (13th-15th century)
Alberti, Leon Battista **1** 113-115
Andrea Pisano **1** 225-226
Arnolfo di Cambio **1** 315-316
Bernini, Gian Lorenzo **2** 214-216
Bramante, Donato **2** 493-494
Brunelleschi, Filippo **3** 70-72
Ghiberti, Lorenzo **6** 291-292
Giotto **6** 342-345
Leonardo da Vinci **9** 337-340
Michelozzo **11** 6-7
Orcagna **11** 526-527
Quercia, Jacopo della **12** 509
Sangallo family **13** 464-466
architects (16th century)
Bramante, Donato **2** 493-494
Leonardo da Vinci **9** 337-340
Maderno, Carlo **10** 117-118
Michelangelo Buonarroti **11** 2-5
Palladio, Andrea **12** 75-77
Porta, Giacomo della **12** 402-403
Primaticcio, Francesco **12** 453-454
Raphael **13** 40-42
Sangallo family **13** 464-466
Sanmicheli, Michele **13** 469-470
Sansovino, Jacopo **13** 470-471
Vasari, Giorgio **15** 442-443
Vignola, Giacomo da **15** 493-494
architects (17th-20th century)
Borromini, Francesco **2** 424-425
Cortona, Pietro da **4** 256
Guarini, Guarino **7** 25-26
Juvara, Filippo **8** 396-397
Maderno, Carlo **10** 117-118
Nervi, Pier Luigi **11** 346-348
Piranesi, Giovanni Battista
12 321-322
architects (20th century)
Piano, Renzo **12** 289-291
Rossi, Aldo **13** 309-310
clothing designers
Gigli, Romeo **6** 312
engravers
Carracci **3** 319-321
Mantegna, Andrea **10** 215-216
Piranesi, Giovanni Battista
12 321-322
Pollaiuolo, Antonio **12** 377-378

fashion designers
Armani, Giorgio **1** 299-301
goldsmiths
Brunelleschi, Filippo **3** 70-72
Cellini, Benvenuto **3** 391-392
Ghiberti, Lorenzo **6** 291-292
Pollaiuolo, Antonio **12** 377-378
medalists
Pisanello **12** 323-324
painters (13th-14th century)
Cimabue **4** 60-61
Duccio di Buoninsegna **5** 121-122
Giotto **6** 342-345
Lorenzetti, Pietro and Ambrogio
9 517-518
Martini, Simone **10** 298-299
Orcagna **11** 526-527
painters (15th century)
Andrea del Castagno **1** 223-224
Angelico **1** 235-236
Antonello da Messina **1** 251-252
Bellini, Giovanni **2** 137-138
Botticelli, Sandro **2** 439-440
Bramante, Donato **2** 493-494
Veneziano, Domenico **15** 459-460
Gentile da Fabriano **6** 266-267
Ghiberti, Lorenzo **6** 291-292
Ghirlandaio, Domenico **6** 292-293
Lippi, Filippo **9** 439
Mantegna, Andrea **10** 215-216
Masaccio **10** 312-313
Piero della Francesca **12** 301-302
Pisanello **12** 323-324
Pollaiuolo, Antonio **12** 377-378
Sassetta **13** 492
Tura, Cosimo **15** 343-344
Uccello, Paolo **15** 378-379
Verrocchio, Andrea del **15** 471-472
painters (15th-16th century)
Leonardo da Vinci **9** 337-340
Perugino **12** 245-246
Signorelli, Luca **14** 221-222
painters (16th century)
Andrea del Sarto **1** 224-225
Bellini, Giovanni **2** 137-138
Bramante, Donato **2** 493-494
Bronzino **3** 19
Carracci **3** 319-321
Correggio **4** 249-251
Giorgione **6** 340-341
Lotto, Lorenzo **9** 520-521
Michelangelo Buonarroti **11** 2-5
Parmigianino **12** 117
Pontormo **12** 394-395
Primaticcio, Francesco **12** 453-454
Raphael **13** 40-42
Rosso, Il **13** 312-313
Tintoretto **15** 232-234
Titian **15** 242-244
Vasari, Giorgio **15** 442-443
Veronese, Paolo **15** 469-470
painters (17th-18th century)
Canaletto **3** 257-258
Caravaggio **3** 282-284
Carracci **3** 319-321

Cortona, Pietro da **4** 256
Gaulli, Giovanni Battista **6** 238-239
Guardi, Francesco **7** 24-25
Guercino **7** 27
Magnasco, Alessandro **10** 127-128
Reni, Guido **13** 97-98
Rosa, Salvator **13** 289-290
Tiepolo, Giovanni Battista
    15 219-220
painters (20th century)
  Balla, Giacomo **1** 473-474
  Boccioni, Umberto **2** 353-354
  Burri, Alberto **3** 159-160
  Chirico, Giorgio de **4** 4
  Levi, Carlo **9** 364
  Modigliani, Amedeo **11** 72-73
  Morandi, Giorgio **11** 152-153
  Severini, Gino **14** 122
sculptors (13th-14th century)
  Andrea Pisano **1** 225-226
  Arnolfo di Cambio **1** 315-316
  Giotto **6** 342-345
  Orcagna **11** 526-527
  Pisano, Giovanni **12** 324-325
  Pisano, Nicola **12** 325
sculptors (15th century)
  Agostino di Duccio **1** 86
  Bernini, Gian Lorenzo **2** 214-216
  Brunelleschi, Filippo **3** 70-72
  da Settignano, Desiderio **4** 509
  Donatello **5** 55-56
  Ghiberti, Lorenzo **6** 291-292
  Leonardo da Vinci **9** 337-340
  Luca della Robbia **10** 19-20
  Michelozzo **11** 6-7
  Pollaiuolo, Antonio **12** 377-378
  Quercia, Jacopo della **12** 509
  Verrocchio, Andrea del **15** 471-472
sculptors (16th century)
  Cellini, Benvenuto **3** 391-392
  Giovanni da Bologna **6** 345-346
  Leonardo da Vinci **9** 337-340
  Michelangelo Buonarroti **11** 2-5
  Primaticcio, Francesco **12** 453-454
  Sansovino, Jacopo **13** 470-471
sculptors (19th-20th century)
  Boccioni, Umberto **2** 353-354
  Canova, Antonio **3** 263-264
  Manzù, Giacomo **10** 224-225
  Marini, Marino **10** 260-262
  Modigliani, Amedeo **11** 72-73
  Rosso, Medardo **13** 313-315
violin makers
  Stradivari, Antonio **14** 488-490

Artists, Japanese
architects
  Isozaki, Arata **8** 152-153
  Maki, Fumihiko **10** 159-161
  Tange, Kenzo **15** 99-101
painters (12th-16th century)
  Eitoku, Kano **5** 242
  Sesshu, Toya **14** 116-117
  Toba Sojo **15** 248-249
painters (17th-19th century)
  Harunobu, Suzuki **7** 188-189

Hiroshige, Ando **7** 412-413
Hokusai, Katsushika **7** 447-448
Sotatsu, Tawaraya **14** 349
printmakers
  Harunobu, Suzuki **7** 188-189
  Hokusai, Katsushika **7** 447-448
  Utamaro, Kitagawa **15** 397

Artists, Lebanese
Gibran, Kahlil **6** 303-305

Artist's Life (waltz)
Strauss, Johann Jr. **14** 498-499

Artists, Mexican
Barragán, Luis **2** 17-19
Kahlo, Frida **8** 406-407
Orozco, José Clemente **12** 1-2
Rivera, Diego **13** 183-184
Siqueiros, David Alfaro **14** 256
Velasco, Luis de **15** 450-451

Artists, Netherlandish
Bosch, Hieronymus **2** 426-428
Bruegel, Pieter the Elder **3** 65-67
Geertgen tot Sint Jans **6** 248
Limbourg brothers, The **9** 412-413
Memling, Hans **10** 476
see also Artists, Dutch

Artists, Nigerian
Ewonwu, Benedict Chuka **5** 351-352

Artists, Norwegian
Munch, Edvard **11** 247-248

Artists, Ottoman
Sinan, Kodja Mimar **14** 245-246

Artists, Persian
Behzad **2** 123

Artists, Philippine
Amorsolo, Fernando **1** 204
Luz, Arturo Rogerio **10** 56-57

Artists, Romanian
Brancusi, Constantin **2** 494-496

Artists, Russian
architects
  Melnikov, Konstantin Stepanovich
    10 470-471
fashion designers
  Erté **5** 314-316
illustrators
  Erté **5** 314-316
painters (20th century)
  Chagall, Marc **3** 406-407
  Goncharova, Natalia **6** 424-426
  Jawlensky, Alexej von **8** 228-229
  Kandinsky, Wassily **8** 420-422
  Larionov, Mikhail **9** 205-206
  Malevich, Kasimir **10** 168-169
  Pevsner, Antoine **12** 263-264
  Popova, Liubov Sergeevna
    12 401-402
  Rodchenko, Alexander Mikhailovich
    13 233-234
  Soutine, Chaim **14** 356-357
  Tatlin, Vladimir Evgrafovich
    15 117-118
photographers

Abe, Kobo **1** 20-22
Rodchenko, Alexander Mikhailovich
    13 233-234
sculptors
  Archipenko, Alexander **1** 280-281
  Gabo, Naum **6** 158-159
  Pevsner, Antoine **12** 263-264
  Rodchenko, Alexander Mikhailovich
    13 233-234
  Tatlin, Vladimir Evgrafovich
    15 117-118
  Zadkine, Ossip Joselyn **16** 484

Artists, Scottish
architects
  Adam, Robert and James **1** 38-40
  Gibbs, James **6** 301-302
  Mackintosh, Charles Rennie
    10 107-108
  Shaw, Richard Norman **14** 167-168
town planners
  Geddes, Patrick **6** 246-247

Artists, Spanish
architects
  Bofill, Ricardo **2** 362-363
  Churriguera, José Benito de **4** 53-54
  Herrera, Juan de **7** 335
fashion designers
  Picasso, Paloma **12** 295-297
painters (15th-17th century)
  Bermejo, Bartolomé **2** 205
  Greco **6** 511-514
  Morales, Luis de **11** 150
  Murillo, Bartolomé Esteban
    11 258-259
  Ribera, Jusepe de **13** 122-123
  Velázquez, Diego Rodríguez de
    Silva y **15** 454-456
  Zurbarán, Francisco de **16** 534-535
painters (18th-20th century)
  Dali, Salvador **4** 376-377
  Goya y Lucientes, Francisco de
    Paula José de **6** 476-478
  Gris, Juan **7** 5-6
  Miró, Joan **11** 53-54
  Picasso, Pablo **12** 292-295
sculptors
  Berruguete, Alonso **2** 223-224
  Churriguera, José Benito de **4** 53-54
  González, Julio **6** 428-429
  Picasso, Pablo **12** 292-295

Artists, Swedish
Asplund, Eric Gunnar **1** 344

Artists, Swiss
architects
  Le Corbusier **9** 274-275
designers
  Taeuber-Arp, Sophie **15** 73-74
painters
  Amiet, Cuno **1** 201-202
  Böcklin, Arnold **2** 354-355
  Fuseli, Henry **6** 153-155
  Giacometti, Alberto **6** 294-295
  Hodler, Ferdinand **7** 434-435
  Klee, Paul **9** 47-49
  Taeuber-Arp, Sophie **15** 73-74

sculptors
  Giacometti, Alberto **6** 294-295
  Oppenheim, Meret **11** 524-525
  Tinguely, Jean **15** 230-232
town planners
  Le Corbusier **9** 274-275

Artois (region, France)
  Foch, Ferdinand **5** 498-499
  Louis XIII **9** 529-531

Arts and Crafts movement (19th century)
functional design
  Richardson, Henry Hobson
  13 139-141
furniture design
  Mies van der Rohe, Ludwig
  11 10-12
  Van de Velde, Henry **15** 419-420
industrial design
  Gropius, Walter **7** 13-14
  Saarinen, Eliel and Eero **13** 396-398
origins
  Burne-Jones, Edward Coley
  3 145-146
  Morris, William **11** 187-188

Arts and Crafts Society (Sweden)
  Asplund, Eric Gunnar **1** 344

Arts, The (book)
  Celsus, Aulus Cornelius **3** 393

Artusi, Giovanni Maria (1550?-1613), Italian composer and music theorist
  Monteverdi, Claudio Giovanni Antonio
  11 126-128

ARU
  see American Railway Union

Arundel, Thomas (1353-1413), English prelate, Archbishop of Canterbury
  Richard II **13** 130-131

Arundel Mill and Castle (painting)
  Constable, John **4** 208-209

Arundell, Henry (3d Baron Arundell of Wardour; 1606?-1694), English statesman
  Charles, I **3** 450-452

Arundell, Isabel
  see Burton, Lady Isabel Arundell

Arusha Declaration (1967)
  Nyerere, Julius Kamberage **11** 447-449

Arverni (Gallic tribe)
  Caesar, Gaius Julius **3** 207-210

Arya (magazine)
  Ghose, Aurobindo **6** 293-294

Arya Samaj Society (India)
  Dayananda Saraswati **4** 431
  Premchand **12** 439
  Rai, Lala Lajpat **13** 5-6

Aryan (ethnic type)
  Gobineau, Comte de **6** 375-376

Aryan (Hindu caste)
  Buddha **3** 97-101

Aryan (language group)
  Chamberlain, Houston Stewart **3** 411

Aryans, The (book)
  Childe, Vere Gordon **3** 521-522

Aryeh, the Gross (novel)
  Bialik, Hayyim Nahman **2** 262-263

As I Ebb'd with the Ocean of Life (poem)
  Whitman, Walt **16** 249-251

As I Lay Dying (novel)
  Faulkner, William **5** 395-397

As the Old Sang, So the Young Pipe (painting)
  Jordaens, Jacob **8** 347-349

As the Time Draws Nigh (poem)
  Whitman, Walt **16** 249-251

As Thousands Cheer (musical)
  Berlin, Irving **2** 200-201

As You Desire Me (film)
  Garbo, Greta **6** 205-207

As You Like It (play; Shakespeare)
  Arne, Thomas Augustine **1** 307-308
  Paine, John Knowles **12** 65
  Shakespeare, William **14** 142-145

Asafiev, Boris (1844-1949), Russian composer
  Prokofiev, Sergei Sergeevich
  12 458-460

Asahi Newspaper (publication)
  Natsume, Soseki **11** 324-325

Asal (literary character)
  ibn Tufayl, Abu Bakr Muhammad **8** 96

Asalefte Zoe (poems)
  Palamas, Kostes **12** 70

ASAM, COSMAS DAMIAN (1686-1739), German artist **1** 323-324

ASAM, EGID QUIRIN (1692-1750), German artist **1** 323-324

Asam, Hans Georg (1649?-1711), German artist
  Asam, Cosmas Damian and Egid Quirin
  1 323-324

Asam Church (Munich)
  Asam, Cosmas Damian and Egid Quirin
  1 323-324

Asanga-Vasubandhu tradition (Buddhism)
  Hsüan Tsang **8** 6-7

ASBURY, FRANCIS (1745-1816), English-born American Methodist bishop
  1 324-325
  Allen, Richard **1** 168
  Cartwright, Peter **3** 344-345
  Otterbein, Philip William **12** 27-28

Ascanio in Alba (opera)
  Mozart, Wolfgang Amadeus
  11 218-221

Ascension (astronomy)
  Hipparchus **7** 407-408

Ascension (mural)
  La Farge, John **9** 149-150

Ascension, Church of the (New York City)
  La Farge, John **9** 149-150

Ascension of Christ (sculpture)
  Luca della Robbia **10** 19-20

Ascension of the Virgin (altarpiece)
  Bellini, Giovanni **2** 137-138

Ascent of Culture (mural)
  Siqueiros, David Alfaro **14** 256

Ascent of F 6, The (play; Audenlsherwood)
  Auden, Wystan Hugh **1** 364-366

Ascent of Mount Carmel (treatise)
  John of the Cross **8** 285

Asceticism (religion)
  Abu-L-Ala al-Maarri **1** 32
  Calvin, John **3** 239-242
  Jerome **8** 249
  John Chrysostom **8** 280-281
  Valla, Lorenzo **15** 406
  Zwingli, Huldreich **16** 537-538
  see also Monasticism

ASCH, SHALOM (1880-1957), Polish-born playwright and novelist **1** 325-326

Ascham, Roger (1515-1568), English scholar
  Edward VI **5** 213-214
  Elizabeth I **5** 263-266

Asclepiades
  see Hippocrates

Asclepius (Greek god)
  Hippocrates **7** 408-410
  Sophocles **14** 343-345

Ascorbic acid
  see Vitamin C

Ascyltus (literary character)
  Petronius Arbiter **12** 262-263

Asepsis (medicine)
  Lister, Joseph **9** 444-445

ASH, MARY KAY WAGNER (born circa 1916), cosmetics tycoon **1** 326-327

Ash Wednesday (poem)
  Eliot, Thomas Stearns **5** 258-261

Ash Wednesday Supper, The (book)
  Bruno, Giordano **3** 75-76

Ashanti (West Africa people)
  Busia, Kofi Abrefa **3** 172-173

Ashanti Empire (West Africa)
  Anokye, Okomfo **1** 242-243
  Maclean, George **10** 108-109

ASHARI, ABU AL- HASAN ALI AL- (873/883-935), Moslem theologian
  1 327-328

Ashcan school (American art)
  Davis, Stuart **4** 424-425
  Glackens, William **6** 355-356
  Kline, Franz **9** 55
  Marsh, Reginald **10** 276-277
  see also Eight, The

ASHE, ARTHUR ROBERT, JR. (1943-1993), world champion athlete, social activist, teacher, and charity worker **1** 328-330

Ashenden (novel)
Maugham, William Somerset **10** 344-345

Ashikaga shogunate
see Japan—1338-1573

ASHIKAGA TAKAUJI (1305-1358), Japanese shogun **1** 330-332
Nobunaga, Oda **11** 413-414
Yoritomo, Minamoto **16** 463-464
see also Japan—1338-1573

Ashikaga Yoshimitsu (1358-1395), Japanese shogun 1367-1395
Ashikaga Takauji **1** 330-332
Yung-lo **16** 482-483
Zeami, Kanze **16** 492-493

Ashikari (play)
Tanizaki, Junichiro **15** 101-102

Ashiqqa party (Sudan)
Azhari, Sayyid Ismail al- **1** 399-401
Khalil, Sayyid Abdullah **8** 531-532

Ashkenazi (Jewish communities)
Caro, Joseph ben Ephraim **3** 316-317

Ashland (house; Lexington, Kentucky)
Latrobe, Benjamin Henry **9** 222-224

Ashley, 1st Baron
see Shaftesbury, 1st Earl of

ASHLEY, LAURA (Mountney; 1925-1985), British designer of women's clothes and home furnishings **1** 332-333

Ashley, Lord
see Shaftesbury, 7th Earl of

ASHLEY, WILLIAM HENRY (circa 1778-1838), American businessman, fur trader, and explorer **1** 333-334
Bridger, James **3** 2-3
Fitzpatrick, Thomas **5** 474-475
Smith, Jedediah S. **14** 294-295

Ashmolean Museum (Oxford University)
Evans, Arthur John **5** 335-336

ASHMORE, HARRY SCOTT (born 1916), American journalist **1** 334-335

ASHMUN, JEHUDI (1794-1828), American governor of Liberia Colony **1** 335-336

ASHRAWI, HANAN MIKHAIL (born 1946), Palestinian spokesperson **1** 336-338

Ashtamahasricaityastotra (poem)
Harsha **7** 181-182

ASHURBANIPAL (died circa 630 B.C.), Assyrian king 669-ca. 630 **1** 338
Taharqa **15** 81-82

Ashur-nirari V (died circa 745 B.C.), Assyrian king
Tiglath-pileser III **15** 221-222

Ashville (painting)
de Kooning, Willem **4** 468-469

Asi que pasen cinco años (play)
Lorca, Federico García **9** 511-513

Asia (continent)
Communist Chinese policy
Chou En-lai **4** 20-22
economic development
Myrdal, Karl Gunnar **11** 284
exploration
Bonvalot, Pierre Gabriel Édouard **2** 396
Hedin, Sven Anders **7** 252-253
narratives of (Southeast)
Conti, Niccolò de' **4** 212-213
ocean commerce (Korea)
Chang Po-go **3** 433-434
papal limits
Leo I **9** 329-330
see also individual countries

Asia-Africa-Latin America People's Solidarity Organization (established 1966)
Castro Ruz, Fidel **3** 365-368

Asia Minor (peninsula, Asia)
Arab raids
Leo III **9** 330-332
Muawiya ibn Abu Sufyan **11** 223-224
Christian missions (1st century)
Paul **12** 141-143
Greco-Persian wars
Agesilaus II **1** 79-80
Turkish rule
Manuel I **10** 218-219
Mehmed the Conqueror **10** 452-454
Castro Ruz, Fidel **3** 365-368

Asian Artists in Crystal (exhibition; 1955)
Luz, Arturo Rogerio **10** 56-57

Asian Development Bank
Johnson, Lyndon Baines **8** 308-312

Asian Drama (book)
Myrdal, Karl Gunnar **11** 284

Asie Centrale (book)
Humboldt, Friedrich Heinrich Alexander von **8** 30-31

ASIMOV, ISAAC (1920-1992), American author **1** 338-341

Asinaria (play)
Plautus **12** 348-350

Askia the Great
see Muhammad Ture, Askia

ASOKA (ruled circa 273-232 B.C.), Indian emperor of the Maurya dynasty **1** 341-342
Buddha **3** 97-101
Chandragupta Maurya **3** 426
Harsha **7** 181-182
Samudragupta **13** 457

Asolani, Gli (book; Bembo)
Bembo, Pietro **2** 144-145
Giorgione **6** 340-341

Aspasios (1st century B.C.), Roman gem cutter
Phidias **12** 265-267

Aspects of the Novel (book)
Forster, Edward Morgan **6** 14-16

Aspern Papers, The (story)
James, Henry **8** 211-212

Asphodel... (poem)
Williams, William Carlos **16** 308-309

ASPIN, LES (1938-1995), United States congressman and secretary of defense **1** 342-344

Aspirations of Jean Servien, The (novel)
France, Anatole **6** 39-40

ASPLUND, ERIC GUNNAR (1885-1945), Swedish architect **1** 344

ASQUITH, HERBERT HENRY (1st Earl of Oxford and Asquith; 1852-1928), English statesman, prime minister 1908-1916 **1** 344-346
Churchill, Winston Leonard Spencer **4** 51-53
George V **6** 273-275
Henderson, Arthur **7** 277-278
Lloyd George, David **9** 469-471
Morley, John **11** 178-179
Pankhurst, Emmeline **12** 85-86
Perth, 16th Earl of **12** 244-245

Asquith Commission (colonial education)
Carr-Saunders, Alexander Morris **3** 333-334

Asrar-i-Khudi (poem)
Iqbal, Muhammad **8** 132-133

ASSAD, HAFIZ (born 1930), president of Syria **1** 346-348

Assam (state; India)
Bhashani, Maulana Abdul Hamid Khan **2** 255-257

Assassinations
Arab Empire
Omar ibn al-Khattab **11** 508-509
Austria
Dollfuss, Engelbert **5** 47
Francis Ferdinand **6** 44
Bangladesh
Ziaur Rahman **16** 515-516
Bolivia
Paz, Octavio **12** 161-162
Brazil
Cunha, Euclides Rodrigues Pimenta da **4** 336-337
Canada
Brown, George **3** 35-36
Chile
Portales Plazazuelos, Diego José Víctor **12** 404
China
Chang Tso-lin **3** 434-435
Colombia
Gaitán, Jorge Eliécer **6** 172-173
Dominican Republic
Trujillo Molina, Rafael Leonidas **15** 313-314
Ecuador
García Moreno, Gabriel **6** 209-210
Sucre, Antonio José de **15** 11-12
Egypt
Sadat, Anwar **13** 412-414

England
    Buckingham, 1st Duke of **3** 93-94
France
    Coligny, Gaspard de **4** 159-160
    Ferry, Jules François Camille **5** 430
    Henry IV **7** 293-295
    Jaurès, Jean **8** 226-227
Germany
    Rathenau, Walther **13** 48-49
Greece
    Alcibiades **1** 119-120
Haiti
    Dessalines, Joan Jacques **4** 511-512
India
    Gandhi, Mohandas Karamchand
        6 201-204
Italy
    Gentile, Giovanni **6** 267
Japan
    Hara, Kei **7** 138
    Inukai, Tsuyoshi **8** 130-131
    Ito, Hirobumi **8** 153-155
    Nobunaga, Oda **11** 413-414
    Okubo, Toshimichi **11** 489-490
    Takahashi, Korekiyo **15** 84-85
Kenya
    Mboya, Thomas Joseph **10** 384-385
Korea
    Chang Po-go **3** 433-434
    Min **11** 46-47
Mexico
    Carranza, Venustiano **3** 321-322
    Madero, Francisco Indalecio
        10 118-119
    Obregón, Álvaro **11** 458-459
    Trotsky, Leon **15** 302-305
Mozambique
    Mondlane, Eduardo Chivambo
        11 100-101
Netherlands
    William the Silent **16** 300-302
Nicaragua
    Sandino, Augusto C. **13** 462-463
    Somoza, Anastasio **14** 335-336
    Somoza Debayle, Anastasio
        14 336-337
Nigeria
    Bello, Ahmadu **2** 139-140
    Tafawa Balewa, Abubakar **15** 75
Pakistan
    Liaquat Ali Khan **9** 397
    Zia ul-Haq, Mohammad
        16 513-515
Palestine
    Abdullah ibn Husein **1** 19-20
Persia
    Nagel, Ernest **11** 291-292
Roman Empire
    Caesar, Gaius Julius **3** 207-210
    Caligula **3** 228-229
    Caracalla **3** 281-282
    Ulpian, Domitius **15** 385-386
Russia
    Alexander II **1** 132-133
    Nicholas II **11** 378-380
    Paul I **12** 143-144

Rasputin, Grigori Efimovich
    13 44-45
Stolypin, Piotr Arkadevich
    14 465-466
Scotland
    James I **8** 206-207
South Africa
    Verwoerd, Hendrik Frensch
        15 472-473
Sweden
    Gustavus III **7** 45-46
Tanzania
    Karume, Abeid Amani **8** 452-453
Togo
    Olympio, Sylvanus E. **11** 506-507
United States
    Garfield, James Abram **6** 213-214
    Kennedy, John Fitzgerald **8** 502-506
    Kennedy, Robert Francis **8** 508-509
    King, Martin Luther Jr. **9** 20-22
    Lincoln, Abraham **9** 415-418
    Long, Huey Pierce **9** 496-497
    Malcolm X **10** 165-166
    McKinley, William **10** 418-420
    Phillips, David Graham **12** 280-281
    White, Stanford **16** 235-236
Yugoslavia
    Alexander of Yugoslavia **1** 136-137
Zululand
    Shaka **14** 141-142
    see also Executions; Murder victims

Assassins (Persian sect)
    Ala-ud-din **1** 102-103
    Hulagu Khan **8** 27-28

Assayer (book)
    Galileo Galilei **6** 180-183

Assemblage (art)
    Archipenko, Alexander **1** 280-281
    Burri, Alberto **3** 159-160
    Nevelson, Louise **11** 356-357

Assembly (stories)
    O'Hara, John **11** 485

Assembly line (industry)
    Ford, Henry **6** 5-6

Assembly of First Nations (Canada)
    Erasmus, Georges Henry **5** 300-301

Assembly of the Clergy (France; 1681)
    Bossuet, Jacques Bénigne **2** 431-432

Assembly of the French Union
(Cameroons)
    Ahidjo, Ahmadou **1** 89-90

Assembly of the Notables (France;
1787-1788)
    du Pont de Nemours, Pierre Samuel
        5 155-156
    Lafayette, Marquis de **9** 151-152

Asséns, Rafael Cansino (born 1883), Spanish author and critic
    Borges, Jorge Luis **2** 411-412

Asser (died 909), Welsh monk
    Alfred **1** 151-153

Assertion of the Seven Sacraments (tract)
    Henry VIII **7** 302-305

Assiniboia (town; Saskatchewan, Canada)
    Lacombe, Albert **9** 147-148

Assisi (city; Italy)
    Carissimi, Giacomo **3** 299-300
    Francis of Assisi **6** 46-47
    Visconti, Gian Galeazzo **15** 510-511
    see also San Francesco (church)

Associated production, theory of (element—chemistry particles)
    Gell-Mann, Murray **6** 257-258

Association (book)
    Brisbane, Albert **3** 9

Association (law)
    Gierke, Otto von **6** 311-312

Association (psychology)
    Guthrie, Edwin Ray **7** 49-50
    Hartley, David **7** 185
    Jung, Carl Gustav **8** 388-389

Association, Articles of (United States; 1774)
    Lee, Richard Henry **9** 291-292
    Sherman, Roger **14** 185-186

**Association for Promoting the Discovery
of the Interior Parts of Africa**
    Burckhardt, Johann Ludwig **3** 133

Association for Social Politics (Germany)
    Tönnies, Ferdinand **15** 266-267

**Association for the Advancement of Psy-
choanalysis**
    Horney, Karen Danielsen **7** 508-509

**Association for the Study of Negro Life
and History**
    Woodson, Carter Godwin **16** 374-376

Association in Defense of Hindu Culture
(established 1830)
    Deb, Radhakant **4** 437

Association of Algerian Muslim 'Ulama
(AAMU)
    Ben Badis, 'Abd al-Hamid **2** 147-148

Association of American Geographers
(established 1904)
    Davis, William Morris **4** 425-426

**Association of German Academic Econo-
mists**
    Schmoller, Gustav Friedrich von **14** 21

Association of God
    see Brahmo Samaj

Association of May (Argentina; established
1838)
    Echeverría, José Estéban **5** 197-198

Association of Saxon Industrialists (established 1902)
    Stresemann, Gustav **14** 508-509

Association of Southeast Asian Nations
(ASEAN)
    Prem Tinsulanonda **12** 437

Association of State Libraries (established
1890)
    Dewey, Melvil **4** 523-524

Association Polytechnique (France)
Carnot, Nicolas Léonard Sadi **3** 315

Assommoir, L' (novel)
Zola, Émile **16** 526-528

Assonance (literature)
Ennius, Quintus **5** 289
Hopkins, Gerard Manley **7** 492-494

Assumption (painting; Titian)
Greco **6** 511-514

Assumption, Basilica of the (Baltimore, Maryland)
Latrobe, Benjamin Henry **9** 222-224

Assumption of Mary Magdalene (painting)
Ribera, Jusepe de **13** 122-123

Assumption of the Virgin (altarpiece)
Riemenschneider, Tilman **13** 166
Rubens, Peter Paul **13** 339-342

Assumption of the Virgin (painting)
Goya y Lucientes, Francisco de Paula José de **6** 476-478
Greco **6** 511-514
Sassetta **13** 492
Titian **15** 242-244

Assumption of the Virgin (sculpture)
Asam, Cosmas Damian and Egid Quirin **1** 323-324

Assya (story)
Turgenev, Ivan Sergeyevich **15** 345-348

Assyria (ancient kingdom; West Asia)
Akkadian conquest
Sargon of Agade **13** 483
Babylonian conquest
Hammurabi **7** 109-110
Egyptian conflict
Ashurbanipal **1** 338
Shabaka **14** 130
Taharqa **15** 81-82
expansion
Sargon II **13** 482
Tiglath-pileser III **15** 221-222
government reforms
Tiglath-pileser III **15** 221-222
Israeli alliance
Hosea **7** 512
Nineveh rebuilt
Sennacherib **14** 108

Assyrian, The (novel)
Saroyan, William **13** 486-487

ASTAIRE, FRED (Frederick Austerlitz; 1899-1987), dancer and choreographer **1** 348-350
Crosby, Harry Lillis **4** 324-326
Garland, Judy **6** 218-219

Astarotte (literary character)
Pulci, Luigi **12** 481

Ästhetik des Reinen Gefühls (book)
Cohen, Hermann **4** 138-139

Astianatte (opera; Bononcini)
Handel, George Frederick **7** 116-119

Aston (literary character)
Pinter, Harold **12** 317-318

ASTON, FRANCIS WILLIAM (1877-1945), English chemist and physicist **1** 350-351

ASTOR, JOHN JACOB (1763-1848), American fur trader, merchant, and capitalist **1** 351-352
Baranov, Aleksandr Andreievich **1** 499-500
Girard, Stephen **6** 347-348
Irving, Washington **8** 141-143
Ogden, Peter Skene **11** 480-481
Thompson, David **15** 194-195

ASTOR, NANCY LANGHORNE (1879-1964), first woman to serve as a member of the British Parliament (1919-1945) **1** 352-354
Lawrence, Thomas Edward **9** 253-254

Astor Place Theater (New York City)
Forrest, Edwin **6** 11-12

Astoria (book)
Irving, Washington **8** 141-143

Astoria (city, Oregon)
Astor, John Jacob **1** 351-352
Thompson, David **15** 194-195

Astraea redux (poem)
Dryden, John **5** 106-107

Astrakhan (city, Union of Soviet Socialist Republics)
Ivan IV **8** 157-159
Potemkin, Grigori Aleksandrovich **12** 411-412

Astrée (play)
La Fontaine, Jean de **9** 156-157

Astrolabe (instrument)
Chaucer, Geoffrey **3** 482-485
Fernel, Jean François **5** 425-426
Peregrinus, Petrus **12** 208

Astrology
Nicholas of Oresme **11** 380
Nostradamus **11** 432-434
Ptolemy, Claudius **12** 473-474

Astronautics (science)
Goddard, Robert Hutchings **6** 376-377
Tsiolkovsky, Konstantin Eduardovich **15** 326-328
see also Rocketry; Space exploration

Astronauts
Armstrong, Neil Alden **1** 304-306
Bluford, Guion Stewart Jr. **2** 341-343
Collins, Eileen **4** 163-165
Gagarin, Yuri Alexeivich **6** 166-167
Glenn, John Herschel Jr. **6** 365-367
Jemison, Mae C. **8** 243-244
Ochoa, Ellen **11** 460-461
Ride, Sally **13** 158-160
Shepard, Alan **14** 178-180
Tereshkova, Valentina **15** 151-152

Astronomer, The (painting)
Vermeer, Jan **15** 466-467

Astronomia magna (book)
Paracelsus, Philippus Aureolus **12** 91-93

Astronomia nova (book)
Kepler, Johannes **8** 514-516

Astronomiae instauratae progymnasmata (book; Brahe)
Brahe, Tycho **2** 489-490
Kepler, Johannes **8** 514-516

Astronomiae pars optica (book)
Kepler, Johannes **8** 514-516

Astronomy (science)
aberration of light
Bradley, James **2** 482-483
astronomical tables
Banneker, Benjamin **1** 490-491
Kepler, Johannes **8** 514-516
Khwarizmi, Muhammad ibn Musa al- **8** 541
big bang theory
Lemaître, Abbè Georges Édouard **9** 315-316
celestial mechanics
Leverrier, Urbain Jean Joseph **9** 361-362
Poincaré, Jules Henri **12** 365-366
see also Celestial mechanics
comets
Halley, Edmund **7** 88-89
Mitchell, Maria **11** 61
Regiomontanus **13** 81-82
Copernican
see heliocentric theory (below)
double stars
Herschel, John Frederick William **7** 340-341
Struve, Friedrich Georg Wilhelm von **14** 513
galaxies
Geller, Margaret Joan **6** 256-257
Kapteyn, Jacobus Cornelis **8** 436-437
Oort, Jan Hendrik **11** 523-524
Shapley, Harlow **14** 155-156
geocentric theory
see Ptolemaic system (below)
heliocentric theory
Aristarchus of Samos **1** 290-291
Copernicus, Nicolaus **4** 226-227
Galileo Galilei **6** 180-183
homocentric theory
Eudoxus of Cnidus **5** 329-330
mathematics in
Apollonius of Perga **1** 261-262
Euclid **5** 327-329
Eudoxus of Cnidus **5** 329-330
nebular hypothesis
Laplace, Marquis de **9** 202-204
observatories
Hale, George Ellery **7** 72-74
photography
Barnard, Edward Emerson **2** 8-9
Fizeau, Hippolyte Armand Louis **5** 475
photometry
Herschel, John Frederick William **7** 340-341
Pickering, Edward Charles **12** 298
Shapley, Harlow **14** 155-156
planetarium

Archimedes **1** 277-280
planetary studies
   Sagan, Carl E. **13** 424-425
planets
  see Planet
Ptolemaic system
   Hasan ibn al-Haytham **7** 190-191
   Nicholas of Oresme **11** 380
   Ptolemy, Claudius **12** 473-474
radio
   Bell Burnell, Susan Jocelyn
    2 133-134
   Lovell, Alfred Charles Bernard
    10 8-9
solar parallax and distance
   Aristarchus of Samos **1** 290-291
   Newcomb, Simon **11** 361-362
   Winthrop, John **16** 341-342
solar spectra
   Moore, Charlotte E. **11** 145-146
star catalogs
   Cannon, Annie Jump **3** 260-261
   Eratosthenes of Cyrene **5** 301-302
   Flamsteed, John **5** 477-478
   Hipparchus **7** 407-408
   Kapteyn, Jacobus Cornelis
    8 436-437
   Pickering, Edward Charles **12** 298
star magnatudes
   Celsius, Anders **3** 392
star streams
   Kapteyn, Jacobus Cornelis
    8 436-437
stellar motion
   Bessel, Friedrich Wilhelm **2** 234-235
   Eddington, Arthur Stanley **5** 201-202
   Halley, Edmund **7** 88-89
stellar spectra classification
   Cannon, Annie Jump **3** 260-261
   Payne-Gaposchkin, Cecilia
    12 159-161
sundial
   Anaximander **1** 209-210
sunspots
   Hale, George Ellery **7** 72-74
Tychonic system
   Brahe, Tycho **2** 489-490
  see also Astrophysics; Scientists—
   astronomers; Universe, systems of

Astronomy (sculpture)
  Giovanni da Bologna **6** 345-346

Astronomy for Everybody (book)
  Newcomb, Simon **11** 361-362

Astrophel (poem)
  Spenser, Edmund **14** 373-376

Astrophel and Stella (sonnets)
  Sidney, Philip **14** 214-215

Astrophysics
  Eddington, Arthur Stanley **5** 201-202
  Geller, Margaret Joan **6** 256-257
  Huggins, William **8** 14-15
  Jeans, James Hopwood **8** 235-236
  Moore, Charlotte E. **11** 145-146
  Payne-Gaposchkin, Cecilia **12** 159-161

ASTURIAS, MIGUEL ANGEL (born 1899),
  Guatemalan novelist and poet **1** 354-355

Astyages (died 550 B.C.), king of Media
  circa 584-550 B.C.
   Cyrus the Great **4** 363-364

Astyanax (literary character)
  Racine, Jean Baptiste **12** 532-535

Asvaghosha (1st-2d century), Indian
  poet-philosopher
   Kalidasa **8** 414-415

Aswan Dam (Egypt)
  Nasser, Gamal Abdel **11** 317-318

Asymptote (mathematics)
  Euler, Leonard **5** 331-332
  Jeffreys, Harold **8** 241-242

At a Solemn Musik (poem)
  Milton, John **11** 43-46

At Five in the Afternoon (painting)
  Motherwell, Robert **11** 210-211

At Home and Abroad (book)
  Kennedy, John Pendleton **8** 506-507

At Lady Molly's (novel)
  Powell, Anthony **12** 422-423

At Melville's Tomb (poem)
  Crane, Hart **4** 291-293

At the Boar's Head (opera)
  Holst, Gustav **7** 459-460

At the Hawk's Well (play)
  Yeats, William Butler **16** 445-447

At the Mill (painting)
  Weber, Max **16** 160

At the Moulin Rouge (painting)
  Toulouse-Lautrec, Henri de **15** 273-274

At the Piano (painting)
  Whistler, James Abbott McNeill
   16 225-226

At the Sign of the Reine Pédauque (novel)
  France, Anatole **6** 39-40

At the Station (poem)
  Carducci, Giosuè **3** 290-291

At the World's End (story)
  Bunin, Ivan Alekseevich **3** 124

ATAHUALPA (circa 1502-1533), Inca
  emperor of Peru 1532-1533 **1** 355-356
   Almagro, Diego de **1** 177-178
   Benalcázar, Sebastián de **2** 145-146
   Manco Capac **10** 184-185

Atala (novel)
  Chateaubriand, Vicomte de **3** 477-479

Atalanta and Hippomenes (painting)
  Reni, Guido **13** 97-98

Atalanta in Calydon (play)
  Swinburne, Algernon Charles **15** 54-55

ATATÜRK, GHAZI MUSTAPHA KEMAL
  (1881-1938), Turkish nationalist, president 1923-1938 **1** 356-357
   Churchill, Winston Leonard Spencer
   4 51-53
   Gökalp, Mehmet Ziya **6** 395-396

John, XXIII **8** 277-280
  Venizelos, Eleutherios **15** 460-461

Atavism (criminology)
  Lombroso, Cesare **9** 493

Atbara River (Northeast Africa)
  Baker, Samuel White **1** 454-455

ATCHISON, DAVID RICE (1807-1886),
  American lawyer and politician
  1 357-358

Atchison Daily Globe (newspaper)
  Howe, Edgar Watson **7** 529

Aten (Egyptian god)
  Amenhotep III **1** 194-195
  Ikhnaton **8** 110-111
  Tutankhamen **15** 359-360

Ateneo de la Juventud (Mexico City)
  Reyes, Alfonso **13** 112-113
  Vasconcelos, José **15** 443-444

Ateneo de Madrid (club)
  Azaña Diaz, Manuel **1** 396-397

Athabasca Department (Canada)
  Fraser, Simon **6** 74-75

Athalaric (516-534), Ostrogothic king in
  Italy 526-534
   Theodoric the Great **15** 175-176

Athalia (oratorio)
  Handel, George Frederick **7** 116-119

Athalie (play)
  Racine, Jean Baptiste **12** 532-535

ATHANASIUS, ST. (circa 296-373), Christ-
  ian theologian, bishop of Alexandria
  1 358-359
   Ambrose **1** 192-193
   Anthony, Susan Brownell **1** 246-248
   Arius **1** 297-298

Atheism (philosophy)
  Bakunin, Mikhail Aleksandrovich
   1 458-460
  Bradlaugh, Charles **2** 478
  Diderot, Denis **5** 1-2
  Holbach, Baron d' **7** 448-449
  O'Hair, Madalyn Murray **11** 484-485

Atheismus triumphatus (book)
  Campanella, Tommaso **3** 249

Athelney, Isle of (England)
  Alfred **1** 151-153

Athelstan (895-940), king of England
  924-940
   Dunstan **5** 151-152
   Edward the Elder **5** 219-220
   Harold I **7** 161-162

Athena (Greek mythology)
  Alexander the Great **1** 137-141
  Ictinus **8** 101
  Sophocles **14** 343-345

Athena (sculpture)
  Myron **11** 285
  Phidias **12** 265-267

Athena Parthenos (sculpture; Phidias)
  Phidias **12** 265-267, 402

Polykleitos **12** 385-386

Athenaeum (journal)
Huxley, Aldous Leonard **8** 74-75
Masaryk, Tomáš Garrigue **10** 314-315
Schlegel, Friedrich von **14** 10-11

Athenagoras I (1886-1972), Eastern Orthodox patriarch of Constantinople 1948-1972
John, XXIII **8** 277-280
Paul VI **12** 146-148

Atheneun (building; New Harmony, Indiana)
Meier, Richard **10** 456-458

Athens (ancient city-state, Greece)
government reform
Cleisthenes **4** 98-99
Solon **14** 327-328
Macedonian control
Demosthenes **4** 495-496
Menander **10** 477-478
Philip II **12** 269-271
Peloponnesian War
see Peloponnesian War
Periclean Age (445-431)
Aristophanes **1** 293-294
Pericles **12** 219-221
Persian wars
see Persian wars
Spartan influence
Cleomenes I **4** 103
Theban war
Epaminondas **5** 291-292
Thirty Tyrants era
Plato **12** 345-347

Athens, University of
Palamas, Kostes **12** 70

Athletes
American
see Athletes, American
Australian
Bradman, Donald George
2 485-486
Brasilian
Pele **12** 190-191
Canadian
Gretzky, Wayne **6** 537-539
Howe, Gordie **7** 532-534
Orr, Bobby **12** 2-4
Panamanian
Carew, Rod **3** 291-292

Athletes, American
baseball players
Aaron, Henry Louis (Hank) **1** 2-3
Carew, Rod **3** 291-292
Cobb, Tyrus Raymond **4** 124-126
DiMaggio, Joe **5** 10-11
Jackson, Reginald Martinez
8 180-182
Mantle, Mickey **10** 216-218
Mays, Willie **10** 376-379
Paige, Satchel **12** 62-65
Rickey, Wesley Branch **13** 153-155
Robinson, Frank Jr. **13** 202-203

Robinson, Jack Roosevelt
13 207-208
Ruth, George Herman Jr. **13** 384
Ryan, Nolan **13** 389-391
Sunday, William Ashley **15** 32-33
Thorpe, Jim **15** 209-211
Ueberroth, Peter Victor **15** 379-381
Zaharias, Mildred Didrikson
16 487-488
basketball players
Bird, Larry **2** 279-281
Chamberlain, Wilt **3** 413-415
Erving, Julius Winfield **5** 317-319
Jabbar, Kareem Abdul **8** 164-165
Johnson, Marietta Louise Pierce
8 312-313
Jordan, Michael **8** 355-357
boxers
Ali, Muhammad **1** 156-158
Dempsey, Jack **4** 496-497
Johnson, Jack **8** 301-304
Louis, Joe **9** 537-538
Marciano, Rocky **10** 237-238
Sullivan, John Lawrence **15** 24-25
football players
Bryant, Paul **3** 82-83
Lombardi, Vince **9** 491-492
Montana, Joe **11** 120-121
Thorpe, Jim **15** 209-211
football coaches
Rockne, Knute **13** 231
golfers
Jones, Robert Tyre **8** 342
Nicklaus, Jack **11** 382-383
Palmer, Arnold Daniel **12** 78-80
judo practitioners
Campbell, Ben Nighthorse
3 252-253
tennis players
Ashe, Arthur Robert Jr. **1** 328-330
Capriati, Jennifer **3** 278-281
Gibson, Althea **6** 305-306
King, Billie Jean **9** 14-15
McEnroe, John Patrick Jr.
10 408-411
Navratilova, Martina **11** 325-327
track coaches
Walker, LeRoy Tashreau **16** 64-65
track and field athletes
Lewis, Carl **9** 377-380
Owens, Jesse **12** 43-44
Rudolph, Wilma **13** 350-352
Thorpe, Jim **15** 209-211
Zaharias, Mildred Didrikson
16 487-488

Athos (literary character)
Dumas, Alexandre **5** 136-138

Atidenu (periodical)
Kaufmann, Ezekiel **8** 460

Atkinson, Henry (1782-1842), American general
Taylor, Zachary **15** 128-130

Atlanta, battle of (1964)
Howard, Oliver Otis **7** 528-529
Johnston, Joseph Eggleston **8** 323

Sherman, William Tecumseh
14 186-187
Thomas, George Henry **15** 190-191

Atlanta Braves (baseball team)
Aaron, Henry Louis (Hank) **1** 2-3

Atlanta Compromise (speech)
Washington, Booker Taliaferro
16 125-126

Atlanta Constitution (newspaper)
Grady, Henry Woodfin **6** 482-483
Harris, Joel Chandler **7** 173-174
McGill, Ralph Emerson **10** 411-412

Atlanta, Georgia
Jackson, Maynard Holbrook Jr.
8 176-178
Woodruff, Robert W. **16** 372-374
Young, Andrew Jackson Jr. **16** 467-469

Atlanta Journal (newspaper)
Caldwell, Erskine **3** 223-224
Mitchell, Margaret **11** 59-60

Atlanta School of Social Work
Frazier, Edward Franklin **6** 77

Atlanta University
Du Bois, William Edward Burghardt
5 116-118
Hope, John **7** 489-490

Atlantic cable (communications)
Cooper, Peter **4** 223-224
Maury, Matthew Fontaine **10** 351-352
Whitman, Walt **16** 249-251

Atlantic Migration, The (book; Hansen)
Schlesinger, Arthur Meier **14** 13

Atlantic Monthly (magazine; estabished 1857)
contributors
Alcott, Louisa May **1** 122
Harte, Francis Brett **7** 184-185
Higginson, Thomas Wentworth
7 380
Holmes, Oliver Wendell **7** 457-458
Howells, William Dean **7** 539-541
James, Henry **8** 211-212
Jewett, Sarah Orne **8** 256
Lampman, Archibald **9** 180-181
Lloyd, Henry Demarest **9** 468-469
Twain, Mark **15** 363-366
Wilder, Thornton Niven **16** 276-277
editors
Howells, William Dean **7** 539-541
Lowell, James Russell **10** 14-15
Page, Walter Hines **12** 60-61

Atlantida (musical composition)
Falla, Manuel de **5** 372-373

Atlantis (mythologic island)
Donnelly, Ignatius **5** 62
Mendaña de Neyra, Álvaro de **10** 483

Atlantis (novel)
Hauptmann, Gerhart Johann Robert
7 199-201

Atlas Enclipticalis (musical composition)
Cage, John **3** 211-214

Atman (Hinduism)
Buddha **3** 97-101
Shankara **14** 150-151

Atmosphere (physics)
Chapman, Sydney **3** 441
Dalton, John **4** 378-379
Guericke, Otto Von **7** 27-28
Rayleigh, 3d Baron **13** 62
Watson-Watt, Robert Alexander **16** 140-141
Wilson, Charles Thomson Rees **16** 317-318

Atmosphere (sculpture)
Nevelson, Louise **11** 356-357

Atom (physics)
atomic clocks
Ramsey, Norman Foster Jr. **13** 25-27
atomic pile
Fermi, Enrico **5** 422-424
atomic weights
Avogadro, Lorenzo Romano Amedeo Carlo **1** 388-389
Berzelius, Jöns Jacob **2** 231-233
Dalton, John **4** 378-379
Dumas, Jean Baptiste André **5** 138-139
Richards, Theodore William **13** 137-138
Brownian motion
Einstein, Albert **5** 228-231
Perrin, Jean Baptiste **12** 233-236
decay
Lee, Tsung-Dao **9** 299-300
fission
Bohr, Niels Henrik David **2** 366-368
Joliot-Curie, Jean Frédéric **8** 327-328
Meitner, Lise **10** 463-466
Thomson, George Paget **15** 198-199
see also Atomic bomb
hydrogen welding
Langmuir, Irving **9** 196-197
isotopes
Urey, Harold Clayton **15** 394-396
K-mesons
Lee, Tsung-Dao **9** 299-300
quantum mechanics
Born, Max **2** 420-421
Dirac, Paul Adrien Maurice **5** 23-24
Heisenberg, Werner Karl **7** 261-263
Schrödinger, Erwin **14** 31-33
see also Quantum theory
radioactivity
Bothe, Walther **2** 438-439
Chadwick, James **3** 405-406
Fermi, Enrico **5** 422-424
Kapitsa, Pyotr Leonidovich **8** 433-435
Rutherford, Ernest **13** 384-387
Soddy, Frederick **14** 321-323
see also Radioactivity
structure
Bohr, Niels Henrik David **2** 366-368
Fermi, Enrico **5** 422-424
Herzberg, Gerhard **7** 349-350

Pauli, Wolfgang Ernst **12** 149
Perrin, Jean Baptiste **12** 233-236
Rutherford, Ernest **13** 384-387
Stern, Otto **14** 435
Thomson, Joseph John **15** 200-201
von Laue, Max **16** 23-24
Walton, Ernest **16** 88-90
Wigner, Eugene Paul **16** 268-269

Atom and Organism (book)
Elsasser, Walter Maurice **5** 277-278

Atomic bomb (weapon)
development
Bethe, Hans Albrecht **2** 238-239
Bush, Vannevar **3** 169-171
Bohr, Niels Henrik David **2** 366-368
Chadwick, James **3** 405-406
Cockcroft, John Douglas **4** 131-132
Compton, Arthur Holly **4** 186-188
Conant, James Bryant **4** 192-193
Fermi, Enrico **5** 422-424
Feynman, Richard Phillips **5** 432-434
Franck, James **6** 49-52
Frisch, Otto Robert **6** 119-120
Goeppert-Mayer, Maria **6** 385-387
Groves, Leslie **7** 21-22
Lawrence, Ernest Orlando **9** 248-250
Oppenheimer, J. Robert **11** 525-526
Quimby, Edith H. **12** 513-514
Sakharov, Andrei **13** 439-441
Stimson, Henry Lewis **14** 457-458
Szilard, Leo **15** 64-66
Teller, Edward **15** 139-141
Wigner, Eugene Paul **16** 268-269
principle
Einstein, Albert **5** 228-231
use
Hirohito **7** 410-412
Truman, Harry S. **15** 314-316

Atomic Energy Commission (India)
Bhabha, Homi Jehangir **2** 253-254

Atomic Energy Commission (United States)
Conant, James Bryant **4** 192-193
Lawrence, Ernest Orlando **9** 248-250
Libby, Willard Frank **9** 397-398
Lilienthal, David Eli **9** 410-411
Rabi, Isidor Isaac **12** 526-527
Ray, Dixy Lee **13** 56-57
Rickover, Hyman George **13** 155-157
Schlesinger, James Rodney **14** 15-16
Seaborg, Glenn Theodore **14** 74-76
Von Neumann, John **16** 27-28

Atomic energy, peaceful use of
see United Nations—atomic energy

Atomic physics
see Atom; Nuclear physics; Quantum theory

Atomic Quest (book)
Compton, Arthur Holly **4** 186-188

Atomic Theory, The (book)
Born, Max **2** 420-421

Atomism (philosophy)
Bradley, Francis Herbert **2** 481-482
Democritus **4** 493-494
Durkheim, Émile **5** 162-163
Epicurus **5** 292-294
Isidore of Seville **8** 149-150
Lucretius **10** 26-27

Atoms, Molecules, and Quanta (book)
Urey, Harold Clayton **15** 394-396

Atonality (music)
Berg, Alban **2** 186-187
Ives, Charles Edward **8** 159-160
Krenek, Ernst **9** 98-99
Schoenberg, Arnold **14** 24-26
Sibelius, Jean Julius Christian **14** 211-212

Atonement (religion)
Anselm of Canterbury **1** 244-245
Bushnell, Horace **3** 171-172

Atossa (6th century B.C.), Persian queen
Aeschylus **1** 70-72
Xerxes **16** 420

Atoxyl (chemistry)
Ehrlich, Paul **5** 225-226

ATP
see Adenosine triphosphate

ATPase
see Adenosine triphosphatase

Atriden tetralogy (verse dramas)
Hauptmann, Gerhart Johann Robert **7** 199-201

Atropine (chemistry)
Loewi, Otto **9** 486-487

Atta Troll (mock epic)
Heine, Heinrich **7** 259-260

Attaché, The (book)
Haliburton, Thomas Chandler **7** 80

Attack of Nerves, An (story)
Chekhov, Anton Pavlovich **3** 494-497

Attainder, Act of (1779)
Butler, John **3** 180

Attalus, Flavius Priscus (died after 416), Roman emperor 409-410
Alaric **1** 101-102

ATTAR, FARID ED-DIN (circa 1140-circa 1234), Persian poet **1** 359-360
Rumi, Jalai ed-Din **13** 362-363

Attaway, William (1912-1986), African American novelist
Lawrence, Jacob **9** 250-251

Attenzione, L' (novel)
Moravia, Alberto **11** 153-155

Atterbury, Francis (1662-1732), English bishop
Pope, Alexander **12** 395-397

Attic Bee
see Sophocles

Attica (ancient state, Greece)
Cleomenes I **4** 103

Atticus (literary character)
Pope, Alexander **12** 395-397

Atticus, Titus Pomponius (109-32 B.C.),
Roman literary patron
Cicero, Marcus Tullius **4** 55-58

ATTILA (died 453), Hun chieftain **1** 360
Gaiseric **6** 172
Leo I **9** 329-330
Odoacer **11** 473

Attila (opera)
Verdi, Giuseppe Fortunino Francesco
15 463-465

Attila Hemicycle (painting)
Delacroix, Ferdinand Victor Eugène
4 469-471

Attis poem (literature)
Catullus, Gaius Valerius **3** 377-378

ATTLEE, CLEMENT RICHARD (1st Earl
Attlee; 1883-1967), English statesman,
prime minister 1945-1951 **1** 361-362
Aung San **1** 374-375
Clapham, John Harold **4** 71

Attorneys
see Jurists—lawyers

Attorneys general
see statesmen, American

ATWOOD, MARGARET ELEANOR (born
1939), Canadian novelist, poet, critic,
and politically committed cultural activist
1 362-364

Au dessus de la melée (essays)
Rolland, Romain **13** 260

Au fil des jours (book)
Clemenceau, Georges **4** 99-101

Au Maroc (book)
Loti, Pierre **9** 519-520

Au pied de Sinai (book)
Clemenceau, Georges **4** 99-101

Au service de la France (memoirs)
Poincaré, Raymond **12** 366-368

Au Service de l'Allemagne (novel)
Barrès, Auguste Maurice **2** 20-21

Au soir de la pensée (book)
Clemenceau, Georges **4** 99-101

Aubert, Étienne
see Innocent VI

AUBERT DE GASPÉ, PHILIPPE
(1786-1871), French-Canadian author
1 364

Aubigné, Agrippa d' (1552-1630), French
author
Hugo, Victor Marie **8** 22-25

Auburn Prison (New York State)
Osborne, Thomas Mott **12** 17-18

Auburn Theological Seminary (New York
State)
Bennett, John Coleman **2** 170-171

Auchinleck, Sir Claude John Eyre
(born 1884), British field marshal

Wavell, Archibald Percival
16 147-148

Auckland (city, New Zealand)
Hobson, William **7** 426

Auckland General Labourers Union (New
Zealand)
Fraser, Peter **6** 73-74

AUDEN, WYSTAN HUGH (1907-1973),
English-born American poet **1** 364-366
Berio, Luciano **2** 194-195
Eliot, Thomas Stearns **5** 258-261
Henze, Hans Werner **7** 314
Lewis, Cecil Day **9** 380
MacNeice, Louis **10** 113-114
Spender, Stephen Harold **14** 370-371
Stravinsky, Igor Fedorovich **14** 502-506

Audenarde, battle of (1745)
Saxe, Comte de **13** 507-508

Audiencia (court)
Zumárraga, Juan de **16** 531-532

Audition colorée (synesthesia)
Rimbaud, Jean Nicolas Arthur
13 172-174

Auditorium Building (Chicago)
Sullivan, Louis Henri **15** 27-28

Audran, Claude III (1658-1734), French
painter
Watteau, Antoine **16** 143-144

AUDUBON, JOHN JAMES (1785-1851),
American artist and ornithologist
1 366-367
Lear, Edward **9** 265-266
Wilson, Alexander **16** 313-314

Auerstädt, battle of (1806)
Napoleon I **11** 306-310

Auf dem See (poems)
Goethe, Johann Wolfgang von
6 388-391

Auf dem Staatshof (novella)
Storm, Theodor **14** 479-480

Auf den Marmorklippen (novel)
Jünger, Ernst **8** 391-392

Aufhaltsame Aufstieg des Arturo Ui, Der
(play)
Brecht, Bertolt **2** 512-514

Aufidius, Bassus (flourished 1st century),
Roman historian
Pliny the Elder **12** 355-356

Aufwecker der teutschen Nation (book)
Hutten, Ulrich von **8** 72-73

**Aufzeichnungen des Malte Laurids Brigge,
Die** (novel)
Rilke, Rainer Maria **13** 171-172

Augier, Émile (1820-1889), French dramatist and poet
Daudet, Alphonse **4** 402-403

Augsburg, League of (1686)
Frederick William **6** 85-86
see also Augsburg, War of the League of

Augsburg, Treaty of (1555)
Charles V **3** 457-459
Ferdinand I **5** 414-415
Paul IV **12** 145-146

Augsburg, War of the League of
(1688-1697)
Louis XIV **9** 531-533
Orléans, Philippe II D' **11** 530-531
Victor Amadeus II **15** 482-483
William III **16** 295-296
see also King William's War for Ameri-
can phase

Augsburg Confession (1530)
Charles V **3** 457-459
Luther, Martin **10** 48-51
Melanchthon, Philip **10** 466-467

Augsburg Interim (1548)
Charles V **3** 457-459

August (novel)
Hamsun, Knut **7** 113-114

Augusta (1811-1890), empress of Germany
Laforgue, Jules **9** 160-161
William I **16** 292-293

Augusta Triumphans (book)
Defoe, Daniel **4** 457-459

Auguste (literary character)
Corneille, Pierre **4** 234-236

Augustenburg, Christian Augustus, Duke of
(1798-1869), claimant to duchy of Hol-
stein
Bismarck, Otto Eduard Leopold von
2 294-296

AUGUSTINE OF CANTERBURY, ST. (died
circa 606), Roman monk, archbishop of
Canterbury **1** 370-371
Bede **2** 109-110
Gregory I **6** 531-532

Augustine of Hippo
see Augustine, St.

AUGUSTINE, ST. (354-430), Christian
philosopher and theologian **1** 367-370
baptized
Ambrose **1** 192-193
biblical criticism
Jerome **8** 249
City of God
Charonton, Enguerrand **3** 471
Otto of Freising **12** 30
concept of mind
Bonaventure **2** 383-384
Malebranche, Nicolas **10** 166-167
editions
Erasmus, Desiderius **5** 298-300
God defined
Anselm of Canterbury **1** 244-245
heresy opposed
Donatus **5** 56-57
Pelagius **12** 189-190
influence of
Dominic **5** 51-52
Jansen, Cornelis **8** 220-221
Karlstadt, Andreas Bodenheim von
8 449

Lombard, Peter **9** 490-491
Machiavelli, Niccolò **10** 97-99
Petrarch **12** 259-261
influenced by
Paul **12** 141-143
Plato **12** 345-347
musical settings
Dallapiccola, Luigi **4** 377-378
quoted
Donatus **5** 56-57
Mies van der Rohe, Ludwig
11 10-12
translations
Alfred **1** 151-153
see also Augustinianism

Augustinian Canons (religious congregation)
Arnold of Brescia **1** 314-315
David I **4** 407
Ruysbroeck, Jan van **13** 388-389

Augustinian Friars (religious order)
Coverdale, Miles **4** 278
Luther, Martin **10** 48-51
Mendel, Johann Gregor **10** 483-486

Augustinianism (philosophy)
Lull, Raymond **10** 39-40
Thomas Aquinas **15** 183-186
see also Augustine, St.

Augustinians, church of the
(Antwerp)
Rubens, Peter Paul **13** 339-342

Augustinus (book)
Jansen, Cornelis **8** 220-221

Augustulus, Romulus
see Romulus Augustulus

AUGUSTUS (Octavian; 63 B.C.-A.D. 14),
Roman emperor 27 B.C.-A.D. 14
1 371-373
and literature
Horace **7** 500-503
Livy **9** 465-467
Ovid **12** 34-36
Virgil **15** 507-510
consorts
Livia **9** 457-460
Egypt and Judea
Cleopatra **4** 105-106
Herod the Great **7** 333-334
republic falls
Cato, the Younger **3** 374-375
Cicero, Marcus Tullius **4** 55-58
Strabo **14** 485-486
successor of
Tiberius Julius Caesar Augustus
15 217-218
Triumvirate
Antony, Mark **1** 253-254
Brutus, Marcus Junius **3** 79-80

Augustus, Forum of (Rome)
Augustus **1** 371-373

AUGUSTUS II (1670-1733), king of Poland
and elector of Saxony **1** 373-374
Charles XII **3** 464-466

Saxe, Comte de **13** 507-508

Augustus II (1696-1763), king of Poland
and elector of Saxony
Anna Ivanovna **1** 240-241

Augustus, Forum of (Rome)
Augustus **1** 371-373

Augustus the Strong
see Augustus II

**AULARD, ALPHONSE FRANÇOIS VICTOR
ALPHONSE** (1849-1928), French historian **1** 374
Mathiez, Albert **10** 333-334
Salvemini, Gaetano **13** 455-456

Auld Farmer's Salutation to His Mare
(poem)
Burns, Robert **3** 155-156

Auld Lang Syne (song)
Burns, Robert **3** 155-156

Auld Licht Idylls (folktales)
Barrie, James Matthew **2** 21-22

Aulnay, Seigneur d'
see Charnisay

Aulularia (play)
Plautus **12** 348-350

AUNG SAN (1915-1947), Burmese politician **1** 374-375
Ba Maw **1** 480-481
Ne Win **11** 364-365
Nu, U **11** 439-441
Thant, U **15** 161-162

AUNG SAN SUU KYI (born 1945), leader
of movement toward democracy in
Burma (Myanmar) and Nobel Peace Prize
winner **1** 375-376

Aung Zeya
see Alaungpaya

Aunt Rhody (song)
Thomson, Virgil **15** 202-203

Aunt's Story, The (novel)
White, Patrick Victor Martindale
16 233-235

Aura (novel)
Fuentes, Carlos **6** 141-142

AURANGZEB (1618-1707), Mogul emperor of India 1658-1707 **1** 377
Shah Jahan **14** 138-139
Śivajī **14** 266-267

Aurélia (autobiography)
Nerval, Gérard de **11** 345-346

Aurelia the Vestal (opera)
Fry, William Henry **6** 136-137

Aurelian (Roman emperor)
Zenobia **16** 500-503

Aurelius, St. (died circa 340), bishop of
Carthage
Pelagius **12** 189-190

Aureng-Zebe (play)
Dryden, John **5** 106-107

Auric, Georges (1899-1983), French composer
Honegger, Arthur **7** 472-473

Aurignacian (geologic era)
Breuil, Henri Edouard Prosper
2 521-522

Auriol, Vincent (1884-1966), French president 1947-1954
John, XXIII **8** 277-280

Aurora (book)
Boehme, Jacob **2** 357

Aurora (fresco)
Reni, Guido **13** 97-98

Aurora (journal)
Duane, William **5** 109

Aurora (ship)
Shackleton, Ernest Henry **14** 132-133

Aurora Leigh (poem)
Browning, Elizabeth Barrett **3** 52-53

Aurora roja (novel)
Baroja y Nessi, Pío **2** 15-16

Auroras of Autumn (poems)
Stevens, Wallace **14** 443-445

Aus Italien (musical composition)
Strauss, Richard **14** 500-501

**Aus meinem Leben, Dichtung und
Wahrheit** (autobiography)
Goethe, Johann Wolfgang von
6 388-391

Ausculta fili (papal bull)
Boniface VIII **2** 392-393

Ausgefragt (poems)
Grass, Günter **6** 496-497

Ausgerechnet und verspielt (television
opera)
Krenek, Ernst **9** 98-99

Ausgleich
see Austro-Hungarian Compromise
(1867)

Ausnahme und die Regel, Die (play)
Brecht, Bertolt **2** 512-514

Ausonius, Decimus Magnus (flourished 4th
century), Roman poet
Juvenal **8** 397-399

AUSTEN, JANE (1775-1817), English novelist **1** 377-379
Cooper, James Fenimore **4** 220-223

Austen Riggs Center (Stockbridge, Massachusetts)
Erikson, Erik Homburger **5** 309-310

Austerlitz, battle of (1805)
Alexander I **1** 130-132
Bernadotte, Jean Baptiste **2** 205-206
Kutuzov, Mikhail Ilarionovich
9 137-138
Napoleon I **11** 306-310
Pitt, William the Younger **12** 329-331

Austin, John (1790-1859), English jurist
Mill, John Stuart **11** 21-23

AUSTIN, JOHN LANGSHAW (1911-1960),
English philosopher **1** 379-380

Austin, Moses (1761-1821), American pioneer
Austin, Stephen Fuller **1** 380-381

AUSTIN, STEPHEN FULLER (1793-1836),
American pioneer **1** 380-381
Borden, Gail **2** 409
Houston, Samuel **7** 526-527

Australia, Commonwealth of (island continent)
Bruce of Melbourne, 1st Viscount
3 61-62
Fisher, Andrew **5** 462
Grey, George **6** 540-541
Commonwealth created
Barton, Edmund **2** 39-40
Deakin, Alfred **4** 432-433
Griffith, Samuel Walker **6** 545-546
Victoria **15** 485-487
constitutional crisis
Lang, John Thomas **9** 192-193
convict reforms
Bigge, John Thomas **2** 272
Parkes, Henry **12** 113
cultural definition
Murray, Leslie Allan **11** 262-263
economic development
Coombs, Herbert Cole **4** 219-220
Forrest, John **6** 12-13
Hawke, Robert James Lee **7** 205-206
Keating, Paul John **8** 469-470
Kidman, Sidney **8** 542-544
Lewis, Essington **9** 382-384
Menzies, Robert Gordon
10 510-511
Monash, John **11** 95-96
Parbo, Arvi **12** 93-94
education system
MacKillop, Mary **10** 106-107
emancipists
Macquarie, Lachlan **10** 115-116
Phillip, Arthur **12** 279-280
Wentworth, William Charles
16 203-204
exploration
Burke, Robert O'Hara **3** 142-143
Tasman, Abel Janszoon **15** 113-114
see also Explorers, Australian;
Explorers, English—of Australia
foreign policy
Evatt, Herbert Vere **5** 341-343
gold rush (1851)
Hargraves, Edward Hammond
7 153-154
Great Depression
Lyons, Joseph Aloysius **10** 69-70
Scullin, James Henry **14** 73
inland medical services
Flynn, John **5** 497-498
Rum Rebellion (1808)
Bligh, William **2** 325-326
Macarthur, John **10** 78
social reforms
Namatjira, Albert **11** 300-301

Whitlam, Edward Gough
16 244-245
sports
Bradman, Donald George
2 485-486
systematic colonization
Wakefield, Edward Gibbon
16 48-49
turn toward conservatism (1970s)
Bjelke-Petersen, Johannes
2 297-299
Fraser, Malcolm **6** 71-73
World Wars
Curtin, John Joseph **4** 348-349
Hughes, William Morris **8** 21-22
see also Australian art; Australian literature
see also World War I; World War II

Australia Felix (novel)
Richardson, Henry Handel **13** 139

Australia Felix (painting)
Streeton, Arthur Ernest **14** 507-508

Australian (newspaper)
Wentworth, William Charles
16 203-204

Australian Agricultural Co. (1824)
Macarthur, John **10** 78

Australian art
Dobell, William **5** 34-35
Drysdale, George Russell **5** 107-109
Namatjira, Albert **11** 300-301
Nolan, Sidney Robert **11** 418
Rees, Lloyd Frederic **13** 78-79
Streeton, Arthur Ernest **14** 507-508

Australian Colonies Act (1850)
Russell, John **13** 380-381

Australian Federated Union of Locomotive Enginemen
Chifley, Joseph Benedict **3** 518

Australian Labor Leader (biography)
Evatt, Herbert Vere **5** 341-343

Australian literature
Carey, Peter **3** 295-297
Clarke, Marcus Andrew Hislop **4** 87-88
Franklin, Stella Maraia Sarah Miles
6 68-69
Furphy, Joseph **6** 152-153
Handke, Peter **7** 119-121
Lawson, Henry **9** 254-255
Lind, Jakov **9** 419-420
Murray, Leslie Allan **11** 262-263
Richardson, Henry Handel **13** 139
White, Patrick Victor Martindale
16 233-235
see also Journalism, Australian

Australian National University (Canberra;
established 1946)
Bruce of Melbourne, 1st Viscount
3 61-62
Florey, Howard Walter **5** 491-492

Australian Workers Union
Scullin, James Henry **14** 73

Australasia (region, Gaul)
Martel, Charles **10** 285

Austria, Republic of (nation, Central
Europe)
Allied occupation (World War II)
Clark, Mark Wayne **4** 80-81
Kreisky, Bruno **9** 97-98
Renner, Karl **13** 98-99
Waldheim, Kurt **16** 54-55
anti-Semitism in
Harand, Irene **7** 139-145
Austrian Netherlands
Frederick II **6** 81-84
Joseph II **8** 359-360
Lafayette, Marquis de **9** 151-152
Leopold II **9** 346
Talleyrand, Charles Maurice de
15 89-90
see also Belgium
Austro-Hungarian Compromise (1867)
Andrássy, Julius **1** 222-223
Deák, Francis **4** 431-432
Francis Joseph **6** 45-46
Austro-Slavism urged
Palacký, František **12** 69-70
Congress of Vienna
see Vienna, Congress of
defeated (World War I)
Badoglio, Pietro **1** 428-429
Renner, Karl **13** 98-99
French Revolutionary Wars
Lafayette, Marquis de **9** 151-152
Louis XVI **9** 534-535
Marie Antoinette **10** 258-259
German Confederation
Metternich, Klemens von
10 533-536
William I **16** 292-293
Germans annex (1938)
Chamberlain, Arthur Neville
3 409-411
Harand, Irene **7** 139-145
Hitler, Adolf **7** 417-420
Horthy de Nagybánya, Nicholas
7 510-512
Schuschnigg, Kurt von **14** 45-46
Holy Alliance (1815-1848)
Metternich, Klemens von
10 533-536
Holy League (1684)
John III **8** 276-277
Italian independence wars
Cavour, Conte di **3** 385-386
Charles Albert, King of Sardinia
3 466
Ferdinand II **5** 415-416
Garibaldi, Giuseppe **6** 215-217
Victor Emmanuel II **15** 483-484
League of Augsburg
Frederick William **6** 85-86
Napoleonic Wars
Bernadotte, Jean Baptiste **2** 205-206
Napoleon I **11** 306-310
Poland partitioned
Catherine the Great **3** 370-372
Francis II **6** 43-44

Polish Succession war
    Eugene of Savoy **5** 330-331
Potato War (1778-1779)
    Joseph II **8** 359-360
Pragmatic Sanction
    Maria Theresa **10** 256-258
republic
    Renner, Karl **13** 98-99
Seven Years War (1756-1763)
    Frederick II **6** 81-84
    Maria Theresa **10** 256-258
Soviets evacuate
    Eisenhower, Dwight David
    5 233-236
Spanish Succession war
    Charles II **3** 454
    Eugene of Savoy **5** 330-331
    Louis XIV **9** 531-533
Thirty Years War
    see Thirty Years War
Treaty of Pillnitz (1792)
    Leopold II **9** 346
Turks besiege Vienna
    Charles V **3** 457-459
    Eugene of Savoy **5** 330-331
    Suleiman I **15** 20-21
    see also Austria-Hungary; Austrian
    art; Austrian literature; Austrian
    music; Austrian Succession, War
    of the; Austro-Prussian War

Austria-Hungary (former kingdom, Central
Europe)
    created
        Andrássy, Julius **1** 222-223
        Deák, Francis **4** 431-432
        Kossuth, Louis **9** 88-90
    Dual Aliance (1879)
        Andrássy, Julius **1** 222-223
        Bismarck, Otto Eduard Leopold von
        2 294-296
    fall (1918)
        Berchtold, Leopold von **2** 183-184
        Ferdinand **5** 413-414
        Horthy de Nagybánya, Nicholas
        7 510-512
        Masaryk, Tomáš Garrigue
        10 314-315
        Renner, Karl **13** 98-99
    German "blank check"
        Bethmann Hollweg, Theobald von
        2 239-240
    nationality issue
        Francis Ferdinand **6** 44
        Francis Joseph **6** 45-46
    Triple Alliance (1882)
        Bismarck, Otto Eduard Leopold von
        2 294-296
        Crispi, Francesco **4** 310-311

Austrian architecture
    Hoffmann, Josef **7** 440-441
    Loos, Adolf **9** 502-503
    Olbrich, Joseph Maria **11** 494-495
    Wagner, Otto **16** 39-40

Austrian art
    Donner, Georg Raphael **5** 63

Hundertwasser, Friedensreich **8** 36-37
Klimt, Gustav **9** 53-55
Kokoschka, Oskar **9** 75-76
Maulbertsch, Franz Anton **10** 345
Schiele, Egon **14** 1-2
Troger, Paul **15** 300
see also Baroque architecture; Baroque
    painting (German and Austrian)

Austrian Federal Railways
    Dollfuss, Engelbert **5** 47

Austrian literature
    Grillparzer, Franz **6** 546-547
    Hofmannsthal, Hugo von **7** 443-444
    Musil, Robert Edler Von **11** 268-269
    Schnitzler, Arthur **14** 23-24
    Werfel, Franz **16** 204-205
    see also Authors, Austrian; German lit-
    erature

Austrian music
    avant-garde
        Ligeti, György **9** 406-407
    classicism
        Haydn, Franz Joseph **7** 219-221
        Mozart, Wolfgang Amadeus
        11 218-221
    contrapuntal theory
        Bruckner, Joseph Anton **3** 64-65
        Fux, Johann Joseph **6** 155-156
    opera
        Gluck, Christoph Willibald
        6 372-374
        Mahler, Gustav **10** 144-145
        Mozart, Wolfgang Amadeus
        11 218-221
        Strauss, Johann Jr. **14** 498-499
    romanticism
        Mahler, Gustav **10** 144-145
        Schoenberg, Arnold **14** 24-26
    songs
        Hofhaimer, Paul **7** 441
    twelve-tone method
        Krenek, Ernst **9** 98-99
        Schoenberg, Arnold **14** 24-26
        Webern, Anton **16** 160-162
    waltzes
        Strauss, Johann Jr. **14** 498-499

Austrian People's Party (established 1930)
    Harand, Irene **7** 139-145

Austrian school (economics)
    Böhm-Bawerk, Eugen von **2** 366
    von Mises, Ludwig **16** 25

Austrian Succession, War of the
(1740-1748)
    American phase
        see King George's War
    British forces
        Amherst, Jeffery **1** 200-201
        Clive, Robert **4** 119-120
        Dupleix **5** 153
        Forbes, John **5** 507-508
    causes and issues
        Frederick II **6** 81-84
        Joseph II **8** 359-360
        Maria Theresa **10** 256-258

French forces
    Montcalm de Saint-Véran, Marquis
    de **11** 122-123
    Rochambeau, Comte de **13** 220-221

Austro-Hungarian Compromise (1867)
    see Austria

Austro-Prussian War (1866)
    Bismarck, Otto Eduard Leopold von
    2 294-296
    Moltke, Helmuth Karl Bernard von
    11 90-91
    Napoleon III **11** 310-312
    Victoria **15** 485-487

Auswahl aus des Teufels Papieren (satires)
    Richter, Johann Paul Friedrich
    13 150-151

Autels de la peur, Les (poem)
    Chénier, André Marie **3** 500-501

Author to Her Book, The (poem)
    Bradstreet, Anne Dudley **2** 486-487

Authors, African
    see African Literature, modern; Authors,
    Cameroonian; Authors, Nigerian, etc.

Authors, American
    advice
        Brown, Helen Gurley **3** 36-37
    advice books
        Brothers, Joyce **3** 26-28
    architecture
        Eisenman, Peter D. **5** 239-240
    art
        Judd, Donald **8** 376-377
    art critics (20th century)
        Greenberg, Clement **6** 521-523
        Kirstein, Lincoln **9** 39-41
    autobiographical fiction
        Angelou, Maya **1** 238-239
        Kerouac, Jean-Louis Lebris de
        8 518-519
    autobiographies
        Chamberlain, Wilt **3** 413-415
        Cobb, Tyrus Raymond **4** 124-126
        Davis, Angela **4** 412-413
        de Mille, Agnes **4** 486-488
        Dunham, Katherine **5** 145-146
        Eastman, Charles A. **5** 183-185
        Evers-Williams, Myrlie **5** 348-350
        Fischer, Bobby **5** 454-456
        Hall, Donald **7** 84-85
        Hearst, Patricia **7** 242-243
        Lindbergh, Anne Morrow **9** 420-421
        Mays, Benjamin E. **10** 374-376
        Means, Russell **10** 441-444
        Robinson, Harriet Hanson
        13 203-207
        Ryan, Nolan **13** 389-391
    biographers (19th century)
        Adams, Henry Brooks **1** 45-47
        Alger, Horatio **1** 153-154
        Ford, Paul Leicester **6** 9-10
        Irving, Washington **8** 141-143
        Peabody, Elizabeth Palmer
        12 167-168
        Weems, Mason Locke **16** 170

biographers (19th-20th century)
  Harris, Frank **7** 172-173
  Masters, Edgar Lee **10** 326-327
biographers (20th century)
  Baker, Ray Stannard **1** 451-452
  Chandler, Alfred Du Pont Jr.
    3 422-423
  Clapp, Margaret Antoinette **4** 71-72
  Croly, Herbert David **4** 316-317
  de Mille, Agnes **4** 486-488
  Eiseley, Loren Corey **5** 232-233
  Forman, James **6** 10-11
  Morison, Samuel Eliot **11** 175-176
  Nevins, Allan **11** 357-359
  Sandburg, Carl **13** 461-462
  Tate, Allen **15** 116
  Terkel, Louis **15** 152-153
children's books
  Baum, L. Frank **2** 73-74
columnists
  Brothers, Joyce **3** 26-28
  Rogers, Will **13** 251-252
  Rowan, Carl T. **13** 329-330
  Royko, Mike **13** 337-339
  Safire, William **13** 422-424
  Steinem, Gloria **14** 418-419
  vos Savant, Marilyn **16** 32-33
  Will, George Frederick **16** 286-287
commentators
  Buchanan, Patrick Joseph **3** 90-91
  Goodman, Ellen Holtz **6** 438-439
  Marty, Martin E. **10** 300-301
  Rogers, Will **13** 251-252
  Thompson, Hunter Stockton
    15 196-198
comparative mythology
  Campbell, Joseph **3** 253-255
cookbooks
  Child, Julia McWilliams **3** 519-520
critics (19th century)
  Brown, Charles Brockden **3** 33
  Norris, Benjamin Franklin Jr.
    11 427-428
  Poe, Edgar Allan **12** 363-365
critics (20th century)
  Aiken, Conrad **1** 90-91
  Allen, Paula Gunn **1** 165-167
  Burke, Kenneth **3** 141-142
  Eliot, Thomas Stearns **5** 258-261
  Farrell, James Thomas **5** 390-391
  Jarrell, Randall **8** 222-223
  Lowell, Amy **10** 13
  Macdonald, Dwight **10** 81-83
  McCarthy, Mary T. **10** 389-391
  Nathan, George Jean **11** 319-321
  Nin, Anais **11** 397-398
  Pound, Ezra Loomis **12** 415-417
  Ransom, John Crowe **13** 39-40
  Rich, Adrienne **13** 128-130
  Richards, Ivor Armstrong **13** 137
  Tate, Allen **15** 116
  White, E. B. **16** 228-230
  Wilder, Amos Niven **16** 273-274
  Wilson, Edmund **16** 318-319
  Young, Stark **16** 474-475

diarists
  Byrd, William II **3** 189-190
  Chesnut, Mary Boykin **3** 506-508
  Lindbergh, Anne Morrow **9** 420-421
  Nin, Anais **11** 397-398
  Rorem, Ned **13** 284-286
  Sewall, Samuel **14** 123-124
essayists (18th century)
  Ames, Fisher **1** 199-200
  Leonard, Daniel **9** 336-337
essayists (19th century)
  Adams, Henry Brooks **1** 45-47
  Alcott, Amos Bronson **1** 121
  Burroughs, John **3** 160-161
  Emerson, Ralph Waldo **5** 278-280
  Holmes, Oliver Wendell **7** 457-458
  Irving, Washington **8** 141-143
  Peabody, Elizabeth Palmer
    12 167-168
essayists (19th-20th century)
  Beecher, Catharine **2** 110-112
  Freneau, Philip Morin **6** 99-100
  Gilman, Charlotte Anna Perkins
    6 323-325
  Page, Thomas Nelson **12** 59-60
essayists (20th century)
  Aiken, Conrad **1** 90-91
  Baker, Russell **1** 452-454
  Baker, Ray Stannard **1** 451-452
  Baldwin, James Arthur **1** 465-466
  Bellow, Saul **2** 141-143
  Bourne, Randolph Silliman
    2 456-457
  Brodsky, Joseph **3** 13-15
  Buckley, William F. Jr. **3** 96-97
  Buechner, Frederick **3** 103-105
  Burroughs, William S. **3** 162-163
  Butler, Octavia E. **3** 182-183
  Cabell, James Branch **3** 195-196
  Chopin, Katherine **4** 18-20
  Coles, Robert Martin **4** 156-157
  Cousins, Norman **4** 274-276
  Davis, Ossie **4** 421-422
  Haley, Alex **7** 76-78
  Himmelfarb, Gertrude **7** 396-398
  hooks, bell **7** 477-481
  Howe, Florence Rosenfeld
    7 530-531
  Jones, Robert Edmond **8** 341-342
  Lasch, Christopher **9** 212-214
  Lovecraft, H. P. **10** 3-6
  Macdonald, Dwight **10** 81-83
  Mamet, David Alan **10** 181-182
  McCarthy, Mary T. **10** 389-391
  Oates, Joyce Carol **11** 454-456
  Riesman, David **13** 167-168
  Rorem, Ned **13** 284-286
  Rowan, Carl T. **13** 329-330
  Smithson, Robert **14** 301-303
  Sontag, Susan **14** 342-343
  Steel, Danielle **14** 404-406
  Updike, John **15** 390-392
  Vidal, Eugene Luther Gore
    15 488-490
  Vonnegut, Kurt Jr. **16** 25-27
  Welty, Eudora **16** 199-201

  White, E. B. **16** 228-230
  Wiesel, Elie **16** 263-264
  Wilder, Amos Niven **16** 273-274
  Wright, Richard **16** 401-402
feminist
  Starhawk **14** 403-404
historical novels
  Mattingly, Garrett **10** 342-344
humorists
  Benchley, Robert **2** 150-151
  Golden, Harry **6** 402-403
  Harte, Francis Brett **7** 184-185
  Lardner, Ringgold Wilmer
    9 204-205
  Parker, Dorothy Rothschild **12** 106
  Sholem Aleichem **14** 202-203
  Thurber, James Grove **15** 213-214
  Twain, Mark **15** 363-366
  Ward, Artemus **16** 112-113
Johnson, James Weldon
  Lindsay, Vachel **9** 424-425
  Lowell, Amy **10** 13
  Lowell, Robert Trail Spence Jr.
    10 16-17
  MacLeish, Archibald **10** 109-110
  McKay, Claude **10** 416
  Millay, Edna St. Vincent **11** 24-25
  Moore, Marianne **11** 148-149
  Nabokov, Vladimir **11** 287-288
  Johnson, James Weldon **8** 304-305
  Pound, Ezra Loomis **12** 415-417
  Ransom, John Crowe **13** 39-40
  Reed, John Silas **13** 76-77
  Robinson, Edwin Arlington
    13 201-202
  Roethke, Theodore **13** 243-244
  Sandburg, Carl **13** 461-462
  Stevens, Wallace **14** 443-445
  Tate, Allen **15** 116
  Warren, Robert Penn **16** 121-122
  Williams, William Carlos
    16 308-309
journalists
  see Journalists, American
lexicographers
  Judson, Adoniram **8** 377-378
  Webster, Noah **16** 164-166
librettists
  Hammerstein, Oscar Clendenning II
    7 104-106
nonfiction writers
  Bailey, F. Lee **1** 441-443
  Bailey, Florence Merriam **1** 443-444
  Beard, Mary Ritter **2** 85-86
  Beecher, Catharine **2** 110-112
  Billington, James Hadley **2** 275-276
  Broudy, Harry Samuel **3** 28-29
  Burroughs, William S. **3** 162-163
  Bush, Vannevar **3** 169-171
  Capote, Truman **3** 273-275
  Carson, Rachel Louise **3** 337-338
  Chomsky, Noam Avram **4** 13-15
  Cole, Johnnetta **4** 147-149
  Commoner, Barry **4** 183-185
  Cosby, William Henry Jr. **4** 257-258
  Counts, George S. **4** 267-269

Cousins, Norman **4** 274-276
Crichton, John Michael **4** 308-310
Cubberley, Ellwood Patterson
  4 329-331
Daly, Mary **4** 380-381
Dana, Richard Henry Jr. **4** 385-386
Deloria, Vine Jr. **4** 481-484
Earle, Sylvia A. **5** 180-181
Eastman, Max **5** 187-188
Eiseley, Loren Corey **5** 232-233
Finkelstein, Rabbi Louis **5** 448-450
Fischer, Bobby **5** 454-456
FitzGerald, Frances **5** 469-470
Forman, James **6** 10-11
Franklin, John Hope **6** 65-67
Friedan, Betty **6** 109-111
Gamow, George **6** 199-200
Green, Constance McLaughlin
  6 518-519
Harrington, Michael **7** 167-169
hooks, bell **7** 477-481
Howe, Florence Rosenfeld
  7 530-531
Hyman, Libbie Henrietta **8** 83-84
Karenga, Maulana **8** 444-447
La Flesche, Francis **9** 152-154
Locke, Alain **9** 475-478
Luhan, Mabel Dodge **10** 32-34
Margulis, Lynn **10** 253-254
McNickle, D'Arcy **10** 433
Morgan, Robin **11** 168-170
Palmer, Arnold Daniel **12** 78-80
Proxmire, William **12** 467-468
Ride, Sally **13** 158-160
Rowan, Carl T. **13** 329-330
Rubenstein, Richard L. **13** 343-344
Sagan, Carl E. **13** 424-425
Salisbury, Harrison Evans
  13 449-451
Schlesinger, Arthur Meier Jr.
  14 13-15
Smith, James McCune **14** 293-294
Snow, Edgar **14** 312-313
Thompson, Dorothy **15** 195-196
Winnemucca, Sarah **16** 336-338
novelists (18th-19th century)
  Brackenridge, Hugh Henry
    2 472-473
  Brown, Charles Brockden **3** 33
  Tyler, Royall **15** 371-372
novelists (19th century)
  Alcott, Louisa May **1** 122
  Alger, Horatio **1** 153-154
  Bellamy, Edward **2** 134-135
  Bird, Robert Montgomery **2** 281-282
  Brown, William Wells **3** 48-49
  Cable, George Washington
    3 198-199
  Cahan, Abraham **3** 214
  Child, Lydia Maria Francis
    3 520-521
  Cooper, James Fenimore **4** 220-223
  Crane, Stephen **4** 293-295
  Donnelly, Ignatius **5** 62
  Dunbar, Paul Laurence **5** 141-142
  Eggleston, Edward **5** 223-224

Ford, Paul Leicester **6** 9-10
Hale, Sarah Josepha **7** 74-75
Harris, Joel Chandler **7** 173-174
Harte, Francis Brett **7** 184-185
Hawthorne, Nathaniel **7** 212-215
Hearn, Lafcadio **7** 240
Jackson, Helen Hunt **8** 172
Jewett, Sarah Orne **8** 256
Kennedy, John Pendleton **8** 506-507
Melville, Herman **10** 472-476
Norris, Benjamin Franklin Jr.
  11 427-428
Phillips, David Graham **12** 280-281
Poe, Edgar Allan **12** 363-365
Simms, William Gilmore
  14 235-236
Stowe, Harriet Elizabeth Beecher
  14 484-485
Tourgée, Albion Winegar
  15 277-278
Twain, Mark **15** 363-366
Wallace, Lewis **16** 74-75
novelists (19th-20th century)
  Davis, Richard Harding **4** 422-423
  Gilman, Charlotte Anna Perkins
    6 323-325
  Howe, Edgar Watson **7** 529
  James, Henry **8** 211-212
  Page, Thomas Nelson **12** 59-60
  Sheldon, Charles M. **14** 172-174
  Tarkington, Newton Booth **15** 109
  Wharton, Edith **16** 221
novelists (20th century)
  Agee, James **1** 78-79
  Aiken, Conrad **1** 90-91
  Alexie, Sherman **1** 141-142
  Algren, Nelson **1** 154-155
  Allen, Paula Gunn **1** 165-167
  Alvarez, Julia **1** 185-187
  Anderson, Sherwood **1** 220-221
  Angelou, Maya **1** 238-239
  Asimov, Isaac **1** 338-341
  Baldwin, James Arthur **1** 465-466
  Bambara, Toni Cade **1** 482-483
  Barnes, Djuna **2** 11-13
  Bellow, Saul **2** 141-143
  Blume, Judy **2** 344-345
  Bradbury, Ray **2** 473-474
  Brownmiller, Susan **3** 56-57
  Buck, Pearl Sydenstricker **3** 91-93
  Buckley, William F. Jr. **3** 96-97
  Buechner, Frederick **3** 103-105
  Bukowski, Charles **3** 113-115
  Burroughs, William S. **3** 162-163
  Butler, Octavia E. **3** 182-183
  Cabell, James Branch **3** 195-196
  Cable, George Washington
    3 198-199
  Caldwell, Erskine **3** 223-224
  Capote, Truman **3** 273-275
  Cather, Willa Sibert **3** 368-369
  Chandler, Raymond Jr. **3** 423-425
  Childress, Alice **3** 522-524
  Chopin, Katherine **4** 18-20
  Churchill, Winston **4** 50-51
  Clancy, Tom **4** 70-71

Crichton, John Michael **4** 308-310
Doolittle, Hilda **5** 65-66
Dos Passos, John Roderigo **5** 69-71
Dreiser, Herman Theodore **5** 98-100
Eiseley, Loren Corey **5** 232-233
Ellison, Ralph Waldo **5** 274-275
Farrell, James Thomas **5** 390-391
Faulkner, William **5** 395-397
Feiffer, Jules Ralph **5** 403-404
Ferber, Edna **5** 413
Fitzgerald, Francis Scott Key
  5 470-472
Glasgow, Ellen **6** 360-361
Greeley, Andrew M. **6** 514-515
Grisham, John **7** 6-8
Haley, Alex **7** 76-78
Hammett, Dashiell **7** 106-108
Heller, Joseph **7** 263-265
Hemingway, Ernest Miller
  7 274-277
Hinojosa, Rolando **7** 403-405
Hinton, Susan Eloise **7** 406-407
Hughes, Langston **8** 18-19
Hurston, Zora Neale **8** 55-56
Johnson, James Weldon **8** 304-305
Kerouac, Jean-Louis Lebris de
  8 518-519
King, Stephen **9** 23-25
Lardner, Ringgold Wilmer
  9 204-205
Larsen, Nella **9** 209-210
Lewis, Harry Sinclair **9** 385-387
Lovecraft, H. P. **10** 3-6
Ludlum, Robert **10** 28-29
Mailer, Norman Kingsley
  10 148-150
Malamud, Bernard **10** 162-163
Mamet, David Alan **10** 181-182
Marshall, Paule Burke **10** 281-282
McCarthy, Mary T. **10** 389-391
McKay, Claude **10** 416
McMillan, Terry **10** 427-428
McNickle, D'Arcy **10** 433
Miller, Arthur **11** 25-26
Miller, Henry **11** 26-27
Mitchell, Margaret **11** 59-60
Momaday, N. Scott **11** 92-94
Morrison, Toni **11** 188-190
Nabokov, Vladimir **11** 287-288
Naylor, Gloria **11** 328-329
Nemerov, Howard **11** 338-340
Nin, Anais **11** 397-398
Oates, Joyce Carol **11** 454-456
O'Connor, Flannery **11** 467-468
O'Hara, John **11** 485
Patchen, Kenneth **12** 128-129
Peck, Robert Newton **12** 177-178
Plath, Sylvia **12** 344-345
Porter, Katherine Anne **12** 406-407
Post, Emily Price **12** 409-410
Proulx, E. Annie **12** 463-465
Pynchon, Thomas **12** 496-498
Rice, Anne **13** 125-126
Rice, Elmer **13** 126-127
Richter, Conrad Michael
  13 148-149

Roth, Philip **13** 318-320
Rölvaag, Ole Edvart **13** 265
Salinger, J. D. **13** 447-448
Salisbury, Harrison Evans
    13 449-451
Saroyan, William **13** 486-487
Silko, Leslie **14** 226-227
Sinclair, Upton Beale Jr. **14** 248-249
Singer, Isaac Bashevis **14** 249-250
Smith, Lillian Eugenia **14** 298-299
Steel, Danielle **14** 404-406
Stein, Gertrude **14** 414-415
Steinbeck, John Ernst **14** 416-417
Stone, Robert Anthony **14** 475-476
Styron, William **15** 6-8
Tan, Amy **15** 95-96
Theroux, Paul **15** 179-180
Tyler, Anne **15** 367-368
Updike, John **15** 390-392
Vidal, Eugene Luther Gore
    15 488-490
Vonnegut, Kurt Jr. **16** 25-27
Walker, Alice Malsenior **16** 59-61
Walker, Margaret **16** 67
Warren, Robert Penn **16** 121-122
Welty, Eudora **16** 199-201
West, Nathanael **16** 213-214
White, T. H. **16** 236-237
Wiesel, Elie **16** 263-264
Wilder, Thornton Niven **16** 276-277
Williams, Tennessee **16** 306-308
Wilson, Harriet E. **16** 320-322
Wolfe, Thomas Clayton **16** 355-356
Wolfe, Thomas Kennerly Jr.
    16 356-357
Wright, Richard **16** 401-402
Young, Stark **16** 474-475
pamphleteers
    Grimké, Archibald Henry **7** 1-2
    Paine, Thomas **12** 66-67
playwrights (18th-19th century)
    Belasco, David **2** 124-125
    Tyler, Royall **15** 371-372
playwrights (19th century)
    Bird, Robert Montgomery **2** 281-282
    Brown, William Wells **3** 48-49
    Lazarus, Emma **9** 260-261
    Miller, Joaquin **11** 27-28
    Payne, John Howard **12** 159
    Tarkington, Newton Booth **15** 109
playwrights (20th century)
    Albee, Edward Franklin III
        1 106-108
    Allen, Woody **1** 169-171
    Anderson, Maxwell **1** 219-220
    Angelou, Maya **1** 238-239
    Auden, Wystan Hugh **1** 364-366
    Baldwin, James Arthur **1** 465-466
    Baraka, Imamu Amiri **1** 498-499
    Bellow, Saul **2** 141-143
    Capote, Truman **3** 273-275
    Childress, Alice **3** 522-524
    Cohan, George Michael **4** 137-138
    Colum, Padraic **4** 174-175
    Davis, Ossie **4** 421-422
    Davis, Richard Harding **4** 422-423

Eliot, Thomas Stearns **5** 258-261
Feiffer, Jules Ralph **5** 403-404
Ferber, Edna **5** 413
Flanagan, Hallie **5** 478-479
Hansberry, Lorraine Vivian
    7 130-131
Hecht, Ben **7** 248-250
Heller, Joseph **7** 263-265
Hellman, Lillian Florence **7** 267-268
Isherwood, Christopher **8** 147-149
Kaufman, George S. **8** 457-458
Luce, Clare Boothe **10** 21-23
MacLeish, Archibald **10** 109-110
Mamet, David Alan **10** 181-182
Merrill, James **10** 521-522
Miller, Arthur **11** 25-26
Oates, Joyce Carol **11** 454-456
Odets, Clifford **11** 470-471
O'Neill, Eugene **11** 514-516
Rice, Elmer **13** 126-127
Robinson, Edwin Arlington
    13 201-202
Saroyan, William **13** 486-487
Shaffer, Peter Levin **14** 133-135
Shepard, Sam **14** 180-181
Sherwood, Robert Emmet
    14 189-190
Trudeau, Garretson Beekman
    15 308-309
Valdez, Luis **15** 399-400
Vidal, Eugene Luther Gore
    15 488-490
Vonnegut, Kurt Jr. **16** 25-27
Wilder, Thornton Niven **16** 276-277
Williams, Tennessee **16** 306-308
Wilson, August **16** 314-316
Young, Stark **16** 474-475
poets (17th-18th century)
    Barlow, Joel **2** 6-7
    Bradstreet, Anne Dudley **2** 486-487
    Taylor, Edward **15** 122-123
    Wheatley, Phillis **16** 221-222
    Wigglesworth, Michael **16** 266-267
poets (19th century)
    Alcott, Amos Bronson **1** 121
    Alvarez, Julia **1** 185-187
    Brown, William Wells **3** 48-49
    Bryant, William Cullen **3** 83-85
    Crane, Stephen **4** 293-295
    Dickinson, Emily **4** 541-543
    Dunbar, Paul Laurence **5** 141-142
    Hale, Sarah Josepha **7** 74-75
    Harte, Francis Brett **7** 184-185
    Holmes, Oliver Wendell **7** 457-458
    Key, Francis Scott **8** 525-527
    Lanier, Sidney **9** 199-200
    Lazarus, Emma **9** 260-261
    Longfellow, Henry Wadsworth
        9 499-500
    Lowell, James Russell **10** 14-15
    Miller, Joaquin **11** 27-28
    Poe, Edgar Allan **12** 363-365
    Riley, James Whitcomb **13** 170-171
    Thoreau, Henry David **15** 203-205
    Whitman, Walt **16** 249-251

Whittier, John Greenleaf
    16 256-257
poets (19th-20th century)
    Bates, Katharine Lee **2** 54-55
    Freneau, Philip Morin **6** 99-100
    Markham, Edwin **10** 267
    Masters, Edgar Lee **10** 326-327
poets (20th century)
    Agee, James **1** 78-79
    Aiken, Conrad **1** 90-91
    Alexie, Sherman **1** 141-142
    Allen, Paula Gunn **1** 165-167
    Angelou, Maya **1** 238-239
    Auden, Wystan Hugh **1** 364-366
    Baraka, Imamu Amiri **1** 498-499
    Barnes, Djuna **2** 11-13
    Benét, Stephen Vincent **2** 157-158
    Bishop, Elizabeth **2** 290-292
    Brodsky, Joseph **3** 13-15
    Brooks, Gwendolyn **3** 24-26
    Bukowski, Charles **3** 113-115
    Cather, Willa Sibert **3** 368-369
    Childress, Alice **3** 522-524
    Chopin, Katherine **4** 18-20
    Cisneros, Sandra **4** 64-65
    Colum, Padraic **4** 174-175
    Crane, Hart **4** 291-293
    Cullen, Countee **4** 333-334
    Cummings, Edward Estlin **4** 334-336
    Doolittle, Hilda **5** 65-66
    Dove, Rita Frances **5** 87-89
    Dugan, Alan **5** 127-128
    Eliot, Thomas Stearns **5** 258-261
    Faulkner, William **5** 395-397
    Frost, Robert Lee **6** 130-133
    Ginsberg, Allen **6** 332-333
    Giovanni, Yolande Cornelia Jr.
        6 346-347
    Hall, Donald **7** 84-85
    Hughes, Langston **8** 18-19
    Jarrell, Randall **8** 222-223
    Jeffers, John Robinson **8** 236-237
    Jordan, June **8** 351-353
    Kunstler, William M. **9** 131-133
    Lorde, Audre **9** 513-515
    Merrill, James **10** 521-522
    Merton, Thomas **10** 523-525
    Momaday, N. Scott **11** 92-94
    Morgan, Robin **11** 168-170
    Nemerov, Howard **11** 338-340
    Oates, Joyce Carol **11** 454-456
    Olson, Charles **11** 505-506
    Ortiz, Simon J. **12** 9-12
    Patchen, Kenneth **12** 128-129
    Plath, Sylvia **12** 344-345
    Peck, Robert Newton **12** 177-178
    Rich, Adrienne **13** 128-130
    Sexton, Anne **14** 125-126
    Silko, Leslie **14** 226-227
    Simpson, Louis Aston Marantz
        14 243-244
    Steel, Danielle **14** 404-406
    Strand, Mark **14** 491-493
    Updike, John **15** 390-392
    Van Duyn, Mona **15** 422-423

Walker, Alice Malsenior **16** 59-61
Walker, Margaret **16** 67
White, E. B. **16** 228-230
Wilbur, Richard Purdy **16** 271-272
Wilder, Amos Niven **16** 273-274
political writers
  Brownmiller, Susan **3** 56-57
  Carroll, Anna Ella **3** 327-331
  Chavez, Linda **3** 489-491
  Gage, Matilda Joslyn **6** 167-169
  Hayden, Thomas Emmet **7** 217-219
  Hoffman, Abbie **7** 437-439
  Jacobs, Harriet A. **8** 190-193
  Kellor, Frances **8** 481-482
  Kreps, Juanita Morris **9** 99-101
  Millett, Kate **11** 31-33
  Moyers, Bill **11** 214-216
  Robinson, Harriet Hanson
    13 203-207
  Safire, William **13** 422-424
  Smith, Lillian Eugenia **14** 298-299
popular science
  Asimov, Isaac **1** 338-341
  Gould, Stephen Jay **6** 472-473
  Kübler-Ross, Elisabeth **9** 118-120
  Sagan, Carl E. **13** 424-425
psychological novels
  Oates, Joyce Carol **11** 454-456
religious writers
  Jung, Leo **8** 390-391
  Marty, Martin E. **10** 300-301
  Merton, Thomas **10** 523-525
  O'Hair, Madalyn Murray
    11 484-485
  Watts, Alan Wilson **16** 144-145
satirists
  Curtis, George William **4** 349-350
  Parker, Dorothy Rothschild **12** 106
scientific writers
  Calderón, Alberto P. **3** 219-220
scriptwriters (20th century)
  Agee, James **1** 78-79
  Angelou, Maya **1** 238-239
  Bambara, Toni Cade **1** 482-483
  Bradbury, Ray **2** 473-474
  Bukowski, Charles **3** 113-115
  Capote, Truman **3** 273-275
  Crichton, John Michael **4** 308-310
  Hecht, Ben **7** 248-250
  Hinton, Susan Eloise **7** 406-407
  King, Stephen **9** 23-25
  Mamet, David Alan **10** 181-182
  Stone, Oliver **14** 472-475
  Tan, Amy **15** 95-96
short-story writers (19th century)
  Bierce, Ambrose Gwinett **2** 269-270
  Garland, Hannibal Hamlin
    6 217-218
  Hale, Edward Everett **7** 71-72
  Harris, Joel Chandler **7** 173-174
  Harte, Francis Brett **7** 184-185
  Hawthorne, Nathaniel **7** 212-215
  Irving, Washington **8** 141-143
short-story writers (19th-20th century)
  Cable, George Washington
    3 198-199

Davis, Richard Harding **4** 422-423
Henry, O. **7** 308-309
Page, Thomas Nelson **12** 59-60
short-story writers (20th century)
  Algren, Nelson **1** 154-155
  Anderson, Sherwood **1** 220-221
  Asimov, Isaac **1** 338-341
  Baldwin, James Arthur **1** 465-466
  Bambara, Toni Cade **1** 482-483
  Barnes, Djuna **2** 11-13
  Bradbury, Ray **2** 473-474
  Bukowski, Charles **3** 113-115
  Burroughs, William S. **3** 162-163
  Caldwell, Erskine **3** 223-224
  Capote, Truman **3** 273-275
  Cather, Willa Sibert **3** 368-369
  Cheever, John **3** 493-494
  Chopin, Katherine **4** 18-20
  Cisneros, Sandra **4** 64-65
  Geisel, Theodor (Dr. Seuss)
    6 255-256
  Faulkner, William **5** 395-397
  Ferber, Edna **5** 413
  Hall, Donald **7** 84-85
  Harris, Frank **7** 172-173
  Heller, Joseph **7** 263-265
  Hemingway, Ernest Miller
    7 274-277
  Hurston, Zora Neale **8** 55-56
  King, Stephen **9** 23-25
  Lardner, Ringgold Wilmer
    9 204-205
  London, Jack **9** 494-495
  Lovecraft, H. P. **10** 3-6
  Malamud, Bernard **10** 162-163
  McMillan, Terry **10** 427-428
  Nemerov, Howard **11** 338-340
  Nin, Anais **11** 397-398
  Oates, Joyce Carol **11** 454-456
  O'Connor, Flannery **11** 467-468
  O'Hara, John **11** 485
  Ortiz, Simon J. **12** 9-12
  Peck, Robert Newton **12** 177-178
  Porter, Katherine Anne **12** 406-407
  Post, Emily Price **12** 409-410
  Proulx, E. Annie **12** 463-465
  Pynchon, Thomas **12** 496-498
  Richter, Conrad Michael
    13 148-149
  Salinger, J. D. **13** 447-448
  Saroyan, William **13** 486-487
  Silko, Leslie **14** 226-227
  Singer, Isaac Bashevis **14** 249-250
  Tan, Amy **15** 95-96
  Tyler, Anne **15** 367-368
  Updike, John **15** 390-392
  Vidal, Eugene Luther Gore
    15 488-490
  Walker, Alice Malsenior **16** 59-61
  Welty, Eudora **16** 199-201
  Wiesel, Elie **16** 263-264
social commentary
  Lasch, Christopher **9** 212-214
social critics
  Coles, Robert Martin **4** 156-157
textbook writers

Bailey, F. Lee **1** 441-443
Brubacher, John Seiler **3** 58-59
Commager, Henry Steele **4** 181-183
Cubberley, Ellwood Patterson
  4 329-331
Rugg, Harold **13** 355-357
translators
  Bloom, Allan David **2** 335-337
  Eastman, Max **5** 187-188
  Hinojosa, Rolando **7** 403-405
  Studi, Wes **15** 1-2
  Wilbur, Richard Purdy **16** 271-272
travel writers
  Isherwood, Christopher **8** 147-149
  Owen, Ruth Bryan **12** 41-43
  Theroux, Paul **15** 179-180

Authors, Angolan
de Andrade, Mario **4** 434-435
Neto, António Agostinho **11** 351-352

Authors, Arab
Abu Nuwas **1** 33-34
Abu-L-Ala al-Maarri **1** 32
Darwish, Mahmud **4** 399-401
Ibn al-Arabi, Muhyi al-Din **8** 91
ibn Battuta, Muhammad **8** 91-92
ibn Tufayl, Abu Bakr Muhammad **8** 96
Mahfuz, Najib **10** 142-144
see also Authors, Egyptian

Authors, Argentine
essayists
  Borges, Jorge Luis **2** 411-412
  Sábato, Ernesto **13** 399-400
novelists
  Güiráldez, Ricardo **7** 38-39
  Mármol, José **10** 274
  Sábato, Ernesto **13** 399-400
poets
  Borges, Jorge Luis **2** 411-412
  Echeverría, José Estéban **5** 197-198
  Güiráldez, Ricardo **7** 38-39
  Hernández, José **7** 328-329
short-story writers
  Borges, Jorge Luis **2** 411-412

Authors, Australian
nonfiction
  Greer, Germaine **6** 528-530
  Murray, Leslie Allan **11** 262-263
novelists
  Carey, Peter **3** 295-297
  Clarke, Marcus Andrew Hislop
    4 87-88
  Franklin, Stella Maraia Sarah Miles
    6 68-69
  Furphy, Joseph **6** 152-153
  Richardson, Henry Handel **13** 139
  White, Patrick Victor Martindale
    16 233-235
playwrights
  White, Patrick Victor Martindale
    16 233-235
poets
  Lawson, Henry **9** 254-255
  Paterson, Andrew Barton
    12 131-132
short-story writers

Lawson, Henry **9** 254-255

Authors, Austrian
essayists
Handke, Peter **7** 119-121
Hofmannsthal, Hugo von **7** 443-444
novelists
Handke, Peter **7** 119-121
Lind, Jakov **9** 419-420
Musil, Robert Edler Von **11** 268-269
Schnitzler, Arthur **14** 23-24
Suttner, Bertha von **15** 42-44
Werfel, Franz **16** 204-205
playwrights
Grillparzer, Franz **6** 546-547
Handke, Peter **7** 119-121
Hofmannsthal, Hugo von **7** 443-444
Lind, Jakov **9** 419-420
Musil, Robert Edler Von **11** 268-269
Schnitzler, Arthur **14** 23-24
Werfel, Franz **16** 204-205
poets
Hofmannsthal, Hugo von **7** 443-444
Werfel, Franz **16** 204-205
political writers
Harand, Irene **7** 139-145
short-story writers
Lind, Jakov **9** 419-420
Musil, Robert Edler Von **11** 268-269

Authors, Belgian
Maeterlinck, Maurice **10** 125-126
Simenon, Georges **14** 233-234

Authors, Brazilian
Amado, Jorge **1** 189-190
Castro Alves, Antônio de **3** 364-365
Cunha, Euclides Rodrigues Pimenta da
4 336-337
Fonseca, Rubem **5** 502-504
Machado de Assis, Joaquim Maria
10 91-92

Authors, British
see Authors, English; Authors, Irish;
Authors, Scottish; Authors, Welsh

Authors, Burmese
Nu, U **11** 439-441

Authors, Cameroonian
Beti, Mongo **2** 242-243

Authors, Canadian
critics
Atwood, Margaret Eleanor
1 362-364
Frye, Northrop **6** 137-139
essayists
Grove, Frederick Philip **7** 20-21
Haliburton, Thomas Chandler **7** 80
MacLennan, Hugh **10** 110-111
McClung, Nellie Letitia **10** 396-397
Moodie, Susanna **11** 140-141
nonfiction writers
McLuhan, Marshall **10** 424-426
Seton, Ernest Thompson **14** 119-120
novelists
Atwood, Margaret Eleanor
1 362-364
Aubert de Gaspé, Philippe **1** 364

Callaghan, Edward Morley
3 229-230
de la Roche, Mazo Louise
4 474-475
Grove, Frederick Philip **7** 20-21
Hémon, Louis **7** 277
Klein, A. M. **9** 49-50
Laurence, Margaret **9** 229-230
MacLennan, Hugh **10** 110-111
Montgomery, Lucy Maud
11 136-138
Moodie, Susanna **11** 140-141
playwrights
de la Roche, Mazo Louise
4 474-475
Fréchette, Louis-Honoré **6** 77-78
Heavysege, Charles **7** 246
poets
Atwood, Margaret Eleanor
1 362-364
Crémazie, Octave **4** 305-306
Fréchette, Louis-Honoré **6** 77-78
Goldsmith, Oliver **6** 411
Heavysege, Charles **7** 246
Klein, A. M. **9** 49-50
Lampman, Archibald **9** 180-181
Moodie, Susanna **11** 140-141
Morin, Paul **11** 174
Scott, Francis Reginald **14** 66-67
Strand, Mark **14** 491-493
prose writers
Carr, Emily **3** 319
Traill, Catharine Parr **15** 291
short-story writers
Callaghan, Edward Morley
3 229-230
Fréchette, Louis-Honoré **6** 77-78
McClung, Nellie Letitia **10** 396-397
Montgomery, Lucy Maud
11 136-138

Authors, Cape Verdean
Sousa, Henrique Teixeira de
14 352-353

Authors, Chilean
Allende, Isabel **1** 172-174
Bombal, María Luisa **2** 380-381
Donoso, José **5** 63-65
Mistral, Gabriela **11** 55-56
Neruda, Pablo **11** 344-345

Authors, Chinese
critics
Liu Hsieh **9** 452-453
Lu Chi **10** 24
essayists
Han Fei Tzu **7** 124-125
Han Yü **7** 136-137
Liu Tsung-Yüan **9** 455-456
Lu Hsün **10** 35-37
Ou-yang Hsiu **12** 33-34
Wang An-shih **16** 95-97
novelists
Lao Shê **9** 200-201
Pa Chin **12** 53-54
playwrights
Kuo Mo-jo **9** 133-134

Lao Shê **9** 200-201
poets (2d century B.C.)
Ssu-ma Hsiang-ju **14** 389-390
poets (3d-8th century)
Hsieh Ling-yün **8** 5-6
Li Po **9** 437-439
Liu Tsung-Yüan **9** 455-456
Lu Chi **10** 24
T'ao Ch'ien **15** 104-105
Tu Fu **15** 335-336
Wang Wei **16** 106-108
poets (9th-11th century)
Han Yü **7** 136-137
Ou-yang Hsiu **12** 33-34
Po Chü-i **12** 362-363
Su Shih **15** 39-40
Wang An-shih **16** 95-97
poets (18th-20th century)
Ch'i Pai-shih **3** 526-527
Lao Shê **9** 200-201
Yüan Mei **16** 479-480
short-story writers
Lao Shê **9** 200-201
Lu Hsün **10** 35-37

Authors, Colombian
García Márquez, Gabriel **6** 208-209
Isaacs, Jorge **8** 144
Rivera, José Eustacio **13** 185-186

Authors, Cuban
Guillén, Nicolás **7** 34-35
Martí, José **10** 285-286

Authors, Czech
Čapek, Karel **3** 271-272
Havel, Vaclav **7** 202-205
Kundera, Milan **9** 128-129

Authors, Danish
Andersen, Hans Christian **1** 212-214
Dinesen Blixen-Finecke, Karen **5** 13-14
Jacobsen, Jens Peter **8** 193-194
Nexø, Martin Anderson **11** 372

Authors, Dominican
Bosch, Juan **2** 428-429

Authors, Dutch
Erasmus, Desiderius **5** 298-300
Kempis, Thomas à **8** 493-494
Vondel, Joost van den **16** 19-20

Authors, Egyptian
Abduh ibn Hasan Khayr Allah, Muham-
mad **1** 16-17
Husayn, Taha **8** 61-62
Mahfuz, Najib **10** 142-144
Sayyid Qutb **13** 509-511
see also Authors, Arab

Authors, English
art critics
Brookner, Anita **3** 23-24
Clark, Kenneth M. **4** 79-80
autobiographers
Dahl, Roald **4** 366-367
Pritchett, V. S. **12** 455-457
autobiographies
Gielgud, John **6** 310-311
biographers

Burgess, Anthony **3** 136-137
Burney, Fanny **3** 147-148
Churchill, Winston Leonard Spencer **4** 51-53
Fraser, Antonia **6** 70-71
Jenkins, Roy Harris **8** 244-245
Johnson, Samuel **8** 315-317
Lawrence, Thomas Edward **9** 253-254
Morley, John **11** 178-179
Nicolson, Harold George **11** 383-384
Pritchett, V. S. **12** 455-457
Spark, Muriel Sarah **14** 361-362
Strachey, Giles Lytton **14** 487-488
Walton, Izaak **16** 90-91
children's-story writers
Carroll, Lewis **3** 332-333
critics (17th century)
Dryden, John **5** 106-107
critics (19th century)
Arnold, Matthew **1** 311-313
Bagehot, Walter **1** 436-437
Hazlitt, William **7** 235-236
Morley, John **11** 178-179
Morris, William **11** 187-188
Shaw, George Bernard **14** 163-164
Stephen, Leslie **14** 429
Swinburne, Algernon Charles **15** 54-55
Wilde, Oscar Fingall O'Flahertie Wills **16** 272-273
critics (20th century)
Betjeman, John **2** 243-245
Burgess, Anthony **3** 136-137
Connolly, Cyril **4** 204-205
Eliot, Thomas Stearns **5** 258-261
Graves, Robert Ranke **6** 504-506
Nicolson, Harold George **11** 383-384
Pritchett, V. S. **12** 455-457
Sitwell, Edith **14** 265-266
Spark, Muriel Sarah **14** 361-362
Spender, Stephen Harold **14** 370-371
Strachey, Giles Lytton **14** 487-488
Wedgwood, Cicely Veronica **16** 167-168
Woolf, Virginia Stephen **16** 381-382
diarists
Burney, Fanny **3** 147-148
Evelyn, John **5** 343-344
Nicolson, Harold George **11** 383-384
Pepys, Samuel **12** 207-208
dramatists
see playwrights (below)
essayists (16th-18th century)
Addison, Joseph **1** 57-58
Bacon, Francis **1** 422-424
Cowley, Abraham **4** 281-282
Fielding, Henry **5** 442-444
Goldsmith, Oliver **6** 411-413
Johnson, Samuel **8** 315-317
Lamb, Charles **9** 176-177
Mandeville, Bernard **10** 192

Steele, Richard **14** 407-409
Swift, Jonathan **15** 51-54
essayists (19th century)
Butler, Samuel **3** 183
Hazlitt, William **7** 235-236
Landor, Walter Savage **9** 186-187
Macaulay, Thomas Babington **10** 79-80
Martineau, Harriet **10** 296-297
Mill, John Stuart **11** 21-23
essayists (20th century)
Belloc, Joseph Hilaire Pierre **2** 141
Chesterton, Gilbert Keith **3** 508-509
Forster, Edward Morgan **6** 14-16
Golding, William **6** 404-406
Huxley, Aldous Leonard **8** 74-75
Lawrence, David Herbert **9** 247-248
Lewis, Cecil Day **9** 380
Lewis, Clive Staples **9** 381-382
Orwell, George **12** 14-15
Priestley, J. B. **12** 451-452
Tolkien, J. R. R. **15** 259-261
Weldon, Fay Birkinshaw **16** 186-188
Woolf, Virginia Stephen **16** 381-382
fantasy
Tolkien, J. R. R. **15** 259-261
lexicographers
Johnson, Samuel **8** 315-317
narrative historians
Wedgwood, Cicely Veronica **16** 167-168
nonfiction writers
Greer, Germaine **6** 528-530
Hockney, David **7** 429-431
nonsense writers
Carroll, Lewis **3** 332-333
Lear, Edward **9** 265-266
novelists (18th century)
Burney, Fanny **3** 147-148
Dahl, Roald **4** 366-367
Defoe, Daniel **4** 457-459
Edgeworth, Maria **5** 205-206
Fielding, Henry **5** 442-444
Goldsmith, Oliver **6** 411-413
Richardson, Samuel **13** 141-142
Smollett, Tobias George **14** 305-307
Sterne, Laurence **14** 435-437
novelists (19th century)
Austen, Jane **1** 377-379
Brontë, Charlotte **3** 17-18
Brontë, Emily **3** 18-19
Butler, Samuel **3** 183
Collins, William Wilkie **4** 169-170
Dickens, Charles John Huffam **4** 538-541
Eliot, George **5** 254-256
Gaskell, Elizabeth **6** 231-232
Kingsley, Charles **9** 28
Lewis, Matthew Gregory **9** 390-391
Meredith, George **10** 512-513
Peacock, Thomas Love **12** 169
Shelley, Mary Wollstonecraft **14** 174-176
Thackeray, William Makepeace **15** 159-161

Trollope, Anthony **15** 300-302
Wilde, Oscar Fingall O'Flahertie Wills **16** 272-273
novelists (19th-20th century)
Barrie, James Matthew **2** 21-22
Doyle, Arthur Conan **5** 91-92
Hardy, Thomas **7** 150-152
James, Henry **8** 211-212
Johnston, Henry Hamilton **8** 322-323
Kipling, Joseph Rudyard **9** 32-33
Shaw, George Bernard **14** 163-164
Wells, Herbert George **16** 195-196
Zangwill, Israel **16** 488-489
novelists (20th century)
Ambler, Eric **1** 191-192
Belloc, Joseph Hilaire Pierre **2** 141
Bennett, Arnold **2** 167-168
Brookner, Anita **3** 23-24
Burgess, Anthony **3** 136-137
Chesterton, Gilbert Keith **3** 508-509
Christie, Agatha **4** 25-26
Churchill, Winston Leonard Spencer **4** 51-53
Connolly, Cyril **4** 204-205
Conrad, Joseph **4** 205-207
Durrell, Lawrence **5** 163-164
Ford, Ford Madox **6** 1-2
Forster, Edward Morgan **6** 14-16
Fowles, John **6** 33-35
Fraser, Antonia **6** 70-71
Galsworthy, John **6** 189-190
Golding, William **6** 404-406
Graves, Robert Ranke **6** 504-506
Greene, Graham **6** 523-524
Huxley, Aldous Leonard **8** 74-75
James, P. D. **8** 213-215
Kundera, Milan **9** 128-129
Lawrence, David Herbert **9** 247-248
Le Carre, John **9** 270-271
Lewis, Clive Staples **9** 381-382
Lodge, David **9** 480-482
Maugham, William Somerset **10** 344-345
Mortimer, John Clifford **11** 194-195
Murdoch, Iris **11** 256-257
Orton, John Kingsley **12** 12-14
Orwell, George **12** 14-15
Potter, Dennis **12** 412-414
Powell, Anthony **12** 422-423
Priestley, J. B. **12** 451-452
Pritchett, V. S. **12** 455-457
Rendell, Ruth **13** 96-97
Snow, Charles Percy **14** 311-312
Spark, Muriel Sarah **14** 361-362
Theroux, Paul **15** 179-180
Tolkien, J. R. R. **15** 259-261
Trevor, William **15** 295-297
Waugh, Evelyn Arthur St. John **16** 145-147
Weldon, Fay Birkinshaw **16** 186-188
Woolf, Virginia Stephen **16** 381-382
playwrights (16th century)
Chapman, George **3** 440-441
Dekker, Thomas **4** 465-466

Heywood, Thomas **7** 373-374
Jonson, Ben **8** 343-345
Kyd, Thomas **9** 140-141
Marlowe, Christopher **10** 272-274
Shakespeare, William **14** 142-145
playwrights (17th century)
   Beaumont, Francis **2** 95
   Burgoyne, John **3** 137-138
   Chapman, George **3** 440-441
   Dryden, John **5** 106-107
   Fletcher, John **5** 487
   Ford, John **6** 7-8
   Heywood, Thomas **7** 373-374
   Massinger, Philip **10** 324-325
   Middleton, Thomas **11** 8-9
   Suckling, John **15** 10-11
   Vanbrugh, John **15** 409-410
   Webster, John **16** 164
   Wycherley, William **16** 411-412
playwrights (18th century)
   Congreve, William **4** 200-201
   Fielding, Henry **5** 442-444
   Gay, John **6** 243-244
   Goldsmith, Oliver **6** 411-413
   Sheridan, Richard Brinsley
     14 183-184
   Steele, Richard **14** 407-409
   Thomson, James **15** 199-200
playwrights (19th century)
   Gilbert, William Schwenck
     6 314-315
   Lewis, Matthew Gregory **9** 390-391
   Wilde, Oscar Fingall O'Flahertie
     Wills **16** 272-273
playwrights (19th-20th century)
   Barrie, James Matthew **2** 21-22
   Hardy, Thomas **7** 150-152
   Shaw, George Bernard **14** 163-164
   Swinburne, Algernon Charles
     15 54-55
playwrights (20th century)
   Auden, Wystan Hugh **1** 364-366
   Bennett, Arnold **2** 167-168
   Bennett, Alan **2** 166-167
   Burgess, Anthony **3** 136-137
   Christie, Agatha **4** 25-26
   Coward, Noel **4** 279-280
   Eliot, Thomas Stearns **5** 258-261
   Galsworthy, John **6** 189-190
   Greene, Graham **6** 523-524
   Isherwood, Christopher **8** 147-149
   Mortimer, John Clifford **11** 194-195
   Osborne, John **12** 16-17
   Pinter, Harold **12** 317-318
   Potter, Dennis **12** 412-414
   Priestley, J. B. **12** 451-452
   Shaffer, Peter Levin **14** 133-135
   Stoppard, Thomas **14** 478-479
   Trevor, William **15** 295-297
   Weldon, Fay Birkinshaw
     16 186-188
poets (12th-13th century)
   Geoffrey of Monmouth **6** 268
   Layamon **9** 256-257
poets (14th century)
   Chaucer, Geoffrey **3** 482-485

Gower, John **6** 475-476
Langland, William **9** 194-195
Lydgate, John **10** 61-62
Rolle of Hampole, Richard
   13 260-261
poets (15th century)
   Skelton, John **14** 268-269
poets (16th century)
   Chapman, George **3** 440-441
   Raleigh, Walter **13** 9-11
   Sidney, Philip **14** 214-215
   Skelton, John **14** 268-269
   Spenser, Edmund **14** 373-376
   Wyatt, Thomas **16** 410-411
poets (16th-17th century)
   Drayton, Michael **5** 97-98
   Jonson, Ben **8** 343-345
   Shakespeare, William **14** 142-145
poets (17th century)
   Butler, Samuel **3** 183-184
   Chapman, George **3** 440-441
   Cowley, Abraham **4** 281-282
   Crashaw, Richard **4** 296
   Donne, John **5** 60-61
   Dryden, John **5** 106-107
   Herbert, George **7** 324-326
   Herrick, Robert **7** 336-339
   Lovelace, Richard **10** 7-8
   Marvell, Andrew **10** 301-303
   Milton, John **11** 43-46
   Suckling, John **15** 10-11
   Vaughan, Henry **15** 444-445
poets (18th century)
   Addison, Joseph **1** 57-58
   Blake, William **2** 316-318
   Chatterton, Thomas **3** 481-482
   Collins, William **4** 168-169
   Cowper, William **4** 282
   Defoe, Daniel **4** 457-459
   Gay, John **6** 243-244
   Goldsmith, Oliver **6** 411-413
   Gray, Thomas **6** 509-510
   Lamb, Charles **9** 176-177
   Pope, Alexander **12** 395-397
   Swift, Jonathan **15** 51-54
   Thomson, James **15** 199-200
poets (19th century)
   Arnold, Matthew **1** 311-313
   Browning, Elizabeth Barrett **3** 52-53
   Browning, Robert **3** 53-55
   Byron, George Gordon Noel
     3 193-194
   Clough, Arthur Hugh **4** 123-124
   Coleridge, Samuel Taylor **4** 154-156
   Crabbe, George **4** 288
   Gilbert, William Schwenck
     6 314-315
   Hopkins, Gerard Manley **7** 492-494
   Keats, John **8** 470-472
   Landor, Walter Savage **9** 186-187
   Meredith, George **10** 512-513
   Morris, William **11** 187-188
   Rossetti, Christina Georgina
     13 307-308
   Rossetti, Dante Gabriel **13** 308-309
   Shelley, Percy Bysshe **14** 176-178

Tennyson, Alfred **15** 144-146
Wordsworth, William **16** 385-388
poets (19th-20th century)
   Hardy, Thomas **7** 150-152
   Housman, Alfred Edward **7** 521-522
   Kipling, Joseph Rudyard **9** 32-33
   Swinburne, Algernon Charles
     15 54-55
poets (20th century)
   Auden, Wystan Hugh **1** 364-366
   Belloc, Joseph Hilaire Pierre **2** 141
   Betjeman, John **2** 243-245
   Brooke, Rupert **3** 22-23
   Chesterton, Gilbert Keith **3** 508-509
   Durrell, Lawrence **5** 163-164
   Eliot, Thomas Stearns **5** 258-261
   Graves, Robert Ranke **6** 504-506
   Hughes, Ted **8** 19-21
   Larkin, Philip **9** 206-207
   Lawrence, David Herbert **9** 247-248
   Lennon, John Winston **9** 326-328
   Lewis, Cecil Day **9** 380
   MacNeice, Louis **10** 113-114
   Sassoon, Siegfried **13** 492-493
   Sitwell, Edith **14** 265-266
   Spark, Muriel Sarah **14** 361-362
   Spender, Stephen Harold
     14 370-371
   Thomas, Dylan Marlais **15** 188-190
political writers
   Fawcett, Millicent Garrett **5** 398-400
   Jenkins, Roy Harris **8** 244-245
   Rushdie, Salman **13** 366-368
popular science
   Huxley, Julian **8** 75-77
   Stopes, Marie **14** 476-478
religious writers (17th century)
   Browne, Thomas **3** 49-50
   Bunyan, John **3** 128-129
religious writers (19th-20th centuries)
   Inge, William Ralph **8** 118-119
   Royden, Agnes Maude **13** 335-337
satirists
   Mandeville, Bernard **10** 192
   Peacock, Thomas Love **12** 169
   Pope, Alexander **12** 395-397
   Swift, Jonathan **15** 51-54
screenwriters
   Ambler, Eric **1** 191-192
   Burgess, Anthony **3** 136-137
   Potter, Dennis **12** 412-414
   Priestley, J. B. **12** 451-452
   Scorsese, Martin **14** 63-65
short-story writers
   Dahl, Roald **4** 366-367
   Huxley, Aldous Leonard **8** 74-75
   Kipling, Joseph Rudyard **9** 32-33
   Lawrence, David Herbert **9** 247-248
   Martineau, Harriet **10** 296-297
   Pritchett, V. S. **12** 455-457
   Rendell, Ruth **13** 96-97
   Shelley, Mary Wollstonecraft
     14 174-176
   Trevor, William **15** 295-297
   Zangwill, Israel **16** 488-489

translators
  Spender, Stephen Harold
    14 370-371
travel writers
  Durrell, Lawrence **5** 163-164
  Pritchett, V. S. **12** 455-457
  Spender, Stephen Harold
    14 370-371
  Theroux, Paul **15** 179-180
  see also Authors, Irish; Authors,
    Scottish; Authors, Welsh

Authors, Ethiopian
  Heruy Wäldä-Sellasé **7** 348-349
  Mäkonnen Endalkačäw **10** 161-162

Authors, Filipino
  Rizal, José **13** 187-189

Authors, French
  autobiographers
    Roland **13** 256-259
  chroniclers
    Froissart, Jean **6** 124-125
    Joinville, Jean de **8** 325
  critics
    Artaud, Antonin **1** 320-321
    Benda, Julien **2** 151-152
    Boileau-Despréaux, Nicholas
      2 369-371
    Foucault, Michel **6** 29-30
    Gide, André **6** 308-309
    Gourmont, Remy de **6** 475
    Sainte-Beuve, Charles Augustin
      13 438
    Taine, Hippolyte Adolphe **15** 82-83
  diarists
    Saint-Simon, Duc de **13** 436
  essayists (16th-18th century)
    La Rochefoucauld, François Duc de
      9 208-209
    Mirabeau, Comte de **11** 51-52
    Montaigne, Michel Eyquem de
      11 116-117
  essayists (19th-20th century)
    Bernanos, Georges **2** 206-207
    Camus, Albert **3** 255-257
    France, Anatole **6** 39-40
    Gourmont, Remy de **6** 475
    Malraux, André **10** 178-180
    Rolland, Romain **13** 260
    Saint-Exupéry, Antoine de
      13 431-432
    Weil, Simone **16** 172-174
    Yourcenar, Marguerite **16** 477-479
  essayists (20th century)
    Sarraute, Nathalie Tcherniak
      13 488-490
  musical works
    Sauguet, Henri **13** 497-498
  nonfiction writers
    Aron, Raymond **1** 316-317
    de Broglie, Louis **4** 442-444
    Servan-Schreiber, Jean-Jacques
      14 113-115
  novelists (16th-17th century)
    La Fayette, Comtesse de **9** 150-151
    Lesage, Alain René **9** 353-354

  Rabelais, François **12** 524-526
  novelists (18th century)
    Diderot, Denis **5** 1-2
    Marivaux, Pierre Carlet de Cham-
      blain de **10** 265-266
    Prévost, Abbé **12** 445-446
    Rousseau, Jean Jacques **13** 324-328
    Sade, Comte de **13** 416-418
    Staël, Germaine de **14** 391-392
  novelists (19th century)
    Balzac, Honoré de **1** 478-480
    Chateaubriand, Vicomte de
      3 477-479
    Daudet, Alphonse **4** 402-403
    Dumas, Alexandre **5** 136-138
    Flaubert, Gustave **5** 480-482
    Goncourt, Edmond de and Jules de
      6 426-427
    Hugo, Victor Marie **8** 22-25
    Huysmans, Joris Karl **8** 81-82
    Maupassant, Henri René Albert Guy
      de **10** 347
    Mérimée, Prosper **10** 517
    Sand, George **13** 459-461
    Stendhal **14** 422-425
    Verne, Jules **15** 467-469
    Zola, Émile **16** 526-528
  novelists (19th-20th century)
    Barrès, Auguste Maurice **2** 20-21
    France, Anatole **6** 39-40
    Loti, Pierre **9** 519-520
    Proust, Marcel **12** 465-467
    Rolland, Romain **13** 260
  novelists (20th century)
    Aragon, Louis **1** 271-272
    Beckett, Samuel **2** 102-104
    Benda, Julien **2** 151-152
    Bernanos, Georges **2** 206-207
    Camus, Albert **3** 255-257
    Céline, Louis Ferdinand **3** 390-391
    Cocteau, Jean **4** 132-133
    Colette, Sidonie Gabrielle
      4 158-159
    de Beauvoir, Simone **4** 440-441
    Genet, Jean **6** 262-263
    Gide, André **6** 308-309
    Giraudoux, Jean **6** 349-350
    Hémon, Louis **7** 277
    Malraux, André **10** 178-180
    Martin du Gard, Roger **10** 295-296
    Mauriac, François **10** 347-348
    Robbe-Grillet, Alain **13** 189-190
    Saint-Exupéry, Antoine de
      13 431-432
    Sarraute, Nathalie Tcherniak
      13 488-490
    Sartre, Jean Paul **13** 491-492
    Yourcenar, Marguerite **16** 477-479
  playwrights (17th century)
    Corneille, Pierre **4** 234-236
    Lesage, Alain René **9** 353-354
    Molière **11** 86-88
    Racine, Jean Baptiste **12** 532-535
  playwrights (18th century)
    Beaumarchais, Pierre August Caron
      de **2** 93-94

  Diderot, Denis **5** 1-2
  Marivaux, Pierre Carlet de Cham-
    blain de **10** 265-266
  Voltaire **16** 14-16
  playwrights (19th century)
    Daudet, Alphonse **4** 402-403
    Dumas, Alexandre **5** 136-138
    Musset, Louis Charles Alfred de
      11 271-272
    Rolland, Romain **13** 260
  playwrights (20th century)
    Anouilh, Jean **1** 243-244
    Beckett, Samuel **2** 102-104
    Camus, Albert **3** 255-257
    Claudel, Paul Louis Charles **4** 90-91
    Cocteau, Jean **4** 132-133
    Genet, Jean **6** 262-263
    Gide, André **6** 308-309
    Giraudoux, Jean **6** 349-350
    Ionesco, Eugène **8** 131-132
    Sarraute, Nathalie Tcherniak
      13 488-490
    Yourcenar, Marguerite **16** 477-479
  poets (12th century)
    Chrestien de Troyes **4** 23-24
    Marie de France **10** 259
  poets (13th century)
    Guillaume de Lorris **7** 33-34
    Jean de Meun **8** 234-235
  poets (14th century)
    Christine de Pisan **4** 29-30
    Froissart, Jean **6** 124-125
    Machaut, Guillaume de **10** 93-94
    Vitry, Philippe de **16** 2
  poets (15th century)
    Christine de Pisan **4** 29-30
    Orléans, Charles D' **11** 530
    Villon, François **15** 499-501
  poets (16th-17th century)
    du Bellay, Joachim **5** 113-114
    La Fontaine, Jean de **9** 156-157
    Malherbe, François de **10** 169-170
    Nostradamus **11** 432-434
    Ronsard, Pierre de **13** 271-273
  poets (18th century)
    Chénier, André Marie **3** 500-501
    Voltaire **16** 14-16
  poets (19th century)
    Baudelaire, Charles Pierre **2** 61-63
    Daudet, Alphonse **4** 402-403
    Hugo, Victor Marie **8** 22-25
    Laforgue, Jules **9** 160-161
    Lamartine, Alphonse Marie Louis de
      9 173-175
    Leconte de Lisle, Charles Marie
      René **9** 273-274
    Mallarmé, Stéphane **10** 172-173
    Musset, Louis Charles Alfred de
      11 271-272
    Nerval, Gérard de **11** 345-346
    Péguy, Charles Pierre **12** 183-184
    Rimbaud, Jean Nicolas Arthur
      13 172-174
    Verlaine, Paul Marie **15** 465-466
    Vigny, Comte de **15** 494-495
  poets (20th century)

Apollinaire, Guillaume **1** 260
Aragon, Louis **1** 271-272
Beckett, Samuel **2** 102-104
Cocteau, Jean **4** 132-133
Péguy, Charles Pierre **12** 183-184
Perse, Saint-John **12** 242-243
Picabia, Francis **12** 291-292
Valéry, Paul Ambroise **15** 405-406
Yourcenar, Marguerite **16** 477-479
pornographers
　Sade, Comte de **13** 416-418
satirists
　Boileau-Despréaux, Nicholas
　2 369-371
　Chénier, André Marie **3** 500-501
　Daudet, Alphonse **4** 402-403
　Montesquieu **11** 123-125
short-story writers
　Maupassant, Henri René Albert Guy
　de **10** 347
　Mérimée, Prosper **10** 517
trouvères
　Marie de France **10** 259
　Thibaut IV **15** 180-181

Authors, German
biographers
　Chamberlain, Houston Stewart
　3 411
critics
　Freytag, Gustav **6** 107-108
　Schlegel, Friedrich von **14** 10-11
diarists
　Frank, Anne **6** 54-56
　Jünger, Ernst **8** 391-392
essayists
　Böll, Heinrich **2** 377-378
　Heine, Heinrich **7** 259-260
　Mann, Heinrich **10** 201-202
　Mann, Thomas **10** 204-207
　Schlegel, Friedrich von **14** 10-11
fairy tale writers
　Grimm, Jakob and Wilhelm Karl
　7 3-4
humorists
　Richter, Johann Paul Friedrich
　13 150-151
lexicographers
　Grimm, Jakob and Wilhelm Karl
　7 3-4
nonfiction writers
　Fromm, Erich **6** 125-127
novelists (17th century)
　Grimmelshausen, Hans Jakob
　Christoffel von **7** 4-5
novelists (18th-19th century)
　Goethe, Johann Wolfgang von
　6 388-391
　Richter, Johann Paul Friedrich
　13 150-151
　Tieck, Ludwig **15** 218-219
　Wieland, Christoph Martin
　16 260-261
novelists (19th century)
　Arnim, Achim von **1** 308-309
　Brentano, Clemens **2** 515-516
　Fontane, Theodor **5** 504

Freytag, Gustav **6** 107-108
Hoffmann, Ernst Theodor Amadeus
　7 439-440
Storm, Theodor **14** 479-480
novelists (19th-20th century)
　Hauptmann, Gerhart Johann Robert
　7 199-201
　Heyse, Paul Johann Ludwig
　7 372-373
　Mann, Thomas **10** 204-207
　Sudermann, Hermann **15** 12-13
　Wassermann, Jakob **16** 130-131
novelists (20th century)
　Böll, Heinrich **2** 377-378
　Feuchtwanger, Lion **5** 430-432
　Grass, Günter **6** 496-497
　Hesse, Hermann **7** 367-369
　Huch, Ricarda **8** 11-12
　Jünger, Ernst **8** 391-392
　Kafka, Franz **8** 403-406
　Mann, Heinrich **10** 201-202
　Remarque, Erich Maria **13** 91
playwrights (18th century)
　Lessing, Gotthold Ephraim
　9 357-359
　Schiller, Johann Christoph Friedrich
　von **14** 4-7
playwrights (18th-19th century)
　Goethe, Johann Wolfgang von
　6 388-391
　Tieck, Ludwig **15** 218-219
playwrights (19th century)
　Freytag, Gustav **6** 107-108
　Hebbel, Friedrich **7** 247
　Kleist, Heinrich von **9** 52-53
playwrights (19th-20th century)
　Hauptmann, Gerhart Johann Robert
　7 199-201
　Sudermann, Hermann **15** 12-13
　Wedekind, Frank **16** 166-167
playwrights (20th century)
　Brecht, Bertolt **2** 512-514
　Grass, Günter **6** 496-497
　Kaiser, Georg **8** 411-412
　Sachs, Nelly **13** 411-412
　Toller, Ernst **15** 261
poets (10th-13th century)
　Gershom ben Judah **6** 283-284
　Gottfried von Strassburg **6** 461-462
　Vogelweide, Walther von der
　16 10-11
　Wolfram von Eschenbach
　16 360-361
poets (16th century)
　Sachs, Hans **13** 410-411
poets (18th century)
　Klopstock, Friedrich Gottlieb
　9 55-56
　Novalis **11** 435
　Schiller, Johann Christoph Friedrich
　von **14** 4-7
poets (18th-19th century)
　Goethe, Johann Wolfgang von
　6 388-391
　Hölderlin, Johann Christian
　Friedrich **7** 451-452

Wieland, Christoph Martin
　16 260-261
poets (19th century)
　Brentano, Clemens **2** 515-516
　Fontane, Theodor **5** 504
　Hebbel, Friedrich **7** 247
　Heine, Heinrich **7** 259-260
　Nietzsche, Friedrich **11** 390-392
　Storm, Theodor **14** 479-480
poets (19th-20th century)
　George, Stefan **6** 277-278
poets (20th century)
　Benn, Gottfried **2** 164
　Brecht, Bertolt **2** 512-514
　Grass, Günter **6** 496-497
　Huch, Ricarda **8** 11-12
　Rilke, Rainer Maria **13** 171-172
　Sachs, Nelly **13** 411-412
　Schwitters, Kurt **14** 60-61
religious writers
　Soelle, Dorothee **14** 324-325
satirists
　Brant, Sebastian **2** 503-504
short-story writers
　Böll, Heinrich **2** 377-378
　Hoffmann, Ernst Theodor Amadeus
　7 439-440
　Kafka, Franz **8** 403-406
translators
　Böll, Heinrich **2** 377-378
trouvères
　Marie de France **10** 259
　Thibaut IV **15** 180-181

Authors, Ghanaian
Hayford, J. E. Casely **7** 228-230

Authors, Greek (ancient)
essayists
　Plutarch **12** 359-360
　Xenophon **16** 418-420
lexicographers
　Galen **6** 178-180
playwrights
　Aeschylus **1** 70-72
　Aristophanes **1** 293-294
　Euripides **5** 332-334
　Menander **10** 477-478
　Sophocles **14** 343-345
poets
　Callimachus **3** 235-236
　Empedocles **5** 282
　Hesiod **7** 361-362
　Homer **7** 465-467
　Pindar **12** 312-313
　Sappho **13** 479-480
　Solon **14** 327-328
　Theocritus **15** 171-172
satirists
　Lucian **10** 25-26
travel reports
　Pytheas **12** 499-500

Authors, Greek (modern)
Cavafy, Constantine P. **3** 381-382
Kazantzakis, Nikos **8** 466-468
Palamas, Kostes **12** 70

Seferis, George **14** 84-85
Authors, Guatemalan
  Asturias, Miguel Angel **1** 354-355
Authors, Hebrew
  Agnon, Shmuel Yoseph **1** 85-86
  Ahad Haam **1** 88-89
  Ben Yehuda, Eliezer **2** 181-182
  Bialik, Hayyim Nahman **2** 262-263
  Judah Halevi **8** 373
  Luzzato, Moses Hayyim **10** 57-58
  Saadia ben Joseph al-Fayumi **13** 396
  Tschernichowsky, Saul **15** 323
Authors, Hungarian
  Koestler, Arthur **9** 71-73
  Lukács, Gyorgy **10** 37-38
  Pázmány, Péter **12** 164-165
Authors, Icelandic
  Sturluson, Snorri **14** 310-311
Authors, Indian (Asia)
  lexicographers
    Ram Camul Sen **13** 16-17
  novelists
    Chatterji, Bankimchandra
      3 480-481
    Narayan, R. K. **11** 313-314
    Premchand **12** 439
    Rushdie, Salman **13** 366-368
    Rabindranath Tagore **12** 529-531
  playwrights
    Harsha **7** 181-182
    Kalidasa **8** 414-415
    Rabindranath Tagore **12** 529-531
  poets
    Das, Chitta Ranjan **4** 401-402
    Harsha **7** 181-182
    Iqbal, Muhammad **8** 132-133
    Kalidasa **8** 414-415
    Naidu, Sarojini **11** 294-295
    Rabindranath Tagore **12** 529-531
  religious writers
    Mawdūdī, Abu-I A'la **10** 353-354
  short-story writers
    Premchand **12** 439
Authors, Iraqi
  Fādil al-Jamālī, Muhammad **5** 361-362
Authors, Irish
  autobiographies
    Adams, Gerald **1** 42-44
  critics
    Shaw, George Bernard **14** 163-164
  essayists
    Goldsmith, Oliver **6** 411-413
    Heaney, Seamus Justin **7** 238-240
    Hyde, Douglas **8** 82-83
    Lecky, William Edward Hartpole
      9 271-272
    Steele, Richard **14** 407-409
    Stoker, Bram **14** 463-464
  nonfiction writers
    Lonsdale, Kathleen **9** 501-502
  novelists
    Beckett, Samuel **2** 102-104
    Bowen, Elizabeth **2** 462-463

Goldsmith, Oliver **6** 411-413
    Joyce, James **8** 365-367
    Murdoch, Iris **11** 256-257
    Shaw, George Bernard **14** 163-164
    Somerville, Edith Anna OEnone
      14 334-335
    Stephens, James **14** 430-431
    Stoker, Bram **14** 463-464
  playwrights
    Beckett, Samuel **2** 102-104
    Colum, Padraic **4** 174-175
    Friel, Bernard Patrick **6** 115-116
    Goldsmith, Oliver **6** 411-413
    Gregory, Augusta **6** 535-536
    Hyde, Douglas **8** 82-83
    O'Casey, Sean **11** 459-460
    Shaw, George Bernard **14** 163-164
    Steele, Richard **14** 407-409
    Synge, Edmund John Millington
      15 61-62
    Yeats, William Butler **16** 445-447
  poets
    Beckett, Samuel **2** 102-104
    Colum, Padraic **4** 174-175
    Goldsmith, Oliver **6** 411-413
    Heaney, Seamus Justin **7** 238-240
    Pearse, Patrick Henry **12** 173-174
    Stephens, James **14** 430-431
    Yeats, William Butler **16** 445-447
  political writers
    Adams, Gerald **1** 42-44
  short-story writers
    Adams, Gerald **1** 42-44
    Somerville, Edith Anna OEnone
      14 334-335
    Stoker, Bram **14** 463-464
    see also Authors, English; Authors,
      Scottish; Authors, Welsh
Authors, Israeli
  Appelfeld, Aharon **1** 262-263
  Oz, Amos **12** 45-47
Authors, Italian
  ancient
    see Authors, Roman
  autobiographical
    Levi, Primo **9** 365-366
  biographers
    Casanova de Seinglat, Giacomo
      Jacopo Girolamo **3** 350-351
    Vasari, Giorgio **15** 442-443
  critics
    Foscolo, Ugo **6** 21
    Montale, Eugenio **11** 117-118
    Pavese, Cesare **12** 154-155
    Pirandello, Luigi **12** 319-321
  essayists
    Ginzburg, Natalia Levi **6** 338-339
    Levi, Carlo **9** 364
    Silone, Ignazio **14** 231-232
  novelists
    Calvino, Italo **3** 243-244
    D'Annunzio, Gabriele **4** 388
    Ginzburg, Natalia Levi **6** 338-339
    Manzoni, Alessandro **10** 222-224
    Moravia, Alberto **11** 153-155

Pavese, Cesare **12** 154-155
    Pirandello, Luigi **12** 319-321
    Silone, Ignazio **14** 231-232
    Svevo, Italo **15** 47-48
    Vittorini, Elio **16** 2-3
  playwrights (15th-16th century)
    Ariosto, Ludovico **1** 289-290
    Machiavelli, Niccolò **10** 97-99
    Porta, Giambattista della
      12 403-404
  playwrights (18th-19th century)
    Alfieri, Vittoria **1** 145-146
    D'Annunzio, Gabriele **4** 388
    Foscolo, Ugo **6** 21
    Goldoni, Carlo **6** 408-409
    Manzoni, Alessandro **10** 222-224
  playwrights (20th century)
    Betti, Ugo **2** 246
    D'Annunzio, Gabriele **4** 388
    Ginzburg, Natalia Levi **6** 338-339
    Moravia, Alberto **11** 153-155
    Pirandello, Luigi **12** 319-321
  poets (13th-14th century)
    Boccaccio, Giovanni **2** 351-353
    Cavalcanti, Guido **3** 382
    Dante Alighieri **4** 389-391
    Guinizzelli, Guido **7** 36-37
    Jacopone da Todi **8** 194
    Landini, Francesco **9** 185-186
    Petrarch **12** 259-261
  poets (15th century)
    Boiardo, Matteo Maria **2** 369
    Medici, Lorenzo de' **10** 450-451
    Poliziano, Angelo **12** 373-374
    Pulci, Luigi **12** 481
  poets (16th century)
    Ariosto, Ludovico **1** 289-290
    Bembo, Pietro **2** 144-145
    Bruno, Giordano **3** 75-76
    Castiglione, Baldassare **3** 360-361
    Tasso, Torquato **15** 114-116
  poets (17th-19th century)
    Campanella, Tommaso **3** 249
    Carducci, Giosuè **3** 290-291
    D'Annunzio, Gabriele **4** 388
    Foscolo, Ugo **6** 21
    Goldoni, Carlo **6** 408-409
    Leopardi, Giacomo **9** 344-345
    Rosa, Salvator **13** 289-290
  poets (20th century)
    D'Annunzio, Gabriele **4** 388
    Montale, Eugenio **11** 117-118
    Pavese, Cesare **12** 154-155
    Quasimodo, Salvatore **12** 506
    Ungaretti, Giuseppe **15** 389-390
  short-story writers
    Vittorini, Elio **16** 2-3
Authors, Japanese
  critics
    Zeami, Kanze **16** 492-493
  essayists
    Abe, Kobo **1** 20-22
    Tanizaki, Junichiro **15** 101-102
  novelists
    Abe, Kobo **1** 20-22

Kawabata, Yasunari **8** 463-464
Mishima, Yukio **11** 54-55
Murasaki Shikibu **11** 252-253
Natsume, Soseki **11** 324-325
Tanizaki, Junichiro **15** 101-102
playwrights
Abe, Kobo **1** 20-22
Mishima, Yukio **11** 54-55
Tanizaki, Junichiro **15** 101-102
Zeami, Kanze **16** 492-493
poets
Basho, Matsuo **2** 45-48
Mabuchi, Kamo **10** 73-74
religious writers
Suzuki, Daisetz Teitaro **15** 46-47
screenwriters
Abe, Kobo **1** 20-22
short-story writers
Abe, Kobo **1** 20-22
Alexie, Sherman **1** 141-142
translators
Alexie, Sherman **1** 141-142

Authors, Jewish
Baeck, Leo **1** 429-430
Fackenheim, Emil Ludwig **5** 359-361
Shestov, Lev **14** 190-191

Authors, Kenyan
Ngugi wa Thiong'o **11** 375-376
Ogot, Grace Emily Akinyi **11** 483-484

Authors, Korean
Sol Ch'ong **14** 325-326
Yi Hwang **16** 457
Yun Sondo **16** 483

Authors, Lebanese
Adonis **1** 64-65
Gibran, Kahlil **6** 303-305

Authors, Lesothoan
Mofolo, Thomas **11** 74

Authors, Malagasy
Rabearivelo, Jean Joseph **12** 523-524

Authors, Mexican
Azuela, Mariano **1** 402
Cosio Villegas, Daniel **4** 260-261
Fernández de Lizardi, José Joaquin **5** 424-425
Fuentes, Carlos **6** 141-142
Juana Inés de la Cruz **8** 367-368
Paz, Octavio **12** 161-162
Poniatowska, Elena **12** 392-393
Reyes, Alfonso **13** 112-113
Vasconcelos, José **15** 443-444

Authors, Moroccan
Allal al-Fasśi, Mohamed **1** 162

Authors, Mozambican
Craveirinha, José **4** 297-299

Authors, Muslim
Mawdūdī, Abu-I A'la **10** 353-354

Authors, New Zealander
Mansfield, Katherine **10** 213-214

Authors, Nicaraguan
Darío, Rubén **4** 393-394

Authors, Nigerian
Achebe, Chinua **1** 35-37
Ekwensi, Cyprian **5** 242-243
Equiano, Olaudah **5** 296-297
Imam, Alhadji Abubakar **8** 114-115
Soyinka, Wole **14** 358-359
Tutuola, Amos **15** 361-362

Authors, Norwegian
Bjørnson, Bjørnstjerne **2** 299-300
Hamsun, Knut **7** 113-114
Ibsen, Henrik **8** 98-100
Undset, Sigrid **15** 388-389

Authors, Palestinian
Darwish, Mahmud **4** 399-401

Authors, Persian
novelists
Hidayat, Sadiq **7** 377-378
poets
Attar, Farid ed-Din **1** 359-360
Firdausi **5** 451-452
Hafiz, Shams al-Din **7** 63
Jami **8** 218-219
Omar Khayyam **11** 510-511
Rumi, Jalai ed-Din **13** 362-363
Sa'di **13** 418-419

Authors, Peruvian
Garcilaso de la Vega, Inca **6** 210-211
González Prada, Manuel **6** 431
Mariátegui, José Carlos **10** 255-256
Palma, Ricardo **12** 77
Vallejo, César Abraham **15** 408-409
Vargas Llosa, Mario **15** 434-436

Authors, Polish
Asch, Shalom **1** 325-326
Milosz, Czeslaw **11** 40-42
Peretz, Isaac Loeb **12** 212
Sienkiewicz, Henryk **14** 216-217

Authors, Portuguese
Anchieta, José de **1** 210-211
Camoëns, Luis Vaz de **3** 247-249
Mendes Pinto, Fernao **10** 493-494
Vicente, Gil **15** 479-480

Authors, Roman (ancient)
biographers
Suetonius Tranquillus, Gaius **15** 13
critics
Horace **7** 500-503
Longinus **9** 500-501
Quintilian **12** 518-519
encylopedists
Cassiodorus, Flavius Magnus Aurelius **3** 357-358
Pliny the Elder **12** 355-356
epigrammatists
Martialis, Marcus Valerius **10** 286-287
essayists
Cicero, Marcus Tullius **4** 55-58
letter writers
Pliny the Younger **12** 356
novelists
Petronius Arbiter **12** 262-263
playwrights

Plautus **12** 348-350
Seneca the Younger, Lucius Annaeus **14** 103-105
Terence **15** 146-148
poets
Catullus, Gaius Valerius **3** 377-378
Cicero, Marcus Tullius **4** 55-58
Ennius, Quintus **5** 289
Horace **7** 500-503
Lucretius **10** 26-27
Ovid **12** 34-36
Virgil **15** 507-510
satirists
Horace **7** 500-503
Juvenal **8** 397-399
Varro, Marcus Terentius **15** 438-439

Authors, Romanian
Blandiana, Ana **2** 321-322
Eliade, Mircea **5** 249-250
Eminescu, Mihail **5** 280-281

Authors, Russian
critics
Bakhtin, Mikhail Mikhailovich **1** 456-458
Belinsky, Grigorievich **2** 128
Chernyshevsky, Nikolai Gavrilovich **3** 504-505
Merezhkovsky, Dmitry Sergeyevich **10** 515-516
Shestov, Lev **14** 190-191
novelists (18th-19th century)
Karamzin, Nikolai Mikhailovich **8** 441-442
novelists (19th century)
Chernyshevsky, Nikolai Gavrilovich **3** 504-505
Dostoevsky, Fyodor **5** 74-77
Gogol, Nikolai **6** 391-393
Goncharov, Ivan Aleksandrovich **6** 424
Lermontov, Mikhail Yurievich **9** 352-353
Pushkin, Aleksandr Sergeevich **12** 489-491
Tolstoy, Leo **15** 262-265
Turgenev, Ivan Sergeyevich **15** 345-348
novelists (19th-20th century)
Aleichem, Sholom **1** 124-125
Merezhkovsky, Dmitry Sergeyevich **10** 515-516
novelists (20th century)
Bulgakov, Mikhail Afanasievich **3** 117
Bunin, Ivan Alekseevich **3** 124
Ehrenburg, Ilya Grigorievich **5** 224-225
Gorky, Maxim **6** 458-460
Pasternak, Boris Leonidovich **12** 124-125
Sholokhov, Mikhail Aleksandrovich **14** 203-204
Simonov, Konstantin Mikhailovich **14** 239-240
Solzhenitsyn, Alexander Isayevich **14** 330-332

playwrights (19th century)
Chekhov, Anton Pavlovich
3 494-497
Gogol, Nikolai **6** 391-393
Pushkin, Aleksandr Sergeevich
12 489-491
Turgenev, Ivan Sergeyevich
15 345-348
playwrights (19th-20th century)
Aleichem, Sholom **1** 124-125
playwrights (20th century)
Afinogenov, Aleksandr Nikolaevich
1 72-73
Bulgakov, Mikhail Afanasievich
3 117
poets (19th century)
Lermontov, Mikhail Yurievich
9 352-353
Merezhkovsky, Dmitry Sergeyevich
10 515-516
Pushkin, Aleksandr Sergeevich
12 489-491
poets (20th century)
Akhmatova, Anna **1** 96-97
Blok, Aleksandr Aleksandrovich
2 335
Brodsky, Joseph **3** 13-15
Bunin, Ivan Alekseevich **3** 124
Ehrenburg, Ilya Grigorievich
5 224-225
Esenin, Sergei Aleksandrovich **5** 321
Mandelstam, Osip Emilyevich
10 191
Mayakovsky, Vladimir Vladimirovich
10 364-365
Pasternak, Boris Leonidovich
12 124-125
Simonov, Konstantin Mikhailovich
14 239-240
Yevtushenko, Yevgeny Alexan-
drovich **16** 455-456
satirists
Bulgakov, Mikhail Afanasievich
3 117
short-story writers
Aleichem, Sholom **1** 124-125
Babel, Isaac Emmanuelovich
1 411-412
Bunin, Ivan Alekseevich **3** 124
Chekhov, Anton Pavlovich
3 494-497
Gogol, Nikolai **6** 391-393
Turgenev, Ivan Sergeyevich
15 345-348
translators
Brodsky, Joseph **3** 13-15
Authors, Scottish
biographers
Boswell, James **2** 432-434
essayists
Carlyle, Thomas **3** 304-305
Hume, David **8** 31-34
Stevenson, Robert Louis **14** 446-448
novelists
Barrie, James Matthew **2** 21-22
Scott, Walter **14** 68-70
Smollett, Tobias George **14** 305-307

Stevenson, Robert Louis **14** 446-448
playwrights
Barrie, James Matthew **2** 21-22
Thomson, James **15** 199-200
poets
Burns, Robert **3** 155-156
Douglas, Gavin **5** 77-78
Dunbar, William **5** 142-143
Lyndsay, David **10** 66-67
Scott, Walter **14** 68-70
Stevenson, Robert Louis **14** 446-448
Thomson, James **15** 199-200
see also Authors, English; Authors,
Irish; Authors, Welsh
Authors, Senegalese
Ousmane, Sembene **12** 32-33
Senghor, Léopold Sédar **14** 106-107
Authors, Sierra Leonean
Wallace-Johnson, Isaac Theophilus
Akunna **16** 76-77
Authors, Somali
Hassan, Muhammad Abdille **7** 194-195
Authors, South African
Biko, Steve **2** 273-274
Brutus, Dennis **3** 77-78
Coetzee, J. M. **4** 133-135
Dube, John Langalibalele **5** 113
First, Ruth **5** 453-454
Fugard, Athol **6** 142-143
Gordimer, Nadine **6** 446-447
Mofolo, Thomas **11** 74
Mphahlele, Ezekiel **11** 221-223
Mqhayi, Samuel Edward Krune **11** 223
Nkosi, Lewis **11** 407-408
Paton, Alan Stewart **12** 134-135
Plaatje, Solomon Tshekisho **12** 341-342
Authors, Spanish
critics
Altamira Y Crevea, Rafael **1** 179
Valera y Alcalá Galiano, Juan
15 403
essayists
Baroja y Nessi, Pío **2** 15-16
Ortega Y Gasset, José **12** 7-8
Ruíz, José Martínez **13** 358
Unamuno y Jugo, Miguel de
15 386-387
humorists
Gracián y Morales, Baltasar Jeróni-
mo **6** 481-482
novelists (16th-18th century)
Alemán, Mateo **1** 126
Cervantes, Miguel de Saavedra
3 395-398
Galdós, Benito Pérez **6** 177-178
Gracián y Morales, Baltasar Jeróni-
mo **6** 481-482
Quevedo Y Villegas, Francisco
Gómez de **12** 511
novelists (19th-20th century)
Alarcón, Pedro Antonio de
1 100-101
Baroja y Nessi, Pío **2** 15-16
Cela y Trulock, Camilo José
3 389-390

Galdós, Benito Pérez **6** 177-178
Ferrer, Gabriel Miró **5** 428
Unamuno y Jugo, Miguel de
15 386-387
Valera y Alcalá Galiano, Juan
15 403
Valle Inclán, Ramón Maria del
15 407-408
playwrights (15th-17th century)
Alarcón, Pedro Antonio de
1 100-101
Calderón, Pedro **3** 221-222
Encina, Juan del **5** 283
Lope Félix de Vega Carpio
9 503-506
Tirso de Molina **15** 237-238
playwrights (18th-20th century)
Benavente y Martinez, Jacinto
2 146-147
Galdós, Benito Pérez **6** 177-178
Lorca, Federico García **9** 511-513
Saavedra, Angel de **13** 398
Valle Inclán, Ramón Maria del
15 407-408
poets (11th-14th century)
Alfonso X **1** 150-151
Gonzalo de Berceo **6** 431-432
ibn Gabirol, Solomon ben Judah
8 92
Judah Halevi **8** 373
López de Ayala, Pedro **9** 508-509
Ruiz, Juan **13** 358-359
poets (15th-17th century)
Calderón, Pedro **3** 221-222
Ercilla y Zúñiga, Alonso de **5** 302
Góngora y Argote, Luis de
6 427-428
John of the Cross **8** 285
Manrique, Jorge **10** 210-211
Quevedo Y Villegas, Francisco
Gómez de **12** 511
poets (19th-20th century)
Bécquer, Gustavo Adolfo
Dominguez **2** 107-108
Guillén, Nicolás **7** 34-35
Ibárruri Gómez, Dolores **8** 88-90
Jiménez, Juan Ramón **8** 261-262
Lorca, Federico García **9** 511-513
Saavedra, Angel de **13** 398
Unamuno y Jugo, Miguel de
15 386-387
Valle Inclán, Ramón Maria del
15 407-408
satirists
Gracián y Morales, Baltasar Jeróni-
mo **6** 481-482
Authors, Swedish
Heidenstam, Carl Gustaf Verner Von
7 258-259
Lagerkvist, Pär Fabian **9** 162-163
Lagerlöf, Selma Ottiliana Lovisa
9 163-164
Strindberg, August **14** 509-511
Authors, Swiss
Dürrenmatt, Friedrich **5** 164-165
Frisch, Max **6** 118-119

Keller, Gottfried **8** 478-479

Authors, Tanzanian
Shaaban Robert **14** 128-129

Authors, Thai
Kukrit Pramoj, Momrajawong (M.R.) **9** 126-127

Authors, Trinidadian
Naipaul, V. S. **11** 295-296

Authors, Turkish
Halide Edip Adivar **7** 80-82
Kemal, Yashar **8** 489-491

Authors, Turkish Cypriot
Denktash, Rauf **4** 500-502

Authors, Ukranian
Ginzberg, Asher **6** 336-337

Authors, Uruguayan
Quiroga, Horacio **12** 520-521
Rodó, José Enrique **13** 240-241
Zorrilla de San Martin, Juan **16** 530-531

Authors, Venezuelan
Bello, Ahmadu **2** 139-140
Gallegos Freire, Rómulo **6** 185-186

Authors, Welsh
Lawrence, Thomas Edward **9** 253-254
Thomas, Dylan Marlais **15** 188-190
Vaughan, Henry **15** 444-445
see also Authors, English; Authors, Irish; Authors, Scottish

Authors, West Indian
Walcott, Derek Alton **16** 50-51

Authors, Yugoslavian
Djilas, Milovan **5** 34

Authors, Zimbabwean (expatriate)
Lessing, Doris **9** 355-357

Autism (psychology)
Bettelheim, Bruno **2** 245-246
Bleuler, Eugen **2** 325

Auto (play)
Vicente, Gil **15** 479-480
see also Autos sacramentales

Auto de Filodemo (poem)
Camoëns, Luis Vaz de **3** 247-249

Auto Icon (book)
Bentham, Jeremy **2** 176-178

Autobiography (B. Franklin)
Bigelow, John **2** 271-272
Franklin, Benjamin **6** 60-64
Sarmiento, Domingo Faustino **13** 484-485

Autobiography of Alice B. Toklas, The (book)
Stein, Gertrude **14** 414-415

Autobiography of an Idea, The (book)
Sullivan, Louis Henri **15** 27-28

Autobiography of Lincoln Steffens, The (autobiography)
Steffens, Lincoln **14** 410-411

Autobiography of Malcolm X, The (autobiography)
Malcolm X **10** 165-166

Autocracy (government)
Karamzin, Nikolai Mikhailovich **8** 441-442
Pobedonostsev, Konstantin Petrovich **12** 360-361
Witte, Sergei Yulyevich **16** 349-350
see also Absolutism (government)

Autocrat of the Breakfast-Table The (essays)
Holmes, Oliver Wendell **7** 457-458

Auto-da-fé (law)
Manasseh ben Israel **10** 183-184

Autoimmunity (medicine)
Burnet, Frank Macfarlane **3** 146-147
Salk, Jonas Edward **13** 451-452

Autolycus, battle of (422 B.C.)
Xenophon **16** 418-420

Automatism (art)
Hofmann, Hans **7** 442-443
Tanguy, Yves **15** 101

Automobile industry
Agnelli, Giovanni **1** 82-83
Benz, Carl **2** 182-183
Chrysler, Walter Percy **4** 36-37
Citroën, André-Gustave **4** 66-68
Daimler, Gottlieb **4** 368
Durant, William Crapo **5** 158
Firestone, Harvey Samuel **5** 452-453
Ford, Henry **6** 5-6
Ford, Henry II **6** 6-7
Honda, Soichiro **7** 469-470
Kaiser, Henry John **8** 412-413
Knudsen, William S. **9** 67-68
Nader, Ralph **11** 290-291
Reuther, Walter Philip **13** 107-108
Sloan, Alfred Pritchard Jr. **14** 274
Toyoda, Eiji **15** 284-286
see also Business and industrial leaders—automobile industry

Automobile racing
Andretti, Mario **1** 228-230
Muldowney, Shirley **11** 236-238

Autonomist party (Puerto Rico)
Muñoz Rivera, Luís **11** 250

Autonomy Bills (Canada; 1905)
Laurier, Wilfrid **9** 232-234

Autos sacramentales (plays)
Calderón, Pedro **3** 221-222
Lope Félix de Vega Carpio **9** 503-506

Autronius Paetus, Publius (1st century B.C.), Roman consul 66-62 B.C.
Crassus Dives, Marcus Licinius **4** 296-297

Autumn (novel)
Pa Chin **12** 53-54

Autumn (painting)
Poussin, Nicolas **12** 418-420

Autumn (poem)
Thomson, James **15** 199-200

Autumn Colors on the Ch'iao... (scroll)
Chao Meng-fu **3** 436-437

Autumn Garden (play)
Hellman, Lillian Florence **7** 267-268

Autumn Leaves (painting)
Millais, John Everett **11** 23-24

Autumn Rhythm (painting)
Pollock, Jackson **12** 379-380

Autumn Wind (novel)
Natsume, Soseki **11** 324-325

Autumnal Tints (essay)
Thoreau, Henry David **15** 203-205

Avalon (colony, Newfoundland)
Calvert, George **3** 238-239

Avanti! (newspaper)
Mussolini, Benito **11** 272-274
Silone, Ignazio **14** 231-232

Avare, L' (play, Molière)
Alarcón, Pedro Antonio de **1** 100-101
Molière **11** 86-88

Avaricum, battle of (52 B.C.)
Caesar, Gaius Julius **3** 207-210

Avars
see Huns

Ave Maria (musical composition)
Gounod, Charles François **6** 473-474
Josquin des Prez **8** 361-363
Verdi, Giuseppe Fortunino Francesco **15** 463-465

Ave Regina caelorum (musical composition)
Dufay, Guillaume **5** 125-126
Dunstable, John **5** 150-151

AVEDON, RICHARD (born 1923), American fashion photographer **1** 381-382
Baldwin, James Arthur **1** 465-466

Aveling, Edward Bibbins (1851-1898), English scientist
Averroës **1** 382-383
Marx, Karl **10** 304-308

Avempace (died 1138), Arab philosopher
Averroës **1** 382-383

Avenarius, Richard (1843-1896), German philosopher
Schrödinger, Erwin **14** 31-33

Avenir, L' (journal)
Lacordaire, Jean Baptiste Henri **9** 148
Lamennais, Hugues Félicité Robert de **9** 179
Montalembert, Comte de **11** 118-119

Aventures d'Arthur Gordon Pym (book, Poe)
Baudelaire, Charles Pierre **2** 61-63

Aventures de M. Robert Chevalier... (novel)
Lesage, Alain René **9** 353-354

Aventures prodigieuses de Tartarin de Tarascon (satire)
Daudet, Alphonse **4** 402-403

Average error, method of (psychophysics)
Fechner, Gustav Theodor **5** 401-402

Avercamp, Hendrick van (1585-1663), Dutch painter
Le Nain, Antoine, Louis and Mathieu **9** 321-322

AVERROËS (1126-1198), Spanish-Arabian philosopher **1** 382-383
influence of
Eckhart, Johann **5** 200-201
Levi ben Gershon **9** 363-364
Thomas Aquinas **15** 183-186
see also Averroism
influenced by
Bitruji, Nur al-Din Abu Ishaq al **2** 296
ibn Tufayl, Abu Bakr Muhammad **8** 96

Averroism (philosophy)
Averroës **1** 382-383
Levi ben Gershon **9** 363-364
Lull, Raymond **10** 39-40
Marsilius of Padua **10** 284
Pomponazzi, Pietro **12** 390-391
Thomas Aquinas **15** 183-186, 422
see also Averroës

AVERY, OSWALD THEODORE (1877-1955), Canadian/American biologist and bacteriologist **1** 384-386

Avery Coonley House (Riverside, Illinois)
Wright, Frank Lloyd **16** 398-401

Avesta (Zoroastrian book)
Zoroaster **16** 528-530, 535

Aveugle, L' (poem)
Chénier, André Marie **3** 500-501

Aveugles, Les (play)
Maeterlinck, Maurice **10** 125-126

Aviation (mural)
Gorky, Arshile **6** 458

Aviation (science)
Banting, Frederick Grant **1** 493-494
Bell, Alexander Graham **2** 129-131
Compton, Arthur Holly **4** 186-188
Coolidge, John Calvin **4** 217-219
Hoover, Herbert Clark **7** 483-485
Nobile, Umberto **11** 411-412
see also Aerodynamics; Aeronautics; Aircraft; Aviators

Aviation industry
Sopwith, Thomas Octave Murdoch **14** 345-346
Trippe, Juan Terry **15** 297-298

Aviators
American
Armstrong, Neil Alden **1** 304-306
Arnold, Henry Harley **1** 310-311
Byrd, Richard Evelyn **3** 186-187
Coleman, Bessie **4** 152-154
Curtiss, Glenn Hammond **4** 350-351
Doolittle, James Harold **5** 66-68
Earhart, Amelia Mary **5** 177-179
Langley, Samuel Pierpont **9** 195-196

Lindbergh, Anne Morrow **9** 420-421
Lindbergh, Charles Augustus **9** 421-423
Rickenbacker, Edward Vernon **13** 152-153
Shepard, Alan **14** 178-180
Wright brothers **16** 394-396
Yeager, Chuck **16** 444-445
Australian
Kingsford Smith, Charles **9** 26-28
Wilkins, George Hubert **16** 281-282
Brazilian
Santos-Dumont, Alberto **13** 477-478
English
Sopwith, Thomas Octave Murdoch **14** 345-346
French
Montgolfier, Joseph and Jacques Michel Étienne **11** 133-134
Saint-Exupéry, Antoine de **13** 431-432
Russian
Gagarin, Yuri Alexeivich **6** 166-167
Swedish
Andrée, Salomon August **1** 226

Avicebrón (Avicembril)
see Ibn Gabirol, Solomon ben Judah

AVICENNA (circa 980-1037), Arabian physician and philosopher **1** 386-387
Akbar, Jalal-ud-din Mohammed **1** 96
Averroës **1** 382-383
Ghazali, Abu Hamid Muhammad al- **6** 290-291
ibn Tufayl, Abu Bakr Muhammad **8** 96
Maimonides **10** 151-152

Avidya (Buddhism)
Buddha **3** 97-101

Avignon, siege of (1793)
Napoleon I **11** 306-310

Avignon papacy (1308-1378)
Catherine of Siena **3** 369-370
Charles IV **3** 455-456
Clement V **4** 101-102
Guy de Chauliac **7** 54
Rienzi, Cola di **13** 166-167
Urban VI **15** 394
Wyclif, John **16** 412-413
see also Great Schism

Avignon Pietà (painting)
Pilon, Germain **12** 305

Ávila, Pedro Arias de
see Pedrarias

ÁVILA CAMACHO, GEN. MANUEL (1897-1955), Mexican president 1940-1946 **1** 387-388
Alemán, Mateo **1** 126
Cárdenas, Lázaro **3** 286-287

Avitus, Marcus Maecilius (died 456), Roman emperor 455-456
Ricimer, Flavius **13** 151-152

AVOGADRO, LORENZO ROMANO AMEDO CARLO (Conte di Quaregna e di

Cerreto; 1776-1865), Italian physicist and chemist **1** 388-389
Gay-Lussac, Joseph Louis **6** 245-246

Avogadro's law (physics)
Avogadro, Lorenzo Romano Amedeo Carlo **1** 388-389

Avvakum (1620-1682), Russian archpriest
Nikon, Nikita Minov **11** 395

Avventura d'un povero cristiano, L' (novel)
Silone, Ignazio **14** 231-232

Awake and Sing (play)
Odets, Clifford **11** 470-471

Awakening (novel)
Galsworthy, John **6** 189-190

Awakening (religious)
see Great Awakening; Revivalism, religious

Awakening Conscience (painting)
Hunt, William Holman **8** 44-45

Awakening of Spring, The (play)
Wedekind, Frank **16** 166-167

Awakening, The (painting)
Courbet, Jean Desiré Gustave **4** 271-273

Awakening, The (sculpture)
Ewonwu, Benedict Chuka **5** 351-352

Awakening the Soul, The (essay)
Maeterlinck, Maurice **10** 125-126

Awami Muslim League (Pakistan)
Bhashani, Maulana Abdul Hamid Khan **2** 255-257
Mujibur Rahman **11** 234-236

Awkward Age, The (novel)
James, Henry **8** 211-212

Awo (autobiography)
Awolowo, Obafemi **1** 389-390

AWOLOWO, CHIEF OBAFEMI (born 1909), Nigerian nationalist and politician **1** 389-390
Macaulay, Herbert **10** 78-79

AX, EMANUEL (born 1949), American pianist **1** 391

Axel's Castle (book)
Wilson, Edmund **16** 318-319

Axiom (logic)
Euclid **5** 327-329
Frege, Gottlob **6** 93-94
Gödel, Kurt **6** 377-379

Axum (ancient kingdom)
see Ethiopia

Ayacucho, battle of (1824)
Bolívar, Simón **2** 375-377
Sucre, Antonio José de **15** 11-12

Ayala, Pedro López de
see López de Ayala, Pedro

Ayala, Plan of (1910-1911)
Madero, Francisco Indalecio **10** 118-119
Zapata, Emiliano **16** 489-490

AYER, ALFRED JULES (1910-1989), English philosopher **1** 391-393
Schlick, Friedrich Albert Moritz **14** 16-17

Aylesford scandal (1876)
Edward VII **5** 214-215

Aylmer Papillon (novel)
Disraeli, Benjamin **5** 27-29

AYLWIN AZÓCAR, PATRICIO (born 1918), leader of the Chilean Christian Democratic party and president of Chile **1** 393-395

Aynhoe Park (Northamptonshire)
Soane, John **14** 314-315

Ayton, Truce of (1497)
Henry VII **7** 300-302

AYUB KHAN, MOHAMMED (1907-1989), Pakistani statesman **1** 395-396

Ayudhya (state, Indochina)
Rama Khamhaeng **13** 11

Ayutla, Plan of (1855)
Álvarez, Juan **1** 184-185
Juárez, Benito **8** 369-372

AZAÑA DIAZ, MANUEL (1880-1940), Spanish statesman, president 1936-1939 **1** 396-397

Azande (African people)
Evans-Pritchard, Edward Evan **5** 340

Azara (opera)
Paine, John Knowles **12** 65

AZARA, FÉLIX DE (1746-1821), Spanish explorer and naturalist **1** 397-398

Azara, José Nicolás de (1731-1804), Spanish diplomat
Azara, Félix de **1** 397-398

Azariah
see Uzziah

AZCONA HOYO, JOSÉ (born 1927), president of Honduras (1986-1990) **1** 398-399

Azerbaijan (Azerbaidzhan)
Hulagu Khan **8** 27-28
Mansur, Abu Jafar ibn Muhammad al- **10** 214-215

Azhar
see Al-Azar

AZHARI, SAYYID ISMAIL AL- (1898-1969), Sudanese president 1965-1968 **1** 399-401
Abboud, Ibrahim **1** 11-12
Khalil, Sayyid Abdullah **8** 531-532

Azharoth (poem)
Saadia ben Joseph al-Fayumi **13** 396

AZIKIWE, NNAMDI (born 1904), Nigerian nationalist, president 1963-1966 **1** 401-402
Macaulay, Herbert **10** 78-79
Nkrumah, Kwame **11** 408-410
Wallace-Johnson, Isaac Theophilus Akunna **16** 76-77

Aziyadé (book)
Loti, Pierre **9** 519-520

Aziz (literary character)
Forster, Edward Morgan **6** 14-16

Azores (island, Atlantic Ocean)
Donne, John **5** 60-61
Henry the Navigator **7** 305-306

Azorin
see Ruíz, José Martinez

Azov (town, Russia)
Mehmed the Conqueror **10** 452-454
Potemkin, Grigori Aleksandrovich **12** 411-412

Aztec Empire (Mexico)
Cortés, Hernán **4** 255-256
Cuauhtemoc **4** 329
Díaz del Castillo, Bernal **4** 536-537
Montezuma, II **11** 128-129
Pizarro, Francisco **12** 340-341
Velázquez de Cuéllar, Diego **15** 459

Azuchi (town, Japan)
Eitoku, Kano **5** 242
Nobunaga, Oda **11** 413-414

AZUELA, MARIANO (1873-1952), Mexican novelist **1** 402

Azul (literary collection)
Darío, Rubén **4** 393-394

Azur, L' (poem)
Mallarmé, Stéphane **10** 172-173

B

BA MAW (1893-1977), Burmese statesman **1** 480-481
  Aung San **1** 374-375
  Ne Win **11** 364-365
  Nu, U **11** 439-441

Baade, Walter (1893-1960),
German-American astronomer
  Lemaître, Abbè Georges Édouard
  9 315-316
  Shapley, Harlow **14** 155-156

BAADER and MEINHOF (1967-1976),
founders of the West German "Red Army
Faction" **1** 403-404

Baader, F.X. von (1765-1841), German
philosopher
  Döllinger, Josef Ignaz von **5** 47-48

Baal (play)
  Brecht, Bertolt **2** 512-514

BAAL SHEM TOV (circa 1700-circa 1760),
founder of modern Hasidism **1** 404-405
  Elijah ben Solomon **5** 251-252

Baath party (Syria)
  Nasser, Gamal Abdel **11** 317-318

Bab Ballads (poems)
  Gilbert, William Schwenck **6** 314-315

BABAR THE CONQUEROR (aka
Zahir-ud-din Muhammad Babur;
1483-1530), Mogul emperor of India
1526-1530 **1** 405-407
  Tamerlane **15** 94-95

BABBAGE, CHARLES (1791-1871), English
inventor and mathematician **1** 407-408

Babbitt (novel)
  Lewis, Harry Sinclair **9** 385-387

BABBITT, BRUCE EDWARD (born 1938),
governor of Arizona (1978-1987) and
United States secretary of the interior
1 408-410

Babbitt, Irving (1865-1933), American
educator
  Eliot, Thomas Stearns **5** 258-261

BABBITT, MILTON (born 1916), American
composer **1** 410
  Sessions, Roger Huntington **14** 117-118

Babbling April (poems)
  Greene, Graham **6** 523-524

BABCOCK, STEPHEN MOULTON
(1843-1931), American agricultural
chemist **1** 410-411

Babcock test (milk)
  Babcock, Stephen Moulton **1** 410-411

BABEL, ISAAC EMMANUELOVICH
(1894-1941), Russian writer **1** 411-412
  Ehrenburg, Ilya Grigorievich **5** 224-225

Baber
  see Babar the Conqueror

Babes in Arms (musical)
  Rodgers, Richard Charles **13** 234-236

BABEUF, FRANÇOIS NOEL ("Caius Gracchus"; 1760-1797), French revolutionist
and writer **1** 412

Babi Yar (poem; Yevtushenko)
  Shostakovich, Dmitri Dmitrievich
  14 204-205
  Yevtushenko, Yevgeny Alexandrovich
  16 455-456

Babington, Anthony (1561-1586), English
Catholic conspirator
  Mary, I **10** 308-309

Babrak Karmal
  see Karmal, Babrak

Babur, Zahir-ud-din Muhammed
  see Babar the Conqueror

Baby and Child Care (book)
  Spock, Benjamin **14** 383-385

Baby Doll (film)
  Williams, Tennessee **16** 306-308

Babylon (ancient city, Mesopotamia)
  Alexander the Great **1** 137-141
  Antiochus IV **1** 250
  Ashurbanipal **1** 338
  Cyrus the Great **4** 363-364
  Tiglath-pileser III **15** 221-222

Babylon Revisited (story)
  Fitzgerald, Francis Scott Key **5** 470-472

Babylonia (ancient nation, Southwest Asia)
  Amorite rule
    Hammurabi **7** 109-110
  Assyrian rule
    Tiglath-pileser III **15** 221-222
  Greek rule
    Alexander the Great **1** 137-141
  Judaism in
    Anan ben David **1** 207-208
  Neo-Babylonian Empire
    Nebuchadnezzar **11** 330
  Seleucid rule
    Antigonus I **1** 248-249
    Seleucus I **14** 92-93
  see also Mesopotamia

Babylonian Captivity (597; 586 B.C.)
  Isaiah **8** 146-147
  Jeremiah **8** 247-248
  Micah **10** 542-543

Babylonian Captivity (1308-1378)
  see Avignon papacy

Babylonian Talmud (Jewish law)
  Abba Arika **1** 3-4

Babylonians, The (play; Aristophanes)
  Aristophanes **1** 293-294
  Cleon **4** 104-105

BACA-BARRAGÁN, POLLY (born 1943),
Hispanic American politician **1** 412-414

Bacall, Lauren (Mrs. Humphrey Bogart;
born 1924), American actress
  Bogart, Humphrey **2** 363-364

Bacatá
  see Bogotá

Baccaneles, La (musical composition)
  Couperin, François **4** 270-271

Bacchae (play)
  Euripides **5** 332-334

Bacchanal (engraving)
  Mantegna, Andrea **10** 215-216

Bacchanals (painting)
  Poussin, Nicolas **12** 418-420

Bacchides (play)
  Plautus **12** 348-350

Bacchus (sculpture)
Michelangelo Buonarroti **11** 2-5
Sansovino, Jacopo **13** 470-471

Bacchus and Ariadne (painting)
Tintoretto **15** 232-234
Titian **15** 242-244

Bacchus et Ariane (ballet)
Roussel, Albert **13** 328-329

Bacchus with a Wine Glass (painting)
Caravaggio **3** 282-284

BACH, CARL PHILIPP EMANUEL
(1714-1788), German composer
1 414-415
Bach, Johann Christian **1** 415-416
Bach, Johann Sebastian **1** 416-419
Schumann, Robert Alexander **14** 41-43

BACH, JOHANN CHRISTIAN
(1735-1782), German composer
1 415-416
Bach, Carl Philipp Emanuel **1** 414-415

Bach, Johann Christoph (1642-1703), German composer
Pachelbel, Johann **12** 52

Bach, Johann Christoph (1671-1721), German musician
Bach, Johann Sebastian **1** 416-419

Bach, Johann Christoph (1732-1795), German musician
Bach, Johann Sebastian **1** 416-419

BACH, JOHANN SEBASTIAN (1685-1750),
German composer and organist
1 416-419
arrangements
Gounod, Charles François **6** 473-474
Mozart, Wolfgang Amadeus **11** 218-221
biographies of
Schweitzer, Albert **14** 55-56
influence of
Franck, César **6** 48-49
Honegger, Arthur **7** 472-473
Mendelssohn, Moses **10** 488-489
influenced by
Buxtehude, Dietrich **3** 185-186
Froberger, Johann Jakob **6** 120-121
Pachelbel, Johann **12** 52
Vivaldi, Antonio **16** 3-4
relatives
Bach, Carl Philipp Emanuel **1** 414-415
Bach, Johann Christian **1** 415-416
techniques
Beethoven, Ludwig van **2** 114-117
Schumann, Robert Alexander **14** 41-43
Telemann, Georg Philipp **15** 137-138

Bach, Wilhelm Friedemann (1710-1784),
German musician
Bach, Johann Sebastian **1** 416-419

B-A-C-H motive (music)
Penderecki, Krzysztof **12** 195-197

Bach-Abel Concerts (1764-1782)
Bach, Johann Christian **1** 415-416

BACHE, ALEXANDER DALLAS
(1806-1867), American educator and scientist **1** 420
Agassiz, Jean Louis Rodolphe **1** 76-78

Bache, Benjamin Franklin (1769-1798),
American journalist
Duane, William **5** 109

Bache, Richard (1737-1811), American merchant
Franklin, Benjamin **6** 60-64

Bachelier de Salamanque, Le (novel)
Lesage, Alain René **9** 353-354

Bachelor of Arts (novel)
Narayan, R. K. **11** 313-314

Bachelorhood of England (political organization)
Edward I **5** 208-210

Bachet, Claude Gaspard (1581-1638),
Swiss mathematician
Fermat, Pierre de **5** 421-422

Bachianas brasileiras (musical composition)
Villa-Lobos, Heitor **15** 496-497

Bachman, John (1790-1874), American
Lutheran clergyman and naturalist
Audubon, John James **1** 366-367

Baciccio
see Gaulli, Giovanni Battista

Bacillus anthracis (bacteriology)
Lwoff, André **10** 58-59

Bacillus tuberculosis (bacteriology)
Lwoff, André **10** 58-59

Back from the Market (painting)
Chardin, Jean Baptiste Siméon **3** 442-443

Back to Bool Bool (novel)
Franklin, Stella Maraia Sarah Miles **6** 68-69

Back to Methuselah (play)
Shaw, George Bernard **14** 163-164

Backer, Jacob Adriaansz (1608-1651),
Dutch painter
Rembrandt Harmensz van Rijn **13** 91-95

Backlight (art technique)
Amorsolo, Fernando **1** 204

Back-of-the-Yards Neighborhood Council
(citizen reform group)
Alinsky, Saul David **1** 161-162

Back-to-Africa movement (African American)
Malcolm X **10** 165-166

BACKUS, ISAAC (1724-1806), American
Baptist leader **1** 420-421

Backwoods of Canada, The (book)
Traill, Catharine Parr **15** 291

BACON, FRANCIS (1561-1626), English
philosopher, statesman, and author
1 422-424
as author
Donnelly, Ignatius **5** 62
as philosopher
Hobbes, Thomas **7** 421-423
Stewart, Dugald **14** 449
Telesio, Bernardino **15** 138-139
Voltaire **16** 14-16
as statesman
Coke, Edward **4** 141-142
Essex, 2d Earl of **5** 321-322
essays about
Eiseley, Loren Corey **5** 232-233

BACON, FRANCIS (1909-1992), English
artist **1** 421-422

Bacon, Henry (1866-1924), American
architect
French, Daniel Chester **6** 98-99

BACON, NATHANIEL (1647-1676), American colonial leader **1** 424-425

Bacon, Nicholas (1509-1579), English
statesman
Bacon, Francis **1** 422-424

BACON, ROGER (circa 1214-1294), English philosopher **1** 425-427
Grosseteste, Robert **7** 15
Skinner, Burrhus Frederic **14** 269-270

Bacon's Laws (colonial Virginia)
Bacon, Nathaniel **1** 424-425

Bacon's Rebellion (Virginia; 1675-1676)
Bacon, Nathaniel **1** 424-425
Berkeley, William **2** 198-199
Byrd, William **3** 188-189

Bacteria (microorganisms)
Domagk, Gerhard Johannes Paul **5** 48-50
Hinshelwood, Cyril Norman **7** 405-406
Leeuwenhoek, Anton van **9** 300-301

Bacteriology (science)
chemical kinetics
Hinshelwood, Cyril Norman **7** 405-406
foundations
Koch, Heinrich Hermann Robert **9** 69-70
immunology
Behring, Emil Adolph von **2** 122-123
Metchnikoff, Élie **10** 532-533
lysogeny
Lwoff, André **10** 58-59
medical
Biggs, Hermann Michael **2** 272-273
Domagk, Gerhard Johannes Paul **5** 48-50
Ehrlich, Paul **5** 225-226
Park, William Hallock **12** 104-105
Welch, William Henry **16** 185-186
penicillin
Fleming, Alexander **5** 483-485
Florey, Howard Walter **5** 491-492
see also Scientists—bacteriologists

Bacteriophage (bacteriology)
Northrop, John Howard **11** 430-431

Bactria (ancient nation, Southwest Asia)
Antiochus III **1** 249-250

Bad Axe River, battle of (1832)
Black Hawk **2** 308

Bad Child's Book of Beasts, The (book)
Belloc, Joseph Hilaire Pierre **2** 141

Bad Hand
see Fitzpatrick, Thomas

BAD HEART BULL, AMOS (1869-1913), Oglala Lakota Sioux tribal historian and artist **1** 427-428

Badajoz, battle of (1812)
Wellington, 1st Duke of **16** 193-195

Badajoz, siege of (1169)
Alfonso I **1** 148

Badarayana (circa 400 B.C.), Hindu sage
Shankara **14** 150-151

Baden, Prince
see Maximilian

Badener Lehrstück vom Einverständnis, Das (play)
Brecht, Bertolt **2** 512-514

Badia, the (church, Florence)
Arnolfo di Cambio **1** 315-316
Bronzino **3** 19
Sangallo family **13** 464-466

Badile, Antonio (1517-1560), Italian painter
Veronese, Paolo **15** 469-470

BADOGLIO, PIETRO (1871-1956), Italian general and statesman **1** 428-429
Victor Emmanuel III **15** 484-485

Badr (flourished 750-756), Greek-born freedman
Abd al-Rahman I **1** 13-14

Bad-tempered Man, The (play)
Menander **10** 477-478

BAECK, LEO (1873-1956), rabbi, teacher, hero of the concentration camps, and Jewish leader **1** 429-430

Baecula, battle of (208 B.C.)
Scipio Africanus Major, Publius Cornelius **14** 61-62

BAEKELAND, LEO HENDRIK (1863-1944), American chemist **1** 430-431

BAER, KARL ERNST VON (1792-1876), Estonian anatomist and embryologist **1** 431-432

BAEYER, (JOHANN FRIEDRICH) ADOLF VON (1835-1917), German chemist
Fischer, Emil **5** 456-457
Hofmann, August Wilhelm von **7** 441-442

BAEZ, BUENAVENTURA (1812-1884), Dominican statesman, five time president **1** 432-433
Santana, Pedro **13** 474-475

BAEZ, JOAN (born 1941), American folk singer and human rights activist **1** 433-435

BAFFIN, WILLIAM (circa 1584-1622), English navigator and explorer **1** 435-436

Baffin Bay (Atlantic Ocean)
Baffin, William **1** 435-436

Baffin Island (Baffin Land; Arctic Ocean)
Boas, Franz **2** 349-351
Davis, John **4** 419
Eric the Red **5** 304
Frobisher, Martin **6** 121-122

Bafokeng (African people)
Moshweshwe **11** 203-205

Bagarre, La (musical composition)
Martinu, Bohuslav **10** 299-300

BAGEHOT, WALTER (1826-1877), English economist **1** 436-437
Nabuco de Araujo, Joaquim Aurelio **11** 288-289

Baghdad (city, Iraq)
architecture
Gropius, Walter **7** 13-14
Wright, Frank Lloyd **16** 398-401
battles
Hulagu Khan **8** 27-28
Suleiman I **15** 20-21
Islamic center
Abu-L-Ala al-Maarri **1** 32
Mamun, Abdallah al- **10** 183
Mansur, Abu Jafar ibn Muhammad al- **10** 214-215

Baghdad Pact (1955)
Nasser, Gamal Abdel **11** 317-318

BAGLEY, WILLIAM CHANDLER (1874-1946), educator and theorist of educational "essentialism" **1** 437-438

Baglione, Giovanni (1571-1644), Italian painter
Caravaggio **3** 282-284

Bagot, Sir Charles (1781-1843), English diplomat
Baldwin, Robert **1** 466-468

Baha ad-Din (1145-1234), Arab writer and statesman
Saladin **13** 441-442

Bahama Channel (Gulf Stream)
Ponce de León, Juan **12** 391-392

Bahama Islands (archipelago, Atlantic Ocean)
Columbus, Christopher **4** 176-179
Dunmore, 4th Earl of **5** 147

Baharistan (book)
Jami **8** 218-219

Bahía Honda (bay and town, Cuba)
Estrada Palma, Tomás **5** 326-327

Bahnwärter Thiel (novella)
Hauptmann, Gerhart Johann Robert **7** 199-201

BAHR, EGON (born 1922), West German politician **1** 438-440

Bahram I (ruled 274-277), king of Persia
Mani **10** 196-197

Baïf, Jean Antoine de (1532-1589), French poet
du Bellay, Joachim **5** 113-114
Le Jeune, Claude **9** 314-315

Baïf, Lazare de (died 1547) French humanist
Ronsard, Pierre de **13** 271-273

BAIKIE, WILLIAM BALFOUR (1825-1864), Scottish explorer and scientist **1** 440
Clapperton, Hugh **4** 72-73

BAILEY, F. LEE (born 1933), American defense attorney and author **1** 441-443

BAILEY, FLORENCE MERRIAM (1863-1948), American ornithologist and author **1** 443-444

BAILEY, GAMALIEL (1807-1859), American editor and politician **1** 444-445

Bailey, James Anthony (1847-1906), American circus owner
Barnum, Phineas Taylor **2** 13-15

BAILLIE, D(ONALD) M(ACPHERSON) (1887-1954), Scottish theologian **1** 445

BAILLIE, JOHN (1886-1960), Scottish theologian and ecumenical churchman **1** 445-447

Bainbridge, William (1774-1833), American naval officer
Lawrence, James **9** 251-252

Baines, Constance and Sophia (literary characters)
Bennett, Arnold **2** 167-168

Bairam Khan (ruled 1556-1560), Mogul regent of India
Akbar, Jalal-ud-din Mohammed **1** 96

Baiser au lépreux, Le (novel)
Mauriac, François **10** 347-348

Baius, Michael (1513-1589), Belgian theologian
Jansen, Cornelis **8** 220-221

Baja California
see Lower California

Bajazet
see Bayezid

Bajazet (play)
Racine, Jean Baptiste **12** 532-535

Bakelite (plastic)
Baekeland, Leo Hendrik **1** 430-431

Baker, George Pierce (1866-1935), American educator
O'Neill, Eugene **11** 514-516

BAKER, JAMES ADDISON III (born 1930), Republican party campaign leader **1** 447-448

BAKER, JOSEPHINE (1906-1975) Parisian dancer and singer from America **1** 448-451

BAKER, NEWTON DIEHL (1871-1937), American statesman **1** 451
   Lippmann, Walter **9** 439-440
   Pershing, John Joseph **12** 243-244
   Wilson, Thomas Woodrow **16** 330-332

BAKER, RAY STANNARD (1870-1946), American author **1** 451-452
   McClure, Samuel Sidney **10** 398-399

BAKER, RUSSELL (born 1925), American writer of personal-political essays **1** 452-454

BAKER, SIR SAMUEL WHITE (1821-1893), English explorer and administrator **1** 454-455
   Gordon, Charles George **6** 448-449

BAKER, SARA JOSEPHINE (1873-1945), American physician **1** 455-456

Baker v. Carr (1962)
   Brennan, William J. Jr. **2** 514-515
   Warren, Earl **16** 117-120

Bakeries
   Rudkin, Margaret Fogarty **13** 346-347

Bakewell, Robert (1725-1795), English agriculturist
   Lyell, Charles **10** 62-63

BAKHTIN, MIKHAIL MIKHAILOVICH (1895-1975), Russian philosopher and literary critic **1** 456-458

Bakongo (African people)
   Kasavubu, Joseph **8** 453-455
   Lumumba, Patrice Emery **10** 43-45
   Youlou, Fulbert **16** 466-467

Bakst, Leon (1866?-1924), Russian painter
   Chagall, Marc **3** 406-407

Bakufu (shogun military government)
   see Japan—1185-1867

BAKUNIN, MIKHAIL ALEKSANDROVICH (1814-1876), Russian anarchist **1** 458-460
   Dostoevsky, Fyodor **5** 74-77
   Marx, Karl **10** 304-308
   Mazzini, Giuseppe **10** 381-383
   Proudhon, Pierre Joseph **12** 461-463
   Turgenev, Ivan Sergeyevich **15** 345-348

Bal des voleurs, Le (play)
   Anouilh, Jean **1** 243-244

Baladas de primavera (poems)
   Jiménez, Juan Ramón **8** 261-262

Baladas peruanas (poems)
   González Prada, Manuel **6** 431

BALAGUER Y RICARDO, JOAQUÍN (born 1907), Dominican statesman **1** 460-461
   Bosch, Juan **2** 428-429
   Trujillo Molina, Rafael Leonidas **15** 313-314

Balakane (literary character)
   Wolfram von Eschenbach **16** 360-361

Balakirev, Mili Alexeyevich (1837-1910), Russian composer
   Borodin, Aleksandr Profirevich **2** 422-423
   Glinka, Mikhail Ivanovich **6** 369-370
   Mussorgsky, Modest Petrovich **11** 274-276
   Rimsky-Korsakov, Nikolai Andreevich **13** 174-175
   Tchaikovsky, Peter Ilyich **15** 130-132

Balakirev Circle
   see Mighty Five

Balali (African people)
   Youlou, Fulbert **16** 466-467

Balance in nature (philosophy)
   Ingenhousz, Jan **8** 119-120
   Linnaeus, Carl **9** 427-429

Balance of power (political)
   Cobden, Richard **4** 127-128
   Elizabeth I **5** 263-266
   Frederick II **6** 81-84
   Montesquieu **11** 123-125

Balanced Discourses (book)
   Wang Ch'ung **16** 98-99

BALANCHINE, GEORGE (1904-1983), Russian-born American choreographer **1** 461-462
   Farrell, Suzanne **5** 391-393
   Kirstein, Lincoln **9** 39-41
   Rodgers, Richard Charles **13** 234-236
   Stravinsky, Igor Fedorovich **14** 502-506
   Tallchief, Maria **15** 88-89
   Weill, Kurt **16** 174-175

Balanchivadze, Georgi Melitonovitch
   see Balanchine, George

Balbiani, Valentine (flourished 16th century), wife of Italian statesman René de Birague
   Pilon, Germain **12** 305

Balbo, Italo (1896-1940), Italian air marshal
   Nobile, Umberto **11** 411-412

BALBOA, VASCO NÚÑEZ DE (circa 1475-1519), Spanish explorer **1** 462-463
   Benalcázar, Sebastián de **2** 145-146
   Magellan, Ferdinand **10** 126-127
   Pedrarias **12** 179
   Pizarro, Francisco **12** 340-341

BALBULUS, NOTKER (circa 840-912), Swiss poet-musician and monk **11** 434-435

BALCH, EMILY GREENE (1867-1961), American pacifist and social reformer **1** 463-464

Balcony, The (play)
   Genet, Jean **6** 262-263

Balder (mythology)
   Arnold, Matthew **1** 311-313

Balder Dead (epic)
   Arnold, Matthew **1** 311-313

Baldomir, Alfredo (1884-1948), Uruguayan president 1938-1943
   Terra, Gabriel **15** 154-155

Baldovinetti, Alessio (1425?-1499), Italian painter
   Ghirlandaio, Domenico **6** 292-293

BALDWIN I (1058-1118), Norman king of Jerusalem 1100-1118 **1** 464-465
   Godfrey of Bouillon **6** 379

Baldwin I (1171?-1205), emperor of Constantinople 1204-1205
   Villehardouin, Geffroi de **15** 499

Baldwin II (died 1131), Norman king of Jerusalem 1118-1131
   Baldwin I **1** 464-465

Baldwin II (1217-1273), emperor of Constantinople 1228-1261
   Montreuil, Pierre de **11** 139

Baldwin III (1130?-1162), king of Jerusalem 1143-1162
   Nureddin **11** 444-445

Baldwin IV (1160-1185), king of Jerusalem 1174-1185
   Saladin **13** 441-442
   William of Tyre **16** 299-300

Baldwin V (died 1067), count of Flanders 1036-1067
   William I **16** 290-291

BALDWIN, JAMES ARTHUR (1924-1987), African American author, poet, and dramatist **1** 465-466
   Wright, Richard **16** 401-402

BALDWIN, ROBERT (1804-1858), Canadian politician **1** 466-468
   Elgin, 8th Earl of **5** 248-249
   Howe, Joseph **7** 534-535
   Lafontaine, Louis-Hippolyte **9** 157-158
   Ryerson, Adolphus Egerton **13** 392-393

BALDWIN, STANLEY (1st Earl Baldwin of Bewdley; 1867-1947), English statesman, three times prime minister **1** 468-469
   Chamberlain, Arthur Neville **3** 409-411
   Churchill, Winston Leonard Spencer **4** 51-53
   Curzon, George Nathaniel **4** 351-352
   George V **6** 273-275

Baldwin of Bewdley, 1st Earl
   see Baldwin, Stanley

Baldwin of Boulogne
   see Baldwin I, king

Bale, John (1495-1563), English author and bishop
   Malory, Thomas **10** 175-176

BALFOUR, ARTHUR JAMES (1st Earl of Balfour; 1848-1930), British statesman and philosopher **1** 469-470
   Cecil, of Chelwood Viscount **3** 388-389
   Curzon, George Nathaniel **4** 351-352
   Lloyd George, David **9** 469-471
   Perth, 16th Earl of **12** 244-245
   Younghusband, Francis Edward **16** 477

Balfour Declaration (1917)
Balfour, Arthur James **1** 469-470
Ben-Gurion, David **2** 160-161
Husein ibn Ali **8** 63
Kuk, Abraham Issac **9** 123-124
Weizmann, Chaim **16** 183-184
Wise, Stephen Samuel **16** 344-345
Zangwill, Israel **16** 488-489

Balfour Report (1926)
Balfour, Arthur James **1** 469-470

Bali (island)
see Indonesia

Bal-i-Jibril (poem)
Iqbal, Muhammad **8** 132-133

Baline, Israel
see Berlin, Irving

Baliol
see Balliol

Balkan Entente (1934)
Atatürk, Ghazi Mustapha Kemal
1 356-357

Balkan States (Southeast Europe)
Roman and Byzantine rule
Diocletian **5** 19-20
Manuel I **10** 218-219
Turkish rule
Charles V **3** 457-459
Gladstone, William Ewart
6 357-360
Mahmud II **10** 145-147
Selim III **14** 95-96
see also Albania; Balkan wars; Bul-
garia; Greece; Romania; Turkey;
Yugoslavia

Balkan wars
Ferdinand **5** 413-414
First (1912-1913)
Alexander of Yugoslavia **1** 136-137
Poincaré, Raymond **12** 366-368
Venizelos, Eleutherios **15** 460-461
Wilkins, George Hubert **16** 281-282
Second (1913)
Alexander of Yugoslavia **1** 136-137
Atatürk, Ghazi Mustapha Kemal
1 356-357
Enver Pasha **5** 290-291
1990s
Bulatovic, Momir **3** 115-116
Gligorov, Kiro **6** 367-369
Izetbegovic, Alija **8** 161-163
Milosevic, Slobodan **11** 39-40
Mladic, Ratko **11** 68-69
Owen, David Anthony Llewellyn
12 37-39
Tudjman, Franjo **15** 333-335

BALL, GEORGE (1909-1994), American
politician and supporter of an economi-
cally united Europe **1** 470-471

BALL, LUCILLE (Lucille Desiree Hunt;
1911-1989), American comedienne
1 472-473

Ball, Thomas (1819-1911), American sculptor
French, Daniel Chester **6** 98-99

BALLA, GIACOMO (1871-1958), Italian
painter **1** 473-474
Boccioni, Umberto **2** 353-354
Severini, Gino **14** 122

Ballad of Baby Doe, The (opera; D. Moore)
Tabor, Horace Austin Warner **15** 70

Ballad of Billie Potts, The (poem)
Warren, Robert Penn **16** 121-122

Ballad of East and West, A (poem)
Kipling, Joseph Rudyard **9** 32-33

Ballad of Everlasting Sorrow (poem)
Po Chü-i **12** 362-363

Ballad of Reading Gaol, The (poem)
Wilde, Oscar Fingall O'Flahertie Wills
16 272-273

Ballad of the Brown Girl (poem)
Cullen, Countee **4** 333-334

Ballad of the Lute (poem)
Po Chü-i **12** 362-363

Ballad of the Sun (musical composition)
Chávez, Carlos **3** 486

Ballad of the White Horse, The (poem)
Chesterton, Gilbert Keith **3** 508-509

Ballad of William Sycamore, A (poem)
Benét, Stephen Vincent **2** 157-158

Ballad upon a Wedding (poem)
Suckling, John **15** 10-11

Ballade (literature)
Musset, Louis Charles Alfred de
11 271-272
Villon, François **15** 499-501
Vitry, Philippe de **16** 2

Ballade (music)
Brahms, Johannes **2** 490-492
Chopin, Frédéric François **4** 16-18
Josquin des Prez **8** 361-363
Machaut, Guillaume de **10** 93-94
Vitry, Philippe de **16** 2

Ballads and Other Poems (literary collection)
Longfellow, Henry Wadsworth
9 499-500

Ballads and Poems (anthology)
Benét, Stephen Vincent **2** 157-158

Ballads and Sonnets (poems)
Rossetti, Dante Gabriel **13** 308-309

Ballads for Sale (poems)
Lowell, Amy **10** 13

BALLADUR, EDOUARD (born 1929), premier of the French Government
1 474-475

Ballance, John (1839-1893), New Zealand
journalist and statesman
Seddon, Richard John **14** 81-82

Ballata (song)
Landini, Francesco **9** 185-186

Ballerina and Lady with Fan (pastel)
Degas, Hilaire Germain Edgar
4 461-462

Balleroy (French château)
Mansart, François **10** 211

Ballet (dance)
Ailey, Alvin **1** 91-94
Balanchine, George **1** 461-462
Baryshnikov, Mikhail **2** 43-44
Cocteau, Jean **4** 132-133
de Mille, Agnes **4** 486-488
Diaghilev, Sergei **4** 525-527
Farrell, Suzanne **5** 391-393
Fonteyn, Dame Margot **5** 504-505
Graham, Martha **6** 485-486
Joffrey, Robert **8** 268-270
Kirstein, Lincoln **9** 39-41
Morris, Mark **11** 184-185
Nijinsky, Vaslav **11** 393-395
Nureyev, Rudolph **11** 445-446
Pavlova, Anna **12** 157-159
Plisetskaya, Maya Mikhailovna
12 356-358
Robbins, Jerome **13** 190-192
Schlemmer, Oskar **14** 12-13
Smuin, Michael **14** 307-309
Taeuber-Arp, Sophie **15** 73-74
Tallchief, Maria **15** 88-89
Tharp, Twyla **15** 164-165
Ulanova, Galina **15** 382-383
see also Modern dance

Ballet (music)
Cesti, Pietro **3** 399-400
Chávez, Carlos **3** 486
Lully, Jean Baptiste **10** 40-41
Malipiero, Gian Francesco **10** 171
Morley, Thomas **11** 179-180
Musgrave, Thea **11** 266-268
Sauguet, Henri **13** 497-498
Stravinsky, Igor Fedorovich **14** 502-506
Tcherepnin, Alexander **15** 132-133
Villa-Lobos, Heitor **15** 496-497

Ballet mécanique (film)
Léger, Fernand **9** 302-303

Ballet of the Twentieth Century
Farrell, Suzanne **5** 391-393

Ballets, Les (dance co.)
Balanchine, George **1** 461-462

Ballets Monte Carlo (paris)
Chirico, Giorgio de **4** 4

Ballets Russes de Sergei Diaghilev
Diaghilev, Sergei **4** 525-527
Goncharova, Natalia **6** 424-426
Nijinsky, Vaslav **11** 393-395
Roussel, Albert **13** 328-329
Tallchief, Maria **15** 88-89

Ballets Suédois (Paris)
Chirico, Giorgio de **4** 4

Ballinger, Richard A. (1858-1922), American statesman
Hapgood, Norman **7** 137-138
Pinchot, Gifford **12** 308-309
Taft, William Howard **15** 78-81

Balliol, Edward de (died 1363), claimant to Scottish throne
Edward III **5** 211-212
Philip VI **12** 277-278
Robert II **13** 194

Balliol, John de (1249-1315), claimant to Scottish throne
Edward I **5** 208-210
Robert I **13** 192-194

Ballistite (explosive)
Nobel, Alfred Bernhard **11** 410-411

BALLIVIÁN, JOSÉ (1805-1852), Bolivian president 1841-1847 **1** 475

Ballo dell' ingrate, Il (opera)
Monteverdi, Claudio Giovanni Antonio **11** 126-128

Ballo in maschera, Un (opera; Verdi)
Anderson, Marian **1** 218-219
Kokoschka, Oskar **9** 75-76
Verdi, Giuseppe Fortunino Francesco **15** 463-465

Balloon (aircraft)
gasoline-powered
Curtiss, Glenn Hammond **4** 350-351
Santos-Dumont, Alberto **13** 477-478
hot air
Montgolfier, Joseph and Jacques Michel Étienne **11** 133-134
hydrogen
Andrée, Salomon August **1** 226
Hopkinson, Francis **7** 496-497
Mendeleev, Dmitrii Ivanovich **10** 486-488
Piccard, Auguste **12** 297-298

Ballroom dancing
Castle, Vernon and Irene **3** 361-363

BALMACEDA FERNÁNDEZ, JOSÉ MANUEL (1840-1891), Chilean president 1886-1891 **1** 475-476

Balmer, Johann Jacob (1825-1898), German mathematician and physicist
Bohr, Niels Henrik David **2** 366-368

Balmoral Castle (Scotland)
Victoria **15** 485-487

Balta, José (1816-1872), Peruvian president 1868-1872
Meiggs, Henry **10** 458-459

BALTHUS (Balthasar Klossowski; born 1908), European painter and stage designer **1** 476-477

Baltic Sea (Northern Europe)
Cook, James **4** 214-215
Peter I **12** 253-256

Baltimore (city, Maryland)
archdiocese
Carroll, John **3** 331-332

Gibbons, James **6** 300-301
architecture
Latrobe, Benjamin Henry **9** 222-224
Mills, Robert **11** 36-37
promoters
Brown, Alexander **3** 31-32

Baltimore, Barons
see Calvert

BALTIMORE, DAVID (born 1938), American virologist **1** 477-478

Baltimore and Ohio Railroad (United States)
Brown, Alexander **3** 31-32
Cooper, Peter **4** 223-224
Garrett, John Work **6** 225
Gould, Jay **6** 470-472

Baltimore Conference (Methodists; 1780)
Asbury, Francis **1** 324-325

Baltimore Orioles (baseball team)
Ruth, George Herman Jr. **13** 384

Balubakat (Baluba association)
Tshombe, Moïse Kapenda **15** 325-326

Baluchistan (region, Western Asia)
Mahmud of Ghazni **10** 147

BALZAC, HONORÉ DE (1799-1850), French novelist **1** 478-480
influence of
Dreiser, Herman Theodore **5** 98-100
Farrell, James Thomas **5** 390-391
Hugo, Victor Marie **8** 22-25
Rabearivelo, Jean Joseph **12** 523-524
Wassermann, Jakob **16** 130-131
statue of
Rodin, Auguste **13** 236-238
universal reality
Proust, Marcel **12** 465-467
Singer, Isaac Bashevis **14** 249-250
Stendhal **14** 422-425

Bamako Conference (1946)
Houphouët-Boigny, Felix **7** 519-520

BAMBA, AMADOU (1850-1927), Senegalese religious leader **1** 481-482

BAMBARA, TONI CADE (1939-1995), African American writer and editor **1** 482-483

Bambi (film)
Disney, Walter Elias **5** 26-27

Bamboccianti (Netherlands artists)
Le Nain, Antoine, Louis and Mathieu **9** 321-322

Bamboo, Rock and Tall Tree (painting)
Ni Tsan **11** 400

Bamboo, Rocks and Lonely Orchids (scroll)
Chao Meng-fu **3** 436-437

Bamboo Sprig Songs (poems)
Po Chü-i **12** 362-363

Bamboula (musical composition)
Gottschalk, Louis Moreau **6** 463-464

Bamokoteli (African people)
Moshweshwe **11** 203-205

Ban Müang (flourished 13th century), Thai king
Rama Khamhaeng **13** 11

Bana (Banabhatta; 7th century), Sanskrit poet
Harsha **7** 181-182

Banana Bottom (novel)
McKay, Claude **10** 416

Banana Cycle (novel)
Asturias, Miguel Angel **1** 354-355

Bananier, Le (musical composition)
Gottschalk, Louis Moreau **6** 463-464

Banco de Avio (Mexico)
Alamán, Lucas **1** 99-100

Banco di Sto Spirito (Rome)
Sangallo family **13** 464-466

Bancroft, Edward (1744-1821), American scientist
Deane, Silas **4** 435-437

Bancroft, Frederick (1860-1945), American historian
Dunning, William Archibald **5** 148-149

BANCROFT, GEORGE (1800-1891), American historian and statesman **1** 483-484
as statesman
Polk, James Knox **12** 374-376
romantic style
Hildreth, Richard **7** 382
Parkman, Francis **12** 113-115
Tucker, George **15** 332-333
students
Bellows, Henry Whitney **2** 143-144
Motley, John Lothrop **11** 211-212

BANCROFT, HUBERT HOWE (1832-1918), American historian **1** 484-485

Band of Angels (novel)
Warren, Robert Penn **16** 121-122

BANDA, HASTINGS KAMUZU (born 1905), Malawi statesman **1** 485-486

Bandanese (Indonesian people)
Coen, Jan Pieterszoon **4** 133

BANDARANAIKE, SIRIMAVO (also Sirima) **RATWATTE DIAS** (born 1916), first woman prime minister in the world as head of the Sri Lankan Freedom party government (1960-1965, 1970-1976) **1** 486-488

Bande Mataram (poem)
Chatterji, Bankimchandra **3** 480-481

Bandinelli, Baccio (1493-1560), Italian sculptor
Cellini, Benvenuto **3** 391-392

Bandinelli, Orlando
see Alexander III, pope

BANERJEE, SURENDRANATH (1848-1925), Indian nationalist **1** 488
Das, Chitta Ranjan **4** 401-402
Mehta, Pherozeshah **10** 455

Bangala (African people)
Mobutu Sese Seko **11** 69-71

Bangkok (city, Thailand)
Chulalongkorn **4** 43-45

Bangla siksa-grantha (book)
Deb, Radhakant **4** 437

Bangladesh (former East Pakistan)
Bhashani, Maulana Abdul Hamid Khan **2** 255-257
Ershad, Hussain Mohammad **5** 312-314
Gandhi, Indira Priyadarshini **6** 200-201
Mujibur Rahman **11** 234-236
Ziaur Rahman **16** 515-516

Banjo
Seeger, Pete **14** 83-84

Banjo (novel)
McKay, Claude **10** 416

Banjo Lesson (painting)
Tanner, Henry Ossawa **15** 102-103

Bank Dick, The (film)
Fields, W. C. **5** 444

Bank of America
Giannini, A. P. **6** 295-297

Bank of Augusta v. Earle (legal case; 1839)
Taney, Roger Brooke **15** 98-99

Bank of England
Keynes, John Maynard **8** 528-530
Soane, John **14** 314-315
William III **16** 295-296

Bank of England (book)
Clapham, John Harold **4** 71

Bank of France
Blum, Léon **2** 343-344

Bank of Japan
Takahashi, Korekiyo **15** 84-85

Bank of North America
Morris, Robert **11** 185-187
Paine, Thomas **12** 66-67

Bank of Stephen Girard (Philadelphia)
Girard, Stephen **6** 347-348

Bank of the United States, First
(1791-1811)
established
Hamilton, Alexander **7** 95-98
Washington, George **16** 126-129
rechartered
Clinton, George **4** 113-114
Crawford, William Harris **4** 299-300
Gallatin, Albert **6** 183-184
Girard, Stephen **6** 347-348
Macon, Nathaniel **10** 114-115
supporters
Gerry, Elbridge **6** 282-283

Bank of the United States, Second
(1816-1836)
charter
Marshall, John **10** 279-281
directors
Biddle, Nicholas **2** 264-265
du Pont, Éleuthère Irénée **5** 154
legal defense
Webster, Daniel **16** 162-164
opponents

Atchison, David Rice **1** 357-358
Benton, Thomas Hart **2** 178-179
Blair, Francis Preston **2** 313-315
Crockett, David **4** 314-316
Duane, William **5** 109
Jackson, Andrew **8** 168-172
Polk, James Knox **12** 374-376
Taney, Roger Brooke **15** 98-99
Tyler, John **15** 368-369
supporters
Adams, John Quincy **1** 52-54
Ashley, William Henry **1** 333-334
Brown, Alexander **3** 31-32
Clay, Henry **4** 94-96
Everett, Edward **5** 344
Gallatin, Albert **6** 183-184
Girard, Stephen **6** 347-348
Monroe, James **11** 111-113

Bankers
see Business and industrial leaders—bankers

Banking, Australian
Chifley, Joseph Benedict **3** 518
Fisher, Andrew **5** 462

Banking, Canadian
Smith, Donald Alexander **14** 288-289

Banking, Chilean
Herrera, Juan de **7** 335

Banking, Indian (Asia)
Gandhi, Indira Priyadarshini **6** 200-201

Banking, international
see Inter-American Development Bank; World Bank

Banking, Mexican
Calles, Plutarco Elías **3** 234-235

Banking, United States
and international relations
Rockefeller, David **13** 224-225
central
Aldrich, Nelson Wilmarth **1** 123-124
Biddle, Nicholas **2** 264-265
Chandler, Zachariah **3** 425-426
Cooke, Jay **4** 215-216
Morgan, John Pierpont **11** 163-165
see also Bank of the United States
Federal Reserve
Hoover, Herbert Clark **7** 483-485
Warburg, Paul Moritz **16** 111-112
Hamiltonian policies
Appleton, Nathan **1** 266-267
reform
Giannini, A. P. **6** 295-297
Senate Committee on
Byrnes, James Francis **3** 191-192
Morgan, John Pierpont II **11** 165

Bankrupt, The (play)
Bjørnson, Bjørnstjerne **2** 299-300

Banks of the Oise (painting)
Daubigny, Charles François **4** 402

BANKS, DENNIS J. (born 1932), Native American leader, teacher, activist, and author **1** 488-489

BANKS, SIR JOSEPH (1743-1820), English naturalist **1** 489-490
Bligh, William **2** 325-326
Burckhardt, Johann Ludwig **3** 133
Cook, James **4** 214-215
Volta, Alessandro **16** 12-14

BANNEKER, BENJAMIN (1731-1806), African American mathematician **1** 490-491

Banner of Jerusalem movement (Palestine)
Kuk, Abraham Issac **9** 123-124

BANNISTER, EDWARD MTICHELL (1828-1901), African American landscape painter **1** 491-493

Bannock (town, Montana)
Bozeman, John M. **2** 471-472

Bannockburn, battle of (1314)
Douglas, James **5** 78
Edward II **5** 210
Robert I **13** 192-194

Banque Royale (Paris)
Law, John **9** 244-245

Banquet in a Park (painting)
Hals, Frans **7** 89-91

Banqueters, The (play)
Aristophanes **1** 293-294

Banqueting House (Whitehall, England)
Rubens, Peter Paul **13** 339-342

Bantamese (people; Western Java)
Coen, Jan Pieterszoon **4** 133

Bantams in Pine-woods (poem)
Stevens, Wallace **14** 443-445

Ban-the-bomb movement (England; 1960s)
Russell, Bertrand Arthur William **13** 373-374

BANTING, FREDERICK GRANT (1891-1941), Canadian physiolgist **1** 493-494
Best, Charles Herbert **2** 236-237

Bantu (language)
Johnston, Henry Hamilton **8** 322-323

Bantu (people; South Africa)
Mobutu Sese Seko **11** 69-71
Plaatje, Solomon Tshekisho **12** 341-342

Bantu Land Act (South Africa)
Mofolo, Thomas **11** 74

Bantustans (South Africa)
Verwoerd, Hendrik Frensch **15** 472-473

Banu Ghaniya (Berbers)
Yakub al-Mansur, Abu Yusuf **16** 426

BANZER SUÁREZ, HUGO (born 1926), Bolivian president (1971-1979) **1** 494-496

BAO DAI (born 1913), emperor of Vietnam 1932-1945 and 1949-1955 **1** 496-497
Diem, Ngo Dinh **5** 6-7

Bapaune, battle of (1871)
Faidherbe, Louis Léon César **5** 366-367

Baptism (religious rite)
Campbell, Alexander **3** 249-250
Cyprianus, Thascius Caecilianus
4 361-362
Ignatius of Antioch **8** 107-108
John the Baptist **8** 290

Baptism of Christ (altarpiece)
Bellini, Giovanni **2** 137-138

Baptism of Christ (painting)
Corot, Jean Baptiste Camille **4** 247-249
Greco **6** 511-514
Piero della Francesca **12** 301-302

Baptism of Christ (painting; Verrocchio)
Leonardo da Vinci **9** 337-340
Verrocchio, Andrea del **15** 471-472

Baptist Missionary Society (England)
Carey, William **3** 297

Baptist Union Theological Seminary
(Chicago)
Harper, William Rainey **7** 163-164

Baptists (religious denomination)
anticreedalism
Campbell, Alexander **3** 249-250
evangelism
Backus, Isaac **1** 420-421
Graham, William Franklin Jr.
6 487-488
Miller, William **11** 30-31
Fundamentalists
Falwell, Jerry **5** 375-376
missions
Carey, William **3** 297

Bar, Confederation of (Polish independence movement)
Pulaski, Casimir **12** 480-481

Bar at the Folies-Bergère, A. (painting)
Manet, Édouard **10** 193-194

BAR KOCHBA, SIMEON (died 135), Jewish
commander of revolt against Romans **2** 5
Akiba ben Joseph **1** 97-98
Hadrian **7** 60-61

Barabas (literary character)
Marlowe, Christopher **10** 272-274

BARAK, EHUD (born 1942), 14th head of
the Israel Defense Forces **1** 497-498

BARAKA, IMAMU AMIRI (Everett LeRoi
Jones; born 1934), African American poet
and playwright **1** 498-499
Wright, Richard **16** 401-402

BARANOV, ALEKSANDR ANDREIEVICH
(1747-1819), Russian explorer **1** 499-500

Barbadori Altar (painting)
Lippi, Filippo **9** 439

Barbara, oder die Frömmigkeit (novel)
Werfel, Franz **16** 204-205

Barbarians (Roman empire)
conversion of
Clovis I **4** 124
defeated

Constantine I **4** 209-211
Marcus Aurelius Antoninus
10 243-245
Ricimer, Flavius **13** 151-152
Valerian **15** 404-405
invasions
Odoacer **11** 473
Stilicho, Flavius **14** 452-453
sack of Rome
Alaric **1** 101-102

Barbarossa, Frederick
see Frederick I

Barbarossa II (Khair al-Din; 1466?-1546),
Algerian pirate
Suleiman I **15** 20-21

Barbarous Odes (poems)
Carducci, Giosuè **3** 290-291

Barbary Shore (novel)
Mailer, Norman Kingsley **10** 148-150

Barbary States (North Africa)
Barry, John **2** 24-25
Decatur, Stephen **4** 448-449
Madison, James **10** 121-123

Barbeau, Marius (1883-1969), Canadian
anthropologist
Carr, Emily **3** 319

Barber of Seville (opera)
Rossini, Gioacchino **13** 311-312

Barber of Seville (play)
Beaumarchais, Pierre August Caron de
2 93-94

BARBER, SAMUEL (1910-1981), American
composer **1** 500-501
Menotti, Gian Carlo **10** 509-510

Barberine (play)
Musset, Louis Charles Alfred de
11 271-272

Barberini, Antonio (1608-1671), Italian
cardinal
Rossi, Luigi **13** 310-311

Barberini, Maffeo
see Urban VIII

BARBIE, KLAUS (Klaus Altmann;
1913-1991), Nazi leader in Vichy France
1 501-503

Barbieri, Giovanni Francesco
see Guercino

Barbizon school (French art)
influence of
Blakelock, Ralph Albert **2** 318
Bonington, Richard Parkes
2 394-395
Inness, George **8** 123-124
Mondrian, Piet **11** 101-102
Pissaro, Camille **12** 326-327
Seurat, Georges Pierre **14** 120-122
leaders
Corot, Jean Baptiste Camille
4 247-249
Daubigny, Charles François **4** 402
Millet, Jean François **11** 31
Rousseau, Théodore **13** 328

plein-air painting
Böcklin, Arnold **2** 354-355
Liebermann, Max **9** 402-403
Monet, Claude **11** 102-104

Barbo, Pietro
see Paul II, pope

BARBOSA, RUY (1849-1923), Brazilian
journalist and politician **1** 503-504

Barcas (plays)
Vicente, Gil **15** 479-480

Barcelona Disputation (1263)
Nahmanides **11** 293-294

Barcelona International Exposition (1929)
Mies van der Rohe, Ludwig **11** 10-12

Barchester Towers (novel)
Trollope, Anthony **15** 300-302

Barclay, Edwin (1882-1955), Liberian
statesman, twice president
Tubman, William Vacanarat Shadrach
15 331

Bard College (Annandale-on-Hudson, New
York State)
Bellow, Saul **2** 141-143
Ellison, Ralph Waldo **5** 274-275

Bard, the (poem)
Gray, Thomas **6** 509-510

Bardamu (literary character)
Céline, Louis Ferdinand **3** 390-391

Bardas, Caesar (died 866), Byzantine core-
gent 842-856
Basil I **2** 49-50
Photius **12** 283-284

Bardas Phocas (died 989), Byzantine general
Basil II **2** 50-51

Bardas Sclerus (flourished 979-989),
Byzantine general
Basil II **2** 50-51

BARDEEN, JOHN (1908-1991), American
Nobel physicist **2** 1-3
Brattain, Walter H. **2** 505-507

Bardi Chapel (Sta Croce, Florence)
Giotto **6** 342-345

Bardi, Donato di Niccolò
see Donatello

Bardi, Giovanni de' (1534?-1612?), Italian
scholar and music patron
Caccini, Giulio **3** 205-206

Bardiya
see Smerdis

Bardoli Satyagraha (Gandhian system)
Patel, Vallabhbhai **12** 129-130

Barefoot Boy, The (poem)
Whittier, John Greenleaf **16** 256-257

Barefoot Contessa, The (film)
Bogart, Humphrey **2** 363-364

Barefoot Saint, The (stories)
Benét, Stephen Vincent **2** 157-158

BARENBOIM, DANIEL (born 1942), Israeli pianist and conductor **2** 3-4

BARENTS, WILLEM (died 1597), Dutch navigator and explorer **2** 4-5
 Chancellor, Richard **3** 422
 Hudson, Henry **8** 12-13

Barents Sea (Arctic Ocean)
 Barents, Willem **2** 4-5

Bargaining for a Horse (painting)
 Mount, William Sidney **11** 213-214

Bargash Sayyid (died 1888), sultan of Zanzibar (1870-1888)
 Tippu Tip **15** 235-236

Barges (painting)
 Vlaminck, Maurice **16** 6

Bari (city, Italy)
 Guiscard, Robert **7** 39-40

Baring, Evelyn
 see Cromer, 1st Earl of

Baring, Thomas George
 see Northbrook, Lord

Barium (element—chemistry)
 Davy, Humphry **4** 426-427
 Scheele, Karl Wilhelm **13** 525-526

Barker, Sir Ernest (1874-1960), English historian
 Laski, Harold J. **9** 215-216

Barkla, Charles Grover (1877-1944), English physicist
 Compton, Arthur Holly **4** 186-188

BARLACH, ERNST (1870-1938), German sculptor **2** 5-6
 Lehmbruck, Wilhelm **9** 307

Barlas (Mongol clan)
 Tamerlane **15** 94-95

BARLOW, JOEL (1754-1812), American poet **2** 6-7
 Freneau, Philip Morin **6** 99-100
 Webster, Noah **16** 164-166

Barnabas (New Testament character)
 Mark **10** 266-267
 Paul **12** 141-143

Barnaby Rudge (novel)
 Dickens, Charles John Huffam **4** 538-541

BARNARD, CHRISTIAAN N. (born 1922), South African heart transplant surgeon **2** 7-8

Barnard College (Columbia University)
 Barnard, Frederick Augustus Porter **2** 9-10
 Hewitt, Abram Stevens **7** 371-372
 MacIver, Robert Morrison **10** 100-101

BARNARD, EDWARD EMERSON (1857-1923), American astronomer **2** 8-9

BARNARD, FREDERICK AUGUSTUS PORTER (1809-1889), American educator and mathematician **2** 9-10

Barnard, George Grey (1863-1938), American sculptor
 Epstein, Jacob **5** 295-296

BARNARD, HENRY (1811-1900), American educator **2** 10
 Willard, Emma Hart **16** 288-289

Barnato, Barney (1852-1897), English speculator
 Morgan, Junius Spencer **11** 166-167
 Rhodes, Cecil John **13** 120-122

Barnave, A.P. (1761-1793), French politician
 Marie Antoinette **10** 258-259

Barndall House (Hollywood, California)
 Wright, Frank Lloyd **16** 398-401

Barnes, Albert C. (1872-1951), American physician and art collector
 Glackens, William **6** 355-356
 Lipchitz, Jacques **9** 432-433
 Matisse, Henri **10** 336-337
 Pippin, Horace **12** 318-319
 Sloan, John **14** 274-275

BARNES, DJUNA (a.k.a. Lydia Steptoe; 1892-1982), American author **2** 11-13

Barnes, Harry Elmer (1889-1968), American historian and sociologist
 Robinson, James Harvey **13** 208

Barnes, Robert (1495-1540), English martyr
 Coverdale, Miles **4** 278

Barnet, battle of (1471)
 Henry VI **7** 298-299
 Margaret of Anjou **10** 249-250
 Warwick and of Salisbury, Earl of **16** 122-123

BARNUM, PHINEAS TAYLOR (1810-1891), American showman **2** 13-15

Barocchio, Giacomo
 see Vignola, Giacomo da

Baroda College (India)
 Ghose, Aurobindo **6** 293-294

BAROJA Y NESSI, PÍO (1872-1956), Spanish novelist **2** 15-16
 Cela y Trulock, Camilo José **3** 389-390

Barometer (instrument)
 Boyle, Robert **2** 469-471
 Gay-Lussac, Joseph Louis **6** 245-246
 Hooke, Robert **7** 475
 Mendeleev, Dmitrii Ivanovich **10** 486-488
 Torricelli, Evangelista **15** 268-269

Barometer Rising (novel)
 MacLennan, Hugh **10** 110-111

BARON, SALO WITTMAYER (1895-1989), Austrian-American educator and Jewish historian **2** 16-17
 Cohen, Morris Raphael **4** 139-140

Baronius, Caesar (1538-1607), Italian historian
 Gregory XIII **6** 534
 Canisius, Peter **3** 258

Barons War (England; 1263-1265)
 Montfort, Simon de **11** 132-133

Baron's Wars, The (poem)
 Drayton, Michael **5** 97-98

Baroque architecture
 England
  Gibbs, James **6** 301-302
  Hawksmoor, Nicholas **7** 211-212
  Jones, Inigo **8** 333-334
  Vanbrugh, John **15** 409-410
  Wren, Christopher **16** 393-394
 France
  Le Nôtre, André **9** 328-329
  Le Vau, Louis **9** 360-361
  Mansart, François **10** 211
  Mansart, Jules Hardouin **10** 212
  Perrault, Claude **12** 232-233
 Germany and Austria
  Artigas, José Gervasio **1** 323
  Fischer von Erlach, Johann Bernhard **5** 459-461
  Hildebrandt, Johann Lucas von **7** 380-381
  Neumann, Balthasar **11** 354-355
  Prandtauer, Jakob **12** 432
  Schlüter, Andreas **14** 18-19
 Italy and Spain
  Bernini, Gian Lorenzo **2** 214-216
  Borromini, Francesco **2** 424-425
  Churriguera, José Benito de **4** 53-54
  Cortona, Pietro da **4** 256
  Guarini, Guarino **7** 25-26
  Juvara, Filippo **8** 396-397
  Maderno, Carlo **10** 117-118
  Perrault, Claude **12** 232-233

Baroque art
 see Baroque architecture; Baroque painting; Baroque sculpture

Baroque literature
 drama and novel
  Corneille, Pierre **4** 234-236
  Gracián y Morales, Baltasar Jerónimo **6** 481-482
 poetry
  Crashaw, Richard **4** 296
  Donne, John **5** 60-61
  Góngora y Argote, Luis de **6** 427-428
  Juana Inés de la Cruz **8** 367-368

Baroque music (Dutch)
 Sweelinck, Jan Pieterszoon **15** 50-51

Baroque music (English)
 Arne, Thomas Augustine **1** 307-308
 Bach, Johann Sebastian **1** 416-419
 Handel, George Frederick **7** 116-119
 Purcell, Henry **12** 484-485

Baroque music (French)
 Charpentier, Marc Antoine **3** 471-472
 Couperin, François **4** 270-271

Lully, Jean Baptiste **10** 40-41
Rameau, Jean Philippe **13** 17-18

Baroque music (German and Austrian)
instrumental
Buxtehude, Dietrich **3** 185-186
Froberger, Johann Jakob **6** 120-121
vocal
Bach, Johann Sebastian **1** 416-419
Fux, Johann Joseph **6** 155-156
Praetorius, Michael **12** 431-432
Schütz, Heinrich **14** 48-49
Telemann, Georg Philipp
15 137-138

Baroque music (Italian)
instrumental
Corelli, Arcangelo **4** 230-231
Frescobaldi, Girolamo **6** 101-102
Gabrieli, Giovanni **6** 161-162
Monteverdi, Claudio Giovanni
Antonio **11** 126-128
Scarlatti, Domenico **13** 515-517
Vivaldi, Antonio **16** 3-4
vocal
Caccini, Giulio **3** 205-206
Carissimi, Giacomo **3** 299-300
Cavalli, Pietro Francesco **3** 382-383
Cesti, Pietro **3** 399-400
Gabrieli, Giovanni **6** 161-162
Monteverdi, Claudio Giovanni
Antonio **11** 126-128
Rossi, Luigi **13** 310-311
Scarlatti, Pietro Alessandro Gaspare
13 517-518

Baroque painting (English)
landscape
Gainsborough, Thomas **6** 170-172
Wilson, Richard **16** 329-330
portraiture
Lely, Peter **9** 315
Reynolds, Joshua **13** 115-116
Van Dyck, Anthony **15** 423-425

Baroque painting (Flemish and Dutch)
genre and portraiture
Brouwer, Adriaen **3** 29-30
Hals, Frans **7** 89-91
Hooch, Pieter de **7** 473-474
Jordaens, Jacob **8** 347-349
Rembrandt Harmensz van Rijn
13 91-95
Rubens, Peter Paul **13** 339-342
Ter Borch, Gerard **15** 146
Van Dyck, Anthony **15** 423-425
Vermeer, Jan **15** 466-467
landscape
Cuyp, Aelbert **4** 360-361
Goyen, Jan van **6** 478-479
Ruisdael, Jacob van **13** 357-358

Baroque painting (French)
genre
La Tour, George de **9** 222
Le Nain, Antoine, Louis and Mathieu **9** 321-322
landscape
Claude Lorrain **4** 89-90

Poussin, Nicolas **12** 418-420

Baroque painting (German and Austrian)
Artigas, José Gervasio **1** 323
Rottmayr, Johann Michael **13** 321

Baroque painting (Italian)
frescoes
Carracci **3** 319-321
Cortona, Pietro da **4** 256
Gaulli, Giovanni Battista **6** 238-239
Guercino **7** 27
Reni, Guido **13** 97-98
Tiepolo, Giovanni Battista
15 219-220
genre
Caravaggio **3** 282-284
landscape
Canaletto **3** 257-258
Guardi, Francesco **7** 24-25
Magnasco, Alessandro **10** 127-128
Rosa, Salvator **13** 289-290

Baroque painting (Spanish)
genre
Ribera, Jusepe de **13** 122-123
Velázquez, Diego Rodríguez de
Silva y **15** 454-456
portraiture
Goya y Lucientes, Francisco de
Paula José de **6** 476-478
Murillo, Bartolomé Esteban
11 258-259
Zurbarán, Francisco de **16** 534-535

Baroque sculpture
Artigas, José Gervasio **1** 323
Bernini, Gian Lorenzo **2** 214-216
Churriguera, José Benito de **4** 53-54
Coysevox, Antoine **4** 287-288
Falconet, Étienne Maurice **5** 372
Girardon, François **6** 348-349
Schlüter, Andreas **14** 18-19

Barozzi, Giacomo
see Vignola, Giacomo da

Barr, Alfred Hamilton, Jr. (1902-1981),
American art historian
Picasso, Pablo **12** 292-295, 433

Barra, Francisco Leon de la (1863-1939),
Mexican statesman
Calles, Plutarco Elías **3** 234-235
Madero, Francisco Indalecio
10 118-119

Barrack-room Ballads (poems)
Kipling, Joseph Rudyard **9** 32-33

Barracuda (ship)
Ewing, William Maurice **5** 350-351

BARRAGÁN, LUIS (1902-1988), Mexican
architect and landscape architect **2** 17-19

BARRAS, VICOMTE DE (Paul François Jean
Nicolas; 1755-1829), French statesman
and revolutionist **2** 19
Napoleon I **11** 306-310

BARRE, RAYMOND (1924-1981), prime
minister of France (1976-1981) **2** 19-20

Barren Genius (novel)
Eminescu, Mihail **5** 280-281

Barren Ground (novel)
Glasgow, Ellen **6** 360-361

BARRÈS, AUGUSTE MAURICE
(1862-1923), French writer and politician
2 20-21
Maurras, Charles Marie Photius
10 350-351

Barrett, Elizabeth
see Browning, Elizabeth Barrett

Barrie, Sir James Matthew (1860-1937;
British author)
Frohman, Charles **6** 123-124

BARRIE, SIR JAMES MATTHEW
(1860-1937), British dramatist and novelist **2** 21-22
Barrymores **2** 28-30
Hapgood, Norman **7** 137-138

BARRIENTOS ORTUÑO, RENÉ
(1919-1969), populist Bolivian president
(1966-1969) **2** 22-23

BARRIOS, JUSTO RUFINO (1835-1885),
Guatemalan general, president
1873-1885 **2** 23-24

Barristers
see Jurists, English

Barron, James (1768-1851), American
naval officer
Decatur, Stephen **4** 448-449

Barros, João de (1496-1570), Portuguese
chronicler
Dias de Novais, Bartolomeu **4** 533-534

Barrow, Isaac (1630-1677), English mathematician
Newton, Isaac **11** 369-372

Barrow, Joe Louis
see Louis, Joe

Barry, Elizabeth (1658-1713), English
actress
Congreve, William **4** 200-201

BARRY, JOHN (1745-1803), American
naval officer **2** 24-25

BARRY, MARION SHEPILOV, JR. (born
1936), African American mayor and civil
rights activist **2** 25-28

Barry, Philip (1896-1949), American playwright
Benét, Stephen Vincent **2** 157-158

Barry, Sir Charles (1795-1860), English
architect
Pugin, Augustus Welby Northmore
12 479-480

Barrymore, Maurice (Herbert Blythe;
1847-1905), English-American actor
Barrymores **2** 28-30

Barrymore, Mrs. Maurice
see Drew, Georgiana Emma

BARRYMORES, American theatrical
dynasty **2** 28-30
Griffith, David Wark **6** 544-545

Kaufman, George S. **8** 457-458

Barsetshire novels (series)
Trollope, Anthony **15** 300-302

Bar-sur-Aube, battle of (1814)
William I **16** 292-293

Bartas, Seigneur du (Guillaume de Sallust; 1544-1590), French poet
Vondel, Joost van den **16** 19-20

Bartered Bride, The (opera)
Smetana, Bedřich **14** 281-282

BARTH, HEINRICH (1821-1865), German explorer **2** 30-31
Clapperton, Hugh **4** 72-73

BARTH, KARL (1886-1968), Swiss Protestant theologian **2** 31-32
Küng, Hans **9** 129-130
Ritschl, Albrecht Benjamin **13** 180
Tillich, Paul Johannes **15** 224-225

BARTHÉ, RICHMOND (1901-1989), African American sculptor **2** 33-34

Bartholdi, F.A. (1834-1904), French sculptor
Eiffel, Alexandre Gustave **5** 227-228

Bartholomew Fair (play)
Jonson, Ben **8** 343-345

Barthou, Louis (1862-1934), French statesman
Alexander of Yugoslavia **1** 136-137

Bartleby (story)
Melville, Herman **10** 472-476

BARTLETT, SIR FREDERIC CHARLES (1886-1969), British psychologist **2** 34-35

BARTÓK, BÉLA (1881-1945), Hungarian composer and pianist **2** 35-36
Copland, Aaron **4** 227-228
Halffter, Christóbal **7** 79-80
Henze, Hans Werner **7** 314
Kodály, Zoltán **9** 71
Lutoslawski, Witold **10** 52-53
Penderecki, Krzysztof **12** 195-197

Bartolini, Lorenzo (1778-1850), Italian sculptor
Ingres, Jean Auguste Dominique **8** 121-123

Bartolommeo, Fra (1475-1517), Italian painter
Andrea del Sarto **1** 224-225
Leonardo da Vinci **9** 337-340

Barton, Benjamin Smith (1766-1815), American naturalist and physician
Bartram, William **2** 41-42

BARTON, BRUCE (1886-1967), American advertising business executive and congressman **2** 36-37

BARTON, CLARA (1821-1912), American humanitarian **2** 37-39
Bellows, Henry Whitney **2** 143-144
Dix, Dorothea Lynde **5** 32-33

BARTON, SIR EDMUND (1849-1920), Australian statesman and jurist **2** 39-40
Deakin, Alfred **4** 432-433

Forrest, Edwin **6**

BARTRAM, JOHN (1699-1777), American botanist **2** 40-41
Bartram, William **2** 41-42

BARTRAM, WILLIAM (1739-1823), American naturalist **2** 41-42
Wilson, Alexander **16** 313-314

Baru, Sunni (ruled 1492-1493), Songhay Empire
Ali, Sunni **1** 158-159
Muhammad, Elijah **11** 230-231

Baruch (Old Testament character)
Jeremiah **8** 247-248

BARUCH, BERNARD MANNES (1870-1965), American statesman and financier **2** 42-43

Baruch of Mainz (poem)
Tschernichowsky, Saul **15** 323

Baruch Plan (1945)
Baruch, Bernard Mannes **2** 42-43

Baruch Report (1942)
Baruch, Bernard Mannes **2** 42-43

Barulcus (book)
Heron of Alexandria **7** 334-335

Bärwalde, Treaty of (1631)
Gustavus II **7** 43-45

Barye, Antoine Louis (1795-1875), French sculptor
Rodin, Auguste **13** 236-238

BARYSHNIKOV, MIKHAIL (born 1948), ballet dancer **2** 43-44

Baryton, (musical instrument)
Haydn, Franz Joseph **7** 219-221

Barzizza, Gasparino da (1359-1431), Italian humanist
Alberti, Leon Battista **1** 113-115

Basaltes (pottery)
Wedgwood, Josiah **16** 168-169

Bascom affair (1861)
Cochise **4** 128

Base (chemistry)
Boyle, Robert **2** 469-471
Lewis, Gilbert Newton **9** 384-385

Base of All Metaphysics, The (poem)
Whitman, Walt **16** 249-251

Baseball Hall of Fame (Cooperstown, New York State)
Aaron, Henry Louis (Hank) **1** 2-3
Cobb, Tyrus Raymond **4** 124-126
Robinson, Jack Roosevelt **13** 207-208

Baseball players
see Athletes

BASEDOW, JOHANN BERNHARD (1724-1790), German educator and reformer **2** 44-45

Basekake (African people)
Moshweshwe **11** 203-205

Basel, Counsil of (1431-1449)
Cusa, Nicholas of **4** 352-353

Martin V **10** 287-288
Pius II **12** 331
Sigismund **14** 220-221

Basel, University of (Switzerland)
Burckhardt, Jacob Christoph **3** 132-133
Jung, Carl Gustav **8** 388-389
Karlstadt, Andreas Bodenheim von **8** 449
Michels, Robert **11** 7
Reichstein, Tadeus **13** 85-87

Basel Museum (Switzerland)
Böcklin, Arnold **2** 354-355

Basement, The (play)
Pinter, Harold **12** 317-318

Bashan and I (book)
Mann, Thomas **10** 204-207

Bashful Man at Court, The (play)
Tirso de Molina **15** 237-238

BASHO, MATSUO (1644-1694), Japanese poet **2** 45-48
Child, Lydia Maria Francis **3** 520-521

Basho Schichibushu (anthology)
Basho, Matsuo **2** 45-48

Basho-an
see Hermitage of the Banana Plant

BASIE, COUNT (William Basie; 1904-1984), pianist and jazz band leader **2** 48-49

Basiez moy (chanson)
Josquin des Prez **8** 361-363

Basil (novel)
Collins, William Wilkie **4** 169-170

BASIL I (circa 812-886), Byzantine emperor 867-886 **2** 49-50
Photius **12** 283-284

BASIL II (circa 958-1025), Byzantine emperor 963-1025 **2** 50-51
Otto III **12** 29-30
Vladimir I **16** 5-6

Basil II (1415-1462), grand duke of Moscow 1425-1462
Ivan III **8** 156-157

Basil III (1479-1533), grand duke of Moscow 1505-1533
Ivan III **8** 156-157
Ivan IV **8** 157-159

BASIL THE GREAT, ST. (329-379), theologian and bishop of Caesarea **2** 51-52

Basil the Macedonian
see Basil I

Basile, Mathieu
see Guesde, Jules

Basilica Palladiana
see Palazzo della Ragione (Vicenza, Italy)

Basilica Porcia (Rome)
Cato, Marcus Porcius the Elder **3** 375

Basilikon Doron (book)
James I **8** 204-206

Basin of San Marco (painting)
Guardi, Francesco **7** 24-25

Basis of Sensation, The (book)
Adrian, Edgar Douglas **1** 67-69

Basketball (United States)
see Athletes

Basque (language)
Humboldt, Wilhelm von **8** 31

Basque Country (trilogy)
Baroja y Nessi, Pío **2** 15-16

Basra (city, Iraq)
Karim Khan Zand **8** 447
Omar ibn al-Khattab **11** 508-509

Bass, George (died 1812?) English explorer
Flinders, Matthew **5** 490

Bass Strait (Australia-Tasmania)
Flinders, Matthew **5** 490

Bassano, Jacopo (1510-1592), Italian painter
Veronese, Paolo **15** 469-470

Bassarids, The (opera)
Henze, Hans Werner **7** 314

Bassein, Treaty of (1802)
Wellesley, Richard Colley **16** 192-193

Bassianus
see Caracalla

Basso continuo (music)
Gabrieli, Giovanni **6** 161-162
Sweelinck, Jan Pieterszoon **15** 50-51

Bassompierre, François, Baron de (1579-1646), marshal of France
Saint-Simon, Duc de **13** 436

Bastard, The (novel)
Caldwell, Erskine **3** 223-224

Bastian, Adolph (1826-1905), German ethnologist
Boas, Franz **2** 349-351

Bastidas, Rodrigo de (born 1460?), Spanish explorer
Balboa, Vasco Núñez de **1** 462-463

Bastien und Bastienne (opera)
Mozart, Wolfgang Amadeus **11** 218-221

Bastille, storming of the (1789)
Barras, Vicomte de **2** 19
Charles X **3** 463-464
Danton, Georges Jacques **4** 391-393
Lafayette, Marquis de **9** 151-152
Louis XVI **9** 534-535
Marie Antoinette **10** 258-259
Necker, Jacques **11** 330-331

Basuto National party (established 1959)
Jonathan, Joseph Leabua **8** 330-331

Basutoland
see Lesotho

Basutos (African people)
Gordon, Charles George **6** 448-449
Jonathan, Joseph Leabua **8** 330-331

Bat, The (operetta)
Strauss, Johann Jr. **14** 498-499

Bat Man (sculpture)
Richier, Germaine **13** 145-146

Bataan (peninsula, Philippines)
MacArthur, Douglas **10** 76-78
Magsaysay, Ramon **10** 130-131
Marcos, Ferdinand **10** 240-242
Wainwright, Jonathan Mayhew **16** 45-46

Bataan, Corner of Hell (painting)
Amorsolo, Fernando **1** 204

Batavia (modern Jakarta, Indonesia)
Coen, Jan Pieterszoon **4** 133
Eijkman, Christian **5** 228
Van Diemen, Anthony Meuza **15** 420

Batavische Gebroeders (play)
Vondel, Joost van den **16** 19-20

Bateau ivre, Le (poem)
Rimbaud, Jean Nicolas Arthur **13** 172-174

Bateau-Lavoir (art studio, Paris)
Modigliani, Amedeo **11** 72-73
Picasso, Pablo **12** 292-295

Bates, Blanche (1873-1941), American singer and actress
Belasco, David **2** 124-125

BATES, DAISY MAE (née O'Dwyer; 1861-1951), Irish-born Australian social worker **2** 52-53

BATES, HENRY WALTER (1825-1892), English explorer and naturalist **2** 53-54
Wallace, Alfred Russel **16** 69-70

BATES, KATHARINE LEE (1859-1929), American poet and educator **2** 54-55

BATESON, WILLIAM (1861-1926), English biologist concerned with evolution **2** 55-57
Vavilov, Nikolai Ivanovich **15** 447-448

Batetela (African people)
Lumumba, Patrice Emery **10** 43-45

Ba'th party (Iraq)
Saddam Hussein **13** 415-416

Ba'th party (Syria)
'Aflaq, Michel **1** 73-74

Bather (sculpture)
Lehmbruck, Wilhelm **9** 307

Bather and Head (sculpture)
Lipchitz, Jacques **9** 432-433

Bather of Valpinçon (painting)
Ingres, Jean Auguste Dominique **8** 121-123

Bathers, The (painting)
Courbet, Jean Desiré Gustave **4** 271-273

Bathhouse, The (play; Mayakovsky)
Meyerhold, Vsevolod Emilievich **10** 539

Bathos (print)
Hogarth, William **7** 446-447

Baths of Diocletian (Rome)
Diocletian **5** 19-20

Bathsheba (Old Testament character)
David, Jacques Louis **4** 407-409
Solomon **14** 326-327

Bathurst, Allen (1st Earl Bathurst; 1684-1775), English politician
Pope, Alexander **12** 395-397

Bathurst, Henry (3d Earl Bathurst; 1762-1834), English colonial secretary 1812-1828
Bigge, John Thomas **2** 272

Bathyscaphe (submersible)
Piccard, Auguste **12** 297-298

Bathythermograph (instrument)
Ewing, William Maurice **5** 350-351

BATISTA Y ZALDÍVAR, FULGENCIO (1901-1973), Cuban political and military leader **2** 57-58
Bosch, Juan **2** 428-429
Castro Ruz, Fidel **3** 365-368
Eisenhower, Dwight David **5** 233-236
Grau San Martin, Ramón **6** 499-500
Guevara, Ernesto **7** 30-31

Batlle, Lorenzo (1812-1872?) Uruguayan president 1868-1872
Batlle y Ordóñez, José **2** 58-59

BATLLE Y ORDÓÑEZ, JOSÉ (1856-1929), Uruguayan statesman and journalist **2** 58-59
Rodó, José Enrique **13** 240-241
Terra, Gabriel **15** 154-155

Batouala (novel; Maran)
Eboué, Adolphe Felix Sylvestre **5** 194

Battani, al- (Albategnius; circa 850-929), Arab astronomer
Regiomontanus **13** 81-82

Battery (electrical cell)
Edison, Thomas Alva **5** 206-208
Volta, Alessandro **16** 12-14

Batthyány, Count Lajos (1806?-1849), Hungarian statesman, premier 1848
Deák, Francis **4** 431-432
Kossuth, Louis **9** 88-90

Batthyány Palace (Vienna)
Fischer von Erlach, Johann Bernhard **5** 459-461

BATTLE, KATHLEEN (born 1948), American opera and concert singer **2** 59-60

Battle as Inner Experience (diary)
Jünger, Ernst **8** 391-392

Battle Casualties ... (book)
DeBakey, Michael Ellis **4** 437-438

Battle Hymn of the Republic, The (song; J.W. Howe)
Howe, Julia Ward **7** 535-536
Howe, Samuel Gridley **7** 537

Battle of Agincourt (poem)
Drayton, Michael **5** 97-98

Battle of Alexander (painting)
Altdorfer, Albrecht **1** 179-180

Battle of Angels (play)
Williams, Tennessee **16** 306-308

Battle of Anghiari (painting; Leonardo da Vinci)
Leonardo da Vinci **9** 337-340
Raphael **13** 40-42

Battle of Bunker's Hill (painting)
Trumbull, John **15** 316-317

Battle of Cascina (painting; Michelangelo)
Michelangelo Buonarroti **11** 2-5
Raphael **13** 40-42
Rosso, Il **13** 312-313

Battle of Lights, Coney Island (painting)
Stella, Joseph **14** 422

Battle of Marathon, The (epic)
Browning, Elizabeth Barrett **3** 52-53

Battle of Taillebourg (painting)
Delacroix, Ferdinand Victor Eugène **4** 469-471

Battle of the Books, The (essay)
Swift, Jonathan **15** 51-54

Battle of the Centaurs (sculpture)
Michelangelo Buonarroti **11** 2-5

Battle of the Frogs and Mice, The (epic)
Homer **7** 465-467

Battle of the Kegs, The (poem)
Hopkinson, Francis **7** 496-497

Battle of the Nudes (engraving)
Pollaiuolo, Antonio **12** 377-378

Battle of the Sea Gods (engraving)
Mantegna, Andrea **10** 215-216

Battle Window (Harvard University)
La Farge, John **9** 149-150

Battle with the Slum, The (book)
Riis, Jacob August **13** 169-170

Battleground, The (novel)
Glasgow, Ellen **6** 360-361

Battle-Pieces (verse cycle)
Melville, Herman **10** 472-476

Battleship Potemkin, The (film; Eisenstein)
Bacon, Francis **1** 421-422

Battló House (Barcelona)
Gaudí i Cornet, Antoni **6** 235-236

BATU KHAN (died 1255), Mongol leader **2** 60-61
Genghis Khan **6** 263-265

Baturin (city, Ukraine)
Mazepa, Ivan Stepanovich **10** 381

Bauakademie (Berlin)
Schinkel, Karl Friedrich **14** 8

Bauchi Discussion Circle (Nigeria)
Tafawa Balewa, Abubakar **15** 75

Baucis (literary character)
Ovid **12** 34-36

Baucis and Philemon (poem)
Swift, Jonathan **15** 51-54

BAUDELAIRE, CHARLES PIERRE
(1821-1867), French poet and art critic **2** 61-63
art criticism
Corot, Jean Baptiste Camille **4** 247-249
Manet, Édouard **10** 193-194
Rousseau, Théodore **13** 328
influence of
Güiráldez, Ricardo **7** 38-39
Rabearivelo, Jean Joseph **12** 523-524
Stevens, Wallace **14** 443-445
Tanizaki, Junichiro **15** 101-102
influenced by
Claudel, Paul Louis Charles **4** 90-91
Hoffmann, Ernst Theodor Amadeus **7** 439-440
Poe, Edgar Allan **12** 363-365
musical settings
Berg, Alban **2** 186-187
portrait busts
Duchamp-Villon, Raymond **5** 123
Rodin, Auguste **13** 236-238
works illustrated
Redon, Odilon **13** 75-76

Baudot, Anatole de (1834-1915), French architect
Nervi, Pier Luigi **11** 346-348

Baudouin (1930-1963), King of Belgium
Leopold III **9** 347-348
Lumumba, Patrice Emery **10** 43-45

Bauer, Bruno (1809-1882), German philosopher
Engels, Friedrich **5** 286-288
Marx, Karl **10** 304-308

Bauer, Georg
see Agricola, Georgius

Bauer, Gustav (1870-1944), German politician
Kapp, Wolfgang **8** 436

Bauer, Otto (1881-1938), Austrian politician
Trotsky, Leon **15** 302-305

Bauernfeld, Eduard von (1802-1890), Viennese playwright
Schubert, Franz Peter **14** 35-37

Bauhaus (art school, Germany)
directors
Gropius, Walter **7** 13-14
Mies van der Rohe, Ludwig **11** 10-12
faculty
Albers, Josef **1** 110
Breuer, Marcel **2** 520-521
Feininger, Lyonel **5** 406-407
Kandinsky, Wassily **8** 420-422
Klee, Paul **9** 47-49
Moholy-Nagy, László **11** 82-83
Oud, Jacobus Johannes Pieter **12** 32

Bauhaus, New (Chicago)
Moholy-Nagy, László **11** 82-83

BAULIEU, ÉTIENNE-ÉMILE (Étienne Blum; born 1926), French physician and biochemist who developed RU 486 **2** 63-66

BAUM, HERBERT (1912-1942), German human/civil rights activist **2** 66-73

BAUM, L. FRANK (1856-1919), author of the Wizard of Oz books **2** 73-74

Baumfree, Isabella
see Truth, Sojourner

BAUR, FERDINAND CHRISTIAN
(1792-1860), German theologian **2** 74-75
Ritschl, Albrecht Benjamin **13** 180

BAUSCH, PINA (born 1940), a controversial German dancer/choreographer **2** 75-76

Bausch and Lomb Co. (Rochester, New York State)
Land, Edwin Herbert **9** 183-184

Bavaria (state, Federal Republic of Germany)
Austrian Succession War
Frederick II **6** 81-84
Maria Theresa **10** 256-258
Bavarian Succession War
Frederick II **6** 81-84
Joseph II **8** 359-360
Carolingian rule
Charlemagne **3** 445-447
Guelphs defeated
Frederick I **6** 78-79
politicians
Hamm-Brücher, Hildegard **7** 101-103
Strauss, Franz Josef **14** 497-498
Swedish invasion
Gustavus II **7** 43-45
see also Thirty Years War

Bavarian Academy of Science
Einstein, Albert **5** 228-231

Bavarian art
see German art

Baxter, Gregory Paul (1876-1953), American chemist
Richards, Theodore William **13** 137-138

Baxter, John (died 1841), Australian explorer
Eyre, Edward John **5** 354

BAXTER, RICHARD (1615-1691), English theologian **2** 76-77

Baxter, Willie (literary character)
Tarkington, Newton Booth **15** 109

Bay Area Women's Philharmonic
Falletta, JoAnn **5** 373-375

Bay of Marseilles from L'Estaque (painting)
Cézanne, Paul **3** 400-402

Bay of Pigs invasion (1961)
Cárdenas, Lázaro **3** 286-287
Castro Ruz, Fidel **3** 365-368
Eisenhower, Dwight David **5** 233-236
Kennedy, John Fitzgerald **8** 502-506
Stevenson, Adlai Ewing **14** 445-446

Bay State (ship)
Cabot, Richard Clarke **3** 200

Bayan (flourished late 13th century), Mongol general
Kublai Khan **9** 115-118
Wen T'ien-hsiang **16** 203

Bayard, James Asheton (1767-1815), American lawyer
Adams, John Quincy **1** 52-54
Gallatin, Albert **6** 183-184

Bayard, Thomas (1828-1898), American statesman
Cleveland, Stephen Grover **4** 108-110

Bayazid
see Bayezid

Bayeux Tapestry
Harold II **7** 162

Bayezid (died 1559), Turkish prince
Suleiman I **15** 20-21

Bayezid II (1447-1513), Ottoman sultan 1481-1512
Mehmed the Conqueror **10** 452-454
Selim I **14** 94-95
Tamerlane **15** 94-95

BAYLE, PIERRE (1647-1706), French philosopher **2** 77-78
Leibniz, Gottfried Wilhelm von **9** 307-310

Bayley, Elizabeth
see Seton, Elizabeth Ann Bayley

Bayley, James Roosevelt (1814-1877), American archbishop
Corrigan, Michael Augustine **4** 253

Bayley, Richard (1745-1801), American physician
Seton, Elizabeth Ann Bayley **14** 118-119

Baylor University (Houston, Texas)
DeBakey, Michael Ellis **4** 437-438

Bayreuth music festival
Chamberlain, Houston Stewart **3** 411
Toscanini, Arturo **15** 270-271

Bazaar of Heraclides (book)
Nestorius **11** 349-350

Bazaine, Achille (1811-1888), marshal of France
Maximilian of Hapsburg **10** 358-360
Moltke, Helmuth Karl Bernard von **11** 90-91

Bazarov (literary character)
Turgenev, Ivan Sergeyevich **15** 345-348

Bazille, Jean Frédéric (1841-1870), French painter
Monet, Claude **11** 102-104
Renoir, Pierre Auguste **13** 101-102

Baziotes, William (born 1912), American painter
Motherwell, Robert **11** 210-211
Newman, Barnett **11** 365
Rothko, Mark **13** 320-321

BBC
see British Broadcasting Corporation

BEA, AUGUSTINUS (1881-1968), German cardinal **2** 79
John, XXIII **8** 277-280
Paul VI **12** 146-148

Beach, Alfred Ely (1826-1896), American journalist
Beach, Moses Yale **2** 79-80

Beach, Moses Sperry (1822-1892), American journalist
Beach, Moses Yale **2** 79-80

BEACH, MOSES YALE (1800-1868), American inventor and newspaperman **2** 79-80

Beach, Paramé, The (painting)
Morrice, James Wilson **11** 181-182

Beach, Sir Michael Hicks (1837-1916), English statesman
Frere, Henry Bartle Edward **6** 100-101

Beach of Falesá, The (story)
Stevenson, Robert Louis **14** 446-448

Beacon Hill school (England)
Russell, Bertrand Arthur William **13** 373-374

Beaconsfield, Earl of
see Disraeli, Benjamin

BEADLE, GEORGE WELLS (1903-1989), American scientist, educator, and administrator **2** 80-81

Beagle (ship)
Darwin, Charles Robert **4** 397-399

BEALE, DOROTHEA (1831-1906), British educator **2** 81-83

Beale Street Blues (song)
Handy, William Christopher **7** 123-124

Bear, The (musical composition)
Walton, William Turner **16** 92-93

Bear, The (play)
Chekhov, Anton Pavlovich **3** 494-497

Bear Flag Revolt (California; 1846-1847)
Bidwell, John **2** 265
Frémont, John Charles **6** 97-98
Larkin, Thomas Oliver **9** 208
Stockton, Robert Field **14** 461-462
Sutter, John Augustus **15** 41-42

Bear Island (Barents Sea)
Barents, Willem **2** 4-5

BEARD, CHARLES AUSTIN (1874-1948), American historian **2** 84
Dewey, John **4** 520-523
Dunning, William Archibald **5** 148-149
Parrington, Vernon Louis **12** 119-120
Robinson, James Harvey **13** 208
Schlesinger, Arthur Meier **14** 13

BEARD, MARY RITTER (1876-1958), American author and activist **2** 85-86
Beard, Charles Austin **2** 84

BEARDEN, ROMARE HOWARD (1914-1988), African American painter-collagist **2** 86-88
Lawrence, Jacob **9** 250-251

Beardmore Glacier (Antarctica)
Shackleton, Ernest Henry **14** 132-133

BEARDSLEY, AUBREY VINCENT (1872-1898), English illustrator **2** 88-89
Klee, Paul **9** 47-49
Nadelman, Elie **11** 289-290

Béarn (region, Southwest France)
Louis XIII **9** 529-531

Beast and the Jungle, The (book)
Lindsey, Benjamin Barr **9** 425-426

Beast with Five Fingers, The (film)
Buñuel, Luis **3** 127-128

Beat Generation (American literature)
Burroughs, William S. **3** 162-163
Ginsberg, Allen **6** 332-333
Kerouac, Jean-Louis Lebris de **8** 518-519

Beat the Devil (film)
Bogart, Humphrey **2** 363-364

Beata Beatrix (painting)
Rossetti, Dante Gabriel **13** 308-309

Beatitudes, The (musical composition)
Franck, César **6** 48-49

BEATLES, THE (1957-1971), British rock and roll band **2** 89-92
Lennon, John Winston **9** 326-328

Beaton, David (1494-1546), Scottish cardinal
Knox, John **9** 65-66

Beatrice (literary character)
Dante Alighieri **4** 389-391
Shakespeare, William **14** 142-145

Beatrice (novel)
Schnitzler, Arthur **14** 23-24

Béatrice et Bénédict (opera)
Berlioz, Louis Hector **2** 203-205

Beatrice-Joanna (literary character)
Middleton, Thomas **11** 8-9

BEATRIX, WILHELMINA VON AMSBERG, QUEEN (born 1938), queen of Netherlands (1980-) **2** 92-93

Beauchamp
see Warwick, Earl of

Beauchamp's Career (novel)
Meredith, George **10** 512-513

Beaufort, English noble family excluded from succession 1397
Henry IV **7** 292-293
Henry VII **7** 300-302

Beaufort, Henry (1377-1447), English cardinal and statesman
Gloucester, Duke of **6** 370-371
Henry VI **7** 298-299

Beaufort, Pierre Roger de
see Gregory XI

Beauharnais, Alexandre de (died 1794),
French army officer
Napoleon I **11** 306-310

Beauharnais, Hortense de (1783-1837),
wife of Louis Bonaparte
Bonaparte, Louis **2** 382-383

Beauharnais, Josephine de
see Josephine

**BEAUMARCHAIS, PIERRE AUGUST
CARON DE** (1732-1799), French play-
wright **2** 93-94
Mozart, Wolfgang Amadeus
11 218-221
Rossini, Gioacchino **13** 311-312

BEAUMONT, FRANCIS (1584/1585-1616),
English playwright **2** 95
Dryden, John **5** 106-107
Fletcher, John **5** 487
Heywood, Thomas **7** 373-374
Jonson, Ben **8** 343-345
Shakespeare, William **14** 142-145

Beaumont, George Howland (1753-1827),
English painter
Constable, John **4** 208-209

BEAUMONT, WILLIAM (1785-1853),
American surgeon **2** 95-96
Drake, Daniel **5** 93-94

**Beaumont de La Bonninière, Gustave
Auguste de** (1802-1866), French publicist
Tocqueville, Alexis Charles Henri Mau-
rice Clérel de **15** 250-251

**BEAUREGARD, PIERRE GUSTAVE
TOUTANT** (1818-1893), Confederate
general **2** 96-97
Davis, Jefferson **4** 416-418
Lee, Robert Edward **9** 292-294

Beauté, La (poem)
Baudelaire, Charles Pierre **2** 61-63

Beauties of Santa Cruz, The (poem)
Freneau, Philip Morin **6** 99-100

Beautiful and the Damned, The (novel)
Fitzgerald, Francis Scott Key **5** 470-472

Beautiful Dreamer (song)
Foster, Stephen Collins **6** 25-27

Beautiful Feathers (novel)
Ekwensi, Cyprian **5** 242-243

Beautiful People, The (play)
Saroyan, William **13** 486-487

Beautiful Sunday in September, A (play)
Betti, Ugo **2** 246

Beauty Within, The (essay)
Maeterlinck, Maurice **10** 125-126

Beaver Coat, The (comedy)
Hauptmann, Gerhart Johann Robert
7 199-201

Beaverbrook, Lord
see Aitken, William Maxwell

Beaverhead Valley (Montana)
Bozeman, John M. **2** 471-472

Bebel, Ferdinand August (1840-1913), German socialist writer
Kautsky, Karl Johann **8** 462-463

Bec, monastery of
see Le Bec-Hellouin

BECARRIA, MARCHESE DI (1738-1794),
Italian jurist and economist **2** 97-98
Catherine the Great **3** 370-372

Becher, Johann Joachim (1635-1682), German chemist
Stahl, Georg Ernst **14** 392-393

BECHTEL, STEPHEN DAVISON
(1900-1989), American construction
engineer and business executive **2** 98-99

Bechtel Corporation
Bechtel, Stephen Davison **2** 98-99
Shultz, George Pratt **14** 209-211

Bechuanaland
see Botswana

Bechuanaland Democratic party
Khama, Seretse M. **8** 532-533

Beck, Józef (1894-1944), Polish statesman
Pilsudski, Joseph **12** 305-306

BECK, LUDWIG AUGUST THEODOR
(1880-1944), German general **2** 99-100
Rundstedt, Karl Rudolf Gerd Von
13 363-364

BECKER, CARL LOTUS (1873-1945), American historian **2** 100-101
Dunning, William Archibald **5** 148-149

Becket (play)
Anouilh, Jean **1** 243-244
Tennyson, Alfred **15** 144-146

BECKET, ST. THOMAS (1128?-1170), Eng-
lish prelate **2** 101-102
Eliot, Thomas Stearns **5** 258-261
Henry II **7** 287-289
John of Salisbury **8** 284-285
Matthew Paris **10** 341-342

BECKETT, SAMUEL (1906-1989), Irish nov-
elist, playwright, and poet **2** 102-104
Berio, Luciano **2** 194-195
Borges, Jorge Luis **2** 411-412
Grass, Günter **6** 496-497

BECKMANN, MAX (1884-1950), German
painter **2** 104-105
Grosz, George **7** 17-18

Beckmesser (literary character)
Wagner, Richard **16** 40-43

BECKNELL, WILLIAM (circa 1797-1865),
American soldier and politician
2 105-106

BECKWOURTH, JIM (James P. Beckwourth;
c. 1800-1866), African American fur trapper and explorer **2** 106-107

**BÉCQUER, GUSTAVO ADOLFO
DOMINGUEZ** (1836-1870), Spanish lyric
poet **2** 107-108

Becquerel, Alexandre Edmond
(1820-1891), French physicist
Becquerel, Antoine Henri **2** 108-109

Becquerel, Antoine César (1788-1878),
French physicist
Becquerel, Antoine Henri **2** 108-109

BECQUEREL, ANTOINE HENRI
(1852-1908), French physicist **2** 108-109
Curie, Marie Sklodowska **4** 339-341
Röntgen,Wilhelm Conrad **13** 273-275
Rutherford, Ernest **13** 384-387

Bed (art work)
Rauschenberg, Robert **13** 52-53

Bed and Board (film)
Truffaut, François **15** 311-313

Bedbug, The (play; Mayakovsky)
Meyerhold, Vsevolod Emilievich **10** 539

BEDE, ST. (672/673-735), English theolo-
gian **2** 109-110
Alcuin of York **1** 122-123
Alfred **1** 151-153
Layamon **9** 256-257

Bedford (ship)
Franklin, John **6** 64-65

Bedford, Duke of
see John of Lancaster

Bedford, John (literary character)
Richardson, Samuel **13** 141-142

Bedford, John Russell, 6th Duke of
(1766-1839), English statesman
Russell, John **13** 380-381

Bedford Park (London)
Shaw, Richard Norman **14** 167-168

Bedouin (Arab nomads)
Glubb, John Bagot **6** 371-372
Ibrahim Pasha **8** 97-98

Bee, Barnard Elliott (1824-1861), American Confederate soldier
Jackson, Shirley Ann **8** 183-184

Beech Aircraft Co.
Fuller, Richard Buckminster **6** 149-150

Beech Tree, The (book)
Buck, Pearl Sydenstricker **3** 91-93

Beecham, Sir Thomas (1879-1961), English
conductor
Saint-Saëns, Charles Camille
13 435-436

BEECHER, CATHARINE (1800-1878),
American author and educator **2** 110-112

BEECHER, HENRY WARD (1813-1887),
American Congregationalist clergyman
2 112-113
Abbott, Lyman **1** 10-11
Evarts, William Maxwell **5** 340-341
Rogers, John **13** 248

BEECHER, LYMAN (1775-1863), Presbyter-
ian clergyman **2** 113
Beecher, Henry Ward **2** 112-113
Stowe, Harriet Elizabeth Beecher
14 484-485
Weld, Theodore Dwight **16** 186

Beeny Cliff (poem)
Hardy, Thomas **7** 150-152

Beer, Jakob Liebmann
see Meyerbeer, Giacomo

Beer Hall Putsch (Munich, 1923)
Göring, Hermann Wilhelm **6** 457-458
Himmler, Heinrich **7** 398-399
Hitler, Adolf **7** 417-420
Ludendorff, Erich Friedrich Wilhelm
10 27-28

Beethoven (biography)
Rolland, Romain **13** 260

Beethoven, Karl (1806-1858), nephew of L.
Beethoven
Beethoven, Ludwig van **2** 114-117

BEETHOVEN, LUDWIG VAN (1770-1827),
German composer **2** 114-117
influence of
Berlioz, Louis Hector **2** 203-205
Bruckner, Joseph Anton **3** 64-65
Eliot, Thomas Stearns **5** 258-261
Mahler, Gustav **10** 144-145
Schumann, Robert Alexander
14 41-43
Wagner, Richard **16** 40-43
influenced by
Bach, Carl Philipp Emanuel
1 414-415
Haydn, Franz Joseph **7** 219-221
Schiller, Johann Christoph Friedrich
von **14** 4-7
interpretations
Barenboim, Daniel **2** 3-4
performances
Heinrich, Anthony Philip **7** 261
Liszt, Franz **9** 445-447
Paganini, Niccolo **12** 58-59
portraits of
Bourdelle, Emile-Antoine **2** 449-450

Beethoven of America
see Heinrich, Anthony Philip

Beetles in Amber (verses)
Bierce, Ambrose Gwinett **2** 269-270

Beeton's Christmas Annual (periodical)
Doyle, Arthur Conan **5** 91-92

Before Dawn (drama)
Hauptmann, Gerhart Johann Robert
7 199-201

Before God (book)
Maeterlinck, Maurice **10** 125-126

Before the Great Silence (book)
Maeterlinck, Maurice **10** 125-126

Before Thy Throne I Stand (hymn)
Bach, Johann Sebastian **1** 416-419

BEGAY, HARRISON (born 1917), Native
American artist **2** 117-118

Beggar's Opera, The (musical composition;
Gay-Pepusch)
Bolingbroke, Viscount **2** 374-375
Brecht, Bertolt **2** 512-514
Britten, Benjamin **3** 10-11
Gay, John **6** 243-244
Handel, George Frederick **7** 116-119

BEGIN, MENACHEM (1913-1992), Israel's
first non-Socialist prime minister
(1977-1983) **2** 118-120

Begin the Beguine (song)
Porter, Cole Albert **12** 405-406

Beginning and the End, The (poems)
Jeffers, John Robinson **8** 236-237

Beginning of the World (sculpture)
Brancusi, Constantin **2** 494-496

Beginning of Wisdom, The (novel)
Benét, Stephen Vincent **2** 157-158

Beginning of Youth (poems)
Jami **8** 218-219

Beginnings of Kabbalism, The (book)
Scholem, Gershom **14** 26

Behavior (psychology)
animal
Frisch, Karl von **6** 117-118
Morgan, Conway Lloyd **11** 159-160
Pavlov, Ivan Petrovich **12** 155-157
Thorndike, Edward Lee **15** 208-209
Wilson, Edward Osborne
16 319-320
defined
Bentley, Arthur F. **2** 178
Tolman, Edward Chace **15** 261-262
see also Behaviorism

Behavior of Organisms (book)
Skinner, Burrhus Frederic **14** 269-270

Behavior System, A (book)
Hull, Clark Leonard **8** 28

Behaviorism (psychology)
associationism
Guthrie, Edwin Ray **7** 49-50
Lashley, Karl Spencer **9** 214-215
Thorndike, Edward Lee **15** 208-209
opponents
Merleau-Ponty, Maurice **10** 518
Montessori, Maria **11** 125-126
sociality
Mead, George Herbert **10** 437-438
theory
Berelson, Bernard **2** 185-186
Hull, Clark Leonard **8** 28
Skinner, Burrhus Frederic
14 269-270
Tolman, Edward Chace **15** 261-262
Watson, John Broadus **16** 138-139

Beheading of John the Baptist (painting)
Lucas van Leyden **10** 20-21

Beheading of John the Baptist (sculpture)
Verrocchio, Andrea del **15** 471-472

Behind the Fence (novel)
Bialik, Hayyim Nahman **2** 262-263

Behistun Inscription (Iran)
Darius I **4** 394-395

Behmen, Jacob
see Boehme, Jacob

Behold, Oh Land (poems)
Tschernichowsky, Saul **15** 323

BEHRENS, HILDEGARD (born 1937), German soprano **2** 120-121

BEHRENS, PETER (1868-1940), German
architect, painter, and designer
2 121-122
Gropius, Walter **7** 13-14
Le Corbusier **9** 274-275
Mies van der Rohe, Ludwig **11** 10-12
Wright, Frank Lloyd **16** 398-401

BEHRING, EMIL ADOLPH VON
(1854-1917), German hygienist and
physician **2** 122-123

BEHZAD (died circa 1530), Persian painter
2 123

Being (philosophy)
Aristotle **1** 295-296
Duns Scotus, John **5** 149-150
Heidegger, Martin **7** 257-258
Lovejoy, Arthur Oncken **10** 6
Parmenides **12** 116-117

Being and Having (book)
Marcel, Gabriel **10** 233-234

Being and Nothingness (book)
Sartre, Jean Paul **13** 491-492

Being and Some Philosophers (book)
Gilson, Étienne Henry **6** 327-328

Being and Time (book)
Heidegger, Martin **7** 257-258

Being Bissextile... (book)
Banneker, Benjamin **1** 490-491

BEISSEL, JOHANN CONRAD (1690-1768),
German-American pietist **2** 123-124

Beja (African people)
Ezana **5** 354-355

Bekehrte, Die (book; Goethe)
Cimarosa, Domenico **4** 61-62

Bekenntnisse des Hochstaplers Felix Krull
(book)
Mann, Thomas **10** 204-207

Belacqua (literary character)
Beckett, Samuel **2** 102-104

Bel-Ami (novel)
Maupassant, Henri René Albert Guy de
10 347

BELASCO, DAVID (1853-1931), American
playwright and director-producer
2 124-125

Belasco Theater (New York City)
Belasco, David **2** 124-125

BELAÚNDE TERRY, FERNANDO (born
1912), president of Peru (1963-1968,
1980-1985) **2** 125-126
Prado Ugarteche, Manuel **12** 430-431

Belch, Sir Toby (literary character)
Shakespeare, William **14** 142-145

Belfagor (story)
Machiavelli, Niccolò **10** 97-99

Belfry of Bruges... (poems)
Longfellow, Henry Wadsworth
9 499-500

Belgae (Gallic tribe)
Caesar, Gaius Julius **3** 207-210

Belgian art
Ensor, James **5** 289-290
Magritte, René **10** 128-130
Van de Velde, Henry **15** 419-420
see also Flemish art

Belgian Democracy (book)
Pirenne, Jean Henri Otto Lucien Marie **12** 322-323

Belgian literature
Maeterlinck, Maurice **10** 125-126
Simenon, Georges **14** 233-234

Belgicae (book)
Baudelaire, Charles Pierre **2** 61-63

Belgium, Kingdom of (nation, Northwestern Europe)
Congo
Davignon **4** 410-411
Doyle, Arthur Conan **5** 91-92
Kasavubu, Joseph **8** 453-455
Leopold II **9** 346-347
Tippu Tip **15** 235-236
German invasions
Albert I **1** 112
Bethmann Hollweg, Theobald von **2** 239-240
Leopold III **9** 347-348
independence
Leopold I **9** 345-346
Palmerston, 3d Viscount **12** 81-83
national unity
Albert II **1** 112-113
Spanish Netherlands
Coligny, Gaspard de **4** 159-160
Louis XIV **9** 531-533
William I **16** 291-292
see also Belgian art; Belgian literature

Belgrade (city, Yugoslavia)
Eugene of Savoy **5** 330-331
Hunyadi, John **8** 51-52
Leopold II **9** 346
Suleiman I **15** 20-21

BELGRANO, MANUEL (1770-1820), Argentine general and politician **2** 126-127
Mitre, Bartolomé **11** 62-63

Belinda (literary character)
Pope, Alexander **12** 395-397

Belinda (novel)
Edgeworth, Maria **5** 205-206

BELINSKY, GRIGORIEVICH (1811-1848), Russian literary critic **2** 128
critical acclaim
Dostoevsky, Fyodor **5** 74-77
Goncharov, Ivan Aleksandrovich **6** 424
Lermontov, Mikhail Yurievich **9** 352-353
influence of
Chernyshevsky, Nikolai Gavrilovich **3** 504-505

Turgenev, Ivan Sergeyevich **15** 345-348

BELISARIUS (circa 506-565), Byzantine general **2** 128-129
Gaiseric **6** 172
Justinian I **8** 393-395
Procopius of Caesarea **12** 457-458

Belisarius Asking for Alms (painting)
David, Jacques Louis **4** 407-409

Belize (district, British Honduras)
Carrera, José Rafael **3** 324-325

Belknap, William Worth (1829-1890), American army officer and politician
Custer, George Armstrong **4** 355-356

Bell (magazine)
Herzen, Aleksandr Ivanovich **7** 351-352

Bell, Acton
see Brontë, Anne

BELL, ALEXANDER GRAHAM (1847-1922), Scottish-born American inventor **2** 129-131
Curtiss, Glenn Hammond **4** 350-351
Edison, Thomas Alva **5** 206-208
Keller, Helen Adams **8** 479-480

BELL, ANDREW (1753-1832), Scottish educator **2** 131-132

Bell, Currer (pseudonym)
see Brontë, Charlotte

BELL, DANIEL (Bolotsky; born 1919), American sociologist **2** 132-133

Bell, Ellis (pseudonym)
see Brontë, Emily

Bell, John (1797-1869), American lawyer
Douglas, Stephen Arnold **5** 80-82

Bell, The (fairy tale)
Andersen, Hans Christian **1** 212-214

Bell, The (novel)
Murdoch, Iris **11** 256-257

Bell Aircraft Corp.
Whittle, Frank **16** 257-258

BELL BURNELL, SUSAN JOCELYN (born 1943), English radio astronomer **2** 133-134

Bell House (pottery factory)
Wedgwood, Josiah **16** 168-169

Bell-Lancaster system (education)
see Madras system

Bell Telephone Co.
Bell, Alexander Graham **2** 129-131
Pupin, Michael Idvorsky **12** 483-484

Bell Telephone Laboratories (research organization)
Brattain, Walter H. **2** 505-507
Shannon, Claude Elwood **14** 153-154

Bell Trade Act (Philippines)
Magsaysay, Ramon **10** 130-131
Roxas, Manuel **13** 331-332

Bella domenica di settembre, Una (play)
Betti, Ugo **2** 246

Bella estate, La (story)
Pavese, Cesare **12** 154-155

BELLAMY, EDWARD (1850-1898), American novelist, propagandist, and reformer **2** 134-135
influence of
De Leon, Daniel **4** 479-480
Furphy, Joseph **6** 152-153
Lawson, Henry **9** 254-255
Parsons, Frank **12** 121-122
Veblen, Thorstein Bunde **15** 449-450
translations
Schindler, Solomon **14** 7-8

Bellamy Clubs (social organization)
Bellamy, Edward **2** 134-135

BELLARMINE, ST. ROBERT (1542-1621), Italian theologian and cardinal **2** 135-136
Galileo Galilei **6** 180-183
Mariana, Juan de **10** 254-255
Pázmány, Péter **12** 164-165

Bellay, Joachim du
see Du Bellay, Joachim

Belle Chair (book; Verhaeren)
Maillol, Aristide **10** 150-151

Belle dame sans merci, La (poem; Keats)
Keats, John **8** 470-472
Nabokov, Vladimir **11** 287-288

Belle de jour (film)
Buñuel, Luis **3** 127-128

Belle Hélène, La (operetta)
Offenbach, Jacques **11** 478-479

Belle Isle, siege of (1761)
Carleton, Guy **3** 300-301

Belle jardinière, La (painting)
Raphael **13** 40-42

Belle saison, La (novel)
Martin du Gard, Roger **10** 295-296

BELLECOURT, CLYDE (born 1939), Native American activist **2** 136-137

Belleli Family (painting)
Degas, Hilaire Germain Edgar **4** 461-462

Bellerophon (play)
Kaiser, Georg **8** 411-412

Bellerophon (ship)
Franklin, John **6** 64-65

Belles Heures du duc de Berry (book)
Limbourg brothers, The **9** 412-413

Belleville manifesto (French politics)
Gambetta, Léon **6** 198-199

Bellevue Hospital (New York City)
Biggs, Hermann Michael **2** 272-273
Park, William Hallock **12** 104-105
Welch, William Henry **16** 185-186

Belleza (poems)
Jiménez, Juan Ramón **8** 261-262

Bellini, Gentile (circa 1429-1507), Italian painter
Bellini, Giovanni **2** 137-138

Lotto, Lorenzo **9** 520-521

BELLINI, GIOVANNI (circa 1435-1516),
Itlaian painter **2** 137-138
Antonello da Messina **1** 251-252
Dürer, Albrecht **5** 159-161
Giorgione **6** 340-341
Lotto, Lorenzo **9** 520-521
Titian **15** 242-244

Bellini, Jacopo (circa 1400-circa 1470),
Italian painter
Bellini, Giovanni **2** 137-138
Mantegna, Andrea **10** 215-216

BELLINI, VINCENZO (1801-1835), Italian
composer **2** 138-139
Chopin, Frédéric François **4** 16-18
Donizetti, Gaetano **5** 59-60

BELLO, ALHAJI SIR AHMADU
(1909-1966), Nigerian politician
2 139-140
Tafawa Balewa, Abubakar **15** 75

BELLO Y LÓPEZ, ANDRÉS (1781-1865),
Venezuelan humanist **2** 140-141

BELLOC, JOSEPH HILAIRE PIERRE
(1870-1953), French-born English author
and historian **2** 141
Chesterton, Gilbert Keith **3** 508-509

Belloc, Marie Adelaide (1868-1947; pen
name Mrs. Belloc Lowndes), English novelist
Belloc, Joseph Hilaire Pierre **2** 141

Bellori, Giovanni Pietro (1636?-1700), Italian art historian
Carracci **3** 319-321

BELLOW, SAUL (born 1915), American
novelist and Nobel Prize winner
2 141-143

BELLOWS, GEORGE WESLEY (1882-1925),
American painter **2** 143

BELLOWS, HENRY WHITNEY
(1814-1882), American Unitarian minister **2** 143-144
Dix, Dorothea Lynde **5** 32-33

Bells, The (play)
Barrymores **2** 28-30

Bells, The (symphony)
Rachmaninov, Sergei Vasilievich
12 531-532

Bells for John Whiteside's Daughter (poem)
Ransom, John Crowe **13** 39-40

Bellum lugurthinum (book)
Sallust **13** 454

Belmont, August (1816-1890),
German-American banker
Sherman, John **14** 184-185

Beloit College (Wisconsin)
Chamberlin, Thomas Chrowder
3 415-416

Belopoeica (book)
Heron of Alexandria **7** 334-335

Beloved (book)
Morrison, Toni **11** 188-190

Beloved Infidel (book; Graham)
Fitzgerald, Francis Scott Key **5** 470-472

Beloved Returns, The (novel)
Mann, Thomas **10** 204-207

Belshazzar (musical composition)
Handel, George Frederick **7** 116-119

Belshazzar's Feast (oratorio)
Walton, William Turner **16** 92-93

Belshazzar's Feast (painting)
Allston, Washington **1** 176-177

Belshazzar's Feast (play)
Calderón, Pedro **3** 221-222

Belshazzar's Feast (play; Procopé)
Sibelius, Jean Julius Christian
14 211-212

Beltov
see Plekhanov, Georgi Valentinovich

Beltrami, Eugenio (1835-1900), Italian
mathematician
Lobachevskii, Nikolai Ivanovich
9 472-474

Belvedere Palace, Upper (Vienna)
Hildebrandt, Johann Lucas von
7 380-381

Bely, Andrei (pseudonym of B.N. Bugayev;
1880-1934), Russian poet
Blok, Aleksandr Aleksandrovich **2** 335

Belzú, Manuel Isidoro (1808-1866), Bolivian president 1848-1855
Ballivián, José **1** 475

BEMBO, PIETRO (1470-1547), Italian
humanist, poet, and historian **2** 144-145
Cajetan **3** 215-216
Camoëns, Luis Vaz de **3** 247-249
Giorgione **6** 340-341

Bemis Heights, battle of (1777)
see Saratoga, battles of

BEN BADIS, ABD AL-HAMID (1889-1940),
leader of the Islamic Reform Movement
in Algeria between the two world wars
2 147-148

BEN BELLA, AHMED (born 1918), first
president of the Algerian Republic
2 148-149
Abbas, Ferhat **1** 6-7
Boumediene, Houari **2** 445-446

BEN-GURION, DAVID (born 1886), Russ-
ian-born Israeli statesman **2** 160-161
Dayan, Moshe **4** 429-431
Hammarskjöld, Dag **7** 100-101
Kuk, Abraham Issac **9** 123-124

BEN-HAIM, PAUL (Frankenburger;
1897-1984), Israeli composer **2** 161-162

Ben-Hur (novel)
Wallace, Lewis **16** 74-75

Ben Lindsey, the Just Judge (article; Steffens)
Lindsey, Benjamin Barr **9** 425-426

Ben the Luggage Boy (book)
Alger, Horatio **1** 153-154

BEN YEHUDA, ELIEZER (1858-1922),
Hebrew lexicographer and editor
2 181-182

Ben Zvi, Yitzhak (1884-1963), Israeli statesman
Ben-Gurion, David **2** 160-161

BENALCÁZAR, SEBASTIÁN DE (died
1551), Spanish conquistador **2** 145-146
Quesada, Gonzalo Jiménez de
12 509-510

Benares (city, India)
Besant, Annie Wood **2** 233-234
Buddha **3** 97-101, 232

BENAVENTE Y MARTINEZ, JACINTO
(1866-1954), Spanish dramatist
2 146-147

BENCHLEY, ROBERT (1889-1945), American humorist **2** 150-151

Bencoelen (region, Southwest Sumatra)
Dampier, William **4** 384

Bend in the River, A (book)
Naipaul, V. S. **11** 295-296

Bend Sinister (novel)
Nabokov, Vladimir **11** 287-288

BENDA, JULIEN (1867-1956), French cultural critic and novelist **2** 151-152

Bendix Corp.
Blumenthal, Werner Michael **2** 345-346

Beneath the Blue Sky of Her Native Land
(poem)
Pushkin, Aleksandr Sergeevich
12 489-491

Beneath the Wheel (novel)
Hesse, Hermann **7** 367-369

Benedetti, Count Vincent (1817-1900),
French diplomat
Bismarck, Otto Eduard Leopold von
2 294-296

Benedick (literary character)
Shakespeare, William **14** 142-145

Benedict IX (1012?-1056), pope
Henry III **7** 290

Benedict XI (Niccolò Boccasini; died
1304), pope 1303-1304
Jacopone da Todi **8** 194

Benedict XII (Jacques Fournier; died 1342),
pope 1334-1342
Froissart, Jean **6** 124-125

Benedict XIII (Pedro de Luna; circa
1328-circa 1423), antipope 1394-1423
Ailly, Pierre d' **1** 94
Martin V **10** 287-288

Benedict XIV (Prospero Lorenzo Lamberti-
ni; 1675-1758), pope 1740-1758
Pius VI **12** 333-334

BENEDICT XV (Giacomo della Chiesa;
1854-1922), pope, 1914-1922 **2** 153-154
John, XXIII **8** 277-280
Pius XI **12** 337-339

BENEDICT, RUTH FULTON (1887-1948),
American cultural anthropologist
2 154-155
  Boas, Franz **2** 349-351
  Mead, Margaret **10** 438-440

BENEDICT, ST. (circa 480-547), Italian
founder of the Benedictines **2** 154-155
  Columban **4** 176
  Dunstan **5** 151-152
  Gregory I **6** 531-532
  see also Benedictines

Benedict of Aniane, St. (circa 750-821),
French abbot
  Louis I **9** 522-523

Benedict of Nursia, St.
  see Benedict, St.

Benedictines (religious order)
  chroniclers
    Lydgate, John **10** 61-62
    Matthew Paris **10** 341-342
  missionaries
    Boniface **2** 391
  rule
    Benedict, Ruth Fulton **2** 154-155
    Stephen Harding **14** 428-429
  scholarship
    Gratian **6** 498-499
    Mabillon, Jean **10** 72
    Muratori, Lodovico Antonio
      11 254-255
  teachers
    Pius VII **12** 334-335
    Prévost, Abbé **12** 445-446

Benediktbeuren (church, near Munich)
  Cuvilliés, François **4** 359-360

Benefial, Marco (1684-1764), Italian
painter
  Mengs, Anton Raphael **10** 505

Benelux customs union (1948)
  Spaak, Paul Henri **14** 359-360

BENEŠ, EDWARD (1884-1948), Czechoslovak president 1935-1938 and 1940-1948
2 155-157

Benét, Rose (1886-1950), American poet
and critic
  Benét, Stephen Vincent **2** 157-158

BENÉT, STEPHEN VINCENT (1898-1943),
American poet and novelist **2** 157-158

BENETTON, Italian family (Luciano, Giu-
liana, Gilberto, Carlo and Mauro) who
organized a world-wide chain of colorful
knitwear stores **2** 158-159

Benevolence of the Deity, The (book)
  Chauncy, Charles **3** 485-486

Benevolent despots
  see Enlightened despots

BENEZET, ANTHONY (1713-1784), American philanthropist and educator
2 159-160

Bengal (region, Northeast India)
  British rule

Chelmsford, Frederic John Napier
  Thesiger **3** 497
Clive, Robert **4** 119-120
Cornwallis, Charles **4** 241-243
Dalhousie, 1st Marquess of
  4 375-376
nationalism
  Banerjee, Surendranath **1** 488
  Bhashani, Maulana Abdul Hamid
    Khan **2** 255-257
  Bose, Subhas Chandra **2** 430-431
  Chatterji, Bankimchandra
    3 480-481
  Das, Chitta Ranjan **4** 401-402
  Mujibur Rahman **11** 234-236
social reform
  Rabindranath Tagore **12** 529-531
  Roy, Ram Mohun **13** 18

Bengalee (newspaper)
  Banerjee, Surendranath **1** 488

Bengali (East Indic language)
  Chatterji, Bankimchandra **3** 480-481
  Ram Camul Sen **13** 16-17
  Rabindranath Tagore **12** 529-531

Bengan Korei
  see Muhammad II, Askia

Beni, El (department, Bolivia)
  Ballivián, José **1** 475

Beni Ouriaghel (Berber people)
  Abd el-Krim el-Khatabi, Mohamed ben
    1 15-16

Benidorm, Pact of (1956)
  Gómez, Máximo **6** 418-419
  Lleras Camargo, Alberto **9** 467

Benin, Bight of (bay, Gulf of Guinea)
  Burton, Richard **3** 163-164

Benito Cereno (story)
  Melville, Herman **10** 472-476

BENJAMIN, ASHER (1773-1845), American
architect **2** 162-163
  Bulfinch, Charles **3** 116-117

BENJAMIN, JUDAH PHILIP (1811-1884),
American statesman **2** 163-164
  Memminger, Christopher Gustavus
    10 476-477
  Soulé, Pierre **14** 351-352

Benjamin, tribe of (Old Testament)
  David, Jacques Louis **4** 407-409
  Paul **12** 141-143
  Saul **13** 498

Benjamin Banneker's ... Almanack (book)
  Banneker, Benjamin **1** 490-491

Benjamin Franklin (sculpture)
  Zorach, William **16** 528

Benjy (literary character)
  Faulkner, William **5** 395-397

BENN, TONY (Anthony Neil Wedgewood
Benn; born 1925), British Labour party
politician **2** 164-166

BENN, GOTTFRIED (1886-1956), German
author **2** 164
  Grass, Günter **6** 496-497

Bennet, Elizabeth (literary character)
  Austen, Jane **1** 377-379

Bennet, Henry
  see Arlington, 1st Earl of

BENNETT, ALAN (born 1934), British playwright **2** 166-167

BENNETT, ENOCH ARNOLD (1867-1931),
English novelist and dramatist **2** 167-168
  Conrad, Joseph **4** 205-207
  Morrice, James Wilson **11** 181-182
  Woolf, Virginia Stephen **16** 381-382

Bennett, Floyd (1890-1952), American aviator
  Byrd, Richard Evelyn **3** 186-187

BENNETT, JAMES GORDON (1795-1872),
Scottish-born American journalist and
publisher **2** 168-169
  Beach, Moses Yale **2** 79-80

BENNETT, JAMES GORDON, JR.
(1841-1918), American newspaper owner
and editor **2** 169-170
  Bennett, James Gordon **2** 168-169
  Mackay, John William **10** 101-102

BENNETT, JOHN COLEMAN (1902-1995),
American theologian **2** 170-171

BENNETT, RICHARD BEDFORD
(1870-1947), Canadian statesman, prime
minister 1930-1935 **2** 171-172
  Meighen, Arthur **10** 459-460

BENNETT, RICHARD RODNEY (born
1936), English composer **2** 172

BENNETT, WILLIAM JOHN (born 1943),
American teacher and scholar and secretary of the Department of Education
(1985-1988) **2** 172-174

**Bennett of Mickleham, Calgary, and
Hopewell, Viscount**
  see Bennett, Richard Bedford

Bennington (sculpture)
  Caro, Anthony **3** 316

Bennington (Vermont)
  Benjamin, Asher **2** 162-163

Bennington, battle of (1777)
  Burgoyne, John **3** 137-138

Bennington College (Vermont)
  Graham, Martha **6** 485-486
  Polanyi, Karl **12** 372
  Roethke, Theodore **13** 243-244

BENNY, JACK (Benjamin Kubelsky;
1894-1974), American comedian and a
star of radio, television, and stage
2 174-176

Benouville, château of (France)
  Ledoux, Claude Nicolas **9** 277-278

Ben's Nugget (book)
Alger, Horatio **1** 153-154

BENTHAM, JEREMY (1748-1832), English philosopher, political theorist, and jurist **2** 176-178
associates
Mill, James **11** 21
Owen, Robert **12** 39-40
Sydenham, Thomas **15** 59-60
influence of
Chadwick, Edwin **3** 404-405
Halévy, Élie **7** 76
Mill, John Stuart **11** 21-23
O'Connell, Daniel **11** 465-467
Rivadavia, Bernardino **13** 182-183
influenced by
Becarria, Marchese di **2** 97-98
Helvétius, Claude Adrien **7** 273-274
Hume, David **8** 31-34
utilitarianism antedated
Carneades **3** 309

Bentinck, Lord William Cavendish
(1774-1839), English governor-general of India
Deb, Radhakant **4** 437

Bentinck, William Cavendish (3d Duke of Portland; 1738-1809), English statesman, prime minister 1807-1809
Canning, George **3** 258-260

Bentivoglio, Guido (1579-1644), Italian cardinal, statesman, and historian
Claude Lorrain **4** 89-90
Frescobaldi, Girolamo **6** 101-102
Van Dyck, Anthony **15** 423-425

BENTLEY, ARTHUR F. (1870-1957), American philosopher and political scientist **2** 178

Bentley, Eric Russell (born 1916), American theater critic and director
Schnitzler, Arthur **14** 23-24

Bentley, Thomas (died 1780), English potter
Wedgwood, Josiah **16** 168-169

Bentley, William (1759-1819), American Unitarian clergyman
McIntire, Samuel **10** 415

Bentley's Miscellany (periodical)
Dickens, Charles John Huffam **4** 538-541

BENTON, SEN. THOMAS HART
(1782-1858), American statesman **2** 178-179
Atchison, David Rice **1** 357-358
Blair, Francis Preston **2** 313-315
Brown, Benjamin Gratz **3** 32-33
Frémont, John Charles **6** 97-98
Hayne, Robert Young **7** 231-232

BENTON, THOMAS HART (1889-1975), American regionalist painter **2** 178-179
Burchfield, Charles **3** 131-132
Pollock, Jackson **12** 379-380

BENTSEN, LLOYD MILLARD (born 1921), senior United States senator from Texas

and Democratic vice-presidential candidate in 1988 **2** 180-181

Benue River (West Africa)
Baikie, William Balfour **1** 440
Barth, Heinrich **2** 30-31

Benvenuto Cellini (opera; Berlioz)
Berlioz, Louis Hector **2** 203-205
Cellini, Benvenuto **3** 391-392

BENZ, CARL (1844-1929), German inventor **2** 182-183

Benzene (chemistry)
Baeyer, Johann Friedrich Adolf von **1** 432
Couper, Archibald Scott **4** 269-270
Faraday, Michael **5** 380
Kekulé, Friedrich August **8** 477-478

Benzoyl radical (chemistry)
Liebig, Justus von **9** 403-404

Beowulf (epic)
Morris, William **11** 187-188

Beppo (satire)
Byron, George Gordon Noel **3** 193-194

Bérard, Christian (1902-1949), French painter
Thomson, Virgil **15** 202-203

Berardi, Gianetto (died 1495), Italian merchant
Vespucci, Amerigo **15** 476-478

Berbers (North African people)
Almohads
Abd al-Mumin **1** 13
ibn Tumart, Muhammad **8** 96-97
Yakub al-Mansur, Abu Yusuf **16** 426
Almoravids
Abdullah ibn Yasin **1** 20
Alfonso VI **1** 149
ibn Tashufin, Yusuf **8** 95-96

Bercerillo (dog)
Ponce de León, Juan **12** 391-392

BERCHTOLD, COUNT LEOPOLD VON
(1863-1942), Austro-Hungarian statesman **2** 183-184

BERDYAEV, NICHOLAS ALEXAN-DROVICH (1874-1948), Russian philosopher **2** 184-185

Berea College (Kentucky)
Fee, John Gregg **5** 402-403

Berea College v. Kentucky (legal case)
Harlan, John Marshall **7** 156-157

Berean, The (book)
Noyes, John Humphrey **11** 437-438

BERELSON, BERNARD (1912-1979), American behavioral scientist **2** 185-186

Bérenger of Tours (Berengarius; 998-1008), French theologian
Lanfranc **9** 189-190
Leo IX **9** 332

Bérénice (play)
Racine, Jean Baptiste **12** 532-535

Berenice (poem)
Theocritus **15** 171-172

BERG, ALBAN (1885-1935), Austrian composer **2** 186-187
Dallapiccola, Luigi **4** 377-378
Krenek, Ernst **9** 98-99
Mahler, Gustav **10** 144-145
Perle, George **12** 223-224
Schoenberg, Arnold **14** 24-26
Webern, Anton **16** 160-162

Berg (former duchy, West Germany)
Frederick William I **6** 86-87

BERG, PAUL (born 1926), American chemist **2** 187-189

Berg am Laim (church, Munich)
Cuvilliés, François **4** 359-360
Zimmermann, Johann Baptist and Domenikus **16** 518

Bergamo (city, Italy)
Bramante, Donato **2** 493-494

Bergen Museum (Norway)
Nansen, Fridtjof **11** 304-305

Berger, Hans (1873-1941), Austrian psychiatrist
Adrian, Edgar Douglas **1** 67-69

BERGER, VICTOR LOUIS (1860-1929), American politician **2** 189-190

Berger et la bergère, Le (musical composition)
Lassus, Roland de **9** 216-218

Berger v. New York (legal case)
Warren, Earl **16** 117-120

Bergerac, Cyrano de
see Cyrano de Bergerac

Bergeret, Monsieur (literary character)
France, Anatole **6** 39-40

BERGMAN, (ERNST) INGMAR (born 1918); Swedish film and stage director **2** 190-191
Chaplin, Charles Spencer **3** 438-440
Stravinsky, Igor Fedorovich **14** 502-506

Bergman, Ingrid (1917-1982), Swedish actress
Bogart, Humphrey **2** 363-364

Bergson, Alexandra (literary character)
Cather, Willa Sibert **3** 368-369

BERGSON, HENRI (1859-1941), French philosopher **2** 191-192
influence of
Burroughs, John **3** 160-161
Čapek, Karel **3** 271-272
Iqbal, Muhammad **8** 132-133
Maritain, Jacques **10** 263
Maurras, Charles Marie Photius **10** 350-351
Ortega Y Gasset, José **12** 7-8
Péguy, Charles Pierre **12** 183-184
Radhakrishnan, Sarvepalli **12** 537-538
vitalism
Driesch, Hans Adolf Eduard **5** 105

BERIA, LAVRENTY PAVLOVICH
(1899-1953), Soviet secret-police chief
and politician **2** 192-193
    Konev, Ivan Stefanovich **9** 81-82
    Molotov, Vyacheslav Mikhailovich
        11 89-90
    Zhukov, Georgi Konstantinovich
        16 512-513

Beriberi (medicine)
    Eijkman, Christian **5** 228

BERING, VITUS (1681-1741), Danish navigator in Russian employ **2** 193-194

Bering Sea (North Pacific Ocean)
    Cook, James **4** 214-215

Bering Sea Arbitration (1892-1893)
    Lansing, Robert **9** 200

Bering Sea Claims Commission
(1896-1897)
    Lansing, Robert **9** 200

Bering Strait
    Bering, Vitus **2** 193-194
    Franklin, John **6** 64-65
    Peter I **12** 253-256

BERIO, LUCIANO (born 1925), Italian
composer **2** 194-195
    Boulez, Pierre **2** 444-445

BERISHA, SALI (born 1944), president of
the Republic of Albania (1992-)
2 195-197

Beritten Hin und Zuruck (play)
    Grass, Günter **6** 496-497

BERKELEY, GEORGE (1685-1753),
Anglo-Irish philosopher and Anglican
bishop **2** 197-198
    Mach, Ernst **10** 90-91
    Malebranche, Nicolas **10** 166-167
    Mandeville, Bernard **10** 192
    Smibert, John **14** 282
    Witherspoon, John **16** 346-348

Berkeley, John (1st Baron Berkeley of Stratton; died 1678), English Royalist
    Berkeley, William **2** 198-199

Berkeley, Lennox Randal Francis
(1903-1989), English composer
    Bennett, Richard Rodney **2** 172

BERKELEY, SIR WILLIAM (1606-1677),
English royal governor of Virginia
2 198-199
    Bacon, Nathaniel **1** 424-425
    Byrd, William **3** 188-189
    Dinwiddie, Robert **5** 18-19
    Dunmore, 4th Earl of **5** 147

Berkman, Alexander (1870-1936),
Polish-born anarchist
    Goldman, Emma **6** 406-407

Berkshire Agricultural Society (Massachusetts)
    Watson, Elkanah **16** 136

Berkshire Hathaway, Inc.
    Buffett, Warren **3** 106-109

Berkshire Music Center (Tanglewood,
Massachusetts)
    Copland, Aaron **4** 227-228
    Schuller, Gunther **14** 37-38

Berkshires (painting)
    Durand, Asher Brown **5** 156-157

Berlage, Hendrick Petrus (1856-1934),
Dutch architect
    Oud, Jacobus Johannes Pieter **12** 32
    Wright, Frank Lloyd **16** 398-401

BERLE, ADOLF AUGUSTUS, JR.
(1895-1971), American educator
2 199-200

Berlin (city, Germany)
    architecture
        Behrens, Peter **2** 121-122
        Schinkel, Karl Friedrich **14** 8
        Schlüter, Andreas **14** 18-19
    lord mayors
        Brandt, Willy **2** 499-500
    revolution (1848)
        Frederick William IV **6** 87-88
    Wall crisis
        Brandt, Willy **2** 499-500
        John, XXIII **8** 277-280
        Kennedy, John Fitzgerald **8** 502-506
        Konev, Ivan Stefanovich **9** 81-82
        Ulbricht, Walter **15** 383-384

Berlin, Congress of (1878)
    Austria-Hungary
        Andrássy, Julius **1** 222-223
    British interests
        Balfour, Arthur James **1** 469-470
        Disraeli, Benjamin **5** 27-29
        Salisbury, 3d Marquess of
            13 448-449
        Victoria **15** 485-487
    chairman
        Bismarck, Otto Eduard Leopold von
            2 294-296
    Ottoman Empire
        Abdul-Hamid II **1** 17-18
        Malkam Khan, Mirza **10** 172

BERLIN, IRVING (1888-1989), American
composer **2** 200-201
    Gershwin, George **6** 284-285
    Oakley, Annie **11** 453-454

BERLIN, ISAIAH (born 1909), British
philosopher **2** 201-203
    Bowen, Elizabeth **2** 462-463

Berlin, University of
    chemistry
        Fischer, Emil **5** 456-457
        Hahn, Otto **7** 64-65
        Hofmann, August Wilhelm von
            7 441-442
        Van't Hoff, Jacobus Hendricus
            15 431-432
    founded
        Humboldt, Wilhelm von **8** 31
    history and philology
        Diels, Otto Paul Hermann **5** 5-6
        Meinecke, Friedrich **10** 460-461
        Mommsen, Theodor **11** 94-95

        Ranke, Leopold von **13** 33-35
        Wolf, Friedrich August **16** 352-353
    law
        Savigny, Friedrich Karl von
            13 502-503
    mathematics
        Von Neumann, John **16** 27-28
    medicine
        Koch, Heinrich Hermann Robert
            9 69-70
        Müller, Johannes Peter **11** 239-240
        Virchow, Rudolf Ludwig Carl
            15 506-507
    philosophy
        Cassirer, Ernst **3** 358-359
        Du Bois-Reymond, Emil **5** 118-119
        Fichte, Johann Gottlieb **5** 435-436
        Hegel, Georg Wilhelm Friedrich
            7 254-256
        Schopenhauer, Arthur **14** 29-31
        Simmel, Georg **14** 234-235
    physics
        Born, Max **2** 420-421
        Clausius, Rudolf Julius Emanuel
            4 92-94
        Debye, Peter Joseph William
            4 447-448
        Einstein, Albert **5** 228-231
        Heisenberg, Werner Karl **7** 261-263
        Helmholtz, Hermann Ludwig Ferdi-
            nand von **7** 268-269
        Hertz, Heinrich Rudolf **7** 346-347
        Planck, Max Karl Ernst Ludwig
            12 342-344
        Schrödinger, Erwin **14** 31-33
    social sciences
        Boas, Franz **2** 349-351
        Ritter, Karl **13** 181-182
        Schmoller, Gustav Friedrich von
            14 21
        Sombart, Werner **14** 332-333
        Wertheimer, Max **16** 207-208
    theology
        Harnack, Adolf von **7** 160
        Schaff, Philip **13** 519-520
        Tillich, Paul Johannes **15** 224-225

Berlin Academy of Sciences
    Alembert, Jean le Rond d' **1** 127-128
    Lagrange, Joseph Louis **9** 164-166

Berlin Conference (1884-1885)
    Brazza, Pierre Paul François Camille
        Savorgnan de **2** 509-510
    Goldie, George Dashwood Taubman
        6 404
    Leopold II **9** 346-347
    Lobengula **9** 474-475
    Tippu Tip **15** 235-236

Berlin Geographical Society
    Ritter, Karl **13** 181-182

Berlin Institute for Jewish Studies
    Cohen, Hermann **4** 138-139

Berlin Observatory
    Fraunhofer, Joseph von **6** 75-76

Berlin Psychoanalytic Institute
Horney, Karen Danielsen **7** 508-509
Klein, Melanie **9** 52

Berlin Schloss (palace)
Schlüter, Andreas **14** 18-19

Berlin Secession (art group)
Corinth, Lovis **4** 234
Liebermann, Max **9** 402-403
Nolde, Emil **11** 419-420
Schiele, Egon **14** 1-2

Berliner, Émile (1851-1929),
German-born American inventor
Bell, Alexander Graham **2** 129-131
Edison, Thomas Alva **5** 206-208

Berliner Ensemble (theater co.)
Brecht, Bertolt **2** 512-514

BERLIOZ, LOUIS HECTOR (1803-1869),
French composer, conductor, and critic
2 203-205
influence of
Chopin, Frédéric François **4** 16-18
Holst, Gustav **7** 459-460
Schumann, Robert Alexander
14 41-43
Strauss, Richard **14** 500-501
influenced by
Cellini, Benvenuto **3** 391-392
Gluck, Christoph Willibald
6 372-374

Berlioz, Mrs. Hector
see Smithson, Harriett

BERMEJO, BARTOLOMÉ (Bartolomé de
Cárdenas; flourished 1474-1498), Spanish painter **2** 205

Bermuda (archipelago; Atlantic Ocean)
Berkeley, George **2** 197-198
Dinwiddie, Robert **5** 18-19
Durham, 1st Earl of **5** 161-162
Leonard, Daniel **9** 336-337
Vespucci, Amerigo **15** 476-478

Bermudas (poem)
Marvell, Andrew **10** 301-303

Bern, University of (Switzerland)
Einstein, Albert **5** 228-231

Bernadette of Lourdes, St. (1844-1879),
French peasant girl, canonized 1933
Werfel, Franz **16** 204-205

Bernadotte, Count Folke (1895-1948),
Swedish diplomat
Bunche, Ralph Johnson **3** 121-122

Bernadotte, Jean Baptiste
see Charles XIV John

Bernadotte dynasty (Sweden; ruled from
1818)
Bernadotte, Jean Baptiste **2** 205-206

BERNANOS, GEORGES (1888-1948),
French novelist and essayist **2** 206-207

Bernard VII (died 1418), Count of
Armagnac, constable of France
Charles VI **3** 460-461

BERNARD, CLAUDE (1813-1878), French
physiologist **2** 208-210

Bernard, Émile (1868-1941), French
painter and engraver
Bonnard, Pierre **2** 395-396
Gauguin, Paul **6** 236-238
Van Gogh, Vincent **15** 427-429

Bernard, Sir Francis (1712-1779), English
colonial governor in America
Otis, James Jr. **12** 25-27

BERNARD OF CLAIRVAUX, ST.
(1090-1153), French theologian, Doctor
of the Church **2** 207-208
Abelard, Peter **1** 23-25
Arnold of Brescia **1** 314-315
Louis VII **9** 524-525
Roger II **13** 244-245
Stephen Harding **14** 428-429

Bernard Shaw (book)
Harris, Frank **7** 172-173
Mencken, Henry Louis **10** 481-483

Bernardes, Arturo da Silva (1875-1955),
Brazilian president 1922-1926
Prestes, Luiz Carlos **12** 442-444

BERNARDIN, CARDINAL JOSEPH
(1928-1996), Roman Catholic Cardinal
and American activist **2** 210-211

Bernardone, Giovanni di
see Francis of Assisi, St.

BERNAYS, EDWARD L. (1891-1995),
American public relations consultant
2 211-212

Bernhard of Lippe-Biesterfeld (born 1911),
German prince
Wilhelmina **16** 278-279

BERNHARDT, SARAH (Henriette-Rosine
Bernard; 1844-1923), French actress
2 212-214

Bernheim, Hippolyte (1837-1919), French
physician
Janet, Pierre Marie Félix **8** 220
Mesmer, Franz Anton **10** 526-527

Berni, Francesco (1497-1536), Italian poet
and satirist
Boiardo, Matteo Maria **2** 369

BERNINI, GIAN LORENZO (1598-1680),
Italian artist **2** 214-216
critics
Rosa, Salvator **13** 289-290
influence of
Churriguera, José Benito de **4** 53-54
Falconet, Étienne Maurice **5** 372
Fischer von Erlach, Johann Bernhard
5 459-461
Schlüter, Andreas **14** 18-19
influenced by
Carracci **3** 319-321
Correggio **4** 249-251
Michelangelo Buonarroti **11** 2-5
rivals
Borromini, Francesco **2** 424-425

Bernini, Pietro (1562-1629), Italian sculptor
Bernini, Gian Lorenzo **2** 214-216

BERNOULLI, DANIEL (1700-1782), Swiss
mathematician and physicist **2** 216
Alembert, Jean le Rond d' **1** 127-128
Ampère, André Marie **1** 205-206
Lagrange, Joseph Louis **9** 164-166
Maxwell, James Clerk **10** 361-364

Bernoulli, Jakob (1654-1705), Swiss math-
ematician
Laplace, Marquis de **9** 202-204
Ohm, Georg Simon **11** 486-487

Bernoulli, Jean (or Johann; 1667-1748),
Swiss mathematician
Bernoulli, Daniel **2** 216
Fermat, Pierre de **5** 421-422

Bernoulli, Johann (1710-1790), Swiss
mathematician
Lagrange, Joseph Louis **9** 164-166

Bernoulli, Nicholas (or Nikolaus;
1695-1726), Swiss mathematician
Bernoulli, Daniel **2** 216

Bernstein, Carl (born 1944), investigative
reporter
Woodward and Bernstein **16** 376-378

BERNSTEIN, DOROTHY LEWIS (born
1914), American mathematician **2** 217

BERNSTEIN, EDUARD (1850-1932), Ger-
man socialist **2** 218
Kautsky, Karl Johann **8** 462-463
Luxemburg, Rosa **10** 55-56
Trotsky, Leon **15** 302-305

BERNSTEIN, LEONARD (1918-1990),
American composer, conductor, and
pianist **2** 218-219
Boulez, Pierre **2** 444-445
Cage, John **3** 211-214
Sondheim, Stephen **14** 337-338

Bernstein, Ludvik
see Namier, Sir Lewis Bernstein

Berrettini, Pietro
see Cortona, Pietroda

Berretto a sonagli, Il (play)
Pirandello, Luigi **12** 319-321

BERRI, NABIH (born 1939), leader of the
Shi'ite Muslims in Lebanon **2** 220-222

BERRIGAN, DANIEL J. (born 1921), activist
American Catholic priest **2** 222-223

Berrio (ship)
Gama, Vasco da **6** 196-198

BERRUGUETE, ALONSO (1486/90-1561),
Spanish sculptor **2** 223-224

Berruguete, Pedro (circa 1450-1504),
Spanish painter
Berruguete, Alonso **2** 223-224

**Berry, Charles Ferdinand de Bourbon,
Duke of** (1778-1820), French statesman
Louis XVIII **9** 535-536

Berry, Jean de France, 1st Duke of (1340-1416), French statesman and art patron
  Charles VI **3** 460-461
  Limbourg brothers, The **9** 412-413
  Machaut, Guillaume de **10** 93-94

BERRY, MARY FRANCES (born 1938), African American human/civil rights activist and official **2** 226-229

Berthelot, Marcelin Pierre Eugène (1827-1907), French chemist
  Duhem, Pierre Maurice Marie **5** 129
  Renan, Ernest **13** 95-96

BERTHOLLET, CLAUDE LOUIS (1748-1822), French chemist **2** 229-230
  Gay-Lussac, Joseph Louis **6** 245-246
  Lavoisier, Antoine Laurent **9** 241-244

BERTILLON, ALPHONSE (1853-1914), French criminologist **2** 230-231

Bertillon, Jacques (1851-1922), French physician and statistician
  Bertillon, Alphonse **2** 230-231

Bertillon, Louis Adolphe (1821-1883), French physician and statistician
  Bertillon, Alphonse **2** 230-231

Bertin, François Edouard (1797-1871), French painter
  Corot, Jean Baptiste Camille **4** 247-249

Bertin, Jean Victor (1775-1842), French painter
  Corot, Jean Baptiste Camille **4** 247-249

Bertrada (died 783), mother of Charlemagne
  Charlemagne **3** 445-447

Bertram, Thomas (literary character)
  Austen, Jane **1** 377-379

Bérulle, Pierre de (1575-1629), French cardinal
  Malebranche, Nicolas **10** 166-167

Beryllium (element—chemistry)
  Chadwick, James **3** 405-406
  Davy, Humphry **4** 426-427

BERZELIUS, JÖNS JACOB (1779-1848), Swedish chemist **2** 231-233
  Dumas, Jean Baptiste André **5** 138-139
  Hare, Robert **7** 152-153
  Liebig, Justus von **9** 403-404

Besançon, Diet of (1157)
  Frederick I **6** 78-79

BESANT, ANNIE WOOD (1847-1933), British social reformer and theosophist **2** 233-234
  Bradlaugh, Charles **2** 478
  Krishnamurti, Jiddu **9** 101-103
  Menon, Vengalil Krishnan Krishna **10** 507-509
  Naidu, Sarojini **11** 294-295
  Nehru, Jawaharlal **11** 332-334

Beschreibung eines Kampfes, Die (book)
  Kafka, Franz **8** 403-406

Besht
  see Baal Shem Tov

Bespiegelingen van Godt en Godtsdienst (poem)
  Vondel, Joost van den **16** 19-20

Bess of Bedlam (song)
  Purcell, Henry **12** 484-485

Bessarabia (region, former Union of Soviet Socialist Republics)
  Ferdinand **5** 413-414
  Gordon, Charles George **6** 448-449
  Mahmud II **10** 145-147

Bessarion, Cardinal (1403-1472), Greek bishop, theologian, and humanist
  Regiomontanus **13** 81-82

BESSEL, FRIEDRICH WILHELM (1784-1846), German astronomer **2** 234-235
  Bradley, James **2** 482-483
  Herschel, William **7** 341-343
  Struve, Friedrich Georg Wilhelm von **14** 513

Bessel functions (mathematics)
  Bessel, Friedrich Wilhelm **2** 234-235

BESSEMER, SIR HENRY (1813-1898), English inventor **2** 235-236

Bessemer process (steel industry)
  Bessemer, Henry **2** 235-236
  Carnegie, Andrew **3** 309-312
  Corning, Erastus **4** 238-239
  Kelly, William **8** 487-488
  Krupp **9** 109-111

BEST, CHARLES HERBERT (1899-1978), Canadian physiologist **2** 236-237
  Banting, Frederick Grant **1** 493-494

Best Times, The (autobiography)
  Dos Passos, John Roderigo **5** 69-71

Best Years of Our Lives, The (film)
  Goldwyn, Samuel **6** 416
  Sherwood, Robert Emmet **14** 189-190

Besuch aus dem Elysium (play)
  Werfel, Franz **16** 204-205

Bet Din Hagadol
  see Sanhedrin, Great

Bet Hillel (Jewish academy)
  Shammai **14** 149

Bet Shammai (Jewish academy)
  Shammai **14** 149

Bet Yosef (book)
  Caro, Joseph ben Ephraim **3** 316-317

Bet Zecharia, battle of (162 B.C.)
  Judas Maccabeus **8** 374-375

Beta
  see Eratosthenes of Cyrene

Beta radiation (physics)
  Chadwick, James **3** 405-406
  Fermi, Enrico **5** 422-424
  Rutherford, Ernest **13** 384-387
  Soddy, Frederick **14** 321-323

BETANCOURT, RÓMULO (1908-1990), Venezuelan statesman **2** 237-238
  Trujillo Molina, Rafael Leonidas **15** 313-314

Beth Sholom Synagogue (Elkins Park, Pennsylvania)
  Wright, Frank Lloyd **16** 398-401

Bethany College (Illinois)
  Campbell, Alexander **3** 249-250

BETHE, HANS ALBRECHT (born 1906), Alsatian-American physicist **2** 238-239
  Oppenheimer, J. Robert **11** 525-526
  Yukawa, Hideki **16** 481-482

Bethel (ancient city, Palestine)
  Jeroboam I **8** 248-249

Bethel Church (Philadelphia)
  Allen, Richard **1** 168

Bethlehem Chapel (Prague)
  Hus, Jan **8** 56-59

Bethlehem Steel Corp.
  Schwab, Charles Michael **14** 50-51

Bethlen, Count István (1874-1947), Hungarian statesman
  Horthy de Nagybánya, Nicholas **7** 510-512

BETHMANN HOLLWEG, THEOBALD VON (1856-1921), German statesman **2** 239-240
  Kapp, Wolfgang **8** 436
  Ludendorff, Erich Friedrich Wilhelm **10** 27-28

Bethune, David
  see Beaton, David

BETHUNE, HENRY NORMAN (1890-1939), Canadian humanitarian physician **2** 240-241

BETHUNE, MARY MCLEOD (1875-1955), African American educator **2** 241-242

Bethune-Cookman College (Daytona Beach, Florida)
  Bethune, Mary McLeod **2** 241-242

Bethune-Volusia Beach Corp.
  Bethune, Mary McLeod **2** 241-242

BETI, MONGO (Alexandre Biyidi; born 1932), Cameroonian novelist **2** 242-243

Betine (play)
  Musset, Louis Charles Alfred de **11** 271-272

BETJEMAN, JOHN (1906-1984), Poet Laureate of Britain 1972-1984 **2** 243-245

Betrachtung (stories)
  Kafka, Franz **8** 403-406

Betrayal of Christ (painting)
  Giotto **6** 342-345
  Van Dyck, Anthony **15** 423-425

Betrothal II (painting)
  Gorky, Arshile **6** 458

Betrothal of the Virgin (painting)
  Campin, Robert **3** 255

Betrothed (story)
Agnon, Shmuel Yoseph **1** 85-86

Betrothed, The (novel)
Manzoni, Alessandro **10** 222-224
Scott, Walter **14** 68-70

Bettar, siege of (135)
Bar Kochba, Simeon **2** 5

BETTELHEIM, BRUNO (1903-1990), Austrian-born American psychoanalyst and educational psychologist **2** 245-246

Better Late than Never (autobiography)
Goncharov, Ivan Aleksandrovich **6** 424

Better Less but Better (article)
Lenin, Vladimir Ilich **9** 323-326

Betterton, Thomas (1635-1710), English actor
Congreve, William **4** 200-201

BETTI, UGO (1892-1953), Italian playwright **2** 246

Betti di Biagio, Bernardino
see Pintoricchio

Betty Crocker (advertising symbol)
Barton, Bruce **2** 36-37

Betty Leicester (book)
Jewett, Sarah Orne **8** 256

Between Man and Man (book)
Buber, Martin **3** 87-89

Between Roads (book)
Kaufmann, Ezekiel **8** 460

Between the Acts (novel)
Woolf, Virginia Stephen **16** 381-382

Between the Light (painting)
Kandinsky, Wassily **8** 420-422

Between Two Worlds (book)
Ferrero, Guglielmo **5** 429-430

Between Two Worlds (play)
Rice, Elmer **13** 126-127

Beust, Count Friedrich Ferdinand von (1809-1886), German statesman and Austrian chancellor
Andrássy, Julius **1** 222-223

BEUYS, JOSEPH (1921-1986), German artist and sculptor **2** 246-248

BEVAN, ANEURIN (1897-1960), Labour minister responsible for the creation of the British National Health Service **2** 248-249
Foot, Michael **5** 505-507
Wilson, James Harold **16** 324-325

Bevatron
see Electron synchrotron

BEVEL, JAMES LUTHER (born 1936), American civil rights activist of the 1960s **2** 250-251

Beveridge, Albert Jeremiah (1862-1927), American politician and historian
Phillips, David Graham **12** 280-281
Roosevelt, Theodore **13** 280-283

Beveridge and the Progressive Era (book)
Bowers, Claude Gernade **2** 463

BEVERIDGE, WILLIAM HENRY (1st Baron Beveridge of Tuccal; 1879-1963), English economist and social reformer **2** 251-252
Wilson, James Harold **16** 324-325

Beveridge Report (1942)
Beveridge, William Henry **2** 251-252

Beverley, Robert (1641-1687), colonial American planter
Beverley, Robert **2** 252

BEVERLEY, ROBERT (circa 1673-1722), colonial American historian **2** 252

Bevilacqua Palace (Verona)
Sanmicheli, Michele **13** 469-470

BEVIN, ERNEST (1881-1951), English trade union leader and politician **2** 252-253

Bewick Finzer (verse)
Robinson, Edwin Arlington **13** 201-202

Beyle, Marie Henri
see Stendhal

Beylism (literature)
Stendhal **14** 422-425

Beyond God the Father (book)
Daly, Mary **4** 380-381

Beyond Horizons (autobiography)
Ellsworth, Lincoln **5** 277

Beyond Life (book)
Cabell, James Branch **3** 195-196

Beyond Our Power (play)
Bjørnson, Bjørnstjerne **2** 299-300

Beyond Painting (book)
Ernst, Max **5** 311-312

Beyond Racism (book)
Young, Whitney Moore Jr. **16** 476-477

Beyond the City (novel)
Doyle, Arthur Conan **5** 91-92

Beyond the Horizon (play)
O'Neill, Eugene **11** 514-516

Beyond Tragedy (book)
Niebuhr, Reinhold **11** 387-388

Bèze, Théodore de (1519-1605), French Protestant theologian
Arminius, Jacobus **1** 301-302
Goudimel, Claude **6** 466
Le Jeune, Claude **9** 314-315
Ronsard, Pierre de **13** 271-273

Bezels of Wisdom (book)
Ibn al-Arabi, Muhyi al-Din **8** 91

Bezhin Meadow (film)
Eisenstein, Sergei Mikhailovich **5** 240-242

BHABHA, HOMI JEHANGIR (1909-1966), Indian atomic physicist **2** 253-254

Bhagavad Gita (Hindu epic)
Besant, Annie Wood **2** 233-234
Bhaktivedanta Prabhupada **2** 254-255
Ghose, Aurobindo **6** 293-294
Oppenheimer, J. Robert **11** 525-526
Radhakrishnan, Sarvepalli **12** 537-538

Bhagavat (poem)
Leconte de Lisle, Charles Marie René **9** 273-274

BHAKTIVEDANTA PRABHUPADA (Abhay Charan De; 1896-1977), Hindu religious teacher who founded the International Society for Krishna Consciousness **2** 254-255

BHASHANI, MAULANA ABDUL HAMID KHAN (1880-1976), Muslim leader who promoted nationalism in Assam, Bengal, and Bangladesh **2** 255-257

BHAVE, VINOBA (born 1895), Indian nationalist and social reformer **2** 257-258
Narayan, Jayaprakash **11** 312-313

Bhoodan movement (India)
Bhave, Vinoba **2** 257-258
Narayan, Jayaprakash **11** 312-313

BHUMIBOL ADULYADEJ (born 1927), king of Thailand (1946-) representing the Chakri Dynasty **2** 258-259
Sarit Thanarat **13** 483-484

Bhutan, Kingdom of (nation; Central Asia)
Dalai Lama **4** 369-371

BHUTTO, BENAZIR (born 1953), prime minister of Pakistan (1988-1990) **2** 259-261

BHUTTO, ZULFIKAR ALI (1928-1979), Pakistan's president and later prime minister (1971-1979) **2** 261-262
Zia ul-Haq, Mohammad **16** 513-515

Biafra (region, Eastern Nigeria)
Dike, Kenneth **5** 7-8
Ekwensi, Cyprian **5** 242-243
Houphouët-Boigny, Felix **7** 519-520
see also Civil war, Nigerian-Biafran

Biafra, Bight of (bay, West Africa)
Burton, Richard **3** 163-164
Johnston, Henry Hamilton **8** 322-323

BIALIK, HAYYIM NAHMAN (1873-1934), Russian-born Hebrew poet **2** 262-263

Bianca e Fernando (opera)
Bellini, Vincenzo **2** 138-139

Biancofiore (literary character)
Boccaccio, Giovanni **2** 351-353

Biathanatos (treatise)
Donne, John **5** 60-61

Bibaculus, Marcus Furius (1st century B.C.), Latin poet
Catullus, Gaius Valerius **3** 377-378

Biberpelz, Der (comedy)
Hauptmann, Gerhart Johann Robert **7** 199-201

Bibiena, Ferdinando (1657-1743), Italian architect
Piranesi, Giovanni Battista **12** 321-322

Bible
• BIBLICAL STUDIES
as literary source
Dickinson, Emily **4** 541-543

Dinesen Blixen-Finecke, Karen **5** 13-14
Furphy, Joseph **6** 152-153
Heavysege, Charles **7** 246
Hugo, Victor Marie **8** 22-25
Lagerlöf, Selma Ottiliana Lovisa **9** 163-164
biblical criticism
Bea, Augustinus **2** 79
Harper, William Rainey **7** 163-164
Kaufmann, Ezekiel **8** 460
Loisy, Alfred Firmin **9** 489-490
Renan, Ernest **13** 95-96
Ritschl, Albrecht Benjamin **13** 180
Wolf, Friedrich August **16** 352-353
Catholic study curbed
Pius X **12** 336-337
Pius XII **12** 339-340
commentaries
Cassiodorus Flavius Magnus Aurelius **3** 357-358
Schaff, Philip **13** 519-520
illustrators
Blake, William **2** 316-318
Chagall, Marc **3** 406-407
translations
Coverdale, Miles **4** 278
Eliot, John **5** 256-258
Saadia ben Joseph al-Fayumi **13** 396
Ulfilas **15** 384
versions
Gutenberg, Johann **7** 48-49
Henry VIII **7** 302-305
Luther, Martin **10** 48-51
Tyndale, William **15** 373-374
• NEW TESTAMENT
Apostles
see Epistolists and Evangelists (below)
commentaries
Barth, Karl **2** 31-32
Baur, Ferdinand Christian **2** 74-75
Erasmus, Desiderius **5** 298-300
Valla, Lorenzo **15** 406
demythologizing
Bultmann, Rudolf Karl **3** 119-120
Harnack, Adolf von **7** 160
Jaspers, Karl **8** 225-226
Epistolists
John, St. **8** 274-275
Paul **12** 141-143
Peter **12** 252-253
Evangelists (Gospel authors)
John, St. **8** 274-275
Luke **10** 38
Mark **10** 266-267
Matthew **10** 340-341
forerunner of Jesus
John the Baptist **8** 290
Holy Family

Jesus of Nazareth **8** 251-255
Mary **10** 308
interpretations
Isidore of Seville **8** 149-150
Marcion **10** 238-239
Ritschl, Albrecht Benjamin **13** 180
Schüssler Fiorenza, Elisabeth **14** 46-48
Waldo, Peter **16** 55-56
Wilder, Amos Niven **16** 273-274
see also demythologizing (above)
Muratorian Canon
Muratori, Lodovico Antonio **11** 254-255
newspaper prints
Medill, Joseph **10** 451-452
translations
Brant, Joseph **2** 500-501
Campbell, Alexander **3** 249-250
Crowther, Samuel Adjai **4** 326
Jerome **8** 249
Palamas, Kostes **12** 70
Sixtus V **14** 267-268
• OLD TESTAMENT
as tradition history
von Rad, Gerhard **16** 29-30
commentaries
Abravanel, Isaac ben Judah **1** 31
Aelfric **1** 69-70
Origen **11** 528-529
Rashi **13** 43
interpretations
Akiba ben Joseph **1** 97-98
Ambrose **1** 192-193
Gershom ben Judah **6** 283-284
Graetz, Heinrich Hirsch **6** 483
Hillel **7** 390-391
Isidore of Seville **8** 149-150
Philo Judaeus **12** 282-283
Marcion **10** 238-239
Nahmanides **11** 293-294
Saadia ben Joseph al-Fayumi **13** 396
Schüssler Fiorenza, Elisabeth **14** 46-48
von Rad, Gerhard **16** 29-30
Kings and Judges
David **4** 406-407
Jeroboam I **8** 248-249
Samuel **13** 457-458
Saul **13** 498
Solomon **14** 326-327
Maccabees
Judas Maccabeus **8** 374-375
prophets
Amos **1** 205
Ezekiel **5** 355-356
Hosea **7** 512
Isaiah **8** 146-147
Jeremiah **8** 247-248
Micah **10** 542-543
Moses **11** 200-201
Samuel **13** 457-458

Protestant Apocrypha
Jesus ben Sira **8** 251
translations
Jerome **8** 249
Origen **11** 528-529
Wisdom literature
Ezra **5** 356-357
Jesus ben Sira **8** 251
Bible against Slavery, The (book)
Weld, Theodore Dwight **16** 186
Bible Commonwealth
see Geneva
Bible Communism and Male Continence (book)
Noyes, John Humphrey **11** 437-438
Bible de l'humanité, La (book)
Michelet, Jules **11** 5-6
Bible of Amiens, The (book; Ruskin)
Proust, Marcel **12** 465-467
Biblia Americana (book)
Mather, Cotton **10** 330-332
Biblia naturae (book)
Swammerdam, Jan **15** 48-49
Biblical Message (painting series)
Chagall, Marc **3** 406-407
Biblical Religion and the Search for Ultimate Reality (book)
Tillich, Paul Johannes **15** 224-225
Biblical studies
see Bible
Bibliografia Kabbalistica (book)
Scholem, Gershom **14** 26
Biblioteca (bibliography)
Photius **12** 283-284
Biblioteca americana (periodical)
Bello, Ahmadu **2** 139-140
Biblioteca Laurenziana (Florence)
Michelangelo Buonarroti **11** 2-5
Biblioteca México
Vasconcelos, José **15** 443-444
Bibliotheca Radcliviana (book)
Gibbs, James **6** 301-302
Bibliotheca universalis (encyclopedia)
Gesner, Konrad von **6** 287
Bibliothèque Nationale (Paris)
Budé, Guillaume **3** 102-103
Labrouste, Pierre François Henri **9** 144
Bibliothèque Ste-Geneviève (Paris)
Labrouste, Pierre François Henri **9** 144
Bibulus, Marcus Calpurnius (died 48 B.C.), Roman politician
Caesar, Gaius Julius **3** 207-210
Bicêtre, l'Hospice de (Paris)
Pinel, Philippe **12** 313-314
BICHAT, MARIE FRANÇOIS XAVIER (1771-1802), French anatomist, pathologist, and physiologist **2** 263-264
Bicinia (musical form)
Praetorius, Michael **12** 431-432

Bicycle Rider in Beverly Hills, The (autobiography)
Saroyan, William **13** 486-487

Bicycle Thief (film; de Sica)
Ray, Satyajit **13** 60-61

Bicycle Wheel (ready-made)
Duchamp, Marcel **5** 122-123

Bid Me to Live (novel)
Doolittle, Hilda **5** 65-66

Bidatsu (ruled 572-585), emperor of Japan
Shotoku Taishi **14** 205-207
Suiko **15** 15-16

Bidault, Georges (1899-1983), French statesman
Schuman, Robert **14** 41

BIDDLE, NICHOLAS (1786-1844), American financier **2** 264-265
Jackson, Andrew **8** 168-172

Bidone, II (film)
Fellini, Federico **5** 408-409

BIDWELL, JOHN (1819-1900), American pioneer and agriculturist **2** 265

BIEBER, OWEN (born 1929), American union executive **2** 266-268

Biedermann and the Incendiaries (play)
Frisch, Max **6** 118-119

Bien Público, El (newspaper)
Zorrilla de San Martin, Juan **16** 530-531

Bienséance (drama)
Corneille, Pierre **4** 234-236

BIENVILLE, SIEUR DE (Jean Baptiste Le Moyne; 1680-1768), French colonizer and administrator **2** 268-269

BIERCE, AMBROSE GWINETT (1842-1914?), American journalist and author **2** 269-270
Hearst, William Randolph **7** 243-244

Biermer, Anton (died 1892), German physician
Addison, Thomas **1** 58-59

Biermer's anemia
see Pernicious anemia

BIERSTADT, ALBERT (1830-1902), American painter **2** 270-271

Biffen, Sir Rowland Harry (1874-1949), English geneticist
Vavilov, Nikolai Ivanovich **15** 447-448

Big Bertha (field gun)
Krupp **9** 109-111

Big Blonde (story)
Parker, Dorothy Rothschild **12** 106

Big Bonanza (ore strike, 1873)
Mackay, John William **10** 101-102

Big Fish Eat Little Fish (drawing)
Bruegel, Pieter the Elder **3** 65-67

Big Four Conference (Geneva; 1955)
Dulles, John Foster **5** 134-135

Big Four Conference (Paris; 1919)
see also Versailles, Treaty of (1919)

Big Geese Pagoda
see Ta-yen-t'a (pagoda)

Big Knife, The (play)
Odets, Clifford **11** 470-471

Big Money, The (novel)
Dos Passos, John Roderigo **5** 69-71

Big Nose George (painting)
Russell, Charles Marion **13** 375-376

Big Sleep, The (film)
Bogart, Humphrey **2** 363-364

Big Split, The (book)
Cocteau, Jean **4** 132-133

Big Store, The (film)
Marx brothers **10** 303-304

Big Sur and the Oranges of Hieronymus Bosch (book)
Miller, Henry **11** 26-27

Big Town, The (book)
Lardner, Ringgold Wilmer **9** 204-205

Big Two-hearted River, The (story)
Hemingway, Ernest Miller **7** 274-277

Big Victory, Great Task (book)
Giap, Vo Nguyen **6** 297-299

Big Wind (poem)
Roethke, Theodore **13** 243-244

BIGELOW, JOHN (1817-1911), American journalist, editor, and diplomat **2** 271-272
Clapp, Margaret Antoinette **4** 71-72

BIGGE, JOHN THOMAS (1780-1843), English judge and royal commissioner **2** 272
Macarthur, John **10** 78
Macquarie, Lachlan **10** 115-116

BIGGS, HERMANN MICHAEL (1859-1923), American physician **2** 272-273

Biglow Papers (periodical)
Lowell, James Russell **10** 14-15

Bigordi, Domenico di Tommaso
see Ghirlandaio, Domenico

Bigot de Morognes, Marie (1786-1820), Alsatian pianist
Mendelssohn, Moses **10** 488-489

Bihar (state, India)
Clive, Robert **4** 119-120
Gandhi, Mohandas Karamchand **6** 201-204

Bihzad
see Behzad

Bijapur, kingdom of (India)
Śivajī **14** 266-267

BIKO, STEVE (Stephen Bantu Biko; 1946-1977), political activist and writer and father of the Black Consciousness movement in the Union of South Africa **2** 273-274

Bilderbuch meiner Jugend, Das (book)
Sudermann, Hermann **15** 12-13

Bildungsroman (educational novel)
Dickens, Charles John Huffam **4** 538-541
Goethe, Johann Wolfgang von **6** 388-391
Joyce, James **8** 365-367
Kafka, Franz **8** 403-406

Bile acids (chemistry)
Diels, Otto Paul Hermann **5** 5-6

Bile pigments (chemistry)
Fischer, Hans **5** 457-459
Whipple, George Hoyt **16** 224-225

Bilingualism and Biculturalism, Royal Commission on (Canada)
Pearson, Lester Bowles **12** 174-175

Bill of Divorcement (film)
Barrymores **2** 28-30

Bill of Rights (Philippines)
Root, Elihu **13** 283-284

Bill of Rights (United States)
Gerry, Elbridge **6** 282-283
Madison, James **10** 121-123
Mason, George **10** 319-320
Washington, George **16** 126-129

Bille, Steen Andersen (1797-1883), Danish admiral
Brahe, Tycho **2** 489-490

BILLINGS, WILLIAM (1746-1800), American composer **2** 274-275

BILLINGTON, JAMES HADLEY (born 1929), American scholar and author **2** 275-276

Billion Dollar Congress (United States; 1890)
Harrison, Benjamin **7** 178-179

Bill-Lee's Delight (painting)
de Kooning, Willem **4** 468-469

Billy Budd (novel)
Melville, Herman **10** 472-476

Billy Budd (opera)
Britten, Benjamin **3** 10-11

Billy Graham Evangelistic Association
Graham, William Franklin Jr. **6** 487-488

Billy the Kid (ballet)
Copland, Aaron **4** 227-228

BILLY THE KID (W.H. Bonney; 1859-1881), American frontiersman and outlaw **2** 277
Chisum, John Simpson **4** 11
Love, Nat **10** 1-2

Biltmore Program (1942)
Ben-Gurion, David **2** 160-161

Bimini (island, Bahamas)
Ponce de León, Juan **12** 391-392

Bin (play)
Frisch, Max **6** 118-119

Binchois, Gilles (circa 1400-1460), Flemish composer
Dufay, Guillaume **5** 125-126
Dunstable, John **5** 150-151
Eyck, Hubert and Jan van **5** 352-354

Bindo Altoviti (sculpture)
Cellini, Benvenuto **3** 391-392

BINET, ALFRED (1857-1911), French psychologist **2** 277-278
Yerkes, Robert Mearns **16** 454-455

Binet Laboratory (Paris)
Piaget, Jean **12** 287-288

BINGHAM, GEORGE CALEB (1811-1879), American painter **2** 278-279

Binomial theorem (mathematics)
Newton, Isaac **11** 369-372

Binz, Karl (1832-1913), German pharmacologist, physician, and chemist
Behring, Emil Adolph von **2** 122-123

Bio Health Resort (Arnhem)
Oud, Jacobus Johannes Pieter **12** 32

Biochemistry (science)
antibiotics
Brown, Rachel Fuller **3** 43-44
Chain, Ernst Boris **3** 407-408
biosynthesis
Bloch, Konrad **2** 330-332
cell respiration
Warburg, Otto **16** 109-111
chlorophyll
Willstätter, Richard **16** 310-312
cholesterol
Bloch, Konrad **2** 330-332
chromatographic methods
Tiselius, Arne Wilhelm Kaurin
15 240-241
DNA
Kornberg, Arthur **9** 85-87
Mintz, Beatrice **11** 49-50
Nirenberg, Marshall Warren
11 399-400
Todd, Alexander **15** 251-253
genetic engineering
Singer, Maxine **14** 251-252
hemoglobin structure
Perutz, Max **12** 246-248
hormones
Kendall, Edward Calvin **8** 495
Pincus, Gregory Goodwin
12 310-312
Sanger, Frederick **13** 466-467
immunochemistry
Avery, Oswald Theodore **1** 384-386
Krebs cycle
Krebs, Hans Adolf **9** 95-97
metabolism
Cori, Gerty T. **4** 231-234
Liebig, Justus von **9** 403-404
Lipmann, Fritz **9** 435-437
Neufeld, Elizabeth F. **11** 352-353
Ochoa, Severo **11** 461-464
muscle chemistry
Meyerhof, Otto Fritz **10** 537-539
Szent-Györgyi, Albert von **15** 62-64
perinatal neurobiochemistry
Mayor Zaragosa, Federico
10 369-371
plant hybrids
Borlaug, Norman Ernest **2** 418-420

protein synthesis
Lipmann, Fritz **9** 435-437
pyrogenic distilled water
Seibert, Florence B. **14** 89-90
radioimmunoassay
Yalow, Rosalyn S. **16** 427-428
recombinant DNA
Berg, Paul **2** 187-189
retrovirus biochemistry
Baltimore, David **1** 477-478
Montagnier, Luc **11** 114-116
RNA
Monod, Jacques **11** 110-111
Ochoa, Severo **11** 461-464
Todd, Alexander **15** 251-253
steroid hormones
Baulieu, Étienne-Émile **2** 63-66
virology
Elion, Gertrude B. **5** 252-254
vitamins
Dam, Carl Peter Henrik **4** 382-383
Hopkins, Frederick Gowland
7 491-492
Szent-Györgyi, Albert von **15** 62-64
Todd, Alexander **15** 251-253
Wald, George **16** 51-53
see also Scientists—biochemists

Biochemistry, Institute of (Uppsala, Sweden)
Tiselius, Arne Wilhelm Kaurin
15 240-241

Biogenetic law (embryology)
Baer, Karl Ernst von **1** 431-432

Biogeography (social science)
Ratzel, Friedrich **13** 50-51

Biograph Co. (films)
Griffith, David Wark **6** 544-545

Biographers
see Authors—biographers

Biographia literaria (book)
Coleridge, Samuel Taylor **4** 154-156

Biographical Memoirs... (book)
Stewart, Dugald **14** 449

Biographies of Virtuous Women (painting)
Ku K'ai-chih **9** 125-126

Biographische Belustigungen ... (book)
Richter, Johann Paul Friedrich
13 150-151

Biography (literary form)
Boswell, James **2** 432-434
Varro, Marcus Terentius **15** 438-439
Vasari, Giorgio **15** 442-443

Biography of the Life of Manuel (saga)
Cabell, James Branch **3** 195-196

Biology (science)
and social behavior
Wilson, Edward Osborne
16 319-320
binomal nomenclature
Linnaeus, Carl **9** 427-429
cell theory
Just, Ernest **8** 392-393

Margulis, Lynn **10** 253-254
Schwann, Theodor **14** 51-52
classification
see Animal systematics
early microscopy
Leeuwenhoek, Anton van **9** 300-301
exobiology
Sagan, Carl E. **13** 424-425
gnotobiology
Northrop, John Howard **11** 430-431
limnology
Patrick, Ruth **12** 137-138
marine
Just, Ernest **8** 392-393
Ray, Dixy Lee **13** 56-57
microbiology
Avery, Oswald Theodore **1** 384-386
molecular
Baltimore, David **1** 477-478
Crick, Francis Harry Crompton
4 310
Delbrück, Max **4** 476-478
Franklin, Rosalind Elsie **6** 67-68
Karle, Isabella **8** 447-449
Lonsdale, Kathleen **9** 501-502
Lwoff, André **10** 58-59
Pauling, Linus Carl **12** 150-152
Szilard, Leo **15** 64-66
Watson, James Dewey **16** 137-138
nerve growth factor
Levi-Montalcini, Rita **9** 366-368
physical foundations
Elsasser, Walter Maurice **5** 277-278
speciation
Mayr, Ernst **10** 372-374
vitalism
Driesch, Hans Adolf Eduard **5** 105
see also Embryology; Evolution;
Genetics; Scientists—biologists

Biometrika (journal)
Galton, Francis **6** 193-194

Biomorphic art
Arp, Jean **1** 317-318
Moore, Henry **11** 146-148

Biophysics (science)
Ingenhousz, Jan **8** 119-120

Biot, Jean Baptiste (1774-1862), French physicist
Pasteur, Louis **12** 125-127

Biquadratic equations (mathematics)
Hasan ibn al-Haytham **7** 190-191

Biquadratic residues theory (mathematics)
Gauss, Karl Friedrich **6** 240-242

Birague chapel (Paris)
Pilon, Germain **12** 305

Birague, René de (1506?-1583), French cardinal and statesman
Pilon, Germain **12** 305

Birches (poem)
Frost, Robert Lee **6** 130-133

Bird
see Parker, Charlie

BIRD, LARRY (born 1956), American basketball player **2** 279-281

BIRD, ROBERT MONTGOMERY (1806-1854), American dramatist and novelist **2** 281-282

Bird, The (book)
Michelet, Jules **11** 5-6

Bird Basket (sculpture)
Moore, Henry **11** 146-148

Bird in Space (sculpture cycle)
Brancusi, Constantin **2** 494-496

Bird Man (sculpture cycle)
Richier, Germaine **13** 145-146

Bird of Time, The (poem)
Naidu, Sarojini **11** 294-295

Birdland (literary site)
Aristophanes **1** 293-294

Birds (United States)
Audubon, John James **1** 366-367
Carson, Rachel Louise **3** 337-338

Birds, The (film)
Hitchcock, Alfred **7** 415-416

Birds, The (play)
Aristophanes **1** 293-294

Birds, Beasts and Flowers (poems)
Lawrence, David Herbert **9** 247-248

Birds of America (book; Audubon)
Audubon, John James **1** 366-367
Wilson, Alexander **16** 313-314

BIRENDRA (Bir Bikram Shah Dev; born 1945), King of Nepal (1972-) **2** 282-283

BIRINGUCCIO, VANNOCCIO (1480-1539), Italian mining engineer and metallurgist **2** 283

Birkenhead, 1st Earl of (1872-1930), English statesman
Chamberlain, Arthur Neville **3** 409-411

Birmingham (city, Alabama)
King, Martin Luther Jr. **9** 20-22

Birmingham (city, England)
Chamberlain, Arthur Neville **3** 409-411
Chamberlain, Joseph **3** 411-413

Birmingham Symphony Orchestra, City of
Rattle, Simon Denis **13** 49-50

Birmingham University (England)
Medawar, Peter Brian **10** 444-445

BIRNEY, JAMES GILLESPIE (1792-1857), American lawyer and abolitionist **2** 283-284
Bailey, Gamaliel **1** 444-445

Biron, Johann Ernst (1690-1772), Russian statesman
Anna Ivanovna **1** 240-241

Birth (philosophy)
Anaxagoras **1** 208-209

Birth-control (medicine)
advocates
Besant, Annie Wood **2** 233-234
Bradlaugh, Charles **2** 478

Comstock, Anthony **4** 188-189
Goldman, Emma **6** 406-407
Lease, Mary Elizebeth Clyens **9** 268
Sanger, Margaret Higgins **13** 467-468
Stopes, Marie **14** 476-478
eugenics
Carr-Saunders, Alexander Morris **3** 333-334
opponents
Malthus, Thomas Robert **10** 180-181
Paul VI **12** 146-148
Spellman, Francis Joseph **14** 367
oral contraceptive
Pincus, Gregory Goodwin **12** 310-312

Birth of a Nation, The (film)
Griffith, David Wark **6** 544-545

Birth of Kumara (epic)
Kalidasa **8** 414-415

Birth of the Virgin (painting)
Altdorfer, Albrecht **1** 179-180
Sassetta **13** 492

Birth of Tragedy, The (book)
Nietzsche, Friedrich **11** 390-392

Birth of Venus (painting)
Botticelli, Sandro **2** 439-440

Birth Project, The (artwork)
Chicago, Judy **3** 515-516

Birth trauma theory (psychology)
Rank, Otto **13** 33

Birthday Ode for Queen Anne (musical composition)
Handel, George Frederick **7** 116-119

Birthday Party, The (play)
Pinter, Harold **12** 317-318

BIRUNI, ABU RAYHAN AL- (973-circa 1050), Arabian scientist and historian **2** 284-285
Mahmud of Ghazni **10** 147

BIRYUKOVA, ALEKSANDRA PAVLOVNA (1929-1990), a secretary of the Central Committee of the Communist party of the Soviet Union and a deputy prime minister (1986-1990) **2** 285-287

BISHARA, ABDULLAH YACCOUB (born 1936), Kuwaiti statesman and first secretary-general of the Gulf Cooperative Council **2** 287-288

BISHOP, BRIDGET (died 1692), Salem, Massachusetts, witch trial defendant **2** 288-290

BISHOP, ELIZABETH (1911-1979), American poet **2** 290-292

Bishop, John Peale (1892-1944), American author
Fitzgerald, Francis Scott Key **5** 470-472
Wilson, Edmund **16** 318-319

BISHOP, MAURICE (1944-1983), leader of the New Jewel Movement and prime

minister of Grenada (1979-1983) **2** 292-293

Bishop, The (story)
Chekhov, Anton Pavlovich **3** 494-497

Bishop Berkeley's Rock (painting)
La Farge, John **9** 149-150

Bishop of Broadway
see Belasco, David

Bishop Orders His Tomb, The (poem)
Browning, Robert **3** 53-55

Bishops, Synod of (Roman Catholic Church)
Paul VI **12** 146-148

Bishop's Bonfire, The (play)
O'Casey, Sean **11** 459-460

Bishop's Palace (Regensburg)
Altdorfer, Albrecht **1** 179-180

Bishops' Program of Social Reconstruction (1919)
Hayes, Patrick Joseph **7** 224-225

Bishop's War (Scotland; 1638)
Harrington, James **7** 166-167

Bismarck (play)
Wedekind, Frank **16** 166-167

BISMARCK, OTTO EDUARD LEOPOLD VON (1815-1898), German statesman **2** 294-296
socialism
Bernstein, Eduard **2** 218
Leo XIII **9** 334-336
European policy
Moltke, Helmuth Karl Bernard von **11** 90-91
Napoleon III **11** 310-312
imperialism
Ismail Pasha **8** 150-151
Peters, Carl **12** 257-258
opponents
Virchow, Rudolf Ludwig Carl **15** 506-507
Palmerston, 3d Viscount
Thiers, Louis Adolphe **15** 181-182
William I **16** 292-293
William II **16** 294-295
supporters
Treitschke, Heinrich von **15** 293-294

Bismarck Archipelago (West Pacific Ocean)
Schouten, William Cornelius **14** 31

Bismarck-Schönhausen, Prince Herbert Nikolaus von (1849-1904), German statesman
Bismarck, Otto Eduard Leopold von **2** 294-296

Bismarck-Schöhausen, Count Wilhelm Albrecht Otto von (1852-1901), German statesman
Bismarck, Otto Eduard Leopold von **2** 294-296

Bissagos Archipelago (West Africa)
Cadamosto, Alvise da **3** 206-207

BITRUJI, NUR AL-DIN ABU ISHAQ AL (circa 1150-1200), Spanish Moslem astronomer **2** 296

Bits of Talk about Home Matters (book)
Jackson, Helen Hunt **8** 172

Bits of Travel (book)
Jackson, Helen Hunt **8** 172

Bitter Sweet (musical)
Coward, Noel **4** 279-280
Ziegfeld, Florenz **16** 516-517

Bitumen (chemistry)
Daguerre, Louis Jacques Mandé **4** 365-366

Biyidi, Alexandre
see Beti, Mongo

Bizerte, battle of (1943)
Bradley, Omar Nelson **2** 483-484

Bizerte crisis (1961)
Bourguiba, Habib **2** 453-455

BIZET, GEORGES (1838-1875), French composer **2** 296-297
Daudet, Alphonse **4** 402-403
Mérimée, Prosper **10** 517

BJELKE-PETERSEN, JOHANNES ("Joh;" born 1911), Australian politician **2** 297-299

BJØRNSON, BJØRNSTJERNE (1832-1910), Norwegian author **2** 299-300
Grieg, Edvard Hagerup **6** 541-542

Blå böcker (diary)
Strindberg, August **14** 509-511

Black, Adam (1784-1874), Scottish publisher
Sheraton, Thomas **14** 181-182

BLACK, CONRAD MOFFAT (born 1944), Canadian-born international press baron **2** 300-301

BLACK, HUGO LAFAYETTE (1886-1971), American jurist **2** 301-303
Douglas, William Orville **5** 83-85
Jackson, Robert Houghwout **8** 182-183

BLACK, JOSEPH (1728-1799), British chemist **2** 303
Cavendish, Henry **3** 383-384
Lavoisier, Antoine Laurent **9** 241-244
Watt, James **16** 141-143

BLACK, SHIRLEY TEMPLE (born 1928), American actress and public servant **2** 303-305

Black Arts Repertory Theater-School (New York City)
Baraka, Imamu Amiri **1** 498-499

Black Banners (novel)
Strindberg, August **14** 509-511

Black Bishop (literary character)
Middleton, Thomas **11** 8-9

Black Bourgeoisie (book)
Frazier, Edward Franklin **6** 77

Black Boy (autobiography)
Wright, Richard **16** 401-402

Black Brunswicker, The (painting)
Millais, John Everett **11** 23-24

Black Christ, The (poems)
Cullen, Countee **4** 333-334

Black Codes (United States)
Bienville, Sieur de **2** 268-269
Johnson, Andrew **8** 294-295

Black comedy (literature)
Dürrenmatt, Friedrich **5** 164-165
Frisch, Max **6** 118-119
Grass, Günter **6** 496-497
Melville, Herman **10** 472-476

Black Consciousness (ideology)
South Africa
Biko, Steve **2** 273-274

Black Cross, New Mexico (painting)
O'Keeffe, Georgia **11** 487-489

Black Death (1348)
Boccaccio, Giovanni **2** 351-353
Edward III **5** 211-212
Guy de Chauliac **7** 54
Langland, William **9** 194-195
Orcagna **11** 526-527
Petrarch **12** 259-261
Philip VI **12** 277-278

Black Docker, The (novel)
Ousmane, Sembene **12** 32-33

Black Dog (ship)
Davis, John **4** 419

Black Dwarf, The (novel)
Scott, Walter **14** 68-70

Black Earth, The (story)
Bunin, Ivan Alekseevich **3** 124

BLACK ELK, NICHOLAS (1863-1950), Oglala Sioux medicine man **2** 305-306

Black Fire (anthology)
Baraka, Imamu Amiri **1** 498-499

Black Flame, The (trilogy)
Du Bois, William Edward Burghardt **5** 116-118

Black Folk, Then and Now (book)
Du Bois, William Edward Burghardt **5** 116-118

Black Friday (1869)
Gould, Jay **6** 470-472

Black Guelphs (Florentine political party)
Cavalcanti, Guido **3** 382
Dante Alighieri **4** 389-391

BLACK HAWK (1767-1838), Native American war chief **2** 308
Taft, Lorado **15** 75-76
Taylor, Zachary **15** 128-130
see also Black Hawk War

Black Hawk War (United States; 1832)
Becknell, William **2** 105-106
Black Hawk **2** 308
Comstock, Henry Tompkins Paige **4** 189
Lincoln, Abraham **9** 415-418
Scott, Winfield **14** 70-71
Taylor, Zachary **15** 128-130

Black Heralds, The (poems)
Vallejo, César Abraham **15** 408-409

Black Hills gold rush (1875)
Crazy Horse **4** 303-304
Sitting Bull **14** 264-265

Black Hole (dungeon, Calcutta)
Clive, Robert **4** 119-120
Hastings, Warren **7** 195-196

Black House (San Francisco)
Cleaver, Leroy Eldridge **4** 97-98

Black Iris (painting)
O'Keeffe, Georgia **11** 487-489

Black is beautiful (philosophy)
Senghor, Léopold Sédar **14** 106-107

Black Jack
see Pershing, John Joseph

Black Kettle (died 1868), American Indian chief
Custer, George Armstrong **4** 355-356

Black Magic Poetry (poems)
Baraka, Imamu Amiri **1** 498-499

Black Majesty (sculpture)
Nevelson, Louise **11** 356-357

Black Man (book)
Brown, William Wells **3** 48-49

Black Man (periodical)
Garvey, Marcus Mosiah **6** 228-229

Black Man Is His Own Worst Enemy, The (book)
Dube, John Langalibalele **5** 113

Black Manhattan (memoir)
Johnson, James Weldon **8** 304-305

Black Manifesto, The (book)
Forman, James **6** 10-11

Black Man's Doom, The (book)
Turner, Henry McNeal **15** 351-352

Black Maria (laboratory)
Edison, Thomas Alva **5** 206-208

Black Maskers, The (musical composition)
Sessions, Roger Huntington **14** 117-118

Black Mass, Great Goodness of Life, A (play)
Baraka, Imamu Amiri **1** 498-499

Black Mischief (novel)
Waugh, Evelyn Arthur St. John **16** 145-147

Black Monk, The (story)
Chekhov, Anton Pavlovich **3** 494-497

Black Mountain College (North Carolina)
Cage, John **3** 211-214
Kline, Franz **9** 55
Lippold, Richard **9** 440-442
Radin, Paul **12** 538-539

Black Music (book)
Baraka, Imamu Amiri **1** 498-499

Black Muslims (Nation of Islam)
Cleaver, Leroy Eldridge **4** 97-98
Farrakhan, Louis **5** 389-390
Malcolm X **10** 165-166

Muhammad, Elijah **11** 230-231

Black Obelisk, The (novel)
Remarque, Erich Maria **13** 91

Black Orpheus (magazine)
Soyinka, Wole **14** 358-359

Black Panther Party (United States; established 1966)
Carmichael, Stokely **3** 305-308
Fonda, Jane **5** 501-502
Forman, James **6** 10-11
Newton, Huey P. **11** 367-369
Seale, Robert George **14** 77-78

Black Patio Door (painting)
O'Keeffe, Georgia **11** 487-489

Black People's Convention (South Africa)
Biko, Steve **2** 273-274

Black Power (book)
Wright, Richard **16** 401-402

Black power (political movement, United States)
Carmichael, Stokely **3** 305-308
Cone, James Hall **4** 196-197
McKissick, Floyd B. **10** 420-422

Black Prince
see Edward the Black Prince

Black Reconstruction in America (book)
Du Bois, William Edward Burghardt
5 116-118

Black Redistribution (Russian revolutionary movement)
Plekhanov, Georgi Valentinovich
12 351-352

Black Riders, The (poems)
Crane, Stephen **4** 293-295

Black Sea (between Europe and Asia)
Catherine the Great **3** 370-372
Peter I **12** 253-256

Black Seated Torso (sculpture)
Archipenko, Alexander **1** 280-281

Black Skin, White Masks (book)
Fanon, Frantz **5** 379-380

Black Snow (novel)
Bulgakov, Mikhail Afanasievich **3** 117

Black Spartacus
see Turner, Nathaniel

Black Spring (novel)
Miller, Henry **11** 26-27

Black Spurgeon
see Turner, Henry McNeal

Black Star Line (shipping co.)
Garvey, Marcus Mosiah **6** 228-229

Black Swan Phonograph Co.
Still, William Grant **14** 455-456

Black Thunder (novel; Bontemps)
Prosser, Gabriel **12** 460-461

Black Warrior incident (Cuba)
Soulé, Pierre **14** 351-352

Black Worker, The (book)
Harris, Abram Lincoln Jr. **7** 169-171

Blackbody radiation
see Radioactivity

Blackburn, Joseph (circa 1700-1765), English painter in America
Copley, John Singleton **4** 228-230

BLACKETT, PATRICK M.S. (1897-1974), British physicist **2** 306-307
Anderson, Carl David **1** 214-215

Blackfoot Indians (North America)
Bozeman, John M. **2** 471-472
Lacombe, Albert **9** 147-148
Lewis, Meriwether **9** 391-392

Blacklist (anti-Communist measure; United States; 1950s)
Seeger, Pete **14** 83-84
Shirer, William L. **14** 198-199

Blackmail (film)
Hitchcock, Alfred **7** 415-416

BLACKMUN, HARRY (born 1908), United States Supreme Court justice **2** 309-310

"Black-robe Voyageur"
see Lacombe, Albert

Blacks
see African American history (United States); Africa

Blacks, The (play)
Genet, Jean **6** 262-263

Blackshirts (Italian politics)
Ferrero, Guglielmo **5** 429-430
Orlando, Vittorio Emmanuele
11 529-530

Blacksmiths, American
Burritt, Elihu **3** 160

BLACKSTONE, SIR WILLIAM (1723-1780), English jurist **2** 310-311
Bentham, Jeremy **2** 176-178

Blackwell, Alice Stone (1857-1950), American editor
Stone, Lucy **14** 471-472

BLACKWELL, ELIZABETH (1821-1910), American physician **2** 311-312
Jacobi, Abraham and Mary Putnam
8 188-189

Blackwell, Henry B. (1825-1909), American editor
Stone, Lucy **14** 471-472

Blackwood's Magazine (London)
Disraeli, Benjamin **5** 27-29
Keats, John **8** 470-472

Bladelin Triptych (painting; van der Weyden)
Schongauer, Martin **14** 26-28
Weyden, Rogier van der **16** 219-221

Bladensburg, of (1814)
Madison, James **10** 121-123

BLAINE, JAMES GILLESPIE (1830-1893), American statesman **2** 312-313
as secretary of state
Garfield, James Abram **6** 213-214
nomination campaigns
Arthur, Chester Alan **1** 321-323

Cleveland, Stephen Grover
4 108-110
Harlan, John Marshall **7** 156-157
Harrison, Benjamin **7** 178-179
Hayes, Rutherford Birchard
7 227-228
opponents
Conkling, Roscoe **4** 201-202
Curtis, George William **4** 349-350
Godkin, Edwin Lawrence **6** 380
Schurz, Carl **14** 44-45
supporters
Ingersoll, Robert Green **8** 120-121
McKinley, William **10** 418-420

Blair, Eric Arthur
see Orwell, George

BLAIR, FRANCIS PRESTON (1791-1876), American journalist and politician
2 313-315

BLAIR, JAMES (1655-1743), British educator and Anglican missionary **2** 315-316
Andros, Edmund **1** 234-235
Dunster, Henry **5** 152-153
Nicholson, Francis **11** 381-382

Blair, John (1732-1800), American jurist
Chase, Samuel **3** 475-476

Blair, Robert (1699-1746), Scottish clergyman
Blake, William **2** 316-318

Blair Athole (ship)
Reading, 1st Marquess of **13** 64

Blaise Hamlet (near Bristol, England)
Nash, John **11** 316

Blake, Edward (1833-1912), Canadian politician
Laurier, Wilfrid **9** 232-234
Mackenzie, Alexander **10** 104

Blake, Francis (1850-1913), American inventor
Bell, Alexander Graham **2** 129-131

Blake, Nicholas
see Lewis, Cecil Day

Blake, Robert (died 1787), English artist
Blake, William **2** 316-318

BLAKE, WILLIAM (1757-1827), English poet, engraver, and painter **2** 316-318
influence of
Crane, Hart **4** 291-293
Ginsberg, Allen **6** 332-333
Lindsay, Vachel **9** 424-425
influenced by
Milton, John **11** 43-46
interpreters
Frye, Northrop **6** 137-139
Nonconformism
Bunyan, John **3** 128-129

BLAKELOCK, RALPH ALBERT (1847-1919), American painter **2** 318
Tanner, Henry Ossawa **15** 102-103

Blame Not My Lute (poem)
Wyatt, Thomas **16** 410-411

BLANC, LOUIS (1811-1882), French journalist, historian, and politician **2** 318-319
   Chernyshevsky, Nikolai Gavrilovich
   3 504-505

BLANC, MEL (1908-1989), American creator of and voice of cartoon characters
2 319-320

Blanche, Duchess of Lancaster (died
1369), wife of John of Gaunt
   Chaucer, Geoffrey **3** 482-485

Blanche of Castile (1187?-1252), queen of
France 1223-1226; regent 1226-1236
and 1248-1252
   Louis IX **9** 525-526

BLANCO, ANTONIO GUZMÁN
(1829-1899), Venezuelan politician,
three-times president **2** 320-321

Blanco party (Uruguayan politics)
   Batlle y Ordóñez, José **2** 58-59
   Rivera, Fructuoso **13** 184-185

Blanco White, José Maria (1775-1841),
Spanish-born British writer and editor
   Bello, Ahmadu **2** 139-140

BLANDIANA, ANA (born Otilia-Valeria
Coman, 1942), Romanian poet
2 321-322

BLANDING, SARAH GIBSON
(1898-1985), American educator
2 322-323

Blank Verse (book)
   Lamb, Charles **9** 176-177

Blank verse (poetry)
   Eliot, Thomas Stearns **5** 258-261
   Frost, Robert Lee **6** 130-133
   Johnson, Samuel **8** 315-317
   Marlowe, Christopher **10** 272-274
   Milton, John **11** 43-46

Blanka von Kastilien (play)
   Grillparzer, Franz **6** 546-547

BLANQUI, LOUIS AUGUSTE (1805-1881),
French revolutionary **2** 323-324
   Maillol, Aristide **10** 150-151
   Mussolini, Benito **11** 272-274

Blashki, Philip
   see Evergood, Philip

Blasphemy (religion)
   Calvin, John **3** 239-242
   Gorton, Samuell **6** 460

Blast (magazine)
   Pound, Ezra Loomis **12** 415-417

Blast furnace (iron industry)
   Cort, Henry **4** 254

Blätter für die Kunst (journal)
   George, Stefan **6** 277-278

Blaue Blume (literary image)
   Novalis **11** 435

Blaue Reiter (art group)
   Arp, Jean **1** 317-318
   Delaunay, Robert **4** 475-476
   Feininger, Lyonel **5** 406-407
   Hartley, Marsden **7** 186

   Kandinsky, Wassily **8** 420-422
   Klee, Paul **9** 47-49
   Macke, August **10** 102-103
   Marc, Franz **10** 231

Blaue Vier (art group)
   Feininger, Lyonel **5** 406-407
   Kandinsky, Wassily **8** 420-422
   Klee, Paul **9** 47-49

Blavatsky, Elena Petrovna (Helena Hahn;
1831-1891), Russian theosophist
   Besant, Annie Wood **2** 233-234

Blaxland, Gregory (1778-1853), Australian
explorer
   Wentworth, William Charles
   16 203-204

Blé en herbe, Le (novel)
   Colette, Sidonie Gabrielle **4** 158-159

Bleaching Tub (painting)
   Millet, Jean François **11** 31

Bleak House (novel; Dickens)
   Dickens, Charles John Huffam
   4 538-541
   Landor, Walter Savage **9** 186-187

Bleda (died 445), Hun chieftain
   Attila **1** 360

BLEDSOE, ALBERT TAYLOR (1809-1877),
American lawyer, educator, and Confederate apologist **2** 324-325

Blei, Franz (1871-1942), Austrian writer in
Germany
   Kafka, Franz **8** 403-406

Blenheim, battle of (1704)
   Anne **1** 241-242
   Eugene of Savoy **5** 330-331
   Marlborough, 1st Duke of **10** 271-272
   Spotswood, Alexander **14** 385

Blenheim Palace (England)
   Churchill, Winston Leonard Spencer
   4 51-53
   Hawksmoor, Nicholas **7** 211-212
   Vanbrugh, John **15** 409-410

Blessed Damozel, The (poem)
   Rossetti, Dante Gabriel **13** 308-309

Blessings of Business, The (book)
   Howe, Edgar Watson **7** 529

Bleter fun mayn Leben (autobiography)
   Cahan, Abraham **3** 214

BLEULER, EUGEN (1857-1939), Swiss psy-
chiatrist **2** 325
   Freud, Sigmund **6** 103-106
   Jung, Carl Gustav **8** 388-389

Bleyl, Fritz (born 1881), German painter
   Kirchner, Ernst Ludwig **9** 34-35

BLIGH, WILLIAM (1754-1817), English
naval officer and colonial governor
2 325-326
   Evatt, Herbert Vere **5** 341-343
   Flinders, Matthew **5** 490
   Macarthur, John **10** 78
   Macquarie, Lachlan **10** 115-116

Blind
   artists
      Kane, Paul **8** 422-423
   authors
      Brentano, Franz Clemens **2** 516-517
      Bulgakov, Mikhail Afanasievich
      3 117
      Galdós, Benito Pérez **6** 177-178
      Goldoni, Carlo **6** 408-409
      Homer **7** 465-467
      Husayn, Taha **8** 61-62
      Keller, Helen Adams **8** 479-480
      Milton, John **11** 43-46
      Tarkington, Newton Booth **15** 109
      Thurber, James Grove **15** 213-214
      Valera y Alcalá Galiano, Juan
      15 403
   education of
      Cardano, Geronimo **3** 285-286
      Howe, Samuel Gridley **7** 537
      Keller, Helen Adams **8** 479-480
   educators
      Braille, Louis **2** 492-493
      Witherspoon, John **16** 346-348
   explorers
      Sturt, Charles **15** 2-3
   journalists
      Pulitzer, Joseph **12** 481-482
   musicians
      Bach, Johann Sebastian **1** 416-419
      Cabezón, Antonio **3** 197-198
      Handel, George Frederick
      7 116-119
      Handy, William Christopher
      7 123-124
      Landini, Francesco **9** 185-186
   reading system for the
      Braille, Louis **2** 492-493
   scientists
      Eratosthenes of Cyrene **5** 301-302
      Euler, Leonard **5** 331-332
      Lamarck, Chevalier de **9** 171-173
   statesmen
      George III **6** 270-272
      Vieira, Antônio **15** 492
   theologians
      Booth, William **2** 405-406

Blind, The (play)
   Dürrenmatt, Friedrich **5** 164-165
   Maeterlinck, Maurice **10** 125-126

Blind Botanist (drawing)
   Shahn, Ben **14** 139-140

Blind Children (poems)
   Zangwill, Israel **16** 488-489

Blind Girl (painting)
   Millais, John Everett **11** 23-24

Blind Highland Piper, The (book)
   Traill, Catharine Parr **15** 291

Blind Man's Buff (triptych)
   Beckmann, Max **2** 104-105

Blind Man's Tale, A (novel)
   Tanizaki, Junichiro **15** 101-102

Blind Owl, The (novel)
Hidayat, Sadiq **7** 377-378

Blindman's World... (anthology)
Bellamy, Edward **2** 134-135

Bliss (novel)
Carey, Peter **3** 295-297

Bliss, Philemon (1814-1889), American jurist
Langston, John Mercer **9** 197

Blithe Spirit (play; film)
Coward, Noel **4** 279-280

Blithedale Romance, The (book)
Hawthorne, Nathaniel **7** 212-215

Blitzkrieg (military tactic)
De Gaulle, Charles André Joseph Marie **4** 463-465
Hitler, Adolf **7** 417-420
Moltke, Helmuth Karl Bernard von **11** 90-91

Blix (novel)
Norris, Benjamin Franklin Jr. **11** 427-428

Blixen-Finecke, Baroness
see Dinesen, Isak

Bloc, Le (magazine)
Clemenceau, Georges **4** 99-101

Bloc Africain (political party; Senegal)
Senghor, Léopold Sédar **14** 106-107

Bloc des Masses Senegalises (political party)
Diop, Cheikh Anta **5** 21-22

Bloc National (France)
Herriot, Édouard **7** 339-340

BLOCH, ERNEST (1880-1959), Swiss-born American composer and teacher **2** 326-327
Sessions, Roger Huntington **14** 117-118

BLOCH, ERNST (1885-1977), German humanistic interpreter of Marxist thought **2** 327-328

BLOCH, FELIX (1905-1983), Swiss/American physicist **2** 328-330

BLOCH, KONRAD (born 1912), American biochemist **2** 330-332

BLOCH, MARC (1886-1944), French historian **2** 332-333
Lefebvre, Georges **9** 301-302

BLOCK, HERBERT (Herblock; born 1909), American newspaper cartoonist **2** 333-334

Bloemenwerf (house; Uccle, Belgium)
Van de Velde, Henry **15** 419-420

Bloemfontein (city, South Africa)
Doyle, Arthur Conan **5** 91-92
Roberts, Frederick Sleigh **13** 195-196

Blois (French chateau)
Mansart, François **10** 211
Mansart, Jules Hardouin **10** 212

BLOK, ALEKSANDR ALEKSANDROVICH (1880-1921), Russian poet **2** 335
Esenin, Sergei Aleksandrovich **5** 321
Merezhkovsky, Dmitry Sergeyevich **10** 515-516

Blomberg, Werner von (1878-1946), German general
Hitler, Adolf **7** 417-420

Blomfield, Sir Reginald (1856-1942), English architect
Shaw, Richard Norman **14** 167-168

Blonde Eckbert, The (story)
Tieck, Ludwig **15** 218-219

Blonde Göttin, Die (play)
Toller, Ernst **15** 261

Blondel, Jacques François (1705-1774), French architect
Cuvilliés, François **4** 359-360
Ledoux, Claude Nicolas **9** 277-278

Blood (animal)
Pavlov, Ivan Petrovich **12** 155-157

Blood (human)
anemia
see Anemia
banks
Drew, Charles Richard **5** 100-101
Rous, Francis Peyton **13** 322-323
capillaries
Krogh, Schack August Steenberg **9** 106
circulation and pressure
Dale, Henry Hallett **4** 371-373
Erlanger, Joseph **5** 310-311
Hales, Stephen **7** 75
Harvey, William **7** 189-190
clotting
Dam, Carl Peter Henrik **4** 382-383
groups
Fisher, Ronald Aylmer **5** 463-464
Landsteiner, Karl **9** 188-189
hemoglobin structure
Perutz, Max **12** 246-248
transfusions
Bethune, Henry Norman **2** 240-241
DeBakey, Michael Ellis **4** 437-438
Tiselius, Arne Wilhelm Kaurin **15** 240-241

Blood, Council of (1567)
Alba, Duke of **1** 103-104

Blood Knot, The (play)
Fugard, Athol **6** 142-143

Blood of the Bambergs, The (play)
Osborne, John **12** 16-17

Blood of the Prophets, The (poems)
Masters, Edgar Lee **10** 326-327

Blood-poisoning victims
Berg, Alban **2** 186-187
Brooke, Rupert **3** 22-23
Duchamp-Villon, Raymond **5** 123
Semmelweis, Ignaz Philipp **14** 101-102

Blood River (South Africa)
Dingane **5** 14-15

Blood Wedding (play)
Lorca, Federico García **9** 511-513

Bloody Era, The (book)
Mäkonnen Endalkačäw **10** 161-162

Bloody Mary
see Mary I

Bloody Run, battle of (1763)
Pontiac **12** 393-394
Rogers, Robert **13** 250-251

Bloody Sunday (London; 1888)
Asquith, Herbert Henry **1** 344-346

Bloody Sunday (Russia; 1905)
Nicholas II **11** 378-380
Trotsky, Leon **15** 302-305

BLOOM, ALLAN DAVID (1930-1992), American political philosopher, professor, and author **2** 335-337

Bloom, Leopold (literary character)
Joyce, James **8** 365-367

BLOOMER, AMELIA JENKS (1818-1894), American reformer and suffrage advocate **2** 337

Bloomers (dress)
Anthony, Susan Brownell **1** 246-248
Bloomer, Amelia Jenks **2** 337

BLOOMFIELD, LEONARD (1887-1949), American linguist **2** 338

Bloomsbury Group (British literature)
Bowen, Elizabeth **2** 462-463
Eliot, Thomas Stearns **5** 258-261
Forster, Edward Morgan **6** 14-16
Strachey, Giles Lytton **14** 487-488
Woolf, Virginia Stephen **16** 381-382

BLOOR, ELLA REEVE ("Mother Bloor"; 1862-1951), American labor organizer and social activist **2** 338-340

Blore Heath, battle of (1459)
Henry VI **7** 298-299

Bloudy Tenent of Persecution, The (book)
Williams, Roger **16** 304-305

Bloudy Tennent Washed, The (book)
Cotton, John **4** 263-265

Blow, John (1648-1708), English composer
Purcell, Henry **12** 484-485

Blow-Up (film)
Antonioni, Michelangelo **1** 252-253

Bloy, Léon (1846-1917), French author
Maritain, Jacques **10** 263
Rouault, Georges **13** 321-322

Blucher (locomotive)
Stephenson, George and Robert **14** 432-433

BLÜCHER, GEBHARD LEBERECHT VON (Prince of Wahlstatt; 1742-1819), Prussian field marshal **2** 340-341
Napoleon I **11** 306-310
Scharnhorst, Gerhard Johann David von **13** 521-522
Wellington, 1st Duke of **16** 193-195

Blue Angel, The (novel; film)
Mann, Heinrich **10** 201-202

Blue-back Speller, The (book)
Webster, Noah **16** 164-166

Blue Bird, The (play; Maeterlinck)
Maeterlinck, Maurice **10** 125-126
Stanislavsky, Constantin **14** 398-399

Blue Book (military manual)
Steuben, Frederick William Augustus
von **14** 438-439

Blue Boy (painting)
Gainsborough, Thomas **6** 170-172

Blue Danube (waltz)
Strauss, Johann Jr. **14** 498-499

Blue flower (literary image)
Novalis **11** 435

Blue Flower, The (poem)
Eminescu, Mihail **5** 280-281

Blue Four
see Blaue Vier

Blue God (ballet)
Cocteau, Jean **4** 132-133

Blue Hotel, The (stories)
Crane, Stephen **4** 293-295

Blue Nile (river, Africa)
Bruce, James **3** 63-64
Speke, John Hanning **14** 366-367

Blue Nude (painting)
Matisse, Henri **10** 336-337

Blue Poles (painting)
Pollock, Jackson **12** 379-380

Blue Rider
see Blaue Reiter

Blue Steel (opera)
Still, William Grant **14** 455-456

Blue-White (painting)
Kelly, Ellsworth **8** 482-483

Bluebeard's Castle (opera)
Bartók, Béla **2** 35-36

Blues (music)
Handy, William Christopher **7** 123-124
Still, William Grant **14** 455-456

Blues for Mr. Charlie (play)
Baldwin, James Arthur **1** 465-466

Blues People (book)
Baraka, Imamu Amiri **1** 498-499

BLUFORD, GUION STEWART, JR. (born
1942), African American aerospace engineer, pilot, and astronaut **2** 341-343

BLUM, LÉON (1872-1950), French statesman **2** 343-344
Daladier, Édouard **4** 369

BLUME, JUDY (born Judy Sussman; b.
1938), American fiction author
2 344-345

Blumenbach, Johann Friedrich
(1752-1840), German zoologist
Burckhardt, Johann Ludwig **3** 133

BLUMENTHAL, WERNER MICHAEL (born
1926), American businessman and treasury secretary **2** 345-346

Blütezeit der Romantik (novel)
Huch, Ricarda **8** 11-12

BLY, NELLIE (born Elizabeth Cochrane Seaman; 1864-1922), American journalist
and reformer **2** 346-348

BLYDEN, EDWARD WILMOT (1832-1912),
Liberian statesman **2** 348-349
Hayford, J. E. Casely **7** 228-230
Williams, Henry Sylvester **16** 303-304

Blythe, Herbert
see Barrymore, Maurice

Blythe, Vernon William
see Castle, I. and V.

Bnei Berak (academy, Jaffa)
Akiba ben Joseph **1** 97-98

Boa Vista (Cape Verde Island)
Cadamosto, Alvise da **3** 206-207

Boanerges
see John, St.

Board of Trade (Great Britain)
Dalhousie, 1st Marquess of **4** 375-376
Sydenham, Thomas **15** 59-60
officials
Beveridge, William Henry
2 251-252
presidents
Bright, John **3** 6-7
Bryce, James **3** 85
Chamberlain, Joseph **3** 411-413
Gladstone, William Ewart
6 357-360

Board of Universities (China)
Ts'ai Yüan-p'ei **15** 322

BOAS, FRANZ (1858-1942), German-born
American anthropologist **2** 349-351
anthropological linguistics
Bloomfield, Leonard **2** 338
Kroeber, Alfred Louis **9** 105-106
Redfield, Robert **13** 73-74
Sapir, Edward **13** 478-479
students
Benedict, Ruth Fulton **2** 154-155
Freyre, Gilberto **6** 106-107
Herskovits, Melville Jean **7** 345
Lowie, Robert Harry **10** 18
Mead, Margaret **10** 438-440
Radin, Paul **12** 538-539

Boat of Longing, The (novel)
Rölvaag, Ole Edvart **13** 265

Bobadilla, Francisco de (died 1502), Spanish officer
Columbus, Christopher **4** 176-179

Bobbies (London police)
Peel, Robert **12** 181-183

Bobbio (town; Italy)
Columban **4** 176

Bobolink Waltz, The (musical composition)
Porter, Cole Albert **12** 405-406

BOCCACCIO, GIOVANNI (1313-1375),
Italian author **2** 351-353
as biographer
Dante Alighieri **4** 389-391
friends
Petrarch **12** 259-261
influence of
Chaucer, Geoffrey **3** 482-485
Lessing, Gotthold Ephraim
9 357-359
Lydgate, John **10** 61-62
translations
Dryden, John **5** 106-107
López de Ayala, Pedro **9** 508-509

Boccaccio 70 (film)
Fellini, Federico **5** 408-409

BOCCIONI, UMBERTO (1882-1916), Ital-
ian artist **2** 353-354
associates
Severini, Gino **14** 122
Stella, Joseph **14** 422
influence of
Archipenko, Alexander **1** 280-281
Balla, Giacomo **1** 473-474
Duchamp-Villon, Raymond **5** 123

Bocconi University (Milan)
Pound, Ezra Loomis **12** 415-417

BÖCKLIN, ARNOLD (1827-1901), Swiss
painter **2** 354-355
Chirico, Giorgio de **4** 4
Nolde, Emil **11** 419-420

Bodas de sangre (play)
Lorca, Federico García **9** 511-513

Bodawpaya (ruled 1782-1819), king of
Burma
Alaungpaya **1** 103

BODE, BOYD HENRY (1873-1953), American philosopher and educator **2** 355-356

Bodenstein, Andreas
see Karlstadt

Bodhi (Buddhism)
Buddha **3** 97-101

Bodhisattva (Buddhism)
Buddha **3** 97-101
Dalai Lama **4** 369-371
Nichiren **11** 376-377

Bodhisattva Emperor
see Liang Wu-ti

BODIN, JEAN (1529/30-1596), French
political philosopher **2** 356-357
Filmer, Robert **5** 448

Bodmer, Johann Jakob (1698-1783);
Swiss-German author
Fuseli, Henry **6** 153-155
Wieland, Christoph Martin **16** 260-261

Boeckh, Philipp August (1785-1867), German classical scholar
Burckhardt, Jacob Christoph **3** 132-133

Boehm, Martin (1725-1812), American
United Brethren bishop
Otterbein, Philip William **12** 27-28

BOEHME, JACOB (1575-1624), German
mystic **2** 357
    Berdyaev, Nicholas Alexandrovich
    2 184-185

BOEING, WILLIAM EDWARD
(1881-1956), American businessman
2 357-358

Boeing Airplane Company
    Boeing, William Edward **2** 357-358

Boeotia (ancient republic; Greece)
    Cleomenes I **4** 103
    Lysander **10** 70

Boeotian League (Greece)
    Agesilaus II **1** 79-80
    Epaminondas **5** 291-292

Boeotian school (Greek literature)
    Hesiod **7** 361-362

Boer War (1899-1902)
    Boer leaders
        Botha, Louis **2** 434-436
        Hertzog, James Barry Munnik
        7 347-348
        Kruger, Stephanus Johannes Paulus
        9 108-109
        Smuts, Jan Christian **14** 309-310
        see also Boers
    British army
        Allenby, Edmund Henry Hynman
        1 171-172
        Kitchener, Horatio Herbert **9** 45-46
        Plaatje, Solomon Tshekisho
        12 341-342
        Rhodes, Cecil John **13** 120-122
        Roberts, Frederick Sleigh
        13 195-196
    British politics
        Chamberlain, Joseph **3** 411-413
        Milner, Alfred **11** 38-39
        Salisbury, 3d Marquess of
        13 448-449
        Victoria **15** 485-487
    Canada in
        Bourassa, Joseph-Henri-Napoleon
        2 446-447
        Laurier, Wilfrid **9** 232-234
        Smith, Donald Alexander
        14 288-289
    journalists
        Churchill, Winston Leonard Spencer
        4 51-53
    medical services
        Doyle, Arthur Conan **5** 91-92
    New Zealand in
        Seddon, Richard John **14** 81-82
    opponents
        Hardie, James Keir **7** 147-148
        Lloyd George, David **9** 469-471
        MacDonald, James Ramsay
        10 84-85

BOERHAAVE, HERMANN (1668-1738),
Dutch physician and chemist **2** 358-359
    La Mettrie, Julien Offray de **9** 179-180
    Linnaeus, Carl **9** 427-429
    Swammerdam, Jan **15** 48-49

Boers (Dutch South Africa)
    African opponents
        Dube, John Langalibalele **5** 113
        Moshweshwe **11** 203-205
    Great Trek
        Botha, Louis **2** 434-436
        Dingane **5** 14-15
        Kruger, Stephanus Johannes Paulus
        9 108-109
        Mzilikazi **11** 285-286
        Pretorius, Andries **12** 444-445
        Retief, Pieter **13** 105-106
    in fiction
        Plaatje, Solomon Tshekisho
        12 341-342
    nationalism
        Malan, Daniel Francois **10** 163-164
        Verwoerd, Hendrik Frensch
        15 472-473
        Vorster, Balthazar Johannes
        16 30-32
    republic
        Frere, Henry Bartle Edward
        6 100-101
        Kruger, Stephanus Johannes Paulus
        9 108-109
    see also Boer War

BOESAK, ALLAN AUBREY (born 1945),
opponent of apartheid in South Africa
and founder of the United Democratic
Front **2** 359-360

**BOETHIUS, ANICIUS MANLIUS SEVERI-
NUS** (480?-524/525), Roman logician
and theologian **2** 360-361
    influence of
        Chaucer, Geoffrey **3** 482-485
        Dante Alighieri **4** 389-391
        Theodoric the Great **15** 175-176
    influenced by
        Varro, Marcus Terentius **15** 438-439
    musical settings
        Dallapiccola, Luigi **4** 377-378
    translations and glosses
        Abelard, Peter **1** 23-25
        Alfred **1** 151-153
        Caxton, William **3** 386-387
        Jean de Meun **8** 234-235
        López de Ayala, Pedro **9** 508-509

Boethius of Dacia (flourished 1st half of
13th century), Scandinavian philosopher
    Lull, Raymond **10** 39-40
    Thomas Aquinas **15** 183-186

Boeuf sur le toit, Le (musical composition)
    Milhaud, Darius **11** 17-18

BOFFRAND, GABRIEL GERMAIN
(1667-1754), French architect and decorator **2** 361
    Neumann, Balthasar **11** 354-355

BOFILL, RICARDO (born 1939), post-modern Spanish architect **2** 362-363

BOGART, HUMPHREY (1899-1957),
American stage and screen actor
2 363-364

Bogatyr Symphony (musical composition)
    Borodin, Aleksandr Profirevich
    2 422-423

Boggs, Lilburn (1792-1860), American
politician
    Ashley, William Henry **1** 333-334

Bogotá (city, Colombia)
    Benalcázar, Sebastián de **2** 145-146
    Castro Ruz, Fidel **3** 365-368
    Gaitán, Jorge Eliécer **6** 172-173
    Quesada, Gonzalo Jiménez de
    12 509-510

Bogotazo (Bogotá riots; 1948)
    Castro Ruz, Fidel **3** 365-368
    Gaitán, Jorge Eliécer **6** 172-173
    Rojas Pinilla, Gustavo **13** 255-256

Bohème, La (opera; Puccini)
    Caruso, Enrico **3** 345
    Puccini, Giacomo **12** 474-476
    Toscanini, Arturo **15** 270-271

Bohemia (former kingdom; province,
Czechoslovakia)
    and Holy Roman Empire
        Charles IV **3** 455-456
        Ferdinand II **5** 415
        Frederick III **6** 84-85
    Czech nationalism
        Wenceslaus **16** 201-202
    German invasions
        Henry I **7** 285-286
        Rudolf I **13** 347-348
    Hussite rebellion
        Hus, Jan **8** 56-59
        Sigismund **14** 220-221
        Wenceslaus **16** 201-202
    Thirty Years War
        Wallenstein, Albrecht Wenzel Euse-
        bius von **16** 80-81

Bohemian life-style
    Diderot, Denis **5** 1-2
    Ehrenburg, Ilya Grigorievich **5** 224-225

Bohemian music
    Smetana, Bedřich **14** 281-282

Bohemian Unity of Brethren (religious
sect)
    Comenius, John Amos **4** 180-181

BOHEMUND I (of Tarantò; circa
1055-1111), Norman Crusader **2** 364
    Alexius I **1** 143-144
    Comnena, Anna **4** 185-186
    Godfrey of Bouillon **6** 379

Bohemud III (died 1201), Norman prince
of Antioch 1163-1199
    Nureddin **11** 444-445

BOHLEN, CHARLES (CHIP) EUSTIS
(1904-1973), United States ambassador
to the Soviet Union, interpreter, and presidential adviser **2** 364-366

Bohlen und Halbach, Gustav von
(1870-1950)
    Krupp **9** 109-111

Böhm.
see also Boehm

Böhm, Georg (1661-1733), German organist
Bach, Johann Sebastian **1** 416-419

BÖHM-BAWERK, EUGEN VON
(1851-1914), Austrian economist **2** 366
Fisher, Irving **5** 462-463
Schumpeter, Joseph Alois **14** 43-44
von Mises, Ludwig **16** 25

Böhme, Jakob
see Boehme, Jacob

BOHR, NIELS HENRIK DAVID
(1885-1962), Danish physicist **2** 366-368
atom
Chadwick, James **3** 405-406
de Broglie, Louis **4** 442-444
Pauli, Wolfgang Ernst **12** 149
Copenhagen institute
Heisenberg, Werner Karl **7** 261-263
Hevesy, George Charles de **7** 371
Landau, Lev Davidovich **9** 184-185
Urey, Harold Clayton **15** 394-396
quantum theory
Bhabha, Homi Jehangir **2** 253-254
Einstein, Albert **5** 228-231
Rutherford, Ernest **13** 384-387

Bohun, Mary de (died 1394), English wife of Henry IV
Henry IV **7** 292-293

BOIARDO, MATTEO MARIA (Conte di Scandiano; 1440/41-1494), Italian poet **2** 369
Ariosto, Ludovico **1** 289-290
Camoëns, Luis Vaz de **3** 247-249

BOILEAU-DESPRÉAUX, NICHOLAS
(1636?-1711), French critic and writer **2** 369-371
Corneille, Pierre **4** 234-236
Juvenal **8** 397-399
La Fontaine, Jean de **9** 156-157
Pope, Alexander **12** 395-397

Bois de Boulogne (Paris)
Haussmann, Baron Georges Eugène **7** 201-202

Boisy, Francis
see Francis of Sales, St.

Boito, Arrigo (1842-1918), Italian composer and librettist
Verdi, Giuseppe Fortunino Francesco **15** 463-465-121

Bojador Cape (Northwest Africa)
Henry the Navigator **7** 305-306

BOK, DEREK CURTIS (born 1930), dean of the Harvard Law School and president of Harvard University **2** 371-372

BOK, SISSELA ANN (born 1934), American moral philosopher **2** 372-374

Bol, Ferdinand (1618-1680), Dutch painter
Rembrandt Harmensz van Rijn **13** 91-95

Boldino (estate, Russia)
Pushkin, Aleksandr Sergeevich **12** 489-491

Boléro (musical composition)
Ravel, Maurice Joseph **13** 54-55

Boleyn, Anne (1507-1536), second wife of Henry VIII
Cranmer, Thomas **4** 295-296
Elizabeth I **5** 263-266
Henry VIII **7** 302-305
Mary, I **10** 308-309
Norfolk, 3d Duke of **11** 423
Wyatt, Thomas **16** 410-411

Bolikango, Jean (born 1909), Congolese politician
Kasavubu, Joseph **8** 453-455

Bolingbroke, Henry
see Henry IV (king of England)

BOLINGBROKE, VISCOUNT (Henry St. John; 1678-1751), English statesman **2** 374-375
associates
Pope, Alexander **12** 395-397
Swift, Jonathan **15** 51-54
Voltaire **16** 14-16
Peace of Urecht (1713)
Anne **1** 241-242
Harley, Robert **7** 159-160

Bolívar (musical composition)
Milhaud, Darius **11** 17-18

BOLÍVAR, SIMÓN (1783-1830), South American general and statesman **2** 375-377
and Bolivia
Sucre, Antonio José de **15** 11-12
and Colombia
Harrison, William Henry **7** 180-181
Mosquera, Tomás Cipriano de **11** 205-206
Nariño, Antonio **11** 314-315
Santander, Franciso de Paula **13** 475
and Ecuador
Flores, Juan José **5** 491
Panama Congress (1826)
Adams, John Quincy **1** 52-54
and Peru
Ballivián, José **1** 475
Castilla, Ramón **3** 361
San Martín, José de **13** 468-469
Santa Cruz, Andrés de **13** 472-473
Unánue, José Hipólito **15** 387-388
tutors
Bello, Ahmadu **2** 139-140
and Venezuela
López, Narciso **9** 508
Miranda, Francisco de **11** 52-53
Páez, José Antonio **12** 58

Bolivia, Republic of (nation; South America)
Acre dispute
Rio Branco, Barão do **13** 177
and Peru
Ballivián, José **1** 475
Santa Cruz, Andrés de **13** 472-473

Chaco War
see Chaco War
Communist guerrillas
Guevara, Ernesto **7** 30-31
economic development
Banzer Suárez, Hugo **1** 494-496
Paz Zamora, Jaime **12** 165-167
Gaucho War
Güemes, Martín **7** 26-27
guerrillas defeated
Barrientos Ortuño, René **2** 22-23
independence movement
Ballivián, José **1** 475
Bolívar, Simón **2** 375-377
San Martín, José de **13** 468-469
Santa Cruz, Andrés de **13** 472-473
Sucre, Antonio José de **15** 11-12
revolution (1951-1952)
Paz, Octavio **12** 161-162
tin mines nationalized (1952)
Patiño, Simón Iturri **12** 133-134
Paz, Octavio **12** 161-162
War of the Pacific
Balmaceda Fernández, José Manuel **1** 475-476

BÖLL, HEINRICH (1917-1985), German writer and translator **2** 377-378

Bologna (city; Italy)
Julius II **8** 384-386
Visconti, Gian Galeazzo **15** 510-511

Bologna, Concordat of (1515)
Francis I **6** 40-43

Bologna, University of (Italy)
Cardano, Geronimo **3** 285-286
Carducci, Giosuè **3** 290-291
Clement V **4** 101-102
Luzzi, Mondino de' **10** 58
Malpighi, Marcello **10** 176-178

Bologna school (music)
Corelli, Arcangelo **4** 230-231

Bolometer (instrument)
Langley, Samuel Pierpont **9** 195-196

Bolshevik (journal)
Bukharin, Nikolai Ivanovich **3** 112-113

Bolshevik Revolution
see Russian Revolution (1917; October)

Bolsheviks (Russian politics)
creation and goals
Lenin, Vladimir Ilich **9** 323-326
leaders
Bukharin, Nikolai Ivanovich **3** 112-113
Frunze, Mikhail Vasilievich **6** 134
Kollontai, Aleksandra Mikhailovna **9** 79
Litvinov, Maxim Maximovich **9** 451-452
Mayakovsky, Vladimir Vladimirovich **10** 364-365
Molotov, Vyacheslav Mikhailovich **11** 89-90
Stalin, Joseph **14** 393-396
Trotsky, Leon **15** 302-305-514

Zhukov, Georgi Konstantinovich **16** 512-513
Zinoviev, Grigori Evseevich **16** 521-522
opponents
  Goldman, Emma **6** 406-407
  Kolchak, Aleksandr Vasilievich **9** 77-78
  Kropotkin, Peter Alekseevich **9** 107-108
  Miliukov, Pavel Nikolayevich **11** 18-19
  Pavlov, Ivan Petrovich **12** 155-157
supporters
  Babel, Isaac Emmanuelovich **1** 411-412
  Dzerzhinsky, Felix Edmundovich **5** 173-174
  Ehrenburg, Ilya Grigorievich **5** 224-225
  Kamenev, Lev Borisovich **8** 417-418
  Meyerhold, Vsevolod Emilievich **10** 539
  see also Mensheviks

Bolshevism and the United States (book)
  Russell, Charles Edward **13** 374-375

Bolts of Melody (poems)
  Dickinson, Emily **4** 541-543

Boltwood, Bertram Borden (1870-1927),
American chemist and physicist
  Rutherford, Ernest **13** 384-387

BOLTWOOD, BERTRAM BORDEN
(1870-1927), American radiochemist
2 378-379

BOLTZMANN, LUDWIG (1844-1906),
Austrian physicist **2** 379-380
  Arrhenius, Svante August **1** 318-320
  Planck, Max Karl Ernst Ludwig **12** 342-344

Bom Jesus de Matozinhos (Congonhas do Campo, Brazil)
  Aleijadinho, O **1** 125-126

Bomani, Paul (born 1925), Tanzanian politician
  Nyerere, Julius Kamberage **11** 447-449

Bomarzo (cantata and opera)
  Ginastera, Alberto Evaristo **6** 328-329

BOMBAL, MARÍA LUISA (1910-1980),
Chilean novelist and story writer **2** 380-381

Bombardment of Fort Sumter (painting)
  Bierstadt, Albert **2** 270-271

Bombay, University of (India)
  Geddes, Patrick **6** 246-247
  Gokhale, Gopal Krishna **6** 396
  Mehta, Pherozeshah **10** 455

Bombay Legislative Council (India)
  Ambedkar, Bhimrao Ramji **1** 190-191
  Gokhale, Gopal Krishna **6** 396
  Mehta, Pherozeshah **10** 455

Bombay Presidency Association (India)
  Mehta, Pherozeshah **10** 455

Bombing, strategic (military)
  Arnold, Henry Harley **1** 310-311

Bombs Away (book)
  Steinbeck, John Ernst **14** 416-417

Bon Bock (painting)
  Manet, Édouard **10** 193-194

Bon Homme Richard (ship)
  Jones, John Paul **8** 337-338

Bon Marché Department Store (Paris)
  Eiffel, Alexandre Gustave **5** 227-228

Bona Dea (Roman goddess)
  Clodius Pulcher, Publius **4** 121-122

Bonagiunta da Lucca (flourished 13th century), Italian poet
  Guinizzelli, Guido **7** 36-37

Bonaparte, Charles Louis Napoleon
  see Napoleon III

Bonaparte, Charles Lucien (1803-1857),
prince of Canino and Musignano
  Wilson, Alexander **16** 313-314

Bonaparte, François Charles Joseph
  see Napoleon II

BONAPARTE, JOSEPH (1768-1844),
French statesman, king of Naples 1806-1808 and of Spain 1808-1813 **2** 381-382
  Bolívar, Simón **2** 375-377
  Charles IV **3** 456-457
  Ferdinand VII **5** 418-420
  Godoy y Álvarez de Faria, Manuel de **6** 381-382
  Goya y Lucientes, Francisco de Paula José de **6** 476-478
  Napoleon I **11** 306-310
  Wellington, 1st Duke of **16** 193-195

Bonaparte, Josephine
  see Josephine

BONAPARTE, LOUIS (1778-1846), French statesman, king of Holland 1806-1810 **2** 382-383

Bonaparte, Napoleon
  see Napoleon I

Bonaparte Crossing the St. Bernard Pass (painting)
  David, Jacques Louis **4** 407-409

Bonaventure (stories)
  Cable, George Washington **3** 198-199

BONAVENTURE, ST. (1217-1274), Italian theologian and philosopher **2** 383-384
  Duns Scotus, John **5** 149-150
  Thomas Aquinas **15** 183-186

Boncompagni, Ugo
  see Gregory XIII

BOND, JULIAN (born 1940), civil rights leader elected to the Georgia House of Representatives **2** 386-387
  Bond, Horace Mann **2** 384-386

BOND, HORACE MANN (1904-1972),
African American educator **2** 384-386

Bond Bill (United States; 1894)
  Coxey, Jacob Sechler **4** 286-287

Bond Head, Sir Francis
  see Head, Sir Francis Bond

Bond Honoured, A (play)
  Osborne, John **12** 16-17

Bond of 1844 (African states)
  Maclean, George **10** 108-109

BONDFIELD, MARGARET GRACE
(1873-1953), British union official and political leader **2** 388-389

Bondi, Hermann (born 1919), Austrian mathematician
  Lemaître, Abbè Georges Édouard **9** 315-316

Bone Ranks (Korean caste system)
  Sol Ch'ong **14** 325-326

Bones (minstrel character)
  Christy, Edwin P. **4** 34-35

Bonesana, Cesare
  see Becarria, Marchese di

Bonfire (poems)
  Aragon, Louis **1** 271-272

Bonham case (1610)
  Coke, Edward **4** 141-142

BONHOEFFER, DIETRICH (1906-1945),
German theologian **2** 389-391
  Barth, Karl **2** 31-32

Boniface (died 432), Roman governor of North Africa
  Gaiseric **6** 172

BONIFACE, ST. (circa 672-754), English monk **2** 391
  Martel, Charles **10** 285

BONIFACE VIII (Benedetto Caetani; 1235?-1303), pope 1294-1303 **2** 392-393
  and Franciscans
    Jacopone da Todi **8** 194
  conflict with Philip IV
    Clement V **4** 101-102
    Duns Scotus, John **5** 149-150
    Edward I **5** 208-210
    Philip IV **12** 274
  Florentine independence
    Dante Alighieri **4** 389-391
  in art
    Arnolfo di Cambio **1** 315-316
    Giotto **6** 342-345

BONIFACIO, ANDRES (1863-1897), Filipino revolutionary hero **2** 393-394
  Del Pilar, Marcelo Hilario **4** 486
  Mabini, Apolinario **10** 72-73
  Rizal, José **13** 187-189

Bonifacius (book)
  Mather, Cotton **10** 330-332

BONINGTON, RICHARD PARKES
(1802-1828), English painter **2** 394-395
  Delacroix, Ferdinand Victor Eugène **4** 469-471
  Hassam, Frederick Childe **7** 192

Bonn, Treaty of (921)
  Henry I **7** 285-286

Bonn, University of (Germany)
  science
    Clausius, Rudolf Julius Emanuel
      4 92-94
    Helmholtz, Hermann Ludwig Ferdinand von **7** 268-269
    Hofmann, August Wilhelm von
      7 441-442
    Kekulé, Friedrich August **8** 477-478
  social science
    Niebuhr, Barthold Georg
      11 385-386
    Schumpeter, Joseph Alois **14** 43-44
  theology
    Barth, Karl **2** 31-32
    Troeltsch, Ernst **15** 299-300

BONNARD, PIERRE (1867-1947), French painter **2** 395-396
  Prendergast, Maurice Brazil **12** 440
  Vuillard, Jean Édouard **16** 36

Bonne chanson, La (poem)
  Verlaine, Paul Marie **15** 465-466

Bonne chanson, La (song cycle)
  Fauré, Gabriel Urbain **5** 397-398

Bonneville Dam (Washington-Oregon)
  Kaiser, Henry John **8** 412-413

Bonney, William Harrison
  see Billy the Kid

Bonnie Prince Charlie
  see Stuart, Prince Charles Edward

Bonny Kingdom (Nigeria)
  Ja Ja of Opobo **8** 201-204

Bononcini, Giovanni Battista (circa 1672-circa 1752), Italian operatic composer
  Handel, George Frederick **7** 116-119

Bonpland, Aimé (1773-1858), French botanist
  Humboldt, Friedrich Heinrich Alexander von **8** 30-31

Bons Amis (French religious group)
  Laval, Francois Xavier de **9** 235-236

Bontemps, Arna Wendell (1902-1973), African American author, librarian, and playwright
  Cullen, Countee **4** 333-334
  Hughes, Langston **8** 18-19

Bontemps, Pierre (1507-1570), French sculptor
  Pilon, Germain **12** 305

Bonus army (United States)
  Hoover, Herbert Clark **7** 483-485

BONVALOT, PIERRE GABRIEL ÉDOUARD (1853-1933), French explorer and author **2** 396

Book about Myself, A (autobiography)
  Dreiser, Herman Theodore **5** 98-100

Book of Ahania, The (poems)
  Blake, William **2** 316-318

Book of American Negro Poetry (anthology)
  Johnson, James Weldon **8** 304-305

Book of American Negro Spirituals (anthology)
  Johnson, James Weldon **8** 304-305

Book of Architecture (book)
  Gibbs, James **6** 301-302

Book of Bahir (Cabalist text)
  Scholem, Gershom **14** 26

Book of Burlesques, A (book)
  Mencken, Henry Louis **10** 481-483

Book of Changes
  see I Ching

Book of Common Prayer
  Cranmer, Thomas **4** 295-296
  Crowther, Samuel Adjai **4** 326

Book of Creatures (book; R. Sebond)
  Montaigne, Michel Eyquem de
    11 116-117

Book of Delight, The (book)
  Abrahams, Israel **1** 29

Book of Documents (Confucius)
  Confucius **4** 197-200
  Mencius **10** 480-481
  Ssu-ma Ch'ien **14** 388-389

Book of Good Love, The (poem) 316, 317
  Ruiz, Juan **13** 358-359

Book of Homage to Shakespeare (book; Gollancz)
  Plaatje, Solomon Tshekisho **12** 341-342

Book of Hours, The (religious poems)
  Rilke, Rainer Maria **13** 171-172

Book of Hours of Étienne Chevalier (religious book)
  Fouquet, Jean **6** 31

Book of Image (book)
  Nahmanides **11** 293-294

Book of Images (poems)
  Rilke, Rainer Maria **13** 171-172

Book of Kings (epic)
  Firdausi **5** 451-452

Book of Lord Shang (treatises)
  Shang Yang **14** 149-150

Book of Mormon (book; Smith)
  Smith, Joseph **14** 297-298
  Young, Brigham **16** 469-470

Book of Music (book)
  Confucius **4** 197-200

Book of Nonsense (book)
  Ray, Satyajit **13** 60-61

Book of Odes (Confucius)
  Confucius **4** 197-200
  Mencius **10** 480-481

Book of Peace (book)
  Christine de Pisan **4** 29-30

Book of Prefaces, A (book)
  Mencken, Henry Louis **10** 481-483

Book of Roger (book)
  Idrisi, Muhammad ibn Muhammad al-
    8 102-103

Book of Secrets (poems; Attar)
  Rumi, Jalai ed-Din **13** 362-363

Book of Secrets (religious book)
  Mani **10** 196-197

Book of Sentences (Lombard)
  see Sentences

Book of Small, The (book)
  Carr, Emily **3** 319

Book of Songs (poems)
  Heine, Heinrich **7** 259-260

Book of Sovereigns (prose epic)
  Firdausi **5** 451-452

Book of the Courtier (book)
  Castiglione, Baldassare **3** 360-361

Book of the Duchess, The (poem)
  Chaucer, Geoffrey **3** 482-485

Book of the Festivals (polemic)
  Saadia ben Joseph al-Fayumi **13** 396

Book of the Foundations, The (autobiography)
  Theresa **15** 178-179

Book of the New Moral World (book)
  Owen, Robert **12** 39-40

Book of the Thousand Nights and a Night, The (English translation)
  Burton, Richard **3** 163-164

Book of the Three Virtues (book)
  Christine de Pisan **4** 29-30

Book of the Two Principles (book)
  Mani **10** 196-197

Book of Thel, The (book)
  Blake, William **2** 316-318

Book of Urizen, The (book)
  Blake, William **2** 316-318

Book of Verse, A (poems)
  Masters, Edgar Lee **10** 326-327

Book of Zohar (book)
  Manasseh ben Israel **10** 183-184

BOOLE, GEORGE (1815-1864), English mathematician **2** 396-397
  Leibniz, Gottfried Wilhelm von
    9 307-310

Boolean algebra
  Boole, George **2** 396-397

Boomerang (newspaper)
  Lawson, Henry **9** 254-255

Boomtown (film)
  Gable, William Clark **6** 157-158

Boon (novel)
  Wells, Herbert George **16** 195-196

BOONE, DANIEL (1734-1820), American frontiersman and explorer **2** 397-398
  Bingham, George Caleb **2** 278-279
  Brown, William Wells **3** 48-49
  Henderson, Richard **7** 278-279
  Porter, Katherine Anne **12** 406-407

Boone's Station (Kentucky)
  Boone, Daniel **2** 397-398

Boonesborough (Kentucky)
Boone, Daniel **2** 397-398

BOORSTIN, DANIEL J. (born 1914), American historian **2** 398-400

Booth, Amelia (literary character)
Fielding, Henry **5** 442-444

Booth, Bramwell (1856-1929), English Salvation Army leader
Booth, William **2** 405-406

BOOTH, CHARLES (1840-1916), English social scientist **2** 400-401
Webb, Beatrice Potter **16** 153-154
Woods, Robert Archey **16** 374

BOOTH, EDWIN (1833-1893), American actor **2** 401-402
Barrymores **2** 28-30
Forrest, John 1st Baron **6** 12-13

BOOTH, EVANGELINE CORY (1865-1950), British/American humanist **2** 402-403

BOOTH, JOHN WILKES (1838-1865), American actor **2** 404
Booth, Edwin **2** 401-402

BOOTH, JOSEPH (1851-1932), English missionary in Africa **2** 404-405

Booth, Junius Brutus (1796-1852), English-born American actor
Booth, Edwin **2** 401-402

Booth, Junius Brutus, Jr. (1821-1883) American actor-manager
Booth, Edwin **2** 401-402

BOOTH, WILLIAM (1829-1912), English evangelist, Salvation Army founder **2** 405-406
Lindsay, Vachel **9** 424-425

Booth Theater (New York City)
Booth, Edwin **2** 401-402

Boothe, Clare
see Luce, Clare Boothe

BOOTHROYD, BETTY (born 1929), first woman speaker in Great Britain's House of Commons **2** 406-407

Bootleg monopoly (United States)
Capone, Al **3** 272-273

Bop (jazz style)
Parker, Charles Christopher Jr. **12** 105-106

Bora, Katherine von (1499-1552), German nun
Luther, Martin **10** 48-51

BORAH, WILLIAM EDGAR (1865-1940), American statesman **2** 408
Johnson, Hiram Warren **8** 300-301

Bordeaux (city; France)
Clement V **4** 101-102
Leclerc, Jacques Philippe **9** 272-273

Bordeaux, University of
Durkheim, Émile **5** 162-163
Sabatier, Paul **13** 398-399

BORDEN, GAIL (1801-1874), American pioneer and inventor of food-processing techniques **2** 409

BORDEN, SIR ROBERT LAIRD (1854-1937), Canadian prime minister, 1911-1920 **2** 409-411
Crerar, Thomas Alexander **4** 306
Laurier, Wilfrid **9** 232-234

Borden Co.
Borden, Gail **2** 409
Meighen, Arthur **10** 459-460

Border Ruffians (United States)
Atchison, David Rice **1** 357-358

Borderers, The (play)
Wordsworth, William **16** 385-388

Bordone, Paris (1500-1571), Italian painter
Tintoretto **15** 232-234

Bordoni, Faustina (1700-1781), Italian singer
Handel, George Frederick **7** 116-119

Boreas (ship)
Nelson, Horatio **11** 336-338

Borelli, Giovanni (1608-1679), Italian physicist
Malpighi, Marcello **10** 176-178

BORGES, JORGE LUIS (1899-1986), Argentine author and critic **2** 411-412
Güiráldez, Ricardo **7** 38-39

Borghese, Camillo
see Paul V, pope

Borghese, Marc' Antonio (died 1658), Italian nobleman
Rossi, Luigi **13** 310-311

Borghese, Pauline (Maria Paulina Buonaparte; 1780-1825), sister of Napoleon I
Canova, Antonio **3** 263-264

Borghese, Scipione (Caffarelli; 1576-1633), Italian cardinal
Bernini, Gian Lorenzo **2** 214-216

Borghesi, Bartolommeo (1781-1860), Italian numismatist
Mommsen, Theodor **11** 94-95

Borgia, Alfonso
see Calixtus III

BORGIA, CESARE (1475-1507), Italian cardinal, general, and administrator **2** 412-413
Alexander VI **1** 134-135
Julius II **8** 384-386
Leonardo da Vinci **9** 337-340
Machiavelli, Niccolò **10** 97-99

Borgia, Giovanni (Juan, or Joan; 1476-1497), 2d Duke of Gandia
Alexander VI **1** 134-135
Borgia, Cesare **2** 412-413

Borgia, Goffredo (1481-1517), prince of Squillace
Alexander VI **1** 134-135
Borgia, Cesare **2** 412-413

BORGIA, LUCREZIA (1480-1519), Italian duchess of Ferrara **2** 413-416
Alexander VI **1** 134-135
Borgia, Cesare **2** 412-413

Borgia, Pier Luigi (circa 1468-88), 1st Duke of Gandia
Borgia, Cesare **2** 412-413

Borgia, Rodrigo
see Alexander VI, pope

BORGLUM, JOHN GUTZON DE LA MOTHE (1867-1941), American sculptor and engineer **2** 416-417

Borglum, Lincoln (1912-1986), American sculptor
Borglum, John Gutzon de la Mothe **2** 416-417

Borinquén
see Puerto Rico

Boris Godunov (opera; Mussorgsky)
Mussorgsky, Modest Petrovich **11** 274-276
Pushkin, Aleksandr Sergeevich **12** 489-491
Rimsky-Korsakov, Nikolai Andreevich **13** 174-175

Boris Godunov (play)
Pushkin, Aleksandr Sergeevich **12** 489-491

Borja
see Borgia

BORJA CEVALLOS, RODRIGO (born 1935), a founder of Ecuador's Democratic Left (Izquierda Democratica) party and president of Ecuador (1988-) **2** 417-418

Borkman, John Gabriel (literary character)
Ibsen, Henrik **8** 98-100

BORLAUG, NORMAN ERNEST (born 1914), American biochemist who developed high yield cereal grains **2** 418-420

BORN, MAX (1882-1970), German physicist **2** 420-421
associates
Heisenberg, Werner Karl **7** 261-263
Kármán, Theodore von **8** 451-452
Pauli, Wolfgang Ernst **12** 149
influence of
Bohr, Niels Henrik David **2** 366-368
Dirac, Paul Adrien Maurice **5** 23-24
Oppenheimer, J. Robert **11** 525-526
opponents
Einstein, Albert **5** 228-231
quantum mechanics
Tomonaga, Sin-itiro **15** 265-266

Born to Rebel (book)
Mays, Benjamin E. **10** 374-376

Borneo (island)
see Indonesia

Bornholm (island, Denmark)
Oersted, Hans Christian **11** 476-478

Bornu (province, Nigeria)
Uthman don Fodio **15** 397-398

BOROCHOV, DOV BER (1881-1917), early Zionist thinker who reconciled Judaism and Marxism **2** 421-422

BORODIN, ALEKSANDR PROFIREVICH (1833-1887), Russian composer **2** 422-423
  Mussorgsky, Modest Petrovich **11** 274-276
  Rimsky-Korsakov, Nikolai Andreevich **13** 174-175
  Tchaikovsky, Peter Ilyich **15** 130-132

Borodin, Mikhail Markovich (1884-1953), Russian diplomat
  Chiang Kai-shek **3** 510-513
  Ho Chi Minh **7** 426-428
  Sun Yat-sen **15** 35-39

Borodino, battle of (1812)
  Kutuzov, Mikhail Ilarionovich **9** 137-138
  Napoleon I **11** 306-310
  Ney, Michel **11** 372-373

Borom Sarat (film)
  Ousmane, Sembene **12** 32-33

Boron (element—chemistry)
  Bothe, Walther **2** 438-439
  Davy, Humphry **4** 426-427
  Gay-Lussac, Joseph Louis **6** 245-246

Borotin, Count (literary character)
  Grillparzer, Franz **6** 546-547

Borough, Stephen (1525-1584), English navigator
  Cabot, Sebastian **3** 200-201

Borough, The (poem)
  Crabbe, George **4** 288

Borowski, Felix (1872-1956), American composer
  Dawson, William Levi **4** 427-428

BORROMEO, ST. CHARLES (1538-1584), Italian cardinal and reformer **2** 423-424
  Bellarmine, Robert **2** 135-136
  Gregory XIII **6** 534
  Neri, Philip **11** 340
  Pius IV **12** 332

BORROMINI, FRANCESCO (1599-1667), Italian architect **2** 424-425
  contemporaries
    Cortona, Pietro da **4** 256
  influence of
    Aleijadinho, O **1** 125-126
    Boffrand, Gabriel Germain **2** 361
    Fischer von Erlach, Johann Bernhard **5** 459-461
    Juvara, Filippo **8** 396-397
    Le Vau, Louis **9** 360-361
  style
    Gentile da Fabriano **6** 266-267
    Guarini, Guarino **7** 25-26

BOSANQUET, BERNARD (1848-1923), English philosopher **2** 425-426

Boscawen, Edward (1711-1761), British admiral
  Adam, Robert and James **1** 38-40
  Rodney, George Brydges **13** 239-240

Bosch, Carl (1874-1940), German industrial chemist
  Haber, Fritz **7** 56-58

BOSCH, HIERONYMUS (1453-1516), Netherlandish painter **2** 426-428
  Brouwer, Adriaen **3** 29-30
  Bruegel, Pieter the Elder **3** 65-67
  Evergood, Philip **5** 345
  Smith, David **14** 287-288
  van der Goes, Hugo **15** 416-417

BOSCH, JUAN (born 1909), Dominican writer, president, 1963 **2** 428-429
  Balaguer y Ricardo, Joaquin **1** 460-461
  Duvalier, François **5** 165-166

Bose Research Institute (Calcutta)
  Bose, Jagadis Chandra **2** 429-430

Bose, S.N. (1894-1974), Indian mathematician
  Einstein, Albert **5** 228-231

BOSE, SIR JAGADIS CHANDRA (1858-1937), Indian physicist and plant physiologist **2** 430-431

BOSE, SUBHAS CHANDRA (1897-1945), Indian nationalist **2** 430-431
  Das, Chitta Ranjan **4** 401-402

Bose-Einstein statistics
  Einstein, Albert **5** 228-231

Bosen Koche, Die (play)
  Grass, Günter **6** 496-497

Bosnia (region; former Yugoslavia)
  Karadzic, Radovan **8** 437-440
  Mahmud II **10** 145-147
  Mehmed the Conqueror **10** 452-454
  Mladic, Ratko **11** 68-69

Bosnia-Herzegovina (nation; former republic, Yugoslavia)
  Francis Ferdinand **6** 44
  Francis Joseph **6** 45-46
  Izetbegovic, Alija **8** 161-163

Boss, The (book; McKean)
  Hague, Frank **7** 63-64

Bossi, Enrico (1861-1925), Italian composer
  Malipiero, Gian Francesco **10** 171

Bossism (United States politics)
  see Political machines (United States)

BOSSUET, JACQUES BÉNIGNE (1627-1704), French bishop and author **2** 431-432
  Condé, Prince de **4** 193-194
  Fénelon, François de Salignac de la Mothe **5** 410-411
  La Bruyère, Jean de **9** 145
  Leibniz, Gottfried Wilhelm von **9** 307-310
  Simon, Jules François **14** 237-238

Boston (city, Massachusetts)
  architecture
    Benjamin, Asher **2** 162-163
    Bulfinch, Charles **3** 116-117
    Faneuil, Peter **5** 377
    Gropius, Walter **7** 13-14
    McKim, Charles Follen **10** 417-418
  British siege
    Allen, Ethan **1** 163-164
    Greene, Nathanael **6** 525-526
    Howe, William **7** 538-539
    Hull, William **8** 29-30
    Knox, Henry **9** 64
    Putnam, Israel **12** 491-492
  Catholic diocese
    Carroll, John **3** 331-332
  colonial period
    Boylston, Zabdiel **2** 471
    Sewall, Samuel **14** 123-124
  officials
    Curley, James Michael **4** 344-345
    Otis, Harrison Gray **12** 25
    Shaw, Lemuel **14** 164-165
    White, Kevin H. **16** 231-232
  police strike (1919)
    Coolidge, John Calvin **4** 217-219
  public schools
    Emerson, Ralph Waldo **5** 278-280
    Mason, Lowell **10** 321-322
    Schindler, Solomon **14** 7-8
  see also Brook Farm; Bunker Hill, Battle of; and entries beginning Boston

Boston (novel)
  Sinclair, Upton Beale Jr. **14** 248-249

Boston Academy of Music
  Mason, Lowell **10** 321-322

Boston American (newspaper)
  Hearst, William Randolph **7** 243-244

Boston Atlas (newspaper)
  Hildreth, Richard **7** 382

Boston Brahmins (American literature)
  Cummings, Edward Estlin **4** 334-336

Boston Braves (baseball team)
  Aaron, Henry Louis (Hank) **1** 2-3

Boston Bruins (U.S. hockey team)
  Orr, Bobby **12** 2-4

Boston Carpet-bag (newspaper)
  Ward, Artemus **16** 112-113

Boston Celtics (basketball team)
  Bird, Larry **2** 279-281

Boston Christian Register (newspaper)
  Bellows, Henry Whitney **2** 143-144

Boston Cooking School
  Farmer, Fannie Merritt **5** 383

Boston Gazette (newspaper)
  Adams, John **1** 48-51
  Adams, Samuel **1** 55-56
  Otis, James Jr. **12** 25-27

Boston Globe (newspaper)
  Schindler, Solomon **14** 7-8

Boston Manufacturing Co.
  Lowell, Francis Cabot **10** 13-14

Boston Massacre (1770)
  Adams, John **1** 48-51
  Adams, Samuel **1** 55-56
  Hancock, John **7** 114-116

Boston Pops (orchestra)
Fiedler, Arthur **5** 437-438

Boston Port Bill
see Intolerable Acts (1774)

Boston Public Library
Garland, Hannibal Hamlin **6** 217-218
Lawrence, Abbott **9** 246
McKim, Charles Follen **10** 417-418
Sargent, John Singer **13** 481-482

Boston Quarterly Review (magazine)
Brownson, Orestes Augustus **3** 57-58

Boston Red Sox (baseball team)
Ruth, George Herman Jr. **13** 384

Boston School of Oratory
Garland, Hannibal Hamlin **6** 217-218

Boston School Song Book, The (anthology)
Mason, Lowell **10** 321-322

Boston Slave Riot (1854)
Burns, Anthony **3** 151

Boston Strong Boy
see Sullivan, John Lawrence

Boston Symphony Orchestra
Chávez, Carlos **3** 486
Ozawa, Seiji **12** 49-51
Piston, Walter **12** 327-328

Boston Tea Party (1773)
British retaliation
Gage, Thomas **6** 169-170
North, Frederick **11** 429-430
see also Intolerable Acts (1774)
participants
Adams, Samuel **1** 55-56
Revere, Paul **13** 110-111
supporters
Adams, John **1** 48-51
Chase, Samuel **3** 475-476
Dickinson, John **4** 543-544
Franklin, Benjamin **6** 60-64
Hancock, John **7** 114-116

Boston University
Adams, Peter Chardon Brooks **1** 54
Bell, Alexander Graham **2** 129-131
Brightman, Edgar Sheffield **3** 8-9
Parsons, Frank **12** 121-122
Silber, John **14** 224-226
Zinn, Howard **16** 520-521

Bostonians, The (novel)
James, Henry **8** 211-212

Boston's Immigrants (book)
Handlin, Oscar **7** 121-122

Boston's Watch and Ward Society
Williams, Tennessee **16** 306-308

BOSWELL, JAMES (1740-1795), Scottish
biographer and diarist **2** 432-434
Burke, Edmund **3** 138-141
Goldsmith, Oliver **6** 411-413
Johnson, Samuel **8** 315-317
Wilkes, John **16** 280-281

Bosworth Field, Battle of (1485)
Henry VII **7** 300-302

Richard III **13** 132-133

Botanical Mission (Columbia; established 1783)
Mutis, José Celestino **11** 278-279

Botany (science)
classification
Bartram, William **2** 41-42
Colden, Cadwallader **4** 145-146
Cutler, Manasseh **4** 356-357
Gray, Asa **6** 506-507
Lamarck, Chevalier de **9** 171-173
Ray, John **13** 57-59
collections (18th century)
Banks, Joseph **1** 489-490
Bartram, John **2** 40-41
Boerhaave, Hermann **2** 358-359
Mutis, José Celestino **11** 278-279
expeditions
Gray, Asa **6** 506-507
Humboldt, Friedrich Heinrich
Alexander von **8** 30-31
plant genetics
de Vries, Hugo **4** 516-518
East, Edward Murray **5** 182-183
Vavilov, Nikolai Ivanovich
15 447-448
see also Plant breeding; Plant physiology; Scientists—botanists

Botany Bay (Australia)
Flinders, Matthew **5** 490
Phillip, Arthur **12** 279-280

Botchan (novel)
Natsume, Soseki **11** 324-325

Both, Jan (1618?-1652), Dutch painter
Cuyp, Aelbert **4** 360-361

Both Your Houses (play)
Anderson, Maxwell **1** 219-220

BOTHA, LOUIS (1862-1919), South
African soldier and statesman **2** 434-436
Hertzog, James Barry Munnik
7 347-348
Plaatje, Solomon Tshekisho **12** 341-342
Roberts, Frederick Sleigh **13** 195-196
Smuts, Jan Christian **14** 309-310

BOTHA, PIETER WILLEM (born 1916),
prime minister (1978-1984) and first
executive state president of the Republic
of South Africa **2** 436-438

BOTHE, WALTHER (1891-1957), German
physicist **2** 438-439

Bothie of Tober-na-Vuolich, a Long Vacation Pastoral, The (narrative poem)
Clough, Arthur Hugh **4** 123-124

Bothwell, 4th Earl of (James Hepburn;
1536?-1578), Scottish Protestant nobleman
James I **8** 204-206
Mary, I **10** 308-309

Botkin, Sergei (1832-1889), Russian physician
Pavlov, Ivan Petrovich **12** 155-157

Boto, Eza
see Beti, Mongo

Botswana (formerly Bechuanaland; nation,
South Africa)
Khama, Seretse M. **8** 532-533
Malan, Daniel Francois **10** 163-164
Masire, Quett Ketumile **10** 318-319
Rhodes, Cecil John **13** 120-122

Botswana Democratic party
Chiepe, Gaositwe Keagakwa Tibe **3** 517

BOTTICELLI, SANDRO (1444-1510), Italian painter **2** 439-440
influence of
Burne-Jones, Edward Coley
3 145-146
Duncan, Isadora **5** 144-145
Modigliani, Amedeo **11** 72-73
Pater, Walter Horatio **12** 130-131
influenced by
Apelles **1** 257
Lippi, Filippo **9** 439
patron
Medici, Lorenzo de' **10** 450-451

Bou Kharouba, Mohammed Ben Brahim
see Boumediene, Houari

Boucher, Catherine (died 1831), wife of
William Blake
Blake, William **2** 316-318

BOUCHER, FRANÇOIS (1703-1770),
French painter **2** 440-442
influence of
Clouet, Jean and François **4** 122-123
David, Jacques Louis **4** 407-409
Fragonard, Jean Honoré **6** 38-39
Renoir, Pierre Auguste **13** 101-102
rococo
Chardin, Jean Baptiste Siméon
3 442-443
Watteau, Antoine **16** 143-144

Boucher, Nicolas (1671-1743), French decorator
Boucher, François **2** 440-442

BOUCICAULT, DION (1820-1890),
Irish-American playwright and actor
2 442-443
Belasco, David **2** 124-125
Jefferson, Joseph **8** 237

Boudeuse (ship)
Bougainville, Louis Antoine de
2 443-444

Boudin, Eugène (1825-1898), French
painter
Monet, Claude **11** 102-104

Boudouin, Pierre Antoine (1723-1769),
French painter
Boucher, François **2** 440-442

BOUGAINVILLE, LOUIS ANTOINE DE
(1729-1811), French soldier and explorer
2 443-444
Cook, James **4** 214-215

Bouguereau, Adolphe William
(1825-1905), French painter
Matisse, Henri **10** 336-337

Bouilhet, Louis (1822-1869), French poet
Flaubert, Gustave **5** 480-482

Boulanger, Georges Ernest J.M.
(1837-1891), French general
Clemenceau, Georges **4** 99-101

Boulanger, N.A. (pseudonym)
see Holbach, Baron d'

Boulanger, Nadia (1887-1979), French
conductor and teacher
Carter, Elliott Cook Jr. **3** 338-339
Copland, Aaron **4** 227-228
Harris, Roy **7** 175-176
Piston, Walter **12** 327-328
Thomson, Virgil **15** 202-203

Boulangists (French politics)
Barrès, Auguste Maurice **2** 20-21

Boule de suif (story)
Maupassant, Henri René Albert Guy de
10 347

Boulevard, Le (painting)
Severini, Gino **14** 122

BOULEZ, PIERRE (born 1925), French
composer, conductor, and teacher
2 444-445
influence of
Berio, Luciano **2** 194-195
Cage, John **3** 211-214
Stockhausen, Karlheinz **14** 460-461
influenced by
Messiaen, Olivier **10** 528-529
Stravinsky, Igor Fedorovich
14 502-506
students
Bennett, Richard Rodney **2** 172

Boulogne, Battle of (1545)
Henry VIII **7** 302-305

Boulton, Matthew (1728-1809), English
industrialist
Watt, James **16** 141-143

Boulton and Watt (co.)
Fulton, Robert **6** 151-152

BOUMEDIENE, HOUARI (born 1932),
Algerian revolutionary, military leader,
and president **2** 445-446
Abbas, Ferhat **1** 6-7
Ben Bella, Ahmed **2** 148-149

Bound East for Cardiff (play)
O'Neill, Eugene **11** 514-516

Bound to Rise (book)
Alger, Horatio **1** 153-154

Bounty (ship)
Bligh, William **2** 325-326

BOURASSA, JOSEPH-HENRI-NAPOLEON
(1868-1952), French-Canadian nationalist
and editor **2** 446-447
Laurier, Wilfrid **9** 232-234

BOURASSA, ROBERT (born 1933), premier
of the province of Quebec (1970-1976
and 1985-) **2** 447-449

Bourbon (dynasty)
French branch (ruled 1589-1795;
1814-30)
Charles X **3** 463-464
Henry IV **7** 293-295

Louis XIII **9** 529-531
Louis XIV **9** 531-533
Louis XV **9** 533-534
Louis XVI **9** 534-535
Louis XVIII **9** 535-536
see also France—1815-1830
Neopolitan branch (ruled 1735-1805;
1815-1860)
Charles III **3** 454-455
Ferdinand II **5** 415-416
Spanish branch (ruled 1700-1868;
1874-1931)
Alfonso XIII **1** 151
Charles III **3** 454-455
Charles IV **3** 456-457
Ferdinand VII **5** 418-420
Isabella II **8** 145-146
Philip V **12** 276-277

Bourbon, Charles de (1490-1527), constable of France
Francis I **6** 40-43

Bourbon-Condé, Louis Antoine Henri de
see Enghein, Duke of

Bourcicault, Dion
see Boucicault, Dion

BOURDELLE, EMILE-ANTOINE
(1861-1929), French sculptor **2** 449-450
Giacometti, Alberto **6** 294-295
Richier, Germaine **13** 145-146
Rodin, Auguste **13** 236-238

Bourdon, Sébastien (1616-1671), French
painter
Claude Lorrain **4** 89-90

BOURGEOIS, LÉON (1851-1925), French
premier 1895-1896 **2** 450-451

Bourgeois, Louis (circa 1510-1561), French
composer
Goudimel, Claude **6** 466

BOURGEOIS, LOUISE (born 1911), American sculptor **2** 451-452

Bourgeois gentilhomme, Le (play; Molière)
Lully, Jean Baptiste **10** 40-41
Molière **11** 86-88

BOURGEOYS, BLESSED MARGUERITE
(1620-1700), French educator and religious founder **2** 452-453

Bourgmestre de Stilmonde, Le (play)
Maeterlinck, Maurice **10** 125-126

Bourgogne, Jean de
see Mandeville, Sir John

BOURGUIBA, HABIB (born 1903),
Tunisian statesman **2** 453-455
Ben Bella, Ahmed **2** 148-149
Zine el Abidine Ben Ali **16** 518-520

Bourignon, Antoinette (1616-1680), Flemish mystic
Swammerdam, Jan **15** 48-49

Bourke, Capt. John Gregory (1846-1896),
American ethnologist
Crazy Horse **4** 303-304

BOURKE-WHITE, MARGARET
(1904-1971), American photographer and
photojournalist **2** 455-456
Caldwell, Erskine **3** 223-224

BOURNE, RANDOLPH SILLIMAN
(1886-1918), American pacifist and cultural critic **2** 456-457

Bourra bienfaisant, Le (play)
Goldoni, Carlo **6** 408-409

Bourse (Brussels)
Rodin, Auguste **13** 236-238

Boursiquot, Dionysius Lardner
see Boucicault, Dion

Bouteille à la mer, La (poem)
Vigny, Comte de **15** 494-495

Boutique Fantasque, La (ballet)
Respighi, Ottorino **13** 103-104

Boutmy, Émile (1835-1906), French educator
Halévy, Élie **7** 76

Bouton, Charles Marie (1781-1853),
French painter
Daguerre, Louis Jacques Mandé
4 365-366

BOUTROS-GHALI, BOUTROS (born
1922), Egyptian diplomat and sixth secretary-general of the United Nations
(1991-) **2** 457-458

Boutroux, Étienne Émile Marie
(1845-1921), French philosopher
Durkheim, Émile **5** 162-163

Bouts, Aelbrecht (1455/60-1549), Dutch
painter
Bouts, Dirk **2** 458-459

BOUTS, DIRK (1415/20-1475), Dutch
painter **2** 458-459
Bermejo, Bartolomé **2** 205
Christus, Petrus **4** 33-34
Eyck, Hubert and Jan van **5** 352-354
Massys, Quentin **10** 325-326
Schongauer, Martin **14** 26-28

Bouts, Dirk, the Younger (1448-1491),
Dutch painter
Bouts, Dirk **2** 458-459

Bouvard and Pécuchet (novel)
Flaubert, Gustave **5** 480-482

Bouvier, Jacqueline Lee
see Kennedy, Jacqueline

Bouvines, Battle of (1214)
Frederick II **6** 79
Innocent, III **8** 125-127
John **8** 274-275

Bovary, Emma and Charles (literary characters)
Flaubert, Gustave **5** 480-482

Boveri, Theodor (1862-1915), German
zoologist
Spemann, Hans **14** 368-369

Bow Street Runners (England)
Fielding, Henry **5** 442-444

BOWDITCH, HENRY INGERSOLL
(1808-1892), American physician
2 459-460

BOWDITCH, NATHANIEL (1773-1838),
American navigator and mathematician
2 460-461
Dunbar, William **5** 143-144

Bowdoin College (Maine)
Longfellow, Henry Wadsworth
9 499-500
MacMillan, Donald Baxter **10** 111-112
Russwurm, John Brown **13** 381-382

BOWDOIN, JAMES (1726-1790), American merchant and politician **2** 461-462

Bowen, Edward George (1911-1991), Australian radio astronomer
Watson-Watt, Robert Alexander
16 140-141

BOWEN, ELIZABETH (1899-1973), British
novelist **2** 462-463

Bowen, Marjorie (pseudonym of Gabrielle
Margaret Vere Long; 1888-1952), English
novelist
Greene, Graham **6** 523-524

BOWERS, CLAUDE GERNADE
(1878-1958), American journalist, historian, and diplomat **2** 463

Bowery (New York City)
Crane, Stephen **4** 293-295

Bowery, The (painting)
Marsh, Reginald **10** 276-277

Bowery Theater (New York City)
Christy, Edwin P. **4** 34-35

Bowes-Lyon, Lady Elizabeth
see Elizabeth, queen of George VI

Bowge of Court, The (satire)
Skelton, John **14** 268-269

Bowie, James (circa 1796-1836), American
soldier
Travis, William Barret **15** 292-293

BOWLES, SAMUEL (1826-1878), American
newspaper publisher **2** 464
Applegate, Jesse **1** 264-265
Dickinson, Emily **4** 541-543

Bowls (poem)
Moore, Marianne **11** 148-149

BOWMAN, ISAIAH (1878-1950), American geographer **2** 464-465

Bowood (Wiltshire, England)
Adam, Robert and James **1** 38-40

Boworadet rebellion (Thailand; 1933)
Phibun Songkhram, Luang **12** 264-265

Box Tunnel (near Bath, England)
Brunel, Isambard Kingdom **3** 69-70

BOXER, BARBARA (born 1940), U.S. Senator from California **2** 465-468

Boxer Rebellion (1898-1900)
Chang Chien **3** 429-430
Chang Chih-tung **3** 430-431
Jellicoe, John Rushworth **8** 242-243
Li Hung-Chang **9** 407-409

Tz'u-hsi **15** 375-376
Yüan Shih-k'ai **16** 480-481

Boxers
see Athletes, American—boxers

Boy bachelor
see Wolsey, Thomas

Boy Bitten by a Lizard (painting)
Caravaggio **3** 282-284

Boy in the House, A (novella)
de la Roche, Mazo Louise **4** 474-475

Boy Leading a Horse (painting)
Picasso, Pablo **12** 292-295

Boy Lighting a Candle (painting)
Greco **6** 511-514

Boy Scouts of America
Seton, Ernest Thompson **14** 119-120

Boy with an Arrow (painting)
Giorgione **6** 340-341

Boy with the Squirrel
Copley, John Singleton **4** 228-230

Boyacá, Battle of (1819)
Bolívar, Simón **2** 375-377
Santander, Franciso de Paula **13** 475

Boyars (Russia)
Ivan IV **8** 157-159-500

Boycott
see Labor unions

Boyd, Sir Alexander (15th century), Scottish
statesman
James III **8** 208-209

Boyd, Nancy
see Millay, Edna St. Vincent

Boyd, Lord (Robert Boyd; died circa 1470),
Scottish statesman
James III **8** 208-209

Boyd Orr, John
see Orr, John Boyd

Boyen, Hermann von (1771-1848), Prussian general
Meinecke, Friedrich **10** 460-461

BOYER, JEAN PIERRE (1776-1850), Haitian
president 1818-1845 **2** 468-469

Boyhood of Christ, The (narrative)
Wallace, Lewis **16** 74-75

Boyle, Richard (1st Earl of Cork;
1566-1643), Irish nobleman
Boyle, Robert **2** 469-471

Boyle, Richard (1694-1753)
see Burlington, 3d Earl of

BOYLE, ROBERT (1627-1691), British
chemist and physicist **2** 469-471
Guericke, Otto Von **7** 27-28
Hooke, Robert **7** 475
Locke, John **9** 478-480
van der Waals, Johannes Diderik
15 417-418)

Boyle family (literary characters)
O'Casey, Sean **11** 459-460

Boyle lectures (sermons)
Boyle, Robert **2** 469-471
Clarke, Samuel **4** 88

Boyle's law (physics)
Boyle, Robert **2** 469-471

BOYLSTON, ZABDIEL (1679-1766), American physician **2** 471
Mather, Cotton **10** 330-332

Boylston market (Boston, Massachusetts)
Bulfinch, Charles **3** 116-117

Boyne, Battle of the (1690)
James II **8** 207-208
William III **16** 295-296

Boys from Syracuse, The (musical)
Rodgers, Richard Charles **13** 234-236

Boys in the Back Room, The (book)
Wilson, Edmund **16** 318-319

Boy's King Arthur, The (book)
Lanier, Sidney **9** 199-200

Boy's Magic Horn, The (folk songs)
Arnim, Achim von **1** 308-309
Brentano, Clemens **2** 515-516

Boy's Town, A (book)
Howells, William Dean **7** 539-541

Boy's Will, A (poems)
Frost, Robert Lee **6** 130-133

Boythorn, Laurence (literary character)
Landor, Walter Savage **9** 186-187

Boz
see Dickens, Charles

BOZEMAN, JOHN M. (1837-1867), American pioneer **2** 471-472

Bozeman Trail (Colorado-Montana)
Bozeman, John M. **2** 471-472
Bridger, James **3** 2-3
Red Cloud **13** 70-71

Bozzie
see Boswell, James

Brabham Moor, Battle of (1408)
Henry IV **7** 292-293

Bracciolini, Poggio (1380-1459), Italian
humanist
Martin V **10** 287-288

Bracebridge Hall (novel)
Irving, Washington **8** 141-143

Bracegirdle, Anne (1663?-1748), English
actress
Congreve, William **4** 200-201

BRACKENRIDGE, HUGH HENRY
(1749-1816), American lawyer and writer
2 472-473
Freneau, Philip Morin **6** 99-100

Bracton, Henry de (died 1268), English
jurist and ecclesiastic
Blackstone, William **2** 310-311
Vinogradoff, Paul Gavrilovitch **15** 503

Bradamante (literary character)
Ariosto, Ludovico **1** 289-290
Boiardo, Matteo Maria **2** 369

BRADBURY, RAY (born 1920), American fantasy and science fiction writer **2** 473-474

Bradby, Lucy Barbara
   see Hammond, Lawrence and Barbara

BRADDOCK, EDWARD (1695-1755), British commander in North America **2** 474-475
   aides-de-camp
      Washington, George **16** 126-129
   French and Indian War
      Forbes, John **5** 507-508
      Lewis, Andrew **9** 376-377
   Ft. Duquesne
      Boone, Daniel **2** 397-398
      Franklin, Benjamin **6** 60-64
      Gist, Christopher **6** 352-353
      Morgan, Daniel **11** 160-161

Bradford, Andrew (1686-1742), American printer
   Bradford, William **2** 477

Bradford, Thomas (1745-1838), American journalist
   Bradford, William **2** 477

BRADFORD, WILLIAM (1590-1657), leader of Plymouth Colony **2** 475-476
   Brewster, William **2** 523-524

BRADFORD, WILLIAM (1663-1752), American printer **2** 476-477
   Zenger, John Peter **16** 497-498

BRADFORD, WILLIAM (1722-1791), American journalist **2** 477

BRADLAUGH, CHARLES (1833-1891), English freethinker and political agitator **2** 478
   Besant, Annie Wood **2** 233-234

Bradley, Andrew Cecil (1851-1935), English literary critic
   Bradley, Francis Herbert **2** 481-482

BRADLEY, ED (born 1941), African American broadcast journalist **2** 478-481

BRADLEY, FRANCIS HERBERT (1846-1924), English philosopher **2** 481-482
   Bosanquet, Bernard **2** 425-426
   Eliot, Thomas Stearns **5** 258-261
   Moore, George Edward **11** 146

BRADLEY, JAMES (1693-1762), English astronomer **2** 482-483
   Flamsteed, John **5** 477-478

BRADLEY, OMAR NELSON (1893-1981), American general **2** 483-484

BRADLEY, TOM (born 1917), first African American mayor of Los Angeles **2** 484-485

BRADMAN, SIR DONALD GEORGE (born 1908), Australian cricketer **2** 485-486

Bradomín, Marquis de (literary character)
   Valle Inclán, Ramón Maria del **15** 407-408

BRADSTREET, ANNE DUDLEY (circa 1612-1672), English-born American poet **2** 486-487

Bradstreet, Simon (1603-1697), English colonial governor of Massachusetts 1630-1636
   Bradstreet, Anne Dudley **2** 486-487

Brady, James (died 1878), American sheriff
   Billy the Kid **2** 277

BRADY, MATHEW B. (circa 1823-1896), American photographer **2** 487-488
   Daguerre, Louis Jacques Mandé **4** 365-366

Braganza dynasty (Portugal, Brazil; 15th century)
   Manuel I **10** 219-220
   Pedro I **12** 179-180
   Pedro II **12** 180-181

Bragg, Braxton (1817-1876), American general
   Forrest, Nathan Bedford **6** 13-14
   Lee, Robert Edward **9** 292-294

BRAGG, SIR WILLIAM HENRY (1862-1942), English physicist **2** 488-489

Bragg, William L. (1890-1971), English physicist
   Bragg, William Henry **2** 488-489

Bragg equation (physics)
   Bragg, William Henry **2** 488-489

Bragg spectrometer (physics)
   Compton, Arthur Holly **4** 186-188

Braggart Warrior, The (play)
   Plautus **12** 348-350

Braggioni (literary character)
   Porter, Katherine Anne **12** 406-407

BRAHE, TYCHO (1546-1601), Danish astronomer **2** 489-490
   Halley, Edmund **7** 88-89
   Heraclides of Pontus **7** 319-320
   Kepler, Johannes **8** 514-516

Brahmanism (religion)
   Kukai **9** 124-125
   Shankara **14** 150-151

Brahmaputra River (Tibet-India)
   Hedin, Sven Anders **7** 252-253

Brahmi script (India)
   Asoka **1** 341-342

Brahmins (Hindu caste)
   Buddha **3** 97-101
   Duff, Alexander **5** 126-127

Brahmo Samaj (Association of God)
   Roy, Ram Mohun **13** 18
   Rabindranath Tagore **12** 529-531
   Vivekananda **16** 4-5

BRAHMS, JOHANNES (1833-1897), German composer **2** 490-492
   influence of
      Dvořák, Antonin **5** 168-169
      Mahler, Gustav **10** 144-145
      Schoenberg, Arnold **14** 24-26

      Schumann, Robert Alexander **14** 41-43
      Strauss, Richard **14** 500-501
   influenced by
      Bach, Johann Sebastian **1** 416-419
      Beethoven, Ludwig van **2** 114-117
   settings of poems
      Heine, Heinrich **7** 259-260

Braid, James (1795?-1860), British surgeon
   Mesmer, Franz Anton **10** 526-527

Braidwood method (sign language)
   Gallaudet, Thomas Hopkins **6** 185

BRAILLE, LOUIS (1809-1852), French teacher and creator of braille system **2** 492-493

Brain (dog)
   Pavlov, Ivan Petrovich **12** 155-157
   Sherrington, Charles Scott **14** 187-189

Brain (human)
   Adrian, Edgar Douglas **1** 67-69
   Cushing, Harvey Williams **4** 353-354
   Penfield, Wilder Graves **12** 198-200

Brain (rat)
   Lashley, Karl Spencer **9** 214-215

Brain hemorrhage victims
   Curtis, Benjamin Robbins **4** 349
   Dewey, Melvil **4** 523-524
   Evatt, Herbert Vere **5** 341-343
   Flaubert, Gustave **5** 480-482
   Francis of Sales **6** 47
   Harding, Warren Gamaliel **7** 148-149
   Jenner, Edward **8** 245-246
   Schumpeter, Joseph Alois **14** 43-44

Brain trust (F. Roosevelt administration)
   Berle, Adolf Augustus Jr. **2** 199-200
   Byrnes, James Francis **3** 191-192
   Hoover, Herbert Clark **7** 483-485
   Tugwell, Rexford Guy **15** 336-339

Brainerd, David (1718-1747), American missionary
   Edwards, Jonathan **5** 220-222

Brake (automobile)
   Sloan, Alfred Pritchard Jr. **14** 274

Brakna Moors (Arab tribe)
   Caillié, Auguste René **3** 214-215

BRAMANTE, DONATO (1444-1514), Italian architect and painter **2** 493-494
   associates
      Leonardo da Vinci **9** 337-340
      Raphael **13** 40-42
   influence of
      Lescot, Pierre **9** 354
      Palladio, Andrea **12** 75-77, 267
      Sangallo family **13** 464-466
      Sanmicheli, Michele **13** 469-470
      Sansovino, Jacopo **13** 470-471
      Vignola, Giacomo da **15** 493-494
   influenced by
      Alberti, Leon Battista **1** 113-115
   patrons
      Sforza, Lodovico **14** 127-128
   St. Peter's (Rome)

Julius II **8** 384-386
Michelangelo Buonarroti **11** 2-5
Sangallo family **13** 464-466

Bramble, Matthew (literary character)
Smollett, Tobias George **14** 305-307

Brancacci, Felice (flourished 15th century), Italian merchant
Masaccio **10** 312-313

Brancacci, Rinaldo (died 1427), Italian cardinal
Donatello **5** 55-56
Michelozzo **11** 6-7

BRANCUSI, CONSTANTIN (1876-1957), Romanian sculptor in France **2** 494-496
associates
Modigliani, Amedeo **11** 72-73
compared to
Arp, Jean **1** 317-318
exhibitions (United States)
Steichen, Edward **14** 411-412
Stieglitz, Alfred **14** 451-452
influence of
Lipchitz, Jacques **9** 432-433
Moore, Henry **11** 146-148
Noguchi, Isamu **11** 416-418

Brand (play)
Ibsen, Henrik **8** 98-100

Brand von Egliswyl, Der (prose tale)
Wedekind, Frank **16** 166-167

BRANDEIS, LOUIS DEMBITZ (1856-1941), American jurist **2** 496-497
and Zionism
Silver, Abba Hillel **14** 232-233
Szold, Henrietta **15** 66-67
Wise, Stephen Samuel **16** 344-345
"Brandeis brief"
Kelley, F. **8** 483-484
fellow justices
Cardozo, Benjamin Nathan **3** 288-290
Stone, Harlan Fiske **14** 468-470
White, Edward Douglass **16** 230-231
influence of
Douglas, William Orville **5** 83-85
nomination to Court
Pound, Roscoe **12** 417-418
Taft, William Howard **15** 78-81
Walsh, Thomas James **16** 85-86
secretaries
Acheson, Dean Gooderham **1** 37-38

Brandeis University (Waltham, Massachusetts)
Bernstein, Leonard **2** 218-219
Krenek, Ernst **9** 98-99
Kroeber, Alfred Louis **9** 105-106
Lawrence, Jacob **9** 250-251
Marcuse, Herbert **10** 245-247
Radin, Paul **12** 538-539

Brandenburg (region, Prussia)
Charles XII **3** 464-466
Frederick William **6** 85-86
Sigismund **14** 220-221

Brandenburg Concertos (music)
Bach, Johann Sebastian **1** 416-419

Brandes, Georg Morris (G.M. Cohen; 1842-1927), Danish critic and historian
Bjørnson, Bjørnstjerne **2** 299-300
Ibsen, Henrik **8** 98-100
Jacobsen, Jens Peter **8** 193-194
Lagerlöf, Selma Ottiliana Lovisa **9** 163-164
Strindberg, August **14** 509-511

BRANDO, MARLON (born 1924), American actor **2** 497-499

BRANDT, WILLY (Herbert Frahm Brandt; 1913-1992), German statesman, chancellor of West Germany **2** 499-500
Bahr, Egon **1** 438-440
King, Martin Luther Jr. **9** 20-22

Brandy, mucho Brandy (play)
Ruíz, José Martínez **13** 358

Brandy Station, Battle of (1863)
Stuart, James Ewell Brown **14** 515-516

Brandywine, Battle of (1777)
Cornwallis, Charles **4** 241-243
Greene, Nathanael **6** 525-526
Howe, William **7** 538-539
Knox, Henry **9** 64
Pulaski, Casimir **12** 480-481

Branković, George (1367-1456), Serbian noble
Hunyadi, John **8** 51-52

Bransfield, Edward (circa 1795-1852), English naval officer
Palmer, Nathaniel Brown **12** 80-81

BRANT, JOSEPH (1742-1807), Mohawk Indian chief **2** 500-501

BRANT, MARY (1736-1796), Native American who guided the Iroquois to a British alliance **2** 501-503

BRANT, SEBASTIAN (1457-1521), German author **2** 503-504
Porter, Katherine Anne **12** 406-407

BRAQUE, GEORGES (1882-1967), French painter **2** 504-505
early Fauve
Matisse, Henri **10** 336-337
friends
Archipenko, Alexander **1** 280-281
Klee, Paul **9** 47-49
Picasso, Pablo **12** 292-295
Staël, Nicolas de **14** 392
Stein, Gertrude **14** 414-415
Ungaretti, Giuseppe **15** 389-390
influence of
Gris, Juan **7** 5-6
Pevsner, Antoine **12** 263-264
Sheeler, Charles **14** 170-171
influenced by
Cézanne, Paul **3** 400-402

Braque Triptych (painting)
Weyden, Rogier van der **16** 219-221

Brasa en el pico del cuervo, La (book)
Gallegos Freire, Rómulo **6** 185-186

Braschi, Gianangelo
see Pius VI

Brasidas (died 422 B.C.), Spartan commander
Cleon **4** 104-105
Thucydides **15** 211-212

Brasile
see Newfoundland

Brasília (city; Brazil)
Kubitschek de Oliveira, Juscelino **9** 113-115
Niemeyer Soares Filho, Oscar **11** 389-390

Brasserie des Martyrs (café, Paris)
Monet, Claude **11** 102-104

Brasserie Reichshoffen (painting)
Manet, Édouard **10** 193-194

Bratsk Station (poems)
Yevtushenko, Yevgeny Alexandrovich **16** 455-456

BRATTAIN, WALTER H. (1902-1987), American physicist and co-inventor of the transistor **2** 505-507
Bardeen, John **2** 1-3

Brattle Square Church (Boston)
Richardson, Henry Hobson **13** 139-141

Bratton, Henry de
see Bracton, Henry de

BRAUDEL, FERNAND (1902-1985), leading exponent of the *Annales* school of history **2** 507-508

Braulion (circa 585-circa 651), Spanish bishop
Isidore of Seville **8** 149-150

BRAUN, FERDINAND (1850-1918), German recipient of the Nobel Prize in Physics for work on wireless telegraphy **2** 508-509
Marconi, Guglielmo **10** 239-240

Braut von Korinth, Die (ballad)
Goethe, Johann Wolfgang von **6** 388-391

Braut von Messina, Die (play)
Schiller, Johann Christoph Friedrich von **14** 4-7

Brave African Huntress, The (book)
Tutuola, Amos **15** 361-362

Brave New World (novel)
Huxley, Aldous Leonard **8** 74-75

Brave New World Revisited (novel)
Huxley, Aldous Leonard **8** 74-75

Bravo, The (novel)
Cooper, James Fenimore **4** 220-223

Brawa (town, East Africa)
Cheng Ho **3** 500

Brazil, Federative Republic of (nation; South America)
Empire (1822-1889)
Andrada e Silva, José Bonifácio de **1** 221-222
Caxias, Duque de **3** 386

Feijó, Diogo Antônio **5** 405-406
Pedro I **12** 179-180
Pedro II **12** 180-181
republic founded (1889)
Deodoro da Fonseca, Manoel **4** 502
Nabuco de Araujo, Joaquim Aurelio
11 288-289
Pedro II **12** 180-181
Peixoto, Floriano **12** 188-189
slavery in
Canot, Theodore **3** 262-263
Nabuco de Araujo, Joaquim Aurelio
11 288-289
1960s
Castelo Branco, Humberto
3 359-360
Goulart, João **6** 467-469
Kubitschek de Oliveira, Juscelino
9 113-115
1970s
Geisel, Ernesto **6** 253-255
and Argentina
Pedro II **12** 180-181
Rio Branco, Barão do **13** 177
Rivadavia, Bernardino **13** 182-183
and Peru
Leguía y Salcedo, Augusto Bernardi-
no **9** 305-306
and Uruguay
Lavalleja, Juan Antonio **9** 238-239
Communist party
Prestes, Luiz Carlos **12** 442-444
Dutch in
John Maurice of Nassau **8** 281-282
economic development
Ludwig, Daniel Keith **10** 29-31
economic reform
Collor de Mello, Fernando
4 170-172
exploration
Cabral, Pedro Álvares **3** 203-204
Dias de Novais, Bartolomeu
4 533-534
Magellan, Ferdinand **10** 126-127
Manuel I **10** 219-220
Rondon, Candido Mariano da Silva
13 271
Vespucci, Amerigo **15** 476-478
French in
Sá, Mem de **13** 395
historians of
Varnhagen, Francisco Adolfo de
15 437-438
literacy programs
Freire, Paulo **6** 95-96
military rule ended (1985)
Figueiredo, João Batista de Oliveira
5 445-446
missionaries in
Anchieta, José de **1** 210-211
Vieira, Antônio **15** 492
Paraguayan war
see Triple Alliance, War of the
Portuguese rule
Pombal, Marquês de **12** 386-387
Sá, Mem de **13** 395

Sousa, Martim Afonso de
14 354-355
Tiradentes **15** 237
Vargas regimes
Aranha, Osvaldo **1** 272-273
Vargas, Getulio Dornelles
15 433-434
see also entries beginning Brazilian

Brazilian Antislavery Society
Nabuco de Araujo, Joaquim Aurelio
11 288-289

Brazilian art and architecture
Aleijadinho, O **1** 125-126
Le Corbusier **9** 274-275
Niemeyer Soares Filho, Oscar
11 389-390
Portinari, Cândido **12** 407-408

Brazilian immigration service (Paris)
Rio Branco, Barão do **13** 177

Brazilian literature
Amado, Jorge **1** 189-190
Castro Alves, Antônio de **3** 364-365
Cunha, Euclides Rodrigues Pimenta da
4 336-337
Freyre, Gilberto **6** 106-107
Machado de Assis, Joaquim Maria
10 91-92

Brazilian music
Villa-Lobos, Heitor **15** 496-497

**BRAZZA, PIERRE PAUL FRANÇOIS
CAMILLE SAVORGNAN DE** (1852-1905),
Italian-born French explorer **2** 509-510

Brazzaville Conferences
1944
Eboué, Adolphe Felix Sylvestre
5 194
1960
Houphouët-Boigny, Felix **7** 519-520
Youlou, Fulbert **16** 466-467

Bread and Wine (elegy)
Hölderlin, Johann Christian Friedrich
7 451-452

Bread and Wine (novel)
Silone, Ignazio **14** 231-232

"Bread or Club" policy (Mexico)
Díaz, José de la Cruz Porfirio **4** 534-536

Breadwinner's Institute (Boston)
Parsons, Frank **12** 121-122

Breakers, The (Newport, Rhode Island)
Hunt, Richard Morris **8** 44

Breakfast cereals
Post, Charles William **12** 408-409

Breakfast Room (painting)
Bonnard, Pierre **2** 395-396

Breaking Heart, The (symphony)
Fry, William Henry **6** 136-137

Breaking New Ground (autobiography)
Pinchot, Gifford **12** 308-309

Breakspear, Nicholas
see Adrian IV, pope

Breakthrough in Burma (book)
Ba Maw **1** 480-481

BREASTED, JAMES HENRY (1865-1935),
American Egyptologist and archeologist
2 510-511

Breastplate of Justice (Jewish law)
see Shulhan Aruk

Breasts of Tiresias, The (play)
Apollinaire, Guillaume **1** 260

Breathless (film)
Truffaut, François **15** 311-313

BRÉBEUF, JEAN DE (1593-1649), French
Jesuit missionary **2** 511-512

BRECHT, BERTOLT (1898-1956), German
playwright **2** 512-514
Frisch, Max **6** 118-119
Gay, John **6** 243-244
Grimmelshausen, Hans Jakob Christof-
fel von **7** 4-5
Osborne, John **12** 16-17
Stravinsky, Igor Fedorovich **14** 502-506
Weill, Kurt **16** 174-175

Brecht, Mrs. Bertolt
see Weigel, Helene

Breckinridge, John Cabell (1821-1875),
American statesman
Buchanan, James **3** 89-90
Douglas, Stephen Arnold **5** 80-82

Bred in the Bone (stories)
Page, Thomas Nelson **12** 59-60

Breda, Battles of (1590; 1625)
Maurice of Nassau **10** 348-349

Breda, Declaration of (1660)
Charles II **3** 452-454

Breda, Treaty of (1667)
Witt, Johan de **16** 348-349

Brède, Baron de la
see Montesquieu, Baron de

Breguet, Louis (1747-1823), French instrument maker
Brunel, Isambard Kingdom **3** 69-70

Breitenfeld, Battle of (1631)
Gustavus II **7** 43-45

Bremen (city; Germany)
Ebert, Friedrich **5** 193-194

Bremsstrahlung process (physics)
Cherenkov, Pavel Alekseevich
3 502-503

Brémule, Battle of (1119)
Henry I **7** 286-287

BRENNAN, WILLIAM J., JR. (born 1906),
United States Supreme Court justice
2 514-515

Brent of Bin Bin
see Franklin, Miles

Brentano, Bettina
see Arnim, Bettina von

BRENTANO, CLEMENS (1778-1842), German poet and novelist **2** 515-516
Arnim, Achim von **1** 308-309

Grimm Brothers **4** 551
Hoffmann, Ernst Theodor Amadeus
   7 439-440
Savigny, Friedrich Karl von **13** 502-503
BRENTANO, FRANZ CLEMENS
(1838-1917), German philosopher
2 516-517
   Husserl, Edmund **8** 67-68
   Meinong, Alexius Ritter von Hand-
      schuchsheim **10** 461-462
Brenzoni tomb (San Fermo, Verona)
   Pisanello **12** 323-324
Br'er Rabbit (literary character)
   Harris, Joel Chandler **7** 173-174
Brera Academy of Fine Arts (Milan)
   Manzù, Giacomo **10** 224-225
   Marini, Marino **10** 260-262
Brereton, John (1572-after 1619), English
author
   Ford, Paul Leicester **6** 9-10
Brescia (city; Italy)
   Henry VII **7** 299-300
BRESHKOVSKY, CATHERINE (1844-1934),
Russian revolutionary **2** 517-519
Breslau (city; Poland)
   Rottmayr, Johann Michael **13** 321
Breslau, University of
   Gierke, Otto von **6** 311-312
   Mommsen, Theodor **11** 94-95
   Schrödinger, Erwin **14** 31-33
   Sombart, Werner **14** 332-333
Bresslau, Helene
   see Schweitzer, Helene Bresslau
Brest-Litovsk, Treaty of (1918)
   Kollontai, Aleksandra Mikhailovna **9** 79
   Ludendorff, Erich Friedrich Wilhelm
      10 27-28
   Trotsky, Leon **15** 302-305
Brethren of the Common Life (Netherlands
religious society)
   Erasmus, Desiderius **5** 298-300
   Groote, Gerard **7** 12-13
   Kempis, Thomas à **8** 493-494
Brétigny, Treaty of (1360)
   Charles V **3** 459-460
   Chaucer, Geoffrey **3** 482-485
   Edward III **5** 211-212
   John II **8** 275-276
   Langland, William **9** 194-195
BRETON, ANDRÉ (1896-1966), French
author **2** 519-520
   and surrealism
      Aragon, Louis **1** 271-272
      Chirico, Giorgio de **4** 4
      Dali, Salvador **4** 376-377
      Picasso, Pablo **12** 292-295
   influence of
      Buñuel, Luis **3** 127-128
      Cage, John **3** 211-214
      Ernst, Max **5** 311-312
      Gorky, Arshile **6** 458
      Tanguy, Yves **15** 101

influenced by
      Duchamp, Marcel **5** 122-123
   quoted
      Chagall, Marc **3** 406-407
   Rayograph portrait
      Ray, Man **13** 59-60
Bretón, Tomás (1850-1923), Spanish com-
poser
   Zorrilla de San Martin, Juan **16** 530-531
Breton contes and fabliaux (literature)
   Marie de France **10** 259
Breton romances (literature)
   Boiardo, Matteo Maria **2** 369
Bretton, Henry de
   see Bracton, Henry de
Bretton Woods Conference (1944)
   Hansen, Alvin **7** 131-132
   Robertson, Dennis Holme **13** 196
Breuer, Joseph (1842-1925), Austrian
physician
   Freud, Sigmund **6** 103-106
BREUER, MARCEL (1902-1981),
Hungarian-born American architect
2 520-521
   Aalto, Hugo Alvar Henrik **1** 1-2
   Gropius, Walter **7** 13-14
   Johnson, Philip **8** 313-314
   Nervi, Pier Luigi **11** 346-348
Breughel
   see Bruegel
BREUIL, HENRI EDOUARD PROSPER
(1877-1961), French archeologist
2 521-522
Breviarium Romanum (religious book)
   Pius V **12** 332-333
Brevis (musical note)
   Franco of Cologne **6** 52
Brewsie and Willie (book)
   Stein, Gertrude **14** 414-415
BREWSTER, KINGMAN, JR. (1919-1988),
president of Yale University (1963-1977)
2 522-523
BREWSTER, WILLIAM (circa 1566-1644),
English-born Pilgrim leader **2** 523-524
   Bradford, William **2** 475-476
   Winslow, Edward **16** 338-339
BREYER, STEPHEN (born 1938), U.S.
Supreme Court justice **2** 524-527
Brézé tomb (Rouen cathedral)
   Goujon, Jean **6** 466-467
BREZHNEV, LEONID ILICH (1906-1982),
general secretary of the Communist party
of the Union of Soviet Socialist Republics
(1964-1982) and president of the Union
of Soviet Socialist Republics (1977-1982)
2 527-528
   Chernenko, Konstantin Ustinovich
      3 503-504
   Kosygin, Aleksei Nikolaevich **9** 90-91
Brhatkatha (play)
   Harsha **7** 181-182

BRIAND, ARISTIDE (1862-1932), French
statesman **2** 528-529
   Bourgeois, Léon **2** 450-451
   Coolidge, John Calvin **4** 217-219
   Stresemann, Gustav **14** 508-509
BRICE, FANNY (1891-1951), vaudeville,
Broadway, film, and radio singer and
comedienne **3** 1-2
   Ziegfeld, Florenz **16** 516-517
Brices Cross Roads, Battle of (1864)
   Forrest, Nathan Bedford **6** 13-14
Brick House Works (pottery factory)
   Wedgwood, Josiah **16** 168-169
Brick Market (Newport, Rhode Island)
   Harrison, Peter **7** 179-180
Bridal Canopy, The (novel)
   Agnon, Shmuel Yoseph **1** 85-86
Bride, The (sculpture)
   Moore, Henry **11** 146-148
Bride Comes to Yellow Sky, The (stories)
   Crane, Stephen **4** 293-295
Bride Elect, The (opera)
   Sousa, John Philip **14** 353-354
Bride of Abydos, The (epic tale)
   Byron, George Gordon Noel **3** 193-194
Bride of Lammermoor, The (novel)
   Scott, Walter **14** 68-70
**Bride Stripped Bare by Her Bachelors,
Even, The** (painting on glass)
   Duchamp, Marcel **5** 122-123
Bride Wore Black, The (film)
   Truffaut, François **15** 311-313
Brideshead Revisited (novel)
   Waugh, Evelyn Arthur St. John
      16 145-147
Bridge, Horatio (1806-1893), American
author
   Hawthorne, Nathaniel **7** 212-215
Bridge (structure)
   Brunel, Isambard Kingdom **3** 69-70
   Eads, James Buchanan **5** 175-176
   Eiffel, Alexandre Gustave **5** 227-228
   Roebling, John Augustus **13** 241-242
Bridge, The (painting)
   Kline, Franz **9** 55
Bridge, The (poem)
   Crane, Hart **4** 291-293
   Longfellow, Henry Wadsworth
      9 499-500
Bridge at Narni (painting)
   Corot, Jean Baptiste Camille **4** 247-249
Bridge of Heaven (painting)
   Sesshu, Toya **14** 116-117
Bridge of San Luis Rey, The (novel)
   Wilder, Thornton Niven **16** 276-277
BRIDGER, JAMES (1804-1881), American
fur trader and scout **3** 2-3
   Bozeman, John M. **2** 471-472
   Fitzpatrick, Thomas **5** 474-475
   Washakie **16** 123-125

BRIDGES, HARRY A.R. (1901-1990), radical American labor leader **3** 3-5

Bridgman, Laura Dewey (1829-1889), sight and hearing impaired American
Howe, Samuel Gridley **7** 537

BRIDGMAN, PERCY WILLIAMS (1882-1961), American physicist **3** 5-6

Brief Account of the Destruction of the Indies (book)
Las Casas, Bartolomé de **9** 211-212

Brief des Lord Chandos (book)
Hofmannsthal, Hugo von **7** 443-444

Brief Encounter (film)
Coward, Noel **4** 279-280

Brief Exposition of ... Geometry ... (treatise)
Lobachevskii, Nikolai Ivanovich **9** 472-474

Brief History of Epidemic and Pestilential Diseases, A (book)
Webster, Noah **16** 164-166

Briefe antiquarischen Inhalts (book)
Lessing, Gotthold Ephraim **9** 357-359

Briefe aus dem Gefängnis (essays)
Toller, Ernst **15** 261

Briefe, die neueste Literatur betreffend (book)
Lessing, Gotthold Ephraim **9** 357-359

Briggs, Henry (1556-1631), English mathematician
Napier, John **11** 306

Bright, Charles Tilson (1832-1888), English telegraph engineer
Field, Cyrus West **5** 438-439

Bright Islands, The (tales)
Colum, Padraic **4** 174-175

BRIGHT, JOHN (1811-1889), English politician **3** 6-7
Cobden, Richard **4** 127-128
Disraeli, Benjamin **5** 27-29

BRIGHT, RICHARD (1789-1858), English physician **3** 7-8
Addison, Thomas **1** 58-59

BRIGHTMAN, EDGAR SHEFFIELD (1884-1953), philosopher of religion and exponent of American Personalism **3** 8-9

Brighton (city, England)
Nash, John **11** 316

Brighton Rock (novel)
Greene, Graham **6** 523-524

Bright's disease (medicine)
Bright, Richard **3** 7-8

Brill, Paul (1554-1626), Flemish painter
Claude Lorrain **4** 89-90

Brindisi, Peace of (40 B.C.)
Antony, Mark **1** 253-254

Brindle, Reginald Smith (born 1917), English critic and composer
Nono, Luigi **11** 420-421

Bringing in the Sheaves (hymn)
Ives, Charles Edward **8** 159-160

Brinkley, David
see Huntley and Brinkley

BRISBANE, ALBERT (1809-1890), American social theorist **3** 9
Greeley, Horace **6** 515-517

Brisbane, Arthur (1864-1936), American newspaper editor
Hearst, William Randolph **7** 243-244

Brise marine (poem)
Mallarmé, Stéphane **10** 172-173

Bristol (city, England)
Butler, Joseph **3** 180-181

Bristol, University of (England)
Broad, Charlie Dunbar **3** 12
Morgan, Conway Lloyd **11** 159-160

BRISTOW, BENJAMIN HELM (1832-1896), American lawyer and Federal official **3** 9-10
Harlan, John Marshall **7** 156-157

Britain, Battle of (1940)
Churchill, Winston Leonard Spencer **4** 51-53)
Hitler, Adolf **7** 417-420
Kesselring, Albert Field Marshal **8** 522-523
Watson-Watt, Robert Alexander **16** 140-141

Britain, history of
see England

Britannicus (41-55), Roman noble
Nero Claudius Caesar **11** 342-344
Seneca the Younger, Lucius Annaeus **14** 103-105
Titus Flavius Vespasianus **15** 247-248

Britannicus (play)
Racine, Jean Baptiste **12** 532-535

British Atomic Energy Authority
Cockcroft, John Douglas **4** 131-132
Thomson, George Paget **15** 198-199

British Broadcasting Corp.
Pinter, Harold **12** 317-318
Thomas, Dylan Marlais **15** 188-190

British Campaigns in France and Flanders, The (book)
Doyle, Arthur Conan **5** 91-92

British Church Missionary Society (Buganda)
Mutesa I **11** 277

British Columbia (province, Canada)
Boas, Franz **2** 349-351
Macdonald, John Alexander **10** 85-87

British Columbia, University of (Vancouver)
Museum of Anthropology
Erickson, Arthur Charles **5** 304-306

British Committee on Atomic Energy
Thomson, George Paget **15** 198-199

British Commonwealth of Nations (established 1931)
Africa (Central Africa)
Smith, Ian Douglas **14** 291-293
Africa (East Africa)
Kenyatta, Jomo **8** 512-514
Mutesa II **11** 277-278
Nyerere, Julius Kamberage **11** 447-449
Obote, Apolo Milton **11** 457
Odinga, Ajuma Jaramogi Oginga **11** 471-473
Africa (South Africa)
Hertzog, James Barry Munnik **7** 347-348
Khama, Seretse M. **8** 532-533
Malan, Daniel Francois **10** 163-164
Verwoerd, Hendrik Frensch **15** 472-473
Africa (West Africa)
Jawara, Dauda Kairaba **8** 227-228
Margai, Milton Augustus Striery **10** 248-249
Nkrumah, Kwame **11** 408-410
Olympio, Sylvanus E. **11** 506-507
Australia
Menzies, Robert Gordon **10** 510-511
Burma
Nu, U **11** 439-441
Canada
King, William Lyon Mackenzie **9** 25-26
Lyons, Joseph Aloysius **10** 69-70
constitutional development
Baldwin, Robert **1** 466-468
Balfour, Arthur James **1** 469-470
Elgin, 8th Earl of **5** 248-249
Harrington, James **7** 166-167
Guyana
Ramphal, Shridath Surendranath **13** 19-20
India
Attlee, Clement Richard **1** 361-362
Menon, Vengalil Krishnan Krishna **10** 507-509
Pandit, Vijaya Lakshmi **12** 83-84
Prasad, Rajendra **12** 433
Middle East
Glubb, John Bagot **6** 371-372
monarchy and
Elizabeth II **5** 266-269
George VI **6** 275
Pakistan
Attlee, Clement Richard **1** 361-362
Westminster Statute (1931)
Balfour, Arthur James **1** 469-470
Hertzog, James Barry Munnik **7** 347-348
see also England and under member nations

British Commonwealth Relations (publication)
Toynbee, Arnold Joseph **15** 283-284

British East Africa (established 1888)
Salisbury, 3d Marquess of **13** 448-449

British East India Co.
see East India Co. (British)

British Economics Association
see Royal Economics Society

British Empire and the United States, The
(book)
Dunning, William Archibald **5** 148-149

British Empire, First (16th century-American Revolution)
American Revolution
see American Revolution
British North America
Amherst, Jeffery **1** 200-201
Carleton, Guy **3** 300-301
see also Canada; United States
chartered companies
see East India Co. (British); Hudson's Bay Co.; Massachusetts Bay Co.; Muscovy Co.; Virginia Co.
colonial policy
Calvert, George **3** 238-239
Pitt, William the Elder **12** 328-329
Rockingham, 2d Marquess of **13** 230-231
East Indies conflict
Coen, Jan Pieterszoon **4** 133
India
Clive, Robert **4** 119-120
Cornwallis, Charles **4** 241-243
Dupleix **5** 153
Haidar Ali **7** 65-66
Hastings, Warren **7** 195-196
see also England; Explorers, English; French and Indian War, King George's War; King William's War; Lord Dunmore's War; Pontiac's Conspiracy

British Empire, Second (American Revolution-1931)
administration
George III **6** 270-272
Salisbury, 3d Marquess of **13** 448-449
Victoria **15** 485-487
Africa (East Africa)
Livingstone, David **9** 463-465
Mwanga **11** 282-283
Africa (Egypt and Sudan)
Cromer, 1st Earl of **4** 317
Fuad I **6** 139
Gordon, Charles George **6** 448-449
Ismail Pasha **8** 150-151
Kitchener, Horatio Herbert **9** 45-46
Tewfik Pasha **15** 157-158
Victoria **15** 485-487
Africa (South Africa)
Frere, Henry Bartle Edward **6** 100-101
Hertzog, James Barry Munnik **7** 347-348
Jameson, Leander Starr **8** 218
Kitchener, Horatio Herbert **9** 45-46
Kruger, Stephanus Johannes Paulus **9** 108-109
Lobengula **9** 474-475

Milner, Alfred **11** 38-39
Moshweshwe **11** 203-205
Pretorius, Andries **12** 444-445
Rhodes, Cecil John **13** 120-122
Roberts, Frederick Sleigh **13** 195-196
Africa (West Africa)
Goldie, George Dashwood Taubman **6** 404
Johnston, Henry Hamilton **8** 322-323
Lugard, Frederick John Dealtry **10** 31-32
Maclean, George **10** 108-109
Australia and New Zealand
Flinders, Matthew **5** 490
Forrest, John **6** 12-13
Hobson, William **7** 426
Macquarie, Lachlan **10** 115-116
Sturt, Charles **15** 2-3
Vogel, Julius **16** 9-10
Wakefield, Edward Gibbon **16** 48-49
Burma
Dalhousie, 1st Marquess of **4** 375-376
Mindon Min **11** 47
Salisbury, 3d Marquess of **13** 448-449
Canada
Durham, 1st Earl of **5** 161-162
Fleming, Sandford **5** 485-486
Gourlay, Robert **6** 474
Howe, Joseph **7** 534-535
Elgin, 8th Earl of **5** 248-249
Macdonald, John Alexander **10** 85-87
Mackenzie, William Lyon **10** 104-106
Metcalfe, Charles Theophilus **10** 531-532
Selkirk, 5th Earl of **14** 96
Sydenham, Thomas **15** 59-60
East Indies
Raffles, Thomas Stamford **13** 1-2
India
Chelmsford, Frederic John Napier Thesiger **3** 497
Dalhousie, 1st Marquess of **4** 375-376
Duff, Alexander **5** 126-127
Frere, Henry Bartle Edward **6** 100-101
Kitchener, Horatio Herbert **9** 45-46
Metcalfe, Charles Theophilus **10** 531-532
Ranjit Singh **13** 32-33
Roberts, Frederick Sleigh **13** 195-196
Salisbury, 3d Marquess of **13** 448-449
Tipu Sultan **15** 236
Wellesley, Richard Colley **16** 192-193
Wellington, 1st Duke of **16** 193-195
Singapore
Raffles, Thomas Stamford **13** 1-2

West Indies
Metcalfe, Charles Theophilus **10** 531-532
see also British East Africa Co.; British South Africa Co.; England; and individual nations

British empiricism
see Empiricism

British Honduras (colony, Central America)
Carrera, José Rafael **3** 324-325

British India
see India (British rule)

British Lying-in Hospital (England)
Hunter, William **8** 48-49

British Magazine (periodical)
Newman, John Henry **11** 365-367
Smollett, Tobias George **14** 305-307

British Medical Association Building (London)
Epstein, Jacob **5** 295-296

British Museum (London)
Leakey, Louis Seymour Bazett **9** 262
Owen, Richard **12** 39
Wilkins, George Hubert **16**

British National Gallery
Clark, Kenneth M. **4** 79-80

British North America (federation)
Brown, George **3** 35-36
Cartier, George-Étienne **3** 342-343
Howe, Joseph **7** 534-535
Macdonald, John Alexander **10** 85-87
Sydenham, Thomas **15** 59-60
see also British Empire, First; British Empire, Second

British North Borneo (former British colony)
Macapagal, Diosdado P. **10** 74-76
see also Indonesia

British Northwest Co.
Astor, John Jacob **1** 351-352

British Prison-Ship, The (poem)
Freneau, Philip Morin **6** 99-100

British Psychoanalytic Society
Jones, Ernest Alfred **8** 331-332

British Royal Society
see Royal Society (Britain)

British South Africa (established 1889)
Jameson, Leander Starr **8** 218
Lobengula **9** 474-475
Rhodes, Cecil John **13** 120-122
Salisbury, 3d Marquess of **13** 448-449

British West Charterland Co.
Lugard, Frederick John Dealtry **10** 31-32

British White Paper (1939)
Ben-Gurion, David **2** 160-161
Meir, Golda **10** 462-463

Brittanicus (Claudius Tiberius Germanicus; 41-55), son of Tiberius Claudius Germanicus, Claudius I
Claudius Germanicus, Tiberius **4** 91-92

Brittany (province, France)
John **8** 274-275

BRITTEN, BENJAMIN (1913-1976), English
composer **3** 10-11
Forster, Edward Morgan **6** 14-16
Ives, Charles Edward **8** 159-160
Stravinsky, Igor Fedorovich **14** 502-506

Brixen Cathedral (now Bressanone, Italy)
Troger, Paul **15** 300

Brizna de hierba en el viento, La (book)
Gallegos Freire, Rómulo **6** 185-186

BROAD, CHARLIE DUNBAR (1887-1971),
English philosopher **3** 12

Broad Churchmen (Church of England)
Hobart, John Henry **7** 420-421
see also England, Church of

Broadacre City (plan; F.L. Wright)
Le Corbusier **9** 274-275
Wright, Frank Lloyd **16** 398-401

Broadcasting
Paley, William S. **12** 72-75
Thomson, Kenneth **15** 201-202

Broadway Journal (magazine)
Poe, Edgar Allan **12** 363-365

Broadway Magazine
Dreiser, Herman Theodore **5** 98-100

Brobdingnag (literary locale)
Swift, Jonathan **15** 51-54

Broca, Paul (1824-1880), French surgeon
Lashley, Karl Spencer **9** 214-215

BROCK, SIR ISAAC (1769-1812), British
general **3** 12-13
Hull, William **8** 29-30
Robinson, John Beverley **13** 210
Tecumseh **15** 133

Brockes, Berthold Heinrich (1680-1747),
German poet
Handel, George Frederick **7** 116-119

Brod, Max (1884-1968), German writer
Kafka, Franz **8** 403-406

Brodrick, St. John (1856-1952), English
statesman
Younghusband, Francis Edward **16** 477

BRODSKY, JOSEPH (Iosif Alexandrovich
Brodsky, 1940-1996), Russian-born
Nobel Prize winner and fifth United
States poet laureate **3** 13-15

Broederbond, Die (established 1919)
Verwoerd, Hendrik Frensch **15** 472-473

Brogan, Sir Denis (1900-1974), British
political scientist
Schlesinger, Arthur Meier **14** 13

Broglie, Louis de
see de Broglie, Louis

Brokaw, Clare Boothe
see Luce, Clare Boothe

Broken Blossoms (film)
Griffith, David Wark **6** 544-545

Broken Hand
see Fitzpatrick, Thomas

Broken Heart, The (play)
Ford, John **6** 7-8

Broken Heart, The (poems)
Aragon, Louis **1** 271-272

Broken Hill Proprietary Co. Ltd. (Australia)
Lewis, Essington **9** 382-384

Broken Journey, A. (novel)
Callaghan, Edward Morley **3** 229-230

Broken Jug, The (play)
Kleist, Heinrich von **9** 52-53

Broken Souls (novel)
Kazantzakis, Nikos **8** 466-468

Broken Straws (play)
Verne, Jules **15** 467-469

Broken Tower, The (poem)
Crane, Hart **4** 291-293

Broken Wing, The, (poem)
Naidu, Sarojini **11** 294-295

Broker of Bogota, The (play)
Bird, Robert Montgomery **2** 281-282
Forrest, Edwin **6** 11-12

Bromine (element—chemistry)
Fizeau, Hippolyte Armand Louis **5** 475

Brömsebro, Treaty of (1645)
Oxenstierna, Axel Gustafsson **12** 44-45

Bronco Buster, The (sculpture)
Rembrandt Harmensz van Rijn
13 91-95

Bronn, Heinrich Georg (1800-1862), German zoologist and paleontologist
Agassiz, Jean Louis Rodolphe **1** 76-78

Bronsted, Johannes Nicolaus (1897-1947),
Danish chemist
Hevesy, George Charles de **7** 371

Bronstein, Lev Davidovich
see Trotsky, Leon

Brontë, Anne (1820-1849), English novelist
Brontë, Charlotte **3** 17-18
Brontë, Emily **3** 18-19

BRONTË, CHARLOTTE (1816-1855), Eng-
lish novelist **3** 17-18
Brontë, Emily **3** 18-19
Gaskell, Elizabeth **6** 231-232

Bronte, Duke of
see Nelson, Viscount

BRONTË, EMILY (1818-1848), English novelist **3** 18-19
Brontë, Charlotte **3** 17-18

Brontë, Patrick Branwell (1817-1848), English painter
Brontë, Emily **3** 18-19

Bronze Age (3000-1200 B.C.)
Breuil, Henri Edouard Prosper
2 521-522
Evans, Arthur John **5** 335-336

Bronze Horseman, The (poem)
Pushkin, Aleksandr Sergeevich
12 489-491

BRONZINO (1503-1572), Italian painter
3 19
Clouet, Jean and François **4** 122-123
Pontormo **12** 394-395

Brook Farm (West Roxbury, Massachusetts)
members
Curtis, George William **4** 349-350
Dana, Charles Anderson **4** 384-385
Hecker, Isaac Thomas **7** 250-251
philosophy
Brisbane, Albert **3** 9
Ripley, George **13** 179-180
visitors
Brownson, Orestes Augustus
3 57-58
Greeley, Horace **6** 515-517
Hawthorne, Nathaniel **7** 212-215

BROOK, PETER (born 1925),
world-renowned theater director **3** 19-21

Brooke, Sir Alan Francis (1883-1963),
British general
Alexander of Tunis, 1st Earl **1** 135-136

Brooke, Sir Charles Anthony Johnson
see Brooke, Capt. James

Brooke, Dorothea (literary character)
Eliot, George **5** 254-256

Brooke, 1st Baron
see Greville, Sir Fulke

Brooke, Capt. James (1829-1917), British
governor in Borneo
Brooke, James **3** 21-22

BROOKE, SIR JAMES (1803-1868), British
governor in Borneo **3** 21-22

Brooke, John Rutter (1838-1926), American general, governor of Puerto Rico
1898 and of Cuba 1899
Muñoz Rivera, Luís **11** 250

BROOKE, RUPERT (1887-1915), English
poet **3** 22-23

Brookhaven National Laboratory (Long
Island, New York State)
Rabi, Isidor Isaac **12** 526-527

Brookline Town Hall (Massachusetts)
Richardson, Henry Hobson **13** 139-141

Brooklyn Bridge (New York City)
Crane, Hart **4** 291-293
Roebling, John Augustus **13** 241-242
Roebling, Washington Augustus **13** 243
Stella, Joseph **14** 422

Brooklyn College (New York City)
Rothko, Mark **13** 320-321

Brooklyn Dodgers (baseball team)
Rickey, Wesley Branch **13** 153-155
Robinson, Jack Roosevelt **13** 207-208

Brooklyn Eagle (newspaper)
Whitman, Walt **16** 249-251

BROOKNER, ANITA (born 1928), British art historian and novelist **3** 23-24

Brooks, Cleanth (1906-1994), American critic and scholar
Tate, Allen **15** 116
Warren, Robert Penn **16** 121-122

BROOKS, GWENDOLYN (born 1917), first African American author to receive the Pulitzer Prize for Literature **3** 24-26

BROOKS, PHILLIPS (1835-1893), American Episcopalian bishop **3** 26
Schindler, Solomon **14** 7-8

Brooks, Preston Smith (1819-1857), American politician
Sumner, Charles **15** 30-31

Brooks, Van Wyck (1886-1963), American author
Bourne, Randolph Silliman **2** 456-457

Broome, William (1689-1745), English scholar
Pope, Alexander **12** 395-397

Brosin, Edith (died 1921), German actress
Benn, Gottfried **2** 164

Brosse, Salomon de (1565?-1627), French architect
Mansart, François **10** 211

Brot und Wein (elegy)
Hölderlin, Johann Christian Friedrich **7** 451-452

Brother Jonathan's Lament for Sister Caroline (poem)
Holmes, Oliver Wendell **7** 457-458

Brother to Dragons (story)
Warren, Robert Penn **16** 121-122

Brotherhood of Locomotive Firemen (labor union)
Debs, Eugene Victor **4** 444-445

Brotherhood of Sleeping Car Porters (labor union)
Randolph, A. Philip **13** 28-29

Brotherhood of the Kingdom (religious society)
Rauschenbusch, Walter **13** 53-54

Brothers (society of wits)
Swift, Jonathan **15** 51-54

Brothers, The (play)
Vondel, Joost van den **16** 19-20

BROTHERS, JOYCE (Joyce Diane Bauer; born 1927), American psychologist who pioneered radio phone-in questions for professional psychological advice **3** 26-28

Brothers Karamazov, The (novel)
Dostoevsky, Fyodor **5** 74-77

Brothers of No Kin... (stories)
Richter, Conrad Michael **13** 148-149

Brothers of the Common Life (Netherlands religious social society)
Groote, Gerard **7** 12-13
Kempis, Thomas à **8** 493-494

Brothers' party (Sudan)
Azhari, Sayyid Ismail al- **1** 399-401

Brotteaux (literary character)
France, Anatole **6** 39-40

BROUDY, HARRY SAMUEL (born 1905), American philosopher, teacher, and author **3** 28-29

Brougham, Henry Peter (Baron Brougham and Vaux; 1778-1868), Scottish jurist
Stewart, Dugald **14** 449

Broun, Heywood (1888-1939), American journalist
Eliot, Thomas Stearns **5** 258-261

BROUWER, ADRIAEN (1605/06-1638), Flemish painter **3** 29-30
Hals, Frans **7** 89-91

Brouwer, Luitzen Egbertus Jan (1881-1966), Dutch mathematician
Tarski, Alfred **15** 110-111

Břovnov Abbey (near Prague)
Asam, Cosmas Damian and Egid Quirin **1** 323-324

BROWDER, EARL RUSSELL (1891-1973), American Communist leader **3** 30-31
Foster, William Zebulon **6** 27-28

BROWN, ALEXANDER (1764-1834), American merchant and banker **3** 31-32

BROWN, BENJAMIN GRATZ (1826-1885), American politician **3** 32-33

BROWN, CHARLES BROCKDEN (1771-1810), American novelist **3** 33

BROWN, CHARLOTTE EUGENIA HAWKINS (born Lottie Hawkins; 1882-1961), African American educator and humanitarian **3** 34

Brown, Ford Madox (1821-1893), English painter
Ford, Ford Madox **6** 1-2
Rossetti, Dante Gabriel **13** 308-309

Brown, Frederick (died 1856), American abolitionist
Brown, John **3** 39-41

Brown, George (1787-1859), American financier
Brown, Alexander **3** 31-32

BROWN, GEORGE (1818-1880), Canadian politician **3** 35-36
Cartier, George-Étienne **3** 342-343

Brown, Sir George Lindor (1903-1971), British physiologist
Dale, Henry Hallett **4** 371-373

BROWN, HELEN GURLEY (born 1922), American author and editor **3** 36-37

Brown, James (1791-1877), American financier
Brown, Alexander **3** 31-32

BROWN, JAMES (born 1928), African American singer **3** 37-39

Brown, John (1736-1803), American merchant
Watson, Elkanah **16** 136

Brown, John (1744-1880), American Revolutionary soldier
Allen, Ethan **1** 163-164

BROWN, JOHN (1800-1859), American abolitionist **3** 39-41
Harpers Ferry uprising
Child, Lydia Maria Francis **3** 520-521
Douglass, Frederick **5** 85-86
Fee, John Gregg **5** 402-403
Jackson, Shirley Ann **8** 183-184
Lee, Robert Edward **9** 292-294
Stuart, James Ewell Brown **14** 515-516
in art and literature
Lawrence, Jacob **9** 250-251
Melville, Herman **10** 472-476
Pippin, Horace **12** 318-319
method criticized
Garrison, William Lloyd **6** 226-228
supporters
Andrew, John Albion **1** 230-231
Higginson, Thomas Wentworth **7** 380
Howe, Samuel Gridley **7** 537
Parker, Theodore **12** 112-113
Purvis, Robert **12** 485-486
Smith, Gerrit **14** 290-291
Still, William **14** 454-455
Thayer, Eli **15** 168
Thoreau, Henry David **15** 203-205
Tubman, Harriet Ross **15** 330-331

Brown, John A. (1788-1872), American merchant and banker
Brown, Alexander **3** 31-32

Brown, John Mason (1900-1969), American drama critic
Chaplin, Charles Spencer **3** 438-440

BROWN, JOSEPH EMERSON (1821-1894), American lawyer and politician **3** 41-42
Gordon, John Brown **6** 449-450
Letcher, John **9** 359-360

Brown, Mather (1761-1831), American painter
Stuart, Gilbert **14** 513-515

BROWN, MOSES (1738-1836), American manufacturer and merchant **3** 42-43
du Pont, Éleuthère Irénée **5** 154
Slater, Samuel **14** 272-273

Brown, Obadiah (1771-1822), American merchant
Brown, Moses **3** 42-43

Brown, Oliver (died 1859), American abolitionist
Brown, John **3** 39-41

Brown, Peter (1784-1863), Scottish-born Canadian journalist
Brown, George **3** 35-36

Brown, Peter McKenzie (born 1924), South African politician
Paton, Alan Stewart **12** 134-135

BROWN, RACHEL FULLER (1898-1980), American biochemist **3** 43-44

Brown, Robert (1773-1858), Scottish botanist
Einstein, Albert **5** 228-231

BROWN, RONALD H. (1941-1996), African American politician, cabinet official **3** 44-47

BROWN, TINA (Christina Hambly Brown; born 1953), British editor who transformed the English magazine *Tatler*, then the United States magazines *Vanity Fair* and the *New Yorker* **3** 47-48

Brown, Watson (died 1859), American abolitionist
Brown, John **3** 39-41

Brown, Sir William (1784-1864), American-born English financier
Brown, Alexander **3** 31-32

BROWN, WILLIAM WELLS (1815/16-1884), African American author and abolitionist **3** 48-49

Brown Decades, The (book)
Mumford, Lewis **11** 246-247

Brown Owl, The (fairy tale)
Ford, Ford Madox **6** 1-2

Brown University (Providence, Rhode Island)
Backus, Isaac **1** 420-421
Brown, Moses **3** 42-43
Scholem, Gershom **14** 26
Ward, Lester Frank **16** 113-114
Wayland, Francis **16** 148-149

Brown v. Board of Education of Topeka (1954)
Clark, Kenneth B. **4** 78-79
Eisenhower, Dwight David **5** 233-236
Marshall, Thurgood **10** 282-284
Warren, Earl **16** 117-120

Brown v. Maryland (1827)
Marshall, John **10** 279-281

Browne, Charles Farrar
see Ward, Artemus

Browne, Hablot Knight (Phiz; 1815-1882), English painter
Dickens, Charles John Huffam **4** 538-541

BROWNE, SIR THOMAS (1605-1682), English author **3** 49-50
Melville, Herman **10** 472-476

BROWNER, CAROL M. (born 1955), U.S. Environmental Protection Agency administrator **3** 50-52

Brownian motion (physics)
Einstein, Albert **5** 228-231

Brownie's Book (publication)
Hughes, Langston **8** 18-19

BROWNING, ELIZABETH BARRETT (1806-1861), English poet **3** 52-53
Browning, Robert **3** 53-55
Naidu, Sarojini **11** 294-295

BROWNING, ROBERT (1812-1889), English poet **3** 53-55
critical studies
Chesterton, Gilbert Keith **3** 508-509
friends
Hardy, Thomas **7** 150-152
influence of
Dickinson, Emily **4** 541-543
Landor, Walter Savage **9** 186-187
Pound, Ezra Loomis **12** 415-417
influenced by
Carlyle, Thomas **3** 304-305
Plutarch **12** 359-360
relatives
Browning, Elizabeth Barrett **3** 52-53

Browning, Robert Wiedeman Barrett (1849-1912), English painter and sculptor
Browning, Elizabeth Barrett **3** 52-53
Browning, Robert **3** 53-55

BROWNLOW, WILLIAM GANNAWAY (1805-1877), American journalist and politician **3** 55-56

BROWNMILLER, SUSAN (born 1935), American activist, journalist, and novelist **3** 56-57

Brown's Descent (poem)
Frost, Robert Lee **6** 130-133

BROWNSON, ORESTES AUGUSTUS (1803-1876), American clergyman and transcendentalist **3** 57-58
Hecker, Isaac Thomas **7** 250-251
Higginson, Thomas Wentworth **7** 380

Brownson's Quarterly Review (journal, 1844-1875)
Brownson, Orestes Augustus **3** 57-58

Broz, Josip
see Tito, Marshal

Bruant, Libéral (circa 1635-1697), French architect
Mansart, Jules Hardouin **10** 212

BRUBACHER, JOHN SEILER (1898-1988), American historian and educator **3** 58-59

BRUBECK, DAVE (born 1920), American pianist, composer, and bandleader **3** 59-61

BRUCE, BLANCHE KELSO (1841-1898), African American politician **3** 62-63

BRUCE, DAVID (1855-1931), Australian parasitologist **3** 63

BRUCE, JAMES (1730-1794), Scottish explorer **3** 63-64
Lalibela **9** 170
Speke, John Hanning **14** 366-367

Bruce, James (1811-1863)
see Elgin, 8th Earl of

Bruce, Marjorie (died 1316), Scottish princess
Robert II **13** 194

Bruce, Robert
see Robert I (king of Scotland)

BRUCE OF MELBOURNE, 1ST VISCOUNT (Stanley Melbourne Bruce; 1883-1967), Australian statesman **3** 61-62
Hughes, William Morris **8** 21-22

Brucellosis
see Undulant fever

Bruch, Max (1838-1920), German composer
Respighi, Ottorino **13** 103-104
Vaughan Williams, Ralph **15** 446-447

Brücke, Ernst Wilhelm von (1819-1892), German physiologist
Freud, Sigmund **6** 103-106

Brücke, Die (German art group)
Amiet, Cuno **1** 201-202
Kandinsky, Wassily **8** 420-422
Kirchner, Ernst Ludwig **9** 34-35
Nolde, Emil **11** 419-420
Pechstein, Hermann Max **12** 176-177

BRUCKNER, JOSEPH ANTON (1824-1896), Austrian composer **3** 64-65
Wagner, Richard **16** 40-43

Bruderhaus Maschinen-Fabrik (Reutlingen, Germany)
Daimler, Gottlieb **4** 368

Bruegel, Jan (1568-1625), Netherlandish painter
Bruegel, Pieter the Elder **3** 65-67

BRUEGEL, PIETER, THE ELDER (1525/30-1569), Netherlandish painter **3** 65-67
Bosch, Hieronymus **2** 426-428
Brouwer, Adriaen **3** 29-30
Evergood, Philip **5** 345
Smith, David **14** 287-288
van der Goes, Hugo **15** 416-417

Bruegel, Pieter, the Younger (1564-1638), Netherlandish painter
Bruegel, Pieter the Elder **3** 65-67

Bruges, Battle of (1745)
Saxe, Comte de **13** 507-508

Brugmann, Karl (1848-1919), German philologist
Bloomfield, Leonard **2** 338

BRÛLÉ, ÉTIENNE (circa 1592-1633), French explorer in North America **3** 67-68

Brum, Baltasar (1883-1933), Uruguayan president 1919-1923
Terra, Gabriel **15** 154-155

Brumaire coup d'etat (France; 1799)
Bonaparte, Joseph **2** 381-382
Bonaparte, Louis **2** 382-383
Bernadotte, Jean Baptiste **2** 205-206
Fouché, Joseph **6** 30-31
Napoleon I **11** 306-310
Talleyrand, Charles Maurice de **15** 89-90

BRUNDTLAND, GRO HARLEM (1939-1989), Norwegian prime minister and chair of the United Nations World

Commission for Environment and Development 3 68-69

Brunei (city, Borneo)
Brooke, James 3 21-22

BRUNEL, ISAMBARD KINGDOM (1806-1859), English civil engineer 3 69-70

Brunel, Marc Isambard (1769-1849), French-born American inventor
Brunel, Isambard Kingdom 3 69-70

BRUNELLESCHI, FILIPPO (1377-1446), Italian architect and sculptor 3 70-72
influence of
Veneziano, Domenico 15 459-460
Masaccio 10 312-313, 241
Michelozzo 11 6-7
Sangallo family 13 464-466
works
Ghiberti, Lorenzo 6 291-292
Medici, Cosimo de' 10 449-450
Quercia, Jacopo della 12 509

BRUNER, JEROME SEYMOUR (born 1915), American psychologist 3 72-73
Piaget, Jean 12 287-288

Brüning, Heinrich (1885-1970), German statesman
Hindenburg, Paul Ludwig Hans von Beneckendorff und von 7 400-401

BRUNNER, ALOIS (born 1912), Nazi German officer who helped engineer the destruction of European Jews 3 73-74

BRUNNER, EMIL (1889-1966), Swiss Reformed theologian 3 74-75

Brunner, Heinrich (1840-1915), Austrian jurist
Vinogradoff, Paul Gavrilovitch 15 503

Brunner, Heinrich Emil (1889-1966), Swiss Protestant theologian
Barth, Karl 2 31-32

Brunner, Sebastian (1814-1893), Austrian priest and writer
Ritschl, Albrecht Benjamin 13 180

Brünnhilde (opera character)
Wagner, Richard 16 40-43

Brünnow, Franz Friedrich Ernst (1821-1891), German astronomer
Hall, Asaph 7 83-84

BRUNO, GIORDANO (1548-1600), Italian philosopher and poet 3 75-76
Hamann, Johann Georg 7 92
Telesio, Bernardino 15 138-139
Toland, John 15 256

Bruno of Cologne, St. (925?-965), German archbishop
Otto I 12 28-29

Bruno of Toul (Egisheim)
see Leo IX, St.

Bruno's Dream (novel)
Murdoch, Iris 11 256-257

Brunswick, Karl Wilhelm Ferdinand, Duke of (1735-1806), German general
Louis XVI 9 534-535

Brussels (city, Belgium)
Saxe, Comte de 13 507-508

Brussels Convention (1902)
Böhm-Bawerk, Eugen von 2 366

Brussels University
Piccard, Auguste 12 297-298

Brussels World's Fair
see World's Fairs—Brussels

Brut (poem)
Layamon 9 256-257

Bruto I (play)
Alfieri, Vittoria 1 145-146

BRUTON, JOHN GERARD (born 1947), prime minister of Ireland 3 76-77

Brutus (legendary character)
Geoffrey of Monmouth 6 268

Brutus (play)
Payne, John Howard 12 159

Brutus (treatise; Cicero)
Brutus, Marcus Junius 3 79-80
Cicero, Marcus Tullius 4 55-58

Brutus, Decimus Junius (died 43 B.C.), Roman governor of Gaul
Antony, Mark 1 253-254

BRUTUS, DENNIS (born 1924), exiled South African poet and political activist opposed to apartheid 3 77-78

Brutus, Lucius Junius (flourished 510 B.C.), Roman praetor
Brutus, Marcus Junius 3 79-80

BRUTUS, MARCUS JUNIUS (circa 85-42 B.C.), Roman statesman 3 79-80
in literature
Shakespeare, William 14 142-145
Philippi (42 B.C.)
Antony, Mark 1 253-254
Augustus 1 371-373
Horace 7 500-503
plot against Caesar
Cato, the Younger 3 374-375
Cleopatra 4 105-106

Brutus, Quintus Caepio
see Brutus, Marcus Junius

Brutus and the Lictors ... (painting)
David, Jacques Louis 4 407-409

Bruyas, Alfred (1821-1877), French art collector
Courbet, Jean Desiré Gustave 4 271-273

Bryan, Bryan, Bryan, Bryan (poem; Lindsay)
Bryan, William Jennings 3 80-82

BRYAN, WILLIAM JENNINGS (1860-1925), American lawyer and politician 3 80-82
Owen, Ruth Bryan 12 41-43
and Populists
Polk, Leonidas Lafayette 12 376-377
Watson, Thomas Edward 16 139
free silver
Altgeld, John Peter 1 180-182

Straus, Isidor 14 496
in Cabinet
Wilson, Thomas Woodrow 16 330-332
opponents
Cleveland, Stephen Grover 4 108-110
Fosdick, Harry Emerson 6 21-22
McKinley, William 10 418-420
Olney, Richard 11 504-505
Taft, William Howard 15 78-81
White, William Allen 16 240-241
Scopes trial
Darrow, Clarence Seward 4 396-397
supporters
Borah, William Edgar 2 408
Daniels, Josephus 4 387
Donnelly, Ignatius 5 62
Hearst, William Randolph 7 243-244
Hitchcock, Gilbert Monell 7 416-417
Weaver, James Baird 16 151-152

Bryanston (Dorset)
Shaw, Richard Norman 14 167-168

BRYANT, PAUL ("Bear;" 1919-1983), American college football coach 3 82-83

BRYANT, WILLIAM CULLEN (1794-1878), American poet and editor 3 83-85
Biddle, Nicholas 2 264-265
Bigelow, John 2 271-272
Durand, Asher Brown 5 156-157
Freneau, Philip Morin 6 99-100
Welles, Gideon 16 188-190

Bryant and May match factory strike (1888)
Besant, Annie Wood 2 233-234

BRYCE, JAMES (1838-1922), British historian, jurist, and statesman 3 85
Brooks, Phillips 3 26

Bryennius, Nicephorus (1062?-1137), Byzantine soldier and historian
Comnena, Anna 4 185-186

Bryher
see Ellerman, Winifred

Brymner, William (1855-1925), Canadian painter
Morrice, James Wilson 11 181-182

Bryn Mawr College (Pennsylvania)
Andrews, Charles McLean 1 231
Carey Thomas, Martha 3 297-298
Giddings, F. 4 391
Morgan, Thomas Hunt 11 170-171
Wilson, Thomas Woodrow 16 330-332

Bryusov, Valery Yakolevich (1873-1924), Russian symbolist poet
Blok, Aleksandr Aleksandrovich 2 335

BRZEZINSKI, ZBIGNIEW (1928-1980), assistant to President Carter for national security affairs (1977-1980) 3 85-87

BSCP
see Brotherhood of Sleeping Car Porters

Bubble sextant (instrument)
Byrd, Richard Evelyn **3** 186-187

Bubbles (painting)
Millais, John Everett **11** 23-24

Bubbles of Canada, The (book)
Haliburton, Thomas Chandler **7** 80

BUBER, MARTIN (1878-1965),
Austrian-born Jewish theologian and
philosopher **3** 87-89
Agnon, Shmuel Yoseph **1** 85-86
Heschel, Abraham Joshua **7** 358-359
Rosenzweig, Franz **13** 294
Tillich, Paul Johannes **15** 224-225

Bucareli Agreement (1923)
Obregón, Álvaro **11** 458-459

Bucareli y Ursúa, Antonio Maria de
(1717-1779), Spanish general
Anza, Juan Bautista de **1** 254-255

Buccleugh
see Monmouth and Buccleugh Duke of

Bucer, Martin (1491-1551), German
Protestant theologian
Melancthon, Philip **10** 466-467
Schwenckfeld, Kasper von **14** 56-57
Servetus, Michael **14** 115-116

Buch Bahir, Das (book)
Scholem, Gershom **14** 26

Buch der Bilder, Das (poems)
Rilke, Rainer Maria **13** 171-172

Buch der Leidenschaft, Das (novel)
Hauptmann, Gerhart Johann Robert
7 199-201

Buch der Lieder (poems)
Heine, Heinrich **7** 259-260

Buch vom mönchischen Leben, Das
(poems)
Rilke, Rainer Maria **13** 171-172

Buchanan, George (1506-1582), Scottish
humanist
James I **8** 204-206
Montaigne, Michel Eyquem de
11 116-117

BUCHANAN, JAMES (1791-1868), Ameri-
can statesman, president 1857-1861
3 89-90
associates
Scott, Winfield **14** 70-71
Cabinet of
Cass, Lewis **3** 355-356
Stanton, Edwin McMasters
14 401-402
in Cabinet
Polk, James Knox **12** 374-376
Kansas issue
Douglas, Stephen Arnold **5** 80-82
Walker, Robert John **16** 67-68
land-grant colleges
Morrill, Justin Smith **11** 182
supporters
Seymour, Horatio **14** 126-127
Slidell, John **14** 273
Van Buren, Martin **15** 410-411

BUCHANAN, PATRICK JOSEPH (born
1938), commentator, journalist, and presidential candidate **3** 90-91

Bucharest (city, Romania)
Ceausescu, Nicolae **3** 387-388
Ferdinand **5** 413-414

Bucharest, Peace of (1918)
Ferdinand **5** 413-414

Bucharest, Treaty of (1812)
Mahmud II **10** 145-147

Bucharest, University of
Titulescu, Nicolae **15** 246-247

Bücher, Karl (1847-1930), German economist
Malinowski, Kaspar Bronislaw
10 170-171

Büchner, Georg (1813-1837), German poet
and playwright
Berg, Alban **2** 186-187
Wedekind, Frank **16** 166-167

Buchon, Max (1818-1869), French author
Courbet, Jean Desiré Gustave
4 271-273

Büchse der Pandora (play)
Wedekind, Frank **16** 166-167

Buck, Dudley (1839-1909), American composer
Lanier, Sidney **9** 199-200

BUCK, PEARL SYDENSTRICKER
(1892-1973), American novelist **3** 91-93

Buck in the Snow (poems)
Millay, Edna St. Vincent **11** 24-25

BUCKINGHAM, 1ST DUKE OF (George
Villiers; 1592-1628), English courtier and
military leader **3** 93-94
Charles, I **3** 450-452
Coke, Edward **4** 141-142
Herrick, Robert **7** 336-339
James I **8** 204-206

BUCKINGHAM, 2D DUKE OF (George
Villiers; 1628-1687), English statesman
3 94-95
Butler, Samuel **3** 183-184
Charles II **3** 452-454
Clarendon, 1st Earl of **4** 73-75
Shaftesbury, 1st Earl of **14** 135-136

Buckingham, Henry Stafford, 2d Duke of
(1454-1483), English statesman
Richard III **13** 132-133

Buckingham Palace (London)
George IV **6** 272-273
Nash, John **11** 316

Buckland, William (1784-1856), English
geologist
Lyell, Charles **10** 62-63

BUCKLE, HENRY THOMAS (1821-1862),
English historian **3** 95-96
Strindberg, August **14** 509-511
Tyler, Moses Coit **15** 369-370

BUCKLEY, WILLIAM F., JR. (born 1925),
conservative American author, editor, and
political activist **3** 96-97

Buckner, Simon B. (1823-1914), American
general
Grant, Ulysses Simpson **6** 492-494

Buckower Elegien (poems)
Brecht, Bertolt **2** 512-514

Bucks County Barn (painting)
Sheeler, Charles **14** 170-171

Bucolics
see Eclogues

Bucolicum carmen (poems)
Petrarch **12** 259-261

Bucoliques (poems)
Chénier, André Marie **3** 500-501

Bucovina (Austrian crownland)
Ferdinand **5** 413-414

Budapest (city, Hungary)
Saarinen, Eliel and Eero **13** 396-398
Semmelweis, Ignaz Philipp **14** 101-102
see also Hungarian revolt (1956)

Budapest, University of
Pázmány, Péter **12** 164-165
Szent-Györgyi, Albert von **15** 62-64

Buddenbrooks (novel)
Mann, Thomas **10** 204-207, 145

BUDDHA (circa 560-480 B.C.), Indian
founder of Buddhism **3** 97-101
Honen **7** 473
Hui-yüan **8** 25-26
Shinran **14** 197
see also Buddhism

Buddha (play)
Kazantzakis, Nikos **8** 466-468

Buddhabhadra (flourished 5th century),
Sarvastivadin Kashmirian monk
Hui-yüan **8** 25-26

BUDDHADĀSA BHIKKHU (Nguam
Phanich; born 1906), founder of Wat
Suan Mokkhabalārama in southern Thailand and interpreter of Theravāda Buddhism **3** 101-102

Buddhism
doctrine
Buddha **3** 97-101
influence of
Hafiz, Shams al-Din **7** 63
Wang An-shih **16** 95-97
Wang Pi **16** 104-105
interpreters
Buddhadāsa Bhikkhu **3** 101-102
Jainism and
Mahavira, Vardhamana **10** 135-137
Neo-Confucianism and
Chu Hsi **4** 40-43
psychological studies
Jung, Carl Gustav **8** 388-389
spread of
Kanishka **8** 428-429

see also Hinayana Buddhism;
   Lamaism; Mahayana Buddhism;
   Zen Buddhism

Buddhism (Burma)
   Mindon Min **11** 47
   Nu, U **11** 439-441

Buddhism (Ceylon)
   Asoka **1** 341-342

Buddhism (China)
   4th century (introduced)
      Hui-yüan **8** 25-26
      Shih Le **14** 195
      Tao-an **15** 103-104
   5th century
      Hsieh Ling-yün **8** 5-6
      Liu Hsieh **9** 452-453
   6th century
      Chih-i **3** 518-519
      Liang Wu-ti **9** 396-397
      Sui Wen-ti **15** 16-18
   7th-8th century
      Han Yü **7** 136-137
      Hsüan Tsang **8** 6-7
   13th century
      Chia Ssu-tao **3** 514-515
      Kublai Khan **9** 115-118
   Lü-tsung (Disciplinary school)
      Tao-hsüan **15** 105

Buddhism (India)
   Ambedkar, Bhimrao Ramji **1** 190-191
   Asoka **1** 341-342
   Harsha **7** 181-182
   Kumarajiva **9** 127
   Shankara **14** 150-151

Buddhism (Indochina)
   Buddha **3** 97-101

Buddhism (Japan)
   introduced (6th century)
      Shotoku Taishi **14** 205-207
      Suiko **15** 15-16
   opposed
      Kammu **8** 420
   sects
      Eisai **5** 231-232
      Ennin **5** 288-289
      Honen **7** 473
      Ikeda, Daisaku **8** 109-110
      Kukai **9** 124-125
      Nichiren **11** 376-377
      Niwano, Nikkyo **11** 400-401
      Saicho **13** 426-428
      Shinran **14** 197

Buddhism (Korea)
   Kwangjong **9** 140
   Sejong **14** 91-92
   Yi Sng-gye **16** 458-459

Buddhism (Thailand)
   Buddhadāsa Bhikkhu **3** 101-102
   Chulalongkorn **4** 43-45
   Mongkut **11** 104

Buddhism (Tibet)
   Dalai Lama **4** 369-371

Buddhism (Vietnam)
   Diem, Ngo Dinh **5** 6-7

BUDÉ, GUILLAUME (1467-1540), French
   humanist **3** 102-103
   Fernel, Jean François **5** 425-426
   Francis I **6** 40-43
   Rabelais, François **12** 524-526

Budyenny, Semyon M. (born 1883), marshal of the Soviet Union
   Rundstedt, Karl Rudolf Gerd Von
      13 363-364

BUECHNER, FREDERICK (born 1926),
   American novelist and theologian
   3 103-105

BUEL, JESSE (1778-1839), American agri-
   culturalist and journalist **3** 105

Buell, Don Carlos (1818-1898), American
   general
   Sherman, William Tecumseh
      14 186-187
   Wallace, Lewis **16** 74-75

Buell, Sarah Josepha
   see Hale, Sarah Josepha

Buena guarda, La (play)
   Lope Félix de Vega Carpio **9** 503-506

Buena Vista, Battle of (1847)
   Davis, Jefferson **4** 416-418
   Lee, Robert Edward **9** 292-294
   Taylor, Zachary **15** 128-130

Buenas conciencias, La (novel)
   Fuentes, Carlos **6** 141-142

Buendía family (literary characters)
   García Márquez, Gabriel **6** 208-209

Buenos Aires (city, Argentina)
   Artigas, José Gervasio **1** 323
   Belgrano, Manuel **2** 126-127
   Rivadavia, Bernardino **13** 182-183
   Rosas, Juan Manuel de **13** 290-291
   Urquiza, Justo José **15** 396-397

Buenos Aires, University of
   Houssay, Bernardo Alberto **7** 522-523

Buenos Aires Conference (1936)
   Hull, Cordell **8** 28-29
   Justo, Agustin Pedro **8** 396
   Welles, Sumner **16** 191-192

Bufera e altro, La (poems)
   Montale, Eugenio **11** 117-118

Buffalo (animal)
   Goodnight, Charles **6** 439

Buffalo (city; New York State)
   Cleveland, Stephen Grover **4** 108-110
   Corning, Erastus **4** 238-239
   Fargo, William George **5** 380-381

BUFFALO BILL (William Frederick Cody;
   1846-1917), American scout and publicist **3** 105-106
   Oakley, Annie **11** 453-454

Buffalo Bill (poem)
   Sandburg, Carl **13** 461-462

Buffalo Bill's (poem; Cummings)
   Sandburg, Carl **13** 461-462

Buffalo Express (newspaper)
   Twain, Mark **15** 363-366

Buffalo soldiers
   Davis, Benjamin O. Sr. **4** 414-415

BUFFETT, WARREN (born 1930), American
   investment salesman **3** 106-109

Buffet, The (painting)
   Chardin, Jean Baptiste Siméon
      3 442-443

BUFFON, COMTE DE (Georges Louis
   Leclerc; 1707-1788), French naturalist
   3 109-111
   Condillac, Étienne Bonnot de
      4 194-195
   Lamarck, Chevalier de **9** 171-173
   Spallanzani, Lazzaro **14** 360-361

Buffoons, War of the (musical)
   Pergolesi, Giovanni Battista **12** 218-219

Buganda
   see Uganda

Bugayev, B.N.
   see Bely, Andrei

**BUGEAUD DE LA PICONNERIE, THOMAS
   ROBERT** (1784-1849), Duke of Isly and
   marshal of France **3** 111
   Abd el-Kadir **1** 15

Buggiano
   see Andrea di Lazzaro Cavalcanti

Bugs Bunny (cartoon character)
   Blanc, Mel **2** 319-320
   Lichtenstein, Roy **9** 398-399

Buick Motor Car Co.
   Chrysler, Walter Percy **4** 36-37
   Durant, William Crapo **5** 158

Build Soil (poem)
   Frost, Robert Lee **6** 130-133

Build-up, The (novel)
   Williams, William Carlos **16** 308-309

Builders of the Bay Colony (book)
   Morison, Samuel Eliot **11** 175-176

Builder's Treasury (book; Langley)
   McIntire, Samuel **10** 415

Building of Carthage (painting; Turner)
   Cole, Thomas **4** 151-152

Building of the City Beautiful, The (novel)
   Miller, Joaquin **11** 27-28

Building of the Earth (book)
   Teilhard de Chardin, Marie Joseph
   Pierre **15** 134-136

Building of the Ship, The (poem)
   Longfellow, Henry Wadsworth
      9 499-500

Bukhara (former emirate; state, Union of
   Soviet Socialist Republics)
   Genghis Khan **6** 263-265
   Mahmud of Ghazni **10** 147

BUKHARI, MUHAMMAD IBN ISMAIL AL-
(810-870), Arab scholar and Moslem
saint **3** 111-112

BUKHARIN, NIKOLAI IVANOVICH
(1858-1938), Russian politician
3 112-113
Katayama, Sen **8** 457
Stalin, Joseph **14** 393-396
Trotsky, Leon **15** 302-305

Bukofzer, Manfred F. (1910-1955),
German-born American musicologist
Corelli, Arcangelo **4** 230-231

BUKOWSKI, CHARLES (1920-1994),
American writer and poet **3** 113-115

BULATOVIC, MOMIR (born 1956), president of Montenegro (1990-1992) and of
the new Federal Republic of Yugoslavia
(1992-) **3** 115-116

BULFINCH, CHARLES (1763-1844), Amer-
ican colonial architect **3** 116-117
Adam, Robert and James **1** 38-40
Benjamin, Asher **2** 162-163
McIntire, Samuel **10** 415
Revere, Paul **13** 110-111

BULGAKOV, MIKHAIL AFANASIEVICH
(1891-1940), Russian novelist and playwright **3** 117

BULGANIN, NIKOLAI (1885-1975), chairman of the Soviet Council of Ministers
(1955-1958) **3** 118-119
Dulles, John Foster **5** 134-135
Khrushchev, Nikita Sergeevich
8 539-540

Bulgaria, People's Republic of (nation,
Southeast Europe)
Alexander II **1** 132-133
Basil II **2** 50-51
Batu Khan **2** 60-61
Dimitrov, Georgi **5** 11-13
Ferdinand **5** 413-414
John, XXIII **8** 277-280
Venizelos, Eleutherios **15** 460-461
Zhivkov, Todor **16** 510-512

Bulgaroctonus (Bulgar-Slayer)
see Basil II

Bulge, Battle of the (1944)
Montgomery, Bernard Law **11** 135-136
Rundstedt, Karl Rudolf Gerd Von
13 363-364

Bull Moose party (United States)
Roosevelt, Theodore **13** 280-283
White, William Allen **16** 240-241

Bull Run, Battle of (First; 1861)
Confederates
Beauregard, Pierre Gustave Toutant
2 96-97
Davis, Jefferson **4** 416-418
Jackson, Shirley Ann **8** 183-184
Johnston, Joseph Eggleston **8** 323
Lee, Robert Edward **9** 292-294
Stuart, James Ewell Brown
14 515-516

Union
Ames, Adelbert **1** 198
McClellan, George Brinton
10 391-392
Sherman, William Tecumseh
14 186-187
Tourgée, Albion Winegar
15 277-278

Bull Run, Battle of (Second; 1862)
Confederates
Davis, Jefferson **4** 416-418
Jackson, Shirley Ann **8** 183-184
Lee, Robert Edward **9** 292-294
Stuart, James Ewell Brown
14 515-516
Union
McClellan, George Brinton
10 391-392
Meade, George Gordon **10** 440-441

Bulldog Drummond (film)
Goldwyn, Samuel **6** 416

Buller, Sir Redvers Henry (1839-1908),
British general
Botha, Louis **2** 434-436

Bulletin (newspaper; Australia)
Furphy, Joseph **6** 152-153
Lawson, Henry **9** 254-255
Paterson, Andrew Barton **12** 131-132

Bulletin (painting)
Miró, Joan **11** 53-54

Bullinger, Heinrich (1504-1575), Swiss
religious reformer
Gesner, Konrad von **6** 287

Bullitt, W.C. (1891-1967), American diplomat
Freud, Sigmund **6** 103-106

Buln Buln and the Brolga, The (novel)
Furphy, Joseph **6** 152-153

Bülow, Hans von (1830-1894), German
pianist and conductor
Brahms, Johannes **2** 490-492

Bülow, Prince Bernhard von (1849-1929),
German diplomat and chancellor
Bethmann Hollweg, Theobald von
2 239-240

BULTMANN, RUDOLF KARL (1884-1976),
German theologian **3** 119-120
Barth, Karl **2** 31-32
Heidegger, Martin **7** 257-258
Soelle, Dorothee **14** 324-325
Tillich, Paul Johannes **15** 224-225

Bulwark, The (novel)
Dreiser, Herman Theodore **5** 98-100

Bulwer-Lytton, Edward George Lytton (1st
Baron Lytton of Knebworth; 1803-1873),
English novelist
Collins, William Wilkie **4** 169-170
Fry, William Henry **6** 136-137

Bumppo, Natty (literary character)
Cooper, James Fenimore **4** 220-223

BUNAU-VARILLA, PHILIPPE JEAN
(1859-1940), French engineer and soldier
3 120-121

BUNCHE, RALPH JOHNSON
(1904-1971), African American diplomat
3 121-122
Carver, George Washington **3** 346-347

Bundesstaat und Einheitsstaat (essay)
Treitschke, Heinrich von **15** 293-294

BUNDY, McGEORGE (born 1919), national
security adviser to two presidents
3 122-124

Bungei Jidai (magazine)
Kawabata, Yasunari **8** 463-464

BUNIN, IVAN ALEKSEEVICH (1870-1953),
Russian poet and novelist **3** 124
Chekhov, Anton Pavlovich **3** 494-497

Bunker Hill, Battle of (1775)
Clinton, Henry **4** 114-115
Gage, Thomas **6** 169-170
Howe, William **7** 538-539
Putnam, Israel **12** 491-492

BUNSEN, ROBERT WILHELM
(1811-1899), German chemist and physi-
cist **3** 124-125
Boltzmann, Ludwig **2** 379-380
Huggins, William **8** 14-15
Kirchhoff, Gustav Robert **9** 33-34
Mendeleev, Dmitrii Ivanovich
10 486-488
Ramsay, William **13** 21-22

Bunsen burner (instrument)
Bunsen, Robert Wilhelm **3** 124-125

BUNSHAFT, GORDON (1909-1990),
American architect **3** 125-127

Buntline, Ned (Edward Zane Carroll;
1823-1886), American inventor
Buffalo Bill **3** 105-106

BUÑUEL, LUIS (1900-1983), Spanish film
director **3** 127-128

BUNYAN, JOHN (1628-1688), English
author and Baptist preacher **3** 128-129
Baxter, Richard **2** 76-77

Buonaparte, Carlo (1746-1785), Corsican
lawyer, father of Napoleon I
Bonaparte, Joseph **2** 381-382
Bonaparte, Louis **2** 382-383
see also Bonaparte

Buonaparte, Maria Paulina
see Borghese, Pauline

Buoyant Billions (play)
Shaw, George Bernard **14** 163-164

Buraimi Oasis
Zayid bin Sultan Al-Nahyan **16** 491-492

BURBANK, LUTHER (1849-1926), Ameri-
can plant breeder **3** 129-131
Carver, George Washington **3** 346-347
East, Edward Murray **5** 182-183

BURCHFIELD, CHARLES (1893-1967),
American painter **3** 131-132

Burckhardt, Georg
see Spalatin, Georg

BURCKHARDT, JACOB CHRISTOPH
(1818-1897), Swiss historian **3** 132-133
Huizinga, Johan **8** 26-27

BURCKHARDT, JOHANN LUDWIG
(1784-1817), Swiss-born explorer **3** 133

Burdon-Sanderson, Sir John Scott
(1828-1905), English physiologist
Titchener, Edward Bradford **15** 241-242

Bureau of Animal Husbandry Act (1884)
Hatch, William Henry **7** 196

Bureau of Investigation
see Federal Bureau of Investigation (FBI)

Bureau of Records (Washington, D.C.)
Barton, Clara **2** 37-39

Bureaucracy
see Civil service

Burger, Die (newspaper)
Malan, Daniel Francois **10** 163-164

Bürger, Gottfried August (1747-1794),
German poet
Klopstock, Friedrich Gottlieb **9** 55-56

Bürger von Calais, Die (play)
Kaiser, Georg **8** 411-412

Bürgerliches Trauerspiel (play)
Lessing, Gotthold Ephraim **9** 357-359

BURGER, WARREN E. (1907-1986), Chief
Justice of the United States Supreme
Court (1969-1986) **3** 133-136

Burgers, Thomas François (1834-1881),
South African politician
Kruger, Stephanus Johannes Paulus
9 108-109

Burges, William (1827-1881), English
architect
Richardson, Henry Hobson **13** 139-141

BURGESS, ANTHONY (John Anthony
Burgess Wilson; 1917-1993), English
author **3** 136-137

Burgess, John William (1844-1931), American educator
Mayo-Smith, Richmond **10** 371-372
Seligman, Edwin Robert Anderson
14 93-94

Burghers of Calais (play)
Kaiser, Georg **8** 411-412

Burghers of Calais (sculpture)
Rodin, Auguste **13** 236-238

Burghley, Lord (Sir William Cecil;
1520-1598), English statesman
Elizabeth I **5** 263-266
Essex, 2d Earl of **5** 321-322

Burghölzi hospital (Switzerland)
Bleuler, Eugen **2** 325

Burgkmair, Hans, the Elder (1473-1531),
German painter
Holbein, Hans the Younger **7** 449-450

Burgo Paper Mill (Mantua)
Nervi, Pier Luigi **11** 346-348

BURGOYNE, JOHN (1723-1792), British
general and statesman **3** 137-138
Canadian campaign
Carleton, Guy **3** 300-301
Clinton, Henry **4** 114-115
Montgomery, Richard **11** 138-139
Saratoga
Arnold, Benedict **1** 309-310
Howe, William **7** 538-539
Lincoln, Benjamin **9** 418-419
Morgan, Daniel **11** 160-161
Ticonderoga
Montgomery, Richard **11** 138-139
Schuyler, Philip John **14** 49-50

Bürgschaft, Die (opera)
Weill, Kurt **16** 174-175

Burgundians (German people)
Ulfilas **15** 384

Burgundy (region, Southeast France)
English ally
Charles VI **3** 460-461
Edward IV **5** 212-213
Holy Roman Empire
Frederick I **6** 78-79
Frederick III **6** 84-85
Otto I **12** 28-29
Valois rule
Charles the Bold **3** 467-469
Philip the Good **12** 278-279

Burial at Ornans (painting)
Courbet, Jean Desiré Gustave
4 271-273

Burial Ground, South (Stockholm)
Asplund, Eric Gunnar **1** 344

Burial of the Conde de Orgaz (painting)
Greco **6** 511-514

Burial of the Queen of Sheba (painting)
Evergood, Philip **5** 345

Buridan, Jean (circa 1297-circa 1358),
French philosopher
Galileo Galilei **6** 180-183

Buried Alive (novel; A. Bennett)
Bennett, Arnold **2** 167-168
Morrice, James Wilson **11** 181-182

Buried Alive (stories)
Hidayat, Sadiq **7** 377-378

Buried Life, The (poem)
Arnold, Matthew **1** 311-313

Burke, Charles (1822-1854), American
actor
Jefferson, Joseph **8** 237

BURKE, EDMUND (1729-1797), British
statesman, political theorist, and philosopher **3** 138-141
associates
Boswell, James **2** 432-434
Goldsmith, Oliver **6** 411-413
Johnson, Samuel **8** 315-317
Sheridan, Richard Brinsley
14 183-184

influence of
Acton, John Emerich Edward Dal-
berg **1** 38
Crabbe, George **4** 288
Maistre, Joseph de **10** 153-154
Metternich, Klemens von
10 533-536
political theory
Godwin, William **6** 383-384
Lecky, William Edward Hartpole
9 271-272
Namier, Lewis Bernstein
11 301-303
Paine, Thomas **12** 66-67
Wilkes, John **16** 280-281

Burke, John Bernard (1814-1892), Irish
genealogist and publicist
Buffalo Bill **3** 105-106

BURKE, KENNETH (born 1897), American
literary theorist and critic **3** 141-142

BURKE, ROBERT O'HARA (1820-1861),
Irish-born Australian policeman and
explorer **3** 142-143

BURKE, SELMA (1900-1995), African
American sculptor **3** 143-144

Burke, Thomas Henry (1829-1882), Irish
politician
Gladstone, William Ewart **6** 357-360

Burlador de Sevilla, El (play)
Tirso de Molina **15** 237-238

BURLINGAME, ANSON (1820-1870),
American diplomat **3** 144-145
Wen-hsiang **16** 202-203

Burlingame Treaty (1868)
Burlingame, Anson **3** 144-145

Burlington, Richard Boyle, 3d Earl of
(1694-1753), English architect
Vanbrugh, John **15** 409-410

Burlington House (Piccadilly)
Gibbs, James **6** 301-302

Burlington Railroad (United States)
Hill, James Jerome **7** 388-389
Schiff, Jacob Henry **14** 2-3

Burma, Union of (nation, Southeastern
Asia; now Myanmar)
annexed to India
Dalhousie, 1st Marquess of
4 375-376
Salisbury, 3d Marquess of
13 448-449
democracy movement in
Aung San Suu Kyi **1** 375-376
exploration
Andrews, Roy Chapman **1** 232-233
Conti, Niccolò de' **4** 212-213
Polo, Marco **12** 380-382
independence
Aung San **1** 374-375
Ba Maw **1** 480-481
Ne Win **11** 364-365
Nu, U **11** 439-441
Thant, U **15** 161-162
Konbaung dynasty

Alaungpaya **1** 103
Mindon Min **11** 47
military coup (1988)
Saw Maung **13** 506-507
missionaries
Judson, Adoniram **8** 377-378
Mongols in
Kublai Khan **9** 115-118
World War II
Ba Maw **1** 480-481
Curtin, John Joseph **4** 348-349
Ne Win **11** 364-365
Stilwell, Joseph Warren **14** 456-457
see also Anglo-Burmese Wars

Burma Boy (magazine)
Thant, U **15** 161-162

Burmese Days (novel)
Orwell, George **12** 14-15

Burmese literature
Nu, U **11** 439-441

Burmese Wars
see Anglo-Burmese Wars

Burn, William (1789-1870), English architect
Shaw, Richard Norman **14** 167-168

BURNE-JONES, SIR EDWARD COLEY
(1833-1898), English painter and designer **3** 145-146
Beardsley, Aubrey Vincent **2** 88-89
Morris, William **11** 187-188
Richardson, Henry Hobson **13** 139-141
Swinburne, Algernon Charles **15** 54-55

BURNET, GILBERT (1643-1715), British bishop and historian **3** 147
Mary II **10** 309-310

BURNET, SIR FRANK MACFARLANE
(1899-1985), Australian virologist **3** 146-147
Medawar, Peter Brian **10** 444-445

Burnet, William (1688-1729), English colonial governor in America
DeLancey, Stephen **4** 473

Burney, Charles (1726-1814), English organist
Arne, Thomas Augustine **1** 307-308
Bach, Carl Philipp Emanuel **1** 414-415

BURNEY, FRANCES "FANNY"
(1752-1840), English novelist and diarist **3** 147-148
Lawrence, Thomas Edward **9** 253-254

BURNHAM, DANIEL HUDSON
(1846-1912), American architect and city planner **3** 148-149

BURNHAM, FORBES (1923-1985), leader of the independence movement in British Guiana and Guyana's first prime minister **3** 149-151

Burnham and Root (architecture firm)
Burnham, Daniel Hudson **3** 148-149
Richardson, Henry Hobson **13** 139-141

Burning bush (Old Testament)
Moses **11** 200-201

Burning Bush, The (novel)
Undset, Sigrid **15** 388-389

Burning City (poems)
Benét, Stephen Vincent **2** 157-158

Burning Grass (book)
Ekwensi, Cyprian **5** 242-243

Burning of the Bones of John the Baptist
(painting)
Geertgen tot Sint Jans **6** 248

Burning Truths from Billy's Bat (book)
Sunday, William Ashley **15** 32-33

BURNS, ANTHONY (1834-1862), African American slave **3** 151
Douglass, Frederick **5** 85-86

BURNS, ARTHUR (1904-1987), American economic statesman **3** 151-153
Mitchell, Wesley Clair **11** 61-62

BURNS, GEORGE (born Nathan Birnbaum; 1896-1996), American comedian and actor **3** 153-155

BURNS, ROBERT (1759-1796), Scottish poet **3** 155-156
Riley, James Whitcomb **13** 170-171
Whittier, John Greenleaf **16** 256-257

Burnside, Ambrose Everett (1824-1881), American army commander
Jackson, Shirley Ann **8** 183-184
Lee, Robert Edward **9** 292-294
Vallandigham, Clement Laird **15** 406-407

Burnt Norton (poem)
Eliot, Thomas Stearns **5** 258-261

Burnt Ones, The (stories)
White, Patrick Victor Martindale **16** 233-235

Burnt-out Case, A (novel)
Greene, Graham **6** 523-524

BURR, AARON (1756-1836), American politician, vice president 1801-1805 **3** 156-159
conspiracy and trial
Jefferson, Thomas **8** 238-241
Livingston, Edward **9** 460-461
Marshall, John **10** 279-281
Martin, Luther **10** 289-290
Randolph, Edmund **13** 29-30
Randolph, John **13** 30
Scott, Winfield **14** 70-71
Wilkinson, James **16** 284-286
political career
Clinton, DeWitt **4** 112-113
Clinton, George **4** 113-114
Hamilton, Alexander **7** 95-98
Jefferson, Thomas **8** 238-241
Livingston, Robert R. **9** 462-463

Burr, Theodosia (Mrs. Joseph Alston; 1783-1813), daughter and agent of Aaron Burr
Burr, Aaron **3** 156-159

BURRI, ALBERTO (1915-1995), Italian painter **3** 159-160

BURRITT, ELIHU (1810-1879), American pacifist, author, and linguist **3** 160
Ladd, William **9** 149

BURROUGHS, JOHN (1837-1921), American naturalist and essayist **3** 160-161
Carver, George Washington **3** 346-347

BURROUGHS, WILLIAM S. (1914-1997), American writer **3** 162-163
Ginsberg, Allen **6** 332-333
Kerouac, Jean-Louis Lebris de **8** 518-519

Burrus, Sextus Afranius (died 62), Roman general
Nero Claudius Caesar **11** 342-344
Seneca the Younger, Lucius Annaeus **14** 103-105

Bursts (art)
Gottlieb, Adolph **6** 462-463

Burton, Lady Isabel Arundell (1831-1896), English author
Burton, Richard **3** 163-164

BURTON, RICHARD (Richard Jenkins; 1925-1984), British actor **3** 163-164
Taylor, Elizabeth Rosemond **15** 124-125

BURTON, SIR RICHARD FRANCIS
(1821-1890), English explorer, author, and diplomat **3** 164-166
Speke, John Hanning **14** 366-367

BURTON, ROBERT (1577-1640), English author and clergyman **3** 166-167
Donne, John **5** 60-61
Jonson, Ben **8** 343-345

Burton's Gentleman's Magazine (journal)
Poe, Edgar Allan **12** 363-365

Bury, John Bagnell (1861-1927), Irish historian
Trevelyan, George Macaulay **15** 294-295

Bury, Richard de (1287-1345), English ecclesiastic
Chaucer, Geoffrey **3** 482-485

Busby, Dr. Richard (1606-1695), English clergyman
Dryden, John **5** 106-107

Busca, Mala hierba, La (novel)
Baroja y Nessi, Pío **2** 15-16

BUSH, GEORGE (George Herbert Walker Bush; born 1924), United States vice president (1981-1989) and president (1989-1993) **3** 167-169
appointees
Baker, James Addison III **1** 447-448
Bennett, William John **2** 172-174
Cheney, Richard B. **3** 497-499
Freeh, Louis J. **6** 90-91
Greenspan, Alan **6** 526-528
Kemp, Jack French Jr. **8** 491-493
Kessler, David A. **8** 523-524
Martin, Lynn Morley **10** 290-292
Souter, David H. **14** 355-356
Thomas, Clarence **15** 186-188

BUSH, VANNEVAR (1890-1974), American scientist and engineer **3** 169-171

Bushell Case (legal case)
Penn, William **12** 200-202

Bushman's River (South Africa)
Dias de Novais, Bartolomeu **4** 533-534

Bushnell, David (1742-1824), American inventor
Holland, John Philip **7** 453-454

BUSHNELL, HORACE (1802-1876), American Congregational clergyman **3** 171-172
Gladden, Washington **6** 356-357

BUSIA, KOFI ABREFA (1914-1978), Ghanaian premier and sociologist **3** 172-173

Business and industrial leaders
American
see Business and industrial leaders, American
Australian
Kidman, Sidney **8** 542-544
Lewis, Essington **9** 382-384
Macarthur, John **10** 78
Monash, John **11** 95-96
Murdoch, Rupert **11** 257-258
Parbo, Arvi **12** 93-94
Bolivian
Patiño, Simón Iturri **12** 133-134
Brazilian
Collor de Mello, Fernando **4** 170-172
British
Westwood, Vivienne **16** 217-218
Canadian
Aitken, William Maxwell **1** 94-96
Black, Conrad Moffat **2** 300-301
Irving, Kenneth Colin **8** 140-141
Smith, Donald Alexander **14** 288-289
Taylor, Edward Plunket **15** 123-124
Thomson, Kenneth **15** 201-202
Van Horne, William Cornelius **15** 429-430
Chilean
Herrera, Juan de **7** 335
Chinese
Li Hung-Chang **9** 407-409
Dutch
Van Diemen, Anthony Meuza **15** 420
Van Rensselaer, Kiliaen **15** 430-431
English
Arkwright, Richard **1** 298
Ashley, Laura **1** 332-333
Bessemer, Henry **2** 235-236
Cort, Henry **4** 254
Goldie, George Dashwood Taubman **6** 404
Goldsmith, James Michael **6** 409-411
Maxwell, Ian Robert **10** 360-361
Newbery, John **11** 360-361
Rhodes, Cecil John **13** 120-122
Sopwith, Thomas Octave Murdoch **14** 345-346

Sydenham, Thomas **15** 59-60
Wedgwood, Josiah **16** 168-169
French
Citroën, André-Gustave **4** 66-68
Dior, Christian **5** 22
Goldsmith, James Michael **6** 409-411
Lagerfeld, Karl **9** 161-162
Montgolfier, Joseph and Jacques Michel Étienne **11** 133-134
Necker, Jacques **11** 330-331
German
Benz, Carl **2** 182-183
Krupp **9** 109-111
Lagerfeld, Karl **9** 161-162
Rathenau, Walther **13** 48-49
Schacht, Hjalmar Horace Greeley **13** 518-519
Schliemann, Heinrich **14** 17-18
Indian (Asia)
Ram Camul Sen **13** 16-17
Italian
Agnelli, Giovanni **1** 82-83
Armani, Giorgio **1** 299-301
Benetton **2** 158-159
Fibonacci, Leonardo **5** 434-435
Lauro, Achille **9** 234-235
Mattei, Enrico **10** 337-339
Olivetti, Adriano **11** 501-502
Japanese
Honda, Soichiro **7** 469-470
Morita, Akio **11** 176-178
Toyoda, Eiji **15** 284-286
Korean
Chang Po-go **3** 433-434
New Zealand
Vogel, Julius **16** 9-10
Paraguayan
Wasmosy, Juan Carlos **16** 129-130
Polish
Rubenstein, Helena **13** 342-343
Scottish
Dinwiddie, Robert **5** 18-19
Law, John **9** 244-245
Nasmyth, James **11** 316-317
see also Labor leaders
Singaporean
Goh Chok Tong **6** 393-395
Spanish
Picasso, Paloma **12** 295-297
Uruguayan
Iglesias, Enrique V. **8** 106-107

Business and industrial leaders, American
advertising
Wells, Mary Georgene Berg **16** 197-198
advertising industry
Barton, Bruce **2** 36-37
Bernays, Edward L. **2** 211-212
Ogilvy, David MacKenzie **11** 481-482
Post, Charles William **12** 408-409
African American entrepreneurs
Johnson, John Harold **8** 306-308
Morgan, Garrett A. **11** 161-162

Spaulding, Charles Clinton **14** 364-365
Walker, C.J. **16** 62-63
Walker, Maggie Lena **16** 65-66
agricultural machinery
Deere, John **4** 455
Deering, William **4** 455-456
McCormick, Cyrus Hall **10** 400-401
Oliver, James **11** 500-501
Whitney, Eli **16** 253-254
air conditioning industry
Carrier, Wills **3** 325-326
air lines
Rickenbacker, Edward Vernon **13** 152-153
aircraft industry
Boeing, William Edward **2** 357-358
Curtiss, Glenn Hammond **4** 350-351
Douglas, Donald Wills **5** 77
Hughes, Howard Robard **8** 16-17
Sikorsky, Igor **14** 223-224
aluminum industry
Davis, Arthur Vining **4** 413-414
armament industry
Ashley, William Henry **1** 333-334
Colt, Samuel **4** 172-173
du Pont, Éleuthère Irénée **5** 154
Whitney, Eli **16** 253-254
automobile industry
Chrysler, Walter Percy **4** 36-37
du Pont, Pierre Samuel **5** 154-155
Durant, William Crapo **5** 158
Ford, Henry **6** 5-6
Ford, Henry II **6** 6-7
Iacocca, Lido (Lee) Anthony **8** 86-88
Kaiser, Henry John **8** 412-413
Kettering, Charles F. **8** 524-525
Knudsen, William S. **9** 67-68
McNamara, Robert S. **10** 429-431
Sloan, Alfred Pritchard Jr. **14** 274
Wilson, Charles Erwin **16** 316-317
aviation industry
Trippe, Juan Terry **15** 297-298
bankers (19th century)
Biddle, Nicholas **2** 264-265
Brown, Alexander **3** 31-32
Cooke, Jay **4** 215-216
Girard, Stephen **6** 347-348
McCulloch, Hugh **10** 404-405
Morgan, John Pierpont **11** 163-165
Morgan, Junius Spencer **11** 166-167
Peabody, George **12** 168
Schiff, Jacob Henry **14** 2-3
Watson, Elkanah **16** 136
bankers (20th century)
Giannini, A. P. **6** 295-297
Greenspan, Alan **6** 526-528
Lehman, Herbert Henry **9** 306-307
McNamara, Robert S. **10** 429-431
Mellon, Andrew William **10** 469-470
Morgan, John Pierpont II **11** 165
Morrow, Dwight Whitney **11** 190-191
Rockefeller, David **13** 224-225

Spaulding, Charles Clinton
14 364-365
Volcker, Paul **16** 11-12
Walker, Maggie Lena **16** 65-66
Warburg, Paul Moritz **16** 111-112
see also financiers (below)
biographies of
Chandler, Alfred Du Pont Jr.
3 422-423
Nevins, Allan **11** 357-359
chemical industry
Grasselli, Caesar Augustin
6 497-498
communications industry
Cornell, Ezra **4** 236-237
Disney, Walter Elias **5** 26-27
Farnsworth, Philo T. **5** 386-387
Field, Cyrus West **5** 438-439
Goldwyn, Samuel **6** 416
Graham, Katharine Meyer
6 483-485
Hefner, Hugh **7** 253-254
Hobby, Oveta Culp **7** 423-425
Morse, Samuel Finley Breese
11 192-193
Newhouse, Samuel Irving
11 362-364
Paley, William S. **12** 72-75
Pupin, Michael Idvorsky **12** 483-484
Robertson, Pat **13** 196-198
Sarnoff, David **13** 485-486
Sarnoff, David **13** 485-486
Sulzberger, Arthur Ochs **15** 28-30
Turner, Ted **15** 355-357
Young, Owen D. **16** 473-474
see also Editors; Journalists; Publishers
computer industry
Cray, Seymour **4** 301-303
Gates, William Henry III **6** 232-234
Jobs, Steven **8** 265-267
Noyce, Robert **11** 436-437
Packard, David **12** 54-56
Wang, An **16** 93-95
Watson, Thomas J. **16** 140
conglomerates
Blumenthal, Werner Michael
2 345-346
construction industry
Bechtel, Stephen Davison **2** 98-99
copier industry
Wilson, Joseph Chamberlain
16 325-326
cosmetics and beauty aids industry
Arden, Elizabeth **1** 281-282
Ash, Mary Kay Wagner **1** 326-327
Lauder, Estee **9** 225-226
Rubenstein, Helena **13** 342-343
Walker, C. J. **16** 61-62
data processing industry
Perot, Henry Ross **12** 230-231
electrical industry
Farmer, Moses Gerrish **5** 385
Insull, Samuel **8** 130
Packard, David **12** 54-56

Steinmetz, Charles Proteus
14 419-420
Swope, Gerard **15** 56-58
Westinghouse, George **16** 215
elevator industry
Otis, Elisha Graves **12** 24
Sprague, Frank Julian **14** 385-386
engineering
Sperry, Elmer A. **14** 377-379
entertainment industry
Capra, Frank **3** 276-278
Frohman, Charles **6** 123-124
Gordy, Berry Jr. **6** 450-451
Loew, Marcus **9** 485-486
Shubert Brothers **14** 207-209
express systems
Butterfield, John **3** 184-185
Fargo, William George **5** 380-381
fashion industry
Carnegie, Hattie **3** 313
Claiborne, Liz **4** 68-69
Johnson, Betsey **8** 295-296
Karan, Donna **8** 442-444
Klein, Calvin **9** 50-52
Lauren, Ralph **9** 228-229
Mizrahi, Isaac **11** 66-67
von Furstenberg, Diane **16** 20-21
financiers (19th century)
Butterfield, John **3** 184-185
Cooper, Peter **4** 223-224
Corning, Erastus **4** 238-239
Drew, Daniel **5** 101-102
Duke, James Buchanan **5** 133-134
Gould, Jay **6** 470-472
Vanderbilt, Cornelius **15** 415-416
financiers (19th-20th century)
Aldrich, Nelson Wilmarth
1 123-124
Frick, Henry Clay **6** 108-109
Kennedy, John Stewart **8** 507-508
financiers (20th century)
Baruch, Bernard Mannes **2** 42-43
Harriman, W. Averell **7** 165-166
see also bankers (above)
food and beverage industry
Armour, Philip Danforth **1** 302
Borden, Gail **2** 409
Goodnight, Charles **6** 439
Keith, Minor Cooper **8** 476-477
Kroc, Raymond Albert **9** 103-104
McCoy, Joseph Geiting **10** 403-404
Pillsbury, Charles Alfred **12** 304
Post, Charles William **12** 408-409
Rudkin, Margaret Fogarty
13 346-347
Woodruff, Robert W. **16** 372-374
Zemurray, Samuel **16** 496-497
foundation managers
Rockefeller, John D. Jr. **13** 225-226
glass and plastics industry
Baekeland, Leo Hendrik **1** 430-431
Stiegel, Henry William **14** 451
Tiffany, Louis Comfort **15** 220-221
hotel industry
Grossinger, Jennie **7** 15-17

Tisch brothers **15** 238-240
industrial management
Gilbreth, Lillian **6** 315-317
insurance
Bethune, Mary McLeod **2** 241-242
Girard, Stephen **6** 347-348
Spaulding, Charles Clinton
14 364-365
investors
Riordan, Richard Joseph **13** 177-179
iron and steel industry (18th-19th century)
Carnegie, Andrew **3** 309-312
Cooper, Peter **4** 223-224
Hanna, Marcus Alonzo **7** 127-128
Hewitt, Abram Stevens **7** 371-372
Kelly, William **8** 487-488
Stiegel, Henry William **14** 451
iron and steel industry (20th century)
Frick, Henry Clay **6** 108-109
Gary, Elbert Henry **6** 229-230
Kaiser, Henry John **8** 412-413
Mellon, Andrew William
10 469-470
Morgan, John Pierpont **11** 163-165
Rockefeller, John Davison
13 226-228
Schwab, Charles Michael **14** 50-51
Stettinius, Edward R. Jr. **14** 437-438
merchants (colonial)
Bowdoin, James **2** 461-462
Brown, Moses **3** 42-43
Byrd, William **3** 188-189
Cuffe, Paul **4** 331-332
DeLancey, Stephen **4** 473
Faneuil, Peter **5** 377
Harrison, Peter **7** 179-180
Laurens, Henry **9** 232
Morris, Robert **11** 185-187
Pepperell, William **12** 206-207
Pinto, Isaac **12** 318
Watson, Elkanah **16** 136
merchants (19th century)
Appleton, Nathan **1** 266-267
Brown, Alexander **3** 31-32
Corning, Erastus **4** 238-239
Field, Cyrus West **5** 438-439
Forbes, Robert Bennet **5** 509-510
Girard, Stephen **6** 347-348
Grace, William Russell **6** 480-481
Harris, Townsend **7** 176-177
Larkin, Thomas Oliver **9** 208
Stewart, Alexander Turney
14 448-449
Tappan brothers **15** 105-106
mining industry
Clark, William Andrews **4** 83-85
Comstock, Henry Tompkins Paige
4 189
Daly, Marcus **4** 379-380
Guggenheim, Meyer **7** 31-32
Hearst, George **7** 242
Mackay, John William **10** 101-102
Tabor, Horace Austin Warner **15** 70
music industry
Gordy, Berry Jr. **6** 450-451

Jones, Quincy Delight Jr. **8** 339-341
oil industry
   Getty, Jean Paul **6** 288-290
   Hunt, H. L. **8** 42-44
   Jones, Samuel Milton **8** 342-343
   Mellon, Andrew William
     10 469-470
   Rockefeller, John Davison
     13 226-228
   Rockefeller, John D. Jr. **13** 225-226
photography
   Eastman, George **5** 186
   Land, Edwin Herbert **9** 183-184
printing industry
   Bradford, William **2** 476-477
   Bradford, William **2** 477
   Forbes, Malcolm **5** 508-509
   Franklin, Benjamin **6** 60-64
   Hoe, Richard March **7** 435-436
   Knopf, Blanche Wolf **9** 61-62
   Mergenthaler, Ottmar **10** 516-517
   Sulzberger, Arthur Ochs **15** 28-30
   Zenger, John Peter **16** 497-498
   see also Publishers
promoters and speculators
   Bernays, Edward L. **2** 211-212
   Fisk, James **5** 464-465
   Hammer, Armand **7** 103-104
   Lawson, Thomas William **9** 255-256
   Vanderbilt, Cornelius **15** 415-416
   Walker, William **16** 68-69
   Watson, Elkanah **16** 136
railroad industry (builders)
   Gordon, John Brown **6** 449-450
   Gould, Jay **6** 470-472
   Hill, James Jerome **7** 388-389
   Judah, Theodore Dehone **8** 373-374
   Keith, Minor Cooper **8** 476-477
   Meiggs, Henry **10** 458-459
   Pullman, George Mortimer
     12 482-483
   Stanford, Leland **14** 397-398
   Vanderbilt, Cornelius **15** 415-416
   Wheelwright, William **16** 223-224
railroad industry (executives)
   Corning, Erastus **4** 238-239
   Durant, Thomas Clark **5** 157-158
   Garrett, John Work **6** 225
   Gould, Jay **6** 470-472
   Harriman, Edward Henry **7** 164-165
   Harriman, W. Averell **7** 165-166
   Huntington, Collis Potter **8** 49
   Vanderbilt, Cornelius **15** 415-416
real estate
   Astor, John Jacob **1** 351-352
   DeBartolo **4** 438-440
   Girard, Stephen **6** 347-348
   Henderson, Richard **7** 278-279
   Hunt, H. L. **8** 42-44
   Tisch brothers **15** 238-240
   Trump, Donald John **15** 318-319
retail marketing
   Field, Marshall **5** 440-441
   Penney, J. C. **12** 202-203
   Rosenwald, Julius **13** 293

Straus, Isidor **14** 496
   von Furstenberg, Diane **16** 20-21
   Walton, Sam Moore **16** 91-92
   Ward, Aaron Montgomery **16** 112
   Wood, Robert Elkington **16** 370-371
   Woolworth, Frank Winfield
     16 383-384
sewing machines
   Singer, Isaac M. **14** 250
shipping industry
   Astor, John Jacob **1** 351-352
   Bechtel, Stephen Davison **2** 98-99
   Forbes, Robert Bennet **5** 509-510
   Forten, James **6** 17-18
   Ludwig, Daniel Keith **10** 29-31
   McKay, Donald **10** 416-417
stock brokers
   Buffett, Warren **3** 106-109
   Merrill, Charles E. **10** 519-520
textile industry
   Appleton, Nathan **1** 266-267
   Brown, Moses **3** 42-43
   Coxe, Tench **4** 285-286
   Evans, Oliver **5** 338
   Gregg, William **6** 530-531
   Lawrence, Abbott **9** 246
   Little, Royal **9** 449-451
   Lowell, Francis Cabot **10** 13-14
   Slater, Samuel **14** 272-273
tire and rubber industry
   Firestone, Harvey Samuel **5** 452-453
   Goodyear, Charles **6** 441
tobacco industry
   Duke, James Buchanan **5** 133-134
transit systems
   Johnson, Tom Loftin **8** 317
   Sprague, Frank Julian **14** 385-386
travel industry
   Trippe, Juan Terry **15** 297-298
   Ueberroth, Peter Victor **15** 379-381
underwriters
   Merrill, Charles E. **10** 519-520

Business and industrial leaders, French
   Chanel, Coco **3** 429
   Lumière Brothers, The **10** 41-43

Business and industry (United States)
administration
   Chandler, Alfred Du Pont Jr.
     3 422-423
   du Pont, Pierre Samuel **5** 154-155
   Field, Marshall **5** 440-441
Federal policy
   Coolidge, John Calvin **4** 217-219
   Harding, Warren Gamaliel
     7 148-149
   Harrison, Benjamin **7** 178-179
   Nixon, Richard Milhous **11** 401-404
   Roosevelt, Theodore **13** 280-283
   Taft, William Howard **15** 78-81
   see also Antitrust laws
history of
   Chandler, Alfred Du Pont Jr.
     3 422-423
industrial research
   Carlson, Chester F. **3** 303-304

Langmuir, Irving **9** 196-197
   Steinmetz, Charles Proteus
     14 419-420
influence on universities
   Veblen, Thorstein Bunde
     15 449-450
mechanization
   Ford, Henry **6** 5-6
   Ford, Henry II **6** 6-7
safety crusade
   Nader, Ralph **11** 290-291
   see also Business and industrial
     leaders, American; Labor unions;
     Mass production; Monopoly

Business cycles (economics)
   Fisher, Irving **5** 462-463
   Hoover, Herbert Clark **7** 483-485
   Kuznets, Simon **9** 138-139
   Mitchell, Wesley Clair **11** 61-62
   Robertson, Dennis Holme **13** 196
   Schumpeter, Joseph Alois **14** 43-44
   von Mises, Ludwig **16** 25

Busiris (speech)
   Isocrates **8** 151

Busnois, Anthoine (died 1492), French
composer
   Dufay, Guillaume **5** 125-126
   Dunstable, John **5** 150-151
   Ockeghem, Johannes **11** 464-465

BUSONI, FERRUCCIO BENVENUTO
(1866-1924) Italian musician **3** 173-174
   Varèse, Edgard **15** 432-433
   Weill, Kurt **16** 174-175

Bussaco, Battle of (1810)
   Wellington, 1st Duke of **16** 193-195

BUSSOTTI, SYLVANO (born 1931) Italian
composer **3** 174-175

Bussy D'Ambois (play)
   Chapman, George **3** 440-441

Bust of a Young Woman (sculpture)
   Verrocchio, Andrea del **15** 471-472

Bustamante, Anastasio (1780-1853), Mexi-
can general, president 1829-1832
   Alamán, Lucas **1** 99-100
   Guerrero, Vicente **7** 28-30
   Santa Ana, Antonio López de
     13 471-472

BUSTAMANTE, WILLIAM ALEXANDER
(1884-1977), Jamaican labor leader and
first prime minister (1962-1967)
3 175-177

Bustamante Industrial Trade Union
(Jamaica)
   Bustamante, William Alexander
     3 175-177

Bustamante y Rivero, Jose Luis
(1894-1989), Peruvian jurist, president
1945-1948
   Prado Ugarteche, Manuel **12** 430-431

Bustan (poems)
   Sa'di **13** 418-419

But Even the Sun Has No Home (poems)
   Sachs, Nelly **13** 411-412

Bute (island, Firth of Clyde)
Bute, 3d Earl of **3** 177-178

BUTE, 3D EARL OF (John Stuart; 1713-1792), British statesman, prime minister 1762-1763 **3** 177-178
Franklin, William **6** 69-70
George III **6** 270-272
Pitt, William the Elder **12** 328-329
Wilkes, John **16** 280-281

BUTHELEZI, MANGOSUTHU GATSHA (born 1928), chief of the Zulu "homeland" and an important figure in the struggle to end apartheid in South Africa **3** 178-179

Butler, Andrew Pickens (1796-1857), American politician
Sumner, Charles **15** 30-31

Butler, Benjamin Franklin (1818-1893), American general and politician
Barton, Clara **2** 37-39
Gatling, Richard Jordan **6** 234-235
Soulé, Pierre **14** 351-352

BUTLER, JOHN (1728-1796), British Indian agent and Loyalist leader **3** 180

BUTLER, JOSEPH (1692-1752), English philosopher and theologian **3** 180-181

BUTLER, NICHOLAS MURRAY (1862-1947), American educator **3** 181
Dewey, Melvil **4** 523-524
Stone, Harlan Fiske **14** 468-470

BUTLER, OCTAVIA E. (born 1947), African American novelist and essayist **3** 182-183

Butler, Pierce (1866-1939), American jurist
Taft, William Howard **15** 78-81
Washington, George **16** 126-129

Butler, Reginald Cotterell (1913-1981), English sculptor
González, Julio **6** 428-429

BUTLER, SAMUEL (1613-1680) English poet **3** 183-184

BUTLER, SAMUEL (1835-1902), English novelist and essayist **3** 183

Butler, Walter (died 1781), American military officer
Butler, John **3** 180

Butler University (Indianapolis, Indiana)
Jordan, David Starr **8** 350-351
Wiley, Harvey Washington **16** 277-278

Butlerov, Aleksandr Miklailovich (1828-1886), Russian chemist
Pavlov, Ivan Petrovich **12** 155-157

Butler's Rangers (Loyalists, American Revolution)
Butler, John **3** 180

Butor, Michel Marie François (born 1926), French writer
Robbe-Grillet, Alain **13** 189-190

Butt, Isaac (1813-1879), Irish nationalist
Gladstone, William Ewart **6** 357-360
Parnell, Charles Stewart **12** 117-119

Butte Miner (newspaper)
Clark, William Andrews **4** 83-85

Buttered Side Down (stories)
Ferber, Edna **5** 413

Butterfat (milk)
Babcock, Stephen Moulton **1** 410-411

Butterfield, Daniel (1831-1901), American general
Butterfield, John **3** 184-185

BUTTERFIELD, JOHN (1801-1869), American financier and politician **3** 184-185

Butterfield, William (1814-1900), English architect
Richardson, Henry Hobson **13** 139-141

Butterfield 8 (novel)
O'Hara, John **11** 485

Butterfield, Wasson and Company
see American Express

Button, Sir Thomas (died 1634), English navigator
Baffin, William **1** 435-436

Butts, Thomas (1757?-1845), English literary patron
Blake, William **2** 316-318

BUXTEHUDE, DIETRICH (1637-1707), Danish composer and organist **3** 185-186
Bach, Johann Sebastian **1** 416-419
Froberger, Johann Jakob **6** 120-121

Buyer's Market, A (novel)
Powell, Anthony **12** 422-423

Buzi (Old Testament character)
Ezekiel **5** 355-356

By Avon River (book)
Doolittle, Hilda **5** 65-66

By Blue Ontario's Shore (poem)
Whitman, Walt **16** 249-251

By-Line Ernest Hemingway (literary collection)
Hemingway, Ernest Miller **7** 274-277

By Night at the Old Market (book)
Peretz, Isaac Loeb **12** 212

By the Road to the Contagious Hospital (poem)
Williams, William Carlos **16** 308-309

By the Seaside and the Fireside (literary collection)
Longfellow, Henry Wadsworth **9** 499-500

By the Waters of Babylon (musical composition)
Bach, Johann Sebastian **1** 416-419

BYRD, RICHARD EVELYN (1888-1957), American admiral and polar explorer **3** 186-187
Ellsworth, Lincoln **5** 277
MacMillan, Donald Baxter **10** 111-112

BYRD, WILLIAM (1543?-1623), English composer **3** 187-188
Dowland, John **5** 90
Isaac, Heinrich **8** 143-144

Morley, Thomas **11** 179-180
Tallis, Thomas **15** 91
Vaughan Williams, Ralph **15** 446-447

BYRD, WILLIAM (1652-1704), English colonial planter and merchant **3** 188-189
Byrd, William II **3** 189-190

BYRD, WILLIAM II (1674-1744), American diarist and government official **3** 189-190
Beverley, Robert **2** 252

Byrne, Donn
see Donn-Byrne, Brian Oswald

BYRNE, JANE (born 1934), first woman mayor of Chicago **3** 190-191

BYRNES, JAMES FRANCIS (1879-1972), American public official **3** 191-192
Baruch, Bernard Mannes **2** 42-43
Truman, Harry S. **15** 314-316

BYRON, GEORGE GORDON NOEL (6th Baron Byron; 1788-1824), English poet **3** 193-194
associates
Lewis, Matthew Gregory **9** 390-391
Melbourne, 2nd Viscount **10** 468-469
Shelley, Percy Bysshe **14** 176-178
influence of
Browning, Elizabeth Barrett **3** 52-53
Bunin, Ivan Alekseevich **3** 124
Echeverría, José Estéban **5** 197-198
Eminescu, Mihail **5** 280-281
Lamartine, Alphonse Marie Louis de **9** 173-175
Lermontov, Mikhail Yurievich **9** 352-353
Pushkin, Aleksandr Sergeevich **12** 489-491
influenced by
Burton, Robert **3** 166-167
Juvenal **8** 397-399
works
Boone, Daniel **2** 397-398
Ryder, Albert Pinkham **13** 391-392
Schumann, Robert Alexander **14** 41-43
Verdi, Giuseppe Fortunino Francesco **15** 463-465

Byron, Harriet (literary character)
Richardson, Samuel **13** 141-142

Byron, John (Mad Jack; 1756-1791), English captain
Byron, George Gordon Noel **3** 193-194

Bystander, The (novel)
Gorky, Maxim **6** 458-460

Byzantine art
see Italo-Byzantine style

Byzantine Church
see Orthodox Eastern Church

Byzantine Empire (395-1453; Eastern Roman Empire 395-474)
and Holy Roman Empire
Irene of Athens **8** 135-138
Bulgaria conquered
Basil II **2** 50-51

crusades (1st)
  Alexius I **1** 143-144
  Bohemund, I **2** 364
  Dandolo, Enrico **4** 386-387
  Godfrey of Bouillon **6** 379
  Innocent, III **8** 125-127
decline and fall
  Constantine XI **4** 211-212
  Frederick I **6** 78-79
  Manuel I **10** 218-219
  Mehmed the Conqueror **10** 452-454
  Michael VIII **11** 1-2
  Zoë **16** 524-525
histories
  Comnena, Anna **4** 185-186
  Procopius of Caesarea **12** 457-458
Islamic campaigns
  Basil I **2** 49-50
  Harun al-Rashid **7** 188

Heraclius **7** 320-321
Leo III **9** 330-332
Mamun, Abdallah al- **10** 183
Muawiya ibn Abu Sufyan
  11 223-224
Omar ibn al-Khattab **11** 508-509
Italy
  Alexius I **1** 143-144
  Basil I **2** 49-50
  Belisarius **2** 128-129
  Gregory I **6** 531-532
  Guiscard, Robert **7** 39-40
  Justinian I **8** 393-395
  Otto I **12** 28-29
legal reforms
  Basil I **2** 49-50
  Justinian I **8** 393-395
peace with Huns (435)
  Attila **1** 360

religious controversies
  Cyril **4** 362
  Eutyches **5** 335
  John of Damascus **8** 282
  Justinian I **8** 393-395
  Leo I **9** 329-330
  Leo III **9** 330-332
  Nestorius **11** 349-350
  Theodora **15** 172-175
Vandal wars
  Alaric **1** 101-102
  Belisarius **2** 128-129
  Gaiseric **6** 172
  Justinian I **8** 393-395
  Ricimer, Flavius **13** 151-152

Byzantine literature
  Photius **12** 283-284

Byzantium
  see Byzantine Empire

C

Ca' Rezzonico (Venice)
Tiepolo, Giovanni Battista **15** 219-220

Cabal (1667-1673; English politics)
Buckingham, 2d Duke of **3** 94-95
Charles II **3** 452-454
Shaftesbury, 1st Earl of **14** 135-136

Cabala (Jewish mysticism)
commentaries
Caro, Joseph ben Ephraim
3 316-317
Elijah ben Solomon **5** 251-252
Leon, Moses de **9** 336
Hasidism
Baal Shem Tov **1** 404-405
Luria, Isaac ben Solomon Ashkenazi
10 47-48
Scholem, Gershom **14** 26
influence of
Kuk, Abraham Issac **9** 123-124
Yeats, William Butler **16** 445-447
Zunz, Leopold **16** 534
Lurianic
Luria, Isaac ben Solomon Ashkenazi
10 47-48
Sabbatai Zevi **13** 400-401
Messianic Age
Luzzato, Moses Hayyim **10** 57-58
Manasseh ben Israel **10** 183-184
Sabbatai Zevi **13** 400-401
Neoplatonism
ibn Gabirol, Solomon ben Judah
8 92
Nahmanides **11** 293-294
Scholem, Gershom **14** 26
see also Mysticism, Jewish

Cabala, The (novel)
Wilder, Thornton Niven **16** 276-277

Cabanel, Alexandre (1823-1889), French
painter
Maillol, Aristide **10** 150-151

Cabbages and Kings (stories)
Henry, O. **7** 308-309

CABELL, JAMES BRANCH (1879-1958),
American essayist and novelist **3** 195-196

CABET, ÉTIENNE (1788-1856), French
political radical **3** 196

CABEZA DE VACA, ÁLVAR NÚÑEZ (circa
1490-circa 1557), Spanish explorer **3** 197
Coronado, Francisco Vásquez de **4** 247
Díaz del Castillo, Bernal **4** 536-537
Estevanico **5** 324-325
Marcos de Niza **10** 240
Narváez, Pánfilo de **11** 315

Cabeza del dragón, La (play)
Valle Inclán, Ramón Maria del
15 407-408

CABEZÓN, ANTONIO (1510-1566), Spanish composer **3** 197-198

Cabezon, Hernando (1541-1602), Spanish
organist
Cabezón, Antonio **3** 197-198

Cabinda (region, Angola)
Kasavubu, Joseph **8** 453-455

Cabinet (government)
Howe, Joseph **7** 534-535
Liverpool, 2nd Earl of **9** 456-457
Perkins, Frances **12** 221-222
Washington, George **16** 126-129

Cabinet of Dr. Caligari, The (film)
Goldwyn, Samuel **6** 416

Cabinet-maker ... Encyclopedia (book)
Sheraton, Thomas **14** 181-182

**Cabinet-maker and Upholsterer's Drawing
Book, The** (book)
Sheraton, Thomas **14** 181-182

**Cabinet-Maker and Upholsterer's Guide,
The** (book)
Hepplewhite, George **7** 317-318

Cabinet-Maker's Director
see Gentleman and Cabinet-Maker's
Director, The

CABLE, GEORGE WASHINGTON
(1844-1925), American novelist
3 198-199

Cable News Network (United States)
Turner, Ted **15** 355-357

Caboose (painting)
Kline, Franz **9** 55

CABOT, JOHN (flourished 1471-1498),
Italian explorer in English service
3 199-200
Cabot, Sebastian **3** 200-201
Cartier, Jacques **3** 343-344
Champlain, Samuel de **3** 419-421
Henry VII **7** 300-302

CABOT, RICHARD CLARKE (1868-1939),
American physician **3** 200

CABOT, SEBASTIAN (circa 1482-1557),
Italian-born explorer for England and
Spain **3** 200-201
Cabot, John **3** 199-200
Chancellor, Richard **3** 422

Caboto, Giovanni
see Cabot, John

CABRAL, AMÍLCAR LOPES (1924-1973),
father of modern African nationalism in
Guinea-Bissau and the Cape Verde
Islands **3** 202-203

CABRAL, PEDRO ÁLVARES
(1467/68-1520), Portuguese navigator
3 203-204
Dias de Novais, Bartolomeu **4** 533-534
Manuel I **10** 219-220
Vespucci, Amerigo **15** 476-478

Cabrera, Manuel Estrada
see Estrada Cabrera, Manuel

CABRILLO, JUAN RODRÍGUEZ (died
1543), Portuguese explorer for Spain
3 204-205

CABRINI, ST. FRANCES XAVIER
(1850-1917), Italian-born founder of the
Missionary Sisters of the Sacred Heart
3 205

Cacau (novel)
Amado, Jorge **1** 189-190

Caccia (song)
Landini, Francesco **9** 185-186

Caccia di Diana (poem)
Boccaccio, Giovanni **2** 351-353

Cacciaguida (died circa 1147), Italian
nobleman
Dante Alighieri **4** 389-391

Cacciatori delle Alpi (Italian corps)
Victor Emmanuel II **15** 483-484

CACCINI, GIULIO (circa 1545-1618), Italian singer and composer **3** 205-206
Monteverdi, Claudio Giovanni Antonio **11** 126-128

Caciques (Aztec chiefs)
Montezuma, II **11** 128-129

Cactus Man (sculpture)
González, Julio **6** 428-429

CADAMOSTO, ALVISE DA (circa 1428-1483), Italian explorer **3** 206-207
Henry the Navigator **7** 305-306

Cade, Jack (died 1450), English rebel leader
Henry VI **7** 298-299

Cadenus and Vanessa (poem)
Swift, Jonathan **15** 51-54

Cader Idris (painting)
Wilson, Richard **16** 329-330

Cadillac, Antoine de la Mothe (1658-1730), French colonial administrator
Bienville, Sieur de **2** 268-269

Cadillac Automobile Co.
Durant, William Crapo **5** 158

Cadiz (city, Spain)
English raids
Buckingham, 1st Duke of **3** 93-94
Charles, I **3** 450-452
Donne, John **5** 60-61
Drake, Francis **5** 94-96
Essex, 2d Earl of **5** 321-322
Raleigh, Walter **13** 9-11
general
Columbus, Christopher **4** 176-179
Murillo, Bartolomé Esteban **11** 258-259

Cadmium (element—chemistry)
Hofmann, August Wilhelm von **7** 441-442

Cadmus (literary character)
Euripides **5** 332-334

Caecilius Statius (219?-166? B.C.), Roman playwright
Terence **15** 146-148

Caedmon (flourished 670), English poet
Bede **2** 109-110

Caelestius (flourished 5th century), British Pelagian heretic
Pelagius **12** 189-190

Caelius Aurelianus (flourished 5th century), North African physician
Celsus, Aulus Cornelius **3** 393

Caelius Rufus, Marcus (died 48 B.C.), Roman statesman
Catullus, Gaius Valerius **3** 377-378

Caen, University of (France)
Poincaré, Jules Henri **12** 365-366

Caepio, Quintus Servilius (flourished circa 105 B.C.), Roman general

Drusus, Marcus Livius **5** 105-106

Caerhayes (house, Cornwall)
Nash, John **11** 316

Caesar (play)
Goethe, Johann Wolfgang von **6** 388-391

Caesar, Irving (1895-1996), American lyricist
Gershwin, George **6** 284-285

Caesar, Julia (died 54 B.C.), wife of Pompey
Caesar, Gaius Julius **3** 207-210

CAESAR, (GAIUS) JULIUS (100-44 B.C.), Roman general and statesman **3** 207-210
adopts Octavian
Augustus **1** 371-373
assassination
Antony, Mark **1** 253-254
Brutus, Marcus Junius **3** 79-80
Catiline conspiracy
Cato, the Younger **3** 374-375
civil war
Cato, the Younger **3** 374-375
Pompey **12** 387-389
Sallust **13** 454
Varro, Marcus Terentius **15** 438-439
Egypt and
Cleopatra **4** 105-106
First Triumvirate
Cato, the Younger **3** 374-375
Cicero, Marcus Tullius **4** 55-58
Clodius Pulcher, Publius **4** 121-122
Crassus Dives, Marcus Licinius **4** 296-297
Pompey **12** 387-389
in literature
Catullus, Gaius Valerius **3** 377-378
Clarke, Samuel **4** 88
Ferrero, Guglielmo **5** 429-430
Shakespeare, William **14** 142-145
Suetonius Tranquillus, Gaius **15** 13
Wilder, Thornton Niven **16** 276-277

CAESAR, SHIRLEY (born 1938), African American singer **3** 210-211

Caesarea (ancient city, Cappadocia)
Basil the Great **2** 51-52

Caesarea (ancient city, Palestine)
Herod the Great **7** 333-334

Caesar's Column (book)
Donnelly, Ignatius **5** 62

Caesura (literature)
Ennius, Quintus **5** 289

Caetani, Benedetto
see Boniface VIII

Caetano, Marcelo (1906-1980), Portuguese statesman
Salazar, António de Oliveira **13** 442-443

Café (painting)
Portinari, Cândido **12** 407-408

Café de artistas (book)
Cela y Trulock, Camilo José **3** 389-390

Caffa (modern Feodosiya, Ukraine)
Mehmed the Conqueror **10** 452-454

Caffarelli
see Borghese, Scipione

CAGE, JOHN (1912-1992), American composer **3** 211-214
influence of
Bussotti, Sylvano **3** 174-175
Cunningham, Merce **4** 337-338
Johns, Jasper **8** 291-293
Stockhausen, Karlheinz **14** 460-461
influenced by
Ives, Charles Edward **8** 159-160
Varèse, Edgard **15** 432-433

Cage, John Milton (1887?-1964), American inventor and engineer
Cage, John **3** 211-214

Cagney, James (1904-1986), American actor
Cohan, George Michael **4** 137-138

CAHAN, ABRAHAM (1860-1951), Lithuanian-American Jewish author **3** 214

Cahiagué (village, Ontario)
Champlain, Samuel de **3** 419-421

Cahier gris, Le (novel)
Martin du Gard, Roger **10** 295-296

Cahiers d'André Walter, Les (book)
Gide, André **6** 308-309

Cahiers de la quinzaine (periodical)
Péguy, Charles Pierre **12** 183-184

Cahiers du cinéma (revolution)
Truffaut, François **15** 311-313

Caillaux, Joseph (1863-1944), French politician
Laval, Pierre **9** 237-238

Caillavet, Madame Arman de (died 1910), French literary figure
France, Anatole **6** 39-40

Caillebotte, Gustave (1848-1894), French painter
Monet, Claude **11** 102-104
Renoir, Pierre Auguste **13** 101-102

CAILLIÉ, AUGUSTE RENÉ (1799-1838), French explorer **3** 214-215
Barth, Heinrich **2** 30-31

Cain (play)
Byron, George Gordon Noel **3** 193-194

Caine Mutiny, The (novel; Wouk)
Bogart, Humphrey **2** 363-364

Cairo (city, Egypt)
Omar ibn Said Tal, Al-Hajj **11** 509-510
Selim I **14** 94-95

Cairo, University of
Hanafi, Hassan **7** 114

CAJETAN, ST. (1480-1547), Italian reformer; cofounder of the Theatines **3** 215-216
Paul IV **12** 145-146

Cajetan, Thomas de Vio (1469-1534), Italian theologian
  Luther, Martin **10** 48-51

Cakes and Ale (novel)
  Maugham, William Somerset **10** 344-345

Calabar (town, Nigeria)
  Macaulay, Herbert **10** 78-79

Calabria, Duke of
  see Guiscard, Robert

Calais, Battle of (1558)
  Mary, I **10** 308-309

Calais, siege of (1346-1347)
  Edward III **5** 211-212
  Edward the Black Prince **5** 217-218
  Philip VI **12** 277-278

Calais Pier (painting)
  Turner, Joseph Mallord William **15** 352-354

Calamba (town, Philippines)
  Rizal, José **13** 187-189

CALAMITY JANE (Martha Jane Cannary; 1852-1903), American frontier woman **3** 216
  Hickok, James Butler **7** 374-375

Calamus (poems)
  Whitman, Walt **16** 249-251

Calatafimi, Battle of (1860)
  Garibaldi, Giuseppe **6** 215-217

Calavar (novel)
  Bird, Robert Montgomery **2** 281-282

Calcar, Jan Stephan van (circa 1499-circa 1550), Dutch painter
  Vesalius, Andreas **15** 473-475

Calcium (element—chemistry)
  Cavendish, Henry **3** 383-384
  Davy, Humphry **4** 426-427

Calculated Risk (book)
  Clark, Mark Wayne **4** 80-81

Calculating machine (mathematics)
  Babbage, Charles **1** 407-408
  Hooke, Robert **7** 475
  Leibniz, Gottfried Wilhelm von **9** 307-310

Calculus (mathematics)
  differential
    Cauchy, Augustin Louis **3** 378-380
    Einstein, Albert **5** 228-231
    Leibniz, Gottfried Wilhelm von **9** 307-310
  infinitesimal
    Laplace, Marquis de **9** 202-204
  integral
    Alembert, Jean le Rond d' **1** 127-128
    Archimedes **1** 277-280-223
    Einstein, Albert **5** 228-231
    Fourier, Jean Baptiste Joseph **6** 32-33
    Leibniz, Gottfried Wilhelm von **9** 307-310
  invention

    Leibniz, Gottfried Wilhelm von **9** 307-310
    Newton, Isaac **11** 369-372
  matrix
    Dirac, Paul Adrien Maurice **5** 23-24
    Heisenberg, Werner Karl **7** 261-263
  of operators
    Boole, George **2** 396-397
  of probability
    Ampère, André Marie **1** 205-206
    Cournot, Antoine Augustin **4** 273
    Demoivre, Abraham **4** 494-495
    Fermat, Pierre de **5** 421-422
  of variations
    Euler, Leonard **5** 331-332
    Lagrange, Joseph Louis **9** 164-166
  propositional and predicate
    Frege, Gottlob **6** 93-94

Calculus, felicific (philosophy)
  Bentham, Jeremy **2** 176-178

Calcutta (city, India)
  Clive, Robert **4** 119-120
  Das, Chitta Ranjan **4** 401-402
  Gandhi, Mohandas Karamchand **6** 201-204
  Teresa **15** 148-151

Calcutta, University of (India)
  Maine, Henry James Sumner **10** 152
  Radhakrishnan, Sarvepalli **12** 537-538
  Raman, Chandrasekhar Venkata **13** 13-14

Calcutta Corp. (politics)
  Das, Chitta Ranjan **4** 401-402

Calcutta School Book Society
  Deb, Radhakant **4** 437

CALDER, ALEXANDER (1898-1976), American sculptor **3** 216-218
  Noguchi, Isamu **11** 416-418

Calder, Sir Robert (1745-1818), British naval officer
  Nelson, Horatio **11** 336-338

Calder Hall (Great Britain)
  Cockcroft, John Douglas **4** 131-132

Calder v. Bull (legal case)
  Chase, Samuel **3** 475-476

CALDERA RODRÍGUEZ, RAFAEL (born 1916), president of Venezuela (1969-1974) **3** 218-219

Calderon, Battle at the bridge of (1811)
  Hidalgo y Costilla, Miguel **7** 375-377

CALDERÓN, ALBERTO P. (born 1920), Hispanic American mathematician **3** 219-220

CALDERÓN, PEDRO (1600-1681), Spanish poet and playwright **3** 221-222
  Cervantes, Miguel de Saavedra **3** 395-398
  Grillparzer, Franz **6** 546-547
  Lope Félix de Vega Carpio **9** 503-506
  Tirso de Molina **15** 237-238
  Wycherley, William **16** 411-412

CALDERÓN FOURNIER, RAFAEL (born 1949), president of Costa Rica (1990-) **3** 222-223

Calderon Guardia, Rafael (1900-1970), Costa Rican politician
  Ferrer, José Figuéres **5** 428-429

CALDWELL, ERSKINE (1903-1987), American novelist **3** 223-224

CALDWELL, SARAH (born 1924), long-time artistic director, conductor, and founder of the Opera Company of Boston **3** 224-226

Calef, Robert (1648-1719), American merchant
  Mather, Cotton **10** 330-332

Calendar (chronology)
  Caesar, Gaius Julius **3** 207-210
  Eudoxus of Cnidus **5** 329-330
  Gregory XIII **6** 534
  Omar Khayyam **11** 510-511
  Shotoku Taishi **14** 205-207

Calendario manual y guía universal (book)
  Bello, Ahmadu **2** 139-140

Caletti-Bruni, Pietro Francesco
  see Cavalli, Pietro Francesco

Calgary (city, Canada)
  Bennett, Richard Bedford **2** 171-172

Calgary Prophetic Bible Institute (Canada)
  Aberhart, William **1** 26-27

CALHOUN, JOHN CALDWELL (1782-1850), American statesman **3** 226-228
  nullification crisis
    Blair, Francis Preston **2** 313-315
    Clay, Henry **4** 94-96
    Jackson, Andrew **8** 168-172
    McDuffie, George **10** 408
    Rhett, Robert Barnwell **13** 120
  political career
    Mason, James Murray **10** 320-321
    McCoy, Isaac **10** 403
    Monroe, James **11** 111-113
    Tyler, John **15** 368-369
  slavery defended
    Atchison, David Rice **1** 357-358
    Dew, Thomas Roderick **4** 519
  states' rights
    Hayne, Robert Young **7** 231-232
    McDuffie, George **10** 408
    Randolph, John **13** 30
    Webster, Daniel **16** 162-164
    Wilmot, David **16** 312-313

Caliari, Paolo
  see Veronese, Paolo

Calicut (city, India)
  Gama, Vasco da **6** 196-198

California (sculpture)
  Powers, Hiram **12** 428-429

California (state, United States)
  Bear Flag Revolt
    Frémont, John Charles **6** 97-98
    Larkin, Thomas Oliver **9** 208

Stockton, Robert Field **14** 461-462
Sutter, John Augustus **15** 41-42
ceded to U.S.
Polk, James Knox **12** 374-376
Sutter, John Augustus **15** 41-42
Congress, members of
Boxer, Barbara **2** 465-468
Panetta, Leon E. **12** 84-85
Waters, Maxine **16** 132-134
exploration
Cabrillo, Juan Rodríguez **3** 204-205
Drake, Francis **5** 94-96
Revillagigedo, Conde de
13 111-112
Franciscan missions
Serra, Junípero **14** 111-112
gold rush
Bidwell, John **2** 265
Comstock, Henry Tompkins Paige
4 189
Foster, Stephen Collins **6** 25-27
Judah, Theodore Dehone **8** 373-374
Mackay, John William **10** 101-102
Sutter, John Augustus **15** 41-42
Vanderbilt, Cornelius **15** 415-416
Walker, Joseph Reddeford **16** 63-64
governors
Wilson, Pete **16** 326-329
legal reforms
Field, David Dudley **5** 439-440
Johnson, Hiram Warren **8** 300-301
Warren, Earl **16** 117-120
mining
Hearst, George **7** 242
paleontology
Leakey, Louis Seymour Bazett **9** 262
Whitney, Josiah Dwight **16** 254-255
railroads
Harriman, Edward Henry **7** 164-165
Stanford, Leland **14** 397-398
settlement
Anza, Juan Bautista de **1** 254-255
Bidwell, John **2** 265
statehood
Clay, Henry **4** 94-96
Fillmore, Millard **5** 447-448

California, University of (all campuses)
Industrial Relations, Institute of
Kerr, Clark **8** 519-521
presidents
Kerr, Clark **8** 519-521

California, University of (Berkeley)
Bancroft Library
Teggart, Frederick J. **15** 133-134
literature
Cleaver, Leroy Eldridge **4** 97-98
music
Bloch, Ernest **2** 326-327
Hofmann, Hans **7** 442-443
Nin-Culmell, Joaquín María **11** 398
Schoenberg, Arnold **14** 24-26
philosophy
Lewis, Clarence Irving **9** 381
presidents
Gilman, Daniel Coit **6** 325-326

sciences
Calvin, Melvin **3** 242-243
Compton, Arthur Holly **4** 186-188
Lawrence, Ernest Orlando
9 248-250
Lewis, Gilbert Newton **9** 384-385
Oppenheimer, J. Robert **11** 525-526
Seaborg, Glenn Theodore **14** 74-76
Stanley, Wendell Meredith
14 400-401
Tarski, Alfred **15** 110-111
Teller, Edward **15** 139-141
Whipple, George Hoyt **16** 224-225
social sciences
Bancroft, Hubert Howe **1** 484-485
Erikson, Erik Homburger **5** 309-310
Kroeber, Alfred Louis **9** 105-106
Lewin, Kurt **9** 375-376
Lowie, Robert Harry **10** 18
Radin, Paul **12** 538-539
Sauer, Carl Ortwin **13** 496-497
Tolman, Edward Chace **15** 261-262
sociology
Teggart, Frederick J. **15** 133-134

California, University of (La Jolla)
Elsasser, Walter Maurice **5** 277-278

California, University of (Los Angeles)
Carnap, Rudolf **3** 308-309
Goodlad, John Inkster **6** 434-436
Libby, Willard Frank **9** 397-398
Popham, William James **12** 399-401

California, University of (San Diego)
Marcuse, Herbert **10** 245-247
Urey, Harold Clayton **15** 394-396

California Institute of Technology (Pasadena)
chemistry
Pauling, Linus Carl **12** 150-152
genetics
Beadle, George Wells **2** 80-81
Morgan, Thomas Hunt **11** 170-171
Watson, James Dewey **16** 137-138
geology
Davis, William Morris **4** 425-426
physics
Anderson, Carl David **1** 214-215
Elsasser, Walter Maurice **5** 277-278
Gell-Mann, Murray **6** 257-258
Kármán, Theodore von **8** 451-452
Millikan, Robert Andrews **11** 33-35
Oppenheimer, J. Robert **11** 525-526

California School of Fine Arts (San Francisco)
Rivera, Diego **13** 183-184
Rothko, Mark **13** 320-321

California Trail (Missouri-California)
Bridger, James **3** 2-3

CALIGULA (12-41), Roman emperor 37-41
3 228-229
Claudius Germanicus, Tiberius **4** 91-92
Philo Judaeus **12** 282-283
Seneca the Younger, Lucius Annaeus
14 103-105
Tacitus **15** 70-72

Zeno of Citium **16** 499-500

Caligula (play)
Camus, Albert **3** 255-257

Călin (poem)
Eminescu, Mihail **5** 280-281

Caliphs
see Statesmen

Calixtus II (Guido of Vienne; died 1124),
pope 1119-1124
Henry V **7** 295-296

Calixtus III (Alfonso Borgia; 1378-1458),
pope 1455-58
Alexander VI **1** 134-135

Call (newspaper)
Wilkins, Roy **16** 282-283

Call-Bulletin (newspaper)
Anderson, Maxwell **1** 219-220

Call Me Madam (musical)
Berlin, Irving **2** 200-201

Call of the Wild, The (stories)
London, Jack **9** 494-495

Call to Arms, A (stories)
Lu Hsün **10** 35-37

CALLAGHAN, EDWARD MORLEY
(1903-1990), Canadian novelist
3 229-230

CALLAGHAN, LEONARD JAMES (born
1912), Labor member of the British Parliament and prime minister, 1976-1979
3 230-231

CALLAHAN, DANIEL (born 1930), American philosopher who focused on biomedical ethics **3** 231-233

Callao (city, Peru)
Meiggs, Henry **10** 458-459

Calleja del Rey, Felix María (1750-1820),
Spanish general
Hidalgo y Costilla, Miguel **7** 375-377

CALLEJAS ROMERO, RAFAEL LEONARDO
(born 1943), president of Honduras
(1990-) **3** 233-234

Callender, James Thomson (1758-1803),
American journalist
Chase, Samuel **3** 475-476

CALLES, PLUTARCO ELÍAS (1877-1945),
Mexican revolutionary leader **3** 234-235
Cárdenas, Lázaro **3** 286-287
Carranza, Venustiano **3** 321-322
Gompers, Samuel **6** 420-422
Morrow, Dwight Whitney **11** 190-191
Obregón, Álvaro **11** 458-459
Villa, Pancho **15** 495-496

Callias (flourished 4th century B.C.), Athenian soldier
Socrates **14** 320-321
Xenophon **16** 418-420

Callias, Peace of (448 B.C.)
Pericles **12** 219-221

Calligrammes (poems)
Apollinaire, Guillaume **1** 260

Calligraphers
see Artists—calligraphers

Calligraphy (Chinese)
Mi Fei **11** 12-13
Ni Tsan **11** 400
Tung Ch'i-ch'ang **15** 339-340
Wu Tao-tzu **16** 405-406

CALLIMACHUS (circa 310-240 B.C.),
Greek poet **3** 235-236
Eratosthenes of Cyrene **5** 301-302
Miltiades **11** 42-43
Poliziano, Angelo **12** 373-374
Theocritus **15** 171-172

Callimachus (speech)
Isocrates **8** 151

Calling of Peter and Andrew (fresco)
Ghirlandaio, Domenico **6** 292-293

Calling of St. Matthew (painting)
Caravaggio **3** 282-284

Calling of the Soldier, The (novel)
Barrès, Auguste Maurice **2** 20-21

Callipides (literary character)
Menander **10** 477-478

Callisthenes (360?-328? B.C.), Greek historian
Ptolemy I **12** 470-472

CALLOWAY, CAB (1907-1994) American
singer, songwriter, and bandleader
3 236-238

Calm, The (poem)
Donne, John **5** 60-61

Calm Sea and Prosperous Voyage (overture)
Mendelssohn, Moses **10** 488-489

Calmecac (Aztec school)
Cuauhtemoc **4** 329

Calonne, Charles Alexandre de
(1734-1802), French statesman
Louis XVI **9** 534-535
Mirabeau, Comte de **11** 51-52

Caloric engine
see Steam engine

Calorimeter (instrument)
Hare, Robert **7** 152-153
Lavoisier, Antoine Laurent **9** 241-244
Richards, Theodore William
13 137-138

Calumny (painting)
Apelles **1** 257

Calumny of Apelles (painting)
Botticelli, Sandro **2** 439-440

Calvaert, Denis (1540?-1619), Flemish
painter
Reni, Guido **13** 97-98

Calvary, Mount (near Jerusalem)
Jesus of Nazareth **8** 251-255

Calvary Church (New York City)
Renwick, James **13** 102-103

Calvert, Cecilius, 2d Baron Baltimore
(1605-1675), American statesman
Calvert, Charles **3** 238

CALVERT, CHARLES (3rd Baron Baltimore;
1637-1715), English proprietor of colonial Maryland **3** 238
Calvert, George **3** 238-239
Penn, William **12** 200-202

Calvert, Charles, 5th Baron Baltimore
(1699-1751), English colonial governor
Calvert, Charles **3** 238

CALVERT, GEORGE (1st Baron Baltimore;
circa 1580-1632), English statesman,
founder of Maryland colony **3** 238-239
Calvert, Charles **3** 238
Strafford, 1st Earl of **14** 490-491

CALVIN, JOHN (1509-1564), French
Protestant reformer **3** 239-242
influence of
Edward VI **5** 213-214
Knox, John **9** 65-66
Lucaris, Cyril **10** 20
McGuffey, William Holmes
10 414-415
Stowe, Harriet Elizabeth Beecher
14 484-485
opponents
Ronsard, Pierre de **13** 271-273
Servetus, Michael **14** 115-116

CALVIN, MELVIN (born 1911), American
chemist **3** 242-243
Lewis, Gilbert Newton **9** 384-385

Calvinism (religion)
doctrine
Backus, Isaac **1** 420-421
Calvin, John **3** 239-242
Chauncy, Charles **3** 485-486
influence of
Jordaens, Jacob **8** 347-349
Knox, John **9** 65-66
Lloyd, Henry Demarest **9** 468-469
Tappan brothers **15** 105-106
Lutherans and
Frederick William III **6** 87
Maximilian II **10** 357-358
opponents
Channing, William Ellery **3** 435-436
Cudworth, Ralph **4** 331
Finney, Charles Grandison
5 450-451
Francis of Sales **6** 47
Louis XIV **9** 531-533
Ronsard, Pierre de **13** 271-273
rigorists
Dudley, Thomas **5** 124-125
Maurice of Nassau **10** 348-349
Oldenbarnevelt, Johan van
11 495-496
William the Silent **16** 300-302
see also Arminianism; Huguenots

CALVINO, ITALO (1923-1985), Italian
author **3** 243-244
Vittorini, Elio **16** 2-3

Calvo, Carlos (1824-1906), Argentine jurist
Drago, Luis María **5** 92-93

Calvus, Gaius Licinius Macer (flourished
1st century B.C.), Roman poet

Catullus, Gaius Valerius **3** 377-378

Calypso Oceanographic Expeditions
Cousteau, Jacques-Yves **4** 276-277

Calzabigi, Ranieri (1714-1795), Italian poet
Gluck, Christoph Willibald **6** 372-374

Cam, Diogo
see Cão, Diogo

Camagüey (province, Cuba)
Céspedes, Carlos Manuel de **3** 398-399

Cambiale de matrimonio, La (opera)
Rossini, Gioacchino **13** 311-312

Cambio, Collegio del (Perugia)
Perugino **12** 245-246

Cambio 90 (Peruvian political party)
Fujimori, Alberto Keinya **6** 143-145

Cambio de piel (novel)
Fuentes, Carlos **6** 141-142

Cambodia (Khmer Republic; nation, South-
east Asia)
Chulalongkorn **4** 43-45
Rannaridh, Norodom **13** 37-39
Sihanouk, Norodom **14** 222-223
see also Vietnam War (1956-1976)

Cambodian People's Republic (now Kam-
puchea; Southeast Asia)
Heng Samrin **7** 283-285
Hun Sen **8** 39-42
Pol Pot **12** 382-384
Sihanouk, Norodom **14** 222-223

Cambrai (city, France)
Dufay, Guillaume **5** 125-126
Edward III **5** 211-212

Cambrai, League of (1508-1510)
Julius II **8** 384-386
Maximilian I **10** 356-357

Cambrai, Peace of (1529)
Charles V **3** 457-459
Henry VIII **7** 302-305

Cambrian system (geology)
Murchison, Roderick Impey **11** 255-256
Sedgwick, Adam **14** 82-83

Cambridge Arts Theatre (established 1936)
Keynes, John Maynard **8** 528-530

Cambridge Platonists (English philosophy)
Cudworth, Ralph **4** 331

Cambridge school (economics)
Fisher, Irving **5** 462-463
Robertson, Dennis Holme **13** 196
von Mises, Ludwig **16** 25

Cambridge University (England)
astronomy
Eddington, Arthur Stanley **5** 201-202
biochemistry
Florey, Howard Walter **5** 491-492
Hopkins, Frederick Gowland
7 491-492
Krebs, Hans Adolf **9** 95-97
biology
Haldane, John Burdon Sanderson
7 70-71

Cavendish Laboratory
  see Cavendish Laboratory
chancellors
  Balfour, Arthur James **1** 469-470
geology
  Sedgwick, Adam **14** 82-83
history
  Kingsley, Charles **9** 28
  Maurice, John Frederick Denison
    10 349-350
  Trevelyan, George Macaulay
    15 294-295
History Faculty Building
  Stirling, James **14** 458-459
languages
  Erasmus, Desiderius **5** 298-300
  Housman, Alfred Edward **7** 521-522
  Maine, Henry James Sumner **10** 152
  Schechter, Solomon **13** 524
mathematics
  Babbage, Charles **1** 407-408
  Dirac, Paul Adrien Maurice **5** 23-24
  Fisher, Ronald Aylmer **5** 463-464
  Ramsey, Frank Plumpton **13** 25
  Russell, Bertrand Arthur William
    13 373-374
  Whitehead, Alfred North
    16 242-244
philosophy
  Broad, Charlie Dunbar **3** 12
  Cudworth, Ralph **4** 331
  Sidgwick, Henry **14** 213
  Wittgenstein, Ludwig **16** 350-351
physics
  Bethe, Hans Albrecht **2** 238-239
  Cockcroft, John Douglas **4** 131-132
  Maxwell, James Clerk **10** 361-364
  Rayleigh, 3d Baron **13** 62
  Thomson, George Paget **15** 198-199
  Thomson, Joseph John **15** 200-201
  Wilson, Charles Thomson Rees
    16 317-318
physiology
  Adrian, Edgar Douglas **1** 67-69
  Hodgkin, Alan Lloyd **7** 431-432
poetry
  Lewis, Cecil Day **9** 380
social sciences
  Bartlett, Frederic Charles **2** 34-35
  Clapham, John Harold **4** 71
  Evans-Pritchard, Edward Evan **5** 340
  Marshall, Alfred **10** 277-278
  Pigou, Arthur Cecil **12** 302
theology
  Ramsey, Arthur Michael **13** 23-25

Cambyses II (died 522 B.C.), king of Persia
529-522
  Cyrus the Great **4** 363-364
  Darius I **4** 394-395

Camden, Battle of (1780)
  Cornwallis, Charles **4** 241-243
  Greene, Nathanael **6** 525-526
  Marion, Francis **10** 262-263

Camden Town group (painters)
  Sickert, Walter Richard **14** 212-213

Camden, William (1551-1623), English historian
  Jonson, Ben **8** 343-345

CAMDESSUS, MICHEL (born 1933),
French civil servant and managing director of the International Monetary Fund
3 244-246

Camel, Battle of (near Basra, 656)
  Ali **1** 155-156

Camel Hsiang-tzu (novel)
  Lao Shê **9** 200-201

Camera
  see Photography

Camera degli Sposi (Ducal Palace, Mantua,
Italy)
  Mantegna, Andrea **10** 215-216

Camera Eye, The (literary technique)
  Dos Passos, John Roderigo **5** 69-71

Camera obscura (photography)
  Canaletto **3** 257-258
  Daguerre, Louis Jacques Mandé
    4 365-366
  Levi ben Gershon **9** 363-364

Camera Work (journal)
  Stieglitz, Alfred **14** 451-452

Cameralists, The (book)
  Small, Albion Woodbury **14** 277

Cameron, Don (1833-1918), American
politician
  Adams, Henry Brooks **1** 45-47

Cameron, Elizabeth Bowen
  see Bowen, Elizabeth

CAMERON, SIMON (1799-1889), American politician **3** 246-247
  Quay, Matthew Stanley **12** 507

Cameron, Verney Lovett (1844-1894), English explorer
  Tippu Tip **15** 235-236

Cameroon, United Republic of (nation,
West Africa)
  Ahidjo, Ahmadou **1** 89-90
  Burton, Richard **3** 163-164
  Mondlane, Eduardo Chivambo
    11 100-101

Cameroon National Union (political party)
  Ahidjo, Ahmadou **1** 89-90

Camilla (novel)
  Burney, Fanny **3** 147-148

Camille (film)
  Garbo, Greta **6** 205-207

Camillus of Lellis, St. (1550-1614), Italian
religious founder
  Neri, Philip **11** 340

Camino de Paros, El (literary collection)
  Rodó, José Enrique **13** 240-241

Camino de perfeccion (novel)
  Baroja y Nessi, Pío **2** 15-16

Camino Real (play)
  Williams, Tennessee **16** 306-308

CAMOËNS, LUIS VAZ DE (1524-1580),
Portuguese poet **3** 247-249
  Lope Félix de Vega Carpio **9** 503-506

Camöens and the Lusiads (book)
  Nabuco de Araujo, Joaquim Aurelio
    11 288-289

Camões Luis Vaz de
  see Camoëns, Luis Vaz de

Camoin, Charles (1879-1965), French
painter
  Matisse, Henri **10** 336-337

Camp David accords (1979)
  Carter, James Earl **3** 339-342
  Sadat, Anwar **13** 412-414
  Vance, Cyrus R. **15** 411-413

Camp Robinson, (Nebraska)
  Crazy Horse **4** 303-304

Campagnola, Domenico (circa 1484-circa
1563), Italian painter
  Watteau, Antoine **16** 143-144

Campaign, The (poem)
  Addison, Joseph **1** 57-58

Campaldino, Battle of (1289)
  Dante Alighieri **4** 389-391

Campaña, Pedro de (1503-1580), Flemish
painter, architect, and sculptor
  Morales, Luis de **11** 150

CAMPANELLA, TOMMASO (Giovanni
Domenico Campanella; 1568-1639), Italian philosopher, political theorist, and
poet **3** 249
  Telesio, Bernardino **15** 138-139

Campania (province; Italy)
  Cato, Marcus Porcius the Elder **3** 375

CAMPBELL, ALEXANDER (1788-1866),
Irish-born American clergyman
3 249-250

**CAMPBELL, AVRIL PHAEDRA DOUGLAS
(KIM)** (born 1947), Canada's first woman
prime minister **3** 250-252

CAMPBELL, BEN NIGHTHORSE (born
1933), Native American United States
senator from Colorado **3** 252-253

Campbell, Colen (died 1729), British archi-
tect
  Benjamin, Asher **2** 162-163
  Gibbs, James **6** 301-302

Campbell, E. Simms (1908-1971), African
American cartoonist and commercial
artist
  Bearden, Romare Howard **2** 86-88

CAMPBELL, JOSEPH (1904-1987), American editor and popularizer of comparative mythology **3** 253-255

Campbell, Thomas (1763-1854), American
Presbyterian minister
  Campbell, Alexander **3** 249-250
  Ryder, Albert Pinkham **13** 391-392

Campbell-Bannerman, Sir Henry
(1836-1908), British statesman
  Asquith, Herbert Henry **1** 344-346
  Cromer, 1st Earl of **4** 317

Morley, John **11** 178-179
Smuts, Jan Christian **14** 309-310

Campeggio, Lorenzo (1472-1539), Italian cardinal
Henry VIII **7** 302-305
Wolsey, Thomas **16** 364-366

Campi Magni, Battle of (203 B.C.)
Scipio Africanus Major, Publius Cornelius **14** 61-62

CAMPIN, ROBERT (circa 1375/80-1444), Flemish painter **3** 255
Charonton, Enguerrand **3** 471
Eyck, Hubert and Jan van **5** 352-354
Massys, Quentin **10** 325-326
Sluter, Claus **14** 275-276
Weyden, Rogier van der **16** 219-221

Campion, Edmund (1540-1581), English Jesuit martyr
Waugh, Evelyn Arthur St. John **16** 145-147

Campion, Thomas (1567-1620), English poet and musician
Catullus, Gaius Valerius **3** 377-378

Campo, Carlos Ibáñez del
see Ibáñez del Campo, Carlos

Campoformio, Treaty of (1797)
Barras, Vicomte de **2** 19
Napoleon I **11** 306-310

Campos, Roberto (born 1917), Brazilian economist
Castelo Branco, Humberto **3** 359-360

Campra, André (1660-1744), French composer
Telemann, Georg Philipp **15** 137-138

CAMUS, ALBERT (1913-1960), French novelist, essayist, and playwright **3** 255-257
Calderón, Pedro **3** 221-222
Céline, Louis Ferdinand **3** 390-391
Cela y Trulock, Camilo José **3** 389-390
Lagerkvist, Pär Fabian **9** 162-163
Robbe-Grillet, Alain **13** 189-190

Can-can (dance)
Offenbach, Jacques **11** 478-479

Can-Can (musical)
Porter, Cole Albert **12** 405-406

Can Such Things Be? (book)
Bierce, Ambrose Gwinett **2** 269-270

Can You Forgive Her? (novel)
Trollope, Anthony **15** 300-302

Cana (village, Northern Palestine)
Mary **10** 308

Canaan (Promised Land)
Moses **11** 200-201

Canada (nation, North America)
agricultural development
Sifton, Clifford **14** 219-220
American Revolution
Arnold, Benedict **1** 309-310
Carleton, Guy **3** 300-301
Johnson, John **8** 305-306
Montgomery, Richard **11** 138-139

Morgan, Daniel **11** 160-161
see also American Revolution
and relations with United States
Mulroney, Martin Brian **11** 242-246
Anglo-French rivalry
Iberville, Sieur d' **8** 90-91
Phips, William **12** 283
anti-separatism (Quebec)
Bourassa, Robert **2** 447-449
Chrétien, Joseph-Jacques-Jean **4** 24-25
Trudeau, Pierre Elliott **15** 309-311
as United States slave and Native American sanctuary
Henson, Josiah **7** 311-312
Joseph **8** 358-359
Tubman, Harriet Ross **15** 330-331
bicultural relations
Baldwin, Robert **1** 466-468
Cartier, George-Étienne **3** 342-343
Lafontaine, Louis-Hippolyte **9** 157-158
Macdonald, John Alexander **10** 85-87
bishops
Laval, François Xavier de **9** 235-236
Strachan, John **14** 486-487
boundary disputes
Gallatin, Albert **6** 183-184
Hay, John **7** 215-216
Roosevelt, Theodore **13** 280-283
Webster, Daniel **16** 162-164
colonial policy
Frontenac et Palluau, Comte de **6** 128-130
Talon, Jean **15** 91-92
confederation
Borden, Robert Laird **2** 409-411
Brown, George **3** 35-36
Cartier, George-Étienne **3** 342-343
Durham, 1st Earl of **5** 161-162
Galt, Alexander Tilloch **6** 190-191
Howe, Joseph **7** 534-535
Macdonald, John Alexander **10** 85-87
Mackenzie, Alexander **10** 104
Tilley, Samuel Leonard **15** 223-224
Tupper, Charles **15** 342-343
see also British North America (federation)
conscription
Bourassa, Joseph-Henri-Napoleon **2** 446-447
Crerar, Thomas Alexander **4** 306
Currie, Arthur William **4** 345
King, William Lyon Mackenzie **9** 25-26
Laurier, Wilfrid **9** 232-234
Meighen, Arthur **10** 459-460
constitutional law
Scott, Francis Reginald **14** 66-67
defense
Diefenbaker, John George **5** 4-5
King, William Lyon Mackenzie **9** 25-26
development of the West

Sifton, Clifford **14** 219-220
Durham Report
Durham, 1st Earl of **5** 161-162
Sydenham, Thomas **15** 59-60
economic development
Irving, Kenneth Colin **8** 140-141
economy
Aberhart, William **1** 26-27
Aitken, William Maxwell **1** 94-96
Bennett, Richard Bedford **2** 171-172
Innis, Harold Adams **8** 124-125
Laurier, Wilfrid **9** 232-234
Smith, Donald Alexander **14** 288-289
St. Laurent, Louis Stephen **13** 434
exploration
Brûlé, Étienne **3** 67-68
Cartier, Jacques **3** 343-344
Champlain, Samuel de **3** 419-421
Fraser, Simon **6** 74-75
Kelsey, Henry **8** 488
la Verendrye, Sieur de **9** 239-240
Maisoneuve, Sieur de **10** 153
Ogden, Peter Skene **11** 480-481
Radisson, Pierre-Esprit **12** 539-540
see also Northwest Passage
French and Indian War
see French and Indian War
fur trade
Jolliet, Louis **8** 328-329
Talon, Jean **15** 91-92
Indian self-determination
Erasmus, Georges Henry **5** 300-301
Métis supporters
Lacombe, Albert **9** 147-148
Riel, Louis **13** 163-164
missionaries
Brecht, Bertolt **2** 512-514
Jogues, Isaac **8** 270-271
Lacombe, Albert **9** 147-148
Laval, François Xavier de **9** 235-236
Marquette, Jacques **10** 274-275
prime ministers
Campbell, Avril Phaedra Douglas **3** 250-252
Quebec independence
Lévesque, René **9** 362-363
Parizeau, Jacques **12** 96-99
railroads
Bennett, Richard Bedford **2** 171-172
Cartier, George-Étienne **3** 342-343
Fleming, Sandford **5** 485-486
Meighen, Arthur **10** 459-460
see also Canadian Pacific Railway
rebellion (1837)
Baldwin, Robert **1** 466-468
Durham, 1st Earl of **5** 161-162
Garneau, François-Xavier **6** 219-220
Lafontaine, Louis-Hippolyte **9** 157-158
Macdonald, John Alexander **10** 85-87
Mackenzie, William Lyon **10** 104-106
Papineau, Louis-Joseph **12** 91
Scott, Winfield **14** 70-71

Sydenham, Thomas **15** 59-60
Van Buren, Martin **15** 410-411
reforms
Bethune, Henry Norman **2** 240-241
Douglas, Thomas Clement **5** 82-83
Gourlay, Robert **6** 474
King, William Lyon Mackenzie
9 25-26
Pitt, William the Younger
12 329-331
Scott, Francis Reginald **14** 66-67
Woodsworth, James Shaver **16** 376
responsible government
Baldwin, Robert **1** 466-468
Elgin, 8th Earl of **5** 248-249
Lafontaine, Louis-Hippolyte
9 157-158
Metcalfe, Charles Theophilus
10 531-532
Sydenham, Thomas **15** 59-60
settlements
Champlain, Samuel de **3** 419-421
Charnisay, Charles de Menou
3 470-471
Kelsey, Henry **8** 488
Maisoneuve, Sieur de **10** 153
Selkirk, 5th Earl of **14** 96
War of 1812
Brock, Isaac **3** 12-13
Robinson, John Beverley **13** 210
see also Canadian art; Canadian lit-
erature; and individual provinces
see also War of 1812

Canadian art
Reid, William Ronald **13** 88-89
genre
Carr, Emily **3** 319
Kane, Paul **8** 422-423
Krieghoff, Cornelius **9** 101
impressionism
Cullen, Maurice Galbraith **4** 334
Milne, David Brown **11** 37-38
landscape
Morrice, James Wilson **11** 181-182
Thomson, Tom **15** 202
see also Artists, Canadian

Canadian Atomic Energy Project
Cockcroft, John Douglas **4** 131-132

Canadian Breweries
Taylor, Edward Plunket **15** 123-124

Canadian Crusoes, The (book)
Traill, Catharine Parr **15** 291

Canadian Embassy (Washington, District of
Columbia)
Erickson, Arthur Charles **5** 304-306

Canadian Institute (Toronto)
Fleming, Sandford **5** 485-486

Canadian Jewish Chronicle
Klein, A. M. **9** 49-50

Canadian literature
animal stories
Seton, Ernest Thompson **14** 119-120
children's books

Montgomery, Lucy Maud
11 136-138
Confederation Poets
Lampman, Archibald **9** 180-181
cosmopolitanism
Morin, Paul **11** 174
modern
Klein, A. M. **9** 49-50
nationalism
Callaghan, Edward Morley
3 229-230
MacLennan, Hugh **10** 110-111
Scott, Francis Reginald **14** 66-67
Patriotic school
Aubert de Gaspé, Philippe **1** 364
Crémazie, Octave **4** 305-306
Fréchette, Louis-Honoré **6** 77-78
Garneau, François-Xavier **6** 219-220
pioneer theme
Goldsmith, Oliver **6** 411
Grove, Frederick Philip **7** 20-21
Haliburton, Thomas Chandler **7** 80
Hémon, Louis **7** 277
Moodie, Susanna **11** 140-141
Traill, Catharine Parr **15** 291
romance
de la Roche, Mazo Louise
4 474-475
Heavysege, Charles **7** 246
see also Authors, Canadian
women's life themes
Atwood, Margaret Eleanor
1 362-364
Laurence, Margaret **9** 229-230

Canadian music
Gould, Glenn **6** 469-470

Canadian National Museum (Ottawa)
Sapir, Edward **13** 478-479

Canadian National Railways
Meighen, Arthur **10** 459-460

Canadian Pacific Railway
building of
Bennett, Richard Bedford **2** 171-172
Fleming, Sandford **5** 485-486
Lacombe, Albert **9** 147-148
Smith, Donald Alexander
14 288-289
Tupper, Charles **15** 342-343
supporters
Cartier, George-Étienne **3** 342-343
Hill, James Jerome **7** 388-389
Macdonald, John Alexander
10 85-87

Canadians of Old, The (novel)
Aubert de Gaspé, Philippe **1** 364

Canaima (novel)
Gallegos Freire, Rómulo **6** 185-186

Canal, Giovanni Antonio
see Canaletto

Canal ring (New York City politics)
Tilden, Samuel Jones **15** 222-223

Canal Zone (Panama)
see Panama; Panama Canal

CANALETTO (1697-1768), Italian painter
3 257-258
Guardi, Francesco **7** 24-25

Canary Islands (Atlantic Ocean)
Cadamosto, Alvise da **3** 206-207
Columbus, Christopher **4** 176-179
Cook, James **4** 214-215
Henry the Navigator **7** 305-306

Canberra (city, Australia)
Saarinen, Eliel and Eero **13** 396-398

Canberra Pact (1944)
Fraser, Peter **6** 73-74

Canção VIII (poem)
Camoëns, Luis Vaz de **3** 247-249

Cancer (medicine)
Banting, Frederick Grant **1** 493-494
Curie, Marie Sklodowska **4** 339-341
Domagk, Gerhard Johannes Paul
5 48-50
Quimby, Edith H. **12** 513-514
Rous, Francis Peyton **13** 322-323

Cancer research
Baltimore, David **1** 477-478
Elion, Gertrude B. **5** 252-254
Love, Susan M. **10** 2-3
Macdonald, Eleanor Josephine
10 83-84
Mintz, Beatrice **11** 49-50
Montagnier, Luc **11** 114-116
Sager, Ruth **13** 425-426
Seibert, Florence B. **14** 89-90
Singer, Maxine **14** 251-252
Slye, Maud **14** 276-277
Varmus, Harold Eliot **15** 436-437

Cancer victims
Benton, Thomas Hart **2** 178-179
Bogart, Humphrey **2** 363-364
Brahms, Johannes **2** 490-492
Cushman, Charlotte **4** 354-355
Debussy, Achille Claude **4** 445-447
Dulles, John Foster **5** 134-135
Dunne, Finley Peter **5** 147-148
Engels, Friedrich **5** 286-288
Fischer, Emil **5** 456-457
Freud, Sigmund **6** 103-106
Frunze, Mikhail Vasilievich **6** 134
Grant, Ulysses Simpson **6** 492-494
Haidar Ali **7** 65-66
Henry, Patrick **7** 309-311
Hill, Benjamin Harvey **7** 386-387
Huysmans, Joris Karl **8** 81-82
John, XXIII **8** 277-280
La Guardia, Fiorello Henry **9** 166-167
Lazarus, Emma **9** 260-261
Lowie, Robert Harry **10** 18
Malevich, Kasimir **10** 168-169
Metcalfe, Charles Theophilus
10 531-532
Napoleon I **11** 306-310
Oppenheimer, J. Robert **11** 525-526
Puccini, Giacomo **12** 474-476
Rossetti, Christina Georgina
13 307-308
Selim I **14** 94-95

Sismondi, Jean Charles Léonard
Simonde de **14** 258-259
Sun Yat-sen **15** 35-39
Turgenev, Ivan Sergeyevich **15** 345-348
Wittgenstein, Ludwig **16** 350-351

Cancer Ward (novel)
Solzhenitsyn, Alexander Isayevich
14 330-332

Cancioneiro geral (book; G. de Resende)
Vicente, Gil **15** 479-480

Cancionero musical de Palacio (musical collection)
Encina, Juan del **5** 283

Canciones (book)
Lorca, Federico García **9** 511-513

Candia (city, Crete)
Köprülü, Ahmed **9** 84-85

Candida (play)
Shaw, George Bernard **14** 163-164

Candidate, The (poem)
Crabbe, George **4** 288

Candide (musical)
Bernstein, Leonard **2** 218-219
Hellman, Lillian Florence **7** 267-268

Candide (novel; Voltaire)
France, Anatole **6** 39-40
Johnson, Samuel **8** 315-317
Voltaire **16** 14-16

Candlestick with the Burning Lights (painting)
Chagall, Marc **3** 406-407

Canio (opera character)
Caruso, Enrico **3** 345

CANISIUS, ST. PETER (1521-1597), Dutch Jesuit **3** 258

Canmore dynasty (Scotland)
Macbeth **10** 81
Malcolm III **10** 164-165

Cannae, Battle of (216 B.C.)
Hannibal Barca **7** 128-130
Scipio Africanus Major, Publius Cornelius **14** 61-62

Cannary, Martha Jane
see Calamity Jane

Cannery Row (novel)
Steinbeck, John Ernst **14** 416-417

Cannibalism (Africa)
Moshweshwe **11** 203-205

Cannibals and Christians (book)
Mailer, Norman Kingsley **10** 148-150

Canning (food industry)
Armour, Philip Danforth **1** 302

CANNING, GEORGE (1770-1827), English orator and statesman **3** 258-260
Catholic question
Castlereagh, Viscount **3** 363-364
George IV **6** 272-273
Peel, Robert **12** 181-183
political associates
Liverpool, 2nd Earl of **9** 456-457

Melbourne, 2nd Viscount
10 468-469
Palmerston, 3d Viscount **12** 81-83
Wellington, 1st Duke of **16** 193-195

Cannizzaro, Stanislao (1826-1910), Italian chemist
Mendeleev, Dmitrii Ivanovich
10 486-488

Cannon (weapon)
Krupp **9** 109-111

CANNON, ANNIE JUMP (1863-1941), American astronomer **3** 260-261

CANNON, JOSEPH GURNEY (1836-1926), American politican **3** 261-262
Hapgood, Norman **7** 137-138
Norris, George William **11** 428-429
Taft, William Howard **15** 78-81

Cannons House (Middlesex)
Gibbs, James **6** 301-302

Cano, Alonso (1601-1667), Spanish painter, sculptor, and architect
Murillo, Bartolomé Esteban **11** 258-259
Velázquez, Diego Rodríguez de Silva y **15** 454-456

Cano, Diego
see Cão, Diogo

Cano, Juan Sebastián del (died 1526), Spanish navigator
Magellan, Ferdinand **10** 126-127

Canobic Inscription (147/146 B.C.)
Ptolemy, Claudius **12** 473-474

Canon (book)
Avicenna **1** 386-387

Canon (music)
Byrd, William **3** 187-188
Gombert, Nicolas **6** 416-417
Isaac, Heinrich **8** 143-144
Landini, Francesco **9** 185-186
Machaut, Guillaume de **10** 93-94

Canon (sculpture; book)
Polykleitos **12** 385-386

Canon law (Roman Catholic)
Boniface VIII **2** 392-393
Clement V **4** 101-102
Gratian **6** 498-499
Innocent, III **8** 125-127
Paul VI **12** 146-148
Pius X **12** 336-337
Urban II **15** 393

Canon Law in England (book)
Maitland, Frederic William **10** 154-155

Canon Lluis Desplà (painting)
Bermejo, Bartolomé **2** 205

Canons Regular of St. Augustine
see Augustinian Canons

Canossa (city, Italy)
Gregory VII **6** 532-534
Henry IV **7** 292

Canossa Palace (Verona)
Sanmicheli, Michele **13** 469-470

CANOT, THEODORE (1804-1860), French-Italian adventurer and slave trader **3** 262-263

CANOVA, ANTONIO (1757-1822), Italian sculptor **3** 263-264
Alfieri, Vittoria **1** 145-146
Clodion **4** 121
Peale, Rembrandt **12** 172-173
Prud'hon, Pierre Paul **12** 469

Canovás (novel)
Galdós, Benito Pérez **6** 177-178

Canso (town, Nova Scotia)
Champlain, Samuel de **3** 419-421

Cantaclaro (novel)
Gallegos Freire, Rómulo **6** 185-186

Cantar de ciegos (book)
Fuentes, Carlos **6** 141-142

Cantar de Mio Cid (anonymous epic)
Camoëns, Luis Vaz de **3** 247-249

Cantare (song)
Vicente, Gil **15** 479-480

Cantata (music)
Bach, Carl Philipp Emanuel **1** 414-415
Bach, Johann Sebastian **1** 416-419, 332
Britten, Benjamin **3** 10-11
Buxtehude, Dietrich **3** 185-186
Cimarosa, Domenico **4** 61-62
Donizetti, Gaetano **5** 59-60
Handel, George Frederick **7** 116-119
Rossi, Luigi **13** 310-311
Scarlatti, Pietro Alessandro Gaspare **13** 517-518
Schoenberg, Arnold **14** 24-26
Schütz, Heinrich **14** 48-49
Tippett, Michael Kemp **15** 234-235
Vivaldi, Antonio **16** 3-4
Webern, Anton **16** 160-162

Cantata Academica (musical composition)
Britten, Benjamin **3** 10-11

Cantata for the...October Revolution (musical composition)
Prokofiev, Sergei Sergeevich **12** 458-460

Cantata profana (musical composition)
Bartók, Béla **2** 35-36

Cantate à trois voix, La (poems)
Claudel, Paul Louis Charles **4** 90-91

Cantatrice chauve, La (play)
Ionesco, Eugène **8** 131-132

Cante hondo (music)
Falla, Manuel de **5** 372-373

Canterbury, see of (England)
archbishops
Anselm of Canterbury **1** 244-245
Augustine of Canterbury **1** 370-371
Becket, Thomas **2** 101-102
Carey, George Leonard **3** 293-294
Cranmer, Thomas **4** 295-296
Dunstan **5** 151-152
Lanfranc **9** 189-190
Laud, William **9** 224-225

Ramsey, Arthur Michael **13** 23-25
Temple, William **15** 141-143
founded
Augustine of Canterbury **1** 370-371
in literature
Chaucer, Geoffrey **3** 482-485
Eliot, Thomas Stearns **5** 258-261
rebuilt
Anselm of Canterbury **1** 244-245
Lanfranc **9** 189-190

Canterbury Female Boarding School (Connecticut)
Crandall, Prudence **4** 291

Canterbury Tales, The (book; Chaucer)
Boccaccio, Giovanni **2** 351-353
Caxton, William **3** 386-387
Chaucer, Geoffrey **3** 482-485
Lydgate, John **10** 61-62

Canterbury University College
(Christchurch, New Zealand)
Popper, Karl Raimund **12** 402

Canti, I (poems)
Leopardi, Giacomo **9** 344-345

Canti de liberazione (musical composition)
Dallapiccola, Luigi **4** 377-378

Canti di prigionia (musical composition)
Dallapiccola, Luigi **4** 377-378

Canticle of Canticles
see Song of Songs (Old Testament)

Canticle of Creatures (poem)
Francis of Assisi **6** 46-47

Canticle of the Rose, The (poems)
Sitwell, Edith **14** 265-266

Canticle of the Sun
see Canticle of Creatures

Canticles (musical composition)
Britten, Benjamin **3** 10-11

Canticles of Holy Mary (poem)
Alfonso X **1** 150-151

Cántico (poems)
Guillén, Nicolás **7** 34-35

Canticum sacrum (oratorio)
Stravinsky, Igor Fedorovich **14** 502-506

Cantiones sacrae (music)
Byrd, William **3** 187-188
Schütz, Heinrich **14** 48-49
Sweelinck, Jan Pieterszoon **15** 50-51
Tallis, Thomas **15** 91

Cantlie, James (1851-1926), Scottish physician
Sun Yat-sen **15** 35-39

Canto de Caliope (poem; Cervantes)
Góngora y Argote, Luis de **6** 427-428

Canto errante, El (book)
Darío, Rubén **4** 393-394

Canto sospeso (musical composition)
Nono, Luigi **11** 420-421

Canton (city, China)
Chang Chih-tung **3** 430-431

Lin Tse-hsü **9** 431-432

CANTOR, EDDIE (Isador Iskowitz; 1892-1964), American singer and comedian **3** 264-265
Ziegfeld, Florenz **16** 516-517

CANTOR, GEORG FERDINAND LUDWIG PHILIPP (1845-1918), German mathematician **3** 265-266
Fourier, Jean Baptiste Joseph **6** 32-33

Cantos (poems)
Pound, Ezra Loomis **12** 415-417

Cantos de vida y esperanza (poems)
Darío, Rubén **4** 393-394

Cantus firmus (music)
Dufay, Guillaume **5** 125-126
Dunstable, John **5** 150-151
Gombert, Nicolas **6** 416-417
Isaac, Heinrich **8** 143-144
Josquin des Prez **8** 361-363
Lassus, Roland de **9** 216-218
Léonin **9** 343-344
Machaut, Guillaume de **10** 93-94
Obrecht, Jacob **11** 457-458
Palestrina, Giovanni Pierluigi da **12** 70-72
Pérotin **12** 231-232
Senfl, Ludwig **14** 105-106
Tallis, Thomas **15** 91

CANUTE I THE GREAT (c. 995-1035), Viking king of England and Denmark **3** 266-269
Edward the Confessor **5** 218-219
Ethelred the Unready **5** 327
Olaf, II **11** 493-494

Canyons of the Colorado (book)
Powell, John Wesley **12** 425-426

Canzona (music)
Gabrieli, Giovanni **6** 161-162
Merulo, Claudio **10** 525-526

Canzonets... (musical composition)
Morley, Thomas **11** 179-180

Canzonette (musical collection)
Monteverdi, Claudio Giovanni Antonio **11** 126-128

Canzoni (literature)
Tasso, Torquato **15** 114-116

Canzoniere (poems)
Boiardo, Matteo Maria **2** 369
Petrarch **12** 259-261

Cão, Diogo (Cam, or Cano; flourished 1480-1486), Portuguese explorer
Affonso I **1** 72
Dias de Novais, Bartolomeu **4** 533-534
Nzinga Nkuwu **11** 451-452

Cap ranks (Japan)
Shotoku Taishi **14** 205-207
Suiko **15** 15-16

CAPA, ROBERT (Endre Friedmann; 1913-1954), Hungarian-American war photographer and photojournalist **3** 269-271
Steinbeck, John Ernst **14** 416-417

Cape (geography)
see under latter term except as listed below

Cape Anne (peninsula, Massachusetts)
Endecott, John **5** 284-285

Cape Blanc (Atlantic Ocean, Northwest Africa)
Cadamosto, Alvise da **3** 206-207
Henry the Navigator **7** 305-306

Cape Bonavista (Newfoundland)
Cartier, Jacques **3** 343-344

Cape Coast Castle (West Africa)
Dalzel, Archibald **4** 381-382

Cape Cod (essays)
Thoreau, Henry David **15** 203-205

Cape Cod (peninsula, Southeast Massachusetts)
Champlain, Samuel de **3** 419-421
Gorges, Ferdinando **6** 455-456

Cape Cod Lighter, The (stories)
O'Hara, John **11** 485

Cape Colony
see Cape Province

Cape Hatteras (poem)
Crane, Hart **4** 291-293

Cape of Good Hope (South West Africa)
Cook, James **4** 214-215
Covilhão, Pedro de **4** 278-279
Dias de Novais, Bartolomeu **4** 533-534
Drake, Francis **5** 94-96

Cape of Good Hope, The (poems)
Cocteau, Jean **4** 132-133

Cape Province (South Africa)
Dingane **5** 14-15
Gordon, Charles George **6** 448-449
Grey, George **6** 540-541
Moshweshwe **11** 203-205
Rhodes, Cecil John **13** 120-122
see also South Africa, Republic of

Cape Verde Islands (North Atlantic Ocean)
Cabral, Amílcar Lopes **3** 202-203
Cadamosto, Alvise da **3** 206-207
Cook, James **4** 214-215
Darwin, Charles Robert **4** 397-399
Dias de Novais, Bartolomeu **4** 533-534
Drake, Francis **5** 94-96
Henry the Navigator **7** 305-306
Sousa, Henrique Teixeira de **14** 352-353

Čapek, Joseph (1887-1945), Czech painter
Čapek, Karel **3** 271-272

ČAPEK, KAREL (1890-1938), Czech novelist, playwright, and essayist **3** 271-272

Čapek, Mrs. Karel
see Scheinpflugova, Olga

Capêo
see Sancho II

Capetian dynasty (France; ruled 987-1328)
Louis VI **9** 523-524
Louis VII **9** 524-525

Louis IX **9** 525-526
Philip II **12** 268-269
Philip IV **12** 274

Capgrave, John (1393-1464), English chronicler
Gloucester, Duke of **6** 370-371

Capillarity (chemistry)
Draper, John William **5** 96-97
Mendeleev, Dmitrii Ivanovich **10** 486-488

Capillary (anatomy)
Adrian, Edgar Douglas **1** 67-69
Dale, Henry Hallett **4** 371-373
Leeuwenhoek, Anton van **9** 300-301
Malpighi, Marcello **10** 176-178

Capital
see Kapital, Das

Capital (economics)
Böhm-Bawerk, Eugen von **2** 366
Walras, Marie Esprit Léon **16** 84-85

Capital punishment (criminology)
Becarria, Marchese di **2** 97-98
Darrow, Clarence Seward **4** 396-397
Livingston, Edward **9** 460-461
Peel, Robert **12** 181-183
Reed, Thomas Brackett **13** 77
Shabaka **14** 130

Capitalism (economics)
critics
Browder, Earl Russell **3** 30-31
Frei Montalva, Eduardo **6** 94-95
Gorky, Maxim **6** 458-460
Johnson, Tom Loftin **8** 317
Morris, William **11** 187-188
effect of Protestantism
Troeltsch, Ernst **15** 299-300
Weber, Max **16** 157-160
historians of
Clapham, John Harold **4** 71
Sombart, Werner **14** 332-333
laissez faire
McCormick, Robert Rutherford **10** 401-402
Polanyi, Karl **12** 372
supporters
Dubinsky, David **5** 114-115
Gompers, Samuel **6** 420-422
Hanna, Marcus Alonzo **7** 127-128
Marshall, John **10** 279-281
Mosquera, Tomás Cipriano de **11** 205-206
theories
Marx, Karl **10** 304-308
Schumpeter, Joseph Alois **14** 43-44
Veblen, Thorstein Bunde **15** 449-450

Capitan, El (opera)
Sousa, John Philip **14** 353-354

Capitán Veneno, El (novel)
Alarcón, Pedro Antonio de **1** 100-101

Capitana (ship)
Cabrillo, Juan Rodríguez **3** 204-205

Capitol (Rome)
Paul III **12** 144-145
Porta, Giacomo della **12** 402-403

Capitol (United States)
see Washington, D.C.—Capitol

Capitoline (sculpture type)
Polykleitos **12** 385-386

CAPONE, AL (Alphonso Caponi, a.k.a. "Scarface;" 1899-1947), American gangster **3** 272-273
Dillinger, John **5** 9

CAPOTE, TRUMAN (born Truman Streckfus Persons; 1924-1984), American author **3** 273-275
Bogart, Humphrey **2** 363-364

CAPP, AL (Alfred Gerald Capp; 1909-1979), American cartoonist and satirist **3** 275-276

Cappacodian fathers (Eastern Orthodox Church)
Basil the Great **2** 51-52

Cappadocia, Battle of (162)
Marcus Aurelius Antoninus **10** 243-245

Cappellari, Bartolommeo Alberto
see Gregory XVI

Capponi, Raffaello
see Raffaellino del Garbo

CAPRA, FRANK (1897-1991), American film director **3** 276-278
Gable, William Clark **6** 157-158

Caprarola (city, Italy)
Vignola, Giacomo da **15** 493-494

CAPRIATI, JENNIFER (born 1976), American tennis player **3** 278-281

Capriccio (musical composition)
Penderecki, Krzysztof **12** 195-197
Stravinsky, Igor Fedorovich **14** 502-506

Capriccio (opera)
Strauss, Richard **14** 500-501

Capriccio burlesco (musical composition)
Walton, William Turner **16** 92-93

Capriccio español (tone poem)
Rimsky-Korsakov, Nikolai Andreevich **13** 174-175

Caprice, Un (play)
Musset, Louis Charles Alfred de **11** 271-272

Caprichos, Los (etching series)
Goya y Lucientes, Francisco de Paula José de **6** 476-478

Caprini Palace (Rome)
Bramante, Donato **2** 493-494

Caps (Swedish politics)
Gustavus III **7** 45-46

Captain (ship)
Nelson, Horatio **11** 336-338

Captain Carpenter (poem)
Ransom, John Crowe **13** 39-40

Captain Craig (poem)
Robinson, Edwin Arlington **13** 201-202

Captain Jinks of the Horse Marines (play)
Barrymores **2** 28-30

Captain Macklin (novel)
Davis, Richard Harding **4** 422-423

Captain of the Gray-Horse Troop, The (book)
Garland, Hannibal Hamlin **6** 217-218

Captain Stormfield's Visit to Heaven (book)
Twain, Mark **15** 363-366

Captain Venom (novel)
Alarcón, Pedro Antonio de **1** 100-101

Captains Courageous (novel)
Kipling, Joseph Rudyard **9** 32-33

Captain's Daughter, The (novel)
Pushkin, Aleksandr Sergeevich **12** 489-491

Captain's Doll, The (novelette)
Lawrence, David Herbert **9** 247-248

Captive, The (novel)
Proust, Marcel **12** 465-467

Captive Woman, The (poem)
Echeverría, José Estéban **5** 197-198

Captives, The (play)
Gay, John **6** 243-244

Captivi (play)
Plautus **12** 348-350

Capture of Oichalia (poem)
Homer **7** 465-467

Capture of the Hessians at Trenton (painting)
Trumbull, John **15** 316-317

Captured Hand (sculpture)
Giacometti, Alberto **6** 294-295

Capua (city, Italy)
Alaric **1** 101-102
Hannibal Barca **7** 128-130

Capuleli ed i Montecchi, I (opera)
Bellini, Vincenzo **2** 138-139

Caput (Mass; Ockeghem)
Dufay, Guillaume **5** 125-126

Cara de plata (play)
Valle Inclán, Ramón Maria del **15** 407-408

Carabobo, Battle of (1821)
Bolívar, Simón **2** 375-377
Flores, Juan José **5** 491
Páez, José Antonio **12** 58

CARACALLA (188-217), Roman emperor **3** 281-282
Septimius Severus, Lucius **14** 109-110
Ulpian, Domitius **15** 385-386

Caracas (city; Venezuela)
Gómez, Juan Vicente **6** 417-418

Caracciolo, Francesco (1752-1799), Italian admiral
Nelson, Horatio **11** 336-338

Caracciolo, Innico (died 1685), Italian archbiship
  Molinos, Miguel de **11** 88-89

Caractères, Les (book)
  La Bruyère, Jean de **9** 145

Carafa, Carlo (1517-1561), Italian adventurer and cardinal
  Paul IV **12** 145-146

Carafa, Giampietro
  see Paul IV (pope)

Carafa, Oliviero (1430-1511), Italian diplomat, jurist, and cardinal
  Paul IV **12** 145-146

CARAVAGGIO (1573-1610), Italian painter **3** 282-284
  influence of
    Bernini, Gian Lorenzo **2** 214-216
    Cézanne, Paul **3** 400-402
    Jordaens, Jacob **8** 347-349
    La Tour, George de **9** 222, 349
    Poussin, Nicolas **12** 418-420
    Reni, Guido **13** 97-98
    Ribera, Jusepe de **13** 122-123
    Tiepolo, Giovanni Battista **15** 219-220
    Velázquez, Diego Rodríguez de Silva y **15** 454-456
    Zurbarán, Francisco de **16** 534-535
  influenced by
    Michelangelo Buonarroti **11** 2-5

Caravaggists (Utrecht art group)
  Vermeer, Jan **15** 466-467

Caravel (ship)
  Cadamosto, Alvise da **3** 206-207

CARAWAY, HATTIE WYATT (1878-1950), first woman elected to the United States Senate in her own right **3** 284-285

Carbo, Gaius Papirius (died 119 B.C.), Roman tribune
  Scipio Africanus Minor, Publius Cornelius Aemilianus **14** 62-63

Carbohydrate (chemistry)
  metabolism
    Banting, Frederick Grant **1** 493-494
    Loewi, Otto **9** 486-487
    Meyerhof, Otto Fritz **10** 537-539
    Reichstein, Tadeus **13** 85-87
  oxidation
    Krebs, Hans Adolf **9** 95-97
    Szent-Györgyi, Albert von **15** 62-64
  structure
    Fischer, Emil **5** 456-457

Carbolic acid
  see Phenol

Carboloy (steel alloy)
  Bridgman, Percy Williams **3** 5-6

Carbon (element—chemistry)
  atomic weight
    Avogadro, Lorenzo Romano Amedeo Carlo **1** 388-389
    Dumas, Jean Baptiste André **5** 138-139
  conductivity
    Priestley, Joseph **12** 452-453
  tetravalency
    Couper, Archibald Scott **4** 269-270
    Kekulé, Friedrich August **8** 477-478

Carbon dioxide (gas)
  Black, Joseph **2** 303
  Cavendish, Henry **3** 383-384

Carbon-14 (radioisotope)
  Calvin, Melvin **3** 242-243
  Diop, Cheikh Anta **5** 21-22

Carbon monoxide (gas)
  Bernard, Claude **2** 208-210

Carbon suboxide (chemistry)
  Diels, Otto Paul Hermann **5** 5-6

Carbonari (secret society; France, Italy, Spain)
  Blanqui, Louis Auguste **2** 323-324
  Cabet, Étienne **3** 196
  Mazzini, Giuseppe **10** 381-383
  Pius VII **12** 334-335

Carcass of Beef (painting)
  Soutine, Chaim **14** 356-357

Carcere, Il (novel)
  Pavese, Cesare **12** 154-155

Carceri d'invenzione (engraving series)
  Piranesi, Giovanni Battista **12** 321-322

Carchemish (ancient city, Asia Minor)
  Lawrence, Thomas Edward **9** 253-254

Carchemish, Battle of (605 B.C.)
  Nebuchadnezzar **11** 330

Card Party, The (ballet)
  Balanchine, George **1** 461-462

Card Players (painting)
  Hooch, Pieter de **7** 473-474

CARDANO, GERONIMO (1501-1576), Italian mathematician, astronomer, and physician **3** 285-286

Cárdenas, Bartolomé de
  see Bermejo, Bartolomé

CÁRDENAS, LÁZARO (1895-1970), Mexican revolutionary president 1934-1940 **3** 286-287
  Ávila Camacho, Manuel **1** 387-388
  Calles, Plutarco Elías **3** 234-235
  Cárdenas Solorzano, Cuauhtémoc **3** 287-288
  Toledano, Vicente Lombardo **15** 256-257

CÁRDENAS SOLORZANO, CUAUHTÉMOC (born 1934), Mexican politician **3** 287-288

Cardillac (opera)
  Hindemith, Paul **7** 399-400

Cardinal (sculpture)
  Manzù, Giacomo **10** 224-225

Cardinal Albrecht of Brandenburg (painting)
  Cranach, Lucas the Elder **4** 289-290

Cardinal Fernando Niño de Guevara (painting)
  Greco **6** 511-514

Cardinal Mindszenty Foundation (United States)
  Schlafly, Phyllis **14** 9-10

Cardinal, The (film)
  Davis, Ossie **4** 421-422

Cardinals, Sacred College of (Roman Catholic)
  Boniface VIII **2** 392-393
  John, XXIII **8** 277-280
  Sixtus V **14** 267-268
  see also Religious leaders—cardinals

Cardinal's First Tale, The (story)
  Dinesen Blixen-Finecke, Karen **5** 13-14

Cardiology (medicine)
  Cabot, Richard Clarke **3** 200
  DeBakey, Michael Ellis **4** 437-438
  Healy, Bernadine Patricia **7** 237-238
  Houssay, Bernardo Alberto **7** 522-523
  Taussig, Helen Brooke **15** 118-120
  see also Heart-attack victims

CARDOZO, BENJAMIN NATHAN (1870-1938), American jurist and legal philosopher **3** 288-290
  Evatt, Herbert Vere **5** 341-343
  Stone, Harlan Fiske **14** 468-470
  Taft, William Howard **15** 78-81
  Wise, Stephen Samuel **16** 344-345

Cardplayers (painting)
  Cézanne, Paul **3** 400-402

CARDUCCI, GIOSUÈ (1835-1907), Italian poet **3** 290-291

Carducci house (near Florence)
  Andrea del Castagno **1** 223-224

Careful and Strict Enquiry ... (book)
  Edwards, Jonathan **5** 220-222

Careless Love (song)
  Handy, William Christopher **7** 123-124

Caretaker, The (play)
  Pinter, Harold **12** 317-318

CAREW, ROD (born 1945), Panamanian baseball player

Carew, Thomas (1595?-1645?), English poet
  Van Dyck, Anthony **15** 423-425

CAREY, GEORGE LEONARD (born 1935), archbishop of Canterbury **3** 293-294

Carey, Harry (1878-1947), American actor
  Buffalo Bill **3** 105-106

CAREY, HENRY CHARLES (1793-1879), American writer on economics **3** 294-295

Carey, Mathew (1760-1839), Irish-born American publisher
  Weems, Mason Locke **16** 170

CAREY, PETER (born 1943), Australian author **3** 295-297

CAREY, WILLIAM (1761-1834), English
Baptist missionary **3** 297
  Duff, Alexander **5** 126-127
  Judson, Adoniram **8** 377-378
  Ram Camul Sen **13** 16-17

CAREY THOMAS, MARTHA (1857-1935),
American educator **3** 297-298

CARÍAS ANDINO, TIBURCIO
(1876-1969), Honduran dictator
(1932-1949) **3** 298-299

Caricature and Charivari (publication)
Daumier, Honoré Victorin **4** 403-405

Carillon, Ft.
  see Ft. Ticonderoga

Carillon, Le (musical group)
Dallapiccola, Luigi **4** 377-378

CARISSIMI, GIACOMO (1605-1674), Ital-
ian composer **3** 299-300
  Cesti, Pietro **3** 399-400
  Charpentier, Marc Antoine **3** 471-472
  Scarlatti, Pietro Alessandro Gaspare
    13 517-518

Carles, Arthur B., Jr. (1882-1952), American painter
Dove, Arthur Garfield **5** 86-87

CARLETON, GUY (1st Baron Dorchester;
1724-1808), British general and statesman **3** 300-301
Clinton, Henry **4** 114-115

Carleton College (Northfield, Minnesota)
Clark, John Bates **4** 76-77

CARLIN, GEORGE (born 1937), American
comedian **3** 301-303

Carlisle Indian School (Pennsylvania)
Moore, Marianne **11** 148-149

Carlisle, John G. (1835-1910), American
politician
Cleveland, Stephen Grover **4** 108-110

Carlists (Spanish politics)
Conrad, Joseph **4** 205-207
Franco Bahamonde, Francisco **6** 52-54
Isabella II **8** 145-146
Talleyrand, Charles Maurice de
  15 89-90

Carloman (751-771), king of Eastern Franks
768-771
Charlemagne **3** 445-447

Carlone, Carlo Antonio (died 1708), Italian
architect
Prandtauer, Jakob **12** 432

Carlos I (1863-1908), king of Portugal
(1889-1908)
Salazar, António de Oliveira
  13 442-443

Carlos, Don (died circa 1543), Indian
cacique of Texcoco
Zumárraga, Juan de **16** 531-532

Carlos, Don (de Austria; 1545-1568), Span-
ish prince
Mary, I **10** 308-309
Philip II **12** 271-273

Carlos, Don, 1st (Carlos María Isidro de
Bourbon; 1788-1855), Spanish pretender
Ferdinand VII **5** 418-420
Isabella II **8** 145-146

Carlos, Don, 3d (Carlos María de los
Dolores; 1848-1909), Spanish pretender
Conrad, Joseph **4** 205-207

Carlos among the Candles (play)
Stevens, Wallace **14** 443-445

Carlotta (1840-1927), empress of Mexico
1864-1867
Maximilian of Hapsburg **10** 358-360

Carlsbad Decrees (1819)
Francis II **6** 43-44
Kotzebue, Otto von **9** 91-92
Metternich, Klemens von **10** 533-536

CARLSON, CHESTER F. (1906-1968),
American inventor of the process of
xerography **3** 303-304
Wilson, Joseph Chamberlain
  16 325-326

Carlstadt
  see Karlstadt

Carlton Club Conference (London, 1922)
Baldwin, Stanley **1** 468-469

CARLYLE, THOMAS (1795-1881), Scottish
essayist and historian **3** 304-305
  associates
    Browning, Robert **3** 53-55
    Turgenev, Ivan Sergeyevich
      15 345-348
  influence of
    Dickens, Charles John Huffam
      4 538-541
    Froude, James Anthony **6** 133-134
    Hertzog, James Barry Munnik
      7 347-348
    Lagerlöf, Selma Ottiliana Lovisa
      9 163-164
    Morris, William **11** 187-188
    Ruskin, John **13** 371-372
    Tawney, Richard Henry **15** 120-121
  influenced by
    Coleridge, Samuel Taylor **4** 154-156
  quoted
    Alcott, Amos Bronson **1** 121
    Harris, Frank **7** 172-173
    Mill, John Stuart **11** 21-23

Carmagnole, La (musical composition)
Paganini, Niccolo **12** 58-59

Carmaux (city, France)
Jaurès, Jean **8** 226-227

Carmelites (religious order)
Gregory XIII **6** 534
John of the Cross **8** 285
Juana Inés de la Cruz **8** 367-368
Langland, William **9** 194-195
Theresa **15** 178-179

Carmen (film)
Goldwyn, Samuel **6** 416

Carmen (novel)
Mérimée, Prosper **10** 517

Carmen (opera)
Bizet, Georges **2** 296-297

Carmen saeculare (poems)
Horace **7** 500-503

CARMICHAEL, STOKELY (born 1941),
African American civil rights activist
3 305-308
Cleaver, Leroy Eldridge **4** 97-98

Carmina (poem; Catullus)
Titian **15** 242-244

Carmina Sacra (musical anthology)
Mason, Lowell **10** 321-322

Carmosine (play)
Musset, Louis Charles Alfred de
  11 271-272

CARNAP, RUDOLF (1891-1970),
German-American philosopher
3 308-309
Nagel, Ernest **11** 291-292
Quine, Willard Van Orman **12** 514-515
Schlick, Friedrich Albert Moritz
  14 16-17

Carnatic (region, India)
Dupleix **5** 153

Carnaval (musical composition)
Schumann, Robert Alexander **14** 41-43

Carnaval romain, Le (overture)
Berlioz, Louis Hector **2** 203-205

Carné, Marcel Albert (1909-1996), French
film director
Antonioni, Michelangelo **1** 252-253

CARNEADES (circa 213-circa 128 B.C.),
Greek philosopher **3** 309
Augustine **1** 367-370

CARNEGIE, ANDREW (1835-1919), American industrialist and philanthropist
3 309-312
  associates
    Frick, Henry Clay **6** 108-109
    Keller, Helen Adams **8** 479-480
    Morgan, Junius Spencer **11** 166-167
    Rockefeller, John Davison
      13 226-228
    Schwab, Charles Michael **14** 50-51
    Spencer, Herbert **14** 369-370
  influenced by
    Cooper, Peter **4** 223-224

CARNEGIE, HATTIE (born Henrietta
Kanengeiser; 1889-1956), American fashion designer **3** 313

Carnegie Co.
Carnegie, Andrew **3** 309-312
Frick, Henry Clay **6** 108-109
Knox, Philander Chase **9** 66-67
after 1901
  see United States Steel Corp.

Carnegie Corp. of New York
Bunche, Ralph Johnson **3** 121-122
Carnegie, Andrew **3** 309-312
Gardner, John W. **6** 211-213
Myrdal, Karl Gunnar **11** 284

Carnegie Endowment for International Peace (established 1910)
Butler, Nicholas Murray **3** 181
Carnegie, Andrew **3** 309-312
Clark, John Bates **4** 76-77
Root, Elihu **13** 283-284

Carnegie Foundation for the Advancement of Teaching
Conant, James Bryant **4** 192-193
Goddard, Robert Hutchings **6** 376-377
Jordan, David Starr **8** 350-351
Thomas, William Isaac **15** 193

Carnegie Hall (New York City)
Carnegie, Andrew **3** 309-312

Carnegie Institute of Technology (Pittsburgh)
Carnegie, Andrew **3** 309-312
Libby, Willard Frank **9** 397-398
Stern, Otto **14** 435
see also Carnegie-Mellon University

Carnegie Institution of Washington, D.C.
established
Carnegie, Andrew **3** 309-312
Gilman, Daniel Coit **6** 325-326
research grants
Burbank, Luther **3** 129-131
Compton, Arthur Holly **4** 186-188
East, Edward Murray **5** 182-183
Kidder, Alfred Vincent **8** 541-542
Sarton, George **13** 490-491

Carnegie International Competition (1926)
Bonnard, Pierre **2** 395-396

Carnegie-Mellon University
Carnegie, Andrew **3** 309-312
Simon, Herbert Alexander **14** 236-237

Carnesecchi Tabernacle (fresco)
Veneziano, Domenico **15** 459-460

Carnets (book)
Camus, Albert **3** 255-257

Carnival (overture)
Dvořák, Antonin **5** 168-169

Carnival Country (novel)
Amado, Jorge **1** 189-190

Carnival of Animals (musical composition)
Saint-Saëns, Charles Camille **13** 435-436

Carnival songs (music)
Isaac, Heinrich **8** 143-144

CARNOT, LAZARE NICOLAS MARGUERITE (1753-1823), French engineer, general, and statesman **3** 313-314
Carnot, Nicolas Léonard Sadi **3** 315

Carnot, Marie François Sadi (1837-1894), French president 1887-1894
Clemenceau, Georges **4** 99-101
Le Bon, Gustave **9** 268-269

CARNOT, NICHOLAS LÉONARD SADI (1796-1832), French physicist **3** 315
Clausius, Rudolf Julius Emanuel **4** 92-94
Diesel, Rudolf **5** 7

Carnot cycle (physics)
Carnot, Nicolas Léonard Sadi **3** 315

CARO, ANTHONY (born 1924), English sculptor **3** 316

CARO, JOSEPH BEN EPHRAIM (1488-1575), Jewish Talmudic scholar **3** 316-317
Elijah ben Solomon **5** 251-252

Carol I (1839-1914), king of Romania 1881-1914
Ferdinand **5** 413-414

Carol II (1893-1953), king of Romania 1930-40
Ferdinand **5** 413-414

Carolina, Wilhelmina
see Caroline of Anspach

Carolina Israelite (newspaper)
Golden, Harry **6** 402-403

Caroline of Anspach (Wilhelmina Carolina; 1683-1727), queen of George II of England
Butler, Joseph **3** 180-181
George II **6** 269-270
Walpole, Robert **16** 82-84

Caroline of Brunswick (Amelia Elizabeth Caroline; 1768-1821), queen of George IV of England
Canning, George **3** 258-260
Castlereagh, Viscount **3** 363-364
George IV **6** 272-273

Caroling Dusk (anthology)
Cullen, Countee **4** 333-334

Carolingian cycle (literature)
Boiardo, Matteo Maria **2** 369

Carolingian dynasty (France; ruled 751-987)
Charlemagne **3** 445-447
Martel, Charles **10** 285
Louis I **9** 522-523
see also France—751-987; Holy Roman Empire

Carolingian minuscule (script)
Charlemagne **3** 445-447

Caron, Pierre August
see Beaumarchais, Pierre August Caron de

CAROTHERS, WALLACE HUME (1896-1937), American chemist **3** 317-318

Carousel (musical)
Rodgers, Richard Charles **13** 234-236

Carpaccio, Vittore (circa 1465-circa 1526), Italian painter
Giorgione **6** 340-341

CARPEAUX, JEAN BAPTISTE (1827-1875), French sculptor and painter **3** 318-319
Rodin, Auguste **13** 236-238

Carpentaria, Gulf of (Australia)
Burke, Robert O'Hara **3** 142-143
Flinders, Matthew **5** 490

Carpenter, Lant (1780-1840), English Unitarian minister
Roy, Ram Mohun **13** 18

Carpenter Visual Arts Center (Cambridge, Massachusetts)
Le Corbusier **9** 274-275

Carpentier, Georges (1894-1975), French boxer
Dempsey, Jack **4** 496-497

Carpet of Life, The (poems)
George, Stefan **6** 277-278

CARR, EMILY (1871-1945), Canadian painter and writer **3** 319

Carr, Eugene Asa (1830-1910), American general
Buffalo Bill **3** 105-106

Carr, John (1723-1807), British architect
Adam, Robert and James **1** 38-40

Carr, Robert
see Somerset, Earl of

CARR-SAUNDERS, SIR ALEXANDER MORRIS (1886-1966), English demographer and sociologist **3** 333-334

Carrà, Carlo (1881-1966), Italian painter
Boccioni, Umberto **2** 353-354
Chirico, Giorgio de **4** 4
Stella, Joseph **14** 422

Carracci Academy (Bologna)
Carracci **3** 319-321
Reni, Guido **13** 97-98

CARRANZA, VENUSTIANO (1859-1920), Mexican revolutionary, president 1914-1920 **3** 321-322
associates
Calles, Plutarco Elías **3** 234-235
Madero, Francisco Indalecio **10** 118-119
Obregón, Álvaro **11** 458-459
Siqueiros, David Alfaro **14** 256
Zapata, Emiliano **16** 489-490
opponents
Díaz, José de la Cruz Porfirio **4** 534-536
Huerta, Victoriano **8** 13-14
Villa, Pancho **15** 495-496

Carré (musical composition)
Stockhausen, Karlheinz **14** 460-461

CARREL, ALEXIS (1873-1944), French-American surgeon **3** 322-323
Lindbergh, Charles Augustus **9** 421-423

Carrel, Nicolas Armand (1800-1836), French journalist and politician
Thiers, Louis Adolphe **15** 181-182

CARRERA, JOSÉ MIGUEL (1785-1821), Chilean revolutionary **3** 323-324
O'Higgins, Bernardo **11** 486

CARRERA, JOSÉ RAFAEL (1814-1865), Guatemalan statesman, president 1851-1865 **3** 324-325
Morazán, José Francisco **11** 155

Carrera, Juan José (died 1818), Chilean revolutionary
    Carrera, José Miguel **3** 323-324

Carrera, Luis (died 1818), Chilean revolutionary
    Carrera, José Miguel **3** 323-324

Carrhae (town, Southeast Turkey)
    Caracalla **3** 281-282

Carrhae, Battle of (53 B.C.)
    Caesar, Gaius Julius **3** 207-210
    Crassus Dives, Marcus Licinius **4** 296-297

Carriage at the Races, A (painting)
    Degas, Hilaire Germain Edgar **4** 461-462

Carrick, Earl of
    see Robert III

Carrick's Ford, Battle of (1861)
    McClellan, George Brinton **10** 391-392

CARRIER, WILLS (1876-1950), American inventor who was the "father of air conditioning" **3** 325-326

Carrier-Belleuse (Albert-Ernest Carrier de Belleuse; 1824-1887), French sculptor
    Rodin, Auguste **13** 236-238

Carrillo, Braulio (1800-1845), Costa Rican jurist and president
    Morazán, José Francisco **11** 155

Carrillo de Albornoz, Gil Álvarez (circa 1295-1367), Spanish archbishop
    Rienzi, Cola di **13** 166-167
    Ruiz, Juan **13** 358-359

CARRINGTON, BARON (born 1919), British politician and secretary-general of the North Atlantic Treaty Organization (1984-1988) **3** 326-327

Carriola, La (story)
    Pirandello, Luigi **12** 319-321

Carrión, Gerónimo (1812-1873), Ecuadorian president 1865-1867
    García Moreno, Gabriel **6** 209-210)

Carrogis, Louis
    see Carmontelle, Louis

CARROLL, ANNA ELLA (1815-1893), American political writer and presidential aide **3** 327-331

Carroll, Charles (1732-1832), American Revolutionary leader
    Carroll, John **3** 331-332

Carroll, Earl (1893-1948), American theatrical producer
    Fields, W. C. **5** 444

Carroll, Edward Zane
    see Buntline, Ned

Carroll, James (1854-1907), English-born American army surgeon
    Reed, Walter **13** 78

CARROLL, JOHN (1735-1815), American Catholic bishop **3** 331-332
    Seton, Elizabeth Ann Bayley **14** 118-119

CARROLL, LEWIS (pseudonym of Charles Lutwidge Dodgson; 1832-1898), English cleric and author **3** 332-333

Carrucci, Jacopo
    see Pontormo

Cars, Jean François (1665/70-1763), French engraver
    Boucher, François **2** 440-442

Cars, Laurent (1699-1771), French painter and engraver
    Boucher, François **2** 440-442

CARSON, JOHNNY (born 1925), American television host and comedian **3** 335-337

CARSON, CHRISTOPHER "KIT" (1809-1868), American frontiersman **3** 334-335
    Fitzpatrick, Thomas **5** 474-475
    Frémont, John Charles **6** 97-98
    Washakie **16** 123-125

CARSON, RACHEL LOUISE (1907-1964), American biologist and author **3** 337-338

Carson Pass (Nevada)
    Carson, Christopher **3** 334-335

Carson Pirie Scott and Company Building (Chicago)
    Sullivan, Louis Henri **15** 27-28

Carsten Curator (novella)
    Storm, Theodor **14** 479-480

Cartagena (city, Colombia)
    Drake, Francis **5** 94-96

Cartas americans (book)
    Valera y Alcalá Galiano, Juan **15** 403

Cartas da Inglaterra (book)
    Barbosa, Ruy **1** 503-504

Cartas de mujeres (book)
    Benavente y Martinez, Jacinto **2** 146-147

Carte, Richard D'Oyly (1844-1901), English impressario
    Gilbert, William Schwenck **6** 314-315

Cartel des Gauches (France; 1824)
    Herriot, Édouard **7** 339-340
    Poincaré, Raymond **12** 366-368

CARTER, ELLIOTT COOK, JR. (born 1908), American composer **3** 338-339
    Stravinsky, Igor Fedorovich **14** 502-506

CARTER, JAMES EARL ("Jimmy" Carter; born 1924), United States president (1977-1981) **3** 339-342
    Blumenthal, Werner Michael **2** 345-346
    Brewster, Kingman Jr. **2** 522-523
    Brzezinski, Zbigniew **3** 85-87
    Christopher, Warren Minor **4** 32-33
    Mondale, Walter. F. **11** 97-99
    Schlesinger, James Rodney **14** 15-16
    Strauss, Robert Schwarz **14** 501-502
    Volcker, Paul **16** 11-12

Carter, Leslie (1862-1937), American actress
    Belasco, David **2** 124-125

Carter, Thomas Henry (1854-1911), American legislator
    Clark, William Andrews **4** 83-85

Carteret, John (1690-1763); English statesman
    George II **6** 269-270

Cartesian Mediations (book)
    Husserl, Edmund **8** 67-68

Cartesianism (philosophy)
    Descartes, René **4** 505-508
    Hobbes, Thomas **7** 421-423
    Hume, David **8** 31-34
    Malebranche, Nicolas **10** 166-167

Carthage (ancient city, North Africa)
    bishops
        Cyprianus, Thascius Caecilianus **4** 361-362
        Donatus **5** 56-57
    Punic Wars
        Cato, Marcus Porcius the Elder **3** 375
        Hamilcar Barca **7** 94-95
        Hannibal Barca **7** 128-130
        Polybios **12** 384-385
        Scipio Africanus Minor, Publius Cornelius Aemilianus **14** 62-63
    Roman colony
        Caesar, Gaius Julius **3** 207-210
        Gracchus, Tiberius and Gaius Sempronius **6** 479-480
    Vandal conquest (439)
        Gaiseric **6** 172
        Leo I **9** 329-330

Carthage, Synod of (411)
    Pelagius **12** 189-190

Carthaginian, The (play)
    Plautus **12** 348-350

CARTIER, SIR GEORGE-ÉTIENNE (1814-1873), Canadian statesman **3** 342-343

CARTIER, JACQUES (1491-1557), French explorer and navigator **3** 343-344
    Cabot, Sebastian **3** 200-201
    Champlain, Samuel de **3** 419-421
    Hakluyt, Richard **7** 70

Cartography (science)
    Champlain, Samuel de **3** 419-421
    Mercator, Gerhardus **10** 511-512
    Tharp, Marie **15** 162-164
    see also Scientists—cartographers

Cartoonists
    see Artists—cartoonists

CARTWRIGHT, PETER (1785-1872), American Methodist preacher **3** 344-345

Cartwright, Thomas (1535?-1603), English Puritan clergyman
    Elizabeth I **5** 263-266

Carus, Carl Gustav (1789-1869), German physiologist and painter
    Friedrich, Caspar David **6** 114-115

CARUSO, ENRICO (1873-1921), Italian operatic tenor **3** 345
De Forest, Lee **4** 459-460

Carvajal, Francisco de (1464-1548), Spanish soldier
Gasca, Pedro de la **6** 230-231

Carvajal, Gaspar de (circa 1504-1584), Spanish missionary and explorer
Orellana, Francisco de **11** 527-528

Carvalho e Mello, Sebastião José de
see Pombal, Marquês de

CARVER, GEORGE WASHINGTON (1864-1943), African American agricultural chemist **3** 346-347
Washington, Booker Taliaferro **16** 125-126

Carver, John (circa 1576-1621), Pilgrim leader in the New World
Bradford, William **2** 475-476

CARVER, JONATHAN (1710-1780), American explorer and writer **3** 347-348

Cary, Elizabeth Cabot
see Agassiz, Elizabeth Cabot Cary

Cary, Lott (circa 1780-1828), African American clergyman
Ashmun, Jehudi **1** 335-336

Cary, Lucius
see Falkland, Lord

Casa Civena (Vicenza, Italy)
Palladio, Andrea **12** 75-77

Casa de Aizgorri, La (novel)
Baroja y Nessi, Pío **2** 15-16

Casa de Bernarda Alba, La (play)
Lorca, Federico García **9** 511-513

Casa del Obrero Mundial (Mexican labor organization)
Madero, Francisco Indalecio **10** 118-119

Casa grande and senzala (book)
Freyre, Gilberto **6** 106-107

Casa Guidi Windows (book)
Browning, Elizabeth Barrett **3** 52-53

Casa in collina, La (novel)
Pavese, Cesare **12** 154-155

Casa Panigarola (Milan, Italy)
Bramante, Donato **2** 493-494

Casa sull'acqua, La (play)
Betti, Ugo **2** 246

Casablanca (city, Morocco)
Marshall, George Catlett **10** 278-279
Patton, George Smith Jr. **12** 140-141

Casablanca (film)
Bogart, Humphrey **2** 363-364

CASALS, PABLO (born Pau Carlos Salvador Casals y Defill; 1876-1973), Spanish cellist, conductor, and composer **3** 348-350

Casamance River (Senegal)
Henry the Navigator **7** 305-306

CASANOVA, GIACOMO JACOPO GIROLAMO, CHEVALIER DE SEINGLAT
(1725-1798), Italian adventurer **3** 350-351

Casanova's Chinese Restaurant (novel)
Powell, Anthony **12** 422-423

Casanova's Homecoming (novel)
Schnitzler, Arthur **14** 23-24

Case is Altered, The (play; B. Jonson)
Plautus **12** 348-350

Case School of Applied Science (Cleveland, Ohio)
Michelson, Albert Abraham **11** 7-8

Case-study method (sociology)
Bosanquet, Bernard **2** 425-426
Stouffer, Samuel A. **14** 482-483

Casein (chemistry)
Babcock, Stephen Moulton **1** 410-411

Casely Hayford, J.E.
see Hayford, J.E. Casely

Casement, Sir Roger David (1864-1916), Irish revolutionary
Colum, Padraic **4** 174-175

Caseros, Battle of (1852)
Rosas, Juan Manuel de **13** 290-291
Urquiza, Justo José **15** 396-397

Cases of Conscience Concerning Evil Spirits (book)
Mather, Increase **10** 332-333

Casey, John
see O'Casey, Sean

Casey, Richard Gardiner (1890-1976), Australian soldier and diplomat
Lyons, Joseph Aloysius **10** 69-70

CASEY, WILLIAM J. (1913-1987), American director of the Central Intelligence Agency (CIA) **3** 351-353

CASH, JOHNNY (born 1932), American singer and songwriter **3** 353-355

Cash balances (economics)
von Mises, Ludwig **16** 25
Walras, Marie Esprit Léon **16** 84-85

Cashel Byron's Profession (novel)
Shaw, George Bernard **14** 163-164

Casibus virorum illustrium, De (book; G. Boccaccio)
Lydgate, John **10** 61-62

Casina (play)
Plautus **12** 348-350

Casket, The (play)
Plautus **12** 348-350

Casket Letters (Scottish history)
Mary, I **10** 308-309

Caspar Hauser (novel)
Wassermann, Jakob **16** 130-131

CASS, LEWIS (1782-1866), American statesman **3** 355-356
Polk, James Knox **12** 374-376
Taylor, Zachary **15** 128-130

Cass Timberlane (novel)
Lewis, Harry Sinclair **9** 385-387

Cassander (350?-297 B.C.), king of Macedon 316-297
Antigonus I **1** 248-249
Seleucus I **14** 92-93

Cassaria, La (play; Ariosto)
Ariosto, Ludovico **1** 289-290
Plautus **12** 348-350

CASSATT, MARY (1845-1926), American painter **3** 356-357

Cassel (town, France)
Edward III **5** 211-212

Cassino, Battle of (1943)
Alexander of Tunis, 1st Earl **1** 135-136

CASSIODORUS, FLAVIUS MAGNUS AURELIUS, SENATOR (circa 480-circa 575), Roman statesman and author **3** 357-358
Theodoric the Great **15** 175-176

CASSIRER, ERNST (1874-1945), German philosopher **3** 358-359

Cassius, Avidius (died 175), Roman general
Marcus Aurelius Antoninus **10** 243-245

Cassius Longinus, Gaius (died 42 B.C.), Roman general
Antony, Mark **1** 253-254
Augustus **1** 371-373
Brutus, Marcus Junius **3** 79-80
Cleopatra **4** 105-106
Herod the Great **7** 333-334
Horace **7** 500-503

Cast-iron construction (architecture)
Labrouste, Pierre François Henri **9** 144

Castagno, Andrea del
see Andrea del Castagno

Castaway, The (poem)
Cowper, William **4** 282

Caste (social system)
Boyer, Jean Pierre **2** 468-469
Chatterji, Bankimchandra **3** 480-481
Nanak **11** 303
Shankara **14** 150-151
Vivekananda **16** 4-5
see also Class (social system)

Castel, Charles Irénée
see Saint-Pierre, Abbé de

Castel, Étienne de (died 1390), French statesman
Christine de Pisan **4** 29-30

Castel Sant' Angelo (Rome)
Hadrian **7** 60-61
Sangallo family **13** 464-466

Castelfranco, Giorgio da
see Giorgione

Castellani, Aldo (1877-1971), Italian physician
Bruce, David **3** 63

Castelli, Benedetto (1578-1643), Italian astronomer and physicist
Galileo Galilei **6** 180-183
Torricelli, Evangelista **15** 268-269

Castelli, Francesco
see Borromini, Francesco

Castelli, Valerio (1625-1659), Italian painter
Magnasco, Alessandro **10** 127-128

CASTELO BRANCO, HUMBERTO (1900-1967), Brazilian general, president 1964-1966 **3** 359-360
Geisel, Ernesto **6** 253-255
Goulart, João **6** 467-469

Castelvetro, Lodovico (1505-1571), Italian critic and philologist
Sidney, Philip **14** 214-215

CASTIGLIONE, BALDASSARE (1478-1529), Italian author and diplomat **3** 360-361
Milán, Luis **11** 15-16
Raphael **13** 40-42

Castiglione, Giovanni Benedetto (1616-1670), Italian painter
Magnasco, Alessandro **10** 127-128

Castigo del Penséque, El (play)
Tirso de Molina **15** 237-238

Castile (province, Spain)
Alfonso I **1** 148
Cid **4** 58-59
Isabella I **8** 144-145

Castile, Council of (1625; Spain)
Tirso de Molina **15** 237-238

Castilian (language)
García Márquez, Gabriel **6** 208-209
Gonzalo de Berceo **6** 431-432

Castilla (book)
Ruíz, José Martínez **13** 358

CASTILLA, RAMÓN (1797-1867), Peruvian military leader and president **3** 361

Castillo, Juan del (1584-1640), Spanish painter
Murillo, Bartolomé Esteban **11** 258-259

CASTLE, IRENE and VERNON (1910-1918), ballroom dancers **3** 361-363

Castle, The (novel)
Kafka, Franz **8** 403-406

Castle Dangerous (novel; Scott)
Douglas, James **5** 78
Scott, Walter **14** 68-70

Castle Howard (Yorkshire, England)
Hawksmoor, Nicholas **7** 211-212
Vanbrugh, John **15** 409-410

Castle of Heavens (observatory, Denmark)
Brahe, Tycho **2** 489-490

Castle of Indolence, The (poem)
Thomson, James **15** 199-200

Castle of Steen (painting)
Rubens, Peter Paul **13** 339-342

Castle Rackrent (novel)
Edgeworth, Maria **5** 205-206

Castle Spectre, The (play)
Lewis, Matthew Gregory **9** 390-391

Castlemaine (town, Australia)
Burke, Robert O'Hara **3** 142-143

CASTLEREAGH, VISCOUNT (Robert Stewart; 1769-1822), British statesman **3** 363-364
associates
Canning, George **3** 258-260
Liverpool, 2nd Earl of **9** 456-457
foreign policy
Aberdeen, 4th Earl of **1** 25-26
Adams, John Quincy **1** 52-54
Metternich, Klemens von **10** 533-536
Raffles, Thomas Stamford **13** 1-2

Castor and Pollux (mythology)
Euripides **5** 332-334

Castor et Pollux (opera)
Rameau, Jean Philippe **13** 17-18

Castorp, Hans (literary character)
Mann, Thomas **10** 204-207

Castrato (music)
Scarlatti, Pietro Alessandro Gaspare **13** 517-518

Castro, Cipriano (1858?-1924), Venezuelan general, president 1902-1908
Gómez, Juan Vicente **6** 417-418

CASTRO ALVES, ANTÔNIO DE (1847-1871), Brazilian poet **3** 364-365

CASTRO RUZ, FIDEL (born 1926), Cuban prime minister **3** 365-368
Batista y Zaldívar, Fulgencio **2** 57-58
Eisenhower, Dwight David **5** 233-236
Gaitán, Jorge Eliécer **6** 172-173
Guevara, Ernesto **7** 30-31
Velasco Ibarra, José María **15** 452-454
see also Bay of Pigs invasion; Cuban missile crisis

Castro Ruz, Raul (born 1931), Cuban lawyer and politician
Castro Ruz, Fidel **3** 365-368

Cat and Mouse (novella)
Grass, Günter **6** 496-497

"Cat and Mouse" Act (England; 1913)
Pankhurst, Emmeline **12** 85-86

Cat in the Hat (book)
Geisel, Theodor (Dr. Seuss) **6** 255-256

Cat on a Hot Tin Roof (play)
Williams, Tennessee **16** 306-308

Cat, Shozo, and Two Women, A (novel)
Tanizaki, Junichiro **15** 101-102

Catalaunian Plains
see Chalônssur-Marne, Battle of (451)

Catalog of Birds (musical composition)
Messiaen, Olivier **10** 528-529

Catalog of Women (poem)
Hesiod **7** 361-362

Catalogus plantarum ... (books)
Ray, John **13** 57-59

Catalonia (region, Spain)
Calderón, Pedro **3** 221-222

Charles II **3** 454

Catalysis (chemistry)
Berzelius, Jöns Jacob **2** 231-233
Sabatier, Paul **13** 398-399

Catanei, Vanozza de' (flourished 1470-1492), Italian mistress of Rodrigo Borgia
Alexander VI **1** 134-135
Borgia, Cesare **2** 412-413

Catastrophe, The (book)
Kerensky, Aleksandr Fedorovich **8** 516-517

Catastrophism (geology)
Cuvier, Georges Léopold **4** 357-359
Lyell, Charles **10** 62-63

Catavi tin mine (Bolivia)
Patiño, Simón Iturri **12** 133-134

Catch (music)
Arne, Thomas Augustine **1** 307-308
Landini, Francesco **9** 185-186

Catch-22 (book)
Heller, Joseph **7** 263-265

Catcher in the Rye (book)
Salinger, J. D. **13** 447-448

Catching the Turkey (painting)
Moses, Grandma **11** 201-202

Cateau-Cambrésis, Treaty of (1559)
Alba, Duke of **1** 103-104
Charles VIII **3** 462-463
Philip II **12** 271-273

Categorical imperative (philosophy)
Kant, Immanuel **8** 430-432

Categories (book; Aristotle)
Abelard, Peter **1** 23-25
Boethius, Anicius Manlius Severinus **2** 360-361

Caterpillar strike (1992)
Bieber, Owen **2** 266-268

Catharsis (painting)
Orozco, José Clemente **12** 1-2

Catharsis (psychology)
Freud, Sigmund **6** 103-106

Cathay (ancient China)
Columbus, Christopher **4** 176-179

Cathay (poems)
Pound, Ezra Loomis **12** 415-417

Cathcart, George (1794-1854), English soldier
Moshweshwe **11** 203-205

Cathedra (painting)
Newman, Barnett **11** 365

Cathedral, The (etching)
Ensor, James **5** 289-290

Cathedral, The (poem)
Lowell, James Russell **10** 14-15

Cathédrale, La (novel)
Huysmans, Joris Karl **8** 81-82

CATHER, WILLA SIBERT (1873-1947),
American writer **3** 368-369
Caldwell, Erskine **3** 223-224
McClure, Samuel Sidney **10** 398-399
Mencken, Henry Louis **10** 481-483

Catherine (novel)
Thackeray, William Makepeace
15 159-161

Catherine I (1684-1727), empress of Russia
1725-1727
Anna Ivanovna **1** 240-241
Elizabeth, the Queen Mother **5** 261-263
Euler, Leonard **5** 331-332
Peter I **12** 253-256

Catherine II (empress of Russia)
see Catherine the Great

Catherine de' Médici
Médici, Catherine de'

Catherine of Aragon (1485-1536), Spanish
princess, first queen of Henry VIII of Eng-
land
Cranmer, Thomas **4** 295-296
Henry VII **7** 300-302
Henry VIII **7** 302-305
Isabella I **8** 144-145
Mary, I **10** 308-309
More, Thomas **11** 156-157
Norfolk, 3d Duke of **11** 423
Tyndale, William **15** 373-374
Wolsey, Thomas **16** 364-366

Catherine of Aragon (book)
Froude, James Anthony **6** 133-134
Mattingly, Garrett **10** 342-344

Catherine of Braganza (1638-1705), Por-
tuguese princess, queen of Charles II of
England
Clarendon, 1st Earl of **4** 73-75

Catherine of France
see Catherine of Valois

CATHERINE OF SIENA, ST. (1347-1380),
Italian mystic **3** 369-370
Dryden, John **5** 106-107

Catherine of Valois (1401-1437), French
princess, queen of England
Henry V **7** 296-297

CATHERINE THE GREAT (1729-1796),
Russian empress 1762-1796 **3** 370-372
domestic policy
Alexander I **1** 130-132, 112
Becarria, Marchese di **2** 97-98
Pugachev, Emelyan Ivanovich
12 478-479
foreign policy
Agha Mohammad Khan **1** 80-81
Gustavus III **7** 45-46
Miranda, Francisco de **11** 52-53
Potemkin, Grigori Aleksandrovich
12 411-412
Suvorov, Aleksandr Vasilievich
15 44-45
patronage
Cimarosa, Domenico **4** 61-62
Diderot, Denis **5** 1-2

Falconet, Étienne Maurice **5** 372
Houdon, Antoine **7** 516-517
relatives
Elizabeth, the Queen Mother
5 261-263
Paul I **12** 143-144

Catherine the Great (biography)
Gooch, George Peabody **6** 432-433

Cathleen Listens In (play)
O'Casey, Sean **11** 459-460

Cathode rays (physics)
Crookes, William **4** 323-324
Hertz, Heinrich Rudolf **7** 346-347
Röntgen, Wilhelm Conrad **13** 273-275
Thomson, Joseph John **15** 200-201

Catholic Action (religious movement)
Benedict XV **2** 153-154
John, XXIII **8** 277-280
Mannix, Daniel **10** 210
Pius XI **12** 337-339
Pius XII **12** 339-340

Catholic Association (Ireland)
O'Connell, Daniel **11** 465-467

Catholic Center party (Germany)
Erzberger, Matthias **5** 319-320
Leo XIII **9** 334-336

Catholic Charities (New York State archdiocese)
Hayes, Patrick Joseph **7** 224-225

Catholic Church
see Roman Catholic Church

Catholic Committee (Ireland)
O'Connell, Daniel **11** 465-467

Catholic emancipation
England
Grey, Charles **6** 539-540
Peel, Robert **12** 181-183
Pitt, William the Younger
12 329-331
Russell, John **13** 380-381
Wellesley, Richard Colley
16 192-193
Wellington, 1st Duke of **16** 193-195
Ireland
Cornwallis, Charles **4** 241-243
George III **6** 270-272
Grattan, Henry **6** 499
Liverpool, 2nd Earl of **9** 456-457
O'Connell, Daniel **11** 465-467
Peel, Robert **12** 181-183
Wellington, 1st Duke of **16** 193-195

Catholic League (France)
see Holy League (1511-1513)

Catholic League (Germany; established
1609)
Ferdinand II **5** 415
Leopold II **9** 346-347
Leopold III **9** 347-348

Catholic People's party (Italy)
De Gasperi, Alcide **4** 462-463

Catholic Popular Democratic party
(France)
Schuman, Robert **14** 41

Catholic Reformation
see Counter Reformation

Catholic Relief Bill (England; 1822)
Liverpool, 2nd Earl of **9** 456-457

Catholic Social Movement (Australia)
Santamaria, Bartholomew Augustine
13 473-474

Catholic University (Chile)
Frei Montalva, Eduardo **6** 94-95

Catholic University of America, The
(Washington, D.C.)
Ireland, John **8** 133-134
Noland, Kenneth **11** 418-419

Catholic University of Argentina
Ginastera, Alberto Evaristo **6** 328-329

Catholic Worker Movement (reform group,
United States)
Day, Dorothy **4** 428-429

Catholicism, Capitalism and Protestantism
(book)
Fanfani, Amintore **5** 378-379

Catholicon (book)
Gutenberg, Johann **7** 48-49

Catilina, Lucius Sergius
see Catiline

Catilinarias (pamphlet)
Montalvo, Juan María **11** 119-120

CATILINE (Lucius Sergius Catilina; circa
108-62 B.C.), Roman politician and revo-
lutionary **3** 372-373
Cato the Younger **3**
Cicero, Marcus Tullius **4** 55-58
Clodius Pulcher, Publius **4** 121-122
Crassus Dives, Marcus Licinius
4 296-297
Sallust **13** 454

Catiline (play)
Ibsen, Henrik **8** 98-100

Catiline His Conspiracy (play)
Jonson, Ben **8** 343-345

CATLIN, GEORGE (1796-1872), American
painter **3** 373-374
Kane, Paul **8** 422-423

Cato (play; Addison)
Addison, Joseph **1** 57-58
Pope, Alexander **12** 395-397

Cato the Censor
see Cato the Elder

CATO, MARCUS PORCIUS, THE ELDER
(234-149 B.C.), Roman soldier, statesman, and historian **3** 375
influence of
Edward VI **5** 213-214
Ennius, Quintus **5** 289
Quintilian **12** 518-519
opposes pro-Hellenism
Scipio Africanus Major, Publius Cornelius **14** 61-62

works
  Celsus, Aulus Cornelius **3** 393
  Logan, James **9** 487-488

CATO THE YOUNGER (Marcus Porcius Cato Uticensis; 95-46 B.C.), Roman politician **3** 374-375
  Brutus, Marcus Junius **3** 79-80
  Caesar, Gaius Julius **3** 207-210
  Clodius Pulcher, Publius **4** 121-122
  Crassus Dives, Marcus Licinius **4** 296-297

Catonsville Nine (political activist group, United States)
  Berrigan, Daniel J. **2** 222-223

Catoptrica (book)
  Heron of Alexandria **7** 334-335

Cats (musical)
  Webber, Andrew Lloyd **16** 155-156

Catskill Mountains (New York State)
  Bartram, John **2** 40-41
  Durand, Asher Brown **5** 156-157

CATT, CARRIE CHAPMAN (1859-1947), American reformer **3** 375-376
  Shaw, Anna Howard **14** 162-163

Cattalo (hybrid animal)
  Goodnight, Charles **6** 439

CATTELL, JAMES McKEEN (1860-1944), American psychologist and editor **3** 376-377

Cattle Driver (painting; Remington)
  Chisum, John Simpson **4** 11

Cattle industry
  cattle diseases
    Koch, Heinrich Hermann Robert **9** 69-70
    Pasteur, Louis **12** 125-127
  ranchers
    Chisum, John Simpson **4** 11
    Goodnight, Charles **6** 439
    Kidman, Sidney **8** 542-544
    Love, Nat **10** 1-2
    McCoy, Joseph Geiting **10** 403-404

CATULLUS, GAIUS VALERIUS (circa 84-circa 54 B.C.), Roman poet **3** 377-378
  Horace **7** 500-503
  Sappho **13** 479-480
  Sulla, Lucius Cornelius I **15** 21-22
  Titian **15** 242-244

Catulus, Gaius Lutatius (flourished 3d century B.C.), Roman naval commander
  Hamilcar Barca **7** 94-95

Catulus, Quintus Lutatius (died 60 B.C.), Roman consul and censor
  Crassus Dives, Marcus Licinius **4** 296-297

Caucasian Captive, The (poem)
  Pushkin, Aleksandr Sergeevich **12** 489-491

Caucasian Chalk Circle, The (play)
  Brecht, Bertolt **2** 512-514

Caucasus (region, Union of Soviet Socialist Republics)
  Godunov, Boris Feodorovich **6** 382-383
  Leo III **9** 330-332

Cauchon, Pierre (died 1442), French bishop
  Joan of Arc **8** 264-265

CAUCHY, AUGUSTIN LOUIS (1789-1857), French mathematician **3** 378-380
  Taylor, Brook **15** 121-122

Cauchy-Riemann equations (mathematics)
  Alembert, Jean le Rond d' **1** 127-128

Caucus Club (Boston)
  Adams, Samuel **1** 55-56

Caudillos (South American politics)
  Portales Plazazuelos, Diego José Víctor **12** 404
  Quiroga, Juan Facundo **12** 521-522
  Roca, Julio Argentino **13** 218
  Rosas, Juan Manuel de **13** 290-291

Caughnawaga Indians (Canada)
  Krieghoff, Cornelius **9** 101

Caupolicán (died 1558), Araucanian chief
  Ercilla y Zúñiga, Alonso de **5** 302
  Valdivia, Pedro de **15** 400-401

Caus, Salomon de (1576?-1626), Norman engineer and architect
  Le Nôtre, André **9** 328-329

Cause for Alarm (book)
  Ambler, Eric **1** 191-192

Causeries du lundi (book)
  Sainte-Beuve, Charles Augustin **13** 438

Cautionary Tales and More Beasts for Worse Children (book)
  Belloc, Joseph Hilaire Pierre **2** 141

Cauvin, John
  see Calvin, John

CAVAFY, CONSTANTINE P. (Konstantinos P. Kabaphēs; 1863-1933), first modernist Greek poet **3** 381-382

Cavagnari, Sir Pierre Louis Napoleon (1841-7189), British military administrator
  Roberts, Frederick Sleigh **13** 195-196

Cavaignac, Godefroy (1853-1905), French politician
  Dreyfus, Alfred **5** 103-105

Cavaignac, Louis Eugène (1802-1857), French general
  Blanc, Louis **2** 318-319

Cavalcade (play)
  Coward, Noel **4** 279-280

CAVALCANTI, GUIDO (circa 1255-1300), Italian poet **3** 382
  Dante Alighieri **4** 389-391

Cavalier, The (novel)
  Cable, George Washington **3** 198-199

Cavalier-Anglican party (England)
  Shaftesbury, 1st Earl of **14** 135-136

Cavalier Parliament (England; 1661)
  Clarendon, 1st Earl of **4** 73-75
  Vane, Henry **15** 425-426

Cavalier poets (England)
  Herrick, Robert **7** 336-339
  Lovelace, Richard **10** 7-8
  Marvell, Andrew **10** 301-303
  Suckling, John **15** 10-11

CAVALLI, PIETRO FRANCESCO (1602-1676), Italian composer **3** 382-383
  Caccini, Giulio **3** 205-206
  Cesti, Pietro **3** 399-400
  Malipiero, Gian Francesco **10** 171

Cavalry Crossing a Ford (poem)
  Whitman, Walt **16** 249-251

Cave, Edward (1691-1754), English printer and editor
  Johnson, Samuel **8** 315-317

Cave, Peace of (1557)
  Paul IV **12** 145-146

Cave, The (novel)
  Warren, Robert Penn **16** 121-122

Cave Inscriptions (India)
  Asoka **1** 341-342

Cave of Vanhest, The (allegory)
  Brackenridge, Hugh Henry **2** 472-473

Cavelier, René Robert
  see La Salle, Sieur de

Cavendish, Lord Frederick Charles (1836-1882), English statesman
  Gladstone, William Ewart **6** 357-360

Cavendish, George (1500-1562?), English biographer
  Wolsey, Thomas **16** 364-366

CAVENDISH, HENRY (1731-1810), English physicist and chemist **3** 383-384

Cavendish, William
  see Devonshire, 4th Duke of

Cavendish Laboratory (Cambridge University, England)
  directors
    Maxwell, James Clerk **10** 361-364
    Rutherford, Ernest **13** 384-387
    Thomson, Joseph John **15** 200-201
  researchers
    Aston, Francis William **1** 350-351, 273
    Bohr, Niels Henrik David **2** 366-368
    Chadwick, James **3** 405-406
    Cockcroft, John Douglas **4** 131-132
    Compton, Arthur Holly **4** 186-188
    Crick, Francis Harry Crompton **4** 310
    Haber, Fritz **7** 56-58
    Kapitsa, Pyotr Leonidovich **8** 433-435

Cavendish Square Madonna and Child (sculpture)
  Epstein, Jacob **5** 295-296

Cavern Club (Liverpool, England)
  Lennon, John Winston **9** 326-328

Caves du Vatican, Les (book)
Gide, André **6** 308-309

CAVOUR, CONTE DI (Camillo Benso; 1810-1861), Italian statesman **3** 385-386
as premier
Crispi, Francesco **4** 310-311
Victor Emmanuel II **15** 483-484
unification of Italy
Charles Albert, King of Sardinia **3** 466
Garibaldi, Giuseppe **6** 215-217
Napoleon III **11** 310-312
Palmerston, 3d Viscount **12** 81-83

CAXIAS, DUQUE DE (Luiz Alves de Lima e Silva; 1803-1880), Brazilian general and statesman **3** 386
Deodoro da Fonseca, Manoel **4** 502
Feijó, Diogo Antônio **5** 405-406

CAXTON, WILLIAM (1422-1491), English printer **3** 386-387
Malory, Thomas **10** 175-176
Spenser, Edmund **14** 373-376

Cayuse Indians (North America)
Ogden, Peter Skene **11** 480-481
Whitman, Marcus **16** 248-249

CBS
see Columbia Broadcasting System

CCP
see Christian Democratic Union; Communist party (China); Cooperative Commonwealth Federation (Canada)

Ceasarion
see Ptolemy XIV

CEAUSESCU, NICOLAE (1918-1989), Romanian statesman **3** 387-388
Dubček, Alexander **5** 112-113
Tito, Marshal **15** 244-246

Cecil, Lord David (1902-1986), English critic
Bowen, Elizabeth **2** 462-463

Cecil, Edward Algernon Robert
see Cecil of Chelwood, Viscount

Cecil, Sir Robert (1563?-1612), English statesman
Calvert, George **3** 238-239
Elizabeth I **5** 263-266
Essex, 2d Earl of **5** 321-322
James I **8** 204-206

Cecil, Sir William
see Burghley, Lord

CECIL OF CHELWOOD, VISCOUNT (Edgar Algernon Robert Cecil; 1864-1958), English statesman **3** 388-389

Cécile (novel)
Fontane, Theodor **5** 504

Cecilia (novel)
Burney, Fanny **3** 147-148

Cecilia, St. (sculpture)
Clodion **4** 121

Cédron (literary character)
Lamartine, Alphonse Marie Louis de **9** 173-175

Cefalù Cathedral
Roger II **13** 244-245

CELA Y TRULOCK, CAMILO JOSÉ (born 1916), Spanish author **3** 389-390

Celaya, Battle of (1915)
Carranza, Venustiano **3** 321-322
Obregón, Álvaro **11** 458-459
Villa, Pancho **15** 495-496

Celebrating Myself (poems)
Rilke, Rainer Maria **13** 171-172

Celebrity (novel)
Churchill, Winston **4** 50-51

Celestial mechanics (astronomy)
Adams, John Couch **1** 51-52
Bowditch, Nathaniel **2** 460-461
Halley, Edmund **7** 88-89
Leverrier, Urbain Jean Joseph **9** 361-362
Poincaré, Jules Henri **12** 365-366

Celestial Omnibus ... (stories)
Forster, Edward Morgan **6** 14-16

Celestine I, St. (died 432), pope 422-432
Nestorius **11** 349-350

Celestine III (1106?-1198), pope 1191-1198
Innocent, III **8** 125-127

Celestine V (Pietro di Murrone; 1215-1296), pope 1294
Boniface VIII **2** 392-393
Jacopone da Todi **8** 194

Celestius
see Caelestius

Celibacy, clerical (religion)
Dunstan **5** 151-152
Feijó, Diogo Antônio **5** 405-406
Paul VI **12** 146-148
Zwingli, Huldreich **16** 537-538

CÉLINE, LOUIS FERDINAND (pen name of Ferdinand Destouches; 1894-1961), French novelist **3** 390-391

Cell respiration (biochemistry)
Szent-Györgyi, Albert von **15** 62-64
Warburg, Otto **16** 109-111

Cell theory (biology)
Schwann, Theodor **14** 51-52
Virchow, Rudolf Ludwig Carl **15** 506-507

Cella (Greek architecture)
Ictinus **8** 101

CELLINI, BENVENUTO (1500-1571), Italian goldsmith and sculptor **3** 391-392
Goujon, Jean **6** 466-467

Cellular pathology (biology)
Ehrlich, Paul **5** 225-226
Virchow, Rudolf Ludwig Carl **15** 506-507

CELSIUS, ANDERS (1701-1744), Swedish astronomer **3** 392

Celsius, Olof (1670-1756), Swedish botanist
Linnaeus, Carl **9** 427-429

CELSUS, AULUS CORNELIUS (circa 25 B.C.-A.D. 45?), Roman medical author **3** 393

Celtes, Conradus (Konrad Pickel; 1459-1508), German humanist
Zwingli, Huldreich **16** 537-538

Celtic renaissance
see Irish literary renaissance

Celtic Twilight, The (literary collection)
Yeats, William Butler **16** 445-447

Celts (European people)
Augustine of Canterbury **1** 370-371
Gobineau, Comte de **6** 375-376

Cemetery (painting)
Ruisdael, Jacob van **13** 357-358

Cena de le Ceneri, La (book)
Bruno, Giordano **3** 75-76

Cena del Rey Baltasar, La (play)
Calderón, Pedro **3** 221-222

Cénacle (French literary group)
Hugo, Victor Marie **8** 22-25
Sainte-Beuve, Charles Augustin **13** 438

Cencerro de cristal, El (poems)
Güiráldez, Ricardo **7** 38-39

Cenci, The (play)
Shelley, Percy Bysshe **14** 176-178

Cendrars, Blaise (1887-1961), French poet
Chagall, Marc **3** 406-407

Cenerentola, La (opera)
Rossini, Gioacchino **13** 311-312

Cenno de' Pepsi
see Cimabue

Censer (print)
Schongauer, Martin **14** 26-28

Censor americano, El (periodical)
Bello, Ahmadu **2** 139-140

Censors, Roman
see Statesmen, Roman

Censorship
Austria
Francis II **6** 43-44
Joseph II **8** 359-360
Metternich, Klemens von **10** 533-536
China
Li Ssu **9** 442-443
Qianlong **12** 502-505
Quin Shi Huang-di **12** 515-518
Czechoslovakia
Dubček, Alexander **5** 112-113
England
Filmer, Robert **5** 448
Lawrence, David Herbert **9** 247-248
Milton, John **11** 43-46
France
Charles X **3** 463-464
Helvétius, Claude Adrien **7** 273-274

Hugo, Victor Marie **8** 22-25
Germany
  Benn, Gottfried **2** 164
  Bonhoeffer, Dietrich **2** 389-391
  Brecht, Bertolt **2** 512-514
  Döllinger, Josef Ignaz von **5** 47-48
  Goebbels, Joseph Paul **6** 384-385
Italy
  Verdi, Giuseppe Fortunino
    Francesco **15** 463-465
Mexico
  Fernández de Lizardi, José Joaquin
    5 424-425
Poland
  Gomulka, Wladislaw **6** 422-424
Prussia
  Frederick William III **6** 87
  Frederick William IV **6** 87-88
Russia
  Akhmatova, Anna **1** 96-97
  Babel, Isaac Emmanuelovich
    1 411-412
  Dostoevsky, Fyodor **5** 74-77
  Gogol, Nikolai **6** 391-393
  Mandelstam, Osip Emilyevich
    10 191
  Pasternak, Boris Leonidovich
    12 124-125
  Solzhenitsyn, Alexander Isayevich
    14 330-332
Spain
  Mariana, Juan de **10** 254-255
Switzerland
  Calvin, John **3** 239-242
United States
  Bradford, William **2** 475-476
  Comstock, Anthony **4** 188-189
  Creel, George **4** 304-305
  Dreiser, Herman Theodore **5** 98-100
  Frankfurter, Felix **6** 57
  see also Civil liberties; Freedom of
    speech; Freedom of the press;
    Index of Forbidden books;
    Obscenity trials (United States);
    Pornography (literature); Religious
    liberty

Censorship (play)
  Wedekind, Frank **16** 166-167

Census (China)
  Hung-wu **8** 38-39

Census (Mongolia)
  Yeh-lü Ch'u-ts'ai **16** 447-449

Census, United States Bureau of the
  Cooley, Charles Horton **4** 216-217
  De Bow, James Dunwoody Brownson
    4 441-442
  McCoy, Joseph Geiting **10** 403-404

Centennial Hymn (musical composition)
  Paine, John Knowles **12** 65

Centennial Meditation of Columbia, The
  (cantata)
  Lanier, Sidney **9** 199-200

Centennial Summer (musical)
  Kern, Jerome David **8** 517-518

Center Academy (Brooklyn)
  Rothko, Mark **13** 320-321

Center for Advanced Musical Studies
  (Buenos Aires)
  Ginastera, Alberto Evaristo **6** 328-329

**Center for Advanced Study in the Behav-
ioral Sciences** (Stanford University, California)
  Berelson, Bernard **2** 185-186
  Tyler, Ralph W. **15** 370-371

**Center for the Study of Democratic Insti-
tutions** (Santa Barbara, California)
  Hutchins, Robert Maynard **8** 68-69
  Pauling, Linus Carl **12** 150-152
  Tugwell, Rexford Guy **15** 336-339

Center for the Study of Responsive Law
  (United States)
  Nader, Ralph **11** 290-291

Center party (Germany)
  Adenauer, Konrad **1** 59-61

Center Station Pumping House (Philadelphia, Pennsylvania)
  Latrobe, Benjamin Henry **9** 222-224

CENTO
  see Central Treaty Organization

Central Aerohydrodynamics Institute (Russia)
  Tupolev, Andrei Nikolaevich
    15 341-342

Central African Republic (nation, Central
Africa)
  Brazza, Pierre Paul François Camille
    Savorgnan de **2** 509-510
  Eboué, Adolphe Felix Sylvestre **5** 194
  Idris I **8** 102
  Leclerc, Jacques Philippe **9** 272-273
  Marchand, Jean-Baptiste **10** 234-237
  Schweitzer, Albert **14** 55-56

Central America
  see Latin America

Central America (book)
  Davis, Richard Harding **4** 422-423

Central American Federation (1825-1838)
  Barrios, Justo Rufino **2** 23-24
  Carrera, José Rafael **3** 324-325
  Morazán, José Francisco **11** 155

Central American International Railroad
  Keith, Minor Cooper **8** 476-477

Central Asia (Steppes-Turkestan)
  Andrews, Roy Chapman **1** 232-233
  Hsüan Tsang **8** 6-7
  Kublai Khan **9** 115-118
  Przhevalsky, Nikolai Mikhailovich
    12 469-470

Central Bank (Chile)
  Herrera, Juan de **7** 335

Central Bank (Germany)
  Schacht, Hjalmar Horace Greeley
    13 518-519

Central Bank (Mexico)
  Calles, Plutarco Elías **3** 234-235

Central Bank (Sweden)
  Hammarskjöld, Dag **7** 100-101

Central Committee (Union of Soviet
Socialist Republics)
  see Statesmen, Russian—Central Com-
    mittee; Communist party (Union of
    Soviet Socialist Republics)

Central Conference of American Rabbis
  Wise, Isaac Mayer **16** 342-343

Central Congregational Church (Boston,
Massachusetts)
  Upjohn, Richard **15** 392

Central Control Commission (Union of
Soviet Socialist Republics)
  Dzerzhinsky, Felix Edmundovich
    5 173-174

Central Europe (journal)
  Mazzini, Giuseppe **10** 381-383

Central Highway (Cuba)
  Machado y Morales, Gerardo **10** 92-93

Central Hindu College (Benares, India)
  Besant, Annie Wood **2** 233-234

Central Intelligence Agency (United States)
  Arbenz Guzmán, Jacobo **1** 274-276
  Casey, William J. **3** 351-353
  Colby, William E. **4** 143-145
  Kennedy, John Fitzgerald **8** 502-506
  Marcos, Ferdinand **10** 240-242
  McCarthy, Eugene Joseph **10** 386-388
  Mobutu Sese Seko **11** 69-71

Central Life Insurance Co. (Tampa, Florida)
  Bethune, Mary McLeod **2** 241-242

Central Pacific Railroad (United States)
  Durant, Thomas Clark **5** 157-158
  Huntington, Collis Potter **8** 49
  Judah, Theodore Dehone **8** 373-374
  Stanford, Leland **14** 397-398

Central Park (New York City)
  Olmsted, Frederick Law **11** 503-504
  Wood, Fernando **16** 367-368

Central Part of the Chain (poems)
  Jami **8** 218-219

Central Powers (WWI)
  see World War I

Central School for Arts and Manufactures
  Dumas, Jean Baptiste André **5** 138-139

Central Treaty Organization (CENTO)
  Ayub Khan, Mohammed **1** 395-396

Central University (Kentucky)
  Saunders, Charles Edward **13** 498-499

Centralism (government; South America)
  Nariño, Antonio **11** 314-315

**Centre National d'Art et Culture Georges
Pompidou** (building; Paris)
  Piano, Renzo **12** 289-291
  Rogers, Richard **13** 248-250

Centrencephalon (brain)
  Penfield, Wilder Graves **12** 198-200

Centrifugal governor (instrument)
  Foucault, Jean Bernard Léon **6** 28-29

Centrosoyus (Moscow)
Le Corbusier **9** 274-275

Centuria prima miscellaneorum (book)
Poliziano, Angelo **12** 373-374

Centuries (series of books)
Nostradamus **11** 432-434

Centuries of Magdeburg, The (book)
Canisius, Peter **3** 258

Century, The (magazine)
Crane, Stephen **4** 293-295
Johnson, James Weldon **8** 304-305
Markham, Edwin **10** 267
McClure, Samuel Sidney **10** 398-399
Rembrandt Harmensz van Rijn
13 91-95

Century Club (New York City)
Bellows, Henry Whitney **2** 143-144

Century Dictionary and Cyclopedia, The
(book)
Whitney, Josiah Dwight **16** 254-255

Century of Dishonor, A (treatise)
Jackson, Helen Hunt **8** 172

Century of Roundels, A (poems)
Swinburne, Algernon Charles **15** 54-55

Cepeda y Ahumada, Teresa de
see Theresa, St.

Cephalic index (anthropology)
Boas, Franz **2** 349-351

Cephas
see Peter, St.

Cepheid stars (astronomy)
Hubble, Edwin Powell **8** 10-11
Shapley, Harlow **14** 155-156

Cercle et Carré (sculpture group)
González, Julio **6** 428-429

Cerebral palsy (medicine)
Freud, Sigmund **6** 103-106

Cerebrospinal fever (medicine)
Domagk, Gerhard Johannes Paul
5 48-50

Cerebrospinal fluid (physiology)
Swedenborg, Emanuel **15** 49-50

Ceremony of Carols, A (musical composition)
Britten, Benjamin **3** 10-11

Cerenkov, Pavel
see Cherenkov, Pavel

Cerenkov effect
see Cherenkov effect

Ceres (asteroid)
Gauss, Karl Friedrich **6** 240-242

CEREZO AREVALO, MARCO VINICIO
(born 1942), president of Guatemala
(1986-1991) **3** 393-395

Cerium (element—chemistry)
Berzelius, Jöns Jacob **2** 231-233

CERN (Conseil Européen pour la
Recherche Nucléaire)

see European Center for Nuclear
Research

Cerne Abbas monastery (Dorset, England)
Aelfric **1** 69-70

Cerro Gordo, Battle of (1847)
Beauregard, Pierre Gustave Toutant
2 96-97

Certain Measure, A (book)
Glasgow, Ellen **6** 360-361

Certains (book)
Huysmans, Joris Karl **8** 81-82

CERVANTES, MIGUEL DE SAAVEDRA
(1547-1616), Spanish novelist **3** 395-398
Golden Age
Calderón, Pedro **3** 221-222
Góngora y Argote, Luis de
6 427-428
Lope Félix de Vega Carpio
9 503-506
influence of
Beaumont, Francis **2** 95
Brackenridge, Hugh Henry
2 472-473
Falla, Manuel de **5** 372-373
Mendelssohn, Moses **10** 488-489
influenced by
Ariosto, Ludovico **1** 289-290
translations of
Merezhkovsky, Dmitry Sergeyevich
10 515-516
Smollett, Tobias George **14** 305-307
Tieck, Ludwig **15** 218-219

Cervini, Marcello
see Marcellus II

César Birotteau (story)
Balzac, Honoré de **1** 478-480

Cesare amante (opera)
Cesti, Pietro **3** 399-400

Cesena (Italian city-state)
Julius II **8** 384-386

Cesium (element—chemistry)
Bunsen, Robert Wilhelm **3** 124-125

CÉSPEDES, CARLOS MANUEL DE
(1819-1874), Cuban lawyer and revolutionary **3** 398-399
Batista y Zaldívar, Fulgencio **2** 57-58
Gómez, Máximo **6** 418-419
Grau San Martin, Ramón **6** 499-500
Maceo, Antonio **10** 88-90

CESTI, PIETRO (Marc'Antonio Cesti;
1623-1669), Italian composer **3** 399-400
Caccini, Giulio **3** 205-206
Cavalli, Pietro Francesco **3** 382-383

CETSHWAYO (Cetewayo; circa
1826-1884), king of Zululand 1873-1879
3 400
Botha, Louis **2** 434-436
Frere, Henry Bartle Edward **6** 100-101

Ceuta (city, Spanish Morocco)
Abd al-Rahman III **1** 14
Camoëns, Luis Vaz de **3** 247-249
Henry the Navigator **7** 305-306

Ceylon (now Sri Lanka; island nation, Indian Ocean)
Buddha **3** 97-101
Rajaraja I **13** 7

CÉZANNE, PAUL (1839-1906), French
painter **3** 400-402
friends
Pissaro, Camille **12** 326-327
Zola, Émile **16** 526-528
influence (France)
Braque, Georges **2** 504-505
Derain, André **4** 503
Léger, Fernand **9** 302-303
Matisse, Henri **10** 336-337
Vlaminck, Maurice **16** 6
influence (Italy)
Modigliani, Amedeo **11** 72-73
influence (Mexico)
Rivera, Diego **13** 183-184
influence (Spain)
Picasso, Pablo **12** 292-295
influence (Switzerland)
Klee, Paul **9** 47-49
influence (United States)
Demuth, Charles **4** 497-498
Gorky, Arshile **6** 458
Hartley, Marsden **7** 186
Hofmann, Hans **7** 442-443
Weber, Max **16** 160
influenced by
Carracci **3** 319-321
Courbet, Jean Desiré Gustave
4 271-273
Delacroix, Ferdinand Victor Eugène
4 469-471
quoted
Monet, Claude **11** 102-104
Poussin, Nicolas **12** 418-420

CGOC
see General Confederation of Workers
and Peasants (Mexico)

CGT
see Confédération Générale des Travailleurs

CGTA
see Confédération Générale du Travail
Africain

Chabas, Paul Émile (1869-1937), French
painter
Comstock, Anthony **4** 188-189

Chacabuco, Battle of (1817)
O'Higgins, Bernardo **11** 486

Chace (music)
see Round (music)

Chaco War (1932-1935)
Bolivia
Paz, Octavio **12** 161-162
mediation
Lamas, Carlos Saavedra **9** 175-176
Paraguay
Justo, Agustin Pedro **8** 396
Morínigo, Higinio **11** 174-175
Stroessner, Alfredo **14** 511-512

Chaconne (musical composition)
Nielsen, Carl August **11** 388-389

Chad, Lake (Africa)
Clapperton, Hugh **4** 72-73

Chad, Republic of (nation, North Central Africa)
Eboué, Adolphe Felix Sylvestre **5** 194

CHADLI BENJEDID (born 1929), president of the Algerian Republic (1979-) **3** 402-404

CHADWICK, SIR EDWIN (1800-1890), English utilitarian reformer **3** 404-405

CHADWICK, SIR JAMES (1891-1974), English physicist **3** 405-406
Lawrence, Ernest Orlando **9** 248-250
Szilard, Leo **15** 64-66

Chadwick, Lynn (born 1914), English sculptor
González, Julio **6** 428-429

Chaerea (literary character)
Terence **15** 146-148

Chaeronea, Battle of (338 B.C.)
Alexander the Great **1** 137-141
Isocrates **8** 151

CHAGALL, MARC (1887-1985), Russian painter **3** 406-407

Chagatai khanate (Mongolian Empire)
Tamerlane **15** 94-95

CHAIN, ERNST BORIS (1906-1979), German-born English biochemist **3** 407-408
Fleming, Alexander **5** 483-485
Florey, Howard Walter **5** 491-492

Chain store (retailing)
Penney, J. C. **12** 202-203
Rosenwald, Julius **13** 293
Stewart, Alexander Turney **14** 448-449
Ward, Aaron Montgomery **16** 112
Woolworth, Frank Winfield **16** 383-384

Chainbearer, The (novel)
Cooper, James Fenimore **4** 220-223

Chained Action (sculpture)
Maillol, Aristide **10** 150-151

Chaises, Les (play)
Ionesco, Eugène **8** 131-132

Chaka (novel)
Mofolo, Thomas **11** 74
see also Shaka

Chakri Dynasty (Thailand)
Bhumibol Adulyadej **2** 258-259

Chalcedon, Council of (451)
Eutyches **5** 335
Justinian I **8** 393-395
Leo I **9** 329-330
Nestorius **11** 349-350

Chalchuapa, Battle of (1885)
Barrios, Justo Rufino **2** 23-24

Chalcidian League (Greece; 379 B.C.)
Agesilaus II **1** 79-80

Chalcidice (peninsula, Greece)
Cleon **4** 104-105

Chalcis (city, Greece)
Cleomenes I **4** 103

Chaldea (ancient region; Persian Gulf, Asia)
Ashurbanipal **1** 338

Chaldiran, Battle of (1514)
Selim I **14** 94-95

Chalgrove Field, Battle of (1643)
Hampden, John **7** 110-111

Challenge of Africa, The (book)
Busia, Kofi Abrefa **3** 172-173

Challenger, Professor (literary character)
Doyle, Arthur Conan **5** 91-92

Challenger Deep (Mariana Trench)
Piccard, Auguste **12** 297-298

CHALMERS, THOMAS (1780-1847), Scottish reformer and theologian **3** 408-409
Duff, Alexander **5** 126-127

Chalôns-sur-Marne, Battle of (451)
Attila **1** 360

Chamber music (ensemble music)
20th century
Bartók, Béla **2** 35-36
Berg, Alban **2** 186-187
Britten, Benjamin **3** 10-11
Harris, Roy **7** 175-176
Hindemith, Paul **7** 399-400
Honegger, Arthur **7** 472-473
Malipiero, Gian Francesco **10** 171
Milhaud, Darius **11** 17-18
Musgrave, Thea **11** 266-268
Poulenc, Francis **12** 414-415
Prokofiev, Sergei Sergeevich **12** 458-460
Schoenberg, Arnold **14** 24-26
Shostakovich, Dmitri Dmitrievich **14** 204-205
Tcherepnin, Alexander **15** 132-133
Tower, Joan **15** 279-281
Zwilich, Ellen Taaffe **16** 536-537
see also specific forms
baroque
Buxtehude, Dietrich **3** 185-186
Carissimi, Giacomo **3** 299-300
Corelli, Arcangelo **4** 230-231
Handel, George Frederick **7** 116-119
Monteverdi, Claudio Giovanni Antonio **11** 126-128
Rameau, Jean Philippe **13** 17-18
Scarlatti, Pietro Alessandro Gaspare **13** 517-518
classic and romantic
Haydn, Franz Joseph **7** 219-221
Mozart, Wolfgang Amadeus **11** 218-221
Schubert, Franz Peter **14** 35-37
Weber, Carl Maria Friedrich Ernst von **16** 156-157
postromantic and nationalism
Brahms, Johannes **2** 490-492
Rimsky-Korsakov, Nikolai Andreevich **13** 174-175

Saint-Saëns, Charles Camille **13** 435-436
Smetana, Bedřich **14** 281-282

Chamber Music (poems)
Joyce, James **8** 365-367

Chamber of Accounts (France)
Philip IV **12** 274

Chamber of Deputies (Belgium)
Albert I **1** 112

Chamber of Deputies (France)
Herriot, Édouard **7** 339-340

Chamber of Deputies (Italy)
Paul VI **12** 146-148

Chamber of Five Hundred (France)
Barras, Vicomte de **2** 19

Chambered Nautilus, The (poem)
Holmes, Oliver Wendell **7** 457-458

CHAMBERLAIN, (ARTHUR) NEVILLE (1869-1940), English statesman **3** 409-411
appeasement policy
Daladier, Édouard **4** 369
Macmillan, Harold **10** 112-113
Perth, 16th Earl of **12** 244-245
domestic policy
Baldwin, Stanley **1** 468-469
Chamberlain, Joseph **3** 411-413
Churchill, Winston Leonard Spencer **4** 51-53
Eden, Anthony **5** 204-205
Lloyd George, David **9** 469-471
influenced by
Disraeli, Benjamin **5** 27-29
relatives
Chamberlain, Joseph **3** 411-413

CHAMBERLAIN, SIR (JOSEPH) AUSTEN (1863-1937), English statesman **3**
Chamberlain, Arthur Neville **3** 409-411
Chamberlain, Joseph **3** 411-413
Chelmsford, Frederic John Napier Thesiger **3** 497

CHAMBERLAIN, HOUSTON STEWART (1855-1927), English-born German writer **3** 411
Gobineau, Comte de **6** 375-376

CHAMBERLAIN, JOSEPH (1836-1914), English politician **3** 411-413
colonial policy
Goldie, George Dashwood Taubman **6** 404
Gooch, George Peabody **6** 432-433
Kruger, Stephanus Johannes Paulus **9** 108-109
Rhodes, Cecil John **13** 120-122
home rule
Gladstone, William Ewart **6** 357-360
Salisbury, 3d Marquess of **13** 448-449
relatives
Chamberlain, Arthur Neville **3** 409-411

CHAMBERLAIN, WILT (born 1936), American basketball player **3** 413-415

Chamberlain's war
see Boer War (1899-1902)

Chamberlin, Edward Hastings (1899-1967), American economist
Clark, John Maurice **4** 77-78

CHAMBERLIN, THOMAS CHROWDER (1843-1928), American geologist **3** 415-416

Chambers, Robert (1802-1871), Scottish publisher
Darwin, Charles Robert **4** 397-399

CHAMBERS, WHITTAKER (Jay Vivian; 1901-1961), magazine editor who helped organize a Communist spy ring in the United States government **3** 416-417
Hiss, Alger **7** 413-415

Chambers, William (1726-1796), British architect
Adam, Robert and James **1** 38-40

Chambers v. Florida (legal case)
Black, Hugo Lafayette **2** 301-303

Chamorro Vargas, Emiliano (1871-1966), Nicaraguan general and politician
Somoza, Anastasio **14** 335-336

CHAMORRO, VIOLETA BARRIOS DE (born 1930), newspaper magnate, publicist, and first woman president of Nicaragua (1990) **3** 417-419

Champ de Mars (park, Paris)
Danton, Georges Jacques **4** 391-393

Champa (ancient king; Indochina)
Cheng Ho **3** 500
Kublai Khan **9** 115-118

Champaran (town, India)
Prasad, Rajendra **12** 433

Champfleury (Jules Fleury-Husson; 1821-1889), French critic and novelist
Courbet, Jean Desiré Gustave **4** 271-273

Champion (story)
Lardner, Ringgold Wilmer **9** 204-205

Champion, The (film)
Chaplin, Charles Spencer **3** 438-440

Champion Bay (Western Australia)
Forrest, John **6** 12-13

Champion des dames, Le (poem; Martin le Franc)
Dufay, Guillaume **5** 125-126
Dunstable, John **5** 150-151

Champion of the Spirit (sculpture)
Barlach, Ernst **2** 5-6

Champlain, Lake (between Vermont and New York State)
Arnold, Benedict **1** 309-310

CHAMPLAIN, SAMUEL DE (circa 1570-1635), French geographer and explorer **3** 419-421
Brébeuf, Jean de **2** 511-512
Brûlé, Étienne **3** 67-68

Champlain Canal (New York State)
Clinton, DeWitt **4** 112-113

CHAMPOLLION, JEAN FRANÇOIS (1790-1832), French Egyptologist **3** 421

Champollion-Figeac, Jacques Joseph (1778-1867), French archeologist
Champollion, Jean François **3** 421

Champs délicieux, Les (art collection)
Ray, Man **13** 59-60

Ch'an sect
see Zen Buddhism

Chanakya
see Kautilya

Chance (novel)
Conrad, Joseph **4** 205-207

Chance, Love and Logic (essays; Pierce)
Cohen, Morris Raphael **4** 139-140

Chance music
see Aleatory music

CHANCELLOR, RICHARD (died 1556), English navigator **3** 422
Cabot, Sebastian **3** 200-201
Ivan IV **8** 157-159

Chancellorsville, Battle of (1863)
Confederates
Davis, Jefferson **4** 416-418
Jackson, Shirley Ann **8** 183-184
Lee, Robert Edward **9** 292-294
Stuart, James Ewell Brown **14** 515-516
Union
Howard, Oliver Otis **7** 528-529
Meade, George Gordon **10** 440-441
Schurz, Carl **14** 44-45

Chandelier, Le (play)
Musset, Louis Charles Alfred de **11** 271-272

Chanderi (town, India)
Ala-ud-din **1** 102-103

Chandernagor (province, India)
Dupleix **5** 153

Chandigarh (city, India)
Le Corbusier **9** 274-275

CHANDLER, ALFRED DU PONT, JR. (born 1918), American historian of American business **3** 422-423

CHANDLER, RAYMOND, JR. (1888-1959), American author of crime fiction **3** 423-425
Bogart, Humphrey **2** 363-364

CHANDLER, ZACHARIAH (1813-1879), American politician **3** 425-426

Chandos Anthems (musical composition)
Handel, George Frederick **7** 116-119

Chandragupta II (ruled 380-413), emperor of India
Kalidasa **8** 414-415

CHANDRAGUPTA MAURYA (died circa 298 B.C.), emperor of India 322?-298 **3** 426
Asoka **1** 341-342
Kautilya **8** 462

CHANEL, COCO (born Gabrielle Chanel; 1882-1971), French fashion designer **3** 429

Chang, John M.
see Chang Myon

Ch'ang-an (city, China)
Liu Pang **9** 453

Chang Chiao
see Chang Chüeh

CHANG CHIEN (1853-1926), Chinese industrialist and social reformer **3** 429-430

CHANG CHIH-TUNG (1837-1909), Chinese official and reformer **3** 430-431
Feng Kuei-fen **5** 411-412
K'ang Yu-wei **8** 426-428

Chang-chou
see Amoy

CHANG CHÜ-CHENG (1525-1582), Chinese statesman **3** 431-432

CHANG CHÜEH (died 184), Chinese religious and revolutionary leader **3** 432-433

Chang Hsü (flourished circa 700), Chinese calligrapher
Wu Tao-tzu **16** 405-406

CHANG HSÜEH-CH'ENG (1738-1801), Chinese scholar and historian **3** 433
Huang Tsung-hsi **8** 9-10

Chang Hsüeh-liang (born 1898), Chinese general
Chang Tso-lin **3** 434-435
Chiang Kai-shek **3** 510-513
Chou En-lai **4** 20-22
Yen Hsi-shan **16** 452-453

Ch'ang-k'ang
see Ku K'ai-chih

Chang Myon (1899-1966), South Korean statesman
Park, Chung Hee **12** 99-102
Rhee, Syngman **13** 117-120

Chang Pin (flourished early 4th century), Chinese statesman
Shih Le **14** 195

CHANG PO-GO (died 846), Korean adventurer and merchant prince **3** 433-434

Chang Shih-ch'eng (flourished mid-14th century), Chinese military leader
Hung-wu **8** 38-39
Wang Fu-chih **16** 99-101

Chang Tsai (1020-1077), Chinese philosopher
Chu Hsi **4** 40-43

CHANG TSO-LIN (1873-1928), Chinese warlord **3** 434-435
Hirohito **7** 410-412
Li Ta-chao **9** 447

Sun Yat-sen **15** 35-39
Wu P'ei-fu **16** 404-405

Change and Habit (book)
Toynbee, Arnold Joseph **15** 283-284

Change of Skin (novel)
Fuentes, Carlos **6** 141-142

Changeling, The (play)
Middleton, Thomas **11** 8-9

Changes of Fortune (poem)
Christine de Pisan **4** 29-30

Changing America (book)
Ross, Edward Alsworth **13** 300

Changsha (city, China)
Chu Hsi **4** 40-43
Tseng Kuo-fan **15** 324-325

Channel Heights (San Pedro, California)
Neutra, Richard Joseph **11** 355-356

CHANNING, EDWARD (1856-1931),
American historian **3** 435
Morison, Samuel Eliot **11** 175-176

Channing, Walter (1786-1876), American
physician
Channing, Edward **3** 435

CHANNING, WILLIAM ELLERY
(1780-1842), Unitarian minister and theologian **3** 435-436
friends
Brownson, Orestes Augustus
3 57-58
Hawthorne, Nathaniel **7** 212-215
Sumner, Charles **15** 30-31
influence of
Peabody, Elizabeth Palmer
12 167-168
Tappan brothers **15** 105-106
influenced by
Child, Lydia Maria Francis
3 520-521
Woolman, John **16** 382-383

Channing, William Ellery (1818-1901),
American poet
Allston, Washington **1** 176-177
Channing, Edward **3** 435

Channing, William Francis (1820-1901),
American inventor
Farmer, Moses Gerrish **5** 385

Chanson (musical form)
Clemens non Papa, Jacobus **4** 101
Dufay, Guillaume **5** 125-126
Gombert, Nicolas **6** 416-417
Goudimel, Claude **6** 466
Josquin des Prez **8** 361-363
Lassus, Roland de **9** 216-218
Le Jeune, Claude **9** 314-315
Obrecht, Jacob **11** 457-458
Ockeghem, Johannes **11** 464-465
Willaert, Adrian **16** 287-288

Chanson d'automne (poem)
Verlaine, Paul Marie **15** 465-466

Chanson d'Eve, La (song cycle)
Fauré, Gabriel Urbain **5** 397-398

Chanson royale (musical composition)
Machaut, Guillaume de **10** 93-94

Chansons a 5 (musical composition)
Sweelinck, Jan Pieterszoon **15** 50-51

Chansons de geste (literary form)
Rabelais, François **12** 524-526
Wolfram von Eschenbach **16** 360-361

Chansons madécasses (musical composition)
Ravel, Maurice Joseph **13** 54-55

Chant du soldat (musical composition)
Gottschalk, Louis Moreau **6** 463-464

Chant tune
see Cantus firmus

Chantal, St. Jeanne Françoise de
see Jane Frances de Chantal, St.

Chantilly (town, France)
Le Nôtre, André **9** 328-329

Chantry (religious post)
Edward VI **5** 213-214

Chants d'ombre (poems)
Senghor, Léopold Sédar **14** 106-107

Chants du crépuscule (literary collection)
Hugo, Victor Marie **8** 22-25

Chants pour Naëtt (poems)
Senghor, Léopold Sédar **14** 106-107

Chanukah (Jewish feast of Dedication)
Judas Maccabeus **8** 374-375

Chanut, La (painting)
Seurat, Georges Pierre **14** 120-122

Chao (ruled 311-278 B.C.), king of Chinese
state of Yen
Tsou Yen **15** 329-330

Chao Chih-ch'ien (1829-1884), Chinese
painter
Ch'i Pai-shih **3** 526-527

Chao ch'ing (city; China)
Ricci, Matteo **13** 124-125

Chao dynasty, Latter (China; ruled
319-349)
Shih Le **14** 195

Chao Kao (died 206 B.C.), Chinese eunuch
of Ch'in empire
Li Ssu **9** 442-443
Quin Shi Huang-di **12** 515-518

Chao K'uang-yin
see Zhao Kuang-yin

Chao Lin (flourished late 13th-early 14th
century), Chinese painter
Chao Meng-fu **3** 436-437

Chao Ling-jan
see Chao Ta-nien

CHAO MENG-FU (1254-1322), Chinese
painter **3** 436-437

Chao Ta-nien (flourished late 11th century),
Chinese landscape painter
Mi Fei **11** 12-13

Chao Tzu-yüeh (novel)
Lao Shê **9** 200-201

Chao Yung (flourished late 13th-early 14th
century), Chinese painter
Chao Meng-fu **3** 436-437

Chao-hua hsi-shih (prose poetry)
Lu Hsün **10** 35-37

Chaos (literary collection)
Lagerkvist, Pär Fabian **9** 162-163

Chapeau de paille, Le (painting)
Rubens, Peter Paul **13** 339-342

CHAPIN, F(RANCIS) STUART
(1888-1974), American sociologist
3 437-438

Chapin, Samuel (1598-1675), American
colonial pioneer
Saint-Gaudens, Augustus **13** 432

Chapin Social Participation Scale
Chapin, (F.) Stuart **3** 437-438

Chapin Social Status Scale
Chapin, (F.) Stuart **3** 437-438

CHAPLIN, CHARLES SPENCER
(1889-1977), Anglo-American film actor,
director, and writer **3** 438-440
Griffith, David Wark **6** 544-545
Lubitsch, Ernst **10** 18-19
O'Neill, Eugene **11** 514-516
Sennett, Mack **14** 108-109

CHAPMAN, GEORGE (1559/60-1634),
English poet, dramatist, and translator
3 440-441
Keats, John **8** 470-472
Kyd, Thomas **9** 140-141
Plutarch **12** 359-360

CHAPMAN, SYDNEY (1888-1970), English
geophysicist **3** 441

Chapman-Ferraro theory (physics)
Chapman, Sydney **3** 441

Chapters in Jewish Literature (book)
Abrahams, Israel **1** 29

Chapters of Isaac the Scribe, The (newspaper series)
Pinto, Isaac **12** 318

Chapultepec Conference (1945)
Plaza Lasso, Galo **12** 350-351

Char, René (1903-1988), French poet
Boulez, Pierre **2** 444-445

**Characteristics of Men, Manners, Opin-
ions, Times** (essays)
Shaftesbury, 3d Earl of **14** 136-137

Characters (book; Overbury)
Webster, John **16** 164

Characters (book; Theophrastus)
Menander **10** 477-478

Characters of Theophrastus... (book)
La Bruyère, Jean de **9** 145

Charcoal Sketches (stories)
Sienkiewicz, Henryk **14** 216-217

CHARCOT, JEAN MARTIN (1825-1893),
French psychiatrist **3** 442
Binet, Alfred **2** 277-278
Freud, Sigmund **6** 103-106

Janet, Pierre Marie Félix **8** 220

CHARDIN, JEAN BAPTISTE SIMÉON
(1699-1779), French painter **3** 442-443
Fragonard, Jean Honoré **6** 38-39
Watteau, Antoine **16** 143-144

Chardón Plan (Puerto Rico)
Muñoz Marín, José Luís Alberto
11 249-250

CHARGAFF, ERWIN (born 1905), American biochemist who worked with DNA
3 444-445

Charge of the Light Brigade, The (poem)
Tennyson, Alfred **15** 144-146

Chariot (sculpture)
Giacometti, Alberto **6** 294-295

Charité Hospital (Paris)
Louis, Pierre Charles Alexandre **9** 540

Charity (painting)
Andrea del Sarto **1** 224-225

Charity (sculpture)
Powers, Hiram **12** 428-429

Charity, Institute of (Monte Clavario, Italy)
Rosmini-Serbati, Antonio **13** 296-297

Charity Hospital (Welfare Island, New York City)
Renwick, James **13** 102-103

Charity Organization Society (London)
Bosanquet, Bernard **2** 425-426

Charity Organization Society (New York City)
Lowell, Josephine Shaw **10** 15-16

Charlatan (etching)
Maulbertsch, Franz Anton **10** 345

CHARLEMAGNE (742-814), king of the Franks, 768-814, and emperor of the West, 800-814 **3** 445-447
Abd al-Rahman I **1** 13-14
Alcuin of York **1** 122-123
Notker Balbulus **11** 434-435
Harun al-Rashid **7** 188
Irene of Athens **8** 135-138
Juvenal **8** 397-399
Louis I **9** 522-523

Charles II (823-877), Holy Roman emperor 875-877 and king of France (as Charles I) 840-877
Erigena, John Scotus **5** 308-309
Louis I **9** 522-523

CHARLES IV (1316-1378), Holy Roman emperor 1346-1378 **3** 455-456
Petrarch **12** 259-261
Rienzi, Cola di **13** 166-167
Sigismund **14** 220-221
Wenceslaus **16** 201-202

CHARLES V (1500-1558), Holy Roman emperor 1519-1556 **3** 457-459
and Catholicism
Castiglione, Baldassare **3** 360-361
Leo X **9** 332-334
Paul III **12** 144-145
Paul IV **12** 145-146

and Lutheranism
Eck, Johann Maier von **5** 200
Ferdinand I **5** 414-415
Hutten, Ulrich von **8** 72-73
Luther, Martin **10** 48-51
Melancthon, Philip **10** 466-467
colonial policy
Benalcázar, Sebastián de **2** 145-146
Cortés, Hernán **4** 255-256
Gasca, Pedro de la **6** 230-231
Mendoza, Antonio de **10** 494-495
Zumárraga, Juan de **16** 531-532
court
Erasmus, Desiderius **5** 298-300
Toledo, Francisco de **15** 257-259
William the Silent **16** 300-302
English policy
Cranmer, Thomas **4** 295-296
Henry VIII **7** 302-305
Wolsey, Thomas **16** 364-366
Wyatt, Thomas **16** 410-411
explorers
Cabot, Sebastian **3** 200-201
Coronado, Francisco Vásquez de **4** 247
de Soto, Hernando **4** 510-511
Magellan, Ferdinand **10** 126-127
Menéndez de Avilés, Pedro **10** 499-500
Mercator, Gerhardus **10** 511-512
French wars (1521-1544)
Alba, Duke of **1** 103-104
Francis I **6** 40-43
Hapsburg branch
Frederick III **6** 84-85
Maximilian II **10** 357-358
patronage
Berruguete, Alonso **2** 223-224
Dürer, Albrecht **5** 159-161
Gombert, Nicolas **6** 416-417
Herrera, Juan de **7** 335
Josquin des Prez **8** 361-363
Titian **15** 242-244
Vesalius, Andreas **15** 473-475
relatives
Ferdinand V **5** 417-418
Isabella I **8** 144-145
John II **8** 275-276
Manuel I **10** 219-220
Maximilian I **10** 356-357
Philip II **12** 271-273
Rome sacked (1527)
Guicciardini, Francesco **7** 32-33
Rosso, Il **13** 312-313
Sangallo family **13** 464-466

Charles VI (1685-1740), Holy Roman emperor, 1711-1740, and king of Hungary (as Charles III)
Eugene of Savoy **5** 330-331
Fischer von Erlach, Johann Bernhard **5** 459-461
Joseph II **8** 359-360
Maria Theresa **10** 256-258
Philip V **12** 276-277

Charles VII (1697-1745), Holy Roman emperor 1742-1745
Maria Theresa **10** 256-258

Charles I (king of Bohemia)
see Charles IV (Holy Roman emperor)

CHARLES I (1600-1649), king of England 1625-1649 **3** 450-452
advisers
Buckingham, 1st Duke of **3** 93-94
Clarendon, 1st Earl of **4** 73-75
Strafford, 1st Earl of **14** 490-491
civil war
Cromwell, Oliver **4** 317-320
Hampden, John **7** 110-111
Lilburne, John **9** 409-410
Milton, John **11** 43-46
Pym, John **12** 495-496
colonial grants
Berkeley, William **2** 198-199
Calvert, George **3** 238-239
Champlain, Samuel de **3** 419-421
Gorges, Ferdinando **6** 455-456
execution
Cromwell, Oliver **4** 317-320
Vane, Henry **15** 425-426
First Bishops' War (1639)
Harrington, James **7** 166-167
Suckling, John **15** 10-11
patronage
Jones, Inigo **8** 333-334
Lovelace, Richard **10** 7-8
Rubens, Peter Paul **13** 339-342, 311
Van Dyck, Anthony **15** 423-425
relatives
Charles II **3** 452-454
James II **8** 207-208
royalists
Filmer, Robert **5** 448
Harvey, William **7** 189-190
Laud, William **9** 224-225

CHARLES II (1630-1685), king of England, Scotland, and Ireland 1660-1685 **3** 452-454
advisers
Godolphin, Sidney **6** 380-381
colonial policy
Bacon, Nathaniel **1** 424-425
Endecott, John **5** 284-285
Phips, William **12** 283
Stuyvesant, Peter **15** 5-6
Winthrop, John **16** 341
Dutch wars
Louis XIV **9** 531-533
Witt, Johan de **16** 348-349
Glorious Revolution
Mary II **10** 309-310
William III **16** 295-296
patronage
Butler, Samuel **3** 183-184
Dryden, John **5** 106-107
Flamsteed, John **5** 477-478
Lely, Peter **9** 315
Milton, John **11** 43-46
Purcell, Henry **12** 484-485
Wren, Christopher **16** 393-394

Wycherley, William **16** 411-412
Popish Plot
  Burnet, Gilbert **3** 147
  Monmouth and Buccleugh, Duke of **11** 108-109
  Oates, Titus **11** 456
Restoration (1660)
  Buckingham, 2d Duke of **3** 94-95
  Clarendon, 1st Earl of **4** 73-75
  Monck, George **11** 96-97
  Shaftesbury, 1st Earl of **14** 135-136
Charles I (king of France)
  see Charles II (Holy Roman emperor)
Charles III (Charles the Simple; 879-929), king of France 898-923
  Henry I **7** 285-286
  Rollo **13** 264-265
Charles IV (1294-1328), king of France 1322-1328
  Philip VI **12** 277-278
CHARLES V (1337-1380), king of France 1364-1380 **3** 459-460
  Charles VI **3** 460-461
  Christine de Pisan **4** 29-30
  Edward III **5** 211-212
  Edward the Black Prince **5** 217-218
  Nicholas of Oresme **11** 380
CHARLES VI (1368-1422), king of France 1380-1422 **3** 460-461
  Charles VII **3** 461-462
  Christine de Pisan **4** 29-30
  Joan of Arc **8** 264-265
  Philip the Good **12** 278-279
CHARLES VII (1403-1461), king of France 1422-1461 **3** 461-462
  Hundred Years War
    Henry VI **7** 298-299
    Joan of Arc **8** 264-265
    Philip the Good **12** 278-279
  patronage
    Fouquet, Jean **6** 31
    Ockeghem, Johannes **11** 464-465
  relatives
    Charles VI **3** 460-461
    Charles VIII **3** 462-463
    Louis XI **9** 526-528
    Margaret of Anjou **10** 249-250
CHARLES VIII (1470-1498), king of France 1483-1498 **3** 462-463
  chroniclers
    Comines, Philippe de **4** 181
  invades Italy
    Alexander VI **1** 134-135
    Borgia, Cesare **2** 412-413
    Ferdinand V **5** 417-418
    Henry VII **7** 300-302
    Louis XII **9** 528-529
    Savonarola, Girolamo **13** 505-506
Charles IX (1550-1574), king of France 1560-1574
  Medici, Catherine de' **10** 445-449
  Clouet, Jean and François **4** 122-123
  Coligny, Gaspard de **4** 159-160
  Lassus, Roland de **9** 216-218

Pilon, Germain **12** 305
Ramus, Petrus **13** 27-28
CHARLES X (1757-1836), king of France 1824-1830 **3** 463-464
  liberal opponents
    Lafayette, Marquis de **9** 151-152
    Soulé, Pierre **14** 351-352
  patronage
    Champlain, Samuel de **3** 419-421
    Champollion, Jean François **3** 421
    Ingres, Jean Auguste Dominique **8** 121-123
  Revolution of 1830
    Chateaubriand, Vicomte de **3** 477-479
    Louis Philippe **9** 536-537
    Louis XVIII **9** 535-536
    Metternich, Klemens von **10** 533-536
  supporters
    Cauchy, Augustin Louis **3** 378-380
    Hugo, Victor Marie **8** 22-25
Charles III (king of Hungary)
  see Charles VI (Holy Roman emperor)
Charles IV (1887-1922), king of Hungary 1916-1918
  Horthy de Nagybánya, Nicholas **7** 510-512
Charles II (1332-1387), king of Navarre 1349-1387
  John II **8** 275-276
Charles (died 810), king of Neustria
  Charlemagne **3** 445-447
  Louis I **9** 522-523
Charles I (king of Spain)
  see Charles V (Holy Roman emperor)
CHARLES II (1661-1700), king of Spain 1665-1700 **3** 454
  Churriguera, José Benito de **4** 53-54
  Louis XIV **9** 531-533
  Philip IV **12** 275
  Philip V **12** 276-277
CHARLES III (1716-1788), king of Spain 1759-1788 **3** 454-455
  Catherine the Great **3** 370-372
  Goya y Lucientes, Francisco de Paula José de **6** 476-478
  Jay, John **8** 230-232
  Portolá, Gaspar de **12** 408
  Tiepolo, Giovanni Battista **15** 219-220
CHARLES IV (1748-1819), king of Spain 1788-1808 **3** 456-457
  Belgrano, Manuel **2** 126-127
  Charles III **3** 454-455
  Ferdinand VII **5** 418-420
  Godoy y Álvarez de Faria, Manuel de **6** 381-382
  Pedro I **12** 179-180
Charles IX (1550-1611), king of Sweden 1604-1611
  Gustavus I **7** 42-43
  Oxenstierna, Axel Gustafsson **12** 44-45

Charles XI (1655-1697), king of Sweden 1660-1697
  Charles XII **3** 464-466
CHARLES XII (1682-1718), king of Sweden 1697-1718 **3** 464-466
  Augustus II **1** 373-374
  Mazepa, Ivan Stepanovich **10** 381
  Peter I **12** 253-256
  Voltaire **16** 14-16
Charles XIII (1748-1818), king of Sweden 1809-1818
  Bernadotte, Jean Baptiste **2**
CHARLES XIV JOHN (1763-1844), king of Sweden 1818-1844 **2** 205-206
Charles I (1226-1285), king of Two Sicilies 1266-1285
  Arnolfo di Cambio **1** 315-316
  Louis IX **9** 525-526
  Michael VIII **11** 1-2
  Peter III **12** 256-257
Charles IV (king of Two Sicilies)
  see Charles III (king of Spain)
Charles (died 1800), prince of Savoy-Carignan
  Charles Albert, King of Sardinia **3** 466
CHARLES (born 1948), Prince of Wales and heir apparent to the British throne **3** 448-450
  Diana, Princess of Wales **4** 529-533
  Elizabeth II **5** 266-269
Charles (died 1590), archduke of Inner Austria
  Elizabeth I **5** 263-266
  Ferdinand II **5** 415
Charles V (1643-1690), duke of Lorraine
  John III **8** 276-277
Charles, Count of Flanders (born 1903), Belgian regent
  Albert I **1** 112
  Leopold III **9** 347-348
Charles, Count of Provence
  see Charles I (king of Two Sicilies)
CHARLES, RAY (Robinson; born 1932), American jazz musician—singer, pianist, and composer **3** 469-470
Charles Albert (1697-1745)
  see Charles VII (Holy Roman emperor)
CHARLES ALBERT (1798-1849), king of Sardinia 1831-1849 **3** 466
  Cavour, Conte di **3** 385-386
  Garibaldi, Giuseppe **6** 215-217
  Manin, Daniele **10** 197-198
  Victor Emmanuel II **15** 483-484
Charles City (Virginia)
  Byrd, William, II **3**
Charles Demailly (novel)
  Goncourt, Edmond de and Jules de **6** 426-427
CHARLES EDWARD LOUIS PHILIP CASIMIR STUART (1720-1788), Scottish

claimant to English and Scottish thrones
3 466-467
Alfieri, Vittoria **1** 145-146
Fielding, Henry **5** 442-444
Rockingham, 2d Marquess of
13 230-231

Charles Emmanuel I (king of Sardinia)
see Charles Emmanuel III, duke of
Savoy

Charles Emmanuel II (1634-1675), duke of
Savoy 1638-1675
Victor Amadeus II **15** 482-483

Charles Emmanuel III (1701-1773), duke
of Savoy
Victor Amadeus II **15** 482-483

Charles Emmanuel IV (1751-1819), duke
of Savoy 1796-1798
Charles Albert, King of Sardinia **3** 466

Charles II Eugene (1728-1793), duke of
Württemberg 1737-1793
Schiller, Johann Christoph Friedrich von
14 4-7

Charles F. Kettering Foundation
Kettering, Charles F. **8** 524-525

Charles Felix (1756-1831), king of Sardinia
1821-1831
Charles Albert, King of Sardinia **3** 466

Charles Ives and His Music (book)
Cowell, Henry Dixon **4** 280-281

Charles' law (physics)
Gay-Lussac, Joseph Louis **6** 245-246

Charles Louis Napoleon
see Napoleon III

Charles Martel
see Martel, Charles

Charles Men, The (stories)
Heidenstam, Carl Gustaf Verner Von
7 258-259

Charles of Anjou
see Charles I (king of Two Sicilies)

Charles of Luxemburg
see Charles IV (Holy Roman emperor)

Charles of Valois (1270-1325), son of
Philip III of France
Philip VI **12** 277-278

Charles Philippe (Count of Artois)
see Charles X (king of France)

Charles River Bridge v. Warren Bridge
(legal case)
Taney, Roger Brooke **15** 98-99

Charles Scribner's Sons (publishing house)
Perkins, William Maxwell Evarts
12 222-223

Charles the Bad
see Charles II (king of Navarre)

Charles the Bald
see Charles II (Holy Roman emperor)

CHARLES THE BOLD (1433-1477), duke of
Burgundy 1467-1477 **3** 467-469
art patronage

Dufay, Guillaume **5** 125-126
van der Goes, Hugo **15** 416-417
councilors
Comines, Philippe de **4** 181
relatives
Frederick III **6** 84-85
Philip the Good **12** 278-279
Wars of the Roses
Edward IV **5** 212-213
Louis XI **9** 526-528
Margaret of Anjou **10** 249-250
Warwick and of Salisbury, Earl of
16 122-123

Charles the Fair
see Charles IV (king of France)

Charles the Great
see Charlemagne

Charles the Mad
see Charles VI (king of France)

Charles the Second (play)
Payne, John Howard **12** 159

Charles the Simple
see Charles III (king of France)

Charles University of Prague
see Prague University

Charleston (city, South Carolina)
American Revolution
Clinton, Henry **4** 114-115
Cornwallis, Charles **4** 241-243
Greene, Nathanael **6** 525-526
Kościuszko, Tadeusz Andrzej
Bonawentura **9** 88
Marion, Francis **10** 262-263
Pinckney, Charles Cotesworth
12 310
Pulaski, Casimir **12** 480-481
Tarleton, Banastre **15** 110
architecture
Harrison, Peter **7** 179-180
Mills, Robert **11** 36-37
Civil War
Barton, Clara **2** 37-39
Beauregard, Pierre Gustave Toutant
2 96-97
Douglas, Stephen Arnold **5** 80-82
England, John **5** 288
see also Ft. Sumter first Catholic
bishop

Charleston Mercury (newspaper)
Rhett, Robert Barnwell **13** 120

Charlie and the Chocolate Factory (book)
Dahl, Roald **4** 366-367

Charlier, Jean
see Gerson, John

Charlotte d'Albret (flourished 1499),
French princess, sister of Jean d'Albret,
king of Navarre
Alexander VI **1** 134-135

Charlotte Sophia (1744-1818), queen of
George III of England
Burney, Fanny **3** 147-148
George III **6** 270-272

Hunter, William **8** 48-49

Charlotte's Web (children's book)
White, E. B. **16** 228-230

Charmides (dialogue)
Plato **12** 345-347

CHARNISAY, CHARLES DE MENOU
(Seigneur d'Aulnay; circa 1604-1650),
French governor of Acadia **3** 470-471

Charnley House (Chicago, Illinois)
Wright, Frank Lloyd **16** 398-401

Charolais, Count of
see Charles the Bold

Charolaise, La (musical composition)
Couperin, François **4** 270-271

Charon (book)
Lucian **10** 25-26

CHARONTON, ENGUERRAND (circa
1410/15-after 1466), French painter
3 471

Charpentier, Georges (flourished 19th century), French publisher
Renoir, Pierre Auguste **13** 101-102

CHARPENTIER, MARC ANTOINE
(1634-1704), French composer
3 471-472

CHARRON, PIERRE (1541-1603), French
philosopher and theologian **3** 472

Charter Oath (1868; Japan)
Mutsuhito **11** 279-282

Charter of 1617 (Sweden)
Gustavus II **7** 43-45

Charter of 1814 (France)
Louis Philippe **9** 536-537
Louis XVIII **9** 535-536

Charter of Charity (religious code)
Stephen Harding **14** 428-429

Charter of Freedom and Exemptions
(Netherlands)
Van Rensselaer, Kiliaen **15** 430-431

Charterhouse, The (painting)
Gainsborough, Thomas **6** 170-172

Charterhouse of Parma, The (novel)
Stendhal **14** 422-425

Chartism (book)
Carlyle, Thomas **3** 304-305

Chartist movement (England)
Disraeli, Benjamin **5** 27-29
Owen, Robert **12** 39-40
Wellington, 1st Duke of **16** 193-195

Chartres Cathedral (painting)
Corot, Jean Baptiste Camille **4** 247-249

Chartres, Duc de (Robert Philippe Louis
Eugène Ferdinand d'Orléans;
1840-1910), French nobleman
Bonvalot, Pierre Gabriel Édouard **2** 396

Charwoman's Daughter, The (novel)
Stephens, James **14** 430-431

Charybdis (whirlpool, Sicily)
Homer **7** 465-467

CHASE, PHILANDER (1775-1852), American Episcopalian bishop and missionary **3** 472-473
    Chase, Salmon Portland **3** 473-475

CHASE, SALMON PORTLAND (1808-1873), American statesman and jurist **3** 473-475
    critics
        Lincoln, Abraham **9** 415-418
        Seward, William Henry **14** 124-125
    national banks
        Cooke, Jay **4** 215-216
        McCulloch, Hugh **10** 404-405
    Supreme Court
        Field, Stephen Johnson **5** 441-442
        Miller, Samuel Freeman **11** 29-30

CHASE, SAMUEL (1741-1811), American politician and jurist **3** 475-476
    Burr, Aaron **3** 156-159
    Carroll, John **3** 331-332
    Martin, Luther **10** 289-290
    Randolph, John **13** 30
    Waite, Morrison Remick **16** 46

CHASE, WILLIAM MERRITT (1849-1916), American painter **3** 476-477
    associates
        Sheeler, Charles **14** 170-171
        Twachtman, John Henry **15** 362-363
    students
        Demuth, Charles **4** 497-498
        Hartley, Marsden **7** 186
        Kent, Rockwell **8** 511
        Stella, Joseph **14** 422
        Tanner, Henry Ossawa **15** 102-103

Chase and Sanborne Hour (radio show)
    Cantor, Eddie **3** 264-265

Chase Manhattan Bank (United States)
    Rockefeller, David **13** 224-225
    Volcker, Paul **16** 11-12

Chasm of the Colorado (painting)
    Moran, Thomas **11** 151-152

Chasseloup-Laubat, Comte de (1805-1873), French statesman
    Garnier, Francis **6** 220-221

Chasseur Officer on Horseback Charging (painting)
    Géricault, Jean Louis André Théodore **6** 280-281

Chaste Maid in Cheapside, A (play)
    Middleton, Thomas **11** 8-9

Chateau de Steen (painting, Rubens)
    Constable, John **4** 208-209

Château d'If (prison, Marseilles)
    Blanqui, Louis Auguste **2** 323-324

Château Thierry (city, France)
    Clemenceau, Georges **4** 99-101

CHATEAUBRIAND, VICOMTE DE (1768-1848), French author **3** 477-479
    Chénier, André Marie **3** 500-501
    Hugo, Victor Marie **8** 22-25
    Sand, George **13** 459-461

Chateaubriand et son groupe littéraire (literary criticism)
    Sainte-Beuve, Charles Augustin **13** 438

Châtelet, Marquise du (Gabrielle Émilie Le Tonnelier de Breteuil; 1706-1749), French writer
    Voltaire **16** 14-16

Chatham, 1st Earl of
    see Pitt, William, the Elder

CHATICHAI CHOONHAVAN (born 1922), prime minister of Thailand (1988-1990) **3** 479-480

Châtillon (commune, France)
    Garibaldi, Giuseppe **6** 215-217

Châtiments, Les (verse)
    Hugo, Victor Marie **8** 22-25

Chatsworth Triptych (painting)
    Memling, Hans **10** 476

Chattanooga, Battle of (1863)
    Sherman, William Tecumseh **14** 186-187
    Thomas, George Henry **15** 190-191

Chattanooga Times (newspaper)
    Ochs, Adolph Simon **11** 464

Chatte, La (ballet; Diaghilev)
    Gabo, Naum **6** 158-159
    Pevsner, Antoine **12** 263-264

CHATTERJI, BANKIMCHANDRA (1838-1894), Bengali novelist **3** 480-481

Chatterton (play)
    Vigny, Comte de **15** 494-495

CHATTERTON, THOMAS (1752-1770), English poet **3** 481-482

Chattopadhyay, Sarojini
    see Naidu, Sarojini

CHAUCER, GEOFFREY (circa 1345-1400), English poet **3** 482-485
    editions and translations
        Caxton, William **3** 386-387
        Dryden, John **5** 106-107
        Pope, Alexander **12** 395-397
    illustrators
        Kent, Rockwell **8** 511
    influence of
        Douglas, Gavin **5** 77-78
        Dunbar, William **5** 142-143
        Lydgate, John **10** 61-62
        Ryder, Albert Pinkham **13** 391-392
        Skelton, John **14** 268-269
        Spenser, Edmund **14** 373-376
    influenced by
        Boccaccio, Giovanni **2** 351-353
        Froissart, Jean **6** 124-125
        Guillaume de Lorris **7** 33-34
        Juvenal **8** 397-399
        Ovid **12** 34-36
    social critics
        Gower, John **6** 475-476
        Langland, William **9** 194-195
        Lyndsay, David **10** 66-67
        Wyclif, John **16** 412-413

Chaucer and His England (book)
    Coulton, George Gordon **4** 267

Chaulieu Abbé de (Guillaume Amfrye; 1639-1720), French abbé, poet, and wit
    Voltaire **16** 14-16

Chaumont (city, France)
    Castlereagh, Viscount **3** 363-364

Chauncy, Charles (1592-1672), English-born American clergyman and educator
    Chauncy, Charles **3** 485-486

CHAUNCY, CHARLES (1705-1787), American Calvinist clergyman and theologian **3** 485-486
    Edwards, Jonathan **5** 220-222

Chausson, Ernest (1855-1899), French composer
    Franck, César **6** 48-49

Chautauqua movement (adult education)
    Harper, William Rainey **7** 163-164
    Holbrook, Josiah **7** 450-451
    Vincent, John Heyl **15** 502-503

Chautauquan (newspaper)
    Tarbell, Ida Minerva **15** 107-108

Chautemps, Camille (1885-1963), French lawyer and politician
    Blum, Léon **2** 343-344

CHÁVEZ, CARLOS (1899-1978), Mexican conductor and composer **3** 486
    Ives, Charles Edward **8** 159-160

CHAVEZ, CESAR (1927-1993), American labor leader **3** 486-487
    Valdez, Luis **15** 399-400

CHÁVEZ, DENNIS (1888-1962), Hispanic American politician **3** 488-489

CHAVEZ, LINDA (born 1947), Hispanic American civil rights activists **3** 489-491

CHAVIS, BENJAMIN (born 1948), African American religious leader, civil rights activist, **3** 491-493 labor organizer, and author

Che school (Chinese art)
    Sesshu, Toya **14** 116-117

Cheat, The (painting)
    La Tour, George de **9** 222

Check-List of American Magazine... (book)
    Ford, Paul Leicester **6** 9-10

Cheerfulness (philosophy)
    Democritus **4** 493-494

Cheirobalistra (machine)
    Heron of Alexandria **7** 334-335

CHEEVER, JOHN (1912-1982), American short-story writer **3** 493-494

Chefs
    Child, Julia McWilliams **3** 519-520

Cheka (secret police, Russia)
    Dzerzhinsky, Felix Edmundovich **5** 173-174

Cheke, Sir John (1514-1557), English classical scholar
Edward VI **5** 213-214

Chekhonte, Antosha (pseudonym)
see Chekhov, Anton Pavlovich

CHEKHOV, ANTON PAVLOVICH
(1860-1904), Russian author **3** 494-497
Bunin, Ivan Alekseevich **3** 124
Gorky, Maxim **6** 458-460
Lermontov, Mikhail Yurievich
9 352-353
Stanislavsky, Constantin **14** 398-399
Turgenev, Ivan Sergeyevich **15** 345-348

Chekiang (province, China)
Chao Meng-fu **3** 436-437
Chu Hsi **4** 40-43

Chelles, Jean de (flourished circa 1250),
French architect and sculptor
Montreuil, Pierre de **11** 139

CHELMSFORD, 1st VISCOUNT (Frederic
John Napier Thesigner Chelmsford;
1868-1933), English statesman **3** 497

Chelsea Girls, The (film)
Warhol, Andy **16** 114-115

Chelsea Hospital (England)
Hawksmoor, Nicholas **7** 211-212

Cheltenham Ladies' College (England)
Beale, Dorothea **2** 81-83

Chemical News (journal)
Crookes, William **4** 323-324

Chemical warfare
Conant, James Bryant **4** 192-193
Haber, Fritz **7** 56-58
Todd, Alexander **15** 251-253
Willstätter, Richard **16** 310-312

Chemistry (science)
agricultural
Babcock, Stephen Moulton
1 410-411
Carver, George Washington
3 346-347
Liebig, Justus von **9** 403-404
chemical engineering
Patrick, Jennie R. **12** 136-137
chemical lasers
Polanyi, John Charles **12** 370-372
chemical reactions
Berthollet, Claude Louis **2** 229-230
Diels, Otto Paul Hermann **5** 5-6
Duhem, Pierre Maurice Marie **5** 129
Hinshelwood, Cyril Norman
7 405-406
Lavoisier, Antoine Laurent
9 241-244
Onsager, Lars **11** 520-523
Sabatier, Paul **13** 398-399
Semenov, Nikolai Nikolaevich
14 101
chemical structure
Arrhenius, Svante August **1** 318-320
Couper, Archibald Scott **4** 269-270
Dalton, John **4** 378-379

Dumas, Jean Baptiste André
5 138-139
Faraday, Michael **5** 380
Fischer, Emil **5** 456-457
Fischer, Hans **5** 457-459
Haber, Fritz **7** 56-58
Hodgkin, Dorothy Crowfoot
7 432-434
Karle, Isabella **8** 447-449
Kekulé, Friedrich August **8** 477-478
Kendrew, John C. **8** 495-496
Lewis, Gilbert Newton **9** 384-385
Mendeleev, Dmitrii Ivanovich
10 486-488
Pauling, Linus Carl **12** 150-152
Perutz, Max **12** 246-248
Van't Hoff, Jacobus Hendricus
15 431-432
Willstätter, Richard **16** 310-312
gas studies
Avogadro, Lorenzo Romano
Amedeo Carlo **1** 388-389
Boyle, Robert **2** 469-471
Gay-Lussac, Joseph Louis **6** 245-246
Helmont, Jan Baptista van
7 269-271
Priestley, Joseph **12** 452-453
Ramsay, William **13** 21-22
industrial
Baekeland, Leo Hendrik **1** 430-431
Carothers, Wallace Hume
3 317-318
Haber, Fritz **7** 56-58
Müller, Paul Hermann **11** 241-242
Nobel, Alfred Bernhard **11** 410-411
instruments
Bunsen, Robert Wilhelm **3** 124-125
Crookes, William **4** 323-324
Hare, Robert **7** 152-153
isotopes
Aston, Francis William **1** 350-351
Calvin, Melvin **3** 242-243
Hahn, Otto **7** 64-65
Hevesy, George Charles de **7** 371
Libby, Willard Frank **9** 397-398
Richards, Theodore William
13 137-138
laws of substitution
Baeyer, Johann Friedrich Adolf von
1 432
Dumas, Jean Baptiste André
5 138-139
Hofmann, August Wilhelm von
7 441-442
macronuclear
Flory, Paul **5** 492-494
phlogiston theory
Cavendish, Henry **3** 383-384
Scheele, Karl Wilhelm **13** 525-526
Stahl, Georg Ernst **14** 392-393
physical see Physical chemistry physiological
Berzelius, Jöns Jacob **2** 231-233
Ehrlich, Paul **5** 225-226
Khorana, Har Gobind **8** 537-538
Reichstein, Tadeus **13** 85-87

solution chemistry
Nernst, Walther **11** 340-342
see also Biochemistry; Electrochemistry; Scientists—chemists

Chemistry, First International Congress of
(Karlsruhe, 1860)
Mendeleev, Dmitrii Ivanovich
10 486-488

Chemistry, Institute of (Heidelberg University)
Bunsen, Robert Wilhelm **3** 124-125

Chemotherapy (medicine)
Domagk, Gerhard Johannes Paul
5 48-50
Ehrlich, Paul **5** 225-226
Fleming, Alexander **5** 483-485
Waksman, Selman Abraham **16** 49-50
see also Antibiotics

Ch'en Chiung-ming (1875-1933), Chinese
military leader
Ch'en Tu-hsiu **3** 501-502
Chiang Kai-shek **3** 510-513
Sun Yat-sen **15** 35-39

Ch'en dynasty (China; ruled 557-589)
Sui Wen-ti **15** 16-18

Ch'en Liang (1143-1194), Chinese philosopher
Chu Hsi **4** 40-43

CH'EN TU-HSIU (1879-1942), Chinese
statesman and editor **3** 501-502
Hu Shih **8** 63-65
Li Ta-chao **9** 447
Ts'ai Yüan-p'ei **15** 322
Yen Fu **16** 452

Ch'en Wang-tao
see Chih-i

Ch'en Yi (1901-1972), Chinese soldier and
politician
Chou En-lai **4** 20-22

CHENEY, RICHARD B(RUCE) (born 1941),
U.S. secretary of defense under George
Bush **3** 497-499

CHENG HO (1371-circa 1433), Chinese
admiral **3** 500
Yung-lo **16** 482-483

Ch'eng I (1033-1107), Chinese Neoconfucian philosopher
Chu Hsi **4** 40-43
Lu Chiu-yuan **10** 24-25

Chengtu (city, China)
Kublai Khan **9** 115-118

CHÉNIER, ANDRÉ MARIE (1762-1794),
French poet **3** 500-501
Hugo, Victor Marie **8** 22-25

Chennault, Claire Lee (1890-1958), American military aviator
Chiang Kai-shek **3** 510-513

Chentan University (Shanghai)
Ku Chieh-kang **9** 120-121

Cheops
see Khufu

Cherbourg (city, France)
Gloucester, Duke of **6** 370-371

Chercheur de trésors, Le (novel; P.I.F. Aubert de Gaspé)
Aubert de Gaspé, Philippe **1** 364

Chercheuses de poux, Les (poem)
Rimbaud, Jean Nicolas Arthur **13** 172-174

CHERENKOV, PAVEL ALEKSEEVICH (1904-1990), Russian physicist **3** 502-503

Cherenkov effect (physics)
Cherenkov, Pavel Alekseevich **3** 502-503

Cherepnin, Nikolai (1873-1945), Russian composer
Mussorgsky, Modest Petrovich **11** 274-276

Chéri (novel)
Colette, Sidonie Gabrielle **4** 158-159

Chermayeff, Serge (1900-1996), American architect
Mendelsohn, Erich **10** 488

CHERNENKO, KONSTANTIN USTI-NOVICH (1911-1985), the Soviet Union general secretary from February 1984 to March 1985 **3** 503-504

Chernigov-Seversk (region, Ukraine)
Ivan III **8** 156-157

Chernov, Viktor Mikhailovich (1876-1952), Russian journalist
Kolchak, Aleksandr Vasilievich **9** 77-78

Chernovtsy, University of (Ukraine)
Schumpeter, Joseph Alois **14** 43-44

CHERNYSHEVSKY, NIKOLAI GAVRILOVICH (1828-1889), Russian journalist, critic, and social theorist **3** 504-505
Lenin, Vladimir Ilich **9** 323-326
Mussorgsky, Modest Petrovich **11** 274-276
Tolstoy, Leo **15** 262-265
Turgenev, Ivan Sergeyevich **15** 345-348

Cherokee Indians (North America)
activism
Mankiller, Wilma **10** 198-199
education
Houston, Samuel **7** 526-527
Sequoyah **14** 110-111
forced migration
Cass, Lewis **3** 355-356
Ross, John **13** 303-304
Scott, Winfield **14** 70-71
land surveys
Frémont, John Charles **6** 97-98
Henderson, Richard **7** 278-279
raids and wars
Boone, Daniel **2** 397-398
Forbes, John **5** 507-508
Marion, Francis **10** 262-263

Cherokee Nation (Oklahoma)
McCoy, Joseph Geiting **10** 403-404

Cherry Orchard, The (play)
Chekhov, Anton Pavlovich **3** 494-497

Cherry Valley massacre (1778)
Brant, Joseph **2** 500-501

Chersonesus Thracica (peninsula, Turkey)
Miltiades **11** 42-43

Cherubin (literary character)
Beaumarchais, Pierre August Caron de **2** 93-94

CHERUBINI, LUIGI CARLO ZANOBI SAL-VATORE MARIA (1760-1842), Italian-born French composer **3** 505-506
Gluck, Christoph Willibald **6** 372-374
Liszt, Franz **9** 445-447
Mendelssohn, Moses **10** 488-489

Chesapeake (ship)
Lawrence, James **9** 251-252

Chesapeake and Ohio Railroad (United States)
Huntington, Collis Potter **8** 49

Chesapeake Bay (inlet between Virginia and Maryland)
Verrazano, Giovanni da **15** 470-471

Chesapeake Bay, Battle of (1781)
Bougainville, Louis Antoine de **2** 443-444

Chesapeake-Leopard affair (United States; 1808)
Decatur, Stephen **4** 448-449

Chess (game)
Fischer, Bobby **5** 454-456

Chester (hymn)
Billings, William **2** 274-275

Chester and Holyhead Railway (England)
Stephenson, George and Robert **14** 432-433

Chesterfield, 4th Earl of (Philip Dormer Stanhope; 1694-1773), English statesman
Johnson, Samuel **8** 315-317

Chesterton, Cecil Edward (1879-1918), English journalist
Belloc, Joseph Hilaire Pierre **2** 141

CHESTERTON, GILBERT KEITH (1874-1936), English author and artist **3** 508-509
Belloc, Joseph Hilaire Pierre **2** 141

CHESNUT, MARY BOYKIN (1823-1886), Civil War diarist **3** 506-508

Chevalier, Étienne (flourished mid-15th century), treasurer of France
Fouquet, Jean **6** 31

Chevalier au Cygne (legendary character)
Godfrey of Bouillon **6** 379

Chevreul, Michel Eugène (1786-1889), French chemist
Seurat, Georges Pierre **14** 120-122

Chevrolet (automobile)
Durant, William Crapo **5** 158
Ford, Henry **6** 5-6
Knudsen, William S. **9** 67-68

Cheyenne, The (sculpture)
Rembrandt Harmensz van Rijn **13** 91-95

Cheyenne Autumn (film)
Ford, John **6** 7-8

Cheyenne Indians (North America)
Crazy Horse **4** 303-304
Custer, George Armstrong **4** 355-356
Dull Knife **5** 135-136
Fitzpatrick, Thomas **5** 474-475
Miles, Nelson Appleton **11** 16-17

Chézy, Helmine von (1783-1855), French poet
Weber, Carl Maria Friedrich Ernst von **16** 156-157

Ch'i (Chinese philosophy)
Chu Hsi **4** 40-43
Wang Fu-chih **16** 99-101
Wang Yang-ming **16** 108-109

Ch'i (Chinese state)
Confucius **4** 197-200
Mencius **10** 480-481

Ch'i dynasty (China; ruled 479-502)
Liu Hsieh **9** 452-453

Chi Fa
see Wu wang

Ch'i Heng
see Ch'i Pai-shih

Chi-hsia (Chinese academy)
Hsün-tzu **8** 8
Mencius **10** 480-481

Ch'i-lu University (Chungking)
Ku Chieh-kang **9** 120-121

CH'I PAI-SHIH (1863-1957), Chinese painter and poet **3** 526-527

Chi Tan
see Chou kung

Ch'i Wei-ch'ing
see Ch'i Pai-shih

CH'I-YING (circa 1786-1858), Chinese statesman and diplomat **4** 12

Chia
see Hui-yüan

Chia (novel)
Pa Chin **12** 53-54

Ch'ia-ch'ing (1760-1820), Chinese emperor 1796-1820
Ho-shen **7** 512-513
Qianlong **12** 502-505

Chia-ku convention (Ch'i state; 500 B.C.)
Confucius **4** 197-200

CHIA SSU-TAO (1213-1275), Chinese statesman **3** 514-515

Chia-yin tsa-chih (magazine)
Ch'en Tu-hsiu **3** 501-502
Li Ta-chao **9** 447

Ch'iang (Asian people)
Fan Chung-yen **5** 376-377

Ch'iang-hsüeh hui (Chinese reform society)
   K'ang Yu-wei **8** 426-428
   Liang Ch'i-ch'ao **9** 395-396

Chiang Ch'ing
   see Jiang Qing

CHIANG CHING-KUO (1910-1988), chairman of the Nationalist party and president of the Republic of China in Taiwan (1978-1988) **3** 509-510

CHIANG KAI-SHEK (1887-1975), Chinese nationalist leader and president **3** 510-513
   Communist policy
      Ch'en Tu-hsiu **3** 501-502
      Lin Piao **9** 429-430
      Mao Zedong **10** 225-227
      Wu P'ei-fu **16** 404-405
   Japan and
      Inukai, Tsuyoshi **8** 130-131
      Saionji, Kimmochi **13** 438-439
   Kuomingtang
      Chou En-lai **4** 20-22
      Sun Yat-sen **15** 35-39, 293
      Wang Ching-wei **16** 98
      Yen Hsi-shan **16** 452-453
   Northern Expedition
      Chang Tso-lin **3** 434-435
      Feng Yü-hsiang **5** 412-413
      Hu Shih **8** 63-65
      Ts'ai Yüan-p'ei **15** 322
   supporters
      Song Sisters **14** 338-341
   United States and
      Marshall, George Catlett **10** 278-279
      Stilwell, Joseph Warren **14** 456-457

Chiang Kai-shek, Mme.
   see Soong Mei-ling

Chiao-ch'ou t'ung-i (essay)
   Chang Hsüeh-ch'eng **3** 433

Chiao-pin-lu k'ang (essays)
   Feng Kuei-fen **5** 411-412

Chiaramonti, Luigi Barnabà
   see Pius VII

CHIARI, ROBERTO (born 1905), president of Panama (1960-1964) **3** 513-514

Chiaroscuro (art technique)
   Andrea del Sarto **1** 224-225
   Bermejo, Bartolomé **2** 205
   Claude Lorrain **4** 89-90
   Cranach, Lucas the Elder **4** 289-290
   Dürer, Albrecht **5** 159-161
   Tanner, Henry Ossawa **15** 102-103

Chibcha Indians (South America)
   Benalcázar, Sebastián de **2** 145-146
   Quesada, Gonzalo Jiménez de **12** 509-510

Chicago (city, Illinois)
   development
      Daley, Richard J. **4** 373-375
      Field, Marshall **5** 440-441
      McCoy, Joseph Geiting **10** 403-404
      Medill, Joseph **10** 451-452

      Ward, Aaron Montgomery **16** 112
   gangsters
      Capone, Al **3** 272-273
   mayors
      Daley, Richard J. **4** 373-375
   Operation Breadbasket
      Jackson, Jesse Louis **8** 174-176
   political reforms
      Byrne, Jane **3** 190-191
      Merriam, Charles Edward **10** 518-519
      Pinkerton, Allan **12** 314-315
   World's Fair
      see World's Columbian Exposition

CHICAGO, JUDY (Judith Cohen; born 1939), American artist and activist **3** 515-516
   Schapiro, Miriam **13** 520-521

Chicago, University of (Illinois)
   anthropology
      Banda, Hastings Kamuzu **1** 485-486
      Bloomfield, Leonard **2** 338
      Harper, William Rainey **7** 163-164
      Radin, Paul **12** 538-539
      Redfield, Robert **13** 73-74
      Sapir, Edward **13** 478-479
   architecture
      Wright, Frank Lloyd **16** 398-401
   Divinity School
      Gilkey, Langdon Brown **6** 318-319
      Greeley, Andrew M. **6** 514-515
      Meland, Bernard Eugene **10** 467-468
      Wieman, Henry Nelson **16** 261-262
      Wilder, Amos Niven **16** 273-274
   economics
      Harris, Abram Lincoln Jr. **7** 169-171
      Johnson, Alvin Saunders **8** 293-294
      Knight, Frank Hyneman **9** 58-59
      Veblen, Thorstein Bunde **15** 449-450
   education
      Judd, Charles Hubbard **8** 375-376
      Tyler, Ralph W. **15** 370-371
   founded
      Field, Marshall **5** 440-441
      Rockefeller, John Davison **13** 226-228
   geology
      Chamberlin, T.C. **3** 415-416
   history
      Breasted, James Henry **2** 510-511
      Eliade, Mircea **5** 249-250
      Franklin, John Hope **6** 65-67
      Woodward, Comer Vann **16** 378-379
   law
      Pound, Roscoe **12** 417-418
   literature
      Bellow, Saul **2** 141-143
      Ellison, Ralph Waldo **5** 274-275
      Wilder, Thornton Niven **16** 276-277
   philosophy
      Carnap, Rudolf **3** 308-309
      Dewey, John **4** 520-523

      Tillich, Paul Johannes **15** 224-225
      Toulmin, Stephen Edelston **15** 271-273
   physics
      Born, Max **2** 420-421
      Compton, Arthur Holly **4** 186-188
      Fermi, Enrico **5** 422-424
      Gell-Mann, Murray **6** 257-258
      Michelson, Albert Abraham **11** 7-8
      Millikan, Robert Andrews **11** 33-35
      Szilard, Leo **15** 64-66
      Urey, Harold Clayton **15** 394-396
      Yang, Chen Ning **16** 437-438
   political science
      Beneš, Edward **2** 155-157
      Merriam, Charles Edward **10** 518-519
      Miliukov, Pavel Nikolayevich **11** 18-19
      Morgenthau, Hans J. **11** 171-172
      Tugwell, Rexford Guy **15** 336-339
   presidents
      Beadle, George Wells **2** 80-81
      Gray, Hannah Holborn **6** 507-508
      Harper, William Rainey **7** 163-164
      Hutchins, Robert Maynard **8** 68-69
   psychology
      Bettelheim, Bruno **2** 245-246
      Lashley, Karl Spencer **9** 214-215
      Mead, George Herbert **10** 437-438
      Thurstone, Louis Leon **15** 215-216
      Watson, John Broadus **16** 138-139
   sociology
      Bentley, Arthur F. **2** 178
      Eliade, Mircea **5** 249-250
      Ogburn, William Fielding **11** 480
      Park, Robert E. **12** 102-104
      Shils, Edward Albert **14** 195-197
      Small, Albion Woodbury **14** 277
      Stouffer, Samuel A. **14** 482-483
      Thomas, William Isaac **15** 193

Chicago American (newspaper)
   Hearst, William Randolph **7** 243-244

Chicago and Alton Railroad (United States)
   Harriman, Edward Henry **7** 164-165
   Van Horne, William Cornelius **15** 429-430

Chicago and North Western Railway (United States)
   Darrow, Clarence Seward **4** 396-397
   Pinkerton, Allan **12** 314-315

Chicago Art Institute (Illinois)
   Bellows, George Wesley **2** 143
   Taft, Lorado **15** 75-76

Chicago Bible Institute
   see Moody Bible Institute

Chicago Bulls (United States basketball team)
   Jordan, Michael **8** 355-357

Chicago, Burlington and Quincy Railroad (United States)
   Corning, Erastus **4** 238-239
   Harriman, Edward Henry **7** 164-165

Chicago Civic Opera House (Illinois)
Insull, Samuel **8** 130

Chicago Civic Orchestra (Illinois)
Dawson, William Levi **4** 427-428

Chicago Defender (newspaper)
Hughes, Langston **8** 18-19

Chicago Examiner (newspaper)
Hearst, William Randolph **7** 243-244

Chicago Globe (newspaper)
Dreiser, Herman Theodore **5** 98-100

Chicago Great Western Railroad (United States)
Chrysler, Walter Percy **4** 36-37

Chicago group (American literature)
Anderson, Sherwood **1** 220-221

Chicago, Milwaukee and St. Paul Railroad (United States)
Van Horne, William Cornelius **15** 429-430

Chicago Poems (literary collection)
Sandburg, Carl **13** 461-462

Chicago Psychoanalytic Institute (Illinois)
Horney, Karen Danielsen **7** 508-509

Chicago Record (newspaper)
Baker, Ray Stannard **1** 451-452

Chicago, Rock Island, and Pacific Railroad (United States)
Durant, Thomas Clark **5** 157-158

Chicago Sanitary District Board (Illinois)
McCormick, Robert Rutherford **10** 401-402

Chicago School of Design (Illinois)
Cage, John **3** 211-214

Chicago Seven (antiwar protesters; United States; 1968)
Dellinger, David **4** 480-481
Kunstler, William M. **9** 131-133
Rubin, Jerry **13** 344-346
Seale, Robert George **14** 77-78

Chicago Sun-Times (newspaper)
Murdoch, Rupert **11** 257-258

Chicago Sunday Tribune (newspaper)
Feininger, Lyonel **5** 406-407

Chicago Symphony Orchestra (Illinois)
Thomas, Theodore **15** 192-193

Chicago Times (newspaper)
Dunne, Finley Peter **5** 147-148

Chicago Tribune (newspaper)
Emerson, Ralph Waldo **5** 278-280
Ford, Henry **6** 5-6
Lloyd, Henry Demarest **9** 468-469
McCormick, Robert Rutherford **10** 401-402
Medill, Joseph **10** 451-452
Royko, Mike **13** 337-339

Chicago Tribune Tower (Illinois)
Saarinen, Eliel and Eero **13** 396-398

Chicago Urban League (Illinois)
Johnson, Charles Spurgeon **8** 296-297

Chicago White Sox (baseball team)
Sunday, William Ashley **15** 32-33

Chicago World's Fair (1893)
see World's Columbian Exposition

Chicherin, Boris Nikolaevich (1830-1904), Russian philosopher
Klyuchevsky, Vasily Osipovich **9** 57-58

CHICHERIN, GEORGI VASILYEVICH (1872-1936), Russian statesman **3** 516-517
Litvinov, Maxim Maximovich **9** 451-452

Chichester (ship)
Smollett, Tobias George **14** 305-307

Chichikov (literary character)
Gogol, Nikolai **6** 391-393

Chickamauga, Battle of (1863)
Forrest, Nathan Bedford **6** 13-14
Garfield, James Abram **6** 213-214
Grant, Ulysses Simpson **6** 492-494
Thomas, George Henry **15** 190-191

Chickasaw Bluffs, Battle of (1862)
Sherman, William Tecumseh **14** 186-187

Chickasaw Indians (North America)
Bienville, Sieur de **2** 268-269

Chicken (fowl)
Dam, Carl Peter Henrik **4** 382-383

Chicken-pox virus (medicine)
Enders, John Franklin **5** 285-286

Chidiock Tichbourne (novel)
Clarke, Marcus Andrew Hislop **4** 87-88

Chief (painting)
Kline, Franz **9** 55

Chief, The (art action)
Beuys, Joseph **2** 246-248

Chief, The (book)
Mann, Heinrich **10** 201-202

Chieh-liu san-pu-ch'ü (trilogy)
Pa Chin **12** 53-54

Chien Andalou, Un (film)
Buñuel, Luis **3** 127-128

Ch'ien Hsuan (circa 1235-1300), Chinese painter
Chao Meng-fu **3** 436-437

Chien-kuo fang-lueh (book)
Sun Yat-sen **15** 35-39

Ch'ien-lung
seeQianlong

CHIEPE, GAOSITWE KEAGAKWA TIBE (born 1926), intellectual, educator, diplomat, politician, and cabinet minister of external affairs of Botswana **3** 517

Chiesa, Giacomo della
see Benedict XV

Chieti, diocese of (Rome)
Cajetan **3** 215-216

CHIFLEY, JOSEPH BENEDICT (1885-1951), Australian statesman **3** 518
Evatt, Herbert Vere **5** 341-343
Menzies, Robert Gordon **10** 510-511

CHIH-I (Chih-k'ai, 538-597), Chinese Buddhist monk **3** 518-519

Ch'ih-pi, Battle of (208)
Ts'ao Ts'ao **15** 322-323

Chihli (province, China)
Tseng Kuo-fan **15** 324-325

Chihli clique (Chinese warlords)
Wu P'ei-fu **16** 404-405

Chihli-Fengtien War (1922)
Chang Tso-lin **3** 434-435

Chiisana Okoku (novel)
Tanizaki, Junichiro **15** 101-102

Chijin no Ai (novel)
Tanizaki, Junichiro **15** 101-102

Child, David Lee (died 1874), American author and editor
Child, Lydia Maria Francis **3** 520-521

CHILD, JULIA McWILLIAMS (born 1912), chef, author, and television personality **3** 519-520

CHILD, LYDIA MARIA FRANCIS (1802-1880), American author and abolitionist **3** 520-521

Child Asleep in Its Own Life, A (poem)
Stevens, Wallace **14** 443-445

Child development
child rearing
King, Frederic Truby **9** 18-19
Spock, Benjamin **14** 383-385
educational theories
Montessori, Maria **11** 125-126
Peabody, Elizabeth Palmer **12** 167-168
Pestalozzi, Johann Heinrich **12** 249-250
physical
Mendenhall, Dorothy Reed **10** 491-492
psychological studies
Bettelheim, Bruno **2** 245-246
Erikson, Erik Homburger **5** 309-310
Gesell, Arnold Lucius **6** 286-287
Klein, Melanie **9** 52
Lewin, Kurt **9** 375-376
Piaget, Jean **12** 287-288

Child in America, The (book)
Thomas, William Isaac **15** 193

Child labor (economics)
Coolidge, John Calvin **4** 217-219
Daudet, Alphonse **4** 402-403
Kelley, F. **8** 483-484
Palmer, Alexander Mitchell **12** 77-78
Slater, Samuel **14** 272-273

Child of Our Time, A (cantata)
Tippett, Michael Kemp **15** 234-235

Child of Pleasure, The (novel)
D'Annunzio, Gabriele **4** 388

Child prodigies
art
Lawrence, Thomas **9** 252-253
Sargent, John Singer **13** 481-482
literature
Anouilh, Jean **1** 243-244
Chatterton, Thomas **3** 481-482
Darío, Rubén **4** 393-394
Peretz, Isaac Loeb **12** 212
Rimbaud, Jean Nicolas Arthur **13** 172-174
Tschernichowsky, Saul **15** 323
mathematics
Pascal, Blaise **12** 122-124
Riemann, Georg Friedrich Bernard **13** 164-165
Wiener, Norbert **16** 262-263
music
Barber, Samuel **1** 500-501
Bartók, Béla **2** 35-36
Bellini, Vincenzo **2** 138-139
Bizet, Georges **2** 296-297
Brahms, Johannes **2** 490-492
Busoni, Ferruccio Benvenuto **3** 173-174
Chopin, Frédéric François **4** 16-18
Fauré, Gabriel Urbain **5** 397-398
Mendelssohn, Moses **10** 488-489
Mozart, Wolfgang Amadeus **11** 218-221
Paganini, Niccolo **12** 58-59
Rodgers, Richard Charles **13** 234-236
Saint-Saëns, Charles Camille **13** 435-436
other
Adams, John Quincy **1** 52-54
Galen **6** 178-180
Grotius, Hugo **7** 18-19
philosophy
Bentham, Jeremy **2** 176-178
Chu Hsi **4** 40-43

Child psychology
see Child development

Child Study Association (New York City)
Adler, Felix **1** 63-64

Child with Cat (sculpture)
Zorach, William **16** 528

Child with Top (painting)
Chardin, Jean Baptiste Siméon **3** 442-443

CHILDE, VERE GORDON (1892-1957), Australian prehistorian and archeologist **3** 521-522

Childe Harold (symphony)
Fry, William Henry **6** 136-137

Childe Harold's Pilgrimage (poem)
Byron, George Gordon Noel **3** 193-194
Mármol, José **10** 274

Childebert I (died 558), Frankish king 511-558
Clovis I **4** 124

Childebert II (ruled 575-596), Frankish king
Columban **4** 176

Childeric I (437?-481), king of Salian Franks 458?-481
Clovis I **4** 124

Childhood (autobiography)
Gorky, Maxim **6** 458-460
Tolstoy, Leo **15** 262-265

Childhood (play)
Wilder, Thornton Niven **16** 276-277

Childhood (poem)
Vaughan, Henry **15** 444-445

Childhood and Society (book)
Erikson, Erik Homburger **5** 309-310

Children (novel)
Tanizaki, Junichiro **15** 101-102

Children (stories)
Chekhov, Anton Pavlovich **3** 494-497

Children in Bondage (book; East Markham)
Lindsey, Benjamin Barr **9** 425-426

Children of Adam (poems)
Whitman, Walt **16** 249-251

Children of Crisis (book series)
Coles, Robert Martin **4** 156-157

Children of Light and Children of Darkness (book)
Niebuhr, Reinhold **11** 387-388

Children of the Bush (book)
Lawson, Henry **9** 254-255

Children of the Ghetto (book)
Zangwill, Israel **16** 488-489

Children of the Soil (novel)
Sienkiewicz, Henryk **14** 216-217

Children of the Tenement (book)
Riis, Jacob August **13** 169-170

Children of Violence series (books)
Lessing, Doris **9** 355-357

Children's Bureau
see Health, Education and Welfare, United States Department of

Children's Corner Suite (musical composition)
Debussy, Achille Claude **4** 445-447

Children's Day at the Camp Meeting (sonata)
Ives, Charles Edward **8** 159-160

Children's Defense Fund
Clinton, Hillary Rodham **4** 115-117
Edelman, Marian Wright **5** 202-204

Children's Games (painting)
Bruegel, Pieter the Elder **3** 65-67

Children's Heads (sculpture)
Brancusi, Constantin **2** 494-496

Children's Hospital (Boston)
Enders, John Franklin **5** 285-286

Children's Hour, The (play; L. Hellman)
Goldwyn, Samuel **6** 416
Hellman, Lillian Florence **7** 267-268

Children's literature
see Literature for children

CHILDRESS, ALICE (1920-1994), African American dramatist, author, and poet **3** 522-524

Child's Garden of Verses, A (poems)
Stevenson, Robert Louis **14** 446-448

Chile (ship)
Wheelwright, William **16** 223-224

Chile, Republic of (nation, South America)
Araucanian revolt
Ercilla y Zúñiga, Alonso de **5** 302
Lautaro **9** 235
dictatorship
Balmaceda Fernández, José Manuel **1** 475-476
Ibáñez del Campo, Carlos **8** 88
Pinochet Ugarte, Augusto **12** 315-317
economic expansion
Hearst, George **7** 242
Meiggs, Henry **10** 458-459
Wheelwright, William **16** 223-224
exploration
Almagro, Diego de **1** 177-178
Drake, Francis **5** 94-96
Valdivia, Pedro de **15** 400-401
independence movement
Carrera, José Miguel **3** 323-324
O'Higgins, Bernardo **11** 486
Portales Plazazuelos, Diego José Víctor **12** 404
San Martín, José de **13** 468-469
Peru and
Ballivián, José **1** 475
González Prada, Manuel **6** 431
Leguía y Salcedo, Augusto Bernardino **9** 305-306
Santa Cruz, Andrés de **13** 472-473
presidents
Allende Gossens, Salvador **1** 174-176
Aylwin Azócar, Patricio **1** 393-395
social reforms
Alessandri Rodriguez, Jorge **1** 129-130
Allende Gossens, Salvador **1** 174-176
Frei Montalva, Eduardo **6** 94-95
Montt Torres, Manuel **11** 139-140
Sarmiento, Domingo Faustino **13** 484-485
see also Chilean literature

Chile, University of (Santiago)
Bello, Ahmadu **2** 139-140

Chilean literature
Allende, Isabel **1** 172-174
Bello, Ahmadu **2** 139-140
Bombal, María Luisa **2** 380-381
Donoso, José **5** 63-65
Mistral, Gabriela **11** 55-56

Chilembwe, John (died 1915), Nyasalander tribesman
Booth, Joseph **2** 404-405

Chill October (painting)
Millais, John Everett **11** 23-24

Chilled plow (farming instrument)
Oliver, James **11** 500-501

Chillington (Staffordshire)
Soane, John **14** 314-315

Chills and Fever (book)
Ransom, John Crowe **13** 39-40

Chilpancingo, Congress of (Mexico; 1813)
Matamoros, Mariano **10** 329-330
Morelos, José María **11** 157-158

Chilperic (561-584), Merovingian king of the Franks
Gregory of Tours **6** 534-535

Chimborazo, Mt. (Ecuador)
Church, Frederick Edwin **4** 49-50

Chimène (literary character)
Corneille, Pierre **4** 234-236

Chimera, The (sculpture)
Brancusi, Constantin **2** 494-496

Chimères, Les (poems)
Nerval, Gérard de **11** 345-346

Chimes, The (stories)
Dickens, Charles John Huffam **4** 538-541

Chimney sweeps (England)
Shaftesbury, 7th Earl of **14** 137-138

Chimpanzees
Goodall, Jane **6** 433-434

Ch'in (ancient state, China)
Han Fei Tzu **7** 124-125
Kim Pusik **9** 8-9
Quin Shi Huang-di **12** 515-518

Chin (Isin dynasty, China; ruled 265-420)
Hsieh Ling-yün **8** 5-6
Shih Le **14** 195

Chin (Jürchen dynasty, China; ruled 1115-1234)
Chu Hsi **4** 40-43
Genghis Khan **6** 263-265
Hui-Tsung **8** 25
Kao-tsung **8** 433
Kim Pusik **9** 8-9
Yeh-lü Ch'u-ts'ai **16** 447-449

Chin (Later Chin dynasty, China; ruled 936-947)
Ch'in Kuei **3** 524-525
Zhao Kuang-yin **16** 505-508

Ch'in dynasty (China; ruled 221-207 B.C.)
Han Fei Tzu **7** 124-125
Li Ssu **9** 442-443
Liu Pang **9** 453
Quin Shi Huang-di **12** 515-518
Shang Yang **14** 149-150

CH'IN KUEI (1090-1155), Chinese official **3** 524-525
Chu Hsi **4** 40-43
Kao-tsung **8** 433
Yo Fei **16** 462

Chin-pu-tang (political party, China)

Liang Ch'i-ch'ao **9** 395-396

Ch'in-shan
see Yüan, Ma

Chin-shih (Chinese degree)
Chang Chü-cheng **3** 431-432
Ch'in Kuei **3** 524-525
Fan Chung-yen **5** 376-377
Wang An-shih **16** 95-97

Ch'in Shih Huang-ti
see Quin Shi Huang-Di

Chin Tatars (Mongolian people)
Ma Yüan **10** 379

Ch'in-Tsung (1100-1161), Chinese emperor
Chu Hsi **4** 40-43
Hui-Tsung **8** 25
Kao-tsung **8** 433

China (nation, East Asia)
• DYNASTIC CHRONOLOGY
1122-256 B.C. (Chou dynasty)
Chou Kung **4** 22-23
Chuang Tzu **4** 40
Han Fei Tzu **7** 124-125
Lao Tzu **9** 201-202
Shang Yang **14** 149-150
Tsou Yen **15** 329-330
Wu wang **16** 408-409
207 B.C.-220 A.D. (Han dynasty)
Liu, Pang **9** 453
Wu-ti **16** 406-408
1279-1369 (Yüan dynasty)
Chia Ssu-tao **3** 514-515
Genghis Khan **6** 263-265
Kublai Khan **9** 115-118
Wen T'ien-hsiang **16** 203
Yeh-lü Ch'u-ts'ai **16** 447-449
1368-1644 (Ming dynasty)
Chang Chü-cheng **3** 431-432
Cheng Ho **3** 500
Hung-wu **8** 38-39
Li Tzu-Ch'eng **9** 452
Shih Ko-fa **14** 194-195
Wang Fu-chih **16** 99-101
Wang Yang-ming **16** 108-109
Yung-lo **16** 482-483
1644-1912 (Ch'ing or Manchu dynasty)
Chang Chien **3** 429-430
Chang Chih-tung **3** 430-431
Ch'i-ying **4** 12
Ho-shen **7** 512-513
Huang Tsung-hsi **8** 9-10
Hung Hsiu-ch'üan **8** 37-38
K'ang-hsi **8** 423-426
Kuang-hsü **9** 111-112
Li Hung-Chang **9** 407-409
Liang Ch'i-ch'ao **9** 395-396
Lin Tse-hsü **9** 431-432
Qianlong **12** 502-505
Sun Yat-sen **15** 35-39
Tseng Kuo-fan **15** 324-325
Tso Tsung-t'ang **15** 328-329
Tz'u-hsi **15** 375-376
Wang Fu-chih **16** 99-101

Wen-hsiang **16** 202-203
Yüan Shih-k'ai **16** 480-481
see also Revolution of 1911 (China) and individual dynasties
207 B.C.-A.D. 220 (Han dynasty)
Chang Chüeh **3** 432-433
Han Wu-ti **7** 136
Kuang-wu-ti **9** 112-113
Liu Pang **9** 453
Shih Le **14** 195
Wang Ch'ung **16** 98-99
Wang Mang **16** 101-103
220-265 (Three Kings.)
Ts'ao Ts'ao **15** 322-323
Wang Pi **16** 104-105
221-207 B.C. (Ch'in dynasty)
Li Ssu **9** 442-443
Quin Shi Huang-Di **12** 515-518
386-581 (Northern dynasty)
Sui Wen-ti **15** 16-18
Hsiao-Wen-ti, Wei **8** 5
420-589 (Southern dynasty)
Liang Wu-ti **9** 396-397
581-617 (Sui dynasty)
Chih-i **3** 518-519
Sui Wen-ti **15** 16-18
618-906 (T'ang dynasty)
An Lu-shan **1** 239-240
Ennin **5** 288-289
Hsüan Tsang **8** 6-7
Hsüan-tsung, T'ang **8** 7-8
Huang Ch'ao **8** 8-9
T'ai-tsung, T'ang **15** 83-84
Wu Tse-t'ien **16** 408
960-1279 (Sung dynasty)
Chia Ssu-tao **3** 514-515
Ch'in Kuei **3** 524-525
Fan Chung-yen **5** 376-377
Hui-Tsung **8** 25
Kao-tsung **8** 433
Ssu-ma kuang **14** 390-391
Wang An-shih **16** 95-97
Wen T'ien-hsiang **16** 203
Yo Fei **16** 462
Zhao Kuang-yin **16** 505-508
• OTHER HISTORY
after 1949
see China, People's Republic of; China, Republic of
art
see Chinese art
Boxer Rebellion
see Boxer Rebellion
Communist-Nationalist Coalition
Ch'en Tu-hsiu **3** 501-502
Chiang Kai-shek **3** 510-513
Chu Teh **4** 54-55
Song Sisters **14** 338-341
Communist Revolution
Chou En-lai **4** 20-22
Mao Zedong **10** 225-227
Confucianism see Confucianism
explorers

Andrews, Roy Chapman
1 232-233
Hedin, Sven Anders **7** 252-253
ibn Battuta, Muhammad **8** 91-92
Polo, Marco **12** 380-382
foreign relations
Ayub Khan, Mohammed
1 395-396
Chang Chih-tung **3** 430-431
Dupleix **5** 153
Garnier, Francis **6** 220-221
Gordon, Charles George
6 448-449
Great Wall
Quin Shi Huang-di **12** 515-518
historians of
Ssu-ma Ch'ien **14** 388-389
Ssu-ma kuang **14** 390-391
Japanese relations
Chang Chien **3** 429-430
Chang Tso-lin **3** 434-435
Chiang Kai-shek **3** 510-513
Ho Chi Minh **7** 426-428
Ito, Hirobumi **8** 153-155
Konoe, Fumimaro **9** 82-83
Shotoku Taishi **14** 205-207
Wang Ching-wei **16** 98
see also Sino-Japanese wars
Korean relations
Clark, Mark Wayne **4** 80-81
Kim Ok-kyun **9** 7-8
Taewŏn'gun, Hŭngsŏn **15** 74-75
literature
Francis Xavier **6** 48
Ricci, Matteo **13** 124-125
also see Chinese literature missionaries
medical services
Bethune, Henry Norman
2 240-241
Nationalist government formed
Chiang Kai-shek **3** 510-513
Wang Ching-wei **16** 98
Opium War
see Opium War
religions in
Xu Guangqi **16** 422-425
Russian relations
Chang Tso-lin **3** 434-435
Tso Tsung-t'ang **15** 328-329
Self-strengthening movement
Li Hung-Chang **9** 407-409
Tso Tsung-t'ang **15** 328-329
Wei Yüan **16** 180-181
Wen-hsiang **16** 202-203
Wo-jen **16** 352
social reforms
Chang Chien **3** 429-430
Chang Chih-tung **3** 430-431
Feng Kuei-fen **5** 411-412
Hu Shih **8** 63-65
K'ang Yu-wei **8** 426-428
Ku Chieh-kang **9** 120-121
Quin Shi Huang-di **12** 515-518
Ts'ai Yüan-p'ei **15** 322
Wen-hsiang **16** 202-203

Taiping Rebellion
see Taiping Rebellion
United States relations
Astor, John Jacob **1** 351-352
Burlingame, Anson **3** 144-145
Coolidge, John Calvin **4** 217-219
Evarts, William Maxwell
5 340-341
Forbes, Robert Bennet **5** 509-510
Fulbright, James William
6 147-149
Harding, Warren Gamaliel
7 148-149
Hay, John **7** 215-216
McKinley, William **10** 418-420
Pound, Roscoe **12** 417-418
Stilwell, Joseph Warren
14 456-457
warlordism
Chang Tso-lin **3** 434-435
Feng Yü-hsiang **5** 412-413
Wu P'ei-fu **16** 404-405
Yen Hsi-shan **16** 452-453
see also Northern Expedition
Westernization
Feng Kuei-fen **5** 411-412
Wo-jen **16** 352
Yen Fu **16** 452
see also May Fourth movement;
May Thirtieth movement

China, People's Republic of (Communist)
Communist Revolution
Chiang Kai-shek **3** 510-513
Chou En-lai **4** 20-22
Lin Piao **9** 429-430
Liu Shao-Ch'i **9** 453-455
Mao Zedong **10** 225-227
Wang Ming **16** 103-104
cultural heroes
Ch'i Pai-shih **3** 526-527
Kuo Mo-jo **9** 133-134
Mao Zedong **10** 225-227
economic reform
Jiang Zemin **8** 260-261
established
Chou En-lai **4** 20-22
Chu Teh **4** 54-55
Kuo Mo-jo **9** 133-134
Liu Shao-Ch'i **9** 453-455
Mao Zedong **10** 225-227
foreign relations
Bhutto, Zulfikar Ali **2** 261-262
Castro Ruz, Fidel **3** 365-368
Dalai Lama **4** 369-371
Hoxha, Enver **8** 1-3
Keita, Modibo **8** 474-475
Mondlane, Eduardo Chivambo
11 100-101
Nehru, Jawaharlal **11** 332-334
Pridi Phanomyong **12** 449
Wang Ming **16** 103-104
Great Proletarian Cultural Revolution
Jiang Qing **8** 256-260
Red Guards
Jiang Qing **8** 256-260

reform movements
Zhao Ziyang **16** 508-509
Tiananmen Square
Li Peng **9** 433-435
United Nations policy
Chiang Kai-shek **3** 510-513
Lie, Trygve Halvdan **9** 400-401
Nixon, Richard Milhous **11** 401-404
United States relations
Acheson, Dean Gooderham **1** 37-38
Dulles, John Foster **5** 134-135
MacArthur, Douglas **10** 76-78
Snow, Edgar **14** 312-313
Song Sisters **14** 338-341
see also Cultural Revolution

China, Republic of (Nationalist)
established
Chiang Kai-shek **3** 510-513
Yen Hsi-shan **16** 452-453
foreign relations
Ho Chi Minh **7** 426-428
Inukai, Tsuyoshi **8** 130-131
presidents
Chiang Ching-kuo **3** 509-510
Lee Teng-hui **9** 283-285
United States relations
Dulles, John Foster **5** 134-135
Eisenhower, Dwight David
5 233-236
Forrestal, James Vincent **6** 14
Song Sisters **14** 338-341

China and Japan (book)
Schliemann, Heinrich **14** 17-18

China Merchants Steam Navigation Co.
Li Hung-Chang **9** 407-409

China Squadron (British)
Brooke, James **3** 21-22

China's Destiny (book)
Chiang Kai-shek **3** 510-513

Chinchow, Battle of (1948)
Lin Piao **9** 429-430

Chinese (language)
Leibniz, Gottfried Wilhelm von
9 307-310
Sol Ch'ong **14** 325-326

Chinese art
calligraphy
Chao Meng-fu **3** 436-437
Hui-Tsung **8** 25
Mi Fei **11** 12-13
Su Shih **15** 39-40
Tung Ch'i-ch'ang **15** 339-340
figure painting
Ku K'ai-chih **9** 125-126
Wu Tao-tzu **16** 405-406
Yen Li-pen **16** 453-454
landscape painting
Ch'i Pai-shih **3** 526-527
Hsia Kuei **8** 4-5
Ma Yüan **10** 379
Mi Fei **11** 12-13
Ni Tsan **11** 400
Wang Wei **16** 106-108

literati painting
  Mi Fei **11** 12-13
  Su Shih **15** 39-40
  Tung Ch'i-ch'ang **15** 339-340
Chinese Communist party
  see Communist party (China)
Chinese Eastern Railway
  Chang Tso-lin **3** 434-435
Chinese Letters (essays)
  Goldsmith, Oliver **6** 411-413
Chinese literature
  1644-1912 (Ch'ing or Manchu dynasty)
    Wang T'ao **16** 105-106
    Yüan Mei **16** 479-480
  1911 Revolution, impact of
    Kuo Mo-jo **9** 133-134
    Lu Hsün **10** 35-37
  207 B.C.-A.D. 220 (Han dynasty)
    Pan Ku **12** 86-87
    Ssu-ma Ch'ien **14** 388-389
    Ssu-ma Hsiang-ju **14** 389-390
  220-265 (Three Kings.)
    Lu Chi **10** 24
  386-581 (Northern dynasty)
    Hsieh Ling-yün **8** 5-6
    Liu Hsieh **9** 452-453
    T'ao Ch'ien **15** 104-105
  618-906 (T'ang dynasty)
    Han Yü **7** 136-137
    Li Po **9** 437-439
    Liu Tsung-Yüan **9** 455-456
    Po Chü-i **12** 362-363
    Tu Fu **15** 335-336
    Wang An-shih **16** 95-97
    Wang Wei **16** 106-108
  960-1279 (Sung dynasty)
    Ou-yang Hsiu **12** 33-34
    Su Shih **15** 39-40
  Communist influence
    Kuo Mo-jo **9** 133-134
    Lao Shê **9** 200-201
    Pa Chin **12** 53-54
  see also Confucian classics
Chinese Nightingale, The (book)
  Lindsay, Vachel **9** 424-425
Chinese Restaurant (painting)
  Weber, Max **16** 160
Chinese Socialist Youth Corps
  Chou En-lai **4** 20-22
Chinese Socialist Youth League
  Chu Teh **4** 54-55
Chinesische Flöte, Die (Chinese poems, translation by Bethge)
  Mahler, Gustav **10** 144-145
Ching (ruled 156-141 B.C.), emperor of China
  Kuang-wu-ti **9** 112-113
Ch'ing (Manchu; Chinese dynasty, ruled 1644-1912)
  decline and overthrow
    Chang Chien **3** 429-430
    Chang Tso-lin **3** 434-435

    Ch'i-ying **4** 12
    Chu Teh **4** 54-55
    Ho-shen **7** 512-513
    Sun Yat-sen **15** 35-39
    Yüan Shih-k'ai **16** 480-481
  emperors
    K'ang-hsi **8** 423-426
    Kuang-hsü **9** 111-112
    Qianlong **12** 502-505
  foreign relations
    Dalai Lama **4** 369-371
    Min **11** 46-47
  historians of
    Chang Hsüeh-ch'eng **3** 433
    Huang Tsung-hsi **8** 9-10
    Wang Fu-chih **16** 99-101
    Wei Yüan **16** 180-181
  Ming dynasty vs.
    Li Tzu-Ch'eng **9** 452
    Shih Ko-fa **14** 194-195
  Self-strengthening movement
    Li Hung-Chang **9** 407-409
    Tso Tsung-t'ang **15** 328-329
    Wei Yüan **16** 180-181
    Wen-hsiang **16** 202-203
    Wo-jen **16** 352
  social reforms
    Chang Chih-tung **3** 430-431
    Feng Kuei-fen **5** 411-412
    K'ang Yu-wei **8** 426-428
    Liang Ch'i-ch'ao **9** 395-396
    Tz'u-hsi **15** 375-376
  Taiping Rebellion
    see Taiping Rebellion
Ch'ing-nien tsa-chih (magazine)
  Ch'en Tu-hsiu **3** 501-502
Chingiz-Khan
  see Genghis Khan
Chinhung (ruled 540-575), Korean king
  Sol Ch'ong **14** 325-326
CHINN, MAY EDWARD (1896-1980), African American physician **3** 525-526
Chino-Japanese War
  see Sino-Japanese War (1937-1945)
Chinoiserie (art)
  Nash, John **11** 316
Chinook (language, North America Indian)
  Kroeber, Alfred Louis **9** 105-106
  Sapir, Edward **13** 478-479
Chios (island, Aegean Sea)
  Columbus, Christopher **4** 176-179
CHIPPENDALE, THOMAS (1718-1779), English cabinetmaker **4** 1-2
  Adam, Robert and James **1** 38-40
  Hepplewhite, George **7** 317-318
Chippendale, Thomas (1749-1822/23), English cabinetmaker
  Chippendale, Thomas **4** 1-2
Chippewa Indians (North America)
  Pontiac **12** 393-394
CHIRAC, JACQUES (born 1932), French prime minister **4** 2-3

Chiricahua Indians (North America)
  Cochise **4** 128
CHIRICO, GIORGIO DE (1888-1978), Italian painter **4** 4
  influence of
    Ernst, Max **5** 311-312
    Tanguy, Yves **15** 101
    Ungaretti, Giuseppe **15** 389-390
    Zadkine, Ossip Joselyn **16** 484
  influenced by
    Böcklin, Arnold **2** 354-355
  symbolism
    Chagall, Marc **3** 406-407
    Dali, Salvador **4** 376-377
Chiriguano Indians (South America)
  Toledo, Francisco de **15** 257-259
Chirlandaio, Benedetto (1458-1497), Italian painter
  Ghirlandaio, Domenico **6** 292-293
Chirurgia magna (book)
  Guy de Chauliac **7** 54
CHISHOLM, SHIRLEY ANITA ST. HILL (born 1924), first African American woman to serve in the United States Congress **4** 7-9
Chisholm v. Georgia (legal case; 1793)
  Wilson, James **16** 323-324
CHISSANO, JOAQUIM ALBERTO (born 1939), a leader of Mozambique's war for independence and later president of Mozambique (1986-) **4** 9-11
CHISUM, JOHN SIMPSON (1824-1884), American rancher **4** 11
Chita (novel)
  Hearn, Lafcadio **7** 240
Chitor (city, India)
  Ala-ud-din **1** 102-103
Chitral (river, Pakistan)
  Bonvalot, Pierre Gabriel Édouard **2** 396
Ch'iu (novel)
  Pa Chin **12** 53-54
Chivalry (book)
  Cabell, James Branch **3** 195-196
Chladni, Ernst Florens Friedrich (1756-1827), German physicist
  Oersted, Hans Christian **11** 476-478
Chloral (chemistry)
  Liebig, Justus von **9** 403-404
Chlorides (chemistry)
  Sabatier, Paul **13** 398-399
Chlorinated hydrocarbons (chemistry)
  Carson, Rachel Louise **3** 337-338
Chlorine (element—chemistry)
  Avogadro, Lorenzo Romano Amedeo Carlo **1** 388-389
  Berthollet, Claude Louis **2** 229-230
  Davy, Humphry **4** 426-427
  Scheele, Karl Wilhelm **13** 525-526
Chloroform (chemistry)
  Liebig, Justus von **9** 403-404
  Wells, Horace **16** 196

Chlorophyll (pigment)
Fischer, Hans **5** 457-459
Willstätter, Richard **16** 310-312

Chloroprene (chemistry)
Carothers, Wallace Hume **3** 317-318

CHMIELNICKI, BOGDAN (1595-1657),
Cossack leader of Ukrainian revolt
4 12-13

CH'OE CH'UNG-HON (1149-1219), Korean general **4** 13
Chong Chung-bu **4** 15

Ch'oe U (died 1249), Korean dictator
Ch'oe Ch'ung-hn **4** 13

Choéphores, Les (musical composition)
Milhaud, Darius **11** 17-18

Choephori, The (play)
Aeschylus **1** 70-72

Choice of Hercules, The (musical composition)
Handel, George Frederick **7** 116-119

Choiseul Praslin, Duc de (1805-1847),
French legislator
Baudelaire, Charles Pierre **2** 61-63

Choju Giga (scrolls)
Toba Sojo **15** 248-249

Chokei Temple (Fukagawa, Japan)
Basho, Matsuo **2** 45-48

Chokushiden (Japanese agriculture)
Kammu **8** 420

Cholera victims
Bugeaud de la Piconnerie, Thomas
Robert **3** 111
Hegel, Georg Wilhelm Friedrich
7 254-256
Rittenhouse, David **13** 180-181
Taylor, Zachary **15** 128-130
Tchaikovsky, Peter Ilyich **15** 130-132

Cholesterol (chemistry)
Dam, Carl Peter Henrik **4** 382-383
Diels, Otto Paul Hermann **5** 5-6

Choline (vitamin)
Best, Charles Herbert **2** 236-237
Dale, Henry Hallett **4** 371-373

Ch'oljong (died 1863), king of Korea
Kojong **9** 74-75
Taewŏn'gun, Hŭngsŏn **15** 74-75

Chomedey, Paul de
see Maisoneuve, Sieur de

CHOMSKY, NOAM AVRAM (born 1928),
American linguist and philosopher
4 13-15

CHONG CHUNG-BU (1106-1179), Korean general **4** 15

Chong Mong-ju (died 1392), Korean Koryo
loyalist
Yi Sng-gye **16** 458-459

CHONGJO (1752-1800), king of Korea
4 15-16

CHOPIN, FRÉDÉRIC FRANÇOIS
(1810-1849), Polish-French composer
and pianist **4** 16-18
friends
Liszt, Franz **9** 445-447
Sand, George **13** 459-461
influence of
Paderewski, Ignace Jan **12** 56-57
Poulenc, Francis **12** 414-415
Scriabin, Alexander Nikolayevich
14 71-72
Szymanowski, Karol **15** 67-68

CHOPIN, KATHERINE ("Kate"; born
Katherine O'Flaherty; 1851-1904), American writer, poet, and essayist **4** 18-20

Chopinel, Jean
see Jean de Meun

Choquet, Victor (1821-1891), French art
collector
Renoir, Pierre Auguste **13** 101-102

Choral Symphony (musical composition)
Beethoven, Ludwig van **2** 114-117,
461, 462

Chorale (music)
Bach, Johann Sebastian **1** 416-419
Buxtehude, Dietrich **3** 185-186
Pachelbel, Johann **12** 52
Sweelinck, Jan Pieterszoon **15** 50-51

Choralis Constantinus (musical collection;
Isaac)
Senfl, Ludwig **14** 105-106
Webern, Anton **16** 160-162

Choreographers
see Actors and entertainers

Chori spezzati (music)
Willaert, Adrian **16** 287-288

Chorus (drama)
Schiller, Johann Christoph Friedrich von
14 4-7

Chorus, role of (music)
Lully, Jean Baptiste **10** 40-41
Penderecki, Krzysztof **12** 195-197

Chosen Country (novel)
Dos Passos, John Roderigo **5** 69-71

Chosen People, Jews as
Paul **12** 141-143
Rosenzweig, Franz **13** 294

Choshu (Nagato province, Japan)
Saigo, Takamori **13** 429
Yamagata, Aritomo **16** 428-429

Choson (Korea)
Yi Sng-gye **16** 458-459

Chosroes
see Khosrow

Chotek, Countess Sophie (1868-1914),
duchess of Hohenberg
Francis Ferdinand **6** 44

Chotin, defeat of (1673)
Köprülü, Ahmed **9** 84-85

Chou, Duke of
see Chou kung

Chou dynasty (China; ruled 1122-256 B.C.)
Confucianism
Confucius **4** 197-200
Hsün-tzu **8** 8
Mencius **10** 480-481
established
Chou Kung **4** 22-23
Wu wang **16** 408-409
Legalism
Han Fei Tzu **7** 124-125
Shang Yang **14** 149-150

Chou dynasty, Later (China; ruled 951-959)
Kwangjong **9** 140
Zhao Kuang-yin **16** 505-508

CHOU EN-LAI (1898-1976), Chinese Communist premier **4** 20-22
Chiang Kai-shek **3** 510-513
Chu Teh **4** 54-55
Dalai Lama **4** 369-371
Liu Shao-Ch'i **9** 453-455

Chou Hsin (flourished circa 1116 B.C.), last
ruler of Shang dynasty
Wu wang **16** 408-409

Chou-i lüeh-li (commentary)
Wang Pi **16** 104-105

CHOU KUNG (flourished circa 1116 B.C.),
Chinese statesman **4** 22-23
Wu wang **16** 408-409

Chou Li (ancient Chinese text)
Chou Kung **4** 22-23
Wang An-shih **16** 95-97

Chou Shu-jen
see Lu Hsün

Chou Tun-i (1017-1073), Chinese Neoconfucian philosopher
Chu Hsi **4** 40-43

Chouans, Les (novel)
Balzac, Honoré de **1** 478-480

Chouinard School of Art (Los Angeles)
Siqueiros, David Alfaro **14** 256

CHRESTIEN DE TROYES (flourished 12th
century), French poet **4** 23-24
Guillaume de Lorris **7** 33-34
Thibaut IV **15** 180-181
Wolfram von Eschenbach **16** 360-361

**CHRÉTIEN, JOSEPH-JACQUES-JEAN
"JEAN"** (born 1934), French Canadian
politician and Canada's 20th prime minister **4** 24-25

Chris Christopherson (play)
O'Neill, Eugene **11** 514-516

Christ, Jesus
see Jesus of Nazareth

Christ (literary work)
Kazantzakis, Nikos **8** 466-468

Christ among the Doctors (painting)
Dürer, Albrecht **5** 159-161
Jordaens, Jacob **8** 347-349
Veronese, Paolo **15** 469-470

Christ and Anti-Christ (trilogy)
Merezhkovsky, Dmitry Sergeyevich
10 515-516

Christ and Culture (book)
Niebuhr, Helmut Richard **11** 386-387

Christ and the Adulteress (painting)
Giorgione **6** 340-341

Christ and the Tribute Money (painting)
Titian **15** 242-244

Christ at the Column (painting)
Bramante, Donato **2** 493-494

Christ at the Pool of Bethesda (painting)
Veronese, Paolo **15** 469-470

Christ before Pilate (painting)
Pontormo **12** 394-395
Titian **15** 242-244

Christ Blessing the Little Children (painting)
Cranach, Lucas the Elder **4** 289-290

Christ Carrying the Cross (painting)
Bosch, Hieronymus **2** 426-428
Greco **6** 511-514
Titian **15** 242-244

Christ Church (Brooklyn, New York State)
Upjohn, Richard **15** 392

Christ Church (Cambridge, Massachusetts)
Harrison, Peter **7** 179-180

Christ Church (Washington, D.C.)
Latrobe, Benjamin Henry **9** 222-224

Christ Church College (Oxford University)
Carroll, Lewis **3** 332-333
Ryle, Gilbert **13** 393-394
Wolsey, Thomas **16** 364-366

Christ Crowned with Thorns (paintings)
Titian **15** 242-244

Christ Giving the Keys to St. Peter (fresco)
Perugino **12** 245-246

Christ Healing the Blind (painting)
Greco **6** 511-514

Christ Healing the Sick (painting)
West, Benjamin **16** 210-212

Christ in Gethsemane (sculpture)
Riemenschneider, Tilman **13** 166

Christ in Glory in the Tetramorph (tapestry)
Sutherland, Graham **15** 40-41

Christ in Majesty (sculpture)
Epstein, Jacob **5** 295-296

Christ in the House of His Parents (painting)
Millais, John Everett **11** 23-24

Christ in the House of Mary and Martha (painting)
Velázquez, Diego Rodríguez de Silva y **15** 454-456
Vermeer, Jan **15** 466-467

Christ Legends (stories)
Lagerlöf, Selma Ottiliana Lovisa **9** 163-164

Christ Lutheran Church (Minneapolis, Minnesota)
Saarinen, Eliel and Eero **13** 396-398

Christ Meditating on the Passion (painting)
Morales, Luis de **11** 150

Christ Mocked by the Soldiers (painting)
Manet, Édouard **10** 193-194

Christ of Velásquez, The (book)
Unamuno y Jugo, Miguel de **15** 386-387

Christ on the Lake of Genesareth (painting)
Delacroix, Ferdinand Victor Eugène **4** 469-471

Christ on the Mount of Olives (painting)
Correggio **4** 249-251

Christ Recrucified (novel)
Kazantzakis, Nikos **8** 466-468

Christ Seated on His Tomb (painting)
Bermejo, Bartolomé **2** 205

Christ Stopped at Eboli (book)
Levi, Carlo **9** 364

Christ Taking Leave of His Mother (painting)
Lotto, Lorenzo **9** 520-521

Christ, Thou Who Art the Bright Day (musical composition)
Bach, Johann Sebastian **1** 416-419

Christ Washing the Feet of the Apostles (painting)
Tintoretto **15** 232-234

Christabel (poem)
Coleridge, Samuel Taylor **4** 154-156

Christchurch, Spitalfields (London)
Hawksmoor, Nicholas **7** 211-212

Christian II (1481-1559), king of Denmark and Norway 1513-1523 and of Sweden 1520-1523
Gustavus I **7** 42-43
Jones, Inigo **8** 333-334

Christian III (1503-1559), king of Denmark and Norway 1534-1559
Gustavus I **7** 42-43

Christian IV (1577-1648), king of Denmark and Norway 1588-1648
Dowland, John **5** 90
Gustavus II **7** 43-45

Christian, Fletcher (flourished 1789), English naval officer and mutineer
Bligh, William **2** 325-326

Christian (literary character)
Bunyan, John **3** 128-129

Christian Association Church (Brush Run, Pennsylvania)
Campbell, Alexander **3** 249-250

Christian Broadcasting Network
Robertson, Pat **13** 196-198

Christian Century, The (magazine)
Marty, Martin E. **10** 300-301

Christian Citizen (periodical)
Burritt, Elihu **3** 160

Christian Council of South Africa
Luthuli, Albert John **10** 51-52

Christian Democratic party (Chile)
Aylwin Azócar, Patricio **1** 393-395
Frei Montalva, Eduardo **6** 94-95

Christian Democratic party (COPEI; Venezuela)
Caldera Rodríguez, Rafael **3** 218-219

Christian Democratic party (El Salvador)
Duarte, José Napoleón **5** 109-111

Christian Democratic party (Italy)
Andreotti, Giulio **1** 226-228
De Gasperi, Alcide **4** 462-463
Fanfani, Amintore **5** 378-379
Moro, Aldo **11** 180-181
Pius X **12** 336-337
Pius XII **12** 339-340
Scalfaro, Oscar Luigi **13** 511-512

Christian Democratic Union (Germany)
Adenauer, Konrad **1** 59-61
Brandt, Willy **2** 499-500
Herzog, Roman **7** 355-357
Kohl, Helmut **9** 73-74

Christian Democratic Union (West Germany)
Kohl, Helmut **9** 73-74

Christian Doctrine (book)
Milton, John **11** 43-46

Christian Doctrine... (book)
Strauss, David Friedrich **14** 496-497

Christian Front (United States politics)
Coughlin, Charles Edward **4** 265-266

Christian Guardian (periodical)
Ryerson, Adolphus Egerton **13** 392-393

Christian Inquirer
Boston Christian Register

Christian Inspiration (mural)
Puvis de Chavannes, Pierre **12** 492-493

Christian Mission (East London)
see Salvation Army

Christian Morals (book)
Browne, Thomas **3** 49-50

Christian Nationalism (South Africa)
Vorster, Balthazar Johannes **16** 30-32

Christian Nurture (book)
Bushnell, Horace **3** 171-172

Christian Philosopher, The (book)
Mather, Cotton **10** 330-332

Christian Register (journal)
Channing, William Ellery **3** 435-436

Christian Science (religion)
Eddy, Mary Baker **5** 202
Mesmer, Franz Anton **10** 526-527

Christian Science Monitor (newspaper)
Eddy, Mary Baker **5** 202

Christian Social Ethics ... (book)
Bennett, John Coleman **2** 170-171

Christian Social Union (Germany)
Herzog, Roman **7** 355-357

Christian Social Union (West Germany)
Strauss, Franz Josef **14** 497-498

Christian socialism (reform movement)
Kingsley, Charles **9** 28
Maurice, John Frederick Denison
  10 349-350
Parsons, Frank **12** 121-122
Rauschenbusch, Walter **13** 53-54
Strong, Josiah **14** 512-513
Thomas, Norman Mattoon **15** 191-192
Woods, Robert Archey **16** 374

Christian Socialist party (Austria)
Dollfuss, Engelbert **5** 47
Hitler, Adolf **7** 417-420
Schuschnigg, Kurt von **14** 45-46

Christian Union, The (periodical)
see Outlook, The

Christian unity
see Ecumenism

Christian Unity, Secretariate for Promoting
(Roman Catholic Church)
Bea, Augustinus **2** 79

Christianity (religion)
Africa (19th century)
  Lavigerie, Charles Martel Allemand
    9 240
  Mwanga **11** 282-283
  Tewodros II **15** 158-159
crusades
  see Crusades
Doctors of the Church
  see Religious leaders, Christian
expansion (England and Ireland)
  Augustine of Canterbury **1** 370-371
  Columba **4** 175-176
  Columban **4** 176
  Patrick, St. **12** 135-136
expansion (France and Germany)
  Boniface **2** 391
  Charlemagne **3** 445-447
  Clovis I **4** 124
expansion (Hungary)
  László I, King of Hungary **9** 219-221
expansion (Mexico)
  Cortés, Hernán **4** 255-256
expansion (Norway and Russia)
  Cyril and Methodius, Saints
    4 362-363
  Olaf, II **11** 493-494
  Vladimir I **16** 5-6
expansion (Roman Empire)
  Constantine I **4** 209-211
  Ezana **5** 354-355
  Leo I **9** 329-330
  Theodosius **15** 176
Fathers of the Church
  see Religious leaders, Christian
foundation and doctrine
  Ficino, Marsilio **5** 436-437
  Jesus of Nazareth **8** 251-255
  John, St. **8** 273-274

John the Baptist **8** 290
Luke **10** 38
Mark **10** 266-267
Mary **10** 308
Matthew **10** 340-341
Paul **12** 141-143
Peter **12** 252-253
Plotinus **12** 358-359
Zeno of Citium **16** 499-500
see also Bible and Greek philoso-
  phies
hagiographies
  Gregory of Tours **6** 534-535
  Grosseteste, Robert **7** 15
heresy
  see Heresy (Christian)
history of
  Pagels, Elaine Hiesey **12** 61-62
oppression
  Diocletian **5** 19-20
  Domitian **5** 52-53
  Julian **8** 378-379
  Marcus Aurelius Antoninus
    10 243-245
  Nero Claudius Caesar **11** 342-344
  Shahpur II **14** 140-141
  Valerian **15** 404-405
  see also Persecutions, religious
Protestantism
  seeProtestant Reformation; Protes-
    tantism
Scholasticism
  see Scholasticism
sectarian deviations
  Averroës **1** 382-383
  Donatus **5** 56-57
  Marcion **10** 238-239
  Montanus **11** 122
theological critics (19th-20th century)
  Harnack, Adolf von **7** 160
  Kierkegaard, Søren Aabye
    8 547-549
  Schaff, Philip **13** 519-520
  Schleiermacher, Friedrich Ernst
    Daniel **14** 11-12
  Söderblom, Nathan **14** 323-324
  Teilhard de Chardin, Marie Joseph
    Pierre **15** 134-136
  see also Orthodox Eastern Church;
    Roman Catholic Church, and
    under names of other Christian
    churches and sects

Christianity and Crisis (periodical)
Bennett, John Coleman **2** 170-171

Christianity, Islam and the Negro Race
(book)
Blyden, Edward Wilmot **2** 348-349

Christianity Not Mysterious (book)
Toland, John **15** 256

**Christians Sheltering a Priest from the
Druids** (painting)
Hunt, William Holman **8** 44-45

CHRISTIE, AGATHA (Agatha Mary Clarissa
Miller; 1890-1976), best selling mystery
author **4** 25-26

CHRISTINA OF SWEDEN (1626-1689),
queen of Sweden 1632-1654 **4** 26-29
Cesti, Pietro **3** 399-400
Oxenstierna, Axel Gustafsson **12** 44-45
Scarlatti, Pietro Alessandro Gaspare
  13 517-518
Vieira, Antônio **15** 492

Christina's World (painting)
Wyeth, Andrew Newell **16** 413-415

CHRISTINE DE PISAN (1364/65-circa
1430), French author **4** 29-30
Caxton, William **3** 386-387

Christmas (hymn)
Manzoni, Alessandro **10** 222-224

Christmas Carol, A (story; Dickens)
Barrymores **2** 28-30
Dickens, Charles John Huffam
  4 538-541

Christmas carols (songs)
Juana Inés de la Cruz **8** 367-368

Christmas Concerto (music)
Corelli, Arcangelo **4** 230-231

Christmas Ghost, The (book)
Buck, Pearl Sydenstricker **3** 91-93

Christmas Island (Indian Ocean)
Cook, James **4** 214-215

Christmas Miniature (book)
Buck, Pearl Sydenstricker **3** 91-93

Christmas Story (book)
Mencken, Henry Louis **10** 481-483

Christmas Story (musical composition)
Schütz, Heinrich **14** 48-49

CHRISTO (Christo Vladimiroff Javacheff;
born 1935), Bulgarian-born sculptor
noted for large-scale environmental artworks **4** 30-31

Christographia (sermons)
Taylor, Edward **15** 122-123

Christology (religion)
Feuerbach, Ludwig Andreas **5** 432
Schwenckfeld, Kasper von **14** 56-57

CHRISTOPHE, HENRI (1767-1820), Hait-
ian patriot and king **4** 32
Boyer, Jean Pierre **2** 468-469
Dessalines, Joan Jacques **4** 511-512
Toussaint L'Ouverture, François
  Dominique **15** 278-279

Christophe Colomb (musical composition)
Milhaud, Darius **11** 17-18

CHRISTOPHER, WARREN MINOR (born
1925), United States secretary of state
4 32-33

Christopher Columbus (play)
Kazantzakis, Nikos **8** 466-468

CHRISTUS, PETRUS (circa 1410-1472/73),
Flemish painter **4** 33-34
Antonello da Messina **1** 251-252
Bouts, Dirk **2** 458-459

Eyck, Hubert and Jan van **5** 352-354

Christus (sacred music)
Liszt, Franz **9** 445-447

Christus, The (book)
Longfellow, Henry Wadsworth
9 499-500

CHRISTY, EDWIN P. (1815-1862), American minstrel **4** 34-35
Foster, Stephen Collins **6** 25-27

Christy, Henry (died 1865), Bristish art collector
Tylor, Edward Burnett **15** 372-373

Christy Minstrels (theatrical group)
Christy, Edwin P. **4** 34-35
Foster, Stephen Collins **6** 25-27

Croats (nationality)
see Yugoslavia

Chromaticism (music)
16th century
Clemens non Papa, Jacobus **4** 101
Gesualdo, Don Carlo **6** 287-288
Le Jeune, Claude **9** 314-315
Willaert, Adrian **16** 287-288
Zarlino, Gioseffo **16** 490-491
17th century
Cavalli, Pietro Francesco **3** 382-383
Schütz, Heinrich **14** 48-49
19th-20th century
Debussy, Achille Claude **4** 445-447
Franck, César **6** 48-49
Schoenberg, Arnold **14** 24-26
Sessions, Roger Huntington
14 117-118
Wagner, Richard **16** 40-43
Webern, Anton **16** 160-162

Chronica majora (book)
Matthew Paris **10** 341-342

Chronicle (book)
Otto of Freising **12** 30
Villani, Giovanni **15** 497-498

Chronicle (newspaper)
Anderson, Maxwell **1** 219-220

Chronicle of a Wandering Scholar (novel)
Brentano, Clemens **2** 515-516

Chroniclers
see Authors—chroniclers; Historiography—chronicles

Chronicles of Japan (book)
Suiko **15** 15-16

Chronique du règne de Charles IX (historical novel)
Mérimée, Prosper **10** 517

Chroniques (poem)
Perse, Saint-John **12** 242-243

Chroniques de France... (book)
Froissart, Jean **6** 124-125

Chronology (dating)
Eratosthenes of Cyrene **5** 301-302
Newton, Isaac **11** 369-372
Petrie, William Matthew Flinders
12 261-262

Tacitus **15** 70-72

Chrysanthemum and the Sword (book)
Benedict, Ruth Fulton **2** 154-155

CHRYSIPPUS (circa 280-circa 206 B.C.), Greek Stoic philosopher **4** 35-36
Carneades **3** 309
Zeno of Citium **16** 499-500

CHRYSLER, WALTER PERCY (1875-1940), American manufacturer **4** 36-37

Chrysler Corp. (automobile firm)
Chrysler, Walter Percy **4** 36-37
Iacocca, Lido (Lee) Anthony **8** 86-88

Chrysoloras, Manuel (circa 1355-1415), Greek scholar
Visconti, Gian Galeazzo **15** 510-511

Chrysostom
see John Chrysostom, St.

Chrysothemis (literary character)
Sophocles **14** 343-345

Ch'u (state, China)
Ch'in Kuei **3** 524-525
Liu Pang 453
Ssu-ma Hsiang-ju **14** 389-390

CHU, PAUL CHING-WU (born 1941), Chinese-American experimentalist in solid-state physics **4** 37-39

Chu-fu (story)
Lu Hsün **10** 35-37

CHU HSI (Chu Fu-tzu; 1130-1200), Chinese scholar and philosopher **4** 40-43
Lu Chiu-yuan **10** 24-25
Ou-yang Hsiu **12** 33-34
Wang Fu-chih **16** 99-101
Wang Yang-ming **16** 108-109
Yi Hwang **16** 457

Chu Kao-chih
see Hung-hsi

CHU TEH (1886-1976), Chinese Communist military leader **4** 54-55
Chou En-lai **4** 20-22
Lin Piao **9** 429-430
Liu Shao-Ch'i **9** 453-455

Chu Ti
see Yung-lo

Ch'u tz'u (poems)
Ssu-ma Hsiang-ju **14** 389-390

Chu Yu-chien
see Ch'ung-chen

Ch'ü-Yüan (flourished 4th century B.C.), Chinese poet
Liu Tsung-Yüan **9** 455-456

Ch'ü Yüan (play)
Kuo Mo-jo **9** 133-134

Chu Yüan-chang
see Hung-wu

Ch'üan-hsing (Chinese philosophy)
Wang Pi **16** 104-105

Ch'uan-shan hsüeh-she (Chinese literary society)
Wang Fu-chih **16** 99-101

Ch'üan T'ang shih (book)
K'ang-hsi **8** 423-426

Ch'uang-tsao Chi-k'an (journal)
Kuo Mo-jo **9** 133-134

Ch'uang-tsao shê (literary group)
Kuo Mo-jo **9** 133-134

Chuang-tzu, Book of (Buddhism)
Hui-yüan **8** 25-26
Tao-an **15** 103-104

Ch'uang-wang
see Kao Ying-hsiang

Chub
see Ward, Artemus

CHULALONGKORN (Rama V; 1853-1910), king of Thailand 1868-1910 **4** 43-45
Mongkut **11** 104

Chulalongkorn University (Thailand)
Pridi Phanomyong **12** 449

Chumash Indians (North America)
Cabrillo, Juan Rodríguez **3** 204-205

Ch'un (novel)
Pa Chin **12** 53-54

Chün (political division, China)
Li Ssu **9** 442-443
Quin Shi Huang-di **12** 515-518

Ch'un Ch'iu (Chinese classic)
Confucius **4** 197-200
Ssu-ma Ch'ien **14** 388-389
Wang An-shih **16** 95-97

Ch'un-Ch'iu fan-lu (essays)
Chung-shu, Tung **4** 48-49

CHUN DOO HWAN (born 1931), army general turned politician and president of the Republic of Korea (South Korea); 1981-1988 **4** 45-47

Chün-tzu (Chinese philosophy)
Confucius **4** 197-200

CHUNG, CONNIE (born 1946), American correspondent and resporter **4** 47-48

Ch'ung-chen (died 1644), Chinese emperor
Li Tzu-Ch'eng **9** 452

Ch'ung Ch'eng
see Shih Ko-fa

Chung-hua ko-ming tang (Chinese Revolution party)
Sun Yat-sen **15** 35-39

Chung-shan
see Sun Yat-sen

CHUNG-SHU, TUNG (circa 179-104 B.C.), Chinese man of letters **4** 48-49
Wang Ch'ung **16** 98-99

Chung-tsung (ruled 685-690, 705-710), Chinese emperor
Hsüan-tsung, T'ang **8** 7-8

Ch'ungnyong, Prince
see Sejong

Chungshan gunboat incident (1926)
Chiang Kai-shek **3** 510-513

Chou En-lai **4** 20-22
CHURCH, FREDERICK EDWIN
(1826-1900), American painter **4** 49-50
Cole, Thomas **4** 151-152
Durand, Asher Brown **5** 156-157
Heade, Martin Johnson **7** 236

Church and State (Algeria)
Chadli Benjedid **3** 402-404

Church and State (Argentina)
Perón, Juan Domingo **12** 228-230

Church and State (Austria)
Joseph II **8** 359-360
Pius VI **12** 333-334

Church and State (Brazil)
Pedro II **12** 180-181

Church and State (Byzantine Empire)
Nestorius **11** 349-350

Church and State (Canada)
Brown, George **3** 35-36

Church and State (Chile)
Montt Torres, Manuel **11** 139-140

Church and State (China)
Chia Ssu-tao **3** 514-515
Han Wu-ti **7** 136
Hui-yüan **8** 25-26

Church and State (Colombia)
Mosquera, Tomás Cipriano de
11 205-206
Santander, Franciso de Paula **13** 475

Church and State (Cuba)
Castro Ruz, Fidel **3** 365-368

Church and State (Cyprus)
Makarios III **10** 157-158

Church and State (Ecuador)
Alfaro, José Eloy **1** 144-145
García Moreno, Gabriel **6** 209-210

Church and State (Egypt)
Egypt
Sayyid Qutb **13** 509-511

Church and State (El Salvador)
Romero, Oscar **13** 265-267

Church and State (England)
church revenues
Grosseteste, Robert **7** 15
Henry III **7** 290-292
Clarendon constitutions
Becket, Thomas **2** 101-102
Henry II **7** 287-289
Investiture Struggle
Anselm of Canterbury **1** 244-245
Henry I **7** 286-287
Lanfranc **9** 189-190
William I **16** 290-291
William II **16** 293-294
nonjurors
Law, William **9** 245-246
Protestantism established
Cranmer, Thomas **4** 295-296
Cromwell, Thomas **4** 320-321
Henry VIII **7** 302-305
Latimer, Hugh **9** 221

More, Thomas **11** 156-157
Wolsey, Thomas **16** 364-366
religious toleration
Charles II **3** 452-454
James I **8** 204-206
James II **8** 207-208
royal absolutism
Charles, I **3** 450-452
Laud, William **9** 224-225
Strafford, 1st Earl of **14** 490-491
see also Civil War, English; Execu-
tions—England; Glorious Revolu-
tion (England)

Church and State (Ethiopia)
Tewodros II **15** 158-159

Church and State (France)
cooperation
Charles VII **3** 461-462
Francis I **6** 40-43
Gregory of Tours **6** 534-535
Leo X **9** 332-334
Louis VI **9** 523-524
Louis IX **9** 525-526
Napoleon I **11** 306-310
Philip IV **12** 274
Pius VI **12** 333-334
Pius VII **12** 334-335
see also Avignon Papacy papal role
limited
Protestants repressed
Louis XIII **9** 529-531
Louis XIV **9** 531-533
Richelieu, Armand Jean du Plessis
de **13** 142-144
Religion, Wars of
see Religion, Wars of
separation movement
Briand, Aristide **2** 528-529
Clemenceau, Georges **4** 99-101
Dreyfus, Alfred **5** 103-105
Ferry, Jules François Camille **5** 430
Montalembert, Comte de
11 118-119
Pius X **12** 336-337

Church and State (Guatemala)
Barrios, Justo Rufino **2** 23-24
Carrera, José Rafael **3** 324-325

Church and State (Holy Roman Empire)
conflict
Charles V **3** 457-459
Frederick I **6** 78-79
Frederick II **6** 79
Henry III **7** 290
Innocent, III **8** 125-127
Louis I **9** 522-523
Rudolf I **13** 347-348
cooperation
Frederick III **6** 84-85
Investiture Struggle
Gregory VII **6** 532-534
Henry IV **7** 292
Henry V **7** 295-296
see also Investiture Struggle
Protestantism

Ferdinand I **5** 414-415
Ferdinand II **5** 415
Ferdinand III **5** 416-417

Church and State (Hungary)
Mindszenty, József **11** 47-49

Church and State (India)
Aurangzeb **1** 377
Bhashani, Maulana Abdul Hamid Khan
2 255-257
Jinnah, Mohammad Ali **8** 262-263

Church and State (Indonesia)
Hatta, Mohammad **7** 197-199

Church and State (Iran)
Khomeini, Ruhollah Musavi **8** 535-537
Reza Shah Pahlavi **13** 116-117

Church and State (Ireland)
Paisley, Ian K. **12** 67-69
see Catholic Emancipation

Church and State (Islamic)
Sayyid Qutb **13** 509-511

Church and State (Israel)
Lee Kuan Yew **9** 281-283

Church and State (Italy)
John Paul I **8** 286-287
Church reforms
Arnold of Brescia **1** 314-315
Gregory I **6** 531-532
taxation issue
Boniface VIII **2** 392-393
Giolitti, Giovanni **6** 339-340
see also Papal States; Vatican City,
State of the

Church and State (Japan)
Suiko **15** 15-16

Church and State (Lebanon)
Berri, Nabih **2** 220-222

Church and State (Mexico)
Calles, Plutarco Elías **3** 234-235
Guerrero, Vicente **7** 28-30

Church and State (Netherlands)
Grotius, Hugo **7** 18-19

Church and State (Norway)
Olaf, II **11** 493-494

Church and State (Oman)
Qaboos ibn Sa'id **12** 501-502

Church and State (Ottoman Empire)
Lucaris, Cyril **10** 20

Church and State (Pakistan)
Mawdūdī, Abu-I A'la **10** 353-354
Zia ul-Haq, Mohammad **16** 513-515

Church and State (Paraguay)
López, Carlos Antonio **9** 506-507

Church and State (Philippines)
Sin, Jaime L. **14** 244-245

Church and State (Poland)
John Paul II **8** 287-290

Church and State (Roman Empire)
Ambrose **1** 192-193
Augustus **1** 371-373

Leo I **9** 329-330

Church and State (Saudi Arabia)
Faisal ibn Abd al Aziz ibn Saud
5 371-372

Church and State (Scotland)
James I **8** 204-206
Laud, William **9** 224-225
Mary, I **10** 308-309

Church and State (Spain)
Ferdinand V **5** 417-418
Lope Félix de Vega Carpio **9** 503-506
Philip II **12** 271-273
see also Inquisition, Spanish

Church and State (Sweden)
Gustavus I **7** 42-43

Church and State (Tunisia)
Bourguiba, Habib **2** 453-455

Church and State (Turkey)
Atatürk, Ghazi Mustapha Kemal
1 356-357

Church and State (United States)
colonial disputes (New England)
Cotton, John **4** 263-265
Hutchinson, Anne Marbury **8** 69-71
Mather, Cotton **10** 330-332
Williams, Roger **16** 304-305
separation
Backus, Isaac **1** 420-421
Gibbons, James **6** 300-301
Jefferson, Thomas **8** 238-241
Kennedy, John Fitzgerald **8** 502-506

Church and State (Venezuela)
Blanco, Antonio Guzmán **2** 320-321

Church and State (Yugoslavia)
Stepinac, Alojzije **14** 433-435

Church and the Second Sex, The (book)
Daly, Mary **4** 380-381

Church Dogmatics (books)
Barth, Karl **2** 31-32

Church law
see Canon law

Church Missionary Society (Sierra Leone)
Crowther, Samuel Adjai **4** 326

Church music
see Sacred music

Church of Auvers (painting)
Van Gogh, Vincent **15** 427-429

Church of Christ, Scientist
see Christian Science Church

Church of Christian Endeavor (Brooklyn, New York State)
Eggleston, Edward **5** 223-224

Church of England
see England, Church of

Church of God in the Spirit (Pietistic sects)
Zinzendorf, Nikolaus Ludwig von
16 522-523

Church of Jesus Christ of Latter Day Saints
see Mormons

Church of Rome
see Roman Catholic Church

Church of the Ascension (New York City)
Upjohn, Richard **15** 392

Church of the Holy Communion (New York City)
Muhlenberg, William Augustus
11 233-234

Church of the United Brethren (United States)
Otterbein, Philip William **12** 27-28

Church Street El (painting)
Sheeler, Charles **14** 170-171

Churchill, John
see Marlborough, Duke of

Churchill, Lord Randolph (1849-1895), British statesman
Churchill, Winston Leonard Spencer
4 51-53
Salisbury, 3d Marquess of **13** 448-449

Churchill, Sarah (1660-1744), duchess of Marlborough
Anne **1** 241-242
Congreve, William **4** 200-201

CHURCHILL, WINSTON (1871-1947), American novelist **4** 50-51

CHURCHILL, SIR WINSTON LEONARD SPENCER (1874-1965), English statesman
4 51-53
Allied policy (World War II)
De Gaulle, Charles André Joseph Marie **4** 463-465
Eisenhower, Dwight David
5 233-236
Wavell, Archibald Percival
16 147-148
coalition government
Attlee, Clement Richard **1** 361-362
Eden, Anthony **5** 204-205
Halifax, 1st Earl of **7** 82-83
Macmillan, Harold **10** 112-113
diplomacy
Hopkins, Harry Lloyd **7** 494-495
Monnet, Jean **11** 109-110
Great Powers councils
Chiang Kai-shek **3** 510-513
Roosevelt, Franklin Delano
13 277-280
Stettinius, Edward R. Jr. **14** 437-438
Truman, Harry S. **15** 314-316
ministerial posts
Chamberlain, Arthur Neville
3 409-411
Elizabeth II **5** 266-269

Churchyard Pottery (factory)
Wedgwood, Josiah **16** 168-169

Churriguera, Alberto de (1676-1750), Spanish architect
Churriguera, José Benito de **4** 53-54

Churriguera, Joaquin de (1674-1724), Spanish architect
Churriguera, José Benito de **4** 53-54

CHURRIGUERA, JOSÉ BENITO DE (1665-1725), Spanish architect and sculptor **4** 53-54

Churriguera, José Simón de (died 1697), Spanish sculptor
Churriguera, José Benito de **4** 53-54

Churriguera, Manuel de (born 1667), Spanish sculptor
Churriguera, José Benito de **4** 53-54

Churriguera, Miguel de (flourished 16th-17th century), Spanish architect
Churriguera, José Benito de **4** 53-54

Churriguera, Nicholas de (flourished 18th century), Spanish architect
Churriguera, José Benito de **4** 53-54

Churrigueresque style (art)
Churriguera, José Benito de **4** 53-54

Chute, La (novel)
Camus, Albert **3** 255-257

Chute d'un ange, La (poem)
Lamartine, Alphonse Marie Louis de
9 173-175

CIA
see Central Intelligence Agency (United States)

CIAM (International Congress of Modern Architecture)
Le Corbusier **9** 274-275
Rietveld, Gerrit Thomas **13** 169

Ciano, Galeatto (1903-1944), Italian statesman
Mussolini, Benito **11** 272-274

Ciascuno a suo modo (play)
Pirandello, Luigi **12** 319-321

Cibber, Colley (1671-1757), English actor and dramatist
Pope, Alexander **12** 395-397

Cibber, Susannah Maria Arne (1714-1766), English actress
Arne, Thomas Augustine **1** 307-308

Cibo, Giovanni Battista
see Innocent VIII

Cíbola (mythologic kingdom, Mexico)
Coronado, Francisco Vásquez de **4** 247
Mendoza, Antonio de **10** 494-495

CICERO, MARCUS TULLIUS (106-43 B.C.), Roman orator and writer **4** 55-58
influence of
Augustine **1** 367-370
Castiglione, Baldassare **3** 360-361
Dante Alighieri **4** 389-391
Machiavelli, Niccolò **10** 97-99
influenced by
Drusus, Marcus Livius **5** 105-106
Ennius, Quintus **5** 289
Isocrates **8** 151
Scipio Africanus Minor, Publius Cornelius Aemilianus **14** 62-63
Varro, Marcus Terentius **15** 438-439
letters and orations
Brutus, Marcus Junius **3** 79-80
Catullus, Gaius Valerius **3** 377-378

Petrarch **12** 259-261
literary styles
  Livy **9** 465-467
  Seneca the Younger, Lucius Annaeus
    14 103-105
  Tacitus **15** 70-72
  Terence **15** 146-148
political opponents
  Antony, Mark **1** 253-254
  Caesar, Gaius Julius **3** 207-210
  Catiline **3** 372-373
  Clodius Pulcher, Publius **4** 121-122
quoted
  Lucretius **10** 26-27
translations
  Leopardi, Giacomo **9** 344-345
  Logan, James **9** 487-488
  Wieland, Christoph Martin
    16 260-261

Cicero, Marcus Tullius, the Younger
(65-after 30 B.C.), Roman statesman
Horace **7** 500-503

CID (Cid Campeador; 1043-1099), Spanish
medieval warrior **4** 58-59
Alfonso VI **1** 149
Corneille, Pierre **4** 234-236

Cien años de soledad (novel)
García Márquez, Gabriel **6** 208-209

Cigar-makers' Union (United States)
Gompers, Samuel **6** 420-422

CILLER, TANSU (born 1946), prime minister of Turkey (1993-) **4** 59-60

CIMABUE (flourished late 13th century),
Italian painter **4** 60-61
Duccio di Buoninsegna **5** 121-122
Giotto **6** 342-345

CIMAROSA, DOMENICO (1749-1801),
Italian opera composer **4** 61-62

Cimarron (novel)
Ferber, Edna **5** 413

Cimarron, El (opera)
Henze, Hans Werner **7** 314

Cimarron Desert (Kansas)
Becknell, William **2** 105-106

Cimbri (German people)
Marius, Gaius **10** 264-265
Sulla, Lucius Cornelius I **15** 21-22

Cimetière marin, La (poem)
Valéry, Paul Ambroise **15** 405-406

Cimon (507?-449 B.C.) Athenian general
Pericles **12** 219-221
Thucydides **15** 211-212

Cinchona
see Quinine

Cincinnati (city; Ohio)
Drake, Daniel **5** 93-94

Cincinnati, University of (Ohio)
Bloomfield, Leonard **2** 338
Chase, Philander **3** 472-473
McGuffey, William Holmes **10** 414-415
Mead, Margaret **10** 438-440

Cincinnati Post (newspaper)
Scripps, Edward Wyllis **14** 72-73

Cinco microformas (musical composition)
Halffter, Christóbal **7** 79-80

Cinema
see Motion pictures

Cinemaphone (film instrument)
Edison, Thomas Alva **5** 206-208

Cinna, Gaius Helvius (flourished 1st century B.C.), Roman poet
Catullus, Gaius Valerius **3** 377-378

Cinna, Lucius Cornelius (died 84 B.C.),
Roman general
Caesar, Gaius Julius **3** 207-210
Crassus Dives, Marcus Licinius
  4 296-297
Marius, Gaius **10** 264-265
Sulla, Lucius Cornelius I **15** 21-22

Cinna (drama)
Corneille, Pierre **4** 234-236

Cinq Grandes Odes (poems)
Claudel, Paul Louis Charles **4** 90-91

Cinq-Mars, Marquis de (Henri Coiffier de
Ruzé; 1620-1642), French conspirator
Richelieu, Armand Jean du Plessis de
  13 142-144

Cinq-Mars (novel)
Vigny, Comte de **15** 494-495

CINQUE, JOSEPH (circa 1813-circa 1879),
West African slave leader **4** 62

Cinque frammenti di Saffo (musical composition)
Dallapiccola, Luigi **4** 377-378

Cinquième livre (book)
Rabelais, François **12** 524-526

CIO
see Congress of Industrial Organizations

Ciociara, La (novel)
Moravia, Alberto **11** 153-155

Cione, Andrea di
see Orcagna

Ciotat, La (painting)
Braque, Georges **2** 504-505

Cipolla (literary character)
Mann, Thomas **10** 204-207

Circe (mythology)
Homer **7** 465-467

Circle (mythology)
Archimedes **1** 277-280
Euclid **5** 327-329
Gauss, Karl Friedrich **6** 240-242

Circles (musical composition)
Berio, Luciano **2** 194-195

Circuit Rider, The (novel)
Eggleston, Edward **5** 223-224

Circular Letter (1768)
Otis, James Jr. **12** 25-27

Circular Letter (1783)
Washington, George **16** 126-129

Circulation (blood)
see Blood—circulation

Circumnutation (botany)
Darwin, Charles Robert **4** 397-399

Circus (entertainment)
Barnum, Phineas Taylor **2** 13-15

Circus (painting)
Seurat, Georges Pierre **14** 120-122
Vlaminck, Maurice **16** 6

Circus, The (book)
Rouault, Georges **13** 321-322

Circus, The (film)
Chaplin, Charles Spencer **3** 438-440

Cirenaica (province, Libya)
Omar al-Mukhtar **11** 507-508

Ciro, II (opera)
Cavalli, Pietro Francesco **3** 382-383

cis-Aconitic acid (biochemistry)
Krebs, Hans Adolf **9** 95-97

Cisalpine Gaul
see Gaul

Cisalpine Republic (Northern Italy)
Murat, Joachim **11** 253-254

Cisneros, Francisco Jiménez de
see Jiménez de Cisneros, Francisco

CISNEROS, HENRY G. (born 1947), first
Hispanic mayor in Texas **4** 62-64

CISNEROS, SANDRA (born 1954), Hispanic American short story writer and poet
4 64-65

CISSÉ, SOULEYMANE (born 1940), Malian
filmmaker **4** 65-66

Cistellaria (play)
Plautus **12** 348-350

Cistercians (religious order)
Alfonso I **1** 148
Bernard of Clairvaux **2** 207-208
David I **4** 407
Joachim of Fiore **8** 263-264
Stephen Harding **14** 428-429

Cistern, The (poem)
Seferis, George **14** 84-85

Citadel (Pisa)
Brunelleschi, Filippo **3** 70-72

Citadel, The (Charleston, South Carolina)
Clark, Mark Wayne **4** 80-81

Cité antique, La (book)
Fustel de Coulanges, Numa Denis
6 155

Cîteaux, abbey of (France)
Bernard of Clairvaux **2** 207-208
Stephen Harding **14** 428-429

Cities and Their Stories (book)
Thant, U **15** 161-162

Cities in Evolution (book)
Geddes, Patrick **6** 246-247

Cities of the Plain (novel)
Proust, Marcel **12** 465-467

Citizen Kane (film)
Welles, Orson **16** 190-191

Citizen of the World (book)
Burritt, Elihu **3** 160
Goldsmith, Oliver **6** 411-413

Citizens' Municipal Reform Assn.
(Philadelphia, Pennsylvania)
Lea, Henry Charles **9** 261-262

Citizens party (United States)
Commoner, Barry **4** 183-185

Citric acid (chemistry)
Krebs, Hans Adolf **9** 95-97
Scheele, Karl Wilhelm **13** 525-526
see also Krebs cycle

CITROËN, ANDRÉ-GUSTAVE (1878-1935),
French automobile manufacturer **4** 66-68

Citrulline (amino acid)
Krebs, Hans Adolf **9** 95-97

Città del mondo, Le (novel)
Vittorini, Elio **16** 2-3

City (painting)
Léger, Fernand **9** 302-303
Luz, Arturo Rogerio **10** 56-57

City, The (book)
Saarinen, Eliel and Eero **13** 396-398

City Affairs (book)
Varro, Marcus Terentius **15** 438-439

City College of New York (CCNY)
see New York, City University of

City government
see Municipal government

City in History, The (book)
Mumford, Lewis **11** 246-247

City Interior (photography)
Sheeler, Charles **14** 170-171

City Lights (film)
Chaplin, Charles Spencer **3** 438-440

City Looking Glass, The (play)
Bird, Robert Montgomery **2** 281-282

City of Cats, The (novel)
Lao Shê **9** 200-201

City of God, The (book; Saint Augustine)
Augustine **1** 367-370, 293
Charonton, Enguerrand **3** 471
Otto of Freising **12** 30
Voegelin, Eric **16** 6-8

City of Ladies (book)
Christine de Pisan **4** 29-30

City of the Sun, The (book)
Campanella, Tommaso **3** 249

City planning
see Town planning

City Shower, The (poem)
Swift, Jonathan **15** 51-54

City Square (sculpture)
Giacometti, Alberto **6** 294-295

Ciudad Juárez (city, Mexico)
Madero, Francisco Indalecio
10 118-119

Ciudad Rodrigo (commune, Spain)
Wellington, 1st Duke of **16** 193-195

Ciujpers and Stuyt (architecture firm)
Oud, Jacobus Johannes Pieter **12** 32

Civil Constitution of the Clergy (France;
1790)
Pius VI **12** 333-334
Talleyrand, Charles Maurice de
15 89-90

Civil Disobedience (essay; Thoreau)
Thoreau, Henry David **15** 203-205

Civil disobedience (political strategy)
England
Pankhurst, Emmeline **12** 85-86
South Africa
Gandhi, Mohandas Karamchand
6 201-204
Luthuli, Albert John **10** 51-52
United States
Farmer, James **5** 383-385
Fonda, Jane **5** 501-502
Forman, James **6** 10-11
Muste, Abraham Johannes
11 276-277
Thoreau, Henry David **15** 203-205
see also Nonviolent protest move-
ments; Passive resistance move-
ments; Student protest

Civil liberties
Evatt, Herbert Vere **5** 341-343
Fox, Charles James **6** 35-37
Kubitschek de Oliveira, Juscelino
9 113-115
Marcos, Ferdinand **10** 240-242
Rivadavia, Bernardino **13** 182-183
Robespierre, Maximilien François Marie
Isidore de **13** 199-201
Ts'ai Yüan-p'ei **15** 322

Civil liberties (United States)
ACLU
Flynn, Elizabeth Gurley **5** 496-497
Ginsburg, Ruth Bader **6** 333-336
Holmes, John Haynes **7** 456-457
see also American Civil Liberties
Union
aliens
Gallatin, Albert **6** 183-184
Palmer, Alexander Mitchell
12 77-78
see also Alien and Sedition Acts
anarchists and
Goldman, Emma **6** 406-407
defenders
Brandeis, Louis Dembitz **2** 496-497
Dees, Morris S. Jr. **4** 456-457
Douglas, William Orville **5** 83-85
Fortas, Abe **6** 16-17
Frankfurter, Felix **6** 57
Hapgood, Norman **7** 137-138
King, Coretta Scott **9** 16-17
Lieber, Francis **9** 401-402

see also Supreme Court (United
States)—civil liberties cases
due process
Hoover, John Edgar **7** 485-487
free speech
Comstock, Anthony **4** 188-189
see also Freedom of speech; Freedom of the press
Reconstruction era
Field, David Dudley **5** 439-440
see also Civil rights; Constitution of
the United States; Minority rights;
Reconstruction (United States)

Civil rights (Brazil)
Castelo Branco, Humberto **3** 359-360

Civil rights (South Africa)
Biko, Steve **2** 273-274
Lembede, Anton **9** 318-319
Mandela, Winnie **10** 187-189

Civil rights (Senegal)
Gueye, Lamine **7** 31

Civil Rights Acts (United States)
1866
Bristow, Benjamin Helm **3** 9-10
Brown, Benjamin Gratz **3** 32-33
Johnson, Andrew **8** 294-295
Stevens, Thaddeus **14** 442-443
1957
Eisenhower, Dwight David
5 233-236
Johnson, Lyndon Baines **8** 308-312
1964
Johnson, Lyndon Baines **8** 308-312
King, Martin Luther Jr. **9** 20-22
Wallace, George Corley **16** 71-72

Civil Rights Cases (1883)
Harlan, John Marshall **7** 156-157
Turner, Henry McNeal **15** 351-352
Waite, Morrison Remick **16** 46

Civil Rights Commission (United States)
Berry, Mary Frances **2** 226-229
Hesburgh, Theodore Martin **7** 357-358

Civil Rights Memorial (Montgomery, Alabama; 1989)
Lin, Maya Ying **9** 413-415

Civil rights movement (United States)
African American leaders
see African American history (United States)
commitment abandoned (1890s)
Harrison, Benjamin **7** 178-179
courts
see Civil Rights Cases (1883);
Supreme Court (United States)—
civil liberties cases
see also African Americn history;
Brown v. Board of Education of
Topeka; Dred Scott decision;
Plessy v. Ferguson; Slaughter
House Cases; United States v. Harris
crises and protests
Bevel, James Luther **2** 250-251
Bond, Julian **2** 386-387

Bunche, Ralph Johnson **3** 121-122
Carmichael, Stokely **3** 305-308
Chavis, Benjamin **3** 491-493
Eisenhower, Dwight David
 5 233-236
Evers, Medgar **5** 345-348
Evers-Williams, Myrlie **5** 348-350
Hamer, Fannie Lou **7** 93-94
Henry, Aaron **7** 306-307
Kennedy, John Fitzgerald **8** 502-506
King, Martin Luther Jr. **9** 20-22
McKissick, Floyd B. **10** 420-422
 see also March on Washington for
 Jobs and Freedom; Nonviolent
 protest movement; Poor People's
 March
employment
 Bundy, McGeorge **3** 122-124
 Ford, Henry II **6** 6-7
 Hill, Herbert **7** 387-388
 Johnson, Lyndon Baines **8** 308-312
 Kirkland, Joseph Lane **9** 35-37
 Meany, George **10** 444
 Rickey, Wesley Branch **13** 153-155
 Truman, Harry S. **15** 314-316
foundation for
 Houston, Charles Hamilton
 7 523-526
 Mays, Benjamin E. **10** 374-376
law
 see Civil Rights Acts; Constitution of
 the United States—Amendments
 see also African American history
legal equality enforcement
 Hoover, John Edgar **7** 485-487
opponents (white)
 McClellan, John Little **10** 392-393
 Tillman, Benjamin Ryan **15** 225-226
 Wallace, George Corley **16** 71-72
 see also Racism (United States)
presidential support
 Eisenhower, Dwight David
 5 233-236
 Johnson, Lyndon Baines **8** 308-312
 Kennedy, John Fitzgerald **8** 502-506
 Truman, Harry S. **15** 314-316
supporters (religious leaders)
 Perry, Harold Robert **12** 236-237
supporters (white)
 Ashmore, Harry Scott **1** 334-335
 Bundy, McGeorge **3** 122-124
 Cable, George Washington
 3 198-199
 Coffin, William Sloane Jr. **4** 135-137
 Humphrey, Hubert Horatio Jr.
 8 34-36
 Johnson, Guy Benton **8** 299-300
 Kennedy, Robert Francis **8** 508-509
 Kirkland, Joseph Lane **9** 35-37
 Kunstler, William M. **9** 131-133
 McGill, Ralph Emerson **10** 411-412
 Ovington, Mary White **12** 36-37
 Phillips, Wendell **12** 281-282
 Rickey, Wesley Branch **13** 153-155
 Roosevelt, Eleanor **13** 275-277
 Smith, Lillian Eugenia **14** 298-299

Stevenson, Adlai Ewing **14** 445-446
Voting Rights Act (1965)
 Bevel, James Luther **2** 250-251
 Johnson, Lyndon Baines **8** 308-312
 King, Martin Luther Jr. **9** 20-22
 see also Civil liberties (United
 States); Minority rights

Civil service (Britain)
 Banerjee, Surendranath **1** 488
 Eaton, Dorman Bridgman **5** 190-191
 Gladstone, William Ewart **6** 357-360
 Jowett, Benjamin **8** 364-365
 Macaulay, Herbert **10** 78-79

Civil service (China)
 merit system
 Chang Chü-cheng **3** 431-432
 Liang Ch'i-ch'ao **9** 395-396
 Zhao Kuang-yin **16** 505-508
 reforms
 Fan Chung-yen **5** 376-377
 Huang Tsung-hsi **8** 9-10
 K'ang-hsi **8** 423-426
 Kuang-hsü **9** 111-112
 Sui Wen-ti **15** 16-18
 Wang An-shih **16** 95-97

Civil service (France)
 Le Play, Guillaume Frédéric **9** 350-351
 Philip II **12** 268-269

Civil service (Korea)
 Kwangjong **9** 140

Civil service (Nigeria)
 Imam, Alhadji Abubakar **8** 114-115

Civil service (Prussia)
 Frederick William I **6** 86-87

Civil service (Roman Empire)
 Augustus **1** 371-373

Civil service (Russia)
 Gogol, Nikolai **6** 391-393

Civil service (United States)
 Civil Service Commission
 Cooley, Charles Horton **4** 216-217
 Eaton, Dorman Bridgman **5** 190-191
 Pendleton, George Hunt **12** 198
 Perkins, Frances **12** 221-222
 Roosevelt, Theodore **13** 280-283
 reforms
 Arthur, Chester Alan **1** 321-323
 Cleveland, Stephen Grover
 4 108-110
 Conkling, Roscoe **4** 201-202
 Curtis, George William **4** 349-350
 Garfield, James Abram **6** 213-214
 Godkin, Edwin Lawrence **6** 380
 Lodge, Henry Cabot **9** 482-483
 Schurz, Carl **14** 44-45

Civil Service Act of 1883 (United States)
 Eaton, Dorman Bridgman **5** 190-191

Civil War, Castilian (1474)
 Isabella I **8** 144-145
 Manrique, Jorge **10** 210-211

Civil War, Chinese (1945-1949)
 Communists

Chou En-lai **4** 20-22
Chu Teh **4** 54-55
Ku Chieh-kang **9** 120-121
Kuo Mo-jo **9** 133-134
Lao Shê **9** 200-201
Lin Piao **9** 429-430
Liu Shao-Ch'i **9** 453-455
Mao Zedong **10** 225-227
Nationalists
 Chiang Kai-shek **3** 510-513
 Hu Shih **8** 63-65
 Yen Hsi-shan **16** 452-453

Civil War, Colombian (1876)
 Isaacs, Jorge **8** 144

Civil War, Dominican (1965)
 Balaguer y Ricardo, Joaquin **1** 460-461
 Bosch, Juan **2** 428-429
 Johnson, Lyndon Baines **8** 308-312

Civil War, English
 • EARLY WARS
 1139-1153
 David I **4** 407
 Stephen **14** 426-427
 1215-1216
 John **8** 274-275
 see also Magna Carta
 1263-1265
 Henry III **7** 290-292
 Louis IX **9** 525-526
 Montfort, Simon de **11** 132-133
 1321-1327
 Edward II **5** 210
 1455-1485
 see Roses, Wars of the
 1485
 Henry VII **7** 300-302
 Richard III **13** 132-133
 • PURITAN REVOLUTION (1642-1646)
 Parliamentarians
 Bunyan, John **3** 128-129
 Cromwell, Oliver **4** 317-320
 Hampden, John **7** 110-111
 Lilburne, John **9** 409-410
 Pym, John **12** 495-496
 Vane, Henry **15** 425-426
 Parliamentarians (literature)
 Marvell, Andrew **10** 301-303
 Milton, John **11** 43-46
 Royalists
 Buckingham, 2d Duke of
 3 94-95
 Charles, I **3** 450-452
 Clarendon, 1st Earl of **4** 73-75
 Lovelace, Richard **10** 7-8
 Strafford, 1st Earl of **14** 490-491
 Royalists (literature)
 Hobbes, Thomas **7** 421-423
 Lovelace, Richard **10** 7-8
 Marvell, Andrew **10** 301-303
 Royalists (supporters)
 Browne, Thomas **3** 49-50
 Gorges, Ferdinando **6** 455-456
 Laud, William **9** 224-225

- PURITAN REVOLUTION (1648-1651)
  Cromwell ascendancy
    Buckingham, 2d Duke of
      3 94-95
    Charles, I **3** 450-452
    Charles II **3** 452-454
    Cromwell, Oliver **4** 317-320
    Monck, George **11** 96-97
  effect on universities
    Cowley, Abraham **4** 281-282
    Crashaw, Richard **4** 296
  historians of
    Gardiner, Samuel Rawson **6** 211
    Macaulay, Thomas Babington
      10 79-80
    see also Executions—England;
    Levellers; Restoration, The
    (England; 1660)

Civil War, Hawaiian (1782-1795)
  Kamehameha I **8** 416

Civil War, Incan (1528-1532)
  Atahualpa **1** 355-356
  Manco Capac **10** 184-185

Civil War, Japanese
  1156-1160
    Goshirakawa **6** 460-461
  1336-1392
    Ashikaga Takauji **1** 330-332
    Daigo II **4** 367-368
  1467-1477
    Nobunaga, Oda **11** 413-414

Civil War, Mexican (1876)
  Díaz, José de la Cruz Porfirio **4** 534-536

Civil War, Nigerian-Biafran (1967-1970)
  Azikiwe, Nnamdi **1** 401-402
  Dike, Kenneth **5** 7-8
  Houphouët-Boigny, Felix **7** 519-520

Civil War, Roman
  44-42 B.C.
    Antony, Mark **1** 253-254
    Augustus **1** 371-373
    Brutus, Marcus Junius **3** 79-80
  49-45 B.C.
    Caesar, Gaius Julius **3** 207-210
    Cato the Younger **3** 374-375
    Pompey **12** 387-389
  53-45 B.C.
    Caesar, Gaius Julius **3** 207-210
    Cato, the Younger **3** 374-375
  88-82 B.C.
    Marius, Gaius **10** 264-265
    Sulla, Lucius Cornelius I **15** 21-22

Civil War, Russian
  see Russian Revolution (1918-1920)

Civil war, Spanish (1833-1839; Isabella and Don Carlos)
  Isabella II **8** 145-146

Civil War, Spanish (1936-1939)
  Axis intervention
    Franco Bahamonde, Francisco
      6 52-54
    Hitler, Adolf **7** 417-420
    Mussolini, Benito **11** 272-274

beginning
  Azaña Diaz, Manuel **1** 396-397
  Franco Bahamonde, Francisco
    6 52-54
in film and fiction
  Afinogenov, Aleksandr Nikolaevich
    1 72-73
  Cela y Trulock, Camilo José
    3 389-390
  Dos Passos, John Roderigo **5** 69-71
  Hemingway, Ernest Miller
    7 274-277
  Malraux, André **10** 178-180
  Orwell, George **12** 14-15
journalists
  Ehrenburg, Ilya Grigorievich
    5 224-225
  Hemingway, Ernest Miller
    7 274-277
Loyalist supporters
  Dos Passos, John Roderigo **5** 69-71
  Goldman, Emma **6** 406-407
  Laski, Harold J. **9** 215-216
  Orwell, George **12** 14-15
  Ulbricht, Walter **15** 383-384
medical assistance
  Bethune, Henry Norman **2** 240-241
neutral nations policy
  Baldwin, Stanley **1** 468-469
  Salazar, António de Oliveira
    13 442-443
photojournalists
  Capa, Robert **3** 269-271
Republican supporters
  Bethune, Henry Norman **2** 240-241
  Ibárruri Gómez, Dolores **8** 88-90
  Malraux, André **10** 178-180
Vatican policy
  Pius XI **12** 337-339
  see also Exiles (political)—from Spain

Civil War, Swiss (1531)
  Zwingli, Huldreich **16** 537-538

Civil War, United States (1861-1865)
- ACCOUNTS OF
  by historians
    Beard, Charles Austin **2** 84
    Dunning, William Archibald
      5 148-149
    Rhodes, James Ford **13** 122
    Welles, Gideon **16** 188-190
  in journalism
    Adams, Henry Brooks **1** 45-47
    Greeley, Horace **6** 515-517
  in literature
    Benét, Stephen Vincent
      2 157-158
    Chesnut, Mary Boykin
      3 506-508
    Crane, Stephen **4** 293-295
    Melville, Herman **10** 472-476
    Mitchell, Margaret **11** 59-60
    Tourgée, Albion Winegar
      15 277-278
    Whitman, Walt **16** 249-251

- ANTISLAVERY MOVEMENT

financing
  Chandler, Zachariah **3** 425-426
  Chase, Salmon Portland
    3 473-475
  Cooke, Jay **4** 215-216
  McCulloch, Hugh **10** 404-405
  Walker, Robert John **16** 67-68
food suppliers
  Armour, Philip Danforth **1** 302
  Borden, Gail **2** 409
Indian role
  Cochise **4** 128
  Ross, John **13** 303-304
ironclad ships
  Eads, James Buchanan
    5 175-176
  Ericsson, John **5** 307-308
memorial sculptures
  Saint-Gaudens, Augustus **13** 432
  White, Stanford **16** 235-236
navy
  Dewey, George **4** 520
  Farragut, David Glasgow
    5 388-389
  Mahan, Alfred Thayer
    10 131-132
President and Cabinet
  Cameron, Simon **3** 246-247
  Chase, Salmon Portland
    3 473-475
  Lincoln, Abraham **9** 415-418
  Seward, William Henry
    14 124-125
  Stanton, Elizabeth Cady
    14 402-403
  Welles, Gideon **16** 188-190
railroads and bridges
  Garrett, John Work **6** 225
  Judah, Theodore Dehone
    8 373-374
  Roebling, Washington Augustus
    13 243
relief programs
  Barton, Clara **2** 37-39
  Bellows, Henry Whitney
    2 143-144
  Blackwell, Elizabeth **2** 311-312
  Dix, Dorothea Lynde **5** 32-33
  Taylor, Susie King **15** 127-128
state and local politics (Mid Atlantic)
  Curtin, Andrew Gregg **4** 347-348
  Seymour, Horatio **14** 126-127
  Wood, Fernando **16** 367-368
state and local politics (Midwest)
  Cass, Lewis **3** 355-356
  Donnelly, Ignatius **5** 62
  Morton, Oliver Hazard Perry
    Throck **11** 197-198
  Pendleton, George Hunt **12** 198
  Vallandigham, Clement Laird
    15 406-407
state and local politics (New England)
  Andrew, John Albion **1** 230-231
  Everett, Edward **5** 344

- CONFEDERACY

army
    Beauregard, Pierre Gustave
      Toutant **2** 96-97
    Forrest, Nathan Bedford **6** 13-14
    Goodnight, Charles **6** 439
    Gordon, John Brown **6** 449-450
    Hampton, Wade III **7** 112
    Jackson, Shirley Ann **8** 183-184
    Johnston, Joseph Eggleston **8** 323
    Lee, Robert Edward **9** 292-294
    Mahone, William **10** 147-148
    Stuart, James Ewell Brown
      14 515-516
    White, Edward Douglass
      16 230-231
conscription
    Brown, Joseph Emerson **3** 41-42
    Davis, Jefferson **4** 416-418
    Hill, Benjamin Harvey
      7 386-387
navy
    Benjamin, Judah Philip
      2 163-164
    Gorgas, Josiah **6** 453-454
    Maury, Matthew Fontaine
      10 351-352
    Semmes, Raphael **14** 102-103
    see also Confederate States of
      America; Reconstruction (Unit-
      ed States); Secession
• UNION
  army
    Grant, Ulysses Simpson
      6 492-494
    McClellan, George Brinton
      10 391-392
    Meade, George Gordon
      10 440-441
    Sheridan, Philip Henry
      14 182-183
    Sherman, William Tecumseh
      14 186-187
    Thomas, George Henry
      15 190-191
  army campaigns
    Bristow, Benjamin Helm **3** 9-10
    Carroll, Anna Ella **3** 327-331
    Carson, Christopher **3** 334-335
    Crook, George **4** 322-323
    Custer, George Armstrong
      4 355-356
    Dow, Neal **5** 89-90
    Harrison, Benjamin **7** 178-179
    Hayes, Rutherford Birchard
      7 227-228
    Hickok, James Butler **7** 374-375
    Holmes, Oliver Wendell Jr.
      7 458-459
    Howard, Oliver Otis **7** 528-529
    Ingersoll, Robert Green
      8 120-121
    Wallace, Lewis **16** 74-75
    Weaver, James Baird **16** 151-152
  black regiments
    Armstrong, Samuel Chapman
      1 306-307

Delany, Martin Robinson
  4 473-474
Douglass, Frederick **5** 85-86
Higginson, Thomas Wentworth
  7 380
Langston, John Mercer **9** 197
Remond, Charles Lennox **13** 95
Revels, Hiram Rhoades
  13 109-110
Turner, Henry McNeal
  15 351-352
Congress
  Chandler, Zachariah **3** 425-426
  Davis, Henry Winter **4** 415-416
  Stevens, Thaddeus **14** 442-443
  Sumner, Charles **15** 30-31
  Trumbull, Lyman **15** 317-318
  Wade, Benjamin Franklin
    16 38-39
  Wilson, Henry **16** 322-323
  see also Radical Republicans
conscription
  Cleveland, Stephen Grover
    4 108-110
diplomacy
  Adams, Charles Francis **1** 41-42
  Bigelow, John **2** 271-272
  Evarts, William Maxwell
    5 340-341
  Hughes, John Joseph **8** 17-18
  Palmerston, 3d Viscount
    12 81-83
  Russell, John **13** 380-381
  see also Alabama claims; Trent
    Affair
Emancipation Proclamation
  see Emancipation Proclamation;
    Abolitionists
Native Americans, role of
  Parker, Ely Samuel **12** 106-108

Civilian Defense, Office of (United States)
  Roosevelt, Eleanor **13** 275-277

Civilis, Julius (or Claudius; flourished
  mid-1st century), German military leader
  Vondel, Joost van den **16** 19-20

Civilization (social science)
  critics (literature)
    Montesquieu **11** 123-125
    More, Thomas **11** 156-157
  evolution of
    Childe, Vere Gordon **3** 521-522
    Fiske, John **5** 465-466
    Frazer, James George **6** 76
    ibn Khaldun, Abd al-Rahman ibn
      Muhammad **8** 93-94
    Spengler, Oswald **14** 372-373
    Veblen, Thorstein Bunde
      15 449-450
  see also Culture; Society

Civilization and Barbarism (book)
  Sarmiento, Domingo Faustino
    13 484-485

**Civilization and Capitalism, 15th-18th
Century** (book)
  Braudel, Fernand **2** 507-508

Civita Castellana (Rome)
  Sangallo family **13** 464-466

Civitas solis (book)
  Campanella, Tommaso **3** 249

Civitate, Battle of (1053)
  Guiscard, Robert **7** 39-40

Clagny (château; France)
  Le Nôtre, André **9** 328-329
  Mansart, Jules Hardouin **10** 212

CLAIBORNE, LIZ (Elizabeth Claiborne
Ortenberg; born 1929), American businesswoman and clothing designer
4 68-69

Clair de lune (musical composition)
  Debussy, Achille Claude **4** 445-447

Clair de lune (poem)
  Verlaine, Paul Marie **15** 465-466

Clairmont, Clare Mary Jane (1798-1879),
mistress of Byron
  Byron, George Gordon Noel **3** 193-194

Clairvaux, Abbey of (France)
  Bernard of Clairvaux **2** 207-208

Clairvoyance (parapsychology)
  Driesch, Hans Adolf Eduard **5** 105

Clamence (literary character)
  Camus, Albert **3** 255-257

Clamor (book)
  Guillén, Nicolás **7** 34-35

Clan system (Scotland)
  Selkirk, 5th Earl of **14** 96

CLANCY, TOM (born 1947), American
author **4** 70-71

Clancy of the Overflow (verse)
  Paterson, Andrew Barton **12** 131-132

Clapeyron, Benoît-Paul-Émile (1799-1864),
French engineer
  Carnot, Nicolas Léonard Sadi **3** 315

CLAPHAM, SIR JOHN HAROLD
(1873-1946), English economic historian
4 71

Clapham sect (English antislavery organiza-
tion)
  Macaulay, Thomas Babington **10** 79-80
  Wilberforce, William **16** 269-270

CLAPP, MARGARET ANTOINETTE
(1910-1974), American author, educator,
and president of Wellesley College
(1949-1966) **4** 71-72

CLAPPERTON, HUGH (1788-1827), Scottish explorer of Africa **4** 72-73

Clara (literary character)
  Alarcón, Pedro Antonio de **1** 100-101

Clara Howard (novel)
  Brown, Charles Brockden **3** 33

Clara Milich (story)
  Turgenev, Ivan Sergeyevich **15** 345-348

Clare, Gilbert de (9th Earl of Clare)
  see Gloucester, 8th Earl of

Clarel (poem)
Melville, Herman **10** 472-476

Claremont (ship)
Stevens, John **14** 439-440

Claremont House (Surrey; England)
Soane, John **14** 314-315
Vanbrugh, John **15** 409-410

Clarence, Duke of (George; 1449-1478),
English noble, son of Richard, Duke of
York
Henry V **7** 296-297
Margaret of Anjou **10** 249-250
Richard III **13** 132-133

Clarence (literary character)
Laye, Camara **9** 257-259

Clarence and Avondale, Duke of (Albert
V.C. Edward; 1864-1892), son of Edward
VII
George V **6** 273-275

CLARENDON, 1ST EARL OF (Edward
Hyde; 1609-1674), English statesman and
historian **4** 73-75
Buckingham, 2d Duke of **3** 94-95
Charles II **3** 452-454
Shaftesbury, 1st Earl of **14** 135-136

Clarendon, Henry Hyde, 2d Earl of
(1638-1709), English statesman
Mary II **10** 309-310

Clarendon, 3d Earl of
see Hyde, Edward

Clarendon, Assize of (1166)
Henry II **7** 287-289

Clarendon, Constitutions of (England;
1164)
Becket, Thomas **2** 101-102
Henry II **7** 287-289

Clarendon code (England; 1661-1665)
Clarendon, 1st Earl of **4** 73-75

Clari (play)
Payne, John Howard **12** 159

Clarinda
see Maclehose, Agnes

Clarinet trio
see Trios (clarinet)

Clarissa Harlowe (novel; Richardson)
Richardson, Samuel **13** 141-142
Smollett, Tobias George **14** 305-307

CLARK, GEORGE ROGERS (1752-1818),
American Revolutionary War soldier
4 75-76
Clark, William **4** 82-83
Henry, Patrick **7** 309-311
Lewis, Andrew **9** 376-377

CLARK, JOHN BATES (1847-1938), American economist **4** 76-77
Clark, John Maurice **4** 77-78

CLARK, JOHN MAURICE (1884-1963),
American economist **4** 77-78
Berle, Adolf Augustus Jr. **2** 199-200
Clark, John Bates **4** 76-77

Clark, Jonas G. (1815-1900), American
merchant
Hall, Granville Stanley **7** 85-86

CLARK, KENNETH B. (born 1914), American social psychologist **4** 78-79

CLARK, KENNETH M. (Lord; 1903-1983),
English art historian **4** 79-80
Fuller, Richard Buckminster **6** 149-150
Turner, Joseph Mallord William
15 352-354

CLARK, MARK WAYNE (1896-1984),
American general **4** 80-81
Alexander of Tunis, 1st Earl **1** 135-136

CLARK, TOM CAMPBELL (1899-1977),
President Harry S. Truman's attorney general and Supreme Court justice **4** 81-82

CLARK, WILLIAM (1770-1838), American
explorer and soldier **4** 82-83
Catlin, George **3** 373-374
Gray, Robert **6** 508-509
Lewis, Meriwether **9** 391-392
Pike, Zebulon **12** 302-304
Sacajawea **13** 405-408

CLARK, WILLIAM ANDREWS (1839-1925),
American copper entrepreneur and politi-
cian **4** 83-85
Daly, Marcus **4** 379-380

Clark and Rockefeller (oil co.)
Rockefeller, John Davison **13** 226-228

Clark College (Atlanta, Georgia)
Tanner, Henry Ossawa **15** 102-103

Clark Memorandum (1928)
Kellogg, Frank Billings **8** 481

Clark University (Worcester, Massachu-
setts)
Boas, Franz **2** 349-351
Freud, Sigmund **6** 103-106
Goddard, Robert Hutchings **6** 376-377
Hall, Granville Stanley **7** 85-86
Michelson, Albert Abraham **11** 7-8
Wright, Carroll Davidson **16** 396

CLARKE, KENNETH HARRY (born 1940),
Conservative politician and Great
Britain's chancellor of the exchequer
(1993-) **4** 85-87

CLARKE, MARCUS ANDREW HISLOP
(1846-1881), English-born Australian
journalist and author **4** 87-88

Clarke, Richard (1711-1795), American
merchant
Copley, John Singleton **4** 228-230

CLARKE, SAMUEL (1675-1729), English
theologian and philosopher **4** 88
Butler, Joseph **3** 180-181
Leibniz, Gottfried Wilhelm von
9 307-310
Price, Richard **12** 447-448

Clarke, E.W., and Co. (banking firm)
Cooke, Jay **4** 215-216

Clarkson, Thomas (1760-1846), English
abolitionist
Cugoano, Ottobah **4** 332-333

Wilberforce, William **16** 269-270

Clash by Night (play)
Odets, Clifford **11** 470-471

Clásicos y modernos (book)
Ruíz, José Martínez **13** 358

Class (social system)
Chih-i **3** 518-519
Engels, Friedrich **5** 286-288
Marx, Karl **10** 304-308
Solon **14** 327-328
Toyotomi Hideyoshi **15** 286-289
Wright, Carroll Davidson **16** 396
see also Caste (social system)

Class Struggles in France, 1848-1850, The
(book)
Marx, Karl **10** 304-308

Classic of the Way and the Power
see Tao te Ching

Classical mechanics (physics)
Alembert, Jean le Rond d' **1** 127-128
Archimedes **1** 277-280
Galileo Galilei **6** 180-183
Heron of Alexandria **7** 334-335
Huygens, Christiaan **8** 79-81
Lagrange, Joseph Louis **9** 164-166
Newton, Isaac **11** 369-372
see also Celestial mechanics

Classical Symphony (music)
Prokofiev, Sergei Sergeevich
12 458-460

Classicism (art)
architecture
Ictinus **8** 101
interpretations
Pater, Walter Horatio **12** 130-131
neoclassicism
see Neoclassicism (art)
painting
Apelles **1** 257
Apollodorus **1** 261
Renaissance
see Renaissance (art)
sculpture
Myron **11** 285
Phidias **12** 265-267
Polykleitos **12** 385-386
Praxiteles **12** 433-434

Classicism (literature)
drama
Aeschylus **1** 70-72
Aristophanes **1** 293-294
Euripides **5** 332-334
Sophocles **14** 343-345
Humanism
see Humanism (literature)
medieval preservation
Cassiodorus, Flavius Magnus Aure-
lius **3** 357-358
neoclassicism
see Neoclassicism (literature)
prose
Aristotle **1** 295-296
Cicero, Marcus Tullius **4** 55-58

Demosthenes **4** 495-496
Herodotus **7** 330-333
Plato **12** 345-347
Thucydides **15** 211-212
Xenophon **16** 418-420
Renaissance
see Renaissance (literature)
verse
Horace **7** 500-503
Ovid **12** 34-36
Pindar **12** 312-313
Virgil **15** 507-510

Classicism (music)
Beethoven, Ludwig van **2** 114-117
Haydn, Franz Joseph **7** 219-221
Mozart, Wolfgang Amadeus
11 218-221
Schubert, Franz Peter **14** 35-37
see also Neoclassicism (music); Renaissance (music)

Classics and Commercials (book)
Wilson, Edmund **16** 318-319

Classification (biology)
see Animal systematics; Plant classification (botany)

Classification and Subject Index... (book)
Dewey, Melvil **4** 523-524

Classroom Management (textbook)
Bagley, William Chandler **1** 437-438

CLAUDE LORRAIN (1600-1682), French painter, draftsman, and etcher **4** 89-90
Cole, Thomas **4** 151-152
Constable, John **4** 208-209
Cuyp, Aelbert **4** 360-361
Durand, Asher Brown **5** 156-157
Ingres, Jean Auguste Dominique
8 121-123
Inness, George **8** 123-124
Moran, Thomas **11** 151-152
Turner, Joseph Mallord William
15 352-354
Wilson, Richard **16** 329-330

CLAUDEL, PAUL LOUIS CHARLES
(1868-1955), French author and diplomat
4 90-91
Gide, André **6** 308-309
Milhaud, Darius **11** 17-18
Perse, Saint-John **12** 242-243

Claudian (Claudius Claudianus; flourished circa 395), Latin poet
Juvenal **8** 397-399

Claudine... (novels)
Colette, Sidonie Gabrielle **4** 158-159

CLAUDIUS GERMANICUS, TIBERIUS
(Claudius I; 10 B.C. -A.D. 54), emperor of Rome 41-54 **4** 91-92
Celsus, Aulus Cornelius **3** 393
Nero Claudius Caesar **11** 342-344
Seneca the Younger, Lucius Annaeus
14 103-105
Tacitus **15** 70-72
Titus Flavius Vespasianus **15** 247-248

Claudius, Matthias (1740-1815), German poet
Schubert, Franz Peter **14** 35-37

Claudius Pulcher, Appius (died 48 B.C.), Roman politician
Brutus, Marcus Junius **3** 79-80

Claudius the God (novel)
Graves, Robert Ranke **6** 504-506

Clausewitz, Karl von (1780-1831), Prussian army officer
Suvorov, Aleksandr Vasilievich **15** 44-45

CLAUSIUS, RUDOLF JULIUS EMANUEL
(1822-1888), German physicist **4** 92-94
Boltzmann, Ludwig **2** 379-380
Kelvin of Largs, Baron **8** 488-489
van der Waals, Johannes Diderik
15 417-418

Clausula (literary technique)
Skelton, John **14** 268-269

Clausula (music)
Pérotin **12** 231-232

CLAVER, ST. PETER (1580-1654), Spanish Jesuit missionary **4** 94

Clavigo (play)
Goethe, Johann Wolfgang von
6 388-391

CLAY, HENRY (1777-1852), American lawyer and statesman **4** 94-96
Ashland
Latrobe, Benjamin Henry **9** 222-224
Compromise of 1850
see Compromise of 1850
political opponents
Blair, Francis Preston **2** 313-315
Crawford, William Harris **4** 299-300
Jackson, Andrew **8** 168-172
Polk, James Knox **12** 374-376
Taylor, Zachary **15** 128-130
supporters
Clayton, John Middleton **4** 96-97
Curtin, Andrew Gregg **4** 347-348
Greeley, Horace **6** 515-517
Lincoln, Abraham **9** 415-418
"War Hawks"
Calhoun, John Caldwell **3** 226-228
see also War of 1812
Whig program
Tyler, John **15** 368-369
Webster, Daniel **16** 162-164

Clayhanger (novel)
Bennett, Arnold **2** 167-168

CLAYTON, JOHN MIDDLETON
(1796-1856), American lawyer and statesman **4** 96-97

Clayton-Bulwer Treaty (1850)
Buchanan, James **3** 89-90
Clayton, John Middleton **4** 96-97
Lawrence, Abbott **9** 246
Salisbury, 3d Marquess of **13** 448-449
Taylor, Zachary **15** 128-130

Cleanthes (circa 301-252/232 B.C.), Stoic philosopher
Chrysippus **4** 35-36
Zeno of Citium **16** 499-500

Clear and Lonely Sound of the Fisherman's Flute (scroll)
Hsia Kuei **8** 4-5

Clearchus (died circa 401 B.C.), Spartan-born professional soldier
Xenophon **16** 418-420

Clearing after Snow over Mountains and River (painting)
Wang Wei **16** 106-108

CLEAVER, LEROY ELDRIDGE (born 1935), American writer and Black Panther leader **4** 97-98

Clef musicale des langages tambourinés et sifflés, La (book)
Eboué, Adolphe Felix Sylvestre **5** 194

CLEISTHENES (flourished 6th century B.C.), Athenian statesman **4** 98-99
Cleomenes I **4** 103
Pericles **12** 219-221

Cleisthenes (flourished 6th century B.C.), tyrant of Sicyon
Cleisthenes **4** 98-99

CLEMENCEAU, GEORGES (1841-1929), French statesman **4** 99-101
domestic policy
Dreyfus, Alfred **5** 103-105
Foch, Ferdinand **5** 498-499
foreign policy
Lloyd George, David **9** 469-471
Orlando, Vittorio Emmanuele
11 529-530
Perth, 16th Earl of **12** 244-245
political opponents
Briand, Aristide **2** 528-529
Laval, Pierre **9** 237-238
Poincaré, Raymond **12** 366-368
portrait busts of
Rodin, Auguste **13** 236-238

CLEMENS NON PAPA, JACOBUS (circa 1510-circa 1556), Flemish composer **4** 101
Gombert, Nicolas **6** 416-417

Clemens, Samuel Langhorne
see Twain, Mark

Clemens, Titus Flavius
see Clement of Alexandria

Clement I, St. (30?-?100), pope 90?-100
Cyril and Methodius, Saints **4** 362-363
Peter **12** 252-253

Clement II (died 1047), pope 1046-1047
Henry III **7** 290

Clement III (died 1191), pope 1187-1191
Innocent, III **8** 125-127

Clement III (Guibert of Ravenna; 1030?-1100), antipope 1080 and 1084-1100
Urban II **15** 393

CLEMENT V (1264-1314), pope 1304-1314
4 101-102
Henry VII **7** 299-300
Philip IV **12** 274

Clement VI (Pierre Roger; 1291-1352),
pope 1342-1352
Charles IV **3** 455-456
Guy de Chauliac **7** 54
Levi ben Gershon **9** 363-364
Petrarch **12** 259-261
Rienzi, Cola di **13** 166-167
Wenceslaus **16** 201-202

Clement VII (1342-1394), antipope
1378-1394
Urban VI **15** 394

Clement VII (Giulio de' Medici;
1478-1534), pope 1523-1534
associates
Bembo, Pietro **2** 144-145
Machiavelli, Niccolò **10** 97-99
church policies
Cajetan **3** 215-216
Cranmer, Thomas **4** 295-296
Wolsey, Thomas **16** 364-366
relatives
Médici, Catherine de' **10** 445-449
temporal policies
Biringuccio, Vannoccio **2** 283
Castiglione, Baldassare **3** 360-361
Charles V **3** 457-459
Guicciardini, Francesco **7** 32-33
Henry VIII **7** 302-305
Mary, I **10** 308-309

Clement VIII (Ippolito Aldobrandini;
1536-1605), pope 1592-1605
Bellarmine, Robert **2** 135-136
Francis of Sales **6** 47
Sixtus V **14** 267-268

Clement XI (1649-1721), pope 1700-1721
Louis XIV **9** 531-533

Clement XIV (1705-1774), pope
1769-1774
Pius VI **12** 333-334

CLEMENT OF ALEXANDRIA (circa
150-circa 215), Christian theologian
4 102-103

Clement of Rome, St.
see Clement I, St.

Clementi, Muzio (1752-1832), Italian
pianist and composer
Meyerbeer, Giacomo **10** 536-537

Clemenza di Tito, La (opera)
Mozart, Wolfgang Amadeus
11 218-221

Clenched Fist, The (book)
Lagerkvist, Pär Fabian **9** 162-163

Cleombrotus I (died 371 B.C.), Spartan
king 380-371
Agesilaus II **1** 79-80

CLEOMENES I (flourished circa 520-490
B.C.), Spartan king **4** 103
Cleisthenes **4** 98-99

CLEOMENES III (circa 260-219 B.C.), king
of Sparta 235-219 **4** 103-104
Agis IV **1** 81-82
Aratus **1** 273-274

Cleomenes (play)
Dryden, John **5** 106-107

Cleomenes of Naucrates (flourished 4th
century B.C.), Egyptian official
Ptolemy I **12** 470-472

CLEON (circa 475-422 B.C.), Athenian
political leader **4** 104-105
Aristophanes **1** 293-294
Thucydides **15** 211-212

CLEOPATRA (69-30 B.C.), queen of Egypt
4 105-106
Antony, Mark **1** 253-254
Augustus **1** 371-373
Caesar, Gaius Julius **3** 207-210
Herod the Great **7** 333-334

Cleopatra (born 357 B.C.), daughter of
Philip II of Macedon
Philip II **12** 269-271

Cleopatra (opera)
Cimarosa, Domenico **4** 61-62

Cleopatra (painting)
Reni, Guido **13** 97-98

Cleopatra (play)
Alfieri, Vittoria **1** 145-146

Cleopatra (sculpture)
Barlach, Ernst **2** 5-6

Cleophil (pseudonym)
see Congreve, William

Cleremont (literary character)
Chapman, George **3** 440-441

**Clergy and Laity Concerned about Viet-
nam** (anti-war organization, United
States)
Coffin, William Sloane Jr. **4** 135-137
Marty, Martin E. **10** 300-301

Clergyman's Daughter, A (novel)
Orwell, George **12** 14-15

Clergymen
see Religious leaders

Clericis laicos (1296; papal bull)
Boniface VIII **2** 392-393
Clement V **4** 101-102

Clérisseau, Charles-Louis (1722-1820),
French architect and painter
Adam, Robert and James **1** 38-40

Clerk Sanders (painting)
Burne-Jones, Edward Coley **3** 145-146

Clerks Regular
see Theatines

Clermont (steamboat)
Fulton, Robert **6** 151-152

Clermont, council of (France; 1095)
Urban II **15** 393

Clermont-Ferrand, University of (France)
Lefebvre, Georges **9** 301-302

Cleve, Joos van (died 1540), Flemish
painter
Clouet, Jean and François **4** 122-123

CLEVELAND, JAMES (1932-1991), African
American singer, songwriter, and pianist
4 106-108

CLEVELAND, STEPHEN GROVER
(1837-1908), American statesman, twice
president **4** 108-110
associates
Keller, Helen Adams **8** 479-480
Straus, Isidor **14** 496
Wood, Leonard **16** 369-370
Cabinet
Lamar, Lucius Quintus Cincinnatus
9 170-171
Olney, Richard **11** 504-505
domestic policy
Altgeld, John Peter **1** 180-182
Geronimo **6** 281-282
Miles, Nelson Appleton **11** 16-17
Morgan, John Pierpont **11** 163-165
foreign policy
Dole, Sanford Ballard **5** 46
Liliuokalani, Lydia Kamakaeha
9 411-412
Lodge, Henry Cabot **9** 482-483
Rio Branco, Barão do **13** 177
Salisbury, 3d Marquess of
13 448-449
in fiction
Ford, Paul Leicester **6** 9-10
political appointments
Johnston, Joseph Eggleston **8** 323
Pendleton, George Hunt **12** 198
White, Edward Douglass
16 230-231
political opponents
Blaine, James Gillespie **2** 312-313
Harrison, Benjamin **7** 178-179
Tillman, Benjamin Ryan **15** 225-226

Cleveland (city, Ohio)
Baker, Newton Diehl **1** 451
Johnson, Tom Loftin **8** 317
Stokes, Carl B. **14** 464-465

Cleveland (novel)
Prévost, Abbé **12** 445-446

Cleveland Bureau of Jewish Education
(Ohio)
Silver, Abba Hillel **14** 232-233

Cleveland Institute of Music (Ohio)
Bloch, Ernest **2** 326-327

Cleveland Leader (newspaper)
Medill, Joseph **10** 451-452

Cleveland Penny Press (newspaper)
Scripps, Edward Wyllis **14** 72-73

Cleveland Plain Dealer (newspaper)
Stokes, Carl B. **14** 464-465
Ward, Artemus **16** 112-113

Cliff Klingenhagen (verse)
Robinson, Edwin Arlington **13** 201-202

Clifford, Clark McAdams (born 1906),
American lawyer and statesman
Truman, Harry S. **15** 314-316

Clifford, William Kingdon (1845-1879),
English mathematician
Lobachevskii, Nikolai Ivanovich
9 472-474

Clifford of Chudleigh, 1st Baron
(1630-1673), English statesman
Buckingham, 2d Duke of **3** 94-95

Clifton bridge (near Bristol, England)
Brunel, Isambard Kingdom **3** 69-70

Cligès (romance)
Chrestien de Troyes **4** 23-24

Climb Every Mountain (song)
Rodgers, Richard Charles **13** 234-236

CLINE, PATSY (born Virginia Patterson
Hensley; 1932-1963), American singer
4 110-112

CLINTON, DeWITT (1769-1828), Ameri-
can lawyer and statesman **4** 112-113
Catlin, George **3** 373-374
Clinton, George **4** 113-114
Marcy, William Learned **10** 247-248
Willard, Emma Hart **16** 288-289

Clinton, George (1686?-1761), British
colonial governor
Clinton, Henry **4** 114-115

CLINTON, GEORGE (1739-1812), Ameri-
can patriot and statesman **4** 113-114
Clinton, DeWitt **4** 112-113
Colden, Cadwallader **4** 145-146
Genet, Edmond Charles **6** 261-262
Livingston, Robert R. **9** 462-463

CLINTON, SIR HENRY (1738?-1795),
British commander in chief during the
American Revolution **4** 114-115
Burgoyne, John **3** 137-138
Cornwallis, Charles **4** 241-243
Lincoln, Benjamin **9** 418-419
Rochambeau, Comte de **13** 220-221
Tarleton, Banastre **15** 110
see also American Revolution

CLINTON, HILLARY RODHAM (born
1947), American politician and first lady
4 115-117

Clinton, James (1733-1812), American
general in the Revolutionary War
Clinton, DeWitt **4** 112-113

CLINTON, WILLIAM JEFFERSON ("Bill"
Clinton; born 1946), 42nd president of
the United States **4** 117-119
appointees
Albright, Madeleine Korbel
1 116-118
Aspin, Les **1** 342-344
Babbitt, Bruce Edward **1** 408-410
Breyer, Stephen **2** 524-527
Brown, Ronald H. **3** 44-47
Browner, Carol M. **3** 50-52
Christopher, Warren Minor **4** 32-33
Deer, Ada E. **4** 452-454
Elders, Joycelyn **5** 243-246

Freeh, Louis J. **6** 90-91
Ginsburg, Ruth Bader **6** 333-336
Jackson, Shirley Ann **8** 183-184
Kessler, David A. **8** 523-524
Panetta, Leon E. **12** 84-85
Perry, William James **12** 240-242
Reno, Janet **13** 99-101
Shalikashvili, John Malchase David
14 145-147
Varmus, Harold Eliot **15** 436-437

Clipper ships
McKay, Donald **10** 416-417
Palmer, Nathaniel Brown **12** 80-81

Clitandre (play)
Corneille, Pierre **4** 234-236

CLIVE, ROBERT (Baron Clive of Plassey;
1725-1774), English soldier and statesman **4** 119-120
Dupleix **5** 153
Hastings, Warren **7** 195-196

Clizia (play)
Machiavelli, Niccolò **10** 97-99

Clock (time-measurement instrument)
Charles IV **3** 456-457
Farmer, Moses Gerrish **5** 385
Huygens, Christiaan **8** 79-81
Rabi, Isidor Isaac **12** 526-527

Clockmaker, The (book)
Haliburton, Thomas Chandler **7** 80

CLODION (1738-1814), French sculptor
4 121
Canova, Antonio **3** 263-264

CLODIUS PULCHER, PUBLIUS (died 52
B.C.), Roman politician **4** 121-122
Antony, Mark **1** 253-254
Caesar, Gaius Julius **3** 207-210
Cicero, Marcus Tullius **4** 55-58
Crassus Dives, Marcus Licinius
4 296-297
Pompey **12** 387-389
Sallust **13** 454

Cloisters (art museum, New York City)
Rockefeller, John D. Jr. **13** 225-226

Clopinel, Jean
see Jean de Meun

Clore Gallery (Tate Gallery, London)
Stirling, James **14** 458-459

Clorinda (literary character)
Tasso, Torquato **15** 114-116

Close Harmony (play)
Parker, Dorothy Rothschild **12** 106

Close of Life (poems)
Jami **8** 218-219

Closed Commercial State, The (book)
Fichte, Johann Gottlieb **5** 435-436

Closing of the American Mind, The (book)
Bloom, Allan David **2** 335-337

Clotelle (novel)
Brown, William Wells **3** 48-49

Clothar I (died 561), king of Soissons
511-558, of all the Franks 558-561
Clovis I **4** 124

Clothed Maja (painting)
Goya y Lucientes, Francisco de Paula
José de **6** 476-478

Clothing industry
Armani, Giorgio **1** 299-301
Ashley, Laura **1** 332-333
Benetton **2** 158-159
Chanel, Coco **3** 429
Gaultier, Jean Paul **6** 239-240
Gigli, Romeo **6** 312
von Furstenberg, Diane **16** 20-21

Clotilde (475?-?545), queen of Franks
Clovis I **4** 124

Cloud chamber (physics)
Anderson, Carl David **1** 214-215
Bothe, Walther **2** 438-439
Chadwick, James **3** 405-406

Cloud in Trousers (book)
Mayakovsky, Vladimir Vladimirovich
10 364-365

Cloud Messenger (elegy)
Kalidasa **8** 414-415

Cloudcuckoobury (fictional city)
Aristophanes **1** 293-294

Clouds (musical composition)
Debussy, Achille Claude **4** 445-447

Clouds, The (play; Aristophanes)
Aristophanes **1** 293-294
Protagoras **12** 461
Socrates **14** 320-321

CLOUET, FRANÇOIS (circa 1516-circa
1572), French portrait painter **4** 122-123

Clouet, Jan (flourished circa 1475-1491),
French painter
Clouet, Jean and François **4** 122-123

CLOUET, JEAN (circa 1485-circa 1541),
French portrait painter **4** 122-123

CLOUGH, ARTHUR HUGH (1819-1861),
English poet **4** 123-124
Arnold, Matthew **1** 311-313

Clovio, Giulio (1498-1578), Italian painter
Bruegel, Pieter the Elder **3** 65-67
Greco **6** 511-514

CLOVIS I (465-511), Frankish king **4** 124

Club, The (literary group, London)
Boswell, James **2** 432-434
Goldsmith, Oliver **6** 411-413

Cluny, abbey of (France)
Bernard of Clairvaux **2** 207-208

Clyens, Mary Elizabeth
see Lease, Mary Elizabeth Clyens

Clytemnestra (mythology)
Aeschylus **1** 70-72
Euripides **5** 332-334
Sophocles **14** 343-345

Cnidus (ancient town, Asia Minor)
Eudoxus of Cnidus **5** 329-330

CNU
see Cameroon National Union

Cnut
see Canute I

Coahuila (state, Mexico)
Carranza, Venustiano **3** 321-322

Coal (fuel)
formation
Logan, William Edmond **9** 488-489
labor unions
Lewis, John Llewellyn **9** 387-388
Mitchell, John **11** 58-59
Roosevelt, Theodore **13** 280-283
mining industry
Baldwin, Stanley **1** 468-469
Mendeleev, Dmitrii Ivanovich
10 486-488
Monnet, Jean **11** 109-110
Schuman, Robert **14** 41

Coal tar (chemistry)
Dumas, Jean Baptiste André **5** 138-139
Hofmann, August Wilhelm von
7 441-442

Coatzacoalcos (town, Mexico)
Díaz del Castillo, Bernal **4** 536-537

Cobb, Howell (1815-1868), American
lawyer
Toombs, Robert Augustus **15** 267-268

COBB, TYRUS RAYMOND (1886-1961),
baseball player **4** 124-126

COBBETT, WILLIAM (1763-1835), English
journalist and politician **4** 126-127
Paine, Thomas **12** 66-67

COBDEN, RICHARD (1804-1865), English
politician **4** 127-128
Bright, John **3** 6-7
Brown, William Wells **3** 48-49

Cobden-Chevalier Treaty (1860)
Cobden, Richard **4** 127-128

Cobwebs from an Empty Skull (book)
Bierce, Ambrose Gwinett **2** 269-270

Coca-Cola Company
Woodruff, Robert W. **16** 372-374

Cocardes (songs)
Poulenc, Francis **12** 414-415

Cocceji, Baron Samuel von (1679-1755),
Prussian jurist
Frederick II **6** 81-84

Cochin, Charles Nicolas (1715-1790),
French engraver
Gabriel, Ange Jacques **6** 160-161

Cochin (region, India)
Cabral, Pedro Álvares **3** 203-204

Cochin China (former republic; Vietnam)
Garnier, Francis **6** 220-221

COCHISE (circa 1825-1874), American
Chiricahua Apache Indian chief **4** 128

COCHRAN, JOHNNIE (born 1937),
African American lawyer **4** 128-131

Cochrane, Thomas (10th Earl of Dundon-
ald; 1775-1860), British naval commander
San Martín, José de **13** 468-469

Cock, Hieronymus (flourished 16th century), Flemish engraver
Bruegel, Pieter the Elder **3** 65-67

Cock (book)
Lucian **10** 25-26

Cock, The (sculpture)
Brancusi, Constantin **2** 494-496

Cock-a-Doodle Dandy (play)
O'Casey, Sean **11** 459-460

Cockaigne (musical composition)
Elgar, Edward **5** 247-248

Cockatoos (novel)
Franklin, Stella Maraia Sarah Miles
6 68-69

COCKCROFT, JOHN DOUGLAS
(1897-1967), English physicist **4** 131-132

Cockerell, Samuel Pepys (1754-1827), English architect
Latrobe, Benjamin Henry **9** 222-224

Cockerill, John Albert (1845-1896), American journalist
Pulitzer, Joseph **12** 481-482

Cocktail Party, The (play)
Eliot, Thomas Stearns **5** 258-261

Cocoa (novel)
Amado, Jorge **1** 189-190

Coconuts (musical)
Marx brothers **10** 303-304

Cocos Islands (Indian Ocean)
Darwin, Charles Robert **4** 397-399

Cocoyé, El (musical composition)
Gottschalk, Louis Moreau **6** 463-464

COCTEAU, JEAN (1889-1963), French
writer **4** 132-133
Genet, Jean **6** 262-263
Milhaud, Darius **11** 17-18
Picasso, Pablo **12** 292-295
Poulenc, Francis **12** 414-415
Satie, Erik **13** 494-495
Stravinsky, Igor Fedorovich **14** 502-506

Coddington, William (1601-1678), British
colonial governor
Williams, Roger **16** 304-305

Codex Argenteus (6th-century manuscript)
Ulfilas **15** 384

Codicil of Master Jean de Meun, The
(poem)
Jean de Meun **8** 234-235

Codomannus
see Darius III

Cody, William Frederick
see Buffalo Bill

Coecke van Aelst, Pieter (1502-1550),
Flemish painter

Bruegel, Pieter the Elder **3** 65-67

Coelho, Gonçalo (flourished early 16th
century), Portuguese mariner
Vespucci, Amerigo **15** 476-478

Coelho, Nicolas (flourished 15th century),
Portuguese explorer
Gama, Vasco da **6** 196-198

COEN, JAN PIETERSZOON (circa
1586-1629), Dutch governor general of
Batavia **4** 133
Schouten, William Cornelius **14** 31
Van Diemen, Anthony Meuza **15** 420

Coercive Acts
see Intolerable Acts

COETZEE, J(OHN) M. (born 1940), white
South African novelist **4** 133-135

Coeur, Jacques (1395?-1456), French mer-
chant
Charles VII **3** 461-462
Louis XI **9** 526-528

Co-Existence (journal)
Polanyi, Karl **12** 372

COFFIN, LEVI (1789-1877), American antislavery reformer **4** 135

Coffin, Lucretia
see Mott, Lucretia Coffin

COFFIN, WILLIAM SLOANE, JR. (born
1924), Yale University chaplain who
spoke out against the Vietnam War
4 135-137

Cognac, League of (1526)
Guicciardini, Francesco **7** 32-33

Cogswell, Joseph Green (1786-1871),
American educator, librarian, and bibli-
ographer
Bancroft, George **1** 483-484

COHAN, GEORGE MICHAEL
(1878-1942), American actor and playwright **4** 137-138
Lardner, Ringgold Wilmer **9** 204-205

Cohen, Felix Solomon (1907-1953), American lawyer
Cohen, Morris Raphael **4** 139-140

Cohen, George Morris
see Brandes, Georg Morris

COHEN, HERMANN (1842-1918),
Jewish-German philosopher **4** 138-139
Cassirer, Ernst **3** 358-359
Ortega Y Gasset, José **12** 7-8
Pasternak, Boris Leonidovich
12 124-125

COHEN, MORRIS RAPHAEL (1880-1947),
American philosopher and teacher
4 139-140
Gierke, Otto von **6** 311-312
Nagel, Ernest **11** 291-292

Cohens v. Virginia (legal case; 1821)
Marshall, John **10** 279-281

Cohn, Roy Marcus (1927-1986), American
lawyer and businessman
McCarthy, Joseph Raymond **10** 388-389

COHN-BENDIT, DANIEL (born 1946), led "new left" student protests in France in 1968 **4** 140-141

Coimbra, University of (Portugal)
Andrada e Silva, José Bonifácio de **1** 221-222
Pombal, Marquês de **12** 386-387
Salazar, António de Oliveira **13** 442-443

Coinage (metal currency)
Abd al-Malik **1** 12-13
Caesar, Gaius Julius **3** 207-210
David I **4** 407
Louis IX **9** 525-526
Muhammad bin Tughluq **11** 229
Quin Shi Huang-di **12** 515-518
see also Currency; Mint

COKE, SIR EDWARD (1552-1634), English jurist and parliamentarian **4** 141-142
James I **8** 204-206

Colantonio (circa 1352-1442), Italian painter
Antonello da Messina **1** 251-252

Colas Breugnon (novel)
Rolland, Romain **13** 260

Colba
see Cuba

Colbath, Jeremiah Jones
see Wilson, Henry

COLBERT, JEAN BAPTISTE (1619-1683), French statesman **4** 142-143
art patronage
Boileau-Despréaux, Nicholas **2** 369-371
Le Brun, Charles **9** 269-270
Le Vau, Louis **9** 360-361
Perrault, Claude **12** 232-233
colonial policy
Frontenac et Palluau, Comte de **6** 128-130
Talon, Jean **15** 91-92
domestic policy
Louis XIV **9** 531-533
Mazarin, Jules **10** 379-380

Colburn, Zerah (1804-1840), American mathematician
Hamilton, William Rowan **7** 99-100

COLBY, WILLIAM E. (1920-1996), American director of the Central Intelligence Agency (CIA) **4** 143-145

Colby College (Waterville, Maine)
Small, Albion Woodbury **14** 277

Colcord, Lincoln Ross (1883-1947), American writer
Rölvaag, Ole Edvart **13** 265

Cold Harbor, Battle of (1863)
Grant, Ulysses Simpson **6** 492-494
Lee, Robert Edward **9** 292-294

Cold Nights (novel)
Pa Chin **12** 53-54

Cold War (international politics)
containment

Acheson, Dean Gooderham **1** 37-38
Dulles, John Foster **5** 134-135
Forrestal, James Vincent **6** 14
Kennan, George F. **8** 496-498
Truman, Harry S. **15** 314-316
end of
Gorbachev, Mikhail Sergeevich **6** 441-444
European attitude
Adenauer, Konrad **1** 59-61
Churchill, Winston Leonard Spencer **4** 51-53
Franco Bahamonde, Francisco **6** 52-54
John, XXIII **8** 277-280
in literature
Simonov, Konstantin Mikhailovich **14** 239-240
opponents (United States)
McGovern, George Stanley **10** 412-414
Stone, I. F. **14** 470-471
Wallace, Henry Agard **16** 73-74
Soviet participants
Gromyko, Andrei Andreevich **7** 9-11
supporters (United States)
Byrnes, James Francis **3** 191-192
Dewey, John **4** 520-523
Jackson, Henry Martin **8** 172-174
Kirkland, Joseph Lane **9** 35-37
MacArthur, Douglas **10** 76-78
McCarthy, Joseph Raymond **10** 388-389
see also Korean War (1950-1953); Vietnam War (1956-1976); and individual countries

COLDEN, CADWALLADER (1688-1776), American botanist and politician **4** 145-146
Bartram, John **2** 40-41

Colden, David (1769-1834), American lawyer and statesman
Colden, Cadwallader **4** 145-146

Colden, Jane (1724-1766), American botanist
Colden, Cadwallader **4** 145-146

COLE, GEORGE DOUGLAS HOWARD (1889-1959), English historian and economist **4** 146-147

COLE, JOHNNETTA (born 1936), African American scholar and educator **4** 147-149

Cole, Margaret Postgate (born 1893), English novelist
Cole, George Douglas Howard **4** 146-147

COLE, NAT (a.k.a. Nat "King" Cole, born Nathaniel Adams Coles; 1919-1965), American jazz musician **4** 149-151

COLE, THOMAS (1801-1848), American painter **4** 151-152
Allston, Washington **1** 176-177
Church, Frederick Edwin **4** 49-50
Durand, Asher Brown **5** 156-157

Colegio de Santa Cruz de Tlatelolco (Mexico)
Zumárraga, Juan de **16** 531-532

Colegio Militar (Argentina)
Justo, Agustin Pedro **8** 396

Colegio Nacional (Mexico)
Azuela, Mariano **1** 402
Reyes, Alfonso **13** 112-113

Colegio Seminario de San Carlos (Paraguay)
López, Carlos Antonio **9** 506-507

COLEMAN, BESSIE (1892-1926), first African American to earn an international pilot's license **4** 152-154

Colère de Samson, La (poem)
Vigny, Comte de **15** 494-495

COLERIDGE, SAMUEL TAYLOR (1772-1834), English poet and critic **4** 154-156
associates
Allston, Washington **1** 176-177
Carlyle, Thomas **3** 304-305
Hamilton, William Rowan **7** 99-100
Owen, Robert **12** 39-40
Wordsworth, William **16** 385-388, 444, 445
influence of
Bryant, William Cullen **3** 83-85
Hawthorne, Nathaniel **7** 212-215
Hazlitt, William **7** 235-236
Lamb, Charles **9** 176-177
Maurice, John Frederick Denison **10** 349-350
O'Neill, Eugene **11** 514-516
Shelley, Percy Bysshe **14** 176-178
influenced by
Bartram, William **2** 41-42
Hartley, David **7** 185
Milton, John **11** 43-46
Schelling, Friedrich Wilhelm Joseph von **13** 526-527
literary criticism on
Pater, Walter Horatio **12** 130-131
Peacock, Thomas Love **12** 169
opponents
Lewis, Matthew Gregory **9** 390-391
quoted
Keats, John **8** 470-472

Coleridge on Imagination (book)
Richards, Ivor Armstrong **13** 137

COLES, ROBERT MARTIN (born 1929), American social psychiatrist, social critic, and humanist **4** 156-157

COLET, JOHN (circa 1446-1519), English theologian **4** 157-158
Erasmus, Desiderius **5** 298-300
More, Thomas **11** 156-157
Tyndale, William **15** 373-374

Colet, Louise (1810-1870), French poet
Flaubert, Gustave **5** 480-482

COLETTE, SIDONIE GABRIELLE (1873-1954), French author **4** 158-159
Claudel, Paul Louis Charles **4** 90-91

Colette Baudoche (novel)
Barrès, Auguste Maurice **2** 20-21

Colfax, Schuyler (1823-1885), American politician
Applegate, Jesse **1** 264-265

COLIGNY, GASPARD DE (1519-1572), French admiral and statesman **4** 159-160
Medici, Catherine de' **10** 445-449
William the Silent **16** 300-302

Coligny, Gaspard de (Seigneur de Châtillon; 1470?-1522), French marshal
Coligny, Gaspard de **4** 159-160

Colin Clout (satire)
Skelton, John **14** 268-269

Colin Clout's Come Home Again (poem)
Spenser, Edmund **14** 373-376

Collage (art form)
Arp, Jean **1** 317-318
Burri, Alberto **3** 159-160
Dove, Arthur Garfield **5** 86-87
Gris, Juan **7** 5-6
Miró, Joan **11** 53-54
Picasso, Pablo **12** 292-295
Rauschenberg, Robert **13** 52-53

Collection, The (play)
Pinter, Harold **12** 317-318

Collective bargaining
see Labor unions

Collective farms (Union of Soviet Socialist Republics)
Sholokhov, Mikhail Aleksandrovich **14** 203-204
Stalin, Joseph **14** 393-396

Collective security (international politics)
Fraser, Peter **6** 73-74
Litvinov, Maxim Maximovich **9** 451-452
Morgenthau, Henry Jr. **11** 172-173
Titulescu, Nicolae **15** 246-247

Collectivism (politics)
Cole, George Douglas Howard **4** 146-147
Merezhkovsky, Dmitry Sergeyevich **10** 515-516
Ulbricht, Walter **15** 383-384

Collector, The (novel)
Fowles, John **6** 33-35

Colleen Bawn, The (play)
Boucicault, Dion **2** 442-443

College campus disorders
see Student rebellions

Collège de Bourg (France)
Ampère, André Marie **1** 205-206

Collège de Coqueret (France)
Ronsard, Pierre de **13** 271-273

Collège de France (Paris)
founded
Budé, Guillaume **3** 102-103
Francis I **6** 40-43
mathematics
Cauchy, Augustin Louis **3** 378-380

natural history
Cuvier, Georges Léopold **4** 357-359
philosophy
Bergson, Henri **2** 191-192
Gilson, Étienne Henry **6** 327-328
Tarde, Jean Gabriel **15** 108-109
physics
Joliot-Curie, Jean Frédéric **8** 327-328
social sciences
Aron, Raymond **1** 316-317
Breuil, Henri Edouard Prosper **2** 521-522
Cabot, Richard Clarke **3** 200
Champollion, Jean François **3** 421
Mauss, Marcel **10** 352-353
Say, Jean Baptiste **13** 508-509

College Entrance Examination Board (established 1906)
Eliot, Charles William **5** 254

College of Assembled Worthies (Korea, 1420)
Sejong **14** 91-92

College of Commissioners (Congo—Kinshasa)
Mobutu Sese Seko **11** 69-71

College of New Art (Vitebsk, Union of Soviet Socialist Republics)
Malevich, Kasimir **10** 168-169

College of Physicians (Milan)
Cardano, Geronimo **3** 285-286

College of Physicians (Rome)
Cardano, Geronimo **3** 285-286

College of the City of New York
see New York, City University of

Collège Royal
see Collège de France

Collegiants (religious sect)
Spinoza, Baruch **14** 381-383

Collegium (Kiev, Ukraine)
Mogila, Peter **11** 74-75

Collegium Musicum (established 1704)
Telemann, Georg Philipp **15** 137-138

Colleoni, Bartolommeo (1400-1475), Italian soldier
Verrocchio, Andrea del **15** 471-472

Collier, Jeremy (1650-1726), English clergyman
Congreve, William **4** 200-201

COLLIER, JOHN (1884-1968), American proponent of Native American culture **4** 160-162

Collier's (magazine)
Dunne, Finley Peter **5** 147-148
Hapgood, Norman **7** 137-138
Hemingway, Ernest Miller **7** 274-277
Lardner, Ringgold Wilmer **9** 204-205
Rembrandt Harmensz van Rijn **13** 91-95

Colline Gate, Battle of (82 B.C.)
Crassus Dives, Marcus Licinius **4** 296-297

Collingwood, Cuthbert (1750-1810), English naval commander
Nelson, Horatio **11** 336-338

COLLINGWOOD, ROBIN GEORGE (1889-1943), English historian and philosopher **4** 162

Collingwood (ship)
George VI **6** 275

COLLINS, EDWARD KNIGHT (1802-1878), American businessman and shipowner **4** 162-163

COLLINS, EILEEN (born 1956), American astronaut **4** 163-165

COLLINS, MARVA (born Marva Deloise Nettles; b. 1936), African American educator **4** 165-167

COLLINS, MICHAEL (1890-1922), Irish revolutionary leader and soldier **4** 167-168

Collins, Michael (born 1930), American astronaut
Armstrong, Neil Alden **1** 304-306

COLLINS, WILLIAM WILKIE (1824-1889), English novelist **4** 169-170
Doyle, Arthur Conan **5** 91-92
Trollope, Anthony **15** 300-302

COLLINS, WILLIAM (1721-1759), English lyric poet **4** 168-169

Collinson, Peter (1694-1768), English naturalist and botanist
Bartram, John **2** 40-41
Colden, Cadwallader **4** 145-146

Collip, James Bertram (1892-1965), Canadian biochemist
Banting, Frederick Grant **1** 493-494

Collodion process (photography)
see Wet-plate process

Colloque sentimental (poem)
Verlaine, Paul Marie **15** 465-466

Colloqui coi personaggi (story)
Pirandello, Luigi **12** 319-321

Colloquia (book)
Erasmus, Desiderius **5** 298-300
Hutten, Ulrich von **8** 72-73

Colloquy (book)
Aelfric **1** 69-70

COLLOR DE MELLO, FERNANDO (born 1949), businessman who became president of Brazil in 1990 **4** 170-172

Colloredo, Hieronymus (1732-1812), prince archbishop of Salzburg
Mozart, Wolfgang Amadeus **11** 218-221

Colman and Guaire (play)
Gregory, Augusta **6** 535-536

Colman, Benjamin (1673-1747), American clergyman
Whitefield, George **16** 241-242

Colocolo (died 1557?), Araucanian chief
Ercilla y Zúñiga, Alonso de **5** 302

Cologne (Köln; city, Germany)
Adenauer, Konrad **1** 59-61

Cologne, University of (Germany)
Driesch, Hans Adolf Eduard **5** 105

Cologne Cathedral (Germany)
Lochner, Stephan **9** 475

Colomba (novel)
Mérimée, Prosper **10** 517

Colombia, Republic of (nation, South
America)
Gaviria Trujillo, Cesar Augusto
6 242-243
1538-1819: New Granada
Almagro, Diego de **1** 177-178
Quesada, Gonzalo Jiménez de
12 509-510
Mutis, José Celestino **11** 278-279
1819-1830: Gran Colombia
Bolívar, Simón **2** 375-377
Nariño, Antonio **11** 314-315
Santander, Franciso de Paula **13** 475
1831-1885: New Granada Republic
Flores, Juan José **5** 491
Isaacs, Jorge **8** 144
Mosquera, Tomás Cipriano de
11 205-206
Páez, José Antonio **12** 58
1886-1930: Conservative era
Bunau-Varilla, Philippe Jean
3 120-121
Gómez. Castro Laureano **6** 418-419
Leguía y Salcedo, Augusto Bernardi-
no **9** 305-306
Reyes, Rafael **13** 113
Rio Branco, Barão do **13** 177
modern era
Lleras Camargo, Alberto **9** 467
see also Bogotazo
see also Colombian literature

Colombian literature
García Márquez, Gabriel **6** 208-209
Isaacs, Jorge **8** 144
Rivera, José Eustacio **13** 185-186

Colón (city, Panama)
Gorgas, William Crawford **6** 454-455

Colonel Banastre Tarleton (painting)
Reynolds, Joshua **13** 115-116

Colonel Starbottle's Client ... (book)
Harte, Francis Brett **7** 184-185

Colonial Social Science Research Council
(1945-1951)
Carr-Saunders, Alexander Morris
3 333-334

Colonial Stock Act (Great Britain; 1877)
Vogel, Julius **16** 9-10

Colonialism
see Imperialism

Colonna, Giovanni (died 1348), Italian cardinal
Petrarch **12** 259-261

Colonna, Oddone
see Martin V

Colonna, Pietro (died 1326), Italian cardinal
Jacopone da Todi **8** 194

Colonna, Stefano (died after 1347), Italian
noble
Rienzi, Cola di **13** 166-167

Colonna, Vittoria (1492?-1547), Italian
poet
Michelangelo Buonarroti **11** 2-5

Coloquio de los perros, El (book)
Cervantes, Miguel de Saavedra
3 395-398

Color (poems)
Cullen, Countee **4** 333-334

Color and Democracy (book)
Du Bois, William Edward Burghardt
5 116-118

Color Curtain, The (book)
Wright, Richard **16** 401-402

Color-field abstraction (art)
Frankenthaler, Helen **6** 56-57
Newman, Barnett **11** 365
Noland, Kenneth **11** 418-419

Color Purple, The (book)
Walker, Alice Malsenior **16** 59-61

Color vision (physiology)
Helmholtz, Hermann Ludwig Ferdinand
von **7** 268-269
Müller, Johannes Peter **11** 239-240

COLORADAS, MANGAS (1797?-1863),
Apache war chief **10** 194-196
Cochise **4** 128

Colorado (state, United States)
Baca-Barragán, Polly **1** 412-414
Carson, Christopher **3**
Lindsey, Benjamin Barr **9** 425-426
Pike, Zebulon **12** 302-304
Tabor, Horace Austin Warner **15** 70

Colorado, University of (Boulder)
Lewis, Clarence Irving **9** 381
Redfield, Robert **13** 73-74
Rothko, Mark **13** 320-321

Colorado and Montana Smelting Co.
Clark, William Andrews **4** 83-85

Colorado College (Colorado Springs)
Clark, John Maurice **4** 77-78

Colorado Fuel and Iron Co.
Rockefeller, John D. Jr. **13** 225-226

Colorado party (Paraguay)
Morínigo, Higinio **11** 174-175
Stroessner, Alfredo **14** 511-512

Colorado party (Uruguay)
Batlle y Ordóñez, José **2** 58-59
Rivera, Fructuoso **13** 184-185
Terra, Gabriel **15** 154-155

Colorado River (United States)
Ashley, William Henry **1** 333-334
Coronado, Francisco Vásquez de **4** 247
Powell, John Wesley **12** 425-426

Coloratura (opera)
Scarlatti, Pietro Alessandro Gaspare
13 517-518

Colored Association (Boston, Massachusetts)
Walker, David **16** 62-63

Colored National League (United States)
Grimké, Archibald Henry **7** 1-2

Colosseum (Rome)
Martialis, Marcus Valerius **10** 286-287
Titus Flavius Vespasianus **15** 247-248
Vespasian **15** 475-476

Colossi of Memnon (statuary)
Amenhotep III **1** 194-195

Colossians, Letter to the (New Testament
book)
Paul **12** 141-143

Colossus of Maroussi, The (book)
Miller, Henry **11** 26-27

Colquitt, Alfred H. (1824-1894), American
politician
Gordon, John Brown **6** 449-450

COLT, SAMUEL (1814-1862), American
inventor and manufacturer **4** 172-173

Colt Industries (gun firm)
Gatling, Richard Jordan **6** 234-235
Ridgway, Matthew Bunker **13** 160-161

COLTRANE, JOHN (1926-1967), African
American jazz saxophonist **4** 173-174

COLUM, PADRAIC (1881-1972),
Irish-American poet and playwright
4 174-175
Edgeworth, Maria **5** 205-206

COLUMBA, ST. (circa 521-597), Irish monk
and missionary **4** 175-176

COLUMBAN, ST. (circa 543-615), Irish
missionary **4** 176

Columbia (spacecraft)
Armstrong, Neil Alden **1** 304-306

Columbia (warship)
Melville, George Wallace **10** 472

Columbia Broadcasting System (communi-
cations)
Bradley, Ed **2** 478-481
Chung, Connie **4** 47-48
Coughlin, Charles Edward **4** 265-266
Cronkite, Walter Leland Jr. **4** 321-322
Paley, William S. **12** 72-75
Tisch brothers **15** 238-240

Columbia College (New York City)
see Columbia University (New York
City)

Columbia Gramophone Co.
Bell, Alexander Graham **2** 129-131

Columbia Rediviva (ship)
Gray, Robert **6** 508-509

Columbia River (Canada-United States)
Clark, William **4** 82-83
Frémont, John Charles **6** 97-98
Gray, Robert **6** 508-509

Thompson, David **15** 194-195

Columbia, the Gem of the Ocean (tune)
Ives, Charles Edward **8** 159-160

Columbia University (New York City)
anthropology
Benedict, Ruth Fulton **2** 154-155
Boas, Franz **2** 349-351
Frazier, Edward Franklin **6** 77
Kroeber, Alfred Louis **9** 105-106
Linton, Ralph **9** 431
Mead, Margaret **10** 438-440
Applied Social Research, Bureau of
Lazarsfeld, Paul F. **9** 259-260
art
Grosz, George **7** 17-18
biochemistry
Chargaff, Erwin **3** 444-445
biology
Morgan, Thomas Hunt **11** 170-171
Muller, Hermann Joseph
11 238-239
economics
Clark, John Bates **4** 76-77
Clark, John Maurice **4** 77-78
Johnson, Alvin Saunders **8** 293-294
Polanyi, Karl **12** 372
Seligman, Edwin Robert Anderson
14 93-94
education
Lloyd-Jones, Esther McDonald
9 471-472
English and comparative literature
Nicolson, Marjorie Hope
11 384-385
geophysics
Ewing, William Maurice **5** 350-351
history
Baron, Salo Wittmayer **2** 16-17
Beard, Charles Austin **2** 84
Dunning, William Archibald
5 148-149
Malone, Dumas **10** 174-175
Osgood, Herbert Levi **12** 18-19
Robinson, James Harvey **13** 208
Jewish studies
Baron, Salo Wittmayer **2** 16-17
journalism
Freeman, Douglas Southall **6** 91-92
Pulitzer, Joseph **12** 481-482
Law School
Berle, Adolf Augustus Jr. **2** 199-200
Douglas, William Orville **5** 83-85
Ginsburg, Ruth Bader **6** 333-336
Stone, Harlan Fiske **14** 468-470
music
Bartók, Béla **2** 35-36
MacDowell, Edward Alexander
10 87-88
paleontology
Simpson, George Gaylord
14 240-242
philosophy
Cassirer, Ernst **3** 358-359
Dewey, John **4** 520-523
Lewis, Clarence Irving **9** 381

MacIver, Robert Morrison
10 100-101
physics
Fermi, Enrico **5** 422-424
Pupin, Michael Idvorsky **12** 483-484
Rabi, Isidor Isaac **12** 526-527
Szilard, Leo **15** 64-66
Urey, Harold Clayton **15** 394-396
Yukawa, Hideki **16** 481-482
political science
Adler, Felix **1** 63-64
Bentley, Arthur F. **2** 178
Lieber, Francis **9** 401-402
presidents
Barnard, Frederick Augustus Porter
2 9-10
Butler, Nicholas Murray **3** 181
Eisenhower, Dwight David
5 233-236
Johnson, Samuel **8** 314-315
Low, Seth **10** 11-12
psychology
Cattell, James McKeen **3** 376-377
Thorndike, Edward Lee **15** 208-209
sociology
Giddings, Franklin Henry **6** 307-308
Lazarsfeld, Paul F. **9** 259-260
Lynd, Robert Staughton **10** 64-65
Mayo-Smith, Richmond **10** 371-372
Merton, Robert K. **10** 522-523
Mills, C. Wright **11** 35-36
Ogburn, William Fielding **11** 480
Znaniecki, Florian **16** 523-524
Teachers College
Bagley, William Chandler **1** 437-438
Counts, George S. **4** 267-269
Dodge, Grace Hoadley **5** 37-38
Kilpatrick, William H. **9** 1-3
Rugg, Harold **13** 355-357
Russell, James Earl **13** 379-380
Strang, Ruth May **14** 493-494
theology
Kaplan, Mordecai Menahem
8 435-436
trustees
Hewitt, Abram Stevens **7** 371-372

Columbia University Library (New York City)
McKim, Charles Follen **10** 417-418

Columbiad (musical composition)
Heinrich, Anthony Philip **7** 261

Columbiad, The (poem)
Barlow, Joel **2** 6-7

Columbian University (Washington, D.C.)
see George Washington University

Columbianum
see Pennsylvania Academy of the Fine Arts

Columbus, Bartolomé (1445?-1514?), Italian navigator
Columbus, Christopher **4** 176-179

COLUMBUS, CHRISTOPHER (1451-1506), Italian navigator, discoverer of America
4 176-179

America named
Waldseemüller, Martin **16** 56
in art and literature
Irving, Washington **8** 141-143
Taft, Lorado **15** 75-76
influence of
Magellan, Ferdinand **10** 126-127
Ponce de León, Juan **12** 391-392
Velázquez de Cuéllar, Diego **15** 459
Vespucci, Amerigo **15** 476-478
influenced by
Ailly, Pierre d' **1** 94
voyages
Ferdinand V **5** 417-418
Isabella I **8** 144-145
Morison, Samuel Eliot **11** 175-176

Columbus, Diego (1450?-1515), Italian voyager and administrator
Columbus, Christopher **4** 176-179

Columbus, Diego (circa 1480-1526), Spanish colonial administrator
Velázquez de Cuéllar, Diego **15** 459

Columbus (city, New Mexico)
Carranza, Venustiano **3** 321-322
Villa, Pancho **15** 495-496

Columbus (city, Ohio)
Gladden, Washington **6** 356-357

Columbus Hospital (Chicago)
Cabrini, Frances Xavier **3** 205

Columbus March and Hymn (musical composition)
Paine, John Knowles **12** 65

Columella (flourished 1st century A.D.), Spanish writer
Celsus, Aulus Cornelius **3** 393

Column (sculpture)
Gabo, Naum **6** 158-159

Colville Reservation (Washington)
Joseph **8** 358-359

COLWELL, RITA R. (born 1934), American marine microbiologist **4** 179-180

Comanche Indians (North America)
Anza, Juan Bautista de **1** 254-255
Fitzpatrick, Thomas **5** 474-475
Goodnight, Charles **6** 439
Linton, Ralph **9** 431
Miles, Nelson Appleton **11** 16-17
Parker, Quanah **12** 109-112
Smith, Jedediah S. **14** 294-295

Combat (newspaper)
Camus, Albert **3** 255-257

Combat of Carnival and Lent (painting)
Bruegel, Pieter the Elder **3** 65-67

Combat of Love and Chastity (painting)
Perugino **12** 245-246

Combattimento di Tancredi e Clorinda, II (cantata)
Monteverdi, Claudio Giovanni Antonio
11 126-128

Combes, Justin Louis Émile (1835-1921), French politician
Jaurès, Jean **8** 226-227

Combine (art)
Rauschenberg, Robert **13** 52-53

Combine (farm machine)
McCormick, Cyrus Hall **10** 400-401

Combines Investigation Act (Canada; 1910)
King, William Lyon Mackenzie **9** 25-26

Combustion (chemistry)
Berthollet, Claude Louis **2** 229-230
Boyle, Robert **2** 469-471
Cavendish, Henry **3** 383-384
Hooke, Robert **7** 475
Lavoisier, Antoine Laurent **9** 241-244, 365
Stahl, Georg Ernst **14** 392-393

Come again, sweet love (song)
Dowland, John **5** 90

Come and Get It (novel)
Ferber, Edna **5** 413

Come In (poem)
Frost, Robert Lee **6** 130-133

Come Up from the Fields Father (poem)
Whitman, Walt **16** 249-251

Comedia do viuvo (poem)
Vicente, Gil **15** 479-480

Comedian as the Letter C, The (poem)
Stevens, Wallace **14** 443-445

Comedians
see Actors and entertainers

Comedians, The (novel)
Greene, Graham **6** 523-524

Comedias (plays)
Calderón, Pedro **3** 221-222

Comédie Française (French state theater)
Lesage, Alain René **9** 353-354
Offenbach, Jacques **11** 478-479

Comédie humaine, La (book; Balzac)
Balzac, Honoré de **1** 478-480
Proust, Marcel **12** 465-467

Comedy (literary form)
Greek and Latin
Aristophanes **1** 293-294
Menander **10** 477-478
Plautus **12** 348-350
Terence **15** 146-148
of menace
Pinter, Harold **12** 317-318
satire
Beaumarchais, Pierre August Caron de **2** 93-94
Beaumont, Francis **2** 95
Goldsmith, Oliver **6** 411-413
Jonson, Ben **8** 343-345
Molière **11** 86-88
see also Black comedy; Commedia dell'arte; Theater of the Absurd

Comedy (sculpture)
Rush, William **13** 365-366

Comedy, The (play)
Kazantzakis, Nikos **8** 466-468

Comedy of Errors, The (play; Shakespeare)
Plaatje, Solomon Tshekisho **12** 341-342
Plautus **12** 348-350
Shakespeare, William **14** 142-145

Comedy of humours (literary form)
Chapman, George **3** 440-441
Jonson, Ben **8** 343-345

Comedy of manners (literary form)
Benavente y Martinez, Jacinto **2** 146-147
Congreve, William **4** 200-201
Terence **15** 146-148
Tyler, Royall **15** 371-372

Comedy of the Asses, The (play)
Plautus **12** 348-350

Comendador Mendoza, El (novel)
Valera y Alcalá Galiano, Juan **15** 403

COMENIUS, JOHN AMOS (1592-1670), Moravian theologian and educational reformer **4** 180-181

Comet (astronomy)
Dias de Novais, Bartolomeu **4** 533-534
Halley, Edmund **7** 88-89
Lovell, Alfred Charles Bernard **10** 8-9
Mitchell, Maria **11** 61
Oort, Jan Hendrik **11** 523-524

Comgall, St. (Circa 520-circa 602), Irish abbot
Columban **4** 176

Comic Theatre, The (play)
Goldoni, Carlo **6** 408-409

Comics (cartoons)
Hearst, William Randolph **7** 243-244
Lichtenstein, Roy **9** 398-399
Luks, George Benjamin **10** 38-39
Schulz, Charles M. **14** 38-39

COMINES, PHILIPPE DE (circa 1445-1511), French chronicler **4** 181
Charles the Bold **3** 467-469
Louis XI **9** 526-528

Coming Ham, The (book)
Merezhkovsky, Dmitry Sergeyevich **10** 515-516

Coming of Age in Samoa (book)
Mead, Margaret **10** 438-440

Coming of the Post-Industrial Society, The (book)
Bell, Daniel **2** 132-133

Coming Storm (painting)
Inness, George **8** 123-124

Coming Up for Air (book)
Orwell, George **12** 14-15

Coming World Civilization, The (book)
Hocking, William Ernest **7** 428-429

Comintern
see International, Third

Comische Erzählungen (book)
Wieland, Christoph Martin **16** 260-261

Comité de l'Unité (Togo)
Olympio, Sylvanus E. **11** 506-507

Comité Dupleix (French colonial organization)
Bonvalot, Pierre Gabriel Édouard **2** 396

Comité National des Métis (political organization; Canada)
Riel, Louis **13** 163-164

COMMAGER, HENRY STEELE (born 1902), American historian, textbook author, and editor **4** 181-183
Morison, Samuel Eliot **11** 175-176
Sullivan, Louis Henri **15** 27-28

Comme on voit sur la branche (poem)
Ronsard, Pierre de **13** 271-273

Commedia (Dante)
see Divine Comedy, The

Commedia dell'arte (Italian literary form)
Goldoni, Carlo **6** 408-409
Sennett, Mack **14** 108-109
Severini, Gino **14** 122

Commedie (literary collection)
Svevo, Italo **15** 47-48

Commentaries (book; Ghiberti)
Giotto **6** 342-345
Vasari, Giorgio **15** 442-443

Commentaries (book; Kent)
Eaton, Dorman Bridgman **5** 190-191

Commentaries (Caesar)
see Gallic War, Commentaries on the

Commentaries on the Laws of England (book)
Blackstone, William **2** 310-311

Commentaries on Virgil (book; Petrarch)
Martini, Simone **10** 298-299

Commentary (magazine)
Greenberg, Clement **6** 521-523

Commentary on Plato's Symposium (Ficino)
Bembo, Pietro **2** 144-145

Commento all'Inferno (book)
Boccaccio, Giovanni **2** 351-353

Commerce (economics)
see Banking; Business and industry; Economics; Free trade; Stock market; Tariff; Transportation

Commerce, U.S. Department of
Brown, Ronald H. **3** 44-47

Commercial Academy (Prague)
Beneš, Edward **2** 155-157

Commercial law (United States)
Benjamin, Judah Philip **2** 163-164
Cardozo, Benjamin Nathan **3** 288-290

Commercial Review of the South and Southwest (magazine)
De Bow, James Dunwoody Brownson **4** 441-442

Committee for a SANE Nuclear Policy (SANE; United States activist group)
Spock, Benjamin **14** 383-385

Committee for Industrial Organization
see Congress of Industrial Organizations

Committee for Non-Violent Action (United States politics)
Muste, Abraham Johannes **11** 276-277

Committee for State Security (KGB; Union of Soviet Socialist Republics)
Andropov, Iury Vladimirovich **1** 233-234

Committee of 15 (United States politics)
Conkling, Roscoe **4** 201-202

Committee of Fifty-one (New York political group)
Jay, John **8** 230-232

Committee of Public Safety (French Revolution)
Hébert, Jacques René **7** 247-248
Napoleon I **11** 306-310
Robespierre, Maximilien François Marie Isidore de **13** 199-201

Committee of Safety (American Revolution)
Pendleton, Edmund **12** 197-198

Committee of Ten (NEA)
Eliot, Charles William **5** 254

Committee of Union and Progress
see Young Turks (Ottoman Empire)

Committee on Youth Organization (Ghana)
Nkrumah, Kwame **11** 408-410

Committees of Correspondence (United States history)
Dunmore, 4th Earl of **5** 147
Putnam, Israel **12** 491-492
Sherman, Roger **14** 185-186
Wilson, James **16** 323-324

Commodus, Lucius Aelius Aurelius
(161-192), Roman emperor 180-192
Galen **6** 178-180
Marcus Aurelius Antoninus **10** 243-245

Commodus, Lucius Ceionius
see Verus, Lucius Aurelius

Common Asphodel, The (poems)
Graves, Robert Ranke **6** 504-506

Common Cause (lobbying group; United States)
Gardner, John W. **6** 211-213

Common law (legal system)
Bentham, Jeremy **2** 176-178
Blackstone, William **2** 310-311
Holmes, Oliver Wendell Jr. **7** 458-459
Shaw, Lemuel **14** 164-165

Common Market (European Economic Community)
and African countries
Luns, Joseph **10** 46-47
Belgium
Davignon **4** 410-411
British entry
De Gaulle, Charles André Joseph Marie **4** 463-465

Heath, Edward Richard George **7** 244-246
Jenkins, Roy Harris **8** 244-245
Macmillan, Harold **10** 112-113
Pym, Francis **12** 494-495
Spaak, Paul Henri **14** 359-360
France and Germany
Adenauer, Konrad **1** 59-61
Barre, Raymond **2** 19-20
Camdessus, Michel **3** 244-246
De Gaulle, Charles André Joseph Marie **4** 463-465
Delors, Jacques **4** 484-486
Kelly, Petra **8** 486-487
Krupp **9** 109-111
Monnet, Jean **11** 109-110
Schuman, Robert **14** 41
Great Britain
Thatcher, Margaret Hilda **15** 165-168
Luxembourg
Thorn, Gaston **15** 207-208
Portuguese entry
Soares, Mário **14** 315-316
Spain
González Márquez, Felipe **6** 429-431
United States supporters
Ball, George **1** 470-471
Yugoslavia
Owen, David Anthony Llewellyn **12** 37-39

Common Market (Latin America)
Plaza Lasso, Galo **12** 350-351

Common Reader, The (essays)
Woolf, Virginia Stephen **16** 381-382

Common School Journal (periodical)
Mann, Horace **10** 202-204

Common Sense (pamphlet; Paine)
Paine, Thomas **12** 66-67
Rush, Benjamin **13** 364-365

Common sense philosophy
see Scottish school of common sense

Common Story, A (novel)
Goncharov, Ivan Aleksandrovich **6** 424

COMMONER, BARRY (born 1917), American biologist and environmental activist **4** 183-185

Commonplace (stories)
Rossetti, Christina Georgina **13** 307-308

Commonplace Book (book)
Milton, John **11** 43-46

COMMONS, JOHN ROGERS (1862-1945), American historian **4** 185

Commonweal of Christ
see Coxey's Army

Commonwealth (England; 1649-1653)
Bunyan, John **3** 128-129
Charles II **3** 452-454
Monck, George **11** 96-97
Vane, Henry **15** 425-426

see also Civil War, English-Puritan Revolution (1648-1651)

Commonwealth Act (Australia; 1900)
Barton, Edmund **2** 39-40

Commonwealth Bank (Australia)
Bruce of Melbourne, 1st Viscount **3** 61-62
Fisher, Andrew **5** 462

Commonwealth, British
see British Commonwealth of Nations

Commonwealth Constitution (Australia; 1901)
Hughes, William Morris **8** 21-22

Commonwealth of Independent States
Yeltsin, Boris Nikolaevich **16** 449-452

Commonwealth-Edison Co. (electric firm)
Insull, Samuel **8** 130

Commotio (musical composition)
Nielsen, Carl August **11** 388-389

Communal Pact (India; 1924)
Das, Chitta Ranjan **4** 401-402

Communal sects (religion)
Noyes, John Humphrey **11** 437-438
Rapp, George **13** 42-43

Commune of Paris
1789-1795
Danton, Georges Jacques **4** 391-393
Hébert, Jacques René **7** 247-248
Louis XVI **9** 534-535
1871
Blanc, Louis **2** 318-319
Clemenceau, Georges **4** 99-101
Courbet, Jean Desiré Gustave **4** 271-273
Crémazie, Octave **4** 305-306
Taine, Hippolyte Adolphe **15** 82-83
Thiers, Louis Adolphe **15** 181-182

Communications industry
see Business and industrial leaders—communications industry; Radio; Telegraph; Television

Communion (religion)
see Eucharist

Communion of the Apostles (painting)
Ribera, Jusepe de **13** 122-123

Communism (social system)
advocates
see Communist party
containment policy (United States)
Acheson, Dean Gooderham **1** 37-38
Dulles, John Foster **5** 134-135
Forrestal, James Vincent **6** 14
in literature
Brecht, Bertolt **2** 512-514
Koestler, Arthur **9** 71-73
Kuo Mo-jo **9** 133-134
opponents (Catholic)
Leo XIII **9** 334-336
Mannix, Daniel **10** 210
Paul VI **12** 146-148
Santamaria, Bartholomew Augustine **13** 473-474

Spellman, Francis Joseph **14** 367
Stepinac, Alojzije **14** 433-435
opponents (Guinea)
Touré, Sékou **15** 275-277
opponents (South Africa)
Vorster, Balthazar Johannes **16** 30-32
opponents (United States)
Clark, Mark Wayne **4** 80-81
Coughlin, Charles Edward **4** 265-266
Dos Passos, John Roderigo **5** 69-71
Kennan, George F. **8** 496-498
MacArthur, Douglas **10** 76-78
MacLeish, Archibald **10** 109-110
Nixon, Richard Milhous **11** 401-404
Thomas, Norman Mattoon **15** 191-192
theory
Althusser, Louis **1** 182-183
Babeuf, François Noel **1** 412
Engels, Friedrich **5** 286-288
Marx, Karl **10** 304-308
Sorel, Georges **14** 347-348
see also Marxism; Socialism, state

Communist China
see China, People's Republic of

Communist International
see International, Third (Comintern)

Communist Labor party (United States)
Reed, John Silas **13** 76-77

Communist League (Brussels)
Marx, Karl **10** 304-308

Communist Manifesto (book; Marx-Engels)
Engels, Friedrich **5** 286-288
Leo XIII **9** 334-336
Marx, Karl **10** 304-308

Communist party
Afghanistan
Karmal, Babrak **8** 449-451
Albania
Alia, Ramiz **1** 159
Hoxha, Enver **8** 1-3
Argentina
Sábato, Ernesto **13** 399-400
Australia
Lang, John Thomas **9** 192-193
Menzies, Robert Gordon **10** 510-511
Brazil
Amado, Jorge **1** 189-190
Prestes, Luiz Carlos **12** 442-444
Bulgaria
Dimitrov, Georgi **5** 11-13
Zhivkov, Todor **16** 510-512
Burma
Nu, U **11** 439-441
Cambodia
Heng Samrin **7** 283-285
Pol Pot **12** 382-384
Sihanouk, Norodom **14** 222-223
China
see Communist party (China)
Costa Rica

Betancourt, Rómulo **2** 237-238
Ferrer, José Figuéres **5** 428-429
Cuba
Batista y Zaldívar, Fulgencio **2** 57-58
Castro Ruz, Fidel **3** 365-368
Czechoslovakia
Beneš, Edward **2** 155-157
Dubček, Alexander **5** 112-113
Gottwald, Klement **6** 464-466
Husák, Gustáv **8** 59-61
Slánský, Rudolf Salzmann **14** 270-271
England
Cole, George Douglas Howard **4** 146-147
Haldane, John Burdon Sanderson **7** 70-71
Orwell, George **12** 14-15
France
see Communist party (France)
Germany
Baum, Herbert **2** 66-73
Hindenburg, Paul Ludwig Hans von Beneckendorff und von **7** 400-401
Luxemburg, Rosa **10** 55-56
Radek, Karl Bernardovich **12** 536-537
Ulbricht, Walter **15** 383-384
Zetkin, Clara **16** 504-505
Germany (East)
Honecker, Erich **7** 471-472
Ulbricht, Walter **15** 383-384
Guatemala
Arévalo, Juan José **1** 285-286
Hungary
Horthy de Nagybánya, Nicholas **7** 510-512
Kádár, János **8** 402-403
Lukács, Gyorgy **10** 37-38
Nagy, Imre **11** 292-293
Szent-Györgyi, Albert von **15** 62-64
India
Menon, Vengalil Krishnan Krishna **10** 507-509
Indonesia
Sukarno **15** 18-20
Iran
Mohammad Reza Shah Pahlavi **11** 75-76
Italy
Gramsci, Antonio **6** 488-489
Nono, Luigi **11** 420-421
Pavese, Cesare **12** 154-155
Pius XII **12** 339-340
Silone, Ignazio **14** 231-232
Togliatti, Palmiro **15** 253-254
Victor Emmanuel III **15** 484-485
Vittorini, Elio **16** 2-3
Laos
Souvanna Phouma **14** 357-358
Mexico
Kahlo, Frida **8** 406-407
North Korea
Kim Il-sung **9** 4-6
Paraguay

Stroessner, Alfredo **14** 511-512
Philippines
Macapagal, Diosdado P. **10** 74-76
Magsaysay, Ramon **10** 130-131
Marcos, Ferdinand **10** 240-242
Poland
Gomulka, Wladislaw **6** 422-424
Jaruzelski, Wojciech Witold **8** 223-225
Romania
Ceausescu, Nicolae **3** 387-388
Iliescu, Ion **8** 111-112
South Africa
First, Ruth **5** 453-454
Spain
Ibárruri Gómez, Dolores **8** 88-90
Vallejo, César Abraham **15** 408-409
United States
see Communist party (United States)
Union of Soviet Socialist Republics
see Communist party (Union of Soviet Socialist Republics)
Vietnam
Diem, Ngo Dinh **5** 6-7
Do Muoi **5** 53-55
Dong, Pham Van **5** 57-59
Giap, Vo Nguyen **6** 297-299
Ho Chi Minh **7** 426-428
Le Duan **9** 278-280
Linh, Nguyen Van **9** 426-427
Thieu, Nguyen Van **15** 182-183
Truong Chinh **15** 319-320
Yugoslavia
Djilas, Milovan **5** 34
Tito, Marshal **15** 244-246
Zanzibar
Nyerere, Julius Kamberage **11** 447-449

Communist party (China)
and Kuomintang
Chiang Kai-shek **3** 510-513
Ho Chi Minh **7** 426-428
Sun Yat-sen **15** 35-39, 293
and United States policy
Dulles, John Foster **5** 134-135
Eisenhower, Dwight David **5** 233-236
Forrestal, James Vincent **6** 14
MacArthur, Douglas **10** 76-78
Truman, Harry S. **15** 314-316
founded
Ch'en Tu-hsiu **3** 501-502
Hu Shih **8** 63-65
Li Ta-chao **9** 447
Mao Zedong **10** 225-227
internationalist group
Wang Ming **16** 103-104
leaders
Chou En-lai **4** 20-22
Chu Teh **4** 54-55
Deng Xiaoping **4** 498-500
Jiang Qing **8** 256-260
Jiang Zemin **8** 260-261
Li Peng **9** 433-435
Lin Piao **9** 429-430

Liu Shao-Ch'i **9** 453-455
Mao Zedong **10** 225-227
Wang Ming **16** 103-104
Xiang Jingyu **16** 421-422
Zhao Ziyang **16** 508-509
reporters on
Snow, Edgar **14** 312-313

Communist party (France)
leaders
Thorez, Maurice **15** 206-207
opponents
Houphouët-Boigny, Felix **7** 519-520
Merleau-Ponty, Maurice **10** 518
Rolland, Romain **13** 260
Schuman, Robert **14** 41
supporters
Aragon, Louis **1** 271-272
Breton, André **2** 519-520
Camus, Albert **3** 255-257
France, Anatole **6** 39-40
Ho Chi Minh **7** 426-428
Joliot-Curie, Jean Frédéric
8 327-328
Malraux, André **10** 178-180

Communist party (Union of Soviet Socialist
Republics)
break-up of
Yeltsin, Boris Nikolaevich
16 449-452
Central Committee
Beria, Lavrenty Pavlovich **2** 192-193
Chicherin, Georgi Vasilyevich
3 516-517
Dzerzhinsky, Felix Edmundovich
5 173-174
Litvinov, Maxim Maximovich
9 451-452
Molotov, Vyacheslav Mikhailovich
11 89-90
Radek, Karl Bernardovich
12 536-537
Zhukov, Georgi Konstantinovich
16 512-513
formation
Lenin, Vladimir Ilich **9** 323-326
Stalin, Joseph **14** 393-396
Trotsky, Leon **15** 302-305
members
Afinogenov, Aleksandr Nikolaevich
1 72-73
Dimitrov, Georgi **5** 11-13
Semenov, Nikolai Nikolaevich
14 101
Sholokhov, Mikhail Aleksandrovich
14 203-204
Simonov, Konstantin Mikhailovich
14 239-240
Politboro (Presidium)
Biryukova, Aleksandra Pavlovna
2 285-287
Gorbachev, Mikhail Sergeevich
6 441-444
Ligachev, Yegor Kuz'mich **9** 404-406
Shevardnadze, Eduard Amvrosevich
14 191-193
Politburo (Presidium)

Andropov, Iury Vladimirovich
1 233-234
Brezhnev, Leonid Ilich **2** 527-528
Bukharin, Nikolai Ivanovich
3 112-113
Bulganin, Nikolai **3** 118-119
Chernenko, Konstantin Ustinovich
3 503-504
Frunze, Mikhail Vasilievich **6** 134
Gorbachev, Mikhail Sergeevich
6 441-444
Gromyko, Andrei Andreevich **7** 9-11
Kamenev, Lev Borisovich **8** 417-418
Khrushchev, Nikita Sergeevich
8 539-540
Konev, Ivan Stefanovich **9** 81-82
Kosygin, Aleksei Nikolaevich
9 90-91
Malenkov, Georgy Maksimil-
ianovich **10** 168
Yeltsin, Boris Nikolaevich
16 449-452
Zinoviev, Grigori Evseevich
16 521-522
science and
Lysenko, Trofim Denisovich **10** 71

Communist party (United States)
government investigations
Chambers, Whittaker **3** 416-417
Hiss, Alger **7** 413-415
Hoover, John Edgar **7** 485-487
Lie, Trygve Halvdan **9** 400-401
McCarthy, Joseph Raymond
10 388-389
Palmer, Alexander Mitchell
12 77-78
see also Red scare (United States)
members
Bloor, Ella Reeve **2** 338-340
Browder, Earl Russell **3** 30-31
Chambers, Whittaker **3** 416-417
Davis, Angela **4** 412-413
Du Bois, William Edward Burghardt
5 116-118
Eastman, Max **5** 187-188
Flynn, Elizabeth Gurley **5** 496-497
Foster, William Zebulon **6** 27-28
Katayama, Sen **8** 457
Odets, Clifford **11** 470-471
Wright, Richard **16** 401-402
opponents
Dubinsky, David **5** 114-115
Eastman, Max **5** 187-188
Murray, Philip **11** 264-265
Thompson, Dorothy **15** 195-196
Wayne, John **16** 150-151
Welch, Robert **16** 184-185

Communist Revolution (1949)
see Civil War, Chinese

Communists, The (novel)
Aragon, Louis **1** 271-272

Community (book)
MacIver, Robert Morrison **10** 100-101

Community Church of New York (established 1919)
Holmes, John Haynes **7** 456-457

Community of the Peace People (peace
group, Northern Ireland)
Corrigan and Williams **4** 251-253

Community Service Organization (CSO)
Chavez, Cesar **3** 486-487

Communium naturalium (book)
Bacon, Roger **1** 425-427

COMNENA, ANNA (1083-1148), Byzantine princess and historian **4** 185-186
Bohemund, I **2**

Comonfort, Ignacio (1812-1863), Mexican
statesman, president 1855
Álvarez, Juan **1** 184-185
Juárez, Benito **8** 369-372
Lerdo de Tejada, Miguel **9** 351-352

Comorin, Cape (Southern India)
Ala-ud-din **1** 102-103

Compagnie des Indes (French firm)
Dupleix **5** 153

Compagnie d'Occident (French firm)
Law, John **9** 244-245

Compagnie du Sénégal, La (book)
Ly, Abdoulaye **10** 60

Compagno, Il (novel)
Pavese, Cesare **12** 154-155

Compagnon du tour de France, Le (novel)
Sand, George **13** 459-461

Companions (Macedonian nobility)
Philip II **12** 269-271

Company of New France (trading co.)
Charnisay, Charles de Menou
3 470-471

Company of One Hundred Associates
(French trade co.)
Champlain, Samuel de **3** 419-421

Company town (United States)
Lowell, Francis Cabot **10** 13-14
Pullman, George Mortimer **12** 482-483

Comparative anatomy (science)
Cuvier, Georges Léopold **4** 357-359
Leeuwenhoek, Anton van **9** 300-301
Malpighi, Marcello **10** 176-178-126
Müller, Johannes Peter **11** 239-240
Owen, Richard **12** 39
Swammerdam, Jan **15** 48-49

Compartment, The (film script)
Pinter, Harold **12** 317-318

Compass (painting)
Léger, Fernand **9** 302-303

**Compendious Dictionary of the English
Language, A** (book)
Webster, Noah **16** 164-166

Competition (economics)
Carnegie, Andrew **3** 309-312, 378
Chernyshevsky, Nikolai Gavrilovich
3 504-505
Clark, John Bates **4** 76-77

Clark, John Maurice **4** 77-78
Ferguson, Adam **5** 420-421
Knight, Frank Hyneman **9** 58-59
Spencer, Herbert **14** 369-370
see also Business and industry; Laissez faire (economics)

Compiègne (town, France)
Joan of Arc **8** 264-265

Compiègne, Treaty of (1918)
Erzberger, Matthias **5** 319-320

Compilaçam (literary collection)
Vicente, Gil **15** 479-480

Complaintes (songs)
Laforgue, Jules **9** 160-161

Complaints (poems)
Spenser, Edmund **14** 373-376

Complaisant Lover, The (play)
Greene, Graham **6** 523-524

Compleat Angler, The (book)
Walton, Izaak **16** 90-91

Compleat View of Episcopacy (book)
Chauncy, Charles **3** 485-486

Complete English Tradesman, The (book)
Defoe, Daniel **4** 457-459

Complex numbers (mathematics)
Cardano, Geronimo **3** 285-286
Cauchy, Augustin Louis **3** 378-380
Lobachevskii, Nikolai Ivanovich **9** 472-474
Riemann, Georg Friedrich Bernard **13** 164-165

Complex variable (mathematics)
Cauchy, Augustin Louis **3** 378-380
Riemann, Georg Friedrich Bernard **13** 164-165

Complexity and Contradiction in Architecture (book)
Venturi, Robert **15** 461-463

Composers
see Musicians-composers

Composition (painting series)
Kandinsky, Wassily **8** 420-422

Composition (sculpture)
Moore, Henry **11** 146-148

Composition 45 (painting)
Staël, Nicolas de **14** 392

Compromise of 1820
see Missouri Compromise

Compromise of 1850 (United States history)
opponents (north)
Benton, Thomas Hart **2** 178-179
Chase, Salmon Portland **3** 473-475
Greeley, Horace **6** 515-517
Lincoln, Abraham **9** 415-418
Seward, William Henry **14** 124-125
Stevens, Thaddeus **14** 442-443
Sumner, Charles **15** 30-31
Wilmot, David **16** 312-313
opponents (south)

Calhoun, John Caldwell **3** 226-228
supporters (north)
Cass, Lewis **3** 355-356
Clay, Henry **4** 94-96
Douglas, Stephen Arnold **5** 80-82
Evarts, William Maxwell **5** 340-341
Fillmore, Millard **5** 447-448
Pierce, Franklin **12** 300-301
Webster, Daniel **16** 162-164
supporters (south)
Davis, Jefferson **4** 416-418
Forbes, John **5** 507-508
Hill, Benjamin Harvey **7** 386-387
Houston, Samuel **7** 526-527
Rhett, Robert Barnwell **13** 120
Stephens, Alexander Hamilton **14** 429-430
Tyler, John **15** 368-369

Compromise of 1867
see Austro-Hungarian Compromise (1867)

Compromise of 1877 (United States history)
Lamar, Lucius Quintus Cincinnatus **9** 170-171

Compson family (literary characters)
Faulkner, William **5** 395-397

COMPTON, ARTHUR HOLLY (1892-1962), American physicist **4** 186-188
Fermi, Enrico **5** 422-424
Millikan, Robert Andrews **11** 33-35
Wilson, Charles Thomson Rees **16** 317-318

Compton, Henry (1632-1713), English bishop
Blair, James **2** 315-316
Mary II **10** 309-310

Compton effect (physics)
Bothe, Walther **2** 438-439
Compton, Arthur Holly **4** 186-188
Schrödinger, Erwin **14** 31-33

Computers and calculating machines
Babbage, Charles **1** 407-408
Bush, Vannevar **3** 169-171
Cage, John **3** 211-214
Cray, Seymour **4** 301-303
Hopper, Grace **7** 498-500
Jobs, Steven **8** 265-267
Lanier, Jaron **9** 198-199
Leibniz, Gottfried Wilhelm von **9** 307-310
Napier, John **11** 306
Noyce, Robert **11** 436-437
Olivetti, Adriano **11** 501-502
Packard, David **12** 54-56
Shannon, Claude Elwood **14** 153-154
Turing, Alan Mathison **15** 349-350
Von Neumann, John **16** 27-28
Wang, An **16** 93-95
applications of
Hounsfield, Godfrey **7** 517-519
used to create art
Gates, William Henry III **6** 232-234

Holzer, Jenny **7** 462-463

Computer industry
see Business and industrial leaders—computer industry

Computerized axial tomography (CAT scan)
Hounsfield, Godfrey **7** 517-519

Computing-Tabulating-Recording Co. (industry firm)
Watson, Thomas J. **16** 140

Comrade (film)
Sennett, Mack **14** 108-109

COMSTOCK, ANTHONY (1844-1915), American antivice crusader **4** 188-189

COMSTOCK, HENRY TOMPKINS PAIGE (1820-1870), American gold prospector **4** 189

Comstock Lode (silver deposit, Nevada)
Comstock, Henry Tompkins Paige **4** 189
Daly, Marcus **4** 379-380
Hearst, George **7** 242
Mackay, John William **10** 101-102

COMTE, AUGUSTE (1798-1857), French philosopher **4** 189-191
influence of
Buckle, Henry Thomas **3** 95-96
Childe, Vere Gordon **3** 521-522
Clemenceau, Georges **4** 99-101
Dewey, John **4** 520-523
Eliot, George **5** 254-256
Lévy-Bruhl, Lucien **9** 374-375
Martineau, Harriet **10** 296-297
Maurras, Charles Marie Photius **10** 350-351
Mill, John Stuart **11** 21-23
Sarton, George **13** 490-491
influenced by
Adams, Henry Brooks **1** 45-47
Díaz, José de la Cruz Porfirio **4** 534-536
Geddes, Patrick **6** 246-247
Saint-Simon, Comte de **13** 436-437
Vico, Giambattista **15** 480-481

Comte de Monte-Cristo, Le (novel)
Dumas, Alexandre **5** 136-138

Comte Ory, Le (opera)
Rossini, Gioacchino **13** 311-312

Comtesse de Tende (novel)
La Fayette, Comtesse de **9** 150-151

Comus (masque)
Arne, Thomas Augustine **1** 307-308

Comus (play; Milton)
Ford, Paul Leicester **6** 9-10
Milton, John **11** 43-46

Comyn, John (died 1306), Scottish statesman
Robert I **13** 192-194

CONABLE, BARBER B., JR. (born 1922), head of the World Bank (1986-1991) **4** 191-192

Conakat
see Confédération des Associations du Katanga

CONANT, JAMES BRYANT (1893-1978), American chemist and educator **4** 192-193

Conca, Sebastiano (1680-1764), Italian painter
Mengs, Anton Raphael **10** 505

Concentration camp (detention center)
Germany
Bettelheim, Bruno **2** 245-246
Goebbels, Joseph Paul **6** 384-385
Himmler, Heinrich **7** 398-399
Hitler, Adolf **7** 417-420
Sachs, Nelly **13** 411-412
South Africa
Milner, Alfred **11** 38-39
United States
Hoover, John Edgar **7** 485-487
Warren, Earl **16** 117-120

Concentration Camp Essen (artwork)
Beuys, Joseph **2** 246-248

Concepción (ship)
Magellan, Ferdinand **10** 126-127

Conceptual analysis (philosophy)
Driesch, Hans Adolf Eduard **5** 105
Lewis, Clarence Irving **9** 381
Moore, George Edward **11** 146

Concerning Ancient Myths (poem)
Leopardi, Giacomo **9** 344-345

Concerning Hired Companions (satire)
Lucian **10** 25-26

Concerning the Cause, Principle, and One (book)
Bruno, Giordano **3** 75-76

Concerning the End for Which God Created the World
Edwards, Jonathan **5** 220-222

Concert champêtre (painting; Giorgione)
Manet, Édouard **10** 193-194

Concert of United Prayer ... (religious revival)
Edwards, Jonathan **5** 220-222

Concert, The (painting)
Vermeer, Jan **15** 466-467

Concert, The (painting; Titian)
Giorgione **6** 340-341
Titian **15** 242-244

Concert with Artillery (cartoon)
Berlioz, Louis Hector **2** 203-205

Concerto (musical form)
for cello
Dvořák, Antonin **5** 168-169
Ginastera, Alberto Evaristo **6** 328-329
Shostakovich, Dmitri Dmitrievich **14** 204-205
Walton, William Turner **16** 92-93
for clarinet

Weber, Carl Maria Friedrich Ernst von **16** 156-157
for double bass
Henze, Hans Werner **7** 314
for flute and harp
Mozart, Wolfgang Amadeus **11** 218-221
for harp
Ginastera, Alberto Evaristo **6** 328-329
for harpsichord
Falla, Manuel de **5** 372-373
Haydn, Franz Joseph **7** 219-221
Poulenc, Francis **12** 414-415
for horns
Chávez, Carlos **3** 486
for orchestra
Arne, Thomas Augustine **1** 307-308
Bartók, Béla **2** 35-36
Berg, Alban **2** 186-187
Carter, Elliott Cook Jr. **3** 338-339
Henze, Hans Werner **7** 314
Lutoslawski, Witold **10** 52-53
Stravinsky, Igor Fedorovich **14** 502-506
Tippett, Michael Kemp **15** 234-235
Webern, Anton **16** 160-162
for organ
Gabrieli, Giovanni **6** 161-162
Hanson, Howard **7** 135-136
Haydn, Franz Joseph **7** 219-221
Hindemith, Paul **7** 399-400
Poulenc, Francis **12** 414-415
for piano
Barber, Samuel **1** 500-501
Barenboim, Daniel **2** 3-4
Bartók, Béla **2** 35-36
Beethoven, Ludwig van **2** 114-117
Bennett, Richard Rodney **2** 172
Brahms, Johannes **2** 490-492
Busoni, Ferruccio Benvenuto **3** 173-174
Carter, Elliott Cook Jr. **3** 338-339
Chávez, Carlos **3** 486
Chopin, Frédéric François **4** 16-18
Copland, Aaron **4** 227-228
Gershwin, George **6** 284-285
Ginastera, Alberto Evaristo **6** 328-329
Hanson, Howard **7** 135-136
Haydn, Franz Joseph **7** 219-221
Henze, Hans Werner **7** 314
Khachaturian, Aram Ilich **8** 530-531
Liszt, Franz **9** 445-447
MacDowell, Edward Alexander **10** 87-88
Malipiero, Gian Francesco **10** 171
Martinu, Bohuslav **10** 299-300
Mendelssohn, Moses **10** 488-489
Mozart, Wolfgang Amadeus **11** 218-221
Paderewski, Ignace Jan **12** 56-57
Poulenc, Francis **12** 414-415
Prokofiev, Sergei Sergeevich **12** 458-460

Rachmaninov, Sergei Vasilievich **12** 531-532
Saint-Saëns, Charles Camille **13** 435-436
Stravinsky, Igor Fedorovich **14** 502-506
Tchaikovsky, Peter Ilyich **15** 130-132
for viola
Bartók, Béla **2** 35-36
Piston, Walter **12** 327-328
Walton, William Turner **16** 92-93
for violin
Bartók, Béla **2** 35-36
Berg, Alban **2** 186-187
Brahms, Johannes **2** 490-492
Chávez, Carlos **3** 486
Ginastera, Alberto Evaristo **6** 328-329
Haydn, Franz Joseph **7** 219-221
Henze, Hans Werner **7** 314
Khachaturian, Aram Ilich **8** 530-531
Mendelssohn, Moses **10** 488-489
Milhaud, Darius **11** 17-18
Mozart, Wolfgang Amadeus **11** 218-221
Nielsen, Carl August **11** 388-389
Paganini, Niccolo **12** 58-59
Sessions, Roger Huntington **14** 117-118
Shostakovich, Dmitri Dmitrievich **14** 204-205
Sibelius, Jean Julius Christian **14** 211-212
Stravinsky, Igor Fedorovich **14** 502-506
Szymanowski, Karol **15** 67-68
Tartini, Giuseppe **15** 112-113
Tchaikovsky, Peter Ilyich **15** 130-132
Walton, William Turner **16** 92-93
for violoncello
Haydn, Franz Joseph **7** 219-221

Concerto Gregoriano (musical composition)
Respighi, Ottorino **13** 103-104

Concerto grosso (musical form)
Bloch, Ernest **2** 326-327
Corelli, Arcangelo **4** 230-231
Handel, George Frederick **7** 116-119
Martinu, Bohuslav **10** 299-300
Vivaldi, Antonio **16** 3-4

Conciliarism (religion)
Ailly, Pierre d' **1** 94
Cusa, Nicholas of **4** 352-353
Döllinger, Josef Ignaz von **5** 47-48
Francis I **6** 40-43
Gerson, John **6** 285-286
Martin V **10** 287-288
Pius II **12** 331

Concón, Battle of (1891)
Balmaceda Fernández, José Manuel **1** 475-476

Concord (sloop)
Perry, Matthew Calbraith **12** 237-239

Concord, Battle of
see Lexington and Concord, Battles of

Concordat of 1801 (France, papal compact)
Napoleon I **11** 306-310
Pius VII **12** 334-335

Concordia, discordantium canonum (book)
Gratian **6** 498-499

Concretion (art form)
Arp, Jean **1** 317-318
Taeuber-Arp, Sophie **15** 73-74

Condé, Henry II de Bourbon, Prince de (1588-1646), French nobleman
Louis XIII **9** 529-531
Richelieu, Armand Jean du Plessis de **13** 142-144

Condé, Louis I de Bourbon, Prince de (1530-1569), Protestant leader and general
Henry IV **7** 293-295

CONDÉ, PRINCE DE (Louis II de Bourbon 1621-1686), French general **4** 193-194
Bossuet, Jacques Bénigne **2** 431-432
Mazarin, Jules **10** 379-380

Condenado por desconfiado, El (play)
Tirso de Molina **15** 237-238

Condensed Novels (parodies)
Harte, Francis Brett **7** 184-185

CONDILLAC, ÉTIENNE BONNOT DE (1715-1780), French philosopher and educator **4** 194-195
La Mettrie, Julien Offray de **9** 179-180
Rousseau, Jean Jacques **13** 324-328

Condition ... of the Colored People of the United States ... (book)
Delany, Martin Robinson **4** 473-474

Condition humaine, La (novel)
Malraux, André **10** 178-180

Condition of the Working Class in England in 1844, The (book; Engels)
Engels, Friedrich **5** 286-288
Kelley, F. **8** 483-484

Conditioned Reflex, The (article)
Pavlov, Ivan Petrovich **12** 155-157

Condivi, Ascanio (circa 1525-1574), Italian art historian
Vasari, Giorgio **15** 442-443

Condon, Edward U. (1902-1974), American physicist
Fermi, Enrico **5** 422-424

CONDORCET, MARQUIS DE (Marie Jean Antoine Nicolas Caritat; 1743-1794), French philosopher and mathematician **4** 195-196
Banneker, Benjamin **1** 490-491
Baudelaire, Charles Pierre **2** 61-63
Comte, Auguste **4** 189-191

Condottiere Guidoriccio da Fogliano (fresco)
Martini, Simone **10** 298-299

Conduct of the Allies, The (book)
Swift, Jonathan **15** 51-54

Conductor eléctrica, El (periodical)
Fernández de Lizardi, José Joaquin **5** 424-425

Conductus (music)
Léonin **9** 343-344
Pérotin **12** 231-232

CONE, JAMES HALL (born 1938), American theologian **4** 196-197

Cone (mathematics)
Archimedes **1** 277-280
Democritus **4** 493-494
Eudoxus of Cnidus **5** 329-330

Confederación Regional Obrera Mexicana (labor group)
Toledano, Vicente Lombardo **15** 256-257

Confederacy, American
see Confederate States of America

Confederacy, The (play)
Vanbrugh, John **15** 409-410

Confederate States of America (1861-1865)
amnesty to supporters
Johnson, Andrew **8** 294-295
Civil War
see Civil War, United States
Congress
Forbes, John **5** 507-508
Hill, Benjamin Harvey **7** 386-387
Rhett, Robert Barnwell **13** 120
Tyler, John **15** 368-369
diplomacy
Mason, James Murray **10** 320-321
Slidell, John **14** 273
Yancey, William Lowndes **16** 436-437
President and Cabinet
Benjamin, Judah Philip **2** 163-164
Bledsoe, Albert Taylor **2** 324-325
Davis, Jefferson **4** 416-418
Fitzhugh, George **5** 474
Memminger, Christopher Gustavus **10** 476-477
Stephens, Alexander Hamilton **14** 429-430
Toombs, Robert Augustus **15** 267-268
secession
see Secession
state and local politics
Brown, Joseph Emerson **3** 41-42
Lamar, Lucius Quintus Cincinnatus **9** 170-171
Letcher, John **9** 359-360
Soulé, Pierre **14** 351-352
Vance, Zebulon Baird **15** 413-414
see also Reconstruction (United States)

Confederated Republic of the Rif Tribes (Morocco)
Abd el-Krim el-Khatabi, Mohamed ben **1** 15-16

Confédération Générale du Travail Africain (Guinea)
Touré, Sékou **15** 275-277

Confederation of Latin American Workers (established 1938)
Toledano, Vicente Lombardo **15** 256-257

Confederation of Mexican Workers (established 1936)
Cárdenas, Lázaro **3** 286-287
Toledano, Vicente Lombardo **15** 256-257

Conference for Progressive Labor Action (established 1929)
Muste, Abraham Johannes **11** 276-277

Conference of the Birds (book)
Attar, Farid ed-Din **1** 359-360

Conference on Jewish Relations (United States)
Cohen, Morris Raphael **4** 139-140

Confesiones de un pequeño filósofo, Las (autobiographical novel)
Ruíz, José Martínez **13** 358

Confessing Church of anti-Nazi German Protestants
Bonhoeffer, Dietrich **2** 389-391

Confessing Church's Barmen Declaration (1934)
Barth, Karl **2** 31-32

Confessio amantis (book; Gower)
Caxton, William **3** 386-387
Gower, John **6** 475-476

Confession (book)
Patrick, St. **12** 135-136
Tolstoy, Leo **15** 262-265
Wyclif, John **16** 412-413

Confession concerning the Lord's Supper (book)
Luther, Martin **10** 48-51

Confession d'un enfant du siècle, La (autobiography)
Musset, Louis Charles Alfred de **11** 271-272

Confession of a Fool, The (novel)
Strindberg, August **14** 509-511

Confessions (book)
Heine, Heinrich **7** 259-260
Rousseau, Jean Jacques **13** 324-328

Confessions, The (book; Augustine)
Augustine **1** 367-370
Pelagius **12** 189-190
Petrarch **12** 259-261

Confessions of an English Opium Eater (book; DeQuincey)
Baudelaire, Charles Pierre **2** 61-63
Musset, Louis Charles Alfred de **11** 271-272

Confessions of Felix Krul ... (book)
Mann, Thomas **10** 204-207

Confessions of Nat Turner (novel; Styron)
Styron, William **15** 6-8

Turner, Nathaniel **15** 354

Confessions of Zeno, The (novel)
Svevo, Italo **15** 47-48

Confidence (novel)
James, Henry **8** 211-212

Confidence-Man, The (novel)
Melville, Herman **10** 472-476

Confidential Agent, The (novel)
Greene, Graham **6** 523-524

Confidential Clerk, The (play)
Eliot, Thomas Stearns **5** 258-261

Confirmatio Cartarum (England)
Edward II **5** 210

Conflict, The (novel)
Phillips, David Graham **12** 280-281

Conformist, The (novel)
Moravia, Alberto **11** 153-155

Confucian classics (Chinese philosophy)
K'ang Yu-wei **8** 426-428
Li Ssu **9** 442-443
Liu Hsieh **9** 452-453
Wang T'ao **16** 105-106
see also I Ching

Confucianism (religious and ethical system)
and Legalism
Li Ssu **9** 442-443
and Taoism
Wang Pi **16** 104-105
see also Neo-Confucianism
communism and
Ch'en Tu-hsiu **3** 501-502
Mao Zedong **10** 225-227
Japan
Inukai, Tsuyoshi **8** 130-131
Katayama, Sen **8** 457
Kukai **9** 124-125
Mabuchi, Kamo **10** 73-74
Makibi, Kibi-no **10** 161
Saicho **13** 426-428
Shotoku Taishi **14** 205-207
Sui Wen-ti **15** 16-18
Korea
Chongjo **4** 15-16
Sejo **14** 90-91
Sejong **14** 91-92
Sŏnjo **14** 341-342
Yi Hwang **16** 457
literary tradition
Kuang-wu-ti **9** 112-113
Po Chü-i **12** 362-363
Wang Mang **16** 101-103
Yeh-lü Ch'u-ts'ai **16** 447-449
modern reinterpretations
K'ang Yu-wei **8** 426-428
Ku Chieh-kang **9** 120-121
Liang Ch'i-ch'ao **9** 395-396
Wo-jen **16** 352
Yen Fu **16** 452
origins
Chung-shu, Tung **4** 48-49
Confucius **4** 197-200
Hsün-tzu **8** 8

Mencius **10** 480-481
reforms
Fan Chung-yen **5** 376-377
Ou-yang Hsiu **12** 33-34
Ssu-ma kuang **14** 390-391
Wang An-shih **16** 95-97
Wang Mang **16** 101-103
scholars of
Chou Kung **4** 22-23
Quin Shi Huang-di **12** 515-518
Sol Ch'ong **14** 325-326
Wo-jen **16** 352
state orthodoxy
Han Wu-ti **7** 136
Sui Wen-ti **15** 16-18

CONFUCIUS (551-479 B.C.), Chinese
teacher and philosopher **4** 197-200
historians of
Ssu-ma Ch'ien **14** 388-389
influence of
Chu Hsi **4** 40-43
Kammu **8** 420
Lao Tzu **9** 201-202
Ou-yang Hsiu **12** 33-34
Yi Hwang **16** 457
veneration of
Chang Chih-tung **3** 430-431
Chung-shu, Tung **4** 48-49
Wang Ch'ung **16** 98-99
see also Confucianism

Congo, Belgian (Léopoldville)
see Congo, Democratic Republic of the

Congo, Democratic Republic of the (Kin-
shasa; formerly Zaire; nation, Central
Africa)
as Congo Free State
Gordon, Charles George **6** 448-449
Leopold II **9** 346-347
Stanley, Henry Morton **14** 399-400
Tippu Tip **15** 235-236
as Zaire (1972)
Mobutu Sese Seko **11** 69-71
independence (Belgium)
Bunche, Ralph Johnson **3** 121-122
Kasavubu, Joseph **8** 453-455
Lumumba, Patrice Emery **10** 43-45
Plaza Lasso, Galo **12** 350-351
Katanga secession
Hammarskjöld, Dag **7** 100-101
Lumumba, Patrice Emery **10** 43-45
Mobutu Sese Seko **11** 69-71
Tshombe, Moïse Kapenda
15 325-326-8
Youlou, Fulbert **16** 466-467
rebellion (1963-1965)
Johnson, Lyndon Baines **8** 308-312
Mobutu Sese Seko **11** 69-71
Tshombe, Moïse Kapenda
15 325-326

Congo, French
see Congo, People's Republic of the
(Brazzaville)

Congo, People's Republic of the (Brazzaville; former nation, Central Africa)

Eboué, Adolphe Felix Sylvestre **5** 194
Marchand, Jean-Baptiste **10** 234-237
Youlou, Fulbert **16** 466-467

Congo Free State
see Congo, Democratic Republic of the
(Kinshasa)

Congo River Basin (Africa)
Brazza, Pierre Paul François Camille
Savorgnan de **2** 509-510
Burton, Richard **3** 163-164
Goodall, Jane **6** 433-434
Stanley, Henry Morton **14** 399-400

Congo, The (poem)
Lindsay, Vachel **9** 424-425

Congregation of Notre Dame of Montreal
(established 1698)
Bourgeoys, Marguerite **2** 452-453

Congregation of the Mission (established
1625)
Vincent de Paul **15** 501-502

Congregation of the Oratory
see Oratorians

Congregational Association (Protestant
organization)
Beecher, Henry Ward **2** 112-113

Congregational Christian Church
see United Church of Christ

Congregational Church (Bennington, Vermont; L. Fillmore)
Benjamin, Asher **2** 162-163

Congregational Way (religion)
Johnson, Samuel **8** 314-315

Congregationalism (religion)
Massachusetts Bay Colony
Bradford, William **2** 475-476
Cotton, John **4** 263-265
Mather, Cotton **10** 330-332
Mather, Increase **10** 332-333
political organization
Dwight, Timothy **5** 169
Hooker, Thomas **7** 476-477

Congregationalist (periodical)
Gladden, Washington **6** 356-357

Congregationalist Kingsley Hall (settlement
house, Japan)
Katayama, Sen **8** 457

Congress (ship)
Stockton, Robert Field **14** 461-462

Congress Alliance (South African political
group)
First, Ruth **5** 453-454

Congress of Industrial Organizations (labor
union)
and ILWU
Bridges, Harry A.R. **3** 3-5
conflict with AFL
Bridges, Harry A.R. **3** 3-5
Green, William R. **6** 521
Perkins, Frances **12** 221-222
founders
Dubinsky, David **5** 114-115

Hillman, Sidney **7** 392-393
Lewis, John Llewellyn **9** 387-388
Murray, Philip **11** 264-265
merger with AFL
Meany, George **10** 444
Reuther, Walter Philip **13** 107-108
see also American Federation of
Labor and Congress of Industrial
Organizations

Congress of Racial Equality (interracial
organization)
Farmer, James **5** 383-385
King, Martin Luther Jr. **9** 20-22
McKissick, Floyd B. **10** 420-422
Muste, Abraham Johannes **11** 276-277
Rustin, Bayard **13** 382-383
see also African American history (Unit-
ed States)

Congress of Vienna
see Vienna, Congress of

Congress party (India)
Singh, Vishwanath Pratap **14** 254-256
see Indian National Congress

Congress party (Malawi)
Banda, Hastings Kamuzu **1** 485-486

Congress party (Nyasaland)
Banda, Hastings Kamuzu **1** 485-486

Congress Socialist party (India; established
1934)
Narayan, Jayaprakash **11** 312-313

Congressional Black Caucus (United States)
Mfume, Kweisi **10** 539-542

Congressional Medal of Honor (United
States)
Ames, Adelbert **1** 198
Cohan, George Michael **4** 137-138
Greely, Adolphus Washington
6 517-518
Lindbergh, Charles Augustus **9** 421-423
Wainwright, Jonathan Mayhew
16 45-46

Congressional Women's Caucus (United
States)
Mikulski, Barbara **11** 13-15

Congressmen
see Statesmen, American—legislative

CONGREVE, WILLIAM (1670-1729), Eng-
lish dramatist **4** 200-201
associates
Byrd, William II **3** 189-190
Swift, Jonathan **15** 51-54
Voltaire **16** 14-16
influence of
Arne, Thomas Augustine **1** 307-308
Coward, Noel **4** 279-280
Hallam, Lewis Sr. and Jr. **7** 87

Conic sections (mathematics)
Apollonius of Perga **1** 261-262
Euclid **5** 327-329
Fermat, Pierre de **5** 421-422

Conics (book)
Apollonius of Perga **1** 261-262

Hasan ibn al-Haytham **7** 190-191

Coningsby (novel)
Disraeli, Benjamin **5** 27-29

Coniston (novel)
Churchill, Winston **4** 50-51

Conjugal Love (novel)
Moravia, Alberto **11** 153-155

Conjurer, The (painting)
Bosch, Hieronymus **2** 426-428
Hofmann, Hans **7** 442-443

CONKLING, ROSCOE (1829-1888), Amer-
ican politician **4** 201-202
Arthur, Chester Alan **1** 321-323
Curtis, George William **4** 349-350
Garfield, James Abram **6** 213-214
Platt, Thomas Collier **12** 347-348

CONNALLY, JOHN BOWDEN, JR. (born
1917), Texas governor, political adviser,
and confidant to presidents **4** 202-204
Strauss, Robert Schwarz **14** 501-502

Connecticut (state, United States)
colonial charter
Andros, Edmund **1** 234-235
Davenport, John **4** 405-406
Hooker, Thomas **7** 476-477
Winthrop, John **16** 341
educators
Barnard, Henry **2** 10
Barnum, Phineas Taylor **2** 13-15
Crandall, Prudence **4** 291
Gallaudet, Thomas Hopkins **6** 185
Johnson, Samuel **8** 314-315 legisla-
tors
Sherman, Roger **14** 185-186
Welles, Gideon **16** 188-190

**Connecticut Agricultural Experiment Sta-
tion** (New Haven)
East, Edward Murray **5** 182-183

**Connecticut General Life Insurance Com-
pany** (Hartford)
Noguchi, Isamu **11** 416-418

Connecticut Wits (American poets)
Barlow, Joel **2** 6-7
Dwight, Timothy **5** 169

**Connecticut Yankee in King Arthur's Court,
A** (novel)
Twain, Mark **15** 363-366

Connelly, Marc (1890-1980), American
playwright
Kaufman, George S. **8** 457-458

Connoisseurs, The (painting)
Daumier, Honoré Victorin **4** 403-405

CONNOLLY, CYRIL (1903-1974), British
novelist and literary and social critic
4 204-205
Bowen, Elizabeth **2** 462-463

Connotations (musical composition)
Copland, Aaron **4** 227-228

Conquerors, The (novel)
Malraux, André **10** 178-180

Conquest of Canaan, The (poem)
Dwight, Timothy **5** 169

Conquest of Granada, The (play)
Dryden, John **5** 106-107

Conquistador (poem)
MacLeish, Archibald **10** 109-110

Conquistadores (Spanish conquerors; 16th
century)
Cortés, Hernán **4** 255-256
Cuauhtemoc **4** 329
Mendoza, Antonio de **10** 494-495
Montezuma, II **11** 128-129
Pizarro, Francisco **12** 340-341
Valdivia, Pedro de **15** 400-401
Velázquez de Cuéllar, Diego **15** 459

Conrad II (Holy Roman emperor)
see Conrad II (king of Germany)

Conrad I (died 918), king of Germany
911-918
Henry I **7** 285-286

Conrad II (990?-1039), king of Germany
and Holy Roman emperor 1024-1039
Canute I, the Great **3** 266-269
Henry III **7** 290
Leo IX **9** 332

Conrad III (1093-1152), king of Germany
1138-1152
Bernard of Clairvaux **2** 207-208
Dante Alighieri **4** 389-391
Frederick I **6** 78-79
Louis VII **9** 524-525
Manuel I **10** 218-219
Roger II **13** 244-245

Conrad IV (1228-1254), king of Germany
and Sicily 1250-1254
Frederick II **6** 79

Conrad, Charles, Jr. (born 1930), American
astronaut
Armstrong, Neil Alden **1** 304-306

CONRAD, JOSEPH (1857-1924),
Polish-born English novelist **4** 205-207
Bennett, Richard Rodney **2** 172
Čapek, Karel **3** 271-272
Epstein, Jacob **5** 295-296
Flaubert, Gustave **5** 480-482
Galsworthy, John **6** 189-190

Conrad von Hötzendorf, Count Franz
(1852-1925), Austrian field marshal
Berchtold, Leopold von **2** 183-184

Conroy Gabriel (literary character)
Joyce, James **8** 365-367

Conscience (literary character)
Langland, William **9** 194-195

Conscience of the Rich, The (novel)
Snow, Charles Percy **14** 311-312

Conscience Whigs (United States politics)
Adams, Charles Francis **1** 41-42
Sumner, Charles **15** 30-31

Conscientious objectors
see Draft resistance

Conscious Lovers, The (play)
   Steele, Richard **14** 407-409

Conscription
   see Draft (military)

Conservation (Canada)
   Sifton, Clifford **14** 219-220

Conservation (United States)
   Federal programs
      Cannon, Joseph Gurney **3** 261-262
      Clark, William Andrews **4** 83-85
      Pinchot, Gifford **12** 308-309
      Roosevelt, Theodore **13** 280-283
      Taft, William Howard **15** 78-81
   supporters
      Adams, Ansel **1** 40-41
      Carson, Rachel Louise **3** 337-338
      Dubos, René Jules **5** 119
      Muir, John **11** 234
      Powell, John Wesley **12** 425-426
      Wright, Elizur **16** 396-397

Conservatism (politics)
   Kent, James **8** 510-511
   Metternich, Klemens von **10** 533-536
   Montt Torres, Manuel **11** 139-140
   Penrose, Boies **12** 203-204
   Root, Elihu **13** 283-284
   Rutledge, John **13** 387-388
   Spengler, Oswald **14** 372-373
   Ssu-ma kuang **14** 390-391
   Will, George Frederick **16** 286-287
   Zhirinovsky, Vladimir Volfovich
      16 509-510
   see also Conservative party; Liberalism;
      Radicalism; Socialism

Conservatism (politics)
   Falwell, Jerry **5** 375-376

Conservatism (religion)
   Moody, Dwight L. **11** 141-142
   Pius IX **12** 335-336
   Pius VII **12** 334-335
   Pius XII **12** 339-340
   Rosmini-Serbati, Antonio **13** 296-297

Conservative Judaism (American religious
   movement)
   Finkelstein, Rabbi Louis **5** 448-450

Conservative party (Argentina)
   Irigoyen, Hipólito **8** 139-140

Conservative party (Australia)
   Massey, William Ferguson **10** 324

Conservative party (Canada)
   Campbell, Avril Phaedra Douglas
      3 250-252
   Mulroney, Martin Brian **11** 242-246
   opponents
      King, William Lyon Mackenzie
         9 25-26
      Mackenzie, Alexander **10** 104
   supporters
      Baldwin, Robert **1** 466-468
      Bennett, Richard Bedford **2** 171-172
      Borden, Robert Laird **2** 409-411
      Bourassa, Joseph-Henri-Napoleon
         2 446-447
      Cartier, George-Étienne **3** 342-343
      Diefenbaker, John George **5** 4-5
      Meighen, Arthur **10** 459-460
      Tupper, Charles **15** 342-343

Conservative party (Chile)
   Frei Montalva, Eduardo **6** 94-95

Conservative party (Colombia)
   Gómez Castro, Laureano **6** 419-420
   Isaacs, Jorge **8** 144
   Lleras Camargo, Alberto **9** 467
   Rojas Pinilla, Gustavo **13** 255-256

Conservative party (Cuba)
   Machado y Morales, Gerardo **10** 92-93
   Menocal, Mario Garcia **10** 506-507

Conservative party (Ecuador)
   Plaza Lasso, Galo **12** 350-351
   Velasco Ibarra, José María **15** 452-454

Conservative party (England)
   19th century
      Chamberlain, Joseph **3** 411-413
      Disraeli, Benjamin **5** 27-29
      Gladstone, William Ewart
         6 357-360
      Salisbury, 3d Marquess of
         13 448-449
      Shaftesbury, 7th Earl of **14** 137-138
   20th century
      Baldwin, Stanley **1** 468-469
      Balfour, Arthur James **1** 469-470
      Carrington **3** 326-327
      Chamberlain, Arthur Neville
         3 409-411
      Clarke, Kenneth Harry **4** 85-87
      Eden, Anthony **5** 204-205
      Heath, Edward Richard George
         7 244-246
      Heseltine, Michael **7** 359-361
      Howe, Geoffrey **7** 531-532
      Hurd, Douglas **8** 52-55
      Macmillan, Harold **10** 112-113
      Major, John **10** 155-157
      Pym, Francis **12** 494-495
      Thatcher, Margaret Hilda
         15 165-168
   see also Tory party (England)

Conservative party (Mexico)
   Álvarez, Juan **1** 184-185
   Alamán, Lucas **1** 99-100
   Juárez, Benito **8** 369-372
   Lerdo de Tejada, Miguel **9** 351-352

Conservative party (Nicaragua)
   Zelaya, José Santos **16** 495-496

Conservative party (United States)
   Buckley, William F. Jr. **3** 96-97

Conservative Republican party (Cuba)
   Estrada Palma, Tomás **5** 326-327

Conservatory (Brighton, England)
   Nash, John **11** 316

Conservatory of Music and Scenic Art
   (established 1948)
   Ginastera, Alberto Evaristo **6** 328-329

Conservatory of Santa Cecilia (Rome)
      Respighi, Ottorino **13** 103-104

Consider Her Ways (fantasy-satire)
   Grove, Frederick Philip **7** 20-21

Considerations on Machiavelli's Discourses
   (book)
   Guicciardini, Francesco **7** 32-33

**Considerations on the ... Grandeur of
   Rome ...** (book)
   Montesquieu **11** 123-125

**Considérations sur le gouvernement de la
   Pologne** (book)
   Rousseau, Jean Jacques **13** 324-328

Consiliador, El (book)
   Manasseh ben Israel **10** 183-184

Consilium de emandanda ecclesia (papal
   review)
   Paul III **12** 144-145

Consolation of Philosophy, The (book;
   Boethius)
   Alfred **1** 151-153
   Boethius, Anicius Manlius Severinus
      2 360-361
   Chaucer, Geoffrey **3** 482-485
   Jean de Meun **8** 234-235
   Varro, Marcus Terentius **15** 438-439

Consolations (poems)
   Echeverría, José Estéban **5** 197-198
   Malherbe, François de **10** 169-170
   Sainte-Beuve, Charles Augustin **13** 438

Consolidator, The (book)
   Defoe, Daniel **4** 457-459

Conspiracy to Murder Bill (1858; England)
   Disraeli, Benjamin **5** 27-29
   Palmerston, 3d Viscount **12** 81-83

Constab Ballads (poems)
   McKay, Claude **10** 416

CONSTABLE, JOHN (1776-1837), English
   landscape painter **4** 208-209
   Delacroix, Ferdinand Victor Eugène
      4 469-471
   Hassam, Frederick Childe **7** 192
   Pissarro, Camille **12** 326-327
   Staël, Nicolas de **14** 392
   Wyant, Alexander Helwig **16** 409-410

Constance, Council of (1414-1418)
   Ailly, Pierre d' **1** 94
   Gerson, John **6** 285-286
   Hus, Jan **8** 56-59
   Martin V **10** 287-288
   Sigismund **14** 220-221
   Wenceslaus **16** 201-202

Constance, Peace of (1183)
   Frederick I **6** 78-79

Constans (323?-350), Roman emperor
   337-350
   Constantine I **4** 209-211

Constant de Rebecque, Benjamin
   (1767-1830), French writer and politician
   Staël, Germaine de **14** 391-392

Constant Prince, The (play)
   Calderón, Pedro **3** 221-222

Constant Wife, The (play)
  Barrymores **2** 28-30

Constantia, Flavia Valeria (died circa 330), half sister of Constantine I
  Constantine I **4** 209-211

Constantine (827-869)
  see Cyril and Methodius, Sts.—Cyril

Constantine (died 879), Byzantine coemperor
  Basil I **2** 49-50

Constantine IV (Pogonatus; 648-685), Byzantine emperor 668-685
  Leo III **9** 330-332

Constantine V (Copronymus; 719-775), Byzantine emperor 741-775
  Leo III **9** 330-332

Constantine VIII (circa 960-1028), Byzantine coemperor 976-1025, emperor 1025-1028
  Basil II **2** 50-51

Constantine IX (Monomachus; 1000?-1055), Byzantine emperor 1042-1055
  Zoë **16** 524-525

CONSTANTINE XI (Palaeologus; 1405-1453), Byzantine emperor 1448-1453 **4** 211-212
  Mehmed the Conqueror **10** 452-454

CONSTANTINE I (circa 274-337), Roman emperor 306-337 **4** 209-211
  and Persia
    Shahpur II **14** 140-141
  Arian controversy
    Anthony, Susan Brownell **1** 246-248
    Arius **1** 297-298
    Athanasius **1** 358-359
    Ulfilas **15** 384

Constantine II (Flavius Claudius Constantinus; 317-340), Roman emperor 337-340
  Constantine I **4** 209-211

Constantine I (1868-1923), king of Greece
  Venizelos, Eleutherios **15** 460-461

Constantine (Flavius Claudius Constantinus; died 411), Roman usurper
  Stilicho, Flavius **14** 452-453

Constantine Paleologos (play)
  Kazantzakis, Nikos **8** 466-468

Constantinople (Byzantine capital, 330-1453)
  after 1453
    see Istanbul
  Arab attacks
    Leo III **9** 330-332
  Early Church in
    John Chrysostom **8** 280-281
    Leo I **9** 329-330
    Nestorius **11** 349-350
  First Crusade (1096)
    Godfrey of Bouillon **6** 379
  founded (330)
    Constantine I **4** 209-211
  Latin conquest and empire

    Dandolo, Enrico **4** 386-387
    Innocent, III **8** 125-127
    Villehardouin, Geffroi de **15** 499
  Nika revolt in
    Theodora **15** 172-175
  Turks capture (1453)
    Constantine XI **4** 211-212
    Hunyadi, John **8** 51-52
    Mehmed the Conqueror **10** 452-454

Constantinople, Councils of
  First (381)
    Ambrose **1** 192-193
    Basil the Great **2** 51-52
    Eutyches **5** 335
  Second (553)
    Justinian I **8** 393-395

Constantius I (Flavius Valerius Constantius Chlorus; 250?-306), Roman emperor 305-306
  Constantine I **4** 209-211
  Diocletian **5** 19-20

Constantius II (Flavius Julius Constantius; 317-361), Roman emperor 337-361
  Constantine I **4** 209-211
  Julian **8** 378-379

Constellations (gouache series)
  Miró, Joan **11** 53-54

Constituent Assembly (France)
  see French Revolution—1789-1791; National Assembly (French Revolution)

Constituent Convention (1861; Ecuador)
  García Moreno, Gabriel **6** 209-210

Constituent Fascists (Italian politics)
  Mussolini, Benito **11** 272-274
  see also Fascism; Fascist regime (Italy)

Constitution (government)
  Alsace-Lorraine (1911)
    Bethmann Hollweg, Theobald von **2** 239-240
  Argentina (1853)
    Alberdi, Juan Bautista **1** 109-110
    Artigas, José Gervasio **1** 323
  Athens (6th century B.C.)
    Cleisthenes **4** 98-99
  Brazil (1824)
    Feijó, Diogo Antônio **5** 405-406
    Pedro I **12** 179-180
  Canada (1867)
    Macdonald, John Alexander **10** 85-87
  Chile (1833)
    Bello, Ahmadu **2** 139-140
  Chile (1925)
    Alessandri Palma, Arturo **1** 128-129
  China (1969)
    Lin Piao **9** 429-430
  Congo (1964)
    Kasavubu, Joseph **8** 453-455
  Cuba (1869)
    Céspedes, Carlos Manuel de **3** 398-399
  Cuba (1940)

    Batista y Zaldívar, Fulgencio **2** 57-58
    Menocal, Mario Garcia **10** 506-507
  Czechoslovakia (1948)
    Beneš, Edward **2** 155-157
  Ecuador (1946)
    Velasco Ibarra, José María **15** 452-454
  Ecuador (1967)
    Velasco Ibarra, José María **15** 452-454
  France (1793)
    Babeuf, François Noel **1** 412
    Saint-Just, Louis Antoine Léon de **13** 433
  Guatemala (1879)
    Barrios, Justo Rufino **2** 23-24
  Hawaii (1840; 1852)
    Kamehameha III **8** 416-417
  India (1888)
    Mehta, Pherozeshah **10** 455
  Indonesia (1945)
    Sukarno **15** 18-20
  Ireland (1937)
    Hyde, Douglas **8** 82-83
  Japan (1889)
    Mutsuhito **11** 279-282
  Japan (604)
    Shotoku Taishi **14** 205-207
    Suiko **15** 15-16
  Korea (1948)
    Rhee, Syngman **13** 117-120
  Mexico (1812)
    Guerrero, Vicente **7** 28-30
  Mexico (1857)
    Juárez, Benito **8** 369-372
  Mexico (1917)
    Carranza, Venustiano **3** 321-322
  Ottoman Empire (1876)
    Enver Pasha **5** 290-291
  Paraguay (1844)
    López, Carlos Antonio **9** 506-507
  Peru (1920)
    Leguía y Salcedo, Augusto Bernardino **9** 305-306
  Spain (1812)
    Ferdinand VII **5** 418-420
  Sweden (1634)
    Gustavus II **7** 43-45
  Uruguay (1918)
    Terra, Gabriel **15** 154-155
  United States
    see Constitution of the United States
  Union of Soviet Socialist Republics (1936)
    Radek, Karl Bernardovich **12** 536-537
  Venezuela (1864)
    Blanco, Antonio Guzmán **2** 320-321
  Venezuela (1960)
    Gallegos Freire, Rómulo **6** 185-186
  Yugoslavia (1931)
    Alexander of Yugoslavia **1** 136-137
    see also Constitutional government

Constitution Bill (Australia; 1891)
  Deakin, Alfred **4** 432-433
  Parkes, Henry **12** 113

Constitution Hall (Washington, D.C.)
Anderson, Marian **1** 218-219

Constitution in Favor of the Princes (1231)
Frederick II **6** 79

Constitution of Church and State, The
(book)
Coleridge, Samuel Taylor **4** 154-156

Constitution of the Athenians (book)
Aristotle **1** 295-296

Constitution of the United States (1787)
Amendments (1st)
Black, Hugo Lafayette **2** 301-303
Douglas, William Orville **5** 83-85
see also Church and State (United
States); Freedom of speech; Free-
dom of the press
Amendments (5th)
Cardozo, Benjamin Nathan
3 288-290
Taney, Roger Brooke **15** 98-99
Amendments (1st-10th; Bill of Rights)
Gerry, Elbridge **6** 282-283
Madison, James **10** 121-123
Mason, George **10** 319-320
Washington, George **16** 126-129
Amendments (12th)
Clinton, DeWitt **4** 112-113
Amendments (13th)
Anthony, Susan Brownell **1** 246-248
Douglas, Stephen Arnold **5** 80-82
Hearst, George **7** 242
Mott, Lucretia Coffin **11** 212-213
Stanton, Elizabeth Cady **14** 402-403
Trumbull, Lyman **15** 317-318
Amendments (14th; controversy)
Anthony, Susan Brownell **1** 246-248
Johnson, Andrew **8** 294-295
Morton, Oliver Hazard Perry Throck
11 197-198
Stevens, Thaddeus **14** 442-443
Sumner, Charles **15** 30-31
Vance, Zebulon Baird **15** 413-414
Amendments (14th; Supreme Court on)
Field, Stephen Johnson **5** 441-442
Harlan, John Marshall **7** 156-157
Miller, Samuel Freeman **11** 29-30
Waite, Morrison Remick **16** 46
Warren, Earl **16** 117-120
Amendments (15th)
Anthony, Susan Brownell **1** 246-248
Coffin, Levi **4** 135
Foster, Abigail Kelley **6** 25
Garrett, Thomas **6** 225-226
Miller, Samuel Freeman **11** 29-30
Morton, Oliver Hazard Perry Throck
11 197-198
see also Suffrage (United States)
Amendments (18th)
Butler, Nicholas Murray **3** 181
see also Temperance movement
(United States)
Amendments (19th)
Anthony, Susan Brownell **1** 246-248
Catt, Carrie Chapman **3** 375-376

see also Suffrage (United States);
Women's suffrage
Amendments (20th)
Norris, George William **11** 428-429
constitutional law
Cardozo, Benjamin Nathan
3 288-290
Frankfurter, Felix **6** 57
Marshall, John **10** 279-281
Taney, Roger Brooke **15** 98-99
and Declaration of Independence
Parrington, Vernon Louis
12 119-120
drafted
see Constitutional Convention (Unit-
ed States; 1787)
nullification crisis
see Nullification crisis
ratification (Middle Colonies; against)
Chase, Samuel **3** 475-476
Clinton, DeWitt **4** 112-113
Clinton, George **4** 113-114
ratification (Middle Colonies; for)
Coxe, Tench **4** 285-286
Dickinson, John **4** 543-544
Franklin, Benjamin **6** 60-64
Hamilton, Alexander **7** 95-98
Morris, Robert **11** 185-187
Pickering, Timothy **12** 298-299
ratification (New England; against)
Gerry, Elbridge **6** 282-283
ratification (New England; for)
Ames, Fisher **1** 199-200
Hancock, John **7** 114-116
ratification (South; against)
Henry, Patrick **7** 309-311
Lee, Arthur **9** 288-289
Macon, Nathaniel **10** 114-115
ratification (South; for)
Pendleton, Edmund **12** 197-198
Randolph, Edmund **13** 29-30
Washington, George **16** 126-129
states' rights
see States' rights; Anti-Federalists;
Articles of Confederation; Federal-
ist party (United States)

Constitutional Act of 1791 (Canada)
Carleton, Guy **3** 300-301

Constitutional Assembly (Brazil; 1823)
Feijó, Diogo Antônio **5** 405-406

Constitutional Convention (Episcopal
Church; 1789)
see General Convention (Protestant
Episcopal Church; 1789)

Constitutional Convention (United States;
1787)
delegate nonsigners
Gerry, Elbridge **6** 282-283
Martin, Luther **10** 289-290
Mason, George **10** 319-320
Randolph, Edmund **13** 29-30
delegate signers (Middle Colonies)
Dickinson, John **4** 543-544
Franklin, Benjamin **6** 60-64
Hamilton, Alexander **7** 95-98

Morris, Gouverneur **11** 182-183
Morris, Robert **11** 185-187
Paterson, William **12** 132-133
Wilson, James **16** 323-324
delegate signers (New England)
King, Rufus **9** 22-23
delegate signers (South)
Madison, James **10** 121-123
Pinckney, Charles **12** 309-310
Pinckney, Charles Cotesworth
12 310
Rutledge, John **13** 387-388
Sherman, Roger **14** 185-186
Washington, George **16** 126-129
essays on
Condorcet, Marquis de **4** 195-196
Great Compromise
Franklin, Benjamin **6** 60-64
Paterson, William **12** 132-133
Sherman, Roger **14** 185-186
supporters
Coxe, Tench **4** 285-286
Jay, John **8** 230-232
see also Constitution of the United
States

Constitutional Democratic party (Russia)
Miliukov, Pavel Nikolayevich **11** 18-19

Constitutional Democratic party (United
States; 1860)
Yancey, William Lowndes **16** 436-437

Constitutional government (politics)
constitutional law
Evatt, Herbert Vere **5** 341-343
development
Carranza, Venustiano **3** 321-322
Francis Joseph **6** 45-46
Huerta, Victoriano **8** 13-14
Isaacs, Jorge **8** 144
Montesquieu **11** 123-125
Montfort, Simon de **11** 132-133
Zapata, Emiliano **16** 489-490
discredited
Farouk I **5** 387-388
established in Japan
Ito, Hirobumi **8** 153-155
Iwakura, Tomomi **8** 160-161
historians of
Curry, Jabez Lamar Monroe
4 346-347
Dunning, William Archibald
5 148-149
Gardiner, Samuel Rawson **6** 211
reforms
Alexander I **1** 130-132
Chang Chien **3** 429-430
see also Monarchy, constitutional

Constitutional History of Athens (book,
Schömann)
Bosanquet, Bernard **2** 425-426

Constitutional monarchy
see Monarchy, constitutional

Constitutional Union party (United States
politics)
Douglas, Stephen Arnold **5** 80-82

Everett, Edward **5** 344
Lincoln, Abraham **9** 415-418
Stephens, Alexander Hamilton **14** 429-430
Toombs, Robert Augustus **15** 267-268

Constitutionalist party (Mexico)
Obregón, Álvaro **11** 458-459

Constitutions of Clarendon
see Clarendon, Constitutions of

Constitutions of Melfi (1231)
Frederick II **6** 79

Construction (sculpture)
Gabo, Naum **6** 158-159

Construction for an Airport (sculpture)
Pevsner, Antoine **12** 263-264

Construction in Metal (musical composition)
Cage, John **3** 211-214

Construction industry
Bechtel, Stephen Davison **2** 98-99

Constructivism (art movement)
Duchamp-Villon, Raymond **5** 123
Gabo, Naum **6** 158-159
González, Julio **6** 428-429
Hepworth, Barbara **7** 318-319
Lippold, Richard **9** 440-442
Malevich, Kasimir **10** 168-169
Marc, Franz **10** 231
Moholy-Nagy, László **11** 82-83
Pevsner, Antoine **12** 263-264
Rodchenko, Alexander Mikhailovich **13** 233-234
Taeuber-Arp, Sophie **15** 73-74
Tatlin, Vladimir Evgrafovich **15** 117-118
Tinguely, Jean **15** 230-232
van Doesburg, Theo **15** 421

Constructivism (literature)
Meyerhold, Vsevolod Emilievich **10** 539

Consuelo (novel)
Sand, George **13** 459-461

Consul, The (opera)
Menotti, Gian Carlo **10** 509-510

Consulate (France; 1799-1804)
see France—1799-1804

Consultation, La (novel)
Martin du Gard, Roger **10** 295-296

Consumer Behavior, Inc.
Chapin, (F.) Stuart **3** 437-438

Consumer Credit Protection Act (United States)
Proxmire, William **12** 467-468

Containment policy (United States)
see Communism

Contarini Fleming (novel)
Disraeli, Benjamin **5** 27-29

Contarini, Gasparo (1483-1542), Italian diplomat and religious leader
Paul III **12** 144-145
Pomponazzi, Pietro **12** 390-391

Contemplation (stories)
Kafka, Franz **8** 403-406

Contemplations (anthology)
Lamartine, Alphonse Marie Louis de **9** 173-175

Contemplations (poem)
Bradstreet, Anne Dudley **2** 486-487

Contemplations, Les (poems)
Hugo, Victor Marie **8** 22-25

Contemporary (periodical)
Belinsky, Grigorievich **2** 128
Chernyshevsky, Nikolai Gavrilovich **3** 504-505
Tolstoy, Leo **15** 262-265
Turgenev, Ivan Sergeyevich **15** 345-348

Contemporary Chamber Players (United States)
Shapey, Ralph **14** 154-155

Contemporary Scene, The (essays)
Mariátegui, José Carlos **10** 255-256

Contes d'Espagne et D'Italie (poems)
Musset, Louis Charles Alfred de **11** 271-272

Contes et Nouvelles en vers (literary collection)
La Fontaine, Jean de **9** 156-157

Contes indiens (book)
Mallarmé, Stéphane **10** 172-173

Conti, Louis François Joseph, Prince de (1734-1814), French nobleman
Rousseau, Jean Jacques **13** 324-328

CONTI, NICCOLÒ DE' (circa 1396-1469), Venetian merchant-adventurer **4** 212-213
Covilhão, Pedro de **4** 278-279

Conti, Rinaldo
see Alexander IV

Conti (literary character)
Lessing, Gotthold Ephraim **9** 357-359

Continental Congress (United States; 1774-1789)
• 1774: FIRST
  members (Middle Colonies)
    Chase, Samuel **3** 475-476
    Dickinson, John **4** 543-544
    Galloway, Joseph **6** 186-187
    Jay, John **8** 230-232
  members (New England)
    Adams, John **1** 48-51
    Adams, Samuel **1** 55-56
    Sherman, Roger **14** 185-186
  members (South)
    Henry, Patrick **7** 309-311
    Lee, Richard Henry **9** 291-292
    Pendleton, Edmund **12** 197-198
    Rutledge, John **13** 387-388
    Washington, George **16** 126-129
• 1775-89: SECOND
  members (Middle Colonies)
    Chase, Samuel **3** 475-476
    Clinton, George **4** 113-114
    Dickinson, John **4** 543-544

    Franklin, Benjamin **6** 60-64
    Galloway, Joseph **6** 186-187
    Hamilton, Alexander **7** 95-98
    Hopkinson, Francis **7** 496-497
    Jay, John **8** 230-232
    Livingston, Robert R. **9** 462-463
    Morris, Gouverneur **11** 182-183
    Morris, Robert **11** 185-187
    Rush, Benjamin **13** 364-365
    Schuyler, Philip John **14** 49-50
    Wilson, James **16** 323-324
  members (New England)
    Deane, Silas **4** 435-437
    Gerry, Elbridge **6** 282-283
    Hancock, John **7** 114-116
    King, Rufus **9** 22-23
    Sherman, Roger **14** 185-186
  members (South)
    Henry, Patrick **7** 309-311
    Jefferson, Thomas **8** 238-241
    Lee, Arthur **9** 288-289
    Lee, Richard Henry **9** 291-292
    Madison, James **10** 121-123
    Pinckney, Charles **12** 309-310
    Randolph, Edmund **13** 29-30
    Rutledge, John **13** 387-388
    Washington, George **16** 126-129
    Wythe, George **16** 415
• GENERAL POLICIES
  diplomatic missions
    Allen, Ethan **1** 163-164
    Carroll, John **3** 331-332
    Deane, Silas **4** 435-437
    Franklin, Benjamin **6** 60-64
    Lee, Arthur **9** 288-289
    Pinckney, Charles Cotesworth **12** 310
  presidents
    Hancock, John **7** 114-116
    Jay, John **8** 230-232
    Laurens, Henry **9** 232
    St. Clair, Arthur **13** 429-430
  supporters
    Bradford, William **2** 477
    Coxe, Tench **4** 285-286
    Montgomery, Richard **11** 138-139
    Morgan, Daniel **11** 160-161
    see also Articles of Confederation (United States; 1781); Constitution of the United States (1787); Intolerable Acts (1774)

Continental Harmony (music collection)
Billings, William **2** 274-275

Continental System (economics blockade; 1806-1807)
Krupp **9** 109-111
Napoleon I **11** 306-310
Selim III **14** 95-96
see also Napoleonic Wars

Continuation du Discours des misères de ce temps (poems)
Ronsard, Pierre de **13** 271-273

Continuations des Amours (poems)
Ronsard, Pierre de **13** 271-273

Continuity (painting)
Sheeler, Charles **14** 170-171

Contraception
see Birth control

Contrafactum (musical form)
Tallis, Thomas **15** 91

Contrapuntal music
see Counterpoint (music)

Contra-Remonstrants (religion)
Maurice of Nassau **10** 348-349
Oldenbarnevelt, Johan van **11** 495-496

Contrast, The (book)
Hildreth, Richard **7** 382

Contrast, The (play; Tyler)
Hallam, Lewis Sr. and Jr. **7** 87
Tyler, Royall **15** 371-372

Contrasting Forms (painting)
Léger, Fernand **9** 302-303

Contrasts (book)
Pugin, Augustus Welby Northmore
12 479-480

Contrasts (musical composition)
Bartók, Béla **2** 35-36

Contrat de mariage, Le (book)
Balzac, Honoré de **1** 478-480

Contre Sainte-Beuve (book)
Proust, Marcel **12** 465-467

Contre-Machiavel (book; Gentillet)
Machiavelli, Niccolò **10** 97-99

Contrition (literary character)
Langland, William **9** 194-195

Controversie concerning Liberty of Conscience ... (book)
Cotton, John **4** 263-265

Controversies (book; Bellarmine)
Pázmány, Péter **12** 164-165

Convention People's party (Ghana)
Nkrumah, Kwame **11** 408-410

Conventuals (Franciscan congregation)
Jacopone da Todi **8** 194

Conversation at Midnight (book)
Millay, Edna St. Vincent **11** 24-25

Conversation Books (books)
Beethoven, Ludwig van **2** 114-117

Conversation with a Beggar (story)
Kafka, Franz **8** 403-406

Conversation with a Drunkard (story)
Kafka, Franz **8** 403-406

Conversazione in Sicilia (novel; Vittorini)
Pavese, Cesare **12** 154-155
Vittorini, Elio **16** 2-3

Conversions, religious
to Baptists
Backus, Isaac **1** 420-421
Bunyan, John **3** 128-129
McCoy, Isaac **10** 403

Miller, William **11** 30-31
to Calvinism
Calvin, John **3** 239-242
Jordaens, Jacob **8** 347-349
to Catholicism (16th-18th century)
Bach, Johann Christian **1** 415-416
Crashaw, Richard **4** 296
Dowland, John **5** 90
Dryden, John **5** 106-107
James II **8** 207-208
Luther, Martin **10** 48-51
Vondel, Joost van den **16** 19-20
Wallenstein, Albrecht Wenzel Eusebius von **16** 80-81
Winckelmann, Johann Joachim
16 332-333
to Catholicism (18th-19th century)
Brownson, Orestes Augustus
3 57-58
Chateaubriand, Vicomte de
3 477-479
Hecker, Isaac Thomas **7** 250-251
Newman, John Henry **11** 365-367
Pugin, Augustus Welby Northmore
12 479-480
Seton, Elizabeth Ann Bayley
14 118-119
to Catholicism (19th-20th century)
Chesterton, Gilbert Keith **3** 508-509
Claudel, Paul Louis Charles **4** 90-91
Diem, Ngo Dinh **5** 6-7
Evans-Pritchard, Edward Evan **5** 340
Greene, Graham **6** 523-524
Hara, Kei **7** 138
Maritain, Jacques **10** 263
Péguy, Charles Pierre **12** 183-184
Undset, Sigrid **15** 388-389
to Christianity (pre-Reformation)
Augustine **1** 367-370
Cyprianus, Thascius Caecilianus
4 361-362
Ezana **5** 354-355
Paul **12** 141-143
Rollo **13** 264-265
Theodosius **15** 176
to Church of England
Eliot, Thomas Stearns **5** 258-261
to Evangelicalism
Equiano, Olaudah **5** 296-297
Wilberforce, William **16** 269-270
to German Reformed Church
Nevin, John Williamson **11** 357
to Islam
Sabbatai Zevi **13** 400-401
Sinan, Kodja Mimar **14** 245-246
Touré, Sékou **15** 275-277
to Lutheranism
Luther, Martin **10** 48-51
to Methodism
Cartwright, Peter **3** 344-345
Feng Yü-hsiang **5** 412-413
McLean, John **10** 422-423
Rhee, Syngman **13** 117-120
Sithole, Ndabaningi **14** 262-264
Whitefield, George **16** 241-242
to Pentecostalism

McPherson, Aimee Semple **10** 434
to Quakerism
Bradford, William **2** 475-476
Lancaster, Joseph **9** 182-183
Mott, Lucretia Coffin **11** 212-213
Penn, William **12** 200-202
to Unitarianism
Ricardo, David **13** 123-124

Conversos (baptized Jews)
Ferdinand V **5** 417-418

Convivio (treatise)
Dante Alighieri **4** 389-391

CONWAY, JILL KATHRYN KER (born 1934), historian interested in the role of women and president of Smith College **4** 213-214

Conway, Treaty of (1277)
Llewelyn ap Gruffydd **9** 468

Cook, Frederick Albert (1865-1940), American physician and Arctic explorer
Cook, James **4** 214-215

COOK, JAMES (1728-1779), English explorer, navigator, and cartographer **4** 214-215
associates
Banks, Joseph **1** 489-490
Bligh, William **2** 325-326
Jenner, Edward **8** 245-246
Vancouver, George **15** 414-415
explorations
Kamehameha I **8** 416
Mendaña de Neyra, Álvaro de
10 483

Cook, The (painting)
Vermeer, Jan **15** 466-467

Cook Islands (South Pacific Ocean)
Seddon, Richard John **14** 81-82

Cooke, Deryck Victor (1919-1976), English musicologist
Mahler, Gustav **10** 144-145

COOKE, JAY (1821-1905), American merchant banker **4** 215-216
Chase, Salmon Portland **3** 473-475
Collins, Edward Knight **4** 162-163

Cookman Institute (Jacksonville, Florida)
Bethune, Mary McLeod **2** 241-242

Cool Million, A (novel)
West, Nathanael **16** 213-214

COOLEY, CHARLES HORTON (1864-1929), American social psychologist, sociologist, and educator **4** 216-217

Cooley, Thomas McIntyre (1824-1898), American jurist
Cooley, Charles Horton **4** 216-217

Cooley v. Board of Wardens (legal case)
Curtis, Benjamin Robbins **4** 349

Coolgardie (district; Australia)
Forrest, John **6** 12-13

COOLIDGE, JOHN CALVIN (1872-1933), president of the United States 1923-1929
4 217-219

biographies of
    Woods, Robert Archey **16** 374
Cabinet
    Hoover, Herbert Clark **7** 483-485
    Kellogg, Frank Billings **8** 481
    Mellon, Andrew William
        10 469-470
    Stone, Harlan Fiske **14** 468-470
diplomatic appointments
    Hearst, William Randolph
        7 243-244
    Morrow, Dwight Whitney
        11 190-191
    Stimson, Henry Lewis **14** 457-458
friends
    Carver, George Washington
        3 346-347
    Keller, Helen Adams **8** 479-480
Teapot Dome scandal
    Walsh, Thomas James **16** 85-86

COOMBS, HERBERT COLE (Nugget; born 1906), Australian economist **4** 219-220

Cooper, Anthony Ashley (1621-1683)
    see Shaftesbury, 1st Earl of

Cooper, Anthony Ashley (1671-1713)
    see Shaftesbury, 3d Earl of

Cooper, Anthony Ashley (1801-1885)
    see Shaftesbury, 7th Earl of

Cooper, Gary (1901-1961), American motion picture actor
    Goldwyn, Samuel **6** 416

COOPER, JAMES FENIMORE (1789-1851), American novelist and social critic **4** 220-223
    Bird, Robert Montgomery **2** 281-282
    Brackenridge, Hugh Henry **2** 472-473
    Parkman, Francis **12** 113-115
    Sarmiento, Domingo Faustino
        13 484-485
    Simms, William Gilmore **14** 235-236

Cooper, Leroy Gordon, Jr. (born 1927), American astronaut
    Armstrong, Neil Alden **1** 304-306

COOPER, PETER (1791-1883), American inventor and manufacturer **4** 223-224
    Hewitt, Abram Stevens **7** 371-372

COOPER, THOMAS (1759-1839), English-born American scientist and educator **4** 224

Cooper, Hewitt and Co. (steel firm)
    Hewitt, Abram Stevens **7** 371-372

Cooper Union School of Design for Women (New York City)
    Rimmer, William **13** 174

Cooper Union, The (New York City; established 1859)
    Cooper, Peter **4** 223-224
    Hewitt, Abram Stevens **7** 371-372

Cooper v. Telfair (legal case)
    Chase, Samuel **3** 475-476

Cooperative Commonwealth Federation (Canada)
    Douglas, Thomas Clement **5** 82-83

King, William Lyon Mackenzie **9** 25-26
Woodsworth, James Shaver **16** 376

Cooperative movement (economics)
    Dubinsky, David **5** 114-115
    Lloyd, Henry Demarest **9** 468-469
    Margai, Milton Augustus Striery
        10 248-249
    Owen, Robert **12** 39-40
    Webb, Beatrice Potter **16** 153-154

Cooperativism and Socialism (book)
    Terra, Gabriel **15** 154-155

Cooper's Creek (Australia)
    Burke, Robert O'Hara **3** 142-143

Cooper's Hill (poem; Denham)
    Pope, Alexander **12** 395-397

Cooperstown (village; New York State)
    Cooper, James Fenimore **4** 220-223

Cooweescoowe
    see Ross, John

COPEAU, JACQUES (1879-1949), French dramatic theorist, director, and actor who established the Vieux Colombier **4** 225

Copenhagen (city, Denmark)
    Charles XII **3** 464-466

Copenhagen, Battle of (1801)
    Bligh, William **2** 325-326
    Brock, Isaac **3** 12-13
    Canning, George **3** 258-260
    Franklin, John **6** 64-65
    Nelson, Horatio **11** 336-338

Copenhagen, University of (Denmark)
    Brahe, Tycho **2** 489-490
    Dam, Carl Peter Henrik **4** 382-383
    Heisenberg, Werner Karl **7** 261-263
    Krogh, Schack August Steenberg **9** 106
    Oersted, Hans Christian **11** 476-478
    Steno, Nicolaus **14** 425-426

COPERNICUS, NICOLAUS (1473-1543), Polish astronomer **4** 226-227
    Brahe, Tycho **2** 489-490
    Bruno, Giordano **3** 75-76
    Hipparchus **7** 407-408
    Kant, Immanuel **8** 430-432
    see also Universe, systems of—Copernican

COPLAND, AARON (1900-1990), American composer **4** 227-228
    Graham, Martha **6** 485-486
    Ives, Charles Edward **8** 159-160
    Sessions, Roger Huntington **14** 117-118

Copland, Robert (1508-1547), English printer
    Brant, Sebastian **2** 503-504

Coplas (elegy)
    Manrique, Jorge **10** 210-211

COPLEY, JOHN SINGLETON (1738-1815), American portrait painter **4** 228-230
    Allston, Washington **1** 176-177
    Eakins, Thomas **5** 176-177
    Revere, Paul **13** 110-111
    Smibert, John **14** 282

Stuart, Gilbert **14** 513-515
Trumbull, John **15** 316-317

Copper mining (industry)
    Daly, Marcus **4** 379-380
    Hearst, George **7** 242
    Kaunda, Kenneth David **8** 460-461
    Schoolcraft, Henry Rowe **14** 29

Copper Sun (poems)
    Cullen, Countee **4** 333-334

Copperhead, The (play)
    Barrymores **2** 28-30

Copperheads (United States politics)
    Barnard, Frederick Augustus Porter
        2 9-10
    Vallandigham, Clement Laird
        15 406-407

Coppermine River (Canada)
    Hearne, Samuel **7** 241-242

Coptos (Qift, town, Egypt)
    Petrie, William Matthew Flinders
        12 261-262

Copyright (law)
    Hand, Billings Learned **7** 116
    Payne, John Howard **12** 159
    Sydenham, Thomas **15** 59-60
    Webster, Noah **16** 164-166

Copyright Act (England; 1735)
    Hogarth, William **7** 446-447

Coral Sea, Battle of the (1942)
    Nimitz, Chester William **11** 395-396

Coral, The (play)
    Kaiser, Georg **8** 411-412

Corbaccio (book)
    Boccaccio, Giovanni **2** 351-353

Corbeau, Le (poem)
    Mallarmé, Stéphane **10** 172-173

Corbett, James John (1866-1933), American professional boxer
    Sullivan, John Lawrence **15** 24-25

Corbie, (town, France)
    Louis XIII **9** 529-531

Corcoran Gallery (Washington, D.C.)
    Clark, William Andrews **4** 83-85

Corday, Charlotte (1768-1793), French patriot
    Marat, Jean Paul **10** 230-231

Cordeliers Club (French Revolution)
    Danton, Georges Jacques **4** 391-393

Cordini, Antonio
    see Sangallo Family (Antonio the Younger)

Córdoba, Francisco Hernandez de (died 1518), Spanish explorer and soldier
    Velázquez de Cuéllar, Diego **15** 459

Cordova (Córdoba; province, Spain)
    Abd al-Rahman I **1** 13-14

Cordova, Treaty of (1821)
    Iturbide, Agustín de **8** 155-156

CORE
see Congress of Racial Equality

CORELLI, ARCANGELO (1653-1713), Italian composer and violinist **4** 230-231
Buxtehude, Dietrich **3** 185-186
Tartini, Giuseppe **15** 112-113

Corfu (island, Ionian Sea)
Guiscard, Robert **7** 39-40

CORI, GERTY T. (born Gerty Theresa Radnitz; 1896-1957), American biochemist **4** 231-234

Corinna (flourished 5th century B.C.), Greek lyric poet
Pindar **12** 312-313

Corinna (literary character)
Ovid **12** 34-36

Corinne ou l'Italie (novel)
Staël, Germaine de **14** 391-392

CORINTH, LOVIS (1838-1925), German artist **4** 234

Corinth, Lovis (1858-1925), German painter and engraver
Beckmann, Max **2** 104-105

Corinth (Greek city-state)
Aratus **1** 273-274
Caesar, Gaius Julius **3** 207-210
Cleomenes III **4** 103-104
Polybios **12** 384-385

Corinthian League (military)
Alexander the Great **1** 137-141, 124
Philip II **12** 269-271
Ptolemy I **12** 470-472

Corinthian War (395-387 B.C.)
Agesilaus II **1** 79-80

Corinthians, Letters to the (New Testament book)
Paul **12** 141-143

Coriolano (opera)
Cavalli, Pietro Francesco **3** 382-383

Coriolanus (play; Shakespeare)
Brecht, Bertolt **2** 512-514
Shakespeare, William **14** 142-145

Coriolanus Overture (musical composition)
Beethoven, Ludwig van **2** 114-117

Coriolis, Gustave (1792-1843), French mathematician
Foucault, Jean Bernard Léon **6** 28-29

Cork, 1st Earl of
see Boyle, Richard

Cormon, Fernand Anne Piestre (1845-1924), French painter
Toulouse-Lautrec, Henri de **15** 273-274
Van Gogh, Vincent **15** 427-429

Corn Husking Bee (painting)
Johnson, Earvin Jr. **8** 297-299

Corn Is Green, The (play)
Barrymores **2** 28-30

Corn Laws (England)
Aberdeen, 4th Earl of **1** 25-26
Bright, John **3** 6-7
Cobden, Richard **4** 127-128
Gladstone, William Ewart **6** 357-360
Liverpool, 2nd Earl of **9** 456-457
Peel, Robert **12** 181-183

Cornaro a San Polo Palace (Venice)
Sanmicheli, Michele **13** 469-470

Cornbury, Viscount
see Hyde, Edward, 3d Earl of Clarendon

CORNEILLE, PIERRE (1606-1684), French playwright **4** 234-236
influence of
Charpentier, Marc Antoine **3** 471-472
Dryden, John **5** 106-107
Racine, Jean Baptiste **12** 532-535
Voltaire **16** 14-16
influenced by
Alarcón, Pedro Antonio de **1** 100-101
Seneca the Younger, Lucius Annaeus **14** 103-105
opponents
La Bruyère, Jean de **9** 145

Cornelia (flourished 2d century B.C.), Roman matron, daughter of Scipio Africanus Major
Gracchus, Tiberius and Gaius Sempronius **6** 479-480

Cornelia (play; Garnier)
Kyd, Thomas **9** 140-141

Cornell, Alonzo (1832-1904), American businessman and politician
Arthur, Chester Alan **1** 321-323
Cornell, Ezra **4** 236-237

CORNELL, EZRA (1807-1874), American financier and philanthropist **4** 236-237
Corning, Erastus **4** 238-239
White, Andrew Dickson **16** 226-227

CORNELL, JOSEPH (1903-1972), American artist **4** 237-238

Cornell Christian Union (religious society)
Mott, John R. **11** 212

Cornell University (Ithaca, New York State)
chemistry
Debye, Peter Joseph William **4** 447-448
founders
Cornell, Ezra **4** 236-237
White, Andrew Dickson **16** 226-227
history
Becker, Carl Lotus **2** 100-101
Tyler, Moses Coit **15** 369-370
literature
Nabokov, Vladimir **11** 287-288
physics
Bethe, Hans Albrecht **2** 238-239
social sciences
Johnson, Alvin Saunders **8** 293-294
Lewin, Kurt **9** 375-376
Malinowski, Kaspar Bronislaw **10** 170-171
Perkins, Frances **12** 221-222

Titchener, Edward Bradford **15** 241-242

Corner Palace (Venice)
Sansovino, Jacopo **13** 470-471

Cornfield with Crows (painting)
Van Gogh, Vincent **15** 427-429

Cornhill Magazine (periodical)
Doyle, Arthur Conan **5** 91-92
Ruskin, John **13** 371-372
Thackeray, William Makepeace **15** 159-161

Cornhuskers (poems)
Sandburg, Carl **13** 461-462

CORNING, ERASTUS (1794-1872), American merchant and financier **4** 238-239

CORNPLANTER (c. 1732-1836), Seneca village leader **4** 239-241

Cornstalk (circa 1720-1777), Shawnee Indian Chief
Dunmore, 4th Earl of **5** 147
Lewis, Andrew **9** 376-377

CORNWALLIS, CHARLES (1st Marquess Cornwallis; 1738-1805), British soldier and statesman **4** 241-243
associates
Clinton, Henry **4** 114-115
Howe, William **7** 538-539
invades Virginia
Jefferson, Thomas **8** 238-241
Morgan, Daniel **11** 160-161
prisoner exchange
Laurens, Henry **9** 232
Yorktown, Battle of
see Yorktown, Battle of (1781)

CORONA, BERT (born 1918), Hispanic American union organizer **4** 243-247

Corona School (Bell, California)
Neutra, Richard Joseph **11** 355-356

Corona trágica, La (poem)
Lope Félix de Vega **9** 503-506

CORONADO, FRANCISCO VÁSQUEZ DE (1510-1554), Spanish explorer and colonial official **4** 247
Cabrillo, Juan Rodríguez **3** 204-205
Estevanico **5** 324-325
Marcos de Niza **10** 240
Mendoza, Antonio de **10** 494-495

Coronado case (legal case)
Taft, William Howard **15** 78-81

Coronation of Napoleon and Josephine (painting)
David, Jacques Louis **4** 407-409

Coronation of the Virgin (altarpiece)
Bellini, Giovanni **2** 137-138
Charonton, Enguerrand **3** 471

Coronation of the Virgin (painting)
Gentile da Fabriano **6** 266-267

Coronea, Battle of (394 B.C.)
Xenophon **16** 418-420

Coronet no tiene quien le escriba, El (stories)
García Márquez, Gabriel **6** 208-209

COROT, JEAN BAPTISTE CAMILLE
(1796-1875), French painter **4** 247-249
influence of
Böcklin, Arnold **2** 354-355
Daubigny, Charles François **4** 402
Gorky, Arshile **6** 458
Hodler, Ferdinand **7** 434-435
Inness, George **8** 123-124
Monet, Claude **11** 102-104
Pissarro, Camille **12** 326-327
Renoir, Pierre Auguste **13** 101-102
influenced by
Bonington, Richard Parkes
2 394-395
Carracci **3** 319-321
Veronese, Paolo **15** 469-470
works compared
Kane, Paul **8** 422-423
Rousseau, Théodore **13** 328

Coroticus (flourished early 5th century),
British military leader
Patrick, St. **12** 135-136

Corporate state (government)
Gómez, Máximo **6** 418-419
Mussolini, Benito **11** 272-274
Salazar, António de Oliveira
13 442-443

Corps de Dames (painting series)
Dubuffet, Jean Philippe Arthur
5 119-120

Corps glorieux, Les (musical composition)
Messiaen, Olivier **10** 528-529

Corpus inscriptionum Latinarum (book)
Mommsen, Theodor **11** 94-95

Corpus juris civilis
see Law codes—Byzantium

Corrario, Angelo
see Gregory XII

CORREGGIO (circa 1494-1534), Italian
painter **4** 249-251
influence of
Carracci **3** 319-321
Lotto, Lorenzo **9** 520-521
Mengs, Anton Raphael **10** 505
Murillo, Bartolomé Esteban
11 258-259
Parmigianino **12** 117
Reynolds, Joshua **13** 115-116
Ribera, Jusepe de **13** 122-123
influenced by
Mantegna, Andrea **10** 215-216
Michelangelo Buonarroti **11** 2-5
Raphael **13** 40-42

Correns, Karl Erich (1864-1933), German
botanist
Vries, Hugo de **16** 33-36

Correspondances (poem)
Baudelaire, Charles Pierre **2** 61-63

Correspondant (newspaper)
Montalembert, Comte de **11** 118-119

Correspondence ... (book)
Child, Lydia Maria Francis **3** 520-521

Correspondence of Menachem Mendel ...
(book)
Sholem Aleichem **14** 202-203

Corridors of Power (book)
Snow, Charles Percy **14** 311-312

Corridors of Time (series; Peake and Fleure)
Sauer, Carl Ortwin **13** 496-497

Corrigan, Mairead (born 1944), founder of
the women's peace movement in Northern Ireland (1976)
Corrigan and Williams **4** 251-253

CORRIGAN, MICHAEL AUGUSTINE
(1839-1902), American Catholic archbishop **4** 253
Hayes, Patrick Joseph **7** 224-225
McCloskey, John **10** 395

CORRIGAN and WILLIAMS founders of
the women's peace movement in Northern Ireland **4** 251-253

Corrupt Practices Bill (Great Britain; 1868)
Disraeli, Benjamin **5** 27-29

Corruption, political (government)
Curley, James Michael **4** 344-345
Godkin, Edwin Lawrence **6** 380
Grant, Ulysses Simpson **6** 492-494
Lloyd, Henry Demarest **9** 468-469
Merriam, Charles Edward **10** 518-519
Ruef, Abraham **13** 352-353
Tweed, William Marcy **15** 366-367
see also Muckraking; Political
machines; Teapot Dome Scandal
Japan
Tanaka, Kakuei **15** 96-98
Latin America
Somoza Debayle, Anastasio
14 336-337
Philippines
Marcos, Ferdinand **10** 240-242
Marcos, Imelda Romualdez
10 242-243
United States
Agnew, Spiro Theodore **1** 83-85
Nixon, Richard Milhous **11** 401-404

Corruption in the Palace of Justice (play)
Betti, Ugo **2** 246

Corsair (journal)
Kierkegaard, Søren Aabye **8** 547-549

Corsair, The (poem)
Byron, George Gordon Noel **3** 193-194
Lermontov, Mikhail Yurievich
9 352-353

Corsaire, Le (overture)
Berlioz, Louis Hector **2** 203-205

CORT, HENRY (1740-1800), English ironmaster **4** 254

Corte de los milagros, La (novel)
Valle Inclán, Ramón Maria del
15 407-408

CORTE REÁL, GASPAR AND MIGUEL,
Portuguese explorers **4** 254-255

Cortenuova, Battle of (1237)
Frederick II **6** 79

CORTÉS, HERNÁN (1485?-1547), Spanish
conquistador **4** 255-256
conquest of Mexico
Cabrillo, Juan Rodríguez **3** 204-205
Díaz del Castillo, Bernal **4** 536-537
Montezuma, II **11** 128-129
Velázquez de Cuéllar, Diego **15** 459
in literature
Prescott, William Hickling
12 440-441
Wallace, Lewis **16** 74-75
prisoners of
Cuauhtemoc **4** 329
Narváez, Pánfilo de **11** 315
Spanish administrators
Mendoza, Antonio de **10** 494-495
Zumárraga, Juan de **16** 531-532

Cortés, José Domingo (1830-1884),
Chilean writer
González Prada, Manuel **6** 431

Cortés, Palace of (Cuernavaca, Mexico)
Rivera, Diego **13** 183-184

Cortés Castro, Leon (1882-1946), Costa
Rican politician
Ferrer, José Figuéres **5** 428-429

Cortesano, El (book)
Milán, Luis **11** 15-16

Cortines, Adolfo Ruiz
see Ruiz Cortines, Adolfo

Cortisone (hormone)
Diels, Otto Paul Hermann **5** 5-6
Kendall, Edward Calvin **8** 495
Reichstein, Tadeus **13** 85-87

Corto viaggio sentimentale (stories)
Svevo, Italo **15** 47-48

CORTONA, PIETRO DA (1596-1669), Italian painter and architect **4** 256
Carracci **3** 319-321
Le Vau, Louis **9** 360-361
Le Brun, Charles **9** 269-270
Poussin, Nicolas **12** 418-420
Rosa, Salvator **13** 289-290

Corvée (forced labor)
Turgot, Anne Robert Jacques
15 348-349
see also Forced labor

Corwin, Norman (born 1910), American
writer-producer-director
Halffter, Christóbal **7** 79-80

Corydon (book)
Gide, André **6** 308-309

COS
see Charity Organization Society

Cosby, William (1690-1735/36), English
royal governor of New York
Morris, Lewis **11** 183-184
Zenger, John Peter **16** 497-498

COSBY, WILLIAM HENRY, JR. ("Bill" Cosby; born 1937), American entertainer **4** 257-258

Coscienza di Zeno, La (novel) Svevo, Italo **15** 47-48

COSGRAVE, LIAM (born 1920), Irish foreign minister and prime minister (1973-1977) **4** 258-260

Così è (se vi pare) (play) Pirandello, Luigi **12** 319-321

Cosi fan tutte (opera) Mozart, Wolfgang Amadeus **11** 218-221

Cosini, Zeno (literary character) Svevo, Italo **15** 47-48

COSIO VILLEGAS, DANIEL (1898-1976), Mexican teacher, civil servant, and author of studies of Mexican history **4** 260-261

Cosmetic industry
Ash, Mary Kay Wagner **1** 326-327
Chanel, Coco **3** 429
Lauder, Estee **9** 225-226
Picasso, Paloma **12** 295-297
Rubenstein, Helena **13** 342-343
Walker, C. J. **16** 61-62

Cosmic rays (physics)
detection
Anderson, Carl David **1** 214-215
Blackett, Patrick M.S. **2** 306-307
Bothe, Walther **2** 438-439
Compton, Arthur Holly **4** 186-188
Kapitsa, Pyotr Leonidovich **8** 433-435
Lovell, Alfred Charles Bernard **10** 8-9
discovered
Hess, Victor Francis **7** 362-363
Millikan, Robert Andrews **11** 33-35
energies
Cherenkov, Pavel Alekseevich **3** 502-503
Fermi, Enrico **5** 422-424

Cosmogony
see Galaxy; Milky Way Galaxy; Planet; Solar system; Star; Universe, origin of; Universe, systems of

Cosmographiae introductio (book) Waldseemüller, Martin **16** 56

Cosmology
Hawking, Stephen William **7** 206-208
see Universe, origin of; Universe, systems of

Cosmonauts (space exploration)
Armstrong, Neil Alden **1** 304-306
Gagarin, Yuri Alexeivich **6** 166-167

Cosmopolitan (magazine)
Brown, Helen Gurley **3** 36-37

Cosmopolitan Magazine (periodical)
Churchill, Winston **4** 50-51
Crane, Stephen **4** 293-295
Hearst, William Randolph **7** 243-244

Cosmopolitanism and Nation State (book) Meinecke, Friedrich **10** 460-461

Cossa, Baldassare
see John XXIII (antipope)

Cossa, Francesco del (1438?-1480), Italian painter
Tura, Cosimo **15** 343-344

Cossacks (Russian people)
Chmielnicki, Bogdan **4** 12-13
Godunov, Boris Feodorovich **6** 382-383
John III **8** 276-277

Cossacks, The (book)
Tolstoy, Leo **15** 262-265

Cost of Discipleship, The (book)
Bonhoeffer, Dietrich **2** 389-391

Costa, Lúcio (1902-1963), Brazilian architect
Le Corbusier **9** 274-275

Costa e Silva, Arthur da (1902-1969), Brazilian marshal, president 1967-1969
Castelo Branco, Humberto **3** 359-360

Costa Rica, Republic of (nation, Central America)
Arias Sanchez, Oscar **1** 287-289
Calderón Fournier, Rafael **3** 222-223
Ferrer, José Figuéres **5** 428-429
Keith, Minor Cooper **8** 476-477
Meiggs, Henry **10** 458-459

Costaguana (literary nation, South America)
Conrad, Joseph **4** 205-207

Costanza e Fortezza (opera)
Fux, Johann Joseph **6** 155-156

Coster, Charles de (1827-1879), Belgian author
Dallapiccola, Luigi **4** 377-378

Coster, Dirk (1889-1950), Dutch physicist
Hevesy, George Charles de **7** 371

Costilla, Miguel Hidalgo y
see Hidalgo y Costilla, Miguel

Cot and Cradle Stories (book)
Traill, Catharine Parr **15** 291

Côté de Guermantes, Le (novel)
Proust, Marcel **12** 465-467

Cotopaxi, Mt. (Ecuador)
Church, Frederick Edwin **4** 49-50

Cottage Door (painting)
Gainsborough, Thomas **6** 170-172

Cottage Residences (book)
Downing, Andrew Jackson **5** 90-91

Cotte, Robert de (1656-1735), French architect
Boffrand, Gabriel Germain **2** 361
Neumann, Balthasar **11** 354-355

COTTEN, ELIZABETH ("Libba"; born Elizabeth Nevills; 1892-1987), African American musician **4** 261-263

Cotter's Saturday Night, The (poem)
Burns, Robert **3** 155-156

COTTON, JOHN (1584-1652), American Congregationalist clergyman **4** 263-265
Davenport, John **4** 405-406
Dudley, Thomas **5** 124-125
Hutchinson, Anne Marbury **8** 69-71
Mather, Cotton **10** 330-332
Williams, Roger **16** 304-305
Winthrop, John **16** 339-341

Cotton (fiber)
Arkwright, Richard **1** 298
Coxe, Tench **4** 285-286
Dunbar, William **5** 143-144
Hampton, Wade **7** 111-112
Slater, Samuel **14** 272-273

Cotton Club (Harlem, New York City)
Ellington, Edward Kennedy **5** 273-274

Cotton Comes to Harlem (film)
Davis, Ossie **4** 421-422

Cotton gin (machine)
Whitney, Eli **16** 253-254

Cotton Whigs (United States politics)
Sumner, Charles **15** 30-31

Coudenberg, Francis van (flourished 1304-1350), Flemish monk
Ruysbroeck, Jan van **13** 388-389

COUGHLIN, CHARLES EDWARD (1891-1979), Canadian-American priest and politician **4** 265-266
Long, Huey Pierce **9** 496-497
Mundelein, George William **11** 248-249
Townsend, Francis Everitt **15** 282-283

Coulanges, Numa Denis Fustel de
see Fustel de Coulanges, Numa Denis

COULOMB, CHARLES AUGUSTIN DE (1736-1806), French physicist **4** 266-267
Cavendish, Henry **3** 383-384

Coulommiers (château, France)
Mansart, François **10** 211

COULTON, GEORGE GORDON (1858-1947), English historian **4** 267

Council for a Livable World (United States)
Szilard, Leo **15** 64-66

Council for New England (politics)
Calvert, George **3** 238-239
Gorges, Ferdinando **6** 455-456

Council of Economic Advisers (United States)
Burns, Arthur **3** 151-153
Heller, Walter **7** 265-266

Council of Elders
see French Revolution—Council of Elders

Council of Five Hundred
see Five Hundred, Council of

Council of Ministers (Union of Soviet Socialist Republics)
Khruschchev, Nikita Sergeevich **8** 539-540
Molotov, Vyacheslav Mikhailovich **11** 89-90
Stalin, Joseph **14** 393-396

Council of National Defense
see National Defense, Council of (United States; World War I)

Council on African Affairs (established 1937)
Du Bois, William Edward Burghardt **5** 116-118
Robeson, Paul Leroy **13** 198-199

Counsellor-at-law (play)
Rice, Elmer **13** 126-127

Count Almaviva (literary character)
Beaumarchais, Pierre August Caron de **2** 93-94

Count Basie Orchestra
Basie **2** 48-49

Count Belisarius (novel)
Graves, Robert Ranke **6** 504-506

Count Filippo (play)
Heavysege, Charles **7** 246

Count Julian (play)
Landor, Walter Savage **9** 186-187

Count Nulin (verse tale)
Pushkin, Aleksandr Sergeevich **12** 489-491

Count Oderland (play)
Frisch, Max **6** 118-119

Count of Carmagnola, The (verse play)
Manzoni, Alessandro **10** 222-224

Count of Monte Cristo, The (novel)
Dumas, Alexandre **5** 136-138

Count Robert of Paris (novel)
Scott, Walter **14** 68-70

Counter-attack (poems)
Sassoon, Siegfried **13** 492-493

Counter Reformation (Roman Catholic church)
and Protestantism
Bossuet, Jacques Bénigne **2** 431-432
Charles V **3** 457-459
Philip II **12** 271-273
see also Protestant Reformation;
Trent, Council of (1545-1563)
apostolic service
Bellarmine, Robert **2** 135-136
Borromeo, Charles **2** 423-424
Cajetan **3** 215-216
Francis of Sales **6** 47
Ignatius of Loyola **8** 108-109
Neri, Philip **11** 340
Canisius, Peter **3** 258
ecumenical councils
Gregory XIII **6** 534
Pázmány, Péter **12** 164-165
Paul III **12** 144-145
Paul IV **12** 145-146
Pius IV **12** 332
Pius V **12** 332-333
influence on the arts
Alemán, Mateo **1** 126
Caravaggio **3** 282-284
Crashaw, Richard **4** 296
Lassus, Roland de **9** 216-218

Marenzio, Luca **10** 248
Morales, Luis de **11** 150
Muratori, Lodovico Antonio **11** 254-255

Counterfeiters, The (book)
Gide, André **6** 308-309

Counterpoint (music)
Austria
Fux, Johann Joseph **6** 155-156
Haydn, Franz Joseph **7** 219-221
Mozart, Wolfgang Amadeus **11** 218-221
Brazil
Villa-Lobos, Heitor **15** 496-497
France
Franck, César **6** 48-49
Josquin des Prez **8** 361-363
Lassus, Roland de **9** 216-218
Le Jeune, Claude **9** 314-315
Germany
Froberger, Johann Jakob **6** 120-121
Schumann, Robert Alexander **14** 41-43
Schütz, Heinrich **14** 48-49
Senfl, Ludwig **14** 105-106
Italy
Zarlino, Gioseffo **16** 490-491
Netherlands
Sweelinck, Jan Pieterszoon **15** 50-51
United States
Fry, William Henry **6** 136-137
Ives, Charles Edward **8** 159-160
Piston, Walter **12** 327-328
see also Cantus firmus; Fugue; Polyphony

Counterrevolution, Russian
see Russian Revolution (1918-1920)

Countess Cathleen, The (verse drama)
Yeats, William Butler **16** 445-447

Countess from Hong Kong, A (film)
Chaplin, Charles Spencer **3** 438-440

Countess of Touron (painting)
Ingres, Jean Auguste Dominique **8** 121-123

Country By-ways (literary collection)
Jewett, Sarah Orne **8** 256

Country Doctor, A (novel)
Jewett, Sarah Orne **8** 256

Country Doctor, The (stories)
Kafka, Franz **8** 403-406

Country Girl, The (play)
Odets, Clifford **11** 470-471

Country House, The (novel)
Galsworthy, John **6** 189-190

Country Houses (book; Downing)
Davis, Alexander Jackson **4** 411

Country Life, A (poem)
Herrick, Robert **7** 336-339

Country Mouse, The (poem)
Bishop, Elizabeth **2** 290-292

Country of Pointed Firs, The (novel)
Jewett, Sarah Orne **8** 256

Country of Strangers, A (novel)
Richter, Conrad Michael **13** 148-149

Country party (Australian politics)
Hughes, William Morris **8** 21-22
Menzies, Robert Gordon **10** 510-511
Scullin, James Henry **14** 73

Country party (English politics)
Buckingham, 2d Duke of **3** 94-95

Country Road with Poplars (drawing)
Rousseau, Théodore **13** 328

Country Town Sayings (book)
Howe, Edgar Watson **7** 529

Country Wife, The (play)
Wycherley, William **16** 411-412

COUNTS, GEORGE S(YLVESTER) (1889-1974), American educator and educational sociologist **4** 267-269

Count's War (Denmark; 1534-1536)
Gustavus I **7** 42-43

County Election (painting)
Bingham, George Caleb **2** 278-279

Coup de dés jamais n'abolira le hasard, Un (book)
Mallarmé, Stéphane **10** 172-173

Coup de lance (painting; Rubens)
Van Dyck, Anthony **15** 423-425

Coup d'etat
see Coups d'etat

Coupe de cendres, La (book)
Rabearivelo, Jean Joseph **12** 523-524

Coupe et les lèvres, La (verse)
Musset, Louis Charles Alfred de **11** 271-272

COUPER, ARCHIBALD SCOTT (1831-1892), British chemist **4** 269-270

COUPER, JAMES HAMILTON (1794-1866), American agriculturist **4** 270

COUPERIN, FRANÇOIS (1668-1733), French composer, organist, and harpsichordist **4** 270-271
Corelli, Arcangelo **4** 230-231
Rameau, Jean Philippe **13** 17-18

Coups d'etat (politics)
Algeria (1965)
Boumediene, Houari **2** 445-446
Angola
Savimbi, Jonas Malheiros **13** 503-505
Argentina (20th century)
Irigoyen, Hipólito **8** 139-140
Perón, Juan Domingo **12** 228-230
Perón, Isabel Martinez de **12** 226-228
Videla, Jorge Rafaél **15** 490-492
Bangladesh
Ziaur Rahman **16** 515-516
Bolivia (1943; 1964)
Paz, Octavio **12** 161-162

Brazil (1889)
  Barbosa, Ruy **1** 503-504
  Deodoro da Fonseca, Manoel **4** 502
  Pedro II **12** 180-181
  Peixoto, Floriano **12** 188-189
Brazil (1937)
  Aranha, Osvaldo **1** 272-273
  Vargas, Getulio Dornelles
    15 433-434
Brazil (1964)
  Castelo Branco, Humberto
    3 359-360
  Kubitschek de Oliveira, Juscelino
    9 113-115
  Prestes, Luiz Carlos **12** 442-444
Buganda (1888)
  Mwanga **11** 282-283
Burma (1962)
  Ne Win **11** 364-365
Cambodia (1970)
  Sihanouk, Norodom **14** 222-223
Chile
  Alessandri Palma, Arturo **1** 128-129
  Carrera, José Miguel **3** 323-324
  Ibáñez del Campo, Carlos **8** 88
  Pinochet Ugarte, Augusto
    12 315-317
China (1898)
  Kuang-hsü **9** 111-112
  Tz'u-hsi **15** 375-376
Colombia (1953)
  Rojas Pinilla, Gustavo **13** 255-256
Congo
  Kasavubu, Joseph **8** 453-455
  Youlou, Fulbert **16** 466-467
Cuba (1952; 1957)
  Batista y Zaldívar, Fulgencio
    2 57-58
Czechoslovakia (1948)
  Beneš, Edward **2** 155-157
Dahomey (1960s)
  Apithy, Sourou Migan **1** 259-260
Dominican Republic
  Bosch, Juan **2** 428-429
  Vázquez, Horacio **15** 448-449
Ecuador (1940s)
  Velasco Ibarra, José María
    15 452-454
Egypt
  Sadat, Anwar **13** 412-414
Egypt (1952)
  Azhari, Sayyid Ismail al- **1** 399-401
El Salvador
  Duarte, José Napoleón **5** 109-111
France (1799)
  Bonaparte, Joseph **2** 381-382
  Bernadotte, Jean Baptiste **2** 205-206
  Napoleon I **11** 306-310
  Sieyès, Comte Emmanuel Joseph
    14 217-218
  Talleyrand, Charles Maurice de
    15 89-90
France (1851)
  Dumas, Alexandre **5** 136-138
  Napoleon III **11** 310-312
  Simon, Jules François **14** 237-238

Germany (20th century)
  Beck, Ludwig August Theoder
    2 99-100
  Kapp, Wolfgang **8** 436
  Schacht, Hjalmar Horace Greeley
    13 518-519
  Ulbricht, Walter **15** 383-384
Ghana (1966)
  Nkrumah, Kwame **11** 408-410
Guatemala
  Arbenz Guzmán, Jacobo **1** 274-276
Haiti
  Duvalier, Jean-Claude **5** 166-168
Haiti (1950)
  Duvalier, François **5** 165-166
Holland (1650)
  Witt, Johan de **16** 348-349
Hungary
  Nagy, Imre **11** 292-293
Indonesia
  Suharto **15** 14-15
Indonesia (1965)
  Sukarno **15** 18-20
Iraq
  Fādil al-Jamālī, Muhammad
    5 361-362
  Nuri al-Sa'id **11**
  Saddam Hussein **13** 415-416
Japan
  Mutsuhito **11** 279-282
  Takahashi, Korekiyo **15** 84-85
  Yamashita, Tomoyuki **16** 435-436
Korea
  Chong Chung-bu **4** 15
  Sejo **14** 90-91
Liberia
  Doe, Samuel Kanyon **5** 38-39
Mali (1968)
  Keita, Modibo **8** 474-475
Mexico (1863)
  Maximilian of Hapsburg
    10 358-360
Nigeria (1966)
  Azikiwe, Nnamdi **1** 401-402
  Bello, Ahmadu **2** 139-140
  Ekwensi, Cyprian **5** 242-243
  Tafawa Balewa, Abubakar **15** 75
Pakistan (1978)
  Zia ul-Haq, Mohammad
    16 513-515
Panama
  Arias, Arnulfo **1** 286-287
Paraguay (20th century)
  Morínigo, Higinio **11** 174-175
  Stroessner, Alfredo **14** 511-512
Peru (20th century)
  Leguía y Salcedo, Augusto Bernardi-
    no **9** 305-306
  Odría Amoretti, Manuel Apolinario
    11 473-474
  Prado Ugarteche, Manuel
    12 430-431
  Velasco, Luis de **15** 450-451
Portugal (1667)
  Vieira, Antônio **15** 492
Russia

Alexander I **1** 130-132
Catherine the Great **3** 370-372
Kolchak, Aleksandr Vasilievich
    9 77-78
Kornilov, Lavr Georgievich **9** 87-88
Paul I **12** 143-144
Saudi Arabia
  Faisal ibn Abd al Aziz ibn Saud
    5 371-372
Senegal (1960s)
  Senghor, Léopold Sédar **14** 106-107
Songhay empire
  Ali, Sunni **1** 158-159
  Muhammad, Elijah **11** 230-231
South Korea (1961)
  Park, Chung Hee **12** 99-102
Spain (1923)
  Primo de Rivera y Orbaneja, Miguel
    12 454-455
Sudan (20th century)
  Abboud, Ibrahim **1** 11-12
  Azhari, Sayyid Ismail al- **1** 399-401
  Khalil, Sayyid Abdullah **8** 531-532
Sweden
  Gustavus III **7** 45-46
  Oxenstierna, Axel Gustafsson
    12 44-45
Thailand (20th century)
  Phibun Songkhram, Luang
    12 264-265
  Pridi Phanomyong **12** 449
  Sarit Thanarat **13** 483-484
Togo (1963)
  Olympio, Sylvanus E. **11** 506-507
Uganda
  Amin Dada, Idi **1** 202-204
Uganda (1971)
  Obote, Apolo Milton **11** 457
Uruguay (1933)
  Terra, Gabriel **15** 154-155
Venezuela
  Pérez Jiménez, Marcos **12** 217-218
Venezuela (1945)
  Betancourt, Rómulo **2** 237-238

Courage to Be, The (book)
  Tillich, Paul Johannes **15** 224-225

Courageous Woman (painting)
  Hodler, Ferdinand **7** 434-435

COURBET, JEAN DESIRÉ GUSTAVE
  (1819-1877), French painter **4** 271-273
  influence of
    Cézanne, Paul **3** 400-402
    Daubigny, Charles François **4** 402
    Pissarro, Camille **12** 326-327
    Renoir, Pierre Auguste **13** 101-102
    Soutine, Chaim **14** 356-357
    Staël, Nicolas de **14** 392
    Whistler, James Abbott McNeill
      16 225-226
  influenced by
    Ingres, Jean Auguste Dominique
      8 121-123
    Ruisdael, Jacob van **13** 357-358

Courcelles, Daniel Rémy, Sieur de (died 1698), French politician, governor of New France
Talon, Jean **15** 91-92

Courier Sud (novel)
Saint-Exupéry, Antoine de **13** 431-432

COURNOT, ANTOINE AUGUSTIN (1801-1877), French mathematician, philosopher, and economist **4** 273
Walras, Marie Esprit Léon **16** 84-85

Cours familier de littérature (review)
Lamartine, Alphonse Marie Louis de **9** 173-175

Course of Empire (painting series; Cole)
Allston, Washington **1** 176-177
Cole, Thomas **4** 151-152

Court masques (theater festivals)
Jones, Inigo **8** 333-334
Jonson, Ben **8** 343-345

Court of Death, The (painting)
Peale, Rembrandt **12** 172-173

Courtenay, William (1342?-1396), English archbishop of Canterbury 1381-1396
Wyclif, John **16** 412-413

Courtier, The (book)
Milán, Luis **11** 15-16

Courtier, The (book; Castiglione)
Raphael **13** 40-42

Courtly love, code of (literature)
Chrestien de Troyes **4** 23-24
Guillaume de Lorris **7** 33-34

Courtship of Miles Standish, The (poem)
Longfellow, Henry Wadsworth **9** 499-500

Cousin Pons, Le (novel)
Balzac, Honoré de **1** 478-480

COUSIN, VICTOR (1792-1867), French educator and philosopher **4** 273-274
Brisbane, Albert **3** 9
Simon, Jules François **14** 237-238

Cousine Bette, La (novel)
Balzac, Honoré de **1** 478-480

COUSINS, NORMAN (1912-1990), editor-in-chief of the *Saturday Review* and advocate for world peace **4** 274-276

COUSTEAU, JACQUES-YVES (1910-1997), undersea explorer, photographer, inventor, writer, television producer, and film-maker **4** 276-277

Couto, Diogo de (1542-1616), Portugese chronicler
Camoëns, Luis Vaz de **3** 247-249

Couture, Thomas (1815-1879), French painter
La Farge, John **9** 149-150
Manet, Édouard **10** 193-194

Couzens, James S. (1872-1936), American industrialist
Ford, Henry **6** 5-6

Cova, Arturo (literary character)
Rivera, José Eustacio **13** 185-186

Covenant, Book of the (Old Testament)
Moses **11** 200-201

Covenant of the Presbyterians (1645)
Lilburne, John **9** 409-410

Covent Garden (London)
Arne, Thomas Augustine **1** 307-308

Covent Garden Journal (periodical)
Fielding, Henry **5** 442-444

Coventry Cathedral (England)
Epstein, Jacob **5** 295-296
Sutherland, Graham **15** 40-41

COVERDALE, MILES (1488-1568), English Puritan **4** 278
Tyndale, William **15** 373-374

Coverley, Sir Roger de (literary character)
Addison, Joseph **1** 57-58

Covetous Knight, The (play)
Pushkin, Aleksandr Sergeevich **12** 489-491

COVILHÃO, PEDRO DE (circa 1455-circa 1530), Portuguese explorer and diplomat **4** 278-279

Covington and Burling (law firm)
Acheson, Dean Gooderham **1** 37-38

Cow and Fish Playing the Violin (painting)
Chagall, Marc **3** 406-407

COWARD, NOEL (1899-1973), English playwright, actor, and composer **4** 279-280
Porter, Cole Albert **12** 405-406

COWELL, HENRY DIXON (1897-1965), American composer and pianist **4** 280-281
Cage, John **3** 211-214
Gershwin, George **6** 284-285
Ives, Charles Edward **8** 159-160

COWLEY, ABRAHAM (1618-1667), English writer **4** 281-282
Crashaw, Richard **4** 296
Johnson, Samuel **8** 315-317
Swift, Jonathan **15** 51-54

Cowley, Malcolm (1898-1989), American author and editor
Faulkner, William **5** 395-397
Fitzgerald, Francis Scott Key **5** 470-472
Morgan, Daniel **11** 160-161
Tarleton, Banastre **15** 110

COWPER, WILLIAM (1731-1800), English poet **4** 282
Fuseli, Henry **6** 153-155

Cowperwood, Frank Algernon (literary character)
Dreiser, Herman Theodore **5** 98-100

Cowpox vaccination
see Inoculation—smallpox

Cow's Skull with Red (painting)
O'Keeffe, Georgia **11** 487-489

COX, ARCHIBALD (born 1912), American lawyer, educator, author, labor arbitrator, and public servant **4** 283-284

COX, HARVEY (born 1929), American theologian and author **4** 284-285

Cox, James Middleton (1870-1957), American newspaperman and politician
Roosevelt, Franklin Delano **13** 277-280

Cox and Box (operetta)
Sullivan, Arthur Seymour **15** 23

COXE, TENCH (1755-1824), American political economist and businessman **4** 285-286

COXEY, JACOB SECHLER (1854-1951), American reformer and businessman **4** 286-287

Coxey's Army (1894 protest)
Baker, Ray Stannard **1** 451-452
Bryan, William Jennings **3** 80-82
Coxey, Jacob Sechler **4** 286-287

Coxinga
see Watonai

Coypel, Antoine (1661-1722), French painter
Watteau, Antoine **16** 143-144

Coypel, Nöel Nicholas (1690-1734), French painter
Chardin, Jean Baptiste Siméon **3** 442-443

COYSEVOX, ANTOINE (1640-1720), French sculptor **4** 287-288
Girardon, François **6** 348-349

Crab Nebula (astronomy)
Oort, Jan Hendrik **11** 523-524

CRABBE, GEORGE (1754-1832), English poet **4** 288
Wordsworth, William **16** 385-388

Crack-up, The (book)
Wilson, Edmund **16** 318-319

Cradle and the Grave, The (book)
Quevedo Y Villegas, Francisco Gómez de **12** 511

Craft, Robert Lawson (born 1923), American conductor
Stravinsky, Igor Fedorovich **14** 502-506

Craft unions
see Labor unions

Craftsmen (periodical)
Bolingbroke, Viscount **2** 374-375

Crafty Widow, The (play)
Goldoni, Carlo **6** 408-409

CRAIG, EDWARD GORDON (1872-1966), European actor, designer, director, and theoretician **4** 288-289
Stanislavsky, Constantin **14** 398-399

Craigie House (Cambridge, Massachusetts)
Longfellow, Henry Wadsworth **9** 499-500

Crainquebille (story)
France, Anatole **6** 39-40

CRANACH, LUCAS, THE ELDER (1472-1553), German painter, engraver, and designer of woodcuts **4** 289-290
Altdorfer, Albrecht **1** 179-180

Dürer, Albrecht **5** 159-161

Cranbrook Academy of Art (Bloomfield Hills, Michigan)
Saarinen, Eliel and Eero **13** 396-398

CRANDALL, PRUDENCE (1803-1890), American educator **4** 291

CRANE, HART (1899-1932), American poet **4** 291-293
Wolfe, Thomas Clayton **16** 355-356

CRANE, STEPHEN (1871-1900), American writer and poet **4** 293-295
Bierce, Ambrose Gwinett **2** 269-270
Conrad, Joseph **4** 205-207
Dreiser, Herman Theodore **5** 98-100
Howells, William Dean **7** 539-541
Norris, Benjamin Franklin Jr. **11** 427-428
Zola, Émile **16** 526-528

Cranford (novel)
Gaskell, Elizabeth **6** 231-232

CRANMER, THOMAS (1489-1556), English reformer, archbishop of Canterbury **4** 295-296
opponents
Mary, I **10** 308-309
supporters
Cromwell, Thomas **4** 320-321
Edward VI **5** 213-214
Henry VIII **7** 302-305
Northumberland, Duke of **11** 431-432
Somerset, Duke of **14** 333-334

Cranshaw (literary character)
Morrice, James Wilson **11** 181-182

CRASHAW, RICHARD (1612/1613-49), English poet **4** 296
Catullus, Gaius Valerius **3** 377-378
Cowley, Abraham **4** 281-282
Donne, John **5** 60-61
Taylor, Edward **15** 122-123

Crashing Thunder (book)
Radin, Paul **12** 538-539

CRASSUS DIVES, MARCUS LICINIUS (circa 115-53 B.C.), Roman financier and politician **4** 296-297
Catiline **3** 372-373
Clodius Pulcher, Publius **4** 121-122
Spartacus **14** 363-364
Sulla, Lucius Cornelius I **15** 21-22
see also Rome—Roman Republic (First Triumvirate)

Crassus, Publius Licinius (flourished 131 B.C.), Roman jurist
Gracchus, Tiberius and Gaius Sempronius **6** 479-480

Crater, The (novel)
Cooper, James Fenimore **4** 220-223

Craterus (died 321 B.C.), Macedonian general
Antigonus I **1** 248-249
Seleucus I **14** 92-93

Crates of Thebes (flourished late 4th century B.C.), Greek philosopher
Diogenes **5** 20-21
Zeno of Citium **16** 499-500

Cratinus (520?-423 B.C.), Greek playwright
Aristophanes **1** 293-294

Cratylus (dialogue)
Plato **12** 345-347

CRAVEIRINHA, JOSÉ (born 1922), Mozambican journalist and lyric poet **4** 297-299

Crawford, Thomas (1813?-1857), American sculptor
Powers, Hiram **12** 428-429

Crawford, William (died circa 1782), American military officer
Girty, Simon **6** 350

CRAWFORD, WILLIAM HARRIS (1772-1834), American politician **4** 299-300
Adams, John Quincy **1** 52-54
Jackson, Andrew **8** 168-172
Monroe, James **11** 111-113

CRAXI, BETTINO (born 1934), statesman and prime minister of the Italian republic (1983-1987) **4** 300-301

CRAY, SEYMOUR (1925-1996), American computer engineer **4** 301-303

Crayon Miscellany, The (literary collection)
Irving, Washington **8** 141-143

Craze for Speaking Latin, The (book)
Quevedo Y Villegas, Francisco Gómez de **12** 511

CRAZY HORSE (circa 1842-1877), American Indian, Oglala Sioux war chief **4** 303-304
American Horse **1** 195-198
Bad Heart Bull, Amos **1** 427-428
Cochise **4** 128
Custer, George Armstrong **4** 355-356
Miles, Nelson Appleton **11** 16-17
Red Cloud **13** 70-71
Sitting Bull **14** 264-265

Creatine phosphate (physiology)
Hill, Archibald Vivian **7** 385-386
Meyerhof, Otto Fritz **10** 537-539

Creation (painting)
Rivera, Diego **13** 183-184
Uccello, Paolo **15** 378-379

Creation (theology)
Augustine **1** 367-370
Bonhoeffer, Dietrich **2** 389-391
Duns Scotus, John **5** 149-150

Creation, The (oratorio)
Haydn, Franz Joseph **7** 219-221

Création du monde, Le (musical composition)
Milhaud, Darius **11** 17-18

Creation of Adam (painting)
Michelangelo Buonarroti **11** 2-5

Creation of Adam (sculpture)
Quercia, Jacopo della **12** 509

Creation Society (literary group)
Kuo Mo-jo **9** 133-134

Creative Credo (book)
Klee, Paul **9** 47-49

Creative Evolution (book)
Bergson, Henri **2** 191-192

Crécy, Battle of (1346)
Charles IV **3** 455-456
Edward III **5** 211-212
Edward the Black Prince **5** 217-218
Philip VI **12** 277-278

Crécy, Château of (France)
Boucher, François **2** 440-442

Credences of Summer (poem)
Stevens, Wallace **14** 443-445

Credit (economics)
Jackson, Andrew **8** 168-172
Morgan, John Pierpont **11** 163-165
Morgan, Junius Spencer **11** 166-167

Crédit Mobilier of America (construction firm)
Durant, Thomas Clark **5** 157-158

Credit union (bank)
Cajetan **3** 215-216

Creditors (play)
Strindberg, August **14** 509-511

Credo (book)
Barth, Karl **2** 31-32

Credo (musical composition)
Isaac, Heinrich **8** 143-144
Machaut, Guillaume de **10** 93-94

Credo in Unam (poem)
Rimbaud, Jean Nicolas Arthur **13** 172-174

Cree Indians (North America)
Lacombe, Albert **9** 147-148

Creed and Deed (book)
Adler, Felix **1** 63-64

Creek Indians (North America)
Jackson, Andrew **8** 168-172
McGillivray, Alexander **10** 412
Osceola **12** 18
Scott, Winfield **14** 70-71
Tecumseh **15** 133

Creek War (United States; 1813)
Crockett, David **4** 314-316

CREEL, GEORGE (1876-1953), American writer and journalist **4** 304-305

Creelman, James (1859-1915), American journalist
Díaz, José de la Cruz Porfirio **4** 534-536
Madero, Francisco Indalecio **10** 118-119

Cremation (novel)
Lao Shê **9** 200-201

CRÉMAZIE, OCTAVE (1827-1879), Canadian poet **4** 305-306
Fréchette, Louis-Honoré **6** 77-78

Creole Rhapsody (jazz composition)
Ellington, Edward Kennedy **5** 273-274

Creole Ulysses, A (autobiography)
Vasconcelos, José **15** 443-444

Creoles (Latin America)
Belgrano, Manuel **2** 126-127
Bello, Ahmadu **2** 139-140
Bolívar, Simón **2** 375-377
Díaz, José de la Cruz Porfirio **4** 534-536
Hidalgo y Costilla, Miguel **7** 375-377
Iturbide, Agustín de **8** 155-156

Crepúsculo sertanejo (poems)
Castro Alves, Antônio de **3** 364-365

Crépy, Peace of (1544)
Charles V **3** 457-459
Francis I **6** 40-43

CRERAR, THOMAS ALEXANDER
(1876-1975), Canadian political leader
4 306

Crescograph (instrument)
Bose, Jagadis Chandra **2** 429-430

Crespi, Fray Juan (1721-1782), Spanish
missionary and explorer
Portolá, Gaspar de **12** 408

Crespi, Giuseppe Maria (1665-1747), Italian painter
Troger, Paul **15** 300

Crespo, Joaquin (1845-1898), Venezuelan
soldier and political leader
Blanco, Antonio Guzmán **2** 320-321

Crespy, Peace of
see Crépy, Peace of (1544)

CRESSON, EDITH (born 1934), first
woman prime minister of France
4 306-307

Crete (Greek island)
Churchill, Winston Leonard Spencer
4 51-53
Evans, Arthur John **5** 335-336
Frontenac et Palluau, Comte de
6 128-130
Köprülü, Ahmed **9** 84-85
Venizelos, Eleutherios **15** 460-461

Crête-à-Pierrot, Battle of (1802)
Dessalines, Joan Jacques **4** 511-512

Crétin, Joseph (1799-1857), American
Roman Catholic bishop
Ireland, John **8** 133-134

CRÈVECOEUR, ST. JOHN DE (1735-1813),
French-American farmer and writer
4 307-308

Crèvecoeur, Le (poems)
Aragon, Louis **1** 271-272

Cribbage (card game)
Suckling, John **15** 10-11

CRICHTON, (JOHN) MICHAEL (a.k.a.
Michael Douglas, Jeffrey Hudson, and

John Lange; b. 1942), American novelist,
screenwriter, and director **4** 308-310

CRICK, FRANCIS HARRY CROMPTON
(born 1916), English molecular biologist
4 310
Watson, James Dewey **16** 137-138

Cricket
Bradman, Donald George **2** 485-486

Cricket on the Hearth, The (play; Boucicault)
Jefferson, Joseph **8** 237

Cricketers (painting)
Drysdale, George Russell **5** 107-109

Crime
see Criminology

Crime (book)
Darrow, Clarence Seward **4** 396-397

Crime and Punishment (novel)
Dostoevsky, Fyodor **5** 74-77

Crime de Sylvestre Bonnard, Le (novel)
France, Anatole **6** 39-40

Crime novel
see Mystery fiction

Crimea (peninsula; Union of Soviet Social-
ist Republics)
Catherine the Great **3** 370-372
Chmielnicki, Bogdan **4** 12-13
Ivan IV **8** 157-159
Potemkin, Grigori Aleksandrovich
12 411-412
see also Crimean War

Crimean War (1853-1856)
British allies
Cavour, Conte di **3** 385-386
Napoleon III **11** 310-312
Victor Emmanuel II **15** 483-484
British military
Gordon, Charles George **6** 448-449
Speke, John Hanning **14** 366-367
British politics
Aberdeen, 4th Earl of **1** 25-26
Albert **1** 110-112
Bright, John **3** 6-7
Cobden, Richard **4** 127-128
Disraeli, Benjamin **5** 27-29
Gladstone, William Ewart
6 357-360
Palmerston, 3d Viscount **12** 81-83
Victoria **15** 485-487
medicine and journalism
Godkin, Edwin Lawrence **6** 380
Nightingale, Florence **11** 392-393
Shaftesbury, 7th Earl of **14** 137-138
Russians
Nesselrode, Karl Robert **11** 348-349
Nicholas I **11** 377-378
Tolstoy, Leo **15** 262-265
United States and
McClellan, George Brinton
10 391-392
Pierce, Franklin **12** 300-301

Criminal, cult of the (French literature)
Genet, Jean **6** 262-263

Criminal law
China
Shang Yang **14** 149-150
Italy
Becarria, Marchese di **2** 97-98
United States
Allen, Florence Ellinwood
1 164-165
Bailey, F. Lee **1** 441-443
Darrow, Clarence Seward
4 396-397
Field, David Dudley **5** 439-440
Murphy, Frank **11** 260-261
Warren, Earl **16** 117-120

Criminals, American
Billy the Kid **2** 277
Capone, Al **3** 272-273
Dillinger, John **5** 9
Hoffa, James R. **7** 436-437
James, Jesse Woodson **8** 212-213
Siegel, Benjamin, **14** 215-216

Criminology
classification and detection
Bertillon, Alphonse **2** 230-231
Lombroso, Cesare **9** 493
Pinkerton, Allan **12** 314-315
studies
Dugdale, Richard Louis **5** 128-129
Lindsey, Benjamin Barr **9** 425-426
Thorndike, Edward Lee **15** 208-209
see also Criminals; Law enforcement

Criminous clerks (English church history)
Becket, Thomas **2** 101-102
Henry II **7** 287-289

Crimthann
see Columba, St.

Criollos
see Creoles (South America)

Crippled Children's Program (United
States)
Johnson, Lyndon Baines **8** 308-312

Cripps, Sir Stafford (1889-1952), English
statesman
Rajagopalachari, Chakravarti **13** 6-7

Crise de vers (essay)
Mallarmé, Stéphane **10** 172-173

Crisis (film)
Bergman, Ernst Ingmar **2** 190-191

Crisis (magazine)
Du Bois, William Edward Burghardt
5 116-118
Hughes, Langston **8** 18-19
Wilkins, Roy **16** 282-283

Crisis, The (book; R.Owen)
Owen, Robert **12** 39-40
Owen, Robert Dale **12** 40-41

Crisis, The (novel)
Churchill, Winston **4** 50-51

Crisis, The (papers)
Paine, Thomas **12** 66-67

Crisis, theology of
see Dialectical theology

CRISPI, FRANCESCO (1819-1901), Italian statesman **4** 310-311

Crispin (literary character)
Stevens, Wallace **14** 443-445

Crispin rival de son maître (comedy)
Lesage, Alain René **9** 353-354

Crispus Flavius Julius (died 326), Roman naval hero
Constantine I **4** 209-211

Cristeros (Mexican rebels)
Ávila Camacho, Manuel **1** 387-388
Calles, Plutarco Elías **3** 234-235

CRISTIANI, ALFREDO ("Fredy" Cristiani; born 1947), president of El Salvador (1989-) **4** 311-313

Cristiano viejo (Spain)
Góngora y Argote, Luis de **6** 427-428

Cristo nella nostra umanità (sculpture reliefs)
Manzù, Giacomo **10** 224-225

Cristo si è fermato a Eboli (book)
Levi, Carlo **9** 364

Criterion (magazine)
Eliot, Thomas Stearns **5** 258-261

Criterion-referenced measurement
Popham, William James **12** 399-401

Critias (flourished late 5th century B.C.), Athenian orator and politician
Plato **12** 345-347

Critic (newspaper)
Porter, Katherine Anne **12** 406-407

Critic, The (novel)
Gracián y Morales, Baltasar Jerónimo **6** 481-482

Critic, The (play)
Sheridan, Richard Brinsley **14** 183-184

Critica, La (periodical)
Croce, Benedetto **4** 313-314
Gentile, Giovanni **6** 267

Critica sociale (journal)
Salvemini, Gaetano **13** 455-456

Critical (English journal)
Goldsmith, Oliver **6** 411-413

Critical Fable (poem)
Lowell, Amy **10** 13

Critical Forests (book)
Herder, Johann Gottfried von **7** 327-328

Critical philosophy
Fries, Jakob Friedrich **6** 116-117

Criticism and Fiction (book)
Howells, William Dean **7** 539-541

Critilo (literary character)
Gracián y Morales, Baltasar Jerónimo **6** 481-482

Critique de l'École des femmes (play)
Molière **11** 86-88

Critique of Political Economy (book)
Marx, Karl **10** 304-308

Critique of Pure Reason (book)
Kant, Immanuel **8** 430-432

Critique of the Gotha Programme (book)
Marx, Karl **10** 304-308

Crito (dialogue)
Plato **12** 345-347
Socrates **14** 320-321

Crittenden Compromise (1860-1861)
Buchanan, James **3** 89-90

Croatia (republic, Yugoslavia)
Alexander of Yugoslavia **1** 136-137
Stepinac, Alojzije **14** 433-435
see also Yugoslavia

Croatia, Republic of
Tudjman, Franjo **15** 333-335

Crociato in Egitto, II (opera)
Meyerbeer, Giacomo **10** 536-537

CROCE, BENEDETTO (1866-1952), Italian philosopher, critic and educator **4** 313-314
Bosanquet, Bernard **2** 425-426
De Sanctis, Francesco **4** 505
Gentile, Giovanni **6** 267
Pirandello, Luigi **12** 319-321
Vico, Giambattista **15** 480-481

Crock of Gold, The (novel)
Stephens, James **14** 430-431

Crocker, Charles (1822-1888), American financier
Huntington, Collis Potter **8** 49
Judah, Theodore Dehone **8** 373-374
Stanford, Leland **14** 397-398

Crocker Land (Arctic)
MacMillan, Donald Baxter **10** 111-112

CROCKETT, DAVID (1786-1836), American frontiersman **4** 314-316

Croesus (died 546 B.C.), king of Lydia 560-546 B.C.
Cyrus the Great **4** 363-364
Herodotus **7** 330-333

Croisilles (story)
Musset, Louis Charles Alfred de **11** 271-272

Croix, Carlos Francisco, Marquis de (1699-1786), Spanish soldier
Gálvez, José de **6** 196

Croker, John Wilson (1780-1857), British Tory leader and essayist
Macaulay, Thomas Babington **10** 79-80

Croly, David Goodman (1829-1889), American author and editor
Croly, Herbert David **4** 316-317

CROLY, HERBERT DAVID (1869-1930), American editor and author **4** 316-317
Bourne, Randolph Silliman **2** 456-457
Lippmann, Walter **9** 439-440

Croly, Jane Cunningham (Jennie June; 1829-1901), English-born American journalist
Croly, Herbert David **4** 316-317

CROM
see Confederación Regional Obrera Mexicana

Crome Yellow (novel)
Huxley, Aldous Leonard **8** 74-75

CROMER, 1ST EARL OF (Evelyn Baring; 1841-1907), English statesman **4** 317
Fuad I **6** 139
Mahdi **10** 137-138
Milner, Alfred **11** 38-39
Tewfik Pasha **15** 157-158
Zaghlul Pasha, Saad **16** 485-486

Cromwell, Nelson William (1854-1948), American lawyer
Bunau-Varilla, Philippe Jean **3** 120-121

CROMWELL, OLIVER (1599-1658), English statesman and general **4** 317-320
foreign campaigns
Condé, Prince de **4** 193-194
Monck, George **11** 96-97
Winslow, Edward **16** 338-339
Witt, Johan de **16** 348-349
in literature
Carlyle, Thomas **3** 304-305
Dryden, John **5** 106-107
Gardiner, Samuel Rawson **6** 211
Guizot, François Pierre Guillaume **7** 40-41
Harrington, James **7** 166-167
Marvell, Andrew **10** 301-303
Long Parliament
Hampden, John **7** 110-111
Pym, John **12** 495-496
Vane, Henry **15** 425-426
opposition to
Berkeley, William **2** 198-199
Buckingham, 2d Duke of **3** 94-95
Charles, I **3** 450-452
Lilburne, John **9** 409-410
Shaftesbury, 1st Earl of **14** 135-136
religious toleration
Manasseh ben Israel **10** 183-184

Cromwell, Richard (1626-1712), English statesman
Cromwell, Oliver **4** 317-320
Monck, George **11** 96-97
Vane, Henry **15** 425-426

CROMWELL, THOMAS (Earl of Essex; circa 1485-1540), English statesman 1532-1540 **4** 320-321
Coverdale, Miles **4** 278
Cranmer, Thomas **4** 295-296
Henry VIII **7** 302-305
Latimer, Hugh **9** 221
Norfolk, 3d Duke of **11** 423
Northumberland, Duke of **11** 431-432

Cromwell (play)
Hugo, Victor Marie **8** 22-25

Cromwell of Oakham, Baron
see Cromwell, Thomas

Cronaca di un amore (film)
Antonioni, Michelangelo **1** 252-253

Crónica de Pedro I (book)
López de Ayala, Pedro **9** 508-509

Cronkhill (house, Shropshire)
Nash, John **11** 316

CRONKITE, WALTER LELAND, JR. (born 1916), American journalist and radio and television news broadcaster **4** 321-322

CROOK, GEORGE (1828-1890), American general and frontiersman **4** 322-323
Calamity Jane **3** 216
Crazy Horse **4** 303-304
Geronimo **6** 281-282
Sitting Bull **14** 264-265

CROOKES, SIR WILLIAM (1832-1919), English chemist and physicist **4** 323-324
Hofmann, August Wilhelm von **7** 441-442

Croome Court (Worcestershire, England)
Adam, Robert and James **1** 38-40

Croquet Game (painting)
Bonnard, Pierre **2** 395-396

Crosby, Caresse (1892-1970), American art dealer, poet, and editor
Bearden, Romare Howard **2** 86-88

CROSBY, HARRY LILLIS (Bing; 1903-1977), American singer and radio and television personality **4** 324-326

Cross Country (essays)
MacLennan, Hugh **10** 110-111

Cross in the Mountains (painting)
Friedrich, Caspar David **6** 114-115

Cross-incompatibility (genetics)
East, Edward Murray **5** 182-183

Cross Keys, Battle of (1862)
Lee, Robert Edward **9** 292-294

Cross of Gold (speech)
Bryan, William Jennings **3** 80-82

Cross of the World (painting)
Cole, Thomas **4** 151-152

Cross-Purpose (play)
Camus, Albert **3** 255-257

Cross-staff (astronomical instrument)
Levi ben Gershon **9** 363-364

Crossing, The (novel)
Churchill, Winston **4** 50-51

Crossing Brooklyn Ferry (poem)
Whitman, Walt **16** 249-251

Crossing the Bar (poem)
Tennyson, Alfred **15** 144-146

Crotchet Castle (novel)
Peacock, Thomas Love **12** 169

Croton (ancient city, Italy)
Pythagoras **12** 498-499

Croton Reservoir (New York State)
Cooper, Peter **4** 223-224

Crotus Rubianus (Johannes Jäger; circa 1480-circa 1545), German humanist
Hutten, Ulrich von **8** 72-73
Reuchlin, Johann **13** 106-107

Crouching Woman (sculpture)
Rodin, Auguste **13** 236-238

Crow Indians (North America)
Beckwourth, Jim **2** 106-107
Plenty Coups **12** 352-355
Crow Indians, The (book)
Lowie, Robert Harry **10** 18

Crowd behavior (sociology)
Le Bon, Gustave **9** 268-269

Crowder, Enoch H. (1859-1932), American general and diplomat
Menocal, Mario Garcia **10** 506-507

Crown Bride (play)
Strindberg, August **14** 509-511

Crown Guardians, The (novel)
Arnim, Achim von **1** 308-309

Crown of Thorns (religious relic)
Montreuil, Pierre de **11** 139

Crown of Wild Olive, The (literary collection)
Ruskin, John **13** 371-372

Crown Point, Battle of (1775)
Johnson, William **8** 319-320
Schuyler, Philip John **14** 49-50

Crown Point County fail (Indiana)
Dillinger, John **5** 9

Crowning Privilege, The (poems)
Graves, Robert Ranke **6** 504-506

Crowninshield, Benjamin Williams (1772-1851), American secretary of the navy 1814-1818
Monroe, James **11** 111-113

Crownland federalism (Austrian politics)
Francis Ferdinand **6** 44

CROWTHER, SAMUEL ADJAI (circa 1806-1891), Nigerian Anglican bishop **4** 326

Crozat, Pierre (1665-1740), French art collector
Watteau, Antoine **16** 143-144

Crucible, The (play)
Miller, Arthur **11** 25-26

Crucified Christ (painting)
Goya y Lucientes, Francisco de Paula José de **6** 476-478

Crucified Christ (sculpture)
Clodion **4** 121

Crucifix (sculpture)
Cellini, Benvenuto **3** 391-392

Crucifixion (fresco)
Andrea del Castagno **1** 223-224
Cimabue **4** 60-61
Orcagna **11** 526-527
Perugino **12** 245-246

Crucifixion (painting)
Antonello da Messina **1** 251-252

Bellows, George Wesley **2** 143
Botticelli, Sandro **2** 439-440
Cranach, Lucas the Elder **4** 289-290
Greco **6** 511-514
Pippin, Horace **12** 318-319
Sassetta **13** 492
Tintoretto **15** 232-234
Titian **15** 242-244
Veronese, Paolo **15** 469-470

Crucifixion (polyptych)
Masaccio **10** 312-313

Crucifixion (sculpture)
Donatello **5** 55-56
Manzù, Giacomo **10** 224-225

Crucifixion Diptych (painting)
Weyden, Rogier van der **16** 219-221

Crucifixion of St. Peter (painting)
Caravaggio **3** 282-284
Reni, Guido **13** 97-98

Crucifixion Triptych (painting)
Weyden, Rogier van der **16** 219-221

Cruel City (novel)
Beti, Mongo **2** 242-243

CRUMB, GEORGE (born 1929), American composer and teacher **4** 326-328

Crumbling Idols (book)
Garland, Hannibal Hamlin **6** 217-218

Crusade for Citizenship (United States)
King, Martin Luther Jr. **9** 20-22

Crusade in Asia (book)
Rómulo, Carlos P. **13** 270-271

Crusade in Europe (book)
Eisenhower, Dwight David **5** 233-236

Crusader, The (play)
Mármol, José **10** 274

Crusades (religious wars)
1096-1099 (First)
Alexius I **1** 143-144
Baldwin I **1** 464-465
Bohemund, I **2** 364
Godfrey of Bouillon **6** 379
Roger II **13** 244-245
Saladin **13** 441-442
Tasso, Torquato **15** 114-116
Urban II **15** 393
1147-1149 (Second)
Bernard of Clairvaux **2** 207-208
Louis VII **9** 524-525
Manuel I **10** 218-219
Nureddin **11** 444-445
Otto of Freising **12** 30
William of Tyre **16** 299-300
1188-1192 (Third)
Chrestien de Troyes **4** 23-24
Frederick I **6** 78-79
Philip II **12** 268-269
Richard I **13** 130
Saladin **13** 441-442
1202-1204 (Fourth)
Constantine XI **4** 211-212
Dandolo, Enrico **4** 386-387

Innocent, III **8** 125-127
Michael VIII **11** 1-2
Villehardouin, Geffroi de **15** 499
1217-1221 (Fifth)
Francis of Assisi **6** 46-47
1248-1254 (Seventh)
Joinville, Jean de **8** 325
Louis IX **9** 525-526
1270 (Eighth)
Louis IX **9** 525-526
1271-1272 (Ninth)
Edward I **5** 208-210

CRUZ, OSWALDO GONÇALVES
(1872-1917), Brazilian microbiologist
and epidemiologist **4** 328-329

Cry, the Beloved Country (novel)
Paton, Alan Stewart **12** 134-135

Crying Woman (painting)
Portinari, Cândido **12** 407-408

Cryogenics (physics)
Kapitsa, Pyotr Leonidovich **8** 433-435
Landau, Lev Davidovich **9** 184-185

Crystal Palace Exhibition (London; 1851)
exhibitors
Borden, Gail **2** 409
Brady, Mathew B. **2** 487-488
Cobden, Richard **4** 127-128
Colt, Samuel **4** 172-173
Ericsson, John **5** 307-308
Krupp **9** 109-111
McCormick, Cyrus Hall **10** 400-401
Powers, Hiram **12** 428-429
sponsors
Albert **1** 110-112
Victoria **15** 485-487

Crystal structure (cyrstalline)
Born, Max **2** 420-421
Bragg, William Henry **2** 488-489
Bridgman, Percy Williams **3** 5-6·
Debye, Peter Joseph William **4** 447-448
Hodgkin, Dorothy Crowfoot **7** 432-434
Karle, Isabella **8** 447-449
Lonsdale, Kathleen **9** 501-502
Pasteur, Louis **12** 125-127
Pauling, Linus Carl **12** 150-152
Perutz, Max **12** 246-248
Steno, Nicolaus **14** 425-426

CTAL
see Confederation of Latin American
Workers

Ctesiphon (flourished 340 B.C.), Athenian
citizen
Demosthenes **4** 495-496

Ctesiphon (Persian capital)
Julian **8** 378-379

CTM
see Confederation of Mexican Workers

Cuaderna via (literary form)
Gonzalo de Berceo **6** 431-432
López de Ayala, Pedro **9** 508-509

CUAUHTEMOC (circa 1496-1525), Aztec
ruler **4** 329

Cuauhtémoc against the Myth (mural)
Siqueiros, David Alfaro **14** 256

Cuautla, Battle of (1912)
Matamoros, Mariano **10** 329-330
Morelos, José María **11** 157-158

Cuba, Republic of (nation, West Indies)
exploration and Spanish rule
Columbus, Christopher **4** 176-179
Cortés, Hernán **4** 255-256
de Soto, Hernando **4** 510-511
Díaz del Castillo, Bernal **4** 536-537
López, Narciso **9** 508
Menéndez de Avilés, Pedro
10 499-500
Narváez, Pánfilo de **11** 315
Velázquez de Cuéllar, Diego **15** 459
see also Spanish American War; Ten
Years War; War of Independence
Republic (to 1959)
Batista y Zaldívar, Fulgencio
2 57-58
Bosch, Juan **2** 428-429
Estrada Palma, Tomás **5** 326-327
Grau San Martin, Ramón **6** 499-500
Machado y Morales, Gerardo
10 92-93
Menocal, Mario Garcia **10** 506-507
revolution and Castro regime (since
1959)
Castro Ruz, Fidel **3** 365-368
Cleaver, Leroy Eldridge **4** 97-98
Duvalier, François **5** 165-166
Guevara, Ernesto **7** 30-31
Louis, Joe **9** 537-538
see also Bay of Pigs invasion; Cuban
missile crisis
United States annexation plans
Buchanan, James **3** 89-90
Cass, Lewis **3** 355-356
Clay, Henry **4** 94-96
Douglas, Stephen Arnold **5** 80-82
Marcy, William Learned **10** 247-248
Smith, Gerrit **14** 290-291
Soulé, Pierre **14** 351-352
United States governors
Wood, Leonard **16** 369-370
United States relations
Eisenhower, Dwight David
5 233-236
Grau San Martin, Ramón **6** 499-500
Menocal, Mario Garcia **10** 506-507
Roosevelt, Theodore **13** 280-283
Root, Elihu **13** 283-284
Welles, Sumner **16** 191-192

Cuban missile crisis (1962)
Castro Ruz, Fidel **3** 365-368
John, XXIII **8** 277-280
Kennedy, John Fitzgerald **8** 502-506
Kennedy, Robert Francis **8** 508-509
Stevenson, Adlai Ewing **14** 445-446

Cuban Revolutionary party (in United
States)
Martí, José **10** 285-286

CUBBERLEY, ELLWOOD PATTERSON
(1868-1941), American educator and university dean **4** 329-331

Cube (mathematics)
Eratosthenes of Cyrene **5** 301-302
Euclid **5** 327-329

Cube houses (architecture, 18th century)
Ledoux, Claude Nicolas **9** 277-278

Cubi (sculpture series)
Smith, David **14** 287-288

Cubic equations (mathematics)
Cardano, Geronimo **3** 285-286
Lagrange, Joseph Louis **9** 164-166

Cubism (art movement)
Goncharova, Natalia **6** 424-426
Laurens, Henri **9** 230-231
Popova, Liubov Sergeevna **12** 401-402
development
Braque, Georges **2** 504-505
Matisse, Henri **10** 336-337
Picasso, Pablo **12** 292-295
elements (architecture)
Le Corbusier **9** 274-275
Wright, Frank Lloyd **16** 398-401
influence (painting)
Amorsolo, Fernando **1** 204
Miró, Joan **11** 53-54
Mondrian, Piet **11** 101-102
Pollock, Jackson **12** 379-380
Zorach, William **16** 528
influence (sculpture)
Giacometti, Alberto **6** 294-295
Moore, Henry **11** 146-148
Nevelson, Louise **11** 356-357
influenced by
Cézanne, Paul **3** 400-402
Severini, Gino **14** 122
painting (Europe)
Arp, Jean **1** 317-318
Bacon, Francis **1** 421-422
Duchamp, Marcel **5** 122-123
Gris, Juan **7** 5-6
Hofmann, Hans **7** 442-443
Léger, Fernand **9** 302-303
Malevich, Kasimir **10** 168-169
Pevsner, Antoine **12** 263-264
painting (Mexico)
Rivera, Diego **13** 183-184
painting (United States)
Davis, Stuart **4** 424-425
Demuth, Charles **4** 497-498
Feininger, Lyonel **5** 406-407
Gorky, Arshile **6** 458
Hartley, Marsden **7** 186
Sheeler, Charles **14** 170-171
Weber, Max **16** 160
sculpture
Archipenko, Alexander **1** 280-281
Duchamp-Villon, Raymond **5** 123
González, Julio **6** 428-429
Lipchitz, Jacques **9** 432-433
Zadkine, Ossip Joselyn **16** 484

Cubism (dance)
Graham, Martha **6** 485-486

Cubism (literature)
Robbe-Grillet, Alain **13** 189-190

Cuchulain (Irish folk hero)
Yeats, William Butler **16** 445-447

Cuchulain of Muirthemne (play)
Gregory, Augusta **6** 535-536

CUDWORTH, RALPH (1617-1688), English philosopher and theologian **4** 331

Cuéllar, Diego Velázquez de
see Velázquez de Cuéllar, Diego

Cuéllar, Juan Velázquez de (flourished early 16th century), Spanish official
Ignatius of Loyola **8** 108-109

Cuento de abril (play)
Valle Inclán, Ramón Maria del
15 407-408

Cuentos de muerte y de sangre (stories)
Güiráldez, Ricardo **7** 38-39

Cuerda Granadina (Spanish art group)
Alarcón, Pedro Antonio de **1** 100-101

CUFFE, PAUL (1759-1817), African American ship captain and merchant
4 331-332

CUGOANO, OTTOBAH (circa 1757-after 1803), African abolitionist in England
4 332-333
Equiano, Olaudah **5** 296-297

Cui, César Antonovich (1853-1918), Russian composer
Borodin, Aleksandr Profirevich
2 422-423
Mussorgsky, Modest Petrovich
11 274-276
Rimsky-Korsakov, Nikolai Andreevich
13 174-175
Tchaikovsky, Peter Ilyich **15** 130-132

Cuijpers, Petrus Josephus Hubertus
(1827-1921), Dutch architect
Oud, Jacobus Johannes Pieter **12** 32

Cuitlahuac (1470?-1520), Aztec prince
Cuauhtemoc **4** 329
Montezuma, II **11** 128-129

Culex (poem; Virgil)
Spenser, Edmund **14** 373-376

Culex fasciatus (mosquito)
Finlay, Carlos Juan **5** 450

Culiacán (city, Mexico)
Cabeza de Vaca, Álvar Núñez **3** 197

CULLEN, COUNTEE (1903-1946), African American poet **4** 333-334
Dunbar, Paul Laurence **5** 141-142

Cullen, Mrs. Countee
see Du Bois, Yolande

Cullen, Frederick Ashbury (died 1946), American clergyman
Cullen, Countee **4** 333-334

CULLEN, MAURICE GALBRAITH
(1866-1934), Canadian painter **4** 334
Morrice, James Wilson **11** 181-182

Cullen, William (1712-1790), Scottish physician
Hunter, William **8** 48-49
Rush, Benjamin **13** 364-365

Culloden Moor, Battle of (1746)
Charles Edward Louis Philip Casimir
Stuart **3** 466-467

Culpepper Minutemen (American Revolution)
Marshall, John **10** 279-281

Cult figures
American
Dean, James **4** 433-434
Leary, Timothy **9** 266-267
Indian
Rajneesh, Bhagwan Shree **13** 7-9

Cult of Personality (Communist)
Mao Zedong **10** 225-227
Prestes, Luiz Carlos **12** 442-444
Stalin, Joseph **14** 393-396

Culte du moi, Le (trilogy)
Barrès, Auguste Maurice **2** 20-21

Culto (poetry)
Góngora y Argote, Luis de **6** 427-428

Cultural anthropology (social science)
applications
Boas, Franz **2** 349-351
Mead, Margaret **10** 438-440
cultural evolution
Morgan, Lewis Henry **11** 167-168
Tylor, Edward Burnett **15** 372-373
White, Leslie A. **16** 232-233
culture of poverty
Lewis, Oscar **9** 392-393
Indian studies
Isaacs, Jorge **8** 144
Kluckhohn, Clyde **9** 56-57
Sapir, Edward **13** 478-479
integrated social systems
Radcliffe-Brown, A. R. **12** 535-536
tribal studies
Douglas, Mary Tew **5** 79-80
Geertz, Clifford **6** 248-249
Radcliffe-Brown, A. R. **12** 535-536
unification
Benedict, Ruth Fulton **2** 154-155
Linton, Ralph **9** 431

Cultural evolution
see Evolution, cultural

Cultural lag (sociology)
Ogburn, William Fielding **11** 480
Veblen, Thorstein Bunde **15** 449-450

Cultural Revolution (China; 1966-1969)
Chernenko, Konstantin Ustinovich
3 503-504
Chou En-lai **4** 20-22
Deng Xiaoping **4** 498-500
Jiang Qing **8** 256-260
Kuo Mo-jo **9** 133-134
Lao Shê **9** 200-201'
Lin Piao **9** 429-430
Liu Shao-Ch'i **9** 453-455
Mao Zedong **10** 225-227

Culture (anthropology)
concepts of
Boas, Franz **2** 349-351
Huizinga, Johan **8** 26-27
Niebuhr, Helmut Richard
11 386-387
Spengler, Oswald **14** 372-373
popular (in art)
Warhol, Andy **16** 114-115
see also Civilization; Cultural
anthropology

Culture area (archeology and ethnology)
Kroeber, Alfred Louis **9** 105-106

Culture media (bacteriology)
Koch, Heinrich Hermann Robert
9 69-70

Cumans (Asian people)
Alexius I **1** 143-144
Batu Khan **2** 60-61

Cumberland, Duke of (William Augustus;
1721-1765), English military commander
Amherst, Jeffery **1** 200-201
Braddock, Edward **2** 474-475
Rockingham, 2d Marquess of
13 230-231

Cumberland Gap (mountain pass, United
States)
Boone, Daniel **2** 397-398

Cummings, Edward (1861-1926), American
theologian
Cummings, Edward Estlin **4** 334-336

CUMMINGS, EDWARD ESTLIN
(1894-1962), American poet **4** 334-336
Berio, Luciano **2** 194-195
Crane, Hart **4** 291-293
Dos Passos, John Roderigo **5** 69-71
Eliot, Thomas Stearns **5** 258-261
Sandburg, Carl **13** 461-462
Stevens, Wallace **14** 443-445

Cummings, Mrs. E.E.
see Morehouse, Marion

Cummings, Homer Stillé (1870-1956),
American lawyer
Cardozo, Benjamin Nathan **3** 288-290

Cuna y la sepultura, La (book)
Quevedo Y Villegas, Francisco Gómez
de **12** 511

Çunacépa (poem)
Leconte de Lisle, Charles Marie René
9 273-274

Cunard, Samuel (1787-1865), British
shipowner
Collins, Edward Knight **4** 162-163

Cunctator
see Fabius, Quintus

Cundina marca (department; Colombia)
Nariño, Antonio **11** 314-315

CUNHA, EUCLIDES RODRIGUES PIMENTA DA (1866-1909), Brazilian writer
4 336-337

Cunha, Tristão da (1460?-1540?), Portuguese navigator
Albuquerque, Afonso de **1** 118-119

Cunning Little Fox, The (opera)
Janáček, Leoš **8** 219

Cunningham, Jane
see Croly, Jane Cunningham

CUNNINGHAM, MERCE (born 1919), American dancer and choreographer **4** 337-338
Cage, John **3** 211-214
Rauschenberg, Robert **13** 52-53

Cunninghame-Graham, R.B. (1852-1936), Scottish writer
Asquith, Herbert Henry **1** 344-346
Hardie, James Keir **7** 147-148

Cuno House (Eppenhausen, Germany)
Behrens, Peter **2** 121-122

CUOMO, MARIO MATTHEW (born 1932), Democratic New York state governor **4** 338-339

Cup of Gold (novel)
Steinbeck, John Ernst **14** 416-417

Cupid (sculpture)
Michelangelo Buonarroti **11** 2-5

Cupid and Commonsense (play)
Bennett, Arnold **2** 167-168

Cupid Sharpening His Bow (painting)
Parmigianino **12** 117

Cupid's Warning (sculpture)
Falconet, Étienne Maurice **5** 372

Curaçao (Caribbean island)
Stuyvesant, Peter **15** 5-6

Curare (medicine)
Bernard, Claude **2** 208-210
Houssay, Bernardo Alberto **7** 522-523

Curculio (play)
Plautus **12** 348-350

Cure, The (film)
Chaplin, Charles Spencer **3** 438-440

Curé de village, Le (literary work)
Balzac, Honoré de **1** 478-480

Cure of Folly (painting)
Bosch, Hieronymus **2** 426-428

Curée, La (novel)
Zola, Émile **16** 526-528

Cures of Love (book; Ovid)
Chrestien de Troyes **4** 23-24

Curfew Must Not Ring Tonight, The (poem, R.H. Thorpe)
Belasco, David **2** 124-125

Curia, Roman (Roman Catholic Church)
Paul VI **12** 146-148
Pius X **12** 336-337
Sixtus V **14** 267-268
Urban II **15** 393

Curiales (Roman government)
Constantine I **4** 209-211

Curie, Ève (born 1904), French musician and playwright
Curie, Marie Sklodowska **4** 339-341

Curie, Irène
see Joliot-Curie, Irène

CURIE, MARIE SKLODOWSKA (1867-1934), Polish-born French physicist **4** 339-341
Becquerel, Antoine Henri **2** 108-109
Cherenkov, Pavel Alekseevich **3** 502-503
Curie, Pierre **4** 341-344
Dumas, Jean Baptiste André **5** 138-139
Joliot-Curie, Jean Frédéric **8** 327-328
Kármán, Theodore von **8** 451-452

CURIE, PIERRE (1859-1906), French physicist **4** 341-344
Curie, Marie Sklodowska **4** 339-341

Curio, Gaius Scribonius (died 49 B.C.), Roman soldier
Antony, Mark **1** 253-254

Curiosités esthétiques (book)
Baudelaire, Charles Pierre **2** 61-63

CURLEY, JAMES MICHAEL (1874-1958), American politician **4** 344-345

Curll, Edmund (1675-1747), English bookseller
Pope, Alexander **12** 395-397

Curran, John Philpot (1750-1817), Irish jurist
Emmet, Robert **5** 281-282

Currency (United States)
bimetallism vs. gold
McKinley, William **10** 418-420
hard currency
Appleton, Nathan **1** 266-267
Jackson, Andrew **8** 168-172
Tucker, George **15** 332-333
paper
Coxey, Jacob Sechler **4** 286-287
Law, John **9** 244-245
McCulloch, Hugh **10** 404-405
Pendleton, George Hunt **12** 198
silver dispute (1890s)
Bryan, William Jennings **3** 80-82
Cleveland, Stephen Grover **4** 108-110
McKinley, William **10** 418-420
see also Greenback party

Currency reform (economics)
Diocletian **5** 19-20
Erhard, Ludwig **5** 302-304
Ito, Hirobumi **8** 153-155
see also Monetary policy

Current (art work)
Rauschenberg, Robert **13** 52-53

Current (electricity)
Ampère, André Marie **1** 205-206
Armstrong, Edwin Howard **1** 302-303
Faraday, Michael **5** 380
Henry, Joseph **7** 307-308

Current History (magazine)
Ochs, Adolph Simon **11** 464

CURRIE, SIR ARTHUR WILLIAM (1875-1933), Canadian general **4** 345

CURRIER AND IVES (1857-1907), American lithographic firm **4** 345-346

CURRY, JABEZ LAMAR MONROE (1815-1903), American politician **4** 346-347

CURTIN, ANDREW GREGG (1815-1894), American politician **4** 347-348

CURTIN, JOHN JOSEPH (1885-1945), Australian statesman, prime minister **4** 348-349
Bruce of Melbourne, 1st
Chifley, Joseph Benedict **3** 518
Evatt, Herbert Vere **5** 341-343
Hughes, William Morris **8** 21-22
Menzies, Robert Gordon **10** 510-511
Bruce of Melbourne, 1st Viscount **3** 61-62

CURTIS, BENJAMIN ROBBINS (1809-1874), American jurist, United States Supreme Court justice **4** 349

CURTIS, GEORGE WILLIAM (1824-1892), American writer and reformer **4** 349-350
Eaton, Dorman Bridgman **5** 190-191

Curtis Institute of Music (Philadelphia, Pennsylvania)
Barber, Samuel **1** 500-501

Curtis turbine (electricity)
Insull, Samuel **8** 130

CURTISS, GLENN HAMMOND (1878-1930), American aviation pioneer **4** 350-351
Bell, Alexander Graham **2** 129-131
Douglas, Donald Wills **5** 77
Langley, Samuel Pierpont **9** 195-196
Lindbergh, Charles Augustus **9** 421-423

Curtiss-Wright Corp.
Curtiss, Glenn Hammond **4** 350-351
Goddard, Robert Hutchings **6** 376-377

Curtiz, Michael (1888-1962), Hungarian-born film director
Bogart, Humphrey **2** 363-364

Curves (mathematics)
Euler, Leonard **5** 331-332
Fermat, Pierre de **5** 421-422
Hamilton, William Rowan **7** 99-100
Huygens, Christiaan **8** 79-81

CURZON, GEORGE NATHANIEL (1st Marquess Curzon of Kedleston; 1859-1925), English statesman **4** 351-352
George V **6** 273-275
Kitchener, Horatio Herbert **9** 45-46
Perth, 16th Earl of **12** 244-245
Younghusband, Francis Edward **16** 477

CUSA, NICHOLAS OF (1401-1464), German prelate and humanist **4** 352-353
Plato **12** 345-347

Cush (ancient kingdom, Sudan)
Ezana **5** 354-355
Piankhi **12** 288-289
Shabaka **14** 130
Taharqa **15** 81-82

Cushing, Caleb (1800-1879), American politician
Evarts, William Maxwell **5** 340-341
Waite, Morrison Remick **16** 46
Webster, Daniel **16** 162-164

CUSHING, HARVEY WILLIAMS (1869-1939), American neurosurgeon **4** 353-354

Cushing, Richard James (1895-1970), American cardinal
Kennedy, John Fitzgerald **8** 502-506

Cushing, Thomas (1725-1788), American lawyer and politician
Adams, Samuel **1** 55-56

CUSHMAN, CHARLOTTE (1816-1876), American actress **4** 354-355
Forrest, Edwin **6** 11-12

Custer, Elizabeth Bacon (Mrs. George A.; 1842-1933), American author
Custer, George Armstrong **4** 355-356

CUSTER, GEORGE ARMSTRONG (1839-1876), American general **4** 355-356
Crazy Horse **4** 303-304
Sitting Bull **14** 264-265
see also Little Bighorn River, Battle of the

Custom House (New Orleans)
Latrobe, Benjamin Henry **9** 222-224

Customs union (Germany; 1834)
Frederick William III **6** 87

Customs Union Journal
List, Georg Friedrich **9** 443-444

CUT
see Comité de l'Unité (Togo)

Cuthbert, St. (635?-687), English monk
Bede **2** 109-110

CUTLER, MANASSEH (1742-1823), American clergyman, scientist, and politician **4** 356-357

Cutler, Timothy (1684-1765), American clergyman
Johnson, Samuel **8** 314-315
Mather, Cotton **10** 330-332

Cutter of Coleman Street, The (play)
Cowley, Abraham **4** 281-282

Cutts, John, Baron (1661-1707), British general
Steele, Richard **14** 407-409

CUVIER, BARON GEORGES LÉOPOLD (1769-1832), French zoologist and biologist **4** 357-359
Agassiz, Jean Louis Rodolphe **1** 76-78
Buffon, Comte de **3** 109-111
Lamarck, Chevalier de **9** 171-173
Lyell, Charles **10** 62-63
Owen, Richard **12** 39

CUVILLIÉS, FRANÇOIS (1695-1768), Flemish architect and designer **4** 359-360
Zimmermann, Johann Baptist and Domenikus **16** 518

Cuvilliés, François, the Younger (1731-1777), French architect and engraver
Cuvilliés, François **4** 359-360

CUYP, AELBERT (1620-1691), Dutch painter **4** 360-361
Wilson, Richard **16** 329-330

Cuyp, Jacob Gerritsz (1594-1651?), Dutch painter
Cuyp, Aelbert **4** 360-361

Cuzzoni, Francesca (1700-1770), Italian singer
Handel, George Frederick **7** 116-119

Cyanogen (chemistry)
Gay-Lussac, Joseph Louis **6** 245-246

Cyanuric acid (chemistry)
Couper, Archibald Scott **4** 269-270

Cybernetics
Leibniz, Gottfried Wilhelm von **9** 307-310
Von Neumann, John **16** 27-28
Wiener, Norbert **16** 262-263

Cyclades offensive (489 B.C.)
Miltiades **11** 42-43

Cyclical form (music)
Franck, César **6** 48-49
Schubert, Franz Peter **14** 35-37

Cyclists No. 2 (painting)
Luz, Arturo Rogerio **10** 56-57

Cycloid (mathematics)
Pascal, Blaise **12** 122-124

Cyclone (meteorology)
Dunbar, William **5** 143-144

Cyclops (literary character)
Homer **7** 465-467

Cyclops (play)
Euripides **5** 332-334

Cyclotron (particle accelerator)
Bothe, Walther **2** 438-439
Lawrence, Ernest Orlando **9** 248-250

Cygnet (ship)
Dampier, William **4** 384

Cylinder (mathematics)
Archimedes **1** 277-280
Eudoxus of Cnidus **5** 329-330

Cylinder, oscillations of (physics)
Kármán, Theodore von **8** 451-452

Cylinder press (newspaper)
Hoe, Richard March **7** 435-436

Cymbeline (play)
Shakespeare, William **14** 142-145

Cynegeticus (book)
Xenophon **16** 418-420

Cynicism (philosophy)
Abravanel, Isaac ben Judah **1** 31

Antisthenes **1** 250-251
Diogenes **5** 20-21
Epictetus **5** 292

Cynic's Word Book, The (book)
Bierce, Ambrose Gwinett **2** 269-270

Cynoscephalae, Battle of (197 B.C.)
Flamininus, Titus Quinctius **5** 477

Cynthia's Revels (play)
Jonson, Ben **8** 343-345

Cypria (poem)
Homer **7** 465-467

CYPRIANUS, THASCIUS CAECILIANUS (died 258), Roman bishop of Carthage **4** 361-362
Erasmus, Desiderius **5** 298-300

Cyprus, Republic of (island nation; Mediterranean)
Abbasids in
Harun al-Rashid **7** 188
and Greece
Karamanlis, Constantine **8** 440-441
Makarios III **10** 157-158
Roman province
Brutus, Marcus Junius **3** 79-80
Cato, the Younger **3** 374-375
Cleopatra **4** 105-106
Clodius Pulcher, Publius **4** 121-122
United Nations mediation (1964)
Bunche, Ralph Johnson **3** 121-122
Kyprianou, Spyros **9** 141-143
Makarios III **10** 157-158
Plaza Lasso, Galo **12** 350-351
Waldheim, Kurt **16** 54-55

Cyprus, Turkish Republic of Northern
Denktash, Rauf **4** 500-502

Cyrano de Bergerac, Savinien de (1619-1655), French soldier and poet
Molière **11** 86-88

Cyrenaica (province, Ottoman Empire)
Idris I **8** 102

Cyrene (Roman province, North Africa)
Brutus, Marcus Junius **3** 79-80
Cleopatra **4** 105-106

CYRIL (OF ALEXANDRIA), ST. (died 444), Egyptian bishop, Doctor of the Church **4** 362
Leo I **9** 329-330
Nestorius **11** 349-350

CYRIL, ST. (827-869), Apostle to the Slavs **4** 362

Cyropaedia (book)
Xenophon **16** 418-420

Cyrus (book)
Antisthenes **1** 250-251

CYRUS THE GREAT (ruled 550-530 B.C.), founder of the Persian Empire **4** 363-364
Darius I **4** 394-395
Herodotus **7** 330-333
Lysander **10** 70
Xenophon **16** 418-420

Cystic fibrosis
Andersen, Dorothy **1** 212

Cythera (Greek island)
Schliemann, Heinrich **14** 17-18

Cytochrome oxidase (enzyme)
Szent-Györgyi, Albert von **15** 62-64

Cytology (biology)
East, Edward Murray **5** 182-183
Schwann, Theodor **14** 51-52
Vries, Hugo de **16** 33-36

Cyzicus (city, Asia Minor)
Eudoxus of Cnidus **5** 329-330

Czaczkes, Shmuel Yoseph
see Agnon, Shmuel Yoseph

Czar Has His Photograph Taken, The
(opera)
Weill, Kurt **16** 174-175

Czech art
Kupka, Frantisek **9** 134-135

Czech Brethren (religious group)
Masaryk, Tomáš Garrigue **10** 314-315

Czech literature
Čapek, Karel **3** 271-272
Comenius, John Amos **4** 180-181
Havel, Vaclav **7** 202-205
Kafka, Franz **8** 403-406
Kundera, Milan **9** 128-129

Czech music
Dvořák, Antonin **5** 168-169
Janáček, Leoš **8** 219
Martinu, Bohuslav **10** 299-300
Smetana, Bedřich **14** 281-282

Czech University (Prague)
Masaryk, Tomáš Garrigue **10** 314-315

Czechoslovakia (Czechoslovak Socialist
Republic; nation, Central Europe)
created (1918)
Beneš, Edward **2** 155-157
Masaryk, Tomáš Garrigue
10 314-315
fall of Communist regime
Havel, Vaclav **7** 202-205
Hungary and

Horthy de Nagybánya, Nicholas
7 510-512
Kádár, János **8** 402-403
Nazi Germany and
see Munich Conference; Sudeten-
land
Union of Soviet Socialist Republics and
Castro Ruz, Fidel **3** 365-368
Dubček, Alexander **5** 112-113
Gottwald, Klement **6** 464-466
Husák, Gustáv **8** 59-61
Litvinov, Maxim Maximovich
9 451-452
Slánský, Rudolf Salzmann
14 270-271
see also Bohemia; Czech art; Czech
literature; Moravia

Czerny, Carl (1791-1857), Austrian pianist
and composer
Liszt, Franz **9** 445-447

Czolgosz, Leon F. (circa 1873-1901), American anarchist
McKinley, William **10** 418-420

D

D-Day
see Normandy invasion (1944)

Da Gama, Vasco
see Gama, Vasco da

DaCapo Chamber Players (United States)
Tower, Joan **15** 279-281

Dacia (ancient nation; Europe)
Domitian **5** 52-53
Leo I **9** 329-330

Dacian Wars (101-102; 105-106)
Trajan **15** 291-292

Dacron (synthetic fiber)
Carothers, Wallace Hume **3** 317-318

Dadaism (art and literature movement)
France
Apollinaire, Guillaume **1** 260
Cocteau, Jean **4** 132-133
Miró, Joan **11** 53-54
Picabia, Francis **12** 291-292
Germany
Arp, Jean **1** 317-318
Ernst, Max **5** 311-312
Grosz, George **7** 17-18
Richter, Hans **13** 149-150
Italy
Burri, Alberto **3** 159-160
Chirico, Giorgio de **4** 4
Switzerland
Taeuber-Arp, Sophie **15** 73-74
Tinguely, Jean **15** 230-232
United States
Cage, John **3** 211-214
Dos Passos, John Roderigo **5** 69-71
Duchamp, Marcel **5** 122-123
Koons, Jeff **9** 83-84
Johns, Jasper **8** 291-293
Motherwell, Robert **11** 210-211
Patchen, Kenneth **12** 128-129
Ray, Man **13** 59-60

Daddi, Bernardo (flourished 1312-1348),
Italian painter
Orcagna **11** 526-527

Dade, Francis L. (died circa 1836), American military officer
Osceola **12** 18

Dagobert I (died 639), king of Franks 628-639
Martel, Charles **10** 285

Dagon (Burma)
see Rangoon

DAGUERRE, LOUIS JACQUES MANDÉ
(1787-1851), French painter and stage designer **4** 365-366
Draper, John William **5** 96-97
Fizeau, Hippolyte Armand Louis **5** 475

Daguerreotype (photography)
Brady, Mathew B. **2** 487-488
Daguerre, Louis Jacques Mandé **4** 365-366
Draper, John William **5** 96-97
Fizeau, Hippolyte Armand Louis **5** 475
Foucault, Jean Bernard Léon **6** 28-29

Dah Sun Cotton Mill (established 1899)
Chang Chien **3** 429-430

Dahl, Johan Christian (1788-1857), Norwegian painter
Friedrich, Caspar David **6** 114-115

DAHL, ROALD (1916-1990), Welsh-born English author **4** 366-367

Dahlmann, Friedrich Christoph
(1785-1860), German politician and historian
Treitschke, Heinrich von **15** 293-294

Dahomets (Haitian soldiers)
Christophe, Henri **4** 32

Dahomey, Republic of (nation, West Africa)
Apithy, Sourou Migan **1** 259-260
Dalzel, Archibald **4** 381-382
Houphouët-Boigny, Felix **7** 519-520

DAIGO II (1288-1339), Japanese emperor **4** 367-368
Ashikaga Takauji **1** 330-332
Goshirakawa **6** 460-461

Daigoji (temple; Japan)
Sotatsu, Tawaraya **14** 349

Daihosshi (religious title)
Ennin **5** 288-289

Dail Eireann (Irish Parliament)
Collins, Michael **4** 167-168

Daily Forward (newspaper)
Cahan, Abraham **3** 214
Singer, Isaac Bashevis **14** 249-250

Daily Republican (newspaper)
Bowles, Samuel **2** 464

Daily Worker (newspaper)
Haldane, John Burdon Sanderson **7** 70-71
Wright, Richard **16** 401-402

DAIMLER, GOTTLIEB (1834-1900), German mechanical engineer **4** 368
Diesel, Rudolf **5** 7

Daimler-Motoren-Gesellschaft MbH (auto firm)
Daimler, Gottlieb **4** 368

Daimyos (Japanese barons)
Ieyasu, Tokugawa **8** 103-106
Nobunaga, Oda **11** 413-414
Toyotomi Hideyoshi **15** 286-289

Dairy industry (United States)
Babcock, Stephen Moulton **1** 410-411
Borden, Gail **2** 409

Daishi (religious title)
Kukai **9** 124-125

Daisy (literary character)
Fitzgerald, Francis Scott Key **5** 470-472

Daisy Miller (novel)
James, Henry **8** 211-212

Daito (newspaper)
Hara, Kei **7** 138

Dakar (city, Senegal)
Faidherbe, Louis Léon César **5** 366-367
Gueye, Lamine **7** 31

Dakiki, Abu Mansur (Daqiqi of Balkh; died 980), Persian poet
Firdausi **5** 451-452

Dakin, Henry Drysdale (1880-1952), English chemist
Carrel, Alexis **3** 322-323

Dakota Wesleyan University (Mitchell, South Dakota)
McGovern, George Stanley **10** 412-414

DALADIER, ÉDOUARD (1884-1970), French statesman **4** 369
Chamberlain, Arthur Neville **3** 409-411
Giraudoux, Jean **6** 349-350

DALAI LAMA (Lhamo Thondup; born 1935), 14th in a line of Buddhist spiritual and temporal leaders of Tibet **4** 369-371

Dalarna (region, Sweden)
Gustavus I **7** 42-43

DALE, SIR HENRY HALLETT (1875-1968), English pharmacologist and neurophysiologist **4** 371-373
Best, Charles Herbert **2** 236-237
Burnet, Frank Macfarlane **3** 146-147
Eccles, John Carew **5** 195-196
Loewi, Otto **9** 486-487

Dale, Sir Thomas (died 1619), English colonial administrator
Pocahontas **12** 361-362
Powhatan **12** 429-430

D'Alembert, Jean
see Alembert, Jean le Rond d'

D'Alembert's principle (physics)
Alembert, Jean le Rond d' **1** 127-128
Lagrange, Joseph Louis **9** 164-166

DALEY, RICHARD J. (1902-1976), Democratic mayor of Chicago (1955-1976) **4** 373-375
Byrne, Jane **3** 190-191

DALHOUSIE, 1ST MARQUESS OF (James Andrew Broun Ramsay; 1812-1860), British statesman **4** 375-376
Papineau, Louis-Joseph **12** 91

DALI, SALVADOR (1904-1989), Spanish painter **4** 376-377
Buñuel, Luis **3** 127-128
Lorca, Federico García **9** 511-513
Miró, Joan **11** 53-54

Dalibor (opera)
Smetana, Bedřich **14** 281-282

Dalin, Olof von (1708-1763), Swedish poet and historian
Gustavus III **7** 45-46

DALLAPICCOLA, LUIGI (1904-1975), Italian composer **4** 377-378
Berio, Luciano **2** 194-195

Dallas, Alexander James (1759-1817), American statesman
Madison, James **10** 121-123

Dallas River (Texas)
Carson, Christopher **3** 334-335

Dalloway, Mrs. (novel and literary character)
Woolf, Virginia Stephen **16** 381-382

Dalmatia (historical region, Yugoslavia)
Basil I **2** 49-50
Wilson, Thomas Woodrow **16** 330-332

DALTON, JOHN (1766-1844), English chemist **4** 378-379

Avogadro, Lorenzo Romano Amedeo Carlo **1** 388-389
Berthollet, Claude Louis **2** 229-230
Berzelius, Jöns Jacob **2** 231-233
Cavendish, Henry **3** 383-384
Joule, James Prescott **8** 363-364

Dalton's law (physics)
Dalton, John **4** 378-379

DALY, MARCUS (1841-1900), American miner and politician **4** 379-380
Clark, William Andrews **4** 83-85

DALY, MARY (born 1928), American feminist theoretician and philosopher **4** 380-381

DALZEL, ARCHIBALD (or Dalziel; 1740-1811), Scottish slave trader **4** 381-382

DAM, CARL PETER HENRIK (1895-1976), Danish biochemist **4** 382-383

Dama duende, La (play)
Calderón, Pedro **3** 221-222

Damascus (city, Syria)
Allenby, Edmund Henry Hynman **1** 171-172
Isaiah **8** 146-147
Omar ibn al-Khattab **11** 508-509

Damascus Protocol (1915)
Faisal I **5** 370-371

Damasus I, St. (304?-384), pope 366-384
Jerome **8** 249

DAMIEN, FATHER (1840-1889), Belgian missionary **4** 383

Damietta (city, Egypt)
Francis of Assisi **6** 46-47
Joinville, Jean de **8** 325
Louis IX **9** 525-526

Damn (book)
Mencken, Henry Louis **10** 481-483

Damnation de Faust, La (dramatic legend)
Berlioz, Louis Hector **2** 203-205

Damned and the Elect (painting)
Signorelli, Luca **14** 221-222

Damon (flourished 5th century B.C.), Greek musician and philosopher
Pericles **12** 219-221

DAMPIER, WILLIAM (1652-1715), English privateer, author, and explorer **4** 384

Damrosch, Walter (1862-1950), American musical director
Gershwin, George **6** 284-285

Damsel in Distress (film)
Gershwin, George **6** 284-285

DANA, CHARLES ANDERSON (1819-1897), American journalist **4** 384-385
Greeley, Horace **6** 515-517

Dana, Francis (1743-1811), American statesman
Adams, John Quincy **1** 52-54

Dana, James Dwight (1813-1895), American geologist
Gray, Asa **6** 506-507

DANA, RICHARD HENRY, JR. (1815-1882), American author and lawyer **4** 385-386
Burns, Anthony **3** 151

Dana, Richard Henry, Sr. (1787-1879), American poet and editor
Dana, Richard Henry Jr. **4** 385-386

Danaids, The (play)
Aeschylus **1** 70-72

Danby, 1st Earl of (Thomas Osborne; 1631-1712), English statesman
Buckingham, 2d Duke of **3** 94-95
Charles II **3** 452-454
Shaftesbury, 1st Earl of **14** 135-136

Dance
see Ballet; Modern dance

Dance, The (painting)
Matisse, Henri **10** 336-337

Dance, The (sculpture)
Carpeaux, Jean Baptiste **3** 318-319

Dance in the Forest, A (play)
Soyinka, Wole **14** 358-359

Dance of Death (woodcuts)
Holbein, Hans the Younger **7** 449-450

Dance of Death, The (musical composition)
Honegger, Arthur **7** 472-473

Dance of Death, The (play)
Strindberg, August **14** 509-511
Wedekind, Frank **16** 166-167

Dance of the Earth (painting)
Rivera, Diego **13** 183-184

Dance Repertory Theater (New York City)
Graham, Martha **6** 485-486

Dance Suite (musical composition)
Khachaturian, Aram Ilich **8** 530-531

Dance to Death, The (play)
Lazarus, Emma **9** 260-261

Dance to the Music of Time, A (novel series)
Powell, Anthony **12** 422-423

Dancer (sculpture)
Marini, Marino **10** 260-262

Dancer, The (painting)
Kline, Franz **9** 55

Dancers
see Actors and entertainers—choreographers, dancers

Dancers Practicing at the Bar (painting)
Degas, Hilaire Germain Edgar **4** 461-462

Dances of Death (poem)
Blok, Aleksandr Aleksandrovich **2** 335

Dances with Wolves (film)
Greene, Graham **6** 524-525

Dancing Girl in Repose (painting)
Rivera, Diego **13** 183-184

Dancing Girl of Izu, The (novel)
Kawabata, Yasunari **8** 463-464

Dancing Nudes (fresco)
Pollaiuolo, Antonio **12** 377-378

Dancing on the Ceiling (song)
Rodgers, Richard Charles **13** 234-236

Dandarah (ancient town, Egypt)
Petrie, William Matthew Flinders
12 261-262

DANDOLO, ENRICO (circa 1107-1205),
Venetian doge 1192-1205 **4** 386-387

Dandy Frightening the Squatter, The (story)
Twain, Mark **15** 363-366

Dangeau, Marquis de (Philippe de Courcil-
lon; 1638-1720), French courtier
Saint-Simon, Duc de **13** 436

Dangling Man (novel)
Bellow, Saul **2** 141-143

Daniel, Gabriel (1649-1728); French Jesuit
historian
Boucher, François **2** 440-442

Daniel, Book of (Old Testament)
Saadia ben Joseph al-Fayumi **13** 396

Daniel Deronda (novel)
Eliot, George **5** 254-256

Daniel Guggenheim Foundation (aeronautics)
Lindbergh, Charles Augustus **9** 421-423

Daniel in the Lion's Den (painting)
Tanner, Henry Ossawa **15** 102-103

DANIELS, JOSEPHUS (1862-1948), American journalist and statesman **4** 387
Roosevelt, Franklin Delano **13** 277-280

Daniels, W. (pseudonym)
see Wallace-Johnson, Isaac

Danish literature and culture
see Denmark—culture

Danish State Lutheran Church
Kierkegaard, Søren Aabye **8** 547-549

Danites of the Sierras, The (play)
Miller, Joaquin **11** 27-28

Dannoura, Battle of (1185)
Yoritomo, Minamoto **16** 463-464

D'ANNUNZIO, GABRIELE (1863-1938),
Italian poet and patriot **4** 388
Carducci, Giosuè **3** 290-291
Valle Inclán, Ramón Maria del
15 407-408

Danny Deever (poem)
Kipling, Joseph Rudyard **9** 32-33

DANQUAH, JOSEPH B. (1895-1965),
Ghanaian nationalist and politician
4 388-389
Nkrumah, Kwame **11** 408-410

Danrin school (Japanese literature)
Basho, Matsuo **2** 45-48

Danse du Pan Pan au Monico (painting)
Severini, Gino **14** 122

Danse macabre (English version)
Lydgate, John **10** 61-62

Danse macabre (musical composition)
Saint-Saëns, Charles Camille
13 435-436

Dante (book)
Blake, William **2** 316-318

DANTE ALIGHIERI (1265-1321), Italian
poet **4** 389-391
Divine Comedy
see Divine Comedy
influence of
Beckett, Samuel **2** 102-104
Cavalcanti, Guido **3** 382
Chaucer, Geoffrey **3** 482-485
Eliot, Thomas Stearns **5** 258-261, 562
Hugo, Victor Marie **8** 22-25
influenced by
Guinizzelli, Guido **7** 36-37
Ibn al-Arabi, Muhyi al-Din **8** 91
parallels and studies
Attar, Farid ed-Din **1** 359-360
Boccaccio, Giovanni **2** 351-353
Bramante, Donato **2** 493-494
Villani, Giovanni **15** 497-498

Dante and Virgil in Hell (painting)
Delacroix, Ferdinand Victor Eugène
4 469-471

Dante's Dream (painting)
Rossetti, Dante Gabriel **13** 308-309

DANTON, GEORGES JACQUES
(1759-1794), French revolutionary leader
4 391-393
Aulard, François Victor Alphonse **1** 374
Mathiez, Albert **10** 333-334
Robespierre, Maximilien François Marie
Isidore de **13** 199-201
Saint-Just, Louis Antoine Léon de
13 433

Danton (book)
Belloc, Joseph Hilaire Pierre **2** 141
Mathiez, Albert **10** 333-334

Danton (play)
Rolland, Romain **13** 260

Dantonists (French political faction)
Danton, Georges Jacques **4** 391-393
Robespierre, Maximilien François Marie
Isidore de **13** 199-201
Saint-Just, Louis Antoine Léon de
13 433

Danube (river, Europe)
Caracalla **3** 281-282

Danube Landscape near Regensburg
(painting)
Altdorfer, Albrecht **1** 179-180

Danube school (German art)
Altdorfer, Albrecht **1** 179-180
Cranach, Lucas the Elder **4** 289-290

Danubian Confederation (1861)
Kossuth, Louis **9** 88-90

Danza (musical composition)
Gottschalk, Louis Moreau **6** 463-464

Danzas argentinas (musical composition)
Ginastera, Alberto Evaristo **6** 328-329

Daphnae (ancient fortress, Egypt)
Petrie, William Matthew Flinders
12 261-262

Daphne (mythology)
Bernini, Gian Lorenzo **2** 214-216

Daphné (book)
Vigny, Comte de **15** 494-495

Daphnis and Chloe (ballet)
Chagall, Marc **3** 406-407

Daphnis and Chloe (book; Verlaine)
Bonnard, Pierre **2** 395-396

Daphnis and Chloe (romance; Loungus)
Merezhkovsky, Dmitry Sergeyevich
10 515-516

Daphnis et Chloë (musical composition)
Ravel, Maurice Joseph **13** 54-55

DAR
see Daughters of the American Revolution

Dar al-Ulum (Cairo)
Abduh ibn Hasan Khayr Allah, Muhammad **1** 16-17

Dara Shikoh (died 1658), Mogul prince
Aurangzeb **1** 377
Shah Jahan **14** 138-139

Darcy, Fitzwilliam (literary character)
Austen, Jane **1** 377-379

Dardanelles (strait, Europe and Turkey)
Alexander the Great **1** 137-141
Catherine the Great **3** 370-372

Darest Thou Now O Soul (poem)
Whitman, Walt **16** 249-251

Daret, Jacques (1427-1470), Flemish
painter
Campin, Robert **3** 255

Darfur (province, Sudan)
Gordon, Charles George **6** 448-449

Dargomyzhsky, Aleksandr (1813-1869),
Russian composer
Glinka, Mikhail Ivanovich **6** 369-370
Mussorgsky, Modest Petrovich
11 274-275
Pushkin, Aleksandr Sergeevich
12 489-491
Rimsky-Korsakov, Nikolai Andreevich
13 174-175

Darién, Isthmus of
see Panama

Daring Young Man on the Flying Trapeze ...
(stories)
Saroyan, William **13** 486-487

DARÍO, RUBÉN (1867-1916), Nicaraguan
poet **4** 393-394
Güiráldez, Ricardo **7** 38-39
Ferrer, Gabriel Miró **5** 428
Lorca, Federico García **9** 511-513
Rodó, José Enrique **13** 240-241
Valera y Alcalá Galiano, Juan **15** 403
Vallejo, César Abraham **15** 408-409

DARIUS I (the Great; ruled 522-486 B.C.), king of Persia **4** 394-395
   Aeschylus **1** 70-72
   Miltiades **11** 42-43
   Xerxes **16** 420
   Zoroaster **16** 528-530

Darius III (Codomannus, died 330 B.C.), king of Persia 336-330
   Alexander the Great **1** 137-141, 124
   Ptolemy I **12** 470-472

Darius and the Family of Alexander (painting)
   Veronese, Paolo **15** 469-470

Dark Child (novel)
   Laye, Camara **9** 257-259

Dark Day (painting)
   Bruegel, Pieter the Elder **3** 65-67

Dark Flower, The (novel)
   Galsworthy, John **6** 189-190

Dark Huntsman, The (poem)
   Heavysege, Charles **7** 246

Dark Laughter (novel)
   Anderson, Sherwood **1** 220-221

Dark Lives (stories)
   Baroja y Nessi, Pío **2** 15-16

Dark Night of the Soul, The (treatise)
   John of the Cross **8** 285

Dark Princess (novel)
   Du Bois, William Edward Burghardt **5** 116-118

Darker America (musical composition)
   Still, William Grant **14** 455-456

Darkness at Noon (book)
   Koestler, Arthur **9** 71-73

Darkwater (literary collection)
   Du Bois, William Edward Burghardt **5** 116-118

Darlan, Jean Louis Xavier François (1881-1942), French naval officer and politician
   Clark, Mark Wayne **4** 80-81
   Laval, Pierre **9** 237-238
   Pétain, Henri Philippe **12** 250-252

Darling, Sir Ralph (ruled 1825-31), Australian governor
   Sturt, Charles **15** 2-3
   Wentworth, William Charles **16** 203-204

Darling of the Gods (play)
   Belasco, David **2** 124-125

Darling River (New South Wales)
   Burke, Robert O'Hara **3** 142-143
   Sturt, Charles **15** 2-3

Darmstadt (city, Germany)
   Behrens, Peter **2** 121-122

Darnley, Lord (Henry Stewart; 1545-1567), Scottish nobleman
   Leicester, Earl of **9** 312-313
   Mary, I **10** 308-309

DARROW, CLARENCE SEWARD (1857-1938), American lawyer **4** 396-397

Bryan, William Jennings **3** 80-82
Debs, Eugene Victor **4** 444-445
Russell, Charles Edward **13** 374-375
see also Scopes trial

D'Artagnan (literary character)
   Dumas, Alexandre **5** 136-138

Dartmouth College (Hanover, New Hampshire)
   Becker, Carl Lotus **2** 100-101
   Holmes, Oliver Wendell **7** 457-458
   Nervi, Pier Luigi **11** 346-348
   Stefansson, Vilhjalmur **14** 409-410
   Thayer, Sylvanus **15** 168-169
   Wheelock, Eleazar **16** 222-223

Dartmouth College v. Woodward (legal case; 1819)
   Marshall, John **10** 279-281
   Story, Joseph **14** 480-481

Darwin, Charles G. (1887-1962), English physicist
   Born, Max **2** 420-421

DARWIN, CHARLES ROBERT (1809-1882), English naturalist **4** 397-399
   associates
      Rosas, Juan Manuel de **13** 290-291
      Wallace, Alfred Russel **16** 69-70
   influence (literature)
      Bjørnson, Bjørnstjerne **2** 299-300
      Hardy, Thomas **7** 150-152
      Hauptmann, Gerhart Johann Robert **7** 199-201
      Jacobsen, Jens Peter **8** 193-194
      London, Jack **9** 494-495
      Norris, Benjamin Franklin Jr. **11** 427-428
   influence (political theory)
      Clemenceau, Georges **4** 99-101
      Engels, Friedrich **5** 286-288
   influence (religion)
      Ingersoll, Robert Green **8** 120-121
      Osler, William **12** 19-20
      Stephen, Leslie **14** 429
   influence (science)
      Burbank, Luther **3** 129-131
      Childe, Vere Gordon **3** 521-522
      Mendel, Johann Gregor **10** 483-486
      Vries, Hugo de **16** 33-36, 194
   influence (social theory)
      Hobhouse, Leonard Trelawny **7** 425-426
      Veblen, Thorstein Bunde **15** 449-450
   influenced by
      Banks, Joseph **1** 489-490
      Humboldt, Friedrich Heinrich Alexander von **8** 30-31
      Rosmini-Serbati, Antonio **13** 296-297
   intellectual history of
      Eiseley, Loren Corey **5** 232-233
   supporters
      Galton, Francis **6** 193-194
      Gray, Asa **6** 506-507
      Huxley, Thomas Henry **8** 77-79
      Spencer, Herbert **14** 369-370

see also Evolution, organic; Social Darwinism

Darwin, Erasmus (1731-1802), English physiologist and poet
   Darwin, Charles Robert **4** 397-399

Darwin, Francis (1848-1925), English botanist
   Darwin, Charles Robert **4** 397-399

Darwin, George Howard (1845-1912), English astronomer and mathematician
   Darwin, Charles Robert **4** 397-399

Darwin, Horace (1851-1928), English civil engineer
   Darwin, Charles Robert **4** 397-399

Darwin, Leonard (1850-1943), English eugenist
   Darwin, Charles Robert **4** 397-399

Darwinism
   see Evolution, organic; Social Darwinism

DARWISH, MAHMUD (born 1942), Palestinian poet **4** 399-401

DAS, CHITTA RANJAN (1870-1925), Indian lawyer, poet, and nationalist **4** 401-402
   Bose, Subhas Chandra **2** 430-431
   Nehru, Motilal **11** 334-335

Dascalzas Reales (convent, Madrid)
   Rubens, Peter Paul **13** 339-342

Dasein (philosophy)
   Heidegger, Martin **7** 257-258

Daser, Ludwig (1525-1589), German composer
   Lassus, Roland de **9** 216-218

Dashti
   see Jami

Dashwood sisters (literary characters)
   Austen, Jane **1** 377-379

Date (chronology)
   Mabillon, Jean **10** 72
   Petrie, William Matthew Flinders **12** 261-262
   see also Calendar

Datta, Narendranath
   see Vivekananda

Dau
   see Landau, Lev Davidovich

Daubenton, Louis Jean Marie (1716-?1800), French naturalist
   Buffon, Comte de **3** 109-111

DAUBIGNY, CHARLES FRANÇOIS (1817-1878), French painter and etcher **4** 402
   Millet, Jean François **11** 31
   Mondrian, Piet **11** 101-102
   Monet, Claude **11** 102-104

Daubigny, Edmé François (1789-1843), French landscape painter
   Daubigny, Charles François **4** 402

DAUDET, ALPHONSE (1840-1897), French novelist and dramatist **4** 402-403

Bizet, Georges **2** 296-297
Flaubert, Gustave **5** 480-482
Turgenev, Ivan Sergeyevich **15** 345-348

Daudi Chwa II, Sir (died 1939), king of
Buganda
Mutesa II **11** 277-278

Daugherty, Harry Micajah (1860-1941),
American lawyer and politician
Coolidge, John Calvin **4** 217-219

Daughter of Jephthah (painting)
Degas, Hilaire Germain Edgar
4 461-462

Daughter of Jorio, The (play)
D'Annunzio, Gabriele **4** 388

Daughter of Proteus (poem)
Theocritus **15** 171-172

Daughter of the Air, The (play)
Calderón, Pedro **3** 221-222

Daughter of the Middle Border, A (autobiography)
Garland, Hannibal Hamlin **6** 217-218

Daughters of Cecrops (painting)
Jordaens, Jacob **8** 347-349

Daughters of Charity (religious congregation)
Vincent de Paul **15** 501-502

Daughters of Edward Darley Boit (painting)
Sargent, John Singer **13** 481-482

Daughters of Pelias (play)
Euripides **5** 332-334

Daughters of Revolution (painting)
Wood, Grant **16** 368-369

Daughters of the American Revolution
(established 1890)
Anderson, Marian **1** 218-219

DAUMIER, HONORÉ VICTORIN
(1808-1879), French lithographer, painter,
and sculptor **4** 403-405
Evergood, Philip **5** 345
Van Gogh, Vincent **15** 427-429

Daun-Kinsky Palace (Vienna)
Hildebrandt, Johann Lucas von
7 380-381

Dauphine (ship)
Verrazano, Giovanni da **15** 470-471

Davaine, Casimir Joseph (1812-1882),
French physician
Koch, Heinrich Hermann Robert
9 69-70

Dave Brubeck Quartet
Brubeck, Dave **3** 59-61

Davenant, Sir William (1606-1668), English poet laureate and dramatist
Dryden, John **5** 106-107

DAVENPORT, JOHN (1597-1670), English
Puritan clergyman **4** 405-406
Cotton, John **4** 263-265

D'Avernon, Edgar Vincent, 1st Viscount
(1857-1941), English financier and diplomat

Stresemann, Gustav **14** 508-509

DAVID (ruled circa 1010-circa 970 B.C.),
Israelite king **4** 406-407
Honegger, Arthur **7** 472-473
Mary **10** 308
Samuel **13** 457-458
Saul **13** 498
Solomon **14** 326-327

DAVID I (1084-1153), king of Scotland
4 407
Malcolm III **10** 164-165
Stephen **14** 426-427

David II (1324-1371), king of Scotland
Edward III **5** 211-212
Philip VI **12** 277-278
Robert II **13** 194

David, Sir Edgeworth (1858-1934), Australian geologist
Mawson, Douglas **10** 354-355

David, Gerard (circa 1450/60-1523),
Dutch painter
Bosch, Hieronymus **2** 426-428

DAVID, JACQUES LOUIS (1748-1825),
French painter **4** 407-409
influence of
Delacroix, Ferdinand Victor Eugène
4 469-471
Peale, Rembrandt **12** 172-173
Prud'hon, Pierre Paul **12** 469
students
Daumier, Honoré Victorin
4 403-405
Gros **7** 14-15
Ingres, Jean Auguste Dominique
8 121-123

David, Pierre Jean
see David d'Angers

David (ballet)
Cocteau, Jean **4** 132-133

David (musical composition)
Machaut, Guillaume de **10** 93-94
Milhaud, Darius **11** 17-18

David (play)
Lawrence, David Herbert **9** 247-248

David (sculpture)
Donatello **5** 55-56
Verrocchio, Andrea del **15** 471-472

David (sculpture; Michelangelo)
Agostino di Duccio **1** 86
Leonardo da Vinci **9** 337-340
Michelangelo Buonarroti **11** 2-5
Perugino **12** 245-246

David Balfour (novel)
Stevenson, Robert Louis **14** 446-448

David Copperfield (novel; Dickens)
Dickens, Charles John Huffam
4 538-541, 369, 370
Fields, W. C. **5** 444

David d'Angers (Pierre Jean David;
1788-1856), French sculptor
Blanqui, Louis Auguste **2** 323-324

David III (book)
Mäkonnen Endalkačäw **10** 161-162

Davideis (epic)
Cowley, Abraham **4** 281-282

Davidsbündler (musical group)
Schumann, Robert Alexander **14** 41-43

Davidson, Thomas (1840-1900), Scottish
philosopher and educator
Cohen, Morris Raphael **4** 139-140

DAVIES, ARTHUR BOWEN (1862-1928),
American painter **4** 409-410
Flannagan, John Bernard **5** 480
Prendergast, Maurice Brazil **12** 440

Davies, Marion (1897-1961), American
film star
Hearst, William Randolph **7** 243-244

Davies (literary character)
Pinter, Harold **12** 317-318

DAVIGNON, VISCOUNT (ETIENNE) (born
1932), an architect of European integration and unity through the Commission of
the European Communities **4** 410-411

DAVIS, ALEXANDER JACKSON
(1803-1892), American architect **4** 411

DAVIS, ANGELA (Angela Yvonne Davis;
born 1944), African American scholar
and activist **4** 412-413

DAVIS, ARTHUR VINING (1867-1962),
general manager of the Aluminum Company of America (ALCOA) **4** 413-414

DAVIS, BENJAMIN O., SR. (1877-1970),
first African American general in the regular United States Armed Services
4 414-415

Davis, Bette (1908-1989), American actress
Bogart, Humphrey **2** 363-364

DAVIS, HENRY WINTER (1817-1865),
American lawyer and politician
4 415-416
Wade, Benjamin Franklin **16** 38-39

Davis, Jeff (1862-1913), American politician
Tillman, Benjamin Ryan **15** 225-226

DAVIS, JEFFERSON (1808-1889), American
statesman, president of the Confederacy
1862-1865 **4** 416-418
biographers
Tate, Allen **15** 116
Cabinet
Benjamin, Judah Philip **2** 163-164
Memminger, Christopher Gustavus
10 476-477
military strategy
Beauregard, Pierre Gustave Toutant
2 96-97
Forrest, Nathan Bedford **6** 13-14
Johnston, Joseph Eggleston **8** 323
Lee, Robert Edward **9** 292-294
see also Civil War, United States
opponents
Blair, Francis Preston **2** 313-315
Brown, Joseph Emerson **3** 41-42
Forbes, John **5** 507-508

Lincoln, Abraham **9** 415-418
Soulé, Pierre **14** 351-352
Taylor, Zachary **15** 128-130
Toombs, Robert Augustus
15 267-268
supporters
Bledsoe, Albert Taylor **2** 324-325
Hill, Benjamin Harvey **7** 386-387
Johnson, Andrew **8** 294-295
Lamar, Lucius Quintus Cincinnatus
9 170-171
Mason, James Murray **10** 320-321

DAVIS, JOHN (circa 1550-1605), English
navigator **4** 419

Davis, John W. (1873-1955), American
lawyer and politician
McAdoo, William Gibbs **10** 385-386
Smith, Alfred Emmanuel **14** 284-285

DAVIS, MILES (1926-1991), jazz trumpeter,
composer, and small-band leader
4 419-421

DAVIS, OSSIE (born 1917), African American playwright, actor, and director
4 421-422
Dee, Ruby **4** 449-452

DAVIS, RICHARD HARDING (1864-1916),
American journalist, novelist, and drama-
tist **4** 422-423
Hearst, William Randolph **7** 243-244
Norris, Benjamin Franklin Jr.
11 427-428

DAVIS, SAMMY, JR. (1925-1990), African
American singer, dancer, and actor
4 423-424

DAVIS, STUART (1894-1964), American
cubist painter **4** 424-425
Gorky, Arshile **6** 458

DAVIS, WILLIAM MORRIS (1850-1934),
American geographer and geologist
4 425-426
Bowman, Isaiah **2** 464-465

Davis Strait (North Atlantic Ocean)
Davis, John **4** 419
Eric the Red **5** 304

Davisson, Clinton Joseph (1881-1958),
American physicist
de Broglie, Louis **4** 442-444
Thomson, George Paget **15** 198-199

Davout, Louis Nicholas (1770-1823),
French marshal
Bernadotte, Jean Baptiste **2** 205-206

DAVY, SIR HUMPHRY (1778-1829), Eng-
lish chemist and natural philosopher
4 426-427
Faraday, Michael **5** 380
Gay-Lussac, Joseph Louis **6** 245-246
Stephenson, George and Robert
14 432-433
Volta, Alessandro **16** 12-14
Young, Thomas **16** 475-476

DAWES, HENRY LAURENS (1816-1903),
American politician **4** 427

Dawes Plan (German reparations; 1924)
MacDonald, James Ramsay **10** 84-85
Poincaré, Raymond **12** 366-368
Stresemann, Gustav **14** 508-509
Young, Owen D. **16** 473-474

Dawes Severalty Act (1887)
Dawes, Henry Laurens **4** 427

Dawn (autobiography)
Dreiser, Herman Theodore **5** 98-100

Dawn (black community, Ontario)
Henson, Josiah **7** 311-312

Dawn (novel)
Fuentes, Carlos **6** 141-142

Dawn, The (periodical)
Ben Yehuda, Eliezer **2** 181-182

Dawn O'Hara (novel)
Ferber, Edna **5** 413

Dawn Society (India)
Prasad, Rajendra **12** 433

Dawn songs (poems)
Wolfram von Eschenbach **16** 360-361

Dawning of Music in Kentucky (music collection)
Heinrich, Anthony Philip **7** 261

Dawning, The (poem)
Vaughan, Henry **15** 444-445

Dawn's Wedding Feast (sculpture)
Nevelson, Louise **11** 356-357

DAWSON, WILLIAM LEVI (1899-1990),
African American composer, performer,
and music educator **4** 427-428

Day and Night (sculpture)
Epstein, Jacob **5** 295-296
Michelangelo Buonarroti **11** 2-5

Day at the Races, A (film)
Marx brothers **10** 303-304

Day, Benjamin Henry (1810-1889), American newspaperman
Beach, Moses Yale **2** 79-80

DAY, DOROTHY (1897-1980), a founder of
the Catholic Worker Movement
4 428-429

Day in the Country, A (symphony)
Fry, William Henry **6** 136-137

Day is Done, The (poem)
Longfellow, Henry Wadsworth
9 499-500

Day of Death (film)
Eisenstein, Sergei Mikhailovich
5 240-242

Day of Doom, The (poem)
Wigglesworth, Michael **16** 266-267

Day of Pleasure, A (stories)
Singer, Isaac Bashevis **14** 249-250

Day of the Locust, The (novel)
West, Nathanael **16** 213-214

Day, Thomas (1748-1789), English author
Edgeworth, Maria **5** 205-206

Dayaks (Asian people)
Brooke, James **3** 21-22

DAYAN, MOSHE (1915-1981), Israeli general and statesman **4** 429-431
Meir, Golda **10** 462-463
see also Arab-Israeli wars

DAYANANDA SARASWATI (1824-1883),
Indian religious leader **4** 431
Rai, Lala Lajpat **13** 5-6

Daybreak (play)
Kazantzakis, Nikos **8** 466-468

Days, The (autobiography)
Husayn, Taha **8** 61-62

Days and Deeds (poems)
George, Stefan **6** 277-278

Days and Nights (novel)
Simonov, Konstantin Mikhailovich
14 239-240

Days Before, The (essays)
Porter, Katherine Anne **12** 406-407

Days of Messiah, The (play)
Asch, Shalom **1** 325-326

Days of the Commune, The (play)
Brecht, Bertolt **2** 512-514

Days of the Turbins, The (play)
Bulgakov, Mikhail Afanasievich **3** 117

Days to Come (play)
Hellman, Lillian Florence **7** 267-268

Days without End (play)
O'Neill, Eugene **11** 514-516

Day's Work, The (story)
Kipling, Joseph Rudyard **9** 32-33

Dayton Engineering Laboratories Company
(Delco; United States)
Kettering, Charles F. **8** 524-525

**Daytona Literary and Industrial School for
Training Negro Girls** (established 1904)
Bethune, Mary McLeod **2** 241-242

DDT (pesticide)
Knipling, Edward Fred **9** 59-60
Müller, Paul Hermann **11** 241-242

De abajo, Los (novel)
Azuela, Mariano **1** 402

DE ANDRADE, MARIO (Mario Coelho
Pinto Andrade; born 1928), Angolan
poet, critic, and political activist
4 434-435

De asse et partibus (book)
Budé, Guillaume **3** 102-103

De augmentis scientiarum (book)
Bacon, Francis **1** 422-424

DE BEAUVOIR, SIMONE (1908-1986),
French writer and leader of the modern
feminist movement **4** 440-441
Knopf, Blanche Wolf **9** 61-62

De Beers Consolidated Mines (established
1888)
Rhodes, Cecil John **13** 120-122

De bello gallico
see Gallic Wars, Commentaries on the

DE BOW, JAMES DUNWOODY BROWN-SON (1820-1867), American editor and statistician **4** 441-442

De Bow's Review (journal)
Fitzhugh, George **5** 474

De Camp, Maria Theresa (Mrs. Charles Kemble; 1774-1838), English actress
Kemble, Frances Anne **8** 491

De casibus virorum illustrium (biography)
Boccaccio, Giovanni **2** 351-353

De causis errorum (book)
Herbert, Edward **7** 324

De civitate Dei
see City of God

De corpore et sanguine Domini (treatise)
Lanfranc **9** 189-190

DE FOREST, LEE (1873-1961), American inventor **4** 459-460
Armstrong, Edwin Howard **1** 302-303
Goddard, Robert Hutchings **6** 376-377

DE GASPERI, ALCIDE (1881-1954), Italian statesman, premier 1945-1953 **4** 462-463

DE GAULLE, CHARLES ANDRÉ JOSEPH MARIE (1890-1970), French general, president 1958-1969 **4** 463-465
colonial policy
Apithy, Sourou Migan **1** 259-260
Eboué, Adolphe Felix Sylvestre **5** 194
Houphouët-Boigny, Felix **7** 519-520
Senghor, Léopold Sédar **14** 106-107
Touré, Sékou **15** 275-277
domestic affairs
Laval, Pierre **9** 237-238
Leclerc, Jacques Philippe **9** 272-273
Monnet, Jean **11** 109-110
Pétain, Henri Philippe **12** 250-252
Pompidou, Georges **12** 389-390
foreign policy
Ben-Gurion, David **2** 160-161
Kennedy, John Fitzgerald **8** 502-506
supporters
Lippmann, Walter **9** 439-440
Malraux, André **10** 178-180

De generatione (book)
Harvey, William **7** 189-190

De genesi ad litteram (book)
Augustine **1** 367-370

De heretico comburendo (statute; England)
Henry IV **7** 292-293

De Humani corporis fabrica ... (book)
Vesalius, Andreas **15** 473-475

De immortalitate animae (book)
Augustine **1** 367-370
Pomponazzi, Pietro **12** 390-391

DE KLERK, FREDRIK WILLEM (born 1936), state president of South Africa (1989-) **4** 466-468

DE KOONING, WILLEM (1904-1997), Dutch-born American painter **4** 468-469
associates
Gorky, Arshile **6** 458
Pollock, Jackson **12** 379-380
influence of
Dubuffet, Jean Philippe Arthur **5** 119-120
Frankenthaler, Helen **6** 56-57
Johns, Jasper **8** 291-293

De la Barra, Francisco (1863-1939), Mexican statesman
Huerta, Victoriano **8** 13-14
Zapata, Emiliano **16** 489-490

De la Huerta rebellion (1923-1924)
Obregón, Álvaro **11** 458-459

De la littérature ... (book)
Staël, Germaine de **14** 391-392

DE LA MADRID HURTADO, MIGUEL (born 1934), president of Mexico (1982-1988) **4** 471-472

De la Mare, Walter John (1873-1956), English poet and novelist
Brooke, Rupert **3** 22-23

De la pirotechnica (encyclopedia)
Biringuccio, Vannoccio **2** 283

DE LA ROCHE, MAZO LOUISE (1879-1961), Canadian author **4** 474-475

De la sagesse (book)
Charron, Pierre **3** 472

De la Warr Pavilion (Boxhill, England)
Mendelsohn, Erich **10** 488

De l'Allemagne (book)
Staël, Germaine de **14** 391-392

De l'Allemagne (essays)
Heine, Heinrich **7** 259-260

DE LEON, DANIEL (1852-1914), American Socialist theoretician and politician **4** 479-480
Hillquit, Morris **7** 393-394

De libero arbitrio (book)
Augustine **1** 367-370
Erasmus, Desiderius **5** 298-300

De l'Influence des passions ... (book)
Staël, Germaine de **14** 391-392

De lingua Latina (book)
Varro, Marcus Terentius **15** 438-439

De Long, George W. (1844-1881), American naval officer
Melville, George Wallace **10** 472

DE L'ORME, PHILIBERT (1510-1570), French architect **9** 519
Lescot, Pierre **9** 354

DE MILLE, AGNES (1905-1993), American dancer, choreographer, and author **4** 486-488

De monarchia (treatise)
Dante Alighieri **4** 389-391

De moneta (treatise)
Nicholas of Oresme **11** 380

De montibus ... (geographical dictionary)
Boccaccio, Giovanni **2** 351-353

De musica (book)
Augustine **1** 367-370
Boethius, Anicius Manlius Severinus **2** 360-361

De natura deorum (essay)
Cicero, Marcus Tullius **4** 55-58

De natura sonoris (musical composition)
Penderecki, Krzysztof **12** 195-197

De oratore (book; Cicero)
Castiglione, Baldassare **3** 360-361
Cicero, Marcus Tullius **4** 55-58
Polykleitos **12** 385-386

De ordine (book)
Augustine **1** 367-370

De otio religioso (book)
Petrarch **12** 259-261

De Profundis (apologia)
Wilde, Oscar Fingall O'Flahertie Wills **16** 272-273

De Profundis (musical composition)
Josquin des Prez **8** 361-363

De Quincey, Thomas (1785-1859), English author
Baudelaire, Charles Pierre **2** 61-63
Musset, Louis Charles Alfred de **11** 271-272

De re metallica (book; Agricola)
Agricola, Georgius **1** 86-87
Biringuccio, Vannoccio **2** 283

De remediis utriusque fortunae (treatise)
Petrarch **12** 259-261

De republica (book; Cicero)
Cicero, Marcus Tullius **4** 55-58
Niebuhr, Barthold Georg **11** 385-386

De rerum natura (poem; Lucretius)
Evelyn, John **5** 343-344
Lucretius **10** 26-27
Virgil **15** 507-510

De Revoire, Paul
see Revere, Paul

De revolutionibus orbium coelestium (book)
Copernicus, Nicolaus **4** 226-227

DE SANCTIS, FRANCESCO (1817-1883), Italian critic, educator, and legislator **4** 505

De sapientia veterum (book)
Bacon, Francis **1** 422-424

DE SMET, PIERRE JEAN (1801-1873), Belgian Jesuit missionary **4** 509-510

De solido intra solidum naturaliter contento dissertationis prodromus
see Prodromus

DE SOTO, HERNANDO (1500-1542), Spanish conqueror and explorer **4** 510-511
Garcilaso de la Vega, Inca **6** 210-211
Velasco, Luis de **15** 450-451

De Stijl (art movement)
Richter, Hans **13** 149-150
Schwitters, Kurt **14** 60-61

De Stijl (art movement)
de Kooning, Willem **4** 468-469
Mies van der Rohe, Ludwig **11** 10-12
Mondrian, Piet **11** 101-102
Oud, Jacobus Johannes Pieter **12** 32
Rietveld, Gerrit Thomas **13** 169
van Doesburg, Theo **15** 421

De Trinitate (book)
Augustine **1** 367-370
Boethius, Anicius Manlius Severinus
2 360-361

DE VALERA, EAMON (1882-1975), American-born Irish revolutionary leader and
statesman **4** 514-515
Collins, Michael **4** 167-168
Schrödinger, Erwin **14** 31-33

De vegetabilibus et plantis (book)
Albertus Magnus **1** 115-116

De veritate (book)
Herbert, Edward **7** 324

De veritate (treatise)
Thomas Aquinas **15** 183-186

De vetula (poem; Ovid)
Ruiz, Juan **13** 358-359

De viris illustribus (book)
Petrarch **12** 259-261
Suetonius Tranquillus, Gaius **15** 13

De Vita Caesarum (biography)
Suetonius Tranquillus, Gaius **15** 13

De vita solitaria (book)
Petrarch **12** 259-261

DE VRIES, HUGO (1848-1935), Belgian
botanist in the fields of heredity and the
origin of species **4** 516-518

De vulgari eloquentia (treatise)
Dante Alighieri **4** 389-391

Dé Wet, Christian Rudolph (1854-1922),
Boer soldier and politician
Roberts, Frederick Sleigh **13** 195-196

Deacon's Masterpiece, The (poem)
Holmes, Oliver Wendell Jr. **7** 458-459

Dead, The (story)
Joyce, James **8** 365-367

Dead Christ (painting)
Holbein, Hans the Younger **7** 449-450
Mantegna, Andrea **10** 215-216

Dead Christ with Angels (painting)
Manet, Édouard **10** 193-194

Dead End (film)
Bogart, Humphrey **2** 363-364

Dead End, The (stories)
Hidayat, Sadiq **7** 377-378

Dead Lecturer, The (poems)
Baraka, Imamu Amiri **1** 498-499

Dead Man Revived ... (painting)
Allston, Washington **1** 176-177

Dead of the Wilderness, The (poem)
Bialik, Hayyim Nahman **2** 262-263

Dead Pan, The (poem)
Browning, Elizabeth Barrett **3** 52-53

Dead Sea Scrolls (ancient manuscripts)
John the Baptist **8** 290
Josephus Flavius **8** 360-361

Dead Secret, The (novel)
Collins, William Wilkie **4** 169-170

Dead Souls (novel; Gogol)
Chagall, Marc **3** 406-407
Gogol, Nikolai **6** 391-393

Deadline at Dawn (film)
Odets, Clifford **11** 470-471

Deadly Game, The (novel)
Dürrenmatt, Friedrich **5** 164-165

Deadwood (city, South Dakota)
Calamity Jane **3** 216

Deadwood Dick
see Love, Nat

Deaf, the
deaf-mutes
Cardano, Geronimo **3** 285-286
Gallaudet, Thomas Hopkins **6** 185
deafness victims
Beethoven, Ludwig van **2** 114-117
Edison, Thomas Alva **5** 206-208
Fauré, Gabriel Urbain **5** 397-398
George III **6** 270-272
Glasgow, Ellen **6** 360-361
Goya y Lucientes, Francisco de
Paula José de **6** 476-478
Keller, Helen Adams **8** 479-480
Martineau, Harriet **10** 296-297
Prendergast, Maurice Brazil **12** 440
Ronsard, Pierre de **13** 271-273
Smetana, Bedřich **14** 281-282
Treitschke, Heinrich von
15 293-294
Vieira, Antônio **15** 492
education of
Gallaudet, Thomas Hopkins **6** 185
Keller, Helen Adams **8** 479-480

DEÁK, FRANCIS (1803-1876), Hungarian
statesman **4** 431-432
Andrássy, Julius **1** 222-223
Kossuth, Louis **9** 88-90

DEAKIN, ALFRED (1856-1919), Australian
statesman **4** 432-433
Fisher, Andrew **5** 462

Deal in Wheat ... (stories)
Norris, Benjamin Franklin Jr.
11 427-428

**Dealings with the Firm of Dombey and
Son** (novel)
see Dombey and Son

DEAN, JAMES (James Byron Dean;
1931-1955), American actor and cult figure **4** 433-434
Taylor, Elizabeth Rosemond **15** 124-125

Deane, Henry (died 1503), English prelate,
archbishop of Canterbury
Wolsey, Thomas **16** 364-366

DEANE, SILAS (1737-1789), American
merchant lawyer and diplomat **4** 435-437
Adams, John **1** 48-51
Franklin, Benjamin **6** 60-64
Lee, Arthur **9** 288-289
Morris, Robert **11** 185-187
Steuben, Frederick William Augustus
von **14** 438-439

**Dean George Berkeley with His Family
and Friends** (painting)
Smibert, John **14** 282

Dear Brutus (play)
Barrie, James Matthew **2** 21-22

Dear Judas and Other Poems (literary collection)
Jeffers, John Robinson **8** 236-237

Dearborn, Henry (1751-1829), American
politician
Pike, Zebulon **12** 302-304

Dearborn Independent (newspaper)
Baruch, Bernard Mannes **2** 42-43
Ford, Henry **6** 5-6

Dearest Enemy (musical)
Rodgers, Richard Charles **13** 234-236

Death (book)
Maeterlinck, Maurice **10** 125-126

Death (philosophy)
Anaxagoras **1** 208-209
Epicurus **5** 292-294
Jones, Ernest Alfred **8** 331-332

Death (poem; Porteus)
Peale, Rembrandt **12** 172-173

Death and Taxes (verses)
Parker, Dorothy Rothschild **12** 106

Death and the Child (stories)
Crane, Stephen **4** 293-295

Death and the Fool (play)
Hofmannsthal, Hugo von **7** 443-444

Death and the Maiden (musical composition)
Schubert, Franz Peter **14** 35-37

Death Blow (novel)
Aragon, Louis **1** 271-272

Death Comes for the Archbishop (novel)
Cather, Willa Sibert **3** 368-369

Death in a Family (book; Agee)
Barber, Samuel **1** 500-501

Death in the Afternoon (book)
Hemingway, Ernest Miller **7** 274-277

Death in the Making (book)
Capa, Robert **3** 269-271

Death in Venice (novella)
Mann, Thomas **10** 204-207

Death of a Salesman (play)
Miller, Arthur **11** 25-26

Death of Abel, The (oratorio)
Arne, Thomas Augustine **1** 307-308

Death of Artemio Cruz, The (novel)
Fuentes, Carlos **6** 141-142

Death of Cuchulain, The (play)
Yeats, William Butler **16** 445-447

Death of Flowers, The (poem)
Bryant, William Cullen **3** 83-85

Death of God theologies
Altizer, Thomas J. J. **1** 183-184
Gilkey, Langdon Brown **6** 318-319
Rubenstein, Richard L. **13** 343-344

Death of Ivan Ilyich, The (story)
Tolstoy, Leo **15** 262-265

Death of Joseph Bara (painting)
David, Jacques Louis **4** 407-409

Death of Lepeletier de Saint-Fargeau
(painting)
David, Jacques Louis **4** 407-409

Death of Major Pearson, The (painting)
Copley, John Singleton **4** 228-230

Death of Marat (painting)
David, Jacques Louis **4** 407-409

**Death of Montgomery in the Attack on
Quebec** (painting)
Trumbull, John **15** 316-317

Death of Pushkin, The (book)
Akhmatova, Anna **1** 96-97

Death of Sardanapalus (painting)
Delacroix, Ferdinand Victor Eugène
4 469-471

Death of Socrates (painting)
David, Jacques Louis **4** 407-409
West, Benjamin **16** 210-212

Death of the Earl of Chatham (painting)
Copley, John Singleton **4** 228-230

Death of the Gods, The (book)
Merezhkovsky, Dmitry Sergeyevich
10 515-516

Death of the Heart, The (novel)
Bowen, Elizabeth **2** 462-463

Death of the Hired Man, The (poem)
Frost, Robert Lee **6** 130-133

Death of the Virgin (painting)
Schongauer, Martin **14** 26-28
van der Goes, Hugo **15** 416-417

Death of Titian (verse play)
Hofmannsthal, Hugo von **7** 443-444

Death of Wolfe, The (painting)
West, Benjamin **16** 210-212

Death on the Installment Plan (novel)
Céline, Louis Ferdinand **3** 390-391

Death on the Pale Horse (painting)
West, Benjamin **16** 210-212

Death the Proud Brother (story)
Wolfe, Thomas Clayton **16** 355-356

Death to the Invader (mural)
Siqueiros, David Alfaro **14** 256

Death under Sail (novel)
Snow, Charles Percy **14** 311-312

Deaths and Entrances (poems)
Thomas, Dylan Marlais **15** 188-190

Death's Duel (sermon)
Donne, John **5** 60-61

Deathwatch (play)
Genet, Jean **6** 262-263

DEB, RADHAKANT (1783-1867), Bengali
reformer and cultural nationalist **4** 437

Débâcle, La (novel)
Zola, Émile **16** 526-528

DEBAKEY, MICHAEL ELLIS (born 1908),
American surgeon **4** 437-438

DEBARTOLO, EDWARD JOHN, SR. and
JR., real estate developers who special-
ized in large regional malls **4** 438-440

Debbie Go Home (book)
Paton, Alan Stewart **12** 134-135

Debit and Credit (novel)
Freytag, Gustav **6** 107-108

Debits and Credits (stories)
Kipling, Joseph Rudyard **9** 32-33

Deborah (oratorio)
Handel, George Frederick **7** 116-119

DE BROGLIE, LOUIS (1892-1987), French
physicist **4** 442-444
Bohr, Niels Henrik David **2** 366-368
Born, Max **2** 420-421
Dirac, Paul Adrien Maurice **5** 23-24
Einstein, Albert **5** 228-231
Schrödinger, Erwin **14** 31-33

DEBS, EUGENE VICTOR (1855-1926),
American union organizer **4** 444-445
associates
Berger, Victor Louis **2** 189-190
Coxey, Jacob Sechler **4** 286-287
Thomas, Norman Mattoon
15 191-192
Watson, Thomas Edward **16** 139
opponents
Cleveland, Stephen Grover
4 108-110
Olney, Richard **11** 504-505
supporters
Darrow, Clarence Seward **4** 396-397
Hillquit, Morris **7** 393-394
Randolph, A. Philip **13** 28-29

Debt (economics)
Crockett, David **4** 314-316
Gallatin, Albert **6** 183-184
Goodyear, Charles **6** 441

Debtors' prisons (England)
Oglethorpe, James Edward **11** 482-483

DEBUSSY, (ACHILLE) CLAUDE
(1862-1918), French composer
4 445-447
critics
Roussel, Albert **13** 328-329
Saint-Saëns, Charles Camille
13 435-436
influence of
Copland, Aaron **4** 227-228
Falla, Manuel de **5** 372-373
Honegger, Arthur **7** 472-473
Lutoslawski, Witold **10** 52-53

Martinu, Bohuslav **10** 299-300
Messiaen, Olivier **10** 528-529
Milhaud, Darius **11** 17-18
Respighi, Ottorino **13** 103-104
Stravinsky, Igor Fedorovich
14 502-506
Szymanowski, Karol **15** 67-68

DEBYE, PETER JOSEPH WILLIAM
(1884-1966), Dutch-born American physical chemist **4** 447-448
Born, Max **2** 420-421

Debye-Hückel theory (chemistry)
Arrhenius, Svante August **1** 318-320

Decadents (literary group)
Beardsley, Aubrey Vincent **2** 88-89
Gourmont, Remy de **6** 475
Huysmans, Joris Karl **8** 81-82
Laforgue, Jules **9** 160-161
Verlaine, Paul Marie **15** 465-466

Decalogue (Old Testament)
Saadia ben Joseph al-Fayumi **13** 396

Decameron (stories; Boccaccio)
Boccaccio, Giovanni **2** 351-353
Lessing, Gotthold Ephraim **9** 357-359

Decatur (ship)
Farragut, David Glasgow **5** 388-389
Nimitz, Chester William **11** 395-396

DECATUR, STEPHEN (1779-1820), American naval officer **4** 448-449
Lawrence, James **9** 251-252

Decazes, Élie (1780-1860), French statesman
Louis XVIII **9** 535-536

Deccan (region, India)
Ala-ud-din **1** 102-103
Aurangzeb **1** 377
Dupleix **5** 153
Frere, Henry Bartle Edward **6** 100-101
Muhammad bin Tughluq **11** 229
Shah Jahan **14** 138-139

Deccan Education Society (India)
Gokhale, Gopal Krishna **6** 396

Decebalus (died circa 107), king of Dacia
Domitian **5** 52-53

Decembrist Rebellion (1825)
Glinka, Mikhail Ivanovich **6** 369-370
Karamzin, Nikolai Mikhailovich
8 441-442
Nicholas I **11** 377-378

Decemviri stilitibus judicandis (Roman
Republic)
Drusus, Marcus Livius **5** 105-106

Décima (poetic stanza)
Guillén, Nicolás **7** 34-35

Decimus Junius Juvenalis
see Juvenal

Decius (Gaius Messius Quintus Trajanus
Decius; 201-251), Roman emperor
249-251
Origen **11** 528-529
Valerian **15** 404-405

Declaration of independence (Israel)
Meir, Golda **10** 462-463

Declaration of Independence (United States)
critics
Dickinson, John **4** 543-544
Douglas, Stephen Arnold **5** 80-82
drafted
Adams, John **1** 48-51
Franklin, Benjamin **6** 60-64
Jefferson, Thomas **8** 238-241
Lee, Richard Henry **9** 291-292
Livingston, Robert R. **9** 462-463
signers (Middle Colonies)
Chase, Samuel **3** 475-476
Franklin, Benjamin **6** 60-64
Hopkinson, Francis **7** 496-497
Morris, Robert **11** 185-187
Rush, Benjamin **13** 364-365
Wilson, James **16** 323-324
Witherspoon, John **16** 346-348
signers (New England)
Adams, John **1** 48-51
Adams, Samuel **1** 55-56
Gerry, Elbridge **6** 282-283
Hancock, John **7** 114-116
Sherman, Roger **14** 185-186
signers (South)
Jefferson, Thomas **8** 238-241
Lee, Richard Henry **9** 291-292
Wythe, George **16** 415

Declaration of Independence, The (book)
Becker, Carl Lotus **2** 100-101

Declaration of Independence, The (painting; Trumbull)
Durand, Asher Brown **5** 156-157

Declaration of Indulgence (1672-1689)
Shaftesbury, 1st Earl of **14** 135-136

Declaration of Love, The (painting)
Fragonard, Jean Honoré **6** 38-39

Declaration of Rights (England; 1689)
James II **8** 207-208
William III **16** 295-296

Declaration of Rights (United States; 1774)
Lee, Richard Henry **9** 291-292
see also Bill of Rights

Declaration of Rights and Privileges (1765)
Dickinson, John **4** 543-544

Declaration of the Independence of the Mind (book)
Rolland, Romain **13** 260

Declaration of the Relationship of the Church to Non-Christian Religions (Vatican II)
Bea, Augustinus **2** 79

Declaration of the Rights of Man (France; 1789)
Bentham, Jeremy **2** 176-178
Houdon, Antoine **7** 516-517
Lafayette, Marquis de **9** 151-152
Louis XVI **9** 534-535
Nariño, Antonio **11** 314-315

Sieyès, Comte Emmanuel Joseph **14** 217-218

Decline and Fall (novel)
Waugh, Evelyn Arthur St. John **16** 145-147

Decline and Fall of the Roman Empire, The (book; Gibbon)
Gibbon, Edward **6** 299-300
Guizot, François Pierre Guillaume **7** 40-41

Decline of Humanism, The (poem)
Blok, Aleksandr Aleksandrovich **2** 335

Decline of the West, The (book; Spengler)
Jeffers, John Robinson **8** 236-237
Spengler, Oswald **14** 372-373

Decoration Day (musical composition)
Ives, Charles Edward **8** 159-160

Decretals
see Canon law; Liber sextus

Dedal, Adrian Florenz
see Adrian VI

Dedalus (literary character; Ovid)
Joyce, James **8** 365-367

Dedham (city, Massachusetts)
Sacco and Vanzetti **13** 408-410

Dedication, Feast of
see Chanukah

Deductive method (logic)
Descartes, René **4** 505-508
Hobbes, Thomas **7** 421-423
Zeno of Elea **16** 500

Dee, John (1527-1608), English mathematician
Chancellor, Richard **3** 422
Ortelius, Abraham **12** 8-9

DEE, RUBY (born Ruby Ann Wallace; b. 1924), African American actor **4** 449-452
Davis, Ossie **4** 421-422

Deeds and Good Morals of Wise King Charles V (book)
Christine de Pisan **4** 29-30

Deeds of Emperor Frederick I, The (book)
Otto of Freising **12** 30

Deeds of the Kings of England (book)
William of Malmesbury **16** 297-298

Deephaven (novel)
Jewett, Sarah Orne **8** 256

DEER, ADA E. (born 1935), Native American social worker, activist, and director of Bureau of Indian Affairs **4** 452-454

Deer Park, The (novel)
Mailer, Norman Kingsley **10** 148-150

DEERE, JOHN (1804-1886), American inventor and manufacturer **4** 455

DEERING, WILLIAM (1826-1913), American manufacturer **4** 455-456

Deerslayer, The (novel)
Cooper, James Fenimore **4** 220-223

DEES, MORRIS S., JR. (born 1936), American civil rights attorney **4** 456-457

Defeat, The (play)
Warren, Mercy Otis **16** 120-121

Defectors (Czechoslovakia to United States)
Navratilova, Martina **11** 325-327

Defectors (Union of Soviet Socialist Republics to United States)
Baryshnikov, Mikhail **2** 43-44

Defence of Poetry (book)
Shelley, Percy Bysshe **14** 176-178

Defender of the Holy Sepulcher (title)
Godfrey of Bouillon **6** 379

Defenders, The (television series)
Davis, Ossie **4** 421-422

Defense, United States Department of
Aspin, Les **1** 342-344
Perry, William James **12** 240-242
Weinberger, Casper Willard **16** 177-178
Wilson, Charles Erwin **16** 316-317

Defense and Foreign Representation Agreement (1964)
Jawara, Dauda Kairaba **8** 227-228

Defense League (Norway)
Nansen, Fridtjof **11** 304-305

Defense of Fortified Places, The (essay)
Carnot, Lazare Nicolas Marguerite **3** 313-314

Defense of Himself (pamphlet)
Milton, John **11** 43-46

Defense of the Country (book)
Saicho **13** 426-428

Defense of the Jews (book)
Manasseh ben Israel **10** 183-184

Defenses of the English People (pamphlet)
Milton, John **11** 43-46

Defensor pacis (treatise)
Marsilius of Padua **10** 284

Defensorium (book)
Pomponazzi, Pietro **12** 390-391

Deffence et illustration de la langue française (book)
du Bellay, Joachim **5** 113-114

Definitions (book)
Heron of Alexandria **7** 334-335

Deflagrator (science instrument)
Hare, Robert **7** 152-153

Deflores (literary character)
Middleton, Thomas **11** 8-9

DEFOE, DANIEL (1660-1731), English novelist, journalist, and poet **4** 457-459
Bunyan, John **3** 128-129
Cervantes, Miguel de Saavedra **3** 395-398
ibn Tufayl, Abu Bakr Muhammad **8** 96
Sienkiewicz, Henryk **14** 216-217
Sterne, Laurence **14** 435-437

DEGANAWIDA (also DeKanahwidah; c. 1550-c. 1600), Native American prophet, leader, and statesman **4** 460-461

DEGAS, (HILAIRE GERMAIN) EDGAR (1834-1917), French painter and sculptor **4** 461-462
  influence of
    Cassatt, Mary **3** 356-357
    Glackens, William **6** 355-356
    Liebermann, Max **9** 402-403
    Prendergast, Maurice Brazil **12** 440
    Sickert, Walter Richard **14** 212-213
    Toulouse-Lautrec, Henri de **15** 273-274
  influenced by
    Daumier, Honoré Victorin **4** 403-405
    Harunobu, Suzuki **7** 188-189
    Ingres, Jean Auguste Dominique **8** 121-123
    Utamaro, Kitagawa **15** 397

Degenerate art (Nazi epithet)
  Barlach, Ernst **2** 5-6
  Beckmann, Max **2** 104-105
  Grosz, George **7** 17-18
  Hindemith, Paul **7** 399-400
  Klee, Paul **9** 47-49
  Nolde, Emil **11** 419-420

Degotti, Ignace Eugène Marie (died 1824), French painter
  Daguerre, Louis Jacques Mandé **4** 365-366

Dehmel, Richard (1863-1920), German poet and playwright
  Schoenberg, Arnold **14** 24-26

Dehn, Siegfried Wilhelm (1799-1858), German music theorist
  Glinka, Mikhail Ivanovich **6** 369-370

Dehydrogenases (biochemistry)
  Hopkins, Frederick Gowland **7** 491-492
  Theorell, Axel Hugo Theodor **15** 176-177

Dei delitti e delle pene (book)
  Becarria, Marchese di **2** 97-98

Deianera (literary character)
  Sophocles **14** 343-345

Deidamia (opera)
  Handel, George Frederick **7** 116-119

Deir el-Bahri temple (Egypt)
  Hatshepsut **7** 196-197

Deirdre (novel)
  Stephens, James **14** 430-431

Deirdre of the Sorrows (play)
  Synge, Edmund John Millington **15** 61-62

Deism (religion)
  Allen, Ethan **1** 163-164
  Bolingbroke, Viscount **2** 374-375
  Buffon, Comte de **3** 109-111
  Franklin, Benjamin **6** 60-64
  Herbert, Edward **7** 324
  Paine, Thomas **12** 66-67
  Toland, John **15** 256

see also Altheism; Freethinkers; Theism

Dejection (ode; Coleridge)
  Coleridge, Samuel Taylor **4** 154-156
  Shelley, Percy Bysshe **14** 176-178
  Wordsworth, William **16** 385-388

DEKKER, THOMAS (circa 1572-circa 1632), English playwright and pamphleteer **4** 465-466
  Brant, Sebastian **2** 503-504
  Ford, John **6** 7-8
  Jonson, Ben **8** 343-345
  Webster, John **16** 164

DELACROIX, (FERDINAND VICTOR) EUGÈNE (1798-1863), French painter **4** 469-471
  associates
    Bonington, Richard Parkes **2** 394-395
    Hugo, Victor Marie **8** 22-25
    Ingres, Jean Auguste Dominique **8** 121-123
  influence of (France)
    Baudelaire, Charles Pierre **2** 61-63
    Cézanne, Paul **3** 400-402
    Degas, Hilaire Germain Edgar **4** 461-462
    Millet, Jean François **11** 31
    Monet, Claude **11** 102-104
    Renoir, Pierre Auguste **13** 101-102
    Seurat, Georges Pierre **14** 120-122
    Van Gogh, Vincent **15** 427-429
  influence of (Germany)
    Beckmann, Max **2** 104-105
  influence of (Switzerland)
    Böcklin, Arnold **2** 354-355
    Hodler, Ferdinand **7** 434-435
  influence of (United States)
    Davies, Arthur Bowen **4** 409-410
    Marsh, Reginald **10** 276-277
  influenced by
    Constable, John **4** 208-209
    Copley, John Singleton **4** 228-230
    Goya y Lucientes, Francisco de Paula José de **6** 476-478
    Gros **7** 14-15
    Prud'hon, Pierre Paul **12** 469
    Veronese, Paolo **15** 469-470

DeLancey, James (1703-1760), American jurist and colonial administrator
  DeLancey, Stephen **4** 473

DeLancey, James (1732-1800), American sportsman and politician
  Clinton, George **4** 113-114
  DeLancey, Stephen **4** 473

DELANCEY, STEPHEN (1663-1741), American merchant and politician **4** 473

DELANY, MARTIN ROBINSON (1812-1885), African American army officer, politician, and judge **4** 473-474

Delaroche, Paul (1797-1856), French painter
  Daubigny, Charles François **4** 402
  Millet, Jean François **11** 31

Delattre, Roland
  see Lassus, Roland de

DELAUNAY, ROBERT (1885-1941), French abstract painter **4** 475-476
  Arp, Jean **1** 317-318
  Chagall, Marc **3** 406-407
  Hofmann, Hans **7** 442-443
  Kandinsky, Wassily **8** 420-422
  Klee, Paul **9** 47-49
  Marc, Franz **10** 231

Delaware (state, United States)
  Asbury, Francis **1** 324-325
  Clayton, John Middleton **4** 96-97
  Dickinson, John **4** 543-544
  Minuit, Peter **11** 50
  Penn, William **12** 200-202

Delaware Bay (Delaware)
  Verrazano, Giovanni da **15** 470-471

Delaware River (Delaware)
  Knox, Henry **9** 64

DELBRÜCK, MAX (1906-1981), German-born American molecular biologist **4** 476-478

DELCASSÉ, THÉOPHILE (1852-1923), French statesman **4** 478-479
  Poincaré, Raymond **12** 366-368

Delco
  see Dayton Engineering Laboratories Co.

Delecluse, Étienne Jean (1781-1863), French art critic and painter
  Corot, Jean Baptiste Camille **4** 247-249

Del Fondo (theater, Naples)
  Rossini, Gioacchino **13** 311-312

Delft (commune, Netherlands)
  Vermeer, Jan **15** 466-467

Delfzijl, Battle of (1591)
  Maurice of Nassau **10** 348-349

Delgado, Humberto (died 1965), Portuguese politician
  Salazar, António de Oliveira **13** 442-443

Delhi (city, India)
  Shah Jahan **14** 138-139

Delhi, siege of
  see Sepoy Mutiny (1857-1858)

Delhi University (India)
  Radhakrishnan, Sarvepalli **12** 537-538

Delights of the Poet (painting)
  Chirico, Giorgio de **4** 4

Deliverance, The (novel)
  Glasgow, Ellen **6** 360-361

Della famiglia (book)
  Alberti, Leon Battista **1** 113-115

Della pittura (treatise)
  Alberti, Leon Battista **1** 113-115

Della Robbia, Luca
  see Robbia, Luca della

Della Rovere, Francesco Maria (1490-1538), duke of Urbino
  Castiglione, Baldassare **3** 360-361

Della tranquillità dellánimo (treatise)
Alberti, Leon Battista **1** 113-115

DELLINGER, DAVID (born 1915), American pacifist **4** 480-481

DELORIA, VINE, JR. (born 1933), Native American author, poet, and activist **4** 481-484

DELORS, JACQUES (born 1925), French president of the European Commission and chief architect of Western Europe's drive toward market unity by 1992 **4** 484-486

Delphi (city, Greece)
Cleomenes I **4** 103
Gorgias **6** 456

Delphine (novel)
Staël, Germaine de **14** 391-392

DEL PILAR, MARCELO H. (1850-1896), Philippine revolutionary propagandist and satirist **4** 486

Delta (town, Mississippi)
Alcorn, James Lusk **1** 120-121

Deluge, The (journal)
Kuo Mo-jo **9** 133-134

Deluge, The (novel)
Sienkiewicz, Henryk **14** 216-217

Delvile (literary character)
Burney, Fanny **3** 147-148

Del vivir (novel)
Ferrer, Gabriel Miró **5** 428

Demaratus (ruled circa 510-491 B.C.), king of Sparta
Cleomenes I **4** 103

Demea (literary character)
Terence **15** 146-148

Dementia praecox
see Schizophrenia

Demeter (mythology)
Callimachus **3** 235-236

Demetrio e Dolibio (opera)
Rossini, Gioacchino **13** 311-312

Demetrius I (Poliorcetes; 337-283 B.C.), king of Macedon 294-283
Antigonus I **1** 248-249
Seleucus I **14** 92-93

Demetrius II (278?-229 B.C.), king of Macedon 239-229
Aratus **1** 273-274

Demetrius I (Soter; died 150 B.C.), king of Syria 162-150
Judas Maccabeus **8** 374-375

Demetrius (flourished 189-231), bishop of Alexandria
Origen **11** 528-529

Demetrius (drama)
Schiller, Johann Christoph Friedrich von **14** 4-7

Demetrius of Phalerum (Demetrius Phalereus; 345-283 B.C.), Athenian statesman, governor 317-307 B.C.

Menander **10** 477-478

Demian (novel)
Hesse, Hermann **7** 367-369

Demidov, Prince Anatoli Nikolaevich (1813-1870), Russian philanthropist and art patron
Corot, Jean Baptiste Camille **4** 247-249

DEMILLE, CECIL BLOUNT (1881-1959), American film director and producer **4** 488-490
Goldwyn, Samuel **6** 416
Griffith, David Wark **6** 544-545
Lubitsch, Ernst **10** 18-19

DeMille, Henry Churchill (1853-1893), American playwright
Belasco, David **2** 124-125

DEMIREL, SÜLEYMAN (born 1924), Turkish politician, prime minister, and leader of the Justice party **4** 490-493

Democracy (government)
ancient Greece
Alcibiades **1** 119-120
Antisthenes **1** 250-251
Cleisthenes **4** 98-99
Cleon **4** 104-105
Demosthenes **4** 495-496
Pericles **12** 219-221, 366
Solon **14** 327-328
England
Lecky, William Edward Hartpole **9** 271-272
Maine, Henry James Sumner **10** 152
Salisbury, 3d Marquess of **13** 448-449
France
Gobineau, Comte de **6** 375-376
Montalembert, Comte de **11** 118-119
Napoleon III **11** 310-312
papal policy
Leo XIII **9** 334-336
Pius X **12** 336-337
Pius XI **12** 337-339
studies on
Acton, John Emerich Edward Dalberg **1** 38
Beneš, Edward **2** 155-157
Giddings, Franklin Henry **6** 307-308
Hobhouse, Leonard Trelawny **7** 425-426
Lowell, James Russell **10** 14-15
Martineau, Harriet **10** 296-297
Tocqueville, Alexis Charles Henri Maurice Clérel de **15** 250-251
Turner, Frederick Jackson **15** 350-351
United States
Dewey, John **4** 520-523
Merriam, Charles Edward **10** 518-519
Pound, Ezra Loomis **12** 415-417
see also Absolutism; Constitutional government; Fascism; Monarchy, constitutional; Totalitarianism

Democracy (novel)
Adams, Herbert Baxter **1** 47

Democracy, parliamentary (government)
Chulalongkorn **4** 43-45
Pridi Phanomyong **12** 449

Democracy, socialist (government)
Tito, Marshal **15** 244-246

Democracy as a Way of Life (book)
Bode, Boyd Henry **2** 355-356

Democrata party (Philippines)
Recto, Claro M. **13** 69-70

Démocrates Camerounais party (Cameroon)
Ahidjo, Ahmadou **1** 89-90

Democratic Conservative party (Romania)
Titulescu, Nicolae **15** 246-247

Democratic Justice Party (South Korea)
Roh Tae Woo **13** 253-255

Democratic Labour party (Australia)
Mannix, Daniel **10** 210
Santamaria, Bartholomew Augustine **13** 473-474

Democratic Left (Ecuador)
Borja Cevallos, Rodrigo **2** 417-418

Democratic party (Albania)
Berisha, Sali **2** 195-197

Democratic party (Botswana)
Masire, Quett Ketumile **10** 318-319

Democratic party (Germany)
Schacht, Hjalmar Horace Greeley **13** 518-519

Democratic party (Uganda)
Kiwanuka, Benedicto Kagima Mugumba **9** 46-47
Mutesa II **11** 277-278
Obote, Apolo Milton **11** 457

Democratic party (United States)
Chicago convention (1968)
Daley, Richard J. **4** 373-375
Humphrey, Hubert Horatio Jr. **8** 34-36
Rubin, Jerry **13** 344-346
Seale, Robert George **14** 77-78
donkey symbol
Nast, Thomas **11** 318-319
leaders (Arizona)
Babbitt, Bruce Edward **1** 408-410
leaders (Arkansas)
Caraway, Hattie Wyatt **3** 284-285
Clinton, William Jefferson **4** 117-119
McClellan, John Little **10** 392-393
leaders (Atlanta)
Jackson, Maynard Holbrook Jr. **8** 176-178
leaders (Baltimore)
Mfume, Kweisi **10** 539-542
leaders (California)
Boxer, Barbara **2** 465-468
Bradley, Tom **2** 484-485
Feinstein, Dianne **5** 407-408
Panetta, Leon E. **12** 84-85

Roybal-Allard, Lucille **13** 332-334
Waters, Maxine **16** 132-134
leaders (Chicago)
Byrne, Jane **3** 190-191
Daley, Richard J. **4** 373-375
Jackson, Jesse Louis **8** 174-176
leaders (Colorado)
Baca-Barragán, Polly **1** 412-414
Campbell, Ben Nighthorse
3 252-253
Hart, Gary W. **7** 182-184
Schroeder, Patricia Scott **14** 33-35
leaders (Connecticut)
Acheson, Dean Gooderham **1** 37-38
Welles, Gideon **16** 188-190
leaders (Florida)
Pepper, Claude Denson **12** 205-206
Rohde, Ruth Bryan Owen
13 252-253
leaders (Georgia)
Bond, Julian **2** 386-387
Carter, James Earl **3** 339-342
McAdoo, William Gibbs
10 385-386
Nunn, Sam **11** 443-444
Young, Andrew Jackson Jr.
16 467-469
leaders (Illinois)
Altgeld, John Peter **1** 180-182
Daley, Richard J. **4** 373-375
Mosely-Braun, Carol **11** 199-200
Simon, Paul **14** 238-239
Stevenson, Adlai Ewing **14** 445-446
leaders (Louisiana)
Long, Huey Pierce **9** 496-497
Soulé, Pierre **14** 351-352
White, Edward Douglass
16 230-231
leaders (Maine)
Mitchell, George John **11** 56-58
Muskie, Edmund Sixtus **11** 269-271
leaders (Maryland)
Mikulski, Barbara **11** 13-15
leaders (Massachusetts)
Bancroft, George **1** 483-484
Dukakis, Michael **5** 130-133
Kennedy, Edward M. **8** 500-502
McCormack, John William
10 399-400
Olney, Richard **11** 504-505
O'Neill, Thomas P. **11** 517-519
White, Kevin H. **16** 231-232
leaders (Michigan)
Young, Coleman Alexander
16 470-471
leaders (Minnesota)
Humphrey, Hubert Horatio Jr.
8 34-36
McCarthy, Eugene Joseph
10 386-388
leaders (Mississippi)
Hamer, Fannie Lou **7** 93-94
Henry, Aaron **7** 306-307
leaders (Missouri)
Atchison, David Rice **1** 357-358

Gephardt, Richard Andrew
6 278-280
leaders (Nebraska)
Kerrey, J. Robert **8** 521-522
leaders (New Jersey)
Rodino, Peter Wallace Jr.
13 238-239
leaders (New Mexico)
Chávez, Dennis **3** 488-489
leaders (New York City)
Dinkins, David **5** 15-18
Powell, Adam Clayton Jr.
12 421-422
Rangel, Charles B. **13** 31-32
leaders (New York State)
Chisholm, Shirley Anita St. Hill
4 7-9
Corning, Erastus **4** 238-239
Cuomo, Mario Matthew **4** 338-339
Farley, James A. **5** 381-383
Ferraro, Geraldine **5** 426-428
Hewitt, Abram Stevens **7** 371-372
Koch, Edward I. **9** 68-69
Marcy, William Learned **10** 247-248
Moynihan, Daniel Patrick
11 216-218
Powell, Adam Clayton Jr.
12 421-422
Roosevelt, Eleanor **13** 275-277
Seymour, Horatio **14** 126-127
Smith, Alfred Emmanuel **14** 284-285
Wagner, Robert Ferdinand Jr.
16 44-45
Wagner, Robert Ferdinand **16** 43
leaders (Ohio)
Pendleton, George Hunt **12** 198
Stanton, Edwin McMasters
14 401-402
leaders (Oregon)
Morse, Wayne L. **11** 193-194
leaders (Pennsylvania)
Gray, William H. III **6** 510-511
leaders (Puerto Rico)
Velázquez, Nydia Margarita
15 456-459
leaders (South Dakota)
McGovern, George Stanley
10 412-414
leaders (South Carolina)
Jackson, Jesse Louis **8** 174-176
Thurmond, James Strom **15** 214-215
leaders (Tennessee)
Gore, Albert Jr. **6** 452-453
Kefauver, Carey Estes **8** 472-474
Rayburn, Samuel Taliaferro **13** 61-62
leaders (Texas)
Bentsen, Lloyd Millard **2** 180-181
Connally, John Bowden Jr.
4 202-204
Richards, Ann Willis **13** 133-134
leaders (Virginia)
Ruffin, Edmund **13** 354-355
Wilder, Lawrence Douglas
16 274-276
leaders (Vermont)
Douglas, Stephen Arnold **5** 80-82

Kunin, Madeleine May **9** 130-131
leaders (Washington)
Foley, Tom **5** 499-501
Hansen, Julia Butler **7** 132-133
Ray, Dixy Lee **13** 56-57
leaders (Wisconsin)
Aspin, Les **1** 342-344
Proxmire, William **12** 467-468
Walsh, Thomas James **16** 85-86
machines
Cameron, Simon **3** 246-247
Curley, James Michael **4** 344-345
Hague, Frank **7** 63-64
Murphy, Charles Francis **11** 259-260
Tweed, William Marcy **15** 366-367
national committee
Brown, Ronald H. **3** 44-47
Strauss, Robert Schwarz **14** 501-502
Populists
see Populist party (United States)
presidential candidates
Dukakis, Michael **5** 130-133
Gephardt, Richard Andrew
6 278-280
Glenn, John Herschel Jr. **6** 365-367
Hart, Gary W. **7** 182-184
Humphrey, Hubert Horatio Jr.
8 34-36
Jackson, Jesse Louis **8** 174-176
Kefauver, Carey Estes **8** 472-474
Kennedy, Edward M. **8** 500-502
Kerrey, J. Robert **8** 521-522
Mondale, Walter. F. **11** 97-99
Muskie, Edmund Sixtus **11** 269-271
Simon, Paul **14** 238-239
presidents (20th century)
Carter, James Earl **3** 339-342
Clinton, William Jefferson
4 117-119
see also Statesmen and political
leaders, American—presidents
Reconstruction policy
Gordon, John Brown **6** 449-450
Polk, Leonidas Lafayette **12** 376-377
Tillman, Benjamin Ryan **15** 225-226
slavery issue
Chase, Salmon Portland **3** 473-475
Clay, Henry **4** 94-96
Douglas, Stephen Arnold **5** 80-82
Lincoln, Abraham **9** 415-418
Polk, James Knox **12** 374-376
Seymour, Horatio **14** 126-127
Tilden, Samuel Jones **15** 222-223
Tourgée, Albion Winegar
15 277-278
Vallandigham, Clement Laird
15 406-407
Walker, Robert John **16** 67-68
strategists
Farley, James A. **5** 381-383
Strauss, Robert Schwarz **14** 501-502
supporters
Bowers, Claude Gernade **2** 463
Creel, George **4** 304-305
Hearst, William Randolph
7 243-244

Schlesinger, Arthur Meier Jr.
14 13-15
Thomas, Norman Mattoon
15 191-192
unit rule (1912)
Baker, Newton Diehl **1** 451
see also Jacksonian Democracy
vice presidents
Gore, Albert Jr. **6** 452-453

Democratic Republic of Vietnam
see Vietnam, North

Democratic Republican party (South Korea)
Park, Chung Hee **12** 99-102

Democratic Review (magazine)
Brownson, Orestes Augustus **3** 57-58

Democratic Union of the Algerian Manifesto (political party)
Abbas, Ferhat **1** 6-7

Democratic Unionist party (Northern Ireland)
Paisley, Ian K. **12** 67-69

Democratic Vistas (book)
Whitman, Walt **16** 249-251

Democratic-Farmer-Labor party (United States)
McCarthy, Eugene Joseph **10** 386-388
Mondale, Walter. F. **11** 97-99

Democratic-Republican party (United States)
Connecticut
Welles, Gideon **16** 188-190
Georgia
Crawford, William Harris **4** 299-300
Massachusetts
Adams, Samuel **1** 55-56
Story, Joseph **14** 480-481
New York
Clinton, DeWitt **4** 112-113
Genet, Edmond Charles **6** 261-262
Livingston, Robert R. **9** 462-463
Van Buren, Martin **15** 410-411
North Carolina
Macon, Nathaniel **10** 114-115
opponents
see Federalist party (United States)
Pennsylvania
Duane, William **5** 109
presidential nominees
Burr, Aaron **3** 156-159
Clinton, George **4** 113-114
Jefferson, Thomas **8** 238-241
Madison, James **10** 121-123
Monroe, James **11** 111-113
South Carolina
Hayne, Robert Young **7** 231-232
Tennessee
Benton, Thomas Hart **2** 178-179
Virginia
Pendleton, Edmund **12** 197-198
Taylor, John **15** 126
Tucker, George **15** 332-333
Tyler, John **15** 368-369

Democrazia Christiana
see Christian Democratic party (Italy)

DEMOCRITUS (circa 494-circa 404 B.C.), Greek natural philosopher **4** 493-494
Epicurus **5** 292-294
Santayana, George **13** 475-477
Zwingli, Huldreich **16** 537-538

Demodokos (literary character)
Homer **7** 465-467

Demography (social science)
Carr-Saunders, Alexander Morris **3** 333-334
Quételet, Lambert Adolphe Jacques **12** 510-511

Demoiselles d'Avignon, Les (painting)
Picasso, Pablo **12** 292-295

DEMOIVRE, ABRAHAM (1667-1754), Franco-English mathematician **4** 494-495

Demon, The (poem)
Lermontov, Mikhail Yurievich **9** 352-353

Demonax (book)
Lucian **10** 25-26

Demonomania of Witches, The (book)
Bodin, Jean **2** 356-357

Demos (literary character)
Aristophanes **1** 293-294

DEMOSTHENES (384-322 B.C.), Greek orator **4** 495-496
Alexander the Great **1** 137-141, 125
Cleon **4** 104-105
Isocrates **8** 151
Philip II **12** 269-271
Wolf, Friedrich August **16** 352-353

Demotikistes (Greek literature school)
Palamas, Kostes **12** 70

DEMPSEY, JACK (William Harrison Dempsey; 1895-1983), American boxer **4** 496-497

DEMUTH, CHARLES (1883-1935), American painter **4** 497-498
Sheeler, Charles **14** 170-171

Demythologizing (theology)
Bultmann, Rudolf Karl **3** 119-120
Harnack, Adolf von **7** 160
Jaspers, Karl **8** 225-226

Denby, Edwin L. (1870-1929), American statesman
Walsh, Thomas James **16** 85-86

Dene Nation (Canadian Indians)
Erasmus, Georges Henry **5** 300-301

DENG XIAOPING (Teng Hsiao-p'ing; 1904-1997), the most powerful leader in the People's Republic of China (PRC) in the 1970s **4** 498-500
Jiang Qing **8** 256-260

Denham, Dixon (1786-1828), Scottish explorer
Clapperton, Hugh **4** 72-73

Denham, Sir John (1615-1669), English poet

Pope, Alexander **12** 395-397

Denial of St. Peter (painting)
La Tour, George de **9** 222

Denikin, Anton Ivanovich (1872-1947), Russian general
Kolchak, Aleksandr Vasilievich **9** 77-78

Denis, Acolyte (literary character)
Beti, Mongo **2** 242-243

Denis Haggarty's Wife (story)
Thackeray, William Makepeace **15** 159-161

Denis, Maurice (1870-1943), French painter
Bonnard, Pierre **2** 395-396
Maillol, Aristide **10** 150-151
Puvis de Chavannes, Pierre **12** 492-493
Vuillard, Jean Édouard **16** 36

Denishawn School of Dancing (established 1914)
St. Denis, Ruth **13** 430-431

Denkart (Zoroastrian book)
Zoroaster **16** 528-530

DENKTASH, RAUF (born 1924), president of the Turkish Republic of Northern Cyprus (1985-) **4** 500-502

Denkyera Empire (West Africa)
Anokye, Okomfo **1** 242-243

Denmark (kingdom, Europe)
and Scandinavian union
Margaret of Denmark **10** 250-252
Austro-Prussian war (1864)
Moltke, Helmuth Karl Bernard von **11** 90-91
culture (literature)
Andersen, Hans Christian **1** 212-214
Dinesen Blixen-Finecke, Karen **5** 13-14
Jacobsen, Jens Peter **8** 193-194
Nexø, Martin Anderson **11** 372
culture (music)
Buxtehude, Dietrich **3** 185-186
Nielsen, Carl August **11** 388-389
invasions of England
Alfred **1** 151-153
Canute I, the Great **3** 266-269
Edward the Elder **5** 219-220
Ethelred the Unready **5** 327
Olaf, II **11** 493-494
Swedish wars
Charles XII **3** 464-466
Gustavus I **7** 42-43
Gustavus II **7** 43-45
Gustavus III **7** 45-46
Oxenstierna, Axel Gustafsson **12** 44-45

Denn du wirst meine Seele nicht in der Hölle lassen (musical composition)
Bach, Johann Sebastian **1** 416-419

Dennis, Ruth
see St. Denis, Ruth

Denshwai incident (Egypt, 1906)
Cromer, 1st Earl of **4** 317

Density 21.5 (musical composition)
Varèse, Edgard **15** 432-433

Dent du Midi (painting)
Kokoschka, Oskar **9** 75-76

Dentist, The (engraving)
Lucas van Leyden **10** 20-21

Dentistry (medical science)
Morton, William Thomas Green
11 198-199
Rush, Benjamin **13** 364-365
Wells, Horace **16** 196

Dentists
see Scientists—dentists

Denver (city, Colorado)
Tabor, Horace Austin Warner **15** 70

Denver Chamber Orchestra
Falletta, JoAnn **5** 373-375

DEODORO DA FONSECA, MANOEL
(1827-1892), Brazilian statesman, president 1890-1891 **4** 502
Barbosa, Ruy **1** 503-504
Peixoto, Floriano **12** 188-189

Deoxycorticosterone (steroid)
Reichstein, Tadeus **13** 85-87

Deoxyribonucleic acid (DNA)
Baltimore, David **1** 477-478
Berg, Paul **2** 187-189
Chargaff, Erwin **3** 444-445
Crick, Francis Harry Crompton **4** 310
Franklin, Rosalind Elsie **6** 67-68
Hershey, Alfred Day **7** 343-345
Khorana, Har Gobind **8** 537-538
Kornberg, Arthur **9** 85-87
Nirenberg, Marshall Warren
11 399-400
Northrop, John Howard **11** 430-431
Singer, Maxine **14** 251-252
Todd, Alexander **15** 251-253 499
Watson, James Dewey **16** 137-138

Department store (retail business)
Field, Marshall **5** 440-441
Stewart, Alexander Turney **14** 448-449
Straus, Isidor **14** 496
see also Chain store

Departmental (poem)
Frost, Robert Lee **6** 130-133

Departmental Ditties (poems)
Kipling, Joseph Rudyard **9** 32-33

Departure (triptych)
Beckmann, Max **2** 104-105

Departure and the Return, The (painting)
Cole, Thomas **4** 151-152

Dephlogisticated air
see Oxygen

Deposition (painting)
Angelico **1** 235-236
Bouts, Dirk **2** 458-459
Lorenzetti, Pietro and Ambrogio
9 517-518
Massys, Quentin **10** 325-326
Pontormo **12** 394-395

Rosso, Il **13** 312-313
Weyden, Rogier van der **16** 219-221

Deposition (sculpture)
Goujon, Jean **6** 466-467
Pilon, Germain **12** 305

Depot of Charts and Instruments
see Naval Observatory and Hydro-
graphic Office (United States)

Depressed Classes Institute of Bombay
(India)
Ambedkar, Bhimrao Ramji **1** 190-191

Depression, Great (economics; United
States)
administration policies
see Hoover, H.; New Deal; Roo-
sevelt, F.D.
African Americans and
Divine, Father **5** 29-32
crime in
Dillinger, John **5** 9
in literature
Agee, James **1** 78-79
Dos Passos, John Roderigo **5** 69-71
Ford, John **6** 7-8
Steinbeck, John Ernst **14** 416-417
industry in
Chrysler, Walter Percy **4** 36-37
Durant, William Crapo **5** 158
Ford, Henry **6** 5-6
Insull, Samuel **8** 130
Sikorsky, Igor **14** 223-224
photographs from
Lange, Dorothea **9** 193-194
Mydans, Carl **11** 283-284
stock market crash (1929)
Coolidge, John Calvin **4** 217-219
Hoover, Herbert Clark **7** 483-485
Morgan, John Pierpont II **11** 165
Silliman, Benjamin **14** 229-230

Depression, Great (economics; world)
Argentina
Irigoyen, Hipólito **8** 139-140
Justo, Agustin Pedro **8** 396
Australia
Chifley, Joseph Benedict **3** 518
Lang, John Thomas **9** 192-193
Lyons, Joseph Aloysius **10** 69-70
Scullin, James Henry **14** 73
Belgium
Albert I **1** 112
Canada
Aberhart, William **1** 26-27
Bennett, Richard Bedford **2** 171-172
Callaghan, Edward Morley
3 229-230
Woodsworth, James Shaver **16** 376
Chile
Ibáñez del Campo, Carlos **8** 88
Cuba
Machado y Morales, Gerardo
10 92-93
England
MacDonald, James Ramsay
10 84-85

Germany
Hindenburg, Paul Ludwig Hans von
Beneckendorff und von **7** 400-401
Hitler, Adolf **7** 417-420
Hungary
Horthy de Nagybánya, Nicholas
7 510-512
Italy
Mussolini, Benito **11** 272-274
Peru
Leguía y Salcedo, Augusto Bernardi-
no **9** 305-306
South Africa
Malan, Daniel Francois **10** 163-164
Uruguay
Terra, Gabriel **15** 154-155

Depression Tityrus (literary character)
Frost, Robert Lee **6** 130-133

Depressions and panics (United States)
1819 (panic)
Monroe, James **11** 111-113
1823 (panic)
Fleming, Sandford **5** 485-486
1837 (panic)
Biddle, Nicholas **2** 264-265
Dana, Charles Anderson **4** 384-385
Duane, William **5** 109
Evans, George Henry **5** 337-338
Forbes, Robert Bennet **5** 509-510
Harrison, William Henry **7** 180-181
Hayne, Robert Young **7** 231-232
McCormick, Cyrus Hall **10** 400-401
Miller, William **11** 30-31
Peabody, George **12** 168
Tappan brothers **15** 105-106
Van Buren, Martin **15** 410-411
1855 (panic)
Fargo, William George **5** 380-381
1857 (panic)
Donnelly, Ignatius **5** 62
McCulloch, Hugh **10** 404-405
McKay, Donald **10** 416-417
Peabody, George **12** 168
1869 (panic)
Gould, Jay **6** 470-472
1873 (panic)
Cooke, Jay **4** 215-216
Garrett, John Work **6** 225
Goodnight, Charles **6** 439
Gould, Jay **6** 470-472
Mahone, William **10** 147-148
1873-1879 (depression)
Carnegie, Andrew **3** 309-312
Drew, Daniel **5** 101-102
Grant, Ulysses Simpson **6** 492-494
1880s (depression)
Cleveland, Stephen Grover
4 108-110
1893 (panic)
Frick, Henry Clay **6** 108-109
Jones, Samuel Milton **8** 342-343
Morgan, John Pierpont **11** 163-165
Tabor, Horace Austin Warner **15** 70
Taft, Lorado **15** 75-76
Young, Owen D. **16** 473-474

1893-1896 (depression)
> Carnegie, Andrew **3** 309-312
> Cleveland, Stephen Grover **4** 108-110, 44
> Coxey, Jacob Sechler **4** 286-287

1901 (panic)
> Schiff, Jacob Henry **14** 2-3

1907 (panic)
> Morgan, John Pierpont **11** 163-165
> Morgan, John Pierpont II **11** 165
> Taft, William Howard **15** 78-81
> Warburg, Paul Moritz **16** 111-112
> Westinghouse, George **16** 215

1920 (panic)
> Durant, William Crapo **5** 158
> Rosenwald, Julius **13** 293

1929
> *see* Depression, Great (United States)

Depth psychology (social science)
> Jung, Carl Gustav **8** 388-389

Der Krieg (etching)
> Dix, Otto **5** 33-34

Déracinés, Les (novel)
> Barrès, Auguste Maurice **2** 20-21

DERAIN, ANDRÉ (1880-1954), French painter **4** 503
> Matisse, Henri **10** 336-337
> Stein, Gertrude **14** 414-415
> Vlaminck, Maurice **16** 6

Derby, Lord (Laurence Shirley; 1720-1760), 4th Earl of Ferrers (Normandy)
> Burgoyne, John **3** 137-138

Derby, 1st Earl of (Thomas Stanley; 1435?-1504), English statesman
> Richard III **13** 132-133

Derby, 14th Earl of (E.G.G. Smith Stanley; 1799-1869), English statesman
> Disraeli, Benjamin **5** 27-29
> Gladstone, William Ewart **6** 357-360
> Victoria **15** 485-487

Derby, 15th Earl of (E.H. Smith Stanley; 1826-1893), English statesman
> Salisbury, 3d Marquess of **13** 448-449

Dernier chant du pélerinage d'Harold, Le (poem)
> Lamartine, Alphonse Marie Louis de **9** 173-175

Dernier Chouan, Le (novel)
> Balzac, Honoré de **1** 478-480

Dernière idole, La (play)
> Daudet, Alphonse **4** 402-403

DERRIDA, JACQUES (born 1930), French philosopher **4** 503-505

Derry, 4th Earl of
> *see* Hervey, Frederick Augustus

Deruet, Claude (1588-1660), French painter
> Claude Lorrain **4** 89-90

Dervish (Islamic religious order)
> Hassan, Muhammad Abdille **7** 194-195
> Mahmud II **10** 145-147

Rumi, Jalai ed-Din **13** 362-363

Des Moines River (Iowa)
> Frémont, John Charles **6** 97-98

Desargues, Gérard (1593-1662), French mathematician
> Guarini, Guarino **7** 25-26

Desastre, El (autobiography)
> Vasconcelos, José **15** 443-444

Désastre de Lisbonne, Le (poem)
> Voltaire **16** 14-16

Desastres de la guerra, Los (etching)
> Goya y Lucientes, Francisco de Paula José de **6** 476-478

Desault, Pierre Joseph (1744-1795), French surgeon
> Bichat, Marie François Xavier **2** 263-264

DESCARTES, RENÉ (1596-1650), French philosopher and mathematician **4** 505-508
> critics
> > Clarke, Samuel **4** 88
> > Condillac, Étienne Bonnot de **4** 194-195
> > Cudworth, Ralph **4** 331
> > Frege, Gottlob **6** 93-94
> > Hobbes, Thomas **7** 421-423
> > Vico, Giambattista **15** 480-481
> influence of
> > Bayle, Pierre **2** 77-78
> > Beckett, Samuel **2** 102-104
> > Comte, Auguste **4** 189-191
> > Cousin, Victor **4** 273-274
> > Huxley, Thomas Henry **8** 77-79
> > Malebranche, Nicolas **10** 166-167
> > Spinoza, Baruch **14** 381-383
> mathematics
> > Fermat, Pierre de **5** 421-422
> > Huygens, Christiaan **8** 79-81
> > Newton, Isaac **11** 369-372
> > Witt, Johan de **16** 348-349
> > *see also* Cartesianism (philosophy)

Descendant, The (novel)
> Glasgow, Ellen **6** 360-361

Descent from the Cross (painting)
> Fouquet, Jean **6** 31
> Rubens, Peter Paul **13** 339-342

Descent of Man ... (book; Darwin)
> Darwin, Charles Robert **4** 397-399
> Jacobsen, Jens Peter **8** 193-194

Deschamps, Eustache (1340?-?1407), French poet
> Machaut, Guillaume de **10** 93-94

Descriptive geometry
> *see* Geometry—descriptive

Descriptive Sketches (poem)
> Wordsworth, William **16** 385-388

Desde mi celda, cartas literarias (letters)
> Bécquer, Gustavo Adolfo Dominguez **2** 107-108

Desdemona (musical character)
> Verdi, Giuseppe Fortunino Francesco **15** 463-465

Desecration of My Kingdom (autobiography)
> Mutesa II **11** 277-278

Deseret, University of
> *see* Utah, University of

Desert Fox
> *see* Rommel, Erwin

Desert Incident, A (play)
> Buck, Pearl Sydenstricker **3** 91-93

Desert Music (poems)
> Williams, William Carlos **16** 308-309

Desert of Love, The (novel)
> Mauriac, François **10** 347-348

Desert Places (poem)
> Frost, Robert Lee **6** 130-133

Desert Trails of Atacama (book)
> Bowman, Isaiah **2** 464-465

Deserted Village, The (poem)
> Goldsmith, Oliver **6** 411-413

Déserts (musical composition)
> Varèse, Edgard **15** 432-433

Desgodetz, Antoine (1653-1728), French architect
> Gabriel, Ange Jacques **6** 160-161

Deshabandhu (Indian title)
> Das, Chitta Ranjan **4** 401-402

Deshays, Jean Baptiste (1729-1765), French painter
> Boucher, François **2** 440-442

Desiccated Embryos (musical composition)
> Satie, Erik **13** 494-495

Desiderio da Settignano
> *see* Settignano, Desiderio da

Desiderius (756-774), king of the Lombards
> Charlemagne **3** 445-447

Desiderius (abbot)
> *see* Victor III

Design (poem)
> Frost, Robert Lee **6** 130-133

Design for Living (play)
> Coward, Noel **4** 279-280

Designers
> clothing
> > Armani, Giorgio **1** 299-301
> > Ashley, Laura **1** 332-333
> > Carnegie, Hattie **3** 313
> > Chanel, Coco **3** 429
> > Claiborne, Liz **4** 68-69
> > Dior, Christian **5** 22
> > Erté **5** 314-316
> > Gaultier, Jean Paul **6** 239-240
> > Gigli, Romeo **6** 312
> > Johnson, Betsey **8** 295-296
> > Karan, Donna **8** 442-444
> > Klein, Calvin **9** 50-52
> > Lagerfeld, Karl **9** 161-162
> > Lauren, Ralph **9** 228-229
> > Mizrahi, Isaac **11** 66-67
> > von Furstenberg, Diane **16** 20-21
> > Westwood, Vivienne **16** 217-218

furniture
  Ashley, Laura **1** 332-333
  Erté **5** 314-316
  Mackintosh, Charles Rennie
    10 107-108
home furnishings
  Lauren, Ralph **9** 228-229
jewelry
  Picasso, Paloma **12** 295-297
stage sets
  Erté **5** 314-316
  Lee, Ming Cho **9** 289-290

Desire under the Elms (play)
  O'Neill, Eugene **11** 514-516

Désirs de Jean Servien, Les (novel)
  France, Anatole **6** 39-40

Deslinde, El (treatise)
  Reyes, Alfonso **13** 112-113

Desmond rebellion (Ireland; 1579-1583)
  Elizabeth I **5** 263-266

Desolation (poems)
  Mistral, Gabriela **11** 55-56

Desperate Remedies (novel)
  Hardy, Thomas **7** 150-152

Despiau, Charles (1874-1946), French
sculptor
  Duchamp-Villon, Raymond **5** 123
  Rodin, Auguste **13** 236-238

Desportes, Philippe (1546-1606), French
poet
  Spenser, Edmund **14** 373-376

Despotism (government)
  see Absolutism; Enlightened despots;
  Monarchy, absolute; Dictatorship

Despotism in America (book)
  Hildreth, Richard **7** 382

Despréaux, Nicholas Boileau
  see Boileau-Despréaux, Nicholas

DESSALINES, JEAN JACQUES
(1758-1806), Haitian nationalist and
politician **4** 511-512
  Boyer, Jean Pierre **2** 468-469
  Christophe, Henri **4** 32
  Toussaint L'Ouverture, François
    Dominique **15** 278-279

Destinées, Les (poem)
  Vigny, Comte de **15** 494-495

Destouches, Louis Ferdinand
  see Céline, Louis Ferdinand

Destour party (Tunisia)
  Bourguiba, Habib **2** 453-455

Destroyer (torpedo boat)
  Ericsson, John **5** 307-308

Destruction (novel)
  Pa Chin **12** 53-54

Destruction of Sodom (painting)
  Corot, Jean Baptiste Camille **4** 247-249

Destruction of the Daughters of Niobe
(painting)
  Wilson, Richard **16** 329-330

**Destutt de Tracy, Count Antoine Louis
Claude** (1754-1836), French philosopher
  Stendhal **14** 422-425

Detective agencies (United States)
  Pinkerton, Allan **12** 314-315

Detective stories
  see Mystery fiction

Determinants (mathematics)
  Cauchy, Augustin Louis **3** 378-380
  Gauss, Karl Friedrich **6** 240-242
  Lagrange, Joseph Louis **9** 164-166
  see also Algebra; Matrix (mathematics)

Determinism (philosophy)
  advocates
    Holbach, Baron d' **7** 448-449
    Holmes, Oliver Wendell **7** 457-458
    Maine, Henry James Sumner **10** 152
    Mill, John Stuart **11** 21-23
  opponents
    Bergson, Henri **2** 191-192
    Claudel, Paul Louis Charles **4** 90-91
    Cudworth, Ralph **4** 331
    Popper, Karl Raimund **12** 402

Determinism (psychology)
  Hartley, David **7** 185
  James, William **8** 215-217

Detroit (city, Michigan)
  British capture (1812)
    Brock, Isaac **3** 12-13
    Hull, William **8** 29-30
    Robinson, John Beverley **13** 210
    Tecumseh **15** 133
  development
    Cass, Lewis **3** 355-356
    Ford, Henry **6** 5-6
  factories
    Kahn, Albert **8** 407-408
  Freedom Walk (1963)
    King, Martin Luther Jr. **9** 20-22
  mayors
    Young, Coleman Alexander
      16 470-471
  Pontiac's Conspiracy
    see Pontiac's Conspiracy
  Red Wings (hockey team)
    Howe, Gordie **7** 532-534

Detroit (ship)
  Perry, Oliver Hazard **12** 239

Detroit Automobile Co. (established 1899)
  Ford, Henry **6** 5-6

Detroit Edison Co.
  Ford, Henry **6** 5-6

Detroit Mosque (Black Muslim)
  Malcolm X **10** 165-166

DETT, ROBERT NATHANIEL (1882-1943),
African American composer, conductor,
and music educator **4** 512

Dettingen, Battle of (1743)
  Amherst, Jeffery **1** 200-201

Dettingen Te Deum (musical composition)
  Handel, George Frederick **7** 116-119

Dettonville, Amos
  see Pascal, Blaise

Deus ex machina (literary technique)
  Euripides **5** 332-334

Deuterium (hydrogen isotope)
  Urey, Harold Clayton **15** 394-396

Deutero-Isaiah (flourished circa 549-538
B.C.), biblical author of Isaiah (chapters
40-55)
  Amos **1** 205
  Isaiah **8** 146-147
  Micah **10** 542-543

Deuteron (physics)
  Rabi, Isidor Isaac **12** 526-527

DEUTSCH, KARL WOLFGANG
(1912-1992), American political scientist
4 512-514

Deutsch, Otto Erich (1883-1967), Austrian
critic and writer
  Schubert, Franz Peter **14** 35-37

Deutsche Fest-und Gedenksprüche (musical composition)
  Brahms, Johannes **2** 490-492

Deutsche Fortschrittpartei (German political party)
  Virchow, Rudolf Ludwig Carl
    15 506-507

Deutsche Gelehrten Republik, Die (book)
  Klopstock, Friedrich Gottlieb **9** 55-56

Deutsche Geschichte (trilogy)
  Huch, Ricarda **8** 11-12

Deutsche Grammatik (book)
  Grimm, Jakob and Wilhelm Karl **7** 3-4

Deutsche Katastrophe, Die (book)
  Meinecke, Friedrich **10** 460-461

Deutsche Messe (musical composition)
  Krenek, Ernst **9** 98-99
  Walter, Johann **16** 86

Deutsche Sagen (folktales)
  Grimm, Jakob and Wilhelm Karl **7** 3-4

Deutsche Soziologische Gesellschaft
(established 1910)
  Weber, Max **16** 157-160

Deutsche Werkbund exposition (Stuttgart;
1927)
  Le Corbusier **9** 274-275

Deutscher Novellenschatz (novellas)
  Heyse, Paul Johann Ludwig **7** 372-373

Deutsches Theater (Berlin)
  Brecht, Bertolt **2** 512-514

Deutschland (ship)
  Hopkins, Gerard Manley **7** 492-494

Deux amis, Les (play)
  Beaumarchais, Pierre August Caron de
    2 93-94

Deux Journées, Les (opera)
  Cherubini, Luigi Carlo Zanobi Salvatore
    Maria **3** 505-506

Devagiri (former kingdom, India)
  Ala-ud-din **1** 102-103

Devaki (Hindu goddess)
Gama, Vasco da **6** 196-198

Developable Column of Victory (sculpture)
Pevsner, Antoine **12** 263-264

Development and Migration Act (1926; Australia)
Bruce of Melbourne, 1st
Bruce of Melbourne, 1st Viscount
3 61-62

Development and Resources Corp. (established 1955)
Lilienthal, David Eli **9** 410-411

Development of a Bottle in Space (sculpture)
Boccioni, Umberto **2** 353-354

Development of a Child, The (paper)
Klein, Melanie **9** 52

Development of a National Literature, The (book)
Carducci, Giosuè **3** 290-291

Development of Capitalism in Russia, The (book)
Lenin, Vladimir Ilich **9** 323-326
Trotsky, Leon **15** 302-305

Development of Socialism from Utopia to Science (book)
Engels, Friedrich **5** 286-288

Development of the Monistic View of History, The (book)
Plekhanov, Georgi Valentinovich **12** 351-352

Developmental Hypothesis, The (essay)
Spencer, Herbert **14** 369-370

Devenir! (novel)
Martin du Gard, Roger **10** 295-296

Deventer, Battle of (1591)
Maurice of Nassau **10** 348-349

Devereux, Penelope (circa 1562-1607), English noblewoman
Sidney, Philip **14** 214-215

Devi (film)
Ray, Satyajit **13** 60-61

Devil and Daniel Webster, The (folk opera)
Benét, Stephen Vincent **2** 157-158

Devil and the Good Lord, The (play)
Sartre, Jean Paul **13** 491-492

Devil and the Lady, The (play)
Tennyson, Alfred **15** 144-146

Devil inside Him, The (play)
Osborne, John **12** 16-17

Devil, The (story)
Tolstoy, Leo **15** 262-265

Devilry (story)
Bulgakov, Mikhail Afanasievich **3** 117

Devil's Elixir, The (novel)
Hoffmann, Ernst Theodor Amadeus **7** 439-440

Devil's Island (French Guiana)
Dreyfus, Alfred **5** 103-105

Devils of Loudon, The (book)
Huxley, Aldous Leonard **8** 74-75

Devils, The (novel)
see Possessed, The (novel)

Devil's Trill (musical composition)
Tartini, Giuseppe **15** 112-113

DEVLIN, BERNADETTE (McAliskey; born 1947), youngest woman ever elected to the British Parliament **4** 515-516

Devin du village, Le (opera)
Rousseau, Jean Jacques **13** 324-328

Devocion de la Cruz, La (play)
Calderón, Pedro **3** 221-222

Devoir, Le (book)
Simon, Jules François **14** 237-238

Devoir, Le (newspaper)
Bourassa, Joseph-Henri-Napoleon **2** 446-447

Devolution, War of (1667-1668)
Philip IV **12** 275
Witt, Johan de **16** 348-349

Devonian system (geology)
Murchison, Roderick Impey **11** 255-256
Sedgwick, Adam **14** 82-83

Devonshire, 4th Duke of (William Cavendish; 1720-1764), English statesman
Pitt, William the Elder **12** 328-329

Devoted Siblings, The (play)
Kuo Mo-jo **9** 133-134

Devotio Moderna (religious movement)
Canisius, Peter **3** 258
Gerson, John **6** 285-286
Groote, Gerard **7** 12-13
Ruysbroeck, Jan van **13** 388-389

Devotion to the Cross (play)
Calderón, Pedro **3** 221-222

DEVRIES, WILLIAM CASTLE (born 1943), American heart surgeon **4** 518-519

DEW, THOMAS RODERICK (1802-1846), American political economist **4** 519

Dewas Senior (state; India)
Forster, Edward Morgan **6** 14-16

DEWEY, GEORGE (1837-1917), American naval officer **4** 520
Aguinaldo, Emilio **1** 88
Dunne, Finley Peter **5** 147-148

DEWEY, JOHN (1859-1952), American philosopher and educator **4** 520-523
colleagues
Bentley, Arthur F. **2** 178
Robinson, James Harvey **13** 208
influence of
Ambedkar, Bhimrao Ramji **1** 190-191
Bourne, Randolph Silliman **2** 456-457
Hu Shih **8** 63-65
Kilpatrick, William H. **9** 1-3
Nagel, Ernest **11** 291-292
Watson, John Broadus **16** 138-139
Wright, Frank Lloyd **16** 398-401

DEWEY, MELVIL (1851-1931), American librarian and reformer **4** 523-524

DEWEY, THOMAS EDMUND (1902-1971), American lawyer and politician **4** 524
Truman, Harry S. **15** 314-316
Warren, Earl **16** 117-120

Dewey, Ballantine, Bushby, Palmer and Wood (law firm)
Dewey, Thomas Edmund **4** 524

Dewey decimal system (library)
Dewey, Melvil **4** 523-524

Dewitt, Cornelius (1623-1672), Dutch statesman
William III **16** 295-296

DeWitt, Jan (1625-1672), Dutch statesman
William III **16** 295-296

DEWSON, MARY WILLIAMS (Molly; 1874-1962), American reformer, government official, and organizer of women for the Democratic party **4** 525

dGe-lugs-pa (Buddhist sect)
see Yellow Hats

Dhammaraja (Buddhism)
Chulalongkorn **4** 43-45

Dhammayutta sect (Buddhism)
Mongkut **11** 104

Dharma (Buddhism)
Asoka **1** 341-342
Buddha **3** 97-101

Dharma Sabha
see Association in Defense of Hindu Culture

Dharmakāya (Buddhism)
Hui-yüan **8** 25-26

D'Hérelle, Félix Hubert (1873-1949), Canadian bacteriologist
Lwoff, André **10** 58-59

Dhlomo, R.R.R. (born 1901), Zulu novelist
Dube, John Langalibalele **5** 113

Dhu'l-Aktaf
see Shahpur II

Diabelli Variations (musical composition)
Beethoven, Ludwig van **2** 114-117

Diabetes (medicine)
Banting, Frederick Grant **1** 493-494
Bernard, Claude **2** 208-210
Best, Charles Herbert **2** 236-237
Houssay, Bernardo Alberto **7** 522-523

Diable boiteux, Le (novel)
Lesage, Alain René **9** 353-354

Diablo conjuelo (novel; A. de Guevara)
Lesage, Alain René **9** 353-354

Diachronic historical linguistics
see Linguistics

Diadochi (Alexander's successors)
Antigonus I **1** 248-249
Ptolemy I **12** 470-472
Seleucus I **14** 92-93

Diadoumenos (sculpture)
Polykleitos **12** 385-386

Diaghilev, Sergei (1872-1929), Russian ballet producer
influence of
Balanchine, George **1** 461-462
Cocteau, Jean **4** 132-133
Roussel, Albert **13** 328-329
influenced by
Beardsley, Aubrey Vincent **2** 88-89
music commissioned
Prokofiev, Sergei Sergeevich **12** 458-460
Respighi, Ottorino **13** 103-104
Satie, Erik **13** 494-495
Stravinsky, Igor Fedorovich **14** 502-506, 250
sets commissioned
Gabo, Naum **6** 158-159
Gris, Juan **7** 5-6
Miró, Joan **11** 53-54
Pevsner, Antoine **12** 263-264
Rouault, Georges **13** 321-322

DIAGHILEV, SERGEI (1872-1929), Russian who inspired artists, musicians, and dancers to take ballet to new heights of public enjoyment **4** 525-527
Goncharova, Natalia **6** 424-426
Larionov, Mikhail **9** 205-206
Nijinsky, Vaslav **11** 393-395

DIAGNE, BLAISE (1872-1934), Senegalese political leader **4** 527

Dial, The (1840-1844; transcendentalist magazine)
Alcott, Amos Bronson **1** 121
Fuller, Sarah Margaret **6** 150-151
Peabody, Elizabeth Palmer **12** 167-168
Ripley, George **13** 179-180
Thoreau, Henry David **15** 203-205

Dial, The (1880-1929; literary magazine)
Moore, Marianne **11** 148-149
Mumford, Lewis **11** 246-247

Dialect (literature)
Dunbar, Paul Laurence **5** 141-142
Eggleston, Edward **5** 223-224
Harris, Joel Chandler **7** 173-174
Kipling, Joseph Rudyard **9** 32-33
Riley, James Whitcomb **13** 170-171
Thackeray, William Makepeace **15** 159-161

Dialectical materialism (philosophy)
Engels, Friedrich **5** 286-288
Kapitsa, Pyotr Leonidovich **8** 433-435
Lenin, Vladimir Ilich **9** 323-326
Marx, Karl **10** 304-308
Plekhanov, Georgi Valentinovich **12** 351-352
Stalin, Joseph **14** 393-396
see also Marxism

Dialectical theology
Barth, Karl **2** 31-32
Schleiermacher, Friedrich Ernst Daniel **14** 11-12

Dialectics (philosophy)
Abelard, Peter **1** 23-25
Gratian **6** 498-499
Hegel, Georg Wilhelm Friedrich **7** 254-256
Kant, Immanuel **8** 430-432
Zeno of Elea **16** 500

Diallo, Yacine (died 1954), Guinean politician
Touré, Sékou **15** 275-277

Dialoghi con Leucò, I (book)
Pavese, Cesare **12** 154-155

Dialogues (book)
Catherine of Siena **3** 369-370
Fénelon, François de Salignac de la Mothe **5** 410-411
Fernel, Jean François **5** 425-426
Rousseau, Jean Jacques **13** 324-328
Seneca the Younger, Lucius Annaeus **14** 103-105

Dialogues (book; Gregory I)
Benedict, Ruth Fulton **2** 154-155
Gregory I **6** 531-532

Dialogues (book; Plato)
Jowett, Benjamin **8** 364-365
Plato **12** 345-347

Dialogues (poem)
Pope, Alexander **12** 395-397

Dialogues des bêtes (novel)
Colette, Sidonie Gabrielle **4** 158-159

Dialogues des Carmélites, Les (opera)
Poulenc, Francis **12** 414-415

Dialogues of Courtesans (satire)
Lucian **10** 25-26

Dialogues of the Gods (satire)
Lucian **10** 25-26

Dialogues on Love (treatise; Hebreo)
Garcilaso de la Vega, Inca **6** 210-211

Dialogus (book)
Justin Martyr **8** 395-396
Tacitus **15** 70-72

Diamagnetism (physics)
Faraday, Michael **5** 380
Landau, Lev Davidovich **9** 184-185
see also Magnetism (physics)

Diamond (mineral)
Bridgman, Percy Williams **3** 5-6
Frere, Henry Bartle Edward **6** 100-101
Morgan, Junius Spencer **11** 166-167
Rhodes, Cecil John **13** 120-122

Diamond (ship)
Hopkins, Esek **7** 490-491

Diamond as Big as the Ritz, The (story)
Fitzgerald, Francis Scott Key **5** 470-472

DIAMOND, DAVID (born 1915), American composer and teacher **4** 527-529

Diana (sculpture)
Powers, Hiram **12** 428-429
Saint-Gaudens, Augustus **13** 432

DIANA, PRINCESS OF WALES (born Diana Frances Spencer; b. 1961), member of British royal family **4** 529-533
Charles, Prince of Wales **3** 448-450

Diana and Actaeon (painting)
Gainsborough, Thomas **6** 170-172
Titian **15** 242-244

Diana and Callisto (painting)
Titian **15** 242-244

Diana and Her Companions (painting)
Vermeer, Jan **15** 466-467

Diana and the Stag (sculpture)
Goujon, Jean **6** 466-467

Diana as Goddess of the Hunt (sculpture)
Houdon, Antoine **7** 516-517

Diana e la Tuda (play)
Pirandello, Luigi **12** 319-321

Diana of the Crossways (novel)
Meredith, George **10** 512-513

Diane, La (musical composition)
Couperin, François **4** 270-271

Diane Chasseresse (painting)
Renoir, Pierre Auguste **13** 101-102

Diane française, La (poems)
Aragon, Louis **1** 271-272

Diario de Puerto Rico, El (newspaper)
Muñoz Rivera, Luís **11** 250

Diario de un poeta reciencasado (poems)
Jiménez, Juan Ramón **8** 261-262

Diario in pubblico (literary collection)
Vittorini, Elio **16** 2-3

Diariong Tagalog (newspaper)
Del Pilar, Marcelo Hilario **4** 486

Diary (literary form)
Pepys, Samuel **12** 207-208
Sewall, Samuel **14** 123-124
Welles, Gideon **16** 188-190
see also Authors—diarists

Diary and Letters of Madame d'Arblay, The (book)
Burney, Fanny **3** 147-148

Diary of a Chambermaid, The (film)
Buñuel, Luis **3** 127-128

Diary of a Country Priest, The (novel)
Bernanos, Georges **2** 206-207

Diary of a Mad Old Man (novel)
Tanizaki, Junichiro **15** 101-102

Diary of a Madman, The (story)
Gogol, Nikolai **6** 391-393

Diary of Anne Frank (book)
Wiesenthal, Simon **16** 264-266

Diary of Private Prayer
Baillie, John **1** 445-447

Diary of Readings, A
Baillie, John **1** 445-447

Diary of the Year Kapsin (book)
Kim Ok-kyun **9** 7-8

DIAS DE NOVAIS, BARTOLOMEU (died 1500), Portuguese explorer **4** 533-534
Gama, Vasco da **6** 196-198

Dias enmascarados, Los (stories)
Fuentes, Carlos **6** 141-142

Diaspora, Jewish
Ben-Gurion, David **2** 160-161
Dubnov, Simon **5** 115-116
Johanan ben Zakkai **8** 271-272
Judah I **8** 372-373
Paul **12** 141-143
Philo Judaeus **12** 282-283
see also Israel; Jewish history—Biblical era; Palestine

Diaspost (Viking symbol)
Eric the Red **5** 304

Diatonic music
Malipiero, Gian Francesco **10** 171
Sessions, Roger Huntington **14** 117-118
Zarlino, Gioseffo **16** 490-491

Diatribe du docteur Akakia (polemic)
Voltaire **16** 14-16

Diavolo sulle colline, Il (story)
Pavese, Cesare **12** 154-155

Díaz, Adolfo (1874-1964), Nicaraguan politician
Somoza, Anastasio **14** 335-336

Díaz, Manuel Azaña
see Azaña Díaz, Manuel

DÍAZ, PORFIRIO (José de la Cruz Porfirio Díaz; 1830-1915), Mexican general and politician **4** 534-536
associates
Huerta, Victoriano **8** 13-14
Juárez, Benito **8** 369-372
Sierra, Justo **14** 217
opponents
Calles, Plutarco Elías **3** 234-235
Carranza, Venustiano **3** 321-322
Madero, Francisco Indalecio **10** 118-119
Villa, Pancho **15** 495-496
Zapata, Emiliano **16** 489-490

Diaz, Rodrigo
see Cid, The

Diaz de la Pena, Narcisse Virgile (1808-1876), French painter of the Barbizon school
Blakelock, Ralph Albert **2** 318
Millet, Jean François **11** 31

DÍAZ DEL CASTILLO, BERNAL (circa 1496-circa 1584), Spanish soldier and historian **4** 536-537
Cortés, Hernán **4** 255-256

DÍAZ ORDAZ, GUSTAVO (1911-1979), president of Mexico (1964-1970) **4** 537-538
Toledano, Vicente Lombardo **15** 256-257

Dichlorodiphenyltrichloroethane
see DDT

Dichterliebe (musical composition)
Schumann, Robert Alexander **14** 41-43

Dichtung und Wahrheit (autobiography)
Goethe, Johann Wolfgang von **6** 388-391

DICKENS, CHARLES JOHN HUFFAM (1812-1870), English author **4** 538-541
associates
Andersen, Hans Christian **1** 212-214
Gaskell, Elizabeth **6** 231-232
critical studies
Chesterton, Gilbert Keith **3** 508-509
Wilson, Edmund **16** 318-319
influence of
Collins, William Wilkie **4** 169-170
Conrad, Joseph **4** 205-207
Farrell, James Thomas **5** 390-391
Freytag, Gustav **6** 107-108
Harte, Francis Brett **7** 184-185
Lao Shê **9** 200-201
Lewis, Harry Sinclair **9** 385-387
Riley, James Whitcomb **13** 170-171
Van Gogh, Vincent **15** 427-429
influenced by
Landor, Walter Savage **9** 186-187
stylistic comparisons
Hidayat, Sadiq **7** 377-378
Thackeray, William Makepeace **15** 159-161
Trollope, Anthony **15** 300-302

DICKINSON, EMILY (1830-1886), American poet **4** 541-543
Crane, Hart **4** 291-293
Frost, Robert Lee **6** 130-133
Graham, Martha **6** 485-486
Howells, William Dean **7** 539-541
Jackson, Helen Hunt **8** 172
Wilder, Thornton Niven **16** 276-277

Dickinson, Goldsworthy Lowes (1862-1932), English essayist
Russell, Bertrand Arthur William **13** 373-374

DICKINSON, JOHN (1732-1808), American lawyer, pamphleteer, and politician **4** 543-544
Ford, Paul Leicester **6** 9-10
Galloway, Joseph **6** 186-187

Dickinson College (Carlisle, Pennsylvania)
Cooper, Thomas **4** 224
Rush, Benjamin **13** 364-365

Dicotyledon (botany)
Malpighi, Marcello **10** 176-178
Ray, John **13** 57-59

Dictadura perpetua, La (pamphlet)
Montalvo, Juan María **11** 119-120

Dictating machine (instrument)
Edison, Thomas Alva **5** 206-208

Dictator, The (play)
Davis, Richard Harding **4** 422-423

Dictatorship (government)
Africa
Amin Dada, Idi **1** 202-204
Asia
Pol Pot **12** 382-384
Iberian Peninsula

Primo de Rivera y Orbaneja, Miguel **12** 454-455
Salazar, António de Oliveira **13** 442-443
Latin America
Banzer Suárez, Hugo **1** 494-496
Batista y Zaldívar, Fulgencio **2** 57-58
Carías Andino, Tiburcio **3** 298-299
Castelo Branco, Humberto **3** 359-360
Díaz, José de la Cruz Porfirio **4** 534-536
Ibáñez del Campo, Carlos **8** 88
Lleras Camargo, Alberto **9** 467
Machado y Morales, Gerardo **10** 92-93
Martínez, Maximiliano Hernández **10** 297-298
Odría Amoretti, Manuel Apolinario **11** 473-474
Peixoto, Floriano **12** 188-189
Pérez Jiménez, Marcos **12** 217-218
Pinochet Ugarte, Augusto **12** 315-317
Somoza Debayle, Anastasio **14** 336-337
Torrijos, Omar **15** 269-270
Trujillo Molina, Rafael Leonidas **15** 313-314
Ubico y Castañeda, Jorge **15** 377-378
Velasco, Luis de **15** 450-451
Videla, Jorge Rafaél **15** 490-492
Rome
Caesar, Gaius Julius **3** 207-210
Sulla, Lucius Cornelius I **15** 21-22
West Indies
Duvalier, Jean-Claude **5** 166-168
Yugoslavia
Tito, Marshal **15** 244-246
see also Absolutism; Despotism; Fascism; Nazism; Totalitarianism

Dictatorship of the proletariat
see Proletariat

Dictatus papae (papal document)
Gregory VII **6** 532-534

Dictionary (reference book)
Grimm, Jakob and Wilhelm Karl **7** 3-4
Johnson, Samuel **8** 315-317
Judson, Adoniram **8** 377-378
Ram Camul Sen **13** 16-17
Seneca the Younger, Lucius Annaeus **14** 103-105
Webster, Noah **16** 164-166

Dictionary of American Biography (encyclopedia)
Malone, Dumas **10** 174-175
Ochs, Adolph Simon **11** 464

Dictionary of National Biography (encyclopedia)
Pollard, Albert Frederick **12** 378
Stephen, Leslie **14** 429

Dictionnaire de musique (book)
Rousseau, Jean Jacques **13** 324-328

Didactic literature
Ennius, Quintus **5** 289
Froissart, Jean **6** 124-125
Hesiod **7** 361-362
Horace **7** 500-503
Lucretius **10** 26-27
Virgil **15** 507-510

Didactic Play of Baden (play)
Brecht, Bertolt **2** 512-514

Didascaliai (book)
Aristotle **1** 295-296

Diderot and the Encyclopaedists (biography)
Morley, John **11** 178-179

DIDEROT, DENIS (1713-1784), French philosopher, playwright, and encyclopedist **5** 1-2
art criticism
Boucher, François **2** 440-442
Fragonard, Jean Honoré **6** 38-39
Greuze, Jean Baptiste **6** 539
Guardi, Francesco **7** 24-25
Pergolesi, Giovanni Battista **12** 218-219
associates
Alembert, Jean le Rond d' **1** 127-128
Condorcet, Marquis de **4** 195-196
Holbach, Baron d' **7** 448-449
Rousseau, Jean Jacques **13** 324-328
influence of
Catherine the Great **3** 370-372
Du Bois-Reymond, Emil **5** 118-119
Houdon, Antoine **7** 516-517
Smith, Adam **14** 283-284
influenced by
Shaftesbury, 3d Earl of **14** 136-137

Dido (literary character)
Virgil **15** 507-510

Dido and Aeneas (opera; Purcell)
Monteverdi, Claudio Giovanni Antonio **11** 126-128
Purcell, Henry **12** 484-485

Dido Queen of Carthage (play)
Marlowe, Christopher **10** 272-274

DIEBENKORN, RICHARD (born 1922), American abstract expressionist painter **5** 2-4

DIEFENBAKER, JOHN GEORGE (1895-1979), Canadian statesman **5** 4-5
Fairclough, Ellen Louks **5** 367-368
Pearson, Lester Bowles **12** 174-175

Diego Martelli (painting)
Degas, Hilaire Germain Edgar **4** 461-462

Diégo-Suarez (naval base, Madagascar)
Joffre, Joseph Jacques Césaire **8** 267-268

DIELS, (OTTO PAUL) HERMANN (1876-1954), German organic chemist **5** 5-6

Diels-alder reaction (chemistry)
Diels, Otto Paul Hermann **5** 5-6

DIEM, NGO DINH (1901-1963), South Vietnamese president 1955-1963 **5** 6-7

Bao Dai **1** 496-497
Thieu, Nguyen Van **15** 182-183

Dien Bien Phu, Battle of (1954)
Bao Dai **1** 496-497
Diem, Ngo Dinh **5** 6-7
Giap, Vo Nguyen **6** 297-299
Leclerc, Jacques Philippe **9** 272-273

Diencephalon
see Hypothalamus

Dienes, cyclic
Diels, Otto Paul Hermann **5** 5-6

Dientzenhofer, Johann (1665?-1726), German architect
Neumann, Balthasar **11** 354-355

Dies Buch gehört dem König (book; B. von Arnim)
Arnim, Achim von **1** 308-309

Dies irae (choral music)
Penderecki, Krzysztof **12** 195-197
see also Requiem (music)

DIESEL, RUDOLF (1858-1913), German mechanical engineer **5** 7

Dieskau, Ludwig August (1701-1767), German general
Vaudreuil-Cavagnal, Marquis de **15** 444

Diesseits (stories)
Hesse, Hermann **7** 367-369

Diessen (church, near Munich)
Cuvilliés, François **4** 359-360

Diet (food)
Hopkins, Frederick Gowland **7** 491-492
Razi **13** 63-64

Dietramszell, church of (Germany)
Zimmermann, Johann Baptist and Domenikus **16** 518

Dietwald und Amelinde (romance)
Grimmelshausen, Hans Jakob Christoffel von **7** 4-5

Dieux ont soif, Les (novel)
France, Anatole **6** 39-40

Difaqane (South African wars)
Mzilikazi **11** 285-286
Shaka **14** 141-142

Differential calculus
see Calculus

Differential equations (mathematics)
Alembert, Jean le Rond d' **1** 127-128
Cauchy, Augustin Louis **3** 378-380
Lagrange, Joseph Louis **9** 164-166
Laplace, Marquis de **9** 202-204

Difficult Gentleman, The (comedy)
Hofmannsthal, Hugo von **7** 443-444

Diffraction (physics)
de Broglie, Louis **4** 442-444
Fresnel, Augustin Jean **6** 102-103

Diff'rent (play)
O'Neill, Eugene **11** 514-516

Digambaras (Jain sect)
Mahavira, Vardhamana **10** 135-137

Digest (book; Justinian)
Ulpian, Domitius **15** 385-386

Digestion (anatomy)
Beaumont, William **2** 95-96
Bernard, Claude **2** 208-210
Pavlov, Ivan Petrovich **12** 155-157
Schwann, Theodor **14** 51-52

Digges, Dudley (1583-1639), English diplomat and judge
Charles, I **3** 450-452

Dijon (city, France)
Garibaldi, Giuseppe **6** 215-217

Dijon Academy (France)
Cournot, Antoine Augustin **4** 273

DIKE, KENNETH (Kenneth Onwuka Dike; 1917-1983), African historian who set up the Nigerian National Archives **5** 7-8

Dikter (poems)
Heidenstam, Carl Gustaf Verner Von **7** 258-259

Dilemmas (book)
Ryle, Gilbert **13** 393-394

DILLINGER, JOHN (1903-1934), American criminal **5** 9

Dillon, Read and Co.
Forrestal, James Vincent **6** 14

DILTHEY, WILHELM CHRISTIAN LUDWIG (1833-1911), German historian and philosopher **5** 10
Ebbinghaus, Hermann **5** 192-193
Lamprecht, Karl **9** 181
Ortega Y Gasset, José **12** 7-8

Diluvio (play)
Betti, Ugo **2** 246

DIMAGGIO, JOE (born Giuseppe Paolo DiMaggio, Jr.; b. 1914), American baseball player **5** 10-11

Dime novels (literary)
Dreiser, Herman Theodore **5** 98-100

Dimensions of My Hope, The (book)
Borges, Jorge Luis **2** 411-412

DIMITROV, GEORGI (1882-1949), head of the Communist International (1935-1943) and prime minister of Bulgaria (1944-1949) **5** 11-13

Dimitry, Prince (1582-1591), son of Ivan IV
Godunov, Boris Feodorovich **6** 382-383

Dimmesdale (literary character)
Hawthorne, Nathaniel **7** 212-215

Dimostrationi harmoniche (music theory)
Zarlino, Gioseffo **16** 490-491

Din, Muslih-al-
see Sadi

Dindenault (literary character)
Rabelais, François **12** 524-526

DINESEN BLIXEN-FINECKE, KAREN (a.k.a. Isak Dinesen; 1885-1962), Danish author **5** 13-14

DINGANE (circa 1795-1840), Zulu king **5** 14-15
   Cetshwayo **3** 400
   Pretorius, Andries **12** 444-445
   Retief, Pieter **13** 105-106
   Shaka **14** 141-142

Dingiswayo (died circa 1818), Mthethwa chief
   Shaka **14** 141-142

Dingley Tariff (United States, 1897)
   McKinley, William **10** 418-420

Din-i-ilahi (religious movement)
   Akbar, Jalal-ud-din Mohammed **1** 96

DINKINS, DAVID (born 1927), African American politician and mayor of New York City **5** 15-18

Dinner at Eight (play; Ferber-Kaufman)
   Ferber, Edna **5** 413
   Kaufman, George S. **8** 457-458

Dinner Party, The (artwork)
   Chicago, Judy **3** 515-516

Dinocerata (paleontology)
   Marsh, Othniel Charles **10** 275-276

Dinosaur (extinct reptile)
   Andrews, Roy Chapman **1** 232-233
   Marsh, Othniel Charles **10** 275-276

Dinuzulu (1868?-1913), Zulu chief
   Botha, Louis **2** 434-436

DINWIDDIE, ROBERT (1693-1770), Scottish merchant and colonial governor **5** 18-19
   Braddock, Edward **2** 474-475
   Dunmore, 4th Earl of **5** 147
   Washington, George **16** 126-129

Dio Cassius (155?-?230), Roman politician and historian
   Nero Claudius Caesar **11** 342-344

Dio Chrysostomos (40?-?115), Greek sophist and scholar
   Phidias **12** 265-267

Dio et anima (book)
   Ficino, Marsilio **5** 436-437

Dio Kurt, II (play)
   Moravia, Alberto **11** 153-155

Dioclesian (opera)
   Purcell, Henry **12** 484-485

DIOCLETIAN (Gaius Aurelius Valerius Diocletianus; 245-circa 313), Roman emperor 284-305 **5** 19-20
   Constantine I **4** 209-211
   Donatus **5** 56-57
   Lope Félix de Vega Carpio **9** 503-506

Diodati, Charles (1608?-1638), English classical scholar
   Milton, John **11** 43-46

Diodorus, Siculus (flourished 1st century B.C.), Greek historian
   Skelton, John **14** 268-269

Diodorus Cronus (flourished 4th century B.C.), Greek philosopher
   Zeno of Citium **16** 499-500

DIOGENES (circa 400-325 B.C.), Greek philosopher **5** 20-21
   Antisthenes **1** 250-251

Diogenes Laërtius (flourished 3d century), Greek biographer
   Aristotle **1** 295-296
   Epicurus **5** 292-294
   Zeno of Citium **16** 499-500

Diogenes of Babylonian (flourished 2d century B.C.), Stoic philosopher
   Zeno of Citium **16** 499-500

Dion (408?-353 B.C.), Syracusan philosopher and politician
   Plato **12** 345-347

Dionysian culture (American Indian)
   Benedict, Ruth Fulton **2** 154-155

Dionysius (letter)
   Isocrates **8** 151

Dionysius I (the Elder; circa 430-367 B.C.), tyrant of Syracuse
   Isocrates **8** 151
   Plato **12** 345-347

Dionysius II (the Younger; flourished mid-4th century B.C.), tyrant of Syracuse
   Plato **12** 345-347

Dionysus (literary character)
   Euripides **5** 332-334

Dionysus the Areopagite
   see Pseudo-Dionysus

DIOP, CHEIKH ANTA (1923-1986), African historian **5** 21-22

Diophantine equation (mathematics)
   Euler, Leonard **5** 331-332
   Lagrange, Joseph Louis **9** 164-166

Diophantus (flourished 3d century), Greek mathematician
   Fermat, Pierre de **5** 421-422
   Fibonacci, Leonardo **5** 434-435
   Regiomontanus **13** 81-82

Diophysitism (religious doctrine)
   Leo I **9** 329-330

DIOR, CHRISTIAN (1905-1957), French fashion designer **5** 22

Dios deseado y deseante (poems)
   Jiménez, Juan Ramón **8** 261-262

Dioscorides, Pedanius (flourished 1st century A.D.), Greek physician
   Avicenna **1** 386-387

Dioscorus (died 454), bishop of Alexandria
   Eutyches **5** 335
   Leo I **9** 329-330

Dioskouro
   see Castor and Pollux

Diotima (literary character)
   Hölderlin, Johann Christian Friedrich **7** 451-452

Diphilus (flourished circa 340-289 B.C.), Greek playwright
   Plautus **12** 348-350
   Terence **15** 146-148

Diphtheria (medicine)
   Behring, Emil Adolph von **2** 122-123
   Ehrlich, Paul **5** 225-226
   Louis, Pierre Charles Alexandre **9** 540
   Park, William Hallock **12** 104-105
   Richet, Charles Robert **13** 144-145

Diplomatic Revolution (1756; Prussia)
   Frederick II **6** 81-84

Diplomats
  American
    see Diplomats, American
  Argentine
    Alberdi, Juan Bautista **1** 109-110
    Lamas, Carlos Saavedra **9** 175-176
    Rivadavia, Bernardino **13** 182-183
    Sarmiento, Domingo Faustino **13** 484-485
  Australian
    Bruce of Melbourne, 1st Viscount **3** 61-62
  Austrian
    Berchtold, Leopold von **2** 183-184
    Metternich, Klemens von **10** 533-536
    Waldheim, Kurt **16** 54-55
  Belgian
    Davignon **4** 410-411
    Spaak, Paul Henri **14** 359-360
  Bolivian
    Patiño, Simón Iturri **12** 133-134
  Botswanan
    Chiepe, Gaositwe Keagakwa Tibe **3** 517
  Brazilian
    Aranha, Osvaldo **1** 272-273
    Nabuco de Araujo, Joaquim Aurelio **11** 288-289
    Varnhagen, Francisco Adolfo de **15** 437-438
  British
    Carrington **3** 326-327
    Nicolson, Harold George **11** 383-384
  Burmese
    Thant, U **15** 161-162
  Canadian
    Galt, Alexander Tilloch **6** 190-191
    McNaughton, Andrew **10** 431-432
    Pearson, Lester Bowles **12** 174-175
    Smith, Donald Alexander **14** 288-289
    Tupper, Charles **15** 342-343
  Chilean
    Balmaceda Fernández, José Manuel **1** 475-476
    Neruda, Pablo **11** 344-345
  Chinese
    Ch'i-ying **4** 12
    Hu Shih **8** 63-65
    Li Hung-Chang **9** 407-409
  Colombian
    Lleras Camargo, Alberto **9** 467
  Dominican
    Balaguer y Ricardo, Joaquin **1** 460-461
  Dutch

Luns, Joseph **10** 46-47
Van Eekelen, Willem Frederik
15 426-427
Ecuadorian
Plaza Lasso, Galo **12** 350-351
Egyptian
Boutros-Ghali, Boutros **2** 457-458
English
Owen, David Anthony Llewellyn
12 37-39
see also Diplomats, English
Ethiopian
Mäkonnen Endalkačäw **10** 161-162
Filipino
Quezon, Manuel Luis **12** 511-513
Rómulo, Carlos P. **13** 270-271
Flemish
Rubens, Peter Paul **13** 339-342
French
see Diplomats, French
German
Humboldt, Wilhelm von **8** 31
Niebuhr, Barthold Georg
11 385-386
Stresemann, Gustav **14** 508-509
Greek
Seferis, George **14** 84-85
Guatemalan
Arévalo, Juan José **1** 285-286
Guyanese
Ramphal, Shridath Surendranath
13 19-20
Indian (Asia)
Menon, Vengalil Krishnan Krishna
10 507-509
Nizami, Khaliq Ahmad **11** 405
Pandit, Vijaya Lakshmi **12** 83-84
Iraqi
Fādil al-Jamālī, Muhammad
5 361-362
Israeli
Eban, Abba **5** 191-192
Herzog, Chaim **7** 354-355
Rabin, Yitzchak **12** 527-529
Italian
Badoglio, Pietro **1** 428-429
Castiglione, Baldassare **3** 360-361
Japanese
Ogata, Sadako **11** 479-480
Yoshida, Shigeru **16** 464-465
Liberian
Blyden, Edward Wilmot **2** 348-349
Mexican
Cosio Villegas, Daniel **4** 260-261
Lerdo de Tejada, Miguel **9** 351-352
Reyes, Alfonso **13** 112-113
Nigerian
Dike, Kenneth **5** 7-8
papal
Boniface VIII **2** 392-393
Borromeo, Charles **2** 423-424
Persian
Malkam Khan, Mirza **10** 172
Peruvian
Pérez de Cuéllar, Javier **12** 214-215
Portuguese

Mendes Pinto, Fernao **10** 493-494
Vieira, Antônio **15** 492
Romanian
Titulescu, Nicolae **15** 246-247
Russian
Kollontai, Aleksandra Mikhailovna
9 79
Litvinov, Maxim Maximovich
9 451-452
Molotov, Vyacheslav Mikhailovich
11 89-90
Nesselrode, Karl Robert **11** 348-349
Witte, Sergei Yulyevich **16** 349-350
Scottish
Lyndsay, David **10** 66-67
South African
Moshweshwe **11** 203-205
Smuts, Jan Christian **14** 309-310
Soviet
Gromyko, Andrei Andreevich **7** 9-11
Shevardnadze, Eduard Amvrosevich
14 191-193
Vyshinsky, Andrei **16** 36-37
Spanish
Valera y Alcalá Galiano, Juan
15 403
Swedish
Hammarskjöld, Dag **7** 100-101
Hedin, Sven Anders **7** 252-253
Wallenberg, Raoul **16** 78-80
Ugandan
Elizabeth Bagaaya Nyabongo of
Toro **5** 269-271
Uruguayan
Terra, Gabriel **15** 154-155
Zorrilla de San Martin, Juan
16 530-531
Venezuelan
Bello, Ahmadu **2** 139-140
see also Statesmen

Diplomats, American
18th century (in England)
Adams, John **1** 48-51
Adams, John Quincy **1** 52-54
18th century (in France)
Deane, Silas **4** 435-437
Franklin, Benjamin **6** 60-64
Jefferson, Thomas **8** 238-241
Lee, Arthur **9** 288-289
Livingston, Robert R. **9** 462-463
Monroe, James **11** 111-113
Morris, Gouverneur **11** 182-183
Pinckney, Charles Cotesworth
12 310
18th century (in Spain)
Jay, John **8** 230-232
19th century (in China)
Burlingame, Anson **3** 144-145
19th century (England)
Adams, Charles Francis **1** 41-42
Bancroft, George **1** 483-484
Everett, Edward **5** 344
Hay, John **7** 215-216
King, Rufus **9** 22-23
Lawrence, Abbott **9** 246
Motley, John Lothrop **11** 211-212

19th century (in France)
Barlow, Joel **2** 6-7
Bigelow, John **2** 271-272
Cass, Lewis **3** 355-356
Gallatin, Albert **6** 183-184
Slidell, John **14** 273
19th century (in Germany)
Pendleton, George Hunt **12** 198
19th century (in Japan)
Harris, Townsend **7** 176-177
19th century (in Latin America)
Gadsden, James **6** 165-166
Grimké, Archibald Henry **7** 1-2
Harrison, William Henry **7** 180-181
Helper, Hinton Rowan **7** 272-273
Langston, John Mercer **9** 197
Larkin, Thomas Oliver **9** 208
Trist, Nicholas Philip **15** 298-299
19th century (in Russia)
Cameron, Simon **3** 246-247
White, Andrew Dickson **16** 226-227
19th century (in Spain)
Irving, Washington **8** 141-143
Lowell, James Russell **10** 14-15
Pinckney, Charles **12** 309-310
Soulé, Pierre **14** 351-352
20th century (ambassadors-at-large)
Haig, Alexander M. Jr. **7** 66-67
Kissinger, Henry Alfred **9** 43-45
Strauss, Robert Schwarz **14** 501-502
20th century (in Czechoslovakia)
Black, Shirley Temple **2** 303-305
Moynihan, Daniel Patrick
11 216-218
20th century (in Denmark)
Hapgood, Norman **7** 137-138
Owen, Ruth Bryan **12** 41-43
Rohde, Ruth Bryan Owen
13 252-253
20th century (in England)
Brewster, Kingman Jr. **2** 522-523
House, Edward Mandell **7** 520-521
Page, Walter Hines **12** 60-61
20th century (in Finland)
Rowan, Carl T. **13** 329-330
20th century (in India)
Moynihan, Daniel Patrick
11 216-218
20th century (in Iran)
Christopher, Warren Minor **4** 32-33
20th century (in Ireland)
Heckler, Margaret Mary O'Shaugh-
nessy **7** 251-252
20th century (in Italy)
Luce, Clare Boothe **10** 21-23
Page, Thomas Nelson **12** 59-60
20th century (in Japan)
Dulles, John Foster **5** 134-135
20th century (in Latin America)
Berle, Adolf Augustus Jr. **2** 199-200
Daniels, Josephus **4** 387
Johnson, James Weldon **8** 304-305
Morrow, Dwight Whitney
11 190-191
Welles, Sumner **16** 191-192
20th century (in Philippines)

Murphy, Frank **11** 260-261
Sayre, Francis Bowes **13** 509
20th century (in South Vietnam)
Taylor, Maxwell **15** 126-127
20th century (in Spain)
Bowers, Claude Gernade **2** 463
20th century (in Union of Soviet Social-
ist Republics)
Bohlen, Charles (Chip) **2** 364-366
Harriman, W. Averell **7** 165-166
Kennan, George F. **8** 496-498
20th century (in United Nations)
Albright, Madeleine Korbel
1 116-118
Black, Shirley Temple **2** 303-305
Bush, George **3** 167-169
Kirkpatrick, Jeane J. **9** 37-39
Lodge, Henry Cabot Jr. **9** 483-485
Roosevelt, Eleanor **13** 275-277
Stevenson, Adlai Ewing **14** 445-446
Young, Andrew Jackson Jr.
16 467-469
20th century (trade negotiators)
Strauss, Robert Schwarz **14** 501-502
20th century (without portfolio)
Carter, James Earl **3** 339-342
see also Statesmen, American

Diplomats, English
Hurd, Douglas **8** 52-55
16th century
Sidney, Philip **14** 214-215
Spenser, Edmund **14** 373-376
Wyatt, Thomas **16** 410-411
19th century
Burton, Richard **3** 163-164
Salisbury, 3d Marquess of
13 448-449
20th century
Bryce, James **3** 85
Halifax, 1st Earl of **7** 82-83
Perth, 16th Earl of **12** 244-245
Reading, 1st Marquess of **13** 64

Diplomats, French
18th century
Bonaparte, Joseph **2** 381-382
Bernadotte, Jean Baptiste **2** 205-206
Genet, Edmond Charles **6** 261-262
Talleyrand, Charles Maurice de
15 89-90
19th century
Chateaubriand, Vicomte de
3 477-479
Claudel, Paul Louis Charles **4** 90-91
Guizot, François Pierre Guillaume
7 40-41
Lamartine, Alphonse Marie Louis de
9 173-175
Maistre, Joseph de **10** 153-154
Sorel, Albert **14** 346-347
20th century
Delcassé, Théophile **4** 478-479
Giraudoux, Jean **6** 349-350
Maritain, Jacques **10** 263
Monnet, Jean **11** 109-110
Perse, Saint-John **12** 242-243

Pétain, Henri Philippe **12** 250-252

Dipole moment (physics)
Debye, Peter Joseph William **4** 447-448

Dipsodes (literary characters)
Rabelais, François **12** 524-526

Dipsychus (poem)
Clough, Arthur Hugh **4** 123-124

DIRAC, PAUL ADRIEN MAURICE
(1902-1984), English physicist **5** 23-24
Anderson, Carl David **1** 214-215
Bohr, Niels Henrik David **2** 366-368
Eddington, Arthur Stanley **5** 201-202
Fermi, Enrico **5** 422-424
Heisenberg, Werner Karl **7** 261-263
Oppenheimer, J. Robert **11** 525-526
Schrödinger, Erwin **14** 31-33
Tomonaga, Sin-itiro **15** 265-266

Directions to Servants (satire)
Swift, Jonathan **15** 51-54

Directive (poem)
Frost, Robert Lee **6** 130-133

Director (book)
see Gentleman and Cabinetmaker's
Director, The

Directors (theater)
see Actors and Entertainers

Directory (France; 1795-1799)
see French Revolution—1795-1799
(Directory)

Dirichlet, Peter Gustav Lejeune
(1805-1859), German mathematician
Riemann, Georg Friedrich Bernard
13 164-165

Dirigible (aeronautics)
Santos-Dumont, Alberto **13** 477-478
Sikorsky, Igor **14** 223-224
Tsiolkovsky, Konstantin Eduardovich
15 326-328

DIRKSEN, EVERETT McKINLEY
(1896-1969), Republican congressman
and senator from Illinois **5** 24-26

Dirty Hands (play)
Sartre, Jean Paul **13** 491-492

Diruta, Girolamo (circa 1560-after 1609),
Italian organist and theorist
Merulo, Claudio **10** 525-526

Disabilities of Black Folk ... (book)
Hayford, J. E. Casely **7** 228-230

Disappeared
see Desaparecidos

Disarmament (internatnational politics)
Borah, William Edgar **2** 408
Borden, Robert Laird **2** 409-411
Coolidge, John Calvin **4** 217-219
Hoover, Herbert Clark **7** 483-485
Titulescu, Nicolae **15** 246-247

Disaster, The (autobiography)
Vasconcelos, José **15** 443-444

Disasters of War, The (etchings)
Goya y Lucientes, Francisco de Paula
José de **6** 476-478

Discalced Carmelites
see Carmelites

Disciples of Christ (religious sect)
Campbell, Alexander **3** 249-250
Garfield, James Abram **6** 213-214

Discordant Encounters (literary collection)
Wilson, Edmund **16** 318-319

Discours (poems; Ronsard)
Hugo, Victor Marie **8** 22-25
Ronsard, Pierre de **13** 271-273

**Discours sur l'origine de l'inégalité des
hommes** (essay; Rousseau)
Mendelssohn, Moses **10** 488-489
Rousseau, Jean Jacques **13** 324-328

**Discourse of the Contests ... in Athens and
Rome** (essay)
Swift, Jonathan **15** 51-54

Discourse on Method (book)
Descartes, René **4** 505-508-350

Discourses of Epictetus (book; Arrian)
Butler, Joseph **3** 180-181
Epictetus **5** 292

Discourses ... of Titus Livius (book; Machi-
avelli)
Alfieri, Vittoria **1** 145-146
Machiavelli, Niccolò **10** 97-99-68

Discovery (book)
Byrd, Richard Evelyn **3** 186-187

Discovery (ship)
Antarctic expeditions
Scott, Robert Falcon **14** 67-68
Shackleton, Ernest Henry **14** 132-133
Arctic expeditions
Baffin, William **1** 435-436
Cook, James **4** 214-215
Hudson, Henry **8** 12-13
Vancouver, George **15** 414-415

Discreet Person, The (book)
Gracián y Morales, Baltasar Jerónimo
6 481-482

Discrimination (social behavior)
racial
Barton, Edmund **2** 39-40
Bose, Subhas Chandra **2** 430-431
Buddha **3** 97-101
see also Apartheid; African American history (United States)
religious
Calvert, Charles **3** 238
Charles II **3** 452-454
see also Anti-Semitism; Persecutions, religious; Religious liberty

Discrimination (United States)
see African American history (United
States); Civil liberties (United States);
Civil rights movement; Minority
rights; Racism

Discus Thrower
see Diskobolos (sculpture)

Disease (medicine)
early theories
Helmont, Jan Baptista van
7 269-271
Morgagni, Giovanni Battista
11 158-159
microbial theory
Koch, Heinrich Hermann Robert
9 69-70
Lwoff, André **10** 58-59
Pasteur, Louis **12** 125-127
molecular
Pauling, Linus Carl **12** 150-152
psychogenic causation
Jones, Ernest Alfred **8** 331-332

Disease of the Century, The (essay)
Kazantzakis, Nikos **8** 466-468

Diskobolos (sculpture)
Myron **11** 285

Diskophoros (sculpture)
Polykleitos **12** 385-386

DISNEY, WALTER ELIAS (1901-1966),
American film maker and entrepreneur
5 26-27

Disneyland (amusement park)
Disney, Walter Elias **5** 26-27

Disorder and Early Sorrow (novella)
Mann, Thomas **10** 204-207

Disowned Son (dialogue)
Lucian **10** 25-26

Disparates (etching)
Goya y Lucientes, Francisco de Paula
José de **6** 476-478

Disprezzo, Il (novel)
Moravia, Alberto **11** 153-155

Disputà (fresco)
Raphael **13** 40-42

DISRAELI, BENJAMIN (1st Earl of Beacons-
field; 1804-1881), English statesman,
prime minister 1868 and 1874-1880
5 27-29
Bolingbroke, Viscount **2** 374-375
Gladstone, William Ewart **6** 357-360
Ismail Pasha **8** 150-151
Morris, William **11** 187-188
Salisbury, 3d Marquess of **13** 448-449
Turgenev, Ivan Sergeyevich **15** 345-348
Victoria **15** 485-487

Dissertation upon Roast Pig, A (essay)
Lamb, Charles **9** 176-177

Dissolute Youth, The (poem)
Eminescu, Mihail **5** 280-281

Dissonance (music)
Boethius, Anicius Manlius Severinus
2 360-361
Franco of Cologne **6** 52

Distant Stars in the Heaven (poems)
Tschernichowsky, Saul **15** 323

**Distinguishing Marks of a Work of the
Spirit of God, The** (book)
Edwards, Jonathan **5** 220-222

Distribution (economics)
Belloc, Joseph Hilaire Pierre **2** 141
Clark, John Bates **4** 76-77
Commons, John Rogers **4** 185
Ricardo, David **13** 123-124
Say, Jean Baptiste **13** 508-509
Smith, Adam **14** 283-284
see also Marketing

Distribution of the Eagles (painting)
David, Jacques Louis **4** 407-409

District of Columbia
see Washington, D.C.

District of Columbia (novel)
Dos Passos, John Roderigo **5** 69-71

Disubbidienza, La (novel)
Moravia, Alberto **11** 153-155

Ditchley House (Oxfordshire)
Gibbs, James **6** 301-302

Ditte, Child of Man (novel)
Nexø, Martin Anderson **11** 372

Diu, Battle of (1509)
Magellan, Ferdinand **10** 126-127

Diu, siege of (1538)
Suleiman I **15** 20-21

Divagations (book)
Mallarmé, Stéphane **10** 172-173

Divan (literary collection)
Hafiz, Shams al-Din **7** 63

Diván del Tamarit (poem)
Lorca, Federico García **9** 511-513

Dive Bomber (mural)
Orozco, José Clemente **12** 1-2

Diver, Dick (literary character)
Fitzgerald, Francis Scott Key **5** 470-472

Divers jeux rustiques (book)
du Bellay, Joachim **5** 113-114

**Divers Voyages Touching the Discovery of
America** (book)
Hakluyt, Richard **7** 70

Diversity of Creatures, A (stories)
Kipling, Joseph Rudyard **9** 32-33

Divertimento (music)
Dallapiccola, Luigi **4** 377-378
Haydn, Franz Joseph **7** 219-221
Stravinsky, Igor Fedorovich **14** 502-506

Divina Commedia (Dante)
see Divine Comedy

Divinas palabras (novel)
Valle Inclán, Ramón Maria del
15 407-408

DIVINE, FATHER (born George Baker?; c.
1877-1965), African American religious
leader **5** 29-32

Divine Comedy, The (poem; Dante)
authorship
Dante Alighieri **4** 389-391
Inferno
Boccaccio, Giovanni **2** 351-353
Boniface VIII **2** 392-393

Carpeaux, Jean Baptiste **3** 318-319
Galileo Galilei **6** 180-183
Joyce, James **8** 365-367
Rodin, Auguste **13** 236-238
Solzhenitsyn, Alexander Isayevich
14 330-332
Paradiso
Henry VII **7** 299-300
illustrators
Botticelli, Sandro **2** 439-440
Galileo Galilei **6** 180-183
influence on art
Carpeaux, Jean Baptiste **3** 318-319
Rodin, Auguste **13** 236-238
influence on literature
Balzac, Honoré de **1** 478-480
Joyce, James **8** 365-367
Solzhenitsyn, Alexander Isayevich
14 330-332
source
Boniface VIII **2** 392-393
Cimabue **4** 60-61
Godfrey of Bouillon **6** 379
translations
Griffith, Samuel Walker **6** 545-546
Kazantzakis, Nikos **8** 466-468
Longfellow, Henry Wadsworth
9 499-500

Divine Comedies (poems)
Merrill, James **10** 521-522

Divine Dance, Church of the (Hollywood,
California)
St. Denis, Ruth **13** 430-431

Divine Intelligences (philosophy)
Erigena, John Scotus **5** 308-309

Divine Milieu, The (book)
Teilhard de Chardin, Marie Joseph
Pierre **15** 134-136

Divine origin (philosophy)
Schopenhauer, Arthur **14** 29-31

Divine Poem (symphony)
Scriabin, Alexander Nikolayevich
14 71-72

Divine purpose (philosophy)
Lotze, Rudolf Hermann **9** 521-522

Divine right of kings (political philosophy)
Coke, Edward **4** 141-142
Comte, Auguste **4** 189-191
Frederick William IV **6** 87-88
Marsilius of Padua **10** 284
Saint-Pierre, Abbé de **13** 434-435
Suárez, Francisco **15** 8
see also Monarchy, absolute

Divine Tragedy, The (book)
Longfellow, Henry Wadsworth
9 499-500

Divine Vengeance Pursuing Crime (painting)
Prud'hon, Pierre Paul **12** 469

Divine Weeks and Works (poem; Du Bartas)
Bradstreet, Anne Dudley **2** 486-487

Diving bell (vessel)
Eads, James Buchanan **5** 175-176

Divino afflante Spiritu (encyclical)
Pius XII **12** 339-340

Divisionism (art style)
Balla, Giacomo **1** 473-474
Boccioni, Umberto **2** 353-354
Matisse, Henri **10** 336-337
Seurat, Georges Pierre **14** 120-122
Severini, Gino **14** 122
see also Pointillism

Divorce (novel)
Lao Shê **9** 200-201

Diwan (book)
Barth, Heinrich **2** 30-31
Sa'di **13** 418-419

Diwan (poems)
Jami **8** 218-219
Rumi, Jalai ed-Din **13** 362-363

DIX, DOROTHEA LYNDE (1802-1887),
American reformer **5** 32-33
Bellows, Henry Whitney **2** 143-144

DIX, OTTO (1891-1969), German painter
and graphic artist **5** 33-34
Grosz, George **7** 17-18

Dixie (song; Emmet)
Christy, Edwin P. **4** 34-35

Dixit Dominus (motet)
Handel, George Frederick **7** 116-119

Dixon, Jeremiah (flourished 1763-1767),
English surveyor
Rittenhouse, David **13** 180-181

Djamileh (opera)
Bizet, Georges **2** 296-297

Djenné (city, Mali)
Ali, Sunni **1** 158-159
Caillié, Auguste René **3** 214-215

DJILAS, MILOVAN (1911-1995), Yugoslavian writer **5** 34

Dmitri (literary character)
Dostoevsky, Fyodor **5** 74-77

Dmitry Kalinin (play)
Belinsky, Grigorievich **2** 128

Dmowski, Roman (1864-1939), Polish
statesman
Pilsudski, Joseph **12** 305-306

DNA
see Deoxyribonucleic acid

Dnieper River (Union of Soviet Socialist
Republics)
Chmielnicki, Bogdan **4** 12-13

DO MUOI (born 1917), prime minister of
the Socialist Republic of Vietnam (1988-)
5 53-55

Do You Want to Know a Secret (song)
Lennon, John Winston **9** 326-328

Doab (region, India)
Muhammad bin Tughluq **11** 229

Dobama Asiayone (Burmese political
group)
Ne Win **11** 364-365

DOBELL, SIR WILLIAM (1899-1970), Aus-
tralian artist **5** 34-35
Drysdale, George Russell **5** 107-109
Nolan, Sidney Robert **11** 418

Dobest (literary character)
Langland, William **9** 194-195

Dobrogea (region; Romania)
Ceausescu, Nicolae **3** 387-388

Dobrolyubov, Nikolai Aleksandrovich
(1836-1861), Russian journalist and critic
Mussorgsky, Modest Petrovich
11 274-276
Turgenev, Ivan Sergeyevich **15** 345-348

Dobrovský, Josepf (1753-1829), Czech
Jesuit philologist
Palacký, František **12** 69-70

Dobson, Frank (1888-1963), English sculptor
Moore, Henry **11** 146-148

Dobuan Indians (North America)
Benedict, Ruth Fulton **2** 154-155

DOBZHANSKY, THEODOSIUS
(1900-1975), Russian-American biologist
who studied natural selection **5** 35-37

Dochet Island (Canada)
Champlain, Samuel de **3** 419-421

Docker, noir, Le (novel)
Ousmane, Sembene **12** 32-33

Dockers Union (Great Britain)
Bevin, Ernest **2** 252-253

Docteur amoureux, Le (play)
Molière **11** 86-88

Docteur Miracle, Le (opera)
Bizet, Georges **2** 296-297

Doctor and the Doctor's Wife, The (story)
Hemingway, Ernest Miller **7** 274-277

Dr. Bartolo (literary character)
Beaumarchais, Pierre August Caron de
2 93-94

Dr. Brodie's Report (stories)
Borges, Jorge Luis **2** 411-412

Doctor Faustus (novel)
Mann, Thomas **10** 204-207

Doctor Faustus (opera)
Busoni, Ferruccio Benvenuto **3** 173-174

Doctor Faustus (play)
Marlowe, Christopher **10** 272-274

Dr. Grimshawe's Secret (romance)
Hawthorne, Nathaniel **7** 212-215

Dr. Heidegger's Experiment (story)
Hawthorne, Nathaniel **7** 212-215

Dr. Katzenbergers Badreise (novel)
Richter, Johann Paul Friedrich
13 150-151

Dr. Kildare (film series)
Barrymores **2** 28-30

Doctor Martino ... (stories)
Faulkner, William **5** 395-397

**Dr. Nicolaas Tulp Demonstrating the
Anatomy of the Arm** (painting)
Rembrandt Harmensz van Rijn
13 91-95

Dr. Rieux (literary character)
Camus, Albert **3** 255-257

Doctor of Salamanca (painting)
Zurbarán, Francisco de **16** 534-535

Dr. Sevier (novel)
Cable, George Washington **3** 198-199

Doctor Thorne (novel)
Trollope, Anthony **15** 300-302

Doctor Zhivago (novel)
Pasternak, Boris Leonidovich
12 124-125

Doctors of the Church
see Religious leaders, Christian—Doctors

Doctor's Religion (book)
Browne, Thomas **3** 49-50

Doctor's Riot (1788)
Jay, John **8** 230-232

Doctor's Son ... (stories)
O'Hara, John **11** 485

Doctrinaires (French political party)
Guizot, François Pierre Guillaume
7 40-41

Doctrine of the Faith, Congregation for the
see Inquisition, Holy Roman and Universal

Documentary films
Flaherty, Robert **5** 476-477
Flanagan, Hallie **5** 478-479

Documentos (periodical)
Toledano, Vicente Lombardo
15 256-257

Dod Grile
see Bierce, Ambrose Gwinett

Dodecachordon (musical collection)
Le Jeune, Claude **9** 314-315

Dodecahedron (mathematics)
Euclid **5** 327-329
see also Polyhedron

Dodecalogos tou Gyftou (poems)
Palamas, Kostes **12** 70

DODGE, GRACE HOADLEY (1856-1914),
American feminist, philanthropist, and
social worker **5** 37-38

Dodge, Grenville Mellen (1831-1916),
American army officer and civil engineer
Durant, Thomas Clark **5** 157-158

Dodgson, Charles Lutwidge
see Carroll, Lewis

Dodsley, Robert (1703-1764), English poet,
playwright, and bookseller
Collins, William **4** 168-169

Dodsworth (novel; S. Lewis)
Goldwyn, Samuel **6** 416

Lewis, Harry Sinclair **9** 385-387

DOE, SAMUEL KANYON (1951-1990),
Liberian statesman **5** 38-39

Doenitz, Karl (1891-1980), German admiral
Hitler, Adolf **7** 417-420

Dog beneath the Skin, The (play)
Auden, Wystan Hugh **1** 364-366

Dog Years (novel)
Grass, Günter **6** 496-497

Dogali, Battle of (1887)
Johannes IV **8** 272-273

Doghdova (Zorastrianism)
Zoroaster **16** 528-530

Dogon (African people)
Ali, Sunni **1** 158-159

Dog's Life, A (film)
Chaplin, Charles Spencer **3** 438-440

DOI TAKAKO (born 1928), chairperson of
the Japan Socialist party **5** 39-41

Doisy, Edward Adelbert (1893-1986),
American biochemist
Dam, Carl Peter Henrik **4** 382-383

Dokimes (essays)
Seferis, George **14** 84-85

Doktor Faust (play fragment)
Lessing, Gotthold Ephraim **9** 357-359

Doktor Faustus (book)
Mann, Thomas **10** 204-207

Dolbear, Amos Emerson (1837-1910),
American physicist
Bell, Alexander Graham **2** 129-131

Dolce, Lodovico (1508-1568), Italian
writer and scholar
Titian **15** 242-244

Dolce stil nuovo (Italian literature)
Cavalcanti, Guido **3** 382
Guinizzelli, Guido **7** 36-37

Dolce vita, La (film)
Fellini, Federico **5** 408-409

DOLE, ELIZABETH HANFORD (born
1936), American lawyer, politician, and
first female United States secretary of
transportation **5** 41-43

DOLE, ROBERT J. (born 1923), Republican
Senator **5** 43-46

DOLE, SANFORD BALLARD (1844-1926),
American statesman **5** 46
Liliuokalani, Lydia Kamakaeha
9 411-412

Dolet, Étienne (1509-1546), French painter
Rabelais, François **12** 524-526

Dollar diplomacy (United States politics)
Knox, Philander Chase **9** 66-67
Marcos, Ferdinand **10** 240-242
Taft, William Howard **15** 78-81

DOLLFUSS, ENGELBERT (1892-1934),
Austrian statesman **5** 47
Renner, Karl **13** 98-99
Schuschnigg, Kurt von **14** 45-46

DÖLLINGER, JOSEF IGNAZ VON
(1799-1890), German historian and theologian **5** 47-48
Acton, John Emerich Edward Dalberg
1 38
Agassiz, Jean Louis Rodolphe **1** 76-78
Baer, Karl Ernst von **1** 431-432

Dolliver Romance, The (book)
Hawthorne, Nathaniel **7** 212-215

Doll's House, A (play; Ibsen)
Ibsen, Henrik **8** 98-100
Shaw, George Bernard **14** 163-164
Wilder, Thornton Niven **16** 276-277

Dolore, Il (poems)
Ungaretti, Giuseppe **15** 389-390

Dolores (poem)
Swinburne, Algernon Charles **15** 54-55

Dolorous Death, The (poem)
Skelton, John **14** 268-269

Dom Casmurro (novel)
Machado de Assis, Joaquim Maria
10 91-92

Dom-ino project (architecture)
Le Corbusier **9** 274-275

Dom Juan (play; Moliére)
Brecht, Bertolt **2** 512-514
Molière **11** 86-88

Doma (African people)
Anokye, Okomfo **1** 242-243

DOMAGK, GERHARD JOHANNES PAUL
(1895-1964), German bacteriologist
5 48-50

Domaine Musical (concert series)
Boulez, Pierre **2** 444-445

Dombey and Son (novel)
Dickens, Charles John Huffam
4 538-541

Dome of Many-coloured Glass, A (poems)
Lowell, Amy **10** 13

Dome of the Rock (Jerusalem)
Abd al-Malik **1** 12-13

Dome Tombs (Mycenae)
Schliemann, Heinrich **14** 17-18

Domenichino, Il (Domenico Zampieri;
1581-1641), Italian painter
Carracci **3** 319-321
David, Jacques Louis **4** 407-409

Domesday Book (England; 1086)
Henry I **7** 286-287
William I **16** 290-291

Domesday Book (poems)
Masters, Edgar Lee **10** 326-327

Domestic Breviary (poems)
Brecht, Bertolt **2** 512-514

Domine Jesu Christe (motet)
Josquin des Prez **8** 361-363

Domine, quo vadis? (painting)
Carracci **3** 319-321

DOMINGO, PLACIDO (born 1941), Spanish-born lyric-dramatic tenor **5** 50-51

DOMINIC, ST. (circa 1170-1221), Spanish
Dominican founder **5** 51-52
Lacordaire, Jean Baptiste Henri **9** 148
Machiavelli, Niccolò **10** 97-99
see also Dominicans

Dominica (island, West Indies)
Columbus, Christopher **4** 176-179

Dominican Republic (nation; West Indies)
and France
Livingston, Robert R. **9** 462-463
Toussaint L'Ouverture, François
Dominique **15** 278-279
and Spain
Baez, Buenaventura **1** 432-433
Balboa, Vasco Núñez de **1** 462-463
Gómez, Máximo **6** 418-419
Santana, Pedro **13** 474-475
Toussaint L'Ouverture, François
Dominique **15** 278-279
dictatorship
Balaguer y Ricardo, Joaquin
1 460-461
Trujillo Molina, Rafael Leonidas
15 313-314
United States annexation plan
Baez, Buenaventura **1** 432-433
Fish, Hamilton **5** 461-462
Sumner, Charles **15** 30-31
United States intervention
Bosch, Juan **2** 428-429
Fulbright, James William **6** 147-149
Johnson, Lyndon Baines **8** 308-312
Roosevelt, Theodore **13** 280-283
Stroessner, Alfredo **14** 511-512
Vázquez, Horacio **15** 448-449
see also Haiti; Hispaniola

Dominican Sisters of Penitence (religious
congregation)
Catherine of Siena **3** 369-370

Dominican War of the Restoration
(1863-1865)
Baez, Buenaventura **1** 432-433

Dominicans (religious order)
art works
Masaccio **10** 312-313
Stoss, Veit **14** 481-482
criticized
Langland, William **9** 194-195
founded
Dominic **5** 51-52
Holy Alliance
Julius II **8** 384-386
Pius V **12** 332-333
reforms
Lacordaire, Jean Baptiste Henri
9 148
Savonarola, Girolamo **13** 505-506
theology
Albertus Magnus **1** 115-116
Campanella, Tommaso **3** 249
Eckhart, Johann **5** 200-201
Thomas Aquinas **15** 183-186

Vitoria, Francisco de **16** 1-2

DOMITIAN (Titus Flavius Domitianus Augustus; 51-96), Roman emperor 81-96 **5** 52-53
associates
Tacitus **15** 70-72
Trajan **15** 291-292
Christian persecutions
John, St. **8** 273-274
critics
Epictetus **5** 292
Zeno of Citium **16** 499-500
in literature
Juvenal **8** 397-399
Massinger, Philip **10** 324-325
patronage
Martialis, Marcus Valerius **10** 286-287
Quintilian **12** 518-519

Domitius Afer (flourished 1st century A.D.), Roman orator
Quintilian **12** 518-519

Domnei (book)
Cabell, James Branch **3** 195-196

Domontovich, Aleksandra M.
see Kollontai, Aleksandra Mikhailovna

Don Álvaro (play)
Saavedra, Angel de **13** 398

Don Carlo (opera)
Verdi, Giuseppe Fortunino Francesco **15** 463-465

Don Carlos (play)
Schiller, Johann Christoph Friedrich von **14** 4-7

Don Flows Home to the Sea, The (novel)
Sholokhov, Mikhail Aleksandrovich **14** 203-204

Don Garcia (literary character)
Alarcón, Pedro Antonio de **1** 100-101

Don Garcia (play)
Alfieri, Vittoria **1** 145-146

Don Gil de las calzas verdes (play)
Tirso de Molina **15** 237-238

Don Giovanni (opera; Mozart)
Chopin, Frédéric François **4** 16-18
Dallapiccola, Luigi **4** 377-378
Haydn, Franz Joseph **7** 219-221
Mozart, Wolfgang Amadeus **11** 218-221

Don Gutierre (literary character)
Calderón, Pedro **3** 221-222

Don Guzman d'Alfarache (novel)
Lesage, Alain René **9** 353-354

Don Juan (born 1913), pretender to Spanish throne
Alfonso XIII **1** 151
Franco Bahamonde, Francisco **6** 52-54

Don Juan (ballet)
Gluck, Christoph Willibald **6** 372-374

Don Juan (musical composition)
Strauss, Richard **14** 500-501

Don Juan (play)
Frisch, Max **6** 118-119

Don Juan (play; Molière)
see Dom Juan

Don Juan (poem; Byron)
Boone, Daniel **2** 397-398
Byron, George Gordon Noel **3** 193-194
Pushkin, Aleksandr Sergeevich **12** 489-491

Don Juan Carlos (born 1938), successor-designate to Spanish throne
Franco Bahamonde, Francisco **6** 52-54

Don Juan de Mendoza (literary character)
Alarcón, Pedro Antonio de **1** 100-101

Don Juan theme (literature)
Echeverría, José Estéban **5** 197-198
Molière **11** 86-88
Tirso de Molina **15** 237-238

Don Manuel (literary character)
Cabell, James Branch **3** 195-196

Don Mendo (literary character)
Alarcón, Pedro Antonio de **1** 100-101

Don Pasquale (opera)
Donizetti, Gaetano **5** 59-60

Don Procupio (opera)
Bizet, Georges **2** 296-297

Don Quixote (novel; Cervantes)
authorship
Cervantes, Miguel de Saavedra **3** 395-398-451
imitations
Wieland, Christoph Martin **16** 260-261
influence of
Beaumont, Francis **2** 95
Howells, William Dean **7** 539-541
Unamuno y Jugo, Miguel de **15** 386-387
musical adaptations
Falla, Manuel de **5** 372-373
Mendelssohn, Moses **10** 488-489
Strauss, Richard **14** 500-501
translations
Kazantzakis, Nikos **8** 466-468
Smollett, Tobias George **14** 305-307
Tieck, Ludwig **15** 218-219

Don Quixote and Sancho Panza (painting)
Daumier, Honoré Victorin **4** 403-405

Don Rodrigo (opera)
Ginastera, Alberto Evaristo **6** 328-329

Don Sebastian (play)
Dryden, John **5** 106-107

Don Segundo Sombra (novel)
Güiráldez, Ricardo **7** 38-39

Don Sylvio von Rosalva (novel)
Wieland, Christoph Martin **16** 260-261

Doña Bárbara (novel)
Gallegos Freire, Rómulo **6** 185-186

Doña Luz (novel)
Valera y Alcalá Galiano, Juan **15** 403

Doña Perfecta (novel)
Galdós, Benito Pérez **6** 177-178

Doña Rosita la soltera (play)
Lorca, Federico García **9** 511-513

Donald Duck (cartoon character)
Disney, Walter Elias **5** 26-27
Lichtenstein, Roy **9** 398-399

Donaldson, Henry Herbert (1857-1938), American neurologist
Watson, John Broadus **16** 138-139

DONATELLO (Donato di Niccolò Bardi; 1386-1466), Italian sculptor **5** 55-56
associates
Ghiberti, Lorenzo **6** 291-292
Masaccio **10** 312-313
Michelozzo **11** 6-7
influence of
Andrea del Castagno **1** 223-224
Bellini, Giovanni **2** 137-138
da Settignano, Desiderio **4** 509
Lippi, Filippo **9** 439
Mantegna, Andrea **10** 215-216
Manzù, Giacomo **10** 224-225
Rodin, Auguste **13** 236-238
Saint-Gaudens, Augustus **13** 432
Veneziano, Domenico **15** 459-460
Verrocchio, Andrea del **15** 471-472
patrons
Medici, Cosimo de' **10** 449-450

Donati, Corso (flourished 1285-1308), Italian politician
Cavalcanti, Guido **3** 382

Donation of Constantine (papal document)
Valla, Lorenzo **15** 406

Donation of Pepin (756)
Borgia, Cesare **2** 412-413

Donatism (Christian schism)
Constantine I **4** 209-211
Donatus **5** 56-57
Montanus **11** 122

DONATUS (died circa 355), schismatic bishop of Carthage **5** 56-57
Constantine I **4** 209-211
Lucretius **10** 26-27
Montanus **11** 122
Terence **15** 146-148

Donets Basin (region, Union of Soviet Socialist Republics)
Chmielnicki, Bogdan **4** 12-13
Mendeleev, Dmitrii Ivanovich **10** 486-488

Dong Minh Hoi (Vietnamese nationalism; China)
Ho Chi Minh **7** 426-428

DONG, PHAM VAN (born 1906), premier first of the Democratic Republic of Vietnam (DRV) and after 1976 of the Socialist Republic of Vietnam (SRV) **5** 57-59

Dongan, Thomas (Earl of Limerick; 1634-1715), colonial governor of New York
Leisler, Jacob **9** 313-314

DONIZETTI, GAETANA (1797-1848), Italian opera composer **5** 59-60
Cimarosa, Domenico **4** 61-62
Scott, Walter **14** 68-70

Donn-Byrne, Brian Oswald (1889-1928), American novelist
Bellows, George Wesley **2** 143

Donna me prega ... (canzone)
Cavalcanti, Guido **3** 382

Donné, Alfred (1801-1878), French bacteriologist
Foucault, Jean Bernard Léon **6** 28-29

DONNE, JOHN (1572-1631), English metaphysical poet **5** 60-61
biographers
Walton, Izaak **16** 90-91
influence of
Cowley, Abraham **4** 281-282
Crashaw, Richard **4** 296
Eliot, Thomas Stearns **5** 258-261
Frost, Robert Lee **6** 130-133
Herbert, George **7** 324-326
Lovelace, Richard **10** 7-8
Marvell, Andrew **10** 301-303
Pope, Alexander **12** 395-397
Suckling, John **15** 10-11
Vaughan, Henry **15** 444-445
students
Herbert, Edward **7** 324

Donne di Messina, Le (novel)
Vittorini, Elio **16** 2-3

DONNELLY, IGNATIUS (1831-1901), American politician and author **5** 62

DONNER, GEORG RAPHAEL (1693-1741), Austrian sculptor **5** 63
Günther, Ignaz **7** 41-42

Donner, Mathias (1704-1756), Austrian sculptor
Günther, Ignaz **7** 41-42

Donor and His Wife, A (painting)
Christus, Petrus **4** 33-34

DONOSO, JOSÉ (1924-1996), Chilean writer **5** 63-65

Don't Be Weary Traveler (musical composition)
Dett, Robert Nathaniel **4** 512

Don't Fence Me In (song)
Porter, Cole Albert **12** 405-406

Don't give up the ship (motto)
Perry, Oliver Hazard **12** 239

Dooley, Mr. Martin (literary character)
Dunne, Finley Peter **5** 147-148

Doolittle, Amos (1754-1832), American engraver
Earl, Ralph **5** 179

DOOLITTLE, HILDA (1886-1961), American poet and novelist **5** 65-66
Moore, Marianne **11** 148-149
Pound, Ezra Loomis **12** 415-417
Williams, William Carlos **16** 308-309

DOOLITTLE, JAMES HAROLD (1896-1993), American transcontinental pilot **5** 66-68
Nimitz, Chester William **11** 395-396

Doomer, Lambert (circa 1622/23-1700), Dutch painter
Rembrandt Harmensz van Rijn **13** 91-95

Doonesbury (comic strip)
Trudeau, Garretson Beekman **15** 308-309

Doornkop (village, South Africa)
Jameson, Leander Starr **8** 218

Doppia notte dei tigli, La (book)
Levi, Carlo **9** 364

Doppler effect (physics)
Fizeau, Hippolyte Armand Louis **5** 475
Hubble, Edwin Powell **8** 10-11
Huggins, William **8** 14-15

Dorados (Villa's cavalry)
Villa, Pancho **15** 495-496

Dorando (song)
Berlin, Irving **2** 200-201

Dorat, Jean (1508-1588), French poet
du Bellay, Joachim **5** 113-114
Ronsard, Pierre de **13** 271-273

Dorchester, 1st Baron
see Carleton, Guy

Dorchester Heights (Boston)
Knox, Henry **9** 64

Dori, La (opera)
Cesti, Pietro **3** 399-400

Dorian, Antoine Aimé (1818-1891), Canadian jurist
Brown, George **3** 35-36

Dorian Short Service (Anglican music)
Tallis, Thomas **15** 91

Dormeur du val, Le (poem)
Rimbaud, Jean Nicolas Arthur **13** 172-174

Dormition of the Virgin (altar piece)
Giotto **6** 342-345

Dormition of the Virgin (sculpture)
Arnolfo di Cambio **1** 315-316

Dorn, Heinrich (1804-1892), German composer
Schumann, Robert Alexander **14** 41-43

Dorotea, La (novel)
Lope Félix de Vega Carpio **9** 503-506-564

Dorothea (ship)
Franklin, John **6** 64-65

Dorpat Observatory (now Tartu, Estonia)
Fraunhofer, Joseph von **6** 75-76
Struve, Friedrich Georg Wilhelm von **14** 513

Dörpfeld, Wilhelm (1853-1940), German archeologist
Schliemann, Heinrich **14** 17-18

Dorset (county, England)
Alfred **1** 151-153

Dorsey, Basil (flourished 1836), American slave
Purvis, Robert **12** 485-486

Doryphoros (sculpture; Apollonios)
Polykleitos **12** 385-386

DOS PASSOS, RODERIGO (1896-1970), American novelist **5** 69-71
Bourne, Randolph Silliman **2** 456-457
Mailer, Norman Kingsley **10** 148-150
Sacco and Vanzetti **13** 408-410
Sandburg, Carl **13** 461-462
Stravinsky, Igor Fedorovich **14** 502-506

Dos Rios, Battle of (1895)
Martí, José **10** 285-286

DOS SANTOS, JOSÉ EDUARDO (born 1942), leader of the Popular Movement for the Liberation of Angola and president of Angola **5** 71-72

DOS SANTOS, MARCELINO (born 1929), Mozambican nationalist insurgent, statesman, and intellectual **5** 72-74

Dostoevsky (literary collection)
Gide, André **6** 308-309

DOSTOEVSKY, FYODOR (1821-1881), Russian novelist **5** 74-77
critics
Turgenev, Ivan Sergeyevich **15** 345-348
film versions
Kurosawa, Akira **9** 135-137
influence of
Beckett, Samuel **2** 102-104
Berdyaev, Nicholas Alexandrovich **2** 184-185
Buber, Martin **3** 87-89
Camus, Albert **3** 255-257
Fontane, Theodor **5** 504
Hamsun, Knut **7** 113-114
Wassermann, Jakob **16** 130-131
Wright, Richard **16** 401-402
influenced by
Belinsky, Grigorievich **2** 128
Stirner, Max **14** 459-460

Dotheboys Hall (literary locale)
Dickens, Charles John Huffam **4** 538-541

Dou, Gerard (1613-1675), Dutch painter
Rembrandt Harmensz van Rijn **13** 91-95

Douai (city, France)
Corot, Jean Baptiste Camille **4** 247-249

Double, The (novel)
Dostoevsky, Fyodor **5** 74-77

Double Axe ... (poems)
Jeffers, John Robinson **8** 236-237

Double Dealer, The (play; Congreve)
Congreve, William **4** 200-201
Purcell, Henry **12** 484-485

Double Helix, The (book; Watson)
Crick, Francis Harry Crompton **4** 310

Watson, James Dewey **16** 137-138

Double Infidelity (play)
Marivaux, Pierre Carlet de Chamblain
de **10** 265-266

Double Life (autobiography)
Benn, Gottfried **2** 164

Double Oval (sculpture)
Moore, Henry **11** 146-148

Double solution, theory of the (physics)
de Broglie, Louis **4** 442-444

Double star (astronomy)
Herschel, John Frederick William
7 340-341
Herschel, William **7** 341-343
Jeans, James Hopwood **8** 235-236

Doubleday, Frank (1862-1934), American
publisher
Dreiser, Herman Theodore **5** 98-100

Doubleday, Page and Co. (publishing)
Dreiser, Herman Theodore **5** 98-100
Page, Walter Hines **12** 60-61

Doubt (philosophy)
Augustine **1** 367-370
Descartes, René **4** 505-508

Doubtful Speech (books)
Pliny the Elder **12** 355-356

Doubting of Thomas (sculpture)
Verrocchio, Andrea del **15** 471-472

Doughboys (United States; World War I)
Pershing, John Joseph **12** 243-244

Doughty, Thomas (died circa 1578), English
explorer
Drake, Francis **5** 94-96

Douglas, 4th Earl of (Archibald Douglas;
1372-1424), Scottish noble
Henry IV **7** 292-293

Douglas, Lord Alfred Bruce (1870-1945),
English author and editor
Wilde, Oscar Fingall O'Flahertie Wills
16 272-273

Douglas, Archibald ("Bell-the-Cat"; circa
1450-circa 1514), Scottish statesman
Douglas, Gavin **5** 77-78

Douglas, Clifford Hugh (1879-1952), English engineer
Aberhart, William **1** 26-27

DOUGLAS, DONALD WILLS (1892-1981),
American aeronautical engineer **5** 77
Kármán, Theodore von **8** 451-452

DOUGLAS, GAVIN (circa 1475-1522),
Scottish poet, prelate, and courtier
5 77-78

DOUGLAS, SIR JAMES (1286?-1330), Scottish patriot **5** 80-82

Douglas, James (1675-1742), British scientist
Hunter, William **8** 48-49

Douglas, Sir John Sholto (8th Marquess of
Queensberry; 1844-1900), English boxing patron
Wilde, Oscar Fingall O'Flahertie Wills
16 272-273

DOUGLAS, MARY TEW (born 1921),
British anthropologist and social thinker
5 79-80

Douglas, Norman (1868-1952), English
writer
Ford, Ford Madox **6** 1-2

DOUGLAS, STEPHEN ARNOLD
(1813-1861), American politician
5 80-82
Kansas-Nebraska Act
see Kansas-Nebraska Act
opponents
Buchanan, James **3** 89-90
Davis, Jefferson **4** 416-418
Lamar, Lucius Quintus Cincinnatus
9 170-171
Lincoln, Abraham **9** 415-418
Schurz, Carl **14** 44-45
Sumner, Charles **15** 30-31
Trumbull, Lyman **15** 317-318
quoted
Blair, Francis Preston **2** 313-315
supporters
Cass, Lewis **3** 355-356
Letcher, John **9** 359-360
Van Buren, Martin **15** 410-411
Walker, Robert John **16** 67-68

Douglas, Thomas
see Selkirk, 5th Earl of

DOUGLAS, THOMAS CLEMENT
(1904-1986), Canadian clergyman and
politician, premier of Saskatchewan
(1944-1961), and member of Parliament
(1962-1979) **5** 82-83

Douglas, Sir William (died 1298), Scottish
patriot
Douglas, James **5** 78

DOUGLAS, WILLIAM ORVILLE
(1898-1980), American jurist **5** 83-85
Jackson, Robert Houghwout **8** 182-183
Kennedy, Robert Francis **8** 508-509

Douglas (play; Home)
Payne, John Howard **12** 159

Douglas Co. (aircraft firm)
Douglas, Donald Wills **5** 77

DOUGLASS, FREDERICK (circa
1817-1895), African American leader and
abolitionist **5** 85-86
associates
Anthony, Susan Brownell **1** 246-248
Bowditch, Henry Ingersoll
2 459-460
Delany, Martin Robinson **4** 473-474
Remond, Charles Lennox **13** 95
influenced by
Jay, William **8** 232-233
Walker, David **16** 62-63
painting of
Lawrence, Jacob **9** 250-251

Doumergue, Gaston (1863-1937), French
president 1924-1931
Herriot, Édouard **7** 339-340
Pétain, Henri Philippe **12** 250-252
Poincaré, Raymond **12** 366-368

DOVE, ARTHUR GARFIELD (1880-1946),
American painter **5** 86-87
Demuth, Charles **4** 497-498
Stella, Joseph **14** 422

DOVE, RITA FRANCES (born 1952), United
States poet laureate **5** 87-89

Dover, Treaty of (1670)
Shaftesbury, 1st Earl of **14** 135-136

Dover Beach (poem)
Arnold, Matthew **1** 311-313

"Doves" (United States politics)
see Vietnam war (1956-1976)—opponents (United States)

Dow, Arthur Wesley (flourished
1887-1916), American painter
O'Keeffe, Georgia **11** 487-489
Weber, Max **16** 160

DOW, NEAL (1804-1897), American temperance reformer **5** 89-90

Dow Chemical Co.
Calvin, Melvin **3** 242-243

Dowel (literary character)
Langland, William **9** 194-195

DOWLAND, JOHN (1562-1626), British
composer and lutenist **5** 90
Tallis, Thomas **15** 91

Down and Out in London and Paris (book)
Orwell, George **12** 14-15

Down in the Valley (opera)
Weill, Kurt **16** 174-175

Down Stream (novel)
Huysmans, Joris Karl **8** 81-82

Down There (novel)
Huysmans, Joris Karl **8** 81-82

Downes v. Bidwell (legal case)
White, Edward Douglass **16** 230-231

DOWNING, ANDREW JACKSON
(1815-1852), American horticulturist and
landscape architect **5** 90-91
Davis, Alexander Jackson **4** 411
Olmsted, Frederick Law **11** 503-504

Downward filter theory (missiology)
Duff, Alexander **5** 126-127

DOYLE, SIR ARTHUR CONAN
(1859-1930), British author **5** 91-92
Simenon, Georges **14** 233-234
Wyeth, Andrew Newell **16** 413-415

D'Oyly Carte
see Carte, Richard D'Oyly

Draco (constellation)
Huggins, William **8** 14-15

Dracula (book)
Stoker, Bram **14** 463-464

Draft (military)
Australia and New Zealand

Curtin, John Joseph **4** 348-349
Fisher, Andrew **5** 462
Fraser, Peter **6** 73-74
Hughes, William Morris **8** 21-22
Mannix, Daniel **10** 210
Canada
  Borden, Robert Laird **2** 409-411
  Bourassa, Joseph-Henri-Napoleon **2** 446-447
  King, William Lyon Mackenzie **9** 25-26
  Laurier, Wilfrid **9** 232-234
  Meighen, Arthur **10** 459-460
England
  Roberts, Frederick Sleigh **13** 195-196
Japan
  Yamagata, Aritomo **16** 428-429
Syria
  Ibrahim Pasha **8** 97-98
United States
  Brown, Joseph Emerson **3** 41-42
  Cleveland, Stephen Grover **4** 108-110
  Davis, Jefferson **4** 416-418
  Goldman, Emma **6** 406-407
  Hill, Benjamin Harvey **7** 386-387
  Holmes, Oliver Wendell Jr. **7** 458-459
  La Follette, Robert Marion **9** 155-156
  Marshall, George Catlett **10** 278-279
Union of Soviet Socialist Republics
  Frunze, Mikhail Vasilievich **6** 134

Draft resistance (military)
conscientious objectors
  Coffin, William Sloane Jr. **4** 135-137
  Dellinger, David **4** 480-481
  Lowell, Robert Trail Spence Jr. **10** 16-17
  Russell, Bertrand Arthur William **13** 373-374
  Tippett, Michael Kemp **15** 234-235
other resisters
  Baez, Joan **1** 433-435
  Browder, Earl Russell **3** 30-31
  Hitler, Adolf **7** 417-420
  Sacco and Vanzetti **13** 408-410
  Thoreau, Henry David **15** 203-205
  see also Draft riots (New York City; 1863)

Draft riots (New York City; 1863)
Gatling, Richard Jordan **6** 234-235
Hughes, John Joseph **8** 17-18
Seymour, Horatio **14** 126-127

Draftsmen
see Artists—draftsmen

Drageoir à épices, Le (novel)
Huysmans, Joris Karl **8** 81-82

DRAGO, LUIS MARÍA (1859-1921), Argentine international jurist and diplomat **5** 92-93

Drago Doctrine (Argentina)
Drago, Luis María **5** 92-93

Roca, Julio Argentino **13** 218

Dragon Seed (novel)
Buck, Pearl Sydenstricker **3** 91-93

Dragonfly (magazine)
Chekhov, Anton Pavlovich **3** 494-497

Dragon's Teeth (novel)
Sinclair, Upton Beale Jr. **14** 248-249

Dragontea, La (poem)
Lope Félix de Vega Carpio **9** 503-506

DRAKE, DANIEL (1785-1852), American physician **5** 93-94
Audubon, John James **1** 366-367

DRAKE, SIR FRANCIS (circa 1541-1596), English navigator **5** 94-96
Elizabeth I **5** 263-266
Frobisher, Martin **6** 121-122
Hakluyt, Richard **7** 70
Hawkins, John **7** 210-211
Lope Félix de Vega Carpio **9** 503-506
Mendaña de Neyra, Álvaro de **10** 483
Oñate, Juan de **11** 513-514
see also Armada, Spanish

Drake the Pirate (poem)
Lope Félix de Vega Carpio **9** 503-506

Drake's Bay (California)
Drake, Francis **5** 94-96

Drama (literature)
Caribbean
  Walcott, Derek Alton **16** 50-51
criticism
  Nathan, George Jean **11** 319-321
  Young, Stark **16** 474-475
psychological
  see Psychological drama
religious
  Calderón, Pedro **3** 221-222
  Lope Félix de Vega Carpio **9** 503-506
techniques
  Artaud, Antonin **1** 320-321
  Fletcher, John **5** 487
  Ibsen, Henrik **8** 98-100
  O'Neill, Eugene **11** 514-516
theory
  Artaud, Antonin **1** 320-321
tragedy
  Euripides **5** 332-334
  Grillparzer, Franz **6** 546-547
  Racine, Jean Baptiste **12** 532-535
  Sophocles **14** 343-345
  see also Authors—playwrights; Theater; Theater of the Absurd

Drama, The (painting)
Daumier, Honoré Victorin **4** 403-405

Dramatic Lyrics (poems)
Browning, Robert **3** 53-55

Dramatic Romances and Lyrics (poems)
Browning, Robert **3** 53-55

Dramatis Personae (book)
Browning, Robert **3** 53-55

Dramatists
see Authors—playwrights

Dramouss (novel)
Laye, Camara **9** 257-259

Drapeau de Carillon, Le (poem)
Crémazie, Octave **4** 305-306

Draper Catalogue (astronomy)
Pickering, Edward Charles **12** 298

DRAPER, JOHN WILLIAM (1811-1882), Anglo-American scientist and historian **5** 96-97

Drapier, M.B.
see Swift, Jonathan

Drapier's Letters (book)
Swift, Jonathan **15** 51-54

Draussen im Heidehof (novella)
Storm, Theodor **14** 479-480

Dravida Munnetra Kazagham (political party, India)
Kamaraj, Kumaraswami **8** 415

Drawbaugh, Daniel (1827-1911), American inventor
Bell, Alexander Graham **2** 129-131

Draymen and Teamsters' Union (United States)
Kearney, Denis **8** 468

DRAYTON, MICHAEL (1563-1631), English poet **5** 97-98
Webster, John **16** 164

Dream (painting)
Rousseau, Henri **13** 323-324

Dream as a Life, The (play)
Grillparzer, Franz **6** 546-547

Dream Children (essay)
Lamb, Charles **9** 176-177

Dream-Crowned (poems)
Rilke, Rainer Maria **13** 171-172

Dream Girl (play)
Rice, Elmer **13** 126-127

Dream in the Alameda, A (mural)
Rivera, Diego **13** 183-184

Dream King and His Love, The (cantata)
Parker, Horatio William **12** 109

Dream Life of Balso Snell, The (novel)
West, Nathanael **16** 213-214

Dream of Africa, A (novel)
Laye, Camara **9** 257-259

Dream of Constantine (mural)
Piero della Francesca **12** 301-302

Dream of Gerontius, The (musical composition)
Elgar, Edward **5** 247-248

Dream of John Ball, The (book)
Morris, William **11** 187-188

Dream of Love, A (play)
Williams, William Carlos **16** 308-309

Dream of Oblomov, The (story)
Goncharov, Ivan Aleksandrovich **6** 424**

Dream of the Doctor (engraving)
Dürer, Albrecht **5** 159-161

Dream of the Red Chamber (novel; Ts'ao Hsüeh-ch'in)
Hu Shih **8** 63-65
Yüan Mei **16** 479-480

Dream Play, A (play)
Strindberg, August **14** 509-511

Dreamer's Journey, A (autobiography)
Cohen, Morris Raphael **4** 139-140

Dreaming Boys, The (book)
Kokoschka, Oskar **9** 75-76

Dreams (book)
Quevedo Y Villegas, Francisco Gómez de **12** 511

Dreams (lithograph series)
Redon, Odilon **13** 75-76

Dreams (psychology)
Freud, Sigmund **6** 103-106
Jung, Carl Gustav **8** 388-389

Dreams of Chang, The (book)
Bunin, Ivan Alekseevich **3** 124

Dreams of Reason, The (book)
Dubos, René Jules **5** 119

Dreams of the Ghetto (book)
Zangwill, Israel **16** 488-489

Dreams That Money Can Buy (film)
Ray, Man **13** 59-60

Dreamtigers (literary sketches)
Borges, Jorge Luis **2** 411-412

Dreary Story, A (story)
Chekhov, Anton Pavlovich **3** 494-497

Dred (novel)
Stowe, Harriet Elizabeth Beecher **14** 484-485

Dred Scott decision (United States Supreme Court; 1857)
case and Court opinions
Curtis, Benjamin Robbins **4** 349
McLean, John **10** 422-423
Scott, Dred **14** 65-66
Taney, Roger Brooke **15** 98-99
critics
Benton, Thomas Hart **2** 178-179
Purvis, Robert **12** 485-486
Remond, Charles Lennox **13** 95
effects
Buchanan, James **3** 89-90
Lincoln, Abraham **9** 415-418

Drei, Ersilia (literary character)
Pirandello, Luigi **12** 319-321

Drei Kameraden (novel)
Remarque, Erich Maria **13** 91

Drei Volkstexte (musical composition)
Webern, Anton **16** 160-162

Dreigroschenoper, Die (musical play; Brecht-Weill)
Brecht, Bertolt **2** 512-514
Weill, Kurt **16** 174-175

Dreise, Johann (died 1716), German musician
Bach, Johann Sebastian **1** 416-419

Dreiser, Paul (1857-1911), American songwriter
Dreiser, Herman Theodore **5** 98-100

DREISER, (HERMAN) THEODORE (1871-1945), American novelist **5** 98-100
Anderson, Sherwood **1** 220-221
Farrell, James Thomas **5** 390-391
Lewis, Harry Sinclair **9** 385-387
Mencken, Henry Louis **10** 481-483
Norris, Benjamin Franklin Jr. **11** 427-428
Twain, Mark **15** 363-366
Woolman, John **16** 382-383
Wright, Richard **16** 401-402

Dreitr Frauen (stories)
Musil, Robert Edler Von **11** 268-269

Dresden (city, Germany)
Bakunin, Mikhail Aleksandrovich **1** 458-460
Courbet, Jean Desiré Gustave **4** 271-273
Tillich, Paul Johannes **15** 224-225

Dresden (ship)
Diesel, Rudolf **5** 7

Dresden, Battle of (1813)
Ney, Michel **11** 372-373

Dresden Boy (sculpture)
Polykleitos **12** 385-386

Dresden Central School (for dance; Germany)
Wigman, Mary **16** 267-268

Dressmaker's Studio (painting)
Vuillard, Jean Édouard **16** 36

DREW, CHARLES RICHARD (1904-1950), African American surgeon **5** 100-101

DREW, DANIEL (1797-1879), American stock manipulator **5** 101-102
Fisk, James **5** 464-465
Gould, Jay **6** 470-472
Vanderbilt, Cornelius **15** 415-416

Drew, Georgiana Emma (Mrs. Maurice Barrymore; 1856-1893), American actress
Barrymores **2** 28-30

Drew, John (1827-1862), Irish-born American actor
Barrymores **2** 28-30

Drew, Mrs. John
see Lane, Louisa

Drew, John, Jr. (1853-1927), American actor
Barrymores **2** 28-30

Drew, Robinson and Co. (financial firm)
Drew, Daniel **5** 101-102

Drew Theological Seminary (Madison, New Jersey)
Drew, Daniel **5** 101-102

Drew University (Madison, New Jersey)
Herberg, Will **7** 322-323

DREXEL, KATHERINE (1858-1955), founded a Catholic order, the Sisters of the Blessed Sacrament **5** 102-103

Drexel, Morgan and Co. (financial firm)
Cooke, Jay **4** 215-216

DREYFUS, ALFRED (1859-1935), French army officer **5** 103-105
see also Dreyfus Affair

Dreyfus Affair (trials; 1894, 1899, 1906)
anti-Dreyfusards
Barrès, Auguste Maurice **2** 20-21
Dreyfusards (literature)
Barbosa, Ruy **1** 503-504
France, Anatole **6** 39-40
Péguy, Charles Pierre **12** 183-184
Zola, Émile **16** 526-528
Dreyfusards (politics)
Clemenceau, Georges **4** 99-101
Daladier, Édouard **4** 369
Herriot, Édouard **7** 339-340
Jaurès, Jean **8** 226-227
influence of
Blum, Léon **2** 343-344
Proust, Marcel **12** 465-467
Rolland, Romain **13** 260
Sorel, Georges **14** 347-348

DRIESCH, HANS ADOLF EDUARD (1867-1941), German biologist and philosopher **5** 105
Maritain, Jacques **10** 263
Morgan, Thomas Hunt **11** 170-171
Spemann, Hans **14** 368-369

Drift indicator (instrument)
Byrd, Richard Evelyn **3** 186-187

Drink Tea ... (book)
Eisai **5** 231-232

Drive (psychology)
Hull, Clark Leonard **8** 28
see also Motivation

Drives toward War (book)
Tolman, Edward Chace **15** 261-262

Driving Mists (painting)
Wyant, Alexander Helwig **16** 409-410

Drogheda, Battle of (1649)
Cromwell, Oliver **4** 317-320

Drogo (died 1051), Count of Apulia
Guiscard, Robert **7** 39-40

Dropsy (medicine)
Bright, Richard **3** 7-8

Drosophila melanogaster (fruit fly)
Beadle, George Wells **2** 80-81
Morgan, Thomas Hunt **11** 170-171
Muller, Hermann Joseph **11** 238-239
Northrop, John Howard **11** 430-431

Drost, Willem (died 1678), Dutch painter
Rembrandt Harmensz van Rijn **13** 91-95

Drouet, Juliette (1806-1883), French actress and courtesan
Hugo, Victor Marie **8** 22-25

Drover's Cottage (Abilene, Kansas)
McCoy, Joseph Geiting **10** 403-404

Drover's Wife (painting)
Drysdale, George Russell **5** 107-109

Drowning victims
Gilbert, William Schwenck **6** 314-315
Holbrook, Josiah **7** 450-451
Menander **10** 477-478
Minuit, Peter **11** 50
Shelley, Percy Bysshe **14** 176-178
Straus, Isidor **14** 496
Woolf, Virginia Stephen **16** 381-382

Droysen, Johann Gustav (1808-1864), German historian
Burckhardt, Jacob Christoph **3** 132-133

Drug culture (United States)
opponents
Rangel, Charles B. **13** 31-32
proponents
Leary, Timothy **9** 266-267

Drumlin Woodchuck, The (poem)
Frost, Robert Lee **6** 130-133

Drummer Boy, The (novella)
Ekwensi, Cyprian **5** 242-243

Drummond, James Eric
see Perth, 16th Earl of

Drummond of Hawthornden, William
(1585-1649), Scottish poet
Jonson, Ben **8** 343-345

Drumont, Édouard (1844-1917), French journalist
Maurras, Charles Marie Photius **10** 350-351

Drums in the Night (play)
Brecht, Bertolt **2** 512-514

Drum-Taps (poems)
Whitman, Walt **16** 249-251

Drunkard's Looking Glass, The (moral tale)
Weems, Mason Locke **16** 170

Drunkards, The (painting)
Velázquez, Diego Rodríguez de Silva y **15** 454-456

Drunken Angel (film)
Kurosawa, Akira **9** 135-137

Drury Lane Theatre (London)
Arne, Thomas Augustine **1** 307-308
Heinrich, Anthony Philip **7** 261
Sheridan, Richard Brinsley **14** 183-184

DRUSUS, MARCUS LIVIUS (circa 124-91 B.C.), Roman statesman **5** 105-106
Brutus, Marcus Junius **3** 79-80
Cato, the Younger **3** 374-375
Gracchus, Tiberius and Gaius Sempronius **6** 479-480

Drusus Senior (Nero Claudius Drusus Germanicus; 38-9 B.C.), Roman general
Claudius Germanicus, Tiberius **4** 91-92

Dry Bones, Valley of (Old Testament)
Ezekiel **5** 355-356

Dry Salvages, The (poem)
Eliot, Thomas Stearns **5** 258-261

DRYDEN, JOHN (1631-1700), English poet, critic, and dramatist **5** 106-107
associates
Buckingham, 2d Duke of **3** 94-95
Marvell, Andrew **10** 301-303
Pepys, Samuel **12** 207-208
biographers
Scott, Walter **14** 68-70
influence of
Congreve, William **4** 200-201
Eliot, Thomas Stearns **5** 258-261
Johnson, Samuel **8** 315-317
Pope, Alexander **12** 395-397
influenced by
Juvenal **8** 397-399
Milton, John **11** 43-46
Ovid **12** 34-36
Plutarch **12** 359-360
musical settings
Handel, George Frederick **7** 116-119

Dry-goods business (United States)
Field, Marshall **5** 440-441
Stewart, Alexander Turney **14** 448-449
see also Chain store; Department store

Dry-plate techniques (photographt)
Eastman, George **5** 186

DRYSDALE, SIR GEORGE RUSSELL
(1912-1981), Australian painter **5** 107-109
Dobell, William **5** 34-35
Nolan, Sidney Robert **11** 418

Du bonheur (poem)
Helvétius, Claude Adrien **7** 273-274

Du contrat social (treatise)
Rousseau, Jean Jacques **13** 324-328

Du Côté de chez Swann (novel)
Proust, Marcel **12** 465-467

Du Sang, du volupté et de la mort (novel)
Barrès, Auguste Maurice **2** 20-21

Du Système industriel (periodical)
Saint-Simon, Comte de **13** 436-437

Du und Du (waltz)
Strauss, Johann Jr. **14** 498-499

Dua al-Karawan (novella)
Husayn, Taha **8** 61-62

Dual Alliance (Austro-German; 1879)
Andrássy, Julius **1** 222-223
Francis Joseph **6** 45-46

Dual Mandate in British Tropical Africa, The (book)
Lugard, Frederick John Dealtry **10** 31-32

Dual Monarchy
see Austria-Hungary

Dualism
literary technique
Mann, Thomas **10** 204-207
philosophy

Cudworth, Ralph **4** 331
Descartes, René **4** 505-508
Epicurus **5** 292-294
Malebranche, Nicolas **10** 166-167
Pythagoras **12** 498-499
Ryle, Gilbert **13** 393-394
psychology
Sherrington, Charles Scott **14** 187-189
religion
Boehme, Jacob **2** 357
Mani **10** 196-197
Zoroaster **16** 528-530

Duan, Le (1908-1986), North Vietnamese politician
Giap, Vo Nguyen **6** 297-299

DUANE, WILLIAM (1760-1835), American journalist **5** 109

Duane, William John (1780-1865), American lawyer
Duane, William **5** 109

Duarte (1391-1438), King of Portugal
Henry the Navigator **7** 305-306

DUARTE, JOSÉ NAPOLEÓN (1926-1990), civilian reformer elected president of El Salvador in 1984 **5** 109-111

Du Barry, Comtesse (Marie Jeanne Bécu; 1746-1793), adventuress and mistress of Louis XV
Fragonard, Jean Honoré **6** 38-39
Ledoux, Claude Nicolas **9** 277-278
Louis XV **9** 533-534

Du Bartas, Guillaume de Salluste
(1544-1590), French Huguenot poet
Bradstreet, Anne Dudley **2** 486-487

DUBČEK, ALEXANDER (1921-1992), Czechoslovak politician **5** 112-113

DUBE, JOHN LANGALIBALELE
(1870-1949), South African writer and Zulu propagandist **5** 113

Du Bellay, Jean (1492-1560), French cardinal, humanist, and diplomat
du Bellay, Joachim **5** 113-114
Rabelais, François **12** 524-526
l'Orme, Philibert de **9** 519

DU BELLAY, JOACHIM (circa 1522-1560), French poet **5** 113-114
Castiglione, Baldassare **3** 360-361
Ronsard, Pierre de **13** 271-273
Sainte-Beuve, Charles Augustin **13** 438
Spenser, Edmund **14** 373-376

DUBINSKY, DAVID (1892-1982), American trade union official **5** 114-115
Hillman, Sidney **7** 392-393
Murray, Philip **11** 264-265

Dubinushka (tone poem)
Rimsky-Korsakov, Nikolai Andreevich **13** 174-175

Dublin (city; Ireland)
Collins, Michael **4** 167-168
see also Abbey Theatre

Dublin (ship)
Rodney, George Brydges **13** 239-240

Dublin Hermetic Society (established 1885)
Yeats, William Butler **16** 445-447

Dublin school (physics)
Schrödinger, Erwin **14** 31-33

Dubliners (stories)
Joyce, James **8** 365-367

DUBNOV, SIMON (1860-1941), Jewish historian, journalist, and political activist **5** 115-116

Du Bois, Guy Pène (1884-1958), American painter
Calder, Alexander **3** 216-218

Dubois, Jacques
see Sylvius, Jacobus

DU BOIS, WILLIAM EDWARD BURGHARDT (1868-1963), African American educator, pan-Africanist, and protest leader **5** 116-118
associates
Cullen, Countee **4** 333-334
Hope, John **7** 489-490
Hughes, Langston **8** 18-19
influence of
Cleaver, Leroy Eldridge **4** 97-98
Herskovits, Melville Jean **7** 345
Plaatje, Solomon Tshekisho **12** 341-342
influenced by
Washington, Booker Taliaferro **16** 125-126
Pan-Africanism
Diagne, Blaise **4** 527
Hayford, J. E. Casely **7** 228-230
Padmore, George **12** 57-58
Williams, Henry Sylvester **16** 303-304

Du Bois, Yolande (Mrs. Countee Cullen; died 1961) African American matron, daughter of W.E.B. Dubois
Cullen, Countee **4** 333-334

DU BOIS-REYMOND, EMIL (1818-1896), German physiologist **5** 118-119
Erlanger, Joseph **5** 310-311
Helmholtz, Hermann Ludwig Ferdinand von **7** 268-269

DUBOS, RENÉ JULES (1901-1982), French-born American microbiologist **5** 119

Dubourg, L. William (1766-1833), French-American priest and educator
Seton, Elizabeth Ann Bayley **14** 118-119

Dubroeucq, Jacques (circa 1500/10-1584), Flemish artist
Giovanni da Bologna **6** 345-346

DUBUFFET, JEAN PHILLIPE ARTHUR (born 1901), French painter **5** 119-120

Ducal Palace (Venice)
see Venice

DUCCIO DI BUONINSEGNA (1255/60-1318/19), Italian painter **5** 121-122
Giotto **6** 342-345
Lorenzetti, Pietro and Ambrogio **9** 517-518
Martini, Simone **10** 298-299

Duce, Il
see Mussolini, Benito

Duchamp, Gaston
see Villon, Jacques

DUCHAMP, MARCEL (1887-1968), French painter **5** 122-123
Cage, John **3** 211-214
Calder, Alexander **3** 216-218
Duchamp-Villon, Raymond **5** 123
Johns, Jasper **8** 291-293
Ray, Man **13** 59-60

DUCHAMP-VILLON, RAYMOND (1876-1918), French sculptor **5** 123
Duchamp, Marcel **5** 122-123

Duchesne, Louis (1843-1922), French church historian
Loisy, Alfred Firmin **9** 489-490

Duchess Eleanora (painting)
Titian **15** 242-244

Duchess of Malfi, The (play)
Webster, John **16** 164

Duchesse de Bourgogne as Diana (painting)
Coysevox, Antoine **4** 287-288

Duck Soup (film)
Marx brothers **10** 303-304

Dudevant, Amandine Aurore Lucie Dupin
see Sand, George

Dudevant, Maurice
see Sand, Maurice

Dudley, Anne
see Bradstreet, Anne Dudley

DUDLEY, BARBARA (born 1947), American director of Greenpeace **5** 123-124

Dudley, John
see Northumberland, Duke of

Dudley, Joseph (1647-1720), American colonial governor
Wise, John **16** 343-344

Dudley, Robert
see Leicester, 1st Earl of

DUDLEY, THOMAS (1576-1653), American colonial governor and Puritan leader **5** 124-125
Bradstreet, Anne Dudley **2** 486-487
Gorges, Ferdinando **6** 455-456
Winthrop, John **16** 339-341

Due Foscari, I (opera)
Verdi, Giuseppe Fortunino Francesco **15** 463-465

Due process of law
see Constitution of the United States-14th Amendment

Duel (combat)
Burr, Aaron **3** 156-159
Canning, George **3** 258-260
Hamilton, Alexander **7** 95-98
Lassalle, Ferdinand **9** 216
Lermontov, Mikhail Yurievich **9** 352-353
Pushkin, Aleksandr Sergeevich **12** 489-491

Duel, The (story)
Chekhov, Anton Pavlovich **3** 494-497

Duelo que fizo la Virgen, El (poem)
Gonzalo de Berceo **6** 431-432

Duenna, The (opera)
Sheridan, Richard Brinsley **14** 183-184

Duet, A (novel)
Doyle, Arthur Conan **5** 91-92

DUFAY, GUILLAUME (circa 1400-1474), Netherlandish composer **5** 125-126
Dunstable, John **5** 150-151
Josquin des Prez **8** 361-363
Obrecht, Jacob **11** 457-458

DUFF, ALEXANDER (1806-1878), Scottish Presbyterian missionary **5** 126-127

Dufy, Raoul (1877-1953), French painter and decorator
Braque, Georges **2** 504-505
Matisse, Henri **10** 336-337
Rivera, Diego **13** 183-184

DUGAN, ALAN (born 1923), American poet **5** 127-128

DUGDALE, RICHARD LOUIS (1841-1883), English-born American sociologist **5** 128-129

Dughet, Gaspard (1613-1675), French-born Italian painter
Cole, Thomas **4** 151-152
Inness, George **8** 123-124
Wilson, Richard **16** 329-330

DUHEM, PIERRE MAURICE MARIE (1861-1916), French physicist, chemist, and historian of science **5** 129

Duhka (Buddhism)
Buddha **3** 97-101

Duineser Elegien (poems)
Rilke, Rainer Maria **13** 171-172

DUKAKIS, MICHAEL (born 1933), American governor of Massachusetts **5** 130-133

Dukas, Paul (1865-1935), French composer
Piston, Walter **12** 327-328

DUKE, JAMES BUCHANAN (1856-1925), American industrialist and philanthropist **5** 133-134
du Pont, Pierre Samuel **5** 154-155

Duke Francesco Maria I della Rovere (painting)
Titian **15** 242-244

Duke University (Durham, North Carolina)
Duke, James Buchanan **5** 133-134

Dukenfield, William Claude
see Fields, W.C.

Duke's Children, The (novel)
Trollope, Anthony **15** 300-302

Duke's Theatre (England)
Dryden, John **5** 106-107

Dulcamara (play)
Gilbert, William Schwenck **6** 314-315

Dulce boca que a gustar convida, La (sonnet)
Góngora y Argote, Luis de **6** 427-428

Dulcy (play)
Kaufman, George S. **8** 457-458

DULL KNIFE (born Morning Star; c. 1810-1883), Northern Cheyenne tribal leader **5** 135-136

Dullaert, Heyman (1636-1684), French painter
Rembrandt Harmensz van Rijn **13** 91-95

Dulle Griet (painting)
Bruegel, Pieter the Elder **3** 65-67

DULLES, JOHN FOSTER (1888-1959), American statesman and diplomat **5** 134-135
Dewey, Thomas Edmund **4** 524
Eisenhower, Dwight David **5** 233-236
Lehman, Herbert Henry **9** 306-307

Dulles International Airport (Chantilly, Virginia)
Saarinen, Eliel and Eero **13** 396-398

Dulness (poem)
Pope, Alexander **12** 395-397

Dulwich College Picture Gallery (London)
Soane, John **14** 314-315

Duma (Russian legislature)
Miliukov, Pavel Nikolayevich **11** 18-19

DUMAS, ALEXANDRE (1803-1870), French playwright and novelist **5** 136-138
Hugo, Victor Marie **8** 22-25
Liszt, Franz **9** 445-447
Verne, Jules **15** 467-469

Dumas, Alexandre (Dumas fils; 1824-1895), French playwright and novelist
Carpeaux, Jean Baptiste **3** 318-319
Daudet, Alphonse **4** 402-403
Dumas, Alexandre **5** 136-138

DUMAS, JEAN BAPTISTE ANDRÉ (1800-1884), French Chemist **5** 138-139
Couper, Archibald Scott **4** 269-270
Hofmann, August Wilhelm von **7** 441-442
Kekulé, Friedrich August **8** 477-478

Dumb Waiter, The (play)
Pinter, Harold **12** 317-318

Dumbarton Oaks (Washington D.C.)
Johnson, Philip **8** 313-314

"Dumbarton Oaks" concerto (musical composition)
Stravinsky, Igor Fedorovich **14** 502-506

Dumbarton Oaks Conference (1944)
Bunche, Ralph Johnson **3** 121-122
Stettinius, Edward R. Jr. **14** 437-438

Dumfries House (Scotland)
Adam, Robert and James **1** 38-40
Chippendale, Thomas **4** 1-2
Duns Scotus, John **5** 149-150

Dumont, Pierre Étienne Louis (1759-1829), Swiss author, editor, and publicist
Bentham, Jeremy **2** 176-178

Dumouriez, Charles François (1739-1823), French general
Louis Philippe **9** 536-537

Dun and Bradstreet (financial firm)
Tappan brothers **15** 105-106

DUNANT, JEAN HENRI (1828-1910), Swiss philanthropist **5** 139-141

DUNBAR, PAUL LAURENCE (1872-1906), African American poet and novelist **5** 141-142

DUNBAR, WILLIAM (circa 1460-circa 1520), Scottish poet and courtier **5** 142-143
Lyndsay, David **10** 66-67

DUNBAR, WILLIAM (1749-1810), Scottish-born American scientist and planter **5** 143-144

Dunbar, Battle of (1650)
Cromwell, Oliver **4** 317-320

Duncan I (died 1040), King of Scotland 1034-1040
Macbeth **10** 81
Malcolm III **10** 164-165

DUNCAN, ISADORA (1878-1927), American dancer **5** 144-145
Esenin, Sergei Aleksandrovich **5** 321
Graham, Martha **6** 485-486
St. Denis, Ruth **13** 430-431

Duncan Gray (song)
Burns, Robert **3** 155-156

Dunciad (poem; Pope)
Bolingbroke, Viscount **2** 374-375
Pope, Alexander **12** 395-397

Dundas, Henry
see Melville, 1st Viscount

Dunes, Battle of the (1658)
Condé, Prince de **4** 193-194
Cromwell, Oliver **4** 317-320

DUNHAM, KATHERINE (born 1910), African American dancer, choreographer, and anthropologist **5** 145-146

Dunkirk (Dunkerque; city, France)
Clarendon, 1st Earl of **4** 73-75

Dunkirk, Battles of
1658
see Dunes, Battle of the
1940
Alexander of Tunis, 1st Earl **1** 135-136
Churchill, Winston Leonard Spencer **4** 51-53
Kesselring, Albert Field Marshal **8** 522-523
Montgomery, Bernard Law **11** 135-136

Dunlap, William (1766-1839), American painter, playwright, and historian
Brown, Charles Brockden **3** 33
Cole, Thomas **4** 151-152

DUNMORE, 4TH EARL OF (John Murray; 1732-1809), British colonial governor **5** 147
Dinwiddie, Robert **5** 18-19
Henry, Patrick **7** 309-311
Lewis, Andrew **9** 376-377

DUNNE, FINLEY PETER (1867-1936), American journalist **5** 147-148

DUNNING, WILLIAM ARCHIBALD (1857-1922), American historian **5** 148-149
Bentley, Arthur F. **2** 178
Merriam, Charles Edward **10** 518-519

Dunois, Comte de (1403?-1468), French general
Joan of Arc **8** 264-265

Duns, Elias (flourished 13th century), Scottish Franciscan
Duns Scotus, John **5** 149-150

DUNS SCOTUS, JOHN (1265/66-1308), Scottish philosopher and theologian **5** 149-150
Bonaventure **2** 383-384
Hopkins, Gerard Manley **7** 492-494
ibn Gabirol, Solomon ben Judah **8** 92
Maimonides **10** 151-152
Suárez, Francisco **15** 8
William of Ockham **16** 298-299

Dunsink, Observatory of (Ireland)
Hamilton, William Rowan **7** 99-100

DUNSTABLE, JOHN (circa 1390-1453), English composer **5** 150-151
Dufay, Guillaume **5** 125-126

DUNSTAN, ST. (circa 909-988), English monk and archbishop **5** 151-152

DUNSTER, HENRY (circa 1609-1659), English-born American clergyman **5** 152-153

Duo (novel)
Colette, Sidonie Gabrielle **4** 158-159

Duo for Flute and Oboe (musical composition)
Ginastera, Alberto Evaristo **6** 328-329

Duo for Violin and Cello (musical composition)
Ravel, Maurice Joseph **13** 54-55

Duong Van Minh (born 1916), Vietnamese general and politician
Thieu, Nguyen Van **15** 182-183

Duparc, Henri (1848-1933), French composer
Franck, César **6** 48-49

Du Perron, Jacques Davy (1556-1618), French cardinal
Malherbe, François de **10** 169-170

Dupin, Armandine Aurore Lucille
see Sand, George

Duple meter (music)
Machaut, Guillaume de **10** 93-94

DUPLEIX, MARQUIS (Joseph François; 1697-1763), French colonial administrator **5** 153
   Clive, Robert **4** 119-120

DU PONT, ÉLEUTHÈRE IRÉNÉE (1771-1834), French-born American manufacturer **5** 154

DU PONT, PIERRE SAMUEL (1870-1954), American industrialist **5** 154-155
   Carothers, Wallace Hume **3** 317-318
   Durant, William Crapo **5** 158
   Sloan, Alfred Pritchard Jr. **14** 274

Du Pont, Victor (1767-1827), French-born American industrialist
   du Pont, Éleuthère Irénée **5** 154

DU PONT DE NEMOURS, PIERRE SAMUEL (1739-1817), French political economist **5** 155-156
   du Pont, Éleuthère Irénée **5** 154

Du Pont de Nemours, E.I., and Co. (industrial firm)
   Conant, James Bryant **4** 192-193
   du Pont, Éleuthère Irénée **5** 154
   Grasselli, Caesar Augustin **6** 497-498
   Sloan, Alfred Pritchard Jr. **14** 274

Dupuy, Charles (1851-1923), French educator and statesman
   Poincaré, Raymond **12** 366-368

Dura-Europos (ancient town, Syria)
   Rostovtzeff, Michael Ivanovich **13** 315

Duralumin (metal)
   Tupolev, Andrei Nikolaevich **15** 341-342

Duran, Carolus (1837-1917), French painter
   Robinson, Theodore **13** 217
   Sargent, John Singer **13** 481-482
   Van de Velde, Henry **15** 419-420

DURAND, ASHER BROWN (1796-1886), American painter and engraver **5** 156-157
   Church, Frederick Edwin **4** 49-50
   Cole, Thomas **4** 151-152

Durand, Charles Auguste Émile
   see Duran, Carolus

Durand de Saint-Pourçain, Guillaume (died 1332), French scholastic and Dominican monk
   Marsilius of Padua **10** 284

Durand-Ruel, Paul (1831-1922), French art dealer
   Monet, Claude **11** 102-104
   Renoir, Pierre Auguste **13** 101-102

Durango (state, Mexico)
   Lamy, Jean Baptiste **9** 181-182

DURANT, THOMAS CLARK (1820-1885), American railroad executive **5** 157-158

DURANT, WILLIAM CRAPO (1861-1947), American industrialist **5** 158
   Chrysler, Walter Percy **4** 36-37
   du Pont, Pierre Samuel **5** 154-155
   Sloan, Alfred Pritchard Jr. **14** 274

Durant Motors (car industry)
   Durant, William Crapo **5** 158

Durant-Dort Co. (carriage firm)
   Durant, William Crapo **5** 158

Durante, Francesco (1684-1755), Italian composer
   Pergolesi, Giovanni Battista **12** 218-219

Duration (philosophy)
   Bergson, Henri **2** 191-192

Durazzo (prefecture, Albania)
   Bohemund, I **2** 364

Durazzo, Battle of (1081)
   Guiscard, Robert **7** 39-40

Durban (city, South Africa)
   Luthuli, Albert John **10** 51-52

DÜRER, ALBRECHT (1471-1528), German painter and graphic artist **5** 159-161
   compared to
      Grünewald, Matthias **7** 23-24
      Hogarth, William **7** 446-447
      Klee, Paul **9** 47-49
      Schongauer, Martin **14** 26-28
   influence of
      Altdorfer, Albrecht **1** 179-180
      Andrea del Sarto **1** 224-225
      Correggio **4** 249-251
      Cranach, Lucas the Elder **4** 289-290
      Hodler, Ferdinand **7** 434-435
      Kirchner, Ernst Ludwig **9** 34-35
      Lotto, Lorenzo **9** 520-521
      Lucas van Leyden **10** 20-21
      Pontormo **12** 394-395
   works
      Brant, Sebastian **2** 503-504
      Gesner, Konrad von **6** 287

Duret, Francisque Joseph (1804-1865), French sculptor
   Carpeaux, Jean Baptiste **3** 318-319

Durey, Louis (1888-1979), French composer
   Honegger, Arthur **7** 472-473

Durga (mother-goddess)
   Chatterji, Bankimchandra **3** 480-481

Durgeshnandini (novel)
   Chatterji, Bankimchandra **3** 480-481

DURHAM, 1ST EARL OF (John George Lambton; 1792-1840), English statesman **5** 161-162
   Baldwin, Robert **1** 466-468
   Sydenham, Thomas **15** 59-60
   Wakefield, Edward Gibbon **16** 48-49

Durham (county, England)
   Butler, Joseph **3** 180-181

Durham Report (Canada)
   Sydenham, Thomas **15** 59-60

Durham Station (city, North Carolina)
   Sherman, William Tecumseh **14** 186-187

DURKHEIM, ÉMILE (1858-1917), French philosopher and sociologist **5** 162-163
   Gökalp, Mehmet Ziya **6** 395-396

   Lévy-Bruhl, Lucien **9** 374-375
   Mathiez, Albert **10** 333-334
   Mauss, Marcel **10** 352-353
   Parsons, Talcott **12** 122
   Tarde, Jean Gabriel **15** 108-109

DURRELL, LAWRENCE (1912-1990), British author of novels, poetry, plays, short stories, and travel books **5** 163-164
   Miller, Henry **11** 26-27

DÜRRENMATT, FRIEDRICH (1921-1990), Swiss playwright **5** 164-165
   Frisch, Max **6** 118-119

Durrës
   see Durazzo (prefecture, Albania)

Durrie, George Henry (1820-1863), American painter
   Currier and Ives **4** 345-346

Durrow, monastery of (Ireland)
   Columba **4** 175-176

Duse, Eleonora (1859-1924), Italian actress
   D'Annunzio, Gabriele **4** 388

Düsseldorf Art Academy
   Beuys, Joseph **2** 246-248
   Klee, Paul **9** 47-49

Düsseldorf school (art)
   Krieghoff, Cornelius **9** 101

Dust Panned Out in California (book)
   Bierce, Ambrose Gwinett **2** 269-270

Dutch art and architecture
   architecture
      Oud, Jacobus Johannes Pieter **12** 32
      Rietveld, Gerrit Thomas **13** 169
   baroque
      see Baroque painting
   de Stijl
      see De Stijl
   expressionism (forerunners)
      Van Gogh, Vincent **15** 427-429
   genre and portrait painting
      Bouts, Dirk **2** 458-459
      Hals, Frans **7** 89-91
      Hooch, Pieter de **7** 473-474
      Rembrandt Harmensz van Rijn **13** 91-95, 140, 141
      Ter Borch, Gerard **15** 146
      van Dongen, Kees **15** 421-422
      Vermeer, Jan **15** 466-467
   graphic arts
      Lucas van Leyden **10** 20-21
   influence of
      Chardin, Jean Baptiste Siméon **3** 442-443
      Daubigny, Charles François **4** 402
      Durand, Asher Brown **5** 156-157
      Rousseau, Théodore **13** 328
   landscapes
      Bouts, Dirk **2** 458-459
      Cuyp, Aelbert **4** 360-361
      Goyen, Jan van **6** 478-479
      Rembrandt Harmensz van Rijn **13** 91-95
      Ruisdael, Jacob van **13** 357-358
   neoplasticism

Mondrian, Piet **11** 101-102
sculpture
    Sluter, Claus **14** 275-276
    see also Flemish art; Netherlandish
    art

Dutch East India Co.
    see East India Co. (Dutch)

Dutch East Indies
    see Indonesia—Dutch East Indies

Dutch Graves (poem)
    Stevens, Wallace **14** 443-445

Dutch Interiors (art series)
    Miró, Joan **11** 53-54

Dutch literature
    Vondel, Joost van den **16** 19-20

Dutch music
    baroque
        see Baroque music
    Renaissance
        Dufay, Guillaume **5** 125-126
        Obrecht, Jacob **11** 457-458
        Ockeghem, Johannes **11** 464-465

Dutch Psalter (Psalms)
    Hopkinson, Francis **7** 496-497

Dutch Reformed Church (religion)
    Arminius, Jacobus **1** 301-302
    Frelinghuysen, Theodorus Jacobus
    6 96-97
    Leisler, Jacob **9** 313-314
    Malan, Daniel Francois **10** 163-164
    Otterbein, Philip William **12** 27-28

Dutch Wars
    First (1652-1654)
        Monck, George **11** 96-97
        Rembrandt Harmensz van Rijn
        13 91-95
        Witt, Johan de **16** 348-349
    Second (1665-1667)
        Charles II **3** 452-454
        Clarendon, 1st Earl of **4** 73-75
        Monck, George **11** 96-97
        Pepys, Samuel **12** 207-208
        Philip II **12** 271-273
        Underhill, John **15** 388
        Witt, Johan de **16** 348-349
    Third (1672-1674)
        Dampier, William **4** 384
        Louis XIV **9** 531-533
        Shaftesbury, 1st Earl of **14** 135-136
        Witt, Johan de **16** 348-349

Dutchman (play)
    Baraka, Imamu Amiri **1** 498-499

Dutilleux, Constant (1807-1865), French
painter and lithographer
    Corot, Jean Baptiste Camille **4** 247-249

Dutra, Eurico (1885-1974), Brazilian
statesman
    Aranha, Osvaldo **1** 272-273

Duty (philosophy)
    Fichte, Johann Gottlieb **5** 435-436
    Halévy, Élie **7** 76

Duval Ranch (Texas)
    Love, Nat **10** 1-2

DUVALIER, FRANÇOIS (Papa Doc;
1907-1971), Haitian president
1957-1971 **5** 165-166

DUVALIER, JEAN CLAUDE (Baby Doc;
born 1949), president of Haiti
(1971-1986) **5** 166-168
    Duvalier, François **5** 165-166

Duveneck, Frank (1848-1919), American
painter, sculptor, and etcher
    Chase, William Merritt **3** 476-477
    Twachtman, John Henry **15** 362-363

Duvergier de Hauranne, Jean (1581-1643),
French theologian
    Jansen, Cornelis **8** 220-221

Dvir (publishing house)
    Bialik, Hayyim Nahman **2** 262-263

DVOŘÁK, ANTONIN (1841-1904), Czech
composer **5** 168-169
    Franck, César **6** 48-49
    Parker, Horatio William **12** 109

DVR
    see Vietnam, North

Dwarfs, The (novel and play)
    Pinter, Harold **12** 317-318

Dwelling-Place of Light, The (novel)
    Churchill, Winston **4** 50-51

DWIGHT, TIMOTHY (1752-1817), American educator and Congregational minister **5** 169
    Beecher, Lyman **2** 113
    Webster, Noah **16** 164-166

Dybbuk and the Golem, The (story)
    Singer, Isaac Bashevis **14** 249-250

Dyck, Abraham van (1635-1672), Dutch
painter
    Rembrandt Harmensz van Rijn
    13 91-95

Dyck, Anthony van
    see Van Dyck, Anthony

Dye (color matter)
    Baeyer, Johann Friedrich Adolf von
    1 432
    Carver, George Washington **3** 346-347

Dyer, Edward (died 1607), English courtier
and poet
    Sidney, Philip **14** 214-215

Dyer Antilynching Bill (United States)
    Johnson, James Weldon **8** 304-305

Dying (novella)
    Schnitzler, Arthur **14** 23-24

Dying Centaur (sculpture)
    Rimmer, William **13** 174

Dying Poet, The (musical composition)
    Gottschalk, Louis Moreau **6** 463-464

Dying Slave (sculpture; Michelangelo)
    Rodin, Auguste **13** 236-238

Dyje
    see Mühlfrauen (Bohemia)

DYLAN, BOB (born Robert Allen Zimmer-
man; b. 1941), American singer, songwriter, and guitarist **5** 170-171

Dymaxion concept (architecture)
    Fuller, Richard Buckminster **6** 149-150

Dynamic Hieroglyphic of the Bal Tabarin
(painting)
    Severini, Gino **14** 122

Dynamic Meditation
    Rajneesh, Bhagwan Shree **13** 7-9

Dynamic Projection in the 30th Degree
(sculpture)
    Pevsner, Antoine **12** 263-264

Dynamic theory (psychology)
    Lewin, Kurt **9** 375-376

Dynamics (physics)
    see Motion

Dynamics of a Human Body (painting)
    Boccioni, Umberto **2** 353-354

Dynamite (explosive)
    Nobel, Alfred Bernhard **11** 410-411

Dynamo (electricity)
    Edison, Thomas Alva **5** 206-208
    Farmer, Moses Gerrish **5** 385
    O'Neill, Eugene **11** 514-516

Dynamo theory (geophysics)
    Elsasser, Walter Maurice **5** 277-278

Dynasoar (experimental craft)
    Armstrong, Neil Alden **1** 304-306

Dynasts, The (play)
    Hardy, Thomas **7** 150-152

Dyrrachium (prefecture, Albania)
    Cato, the Younger **3** 374-375
    see also Pharsalus, Battle of

Dyskolos (play)
    Menander **10** 477-478

Dyson, F.J. (born 1923), American physicist
    Tomonaga, Sin-itiro **15** 265-266

Dyson, Frank Watson (1868-1939), British
astronomer
    Chapman, Sydney **3** 441

DYSON, FREEMAN JOHN (born 1923),
British-American physicist **5** 171-173

DZERZHINSKY, FELIX EDMUNDOVICH
(1877-1926), Soviet politician and revolutionary **5** 173-174
    Bukharin, Nikolai Ivanovich **3** 112-113

Dzhugashvili, Iosif Vissarionovich
    see Stalin, Joseph

E

Each in His Own Way (play)
Pirandello, Luigi **12** 319-321

Each Man's Son (novel)
MacLennan, Hugh **10** 110-111

Eadmer (circa 1055-circa 1124), English theologian and historian
Anselm of Canterbury **1** 244-245

EADS, JAMES BUCHANAN (1820-1887), American engineer and inventor **5** 175-176

Eagle (balloon)
Andrée, Salomon August **1** 226

Eagle (lunar module)
Armstrong, Neil Alden **1** 304-306

Eagle (ship)
Cook, James **4** 214-215
Rodney, George Brydges **13** 239-240

Eagle Forum (ultraconservative group; United States)
Schlafly, Phyllis **14** 9-10

Eagle Pass (Canada)
Fleming, Sandford **5** 485-486

Eagle That Is Forgotten, The (poem)
Lindsay, Vachel **9** 424-425

Eagle's Gift, The (book)
Rasmussen, Knud Johan Victor **13** 44

Eagle's Shadow, The (book)
Cabell, James Branch **3** 195-196

EAKINS, THOMAS (1844-1916), American painter **5** 176-177
Bellows, George Wesley **2** 143
Tanner, Henry Ossawa **15** 102-103

Eannes, Gil (flourished 1433), Portuguese navigator
Henry the Navigator **7** 305-306

EARHART, AMELIA MARY (1897-1937), American aviator **5** 177-179

EARL, RALPH (1751-1801), American painter **5** 179

EARLE, SYLVIA A. (Born Sylvia Alice Reade; b. 1935), American marine biologist and oceanographer **5** 180-181

Early Americana (stories)
Richter, Conrad Michael **13** 148-149

Early, Jubal (1816-1894), American army officer
Sheridan, Philip Henry **14** 182-183

EARP, WYATT BARRY STEPP (1848-1929), gun-fighting marshal of the American West **5** 181-182

Earth (planet)
circumference
Eratosthenes of Cyrene **5** 301-302
electrostatic force
Cavendish, Henry **3** 383-384
Gilbert, William **6** 313-314
geochronology
Holmes, Arthur **7** 455-456
motion of
Bradley, James **2** 482-483
Elsasser, Walter Maurice **5** 277-278
Foucault, Jean Bernard Léon **6** 28-29
Galileo Galilei **6** 180-183
Heraclides of Pontus **7** 319-320
Jeffreys, Harold **8** 241-242
see also Geology; Geophysics; Moon (Earth's); Universe, systems of

Earth Is the Lord's, The (book)
Heschel, Abraham Joshua **7** 358-359

"Earth, My Mother" (poem)
Kuo Mo-jo **9** 133-134

Earth science
see Geology; Geophysics

Earth Spirit (play)
Wedekind, Frank **16** 166-167

Earthenware (pottery)
Wedgwood, Josiah **16** 168-169

Earthquake (seismology)
Alessandri Rodriguez, Jorge **1** 129-130
Croce, Benedetto **4** 313-314

Jeffreys, Harold **8** 241-242
Pombal, Marquês de **12** 386-387
Richter, Charles F. **13** 146-148
Tharp, Marie **15** 162-164
Winthrop, John (1714-1779) **16** 341-342
see also Seismology

Earthy Paradise, The (poems)
Morris, William **11** 187-188

Earwicker family (literary characters)
Joyce, James **8** 365-367

EAST, EDWARD MURRAY (1879-1938), American plant geneticist **5** 182-183

East African Association (Kenya)
Kenyatta, Jomo **8** 512-514
Thuku, Harry **15** 212-213

East and West Association (established 1941)
Buck, Pearl Sydenstricker **3** 91-93

East Anglia (region, England)
Alfred **1** 151-153
Cromwell, Oliver **4** 317-320
Edward the Elder **5** 219-220

East Coker (poem)
Eliot, Thomas Stearns **5** 258-261

East Cowes Castle (Isle of Wight)
Nash, John **11** 316

East German revolt (1953)
Dulles, John Foster **5** 134-135

East India Bill (Great Britain, 1783)
Boswell, James **2** 432-434

East India Co. (British)
critics
Dalhousie, 1st Marquess of **4** 375-376
Duane, William **5** 109
Fox, Charles James **6** 35-37
Victoria **15** 485-487
Wellesley, Richard Colley **16** 192-193
Dutch disputes
Grotius, Hugo **7** 18-19
employees
Baffin, William **1** 435-436

Brooke, James **3** 21-22
Frere, Henry Bartle Edward **6** 100-101
Mill, James **11** 21
Raffles, Thomas Stamford **13** 1-2
hostility to missionaries
Judson, Adoniram **8** 377-378
officials
Clive, Robert **4** 119-120
Cornwallis, Charles **4** 241-243
Hastings, Warren **7** 195-196
Metcalfe, Charles Theophilus **10** 531-532
Peacock, Thomas Love **12** 169
Roy, Ram Mohun **13** 18
Sandys, Edwin **13** 463-464
wars
Aurangzeb **1** 377
Tipu Sultan **15** 236

East India Co. (Dutch)
Coen, Jan Pieterszoon **4** 133
Grotius, Hugo **7** 18-19
Oldenbarnevelt, Johan van **11** 495-496
Schouten, William Cornelius **14** 31
Tasman, Abel Janszoon **15** 113-114

East India Company's College (Haileybury)
Malthus, Thomas Robert **10** 180-181

East Indian, The (play)
Lewis, Matthew Gregory **9** 390-391

East Indian Association (established 1862)
Naoroji, Dadabhai **11** 305

East of Eden (film)
Dean, James **4** 433-434

East Wind (poems)
Lowell, Amy **10** 13

East Wind: West Wind (novel)
Buck, Pearl Sydenstricker **3** 91-93

Eastbury (Dorset)
Vanbrugh, John **15** 409-410

Easter (play)
Strindberg, August **14** 509-511

Easter Day (poem)
Clough, Arthur Hugh **4** 123-124

Easter Island (South Pacific Ocean)
Cook, James **4** 214-215
Kotzebue, Otto von **9** 91-92

Easter liturgy (Roman Catholic)
Pius XII **12** 339-340

Easter Memoir (paper)
Lavoisier, Antoine Laurent **9** 241-244

Easter Rebellion (Ireland; 1916)
Collins, Michael **4** 167-168
De Valera, Eamon **4** 514-515
Emmet, Robert **5** 281-282
Hyde, Douglas **8** 82-83
Markievicz, Constance **10** 267-271
O'Casey, Sean **11** 459-460
Pearse, Patrick Henry **12** 173-174
Yeats, William Butler **16** 445-447

Easter Story (oratorio)
Schütz, Heinrich **14** 48-49

Easter Synod (1050)
Leo IX **9** 332

Eastern Air Lines
Rickenbacker, Edward Vernon **13** 152-153

Eastern Asia Minor, Committee for the Defense of (established 1919)
Atatürk, Ghazi Mustapha Kemal **1** 356-357

Eastern Catholic Church
see Orthodox Eastern Church

Eastern Grove Society (China)
Huang Tsung-hsi **8** 9-10

Eastern Learning rebellions (Korea; 1894)
Kim Ok-kyun **9** 7-8
Kojong **9** 74-75

Eastern Mediterranean School (music)
Ben-Haim, Paul **2** 161-162

Eastern Orthodox Church
see Orthodox Eastern Church

Eastern question (British; 1870s)
Disraeli, Benjamin **5** 27-29

Eastern question (Roman Empire)
Marcus Aurelius Antoninus **10** 243-245

Eastern Roman Empire
see Byzantine Empire

Eastern Schism (religion)
Alexius I **1** 143-144
Boethius, Anicius Manlius Severinus **2** 360-361

EASTMAN, CHARLES A. (1858-1939), Native American author **5** 183-185

EASTMAN, GEORGE (1854-1932), American inventor and industrialist **5** 186
Ford, Henry **6** 5-6
Land, Edwin Herbert **9** 183-184

EASTMAN, MAX (Max Forrester Eastman; 1883-1969), American poet, radical editor, translator, and author **5** 187-188

Eastman House (New York City)
Kelly, Ellsworth **8** 482-483

Eastman Kodak Co. (photography)
Baekeland, Leo Hendrik **1** 430-431
Eastman, George **5** 186
Land, Edwin Herbert **9** 183-184

Eastman School of Music (Rochester, New York State)
Eastman, George **5** 186
Graham, Martha **6** 485-486
Hanson, Howard **7** 135-136

Easton Neston (Northamptonshire)
Hawksmoor, Nicholas **7** 211-212

Eastward Ho! (play)
Chapman, George **3** 440-441

EASTWOOD, CLINT (born 1930), American movie star and director **5** 188-190

Easy Street (film)
Chaplin, Charles Spencer **3** 438-440

EATON, DORMAN BRIDGMAN (1823-1899), American lawyer and author **5** 190-191

Eaton, Peggy O'Neale (1796-1879), American matron, wife of J.H. Eaton
Calhoun, John Caldwell **3** 226-228

Eaton, Theophilus (1590-1658), English colonist and administrator
Davenport, John **4** 405-406

Eau, L' (sculpture)
Richier, Germaine **13** 145-146

EBAN, ABBA (Abba Solomon Eban; born 1915), Israeli statesman, diplomat, and scholar **5** 191-192

EBBINGHAUS, HERMANN (1850-1909) German psychologist **5** 192-193

Eben (literary character)
O'Neill, Eugene **11** 514-516

Eben ha-Ezer (Jewish law)
see Shulhan Aruk

EBERT, FRIEDRICH (1871-1925), German president 1919-1925 **5** 193-194
Kapp, Wolfgang **8** 436
Luxemburg, Rosa **10** 55-56

Ebert-Groener Deal (Germany)
Ebert, Friedrich **5** 193-194

Ebony (magazine)
Johnson, John Harold **8** 306-308

Ebony Concerto (musical composition)
Stravinsky, Igor Fedorovich **14** 502-506

EBOUÉ, ADOLPHE FELIX SYLVESTRE (1885-1944), African statesman, governor of French Equatorial Africa **5** 194

ECA
see Economic Commission for Africa

Ecbatana (ancient city, Media)
Alexander the Great **1** 137-141
Antiochus IV **1** 250
Cyrus the Great **4** 363-364

Ecce Ancilla Domini (painting)
Rossetti, Dante Gabriel **13** 308-309

Ecce Homo (autobiography)
Nietzsche, Friedrich **11** 390-392

Ecce Homo (graphics series)
Grosz, George **7** 17-18
Lucas van Leyden **10** 20-21
Rembrandt Harmensz van Rijn **13** 91-95

Ecce Puer (poem)
Joyce, James **8** 365-367

Eccentric, The (play)
Afinogenov, Aleksandr Nikolaevich **1** 72-73

ECCLES, SIR JOHN CAREW (1903-1997), Australian neurophysiologist **5** 195-196

Ecclesiam suam (encyclical)
Paul VI **12** 146-148

Écclésiaste, L' (poem)
Leconte de Lisle, Charles Marie René **9** 273-274

Ecclesiastes, Book of (Old Testament)
Isidore of Seville **8** 149-150
Solomon **14** 326-327

Ecclesiastical History... (book; Bede)
Alfred **1** 151-153
Bede **2** 109-110

Ecclesiastical Sonnets (poems)
Wordsworth, William **16** 385-388

Ecclesiastical Titles Bill (England; 1851)
Gladstone, William Ewart **6** 357-360
Russell, John **13** 380-381

Ecclesiasticus (Sirach; Old Testament)
Augustine **1** 367-370
Jesus ben Sira **8** 251

Ecclesiazousai, The (play)
Aristophanes **1** 293-294

ECEVIT, BÜLENT (born 1925), Turkish statesman and prime minister **5** 196-197

Echaurren, Roberto Matta
see Matta Echaurren, Roberto

Echegaray, José y Elizaquirre (1832-1916), Spanish dramatist and engineer
Benavente y Martinez, Jacinto **2** 146-147
Galdós, Benito Pérez **6** 177-178

ECHEVERRÍA, JOSÉ ESTÉBAN (1805-1851), Argentine author and political theorist **5** 197-198
Alberdi, Juan Bautista **1** 109-110

ECHEVERRIA ALVAREZ, LUIS (born 1922), president of Mexico (1970-1976) **5** 198-200

Echo of a Scream (painting)
Siqueiros, David Alfaro **14** 256

ECK, JOHANN MAIER VON (1486-1543), German theologian **5** 200
Karlstadt, Andreas Bodenheim von **8** 449
Luther, Martin **10** 48-51
Melancthon, Philip **10** 466-467

Eckart, Carl (1902-1973), American geophysicist
Einstein, Albert **5** 228-231

ECKHART, (JOHANN) MEISTER (circa 1260-circa 1327), German Dominican theologian **5** 200-201
Ruysbroeck, Jan van **13** 388-389

Eclectic Readers (textbooks)
McGuffey, William Holmes **10** 414-415

Eclecticism (philosophy)
Cousin, Victor **4** 273-274
Philo Judaeus **12** 282-283

Eclipse (astronomy)
lunar
Aristarchus of Samos **1** 290-291
Hasan ibn al-Haytham **7** 190-191
Hipparchus **7** 407-408
solar
Aston, Francis William **1** 350-351
Flamsteed, John **5** 477-478
Hasan ibn al-Haytham **7** 190-191

Eclipse (film)
Antonioni, Michelangelo **1** 252-253

Eclipse of the Stars (poems)
Sachs, Nelly **13** 411-412

Eclogues (poems; Virgil)
Claude Lorrain **4** 89-90
Frost, Robert Lee **6** 130-133
Horace **7** 500-503
Maillol, Aristide **10** 150-151
Virgil **15** 507-510

École, d'Art (New York City)
Archipenko, Alexander **1** 280-281

École de Dessin (Paris)
Viollet-le-Duc, Eugène Emmanuel **15** 505-506

École de Guerre (France)
Foch, Ferdinand **5** 498-499
Pétain, Henri Philippe **12** 250-252

École de l'Europe Libre (Paris)
Berle, Adolf Augustus Jr. **2** 199-200

École de Quebec
see École Patriotique

École des Beaux-Arts (Paris)
Courbet, Jean Desiré Gustave **4** 271-273
Ingres, Jean Auguste Dominique **8** 121-123
Viollet-le-Duc, Eugène Emmanuel **15** 505-506

École des femmes, L' (play)
Molière **11** 86-88

École des indifférents, L' (novellas)
Giraudoux, Jean **6** 349-350

École des Sciences Politiques (France)
Sorel, Albert **14** 346-347

École Militaire (Paris)
Gabriel, Ange Jacques **6** 160-161

École Niedermeyer (France)
Saint-Saëns, Charles Camille **13** 435-436

École Normale Supérieure (Paris)
Althusser, Louis **1** 182-183
Beckett, Samuel **2** 102-104
Fustel de Coulanges, Numa Denis **6** 155
Michelet, Jules **11** 5-6

École Patriotique (literary group)
Crémazie, Octave **4** 305-306

École Polytechnique (Paris)
Ampère, André Marie **1** 205-206
Becquerel, Antoine Henri **2** 108-109
Dumas, Jean Baptiste André **5** 138-139
Fourier, Jean Baptiste Joseph **6** 32-33
Gay-Lussac, Joseph Louis **6** 245-246
Lagrange, Joseph Louis **9** 164-166

École Pratique des Hautes Études (Paris)
Binet, Alfred **2** 277-278

École Romane (French literary group)
Maurras, Charles Marie Photius **10** 350-351

Ecology (science)
founded as discipline
Linnaeus, Carl **9** 427-429
in United States
see Conservation (United States)

Econometrics (economics)
Cournot, Antoine Augustin **4** 273
Marshall, Alfred **10** 277-278
Tinbergen, Jan **15** 228-229

Economic Commission for Africa (Nairobi, 1965)
Kenyatta, Jomo **8** 512-514

Economic Commission for Latin America (United Nations)
Prebisch, Raúl **12** 434-436

Economic Consequences of the Peace, The (book)
Keynes, John Maynard **8** 528-530

Economic Cooperation among Negro Americans (book)
Du Bois, William Edward Burghardt **5** 116-118

Economic crises (United States)
see Depression, Great (economics; United States); Depressions and panics (United States)

Economic History Society (England)
Tawney, Richard Henry **15** 120-121

Economic planning
Castelo Branco, Humberto **3** 359-360
Catherine the Great **3** 370-372
Clapham, John Harold **4** 71
Curtin, John Joseph **4** 348-349
Franco Bahamonde, Francisco **6** 52-54
Kubitschek de Oliveira, Juscelino **9** 113-115
Monnet, Jean **11** 109-110

Economic Reconstruction in Nigeria (book)
Azikiwe, Nnamdi **1** 401-402

Economics (book; Aristotle)
Nicholas of Oresme **11** 380

Economics (social science)
and aging
Epstein, Abraham **5** 294-295
business cycles
see Business cycles
capitalism
see Capitalism
classical school
Carey, Henry Charles **3** 294-295
Keynes, John Maynard **8** 528-530
Malthus, Thomas Robert **10** 180-181
Say, Jean Baptiste **13** 508-509
Tucker, George **15** 332-333
competition
see competition
demographic economics
Kuznets, Simon **9** 138-139
depressions
see Depression, Great; Depressions and panics (United States)
developing countries

Prebisch, Raúl **12** 434-436
distribution
 see Distribution
dynamic analysis
 Clark, John Bates **4** 76-77
 Schmoller, Gustav Friedrich von
  14 21
econometrics
 see Econometrics
economic anthropology
 Harris, Abram Lincoln Jr. **7** 169-171
economic planning
 Kuznets, Simon **9** 138-139
free market
 Hayek, Friedrich A. von **7** 221-223
imperfect competition theory
 Robinson, Joan Violet Maurice
  13 209-210
influence on history
 Adams, Peter Chardon Brooks **1** 54
 Beard, Charles Austin **2** 84
institutional
 Schmoller, Gustav Friedrich von
  14 21
Institutionalist school
 Galbraith, John Kenneth **6** 174-177
 Harris, Abram Lincoln Jr. **7** 169-171
international
 Ball, George **1** 470-471
 Coombs, Herbert Cole **4** 219-220
 Herrera, Juan de **7** 335
 Myrdal, Karl Gunnar **11** 284
 Prebisch, Raúl **12** 434-436
 Rostow, Walt Whitman **13** 315-317
Keynesian
 see Keynesian economics
laissez faire
 Berle, Adolf Augustus Jr. **2** 199-200
 Polanyi, Karl **12** 372
 Smith, Adam **14** 283-284
 von Mises, Ludwig **16** 25
 see also Laissez faire
mathematical
 Clark, John Maurice **4** 77-78
 Cournot, Antoine Augustin **4** 273
 Jevons, William Stanley **8** 255-256
 Mitchell, Wesley Clair **11** 61-62
 Ramsey, Frank Plumpton **13** 25
 Samuelson, Paul Anthony
  13 458-459
 Tinbergen, Jan **15** 228-229
medieval treatises
 Nicholas of Oresme **11** 380
mercantilism
 see Mercantilism
monetary theory
 Bagehot, Walter **1** 436-437
 Becarria, Marchese di **2** 97-98
 Böhm-Bawerk, Eugen von **2** 366
 Burns, Arthur **3** 151-153
 Fisher, Irving **5** 462-463
 Friedman, Milton **6** 111-112
 Heller, Walter **7** 265-266
 Herrera, Juan de **7** 335
 Law, John **9** 244-245
 Mayo-Smith, Richmond **10** 371-372

Ricardo, David **13** 123-124
Robertson, Dennis Holme **13** 196
Schacht, Hjalmar Horace Greeley
 13 518-519
Walras, Marie Esprit Léon **16** 84-85
neoclassic
 Knight, Frank Hyneman **9** 58-59
 Pigou, Arthur Cecil **12** 302
Prebisch thesis
 Prebisch, Raúl **12** 434-436
reforms
 Allende Gossens, Salvador
  1 174-176
 Bruce of Melbourne, 1st Viscount
  3 61-62
 Castilla, Ramón **3** 361
 Coombs, Herbert Cole **4** 219-220
 Goulart, João **6** 467-469
 Louis XV **9** 533-534
 Shang Yang **14** 149-150
 Wang An-shih **16** 95-97
 Wang Mang **16** 101-103
 Yeh-lü Ch'u-ts'ai **16** 447-449
social theories
 Aberhart, William **1** 26-27
 Bellamy, Edward **2** 134-135
 Chernyshevsky, Nikolai Gavrilovich
  3 504-505
 Cole, George Douglas Howard
  4 146-147
 Erhard, Ludwig **5** 302-304
 Galbraith, John Kenneth **6** 174-177
 George, Henry **6** 276
 Harris, Abram Lincoln Jr. **7** 169-171
 Hayek, Friedrich A. von **7** 221-223
 Marx, Karl **10** 304-308
 Patten, Simon Nelson **12** 138-139
 Schmoller, Gustav Friedrich von
  14 21
 Schumpeter, Joseph Alois **14** 43-44
 Simon, Herbert Alexander
  14 236-237
 Veblen, Thorstein Bunde
  15 449-450
"staple theory" (Canada)
 Innis, Harold Adams **8** 124-125
tariff policy
 see Tariff; Social scientists—econo-
  mists

Économie politique (article)
 Rousseau, Jean Jacques **13** 324-328

Economy (town, Pennsylvania)
 Rapp, George **13** 42-43

Economy and Society (encyclopedia volume)
 Weber, Max (social scientist)
  16 157-160

Ecorche (sculpture)
 Brancusi, Constantin **2** 494-496

Ecuador, Republic of (nation, South America)
 Borja Cevallos, Rodrigo **2** 417-418
 border disputes
  Prado Ugarteche, Manuel
   12 430-431

Rio Branco, Barão do **13** 177
culture
 Montalvo, Juan María **11** 119-120
economic growth
 García Moreno, Gabriel **6** 209-210
 Plaza Lasso, Galo **12** 350-351
exploration
 Almagro, Diego de **1** 177-178
independence movement
 Bolívar, Simón **2** 375-377
 Flores, Juan José **5** 491
Political reform
 Alfaro, José Eloy **1** 144-145
 Montalvo, Juan María **11** 119-120
 Velasco Ibarra, José María
  15 452-454
United States relations
 Velasco Ibarra, José María
  15 452-454
 Wheelwright, William **16** 223-224

Ecumenical councils
 see individual councils

Ecumenism (religion)
 Buddhist
  Niwano, Nikkyo **11** 400-401
 Catholic
  Bea, Augustinus **2** 79
  John, XXIII **8** 277-280
  Paul VI **12** 146-148
  Soloviev, Vladimir Sergeevich
   14 329-330
 Jewish
  Herberg, Will **7** 322-323
 Protestant
  Baillie, D. (Donald) M. (Macpher-
   son) **1** 445
  Baillie, John **1** 445-447
  Baxter, Richard **2** 76-77
  Bennett, John Coleman **2** 170-171
  Brunner, Emil **3** 74-75
  Grotius, Hugo **7** 18-19
  Harkness, Georgia **7** 155-156
  Mott, John R. **11** 212
  Nygren, Anders **11** 449-451
  Pusey, Edward Bouverie **12** 488-489
  Schaff, Philip **13** 519-520
  Söderblom, Nathan **14** 323-324
  Strong, Josiah **14** 512-513
  Temple, William **15** 141-143
  Visser't Hooft, Willem Adolf
   15 511-512
  see also World Council of Churches

Ed è subito sera (poems)
 Quasimodo, Salvatore **12** 506

Edad de oro (children's magazine)
 Martí, José **10** 285-286

Edda
 see Prose Edda

EDDINGTON, SIR ARTHUR STANLEY
(1882-1944), English astronomer
5 201-202
 Jeans, James Hopwood **8** 235-236
 Lemaître, Abbè Georges Édouard
  9 315-316

Eddy, Asa (died 1882), American
 Christian Scientist
  Eddy, Mary Baker **5** 202

EDDY, MARY BAKER (1821-1910), Ameri-
 can founder of the Christian Science
 Church **5** 202
  Mesmer, Franz Anton **10** 526-527

Eddy, E.B., Co. (Calgary, Canada)
 Bennett, Richard Bedford **2** 171-172

Eddystone Lighthouse (English Channnel)
 Smeaton, John **14** 280-281

EDELMAN, MARIAN WRIGHT (born
 1939), lobbyist, lawyer, civil rights
 activist, and founder of the Children's
 Defense Fund **5** 202-204

Edema (medicine)
 Eijkman, Christian **5** 228

EDEN, ANTHONY (1897-1977), English
 statesman, prime minister 1955-1957
 5 204-205
  Chamberlain, Arthur Neville **3** 409-411
  Dulles, John Foster **5** 134-135
  Elizabeth II **5** 266-269
  Halifax, 1st Earl of **7** 82-83
  Macmillan, Harold **10** 112-113

Edessa, fall of (1142)
 Bernard of Clairvaux **2** 207-208

Edgar (944-975), king of England 959-975
 Dunstan **5** 151-152
 Ethelred the Unready **5** 327

Edgar (opera)
 Puccini, Giacomo **12** 474-476

Edgar Huntly (novel)
 Brown, Charles Brockden **3** 33

Edgar the Atheling (1050?-1130?), English
 prince
  Margaret of Scotland **10** 252-253

Edgbaston oratory (England)
 Newman, John Henry **11** 365-367

Edge of the Sword, The (book)
 De Gaulle, Charles André Joseph Marie
 4 463-465

EDGEWORTH, MARIA (1767-1849),
 British author **5** 205-206

Edict by the King of Prussia, An (satire)
 Franklin, Benjamin **6** 60-64

Edict of Nantes (1598)
 Frederick William **6** 85-86
 Henry IV **7** 293-295
 Louis XIV **9** 531-533
 Orléans, Philippe II D' **11** 530-531
 Victor Amadeus II **15** 482-483

Edict of Toleration (China; 1705)
 K'ang-hsi **8** 423-426

Edifying Discourses (book)
 Kierkegaard, Søren Aabye **8** 547-549

Edinburgh (city, Scotland)
 Robert II **13** 194

Edinburgh, Treaty of (1560)
 Elizabeth I **5** 263-266

 Mary, I **10** 308-309

Edinburgh, University of (Scotland)
 Adam, Robert and James **1** 38-40
 Balfour, Arthur James **1** 469-470
 Chalmers, Thomas **3** 408-409
 Childe, Vere Gordon **3** 521-522
 Domagk, Gerhard Johannes Paul
 5 48-50
 Ferguson, Adam **5** 420-421
 Fleming, Alexander **5** 483-485
 Holmes, Arthur **7** 455-456
 Stewart, Dugald **14** 449

Edinburgh Missionary Conference (1910)
 Mott, John R. **11** 212

Edinburgh Review (periodical)
 Byron, George Gordon Noel **3** 193-194
 Carlyle, Thomas **3** 304-305
 Hazlitt, William **7** 235-236
 Macaulay, Thomas Babington **10** 79-80
 Owen, Richard **12** 39

Edinburgh Social Union (established 1886)
 Geddes, Patrick **6** 246-247

Edington (village, England)
 Alfred **1** 151-153

Ediphone (dictating machine)
 Edison, Thomas Alva **5** 206-208

EDISON, THOMAS ALVA (1847-1931),
 American inventor **5** 206-208
 associates
  Carver, George Washington
  3 346-347
  Eastman, George **5** 186
  Ford, Henry **6** 5-6
  Insull, Samuel **8** 130
  Sprague, Frank Julian **14** 385-386
  Tesla, Nikola **15** 156-157
  Thurstone, Louis Leon **15** 215-216
 sketches of
  Dos Passos, John Roderigo **5** 69-71
  Dreiser, Herman Theodore **5** 98-100

Edison battery (electricity)
 Edison, Thomas Alva **5** 206-208

Edison Botanic Research Co. (established
 1927)
  Edison, Thomas Alva **5** 206-208

Edison effect (science)
 Edison, Thomas Alva **5** 206-208

Edison General Electric Co. (established
 1899)
  Insull, Samuel **8** 130

Edison Illuminating Company
 see Detroit Edison Company

Editors
 American
  see Editors, American
 Arab
  Haykal, Muhammad Husain
  7 230-231
 Canadian
  Bourassa, Joseph-Henri-Napoleon
  2 446-447
  Brown, George **3** 35-36

 Chinese
  Ch'en Tu-hsiu **3** 501-502
 Colombian
  García Márquez, Gabriel **6** 208-209
 English
  Brown, Tina **3** 47-48
  Ford, Ford Madox **6** 1-2
  Morley, John **11** 178-179
  Spender, Stephen Harold
  14 370-371
  Stephen, Leslie **14** 429
 Hebrew
  Ben Yehuda, Eliezer **2** 181-182
 Indian
  Das, Chitta Ranjan **4** 401-402
 Irish
  Heaney, Seamus Justin **7** 238-240
 Italian
  Vittorini, Elio **16** 2-3
 Mexican
  Cosio Villegas, Daniel **4** 260-261
 Russian
  Bukharin, Nikolai Ivanovich
  3 112-113

Editors, American
 book editors
  Allen, Paula Gunn **1** 165-167
  Bambara, Toni Cade **1** 482-483
  Campbell, Joseph **3** 253-255
  Commager, Henry Steele **4** 181-183
  Ford, Paul Leicester **6** 9-10
  Hall, Donald **7** 84-85
  Locke, Alain **9** 475-478
  Morgan, Robin **11** 168-170
  Onassis, Jacqueline Lee Bouvier
  Kennedy **11** 511-513
  Perkins, William Maxwell Evarts
  12 222-223
  Terkel, Louis **15** 152-153
 magazines and journals (18th century)
  Beecher, Lyman **2** 113
  Brown, Charles Brockden **3** 33
 magazines and journals (19th century)
  Abbott, Lyman **1** 10-11
  Beecher, Henry Ward **2** 112-113
  Bellows, Henry Whitney **2** 143-144
  Bigelow, John **2** 271-272
  Curtis, George William **4** 349-350
  Debs, Eugene Victor **4** 444-445
  Hale, Sarah Josepha **7** 74-75
  Higginson, Thomas Wentworth
  7 380
  Howells, William Dean **7** 539-541
  Poe, Edgar Allan **12** 363-365
  Silliman, Benjamin **14** 229-230
 magazines and journals (19th-20th cen-
 tury)
  Cahan, Abraham **3** 214
  Croly, Herbert David **4** 316-317
  Harris, Frank **7** 172-173
  McClure, Samuel Sidney
  10 398-399
  Seligman, Edwin Robert Anderson
  14 93-94
 magazines and journals (20th century)
  Bagley, William Chandler **1** 437-438

Bell, Daniel **2** 132-133
Brown, Helen Gurley **3** 36-37
Brown, Tina **3** 47-48
Buckley, William F. Jr. **3** 96-97
Cattell, James McKeen **3** 376-377
Chambers, Whittaker **3** 416-417
Cousins, Norman **4** 274-276
Du Bois, William Edward Burghardt
     5 116-118
Eastman, Max **5** 187-188
Hapgood, Norman **7** 137-138
Johnson, Alvin Saunders **8** 293-294
Lovecraft, H. P. **10** 3-6
Luce, Henry Robinson **10** 23-24
Macdonald, Dwight **10** 81-83
Marty, Martin E. **10** 300-301
Mencken, Henry Louis **10** 481-483
Pound, Ezra Loomis **12** 415-417
Ross, Harold **13** 300-302
Rugg, Harold **13** 355-357
Smith, Lillian Eugenia **14** 298-299
Steinem, Gloria **14** 418-419
Tate, Allen **15** 116
Villard, Oswald Garrison
     15 498-499
Wallace, DeWitt **16** 70-71
Wilson, Edmund **16** 318-319
Woodson, Carter Godwin
     16 374-376
Young, Stark **16** 474-475
newspapers (18th century)
     Zenger, John Peter **16** 497-498
newspapers (19th century)
     Bailey, Gamaliel **1** 444-445
     Bowles, Samuel **2** 464
     Bryant, William Cullen **3** 83-85
     Cameron, Simon **3** 246-247
     Garrison, William Lloyd **6** 226-228
     Greeley, Horace **6** 515-517
     Grimké, Archibald Henry **7** 1-2
     Lovejoy, Elijah Parish **10** 6-7
     Lowell, James Russell **10** 14-15
     Medill, Joseph **10** 451-452
     Polk, Leonidas Lafayette **12** 376-377
newspapers (19th-20th century)
     Berger, Victor Louis **2** 189-190
     Bryan, William Jennings **3** 80-82
     Fortune, Timothy Thomas **6** 18-21
     Howe, Edgar Watson **7** 529
     Ochs, Adolph Simon **11** 464
     Scripps, Edward Wyllis **14** 72-73
     Wallace, Henry **16** 73
     see also Journalists, American; Pub-
          lishers, American
newspapers (20th century)
     Maynard, Robert Clyve **10** 366-367
     Proulx, E. Annie **12** 463-465
     Salisbury, Harrison Evans
          13 449-451
     Stone, I. F. **14** 470-471
     Trotter, William Monroe **15** 306-307
textbooks
     Cubberley, Ellwood Patterson
          4 329-331

Edlund, Erik (1819-1888), Swedish physi-
     cist
     Arrhenius, Svante August **1** 318-320
Edmonton (Canada) Oilers (hockey team)
     Gretzky, Wayne **6** 537-539
Edmund I (921-946), king of the Anglo-Sax-
     ons
     Dunstan **5** 151-152
Edmund II (Edmund Ironside; 980?-1016),
     king of the Anglo-Saxons
     Clovis I **4** 124
     Edward the Confessor **5** 218-219
     Ethelred the Unready **5** 327
Edmund Rich, St. (circa 1170-1240), Eng-
     lish archbishop
     Matthew Paris **10** 341-342
Edo
     see Tokyo
Edo and Enam (story)
     Agnon, Shmuel Yoseph **1** 85-86
Edomites (ancient Semitic tribe)
     Saul **13** 498
Édouard (literary character)
     Gide, André **6** 308-309
Edred (died 955), king of the English
     Dunstan **5** 151-152
Education (Africa)
     Faidherbe, Louis Léon César **5** 366-367
     Hayford, J. E. Casely **7** 228-230
     Kawawa, Rashidi Mfaume **8** 464-465
     Marāghī, Mustafā al- **10** 228-229
Education (Asia)
     Chang Chih-tung **3** 430-431
     Chulalongkorn **4** 43-45
     Hastings, Warren **7** 195-196
     Ts'ai Yüan-p'ei **15** 322
Education (Australia)
     MacKillop, Mary **10** 106-107
     Parkes, Henry **12** 113
Education (Europe)
     Belgium
          Leopold II **9** 346-347
     England
          Arnold, Thomas **1** 313-314
          Balfour, Arthur James **1** 469-470
          Beale, Dorothea **2** 81-83
          Bell, Andrew **2** 131-132
          Elizabeth II **5** 266-269
          Garrett (Anderson), Elizabeth
               6 222-225
          Lancaster, Joseph **9** 182-183
          Neill, Alexander Sutherland
               11 335-336
     France
          Braille, Louis **2** 492-493
          Budé, Guillaume **3** 102-103
          Condorcet, Marquis de **4** 195-196
          Cuvier, Georges Léopold **4** 357-359
          Ferry, Jules François Camille **5** 430
          Fourier, François Charles Marie
               6 31-32

          Guizot, François Pierre Guillaume
               7 40-41
          Lavisse, Ernest **9** 241
          Montalembert, Comte de
               11 118-119
     Germany
          Goebbels, Joseph Paul **6** 384-385
          Graetz, Heinrich Hirsch **6** 483
          Herbart, Johann Friedrich **7** 321-322
     Italy
          Gentile, Giovanni **6** 267
          Montessori, Maria **11** 125-126
     Prussia
          Humboldt, Wilhelm von **8** 31
          Stolypin, Piotr Arkadevich
               14 465-466
          Tolstoy, Leo **15** 262-265
     Russia
          Catherine the Great **3** 370-372
     Scotland
          Geddes, Patrick **6** 246-247
     Switzerland
          Pestalozzi, Johann Heinrich
               12 249-250
Education (Latin America)
     Brazil
          Freire, Paulo **6** 95-96
     Cuba
          Castro Ruz, Fidel **3** 365-368
          Estrada Palma, Tomás **5** 326-327
     Guatemala
          Barrios, Justo Rufino **2** 23-24
          Estrada Cabrera, Manuel **5** 325-326
     Mexico
          Calles, Plutarco Elías **3** 234-235
          Cosio Villegas, Daniel **4** 260-261
          Sierra, Justo **14** 217
          Vasconcelos, José **15** 443-444
     South America
          García Moreno, Gabriel **6** 209-210
          López, Carlos Antonio **9** 506-507
          Sarmiento, Domingo Faustino
               13 484-485
Education (United States)
     acting
          Strasberg, Lee **14** 494-495
     administrative structure
          Cubberley, Ellwood Patterson
               4 329-331
     adult
          Cooper, Peter **4** 223-224
          Holbrook, Josiah **7** 450-451
          Knowles, Malcolm Shepherd
               9 62-64
     African American studies programs
          Locke, Alain **9** 475-478
     and integration
          Meredith, James H. **10** 514-515
     and philosophy
          see Education, philosophy of
     and religion
          see Education, religious
     architecture
          Moore, Charles Willard **11** 143-145
          Pelli, Cesar **12** 191-192

art and music
    Albers, Josef **1** 110
    Chase, William Merritt **3** 476-477
    Diamond, David **4** 527-529
    Eakins, Thomas **5** 176-177
    Moholy-Nagy, László **11** 82-83
    Piston, Walter **12** 327-328
    Savage, Augusta Christine
      13 499-501
assessment
    Tyler, Ralph W. **15** 370-371
Chautauqua and lyceum movements
    Harper, William Rainey **7** 163-164
    Holbrook, Josiah **7** 450-451
    Vincent, John Heyl **15** 502-503
computer science
    Shaw, Mary **14** 165-167
conflict resolution
    Andrews, Fannie Fern Phillips
      1 231-232
curriculum
    Bagley, William Chandler **1** 437-438
    Bruner, Jerome Seymour **3** 72-73
    Bryan, William Jennings **3** 80-82
    Escalante, Jaime **5** 320-321
    Gagné, Robert Mills **6** 170
    McGuffey, William Holmes
      10 414-415
    Morse, Jedidiah **11** 191-192
    Rugg, Harold **13** 355-357
    Smith, Dora **14** 289-290
    Tyler, Ralph W. **15** 370-371
elective system
    Eliot, Charles William **5** 254
    Jordan, David Starr **8** 350-351
elementary and kindergarten
    Curry, Jabez Lamar Monroe
      4 346-347
    Harris, William Torrey **7** 177-178
equal opportunity
    Bok, Derek Curtis **2** 371-372
European influences
    Bache, Alexander Dallas **1** 420
    Harris, William Torrey **7** 177-178
    Rice, Joseph Mayer **13** 127-128
experimental schools
    Collins, Marva **4** 165-167
    Johnson, Marietta Louise Pierce
      8 312-313
Federal programs
    Baron, Salo Wittmayer **2** 16-17
    Johnson, Lyndon Baines **8** 308-312
    Morrill, Justin Smith **11** 182
foundations and
    Carnegie, Andrew **3** 309-312
    Rockefeller, John D. Jr. **13** 225-226
higher
    Angell, James Rowland **1** 236-237
    Bagley, William Chandler **1** 437-438
    Bennett, William John **2** 172-174
    Blanding, Sarah Gibson **2** 322-323
    Bloom, Allan David **2** 335-337
    Bok, Derek Curtis **2** 371-372
    Brewster, Kingman Jr. **2** 522-523
    Brooks, Gwendolyn **3** 24-26
    Broudy, Harry Samuel **3** 28-29

Brubacher, John Seiler **3** 58-59
Clapp, Margaret Antoinette **4** 71-72
Cole, Johnnetta **4** 147-149
Conway, Jill Kathryn Ker **4** 213-214
Cubberley, Ellwood Patterson
    4 329-331
Eisenhower, Milton **5** 237-238
Gilman, Daniel Coit **6** 325-326
Gray, Hannah Holborn **6** 507-508
Harper, William Rainey **7** 163-164
Hesburgh, Theodore Martin
    7 357-358
Horner, Matina Souretis **7** 506-508
Hutchins, Robert Maynard **8** 68-69
Jordan, David Starr **8** 350-351
Locke, Alain **9** 475-478
Lowell, Abbott Lawrence **10** 12-13
Lyon, Mary **10** 67-69
Nicolson, Marjorie Hope
    11 384-385
Odum, Howard Washington
    11 474-476
Patterson, Frederick Douglas
    12 139-140
Revel, Bernard **13** 108-109
Riesman, David **13** 167-168
Russell, James Earl **13** 379-380
Silber, John **14** 224-226
Teggart, Frederick J. **15** 133-134
Wayland, Francis **16** 148-149
home economics
    Blanding, Sarah Gibson **2** 322-323
    Dodge, Grace Hoadley **5** 37-38
    Richards, Ellen H. **13** 134-136
instructional systems design
    Gagné, Robert Mills **6** 170
language arts
    Smith, Dora **14** 289-290
legislation
    Green, Edith Starrett **6** 519-520
mathematics
    Bernstein, Dorothy Lewis **2** 217
    Granville, Evelyn Boyd **6** 494-496
medical
    Apgar, Virginia **1** 257-259
    Mayo, William J. and Charles H.
      10 367-369
music
    Crumb, George **4** 326-328
of African Americans
    Armstrong, Samuel Chapman
      1 306-307
    Benezet, Anthony **2** 159-160
    Bond, Horace Mann **2** 384-386
    Brown, Charlotte Eugenia Hawkins
      3 34
    Cole, Johnnetta **4** 147-149
    Lowell, Josephine Shaw **10** 15-16
    Mays, Benjamin E. **10** 374-376
    Patterson, Frederick Douglas
      12 139-140
    Revels, Hiram Rhoades **13** 109-110
    Rockefeller, John D. Jr. **13** 225-226
    Talbert, Mary Morris Burnett
      15 86-88

    see also African American history
      (United States)
of Hispanic Americans
    Escalante, Jaime **5** 320-321
    Prichard, Diana García **12** 448-449
of Native Americans
    Banks, Dennis J. **1** 488-489
    Deloria, Vine Jr. **4** 481-484
    Peabody, Elizabeth Palmer
      12 167-168
    Sequoyah **14** 110-111
    Wheelock, Eleazar **16** 222-223
    Zah, Peterson **16** 486-487
of physically disabled
    Cardano, Geronimo **3** 285-286
    Gallaudet, Thomas Hopkins **6** 185
    Keller, Helen Adams **8** 479-480
of teachers
    Bagley, William Chandler **1** 437-438
    Beecher, Catharine **2** 110-112
    Brubacher, John Seiler **3** 58-59
    Goodlad, John Inkster **6** 434-436
    Hunter, Madeline Cheek **8** 47-48
    Russell, James Earl **13** 379-380
of voters
    Park, Maud Wood **12** 102
of women
    Beecher, Catharine **2** 110-112
    Benezet, Anthony **2** 159-160
    Cole, Johnnetta **4** 147-149
    Conway, Jill Kathryn Ker **4** 213-214
    Dodge, Grace Hoadley **5** 37-38
    Hale, Sarah Josepha **7** 74-75
    Lloyd-Jones, Esther McDonald
      9 471-472
    Lynd, Helen Merrell **10** 63-64
    Lyon, Mary **10** 67-69
    Richards, Ellen H. **13** 134-136
    Willard, Emma Hart **16** 288-289
    see also Reformers, educational;
      Social scientists—educators
parochial schools
    Black, Hugo Lafayette **2** 301-303
    Hughes, John Joseph **8** 17-18
    Ireland, John **8** 133-134
    Seton, Elizabeth Ann Bayley
      14 118-119
    Seward, William Henry **14** 124-125
    see also Education, religious
performance testing
    Popham, William James **12** 399-401
personnel development
    Lloyd-Jones, Esther McDonald
      9 471-472
poetry
    Brooks, Gwendolyn **3** 24-26
professional
    Morgan, John **11** 162-163
    Perry, Matthew Calbraith
      12 237-239
    Reeve, Tapping **13** 79-80
    Waterhouse, Benjamin **16** 131-132
    see also Medical schools
school psychology
    Hunter, Madeline Cheek **8** 47-48
science

Richards, Ellen H. **13** 134-136
state and local
  Barnard, Henry **2** 10
  Cubberley, Ellwood Patterson
    4 329-331
  Curtin, Andrew Gregg **4** 347-348
  Everett, Edward **5** 344
  Fish, Hamilton **5** 461-462
  Haley, Margaret A. **7** 78-79
  Harris, William Torrey **7** 177-178
  Houston, Charles Hamilton
    7 523-526
  Long, Huey Pierce **9** 496-497
  Mann, Horace **10** 202-204
student personnel work
  Strang, Ruth May **14** 493-494
teachers unions
  Shanker, Albert **14** 151-153

Education Act (England; 1870, 1902)
  Balfour, Arthur James **1** 469-470
  Gladstone, William Ewart **6** 357-360

Education and Living (book)
  Bourne, Randolph Silliman **2** 456-457

Education, International Bureau of
  Piaget, Jean **12** 287-288

Education, medieval
  Alcuin of York **1** 122-123
  Charlemagne **3** 445-447
  Charles IV **3** 455-456

Education, Ministry of (Peking, China)
  Chang Chih-tung **3** 430-431

Education of Cupid (painting)
  Correggio **4** 249-251

Education of Henry Adams, The (autobiography)
  Adams, Henry Brooks **1** 45-47

Education, philosophy of
  behavioral theories
    Tyler, Ralph W. **15** 370-371
  child-centered
    Strang, Ruth May **14** 493-494
  general theories
    Alcott, Amos Bronson **1** 121
    Basedow, Johann Bernhard **2** 44-45
    Bloom, Allan David **2** 335-337
    Broudy, Harry Samuel **3** 28-29
    Brubacher, John Seiler **3** 58-59
    Counts, George S. **4** 267-269
    Goodlad, John Inkster **6** 434-436
    Horne, Herman Harrell **7** 503-504
    Huxley, Thomas Henry **8** 77-79
  individual development theories
    Bruner, Jerome Seymour **3** 72-73
    Collins, Marva **4** 165-167
    Comenius, John Amos **4** 180-181
    Froebel, Friedrich Wilhelm August
      6 122-123
    Lloyd-Jones, Esther McDonald
      9 471-472
    Montessori, Maria **11** 125-126
    Pestalozzi, Johann Heinrich
      12 249-250
    Rousseau, Jean Jacques **13** 324-328

liberal defended
  Vico, Giambattista **15** 480-481
progressive
  Bancroft, George **1** 483-484
  Counts, George S. **4** 267-269
  Dewey, John **4** 520-523
  Flexner, Abraham **5** 489-490
  Johnson, Marietta Louise Pierce
    8 312-313
  Judd, Charles Hubbard **8** 375-376
  Kilpatrick, William H. **9** 1-3
  Neill, Alexander Sutherland
    11 335-336
  Ross, Edward Alsworth **13** 300
  Rugg, Harold **13** 355-357
  Russell, Bertrand Arthur William
    13 373-374
  Russell, James Earl **13** 379-380
role in society
  Bode, Boyd Henry **2** 355-356
  Carnegie, Andrew **3** 309-312
  Counts, George S. **4** 267-269
  Cubberley, Ellwood Patterson
    4 329-331
  Freire, Paulo **6** 95-96
  Illich, Ivan **8** 112-114
  Mead, Margaret **10** 438-440
  Ward, Lester Frank **16** 113-114
teaching models
  Hunter, Madeline Cheek **8** 47-48
theories of adult education
  Knowles, Malcolm Shepherd
    9 62-64

Education, religious
Christian
  Borromeo, Charles **2** 423-424
  Calvin, John **3** 239-242
  Laval, Francois Xavier de **9** 235-236
  Morton, Nelle Katherine
    11 195-197
  Ruether, Rosemary Radford
    13 353-354
  see also Education (United States)—
    parochial schools
comparative religions
  Renan, Ernest **13** 95-96
Jewish
  Abba Arika **1** 3-4
  Abrahams, Israel **1** 29
  Ginzberg, Louis **6** 337-338
  Heschel, Abraham Joshua
    7 358-359
  Revel, Bernard **13** 108-109
Zen Buddhist
  Suzuki, Daisetz Teitaro **15** 46-47

Educational psychologists
  see Social scientists—psychologists

Educational Science, Institute for (Geneva)
  Piaget, Jean **12** 287-288

Edusei, Krobo (born 1915), Ghanaian political leader
  Busia, Kofi Abrefa **3** 172-173

Edward (died 978), pre-Norman king of England
  Ethelred the Unready **5** 327

Edward (died 1484), Prince of Wales
  Richard III **13** 132-133

EDWARD I (1239-1307), king of England
1272-1307 **5** 208-210
  Douglas, James **5** 78
  Edward II **5** 210
  Henry III **7** 290-292
  Llewelyn ap Gruffydd **9** 468
  Montfort, Simon de **11** 132-133
  Robert I **13** 192-194
  Wallace, William **16** 75-76

EDWARD II (Edward of Carnarvon;
1284-1327), king of England 1307-27
5 210
  Edward III **5** 211-212
  Langland, William **9** 194-195
  Robert I **13** 192-194

EDWARD III (1312-1377), king of England
1327-77 **5** 211-212
  Chaucer, Geoffrey **3** 482-485
  Douglas, James **5** 78
  Edward the Black Prince **5** 217-218
  Froissart, Jean **6** 124-125
  John of Gaunt **8** 282-283
  Philip VI **12** 277-278
  Richard II **13** 130-131
  Wyclif, John **16** 412-413

Edward IV (1330-1376)
  see Edward the Black Prince

EDWARD IV (1442-1483), king of England
1461-70 **5** 212-213
  accession
    Henry VI **7** 298-299
    Warwick and of Salisbury, Earl of
      16 122-123
  opponents
    James III **8** 208-209
    Louis XI **9** 526-528
    Margaret of Anjou **10** 249-250
  relatives
    Charles the Bold **3** 467-469
    Henry VII **7** 300-302
    Richard III **13** 132-133

Edward V (1471-1483), king of England
1483
  Edward IV **5** 212-213
  Henry VII **7** 300-302
  Richard III **13** 132-133

EDWARD VI (1537-1553), king of England
and Ireland 1547-53 **5** 213-214
  and exploration
    Cabot, Sebastian **3** 200-201
    Chancellor, Richard **3** 422
  and Protestantism
    Cranmer, Thomas **4** 295-296
    Latimer, Hugh **9** 221
    Mary, I **10** 308-309
  physicians
    Recorde, Robert **13** 68-69
  prisoners
    Norfolk, 3d Duke of **11** 423
  succession issue
    Elizabeth I **5** 263-266
    Henry VIII **7** 302-305

Northumberland, Duke of
11 431-432
Somerset, Duke of 14 333-334

EDWARD VII (1841-1910), king of Great
Britian and Ireland 1901-10 5 214-215
Aga Khan 1 74-76
George V 6 273-275
Joyce, James 8 365-367
Kingsley, Charles 9 28
Victoria 15 485-487

EDWARD VIII (1894-1972), King of Eng-
land (1936) and Duke of Windsor after
abdicating his throne 5 215-217
Baldwin, Stanley 1 468-469
Churchill, Winston Leonard Spencer
4 51-53
Elizabeth II 5 266-269
George VI 6 275

Edward of Carnarvon
see Edward II

Edward of Lancaster, Prince (1453-1471),
claimant to English throne
Warwick and of Salisbury, Earl of
16 122-123

EDWARD THE BLACK PRINCE
(1330-1376), English soldier-statesman
5 217-218
Chaucer, Geoffrey 3 482-485
Edward III 5 211-212
John II 8 275-276
John of Gaunt 8 282-283
López de Ayala, Pedro 9 508-509
Richard III 13 132-133

EDWARD THE CONFESSOR (died 1066,
last king of the house of Wessex, reigned
1042-1066) 5 218-219
Ethelred the Unready 5 327
Harold II 7 162
Leo IX 9 332
Matthew Paris 10 341-342
William I 16 290-291

EDWARD THE ELDER (died 924), king of
England 899-924 5 219-220

Edward, Earl of Warwick
see Warwick, Edward, Earl of

Edward and Eleanora (play)
Thomson, James 15 199-200

Edward Bonaventure (ship)
Chancellor, Richard 3 422

Edwards, Eli
see McKay, Claude

Edwards, George (1693-1733), English naturalist
Bartram, William 2 41-42

EDWARDS, JONATHAN (1703-1758),
American Puritan theologian 5 220-222
Burr, Aaron 3 156-159
Chauncy, Charles 3 485-486
Dwight, Timothy 5 169
Frelinghuysen, Theodorus Jacobus
6 96-97
Hopkins, Samuel 7 496
Mather, Cotton 10 330-332

Stoddard, Solomon 14 462-463

EDWARDS, MELVIN (born 1937),
African-American sculptor 5 222-223

Edwards Air Force Base (California)
Armstrong, Neil Alden 1 304-306

Edwy (died 959), king of the English
955-959
Dunstan 5 151-152

Eeckhout, Albert van der (flourished 17th
century), Dutch painter
John Maurice of Nassau 8 281-282

Eeckhout, Gerbrand van den (1621-1674),
Dutch painter
Rembrandt Harmensz van Rijn
13 91-95

EEG
see Electroencephalogram

Eekenhof (novella)
Storm, Theodor 14 479-480

Eendracht (ship)
Schouten, William Cornelius 14 31

Effi Briest (novel)
Fontane, Theodor 5 504

Effingham (ship)
Barry, John 2 24-25

Efflux, law of (physics)
Torricelli, Evangelista 15 268-269

Effner, Joseph (1687-1745), German archi-
tect
Cuvilliés, François 4 359-360
Zimmermann, Johann Baptist and
Domenikus 16 518

Effort Moderne (art group)
Severini, Gino 14 122

Égarements de Minne, Les (novel)
Colette, Sidonie Gabrielle 4 158-159

Egbe Omo Oduduwa (Yoruba cultural society)
Awolowo, Obafemi 1 389-390

Egbert (died 766), archbishop of York
Alcuin of York 1 122-123

Egell, Paul (1691-1752), German sculptor
Günther, Ignaz 7 41-42

Egerton, Sir Thomas (1540?-1617), English
statesman and judge
Donne, John 5 60-61

Egg, The (story)
Anderson, Sherwood 1 220-221

Eggbeater Series (painting)
Davis, Stuart 4 424-425

EGGLESTON, EDWARD (1837-1902),
American Methodist minister and histori-
an 5 223-224
Howells, William Dean 7 539-541

Egil's Saga (saga)
Sturluson, Snorri 14 310-311

Egisto, L' (opera)
Cavalli, Pietro Francesco 3 382-383

Eglinton, Earl of (Hugh Montgomerie;
1460?-1545), Scottish statesman
Boswell, James 2 432-434

Egmont (play)
Goethe, Johann Wolfgang von
6 388-391

Egmont, Lamoral, Comte d' (1522-1568),
Flemish statesman and general
Alba, Duke of 1 103-104

Egnatius (literary character)
Catullus, Gaius Valerius 3 377-378

Ego (psychology)
Erikson, Erik Homburger 5 309-310
Freud, Sigmund 6 103-106

Egoist (magazine)
Doolittle, Hilda 5 65-66
Eliot, Thomas Stearns 5 258-261

Egoist, The (novel)
Meredith, George 10 512-513

Egorushka (literary character)
Chekhov, Anton Pavlovich 3 494-497

Eguchi (play)
Zeami, Kanze 16 492-493

Egypt (United Arab Republic; nation, North
Africa)
pre-2664 B.C. (first dynasty)
Menes 10 500-502
2664-1786 B.C. (Old and Mid. King-
dom)
Amenemhet I 1 193-194
Imhotep 8 116-117
Khufu 8 540-541
Zoser 16 531
1570-1075 B.C. (New Kingdom)
Amenhotep III 1 194-195
Hatshepsut 7 196-197
Ikhnaton 8 110-111
Moses 11 200-201
Nefertiti 11 331-332
Ramses II 13 22-23
Thutmose III 15 216-217
Tutankhamen 15 359-360
1075-322 B.C. (Late Period)
Ashurbanipal 1 338
Darius I 4 394-395
Hosea 7 512
Isaiah 8 146-147
Piankhi 12 288-289
Shabaka 14 130
Taharqa 15 81-82
332-30 B.C. (Hellenistic)
Alexander the Great 1 137-141
Antiochus III 1 249-250
Cleomenes III 4 103-104
Ptolemy I 12 470-472
Ptolemy II 12 472-473
30 B.C.-A.D. 640 (Roman and Byzan-
tine)
Antony, Mark 1 253-254
Augustus 1 371-373
Caesar, Gaius Julius 3 207-210
Cleopatra 4 105-106
Diocletian 5 19-20

Heraclius **7** 320-321
Justinian I **8** 393-395
640-1258 (Islamic)
Louis IX **9** 525-526
Maimonides **10** 151-152
Muawiya ibn Abu Sufyan
11 223-224
Omar ibn al-Khattab **11** 508-509
Saladin **13** 441-442
see also Crusades; Islamic Empire
1517-1918 (Ottoman)
Fuad I **6** 139
Ibrahim Pasha **8** 97-98
Ismail Pasha **8** 150-151
Johannes IV **8** 272-273
Mahdi **10** 137-138
Mohammed Ali **11** 81-82
Zaghlul Pasha, Saad **16** 485-486
see also Ottoman Empire
1800-80 (British and French)
Baker, Samuel White **1** 454-455
Disraeli, Benjamin **5** 27-29
Gordon, Charles George **6** 448-449
Ibrahim Pasha **8** 97-98
Ismail Pasha **8** 150-151
Lesseps, Vicomte de **9** 354-355
Mohammed Ali **11** 81-82
Napoleon I **11** 306-310
Thiers, Louis Adolphe **15** 181-182
1880-1920 (British)
Allenby, Edmund Henry Hynman
1 171-172
Bright, John **3** 6-7
Cromer, 1st Earl of **4** 317
Fuad I **6** 139
Gladstone, William Ewart
6 357-360
Gordon, Charles George **6** 448-449
Kitchener, Horatio Herbert **9** 45-46
Lawrence, Thomas Edward
9 253-254
Mahdi **10** 137-138
Tewfik Pasha **15** 157-158
Zaghlul Pasha, Saad **16** 485-486
since 1920
Abboud, Ibrahim **1** 11-12
Al-Banna, Hassan **1** 104-106
Azhari, Sayyid Ismail al- **1** 399-401
Boutros-Ghali, Boutros **2** 457-458
Farouk I **5** 387-388
Fuad I **6** 139
Haykal, Muhammad Husain
7 230-231
Idris I **8** 102
Khalil, Sayyid Abdullah **8** 531-532
Marāghī, Mustafā al- **10** 228-229
Mubarak, Hosni **11** 225-226
Nasser, Gamal Abdel **11** 317-318
Sadat, Anwar **13** 412-414
Sadat, Jihan **13** 414-415
Zaghlul Pasha, Saad **16** 485-486
see also Alexandria; Egyptology
see also Arab-Israeli wars; Suez crisis (1956)

Egypta (dance program)
St. Denis, Ruth **13** 430-431
Egyptian Church
Mark **10** 266-267
Egyptian literature
Husayn, Taha **8** 61-62
Egyptian revolutions
first (1879-1882)
Fuad I **6** 139
Zaghlul Pasha, Saad **16** 485-486
second (1919)
Fuad I **6** 139
Zaghlul Pasha, Saad **16** 485-486
Egyptian University
Evans-Pritchard, Edward Evan **5** 340
Husayn, Taha **8** 61-62
Egyptians, The (play)
Aeschylus **1** 70-72
Egyptology (archeology)
Breasted, James Henry **2** 510-511
Champollion, Jean François **3** 421
Petrie, William Matthew Flinders
12 261-262
Ehime Convention Center (Matsuyama, Japan)
Tange, Kenzo **15** 99-101
Ehre, Die (play)
Sudermann, Hermann **15** 12-13
EHRENBURG, ILYA GRIGORIEVICH
(1891-1967), Russian author **5** 224-225
EHRLICH, PAUL (1854-1915), German
bacteriologist **5** 225-226
Dale, Henry Hallett **4** 371-373
Domagk, Gerhard Johannes Paul
5 48-50
Fleming, Alexander **5** 483-485
Landsteiner, Karl **9** 188-189
Weidenreich, Franz **16** 171-172
Eichenberg, Fritz (1901-1990), American
book illustrator
Kent, Rockwell **8** 511
Eichendorff, Joseph von (1788-1857), German Catholic poet
Schumann, Robert Alexander **14** 41-43
Eichhorn, Karl Friedrich (1781-1854), German jurist
Savigny, Friedrich Karl von **13** 502-503
EICHMANN, ADOLF (1906-1962), German Nazi war criminal **5** 226-227
Arendt, Hannah **1** 282-284
Baron, Salo Wittmayer **2** 16-17
Wiesenthal, Simon **16** 264-266
Eickemeyer, Rudolph (1831-1895), German-American inventor
Steinmetz, Charles Proteus **14** 419-420
EIFFEL, ALEXANDRE GUSTAVE
(1832-1923), French engineer **5** 227-228
Eight, The (art group)
Davies, Arthur Bowen **4** 409-410
Glackens, William **6** 355-356
Luks, George Benjamin **10** 38-39

Prendergast, Maurice Brazil **12** 440
Sloan, John **14** 274-275
8 1/2 (film)
Fellini, Federico **5** 408-409
Eight Bells (painting)
Homer, Winslow **7** 468-469
Eight Men (stories)
Wright, Richard **16** 401-402
Eight Prose Masters (Chinese literature)
Wang An-shih **16** 95-97
Eight Views of Lake Biwa (prints)
Hiroshige, Ando **7** 412-413
18th Amendment
see Constitution of the United States—Amendments
Eightfold Path (Buddhism)
Buddha **3** 97-101
Eighth Day, The (novel)
Wilder, Thornton Niven **16** 276-277
Eiheiji (temple, Japan)
Basho, Matsuo **2** 45-48
EIJKMAN, CHRISTIAN (1858-1930), Dutch
physician and biologist **5** 228
Eikonoklastes (pamphlet)
Milton, John **11** 43-46
Eilhart von Oberge (flourished late
12th-ear. 13th century), German poet
Gottfried von Strassburg **6** 461-462
Eimi (book)
Cummings, Edward Estlin **4** 334-336
Einaudi (publishing house)
Pavese, Cesare **12** 154-155
Einaudi, Luigi (1874-1961), Italian economist and statesman
Orlando, Vittorio Emmanuele
11 529-530
Einhard (770?-840), Frankish secretary and
biographer
Charlemagne **3** 445-447
Einsame Menschen (drama)
Hauptmann, Gerhart Johann Robert
7 199-201
Einsiedeln, pilgrimage church of (Switzerland)
Asam, Cosmas Damian and Egid Quirin
1 323-324
EINSTEIN, ALBERT (1879-1955),
German-born American physicist
5 228-231
colleagues
Born, Max **2** 420-421
Rutherford, Ernest **13** 384-387
Szilard, Leo **15** 64-66
friends
Schlick, Friedrich Albert Moritz
14 16-17
Urey, Harold Clayton **15** 394-396
influence of
Aston, Francis William **1** 350-351
Compton, Arthur Holly **4** 186-188
de Broglie, Louis **4** 442-444

Debye, Peter Joseph William
4 447-448
Eddington, Arthur Stanley **5** 201-202
Lemaître, Abbè Georges Édouard
9 315-316
Millikan, Robert Andrews **11** 33-35
Stern, Otto **14** 435
Wigner, Eugene Paul **16** 268-269
influenced by
Leibniz, Gottfried Wilhelm von
9 307-310
Leverrier, Urbain Jean Joseph
9 361-362
Lorentz, Hendrik Antoon **9** 515-516
Michelson, Albert Abraham **11** 7-8
pacifist appeal
Muller, Hermann Joseph
11 238-239
quoted
Curie, Marie Sklodowska **4** 339-341
relativity
see Relativity (physics)

Einstein on the Beach (opera)
Glass, Philip **6** 362-364

Einstein Tower (observatory; Potsdam, Germany)
Mendelsohn, Erich **10** 488

Eirenicon (book)
Pusey, Edward Bouverie **12** 488-489

Eisagoge (book; Porphyry)
Boethius, Anicius Manlius Severinus
2 360-361

EISAI (1141-1215), Japanese Buddhist
monk **5** 231-232

EISELEY, LOREN COREY (1907-1977),
American interpreter of science for the
layman **5** 232-233

EISENHOWER, DWIGHT DAVID
(1890-1969), American general and
statesman, president 1953-61 **5** 233-236
Eisenhower, Mamie Doud **5** 236-237
Allied command
Bradley, Omar Nelson **2** 483-484
Marshall, George Catlett
10 278-279
Montgomery, Bernard Law
11 135-136
Ridgway, Matthew Bunker
13 160-161
appointees
Bohlen, Charles (Chip) **2** 364-366
Burns, Arthur **3** 151-153
Eisenhower, Milton **5** 237-238
Hobby, Oveta Culp **7** 423-425
Priest, Ivy Maude Baker **12** 450-451
Shultz, George Pratt **14** 209-211
Stewart, Potter **14** 449-451
Whittaker, Charles Evans
16 255-256
Wilson, Charles Erwin **16** 316-317
Asian policy
Johnson, Lyndon Baines **8** 308-312
Kennedy, John Fitzgerald **8** 502-506
Kishi, Nobusuke **9** 41-43
MacArthur, Douglas **10** 76-78

Nixon, Richard Milhous **11** 401-404
Cabinet
Dulles, John Foster **5** 134-135
Cuba and
Castro Ruz, Fidel **3** 365-368
papers edited
Chandler, Alfred Du Pont Jr.
3 422-423
political appointments
Anderson, Marian **1** 218-219
Ford, Henry II **6** 6-7
Hoover, Herbert Clark **7** 483-485
Johnson, Lyndon Baines **8** 308-312
Warren, Earl **16** 117-120
Spain and
Franco Bahamonde, Francisco
6 52-54

Eisenhower, John (born 1923), American
author and diplomat
Eisenhower, Dwight David **5** 233-236

EISENHOWER, MAMIE DOUD
(1896-1979), American First Lady
5 236-237

EISENHOWER, MILTON (Milton Stover
Esisenhower; 1899-1985), American
adviser to U.S. presidents and college
president **5** 237-238

EISENMAN, PETER D. (born 1932), American architect **5** 239-240

Eisenstein, Ferdinand Gottfried Max
(1823-1852), German mathematician
Riemann, Georg Friedrich Bernard
13 164-165

EISENSTEIN, SERGEI MIKHAILOVICH
(1898-1948), Russian film director and
cinema theoretician **5** 240-242
Bacon, Francis **1** 421-422
Ford, John **6** 7-8
Prokofiev, Sergei Sergeevich
12 458-460
Ray, Satyajit **13** 60-61

Eisler, Hanns (1878-1962), German composer
Brecht, Bertolt **2** 512-514

Either/Or (book; Kierkegaard)
Ibsen, Henrik **8** 98-100
Kierkegaard, Søren Aabye **8** 547-549

EITOKU, KANO (1543-1590), Japanese
painter of the Momoyama period **5** 242

Eji (Korean high priest)
Shotuku Taishi **14** 205-207

Ejidos (communal farms, Mexico)
Cárdenas, Lázaro **3** 286-287

Eklogá (Byzantine law)
Leo III **9** 330-332

EKWENSI, CYPRIAN (born 1921), Nigerian
writer **5** 242-243
Achebe, Chinua **1** 35-37

El (film)
Buñuel, Luis **3** 127-128

El Alamein
see Alamein, El, Battle of

El Dorado (mythologic city, South America)
Mendaña de Neyra, Álvaro de **10** 483

El Mansûra (city, Egypt)
Louis IX **9** 525-526

El Paso (city, Texas)
Butterfield, John **3** 184-185

El Popular (newspaper)
Toledano, Vicente Lombardo
15 256-257

El Salvador, Republic of (nation, Central
America)
Cristiani, Alfredo **4** 311-313
Daly, Mary **4** 380-381
Duarte, José Napoleón **5** 109-111
Estrada Cabrera, Manuel **5** 325-326
Martínez, Maximiliano Hernández
10 297-298
Romero, Oscar **13** 265-267

Elagabalus (Heliogabalus; 204-222),
Roman emperor 218-222
Ulpian, Domitius **15** 385-386

Elam (ancient king; Asia)
Sargon of Agade **13** 483

Elamites (ancient Asiatic people)
Ashurbanipal **1** 338
Sennacherib **14** 108

Elasticity (painting)
Boccioni, Umberto **2** 353-354

Elchingen, Battle of (1805)
Ney, Michel **11** 372-373

Elchingen, Duke of
see Ney, Michel

Elder Conklin (stories)
Harris, Frank **7** 172-173

Elder Statesman, The (play)
Eliot, Thomas Stearns **5** 258-261

ELDERS, JOYCELYN (born 1933), first
African American and second woman
U.S. surgeon general **5** 243-246

ELEANOR OF AQUITAINE (circa
1122-1204), queen of France 1137-52,
and of England 1154-1204 **5** 246-247
Henry II **7** 287-289
John **8** 274-275
Louis VII **9** 524-525
Marie de France **10** 259
Richard I **13** 130

Eleanor of Toledo and Her Son (painting)
Bronzino **3** 19

Eleatic school (philosophy)
Parmenides **12** 116-117
Zeno of Elea **16** 500

Elect, The (Calvinism)
Calvin, John **3** 239-242

Election Entertainment, An (prints)
Hogarth, William **7** 446-447

Electra (ballet)
Graham, Martha **6** 485-486

Electra (Greek mythology)
Aeschylus **1** 70-72

Electra (play)
  Galdós, Benito Pérez **6** 177-178
  Giraudoux, Jean **6** 349-350

Electra (play; Euripides)
  Euripides **5** 332-334
  Sophocles **14** 343-345

Electric battery
  see Battery (electrical cell)

Electrical industry
  see Business and industrial leaders—
    electrical industry

Electricity (physics)
  and magnetism
    Duhem, Pierre Maurice Marie **5** 129
    Faraday, Michael **5** 380
    Henry, Joseph **7** 307-308
    Maxwell, James Clerk **10** 361-364
    Tesla, Nikola **15** 156-157
  applications
    Edison, Thomas Alva **5** 206-208
    Sprague, Frank Julian **14** 385-386
  atomic structure
    Helmholtz, Hermann Ludwig Ferdi-
     nand von **7** 268-269
    Thomson, Joseph John **15** 200-201
  conductivity
    Cavendish, Henry **3** 383-384
    Dirac, Paul Adrien Maurice **5** 23-24
    Röntgen, Wilhelm Conrad
     13 273-275
  in animals
    Galvani, Luigi **6** 194-195
    Volta, Alessandro **16** 12-14
  lightning
    Franklin, Benjamin **6** 60-64
  superconductivity
    Bardeen, John **2** 1-3
  transistors
    Bardeen, John **2** 1-3
  units
    Ampère, André Marie **1** 205-206
    Coulomb, Charles Augustin de
     4 266-267
    Faraday, Michael **5** 380
    Gauss, Karl Friedrich **6** 240-242
    Gilbert, William **6** 313-314
    Henry, Joseph **7** 307-308
    Hertz, Heinrich Rudolf **7** 346-347
    Joule, James Prescott **8** 363-364
    Maxwell, James Clerk **10** 361-364
    Ohm, Georg Simon **11** 486-487
    Rayleigh, 3d Baron **13** 62
    Volta, Alessandro **16** 12-14
    see also Induction (electricity)

Electrochemistry
  Berzelius, Jöns Jacob **2** 231-233
  Haber, Fritz **7** 56-58
  Onsager, Lars **11** 520-523

Electrode, needle (instrument)
  Hess, Walter Rudolf **7** 365

Electrodynamics (physics)
  Ampère, André Marie **1** 205-206
  Einstein, Albert **5** 228-231

Fermi, Enrico 5 422-424
  Helmholtz, Hermann Ludwig Ferdinand
   von **7** 268-269

Electroencephalogram (medicine)
  Adrian, Edgar Douglas **1** 67-69

Electrolysis (chemistry)
  Berzelius, Jöns Jacob **2** 231-233
  Du Bois-Reymond, Emil **5** 118-119
  Faraday, Michael **5** 380
  Gay-Lussac, Joseph Louis **6** 245-246

Electrolyte (chemistry)
  Arrhenius, Svante August **1** 318-320
  Debye, Peter Joseph William **4** 447-448
  Onsager, Lars **11** 520-523

Electromagnetism (physics)
  applications
    Curie, Pierre **4** 341-344
    Marconi, Guglielmo **10** 239-240
    Morse, Samuel Finley Breese
     11 192-193
    Townes, Charles Hard **15** 281-282
  theory
    Anderson, Carl David **1** 214-215
    Bohr, Niels Henrik David **2** 366-368
    Boltzmann, Ludwig **2** 379-380
    Duhem, Pierre Maurice Marie **5** 129
    Eddington, Arthur Stanley **5** 201-202
    Hertz, Heinrich Rudolf **7** 346-347
    Lorentz, Hendrik Antoon **9** 515-516
    Maxwell, James Clerk **10** 361-364
    Oersted, Hans Christian **11** 476-478
    Rutherford, Ernest **13** 384-387

Electrometer (instrument)
  Volta, Alessandro **16** 12-14

Electron (physics)
  discovery
    Crookes, William **4** 323-324
    Thomson, Joseph John **15** 200-201
  physical properties
    Bothe, Walther **2** 438-439
    Bragg, William Henry **2** 488-489
    Landau, Lev Davidovich **9** 184-185
    Langmuir, Irving **9** 196-197
    Millikan, Robert Andrews **11** 33-35
    Rabi, Isidor Isaac **12** 526-527
    Rutherford, Ernest **13** 384-387
  showers (cascade theory)
    Bhabha, Homi Jehangir **2** 253-254
  theory
    Bethe, Hans Albrecht **2** 238-239
    Bohr, Niels Henrik David **2** 366-368
    de Broglie, Louis **4** 442-444
    Dirac, Paul Adrien Maurice **5** 23-24
    Eddington, Arthur Stanley **5** 201-202
    Fermi, Enrico **5** 422-424
    Lorentz, Hendrik Antoon **9** 515-516
    Schrödinger, Erwin **14** 31-33
    Thomson, George Paget **15** 198-199

Electron microscope (instrument)
  Zworykin, Vladimir Kosma **16** 539-540

Electron synchrotron (particle accelerator)
  Lawrence, Ernest Orlando **9** 248-250

Electronic Data Systems (United States
 company)
  Perot, Henry Ross **12** 230-231

Electronic music
  Babbitt, Milton **1** 410
  Berio, Luciano **2** 194-195
  Boulez, Pierre **2** 444-445
  Cage, John **3** 211-214
  Cowell, Henry Dixon **4** 280-281
  Cunningham, Merce **4** 337-338
  Edison, Thomas Alva **5** 206-208
  Halffter, Christóbal **7** 79-80
  Krenek, Ernst **9** 98-99
  Varèse, Edgard **15** 432-433

Electronic studies (musical composition)
  Stockhausen, Karlheinz **14** 460-461

Electrophoresis (chemistry)
  Tiselius, Arne Wilhelm Kaurin
   15 240-241

Electrophorus (science device)
  Volta, Alessandro **16** 12-14

Electrophysiology (medicine)
  Du Bois-Reymond, Emil **5** 118-119

Electroscope (science device)
  Volta, Alessandro **16** 12-14

Electrostatics (physics)
  Cavendish, Henry **3** 383-384
  Coulomb, Charles Augustin de
   4 266-267
  Gilbert, William **6** 313-314

Elegant Amusements of the Four Seasons
 (prints)
  Utamaro, Kitagawa **15** 397

Elegia de madonna Flammetta, L' (book)
  Boccaccio, Giovanni **2** 351-353

Elegia VI (poem)
  Camoëns, Luis Vaz de **3** 247-249

Elegies (poems)
  Chénier, André Marie **3** 500-501
  Theocritus **15** 171-172

Elegy (literature)
  Europe
    Arnold, Matthew **1** 311-313
    Collins, William **4** 168-169
    Donne, John **5** 60-61
    Gray, Thomas **6** 509-510
    Hölderlin, Johann Christian
     Friedrich **7** 451-452
    Hugo, Victor Marie **8** 22-25
    Milton, John **11** 43-46
    Pope, Alexander **12** 395-397
    Shelley, Percy Bysshe **14** 176-178
    Tennyson, Alfred **15** 144-146
  Latin literature
    Catullus, Gaius Valerius **3** 377-378
    Ovid **12** 34-36
  U.S.
    Whitman, Walt **16** 249-251

Elegy for J. F. K. (poem; Auden)
  Stravinsky, Igor Fedorovich **14** 502-506

Elegy for Young Lovers (musical composition)
Henze, Hans Werner **7** 314

Elegy to the Memory of an Unfortunate Lady (poem)
Pope, Alexander **12** 395-397

Elegy Written in a Country Churchyard (poem; Gray)
Gainsborough, Thomas **6** 170-172
Gray, Thomas **6** 509-510

Elejías (poems)
Jiménez, Juan Ramón **8** 261-262

Elektra (opera; Strauss)
Hofmannsthal, Hugo von **7** 443-444
Strauss, Richard **14** 500-501

Element (chemistry)
atomic weight
Avogadro, Lorenzo Romano Amedeo Carlo **1** 388-389
Berzelius, Jöns Jacob **2** 231-233
Dalton, John **4** 378-379
Dumas, Jean Baptiste André **5** 138-139
Richards, Theodore William **13** 137-138
hypothetical
Mendeleev, Dmitrii Ivanovich **10** 486-488
inert
Mendeleev, Dmitrii Ivanovich **10** 486-488
Rutherford, Ernest **13** 384-387
Soddy, Frederick **14** 321-323
isotopic complexity
Aston, Francis William **1** 350-351
see also Isotope (chemistry)
periodic table
Mendeleev, Dmitrii Ivanovich **10** 486-488
Rayleigh, 3d Baron **13** 62
radioactive
Hahn, Otto **7** 64-65
Rutherford, Ernest **13** 384-387
Seaborg, Glenn Theodore **14** 74-76
see also individual elements

Element (philosophy)
Helmont, Jan Baptista van **7** 269-271
Paracelsus, Philippus Aureolus **12** 91-93

Elementargeister (essay)
Heine, Heinrich **7** 259-260

Elementary and Secondary Education Act (United States)
Johnson, Lyndon Baines **8** 308-312

Elementary Forms of Religious Life, The (book; Durkheim)
Durkheim, Émile **5** 162-163
Mauss, Marcel **10** 352-353

Elementary particles (physics)
Anderson, Carl David **1** 214-215
Cherenkov, Pavel Alekseevich **3** 502-503
Fermi, Enrico **5** 422-424
Gell-Mann, Murray **6** 257-258

Heisenberg, Werner Karl **7** 261-263
Millikan, Robert Andrews **11** 33-35
Wigner, Eugene Paul **16** 268-269
Yukawa, Hideki **16** 481-482
see also Electron; Hyperon; Meson; Neutrino; Neutron; Particle accelerators; Particle detectors; Proton; Radioactivity

Elements (book; Euclid)
see Euclidian geometry—*Elements*

Elements of Style, The (book)
White, E. B. **16** 228-230

Elephant (animal)
Hannibal Barca **7** 128-130

Elephant Island (Antarctica)
Shackleton, Ernest Henry **14** 132-133

Elephant on the Moon, The (satire)
Butler, Samuel (poet) **3** 183-184

Éléphants, Les (poem)
Leconte de Lisle, Charles Marie René **9** 273-274

Elevator industry
see Business and industrial leaders—elevator industry

ELGAR, SIR EDWARD (1857-1934), English composer **5** 247-248

Elgin, Frank (literary character)
Odets, Clifford **11** 470-471

ELGIN, 8TH EARL OF (James Bruce; 1811-63), English governor general of Canada **5** 248-249
Baldwin, Robert **1** 466-468
Lafontaine, Louis-Hippolyte **9** 157-158

El-Hajj Malik El-Shabazz
see Malcolm X

Elhanan (Old Testament character)
David, Jacques Louis **4** 407-409

Eli (Old Testament judge)
Samuel **13** 457-458

Eli (play)
Sachs, Nelly **13** 411-412

Elia
see Lamb, Charles

ELIADE, MIRCEA (1907-1986), Rumanian-born historian of religions and novelist **5** 249-250

Elias
see Elijah

ELIAS, TASLIM OLAWALE (1914-1991), Nigerian academic and jurist and president of the International Court of Justice **5** 250-251

Eliezer, Israel ben
see Baal Shem Tov

Elijah (Elias; 9th century B.C.), Biblical prophet
John, St. **8** 273-274

Elijah (oratorio)
Mendelssohn, Moses **10** 488-489

ELIJAH BEN SOLOMON (1720-1797), Jewish scholar **5** 251-252

Elijah Fed by Ravens (painting)
Allston, Washington **1** 176-177
Guercino **7** 27

Elinor and Marianne
see Sense and Sensibility (novel)

ELION, GERTRUDE B. (born 1918), American biochemist and Nobel Prize winner **5** 252-254

ELIOT, CHARLES WILLIAM (1834-1926), American educator **5** 254
Channing, Edward **3** 435
Lowell, Abbott Lawrence **10** 12-13

ELIOT, GEORGE (pen name of Mary Ann Evans; 1819-80), English novelist **5** 254-256
Meredith, George **10** 512-513
Van Gogh, Vincent **15** 427-429

ELIOT, JOHN (1604-1690), English-born missionary to the Massachusetts Indians **5** 256-258

Eliot, Sir John (1592-1632), English statesman
Buckingham, 1st Duke of **3** 93-94
Hampden, John **7** 110-111

ELIOT, THOMAS STEARNS (1888-1965), American-English poet, critic, and playwright **5** 258-261
as critic
Miller, Henry **11** 26-27
Milton, John **11** 43-46
Shelley, Percy Bysshe **14** 176-178
associates
Doolittle, Hilda **5** 65-66
Ford, Ford Madox **6** 1-2
Woolf, Virginia Stephen **16** 381-382
influence of
Auden, Wystan Hugh **1** 364-366
Betjeman, John **2** 243-245
Crane, Hart **4** 291-293
Ellison, Ralph Waldo **5** 274-275
Lowell, Amy **10** 13
MacLeish, Archibald **10** 109-110
Sandburg, Carl **13** 461-462
Tate, Allen **15** 116
Williams, William Carlos **16** 308-309
influenced by
Browning, Robert **3** 53-55
Euripides **5** 332-334
Gourmont, Remy de **6** 475
Laforgue, Jules **9** 160-161
Pound, Ezra Loomis **12** 415-417
Sitwell, Edith **14** 265-266
musical settings
Stravinsky, Igor Fedorovich **14** 502-506
papal theater
John, XXIII **8** 277-280

Eliott, George Augustus
see Heathfield, 1st Baron

Elis (ancient nation, Greece)
    Epaminondas **5** 291-292

Elisabetta, regina d'Inghilterra (opera)
    Rossini, Gioacchino **13** 311-312

Elisir d'amore, L' (opera)
    Donizetti, Gaetano **5** 59-60

Elitism (political science)
    Mills, C. Wright **11** 35-36
    Pareto, Vilfredo **12** 95-96
    Spengler, Oswald **14** 372-373
    Stendhal **14** 422-425
    Tarde, Jean Gabriel **15** 108-109
    Wallas, Graham **16** 77-78

Elixiere des Teufels, Die (novel)
    Hoffmann, Ernst Theodor Amadeus
        7 439-440

Eliza (literary character)
    Stowe, Harriet Elizabeth Beecher
        14 484-485

Eliza (opera)
    Cherubini, Luigi Carlo Zanobi Salvatore
        Maria **3** 505-506

Elizabeth (Elizabeth Angela Marguerite
    Bowes-Lyon; born 1900), queen of
    George VI of England
        George VI **6** 275

Elizabeth (Elizabeth Farnese; 1692-1766),
    Italian queen of Philip V of Spain
        Charles III **3** 454-455
        Philip V **12** 276-277

Elizabeth (Elizabeth of Bourbon; died
    1644), queen of Philip IV of Spain
        Philip IV **12** 275

Elizabeth (Elizabeth of Valois; 1545-68),
    French princess, queen of Philip II of
    Spain
        Philip II (king of Spain) **12** 271-273

ELIZABETH (Elizabeth Petrovna; 1709-61),
    empress of Russia 1741-61 **5** 261-263
        Catherine the Great **3** 370-372
        Frederick II **6** 81-84
        Maria Theresa **10** 256-258
        Paul I **12** 143-144

Elizabeth (Elizabeth Woodville; 1437?-92),
    queen of Edward IV of England
        Richard III **13** 132-133
        Warwick and of Salisbury, Earl of
            16 122-123

ELIZABETH I (1533-1603), queen of Eng-
    land and Ireland 1558-1603 **5** 263-266
        court
            Bacon, Francis **1** 422-424
            Coke, Edward **4** 141-142
            Essex, 2d Earl of **5** 321-322
            Mary, I **10** 308-309
            Raleigh, Walter **13** 9-11
            Sidney, Philip **14** 214-215
        explorations
            Frobisher, Martin **6** 121-122
            Gilbert, Humphrey **6** 313
        historians of
            Clarendon, 1st Earl of **4** 73-75
            Froude, James Anthony **6** 133-134

    in literature and art
        Hilliard, Nicholas **7** 391-392
        Lope Félix de Vega Carpio **9**
        Schiller, Johann Christoph Friedrich
            von **14** 4-7
        Spenser, Edmund **14** 373-376
    Netherlands and
        Leicester, Earl of **9** 312-313
        Oldenbarnevelt, Johan van
            11 495-496
    Protestantism
        Coligny, Gaspard de **4** 159-160
        Cranmer, Thomas **4** 295-296
        Edward VI **5** 213-214
        Pius V **12** 332-333
    Spain and
        Drake, Francis **5** 94-96
        Gorges, Ferdinando **6** 455-456
        Hawkins, John **7** 210-211
        Philip II (king, Spain) **12** 271-273
        see also Armada, Spanish
    succession issue
        Henry VIII **7** 302-305
        James I **8** 204-206
        Mary, I **10** 308-309
        Northumberland, Duke of
            11 431-432

ELIZABETH II (born 1926), queen of Great
    Britain and Ireland **5** 266-269
        Britten, Benjamin **3** 10-11
        Charles, Prince of Wales **3** 448-450
        Coward, Noel **4** 279-280
        George VI **6** 275
        John, XXIII **8** 277-280
        Lennon, John Winston **9** 326-328

Elizabeth, St. (New Testament character)
    Mary **10** 308

Elizabeth Appleton (novel)
    O'Hara, John **11** 485

Elizabeth Bonaventure (ship)
    Drake, Francis **5** 94-96

ELIZABETH BOWES-LYON (Elizabeth
    Angela Marguerite Bowes-Lyon; born
    1900), queen of Great Britain and Ireland
    (1936-1952) and Queen Mother after
    1952 **5** 261-263

Elizabeth Furnace (ironworks)
    Stiegel, Henry William **14** 451

Elizabeth Kenny Institute (Minneapolis,
    Minnesota)
        Kenny, Elizabeth **8** 509-510

ELIZABETH OF HUNGARY (1207-1231),
    saint and humanitarian **5** 271-272

**ELIZABETH BAGAAYA NYABONGO OF
    TORO** (born 1940), Ugandan ambassa-
    dor **5** 269-271

Elizabeth the Queen (play)
    Anderson, Maxwell **1** 219-220

Elizabethan literature
    see English literature—Elizabethan

Elkins Antirebate Bill (1903)
    Roosevelt, Theodore **13** 280-283

Ellen (ship)
    Davis, John **4** 419

Ellerman, Winifred (1894-1983), English
    novelist
        Doolittle, Hilda **5** 65-66
        Moore, Marianne **11** 148-149

Ellesmere, Baron Thomas (1540?-1617),
    British statesman
        Coke, Edward **4** 141-142

Ellesmere Island (Greenland)
    Byrd, Richard Evelyn **3** 186-187
    MacMillan, Donald Baxter **10** 111-112

Ellet, Charles, Jr. (1810-1862), American
    civil engineer
        Roebling, John Augustus **13** 241-242

Ellicott, Maj. Andrew (1754-1820), Ameri-
    can surveyor
        Banneker, Benjamin **1** 490-491

**ELLINGTON, "DUKE" EDWARD
    KENNEDY** (born 1899), American jazz
    composer **5** 273-274

Elliot, Anne (literary character)
    Austen, Jane **1** 377-379

Elliot-Murray-Kynynmond, Gilbert
    see Minto, 1st Earl of

Ellipse (math)
    Euclid **5** 327-329
    Gauss, Karl Friedrich **6** 240-242

Ellipsis (grammar)
    Gracián y Morales, Baltasar Jerónimo
        6 481-482
    Hopkins, Gerard Manley **7** 492-494

Ellis Island (New York City)
    La Guardia, Fiorello Henry **9** 166-167

ELLISON, RALPH WALDO (1914-1994),
    African American author and spokesper-
    son for racial identity **5** 274-275
        Bearden, Romare Howard **2** 86-88

ELLSBERG, DANIEL (born 1931), U.S. gov-
    ernment official and Vietnam peace
    activist **5** 275-277

ELLSWORTH, LINCOLN (1880-1951),
    American adventurer and polar explorer
    5 277
        Amundsen, Roald **1** 206-207
        Nobile, Umberto **11** 411-412

Elmer Gantry (novel)
    Lewis, Harry Sinclair **9** 385-387

Elmer the Great (play)
    Lardner, Ringgold Wilmer **9** 204-205

Elmhurst College (Illinois)
    Niebuhr, Helmut Richard **11** 386-387

Eloges (poems)
    Perse, Saint-John **12** 242-243

Eloisa to Abelard (poem)
    Pope, Alexander **12** 395-397

Elpenor (play)
    Goethe, Johann Wolfgang von
        6 388-391

ELSASSER, WALTER MAURICE
(1904-1991), American physicist
5 277-278

Elsheimer, Adam (1578-1610), German
painter
Claude Lorrain **4** 89-90
Rembrandt Harmensz van Rijn
13 91-95

Elsie Venner (novel)
Holmes, Oliver Wendell **7** 457-458

Elsner, Joseph (1769-1854), Polish musician
Chopin, Frédéric François **4** 16-18

Eltham Ordinaces (1526)
Wolsey, Thomas **16** 364-366

Eluard, Paul (1895-1952), French poet
Breton, André **2** 519-520
Chirico, Giorgio de **4** 4
Poulenc, Francis **12** 414-415

Elvira, or the Bride of the Plate (poem)
Echeverría, José Estéban **5** 197-198

Ely, Richard Theodore (1854-1943), American economist
Commons, John Rogers **4** 185

Emanation (philosophy)
Erigena, John Scotus **5** 308-309
ibn Gabirol, Solomon ben Judah **8** 92

Emanations (musical composition)
Metcalfe, Charles Theophilus
10 531-532
Penderecki, Krzysztof **12** 195-197
Wilberforce, William **16** 269-270

Emancipation of Serfs (Russia; 1861)
Alexander II **1** 132-133

Emancipation Proclamation (United States;
1863)
author
Lincoln, Abraham **9** 415-418
critics
Brown, Benjamin Gratz **3** 32-33
Chase, Salmon Portland **3** 473-475
Curtis, Benjamin Robbins **4** 349
Seymour, Horatio **14** 126-127
Weed, Thurlow **16** 169-170
Wood, Fernando **16** 367-368
supporters
Emerson, Ralph Waldo **5** 278-280
Garrison, William Lloyd **6** 226-228
Morton, Oliver Hazard Perry Throck
11 197-198
Phillips, Wendell **12** 281-282

Emancipists (Australia)
Macquarie, Lachlan **10** 115-116
Phillip, Arthur **12** 279-280
Wentworth, William Charles
16 203-204

Embargo (satire)
Bryant, William Cullen **3** 83-85

Embargo Act (United States; 1807)
Clinton, DeWitt **4** 112-113
Crawford, William Harris **4** 299-300
Gallatin, Albert **6** 183-184

Madison, James **10** 121-123

Embarkation of Cythera (painting)
Watteau, Antoine **16** 143-144

Embden-Meyerhof theory (glycolysis)
Meyerhof, Otto Fritz **10** 537-539

Embraceable You (song)
Parker, Charles Christopher Jr.
12 105-106

Embryology (science)
and cancer
Mintz, Beatrice **11** 49-50
developments in
Baer, Karl Ernst von **1** 431-432
Huxley, Thomas Henry **8** 77-79
Schwann, Theodor **14** 51-52
Stevens, Nettie Maria **14** 441-442
Weismann, August Freidrich
Leopold **16** 178-180
evolutionary
Metchnikoff, Élie **10** 532-533
founders
Harvey, William **7** 189-190
Malpighi, Marcello **10** 176-178
Müller, Johannes Peter **11** 239-240
Spallanzani, Lazzaro **14** 360-361
Spemann, Hans **14** 368-369
see also Scientists—embryologists

Emérillon (ship)
Cartier, Jacques **3** 343-344

Emergence of Novelty, The (book)
Morgan, Conway Lloyd **11** 159-160

Emergency Committee of Atomic Scientists
(established 1947)
Szilard, Leo **15** 64-66

Emergency Fleet Corp. (United States; WW
I)
Schwab, Charles Michael **14** 50-51

Emerson (musical composition)
Ives, Charles Edward **8** 159-160

EMERSON, RALPH WALDO (1803-1882),
American poet, essayist, and philosopher
5 278-280
admires others' works
Allston, Washington **1** 176-177
Carlyle, Thomas **3** 304-305
Heavysege, Charles **7** 246
biographers
Holmes, Oliver Wendell **7** 457-458
friends
Alcott, Louisa May **1** 122
Clough, Arthur Hugh **4** 123-124
Hawthorne, Nathaniel **7** 212-215
Lazarus, Emma **9** 260-261
influence of
Burroughs, John **3** 160-161
Curtis, George William **4** 349-350
French, Daniel Chester **6** 98-99
Frost, Robert Lee **6** 130-133
Holmes, Oliver Wendell **7** 457-458
Howells, William Dean **7** 539-541
Pound, Ezra Loomis **12** 415-417
Vivekananda **16** 4-5
Warren, Robert Penn **16** 121-122

Williams, William Carlos
16 308-309
Wright, Frank Lloyd **16** 398-401
influenced by
Mather, Cotton **10** 330-332
Plutarch **12** 359-360
quoted
Brown, John **3** 39-41
Whitman, Walt **16** 249-251
transcendentalism
Adler, Felix **1** 63-64
Alcott, Amos Bronson **1** 121
Brownson, Orestes Augustus
3 57-58
Crane, Hart **4** 291-293
Cummings, Edward Estlin **4** 334-336
Fuller, Sarah Margaret **6** 150-151
Parker, Theodore **12** 112-113
Thoreau, Henry David **15** 203-205

Emerson, Rollins Adams (1873-1947),
American geneticist
Beadle, George Wells **2** 80-81

Emigrant Aid Journal (periodical)
Donnelly, Ignatius **5** 62

Emigration of Daniel Boone (painting)
Bingham, George Caleb **2** 278-279

Émile, L' (treatise)
Rousseau, Jean Jacques **13** 324-328

Emilia Galotti (play)
Lessing, Gotthold Ephraim **9** 357-359

Emin Pasha, Mehmed (Eduard Schnitzer;
1840-92), German explorer in Africa
Stanley, Henry Morton **14** 399-400
Tippu Tip **15** 235-236

Eminent People (play)
Benavente y Martinez, Jacinto
2 146-147

Eminent Victorians (book; Strachey)
Arnold, Matthew **1** 311-313

EMINESCU, MIHAIL (1850-1889), Romanian poet **5** 280-281

Emma (novel)
Austen, Jane **1** 377-379

Emma of Normandy
see Aelfgyfu

Emmeline (story)
Musset, Louis Charles Alfred de
11 271-272

Emmerich, Anna Katharina (1774-1824),
German stigmatic and visionary
Brentano, Clemens **2** 515-516

EMMET, ROBERT (1778-1803), Irish
nationalist and revolutionary **5** 281-282

Emmett, Dan (1815-1904), American songwriter
Christy, Edwin P. **4** 34-35

Empedocle (play)
Rolland, Romain **13** 260

EMPEDOCLES (circa 493-circa 444 B.C.),
Greek philosopher, poet, and scientist
5 282

Lucretius **10** 26-27

Empedocles on Etna ... (poems)
Arnold, Matthew **1** 311-313

Empedokles (tragedy)
Hölderlin, Johann Christian Friedrich
7 451-452

Emperor and Galilean (play)
Ibsen, Henrik **8** 98-100

Emperor and Proletarian (poem)
Eminescu, Mihail **5** 280-281

Emperor Charles VI (sculpture)
Donner, Georg Raphael **5** 63

Emperor Concerto (musical composition)
Beethoven, Ludwig van **2** 114-117

Emperor Heinrich (sculpture)
Günther, Ignaz **7** 41-42

Emperor Jones, The (play and film)
O'Neill, Eugene **11** 514-516
Robeson, Paul Leroy **13** 198-199

Emperor of Ice Cream, The (poem)
Stevens, Wallace **14** 443-445

Emperor of Portugallia, The (novel)
Lagerlöf, Selma Ottiliana Lovisa
9 163-164

Emperor Quartet (musical composition)
Haydn, Franz Joseph **7** 219-221

Emperors
see Statesmen

Empfang bei der Welt (book)
Mann, Heinrich **10** 201-202

Desaparecidos (Argentina "disappeared" or
"missing ones")
Alfonsín, Raúl Ricardo **1** 146-148
Timerman, Jacobo **15** 226-228

Empiricism (philosophy)
and rationalism
Kant, Immanuel **8** 430-432-123
British
Berkeley, George **2** 197-198
Hobbes, Thomas **7** 421-423
Hume, David **8** 31-34
Locke, John **9** 478-480
Mill, John Stuart **11** 21-23
in historiography
Buckle, Henry Thomas **3** 95-96
Namier, Lewis Bernstein
11 301-303
in psychology and politics
Fries, Jakob Friedrich **6** 116-117
Maurras, Charles Marie Photius
10 350-351
influence of
Condillac, Étienne Bonnot de
4 194-195
Husserl, Edmund **8** 67-68
Lotze, Rudolf Hermann **9** 521-522
Mach, Ernst **10** 90-91
Meinong, Alexius Ritter von Hand-
schuchsheim **10** 461-462
influenced by
Malebranche, Nicolas **10** 166-167

opposition
Bradley, Francis Herbert **2** 481-482
Green, Thomas Hill **6** 520-521
Stirner, Max **14** 459-460
precursors
Campanella, Tommaso **3** 249
Carneades **3** 309
Duns Scotus, John **5** 149-150
William of Ockham **16** 298-299
radical
James, William **8** 215-217
20th-century development
Russell, Bertrand Arthur William
13 373-374

Employment (economics)
Hansen, Alvin **7** 131-132
Keynes, John Maynard **8** 528-530

Employment Act (United States; 1946)
Wagner, Robert Ferdinand **16** 43

Emporia, College of (Kansas)
Parrington, Vernon Louis **12** 119-120

Empress Kunigunde (sculpture)
Günther, Ignaz **7** 41-42

Empress Zoe, The (novel)
Kazantzakis, Nikos **8** 466-468

Empresses
see Statesmen

Empty Canvas, The (novel)
Moravia, Alberto **11** 153-155

Empty House, The (story)
Doyle, Arthur Conan **5** 91-92

Empty Mirror (poems)
Ginsberg, Allen **6** 332-333

Empty Space, The (book)
Brook, Peter **3** 19-21

En blanc et noir (musical composition)
Debussy, Achille Claude **4** 445-447

En Camarades (play)
Colette, Sidonie Gabrielle **4** 158-159

En el mes era de abril (ballad)
Vicente, Gil **15** 479-480

En ménage (novel)
Huysmans, Joris Karl **8** 81-82

En route (novel)
Huysmans, Joris Karl **8** 81-82

Enabling Act (Germany; 1933)
Hitler, Adolf **7** 417-420

Enamel Peacock, The (poems)
Morin, Paul **11** 174

Encantadas, The (story)
Melville, Herman **10** 472-476

Encarnacion, Church of the (Madrid)
Churriguera, José Benito de **4** 53-54

Enchanted Soul, The (novel)
Rolland, Romain **13** 260

ENCINA, JUAN DEL (1468-1529?), Spanish
author and composer **5** 283
Vicente, Gil **15** 479-480

Encolpius (literary character)
Petronius Arbiter **12** 262-263

Encomia (rhetoric)
Isocrates **8** 151

Encomienda system (Spanish America)
Gasca, Pedro de la **6** 230-231
Las Casas, Bartolomé de **9** 211-212
Velasco, Luis de **15** 450-451
Velázquez de Cuéllar, Diego **15** 459
Zumárraga, Juan de **16** 531-532

Encomium moriae (book)
Erasmus, Desiderius **5** 298-300

Encounter (magazine)
Spender, Stephen Harold **14** 370-371

Encounter Bay (Australia)
Flinders, Matthew **5** 490

Encyclopedia (reformer book)
Africana
Du Bois, William Edward Burghardt
5 116-118
Americana
Lieber, Francis **9** 401-402
Britannica
Bellows, George Wesley **2** 143
Mill, James **11** 21
Whitney, Josiah Dwight **16** 254-255
Brockhaus
Lieber, Francis **9** 401-402
Encyclopédie
Alembert, Jean le Rond d'
1 127-128
Diderot, Denis **5** 1-2
Holbach, Baron d' **7** 448-449
Rousseau, Jean Jacques **13** 324-328
Turgot, Anne Robert Jacques
15 348-349
Italiana
Gentile, Giovanni **6** 267
of Mathematical Sciences
Pauli, Wolfgang Ernst **12** 149
of the Social Sciences
Johnson, Alvin Saunders **8** 293-294
Seligman, Edwin Robert Anderson
14 93-94
of mythological science
Boccaccio, Giovanni **2** 351-353

End of Ideology, The (book)
Bell, Daniel **2** 132-133

End of Norma, The (novel)
Alarcón, Pedro Antonio de **1** 100-101

End of Something, The (story)
Hemingway, Ernest Miller **7** 274-277

End of the Affair, The (novel)
Greene, Graham **6** 523-524

End of the Battle, The (novel)
Waugh, Evelyn Arthur St. John
16 145-147

End of the War (painting)
Pippin, Horace **12** 318-319

End of the World (painting)
Signorelli, Luca **14** 221-222

End of the World, The (novel)
Eggleston, Edward **5** 223-224

ENDARA, GUILLERMO (born 1936), installed as president of Panama by the U.S. Government in 1989 **5** 283-284

Endeavor (magazine)
Hu Shih **8** 63-65

Endeavour (ship)
Banks, Joseph **1** 489-490
Cook, James **4** 214-215

ENDECOTT, JOHN (1588-1655), English colonial governor of Massachusetts **5** 284-285

Enderby Land (Antarctica)
Shackleton, Ernest Henry **14** 132-133

ENDERS, JOHN FRANKLIN (1897-1985), American virologist **5** 285-286

Endgame (play)
Beckett, Samuel **2** 102-104

Endicott, William Crowninshield (1860-1936), American lawyer and statesman
Cleveland, Stephen Grover **4** 108-110

Endless Column (sculpture cycle)
Brancusi, Constantin **2** 494-496

Endocrinology (science)
Addison, Thomas **1** 58-59
Houssay, Bernardo Alberto **7** 522-523
Pincus, Gregory Goodwin **12** 310-312

Endurance (ship)
Shackleton, Ernest Henry **14** 132-133

Endymion (novel)
Disraeli, Benjamin **5** 27-29

Endymion (poem)
Keats, John **8** 470-472

Endymion (ship)
Decatur, Stephen **4** 448-449

Enemy of the People, An (play)
Ibsen, Henrik **8** 98-100

Energy resources
policy
Davignon **4** 410-411

Enfance du Christ, L' (oratorio)
Berlioz, Louis Hector **2** 203-205

Enfant noir, L' (novel)
Laye, Camara **9** 257-259

Enfant prodigue, L' (musical composition)
Debussy, Achille Claude **4** 445-447
Milhaud, Darius **11** 17-18

Enfant prodigue, L' (play)
Voltaire **16** 14-16

Enfants anormaux, Les (book)
Binet, Alfred **2** 277-278

Engastrimythes (literary characters)
Rabelais, François **12** 524-526

Engelbrechtsz, Cornelis (1468-1533), Dutch painter
Lucas van Leyden **10** 20-21

ENGELS, FRIEDRICH (1820-1895), German revolutionist and social theorist **5** 286-288
Althusser, Louis **1** 182-183
Bernstein, Eduard **2** 218
Fourier, François Charles Marie **6** 31-32
Kelley, Florence **8** 483-484
Leo XIII **9** 334-336
Marx, Karl **10** 304-308
Morris, William **11** 187-188
Mussolini, Benito **11** 272-274
Rosmini-Serbati, Antonio **13** 296-297
Stirner, Max **14** 459-460
see also Socialism

Enghien, Duke of (Louis Antoine Henri de Bourbon-Condé; 1772-1804), French general
Chateaubriand, Vicomte de **3** 477-479
Talleyrand, Charles Maurice de **15** 89-90

Engine (machine)
Daimler, Gottlieb **4** 368
Diesel, Rudolf **5** 7
Ericsson, John **5** 307-308
Whittle, Frank **16** 257-258

Engineering
aeronautical
see Aeronautics
ancient
Heron of Alexandria **7** 334-335
chemical
Patrick, Jennie R. **12** 136-137
civil
Bechtel, Stephen Davison **2** 98-99
Brunel, Isambard Kingdom **3** 69-70
Imhotep **8** 116-117
Smeaton, John **14** 280-281
Thayer, Sylvanus **15** 168-169
computer
Cray, Seymour **4** 301-303
Hounsfield, Godfrey **7** 517-519
Lanier, Jaron **9** 198-199
Jobs, Steven **8** 265-267
Shaw, Mary **14** 165-167
electrical
Armstrong, Edwin Howard **1** 302-303
Ochoa, Ellen **11** 460-461
Tesla, Nikola **15** 156-157
mechanical
Bush, Vannevar **3** 169-171
Carrier, Wills **3** 325-326
Diesel, Rudolf **5** 7
military
Leonardo da Vinci **9** 337-340
Peregrinus, Petrus **12** 208
see also Marine engineering; Scientists—engineers

England
• 55 B.C.-A.D. 5TH CENTURY (ROMAN)
Caesar, Gaius Julius **3** 207-210
Diocletian **5** 19-20
Domitian **5** 52-53
Frontinus, Sextus Julius **6** 130
Hadrian **7** 60-61
• 5TH CENTURY-1066 (ANGLO-SAXON)
Christianity
Aelfric **1** 69-70
Alcuin of York **1** 122-123
Augustine of Canterbury **1** 370-371
Bede **2** 109-110
Dunstan **5** 151-152
Gregory I **6** 531-532
Danes and
Alfred **1** 151-153
Canute I, the Great **3** 266-269
Edward the Confessor **5** 218-219
Edward the Elder **5** 219-220
Ethelred the Unready **5** 327
Normans and
Harold II **7** 162
William I **16** 290-291
• 1066-1154 (NORMAN)
Church and State
Anselm of Canterbury **1** 244-245
Henry I **7** 286-287
Lanfranc **9** 189-190
William II **16** 293-294
see also Investiture Struggle
Civil War
Stephen **14** 426-427
conquest
Harold II **7** 162
Harold III **7** 163
William I **16** 290-291
France and
Henry I **7** 286-287
Louis VI **9** 523-524
Scotland and
David I **4** 407
Malcolm III **10** 164-165
• 1154-1216 (PLANTAGENET)
Church and State
Becket, Thomas **2** 101-102
Henry II **7** 287-289
Innocent, III **8** 125-127
John **8** 274-275
see also Crusades—Third
French wars
Eleanor of Aquitaine **5** 246-247
Henry II **7** 287-289
Louis VII **9** 524-525
Philip II **12** 268-269
Richard I **13** 130
legal reform
Henry II **7** 287-289
John **8** 274-275
see also Magna Carta
• 1216-1307 (PLANTAGENET)
barons' war (1263-1265)
Henry III **7** 290-292
Montfort, Simon de **11** 132-133
Church and State
Grosseteste, Robert **7** 15
Henry III **7** 290-292

French wars (1295-1298)
  Edward I **5** 208-210
  Philip IV **12** 274
Scotland and Wales
  Edward I **5** 208-210
  Llewelyn ap Gruffydd **9** 468
  Wallace, William **16** 75-76

- 1307-99 (PLANTAGENET)
Hundred Years War
  Edward III **5** 211-212
  Edward the Black Prince
    5 217-218
  see also Hundred Years War
Peasants' Revolt (1381)
  John of Gaunt **8** 282-283
  Richard II **13** 130-131
  Wyclif, John **16** 412-413
Scottish wars
  Douglas, James **5** 78
  Edward II **5** 210
  Robert I **13** 192-194
  Robert II **13** 194

- 1399-1461 (LANCASTRIAN)
France and
  Gloucester, Duke of **6** 370-371
  Henry V **7** 296-297
  Henry VI **7** 298-299
  see also Hundred Years War
rise of parliament
  Henry IV **7** 292-293
Scotland and
  James I **8** 206-207
  Robert III **13** 194-195
Wars of the Roses
  Henry VI **7** 298-299
  Margaret of Anjou **10** 249-250
  see also Roses, Wars of the
Welsh rebellion
  Glendower, Owen **6** 364-365

- 1461-85 (YORKIST)
France and
  Charles the Bold **3** 467-469
  Edward IV **5** 212-213
  Louis XI **9** 526-528
Scotland and
  James III **8** 208-209
Wars of the Roses
  Edward IV **5** 212-213
  Richard III **13** 132-133
  Warwick and of Salisbury, Earl of
    16 122-123
  see also Roses, Wars of the

- 1485-1603 (TUDOR)
1485-1509 (Henry VII)
  Henry VII **7** 300-302
  Richard III **13** 132-133
1509-47 (Henry VIII)
  Cranmer, Thomas **4** 295-296
  Cromwell, Thomas **4** 320-321
  Henry VIII **7** 302-305
  Julius II **8** 384-386
  Louis XII **9** 528-529
  More, Thomas **11** 156-157
  Norfolk, 3d Duke of **11** 423

Wolsey, Thomas **16** 364-366
  see also Church and State (England); Protestant
1547-53 (Edward VI)
  Chancellor, Richard **3** 422
  Edward VI **5** 213-214
  Ivan IV **8** 157-159
  Northumberland, Duke of
    11 431-432
  Somerset, Duke of **14** 333-334
1553-58 (Mary I)
  Mary, I **10** 308-309
  Philip II (king, Spain)
    12 271-273
1558-1603 (Elizabeth I)
  Bacon, Francis **1** 422-424
  Coke, Edward **4** 141-142
  Drake, Francis **5** 94-96
  Elizabeth I **5** 263-266
  Essex, 2d Earl of **5** 321-322
  Godunov, Boris Feodorovich
    6 382-383
  Hawkins, John **7** 210-211
  Leicester, Earl of **9** 312-313
  Mary, I **10** 308-309
  Pius V **12** 332-333
  Raleigh, Walter **13** 9-11
  see also Armada, Spanish;
    Church and State (England)
  see also British Empire, First;
    Church and State (England);
    English art and architecture;
    English literature; English
    music; Explorers, English

- 1603 AND AFTER
  see Great Britain

England, Church of
and ecumenism
  Temple, William **15** 141-143
and women
  Royden, Agnes Maude **13** 335-337
Anglican mysticism
  Inge, William Ralph **8** 118-119
Calvinism opposed
  Hooker, Richard **7** 475-476
  Laud, William **9** 224-225
  Seabury, Samuel **14** 76
in Colonial America
  Asbury, Francis **1** 324-325
Methodist movement
  Wesley, Charles **16** 208-209
  Wesley, John **16** 209-210
modernization
  Carey, George Leonard **3** 293-294
Oxford Movement
  see Oxford Movement
separation from Rome
  Coverdale, Miles **4** 278
  Cranmer, Thomas **4** 295-296
  Cromwell, Thomas **4** 320-321
  Edward VI **5** 213-214
  Henry VIII **7** 302-305
  More, Thomas **11** 156-157
  Tyndale, William **15** 373-374
supporters

Gladstone, William Ewart
    6 357-360
  Milton, John **11** 43-46
West African bishops
  Crowther, Samuel Adjai **4** 326
  see also Anglicanism; Protestant
    Episcopal Church (United States);
    Thirty-nine articles

ENGLAND, JOHN (1786-1842), Irish
Catholic bishop in America **5** 288

England's Heroical Epistles (book)
  Drayton, Michael **5** 97-98

English (language)
  Caxton, William **3** 386-387
  David I **4** 407
  Rolle of Hampole, Richard **13** 260-261
  Webster, Noah **16** 164-166
  see also English literature

English art and architecture
abstract
  Caro, Anthony **3** 316
  Epstein, Jacob **5** 295-296
  Hepworth, Barbara **7** 318-319
  Moore, Henry **11** 146-148
  Nicholson, Ben **11** 380-381
architecture
  Gibbs, James **6** 301-302
  Hockney, David **7** 429-431
  Jones, Inigo **8** 333-334
  Lutyens, Edwin Landseer **10** 54-55
  Palladio, Andrea **12** 75-77
  Rogers, Richard **13** 248-250
  Shaw, Richard Norman **14** 167-168
  Stirling, James **14** 458-459
  Wren, Christopher **16** 393-394
(art)-England
  Soane, John **14** 314-315
baroque
  see Baroquearchitecture; Baroque
    painting; Baroque sculpture
figure painting
  Bacon, Francis **1** 421-422
  John, Augustus Edwin **8** 291
graphics
  Beardsley, Aubrey Vincent **2** 88-89
  Lear, Edward **9** 265-266
  Sutherland, Graham **15** 40-41
impressionism
  see impressionism (art)—England
miniatures
  Hilliard, Nicholas **7** 391-392
neoclassicism
  see Neoclassicism
photography
  Hockney, David **7** 429-431
Pre-Raphaelites
  see PreRaphaelites
Renaissance
  Hilliard, Nicholas **7** 391-392
  Holbein, Hans the Younger
    7 449-450
romanticism
  see Romanticism (art)—English

English Bards and Scotch Reviewers (satire)

Byron, George Gordon Noel **3** 193-194

English Bible
   Cranmer, Thomas **4** 295-296

English Flag, The (poem)
   Kipling, Joseph Rudyard **9** 32-33

English in Ireland ... (book; Froude)
   Froude, James Anthony **6** 133-134
   Lecky, William Edward Hartpole
      9 271-272

English language literature
   Trinidad
      Naipaul, V. S. **11** 295-296
      see also African literature, modern

English literature
   Age of Johnson
      Collins, William **4** 168-169
      Crabbe, George **4** 288
      Goldsmith, Oliver **6** 411-413
      Johnson, Samuel **8** 315-317
      Sheridan, Richard Brinsley
         14 183-184
      Sterne, Laurence **14** 435-437
   allegory
      Bunyan, John **3** 128-129
      Langland, William **9** 194-195
      Lewis, Clive Staples **9** 381-382
   Anglo-Norman
      Geoffrey of Monmouth **6** 268
      Grosseteste, Robert **7** 15
      John of Salisbury **8** 284-285
      Layamon **9** 256-257
   Anglo-Saxon
      Aelfric **1** 69-70
      Alfred **1** 151-153
   Arthurian legend
      see Arthurian legend
   Augustan Age
      Defoe, Daniel **4** 457-459
      Gray, Thomas **6** 509-510
      Pope, Alexander **12** 395-397
   baroque
      see Baroque literature
   biography
      Fraser, Antonia **6** 70-71
      Spark, Muriel Sarah **14** 361-362
      Strachey, Giles Lytton **14** 487-488
   Bloomsbury group
      Bowen, Elizabeth **2** 462-463
      Eliot, Thomas Stearns **5** 258-261
      Forster, Edward Morgan **6** 14-16
      Woolf, Virginia Stephen **16** 381-382
   Cavalier poetry
      see Cavalier
   children's literature
      Dahl, Roald **4** 366-367
      Newbery, John **11** 360-361
   development of novel
      Fielding, Henry **5** 442-444
      James, Henry **8** 211-212
      Richardson, Samuel **13** 141-142
      Smollett, Tobias George **14** 305-307
   diaries and journals
      Boswell, James **2** 432-434
      Evelyn, John **5** 343-344

Pepys, Samuel **12** 207-208
Elizabethan
      Chapman, George **3** 440-441
      Cowley, Abraham **4** 281-282
      Drayton, Michael **5** 97-98
      Heywood, Thomas **7** 373-374
      Kyd, Thomas **9** 140-141
      Marlowe, Christopher **10** 272-274
      Shakespeare, William **14** 142-145
      Sidney, Philip **14** 214-215
      Spenser, Edmund **14** 373-376
   essays (16th-18th century)
      Addison, Joseph **1** 57-58
      Bacon, Francis **1** 422-424
      Fielding, Henry **5** 442-444
      Goldsmith, Oliver **6** 411-413
      Mandeville, Bernard **10** 192
      Steele, Richard **14** 407-409
   essays (19th-20th century)
      Arnold, Matthew **1** 311-313
      Carlyle, Thomas **3** 304-305
      Forster, Edward Morgan **6** 14-16
      Golding, William **6** 404-406
      Hazlitt, William **7** 235-236
      Lamb, Charles **9** 176-177
      Landor, Walter Savage **9** 186-187
      Lewis, Cecil Day **9** 380
      Macaulay, Thomas Babington
         10 79-80
      Orwell, George **12** 14-15
      Priestley, J. B. **12** 451-452
      Tolkien, J. R. R. **15** 259-261
      Weldon, Fay Birkinshaw
         16 186-188
   esthetic movement
      Pater, Walter Horatio **12** 130-131
      Wilde, Oscar Fingall O'Flahertie
         Wills **16** 272-273
   fantasy
      Tolkien, J. R. R. **15** 259-261
   Georgian
      Brooke, Rupert **3** 22-23
      Burney, Fanny **3** 147-148
      Graves, Robert Ranke **6** 504-506
      Sassoon, Siegfried **13** 492-493
   Jacobean
      Beaumont, Francis **2** 95
      Chapman, George **3** 440-441
      Dekker, Thomas **4** 465-466
      Fletcher, John **5** 487
      Heywood, Thomas **7** 373-374
      Massinger, Philip **10** 324-325
      Middleton, Thomas **11** 8-9
      Webster, John **16** 164
   Latin
      Alcuin of York **1** 122-123
      Bacon, Roger **1** 425-427
      Bede **2** 109-110
      Matthew Paris **10** 341-342
      William of Malmesbury **16** 297-298
   literary criticism
      Connolly, Cyril **4** 204-205
      Dryden, John **5** 106-107
      Eliot, Thomas Stearns **5** 258-261
      Graves, Robert Ranke **6** 504-506

Hazlitt, William **7** 235-236
      Landor, Walter Savage **9** 186-187
      Morley, John **11** 178-179
      Pater, Walter Horatio **12** 130-131
      Pritchett, V. S. **12** 455-457
      Sitwell, Edith **14** 265-266
      Spark, Muriel Sarah **14** 361-362
      Spender, Stephen Harold
         14 370-371
      Strachey, Giles Lytton **14** 487-488
      Wells, Herbert George **16** 195-196
   medieval
      Chaucer, Geoffrey **3** 482-485
      Gower, John **6** 475-476
      Langland, William **9** 194-195
      Lydgate, John **10** 61-62
      Malory, Thomas **10** 175-176
   metaphysical poetry
      see Metaphysical poetry
   modern (drama)
      Barrie, James Matthew **2** 21-22
      Bennett, Alan **2** 166-167
      Burgess, Anthony **3** 136-137
      Christie, Agatha **4** 25-26
      Coward, Noel **4** 279-280
      Eliot, Thomas Stearns **5** 258-261
      Greene, Graham **6** 523-524
      Mortimer, John Clifford **11** 194-195
      Orton, John Kingsley **12** 12-14
      Osborne, John **12** 16-17
      Pinter, Harold **12** 317-318
      Priestley, J. B. **12** 451-452
      Shaffer, Peter Levin **14** 133-135
      Shaw, George Bernard **14** 163-164
      Stoppard, Thomas **14** 478-479
      Trevor, William **15** 295-297
      Weldon, Fay Birkinshaw
         16 186-188
   modern (novel)
      Ambler, Eric **1** 191-192
      Bowen, Elizabeth **2** 462-463
      Brookner, Anita **3** 23-24
      Burgess, Anthony **3** 136-137
      Christie, Agatha **4** 25-26
      Connolly, Cyril **4** 204-205
      Conrad, Joseph **4** 205-207
      Ford, Ford Madox **6** 1-2
      Fowles, John **6** 33-35
      Fraser, Antonia **6** 70-71
      Galsworthy, John **6** 189-190
      Golding, William **6** 404-406
      Greene, Graham **6** 523-524
      Huxley, Aldous Leonard **8** 74-75
      James, P. D. **8** 213-215
      Joyce, James **8** 365-367
      Lawrence, David Herbert **9** 247-248
      Lodge, David **9** 480-482
      Maugham, William Somerset
         10 344-345
      Murdoch, Iris **11** 256-257
      Orwell, George **12** 14-15
      Powell, Anthony **12** 422-423
      Priestley, J. B. **12** 451-452
      Pritchett, V. S. **12** 455-457
      Rendell, Ruth **13** 96-97

Snow, Charles Percy **14** 311-312
Wells, Herbert George **16** 195-196
Zangwill, Israel **16** 488-489
modern (novels)
Mortimer, John Clifford **11** 194-195
Spark, Muriel Sarah **14** 361-362
Weldon, Fay Birkinshaw
16 186-188
modern (poetry)
Auden, Wystan Hugh **1** 364-366
Eliot, Thomas Stearns **5** 258-261
Housman, Alfred Edward **7** 521-522
Hughes, Ted **8** 19-21
Kipling, Joseph Rudyard **9** 32-33
Larkin, Philip **9** 206-207
Lennon, John Winston **9** 326-328
MacNeice, Louis **10** 113-114
Sitwell, Edith **14** 265-266
Spark, Muriel Sarah **14** 361-362
Spender, Stephen Harold
14 370-371
Thomas, Dylan Marlais **15** 188-190
modern (short stories)
Pritchett, V. S. **12** 455-457
Trevor, William **15** 295-297
mysticism
Blake, William **2** 316-318
neoclassicism
Arnold, Matthew **1** 311-313
Dryden, John **5** 106-107
Gray, Thomas **6** 509-510
Herrick, Robert **7** 336-339
Jonson, Ben **8** 343-345
poet laureates
Betjeman, John **2** 243-245
Hughes, Ted **8** 19-21
political parables
Rushdie, Salman **13** 366-368
popular science
Stopes, Marie **14** 476-478
religious
Browne, Thomas **3** 49-50
Burton, Robert **3** 166-167
Coverdale, Miles **4** 278
Donne, John **5** 60-61
Hooker, Richard **7** 475-476
Lewis, Clive Staples **9** 381-382
Rossetti, Christina Georgina
13 307-308
Tyndale, William **15** 373-374
Renaissance
see Renaissance, English (literature)
Restoration
Bunyan, John **3** 128-129
Congreve, William **4** 200-201
Dryden, John **5** 106-107
Milton, John **11** 43-46
Pepys, Samuel **12** 207-208
Wycherley, William **16** 411-412
romanticism
see Romanticism
satire (prose)
Mandeville, Bernard **10** 192
Peacock, Thomas Love **12** 169
Smollett, Tobias George **14** 305-307

Swift, Jonathan **15** 51-54
Waugh, Evelyn Arthur St. John
16 145-147
satire (verse)
Butler, Samuel **3** 183-184
Dryden, John **5** 106-107
Gay, John **6** 243-244
Pope, Alexander **12** 395-397
Skelton, John **14** 268-269
Wyatt, Thomas **16** 410-411
science fiction
Lewis, Clive Staples **9** 381-382
screen plays
Priestley, J. B. **12** 451-452
social protest
Spender, Stephen Harold
14 370-371
spy novels
Le Carre, John **9** 270-271
travel
Lawrence, David Herbert **9** 247-248
Mandeville, John **10** 192-193
Martineau, Harriet **10** 296-297
Pritchett, V. S. **12** 455-457
Spender, Stephen Harold
14 370-371
Theroux, Paul **15** 179-180
utopian
see Utopian literature—England
Victorian (prose)
Brontë, Charlotte **3** 17-18
Brontë, Emily **3** 18-19
Carroll, Lewis **3** 332-333
Dickens, Charles John Huffam
4 538-541
Eliot, George **5** 254-256
Frazer, James George **6** 76
Gaskell, Elizabeth **6** 231-232
Hardy, Thomas **7** 150-152
Kingsley, Charles **9** 28
Meredith, George **10** 512-513
Ruskin, John **13** 371-372
Shelley, Mary Wollstonecraft
14 174-176
Stephen, Leslie **14** 429
Thackeray, William Makepeace
15 159-161
Trollope, Anthony **15** 300-302
Victorian (verse)
Arnold, Matthew **1** 311-313
Browning, Elizabeth Barrett **3** 52-53
Browning, Robert **3** 53-55
Clough, Arthur Hugh **4** 123-124
Cowper, William **4** 282
Hopkins, Gerard Manley **7** 492-494
Kipling, Joseph Rudyard **9** 32-33
Lear, Edward **9** 265-266
Rossetti, Christina Georgina
13 307-308
Swinburne, Algernon Charles
15 54-55
Tennyson, Alfred **15** 144-146
see also Irish literature; Mystery fic-
tion; Scottish literature

English music
baroque

see Baroque music (England)
conservative idiom
Britten, Benjamin **3** 10-11
Walton, William Turner **16** 92-93
hymns
Wesley, Charles **16** 208-209
madrigals
Bach, Johann Christian **1** 415-416
Marenzio, Luca **10** 248
Morley, Thomas **11** 179-180
musicals
Webber, Andrew Lloyd **16** 155-156
nationalism
Elgar, Edward **5** 247-248
Holst, Gustav **7** 459-460
Sullivan, Arthur Seymour **15** 23
Vaughan Williams, Ralph
15 446-447
neoclassicism
Tippett, Michael Kemp **15** 234-235
Renaissance
see Renaissance (music)
rock-'n'-roll
Beatles, The **2** 89-92
Lennon, John Winston **9** 326-328
theatrical music
Coward, Noel **4** 279-280
Sullivan, Arthur Seymour **15** 23

English Prayer Book
Edward VI **5** 213-214

English Review (periodical)
Ford, Ford Madox **6** 1-2
Lawrence, David Herbert **9** 247-248

English theater
Craig, Edward Gordon **4** 288-289
Evans, Edith **5** 336-337
Gielgud, John **6** 310-311
Guinness, Alec **7** 37-38

English Traits (book)
Emerson, Ralph Waldo **5** 278-280

English Traveller, The (play)
Heywood, Thomas **7** 373-374

Englishman (periodical)
Sheridan, Richard Brinsley **14** 183-184
Steele, Richard **14** 407-409

Engravers
see Artists—engravers

Enigma of Isidore Ducasse (ready-made)
Ray, Man **13** 59-60

Enigma of the Collective American Soul
(painting)
Evergood, Philip **5** 345

Enigma of the Oracle (painting)
Chirico, Giorgio de **4** 4

Enigma Variations (musical composition)
Elgar, Edward **5** 247-248

Enlightened despots (European politics)
15th century
Medici, Cosimo de' **10** 449-450
18th century
Catherine the Great **3** 370-372
Charles III **3** 454-455

Frederick II **6** 81-84
Gustavus III **7** 45-46
Joseph II **8** 359-360
Victor Amadeus II **15** 482-483
18th century (opposed)
Pius VI **12** 333-334
19th-20th century
Francis Joseph **6** 45-46
William I **16** 291-292

Enlightenment (Buddhism)
Buddha **3** 97-101

Enlightenment (philosophy)
critics
Greuze, Jean Baptiste **6** 539
Hamann, Johann Georg **7** 92
Herder, Johann Gottfried von **7** 327-328
Jacobi, Friedrich Heinrich **8** 189-190
Maistre, Joseph de **10** 153-154
Pius VI **12** 333-334
enlightened despots
see Enlightened despots
influence (England)
Morley, John **11** 178-179
influence (France)
Lafayette, Marquis de **9** 151-152
Louis XVIII **9** 535-536
influence (German and Jewish)
Basedow, Johann Bernhard **2** 44-45
Dubnov, Simon **5** 115-116
Graetz, Heinrich Hirsch **6** 483
Krochmal, Nachman Kohen **9** 104-105
Luzzato, Moses Hayyim **10** 57-58
Schleiermacher, Friedrich Ernst Daniel **14** 11-12
Zunz, Leopold **16** 534
influence (Irish)
Emmet, Robert **5** 281-282
O'Connell, Daniel **11** 465-467
influence (Italy)
Becarria, Marchese di **2** 97-98
Leopold II **9** 346
Manzoni, Alessandro **10** 222-224
Vico, Giambattista **15** 480-481
influence (Mexico)
Fernández de Lizardi, José Joaquin **5** 424-425
Juana Inés de la Cruz **8** 367-368
influence (Russia)
Alexander I **1** 130-132
influence (South America)
Tiradentes **15** 237
Unánue, José Hipólito **15** 387-388
influence (United States)
Jefferson, Thomas **8** 238-241
Madison, James **10** 121-123
philosophy (France)
Buffon, Comte de **3** 109-111
Condorcet, Marquis de **4** 195-196
Diderot, Denis **5** 1-2
Fragonard, Jean Honoré **6** 38-39
Helvétius, Claude Adrien **7** 273-274
Holbach, Baron d' **7** 448-449

La Mettrie, Julien Offray de **9** 179-180
Montesquieu **11** 123-125
Rousseau, Jean Jacques **13** 324-328
Saint-Pierre, Abbé de **13** 434-435
Turgot, Anne Robert Jacques **15** 348-349
Voltaire **16** 14-16
philosophy (Germany)
Kant, Immanuel **8** 430-432
Leibniz, Gottfried Wilhelm von **9** 307-310
Lessing, Gotthold Ephraim **9** 357-359
Mendelssohn, Moses **10** 488-489
Thomasius **15** 193-194
Wolff, Christian von **16** 358
philosophy (United States)
Franklin, Benjamin **6** 60-64
Paine, Thomas **12** 66-67
see also Philosophes

Enneads (book; Plotinus)
Plotinus **12** 358-359
Proclus Diadochus **12** 457

ENNIN (794-864), Japanese Buddhist monk **5** 288-289
Chang Po-go **3** 433-434

ENNIUS, QUINTUS (239-169 B.C.).Roman poet **5** 289

Ennui (painting)
Sickert, Walter Richard **14** 212-213

Enoch Arden (book; Tennyson)
La Farge, John **9** 149-150

Enormous Room, The (book)
Cummings, Edward Estlin **4** 334-336

Enough Rope (poems)
Parker, Dorothy Rothschild **12** 106

Enrico IV (play)
Pirandello, Luigi **12** 319-321

Enrico di Borgogna (opera)
Donizetti, Gaetano **5** 59-60

Enryaku-ji (Buddhist temple)
Saicho **13** 426-428

Enseigne de Gersaint (signboard)
Watteau, Antoine **16** 143-144

ENSOR, JAMES (1860-1949), Belgian painter and graphic artist **5** 289-290

Entente Cordiale (British-French; 1904)
Balfour, Arthur James **1** 469-470
Delcassé, Théophile **4** 478-479

Enterprise (ship)
Decatur, Stephen **4** 448-449
McClintock, Francis Leopold **10** 394-395
Ross, James Clark **13** 302-303
Shreve, Henry Miller **14** 207
Smith, Jedediah S. **14** 294-295

Entertainer, The (play)
Osborne, John **12** 16-17

Entführung aus dem Serail, Die (opera)

Mozart, Wolfgang Amadeus **11** 218-221

Enthroned Madonna (painting)
Massys, Quentin **10** 325-326

Entombment (engraving)
Mantegna, Andrea **10** 215-216

Entombment (painting)
Andrea del Castagno **1** 223-224
Bouts, Dirk **2** 458-459
Lorenzetti, Pietro and Ambrogio **9** 517-518
Raphael **13** 40-42
Titian **15** 242-244

Entombment (painting; Weyden)
Massys, Quentin **10** 325-326
Weyden, Rogier van der **16** 219-221

Entomology (science)
Bates, Henry Walter **2** 53-54
Knipling, Edward Fred **9** 59-60
Malpighi, Marcello **10** 176-178
Swammerdam, Jan **15** 48-49
Weismann, August Freidrich Leopold **16** 178-180
see also Scientists—entomologists

Entropy (physics)
Boltzmann, Ludwig **2** 379-380
Clausius, Rudolf Julius Emanuel **4** 92-94

Entry of Christ into Jerusalem (sculpture)
Riemenschneider, Tilman **13** 166

Entry of the Crusaders into Constantinople (painting)
Delacroix, Ferdinand Victor Eugène **4** 469-471

Envers et l'endroit, L' (essays)
Camus, Albert **3** 255-257

Environment (nation)
Ford, Henry II **6** 6-7
Fuller, Richard Buckminster **6** 149-150
see also Conservation

Environment (sculpture)
Nevelson, Louise **11** 356-357

Environment (sociology)
Dugdale, Richard Louis **5** 128-129
Giddings, Franklin Henry **6** 307-308

Environmental activists (United States)
Commoner, Barry **4** 183-185
Dudley, Barbara **5** 123-124

Environmental Protection Agency (U.S.)
Browner, Carol M. **3** 50-52

Environmental sciences
limnology
Patrick, Ruth **12** 137-138

Environmental sculpture
Christo Vladimiroff Javacheff **4** 30-31
Grooms, Red **7** 11-12
Smithson, Robert **14** 301-303

Envoys from Agamemnon (painting)
Ingres, Jean Auguste Dominique **8** 121-123

Enzio (circa 1220-1272), king of Sardinia
Frederick II **6** 79

Enzyme (chemistry)
Haldane, John Burdon Sanderson
7 70-71
Northrop, John Howard **11** 430-431
Pasteur, Louis **12** 125-127
Theorell, Axel Hugo Theodor
15 176-177
Tiselius, Arne Wilhelm Kaurin
15 240-241

Eolian Harp, The (poem)
Coleridge, Samuel Taylor **4** 154-156

Eonta (musical composition)
Xenakis, Iannis **16** 416-418

Eötvös, Baron Joseph (1813-1871), Hungarian writer and statesman
Deák, Francis **4** 431-432

EPAMINONDAS (c. 425-362 B.C.), Theban general and statesman **5** 291-292
Agesilaus II **1** 79-80

Epaphroditus (died 95), Greek freedman, secretary to Nero
Epictetus **5** 292

Ephesians, Letter to the (NT)
Paul **12** 141-143

Ephesus, Councils of
431 (First)
Cyril **4** 362
Leo I **9** 329-330
Nestorius **11** 349-350
449 (Second)
Eutyches **5** 335
Leo I **9** 329-330

Ephialtes (died 462/461 B.C.), Athenian statesman
Pericles **12** 219-221

Ephor (title)
Agis IV **1** 81-82
Cleomenes III **4** 103-104

Ephraim (literary character)
O'Neill, Eugene **11** 514-516

Ephrata Cloisters (Pennsylvania)
Beissel, Johann Conrad **2** 123-124

Epic (poem)
English
Dryden, John **5** 106-107
Milton, John **11** 43-46
Spenser, Edmund **14** 373-376
French
Boileau-Despréaux, Nicholas
2 369-371
Hugo, Victor Marie **8** 22-25
Greek
Callimachus **3** 235-236
Homer **7** 465-467
Indian
Kalidasa **8** 414-415
Italian
Ariosto, Ludovico **1** 289-290
Dante Alighieri **4** 389-391
Tasso, Torquato **15** 114-116

Latin
Ennius, Quintus **5** 289
Ovid **12** 34-36
Virgil **15** 507-510
Portuguese
Camoëns, Luis Vaz de **3** 247-249
Spanish
Cid **4** 58-59

Epicharmus (poems)
Ennius, Quintus **5** 289

Epicoene (play)
Jonson, Ben **8** 343-345

EPICTETUS (circa 50-circa 135), Greek philosopher **5** 292
Butler, Joseph **3** 180-181
Chrysippus **4** 35-36
Poliziano, Angelo **12** 373-374

Epicureanism (philosophy)
Cicero, Marcus Tullius **4** 55-58
Epicurus **5** 292-294
Isidore of Seville **8** 149-150
Lucretius **10** 26-27
Menander **10** 477-478

EPICURUS (circa 342-270 B.C.), Greek philosopher, founder of Epicureanism
5 292-294
see also Epicureanism

Epicycle (astronomy)
Apollonius of Perga **1** 261-262
Hipparchus **7** 407-408

Epidemia, L' (book)
Moravia, Alberto **11** 153-155

Epidemiology (medical)
Cruz, Oswaldo Gonçalves **4** 328-329
Finlay, Carlos Juan **5** 450
Gayle, Helene Doris **6** 244-245
Macdonald, Eleanor Josephine
10 83-84
Rush, Benjamin **13** 364-365
Schopenhauer, Arthur **14** 29-31
Sydenham, Thomas **15** 59-60
see also Scientists—epidemiologists

Epidicus (play)
Plautus **12** 348-350

Epigones, The (poem)
Eminescu, Mihail **5** 280-281

Epigram (literature)
Donne, John **5** 60-61
Ennius, Quintus **5** 289
Martialis, Marcus Valerius **10** 286-287
Theocritus **15** 171-172

Epilepsy (medicine)
Penfield, Wilder Graves **12** 198-200

Épilogue (novel)
Martin du Gard, Roger **10** 295-296

Epimanes
see Antiochus IV Epiphanes

**Épinay, Louise Florence Pétronille de la
Live** (1726-1783), French author
Rousseau, Jean Jacques **13** 324-328

Epinikion (ode)
Pindar **12** 312-313

Epiphanius, St. (315?-403), Eastern church father and writer
Marcion **10** 238-239

Epiphany (literary technique)
Joyce, James **8** 365-367

Epiphany (triptych)
Bosch, Hieronymus **2** 426-428

Epirus (ancient nation, Greece)
Michael VIII **11** 1-2

Episcopal Church
see Protestant Episcopal Church (United States)

Episode in Palmetto (book)
Caldwell, Erskine **3** 223-224

Episodios nacionales (novel cycle)
Galdós, Benito Pérez **6** 177-178

Epistemology (philosophy)
see Knowledge, theories of

Epistle from Othea (book)
Christine de Pisan **4** 29-30

Epistle to Arbuthnot (poem)
Pope, Alexander **12** 395-397

Epistle to Bathurst (poem)
Pope, Alexander **12** 395-397

Epistle to Burlington, The (poem)
Pope, Alexander **12** 395-397

Epistle to Huet (poem)
La Fontaine, Jean de **9** 156-157

Epistle to the God of Love (book)
Christine de Pisan **4** 29-30

Epistles (book)
Boileau-Despréaux, Nicholas
2 369-371
Seneca the Younger, Lucius Annaeus
14 103-105

Epistles (book; Horace)
Condorcet, Marquis de **4** 195-196
Horace **7** 500-503

Epistles (New Testament)
see Bible—New Testament (Epistolists)

Epistles (poem)
Eminescu, Mihail **5** 280-281

Epistolae obscurorum virorum (book; Hutten-Crotus Rubianus)
Hutten, Ulrich von **8** 72-73
Reuchlin, Johann **13** 106-107

Epistolae sine nomine (letters)
Petrarch **12** 259-261

Epitaph (ballade)
Villon, François **15** 499-501

Epitaph for a Small Winner (novel)
Machado de Assis, Joaquim Maria
10 91-92

Epitaph for a Spy (book)
Ambler, Eric **1** 191-192

Epitaph for George Dillon (play)
Osborne, John **12** 16-17

Epitaph on the Marchioness of Winchester, An (poem)
Milton, John **11** 43-46

Epithalamion (literature)
Donne, John **5** 60-61

Epithalamion (musical composition)
Bennett, Richard Rodney **2** 172

Epithalamion (poem)
Spenser, Edmund **14** 373-376

Epithet (literary technique)
Gracián y Morales, Baltasar Jerónimo **6** 481-482

Epitrepontes (play)
Menander **10** 477-478

Epopeya de Artigas, La (book)
Zorrilla de San Martin, Juan **16** 530-531

EPSTEIN, ABRAHAM (1892-1945), Russian-born American economist **5** 294-295

Epstein, Jean (1899-1953), French film director and critic
Buñuel, Luis **3** 127-128

EPSTEIN, SIR JACOB (1880-1959), American-born English sculptor **5** 295-296
Alexander, Samuel **1** 141
Moore, Henry **11** 146-148

Epyllion (poem)
Catullus, Gaius Valerius **3** 377-378
Theocritus **15** 171-172

Equal Employment Opportunity Commission (United States)
Thomas, Clarence **15** 186-188

Equal Rights Amendment (United States; proposed constitutional amendment)
Smeal, Eleanor **14** 278-280

Equality (essay)
Tawney, Richard Henry **15** 120-121

Equality (novel)
Bellamy, Edward **2** 134-135

Equatorial (musical composition)
Varèse, Edgard **15** 432-433

Equatorium (instrument)
Chaucer, Geoffrey **3** 482-485

EQUIANO, OLAUDAH (1745-circa 1801), African author and former slave **5** 296-297
Cinque, Joseph **4** 62
Cugoano, Ottobah **4** 332-333

Equilibrists, The (poem)
Ransom, John Crowe **13** 39-40

Equinoxes, precession of the
see Precession of the equinoxes

Equitable Labour Exchange (England)
Owen, Robert **12** 39-40

Equitable Life Assurance Society (United States)
Cleveland, Stephen Grover **4** 108-110
Westinghouse, George **16** 215

Equites (equestrian order)
Drusus, Marcus Livius **5** 105-106

Gracchus, Tiberius and Gaius Sempronius **6** 479-480

Equivoci nel sembiante, Gli (opera)
Scarlatti, Pietro Alessandro Gaspare **13** 517-518

Erasers, The (novel)
Robbe-Grillet, Alain **13** 189-190

ERASISTRATUS (c. 304 B.C.- c. 250 B.C.), Greek physician and anantomist **5** 297-298

ERASMUS, DESIDERIUS (1466-1536), Dutch author, scholar, and humanist **5** 298-300
art patronage
Holbein, Hans the Younger **7** 449-450
Massys, Quentin **10** 325-326
associates
Hutten, Ulrich von **8** 72-73
More, Thomas **11** 156-157
influence of
Burton, Robert **3** 166-167
Cervantes, Miguel de Saavedra **3** 395-398
Dürer, Albrecht **5** 159-161
Ferdinand I **5** 414-415
Fernel, Jean François **5** 425-426
Huizinga, Johan **8** 26-27
Tyndale, William **15** 373-374
William the Silent **16** 300-302
Zumárraga, Juan de **16** 531-532
Zwingli, Huldreich **16** 537-538
influenced by
Colet, John **4** 157-158
Quintilian **12** 518-519
Valla, Lorenzo **15** 406

ERASMUS, GEORGES HENRY (born 1948), Canadian Indian leader **5** 300-301

Erato e Apòllion (verse)
Quasimodo, Salvatore **12** 506

ERATOSTHENES OF CYRENE (circa 284-circa 205 B.C.), Greek mathematician, geographer, and astronomer **5** 301-302
Callimachus **3** 235-236
Hipparchus **7** 407-408
Strabo **14** 485-486

ERCILLA Y ZÚÑIGA, ALONSO DE (1533-1594), Spanish poet, soldier, and diplomat **5** 302
Camoëns, Luis Vaz de **3** 247-249
Lautaro **9** 235

Ercole amante (opera)
Cavalli, Pietro Francesco **3** 382-383

Erdgeist (play)
Wedekind, Frank **16** 166-167

Erebus (ship)
Franklin, John **6** 64-65
Ross, James Clark **13** 302-303

Erebus, Mt. (Antarctica)
Mawson, Douglas **10** 354-355
Shackleton, Ernest Henry **14** 132-133

Erec and Enide (romance)
Chrestien de Troyes **4** 23-24

Eretria (city, ancient Greece)
Darius I **4** 394-395

Erewhon (book)
Butler, Samuel **3** 183

Erfurt (city, Germany)
Kautsky, Karl Johann **8** 462-463
Luther, Martin **10** 48-51

Erfurt, University of (Germany)
Luther, Martin **10** 48-51
Wieland, Christoph Martin **16** 260-261

Erga kai Hemerai (poem)
Hesiod **7** 361-362

Ergot (fungus)
Dale, Henry Hallett **4** 371-373

Erh Ma (novel)
Lao Shê **9** 200-201

ERHARD, LUDWIG (1897-1977), German statesman, West German chancellor 1963-66 **5** 302-304
Adenauer, Konrad **1** 59-61

Eric XIV (1533-1577), king of Sweden
Elizabeth I **5** 263-266

ERIC THE RED (Eric Thorvaldsson; flourished late 10th century), Norwegian explorer **5** 304
Ericson, Leif **5** 306-307

Erichsen, Ludwig Mylius
see Mylius-Erichsen, Ludwig

ERICKSON, ARTHUR CHARLES (born 1924), Canadian architect and landscape architect **5** 304-306

ERICSON, LEIF (971-circa 1015), Norse mariner and adventurer **5** 306-307
Eric the Red **5** 304

ERICSSON, JOHN (1803-1889), Swedish-born American engineer and inventor **5** 307-308

Erie (ship)
Stockton, Robert Field **14** 461-462

Erie, Lake, Battle of (1813)
Madison, James **10** 121-123
Perry, Oliver Hazard **12** 239

Erie Canal (New York State)
Clinton, DeWitt **4** 112-113

Erie Railroad "War" (1866-1868)
Drew, Daniel **5** 101-102
Fisk, James **5** 464-465
Gould, Jay **6** 470-472
Vanderbilt, Cornelius **15** 415-416

ERIGENA, JOHN SCOTUS (circa 810-circa 877), Irish scholastic philosopher **5** 308-309
Scholem, Gershom **14** 26

Erigone (elegy)
Eratosthenes of Cyrene **5** 301-302

Erik "Bloody Axe" (died 954?), king of Norway 930-934
Harold I **7** 161-162

Erikönig, Der (ballad)
Goethe, Johann Wolfgang von
6 388-391

ERIKSON, ERIK HOMBURGER
(1902-1994), German-born American
psychoanalyst and educator **5** 309-310
Benedict, Ruth Fulton **2** 154-155

Erinnerungen von Ludolf Ursleu dem Jün-geren (novel)
Huch, Ricarda **8** 11-12

Ériphyle (play)
Voltaire **16** 14-16

Erismena, L' (opera)
Cavalli, Pietro Francesco **3** 382-383

Eritrea (former Italian colony, East Africa)
Haile Selassie **7** 68-70

Erlangen, University of (Germany)
Fichte, Johann Gottlieb **5** 435-436
Ohm, Georg Simon **11** 486-487
Schelling, Friedrich Wilhelm Joseph von
13 526-527

ERLANGER, JOSEPH (1874-1965), Ameri-can physiologist **5** 310-311

Erlkönig (song)
Schubert, Franz Peter **14** 35-37

Erman, Adolf (1854-1937), German Egyp-tologist and lexicographer
Breasted, James Henry **2** 510-511

Ernani (opera)
Verdi, Giuseppe Fortunino Francesco
15 463-465

Ernest I (1784-1844; Ernest III of
Saxe-Coburg-Saalfeld, 1806-26), Duke of
Saxe-Coburg-Gotha
Albert **1** 110-112

ERNST, MAX (born 1891), German painter
5 311-312
Arp, Jean **1** 317-318
Cage, John **3** 211-214
Dubuffet, Jean Philippe Arthur
5 119-120
Miró, Joan **11** 53-54
Motherwell, Robert **11** 210-211

Eroica (sonata)
MacDowell, Edward Alexander
10 87-88

Eroica Symphony (musical composition)
Beethoven, Ludwig van **2** 114-117

Eros (asteroid)
Pickering, Edward Charles **12** 298

Eros (Greek god)
Plato **12** 345-347

Eros (sculpture)
Praxiteles **12** 433-434

Eros and Civilization (book)
Marcuse, Herbert **10** 245-247

Eros Turannos (verse)
Robinson, Edwin Arlington **13** 201-202

Eroticism (philosophy)
Marcuse, Herbert **10** 245-247

Eroticus (book)
Aristotle **1** 295-296

Erring Nun, The (play)
Lope Félix de Vega Carpio **9** 503-506

Error (philosophy)
Augustine **1** 367-370
Descartes, René **4** 505-508

Error, law of (mathematics)
Gauss, Karl Friedrich **6** 240-242

Erse (language)
see Irish language revival movement

ERSHAD, HUSSAIN MOHAMMAD (born
1930), Bengali military leader and presi-dent of Bangladesh (1982-1990)
5 312-314

ERTÉ (Romain de Tirtoff; 1892-1990), Russ-ian fashion illustrator and stage set
designer **5** 314-316

ERVIN, SAM J., JR. (1896-1985), lawyer,
judge, U.S. senator, and chairman of the
Senate Watergate Committee **5** 316-317

ERVING, JULIUS WINFIELD (a.k.a. Dr. J.;
b. 1950), African American basketball
player **5** 317-319

Erysichthon (Greek mythology)
Callimachus **3** 235-236

Eryx (mountain, Sicily)
Hamilcar Barca **7** 94-95

Erzählungen (stories)
Kleist, Heinrich von **9** 52-53

ERZBERGER, MATTHIAS (1875-1921),
German statesman **5** 319-320

Erziehung des Menschengeschlechts, Die
(book)
Lessing, Gotthold Ephraim **9** 357-359

Esa sangre (novel)
Azuela, Mariano **1** 402

Esarhaddon (died 669 B.C.), king of Assyria
681-669
Ashurbanipal **1** 338
Taharqa **15** 81-82

ESCALANTE, JAIME (born 1930), Hispanic
American educator **5** 320-321

Escándalo, El (novel)
Alarcón, Pedro Antonio de **1** 100-101

Escape, The (play)
Brown, William Wells **3** 48-49

Eschatological movement (Roman
Catholic)
Joachim of Fiore **8** 263-264

Escherichia coli (bacterium)
Khorana, Har Gobind **8** 537-538

Esclusa, L' (novel)
Pirandello, Luigi **12** 319-321

Escobedo, Mariano (1827-1902), Mexican
soldier
Maximilian of Hapsburg **10** 358-360

Escoiquiz, Juan (1762-1820), Spanish
ecclesiastic and politician
Ferdinand VII **5** 418-420

Escorial, El (monastery; Spain)
Greco **6** 511-514
Herrera, Juan de **7** 335
Philip II **12** 271-273
Titian **15** 242-244

Escot, Mr. (literary character)
Peacock, Thomas Love **12** 169

Escritor y sus fantasmas, El (essay)
Sábato, Ernesto **13** 399-400

ESENIN, SERGEI ALEKSANDROVICH
(1895-1925), Russian poet **5** 321

Esfahan (Isfahan/Ispahan; city, Iran)
Abbas I **1** 4-6

Eshkol (Jewish encyclopedia)
Kaufmann, Ezekiel **8** 460

Eshkol, Levi (1895-1969), Israeli political
leader
Meir, Golda **10** 462-463

Eshnunna (Mesopotamian city-state)
Hammurabi **7** 109-110

Eskimos (Arctic people)
Frobisher, Martin **6** 121-122
MacMillan, Donald Baxter **10** 111-112
Peary, Robert Edwin **12** 175-176
Rasmussen, Knud Johan Victor **13** 44
Stefansson, Vilhjalmur **14** 409-410

Esmail, Shah
see Ismail I

Esmeralda (literary character)
Hugo, Victor Marie **8** 22-25

Esmond (novel)
Thackeray, William Makepeace
15 159-161

Esoteric Buddhism
see Shingon sect

Española
see Hispaniola

Espartero, Baldomero (1792-1879), Span-ish general and statesman
Isabella II **8** 145-146

Espejos (musical composition)
Halffter, Christóbal **7** 79-80

Espinel, Vicente Martínez (1551?-1624),
Spanish author and musician
Alemán, Mateo **1** 126

Espinosa, Gaspar de (1484?-1537), Spanish
soldier and lawyer
Almagro, Diego de **1** 177-178

Espionage Act (United States; 1917)
Debs, Eugene Victor **4** 444-445
Hand, Billings Learned **7** 116
Haywood, William Dudley **7** 232-233
La Follette, Robert Marion **9** 155-156
Watson, Thomas Edward **16** 139

Espoir, L' (novel)
Malraux, André **10** 178-180

Espolio (painting)
Greco **6** 511-514

Esposito, Elena (literary character)
Mailer, Norman Kingsley **10** 148-150

Esprit nouveau, L' (magazine)
Le Corbusier **9** 274-275

Espumas flutuantes (poems)
Castro Alves, Antônio de **3** 364-365

Essais (book)
Montaigne, Michel Eyquem de
11 116-117

Essanay Studios (films)
Chaplin, Charles Spencer **3** 438-440

Essay (literary form)
Cowley, Abraham **4** 281-282
Montaigne, Michel Eyquem de
11 116-117
see also Authors—essayists

Essay concerning Human Understanding
(book; Locke)
Leibniz, Gottfried Wilhelm von
9 307-310
Locke, John **9** 478-480

Essay of Dramatic Poesy, An (essay)
Dryden, John **5** 106-107

Essay on Criticism (book)
Pope, Alexander **12** 395-397

Essay on Liberation (book)
Marcuse, Herbert **10** 245-247

Essay on Man, An (book; Pope)
Bolingbroke, Viscount **2** 374-375
Pope, Alexander **12** 395-397

Essay on Mind ... (poems)
Browning, Elizabeth Barrett **3** 52-53

Essayists
see Authors—essayists

Essays for Orchestra (musical composition)
Barber, Samuel **1** 500-501

Essays in Criticism (book)
Arnold, Matthew **1** 311-313

Esse est percipi (philosophic thesis)
Berkeley, George **2** 197-198

Essence (philosophy)
Santayana, George **13** 475-477

Essence of Christianity (book; Feuerbach)
Eliot, George **5** 254-256
Feuerbach, Ludwig Andreas **5** 432

Essenes (Jewish sect)
Josephus Flavius **8** 360-361

Essex (ship)
Farragut, David Glasgow **5** 388-389

Essex, Earl of (circa 1485-1540)
see Cromwell, Thomas

Essex, 1st Earl of (Walter Devereux;
1541-76), English statesman
Essex, 2d Earl of **5** 321-322

ESSEX, 2D EARL OF (Robert Devereux;
1567-1601), English courtier **5** 321-322
Bacon, Francis **1** 422-424
Coke, Edward **4** 141-142
Elizabeth I **5** 263-266

Gorges, Ferdinando **6** 455-456
Raleigh, Walter **13** 9-11

Essex, 3d Earl of (Robert Devereux;
1591-1646), English statesman
Hampden, John **7** 110-111
Pym, John **12** 495-496

Estabanico
see Estevan

Established Church (Scotland)
see Scotland, Church of

Establishment (Harwell, England)
Cockcroft, John Douglas **4** 131-132

"Establishment" (United States)
Douglas, William Orville **5** 83-85
Marcuse, Herbert **10** 245-247

Estado Novo (Brazil; 1937)
Kubitschek de Oliveira, Juscelino
9 113-115
Vargas, Getulio Dornelles **15** 433-434

Estampe et l'affiche, L' (poster)
Bonnard, Pierre **2** 395-396

Estancia (ballet)
Ginastera, Alberto Evaristo **6** 328-329

Estates General (France)
Church and State (1614)
Louis XIII **9** 529-531
Richelieu, Armand Jean du Plessis
de **13** 142-144
established (1302)
Boniface VIII **2** 392-393
Philip IV **12** 274
final sessions (1788-1789)
Lafayette, Marquis de **9** 151-152
Louis XVI **9** 534-535
Marie Antoinette **10** 258-259
Mirabeau, Comte de **11** 51-52
Necker, Jacques **11** 330-331
as National Assembly (1789)
Robespierre, Maximilien François
Marie Isidore de **13** 199-201
Talleyrand, Charles Maurice de
15 89-90
see also French Revolution—Nation-
al Assembly

Este, Alfonso I d' (1486-1534), duke
of Ferrara
Ariosto, Ludovico **1** 289-290
Willaert, Adrian **16** 287-288

Este, Baldassare d'
see Vicino da Ferrara

Este, Borso d' (1413-1471), duke of Modena and of Ferrara
Tura, Cosimo **15** 343-344

Este, Ercole I d' (1431-1505), duke of Mod-
ena and of Ferrara
Boiardo, Matteo Maria **2** 369
Josquin des Prez **8** 361-363
Obrecht, Jacob **11** 457-458

Este, Ippolito I d' (1479-1520), Italian cardinal
Ariosto, Ludovico **1** 289-290

Este, Ippolito II d' (1509-1572), Italian car-
dinal
Cellini, Benvenuto **3** 391-392
Palestrina, Giovanni Pierluigi da
12 70-72
Willaert, Adrian **16** 287-288

Este, Isabella d' (1474-1539), marchioness
of Mantua
Boiardo, Matteo Maria **2** 369
Correggio **4** 249-251
Mantegna, Andrea **10** 215-216
Perugino **12** 245-246

Este, Leonello d' (died 1450), ruler of Fer-
rara
Alberti, Leon Battista **1** 113-115
Pisanello **12** 323-324

Este, Luigi d' (1538-1586), Italian cardinal
Marenzio, Luca **10** 248
Porta, Giambattista della **12** 403-404
Tasso, Torquato **15** 114-116

Este, Niccolo III d' (died 1441), ruler of
Ferrara
Alberti, Leon Battista **1** 113-115

Estelle Musson (painting)
Degas, Hilaire Germain Edgar
4 461-462

Estenssoro, Victor Paz
see Paz Estenssoro, Victor

Esterházy, Miklós
see Esterházy, Nicholas

Esterházy, Nicholas (1714-1790), Hungarian prince
Haydn, Franz Joseph **7** 219-221

Esterházy, Nicholas (Fürst Esterházy von
Galantha; 1765-1833), Hungarian prince
Schubert, Franz Peter **14** 35-37

Esterhazy, Ferdinand Walsin (1847-1923),
French army officer
Dreyfus, Alfred **5** 103-105

ESTES, RICHARD (born 1932), American
realist painter **5** 322-323

ESTEVAN (a.k.a. Estabanico, Estevanico the
Black; c. 1500-1539), Moroccan explorer
5 324-325
Cabeza de Vaca, Álvar Núñez **3** 197
Marcos de Niza **10** 240

Esthétique du Mal (poem)
Stevens, Wallace **14** 443-445

Esther (oratorio)
Handel, George Frederick **7** 116-119

Esther (play)
Racine, Jean Baptiste **12** 532-535

Esther the Beautiful (play)
Lope Félix de Vega Carpio **9** 503-506

Esthetics (philosophy)
ethical values and
Croce, Benedetto **4** 313-314
Kierkegaard, Søren Aabye
8 547-549
romanticism
Baudelaire, Charles Pierre **2** 61-63

utilitarian view
  Chernyshevsky, Nikolai Gavrilovich
    3 504-505
value judgments
  Bosanquet, Bernard 2 425-426
  Brentano, Franz Clemens 2 516-517
  Meinong, Alexius Ritter von Hand-
    schuchsheim 10 461-462
  Pater, Walter Horatio 12 130-131
  Shaftesbury, 3d Earl of 14 136-137

Estigarribia, José Félix (1888-1940),
Paraguayan general
  Morínigo, Higinio 11 174-175

Estonia (Estonian Soviet Socialist Republic)
  Litvinov, Maxim Maximovich
    9 451-452
  Saarinen, Eliel and Eero 13 396-398

ESTRADA CABRERA, MANUEL
(1857-1924), Guatemalan president
1898-1920 5 325-326
  Asturias, Miguel Angel 1 354-355

ESTRADA PALMA, TOMÁS (1835-1908),
Cuban president 1902-1906 5 326-327
  Gómez, Máximo 6 418-419
  Martí, José 10 285-286

E.T., The Extra-Terrestrial (film)
  Spielberg, Steven 14 379-381

Et nunc manet in te (book)
  Gide, André 6 308-309

Étaples, Treaty of (1492)
  Henry VII 7 300-302

État de siège, L' (play)
  Camus, Albert 3 255-257

Etched in Moonlight (stories)
  Stephens, James 14 430-431

Etchers
  see Artists—etchers

Été, L' (novel)
  Martin du Gard, Roger 10 295-296

Eteocles (mythology)
  Aeschylus 1 70-72
  Sophocles 14 343-345

Eternal Goodness, The (poem)
  Whittier, John Greenleaf 16 256-257

Eternal rejection (religious doctrine)
  Julian of Norwich 8 381

Eternal Smile, The (story)
  Lagerkvist, Pär Fabian 9 162-163

Eternidades (poems)
  Jiménez, Juan Ramón 8 261-262

Eternity (philosophy)
  Bonaventure 2 383-384

Ethan Frome (novella)
  Wharton, Edith 16 221

Ethelbert (552?-616), King of Kent 560-616
  Augustine of Canterbury 1 370-371

Ethelbert of York
  see Aelbert

Ethelred, St.
  see Ailred, St.

ETHELRED THE UNREADY (968?-1016),
Anglo-Saxon king of England 978-1016
5 327
  Canute I, the Great 3 266-269
  Edward the Confessor 5 218-219
  Olaf, II 11 493-494

Ethelwulf (died 858), king of West Saxons
and Kentishmen and bishop of Winchester
  Alfred 1 151-153

Ether (anesthesia)
  Long, Crawford Williamson 9 495-496
  Morton, William Thomas Green
    11 198-199
  Wells, Horace 16 196

Ethical Culture (religious movement)
  Adler, Felix 1 63-64
  Schleiermacher, Friedrich Ernst Daniel
    14 11-12
  Tönnies, Ferdinand 15 266-267

Ethics (book)
  Bonhoeffer, Dietrich 2 389-391
  Spinoza, Baruch 14 381-383
  Wundt, Wilhelm Max 16 402-403

Ethics (book; Aristotle)
  Aristotle 1 295-296
  Grosseteste, Robert 7 15
  Nicholas of Oresme 11 380

Ethics (philosophy)
and political imperatives
  Clarke, Samuel 4 88
  Cudworth, Ralph 4 331
  Meinecke, Friedrich 10 460-461
  Spinoza, Baruch 14 381-383
  see also Political theory rationalistic
applied ethics
  Bok, Sissela Ann 2 372-374
bioethics
  Singer, Peter Albert David
    14 253-254
biomedical
  Callahan, Daniel 3 231-233
  Fletcher, Joseph Francis 5 488-489
Christian
  Adams, James Luther 1 47-48
  Bennett, John Coleman 2 170-171
  Butler, Joseph 3 180-181
  Charron, Pierre 3 472
  Niebuhr, Helmut Richard
    11 386-387
  Pascal, Blaise 12 122-124
corporate
  Knight, Frank Hyneman 9 58-59
  Nader, Ralph 11 290-291
Cynics
  Antisthenes 1 250-251
existential
  Kierkegaard, Søren Aabye
    8 547-549
Hindu (20th century)
  Radhakrishnan, Sarvepalli
    12 537-538
history of

MacIntyre, Alasdair Chalmers
    10 99-100
  Warnock, Helen Mary Wilson
    16 115-117
human motivation
  Midgely, Mary Burton 11 9-10
Jewish
  Levinas, Emmanuel 9 368-369
loyalty as basis
  Royce, Josiah 13 334-335
moral-sense school
  Hume, David 8 31-34
  Kolakowski, Leszek 9 76-77
  Mandeville, Bernard 10 192
  Price, Richard 12 447-448
  Shaftesbury, 3d Earl of 14 136-137
  Smith, Adam 14 283-284
  Toulmin, Stephen Edelston
    15 271-273
Neo-Kantianism
  Cohen, Hermann 4 138-139
non-Eudamonistic
  Sidgwick, Henry 14 213
sympathy as basis
  Smith, Adam 14 283-284
utilitarianism
  Chernyshevsky, Nikolai Gavrilovich
    3 504-505
  Paley, William 12 72
  Toulmin, Stephen Edelston
    15 271-273
values
  Brentano, Franz Clemens 2 516-517
  Meinong, Alexius Ritter von Hand-
    schuchsheim 10 461-462
  Perry, Ralph Barton 12 239-240

Ethiopia, Empire of (nation, East Africa)
Axumite period
  Ezana 5 354-355
exploration
  Bonvalot, Pierre Gabriel Édouard
    2 396
  Bruce, James 3 63-64
  Burton, Richard 3 163-164
  Dias de Novais, Bartolomeu
    4 533-534
frontier disputes
  Gordon, Charles George 6 448-449
Italy and
  Badoglio, Pietro 1 428-429
  Crispi, Francesco 4 310-311
  Haile Selassie 7 68-70
  Heruy Wäldä-Sellasé 7 348-349
  Hitler, Adolf 7 417-420
  Mäkonnen Endalkačäw 10 161-162
  Menelik II 10 495-497
  Mussolini, Benito 11 272-274
  Schuschnigg, Kurt von 14 45-46
military government (after 1974)
  Mengistu Haile Mariam 10 503-505
rulers (to 15th century)
  Ezana 5 354-355
  Lalibela 9 170
  Menelik II 10 495-497
  Piankhi 12 288-289
  Shabaka 14 130

Taharqa **15** 81-82
Yekuno Amlak **16** 449
rulers (19th-20th century)
Haile Selassie **7** 68-70
Johannes IV **8** 272-273
Menelik II **10** 495-497
Tewodros II **15** 158-159
unification
Johannes IV **8** 272-273
Menelik II **10** 495-497
Tewodros II **15** 158-159

Ethiopian Church
Ezana **5** 354-355
Lalibela **9** 170

Ethiopian literature
Heruy Wäldä-Sellasé **7** 348-349
Mäkonnen Endalkačäw **10** 161-162

Ethiopian Prodigy, The (play)
Lope Félix de Vega Carpio **9** 503-506

Ethiopian War (1935)
see Ethiopia—Italy and

Éthiopiques (poems)
Senghor, Léopold Sédar **14** 106-107

Ethnocentrism (sociology)
Gumplowicz, Ludwig **7** 41
Sumner, William Graham **15** 32

Ethnography (social science)
Durkheim, Émile **5** 162-163
Faye, Safi **5** 400-401
Kluckhohn, Clyde **9** 56-57
Mauss, Marcel **10** 352-353
Morgan, Lewis Henry **11** 167-168
Radin, Paul **12** 538-539
Sapir, Edward **13** 478-479
see also Ethnology

Ethnography, Institute of (France)
Mauss, Marcel **10** 352-353

Ethnology (social science)
Boas, Franz **2** 349-351
Fletcher, Alice Cunningham **5** 486-487
Herskovits, Melville Jean **7** 345
Kroeber, Alfred Louis **9** 105-106
La Flesche, Francis **9** 152-154
Linton, Ralph **9** 431
Rasmussen, Knud Johan Victor **13** 44
see also Ethnography

Ethology (science)
Fossey, Dian **6** 23-24
Tinbergen, Nikolaas **15** 229-230

Étienne Jeaurat (painting)
Greuze, Jean Baptiste **6** 539

Étoile (ship)
Bougainville, Louis Antoine de
2 443-444

Étoile de mer, L' (film)
Ray, Man **13** 59-60

Étoile du Nord, L' (opera)
Meyerbeer, Giacomo **10** 536-537

Étoile vesper, L' (novel)
Colette, Sidonie Gabrielle **4** 158-159

Étranger, L' (novel)
Camus, Albert **3** 255-257

Étrennes des orphelins, Les (poems)
Rimbaud, Jean Nicolas Arthur
13 172-174

Etiquette
Post, Emily Price **12** 409-410

Etruria (ancient city, Italy)
Catiline **3** 372-373

Étude (musical form)
Chopin, Frédéric François **4** 16-18
Debussy, Achille Claude **4** 445-447
Rachmaninov, Sergei Vasilievich
12 531-532
Scriabin, Alexander Nikolayevich
14 71-72
Szymanowski, Karol **15** 67-68

Études symphoniques musical composition)
Schumann, Robert Alexander **14** 41-43

Etymologies (book)
Isidore of Seville **8** 149-150

Etzel Andergast (novel)
Wassermann, Jakob **16** 130-131

Eucharist (religion)
institution and early views
Ignatius of Antioch **8** 107-108
Jesus of Nazareth **8** 251-255
medieval controversies
Erigena, John Scotus **5** 308-309
Leo IX **9** 332
William of Ockham **16** 298-299
Reformation views
Karlstadt, Andreas Bodenheim von
8 449
Luther, Martin **10** 48-51
Schwenckfeld, Kasper von **14** 56-57
Zwingli, Huldreich **16** 537-538
transubstantiation
Innocent, III **8** 125-127
Lanfranc **9** 189-190
Paul VI **12** 146-148
Wyclif, John **16** 412-413

Eucharistic Congress (Bergamo; 1920)
John, XXIII **8** 277-280

Eucharistic Congress (Chicago; 1926)
Mundelein, George William
11 248-249

Euclid (Euclides of Mezara; 450?-374 B.C.),
Greek philosopher
Plato **12** 345-347

EUCLID (flourished 300 B.C.), Greek mathematician **5** 327-329
Aristarchus of Samos **1** 290-291
Einstein, Albert **5** 228-231
Fibonacci, Leonardo **5** 434-435
Hobbes, Thomas **7** 421-423
Tartaglia, Niccolo **15** 111-112
see also Euclidean geometry

Euclidean geometry (mathematics)
a priori validity
Kant, Immanuel **8** 430-432

and non-Euclidean
Gauss, Karl Friedrich **6** 240-242
Lobachevskii, Nikolai Ivanovich
9 472-474
Riemann, Georg Friedrich Bernard
13 164-165
Elements
Apollonius of Perga **1** 261-262
Archimedes **1** 277-280-222
Euclid **5** 327-329-27
Eudoxus of Cnidus **5** 329-330
Lobachevskii, Nikolai Ivanovich
9 472-474
Omar Khayyam **11** 510-511
Proclus Diadochus **12** 457
Recorde, Robert **13** 68-69
Russell, Bertrand Arthur William
13 373-374

Euclio (literary character)
Plautus **12** 348-350

Eudemian Ethics
see Ethics (book; Aristotle)

Eudiometer (instrument)
Volta, Alessandro **16** 12-14

Eudoxia (died 404), Byzantine empress
John Chrysostom **8** 280-281

Eudoxia (Evdokiya Fëdorovna Lopukhina;
1669?-1731), czarina of Russia
Peter I **12** 253-256

EUDOXUS OF CNIDUS (circa 408-circa
355 B.C.), Greek astronomer, mathematician, and physician **5** 329-330
Archimedes **1** 277-280
Bitruji, Nur al-Din Abu Ishaq al **2** 296
Euclid **5** 327-329

Eugénie (1826-1920), empress of the
French 1853-71
Daudet, Alphonse **4** 402-403
Maximilian of Hapsburg **10** 358-360
Mérimée, Prosper **10** 517
Victoria **15** 485-487

Eugénie (play)
Beaumarchais, Pierre August Caron de
2 93-94

Eugénie Grandet (novel)
Balzac, Honoré de **1** 478-480

Eugène de Beauharnais (1781-1824), duke
of Leuchtenberg and prince of Eichstätt
Pedro I **12** 179-180

Eugene (popes)
see Eugenius

Eugene Maurice of Soissons (died 1673),
French nobleman
Eugene of Savoy **5** 330-331

Eugene of Litchenberg
see Eugène de Beauharnais

EUGENE OF SAVOY (1663-1736),
French-born Austrian general and diplomat **5** 330-331
Fischer von Erlach, Johann Bernhard
5 459-461

Hildebrandt, Johann Lucas von
7 380-381
Maria Theresa **10** 256-258
Saxe, Comte de **13** 507-508

Eugene Onegin (novel)
Pushkin, Aleksandr Sergeevich
12 489-491

Eugene Onegin (opera)
Tchaikovsky, Peter Ilyich **15** 130-132

Eugenics (biology)
Carrel, Alexis **3** 322-323
Carr-Saunders, Alexander Morris
3 333-334
Fisher, Ronald Aylmer **5** 463-464
Galton, Francis **6** 193-194
Muller, Hermann Joseph **11** 238-239

Eugenie, Sir Dauphine (literary character)
Jonson, Ben **8** 343-345

Eugenius (died 394), Roman emperor
392-394
Stilicho, Flavius **14** 452-453
Theodosius **15** 176

Eugenius III (Bernando Paganelli; died
1153), pope 1145-53
Arnold of Brescia **1** 314-315
Bernard of Clairvaux **2** 207-208
Lombard, Peter **9** 490-491
Louis VII **9** 524-525

Eugenius IV (1383-1447), pope 1431-47
Alberti, Leon Battista **1** 113-115
Conti, Niccolò de' **4** 212-213
Cusa, Nicholas of **4** 352-353
Fouquet, Jean **6** 31
Pisanello **12** 323-324

Euhemerus (poems)
Ennius, Quintus **5** 289

EULER, LEONARD (1707-1783), Swiss
mathematician **5** 331-332
Ampère, André Marie **1** 205-206
Bernoulli, Daniel **2** 216
Colden, Cadwallader **4** 145-146
Fermat, Pierre de **5** 421-422
Gauss, Karl Friedrich **6** 240-242
Lagrange, Joseph Louis **9** 164-166, 303
Laplace, Marquis de **9** 202-204

Euménides, Les (musical composition)
Milhaud, Darius **11** 17-18

Eumenes (360-416 B.C.), Macedonian general
Antigonus I **1** 248-249

Eumenides, The (play)
Aeschylus **1** 70-72

Eunuch (book; Terence)
La Fontaine, Jean de **9** 156-157

Eunuchs (Chinese)
political power
Cheng Ho **3** 500
Hsüan-tsung, T'ang **8** 7-8
Yung-lo **16** 482-483
power opposed
Huang Tsung-hsi **8** 9-10
Liu Tsung-Yüan **9** 455-456

Po Chü-i **12** 362-363
Zhao Kuang-yin **16** 505-508

Eunuchus (play)
Terence **15** 146-148

Eureka (novel; Poe)
Baudelaire, Charles Pierre **2** 61-63
Poe, Edgar Allan **12** 363-365

Eurhythmics (music)
Jaques-Dalcroze, Emile **8** 221-222

Euric (died circa 484), king of the Visigoths
466-484
Odoacer **11** 473

Euridice (opera)
Caccini, Giulio **3** 205-206

Euripidaristophanize (term)
Aristophanes **1** 293-294

EURIPIDES (480-406 B.C.), Greek play-
wright **5** 332-334
Anaxagoras **1** 208-209
Aristophanes **1** 293-294
Doolittle, Hilda **5** 65-66
Ennius, Quintus **5** 289
Gluck, Christoph Willibald **6** 372-374
Leconte de Lisle, Charles Marie René
9 273-274
Seneca the Younger, Lucius Annaeus
14 103-105
Sophocles **14** 343-345
Werfel, Franz **16** 204-205

Euripides (sculpture)
Noguchi, Isamu **11** 416-418

Europe (continent)
aid to Ottoman Empire
Mohammed Ali **11** 81-82
Palmerston, 3d Viscount **12** 81-83
constitutional movements
Canning, George **3** 258-260
Castlereagh, Viscount **3** 363-364
see also Nationalism, European
literature
Casanova de Seinglat, Giacomo
Jacopo Girolamo **3** 350-351
Cervantes, Miguel de Saavedra
3 395-398
D'Annunzio, Gabriele **4** 388
Dostoevsky, Fyodor **5** 74-77
Hamsun, Knut **7** 113-114
Saint-Simon, Comte de **13** 436-437
Staël, Germaine de **14** 391-392
see also English literature; French lit-
erature; etc.
overseas trade
Abbas I **1** 4-6
Frederick II **6** 81-84
Roman influence
Charlemagne **3** 445-447
Fustel de Coulanges, Numa Denis
6 155
unification of (post-WW II)
Davignon **4** 410-411
Monnet, Jean **11** 109-110
Spaak, Paul Henri **14** 359-360
see also Europe, Council of

Europe, Allied invasion of
see Normandy invasion (1944)

Europe, Council of (established 1949)
Adenauer, Konrad **1** 59-61
Spaak, Paul Henri **14** 359-360

European Center for Nuclear Research
(Meyrin, Switzerland)
Bohr, Niels Henrik David **2** 366-368
Rabi, Isidor Isaac **12** 526-527

European Coal and Steel Community
(established 1951)
Monnet, Jean **11** 109-110
Schuman, Robert **14** 41
Spaak, Paul Henri **14** 359-360

European Commission
Delors, Jacques **4** 484-486

European Defense Community (established
1951)
Adenauer, Konrad **1** 59-61

European Discovery of America (book)
Morison, Samuel Eliot **11** 175-176

European Economic Community
see Common Market

European Equilibrium (lithograph)
Daumier, Honoré Victorin **4** 403-405

European Messenger (journal)
Karamzin, Nikolai Mikhailovich
8 441-442

**European Organization of Molecular Biol-
ogy** (established 1964)
Lwoff, André **10** 58-59

European Recovery Program (established
1947)
Harriman, W. Averell **7** 165-166

Europeans, The (novel)
James, Henry **8** 211-212

Euryanthe (opera)
Weber, Carl Maria Friedrich Ernst von
16 156-157

Eurydice (literary character)
Virgil **15** 507-510

Eurydice (painting)
Delacroix, Ferdinand Victor Eugène
4 469-471

Eusebius of Caesarea (circa 260-340),
Roman theologian and historian
Constantine I **4** 209-211

Eusebius of Nicomedia (died circa 342),
Arian leader and bishop
Arius **1** 297-298
Ulfilas **15** 384

Eustace III (died circa 1125), count of
Boulogne
Baldwin I **1** 464-465

Eustace Conway (novel)
Maurice, John Frederick Denison
10 349-350

Eustace Diamonds, The (novel)
Trollope, Anthony **15** 300-302

Eutaw (novel)
Simms, William Gilmore **14** 235-236

Eutaw Springs, Battle of (1781)
Greene, Nathanael **6** 525-526
Marion, Francis **10** 262-263

Euterpe Society (established 1865)
Grieg, Edvard Hagerup **6** 541-542

Euthydemus (book; Plato)
Antisthenes **1** 250-251
Plato **12** 345-347

Euthyphro (dialogue)
Plato **12** 345-347

Eutopia (neologism)
Geddes, Patrick **6** 246-247

EUTYCHES (circa 380-455), Byzantine
monk **5** 335
Cyril **4** 362
Leo I **9** 329-330

Eva Trout (novel)
Bowen, Elizabeth **2** 462-463

Evan Harrington (novel)
Meredith, George **10** 512-513

Evangelical and Reformed Church (United
States)
Niebuhr, Helmut Richard **11** 386-387

Evangelical Church (Germany)
Praetorius, Michael **12** 431-432

Evangelical Lutheran Church (Germany)
Tillich, Paul Johannes **15** 224-225

Evangelicalism (religion)
Chalmers, Thomas **3** 408-409
Eliot, George **5** 254-256
Wilberforce, William **16** 269-270

Evangelical-Social Congress (established
1902)
Harnack, Adolf von **7** 160

Evangeline (poem)
Longfellow, Henry Wadsworth
9 499-500
Tschernichowsky, Saul **15** 323

Evangelism (religion)
Great Awakening
see Great Awakening
missionaries
Booth, Joseph **2** 404-405
Carey, William **3** 297
reforms
Backus, Isaac **1** 420-421
revivalism
Aberhart, William **1** 26-27
Cartwright, Peter **3** 344-345
Finney, Charles Grandison
5 450-451
McPherson, Aimee Semple **10** 434
Miller, William **11** 30-31
Moody, Dwight L. **11** 141-142
see also Revivalism, religious

Evangelists (New Testament)
see Bible—New Testament

Evangelists, The (painting)
Cimabue **4** 60-61

EVANS, EDITH (1888-1976), English
actress who portrayed comic characters
5 336-337

EVANS, GEORGE HENRY (1805-1856),
American labor and agrarian reformer
5 337-338

Evans, Mary Ann
see Eliot, George

EVANS, OLIVER (1755-1819), American
inventor **5** 338

EVANS, SIR ARTHUR JOHN (1851-1941),
English archeologist **5** 335-336
Childe, Vere Gordon **3** 521-522

Evans, Sir John (1823-1908), English archeologist
Evans, Arthur John **5** 335-336

EVANS, WALKER (1903-1975), American
photographer of American life between
the world wars **5** 339

EVANS-PRITCHARD, SIR EDWARD EVAN
(1902-1973), English social anthropologist **5** 340

Evaristo Carriego (book)
Borges, Jorge Luis **2** 411-412

EVARTS, WILLIAM MAXWELL
(1818-1901), American lawyer and statesman **5** 340-341
Curtis, Benjamin Robbins **4** 349
Waite, Morrison Remick **16** 46

EVATT, HERBERT VERE (1894-1965), Aus-
tralian statesman and jurist **5** 341-343
Curtin, John Joseph **4** 348-349
Mannix, Daniel **10** 210
Santamaria, Bartholomew Augustine
13 473-474

Eve Disconsolate (sculpture)
Powers, Hiram **12** 428-429

Eve of St. Agnes, The (poem; Keats)
Hunt, William Holman **8** 44-45
Keats, John **8** 470-472

Eve of St. Mark, The (play)
Anderson, Maxwell **1** 219-220

Eve Tempted (sculpture)
Powers, Hiram **12** 428-429

Evelina (novel)
Burney, Fanny **3** 147-148

EVELYN, JOHN (1620-1706), English
author **5** 343-344
Pepys, Samuel **12** 207-208

Evening (book)
Akhmatova, Anna **1** 96-97

Evening before the Holiday, The (poem)
Leopardi, Giacomo **9** 344-345

Evening Calm (painting)
Goyen, Jan van **6** 478-479

Evening Harmony (poem)
Baudelaire, Charles Pierre **2** 61-63

Evening Mooring by a Misty Bank (scroll)
Hsia Kuei **8** 4-5

Evening of Life (painting)
Durand, Asher Brown **5** 156-157

Evening Star, The (poem)
Eminescu, Mihail **5** 280-281

Evening Walk, An (poem)
Wordsworth, William **16** 385-388

Evening with Monsieur Teste, The (book)
Valéry, Paul Ambroise **15** 405-406

Evenings on a Farm near Dikanka (stories)
Gogol, Nikolai **6** 391-393

Everdingen, Allaert van (1621-1675),
Dutch painter and etcher
Ruisdael, Jacob van **13** 357-358

EVERETT, EDWARD (1794-1865), American statesman and orator **5** 344

EVERGOOD, PHILIP (1901-1973), American painter **5** 345

EVERS, MEDGAR (1925-1963), African
American civil rights leader **5** 345-348
Evers-Williams, Myrlie **5** 348-350

EVERS-WILLIAMS, MYRLIE (born Myrlie
Louise Beasley; b. 1933), civil rights
leader, lecturer, and writer **5** 348-350
Evers, Medgar **5** 345-348

Everson v. Board of Education (legal case)
Black, Hugo Lafayette **2** 301-303

Every Man in His Humour (play)
Jonson, Ben **8** 343-345

Every Man out of His Humour (play)
Jonson, Ben **8** 343-345

Every Soul Is a Circus (dance)
Cunningham, Merce **4** 337-338

Everybody's Autobiography (book)
Stein, Gertrude **14** 414-415

Everybody's Magazine (periodical)
Lawson, Thomas William **9** 255-256
Lippmann, Walter **9** 439-440

Everybody's Secret (play)
Calderón, Pedro **3** 221-222

Everyman (play)
Hofmannsthal, Hugo von **7** 443-444

Eve's Diary (book)
Twain, Mark **15** 363-366

Evesham Abbey (England)
Montfort, Simon de **11** 132-133

Evesham, Battle of (1265)
Edward I **5** 208-210
Henry III **7** 290-292
Montfort, Simon de **11** 132-133

Évian (Évian-les-Bains, France)
Abbas, Ferhat **1** 6-7
Ben Bella, Ahmed **2** 148-149

Evil (philosophy)
Erigena, John Scotus **5** 308-309
Nazzam, Ibrahim ibn Sayyar al- **11** 329

Evil Tales (stories)
Lagerkvist, Pär Fabian **9** 162-163

Evolución politica del pueblo mexicano, La (book)
Sierra, Justo **14** 217

Evolution and Ethics (book; Huxley)
Hu Shih **8** 63-65
Yen Fu **16** 452

Evolution, cultural
Morgan, Lewis Henry **11** 167-168
Tylor, Edward Burnett **15** 372-373
White, Leslie A. **16** 232-233

Evolution, organic
and nationalism
Keith, Arthur **8** 475-476
applied to society
Abbott, Lyman **1** 10-11
Beecher, Henry Ward **2** 112-113
Fiske, John **5** 465-466
Gladden, Washington **6** 356-357
Gray, Asa **6** 506-507
Gumplowicz, Ludwig **7** 41
McCosh, James **10** 402-403
Spencer, Herbert **14** 369-370
Wallas, Graham **16** 77-78
Ward, Lester Frank **16** 113-114
see also Social Darwinism compatibility with religion
cosmogenesis
Teilhard de Chardin, Marie Joseph Pierre **15** 134-136
Darwinism
Agassiz, Jean Louis Rodolphe **1** 76-78, 68
Butler, Samuel **3** 183
Cuvier, Georges Léopold **4** 357-359
Darwin, Charles Robert **4** 397-399
Dobzhansky, Theodosius **5** 35-37
Fisher, Ronald Aylmer **5** 463-464
Gladden, Washington **6** 356-357
Huxley, Julian **8** 75-77
Huxley, Thomas Henry **8** 77-79
James, William **8** 215-217
Owen, Richard **12** 39
Schrödinger, Erwin **14** 31-33
Wallace, Alfred Russel **16** 69-70
Weismann, August Freidrich Leopold **16** 178-180
see also Natural selection Darwinism (critics)
Darwinism (critics)
Bateson, William **2** 55-57
discontinuity theories
Galton, Francis **6** 193-194
Gould, Stephen Jay **6** 472-473
Morgan, Conway Lloyd **11** 159-160
Vries, Hugo de **16** 33-36
fossil studies
Howells, William White **7** 541-542
Hrdlička, Aleš **8** 3-4
Leakey, Louis Seymour Bazett **9** 262
Simpson, George Gaylord **14** 240-242
Weidenreich, Franz **16** 171-172
genetics and
de Vries, Hugo **4** 516-518

Haldane, John Burdon Sanderson **7** 70-71
Huxley, Julian **8** 75-77
Lamarck, Chevalier de **9** 171-173
Margulis, Lynn **10** 253-254
Morgan, Thomas Hunt **11** 170-171
Sturtevant, A. H. **15** 3-5
Vries, Hugo de **16** 33-36
see also Eugenics; Genetics materialistic theory
materialistic theory
Haeckel, Ernst Heinrich Philipp August **7** 61-62
neo-Darwinism
Mayr, Ernst **10** 372-374
philosophy and
Bergson, Henri **2** 191-192
Dobzhansky, Theodosius **5** 35-37
Haeckel, Ernst Heinrich Philipp August **7** 61-62
Morgan, Conway Lloyd **11** 159-160
Whitehead, Alfred North **16** 242-244
precursors
Anaximander **1** 209-210
Cardano, Geronimo **3** 285-286
Hooke, Robert **7** 475
Schleiermacher, Friedrich Ernst Daniel **14** 11-12
Scopes trial
see Scopes trial
speciation theory
Mayr, Ernst **10** 372-374

Evolutionism (psychology)
Hall, Granville Stanley **7** 85-86

Ewe (Togolese people)
Olympio, Sylvanus E. **11** 506-507

Ewell, Richard S. (1817-1872), American Confederate general
Lee, Robert Edward **9** 292-294

Ewige Jude, Der (epic)
Goethe, Johann Wolfgang von **6** 388-391

EWING, WILLIAM MAURICE (1906-1974), American oceanographer **5** 350-351

Ewins, Arthur James (1882-1957), English chemist
Dale, Henry Hallett **4** 371-373

EWONWU, BENEDICT CHUKA (born 1921), Nigerian sculptor and painter **5** 351-352

Ex parte Yarbrough (legal case)
Miller, Samuel Freeman **11** 29-30

Ex post facto laws (United States)
Chase, Samuel **3** 475-476

Examination, The (story)
Pinter, Harold **12** 317-318

Examiner (periodical)
Addison, Joseph **1** 57-58
Hazlitt, William **7** 235-236
Swift, Jonathan **15** 51-54

Excavation (painting)
de Kooning, Willem **4** 468-469

Excelente Balade of Charitie, An (poem)
Chatterton, Thomas **3** 481-482

Exception and the Rule, The (play)
Brecht, Bertolt **2** 512-514

Exclusion Bill (1679; England)
James II **8** 207-208
Monmouth and Buccleugh, Duke of **11** 108-109

Exclusion principle (physics)
Fermi, Enrico **5** 422-424
Pauli, Wolfgang Ernst **12** 149

Exclusives (Australian politics)
Macquarie, Lachlan **10** 115-116
Wentworth, William Charles **16** 203-204

Excommunication (religion)
in Jewish law
Gershom ben Judah **6** 283-284
Spinoza, Baruch **14** 381-383
of Christian dissidents
Arnold of Brescia **1** 314-315
Döllinger, Josef Ignaz von **5** 47-48
Loisy, Alfred Firmin **9** 489-490
Montanus **11** 122
Tolstoy, Leo **15** 262-265
Waldo, Peter **16** 55-56
of rulers
Henry IV **7** 292
Henry VIII **7** 302-305
John **8** 274-275
Pius VII **12** 334-335
Robert I **13** 192-194
see also Exiles, religious; Heresy

Excursion, The (poems)
Wordsworth, William **16** 385-388

Execrabilis (papal bull)
Pius II **12** 331

Execution of Maximilian (painting)
Manet, Édouard **10** 193-194

Executions
Argentina
Urquiza, Justo José **15** 396-397
Bohemia
Hus, Jan **8** 56-59
Bolivia
Guevara, Ernesto **7** 30-31
Brazil
Tiradentes **15** 237
Canada
Riel, Louis **13** 163-164
Chile
Carrera, José Miguel **3** 323-324
Lautaro **9** 235
China
Chu Hsi **4** 40-43
Costa Rica
Morazán, José Francisco **11** 155
Cuba
López, Narciso **9** 508
Czechoslovakia
Slánský, Rudolf Salzmann **14** 270-271
Egypt

Sayyid Qutb **13** 509-511
England
  Charles, I **3** 450-452
  Cranmer, Thomas **4** 295-296
  Cromwell, Thomas **4** 320-321
  Essex, 2d Earl of **5** 321-322
  Latimer, Hugh **9** 221
  Laud, William **9** 224-225
  Monmouth and Buccleugh, Duke of **11** 108-109
  More, Thomas **11** 156-157
  Northumberland, Duke of **11** 431-432
  Raleigh, Walter **13** 9-11
  Somerset, Duke of **14** 333-334
  Strafford, 1st Earl of **14** 490-491
  Tyndale, William **15** 373-374
  Vane, Henry **15** 425-426
  Wallace, William **16** 75-76
France
  Bloch, Marc **2** 332-333
  Chénier, André Marie **3** 500-501
  Hébert, Jacques René **7** 247-248
  Houdon, Antoine **7** 516-517
  Joan of Arc **8** 264-265
  Laval, Pierre **9** 237-238
  Lavoisier, Antoine Laurent **9** 241-244
  Louis XVI **9** 534-535
  Ney, Michel **11** 372-373
  Robespierre, Maximilien François Marie Isidore de **13** 199-201
  Saint-Just, Louis Antoine Léon de **13** 433
Germany
  Bonhoeffer, Dietrich **2** 389-391
  Münzer, Thomas **11** 251-252
Greece
  Socrates **14** 320-321
Honduras
  Walker, William **16** 68-69
Hungary
  Nagy, Imre **11** 292-293
Iran
  Taqi Khan Amir-e Kabir, Mirza **15** 106-107
Iraq
  Hallaj, Al-Husayn ibn Mansur al- **7** 86-87
  Nuri al-Sa'id **11** 446-447
Ireland
  Emmet, Robert **5** 281-282
  Pearse, Patrick Henry **12** 173-174
Israel
  Eichmann, Adolf **5** 226-227
Italy
  Arnold of Brescia **1** 314-315
  Bruno, Giordano **3** 75-76
  Murat, Joachim **11** 253-254
  Mussolini, Benito **11** 272-274
  Savonarola, Girolamo **13** 505-506
Japan
  Tojo, Hideki **15** 254-256
  Yamashita, Tomoyuki **16** 435-436
Mexico
  Cuauhtemoc **4** 329

  Guerrero, Vicente **7** 28-30
  Hidalgo y Costilla, Miguel **7** 375-377
  Iturbide, Agustín de **8** 155-156
  Matamoros, Mariano **10** 329-330
  Maximilian of Hapsburg **10** 358-360
  Morelos, José María **11** 157-158
Netherlands
  Oldenbarnevelt, Johan van **11** 495-496
Ostrogothic Empire
  Boethius, Anicius Manlius Severinus **2** 360-361
Ottoman Empire
  Selim III **14** 95-96
Pakistan
  Bhutto, Zulfikar Ali **2** 261-262
Palestine
  Jesus of Nazareth **8** 251-255
Panama
  Balboa, Vasco Núñez de **1** 462-463
Peru
  Almagro, Diego de **1** 177-178
  Atahualpa **1** 355-356
  Túpac Amaru, José Gabriel **15** 341
Philippines
  Bonifacio, Andres **2** 393-394
  Rizal, José **13** 187-189
Roman Empire
  Stilicho, Flavius **14** 452-453
Russia
  Beria, Lavrenty Pavlovich **2** 192-193
  Bukharin, Nikolai Ivanovich **3** 112-113
  Kamenev, Lev Borisovich **8** 417-418
  Kolchak, Aleksandr Vasilievich **9** 77-78
  Paul I **12** 143-144
  Pugachev, Emelyan Ivanovich **12** 478-479
  Zinoviev, Grigori Evseevich **16** 521-522
Spain
  Lorca, Federico García **9** 511-513
Switzerland
  Servetus, Michael **14** 115-116
Tunisia
  Lull, Raymond **10** 39-40
U.S.
  Billy the Kid **2** 277
  Brown, John **3** 39-41
  Leisler, Jacob **9** 313-314
  Philip **12** 267-268
  Prosser, Gabriel **12** 460-461
  Sacco and Vanzetti **13** 408-410
  Turner, Nathaniel **15** 354
  Vesey, Denmark **15** 475
  see also Assassinations; Murder victims
Executions of May 3, 1808 (painting; Goya)
  Goya y Lucientes, Francisco de Paula José de **6** 476-478
  Manet, Édouard **10** 193-194
Exegesis, biblical
  see Bible

Exemplarism (philosophy)
  Bonaventure **2** 383-384
Exhaustion, method of (mathematics)
  Archimedes **1** 277-280
  Euclid **5** 327-329
  Eudoxus of Cnidus **5** 329-330
Exhortação da guerra (play)
  Vicente, Gil **15** 479-480
Exhuming of the Mastodon, The (painting)
  Peale, Charles Willson **12** 169-171
Exilarch (Jewish office)
  Anan ben David **1** 207-208
Exile (poems)
  Perse, Saint-John **12** 242-243
Exile, The (biography)
  Buck, Pearl Sydenstricker **3** 91-93
Exile and the Kingdom (stories)
  Camus, Albert **3** 255-257
Exiles (literary)
  from Asia
    Su Shih **15** 39-40
    Yun Sondo **16** 483
  from England and Ireland
    Joyce, James **8** 365-367
    O'Casey, Sean **11** 459-460
    Shelley, Percy Bysshe **14** 176-178
    Synge, Edmund John Millington **15** 61-62
  from France
    Hugo, Victor Marie **8** 22-25
    Prévost, Abbé **12** 445-446
    Rousseau, Jean Jacques **13** 324-328
    Staël, Germaine de **14** 391-392
    Voltaire **16** 14-16
  from Germany
    Storm, Theodor **14** 479-480
  from Latin America
    Mármol, José **10** 274
    Vallejo, César Abraham **15** 408-409
    Zorrilla de San Martin, Juan **16** 530-531
  from North America
    Fréchette, Louis-Honoré **6** 77-78
    Miller, Henry **11** 26-27
  from Poland
    Sienkiewicz, Henryk **14** 216-217
  from Roman Empire
    Ovid **12** 34-36
  from Russia
    Nabokov, Vladimir **11** 287-288
  from Scandinavia
    Ibsen, Henrik **8** 98-100
    Strindberg, August **14** 509-511
  see also Exiles (political)
Exiles (political)
  from Angola
    de Andrade, Mario **4** 434-435
  from Argentina
    Alberdi, Juan Bautista **1** 109-110
    Echeverría, José Estéban **5** 197-198
    Perón, Juan Domingo **12** 228-230
    Perón, Isabel Martinez de **12** 226-228

Rosas, Juan Manuel de **13** 290-291
Sarmiento, Domingo Faustino **13** 484-485
Timerman, Jacobo **15** 226-228
from Athens
Demosthenes **4** 495-496
Solon **14** 327-328
Thucydides **15** 211-212
from Bolivia
Ballivián, José **1** 475
Paz, Octavio **12** 161-162
from Brazil
Andrada e Silva, José Bonifácio de **1** 221-222
Goulart, João **6** 467-469
Kubitschek de Oliveira, Juscelino **9** 113-115
Pedro II **12** 180-181
Prestes, Luiz Carlos **12** 442-444
from Buganda
Mutesa II **11** 277-278
Mwanga **11** 282-283
from Burma
Nu, U **11** 439-441
from Cambodia
Sihanouk, Norodom **14** 222-223
from Cameroons
Beti, Mongo **2** 242-243
from Canada
Mackenzie, William Lyon **10** 104-106
Papineau, Louis-Joseph **12** 91
from Chile
O'Higgins, Bernardo **11** 486
from China
Hsüan Tsang **8** 6-7
K'ang Yu-wei **8** 426-428
Kuo Mo-jo **9** 133-134
Liu Tsung-Yüan **9** 455-456
Po Chü-i **12** 362-363
Sun Yat-sen **15** 35-39
Wang T'ao **16** 105-106
Wang Yang-ming **16** 108-109
from Colombia
Gómez, Máximo **6** 418-419
Mosquera, Tomás Cipriano de **11** 205-206
Nariño, Antonio **11** 314-315
Rojas Pinilla, Gustavo **13** 255-256
from Costa Rica
Ferrer, José Figuéres **5** 428-429
from Cuba
Estrada Palma, Tomás **5** 326-327
Gómez, Máximo **6** 418-419
Maceo, Antonio **10** 88-90
Martí, José **10** 285-286
from Dominican Republic
Baez, Buenaventura **1** 432-433
Balaguer y Ricardo, Joaquin **1** 460-461
Bosch, Juan **2** 428-429
Santana, Pedro **13** 474-475
from Ecuador
Velasco Ibarra, José María **15** 452-454
from Egypt

Zaghlul Pasha, Saad **16** 485-486
from England
Byron, George Gordon Noel **3** 193-194
Lilburne, John **9** 409-410
Margaret of Scotland **10** 252-253
Monmouth and Buccleugh, Duke of **11** 108-109
Suckling, John **15** 10-11
from Ethiopia
Haile Selassie **7** 68-70
Heruy Wäldä-Sellasé **7** 348-349
from Finland
Nordenskjöld, Nils Adolf Erik **11** 421-422
from France
Cabet, Étienne **3** 196
Carnot, Lazare Nicolas Marguerite **3** 313-314
Cauchy, Augustin Louis **3** 378-380
Charles X **3** 463-464
du Pont, Éleuthère Irénée **5** 154
Dumas, Alexandre **5** 136-138
Fouché, Joseph **6** 30-31
Louis Philippe **9** 536-537
Maistre, Joseph de **10** 153-154
Napoleon I **11** 306-310
Napoleon III **11** 310-312
Sieyès, Comte Emmanuel Joseph **14** 217-218
Soulé, Pierre **14** 351-352
Staël, Germaine de **14** 391-392
Talleyrand, Charles Maurice de **15** 89-90
Thiers, Louis Adolphe **15** 181-182
Zola, Émile **16** 526-528
from Germany
Brandt, Willy **2** 499-500
Brecht, Bertolt **2** 512-514
Feuchtwanger, Lion **5** 430-432
Frisch, Otto Robert **6** 119-120
List, Georg Friedrich **9** 443-444
Mann, Heinrich **10** 201-202
Mann, Thomas **10** 204-207
Mannheim, Karl **10** 208-209
Marx, Karl **10** 304-308
Mies van der Rohe, Ludwig **11** 10-12
Salomon, Charlotte **13** 454-455
Schindler, Solomon **14** 7-8
Schrödinger, Erwin **14** 31-33
Ulbricht, Walter **15** 383-384
Voegelin, Eric **16** 6-8
Wagner, Richard **16** 40-43
Weill, Kurt **16** 174-175
from Ghana
Busia, Kofi Abrefa **3** 172-173
Nkrumah, Kwame **11** 408-410
from Gran Colombia
Santander, Franciso de Paula **13** 475
from Greece
Seferis, George **14** 84-85
from Guatemala
Arévalo, Juan José **1** 285-286
Asturias, Miguel Angel **1** 354-355

Ubico y Castañeda, Jorge **15** 377-378
from Haiti
Boyer, Jean Pierre **2** 468-469
from Hungary
Andrássy, Julius **1** 222-223
Lukács, Gyorgy **10** 37-38
from India
Chandragupta Maurya **3** 426
from Indonesia
Sukarno **15** 18-20
from Italy
Cavalcanti, Guido **3** 382
Dante Alighieri **4** 389-391
Foscolo, Ugo **6** 21
Garibaldi, Giuseppe **6** 215-217
Leo X **9** 332-334
Levi, Carlo **9** 364
Manin, Daniele **10** 197-198
Mazzini, Giuseppe **10** 381-383
Medici, Cosimo de' **10** 449-450
Silone, Ignazio **14** 231-232
Victor Emmanuel III **15** 484-485
from Japan
Katayama, Sen **8** 457
from Jerusalem
Jeroboam I **8** 248-249
from Kenya
Ngugi wa Thiong'o **11** 375-376
Thuku, Harry **15** 212-213
from Libya
Idris I **8** 102
from Mexico
Calles, Plutarco Elías **3** 234-235
Juárez, Benito **8** 369-372
Madero, Francisco Indalecio **10** 118-119
Santa Ana, Antonio López de **13** 471-472
Siqueiros, David Alfaro **14** 256
Vasconcelos, José **15** 443-444
from Morocco
Abd el-Krim el-Khatabi, Mohamed ben **1** 15-16
Mohammed V **11** 79-81
from Nicaragua
Zelaya, José Santos **16** 495-496
from Nigeria
Soyinka, Wole **14** 358-359
from Norway
Undset, Sigrid **15** 388-389
from Paraguay
Morínigo, Higinio **11** 174-175
from Peru
Castilla, Ramón **3** 361
Haya de la Torre, Victor Raul **7** 216-217
Palma, Ricardo **12** 77
Prado Ugarteche, Manuel **12** 430-431
from Poland
Dubinsky, David **5** 114-115
Kościuszko, Tadeusz Andrzej Bonawentura **9** 88
from Portuguese colonies
de Andrade, Mario **4** 434-435

from Prussia
    Stein, Heinrich Friedrich Karl vom
        und zum **14** 415-416
from Roman Empire
    Seneca the Younger, Lucius Annaeus
        14 103-105
from Russia
    Bakunin, Mikhail Aleksandrovich
        1 458-460
    Berdyaev, Nicholas Alexandrovich
        2 184-185
    Borochov, Dov Ber **2** 421-422
    Bunin, Ivan Alekseevich **3** 124
    Chernyshevsky, Nikolai Gavrilovich
        3 504-505
    Dzerzhinsky, Felix Edmundovich
        5 173-174
    Ehrenburg, Ilya Grigorievich
        5 224-225
    Herzen, Aleksandr Ivanovich
        7 351-352
    Kollontai, Aleksandra Mikhailovna
        9 79
    Kropotkin, Peter Alekseevich
        9 107-108
    Lenin, Vladimir Ilich **9** 323-326
    Lermontov, Mikhail Yurievich
        9 352-353
    Mandelstam, Osip Emilyevich
        10 191
    Miliukov, Pavel Nikolayevich
        11 18-19
    Molotov, Vyacheslav Mikhailovich
        11 89-90
    Pavlova, Anna **12** 157-159
    Pevsner, Antoine **12** 263-264
    Solzhenitsyn, Alexander Isayevich
        14 330-332
    Sorokin, Pitirim A. **14** 348-349
    Staël, Nicolas de **14** 392
    Stalin, Joseph **14** 393-396
    Trotsky, Leon **15** 302-305
from Serbia
    Peter I **12** 256
from South Africa
    Booth, Joseph **2** 404-405
    Brutus, Dennis **3** 77-78
    First, Ruth **5** 453-454
    Tambo, Oliver Reginald **15** 92-94
from Spain
    Alfonso XIII **1** 151
    Azaña Diaz, Manuel **1** 396-397
    Franco Bahamonde, Francisco
        6 52-54
    Isabella II **8** 145-146
    Ortega Y Gasset, José **12** 7-8
    Primo de Rivera y Orbaneja, Miguel
        12 454-455
    Saavedra, Angel de **13** 398
    Unamuno y Jugo, Miguel de
        15 386-387
from Sudan
    Azhari, Sayyid Ismail al- **1** 399-401
    Touré, Sékou **15** 275-277
from Switzerland
    Mazzini, Giuseppe **10** 381-383
from Thailand

Phibun Songkhram, Luang
    12 264-265
Pridi Phanomyong **12** 449
from the Netherlands
    William I **16** 291-292
    William the Silent **16** 300-302
from the Philippines
    Mabini, Apolinario **10** 72-73
    Rizal, José **13** 187-189
from Turkey
    Atatürk, Ghazi Mustapha Kemal
        1 356-357
    Gökalp, Mehmet Ziya **6** 395-396
from Uruguay
    Artigas, José Gervasio **1** 323
    Lavalleja, Juan Antonio **9** 238-239
    Rivera, Fructuoso **13** 184-185
from U.S.
    Chaplin, Charles Spencer **3** 438-440
    Galloway, Joseph **6** 186-187
    Johnson, John **8** 305-306
    Leonard, Daniel **9** 336-337
from Venezuela
    Betancourt, Rómulo **2** 237-238
    Páez, José Antonio **12** 58
from Zimbabwe
    Nkomo, Joshua Mqabuko
        11 405-407
from Zulu kingdom
    Shaka **14** 141-142
    see also Exiles (literary)

Exiles (religious)
    from Alexandria
        Arius **1** 297-298
        Athanasius **1** 358-359
    from Constantinople
        John Chrysostom **8** 280-281
        Photius **12** 283-284
    from England
        Eliot, John **5** 256-258
        John of Salisbury **8** 284-285
        Tyndale, William **15** 373-374
    from France
        Arnold of Brescia **1** 314-315
        Calvin, John **3** 239-242
        Frederick William **6** 85-86
        Teilhard de Chardin, Marie Joseph
            Pierre **15** 134-136
        William of Ockham **16** 298-299
    from Germany
        Mendelsohn, Erich **10** 488
        Meyerhof, Otto Fritz **10** 537-539
        Schwenckfeld, Kasper von **14** 56-57
        Zinzendorf, Nikolaus Ludwig von
            16 522-523
    from Japan
        Honen **7** 473
        Shinran **14** 197
    from Senegal
        Bamba, Amadou **1** 481-482
    from Spain
        Abravanel, Isaac ben Judah **1** 31
    from Switzerland
        Servetus, Michael **14** 115-116
    from U.S.

Hutchinson, Anne Marbury **8** 69-71
Existence (philosophy)
    Heidegger, Martin **7** 257-258
    Ibn al-Arabi, Muhyi al-Din **8** 91
    Santayana, George **13** 475-477
    see also Being (philosophy)

Existentialism (philosophy)
    and ethics
        Warnock, Helen Mary Wilson
            16 115-117
    and religion
        Berdyaev, Nicholas Alexandrovich
            2 184-185
        Buber, Martin **3** 87-89
        Bultmann, Rudolf Karl **3** 119-120
        Heschel, Abraham Joshua
            7 358-359
        Marcel, Gabriel **10** 233-234
        Rahner, Karl **13** 4-5
        Soloveitchik, Joseph Baer
            14 328-329
        Tillich, Paul Johannes **15** 224-225
    forerunners
        Rosenzweig, Franz **13** 294
        Schelling, Friedrich Wilhelm Joseph
            von **13** 526-527
        Simmel, Georg **14** 234-235
        Weber, Max (social scientist)
            16 157-160
    in literature and film
        Beckett, Samuel **2** 102-104
        Bogart, Humphrey **2** 363-364
        Grass, Günter **6** 496-497
        Mailer, Norman Kingsley
            10 148-150
        Melville, Herman **10** 472-476
        Sartre, Jean Paul **13** 491-492
        T'ao Ch'ien **15** 104-105
        Unamuno y Jugo, Miguel de
            15 386-387
        see also Absurd (literature)
    influence of
        Wright, Richard **16** 401-402
    philosophers
        Heidegger, Martin **7** 257-258
        Jaspers, Karl **8** 225-226
        Kierkegaard, Søren Aabye
            8 547-549
        Merleau-Ponty, Maurice **10** 518
        Ortega Y Gasset, José **12** 7-8
        Sartre, Jean Paul **13** 491-492
        Shestov, Lev **14** 190-191

Exner, Franz (1802-1853), Austrian
philosopher
    Schrödinger, Erwin **14** 31-33

Exner, Sigmund (1846-1926), Austrian
physiologist
    Frisch, Karl von **6** 117-118

Exodion (literary form)
    Pindar **12** 312-313

Exóticos (poems)
    González Prada, Manuel **6** 431

Expansionism (politics)
    see Imperialism

Expedition of Humphrey Clinker, The
see Humphrey Clinker

Experience (essay)
Emerson, Ralph Waldo **5** 278-280

Experience, school of (philosophy)
see Empiricism

Experimental Death Unit # 1 (play)
Baraka, Imamu Amiri **1** 498-499

Experimental farms (Canada)
Saunders, Charles Edward **13** 498-499

Experimental Medicine, Institute of (St. Petersburg, Russia)
Pavlov, Ivan Petrovich **12** 155-157

Experimentalism (philosophy)
Hu Shih **8** 63-65

Explorer I (satellite)
von Braun, Wernher **16** 17-18

Explorers, American
circumnavigation
Gray, Robert **6** 508-509
of American Northwest
Carver, Jonathan **3** 347-348
Clark, William **4** 82-83
Fitzpatrick, Thomas **5** 474-475
Gray, Robert **6** 508-509
Lewis, Meriwether **9** 391-392
of American West
Ashley, William Henry **1** 333-334
Boone, Daniel **2** 397-398
Frémont, John Charles **6** 97-98
Pike, Zebulon **12** 302-304
Powell, John Wesley **12** 425-426
Sacajawea **13** 405-408
Schoolcraft, Henry Rowe **14** 29
Smith, Jedediah S. **14** 294-295
Walker, Joseph Reddeford **16** 63-64
of Antarctic
Byrd, Richard Evelyn **3** 186-187
Ellsworth, Lincoln **5** 277
Palmer, Nathaniel Brown **12** 80-81
Wilkes, Charles **16** 279-280
of Arctic
Byrd, Richard Evelyn **3** 186-187
Ellsworth, Lincoln **5** 277
Greely, Adolphus Washington **6** 517-518
Henson, Matthew A. **7** 312-314
MacMillan, Donald Baxter **10** 111-112
Melville, George Wallace **10** 472
Peary, Robert Edwin **12** 175-176
of Asia
Andrews, Roy Chapman **1** 232-233
of moon
Armstrong, Neil Alden **1** 304-306

Explorers, Australian
Giles, Ernest **6** 317-318
Mawson, Douglas **10** 354-355
Wentworth, William Charles **16** 203-204
Wilkins, George Hubert **16** 281-282

Explorers, Brazilian
Rondon, Candido Mariano da Silva **13** 271

Explorers, British
see Explorers, English; Explorers, Irish; Explorers, Scottish

Explorers, Canadian
Fraser, Simon **6** 74-75
Jolliet, Louis **8** 328-329
la Verendrye, Sieur de **9** 239-240
Ogden, Peter Skene **11** 480-481
Stefansson, Vilhjalmur **14** 409-410
Thompson, David **15** 194-195

Explorers, Chinese
Ssu-ma Hsiang-ju **14** 389-390

Explorers, Danish
Bering, Vitus **2** 193-194
Rasmussen, Knud Johan Victor **13** 44

Explorers, Dutch
Barents, Willem **2** 4-5
Schouten, William Cornelius **14** 31
Tasman, Abel Janszoon **15** 113-114

Explorers, English
circumnavigation
Cook, James **4** 214-215
of Africa
Baker, Samuel White **1** 454-455
Burton, Richard **3** 163-164
Galton, Francis **6** 193-194
Johnston, Henry Hamilton **8** 322-323
Speke, John Hanning **14** 366-367
Stanley, Henry Morton **14** 399-400
of Antarctica
Cook, James **4** 214-215
Fuchs, Vivian **6** 140
Scott, Robert Falcon **14** 67-68
of Arctic
Baffin, William **1** 435-436
Franklin, John **6** 64-65
Hearne, Samuel **7** 241-242
of Asia
Baker, Samuel White **1** 454-455
Burton, Richard **3** 163-164
of Australia
Cook, James **4** 214-215
Dampier, William **4** 384
Drake, Francis **5** 94-96
Eyre, Edward John **5** 354
Flinders, Matthew **5** 490
Forrest, John **6** 12-13
Franklin, John **6** 64-65
Grey, George **6** 540-541
Sturt, Charles **15** 2-3
of Canada
Kelsey, Henry **8** 488
of North America
Cabot, John **3** 199-200
Cook, James **4** 214-215
Drake, Francis **5** 94-96
Gilbert, Humphrey **6** 313
Hudson, Henry **8** 12-13
Raleigh, Walter **13** 9-11
Vancouver, George **15** 414-415

of Northeast Passage and Russia
Chancellor, Richard **3** 422
of Northwest Passage
Davis, John **4** 419
Franklin, John **6** 64-65
Frobisher, Martin **6** 121-122
McClure, Robert **10** 397-398
Raleigh, Walter **13** 9-11
of Pacific
Cook, James **4** 214-215
of South America
Bates, Henry Walter **2** 53-54
of Tibet
Younghusband, Francis Edward **16** 477

Explorers, French
circumnavigation
Bougainville, Louis Antoine de **2** 443-444
of Africa
Brazza, Pierre Paul François Camille Savorgnan de **2** 509-510
Caillié, Auguste René **3** 214-215
Marchand, Jean-Baptiste **10** 234-237
of Canada
Maisoneuve, Sieur de **10** 153
Radisson, Pierre-Esprit **12** 539-540
of Central Asia
Bonvalot, Pierre Gabriel Édouard **2** 396
of Indochina
Garnier, Francis **6** 220-221
of North America
Bienville, Sieur de **2** 268-269
Brûlé, Étienne **3** 67-68
Cartier, Jacques **3** 343-344
Champlain, Samuel de **3** 419-421
La Salle, Sieur de **9** 210-211
Marquette, Jacques **10** 274-275
of Pacific Ocean
Bougainville, Louis Antoine de **2** 443-444

Explorers, German
Barth, Heinrich **2** 30-31
Peters, Carl **12** 257-258
Wegener, Alfred Lothar **16** 170-171

Explorers, Greek
Pytheas **12** 499-500

Explorers, Irish
Burke, Robert O'Hara **3** 142-143
McClintock, Francis Leopold **10** 394-395
Shackleton, Ernest Henry **14** 132-133

Explorers, Italian
of Africa
Cadamosto, Alvise da **3** 206-207
of Arctic
Nobile, Umberto **11** 411-412
of Asia
Conti, Niccolò de' **4** 212-213
John of Piano Carpini **8** 284
Polo, Marco **12** 380-382
Varthema, Ludovico di **15** 439-440

of North America
  Cabot, Sebastian **3** 200-201
  Columbus, Christopher **4** 176-179
  Verrazano, Giovanni da **15** 470-471
of Northeast Passage
  Cabot, Sebastian **3** 200-201
of South America
  Vespucci, Amerigo **15** 476-478

Explorers, Moroccan
  Estevanico **5** 324-325

Explorers, New Zealander
  Hillary, Edmund **7** 389-390

Explorers, Norwegian
  Amundsen, Roald **1** 206-207
  Eric the Red **5** 304
  Ericson, Leif **5** 306-307
  Nansen, Fridtjof **11** 304-305

Explorers, Portuguese
  circumnavigation
    Magellan, Ferdinand **10** 126-127
  of Africa
    Covilhão, Pedro de **4** 278-279
    Dias de Novais, Bartolomeu
      4 533-534
    Gama, Vasco da **6** 196-198
    Henry the Navigator **7** 305-306
  of North America
    Cabrillo, Juan Rodríguez **3** 204-205
    Corte Reál, Gaspar and Miguel
      4 254-255
  of South America
    Cabral, Pedro Álvares **3** 203-204
    Dias de Novais, Bartolomeu
      4 533-534
  of the Far East
    Mendes Pinto, Fernao **10** 493-494

Explorers, Russian
  Baranov, Aleksandr Andreievich
    1 499-500
  Gagarin, Yuri Alexeivich **6** 166-167
  Kotzebue, Otto von **9** 91-92
  Przhevalsky, Nikolai Mikhailovich
    12 469-470

Explorers, Scottish
  Baikie, William Balfour **1** 440
  Bruce, James **3** 63-64
  Clapperton, Hugh **4** 72-73
  Livingstone, David **9** 463-465
  Mackenzie, Alexander **10** 103-104
  Ross, James Clark **13** 302-303

Explorers, Spanish
  of Central America
    Balboa, Vasco Núñez de **1** 462-463
    Benalcázar, Sebastián de **2** 145-146
    Díaz del Castillo, Bernal **4** 536-537
    Pedrarias **12** 179
  of South America
    Almagro, Diego de **1** 177-178
    Azara, Félix de **1** 397-398
    Quesada, Gonzalo Jiménez de
      12 509-510
    Orellana, Francisco de **11** 527-528
    Pizarro, Francisco **12** 340-341
    Solís, Juan Díaz de **14** 326

of Southeastern North America
  de Soto, Hernando **4** 510-511
  Menéndez de Avilés, Pedro
    10 499-500
  Narváez, Pánfilo de **11** 315
  Ponce de León, Juan **12** 391-392
of Southwestern North America
  Anza, Juan Bautista de **1** 254-255
  Cabeza de Vaca, Álvar Núñez **3** 197
  Coronado, Francisco Vásquez de
    4 247
  Kino, Eusebio Francisco **9** 30-31
  Marcos de Niza **10** 240
  Oñate, Juan de **11** 513-514
  Portolá, Gaspar de **12** 408
of the Pacific
  Mendaña de Neyra, Álvaro de
    10 483

Explorers, Swedish
  Andrée, Salomon August **1** 226
  Hedin, Sven Anders **7** 252-253
  Nordenskold, Nils Otto Gustaf
    11 422-423

Explorers, Swiss
  Burckhardt, Johann Ludwig **3** 133

Explorers, underwater
  Cousteau, Jacques-Yves **4** 276-277

Expo 67 (Montreal)
  Calder, Alexander **3** 216-218
  Fuller, Richard Buckminster **6** 149-150

Express systems
  see Business and industrial leaders—
    express systems

Expressionism (architecture)
  Behrens, Peter **2** 121-122

Expressionism (film)
  Fellini, Federico **5** 408-409

Expressionism (literature)
  drama
    Hauptmann, Gerhart Johann Robert
      7 199-201
    Kaiser, Georg **8** 411-412
    O'Casey, Sean **11** 459-460
    O'Neill, Eugene **11** 514-516
    Strindberg, August **14** 509-511
    Toller, Ernst **15** 261
  prose and poetry
    Benn, Gottfried **2** 164
    Lagerkvist, Pär Fabian **9** 162-163
    Werfel, Franz **16** 204-205
    Zola, Émile **16** 526-528

Expressionism (music)
  Strauss, Richard **14** 500-501

Expressionism (painting)
  antecedents
    Church, Frederick Edwin **4** 49-50
    Friedrich, Caspar David **6** 114-115
    Gauguin, Paul **6** 236-238
    Goya y Lucientes, Francisco de
      Paula José de **6** 476-478
    Grünewald, Matthias **7** 23-24
    Hodler, Ferdinand **7** 434-435
    Munch, Edvard **11** 247-248

Van Gogh, Vincent **15** 427-429
Australian
  Nolan, Sidney Robert **11** 418
Austrian
  Kokoschka, Oskar **9** 75-76
  Schiele, Egon **14** 1-2
Brazilian
  Portinari, Cândido **12** 407-408
French
  Vlaminck, Maurice **16** 6
German
  Beckmann, Max **2** 104-105
  Grosz, George **7** 17-18
  Hodler, Ferdinand **7** 434-435
  Kirchner, Ernst Ludwig **9** 34-35
  Kokoschka, Oskar **9** 75-76
  Lehmbruck, Wilhelm **9** 307
  Macke, August **10** 102-103
  Marc, Franz **10** 231
  Mendelsohn, Erich **10** 488
  Mueller, Otto **11** 226-227
  Nolde, Emil **11** 419-420
  Pechstein, Hermann Max
    12 176-177
Russian
  Jawlensky, Alexej von **8** 228-229
  Kandinsky, Wassily **8** 420-422
  Larionov, Mikhail **9** 205-206
  Soutine, Chaim **14** 356-357
Spanish
  Greco **6** 511-514
U.S.
  Hartley, Marsden **7** 186
  Johns, Jasper **8** 291-293
  Pollock, Jackson **12** 379-380

Expressionism (sculpture)
  González, Julio **6** 428-429
  Kollwitz, Käthe **9** 79-81
  Lehmbruck, Wilhelm **9** 307
  Lipchitz, Jacques **9** 432-433

Expulsion of Heliodorus (fresco)
  Raphael **13** 40-42

Exsurge Domine (papal decree)
  Leo X **9** 332-334

Exterminating Angel, The (film)
  Buñuel, Luis **3** 127-128

**Extraordinary Adventures of Julio Juren-
  tio...** (novel)
  Ehrenburg, Ilya Grigorievich **5** 224-225

Extroversion (psychology)
  Jung, Carl Gustav **8** 388-389

Exultations ... (poems)
  Pound, Ezra Loomis **12** 415-417

EYCK, HUBERT VAN (died 1426), Flemish
  painter **5** 352-354
  Bermejo, Bartolomé **2** 205
  Limbourg brothers, The **9** 412-413
  van der Goes, Hugo **15** 416-417

EYCK, JAN VAN (circa 1390-1441), Flemish painter **5** 352-354
  influence of
    Antonello da Messina **1** 251-252
    Bermejo, Bartolomé **2** 205

Christus, Petrus **4** 33-34
Massys, Quentin **10** 325-326
Memling, Hans **10** 476
Schongauer, Martin **14** 26-28
van der Goes, Hugo **15** 416-417
Weyden, Rogier van der **16** 219-221
influenced by
Campin, Robert **3** 255
Limbourg brothers, The **9** 412-413
Sluter, Claus **14** 275-276

Eye (anatomy)
Spemann, Hans **14** 368-369

Eyeless in Gaza (novel)
Huxley, Aldous Leonard **8** 74-75

Eyes of the Interred, The (novel)
Asturias, Miguel Angel **1** 354-355

Eyes of the Mummy, The (film)
Lubitsch, Ernst **10** 18-19

Eylau, Battle of (1807)
Murat, Joachim **11** 253-254
Napoleon I **11** 306-310

Eynsham, Abbey of (England)
Aelfric **1** 69-70

EYRE, EDWARD JOHN (1815-1901), English explorer of Australia **5** 354

EZANA (flourished 4th century), Ethiopian king **5** 354-355

EZEKIEL (flourished 6th century B.C.), Hebrew priest and prophet **5** 355-356

Ezekiel (painting)
Michelangelo Buonarroti **11** 2-5

Ezo
see Ainu

Ezpeleta, Gaspar de (died 1605), Navarese gentleman
Cervantes, Miguel de Saavedra **3** 395-398

EZRA (flourished 5th century B.C.), Hebrew priest, scribe, and reformer **5** 356-357

Ezra (Zionist youth club)
Ben-Gurion, David **2** 160-161

Ezzelino da Romana (1194-1259), Italian Ghibelline leader
Frederick II **6** 79

F

Faber (literary character)
Frisch, Max **6** 118-119

Faber, Jacobus
see Lefèvre d'Étaples, Jacques

Fabian socialism (England)
Glasgow, Ellen **6** 360-361
Tawney, Richard Henry **15** 120-121
Webb, Beatrice Potter **16** 153-154
see also Fabian Society

Fabian Society (England)
executives
Cole, George Douglas Howard **4** 146-147
MacDonald, James Ramsay **10** 84-85
Shaw, George Bernard **14** 163-164
Wallas, Graham **16** 77-78
influence of
Bernstein, Eduard **2** 218
Nehru, Jawaharlal **11** 332-334
members
Attlee, Clement Richard **1** 361-362
Besant, Annie Wood **2** 233-234
Pankhurst, Emmeline **12** 85-86
Webb, Beatrice Potter **16** 153-154
Webb, Sidney James **16** 154-155
Wells, Herbert George **16** 195-196
Wilkinson, Ellen **16** 283-284
Williams, Shirley Vivien Teresa Brittain **16** 305-306
opponents
Bosanquet, Bernard **2** 425-426

FABIUS, LAURENT (born 1946), prime minister of France in the 1980s **5** 358-359

Fabius, Quintus (died 203 B.C.), Roman general
Hannibal Barca **7** 128-130

Fable (literary form)
La Fontaine, Jean de **9** 156-157
Lessing, Gotthold Ephraim **9** 357-359

Fable, A (novel)
Faulkner, William **5** 395-397

Fable for Critics, A (poem; J.R. Lowell)
Lowell, Amy **10** 13
Lowell, James Russell **10** 14-15

Fable of Polyphemus and Galatea, The (poem)
Góngora y Argote, Luis de **6** 427-428

Fable of the Bees... (book; Mandeville)
Law, William **9** 245-246
Mandeville, Bernard **10** 192

Fables (book)
Gay, John **6** 243-244

Fables (book; La Fontaine)
Calder, Alexander **3** 216-218
Chagall, Marc **3** 406-407
La Fontaine, Jean de **9** 156-157
Moore, Marianne **11** 148-149

Fabricius ab Aquapendente, Hieronymus (1537-1619), Italian anatomist
Harvey, William **7** 189-190

Fabritius, Carel (circa 1624-1654), Dutch painter
Rembrandt Harmensz van Rijn **13** 91-95
Vermeer, Jan **15** 466-467

Fabrizi, Aldo (1905-1990), Italian actor
Fellini, Federico **5** 408-409

Façade (musical composition)
Walton, William Turner **16** 92-93

Façade (poems)
Sitwell, Edith **14** 265-266

Fa-ch'ang
see Mu Ch'i

Fa-chia
see Legalism (Chinese philosophy)

FACKENHEIM, EMIL LUDWIG (born 1916), liberal post-World War II Jewish theologian **5** 359-361

Factory Acts (England)
Asquith, Herbert Henry **1** 344-346
Chadwick, Edwin **3** 404-405
Disraeli, Benjamin **5** 27-29

Factory system (manufacturing)
see Industrial Revolution—factory system

Factory, The (poem)
Blok, Aleksandr Aleksandrovich **2** 335

Facundo, Juan
see Quiroga, Juan Facundo

FADIL AL-JAMALI, MUHAMMAD (born 1903), Iraqi educator, writer, diplomat, and politician **5** 361-362

FADLALLAH, SAYYID MUHAMMAD HUSAYN (born 1935), Shi'i Muslim cleric and Lebanese political leader **5** 362-364

Faenza (Italy)
Julius II **8** 384-386

Faenza, Francesco (flourished 15th century), Italian painter
Andrea del Castagno **1** 223-224

Faerie Queen, The (poem; Spenser)
Allston, Washington **1** 176-177
Keats, John **8** 470-472
Spenser, Edmund **14** 373-376
Tasso, Torquato **15** 114-116

Faeroes (Greek island; Northern Atlantic Ocean)
Harold I **7** 161-162

Fagin (literary character)
Dickens, Charles John Huffam **4** 538-541

Faguibine, Lake (West Africa)
Ali, Sunni **1** 158-159

FAHD IBN ABDUL AZIZ AL-SAUD (born 1920), son of the founder of modern Saudi Arabia and king **5** 364-366

Fähnlein der sieben Aufrechten, Das (story)
Keller, Gottfried **8** 478-479

Fahrend schüler im Paradies, Der (play)
Sachs, Hans **13** 410-411

Fahrenheit 451 (film)
Truffaut, François **15** 311-313

FAHRENHEIT, GABRIEL DANIEL (1686-1736), German physicist **5** 366

FAIDHERBE, LOUIS LÉON CÉSAR (1818-1889), French colonial governor **5** 366-367
Omar ibn Said Tal, Al-Hajj **11** 509-510

317

Failures, The (novel)
Azuela, Mariano **1** 402

Faint Heart, The (story)
Dostoevsky, Fyodor **5** 74-77

Fair, James G. (1831-1894), American financier
Mackay, John William **10** 101-102

Fair Employment Act (United States)
Truman, Harry S. **15** 314-316

Fair Employment Practices Committee (established 1941)
Chávez, Dennis **3** 488-489
Randolph, A. Philip **13** 28-29

Fair God, The (novel)
Wallace, Lewis **16** 74-75

Fair Haven, The (book)
Butler, Samuel **3** 183

Fair Maid of Kent
see Joan, Countess of Kent

Fair Maid of Perth, The (novel)
Scott, Walter **14** 68-70

Fair Oaks, battle of
see Seven Days, battle of the

Fair Penitent (book; Nicholas Rowe)
Richardson, Samuel **13** 141-142

Fairbanks, Douglas (1883-1939), American actor
Chaplin, Charles Spencer **3** 438-440
Griffith, David Wark **6** 544-545

FAIRCLOUGH, ELLEN LOUKS (born 1905), Canadian Cabinet minister **5** 367-368

Fairest of the Rural Maids (poem)
Bryant, William Cullen **3** 83-85

Fairfax, Edward (died 1635), English translator
Tasso, Torquato **15** 114-116

Fairfax Resolves (United States politics)
Mason, George **10** 319-320
Washington, George **16** 126-129

Fairfax, Thomas (3rd Baron Fairfax; 1612-1671), Scottish soldier and statesman
Buckingham, 2d Duke of **3** 94-95
Marvell, Andrew **10** 301-303

Fairfax, Thomas (6th Baron Fairfax; 1692-1782), Scottish colonial proprietor
Washington, George **16** 126-129

Fairies, The (opera)
Wagner, Richard **16** 40-43

Fairly Honourable Defeat, A (novel)
Murdoch, Iris **11** 256-257

FAIRUZ (née Nuhad Haddad; born 1933), Arabic singer **5** 368-369

Fairy Queen, The (opera)
Purcell, Henry **12** 484-485

Fairy tale (literary form)
Andersen, Hans Christian **1** 212-214
Čapek, Karel **3** 271-272
Grimm, Jakob and Wilhelm Karl **7** 3-4

Jung, Carl Gustav **8** 388-389
Yeats, William Butler **16** 445-447

Fairyland (opera)
Parker, Horatio William **12** 109

Fairy's Kiss, The (ballet; Stravinsky)
Balanchine, George **1** 461-462
Stravinsky, Igor Fedorovich **14** 502-506

FAISAL I (1883-1933), king of Iraq 1921-33 **5** 370-371
Abdullah ibn Husein **1** 19-20
Husein ibn Ali **8** 63
Lawrence, Thomas Edward **9** 253-254
Nuri al-Sa'id **11** 446-447

FAISAL IBN ABD AL AZIZ IBN SAUD (1904-1975), Saudi Arabian king and prominent Arab leader **5** 371-372

Faistenberger, Andreas (1647-1736), Austrian sculptor
Asam, Cosmas Damian and Egid Quirin **1** 323-324

Faith (religion)
Fries, Jakob Friedrich **6** 116-117
Hamann, Johann Georg **7** 92
Jansen, Cornelis **8** 220-221
Kierkegaard, Søren Aabye **8** 547-549

Faith (sculpture)
Powers, Hiram **12** 428-429

Faithful Wife, The (novel)
Undset, Sigrid **15** 388-389

Faithfull Shepherdess, The (play)
Fletcher, John **5** 487

Faits d'armes et de chevalrie (book; C. de Pisan)
Caxton, William **3** 386-387

Faiyûm, El (town; Egypt)
Petrie, William Matthew Flinders **12** 261-262

Faizi, Abul Feis ibn Mubarak (1547-1595), Indo-Persian poet
Akbar, Jalal-ud-din Mohammed **1** 96

Falaise, Treaty of (1174)
Henry II **7** 287-289

Falange party (Spain)
Franco Bahamonde, Francisco **6** 52-54
Primo de Rivera y Orbaneja, Miguel **12** 454-455
Unamuno y Jugo, Miguel de **15** 386-387

Falcón, Juan (1820-1870), Venezuelan soldier and politician
Blanco, Antonio Guzmán **2** 320-321

Falcone, Aniello (1600-1650), Italian painter
Rosa, Salvator **13** 289-290

FALCONET, ÉTIENNE MAURICE (1716-1791), French sculptor **5** 372
Canova, Antonio **3** 263-264

Falke, Konrad (1880-1942), Swiss novelist
Mann, Thomas **10** 204-207

Falkenhayn, Erich von (1861-1922), German general
Ludendorff, Erich Friedrich Wilhelm **10** 27-28

Falkirk, battle of
1298
Robert I **13** 192-194
Wallace, William **16** 75-76
1745
Charles Edward Louis Philip Casimir Stuart **3** 466-467

Falkland, 2nd Viscount (Lucius Cary; 1610-1643), English statesman
Clarendon, 1st Earl of **4** 73-75

Falkland Islands (Southern Atlantic Ocean)
Bougainville, Louis Antoine de **2** 443-444
Davis, John **4** 419

Falkland Islands War (1982)
Galtieri, Leopoldo Fortunato **6** 191-193
Pym, Francis **12** 494-495
Sopwith, Thomas Octave Murdoch **14** 345-346
Thatcher, Margaret Hilda **15** 165-168

Falkner, William Cuthbert (1825-1889), American author and lawyer
Faulkner, William **5** 395-397

Fall, Albert B. (1861-1944), American lawyer and politician
Harding, Warren Gamaliel **7** 148-149
Walsh, Thomas James **16** 85-86

Fall and Salvation (painting)
Cranach, Lucas the Elder **4** 289-290

Fall Daruga, Der (novel)
Huch, Ricarda **8** 11-12

Fall Maurizius, Der (novel)
Wassermann, Jakob **16** 130-131

Fall of an Angel, The (poem)
Lamartine, Alphonse Marie Louis de **9** 173-175

Fall of Hyperion, The (poem)
Keats, John **8** 470-472

Fall of Man (painting)
van der Goes, Hugo **15** 416-417

Fall of Man in Paradise, The (miniature)
Limbourg brothers, The **9** 412-413

Fall of the House of Usher, The (story)
Poe, Edgar Allan **12** 363-365

Fall of the Niblungs (book)
Morris, William **11** 187-188

Fall, The (novel)
Camus, Albert **3** 255-257

FALLA, MANUEL DE (1876-1946), Spanish composer **5** 372-373
Alarcón, Pedro Antonio de **1** 100-101

Fallen (story)
Mann, Thomas **10** 204-207

Fallen Angel, The (poem)
Echeverría, José Estéban **5** 197-198

Fallen Timbers, battle of (1794)
  Clark, William **4** 82-83
  Harrison, William Henry **7** 180-181
  Wayne, Anthony **16** 149-150

FALLETTA, JOANN (born 1954), American
  conductor **5** 373-375

Falling Gladiator (sculpture)
  Rimmer, William **13** 174

Falling Leaves (poems)
  Bunin, Ivan Alekseevich **3** 124

Falling Rocket (painting)
  Whistler, James Abbott McNeill
  16 225-226

Falling Warrior (sculpture)
  Moore, Henry **11** 146-148

Falling Water (Kaufmann House; Bear Run,
  Pennsylvania)
  Neutra, Richard Joseph **11** 355-356
  Wright, Frank Lloyd **16** 398-401

Fallopio, Gabriele (1523-1562), Italian
  anatomist
  Vesalius, Andreas **15** 473-475

Falstaff (literary character)
  Shakespeare, William **14** 142-145

Falstaff (opera)
  Verdi, Giuseppe Fortunino Francesco
  15 463-465

Falstaff (overture)
  Elgar, Edward **5** 247-248

FALWELL, JERRY (born 1933), fundamentalist religious leader who also promoted
  right-wing political causes **5** 375-376

Fame and Fortune (book)
  Alger, Horatio **1** 153-154

Familia (Romanian review)
  Eminescu, Mihail **5** 280-281

Familiar Pictures (literary collection)
  Peretz, Isaac Loeb **12** 212

Familie Schroffenstein, Die (play)
  Kleist, Heinrich von **9** 52-53

Family Compact (1761)
  Charles III **3** 454-455

Family Compact (Canadian power elite)
  Robinson, John Beverley **13** 210

Family Group (sculpture)
  Moore, Henry **11** 146-148

Family Moskat, The (novel)
  Singer, Isaac Bashevis **14** 249-250

Family of Love, The (play)
  Middleton, Thomas **11** 8-9

Family of Man, The (photography exhibition; book)
  Steichen, Edward **14** 411-412

Family of Pascual Duarte, The (novel)
  Cela y Trulock, Camilo José **3** 389-390

Family of Saltimbanques (painting)
  Picasso, Pablo **12** 292-295

Family planning (social science)
  Noyes, John Humphrey **11** 437-438

see also Birth control

Family Reunion (painting)
  Le Nain, Antoine, Louis and Mathieu
  9 321-322

Family Reunion, The (play)
  Eliot, Thomas Stearns **5** 258-261

Family, The (novel)
  Pa Chin **12** 53-54

Family, The (painting)
  Murillo, Bartolomé Esteban **11** 258-259

Famine (food shortage)
  Colum, Padraic **4** 174-175
  Godunov, Boris Feodorovich **6** 382-383
  Li Tzu-Ch'eng **9** 452
  O'Connell, Daniel **11** 465-467
  Plekhanov, Georgi Valentinovich
  12 351-352
  Russell, John **13** 380-381
  Victoria **15** 485-487

Famous Asturian Women, The (play)
  Lope Félix de Vega Carpio **9** 503-506

FAN CHUNG-YEN (989-1052), Chinese
  statesman **5** 376-377
  Ou-yang Hsiu **12** 33-34
  Wang An-shih **16** 95-97

Fan K'uan (flourished before 1030), Chinese painter
  Chao Meng-fu **3** 436-437

Fan, The (poem)
  Gay, John **6** 243-244

Fanal bleu, Le (novel)
  Colette, Sidonie Gabrielle **4** 158-159

Fanatics, The (novel)
  Dunbar, Paul Laurence **5** 141-142

Fan-ch'eng (city; China)
  Kublai Khan **9** 115-118

Fanciulla del West, La (opera)
  Puccini, Giacomo **12** 474-476

Faneuil Hall (Boston, Massachusetts)
  Bulfinch, Charles **3** 116-117
  Faneuil, Peter **5** 377

FANEUIL, PETER (1700-1743), American
  colonial merchant and philanthropist
  5 377

FANFANI, AMINTORE (born 1908), Italian
  statesman and prime minister **5** 378-379

Fanfarlo, La (book)
  Baudelaire, Charles Pierre **2** 61-63

Fang (West African people)
  Burton, Richard **3** 163-164

Fang-la Rebellion (1120-1122)
  Hui-Tsung **8** 25

Fanny Herself (novel)
  Ferber, Edna **5** 413

FANON, FRANTZ (1925-1961), Algerian
  political theorist and psychiatrist
  5 379-380

Fanshawe (novel)
  Hawthorne, Nathaniel **7** 212-215

Fantasia (film)
  Disney, Walter Elias **5** 26-27

Fantasia (musical composition)
  Bach, Carl Philipp Emanuel **1** 414-415
  Busoni, Ferruccio Benvenuto **3** 173-174
  Byrd, William **3** 187-188
  Chopin, Frédéric François **4** 16-18
  Falla, Manuel de **5** 372-373
  Schumann, Robert Alexander **14** 41-43
  Tippett, Michael Kemp **15** 234-235
  Vaughan Williams, Ralph **15** 446-447

Fantasia (painting)
  Hofmann, Hans **7** 442-443

Fantasiestücke in Callots Manier (stories)
  Hoffmann, Ernst Theodor Amadeus
  7 439-440

Fantasio (play)
  Musset, Louis Charles Alfred de
  11 271-272

Fantastic art
  Bosch, Hieronymus **2** 426-428
  Miró, Joan **11** 53-54

Fantastic Fables (book)
  Bierce, Ambrose Gwinett **2** 269-270

Fantasy (drama technique)
  O'Casey, Sean **11** 459-460

Fantasy (music)
  see Fantasia

Fantasy (psychology)
  Jung, Carl Gustav **8** 388-389

Fanti (African people)
  Cugoano, Ottobah **4** 332-333

**Fantin-Latour, Ignace Henri Joseph
  Théodore** (1836-1904), French painter
  Redon, Odilon **13** 75-76
  Whistler, James Abbott McNeill
  16 225-226

Far Country, A (novel)
  Churchill, Winston **4** 50-51

Far from the Madding Crowd (novel)
  Hardy, Thomas **7** 150-152

Farabi, al- (870-950), Arab philosopher
  Averroës **1** 382-383
  Ghazali, Abu Hamid Muhammad al-
  6 290-291
  Mahmud of Ghazni **10** 147
  Maimonides **10** 151-152

Farad (electrical unit)
  Faraday, Michael **5** 380

Faraday (unit)
  Faraday, Michael **5** 380

FARADAY, MICHAEL (1791-1867), English
  physicist and chemist **5** 380
  compared to
    Rutherford, Ernest **13** 384-387
  critics
    Hare, Robert **7** 152-153
  influence of
    Arrhenius, Svante August **1** 318-320
    Bunsen, Robert Wilhelm **3** 124-125
    Maxwell, James Clerk **10** 361-364

Tyndall, John **15** 374
influenced by
Avogadro, Lorenzo Romano
Amedeo Carlo **1** 388-389
Cavendish, Henry **3** 383-384
Davy, Humphry **4** 426-427
Volta, Alessandro **16** 12-14

Farago, Captain (literary character)
Brackenridge, Hugh Henry **2** 472-473

Faramushkhaneh (Masonic Lodge; Persia)
Malkam Khan, Mirza **10** 172

Farben, I.G., Co. (German company)
Behrens, Peter **2** 121-122
Domagk, Gerhard Johannes Paul
5 48-50

Farel, Guillaume (1489-1565), French
Reformation leader
Calvin, John **3** 239-242

Farewell My Friend (novel)
Rabindranath Tagore **12** 529-531

Farewell, My Lovely (novel)
Chandler, Raymond Jr. **3** 423-425

Farewell Symphony (musical composition)
Haydn, Franz Joseph **7** 219-221

Farewell to Arms, A (novel)
Hemingway, Ernest Miller **7** 274-277

FARGO, WILLIAM GEORGE (1818-1881),
American businessman **5** 380-381

Farias, Valentin Gómez
see Gómez Farias, Valentin

FARLEY, JAMES A. (1888-1976), Democratic Party organizer and political strategist
5 381-383

Farley, John M. (1842-1918), American cardinal
Hayes, Patrick Joseph **7** 224-225

Farll (literary character)
Morrice, James Wilson **11** 181-182

Farm Credit Administration (United States)
Morgenthau, Henry Jr. **11** 172-173

Farm policy (United States)
Coolidge, John Calvin **4** 217-219
Norris, George William **11** 428-429

Farm Security Administration (United
States)
Lange, Dorothea **9** 193-194

Farm system (baseball)
Rickey, Wesley Branch **13** 153-155

FARMER, FANNIE MERRITT (1857-1915),
American authority on cookery **5** 383

FARMER, JAMES (born 1920), civil rights
activist who helped organize the 1960s
"freedom rides" **5** 383-385

FARMER, MOSES GERRISH (1820-1893),
American inventor and manufacturer
5 385

Farmer-Labor party (United States)
Coxey, Jacob Sechler **4** 286-287
Steinmetz, Charles Proteus **14** 419-420

Farmers
see Agriculturists

Farmers' Alliance (United States; politics)
Donnelly, Ignatius **5** 62
Gordon, John Brown **6** 449-450
Watson, Thomas Edward **16** 139
Weaver, James Baird **16** 151-152

Farmers' Alliance-People's party (United
States; politics)
Lease, Mary Elizabeth Clyens **9** 268

Farmers' Association (United States)
Tillman, Benjamin Ryan **15** 225-226

Farmers Cooperative Work Division (United States; Department of Agriculture)
Knapp, Seaman Asahel **9** 58

Farmers' National Grange (United States)
Ward, Aaron Montgomery **16** 112

Farnah (Zoroastrianism)
Zoroaster **16** 528-530

Farnam, Henry (1803-1888), American
engineer
Durant, Thomas Clark **5** 157-158

Farnese, Alessandro (1468-1549)
see Paul III

Farnese, Alessandro (1520-1589), Italian
cardinal
Greco **6** 511-514
William the Silent **16** 300-302

Farnese, Alessandro (1545-1592), Italian
general and diplomat
Maurice of Nassau **10** 348-349

Farnese Palace (Rome)
Carracci **3** 319-321
Porta, Giacomo della **12** 402-403
Sangallo family **13** 464-466

Farnese, Pierluigi (1503-1547), duke of
Parma and of Piacenza
Paul III **12** 144-145

FARNSWORTH, PHILO T. (1906-1971),
American inventor of the television
5 386-387

Farnsworth House (Plano, Illinois)
Mies van der Rohe, Ludwig **11** 10-12

Faro de Malta, El (poem)
Saavedra, Angel de **13** 398

FAROUK I (1920-1965), king of Egypt
1937-1952 **5** 387-388
Abd el-Krim el-Khatabi, Mohamed ben
1 15-16
Azhari, Sayyid Ismail al- **1** 399-401
Fuad I **6** 139
Nasser, Gamal Abdel **11** 317-318

FARRAGUT, DAVID GLASGOW
(1801-1870), American naval officer
5 388-389
Semmes, Raphael **14** 102-103

Farragut Monument (New York City)
Saint-Gaudens, Augustus **13** 432
White, Stanford **16** 235-236

FARRAKHAN, LOUIS (Louis Eugene Walcott, born 1933), a leader of one branch
of the Nation of Islam popularly known
as Black Muslims and militant spokesman
for Black Nationalism **5** 389-390

FARRELL, JAMES THOMAS (1904-1979),
American novelist and social and literary
critic **5** 390-391
Mailer, Norman Kingsley **10** 148-150

FARRELL, SUZANNE (née Roberta Sue
Ficker; born 1945), American classical
ballerina **5** 391-393

Farropos, War of the (Brazil; 1835-45)
Caxias, Duque de **3** 386
Feijó, Diogo Antônio **5** 405-406

Fars (region; Iran)
Hulagu Khan **8** 27-28

Farsa de Ines Pereira (play)
Vicente, Gil **15** 479-480

Farther Spain (Roman province)
Caesar, Gaius Julius **3** 207-210

Faru (African people)
Ali, Sunni **1** 158-159

Farwell, Arthur (1872-1952), American
composer
Harris, Roy **7** 175-176

Fascism (political doctrine)
adherents
Dollfuss, Engelbert **5** 47
Franco Bahamonde, Francisco
6 52-54
Hitler, Adolf **7** 417-420
Mussolini, Benito **11** 272-274
Salazar, António de Oliveira
13 442-443
Vargas, Getulio Dornelles
15 433-434
antifascist organizations
Aung San **1** 374-375
Ceausescu, Nicolae **3** 387-388
Sábato, Ernesto **13** 399-400
Thant, U **15** 161-162
in literature
Jünger, Ernst **8** 391-392
Mann, Thomas **10** 204-207
Montale, Eugenio **11** 117-118
Moravia, Alberto **11** 153-155
influenced by
Sorel, Georges **14** 347-348
opponents
Foster, William Zebulon **6** 27-28
Gooch, George Peabody **6** 432-433
MacLeish, Archibald **10** 109-110
Marcuse, Herbert **10** 245-247
see also Fascist regime; Nazism

Fascist regime (Italy)
anticipated
Pareto, Vilfredo **12** 95-96
observers of
Michels, Robert **11** 7
Perth, 16th Earl of **12** 244-245
opponents
Croce, Benedetto **4** 313-314
Ferrero, Guglielmo **5** 429-430
Giolitti, Giovanni **6** 339-340

Levi, Carlo **9** 364
Matteotti, Giacomo **10** 339-340
Orlando, Vittorio Emmanuele
   11 529-530
Pavese, Cesare **12** 154-155
Salvemini, Gaetano **13** 455-456
Silone, Ignazio **14** 231-232
revolution
   Mussolini, Benito **11** 272-274
supporters
   Coughlin, Charles Edward
      4 265-266
   D'Annunzio, Gabriele **4** 388
   Gentile, Giovanni **6** 267
   Mussolini, Benito **11** 272-274
   Pirandello, Luigi **12** 319-321
   Pius XI **12** 337-339
   Pound, Ezra Loomis **12** 415-417
   Victor Emmanuele III **15** 484-485
   see also Fascism

**Fashionable Adventures of Joshua Craig,
The** (novel)
   Phillips, David Graham **12** 280-281

Fashoda crisis (1898; Sudan)
   Delcassé, Théophile **4** 478-479
   Kitchener, Horatio Herbert **9** 45-46

Fast food industry
   Kroc, Raymond Albert **9** 103-104

Fast, Howard (born 1914), American novelist
   Spartacus **14** 363-364

Fasti (poem; Ovid)
   Ovid **12** 34-36
   Titian **15** 242-244

Fatal Eggs, The (story)
   Bulgakov, Mikhail Afanasievich **3** 117

Fatal Interview (poems)
   Millay, Edna St. Vincent **11** 24-25

Fate of a Man, The (story)
   Sholokhov, Mikhail Aleksandrovich
      14 203-204

Fate-tragedy (literary form)
   Grillparzer, Franz **6** 546-547

Fath Ali (1762?-1835), Kajar shah of Persia
1797-1835
   Aga Khan **1** 74-76

Father and Son (novel)
   Farrell, James Thomas **5** 390-391

Father Brown (literary character)
   Chesterton, Gilbert Keith **3** 508-509

Father Donissan (literary character)
   Bernanos, Georges **2** 206-207

Father Dowling (literary character)
   Callaghan, Edward Morley **3** 229-230

"Father of..."
   see Nicknames

Father Sergius (story)
   Tolstoy, Leo **15** 262-265

Father Superior Drumont (literary character)
   Beti, Mongo **2** 242-243

Father, The (play)
   Strindberg, August **14** 509-511

Fatherland and Liberty (Turkish political
organization)
   Atatürk, Ghazi Mustapha Kemal
      1 356-357

Fathers and Sons (novel)
   Turgenev, Ivan Sergeyevich **15** 345-348

Father's Curse, The (painting)
   Greuze, Jean Baptiste **6** 539

Fathers of the Church
   see Religious leaders, Christian—Fathers

Fathers, The (novel)
   Tate, Allen **15** 116

Fatih
   see Mehmed the Conqueror

Fatima (606-632), daughter of Mohammed
   Aga Khan **1** 74-76
   Ali **1** 155-156

Fatum (symphony poem)
   Tchaikovsky, Peter Ilyich **15** 130-132

Faubourg Saint-Antoine, battle of (1652)
   La Rochefoucauld, François Duc de
      9 208-209

Faubus, Orval (1910-1994), American
politician
   Eisenhower, Dwight David **5** 233-236

FAULKNER, BRIAN (1921-1977), prime
minister of Northern Ireland (1971-1972)
5 393-395

FAULKNER, WILLIAM (1897-1962), Ameri-
can novelist **5** 395-397
   Bogart, Humphrey **2** 363-364
   Caldwell, Erskine **3** 223-224
   Dos Passos, John Roderigo **5** 69-71
   Lewis, Harry Sinclair **9** 385-387
   Tate, Allen **15** 116

Faure, Edgar (1908-1988), French states-
man, prime minister 1955-56
   Dulles, John Foster **5** 134-135
   Senghor, Léopold Sédar **14** 106-107

FAURÉ, GABRIEL URBAIN (1845-1924),
French composer **5** 397-398
   Ravel, Maurice Joseph **13** 54-55
   Saint-Saëns, Charles Camille
      13 435-436
   Sessions, Roger Huntington **14** 117-118

Fausse prude, La (play)
   Watteau, Antoine **16** 143-144

Fausses confidences, Les (play)
   Marivaux, Pierre Carlet de Chamblain
      de **10** 265-266

Faust (dramatic poem; Goethe)
   authorship
      Goethe, Johann Wolfgang von
         6 388-391, 445-446
   influence of
      Clough, Arthur Hugh **4** 123-124
      Joyce, James **8** 365-367
   musical settings
      Berlioz, Louis Hector **2** 203-205

Gounod, Charles François
   6 473-474
   Mahler, Gustav **10** 144-145
   Sachs, Hans **13** 410-411
   Schubert, Franz Peter **14** 35-37
sculpture based on
   Rogers, John **13** 248
translations
   Nerval, Gérard de **11** 345-346

Faust legend (literary theme)
   Goethe, Johann Wolfgang von
      6 388-391
   Mann, Thomas **10** 204-207
   Marlowe, Christopher **10** 272-274
   see also Dr. Faustus

Faustin, La (novel)
   Goncourt, Edmond de and Jules de
      6 426-427

Faustine (poem)
   Swinburne, Algernon Charles **15** 54-55

Fauvism (art movement)
   influence of
      Carr, Emily **3** 319
      Davis, Stuart **4** 424-425
      Demuth, Charles **4** 497-498
      Dove, Arthur Garfield **5** 86-87
      Hofmann, Hans **7** 442-443
      Léger, Fernand **9** 302-303
      Malevich, Kasimir **10** 168-169
      Marc, Franz **10** 231
      Milne, David Brown **11** 37-38
      Mondrian, Piet **11** 101-102
      Pevsner, Antoine **12** 263-264
      Sheeler, Charles **14** 170-171
      Weber, Max **16** 160
   influenced by
      Gauguin, Paul **6** 236-238
   originators
      Braque, Georges **2** 504-505
      Derain, André **4** 503
      Matisse, Henri **10** 336-337
      Miró, Joan **11** 53-54
      van Dongen, Kees **15** 421-422
      Vlaminck, Maurice **16** 6

Faux-monnayeurs, Les (novel)
   Gide, André **6** 308-309

Favola di Orfeo, La (play)
   Poliziano, Angelo **12** 373-374

Favola d'Orfeo, La (opera)
   see Orfeo (opera)

Favre, Pierre (1506-1546), Savoyard
cofounder of Jesuits
   Canisius, Peter **3** 258

Favrile (glass)
   Tiffany, Louis Comfort **15** 220-221

FAWCETT, MILLICENT GARRETT
(1847-1929), British feminist **5** 398-400

Fawkes, Guy (1570-1606), English conspirator
   James I **8** 204-206

Fay, Frank (1897-1961), Irish actor
   Colum, Padraic **4** 174-175

FAYE, SAFI (born 1943), Senegalese film-maker and ethnologist **5** 400-401

Fayyum (province; Egypt)
Ptolemy II **12** 472-473

FBI
see Federal Bureau of Investigation

Fear (pamphlet)
Millay, Edna St. Vincent **11** 24-25

Fear (play)
Afinogenov, Aleksandr Nikolaevich **1** 72-73

Fear and Trembling (book)
Kierkegaard, Søren Aabye **8** 547-549

Fearful Symmetry (book)
Frye, Northrop **6** 137-139

Fears in Solitude (poem)
Coleridge, Samuel Taylor **4** 154-156

Feast at Solhaug, The (play)
Ibsen, Henrik **8** 98-100

Feast during the Plague, The (play)
Pushkin, Aleksandr Sergeevich **12** 489-491

Feast in the House of Levi (painting)
Veronese, Paolo **15** 469-470

Feast in the House of Simon (painting)
Veronese, Paolo **15** 469-470

Feast of Herod (painting)
Giotto **6** 342-345
Lippi, Filippo **9** 439

Feast of Herod (sculpture)
Donatello **5** 55-56

Feast of Saint Gregory the Great (painting)
Veronese, Paolo **15** 469-470

Feast of Swans (English history)
Robert I **13** 192-194

Feast of the Gods (painting)
Bellini, Giovanni **2** 137-138

Feast of the Rose Garlands (painting)
Dürer, Albrecht **5** 159-161

Feast of Venus (painting)
Rubens, Peter Paul **13** 339-342

Feather of the Dawn, The (poems)
Naidu, Sarojini **11** 294-295

Feather Woman of the Jungle, The (book)
Tutuola, Amos **15** 361-362

Febrerista revolts (1936; 1937)
Morínigo, Higinio **11** 174-175

February Patent (1861; Austria)
Francis Joseph **6** 45-46

February Revolution
see Revolution of 1848 (France); Russian Revolution (1917)

Febvre, Lucien Victor Paul (1878-1956), French historian
Bloch, Marc **2** 332-333

FECHNER, GUSTAV THEODOR (1801-1887), German experimental psychologist **5** 401-402
Ebbinghaus, Hermann **5** 192-193

Federal Arts Project (United States)
Bearden, Romare Howard **2** 86-88
Davis, Stuart **4** 424-425
Evergood, Philip **5** 345
Gorky, Arshile **6** 458
Lawrence, Jacob **9** 250-251
Pollock, Jackson **12** 379-380
Rothko, Mark **13** 320-321
Shahn, Ben **14** 139-140

Federal Australasian Council (established 1883)
Griffith, Samuel Walker **6** 545-546

Federal Bill of Rights
see Bill of Rights (United States)

Federal Bureau of Investigation (United States)
Freeh, Louis J. **6** 90-91
Hoover, John Edgar **7** 485-487

Federal Center (Chicago)
Mies van der Rohe, Ludwig **11** 10-12

Federal Communications Commission (United States)
Hooks, Benjamin Lawson **7** 481-483

Federal Constitution (United States)
see Constitution of the United States

Federal Convention (1787)
see Constitutional Convention (1787; United States)

Federal Farm Loan Board (United States)
McAdoo, William Gibbs **10** 385-386

Federal Hall (New York City)
L'Enfant, Pierre Charles **9** 322-323

Federal Home Loan Bank Act (1932)
Hoover, Herbert Clark **7** 483-485

Federal Housing Administration (United States)
Johnson, Lyndon Baines **8** 308-312

Federal Institute of Technology (FIT; Zurich)
Einstein, Albert **5** 228-231
Jung, Carl Gustav **8** 388-389
Pauli, Wolfgang Ernst **12** 149

Federal Judicial Center (United States)
Warren, Earl **16** 117-120

Federal Labor Code (Mexico)
Calles, Plutarco Elías **3** 234-235

Federal party (Brazil)
Vargas, Getulio Dornelles **15** 433-434

Federal party (Puerto Rico)
Muñoz Rivera, Luís **11** 250

Federal Republic of Germany
see Germany, West

Federal Reserve Act (United States; 1913)
Aldrich, Nelson Wilmarth **1** 123-124
Bryan, William Jennings **3** 80-82
Hitchcock, Gilbert Monell **7** 416-417

Polk, James Knox **12** 374-376
Warburg, Paul Moritz **16** 111-112
Wilson, Thomas Woodrow **16** 330-332

Federal Reserve banks (United States)
Biddle, Nicholas **2** 264-265

Federal Reserve Board (United States)
Burns, Arthur **3** 151-153
Greenspan, Alan **6** 526-528
Hansen, Alvin **7** 131-132
Hoover, Herbert Clark **7** 483-485
Martin, William McChesney Jr. **10** 293-295
McAdoo, William Gibbs **10** 385-386
Volcker, Paul **16** 11-12
Warburg, Paul Moritz **16** 111-112

Federal Reserve System (United States)
Hoover, Herbert Clark **7** 483-485
Morgan, John Pierpont **11** 163-165
Warburg, Paul Moritz **16** 111-112

Federal Steel Co.
Gary, Elbert Henry **6** 229-230

Federal Street Church (Boston, Massachusetts)
Bulfinch, Charles **3** 116-117
Channing, William Ellery **3** 435-436

Federal style (architecture)
Benjamin, Asher **2** 162-163

Federal Theatre Project (United States)
Flanagan, Hallie **5** 478-479
Welles, Orson **16** 190-191

Federal Trade Commission Act (1913)
Wilson, Thomas Woodrow **16** 330-332

Federal War (Venezuela)
Páez, José Antonio **12** 58

Federalism (government)
advocates
Artigas, José Gervasio **1** 323
Awolowo, Obafemi **1** 389-390
Epaminondas **5** 291-292
Palacký, František **12** 69-70
Proudhon, Pierre Joseph **12** 461-463
Urquiza, Justo José **15** 396-397
opponents
Nariño, Antonio **11** 314-315
see also Federalist party (United States)

Federalist party (United States)
foreign policy
Jay, John **8** 230-232
Morris, Gouverneur **11** 182-183
Pickering, Timothy **12** 298-299
former supporters
Buchanan, James **3** 89-90
Dickinson, John **4** 543-544
Madison, James **10** 121-123
Pinckney, Charles **12** 309-310
Shaw, Lemuel **14** 164-165
Taney, Roger Brooke **15** 98-99
Webster, Daniel **16** 162-164
in Supreme Court
Chase, Samuel **3** 475-476
Jay, John **8** 230-232

Marshall, John **10** 279-281
opponents
  Adams, Samuel **1** 55-56
  Coxe, Tench **4** 285-286
  Freneau, Philip Morin **6** 99-100
  Gallatin, Albert **6** 183-184
  Henry, Patrick **7** 309-311
  see also Antifederalists;
    Democratic-Republican party
    (United States)
presidential nominees
  Adams, John **1** 48-51
  Clinton, DeWitt **4** 112-113
  Jay, John **8** 230-232
  King, Rufus **9** 22-23
  Pinckney, Charles Cotesworth
    12 310
  Washington, George **16** 126-129
supporters
  Ames, Fisher **1** 199-200
  Hamilton, Alexander **7** 95-98
  Martin, Luther **10** 289-290
  Otis, Harrison Gray **12** 25
  Shippen, Edward **14** 197-198
  Webster, Noah **16** 164-166

Federalist, The (essays)
  Ford, Paul Leicester **6** 9-10
  Hamilton, Alexander **7** 95-98
  Jay, John **8** 230-232
  Madison, James **10** 121-123
  Washington, George **16** 126-129

Federalist War (Venezuela; 1859)
  Blanco, Antonio Guzmán **2** 320-321

Federazione Universitaria Cattolica Italiana
  Paul VI **12** 146-148

Federmann, Nikolaus (circa 1501-1543),
German explorer
  Benalcázar, Sebastián de **2** 145-146
  Quesada, Gonzalo Jiménez de
    12 509-510

Fedora (opera; Giordano)
  Caruso, Enrico **3** 345

Fedorovna (ruled 1796-1801), Russian
empress
  Paul I **12** 143-144

FEE, JOHN GREGG (1816-1901), American abolitionist and clergyman
  5 402-403

Feedback (information system)
  Armstrong, Edwin Howard **1** 302-303
  Babbage, Charles **1** 407-408
  De Forest, Lee **4** 459-460
  Wiener, Norbert **16** 262-263

Feen, Die (opera)
  Wagner, Richard **16** 40-43

Fei Kuo-yü (book)
  Liu Tsung-Yüan **9** 455-456

FEIFFER, JULES RALPH (born 1929), American satirical cartoonist and playwright
and novelist **5** 403-404

FEIGENBAUM, MITCHELL JAY (born 1944), American physicist **5** 404-405

Feigl, Herbert (born 1902), German
philosopher
  Schlick, Friedrich Albert Moritz
    14 16-17

FEIJÓ, DIOGO ANTÔNIO (1784-1843),
Brazilian priest and statesman **5** 405-406

FEININGER, LYONEL (1871-1956), American painter **5** 406-407
  Kandinsky, Wassily **8** 420-422

FEINSTEIN, DIANNE (Goldman; born
1933), politician, public official, and San
Francisco's first female mayor **5** 407-408

Feisi
  see Faizi

Fei-tsao (story)
  Lu Hsün **10** 35-37

Félibrige de Paris (French literary group)
  Maurras, Charles Marie Photius
    10 350-351

Felicific calculus (philosophy)
  Bentham, Jeremy **2** 176-178

Félicité (literary character)
  Flaubert, Gustave **5** 480-482

Feliks
  see Litvinov, Maxim Maximovich

Felix, Antonius (flourished 1st century),
Greek procurator of Judea ca. 52-60
  Paul **12** 141-143

Felix V (1383-1451), antipope 1439-49
  Pius II **12** 331

Felix Holt (novel)
  Eliot, George **5** 254-256

Felix namque (musical composition)
  Tallis, Thomas **15** 91

Felix of Cantalice, Saint (1515-1587), Italian Capuchin laybrother
  Neri, Philip **11** 340

Fellahin (Arab farmers)
  Mohammed Ali **11** 81-82

Felling (poems)
  Mistral, Gabriela **11** 55-56

FELLINI, FEDERICO (1920-1993), Italian
film director **5** 408-409
  Antonioni, Michelangelo **1** 252-253

Fellowship of Reconciliation (religious
organization)
  Muste, Abraham Johannes **11** 276-277
  Rustin, Bayard **13** 382-383
  Thomas, Norman Mattoon **15** 191-192

Felpham (Sussex, England)
  Blake, William **2** 316-318

Felton, John (1595?-1628), English sailor
  Buckingham, 1st Duke of **3** 93-94

FELTRE, VITTORINO DA (1378-1446), Italian humanist and teacher **5** 409-410

Female Eunuch, The (book)
  Greer, Germaine **6** 528-530

Feminine Mystique, The (book)
  Friedan, Betty **6** 109-111

Feminine Shrewdness (play)
  Tirso de Molina **15** 237-238

Feminism
  in literature
    Rich, Adrienne **13** 128-130

Feminist Art Movement
  Schapiro, Miriam **13** 520-521

Feminist movement
  see Women's rights

Feminist theology
  Morton, Nelle Katherine **11** 195-197
  Ruether, Rosemary Radford **13** 353-354

Feminists
  American
    Brownmiller, Susan **3** 56-57
    Chicago, Judy **3** 515-516
    Daly, Mary **4** 380-381
    Dewson, Mary Williams **4** 525
    hooks, bell **7** 477-481
    Schüssler Fiorenza, Elisabeth
      14 46-48
    Smeal, Eleanor **14** 278-280
    Starhawk **14** 403-404
    Yard, Mary Alexander **16** 438-439
  Canadian
    McClung, Nellie Letitia **10** 396-397
  English
    Fawcett, Millicent Garrett **5** 398-400
    Lessing, Doris **9** 355-357
    Rathbone, Eleanor **13** 47-48
    Weldon, Fay Birkinshaw
      16 186-188
  French
    de Beauvoir, Simone **4** 440-441
    Friedan, Betty **6** 109-111
  German
    Gilman, Charlotte Anna Perkins
      6 323-325
    Greer, Germaine **6** 528-530
    Horner, Matina Souretis **7** 506-508
    Howe, Florence Rosenfeld
      7 530-531
    Schüssler Fiorenza, Elisabeth
      14 46-48
    Soelle, Dorothee **14** 324-325
  Irish
    Devlin, Bernadette **4** 515-516
    Millett, Kate **11** 31-33
    Morgan, Robin **11** 168-170
  South African
    Lessing, Doris **9** 355-357
    Talbert, Mary Morris Burnett
      15 86-88

Femme Osage Creek (Missouri)
  Boone, Daniel **2** 397-398

Fen (book)
  Lu Hsün **10** 35-37

Fen (philosophy)
  Wang Pi **16** 104-105

FÉNELON, FRANÇOIS DE SALIGNAC DE LA MOTHE (1651-1715), French archbishop and theologian **5** 410-411
Bossuet, Jacques Bénigne **2** 431-432

Fenêtres, Les (poem)
Mallarmé, Stéphane **10** 172-173

Feng (442-490), Chinese regent 471-490
Hsiao-Wen-ti, Wei **8** 5

Feng and Shan sacrifices (Mt.T'ai; Shantung Province)
T'ai-tsung, T'ang **15** 83-84

FENG KUEI-FEN (1809-1874), Chinese scholar and official **5** 411-412

FENG YÜ-HSIANG (1882-1948), Chinese warlord **5** 412-413
Chang Tso-lin **3** 434-435
Chiang Kai-shek **3** 510-513
Wu P'ei-fu **16** 404-405
Yen Hsi-shan **16** 452-453

Feng-chien lun (book)
Liu Tsung-Yüan **9** 455-456

Fenian Ram (submarine)
Holland, John Philip **7** 453-454

Fenians (Irish political movement)
Collins, Michael **4** 167-168
Emmet, Robert **5** 281-282
Gladstone, William Ewart **6** 357-360
Holland, John Philip **7** 453-454
Pearse, Patrick Henry **12** 173-174

Fenice (literary character)
Chrestien de Troyes **4** 23-24

Fenton, Elijah (1683-1730), English poet
Pope, Alexander **12** 395-397

Feodor I (1557-1598), czar of Russia 1584-1598
Godunov, Boris Feodorovich **6** 382-383
Ivan IV **8** 157-159
Rurik **13** 364

Feodor II (1589-1605), czar of Russia 1605
Godunov, Boris Feodorovich **6** 382-383

Feodor III (1656-1682), czar of Russia 1676-1682
Alexis Mikhailovich Romanov **1** 142-143
Peter I **12** 253-256

Feodorovich, Pëtr
see Peter III

FERBER, EDNA (1887-1968), American author **5** 413
Kaufman, George S. **8** 457-458
Kern, Jerome David **8** 517-518

FERDINAND (1865-1927), king of Romania 1914-1927 **5** 413-414

Ferdinand de la Cerda (died 1275), Spanish prince
Alfonso X **1** 150-151

Ferdinand I (died 1065), king of Castile 1033-65 and of Leéon 1037-1065
Alfonso VI **1** 149

Ferdinand I (1423-1494), king of Naples 1458-1494
Alexander II **1** 132-133
Medici, Lorenzo de' **10** 450-451

FERDINAND I (1503-1564), Holy Roman emperor 1555-1564, king of Hungary and Bohemia 1526-64 and of Germany 1531-1564 **5** 414-415
Charles V **3** 457-459, 501, 502
Maximilian II **10** 357-358
Paul IV **12** 145-146
Philip II (king of Spain) **12** 271-273

Ferdinand I (1751-1825), king of the Two Sicilies 1816-1825
Charles III **3** 454-455

Ferdinand I (1793-1875), emperor of Austria 1835-1848
Francis II **6** 43-44
Francis Joseph **6** 45-46
Metternich, Klemens von **10** 533-536

Ferdinand II (died 1188), king of Leéon 1157-1188
Alfonso I **1** 148

FERDINAND II (1578-1637), Holy Roman emperor 1619-1637, king of Bohemia 1617-1637 and of Hungary 1618-1637 **5** 415
Wallenstein, Albrecht Wenzel Eusebius von **16** 80-81

FERDINAND II (1810-1859), king of the Two Sicilies 1830-1859 **5** 415-416

Ferdinand II (king of Aragon)
see Ferdinand V (king of Castile)

Ferdinand II, grand duke of Tuscany
see Medici, Ferdinand II de'

Ferdinand III (1199-1252), king of Castile 1217-1252
Alfonso X **1** 150-151
Gonzalo de Berceo **6** 431-432

FERDINAND III (1608-1657), Holy Roman emperor 1637-1657, king of Hungary 1626-1657 and of Bohemia 1627-1657 **5** 416-417
Froberger, Johann Jakob **6** 120-121

Ferdinand III (king of Naples)
see Ferdinand V (king of Castile)

Ferdinand III (king of Sicily)
see Ferdinand I (king of Two Sicilies)

Ferdinand IV (1285-1312), king of Castile and León 1295-1312
Tirso de Molina **15** 237-238

Ferdinand IV (king of Naples)
see Ferdinand I (king of Two Sicilies)

FERDINAND V (1452-1516), king of Castile 1474-1504, of Sicily 1468-1516, and of Aragon 1479-1516 **5** 417-418
alliances
Henry VII **7** 300-302
Louis XII **9** 528-529
Church relations
Borgia, Cesare **2** 412-413
Leo X **9** 332-334
colonial ventures

Balboa, Vasco Núñez de **1** 462-463
Columbus, Christopher **4** 176-179
Pedrarias **12** 179
Solís, Juan Díaz de **14** 326
Vespucci, Amerigo **15** 476-478
Inquisition
Abravanel, Isaac ben Judah **1** 31
opponents
Julius II **8** 384-386
relatives
Charles V **3** 457-459
Isabella I **8** 144-145
Manuel I **10** 219-220

Ferdinand V (king of Spain)
see Ferdinand V (king of Castile)

Ferdinand VI (1713-1759), king of Spain 1746-1759
Charles III **3** 454-455
Charles IV **3** 456-457
Philip V **12** 276-277

FERDINAND VII (1784-1833), king of Spain 1808 and 1814-1833 **5** 418-420
colonial revolts
Guerrero, Vicente **7** 28-30
Hidalgo y Costilla, Miguel **7** 375-377
Nariño, Antonio **11** 314-315
opponents
Godoy y Álvarez de Faria, Manuel de **6** 381-382
Goya y Lucientes, Francisco de Paula José de **6** 476-478
Saavedra, Angel de **13** 398
relatives
Charles IV **3** 456-457
Isabella II **8** 145-146
supporters
Azara, Félix de **1** 397-398

Ferdinand Maria (died 1654), Austrian prince
Ferdinand III **5** 416-417

Ferdinand von Hohenzollern-Sigmaringen
see Ferdinand (king of Romania)

Fergus, King (Irish folk hero)
Yeats, William Butler **16** 445-447

FERGUSON, ADAM (1723-1816), Scottish philosopher, moralist, and historian **5** 420-421
Stewart, Dugald **14** 449

Ferguson, Howard (born 1908), Northern-Irish composer
Bennett, Richard Rodney **2** 172

Ferguson, Robert (died 1714), Scottish conspirator
Monmouth and Buccleugh, Duke of **11** 108-109

Feria d'agosto (poems)
Pavese, Cesare **12** 154-155

Feria de los discretos, La (novel)
Baroja y Nessi, Pío **2** 15-16

FERMAT, PIERRE DE (1601-1665), French mathematician **5** 421-422
Euler, Leonard **5** 331-332

Lagrange, Joseph Louis **9** 164-166
Pascal, Blaise **12** 122-124

Fermentation (chemistry)
Cavendish, Henry **3** 383-384
Helmholtz, Hermann Ludwig Ferdinand
von **7** 268-269
Helmont, Jan Baptista van **7** 269-271
Liebig, Justus von **9** 403-404
Pasteur, Louis **12** 125-127
Schwann, Theodor **14** 51-52

FERMI, ENRICO (1901-1954),
Italian-American physicist **5** 422-424
associates
Bethe, Hans Albrecht **2** 238-239
Compton, Arthur Holly **4** 186-188
Hahn, Otto **7** 64-65
Lawrence, Ernest Orlando
9 248-250
Pauli, Wolfgang Ernst **12** 149
Szilard, Leo **15** 64-66
Tomonaga, Sin-itiro **15** 265-266
influence of
Dirac, Paul Adrien Maurice **5** 23-24
Yang, Chen Ning **16** 437-438

Fermi-Dirac statistics (physics)
Dirac, Paul Adrien Maurice **5** 23-24
Fermi, Enrico **5** 422-424

Fermoselle
see Encina, Juan del

Fern Hill (poem)
Thomas, Dylan Marlais **15** 188-190

Fernandes, John (flourished 15th century),
Portuguese navigator
Corte Reál, Gaspar and Miguel
4 254-255

Fernández, José Manuel Balmaceda
see Balmaceda Fernández, José Manuel

Fernández, Manuel Felix
see Guadalupe, Victoria

Fernández de Enciso, Martin
(1470-1528), Spanish colonizer
Balboa, Vasco Núñez de **1** 462-463

**FERNÁNDEZ DE LIZARDI, JOSÉ
JOAQUIN** (1776-1827), Mexican journalist and novelist **5** 424-425

Fernando
see Ferdinand

Fernando Po (island; West Africa)
Burton, Richard **3** 163-164

FERNEL, JEAN FRANÇOIS (circa
1497-1558), French physician **5** 425-426

Ferrante
see Ferdinand

Ferrara (city; Italy)
Borgia, Lucrezia Duchess of Ferrara
2 413-416
Frescobaldi, Girolamo **6** 101-102
Tura, Cosimo **15** 343-344

Ferrara-Florence, Council of (1437-1440)
Constantine XI **4** 211-212

FERRARO, GERALDINE (born 1935), first
woman candidate for the vice presidency
of a major U.S. political party **5** 426-428

FERRER, GABRIEL MIRÓ (1879-1930),
Spanish author **5** 428
Ruíz, José Martínez **13** 358

FERRER, JOSÉ FIGUÉRES (born 1906),
Costa Rican politician **5** 428-429

FERRERO, GUGLIELMO (1871-1942), Italian journalist and historian **5** 429-430

Ferret (schooner)
Farragut, David Glasgow **5** 388-389

Ferri, Enrico (1856-1929), Italian criminol-
ogist
Gaitán, Jorge Eliécer **6** 172-173
Lombroso, Cesare **9** 493

Ferrier, Sir David (1843-1928), Scottish
anatomist
Lashley, Karl Spencer **9** 214-215

Ferromagnetism (physics)
Compton, Arthur Holly **4** 186-188

FERRY, JULES FRANÇOIS CAMILLE
(1832-1893), French statesman **5** 430
Brazza, Pierre Paul François Camille
Savorgnan de **2** 509-510
Clemenceau, Georges **4** 99-101
Simon, Jules François **14** 237-238

Fertilization (biology)
Spallanzani, Lazzaro **14** 360-361

Fertilizers (agriculture)
Carver, George Washington **3** 346-347
Crookes, William **4** 323-324
Liebig, Justus von **9** 403-404

Fervor of Buenos Aires (poems)
Borges, Jorge Luis **2** 411-412

Fest auf Haderslevhuus, Ein (novella)
Storm, Theodor **14** 479-480

Feste Burg, Ein (hymn)
Luther, Martin **10** 48-51

Festin de l'araignée, Le (ballet)
Roussel, Albert **13** 328-329

Festival March (musical composition)
Strauss, Richard **14** 500-501

Festival of Two Worlds (Spoleto, Italy)
Menotti, Gian Carlo **10** 509-510

Festivities (essays)
Camus, Albert **3** 255-257

Festus, Sextus Pompeius (flourished 2nd
century A.D.), Roman grammarian
Plautus **12** 348-350

Fet, A.A. (1820-1892), Russian poet
Tolstoy, Leo **15** 262-265

Fête at Saint-Cloud (painting)
Fragonard, Jean Honoré **6** 38-39

Fête de l'Être Supreme, La (poem)
Chénier, André Marie **3** 500-501

Fêtes galantes (poems)
Verlaine, Paul Marie **15** 465-466

Fetishism (psychology)
Machado de Assis, Joaquim Maria
10 91-92

Fetterman massacre (United States; 1866)
Bozeman, John M. **2** 471-472
Red Cloud **13** 70-71

Fetterman, W.J. (circa 1833-1866), American army captain
Red Cloud **13** 70-71

Feu de joie (poems)
Aragon, Louis **1** 271-272

FEUCHTWANGER, LION (1884-1958),
post-World War I German literary figure
5 430-432
Mann, Thomas **10** 204-207

Feudalism (social system)
China
Han Kao-tsu **7** 125-126
Li Ssu **9** 442-443
Quin Shi Huang-Di **12** 515-518
England
Edward I **5** 208-210
John of Salisbury **8** 284-285
Ethiopia
Johannes IV **8** 272-273
France
Lefebvre, Georges **9** 301-302
Germany
Frederick I **6** 78-79
Henry V **7** 295-296
Greece
Philip II **12** 269-271
Inca Empire
Pizarro, Francisco **12** 340-341
Japan
Ieyasu, Tokugawa **8** 103-106
Okubo, Toshimichi **11** 489-490
Yoritomo, Minamoto **16** 463-464
Ottoman Empire
Mahmud II **10** 145-147
Prussia
Frederick William I **6** 86-87
see also Serf

Feuer aus den Kesseln (play)
Toller, Ernst **15** 261

FEUERBACH, LUDWIG ANDREAS
(1804-1872), German philosopher **5** 432
Eliot, George **5** 254-256
Engels, Friedrich **5** 286-288
Keller, Gottfried **8** 478-479
Marx, Karl **10** 304-308

Feuersnot (opera)
Strauss, Richard **14** 500-501

Feuilles d'automne, Les (poems)
Hugo, Victor Marie **8** 22-25

Feuilletonists (French politics)
Lessing, Gotthold Ephraim **9** 357-359

Févret de Saint-Mémin
see Saint-Mémin, Charles Balthazar
Julien Févret de

Few Figs from Thistles, A (poems)
Millay, Edna St. Vincent **11** 24-25

FEYNMAN, RICHARD PHILLIPS
(1918-1988), American physicist
5 432-434
Tomonaga, Sin-itiro **15** 265-266

Fez (city; Morocco)
Caillié, Auguste René **3** 214-215

Fez Declaration (Middle East, 1981)
Fahd ibn Abdul Aziz Al-Saud **5** 364-366

Fezzan (province; Libya)
Idris I **8** 102

Fiamma, La (opera)
Respighi, Ottorino **13** 103-104

Fiançailles, Les (play)
Maeterlinck, Maurice **10** 125-126

Fiancée, The (story)
Chekhov, Anton Pavlovich **3** 494-497

Fianna Fail (Irish political party)
De Valera, Eamon **4** 514-515

Fianna Fail Party (Ireland)
Reynolds, Albert **13** 113-115

Fianza satisfecha, La (play; Lope de Vega)
Osborne, John **12** 16-17

FIAT (Fabrica Italiana Automobili Torino)
Agnelli, Giovanni **1** 82-83

Fiat nox (poem)
Leconte de Lisle, Charles Marie René
9 273-274

Fibel, Die (book)
George, Stefan **6** 277-278

Fibers, synthetic (textiles)
Carothers, Wallace Hume **3** 317-318

FIBONACCI, LEONARDO (circa
1180-circa 1250), Italian mathematician
5 434-435

Ficciones (stories)
Borges, Jorge Luis **2** 411-412

FICHTE, JOHANN GOTTLIEB
(1762-1814), German philosopher
5 435-436
compared to
Krochmal, Nachman Kohen
9 104-105
influence of
Bakunin, Mikhail Aleksandrovich
1 458-460
Coleridge, Samuel Taylor **4** 154-156
Herbart, Johann Friedrich **7** 321-322
Hölderlin, Johann Christian
Friedrich **7** 451-452
Novalis **11** 435
Schelling, Friedrich Wilhelm Joseph
von **13** 526-527
Schlegel, Friedrich von **14** 10-11
Schleiermacher, Friedrich Ernst
Daniel **14** 11-12
Schopenhauer, Arthur **14** 29-31
influenced by
Kant, Immanuel **8** 430-432
opponent
Fries, Jakob Friedrich **6** 116-117
study of

Hegel, Georg Wilhelm Friedrich
7 254-256

FICINO, MARSILIO (1433-1499), Italian
philosopher and humanist **5** 436-437
Bembo, Pietro **2** 144-145
Medici, Cosimo de' **10** 449-450
Medici, Lorenzo de' **10** 450-451
Pulci, Luigi **12** 481

Fiddler on the Roof (musical)
Aleichem, Sholom **1** 124-125

Fiddler on the Roof (painting)
Chagall, Marc **3** 406-407

Fiddler's House, The (play)
Colum, Padraic **4** 174-175

Fidelio (opera; Beethoven)
Beethoven, Ludwig van **2** 114-117
Cherubini, Luigi Carlo Zanobi Salvatore
Maria **3** 505-506

FIEDLER, ARTHUR (1894-1979), American
conductor of the Boston Pops **5** 437-438

FIELD, CYRUS WEST (1819-1892), Ameri-
can merchant **5** 438-439
Cooper, Peter **4** 223-224
Cornell, Ezra **4** 236-237
Field, David Dudley **5** 439-440
Field, Stephen Johnson **5** 441-442
Grady, Henry Woodfin **6** 482-483

FIELD, DAVID DUDLEY (1805-1894),
American jurist **5** 439-440
Field, Cyrus West **5** 438-439
Field, Stephen Johnson **5** 441-442
Welles, Gideon **16** 188-190

Field emission (physics)
Millikan, Robert Andrews **11** 33-35

Field, John (1782-1837), Irish composer
Chopin, Frédéric François **4** 16-18
Glinka, Mikhail Ivanovich **6** 369-370

FIELD, MARSHALL (1834-1906), American
merchant **5** 440-441
Dreiser, Herman Theodore **5** 98-100

Field Museum of Natural History
Field, Marshall **5** 440-441

Field, Nathan (1587-1633), English actor
and playwright
Fletcher, John **5** 487

Field of Cloth of Gold (Flanders)
Henry VIII **7** 302-305
Wolsey, Thomas **16** 364-366

FIELD, STEPHEN JOHNSON (1816-1899),
American jurist **5** 441-442
Field, Cyrus West **5** 438-439
Field, David Dudley **5** 439-440
Harlan, John Marshall **7** 156-157
White, Edward Douglass **16** 230-231

Field theory (physics)
Faraday, Michael **5** 380
Lewin, Kurt **9** 375-376

Fielding (literary character)
Forster, Edward Morgan **6** 14-16

Fielding, Copley (1787-1855), English
painter
Bonington, Richard Parkes **2** 394-395

FIELDING, HENRY (1707-1754), English
novelist **5** 442-444
influence of
Brackenridge, Hugh Henry
2 472-473
Dickens, Charles John Huffam
4 538-541
Hogarth, William **7** 446-447
influenced by
Cervantes, Miguel de Saavedra
3 395-398
satires
Braddock, Edward **2** 474-475
Richardson, Samuel **13** 141-142
Smollett, Tobias George **14** 305-307
Sterne, Laurence **14** 435-437

Fielding, Sir John (1722-1780), English justice of the peace
Fielding, Henry **5** 442-444

Fields, The (novel)
Richter, Conrad Michael **13** 148-149

FIELDS, W. C. (stage name of William
Claude Dukenfield; 1879-1946), Ameri-
can comedian **5** 444
Ziegfeld, Florenz **16** 516-517

Fiend's Delight (book)
Bierce, Ambrose Gwinett **2** 269-270

Fierabras (opera)
Schubert, Franz Peter **14** 35-37

Fieschi, Ottoboni
see Adrian V

Fieschi, Sinibaldo de'
see Innocent IV

Fieser, L.F. (1899-1977), American chemist
Dam, Carl Peter Henrik **4** 382-383

Fiesko (literary character)
Schiller, Johann Christoph Friedrich von
14 4-7

Fiesole, cloisters of (Italy)
Medici, Cosimo de' **10** 449-450

Fiesole, Mino da (circa 1431-1481), Italian
sculptor
Verrocchio, Andrea del **15** 471-472

15th Amendment
see Constitution of the United States—
Amendments

5th Amendment
see Constitution of the United States—
Amendments

Fifth Column, The (play)
Hemingway, Ernest Miller **7** 274-277

Fifth Crusade
see Crusades—Fifth

Fifth Monarch Men (English millennialists)
Sabbatai Zevi **13** 400-401

Fifth Seal of the Apocalypse (painting)
Greco **6** 511-514

Figaro (literary character)
Beaumarchais, Pierre August Caron de **2** 93-94

Fighting Angel (biography)
Buck, Pearl Sydenstricker **3** 91-93

Fighting Lions (sculpture)
Rimmer, William **13** 174

Fighting Téméraire (painting)
Turner, Joseph Mallord William **15** 352-354

Figlia di Jorio, La (play)
D'Annunzio, Gabriele **4** 388

FIGUEIREDO, JOÃO BATISTA DE OLIVEIRA (born 1918), Brazilian army general and president (1979-1985) **5** 445-446

Figuéres Ferrer, José
see Ferrer, José Figuéres

Figura II (sculpture)
Luz, Arturo Rogerio **10** 56-57

Figuras de la pasión del señor (biography)
Ferrer, Gabriel Miró **5** 428

Figurative manner (art)
Balthus **1** 476-477
Guston, Philip **7** 47-48
Mondrian, Piet **11** 101-102
Nolan, Sidney Robert **11** 418
Shahn, Ben **14** 139-140

Figure (sculpture)
Lipchitz, Jacques **9** 432-433

Figure of Dignity (sculpture)
Flannagan, John Bernard **5** 480

Figured bass
see Basso continuo

Figures doubles prismes (musical composition)
Boulez, Pierre **2** 444-445

Figures of Earth (book)
Cabell, James Branch **3** 195-196

Fihri, Yusuf al- (ruled 746-756), Abbasid governor Spain
Abd al-Rahman I **1** 13-14

Fiji Islands (South Western Pacific Ocean)
Tasman, Abel Janszoon **15** 113-114

Filarete, Antonio (1400-1470), Italian architect and sculptor
Fouquet, Jean **6** 31

Filelfo, Francesco (1398-1481), Italian humanist
Sforza, Lodovico **14** 127-128

Files on Parade (stories)
O'Hara, John **11** 485

Fili mi, Absalon (musical composition)
Schütz, Heinrich **14** 48-49

Filibuster (Southern politics)
Reed, Thomas Brackett **13** 77

Filibusterismo, El (book)
Rizal, José **13** 187-189

Filioque (Roman Catholic theology)
Charonton, Enguerrand **3** 471

Filippo (play)
Alfieri, Vittoria **1** 145-146

Fille du régiment, La (opera)
Donizetti, Gaetano **5** 59-60

Fille Élissa, La (novel)
Goncourt, Edmond de and Jules de **6** 426-427

Filles du feu, Les (book)
Nerval, Gérard de **11** 345-346

Fillmore, Lavius (flourished early 19th century), American architect
Benjamin, Asher **2** 162-163

FILLMORE, MILLARD (1800-1874), American statesman, president 1850-1853 **5** 447-448
Curtis, Benjamin Robbins **4** 349
Everett, Edward **5** 344
Kennedy, John Pendleton **8** 506-507
Webster, Daniel **16** 162-164

FILMER, SIR ROBERT (died 1653), English political theorist **5** 448

Film directors, stars, and writers
see Actors and entertainers; motion pictures

Filocolo (book)
Boccaccio, Giovanni **2** 351-353

Filostrato (poem)
Boccaccio, Giovanni **2** 351-353

Fin de Chéri, La (novel)
Colette, Sidonie Gabrielle **4** 158-159

Fin de Satan, La (poem)
Hugo, Victor Marie **8** 22-25

Final de Norma, El (novel)
Alarcón, Pedro Antonio de **1** 100-101

Final Harvest (poems)
Dickinson, Emily **4** 541-543

Final Problem, The (story)
Doyle, Arthur Conan **5** 91-92

Financial Expert, The (novel)
Narayan, R. K. **11** 313-314

Financier, The (novel)
Dreiser, Herman Theodore **5** 98-100

Financiers
see Business and industrial leaders—financiers

Finck, Hermann (1527-1558), German music theorist
Gombert, Nicolas **6** 416-417

Fin-de-siècle literature
Chekhov, Anton Pavlovich **3** 494-497
D'Annunzio, Gabriele **4** 388
George, Stefan **6** 277-278
Huysmans, Joris Karl **8** 81-82
Loti, Pierre **9** 519-520

Fin-de-siècle movement (art)
Beardsley, Aubrey Vincent **2** 88-89

Finding of the Body of Saint Florian (painting)
Altdorfer, Albrecht **1** 179-180

Finding of the Body of Saint Mark (painting)
Tintoretto **15** 232-234

Fine Clothes to the Jew (book)
Hughes, Langston **8** 18-19

Fine Gael Party (political party; Northern Ireland)
Bruton, John Gerard **3** 76-77
Cosgrave, Liam **4** 258-260
Fitzgerald, Garret **5** 472-474

Fine Work with Pitch and Copper (poem)
Williams, William Carlos **16** 308-309

Finer Grain, The (stories)
James, Henry **8** 211-212

Fingal's Cave (overture)
Mendelssohn, Moses **10** 488-489

Fingerprints (criminology)
Bertillon, Alphonse **2** 230-231
Galton, Francis **6** 193-194

Finian of Clonard, Saint (circa 470-552), Irish monk and scholar
Columba **4** 175-176

Finisterre (poems)
Montale, Eugenio **11** 117-118

Finisterre, Cape (Spain)
Rodney, George Brydges **13** 239-240

Finite differences (mathematics)
Babbage, Charles **1** 407-408
Taylor, Brook **15** 121-122

FINKELSTEIN, RABBI LOUIS (born 1895), American Jewish scholar and head of Conservative Judaism **5** 448-450

Finland, Republic of (nation; Northern Europe)
Aalto, Hugo Alvar Henrik **1** 1-2
Mannerheim, Carl Gustav Emil Von **10** 207-208
Nicholas II **11** 378-380
see also Finnish architecture; Finnish music

Finlandia (musical composition)
Sibelius, Jean Julius Christian **14** 211-212

FINLAY, CARLOS JUAN (1833-1915), Cuban biologist and physician **5** 450
Reed, Walter **13** 78

Finley, John H., Jr. (1863-1940), American educator and editor
Pindar **12** 312-313

Finnegans Wake (novel; Joyce)
Beckett, Samuel **2** 102-104
Joyce, James **8** 365-367-73
Stephens, James **14** 430-431
Wilder, Thornton Niven **16** 276-277

FINNEY, CHARLES GRANDISON (1792-1875), American theologian and educator **5** 450-451
Weld, Theodore Dwight **16** 186

Finnish architecture
Aalto, Hugo Alvar Henrik **1** 1-2
Saarinen, Eliel and Eero **13** 396-398

Finnish music
Sibelius, Jean Julius Christian
14 211-212

Finta giardiniera, La (opera)
Mozart, Wolfgang Amadeus
11 218-221

Finta semplice, La (opera)
Mozart, Wolfgang Amadeus
11 218-221

Fiore, Il (sonnets)
Dante Alighieri **4** 389-391

Fiorelli, Tiberio
see Scaramouche

Fiorentino, P.A. (1806-1864), Italian writer
and critic
Dumas, Alexandre **5** 136-138

FIRDAUSI (934-1020), Persian poet
5 451-452
Jami **8** 218-219
Mahmud of Ghazni **10** 147

Fire (philosophy)
Heraclitus **7** 320
Pythagoras **12** 498-499

Fire alarm (electrical system)
Farmer, Moses Gerrish **5** 385

Fire and Ice (poem)
Frost, Robert Lee **6** 130-133

Fire in the Lake (book)
FitzGerald, Frances **5** 469-470

Fire Next Time, The (book)
Baldwin, James Arthur **1** 465-466

Fire of Egliswyl, The (prose tale)
Wedekind, Frank **16** 166-167

Firebell in the Night (book)
Handlin, Oscar **7** 121-122

Firebird, The (ballet; Stravinsky)
Chagall, Marc **3** 406-407
Stravinsky, Igor Fedorovich **14** 502-506

FIRESTONE, HARVEY SAMUEL
(1868-1938), American industrialist
5 452-453
Carver, George Washington **3** 346-347
du Pont, Pierre Samuel **5** 154-155
Duke, James Buchanan **5** 133-134
Ford, Henry **6** 5-6
Garvey, Marcus Mosiah **6** 228-229

Firestone Co. (tires; industry)
Edison, Thomas Alva **5** 206-208
Firestone, Harvey Samuel **5** 452-453

Fireworks (musical composition)
Stravinsky, Igor Fedorovich **14** 502-506

Firing Line (television program)
Buckley, William F. Jr. **3** 96-97

Firle Place (Sussex)
Chippendale, Thomas **4** 1-2

Firm, The (book)
Grisham, John **7** 6-8

FIRST, RUTH (1925-1982), South African
socialist, anti-apartheid activist, and
scholar **5** 453-454

1st Amendment
see Constitution of the United States—
Amendments

First Battle, The (book)
Bryan, William Jennings **3** 80-82

First Church (Boston)
Benjamin, Asher **2** 162-163
Chauncy, Charles **3** 485-486

First Church of Christ, Scientist (Boston)
Eddy, Mary Baker **5** 202

First Circle, The (novel)
Solzhenitsyn, Alexander Isayevich
14 330-332

First Impressions
see Pride and Prejudice (novel)

First International
see International, First

First Ladies
Clinton, Hillary Rodham **4** 115-117
Eisenhower, Mamie Doud **5** 236-237
Gorbachev, Raisa Maximovna Titorenko
6 444-446
Madison, Dolly **10** 119-121
Onassis, Jacqueline Lee Bouvier
Kennedy **11** 511-513

First Lady (play)
Kaufman, George S. **8** 457-458

First Love (story)
Turgenev, Ivan Sergeyevich **15** 345-348

First Man, The (play)
O'Neill, Eugene **11** 514-516

First Men in the Moon, The (book)
Wells, Herbert George **16** 195-196

First Rapprochement (England-United
States)
King, Rufus **9** 22-23

First Triumvirate
see Roman Republic

First Wife... (stories)
Buck, Pearl Sydenstricker **3** 91-93

Firth, Charles (1857-1936), English historian
Gardiner, Samuel Rawson **6** 211

Firth, Pond and Company (music publishing)
Foster, Stephen Collins **6** 25-27

FISCHER, BOBBY (born 1943), American
chess player **5** 454-456

FISCHER, EMIL (1852-1919), German
organic chemist **5** 456-457
Baeyer, Johann Friedrich Adolf von
1 432
Diels, Otto Paul Hermann **5** 5-6
Fischer, Hans **5** 457-459
Hahn, Otto **7** 64-65
Pregl, Fritz **12** 436-437
Sanger, Frederick **13** 466-467

FISCHER, HANS (1881-1945), German
organic chemist **5** 457-459

Fischer, Otto Philip (1852-1932), German
chemist
Baeyer, Johann Friedrich Adolf von
1 432

**FISCHER VON ERLACH, JOHANN BERN-
HARD** (1656-1723), Austrian architect
5 459-461
Hildebrandt, Johann Lucas von
7 380-381
Neumann, Balthasar **11** 354-355
Prandtauer, Jakob **12** 432
Rottmayr, Johann Michael **13** 321

**FISCHER VON ERLACH, JOSEPH
EMMANUEL** (1693-1742), Austrian architect Fischer von Erlach, J.B. **5** 459-461

Fischerin, Die (song)
Goethe, Johann Wolfgang von
6 388-391

Fish (sculpture cycle)
Brancusi, Constantin **2** 494-496

Fish and Wildlife Service (United States)
Carson, Rachel Louise **3** 337-338

FISH, HAMILTON (1808-1893), American
statesman **5** 461-462
Grant, Ulysses Simpson **6** 492-494
Sumner, Charles **15** 30-31

Fish, Stuyvesant (1851-1923), American
railroad executive
Harriman, Edward Henry **7** 164-165

Fish, The (poem)
Bishop, Elizabeth **2** 290-292
Moore, Marianne **11** 148-149

FISHER, ANDREW (1862-1928), Australian
statesman and labor leader **5** 462
Hughes, William Morris **8** 21-22

Fisher, Geoffrey Francis (Baron Fisher of
Lambeth; born 1887-1972), English
Archibishop of Canterbury
John, XXIII **8** 277-280

Fisher, Herbert Albert Laurens
(1865-1940), English historian
Laski, Harold J. **9** 215-216

FISHER, IRVING (1867-1947), American
economist **5** 462-463

Fisher, John (1459-1535), English Catholic
bishop
Henry VIII **7** 302-305

Fisher of Kilverstone, 1st Baron (John
Arbuthnot; 1841-1920), British admiral of
the fleet
Edward VIII **5** 215-217

FISHER, SIR RONALD AYLMER
(1890-1962), English statistician
5 463-464
Mendel, Johann Gregor **10** 483-486

Fisheries, U.S. Bureau of
Carson, Rachel Louise **3** 337-338

Fisherman at Sea (painting)
Turner, Joseph Mallord William
15 352-354

Fisherman's Songs ... (poems)
Yun Sondo **16** 483

Fishing Boats ... (painting)
Van Gogh, Vincent **15** 427-429

FISK, JAMES (1834-1872), American financial speculator **5** 464-465
Drew, Daniel **5** 101-102
Field, David Dudley **5** 439-440
Gould, Jay **6** 470-472
Vanderbilt, Cornelius **15** 415-416

Fisk University (Nashville, Tennessee)
Frazier, Edward Franklin **6** 77
Johnson, Charles Spurgeon **8** 296-297
Radin, Paul **12** 538-539

Fiske, Helen Marie
see Jackson, Helen Hunt

FISKE, JOHN (1842-1901), American philosopher and historian **5** 465-466

FISKE, MINNIE MADDERN (Mary Augusta Davey; 1865-1932), American "realistic" actress who portrayed Ibsen heroines **5** 466-467

Fission
see Nuclear fission

FIT
see Federal Institute of Technology (Zurich)

FITCH, JOHN (1743-1798), American mechanic and inventor **5** 467-468
Fulton, Robert **6** 151-152
Stevens, John **14** 439-440

Fitnah al-Kubra, Al- (book)
Husayn, Taha **8** 61-62

Fittig, Rudolf (1835-1910), German chemist
Ramsay, William **13** 21-22

Fitz-Boodle, George Savage (pseudonym)
see Thackeray, William Makepeace

FitzGerald, Edward (1809-1883), English poet
Omar Khayyam **11** 510-511

FITZGERALD, ELLA (1918-1996), American jazz singer **5** 468-469

FITZGERALD, FRANCES (born 1940), American author **5** 469-470

FITZGERALD, FRANCIS SCOTT KEY (1896-1940), American author **5** 470-472
Lardner, Ringgold Wilmer **9** 204-205
Lewis, Harry Sinclair **9** 385-387
Perkins, William Maxwell Evarts **12** 222-223
Stein, Gertrude **14** 414-415
Wilson, Edmund **16** 318-319

FITZGERALD, GARRET (born 1926), Irish prime minister (1981-1987) **5** 472-474

Fitzgerald, John Francis (1863-1950), American politician
Kennedy, John Fitzgerald **8** 502-506

Fitzgerald, Zelda Sayre (1900-1947), American author
Fitzgerald, Francis Scott Key **5** 470-472

Fitzherbert, Mrs. (Maria Anne Smythe; 1756-1837), wife of George IV of England
George IV **6** 272-273

FITZHUGH, GEORGE (1806-1881), American polemicist and sociologist **5** 474

Fitzmaurice confederacy (Irish, 1569-1572)
Elizabeth I **5** 263-266

FITZPATRICK, THOMAS (1799-1854), American trapper, guide, and Indian agent **5** 474-475
Carson, Christopher **3** 334-335

Fiume (Rieka; seaport, Yugoslavia)
Orlando, Vittorio Emmanuele **11** 529-530
Peter I **12** 256

Fiumi, I (poem)
Ungaretti, Giuseppe **15** 389-390

Fiuri de Tapo (songs)
Dallapiccola, Luigi **4** 377-378

Five Dynasties (China; ruled 907-960)
Ch'in Kuei **3** 524-525
Kwangjong **9** 140
Zhao Kuang-yin **16** 505-508

Five Element theory (philosophy)
Chung-shu, Tung **4** 48-49
Tsou Yen **15** 329-330
Wang Ch'ung **16** 98-99

500, Council of (Athens)
Cleisthenes **4** 98-99

Five Hundred, Council of (France)
Bonaparte, Joseph **2** 381-382
Carnot, Lazare Nicolas Marguerite **3** 313-314
Murat, Joachim **11** 253-254
Sieyès, Comte Emmanuel Joseph **14** 217-218

Five Nations, The (poems)
Kipling, Joseph Rudyard **9** 32-33

Five Pillars (political philosophy)
Sukarno **15** 18-20

Five Points gang (Brooklyn, New York)
Capone, Al **3** 272-273

Five Weeks in a Balloon (novel)
Verne, Jules **15** 467-469

Five Year Plan (China)
Mao Zedong **10** 225-227

Five Years' Campaign (1392-1397; Western Asia)
Tamerlane **15** 94-95

Five-Year Plans (India)
Nehru, Jawaharlal **11** 332-334

Five-Year Plans (Union of Soviet Socialist Republics)
Stalin, Joseph **14** 393-396

FIZEAU, HIPPOLYTE ARMAND LOUIS (1819-1896), French physicist **5** 475
Foucault, Jean Bernard Léon **6** 28-29

Flaccus, Lucius Valerius (died 180 B.C.), Roman statesman
Cato, Marcus Porcius the Elder **3** 375

Flaccus, Marcus Fulvius (flourished 2nd century B.C.), Roman statesman
Gracchus, Tiberius and Gaius Sempronius **6** 479-480

Flaccus, Marcus Verrius (flourished late 1st-early 2nd century A.D.), Roman scholar
Ovid **12** 34-36

Flaccus, Quintus Horatius
see Horace

Flagellation (painting)
Piero della Francesca **12** 301-302
Signorelli, Luca **14** 221-222

Flagler, Henry M. (1830-1913), American businessman
Rockefeller, John Davison **13** 226-228

FLAHERTY, ROBERT (1884-1951), American documentary filmmaker **5** 476-477

Flajoulot, Charles (1774-1840), French painter
Courbet, Jean Desiré Gustave **4** 271-273

Flambard, Ranulf (died 1128), English bishop and justiciar
Henry I **7** 286-287
William II **16** 293-294

Flame of Life, The (novel)
D'Annunzio, Gabriele **4** 388

Flamen dialis (Priest of Jove)
Caesar, Gaius Julius **3** 207-210

Flamenco (music)
Falla, Manuel de **5** 372-373

Flames (musical composition)
Chávez, Carlos **3** 486

Flaming Angel (opera)
Prokofiev, Sergei Sergeevich **12** 458-460

FLAMININUS, TITUS QUINCTIUS (circa 228-174 B.C.), Roman general and diplomat **5** 477
Halley, Edmund **7** 88-89

Flaminius, Gaius (died 217 B.C.), Roman general and statesman
Hannibal Barca **7** 128-130

FLAMSTEED, JOHN (1646-1719), English astronomer **5** 477-478
Halley, Edmund **7** 88-89

FLANAGAN, HALLIE (1890-1969), American director, playwright, and educator **5** 478-479

Flanders (province; French-Belgian)
Clemens non Papa, Jacobus **4** 101
Cornwallis, Charles **4** 241-243
Edward III **5** 211-212
Philip VI **12** 277-278
see also Flemish art; Franco-Flemish music

Flandin, P.E. (1889-1958), French statesman
Herriot, Édouard **7** 339-340

FLANNAGAN, JOHN BERNARD
(1895-1942), American sculptor **5** 480

Flappers and Philosophers (stories)
Fitzgerald, Francis Scott Key **5** 470-472

Flast v.Cohen (legal case)
Warren, Earl **16** 117-120

Flathead Indians (North America)
Fitzpatrick, Thomas **5** 474-475

FLAUBERT, GUSTAVE (1821-1880), French
novelist **5** 480-482
associates
Daudet, Alphonse **4** 402-403
Mérimée, Prosper **10** 517
Turgenev, Ivan Sergeyevich
15 345-348
commentary on
Proust, Marcel **12** 465-467
illustrators
Redon, Odilon **13** 75-76
influence of
D'Annunzio, Gabriele **4** 388
Fontane, Theodor **5** 504
Güiráldez, Ricardo **7** 38-39
Kafka, Franz **8** 403-406
Maupassant, Henri René Albert Guy
de **10** 347
Stein, Gertrude **14** 414-415
musical adaptations
Mussorgsky, Modest Petrovich
11 274-276
translation
Merezhkovsky, Dmitry Sergeyevich
10 515-516

Flavian (died 449), bishop of Constantino-
ple
Eutyches **5** 335
Leo I **9** 329-330

Flavio (opera)
Handel, George Frederick **7** 116-119

Flavius Claudius Julianus
see Julian the Apostate

Flaxman, John (1755-1826), English sculptor
Wedgwood, Josiah **16** 168-169

Flayed Man, The (sculpture)
Houdon, Antoine **7** 516-517

Fleck, Sir Alexander (1889-1968), British
industrial scientist
Soddy, Frederick **14** 321-323

Fledermaus, Die (operetta)
Strauss, Johann Jr. **14** 498-499

Fleet in Being, A (story)
Kipling, Joseph Rudyard **9** 32-33

Fleg, Edmond (1874-1963), French author
and composer
Bloch, Ernest **2** 326-327

FLEISCHMANN, GISI (1894-1944),
Czechoslovakian leader who rescued

many Jews from the Nazi Holocaust
5 482-483

FLEMING, SIR ALEXANDER (1881-1955),
Scottish bacteriologist **5** 485-486
Florey, Howard Walter **5** 491-492
Waksman, Selman Abraham **16** 49-50

Fleming, Sir John Ambrose (1849-1945),
English engineer
De Forest, Lee **4** 459-460

FLEMING, SIR SANDFORD (1827-1915),
Scottish-born Canadian railway engineer
5 485-486

Flemish art
baroque
see Baroque painting (Flemish and
Dutch)
influence of
Antonello da Messina **1** 251-252
Bermejo, Bartolomé **2** 205
Chardin, Jean Baptiste Siméon
3 442-443
Clouet, Jean and François **4** 122-123
Cranach, Lucas the Elder **4** 289-290
Morales, Luis de **11** 150
Piero della Francesca **12** 301-302
painting (15th century)
Campin, Robert **3** 255
Christus, Petrus **4** 33-34
Eyck, Hubert and Jan van **5** 352-354
Massys, Quentin **10** 325-326
van der Goes, Hugo **15** 416-417
Weyden, Rogier van der **16** 219-221
painting (17th century)
Brouwer, Adriaen **3** 29-30
Jordaens, Jacob **8** 347-349
Rubens, Peter Paul **13** 339-342
Van Dyck, Anthony **15** 423-425
see also Dutch art and architecture;
Netherlandish art

Flemish music
see Franco-Flemish music

Flesh (poems)
Benn, Gottfried **2** 164

Flesh and the Devil, The (film)
Garbo, Greta **6** 205-207

Flesh and the Spirit, The (poem)
Bradstreet, Anne Dudley **2** 486-487

FLETCHER, ALICE CUNNINGHAM
(1838-1923), American anthropologist
5 486-487

Fletcher, James C. (1823-1901), American
Presbyterian missionary
Heade, Martin Johnson **7** 236

FLETCHER, JOHN (1579-1625), English
playwright **5** 487
Beaumont, Francis **2** 95
Dryden, John **5** 106-107
Jonson, Ben **8** 343-345
Massinger, Philip **10** 324-325
Shakespeare, William **14** 142-145

FLETCHER, JOSEPH FRANCIS
(1905-1991), American philosopher who

was the father of modern biomedical
ethics **5** 488-489

Fletcher, Sir Walter Morley (1873-1933),
English physician
Hill, Archibald Vivian **7** 385-386
Meyerhof, Otto Fritz **10** 537-539

Fletcher v. Peck (legal case)
Marshall, John **10** 279-281
Martin, Luther **10** 289-290

Fleurs boréales, Les (poems)
Fréchette, Louis-Honoré **6** 77-78

Fleurs du mal, Les (poems; Baudelaire)
Baudelaire, Charles Pierre **2** 61-63
Redon, Odilon **13** 75-76
Rouault, Georges **13** 321-322

Fleurus, battle of (1794)
Carnot, Lazare Nicolas Marguerite
3 313-314
Saint-Just, Louis Antoine Léon de
13 433

Fleury, André Hercule de (1653-1743),
French statesman and cardinal
Louis XV **9** 533-534
Montesquieu **11** 123-125
Saint-Pierre, Abbé de **13** 434-435

FLEXNER, ABRAHAM (1866-1959), American educational reformer **5** 489-490
Einstein, Albert **5** 228-231

Fliegende Holländer, Der (opera)
Wagner, Richard **16** 40-43

Flies, The (play)
Sartre, Jean Paul **13** 491-492

Flight and Metamorphosis (poems)
Sachs, Nelly **13** 411-412

Flight from Broadway, The (essay)
Davis, Ossie **4** 421-422

Flight from the Enchanter, The (novel)
Murdoch, Iris **11** 256-257

Flight into Egypt (painting)
Carracci **3** 319-321

Flight of Florimell (painting)
Allston, Washington **1** 176-177

Flight of the Bird (sculpture)
Pevsner, Antoine **12** 263-264

Flight to Arras (book)
Saint-Exupéry, Antoine de **13** 431-432

Flinck, Govaert (1615-1660), Dutch
painter
Rembrandt Harmensz van Rijn
13 91-95

FLINDERS, MATTHEW (1774-1814), English naval captain and hydrographer
5 490
Franklin, John **6** 64-65

Flintstones, The (animated television show)
Blanc, Mel **2** 319-320

FLN
see National Liberation Front

Floating Bear (newsletter)
Baraka, Imamu Amiri **1** 498-499

Flodden Field, battle of (1513)
Douglas, Gavin **5** 77-78
Dunbar, William (poet) **5** 142-143
Henry VIII **7** 302-305
Norfolk, 3d Duke of **11** 423

Flogera tou Vasilia, I (poems)
Palamas, Kostes **12** 70

Flood (play)
Betti, Ugo **2** 246

Flood, Henry (1732-1791), Irish politician
Grattan, Henry **6** 499

Flood, Ivry, The (painting)
Vlaminck, Maurice **16** 6

Flood of Years, The (poem)
Bryant, William Cullen **3** 83-85

Flood, The (book)
Sholem Aleichem **14** 202-203
Warren, Robert Penn **16** 121-122

Flor de Santidad (novel)
Valle Inclán, Ramón Maria del
15 407-408

Flora (painting)
Titian **15** 242-244

Flora Lyndsay (novel)
Moodie, Susanna **11** 140-141

Florence (city; Italy)
- ARTS
  architecture
    Alberti, Leon Battista **1** 113-115
    Arnolfo di Cambio **1** 315-316
    Brunelleschi, Filippo **3** 70-72
    Medici, Cosimo de' **10** 449-450
    Sangallo family **13** 464-466
  goldsmithery
    Cellini, Benvenuto **3** 391-392
    Isaac, Heinrich **8** 143-144
  painting
    Andrea del Castagno **1** 223-224
    Andrea del Sarto **1** 224-225
    Angelico **1** 235-236
    Botticelli, Sandro **2** 439-440
    Bronzino **3** 19
    Correggio **4** 249-251
    Duccio di Buoninsegna
    5 121-122
    Orcagna **11** 526-527
    Pontormo **12** 394-395
    Uccello, Paolo **15** 378-379
    Veneziano, Domenico
    15 459-460
  sculpture
    Andrea Pisano **1** 225-226
    Donatello **5** 55-56
    Luca della Robbia **10** 19-20
    Michelangelo Buonarroti **11** 2-5
    Pollaiuolo, Antonio **12** 377-378
    see also Badia, The; Florence
    Cathedral
- HISTORY
  Guelf-Ghibelline wars
    Cavalcanti, Guido **3** 382
    Dante Alighieri **4** 389-391

histories of
Salvemini, Gaetano **13** 455-456
Villani, Giovanni **15** 497-498
Medici rule
Machiavelli, Niccolò **10** 97-99
Medici, Cosimo de' **10** 449-450
Medici, Lorenzo de' **10** 450-451
Savonarola, Girolamo
13 505-506
papal conflict
Catherine of Siena **3** 369-370
Julius II **8** 384-386

Florence Cathedral (Santa Maria del Fiore)
architecture
Arnolfo di Cambio **1** 315-316
Brunelleschi, Filippo **3** 70-72
Ghiberti, Lorenzo **6** 291-292
Michelozzo **11** 6-7
Perugino **12** 245-246
Baptistery
Andrea Pisano **1** 225-226
Borromini, Francesco **2** 424-425
Ghiberti, Lorenzo **6** 291-292
Quercia, Jacopo della **12** 509
Rodin, Auguste **13** 236-238
Sansovino, Jacopo **13** 470-471
Uccello, Paolo **15** 378-379
campanile
Andrea Pisano **1** 225-226
Giotto **6** 342-345
Luca della Robbia **10** 19-20
Veneziano, Domenico **15** 459-460
minor works
Andrea del Castagno **1** 223-224

Florence Triumphant over Pisa (sculpture)
Giovanni da Bologna **6** 345-346

Florensians (religious order)
Joachim of Fiore **8** 263-264

FLORES, JUAN JOSÉ (1801-1864), South
American general, president of Ecuador
5 491
García Moreno, Gabriel **6** 209-210

Flores, Venancio (1809-1868), Uruguayan
general and politician
Rivera, Fructuoso **13** 184-185

Floresta de enganos (play)
Vicente, Gil **15** 479-480

FLOREY, HOWARD WALTER (Baron Florey
of Adelaide; 1898-1968), Australian
pathologist **5** 491-492
Domagk, Gerhard Johannes Paul
5 48-50
Fleming, Alexander **5** 483-485

Florey units
see Oxford units

Florian Geyer (drama)
Hauptmann, Gerhart Johann Robert
7 199-201

Florida (ship)
Adams, Charles Francis **1** 41-42

Florida (state; United States)
colonial rule (Spain)

Charles III **3** 454-455
Gálvez, Bernardo de **6** 195-196
Menéndez de Avilés, Pedro
10 499-500
Narváez, Pánfilo de **11** 315
Velasco, Luis de **15** 450-451
exploration (Spanish)
Cabeza de Vaca, Álvar Núñez **3** 197
de Soto, Hernando **4** 510-511
Ponce de León, Juan **12** 391-392
Indian wars
McGillivray, Alexander **10** 412
see also Seminole Wars
legislators
Rohde, Ruth Bryan Owen
13 252-253
U.S. acquisition
Adams, John Quincy **1** 52-54
Burr, Aaron **3** 156-159
Calhoun, John Caldwell **3** 226-228
Jackson, Andrew **8** 168-172
Monroe, James **11** 111-113
Randolph, John **13** 30

Florida Southern College (Lakeland)
Wright, Frank Lloyd **16** 398-401

Florida State University (Tallahassee)
Ogburn, William Fielding **11** 480

Florida, University of (Gainesville)
Woodward, Comer Vann **16** 378-379

Floridablanca, Count of (José Moñino y
Redondo; 1728-1808), Spanish statesman
Charles III **3** 454-455
Goya y Lucientes, Francisco de Paula
José de **6** 476-478

Floridante (opera)
Handel, George Frederick **7** 116-119

Florindo and Daphne (opera)
Handel, George Frederick **7** 116-119

Florio, John (1553?-1625), English lexicographer
Hakluyt, Richard **7** 70
Montaigne, Michel Eyquem de
11 116-117

FLORY, PAUL (1910-1985), American
chemist and educator **5** 492-494

Flos (book)
Fibonacci, Leonardo **5** 434-435

Floss der Medusa, Das (oratorio)
Henze, Hans Werner **7** 314

Flotsam (novel)
Remarque, Erich Maria **13** 91

Flour milling (United States)
Evans, Oliver **5** 338
Pillsbury, Charles Alfred **12** 304

Flourens, Pierre Jean Marie (1794-1867),
French physiologist
Lashley, Karl Spencer **9** 214-215

Fluorescence (physics)
Mössbauer, Rudolf **11** 208-209

Flourishing Beauties of the Present Day
(prints)
Utamaro, Kitagawa **15** 397

Flow my tears (song)
Dowland, John **5** 90

Flower Fables (book)
Alcott, Louisa May **1** 122

Flower King's Warning, The (book)
Sol Ch'ong **14** 325-326

Flower, W.H. (1831-1899), English zoologist
Huxley, Thomas Henry **8** 77-79

Flowering Judas (stories)
Porter, Katherine Anne **12** 406-407

Flowering Peach, The (play)
Odets, Clifford **11** 470-471

Flowering Wilderness (novel)
Galsworthy, John **6** 189-190

Flowers of Evil
see Fleurs du mal, Les

Flowers of the North (poems)
Fréchette, Louis-Honoré **6** 77-78

FLOYD, CARLISLE (born 1926), American composer of operas **5** 494-496

Fluorescence (physics)
Cherenkov, Pavel Alekseevich **3** 502-503

Fluorescent lamp
Edison, Thomas Alva **5** 206-208
Tesla, Nikola **15** 156-157

Fluorine (element; chemistry)
Avogadro, Lorenzo Romano Amedeo Carlo **1** 388-389
Davy, Humphry **4** 426-427

Fluoroscope (instrument)
Edison, Thomas Alva **5** 206-208

Fluxus Group (German art group)
Beuys, Joseph **2** 246-248

Flying Cloud (ship)
McKay, Donald **10** 416-417

Flying Doctor Service (Australia)
Flynn, John **5** 497-498

Flying Dutchman, The (opera; Wagner)
Dallapiccola, Luigi **4** 377-378
Wagner, Richard **16** 40-43

Flying Inn, The (songs)
Chesterton, Gilbert Keith **3** 508-509

Flying Tigers (United States airmen)
Chiang Kai-shek **3** 510-513

FLYNN, ELIZABETH GURLEY (1890-1964), American labor organizer **5** 496-497

FLYNN, JOHN (1880-1951), founder and superintendent of the Australian Inland Mission **5** 497-498

FM
see Frequency modulation

FNRS (balloon)
Piccard, Auguste **12** 297-298

FNRS 2 (bathyscaphe)
Piccard, Auguste **12** 297-298

FOCH, FERDINAND (1851-1929), French marshal **5** 498-499
Clemenceau, Georges **4** 99-101
Pershing, John Joseph **12** 243-244
Pétain, Henri Philippe **12** 250-252
Poincaré, Raymond **12** 366-368

Focus (novel)
Miller, Arthur **11** 25-26

Fog (poem)
Sandburg, Carl **13** 461-462
Seferis, George **14** 84-85

Fog Horns (painting)
Dove, Arthur Garfield **5** 86-87

Fog Warning, The (painting)
Homer, Winslow **7** 468-469

Fogg, Phineas, (literary character)
Verne, Jules **15** 467-469

Foix, Germaine de (1488-1538), queen of Aragon and Naples
Ferdinand V **5** 417-418

Fokine, Michel (1880-1942), Russian-American choreographer
Stravinsky, Igor Fedorovich **14** 502-506

FOLEY, TOM (born 1929), Democratic representative from the state of Washington and Speaker of the U.S. House of Representatives (1989-1995) **5** 499-501

Folies-Bergère (Paris)
Ziegfeld, Florenz **16** 516-517

Folk art
Johnson, William H. **8** 320-322

Folk music
Brazil
Villa-Lobos, Heitor **15** 496-497
Cuba
Guillén, Nicolás **7** 34-35
Czechoslovakia
Dvořák, Antonin **5** 168-169
Janáček, Leoš **8** 219
Smetana, Bedřich **14** 281-282
England
Britten, Benjamin **3** 10-11
Vaughan Williams, Ralph **15** 446-447
Germany
Arnim, Achim von **1** 308-309
Hungary
Bartók, Béla **2** 35-36-406
Kodály, Zoltán **9** 71
Liszt, Franz **9** 445-447
Israel
Ben-Haim, Paul **2** 161-162
Mexico
Chávez, Carlos **3** 486
Poland
Szymanowski, Karol **15** 67-68
Russia
Borodin, Aleksandr Profirevich **2** 422-423
Glinka, Mikhail Ivanovich **6** 369-370
Spain
Albéniz, Issac **1** 108-109

Falla, Manuel de **5** 372-373
United States (19th century)
Foster, Stephen Collins **6** 25-27
Gottschalk, Louis Moreau **6** 463-464
United States (20th century)
Baez, Joan **1** 433-435
Copland, Aaron **4** 227-228
Cotten, Elizabeth **4** 261-263
Dawson, William Levi **4** 427-428
Dett, Robert Nathaniel **4** 512
Guthrie, Woodrow Wilson **7** 51-52
Handy, William Christopher **7** 123-124
Harris, Roy **7** 175-176
Ives, Charles Edward **8** 159-160
Seeger, Pete **14** 83-84
Still, William Grant **14** 455-456

Folklore (literature)
Calvino, Italo **3** 243-244
Gregory, Augusta **6** 535-536
Grimm, Jakob and Wilhelm Karl **7** 3-4
Herskovits, Melville Jean **7** 345
Hurston, Zora Neale **8** 55-56
Kemal, Yashar **8** 489-491
Laurence, Margaret **9** 229-230
see also Fable (literature); Fairy tale (literature); Mythology

Follow the Fleet (film score)
Berlin, Irving **2** 200-201

Following the Equator (book)
Twain, Mark **15** 363-366

Folsom, Marion B. (1893-1976), American politician
Eisenhower, Dwight David **5** 233-236

Foma Gordeyev (novel)
Gorky, Maxim **6** 458-460

Fon (West African people)
Burton, Richard **3** 163-164

Fond youth is a bubble (musical composition)
Tallis, Thomas **15** 91

FONDA, JANE (born 1937), actress whose career included films, television, exercise videocassettes, and writing **5** 501-502

Fondo de Cultura Económica (publishing house)
Cosio Villegas, Daniel **4** 260-261

Fonseca, Gulf of (Pacific Ocean)
Pedrarias **12** 179

Fonseca, Hermes da (1855-1923), Brazilian president 1910-14
Barbosa, Ruy **1** 503-504

Fonseca, Manoel Deodoro da
see Deodoro da Fonseca, Manoel

FONSECA, RUBEM (born 1925), Brazilian author **5** 502-504

Fontainebleau (art college)
see Barbizon school

Fontainebleau, château of (France)
Cellini, Benvenuto **3** 391-392
Gabriel, Ange Jacques **6** 160-161

Le Nôtre, André **9** 328-329
Primaticcio, Francesco **12** 453-454
Rosso, Il **13** 312-313
see also Bibliothèque Nationale

Fontanebleu, Edict of (1540)
Francis I **6** 40-43

Fontamara (novel)
Silone, Ignazio **14** 231-232

Fontana, Carlo (1634-1714), Italian architect
Gibbs, James **6** 301-302
Hildebrandt, Johann Lucas von
7 380-381
Juvara, Filippo **8** 396-397

Fontana de oro, La (novel)
Galdós, Benito Pérez **6** 177-178

Fontana, Domenico (1543-1607), Italian architect
Maderno, Carlo **10** 117-118
Porta, Giacomo della **12** 402-403

Fontana, Giovanni (1540-1614), Italian architect
Maderno, Carlo **10** 117-118

Fontana Maggiore (Perugia)
Pisano, Giovanni **12** 324-325
Pisano, Nicola **12** 325

Fontana, Niccolo
see Tartaglia, Niccolo

FONTANE, THEODOR (1819-1898), German author **5** 504
Mann, Thomas **10** 204-207

Fontanes, Louis de (1757-1821), French statesman and author
Chateaubriand, Vicomte de **3** 477-479

Fontanin, Daniel de (literary character)
Martin du Gard, Roger **10** 295-296

Font-de-Gaume (French commune)
Breuil, Henri Edouard Prosper
2 521-522

Fonte Gaia (sculpture)
Quercia, Jacopo della **12** 509

Fontenelle, Bernard Le Bovier de
(1657-1757), French man of letters
Leibniz, Gottfried Wilhelm von
9 307-310

Fotenoy, battle of (1745)
Amherst, Jeffery **1** 200-201

FONTEYN, DAME MARGOT (Margaret "Peggy" Hookham; 1919-1991), classical ballerina who devoted her career to the Royal Ballet in England **5** 504-505

Food and Agriculture Organization (United Nations)
Bruce of Melbourne, 1st Viscount
3 61-62
Orr, John Boyd **12** 4-5

Food and Drug Administration (United States)
Kessler, David A. **8** 523-524
Wiley, Harvey Washington **16** 277-278
see also Pure Food and Drug Act

Food for Centaurs (poems)
Graves, Robert Ranke **6** 504-506

Food for Peace (United States program)
McGovern, George Stanley **10** 412-414

Food industry
Goldsmith, James Michael **6** 409-411

Food industry leaders
see Business and industrial leaders— food industry

Food industry reforms (United States)
Hatch, William Henry **7** 196
Sinclair, Upton Beale Jr. **14** 248-249
see also Pure Food and Drug Act

Food Stamp Program (United States)
Johnson, Lyndon Baines **8** 308-312

Fool and a Girl, A (play)
Griffith, David Wark **6** 544-545

Foolish Virgins (print)
Schongauer, Martin **14** 26-28

Fool's Errand... (novel)
Tourgée, Albion Winegar **15** 277-278

Fool's Love, A (novel)
Tanizaki, Junichiro **15** 101-102

FOOT, MICHAEL (born 1913), left-wing journalist and British Labour Party member of Parliament **5** 505-507

Football (sport)
Bryant, Paul **3** 82-83
Lombardi, Vince **9** 491-492
Montana, Joe **11** 120-121
Rockne, Knute **13** 231
Thorpe, Jim **15** 209-211

Foote, Andrew Hull (1806-1863), American commodore
Canot, Theodore **3** 262-263

Foote, Irene
see Castle, I. and V.

Foote, Samuel (1720-1777), English actor and playwright
Sheridan, Richard Brinsley **14** 183-184

For America (political organization)
McCormick, Robert Rutherford
10 401-402

For My People (poetry collection)
Walker, Margaret **16** 67

For Once, Then Something (poem)
Frost, Robert Lee **6** 130-133

For the Good of the Cause (story)
Solzhenitsyn, Alexander Isayevich
14 330-332

For the Term of His Natural Life (novel)
Clarke, Marcus Andrew Hislop **4** 87-88

For the Union Dead (book)
Lowell, Robert Trail Spence Jr. **10** 16-17

For Whom the Bell Tolls (book)
Donne, John **5** 60-61
Hemingway, Ernest Miller **7** 274-277

For You Departed (book)
Paton, Alan Stewart **12** 134-135

Foraker, Joseph (1946-1917), American politician
McKinley, William **10** 418-420

Forbes (magazine)
Forbes, Malcolm **5** 508-509

Forbes, Charles
see Montalembert, Comte de

Forbes, George (1869-1947), New Zealand prime minister
Ngata, Apirana Turupa **11** 374-375

FORBES, JOHN (1710-1759), British general **5** 507-508

FORBES, MALCOLM (1919-1990), American businessman and publisher
5 508-509

FORBES, ROBERT BENNET (1804-1889), American merchant and shipowner
5 509-510

Forbidden Forest, The (book)
Eliade, Mircea **5** 249-250

Forbidden Love (opera)
Wagner, Richard **16** 40-43

Forbidden Paradise (film)
Lubitsch, Ernst **10** 18-19

Force Bill (United States; 1890s)
Lodge, Henry Cabot **9** 482-483

Force of Destiny (play)
Saavedra, Angel de **13** 398

Forced labor (society)
Clarke, Marcus Andrew Hislop **4** 87-88
Cromer, 1st Earl of **4** 317
Diagne, Blaise **4** 527
Las Casas, Bartolomé de **9** 211-212
Turgot, Anne Robert Jacques
15 348-349
Wakefield, Edward Gibbon **16** 48-49
see also Serf; Slavery

Forces of a Street (painting)
Boccioni, Umberto **2** 353-354

Ford, Betty (born 1921; United States; First Lady)
Ford, Gerald **6** 2-5

Ford, Edsel (1893-1943), American industrialist
Ford, Henry **6** 5-6

FORD, FORD MADOX (1873-1939), English author and editor **6** 1-2
Callaghan, Edward Morley **3** 229-230
Conrad, Joseph **4** 205-207
Lawrence, David Herbert **9** 247-248
Stein, Gertrude **14** 414-415

FORD, GERALD (Leslie Lynch King, Junior; born 1913), U.S. Republican vice president (1973) and president (1974-1976)
6 2-5
Boorstin, Daniel J. **2** 398-400
Cheney, Richard B. **3** 497-499
Moynihan, Daniel Patrick **11** 216-218
Rockefeller, Nelson Aldrich **13** 228-230
Schlesinger, James Rodney **14** 15-16
Weinberger, Casper Willard **16** 177-178

FORD, HENRY (1863-1947), American industrialist **6** 5-6
    Baruch, Bernard Mannes **2** 42-43
    Carver, George Washington **3** 346-347
    Chrysler, Walter Percy **4** 36-37
    Edison, Thomas Alva **5** 206-208
    Firestone, Harvey Samuel **5** 452-453
    Hapgood, Norman **7** 137-138
    see also Ford Motor Co.

FORD, HENRY, II (born 1917), American industrialist **6** 6-7

FORD, JOHN (1586-1639?), English playwright **6** 7-8
    Dekker, Thomas **4** 465-466

FORD, JOHN SEAN O'FEENEY (circa 1890-1973), American film director **6** 8-9
    Goldwyn, Samuel **6** 416
    Ray, Satyajit **13** 60-61

FORD, PAUL LEICESTER (1865-1902), American bibliographer and novelist **6** 9-10

Ford, Richard (1796-1858), English author
    Ferdinand VII **5** 418-420

Ford Foundation (established 1936)
    Bundy, McGeorge **3** 122-124
    Ford, Henry **6** 5-6
    Hutchins, Robert Maynard **8** 68-69

Ford in the Forest of Fontainebleau (painting)
    Corot, Jean Baptiste Camille **4** 247-249

Ford Motor Co. (automobile firm)
    Durant, William Crapo **5** 158
    Ford, Henry **6** 5-6
    Ford, Henry II **6** 6-7
    Fuller, Richard Buckminster **6** 149-150
    Iacocca, Lido (Lee) Anthony **8** 86-88
    Knudsen, William S. **9** 67-68
    McNamara, Robert S. **10** 429-431
    Reuther, Walter Philip **13** 107-108
    Ruth, George Herman Jr. **13** 384
    Sloan, Alfred Pritchard Jr. **14** 274

Ford Museum (Dearborn, Michigan)
    Ford, Henry **6** 5-6

Fordham University (New York City)
    Hess, Victor Francis **7** 362-363
    McCloskey, John **10** 395
    Mead, Margaret **10** 438-440

Fordney-McCumber Tariff Bill (1922)
    Carver, George Washington **3** 346-347

Ford's Theater (Washington D.C.)
    Booth, John Wilkes **2** 404

Fordun, John of (died circa 1384), Scottish chronicler
    Macbeth **10** 81

Foreign Legion (French)
    Staël, Nicolas de **14** 392

Foreign Legion (Spanish)
    Franco Bahamonde, Francisco **6** 52-54

Forel, Auguste Henri (1848-1931), Swiss entomologist and psychiatrist
    Kokoschka, Oskar **9** 75-76

Forelle, Die (musical composition)
    Schubert, Franz Peter **14** 35-37

Forest Hymn, A (poem)
    Bryant, William Cullen **3** 83-85

Forest is Young ... (musical composition)
    Nono, Luigi **11** 420-421

Forest of Fontainebleau, Bas-Bréau (painting)
    Rousseau, Théodore **13** 328

Forest, The (play; Ostrovsky)
    Meyerhold, Vsevolod Emilievich **10** 539

Forest, The (sculpture)
    Nevelson, Louise **11** 356-357

Forey, Élie Frédéric (1804-1872), French general
    Maximilian of Hapsburg **10** 358-360

Forgács, Ferenc (died 1615), Hungarian bishop
    Pázmány, Péter **12** 164-165

Forge of Vulcan (painting)
    Velázquez, Diego Rodríguez de Silva y **15** 454-456

Forged Classics ... (book)
    K'ang Yu-wei **8** 426-428

Forget Not Yet (poem)
    Wyatt, Thomas **16** 410-411

Forgiveness and Law (book)
    Bushnell, Horace **3** 171-172

Forgotten First Citizen: John Bigelow (biography)
    Clapp, Margaret Antoinette **4** 71-72

Forkbeard, Sweyn I
    see Swein

Forli (Italian city-state)
    Julius II **8** 384-386

Form (Platonism)
    Plato **12** 345-347
    Plotinus **12** 358-359

Formaldehyde (chemistry)
    Hofmann, August Wilhelm von **7** 441-442

Formalism (mathematics)
    Tarski, Alfred **15** 110-111
    Wittgenstein, Ludwig **16** 350-351

FORMAN, JAMES (born 1928), writer, journalist, political philosopher, and leader of the Student Nonviolent Coordinating Committee **6** 10-11

Formantes (musical composition)
    Halffter, Christóbal **7** 79-80

Formosa (Taiwan; island; China)
    Ito, Hirobumi **8** 153-155
    Joffre, Joseph Jacques Césaire **8** 267-268
    K'ang-hsi **8** 423-426
    see also China, Republic of

Fornovo, battle of (1495)
    Charles VIII **3** 462-463
    Mantegna, Andrea **10** 215-216

FORREST, EDWIN (1806-1872), American actor **6** 11-12
    Bird, Robert Montgomery **2** 281-282
    Booth, Edwin **2** 401-402

FORREST, JOHN (1st Baron Forrest of Bunbury; 1847-1918), Australian explorer and politician **6** 12-13
    Giles, Ernest **6** 317-318

FORREST, NATHAN BEDFORD (1821-1877), American Confederate general **6** 13-14

FORRESTAL, JAMES VINCENT (1892-1949), American statesman **6** 14

FORSTER, EDWARD MORGAN (1879-1970), English novelist and essayist **6** 14-16
    Woolf, Virginia Stephen **16** 381-382

Forsyte Saga, The (novel; Galsworthy)
    Galsworthy, John **6** 189-190
    Mann, Thomas **10** 204-207

Forsyth, John (1780-1841), American statesman
    Cinque, Joseph **4** 62

Fort Apache (film)
    Ford, John **6** 7-8

Fort Benning (Georgia)
    Marshall, George Catlett **10** 278-279

Fort Bridger (Wyoming)
    Bridger, James **3** 2-3

Fort Buchanan (Arizona)
    Cochise **4** 128

Fort Caroline (Florida)
    Menéndez de Avilés, Pedro **10** 499-500

Fort Christina (Delaware)
    Minuit, Peter **11** 50

Fort Clatsop (Oregon)
    Lewis, Meriwether **9** 391-392

Fort Conger (Arctic)
    Greely, Adolphus Washington **6** 517-518

Fort Cumberland (French and Indian wars)
    Braddock, Edward **2** 474-475

Fort Donelson (Tennessee)
    Forrest, Nathan Bedford **6** 13-14
    Grant, Ulysses Simpson **6** 492-494
    Sherman, William Tecumseh **14** 186-187

Fort Donelson, battle of (1862)
    Weaver, James Baird **16** 151-152

Fort Dunmore (Virginia)
    Dunmore, 4th Earl of **5** 147

Fort Duquesne, battles of (French and Indian wars)
    Braddock, Edward **2** 474-475
    Forbes, John **5** 507-508
    Franklin, Benjamin **6** 60-64
    Gist, Christopher **6** 352-353
    Morgan, Daniel **11** 160-161

Fort Fisher (North Carolina)
    Dewey, George **4** 520

Fort Henry (Montana)
Smith, Jedediah S. **14** 294-295

Fort Henry (Tennessee)
Grant, Ulysses Simpson **6** 492-494
Sherman, William Tecumseh
14 186-187

Fort Hill (South Carolina)
Calhoun, John Caldwell **3** 226-228

Fort Liberty (Ohio valley)
Girty, Simon **6** 350

Fort Mackinac (Michigan Territory)
Beaumont, William **2** 95-96

Fort Mandan (North Dakota)
Lewis, Meriwether **9** 391-392

Fort Maurepas (Biloxi, Mississippi)
Iberville, Sieur d' **8** 90-91

Fort Mims (Alabama)
Crockett, David **4** 314-316

Fort Necessity (Pennsylvania)
Gist, Christopher **6** 352-353
Lewis, Andrew **9** 376-377

Fort Niagara (New York State)
Johnson, William **8** 319-320

Fort Pillow Massacre (Tennessee; 1864)
Forrest, Nathan Bedford **6** 13-14

Fort Riley (Kansas)
Hickok, James Butler **7** 374-375

Fort Sill (Oklahoma)
Park, Chung Hee **12** 99-102

Fort Saint David (India)
Dupleix **5** 153

Fort Saint Philip, siege of (1781-1782)
Murray, James **11** 261-262

Fort Stanwix, battle of (1777)
Johnson, John **8** 305-306

Fort Stanwix, Treaty of (1768)
Johnson, William **8** 319-320

Fort Sumter (Charleston, South Carolina)
Beauregard, Pierre Gustave Toutant
2 96-97
Douglas, Stephen Arnold **5** 80-82
Lincoln, Abraham **9** 415-418
Ruffin, Edmund **13** 354-355

Fort Ternan (village; Kenya)
Leakey, Louis Seymour Bazett **9** 262

Fort Ticonderoga, battles of
1775 (American Revolutionary War)
Allen, Ethan **1** 163-164
Arnold, Benedict **1** 309-310
1777 (American Revolutionary War)
Burgoyne, John **3** 137-138
Kościuszko, Tadeusz Andrzej
Bonawentura **9** 88
Schuyler, Philip John **14** 49-50
St. Clair, Arthur **13** 429-430
French and Indian wars
Amherst, Jeffery **1** 200-201
Carver, Jonathan **3** 347-348
Gage, Thomas **6** 169-170

Montcalm de Saint-Véran, Marquis
de **11** 122-123

Fort Vancouver
see Vancouver (city; Washington state)

Fort William Henry, siege of (1757)
Carver, Jonathan **3** 347-348
Montcalm de Saint-Véran, Marquis de
11 122-123

Fort Worth (city; Texas)
Noguchi, Isamu **11** 416-418

FORTAS, ABE (1910-1982), noted civil libertarian who served four years on the Supreme Court (1965-1969) **6** 16-17
Arnold, Thurman Wesley **1** 314

Forte di San Andrea a Lido (Venice)
Sanmicheli, Michele **13** 469-470

Forteguerri, Niccolo (Carteromace; 1674-1735), Italian cardinal and poet
Verrocchio, Andrea del **15** 471-472

FORTEN, JAMES (1766-1842), African American abolitionist and inventor
6 17-18
Douglass, Frederick **5** 85-86

Fortenay, battle of (1744)
Gage, Thomas **6** 169-170

Fortitude (painting)
Botticelli, Sandro **2** 439-440

Fortner, Wolfgang (1907-1987), German composer
Henze, Hans Werner **7** 314

Fortnightly Review (periodical)
Harris, Frank **7** 172-173
Morley, John **11** 178-179
Pater, Walter Horatio **12** 130-131
Wells, Herbert George **16** 195-196

Fortunata y Jacinta (novel)
Galdós, Benito Pérez **6** 177-178

Fortunate Mistress, The (novel)
Defoe, Daniel **4** 457-459

Fortune (magazine)
Agee, James **1** 78-79
Luce, Henry Robinson **10** 23-24
MacLeish, Archibald **10** 109-110

FORTUNE, TIMOTHY THOMAS
(1856-1928), African American journalist
6 18-21

Fortune Teller, The (painting)
Caravaggio **3** 282-284

Fortunes and Misfortunes of the Famous Moll Flanders
see Moll Flanders

Fortunes of Nigel, The (novel)
Scott, Walter **14** 68-70

Fortunes of Richard Mahony (trilogy)
Richardson, Henry Handel **13** 139

Forty Fort (Pennsylvania)
Butler, John **3** 180

Forty-five Minutes from Broadway (play)
Cohan, George Michael **4** 137-138

Forty-niners
see California-gold rush (1849)

42nd Parallel, The (novel)
Dos Passos, John Roderigo **5** 69-71

Forty-two Articles of Religion (treatise)
Cranmer, Thomas **4** 295-296
Edward VI **5** 213-214

Forward (ship)
Nansen, Fridtjof **11** 304-305

Forza del destino, La (opera)
Verdi, Giuseppe Fortunino Francesco
15 463-465

Foscarini, Marco (1696-1763), Italian statesman
Piranesi, Giovanni Battista **12** 321-322

FOSCOLO, UGO (1778-1827), Italian author, poet, and patriot **6** 21

FOSDICK, HARRY EMERSON
(1878-1969), American Presbyterian minister **6** 21-22
Rauschenbusch, Walter **13** 53-54

FOSSE, BOB (1927-1987), American director, choreographer, and dancer **6** 22-23

FOSSEY, DIAN (1932-1985), world's leading authority on the mountain gorilla
6 23-24

Fossils
see Paleontology

FOSTER, ABIGAIL KELLEY (1810-1887), American reformer **6** 25

Foster, John W. (1836-1917), American statesman
Dulles, John Foster **5** 134-135
Lansing, Robert **9** 200

FOSTER, STEPHEN COLLINS (1826-1864), American composer **6** 25-27
Christy, Edwin P. **4** 34-35
Fry, William Henry **6** 136-137
Ives, Charles Edward **8** 159-160

FOSTER, WILLIAM ZEBULON
(1881-1961), American Communist party leader **6** 27-28
Browder, Earl Russell **3** 30-31

Fothergill, John (1712-1780), British physician
Bartram, William **2** 41-42
Waterhouse, Benjamin **16** 131-132

Fo-t'u-teng (flourished 4th century), Chinese Buddhist monk
Shih Le **14** 195
Tao-an **15** 103-104

FOUCAULT, JEAN BERNARD LÉON
(1819-1868), French physicist **6** 28-29
Fizeau, Hippolyte Armand Louis **5** 475

FOUCAULT, MICHEL (1926-1984), French philosopher, critic, and historian **6** 29-30

FOUCHÉ, JOSEPH (1759-1820), French statesman **6** 30-31
Napoleon I **11** 306-310

Foundation for the Advancement of Teaching (United States)
Carnegie, Andrew **3** 309-312

Foundation Trilogy, The
Asimov, Isaac **1** 338-341

Foundling Hospital (painting)
Wilson, Richard **16** 329-330

Foundling, The (novel)
Spellman, Francis Joseph **14** 367

Fountain (ready-made)
Duchamp, Marcel **5** 122-123

Fountain of Arethusa (musical composition)
Szymanowski, Karol **15** 67-68

Fountain of Bakhchisarai, The (poem)
Pushkin, Aleksandr Sergeevich **12** 489-491

Fountain of the Great Lakes (Chicago)
Taft, Lorado **15** 75-76

Fountain of the Innocents (sculpture)
Goujon, Jean **6** 466-467
Lescot, Pierre **9** 354

Fountain of the World's Four Corners (sculpture)
Carpeaux, Jean Baptiste **3** 318-319

Fountain of Time (Chicago)
Taft, Lorado **15** 75-76

Fountain of Youth (mythology)
Ponce de León, Juan **12** 391-392

Fountain of Youth (painting)
Cranach, Lucas the Elder **4** 289-290

Fountain, The (play)
O'Neill, Eugene **11** 514-516

Fountains of Rome (tone poem)
Respighi, Ottorino **13** 103-104

FOUQUET, JEAN (ca. 1420- ca. 1480), French painter **6** 31
Clouet, Jean and François **4** 122-123

Fouquet, Nicolas (1615-1680), French superintendent of finance
La Fontaine, Jean de **9** 156-157
Le Brun, Charles **9** 269-270
Le Nôtre, André **9** 328-329
Le Vau, Louis **9** 360-361
Louis XIV **9** 531-533

Four Ages of Man, The (poem)
Bradstreet, Anne Dudley **2** 486-487

Four Apostles (painting)
Dürer, Albrecht **5** 159-161

Four Black Revolutionary Plays (book)
Baraka, Imamu Amiri **1** 498-499

Four Church Fathers (altarpiece)
Pacher, Michael **12** 53

Four Elements, The (poem)
Bradstreet, Anne Dudley **2** 486-487

Four Great Masters (Chinese art)
see Huang Kung-wang; Ni Tsan; Wang Meng; Wu Chen

Four Hundred, Council of (Athens)
Solon **14** 327-328

400 Blows, The (film)
Truffaut, François **15** 311-313

Four Hymns (poem)
Spenser, Edmund **14** 373-376

Four Legends of Lemminkäinen (musical composition)
Sibelius, Jean Julius Christian **14** 211-212

Four Million, The (stories)
Henry, O. **7** 308-309

Four Philosophers (painting)
Rubens, Peter Paul **13** 339-342

Four Prentices of London, The (play)
Heywood, Thomas **7** 373-374

Four Quartets (poems; Eliot)
Eliot, Thomas Stearns **5** 258-261
Stravinsky, Igor Fedorovich **14** 502-506

Four Rows, The (Jewish code)
Caro, Joseph ben Ephraim **3** 316-317

Four Saints in Three Acts (opera)
Stein, Gertrude **14** 414-415
Thomson, Virgil **15** 202-203

Four Seasons of the Year, The (poem)
Bradstreet, Anne Dudley **2** 486-487

Four Sons (film)
Ford, John **6** 7-8

Four Stages of Cruelty (print)
Hogarth, William **7** 446-447

Four Stations of the Cross (sculpture relief)
Manzù, Giacomo **10** 224-225

Four Temperaments, The (musical composition)
Nielsen, Carl August **11** 388-389

Four Treasuries (anthology)
Qianlong **12** 502-505

Four Zoas, The (poem)
Blake, William **2** 316-318

Fourberies de Scapin, Les (play)
Molière **11** 86-88

Fourcroy, Antoine François de (1755-1809), French chemist
Lavoisier, Antoine Laurent **9** 241-244

FOURIER, FRANÇOIS CHARLES MARIE (1772-1837), French socialist writer **6** 31-32
Chernyshevsky, Nikolai Gavrilovich **3** 504-505
Engels, Friedrich **5** 286-288
Herzen, Aleksandr Ivanovich **7** 351-352
Proudhon, Pierre Joseph **12** 461-463
see also Fourierism

FOURIER, BARON JEAN BAPTISTE JOSEPH (1768-1830), French mathematical physicist **6** 32-33
Cauchy, Augustin Louis **3** 378-380
Lagrange, Joseph Louis **9** 164-166

Fourierism (political philosophy)
Brisbane, Albert **3** 9

Dana, Charles Anderson **4** 384-385
Fourier, François Charles Marie **6** 31-32

Four-Power Peace Pact (1933)
Daladier, Édouard **4** 369

Foursquare Gospel, International Church of the (Angelus Temple)
McPherson, Aimee Semple **10** 434

Fourteen Points (United States politics; 1918)
Ho Chi Minh **7** 426-428
House, Edward Mandell **7** 520-521
Lippmann, Walter **9** 439-440
Mao Zedong **10** 225-227
Paderewski, Ignace Jan **12** 56-57
Wilson, Thomas Woodrow **16** 330-332

14th Amendment
see Constitution of the United States—Amendments

Fourteenth of July, The (play)
Rolland, Romain **13** 260

Fourth Dynasty (Egypt; circa 2613-2494 B.C.)
Khufu **8** 540-541

Fourth Gospel (New Testament)
see John, Gospel according to Saint

4th of July, The (symphony)
Ives, Charles Edward **8** 159-160

Fowey (frigate)
Dunmore, 4th Earl of **5** 147

FOWLES, JOHN (born 1926), English novelist **6** 33-35

Fox (ship)
Franklin, John **6** 64-65
McClintock, Francis Leopold **10** 394-395

Fox and the Camellias, The (novel)
Silone, Ignazio **14** 231-232

FOX, CHARLES JAMES (1749-1806), English parliamentarian **6** 35-37
associates
George IV **6** 272-273
Johnson, Samuel **8** 315-317
North, Frederick **11** 429-430
opponents
Boswell, James **2** 432-434
George III **6** 270-272
Pitt, William the Younger **12** 329-331
supporters
Burgoyne, John **3** 137-138
Grey, Charles **6** 539-540
Melbourne, 2nd Viscount **10** 468-469
Sheridan, Richard Brinsley **14** 183-184
Wilberforce, William **16** 269-270

Fox, Dixon Ryan (1887-1945), American historian
Schlesinger, Arthur Meier **14** 13

FOX, GEORGE (1624-1691), English spiritual reformer **6** 37-38
Boehme, Jacob **2** 357

Bradford, William (printer) **2** 475-476
Bunyan, John **3** 128-129

Fox, Henry (1st Baron Holland;
1705-1774), English statesman
Fox, Charles James **6** 35-37

Fox Indians (North America)
Black Hawk **2** 308

Fox River (Wisconsin)
Jolliet, Louis **8** 328-329

Fox, Sir William (1812-1893), New
Zealand statesman
Vogel, Julius **16** 9-10

Fox, The (novelette)
Lawrence, David Herbert **9** 247-248

Fracasados, Los (novel)
Azuela, Mariano **1** 402

Fractals (mathematics)
Mandelbrot, Benoit B. **10** 189-191

Fragmenta aurea (poems)
Suckling, John **15** 10-11

FRAGONARD, JEAN HONORÉ
(1732-1806), French painter **6** 38-39
Chardin, Jean Baptiste Siméon
3 442-443
Renoir, Pierre Auguste **13** 101-102

Frain Castle (Vranov, Moravia)
Rottmayr, Johann Michael **13** 321

Fram (ship)
Nansen, Fridtjof **11** 304-305

Frame of Government (Pennsylvania;
1682)
Penn, William **12** 200-202

Framley Parsonage (novel)
Trollope, Anthony **15** 300-302

Frammento (musical composition)
Bussotti, Sylvano **3** 174-175

Frana allo scalo Nord (play)
Betti, Ugo **2** 246

Franc, Martin le (1410-1461), French poet
Dufay, Guillaume **5** 125-126

FRANCE, ANATOLE (1844-1924), French
novelist **6** 39-40
Ford, Ford Madox **6** 1-2
Proust, Marcel **12** 465-467

France (French Republic; nation, Western
Europe)

• 51 B.C.-A.D. 987 (ANCIENT - CAR-
OLINGIAN)
51 B.C.- 481 A.D. (Roman)
see Gaul
481-751 (Merovingians)
Clovis I **4** 124
Gregory of Tours **6** 534-535
Martel, Charles **10** 285
751-987 (Carolingians)
Charlemagne **3** 445-447
Leo III **9** 330-332
Louis I **9** 522-523
see also Roncesvalles, battle of
(778)

• 987-1328 (CAPETIAN)
Crown prestige
Louis VI **9** 523-524
Louis IX **9** 525-526
Philip II (king of France)
12 268-269
Philip IV **12** 274
Crusades
see Crusades
English wars
Eleanor of Aquitaine **5** 246-247
Henry I **7** 286-287
Henry II **7** 287-289
Henry III **7** 290-292
Innocent, III **8** 125-127
John **8** 274-275
Louis VI **9** 523-524
Louis VII **9** 524-525
Philip II **12** 268-269
Richard I **13** 130
William I **16** 290-291
papacy and
Boniface VIII **2** 392-393
Clement V **4** 101-102
Edward I **5** 208-210
Philip IV **12** 274
see also Avignon Papacy
see also Capetian dynasty

• 1328-1589 (VALOIS)
Burgundy and
Charles the Bold **3** 467-469
Comines, Philippe de **4** 181
Louis XI **9** 526-528
England and
Henry VII **7** 300-302
Henry VIII **7** 302-305, 206
Louis XII **9** 528-529
Franco-Hapsburg wars
Charles V **3** 457-459
Charles VIII **3** 462-463
Francis I **6** 40-43, 184
Hundred Years War
Charles V **3** 459-460
Charles VI **3** 460-461
Charles VII **3** 461-462
Gloucester, Duke of **6** 370-371
Henry V **7** 296-297
Henry VI **7** 298-299
Joan of Arc **8** 264-265
John II **8** 275-276
Philip VI **12** 277-278
see also Hundred Years War
Italian wars
Charles VIII **3** 462-463
Comines, Philippe de **4** 181
Louis XII **9** 528-529
papacy and
Julius II **8** 384-386
Leo X **9** 332-334
royal authority
Francis I **6** 40-43
Louis XI **9** 526-528
Scotland and
Elizabeth I **5** 263-266
Mary, I **10** 308-309

Wars of Religion (1562-1598)
Coligny, Gaspard de **4** 159-160
Medici, Catherine de'
10 445-449
see also Religion, Wars of

• 1589-1789 (BOURBONS)
1589-1610 (Henry IV)
Henry IV **7** 293-295
see also Edict of Nantes; Reli-
gion, Wars of
1610-43 (Louis XIII)
Charles, I **3** 450-452
Louis XIII **9** 529-531
Richelieu, Armand Jean du
Plessis de **13** 142-144
see also Thirty Years War
1643-1715 (Louis XIV)
Colbert, Jean Baptiste **4** 142-143
Condé, Prince de **4** 193-194
Cromwell, Oliver **4** 317-320
Louis XIV **9** 531-533
Mazarin, Jules **10** 379-380
see also Augsburg, War of the
League of (1688-1697); Dutch
wars—1672-78; Fronde, Wars
of the (1649-1653); Spanish
Succession, War of the
(1701-1714); Thirty Years War
(1614-1648)
1715-1774 (Louis XV)
Law, John **9** 244-245
Louis XV **9** 533-534
Orléans, Philippe II D'
11 530-531
Rochambeau, Comte de
13 220-221
Saxe, Comte de **13** 507-508
see also Austrian Succession,
War of the (1740-1748); Polish
Succession, War of the
(1733-1735); Seven Years War
(1756-1763)
1774-92 (Louis XVI)
Louis XVI **9** 534-535
Marie Antoinette **10** 258-259
Necker, Jacques **11** 330-331
Rochambeau, Comte de
13 220-221
Turgot, Anne Robert Jacques
15 348-349
see also American Revolution;
French Revolution

• 1789-1815 (REVOLUTion—1ST
EMPIRE)
1789-99 (Revolution-Directory)
see French Revolution
(1789-1799)
1792-1802 (French Revolutionary
Wars)
see French Revolutionary Wars
1799-1804 (Consulate)
Barras, Vicomte de **2** 19
Bonaparte, Joseph **2** 381-382
Bernadotte, Jean Baptiste
2 205-206
Fouché, Joseph **6** 30-31
Murat, Joachim **11** 253-254

Napoleon I **11** 306-310
Say, Jean Baptiste **13** 508-509
Sieyès, Comte Emmanuel Joseph
14 217-218
Talleyrand, Charles Maurice de
15 89-90
1803-15 (Napoleonic Wars)
see Napoleonic Wars
1804-14 (1st Empire)
Barras, Vicomte de **2** 19
Bonaparte, Joseph **2** 381-382
Bonaparte, Louis **2** 382-383
Fouché, Joseph **6** 30-31
Murat, Joachim **11** 253-254
Napoleon I **11** 306-310
Ney, Michel **11** 372-373
Stendhal **14** 422-425
Talleyrand, Charles Maurice de
15 89-90
see also Vienna, Congress of
(1814-1815)
1815
see Hundred Days
• 1815-70 (BOURBONS-2ND EMPIRE)
1815-30 (Bourbon Restoration)
Canning, George **3** 258-260
Charles X **3** 463-464
Fouché, Joseph **6** 30-31
Guizot, François Pierre Guil-
laume **7** 40-41
Lafayette, Marquis de **9** 151-152
Louis XVIII **9** 535-536
Sieyès, Comte Emmanuel Joseph
14 217-218
Talleyrand, Charles Maurice de
15 89-90
Wellington, 1st Duke of
16 193-195
see also Revolution of 1830
(France; July Revolution)
1830-48 (Orléans, or July, Monar-
chy)
Blanc, Louis **2** 318-319
Blanqui, Louis Auguste
2 323-324
Charles X **3** 463-464
Daumier, Honoré Victorin
4 403-405
Guizot, François Pierre Guil-
laume **7** 40-41
Hugo, Victor Marie **8** 22-25
Ibrahim Pasha **8** 97-98
Louis Philippe **9** 536-537
Stendhal **14** 422-425
Thiers, Louis Adolphe
15 181-182
see also Revolution of 1848
(France; February Revolution)
1848-52 (2nd Republic)
Blanc, Louis **2** 318-319
Lamartine, Alphonse Marie Louis
de **9** 173-175
Napoleon III **11** 310-312
1852-70 (2nd Empire)
Blanqui, Louis Auguste
2 323-324

Courbet, Jean Desiré Gustave
4 271-273
Garibaldi, Giuseppe **6** 215-217
Montalembert, Comte de
11 118-119
Napoleon III **11** 310-312
Thiers, Louis Adolphe
15 181-182
see also Crimean War;
Franco-Prussian War
(1870-1871)
• 1870-1940 (3RD REPUBLIC)
created (1870)
Gambetta, Léon **6** 198-199
Napoleon III **11** 310-312
Simon, Jules François
14 237-238
Thiers, Louis Adolphe
15 181-182
Dreyfus Affair
see Dreyfus Affair
Entente Cordiale (1904)
Balfour, Arthur James **1** 469-470
Delcassé, Théophile **4** 478-479
interwar years
Bourgeois, Léon **2** 450-451
Briand, Aristide **2** 528-529
Daladier, Édouard **4** 369
Herriot, Édouard **7** 339-340
Laval, Pierre **9** 237-238
Leopold III **9** 347-348
Pétain, Henri Philippe
12 250-252
Poincaré, Raymond **12** 366-368
see also Kellogg-Briand Pact
(1928); League of Nations;
Munich Conference (1938);
Washington Conference
(1921-1922)
overseas empire
Clemenceau, Georges **4** 99-101
Ferry, Jules François Camille
5 430
Marchand, Jean-Baptiste
10 234-237
see also French Overseas Empire
papacy and
Benedict XV **2** 153-154
Leo XIII **9** 334-336
Paris Commune
see Commune of Paris—1871
Prussian war
see Franco-Prussian War; Frank-
furt, Treaty of
Socialist movement
Blanqui, Louis Auguste
2 323-324
Blum, Léon **2** 343-344
Briand, Aristide **2** 528-529
Jaurès, Jean **8** 226-227
see also Socialism—France
Triple Entente (1907)
Berchtold, Leopold von
2 183-184
Delcassé, Théophile **4** 478-479
Poincaré, Raymond **12** 366-368
U.S.S.R. and

Herriot, Édouard **7** 339-340
Litvinov, Maxim Maximovich
9 451-452
World War I
see Versailles, Treaty of (1919);
World War I
• 1940-46 (WORLD WAR II TO 4TH
REPUBLIC)
Free French
Baker, Josephine **1** 448-451
De Gaulle, Charles André Joseph
Marie **4** 463-465
Eboué, Adolphe Felix Sylvestre
5 194
Leclerc, Jacques Philippe
9 272-273
Mendès France, Pierre
10 492-493
Mitterrand, François **11** 63-66
Saint-Exupéry, Antoine de
13 431-432
see also French Resistance
Vichy regime
Barbie, Klaus **1** 501-503
Laval, Pierre **9** 237-238
Maurras, Charles Marie Photius
10 350-351
Pétain, Henri Philippe
12 250-252
Vichy regime critics
Daladier, Édouard **4** 369
Herriot, Édouard **7** 339-340
Houphouët-Boigny, Felix
7 519-520
World War II
see World War II
• SINCE 1946
1946-58 (4th Republic)
Blum, Léon **2** 343-344
De Gaulle, Charles André Joseph
Marie **4** 463-465
Dulles, John Foster **5** 134-135
Franco Bahamonde, Francisco
6 52-54
Mendès France, Pierre
10 492-493
Mitterrand, François **11** 63-66
Monnet, Jean **11** 109-110
Schuman, Robert **14** 41
Youlou, Fulbert **16** 466-467
see also Cold War; Common
Market; French Overseas
Empire; North Atlantic Treaty
Organization; United Nations;
Vietnam War (1946-1954)
since 1959 (5th Republic)
Balladur, Edouard **1** 474-475
Barre, Raymond **2** 19-20
Chirac, Jacques **4** 2-3
De Gaulle, Charles André Joseph
Marie **4** 463-465
Delors, Jacques **4** 484-486
Fabius, Laurent **5** 358-359
Giscard d'Estaing, Valéry
6 350-352
Kennedy, John Fitzgerald
8 502-506

Mendès France, Pierre
  10 492-493
Mitterrand, François **11** 63-66
Pompidou, Georges **12** 389-390
Rocard, Michel **13** 218-220
student protests (1968)
  Cohn-Bendit, Daniel **4** 140-141
see also Church and State
  (France); Franco-Flemish
  music, French architecture;
  French art; French literature;
  French music

France Antartique (French colony; Brazil;
1565-67)
  Sá, Mem de **13** 395

France Champagne (poster)
  Bonnard, Pierre **2** 395-396

France de demain, La (periodical)
  Bonvalot, Pierre Gabriel Édouard **2** 396

France, Jean de
  see Berry, 1st Duke of

Francesca (sculpture)
  Manzù, Giacomo **10** 224-225

Francesca da Rimini (play)
  D'Annunzio, Gabriele **4** 388

Francesco Sassetti and His Son (painting)
  Ghirlandaio, Domenico **6** 292-293

Franche-Comté (historical region; Eastern
Central France)
  Condé, Prince de **4** 193-194
  Louis XIV **9** 531-533

Franchise
  see Suffrage

Francia
  see France

Francia, Francesco (circa 1450-circa 1517),
Italian painter
  Parmigianino **12** 117

Francia, José Rodriguez (circa 1761-1840),
Paraguayan dictator
  López, Carlos Antonio **9** 506-507

Francia, Louis (1772-1839), French painter
  Bonington, Richard Parkes **2** 394-395

Franciabigio (1482-1525), Italian painter
  Andrea del Sarto **1** 224-225
  Ronsard, Pierre de **13** 271-273

Francione, Il (1428-1495), Italian architect
  Sangallo family **13** 464-466

Francis Charles (1802-1878), archduke of
Austria
  Francis Joseph **6** 45-46

FRANCIS FERDINAND (1863-1914), archduke of Austria **6** 44
  Berchtold, Leopold von **2** 183-184

FRANCIS I (1494-1547), king of France
1515-1547 **6** 40-43 art patronage
  Andrea del Sarto **1** 224-225
  Cellini, Benvenuto **3** 391-392
  Leonardo da Vinci **9** 337-340
  Lescot, Pierre **9** 354
  Primaticcio, Francesco **12** 453-454

Rosso, Il **13** 312-313
and education
  Budé, Guillaume **3** 102-103
  Ramus, Petrus **13** 27-28
court
  Clouet, Jean and François **4** 122-123
  Coligny, Gaspard de **4** 159-160
  Ronsard, Pierre de **13** 271-273
exploration
  Cartier, Jacques **3** 343-344
  Verrazano, Giovanni da **15** 470-471
foreign policy
  Charles V **3** 457-459, 501
  Henry VIII **7** 302-305
  Northumberland, Duke of
    11 431-432
  Suleiman I **15** 20-21
  Wolsey, Thomas **16** 364-366
relatives
  Louis XII **9** 528-529
  Medici, Catherine de' **10** 445-449
religious affairs
  Calvin, John **3** 239-242
  Leo X **9** 332-334
  Paul III **12** 144-145

Francis I (1708-1765), Holy Roman emper-
or 1745-1765
  Leopold II **9** 346
  Louis XVI **9** 534-535

Francis I (emperor of Austria)
  see Francis II (Holy Roman emperor)

Francis II (1435-1488), duke of Brittany
1459-1488
  Charles VIII **3** 462-463

Francis II (1544-1560), king of France
1559-1560
  Clouet, Jean and François **4** 122-123
  Henry IV **7** 293-295
  Mary, I **10** 308-309
  Medici, Catherine de' **10** 445-449
  Somerset, Duke of **14** 333-334

FRANCIS II (1768-1835), Holy Roman
emperor 1792-1806 and emperor of Aus-
tria 1804-1835 **6** 43-44
  Ferdinand II **5** 415-416
  Francis Joseph **6** 45-46
  Leopold II **9** 346
  Metternich, Klemens von **10** 533-536
  Napoleon I **11** 306-310

FRANCIS JOSEPH (1830-1916), emperor of
Austria 1868-1916 and king of Hungary
1867-1916 **6** 45-46
  Deák, Francis **4** 431-432
  Freud, Sigmund **6** 103-106
  Horthy de Nagybánya, Nicholas
    7 510-512
  Maximilian of Hapsburg **10** 358-360
  Metternich, Klemens von **10** 533-536

Francis, Lydia Maria
  see Child, Lydia Maria Francis

Francis of Angoulême
  see Francis I (king of France)

FRANCIS OF ASSISI, SAINT (1182-1226),
Italian mystic and religious founder
6 46-47
  Bonaventure **2** 383-384
  John of Piano Carpini **8** 284
  Machiavelli, Niccolò **10** 97-99
  Serra, Junípero **14** 111-112
  see also Franciscans

FRANCIS OF SALES, SAINT (1567-1622),
French bishop **6** 47
  Neri, Philip **11** 340

Francis Renouncing His Patrimony (fresco)
  Giotto **6** 342-345

Francis Sauveur (novel)
  Walras, Marie Esprit Léon **16** 84-85

Francis Stephen of Lorraine, Duke
  see Francis I (Holy Roman emperor)

FRANCIS XAVIER, SAINT (1506-1552),
Spanish Jesuit missionary **6** 48
  Damien **4** 383
  Mendes Pinto, Fernao **10** 493-494

Franciscans (Order of Friars Minor) in alle-
gory
  Langland, William **9** 194-195
American missions
  Marcos de Niza **10** 240
  Serra, Junípero **14** 111-112
and papacy
  Innocent, III **8** 125-127
  John of Piano Carpini **8** 284
foundation and theology
  Bonaventure **2** 383-384
  Duns Scotus, John **5** 149-150
  Francis of Assisi **6** 46-47
poverty issue
  Bacon, Roger **1** 425-427
  Bonaventure **2** 383-384
  Jacopone da Todi **8** 194
  Thomas Aquinas **15** 183-186
  William of Ockham **16** 298-299

FRANCK, CÉSAR (1822-1890), French
composer **6** 48-49
  Sessions, Roger Huntington **14** 117-118

FRANCK, JAMES (1882-1964), German
physicist **6** 49-52
  Heisenberg, Werner Karl **7** 261-263
  Planck, Max Karl Ernst Ludwig
    12 342-344
  Szilard, Leo **15** 64-66
  Urey, Harold Clayton **15** 394-396

Franck, Salamon (1659-1725), German
poet
  Bach, Johann Sebastian **1** 416-419

Francke, August Hermann (1663-1727),
German pietistic preacher
  Wieland, Christoph Martin **16** 260-261

FRANCO BAHAMONDE, FRANCISCO
(1892-1975), Spanish general and dicta-
tor **6** 52-54
  Alfonso XIII **1** 151
  Gómez, Juan Vicente **6** 417-418
  Ibárruri Gómez, Dolores **8** 88-90
  Juan Carlos I **8** 368-369

Mussolini, Benito **11** 272-274
Pius XI **12** 337-339
Salazar, António de Oliveira
13 442-443
Unamuno y Jugo, Miguel de
15 386-387
see also Civil War, Spanish

FRANCO OF COLOGNE (Franco of Paris;
flourished circa 1250-1260), French
music theorist **6** 52

Franco-American Convention (1800)
Gerry, Elbridge **6** 282-283

Franco-Flemish music (15th-16th century)
Gombert, Nicolas **6** 416-417
Isaac, Heinrich **8** 143-144
Josquin des Prez **8** 361-363
Lassus, Roland de **9** 216-218
Palestrina, Giovanni Pierluigi da
12 70-72
Senfl, Ludwig **14** 105-106
Willaert, Adrian **16** 287-288

Franco-German War
see Franco-Prussian War

Franconian house (Germany)
see Salian emperors

Franco-Prussian War (1870-1871) England
and
Victoria **15** 485-487
French forces
Faidherbe, Louis Léon César
5 366-367
Foch, Ferdinand **5** 498-499
Garibaldi, Giuseppe **6** 215-217
Joffre, Joseph Jacques Césaire
8 267-268
Peter I **12** 256
Rousseau, Henri **13** 323-324
French strategy
Gambetta, Léon **6** 198-199
Napoleon III **11** 310-312
Sorel, Albert **14** 346-347
in literature
Fontane, Theodor **5** 504
Taine, Hippolyte Adolphe **15** 82-83
Zola, Émile **16** 526-528
influence of
Blanqui, Louis Auguste **2** 323-324
Courbet, Jean Desiré Gustave
4 271-273
Krupp **9** 109-111
Pasteur, Louis **12** 125-127
opponents
Schindler, Solomon **14** 7-8
Simon, Jules François **14** 237-238
Prussian forces
Bismarck, Otto Eduard Leopold von
2 294-296
Hindenburg, Paul Ludwig Hans von
Beneckendorff und von **7** 400-401
Koch, Heinrich Hermann Robert
9 69-70
Moltke, Helmuth Karl Bernard von
11 90-91
U.S. and
Barton, Clara **2** 37-39

Howe, Julia Ward **7** 535-536
Lieber, Francis **9** 401-402
Morgan, Junius Spencer **11** 166-167

Franco-Thai War (1893)
Chulalongkorn **4** 43-45

Francs-Juges, Les (opera)
Berlioz, Louis Hector **2** 203-205

Frangulis, A.F. (1888-1975), Greek diplomat
Titulescu, Nicolae **15** 246-247

Frank (novel)
Edgeworth, Maria **5** 205-206

FRANK, ANNE (1929-1945), 16-year-old
holocaust victim who kept a famous diary
6 54-56

Frank, Bruno (1887-1945), German poet
Mann, Thomas **10** 204-207

Frank, Ilya Mikhailovich (1908-1990),
Russian physicist
Cherenkov, Pavel Alekseevich
3 502-503

Frank, Lawrence K, (1890-1968), American
educator
Erikson, Erik Homburger **5** 309-310

Frank V (play)
Dürrenmatt, Friedrich **5** 164-165

FRANKENTHALER, HELEN (born 1928),
American painter **6** 56-57
Hofmann, Hans **7** 442-443
Noland, Kenneth **11** 418-419

Frankfurt, Congress of (1848-1849)
Döllinger, Josef Ignaz von **5** 47-48

Frankfurt School (intellectual movement)
Adorno, Theodor W. **1** 65-67

Frankfurt, Treaty of (1871)
Bismarck, Otto Eduard Leopold von
2 294-296
Clemenceau, Georges **4** 99-101
Moltke, Helmuth Karl Bernard von
11 90-91
Thiers, Louis Adolphe **15** 181-182
William I **16** 292-293
see also Franco-Prussian War
(1870-1871)

Frankfurt, University of (Germany)
philosophy and religion
Habermas, Jürgen **7** 58-60
social sciences
Buber, Martin **3** 87-89
Habermas, Jürgen **7** 58-60
Mannheim, Karl **10** 208-209
Tillich, Paul Johannes **15** 224-225
Wertheimer, Max **16** 207-208
sciences
Bethe, Hans Albrecht **2** 238-239
Born, Max **2** 420-421
Stern, Otto **14** 435
Weidenreich, Franz **16** 171-172

FRANKFURTER, FELIX (1882-1965), American jurist **6** 57
civil liberties
Black, Hugo Lafayette **2** 301-303

Jackson, Robert Houghwout
8 182-183
friends
Acheson, Dean Gooderham **1** 37-38
Cohen, Morris Raphael **4** 139-140
Evatt, Herbert Vere **5** 341-343
Laski, Harold J. **9** 215-216
quoted
Cardozo, Benjamin Nathan
3 288-290
Hand, Billings Learned **7** 116

Frankish empire
see Holy Roman Empire

Frankland, Edward (1825-1899), English
chemist
Bunsen, Robert Wilhelm **3** 124-125

FRANKLIN, ARETHA (born 1942), African
American singer and songwriter **6** 58-60

FRANKLIN, BENJAMIN (1706-1790),
American statesman, diplomat, and
inventor **6** 60-64
biographers
Ford, Paul Leicester **6** 9-10
Sparks, Jared **14** 363
Weems, Mason Locke **16** 170
colonial politics
Braddock, Edward **2** 474-475
Dickinson, John **4** 543-544
Galloway, Joseph **6** 186-187
Hutchinson, Thomas **8** 71-72
diplomacy
Carroll, John **3** 331-332
Deane, Silas **4** 435-437
Jefferson, Thomas **8** 238-241
Lee, Arthur **9** 288-289
friends
Hopkinson, Francis **7** 496-497
Houdon, Antoine **7** 516-517
Peale, Charles Willson **12** 169-171
Smith, Adam **14** 283-284
influence of
Ingenhousz, Jan **8** 119-120
Jones, John Paul **8** 337-338
McGuffey, William Holmes
10 414-415
Paine, Thomas **12** 66-67
Sarmiento, Domingo Faustino
13 484-485
Smith, William **14** 301
Steuben, Frederick William Augustus
von **14** 438-439
influenced by
Mather, Cotton **10** 330-332
Winthrop, John **16** 341-342
journalism
Bradford, William **2** 477
relatives
Bache, Alexander Dallas **1** 420
Franklin, William **6** 69-70
scientific studies
Galvani, Luigi **6** 194-195
Lamarck, Chevalier de **9** 171-173
Priestley, Joseph **12** 452-453
see also American Revolution

Franklin, District of (Arctic region)
Franklin, John **6** 64-65

FRANKLIN, JOHN HOPE (born 1915), pioneer African American historian **6** 65-67

FRANKLIN, MILES (1879-1954), Australian novelist **6** 68-69
Clarke, Marcus Andrew Hislop **4** 87-88

FRANKLIN, ROSALIND ELSIE (1920-1958), British physical chemist and molecular biologist **6** 67-68

FRANKLIN, SIR JOHN (1786-1847), English explorer **6** 68-69
Kennedy, John Pendleton **8** 506-507
McClintock, Francis Leopold **10** 394-395
Ross, James Clark **13** 302-303

FRANKLIN, WILLIAM (circa 1731-1813), American colonial administrator **6** 69-70
Franklin, Benjamin **6** 60-64

Franklin, William Temple (1760-1823), American writer
Adams, John **1** 48-51

Franklin and Marshall College (Lancaster, Pennsylvania)
Nevin, John Williamson **11** 357

Franklin Evans (novel)
Whitman, Walt **16** 249-251

Franklin stove (iron fireplace)
Franklin, Benjamin **6** 60-64

Franks (German tribe)
see France—481-751, 751-987; Holy Roman Empire—800-840

Franz Josef
see Francis Joseph

Franz, Shephard Ivory (1874-1933), American psychologist
Lashley, Karl Spencer **9** 214-215

Franziska (literary character)
Lessing, Gotthold Ephraim **9** 357-359

FRAP (political group; Chile)
Frei Montalva, Eduardo **6** 94-95

Frasch, Herman (1851-1914), American chemist
Rockefeller, John Davison **13** 226-228

FRASER (PINTER), LADY ANTONIA (born 1932), popular British biographer, historian, and mystery novelist **6** 70-71

FRASER, MALCOLM (born 1930), prime minister of Australia (1975-1983) **6** 71-73

FRASER, PETER (1884-1950), New Zealand prime minister 1940-49 **6** 73-74
Savage, Michael Joseph **13** 501-502

Fraser River (Canada)
Fraser, Simon **6** 74-75
Mackenzie, Alexander **10** 103-104

FRASER, SIMON (1776-1862), Canadian explorer and fur trader **6** 74-75

Fraser's Magazine (periodical)
Carlyle, Thomas **3** 304-305
Ruskin, John **13** 371-372

Thackeray, William Makepeace **15** 159-161

Frate 'nnammorato, Lo (opera)
Pergolesi, Giovanni Battista **12** 218-219

Fraternity (novel)
Galsworthy, John **6** 189-190

Fratricides, The (novel)
Kazantzakis, Nikos **8** 466-468

Frau Bauman, Frau Schmidt, and Frau Schwartze (poem)
Roethke, Theodore **13** 243-244

Frau Beate und ihr Sohn (novel)
Schnitzler, Arthur **14** 23-24

Frau Jenny Treibel (novel)
Fontane, Theodor **5** 504

Frau ohne Schatten, Die (opera)
Hofmannsthal, Hugo von **7** 443-444
Strauss, Richard **14** 500-501

Frau Sorge (novel)
Sudermann, Hermann **15** 12-13

Frauenliebe und Leben (musical composition)
Schumann, Robert Alexander **14** 41-43

Fräulein Else (story)
Schnitzler, Arthur **14** 23-24

Fraunhofer equatorial telescope (astronomy)
Struve, Friedrich Georg Wilhelm von **14** 513

FRAUNHOFER, JOSEPH VON (1787-1826), German physicist **6** 75-76
Bunsen, Robert Wilhelm **3** 124-125
Rowland, Henry Augustus **13** 330-331

Fraunhofer lines (physics)
Fraunhofer, Joseph von **6** 75-76
Kirchhoff, Gustav Robert **9** 33-34

Fray Hortensio Paravicino (painting)
Greco **6** 511-514

Frazer, Joseph W. (1892-1971), American industrialist
Kaiser, Henry John **8** 412-413

FRAZER, SIR JAMES GEORGE (1854-1941), Scottish classicist and anthropologist **6** 76
Malinowski, Kaspar Bronislaw **10** 170-171

FRAZIER, EDWARD FRANKLIN (1894-1962), African American sociologist **6** 77
Herskovits, Melville Jean **7** 345

FRÉCHETTE, LOUIS-HONORÉ (1839-1908), French-Canadian poet **6** 77-78
Crémazie, Octave **4** 305-306

Frédéric et Bernerette (story)
Musset, Louis Charles Alfred de **11** 271-272

Frederick (king of Bohemia)
see Frederick V (elector Palatin)

FREDERICK I (1123-1190), Holy Roman emperor 1152-1190 **6** 78-79
and Italy
Arnold of Brescia **1** 314-315
Innocent, III **8** 125-127
Manuel I **10** 218-219
histories of
Otto of Freising **12** 30
in art
Tiepolo, Giovanni Battista **15** 219-220
Third Crusade
Philip II **12** 268-269

Frederick I (1657-1713), king of Prussia 1701-1713 and elector of Brandenburg 1688-1701
Frederick William I **6** 86-87
Schlüter, Andreas **14** 18-19
Spencer, Herbert **14** 369-370
Stahl, Georg Ernst **14** 392-393
Thomasius **15** 193-194

Frederick II (1090-1147), duke of Swabia 1105-1147
Frederick I **6** 78-79

FREDERICK II (1194-1250), Holy Roman emperor 1215-1250 **6** 79
and papacy
Innocent, III **8** 125-127
Rudolf I **13** 347-348
court
Pisano, Nicola **12** 325
Thomas Aquinas **15** 183-186
Vogelweide, Walther von der **16** 10-11
relatives
Frederick I **6** 78-79
Peter III **12** 256-257

FREDERICK II (1712-1786), king of Prussia 1740-1786 **6** 81-84
and Austria
Joseph II **8** 359-360
Maria Theresa **10** 256-258
and the arts
Bach, Carl Philipp Emanuel **1** 414-415
Bach, Johann Sebastian **1** 416-419
Houdon, Antoine **7** 516-517
La Mettrie, Julien Offray de **9** 179-180
Voltaire **16** 14-16
army
Blücher, Gebhard Leberecht von **2** 340-341
Scharnhorst, Gerhard Johann David von **13** 521-522
Steuben, Frederick William Augustus von **14** 438-439
biographers
Carlyle, Thomas **3** 304-305
Gooch, George Peabody **6** 432-433
Lavisse, Ernest **9** 241
influenced by
Beccaria, Marchese di **2** 97-98
Frederick William **6** 85-86
mathematicians

Euler, Leonard **5** 331-332
Wolff, Christian von **16** 358

FREDERICK III (1415-1493), Holy Roman
emperor and German king 1440-1493
6 84-85
Charles the Bold **3** 467-469
Pius II **12** 331

Frederick III (1463-1525), elector and duke
of Saxony 1486-1525
Cranach, Lucas the Elder **4** 289-290
Hofhaimer, Paul **7** 441
Luther, Martin **10** 48-51
Walter, Johann **16** 86

Frederick III (1609-1670), king of Denmark
and Norway 1648-1670
Charles XII **3** 464-466

Frederick III (1831-1888), king of Prussia
and German emperor 1888
Bismarck, Otto Eduard Leopold von
2 294-296
Victoria **15** 485-487
William I **16** 292-293
William II **16** 294-295

Frederick III (duke of Saxony)
see Frederick III (elector of Saxony)

Frederick III (duke of Swabia)
see Frederick I (Holy Roman emperor)

Frederick III (elector of Brandenburg-Prus-
sia)
see Frederick I (king of Prussia)

Frederick III (emperor of Germany)
see Frederick III (king of Prussia)

Frederick IV (1671-1730), king of Denmark
and Norway 1699-1730
Charles XII **3** 464-466

Frederick V (1596-1632), elector of Palatin
1610-1623 and king of Bohemia
1619-1620
Buckingham, 1st Duke of **3** 93-94
Charles, I **3** 450-452

Frederick V (archduke of Austria)
see Frederick III (Holy Roman emperor)

Frederick Augustus I-II (elector of Saxony)
see Augustus II-III (king of Poland)

Frederick Barbarossa
see Frederick I (Holy Roman emperor)

Frederick Henry (1584-1647), prince of
Orange-Nassau and Dutch stadtholder
1625-1647
Maurice of Nassau **10** 348-349
Rembrandt Harmensz van Rijn
13 91-95
Van Dyck, Anthony **15** 423-425

Frederick Louis (1707-1751), prince of
Wales
Bolingbroke, Viscount **2** 374-375
George II **6** 269-270
George III **6** 270-272

Frederick of Hohenstaufen
see Frederick II (Holy Roman emperor)

Frederick the Great
see Frederick II (king of Prussia)

Frederick the Winter King
see Frederick V (elector of Palatin)

Frederick the Wise
see Frederick III (elector of Saxony)

FREDERICK WILLIAM (1620-1688), elector
of Brandenburg 1640-1688 **6** 85-86
John III **8** 276-277
Pufendorf, Samuel von **12** 477-478
Schlüter, Andreas **14** 18-19

Frederick William (died 1711), duke of
Courland
Anna Ivanovna **1** 240-241

FREDERICK WILLIAM I (1688-1740), king
of Prussia 1713-1740 **6** 86-87
Frederick II **6** 81-84
Frederick William **6** 85-86
Wolff, Christian von **16** 358

Frederick William II (1744-1797), king of
Prussia 1786-1797
Beethoven, Ludwig van **2** 114-117
Frederick II **6** 81-84
Frederick William III **6** 87
Mozart, Wolfgang Amadeus
11 218-221

FREDERICK WILLIAM III (1770-1840),
king of Prussia 1797-1840 **6** 87
associates
Alexander I **1** 130-132
Metternich, Klemens von
10 533-536
ministers
Hardenberg, Karl August von
7 146-147
Stein, Heinrich Friedrich Karl vom
und zum **14** 415-416
relatives
Frederick William IV **6** 87-88
William I **16** 292-293
state architect
Schinkel, Karl Friedrich **14** 8

FREDERICK WILLIAM IV (1795-1861),
king of Prussia 1840-1861 **6** 87-88
political appointees
Bismarck, Otto Eduard Leopold von
2 294-296
Moltke, Helmuth Karl Bernard von
11 90-91
relatives
Frederick William III **6** 87
William I **16** 292-293

Fredericksburg, battle of (1862)
Barton, Clara **2** 37-39
Davis, Jefferson **4** 416-418
Jackson, Shirley Ann **8** 183-184
Lee, Robert Edward **9** 292-294
Meade, George Gordon **10** 440-441
Stuart, James Ewell Brown **14** 515-516

Fredericq, Paul (1850-1920), Flemish historian
Pirenne, Jean Henri Otto Lucien Marie
12 322-323

Fredriksten, siege of (1718)
Charles XII **3** 464-466

Free African Society (United States)
Allen, Richard **1** 168

Free and Accepted Masons
see Freemasonry

Free association (psychology)
Freud, Sigmund **6** 103-106

Free Church of Scotland
Chalmers, Thomas **3** 408-409
McCosh, James **10** 402-403

Free companies (English soldiers)
Edward III **5** 211-212
Edward the Black Prince **5** 217-218

Free Democratic party (Germany)
Brandt, Willy **2** 499-500
Erhard, Ludwig **5** 302-304
Hamm-Brücher, Hildegard **7** 101-103
Lambsdorff, Otto Graf **9** 177-179

Free Education Act (England; 1891)
Salisbury, 3d Marquess of **13** 448-449

Free Enquirers (new Harmony, Indiana)
Owen, Robert Dale **12** 40-41

Free fall, law of (physics)
Galileo Galilei **6** 180-183

Free French (World War II)
see France—1940-46

Free Joe (stories)
Harris, Joel Chandler **7** 173-174

Free Lance, The (opera)
Sousa, John Philip **14** 353-354

Free love
Kollontai, Aleksandra Mikhailovna **9** 79
Wright, Frances **16** 397-398

Free Man, A (novel)
Barrès, Auguste Maurice **2** 20-21

Free Negro Family, The (book)
Frazier, Edward Franklin **6** 77

Free Russian Press (London)
Herzen, Aleksandr Ivanovich **7** 351-352

Free Soil party (United States)
1848 election
Adams, Charles Francis **1** 41-42
Burlingame, Anson **3** 144-145
Polk, James Knox **12** 374-376
Van Buren, Martin **15** 410-411
formed
Andrew, John Albion **1** 230-231
Dana, Richard Henry Jr. **4** 385-386
Sumner, Charles **15** 30-31
state elections
Chase, Salmon Portland **3** 473-475
Mann, Horace **10** 202-204
Sumner, Charles **15** 30-31
Wade, Benjamin Franklin **16** 38-39
supporters
Blair, Francis Preston **2** 313-315
Field, David Dudley **5** 439-440
Greeley, Horace **6** 515-517

Free Soul, A (film)
Barrymores **2** 28-30

Free Space (paper)
Tsiolkovsky, Konstantin Eduardovich
15 326-328

Free Synagogue (New York City)
Wise, Stephen Samuel **16** 344-345

Free trade (economics)
Australia
Parkes, Henry **12** 113
Britain
Balfour, Arthur James **1** 469-470
Disraeli, Benjamin **5** 27-29
Jevons, William Stanley **8** 255-256
Liverpool, 2nd Earl of **9** 456-457
Peel, Robert **12** 181-183
Smith, Adam **14** 283-284
Sydenham, Thomas **15** 59-60
France
Colbert, Jean Baptiste **4** 142-143
Turgot, Anne Robert Jacques
15 348-349
United States
Carey, Henry Charles **3** 294-295
List, Georg Friedrich **9** 443-444
Lloyd, Henry Demarest **9** 468-469
see also Tariff

Free verse (literature)
Laforgue, Jules **9** 160-161
Rimbaud, Jean Nicolas Arthur
13 172-174
Whitman, Walt **16** 249-251

Free-bank movement (United States)
Hildreth, Richard **7** 382

FREED, JAMES INGO (born 1930), American architect **6** 88-90

Freedmen's Bureau (United States; 1865-72)
Armstrong, Samuel Chapman
1 306-307
Fitzhugh, George **5** 474
Howard, Oliver Otis **7** 528-529
Langston, John Mercer **9** 197
Revels, Hiram Rhoades **13** 109-110
Sumner, Charles **15** 30-31
Trumbull, Lyman **15** 317-318
Turner, Henry McNeal **15** 351-352

Freedmen's Bureau Bill (United States; 1866)
Brown, Benjamin Gratz **3** 32-33
Johnson, Andrew **8** 294-295
Stevens, Thaddeus **14** 442-443
see also Reconstruction (United States)

Freedmen's Hospital (Washington D.C.)
Drew, Charles Richard **5** 100-101
Williams, Daniel Hale **16** 302-303

Freedom (philosophy)
Bakunin, Mikhail Aleksandrovich
1 458-460
Bosanquet, Bernard **2** 425-426
Epictetus **5** 292
Hegel, Georg Wilhelm Friedrich
7 254-256

James, William **8** 215-217
Jansen, Cornelis **8** 220-221

Freedom and People's Rights movement
(Japan, 1881)
Saionji, Kimmochi **13** 438-439

Freedom Bloc (Burma)
Aung San **1** 374-375
Ba Maw **1** 480-481

Freedom of religion
see Religious liberty

Freedom of speech (United States)
Brandeis, Louis Dembitz **2** 496-497
Hand, Billings Learned **7** 116
Holmes, Oliver Wendell Jr. **7** 458-459
Lovejoy, Elijah Parish **10** 6-7
Zenger, John Peter **16** 497-498

Freedom of the press (Spain)
Fernández de Lizardi, José Joaquin
5 424-425

Freedom of the press (Sweden)
Gustavus III **7** 45-46

Freedom of the press (United States)
Bradford, William **2** 476-477
Creel, George **4** 304-305
Hughes, Charles Evans **8** 15-16
Jefferson, Thomas **8** 238-241
Lovejoy, Elijah Parish **10** 6-7
McCormick, Robert Rutherford
10 401-402
Zenger, John Peter **16** 497-498

Freedom or Death (novel)
Kazantzakis, Nikos **8** 466-468

Freedom party (India)
Nehru, Motilal **11** 334-335

Freedom Riders (United States; 1960s)
Farmer, James **5** 383-385
Forman, James **6** 10-11
Henry, Aaron **7** 306-307
Kennedy, John Fitzgerald **8** 502-506
King, Martin Luther Jr. **9** 20-22
Morton, Nelle Katherine **11** 195-197
see also African American history (United States)—Sixties and Seventies

Freedom Walk (Detroit, Michigan; 1963)
King, Martin Luther Jr. **9** 20-22

Freedom's Journal (newspaper)
Russwurm, John Brown **13** 381-382
Walker, David **16** 62-63

FREEH, LOUIS J. (born 1950), director of the Federal Bureau of Investigation (FBI) **6** 90-91

FREEMAN, DOUGLAS SOUTHALL (1886-1953), American journalist **6** 91-92

Freeman, Edward (1823-1892), English historian
Froude, James Anthony **6** 133-134

FREEMAN, ROLAND L. (born 1936), American photographer of rural and urban African Americans **6** 92-93

Freeman's Farm, battle of (1777)
see Saratoga, battles of

Freeman's Journal (newspaper)
Freneau, Philip Morin **6** 99-100
Grattan, Henry **6** 499

Freemasonry (Masonic Fraternity)
Casanova de Seinglat, Giacomo Jacopo Girolamo **3** 350-351
Del Pilar, Marcelo Hilario **4** 486
Karamzin, Nikolai Mikhailovich
8 441-442
Malkam Khan, Mirza **10** 172
Mozart, Wolfgang Amadeus
11 218-221
Pedro II **12** 180-181

Freeshooter, The (opera)
Weber, Carl Maria Friedrich Ernst von
16 156-157

Free-silver issue (United States)
Bryan, William Jennings **3** 80-82
Donnelly, Ignatius **5** 62
McKinley, William **10** 418-420
Straus, Isidor **14** 496
see also Currency; Populist party

Freethinkers (religion)
Condé, Prince de **4** 193-194
Holbach, Baron d' **7** 448-449

FREGE, GOTTLOB (1848-1925), German mathematician and philosopher **6** 93-94
Carnap, Rudolf **3** 308-309
Husserl, Edmund **8** 67-68
Schlick, Friedrich Albert Moritz
14 16-17

FREI MONTALVA, EDUARDO (born 1911), Chilean statesman **6** 94-95
Alessandri Rodriguez, Jorge **1** 129-130

Freiberg, Mining Academy of
Werner, Abraham Gottlob **16** 205-207

Freiburg, University of (Germany)
Eck, Johann Maier von **5** 200
Heidegger, Martin **7** 257-258
Spemann, Hans **14** 368-369
Treitschke, Heinrich von **15** 293-294
Weber, Max **16** 157-160
Weismann, August Freidrich Leopold
16 178-180

Freies Jüdisches Lehrhaus (Frankfurt am Main)
Rosenzweig, Franz **13** 294

Freight Train (song)
Cotten, Elizabeth **4** 261-263

FREIRE, PAULO (born 1921), Brazilian philosopher and educator **6** 95-96

Freire, Ramón (1787-1851), Chilean general and statesman
Portales Plazazuelos, Diego José Víctor
12 404

Freire, Rómulo Gallegos
see Gallegos Freire, Rómulo

Freischütz, Der (opera)
Weber, Carl Maria Friedrich Ernst von
16 156-157

FRELIMO (Mozambique political party)
Chissano, Joaquim Alberto **4** 9-11
see also Mozambique Liberation Front

FRELINGHUYSEN, THEODORUS JACOBUS (1691-circa 1748), Dutch Reformed clergyman and revivalist **6** 96-97
Tennent, Gilbert **15** 143-144

FRÉMONT, JOHN CHARLES (1813-1890), American explorer and politician **6** 97-98
1856 campaign
Bailey, Gamaliel **1** 444-445
Schurz, Carl **14** 44-45
antislavery issue
Brown, Benjamin Gratz **3** 32-33
Lincoln, Abraham **9** 415-418
exploration
Carson, Christopher **3** 334-335
Fitzpatrick, Thomas **5** 474-475
in California
Kearney, Denis **8** 468
Olmsted, Frederick Law **11** 503-504
Stockton, Robert Field **14** 461-462

FRENCH, DANIEL CHESTER (1850-1931), American sculptor **6** 98-99

French, Sir John (Earl of Ypres; 1852-1925), British field marshal
Haig, Douglas **7** 67-68
Jellicoe, John Rushworth **8** 242-243

French Academy (established 1635)
Richelieu, Armand Jean du Plessis de **13** 142-144

French Academy of Sciences (established 1666)
Cuvier, Georges Léopold **4** 357-359
Huygens, Christiaan **8** 79-81

French and Indian War (1754-1763)
American forces
Arnold, Benedict **1** 309-310
Carver, Jonathan **3** 347-348
Franklin, Benjamin **6** 60-64
Lewis, Andrew **9** 376-377
Pepperell, William **12** 206-207
Putnam, Israel **12** 491-492
Rogers, Robert **13** 250-251
Washington, George **16** 126-129
British forces
Amherst, Jeffery **1** 200-201
Braddock, Edward **2** 474-475
Butler, John **3** 180
Clinton, Henry **4** 114-115
Cook, James **4** 214-215
Forbes, John **5** 507-508
Gage, Thomas **6** 169-170
Howe, William **7** 538-539
Montgomery, Richard **11** 138-139
Murray, James **11** 261-262
Wolfe, James **16** 354-355
British-Indian relations
Johnson, William **8** 319-320
Pontiac **12** 393-394
causes
Dinwiddie, Robert **5** 18-19
Howe, Richard **7** 536-537

European phase
see Seven Years War
French forces
Bougainville, Louis Antoine de **2** 443-444
Montcalm de Saint-Véran, Marquis de **11** 122-123
Vaudreuil-Cavagnal, Marquis de **15** 444

French and Indian wars
see French and Indian War; King George's War; King William's War

French architecture
baroque
see Baroque architecture
classical
l'Orme, Philibert de **9** 519
Labrouste, Pierre François Henri **9** 144
Le Vau, Louis **9** 360-361
Lescot, Pierre **9** 354
Mansart, François **10** 211
Mansart, Jules Hardouin **10** 212
Gothic
Montreuil, Pierre de **11** 139
Viollet-le-Duc, Eugène Emmanuel **15** 505-506
landscape
Le Nôtre, André **9** 328-329
modern
Le Corbusier **9** 274-275
Perret, Auguste **12** 233
neobaroque
Garnier, Jean Louis Charles **6** 221-222
neoclassical
Ledoux, Claude Nicolas **9** 277-278
Soufflot, Jacques Germain **14** 349-350
rococo
Boffrand, Gabriel Germain **2** 361
Gabriel, Ange Jacques **6** 160-161

French art
abstract art
Delaunay, Robert **4** 475-476
art brut
Dubuffet, Jean Philippe Arthur **5** 119-120
Barbizon school
see Barbizon school
baroque
Claude Lorrain **4** 89-90
David, Jacques Louis **4** 407-409
La Tour, George de **9** 222
Le Brun, Charles **9** 269-270
Le Nain, Antoine, Louis and Mathieu **9** 321-322
Poussin, Nicolas **12** 418-420
see also Baroque painting (French); Baroque sculpture
cubism
Braque, Georges **2** 504-505
Duchamp-Villon, Raymond **5** 123
Gris, Juan **7** 5-6
Laurens, Henri **9** 230-231

Léger, Fernand **9** 302-303
Picasso, Pablo **12** 292-295
Dada and surrealism
Arp, Jean **1** 317-318
Duchamp, Marcel **5** 122-123
Picabia, Francis **12** 291-292
Tanguy, Yves **15** 101
English influence
Bonington, Richard Parkes **2** 394-395
Fauvism
Derain, André **4** 503
Matisse, Henri **10** 336-337
Rouault, Georges **13** 321-322
van Dongen, Kees **15** 421-422
Vlaminck, Maurice **16** 6
figurative
Balthus **1** 476-477
impressionism
see Impressionism (art)—France
Intimism
Bonnard, Pierre **2** 395-396
Vuillard, Jean Édouard **16** 36
modern sculpture
Maillol, Aristide **10** 150-151
Richier, Germaine **13** 145-146
Rodin, Auguste **13** 236-238
monumental sculpture
Bourdelle, Emile-Antoine **2** 449-450
neoclassicism
see Neoclassicism (art)—France
Op Art
Vasarely, Victor **15** 440-442
postimpressionism
see Postimpressionism (art)
primitivism
Rousseau, Henri **13** 323-324
realism
see Realism (art)—French
Renaissance
see Renaissance (art)—France
rococo
see Rococo-French
romanticism
see Romanticism (art)—French
School of Paris
Chagall, Marc **3** 406-407
Miró, Joan **11** 53-54
Modigliani, Amedeo **11** 72-73
Soulages, Pierre **14** 350-351
Soutine, Chaim **14** 356-357
Staël, Nicolas de **14** 392
symbolism
Brancusi, Constantin **2** 494-496
Puvis de Chavannes, Pierre **12** 492-493
Redon, Odilon **13** 75-76

French Cameroon Trust Territory
see Cameroon Republic

French Community (Africa)
Houphouët-Boigny, Felix **7** 519-520
Senghor, Léopold Sédar **14** 106-107
Touré, Sékou **15** 275-277
Youlou, Fulbert **16** 466-467

French Congo
see Central African Republic; Congo, People's Republic of the

French cuisine
Child, Julia McWilliams **3** 519-520

French Diana, The (poems)
Aragon, Louis **1** 271-272

French Equatorial Africa
see Central African Republic

French Fury (1583)
William the Silent **16** 300-302

French Huguenots
see Huguenots

French Indochina
see Indochina, French

French Lieutenant's Woman, The (novel)
Fowles, John **6** 33-35

French literature
allegory
Guillaume de Lorris **7** 33-34
Jean de Meun **8** 234-235
La Fontaine, Jean de **9** 156-157
baroque
see Baroque literature
chronicles and memoirs
Comines, Philippe de **4** 181
Froissart, Jean **6** 124-125
Joinville, Jean de **8** 325
Saint-Simon, Duc de **13** 436
Villehardouin, Geffroi de **15** 499
criticism
Foucault, Michel **6** 29-30
Dadaist
Picabia, Francis **12** 291-292
drama (17th-18th century)
Corneille, Pierre **4** 234-236
Diderot, Denis **5** 1-2
Lesage, Alain René **9** 353-354
Marivaux, Pierre Carlet de Chamblain de **10** 265-266
Molière **11** 86-88
Racine, Jean Baptiste **12** 532-535
Voltaire **16** 14-16
drama (19th-20th century)
Anouilh, Jean **1** 243-244
Beckett, Samuel **2** 102-104
Camus, Albert **3** 255-257
Cocteau, Jean **4** 132-133
Dumas, Alexandre **5** 136-138
Genet, Jean **6** 262-263
Giraudoux, Jean **6** 349-350
Gourmont, Remy de **6** 475
Ionesco, Eugène **8** 131-132
Rolland, Romain **13** 260
Sartre, Jean Paul **13** 491-492
Sarraute, Nathalie Tcherniak **13** 488-490
Yourcenar, Marguerite **16** 477-479
essays
Giraudoux, Jean **6** 349-350
Gourmont, Remy de **6** 475
La Rochefoucauld, François Duc de **9** 208-209

Malraux, André **10** 178-180
Mirabeau, Comte de **11** 51-52
Montaigne, Michel Eyquem de **11** 116-117
Rousseau, Jean Jacques **13** 324-328
Yourcenar, Marguerite **16** 477-479
literary theory
Boileau-Despréaux, Nicholas **2** 369-371
Kundera, Milan **9** 128-129
Sainte-Beuve, Charles Augustin **13** 438
Sarraute, Nathalie Tcherniak **13** 488-490
Taine, Hippolyte Adolphe **15** 82-83
Nouveau Roman (New Novel)
Sarraute, Nathalie Tcherniak **13** 488-490
novel (16th-18th century)
Diderot, Denis **5** 1-2
La Fayette, Comtesse de **9** 150-151
Prévost, Abbé **12** 445-446
Rabelais, François **12** 524-526
Rousseau, Jean Jacques **13** 324-328
Sade, Comte de **13** 416-418
Voltaire **16** 14-16
novel (19th century)
Balzac, Honoré de **1** 478-480
Barrès, Auguste Maurice **2** 20-21
Daudet, Alphonse **4** 402-403
Dumas, Alexandre **5** 136-138
Flaubert, Gustave **5** 480-482
Goncourt, Edmond de and Jules de **6** 426-427
Hugo, Victor Marie **8** 22-25
Huysmans, Joris Karl **8** 81-82
Maupassant, Henri René Albert Guy de **10** 347
Stendhal **14** 422-425
Verne, Jules **15** 467-469
Zola, Émile **16** 526-528
novel (19th-20th century)
Gourmont, Remy de **6** 475
Loti, Pierre **9** 519-520
Proust, Marcel **12** 465-467
Rolland, Romain **13** 260
novel (20th century)
Barrès, Auguste Maurice **2** 20-21
Beckett, Samuel **2** 102-104
Benda, Julien **2** 151-152
Bernanos, Georges **2** 206-207
Céline, Louis Ferdinand **3** 390-391
Cocteau, Jean **4** 132-133
Colette, Sidonie Gabrielle **4** 158-159
Genet, Jean **6** 262-263
Giraudoux, Jean **6** 349-350
Malraux, André **10** 178-180
Martin du Gard, Roger **10** 295-296
Mauriac, François **10** 347-348
Robbe-Grillet, Alain **13** 189-190
Sartre, Jean Paul **13** 491-492
Sarraute, Nathalie Tcherniak **13** 488-490
Simenon, Georges **14** 233-234
Yourcenar, Marguerite **16** 477-479

poetry (12th-14th century)
Jean de Meun **8** 234-235
Machaut, Guillaume de **10** 93-94
Marie de France **10** 259
Thibaut IV **15** 180-181
Vitry, Philippe de **16** 2
poetry (15th-18th century)
Boileau-Despréaux, Nicholas **2** 369-371
Chénier, André Marie **3** 500-501
du Bellay, Joachim **5** 113-114
La Fontaine, Jean de **9** 156-157
Malherbe, François de **10** 169-170
Orléans, Charles D' **11** 530
Ronsard, Pierre de **13** 271-273
Villon, François **15** 499-501
poetry (19th-20th century)
Apollinaire, Guillaume **1** 260
Claudel, Paul Louis Charles **4** 90-91
Dunbar, William (poet) **5** 142-143
Laforgue, Jules **9** 160-161
Leconte de Lisle, Charles Marie René **9** 273-274
Péguy, Charles Pierre **12** 183-184
Rimbaud, Jean Nicolas Arthur **13** 172-174
Valéry, Paul Ambroise **15** 405-406
poetry (20th century)
Cocteau, Jean **4** 132-133
Perse, Saint-John **12** 242-243
Picabia, Francis **12** 291-292
Rabearivelo, Jean Joseph **12** 523-524
Saint-Exupéry, Antoine de **13** 431-432
Yourcenar, Marguerite **16** 477-479
prophesies
Nostradamus **11** 432-434
romanticism
see Romanticism (literature)
satire
Boileau-Despréaux, Nicholas **2** 369-371
du Bellay, Joachim **5** 113-114
France, Anatole **6** 39-40
La Bruyère, Jean de **9** 145
Lesage, Alain René **9** 353-354
Molière **11** 86-88
Montesquieu **11** 123-125
Rabelais, François **12** 524-526
Voltaire **16** 14-16
surrealism
see Surrealism (literature)
symbolism
Baudelaire, Charles Pierre **2** 61-63
Gide, André **6** 308-309
Gourmont, Remy de **6** 475
Mallarmé, Stéphane **10** 172-173
Valéry, Paul Ambroise **15** 405-406
Verlaine, Paul Marie **15** 465-466
see also Pléiade

French music
ars nova
Machaut, Guillaume de **10** 93-94
Vitry, Philippe de **16** 2

baroque
   see Baroque music
electronic
   Boulez, Pierre **2** 444-445
   Varèse, Edgard **15** 432-433
impressionism
   Debussy, Achille Claude **4** 445-447
   Ravel, Maurice Joseph **13** 54-55
   Roussel, Albert **13** 328-329
Les Six
   Honegger, Arthur **7** 472-473
   Milhaud, Darius **11** 17-18
   Poulenc, Francis **12** 414-415
   Satie, Erik **13** 494-495
Notre Dame School
   Franco of Cologne **6** 52
   Léonin **9** 343-344
   Pérotin **12** 231-232
postimpressionism
   Bizet, Georges **2** 296-297
   Franck, César **6** 48-49
   Gounod, Charles François
      6 473-474
   Offenbach, Jacques **11** 478-479
   Saint-Saëns, Charles Camille
      13 435-436
Renaissance
   see Renaissance(music)—France
romanticism
   Berlioz, Louis Hector **2** 203-205
   Cherubini, Luigi Carlo Zanobi Sal-
      vatore Maria **3** 505-506
   Chopin, Frédéric François **4** 16-18
   Meyerbeer, Giacomo **10** 536-537
song cycles
   Debussy, Achille Claude **4** 445-447
   Fauré, Gabriel Urbain **5** 397-398
   Poulenc, Francis **12** 414-415
   Ravel, Maurice Joseph **13** 54-55
stochastic music
   Xenakis, Iannis **16** 416-418
trouvère songs
   Thibaut IV **15** 180-181
twelve-tone method
   Boulez, Pierre **2** 444-445
   Messiaen, Olivier **10** 528-529
   Stravinsky, Igor Fedorovich
      14 502-506
   see also Opera, French

French Overseas Empire
• AFRICA
   North Africa (Algeria)
      Abbas, Ferhat **1** 6-7
      Abd el-Kadir **1** 15
      Bugeaud de la Piconnerie,
         Thomas Robert **3** 111
      De Gaulle, Charles André Joseph
         Marie **4** 463-465
   North Africa (Morocco)
      Allal al-Fassi, Mohamed **1** 162
      Bugeaud de la Piconnerie,
         Thomas Robert **3** 111
      Lyautey, Louis Hubert Gonzalve
         10 60-61
      Mohammed V **11** 79-81

North Africa (Tunisia)
   Bourguiba, Habib **2** 453-455
   see also Nationalism, African
      (North Africa); and individual
      countries
Subsaharan Africa
   Diagne, Blaise **4** 527
   Eboué, Adolphe Felix Sylvestre
      5 194
   Houphouët-Boigny, Felix
      7 519-520
   Ly, Abdoulaye **10** 60
   Olympio, Sylvanus E.
      11 506-507
   Senghor, Léopold Sédar
      14 106-107
   Touré, Sékou **15** 275-277
   Touré, Sékou **15** 275-277
   Youlou, Fulbert **16** 466-467
   see also French Community;
      Nationalism, African; and indi-
      vidual countries
• ASIA
   China
      Feng Kuei-fen **5** 411-412
      Ts'ai Yüan-p'ei **15** 322
      Wen-hsiang **16** 202-203
   India
      Clinton, Henry **4** 11 4-115
      Dupleix **5** 153
      Haidar Ali **7** 65-66
      Wellesley, Richard Colley
         16 192-193
   Indochina
      see Indochina, French; Vietnam
         War (1946-1954)
• MIDDLE EAST
   Egypt
      Cromer, 1st Earl of **4** 317
      Hammarskjöld, Dag **7** 100-101
      Husein ibn Ali **8** 63
      Ismail Pasha **8** 150-151
      Thiers, Louis Adolphe
         15 181-182
      see also Suez Crisis (1956)
   Syria
      Faisal I **5** 370-371
      Husein ibn Ali **8** 63
      Lawrence, Thomas Edward
         9 253-254
   Turkey
      Atatürk, Ghazi Mustapha Kemal
         1 356-357
      Husein ibn Ali **8** 63
• NEW WORLD
   Brazil
      Sá, Mem de **13** 395
   Haiti
      Boyer, Jean Pierre **2** 468-469
      Christophe, Henri **4** 32
      Toussaint L'Ouverture, François
         Dominique **15** 278-279
   North America (Canada and United
      States)
      Champlain, Samuel de
         3 419-421

Charnisay, Charles de Menou
   3 470-471
Frontenac et Palluau, Comte de
   6 128-130
Jolliet, Louis **8** 328-329
La Salle, Sieur de **9** 210-211
Maisoneuve, Sieur de **10** 153
Marquette, Jacques **10** 274-275
Radisson, Pierre-Esprit
   12 539-540
Talon, Jean **15** 91-92
Vaudreuil-Cavagnal, Marquis de
   15 444
Verrazano, Giovanni da
   15 470-471
see also French and Indian War;
   King George's War; King
   William's War; Louisiana Pur-
   chase
North America (Mexico)
   Álvarez, Juan **1** 184-185
   Díaz, José de la Cruz Porfirio
      4 534-536
   Juárez, Benito **8** 369-372
   Maximilian of Hapsburg
      10 358-360
   Napoleon III **11** 310-312
   see also Explorers, French; Impe-
      rialism, French; and individual
      countries

French Paleontological Mission (China;
established 1923)
   Teilhard de Chardin, Marie Joseph
      Pierre **15** 134-136

French Panama Canal Co. (established
1880)
   Lesseps, Vicomte de **9** 354-355

French Psalter (Marot-De Bèze)
   Goudimel, Claude **6** 466
   Le Jeune, Claude **9** 314-315

French Resistance (World War II)
   literary activity
      Aragon, Louis **1** 271-272
      Camus, Albert **3** 255-257
      Mauriac, François **10** 347-348
      Sartre, Jean Paul **13** 491-492
   political activity
      Beckett, Samuel **2** 102-104
      Bloch, Marc **2** 332-333
      Malraux, André **10** 178-180
      Merleau-Ponty, Maurice **10** 518
      Schuman, Robert **14** 41

French Revolution (1789-1799)
• 1789-1791 (CONSTITUTIONAL
   MONARCHY)
   causes
      Louis XV **9** 533-534
      Louis XVI **9** 534-535
      Marie Antoinette **10** 258-259
      Necker, Jacques **11** 330-331
   Legislative Assembley (1791)
      Carnot, Lazare Nicolas Mar-
         guerite **3** 313-314
      Condorcet, Marquis de
         4 195-196

Louis XVI **9** 534-535
National (Constituent) Assembley
du Pont de Nemours, Pierre
Samuel **5** 155-156
Louis XVI **9** 534-535
Mirabeau, Comte de **11** 51-52
Robespierre, Maximilien
François Marie Isidore de
13 199-201
Sieyès, Comte Emmanuel Joseph
14 217-218
Talleyrand, Charles Maurice de
15 89-90
National Guard in
Lafayette, Marquis de **9** 151-152
Paris Commune
see Commune of Paris—
1789-1795
see also Bastille, storming of the
(1789); Declaration of the
Rights of Man (1789); Estates
General
• 1792-1795(1ST REPUBLIC)
Committee of Public Safety
Hébert, Jacques René **7** 247-248
Napoleon I **11** 306-310
Robespierre, Maximilien
François Marie Isidore de
13 199-201
see also Reign of Terror (below)
Girondists
see Girondists
Hébertists
see Hébertists
Jacobins
see Jacobins
National Convention (1792-1795)
Barras, Vicomte de **2** 19
Carnot, Lazare Nicolas Mar-
guerite **3** 313-314
Condorcet, Marquis de
4 195-196
Danton, Georges Jacques
4 391-393
Louis XVI **9** 534-535
Marat, Jean Paul **10** 230-231
Sade, Comte de **13** 416-418
Paris Commune
see Commune of Paris—
1789-1795
Reign of Terror (1793-1794)
Danton, Georges Jacques
4 391-393
Hébert, Jacques René **7** 247-248
Robespierre, Maximilien
François Marie Isidore de
13 199-201
Saint-Just, Louis Antoine Léon de
13 433
Sieyès, Comte Emmanuel Joseph
14 217-218
Terror victims
Condorcet, Marquis de
4 195-196
Paine, Thomas **12** 66-67
Saint-Simon, Comte de
13 436-437

Staël, Germaine de **14** 391-392
see also Executions—France;
Exiles—France
Thermidorian Reaction
see Thermidorian Reaction
• 1795-1799 (DIRECTORY)
Council of Elders
du Pont de Nemours, Pierre
Samuel **5** 155-156
Council of Five Hundred
Bonaparte, Joseph **2** 381-382
Carnot, Lazare Nicolas Mar-
guerite **3** 313-314
Murat, Joachim **11** 253-254
Sieyès, Comte Emmanuel Joseph
14 217-218
critics
Babeuf, François Noel **1** 412
du Pont de Nemours, Pierre
Samuel **5** 155-156
Directors
Barras, Vicomte de **2** 19
foreign ministers
Bonaparte, Joseph **2** 381-382
Fouché, Joseph **6** 30-31
Talleyrand, Charles Maurice de
15 89-90
overthrown
Murat, Joachim **11** 253-254
Napoleon I **11** 306-310
see also Brumaire coup d'etat;
France—1789-1815; French
Revolutionary Wars
(1792-1802); XYZ Affair (1797)
• REACTION TO
historians of
Aulard, François Victor Alphonse
1 374
Carlyle, Thomas **3** 304-305
Kropotkin, Peter Alekseevich
9 107-108
Lefebvre, Georges **9** 301-302
Mathiez, Albert **10** 333-334
Michelet, Jules **11** 5-6
Morris, Gouverneur **11** 182-183
Salvemini, Gaetano **13** 455-456
Sorel, Albert **14** 346-347
influence of
Emmet, Robert **5** 281-282
Washington, George **16** 126-129
in literature
Blake, William **2** 316-318
Conrad, Joseph **4** 205-207
Dickens, Charles John Huffam
4 538-541
Rolland, Romain **13** 260
Wordsworth, William
16 385-388, 445
opponents
Burke, Edmund **3** 138-141
Cobbett, William **4** 126-127
Gobineau, Comte de **6** 375-376
Le Play, Guillaume Frédéric
9 350-351
Maistre, Joseph de **10** 153-154
Pickering, Timothy **12** 298-299

Pius VI **12** 333-334
Pius VII **12** 334-335
supporters
Coleridge, Samuel Taylor
4 154-156
Fox, Charles James **6** 35-37
Landor, Walter Savage
9 186-187
Madison, James **10** 121-123
Price, Richard **12** 447-448
Priestley, Joseph **12** 452-453
Schelling, Friedrich Wilhelm
Joseph von **13** 526-527

French Revolutionary Wars (1792-1802)
Egyptian campaign (1798-1800)
Bonaparte, Louis **2** 382-383
Murat, Joachim **11** 253-254
Napoleon I **11** 306-310
Nelson, Horatio **11** 336-338
First Coalition (1792-1797)
Charles IV **3** 456-457
Francis II **6** 43-44
Godoy y Álvarez de Faria, Manuel
de **6** 381-382
Howe, Richard **7** 536-537
Murat, Joachim **11** 253-254
Napoleon I **11** 306-310
Nelson, Horatio **11** 336-338
Pitt, William the Younger
12 329-331
French forces
Bernadotte, Jean Baptiste **2** 205-206
Murat, Joachim **11** 253-254
Napoleon I **11** 306-310
Ney, Michel **11** 372-373
Rochambeau, Comte de **13** 220-221
French ministers
Carnot, Lazare Nicolas Marguerite
3 313-314
Genet, Edmond Charles **6** 261-262
Second Coalition (1799-1801)
Cornwallis, Charles **4** 241-243
Francis II **6** 43-44
Frederick William III **6** 87
Murat, Joachim **11** 253-254
Napoleon I **11** 306-310
Nelson, Horatio **11** 336-338
Pitt, William the Younger
12 329-331
Suvorov, Aleksandr Vasilievich
15 44-45
see also French Revolution
(1789-1799)

French River (Canada)
Champlain, Samuel de **3** 419-421

French Set (etching series)
Whistler, James Abbott McNeill
16 225-226

French Socialist party (Senegal)
Gueye, Lamine **7** 31

French-Hater, The (book)
Alfieri, Vittoria **1** 145-146

FRENEAU, PHILIP MORIN (1752-1832), American poet and journalist **6** 99-100
Brackenridge, Hugh Henry **2** 472-473
Duane, William **5** 109

Frente Ampla (Brazilian politics)
Kubitschek de Oliveira, Juscelino **9** 113-115

Frequency modulation
Armstrong, Edwin Howard **1** 302-303

Frequens (papal decree)
Martin V **10** 287-288

Frere, John Hookham (1769-1846), English diplomat
Saavedra, Angel de **13** 398

FRERE, SIR HENRY BARTLE EDWARD (1815-1884), English colonial administrator **6** 100-101

Frère-Orban Law (Belgium; 1879)
Leopold II **9** 346-347

FRESCOBALDI, GIROLAMO (1583-1643), Italian composer and organist **6** 101-102
Froberger, Johann Jakob **6** 120-121

Frescoes for Mr. Rockefeller's City (poem)
MacLeish, Archibald **10** 109-110

FRESNEL, AUGUSTIN JEAN (1788-1827), French physicist **6** 102-103
Fizeau, Hippolyte Armand Louis **5** 475

Freud, Anna (1895-1982), British psychoanalyst
Erikson, Erik Homburger **5** 309-310
Freud, Sigmund **6** 103-106

FREUD, SIGMUND (1856-1939), Viennese psychiatrist, founder of psychoanalysis **6** 103-106
dissenters
Adler, Alfred **1** 61-63
Bleuler, Eugen **2** 325
Cooley, Charles Horton **4** 216-217
Fromm, Erich **6** 125-127
Horney, Karen Danielsen **7** 508-509
Jung, Carl Gustav **8** 388-389
Sullivan, Harry Stack **15** 23-24
influence in literature
Auden, Wystan Hugh **1** 364-366
Lawrence, David Herbert **9** 247-248
O'Neill, Eugene **11** 514-516
Strindberg, August **14** 509-511
Svevo, Italo **15** 47-48
Thomas, Dylan Marlais **15** 188-190
influence on social sciences
Bettelheim, Bruno **2** 245-246
Erikson, Erik Homburger **5** 309-310
Lasswell, Harold Dwight **9** 218-219
Marcuse, Herbert **10** 245-247
Mead, Margaret **10** 438-440
Montessori, Maria **11** 125-126
Tolman, Edward Chace **15** 261-262
influenced by
Charcot, Jean Martin **3** 442
Ebbinghaus, Hermann **5** 192-193
Leibniz, Gottfried Wilhelm von **9** 307-310

Rosmini-Serbati, Antonio **13** 296-297
quoted
Dostoevsky, Fyodor **5** 74-77
supporters
James, William **8** 215-217
Jones, Fay **8** 332-333
Rank, Otto **13** 33
White, William Alanson **16** 239-240

Freycinet, Charles Louis de Saulces de (1828-1923), French statesman
Clemenceau, Georges **4** 99-101

FREYRE, GILBERTO (1900-1987), Brazilian sociologist and writer **6** 106-107

FREYTAG, GUSTAV (1816-1895), German novelist, dramatist, and critic **6** 107-108

Friars by a Stormy Sea (painting)
Magnasco, Alessandro **10** 127-128

Friars Minor, Order of
see Franciscans

Fribourg, University of (France)
Breuil, Henri Edouard Prosper **2** 521-522

FRICK, HENRY CLAY (1849-1919), American industrialist and financier **6** 108-109
Carnegie, Andrew **3** 309-312
Goldman, Emma **6** 406-407

Frick Museum (New York City)
Frick, Henry Clay **6** 108-109

Frick, Wilhelm (1877-1946), German politician
Hitler, Adolf **7** 417-420

Friday (literary character)
Defoe, Daniel **4** 457-459

FRIEDAN, BETTY (Betty Naomi Goldstein; born 1921), women's rights activist and author **6** 109-111

Friedericke Songs (music)
Goethe, Johann Wolfgang von **6** 388-391

Friedheim, Arthur (1859-1932), German pianist
Liszt, Franz **9** 445-447

Friedjung Treason Trial (1909)
Masaryk, Tomáš Garrigue **10** 314-315

Friedland, battle of (1807)
Murat, Joachim **11** 253-254
Napoleon I **11** 306-310

Friedländer, Max J. (1867-1958), German scholar
Dürer, Albrecht **5** 159-161

FRIEDMAN, MILTON (born 1912), American economist **6** 111-112

FRIEDRICH, CARL JOACHIM (1901-1984), German-born educator who became a leading American political theorist **6** 113-114

FRIEDRICH, CASPAR DAVID (1774-1840), German romantic painter **6** 114-115

Friedrich Krupp (German industry)
Diesel, Rudolf **5** 7

Friedrich Werder Church (Berlin)
Schinkel, Karl Friedrich **14** 8

Friedrich Werder Gymnasium (Berlin)
Clausius, Rudolf Julius Emanuel **4** 92-94

FRIEL, BERNARD PATRICK (born 1929), author, teacher, and playwright from Northern Ireland **6** 115-116

Friend (periodical)
Coleridge, Samuel Taylor **4** 154-156
Kipling, Joseph Rudyard **9** 32-33

Friend of Kafka, A (stories)
Singer, Isaac Bashevis **14** 249-250

Friendly Call, A (painting)
Chase, William Merritt **3** 476-477

Friends (poem)
Yeats, William Butler **16** 445-447

Friends and Relations (novel)
Bowen, Elizabeth **2** 462-463

Friends of the Manifesto (Algerian organization)
Abbas, Ferhat **1** 6-7

Friends, Society of
see Quakers

FRIES, JAKOB FRIEDRICH (1773-1843), German philosopher **6** 116-117

Fries, John (1750?-1818), American insurgent
Chase, Samuel **3** 475-476

Friesz, Othon (1879-1949), French painter
Braque, Georges **2** 504-505
Matisse, Henri **10** 336-337

Frieze of Life (series of paintings)
Munch, Edvard **11** 247-248

FRISCH, KARL VON (1886-1982), Austrian zoologist **6** 117-118

FRISCH, MAX (born 1911), Swiss novelist and dramatist **6** 118-119
Dürrenmatt, Friedrich **5** 164-165

FRISCH, OTTO ROBERT (1904-1979), Austrian-British nuclear physicist **6** 119-120

Frisch, Ragnar (1895-1973), Norwegian economist
Tinbergen, Jan **15** 228-229

Frisson d'hiver (prose poem)
Mallarmé, Stéphane **10** 172-173

Froben, Johannes (circa 1460-1527), German printer and scholar
Erasmus, Desiderius **5** 298-300

FROBERGER, JOHANN JAKOB (1616-1667), German composer and organist **6** 120-121
Buxtehude, Dietrich **3** 185-186

FROBISHER, SIR MARTIN (circa 1538-1594), English explorer **6** 121-122
Cabot, Sebastian **3** 200-201
Drake, Francis **5** 94-96
Hawkins, John **7** 210-211

FROEBEL, FRIEDRICH WILHELM AUGUST
(1782-1852), German educator and psychologist **6** 122-123
  Peabody, Elizabeth Palmer **12** 167-168
  Wright, Frank Lloyd **16** 398-401

Frogs, The (play)
  Aristophanes **1** 293-294

FROHMAN, CHARLES (1860-1915), American theatrical producer **6** 123-124

FROISSART, JEAN (circa 1337-after 1404), French priest, poet, and chronicler.
6 124-125
  Chaucer, Geoffrey **3** 482-485
  Kaiser, Georg **8** 411-412

Frollo (literary character)
  Hugo, Victor Marie **8** 22-25

From a View to a Death (novel)
  Powell, Anthony **12** 422-423

From Bohemia's Meadows and Forests
(symphony poem)
  Smetana, Bedřich **14** 281-282

From Death to Morning (literary collection)
  Wolfe, Thomas Clayton **16** 355-356

From Evil Good Always Springs (play)
  Alarcón, Pedro Antonio de **1** 100-101

From Make-believe to Reality (play)
  Lope Félix de Vega Carpio **9** 503-506

From Morn till Midnight (play)
  Kaiser, Georg **8** 411-412

From Slavery to Freedom: A History of Negro Americans (book)
  Franklin, John Hope **6** 65-67

From the Earth to the Moon (novel)
  Verne, Jules **15** 467-469

From the Land of Dreams (musical composition)
  Still, William Grant **14** 455-456

From the Terrace (novelist)
  O'Hara, John **11** 485

Froment jeune et Risler aîné (novel)
  Daudet, Alphonse **4** 402-403

FROMM, ERICH (1900-1980), German writer in the fields of psychoanalysis, psychology, and social philosophy
6 125-127

Fronde, Wars of the (France; 1648-53)
  La Rochefoucauld, François Duc de
  9 208-209
  Louis XIV **9** 531-533
  Mazarin, Jules **10** 379-380
  Philip IV **12** 275

FRONDIZI, ARTURO (1908-1995), leader of the Argentine Radical Party and Argentine president (1958-1962) **6** 127-128
  Sábato, Ernesto **13** 399-400

Front National (French political party)
  Le Pen, Jean Marie **9** 348-350

Front Nationale Senegalaise (political party)
  Diop, Cheikh Anta **5** 21-22

Front Page, The (play)
  Hecht, Ben **7** 248-250

Front Royal (town, Virginia)
  Jackson, Shirley Ann **8** 183-184

FRONTENAC ET PALLUAU, COMTE DE
(Louis de Buade; 1622-1698), French colonial governor **6** 128-130
  Jolliet, Louis **8** 328-329
  La Salle, Sieur de **9** 210-211
  Parkman, Francis **12** 113-115

Frontier (Australia)
  Furphy, Joseph **6** 152-153

Frontier (ballet)
  Graham, Martha **6** 485-486

Frontier (United States)
  Fitzpatrick, Thomas **5** 474-475
  Goodnight, Charles **6** 439
  Oakley, Annie **11** 453-454
  Sevier, John **14** 122-123
  Turner, Frederick Jackson **15** 350-351
  see also Frontiersmen, American

Frontiersmen, American
  folk heroes
    Billy the Kid **2** 277
    Boone, Daniel **2** 397-398
    Calamity Jane **3** 216
    Crockett, David **4** 314-316
    Earp, Wyatt Barry Stepp **5** 181-182
    Hickok, James Butler **7** 374-375
    James, Jesse Woodson **8** 212-213
    Love, Nat **10** 1-2
  explorers, guides, and scouts
    Applegate, Jesse **1** 264-265
    Ashley, William Henry **1** 333-334
    Austin, Stephen Fuller **1** 380-381
    Becknell, William **2** 105-106
    Beckwourth, Jim **2** 106-107
    Bidwell, John **2** 265
    Boone, Daniel **2** 397-398
    Bozeman, John M. **2** 471-472
    Bridger, James **3** 2-3
    Buffalo Bill **3** 105-106
    Carson, Christopher **3** 334-335
    Crook, George **4** 322-323
    Fitzpatrick, Thomas **5** 474-475
    Frémont, John Charles **6** 97-98
    Gist, Christopher **6** 352-353
    Rogers, Robert **13** 250-251
    Smith, Jedediah S. **14** 294-295
    Walker, Joseph Reddeford **16** 63-64
    Washakie **16** 123-125
    Whitman, Marcus **16** 248-249
  renegades
    Girty, Simon **6** 350

Frontiersmen, Canadian
  McLoughlin, John **10** 423-424

FRONTINUS, SEXTUS JULIUS (circa 35-circa 104), Roman magistrate, soldier, and writer **6** 130
  Martialis, Marcus Valerius **10** 286-287

FROST, ROBERT LEE (1874-1963), American poet **6** 130-133
  Ford, Ford Madox **6** 1-2

  Kennedy, John Fitzgerald **8** 502-506
  Lowell, Amy **10** 13

Frost, Stephen S. (1718?-1749), African American educator
  Carver, George Washington **3** 346-347

Frothingham, Octavius Brooks
(1822-1895), American Unitarian clergyman
  Adler, Felix **1** 63-64

Frottage (art technique)
  Ernst, Max **5** 311-312

Frottola (music)
  Josquin des Prez **8** 361-363

FROUDE, JAMES ANTHONY (1818-1894), English historian **6** 133-134
  Carlyle, Thomas **3** 304-305
  Lecky, William Edward Hartpole
  9 271-272

Froude, Richard Hurrell (1803-1836), English Anglo-Catholic theologian
  Newman, John Henry **11** 365-367

Fructose (sugar)
  Fischer, Emil **5** 456-457

Frühlings Erwachen (play)
  Wedekind, Frank **16** 166-167

Frühlingsfeier, Die (poem)
  Klopstock, Friedrich Gottlieb **9** 55-56

Fruit Bowl on Checkered Cloth (painting)
  Gris, Juan **7** 5-6

Fruit Dish (painting)
  Picasso, Pablo **12** 292-295

Fruit fly
  see Drosophila

Fruit Garden (poems)
  Sadi, Shaikh Muslih-al-Din **13** 419-420

Fruitlands (Massachusetts)
  Alcott, Amos Bronson **1** 121
  Alcott, Louisa May **1** 122
  Hecker, Isaac Thomas **7** 250-251

Fruits of the Earth (book)
  Gide, André **6** 308-309
  Grove, Frederick Philip **7** 20-21

Frumentius, Saint (died circa 380), Phoenician apostle to Ethiopia
  Ezana **5** 354-355

FRUNZE, MIKHAIL VASILIEVICH
(1885-1925), Soviet military leader **6** 134

Fry, E. Maxwell (1899-1987), English architect
  Gropius, Walter **7** 13-14

FRY, ELIZABETH (1780-1845), British reformer **6** 134-136

Fry, Roger (1866-1934), English painter and critic
  Moore, Henry **11** 146-148
  Woolf, Virginia Stephen **16** 381-382

FRY, WILLIAM HENRY (1813-1864), American composer **6** 136-137

FRYE, NORTHROP (Herman Northrop Frye; born 1912), Canadian literary scholar **6** 137-139

Fu (literary form)
Lu Chi **10** 24
Pan Ku **12** 86-87
Ssu-ma Hsiang-ju **14** 389-390
Su Shih **15** 39-40
Tu Fu **15** 335-336

Fu Chien (flourished 4th century), Chinese emperor
Kumarajiva **9** 127
Tao-an **15** 103-104

Fu Mattia Pascal, II (novel)
Pirandello, Luigi **12** 319-321

FUAD I (1868-1936), king of Egypt 1922-1936 **6** 139
Zaghlul Pasha, Saad **16** 485-486

FUCHS, SIR VIVIAN (born 1908), English explorer and geologist **6** 140

FUCI
see Federazione Universitaria Cattolica Italiana

Fuego nuevo, El (ballet)
Chávez, Carlos **3** 486

Fuenteovejuna (play)
Lope Félix de Vega Carpio **9** 503-506

FUENTES, CARLOS (born 1928), Mexican author and political activist **6** 141-142

Fuentes, Miguel Y digoras
see Ydigoras Fuentes, Miguel

FUGARD, ATHOL (born 1932), South African playwright **6** 142-143

Fuggilotio musicale (musical collection)
Caccini, Giulio **3** 205-206

Fugitive (periodical)
Ransom, John Crowe **13** 39-40
Tate, Allen **15** 116
Warren, Robert Penn **16** 121-122

Fugitive Slave Act (United States; 1850)
drafted
Clay, Henry **4** 94-96
Mason, James Murray **10** 320-321
opponents
Emerson, Ralph Waldo **5** 278-280
Frémont, John Charles **6** 97-98
Greeley, Horace **6** 515-517
Howe, Samuel Gridley **7** 537
Seward, William Henry **14** 124-125
Smith, Gerrit **14** 290-291
supporters
Cass, Lewis **3** 355-356
Curtis, Benjamin Robbins **4** 349
Fillmore, Millard **5** 447-448
Pierce, Franklin **12** 300-301
Shaw, Lemuel **14** 164-165
Stephens, Alexander Hamilton **14** 429-430
Webster, Daniel **16** 162-164

Fugitive slaves
see African American history (United States)

Fugitive, The (poem)
Lermontov, Mikhail Yurievich **9** 352-353

Fugue (music)
Bach, Johann Sebastian **1** 416-419
Beethoven, Ludwig van **2** 114-117
Harris, Roy **7** 175-176
Shostakovich, Dmitri Dmitrievich **14** 204-205
Villa-Lobos, Heitor **15** 496-497

Fuhrmann Henschel (drama)
Hauptmann, Gerhart Johann Robert **7** 199-201

Fuji, Mount (Japan)
Hiroshige, Ando **7** 412-413
Hokusai, Katsushika **7** 447-448

FUJIMORI, ALBERTO KEINYA (born 1938), president of Peru **6** 143-145

Fujiwara clan (Japanese nobles; ruled circa 8th-12th century)
Ashikaga Takauji **1** 330-332
Fujiwara Kamatari **6** 145
Fujiwara Michinaga **6** 145-146
Goshirakawa **6** 460-461
Konoe, Fumimaro **9** 82-83
Yoritomo, Minamoto **16** 463-464

FUJIWARA KAMATARI (614-669), Japanese imperial official **6** 145

Fujiwara Korechika (975-1010), Japanese nobleman
Murasaki Shikibu **11** 252-253

FUJIWARA MICHINAGA (966-1027), Japanese statesman **6** 145-146
Murasaki Shikibu **11** 252-253

Fujiwara Nakamaro (flourished 8th century), Japanese noble
Makibi, Kibi-no **10** 161

Fujiwara-no Daijin
see Fujiwara Kamatari

FUKUYAMA, FRANCIS (born 1952), American philosopher and foreign policy expert **6** 146-147

Fukuzawa, Yukichi (1834-1901), Japanese educator and author
Inukai, Tsuyoshi **8** 130-131

Fulani (African people)
Ali, Sunni **1** 158-159
Clapperton, Hugh **4** 72-73
Ekwensi, Cyprian **5** 242-243

Fulbert (flourished circa 1083-1119), French canon of Notre Dame
Abelard, Peter **1** 23-25

FULBRIGHT, JAMES WILLIAM (1905-1995), American statesman **6** 147-149
Johnson, Lyndon Baines **8** 308-312
Kennedy, John Fitzgerald **8** 502-506

Fulbright Act (1946)
Fulbright, James William **6** 147-149

Fulda, monastery of (Germany)
Boniface **2** 391

Full Fathom Five (painting)
Pollock, Jackson **12** 379-380

Full Moon in March, A (poems)
Yeats, William Butler **16** 445-447

Fuller, Melville W. (1833-1910), American jurist
Taft, William Howard **15** 78-81

FULLER, RICHARD BUCKMINISTER (born 1895), American architect and engineer **6** 149-150
Cage, John **3** 211-214

FULLER, SARAH MARGARET (1810-1850), American feminist **6** 150-151
Alcott, Louisa May **1** 122
Peabody, Elizabeth Palmer **12** 167-168

Fulton II (ship)
Perry, Matthew Calbraith **12** 237-239

FULTON, ROBERT (1765-1815), American inventor, engineer, and artist **6** 151-152
associates
Barlow, Joel **2** 6-7
Fitch, John **5** 467-468
Owen, Robert **12** 39-40
steamboat
Livingston, Robert R. **9** 462-463
Shreve, Henry Miller **14** 207
Stevens, John **14** 439-440
Vanderbilt, Cornelius **15** 415-416
submarine
Holland, John Philip **7** 453-454

Fulton, Ruth
see Benedict, Ruth Fulton

Fumaric acid (chemistry)
Krebs, Hans Adolf **9** 95-97

Fun (magazine)
Bierce, Ambrose Gwinett **2** 269-270

Functions, theory of (mathematics)
Cournot, Antoine Augustin **4** 273
Euler, Leonard **5** 331-332
Lagrange, Joseph Louis **9** 164-166

Fundamental Orders (Connecticut; 1639)
Hooker, Thomas **7** 476-477

Fundamentalism (religion)
Falwell, Jerry **5** 375-376
Graham, William Franklin Jr. **6** 487-488
Sunday, William Ashley **15** 32-33

Fundy, Bay of (southeast Canada)
Champlain, Samuel de **3** 419-421

Funeral Anthem ... (musical composition)
Handel, George Frederick **7** 116-119

Funeral March (musical composition)
Chopin, Frédéric François **4** 16-18

Funeral March for a Marionette (musical composition)
Gounod, Charles François **6** 473-474

Funeral of Saint Fina (fresco)
Ghirlandaio, Domenico **6** 292-293

Funeral Rites (novel)
Genet, Jean **6** 262-263

Funeral, The (play)
Steele, Richard **14** 407-409

Funerales de la Mama Grande, Los (stories)
García Márquez, Gabriel **6** 208-209

Funivia del Faloria, La (film)
Antonioni, Michelangelo **1** 252-253

Funk, Casimir (1884-1967), Polish-American biochemist
Eijkman, Christian **5** 228

Funke Leben, Der (novel)
Remarque, Erich Maria **13** 91

Funny Face (musical)
Gershwin, George **6** 284-285

Funston, Frederick (1865-1917), American general
Aguinaldo, Emilio **1** 88

Fuoco grande (novel)
Pavese, Cesare **12** 154-155

Fuoco, Il (novel)
D'Annunzio, Gabriele **4** 388

Fur trade
American West
Ashley, William Henry **1** 333-334
Astor, John Jacob **1** 351-352
Baranov, Aleksandr Andreievich **1** 499-500
Becknell, William **2** 105-106
Beckwourth, Jim **2** 106-107
Bridger, James **3** 2-3
Fitzpatrick, Thomas **5** 474-475
Ogden, Peter Skene **11** 480-481
Smith, Jedediah S. **14** 294-295
Walker, Joseph Reddeford **16** 63-64
Canada
Champlain, Samuel de **3** 419-421
Fraser, Simon **6** 74-75
Frontenac et Palluau, Comte de **6** 128-130
Jolliet, Louis **8** 328-329
la Verendrye, Sieur de **9** 239-240
McLoughlin, John **10** 423-424
Ogden, Peter Skene **11** 480-481
Radisson, Pierre-Esprit **12** 539-540
Selkirk, 5th Earl of **14** 96

Smith, Donald Alexander **14** 288-289

Fur Traders Descending the Missouri (painting)
Bingham, George Caleb **2** 278-279

Furies, The (Greek mythology)
Aeschylus **1** 70-72
Euripides **5** 332-334

Fur-lined Teacup, Saucer, and Spoon (sculpture)
Oppenheim, Meret **11** 524-525

Furniture design
Aalto, Hugo Alvar Henrik **1** 1-2
Ashley, Laura **1** 332-333
Breuer, Marcel **2** 520-521
Chippendale, Thomas **4** 1-2
Hepplewhite, George **7** 317-318
Mackintosh, Charles Rennie **10** 107-108
Mies van der Rohe, Ludwig **11** 10-12
Phyfe, Duncan **12** 284-285
Rietveld, Gerrit Thomas **13** 169
Sheraton, Thomas **14** 181-182

FURPHY, JOSEPH (1843-1912), Australian novelist **6** 152-153
Clarke, Marcus Andrew Hislop **4** 87-88
Franklin, William **6** 69-70
Lawson, Henry **9** 254-255

Furtado, Celso (born 1920), Brazilian statesman
Goulart, João **6** 467-469

Further Range, A (literary collection)
Frost, Robert Lee **6** 130-133

Furtwängler, A. (1853-1907), German archeologist and art critic
Phidias **12** 265-267

Furtwängler, Wilhelm (1886-1954), German opera conductor
Archipenko, Alexander **1** 280-281

Fury (ship)
Ross, James Clark **13** 302-303

FUSELI, HENRY (1741-1825), Swiss painter **6** 153-155
Friedrich, Caspar David **6** 114-115

Romney, George **13** 269-270

Fu-she (Chinese society)
Huang Tsung-hsi **8** 9-10

Fust, Johann (1400?-1466), German printer
Gutenberg, Johann **7** 48-49

Fustât
see Cairo

FUSTEL DE COULANGES, NUMA DENIS (1830-1889), French historian **6** 155
Durkheim, Émile **5** 162-163

Fu-su (died 210 B.C.), heir apparent to Ch'in empire
Li Ssu **9** 442-443

Fusuma (painting)
Eitoku, Kano **5** 242

Futen Rojin Nikki (novel)
Tanizaki, Junichiro **15** 101-102

Future Generation (sculpture)
Zorach, William **16** 528

Futurism (art)
Archipenko, Alexander **1** 280-281
Balla, Giacomo **1** 473-474
Boccioni, Umberto **2** 353-354
Duchamp-Villon, Raymond **5** 123
Goncharova, Natalia **6** 424-426
Popova, Liubov Sergeevna **12** 401-402
Severini, Gino **14** 122
Stella, Joseph **14** 422

Futurism (literature)
Kaiser, Georg **8** 411-412
Mayakovsky, Vladimir Vladimirovich **10** 364-365
Pasternak, Boris Leonidovich **12** 124-125

FUX, JOHANN JOSEPH (1660-1741), Austrian composer, conductor, and theoretician **6** 155-156

Fuyu no Hi (poems)
Basho, Matsuo **2** 45-48

Fuzzy-Wuzzy (poem)
Kipling, Joseph Rudyard **9** 32-33

Fyodor (literary character)
Dostoevsky, Fyodor **5** 74-77

G

G. and Z.C. Jewelry Store (Amsterdam)
Rietveld, Gerrit Thomas **13** 169

G.K.'s Weekly (periodical)
Belloc, Joseph Hilaire Pierre **2** 141
Chesterton, Gilbert Keith **3** 508-509

Gabinius, Aulus (died 48 B.C.), Roman
statesman and general
Antony, Mark **1** 253-254

GABLE, WILLIAM CLARK (1901-1960),
American film actor **6** 157-158

GABO, NAUM (1890-1977), Russian
sculptor and designer **6** 158-159
Pevsner, Antoine **12** 263-264

Gabon Republic (nation; west-central
Africa)
Brazza, Pierre Paul François Camille
Savorgnan de **2** 509-510
Burton, Richard **3** 163-164
Schweitzer, Albert **14** 55-56

GABOR, DENNIS (1900-1979),
Hungarian-British physicist who invented
holographic photography **6** 159-160

Gabriel (archangel)
Ashari, Abu al- Hasan Ali al- **1** 327-328

Gabriel (ship)
Bering, Vitus **2** 193-194

GABRIEL, ANGE JACQUES (1698-1782),
French architect **6** 160-161
Ledoux, Claude Nicolas **9** 277-278
Perrault, Claude **12** 232-233

Gabriel, Jacques IV (1630-1686), French
architect
Gabriel, Ange Jacques **6** 160-161

Gabriel, Jacques V (1667-1742), French
architect
Gabriel, Ange Jacques **6** 160-161

Gabriel Conroy (novel)
Harte, Francis Brett **7** 184-185

Gabriel Schillings Flucht (drama)
Hauptmann, Gerhart Johann Robert
7 199-201

Gabriel Tolliver (novel)
Harris, Joel Chandler **7** 173-174

Gabriela... (novel)
Amado, Jorge **1** 189-190

Gabrieli, Andrea (1510?-1586), Italian
composer and organist
Gabrieli, Giovanni **6** 161-162
Merulo, Claudio **10** 525-526
Willaert, Adrian **16** 287-288

GABRIELI, GIOVANNI (circa 1557-1612),
Italian composer **6** 161-162
Frescobaldi, Girolamo **6** 101-102
Praetorius, Michael **12** 431-432
Schütz, Heinrich **14** 48-49
Willaert, Adrian **16** 287-288

Gabriel's Rebellion (1800)
Monroe, James **11** 111-113
Prosser, Gabriel **12** 460-461

Gabriel's Wing (poem)
Iqbal, Muhammad **8** 132-133

Gabrini, Niccola di Lorenzo
see Rienzi, Cola di

Gad (Old Testament)
Moses **11** 200-201

GADAMER, HANS-GEORG (born 1900),
German philosopher, classicist, and interpretation theorist **6** 162-163

GADDAFI, MUAMMAR AL- (born 1942),
head of the revolution that set up the
Libyan Republic in 1969 **6** 163-165

Gaddum, John Henry (1900-1965), English
physiologist
Dale, Henry Hallett **4** 371-373
Loewi, Otto **9** 486-487

Gade, Niels Vilhelm (1817-1890), Danish
composer
Grieg, Edvard Hagerup **6** 541-542

GADSDEN, JAMES (1788-1858), American
soldier and diplomat **6** 165-166

Gadsen Purchase (1853)
Davis, Jefferson **4** 416-418
Gadsden, James **6** 165-166
Polk, James Knox **12** 374-376

Santa Ana, Antonio López de
13 471-472

Gaelic (language)
see Irish language revival movement

Gaelic League (established 1893)
Hyde, Douglas **8** 82-83

Gaeta, siege of (1734)
Charles Edward Louis Philip Casimir
Stuart **3** 466-467

GAGARIN, YURI ALEXEIVICH
(1934-1968), Russian cosmonaut
6 166-167

GAGE, MATILDA JOSLYN (1826-1898),
American reformer and suffragist
6 167-169

GAGE, THOMAS (1719/20-1787), English
general **6** 169-170
Adams, Samuel **1** 55-56
Carleton, Guy **3** 300-301
Carver, Jonathan **3** 347-348
Hancock, John **7** 114-116
Hutchinson, Thomas **8** 71-72

GAGNÉ, ROBERT MILLS (born 1916),
American educator **6** 170

Gaines' Mill
see Seven Days, battle of the

GAINSBOROUGH, THOMAS
(1727-1788), English painter **6** 170-172
Constable, John **4** 208-209
Lawrence, Thomas **9** 252-253
Ruisdael, Jacob van **13** 357-358
Stuart, Gilbert **14** 513-515
Turner, Joseph Mallord William
15 352-354

Gainsborough, battle of (1643)
Cromwell, Oliver **4** 317-320

Gainsborough Film Studios (England)
Hitchcock, Alfred **7** 415-416

Gainsborough's Forest (painting)
Gainsborough, Thomas **6** 170-172

GAISERIC (died 477), king of the Vandals
428-477 **6** 172
Attila **1** 360
Leo I **9** 329-330

Odoacer **11** 473
Ricimer, Flavius **13** 151-152

GAITÁN, JORGE ELIÉCER (1898-1948),
Colombian politician **6** 172-173
Castro Ruz, Fidel **3** 365-368
Gómez Castro, Laureano Eleuterio
6 419-420

GAITSKELL, HUGH (1906-1963), British
chancellor of the exchequer (1950-1951)
and leader of the Labour Party
(1955-1963) **6** 173-174

Gaitskell, Hugh Todd Naylor (1903-1963),
British statesman
Cole, George Douglas Howard
4 146-147
Wilson, James Harold **16** 324-325

Gaius Sallustius Crispus
see Sallust

Gaius Sempronius (circa 154-121 B.C.),
Roman reformer
Clodius Pulcher, Publius **4** 121-122
Drusus, Marcus Livius **5** 105-106
Gracchus, Tiberius and Gaius Sempro-
nius **6** 479-480
Pompey **12** 387-389
Scipio Africanus Minor, Publius Cor-
nelius Aemilianus **14** 62-63

Galápagos Islands (Pacific Ocean; near
Ecuador)
Darwin, Charles Robert **4** 397-399
Melville, Herman **10** 472-476

Galatea (mythology)
Góngora y Argote, Luis de **6** 427-428

Galatea (novel)
Cervantes, Miguel de Saavedra
3 395-398

Galatea e Polifemo (musical composition)
Handel, George Frederick **7** 116-119

Galatians, Epistle to the (New Testament)
Luther, Martin **10** 48-51
Paul **12** 141-143

Galaxy (astronomy)
Hubble, Edwin Powell **8** 10-11
Shapley, Harlow **14** 155-156
see also Milky Way Galaxy

Galba (circa 5 B.C.- 69 A.D.), Roman
emperor 68-69
Nero Claudius Caesar **11** 342-344
Tacitus **15** 70-72
Titus Flavius Vespasianus **15** 247-248
Vespasian **15** 475-476

GALBRAITH, JOHN KENNETH (born
1908), economist and scholar of the
American Institutionalist school
6 174-177
Luce, Henry Robinson **10** 23-24

GALDÓS, BENITO PÉREZ (1843-1920),
Spanish novelist and dramatist **6** 177-178

GALEN (130-200), Greek physician
6 178-180
influence of
Avicenna **1** 386-387

Fernel, Jean François **5** 425-426
Rabelais, François **12** 524-526
influenced by
Hippocrates **7** 408-410
theories disputed
Cardano, Geronimo **3** 285-286
Harvey, William **7** 189-190
Paracelsus, Philippus Aureolus
12 91-93
Vesalius, Andreas **15** 473-475
translations of
Poliziano, Angelo **12** 373-374

Galerius (died 311), Roman emperor
305-311
Constantine I **4** 209-211
Diocletian **5** 19-20, 387

Galicia (region; eastern-central Europe)
Joseph II **8** 359-360

Galicia (region; Spain)
Alfonso I **1** 148

Galilee (region; Palestine)
Jesus of Nazareth **8** 251-255

Galilei, Galileo
see Galileo Galilei

Galilei, Vincenzio (1520-1591), Italian
composer, lutenist, and music theorist
Galileo Galilei **6** 180-183
Zarlino, Gioseffo **16** 490-491

GALILEO GALILEI (1564-1642), Italian
astronomer and physicist **6** 180-183
associates
Porta, Giambattista della
12 403-404
Sarpi, Paolo **13** 487-488
Torricelli, Evangelista **15** 268-269
Church condemns
Bellarmine, Robert **2** 135-136
Campanella, Tommaso **3** 249
influence of
Boyle, Robert **2** 469-471
Donne, John **5** 60-61
Hobbes, Thomas **7** 421-423
Tönnies, Ferdinand **15** 266-267
influenced by
Copernicus, Nicolaus **4** 226-227
Tartaglia, Niccolo **15** 111-112

Galileo (play; Brecht)
Brecht, Bertolt **2** 512-514
Osborne, John **12** 16-17

Gall (1840?-1894), American Sioux Indian
chief
Sitting Bull **14** 264-265

Gall, Franz Joseph (1758-1828), German
founder of phrenology
Lashley, Karl Spencer **9** 214-215

Gallantry (book)
Cabell, James Branch **3** 195-196

GALLATIN, ALBERT (1761-1849),
Swiss-born American statesman, banker,
and diplomat **6** 183-184
Adams, John Quincy **1** 52-54
Madison, James **10** 121-123

Gallatin Valley (Montana)
Bozeman, John M. **2** 471-472

Gallaudet College (Washington D.C.)
Gallaudet, Thomas Hopkins **6** 185

Gallaudet, Edward Miner (1837-1917),
American educator
Gallaudet, Thomas Hopkins **6** 185

GALLAUDET, THOMAS HOPKINS
(1787-1851), American educator **6** 185

Galle, Johann Gottfried (1812-1910), German astronomer
Leverrier, Urbain Jean Joseph **9** 361-362

Gallegher... (stories)
Davis, Richard Harding **4** 422-423

Gallego y su cuadrilla, El (book)
Cela y Trulock, Camilo José **3** 389-390

GALLEGOS FREIRE, RÓMULO
(1884-1969), Venezuelan novelist, president 1948 **6** 185-186
Betancourt, Rómulo **2** 237-238

Gallic Wars, Commentaries on the (book,
Caesar)
Caesar, Gaius Julius **3** 207-210
Clarke, Samuel **4** 88

Gallicanism (theology)
Gerson, John **6** 285-286

Galliéni, Joseph Simon (1849-1916),
French general and statesman
Joffre, Joseph Jacques Césaire
8 267-268
Lyautey, Louis Hubert Gonzalve
10 60-61

Gallienus (died 268), Roman emperor
253-268
Plotinus **12** 358-359
Valerian **15** 404-405

Gallina, La (musical composition)
Gottschalk, Louis Moreau **6** 463-464

Gallinas River (West Africa)
Canot, Theodore **3** 262-263

Gallipoli campaign (World War I)
Churchill, Winston Leonard Spencer
4 51-53
Hughes, William Morris **8** 21-22

Gallium (element—chemistry)
Mendeleev, Dmitrii Ivanovich
10 486-488

GALLOWAY, JOSEPH (circa 1731-1803),
American politician **6** 186-187

Galloway Plan (United States; 1774)
Jay, John **8** 230-232
Rutledge, John **13** 387-388

GALLUP, GEORGE (1901-1984), pioneer
in the field of public opinion polling and
a proponent of educational reform
6 187-189

Gallus, Gaius Vibius Trebonianus
(205?-253?), Roman emperor 251-253
Valerian **15** 404-405

Galois, Évariste (1811-1832), French mathematician

Cauchy, Augustin Louis **3** 378-380
Lagrange, Joseph Louis **9** 164-166

Galop (musical form)
Strauss, Johann Jr. **14** 498-499

Galotti, Odoardo (literary character)
Lessing, Gotthold Ephraim **9** 357-359

GALSWORTHY, JOHN (1867-1933), English novelist and playwright **6** 189-190
Conrad, Joseph **4** 205-207
de la Roche, Mazo Louise **4** 474-475
Ford, Ford Madox **6** 1-2
Mann, Thomas **10** 204-207

Galt, John (1779-1839), Scottish novelist
Galt, Alexander Tilloch **6** 190-191

GALT, SIR ALEXANDER TILLOCH (1817-1893), Canadian politician **6** 190-191

GALTIERI, LEOPOLDO FORTUNATO (born 1926), president of Argentina (1981-1982) **6** 191-193

GALTON, SIR FRANCIS (1822-1911), English scientist, biometrician, and explorer **6** 193-194
Bertillon, Alphonse **2** 230-231

GALVANI, LUIGI (1737-1798), Italian physiologist **6** 194-195
Du Bois-Reymond, Emil **5** 118-119
Volta, Alessandro **16** 12-14

Galvanometer (instrument)
Hill, Archibald Vivian **7** 385-386
Kelvin of Largs **8** 488-489

Galveston (city; Texas)
Borden, Gail **2** 409

Galveston Island (Gulf of Mexico)
Cabeza de Vaca, Álvar Núñez **3** 197

GÁLVEZ, BERNARDO DE (1746-1786), Spanish colonial administrator **6** 195-196

GÁLVEZ, JOSÉ DE (1720-1787), Spanish statesman in Mexico **6** 196
Portolá, Gaspar de **12** 408
Revillagigedo, Conde de **13** 111-112

Galvino (died circa 1557), Araucanian chief
Ercilla y Zúñiga, Alonso de **5** 302

Gama, Paula de (died 1499), Portugese explorer
Gama, Vasco da **6** 196-198

GAMA, VASCO DA (circa 1460-1524), Portuguese navigator **6** 196-198
Indian voyage
Dias de Novais, Bartolomeu **4** 533-534
Manuel I **10** 219-220
Nzinga Nkuwu **11** 451-452
influence of
Cabral, Pedro Álvares **3** 203-204
Camoëns, Luis Vaz de **3** 247-249
Columbus, Christopher **4** 176-179

Gamaliel (died A.D. 50), Jewish rabbi
Paul **12** 141-143

Gamaliel II (circa 80-115), Jewish rabbi
Judah I **8** 372-373

Gamarra, Agustin (1785-1841), Peruvian general and politician
Ballivián, José **1** 475

GAMBETTA, LÉON (1838-1882), French premier 1881-1882 **6** 198-199
Delcassé, Théophile **4** 478-479
Simon, Jules François **14** 237-238

Gambia (The Gambia; nation, West Africa)
Jawara, Dauda Kairaba **8** 227-228

Gambia River (Africa)
Cadamosto, Alvise da **3** 206-207
Henry the Navigator **7** 305-306

Gambrill and Richardson (architectural firm)
McKim, Charles Follen **10** 417-418]

Game and Playe of the Chesse, The (book)
Caxton, William **3** 386-387

Game at Chess, A (play)
Middleton, Thomas **11** 8-9

Game of Cards, A. (musical composition)
Stravinsky, Igor Fedorovich **14** 502-506

Game of Love and Chance, The (play)
Marivaux, Pierre Carlet de Chamblain de **10** 265-266

Gamelin, Évariste (literary character)
France, Anatole **6** 39-40

Games, theory of (math)
Von Neumann, John **16** 27-28

Gamma radiation (physics)
Anderson, Carl David **1** 214-215
Bothe, Walther **2** 438-439
Cherenkov, Pavel Alekseevich **3** 502-503
Hess, Victor Francis **7** 362-363
Mössbauer, Rudolf **11** 208-209

GAMOW, GEORGE (1904-1968), Russian-American nuclear physicist, astrophysicist, biologist, and author of books popularizing science **6** 199-200
Fermi, Enrico **5** 422-424

Ganda (African people)
Johnston, Henry Hamilton **8** 322-323
Mutesa I **11** 277
Mutesa II **11** 277-278
Mwanga **11** 282-283

Gandhi, Feroze (died 1960) Indian lawyer and newspaper executive
Gandhi, Indira Priyadarshini **6** 200-201

GANDHI, INDIRA PRIYADARSHINI (1917-1984), Indian political leader **6** 200-201
Kamaraj, Kumaraswami **8** 415
Nehru, Jawaharlal **11** 332-334

GANDHI, MOHANDAS KARAMCHAND (1869-1948), Indian political and religious leader **6** 201-204
influence of
Holmes, John Haynes **7** 456-457
Kamaraj, Kumaraswami **8** 415
Kaunda, Kenneth David **8** 460-461
King, Martin Luther Jr. **9** 20-22

Muste, Abraham Johannes **11** 276-277
Nehru, Jawaharlal **11** 332-334
Nkrumah, Kwame **11** 408-410
Pandit, Vijaya Lakshmi **12** 83-84
Premchand **12** 439
Radhakrishnan, Sarvepalli **12** 537-538
influenced by
Gokhale, Gopal Krishna **6** 396
Thoreau, Henry David **15** 203-205
nonviolent resistance
Botha, Louis **2** 434-436
Chelmsford, Frederic John Napier Thesiger **3** 497
Das, Chitta Ranjan **4** 401-402
Narayan, Jayaprakash **11** 312-313
Patel, Vallabhbhai **12** 129-130
Reading, 1st Marquess of **13** 64
supporters
Bhave, Vinoba **2** 257-258
Naidu, Sarojini **11** 294-295
Nehru, Motilal **11** 334-335
Prasad, Rajendra **12** 433
Rajagopalachari, Chakravarti **13** 6-7
untouchables issue
Ambedkar, Bhimrao Ramji **1** 190-191
see also Indian National Congress

GANDHI, RAJIV (1944-1991), Indian member of Parliament and prime minister **6** 204-205

Gandhi-Irwin Pact (1931)
Sapru, Tej Bahadur **13** 480-481

Gandhi's Truth (book)
Erikson, Erik Homburger **5** 309-310

Gangaikondacolapuram (city; India)
Rajaraja I **13** 7

Ganges River (India)
Alexander the Great **1** 137-141

Gangrene (medicine)
Fleming, Alexander **5** 483-485
Welch, William Henry **16** 185-186

Gänsemännchen, Das (novel)
Wassermann, Jakob **16** 130-131

Gant, Eugene (literary character)
Wolfe, Thomas Clayton **16** 355-356

Gants, Kiukhelgarten (poem)
Gogol, Nikolai **6** 391-393

Ganymed (poem)
Goethe, Johann Wolfgang von **6** 388-391

Gao (town; Sudan)
Ali, Sunni **1** 158-159

Gaon (Jewish title)
Elijah ben Solomon **5** 251-252
Kuk, Abraham Issac **9** 123-124

Gaon, Saadia (flourished 9th century), Jewish scholar
Schechter, Solomon **13** 524

Gaonic sources (Jewish law)
Caro, Joseph ben Ephraim **3** 316-317

Gapon, George (1870-1906), Russian priest
Nicholas II **11** 378-380

Garabit viaduct (Ruines; France)
Eiffel, Alexandre Gustave **5** 227-228

GARBO, GRETA (1905-1990), Swedish-born American film star **6** 205-207
Barrymores **2** 28-30
Gable, William Clark **6** 157-158
Lubitsch, Ernst **10** 18-19

Garcia (died 1071), king of Galicia 1065-1071
Alfonso VI **1** 149

GARCIA, CARLOS P. (1896-1971), Philippine statesman, president 1957-61 **6** 207-208
Macapagal, Diosdado P. **10** 74-76

Garciá Godoy, Hector (1921-1970), Dominican statesman
Balaguer y Ricardo, Joaquin **1** 460-461
Bosch, Juan **2** 428-429

Garcia Iñiguez, Calixto (1836-1898), Cuban lawyer and revolutionist
Gómez, Máximo **6** 418-419
Menocal, Mario Garcia **10** 506-507

GARCÍA MÁRQUEZ, GABRIEL (born 1928), Colombian author **6** 208-209

GARCÍA MORENO, GABRIEL (1821-1875), Ecuadorian politician, president 1861-1865 and 1869-1875 **6** 209-210
Flores, Juan José **5** 491
Montalvo, Juan María **11** 119-120

Garcia y Sarmientc, Félix Rubén
see Dario, Rubén

GARCILASO DE LA VEGA, INCA (1539-1616), Peruvian chronicler **6** 210-211

Garcilaso de la Vega, Sebastián (circa 1500-1559), Spanish colonial administrator
Garcilaso de la Vega, Inca **6** 210-211

Gardano, Antonio (1509-1569), French-Italian music publisher and composer
Lassus, Roland de **9** 216-218

Garden, Alexander (circa 1730-1791), Scottish-born American naturalist and physician
Bartram, John **2** 40-41

Garden, The (poem)
Marvell, Andrew **10** 301-303

Garden and Forest (journal)
Olmsted, Frederick Law **11** 503-504

Garden City (city; New York State)
Stewart, Alexander Turney **14** 448-449

Garden District (play)
Williams, Tennessee **16** 306-308

Garden in Sochi (painting)
Gorky, Arshile **6** 458

Garden of Bérénice, The (novel)
Barrès, Auguste Maurice **2** 20-21

Garden of Cyrus, The (book)
Browne, Thomas **3** 49-50

Garden of Earthly Delights (triptych)
Bosch, Hieronymus **2** 426-428

Garden of Epicurus, The (literary collection)
France, Anatole **6** 39-40

Garden of Love (painting; Rubens)
Rubens, Peter Paul **13** 339-342
Watteau, Antoine **16** 143-144

Garden Party, The (book)
Moravia, Alberto **11** 153-155

Gardener, The (painting)
Le Nain, Antoine, Louis and Mathieu **9** 321-322

Gardener's Year (book)
Čapek, Karel **3** 271-272

Gardens of Chatou (painting)
Vlaminck, Maurice **16** 6

Gardens of the Luxembourg (painting)
David, Jacques Louis **4** 407-409

GARDINER, SAMUEL RAWSON (1829-1902), English historian **6** 211
Macaulay, Thomas Babington **10** 79-80

Gardiner, Stephen (1483?-1555), English prelate and statesman
Cromwell, Thomas **4** 320-321
Henry VIII **7** 302-305

GARDNER, JOHN W. (born 1912), American educator, public official, and political reformer **6** 211-213

GARFIELD, JAMES ABRAM (1831-1881), American general, president 1881 **6** 213-214
assassination
Arthur, Chester Alan **1** 321-323
Eaton, Dorman Bridgman **5** 190-191
Pendleton, George Hunt **12** 198
biographers
Alger, Horatio **1** 153-154
Cabinet
Blaine, James Gillespie **2** 312-313
opponents
Conkling, Roscoe **4** 201-202
Platt, Thomas Collier **12** 347-348
Sherman, John **14** 184-185
supporters
Arthur, Chester Alan **1** 321-323
Hanna, Marcus Alonzo **7** 127-128
Harrison, Benjamin **7** 178-179

Gargantua (novel)
Rabelais, François **12** 524-526-70

GARIBALDI, GIUSEPPE (1807-1882), Italian patriot **6** 215-217
Cavour, Conte di **3** 385-386
Crispi, Francesco **4** 310-311
Dumas, Alexandre **5** 136-138
Mazzini, Giuseppe **10** 381-383
Trevelyan, George Macaulay **15** 294-295

Victor Emmanuel II **15** 483-484

Garibaldina, La (novel)
Vittorini, Elio **16** 2-3

Garine (literary character)
Malraux, André **10** 178-180

GARLAND, HANNIBAL HAMLIN (1860-1940), American author **6** 217-218
Crane, Stephen **4** 293-295

GARLAND, JUDY (1922-1969), super star of films, musicals, and concert stage **6** 218-219

Garland of Laurel, The (book)
Skelton, John **14** 268-269

Garment Cutters' Association of Philadelphia (established 1862)
Stephens, Uriah **14** 431-432

Garment industry (United States)
Hillman, Sidney **7** 392-393
Howe, Elias **7** 529-530
Stephens, Uriah **14** 431-432
see also International Ladies' Garment Workers' Union

GARNEAU, FRANÇOIS-XAVIER (1809-1866), French-Canadian historian **6** 219-220

Garnet, Henry Highland (1815-1882), African American clergyman, abolitionist, and diplomat
Remond, Charles Lennox **13** 95
Walker, David **16** 62-63

Garnet wheat (grain)
Saunders, Charles Edward **13** 498-499

GARNIER, FRANCIS (Marie Joseph François Garnier; 1839-1873), French naval officer **6** 220-221

GARNIER, JEAN LOUIS CHARLES (1825-1898), French architect **6** 221-222
Carpeaux, Jean Baptiste **3** 318-319

Garnier, Robert (1534-1590), French playwright
Kyd, Thomas **9** 140-141

Garnier, Tony (1869-1948), French architect
Le Corbusier **9** 274-275

Garofano rosso, II (novel)
Vittorini, Elio **16** 2-3

GARRETT, JOHN WORK (1820-1884), American railroad magnate **6** 225

Garrett, Patrick Floyd (1850-1908), American sheriff
Billy the Kid **2** 277
Love, Nat **10** 1-2

GARRETT, THOMAS (1789-1871), American abolitionist **6** 225-226
Coffin, Levi **4** 135

Garrett (Anderson), Elizabeth (1836-1917), English physician and women's rights advocate **6** 222-225

Garrick, David (1717-1779), English actor
Collins, William **4** 168-169
Fuseli, Henry **6** 153-155
Johnson, Samuel **8** 315-317

Sheridan, Richard Brinsley **14** 183-184
Smollett, Tobias George **14** 305-307

Garrick Gaieties (musical review)
Rodgers, Richard Charles **13** 234-236

Garrigue, Charlotte (1850-1923), American wife of Masaryk
Masaryk, Tomáš Garrigue **10** 314-315

Garrison, Cornelius K. (1809-1885), American financier
Walker, William **16** 68-69

GARRISON, WILLIAM LLOYD
(1805-1879), American editor and abolitionist **6** 226-228
abolitionist journalism
Bailey, Gamaliel **1** 444-445
Grimké, Sarah Moore and Angelina Emily **7** 2-3
Lundy, Benjamin **10** 45-46
Walker, David **16** 62-63
associates
Foster, Abigail Kelley **6** 25
Mott, Lucretia Coffin **11** 212-213
Phillips, Wendell **12** 281-282
colonization movement
Birney, James Gillespie **2** 283-284
Forten, James **6** 17-18
influence of
Anthony, Susan Brownell **1** 246-248
Child, Lydia Maria Francis **3** 520-521
Crandall, Prudence **4** 291
Purvis, Robert **12** 485-486
Remond, Charles Lennox **13** 95
Tappan brothers **15** 105-106
Whittier, John Greenleaf **16** 256-257
Wright, Elizur **16** 396-397
relatives
Villard, Oswald Garrison **15** 498-499

Garuda (celestial bird; India)
Harsha **7** 181-182

GARVEY, MARCUS MOSIAH (1887-1940), Jamaican leader and African nationalist **6** 228-229
influence of
Diagne, Blaise **4** 527
Malcolm X **10** 165-166
Nkrumah, Kwame **11** 408-410
pan-Africanism
Hayford, J. E. Casely **7** 228-230
Padmore, George **12** 57-58
Williams, Henry Sylvester **16** 303-304
see also Nationalism, African; pan-Africanism

GARY, ELBERT HENRY (1846-1927), American lawyer and industrialist **6** 229-230
Tarbell, Ida Minerva **15** 107-108

Gas (chemistry)
concept of developed
Helmont, Jan Baptista van **7** 269-271
inert

Rutherford, Ernest **13** 384-387
Soddy, Frederick **14** 321-323
Kinetic theory
see Kinetic theory of gases
physical properties
Cavendish, Henry **3** 383-384
Chapman, Sydney **3** 441
Dalton, John **4** 378-379
Fermi, Enrico **5** 422-424
Gay-Lussac, Joseph Louis **6** 245-246

Gas, natural
Westinghouse, George **16** 215

Gas, poison
see Poison gas

Gas I and II (plays)
Kaiser, Georg **8** 411-412

GASCA, PEDRO DE LA (circa 1496-1567), Spanish priest and statesman **6** 230-231
Valdivia, Pedro de **15** 400-401

Gascony (region; France)
English conflicts
Edward I **5** 208-210
Edward III **5** 211-212
Edward the Black Prince **5** 217-218
Henry III **7** 290-292
French conflicts
Charles VII **3** 461-462
Philip VI **12** 277-278

Gascoyne River (Australia)
Grey, George **6** 540-541

Gascoyne-Cecil, Robert Arthur Talbot
see Salisbury, 3rd Marquess of

GASKELL, ELIZABETH (1810-1865), English novelist **6** 231-232
Dickens, Charles John Huffam **4** 538-541

Gaskia Corp. (established 1945)
Imam, Alhadji Abubakar **8** 114-115

Gasmotor-en-Fabrik (auto firm)
Daimler, Gottlieb **4** 368

Gaspard de la nuit (musical composition)
Ravel, Maurice Joseph **13** 54-55

Gaspard-Poussin
see Dughet, Gaspard

Gasparini, Francesco (1668-1727), Italian composer
Scarlatti, Domenico **13** 515-517

Gaspé, Philippe Aubert de
see Aubert de Gaspé, Philippe

Gassendi, Pierre (1592-1655), French philosopher
Hobbes, Thomas **7** 421-423
Molière **11** 86-88

Gasser, Herbert S. (1888-1963), American physiologist
Erlanger, Joseph **5** 310-311
Hill, Archibald Vivian **7** 385-386

Gastein Convention (1865)
Bismarck, Otto Eduard Leopold von **2** 294-296

Gaston Latour (novel)
Pater, Walter Horatio **12** 130-131

Gastrolates (literary characters)
Rabelais, François **12** 524-526

Gat (slang)
Gatling, Richard Jordan **6** 234-235

Gate... (poems)
Lewis, Cecil Day **9** 380

Gate, The (novel)
Natsume, Soseki **11** 324-325

Gate, The (painting)
Hofmann, Hans **7** 442-443

Gate of the Heroes (sculpture)
Brancusi, Constantin **2** 494-496

Gates, Horatio (1728?-1806), American Revolutionary general
Greene, Nathanael **6** 525-526
Lincoln, Benjamin **9** 418-419
Marion, Francis **10** 262-263
Morgan, Daniel **11** 160-161
Stuart, Gilbert **14** 513-515
Tarleton, Banastre **15** 110
Wilkinson, James **16** 284-286

GATES, WILLIAM HENRY, III ("Bill"; born 1955), computer software company co-founder and executive **6** 232-234

Gates of Hell (sculpture; Rodin)
Epstein, Jacob **5** 295-296
Rodin, Auguste **13** 236-238

Gates of Paradise (poems)
Markham, Edwin **10** 267

Gates of Paradise (sculpture)
see Florence Cathedral—Baptistery

Gathas Hymns (book)
Zoroaster **16** 528-530, 535

"Gather, ye rosebuds...," (sonnet; Herrick)
Góngora y Argote, Luis de **6** 427-428

GATLING, RICHARD JORDAN
(1818-1903), American inventor of multiple-firing guns **6** 234-235

Gatsby, Jay (literary character)
Fitzgerald, Francis Scott Key **5** 470-472

Gattamelata, Erasmo (1370?-1443), Venetian condottiere
Bellini, Giovanni **2** 137-138
Donatello **5** 55-56
Saint-Gaudens, Augustus **13** 432

Gatti-Casazza, Giulio (1869-1940), Italian operatic director
Caruso, Enrico **3** 345

Gaucho War (Argentina; 1814-21)
Güemes, Martín **7** 26-27

Gaude Virgo (motet)
Tallis, Thomas **15** 91

GAUDÍ I CORNET, ANTONI (1852-1926), Catalan architect and designer **6** 235-236

Gaugamela, battle of (331 B.C.)
Alexander the Great **1** 137-141
Ptolemy I **12** 470-472

GAUGUIN, PAUL (1848-1903), French painter and sculptor **6** 236-238
  associates
    Rousseau, Henri **13** 323-324
  influence of
    Amiet, Cuno **1** 201-202
    Bonnard, Pierre **2** 395-396
    Derain, André **4** 503
    Glackens, William **6** 355-356
    Maillol, Aristide **10** 150-151
    Matisse, Henri **10** 336-337
    Rivera, Diego **13** 183-184
    Van Gogh, Vincent **15** 427-429
    Vuillard, Jean Édouard **16** 36
  influenced by
    Hokusai, Katsushika **7** 447-448
    Puvis de Chavannes, Pierre **12** 492-493
    Seurat, Georges Pierre **14** 120-122

Gaul (ancient European nation)
  Merovingians in
    Clovis I **4** 124
    Martel, Charles **10** 285
  Roman rule (3rd-5th century)
    Diocletian **5** 19-20
    Julian **8** 378-379
    Stilicho, Flavius **14** 452-453
  Roman rule (Caesar)
    Antony, Mark **1** 253-254
    Brutus, Marcus Junius **3** 79-80
    Caesar, Gaius Julius **3** 207-210
    Clodius Pulcher, Publius **4** 121-122
    Crassus Dives, Marcus Licinius **4** 296-297
  Vikings in
    Rollo **13** 264-265

GAULLI, GIOVANNI BATTISTA (1639-1709), Italian painter **6** 238-239
  Cortona, Pietro da **4** 256

GAULTIER, JEAN PAUL (born 1952), French avant-garde designer **6** 239-240

Gaumata (died 521 B.C.), Magian priest from Media
  Darius I **4** 394-395

Gauntlet, A (play)
  Bjørnson, Bjørnstjerne **2** 299-300

GAUSS, KARL FRIEDRICH (1777-1855), German mathematician and astronomer **6** 240-242
  Lobachevskii, Nikolai Ivanovich **9** 472-474
  Riemann, Georg Friedrich Bernard **13** 164-165

Gautama, Prince
  see Buddha

Gautier, Théophile (1811-1872), French writer
  Flaubert, Gustave **5** 480-482
  Hearn, Lafcadio **7** 240
  Hugo, Victor Marie **8** 22-25
  Manet, Édouard **10** 193-194
  Nerval, Gérard de **11** 345-346
  Pater, Walter Horatio **12** 130-131

Gaveston, Piers (died 1312), English courtier
  Edward II **5** 210

GAVIRIA TRUJILLO, CESAR AUGUSTO (born 1947), president of Colombia **6** 242-243

Gavroche (literary character)
  Hugo, Victor Marie **8** 22-25

Gawain (Gauvain; literary character)
  Chrestien de Troyes **4** 23-24
  see also Arthurian legend

GAY, JOHN (1685-1732), English playwright and poet **6** 243-244
  associates
    Bolingbroke, Viscount **2** 374-375
    Congreve, William **4** 200-201
    Pope, Alexander **12** 395-397
    Swift, Jonathan **15** 51-54
  influence of
    Brecht, Bertolt **2** 512-514
    Handel, George Frederick **7** 116-119

GAY-LUSSAC, JOSEPH LOUIS (1778-1850), French chemist and physicist **6** 245-246
  Avogadro, Lorenzo Romano Amedeo Carlo **1** 388-389
  Bernard, Claude **2** 208-210
  Liebig, Justus von **9** 403-404

Gaya Congress (India)
  Das, Chitta Ranjan **4** 401-402

GAYLE, HELENE DORIS (born 1955), African American epidemiologist and pediatrician **6** 244-245

Gayne (ballet)
  Khachaturian, Aram Ilich **8** 530-531

Gbedemah, Komla Agbell (born 1912), Ghanaian political leader
  Busia, Kofi Abrefa **3** 172-173

GCBA
  see General Council of Burmese Associations

Gdansk (city; Poland)
  Gomulka, Wladislaw **6** 422-424

GE
  see General Electric

Geba River (Port Guinea)
  Cadamosto, Alvise da **3** 206-207
  Henry the Navigator **7** 305-306

Geber
  see Jabir ibn Hayyan

Gebir (poem)
  Landor, Walter Savage **9** 186-187

Gebroeders, De (play)
  Vondel, Joost van den **16** 19-20

GEDDES, SIR PATRICK (1854-1932), Scottish sociologist and biologist **6** 246-247
  Mumford, Lewis **11** 246-247

Gedichte (poems)
  Heine, Heinrich **7** 259-260
  Huch, Ricarda **8** 11-12

  Keller, Gottfried **8** 478-479

GEERTGEN TOT SINT JANS (Geertgen van Haarlem; circa 1460/65-1490/95), Netherlandish painter **6** 248
  Massys, Quentin **10** 325-326
  van der Goes, Hugo **15** 416-417

Geertruidenberg (city; Netherlands)
  Maurice of Nassau **10** 348-349

GEERTZ, CLIFFORD (born 1926), American cultural anthropologist **6** 248-249

Geez (Old Ethiopian language)
  Yekuno Amlak **16** 449

Gefallen (story)
  Mann, Thomas **10** 204-207

Geheime Staatspolizei
  see Gestapo (Nazi, Germany)

Geheimnisse, Die (epic)
  Goethe, Johann Wolfgang von **6** 388-391

GEHRY, FRANK O. (née Goldberg; born 1929), American architect **6** 250-251

GEIGER, HANS (born Johannes Wilhelm Geiger; 1882-1945), German physicist **6** 251-253
  Bothe, Walther **2** 438-439
  Chadwick, James **3** 405-406
  Rutherford, Ernest **13** 384-387

Geiger counter
  Geiger, Hans **6** 251-253

Geischt der herrschenden Klasse, Das (lithograph series)
  Grosz, George **7** 17-18

GEISEL, ERNESTO (1908-1996), Brazilian army general, president of Brazil's national oil company (Petrobras), and president of the republic (1974-1979) **6** 253-255

GEISEL, THEODOR (a.k.a. Dr. Seuss; 1904-1991), American author of children's books **6** 255-256

Geiseric
  see Gaiseric

Geissler, Heinrich (1814-1879), German inventor
  Röntgen, Wilhelm Conrad **13** 273-275

Geistliche Chormusik (music collection)
  Schütz, Heinrich **14** 48-49

Geistliche Lieder (literary collection)
  Novalis **11** 435

Gelder, Aert de (1645-1727), Dutch painter
  Rembrandt Harmensz van Rijn **13** 91-95

Gelignite (explosive)
  Nobel, Alfred Bernhard **11** 410-411

Gellée, Claude
  see Claude Lorrain

GELLER, MARGARET JOAN (born 1947), American astronomer **6** 256-257

Geller House (Lawrence, New York)
Breuer, Marcel **2** 520-521

Gellert, Christian Fürchtegott (1715-1769),
German poet
Lessing, Gotthold Ephraim **9** 357-359

GELL-MANN, MURRAY (born 1929),
American physicist **6** 257-258

Gemara
see Talmud

GEMAYEL, AMIN (born 1942), Lebanese
nationalist and Christian political leader;
president of the Republic of Lebanon
(1982-1988) **6** 258-259

GEMAYEL, PIERRE (1905-1984), leader of
the Lebanese Phalangist Party **6** 259-261

Gemini
seeCastor and Pollux

Gemini (spacecraft)
Armstrong, Neil Alden **1** 304-306

Geminiani, Francesco (1674?-1762?), Italian violinist and composer
Corelli, Arcangelo **4** 230-231

Gene (biology)
see Genetics

Gene Wesleyan Seminary (New York State)
Willard, Frances Elizabeth Caroline
16 289-290

Genealogia di casa Gonzaga (poem)
Tasso, Torquato **15** 114-116

Genealogy of Morals, A (book)
Nietzsche, Friedrich **11** 390-392

Genealogy of the Gods (poem)
Hesiod **7** 361-362

General Allotment Act (1887)
Fletcher, Alice Cunningham **5** 486-487

General Archives (Mexico)
Revillagigedo, Conde de **13** 111-112

General Association of German Workers
see Social Democratic party (Germany)

General Booth (poem)
Lindsay, Vachel **9** 424-425

**General Confederation of Workers and
Peasants** (Mexico)
Toledano, Vicente Lombardo
15 256-257

General Convention (Protestant Episcopal
Church; 1789)
Seabury, Samuel **14** 76

General Council of Burmese Associations
Ba Maw **1** 480-481

General Died at Dawn, The (film)
Odets, Clifford **11** 470-471

General Education Board (United States)
Rockefeller, John D. Jr. **13** 225-226

General Electric Company (Berlin)
Behrens, Peter **2** 121-122

General Electric Company (Schenectady;
New York State)
Swope, Gerard **15** 56-58

chairmen
Young, Owen D. **16** 473-474
industrial research
Bridgman, Percy Williams **3** 5-6
Fuller, Richard Buckminster
6 149-150
Langmuir, Irving **9** 196-197
Steinmetz, Charles Proteus
14 419-420
Whittle, Frank **16** 257-258
organized
Edison, Thomas Alva **5** 206-208

General Foods Corporation
Post, Charles William **12** 408-409

General Historie of Virginia... (book)
Beverley, Robert **2** 252
Smith, John **14** 295-297

General Line, The (film)
Eisenstein, Sergei Mikhailovich
5 240-242

General Military Academy (Saragossa,
Spain)
Franco Bahamonde, Francisco **6** 52-54

General Motors Corporation
competition
Chrysler, Walter Percy **4** 36-37
du Pont, Pierre Samuel **5** 154-155
Ford, Henry **6** 5-6
founded
Durant, William Crapo **5** 158
officials
du Pont, Pierre Samuel **5** 154-155
Knudsen, William S. **9** 67-68
Sloan, Alfred Pritchard Jr. **14** 274
Stettinius, Edward R. Jr. **14** 437-438
research
Kettering, Charles F. **8** 524-525
Wilson, Charles Erwin **16** 316-317
strikes
Lewis, John Llewellyn **9** 387-388
Murphy, Frank **11** 260-261
Reuther, Walter Philip **13** 107-108
suits against
Nader, Ralph **11** 290-291
Technical Center (Warren, Michigan)
Saarinen, Eliel and Eero **13** 396-398

General Privilege (1283)
Peter III **12** 256-257

Generation of 1837 (Argentine literary
exiles)
Alberdi, Juan Bautista **1** 109-110
Mitre, Bartolomé **11** 62-63

Generation of 1898 (Spanish literature)
Azaña Diaz, Manuel **1** 396-397
Baroja y Nessi, Pío **2** 15-16
Benavente y Martinez, Jacinto
2 146-147
Ruíz, José Martínez **13** 358
Valle Inclán, Ramón Maria del
15 407-408
see also Modernista movement

Generation of 1927 (Spanish literature)
Guillén, Nicolás **7** 34-35

Lorca, Federico García **9** 511-513

Genesis (Old Testament book)
Augustine **1** 367-370
Bonhoeffer, Dietrich **2** 389-391
Isidore of Seville **8** 149-150

GENET, EDMOND CHARLES (1763-1834),
French diplomat **6** 261-262
Jefferson, Thomas **8** 238-241
Washington, George **16** 126-129

GENET, JEAN (1910-1986), French novelist
and playwright **6** 262-263
Sartre, Jean Paul **13** 491-492

Genetic psychology
see Evolutionism (psychology)

Genetics (biology)
DNA
Nirenberg, Marshall Warren
11 399-400
foundations
Avery, Oswald Theodore **1** 384-386
Chargaff, Erwin **3** 444-445
Galton, Francis **6** 193-194
Hershey, Alfred Day **7** 343-345
Kornberg, Arthur **9** 85-87
Lederberg, Joshua **9** 275-277
Mendel, Johann Gregor **10** 483-486
Vries, Hugo de **16** 33-36
Weismann, August Freidrich
Leopold **16** 178-180
gene action
Beadle, George Wells **2** 80-81
Haldane, John Burdon Sanderson
7 70-71
Lwoff, André **10** 58-59
McClintock, Barbara **10** 393-394
Mintz, Beatrice **11** 49-50
Muller, Hermann Joseph
11 238-239
Neufeld, Elizabeth F. **11** 352-353
gene mapping
Sturtevant, A. H. **15** 3-5
gene therapy
Berg, Paul **2** 187-189
molecular
Delbrück, Max **4** 476-478
nucleoproteins
Crick, Francis Harry Crompton
4 310
Khorana, Har Gobind **8** 537-538
Monod, Jacques **11** 110-111
Watson, James Dewey **16** 137-138
sex determination
Stevens, Nettie Maria **14** 441-442
theories
Bateson, William **2** 55-57
de Vries, Hugo **4** 516-518
East, Edward Murray **5** 182-183
Lysenko, Trofim Denisovich **10** 71
Margulis, Lynn **10** 253-254
Morgan, Thomas Hunt **11** 170-171
Stevens, Nettie Maria **14** 441-442
Sturtevant, A. H. **15** 3-5
see also Natural selection; Plant
breeding; Scientists—geneticists

Geneva (city; Switzerland)
Calvin, John **3** 239-242
Francis of Sales **6** 47
Knox, John **9** 65-66
Mary I **10** 308-309

Geneva, University of
Piaget, Jean **12** 287-288
Weizmann, Chaim **16** 183-184

Geneva Conferences 1864 (Red Cross)
Barton, Clara **2** 37-39
1932 (disarmament)
Henderson, Arthur **7** 277-278
Hoover, Herbert Clark **7** 483-485
1954 (Vietnam)
Chou En-lai **4** 20-22
Diem, Ngo Dinh **5** 6-7
Ho Chi Minh **7** 426-428
Menon, Vengalil Krishnan Krishna **10** 507-509
Sihanouk, Norodom **14** 222-223
1955 (Germany)
Dulles, John Foster **5** 134-135
Eisenhower, Dwight David **5** 233-236
1962 (Laos)
Souvanna Phouma **14** 357-358

Geneva Medical College (New York State)
Blackwell, Elizabeth **2** 311-312

Geneva Protocol (1924)
Beneš, Edward **2** 155-157

Genga, Annibale Francesco della
see Leo XII

GENGHIS KHAN (1167-1227), Mongol chief, creator of the Mongol empire **6** 263-265
Babar the Conqueror **1** 405-407
Batu Khan **2** 60-61
Hulagu Khan **8** 27-28
Kublai Khan **9** 115-118
Yeh-lü Ch'u-ts'ai **16** 447-449

Genitrix (novel)
Mauriac, François **10** 347-348

Genius (literary character)
Gower, John **6** 475-476

Genius, The (autobiography)
Dreiser, Herman Theodore **5** 98-100

Genius of Christianity, The (book)
Chateaubriand, Vicomte de **3** 477-479

Genius of Universal Emancipation (newspaper)
Garrison, W.L.
Lundy, Benjamin **10** 45-46

Genizah Studies... (book)
Ginzberg, Louis **6** 337-338

Genji, Hikaru (literary character)
Murasaki Shikibu **11** 252-253

Genji monogatari
see Tale of Genji, The

Genlis, Comtesse de (1746-1830), French writer
Edgeworth, Maria **5** 205-206

Genoa (Italian city-state)
Julius II **8** 384-386
Manuel I **10** 218-219
Polo, Marco **12** 380-382

Genoa Conference (1922)
Rathenau, Walther **13** 48-49

Genossenschaft theory (law)
Gierke, Otto von **6** 311-312

Genoveva (opera)
Schumann, Robert Alexander **14** 41-43

Genoveva (play)
Hebbel, Friedrich **7** 247
Tieck, Ludwig **15** 218-219

Genroku era (Japan; circa 1680-1730)
Basho, Matsuo **2** 45-48

GENSCHER, HANS-DIETRICH (born 1927), leader of West Germany's liberal party (the FDP) and foreign minister **6** 265-266

Genseric
see Gaiseric

Gente conocida (play)
Benavente y Martinez, Jacinto **2** 146-147

Gente del Po (film)
Antonioni, Michelangelo **1** 252-253

GENTILE DA FABRIANO (Gentile di Niccolò di Giovanni di Massio; circa 1370-1427), Italian painter **6** 266-267
Bellini, Giovanni **2** 137-138
Pisanello **12** 323-324
Tura, Cosimo **15** 343-344

GENTILE, GIOVANNI (1875-1944), Italian philosopher and politician **6** 267
Croce, Benedetto **4** 313-314
Vico, Giambattista **15** 480-481

Gentileschi, Orazio (1563-1647), Italian-born painter in England
Le Nain, Antoine, Louis and Mathieu **9** 321-322

Gentili, Luigi (1801-1848), Italian missionary in England
Rosmini-Serbati, Antonio **13** 296-297

Gentiloni Pact (1913)
Pius X **12** 336-337

Gentle Grafter, The (stories)
Henry, O. **7** 308-309

Gentle Shepherds, ye that know (elegy)
Purcell, Henry **12** 484-485

Gentleman and a Lady, A (painting)
Campin, Robert **3** 255

Gentleman and Cabinet-Maker's Director, The (book; Chippendale)
Chippendale, Thomas **4** 1-2
Hepplewhite, George **7** 317-318

Gentleman Dancing Master, The (play)
Wycherley, William **16** 411-412

Gentleman from Indiana, The (novel)
Tarkington, Newton Booth **15** 109

Gentleman from San Francisco, The (book)

Bunin, Ivan Alekseevich **3** 124

Gentleman in Blue (painting)
Titian **15** 242-244

Gentleman's Magazine (periodical)
Collins, William **4** 168-169
Johnson, Samuel **8** 315-317
Sterne, Laurence **14** 435-437

Gentlemen at Gyang Gyang (novel)
Franklin, Stella Maraia Sarah Miles **6** 68-69

Gentner, W. (1906-1980), German physicist
Bothe, Walther **2** 438-439

Gentz, Friedrich von (1764-1832), German diplomat
Metternich, Klemens von **10** 533-536
Ranke, Leopold von **13** 33-35

Geocentric theory (astronomy)
see Universe, systems of—geocentric

Geochemistry (science)
Urey, Harold Clayton **15** 394-396
see also Scientists—geochemists

Geochronology (geology)
Holmes, Arthur **7** 455-456

Geodesic domes (architecture)
Fuller, Richard Buckminster **6** 149-150

Geodesy (science)
Meinesz, Felix Andries Vening **10** 461
see also Scientists—geodesists

Geoffrey IV (the Handsome; 1113-1151), Count of Anjou 1129-1149
Henry I **7** 286-287
Henry II **7** 287-289
Stephen **14** 426-427

Geoffrey Moncton (novel)
Moodie, Susanna **11** 140-141

GEOFFREY OF MONMOUTH (circa 1100-1155), English pseudohistorian **6** 268
Chrestien de Troyes **4** 23-24
Layamon **9** 256-257

Geography
ancient and medieval
Eratosthenes of Cyrene **5** 301-302
Hipparchus **7** 407-408
Idrisi, Muhammad ibn Muhammad al- **8** 102-103
Khwarizmi, Muhammad ibn Musa al- **8** 541
Mercator, Gerhardus **10** 511-512
Ortelius, Abraham **12** 8-9
Ptolemy, Claudius **12** 473-474
Strabo **14** 485-486
Waldseemüller, Martin **16** 56
modern schools
Bowman, Isaiah **2** 464-465
Davis, William Morris **4** 425-426
Morse, Jedidiah **11** 191-192
Ritter, Karl **13** 181-182
Vidal de la Blache, Paul **15** 490
see also Scientists—cartographers, geographers

Geography (book; Ptolemy)
    Mendaña de Neyra, Álvaro de **10** 483
    Mercator, Gerhardus **10** 511-512
    Ortelius, Abraham **12** 8-9
    Ptolemy, Claudius **12** 473-474

Geography (book; Strabo)
    Phidias **12** 265-267
    Strabo **14** 485-486

Geological Survey (Canada)
    Logan, William Edmond **9** 488-489

Geological Survey (England)
    Huxley, Thomas Henry **8** 77-79

Geological Survey (United States)
    Chamberlin, Thomas Chrowder
      3 415-416
    Ward, Lester Frank **16** 113-114

Geology (science)
    continental drift
      Wegener, Alfred Lothar **16** 170-171
    cosmogony
      Chamberlin, Thomas Chrowder
        3 415-416
      Werner, Abraham Gottlob
        16 205-207
    dating methods
      Boltwood, Bertram Borden
        2 378-379
      Hahn, Otto **7** 64-65
    economic
      Humboldt, Friedrich Heinrich
        Alexander von **8** 30-31
      Logan, William Edmond **9** 488-489
      Whitney, Josiah Dwight **16** 254-255
    historical
      Davis, William Morris **4** 425-426
      Holmes, Arthur **7** 455-456
      Murchison, Roderick Impey
        11 255-256
      Sedgwick, Adam **14** 82-83
    of Antarctica
      Fuchs, Vivian **6** 140
    paleontology
      Cuvier, Georges Léopold **4** 357-359
      Steno, Nicolaus **14** 425-426
    petrology
      Holmes, Arthur **7** 455-456
    uniformitarianism
      Darwin, Charles Robert **4** 397-399
      Hutton, James **8** 73-74
      Lamarck, Chevalier de **9** 171-173
      Lyell, Charles **10** 62-63
      see also Scientists—geologists

Geomagnetism (geophysics)
    Chapman, George **3** 440-441
    Elsasser, Walter Maurice **5** 277-278
    Gauss, Karl Friedrich **6** 240-242
    Gay-Lussac, Joseph Louis **6** 245-246
    Humboldt, Friedrich Heinrich Alexan-
      der von **8** 30-31

Geometry (mathematics)
    analytic
      Apollonius of Perga **1** 261-262
      Descartes, René **4** 505-508
      Euler, Leonard **5** 331-332

      Fermat, Pierre de **5** 421-422
    descriptive
      Cauchy, Augustin Louis **3** 378-380
    development
      Archimedes **1** 277-280
      Democritus **4** 493-494
      Euclid **5** 327-329
      Eudoxus of Cnidus **5** 329-330
      Thales **15** 161
    Euclidean
      see Euclidean
    hypergeometric series
      Gauss, Karl Friedrich **6** 240-242
      Ramanujan Aiyangar, Srinivasa
        13 14-15
    non-Euclidean
      Gauss, Karl Friedrich **6** 240-242
      Lobachevskii, Nikolai Ivanovich
        9 472-474
      Riemann, Georg Friedrich Bernard
        13 164-165
    plane
      Euclid **5** 327-329
      Heron of Alexandria **7** 334-335
    projective
      Pascal, Blaise **12** 122-124
    Pythagorean theorem
      Pythagoras **12** 498-499
    Riemannian
      Riemann, Georg Friedrich Bernard
        13 164-165
    solid
      Euclid **5** 327-329

Geomorphology (science)
    Hutton, James **8** 73-74

Geonica (book)
    Ginzberg, Louis **6** 337-338

Geophysics (science)
    Chapman, Sydney **3** 441
    Elsasser, Walter Maurice **5** 277-278
    Ewing, William Maurice **5** 350-351
    Jeffreys, Harold **8** 241-242
    Meinesz, Felix Andries Vening **10** 461
    see also International Geophysical Year
      (1957-1958); Scientists—geophysicists

Geopolitics (social science)
    Haushofer, Karl **7** 201

George (1869-1957), prince of Greece
    Venizelos, Eleutherios **15** 460-461

George (born 1909), prince of Yugoslavia
    Alexander of Yugoslavia **1** 136-137

George (literary character)
    Stowe, Harriet Elizabeth Beecher
      14 484-485

GEORGE I (1660-1727), king of Great
Britain and Ireland 1714-1727 **6** 268-269
    accession
      Anne **1** 241-242
      Bolingbroke, Viscount **2** 374-375
    domestic policies
      Marlborough, 1st Duke of
        10 271-272
      Swift, Jonathan **15** 51-54
      Walpole, Robert **16** 82-84

    opponents
      Law, William **9** 245-246
      Leibniz, Gottfried Wilhelm von
        9 307-310
    patronage
      Handel, George Frederick
        7 116-119
      Steele, Richard **14** 407-409

George I (1845-1913), king of Greece
1863-1913
    Venizelos, Eleutherios **15** 460-461

GEORGE II (1683-1760), king of Great
Britain and Ireland and elector of
Hanover 1727-1760 **6** 269-270
    Butler, Joseph **3** 180-181
    Pitt, William the Elder **12** 328-329
    Walpole, Robert **16** 82-84

George II (1890-1947), king of Greece
1922-1923 and 1935-1947
    Venizelos, Eleutherios **15** 460-461

GEORGE III (1738-1820), king of Great
Britain and Ireland 1760-1820 **6** 270-272
    American opponents
      Adams, Samuel **1** 55-56
      Franklin, Benjamin **6** 60-64
      Jefferson, Thomas **8** 238-241
      Paine, Thomas **12** 66-67
    American supporters
      Dickinson, John **4** 543-544
      Leonard, Daniel **9** 336-337
    Chinese edict to
      Qianlong **12** 502-505
    domestic policies
      Banks, Joseph **1** 489-490
      Bentham, Jeremy **2** 176-178
      Castlereagh, Viscount **3** 363-364
      Herschel, William **7** 341-343
      Liverpool, 2nd Earl of **9** 456-457
    influenced by
      Bolingbroke, Viscount **2** 374-375
      Bute, 3d Earl of **3** 177-178
    ministers
      Amherst, Jeffery **1** 200-201
      Fox, Charles James **6** 35-37
      North, Frederick **11** 429-430
      Pitt, William the Elder **12** 328-329
      Pitt, William the Younger
        12 329-331
      Rockingham, 2d Marquess of
        13 230-231
      Rumford **13** 360-362
    patronage
      Johnson, Samuel **8** 315-317
      Rousseau, Jean Jacques **13** 324-328
      West, Benjamin **16** 210-212
    relatives
      George IV **6** 272-273
      William IV **16** 296-297

GEORGE IV (1762-1830), king of Great
Britain and Ireland 1820-1830 **6** 272-273
    Byron, George Gordon Noel **3** 193-194
    Castlereagh, Viscount **3** 363-364
    Leopold I **9** 345-346
    Liverpool, 2nd Earl of **9** 456-457
    Nash, John **11** 316

Sheridan, Richard Brinsley **14** 183-184
William IV **16** 296-297

GEORGE V (1865-1936), king of Great
Britain and Northern Ireland and emperor
of India 1910-1936 **6** 273-275
Edward VII **5** 214-215
Hirohito **7** 410-412
Reading, 1st Marquess of **13** 64

GEORGE VI (1895-1952), king of Great
Britain and Northern Ireland 1936-1952
6 275
Elizabeth, the Queen Mother **5** 261-263
Elizabeth II **5** 266-269

George, David Lloyd
see Lloyd George, David

GEORGE, HENRY (1839-1897), American
economist and social reformer **6** 276
influence of
Furphy, Joseph **6** 152-153
Glasgow, Ellen **6** 360-361
Johnson, Tom Loftin **8** 317
Lawson, Henry **9** 254-255
Shaw, George Bernard **14** 163-164
Sun Yat-sen **15** 35-39
opponents
Hewitt, Abram Stevens **7** 371-372
supporters
Corrigan, Michael Augustine **4** 253
De Leon, Daniel **4** 479-480
Dewey, John **4** 520-523

GEORGE, JAMES ZACHARIAH
(1826-1897), American politician and
jurist **6** 276-277

GEORGE, STEFAN (1868-1933), German
symbolist poet **6** 277-278
Berg, Alban **2** 186-187
Webern, Anton **16** 160-162

George Burns and Gracie Allen Show, The
Burns, George **3** 153-155

George Crabbe (poem)
Robinson, Edwin Arlington **13** 201-202

George Moore (poem)
Moore, Marianne **11** 148-149

George of Podebrad (1420-1471), king of
Bohemia
Pius II **12** 331

George Speyer-Haus Institute (Frankfurt)
Ehrlich, Paul **5** 225-226

George Villiers... (painting; Van Dyck)
Gainsborough, Thomas **6** 170-172

George Washington Bridge (New York City)
Goethals, George Washington
6 387-388
Nervi, Pier Luigi **11** 346-348

George Washington, Jr. (play)
Cohan, George Michael **4** 137-138

George Washington University (Washing-
ton D.C.)
Fulbright, James William **6** 147-149
Gamow, George **6** 199-200
White, William Alanson **16** 239-240
Wright, Carroll Davidson **16** 396

George William (died 1640), elector of
Brandenberg
Frederick William **6** 85-86

George's Mother (novel)
Crane, Stephen **4** 293-295

Georgetown University (Washington D.C.)
Sullivan, Harry Stack **15** 23-24
White, William Alanson **16** 239-240

Georgia (ancient Iberia; now Georgian
Soviet Socialist Republic)
Alp Arslan **1** 178-179
Godunov, Boris Feodorovich **6** 382-383
Mansur, Abu Jafar ibn Muhammad al-
10 214-215

Georgia (state; United States)
Civil War period
Brown, Joseph Emerson **3** 41-42
Hill, Benjamin Harvey **7** 386-387
Howard, Oliver Otis **7** 528-529
Sherman, William Tecumseh
14 186-187
Stephens, Alexander Hamilton
14 429-430
constitutional convention
Turner, Henry McNeal **15** 351-352
exploration and colonization
de Soto, Hernando **4** 510-511
Franklin, Benjamin **6** 60-64
Oglethorpe, James Edward
11 482-483
Wesley, John **16** 209-210
Whitefield, George **16** 241-242
governors
Carter, James Earl **3** 339-342
Indian policy
Ross, John **13** 303-304
legislators
Bond, Julian **2** 386-387
Brown, Joseph Emerson **3** 41-42
Crawford, William Harris **4** 299-300
Gingrich, Newt **6** 329-332
Hill, Benjamin Harvey **7** 386-387
Stephens, Alexander Hamilton
14 429-430
Toombs, Robert Augustus
15 267-268
Reconstruction period
Gordon, John Brown **6** 449-450
Hill, Benjamin Harvey **7** 386-387

Georgia Boy (novel)
Caldwell, Erskine **3** 223-224

Georgian Bay (Canada)
Champlain, Samuel de **3** 419-421

Georgian poetry (literary movement)
Brooke, Rupert **3** 22-23
Sassoon, Siegfried **13** 492-493

Georgics (poems; Virgil)
Claude Lorrain **4** 89-90
Varro, Marcus Terentius **15** 438-439
Virgil **15** 507-510

Georgium sidus
see Uranus (planet)

GEPHARDT, RICHARD ANDREW (born
1941), Democratic majority leader in the
House of Representatives **6** 278-280

Gérard, Balthasar (1558-1584), French
assassin
William the Silent **16** 300-302

Gérard, François Pascal Simon
(1770-1837), French painter
Peale, Rembrandt **12** 172-173

Gerard of Cremona (1147?-1187), Italian
translator
Avicenna **1** 386-387
Khwarizmi, Muhammad ibn Musa al-
8 541

Gerbert of Aurillac
see Sylvester II

Gergovia, battle of (44 B.C.)
Caesar, Gaius Julius **3** 207-210

Gerhardt, Charles F. (1816-1856), French
chemist
Hofmann, August Wilhelm von
7 441-442
Kekulé, Friedrich August **8** 477-478

GÉRICAULT, JEAN LOIS ANDRÉ
THÉODORE (1791-1824), French painter
6 280-281
Aragon, Louis **1** 271-272
Bonington, Richard Parkes **2** 394-395
Copley, John Singleton **4** 228-230
Delacroix, Ferdinand Victor Eugène
4 469-471
Gros **7** 14-15

Gérin, Jacques Albert (died 1702), French
painter
Watteau, Antoine **16** 143-144

Gerlach, Walter (1889-1979), German
physicist
Stern, Otto **14** 435

Germ theory (medicine)
Behring, Emil Adolph von **2** 122-123
Pasteur, Louis **12** 125-127

Germ theory (United States politics)
Adams, Herbert Baxter **1** 47
Andrews, Charles McLean **1** 231

Germaine, George Sackville (1716-1785),
British general and statesman
Clinton, Henry **4** 114-115
Cornwallis, Charles **4** 241-243

German (language)
Grimm, Jakob and Wilhelm Karl **7** 3-4
Thomasius **15** 193-194

German architecture
baroque
see Baroque architecture
Bauhaus
Gropius, Walter **7** 13-14
see also Bauhaus
International Style
Mendelsohn, Erich **10** 488
Mies van der Rohe, Ludwig
11 10-12
see also International Style

modernist-traditional
Jahn, Helmut **8** 199-201
neoclassicism
Behrens, Peter **2** 121-122
Schinkel, Karl Friedrich **14** 8
rococo
Cuvilliés, François **4** 359-360
Zimmermann, Johann Baptist and
Domenikus **16** 518

German art
abstract cinema
Richter, Hans **13** 149-150
autobiographical
Salomon, Charlotte **13** 454-455
baroque
see Baroque painting; Baroque
sculpture
Bauhaus
see Bauhaus
Blaue Reiter
see Blaue Reiter
Dada
Ernst, Max **5** 311-312
Grosz, George **7** 17-18
Richter, Hans **13** 149-150
Danube school
Altdorfer, Albrecht **1** 179-180
Cranach, Lucas the Elder **4** 289-290
Die Neue Sachlichkeit (The New
Objectivity)
Dix, Otto **5** 33-34
expressionism
see Expressionism (art)—Germany
Gothic
Lochner, Stephan **9** 475
Pacher, Michael **12** 53
Riemenschneider, Tilman **13** 166
Stoss, Veit **14** 481-482
graphics
Barlach, Ernst **2** 5-6
Dürer, Albrecht **5** 159-161
Holbein, Hans the Younger
7 449-450
Kollwitz, Käthe **9** 79-81
Pechstein, Hermann Max
12 176-177
Schongauer, Martin **14** 26-28
human figure
Schlemmer, Oskar **14** 12-13
impressionism
see Impressionism (art)—Germany
International Constructivism
Richter, Hans **13** 149-150
MERZ-art
Schwitters, Kurt **14** 60-61
naturalism
Witz, Konrad **16** 351-352
neoclassicism
Mengs, Anton Raphael **10** 505
Schinkel, Karl Friedrich **14** 8
photography
Riefenstahl, Leni **13** 161-163
political themes
Kiefer, Anselm **8** 544-546
portraits

Corinth, Lovis **4** 234
post-Impressionism
Modersohn-Becker, Paula **11** 71-72
process art
Kiefer, Anselm **8** 544-546
Renaissance
see Renaissance (art)—Germany
rococo
Günther, Ignaz **7** 41-42
Zimmermann, Johann Baptist and
Domenikus **16** 518
romanticism
Friedrich, Caspar David **6** 114-115
Hoffmann, Ernst Theodor Amadeus
7 439-440
stained glass
Macke, August **10** 102-103

German Bund (established 1815)
Metternich, Klemens von **10** 533-536

German Chemical Society (established
1868)
Hofmann, August Wilhelm von
7 441-442

German Colonization Society (established
1884)
Peters, Carl **12** 257-258

German Confederation (1815-1866)
see Germany—German Confederation

German Customs Union (1834)
Krupp **9** 109-111
Schmoller, Gustav Friedrich von **14** 21

German Democratic Republic
see Germany, East

German East Africa
see Tanzania

German Fatherland party (established
1917)
Kapp, Wolfgang **8** 436

German films
directors
Lang, Fritz **9** 190-192

German General Electric Company
see Allgemeine Elektrizitätsgesellschaft

German Ideology, The (book; Engels-Marx)
Engels, Friedrich **5** 286-288
Marx, Karl **10** 304-308

German literature
chivalric romances
Gottfried von Strassburg **6** 461-462
Wolfram von Eschenbach
16 360-361
diaries
Frank, Anne **6** 54-56
Enlightenment
Herder, Johann Gottfried von
7 327-328
Kant, Immanuel **8** 430-432
Lessing, Gotthold Ephraim
9 357-359
Wieland, Christoph Martin
16 260-261
Winckelmann, Johann Joachim
16 332-333

experimental theater
Brecht, Bertolt **2** 512-514
Tieck, Ludwig **15** 218-219
Wedekind, Frank **16** 166-167
folktales
Grimm, Jakob and Wilhelm Karl
7 3-4
humanism
see Humanism (cultural move-
ment)—German literature
lyric poetry (15th-19th century)
Brentano, Clemens **2** 515-516
Heine, Heinrich **7** 259-260
Klopstock, Friedrich Gottlieb
9 55-56
Sachs, Hans **13** 410-411
Storm, Theodor **14** 479-480
lyric poetry (19th-20th century)
Brecht, Bertolt **2** 512-514
George, Stefan **6** 277-278
Hofmannsthal, Hugo von **7** 443-444
Huch, Ricarda **8** 11-12
Rilke, Rainer Maria **13** 171-172
Werfel, Franz **16** 204-205
Minnesingers
Gottfried von Strassburg **6** 461-462
Sachs, Hans **13** 410-411
Vogelweide, Walther von der
16 10-11
modern
Feuchtwanger, Lion **5** 430-432
Huch, Ricarda **8** 11-12
Jünger, Ernst **8** 391-392
Mann, Thomas **10** 204-207
Sachs, Nelly **13** 411-412
moral tales
Böll, Heinrich **2** 377-378
naturalism (drama)
Hauptmann, Gerhart Johann Robert
7 199-201
Hebbel, Friedrich **7** 247
Sachs, Nelly **13** 411-412
Sudermann, Hermann **15** 12-13
neoromanticism
George, Stefan **6** 277-278
Hauptmann, Gerhart Johann Robert
7 199-201
Hofmannsthal, Hugo von **7** 443-444
Rilke, Rainer Maria **13** 171-172
Schnitzler, Arthur **14** 23-24
picaresque novels
Grimmelshausen, Hans Jakob
Christoffel von **7** 4-5
Hesse, Hermann **7** 367-369
psychological experimentalism
Kafka, Franz **8** 403-406
Nietzsche, Friedrich **11** 390-392
Wassermann, Jakob **16** 130-131
realism (19th century)
Fontane, Theodor **5** 504
Freytag, Gustav **6** 107-108
Heine, Heinrich **7** 259-260
Keller, Gottfried **8** 478-479
Storm, Theodor **14** 479-480
realism (19th-20th century)

Heyse, Paul Johann Ludwig
7 372-373
Mann, Heinrich **10** 201-202
Remarque, Erich Maria **13** 91
Schnitzler, Arthur **14** 23-24
Werfel, Franz **16** 204-205
romanticism
see Romanticism (literature)—German
social commentary
Böll, Heinrich **2** 377-378
Sturm und Drang
see Sturm und Drang
theater of the absurd
Grass, Günter **6** 496-497
see also Expressionism (literature)

German music
art music
Zimmermann, Bernd Alois
16 517-518
baroque
see Baroque music
classical
Wolpe, Stefan **16** 362-364
instrumental
Beethoven, Ludwig van **2** 114-117
Froberger, Johann Jakob **6** 120-121
Pachelbel, Johann **12** 52
Stockhausen, Karlheinz **14** 460-461
Minnisingers
Sachs, Hans **13** 410-411
Vogelweide, Walther von der
16 10-11
Wolfram von Eschenbach
16 360-361
nationalism
Brahms, Johannes **2** 490-492
Wagner, Richard **16** 40-43
neoclassicism
Henze, Hans Werner **7** 314
Hindemith, Paul **7** 399-400
rococo
Bach, Carl Philipp Emanuel
1 414-415
Bach, Johann Christian **1** 415-416
romanticism
see Romanticism (music)—German
sacred
see Sacred music—German
songs
Hofhaimer, Paul **7** 441
Schubert, Franz Peter **14** 35-37
vocal
Bach, Johann Christian **1** 415-416
Meyerbeer, Giacomo **10** 536-537
Strauss, Richard **14** 500-501
Wagner, Richard **16** 40-43
see also Opera

German People's party (established 1919)
Stresemann, Gustav **14** 508-509

German Reformed Church (Mercersburg,
Pennsylvania)
Nevin, John Williamson **11** 357
Schaff, Philip **13** 519-520

German Requiem (musical composition)
Brahms, Johannes **2** 490-492
German Sociological Association (established 1910)
Simmel, Georg **14** 234-235
Tönnies, Ferdinand **15** 266-267
Weber, Max **16** 157-160
German Workers' party (Brussels; 1840s)
Marx, Karl **10** 304-308
Germanicus, Julius Caesar
see Caligula
Germanicus, Tiberius Claudius
see Brittanicus; Claudius Germanicus,
T.
Germanium (element—chemistry)
Mendeleev, Dmitrii Ivanovich
10 486-488
Germantown (Philadelphia, Pennsylvania)
Beissel, Johann Conrad **2** 123-124
Germantown, battle of (1777)
Greene, Nathanael **6** 525-526
Knox, Henry **9** 64
Germany (nation; Europe)
• EARLY HISTORY
Carolingian Empire
Charlemagne **3** 445-447
Leo III **9** 330-332
Louis I **9** 522-523
Martel, Charles **10** 285
Roman Empire
Diocletian **5** 19-20
Gregory I **6** 531-532
Julian **8** 378-379
Marcus Aurelius Antoninus
10 243-245
Odoacer **11** 473
Saxon dynasty
Henry I **7** 285-286
Otto I **12** 28-29
Otto III **12** 29-30
see also Saxony
• EMPIRE (HOLY ROMAN)
Burgundy and
Charles the Bold **3** 467-469
church and
see Church and State (Holy
Roman Empire); Investiture
Struggle
Franconian dynasty
Henry III **7** 290
Henry IV **7** 292
Henry V **7** 295-296
Hapsburg dynasty
Charles V **3** 457-459
Ferdinand I **5** 414-415
Ferdinand II **5** 415
Ferdinand III **5** 416-417
Frederick III **6** 84-85
Maximilian I **10** 356-357
Maximilian II **10** 357-358
Rudolf I **13** 347-348
Hohenstauffen dynasty
Frederick I **6** 78-79

Frederick II **6** 79
Luxemburg dynasty
Henry VII **7** 299-300
Napoleonic Wars
see Napoleonic Wars
Prussian growth
Frederick II **6** 81-84
Frederick William **6** 85-86
Frederick William I **6** 86-87
Frederick William III **6** 87
and Sweden
Gustavus I **7** 42-43
Thirty Years War
see Thirty Years War
see also Augsburg, Peace of
(1555); Austria; Austrian Succession, War of the; Prussia
• GERMAN CONFEDERATION
Bismarck, Otto Eduard Leopold von
2 294-296
Frederick William IV **6** 87-88
Metternich, Klemens von
10 533-536
Treitschke, Heinrich von
15 293-294
see also Vienna, Congress of
(1814-1815)
• GERMAN EMPIRE
and Austria
Dollfuss, Engelbert **5** 47
Francis Ferdinand **6** 44
Francis Joseph **6** 45-46
William I **16** 292-293
see also Austria-Hungary
colonization
Peters, Carl **12** 257-258
Congress of Berlin
see Berlin, Congress of (1878)
Dual Alliance
see Dual Alliance (1879)
empire founded
Bethmann Hollweg, Theobald
von **2** 239-240
Moltke, Helmuth Karl Bernard
von **11** 90-91
William I **16** 292-293
foreign relations
Abdul-Hamid II **1** 17-18
Chicherin, Georgi Vasilyevich
3 516-517
Clemenceau, Georges **4** 99-101
Delcassé, Théophile **4** 478-479
Drago, Luis María **5** 92-93
Enver Pasha **5** 290-291
Leo XIII **9** 334-336
William II **16** 294-295
military expansion
Gladstone, William Ewart
6 357-360
and Socialism
Kautsky, Karl Johann **8** 462-463
Luxemburg, Rosa **10** 55-56
William II **16** 294-295
Triple Alliance
see Triple Alliance (1882)
unification

Bismarck, Otto Eduard Leopold
von **2** 294-296
United States ministers
Pendleton, George Hunt **12** 198
White, Andrew Dickson
16 226-227
World War I
see World War I
• REPUBLIC
and Nationalist China
Chiang Kai-shek **3** 510-513
Nazi recognition
Hindenburg, Paul Ludwig Hans
von Beneckendorff und von
7 400-401
von Papen, Franz **16** 28-29
reconstruction
Ebert, Friedrich **5** 193-194
Erzberger, Matthias **5** 319-320
Rathenau, Walther **13** 48-49
Schacht, Hjalmar Horace Gree-
ley **13** 518-519
Stresemann, Gustav **14** 508-509
republic established
William II **16** 294-295
revolutions
Kapp, Wolfgang **8** 436
Kautsky, Karl Johann **8** 462-463
see also Social Democratic party
(Germany)
• THIRD REICH
Austria annexed
Dollfuss, Engelbert **5** 47
von Papen, Franz **16** 28-29
British appeasement
Chamberlain, Arthur Neville
3 409-411
dictatorship
Goebbels, Joseph Paul
6 384-385
Göring, Hermann Wilhelm
6 457-458
Himmler, Heinrich **7** 398-399
Hitler, Adolf **7** 417-420
economic recovery
Schacht, Hjalmar Horace Gree-
ley **13** 518-519
Finland and
Mannerheim, Carl Gustav Emil
Von **10** 207-208
France and
Barbie, Klaus **1** 501-503
Hess, Walter Richard Rudolf
7 363-365
Italy and
Mussolini, Benito **11** 272-274
Japanese Alliance (1939)
Hirohito **7** 410-412
papal relations
Pius XI **12** 337-339
Polish nonaggression threaty (1934)
Pilsudski, Joseph **12** 305-306
rearmament
Beck, Ludwig August Theoder
2 99-100
World War II

see World War II
• REUNIFICATION
Bahr, Egon **1** 438-440
Kohl, Helmut **9** 73-74
Lafontaine, Oskar **9** 158-160
see also Anti-Semitism; Germany,
East; Germany, West; Munich
Conference (1938); Nazism; Holo-
caust
• SINCE REUNIFICATION (1990-)
politicians
Rau, Johannes **13** 51-52
presidents
Herzog, Roman **7** 355-357
reunification problems
Scharping, Rudolf **13** 522-524

Germany, culture
see German architecture; German art;
German literature; German music
Germany, East (German Democratic
Republic; former nation; Europe)
Dulles, John Foster **5** 134-135
Eisenhower, Dwight David **5** 233-236
Honecker, Erich **7** 471-472
Ulbricht, Walter **15** 383-384
see also Berlin—Wall Crisis
Germany, West (Federal Republic of Ger-
many; former nation; Europe)
and defense
Wörner, Manfred **16** 389-390
and detente
Genscher, Hans-Dietrich **6** 265-266
economic recovery
Adenauer, Konrad **1** 59-61
Brandt, Willy **2** 499-500
Erhard, Ludwig **5** 302-304
Kohl, Helmut **9** 73-74
Krupp **9** 109-111
Lambsdorff, Otto Graf **9** 177-179
Schmidt, Helmut **14** 19-21
Geneva Conference (1955)
Eisenhower, Dwight David
5 233-236
judicial code reform
Vogel, Hans-Jochen **16** 8-9
and national unity
Schumacher, Kurt **14** 40-41
and NATO
Dulles, John Foster **5** 134-135
Schmidt, Helmut **14** 19-21
Strauss, Franz Josef **14** 497-498
see also Berlin—Wall Crisis
and reunification
Bahr, Egon **1** 438-440
right-wing movements
Schönhuber, Franz Xaver **14** 28-29
urban guerrillas
Baader and Ulrike Meinhof, Andreas
1 403-404

Germer, Lester Halbert (1896-1971),
American physicist
de Broglie, Louis **4** 442-444

Germfree animals
see Gnotobiology

Germinal (novel)
Zola, Émile **16** 526-528
Germinie Lacerteux (novel)
Goncourt, Edmond de and Jules de
6 426-427
Gero (died 965), German duke of Ostmark
Otto I **12** 28-29
Gérôme, Jean Léon (1824-1904), French
painter
Eakins, Thomas **5** 176-177
Maillol, Aristide **10** 150-151
Robinson, Theodore **13** 217
Rousseau, Henri **13** 323-324
Gerona (Catalonia, Spain)
Scholem, Gershom **14** 26
GERONIMO (1829-1909), American
Apache Indian warrior **6** 281-282
Crook, George **4** 322-323
Miles, Nelson Appleton **11** 16-17
Géronte et son miroir (poems)
Morin, Paul **11** 174
Gerontion (poem)
Eliot, Thomas Stearns **5** 258-261
GERRY, ELBRIDGE (1744-1814), American
patriot and statesman **6** 282-283
Pinckney, Charles Cotesworth **12** 310
Gerrymander (politics)
Gerry, Elbridge **6** 282-283
Vallandigham, Clement Laird
15 406-407
GERSHOM BEN JUDAH (circa 950-1028),
German rabbi, scholar, and poet
6 283-284
Gershon
see Levi ben Gershon
GERSHWIN, GEORGE (1898-1937), Amer-
ican composer **6** 284-285
Porter, Cole Albert **12** 405-406
Gershwin, Ira (1896-1983), American lyri-
cist
Gershwin, George **6** 284-285
GERSON, JOHN (1363-1429), French the-
ologian **6** 285-286
Ailly, Pierre d' **1** 94
Martin V **10** 287-288
Gersonides
see Levi ben Gershon
Gerstern (verse play)
Hofmannsthal, Hugo von **7** 443-444
Gertrude (novel)
Hesse, Hermann **7** 367-369
Gerusalemme conquistata (poem)
Tasso, Torquato **15** 114-116
Gerusalemme liberata (poem)
Tasso, Torquato **15** 114-116
Gesammelte Gedichte (poems)
Hesse, Hermann **7** 367-369
Gesammelte Schriften (book)
Mommsen, Theodor **11** 94-95
Zunz, Leopold **16** 534

Gesang der Geister über den Wassern (lyrics)
Goethe, Johann Wolfgang von **6** 388-391

Gesang vom Kindchen (poem)
Mann, Thomas **10** 204-207

Geschichte der Abderiten, Die (satire)
Wieland, Christoph Martin **16** 260-261

Geschwister, Die (play)
Goethe, Johann Wolfgang von **6** 388-391

Geschwister von Neapel, Die (novel)
Werfel, Franz **16** 204-205

GESELL, ARNOLD LUCIUS (1880-1961), American psychologist and pediatrician **6** 286-287

Gesell Institute of Child Development
Gesell, Arnold Lucius **6** 286-287

Gesellius, Herman (1874-1916), Finnish architect
Saarinen, Eliel and Eero **13** 396-398

Gesellschaft für Deutsche Kolonisation (established 1884)
Peters, Carl **12** 257-258

Gesellschaft für Soziale Reform (political organization)
Tönnies, Ferdinand **15** 266-267

GESNER, KONRAD VON (1516-1565), Swiss naturalist **6** 287

Gessler (literary character)
Schiller, Johann Christoph Friedrich von **14** 4-7

Gesta abbatum (book)
Matthew Paris **10** 341-342

Gesta pontificum (book)
William of Malmesbury **16** 297-298

Gesta regum Anglorum (book)
William of Malmesbury **16** 297-298

Gestalt psychology (social science)
Hull, Clark Leonard **8** 28
Lewin, Kurt **9** 375-376
Merleau-Ponty, Maurice **10** 518
Tolman, Edward Chace **15** 261-262
Wertheimer, Max **16** 207-208

Gestapo (political police)
Freud, Sigmund **6** 103-106
Himmler, Heinrich **7** 398-399
Jünger, Ernst **8** 391-392
Kádár, János **8** 402-403

Geste (poem; Wace)
Layamon **9** 256-257

Gestiefelte Kater, Der (play)
Tieck, Ludwig **15** 218-219

Gesù, Church of the (Rome)
Alberti, Leon Battista **1** 113-115
Gaulli, Giovanni Battista **6** 238-239
Maderno, Carlo **10** 117-118
Vignola, Giacomo da **15** 493-494

GESUALDO, DON CARLO (Prince of Venosa; circa 1560-1613), Italian composer **6** 287-288
Frescobaldi, Girolamo **6** 101-102

Stravinsky, Igor Fedorovich **14** 502-506

Get Away Old Man (play)
Saroyan, William **13** 486-487

Geta, Publius Septimus (189-212), coruler of Roman Empire 211-212
Caracalla **3** 281-282

Gethsemane, Garden of (near Jerusalem)
Jesus of Nazareth **8** 251-255
John, Saint **8** 273-274
Peter **12** 252-253

Géthsémani (poem)
Lamartine, Alphonse Marie Louis de **9** 173-175

Getting of Wisdom, The (novel)
Richardson, Henry Handel **13** 139

GETTY, JEAN PAUL (1892-1976), billionaire independent oil producer **6** 288-290

Getty Oil Company
Getty, Jean Paul **6** 288-290

Getty Tomb (Chicago)
Sullivan, Louis Henri **15** 27-28

Gettysburg, battle of
Confederate forces
Davis, Jefferson **4** 416-418
Lee, Robert Edward **9** 292-294
Stuart, James Ewell Brown **14** 515-516
Union forces
Armstrong, Samuel Chapman **1** 306-307
Grant, Ulysses Simpson **6** 492-494
Howard, Oliver Otis **7** 528-529
Meade, George Gordon **10** 440-441
Schurz, Carl **14** 44-45

Gettysburg Address (1863)
Everett, Edward **5** 344
Lincoln, Abraham **9** 415-418

Gettysburg Address (symphony)
Harris, Roy **7** 175-176

Geulincx, Arnold (1625-1669), Dutch Cartesian philosopher
Malebranche, Nicolas **10** 166-167

Gewandhaus (Leipzig)
Mendelssohn, Moses **10** 488-489

Gewerbe Institute (Berlin)
Baeyer, Johann Friedrich Adolf von **1** 432

Geystliche gesangk Buchleyn (musical collection)
Walter, Johann **16** 86

Gezeichneten, Die (lithograph series)
Grosz, George **7** 17-18

Ghana (ancient empire; West Africa)
Abdullah ibn Yasin **1** 20
Sundiata Keita **15** 33-34

Ghana, Republic of (nation; West Africa)
Ashanti heritage
Anokye, Okomfo **1** 242-243
colonization
Frederick William **6** 85-86
Maclean, George **10** 108-109

independence movement
Busia, Kofi Abrefa **3** 172-173
Danquah, Joseph B. **4** 388-389
Fanon, Frantz **5** 379-380
Nkrumah, Kwame **11** 408-410
Padmore, George **12** 57-58
nationalism
Du Bois, William Edward Burghardt **5** 116-118
Hayford, J. E. Casely **7** 228-230
Houphouët-Boigny, Felix **7** 519-520
republic created (1960)
Nkrumah, Kwame **11** 408-410

Ghana, University of
Busia, Kofi Abrefa **3** 172-173

Ghare baire (novel)
Rabindranath Tagore **12** 529-531

Ghazal (literary form)
Hafiz, Shams al-Din **7** 63

GHAZALI, ABU HAMID MUHAMMAD AL- (1058-1111), Arab philosopher and Islamic theologian **6** 290-291
Averroës **1** 382-383

Ghaznavids (Muslim dynasty; Afghanistan; ruled 962-1186)
Mahmud of Ghazni **10** 147

Ghent (city; Belgium)
Edward III **5** 211-212
Saxe, Comte de **13** 507-508
van der Goes, Hugo **15** 416-417
William the Silent **16** 300-302

Ghent, Treaty of (1814)
Clay, Henry **4** 94-96
Dunning, William Archibald **5** 148-149
Gallatin, Albert **6** 183-184
Madison, James **10** 121-123

Ghent, University of (Belgium)
Pirenne, Jean Henri Otto Lucien Marie **12** 322-323
Van de Velde, Henry **15** 419-420

Ghent Altarpiece (painting; H. and J. van Eyck)
Eyck, Hubert and Jan van **5** 352-354
van der Goes, Hugo **15** 416-417

Ghetto Tragedies (book)
Zangwill, Israel **16** 488-489

Ghibellines (political faction; Germany and Italy)
Cavalcanti, Guido **3** 382
Frederick II **6** 79
see also Guelphs, House of

GHIBERTI, LORENZO (circa 1381-1455), Italian sculptor, goldsmith, and painter **6** 291-292
Commentaries
Cimabue **4** 60-61
Giotto **6** 342-345
Vasari, Giorgio **15** 442-443
contemporaries
Brunelleschi, Filippo **3** 70-72

Donatello **5** 55-56
Quercia, Jacopo della **12** 509
influence of
Michelozzo **11** 6-7
Rodin, Auguste **13** 236-238
Uccello, Paolo **15** 378-379
Veneziano, Domenico **15** 459-460

Ghiberti, Vittorio (1416-1496), Italian artist
Ghiberti, Lorenzo **6** 291-292

Ghirlandaio, Davide (1452-1525), Italian painter
Ghirlandaio, Domenico **6** 292-293

GHIRLANDAIO, DOMENICO
(1449-1494), Italian painter **6** 292-293
Botticelli, Sandro **2** 439-440
Medici, Lorenzo de' **10** 450-451
Michelangelo Buonarroti **11** 2-5
Vespucci, Amerigo **15** 476-478

Ghirlandaio, Ridolfo (1483-1561), Italian painter
Ghirlandaio, Domenico **6** 292-293

Ghislieri, Antonio
see Pius V

Ghiyas-ud-din Tughluq (ruled 1321-1325), Moslem sultan of Delhi
Muhammad bin Tughluq **11** 229

Ghor (ancient Kingdom; southwest Asia)
Mahmud of Ghazni **10** 147

GHOSE, AUROBINDO (1872-1950), Indian nationalist and philosopher **6** 293-294
Das, Chitta Ranjan **4** 401-402

Ghost at Noon, A (novel)
Moravia, Alberto **11** 153-155

Ghost dance (Sioux Indians)
Miles, Nelson Appleton **11** 16-17
Sitting Bull **14** 264-265

Ghost Sonata, The (play)
Strindberg, August **14** 509-511

Ghosts (play)
Ibsen, Henrik **8** 98-100

GIACOMETTI, ALBERTO (1901-1966), Swiss sculptor and painter **6** 294-295
Lehmbruck, Wilhelm **9** 307
Noguchi, Isamu **11** 416-418
Richier, Germaine **13** 145-146
Smith, David **14** 287-288

Giacosa, Giuseppe (1847-1906), Italian dramatist
Puccini, Giacomo **12** 474-476

Giambi ed epodi (poems)
Carducci, Giosuè **3** 290-291

Giambologna
see Giovanni da Bologna

Gianni Schicchi (opera)
Puccini, Giacomo **12** 474-476

GIANNINI, A. P. (Amadeo Peter; 1870-1949), Italian-American financier and banker **6** 295-297

Giant (film)
Dean, James **4** 433-434

Giant (novel)
Ferber, Edna **5** 413

Giant (opera)
Prokofiev, Sergei Sergeevich **12** 458-460

Giants in the Earth (novel)
Rölvaag, Ole Edvart **13** 265

Giaor, The (epic)
Byron, George Gordon Noel **3** 193-194

GIAP, VO NGUYEN (born 1912), Vietnamese Communist general and statesman **6** 297-299
Diem, Ngo Dinh **5** 6-7
Ho Chi Minh **7** 426-428

Giara, La (story and play)
Pirandello, Luigi **12** 319-321

Giasone (opera)
Cavalli, Pietro Francesco **3** 382-383

Giauque, William Francis (1895-1982), American chemist
Lewis, Gilbert Newton **9** 384-385

GIBBON, EDWARD (1737-1794), English historian **6** 299-300
Guizot, François Pierre Guillaume **7** 40-41
Johnson, Samuel **8** 315-317
Law, William **9** 245-246
Wilkes, John **16** 280-281

GIBBONS, JAMES (1834-1921), American Roman Catholic cardinal **6** 300-301
Ireland, John **8** 133-134

Gibbons, Thomas
see Ogden, Aaron

Gibbons v. Ogden (legal case)
Marshall, John **10** 279-281
Webster, Daniel **16** 162-164

GIBBS, JAMES (1682-1754), British architect **6** 301-302
Adam, Robert and James **1** 38-40
Benjamin, Asher **2** 162-163

GIBBS, JOSIAH WILLARD (1839-1903), American mathematical physicist **6** 302-303
Fisher, Irving **5** 462-463
Wiener, Norbert **16** 262-263

Gibbs-Duhem equation (chemistry)
Duhem, Pierre Maurice Marie **5** 129

Gibraltar (British colony; Spain)
Clinton, Henry **4** 114-115
Rodney, George Brydges **13** 239-240

Gibraltar, Strait of (Mediterranean - Atlantic Ocean)
Columbus, Christopher **4** 176-179

GIBRAN, KAHLIL (1883-1931), Lebanese writer and artist **6** 303-305

Gibson, Alfred (died 1873), Australian explorer
Giles, Ernest **6** 317-318

GIBSON, ALTHEA (born 1927), African American tennis player **6** 305-306

Gibson, John (1740-1822), American Revolutionary officer
Girty, Simon **6** 350

Gibson, Kenneth Allen (born 1932), African American statesman
Baraka, Imamu Amiri **1** 498-499

Gibson Desert (Australia)
Giles, Ernest **6** 317-318

GIDDINGS, FRANKLIN HENRY
(1855-1931), American sociologist **6** 307-308
Clark, John Bates **4** 76-77
Dugdale, Richard Louis **5** 128-129

GIDE, ANDRÉ (1869-1951), French author **6** 308-309
Proust, Marcel **12** 465-467
Rilke, Rainer Maria **13** 171-172
Stirner, Max **14** 459-460
Valéry, Paul Ambroise **15** 405-406

Gideon Planish (novel)
Lewis, Harry Sinclair **9** 385-387

Gideon v. Wainwright (legal case)
Fortas, Abe **6** 16-17
Warren, Earl **16** 117-120

Gideon's Band (novel)
Cable, George Washington **3** 198-199

Giebenrath, Hans (literary character)
Hesse, Hermann **7** 367-369

GIELGUD, JOHN (born 1904), English Shakespearean actor **6** 310-311

Gierek, Edward (born 1913), Polish politician
Gomulka, Wladislaw **6** 422-424

GIERKE, OTTO VON (1841-1921), German jurist **6** 311-312
Gooch, George Peabody **6** 432-433

Giessen, University of (Germany)
Bothe, Walther **2** 438-439
Liebig, Justus von **9** 403-404
Röntgen, Wilhelm Conrad **13** 273-275

Gift, The (book)
Mauss, Marcel **10** 352-353

Gift of Black Folk, The (literary collection)
Du Bois, William Edward Burghardt **5** 116-118

Gift of the Magi, The (story)
Henry, O. **7** 308-309

Gift Outright, The (poem)
Frost, Robert Lee **6** 130-133

Giganti della montagna, I (play)
Pirandello, Luigi **12** 319-321

Gigi (novel)
Colette, Sidonie Gabrielle **4** 158-159

GIGLI, ROMEO (born 1949), Italian designer **6** 312

Gigolo (novel)
Ferber, Edna **5** 413

Gijsbrecht van Aemstel (play)
Vondel, Joost van den **16** 19-20

Gikatilla, Joseph ben Abraham (1248-circa 1305), Spanish mystic
Leon, Moses de **9** 336

Gil Blas (novel; Lesage)
Alemán, Mateo **1** 126
Lesage, Alain René **9** 353-354
Smollett, Tobias George **14** 305-307

Gilbert (unit)
Gilbert, William **6** 313-314

Gilbert, John (1897-1936), American film actor
Garbo, Greta **6** 205-207

GILBERT, SIR HUMPHREY (circa 1537-1583), English soldier and colonizer **6** 313
Hakluyt, Richard **7** 70
Raleigh, Walter **13** 9-11

GILBERT, WILLIAM (1544-1603), English physician and physicist **6** 313-314

GILBERT, SIR WILLIAM SCHWENCK (1836-1911), English playwright and poet **6** 314-315
Sousa, John Philip **14** 353-354
Sullivan, Arthur Seymour **15** 23
Tennyson, Alfred **15** 144-146

GILBRETH, LILLIAN (born Lillian Evelyn Moller; 1878-1972), American psychologist and industrial management consultant **6** 315-317

Gilded Age, The (satire)
Twain, Mark **15** 363-366

Gilder, Richard Watson (1844-1909), American poet and editor
Crane, Stephen **4** 293-295

Gildon, Charles (1665-1724), English historical writer
Congreve, William **4** 200-201

GILES, ERNEST (1835-1897), Australian explorer **6** 317-318

Gilgamesh Epic (Babylonia)
Tschernichowsky, Saul **15** 323

Gilgul (religion)
Luria, Isaac ben Solomon Ashkenazi **10** 47-48

GILKEY, LANGDON BROWN (born 1919), American ecumenical Protestant theologian **6** 318-319

Gill, Eric (1882-1940), English sculptor and engraver
Moore, Henry **11** 146-148

Gill, Sir David (1843-1914), Scottish astronomer
Kapteyn, Jacobus Cornelis **8** 436-437

Gilles (painting)
Watteau, Antoine **16** 143-144

GILLESPIE, DIZZY (born John Birks Gillespie; 1917-1993), African American jazz

trumpeter, composer, and band leader **6** 320-322
Parker, Charles Christopher Jr. **12** 105-106

GILLIAM, SAM (born 1933), American artist **6** 322-323

Gillot, Claude (1673-1722), French engraver
Watteau, Antoine **16** 143-144

Gilly, Friedrich (1772-1800), German architect
Schinkel, Karl Friedrich **14** 8

GILMAN, CHARLOTTE ANNA PERKINS (1860-1935), American writer and lecturer **6** 323-325

GILMAN, DANIEL COIT (1831-1908), educator and pioneer in the American university movement **6** 325-326
Eliot, Charles William **5** 254
Maxwell, James Clerk **10** 361-364
White, Andrew Dickson **16** 226-227

Gilmore, Patrick (1829-1892), American bandmaster
Sousa, John Philip **14** 353-354

Gilpin, Charles (1878-1930), African American actor
Robeson, Paul Leroy **13** 198-199

GILPIN, LAURA (1891-1979), American photographer **6** 326-327

GILSON, ÉTIENNE HENRY (1884-1978), French Catholic philosopher **6** 327-328

Gimpel... (stories)
Singer, Isaac Bashevis **14** 249-250

GINASTERA, ALBERTO EVARISTO (1916-1983), Argentine composer **6** 328-329

Ginés (literary character)
Lope Félix de Vega Carpio **9** 503-506

Ginestra, La (poem)
Leopardi, Giacomo **9** 344-345

Ginevra (sculpture)
Powers, Hiram **12** 428-429

Ginevra de' Benci (painting)
Leonardo da Vinci **9** 337-340

Ginevra d'Este (painting)
Pisanello **12** 323-324

Gingertown (stories)
McKay, Claude **10** 416

GINGRICH, NEWT (born 1943), Republican congressman from Georgia **6** 329-332

Gino (literary character)
Forster, Edward Morgan **6** 14-16

GINSBERG, ALLEN (1926-1997), American poet **6** 332-333
Burroughs, William S. **3** 162-163
Lennon, John Winston **9** 326-328
Whitman, Walt **16** 249-251

GINSBURG, RUTH BADER (born 1933), second woman appointed to the United States Supreme Court **6** 333-336

GINZBERG, ASHER (Ahad Ha-Am; means "one of the people;" 1856-1927), Jewish intellectual leader **6** 336-337
see also Ahad Haam

GINZBERG, LOUIS (1873-1953), Lithuanian-American Talmudic scholar **6** 337-338

GINZBURG, NATALIA LEVI (1916-1991), Italian novelist, essayist, playwright, and translator **6** 338-339

GIOLITTI, GIOVANNI (1842-1928), Italian statesman **6** 339-340

Giordani, Pietro (1774-1848), Italian writer
Leopardi, Giacomo **9** 344-345

Giordano, Luca (1632-1705), Italian painter
Troger, Paul **15** 300

Giordano, Umberto (1867-1948), Italian composer
Caruso, Enrico **3** 345

GIORGIONE (1477-1510), Italian painter **6** 340-341
collaborators
Titian **15** 242-244
Influence of
Claude Lorrain **4** 89-90
Correggio **4** 249-251
Lotto, Lorenzo **9** 520-521
Manet, Édouard **10** 193-194
Vanderlyn, John **15** 417
influenced by
Bellini, Giovanni **2** 137-138

Giorno di regno, Un (opera)
Verdi, Giuseppe Fortunino Francesco **15** 463-465

Giorno dopo giorno (poem)
Quasimodo, Salvatore **12** 506

GIOTTO (circa 1267-1337), Italian painter, architect, and sculptor **6** 342-345
associates
Cimabue **4** 60-61
Dante Alighieri **4** 389-391
compared to
Duccio di Buoninsegna **5** 121-122
Veneziano, Domenico **15** 459-460
influence of
Andrea Pisano **1** 225-226
Lorenzetti, Pietro and Ambrogio **9** 517-518
Masaccio **10** 312-313
Moore, Henry **11** 146-148
Orcagna **11** 526-527

Giovanni Arnolfini and His Wife (painting)
Eyck, Hubert and Jan van **5** 352-354

Giovanni d'Alemagna (died 1450), Italian painter
Mantegna, Andrea **10** 215-216

GIOVANNI DA BOLOGNA (1529-1608), Italian sculptor **6** 345-346
Cellini, Benvenuto **3** 391-392
Michelangelo Buonarroti **11** 2-5

Giovanni da Fiesole, Fra
see Angelica, Fra

Giovanni di Stefano (circa 1446-circa 1506), Italian sculptor
Sassetta **13** 492

GIOVANNI, YOLANDE CORNELIA, JR. (born 1943), African American poet **6** 346-347

Giovanni Pisano
see Pisano, Giovanni

Giovanni's Room (book)
Baldwin, James Arthur **1** 465-466

Giovine Italia, La
see Young Italy

Giraldus de Barri (Giraldus Cambrensis; 1146?-1222?), Welsh scholar and geographer
Jean de Meun **8** 234-235

Girard, Albert (1595-1632), Dutch mathematician
Gauss, Karl Friedrich **6** 240-242

GIRARD, STEPHEN (1750-1831), American merchant and philanthropist **6** 347-348
Bache, Alexander Dallas **1** 420

Girard College (Philadelphia)
Bache, Alexander Dallas **1** 420
Girard, Stephen **6** 347-348

GIRARDON, FRANÇOIS (1628-1715), French sculptor **6** 348-349
Boffrand, Gabriel Germain **2** 361
Coysevox, Antoine **4** 287-288
Schlüter, Andreas **14** 18-19

Giraud, Henri (1879-1949), French general
Monnet, Jean **11** 109-110

GIRAUDOUX, JEAN (1882-1944), French novelist, playwright, and diplomat **6** 349-350
Anouilh, Jean **1** 243-244

Giri, Varahgiri Venkata (1894-1980), Indian diplomatist and lawyer
Gandhi, Indira Priyadarshini **6** 200-201

Girl Asleep at a Table (painting)
Vermeer, Jan **15** 466-467

Girl before a Mirror (painting)
Picasso, Pablo **12** 292-295

Girl Crazy (musical)
Gershwin, George **6** 284-285

Girl from Persia, The (play)
Plautus **12** 348-350

Girl from Samos, The (play)
Menander **10** 477-478

Girl of the Golden West (play and opera)
Belasco, David **2** 124-125
Puccini, Giacomo **12** 474-476

Girl Reading (painting)
Sickert, Walter Richard **14** 212-213

Girl Scouts of America
Low, Juliette Gordon **10** 10-11

Girl Who Had Her Hair Cut Off, The (play)
Menander **10** 477-478

Girl with a Wreath (painting)
Reni, Guido **13** 97-98

Girl with the Flaxen Hair (musical composition)
Debussy, Achille Claude **4** 445-447

Girlhood of Mary Virgin (painting)
Rossetti, Dante Gabriel **13** 308-309

Girls, The (novel)
Ferber, Edna **5** 413

Girondists (French Revolution; political group)
Danton, Georges Jacques **4** 391-393
Genet, Edmond Charles **6** 261-262
Marat, Jean Paul **10** 230-231
Robespierre, Maximilien François Marie Isidore de **13** 199-201
Saint-Just, Louis Antoine Léon de **13** 433

Girtin, Thomas (1775-1802), English painter
Bonington, Richard Parkes **2** 394-395
Constable, John **4** 208-209
Turner, Joseph Mallord William **15** 352-354

GIRTY, SIMON (1741-1818), American frontiersman **6** 350

GISCARD D'ESTAING, VALÉRY (born 1926), third president of the French Fifth Republic **6** 350-352
Barre, Raymond **2** 19-20

Gish, Dorothy (1898-1968), American film and stage actress
Griffith, David Wark **6** 544-545

Gish, Lillian (1896-1993), American film and stage actress
Griffith, David Wark **6** 544-545

Gismondo (literary character)
Bembo, Pietro **2** 144-145

GIST, CHRISTOPHER (circa 1706-1759), American frontiersman **6** 352-353

Gitanjali (poems)
Rabindranath Tagore **12** 529-531

Giton (literary character)
Petronius Arbiter **12** 262-263

Giuliani, Giovanni (1663-1714), Austrian sculptor
Donner, Georg Raphael **5** 63

GIULIANI, RUDOLPH WILLIAM (born 1944), mayor of New York City **6** 353-355

Giulio Cesare (opera)
Handel, George Frederick **7** 116-119

Giulio Clovio (painting)
Greco **6** 511-514

Giustino Roncella nato Boggiòlo (novel)
Pirandello, Luigi **12** 319-321

Giustizia e Libertà (Italian political organization)
Levi, Carlo **9** 364

Pavese, Cesare **12** 154-155

Give My Regards to Broadway (song)
Cohan, George Michael **4** 137-138

Gjöa (ship)
Amundsen, Roald **1** 206-207

Glaciologists
see Scientists—glaciologists

GLACKENS, WILLIAM (1870-1938), American painter **6** 355-356
Morrice, James Wilson **11** 181-182
Sloan, John **14** 274-275

GLADDEN, WASHINGTON (1836-1918), American clergyman **6** 356-357
Holmes, John Haynes **7** 456-457

Gladiator, The (march)
Sousa, John Philip **14** 353-354

Gladiator, The (play)
Bird, Robert Montgomery **2** 281-282
Forrest, Edwin **6** 11-12

Gladiators, The (book; Koestler)
Spartacus **14** 363-364

Gladstone, John Hall (1827-1902), English chemist
MacDonald, James Ramsay **10** 84-85

GLADSTONE, WILLIAM EWART (1809-1898), English statesman **6** 357-360
as Cabinet member
Aberdeen, 4th Earl of **1** 25-26
Palmerston, 3d Viscount **12** 81-83
Peel, Robert **12** 181-183
Russell, John **13** 380-381
biographers
Morley, John **11** 178-179
Cabinet of
Asquith, Herbert Henry **1** 344-346
Chamberlain, Joseph **3** 411-413
foreign policies
Gordon, Charles George **6** 448-449
Roberts, Frederick Sleigh **13** 195-196
influence of
Bryce, James **3** 85
Cobden, Richard **4** 127-128
MacDonald, James Ramsay **10** 84-85
Victoria **15** 485-487
Irish home rule
Parnell, Charles Stewart **12** 117-119
political opponents
Disraeli, Benjamin **5** 27-29
Salisbury, 3d Marquess of **13** 448-449
quoted
Ferdinand II **5** 415-416
Seward, William Henry **14** 124-125

Glamorganshire (county; Wales)
Logan, William Edmond **9** 488-489

Glarentza (city; Peloponnesus)
Constantine XI **4** 211-212

Glasgow (ship)
Hopkins, Esek **7** 490-491

GLASGOW, ELLEN (1873-1945), American novelist **6** 360-361

Glasgow Infirmary (Scotland)
Adam, Robert and James **1** 38-40

Glasgow University (Scotland)
chancellors
Orr, John Boyd **12** 4-5
faculty
Burnet, Gilbert **3** 147
Perry, Ralph Barton **12** 239-240
Reid, Thomas **13** 87-88
Smith, Adam **14** 283-284
Soddy, Frederick **14** 321-323

GLASHOW, SHELDON LEE (born 1932), American Nobel Prize winner in physics **6** 361-362

Glass Bead Game, The (novel)
Hesse, Hermann **7** 367-369

Glass Bees (novel)
Jünger, Ernst **8** 391-392

Glass box (architecture)
Johnson, Philip **8** 313-314

Glass designers
see Artists—glass designers

Glass Industry
see Business and industrial leaders—glass and plastics industries

Glass Menagerie, The (play)
Williams, Tennessee **16** 306-308

GLASS, PHILIP (born 1937), American composer of minimalist music **6** 362-364

Glass-Steagall Act (1932)
Hoover, Herbert Clark **7** 483-485

Glaucus (book)
Kingsley, Charles **9** 28

Glaucus of Potniae (play)
Aeschylus **1** 70-72

Gläserne Bienen (novel)
Jünger, Ernst **8** 391-392

Glazunov, Aleksandr (1865-1936), Russian composer
Borodin, Aleksandr Profirevich **2** 422-423
Rimsky-Korsakov, Nikolai Andreevich **13** 174-175
Shostakovich, Dmitri Dmitrievich **14** 204-205

Gleaners (painting)
Millet, Jean François **11** 31

Gleanings in Buddha-fields (book)
Hearn, Lafcadio **7** 240

Glee (musical form)
Arne, Thomas Augustine **1** 307-308

Gleiches, Ein (poem)
Goethe, Johann Wolfgang von **6** 388-391

Gleisdreieck (poem)
Grass, Günter **6** 496-497

Gleizes, Albert Léon (1881-1953), French painter
Weber, Max **16** 160

Glendale, battle of (1862)
Meade, George Gordon **10** 440-441

GLENDOWER, OWEN (1359?-1415?), Welsh national leader **6** 364-365
Henry IV **7** 292-293

Glenkiln Cross (sculpture)
Moore, Henry **11** 146-148

GLENN, JOHN HERSCHEL, JR. (born 1921), military test pilot, astronaut, businessman, and United States senator from Ohio **6** 365-367

Glenwood Institute (Matawan, New Jersey)
Borden, Robert Laird **2** 409-411

Glessner House (Chicago)
Richardson, Henry Hobson **13** 139-141

Gleyre, Charles (1808-1874), Swiss painter
Monet, Claude **11** 102-104
Whistler, James Abbott McNeill **16** 225-226

Glière, Reinhold Moritsevich (1875-1956), Russian composer
Prokofiev, Sergei Sergeevich **12** 458-460

GLIGOROV, KIRO (born 1917), first president of the Republic of Macedonia **6** 367-369

Glimpses of Unfamiliar Japan (book)
Hearn, Lafcadio **7** 240

GLINKA, MIKHAIL IVANOVICH (1804-1857), Russian composer **6** 369-370
Pushkin, Aleksandr Sergeevich **12** 489-491
Rimsky-Korsakov, Nikolai Andreevich **13** 174-175
Stravinsky, Igor Fedorovich **14** 502-506

Glissando (musical technique)
Xenakis, Iannis **16** 416-418

Globe (cartography)
Mercator, Gerhardus **10** 511-512

Globe Theater (London)
Shakespeare, William **14** 142-145

Globolinks (literary characters)
Menotti, Gian Carlo **10** 509-510

Gloomy People (stories)
Chekhov, Anton Pavlovich **3** 494-497

Gloria (novel)
Galdós, Benito Pérez **6** 177-178

Gloria, La (painting)
Titian **15** 242-244

Gloriana (opera)
Britten, Benjamin **3** 10-11

Glorification of Pope Urban VIII (painting)
Cortona, Pietro da **4** 256

Glorification of Saint Charles Borromeo (painting)
Rottmayr, Johann Michael **13** 321

Glorious Revolution (England; 1688)
and Catholic question
Dryden, John **5** 106-107
Godolphin, Sidney **6** 380-381
Oates, Titus **11** 456
historians of
Macaulay, Thomas Babington **10** 79-80
Pepys, Samuel **12** 207-208
James II deposed
Anne **1** 241-242
James II **8** 207-208
Marlborough, 1st Duke of **10** 271-272
Mary II **10** 309-310
William III **16** 295-296
supporters
Calvert, Charles **3** 238
Livingston, Robert **9** 461-462
Taylor, Edward **15** 122-123

Glory of the Seas (ship)
McKay, Donald **10** 416-417

Gloster Aircraft Company
Whittle, Frank **16** 257-258

Gloucester, Duke of (Thomas of Woodstock; 1355-1397), regent of England 1386-1389
Richard II **13** 130-131

Gloucester, Gilbert de Clare, 8th Earl of (1243-1295), English nobleman
Montfort, Simon de **11** 132-133

GLOUCESTER, DUKE OF (1391-1447), English statesman **6** 370-371
Henry VI **7** 298-299

Gloucester, Richard, Duke of
see Richard III

Gloucester, Robert, Earl of (died 1147), English soldier
Stephen **14** 426-427

Gloucester, Statute of (1278; England)
Edward I **5** 208-210

Gloucester Abbey (England)
Edward II **5** 210

Gloucester Street (painting)
Davis, Stuart **4** 424-425

GLUBB, SIR JOHN BAGOT (1897-1986), British commander of the Arab Legion 1939-56 **6** 371-372

GLUCK, CHRISTOPH WILLIBALD (1714-1787), Austrian composer and opera reformer **6** 372-374
Berlioz, Louis Hector **2** 203-205
Euripides **5** 332-334
Monteverdi, Claudio Giovanni Antonio **11** 126-128
Mozart, Wolfgang Amadeus **11** 218-221

GLUCKMAN, MAX (1911-1975), British anthropologist **6** 374-375

Glück im Winkel, Das (play)
Sudermann, Hermann **15** 12-13

Glycogen (physiology)
Bernard, Claude **2** 208-210
Hill, Archibald Vivian **7** 385-386

Glycolysis (biochemistry)
Meyerhof, Otto Fritz **10** 537-539

Glyndyfrdwy, Lord of Giyndwr and Sycharth
see Glendower, O.

Glyoxylic test (biochemistry)
Hopkins, Frederick Gowland **7** 491-492

GM
see General Motors Corporation

Gmelin, Leopold (1788-1853), German chemist
Bunsen, Robert Wilhelm **3** 124-125

Gnarled Trees (painting)
Soutine, Chaim **14** 356-357

Gneisenau, Count August Neithardt von (1760-1831), Prussian field marshal
Blücher, Gebhard Leberecht von **2** 340-341

Gnessin, Mikhail Fabianovich (1883-1957), Russian composer
Khachaturian, Aram Ilich **8** 530-531

Gnomic poems (German literature)
Gottfried von Strassburg **6** 461-462

Gnomon (instrument)
Anaximander **1** 209-210

Gnostic Gospels, The (book)
Pagels, Elaine Hiesey **12** 61-62

Gnosticism (religion)
and Cabalism
Nahmanides **11** 293-294
Scholem, Gershom **14** 26
influence of
Bultmann, Rudolf Karl **3** 119-120
Jung, Carl Gustav **8** 388-389
Origen **11** 528-529
Manichaean
Mani **10** 196-197
opponents
Clement of Alexandria **4** 102-103
Tertullian **15** 155-156

Gnotobiology (science)
Northrop, John Howard **11** 430-431

Go Down, Moses... (stories)
Faulkner, William **5** 395-397

Go Quietly ... Or Else (book)
Agnew, Spiro Theodore **1** 83-85

Go Tell It on the Mountain (novel)
Baldwin, James Arthur **1** 465-466

Go West (film)
Marx brothers **10** 303-304

Goa (district; India)
Albuquerque, Afonso de **1** 118-119
Francis Xavier **6** 48
Manuel I **10** 219-220

Gobelins (tapestry works; France)
Berthollet, Claude Louis **2** 229-230
Boucher, François **2** 440-442

Le Brun, Charles **9** 269-270

Gobernadora, La (play)
Benavente y Martinez, Jacinto **2** 146-147

Gobi Desert (Asia)
Andrews, Roy Chapman **1** 232-233
Hedin, Sven Anders **7** 252-253
Przhevalsky, Nikolai Mikhailovich **12** 469-470

GOBINEAU, COMTE DE (Joseph Arthur Gobineau; 1816-1882), French diplomat **6** 375-376
Chamberlain, Houston Stewart **3** 411

Goblin Market... (poems)
Rossetti, Christina Georgina **13** 307-308

Goblins, The (play)
Suckling, John **15** 10-11

God (philosophy)
Augustinianism
Augustine **1** 367-370
Duns Scotus, John **5** 149-150
Lull, Raymond **10** 39-40
William of Ockham **16** 298-299
Death of God
Altizer, Thomas J. J. **1** 183-184
Rubenstein, Richard L. **13** 343-344
Greek views
Aristotle **1** 295-296
Epicurus **5** 292-294
Plato **12** 345-347
interpretations
Feuerbach, Ludwig Andreas **5** 432
Nietzsche, Friedrich **11** 390-392
Paley, William **12** 72
Tillich, Paul Johannes **15** 224-225
Islamic views
Ashari, Abu al- Hasan Ali al- **1** 327-328
Nazzam, Ibrahim ibn Sayyar al- **11** 329
Jewish views
Philo Judaeus **12** 282-283
kingdom of
Jesus of Nazareth **8** 251-255
Neoplatonism
Anselm of Canterbury **1** 244-245
Averroës **1** 382-383
Erigena, John Scotus **5** 308-309
rationalist view
Descartes, René **4** 505-508
Locke, John **9** 478-480
Reformation views
Calvin, John **3** 239-242
Luther, Martin **10** 48-51
Thomistic view
Thomas Aquinas **15** 183-186

God, Society of (India)
Roy, Ram Mohun **13** 18

God Bless America (song)
Berlin, Irving **2** 200-201

God in Search of Man (book)
Heschel, Abraham Joshua **7** 358-359

God Is My King (cantata)
Bach, Johann Sebastian **1** 416-419

God Moves in a Mysterious Way (hymn)
Cowper, William **4** 282

God of Intercourse with a Full Stomach, The (Japanese pillow book)
Hokusai, Katsushika **7** 447-448

God of Vengeance (play)
Asch, Shalom **1** 325-326

God-Seeker, The (novel)
Lewis, Harry Sinclair **9** 385-387

God That Failed, The (book; Crossman, editor)
Wright, Richard **16** 401-402

God Was in Christ (essay)
Baillie, D. (Donald) M. (Macpherson) **1** 445

God without Thunder (book)
Ransom, John Crowe **13** 39-40

God Worshipers Society
see Taiping sect

Godan (novel)
Premchand **12** 439

Godard, Jean-Luc (born 1930), French film director
Bogart, Humphrey **2** 363-364
Truffaut, François **15** 311-313

GODDARD, ROBERT HUTCHINGS (1882-1945), American pioneer in rocketry **6** 376-377

Goddard, William (1740-1817), American printer
Bradford, William **2** 477

Goddesses (poems)
Kuo Mo-jo **9** 133-134

GÖDEL, KURT (1906-1978), Austrian-American mathematician **6** 377-379
Schlick, Friedrich Albert Moritz **14** 16-17

Goderich Viscount
see Ripon, Frederick John Robinson, Earl of

Godey, Louis Antoine (1804-1878), American publisher
Hale, Sarah Josepha **7** 74-75

Godey's Lady's Book (magazine)
Hale, Sarah Josepha **7** 74-75
Munsey, Frank Andrew **11** 251
Poe, Edgar Allan **12** 363-365

Godfrey, Thomas (1736-1763), American poet and playwright Hallam Family
Hallam, Lewis Sr. and Jr. **7** 87

GODFREY OF BOUILLON (circa 1060-1100), French lay leader of First Crusade **6** 379
Baldwin I **1** 464-465
Tasso, Torquato **15** 114-116

GODKIN, EDWIN LAWRENCE (1831-1902), British-born American journalist **6** 380

God-Man (novel)
Kazantzakis, Nikos **8** 466-468

GODOLPHIN, SIDNEY (1st Earl of Godolphin; 1645-1712), English statesman **6** 380-381
Anne **1** 241-242
Harley, Robert **7** 159-160
Marlborough, 1st Duke of **10** 271-272

GODOY Y ÁLVAREZ DE FARIA, MANUEL DE (1767-1851), Spanish statesman **6** 381-382
Charles IV **3** 456-457
Ferdinand VII **5** 418-420

Gods Are Athirst, The (novel)
France, Anatole **6** 39-40

God's Bit of Wood (novel)
Ousmane, Sembene **12** 32-33

God's Controversy with New England (poem)
Wigglesworth, Michael **16** 266-267

God's Determinations Touching His Elect (poems)
Taylor, Edward **15** 122-123

God's Grandeur (poem)
Hopkins, Gerard Manley **7** 492-494

God's Little Acre (novel)
Caldwell, Erskine **3** 223-224

Gods of the Lightning (play)
Anderson, Maxwell **1** 219-220

God's Trombones (poems)
Johnson, James Weldon **8** 304-305

GODUNOV, BORIS FEODOROVICH (circa 1551-1605), czar of Russia 1598-1605 **6** 382-383
Ivan IV **8** 157-159

Godwi (novel)
Brentano, Clemens **2** 515-516

Godwin, Edward W. (1833-1886), British architect
Richardson, Henry Hobson **13** 139-141
Whistler, James Abbott McNeill **16** 225-226

Godwin, Mary Wollstonecraft (1759-1797), English author
Barlow, Joel **2** 6-7
Godwin, William **6** 383-384

GODWIN, WILLIAM (1756-1836), English political theorist and writer **6** 383-384
Brown, Charles Brockden **3** 33
O'Connell, Daniel **11** 465-467
Shelley, Percy Bysshe **14** 176-178
Wordsworth, William **16** 385-388

Godwin of Wessex, Earl (died 1053), English nobleman
Edward the Confessor **5** 218-219
Harold II **7** 162

GOEBBELS, JOSEPH PAUL (1897-1945), German politician and Nazi propagandist **6** 384-385
Hitler, Adolf **7** 417-420

Goerdeler, Carl (1884-1945), German politician
Beck, Ludwig August Theodor **2** 99-100

GOEPPERT-MAYER, MARIA (1906-1972), American physicist **6** 385-387

GOETHALS, GEORGE WASHINGTON (1858-1928), American Army officer and engineer **6** 387-388
Gorgas, William Crawford **6** 454-455
Lesseps, Vicomte de **9** 354-355

GOETHE, JOHANN WOLFGANG VON (1749-1832), German poet **6** 388-391
friends
Arnim, Achim von **1** 308-309
Herder, Johann Gottfried von **7** 327-328
Jacobi, Friedrich Heinrich **8** 189-190
Schiller, Johann Christoph Friedrich von **14** 4-7
influence of (Argentina and United States)
Echeverría, José Estéban **5** 197-198
Emerson, Ralph Waldo **5** 278-280
Longfellow, Henry Wadsworth **9** 499-500
influence of (China)
Kuo Mo-jo **9** 133-134
influence of (France)
Cousin, Victor **4** 273-274
influence of (Germany; 19th century)
Arnim, Achim von **1** 308-309
Fichte, Johann Gottlieb **5** 435-436
Hölderlin, Johann Christian Friedrich **7** 451-452
Lewis, Matthew Gregory **9** 390-391
Schelling, Friedrich Wilhelm Joseph von **13** 526-527
Schopenhauer, Arthur **14** 29-31
influence of (Germany; 20th century)
Hauptmann, Gerhart Johann Robert **7** 199-201
Kafka, Franz **8** 403-406
Mann, Thomas **10** 204-207
influence of (Great Britain)
Carlyle, Thomas **3** 304-305
Clough, Arthur Hugh **4** 123-124
Joyce, James **8** 365-367
Thackeray, William Makepeace **15** 159-161
influenced by (German and Swiss)
Fuseli, Henry **6** 153-155
Grimmelshausen, Hans Jakob Christoffel von **7** 4-5
Klopstock, Friedrich Gottlieb **9** 55-56
Lessing, Gotthold Ephraim **9** 357-359
Sachs, Hans **13** 410-411
Wieland, Christoph Martin **16** 260-261
Winckelmann, Johann Joachim **16** 332-333
Wolf, Friedrich August **16** 352-353
influenced by (Italian and Greek)
Cellini, Benvenuto **3** 391-392
Cimarosa, Domenico **4** 61-62
Plutarch **12** 359-360
Tasso, Torquato **15** 114-116
musical settings
Berlioz, Louis Hector **2** 203-205
Gounod, Charles François **6** 473-474
Mahler, Gustav **10** 144-145
Schubert, Franz Peter **14** 35-37-465
quoted
Klopstock, Friedrich Gottlieb **9** 55-56
Niebuhr, Barthold Georg **11** 385-386
translations of
Pasternak, Boris Leonidovich **12** 124-125
Scott, Walter **14** 68-70

Goeze, Johann Melchior (1717-1786), German Lutheran theologian
Lessing, Gotthold Ephraim **9** 357-359

Goffredo (literary character)
Tasso, Torquato **15** 114-116

Gog (Old Testament character)
Ezekiel **5** 355-356

Gogarten, Friedrich (1887-1967), German Protestant theologian
Barth, Karl **2** 31-32

GOGOL, NIKOLAI (1809-1852), Russian author **6** 391-393
Belinsky, Grigorievich **2** 128
Chagall, Marc **3** 406-407
Dostoevsky, Fyodor **5** 74-77
Mérimée, Prosper **10** 517
Meyerhold, Vsevolod Emilievich **10** 539
Turgenev, Ivan Sergeyevich **15** 345-348

GOH CHOK TONG (born 1941), leader of the People's Action Party and Singapore's prime minister **6** 393-395

Goin' Fishin' (collage)
Dove, Arthur Garfield **5** 86-87

Goin' Home (song)
Dvořák, Antonin **5** 168-169

Going to Meet the Man (stories)
Baldwin, James Arthur **1** 465-466

Gojjam (province; Ethiopia)
Haile Selassie **7** 68-70

GÖKALP, MEHMET ZIYA (1875/76-1924), Turkish publicist and sociologist **6** 395-396

GOKHALE, GOPAL KRISHNA (1866-1915), Indian nationalist leader **6** 396
Jinnah, Mohammad Ali **8** 262-263
Mehta, Pherozeshah **10** 455

Golah ve nekar (book)
Kaufmann, Ezekiel **8** 460

Gold (currency)
Cadamosto, Alvise da **3** 206-207
Fisk, James **5** 464-465
Gould, Jay **6** 470-472
Law, John **9** 244-245

Morgan, John Pierpont **11** 163-165
see also Gold standard

Gold (play)
O'Neill, Eugene **11** 514-516

Gold Bug, The (story)
Poe, Edgar Allan **12** 363-365

Gold Coast
see Ghana

Gold Coast (book)
Danquah, Joseph B. **4** 388-389

Gold Coast Customs (poems)
Sitwell, Edith **14** 265-266

Gold Coast Leader (newspaper)
Hayford, J. E. Casely **7** 228-230

Gold Democrats (United States politics)
Bryan, William Jennings **3** 80-82
Straus, Isidor **14** 496

Gold rush (Australia)
Hargraves, Edward Hammond
7 153-154
Vogel, Julius **16** 9-10

Gold rush (California; 1849)
Comstock, Henry Tompkins Paige **4** 189
Hargraves, Edward Hammond
7 153-154
Harte, Francis Brett **7** 184-185
Hearst, George **7** 242
Judah, Theodore Dehone **8** 373-374
Mackay, John William **10** 101-102
Miller, Joaquin **11** 27-28
Sutter, John Augustus **15** 41-42
Vanderbilt, Cornelius **15** 415-416

Gold Rush, The (film)
Chaplin, Charles Spencer **3** 438-440

Gold solidus (coins)
Constantine I **4** 209-211

Gold standard
Churchill, Winston Leonard Spencer
4 51-53
Díaz, José de la Cruz Porfirio **4** 534-536
Hanna, Marcus Alonzo **7** 127-128
Leopold III **9** 347-348
Peel, Robert **12** 181-183
Witte, Sergei Yulyevich **16** 349-350
see also Currency (United States)

Gold Standard Act (United States; 1900)
McKinley, William **10** 418-420

Gold, Thomas (born 1920), American
astronomer
Lemaître, Abbè Georges Édouard
9 315-316

Goldberg (literary character)
Pinter, Harold **12** 317-318

GOLDBERG, ARTHUR JOSEPH
(1908-1990), U.S. secretary of labor,
ambassador to the United Nations, and

activist justice of the U.S. Supreme Court
6 397-398

GOLDBERG, WHOOPI (born Caryn E.
Johnson; born 1949), African American
actress **6** 398-402

Golden Age (Spanish literature; 1580-1680)
Calderón, Pedro **3** 221-222
Gracián y Morales, Baltasar Jerónimo
6 481-482
Quevedo Y Villegas, Francisco Gómez
de **12** 511

Golden Age, The (ballet)
Shostakovich, Dmitri Dmitrievich
14 204-205

Golden Argosy (magazine)
Munsey, Frank Andrew **11** 251

Golden Ass, The (book; Apuleius)
La Fontaine, Jean de **9** 156-157

Golden Bough, The (book; Frazer)
Frazer, James George **6** 76
Malinowski, Kaspar Bronislaw
10 170-171
Tylor, Edward Burnett **15** 372-373

Golden Bowl, The (novel)
James, Henry **8** 211-212

Golden Boy (play)
Odets, Clifford **11** 470-471

Golden Bull (imperial ordinances)
Charles IV **3** 455-456

Golden Chain (book)
Thomas Aquinas **15** 183-186

Golden Chain, The (play)
Peretz, Isaac Loeb **12** 212

Golden Cockerel, The (book and opera)
Pushkin, Aleksandr Sergeevich
12 489-491
Rimsky-Korsakov, Nikolai Andreevich
13 174-175

Golden Fleece (magazine)
Blok, Aleksandr Aleksandrovich **2** 335

Golden Fleece, The (play)
Grillparzer, Franz **6** 546-547

Golden Gloves (boxing)
Ali, Muhammad **1** 156-158
Louis, Joe **9** 537-538

GOLDEN, HARRY (1902-1981),
Jewish-American humorist, writer, and
publisher **6** 402-403

Golden Hind (ship)
Drake, Francis **5** 94-96

Golden Horde (Mongolian state;
1223-circa 1400)
Batu Khan **2** 60-61
Godunov, Boris Feodorovich **6** 382-383
Hulagu Khan **8** 27-28
ibn Battuta, Muhammad **8** 91-92
Ivan III **8** 156-157
Kublai Khan **9** 115-118

Golden Legend, The (book)
Longfellow, Henry Wadsworth
9 499-500

Golden Legend, The (hagiographic collection)
Caxton, William **3** 386-387

Golden Notebook, The (book)
Lessing, Doris **9** 355-357

Golden Pot, The (story)
Hoffmann, Ernst Theodor Amadeus
7 439-440

Golden Rule
Hillel **7** 390-391
Jesus of Nazareth **8** 251-255

Golden Six, The (play)
Anderson, Maxwell **1** 219-220

Golden Speech (1601)
Elizabeth I **5** 263-266

Golden Summer (painting)
Streeton, Arthur Ernest **14** 507-508

Golden Threshold, The (poems)
Naidu, Sarojini **11** 294-295

Golden Whales of California, The (poem)
Lindsay, Vachel **9** 424-425

Goldene Kait, Die (play)
Peretz, Isaac Loeb **12** 212

Goldenrod (botany)
Edison, Thomas Alva **5** 206-208

Goldfish, Samuel
see Goldwyn, Samuel

**GOLDIE, SIR GEORGE DASHWOOD
TAUBMAN** (1846-1925), British trader
and empire builder **6** 404

GOLDING, WILLIAM (1911-1993), English
novelist and essayist **6** 404-406

GOLDMAN, EMMA (1869-1940), Lithuanian-born American anarchist **6** 406-407

Goldmann, Max
see Reinhardt, Max

GOLDMARK, JOSEPHINE (1877-1950),
advocate of government assistance in
improving the lot of women and children
6 407-408

Goldmark, Rubin (1872-1936), American
composer
Copland, Aaron **4** 227-228

**Goldne Spiegel oder die Könige von
Scheschian, Der** (novel)
Wieland, Christoph Martin **16** 260-261

Goldne Topf, Der (story)
Hoffmann, Ernst Theodor Amadeus
7 439-440

Goldne Vliess, Das (play)
Grillparzer, Franz **6** 546-547

GOLDONI, CARLO (1707-1793), Italian
dramatist, poet, and librettist **6** 408-409
Howells, William Dean **7** 539-541

GOLDSMITH, JAMES MICHAEL (born
1933), British-French industrialist and financier **6** 409-411

GOLDSMITH, OLIVER (1730-1774), British poet, dramatist, and novelist **6** 411-413
     Boswell, James **2** 432-434
     Goldsmith, Oliver **6** 411
     Irving, Washington **8** 141-143
     Johnson, Samuel **8** 315-317
     Smollett, Tobias George **14** 305-307

GOLDSMITH, OLIVER (1794-1861), Canadian poet **6** 411

Goldsmiths
     see Artists—goldsmiths

Goldstein, Eugen (1850-1930), German physicist
     Röntgen, Wilhelm Conrad **13** 273-275

GOLDWATER, BARRY (born 1909), conservative Republican U.S. senator from Arizona (1952-1987) **6** 413-415
     Johnson, Lyndon Baines **8** 308-312
     Wallace, George Corley **16** 71-72

GOLDWYN, SAMUEL (1882-1974), Polish-born American film producer **6** 416
     Disney, Walter Elias **5** 26-27

Golf
     Nicklaus, Jack **11** 382-383
     Palmer, Arnold Daniel **12** 78-80
     Zaharias, Mildred Didrikson **16** 487-488

Golfo da Roca (bay; South Africa)
     Dias de Novais, Bartolomeu **4** 533-534

Golgotha
     see Calvary

Goliath (biblical character)
     David, Jacques Louis **4** 407-409

Gollancz, Sir Israel (1864-1930), English scholar
     Plaatje, Solomon Tshekisho **12** 341-342

Golliwog's Cake Walk (musical composition)
     Debussy, Achille Claude **4** 445-447

Golpejera, battle of (1072)
     Alfonso VI **1** 149
     Cid **4** 58-59

Goltz, Friedrich Leopold (1834-1902), German physiologist
     Lashley, Karl Spencer **9** 214-215

Gomarians (religion)
     see Contra-Remonstrants (religion)

Gomarus, Francis (1563-1641), Dutch Calvinistic theologian
     Arminius, Jacobus **1** 301-302

Gombe Stream Research Center (Zaire)
     Goodall, Jane **6** 433-434

GOMBERT, NICOLAS (circa 1500-1556/57), Franco-Flemish composer **6** 416-417
     Josquin des Prez **8** 361-363

Gömbös, Gyula (1886-1936), Hungarian general and statesman

Horthy de Nagybánya, Nicholas **7** 510-512

Gomes, Diogo (flourished 15th), Portuguese explorer
     Cadamosto, Alvise da **3** 206-207
     Henry the Navigator **7** 305-306

Gómez, José Miguel (1858-1921), Cuban general and politician
     Machado y Morales, Gerardo **10** 92-93
     Menocal, Mario Garcia **10** 506-507

GÓMEZ, JUAN VICENTE (1857-1935), Venezuelan dictator **6** 417-418
     Betancourt, Rómulo **2** 237-238
     Gallegos Freire, Rómulo **6** 185-186

GÓMEZ, MÁXIMO (1836-1905), Dominican-born Cuban general and independence hero **6** 418-419
     Céspedes, Carlos Manuel de **3** 398-399
     Maceo, Antonio **10** 88-90
     Martí, José **10** 285-286

GÓMEZ CASTRO, LAUREANO ELEUTERIO (1889-1965), Colombian statesman, president **6** 419-420
     Lleras Camargo, Alberto **9** 467
     Rojas Pinilla, Gustavo **13** 255-256

Gómez Farias, Valentin (1781-1858), Mexican politician
     Santa Ana, Antonio López de **13** 471-472

Gómez y Báez, Máximo (1826-1905), Cuban patriot and general
     Menocal, Mario Garcia **10** 506-507

GOMPERS, SAMUEL (1850-1924), American labor leader **6** 420-422
     Coolidge, John Calvin **4** 217-219
     Coxey, Jacob Sechler **4** 286-287
     Green, William R. **6** 521
     Lewis, John Llewellyn **9** 387-388
     Roosevelt, Theodore **13** 280-283

GOMULKA, WLADISLAW (1905-1982), Polish politician **6** 422-424

GONCHAROV, IVAN ALEKSANDROVICH (1812-1891), Russian novelist **6** 424
     Turgenev, Ivan Sergeyevich **15** 345-348

GONCHAROVA, NATALIA (1881-1962), Russian painter and theatrical scenery designer **6** 424-426
     Larionov, Mikhail **9** 205-206

Goncourt Academy (Paris)
     Goncourt, Edmond de and Jules de **6** 426-427

GONCOURT BROTHERS (19th-century French writers) **6** 426-427

Gondar (city; Ethiopia)
     Bruce, James **3** 63-64

Gondi Palace (Florence)
     Sangallo family **13** 464-466

Gondola, Andrea di Pietro dalla
     see Palladio, Andrea

Gondoleiro do amôr, O (poems)
     Castro Alves, Antônio de **3** 364-365

Gondoliers, The (operetta)
     Gilbert, William Schwenck **6** 314-315
     Sullivan, Arthur Seymour **15** 23

Gone Are the Days (film)
     Davis, Ossie **4** 421-422

Gone with the Wind (book)
     Mitchell, Margaret **11** 59-60

Gone with the Wind (film)
     Gable, William Clark **6** 157-158
     McDaniel, Hattie **10** 405-408
     McQueen, Butterfly **10** 434-437

Gongon Musa
     see Musa Mansa

GÓNGORA Y ARGOTE, LUIS DE (1561-1627), Spanish poet **6** 427-428
     Greco **6** 511-514
     Michelangelo Buonarroti **11** 2-5
     Velázquez, Diego Rodríguez de Silva y **15** 454-456

Gongorism (literary style)
     Góngora y Argote, Luis de **6** 427-428
     Quevedo Y Villegas, Francisco Gómez de **12** 511

Gonne, Maud (1866-1953), Irish patriot and philanthropist
     Yeats, William Butler **16** 445-447

Gontcharova, Nathalie (1881-1962), Russian painter
     Malevich, Kasimir **10** 168-169

Gontenbein (literary character)
     Frisch, Max **6** 118-119

Gonzaga, Francesco (died 1483), Italian cardinal and literary patron
     Mantegna, Andrea **10** 215-216
     Poliziano, Angelo **12** 373-374

Gonzaga, Gianfrancesco (died 1444), Italian art patron, marquis of Mantua 1407-1444
     Alberti, Leon Battista **1** 113-115
     Feltre, Vittorino da **5** 409-410

Gonzaga, Giovanni Francesco II
     see Mantua, Duke of

Gonzaga, Lodovico (died 1478), Italian art patron, marquis of Mantua 1444-78
     Alberti, Leon Battista **1** 113-115
     Mantegna, Andrea **10** 215-216

Gonzaga, Vincenzo I (ruled 1587-1612), duke of Mantua
     Monteverdi, Claudio Giovanni Antonio **11** 126-128
     Rubens, Peter Paul **13** 339-342

González, Gil (died circa 1527), Spanish explorer
     Pedrarias **12** 179

González, Joan (died 1908), Spanish painter
     González, Julio **6** 428-429

Gonzalez, José Victoriano
     see Gris, Juan

GONZÁLEZ, JULIO (1876-1942), Spanish sculptor **6** 428-429
     Miró, Joan **11** 53-54

González, Manuel (1833-1893), Mexican general, president 1880-1884
  Díaz, José de la Cruz Porfirio **4** 534-536

GONZÁLEZ MARQUEZ, FELIPE (born 1942), Socialist leader of Spain
  6 429-431

GONZÁLEZ PRADA, MANUEL (1848-1918), Peruvian essayist and poet
  6 431

GONZALO DE BERCEO (circa 1195-after 1252), Spanish author **6** 431-432

GOOCH, GEORGE PEABODY (1873-1968), British historian and political journalist **6** 432-433

Good Afternoon, Mrs. Lincoln (painting)
  Gorky, Arshile **6** 458

Good Bye, Earth (poem)
  Richards, Ivor Armstrong **13** 137

Good Conscience, The (novel)
  Fuentes, Carlos **6** 141-142

Good Earth, The (novel)
  Buck, Pearl Sydenstricker **3** 91-93

Good Family, The (book)
  Mäkonnen Endalkačäw **10** 161-162

Good Gray Poet, The (book; O'Connor)
  Whitman, Walt **16** 249-251

Good Hope (ship)
  Hudson, Henry **8** 12-13

Good Hope, Cape of (South Africa)
  Magellan, Ferdinand **10** 126-127
  Schouten, William Cornelius **14** 31

Good Housekeeping (magazine)
  Hearst, William Randolph **7** 243-244
  Wiley, Harvey Washington **16** 277-278

Good Learning (book)
  Chu Hsi **4** 40-43

Good Life, A (book)
  Bunin, Ivan Alekseevich **3** 124

Good Morning America (poem)
  Sandburg, Carl **13** 461-462

Good Natur'd Man, The (play)
  Goldsmith, Oliver **6** 411-413

Good Parliament (1376; England)
  Edward the Black Prince **5** 217-218
  John of Gaunt **8** 282-283

Good Roads Bill (United States; 1894)
  Coxey, Jacob Sechler **4** 286-287

Good Soldier, The (novel)
  Ford, Ford Madox **6** 1-2

Good Woman of Setzuan, The (play)
  Brecht, Bertolt **2** 512-514

GOODALL, JANE (born 1934), British scientist who studied primates **6** 433-434

Goodhue, Bertram Grosvenor (1869-1924), American architect
  Renwick, James **13** 102-103

GOODLAD, JOHN INKSTER (born 1917), American education researcher and prophet **6** 434-436

GOODMAN, BENNY (Benjamin David Goodman; 1909-1986), jazz clarinetist and big band leader (1935-1945)
  6 436-438

GOODMAN, ELLEN HOLTZ (born 1941), American journalist **6** 438-439

Good-neighbor policy (United States politics)
  Hoover, Herbert Clark **7** 483-485
  Hull, Cordell **8** 28-29
  Lamas, Carlos Saavedra **9** 175-176
  Morrow, Dwight Whitney **11** 190-191
  Stimson, Henry Lewis **14** 457-458
  Welles, Sumner **16** 191-192

GOODNIGHT, CHARLES (1836-1926), American cattleman **6** 439
  Chisum, John Simpson **4** 11

Goodnight College (Texas)
  Goodnight, Charles **6** 439

Goodnight-Loving Trail (western United States)
  Goodnight, Charles **6** 439

Goodnow, Frank Johnson (1859-1939), American political scientist
  Yüan Shih-k'ai **16** 480-481

GOODPASTER, ANDREW JACKSON (born 1915), American Army officer active in organizing NATO forces in Europe and adviser to three presidents **6** 439-441

Goodwill, Fanny (literary character)
  Fielding, Henry **5** 442-444

Goodwin, Hannibal W. (1822-1900), American Episcopalian clergyman and inventor
  Eastman, George **5** 186

GOODYEAR, CHARLES (1800-1860), American inventor **6** 441
  Kármán, Theodore von **8** 451-452

Goon on Earth
  see Antiochus IV Epiphanes

Goose Man, The (novel)
  Wassermann, Jakob **16** 130-131

Gooseberry, The (story)
  Chekhov, Anton Pavlovich **3** 494-497

Gopher Prairie (American Midwest)
  Cather, Willa Sibert **3** 368-369

Gopher Prairie, Minnesota (literary town)
  Lewis, Harry Sinclair **9** 385-387

Gora (novel)
  Rabindranath Tagore **12** 529-531

GORBACHEV, MIKHAIL SERGEEVICH (born 1931), general secretary of the Communist Party and later (1990) president of the Union of Soviet Socialist Republics. **6** 441-444
  August 1991 coup
    Yeltsin, Boris Nikolaevich **16** 449-452
  opponents
    Ligachev, Yegor Kuz'mich **9** 404-406

GORBACHEV, RAISA MAXIMOVNA (née Titorenko; born 1932), first lady of the Soviet Union **6** 444-446

Gorchakov, Aleksandr Mikhailovich (1798-1883), Russian prince and statesman
  Bismarck, Otto Eduard Leopold von **2** 294-296

Gordian III (Gordianus Pius; 224?-244), Roman emperor
  Plotinus **12** 358-359

Gordian Knot (mythology)
  Alexander the Great **1** 137-141

GORDIMER, NADINE (born 1923), South African author of short stories and novels **6** 446-447

Gordium (ancient city; Phrygia)
  Alexander the Great **1** 137-141

GORDON, AARON DAVID (1856-1922), Russian-born Palestinian Zionist **6** 447-448

GORDON, CHARLES GEORGE (1833-1885), English soldier and adventurer **6** 448-449
  Cromer, 1st Earl of **4** 317
  Gladstone, William Ewart **6** 357-360
  Kitchener, Horatio Herbert **9** 45-46
  Mahdi **10** 137-138
  Victoria **15** 485-487

Gordon, George (6th Earl of Huntly; 1562-1636), Scottish statesman
  James I **8** 204-206

Gordon, George Hamilton
  see Aberdeen, 4th Earl of

GORDON, JOHN BROWN (1832-1904), American businessman and politician **6** 449-450

Gordon, Richard F. (born 1929), American astronaut
  Armstrong, Neil Alden **1** 304-306

Gordon riots (England; 1780)
  Amherst, Jeffery **1** 200-201
  Dickens, Charles John Huffam **4** 538-541
  Wilkes, John **16** 280-281

GORDY, BERRY, JR. (born 1929), founder of the Motown Sound **6** 450-451
  Jackson, Michael Joe **8** 178-180
  Jones, Quincy Delight Jr. **8** 339-341

GORE, ALBERT, JR. (born 1948), Democratic U.S. representative, senator, and 45th vice president of the United States **6** 452-453

Gorée (island; Senegal)
  Diagne, Blaise **4** 527

Gorenko, Anna Andreyevna
  see Akhmatova, Anna

GORGAS, JOSIAH (1818-1883), American soldier and educator **6** 453-454

GORGAS, WILLIAM CRAWFORD
(1854-1920), American general and sanitarian **6** 454-455
Finlay, Carlos Juan **5** 450
Goethals, George Washington
6 387-388

GORGES, SIR FERDINANDO (1568-1647),
English colonizer and soldier **6** 455-456
Bradford, William **2** 475-476
Smith, John **14** 295-297

Görgey, Arthur von (1818-1916), Hungarian general and dictator
Kossuth, Louis **9** 88-90

GORGIAS (circa 480-circa 376 B.C.),
Greek sophist philosopher and rhetorician **6** 456
Antisthenes **1** 250-251
Isocrates **8** 151
Xenophon **16** 418-420

Gorgias (dialogue)
Plato **12** 345-347

Gorgias (literary character)
Menander **10** 477-478

Gorham Building (New York City)
White, Stanford **16** 235-236

Gorham, George Cornelius (1787-1857),
Anglican divine
Manning, Henry Edward **10** 209-210

Gorillas
Fossey, Dian **6** 23-24

GÖRING, HERMANN WILHELM
(1893-1946), German politician and air
force commander **6** 457-458
Goebbels, Joseph Paul **6** 384-385
Himmler, Heinrich **7** 398-399
Hitler, Adolf **7** 417-420
Kesselring, Albert Field Marshal
8 522-523
Lindbergh, Charles Augustus **9** 421-423

GORKY, ARSHILE (1905-1948), American
painter **6** 458

GORKY, MAXIM (1868-1936), Russian
author **6** 458-460
Babel, Isaac Emmanuelovich **1** 411-412
Bunin, Ivan Alekseevich **3** 124
Chekhov, Anton Pavlovich **3** 494-497
Kurosawa, Akira **9** 135-137
Stanislavsky, Constantin **14** 398-399

Görres, Johann Josef von (1776-1848),
German journalist
Arnim, Achim von **1** 308-309
Brentano, Clemens **2** 515-516
Döllinger, Josef Ignaz von **5** 47-48

GORTON, SAMUELL (circa 1592-1677),
English colonizer **6** 460
Winslow, Edward **16** 338-339

Goschen, George Joachim (1st Viscount
Goschen; 1831-1907), British statesman
Milner, Alfred **11** 38-39
Salisbury, 3d Marquess of **13** 448-449

Gosford, 2nd Earl of (1776-1849), Irish
statesman

Papineau, Louis-Joseph **12** 91

GOSHIRAKAWA (1127-1192), Japanese
emperor **6** 460-461

Gosnold, Bartholomew (died 1607), English navigator
Smith, John **14** 295-297

Gospels
see Bible—New Testament

Gospel music
Caesar, Shirley **3** 210-211
Cleveland, James **4** 106-108
Franklin, Aretha **6** 58-60

Gossart, Jan (1478?-1533?), Flemish
painter
Clouet, Jean and François **4** 122-123

Gosse, Edmund W. (1849-1928), English
poet
Naidu, Sarojini **11** 294-295

Gossip on Romance, A (essay)
Stevenson, Robert Louis **14** 446-448

Gosson, Stephen (1554-1624), English
ecclesiastic and writer
Sidney, Philip **14** 214-215

Gösta
see Gustavus II Adolphus

Gösta Berling's Saga (novel and film)
Garbo, Greta **6** 205-207
Lagerlöf, Selma Ottiliana Lovisa
9 163-164

Got, Bertrand de
see Clement V

Göta Canal (Sweden)
Ericsson, John **5** 307-308

Göteborg (city; Sweden)
Asplund, Eric Gunnar **1** 344
Gustavus II **7** 43-45

Göteborg, University of (Sweden)
Cassirer, Ernst **3** 358-359
Nordenskold, Nils Otto Gustaf
11 422-423

Gothart, Mathis Neithart
see Grünewald, Matthias

Gothenburg
see Göteborg

Gothic (East Germanic language)
Ulfilas **15** 384

Gothic art and architecture
England
Chippendale, Thomas **4** 1-2
Pugin, Augustus Welby Northmore
12 479-480
Ruskin, John **13** 371-372
Shaw, Richard Norman **14** 167-168
France
Goujon, Jean **6** 466-467
Montreuil, Pierre de **11** 139
Viollet-le-Duc, Eugène Emmanuel
15 505-506
Germany
Riemenschneider, Tilman **13** 166
Stoss, Veit **14** 481-482

Italy
Andrea Pisano **1** 225-226
Arnolfo di Cambio **1** 315-316
Donatello **5** 55-56
Duccio di Buoninsegna **5** 121-122
Giotto **6** 342-345
Lorenzetti, Pietro and Ambrogio
9 517-518
Martini, Simone **10** 298-299
Pisano, Giovanni **12** 324-325
Pisano, Nicola **12** 325
Tura, Cosimo **15** 343-344
Netherlands
Bosch, Hieronymus **2** 426-428
Bruegel, Pieter the Elder **3** 65-67

Gothic revival (American architecture)
Davis, Alexander Jackson **4** 411-411
Latrobe, Benjamin Henry **9** 222-224
Richardson, Henry Hobson **13** 139-141
Sullivan, Louis Henri **15** 27-28
Upjohn, Richard **15** 392

Goths (German people)
Leo I **9** 329-330
see also Ostrogoths; Visigoths

Gotoba (ruled 1184-1198), Japanese
emperor
Goshirakawa **6** 460-461

Gott ist mein König (cantata)
Bach, Johann Sebastian **1** 416-419

Gott und die Bajadere, Der (ballad)
Goethe, Johann Wolfgang von
6 388-391

Gott und die Natur (oratorio)
Meyerbeer, Giacomo **10** 536-537

Götter Griechenlands, Die (poem)
Schiller, Johann Christoph Friedrich von
14 4-7

Götterdämmerung, Die (opera)
Wagner, Richard **16** 40-43

Gottesreich, Das (book)
Cohen, Hermann **4** 138-139

GOTTFRIED VON STRASSBURG (circa
1165-circa 1215), German poet and
romancer **6** 461-462

Göttingen, University of (Germany)
linguistics
Grimm, Jakob and Wilhelm Karl
7 3-4
philosophy
Husserl, Edmund **8** 67-68
Lotze, Rudolf Hermann **9** 521-522
sciences
Born, Max **2** 420-421
Debye, Peter Joseph William
4 447-448
Gauss, Karl Friedrich **6** 240-242
Haller, Albrecht Von **7** 87-88
Kármán, Theodore von **8** 451-452
theology
Barth, Karl **2** 31-32
Ritschl, Albrecht Benjamin **13** 180
Troeltsch, Ernst **15** 299-300

Göttinnen, Die (novel)
Mann, Heinrich **10** 201-202

GOTTLIEB, ADOLPH (1903-1974), American Abstract Expressionist painter **6** 462-463

Gottrecht, Friedman
see Beissel, Johann Conrad

GOTTSCHALK, LOUIS MOREAU (1829-1869), American composer **6** 463-464

Gottschalk of Orbais (circa 805-circa 868), German monk and theologian
Erigena, John Scotus **5** 308-309

Gottsched, Johann Christoph (1700-1766), German author and critic
Fuseli, Henry **6** 153-155
Klopstock, Friedrich Gottlieb **9** 55-56
Lessing, Gotthold Ephraim **9** 357-359

GOTTWALD, KLEMENT (1896-1953), first Communist president of Czechoslovakia (1948-1953) **6** 464-466
Beneš, Edward **2** 155-157

Göttweig, monastery of (Austria)
Hildebrandt, Johann Lucas von **7** 380-381

Götz von Berlichingen (play; Goethe)
Goethe, Johann Wolfgang von **6** 388-391
Klopstock, Friedrich Gottlieb **9** 55-56
Scott, Walter **14** 68-70

GOUDIMEL, CLAUDE (circa 1514-1572), French composer **6** 466
Le Jeune, Claude **9** 314-315

Goudsmit, Samuel Abraham (1902-1978), American physicist
Pauli, Wolfgang Ernst **12** 149

Goudt, Hendrick (1585/88-circa 1630), Dutch engraver
Rembrandt Harmensz van Rijn **13** 91-95

GOUJON, JEAN (circa 1510-1568), French sculptor **6** 466-467
Cellini, Benvenuto **3** 391-392
Lescot, Pierre **9** 354

GOULART, JOÃO (1918-1976), Brazilian statesman **6** 467-469
Castelo Branco, Humberto **3** 359-360
Kubitschek de Oliveira, Juscelino **9** 113-115
Prestes, Luiz Carlos **12** 442-444
Vargas, Getulio Dornelles **15** 433-434

GOULD, GLENN (1932-1982), Canadian musician **6** 469-470

Gould, James (1770-1838), American jurist and law professor
Reeve, Tapping **13** 79-80

GOULD, JAY (1836-1892), American financier and railroad builder **6** 470-472
associates
Drew, Daniel **5** 101-102
Field, Cyrus West **5** 438-439
Fisk, James **5** 464-465

contemporaries
Cooke, Jay **4** 215-216
Pulitzer, Joseph **12** 481-482
rivals
Bennett, James Gordon Jr. **2** 169-170
Field, David Dudley **5** 439-440
Mackay, John William **10** 101-102
Powderly, Terence Vincent **12** 420-421
Vanderbilt, Cornelius **15** 415-416

GOULD, STEPHEN JAY (born 1941), American paleontologist **6** 472-473

Goulden, Emmeline
see Pankhurst, Emmeline

GOUNOD, CHARLES FRANÇOIS (1818-1893), French composer **6** 473-474
Bizet, Georges **2** 296-297

Gounod Choir
see Royal Choral Society

Gourd, The (anthology; Chinseki)
Basho, Matsuo **2** 45-48

Gouritz River (South Africa)
Dias de Novais, Bartolomeu **4** 533-534

GOURLAY, ROBERT (1778-1863), British reformer in Canada **6** 474

GOURMONT, REMY DE (1858-1915), French author, critic, and essayist **6** 475
Mencken, Henry Louis **10** 481-483

Gournay, Marie de (1565-1645), French editor
Montaigne, Michel Eyquem de **11** 116-117

Government (political science)
constitutionalism
Ames, Fisher **1** 199-200
Madison, James **10** 121-123
Maistre, Joseph de **10** 153-154
Paterson, William **12** 132-133
Washington, George **16** 126-129
parliamentary
Leopold I **9** 345-346
Le Play, Guillaume Frédéric **9** 350-351
representative
Wallas, Graham **16** 77-78
Warren, Earl **16** 117-120
responsible
Hansen, Alvin **7** 131-132
Metcalfe, Charles Theophilus **10** 531-532
Ward, Lester Frank **16** 113-114
theories
Bagehot, Walter **1** 436-437
Bentley, Arthur F. **2** 178
Chu Hsi **4** 40-43
Filmer, Robert **5** 448
Machiavelli, Niccolò **10** 97-99
Rousseau, Jean Jacques **13** 324-328
see also Political science; and types of government (ex. Democracy; Dictatorship; Monarchy)

Government Hospital for the Insane (United States)
see Saint Elizabeths Hospital

Government of India Act (1919; 1935)
Ambedkar, Bhimrao Ramji **1** 190-191
Chelmsford, Frederic John Napier Thesiger **3** 497

Governors (politics)
see Statesmen

Governor's Son, The (play)
Cohan, George Michael **4** 137-138

Governor's Wife (play)
Benavente y Martinez, Jacinto **2** 146-147

GOWER, JOHN (circa 1330-1408), English poet **6** 475-476
Caxton, William **3** 386-387
Skelton, John **14** 268-269

GOYA Y LUCIENTES, FRANCISCO DE PAULA JOSÉ DE (1746-1828), Spanish painter and printmaker **6** 476-478
influence of
Daumier, Honoré Victorin **4** 403-405
Evergood, Philip **5** 345
Glackens, William **6** 355-356
Klee, Paul **9** 47-49
Manet, Édouard **10** 193-194
Shahn, Ben **14** 139-140
Smith, David **14** 287-288
influenced by
Velázquez, Diego Rodríguez de Silva y **15** 454-456

Goyakla
see Geronimo

GOYEN, JAN VAN (1596-1656), Dutch painter **6** 478-479
Cuyp, Aelbert **4** 360-361

Goyescas (piano suite)
Granados, Enrique **6** 489-490

Gozzi, Count Carlo (1720-1806), Italian dramatist
Goldoni, Carlo **6** 408-409

Gozzoli, Benozzo (1420-1497), Italian painter
Signorelli, Luca **14** 221-222

Graaf, Regnier de (1641-1673), Dutch physician and anatomist
Leeuwenhoek, Anton van **9** 300-301

GRACCHUS, GAIUS SEMPRONIUS (ca. 154-121 B.C.) member of a Roman plebeian family referred to as the Gracchi; flourished 3rd-2nd century B.C. **6** 479-480
Clodius Pulcher, Publius **4** 121-122
Drusus, Marcus Livius **5** 105-106
Pompey **12** 387-389
Scipio Africanus Minor, Publius Cornelius Aemilianus **14** 62-63

GRACCHUS, TIBERIUS SEMPRONIUS (ca. 163-133 B.C.) member of a Roman plebeian family referred to as the Gracchi;

flourished 3rd-2nd century B.C.
6 479-480
   Drusus, Marcus Livius **5** 105-106
   Scipio Africanus Minor, Publius Cornelius Aemilianus **14** 62-63

Grace, The (painting)
   Chardin, Jean Baptiste Siméon
   3 442-443

GRACE, WILLIAM RUSSELL (1832-1904),
Irish-born American entrepreneur and
politician **6** 480-481

Grace Abounding (book)
   Bunyan, John **3** 128-129

Grace after Meat (book)
   Ransom, John Crowe **13** 39-40

Grace Church (New York City)
   Renwick, James **13** 102-103

Grace Church (Providence, Rhode Island)
   Upjohn, Richard **15** 392

Grace Church (Utica, New York)
   Upjohn, Richard **15** 392

Grace Church (West Medford, Massachusetts)
   Richardson, Henry Hobson **13** 139-141

Graces, The (hymns)
   Foscolo, Ugo **6** 21

Graces Adorning a Term of Hymen (painting)
   Reynolds, Joshua **13** 115-116

**GRACIÁN Y MORALES, BALTASAR
JERÓNIMO** (1601-1658), Spanish writer
6 481-482

Gradualia (musical collection)
   Byrd, William **3** 187-188

Graduates' General Congress (political
party; Sudan)
   Azhari, Sayyid Ismail al- **1** 399-401

GRADY, HENRY WOODFIN (1850-1889),
American editor and orator **6** 482-483
   Hill, Benjamin Harvey **7** 386-387

GRAETZ, HEINRICH HIRSCH
(1817-1891), German historian and biblical exegete **6** 483

Graf Egmont (literary character)
   Goethe, Johann Wolfgang von
   6 388-391

Graf Waldemar (play)
   Freytag, Gustav **6** 107-108

Graf Zeppelin (airship)
   Ellsworth, Lincoln **5** 277

Gräfin Dolores (novel)
   Arnim, Achim von **1** 308-309

Graft
   see Corruption, political

Grafton, Augustus Henry, Duke of
(1735-1811), English statesman
   George III **6** 270-272

GRAHAM, WILLIAM FRANKLIN, JR.
("Billy"; born 1918), American evangelist
6 487-488

Graham, John
   see Phillips, David Graham

GRAHAM, KATHARINE MEYER (born
1917), publisher who managed The
Washington Post **6** 483-485

GRAHAM, MARTHA (1894-1991), American dancer and choreographer **6** 485-486
   Calder, Alexander **3** 216-218

Graham, Sheilah (born 1905?),
English-born American columnist
   Fitzgerald, Francis Scott Key **5** 470-472

Graham, Sir James Robert George
(1792-1861), English politician
   Mazzini, Giuseppe **10** 381-383

GRAHAM, SYLVESTER (1794-1851), American reformer and temperance minister
6 486-487

Graham cracker
   Graham, Sylvester **6** 486-487

Grail, Holy (legend)
   Chrestien de Troyes **4** 23-24
   Gottfried von Strassburg **6** 461-462
   Wolfram von Eschenbach **16** 360-361

Grain (agriculture)
   Borlaug, Norman Ernest **2** 418-420
   Deering, William **4** 455-456
   McCormick, Cyrus Hall **10** 400-401
   Saunders, Charles Edward **13** 498-499

Gramicidin (antibiotic)
   Dubos, René Jules **5** 119

Grammar of Assent, The (book)
   Newman, John Henry **11** 365-367

Grammar of Motives, A (book)
   Burke, Kenneth **3** 141-142

GRAMSCI, ANTONIO (1891-1937), Italian
writer and Communist leader **6** 488-489
   Victor Emmanuel III **15** 484-485

Gran Chaco War
   see Chaco War

Gran Colombia
   see Colombia; Ecuador; Panama;
   Venezuela

Gran teatro del mundo, El (play)
   Calderón, Pedro **3** 221-222

Granada (province; Spain)
   Abd al-Mumin **1** 13
   Ferdinand V **5** 417-418
   Isabella I **8** 144-145

Granada Club (group; Spanish artists)
   Alarcón, Pedro Antonio de **1** 100-101

Granada, Treaty of (1500)
   Borgia, Cesare **2** 412-413
   Louis XII **9** 528-529

GRANADOS, ENRIQUE (1867-1916),
Spanish composer and pianist **6** 489-490

Grand Alliance
   see Augsburg, War of the League of
   (1688-1697); Holy Alliance (1815)

Grand Canal (China)
   K'ang-hsi **8** 423-426

   Kublai Khan **9** 115-118
   Yung-lo **16** 482-483

Grand Canal (Venice)
   Canaletto **3** 257-258

Grand Canyon (Arizona)
   Coronado, Francisco Vásquez de **4** 247
   Powell, John Wesley **12** 425-426

Grand Canyon of the Yellowstone (painting)
   Moran, Thomas **11** 151-152

Grand Coulee Dam (Washington)
   Kaiser, Henry John **8** 412-413

Grand déjeuner, Le (painting)
   Léger, Fernand **9** 302-303

Grand Design, The (novel)
   Dos Passos, John Roderigo **5** 69-71

Grand Hotel (film)
   Barrymores **2** 28-30
   Garbo, Greta **6** 205-207

Grand Inquisitor (literary character)
   Dostoevsky, Fyodor **5** 74-77

Grand National Assembly (Romania)
   Ceausescu, Nicolae **3** 387-388

**Grand National Consolidated Trades
Union** (England)
   Owen, Robert **12** 39-40

Grand nu, Le (painting)
   Modigliani, Amedeo **11** 72-73

Grand Remonstrance (1641)
   Pym, John **12** 495-496

Grand River (Canada)
   Brant, Joseph **2** 500-501

Grand testament (poem)
   Villon, François **15** 499-501

Grand Theater Opera (Moscow)
   Rachmaninov, Sergei Vasilievich
   12 531-532

Grand Trunk Herald (newspaper)
   Edison, Thomas Alva **5** 206-208

Grand Trunk Railroad (United States)
   Edison, Thomas Alva **5** 206-208

Grand Trunk Railway (Canada)
   Cartier, George-Étienne **3** 342-343
   Galt, Alexander Tilloch **6** 190-191

Grande Hermine (ship)
   Cartier, Jacques **3** 343-344

Grande Jatte, La (painting)
   see Sunday Afternoon on the Island at
   La Grande latte, A

Grande Messe des morts (requiem)
   Berlioz, Louis Hector **2** 203-205

Grande odalisque (painting)
   Ingres, Jean Auguste Dominique
   8 121-123

Grande revue, La (periodical)
   Matisse, Henri **10** 336-337

Grandes baigneuses (painting)
   Renoir, Pierre Auguste **13** 101-102

Grandes chroniques de France (book)
Fouquet, Jean **6** 31

Grandes et inestimables croniques du grand et énorme géant Gargantua, Les
see Gargantua (novel)

Grandfather with His Grandson (painting)
Ghirlandaio, Domenico **6** 292-293

Grandfather-Father-Grandson (book)
Kazantzakis, Nikos **8** 466-468

Grandfather's Chair (book)
Hawthorne, Nathaniel **7** 212-215

Grandfathers, The (novel)
Richter, Conrad Michael **13** 148-149

Grandison, Sir Charles (literary character)
Richardson, Samuel **13** 141-142

Grandissimes, The (novel)
Cable, George Washington **3** 198-199

Grandson, battle of (1476)
Charles the Bold **3** 467-469

Grange of the Patrons of Husbandry (agricultural society)
Kelley, Oliver Hudson **8** 480-481

Granger party (United States politics)
Donnelly, Ignatius **5** 62

Grania (play)
Gregory, Augusta **6** 535-536

Granicus River (northwest Asia)
Alexander the Great **1** 137-141

Graniteville Manufacturing Company (textile mill)
Gregg, William **6** 530-531

GRANT, CARY (born Archibald Alexander Leach; 1904-1986), English actor **6** 490-492

Grant, James Augustus (1827-1892), British soldier and explorer
Baker, Samuel White **1** 454-455
Mutesa I **11** 277
Speke, John Hanning **14** 366-367

GRANT, ULYSSES SIMPSON (1822-1885), American general, president 1869-1877 **6** 492-494
Cabinet
Bristow, Benjamin Helm **3** 9-10
Chandler, Zachariah **3** 425-426
Fish, Hamilton **5** 461-462
Stewart, Alexander Turney **14** 448-449
Indian policy
Cochise **4** 128
Crook, George **4** 322-323
Custer, George Armstrong **4** 355-356
Joseph **8** 358-359
Parker, Ely Samuel **12** 106-108
military role
Lincoln, Abraham **9** 415-418
political opponents
Lea, Henry Charles **9** 261-262
Lloyd, Henry Demarest **9** 468-469
Schurz, Carl **14** 44-45

Seymour, Horatio **14** 126-127
Sumner, Charles **15** 30-31
Trumbull, Lyman **15** 317-318
political supporters
Arthur, Chester Alan **1** 321-323
Carroll, Anna Ella **3** 327-331
Conkling, Roscoe **4** 201-202
Stanton, Edwin McMasters **14** 401-402
see also Alabama Claims; Civil War, United States

Grantham, battle of (1643)
Cromwell, Oliver **4** 317-320

Grant's Tomb (New York City)
Grant, Ulysses Simpson **6** 492-494

Granvelle, Antoine Perrenot de (1517-1586), Spanish statesman and cardinal
William the Silent **16** 300-302

GRANVILLE, EVELYN BOYD (born 1924), African American mathematician **6** 494-496

Grao-Para Company (Portugal)
Pombal, Marquês de **12** 386-387

Grape and Melon Eaters (painting)
Murillo, Bartolomé Esteban **11** 258-259

Grapes of Wrath, The (film and novel)
Ford, John **6** 7-8
Steinbeck, John Ernst **14** 416-417

Graphic arts
Kollwitz, Käthe **9** 79-81

GRASS, GÜNTER (born 1927), German novelist, playwright, and poet **6** 496-497

Grasse, Comte François Joseph de (Marquis de Grasse-Tilly; 1722-1788), French admiral
Bougainville, Louis Antoine de **2** 443-444
Rochambeau, Comte de **13** 220-221
Rodney, George Brydges **13** 239-240

GRASSELLI, CAESAR AUGUSTIN (1850-1927), third generation to head the Grasselli Chemical Company **6** 497-498

Grasselli Chemical Company
Grasselli, Caesar Augustin **6** 497-498

Grasshopper Creek (Montana)
Bozeman, John M. **2** 471-472

Grasshopper, The (poem)
Lovelace, Richard **10** 7-8

Grasshopper, The (story)
Chekhov, Anton Pavlovich **3** 494-497

GRATIAN (died circa 1155), Italian scholar, father of canon law **6** 498-499
Lombard, Peter **9** 490-491
Urban II **15** 393

GRATTAN, HENRY (1746-1820), Irish statesman and orator **6** 499

GRAU SAN MARTIN, RAMÓN (1887-1969), Cuban statesman and physician **6** 499-500
Batista y Zaldívar, Fulgencio **2** 57-58

Welles, Sumner **16** 191-192

Graupner, Johann Christoph (1683-1760), German composer
Bach, Johann Sebastian **1** 416-419

Grave of William Penn (painting)
Hicks, Edward **7** 375

Grave, The (book; Blair)
Blake, William **2** 316-318

Gravelot, Hubert François (1699-1773), French engraver
Gainsborough, Thomas **6** 170-172

GRAVES, MICHAEL (born 1934), American Post-Modernist architect **6** 500-502

GRAVES, NANCY STEVENSON (1940-1995), American sculptor **6** 502-504

GRAVES, ROBERT RANKE (1895-1985), English author **6** 504-506

Graves, Thomas (1st Baron Graves; 1725-1802), British admiral
Rochambeau, Comte de **13** 220-221

Graveyard by the Sea, The (poem)
Valéry, Paul Ambroise **15** 405-406

Graveyard school (English literature)
Bryant, William Cullen **3** 83-85
Gray, Thomas **6** 509-510

Gravitation (physics)
and magnetism
Gilbert, William **6** 313-314
and planetary orbits
Einstein, Albert **5** 228-231
Halley, Edmund **7** 88-89
law of gravity
Galileo Galilei **6** 180-183
Hooke, Robert **7** 475
Newton, Isaac **11** 369-372
measurement
Bernoulli, Daniel **2** 216
Meinesz, Felix Andries Vening **10** 461
Tsiolkovsky, Konstantin Eduardovich **15** 326-328
universal constant
Cavendish, Henry **3** 383-384
see also Relativity—general theory

Gravity's Rainbow (book)
Pynchon, Thomas **12** 496-498

Gray and Batton Manufacturing Company
see Western Electric Company

GRAY, ASA (1810-1888), American botanist **6** 506-507
Wilkes, Charles **16** 279-280

Gray, Dorian (literary character)
Wilde, Oscar Fingall O'Flahertie Wills **16** 272-273

Gray, Elisha (1835-1901), American inventor
Bell, Alexander Graham **2** 129-131

GRAY, HANNAH HOLBORN (born 1930), university administrator **6** 507-508

GRAY, ROBERT (1755-1806), American explorer **6** 508-509

GRAY, THOMAS (1716-1771), English poet **6** 509-510
Bryant, William Cullen **3** 83-85

GRAY, WILLIAM H., III (born 1941), first African American to be elected House Whip for the U.S. House of Representatives **6** 510-511

Gray's Harbor (Washington)
Gray, Robert **6** 508-509

Grayson, Betty (Mrs. Clifford Odets; died 1954), American actress
Odets, Clifford **11** 470-471

Grayson, David (pseudonym)
see Baker, Ray Stannard

Graysons, The (novel)
Eggleston, Edward **5** 223-224

Graz, University of (Austria)
economics
Schumpeter, Joseph Alois **14** 43-44
philosophy
Meinong, Alexius Ritter von Hand-schuchsheim **10** 461-462
Pázmány, Péter **12** 164-165
sciences
Boltzmann, Ludwig **2** 379-380
Hess, Victor Francis **7** 362-363
Loewi, Otto **9** 486-487
Mach, Ernst **10** 90-91
Pregl, Fritz **12** 436-437
Schrödinger, Erwin **14** 31-33
Wegener, Alfred Lothar **16** 170-171

Graziella (literary character)
Lamartine, Alphonse Marie Louis de **9** 173-175

Great Australian Bight (bay; Indian Ocean)
Eyre, Edward John **5** 354
Flinders, Matthew **5** 490
Forrest, John **6** 12-13

Great Awakening (religious revivals; United States)
evangelist preachers
Edwards, Jonathan **5** 220-222
Frelinghuysen, Theodorus Jacobus **6** 96-97
Tennent, Gilbert **15** 143-144
Wheelock, Eleazar **16** 222-223
Whitefield, George **16** 241-242
separatist sects
Backus, Isaac **1** 420-421
Chauncy, Charles **3** 485-486
see also Evangelism; Revivalism, religious

Great Bathers (painting)
Cézanne, Paul **3** 400-402

Great Betrayal, The (book)
Wise, Stephen Samuel **16** 344-345

Great Bible (1539)
Coverdale, Miles **4** 278

Great Book of Organa (musical collection)
Léonin **9** 343-344

Pérotin **12** 231-232

Great Britain (United Kingdom of Great Britain and Northern Ireland; island kingdom; northwestern Europe)
• TO 1603
England
see England
Ireland
see Ireland
Scotland
see Scotland
Wales
see Wales
• 1603-1714 (STUART and COMMONWEALTH)
1603-1625 (James I)
Bacon, Francis **1** 422-424
Buckingham, 1st Duke of **3** 93-94
Coke, Edward **4** 141-142
James I **8** 204-206
Raleigh, Walter **13** 9-11
see also Gunpowder Plot; Thirty Years War
1625-1649 (Charles I)
Buckingham, 1st Duke of **3** 93-94
Charles I **3** 450-452
Clarendon, 1st Earl of **4** 73-75
Cromwell, Oliver **4** 317-320
Hampden, John **7** 110-111
Harrington, James **7** 166-167
Laud, William **9** 224-225
Lilburne, John **9** 409-410
Pym, John **12** 495-496
Strafford, 1st Earl of **14** 490-491
see also Civil War, English-Puritan Revolutions; Thirty Years War
1649-1660 (Commonwealth and Protectorate)
Clarendon, 1st Earl of **4** 73-75
Cromwell, Oliver **4** 317-320
Harrington, James **7** 166-167
Lilburne, John **9** 409-410
Monck, George **11** 96-97
Vane, Henry **15** 425-426
see also Commonwealth (England; 1649-60); Dutch Wars
1660-1685 (Charles II)
Buckingham, 2d Duke of **3** 94-95
Charles II **3** 452-454
Clarendon, 1st Earl of **4** 73-75
Monck, George **11** 96-97
Oates, Titus **11** 456
Shaftesbury, 1st Earl of **14** 135-136
see also Dutch Wars—1665-67, 1672-74; London—Great Fire (1666); Popish Plot (1678); Restoration, The
1685-1688 (James II)
James II **8** 207-208
Monmouth and Buccleugh, Duke of **11** 108-109

see also Glorious Revolution (1688)
1689-1714 (William and Mary; Anne)
Anne **1** 241-242
Bolingbroke, Viscount **2** 374-375
Burnet, Gilbert **3** 147
Charles II **3** 454
Godolphin, Sidney **6** 380-381
Harley, Robert **7** 159-160
Livingston, Robert **9** 461-462
Marlborough, 1st Duke of **10** 271-272
Mary II **10** 309-310
William III **16** 295-296
see also Augsburg, War of the League of; Glorious Revolution; King William's War; Spanish Succession, War of the
• 1714-1901 (HANOVER)
1714-1727 (George I)
Bolingbroke, Viscount **2** 374-375
George I **6** 268-269
Walpole, Robert **16** 82-84
1727-1760 (George II)
Cook, James **4** 214-215
Frederick II **6** 81-84
George II **6** 269-270
Oglethorpe, James Edward **11** 482-483
Pitt, William the Elder **12** 328-329
Rodney, George Brydges **13** 239-240
Saxe, Comte de **13** 507-508
Charles Edward Louis Philip Casimir Stuart **3** 466-467
Walpole, Robert **16** 82-84
see also Austrian Succession, War of the; French and Indian War; Jacobites; King George's War; Seven Years War
1760-1820 (George III)
Burke, Edmund **3** 138-141
Castlereagh, Viscount **3** 363-364
Charles IV **3** 456-457
Emmet, Robert **5** 281-282
Fox, Charles James **6** 35-37
George III **6** 270-272
Grattan, Henry **6** 499
Grey, Charles **6** 539-540
Metternich, Klemens von **10** 533-536
Napoleon I **11** 306-310
Nelson, Horatio **11** 336-338
O'Connell, Daniel **11** 465-467
Selim III **14** 95-96
Wellesley, Richard Colley **16** 192-193
Wilkes, John **16** 280-281
1760-1820 (prime ministers)
Bute, 3d Earl of **3** 177-178
Liverpool, 2nd Earl of **9** 456-457
North, Frederick **11** 429-430
Pitt, William the Elder **12** 328-329

Pitt, William the Younger
12 329-331
Rockingham, 2d Marquess of
13 230-231
see also American Revolution;
French Revolutionary Wars;
Gordon Riots; Jay's Treaty;
Napoleonic Wars; Paris, Treaty
of (1763; 1783; 1814; 1815);
Seven Years War; Union, Act
of; Vienna, Congress of; War of
1812
1820-1830 (George IV)
Canning, George **3** 258-260
George IV **6** 272-273
Peel, Robert **12** 181-183
Said, Seyyid **13** 428-429
Wellesley, Richard Colley
16 192-193
Wellington, 1st Duke of
16 193-195
Wilberforce, William
16 269-270
see also Antislavery movement
(England); Catholic emancipa-
tion
1830-1837 (William IV)
Cobbett, William **4** 126-127
Grey, Charles **6** 539-540
Melbourne, 2nd Viscount
10 468-469
Peel, Robert **12** 181-183
Russell, John **13** 380-381
Wellington, 1st Duke of
16 193-195
William IV **16** 296-297
1837-1870 (Victoria)
Aberdeen, 4th Earl of **1** 25-26
Albert **1** 110-112
Baldwin, Robert **1** 466-468
Bright, John **3** 6-7
Carrera, José Rafael **3** 324-325
Chadwick, Edwin **3** 404-405
Cobden, Richard **4** 127-128
Disraeli, Benjamin **5** 27-29
Gladstone, William Ewart
6 357-360
Melbourne, 2nd Viscount
10 468-469
O'Connell, Daniel **11** 465-467
Palmerston, 3d Viscount
12 81-83
Pedro II **12** 180-181
Peel, Robert **12** 181-183
Russell, John **13** 380-381
Shaftesbury, 7th Earl of
14 137-138
Victoria **15** 485-487
see also Arrow War; Civil War,
United States; Crimean War;
Crystal Palace Exhibition;
Opium War; Taiping Rebellion
1870-1901 (Victoria)
Chamberlain, Arthur Neville
3 409-411
Chamberlain, Joseph **3** 411-413
Chulalongkorn **4** 43-45

Cleveland, Stephen Grover
4 108-110
Curzon, George Nathaniel
4 351-352
Disraeli, Benjamin **5** 27-29
Gladstone, William Ewart
6 357-360
Hardie, James Keir **7** 147-148
Hay, John **7** 215-216
Maine, Henry James Sumner
10 152
Parnell, Charles Stewart
12 117-119
Salisbury, 3d Marquess of
13 448-449
Victoria **15** 485-487
see also Berlin, Congress of
(1878); Boer War; Boxer Rebel-
lion; Home Rule Bill (Ireland);
India
• SINCE 1901 (WINDSOR)
1901-1910 (Edward VII;
Saxe-Coburg-Gotha)
Aga Khan **1** 74-76
Asquith, Herbert Henry
1 344-346-271
Balfour, Arthur James **1** 469-470
Curzon, George Nathaniel
4 351-352
Delcassé, Théophile **4** 478-479
Drago, Luis María **5** 92-93
Edward VII **5** 214-215
Hardie, James Keir **7** 147-148
1910-1936 (George V)
Baldwin, Stanley **1** 468-469
Balfour, Arthur James **1** 469-470
Benedict XV **2** 153-154
Chamberlain, Arthur Neville
3 409-411
Collins, Michael **4** 167-168
Curzon, George Nathaniel
4 351-352
George V **6** 273-275
Henderson, Arthur **7** 277-278
Laval, Pierre **9** 237-238
Lloyd George, David **9** 469-471
Macaulay, Herbert **10** 78-79
MacDonald, James Ramsay
10 84-85
Pankhurst, Emmeline **12** 85-86
Perth, 16th Earl of **12** 244-245
see also Ireland; Kellogg-Briand
Pact; Northern Ireland; Wash-
ington Conference
(1921-1922); World War I
1910-1936 (Middle East and Asia)
Abdullah ibn Husein **1** 19-20
Aga Khan **1** 74-76
Atatürk, Ghazi Mustapha Kemal
1 356-357
Churchill, Winston Leonard
Spencer **4** 51-53
Dalai Lama **4** 369-371
Faisal I **5** 370-371
Husein ibn Ali **8** 63
Jabotinsky, Vladimir Evgenevich
8 167-168

Lawrence, Thomas Edward
9 253-254
Reading, 1st Marquess of **13** 64
Weizmann, Chaim **16** 183-184
Zaghlul Pasha, Saad **16** 485-486
1936 (Edward VIII)
Edward VIII **5** 215-217
1936-1952 (George VI)
Attlee, Clement Richard
1 361-362
Baldwin, Stanley **1** 468-469
Bevin, Ernest **2** 252-253
Bruce of Melbourne, 1st Vis-
count **3** 61-62
Chamberlain, Arthur Neville
3 409-411
Churchill, Winston Leonard
Spencer **4** 51-53
Daladier, Édouard **4** 369
Elizabeth, the Queen Mother
5 261-263
George VI **6** 275
Halifax, 1st Earl of **7** 82-83
Hitler, Adolf **7** 417-420
see also Munich Conference;
North Atlantic Treaty Organiza-
tion; United Nations; World
War II
1936-1952 (Middle East and Asia)
Abdullah ibn Husein **1** 19-20
Aung San **1** 374-375
Farouk I **5** 387-388
Gandhi, Mohandas Karamchand
6 201-204
Liaquat Ali Khan **9** 397
Mohammad Reza Shah Pahlavi
11 75-76
Nu, U **11** 439-441
Reza Shah Pahlavi **13** 116-117
Weizmann, Chaim **16** 183-184
since 1952 (Elizabeth II)
Azhari, Sayyid Ismail al-
1 399-401
Bello, Ahmadu **2** 139-140
Boothroyd, Betty **2** 406-407
Callaghan, Leonard James
3 230-231
Carrington **3** 326-327
Charles, Prince of Wales
3 448-450
Churchill, Winston Leonard
Spencer **4** 51-53
Clarke, Kenneth Harry **4** 85-87
Diana, Princess of Wales
4 529-533
Dulles, John Foster **5** 134-135
Eden, Anthony **5** 204-205
Elizabeth, the Queen Mother
5 261-263
Elizabeth II **5** 266-269
Gaitskell, Hugh **6** 173-174
Hammarskjöld, Dag **7** 100-101
Heath, Edward Richard George
7 244-246
Howe, Geoffrey **7** 531-532
Macmillan, Harold **10** 112-113
Major, John **10** 155-157

Pym, Francis **12** 494-495
Thatcher, Margaret Hilda
15 165-168
Wilson, James Harold
16 324-325
since 1952 (and Northern Ireland)
Faulkner, Brian **5** 393-395
Fitzgerald, Garret **5** 472-474
Foot, Michael **5** 505-507
see also British Commonwealth
of Nations; British Empire,
First; British Empire, Second;
Church and State (England);
English art and architecture;
English literature; English
music; Imperialism, British

Great Britain (ship)
Brunel, Isambard Kingdom **3** 69-70

Great Buddhist Synod, Sixth (1954-1956)
Nu, U **11** 439-441

Great Catechism (book)
Luther, Martin **10** 48-51

Great Chain of Being, The (book)
Lovejoy, Arthur Oncken **10** 6

Great Charter (England)
see Magna Carta

Great Compromise (United States Constitu-
tional Convention; 1787)
Franklin, Benjamin **6** 60-64
Paterson, William **12** 132-133
Sherman, Roger **14** 185-186

Great Death Scene (painting)
Beckmann, Max **2** 104-105

Great Depression (economics)
see Depression, Great (economics;
world); Depression, Great (economics; United States)

Great Dictator, The (film)
Chaplin, Charles Spencer **3** 438-440

Great Eastern (ship)
Brunel, Isambard Kingdom **3** 69-70
Field, Cyrus West **5** 438-439

Great Exhibition (London, 1851)
see Crystal Palace Exhibition

Great Expectations (novel)
Dickens, Charles John Huffam
4 538-541

Great Fear of 1789, The (book)
Lefebvre, Georges **9** 301-302

Great Gatsby, The (novel)
Fitzgerald, Francis Scott Key **5** 470-472

Great God Brown, The (play)
O'Neill, Eugene **11** 514-516

Great God Success, The (novel)
Phillips, David Graham **12** 280-281

Great Highway, The (play)
Strindberg, August **14** 509-511

Great Instauration, The (book)
Bacon, Francis **1** 422-424

Great Lakes (East Africa)
Speke, John Hanning **14** 366-367

Great Lakes (United States)
Brûlé, Étienne **3** 67-68
Champlain, Samuel de **3** 419-421
Chateaubriand, Vicomte de **3** 477-479
La Salle, Sieur de **9** 210-211
Pontiac **12** 393-394

Great Leap Forward (1958-60; People's
Republic of China)
Liu Shao-Ch'i **9** 453-455
Mao Zedong **10** 225-227

Great Lover, The (poem)
Brooke, Rupert **3** 22-23

Great Mystery (book)
Boehme, Jacob **2** 357

Great Northern Railroad (United States)
Debs, Eugene Victor **4** 444-445
Harriman, Edward Henry **7** 164-165
Hill, James Jerome **7** 388-389
Knox, Philander Chase **9** 66-67
Schiff, Jacob Henry **14** 2-3

Great Northern Steamship Company
Hill, James Jerome **7** 388-389

Great Northern War (1700-1721)
Augustus II **1** 373-374
Charles XII **3** 464-466
Frederick William I **6** 86-87
Mazepa, Ivan Stepanovich **10** 381
Peter I **12** 253-256

Great Passion (prints)
Dürer, Albrecht **5** 159-161

Great Peace, War of (circa 170)
Chang Chüeh **3** 432-433

Great Portal, The (book)
Maeterlinck, Maurice **10** 125-126

Great Prize, The (play)
Sholem Aleichem **14** 202-203

Great Proletarian Cultural Revolution
see Cultural Revolution (China)

Great Purge (1936-38; Union of Soviet
Socialist Republics)
fictional description
Koestler, Arthur **9** 71-73
perpetrators
Beria, Lavrenty Pavlovich **2** 192-193
Stalin, Joseph **14** 393-396
Vyshinsky, Andrei **16** 36-37
survivors
Khrushchev, Nikita Sergeevich
8 539-540
Konev, Ivan Stefanovich **9** 81-82
Litvinov, Maxim Maximovich
9 451-452
victims
Bukharin, Nikolai Ivanovich
3 112-113
Kamenev, Lev Borisovich **8** 417-418
Radek, Karl Bernardovich
12 536-537
Zinoviev, Grigori Evseevich
16 521-522

Great Reform Act
see Reform Bill of 1832

Great Republic (ship)
McKay, Donald **10** 416-417

Great Rosary (sculpture)
Stoss, Veit **14** 481-482

Great Salt Lake (Utah)
Bridger, James **3** 2-3

Great Schism (1387-1417; Roman Catholic
Church)
adherents of Roman papal line
Catherine of Siena **3** 369-370
Urban VI **15** 394
Wenceslaus **16** 201-202
conciliar movement
Ailly, Pierre d' **1** 94
Gerson, John **6** 285-286
Martin V **10** 287-288
Sigismund **14** 220-221
see also Conciliarism
influence of
Hus, Jan **8** 56-59
Visconti, Gian Galeazzo
15 510-511

Great Schism (Presbyterian Church; Colonial America)
Tennent, Gilbert **15** 143-144

Great Secret, The (book)
Maeterlinck, Maurice **10** 125-126

Great Shadow, The (novel)
Doyle, Arthur Conan **5** 91-92

Great Slave Lake (Canada)
Mackenzie, Alexander **10** 103-104

Great Society (United States history;
1960s)
Johnson, Lyndon Baines **8** 308-312

Great Society, The (book)
Wallas, Graham **16** 77-78

Great Son (novel)
Ferber, Edna **5** 413

Great Soviet Encyclopedia (reformer book)
Bukharin, Nikolai Ivanovich **3** 112-113

Great Stage, the World, The (play)
Calderón, Pedro **3** 221-222

Great Time of Troubles, The (book)
Husayn, Taha **8** 61-62

Great Train Robbery (film; E.S. Porter)
Griffith, David Wark **6** 544-545

Great Transformation, The (book)
Polanyi, Karl **12** 372

Great Trebnik (book)
Mogila, Peter **11** 74-75

Great Trek (South Africa; 1835)
see Boers

Great War (Uruguay; 1842)
Rivera, Fructuoso **13** 184-185

Great Wave at Kanagawa (print)
Hokusai, Katsushika **7** 447-448

Great Western (ship)
Brunel, Isambard Kingdom **3** 69-70

Great Western Railway (England)
Brunel, Isambard Kingdom **3** 69-70

Greater Inclination, The (stories)
Wharton, Edith **16** 221

Greater New York
see New York City (New York State)

Greater Romania
see Romania

Grechko, Andrey A. (1903-1976), Soviet marshal
Konev, Ivan Stefanovich **9** 81-82

Greco, Domenico (circa 1541-1614), Greek painter
Rosa, Salvator **13** 289-290

GRECO, EL (1541-1614), Greek-born Spanish painter **6** 511-514
Evergood, Philip **5** 345
Magnasco, Alessandro **10** 127-128
Soutine, Chaim **14** 356-357
Toulouse-Lautrec, Henri de **15** 273-274

Greco or the Secret of Toledo (novel)
Barrès, Auguste Maurice **2** 20-21

Greece (ancient)
Athens
see Athens
cultural studies
Rostovtzeff, Michael Ivanovich **13** 315
Toynbee, Arnold Joseph **15** 283-284
expansion of empire
Alexander the Great **1** 137-141
Antigonus I **1** 248-249
Philip II **12** 269-271
Ptolemy I **12** 470-472
Seleucus I **14** 92-93
foreign relations
Antiochus III **1** 249-250
Chandragupta Maurya **3** 426
and Rome
Flamininus, Titus Quinctius **5** 477
Philo Judaeus **12** 282-283
Polybios **12** 384-385
Sparta
see Sparta
Visigoths invade (395)
Alaric **1** 101-102
see also Greek art; Greek literature; Mythology, Greco-Roman; Philosophers, Greek

Greece (Hellenic Republic)
Karamanlis, Constantine **8** 440-441
Papandreou, Andreas **12** 88-91

Greece, Kingdom of (modern nation; southeast Europe)
Atatürk, Ghazi Mustapha Kemal **1** 356-357
Crane, Stephen **4** 293-295
Venizelos, Eleutherios **15** 460-461
see also Greek War of Independence (1821-1830)

Greed (film)
Norris, Benjamin Franklin Jr. **11** 427-428

Greek art and architecture (classical)
architecture
Ictinus **8** 101
influence of
Canova, Antonio **3** 263-264
Duncan, Isadora **5** 144-145
see also Greek revival style
painting
Apelles **1** 257
Apollodorus **1** 261
sculpture
Myron **11** 285
Phidias **12** 265-267-403
Polykleitos **12** 385-386
Praxiteles **12** 433-434
see also Classicism (art)

Greek Literature (classical)
comedy and satire
Aristophanes **1** 293-294
Lucian **10** 25-26
Menander **10** 477-478
drama
Aeschylus **1** 70-72
Euripides **5** 332-334
Sophocles **14** 343-345
essays
Plutarch **12** 359-360
Xenophon **16** 418-420
historical narrative
Herodotus **7** 330-333
Polybios **12** 384-385
Strabo **14** 485-486
Thucydides **15** 211-212
Xenophon **16** 418-420
influence of
Carducci, Giosuè **3** 290-291
poetry
Callimachus **3** 235-236
Empedocles **5** 282
Hesiod **7** 361-362
Homer **7** 465-467
Pindar **12** 312-313
Sappho **13** 479-480
Solon **14** 327-328
Theocritus **15** 171-172
see also Classicism (literature)

Greek literature (modern)
Cavafy, Constantine P. **3** 381-382
Kazantzakis, Nikos **8** 466-468
Palamas, Kostes **12** 70
Seferis, George **14** 84-85

Greek music (modern)
Xenakis, Iannis **16** 416-418

Greek mythology
see Mythology, Greco-Roman

Greek New Comedy (Latin translation)
Plautus **12** 348-350
Terence **15** 146-148

Greek Orthodox Church
Joseph II **8** 359-360
Lucaris, Cyril **10** 20

Greek Passion, The (novel; Kazantzakis)
Kazantzakis, Nikos **8** 466-468

Martinu, Bohuslav **10** 299-300

Greek philosophy
see Philosophers, Greek; Philosophy

Greek revival style (architecture)
Benjamin, Asher **2** 162-163
Latrobe, Benjamin Henry **9** 222-224
Mills, Robert **11** 36-37
Upjohn, Richard **15** 392

Greek Slave (sculpture)
Powers, Hiram **12** 428-429

Greek War of Independence (1821-1830)
diplomacy
Aberdeen, 4th Earl of **1** 25-26
Canning, George **3** 258-260
Castlereagh, Viscount **3** 363-364
Metternich, Klemens von **10** 533-536
foreign participants
Byron, George Gordon Noel **3** 193-194
Howe, Samuel Gridley **7** 537
Lieber, Francis **9** 401-402
in literature
Hölderlin, Johann Christian Friedrich **7** 451-452
Shelley, Percy Bysshe **14** 176-178
Turks
Ibrahim Pasha **8** 97-98
Mahmud II **10** 145-147

Greek Youth Seeks a Greek Maid (novel)
Dürrenmatt, Friedrich **5** 164-165

GREELEY, ANDREW M. (born 1928), American Catholic priest, sociologist, and author **6** 514-515

GREELEY, HORACE (1811-1872), American editor and reformer **6** 515-517
associates
Brisbane, Albert **3** 9
Dana, Charles Anderson **4** 384-385
Fuller, Sarah Margaret **6** 150-151
Smith, Gerrit **14** 290-291
Twain, Mark **15** 363-366
opponents
Beach, Moses Yale **2** 79-80
Bennett, James Gordon **2** 168-169
Grant, Ulysses Simpson **6** 492-494
presidential candidacy
Blair, Francis Preston **2** 313-315
Brown, Benjamin Gratz **3** 32-33
Curtin, Andrew Gregg **4** 347-348
Grant, Ulysses Simpson **6** 492-494
Schurz, Carl **14** 44-45
Trumbull, Lyman **15** 317-318

GREELY, ADOLPHUS WASHINGTON (1844-1935), American soldier, explorer, and writer **6** 517-518

GREEN, CONSTANCE McLAUGHLIN (1897-1975), American author and historian **6** 518-519

GREEN, EDITH STARRETT (1910-1987), United States congresswoman from Oregon (1954-1974) **6** 519-520

Green, John Richard (1837-1883), English historian
Lecky, William Edward Hartpole **9** 271-272

Green, Paul (1894-1981), American playwright
Weill, Kurt **16** 174-175

GREEN, THOMAS HILL (1836-1882), British philosopher **6** 520-521
Bosanquet, Bernard **2** 425-426
Hobhouse, Leonard Trelawny **7** 425-426

GREEN, WILLIAM R. (1872-1952), American labor union leader **6** 521

Green Berets (United States special forces)
Kennedy, John Fitzgerald **8** 502-506

Green Bough, The (poems)
Faulkner, William **5** 395-397

Green Eggs and Ham (book)
Geisel, Theodor (Dr. Seuss) **6** 255-256

Green Gang (Chinese secret society)
Chiang Kai-shek **3** 510-513

Green Grow the Rushes, O (song lyrics)
Burns, Robert **3** 155-156

Green Helmet, The (play)
Yeats, William Butler **16** 445-447

Green Hills of Africa, The (book)
Hemingway, Ernest Miller **7** 274-277

Green Mountain Boys (United States history)
Allen, Ethan **1** 163-164
Arnold, Benedict **1** 309-310

Green Party (West Germany)
Kelly, Petra **8** 486-487

Green Pope, The (novel)
Asturias, Miguel Angel **1** 354-355

Green River (poem)
Bryant, William Cullen **3** 83-85

Greenaway, Kate (Catherine; 1846-1901), English painter and illustrator
Beardsley, Aubrey Vincent **2** 88-89

Greenback party (United States politics)
members
Coxey, Jacob Sechler **4** 286-287
Donnelly, Ignatius **5** 62
Kearney, Denis **8** 468
Powderly, Terence Vincent **12** 420-421
Stephens, Uriah **14** 431-432
presidential nominees
Cooper, Peter **4** 223-224
Weaver, James Baird **16** 151-152

Greenback-Labor party (United States)
see Greenback party

Greenbacks
see Currency; Greenback party

GREENBERG, CLEMENT (1909-1994), American art critic **6** 521-523

GREENE, GRAHAM (born 1904), English novelist and dramatist **6** 523-524
Coward, Noel **4** 279-280
Narayan, R.K. **11** 313-314
Robbe-Grillet, Alain **13** 189-190

GREENE, GRAHAM (born ca. 1952), Canadian-Native American actor **6** 524-525

GREENE, NATHANAEL (1742-1786), American Revolutionary War general **6** 525-526
Marion, Francis **10** 262-263
Morgan, Daniel **11** 160-161

Greene, Robert (1560?-1592), English poet, playwright, and novelist
Shakespeare, William **14** 142-145

Greene, Stephen (born 1918), American painter
Stella, Frank **14** 420-422

Greenfield Village (Michigan)
Edison, Thomas Alva **5** 206-208
Ford, Henry **6** 5-6

Greenland (island; Arctic Ocean /Atlantic Ocean; Danish province)
exploration (10th-17th century)
Corte Reál, Gaspar and Miguel **4** 254-255
Eric the Red **5** 304
Ericson, Leif **5** 306-307
Hudson, Henry **8** 12-13
exploration (19th-20th century)
Byrd, Richard Evelyn **3** 186-187
Nansen, Fridtjof **11** 304-305
Nordenskjöld, Nils Adolf Erik **11** 421-422
Nordenskold, Nils Otto Gustaf **11** 422-423
Peary, Robert Edwin **12** 175-176
Rasmussen, Knud Johan Victor **13** 44
Wegener, Alfred Lothar **16** 170-171

Greenough, Horatio (1805-1852), American sculptor
Allston, Washington **1** 176-177
Powers, Hiram **12** 428-429
Wright, Frank Lloyd **16** 398-401

Greenpeace (environmental organization)
Dudley, Barbara **5** 123-124

Greensboro (city; North Carolina)
King, Martin Luther Jr. **9** 20-22

Greensleeves (song)
Vaughan Williams, Ralph **15** 446-447

GREENSPAN, ALAN (born 1926), American economist **6** 526-528

Greenville, Treaty of (1795)
Tecumseh **15** 133
Wayne, Anthony **16** 149-150

Greenwich Hospital (England)
Hawksmoor, Nicholas **7** 211-212
Mary II **10** 309-310
Vanbrugh, John **15** 409-410

Greenwich Observatory (England)
Bradley, James **2** 482-483
Chapman, Sydney **3** 441
Conrad, Joseph **4** 205-207
Flamsteed, John **5** 477-478

GREER, GERMAINE (born 1939), author and authoritative commentator on women's liberation and sexuality **6** 528-530

GREGG, WILLIAM (1800-1867), American manufacturer **6** 530-531

Grégoire, Henri (1750-1831), French Catholic abbé and revolutionary
Cugoano, Ottobah **4** 332-333
Louis XVIII **9** 535-536

Gregorian chant (music)
Guido d'Arezzo **7** 33
Léonin **9** 343-344
Malipiero, Gian Francesco **10** 171
Notker Balbulus **11** 434-435

Gregorian modes (music)
Satie, Erik **13** 494-495

Gregorian reflector (telescope)
Herschel, William **7** 341-343

GREGORY I, SAINT (circa 540-604), pope 590-604 **6** 531-532
Alfred **1** 151-153
Augustine of Canterbury **1** 370-371
Benedict, Ruth Fulton **2** 154-155
Douglas, Gavin **5** 77-78
López de Ayala, Pedro **9** 508-509

Gregory II (circa 669-731), pope 715-731
Boniface **2** 391

Gregory III, Saint (died 741), pope 731-741
Martel, Charles **10** 285

Gregory V (died 999), pope 996-999
Otto III **12** 29-30

Gregory VI (died 1048?), pope 1045-46
Henry III **7** 290

GREGORY VII (circa 1020-1085), pope 1073-85 **6** 532-534
Guiscard, Robert **7** 39-40
Henry IV **7** 292
Lanfranc **9** 189-190
Matilda of Tuscany **10** 334-336
Urban II **15** 393
William I **16** 290-291

Gregory IX (1170?-1241), pope 1227-41
Frederick II **6** 79
Vogelweide, Walther von der **16** 10-11

Gregory X (Teobaldo Visconti; 1210-1276), pope 1271-1276
Bonaventure **2** 383-384
Kublai Khan **9** 115-118
Michael VIII **11** 1-2

Gregory XI (Pierre Roger de Beaufort; 1329-1378), pope 1370-1378
Catherine of Siena **3** 369-370
Urban VI **15** 394

Gregory XII (Angelo Corrario; circa 1325-1417), pope 1406-1415
  Ailly, Pierre d' **1** 94
  Martin V **10** 287-288

GREGORY XIII (1502-1585), pope 1572-1585 **6** 534
  Cardano, Geronimo **3** 285-286
  Lassus, Roland de **9** 216-218
  Neri, Philip **11** 340
  Theresa **15** 178-179

Gregory XV (1554-1623), pope 1621-1623
  Ignatius of Loyola **8** 108-109

Gregory XVI (Bartolommeo Alberto Cappellari; 1765-1846), pope 1831-1846
  Feijó, Diogo Antônio **5** 405-406
  Lacordaire, Jean Baptiste Henri **9** 148
  Lamennais, Hugues Félicité Robert de **9** 179
  Montalembert, Comte de **11** 118-119
  Pius IX **12** 335-336
  Rosmini-Serbati, Antonio **13** 296-297

GREGORY, DICK (Richard Claxton Gregory; born 1932), comedian and civil rights and world peace activist **6** 536-537

GREGORY, LADY AUGUSTA (1852-1932), Irish dramatist **6** 535-536
  Colum, Padraic **4** 174-175
  O'Casey, Sean **11** 459-460
  Synge, Edmund John Millington **15** 61-62
  Yeats, William Butler **16** 445-447

Gregory of Nazianzus, Saint (circa 329-389), Cappadocian theologian, bishop, and father of the Church
  Basil the Great **2** 51-52
  Jerome **8** 249

Gregory of Nyssa, Saint (circa 331-circa 396), Cappadocian theologian, bishop, and father of the Church
  Ambrose **1** 192-193
  Basil the Great **2** 51-52
  Erigena, John Scotus **5** 308-309

GREGORY OF TOURS, SAINT (538-594), Frankish bishop and historian **6** 534-535
  Clovis I **4** 124

Gregory the Great, Saint
  see Gregory I

Grenada (island nation; Caribbean)
  independence
    Bishop, Maurice **2** 292-293
    Reagan, Ronald W. **13** 65-68

Grenfell, George (1849-1906), English Baptist missionary and explorer
  Johnston, Henry Hamilton **8** 322-323

Grenoble Academy (France)
  Champollion, Jean François **3** 421
  Cournot, Antoine Augustin **4** 273

Grenville, George (1712-1770), English statesman
  George III **6** 270-272
  Pitt, William the Elder **12** 328-329

Grenville, Richard Temple (1st Earl Temple; 1711-1779), English statesman

North, Frederick **11** 429-430
Pitt, William the Elder **12** 328-329

Grenville, Sir Richard (1541-1591), English naval commander
  Raleigh, Walter **13** 9-11

Grenville, William Wyndham
  Baron Grenville; 1759-1834, English statesman
    Fox, Charles James **6** 35-37
    Jay, John **8** 230-232

Grenville (ship)
  Cook, James **4** 214-215

Gresham, Walter (1832-1895), American statesman
  Cleveland, Stephen Grover **4** 108-110

Gretchen (literary character)
  Goethe, Johann Wolfgang von **6** 388-391

Gretchen am Spinnrade (song)
  Schubert, Franz Peter **14** 35-37

Grettis Sage (poem)
  Morris, William **11** 187-188

GRETZKY, WAYNE (born 1961), Canadian hockey star **6** 537-539

GREUZE, JEAN BAPTISTE (1725-1805), French painter **6** 539
  Chardin, Jean Baptiste Siméon **3** 442-443
  Le Nain, Antoine, Louis and Mathieu **9** 321-322

Greville, Sir Fulke (1st Baron Brooke; 1554-1628), English poet and statesman
  Sidney, Philip **14** 214-215

Grévin Museum, The (poems)
  Aragon, Louis **1** 271-272

Grévy, François Paul Jules (1807-1891), French statesman, president 1879-1887
  Clemenceau, Georges **4** 99-101

Grew, Nehemiah (1641-1712), English plant physiologist
  Malpighi, Marcello **10** 176-178

Grey, Arthur (14th Baron Grey de Wilton; 1536-1593), English lord deputy of Ireland
  Spenser, Edmund **14** 373-376

GREY, CHARLES (2nd Earl Grey; 1764-1845), English statesman, prime minister 1830-1834 **6** 539-540
  Cabinet members
    Melbourne, 2nd Viscount **10** 468-469
    Palmerston, 3d Viscount **12** 81-83
    Russell, John **13** 380-381
  Reform Bill (1832)
    Cobbett, William **4** 126-127
    Peel, Robert **12** 181-183
    William IV **16** 296-297

Grey, Gilda (1899?-1959), Polish-born American actress
  Ziegfeld, Florenz **16** 516-517

Grey, Henry George Grey, 3rd Earl (1802-1894), English statesman, colonial secretary 1846-1852
  Elgin, 8th Earl of **5** 248-249

Grey, John, 7th Baron Ferrers of Groby (1432-1461), English noble
  Edward IV **5** 212-213

Grey, Lady Jane (1537-1554), queen of England 1553
  Edward VI **5** 213-214
  Leicester, Earl of **9** 312-313
  Mary I **10** 308-309
  Northumberland, Duke of **11** 431-432

Grey, Reginald de, 3rd Baron Grey (1362?-1440), English statesman
  Glendower, Owen **6** 364-365

Grey, Sir Edward (1862-1933), English statesman
  Cecil, of Chelwood Viscount **3** 388-389
  Perth, 16th Earl of **12** 244-245

Grey, Sir George (1799-1882), English statesman
  Moshweshwe **11** 203-205

GREY, SIR GEORGE (1812-1898), English explorer and colonial governor **6** 540-541
  Eyre, Edward John **5** 354
  Wakefield, Edward Gibbon **16** 48-49

Gridley, Jeremiah (circa 1701-1767), American lawyer
  Otis, James Jr. **12** 25-27

Grido e paesaggi, Un (poems)
  Ungaretti, Giuseppe **15** 389-390

Grido, Il (film)
  Antonioni, Michelangelo **1** 252-253

Grief (sculpture)
  Saint-Gaudens, Augustus **13** 432

GRIEG, EDVARD HAGERUP (1843-1907), Norwegian composer **6** 541-542
  MacDowell, Edward Alexander **10** 87-88

GRIERSON, JOHN (1898-1972), Canadian and British filmmaker **6** 542-543

Griess, Peter Johann (1829-1888), German chemist
  Hofmann, August Wilhelm von **7** 441-442

GRIFFES, CHARLES TOMLINSON (1884-1920), American composer **6** 543-544

Griffin v. Illinois (legal case)
  Warren, Earl **16** 117-120

Griffith, Arthur (1872-1922), Irish political leader
  Collins, Michael **4** 167-168
  Colum, Padraic **4** 174-175

GRIFFITH, DAVID WARK (1875-1948), American film maker **6** 544-545
  Barrymores **2** 28-30
  Chaplin, Charles Spencer **3** 438-440
  Eisenstein, Sergei Mikhailovich **5** 240-242

Ford, John **6** 7-8
Sennett, Mack **14** 108-109

GRIFFITH, SIR SAMUEL WALKER
(1845-1920), Australian statesman and
jurist **6** 545-546

Griffiths, Clyde (literary character)
Dreiser, Herman Theodore **5** 98-100

Grijalva, Juan de (circa 1489-1527), Spanish explorer
Velázquez de Cuéllar, Diego **15** 459

Grijns, Gerrit (1865-1944), Dutch biologist
Eijkman, Christian **5** 228

Grillet, Alain Robbe
see Robbe-Grillet, Alain

Grillo, El (musical composition)
Josquin des Prez **8** 361-363

GRILLPARZER, FRANZ (1791-1872), Austrian playwright **6** 546-547
Schubert, Franz Peter **14** 35-37

Grimani Palace (Venice)
Sanmicheli, Michele **13** 469-470

GRIMKÉ, ANGELINA EMILY (1805-1879)
AND SARAH MOORE (1792-1873),
American abolitionists and women's
rights agitators **7** 1-2
Foster, Abigail Kelley **6** 25
Grimké, Archibald Henry **7** 1-2

GRIMKÉ, ARCHIBALD HENRY
(1849-1930), American editor, author,
and diplomat **7** 1-2

Grimm, Baron Melchior von (1723-1807),
German journalist and critic
Houdon, Antoine **7** 516-517
Pergolesi, Giovanni Battista **12** 218-219
Rousseau, Jean Jacques **13** 324-328

GRIMM, JAKOB KARL (1785-1863) **AND
WILHELM KARL** (1786-1859), German
scholars, linguists, and authors **7** 3-4
Brentano, Clemens **2** 515-516
Mencken, Henry Louis **10** 481-483

**GRIMMELSHAUSEN, HANS JAKOB
CHRISTOFFEL VON** (1621/22-1676),
German author **7** 4-5

Grimm's law (linguistics)
Grimm, Jakob and Wilhelm Karl **7** 3-4

Grimsthorpe Castle (Lincolnshire)
Vanbrugh, John **15** 409-410

Grinnell Land (Arctic)
Greely, Adolphus Washington
6 517-518

GRIS, JUAN (1887-1927), Spanish painter
7 5-6
Lipchitz, Jacques **9** 432-433
Miró, Joan **11** 53-54
Picasso, Pablo **12** 292-295
Stein, Gertrude **14** 414-415

Griselda (play and opera)
Hauptmann, Gerhart Johann Robert
7 199-201
Scarlatti, Pietro Alessandro Gaspare
13 517-518

GRISHAM, JOHN (born 1955), American
author and attorney **7** 6-8

Grito de Yara (manifesto)
Céspedes, Carlos Manuel de **3** 398-399

Grobnik, Slats (fictional character)
Royko, Mike **13** 337-339

GROMYKO, ANDREI ANDREEVICH
(1909-1988), minister of foreign affairs
and president of the Union of Soviet
Socialist Republic (1985-1988) **7** 9-11
Paul VI **12** 146-148

Grona, Treaty of (915)
Henry I **7** 285-286

Groningen University (Netherlands)
Huizinga, Johan **8** 26-27
Kapteyn, Jacobus Cornelis **8** 436-437
Szent-Györgyi, Albert von **15** 62-64

Grönländische Prozesse (satires)
Richter, Johann Paul Friedrich
13 150-151

Groombridge Catalog (astronomy)
Eddington, Arthur Stanley **5** 201-202

GROOMS, RED (born 1937), American
artist **7** 11-12

Groot, Huig de
see Grotius, Hugo

GROOTE, GERARD (1340-1384), Dutch
evangelical preacher **7** 12-13
Kempis, Thomas à **8** 493-494

Gropius, Manon (1916-1935), daughter of
Walter and Alma (Mahler) Gropius
Berg, Alban **2** 186-187

GROPIUS, WALTER (1883-1969),
German-American architect, educator,
and designer **7** 13-14
Bauhaus
Breuer, Marcel **2** 520-521
Feininger, Lyonel **5** 406-407
Moholy-Nagy, László **11** 82-83
Oud, Jacobus Johannes Pieter **12** 32
influenced by
Behrens, Peter **2** 121-122
Morris, William **11** 187-188
Van de Velde, Henry **15** 419-420
Wright, Frank Lloyd **16** 398-401

GROS, BARON (Antoine Jean Gros;
1771-1835), French romantic painter
7 14-15
Bonington, Richard Parkes **2** 394-395

Gros Michel (banana)
Keith, Minor Cooper **8** 476-477

Groseilliers, Medard Chouart des
(1618?-circa 1690), French explorer in
Canada
Radisson, Pierre-Esprit **12** 539-540

Gross, Samuel D. (1805-1884), American
physician
Eakins, Thomas **5** 176-177

Gross Clinic (painting)
Eakins, Thomas **5** 176-177

Grosses Schauspielhaus (theater; Berlin)
Reinhardt, Max **13** 89-90

GROSSETESTE, ROBERT (1175-1253), English bishop and statesman **7** 15
Montfort, Simon de **11** 132-133

GROSSINGER, JENNIE (1892-1972),
American hotel executive and philanthropist **7** 15-17

GROSZ, GEORGE (1893-1959),
German-American painter and graphic
artist **7** 17-18
Bearden, Romare Howard **2** 86-88

Grote, George (1794-1871), English histo-
rian
Mill, James **11** 21
Mill, John Stuart **11** 21-23

Grotesques (etching)
Piranesi, Giovanni Battista **12** 321-322

GROTIUS, HUGO (1583-1645), Dutch
jurist, statesman, and historian **7** 18-19
Maurice of Nassau **10** 348-349
Oldenbarnevelt, Johan van **11** 495-496
Pufendorf, Samuel von **12** 477-478
Suárez, Francisco **15** 8
Vondel, Joost van den **16** 19-20

GROTOWSKI, JERZY (born 1933), founder
of the experimental Laboratory Theatre in
Wroclaw, Poland **7** 19-20

Grotto with Cascades (painting)
Rosa, Salvator **13** 289-290

Ground of Artes, The (book)
Recorde, Robert **13** 68-69

Ground We Stand On, The (book)
Dos Passos, John Roderigo **5** 69-71

Group, The (play)
Warren, Mercy Otis **16** 120-121

Group for Contemporary Music (United
States)
Wuorinen, Charles **16** 404

Group for the Emancipation of Labor (Russia)
Plekhanov, Georgi Valentinovich
12 351-352

Group of Seven (Canadian artists)
Carr, Emily **3** 319
Thomson, Tom **15** 202

Group Theater (New York City)
Odets, Clifford **11** 470-471

Group Theatre (New York City)
Strasberg, Lee **14** 494-495

GROVE, FREDERICK PHILIP (circa
1871-1948), Canadian novelist and
essayist **7** 20-21

GROVES, LESLIE (1896-1970), military
director of the Manhattan Project (atom
bomb) during World War II **7** 21-22

Groves v. Slaughter (legal case)
McLean, John **10** 422-423

Growing Up (autobiography)
Baker, Russell **1** 452-454

Growing Up in New Guinea (book)
Mead, Margaret **10** 438-440

Growth of the American Republic, The
(book)
Commager, Henry Steele **4** 181-183

Growth of the Soil (novel)
Hamsun, Knut **7** 113-114

Grumbling Hive (poem)
Mandeville, Bernard **10** 192

Grünberg (Czech manuscript)
Masaryk, Tomáš Garrigue **10** 314-315

Grundy, Felix (1777-1840), American
politician
Polk, James Knox **12** 374-376

Grüne Heinrich, Der (novel)
Keller, Gottfried **8** 478-479

Grünes Blatt, Ein (novella)
Storm, Theodor **14** 479-480

GRÜNEWALD, MATTHIAS (circa
1475-1528), German painter **7** 23-24
Dürer, Albrecht **5** 159-161
Evergood, Philip **5** 345
Hindemith, Paul **7** 399-400

Grunitzky, Nicholas (1913-1969), Togolese
statesman
Olympio, Sylvanus E. **11** 506-507

Grupo Nueva Musica (music society)
Halffter, Christóbal **7** 79-80

Gruppe 47 (Germany; literary organization)
Grass, Günter **6** 496-497

Gruppe aus dem Tartarus (poem; Schiller)
Schubert, Franz Peter **14** 35-37

Gruppen (musical composition)
Stockhausen, Karlheinz **14** 460-461

Gryll Grange (novel)
Peacock, Thomas Love **12** 169

Guadalcanal, battle of (1943)
Halsey, William Frederick **7** 91-92
Nimitz, Chester William **11** 395-396

Guadalupe Hidalgo, Treaty of (1848)
Buchanan, James **3** 89-90
Polk, James Knox **12** 374-376
Trist, Nicholas Philip **15** 298-299

Guadalupe, Victoria (1786?-1843), Mexican general, president 1824-29
Guerrero, Vicente **7** 28-30

Guadeloupe (islands; West Indies)
Columbus, Christopher **4** 176-179
Faidherbe, Louis Léon César **5** 366-367

Guadet, Julien (1834-1908), French architect
Perret, Auguste **12** 233

Guáimaro (city; Cuba)
Céspedes, Carlos Manuel de **3** 398-399

Guam (island; western Pacific Ocean)
Magellan, Ferdinand **10** 126-127
McKinley, William **10** 418-420

Guanabara Bay (Rio de Janeiro)
Vespucci, Amerigo **15** 476-478

Guanahani (Bahamas)
see San Salvador

Guanaja Island (Caribbean)
Columbus, Christopher **4** 176-179

Guanajuato (city; Mexico)
Hidalgo y Costilla, Miguel **7** 375-377

Guantánamo (town; Cuba)
Estrada Palma, Tomás **5** 326-327
Gómez, Máximo **6** 418-419

Guapuré River (South America)
Azara, Félix de **1** 397-398

Guaranty Building (Buffalo, New York)
Sullivan, Louis Henri **15** 27-28

Guard House (Dresden, Germany)
Schinkel, Karl Friedrich **14** 8

GUARDI, FRANCESCO (1712-1793), Ital-
ian painter **7** 24-25
Canaletto **3** 257-258
Magnasco, Alessandro **10** 127-128

Guardi, Gian Antonio (1699-1760), Italian
painter
Guardi, Francesco **7** 24-25

Guardia, Tomás (1832-1882), Costa Rican
general, president 1870-1882
Meiggs, Henry **10** 458-459

Guardian (newspaper)
Trotter, William Monroe **15** 306-307

Guardian (periodical)
Steele, Richard **14** 407-409

Guardian, The (play)
Cowley, Abraham **4** 281-282

Guardian Angel (sculpture)
Günther, Ignaz **7** 41-42

Guardian Angel, The (novel)
Holmes, Oliver Wendell **7** 457-458

Guardiola, Santos (1812?-1862), Honduran
politician, president 1856-1858
Estrada Palma, Tomás **5** 326-327

Guardo, Juana de (died 1613), Spanish
wife of Lope de Vega
Lope Félix de Vega Carpio **9** 503-506

Guarini, Giovanni Battista (1538-1612)
Italian poet
Marenzio, Luca **10** 248
Monteverdi, Claudio Giovanni Antonio
11 126-128

GUARINI, GUARINO (1624-1683), Italian
architect, priest, and philosopher **7** 25-26
Aleijadinho, O **1** 125-126
Juvara, Filippo **8** 396-397

Guarino da Verona (1370-1460), Italian
humanist
Feltre, Vittorino da **5** 409-410

Guastalla (commune; Italian)
Maria Theresa **10** 256-258

Guatamozin (circa 1495-1525), last Aztec
emperor of Mexico
Wallace, Lewis **16** 74-75

Guatemala, Republic of (nation; Central
America)
colonization
Cabrillo, Juan Rodríguez **3** 204-205
Díaz del Castillo, Bernal **4** 536-537
culture
Asturias, Miguel Angel **1** 354-355
foreign intervention
Arbenz Guzmán, Jacobo **1** 274-276
Dulles, John Foster **5** 134-135
Evarts, William Maxwell **5** 340-341
Guevara, Ernesto **7** 30-31
heads of state
Arbenz Guzmán, Jacobo **1** 274-276
Arévalo, Juan José **1** 285-286
Barrios, Justo Rufino **2** 23-24
Carrera, José Rafael **3** 324-325
Cerezo Arevalo, Marco Vinicio
3 393-395
Estrada Cabrera, Manuel **5** 325-326
Morazán, José Francisco **11** 155
Ubico y Castañeda, Jorge
15 377-378
human rights
Menchú, Rigoberta **10** 479-480
human rights abuses
Serrano Elías, Jorge Antonio
14 112-113
railroad
Van Horne, William Cornelius
15 429-430

Guayaquil (seaport; Ecuador)
Benalcázar, Sebastián de **2** 145-146
Nast, Thomas **11** 318-319
Orellana, Francisco de **11** 527-528

Guayaquil Conference (1822)
Bolívar, Simón **2** 375-377
San Martín, José de **13** 468-469

GUCCIONE, BOB, JR. (born ca. 1956),
American publisher **7** 26

Guchkov, Aleksandr (1861?-1936), Russian
politician
Kerensky, Aleksandr Fedorovich
8 516-517

Gude, Hans (1825-1903), Norwegian
painter
Wyant, Alexander Helwig **16** 409-410

Guelfs
see Guelph, House of

Güell Palace (Barcelona)
Gaudí i Cornet, Antoni **6** 235-236

Guelph, House of (flourished 12th-15th
century), European princely family
Cavalcanti, Guido **3** 382
Dante Alighieri **4** 389-391
Frederick I **6** 78-79
Frederick II **6** 79
Henry V **7** 295-296

GÜEMES, MARTÍN (1785-1821), Argentine
independence fighter **7** 26-27

Guenther von Andernach, Johann
(1487-1574), German physician
Vesalius, Andreas **15** 473-475

GUERCINO (Giovanni Francesco Barbieri;
1591-1666), Italian painter **7** 27

Ribera, Jusepe de **13** 122-123
GUERICKE, OTTO VON (1602-1686), German physicist **7** 27-28
  Boyle, Robert **2** 469-471
  Hooke, Robert **7** 475

Guérin, Pierre Narcisse (1774-1833), French painter
  Delacroix, Ferdinand Victor Eugène **4** 469-471
  Géricault, Jean Louis André Théodore **6** 280-281

Guermantes Way, The (novel)
  Proust, Marcel **12** 465-467

Guernica (painting)
  Picasso, Pablo **12** 292-295

Guerra Chiquita (Cuba; 1879-80)
  Gómez, Máximo **6** 418-419

Guerra Grande (Uruguay; 1842)
  Rivera, Fructuoso **13** 184-185

Guerre (book)
  Rouault, Georges **13** 321-322

Guerre de Troie n'aura pas lieu, La (play)
  Giraudoux, Jean **6** 349-350

Guerre folle (1487-88; France)
  Louis XII **9** 528-529

Guerrero (state; Mexico)
  Álvarez, Juan **1** 184-185
  Guerrero, Vicente **7** 28-30

GUERRERO, VICENTE (1783-1831), Mexican independence fighter, president 1829 **7** 28-30
  Álvarez, Juan **1** 184-185
  Iturbide, Agustín de **8** 155-156
  Santa Ana, Antonio López de **13** 471-472

Guerriere (ship)
  Wilkes, Charles **16** 279-280

Guerrilla warfare (ancient)
  Antiochus IV **1** 250
  Judas Maccabeus **8** 374-375
  Pompey **12** 387-389

Guerrilla warfare (modern)
  Africa
    Hassan, Muhammad Abdille **7** 194-195
    Mondlane, Eduardo Chivambo **11** 100-101
    Roberts, Frederick Sleigh **13** 195-196
    Touré, Sékou **15** 275-277
  China
    Lin Piao **9** 429-430
    Liu Shao-Ch'i **9** 453-455
  Germany
    Baader and Ulrike Meinhof, Andreas **1** 403-404
  Guinea-Bissau
    Cabral, Amílcar Lopes **3** 202-203
  India
    Śivajī **14** 266-267
  Indochina
    Giap, Vo Nguyen **6** 297-299

    Ho Chi Minh **7** 426-428
    Leclerc, Jacques Philippe **9** 272-273
  Latin America
    Díaz, José de la Cruz Porfirio **4** 534-536
    Gómez, Máximo **6** 418-419
    Guevara, Ernesto **7** 30-31
    Juárez, Benito **8** 369-372
    Lautaro **9** 235
    Maceo, Antonio **10** 88-90
    Manco Capac **10** 184-185
    Prestes, Luiz Carlos **12** 442-444
    Sandino, Augusto C. **13** 462-463
    Villa, Pancho **15** 495-496
    Zapata, Emiliano **16** 489-490
    see also Caudillos
  Middle East
    Abu Musa **1** 32-33
    Arafat, Yasser **1** 270-271
  North America
    Frontenac et Palluau, Comte de **6** 128-130
    Marion, Francis **10** 262-263
    Morgan, Daniel **11** 160-161
  Philippines
    Macapagal, Diosdado P. **10** 74-76
    Magsaysay, Ramon **10** 130-131
    Marcos, Ferdinand **10** 240-242
    Osmeña, Sergio **12** 22-24
  Scotland
    Douglas, James **5** 78
  South Africa
    Tambo, Oliver Reginald **15** 92-94
  theories
    Giap, Vo Nguyen **6** 297-299
    Guevara, Ernesto **7** 30-31
    Lieber, Francis **9** 401-402

Guerrillero (painting)
  Rivera, Diego **13** 183-184

Guesclin, Bertrand du (1320?-1380), French military commander
  Charles V **3** 459-460

Guesde, Jules (1845-1922), French Socialist editor and writer
  Jaurès, Jean **8** 226-227
  Lefebvre, Georges **9** 301-302

Guess, George
  see Sequoyah

Guest for the Night, A (book)
  Agnon, Shmuel Yoseph **1** 85-86

Guest of Reality (novel)
  Lagerkvist, Pär Fabian **9** 162-163

Guevara, Antonia de (circa 1480-1545), Spanish chronicler
  Lesage, Alain René **9** 353-354

GUEVARA, ERNESTO ("Che"; 1924-1967) Argentine revolutionary and guerrilla theoretician **7** 30-31
  Castro Ruz, Fidel **3** 365-368

GUEYE, LAMINE (1891-1968), Senegalese statesman **7** 31
  Diagne, Blaise **4** 527
  Senghor, Léopold Sédar **14** 106-107

Guggenheim Aeronautical Laboratory
  Kármán, Theodore von **8** 451-452

GUGGENHEIM, MEYER (1828-1905), Swiss-born American industrialist **7** 31-32

Guggenheim, Peggy (1898-1979), American art collector and dealer
  Ernst, Max **5** 311-312
  Motherwell, Robert **11** 210-211
  Pollock, Jackson **12** 379-380

Guggenheim Exploration Co. Inc. (New York City)
  Guggenheim, Meyer **7** 31-32

Guggenheim Museum, The Solomon R. (New York City)
  Wright, Frank Lloyd **16** 398-401

Guibert (Ravenna)
  see Clement III

GUICCIARDINI, FRANCESCO (1483-1540), Italian historian and statesman **7** 32-33
  Bruegel, Pieter the Elder **3** 65-67
  Castiglione, Baldassare **3** 360-361
  Machiavelli, Niccolò **10** 97-99

Guiccioli, Teresa (1801?-1873), Italian author
  Byron, George Gordon Noel **3** 193-194

Guide, The (novel)
  Narayan, R.K. **11** 313-314

Guided democracy (politics)
  Stroessner, Alfredo **14** 511-512
  Sukarno **15** 18-20

GUIDO D'AREZZO (circa 995-circa 1050), Italian music theorist **7** 33

Guido de Cauliaco
  see Guy de Chauliac

Guido di Pietro
  see Angelico, Fra

Guienne (region; France)
  Henry VI **7** 298-299

Guild socialism (England)
  Cole, George Douglas Howard **4** 146-147
  Hobhouse, Leonard Trelawny **7** 425-426

Guilford Court House, battle of (1781)
  Greene, Nathanael **6** 525-526

GUILLAUME DE LORRIS (circa 1210-1237), French poet **7** 33-34
  Chaucer, Geoffrey **3** 482-485
  Jean de Meun **8** 234-235
  Orléans, Charles D' **11** 530

Guillaume Jouvenal des Ursins (painting)
  Fouquet, Jean **6** 31

Guillaume Tell (opera; Rossini)
  Meyerbeer, Giacomo **10** 536-537
  Rossini, Gioacchino **13** 311-312

GUILLÉN, NICOLÁS (born 1902), Cuban author **7** 34-35

GUILLÉN Y ALVAREZ, JORGE
(1893-1984), Spanish poet **7** 35-36
Lorca, Federico García **9** 511-513

Guilt and Sorrow (poem)
Wordsworth, William **16** 385-388

Guimard, Maria Madeleine (1743-1816),
French dancer
Ledoux, Claude Nicolas **9** 277-278

Guinea Coast (West Africa)
Canot, Theodore **3** 262-263
Dias de Novais, Bartolomeu **4** 533-534
Frobisher, Martin **6** 121-122

Guinea, Republic of (nation; West Africa)
Houphouët-Boigny, Felix **7** 519-520
Touré, Sékou **15** 275-277

Guinea-Bissau (West Africa)
independence
Cabral, Amílcar Lopes **3** 202-203

Guinean literature
Laye, Camara **9** 257-259

Guinevere, Queen (literary character)
Chrestien de Troyes **4** 23-24
Peacock, Thomas Love **12** 169
Tennyson, Alfred **15** 144-146

GUINIZZELLI, GUIDO (1230/40-1276),
Italian poet **7** 36-37
Cavalcanti, Guido **3** 382

GUINNESS, ALEC (born 1914), British
actor of the stage, films, and television
7 37-38

GÜIRÁLDEZ, RICARDO (1886-1927),
Argentine poet and novelist **7** 38-39

GUISCARD, ROBERT (1016-1085), Nor-
man adventurer **7** 39-40
Alexius I **1** 143-144
Bohemund, I **2** 364
Roger II **13** 244-245

Guise, François de Lorraine, 2nd Duke
(1519-1563), French soldier and statesman
Coligny, Gaspard de **4** 159-160

Guise, House of (flourished 16th-17th cen-
tury), French noble family
Coligny, Gaspard de **4** 159-160
Henry IV **7** 293-295

Guitar and Flowers (painting)
Gris, Juan **7** 5-6

Guitar, Glasses, and Bottle (painting)
Gris, Juan **7** 5-6

Guitar, The (poem)
Echeverría, José Estéban **5** 197-198

Guitarrero, Le (painting)
Courbet, Jean Desiré Gustave
4 271-273

Guiteau, Charles (1840?-1882), American
lawyer
Garfield, James Abram **6** 213-214

Guittone d'Arezzo (died 1294), Italian poet
Guinizzelli, Guido **7** 36-37

GUIZOT, FRANÇOIS PIERRE GUILLAUME
(1787-1874), French statesman and histo-
rian **7** 40-41
Aberdeen, 4th Earl of **1** 25-26
Brisbane, Albert **3** 9
Louis Philippe **9** 536-537
Sorel, Albert **14** 346-347
Thiers, Louis Adolphe **15** 181-182

Guizot Law of 1833 (France)
Cousin, Victor **4** 273-274

Gujarat (region; India)
Ala-ud-din **1** 102-103
Aurangzeb **1** 377

Gujarat, battle of (1849)
Dalhousie, 1st Marquess of **4** 375-376

Gujarat rebellion (1345)
Muhammad bin Tughluq **11** 229

Gulf Cooperative Council (Middle East)
Bishara, Abdullah Yaccoub **2** 287-288

Gulf Oil Corp. (established 1901)
Mellon, Andrew William **10** 469-470

Gulistan (book; Sadi)
Jami **8** 218-219
Sadi, Shaikh Muslih-al-Din **13** 419-420

Gullible's Travels (book)
Lardner, Ringgold Wilmer **9** 204-205

Gulliver's Travels (satire; Swift)
Bolingbroke, Viscount **2** 374-375
Johnson, Samuel **8** 315-317
Pope, Alexander **12** 395-397
Swift, Jonathan **15** 51-54

Gulls (poem)
Williams, William Carlos **16** 308-309

Gull's Hornbook, The (pamphlet)
Dekker, Thomas **4** 465-466

Gumilev, Nikolai (died 1921), Russian
Akhmatova, Anna **1** 96-97

GUMPLOWICZ, LUDWIG (1838-1909),
Polish-Austrian sociologist and political
theorist **7** 41
Small, Albion Woodbury **14** 277

Gunderic (died 473?), king of Burgundy
436-473?
Gaiseric **6** 172

Gunfight at the O.K. Corral (movie)
Earp, Wyatt Barry Stepp **5** 181-182

Gunga Din (poem)
Kipling, Joseph Rudyard **9** 32-33

Gunpowder Commission (France)
Lavoisier, Antoine Laurent **9** 241-244

Gunpowder industry (United States)
du Pont, Éleuthère Irénée **5** 154

Gunpowder Plot (England; 1605)
Coke, Edward **4** 141-142
James I **8** 204-206
Milton, John **11** 43-46

Guns
see Weapons and explosives

Gunsmoke (TV series)
Still, William Grant **14** 455-456

GÜNTHER, IGNAZ (1725-1775), German
sculptor **7** 41-42

Guntram (opera)
Strauss, Richard **14** 500-501

Gupta dynasty (India; 320-540)
Harsha **7** 181-182
Samudragupta **13** 457

Gurley, Ralph R. (1797-1872), American
philanthropist
Ashmun, Jehudi **1** 335-336

Gurme (African people)
Ali, Sunni **1** 158-159

Gurre-Lieder (cantata)
Schoenberg, Arnold **14** 24-26

Gustaf Vasa (play)
Strindberg, August **14** 509-511

Gustafsson, Greta Lovisa
see Garbo, Greta

GUSTAVUS I (Gustavus Eriksson;
1496-1560), king of Sweden 1523-1560
7 42-43

GUSTAVUS II (Gustavus Adolphus;
1594-1632), king of Sweden 1611-1632
7 43-45
Oxenstierna, Axel Gustafsson **12** 44-45
Pázmány, Péter **12** 164-165
Richelieu, Armand Jean du Plessis de
13 142-144
Wallenstein, Albrecht Wenzel Eusebius
von **16** 80-81

GUSTAVUS III (1746-1792), king of Sweden 1771-1792 **7** 45-46

GUSTON, PHILIP (1913-1980), American
painter and a key member of the New
York School **7** 47-48

Gute Mensch von Sezuan, Der (play)
Brecht, Bertolt **2** 512-514

Gutenberg Bible
Gutenberg, Johann **7** 48-49

GUTENBERG, JOHANN (circa
1398-1468), German inventor and printer
7 48-49

Gutenberg Museum (established 1900;
Mainz)
Gutenberg, Johann **7** 48-49

Guthorm (flourished 9th century), Norwegian nobleman
Harold I **7** 161-162

GUTHRIE, EDWIN RAY (1886-1959),
American psychologist **7** 49-50

GUTHRIE, TYRONE (1900-1971), English
theater director **7** 50-51

GUTHRIE, WOODROW WILSON
("Woody"; 1912-1967), writer and performer of folk songs **7** 51-52

Guthrie Theatre (Minneapolis, Minnesota)
Guthrie, Tyrone **7** 50-51

Guthrum (died 890), Danish king of East Anglia
Alfred **1** 151-153

GUTIÉRRÉZ, GUSTAVO (born 1928), Peruvian who was the father of liberation theology **7** 52-53

GUY DE CHAULIAC (circa 1295-1368), French surgeon **7** 54

Guy Domville (play)
James, Henry **8** 211-212

Guy Mannering (novel and play)
Cushman, Charlotte **4** 354-355
Scott, Walter **14** 68-70

Guy Rivers (novel)
Simms, William Gilmore **14** 235-236

Guyana, Co-Operative Republic of (formerly British Guiana; South America)
Burnham, Forbes **3** 149-151
Ramphal, Shridath Surendranath **13** 19-20

Guyon, Jeanne Marie Bouvier de la Motte (1648-1717), French spiritual writer
Fénelon, François de Salignac de la Mothe **5** 410-411

Guys and Dolls (film)
Goldwyn, Samuel **6** 416

Guy's Hospital (London)
Addison, Thomas **1** 58-59
Bright, Richard **3** 7-8

Guyton de Morveau, Louis Bernard (1737-1816), French chemist
Lavoisier, Antoine Laurent **9** 241-244

Güyük (died 1248), Mongol khan 1246-1248
Kublai Khan **9** 115-118
Yeh-lü Ch'u-ts'ai **16** 447-449

Guzman, Gaspar de
see Olivares, Conde-Duque de

Guzmán Blanco, Antonio
see Blanco, Antonio Guzmán

Guzmán de Alfarache (novel)
Alemán, Mateo **1** 126

Gyges und sein Ring (verse drama)
Hebbel, Friedrich **7** 247

Gymnopédies (musical composition)
Satie, Erik **13** 494-495

Gyn/Ecology (book)
Daly, Mary **4** 380-381

Gypsies, The (poem)
Pushkin, Aleksandr Sergeevich **12** 489-491

Gypsy Ballads (book)
Lorca, Federico García **9** 511-513

Gypsy Baron, The (operetta)
Strauss, Johann Jr. **14** 498-499

Gypsy Blood (film)
Lubitsch, Ernst **10** 18-19

Gypsy Madonna (painting)
Titian **15** 242-244

Gypsy music
see Folk music—Hungarian

Gyroscope (instrument)
Foucault, Jean Bernard Léon **6** 28-29
Sperry, Elmer A. **14** 377-379

Gyroscopic stabilizer (rockets)
Goddard, Robert Hutchings **6** 376-377

Gyrowetz, Adalbert (1763-1850), Austrian composer
Chopin, Frédéric François **4** 16-18

H

H.D.
see Doolittle, Hilda

H.H.
see Jackson, Helen Hunt

H.M.S. Pinafore (operetta)
Gilbert, William Schwenck **6** 314-315
Sullivan, Arthur Seymour **15** 23

Haakon I (the Good; 914?-961), king of
Norway 935-961
Harold I **7** 161-162

Haakon IV (the Old; 1204-1263), king of
Norway 1217-1263
Matthew Paris **10** 341-342
Sturluson, Snorri **14** 310-311

Haarlem school (art)
Goyen, Jan van **6** 478-479
Ruisdael, Jacob van **13** 357-358

Haas, Jacob de (1872-1937), English and
American Jewish journalist
Wise, Stephen Samuel **16** 344-345

Habakkuk (Old Testament prophet)
Donatello **5** 55-56

Habakuk Jephson's Statement (story)
Doyle, Arthur Conan **5** 91-92

Habañera (musical composition)
Ravel, Maurice Joseph **13** 54-55

HABASH, GEORGE (born 1926), founder
of the Arab Nationalists' Movement
(1952) and of the Popular Front for the
Liberation of Palestine (PFLP; 1967)
7 55-56

Habeas corpus (law)
Curtis, Benjamin Robbins **4** 349
Hill, Benjamin Harvey **7** 386-387
Solon **14** 327-328

Habeas Corpus Act (England)
Fox, Charles James **6** 35-37
Pitt, William the Younger **12** 329-331

HABER, FRITZ (1868-1934), German
chemist **7** 56-58

HABERMAS, JÜRGEN (born 1929), German philosopher and sociologist **7** 58-60

Habit (psychology)
James, William **8** 215-217
Lashley, Karl Spencer **9** 214-215

Habitat for Humanity
Carter, James Earl **3** 339-342

Haboku sansui (painting)
Sesshu, Toya **14** 116-117

Habsburg
see Hapsburg

Hacienda (stories)
Porter, Katherine Anne **12** 406-407

Hackett, James K. (1869-1926), American
actor
Griffith, David Wark **6** 544-545

Hadassah (Jewish organization; United
States)
Szold, Henrietta **15** 66-67

Hadefan (flourished 4th century), Ethiopian
noble
Ezana **5** 354-355

Hadi, Musa al- (died 786), Abbasid caliph
785-786
Harun al-Rashid **7** 188

Hadith (Islam)
Bukhari, Muhammad ibn Ismail al-
3 111-112
ibn Tumart, Muhammad **8** 96-97

Hadji Murad (story)
Tolstoy, Leo **15** 262-265

Hadleigh Castle (painting)
Constable, John **4** 208-209

HADRIAN (76-138), Roman emperor
117-138 **7** 60-61
historians of
Suetonius Tranquillus, Gaius **15** 13
Tacitus **15** 70-72
Ulpian, Domitius **15** 385-386
influence of
Juvenal **8** 397-399
Marcus Aurelius Antoninus
10 243-245
influenced by

Epictetus **5** 292
Zeno of Citium **16** 499-500
Jewish rebellion
Bar Kochba, Simeon **2** 5
Trajan **15** 291-292

Hadrian (popes)
see Adrian

Hadrian's Memoires (book)
Yourcenar, Marguerite **16** 477-479

Hadrian's Wall (Great Britain)
Hadrian **7** 60-61

Haecht, Tobias van
see Verhaecht, Tobias van

**HAECKEL, ERNST HEINRICH PHILIPP
AUGUST** (1834-1919), German biologist
and natural philosopher **7** 61-62
Driesch, Hans Adolf Eduard **5** 105

Haffner Serenade (musical composition)
Mozart, Wolfgang Amadeus
11 218-221

HAFIZ, SHAMS AL-DIN (circa 1320-1390),
Persian mystical poet and Koranic
exegete **7** 63
Goethe, Johann Wolfgang von
6 388-391

Hafiz wa-Shawqi (book)
Husayn, Taha **8** 61-62

Hafnium (element—chemistry)
Hevesy, George Charles de **7** 371

Hafrisfjord, battle of (872)
Harold I **7** 161-162

Hafsid dynasty (Hasfite, Tunis and Tripoli;
ruled 1228-1574)
ibn Khaldun, Abd al-Rahman ibn
Muhammad **8** 93-94

Hafsun, Umar ibn (flourished circa
880-928), Moslem revolutionary in Spain
Abd al-Rahman III **1** 14

Haganah (underground organization;
Israel)
Dayan, Moshe **4** 429-431
Jabotinsky, Vladimir Evgenevich
8 167-168

Hageladas (flourished late 6th-early 5th century B.C.), Greek sculptor
Myron **11** 285

Hagenau, Nikolaus von (ca. 1445-ca. 1526), Alsatian sculptor
Grünewald, Matthias **7** 23-24

Hage's Klage (ballad)
Schubert, Franz Peter **14** 35-37

Haggard, Rider (1856-1925), English novelist
Greene, Graham **6** 523-524

Hagia Sophia (Istanbul)
Constantine XI **4** 211-212
Cyril and Methodius, Saints **4** 362-363
Justinian I **8** 393-395
Sinan, Kodja Mimar **14** 245-246

Hagith (opera)
Szymanowski, Karol **15** 67-68

HAGUE, FRANK (1876-1956), American politician **7** 63-64
Curley, James Michael **4** 344-345

Hague Conferences
1899
Bourgeois, Léon **2** 450-451
Ladd, William **9** 149
Low, Seth **10** 11-12
Salisbury, 3d Marquess of **13** 448-449
Suttner, Bertha von **15** 42-44
White, Andrew Dickson **16** 226-227
1907
Barbosa, Ruy **1** 503-504
Bourgeois, Léon **2** 450-451
Kojong **9** 74-75
Ladd, William **9** 149
Roosevelt, Theodore **13** 280-283
Root, Elihu **13** 283-284
1921, 1930 (disarmament)
Mahan, Alfred Thayer **10** 131-132
Schacht, Hjalmar Horace Greeley **13** 518-519

Hague Court
see Permanent Court of Arbitration; *see also* International Court of Justice; Permanent Court of International Justice

Haha o Kouru-ki (novel)
Tanizaki, Junichiro **15** 101-102

HAHN, OTTO (1879-1968), German chemist **7** 64-65
Szilard, Leo **15** 64-66

Haida Indians (Canada)
Reid, William Ronald **13** 88-89

HAIDAR ALI (1721/22-1782), Indian prince, ruler of Mysore 1759-1782 **7** 65-66
Tipu Sultan **15** 236

Haifa (district; Palestine)
Edward I **5** 208-210
Neutra, Richard Joseph **11** 355-356

HAIG, ALEXANDER M., JR. (born 1924), American military leader, diplomat, secretary of state, and presidential adviser **7** 66-67

HAIG, DOUGLAS (1st Earl Haig; 1861-1928), British field marshal **7** 67-68
Allenby, Edmund Henry Hynman **1** 171-172

Haiku (haikai; literary form)
Basho, Matsuo **2** 45-48
Pound, Ezra Loomis **12** 415-417

Hail to the Mother (poem)
Chatterji, Bankimchandra **3** 480-481

HAILE SELASSIE (1892-1975), emperor of Ethiopia **7** 68-70
Epstein, Jacob **5** 295-296
Heruy Wäldä-Sellasé **7** 348-349
Mäkonnen Endalkačäw **10** 161-162
Tewodros II **15** 158-159

Hairy Ape, The (play)
O'Neill, Eugene **11** 514-516

Haiti, Republic of (nation; West Indies)
aid to Venezuela
Bolívar, Simón **2** 375-377
independence struggle
Boyer, Jean Pierre **2** 468-469
Christophe, Henri **4** 32
Dessalines, Joan Jacques **4** 511-512
Toussaint L'Ouverture, François Dominique **15** 278-279
rulers
Boyer, Jean Pierre **2** 468-469
Christophe, Henri **4** 32
Dessalines, Joan Jacques **4** 511-512
Duvalier, François **5** 165-166
Duvalier, Jean-Claude **5** 166-168
struggle for democracy
Aristide, Jean-Bertrand **1** 291-293
U.S. diplomacy
Douglass, Frederick **5** 85-86
Langston, John Mercer **9** 197
see also Dominican Republic; Hispaniola

Hajjaj ibn-Yusuf, al- (661-716?), Moslem general, governor of Iraq
Abd al-Malik **1** 12-13

Ha-Kadosh (Jewish title)
Judah I **8** 372-373

HAKLUYT, RICHARD (1552/53-1616), English geographer and author **7** 70
Ortelius, Abraham **12** 8-9
Raleigh, Walter **13** 9-11
Smith, John **14** 295-297

Hakluyt, Richard (circa 1535-1591), English geographer
Hakluyt, Richard **7** 70

Hakodate (port; Japan)
Perry, Matthew Calbraith **12** 237-239

Halakah (Jewish Oral Law)
see Midrash; Talmud

HALDANE, JOHN BURDON SANDERSON (1892-1964), English biologist **7** 70-71
Krogh, Schack August Steenberg **9** 106

Mendel, Johann Gregor **10** 483-486

Haldane, John Scott (1860-1936), English physiologist
Haldane, John Burdon Sanderson **7** 70-71

Haldane, Richard Burdon (Viscount Haldane of Cloan; 1856-1928), English statesman
Bethmann Hollweg, Theobald von **2** 239-240
Edward VII **5** 214-215
Haig, Douglas **7** 67-68

Haldimand, Sir Frederick (1718-1791), Swiss-born British general
Brant, Joseph **2** 500-501

Haldin (literary character)
Conrad, Joseph **4** 205-207

HALE, EDWARD EVERETT (1822-1909), American Unitarian minister and author **7** 71-72
Barnard, Edward Emerson **2** 8-9
Schindler, Solomon **14** 7-8

HALE, GEORGE ELLERY (1868-1938), American astronomer **7** 72-74
Hubble, Edwin Powell **8** 10-11

HALE, SARAH JOSEPHA (née Buell; 1788-1879), American editor **7** 74-75

Hale, Sir Matthew (1609-1676), English jurist
Blackstone, William **2** 310-311

Hale, sterne superne... (hymn)
Dunbar, William **5** 142-143

Hale telescope (Mount Palomar)
Hubble, Edwin Powell **8** 10-11

HALÉVY, ÉLIE (1870-1937), French philosopher and historian **7** 76

Halévy, Jacques (Jacques Fromental Élie Lévy; 1799-1866), French composer, great uncle of Élie Halévy
Bizet, Georges **2** 296-297
Caruso, Enrico **3** 345
Gounod, Charles François **6** 473-474
Saint-Saëns, Charles Camille **13** 435-436

Halévy, Ludovic (1834-1908), French playwright and novelist
Halévy, Élie **7** 76

HALES, STEPHEN (1677-1761), English scientist and clergyman **7** 75

HALEY, ALEX (1921-1992), African American journalist and author **7** 76-78

HALEY, MARGARET A. (1861-1939), American educator and labor activist **7** 78-79

Half Moon (ship)
Hudson, Henry **8** 12-13

Halfdan the Black (died 860), king of Norway
Harold I **7** 161-162

HALFFTER, CHRISTÓBAL (born 1930), Spanish composer **7** 79-80

Halffter, Ernesto (1905-1989), Spanish composer and conductor in Portugal Halffter, Christóbal **7** 79-80

Halffter, Rodolfo (1900-1987), Spanish composer in Mexico Halffter, Christóbal **7** 79-80

Half-time (musical composition) Martinu, Bohuslav **10** 299-300

Halfway Covenant (Boston; 1657) Edwards, Jonathan **5** 220-222 Mather, Increase **10** 332-333

Halhead, Nathaniel Brassey (1751-1830), English Orientalist Sheridan, Richard Brinsley **14** 183-184

Haliartus, battle of (395 B.C.) Lysander **10** 70

HALIBURTON, THOMAS CHANDLER (1796-1865), Canadian judge and author **7** 80 Goldsmith, Oliver **6** 411

Halicarnassus (ancient city; Turkey) Alexander the Great **1** 137-141

HALIDE EDIP ADIVAR (1884-1964), Turkish woman writer, scholar, and public figure **7** 80-82

Halidon Hill, battle of (1333) Edward III **5** 211-212 Robert II **13** 194

Halieutica (poem) Ovid **12** 34-36

HALIFAX, 1ST EARL OF (Edward Frederick Lindley Wood; 1881-1959), English statesman **7** 82-83 Swift, Jonathan **15** 51-54

Halifax, 3rd Viscount see Halifax, 1st Earl of

HALL, ASAPH (1829-1907), American astronomer **7** 83-84

HALL, DONALD (born 1928), New England memoirist, short story writer, essayist, dramatist, critic, and anthologist as well as poet **7** 84-85

HALL, GRANVILLE STANLEY (1844-1924), American psychologist and educator **7** 85-86 Crandall, Prudence **4** 291 Wundt, Wilhelm Max **16** 402-403

HALLAJ, AL-HUSAYN IBN MANSUR AL (857-922), Persian Moslem mystic and martyr **7** 86-87 Junayd, Abu al-Qasim ibn Muhammad al **8** 388

Hallam, Arthur (died 1833), English poet Tennyson, Alfred **15** 144-146

HALLAM, LEWIS AND LEWIS, SR. AND JR. (Lewis Sr. ca. 1705-55; Lewis Jr.

1740-1808), American actors and theatrical managers **7** 87

Halle, University of (Germany) economics Schmoller, Gustav Friedrich von **14** 21 philosophy Thomasius **15** 193-194 Wolf, Friedrich August **16** 352-353 Wolff, Christian von **16** 358 sciences Cantor, Georg Ferdinand Ludwig Philipp **3** 265-266 Stahl, Georg Ernst **14** 392-393 theology Schleiermacher, Friedrich Ernst Daniel **14** 11-12 Spener, Philipp Jakob **14** 372

Hallé, Sir Charles (1819-1895), English pianist and conductor Liszt, Franz **9** 445-447

HALLER, ALBRECHT VON (1708-1777), Swiss physician **7** 87-88 Bichat, Marie François Xavier **2** 263-264 La Mettrie, Julien Offray de **9** 179-180

HALLEY, EDMUND (1656-1742), English astronomer **7** 88-89 Demoivre, Abraham **4** 494-495 Lagrange, Joseph Louis **9** 164-166 Newton, Isaac **11** 369-372

Halley's comet (astronomy) Bessel, Friedrich Wilhelm **2** 234-235 Compton, Arthur Holly **4** 186-188 Halley, Edmund **7** 88-89 Winthrop, John **16** 341-342

Halliday, Simeon (literary character) Garrett, Thomas **6** 225-226

Haloid Company (United States) Wilson, Joseph Chamberlain **16** 325-326

Halpert's Downtown Gallery (New York City) Lawrence, Jacob **9** 250-251

Hals, Dirck (died 1656), Dutch painter Hals, Frans **7** 89-91

HALS, FRANS (1581/85-1666), Dutch painter **7** 89-91 Brouwer, Adriaen **3** 29-30 Liebermann, Max **9** 402-403 Manet, Édouard **10** 193-194 Stella, Joseph **14** 422

HALSEY, WILLIAM FREDERICK (1882-1959), American admiral **7** 91-92 Nimitz, Chester William **11** 395-396

Halsted, William Stewart (1852-1922), American surgeon Cushing, Harvey Williams **4** 353-354 Osler, William **12** 19-20

Halt during the Chase, The (painting) Watteau, Antoine **16** 143-144

Ham Funeral, The (play) White, Patrick Victor Martindale **16** 233-235

HAMANN, JOHANN GEORG (1730-1788), German philosopher **7** 92 Herder, Johann Gottfried von **7** 327-328 Jacobi, Friedrich Heinrich **8** 189-190 Vico, Giambattista **15** 480-481

Hambidge, Jay (Edward John Hambidge, 1867-1924), Canadian-born American artist Bellows, George Wesley **2** 143

Hamburg, University of (Germany) Cassirer, Ernst **3** 358-359 Pauli, Wolfgang Ernst **12** 149 Stern, Otto **14** 435 Von Neumann, John **16** 27-28

HAMER, FANNIE LOU (born Townsend; 1917-1977), American civil rights activist **7** 93-94

HAMILCAR BARCA (circa 285-229/228 B.C.), Carthaginian general and statesman **7** 94-95 Hannibal Barca **7** 128-130

HAMILTON, ALEXANDER (1755-1804), American statesman **7** 95-98 as Cabinet member Jefferson, Thomas **8** 238-241 Washington, George **16** 126-129 associates Brown, Moses **3** 42-43 Coxe, Tench **4** 285-286 Livingston, Robert R. **9** 462-463 Miranda, Francisco de **11** 52-53 Morris, Robert **11** 185-187 Schuyler, Philip John **14** 49-50 duel Burr, Aaron **3** 156-159 fiscal opponents Macon, Nathaniel **10** 114-115 Taylor, John **15** 126 historians of Ford, Paul Leicester **6** 9-10 Warren, Mercy Otis **16** 120-121 political opponents Adams, John **1** 48-51 Chase, Samuel **3** 475-476 Henry, Patrick **7** 309-311 Madison, James **10** 121-123 Monroe, James **11** 111-113 Randolph, Edmund **13** 29-30 quoted Steuben, Frederick William Augustus von **14** 438-439 Washington, George **16** 126-129 statue of Rimmer, William **13** 174 supporters Ames, Fisher **1** 199-200 King, Rufus **9** 22-23 Marshall, John **10** 279-281 Pickering, Timothy **12** 298-299

HAMILTON, ALICE (1869-1970), American physician 7 98-99

Hamilton, Andrew (died 1703), American pioneer and statesman
Morris, Lewis **11** 183-184
Zenger, John Peter **16** 497-498

Hamilton College (New York State)
Kirkland, Samuel **9** 37

Hamilton, Gavin (1723-1798), English painter
West, Benjamin **16** 210-212

Hamilton, James (1786-1857), American political leader
Couper, James Hamilton **4** 270

Hamilton, James Douglas (1658-1712), 4th Duke of Hamilton
Burnet, Gilbert **3** 147

Hamilton, Lady (Emma Hart; 1761?-1815), mistress of Lord Nelson
Nelson, Horatio **11** 336-338
Romney, George **13** 269-270

Hamilton, Sir William (1730-1803), British diplomat
Nelson, Horatio **11** 336-338

HAMILTON, SIR WILLIAM ROWAN (1805-1865), Irish mathematical physicist 7 99-100

Hamilton's Bawn (poem)
Swift, Jonathan **15** 51-54

Hamlet (play; Shakespeare)
Barrymores **2** 28-30
Booth, Edwin **2** 401-402
Eliot, Thomas Stearns **5** 258-261
Kyd, Thomas **9** 140-141
Lessing, Gotthold Ephraim **9** 357-359
Plautus **12** 348-350
Shakespeare, William **14** 142-145
Stanislavsky, Constantin **14** 398-399

Hamlet, The (novel)
Faulkner, William **5** 395-397

Hamlet and Ophelia (tone poem)
MacDowell, Edward Alexander **10** 87-88

Hamlet in the Snow (painting)
Vlaminck, Maurice **16** 6

Hamlet of A. MacLeish, The (poems)
MacLeish, Archibald **10** 109-110

Hamlin, Hannibal (1809-1891), American politician
Howells, William Dean **7** 539-541

HAMMARSKJÖLD, DAG (1905-1961), Swedish diplomat 7 100-101
Bunche, Ralph Johnson **3** 121-122
Lie, Trygve Halvdan **9** 400-401
Thant, U **15** 161-162

Hammarskjöld Memorial (sculpture)
Hepworth, Barbara **7** 318-319

HAMM-BRÜCHER, HILDEGARD (born 1921), Free Democratic Party's candidate for the German presidency in 1994 7 101-103

HAMMER, ARMAND (1898-1990), American entrepreneur and art collector 7 103-104

Hammerklavier Sonata (musical composition)
Beethoven, Ludwig van **2** 114-117

HAMMERSTEIN, OSCAR CLENDENNING II (1895-1960), lyricist and librettist of the American theater 7 104-106
Kern, Jerome David **8** 517-518
Martin, Mary **10** 292-293
Rodgers, Richard Charles **13** 234-236

HAMMETT, (SAMUEL) DASHIELL (1894-1961), American author 7 106-108
Bogart, Humphrey **2** 363-364
Hellman, Lillian Florence **7** 267-268

HAMMOND, JAMES HENRY (1807-1864), American statesman 7 108-109

HAMMOND, JOHN LAWRENCE LE BRETON (1872-1952), English historian 7 108-109

HAMMOND, LUCY BARBARA (1873-1961), English historian 7 109

HAMMURABI (1792-1750 B.C.), king of Babylonia 7 109-110

HAMPDEN, JOHN (1594-1643), English statesman 7 110-111
Cromwell, Oliver **4** 317-320

Hampshire (ship)
Kitchener, Horatio Herbert **9** 45-46

HAMPTON, WADE (circa 1751-1835), American planter 7 111-112

HAMPTON, WADE III (1818-1902), American statesman and Confederate general 7 112
Delany, Martin Robinson **4** 473-474

Hampton Choral Union (Virginia)
Dett, Robert Nathaniel **4** 512

Hampton Court Palace (England)
Mary I **10** 308-309
Wolsey, Thomas **16** 364-366
Wren, Christopher **16** 393-394

Hampton Institute (Virginia)
Armstrong, Samuel Chapman **1** 306-307
Dett, Robert Nathaniel **4** 512
Eastman, George **5** 186
Washington, Booker Taliaferro **16** 125-126

Hampton Normal and Industrial Institution
see Hampton Institute

Hampton Roads Conference (1865)
Blair, Francis Preston **2** 313-315
Davis, Jefferson **4** 416-418

HAMSUN, KNUT (1859-1952), Norwegian novelist 7 113-114

Han ("barbarian" dynasty; 4th century)
Shih Le **14** 195

Han Ch'i (flourished 11th century), Chinese statesman
Fan Chung-yen **5** 376-377
Ou-yang Hsiu **12** 33-34
Wang An-shih **16** 95-97

Han dynasty (China; ruled 207 B.C. - 220 A.D.)
Former (Western; ruled 207 B.C. -A.D. 9)
Confucius **4** 197-200
Han Kao-tsu **7** 125-126
Han Wu-ti **7** 136
K'ang Yu-wei **8** 426-428
Kuang-wu-ti **9** 112-113
Pan Ku **12** 86-87
Wang Mang **16** 101-103
Wu-ti **16** 406-408
Hsin (ruled 9-23)
Kuang-wu-ti **9** 112-113
Wang Mang **16** 101-103
Later (Eastern; ruled 25-220)
Chang Chüeh **3** 432-433
Hsüan Tsang **8** 6-7
Kuang-wu-ti **9** 112-113
Pan Ku **12** 86-87
Ts'ao Ts'ao **15** 322-323

Han dynasty, Later (China; ruled 947-951)
Zhao Kuang-yin **16** 505-508

HAN FEI TZU (circa 280-233 B.C.), Chinese statesman and philosopher 7 124-125
Hsün-tzu **8** 8
Li Ssu **9** 442-443

Han Kao-tsu
see Liu Pang

Han Kyu-jik (died circa 1894), Korean politician
Kim Ok-kyun **9** 7-8

HAN WU-TI (157-87 B.C.), Chinese emperor 7 136
Chung-shu, Tung **4** 48-49
Ssu-ma Hsiang-ju **14** 389-390

HAN YÜ (768-824), Chinese author 7 136-137
Liu Tsung-Yüan **9** 455-456
Ou-yang Hsiu **12** 33-34

HANAFI, HASSAN (born 1935), Egyptian philosopher 7 114

Hanbal, Ibn (died 855), Moslem religious scholar
Tabari, Muhammad ibn Jarir al- **15** 69-70

HANCOCK, JOHN (1737-1793), American statesman 7 114-116
Adams, John **1** 48-51
Adams, Samuel **1** 55-56
Bowdoin, James **2** 461-462
Burr, Aaron **3** 156-159
Gage, Thomas **6** 169-170
Otis, James Jr. **12** 25-27
Revere, Paul **13** 110-111

HAND, BILLINGS LEARNED (1872-1961),
American jurist **7** 116
   Cardozo, Benjamin Nathan **3** 288-290
   Taft, William Howard **15** 78-81

Hand of Ethelberta, The (novel)
   Hardy, Thomas **7** 150-152

Händel, Georg Friedrich
   see Handel, George Frederick

HANDEL, GEORGE FREDERICK
(1685-1759), German-born English com-
poser and organist **7** 116-119
   Chopin, Frédéric François **4** 16-18
   Corelli, Arcangelo **4** 230-231
   Froberger, Johann Jakob **6** 120-121
   Gay, John **6** 243-244
   Mozart, Wolfgang Amadeus
   11 218-221
   Scarlatti, Domenico **13** 515-517
   Scarlatti, Pietro Alessandro Gaspare
   13 517-518

Handful of Dust, A (novel)
   Waugh, Evelyn Arthur St. John
   16 145-147

HANDKE, PETER (born 1942), Austrian
playwright, novelist, screenwriter, essayist, and poet **7** 119-121

HANDLIN, OSCAR (born 1915), American
historian **7** 121-122
   Schlesinger, Arthur Meier **14** 13

Hands Holding the Void (sculpture)
   Giacometti, Alberto **6** 294-295

Handschuchsheim, Ritter von
   see Meinong, Alexius

HANDSOME LAKE (a.k.a. Hadawa' Ko; ca.
1735-1815), Seneca spiritual leader
7 122-123

HANDY, WILLIAM CHRISTOPHER
(1873-1958), African American songwriter **7** 123-124
   Still, William Grant **14** 455-456

Handy Guide for Beggars (book)
   Lindsay, Vachel **9** 424-425

Hanga, Sheikh Abdulla Kassim (born
1931), Tanzanian politician
   Karume, Abeid Amani **8** 452-453

Hangchow (city; China)
   Chu Hsi **4** 40-43

Hanging Gardens (Babylon)
   Nebuchadnezzar **11** 330

Hangman, The (play)
   Lagerkvist, Pär Fabian **9** 162-163

HANKS, NANCY (1927-1983), called the
"mother of a million artists" for her work
in building federal financial support for
the arts and artists **7** 126-127

Hanlin Academy (China)
   Chang Chü-cheng **3** 431-432
   Chao Meng-fu **3** 436-437
   Feng Kuei-fen **5** 411-412
   Ou-yang Hsiu **12** 33-34
   Wang An-shih **16** 95-97

HANNA, MARCUS ALONZO (1837-1904),
American businessman and politician
7 127-128
   Johnson, Tom Loftin **8** 317
   McKinley, William **10** 418-420
   Sherman, John **14** 184-185

Hanneles Himmelfahrt (play)
   Hauptmann, Gerhart Johann Robert
   7 199-201

Hanneman, Adriaen (ca. 1600-1671),
Dutch painter
   Clarendon, 1st Earl of **4** 73-75

HANNIBAL BARCA (247-183 B.C.),
Carthaginian general **7** 128-130
   Antiochus III **1** 249-250
   Flamininus, Titus Quinctius **5** 477
   Hamilcar Barca **7** 94-95
   Scipio Africanus Major, Publius Cor-
   nelius **14** 61-62
   Sherwood, Robert Emmet **14** 189-190

Hannibal Crossing the Alps (painting)
   Turner, Joseph Mallord William
   15 352-354

Hannibal, Huck, and Tom (stories)
   Twain, Mark **15** 363-366

**Hannibal in the Alps Contemplating the
Italian Lands** (painting)
   Goya y Lucientes, Francisco de Paula
   José de **6** 476-478

Hanno (flourished 3rd century B.C.),
Carthaginian politician
   Hamilcar Barca **7** 94-95

Hanno (literary character)
   Mann, Thomas **10** 204-207

Hanoi (city; North Vietnam)
   Bonvalot, Pierre Gabriel Édouard **2** 396
   Garnier, Francis **6** 220-221
   Qianlong **12** 502-505

Hanover (city; Germany)
   Bismarck, Otto Eduard Leopold von
   2 294-296

Hanover dynasty (Great Britain)
   see Great Britain—1714-1901 (Hanover)

Hans Alienus (novelist)
   Heidenstam, Carl Gustaf Verner Von
   7 258-259

Hans Christian Andersen (film)
   Goldwyn, Samuel **6** 416

Hans und Heinz Kirch (novella)
   Storm, Theodor **14** 479-480

HANSBERRY, LORRAINE VIVIAN
(1930-1965), American writer and a
major figure on Broadway **7** 130-131

Hanseatic League (Hansa)
   Chancellor, Richard **3** 422
   Godunov, Boris Feodorovich **6** 382-383

HANSEN, ALVIN (1887-1975), American
economist **7** 131-132

Hansen, Emil
   see Nolde, Emil

Hansen, Hans (literary character)
   Mann, Thomas **10** 204-207

HANSEN, JULIA BUTLER (1907-1988),
American politician **7** 132-133

Hansen, Marcus Lee (1892-1938), American historian
   Schlesinger, Arthur Meier **14** 13

Han-shu (book)
   Pan Ku **12** 86-87

Hanslick, Eduard (1825-1904), Austrian
music critic
   Brahms, Johannes **2** 490-492
   Bruckner, Joseph Anton **3** 64-65
   Wagner, Richard **16** 40-43

HANSON, DUANE (1925-1990), American
super-realist sculptor **7** 133-135

HANSON, HOWARD (born 1896), American composer and educator **7** 135-136
   Still, William Grant **14** 455-456

Hanukkah
   see Chanukah

Hanuman (Hindu deity)
   Ramakrishna, Sri **13** 11-13

Han-yeh (novel)
   Pa Chin **12** 53-54

HAPGOOD, NORMAN (1868-1937),
American author and editor **7** 137-138

Happenings (art)
   Oldenburg, Claes **11** 496-498

Happenings (theater)
   Rauschenberg, Robert **13** 52-53

Happiness (poem)
   Sandburg, Carl **13** 461-462

Happiness... (poem)
   Frost, Robert Lee **6** 130-133

Happy Days (play)
   Beckett, Samuel **2** 102-104

Happy End (musical play)
   Weill, Kurt **16** 174-175

Happy Journey... (play)
   Wilder, Thornton Niven **16** 276-277

Happy Prince... (stories, Wilde)
   Borges, Jorge Luis **2** 411-412
   Wilde, Oscar Fingall O'Flahertie Wills
   16 272-273

Happy Times in Norway (book)
   Undset, Sigrid **15** 388-389

Happy Valley (novel)
   White, Patrick Victor Martindale
   16 233-235

Hapsburg (European dynasty; ruled
1273-1918)
   Austria (ruled 1278-1918)
      Francis Ferdinand **6** 44
      Francis II **6** 43-44
      Francis Joseph **6** 45-46
      Maria Theresa **10** 256-258
      Maximilian of Hapsburg
      10 358-360
      see also Holy Roman Empire below

Germany
see Holy Roman Empire below
Holy Roman Empire (ruled 1273-1308; 1438-1806)
Charles V **3** 457-459
Ferdinand I **5** 414-415
Ferdinand II **5** 415
Ferdinand III **5** 416-417
Francis II **6** 43-44
Frederick III **6** 84-85
Joseph II **8** 359-360
Leopold II **9** 346
Maximilian I **10** 356-357
Maximilian II **10** 357-358
Rudolf I **13** 347-348
Spain (ruled 1516-1700)
Charles II **3** 454
Charles V **3** 457-459
Philip II **12** 271-273
Philip III **12** 273-274
Philip IV **12** 275
see also Austrian Succession, War of the; Spanish Succession, War of the

HARA, KEI (1856-1921), Japanese statesman and prime minister 1918-1921 **7** 138
Takahashi, Korekiyo **15** 84-85

Harambee (book)
Kenyatta, Jomo **8** 512-514

Haran
see Carrhae

HARAND, IRENE (born Irene Wedl; 1900-1975), Austrian political and human rights activist **7** 139-145

Harar (province; Ethiopia)
Burton, Richard **3** 163-164
Mengs, Anton Raphael **10** 505

HARAWI, ILYAS AL- (Elias Harawi; born 1930), president of Lebanon **7** 145-146

Harbinger of Peace (journal)
Ladd, William **9** 149
Ripley, George **13** 179-180

Harbor Hotel (play)
Betti, Ugo **2** 246

Hard Day's Night, A (film)
Lennon, John Winston **9** 326-328

Hard Times (novel)
Dickens, Charles John Huffam **4** 538-541

Hardenberg, Baron Friedrich Leopold von
see Novalis

HARDENBERG, PRINCE KARL AUGUST VON (1750-1822), Prussian statesman **7** 146-147
Blücher, Gebhard Leberecht von **2** 340-341
Frederick William III **6** 87
Metternich, Klemens von **10** 533-536
Scharnhorst, Gerhard Johann David von **13** 521-522

Harder They Fall, The (film)
Bogart, Humphrey **2** 363-364

HARDIE, JAMES KEIR (1856-1915), Scottish politician **7** 147-148
Cobbett, William **4** 126-127

Harding, Chester (1792-1866), American painter
Stuart, Gilbert **14** 513-515

Harding, Stephen, Saint
see Stephen Harding, Saint

HARDING, WARREN GAMALIEL (1865-1923), American statesman, president 1921-1923 **7** 148-149
associates
Curie, Marie Sklodowska **4** 339-341
Hughes, Charles Evans **8** 15-16
Lodge, Henry Cabot **9** 482-483
Cabinet
Coolidge, John Calvin **4** 217-219
Hoover, Herbert Clark **7** 483-485
Mellon, Andrew William **10** 469-470
domestic policy
Debs, Eugene Victor **4** 444-445
Gary, Elbert Henry **6** 229-230
La Follette, Robert Marion **9** 155-156
political appointments
Taft, William Howard **15** 78-81
Wood, Leonard **16** 369-370
see also Teapot Dome Scandal

Hardinge of Penshurst, Lord Charles (1858-1944), British diplomat
Chelmsford, Frederic John Napier Thesiger **3** 497

Hardouin, Jules
see Mansart, Jules Hardouin

Hardy, Godfrey Harold (1877-1947), English mathematician
Ramanujan Aiyangar, Srinivasa **13** 14-15
Wiener, Norbert **16** 262-263

HARDY, HARRIET (1905-1993), American pathologist **7** 150

HARDY, THOMAS (1840-1928), English novelist, poet, and dramatist **7** 150-152
Ford, Ford Madox **6** 1-2
Frost, Robert Lee **6** 130-133
Kipling, Joseph Rudyard **9** 32-33
Maugham, William Somerset **10** 344-345

HARE, ROBERT (1781-1858), American chemist **7** 152-153
Silliman, Benjamin **14** 229-230
Whitney, Josiah Dwight **16** 254-255

Hare-Hawes-Cutting Act (1933)
Osmeña, Sergio **12** 22-24
Quezon, Manuel Luis **12** 511-513
Quirino, Elpidio **12** 519-520
Roxas, Manuel **13** 331-332

Harewood House (Yorkshire)
Adam, Robert and James **1** 38-40
Chippendale, Thomas **4** 1-2

Harfleur, battle of (1415)
Gloucester, Duke of **6** 370-371

Henry V **7** 296-297

HARGRAVES, EDWARD HAMMOND (1816-1891), Australian publicist **7** 153-154

Harijans
see Untouchables

HARING, KEITH (1958-1990), American artist tied to New York graffiti art of the 1980s **7** 154-155

Hark! The Herald Angels Sing (hymn)
Wesley, Charles **16** 208-209

HARKNESS, GEORGIA (1891-1974), American Methodist and ecumenical theologian **7** 155-156

Harkness, Stephen Vanderburg (1838?-1926), American oil magnate
Rockefeller, John Davison **13** 226-228

HARLAN, JOHN MARSHALL (1833-1911), American jurist **7** 156-157
White, Edward Douglass **16** 230-231

HARLAN, JOHN MARSHALL (1899-1971), U.S. Supreme Court justice **7** 157-159

Harlem (New York City)
Ellington, Edward Kennedy **5** 273-274
Lawrence, Jacob **9** 250-251
Malcolm X **10** 165-166
Powell, Adam Clayton Jr. **12** 421-422
Rangel, Charles B. **13** 31-32
Ringgold, Faith **13** 175-177
VanDer Zee, James **15** 418-419

Harlem Globetrotters (basketball team)
Owens, Jesse **12** 43-44

Harlem Hospital Center (New York City)
Drew, Charles Richard **5** 100-101

Harlem renaissance (American literature)
Cullen, Countee **4** 333-334
Hughes, Langston **8** 18-19
Johnson, Charles Spurgeon **8** 296-297
Knopf, Blanche Wolf **9** 61-62
Larsen, Nella **9** 209-210
McKay, Claude **10** 416

Harlequin (sculpture)
Gris, Juan **7** 5-6

Harlequin's Carnival (painting)
Miró, Joan **11** 53-54

HARLEY, ROBERT (1st Earl of Oxford and Earl Mortimer; 1661-1724), English statesman **7** 159-160
Anne **1** 241-242
Godolphin, Sidney **6** 380-381
Marlborough, 1st Duke of **10** 271-272
Swift, Jonathan **15** 51-54

Harlot's Progress (prints)
Hogarth, William **7** 446-447

Harlow, Jean (1911-1937), American film actress
Gable, William Clark **6** 157-158

Harmattan, L' (novel)
Ousmane, Sembene **12** 32-33

Harmodius (died 514 B.C.), Athenian tyrannicide
Horace **7** 500-503

Harmoniae poeticae (musical collection; Senfl)
Hofhaimer, Paul **7** 441

Harmonic analysis (mathematics)
Wiener, Norbert **16** 262-263

Harmonica (mustical instrument)
Franklin, Benjamin **6** 60-64

Harmonice mundi (book)
Kepler, Johannes **8** 514-516

Harmonie du soir (poem)
Baudelaire, Charles Pierre **2** 61-63

Harmonies (poem)
Palma, Ricardo **12** 77

Harmonies poétiques et religieuses (poems)
Lamartine, Alphonse Marie Louis de **9** 173-175

Harmonists
see Harmony Society

Harmonium (poems)
Stevens, Wallace **14** 443-445

Harmony (borough; Pennsylvania)
Rapp, George **13** 42-43

Harmony (music)
Alembert, Jean le Rond d' **1** 127-128
Fry, William Henry **6** 136-137
Ives, Charles Edward **8** 159-160
Piston, Walter **12** 327-328
Rameau, Jean Philippe **13** 17-18
Xenakis, Iannis **16** 416-418

Harmony (town; Indiana)
Rapp, George **13** 42-43

Harmony Hall (Hampshire, England)
Owen, Robert **12** 39-40

Harmony of the World, The (opera)
Hindemith, Paul **7** 399-400

Harmony Society (religious sect)
Rapp, George **13** 42-43

HARNACK, ADOLF VON (1851-1930), German theologian **7** 160
Gooch, George Peabody **6** 432-433
Loisy, Alfred Firmin **9** 489-490

Harnack, Theodosius (1817-1889), German theologian
Harnack, Adolf von **7** 160

Harnassie (ballet-opera)
Szymanowski, Karol **15** 67-68

HARNETT, WILLIAM MICHAEL (1848-1892), American painter **7** 160-161
Peto, John Frederick **12** 259

Haro, Luis de, Duke of Carpio (1598-1661), Spanish diplomat
Philip IV **12** 275

Harold (died 1018/19), king of Denmark 1014-1018
Cobbett, William **4** 126-127

Harold (verse play)
Tennyson, Alfred **15** 144-146

Harold en Italie (musical composition; Berlioz)
Berlioz, Louis Hector **2** 203-205
Paganini, Niccolo **12** 58-59

Harold "Fairhair"
see Harold I

Harold Haardraade
see Harold III

HAROLD I (circa 840-933), king of Norway 860-930 **7** 161-162

HAROLD II (Harold Godwinson; died 1066), Anglo-Saxon king of England of 1066 **7** 162
Harold III **7** 163
William I **16** 290-291

HAROLD III (1015-1066), king of Norway 1047-1066 **7** 163
Cobbett, William **4** 126-127
Harold II **7** 162
William I **16** 290-291

Harold the Ruthless
see Harold III

Harp Weaver... (book)
Millay, Edna St. Vincent **11** 24-25

Harpalus (died 324 B.C.), governor of Babylon and treasurer of Alexander the Great
Demosthenes **4** 495-496

HARPER, WILLIAM RAINEY (1856-1906), American educator and biblical scholar **7** 163-164
Barnard, Edward Emerson **2** 8-9
Breasted, James Henry **2** 510-511
Dewey, John **4** 520-523
Rockefeller, John Davison **13** 226-228

Harper's Bazaar (magazine)
Erté **5** 314-316
Hearst, William Randolph **7** 243-244
Warhol, Andy **16** 114-115

Harpers Ferry (town; West Virginia)
Brown, John **3** 39-41
Douglass, Frederick **5** 85-86
Howe, Samuel Gridley **7** 537
Jackson, Shirley Ann **8** 183-184
Lee, Robert Edward **9** 292-294

Harper's Magazine (formerly Harper's New Monthly Magazine)
Abbott, Lyman **1** 10-11
Curtis, George William **4** 349-350
Hickok, James Butler **7** 374-375
Homer, Winslow **7** 468-469
Lampman, Archibald **9** 180-181
Rembrandt Harmensz van Rijn **13** 91-95
Ripley, George **13** 179-180

Harper's Weekly (magazine; 1857-1916)
Curtis, George William **4** 349-350
Davis, Richard Harding **4** 422-423
Hapgood, Norman **7** 137-138
Nast, Thomas **11** 318-319

Rembrandt Harmensz van Rijn **13** 91-95
Schurz, Carl **14** 44-45

Harpignies, Henri Joseph (1819-1916), French painter
Morrice, James Wilson **11** 181-182

Harral House (Bridgeport, Connecticut)
Davis, Alexander Jackson **4** 411

Harrich, Jobst (circa 1580-1617), German painter
Dürer, Albrecht **5** 159-161

HARRIMAN, EDWARD HENRY (1848-1909), American railroad executive **7** 164-165
Cooke, Jay **4** 215-216
Durant, Thomas Clark **5** 157-158
Harriman, W. Averell **7** 165-166
Hill, James Jerome **7** 388-389
Morgan, John Pierpont **11** 163-165
Schiff, Jacob Henry **14** 2-3

Harriman Park (Orange County, New York)
Harriman, Edward Henry **7** 164-165

HARRIMAN, W. AVERELL (1891-1986), American industrialist, financier, and diplomat **7** 165-166
Harriman, Edward Henry **7** 164-165

HARRINGTON, JAMES (1611-1677), English political theorist **7** 166-167
Toland, John **15** 256

HARRINGTON, MICHAEL (1928-1989), American political activist and educator **7** 167-169

Harriott, Thomas (1560-1621), English mathematician
Bessel, Friedrich Wilhelm **2** 234-235

HARRIS, ABRAM LINCOLN, JR. (1899-1963), African American economist **7** 169-171

HARRIS, BARBARA CLEMENTINE (born 1930), African American activist and Anglican bishop **7** 171-172

Harris, Charles (1865-1930), American songwriter
Sousa, John Philip **14** 353-354

HARRIS, FRANK (1856-1931), Irish-American author and editor **7** 172-173
Shaw, George Bernard **14** 163-164

HARRIS, JOEL CHANDLER (1848-1908), American writer **7** 173-174

Harris, Lawren (1885-1970), Canadian painter
Carr, Emily **3** 319

HARRIS, PATRICIA ROBERTS (1924-1985), first African American woman in the U.S. Cabinet **7** 174-175

HARRIS, ROY (1898-1979), American composer **7** 175-176

HARRIS, TOWNSEND (1804-1878), American merchant and diplomat **7** 176-177

HARRIS, WILLIAM TORREY (1835-1909), American educator and philosopher **7** 177-178
 Dewey, John **4** 520-523

Harrison, Benjamin (1726?-1791), American statesmen and Revolutionary leader
 Harrison, William Henry **7** 180-181

HARRISON, BENJAMIN (1833-1901), American statesman, president 1889-1893 **7** 178-179
 Blaine, James Gillespie **2** 312-313
 Cleveland, Stephen Grover **4** 108-110
 Quay, Matthew Stanley **12** 507
 Roosevelt, Theodore **13** 280-283

Harrison, Carter, II (1860-1953), American politician
 Altgeld, John Peter **1** 180-182

Harrison, George (born 1943), English singer
 Beatles, The **2** 89-92

HARRISON, PETER (1716-1775), American architect and merchant **7** 179-180

HARRISON, WILLIAM HENRY (1773-1841), American statesman, president 1841 **7** 180-181
 as territorial governor
  Black Hawk **2** 308
  Taylor, Zachary **15** 128-130
  Tecumseh **15** 133
 military service
  Madison, James **10** 121-123
  Perry, Oliver Hazard **12** 239
 presidency
  Clay, Henry **4** 94-96
  Everett, Edward **5** 344
  Tyler, John **15** 368-369
  Van Buren, Martin **15** 410-411
 relatives
  Harrison, Benjamin **7** 178-179
 supporters
  Clayton, John Middleton **4** 96-97
  Curtin, Andrew Gregg **4** 347-348
  Stockton, Robert Field **14** 461-462
  Webster, Daniel **16** 162-164

Harrod, James (1742-1793), American soldier and pioneer
 Boone, Daniel **2** 397-398

HARSHA (Harshavardhana; circa 590-647), king of Northern India 606-612 **7** 181-182
 Hsüan Tsang **8** 6-7

Hart, Emma
 see Hamilton, Lady; Willard, Emma Hart

HART, GARY W. (born 1936), American political campaign organizer, U.S. senator, and presidential candidate **7** 182-184

Hart, Lorenz (1895-1943), American lyricist
 O'Hara, John **11** 485
 Rodgers, Richard Charles **13** 234-236

Hart, Moss (1904-1961), American librettist and playwright
 Kaufman, George S. **8** 457-458
 Weill, Kurt **16** 174-175

Hart, William S. (1872-1946), American actor
 Buffalo Bill **3** 105-106

HARTE, FRANCIS BRET (1837-1902), American poet and fiction writer **7** 184-185
 Howells, William Dean **7** 539-541
 Kipling, Joseph Rudyard **9** 32-33
 Lawson, Henry **9** 254-255
 Strindberg, August **14** 509-511
 Twain, Mark **15** 363-366

Hartford Convention (1814)
 Hayne, Robert Young **7** 231-232
 Morris, Gouverneur **11** 182-183
 Otis, Harrison Gray **12** 25

Hartford statehouse (Connecticut)
 Bulfinch, Charles **3** 116-117

Hartford Wits
 see Connecticut Wits

Harthacnut (1019?-1042), king of Denmark 1035-1042 and of England 1040-1042
 Cobbett, William **4** 126-127

HARTLEY, DAVID (1705-1757), British physician and philosopher **7** 185
 Mill, James **11** 21

HARTLEY, MARSDEN (1877-1943), American painter **7** 186
 Demuth, Charles **4** 497-498

Hartley, Sir Harold (1878-1972), British chemist
 Hinshelwood, Cyril Norman **7** 405-406

Hartmann, Eduard von (1842-1906), German philosopher
 Ebbinghaus, Hermann **5** 192-193
 Laforgue, Jules **9** 160-161

Hartmann, Viktor (1834-1873), Russian painter and architect
 Mussorgsky, Modest Petrovich **11** 274-276

HARTSHORNE, CHARLES (born 1897), American theologian **7** 186-187

Haru no Hi (poems)
 Basho, Matsuo **2** 45-48

HARUN AL-RASHID (766-809), Abbasid caliph of Baghdad 786-809 **7** 188
 Abu Nuwas **1** 33-34
 Mamun, Abdallah al- **10** 183
 Mansur, Abu Jafar ibn Muhammad al- **10** 214-215

HARUNOBU, SUZUKI (ca. 1725-1770), Japanese painter and printmaker **7** 188-189
 Hiroshige, Ando **7** 412-413

Harurites (Moslem sect)
 Ali **1** 155-156

Harvard Club (New York City)
 Bellows, Henry Whitney **2** 143-144

Harvard College
 see Harvard University

Harvard Law Review (journal)
 Frankfurter, Felix **6** 57
 Hand, Billings Learned **7** 116

Harvard Law School Association (established 1886)
 Brandeis, Louis Dembitz **2** 496-497

Harvard Socialist Club
 Lippmann, Walter **9** 439-440

Harvard Society for Contemporary Art
 Kirstein, Lincoln **9** 39-41

Harvard University (Cambridge, Massachusetts)
 architecture
  Breuer, Marcel **2** 520-521
  Gabo, Naum **6** 158-159
  Gropius, Walter **7** 13-14
  Le Corbusier **9** 274-275
 astronomy
  Cannon, Annie Jump **3** 260-261
  Shapley, Harlow **14** 155-156
  Winthrop, John **16** 341-342
  see also Observatory (below)
 biology
  Beadle, George Wells **2** 80-81
  East, Edward Murray **5** 182-183
  Watson, James Dewey **16** 137-138
 Board of Overseers
  Bunche, Ralph Johnson **3** 121-122
  Chauncy, Charles **3** 485-486
 Center for Cognitive Studies
  Bruner, Jerome Seymour **3** 72-73
 chemistry
  Lewis, Gilbert Newton **9** 384-385
  Richards, Theodore William **13** 137-138
 Divinity School
  Cox, Harvey **4** 284-285
  Wilder, Amos Niven **16** 273-274
 economics
  Parsons, Talcott **12** 122
  Schumpeter, Joseph Alois **14** 43-44
 endowments
  Eaton, Dorman Bridgman **5** 190-191
  Lawrence, Abbott **9** 246
  Schiff, Jacob Henry **14** 2-3
 foreign affairs
  Kissinger, Henry Alfred **9** 43-45
 geology
  Davis, William Morris **4** 425-426
  Whitney, Josiah Dwight **16** 254-255
 historians (19th-20th century)
  Adams, Henry Brooks **1** 45-47
  Bancroft, George **1** 483-484
  Channing, Edward **3** 435
  Haskins, Charles Homer **7** 191-192
  Sarton, George **13** 490-491
 historians (20th century)

Laski, Harold J. **9** 215-216
Morison, Samuel Eliot **11** 175-176
Salvemini, Gaetano **13** 455-456
Schlesinger, Arthur Meier **14** 13
Woodward, Comer Vann
　16 378-379
Law School
　Bok, Derek Curtis **2** 371-372
　Cox, Archibald **4** 283-284
　Eliot, Charles William **5** 254
　Frankfurter, Felix **6** 57
　Holmes, Oliver Wendell Jr.
　　7 458-459
　Pound, Roscoe **12** 417-418
　Sayre, Francis Bowes **13** 509
　Story, Joseph **14** 480-481
librarians
　Fiske, John **5** 465-466
　Stoddard, Solomon **14** 462-463
literature
　Cummings, Edward Estlin **4** 334-336
　Frost, Robert Lee **6** 130-133
　Howells, William Dean **7** 539-541
　Lewis, Cecil Day **9** 380
　Longfellow, Henry Wadsworth
　　9 499-500
　MacLeish, Archibald **10** 109-110
　Richards, Ivor Armstrong **13** 137
　Shahn, Ben **14** 139-140
mathematics
　Tarski, Alfred **15** 110-111
　Winthrop, John **16** 341-342
Medical School
　Bowditch, Henry Ingersoll
　　2 459-460
　Cushing, Harvey Williams
　　4 353-354
　Dubos, René Jules **5** 119
　Enders, John Franklin **5** 285-286
　Erikson, Erik Homburger **5** 309-310
　Hamilton, Alice **7** 98-99
　Holmes, Oliver Wendell **7** 457-458
　Theiler, Max **15** 169-170
　Waterhouse, Benjamin **16** 131-132
music
　Chávez, Carlos **3** 486
　Copland, Aaron **4** 227-228
　Holst, Gustav **7** 459-460
　Paine, John Knowles **12** 65
　Piston, Walter **12** 327-328
natural history
　Agassiz, Jean Louis Rodolphe
　　1 76-78
　Gray, Asa **6** 506-507
observatory
　Elsasser, Walter Maurice **5** 277-278
　Pickering, Edward Charles **12** 298
　Shapley, Harlow **14** 155-156
philosophy (19th-20th century)
　Perry, Ralph Barton **12** 239-240
　Royce, Josiah **13** 334-335
　Santayana, George **13** 475-477
　Whitehead, Alfred North
　　16 242-244
philosophy (20th century)
　Gilson, Étienne Henry **6** 327-328

Lewis, Clarence Irving **9** 381
Marcel, Gabriel **10** 233-234
Nozick, Robert **11** 438-439
Popper, Karl Raimund **12** 402
Quine, Willard Van Orman
　12 514-515
Tillich, Paul Johannes **15** 224-225
Wolfson, Harry Austryn **16** 361-362
physics
　Bridgman, Percy Williams **3** 5-6
political science
　Deutsch, Karl Wolfgang **4** 512-514
　Friedrich, Carl Joachim **6** 113-114
presidents
　Bok, Derek Curtis **2** 371-372
　Conant, James Bryant **4** 192-193
　Dunster, Henry **5** 152-153
　Eliot, Charles William **5** 254
　Everett, Edward **5** 344
　Lowell, Abbott Lawrence **10** 12-13
　Mather, Increase **10** 332-333
　Sparks, Jared **14** 363
psychology
　James, William **8** 215-217
　Lashley, Karl Spencer **9** 214-215
　Lewin, Kurt **9** 375-376
　Skinner, Burrhus Frederic
　　14 269-270
　Yerkes, Robert Mearns **16** 454-455
Sackler Museum
　Stirling, James **14** 458-459
sociology and anthropology
　Fletcher, Alice Cunningham
　　5 486-487
　Homans, George Caspar **7** 463-465
　Howells, William White **7** 541-542
　Kroeber, Alfred Louis **9** 105-106
　Sorokin, Pitirim A. **14** 348-349
　Stouffer, Samuel A. **14** 482-483
student policy
　Horner, Matina Souretis **7** 506-508

Harvest on the Don (novel)
　Sholokhov, Mikhail Aleksandrovich
　　14 203-204

Harvest Poems (book)
　Sandburg, Carl **13** 461-462

Harvey, Gabriel (1545?-1630?), English
poet
　Machiavelli, Niccolò **10** 97-99
　Spenser, Edmund **14** 373-376

HARVEY, WILLIAM (1578-1657), English
physician **7** 189-190
　Vesalius, Andreas **15** 473-475

Hary Janos (opera)
　Kodály, Zoltán **9** 71

Harzburg Front (Germany)
　Schacht, Hjalmar Horace Greeley
　　13 518-519

Harzreise im Winter (poem)
　Goethe, Johann Wolfgang von
　　6 388-391

Hasan (ca. 624-ca. 669), Arab caliph
　Aga Khan **1** 74-76
　Ali **1** 155-156

Muawiya ibn Abu Sufyan **11** 223-224

HASAN, IBN AL-HAYTHAM (ca.
966-1039), Arab physicist, astronomer,
and mathematician **7** 190-191

Hasan, Mansur ben
　see Firdausi

Hasan Ali Shah
　see Aga Khan I

Hasan ibn-Hani, al-
　see Abu Nuwas

Hasdrubal (died 221 B.C.), Carthaginian
general
　Hannibal Barca **7** 128-130

Hasdrubal Barca (died 207 B.C.),
Carthaginian general
　Hannibal Barca **7** 128-130
　Scipio Africanus Major, Publius Cor-
　　nelius **14** 61-62

Hasenöhrl, F. (1874-1915), Austrian mathematician and physicist
　Schrödinger, Erwin **14** 31-33

Hashemite (Arab dynasty; Mohammed's
clan)
　Husein ibn Ali **8** 63
　Mohammed **11** 76-78

Hashemite Kingdom
　see Jordan

Hashiloach (periodical)
　Ahad Haam **1** 88-89
　Bialik, Hayyim Nahman **2** 262-263
　Dubnov, Simon **5** 115-116

Hasidism (Jewish religious movement)
　Agnon, Shmuel Yoseph **1** 85-86
　Baal Shem Tov **1** 404-405
　Buber, Martin **3** 87-89
　Elijah ben Solomon **5** 251-252
　Heschel, Abraham Joshua **7** 358-359
　Judas Maccabeus **8** 374-375
　Luria, Isaac ben Solomon Ashkenazi
　　10 47-48
　Sachs, Nelly **13** 411-412
　Scholem, Gershom **14** 26
　Weber, Max **16** 160

Haskalah (Jewish movement)
　Scholem, Gershom **14** 26

Haskell Oriental Museum (University of
Chicago)
　Breasted, James Henry **2** 510-511

HASKINS, CHARLES HOMER (1870-1937),
American historian **7** 191-192

Hasmonean (dynasty of independent Jew-
ish nation; ruled 1st and 2nd century
B.C.)
　Herod the Great **7** 333-334

Hasong, Prince
　see Sonjo

HASSAM, FREDERICK CHILDE
(1859-1935), American impressionist
painter **7** 192
　Twachtman, John Henry **15** 362-363

HASSAN, MOULEY (King Hassan II; born 1929), inherited the throne of Morocco in 1961 **7** 194-195
   Allal al-Fassi, Mohamed **1** 162
   Mohammed V **11** 79-81

HASSAN, MUHAMMAD ABDILLE (1864-1920), Somali politico-religious leader and poet **7** 194-195

Hasse, Johann Adolf (1699-1783), German singer and composer
   Scarlatti, Pietro Alessandro Gaspare **13** 517-518

Hastenbeck, battle of (1757)
   Amherst, Jeffery **1** 200-201

Hastings, battle of (1066)
   Harold II **7** 162
   William I **16** 290-291

Hastings Center
   Callahan, Daniel **3** 231-233

HASTINGS, WARREN (1732-1818), English statesman **7** 195-196
   Burke, Edmund **3** 138-141
   Fox, Charles James **6** 35-37
   Metternich, Klemens von **10** 533-536
   Sheridan, Richard Brinsley **14** 183-184

Hastings, William Hastings, Baron (1430?-1483), English ambassador
   Richard III **13** 132-133

Hasty Pudding, The (poem)
   Barlow, Joel **2** 6-7

Hat on the Bed, The (stories)
   O'Hara, John **11** 485

Hatch Act (1887)
   Hatch, William Henry **7** 196

HATCH, WILLIAM HENRY (1833-1896), American reformer and politician **7** 196

Hatchlands (Surrey)
   Adam, Robert and James **1** 38-40

Hathorne, Nathaniel
   see Hawthorne, Nathaniel

Hatoyama, Ichiro (1883-1959), Japanese politician
   Kishi, Nobusuke **9** 41-43
   Sato, Eisaku **13** 495-496
   Yoshida, Shigeru **16** 464-465

Hats (political faction; Sweden)
   Gustavus III **7** 45-46

HATSHEPSUT (ruled 1503-1482 B.C.), Egyptian queen **7** 196-197
   Thutmose III **15** 216-217

HATTA, MOHAMMAD (1902-1980), a leader of the Indonesian nationalist movement (1920s-1945) and a champion of non-alignment and of socialism grounded in Islam **7** 197-199

Hattin, battle of (1187)
   Saladin **13** 441-442

Hatton, Sir Christopher (1540-1591), English statesman
   Raleigh, Walter **13** 9-11

Haugtussa (song cycle)
   Grieg, Edvard Hagerup **6** 541-542

Haulers, The (painting)
   Weber, Max **16** 160

Haunted Furniture (graphic art)
   Ensor, James **5** 289-290

Haunted House (play)
   Plautus **12** 348-350

HAUPTMANN, GERHART JOHANN ROBERT (1862-1946), German dramatist and novelist **7** 199-201
   Grillparzer, Franz **6** 546-547
   Lehmbruck, Wilhelm **9** 307
   Mann, Thomas **10** 204-207

Hausaland (region; northern Nigeria)
   Achebe, Chinua **1** 35-37
   Goldie, George Dashwood Taubman **6** 404
   Imam, Alhadji Abubakar **8** 114-115
   Muhammad, Elijah **11** 230-231
   Uthman don Fodio **15** 397-398
   see also Nigeria, Federal Republic of

HAUSHOFER, KARL (1869-1946), German general and geopolitician **7** 201

Hauspostille (poems)
   Brecht, Bertolt **2** 512-514

HAUSSMANN, BARON GEORGES EUGÈNE (1809-1891), French prefect of the Seine **7** 201-202

Hauteclocque, Philippe Marie de
   see Leclerc, Jacques Philippe

Havana (city; Cuba)
   Carleton, Guy **3** 300-301
   Howe, William **7** 538-539

Havana, University of
   Castro Ruz, Fidel **3** 365-368
   Machado y Morales, Gerardo **10** 92-93

Havana Conferences (1940; 1964)
   Castro Ruz, Fidel **3** 365-368
   Welles, Sumner **16** 191-192

HAVEL, VACLAV (born 1936), playwright and human rights activist who became the president of Czechoslovakia **7** 202-205

Hawaii (island chain; Pacific Ocean; state; United States)
   discovered
      Cook, James **4** 214-215
   dynasty established
      Kamehameha I **8** 416
      Kamehameha III **8** 416-417
   end of kingdom
      Kalakaua, David **8** 413-414
   exploration
      Kotzebue, Otto von **9** 91-92
   in literature
      Colum, Padraic **4** 174-175
   revolution (1893)
      Cleveland, Stephen Grover **4** 108-110
      Dole, Sanford Ballard **5** 46

      Liliuokalani, Lydia Kamakaeha **9** 411-412
   U.S. annexation
      Lodge, Henry Cabot **9** 482-483
      Dole, Sanford Ballard **5** 46

Hawaii, University of
   Krenek, Ernst **9** 98-99
   Wilder, Thornton Niven **16** 276-277

Hawaii Kai ("dream" city, Hawaii)
   Kaiser, Henry John **8** 412-413

Hawara (ancient site; Egypt)
   Petrie, William Matthew Flinders **12** 261-262

Hawikuh (Zuñi pueblo; New Mexico)
   Coronado, Francisco Vásquez de **4** 247
   Marcos de Niza **10** 240

Hawke, Edward, 1st Baron Hawke (1705-1781), English admiral
   Rodney, George Brydges **13** 239-240

HAWKE, ROBERT JAMES LEE (born 1929), Australian Labor prime minister **7** 205-206

Hawker Aircraft company
   Sopwith, Thomas Octave Murdoch **14** 345-346

Hawkesbury, Baron
   see Liverpool, 2nd Earl of

HAWKING, STEPHEN WILLIAM (born 1942), British physicist and mathematician **7** 206-208

HAWKINS, COLEMAN (1904-1969), American jazz musician **7** 208-210

HAWKINS, SIR JOHN (1532-1595), English naval commander **7** 210-211
   Drake, Francis **5** 94-96, 435
   Elizabeth I **5** 263-266

Hawks, Howard W. (1896-1977), American film director
   Bogart, Humphrey **2** 363-364

Hawks of Hawk-Hollow, The (novel)
   Bird, Robert Montgomery **2** 281-282

HAWKSMOOR, NICHOLAS (1661-1736), English architect **7** 211-212
   Gibbs, James **6** 301-302
   Vanbrugh, John **15** 409-410
   Wren, Christopher **16** 393-394

Hawkwood, Sir John de (died 1394), English soldier of fortune
   Andrea del Castagno **1** 223-224
   Uccello, Paolo **15** 378-379

Hawley-Smoot Tariff (1930)
   Hoover, Herbert Clark **7** 483-485

Haworth, Sir Walter Norman (1883-1950), English chemist
   Reichstein, Tadeus **13** 85-87
   Szent-Györgyi, Albert von **15** 62-64

HAWTHORNE, NATHANIEL (1804-1864), American novelist **7** 212-215
   Brown, Charles Brockden **3** 33
   Heavysege, Charles **7** 246
   Howells, William Dean **7** 539-541

Lowell, Robert Trail Spence Jr. **10** 16-17
Mather, Cotton **10** 330-332
Melville, Herman **10** 472-476
Warren, Robert Penn **16** 121-122
Wright, Frank Lloyd **16** 398-401

Hay Harvest (painting)
Bruegel, Pieter the Elder **3** 65-67

HAY, JOHN (1838-1905), American states-
man **7** 215-216
Adams, Henry Brooks **1** 45-47
Mahan, Alfred Thayer **10** 131-132

Hay Wain, The (oil painting)
Constable, John **4** 208-209

HAYA DE LA TORRE, VICTOR RAUL (born
1895), Peruvian political leader and theorist **7** 216-217
Leguía y Salcedo, Augusto Bernardino
9 305-306
Prado Ugarteche, Manuel **12** 430-431
Vallejo, César Abraham **15** 408-409

Hay-Bunau-Varilla Treaty (1903)
Bunau-Varilla, Philippe Jean **3** 120-121

HAYDEN, THOMAS EMMET (born 1939),
American writer and political activist
7 217-219
Fonda, Jane **5** 501-502

HAYDN, FRANZ JOSEPH (1732-1809),
Austrian composer **7** 219-221
Bach, Carl Philipp Emanuel **1** 414-415
Beethoven, Ludwig van **2** 114-117
Mozart, Wolfgang Amadeus
11 218-221
Schubert, Franz Peter **14** 35-37
Schumann, Robert Alexander **14** 41-43

Haydn, Johann Michael (1737-1806), Austrian composer
Weber, Carl Maria Friedrich Ernst von
16 156-157

HAYEK, FRIEDRICH A. VON (1899-1992),
Austrian-born British free market economist, social philosopher, and Nobel Laureate **7** 221-223

HAYES, HELEN (1900-1993), American
actress **7** 223-224

HAYES, CARDINAL PATRICK JOSEPH
(1867-1938), American cardinal
7 224-225

HAYES, ROLAND (1887-1977), African
American classical singer **7** 225-227
Anderson, Marian **1** 218-219

HAYES, RUTHERFORD BIRCHARD
(1822-1893), American statesman, presi-
dent 1877-1881 **7** 227-228
appointments (non-Cabinet)
Douglass, Frederick **5** 85-86
Harlan, John Marshall **7** 156-157
Cabinet
Evarts, William Maxwell **5** 340-341
Schurz, Carl **14** 44-45
Sherman, John **14** 184-185
domestic policies
Eaton, Dorman Bridgman **5** 190-191
Garrett, John Work **6** 225

Hampton, Wade III **7** 112
Lamar, Lucius Quintus Cincinnatus
9 170-171
election campaign (1876)
Chandler, Zachariah **3** 425-426
Hoe, Richard March **7** 435-436
Tilden, Samuel Jones **15** 222-223
political opponents
Conkling, Roscoe **4** 201-202
Field, David Dudley **5** 439-440
Pendleton, George Hunt **12** 198

HAYFORD, J. E. CASELY (1866-1903),
Gold Coast politician, journalist, and
educator **7** 228-230

HAYKAL, MUHAMMAD HUSAIN (born
1923), Egyptian journalist and editor of
al-Ahram(1957-1974) **7** 230-231

Hayley, William (1745-1820), English poet
Blake, William **2** 316-318
Romney, George **13** 269-270

Hayman, Francis (1708-1776), British
painter
Gainsborough, Thomas **6** 170-172

Haymarket Riot (Chicago; 1886)
Altgeld, John Peter **1** 180-182
Darrow, Clarence Seward **4** 396-397
Howells, William Dean **7** 539-541

HAYNE, ROBERT YOUNG (1791-1839),
American politician **7** 231-232
Jackson, Andrew **8** 168-172
Webster, Daniel **16** 162-164

Hay-Pauncefote treaties (1900; 1901)
Hay, John **7** 215-216

Haystacks (painting series)
Monet, Claude **11** 102-104

Haywain (triptych)
Bosch, Hieronymus **2** 426-428

Hayward, Nathaniel M. (1808-1865),
American inventor
Goodyear, Charles **6** 441

HAYWOOD, WILLIAM DUDLEY
(1869-1928), American labor leader
7 232-233
Darrow, Clarence Seward **4** 396-397

HAYWORTH, RITA (born Margarita Carmen Cansino; 1918-1987), American
actress **7** 233-235

Hazaken (Elder)
see Shammai

Hazard of New Fortunes, A (book)
Howells, William Dean **7** 539-541

HAZLITT, WILLIAM (1778-1830), English
literary and social critic **7** 235-236
Lamb, Charles **9** 176-177

He Left and Returned (play)
Asch, Shalom **1** 325-326

Head (sculpture)
González, Julio **6** 428-429

Head and House and Light (sculpture)
Boccioni, Umberto **2** 353-354

Head of a Woman (sculpture)
Gabo, Naum **6** 158-159

Head of a Young Woman (painting)
Degas, Hilaire Germain Edgar
4 461-462

Head of Baudelaire (sculpture)
Rodin, Auguste **13** 236-238

Head of Christ (painting)
Rouault, Georges **13** 321-322

Head of Christ (sculpture)
Zorach, William **16** 528

Head of Kofi (sculpture)
Ewonwu, Benedict Chuka **5** 351-352

Head, Sir Francis Bond (1793-1875), Eng-
lish soldier and colonial administrator
Baldwin, Robert **1** 466-468
Mackenzie, William Lyon **10** 104-106

Head Start program (United States education)
Johnson, Lyndon Baines **8** 308-312

HEADE, MARTIN JOHNSON (1819-1904),
American painter **7** 236
Lane, Fitz Hugh **9** 189

Headless Horseman (folk opera)
Benét, Stephen Vincent **2** 157-158

Headlong Hall (novel)
Peacock, Thomas Love **12** 169

Headsman, The (novel)
Cooper, James Fenimore **4** 220-223

Health and beauty aids
Arden, Elizabeth **1** 281-282
Rubenstein, Helena **13** 342-343

**Health and Human Services, United States
Department of**
Heckler, Margaret Mary O'Shaughnessy
7 251-252

Health care
ethics
Callahan, Daniel **3** 231-233
proposals, United States
Clinton, Hillary Rodham **4** 115-117

**Health, Education and Welfare, United
States Department of**
Abbott, Grace **1** 9-10
Berry, Mary Frances **2** 226-229
Eisenhower, Dwight David **5** 233-236
Hobby, Oveta Culp **7** 423-425
Perkins, Frances **12** 221-222
Switzer, Mary E. **15** 55-56
Wald, L. **11** 207
Weinberger, Casper Willard **16** 177-178

HEALY, BERNADINE (born 1944) American
physician and administrator **7** 237-238

HEANEY, SEAMUS JUSTIN (born 1939),
Irish poet, author, and editor **7** 238-240

Heard, Gerald (1889-1971), English writer
Huxley, Aldous Leonard **8** 74-75

HEARN, LAFCADIO (1850-1904), Euro-
pean-born American author **7** 240

HEARNE, SAMUEL (1745-1792), English explorer **7** 241-242

HEARST, GEORGE (1820-1891), American publisher and politician **7** 242

HEARST, PATRICIA (born 1954), kidnapped heiress who became a bank robber **7** 242-243

HEARST, WILLIAM RANDOLPH (1863-1951), American publisher and politician **7** 243-244
  Bennett, James Gordon Jr. **2** 169-170
  Bierce, Ambrose Gwinett **2** 269-270
  Dana, Charles Anderson **4** 384-385
  Hearst, George **7** 242
  Hughes, Charles Evans **8** 15-16
  Pulitzer, Joseph **12** 481-482

Heart (human)
  Harvey, William **7** 189-190

Heart (mechanical)
  DeBakey, Michael Ellis **4** 437-438

Heart, The (novel)
  Natsume, Soseki **11** 324-325

Heart disease
  Andersen, Dorothy **1** 212
  Barnard, Christiaan N. **2** 7-8
  Cabot, Richard Clarke **3** 200
  DeVries, William Castle **4** 518-519
  Houssay, Bernardo Alberto **7** 522-523
  see also Heart-attack victims

Heart disease victims
  Boerhaave, Hermann **2** 358-359
  Bright, Richard **3** 7-8
  Burns, Robert **3** 155-156
  Martineau, Harriet **10** 296-297
  see also Heart-attack victims

Heart of a Dog, The (novel)
  Bulgakov, Mikhail Afanasievich **3** 117

Heart of a Man, The (novel)
  Simenon, Georges **14** 233-234

Heart of Darkness, The (novel)
  Conrad, Joseph **4** 205-207

Heart of Happy Hollow, The (stories)
  Dunbar, Paul Laurence **5** 141-142

Heart of Maryland, The (play)
  Belasco, David **2** 124-125

Heart of Midlothian, The (novel)
  Edgeworth, Maria **5** 205-206
  Scott, Walter **14** 68-70

Heart of the Matter, The (novel)
  Greene, Graham **6** 523-524

Heart of the West (stories)
  Henry, O. **7** 308-309

Heart-attack victims
  Africa
    Danquah, Joseph B. **4** 388-389
  Australia
    Chifley, Joseph Benedict **3** 518
  China
    Hu Shih **8** 63-65
  Colombia
    Gómez, Máximo **6** 418-419

Egypt
    Farouk I **5** 387-388
England
    Arnold, Matthew **1** 311-313
    Chelmsford, Frederic John Napier Thesiger **3** 497
    Doyle, Arthur Conan **5** 91-92
    Edward VII **5** 214-215
    George II **6** 269-270
    Henderson, Arthur **7** 277-278
    Keynes, John Maynard **8** 528-530
    Pater, Walter Horatio **12** 130-131
    Robertson, Dennis Holme **13** 196
France
    Le Corbusier **9** 274-275
    Merleau-Ponty, Maurice **10** 518
    Michelet, Jules **11** 5-6
Germany
    Brecht, Bertolt **2** 512-514
Italy
    Marconi, Guglielmo **10** 239-240
Poland
    Peretz, Isaac Loeb **12** 212
Russia
    Berdyaev, Nicholas Alexandrovich **2** 184-185
    Dzerzhinsky, Felix Edmundovich **5** 173-174
    Eisenstein, Sergei Mikhailovich **5** 240-242
Spain
    Unamuno y Jugo, Miguel de **15** 386-387
United States (19th-20th century)
    Baker, Ray Stannard **1** 451-452
    Dreiser, Herman Theodore **5** 98-100
    Stettinius, Edward R. Jr. **14** 437-438
    Sumner, Charles **15** 30-31
    Sunday, William Ashley **15** 32-33
    Wharton, Edith **16** 221
United States (20th century)
    Fitzgerald, Francis Scott Key **5** 470-472
    Hillman, Sidney **7** 392-393
    Hubble, Edwin Powell **8** 10-11
    Kroeber, Alfred Louis **9** 105-106
    Lardner, Ringgold Wilmer **9** 204-205
    Lewis, Harry Sinclair **9** 385-387
    Rice, Elmer **13** 126-127

Heartbreak House (play)
  Shaw, George Bernard **14** 163-164

Hearts of Oak (play)
  Belasco, David **2** 124-125

Hearts of the World (film)
  Griffith, David Wark **6** 544-545

Heat (physics)
  conduction
    Fourier, Jean Baptiste Joseph **6** 32-33
  kinetic theory
    Born, Max **2** 420-421
    Debye, Peter Joseph William **4** 447-448
    Hooke, Robert **7** 475

    Lomonosov, Mikhail Vasilevich **9** 494
  mechanical theory
    Cavendish, Henry **3** 383-384
    Clausius, Rudolf Julius Emanuel **4** 92-94
    Hare, Robert **7** 152-153
    Joule, James Prescott **8** 363-364
    Rumford **13** 360-362
    see also Thermodynamics

Heat of the Day, The (novel)
  Bowen, Elizabeth **2** 462-463

HEATH, EDWARD RICHARD GEORGE (born 1916), prime minister of Great Britain (1970-1974) **7** 244-246

Heathcliff (literary character)
  Brontë, Emily **3** 18-19

Heauton Timorumenos (play)
  Terence **15** 146-148

Heaven Can Wait (film)
  Lubitsch, Ernst **10** 18-19

Heaven Has No Favorites (novel)
  Remarque, Erich Maria **13** 91

Heavenly mandate
  see Mandate of Heaven

Heaven's My Destination (novel)
  Wilder, Thornton Niven **16** 276-277

Heavy Odds (novel)
  Clarke, Marcus Andrew Hislop **4** 87-88

Heavy water (physics)
  Hevesy, George Charles de **7** 371

HEAVYSEGE, CHARLES (1816-1876), Canadian poet and dramatist **7** 246

HEBBEL, FRIEDRICH (1813-1863), German poet and playwright **7** 247

Hébert, Abbé Marcel (died 1916), French Catholic priest
  Martin du Gard, Roger **10** 295-296

HEBERT, JACQUES RENÉ (1757-1794), French journalist and revolutionist **7** 247-248
  Danton, Georges Jacques **4** 391-393
  see also Hébertists

Hébert, Louis Philippe (1850-1917), Canadian sculptor
  Cullen, Maurice Galbraith **4** 334

Hébertists (group; French Revolution)
  Danton, Georges Jacques **4** 391-393
  Hébert, Jacques René **7** 247-248
  Robespierre, Maximilien François Marie Isidore de **13** 199-201
  Saint-Just, Louis Antoine Léon de **13** 433

Hebrew (language)
  Abrahams, Israel **1** 29
  Ben Yehuda, Eliezer **2** 181-182
  Elijah ben Solomon **5** 251-252
  Pinto, Isaac **12** 318

Hebrew literature
  humanist influences
    Luzzato, Moses Hayyim **10** 57-58

Reuchlin, Johann **13** 106-107
medieval religious poetry
   ibn Gabirol, Solomon ben Judah
      8 92
   Judah Halevi **8** 373
nationalism
   Agnon, Shmuel Yoseph **1** 85-86
   Ahad Haam **1** 88-89
   Bialik, Hayyim Nahman **2** 262-263
   Tschernichowsky, Saul **15** 323 stud-
      ies of
   Zunz, Leopold **16** 534
   see also Jewish literature; Yiddish lit-
      erature

Hebrew Union College (established 1875,
Cincinnati)
   Heschel, Abraham Joshua **7** 358-359
   Wise, Isaac Mayer **16** 342-343

Hebrew Union College (New York City)
   Wise, Stephen Samuel **16** 344-345

Hebrew University (Jerusalem)
established
   Bialik, Hayyim Nahman **2** 262-263
   Weizmann, Chaim **16** 183-184
faculty
   Buber, Martin **3** 87-89
   Kaplan, Mordecai Menahem
      8 435-436
   Kaufmann, Ezekiel **8** 460
   Scholem, Gershom **14** 26

Hebrews, Epistle to the (New Testament)
   Luther, Martin **10** 48-51
   Paul **12** 141-143

Hebrides (overture)
   Mendelssohn, Moses **10** 488-489

Hecale (book)
   Callimachus **3** 235-236

Hecataeus of Miletus (flourished 500 B.C.),
Greek historian
   Herodotus **7** 330-333

HECHT, BEN (1894-1964), American journalist, playwright, and Hollywood
scriptwriter **7** 248-250
   Goldwyn, Samuel **6** 416

Heckel, Erich (1883-1970), German
painter
   Kirchner, Ernst Ludwig **9** 34-35

HECKER, ISAAC THOMAS (1819-1888),
American Catholic religious founder
7 250-251

Heckewelder, John Gottlieb Ernestus
(1743-1823), American Moravian Church
missionary
   Cooper, James Fenimore **4** 220-223

**HECKLER, MARGARET MARY
O'SHAUGHNESSY** (born 1931), American attorney, congressional representative, secretary of health and human services, and ambassador **7** 251-252

Hecla (ship)
   Ross, James Clark **13** 302-303

Hector and Andromache (painting)
   Chirico, Giorgio de **4** 4

Hector Imploring the Gods... (sculpture)
   Carpeaux, Jean Baptiste **3** 318-319

Hecuba (play)
   Euripides **5** 332-334

Hecyra (play)
   Terence **15** 146-148

Hedda Gabler (play)
   Ibsen, Henrik **8** 98-100

Hedgehog, The (novel)
   Doolittle, Hilda **5** 65-66

HEDIN, SVEN ANDERS (1865-1952),
Swedish explorer and geographer
7 252-253
   Przhevalsky, Nikolai Mikhailovich
      12 469-470

Hedonism (philosophy)
   Epicurus **5** 292-294
   Green, Thomas Hill **6** 520-521
   Sidgwick, Henry **14** 213
   Yüan Mei **16** 479-480
   see also Utilitarianism

Hedylus (novel)
   Doolittle, Hilda **5** 65-66

Hedyphagetica (poem)
   Ennius, Quintus **5** 289

Heemskerck, Jacob van (1567-1607),
Dutch navigator
   Barents, Willem **2** 4-5

Heemskerk (ship)
   Tasman, Abel Janszoon **15** 113-114

HEFNER, HUGH (born 1926), founder and
publisher of Playboy magazine
7 253-254

HEGEL, GEORG WILHELM FRIEDRICH
(1770-1831), German philosopher and
educator **7** 254-256
critics
   Feuerbach, Ludwig Andreas **5** 432
   Fries, Jakob Friedrich **6** 116-117
   Hobhouse, Leonard Trelawny
      7 425-426
   Kierkegaard, Søren Aabye
      8 547-549
   Popper, Karl Raimund **12** 402
   Schelling, Friedrich Wilhelm Joseph
      von **13** 526-527
   Schopenhauer, Arthur **14** 29-31
influence of (England)
   Bosanquet, Bernard **2** 425-426
   Bradley, Francis Herbert **2** 481-482
   Green, Thomas Hill **6** 520-521
   Jowett, Benjamin **8** 364-365
influence of (France)
   Comte, Auguste **4** 189-191
   Cousin, Victor **4** 273-274
influence of (Germany)
   Baur, Ferdinand Christian **2** 74-75
   Engels, Friedrich **5** 286-288
   Hölderlin, Johann Christian
      Friedrich **7** 451-452
   Lassalle, Ferdinand **9** 216
   Marx, Karl **10** 304-308
   Ritschl, Albrecht Benjamin **13** 180

Strauss, David Friedrich **14** 496-497
   Weber, Max **16** 157-160
influence of (Hungary)
   Lukács, Gyorgy **10** 37-38
influence of (Italy)
   Croce, Benedetto **4** 313-314
   Gentile, Giovanni **6** 267
influence of (Norway)
   Ibsen, Henrik **8** 98-100
influence of (Russia)
   Bakunin, Mikhail Aleksandrovich
      1 458-460
   Belinsky, Grigorievich **2** 128
   Cohen, Morris Raphael **4** 139-140
   Herzen, Aleksandr Ivanovich
      7 351-352
   Plekhanov, Georgi Valentinovich
      12 351-352
   Turgenev, Ivan Sergeyevich
      15 345-348
influence of (United States)
   Dewey, John **4** 520-523
   Harris, William Torrey **7** 177-178
   Krochmal, Nachman Kohen
      9 104-105
   Marcuse, Herbert **10** 245-247
   Wright, Frank Lloyd **16** 398-401
influenced by
   Boehme, Jacob **2** 357
   Kant, Immanuel **8** 430-432
   Vico, Giambattista **15** 480-481
students
   Brisbane, Albert **3** 9
   Feuerbach, Ludwig Andreas **5** 432
   Heine, Heinrich **7** 259-260

Hegira (622)
   Abu Bakr **1** 31-32
   Ali **1** 155-156
   Mohammed **11** 76-78
   Tabari, Muhammad ibn Jarir al-
      15 69-70

Heian period (Japan; 784-1184)
   Eisai **5** 231-232
   Ennin **5** 288-289
   Fujiwara Michinaga **6** 145-146
   Goshirakawa **6** 460-461
   Kammu **8** 420

Heidegger, John James (1659-1749), English theater manager
   Handel, George Frederick **7** 116-119

HEIDEGGER, MARTIN (1889-1976), Ger-
man philosopher **7** 257-258
influence of
   Arendt, Hannah **1** 282-284
   Bultmann, Rudolf Karl **3** 119-120
   Merleau-Ponty, Maurice **10** 518
   Ortega Y Gasset, José **12** 7-8
   Rahner, Karl **13** 4-5
   Sartre, Jean Paul **13** 491-492
influenced by
   Dilthey, Wilhelm Christian Ludwig
      5 10
   Kierkegaard, Søren Aabye
      8 547-549

Heidelberg, University of (Germany)
  chemistry
    Bunsen, Robert Wilhelm **3** 124-125
    Mendeleev, Dmitrii Ivanovich
      10 486-488
  historians
    Gierke, Otto von **6** 311-312
    Pufendorf, Samuel von **12** 477-478
    Troeltsch, Ernst **15** 299-300
  philosophy
    Driesch, Hans Adolf Eduard **5** 105
    Fries, Jakob Friedrich **6** 116-117
    Hegel, Georg Wilhelm Friedrich
      7 254-256
  physics
    Bothe, Walther **2** 438-439
  physiology
    Meyerhof, Otto Fritz **10** 537-539
    Wundt, Wilhelm Max **16** 402-403
  social sciences
    Mannheim, Karl **10** 208-209
    Weber, Max **16** 157-160
    Weidenreich, Franz **16** 171-172

Heidenmauer, The (novel)
  Cooper, James Fenimore **4** 220-223

**HEIDENSTAM, CARL GUSTAF VERNER
VON** (1859-1940), Swedish author
7 258-259

Heifer (sculpture)
  Myron **11** 285

Heiji Monogatari (chronicle)
  Toba Sojo **15** 248-249

Heilige Johanna der Schlachthofe, Die
(play)
  Brecht, Bertolt **2** 512-514

Heiligenkreuz-Gutenbrunn (Hungary)
  Maulbertsch, Franz Anton **10** 345

Heiligenstadt Testament (document)
  Beethoven, Ludwig van **2** 114-117

Heilner, Hermann (literary character)
  Hesse, Hermann **7** 367-369

Heimat (play and film)
  Sudermann, Hermann **15** 12-13

Heimkehr (poems)
  Heine, Heinrich **7** 259-260

Heimskringla (saga)
  Sturluson, Snorri **14** 310-311

HEINE, HEINRICH (1797-1856), German
poet and essayist **7** 259-260
  Arnold, Matthew **1** 311-313
  Byron, George Gordon Noel **3** 193-194
  Lazarus, Emma **9** 260-261
  Liszt, Franz **9** 445-447
  Rilke, Rainer Maria **13** 171-172
  Schubert, Franz Peter **14** 35-37
  Schumann, Robert Alexander **14** 41-43

HEINRICH, ANTHONY PHILIP
(1781-1861), American composer **7** 261

Heinrich von Ofterdingen (novel)
  Novalis **11** 435

Heir of Heaven, The (play)
  Lope Félix de Vega Carpio **9** 503-506

Heiress of Red Dog... (literary collection)
  Harte, Francis Brett **7** 184-185

Heiress, The (film; play)
  Burgoyne, John **3** 137-138
  Copland, Aaron **4** 227-228

HEISENBERG, WERNER KARL (born 1901),
German physicist **7** 261-263
  influence of
    Born, Max **2** 420-421
    Dirac, Paul Adrien Maurice **5** 23-24
    Einstein, Albert **5** 228-231
    Oppenheimer, J. Robert **11** 525-526
    Pauli, Wolfgang Ernst **12** 149
    Schrödinger, Erwin **14** 31-33
    Yukawa, Hideki **16** 481-482
  students
    Rabi, Isidor Isaac **12** 526-527
    Tomonaga, Sin-itiro **15** 265-266

Heiss Eisen, Das (play)
  Sachs, Hans **13** 410-411

Heitler, Walter (1904-1981), Irish physicist
  Bhabha, Homi Jehangir **2** 253-254

Heizer, Der (story)
  Kafka, Franz **8** 403-406

Hela (Norse mythology)
  Arnold, Matthew **1** 311-313

Held, Anna (1873-1918), French comedienne
  Ziegfeld, Florenz **16** 516-517

Helen in Egypt (novel)
  Doolittle, Hilda **5** 65-66

Helen of Troy (mythology)
  Euripides **5** 332-334
  Isocrates **8** 151
  Lindsay, Vachel **9** 424-425
  Yeats, William Butler **16** 445-447

Helena (novel)
  Waugh, Evelyn Arthur St. John
  16 145-147

Helene (literary character)
  Hauptmann, Gerhart Johann Robert
  7 199-201

Hélène (poem)
  Leconte de Lisle, Charles Marie René
  9 273-274

Helfferich, Karl (1872-1924), German
politician
  Erzberger, Matthias **5** 319-320

Helgoland (island; North Sea)
  Salisbury, 3d Marquess of **13** 448-449

Heliaea (Greek courts)
  Pericles **12** 219-221

Helicopter (aircraft)
  Kármán, Theodore von **8** 451-452
  Sikorsky, Igor **14** 223-224

Heliocentric theory (astronomy)
  see Universe, systems of—heliocentric

Heliodora (book)
  Doolittle, Hilda **5** 65-66

Heliogabius (book)
  Mencken, Henry Louis **10** 481-483

Heliography (photography)
  Daguerre, Louis Jacques Mandé
  4 365-366

Heliopolis (novel)
  Jünger, Ernst **8** 391-392

Helios (journal)
  Jiménez, Juan Ramón **8** 261-262

Helios (overture)
  Nielsen, Carl August **11** 388-389

Helium (element—chemistry)
  Kapitsa, Pyotr Leonidovich **8** 433-435
  Landau, Lev Davidovich **9** 184-185
  Mendeleev, Dmitrii Ivanovich
  10 486-488
  Soddy, Frederick **14** 321-323
  Stern, Otto **14** 435

Hell (painting)
  Limbourg brothers, The **9** 412-413
  Orcagna **11** 526-527

Hellancius (flourished 5th century B.C.),
Greek historian
  Thucydides **15** 211-212

Hellas (poem)
  Shelley, Percy Bysshe **14** 176-178

Hellenic League (Greek federation)
  Aratus **1** 273-274
  Cleomenes III **4** 103-104

Hellenica (book)
  Xenophon **16** 418-420

Hellenistic culture
  arts
    Praxiteles **12** 433-434
    see also Greek art and architecture
      (classical);Greek literature (classi-
      cal)
  Christianity and
    Clement of Alexandria **4** 102-103
  Egypt and Macedonia
    Alexander the Great **1** 137-141, 125
    Ptolemy I **12** 470-472
    Ptolemy II **12** 472-473
    Seleucus I **14** 92-93
  Roman Republic
    Cato, Marcus Porcius the Elder
      3 375
    Scipio Africanus Major, Publius Cor-
      nelius **14** 61-62
  science and
    Jabir ibn Hayyan **8** 167

HELLER, JOSEPH (born 1923), American
author **7** 263-265

HELLER, WALTER (1915-1987), chairman
of the Council of Economic Advisors
(1961-1964) and chief spokesman of the
"New Economics" **7** 265-266

Heller Altarpiece (painting)
  Dürer, Albrecht **5** 159-161

Hellespont
see Dardanelles

HELLMAN, LILLIAN FLORENCE (born 1905), American playwright **7** 267-268
Goldwyn, Samuel **6** 416

Hello, Dolly! (musical)
Wilder, Thornton Niven **16** 276-277

Hello Out There (play)
Saroyan, William **13** 486-487

Hello, Young Lovers (song)
Rodgers, Richard Charles **13** 234-236

Helmet, The (sculpture)
Moore, Henry **11** 146-148

HELMHOLTZ, HERMANN LUDWIG FERDINAND VON (1821-1894), German physicist and physiologist **7** 268-269
associates
Boltzmann, Ludwig **2** 379-380
Du Bois-Reymond, Emil **5** 118-119
Wundt, Wilhelm Max **16** 402-403
influence of
Bell, Alexander Graham **2** 129-131
Erlanger, Joseph **5** 310-311
Hill, Archibald Vivian **7** 385-386
Seurat, Georges Pierre **14** 120-122
students
Hertz, Heinrich Rudolf **7** 346-347
James, William **8** 215-217
Planck, Max Karl Ernst Ludwig **12** 342-344

HELMONT, JAN BAPTISTA VAN (1579-1644), Flemish chemist and physician **7** 269-271
Hales, Stephen **7** 75

HELMS, JESSE (born 1921), United States Senator from North Carolina **7** 271-272

Heloise (died 1163), French abbess
Abelard, Peter **1** 23-25-21

Help! (film)
Lennon, John Winston **9** 326-328

Help, Help, the Globolinks! (opera)
Menotti, Gian Carlo **10** 509-510

Help in Adversity (play)
Lope Félix de Vega Carpio **9** 503-506

HELPER, HINTON ROWAN (1829-1909), American author and railroad promoter **7** 272-273

Helsinki Central Railroad Station (Finland)
Saarinen, Eliel and Eero **13** 396-398

Helsinki Watch Group (Soviet Union)
Shcharansky, Anatoly Borisovich **14** 168-170

Helvering v. Davis (legal case)
Cardozo, Benjamin Nathan **3** 288-290

Helvetic Confession, First (Swiss religious statement)
Knox, John **9** 65-66

Helvetii (ancient Celtic tribe)
Caesar, Gaius Julius **3** 207-210

HELVÉTIUS, CLAUDE ADRIEN (1715-1771), French philosopher **7** 273-274
Baudelaire, Charles Pierre **2** 61-63
Smith, Adam **14** 283-284

HEMINGWAY, ERNEST MILLER (1898-1961), American novelist and journalist **7** 274-277
associates
Fitzgerald, Francis Scott Key **5** 470-472
Ford, Ford Madox **6** 1-2
Perkins, William Maxwell Evarts **12** 222-223
Stein, Gertrude **14** 414-415
film adaptations
Bogart, Humphrey **2** 363-364
Dos Passos, John Roderigo **5** 69-71
influence of
Callaghan, Edward Morley **3** 229-230
Ellison, Ralph Waldo **5** 274-275
Mailer, Norman Kingsley **10** 148-150
influenced by
Anderson, Sherwood **1** 220-221
Baroja y Nessi, Pío **2** 15-16
Donne, John **5** 60-61
Twain, Mark **15** 363-366

Hemoglobin (physiology)
Bernard, Claude **2** 208-210
Pauling, Linus Carl **12** 150-152
Whipple, George Hoyt **16** 224-225

HÉMON, LOUIS (1880-1913), French-Canadian novelist **7** 277

Hemophilia (medicine)
Haldane, John Burdon Sanderson **7** 70-71

Hench, Philip Showalter (1896-1965), American physician
Kendall, Edward Calvin **8** 495
Reichstein, Tadeus **13** 85-87

Henderson ... (novel)
Bellow, Saul **2** 141-143

HENDERSON, ARTHUR (1863-1935), British statesman **7** 277-278

HENDERSON, RICHARD (1735-1785), American jurist and land speculator **7** 278-279
Boone, Daniel **2** 397-398

HENDRIX, JIMI (born Johnny Allen Hendrix; 1942-1970), African american guitarist, singer, and composer **7** 279-283

Henéage Lloyd and His Sister (painting)
Gainsborough, Thomas **6** 170-172

HENG SAMRIN (born 1934), Cambodian Communist leader who became president of the People's Republic of Kampuchea (PRK) in 1979 **7** 283-285
Pol Pot **12** 382-384

Henley, William Ernest (1849-1903), English man of letters
Ford, Ford Madox **6** 1-2
Kipling, Joseph Rudyard **9** 32-33

Yeats, William Butler **16** 445-447

Hennebique, François (1842-1921), French engineer
Nervi, Pier Luigi **11** 346-348

Henotheism (religion)
Aeschylus **1** 70-72

Henri d'Orléans (1867-1901), French explorer
Bonvalot, Pierre Gabriel Édouard **2** 396

Henri I (king of Haiti)
see Christophe, Henri

Henri III et sa cour (play)
Dumas, Alexandre **5** 136-138

Henri, Robert (1865-1929), American painter
associates
Davies, Arthur Bowen **4** 409-410
Glackens, William **6** 355-356
Morrice, James Wilson **11** 181-182
influence of
Hopper, Edward **7** 497-498
Sloan, John **14** 274-275
students
Bellows, George Wesley **2** 143
Davis, Stuart **4** 424-425
Kent, Rockwell **8** 511

Henriade (epic)
Voltaire **16** 14-16

Henrietta Anne, Duchesse d'Orléans (1644-1670), daughter of Charles I of England
Bossuet, Jacques Bénigne **2** 431-432

Henrietta Maria (1609-1669), queen consort 1625-1649 of Charles I of England
Bossuet, Jacques Bénigne **2** 431-432
Charles I **3** 450-452
Charles II **3** 452-454
Jones, Inigo **8** 333-334

Henrique, Dom (died 1520), prince of Kongo and bishop of Mbanza (now São Salvador)
Affonso I **1** 72

HENRY I (876-936), king of Germany 919-936 **7** 285-286
Otto I **12** 28-29

HENRY I (1068-1135), king of England 1100-1135 **7** 286-287
Anselm of Canterbury **1** 244-245
David I **4** 407
Stephen **14** 426-427
William I **16** 290-291

Henry I (Holy Roman emperor)
see Henry I (king of Germany)

Henry II (973-1024), Holy Roman emperor and king of Germany 1002-1024
Riemenschneider, Tilman **13** 166

HENRY II (1133-1189), king of England 1154-1189 **7** 287-289
Church-State conflict
Becket, Thomas **2** 101-102
John of Salisbury **8** 284-285
French wars

Louis VII **9** 524-525
Philip II **12** 268-269
relatives
Eleanor of Aquitaine **5** 246-247
John **8** 274-275
Richard I **13** 130

Henry II (1333-1379), king of Castile and León 1369-1379
Edward III **5** 211-212
Edward the Black Prince **5** 217-218
López de Ayala, Pedro **9** 508-509

Henry II (1503-1555), king of Navarre 1517-1555
Henry IV **7** 293-295

Henry II (1519-1559), king of France 1547-1559
court
Clouet, Jean and François **4** 122-123
Coligny, Gaspard de **4** 159-160
Fernel, Jean François **5** 425-426
Paré, Ambroise **12** 94-95
opponents
Charles V **3** 457-459
patronage
l'Orme, Philibert de **9** 519
Lescot, Pierre **9** 354
Pilon, Germain **12** 305
Primaticcio, Francesco **12** 453-454
relatives
Marie de France **10** 259
Medici, Catherine de' **10** 445-449

Henry II-VII (kings of Germany)
see Henry II-VII (Holy Roman emperors)

HENRY III (1017-1056), Holy Roman emperor and king of Germany 1039-1056 **7** 290
Leo IX **9** 332

HENRY III (1207-1272), king of England 1216-1272 **7** 290-292
Alfonso III **1** 148-149
Edward I **5** 208-210
Grosseteste, Robert **7** 15
John **8** 274-275
Llewelyn ap Gruffydd **9** 468
Louis IX **9** 525-526
Montfort, Simon de **11** 132-133

Henry III (1379-1406), king of Castile and León 1390-1406
López de Ayala, Pedro **9** 508-509

Henry III (1551-1589), king of France 1574-1589
Bodin, Jean **2** 356-357
Coligny, Gaspard de **4** 159-160
Henry IV **7** 293-295
Medici, Catherine de' **10** 445-449

Henry III (king of Navarre)
see Henry IV (king of France)

HENRY IV (1050-1106), Holy Roman emperor and king of Germany 1056-1106 **7** 292
Godfrey of Bouillon **6** 379
Gregory VII **6** 532-534

Guiscard, Robert **7** 39-40
Matilda of Tuscany **10** 334-336
Urban II **15** 393

HENRY IV (1367-1413), king of England 1399-1413 **7** 292-293
associates
Chaucer, Geoffrey **3** 482-485
Glendower, Owen **6** 364-365
Gower, John **6** 475-476
relatives
Edward III **5** 211-212
Gloucester, Duke of **6** 370-371
John of Gaunt **8** 282-283
Richard II deposed
Charles VI **3** 460-461
Richard II **13** 130-131
Scottish conflict
James I **8** 206-207
Robert III **13** 194-195

HENRY IV (1425-1474), king of Castile and León 1454-1474
Isabella I **8** 144-145
Manrique, Jorge **10** 210-211

HENRY IV (1553-1610), king of France 1589-1610 **7** 293-295
patronage
Caccini, Giulio **3** 205-206
Champlain, Samuel de **3** 419-421
Le Jeune, Claude **9** 314-315
Rubens, Peter Paul **13** 339-342
relatives
Louis XIII **9** 529-531
Louis XIV **9** 531-533
struggle for throne
Essex, 2d Earl of **5** 321-322
Gorges, Ferdinando **6** 455-456
Mariana, Juan de **10** 254-255
Oldenbarnevelt, Johan van **11** 495-496

Henry IV (play)
Pirandello, Luigi **12** 319-321

Henry IV-VI; VIII (plays; Shakespeare)
see King Henry IV-VI; VIII

HENRY V (1081-1125), Holy Roman emperor and king of Germany 1106-1125 **7** 295-296
Frederick I **6** 78-79
Henry I **7** 286-287
Louis VI **9** 523-524

HENRY V (1387-1422), king of England 1413-1422 **7** 296-297
domestic conflicts
Glendower, Owen **6** 364-365
James I **8** 206-207
French wars
Charles VI **3** 460-461
Charles VII **3** 461-462
Gloucester, Duke of **6** 370-371
Joan of Arc **8** 264-265
Philip the Good **12** 278-279

HENRY VI (1165-1197), Holy Roman emperor and king of Germany 1190-1197
Frederick I **6** 78-79

Frederick II **6** 79
Innocent III **8** 125-127
Richard I **13** 130

HENRY VI (1421-1471), king of England 1422-61 and 1470-1471 **7** 298-299
Gloucester, Duke of **6** 370-371
Henry VII **7** 300-302
Joan of Arc **8** 264-265
Margaret of Anjou **10** 249-250
see also Roses, Wars of the

HENRY VII (1274-1313), Holy Roman emperor and king of Germany 1308-1313 **7** 299-300
Clement V **4** 101-102
Dante Alighieri **4** 389-391

HENRY VII (1457-1509), king of England 1485-1509 **7** 300-302
overseas exploration
Cabot, John **3** 199-200
Cabot, Sebastian **3** 200-201
Hawkins, John **7** 210-211
patronage
Caxton, William **3** 386-387
relatives
John of Gaunt **8** 282-283
Mary I **10** 308-309
Richard III **13** 132-133

HENRY VIII (1491-1547), king of England 1509-1547 **7** 302-305
Church and state
Coverdale, Miles **4** 278
Cranmer, Thomas **4** 295-296
More, Thomas **11** 156-157
Tyndale, William **15** 373-374
divorce issue
Charles V **3** 457-459
Henry VII **7** 300-302
Latimer, Hugh **9** 221
Norfolk, 3d Duke of **11** 423
Wolsey, Thomas **16** 364-366
French wars
Cromwell, Thomas **4** 320-321
Leo X **9** 332-334
Louis XII **9** 528-529
ministers and diplomats
Cromwell, Thomas **4** 320-321
Northumberland, Duke of **11** 431-432
Somerset, Duke of **14** 333-334
Wyatt, Thomas **16** 410-411
patronage
Cabot, Sebastian **3** 200-201
Holbein, Hans the Younger **7** 449-450
Skelton, John **14** 268-269
relatives
Edward VI **5** 213-214
Elizabeth I **5** 263-266
Mary I **10** 308-309

Henry (1519-1534), duke of Richmond and Somerset
Mary I **10** 308-309

Henry (died 1612), English prince, eldest son of James I
Chapman, George **3** 440-441
Raleigh, Walter **13** 9-11

Henry (1876-1934), prince of Mecklenburg-Schwerin
Wilhelmina **16** 278-279

Henry (IV, count of Luxemburg)
see Henry VII (Holy Roman emperor)

Henry (prince, Portugal)
see Henry the Navigator

HENRY, AARON (born 1922), African American civil rights activist **7** 306-307

Henry, Andrew (ca. 1775-1833), American trapper and miner
Ashley, William Henry **1** 333-334
Smith, Jedediah S. **14** 294-295

Henry, Edward Richard (1850-1931), British criminologist
Bertillon, Alphonse **2** 230-231

HENRY, JOSEPH (1797-1878), American physicist and electrical experimenter **7** 307-308
Morse, Samuel Finley Breese **11** 192-193

Henry, Joseph (1848-1898), French soldier
Dreyfus, Alfred **5** 103-105

HENRY, O. (pseudonym of William Sydney Porter; 1862-1910), American short-story writer **7** 308-309
McClure, Samuel Sidney **10** 398-399
Porter, Katherine Anne **12** 406-407

HENRY, PATRICK (1736-1799), American orator and revolutionary **7** 309-311
Clinton, George **4** 113-114
Lee, Richard Henry **9** 291-292
Madison, James **10** 121-123
Mason, George **10** 319-320
Tyler, Moses Coit **15** 369-370
Warren, Mercy Otis **16** 120-121
Washington, George **16** 126-129

Henry of Anjou
see Henry II (king of England)

Henry of Bolingbroke
see Henry IV (king of England)

Henry of Bracton (Bratton)
see Bracton, Henry de

Henry of Burgundy (1057?-1112), count of Portugal
Alfonso I **1** 148

Henry of Derby
see Henry IV (king of England)

Henry of Lancaster
see Henry IV (king of England)

Henry of Navarre
see Henry IV (king of France)

Henry of Trastamare
see Henry II (king of Castile and León)

Henry Plantagenet (duke of Normandy)
see Henry II (king of England)

Henry the Fowler
see Henry I (king of Germany)

Henry the Lion (1129-1195), duke of Saxony and Bavaria
Frederick I **6** 78-79

HENRY THE NAVIGATOR (1394-1460), Portuguese prince **7** 305-306
Cadamosto, Alvise da **3** 206-207
Manuel I **10** 219-220

Henry the Pious (1473-1541), duke of Saxony 1539-1541
Cranach, Lucas the Elder **4** 289-290

Henry the Proud (circa 1108-1139), duke of Saxony and Bavaria
Frederick I **6** 78-79

Henry Draper Catalogue, The (star catalog)
Cannon, Annie Jump **3** 260-261

Henry Street Settlement House (New York City)
Kelly, Florence **8** 483-484
Wald, Lillian **16** 53-54

Henslow, John Stevens (1796-1861), English botanist
Darwin, Charles Robert **4** 397-399

Henslowe, Philip (died 1616), English theatrical manager
Jonson, Ben **8** 343-345
Webster, John **16** 164

HENSON, JOSIAH (1789-1883), African American preacher and former slave **7** 311-312
Douglass, Frederick **5** 85-86

HENSON, MATTHEW A. (1866-1955), African American Arctic explorer **7** 312-314
Peary, Robert Edwin **12** 175-176

HENZE, HANS WERNER (born 1926), German composer **7** 314

Hepburn Act (United States; 1906)
Lodge, Henry Cabot **9** 482-483
Roosevelt, Theodore **13** 280-283
Tillman, Benjamin Ryan **15** 225-226

HEPBURN, AUDREY (born Edda Van Heemstra Hepburn-Ruston; 1929-1993), Swiss actress and humanitarian **7** 314-316

HEPBURN, KATHARINE (born 1907), American actress on the stage and on the screen **7** 316-317
Bogart, Humphrey **2** 363-364
Tracy, Spencer Bonaventure **15** 289-290

HEPPLEWHITE, GEORGE (died 1786), English furniture designer **7** 317-318
Sheraton, Thomas **14** 181-182

HEPWORTH, BARBARA (1903-1975), English sculptor **7** 318-319
Nicholson, Ben **11** 380-381

Hera (mythology)
Polykleitos **12** 385-386

Heracles (mythology)
see Hercules

HERACLIDES OF PONTUS (circa 388-310 B.C.), Greek philosopher **7** 319-320

HERACLITUS (flourished 500 B.C.), Greek philosopher **7** 320
Lucretius **10** 26-27
Schrödinger, Erwin **14** 31-33
Zeno of Citium **16** 499-500

HERACLIUS (circa 575-641), Byzantine emperor 610-641 **7** 320-321

Herakles (mythology)
see Hercules

Herald Building (New York City)
White, Stanford **16** 235-236

Heraldos negros, Los (poems)
Vallejo, César Abraham **15** 408-409

HERBART, JOHANN FRIEDRICH (1776-1841), German philosopher-psychologist and educator **7** 321-322
Fries, Jakob Friedrich **6** 116-117

HERBERG, WILL (1906-1977), Jewish theologian, social thinker, and biblical exegete **7** 322-323

HERBERT, EDWARD (1st Baron Herbert of Cherbury; 1583-1648), English philosopher, poet, diplomat, and historian **7** 324
Herbert, George **7** 324-326

HERBERT, GEORGE (1593-1633), English metaphysical poet and Anglican priest **7** 324-326
Crashaw, Richard **4** 296
Donne, John **5** 60-61
Herbert, Edward **7** 324
Milton, John **11** 43-46
Taylor, Edward **15** 122-123
Vaughan, Henry **15** 444-445
Walton, Izaak **16** 90-91

Herbert, Victor (1859-1924), Irish-American composer and conductor
Rodgers, Richard Charles **13** 234-236

Herblock
see Block, Herbert

Hercules (mythology)
as god
Diocletian **5** 19-20
in art
Apollodorus **1** 261
Giovanni da Bologna **6** 345-346
Pollaiuolo, Antonio **12** 377-378
Polykleitos **12** 385-386
in literature
Aeschylus **1** 70-72
Euripides **5** 332-334
Homer **7** 465-467
Kazantzakis, Nikos **8** 466-468
Seneca the Younger, Lucius Annaeus **14** 103-105
Sophocles **14** 343-345
in music
Handel, George Frederick **7** 116-119

Herculis, Marcus Aurelius Valerius Maximianus
see Maximian

HERDER, JOHANN GOTTFRIED VON
(1744-1803), German philosopher, the-
ologian, and critic **7** 327-328
  Goethe, Johann Wolfgang von
    6 388-391
  Hamann, Johann Georg **7** 92
  Jacobi, Friedrich Heinrich **8** 189-190
  Karamzin, Nikolai Mikhailovich
    8 441-442
  Klopstock, Friedrich Gottlieb **9** 55-56
  Richter, Johann Paul Friedrich
    13 150-151
  Schubert, Franz Peter **14** 35-37
  Vico, Giambattista **15** 480-481

Here at Home (book)
  Riley, James Whitcomb **13** 170-171

Heredero del cielo, El (play)
  Lope Félix de Vega Carpio **9** 503-506

Heredia, José Maria de (1842-1905),
French poet of Spanish parentage
  Gide, André **6** 308-309

Heredity
  see Eugenics; Genetics

Herenigde Nasionale
  see Volksparty (South Africa)

Herero (nation; southwest Africa)
  Maherero, Samuel **10** 139-142

Heresy (Atenist)
  Tutankhamen **15** 359-360

Heresy (Christian)
  12th-15th century
    Eckhart, Johann **5** 200-201
    Hus, Jan **8** 56-59
    Innocent III **8** 125-127
    Pius II **12** 331
    Waldo, Peter **16** 55-56
    William of Ockham **16** 298-299
    Wyclif, John **16** 412-413
  16th century
    Bruno, Giordano **3** 75-76
    Calvin, John **3** 239-242
    Cardano, Geronimo **3** 285-286
    Francis I **6** 40-43
    Latimer, Hugh **9** 221
    Paul IV **12** 145-146
    Tyndale, William **15** 373-374
    Zumárraga, Juan de **16** 531-532
  17th century
    Cotton, John **4** 263-265
    Dudley, Thomas **5** 124-125
    Hutchinson, Anne Marbury **8** 69-71
    Toland, John **15** 256
  19th-20th century
    Beecher, Henry Ward **2** 112-113
    Bushnell, Horace **3** 171-172
    Ireland, John **8** 133-134
    Teilhard de Chardin, Marie Joseph
      Pierre **15** 134-136
  Albigensian
    Dominic **5** 51-52
    Frederick II **6** 79
    Innocent III **8** 125-127
    Thibaut IV **15** 180-181

Arianism *see* Arianism Gnostic sects
  Clement of Alexandria **4** 102-103
  Donatus **5** 56-57
  Marcion **10** 238-239
  Montanus **11** 122
  Origen **11** 528-529
  Tertullian **15** 155-156
historians of
  Renan, Ernest **13** 95-96
iconoclastic controversy
  see Iconoclastic controversy
Jansenism
  see Jansenism
Manichaeism
  see Manichaeism
Nestorian
  see Nestorian controversy
Pelagianism
  Augustine **1** 367-370
  Jerome **8** 249
  Pelagius **12** 189-190
quietism
  Bossuet, Jacques Bénigne **2** 431-432
  Fénelon, François de Salignac de la
    Mothe **5** 410-411
  Molinos, Miguel de **11** 88-89

Heresy (Islam)
  Abu-L-Ala al-Maarri **1** 32
  Bukhari, Muhammad ibn Ismail al-
    3 111-112
  Tabari, Muhammad ibn Jarir al-
    15 69-70

Heretic (ballet)
  Graham, Martha **6** 485-486

Heretics (book)
  Chesterton, Gilbert Keith **3** 508-509

Heritage (poem)
  Cullen, Countee **4** 333-334

Heritage of the Kurts, The (novel)
  Bjørnson, Bjørnstjerne **2** 299-300

Herman, Woody (1913-1987), American
musician
  Stravinsky, Igor Fedorovich **14** 502-506

Hermandad (Spanish police)
  Ferdinand V **5** 417-418
  Manrique, Jorge **10** 210-211

Hermandad Mexicana Nacional, La (United States; Mexican American union)
  Corona, Bert **4** 243-247

Hermann (epic)
  Wieland, Christoph Martin **16** 260-261

Hermann I (died 1217), landgrave of
Thuringia
  Vogelweide, Walther von der **16** 10-11
  Wolfram von Eschenbach **16** 360-361

Hermann und Dorothea (epic)
  Goethe, Johann Wolfgang von
    6 388-391

Hermanns Tod (book)
  Klopstock, Friedrich Gottlieb **9** 55-56

Herman's Battle (play)
  Kleist, Heinrich von **9** 52-53

Hermeneutics
  Ricoeur, Paul **13** 157-158
  Schüssler Fiorenza, Elisabeth **14** 46-48

Hermes (mythology)
  Polykleitos **12** 385-386

Hermes Holding the Infant Dionysos
(sculpture)
  Praxiteles **12** 433-434

Hermetic poetry, Italian
  Montale, Eugenio **11** 117-118
  Quasimodo, Salvatore **12** 506
  Ungaretti, Giuseppe **15** 389-390

Herminie et Tancrède (cantata)
  Berlioz, Louis Hector **2** 203-205

Hermione (literary character)
  Racine, Jean Baptiste **12** 532-535

Hermitage (mansion; near Nashville, Tennessee)
  Jackson, Andrew **8** 168-172

Hermitage of the Banana Plant (Fukagawa,
Japan)
  Basho, Matsuo **2** 45-48

Hermits of Saint Augustine
  see Augustinian Friars

Hermod (Norse mythology)
  Arnold, Matthew **1** 311-313

Hermosa Ester, La (play)
  Lope Félix de Vega Carpio **9** 503-506

HERNÁNDEZ, JOSÉ (1834-1886), Argentine poet **7** 328-329

HERNÁNDEZ COLÓN, RAFAEL (born
1936), Puerto Rican governor **7** 329-330

Hernani (play; Hugo)
  Hugo, Victor Marie **8** 22-25
  Saavedra, Angel de **13** 398

Herne, James A. (1839-1901), American
actor and playwright
  Belasco, David **2** 124-125

Hero (ship)
  Palmer, Nathaniel Brown **12** 80-81

Hero, The (book)
  Gracián y Morales, Baltasar Jerónimo
    6 481-482

Hero and Leander (painting)
  Turner, Joseph Mallord William
    15 352-354

Hero and Leander (poem; Marlowe)
  Chapman, George **3** 440-441
  Marlowe, Christopher **10** 272-274

Hero of Alexandria
  see Heron of Alexandria

Hero of Our Times, A (novel)
  Lermontov, Mikhail Yurievich
    9 352-353

Herod Agrippa I (10? B.C.-44 A.D.), king of
Judea 41-44
  Paul **12** 141-143
  Peter **12** 252-253

Herod Antipas (circa 21 B.C.-39 A.D.), ruler of Judea
Jesus of Nazareth **8** 251-255
John the Baptist **8** 290

HEROD THE GREAT (circa 73-4 B.C.), king of Judea **7** 333-334

Herodes und Mariamne (play)
Hebbel, Friedrich **7** 247

Hérodiade (poem)
Mallarmé, Stéphane **10** 172-173

Herodias (14 B.C. -circa 40 A.D.), sister of Herod Agrippa I
John the Baptist **8** 290

Hérodias (story)
Flaubert, Gustave **5** 480-482

HERODOTUS (circa 484-circa 425 B.C.), Greek historian **7** 330-333
historical critics
Polybios **12** 384-385
Thucydides **15** 211-212
quoted
Cyrus the Great **4** 363-364
Darius I **4** 394-395
Miltiades **11** 42-43
Shabaka **14** 130
Thales **15** 161
Xerxes **16** 420

Héroe, El (book)
Gracián y Morales, Baltasar Jerónimo **6** 481-482

Heroic couplet (literary form)
Goldsmith, Oliver **6** 411-413
Pope, Alexander **12** 395-397

Heroic Symphony (musical composition)
Borodin, Aleksandr Profirevich **2** 422-423

Heroides (poem; Ovid)
Drayton, Michael **5** 97-98
Ovid **12** 34-36

Heroines (poem)
Theocritus **15** 171-172

HERON OF ALEXANDRIA (flourished circa 60), Greek engineer, mathematician, and inventor **7** 334-335
Fermat, Pierre de **5** 421-422

Herr Puntila und sein Knecht Matti (play)
Brecht, Bertolt **2** 512-514

Herr und Hund (book)
Mann, Thomas **10** 204-207

Herr Vogt (brochure)
Marx, Karl **10** 304-308

HERRERA, JUAN DE (circa 1530-1597), Spanish architect **7** 335
Churriguera, José Benito de **4** 53-54

HERRERA LANE, FELIPE (1922-1996), Chilean banker and economist **7** 336

Herrera the Elder, Francisco de (1576-1656), Spanish painter
Velázquez, Diego Rodríguez de Silva y **15** 454-456

HERRICK, ROBERT (1591-1674), English poet and Anglican parson **7** 336-339
Donne, John **5** 60-61
Góngora y Argote, Luis de **6** 427-428
Milton, John **11** 43-46
Plutarch **12** 359-360
Suckling, John **15** 10-11

Herridge, William Duncan (1888-1961), Canadian diplomat
Bennett, Richard Bedford **2** 171-172

HERRIOT, ÉDOUARD (1872-1957), French statesman and author **7** 339-340
Daladier, Édouard **4** 369

HERSCHEL, SIR JOHN FREDERICK WILLIAM (1792-1871), English astronomer **7** 340-341
Herschel, William **7** 341-343

HERSCHEL, SIR WILLIAM (1738-1822), German-born English astronomer **7** 341-343
Adams, John Couch **1** 51-52
Herschel, John Frederick William **7** 340-341
Laplace, Marquis de **9** 202-204

HERSHEY, ALFRED DAY (born 1908), American microbiologist **7** 343-345

HERSKOVITS, MELVILLE JEAN (1895-1963), American anthropologist **7** 345
Boas, Franz **2** 349-351

Hertford, 1st Earl of
see Somerset, Duke of

Hertford, 7th Earl of
see Gloucester, 8th Earl of

Hertwig, Richard von (1850-1937), German zoologist
Frisch, Karl von **6** 117-118

HERTZ, HEINRICH RUDOLF (1857-1894), German physicist **7** 346-347
Bose, Jagadis Chandra **2** 429-430
Einstein, Albert **5** 228-231
Helmholtz, Hermann Ludwig Ferdinand von **7** 268-269
Marconi, Guglielmo **10** 239-240

Hertzian waves
see Electromagnetic waves (physics)

Hertzog, Albert (born 1899), South African politician
Vorster, Balthazar Johannes **16** 30-32

HERTZOG, JAMES BARRY MUNNIK (1866-1942), South African prime minister 1924-39 **7** 347-348
Botha, Louis **2** 434-436
Luthuli, Albert John **10** 51-52
Malan, Daniel Francois **10** 163-164
Smuts, Jan Christian **14** 309-310
Verwoerd, Hendrik Frensch **15** 472-473

HERUY WÄLDÄ-SELLASÉ (1878-1938), Ethiopian writer and government press director **7** 348-349
Mäkonnen Endalkačäw **10** 161-162

Hervey, Frederick Augustus (1730-1803), English bishop
Soane, John **14** 314-315

Hervey, John (Baron Hervey of Ickworth; 1696-1743), English politician
Pope, Alexander **12** 395-397

HERZBERG, GERHARD (born 1904), German-born Canadian chemist/physicist **7** 349-350

Herzegovina (former province, Yugoslavia)
Mehmed the Conqueror **10** 452-454
Peter I **12** 256
see also Yugoslavia

HERZEN, ALEKSANDR IVANOVICH (1812-1870), Russian author and political agitator **7** 351-352
Bakunin, Mikhail Aleksandrovich **1** 458-460
Fourier, François Charles Marie **6** 31-32
Lermontov, Mikhail Yurievich **9** 352-353

HERZL, THEODOR (1860-1904), Hungarian-born Austrian Zionist author **7** 352-354
Ahad Haam **1** 88-89
Wise, Stephen Samuel **16** 344-345
Zangwill, Israel **16** 488-489

Herzog (novel)
Bellow, Saul **2** 141-143

HERZOG, CHAIM (1918-1997), president of the state of Israel **7** 354-355

Herzog Ernst von Schwaben (opera)
Mahler, Gustav **10** 144-145

HERZOG, ROMAN (born 1934), president of the German Federal Constitutional Court (1987-1994) and president of Germany **7** 355-357

HESBURGH, THEODORE MARTIN (born 1917), activist American Catholic priest who was president of Notre Dame (1952-1987) **7** 357-358

HESCHEL, ABRAHAM JOSHUA (1907-1972), Polish-American Jewish theologian **7** 358-359

HESELTINE, MICHAEL (born 1933), British Conservative politician **7** 359-361

Hesilrige, Sir Arthur (died 1661), English Parliamentarian soldier
Lilburne, John **9** 409-410

HESIOD (flourished circa 700 B.C.), Greek poet **7** 361-362
Aeschylus **1** 70-72
Augustine **1** 367-370
Braque, Georges **2** 504-505
Ficino, Marsilio **5** 436-437
Leconte de Lisle, Charles Marie René **9** 273-274
Proclus Diadochus **12** 457
Virgil **15** 507-510
Wolf, Friedrich August **16** 352-353

Hesiodic school
see Boeotian school (Greek literature)

Hesperides (poems)
Herrick, Robert **7** 336-339

HESS, VICTOR FRANCIS (1883-1964),
Austrian-American physicist **7** 362-363
Anderson, Carl David **1** 214-215
Millikan, Robert Andrews **11** 33-35

HESS, WALTER RICHARD RUDOLF
(1894-1987), deputy reichsführer for
Adolf Hitler (1933-1941) **7** 363-365
Hitler, Adolf **7** 417-420

HESS, WALTER RUDOLF (1881-1973),
Swiss neurophysiologist **7** 365

HESSE, EVA (1936-1970), American sculptor **7** 365-367

HESSE, HERMANN (1877-1962), German
novelist **7** 367-369

HESSE, MARY B. (born 1924), British
philosopher **7** 369-371

Hesselius, Gustavus (1682-1755),
Swedish-American painter
West, Benjamin **16** 210-212

Hesselius, John (1728-1778), American
painter
Peale, Charles Willson **12** 169-171

Hester (literary character)
Hawthorne, Nathaniel **7** 212-215

Het Volk (political party; South Africa)
Botha, Louis **2** 434-436
Smuts, Jan Christian **14** 309-310

Hetch Hetchie Canyon (painting)
Bierstadt, Albert **2** 270-271

Heterodoxia (essay)
Sábato, Ernesto **13** 399-400

Heth, Joice (died 1836), African American
entertainer
Barnum, Phineas Taylor **2** 13-15

Hettner, Hermann (1821-1882), German
art historian
Keller, Gottfried **8** 478-479

Heure espagnole, L' (opera)
Ravel, Maurice Joseph **13** 54-55

Heureaux, Ulises (circa 1846-1899),
Dominican president
Vázquez, Horacio **15** 448-449

Heureux qui comme Ulysse (sonnet)
du Bellay, Joachim **5** 113-114

Hevelius, Johannes (1611-1687), German
astronomer
Halley, Edmund **7** 88-89

HEVESY, GEORGE CHARLES DE
(1885-1966), Hungarian chemist **7** 371

HEWITT, ABRAM STEVENS (1822-1903),
American politician and manufacturer
7 371-372
Cooper, Peter **4** 223-224
George, Henry **6** 276

Hexachord system (music)
Guido d'Arezzo **7** 33

Hexapla (Old Testament work)
Origen **11** 528-529

Hexham, battle of (1464)
Henry VI **7** 298-299

Hexuronic acid
see Vitamin C

Heymann, Karl (1854-1922), German
pianist and composer
MacDowell, Edward Alexander
10 87-88

HEYSE, PAUL JOHANN LUDWIG
(1830-1914), German author **7** 372-373

Heyst (literary character)
Conrad, Joseph **4** 205-207

Heywood, John (1497-1580?), English epigrammatist
Donne, John **5** 60-61

HEYWOOD, THOMAS (1573/1574-1641),
English playwright **7** 373-374

Hezekiah (740?-686 B.C.), King of Judah
720?-686
Isaiah **8** 146-147
Sennacherib **14** 108

Hiawatha
see Song of Hiawatha, The

Hiawatha (sculpture)
Saint-Gaudens, Augustus **13** 432

Hibernia (ship)
Wilkes, Charles **16** 279-280

HICKOK, JAMES BUTLER ("Wild Bill";
1837-1876), American gunfighter, scout,
and spy **7** 374-375
Calamity Jane **3** 216

HICKS, EDWARD (1780-1849), American
folk painter **7** 375

Hicks, Elias (1748-1830), American Quaker
minister
Hicks, Edward **7** 375

Hicks, William (1830-1883), British general
in Egyptian army
Mahdi **10** 137-138

Hicks Beach, Sir Michael Edward
see Beach, Sir Michael Hicks

HIDALGO Y COSTILLA, MIGUEL
(1753-1811), Mexican revolutionary
priest **7** 375-377
Alamán, Lucas **1** 99-100
Guerrero, Vicente **7** 28-30
Iturbide, Agustín de **8** 155-156
Morelos, José María **11** 157-158
Santa Ana, Antonio López de
13 471-472

Hidalla (play)
Wedekind, Frank **16** 166-167

HIDAYAT, SADIQ (1903-1951), Persian
author **7** 377-378

Hidden Fortress, The (film)
Kurosawa, Akira **9** 135-137

Hide and Seek (novel)
Collins, William Wilkie **4** 169-170

Hideyoshi
see Toyotomi Hideyoshi

Hiero I (died 466 B.C.), tyrant of Syracuse
Pindar **12** 312-313
Xenophon **16** 418-420

Hiero II (308?-215 B.C.), king of Syracuse
270/65-215
Archimedes **1** 277-280
Theocritus **15** 171-172

Hieroglyph (Egyptian writing)
Champollion, Jean François **3** 421

Hieron (book)
Xenophon **16** 418-420

Hierusalem Verwoest (play)
Vondel, Joost van den **16** 19-20

Higgins, Margaret
see Sanger, Margaret

HIGGINS, MARGUERITE (1920-1966),
American journalist **7** 378-380

Higgins, William (1768?-1825), Irish
chemist
Dalton, John **4** 378-379

HIGGINSON, THOMAS WENTWORTH
(1823-1911), American reformer and editor **7** 380
Brown, John **3** 39-41
Burns, Anthony **3** 151
Dickinson, Emily **4** 541-543
Jackson, Helen Hunt **8** 172

High and Low (film)
Kurosawa, Akira **9** 135-137

High Museum of Art (Atlanta)
Meier, Richard **10** 456-458

High Place, The (book)
Cabell, James Branch **3** 195-196

High School Cadets, The (march)
Sousa, John Philip **14** 353-354

High Tor (play)
Anderson, Maxwell **1** 219-220

Highland Mary (song lyrics)
Burns, Robert **3** 155-156

Hija del aire, La (play)
Calderón, Pedro **3** 221-222

Hijo pródigo, El (play)
Lope Félix de Vega Carpio **9** 503-506

Hijra
see Hegira

Hilary (flourished 5th century), bishop of
Arles 429-449
Leo I **9** 329-330

Hilbert, David (1862-1943), German mathematician
Heisenberg, Werner Karl **7** 261-263
Kármán, Theodore von **8** 451-452
Tarski, Alfred **15** 110-111
Von Neumann, John **16** 27-28

Hilda Lessways (novel)
Bennett, Arnold **2** 167-168

Hildebrand
see Gregory VII, Pope

HILDEBRANDT, JOHANN LUCAS VON
(1663-1745), Austrian architect
7 380-381
  Donner, Georg Raphael **5** 63
  Fischer von Erlach, Johann Bernhard
    5 459-461
  Neumann, Balthasar **11** 354-355
  Prandtauer, Jakob **12** 432

HILDRETH, RICHARD (1807-1865), American historian and political theorist **7** 382

Hilferding, Rudolph (1877-1941), German Marxist writer
  Trotsky, Leon **15** 302-305

Hill, Aaron (1685-1750), English poet and playwright
  Gay, John **6** 243-244

Hill, Ambrose Powell (1825-1865), American Army officer
  Lee, Robert Edward **9** 292-294

HILL, ANITA (born 1956), African American lawyer and professor **7** 382-385

HILL, ARCHIBALD VIVIAN (1886-1977), English physiologist **7** 385-386
  Hodgkin, Alan Lloyd **7** 431-432
  Meyerhof, Otto Fritz **10** 537-539

HILL, BENJAMIN HARVEY (1823-1882), American politician **7** 386-387
  Yancey, William Lowndes **16** 436-437

HILL, HERBERT (born 1924), American scholar and civil rights activist **7** 387-388

HILL, JAMES JEROME (1838-1916), American railroad builder **7** 388-389
  Cooke, Jay **4** 215-216
  Durant, Thomas Clark **5** 157-158
  Harriman, Edward Henry **7** 164-165
  Knox, Philander Chase **9** 66-67
  Morgan, John Pierpont **11** 163-165
  Schiff, Jacob Henry **14** 2-3

Hill Wife, The (poem)
  Frost, Robert Lee **6** 130-133

HILLARY, EDMUND (born 1919), New Zealander explorer and mountaineer
7 389-390

Hillebrandt House (The Hague)
  Rietveld, Gerrit Thomas **13** 169

Hillel Hazaken
  see Hillel I

HILLEL I (circa 60 B.C. -circa 10 A.D.), Jewish scholar and teacher **7** 390-391
  Akiba ben Joseph **1** 97-98
  Johanan ben Zakkai **8** 271-272
  Judah I **8** 372-373
  Shammai **14** 149

Hillel II (flourished mid-4th century), Jewish patriarch
  Anan ben David **1** 207-208

HILLIARD, NICHOLAS (circa 1547-1619), English painter **7** 391-392
  Holbein, Hans the Younger **7** 449-450

HILLMAN, SIDNEY (1887-1946), Lithuanian-born American labor leader
7 392-393

  Dubinsky, David **5** 114-115
  Murray, Philip **11** 264-265

HILLQUIT, MORRIS (1869-1933), Russian-born American lawyer and author **7** 393-394

Hills Beyond, The (stories)
  Wolfe, Thomas Clayton **16** 355-356

HILLS, CARLA ANDERSON (born 1934), Republican who served three presidents as lawyer, cabinet member, and U.S. trade representative **7** 394-396

Hillside Home School (Spring Green, Wisconsin)
  Wright, Frank Lloyd **16** 398-401

Hillyer, Robert Silliman (1895-1961), American poet
  Roethke, Theodore **13** 243-244

Hilton, Walter (died circa 1396), English devotional author
  Rolle of Hampole, Richard **13** 260-261

Hilton Young Commission (1928)
  Kenyatta, Jomo **8** 512-514

Him (play)
  Cummings, Edward Estlin **4** 334-336

Himerologion katastromatos (poems)
  Seferis, George **14** 84-85

Himmel kennt keine Günstlinge, Der
(novel)
  Remarque, Erich Maria **13** 91

HIMMELFARB, GERTRUDE (born 1922), American professor, writer, and scholar
7 396-398

HIMMLER, HEINRICH (1900-1945), German Nazi leader **7** 398-399
  Goebbels, Joseph Paul **6** 384-385
  Göring, Hermann Wilhelm **6** 457-458
  Hitler, Adolf **7** 417-420

Hinayana (Buddhism)
  Buddha **3** 97-101
  Hsüan Tsang **8** 6-7
  Kukai **9** 124-125
  Kumarajiva **9** 127

Hincks, Francis (1807-1885), Irish-born Canadian statesman
  Baldwin, Robert **1** 466-468
  Lafontaine, Louis-Hippolyte **9** 157-158

Hind and the Panther, The (book)
  Dryden, John **5** 106-107

HINDEMITH, PAUL (1895-1963), German composer **7** 399-400
  Brecht, Bertolt **2** 512-514
  Grünewald, Matthias **7** 23-24
  Henze, Hans Werner **7** 314
  Stravinsky, Igor Fedorovich **14** 502-506
  Walton, William Turner **16** 92-93

HINDENBURG, PAUL LUDWIG HANS VON BENECKENDORFF UND VON
(1847-1934), German field marshal, president 1925-1934 **7** 400-401
  Bethmann Hollweg, Theobald von
    2 239-240
  Hitler, Adolf **7** 417-420

  Ludendorff, Erich Friedrich Wilhelm
    10 27-28
  Schacht, Hjalmar Horace Greeley
    13 518-519
  Victor Emmanuel III **15** 484-485

Hindu College (established 1816)
  Deb, Radhakant **4** 437

Hindu Orphan Relief Movement (established 1897)
  Rai, Lala Lajpat **13** 5-6

Hinduism (religion)
  and Jainism
    Mahavira, Vardhamana **10** 135-137
  and Sikhism
    Nanak **11** 303
  and Western civilization
    Bhaktivedanta Prabhupada
      2 254-255
    Bose, Jagadis Chandra **2** 429-430
    Carey, William **3** 297
    Jung, Carl Gustav **8** 388-389
    Roy, Ram Mohun **13** 18
    Yogananda **16** 462-463
  kriya yoga
    Yogananda **16** 462-463
  Moslem reaction
    Ala-ud-din **1** 102-103
    Aurangzeb **1** 377
    Chatterji, Bankimchandra
      3 480-481
    Gandhi, Mohandas Karamchand
      6 201-204
    Iqbal, Muhammad **8** 132-133
    Sapru, Tej Bahadur **13** 480-481
    Shah Jahan **14** 138-139
    see also India
  reformers
    Ambedkar, Bhimrao Ramji
      1 190-191
    Dayananda Saraswati **4** 431
    Deb, Radhakant **4** 437
    Radhakrishnan, Sarvepalli
      12 537-538
    Ramakrishna, Sri **13** 11-13
    Shankara **14** 150-151
    Rabindranath Tagore **12** 529-531
    Vivekananda **16** 4-5

Hiner, Cincinnatus
  see Miller, Joaquin

Hines, Earl Fatha (1905-1983), African American pianist
  Armstrong, Louis Daniel **1** 303-304

HINES, GREGORY OLIVER (born 1946), American dancer and actor **7** 401-403

Hinkemann (play)
  Toller, Ernst **15** 261

Hinks, Roger Packman (1903-1963), English art historian
  Caravaggio **3** 282-284

HINOJOSA, ROLANDO (born 1929), Hispanic-American author **7** 403-405

HINSHELWOOD, SIR CYRIL NORMAN
(1897-1967), English chemist **7** 405-406
Semenov, Nikolai Nikolaevich **14** 101

HINTON, SUSAN ELOISE (born 1950),
American novelist and screenwriter
7 406-407

HIPPARCHUS (flourished 162-126 B.C.),
Greek astronomer **7** 407-408
Aristarchus of Samos **1** 290-291
Ptolemy, Claudius **12** 473-474
Xenophon **16** 418-420

Hippies
see Bohemian life-style

Hippius, Zinaida (Zinaida Merezhkovsky;
1869-1945), Russian poet, novelist, and
critic
Merezhkovsky, Dmitry Sergeyevich
10 515-516

Hippo (modern Bône, Algeria)
Augustine **1** 367-370
Gaiseric **6** 172

HIPPOCRATES (circa 460-circa 377 B.C.),
Greek physician **7** 408-410
Cardano, Geronimo **3** 285-286
Celsus, Aulus Cornelius **3** 393
Galen **6** 178-180
Poliziano, Angelo **12** 373-374
Rabelais, François **12** 524-526
Sydenham, Thomas **15** 59-60

Hippocratic Corpus (book; Hippocrates)
Avicenna **1** 386-387
Galen **6** 178-180
Hippocrates **7** 408-410

Hippocratic oath (medicine)
Hippocrates **7** 408-410

Hippodrome (Constantinople)
Justinian I **8** 393-395

Hippolyte (literary character)
Racine, Jean Baptiste **12** 532-535

Hippolyte et Aricie (opera)
Rameau, Jean Philippe **13** 17-18

Hippolytus (play)
Euripides **5** 332-334

Hippolytus, Saint (died circa 236), Early
Christian writer
Marcion **10** 238-239

Hippolytus Temporizes (verse play)
Doolittle, Hilda **5** 65-66

HIROHITO (1901-1989), emperor of Japan
7 410-412

HIROSHIGE, ANDO (1797-1858), Japan-
ese painter and printmaker **7** 412-413
Burchfield, Charles **3** 131-132
Hartley, Marsden **7** 186

Hiroshima (city; Japan)
Compton, Arthur Holly **4** 186-188
Einstein, Albert **5** 228-231
Hirohito **7** 410-412
Oppenheimer, J. Robert **11** 525-526
Roosevelt, Franklin Delano **13** 277-280
Szilard, Leo **15** 64-66

Truman, Harry S. **15** 314-316

Hiroshima Peace Hall (1949)
Tange, Kenzo **15** 99-101

Hirota, Koki (1878-1948), Japanese diplomat and politician
Yoshida, Shigeru **16** 464-465

Hirsch, Emil Gustav (1851-1923), rabbi
and Talmudic scholar
Graetz, Heinrich Hirsch **6** 483

His Eye on the Main Chance (play)
Alarcón, Pedro Antonio de **1** 100-101

His New Job (film)
Chaplin, Charles Spencer **3** 438-440

His Noble Numbers (poems)
Herrick, Robert **7** 336-339

Hisab al-Jabr wa-al-Muqabala (book)
Khwarizmi, Muhammad ibn Musa al-
8 541

Hisago (anthology ; Chinseki)
Basho, Matsuo **2** 45-48

Hisinger, Wilhelm (1766-1852), Swedish
geologist and mineralogist
Berzelius, Jöns Jacob **2** 231-233

Hispaniola (island; West Indies)
exploration
Benalcázar, Sebastián de **2** 145-146
Columbus, Christopher **4** 176-179
Cortés, Hernán **4** 255-256
Drake, Francis **5** 94-96
Ponce de León, Juan **12** 391-392
slave revolts
Dessalines, Joan Jacques **4** 511-512
Toussaint L'Ouverture, François
Dominique **15** 278-279
see Dominican Republic; Haiti; for
later period

HISS, ALGER (1904-1996), U.S. State
Department official convicted of having
provided classified documents to an
admitted Communist **7** 413-415
Acheson, Dean Gooderham **1** 37-38
Chambers, Whittaker **3** 416-417
Nixon, Richard Milhous **11** 401-404

Hissarlik (ancient Troy; Turkey)
Homer **7** 465-467

Histadruth
see Jewish Federation of Labor

Histamine (biochemistry)
Best, Charles Herbert **2** 236-237
Dale, Henry Hallett **4** 371-373

Histoire contemporaine, L' (book)
France, Anatole **6** 39-40

Histoire de Juliette (novel)
Sade, Comte de **13** 416-418

Histoire de la Princesse de Montpensier, L'
(story)
La Fayette, Comtesse de **9** 150-151

Histoire de Port-Royal (book)
Sainte-Beuve, Charles Augustin **13** 438

Histoire d'eau, Une (film)
Truffaut, François **15** 311-313

**Histoire du chevalier des Grieux et de
Manon Lescaut, L'**
see Manon Lescaut (novel)

Histoire d'un merle blanc (story)
Musset, Louis Charles Alfred de
11 271-272

Histoire naturelle... (books)
Buffon, Comte de **3** 109-111

Histology (science)
Ehrlich, Paul **5** 225-226
Malpighi, Marcello **10** 176-178
Schwann, Theodor **14** 51-52

Historia Anglorum (book)
Matthew Paris **10** 341-342

Historia animalium (book; Aristotle)
Linnaeus, Carl **9** 427-429

Historia animalium (encyclopedia)
Gesner, Konrad von **6** 287

Historia arcana
see Secret History (book)

Historia Brutonum
see Brut (poem)

Historia de las Indias (book)
Las Casas, Bartolomé de **9** 211-212

Historia ecclesiastica gentis anglorum
(book)
Bede **2** 109-110

Historia regum Britanniae
see History of the Kings of Britain

Historical Association (Great Britain)
Pollard, Albert Frederick **12** 378

Historical linguistics
see Linguistics

**Historical Materialism and Marxist Eco-
nomics** (book)
Croce, Benedetto **4** 313-314

Historical Register...1736, The (political
satire)
Fielding, Henry **5** 442-444

Historicism (philosophy)
Croce, Benedetto **4** 313-314
Dilthey, Wilhelm Christian Ludwig **5** 10
Herder, Johann Gottfried von **7** 327-328
Meinecke, Friedrich **10** 460-461
Troeltsch, Ernst **15** 299-300

Historicopositivism (theology)
Harnack, Adolf von **7** 160

Historietas nacionales (stories)
Alarcón, Pedro Antonio de **1** 100-101

Historiography (social science)
African American experience
Franklin, John Hope **6** 65-67
Woodson, Carter Godwin
16 374-376
and politics
Zinn, Howard **16** 520-521
Annales School
Braudel, Fernand **2** 507-508

art
    Brookner, Anita **3** 23-24
    Clark, Kenneth M. **4** 79-80
Biblical *see* Bible chronicles
    Chaucer, Geoffrey **3** 482-485
    Comines, Philippe de **4** 181
    Froissart, Jean **6** 124-125
    Joinville, Jean de **8** 325
    Matthew Paris **10** 341-342
    Muratori, Lodovico Antonio
      11 254-255
    Villehardouin, Geffroi de **15** 499
    William of Tyre **16** 299-300
Canada
    Innis, Harold Adams **8** 124-125
Christianity
    Pagels, Elaine Hiesey **12** 61-62
classical (ancient Greece)
    Herodotus **7** 330-333
    Plutarch **12** 359-360
    Polybios **12** 384-385
    Procopius of Caesarea **12** 457-458
    Thucydides **15** 211-212
    Xenophon **16** 418-420
classical (ancient Rome)
    Caesar, Gaius Julius **3** 207-210
    Cato, Marcus Porcius the Elder
      3 375
    Livy **9** 465-467
    Sallust **13** 454
    Suetonius Tranquillus, Gaius **15** 13
    Tacitus **15** 70-72
classical (Jewish)
    Josephus Flavius **8** 360-361
Cold War
    Kennan, George F. **8** 496-498
communications
    McLuhan, Marshall **10** 424-426
cultural history
    Altamira Y Crevea, Rafael **1** 179
    Burckhardt, Jacob Christoph
      3 132-133
    Foucault, Michel **6** 29-30
    Garneau, François-Xavier **6** 219-220
    Huizinga, Johan **8** 26-27
    Ssu-ma Ch'ien **14** 388-389
    Wagner, Richard **16** 40-43
England (16th-18th century)
    Gibbon, Edward **6** 299-300
    Hakluyt, Richard **7** 70
    Wedgwood, Cicely Veronica
      16 167-168
England (19th-20th century)
    Acton, John Emerich Edward Dal-
      berg **1** 38
    Buckle, Henry Thomas **3** 95-96
    Carlyle, Thomas **3** 304-305
    Froude, James Anthony **6** 133-134
    Gardiner, Samuel Rawson **6** 211
    Gooch, George Peabody **6** 432-433
    Lecky, William Edward Hartpole
      9 271-272
    Maitland, Frederic William
      10 154-155
    Namier, Lewis Bernstein
      11 301-303

Pollard, Albert Frederick **12** 378
Toynbee, Arnold Joseph **15** 283-284
Trevelyan, George Macaulay
    15 294-295
federalism
    Palacký, František **12** 69-70
France
    Aulard, François Victor Alphonse
      1 374
    Guizot, François Pierre Guillaume
      7 40-41
    Halévy, Élie **7** 76
    Lefebvre, Georges **9** 301-302
    Mathiez, Albert **10** 333-334
    Thiers, Louis Adolphe **15** 181-182
Germany
    Meinecke, Friedrich **10** 460-461
    see also Objective school(below)
intellectual history
    Commager, Henry Steele **4** 181-183
    Lasch, Christopher **9** 212-214
Italy
    Ferrero, Guglielmo **5** 429-430
    Guicciardini, Francesco **7** 32-33
    Sarpi, Paolo **13** 487-488
    Vasari, Giorgio **15** 442-443
Latin America
    Sierra, Justo **14** 217
    Varnhagen, Francisco Adolfo de
      15 437-438
liberal theology
    Meland, Bernard Eugene
      10 467-468
medieval
    Alexius I **1** 143-144
    Comnena, Anna **4** 185-186
    Gregory of Tours **6** 534-535
    ibn Khaldun, Abd al-Rahman ibn
      Muhammad **8** 93-94
    Kim Pusik **9** 8-9
    Otto of Freising **12** 30
    Ou-yang Hsiu **12** 33-34
Mexico
    Cosio Villegas, Daniel **4** 260-261
nationalism
    Karamzin, Nikolai Mikhailovich
      8 441-442
New England
    Miller, Perry **11** 28-29
New History movement
    Beard, Charles Austin **2** 84
    Parrington, Vernon Louis
      12 119-120
    Robinson, James Harvey **13** 208
    Spencer, Herbert **14** 369-370
Nigeria
    Dike, Kenneth **5** 7-8
Objective School
    Lavisse, Ernest **9** 241
    Mommsen, Theodor **11** 94-95
    Niebuhr, Barthold Georg
      11 385-386
    Ranke, Leopold von **13** 33-35
    Treitschke, Heinrich von
      15 293-294
of medieval society

Coulton, George Gordon **4** 267
Fustel de Coulanges, Numa Denis
    6 155
Haskins, Charles Homer **7** 191-192
Montesquieu **11** 123-125
Pirenne, Jean Henri Otto Lucien
    Marie **12** 322-323
Vinogradoff, Paul Gavrilovitch
    15 503
philosophy
    MacIntyre, Alasdair Chalmers
      10 99-100
Protestant bias
    Motley, John Lothrop **11** 211-212
Puritanism
    Miller, Perry **11** 28-29
religion
    Eliade, Mircea **5** 249-250
religion in America
    Marty, Martin E. **10** 300-301
Renaissance diplomacy
    Mattingly, Garrett **10** 342-344
Russia
    Billington, James Hadley **2** 275-276
science
    Kuhn, Thomas Samuel **9** 121-123
socioeconomic approach
    Beard, Mary Ritter **2** 85-86
    Klyuchevsky, Vasily Osipovich
      9 57-58
    Nevins, Allan **11** 357-359
    Salvemini, Gaetano **13** 455-456
sociological conception
    Dubnov, Simon **5** 115-116
    Hammond, Lawrence and Lucy
      7 109
    ibn Khaldun, Abd al-Rahman ibn
      Muhammad **8** 93-94
    McMaster, John Bach **10** 426-427
    Schlesinger, Arthur Meier **14** 13
    Sorel, Albert **14** 346-347
source research
    Bancroft, Hubert Howe **1** 484-485
    Gardiner, Samuel Rawson **6** 211
    Huang Tsung-hsi **8** 9-10
    Pan Ku **12** 86-87
    Sparks, Jared **14** 363
    Ssu-ma kuang **14** 390-391
    Wei Yüan **16** 180-181
Spain
    Altamira Y Crevea, Rafael **1** 179
    Mattingly, Garrett **10** 342-344
urban culture
    Green, Constance McLaughlin
      6 518-519
United States (18th-19th century)
    Ramsay, David **13** 21
    Tucker, George **15** 332-333
United States (19th century)
    Adams, Peter Chardon Brooks **1** 54
    Adams, Herbert Baxter **1** 47
    Bancroft, George **1** 483-484
    Hildreth, Richard **7** 382
    Irving, Washington **8** 141-143
    Lea, Henry Charles **9** 261-262
    Motley, John Lothrop **11** 211-212

Parkman, Francis **12** 113-115
Prescott, William Hickling **12** 440-441
Tyler, Moses Coit **15** 369-370
United States (19th-20th century)
 Andrews, Charles McLean **1** 231
 Bancroft, Hubert Howe **1** 484-485
 Du Bois, William Edward Burghardt **5** 116-118
 Dunning, William Archibald **5** 148-149
 Green, Constance McLaughlin **6** 518-519
 Morison, Samuel Eliot **11** 175-176
 Motley, John Lothrop **11** 211-212
 Nevins, Allan **11** 357-359
 Osgood, Herbert Levi **12** 18-19
 Potter, David M. **12** 412
 Rhodes, James Ford **13** 122
 Rostovtzeff, Michael Ivanovich **13** 315
 Turner, Frederick Jackson **15** 350-351
United States (20th century)
 Becker, Carl Lotus **2** 100-101
 Boorstin, Daniel J. **2** 398-400
 Commager, Henry Steele **4** 181-183
 Handlin, Oscar **7** 121-122
 Hofstadter, Richard **7** 444-445
 Kennan, George F. **8** 496-498
 Wolfson, Harry Austryn **16** 361-362
 Woodson, Carter Godwin **16** 374-376
Victorian England
 Himmelfarb, Gertrude **7** 396-398
women's roles
 Conway, Jill Kathryn Ker **4** 213-214
 see also History; Jewish history; Social scientists—historians; New History movement (above)

History
 development and scope
  Bloch, Marc **2** 332-333
  Gumplowicz, Ludwig **7** 41
  Lovejoy, Arthur Oncken **10** 6
  Meinecke, Friedrich **10** 460-461
  Montesquieu **11** 123-125
 evolutionary process
  Chang Hsüeh-ch'eng **3** 433
  Fiske, John **5** 465-466
  Saint-Simon, Comte de **13** 436-437
  Wang Fu-chih **16** 99-101
 philosophy of
  Augustine **1** 367-370
  Fichte, Johann Gottlieb **5** 435-436
  Herder, Johann Gottfried von **7** 327-328
  Huizinga, Johan **8** 26-27
  Joachim of Fiore **8** 263-264
  Marx, Karl **10** 304-308
  Ortega Y Gasset, José **12** 7-8
  Radhakrishnan, Sarvepalli **12** 537-538
  Toynbee, Arnold Joseph **15** 283-284
  Vico, Giambattista **15** 480-481

psychoanalytic and psychogenetic theories
 Freud, Sigmund **6** 103-106
 Lamprecht, Karl **9** 181
racial theories
 Chamberlain, Houston Stewart **3** 411
 Gobineau, Comte de **6** 375-376
scientific approach
 Buckle, Henry Thomas **3** 95-96
 Draper, John William **5** 96-97
 Ku Chieh-kang **9** 120-121
 Popper, Karl Raimund **12** 402
 Spengler, Oswald **14** 372-373
 see also Historiography; Social scientists—historians

History and Adventures of the Renowned Don Quixote, The
 see Don Quixote

History and Remarkable Life of the Truly Honourable Col. Jacque, The (book)
 Defoe, Daniel **4** 457-459

History of a Contra-octave, The (story)
 Pasternak, Boris Leonidovich **12** 124-125

History of a Good Warm Watch, The (book)
 Sterne, Laurence **14** 435-437

History of a Literary Radical (book)
 Bourne, Randolph Silliman **2** 456-457

History of Communication (mural)
 Davis, Stuart **4** 424-425

History of Constantine the Great (tapestry series)
 Rubens, Peter Paul **13** 339-342

History of Deeds Done beyond the Sea (book)
 William of Tyre **16** 299-300

History of Egypt (book)
 Breasted, James Henry **2** 510-511
 Petrie, William Matthew Flinders **12** 261-262

History of England (book)
 Hume, David **8** 31-34
 Macaulay, Thomas Babington **10** 79-80

History of Eternity (book)
 Borges, Jorge Luis **2** 411-412

History of Henry Esmond, The (novel)
 Thackeray, William Makepeace **15** 159-161

History of Henry VII (book)
 Bacon, Francis **1** 422-424

History of Mr. Polly, The (novel)
 Wells, Herbert George **16** 195-196

History of New England, The (book)
 Winthrop, John **16** 339-341

History of Samuel Titmarsh... (story)
 Thackeray, William Makepeace **15** 159-161

History of the Adventures of Joseph Andrews... (novel)

Fielding, Henry **5** 442-444

History of the Dividing Line... (book; Byrd)
 Byrd, William II **3** 189-190
 Crèvecoeur, John de **4** 307-308

History of the Kings of Britain (book; Geoffrey of Monmouth)
 Geoffrey of Monmouth **6** 268
 Layamon **9** 256-257

History of the Life of the Late Mr. Jonathan Wild, the Great, The (book)
 Fielding, Henry **5** 442-444

History of the Remarkable Life of John Sheppard, The (book)
 Defoe, Daniel **4** 457-459

History of the Three Kingdoms (book)
 Kim Pusik **9** 8-9
 Sol Ch'ong **14** 325-326

History of Tom Jones, a Foundling, The (novel)
 see Tom Jones

History of Vanbrugh's House, The (poem)
 Swift, Jonathan **15** 51-54

Hitchcock (film)
 Truffaut, François **15** 311-313

HITCHCOCK, ALFRED (1899-1980), English-born film director **7** 415-416
 Truffaut, François **15** 311-313

HITCHCOCK, GILBERT MONELL (1859-1934), American publisher and politician **7** 416-417
 Johnson, Hiram Warren **8** 300-301

Hitchcock, Henry Russell (1903-1987), American architectural historian
 Johnson, Philip **8** 313-314
 Mies van der Rohe, Ludwig **11** 10-12
 Richardson, Henry Hobson **13** 139-141

Hitchy-Koo (musical)
 Porter, Cole Albert **12** 405-406

HITLER, ADOLF (1889-1945), German dictator, chancellor-president 1933-1945 **7** 417-420
 appeasement policy
  Chamberlain, Arthur Neville **3** 409-411
  Daladier, Édouard **4** 369
  Eden, Anthony **5** 204-205
  Lloyd George, David **9** 469-471
  Macmillan, Harold **10** 112-113
 assassination plot
  Beck, Ludwig August Theoder **2** 99-100
  Himmler, Heinrich **7** 398-399
  Rommel, Erwin **13** 268-269
  Schacht, Hjalmar Horace Greeley **13** 518-519
 field marshals
  Rommel, Erwin **13** 268-269
  Rundstedt, Karl Rudolf Gerd Von **13** 363-364
 foreign policy
  Franco Bahamonde, Francisco **6** 52-54
  Laval, Pierre **9** 237-238

Litvinov, Maxim Maximovich
9 451-452
Mussolini, Benito **11** 272-274
Pius XI **12** 337-339
Schuschnigg, Kurt von **14** 45-46
Szent-Györgyi, Albert von **15** 62-64
see also appeasement policy (above)
influenced by
Chamberlain, Houston Stewart
3 411
Haushofer, Karl **7** 201
Spengler, Oswald **14** 372-373
Jews under
Dubnov, Simon **5** 115-116
ministers
Goebbels, Joseph Paul **6** 384-385
Göring, Hermann Wilhelm
6 457-458
Hess, Walter Richard Rudolf
7 363-365
opponents (Germany)
Bonhoeffer, Dietrich **2** 389-391
Huch, Ricarda **8** 11-12
Mann, Thomas **10** 204-207
Schrödinger, Erwin **14** 31-33
Tillich, Paul Johannes **15** 224-225
opponents (scientists)
Driesch, Hans Adolf Eduard **5** 105
Kármán, Theodore von **8** 451-452
Planck, Max Karl Ernst Ludwig
12 342-344
opponents (United States)
Dewey, John **4** 520-523
Marshall, George Catlett
10 278-279
Mundelein, George William
11 248-249
propagandists for
Riefenstahl, Leni **13** 161-163
rise to power
Hindenburg, Paul Ludwig Hans von
Beneckendorff und von
7 400-401, 280
Krupp **9** 109-111
von Papen, Franz **16** 28-29
supporters
Heidegger, Martin **7** 257-258
Ludendorff, Erich Friedrich Wilhelm
10 27-28

Hittites (ancient people, Asia Minor)
Ramses II **13** 22-23

Hittorf, Johann Wilhelm (1824-1914), German physicist
Crookes, William **4** 323-324
Röntgen, Wilhelm Conrad **13** 273-275

Hive, The (novel)
Cela y Trulock, Camilo José **3** 389-390

Hiver Printemps (musical composition)
Bloch, Ernest **2** 326-327

HO CHI MINH (1890-1969), Vietnamese revolutionary and statesman **7** 426-428
associates
Dong, Pham Van **5** 57-59
Souvanna Phouma **14** 357-358
Truong Chinh **15** 319-320

French defeat and partition
Bao Dai **1** 496-497
Giap, Vo Nguyen **6** 297-299
opponents
Diem, Ngo Dinh **5** 6-7
Leclerc, Jacques Philippe **9** 272-273
Thieu, Nguyen Van **15** 182-183
profiles of
Greene, Graham **6** 523-524

Hoare-Laval Agreement (England-France; 1935)
Laval, Pierre **9** 237-238

Hoban, James (1762?-1831), Irish-American architect
Mills, Robert **11** 36-37

HOBART, JOHN HENRY (1775-1830), American Episcopal bishop **7** 420-421
Seton, Elizabeth Ann Bayley
14 118-119

Hobbemma, Meindert (1638-1709), Dutch landscape painter
Inness, George **8** 123-124
Ruisdael, Jacob van **13** 357-358

HOBBES, THOMAS (1588-1679), English philosopher and political theorist
7 421-423
Bodin, Jean **2** 356-357
Cudworth, Ralph **4** 331
Filmer, Robert **5** 448
Mandeville, Bernard **10** 192
Marsilius of Padua **10** 284
Pufendorf, Samuel von **12** 477-478
Tönnies, Ferdinand **15** 266-267

Hobbit, The (book)
Tolkien, J. R. R. **15** 259-261

HOBBY, OVETA CULP (1905-1995), American government official and businesswoman **7** 423-425

HOBHOUSE, LEONARD TRELAWNY
(1864-1929), English sociologist and philosopher **7** 425-426

Hobkirk's Hill, battle of (1781)
Greene, Nathanael **6** 525-526

Hoboken (city, New Jersey)
Stevens, John **14** 439-440

Hobomok (novel)
Child, Lydia Maria Francis **3** 520-521

Hobrecht, Jacob
see Obrecht, Jacob

HOBSON, WILLIAM (1793-1842), British naval commander and colonial governor
7 426

Hobun
see Yamashita, Tomoyuki

Hochelaga (Indian village)
see Montreal

Hochi (newspaper)
Hara, Kei **7** 138
Inukai, Tsuyoshi **8** 130-131

Hochi Shimbun (journal)
Okuma, Shigenobu **11** 490

Hochwasser (play)
Grass, Günter **6** 496-497

Hochzeit des Camacho, Die (opera)
Mendelssohn, Moses **10** 488-489

Hocket (musical form)
Machaut, Guillaume de **10** 93-94

Hockey
Gretzky, Wayne **6** 537-539
Howe, Gordie **7** 532-534
Orr, Bobby **12** 2-4

HOCKING, WILLIAM ERNEST
(1873-1966), American philosopher
7 428-429

HOCKNEY, DAVID (born 1937), English photographer and artist **7** 429-431

HODGKIN, ALAN LLOYD (born 1914), English physiologist **7** 431-432
Adrian, Edgar Douglas **1** 67-69

HODGKIN, DOROTHY CROWFOOT
(1910-1964), English chemist **7** 432-434

Hodgkin's Disease
Mendenhall, Dorothy Reed **10** 491-492

HODLER, FERDINAND (1853-1918),
Swiss painter **7** 434-435
Ensor, James **5** 289-290
influence of
Amiet, Cuno **1** 201-202

HOE, RICHARD MARCH (1812-1886),
American inventor and manufacturer
7 435-436

Hoedown (minstrel shows)
Christy, Edwin P. **4** 34-35

HOFFA, JAMES R. ("Jimmy"; 1913-1975)
American union leader **7** 436-437
Kennedy, Robert Francis **8** 508-509

HOFFMAN, ABBIE (1936-1989), American writer, activist, and leader of the Youth International Party **7** 437-439

HOFFMANN, ERNST THEODOR AMADEUS (1776-1822), German author, composer, and artist **7** 439-440
Wassermann, Jakob **16** 130-131

Hoffmann, Friedrich (1660-1742), German physician
Stahl, Georg Ernst **14** 392-393

HOFFMANN, JOSEF (1870-1956), Austrian architect and decorator **7** 440-441

Hoffmeister Quartet (musical composition)
Mozart, Wolfgang Amadeus
11 218-221

HOFHAIMER, PAUL (1459-1537), Austrian composer, and organist **7** 441

HOFMANN, AUGUST WILHELM VON
(1818-1892), German organic chemist
7 441-442
Baeyer, Johann Friedrich Adolf von
1 432
Crookes, William **4** 323-324
Liebig, Justus von **9** 403-404

HOFMANN, HANS (1880-1966),
German-American painter **7** 442-443

Nevelson, Louise **11** 356-357

HOFMANNSTHAL, HUGO VON
(1874-1929), Austrian poet and dramatist
7 443-444
Schnitzler, Arthur **14** 23-24
Varèse, Edgard **15** 432-433

Hofmeyr (book)
Paton, Alan Stewart **12** 134-135

HOFSTADTER, RICHARD (1916-1970),
American historian **7** 444-445

Hogarth, David George (1862-1927), English archeologist
Lawrence, Thomas Edward **9** 253-254

Hogarth Press (established 1917)
Woolf, Virginia Stephen **16** 381-382

HOGARTH, WILLIAM (1697-1764), Eng-
lish painter and engraver **7** 446-447
Bearden, Romare Howard **2** 86-88
Dobell, William **5** 34-35
Reynolds, Joshua **13** 115-116
Stravinsky, Igor Fedorovich **14** 502-506

Hogarth's Act (1735)
Hogarth, William **7** 446-447

Hogg, Thomas Jefferson (1792-1862), English lawyer
Shelley, Percy Bysshe **14** 176-178

Hogson House (New Canaan, Connecticut)
Johnson, Philip **8** 313-314

Hohe Lied, Das (novel)
Sudermann, Hermann **15** 12-13

Hohenheim, Theophrastus Bombastus von
see Paracelsus, Philippus Aureolus

Hohenstaufen dynasty (Germany; ruled
circa 1094-1268)
Frederick I **6** 78-79
Frederick II **6** 79
Henry V **7** 295-296
Manuel I **10** 218-219
Otto of Freising **12** 30
Peter III **12** 256-257

Hohenzollern dynasty
Brandenburg (ruled 1417-1918)
Frederick William **6** 85-86
Sigismund **14** 220-221
Germany (ruled 1871-1918)
William I **16** 292-293
William II **16** 294-295
Prussia (ruled 1525-1918)
Frederick II **6** 81-84
Frederick William I **6** 86-87
Frederick William III **6** 87
Frederick William IV **6** 87-88
William I **16** 292-293
William II **16** 294-295

Hohenzollern-Sigmaringen dynasty (Romania; ruled 1866-1947)
Ferdinand **5** 413-414

Hojarasca, La (novel)
García Márquez, Gabriel **6** 208-209

Hojo (Japanese princely family; ruled
1219-1333)

Ashikaga Takauji **1** 330-332
Daigo II **4** 367-368
Yoritomo, Minamoto **16** 463-464

Hokhmat Ben Sira
see Ecclesiasticus

Hokke (Buddhist sutra)
Shotoku Taishi **14** 205-207

Hokoji (Buddhist temple; Japan)
Suiko **15** 15-16

HOKUSAI, KATSUSHIKA (1760-1849),
Japanese painter and printmaker
7 447-448
Burchfield, Charles **3** 131-132
Hiroshige, Ando **7** 412-413

Holabird and Roche (architectural firm)
Neutra, Richard Joseph **11** 355-356

HOLBACH, BARON D' (Paul Henri Thiry;
1723-1789), German-born French encyclopedist and philosopher **7** 448-449
La Mettrie, Julien Offray de **9** 179-180
Smith, Adam **14** 283-284

Holbein, Hans, the Elder (1465?-1524),
German painter
Holbein, Hans the Younger **7** 449-450

HOLBEIN, HANS, THE YOUNGER
(1497/98-1543), German painter and
graphic artist **7** 449-450
Hilliard, Nicholas **7** 391-392
Hodler, Ferdinand **7** 434-435

Holberg Suite (musical composition)
Grieg, Edvard Hagerup **6** 541-542

HOLBROOK, JOSIAH (1788-1854), American educator **7** 450-451

**HÖLDERLIN, JOHANN CHRISTIAN
FRIEDRICH** (1770-1843), German poet
7 451-452
Hegel, Georg Wilhelm Friedrich
7 254-256
Heidegger, Martin **7** 257-258
Schelling, Friedrich Wilhelm Joseph von
13 526-527
Strauss, David Friedrich **14** 496-497

Holdup (painting)
Russell, Charles Marion **13** 375-376

HOLIDAY, BILLIE (1915-1959), American
jazz vocalist **7** 452-453

Holiday Inn (film score)
Berlin, Irving **2** 200-201

Holiday Overture (musical composition)
Carter, Elliott Cook Jr. **3** 338-339

Holidays Symphony (musical composition)
Ives, Charles Edward **8** 159-160

Holinshed, Raphael (died circa 1580), English chronicler
Macbeth **10** 81

Holland
see Netherlands, The

Holland (submarine)
Holland, John Philip **7** 453-454

Holland, Harvey E. (died 1933), New
Zealand politician

Fraser, Peter **6** 73-74
Savage, Michael Joseph **13** 501-502

Holland, Henry (1745-1806), English archi-
tect
Adam, Robert and James **1** 38-40
Sheraton, Thomas **14** 181-182
Soane, John **14** 314-315

HOLLAND, JOHN PHILIP (1840-1914),
Irish-American inventor **7** 453-454

Holland Tunnel (New York State -New Jersey)
Goethals, George Washington
6 387-388

Holles, Denzil, 1st Baron Holles of Ifield
(1599-1680), English statesman
Strafford, 1st Earl of **14** 490-491

Holley, Robert W. (1922-1993), American
scientist
Khorana, Har Gobind **8** 537-538

Hollis Street Church (Boston)
Bulfinch, Charles **3** 116-117

Hollow Men, The (poem)
Eliot, Thomas Stearns **5** 258-261

Hollweg, Theobald von Bethmann
see Bethmann Hollweg, Theobald von

Holly Springs, battle of (1862)
Davis, Jefferson **4** 416-418

HOLM, HANYA (née Johanna Eckert; born
1893), German-American dancer and
teacher **7** 454-455

Holm, Ingeborg (literary character)
Mann, Thomas **10** 204-207

Holm, Saxe
see Jackson, Helen Hunt

HOLMES, ARTHUR (1890-1965), English
geologist and petrologist **7** 455-456

HOLMES, JOHN HAYNES (1879-1964),
American Unitarian clergyman
7 456-457
Fosdick, Harry Emerson **6** 21-22
Wise, Stephen Samuel **16** 344-345

HOLMES, OLIVER WENDELL (1809-1894),
American physician and author
7 457-458
Frost, Robert Lee **6** 130-133
Motley, John Lothrop **11** 211-212

HOLMES, OLIVER WENDELL, JR.
(1841-1935), American jurist **7** 458-459
Baker, Newton Diehl **1** 451
Brandeis, Louis Dembitz **2** 496-497
Cardozo, Benjamin Nathan **3** 288-290
Harlan, John Marshall **7** 156-157
Laski, Harold J. **9** 215-216
Shaw, Lemuel **14** 164-165
Stone, Harlan Fiske **14** 468-470
Taft, William Howard **15** 78-81
White, Edward Douglass **16** 230-231

Holmes, Sherlock (literary character;
Doyle)
Doyle, Arthur Conan **5** 91-92
Simenon, Georges **14** 233-234

Holocaust
and Jewish philosophy
Fackenheim, Emil Ludwig
5 359-361
Rubenstein, Richard L. **13** 343-344
Wiesel, Elie **16** 263-264
avengers
Wiesenthal, Simon **16** 264-266
commemorators
Freed, James Ingo **6** 88-90
heroes
Fleischmann, Gisi **5** 482-483
Wallenberg, Raoul **16** 78-80
opponents (English)
Rathbone, Eleanor **13** 47-48
perpetrators
Barbie, Klaus **1** 501-503
Brunner, Alois **3** 73-74
Eichmann, Adolf **5** 226-227
Hess, Walter Richard Rudolf
7 363-365
Mengele, Josef **10** 502-503
survivors
Levi, Primo **9** 365-366
victims
Arendt, Hannah **1** 282-284
Baeck, Leo **1** 429-430
Baum, Herbert **2** 66-73
Feuchtwanger, Lion **5** 430-432
Fleischmann, Gisi **5** 482-483
Frank, Anne **6** 54-56
Salomon, Charlotte **13** 454-455
Stein, Edith **14** 412-414
Wiesenthal, Simon **16** 264-266
writers about
Appelfeld, Aharon **1** 262-263

Holofernes (sculpture)
Donatello **5** 55-56

Holography
Gabor, Dennis **6** 159-160

HOLST, GUSTAV (1874-1934), English
composer **7** 459-460
Elgar, Edward **5** 247-248

Holty, Carl (1900-1973), American painter
Hofmann, Hans **7** 442-443

Holy Alliance (Russia, Austria, and Prussia;
1815)
Alexander I **1** 130-132
Metternich, Klemens von **10** 533-536

Holy Club (later Methodists)
Wesley, Charles **16** 208-209
Wesley, John **16** 209-210
Whitefield, George **16** 241-242

Holy Cross Church (Boston)
Bulfinch, Charles **3** 116-117

Holy Fair, The (poem)
Burns, Robert **3** 155-156

Holy Family (painting)
Carracci **3** 319-321
Giorgione **6** 340-341
Greco **6** 511-514
Martini, Simone **10** 298-299
Morales, Luis de **11** 150

Poussin, Nicolas **12** 418-420
Rembrandt Harmensz van Rijn
13 91-95
Schongauer, Martin **14** 26-28
Veronese, Paolo **15** 469-470

Holy Family, The (book)
Engels, Friedrich **5** 286-288
Marx, Karl **10** 304-308

Holy Grail (legend)
Wolfram von Eschenbach **16** 360-361

Holy Kindred (painting)
Maulbertsch, Franz Anton **10** 345

Holy Kinship (painting)
Geertgen tot Sint Jans **6** 248
Massys, Quentin **10** 325-326

Holy Kinship (painting; Massys)
see Saint Anne Altarpiece (painting)

Holy Kinship Altarpiece (painting)
Cranach, Lucas the Elder **4** 289-290

Holy League
1511-1513
Ferdinand V **5** 417-418
Henry VIII **7** 302-305
Julius II **8** 384-386
Louis XII **9** 528-529
Maximilian I **10** 356-357
1571
Pius V **12** 332-333
1576-98
Champlain, Samuel de **3** 419-421
Henry IV **7** 293-295
1684
John III **8** 276-277

Holy Night (painting)
Altdorfer, Albrecht **1** 179-180

Holy Office, Congregation of the
see Inquisition, Holy Roman and Universal

Holy Roman Empire
800-840 (Carolingian dynasty)
Charlemagne **3** 445-447
Louis I **9** 522-523
936-1024 (Saxon dynasty)
Henry I **7** 285-286
Otto I **12** 28-29
Otto III **12** 29-30
1024-1125 (Franconian dynasty)
Henry III **7** 290
Henry IV **7** 292
Henry V **7** 295-296
1138-1254 (Hohenstaufen dynasty)
Frederick I **6** 78-79
Frederick II **6** 79
1273-1291; 1438-1740 (Hapsburg
dynasty)
Charles V **3** 457-459
Ferdinand I **5** 414-415
Ferdinand II **5** 415
Ferdinand III **5** 416-417
Frederick III **6** 84-85
Maximilian I **10** 356-357
Maximilian II **10** 357-358

Rudolf I **13** 347-348
see also Spanish Succession, War of
the (1701-1714)
1308-1437 (Luxemburg dynasty)
Charles IV **3** 455-456
Henry VII **7** 299-300
Sigismund **14** 220-221
Wenceslaus **16** 201-202
1745-1806 (Hapsburg-Lorraine dynasty)
Francis II **6** 43-44
Joseph II **8** 359-360
Leopold II **9** 346
Maria Theresa **10** 256-258
see also Austrian Succession, War of
the
foundation and administration
Charlemagne **3** 445-447
Otto I **12** 28-29
Investiture Struggle
see Investiture Struggle
papal relations
Henry III **7** 290
Julius II **8** 384-386
Rudolf I **13** 347-348
see also Byzantine Empire; Thirty
Years War

Holy See
see Papacy

Holy Shroud, Chapel of the (Turin Cathedral)
Guarini, Guarino **7** 25-26

Holy Sonnets (poems)
Donne, John **5** 60-61

Holy Trinity
see Trinity Church (Boston)

Holy Trinity (sculpture)
Günther, Ignaz **7** 41-42

Holy Trinity, Church of the (Salzburg)
Fischer von Erlach, Johann Bernhard
5 459-461

Holy War
see Jihad (holy war)

Holy War, The (allegory)
Bunyan, John **3** 128-129

Holy Week (novel)
Aragon, Louis **1** 271-272

Holy Willie's Prayer (poem)
Burns, Robert **3** 155-156

Holyoake, George Jacob (1817-1906), English social reformer
Bradlaugh, Charles **2** 478

HOLYOAKE, KEITH JACKA (1904-1983),
New Zealand prime minister and leader
of the National Party **7** 460-462

HOLZER, JENNY (born 1950), American
Neo-Conceptualist artist **7** 462-463

Homage to 6,000,000 I (relief)
Nevelson, Louise **11** 356-357

Homage to Catalonia (book)
Orwell, George **12** 14-15

Homage to David (painting)
Léger, Fernand **9** 302-303

Homage to Emerson (poem)
Warren, Robert Penn **16** 121-122

Homage to Goya (lithograph series)
Redon, Odilon **13** 75-76

Homage to John Dryden (essay)
Eliot, Thomas Stearns **5** 258-261

Homage to Joyce (musical composition)
Berio, Luciano **2** 194-195

Homage to Sextus Propertius (poem)
Pound, Ezra Loomis **12** 415-417

Homage to the Square (art works)
Albers, Josef **1** 110

Homage to the World (relief)
Nevelson, Louise **11** 356-357

HOMANS, GEORGE CASPAR (1910-1989),
American sociologist **7** 463-465

Hombori (African people)
Ali, Sunni **1** 158-159

Hombres y engranajes (essay)
Sábato, Ernesto **13** 399-400

Home (essays)
Baraka, Imamu Amiri **1** 498-499

Home, John (1722-1808), Scottish clergy-
man and playwright
Collins, William **4** 168-169
Payne, John Howard **12** 159

Home and the World, The (novel)
Rabindranath Tagore **12** 529-531

Home as Found (novel)
Cooper, James Fenimore **4** 220-223

Home Burial (poem)
Frost, Robert Lee **6** 130-133

Home Co. (Louisiana land development
firm)
Knapp, Seaman Asahel **9** 58

Home Rule Bill (Ireland)
1886
Chamberlain, Joseph **3** 411-413
Gladstone, William Ewart
6 357-360
1893
Gladstone, William Ewart
6 357-360
Lecky, William Edward Hartpole
9 271-272
1912
George V **6** 273-275
Pearse, Patrick Henry **12** 173-174

Home Rule Leagué (India)
Nehru, Jawaharlal **11** 332-334

Home, Sweet Home (song)
Payne, John Howard **12** 159

Home to Harlem (novel)
McKay, Claude **10** 416

Home Town (painting)
Drysdale, George Russell **5** 107-109

Homecoming (novel)
Snow, Charles Percy **14** 311-312

Homecoming, The (play)
Pinter, Harold **12** 317-318

Homenaje (poems)
Guillén, Nicolás **7** 34-35

Homeopathy (medicine)
Madero, Francisco Indalecio
10 118-119
Paracelsus, Philippus Aureolus **12** 91-93

HOMER (ancient Greek epic poet)
7 468-469
influence of
Aeschylus **1** 70-72
Aristophanes **1** 293-294
Chénier, André Marie **3** 500-501
Dinesen Blixen-Finecke, Karen
5 13-14
Goethe, Johann Wolfgang von
6 388-391
Hugo, Victor Marie **8** 22-25
Keats, John **8** 470-472
Lessing, Gotthold Ephraim
9 357-359
Ronsard, Pierre de **13** 271-273
Tasso, Torquato **15** 114-116
Zwingli, Huldreich **16** 537-538
translations of
Arnold, Matthew **1** 311-313
Chapman, George **3** 440-441
Congreve, William **4** 200-201
Cowper, William **4** 282
Ficino, Marsilio **5** 436-437
Hobbes, Thomas **7** 421-423
Leconte de Lisle, Charles Marie
René **9** 273-274
see also Iliad; Odyssey

Homer (book; Pope)
Browning, Elizabeth Barrett **3** 52-53
Swift, Jonathan **15** 51-54

HOMER, WINSLOW (1836-1910), American painter **7** 468-469

Homeric Questions (book)
Aristotle **1** 295-296

Homestake gold mine (South Dakota)
Hearst, George **7** 242

Homestead strike (Pennsylvania; 1892)
Bryan, William Jennings **3** 80-82
Carnegie, Andrew **3** 309-312
Cleveland, Stephen Grover **4** 108-110
Frick, Henry Clay **6** 108-109
Goldman, Emma **6** 406-407

Homeward Bound (novel)
Cooper, James Fenimore **4** 220-223

Homma, Masaharu (1888?-1946), Japanese
general
Wainwright, Jonathan Mayhew
16 45-46

Homme, L' (poem)
Voltaire **16** 14-16

Homme libre, Un (novel)
Barrès, Auguste Maurice **2** 20-21

Homme machine, L' (book)
La Mettrie, Julien Offray de **9** 179-180

Homme qui regardait passer les trains, L'
(novel)
Simenon, Georges **14** 233-234

Homme Revolte, L' (essay)
Camus, Albert **3** 255-257

Homo Faber (novel)
Frisch, Max **6** 118-119

Homocentric theory (astronomy)
see Universe, systems of—homocentric

Homografts (medicine)
Medawar, Peter Brian **10** 444-445

Homosexual rights movement
Milk, Harvey Bernard **11** 19-21

Homosexuality (in literature)
Baldwin, James Arthur **1** 465-466
Gide, André **6** 308-309
Lorca, Federico García **9** 511-513

HONDA, SOICHIRO (1906-1991), Japanese automaker **7** 469-470

Honduran National Party
Carías Andino, Tiburcio **3** 298-299

Honduras, Republic of (nation; Central
America)
Azcona Hoyo, José **1** 398-399
Callejas Romero, Rafael Leonardo
3 233-234
Carías Andino, Tiburcio **3** 298-299
Columbus, Christopher **4** 176-179
Cuauhtemoc **4** 329
Suazo Córdova, Roberto **15** 8-10
Walker, William **16** 68-69
Zemurray, Samuel **16** 496-497

HONECKER, ERICH (1912-1994), German
Communist Party leader and head of the
German Democratic Republic (1971-80s)
7 471-472
Ulbricht, Walter **15** 383-384

HONEGGER, ARTHUR (1892-1955), Swiss
composer identified with France
7 472-473
Milhaud, Darius **11** 17-18
Poulenc, Francis **12** 414-415
Stravinsky, Igor Fedorovich **14** 502-506
Xenakis, Iannis **16** 416-418

HONEN (1133-1212), Japanese Buddhist
monk **7** 473
Nichiren **11** 376-377
Shinran **14** 197

Honest Whore, The (play)
Dekker, Thomas **4** 465-466

Honestà negli amori, L' (opera)
Scarlatti, Pietro Alessandro Gaspare
13 517-518

Honey and Salt (poem)
Sandburg, Carl **13** 461-462

Honeybees
Frisch, Karl von **6** 117-118

Hong Kong (British colony; island, China)
Carr-Saunders, Alexander Morris
3 333-334
Ch'i-ying **4** 12
Ho Chi Minh **7** 426-428

Honorable Peter Stirling, The (novelist)
Ford, Paul Leicester **6** 9-10

Honorius, Flavius (384-423), Roman
emperor of the West 395-423
Alaric **1** 101-102
Stilicho, Flavius **14** 452-453
Theodosius **15** 176

Honorius II (Pietro Cadalous; died 1072),
antipope (1061-1064)
Roger II **13** 244-245

Honorius III (Cencio Savelli; flourished
early 13th century), pope 1216-1227
Francis of Assisi **6** 46-47
Frederick II **6** 79

Honorius IV (Giacomo Savelli;
1210?-1287), pope 1285-1287
Arnolfo di Cambio **1** 315-316

Honthorst, Gerrit van (1590-1656), Dutch
painter
Vermeer, Jan **15** 466-467

HOOCH, PIETER DE (1629-after 1684),
Dutch artist **7** 473-474
Vermeer, Jan **15** 466-467

Hood, John Bell (1831-1879), American
Confederate general
Davis, Jefferson **4** 416-418
Sherman, William Tecumseh
14 186-187

Hood, Samuel (1st Viscount Hood;
1724-1814), British admiral
Nelson, Horatio **11** 336-338

Hood's Comic Almanac (magazine)
Bierce, Ambrose Gwinett **2** 269-270

Hoogstraten, Samuel van (1627-1678),
Dutch painter
Rembrandt Harmensz van Rijn
13 91-95

Hook of Desire (point, Novaya Zemlya
islands)
Barents, Willem **2** 4-5

HOOK, SIDNEY (1902-1989), American
philosopher and exponent of classical
American pragmatism **7** 474-475

HOOKE, ROBERT (1635-1703), English
physicist **7** 475
Boyle, Robert **2** 469-471
Malpighi, Marcello **10** 176-178
Newton, Isaac **11** 369-372

Hooker, Henry Clay (1828-1907), American rancher
Cochise **4** 128

Hooker, Joseph (1814-1879), American
general
Davis, Jefferson **4** 416-418
Jackson, Shirley Ann **8** 183-184
Lee, Robert Edward **9** 292-294
Stuart, James Ewell Brown **14** 515-516

HOOKER, RICHARD (1554-1600), English
theologian and Church of England clergyman **7** 475-476

Hooker, Sir Joseph Dalton (1817-1911),
English botanist
Darwin, Charles Robert **4** 397-399
Wallace, Alfred Russel **16** 69-70

HOOKER, THOMAS (1586-1647), English
Puritan theologian, founder of Connecti-
cut Colony **7** 476-477
Cotton, John **4** 263-265
Eliot, John **5** 256-258
Walton, Izaak **16** 90-91

HOOKS, BELL (born Gloria Jean Watkins,
born 1952) African American social
activist, feminist, and author **7** 477-481

HOOKS, BENJAMIN LAWSON (born
1925), executive director of the NAACP
and first African American commissioner
of the FCC **7** 481-483

Hoorn (ship)
Schouten, William Cornelius **14** 31

Hoorn, Philip de Montmorency, Count of
(1518-1568), Flemish soldier and statesman
Alba, Duke of **1** 103-104

Hoosier School-Master, The (novel)
Eggleston, Edward **5** 223-224

Hoover Dam (Colorado River)
Kaiser, Henry John **8** 412-413

HOOVER, HERBERT CLARK (1874-1964),
American statesman, president
1929-1933 **7** 483-485
Cabinet
Mellon, Andrew William
10 469-470
Stimson, Henry Lewis **14** 457-458
domestic policy
Capone, Al **3** 272-273
Johnson, Charles Spurgeon
8 296-297
Merriam, Charles Edward
10 518-519
Morgenthau, Henry Jr. **11** 172-173
foreign policy
MacDonald, James Ramsay
10 84-85
Osmeña, Sergio **12** 22-24
opponents
Coughlin, Charles Edward
4 265-266
Smith, Alfred Emmanuel **14** 284-285
Walsh, Thomas James **16** 85-86
Supreme Court and
Cardozo, Benjamin Nathan
3 288-290
Hughes, Charles Evans **8** 15-16
see also Depression, Great (econo-
my)

HOOVER, JOHN EDGAR (1895-1972),
American lawyer, criminologist, and FBI
director **7** 485-487
Dillinger, John **5** 9
Palmer, Alexander Mitchell **12** 77-78

Stone, Harlan Fiske **14** 468-470

Hoover, Lou Henry (Mrs. Herbert C.
Hoover; 1874-1944), American translator
Biringuccio, Vannoccio **2** 283

Hope (painting)
Friedrich, Caspar David **6** 114-115
Puvis de Chavannes, Pierre **12** 492-493

Hope (sculpture)
Powers, Hiram **12** 428-429

HOPE, BOB (born Leslie Townes Hope;
born 1903), entertainer in vaudeville,
radio, television, and movies **7** 487-489

Hope, Harry (literary character)
O'Neill, Eugene **11** 514-516

HOPE, JOHN (1868-1936), African American educator and religious leader
7 489-490
Washington, Booker Taliaferro
16 125-126

Hope, Thomas (1770?-1831), English antiquarian and writer
Sheraton, Thomas **14** 181-182

Hope for Poetry, A (book)
Lewis, Cecil Day **9** 380

Hope for South Africa (book)
Paton, Alan Stewart **12** 134-135

Hope of Heaven (novel)
O'Hara, John **11** 485

Hopeless, Mount (Australia)
Eyre, Edward John **5** 354

Hopes (poem)
Theocritus **15** 171-172

Hopetoun House (West Lothian, Scotland)
Adam, Robert and James **1** 38-40

Hopi Indians (North America)
Coronado, Francisco Vásquez de **4** 247

Hopkins, Arthur Melancthon (1878-1950),
American theatrical producer
Barrymores **2** 28-30

HOPKINS, ESEK (1718-1802), American
Revolutionary patriot **7** 490-491

HOPKINS, GERARD MANLEY
(1844-1889), English Jesuit poet
7 492-494
Rossetti, Christina Georgina
13 307-308

HOPKINS, HARRY LLOYD (1890-1946),
American statesman **7** 494-495
Morgenthau, Henry Jr. **11** 172-173

HOPKINS, MARK (1802-1887), American
educator **7** 495-496
Burritt, Elihu **3** 160
Huntington, Collis Potter **8** 49
Judah, Theodore Dehone **8** 373-374
Stanford, Leland **14** 397-398

HOPKINS, SAMUEL (1721-1803), American clergyman and theologian **7** 496

HOPKINS, SIR FREDERICK GOWLAND
(1861-1947), English biochemist **7** 496
Dale, Henry Hallett **4** 371-373

Eijkman, Christian **5** 228
Hill, Archibald Vivian **7** 385-386
Krebs, Hans Adolf **9** 95-97
Meyerhof, Otto Fritz **10** 537-539
Szent-Györgyi, Albert von **15** 62-64

Hopkins, Stephen (1707-1785), American colonial administrator
Hopkins, Esek **7** 490-491

HOPKINSON, FRANCIS (1737-1791), American politician, writer, and composer **7** 496-497

HOPPER, GRACE (born Grace Brewster Murray; 1906-1992), American computer scientist **7** 498-500

HOPPER, EDWARD (1882-1967), American realist painter **7** 497-498

Hoppe-Seyler, Ernest Felix Immanuel (1825-1895), German physiologist and chemist
Bernard, Claude **2** 208-210

Hoppla wir leben! (play)
Toller, Ernst **15** 261

Hora Novissima (oratorio)
Parker, Horatio William **12** 109

Horace (play)
Corneille, Pierre **4** 234-236

HORACE (Quintus Horatius Flaccus; 65-8 B.C.), Roman poet and satirist **7** 500-503
contemporaries
Virgil **15** 507-510
influence of
Boileau-Despréaux, Nicholas **2** 369-371
Camoëns, Luis Vaz de **3** 247-249
Condorcet, Marquis de **4** 195-196
Herrick, Robert **7** 336-339
Marvell, Andrew **10** 301-303
Milton, John **11** 43-46
Pope, Alexander **12** 395-397
musical settings
Hofhaimer, Paul **7** 441
patron
Augustus **1** 371-373
translations of
Congreve, William **4** 200-201
Dryden, John **5** 106-107
Wieland, Christoph Martin **16** 260-261

Horas de lucha (book)
González Prada, Manuel **6** 431

Horatian Ode ... (poem)
Marvell, Andrew **10** 301-303

Hordubal (novel)
Čapek, Karel **3** 271-272

Horeb, Mount
see Sinai, Mount

Horizon (journal)
Du Bois, William Edward Burghardt **5** 116-118

Horloge, L' (poem)
Baudelaire, Charles Pierre **2** 61-63

Hormuz, Strait of
see Ormuz, Strait of

Horn, Cape (southern South America)
Cook, James **4** 214-215
Drake, Francis **5** 94-96
Schouten, William Cornelius **14** 31

Horn, Count of
see Hoorn

Horn Blows at Midnight, The (film)
Benny, Jack **2** 174-176

HORNE, HERMAN HARRELL (1874-1946), American philosopher and educator **7** 503-504

HORNE, LENA (born 1917), popular entertainer **7** 504-506

HORNER, MATINA SOURETIS (born 1939), American scholar and administrator **7** 506-508

Hornet (ship)
Lawrence, James **9** 251-252

HORNEY, KAREN DANIELSEN (1885-1952), German-born American psychoanalyst **7** 508-509

HOROWITZ, VLADIMIR (1904-1989), American pianist **7** 509-510

Horribles et espouventables faictz et prouesse de tres renommé Pantagruel...
see Pantagruel (novel)

Horse (sculpture)
Duchamp-Villon, Raymond **5** 123

Horse and Rider (sculpture)
Marini, Marino **10** 260-262

Horse Knows the Way, The (stories)
O'Hara, John **11** 485

Horse Power (ballet)
Chávez, Carlos **3** 486

Horse racing/breeding
Taylor, Edward Plunket **15** 123-124

Horsefeathers (film)
Marx Brothers **10** 303-304
Perelman, S. J. **12** 209-210

Horseman (sculpture)
Marini, Marino **10** 260-262

Horses and Men (stories)
Anderson, Sherwood **1** 220-221

Horseshoe Bend, battle of (1814)
Houston, Samuel **7** 526-527
Jackson, Andrew **8** 168-172

Horse-Shoe Robinson (novel)
Kennedy, John Pendleton **8** 506-507

Horst, Louis (1884-1964), American composer
Graham, Martha **6** 485-486

Hortensius, Quintus (114-50 B.C.), Roman lawyer
Brutus, Marcus Junius **3** 79-80
Catullus, Gaius Valerius **3** 377-378
Cicero, Marcus Tullius **4** 55-58

HORTHY DE NAGYBÁNYA, NICHOLAS (1868-1957), Hungarian admiral and statesman, regent 1920-44 **7** 510-512

Horticulture
see Plant breeding; Scientists—horticulturists

Horus Neteryerkhet
see Zoser

Horyuji (Buddhist temple; near Nara, Japan)
Shotoku Taishi **14** 205-207
Suiko **15** 15-16

HOSEA (flourished 750-722 B.C.), Hebrew prophet of the kingdom of Israel **7** 512
Micah **10** 542-543

Hoseyn Beyqara, Sultan (died 1506), Timurid king of Khurasan
Behzad **2** 123

HO-SHEN (1750-1799), Manchu official in China **7** 512-513
Qianlong **12** 502-505

Hoshen ha-Mishpat (Jewish law)
see Shulhan Aruk

Hosius, Stanislaus (1504-1579), Polish Roman Catholic prelate
Pius IV **12** 332

Hospital (medical institution)
Aalto, Hugo Alvar Henrik **1** 1-2
Asoka **1** 341-342
Dix, Dorothea Lynde **5** 32-33
Flynn, John **5** 497-498
Nightingale, Florence **11** 392-393
White, William Alanson **16** 239-240

Hospital of Jesus (Mexico)
Cortés, Hernán **4** 255-256

Hospital of Saint John (Toledo, Spain)
Berruguete, Alonso **2** 223-224
Greco **6** 511-514

Hospital Sketches (book)
Alcott, Louisa May **1** 122

Hospitalers
see Knights of Saint John

Hosso (Japanese Buddhist sect)
Kukai **9** 124-125
Saicho **13** 426-428

Hostages
Waite, Terry **16** 47-48

Hosties noires (poems)
Senghor, Léopold Sédar **14** 106-107

Hostilius Mancinus, G. (flourished 137 B.C.), Roman consul
Gracchus, Tiberius and Gaius Sempronius **6** 479-480

HOSTOS, EUGENIO MARÍA DE (1839-1903), Puerto Rican philosopher, educator, and writer **7** 513-514

Hot Chocolates (revue)
Armstrong, Louis Daniel **1** 303-304

Hot Five (jazz record)
Armstrong, Louis Daniel **1** 303-304

Hot Iron, The (play)
Sachs, Hans **13** 410-411

Hot Stillscape for Six Colors (painting)
Davis, Stuart **4** 424-425

Hot Time in the Old Town Tonight (song)
Thomson, Virgil **15** 202-203

Hôtel
Carnavelet (Paris)
Lescot, Pierre **9** 354
de Hallwyl (Paris)
Ledoux, Claude Nicolas **9** 277-278
de la Vrillière (Paris)
Mansart, François **10** 211
de Lorge (Paris)
Mansart, Jules Hardouin **10** 212
de Noailles (Saint-Germain-en-Laye)
Mansart, Jules Hardouin **10** 212
de Parabère (Paris)
Boffrand, Gabriel Germain **2** 361
de Villars (Paris)
Boffrand, Gabriel Germain **2** 361
Dieu (Lyons)
Soufflot, Jacques Germain
14 349-350
d'Uzés (Paris)
Ledoux, Claude Nicolas **9** 277-278
Lambert (Paris)
Le Vau, Louis **9** 360-361
Le Jars (Paris)
Mansart, François **10** 211
Reforma (Mexico City)
Rivera, Diego **13** 183-184
Soubise (Paris)
Boffrand, Gabriel Germain **2** 361

Hotel, The (novel)
Bowen, Elizabeth **2** 462-463

Hotel in Amsterdam, The (play)
Osborne, John **12** 16-17

Hothouses (poems)
Maeterlinck, Maurice **10** 125-126

Hottentots (African people)
Dias de Novais, Bartolomeu **4** 533-534

Hötzendorf, Count Franz Conrad von
see Conrad von Hötzendorf, Count
Franz

Houasse, Michel Ange (1680-1730), French
painter
Goya y Lucientes, Francisco de Paula
José de **6** 476-478

HOUDINI, HARRY (born Erich Weiss;
1874-1926), American magician and illu-
sionist **7** 514-516

HOUDON, ANTOINE (1741-1828),
French sculptor **7** 516-517

Hough, Emerson (1857-1923), American
journalist
Billy the Kid **2** 277

Hound of Heaven, The (poem)
Kuo Mo-jo **9** 133-134

Hound of the Baskervilles, The (novel)
Doyle, Arthur Conan **5** 91-92

HOUNSFIELD, GODFREY (born 1919),
English biomedical engineer **7** 517-519

HOUPHOUËT-BOIGNY, FELIX
(1905-1993), Ivorian statesman 1960
7 519-520
Touré, Sékou **15** 275-277

Hour of the Wolf, The (film)
Bergman, Ernst Ingmar **2** 190-191

Hourloupe, L' (painting series)
Dubuffet, Jean Philippe Arthur
5 119-120

Hours of Idleness (poems)
Byron, George Gordon Noel **3** 193-194

House Divided, A (book)
Buck, Pearl Sydenstricker **3** 91-93

HOUSE, EDWARD MANDELL
(1858-1938), American diplomat
7 520-521
Page, Walter Hines **12** 60-61

House for Mr. Biswas, A (book)
Naipaul, V. S. **11** 295-296

House in Paris, The (novel)
Bowen, Elizabeth **2** 462-463

House of Aizgorri, The (novel)
Baroja y Nessi, Pío **2** 15-16

House of Bernarda Alba, The (play)
Lorca, Federico García **9** 511-513

House of Mirth, The (novel)
Wharton, Edith **16** 221

House of Mist, The (book)
Bombal, María Luisa **2** 380-381

House of Night, The (poem)
Freneau, Philip Morin **6** 99-100

House of Pomegranates, The (stories)
Wilde, Oscar Fingall O'Flahertie Wills
16 272-273

House of Representatives, U.S.
see U.S. House of Representatives

House of the Dead, The (opera)
Janáček, Leoš **8** 219

House of the Hanged Man (painting)
Cézanne, Paul **3** 400-402

House of the Seven Gables, The (novel)
Hawthorne, Nathaniel **7** 212-215, 144

House of the Spirits, The (book)
Allende, Isabel **1** 172-174

House of Wisdom (academy; Baghdad,
Iraq)
Khwarizmi, Muhammad ibn Musa al-
8 541
Mamun, Abdallah al- **10** 183

House on the Water, The (play)
Betti, Ugo **2** 246

House with the Balcony, The (story)
Chekhov, Anton Pavlovich **3** 494-497

Household Words (magazine)
Collins, William Wilkie **4** 169-170
Dickens, Charles John Huffam
4 538-541

Gaskell, Elizabeth **6** 231-232

Houses at L'Estaque (painting)
Braque, Georges **2** 504-505

**Housing and Urban Development, Depart-
ment of** (United States)
Kemp, Jack French Jr. **8** 491-493
Weaver, Robert C. **16** 152-153

HOUSMAN, ALFRED EDWARD
(1859-1936), English poet **7** 521-522
Harris, Frank **7** 172-173
Vaughan Williams, Ralph **15** 446-447

HOUSSAY, BERNARDO ALBERTO
(1887-1971), Argentine physiologist
7 522-523

HOUSTON, CHARLES HAMILTON
(1895-1950), African American lawyer
and civil rights leader **7** 523-526

HOUSTON, SAMUEL (1793-1863), Ameri-
can statesman and soldier **7** 526-527
Austin, Stephen Fuller **1** 380-381
Borden, Gail **2** 409
Santa Ana, Antonio López de
13 471-472

Houston, Texas
Whitmire, Kathryn Jean Niederhofer
16 252-253

Houyhnhnms (literary people)
Swift, Jonathan **15** 51-54

Hovering Angel (sculpture)
Barlach, Ernst **2** 5-6

Hovhaness, Alan (born 1911), American
composer
Cunningham, Merce **4** 337-338

HOVLAND, CARL I. (1912-1961), American psychologist **7** 527-528

How Deep Is the Ocean (song)
Parker, Charles Christopher Jr.
12 105-106

How Green Was My Valley (film)
Ford, John **6** 7-8

How I Won the War (film)
Lennon, John Winston **9** 326-328

How It Is (novel)
Beckett, Samuel **2** 102-104

How Soon hath Time (sonnet)
Milton, John **11** 43-46

How To Explain Paintings to a Dead Hare
(art action)
Beuys, Joseph **2** 246-248

Howard, Catherine (1520?-1542), fifth wife
of Henry VIII
Henry VIII **7** 302-305
Mary I **10** 308-309
Norfolk, 3d Duke of **11** 423

Howard, Charles, 1st Earl of Nottingham
(1536-1624), English admiral
Drake, Francis **5** 94-96

Howard, Charles, 3d Earl of Carlisle
(1674-1738), English art patron
Vanbrugh, John **15** 409-410

Howard, Ebenezer (1850-1928), English shorthand reporter and social reformer
Mumford, Lewis **11** 246-247

Howard, Henry, 1st Earl of Northampton (1540-1614), English statesman
James I **8** 204-206

Howard, Henry, Earl of Surrey (1517?-1547), English soldier and poet
Henry VIII **7** 302-305
Norfolk, 3d Duke of **11** 423
Wyatt, Thomas **16** 410-411

Howard, Leslie (1893-1943), British actor
Bogart, Humphrey **2** 363-364

Howard, Luke (1772-1864), English meteorologist
Constable, John **4** 208-209

HOWARD, OLIVER OTIS (1830-1909), American Union general **7** 528-529
Cochise **4** 128
Joseph **8** 358-359

Howard, Sidney (1891-1939), American dramatist
Goldwyn, Samuel **6** 416

Howard, Thomas
see James, Jesse; Norfolk, 2nd-4th Dukes of; Walden, 1st Baron Howard de

Howard College (Alabama)
Curry, Jabez Lamar Monroe **4** 346-347

Howard University (Washington D.C.)
Bunche, Ralph Johnson **3** 121-122
Drew, Charles Richard **5** 100-101
Frazier, Edward Franklin **6** 77
Houston, Charles Hamilton **7** 523-526
Howard, Oliver Otis **7** 528-529
Langston, John Mercer **9** 197
Locke, Alain **9** 475-478

Howard's End (novel)
Forster, Edward Morgan **6** 14-16

Howe, Clarence Decatur (1886-1960), Canadian engineer and statesman
St. Laurent, Louis Stephen **13** 434

HOWE, EDGAR WATSON (1853-1937), American author and editor **7** 529

HOWE, ELIAS (1819-1867), American inventor **7** 529-530

HOWE, FLORENCE ROSENFELD (born 1929), feminist American author, publisher, literary scholar, and historian **7** 530-531

HOWE, GORDIE (born 1928), Canadian hockey player **7** 532-534

HOWE, JOSEPH (1804-1873), Canadian journalist, reformer, and politician **7** 534-535
Dwight, Timothy **5** 169
Tupper, Charles **15** 342-343

HOWE, JULIA WARD (1819-1910), American author and reformer **7** 535-536

Howe, Louis McHenry (1871-1936), American journalist
Roosevelt, Franklin Delano **13** 277-280

HOWE, RICHARD (Earl Howe; 1726-1799), English admiral **7** 536-537
Howe, William **7** 538-539

HOWE, SAMUEL GRIDLEY (1801-1876), American physician and reformer **7** 537
Brown, John **3** 39-41
Dix, Dorothea Lynde **5** 32-33
Howe, Julia Ward **7** 535-536
Sumner, Charles **15** 30-31

HOWE, GEOFFREY (Richard Edward; born 1926), British foreign secretary **7** 531-532

HOWE, WILLIAM (5th Viscount Howe; 1729-1814), British general **7** 538-539
Coxe, Tench **4** 285-286
Galloway, Joseph **6** 186-187
Howe, Richard **7** 536-537
see also American Revolution

HOWELLS, WILLIAM DEAN (1837-1920), American writer **7** 539-541
Dreiser, Herman Theodore **5** 98-100
Dunbar, Paul Laurence **5** 141-142
Garland, Hannibal Hamlin **6** 217-218
Jewett, Sarah Orne **8** 256
Markham, Edwin **10** 267
Norris, Benjamin Franklin Jr. **11** 427-428

HOWELLS, WILLIAM WHITE (born 1908), American anthropologist **7** 541-542

Howl ... (book; Ginsberg)
Ginsberg, Allen **6** 332-333
Lennon, John Winston **9** 326-328

HOXHA, ENVER (1908-1985), leader of the Communist Party of Albania from its formation in 1941 until his death **8** 1-3
Alia, Ramiz **1** 159

Hoyle, Fred (born 1915), English astronomer
Lemaître, Abbè Georges Édouard **9** 315-316

HRDLIČKA, ALEŠ (1869-1943), American physical anthropologist **8** 3-4

HSIA KUEI (flourished 1190-1225), Chinese painter **8** 4-5
Sesshu, Toya **14** 116-117
Tung Ch'i-ch'ang **15** 339-340
Ma Yüan **10** 379

Hsiang (died 1101), Chinese empress dowager
Hui-Tsung **8** 25

Hsiang Yüan-pien (1525-1590), Chinese art collector
Tung Ch'i-ch'ang **15** 339-340

Hsiang-yang (city; China)
Kublai Khan **9** 115-118

Hsiao, Duke (died 338 B.C.), Chinese statesman
Shang Yang **14** 149-150

Hsiao-jen hsiao-shih (stories)
Pa Chin **12** 53-54

Hsiao Yen
see Liang Wu-ti

HSIEH LING-YÜN (385-433), duke of K'ang-lo, Chinese poet **8** 5-6
Liu Hsieh **9** 452-453

Hsieh-i (art style)
Ch'i Pai-shih **3** 526-527

Hsien (political division; China)
Li Ssu **9** 442-443
Quin Shi Huang-Di **12** 515-518

Hsien-feng (1831-1861), Chinese emperor 1851-1861
Tz'u-hsi **15** 375-376
Wen-hsiang **16** 202-203
Wo-jen **16** 352

Hsien-tze
see Shih Ko-fa

Hsin Ch'ing-nien (magazine)
Ch'en Tu-hsiu **3** 501-502
Hu Shih **8** 63-65
Li Ta-chao **9** 447
Lu Hsün **10** 35-37

Hsin dynasty
see Han dynasty—Hsin

Hsin Shun Wang
see Li Tzu-ch'eng

Hsinbyushin (ruled 1763-1776), king of Burma
Alaungpaya **1** 103

Hsin-chien, Earl of
see Wang Yangming

Hsiung-nu (Asian people)
Han Kao-tsu **7** 125-126
Han Wu-ti **7** 136
Kuang-wu-ti **9** 112-113
Quin Shi Huang-Di **12** 515-518
Wang Mang **16** 101-103

Hsi-yü Chi (book)
Hsüan Tsang **8** 6-7

Hsüan (ruled 319-310 B.C.), Chinese king of Ch'i
Mencius **10** 480-481

Hsüan (ruled 73-47 B.C.), Chinese emperor
Wang Mang **16** 101-103

HSÜAN TSANG (circa 602-664), Chinese Buddhist in India **8** 6-7
Tao-hsüan **15** 105

HSÜAN-TSUNG, T'ANG (685-762), Chinese emperor **8** 7-8
An Lu-shan **1** 239-240
Li Po **9** 437-439
Wu Tao-tzu **16** 405-406

HSÜN-TZU (Hsün Ch'ing; circa 312-circa 235 B.C.), Chinese philosopher **8** 8
Han Fei Tzu **7** 124-125
Li Ssu **9** 442-443
Mencius **10** 480-481

HU SHIH (1891-1962), Chinese philosopher **8** 63-65
Ku Chieh-kang **9** 120-121
Lu Hsün **10** 35-37
Ts'ai Yüan-p'ei **15** 322
Yen Fu **16** 452

Hu Wei-yung (died 1380), Chinese statesman
Hung-wu **8** 38-39

Hua shih (book)
Mi Fei **11** 12-13

HUAC
see Un-American Activities, House
Committee on

Huancayo (region; Peru)
Meiggs, Henry **10** 458-459

HUANG CH'AO (died 884), Chinese rebel
leader **8** 8-9
Zhao Kuang-yin **16** 505-508

Huang Hsing (1873-1916), Chinese general
Sun Yat-sen **15** 35-39
Wang Fu-chih **16** 99-101
Yüan Shih-k'ai **16** 480-481

Huang Kung-wang (1269-1354), Chinese
painter
Chao Meng-fu **3** 436-437
Tung Ch'i-ch'ang **15** 339-340

HUANG TSUNG-HSI (1610-1695), Chinese scholar and philosopher **8** 9-10

Huáscar (1495?-1533), Inca prince
Atahualpa **1** 355-356
Manco Capac **10** 184-185
Pizarro, Francisco **12** 340-341

Huayna Cápac (1450?-ca 1528), Inca
emperor
Atahualpa **1** 355-356
Garcilaso de la Vega, Inca **6** 210-211
Manco Capac **10** 184-185

HUBBLE, EDWIN POWELL (1889-1953),
American astronomer **8** 10-11
Eddington, Arthur Stanley **5** 201-202
Lemaître, Abbè Georges Édouard
9 315-316

Hubertusberg, Peace of (1763)
Frederick II **6** 81-84

HUCH, RICARDA (1864-1947), German
novelist, poet, and historian **8** 11-12

Huckleberry Finn (novel)
Twain, Mark **15** 363-366

Hudibras (poem)
Butler, Samuel **3** 183-184

HUDSON, HENRY (flourished 1607-1611),
English navigator **8** 12-13
Baffin, William **1** 435-436

Hudson, Thomas (1701-1779), British
painter
Reynolds, Joshua **13** 115-116

Hudson, W.H. (1841-1922), English author
and naturalist
Epstein, Jacob **5** 295-296
Ford, Ford Madox **6** 1-2

Hudson Bay (New York State)
Cabot, Sebastian **3** 200-201
Hudson, Henry **8** 12-13

Hudson River (New York State)
Hudson, Henry **8** 12-13
McAdoo, William Gibbs **10** 385-386

Verrazano, Giovanni da **15** 470-471

Hudson River Landscape (sculpture)
Smith, David **14** 287-288

Hudson River school (American art)
Allston, Washington **1** 176-177
Blakelock, Ralph Albert **2** 318
Church, Frederick Edwin **4** 49-50
Cole, Thomas **4** 151-152
Durand, Asher Brown **5** 156-157

Hudson Strait (Northeastern Canada)
Frobisher, Martin **6** 121-122
Hudson, Henry **8** 12-13

Hudson's Bay Co.
and French attacks
Iberville, Sieur d' **8** 90-91
land acquisitions
Cartier, George-Étienne **3** 342-343
Selkirk, 5th Earl of **14** 96
mineral and fur expeditions
Hearne, Samuel **7** 241-242
Ogden, Peter Skene **11** 480-481
Smith, Jedediah S. **14** 294-295
North West Company
see North West Company (Montreal)
officials
Fleming, Sandford **5** 485-486
Kelsey, Henry **8** 488
Radisson, Pierre-Esprit **12** 539-540
Smith, Donald Alexander
14 288-289
Oregon policy
Applegate, Jesse **1** 264-265
McLoughlin, John **10** 423-424

Hue (city; Vietnam)
Diem, Ngo Dinh **5** 6-7

Hueffer, Ford Madox
see Ford, Ford Madox

Hueffer, Francis (1845-1889),
German-English music critic
Ford, Ford Madox **6** 1-2

Huerta, Adolfo de la (died 1955), Mexican
politician
Calles, Plutarco Elías **3** 234-235
Obregón, Álvaro **11** 458-459
Villa, Pancho **15** 495-496

HUERTA, VICTORIANO (1854-1916),
Mexican general and politician **8** 13-14
political opponents
Calles, Plutarco Elías **3** 234-235
Carranza, Venustiano **3** 321-322
Díaz, José de la Cruz Porfirio
4 534-536
Madero, Francisco Indalecio
10 118-119
Obregón, Álvaro **11** 458-459
Villa, Pancho **15** 495-496
Zapata, Emiliano **16** 489-490
U.S. intervention
Wilson, Thomas Woodrow
16 330-332

Huet, Pierre Daniel (1630-1721), French
bishop
La Fayette, Comtesse de **9** 150-151

Huggins, Charles Brenton (born 1901),
American physician
Rous, Francis Peyton **13** 322-323

**Huggins, Sir Godfrey Martin, 1st Viscount
Malvern** (1883-1971), Rhodesian states-
man
Welensky, Roy **16** 188

HUGGINS, SIR WILLIAM (1824-1910),
English astronomer **8** 14-15

Hugh Selwyn Mauberley (poems)
Pound, Ezra Loomis **12** 415-417

Hugh the Drover (opera)
Vaughan Williams, Ralph **15** 446-447

Hughes, Arthur (1832-1915), English illustrator
Rossetti, Christina Georgina
13 307-308

HUGHES, CHARLES EVANS (1862-1948),
American jurist and statesman **8** 15-16
Coolidge, John Calvin **4** 217-219
Harding, Warren Gamaliel **7** 148-149
Stone, Harlan Fiske **14** 468-470
Taft, William Howard **15** 78-81
White, Edward Douglass **16** 230-231

HUGHES, HOWARD ROBARD
(1905-1976), flamboyant American entrepreneur **8** 16-17

HUGHES, JOHN JOSEPH (1797-1864),
Irish-American Catholic archbishop
8 17-18
McCloskey, John **10** 395

HUGHES, LANGSTON (1902-1967),
African American author **8** 18-19
Ellison, Ralph Waldo **5** 274-275
Johnson, James Weldon **8** 304-305
Knopf, Blanche Wolf **9** 61-62.
Weill, Kurt **16** 174-175

HUGHES, TED (born 1930), English poet
laureate **8** 19-21
Plath, Sylvia **12** 344-345

HUGHES, WILLIAM MORRIS
(1864-1952), Australian prime minister
1915-1923 **8** 21-22
Bruce of Melbourne, 1st Viscount
3 61-62
Curtin, John Joseph **4** 348-349
Forrest, John **6** 12-13
Lyons, Joseph Aloysius **10** 69-70

Hughie (play)
O'Neill, Eugene **11** 514-516

HUGO, VICOMTE VICTOR MARIE
(1802-1885), French author **8** 22-25
associates
Brown, William Wells **3** 48-49
Liszt, Franz **9** 445-447
Sainte-Beuve, Charles Augustin
13 438
Verlaine, Paul Marie **15** 465-466
influence of
Bonifacio, Andres **2** 393-394
Castro Alves, Antônio de **3** 364-365
Crémazie, Octave **4** 305-306

Leconte de Lisle, Charles Marie
  René **9** 273-274
Lermontov, Mikhail Yurievich
  9 352-353
Nerval, Gérard de **11** 345-346
Saavedra, Angel de **13** 398
Verdi, Giuseppe Fortunino
  Francesco **15** 463-465
influenced by
  Byron, George Gordon Noel
    3 193-194
  Chénier, André Marie **3** 500-501
monument to
  Rodin, Auguste **13** 236-238

Huguenot and Ophelia (painting)
  Millais, John Everett **11** 23-24

Huguenots (religion)
  Coligny, Gaspard de **4** 159-160
  Frederick William **6** 85-86
  Henry IV **7** 293-295
  Medici, Catherine de' **10** 445-449
  Menéndez de Avilés, Pedro **10** 499-500
  William the Silent **16** 300-302
  see also Religion, Wars of; Saint
    Bartholomew's Day Massacre

Huguenots, Les (opera)
  Meyerbeer, Giacomo **10** 536-537

Hui (ruled 370-319 B.C.), king of Chinese
  state of Wei
  Mencius **10** 480-481
  Tsou Yen **15** 329-330

Hui-ti (ruled 290-306), Western Chin
  emperor
  Lu Chi **10** 24

HUI-TSUNG (1082-1135), Chinese emper-
  or and artist **8** 25
  Chu Hsi **4** 40-43
  Kao-tsung **8** 433
  Su Shih **15** 39-40
  Wang Wei **16** 106-108

Huitzilopochtli (Aztec god)
  Montezuma, II **11** 128-129

HUI-YÜAN (334-416), Chinese Buddhist
  monk **8** 25-26
  Hsieh Ling-yün **8** 5-6
  Kumarajiva **9** 127
  Tao-an **15** 103-104

HUIZINGA, JOHAN (1872-1945), Dutch
  historian **8** 26-27

Huks (Hukbalahap rebellion)
  Magsaysay, Ramon **10** 130-131
  Quirino, Elpidio **12** 519-520

HULAGU KHAN (Hüle'ü; circa
  1216-1265), Mongol ruler in Persia
  8 27-28
  Genghis Khan **6** 263-265
  Kublai Khan **9** 115-118

HULL, CLARK LEONARD (1884-1952),
  American psychologist **8** 28
  Hovland, Carl I. **7** 527-528
  Watson, John Broadus **16** 138-139

HULL, CORDELL (1871-1955), American
  statesman **8** 28-29

Daniels, Josephus **4** 387
Konoe, Fumimaro **9** 82-83
Lamas, Carlos Saavedra **9** 175-176
Stettinius, Edward R. Jr. **14** 437-438
Welles, Sumner **16** 191-192

Hull House (Chicago)
  founded
    Addams, Jane **1** 56-57
  social workers
    Abbott, Grace **1** 9-10
    Hamilton, Alice **7** 98-99
    Kelly, Florence **8** 483-484
    Perkins, Frances **12** 221-222
  supporters
    Beard, Charles Austin **2** 84
    Dewey, John **4** 520-523
    King, William Lyon Mackenzie
      9 25-26
    Lloyd, Henry Demarest **9** 468-469
    Swope, Gerard **15** 56-58
    Wright, Frank Lloyd **16** 398-401

HULL, WILLIAM (1753-1825), American
  military commander **8** 29-30
  Brock, Isaac **3** 12-13
  Harrison, William Henry **7** 180-181

Hulst, battle of (1591)
  Maurice of Nassau **10** 348-349

Human Comedy, The (books)
  Balzac, Honoré de **1** 478-480

Human Comedy, The (essays)
  Robinson, James Harvey **13** 208

Human Comedy, The (novel and film)
  Saroyan, William **13** 486-487

Human Condition, The (book)
  Arendt, Hannah **1** 282-284

Human Drift, The (book)
  London, Jack **9** 494-495

Human figure
  in art
    Segal, George **14** 85-87

Human Genome Project (gene mapping)
  Sturtevant, A. H. **15** 3-5

Human Group, The (book)
  Homans, George Caspar **7** 463-465

Human rights
  activists for
    Harand, Irene **7** 139-145
    Havel, Vaclav **7** 202-205
    Menchú, Rigoberta **10** 479-480
    Pérez Esquivel, Adolfo **12** 215-217
    Timerman, Jacobo **15** 226-228
    Wallenberg, Raoul **16** 78-80
    White, Walter Francis **16** 238-239
    Wiesel, Elie **16** 263-264
  defenders of
    Alfonsín, Raúl Ricardo **1** 146-148
    First, Ruth **5** 453-454
    Forman, James **6** 10-11
    Neruda, Pablo **11** 344-345
    Ngugi wa Thiong'o **11** 375-376
    Ramphal, Shridath Surendranath
      13 19-20

Romero, Oscar **13** 265-267
Sakharov, Andrei **13** 439-441
Scott, Francis Reginald **14** 66-67
Shcharansky, Anatoly Borisovich
  14 168-170
Sin, Jaime L. **14** 244-245
Soelle, Dorothee **14** 324-325
Suzman, Helen **15** 45-46
violators of
  Amin Dada, Idi **1** 202-204
  Daly, Mary **4** 380-381
  Duvalier, Jean-Claude **5** 166-168
  Pinochet Ugarte, Augusto
    12 315-317
  Pol Pot **12** 382-384
  Somoza Debayle, Anastasio
    14 336-337
  Suazo Córdova, Roberto **15** 8-10
  Videla, Jorge Rafaél **15** 490-492

Human Sexual Response (book)
  Johnson, Virginia E. **8** 317-319
  Masters, William Howell **10** 327-328

Human Shows (poems)
  Hardy, Thomas **7** 150-152

Humanae vitae (encyclical)
  Paul VI **12** 146-148

Humani generis (encyclical)
  Pius XII **12** 339-340

Humanism (cultural movement)
  • MIDDLE AGES and RENAISSANCE
    and science
      Fernel, Jean François **5** 425-426
      Waldseemüller, Martin **16** 56
    literature: English
      see Renaissance (literature)—
        England
    literature: French
      Christine de Pisan **4** 29-30
      Orléans, Charles D' **11** 530
      Rabelais, François **12** 524-526
      Villon, François **15** 499-501
    literature: German
      Brant, Sebastian **2** 503-504
      Goethe, Johann Wolfgang von
        6 388-391
      Hutten, Ulrich von **8** 72-73
      Luther, Martin **10** 48-51
      Reuchlin, Johann **13** 106-107
      Sachs, Hans **13** 410-411
    literature: Italian
      Bembo, Pietro **2** 144-145
      Boccaccio, Giovanni **2** 351-353
      Boiardo, Matteo Maria **2** 369
      Castiglione, Baldassare
        3 360-361
      Dante Alighieri **4** 389-391
      Machiavelli, Niccolò **10** 97-99
      Plutarch **12** 359-360
      Poliziano, Angelo **12** 373-374
      Pulci, Luigi **12** 481
    literature: Latin
      Budé, Guillaume **3** 102-103
      Colet, John **4** 157-158
      Erasmus, Desiderius **5** 298-300

Ficino, Marsilio **5** 436-437
Kempis, Thomas à **8** 493-494
Petrarch **12** 259-261
William of Ockham **16** 298-299
literature: Spanish
Encina, Juan del **5** 283
López de Ayala, Pedro
9 508-509
Vicente, Gil **15** 479-480
patrons
Charles IV **3** 455-456
Francis I **6** 40-43
Medici, Cosimo de' **10** 449-450
Medici, Lorenzo de' **10** 450-451
Pius II **12** 331
philosophy: English
John of Salisbury **8** 284-285
More, Thomas **11** 156-157
philosophy: French
Montaigne, Michel Eyquem de
11 116-117
Ramus, Petrus **13** 27-28
philosophy: Italian
Campanella, Tommaso **3** 249
Ficino, Marsilio **5** 436-437
Cusa, Nicholas of **4** 352-353
Pico della Mirandola, Giovanni
12 299-300
Poliziano, Angelo **12** 373-374
Pomponazzi, Pietro **12** 390-391
Porta, Giambattista della
12 403-404
Valla, Lorenzo **15** 406
Feltre, Vittorino da **5** 409-410
philosophy: Dutch
Erasmus, Desiderius **5** 298-300
source
see Classicism (literature)

• MODERN
and psychiatry
Coles, Robert Martin **4** 156-157
and science
Eiseley, Loren Corey **5** 232-233
Schrödinger, Erwin **14** 31-33
literature
Bello, Ahmadu **2** 139-140
Pasternak, Boris Leonidovich
12 124-125
Pater, Walter Horatio
12 130-131
Rolland, Romain **13** 260
philosophy
Block, Herbert **2** 333-334
Croce, Benedetto **4** 313-314
Fromm, Erich **6** 125-127
Gadamer, Hans-Georg
6 162-163
Santayana, George **13** 475-477

Humanism, Christian
Catholics (churchmen)
John of Salisbury **8** 284-285
Justin Martyr **8** 395-396
Cusa, Nicholas of **4** 352-353
Thomas Aquinas **15** 183-186
William of Malmesbury **16** 297-298

William of Ockham **16** 298-299
Zumárraga, Juan de **16** 531-532
Catholics (laymen)
Ficino, Marsilio **5** 436-437
Maritain, Jacques **10** 263
More, Thomas **11** 156-157
Pico della Mirandola, Giovanni
12 299-300
Reuchlin, Johann **13** 106-107
Protestants
Bunyan, John **3** 128-129
Eliade, Mircea **5** 249-250
Melancthon, Philip **10** 466-467
Zwingli, Huldreich **16** 537-538
see also Classicism (literature)

Humanitarians
Diana, Princess of Wales **4** 529-533
Elizabeth of Hungary **5** 271-272

Humason, M.L. (1891-1972), American
astronomer
Hubble, Edwin Powell **8** 10-11

Humayun (1508-1556), Mogul emperor of
India 1530-1556
Akbar, Jalal-ud-din Mohammed **1** 96

Humble Petition and Advice (English constitution; 1657)
Cromwell, Oliver **4** 317-320

Humble Remonstrance, A (essay)
Stevenson, Robert Louis **14** 446-448

**HUMBOLDT, BARON FRIEDRICH HEIN-
RICH ALEXANDER VON** (1769-1859),
German naturalist and explorer **8** 30-31
influence of
Bolívar, Simón **2** 375-377
Church, Frederick Edwin **4** 49-50
Dumas, Jean Baptiste André
5 138-139
Frederick William IV **6** 87-88
Liebig, Justus von **9** 403-404
scientific expeditions
Gay-Lussac, Joseph Louis **6** 245-246
Mutis, José Celestino **11** 278-279

HUMBOLDT, BARON WILHELM VON
(1767-1835), German statesman and
philologist **8** 31
Catlin, George **3** 373-374
Gay-Lussac, Joseph Louis **6** 245-246
Herbart, Johann Friedrich **7** 321-322
Humboldt, Friedrich Heinrich Alexan-
der von **8** 30-31
Savigny, Friedrich Karl von **13** 502-503

Humboldt River (Nevada)
Carson, Christopher **3** 334-335
Ogden, Peter Skene **11** 480-481

HUME, DAVID (1711-1776), Scottish
philosopher **8** 31-34
associates
Ferguson, Adam **5** 420-421
Price, Richard **12** 447-448
Rousseau, Jean Jacques **13** 324-328
Smith, Adam **14** 283-284
editions of
Green, Thomas Hill **6** 520-521
influence of

Cohen, Morris Raphael **4** 139-140
Gibbon, Edward **6** 299-300
Huxley, Thomas Henry **8** 77-79
Kant, Immanuel **8** 430-432
Mach, Ernst **10** 90-91
Masaryk, Tomáš Garrigue
10 314-315
Meinong, Alexius Ritter von Hand-
schuchsheim **10** 461-462
Mill, James **11** 21
Mill, John Stuart **11** 21-23
Reid, Thomas **13** 87-88
influenced by
Malebranche, Nicolas **10** 166-167
Shaftesbury, 3d Earl of **14** 136-137

Hume, Joseph (1777-1855), English physician
Sydenham, Thomas **15** 59-60

Hummel, Johann Nepomuk (1778-1837),
German pianist-composer
Chopin, Frédéric François **4** 16-18

Humoresque (film)
Odets, Clifford **11** 470-471

Humorists
see Authors—humorists

Humorous Day's Mirth, A (play)
Chapman, George **3** 440-441

Humorous Lieutenant, The (play)
Fletcher, John **5** 487

Humphrey (died 1057), Count of Apulia
Guiscard, Robert **7** 39-40

Humphrey Clinker (novel)
Smollett, Tobias George **14** 305-307

Humphrey, Duke of Gloucester
see Gloucester, Duke of

Humphrey, George M. (1890-1970), American industrialist and lawyer
Eisenhower, Dwight David **5** 233-236

HUMPHREY, HUBERT HORATIO, JR.
(1911-1978), mayor of Minneapolis, U.S.
senator from Minnesota, and vice-president of the U.S. **8** 34-36
McCarthy, Eugene Joseph **10** 386-388
McGovern, George Stanley **10** 412-414
Nixon, Richard Milhous **11** 401-404

Humplik, Josef (born 1888), Austrian sculptor
Webern, Anton **16** 160-162

HUN SEN (born 1951), Cambodian prime
minister **8** 39-42

Hunayn, victory of (630)
Mohammed **11** 76-78

HUNDERTWASSER, FRIEDENSREICH
(Friedrich Stowasser; born 1928),
Austrian-born visionary painter and spiri-
tualist **8** 36-37

Hundred Days (France; March-June, 1815)
Allies against Napoleon
Castlereagh, Viscount **3** 363-364
Metternich, Klemens von
10 533-536

see also Vienna, Congress of
(1814-1815)
Bourbon restoration after
Fouché, Joseph **6** 30-31
Lafayette, Marquis de **9** 151-152
Louis XVIII **9** 535-536
supporters of Napoleon
Bonaparte, Joseph **2** 381-382
Carnot, Lazare Nicolas Marguerite
3 313-314
Napoleon I **11** 306-310
Talleyrand, Charles Maurice de
15 89-90
Waterloo
see Waterloo, Battle of (1815)

Hundred Days Reform (China; 1898)
Chang Chih-tung **3** 430-431
K'ang Yu-wei **8** 426-428
Liang Ch'i-ch'ao **9** 395-396
Sun Yat-sen **15** 35-39
Yüan Shih-k'ai **16** 480-481

Hundred Guilder Print (etching)
Rembrandt Harmensz van Rijn
13 91-95

Hundred Years War (1337-1453)
1337-1359 (1st phase)
Charles IV **3** 455-456
Charles V **3** 459-460
Edward III **5** 211-212
Edward the Black Prince **5** 217-218
John II **8** 275-276
Philip VI **12** 277-278
1369-1388 (2nd phase)
Charles V **3** 459-460
John of Gaunt **8** 282-283
1388-1415 (3rd phase)
Charles VI **3** 460-461
Henry IV **7** 292-293
John of Gaunt **8** 282-283
Richard II **13** 130-131
1415-1435 (4th phase)
Henry V **7** 296-297
Joan of Arc **8** 264-265
Philip the Good **12** 278-279
1435-1453 (5th phase)
Charles the Bold **3** 467-469
Charles VII **3** 461-462
Henry VI **7** 298-299
chronicles
Froissart, Jean **6** 124-125
French economics
Louis XI **9** 526-528
Nicholas of Oresme **11** 380
papacy and
Martin V **10** 287-288

Hung-hsi (ruled 1424-1425), Chinese Ming
emperor
Yung-lo **16** 482-483

HUNG HSIU-CH'ÜAN (1814-1864), Chinese religious leader, founder of Taiping
sect **8** 37-38

Hung-li
see Qianlong

Hung-lou meng (novel; Hu Shih)
Hu Shih **8** 63-65

Hung-lou meng (novel; Ts'ao Hsüeh-ch'in)
Yüan Mei **16** 479-480

HUNG-WU (1328-1398), Chinese Ming
emperor 1368-98 **8** 38-39
Kuang-wu-ti **9** 112-113
Yung-lo **16** 482-483

Hungarian revolt (1956)
Dulles, John Foster **5** 134-135
Eisenhower, Dwight David **5** 233-236
Foster, William Zebulon **6** 27-28
Kádár, János **8** 402-403
Mindszenty, József **11** 47-49
Nagy, Imre **11** 292-293
Pandit, Vijaya Lakshmi **12** 83-84
Zhukov, Georgi Konstantinovich
16 512-513

Hungarian revolution (1848)
Francis Joseph **6** 45-46
Kossuth, Louis **9** 88-90

Hungarian Rhapsodies (musical composition)
Liszt, Franz **9** 445-447

Hungary (Hungarian People's Republic;
nation, East-Central Europe)
and Christianity
László I, King of Hungary **9** 219-221
Stephen I **14** 427-428
and the holocaust
Wallenberg, Raoul **16** 78-80
anti-Hapsburg rebellions
Francis Joseph **6** 45-46
Joseph II **8** 359-360
Kossuth, Louis **9** 88-90
Leopold II **9** 346
culture
Bartók, Béla **2** 35-36
Kodály, Zoltán **9** 71
Liszt, Franz **9** 445-447
Moholy-Nagy, László **11** 82-83
Pázmány, Péter **12** 164-165
Vasarely, Victor **15** 440-442
1867-1918
see Austria-Hungary
since World War I
Chou En-lai **4** 20-22
Horthy de Nagybánya, Nicholas
7 510-512
Kádár, János **8** 402-403
see also Hungarian revolt (1956)
Turks and
Augustus II **1** 373-374
Charles V **3** 457-459
Eugene of Savoy **5** 330-331
Ferdinand I **5** 414-415
Hunyadi, John **8** 51-52
Köprülü, Ahmed **9** 84-85
Maximilian II **10** 357-358
Sigismund **14** 220-221
Suleiman I **15** 20-21

Hunger (novel)
Hamsun, Knut **7** 113-114

Hunger Artist, The (story)
Kafka, Franz **8** 403-406

Hungerfield ... (poems)
Jeffers, John Robinson **8** 236-237

Hungry Heart, The (novel)
Phillips, David Graham **12** 280-281

Hungson, Prince
see Taewon'gun, Hungson

Hunkiar Iskelesi, Treaty of (1833)
Mahmud II **10** 145-147

Huns (Asiatic nomads)
Alaric **1** 101-102
Belisarius **2** 128-129
Charlemagne **3** 445-447
Harsha **7** 181-182
Heraclius **7** 320-321
Shahpur II **14** 140-141

HUNT, H. L. (1889-1974), American entrepreneur **8** 42-44

Hunt, Leigh (1784-1859), English poet
Byron, George Gordon Noel **3** 193-194
Keats, John **8** 470-472
Lamb, Charles **9** 176-177
Shelley, Percy Bysshe **14** 176-178

HUNT, RICHARD MORRIS (1827-1895),
American architect **8** 44
Richardson, Henry Hobson **13** 139-141

HUNT, WILLIAM HOLMAN (1827-1910),
English painter **8** 44-45
Lear, Edward **9** 265-266
Millais, John Everett **11** 23-24
Rossetti, Dante Gabriel **13** 308-309

Hunt, William Morris (1824-1879), Ameri-
can painter
French, Daniel Chester **6** 98-99
La Farge, John **9** 149-150

Hunt for Red October, The (book)
Clancy, Tom **4** 70-71

Hunted by Every Hound (play)
Wedekind, Frank **16** 166-167

HUNTER, FLOYD (born 1912), American
social worker and administrator, community worker, professor, and author
8 45-46

Hunter, John (1728-1793), Scottish surgeon
Hunter, William **8** 48-49
Ingenhousz, Jan **8** 119-120
Jenner, Edward **8** 245-246

HUNTER, MADELINE CHEEK (1916-1994),
American educator **8** 47-48

Hunter, Robert (died 1734), British colo-
nial governor
Colden, Cadwallader **4** 145-146
Morris, Lewis **11** 183-184

HUNTER, WILLIAM (1718-1783), Scottish
anatomist **8** 48-49
St. Clair, Arthur **13** 429-430

Hunters in the Snow (painting)
Bruegel, Pieter the Elder **3** 65-67

Hunters of Men, The (poem)
Whittier, John Greenleaf **16** 256-257

Hunter's Sketches (stories)
Turgenev, Ivan Sergeyevich **15** 345-348

Hunting of the Snark, The (verses)
Carroll, Lewis **3** 332-333

HUNTINGTON, COLLIS POTTER
(1821-1900), American railroad builder
8 49
Judah, Theodore Dehone **8** 373-374
Stanford, Leland **14** 397-398

Huntington's disease
Wexler, Nancy **16** 218-219

HUNTLEY AND BRINKLEY (1956-1970),
American journalists and radio and television news team **8** 49-51

Huntley, Chester Robert (Chet;
1911-1974), American journalist and
radio and television news broadcaster
see Huntley and Brinkley

Huntly, 6th Earl of
see Gordon, George

Huntsman, What Quarry (poems)
Millay, Edna St. Vincent **11** 24-25

HUNYADI, JOHN (1385-1456), Hungarian
military leader, regent 1446-1452
8 51-52
Mehmed the Conqueror **10** 452-454

Huong, Tran Van (born 1904), Vietnamese
politician
Thieu, Nguyen Van **15** 182-183

HURD, DOUGLAS (born 1930), English
Conservative Party politician and foreign
secretary **8** 52-55

Hurler Syndrome
Neufeld, Elizabeth F. **11** 352-353

Hurleurs, Les (poem)
Leconte de Lisle, Charles Marie René
9 273-274

Hurley, Patrick J. (1883-1963), American
statesman
Chou En-lai **4** 20-22

Huron Indians (North America)
Brébeuf, Jean de **2** 511-512
Brûlé, Étienne **3** 67-68
Champlain, Samuel de **3** 419-421
Jogues, Isaac **8** 270-271

Huron, Lake (Canada-United States)
Champlain, Samuel de **3** 419-421

Hurrahing in Harvest (poem)
Hopkins, Gerard Manley **7** 492-494

Hurricane (sculpture)
Richier, Germaine **13** 145-146

HURSTON, ZORA NEALE (1903-1960),
African American folklorist and novelist
8 55-56

HUS, JAN (a.k.a. John Hus; ca.1369-1415),
Bohemian religious reformer
Ailly, Pierre d' **1** 94
Knox, John **9** 65-66
Wenceslaus **16** 201-202

see also Hussites

Husain (circa 629-680), grandson of
Mohammed
Aga Khan **1** 74-76

HUSÁK, GUSTÁV (born 1913), president
of the Czechoslovak Socialist Republic
(1975-1987) **8** 59-61

HUSAYN, TAHA (1889-1973), Egyptian
author, educator, and statesman **8** 61-62

HUSAYNI, AL-HAJJ AMIN AL-
(1895-1974), Moslem scholar/leader and
mufti of Jerusalem (1922-1948) **8** 62-63

Husband and Wife (play)
Betti, Ugo **2** 246

HUSEIN IBN ALI (circa 1854-1931), Arab
nationalist, king of Hejaz 1916-1924
8 63
Abdullah ibn Husein **1** 19-20
Faisal I **5** 370-371
ibn Saud, Abd al-Aziz **8** 94-95

Huseyn, Sultan
see Hoseyn Beyqara, Sultan

Huskisson, William (1770-1830), English
financier and statesman
Canning, George **3** 258-260
Liverpool, 2nd Earl of **9** 456-457

Huss, John
see Hus, John

HUSSEIN IBN TALAL (born 1935), king of
the Hashemite Kingdom of Jordan
(1953-80s) **8** 65-67

Husser House (Chicago)
Wright, Frank Lloyd **16** 398-401

HUSSERL, EDMUND (1859-1938), Ger-
man philosopher **8** 67-68
Brentano, Franz Clemens **2** 516-517
Heidegger, Martin **7** 257-258
Merleau-Ponty, Maurice **10** 518
Ortega Y Gasset, José **12** 7-8
Sartre, Jean Paul **13** 491-492
Stein, Edith **14** 412-414

Hussey, Obed (1792-1860), American
inventor
McCormick, Cyrus Hall **10** 400-401

Hussites (Bohemian religious movement)
Hus, Jan **8** 56-59
Masaryk, Tomáš Garrigue **10** 314-315
Palacký, František **12** 69-70
Pius II **12** 331
Sigismund **14** 220-221
Wyclif, John **16** 412-413

Huston, John (1906-1987), American film
director
Bogart, Humphrey **2** 363-364

Hutcheson, Francis (1694-1746), Scottish
philosopher
Mandeville, Bernard **10** 192
Smith, Adam **14** 283-284

HUTCHINS, ROBERT MAYNARD
(1899-1977), American educator **8** 68-69
Dewey, John **4** 520-523
Douglas, William Orville **5** 83-85

Flexner, Abraham **5** 489-490
Urey, Harold Clayton **15** 394-396

HUTCHINSON, ANNE MARBURY
(1591-1643), English-born American reli-
gious leader **8** 69-71
heresy charged
Cotton, John **4** 263-265
Davenport, John **4** 405-406
Dudley, Thomas **5** 124-125
Gorton, Samuell **6** 460
Hooker, Thomas **7** 476-477
Winthrop, John **16** 339-341
Puritan supporters
Vane, Henry **15** 425-426

HUTCHINSON, THOMAS (1711-1780),
American colonial governor **8** 71-72
Adams, Samuel **1** 55-56
Franklin, Benjamin **6** 60-64
Leonard, Daniel **9** 336-337
Otis, James Jr. **12** 25-27
Warren, Mercy Otis **16** 120-121

Hutchinson, William (died 1642),
English-born American merchant
Hutchinson, Anne Marbury **8** 69-71

Hu-t'ou
see Ku K'ai-chih

HUTTEN, ULRICH VON (1488-1523), German humanist **8** 72-73
Reuchlin, Johann **13** 106-107

HUTTON, JAMES (1726-1797), Scottish
geologist **8** 73-74
Darwin, Charles Robert **4** 397-399
Lyell, Charles **10** 62-63

HUXLEY, ALDOUS LEONARD
(1894-1963), English novelist and essayist
8 74-75
Stravinsky, Igor Fedorovich **14** 502-506

Huxley, Andrew Fielding (born 1918), English physiologist
Hodgkin, Alan Lloyd **7** 431-432

HUXLEY, JULIAN (1887-1975), English
biologist and author **8** 75-77
Eyre, Edward John **5** 354

Huxley, Leonard (1860-1933), English
author
Huxley, Aldous Leonard **8** 74-75

HUXLEY, THOMAS HENRY (1825-1895),
English biologist **8** 77-79
and evolution
Darwin, Charles Robert **4** 397-399
Owen, Richard **12** 39
influence of
Burroughs, John **3** 160-161
Dewey, John **4** 520-523
Dreiser, Herman Theodore **5** 98-100
Geddes, Patrick **6** 246-247
Hu Shih **8** 63-65
Ingersoll, Robert Green **8** 120-121
Osler, William **12** 19-20
Titchener, Edward Bradford
15 241-242
Yen Fu **16** 452
students

Wells, Herbert George **16** 195-196

HUYGENS, CHRISTIAAN (1629-1695), Dutch mathematician, astronomer, and physicist **8** 79-81
    Bernoulli, Daniel **2** 216
    Fresnel, Augustin Jean **6** 102-103
    Froberger, Johann Jakob **6** 120-121
    Galileo Galilei **6** 180-183
    Leibniz, Gottfried Wilhelm von **9** 307-310
    Newton, Isaac **11** 369-372
    Pascal, Blaise **12** 122-124

Huygens, Constantin (1596-1687), Dutch poet and diplomat
    Huygens, Christiaan **8** 79-81

Huysmans, Charles Marie Georges
    see Huysmans, Joris Karl

HUYSMANS, JORIS KARL (1848-1907), French novelist **8** 81-82
    Gourmont, Remy de **6** 475
    Mallarmé, Stéphane **10** 172-173
    Redon, Odilon **13** 75-76
    Rouault, Georges **13** 321-322
    Zola, Émile **16** 526-528

Hybridization
    see Plant breeding

HYDE, DOUGLAS (1860-1949), Irish author, president 1938-45 **8** 82-83
    Yeats, William Butler **16** 445-447

Hyde, Edward
    see Clarendon, 1st Earl of

Hyde, Edward (3rd Earl of Clarendon; 1661-1723), English colonial governor
    Makemie, Francis **10** 158-159
    Morris, Lewis **11** 183-184

Hyde, Henry
    see Clarendon, 2d Earl of

Hyde, Mr. (literary character)
    Stevenson, Robert Louis **14** 446-448

Hyde Park Agreement (1941)
    King, William Lyon Mackenzie **9** 25-26

Hydra (biology)
    Leeuwenhoek, Anton van **9** 300-301

Hydrodynamics (physics)
    Bernoulli, Daniel **2** 216
    Duhem, Pierre Maurice Marie **5** 129
    Euler, Leonard **5** 331-332
    Kármán, Theodore von **8** 451-452
    Pascal, Blaise **12** 122-124
    Torricelli, Evangelista **15** 268-269

Hydrogen (element—chemistry)
    Aston, Francis William **1** 350-351
    Bohr, Niels Henrik David **2** 366-368
    Cavendish, Henry **3** 383-384
    Hinshelwood, Cyril Norman **7** 405-406
    Millikan, Robert Andrews **11** 33-35

    Pauli, Wolfgang Ernst **12** 149
    Stern, Otto **14** 435
    Tsiolkovsky, Konstantin Eduardovich **15** 326-328
    Volta, Alessandro **16** 12-14

Hydrogen bomb
    Muller, Hermann Joseph **11** 238-239
    Russell, Bertrand Arthur William **13** 373-374

Hydrographers
    see Scientists—hydrographers

Hydrometer (instrument)
    Fahrenheit, Gabriel Daniel **5** 366

Hydrophobia (medicine)
    Pasteur, Louis **12** 125-127

Hydroplane (aeronautics)
    Bell, Alexander Graham **2** 129-131

Hylton v. United States (legal case)
    Chase, Samuel **3** 475-476

HYMAN, LIBBIE HENRIETTA (1888-1969), American zoologist **8** 83-84

Hymen (book)
    Doolittle, Hilda **5** 65-66

Hymen (musical composition)
    Handel, George Frederick **7** 116-119

Hymn (music)
    Czechoslovakia
        Dvořák, Antonin **5** 168-169
    Denmark
        Nielsen, Carl August **11** 388-389
    England
        Cowper, William **4** 282
        Holst, Gustav **7** 459-460
        Vaughan Williams, Ralph **15** 446-447
        Wesley, Charles **16** 208-209
        Wesley, John **16** 209-210
    Germany
        Beissel, Johann Conrad **2** 123-124
        Luther, Martin **10** 48-51
        Mendelssohn, Moses **10** 488-489
        Notker Balbulus **11** 434-435
        Stockhausen, Karlheinz **14** 460-461
        Walter, Johann **16** 86
    Italy
        Palestrina, Giovanni Pierluigi da **12** 70-72
        Vivaldi, Antonio **16** 3-4
    Spain
        Cabezón, Antonio **3** 197-198
        Victoria, Tomás Luis de **15** 487-488
    United States
        Billings, William **2** 274-275
        Ives, Charles Edward **8** 159-160
        Paine, John Knowles **12** 65
        see also Chorale (music)

Hymn (poem)
    Baudelaire, Charles Pierre **2** 61-63
    Carducci, Giosuè **3** 290-291
    Longfellow, Henry Wadsworth **9** 499-500
    Shelley, Percy Bysshe **14** 176-178
    Swinburne, Algernon Charles **15** 54-55

Hymns (poems)
    D'Annunzio, Gabriele **4** 388
    George, Stefan **6** 277-278
    Novalis **11** 435
    Ronsard, Pierre de **13** 271-273
    Theocritus **15** 171-172

Hypatia (novel)
    Kingsley, Charles **9** 28

HYPATIA OF ALEXANDRIA (370-415), Greek mathematician and philosopher **8** 85

Hyperbolic geometry
    see Non-Euclidean geometry

Hyperides (died 322 B.C.), Athenian statesman
    Isocrates **8** 151

Hyperion (novel)
    Hölderlin, Johann Christian Friedrich **7** 451-452
    Longfellow, Henry Wadsworth **9** 499-500

Hyperion (poem)
    Keats, John **8** 470-472

Hyperon (element—chemistry particle)
    Gell-Mann, Murray **6** 257-258

Hyperprism (musical composition)
    Varèse, Edgard **15** 432-433

Hypnosis (psychology)
    Binet, Alfred **2** 277-278
    Charcot, Jean Martin **3** 442
    Freud, Sigmund **6** 103-106
    Hull, Clark Leonard **8** 28
    Mesmer, Franz Anton **10** 526-527

Hypochondriack
    see Boswell, James

Hypophysis (anatomy)
    Houssay, Bernardo Alberto **7** 522-523

Hypothalamus (anatomy)
    Hess, Walter Rudolf **7** 365

Hystaspes
    see Vishtaspa

Hysteria (psychology)
    Binet, Alfred **2** 277-278
    Charcot, Jean Martin **3** 442
    Freud, Sigmund **6** 103-106
    Sydenham, Thomas **15** 59-60

I

i (lectures)
  Cummings, Edward Estlin **4** 334-336

I! (poems)
  Mayakovsky, Vladimir Vladimirovich **10** 364-365

I Am a Cat (novel)
  Natsume, Soseki **11** 324-325

I Am the People, the Mob (poem)
  Sandburg, Carl **13** 461-462

I and My Village (painting)
  Chagall, Marc **3** 406-407

I and Thou (book)
  Buber, Martin **3** 87-89

I Ching (ancient Chinese book)
  Cage, John **3** 211-214
  Chu Hsi **4** 40-43
  Confucius **4** 197-200
  Kublai Khan **9** 115-118
  Wang Pi **16** 104-105
  Yi Hwang **16** 457

I Claudius (novel)
  Graves, Robert Ranke **6** 504-506

I Confess (film)
  Hitchcock, Alfred **7** 415-416

I Dream of Jeanie ... (song)
  Foster, Stephen Collins **6** 25-27

I.F. Stone's Weekly (newsletter)
  Stone, I. F. **14** 470-471

I Get a Kick out of You (song)
  Porter, Cole Albert **12** 405-406

I hate and I love (poem)
  Catullus, Gaius Valerius **3** 377-378

I Have a Dream (literary collection)
  King, Martin Luther Jr. **9** 20-22

I Know Why the Caged Bird Sings (autobiography)
  Angelou, Maya **1** 238-239

I Live under a Black Sun (novel)
  Sitwell, Edith **14** 265-266

I Love Lucy
  Ball, Lucille **1** 472-473

I promessi sposi (novel)
  Manzoni, Alessandro **10** 222-224

I Saw in Louisiana a Live-Oak Growing (poem)
  Whitman, Walt **16** 249-251

I saw my lady weep (song)
  Dowland, John **5** 90

I Saw the Figure 5 in Gold (poster-portrait)
  Demuth, Charles **4** 497-498

I shall return (oath)
  MacArthur, Douglas **10** 76-78

I Sing the Body Electric (poem)
  Whitman, Walt **16** 249-251

I Sit and Look Out (poem)
  Whitman, Walt **16** 249-251

I stood tiptoe (poem)
  Keats, John **8** 470-472

I taste a liquor never brewed (poem)
  Dickinson, Emily **4** 541-543

I think, therefore, I am (philosophy)
  Descartes, René **4** 505-508

I Thought of Daisy (novel)
  Wilson, Edmund **16** 318-319

I Wake and Feel the Fell of Dark (sonnet)
  Hopkins, Gerard Manley **7** 492-494

I wandered lonely as a cloud (poem)
  Wordsworth, William **16** 385-388

I Want to Hold Your Hand (song)
  Lennon, John Winston **9** 326-328

I Write What I Like (book)
  Biko, Steve **2** 273-274

IACOCCA, LIDO (LEE) ANTHONY (born 1924), American automobile magnate **8** 86-88

Iago (literary character)
  Shakespeare, William **14** 142-145
  Verdi, Giuseppe Fortunino Francesco **15** 463-465

Iambics (poem)
  Theocritus **15** 171-172

Iamblichus (died circa 333), Greek philosopher
  Plotinus **12** 358-359

Iambs and Anapaests (poems)
  Palamas, Kostes **12** 70

Iaroslav (Yaroslav; died 1054), grand prince of Kiev
  Vladimir I **16** 5-6

Iaşi, Treaty of (1792)
  Catherine the Great **3** 370-372
  Potemkin, Grigori Aleksandrovich **12** 411-412
  Selim III **14** 95-96

Iaşi, University of (Romania)
  Titulescu, Nicolae **15** 246-247

IBÁÑEZ DEL CAMPO, CARLOS (1877-1960), Chilean general and president **8** 88
  Alessandri Palma, Arturo **1** 128-129
  Herrera, Juan de **7** 335

ÍBARRURI GÓMEZ, DOLORES (1895-1989), voice of the Republican cause in the Spanish Civil War **8** 88-90

Iberia (musical composition)
  Debussy, Achille Claude **4** 445-447

Iberia (piano suite)
  Albéniz, Issac **1** 108-109

IBERVILLE, SIEUR D' (Pierre le Moyne; 1661-1706), Canadian soldier, naval captain, and adventurer **8** 90-91
  Bienville, Sieur de **2** 268-269
  Kelsey, Henry **8** 488

Ibis (poem)
  Callimachus **3** 235-236
  Ovid **12** 34-36

IBM
  see International Business Machines

IBN AL-ARABI, MUHYI AL-DIN (1165-1240), Spanish-born Moslem poet, philosopher, and mystic **8** 91

Ibn al-Khatib (1313-1374), Arab poet and man of letters
  ibn Khaldun, Abd al-Rahman ibn Muhammad **8** 93-94

IBN BATTUTA, MUHAMMAD
(1304-1368/69), Moslem traveler and
author **8** 91-92
Muhammad bin Tughluq **11** 229
Musa Mansa **11** 266

IBN GABIROL, SOLOMON BEN JUDAH
(circa 1021-circa 1058), Spanish Hebrew
poet and philosopher **8** 92
Zangwill, Israel **16** 488-489

IBN HAZM, ABU MUHAMMAD ALI
(994-1064), Spanish-born Arab theologian and jurist **8** 93

**IBN KHALDUN, ABD AL-RAHMAN IBN
MUHAMMAD** (1332-1406), Arab historian, philosopher, and statesman **8** 93-94

Ibn Nagdala (or Nagrela)
see Samuel ha-Nagid

Ibn Rushd
see Averroës

IBN SAUD, ABD AL-AZIZ (1880-1953),
Arab politician, founder of Saudi Arabia
8 94-95

Ibn Sina
see Avicenna

IBN TASHUFIN, YUSUF (died 1106), North
African Almoravid ruler **8** 95-96

IBN TUFAYL, ABU BAKR MUHAMMAD
(circa 1110-1185), Spanish Moslem
philosopher and physician **8** 96
Bitruji, Nur al-Din Abu Ishaq al **2** 296

IBN TUMART, MUHAMMAD (circa
1080-1130), North African Islamic theologian **8** 96-97
Abd al-Mumin **1** 13

Ibn-Hanbal, Ahmad (780-855), Arab jurist
Mamun, Abdallah al- **10** 183

Ibo (African people)
Achebe, Chinua **1** 35-37
Azikiwe, Nnamdi **1** 401-402

Ibrahim Lodi (died 1526), Afghan king
1517-1526
Babar the Conqueror **1** 405-407

Ibrahim Pasha (1493?-1536), Turkish grand
vizier
Suleiman I **15** 20-21

IBRAHIM PASHA (1789-1848), Turkish
military and administrative leader
8 97-98
Mohammed Ali **11** 81-82

IBSEN, HENRIK (1828-1906), Norwegian
playwright **8** 98-100
associates
Bjørnson, Bjørnstjerne **2** 299-300
Grieg, Edvard Hagerup **6** 541-542
influence of
Hauptmann, Gerhart Johann Robert
7 199-201
Joyce, James **8** 365-367
Merezhkovsky, Dmitry Sergeyevich
10 515-516
Miller, Arthur **11** 25-26
Pirandello, Luigi **12** 319-321
Strindberg, August **14** 509-511

works adapted
Fiske, Minnie Maddern **5** 466-467
Wilder, Thornton Niven **16** 276-277

Ibsenism (literature)
Hu Shih **8** 63-65
Ibsen, Henrik **8** 98-100

Icaria (utopian community; Texas)
Cabet, Étienne **3** 196

Ice Palace (novel)
Ferber, Edna **5** 413

Ice Palace, The (story)
Fitzgerald, Francis Scott Key **5** 470-472

Iceland (Republic of Iceland, North
Atlantic)
Harold I **7** 161-162
Sturluson, Snorri **14** 310-311

Iceman Cometh, The (play)
O'Neill, Eugene **11** 514-516

Ich hatte viel Bekümmernis (cantata)
Bach, Johann Sebastian **1** 416-419

Ichabod (poem)
Whittier, John Greenleaf **16** 256-257

Ichijo (died 1011), emperor of Japan
Fujiwara Michinaga **6** 145-146
Murasaki Shikibu **11** 252-253

Ichthyologists
see Scientists—ichthyologists

Île de la Cité (Paris)
Haussmann, Baron Georges Eugène
7 201-202

Île des Pingouins, L' (novel)
France, Anatole **6** 39-40

ICKES, HAROLD LECLAIRE (1874-1952),
American statesman **8** 100-101
Lilienthal, David Eli **9** 410-411

Iconoclasm (religion)
Alcuin of York **1** 122-123
Holbach, Baron d' **7** 448-449
William the Silent **16** 300-302

Iconoclastic Controversy (circa 725-842)
Charlemagne **3** 445-447
John of Damascus **8** 282
Leo III **9** 330-332

Iconography (art)
Charonton, Enguerrand **3** 471
Cranach, Lucas the Elder **4** 289-290
Gorky, Arshile **6** 458
Lippi, Filippo **9** 439
O'Keeffe, Georgia **11** 487-489

Iconoscope (electronics)
Zworykin, Vladimir Kosma **16** 539-540

Icosameron (novel)
Casanova de Seingalt, Giacomo Jacopo
Girolamo **3** 350-351

ICTINUS (flourished 2nd half of 5th century B.C.), Greek architect **8** 101

I'd Rather Be Right (satire)
Cohan, George Michael **4** 137-138

Ida Elisabeth (novel)
Undset, Sigrid **15** 388-389

Idaho (state, United States)
Borah, William Edgar **2** 408
Harrison, Benjamin **7** 178-179

Idanre ... (poems)
Soyinka, Wole **14** 358-359

Idea (philosophy)
Bonaventure **2** 383-384
Descartes, René **4** 505-508
Hume, David **8** 31-34
Husserl, Edmund **8** 67-68
Philo Judaeus **12** 282-283
Locke, John **9** 478-480
Plotinus **12** 358-359

Idea (poems)
Drayton, Michael **5** 97-98

Idea of the Holy, The (book)
Otto, Louis Karl Rudolf **12** 30-32

Idéal, L' (poem)
Baudelaire, Charles Pierre **2** 61-63

Ideal Husband, An (play)
Wilde, Oscar Fingall O'Flahertie Wills
16 272-273

Idealism (philosophy)
absolute
Bosanquet, Bernard **2** 425-426
Bradley, Francis Herbert **2** 481-482
Fichte, Johann Gottlieb **5** 435-436
Gentile, Giovanni **6** 267
Green, Thomas Hill **6** 520-521
Hegel, Georg Wilhelm Friedrich
7 254-256
Horne, Herman Harrell **7** 503-504
Royce, Josiah **13** 334-335
Schelling, Friedrich Wilhelm Joseph
von **13** 526-527
Schleiermacher, Friedrich Ernst
Daniel **14** 11-12
and science
Lotze, Rudolf Hermann **9** 521-522
influence of
Harris, William Torrey **7** 177-178
Santayana, George **13** 475-477
opponents
Fries, Jakob Friedrich **6** 116-117
McCosh, James **10** 402-403
Perry, Ralph Barton **12** 239-240
Rosenzweig, Franz **13** 294
Stirner, Max **14** 459-460
subjective
Berkeley, George **2** 197-198
Croce, Benedetto **4** 313-314
Schopenhauer, Arthur **14** 29-31
transcendental
Cassirer, Ernst **3** 358-359
Cohen, Hermann **4** 138-139
Kant, Immanuel **8** 430-432
Rosmini-Serbati, Antonio
13 296-297

Idea's Mirror (sonnets)
Drayton, Michael **5** 97-98

Ideas of Order (poems)
Stevens, Wallace **14** 443-445

Identity (psych).
Erikson, Erik Homburger **5** 309-310

Ides of March, The (novel)
Wilder, Thornton Niven **16** 276-277

Idiopathic anemia
see Pernicious anemia

Idiot, The (ballet)
Henze, Hans Werner **7** 314

Idiot, The (novel and film)
Dostoevsky, Fyodor **5** 74-77
Kurosawa, Akira **9** 135-137

Idiot's Delight (play)
Sherwood, Robert Emmet **14** 189-190

Idomeneo (opera)
Mozart, Wolfgang Amadeus
11 218-221

Idomeneus (circa 325-circa 270 B.C.),
Greek biographer and politician
Epicurus **5** 292-294

IDRIS I (1889-1983), king of Libya
1950-69 **8** 102

**IDRISI, MUHAMMAD IBN MUHAMMAD
AL-** (1100-1165?), Arab geographer
8 102-103
Roger II **13** 244-245

Idyll of Theocritus (musical composition)
Sessions, Roger Huntington **14** 117-118

Idylles (poems)
Chénier, André Marie **3** 500-501

Idylls (poems; Theocritus)
Theocritus **15** 171-172
Virgil **15** 507-510

Idylls of the King (poem)
Tennyson, Alfred **15** 144-146

If I Loved You (song)
Rodgers, Richard Charles **13** 234-236

If Thou Wouldst Know (poem)
Bialik, Hayyim Nahman **2** 262-263

If We Must Die (poem)
McKay, Claude **10** 416

If ye love me (anthem)
Tallis, Thomas **15** 91

If, Yes, and Perhaps (literary collection)
Hale, Edward Everett **7** 71-72

Igitur ... (book)
Mallarmé, Stéphane **10** 172-173

IGLESIAS, ENRIQUE V. (born 1930),
Uruguayan economist, banker, and public official **8** 106-107

IGNATIUS OF ANTIOCH, SAINT (died
circa 115), Early Christian bishop and
theologian **8** 107-108
Peter **12** 252-253

Ignatius of Constantinople, Saint (Nicetas;
799?-878), patriarch of Constantinople
Cyril and Methodius, Saints **4** 362-363
Photius **12** 283-284

IGNATIUS OF LOYOLA, SAINT
(1491-1556), Spanish soldier, founder of
Jesuits **8** 108-109
influence of
Bernini, Gian Lorenzo **2** 214-216
Canisius, Peter **3** 258
Caravaggio **3** 282-284
Hopkins, Gerard Manley **7** 492-494
Neri, Philip **11** 340
Velázquez, Diego Rodríguez de
Silva y **15** 454-456
Jesuits founded
Francis Xavier **6** 48

Iguala, Plan of (Mexico; 1821)
Álvarez, Juan **1** 184-185
Guerrero, Vicente **7** 28-30
Iturbide, Agustín de **8** 155-156

Ihara Saikaku (1642-1693), Japanese novelist and poet
Basho, Matsuo **2** 45-48

Ike and Tina Turner Revue
Turner, Tina **15** 357-359

IKEDA, DAISAKU (born 1928), Japanese
Buddhist writer and religious leader
8 109-110

Ikeda, Hayato (1899-1965), Japanese
statesman
Sato, Eisaku **13** 495-496

IKHNATON (ruled 1379-1362 B.C.),
pharaoh of Egypt **8** 110-111
Amenhotep III **1** 194-195
Tutankhamen **15** 359-360

Ikiru (film)
Kurosawa, Akira **9** 135-137

Il falso e vero verde (poem)
Quasimodo, Salvatore **12** 506

Il faut qu'une porte soit ouverte ou fermée
(play)
Musset, Louis Charles Alfred de
11 271-272

Il ne faut jurer de rien (play)
Musset, Louis Charles Alfred de
11 271-272

Il pleure dans mon coeur (poem)
Verlaine, Paul Marie **15** 465-466

Ildefonso Altarpiece (painting)
Rubens, Peter Paul **13** 339-342

ILGWU
see International Ladies' Garment
Workers' Union

Ili crisis (China-Russia; 1879-80)
Chang Chih-tung **3** 430-431

Iliad (epic poem; Homer)
authorship
Homer **7** 465-467
influence of
Alexander the Great **1** 137-141
Sophocles **14** 343-345
Virgil **15** 507-510
Wolf, Friedrich August **16** 352-353
translations
Bryant, William Cullen **3** 83-85

Casanova de Seinglat, Giacomo
Jacopo Girolamo **3** 350-351
Chapman, George **3** 440-441
Clarke, Samuel **4** 88
Kazantzakis, Nikos **8** 466-468
Poliziano, Angelo **12** 373-374
Pope, Alexander **12** 395-397
Tschernichowsky, Saul **15** 323

ILIESCU, ION (born 1930), president of
Romania (1990-) **8** 111-112

I'll Follow My Secret Heart (song)
Coward, Noel **4** 279-280

I'll Say She Is (musical)
Marx brothers **10** 303-304

I'll See You Again (song)
Coward, Noel **4** 279-280

I'll Take My Stand (book)
Ransom, John Crowe **13** 39-40
Warren, Robert Penn **16** 121-122

Illahun (ancient site; Egypt)
Petrie, William Matthew Flinders
12 261-262

Illibata Dei virgo (poem)
Josquin des Prez **8** 361-363

Illica, Luigi (1857-1919), Italian librettist
Puccini, Giacomo **12** 474-476

ILLICH, IVAN (born 1926), theologian,
educator, and social critic **8** 112-114

Illinois (state, United States)
governors
Altgeld, John Peter **1** 180-182
Stevenson, Adlai Ewing **14** 445-446
legislators
Cannon, Joseph Gurney **3** 261-262
Cartwright, Peter **3** 344-345
Lincoln, Abraham **9** 415-418
Trumbull, Lyman **15** 317-318
senators
Mosely-Braun, Carol **11** 199-200
State Supreme Court
Douglas, Stephen Arnold **5** 80-82

Illinois Central Railroad
Harriman, Edward Henry **7** 164-165
McClellan, George Brinton **10** 391-392
Pinkerton, Allan **12** 314-315
Van Horne, William Cornelius
15 429-430

Illinois Indians (North America)
Marquette, Jacques **10** 274-275

Illinois Institute of Technology (Chicago)
Mies van der Rohe, Ludwig **11** 10-12

Illinois River
Marquette, Jacques **10** 274-275

Illinois, University of (Urbana)
Bagley, William Chandler **1** 437-438
Bloomfield, Leonard **2** 338
Broudy, Harry Samuel **3** 28-29
Znaniecki, Florian **16** 523-524

Illumination (poems)
Crane, Hart **4** 291-293

Rimbaud, Jean Nicolas Arthur
13 172-174

Illuminators
see Artists—illuminators

Illuminés, Les (book)
Nerval, Gérard de **11** 345-346

Illusion comique, L' (play)
Corneille, Pierre **4** 234-236

Illusionism (art)
Cézanne, Paul **3** 400-402
Dali, Salvador **4** 376-377
Ernst, Max **5** 311-312
Gaulli, Giovanni Battista **6** 238-239
Harnett, William Michael **7** 160-161
Ingres, Jean Auguste Dominique
8 121-123
Monet, Claude **11** 102-104

Illusions perdues (book)
Balzac, Honoré de **1** 478-480

Illustrators
see Artists—illustrators

Ilmenau (poem)
Goethe, Johann Wolfgang von
6 388-391

ILP
see Independent Labour party

Ilusiones del doctor Faustino, Las (novel)
Valera y Alcalá Galiano, Juan **15** 403

I'm a Fool (story)
Anderson, Sherwood **1** 220-221

I'm a Yankee Doodle Dandy (song)
Cohan, George Michael **4** 137-138

Im Dickicht der Stadte (play)
Brecht, Bertolt **2** 512-514

I'm Not Stiller (novel)
Frisch, Max **6** 118-119

Im Paradiese (novel)
Heyse, Paul Johann Ludwig **7** 372-373

Im Schlaraffenland (novel)
Mann, Heinrich **10** 201-202

Im Schloss (novella)
Storm, Theodor **14** 479-480

Im Westen nichts Neues (novel)
Remarque, Erich Maria **13** 91

Im Wirbel der Berufung (novel)
Hauptmann, Gerhart Johann Robert
7 199-201

Image of Xhorkhom (painting)
Gorky, Arshile **6** 458

Images (musical composition)
Debussy, Achille Claude **4** 445-447

Images of Departure (poems)
Colum, Padraic **4** 174-175

Imaginary Conversations (book)
Landor, Walter Savage **9** 186-187

Imaginary geometry
see Non-Euclidean geometry

Imaginary Prisons (engraving series)
Piranesi, Giovanni Battista **12** 321-322

Imagination (philosophy)
Santayana, George **13** 475-477

Imagism (literature)
Doolittle, Hilda **5** 65-66
Esenin, Sergei Aleksandrovich **5** 321
Lowell, Amy **10** 13
Pound, Ezra Loomis **12** 415-417
Sandburg, Carl **13** 461-462
Williams, William Carlos **16** 308-309
Yeats, William Butler **16** 445-447

IMAM, ALHADJI ABUBAKAR (1911-1981),
Nigerian writer and teacher **8** 114-115

IMAOKA, SHINICHIRO (1881-1988), progressive and liberal religious leader in
Japan **8** 115

Imbroglio, L' (literary collection)
Moravia, Alberto **11** 153-155

Imbros (Turkish island)
Homer **7** 465-467

Imeneo (opera)
Handel, George Frederick **7** 116-119

IMF
see International Monetary Fund

IMHOTEP (ca. 3000 B.C. - ca. 2950 B.C.),
Egyptian vizier, architect, priest,
astronomer, and magician-physician
8 116-117
Zoser **16** 531

Imitation de Notre-Dame la Lune, L'
(poems)
Laforgue, Jules **9** 160-161

Imitation of Christ, The (book; Thomas à
Kempis)
Groote, Gerard **7** 12-13
Kempis, Thomas à **8** 493-494

Imitation of Spenser (poem)
Keats, John **8** 470-472

Imitations of Horace (book)
Pope, Alexander **12** 395-397

Immaculate ... (sculpture)
Günther, Ignaz **7** 41-42

Immaculate Conception (painting)
Murillo, Bartolomé Esteban **11** 258-259

Immaculate Conception (religious doctrine)
Duns Scotus, John **5** 149-150

Immaterialism (philosophy)
Berkeley, George **2** 197-198

Immaturity (novel)
Shaw, George Bernard **14** 163-164

Immense Journey, The (book)
Eiseley, Loren Corey **5** 232-233

Immensee (novella)
Storm, Theodor **14** 479-480

Immigrant and the Community, The (book)
Abbott, Grace **1** 9-10

Immigrant, The (film)
Chaplin, Charles Spencer **3** 438-440

Immigrant, The (poem)
Soyinka, Wole **14** 358-359

Immigrants
to Australia
Bates, Daisy Mae **2** 52-53
Burke, Robert O'Hara **3** 142-143
Hargraves, Edward Hammond
7 153-154
Macarthur, John **10** 78
to Austria
Gumplowicz, Ludwig **7** 41
to Canada
Brown, George **3** 35-36
Butler, John **3** 180
Macdonald, John Alexander
10 85-87
Mackenzie, Alexander **10** 104
Mackenzie, William Lyon
10 104-106
Penfield, Wilder Graves **12** 198-200
Selkirk, 5th Earl of **14** 96
Strachan, John **14** 486-487
Tilley, Samuel Leonard **15** 223-224
Van Horne, William Cornelius
15 429-430
to England
Belloc, Joseph Hilaire Pierre **2** 141
Epstein, Jacob **5** 295-296
Handel, George Frederick
7 116-119
Malinowski, Kaspar Bronislaw
10 170-171
Williams, Henry Sylvester
16 303-304
to France
Berdyaev, Nicholas Alexandrovich
2 184-185
Bunin, Ivan Alekseevich **3** 124
Mann, Heinrich **10** 201-202
Mazarin, Jules **10** 379-380
Miliukov, Pavel Nikolayevich
11 18-19
Offenbach, Jacques **11** 478-479
Rousseau, Jean Jacques **13** 324-328
Stravinsky, Igor Fedorovich
14 502-506
to India
Haldane, John Burdon Sanderson
7 70-71
to Ireland
De Valera, Eamon **4** 514-515
to Israel
Agnon, Shmuel Yoseph **1** 85-86
Asch, Shalom **1** 325-326
Ben-Gurion, David **2** 160-161
Ben Yehuda, Eliezer **2** 181-182
Bialik, Hayyim Nahman **2** 262-263
Meir, Golda **10** 462-463
Scholem, Gershom **14** 26
Steffens, Lincoln **14** 410-411
Stendhal **14** 422-425
Tschernichowsky, Saul **15** 323
to Liberia
Blyden, Edward Wilmot **2** 348-349

to New Zealand
    Savage, Michael Joseph **13** 501-502
to Norway
    Brandt, Willy **2** 499-500
to Peru
    Meiggs, Henry **10** 458-459
to Russia
    Lukács, Gyorgy **10** 37-38
    Struve, Friedrich Georg Wilhelm von
      14 513
to South Africa
    Verwoerd, Hendrik Frensch
      15 472-473
to Sweden
    Nordenskjöld, Nils Adolf Erik
      11 421-422
    Sachs, Nelly **13** 411-412
to Switzerland
    Reichstein, Tadeus **13** 85-87
to Uruguay
    Laforgue, Jules **9** 160-161
to United States
    see Immigrants to the United States

Immigrant's Protective League
    Abbott, Grace **1** 9-10

Immigrants to the United States
    from Alsace-Lorraine
      Bethe, Hans Albrecht **2** 238-239
    from Austria
      Adler, Alfred **1** 61-63
      Berger, Victor Louis **2** 189-190
      Bettelheim, Bruno **2** 245-246
      Landsteiner, Karl **9** 188-189
      Neutra, Richard Joseph **11** 355-356
      Rank, Otto **13** 33
      Schumpeter, Joseph Alois **14** 43-44
      Schuschnigg, Kurt von **14** 45-46
    from Belgium
      Baekeland, Leo Hendrik **1** 430-431
      Sarton, George **13** 490-491
    from Bermuda
      Tucker, George **15** 332-333
    from Bohemia
      Cather, Willa Sibert **3** 368-369
    from British West Indies
      Benjamin, Judah Philip **2** 163-164
      Hamilton, Alexander **7** 95-98
    from Canada
      Bellow, Saul **2** 141-143
      Prendergast, Maurice Brazil **12** 440
      Sennett, Mack **14** 108-109
    from China
      Yang, Chen Ning **16** 437-438
    from Croatia
      Tesla, Nikola **15** 156-157
    from Denmark
      Riis, Jacob August **13** 169-170
    from England (17th-19th century)
      Bacon, Nathaniel **1** 424-425
      Bradford, William **2** 475-476
      Cotton, John **4** 263-265
      Harrison, Peter **7** 179-180
      Latrobe, Benjamin Henry **9** 222-224
      Paine, Thomas **12** 66-67
      Priestley, Joseph **12** 452-453

Slater, Samuel **14** 272-273
      Taylor, Edward **15** 122-123
    from England (19th-20th century)
      Auden, Wystan Hugh **1** 364-366
      Evans, George Henry **5** 337-338
      Gompers, Samuel **6** 420-422
      Rimmer, William **13** 174
      Upjohn, Richard **15** 392
    from France
      Audubon, John James **1** 366-367
      Benezet, Anthony **2** 159-160
      Cabet, Étienne **3** 196
      du Pont, Éleuthère Irénée **5** 154
      Genet, Edmond Charles **6** 261-262
      Girard, Stephen **6** 347-348
      Soulé, Pierre **14** 351-352
      Varèse, Edgard **15** 432-433
    from Germany (17th-18th century)
      Astor, John Jacob **1** 351-352
      Beissel, Johann Conrad **2** 123-124
      Leisler, Jacob **9** 313-314
      Mühlenberg, Heinrich Melchior
        11 232-233
      Otterbein, Philip William **12** 27-28
      Stiegel, Henry William **14** 451
      Zinzendorf, Nikolaus Ludwig von
        16 522-523
    from Germany (19th century)
      Altgeld, John Peter **1** 180-182
      Bierstadt, Albert **2** 270-271
      Lieber, Francis **9** 401-402
      Mergenthaler, Ottmar **10** 516-517
      Rapp, George **13** 42-43
      Roebling, John Augustus
        13 241-242
      Schurz, Carl **14** 44-45
      Sutter, John Augustus **15** 41-42
      Thomas, Theodore **15** 192-193
    from Germany (19th-20th century)
      Boas, Franz **2** 349-351
      Schiff, Jacob Henry **14** 2-3
      Schindler, Solomon **14** 7-8
      Steinmetz, Charles Proteus
        14 419-420
      Warburg, Paul Moritz **16** 111-112
    from Germany (20th century)
      Carnap, Rudolf **3** 308-309
      Erikson, Erik Homburger **5** 309-310
      Grosz, George **7** 17-18
      Lewin, Kurt **9** 375-376
      Lovejoy, Arthur Oncken **10** 6
      Mann, Heinrich **10** 201-202
      Mann, Thomas **10** 204-207
      Marcuse, Herbert **10** 245-247
      Mendelsohn, Erich **10** 488
      Meyerhof, Otto Fritz **10** 537-539
      Mies van der Rohe, Ludwig
        11 10-12
      Stern, Otto **14** 435
      Tillich, Paul Johannes **15** 224-225
      von Braun, Wernher **16** 17-18
      Weill, Kurt **16** 174-175
    from Hungary
      Bartók, Béla **2** 35-36
      Breuer, Marcel **2** 520-521
      Pulitzer, Joseph **12** 481-482

Szent-Györgyi, Albert von **15** 62-64
      Szilard, Leo **15** 64-66
      Von Neumann, John **16** 27-28
      Wigner, Eugene Paul **16** 268-269
    from Ireland (17th-18th century)
      Lewis, Andrew **9** 376-377
      Makemie, Francis **10** 158-159
      Montgomery, Richard **11** 138-139
    from Ireland (19th-20th century)
      Brown, Alexander **3** 31-32
      Campbell, Alexander **3** 249-250
      Daly, Marcus **4** 379-380
      Grace, William Russell **6** 480-481
      Harris, Frank **7** 172-173
      Hearn, Lafcadio **7** 240
      Holland, John Philip **7** 453-454
      Hughes, John Joseph **8** 17-18
      Ireland, John **8** 133-134
      Kearney, Denis **8** 468
      Stewart, Alexander Turney
        14 448-449
    from Italy
      Cabrini, Frances Xavier **3** 205
      Capone, Al **3** 272-273
      Menotti, Gian Carlo **10** 509-510
      Sacco and Vanzetti **13** 408-410
      Stella, Joseph **14** 422
    from Lithuania
      Cahan, Abraham **3** 214
      Ginzberg, Louis **6** 337-338
      Lipchitz, Jacques **9** 432-433
      Shahn, Ben **14** 139-140
      Silver, Abba Hillel **14** 232-233
    from Norway
      Rockne, Knute **13** 231
      Rölvaag, Ole Edvart **13** 265
    from Poland
      Asch, Shalom **1** 325-326
      Heschel, Abraham Joshua
        7 358-359
      Nadelman, Elie **11** 289-290
      Singer, Isaac Bashevis **14** 249-250
      Tarski, Alfred **15** 110-111
      Znaniecki, Florian **16** 523-524
    from Portugal
      Pinto, Isaac **12** 318
    from Romania
      Schechter, Solomon **13** 524
    from Russia (19th-20th century)
      Sholem Aleichem **14** 202-203
      Weber, Max **16** 160
    from Russia (20th century)
      Archipenko, Alexander **1** 280-281
      Balanchine, George **1** 461-462
      Berlin, Irving **2** 200-201
      Dubinsky, David **5** 114-115
      Nabokov, Vladimir **11** 287-288
      Prokofiev, Sergei Sergeevich
        12 458-460
      Rostovtzeff, Michael Ivanovich
        13 315
      Rothko, Mark **13** 320-321
      Sarnoff, David **13** 485-486
      Sikorsky, Igor **14** 223-224
      Sorokin, Pitirim A. **14** 348-349

Stravinsky, Igor Fedorovich
14 502-506
Waksman, Selman Abraham
16 49-50
Zworykin, Vladimir Kosma
16 539-540
from Scotland (17th-19th century)
Bennett, James Gordon **2** 168-169
Brackenridge, Hugh Henry
2 472-473
Livingston, Robert **9** 461-462
McCosh, James **10** 402-403
Phyfe, Duncan **12** 284-285
Pinkerton, Allan **12** 314-315
Smibert, John **14** 282
Wilson, Alexander **16** 313-314
Witherspoon, John **16** 346-348
from Scotland (19th-20th century)
Carnegie, Andrew **3** 309-312
Kane, John **8** 422
MacIver, Robert Morrison
10 100-101
Murray, Philip **11** 264-265
from Serbia
Pupin, Michael Idvorsky **12** 483-484
from South Africa
Theiler, Max **15** 169-170
from Spain
Santayana, George **13** 475-477
from Sweden
Ericsson, John **5** 307-308
from Switzerland
Bloch, Ernest **2** 326-327
Gallatin, Albert **6** 183-184
Guggenheim, Meyer **7** 31-32
Schaff, Philip **13** 519-520

Immigration (United States)
Burlingame, Anson **3** 144-145
Handlin, Oscar **7** 121-122
Harding, Warren Gamaliel **7** 148-149
Hoover, John Edgar **7** 485-487
Kenny, Elizabeth **8** 509-510
Ross, Edward Alsworth **13** 300

Immigration Restriction Act (Australia)
Barton, Edmund **2** 39-40

Immoraliste, L' (book)
Gide, André **6** 308-309

Immortal, The (film)
Robbe-Grillet, Alain **13** 189-190

Immortale Dei (encyclical)
Leo XIII **9** 334-336

Immortel, L' (novel)
Daudet, Alphonse **4** 402-403

Immunology (medicine)
immunochemistry
Arrhenius, Svante August **1** 318-320
Ehrlich, Paul **5** 225-226
Landsteiner, Karl **9** 188-189
immunological tolerance
Behring, Emil Adolph von
2 122-123
Burnet, Frank Macfarlane **3** 146-147
Medawar, Peter Brian **10** 444-445
Metchnikoff, Élie **10** 532-533

inoculation
see Inoculation
see also Scientists—immunologists

Imouthes
see Imhotep

Impeachment (United States)
Chandler, Zachariah **3** 425-426
Chase, Samuel **3** 475-476
Johnson, Andrew **8** 294-295
Sumner, Charles **15** 30-31

Imperative Duty, An (novella)
Howells, William Dean **7** 539-541

Imperial Conference (London ; 1926, 1937)
Balfour, Arthur James **1** 469-470
Hertzog, James Barry Munnik
7 347-348
Lyons, Joseph Aloysius **10** 69-70
Savage, Michael Joseph **13** 501-502

Imperial Diet (Germany)
see Reichstag (Germany)

Imperial Hotel (Tokyo, Japan)
Wright, Frank Lloyd **16** 398-401

Imperial Legislative Council (India)
Gokhale, Gopal Krishna **6** 396
Mehta, Pherozeshah **10** 455

Imperialism (political theory)
Froude, James Anthony **6** 133-134
Pius XI **12** 337-339

Imperialism, American
opponents
Bryan, William Jennings **3** 80-82
Bunche, Ralph Johnson **3** 121-122
Du Bois, William Edward Burghardt
5 116-118
Fulbright, James William **6** 147-149
Schurz, Carl **14** 44-45
Sumner, William Graham **15** 32
Villard, Oswald Garrison
15 498-499
Webster, Daniel **16** 162-164
supporters
Blaine, James Gillespie **2** 312-313
Buchanan, James **3** 89-90
Frémont, John Charles **6** 97-98
Lodge, Henry Cabot **9** 482-483
Mahan, Alfred Thayer **10** 131-132
McKinley, William **10** 418-420
Strong, Josiah **14** 512-513
see also Spanish-American War
(1898)

Imperialism, Belgian
Leopold II **9** 346-347

Imperialism, British
in Africa
Ismail Pasha **8** 150-151
Johnston, Henry Hamilton
8 322-323
Maclean, George **10** 108-109
Milner, Alfred **11** 38-39
Rhodes, Cecil John **13** 120-122
Tewfik Pasha **15** 157-158

in Asia
Brooke, James **3** 21-22
Chulalongkorn **4** 43-45
Mindon Min **11** 47
opponents
Chesterton, Gilbert Keith **3** 508-509
Gladstone, William Ewart
6 357-360
Hobhouse, Leonard Trelawny
7 425-426
Morley, John **11** 178-179
Nehru, Jawaharlal **11** 332-334
supporters
Disraeli, Benjamin **5** 27-29
Gloucester, Duke of **6** 370-371
Victoria **15** 485-487

Imperialism, Dutch
John Maurice of Nassau **8** 281-282

Imperialism, Egyptian
Isaiah **8** 146-147
Mohammed Ali **11** 81-82

Imperialism, Ethiopian
Hassan, Muhammad Abdille **7** 194-195

Imperialism, European
in Asia
Chang Chien **3** 429-430
Chang Chih-tung **3** 430-431
Heruy Wäldä-Sellasé **7** 348-349
Qianlong **12** 502-505
in Latin America
Drago, Luis María **5** 92-93

Imperialism, French
in Africa
Brazza, Pierre Paul François Camille
Savorgnan de **2** 509-510
Diagne, Blaise **4** 527
Faidherbe, Louis Léon César
5 366-367
in Asia
Chulalongkorn **4** 43-45
Colbert, Jean Baptiste **4** 142-143
in Mexico
Juárez, Benito **8** 369-372
opponents
Clemenceau, Georges **4** 99-101
Fanon, Frantz **5** 379-380
Ho Chi Minh **7** 426-428
Ly, Abdoulaye **10** 60
Malraux, André **10** 178-180
Montalembert, Comte de
11 118-119
supporters
Crémazie, Octave **4** 305-306
Ferry, Jules François Camille **5** 430
Francis I **6** 40-43

Imperialism, German
Hitler, Adolf **7** 417-420

Imperialism, Italian
Michels, Robert **11** 7

Imperialism, Japanese
Chang Tso-lin **3** 434-435
Hull, Cordell **8** 28-29
Ito, Hirobumi **8** 153-155

Imperialism, Portuguese
Manuel I **10** 219-220

Imperialism, Roman
Flamininus, Titus Quinctius **5** 477
Scipio Africanus Major, Publius Cornelius **14** 61-62

Imperialism, Russian
Nicholas II **11** 378-380

Imperialism, Spanish
González Prada, Manuel **6** 431
Rizal, José **13** 187-189

Impington College (Cambridgeshire)
Gropius, Walter **7** 13-14

Importance of Being Earnest, The (play)
Evans, Edith **5** 336-337
Wilde, Oscar Fingall O'Flahertie Wills **16** 272-273

Imported Bridegroom ... (stories)
Cahan, Abraham **3** 214

Impresiones y paisajes (book)
Lorca, Federico García **9** 511-513

Impression: Sunrise, Red Boats at Argenteuil (painting)
Monet, Claude **11** 102-104

Impressionism (art)
Australia
Drysdale, George Russell **5** 107-109
Streeton, Arthur Ernest **14** 507-508
England
Constable, John **4** 208-209
Gainsborough, Thomas **6** 170-172
Sargent, John Singer **13** 481-482
Sickert, Walter Richard **14** 212-213
Whistler, James Abbott McNeill **16** 225-226
France (19th century)
Cézanne, Paul **3** 400-402
Corot, Jean Baptiste Camille **4** 247-249
Daubigny, Charles François **4** 402
Ingres, Jean Auguste Dominique **8** 121-123
Manet, Édouard **10** 193-194
Pissaro, Camille **12** 326-327
Renoir, Pierre Auguste **13** 101-102
France (19th-20th century)
Cassatt, Mary **3** 356-357
Degas, Hilaire Germain Edgar **4** 461-462
Matisse, Henri **10** 336-337
Monet, Claude **11** 102-104
Germany
Beckmann, Max **2** 104-105
Hofmann, Hans **7** 442-443
Liebermann, Max **9** 402-403
Marc, Franz **10** 231
Nolde, Emil **11** 419-420
influence of
Amorsolo, Fernando **1** 204
Balla, Giacomo **1** 473-474
Cullen, Maurice Galbraith **4** 334
Ensor, James **5** 289-290
John, Augustus Edwin **8** 291

Kandinsky, Wassily **8** 420-422
Pevsner, Antoine **12** 263-264
Italy
Rosso, Medardo **13** 313-315
Netherlands
Hals, Frans **7** 89-91
Van Gogh, Vincent **15** 427-429
United States
Dove, Arthur Garfield **5** 86-87
Glackens, William **6** 355-356
Hartley, Marsden **7** 186
Hassam, Frederick Childe **7** 192
Homer, Winslow **7** 468-469
Inness, George **8** 123-124
Robinson, Theodore **13** 217
Twachtman, John Henry **15** 362-363
Wood, Grant **16** 368-369

Impressionism (literature)
Crane, Stephen **4** 293-295
Ferrer, Gabriel Miró **5** 428
Ruíz, José Martínez **13** 358
Schnitzler, Arthur **14** 23-24
Woolf, Virginia Stephen **16** 381-382

Impressionism (music)
Debussy, Achille Claude **4** 445-447
Grieg, Edvard Hagerup **6** 541-542
Milhaud, Darius **11** 17-18
Ravel, Maurice Joseph **13** 54-55
Roussel, Albert **13** 328-329
Saint-Saëns, Charles Camille **13** 435-436
Szymanowski, Karol **15** 67-68
see also Anti-impressionism (music)

Impressment (England)
Madison, James **10** 121-123
Oglethorpe, James Edward **11** 482-483

Impromptu (musical composition)
Chopin, Frédéric François **4** 16-18
Gottschalk, Louis Moreau **6** 463-464
Schubert, Franz Peter **14** 35-37

Improvisatore, The (novel)
Andersen, Hans Christian **1** 212-214

In a Station of the Metro (poem)
Pound, Ezra Loomis **12** 415-417

In Autumn (orchestra overture)
Grieg, Edvard Hagerup **6** 541-542

In Chancery (novel)
Galsworthy, John **6** 189-190

In Cold Blood: A True Account of a Multiple Murder and Its Consequences (book)
Capote, Truman **3** 273-275

In Country Sleep (poems)
Thomas, Dylan Marlais **15** 188-190

In der Strafkolonie (novella)
Kafka, Franz **8** 403-406

In Desert and Wilderness (story)
Sienkiewicz, Henryk **14** 216-217

In Distrust of Merit (poem)
Moore, Marianne **11** 148-149

In Dubious Battle (novel)
Steinbeck, John Ernst **14** 416-417

In einer Familie (novel)
Mann, Heinrich **10** 201-202

In His Own Write (book)
Lennon, John Winston **9** 326-328

In His Steps (novel)
Sheldon, Charles M. **14** 172-174

In limine (poem)
Montale, Eugenio **11** 117-118

In May ... (poem)
Dunbar, William **5** 142-143

In Memoriam (poem)
Tennyson, Alfred **15** 144-146

In Ole Virginia (stories)
Page, Thomas Nelson **12** 59-60

In Our Time (stories)
Hemingway, Ernest Miller **7** 274-277

In Praise of Darkness (book)
Borges, Jorge Luis **2** 411-412

In quintum Novembris (epic poem)
Milton, John **11** 43-46

In Savoy (book)
Stein, Gertrude **14** 414-415

In Search of Character (book)
Greene, Graham **6** 523-524

In te, Domine (musical composition)
Josquin des Prez **8** 361-363

In the Bar of a Tokyo Hotel (play)
Williams, Tennessee **16** 306-308

In the Cage (story)
James, Henry **8** 211-212

In the Circus Fernando (painting)
Toulouse-Lautrec, Henri de **15** 273-274

In the City of Slaughter (poem)
Bialik, Hayyim Nahman **2** 262-263

In the Clearing (literary collection)
Frost, Robert Lee **6** 130-133

In the Days When the World Was Wide (literary collection)
Lawson, Henry **9** 254-255

In the Dream (lithograph series)
Redon, Odilon **13** 75-76

In the Heart of the Seas (novel)
Agnon, Shmuel Yoseph **1** 85-86

In the Labyrinth (book)
Robbe-Grillet, Alain **13** 189-190

In the Land of Cockaigne (novel)
Mann, Heinrich **10** 201-202

In the Lena Delta (book)
Melville, George Wallace **10** 472

In the Midst of Life (book)
Bierce, Ambrose Gwinett **2** 269-270

In the Money (novel)
Williams, William Carlos **16** 308-309

In the Open Air (poems)
Bunin, Ivan Alekseevich **3** 124

In the Penal Colony (novella)
Kafka, Franz **8** 403-406

In the Presence of the Sea (poem)
Tschernichowsky, Saul **15** 323

In the Ravine (story)
Chekhov, Anton Pavlovich **3** 494-497

In the Restaurant (poem)
Blok, Aleksandr Aleksandrovich **2** 335

In the Seven Woods (poems)
Yeats, William Butler **16** 445-447

In the South Seas (essays)
Stevenson, Robert Louis **14** 446-448

In the Still of the Night (song)
Porter, Cole Albert **12** 405-406

In the Zone (play)
O'Neill, Eugene **11** 514-516

In This Our Life (novel)
Glasgow, Ellen **6** 360-361

In Which We Serve (film)
Coward, Noel **4** 279-280

Inadmissible Evidence (play)
Osborne, John **12** 16-17

Inauguration of the Second Vatican Council (frieze)
Manzù, Giacomo **10** 224-225

Inca Indians (South American)
Atahualpa **1** 355-356
Garcilaso de la Vega, Inca **6** 210-211
Manco Capac **10** 184-185
Túpac Amaru, José Gabriel **15** 341
see also Peru—Spanish conquest

Incandescent lamp (elec. light)
Eastman, George **5** 186
Edison, Thomas Alva **5** 206-208
Langmuir, Irving **9** 196-197
Maxim, Hiram Stevens **10** 355-356

Incarnation (theology)
Anselm of Canterbury **1** 244-245

Incarnation, Convent of the (Ávila, Spain)
Theresa **15** 178-179

Ince Hall Madonna (painting)
Eyck, Hubert and Jan van **5** 352-354

Incessament livré (chanson)
Josquin des Prez **8** 361-363

Inchon, battle of (1950)
MacArthur, Douglas **10** 76-78

Incident at Krechetovka Station (story)
Solzhenitsyn, Alexander Isayevich
14 330-332

Incident at Vichy (play)
Miller, Arthur **11** 25-26

Incognita (novel)
Congreve, William **4** 200-201

Incoherence of the Philosophers, The (book)
Ghazali, Abu Hamid Muhammad al-
6 290-291

Incomparable Chamber (France; 1816)
Louis XVIII **9** 535-536

Inconstant World, The (book)
Mäkonnen Endalkačäw **10** 161-162

Incoronazione de Poppea, L'
see Poppea (opera)

Incredible Flutist, The (musical composition)
Piston, Walter **12** 327-328

Incredible Jewel Robbery, The (film)
Marx brothers **10** 303-304

Indefinite Divisibility (painting)
Tanguy, Yves **15** 101

Independence Hall (Philadelphia)
Mills, Robert **11** 36-37

Independence movements
see Nationalism

Independent Commission on International Humanitarian Issues
Ogata, Sadako **11** 479-480

Independent Labour party (Great Britain)
Hardie, James Keir **7** 147-148
Henderson, Arthur **7** 277-278
MacDonald, James Ramsay **10** 84-85
Orwell, George **12** 14-15

Independent Order of Saint Luke (fraternal order; United States)
Walker, Maggie Lena **16** 65-66

Independent Socialists (political party; Germany)
Kautsky, Karl Johann **8** 462-463

Indes galantes, Les (opera)
Rameau, Jean Philippe **13** 17-18

Index of Forbidden Books (Roman Catholic Church)
Bayle, Pierre **2** 77-78
France, Anatole **6** 39-40
Machiavelli, Niccolò **10** 97-99
Mariana, Juan de **10** 254-255
Moravia, Alberto **11** 153-155
Paul IV **12** 145-146
Pius IV **12** 332
Pius X **12** 336-337
Rosa, Salvator **13** 289-290
Rosmini-Serbati, Antonio **13** 296-297

India, Republic of (nation, southern Asia)
• TO ca. 1000 (ANCIENT and MEDIEVAL)
Cola (Chola) rule
Rajaraja I **13** 7
Greek conquest (326 B.C.)
Alexander the Great **1** 137-141
Gupta Period
Harsha **7** 181-182
Samudragupta **13** 457
Kashan Empire
Kanishka **8** 428-429
Maurya dynasty
Asoka **1** 341-342
Chandragupta Maurya **3** 426
Kautilya **8** 462
religion
see Buddhism; Hinduism; Jainism; Sikhs (religious sect)
• CA 1000-1600 (MOSLEM)
conquest

Mahmud of Ghazni **10** 147
Delhi Sultanate (1192-1398)
Ala-ud-din **1** 102-103
Kublai Khan **9** 115-118
Muhammad bin Tughluq **11** 229
history of
Nizami, Khaliq Ahmad **11** 405
Mogul dynasty (1526-1857)
Akbar, Jalal-ud-din Mohammed
1 96
Aurangzeb **1** 377
Babar the Conqueror **1** 405-407
Jahangir **8** 196-199
Nanak **11** 303
Shah Jahan **14** 138-139
Śivají **14** 266-267
Portuguese exploration
Albuquerque, Afonso de
1 118-119
Corte Reál, Gaspar and Miguel
4 254-255
Dias de Novais, Bartolomeu
4 533-534
Gama, Vasco da **6** 196-198
Sousa, Martim Afonso de
14 354-355
Venetian exploration
Conti, Niccolò de' **4** 212-213
• Circa 1600-1947 (BRITISH)
allies (of British)
Aga Khan **1** 74-76
Ranjit Singh **13** 32-33
Bengal partitioned
Banerjee, Surendranath **1** 488
Curzon, George Nathaniel
4 351-352
Bengal renaissance
Deb, Radhakant **4** 437
Ram Camul Sen **13** 16-17
British vs. French
Clive, Robert **4** 119-120
Dupleix **5** 153
Haidar Ali **7** 65-66
Christian missionaries
Carey, William **3** 297
Duff, Alexander **5** 126-127
Judson, Adoniram **8** 377-378
commanders in chief
Roberts, Frederick Sleigh
13 195-196
Wellington, 1st Duke of
16 193-195
Council of Viceroys
Aga Khan **1** 74-76
Cromer, 1st Earl of **4** 317
Frere, Henry Bartle Edward
6 100-101
governors general
Canning, George **3** 258-260
Cornwallis, Charles **4** 241-243
Dalhousie, 1st Marquess of
4 375-376
Hastings, Warren **7** 195-196
Metcalfe, Charles Theophilus
10 531-532

Wellesley, Richard Colley
16 192-193
India Acts
Disraeli, Benjamin **5** 27-29
Hastings, Warren **7** 195-196
Jinnah, Mohammad Ali
8 262-263
Mysore wars
see Mysore wars
nationalism
Aga Khan **1** 74-76
Ambedkar, Bhimrao Ramji
1 190-191
Chelmsford, Frederic John Napi-
er Thesiger **3** 497
Ghose, Aurobindo **6** 293-294
Reading, 1st Marquess of **13** 64
Wavell, Archibald Percival
16 147-148
see also Indian National Congress;
Nationalism, Asian—India
reforms
Besant, Annie Wood **2** 233-234
Dayananda Saraswati **4** 431
Kitchener, Horatio Herbert
9 45-46
Macaulay, Thomas Babington
10 79-80
Pitt, William the Younger
12 329-331
secretaries of state
Chamberlain, Arthur Neville
3 409-411
Morley, John **11** 178-179
Salisbury, 3d Marquess of
13 448-449
Sepoy Mutiny
see Sepoy Mutiny
sovereigns
Edward VII **5** 214-215
George V **6** 273-275
George VI **6** 275
Victoria **15** 485-487
viceroys
Chelmsford, Frederic John Napi-
er Thesiger **3** 497
Curzon, George Nathaniel
4 351-352
Elgin, 8th Earl of **5** 248-249
Halifax, 1st Earl of **7** 82-83
Reading, 1st Marquess of **13** 64
Westernization
Chatterji, Bankimchandra
3 480-481
Roy, Ram Mohun **13** 18
Syed Ahmed Khan **15** 60
see also British Commonwealth
of Nations; British Empire, Sec-
ond; East India Company
(British)
• SINCE 1947 (REPUBLIC)
independence
Attlee, Clement Richard
1 361-362
Gandhi, Mohandas Karamchand
6 201-204
Nehru, Jawaharlal **11** 332-334

Pandit, Vijaya Lakshmi **12** 83-84
Patel, Vallabhbhai **12** 129-130
nonalignment policy
Menon, Vengalil Krishnan Krish-
na **10** 507-509
Nehru, Jawaharlal **11** 332-334
Pakistan created
Ayub Khan, Mohammed
1 395-396
Gandhi, Indira Priyadarshini
6 200-201
Jinnah, Mohammad Ali
8 262-263
Liaquat Ali Khan **9** 397
Sapru, Tej Bahadur **13** 480-481
see also Pakistan
party leaders
Kamaraj, Kumaraswami **8** 415
presidents
Prasad, Rajendra **12** 433
prime ministers
Gandhi, Indira Priyadarshini
6 200-201
Gandhi, Rajiv **6** 204-205
Nehru, Jawaharlal **11** 332-334
Singh, Vishwanath Pratap
14 254-256
reforms
Bhave, Vinoba **2** 257-258
Narayan, Jayaprakash
11 312-313
South Africa and
Malan, Daniel Francois
10 163-164
Tibetan refugees
Dalai Lama **4** 369-371
see also Bengal; Indian literature;
Indian National Congress;
Moslem League (India)

Indian Affairs, United States Bureau of
Deer, Ada E. **4** 452-454

Indian art and architecture (Asian)
Jahangir **8** 196-199

**Indian Brotherhood of the Northwest Ter-
ritories** (Canada)
Erasmus, Georges Henry **5** 300-301

Indian Burying Ground, The (poem)
Freneau, Philip Morin **6** 99-100

Indian Camp (story)
Hemingway, Ernest Miller **7** 274-277

Indian Emperor, The (play)
Dryden, John **5** 106-107

Indian Fantasy (musical composition)
Busoni, Ferruccio Benvenuto **3** 173-174

Indian Home Rule League (New York City)
Rai, Lala Lajpat **13** 5-6

Indian Institute of Science (Bangalore)
Bhabha, Homi Jehangir **2** 253-254
Raman, Chandrasekhar Venkata
13 13-14

Indian Journals (book)
Ginsberg, Allen **6** 332-333

Indian literature (Asia)
drama and poetry
Das, Chitta Ranjan **4** 401-402
Harsha **7** 181-182
Iqbal, Muhammad **8** 132-133
Kalidasa **8** 414-415
Naidu, Sarojini **11** 294-295
Rabindranath Tagore **12** 529-531
fiction
Chatterji, Bankimchandra
3 480-481
Narayan, R. K. **11** 313-314
Premchand **12** 439
Ram Camul Sen **13** 16-17
Rabindranath Tagore **12** 529-531

Indian Mutiny
see Sepoy Mutiny (1857-1858)

Indian National Congress (Asia)
founders
Banerjee, Surendranath **1** 488
Mehta, Pherozeshah **10** 455
Naoroji, Dadabhai **11** 305
leaders
Besant, Annie Wood **2** 233-234
Menon, Vengalil Krishnan Krishna
10 507-509
Narayan, Jayaprakash **11** 312-313
Nehru, Jawaharlal **11** 332-334
Pandit, Vijaya Lakshmi **12** 83-84
Rajagopalachari, Chakravarti **13** 6-7
Sapru, Tej Bahadur **13** 480-481
opponents
Syed Ahmed Khan **15** 60
presidents
Banerjee, Surendranath **1** 488
Bose, Subhas Chandra **2** 430-431
Gandhi, Indira Priyadarshini
6 200-201
Gokhale, Gopal Krishna **6** 396
Kamaraj, Kumaraswami **8** 415
Naidu, Sarojini **11** 294-295
Prasad, Rajendra **12** 433
see also Moslem League (India);
Satyagraha method; Swaraj move-
ment

Indian Ocean
Dias de Novais, Bartolomeu **4** 533-534
Drake, Francis **5** 94-96

Indian Queen, The (play and opera)
Dryden, John **5** 106-107
Purcell, Henry **12** 484-485

Indian Suite (musical composition)
MacDowell, Edward Alexander
10 87-88

Indian Summer of a Forsyte (novel)
Galsworthy, John **6** 189-190

Indiana (novel)
Sand, George **13** 459-461

Indiana (state, United States)
Debs, Eugene Victor **4** 444-445
Eggleston, Edward **5** 223-224
Harrison, William Henry **7** 180-181

Morton, Oliver Hazard Perry Throck
  11 197-198
Owen, Robert Dale **12** 40-41
Indiana University (Bloomington)
  Commons, John Rogers **4** 185
  Jordan, David Starr **8** 350-351
  Lewis, Clarence Irving **9** 381
  Muller, Hermann Joseph **11** 238-239
  Skinner, Burrhus Frederic **14** 269-270
  Smith, David **14** 287-288
  Xenakis, Iannis **16** 416-418
Indians (North American)
  artists
    Campbell, Ben Nighthorse
      3 252-253
  assimilation of
    Brant, Mary (Molly) **2** 501-503
    Collier, John **4** 160-162
    Deer, Ada E. **4** 452-454
    La Flesche, Francis **9** 152-154
    Montezuma, Carlos **11** 129-132
    Parker, Quanah **12** 109-112
    Plenty Coups **12** 352-355
    Zah, Peterson **16** 486-487
  athletes
    Campbell, Ben Nighthorse
      3 252-253
  Bacon's Rebellion
    seeBacon's Rebellion
  battle of the Thames
    seeThames, battle of the (1813)
  battle of Tippecanoe
    seeTippecanoe, battle of
  Canadian relations
    Cartier, Jacques **3** 343-344
    Fairclough, Ellen Louks **5** 367-368
    Lacombe, Albert **9** 147-148
    Laval, Francois Xavier de **9** 235-236
  captives
    Estevanico **5** 324-325
    Mangas Coloradas **10** 194-196
    Pocahontas **12** 361-362
    Smith, John **14** 295-297
  Christianity and
    Red Jacket **13** 71-73
  culture
    Alexie, Sherman **1** 141-142
    Bad Heart Bull, Amos **1** 427-428
    Begay, Harrison **2** 117-118
    Benedict, Ruth Fulton **2** 154-155
    Black Elk, Nicholas **2** 305-306
    Collier, John **4** 160-162
    Deloria, Vine Jr. **4** 481-484
    Eastman, Charles A. **5** 183-185
    Fletcher, Alice Cunningham
      5 486-487
    Handsome Lake **7** 122-123
    La Flesche, Francis **9** 152-154
    Linton, Ralph **9** 431
    Lowie, Robert Harry **10** 18
    Malinowski, Kaspar Bronislaw
      10 170-171
    Momaday, N. Scott **11** 92-94
    Ortiz, Simon J. **12** 9-12
    Parker, Quanah **12** 109-112

Radin, Paul **12** 538-539
Reid, William Ronald **13** 88-89
Schoolcraft, Henry Rowe **14** 29
White, Leslie A. **16** 232-233
Wovoka **16** 390-393
Zah, Peterson **16** 486-487
  ethnographies of
    Parker, Ely Samuel **12** 106-108
  French and Indian War
    seeFrench and Indian War
  guides and interpreters
    Squanto **14** 386-388
    Washakie **16** 123-125
    Winnemucca, Sarah **16** 336-338
  historians of
    Bad Heart Bull, Amos **1** 427-428
    Catlin, George **3** 373-374
    McNickle, D'Arcy **10** 433-433
  Indian agents
    Carson, Christopher **3** 334-335
    Fitzpatrick, Thomas **5** 474-475
    McCoy, Isaac **10** 403
  Iroquois Confederacy
    seeIroquois Confederacy
  Keresan-speaking Indians
    White, Leslie A. **16** 232-233
  King Philip's War
    seeKing Philip's War
  kinship terminology
    Morgan, Lewis Henry **11** 167-168
  language studies
    Boas, Franz **2** 349-351
    Dunbar, William **5** 143-144
    Eliot, John **5** 256-258
    Kluckhohn, Clyde **9** 56-57
    Kroeber, Alfred Louis **9** 105-106
    Sapir, Edward **13** 478-479
    Sequoyah **14** 110-111
  Lord Dunmore's War
    seeLord Dunmore's War
  missionaries to
    Brébeuf, Jean de **2** 511-512
    De Smet, Pierre Jean **4** 509-510
    Drexel, Katherine **5** 102-103
    Eliot, John **5** 256-258
    Hobart, John Henry **7** 420-421
    Jogues, Isaac **8** 270-271
    Kino, Eusebio Francisco **9** 30-31
    Kirkland, Samuel **9** 37
    Lacombe, Albert **9** 147-148
    Oñate, Juan de **11** 513-514
    Schoolcraft, Henry Rowe **14** 29
    Serra, Junípero **14** 111-112
    Wheelock, Eleazar **16** 222-223
    Whitman, Marcus **16** 248-249
    Zinzendorf, Nikolaus Ludwig von
      16 522-523
  origin of name
    Columbus, Christopher **4** 176-179
  photographs of
    Gilpin, Laura **6** 326-327
  political leaders
    Erasmus, Georges Henry **5** 300-301
  Pontiac's Conspiracy
    seePontiac's Conspiracy

removal policy
  Cornplanter **4** 239-241
  Crockett, David **4** 314-316
  Dull Knife **5** 135-136
  Harrison, William Henry **7** 180-181
  Jackson, Andrew **8** 168-172
  Manuelito **10** 220-222
  Ross, John **13** 303-304
  Scott, Winfield **14** 70-71
rights defended
  Banks, Dennis J. **1** 488-489
  Crook, George **4** 322-323
  Cuffe, Paul **4** 331-332
  Dawes, Henry Laurens **4** 427
  Fletcher, Alice Cunningham
    5 486-487
  La Flesche, Francis **9** 152-154
  Means, Russell **10** 441-444
  Montezuma, Carlos **11** 129-132
  Penn, William **12** 200-202
  Plenty Coups **12** 352-355
  Quay, Matthew Stanley **12** 507
  see alsoGeneral Allotment Act;
    Omaha Allotment Act
Seminole Wars
  seeSeminole Wars
Sioux wars
  seeSioux wars
statesmen
  Campbell, Ben Nighthorse
    3 252-253
treaty rights issues
  Adams, Hank **1** 45
  Bellecourt, Clyde **2** 136-137
treaties
  Massasoit **10** 322-324
  Red Jacket **13** 71-73
  see alsoAmerican Revolution; indi-
    vidual tribes; Statesmen, Ameri-
    can—Indian chiefs; War of 1812
Indians (South American)
  Araucanians
    see Araucanian Indians
  as labor force
    Roca, Julio Argentino **13** 218
    Sá, Mem de **13** 395
    see also Encomienda system (Span-
      ish American)
  Chibcha
    see Chibcha Indians
  chroniclers of
    Garcilaso de la Vega, Inca
      6 210-211
  culture
    Isaacs, Jorge **8** 144
    Lévi-Strauss, Claude Gustave
      9 371-372
    Rondon, Candido Mariano da Silva
      13 271
  Incas
    see Inca Indians
  missionaries to
    Anchieta, José de **1** 210-211
    Las Casas, Bartolomé de **9** 211-212
    Marcos de Niza **10** 240
  reforms

Castilla, Ramón **3** 361
Gasca, Pedro de la **6** 230-231
Hidalgo y Costilla, Miguel
7 375-377
Mendoza, Antonio de **10** 494-495
Toledo, Francisco de **15** 257-259
Vieira, Antônio **15** 492
see also Conquistadores; individual
countries
see also New Laws of the Indies

Indifférent, L' (painting)
Watteau, Antoine **16** 143-144

Indifferenti, Gli (novel)
Moravia, Alberto **11** 153-155

Indigo (chemistry)
Baeyer, Johann Friedrich Adolf von
1 432
Hofmann, August Wilhelm von
7 441-442

Indipohdi (poem)
Hauptmann, Gerhart Johann Robert
7 199-201

Individual liberties
see Civil liberties

Individualism (social theory)
as social value
Hobbes, Thomas **7** 421-423
Hoover, Herbert Clark **7** 483-485
Spencer, Herbert **14** 369-370
critics
Bradley, Francis Herbert **2** 481-482
Cudworth, Ralph **4** 331
Dewey, John **4** 520-523
Dostoevsky, Fyodor **5** 74-77
in poetry
Frost, Robert Lee **6** 130-133

Individualists ... (novel)
Richter, Conrad Michael **13** 148-149

Individuals (book)
Strawson, Peter Fredrick **14** 506-507

Indochina
see Burma; Cambodia; Indochina,
French; Laos; Malaysia; Thailand; Vietnam

Indochina, French (former nation, south-
east Asia)
French rule
Chang Chih-tung **3** 430-431
Chulalongkorn **4** 43-45
Clemenceau, Georges **4** 99-101
Ferry, Jules François Camille **5** 430
Garnier, Francis **6** 220-221
Joffre, Joseph Jacques Césaire
8 267-268
Phibun Songkhram, Luang
12 264-265
Qianlong **12** 502-505
Tso Tsung-t'ang **15** 328-329
independence movement
see Vietnam War (1946-1954)
since 1954
see Cambodia; Laos; Vietnam

Indonesia, Republic of (nation, southeast
Asia)
Bali
Mead, Margaret **10** 438-440
Borneo
Brooke, James **3** 21-22
Rizal, José **13** 187-189
Dutch East Indies
Coen, Jan Pieterszoon **4** 133
Eijkman, Christian **5** 228
Ho Chi Minh **7** 426-428
Schouten, William Cornelius **14** 31
Van Diemen, Anthony Meuza
15 420
in fiction
Conrad, Joseph **4** 205-207
independence (1945)
Hatta, Mohammad **7** 197-199
Suharto **15** 14-15
Sukarno **15** 18-20
Japanese rule (1942-1945)
Sukarno **15** 18-20
Java
Cheng Ho **3** 500
Conti, Niccolò de' **4** 212-213
Cook, James **4** 214-215
Eijkman, Christian **5** 228
Raffles, Thomas Stamford **13** 1-2
Sumatra
Cheng Ho **3** 500
Conti, Niccolò de' **4** 212-213
Dampier, William **4** 384
ibn Battuta, Muhammad **8** 91-92

Induction (electricity)
Bell, Alexander Graham **2** 129-131
Faraday, Michael **5** 380
Fizeau, Hippolyte Armand Louis **5** 475
Henry, Joseph **7** 307-308

Inductive method (logic)
Hobbes, Thomas **7** 421-423
Mill, John Stuart **11** 21-23
Stewart, Dugald **14** 449
William of Ockham **16** 298-299

Indulgence, Declaration of (England, 1672)
Buckingham, 2d Duke of **3** 94-95
Bunyan, John **3** 128-129
Charles II **3** 452-454

Indulgences (Roman Catholic Church)
Boniface VIII **2** 392-393
Leo X **9** 332-334
Luther, Martin **10** 48-51

Indulgents
see Dantonists

Indus River (India)
Hedin, Sven Anders **7** 252-253

Industrial and Commercial Worker's Union
(South Africa)
Kadalie, Clements **8** 401-402

Industrial Areas Foundation (citizens'
organization)
Alinsky, Saul David **1** 161-162

Industrial Disputes Investigation Act
(1907; Canada)

King, William Lyon Mackenzie **9** 25-26

Industrial management
Gilbreth, Lillian **6** 315-317

Industrial plants (design)
Rogers, Richard **13** 248-250

Industrial revolution
factory system
Arkwright, Richard **1** 298
Phyfe, Duncan **12** 284-285
Whitney, Eli **16** 253-254
histories of
Hammond, Lawrence and Lucy
7 109
iron industry
Cort, Henry **4** 254
Watt, James **16** 141-143
materialism and
Carlyle, Thomas **3** 304-305
steam engine
Newcomen, Thomas **11** 362
Watt, James **16** 141-143
steam hammer
Nasmyth, James **11** 316-317
see also Industrialization; Mass pro-
duction

Industrial Workers of the World (estab-
lished 1905)
Darrow, Clarence Seward **4** 396-397
De Leon, Daniel **4** 479-480
Flynn, Elizabeth Gurley **5** 496-497
Foster, William Zebulon **6** 27-28
Haywood, William Dudley **7** 232-233

Industrialization (mass production)
Alemán, Mateo **1** 126
Boumediene, Houari **2** 445-446
Esenin, Sergei Aleksandrovich **5** 321
Niebuhr, Reinhold **11** 387-388
Saint-Simon, Comte de **13** 436-437
Stalin, Joseph **14** 393-396
Witte, Sergei Yulyevich **16** 349-350
see also Mass production

Industry and Idleness (prints)
Hogarth, William **7** 446-447

Indy, Vincent d' (1851-1931), French com-
poser
Franck, César **6** 48-49
Porter, Cole Albert **12** 405-406
Roussel, Albert **13** 328-329
Varèse, Edgard **15** 432-433

Inebriety (poem)
Crabbe, George **4** 288

Inextinguishable, The (musical composition)
Nielsen, Carl August **11** 388-389

Infallibility, papal (Roman Catholic
Church)
Döllinger, Josef Ignaz von **5** 47-48
John, XXIII **8** 277-280
Küng, Hans **9** 129-130
Manning, Henry Edward **10** 209-210
McCloskey, John **10** 395
Pius IX **12** 335-336

Infancy (play)
Wilder, Thornton Niven **16** 276-277

Infancy Altarpiece (painting)
Bouts, Dirk **2** 458-459

Infant health
Apgar, Virginia **1** 257-259
Baker, Sara Josephine **1** 455-456
King, Frederic Truby **9** 18-19

Infant Hercules (painting)
Reynolds, Joshua **13** 115-116

Infantas (painting; Velázquez)
Ter Borch, Gerard **15** 146

Infante Don Luis (painting)
Goya y Lucientes, Francisco de Paula
José de **6** 476-478

Infantile autism
see Autism

Infantile paralysis
see Poliomyelitis

Inferiority complex (psychology)
Adler, Alfred **1** 61-63

Inferno (book)
Strindberg, August **14** 509-511

Inferno (Dante)
see Divine Comedy

Infidel, The (novel)
Bird, Robert Montgomery **2** 281-282

Infinite, The (poem)
Leopardi, Giacomo **9** 344-345

Inflation (economics)
Brazil
Castelo Branco, Humberto
3 359-360
Goulart, João **6** 467-469
China
Chiang Kai-shek **3** 510-513
Germany (1920s)
Hitler, Adolf **7** 417-420
Schacht, Hjalmar Horace Greeley
13 518-519
Stresemann, Gustav **14** 508-509
Roman Empire
Diocletian **5** 19-20
United States
Hansen, Alvin **7** 131-132
Jackson, Andrew **8** 168-172
Memminger, Christopher Gustavus
10 476-477
Nixon, Richard Milhous **11** 401-404

Influence d'un livre, L' (novel; P.I.F. Aubert
de Gaspé)
Aubert de Gaspé, Philippe **1** 364

Influenza (medicine)
Burnet, Frank Macfarlane **3** 146-147
Salk, Jonas Edward **13** 451-452
Waksman, Selman Abraham **16** 49-50

Información (book)
Cervantes, Miguel de Saavedra
3 395-398

Information theory (mathematics)
Boole, George **2** 396-397

Shannon, Claude Elwood **14** 153-154

Informed Heart, The (book)
Bettelheim, Bruno **2** 245-246

Informer, The (film)
Ford, John **6** 7-8

Infralapsarianism (religion)
Arminius, Jacobus **1** 301-302

INGE, WILLIAM RALPH (1860-1954),
Church of England clergyman, scholar,
social critic, and writer **8** 118-119

Ingegneri, M.A. (1545?-1592), Italian composer
Monteverdi, Claudio Giovanni Antonio
11 126-128

INGENHOUSZ, JAN (1730-1799), Dutch
physician, chemist, and engineer
8 119-120

Ingénue libertine, L' (novel)
Colette, Sidonie Gabrielle **4** 158-159

Ingersoll, Charles (1782-1862), American
lawyer
List, Georg Friedrich **9** 443-444

INGERSOLL, ROBERT GREEN
(1833-1899), American lawyer and lecturer **8** 120-121
Blaine, James Gillespie **2** 312-313

Ingham, Frederick (literary character)
Hale, Edward Everett **7** 71-72

Ingolstadt, University of (West Germany)
Canisius, Peter **3** 258
Eck, Johann Maier von **5** 200

Ingraham, Prentiss (1843-1904), American
publicist
Buffalo Bill **3** 105-106

INGRES, JEAN AUGUSTE DOMINIQUE
(1780-1867), French painter **8** 121-123
Bearden, Romare Howard **2** 86-88
Cherubini, Luigi Carlo Zanobi Salvatore
Maria **3** 505-506
Degas, Hilaire Germain Edgar
4 461-462
Gorky, Arshile **6** 458
Hodler, Ferdinand **7** 434-435
Seurat, Georges Pierre **14** 120-122

Inhale and Exhale (stories)
Saroyan, William **13** 486-487

Inheritors, The (book)
Ford, Ford Madox **6** 1-2

Inishfallen ... (autobiography)
O'Casey, Sean **11** 459-460

Injong (ruled 1544-1545), king of Korea
Kim Pusik **9** 8-9
Sŏnjo **14** 341-342

Injun Joe (literary character)
Twain, Mark **15** 363-366

Inkatha
Buthelezi, Mangosuthu Gatsha
3 178-179

Inland Voyage, An (book)
Stevenson, Robert Louis **14** 446-448

Inman, Henry (1801-1846), American
painter
Mount, William Sidney **11** 213-214

INNESS, GEORGE (1825-1894), American
painter **8** 123-124
Tiffany, Louis Comfort **15** 220-221
Wyant, Alexander Helwig **16** 409-410

Inni sacri (book)
Manzoni, Alessandro **10** 222-224

INNIS, HAROLD ADAMS (1894-1952),
Canadian political economist **8** 124-125

Inno delle nazioni (opera)
Verdi, Giuseppe Fortunino Francesco
15 463-465

Innocent I, Saint (died 417), pope 401-417
Pelagius **12** 189-190

Innocent II (Gregorio Papareschi; died
1143), pope 1130-1143
Arnold of Brescia **1** 314-315
Bernard of Clairvaux **2** 207-208
Roger II **13** 244-245

INNOCENT III (Lothar of Segni;
1160/1161-1216), pope 1198-1216
8 125-127
Dominic **5** 51-52
Francis of Assisi **6** 46-47
Frederick II **6** 79
Joachim of Fiore **8** 263-264
John **8** 274-275
Philip II **12** 268-269
Vogelweide, Walther von der **16** 10-11
see also Crusades—Fourth

Innocent IV (Sinibaldo de' Fieschi; died
1254), pope 1243-1254
Alfonso III **1** 148-149
Frederick II **6** 79
John of Piano Carpini **8** 284
Matthew Paris **10** 341-342

Innocent VI (Étienne Aubert; died 1362),
pope 1352-1362
Guy de Chauliac **7** 54
Rienzi, Cola di **13** 166-167

Innocent VII (Cosimo de' Migliorati;
1336?-1406), pope 1404-1406
Martin V **10** 287-288

Innocent VIII (Giovanni Battista Cibo;
1432-1492), pope 1484-1492
Alexander VI **1** 134-135
Julius II **8** 384-386
Leo X **9** 332-334
Mantegna, Andrea **10** 215-216
Pollaiuolo, Antonio **12** 377-378
Savonarola, Girolamo **13** 505-506

Innocent X (Giovanni Battista Pamfili;
1574-1655), pope 1644-1655
Bernini, Gian Lorenzo **2** 214-216
Velázquez, Diego Rodríguez de Silva y
15 454-456

Innocent XI (Benedetto Odescalchi;
1611-1689), pope 1676-1689
Steno, Nicolaus **14** 425-426

Innocent XII (Antonio Pigratelli; 1615-1700), pope 1691-1700
Fénelon, François de Salignac de la Mothe **5** 410-411
Malpighi, Marcello **10** 176-178

Innocent Irene (play)
Betti, Ugo **2** 246

Innocente, L' (novel)
D'Annunzio, Gabriele **4** 388

Innocents Abroad (book)
Twain, Mark **15** 363-366

Innsbruck ich muss dich lassen (song)
Isaac, Heinrich **8** 143-144

Innsbruck, University of (Austria)
Fischer, Hans **5** 457-459
Hess, Victor Francis **7** 362-363
Pregl, Fritz **12** 436-437

Inoculation (immunology)
anthrax
Koch, Heinrich Hermann Robert **9** 69-70
Pasteur, Louis **12** 125-127
diphtheria
Behring, Emil Adolph von **2** 122-123
Ehrlich, Paul **5** 225-226
influenza
Burnet, Frank Macfarlane **3** 146-147
poliomyelitis
Enders, John Franklin **5** 285-286
Salk, Jonas Edward **13** 451-452
smallpox
Boylston, Zabdiel **2** 471
Cruz, Oswaldo Gonçalves **4** 328-329
Edwards, Jonathan **5** 220-222
Jenner, Edward **8** 245-246
Mather, Cotton **10** 330-332
Mather, Increase **10** 332-333
Waterhouse, Benjamin **16** 131-132
yellow fever
Reed, Walter **13** 78
Theiler, Max **15** 169-170

INÖNÜ, ISMET (1884-1973), Turkish military man, statesman, and second president **8** 127-129

Inoue, Kaoru (1835-1915), Japanese statesman
Hara, Kei **7** 138

Inquiry into the Nature and Causes of the Wealth of Nations, An (book)
see Wealth of Nations

Inquisition (Islam Empire)
see Islam—Mihna

Inquisition, Holy Roman and Universal (now Congolese for the Doctrine of the Faith)
foundations
Innocent III **8** 125-127
Paul III **12** 144-145
investigated
Goya y Lucientes, Francisco de Paula José de **6** 476-478

Valla, Lorenzo **15** 406
prefects
Pius IV **12** 332
Pius V **12** 332-333
trials
Galileo Galilei **6** 180-183
Joan of Arc **8** 264-265
Porta, Giambattista della **12** 403-404
Waldo, Peter **16** 55-56

Inquisition, Spanish (1478-1834)
commissioners
Serra, Junípero **14** 111-112
heresy trials
Morelos, José María **11** 157-158
histories of
Lea, Henry Charles **9** 261-262
investigated
Mariana, Juan de **10** 254-255
opponents
William the Silent **16** 300-302
persecution of Jews
Abravanel, Isaac ben Judah **1** 31
Ferdinand V **5** 417-418
Isabella I **8** 144-145
Manuel I **10** 219-220
Vieira, Antônio **15** 492

Inquisitions (book)
Borges, Jorge Luis **2** 411-412

Insanity
see Mental illness

Inscape (musical composition)
Copland, Aaron **4** 227-228

Inscription for the Entrance to a Wood (poem)
Bryant, William Cullen **3** 83-85

Insect, The (book)
Michelet, Jules **11** 5-6

Insecticide
see Pesticide

Insectivorous Plants (book)
Darwin, Charles Robert **4** 397-399

Insects
see Entomology

Insei system (Japan)
Goshirakawa **6** 460-461

Insel der grossen Mutter, Die (novel)
Hauptmann, Gerhart Johann Robert **7** 199-201

Inside the Whale (essay)
Orwell, George **12** 14-15

Insila kaTshaka (novel)
Dube, John Langalibalele **5** 113

Inspection (play)
Betti, Ugo **2** 246

Inspector General, The (play; Gogol)
Gogol, Nikolai **6** 391-393
Meyerhold, Vsevolod Emilievich **10** 539

Inspiration of the Poet, The (painting)
Poussin, Nicolas **12** 418-420

Instauratio magna (book)
Bacon, Francis **1** 422-424

Institut Catholique (Paris)
Loisy, Alfred Firmin **9** 489-490
Teilhard de Chardin, Marie Joseph Pierre **15** 134-136

Institut de France (established 1795)
see French Academy; French Academy of Sciences

Institut d'Égypte (France)
Fourier, Jean Baptiste Joseph **6** 32-33
Napoleon I **11** 306-310

Institut, L' (journal)
Garneau, François-Xavier **6** 219-220

Instituta patrum (Council of Aachen, 816)
Louis I **9** 522-523

Institute for Advanced Study (Princeton, New Jersey)
Carnap, Rudolf **3** 308-309
Einstein, Albert **5** 228-231
Flexner, Abraham **5** 489-490
Gödel, Kurt **6** 377-379
Oppenheimer, J. Robert **11** 525-526
Pauli, Wolfgang Ernst **12** 149
Tarski, Alfred **15** 110-111
Von Neumann, John **16** 27-28
Yang, Chen Ning **16** 437-438
Yukawa, Hideki **16** 481-482

Institute for Infectious Diseases (Germany)
Ehrlich, Paul **5** 225-226
Koch, Heinrich Hermann Robert **9** 69-70

Institute of Charity (Rosminians; established 1828)
Rosmini-Serbati, Antonio **13** 296-297

Institute of Experimental Psychology (Graz, Austria)
Meinong, Alexius Ritter von Handschuchsheim **10** 461-462

Institute of Organic Chemistry (Basel)
Reichstein, Tadeus **13** 85-87

Institutio oratoria (book; Quintilian)
Phidias **12** 265-267
Quintilian **12** 518-519

Institutio principis Christiani (book)
Erasmus, Desiderius **5** 298-300

Institutional Revolutionary party (Mexico)
Zedillo Ponce de Leon, Ernesto **16** 493-495

Institutiones (literary collection)
Cassiodorus, Flavius Magnus Aurelius **3** 357-358

Instituto de Humanidades (Madrid, Spain)
Ortega Y Gasset, José **12** 7-8

Instructions of 13 (Argentina; politics)
Artigas, José Gervasio **1** 323

Instrument makers
see Scientists—instrument makers

Instrument of Government (England; 1653)
Cromwell, Oliver **4** 317-320

Instrumentalism (philosophy)
　Dewey, John **4** 520-523
　Hu Shih **8** 63-65

Insulin (hormone)
　Banting, Frederick Grant **1** 493-494
　Best, Charles Herbert **2** 236-237
　Sanger, Frederick **13** 466-467

INSULL, SAMUEL (1859-1938),
　English-born American entrepreneur
　8 130

Insulted and the Injured, The (novel)
　Dostoevsky, Fyodor **5** 74-77

Insurance (business)
　Bethune, Mary McLeod **2** 241-242
　Girard, Stephen **6** 347-348

Insurrection in Dublin, The (novel)
　Stephens, James **14** 430-431

Insurrections (poems)
　Stephens, James **14** 430-431

Intégrales (musical composition)
　Varèse, Edgard **15** 432-433

Integrated Revolutionary Organizations
　see Communist Party of Cuba

Integration (racial, United States)
　see African American history

Intel Corporation
　Noyce, Robert **11** 436-437

Intelligence tests (psychology)
　Binet, Alfred **2** 277-278
　Terman, Lewis Madison **15** 153-154
　Yerkes, Robert Mearns **16** 454-455

Intendant system (government institution)
　Gálvez, José de **6** 196
　Louis XIV **9** 531-533
　Turgot, Anne Robert Jacques
　　15 348-349

Intentions (book)
　Wilde, Oscar Fingall O'Flahertie Wills
　　16 272-273

Interaction of Color (book)
　Albers, Josef **1** 110

Inter-American Conference
　see International Conference of Ameri-
　can States

Inter-American Defense Board
　Ridgway, Matthew Bunker **13** 160-161
　Rojas Pinilla, Gustavo **13** 255-256

Inter-American Development Bank (estab-
　lished 1960)
　Herrera, Juan de **7** 335
　Iglesias, Enrique V. **8** 106-107

Inter-American Indigenist Congress, First
　(Mexico)
　Cárdenas, Lázaro **3** 286-287

Interborough Organization (Russian politi-
　cal organization)
　Trotsky, Leon **15** 302-305

Interbrain
　see Hypothalamus

Intercolonial Conference (Sydney; 1883)
　Griffith, Samuel Walker **6** 545-546

Intercolonial Union (exiles; French
　colonies)
　Ho Chi Minh **7** 426-428

Interdiction, L' (book)
　Balzac, Honoré de **1** 478-480

Intereses creados, Los (play)
　Benavente y Martinez, Jacinto
　　2 146-147

Interest theory (economics)
　Böhm-Bawerk, Eugen von **2** 366
　Fisher, Irving **5** 462-463
　Hansen, Alvin **7** 131-132
　Keynes, John Maynard **8** 528-530
　Robertson, Dennis Holme **13** 196

Interest theory of value (philosophy)
　Perry, Ralph Barton **12** 239-240

Intérieur (play)
　Maeterlinck, Maurice **10** 125-126

Interior, United States Department of the
　Babbitt, Bruce Edward **1** 408-410
　Carson, Rachel Louise **3** 337-338
　Chandler, Zachariah **3** 425-426
　Daniels, Josephus **4** 387
　Deer, Ada E. **4** 452-454
　Ickes, Harold LeClaire **8** 100-101
　Schurz, Carl **14** 44-45
　Walker, Robert John **16** 67-68

Interior with Stove (drawing)
　Sheeler, Charles **14** 170-171

Internal combustion engine (machine)
　Daimler, Gottlieb **4** 368
　Diesel, Rudolf **5** 7
　Ford, Henry **6** 5-6
　Santos-Dumont, Alberto **13** 477-478

Internal External Forms (sculpture)
　Moore, Henry **11** 146-148

International, First (International Working-
　men's Association; 1864-76)
　Kropotkin, Peter Alekseevich **9** 107-108
　Marx, Karl **10** 304-308
　Proudhon, Pierre Joseph **12** 461-463
　Sylvis, William **15** 60-61

International, Second (1889-1920)
　Cahan, Abraham **3** 214
　Haywood, William Dudley **7** 232-233
　Jaurès, Jean **8** 226-227
　Katayama, Sen **8** 457

International, Third (Comintern; 1919-43)
　and Asia
　　Ch'en Tu-hsiu **3** 501-502
　　Ho Chi Minh **7** 426-428
　　Katayama, Sen **8** 457
　　Li Ta-chao **9** 447
　　Lin Piao **9** 429-430
　　Mao Zedong **10** 225-227
　founded
　　Lenin, Vladimir Ilich **9** 323-326
　leaders
　　Bukharin, Nikolai Ivanovich
　　　3 112-113

　　Dimitrov, Georgi **5** 11-13
　　Prestes, Luiz Carlos **12** 442-444
　　Radek, Karl Bernardovich
　　　12 536-537
　　Zinoviev, Grigori Evseevich
　　　16 521-522

International African Service Bureau
　(established 1937)
　Padmore, George **12** 57-58
　Wallace-Johnson, Isaac Theophilus
　Akunna **16** 76-77

**International Association for the Explo-
　ration and Civilization of the Congo**
　(established 1876)
　Leopold II **9** 346-347

International Atomic Energy Agency
　(established 1957)
　von Mehren, Robert Brandt **16** 24-25

International Atomic Energy Conference
　(Vienna)
　Molotov, Vyacheslav Mikhailovich
　　11 89-90

**International Bank for Reconstruction and
　Development**
　see World Bank

International Brigades (Spanish Civil War)
　Ibárruri Gómez, Dolores **8** 88-90

International Brotherhood of Teamsters
　Hoffa, James R. **7** 436-437

International Business Machines (IBM)
　Gates, William Henry III **6** 232-234
　Mandelbrot, Benoit B. **10** 189-191
　Müller, Karl Alexander **11** 240-241
　Watson, Thomas J. **16** 140

International Composers' Guild
　(1921-1927)
　Varèse, Edgard **15** 432-433

**International Confederation of Free Trade
　Unions** (labor group)
　Mboya, Thomas Joseph **10** 384-385
　Meany, George **10** 444

**International Conference of American
　States**
　Bogotá (1948)
　　Castro Ruz, Fidel **3** 365-368
　　Gaitán, Jorge Eliécer **6** 172-173
　　see also Organization of American
　　States
　Buenos Aires (1936)
　　Berle, Adolf Augustus Jr. **2** 199-200
　　Justo, Agustín Pedro **8** 396
　　Lamas, Carlos Saavedra **9** 175-176
　Havana (1940)
　　Berle, Adolf Augustus Jr. **2** 199-200
　Lima (1938)
　　Berle, Adolf Augustus Jr. **2** 199-200
　Montevideo (1933)
　　Lamas, Carlos Saavedra **9** 175-176
　Rio de Janeiro (1906)
　　Drago, Luis María **5** 92-93
　　Nabuco de Araujo, Joaquim Aurelio
　　　11 288-289

International Congress of Modern Architecture
see CIAM

International Court of Justice (The Hague; established 1945)
Elias, Taslim Olawale **5** 250-251
Haya de la Torre, Victor Raul **7** 216-217
Jennings, Robert Yewdall **8** 246-247
see also Permanent Court of International Justice

International Danube Commission (1856-1940)
Gordon, Charles George **6** 448-449

International Encyclopedia of Unified Science (reformer book)
Carnap, Rudolf **3** 308-309

International Exhibition of Modern Art (New York City; 1913)
see Armory Show

International exhibitions (expositions)
see World's Fairs

International Geophysical Year (1957-1958)
Chapman, Sydney **3** 441

International Gothic style (painting)
Bellini, Giovanni **2** 137-138
Gentile da Fabriano **6** 266-267
Ghiberti, Lorenzo **6** 291-292
Limbourg brothers, The **9** 412-413
Martini, Simone **10** 298-299
Pisanello **12** 323-324

International Harvester Co. (established 1902)
Deering, William **4** 455-456

International House (film)
Fields, W. C. **5** 444

International Labor Conference (Geneva)
Curtin, John Joseph **4** 348-349
Lamas, Carlos Saavedra **9** 175-176

International Ladies' Garment Workers' Union
Dubinsky, David **5** 114-115
Herberg, Will **7** 322-323
Hillman, Sidney **7** 392-393
Pesotta, Rose **12** 248-249
Schniederman, Rose **14** 22-23

International law
practitioners
Chamberlain, Arthur Neville **3** 409-411
Drago, Luis María **5** 92-93
Jennings, Robert Yewdall **8** 246-247
Lansing, Robert **9** 200
Monnet, Jean **11** 109-110
Perth, 16th Earl of **12** 244-245
Titulescu, Nicolae **15** 246-247
von Mehren, Robert Brandt **16** 24-25
scholars
Boutros-Ghali, Boutros **2** 457-458
Field, David Dudley **5** 439-440
Grotius, Hugo **7** 18-19
Lieber, Francis **9** 401-402

Maine, Henry James Sumner **10** 152
Pufendorf, Samuel von **12** 477-478
Suárez, Francisco **15** 8
Vitoria, Francisco de **16** 1-2

International League (baseball)
Robinson, Jack Roosevelt **13** 207-208

International Longshoremen and Warehousemen's Union (ILWU)
Bridges, Harry A.R. **3** 3-5

International Maize and Wheat Improvement Center (research organization)
Borlaug, Norman Ernest **2** 418-420

International Military Tribunal for the Far East (1946-1948)
Tojo, Hideki **15** 254-256
see also War crimes trials

International Missionary Council (established 1921)
Luthuli, Albert John **10** 51-52
Mott, John R. **11** 212
see also World Council of Churches

International Monetary Bank
Coombs, Herbert Cole **4** 219-220

International Monetary Fund (established 1945)
Camdessus, Michel **3** 244-246
Herrera, Juan de **7** 335
Keynes, John Maynard **8** 528-530

International of Labor Unions (Moscow; 1921)
Browder, Earl Russell **3** 30-31

International Planned Parenthood Federation (established 1946)
Sanger, Margaret Higgins **13** 467-468

International Prime Meridian Conference (1884)
Fleming, Sandford **5** 485-486

International Psycho-Analytic Congress (Salzburg; 1908)
Bleuler, Eugen **2** 325
Freud, Sigmund **6** 103-106

International Red Cross (established 1864)
Barton, Clara **2** 37-39
Bellows, Henry Whitney **2** 143-144
Dunant, Jean Henri **5** 139-141

International Sanitary Conference (1881; 1901)
Finlay, Carlos Juan **5** 450

International Socialist Congress
see International, Second

International Society for Contemporary Music (established 1922)
Lutoslawski, Witold **10** 52-53

International Society for Krishna Consciousness
Bhaktivedanta Prabhupada **2** 254-255

International Style (architecture)
Breuer, Marcel **2** 520-521
Bunshaft, Gordon **3** 125-127
Johnson, Philip **8** 313-314
Meier, Richard **10** 456-458

Mendelsohn, Erich **10** 488
Mies van der Rohe, Ludwig **11** 10-12
Neutra, Richard Joseph **11** 355-356
Niemeyer Soares Filho, Oscar **11** 389-390
Oud, Jacobus Johannes Pieter **12** 32
Pei, I. M. **12** 184-187
Perret, Auguste **12** 233

International Style (painting)
see International Gothic style

International Union of Geodesy and Geophysics (established 1919)
Meinesz, Felix Andries Vening **10** 461

International Woman Suffrage Alliance (1904)
Catt, Carrie Chapman **3** 375-376

International Women's Day (Russia; 1917)
Nicholas II **11** 378-380

International Workingmen's Association
see International, First

Interpretation of Dreams, The (book; Freud)
Freud, Sigmund **6** 103-106
Jung, Carl Gustav **8** 388-389

Interstate Commerce Commission (United States)
Harriman, Edward Henry **7** 164-165
Taft, William Howard **15** 78-81
Tillman, Benjamin Ryan **15** 225-226

Interstate Commerce Omission [sic], The (publication)
Nader, Ralph **11** 290-291

Intervista, L' (play)
Moravia, Alberto **11** 153-155

Intimations of Immortality (poem)
Wordsworth, William **16** 385-388

Into My Own (poem)
Frost, Robert Lee **6** 130-133

Intolerable Acts (1774)
American reaction
Adams, John **1** 48-51
Clinton, George **4** 113-114
Franklin, Benjamin **6** 60-64
Gerry, Elbridge **6** 282-283
Boston Port Bill
Adams, Samuel **1** 55-56
Hancock, John **7** 114-116
Washington, George **16** 126-129
causes
North, Frederick **11** 429-430
see also Boston Tea Party
Massachusetts Government Act
Leonard, Daniel **9** 336-337
Quebec Act
Carleton, Guy **3** 300-301
Lewis, Andrew **9** 376-377

Intolerance (film)
Griffith, David Wark **6** 544-545

Intolleranza (opera)
Nono, Luigi **11** 420-421

Intoxicated Tide (poems)
Benn, Gottfried **2** 164

Introduction to Philosophy (book)
Brightman, Edgar Sheffield **3** 8-9

Introspection (psychology)
Titchener, Edward Bradford **15** 241-242
Watson, John Broadus **16** 138-139
Wundt, Wilhelm Max **16** 402-403

Intruder in the Dust (novel)
Faulkner, William **5** 395-397

Intruder, The (novel)
D'Annunzio, Gabriele **4** 388

Intruder, The (play)
Maeterlinck, Maurice **10** 125-126

Intuition (philosophy)
Bergson, Henri **2** 191-192
Descartes, René **4** 505-508
Kant, Immanuel **8** 430-432
McCosh, James **10** 402-403
Mill, John Stuart **11** 21-23
Sidgwick, Henry **14** 213
Spinoza, Baruch **14** 381-383
William of Ockham **16** 298-299

Intuition (psychology)
Jung, Carl Gustav **8** 388-389

INUKAI, TSUYOSHI (1855-1932), Japanese
journalist and statesman **8** 130-131
Takahashi, Korekiyo **15** 84-85

Invalides, Les (church of, Paris)
Mansart, Jules Hardouin **10** 212

Invective (book)
Petrarch **12** 259-261

Inventors
see Scientists—inventors

Inverse square law (physics)
Hooke, Robert **7** 475
Hubble, Edwin Powell **8** 10-11
Pauli, Wolfgang Ernst **12** 149

Investigator (ship)
Franklin, John **6** 64-65
Ross, James Clark **13** 302-303

Investiture Struggle (Roman Catholic
Church; 11th-12th century)
Anselm of Canterbury **1** 244-245
Gregory VII **6** 532-534
Henry I **7** 286-287
Henry IV **7** 292
Henry V **7** 295-296
Matilda of Tuscany **10** 334-336
Urban II **15** 393

Invisible City of Kitezh, The (opera)
Rimsky-Korsakov, Nikolai Andreevich
13 174-175

Invisible Man (novel)
Ellison, Ralph Waldo **5** 274-275
Wells, Herbert George **16** 195-196

Invisible One, The (play)
Lagerkvist, Pär Fabian **9** 162-163

Invitation au château, L' (play)
Anouilh, Jean **1** 243-244

Inzuzo (poems)
Mqhayi, Samuel Edward Krune **11** 223

Io (mythology)
Aeschylus **1** 70-72

Io Approached by Jupiter... (painting)
Correggio **4** 249-251

Iodine (element—chemistry)
Davy, Humphry **4** 426-427
Fizeau, Hippolyte Armand Louis **5** 475
Gay-Lussac, Joseph Louis **6** 245-246

Iolanthe (operetta)
Gilbert, William Schwenck **6** 314-315
Sullivan, Arthur Seymour **15** 23

Iole, Princess (literary character)
Sophocles **14** 343-345

Ion (play and dialogue)
Euripides **5** 332-334
Plato **12** 345-347

Ion of Chios (flourished 5th century B.C.),
Greek poet
Aeschylus **1** 70-72

Iona (island, Hebrides)
Columba **4** 175-176

IONESCO, EUGÈNE (1912-1994),
Franco-Romanian author **8** 131-132

Ionian Revolt (499-494 B.C.)
Cleomenes I **4** 103
Darius I **4** 394-395
Herodotus **7** 330-333
Miltiades **11** 42-43
see also Persian Wars (500-449 B.C.)

Ionian school (philosophy)
Anaxagoras **1** 208-209
Anaximander **1** 209-210
Anaximenes **1** 210
Heraclitus **7** 320
Thales **15** 161

Ionic order (Greek architecture)
Ictinus **8** 101

Ionisation (musical composition)
Varèse, Edgard **15** 432-433

Ionosphere (physics)
Chapman, Sydney **3** 441
Lovell, Alfred Charles Bernard **10** 8-9

Ionych (story)
Chekhov, Anton Pavlovich **3** 494-497

Iowa, State University of (Iowa City)
Lewin, Kurt **9** 375-376
Schlesinger, Arthur Meier **14** 13

Iowa State College (Ames)
Carver, George Washington **3** 346-347

Iphigenia (Iphigenie; mythology)
Euripides **5** 332-334
Gluck, Christoph Willibald **6** 372-374
Goethe, Johann Wolfgang von
6 388-391
Racine, Jean Baptiste **12** 532-535

Ipsus, battle of (301 B.C.)
Antigonus I **1** 248-249

Ipswich (town, Massachusetts)
Winthrop, John **16** 339-341

IQBAL, MUHAMMAD (1877?-1938), Indian Moslem poet and philosopher
8 132-133
Jinnah, Mohammad Ali **8** 262-263

IRA
see Irish Republican Army

Iran (kingdom, southwestern Asia)
Islamic rule
Khomeini, Ruhollah Musavi
8 535-537
kings
Mohammad Reza Shah Pahlavi
11 75-76
Reza Shah Pahlavi **13** 116-117
nationalism
Mossadegh, Mohammad
11 206-207
since 1979
Khamenei, Sayyid Ali **8** 533-535
Khomeini, Ruhollah Musavi
8 535-537
Rafsanjani, Akbar Hashemi **13** 3-4
Shariati, Ali **14** 156-157
United Nations
Lie, Trygve Halvdan **9** 400-401
U.S. hostages
Christopher, Warren Minor **4** 32-33
seePersia (for period before 1935)

Iran-Contra affair (United States; 1980s)
Casey, William J. **3** 351-353

Iraq, Republic of (nation, southwestern
Asia)
ancient era
see Assyria; Babylonia;
Mesopotamia; Persia
Islamic rule
Abu Bakr **1** 31-32
Ali **1** 155-156
Alp Arslan **1** 178-179
Chelmsford, Frederic John Napier
Thesiger **3** 497
Mahmud II **10** 145-147
Muawiya ibn Abu Sufyan
11 223-224
see also Islamic Empire; Ottoman
Empire; Persia
since 1920
Abdullah ibn Husein **1** 19-20
Dayan, Moshe **4** 429-431
Fādil al-Jamālī, Muhammad
5 361-362
Faisal I **5** 370-371
Glubb, John Bagot **6** 371-372
Husein ibn Ali **8** 63
Lawrence, Thomas Edward
9 253-254
Nuri al-Sa'id **11** 446-447
Saddam Hussein **13** 415-416

IRB (Irish Republican Brotherhood)
see Fenians

Ireland (Eire; republic, British Isles)
• EARLY HISTORY TO UNION

Anglicization policy
  Charles I **3** 450-452
  Cromwell, Oliver **4** 317-320
  Strafford, 1st Earl of **14** 490-491
Christianity and
  Columba **4** 175-176
  Columban **4** 176
  Innocent III **8** 125-127
  Patrick, Saint **12** 135-136
English conquest
  Henry II **7** 287-289
  Henry VIII **7** 302-305
legislative independence
  Fox, Charles James **6** 35-37
  George III **6** 270-272
  Grattan, Henry **6** 499
rebellion (1641)
  Charles I **3** 450-452
  Monck, George **11** 96-97
  Pym, John **12** 495-496
Tudor domination
  Drake, Francis **5** 94-96
  Edward VI **5** 213-214
  Elizabeth I **5** 263-266
  Essex, 2d Earl of **5** 321-322
  Henry VII **7** 300-302
  Henry VIII **7** 302-305
  Raleigh, Walter **13** 9-11
  Spenser, Edmund **14** 373-376
Tyrone's rebellion
  Elizabeth I **5** 263-266
  Essex, 2d Earl of **5** 321-322
  Spenser, Edmund **14** 373-376
  see also England
• ENGLAND: UNION
Act of Union (1800)
  Castlereagh, Viscount **3** 363-364
  Cornwallis, Charles **4** 241-243
  Emmet, Robert **5** 281-282
  Pitt, William the Younger
    12 329-331
Catholic emancipation
  see Catholic emancipation
Easter Rebellion
  see Easter Rebellion
Fenians
  see Fenians
Great Famine (1845-1848)
  Colum, Padraic **4** 174-175
  O'Connell, Daniel **11** 465-467
  Peel, Robert **12** 181-183
  Russell, John **13** 380-381
  Victoria **15** 485-487
home rule issue
  Asquith, Herbert Henry
    1 344-346
  Bright, John **3** 6-7
  Gladstone, William Ewart
    6 357-360
  Morley, John **11** 178-179
  Parnell, Charles Stewart
    12 117-119
  Pearse, Patrick Henry
    12 173-174
  Victoria **15** 485-487

Irish Land Act (1903)
  Balfour, Arthur James **1** 469-470
Irish Republican Brotherhood
  see Fenians
reforms
  O'Connell, Daniel **11** 465-467
  Salisbury, 3d Marquess of
    13 448-449
Sinn Fein
  see Sinn Fein
  see also Great Britain
• FREE STATE and REPUBLIC
as Irish Free State (1922-1937)
  Collins, Michael **4** 167-168
  De Valera, Eamon **4** 514-515
  Lloyd George, David **9** 469-471
  Mannix, Daniel **10** 210
Civil War (1922)
  Collins, Michael **4** 167-168
  De Valera, Eamon **4** 514-515
  Markievicz, Constance
    10 267-271
Eire (1937-1949)
  Hyde, Douglas **8** 82-83
Republic (1949)
  Bruton, John Gerard **3** 76-77
  Cosgrave, Liam **4** 258-260
  De Valera, Eamon **4** 514-515
  Fitzgerald, Garret **5** 472-474
  Reynolds, Albert **13** 113-115
  Robinson, Mary Bourke
    13 211-213
  see also Great Britain; Irish liter-
  ature; Northern Ireland

IRELAND, JOHN (1838-1918), American
Catholic archbishop **8** 133-134
  Corrigan, Michael Augustine **4** 253

IRELAND, PATRICIA (born 1945), president of the National Organization for
Women (NOW) **8** 134-135

IRENE OF ATHENS (ca. 752-803), Byzantine empress 797-802 **8** 135-138
  Charlemagne **3** 445-447
  Harun al-Rashid **7** 188
  see also Iconoclastic controversy

Irene (Ducas; 1066?-1120?), Byzantine
empress
  Comnena, Anna **4** 185-186

Irene (play)
  Johnson, Samuel **8** 315-317
  Voltaire **16** 14-16

Irene innocente (play)
  Betti, Ugo **2** 246

Ireton, Henry (1611-1651), English Parliamentary commander
  Charles I **3** 450-452

IRIGOYEN, HIPÓLITO (circa 1850-1933),
Argentine statesman, twice president
8 139-140
  Justo, Agustin Pedro **8** 396

Iris (novel)
  Hesse, Hermann **7** 367-369

Irish Airman... (poem; Yeats)
  Gregory, Augusta **6** 535-536

Irish Elegies (poems)
  Colum, Padraic **4** 174-175

Irish Fairy Tales (stories)
  Stephens, James **14** 430-431

Irish Free State
  see Ireland—Free State and Republic

Irish language revival movement
(19th-20th century)
  De Valera, Eamon **4** 514-515
  Hyde, Douglas **8** 82-83
  Pearse, Patrick Henry **12** 173-174

Irish literary renaissance (19th-20th centu-
ry)
  Colum, Padraic **4** 174-175
  Gregory, Augusta **6** 535-536
  John, Augustus Edwin **8** 291
  Synge, Edmund John Millington
    15 61-62
  Yeats, William Butler **16** 445-447

Irish literature
drama and poetry
  Boucicault, Dion **2** 442-443
  Colum, Padraic **4** 174-175
  Gregory, Augusta **6** 535-536
  Heaney, Seamus Justin **7** 238-240
  O'Casey, Sean **11** 459-460
  Stephens, James **14** 430-431
  Synge, Edmund John Millington
    15 61-62
  Yeats, William Butler **16** 445-447
fiction
  Bowen, Elizabeth **2** 462-463
  Joyce, James **8** 365-367
  Somerville, Edith Anna OEnone
    14 334-335
  Stephens, James **14** 430-431
  Stoker, Bram **14** 463-464
plays
  Friel, Bernard Patrick **6** 115-116

Irish National League (United States)
  Lease, Mary Elizabeth Clyens **9** 268

Irish National Theatre Society
  see Abbey Theatre

Irish Republican Army (IRA)
  Adams, Gerald **1** 42-44
  Collins, Michael **4** 167-168

Irish Republican Brotherhood
  see Fenians

Irish Sea (England-Ireland)
  Jones, John Paul **8** 337-338

Irish Sketch Book, The (book)
  Thackeray, William Makepeace
    15 159-161

Irish Symphony (musical composition)
  Sullivan, Arthur Seymour **15** 23

Irish Volunteers (nationalist militia)
  De Valera, Eamon **4** 514-515
  Pearse, Patrick Henry **12** 173-174

Iron Chancellor
see Bismarck, Otto von

Iron Duke
see Alba, Duke of; Wellington, 1st
Duke of

Iron Heel, The (book)
London, Jack **9** 494-495

Iron Horse, The (film)
Ford, John **6** 7-8

Iron Industry
see Business and industrial leaders—
iron and steel industry

Iron Molders International Union (established 1859)
Sylvis, William **15** 60-61

Ironclads (ships)
Eads, James Buchanan **5** 175-176
Ericsson, John **5** 307-308
Welles, Gideon **16** 188-190

Ironside, Edmund
see Edmund II

Irony (literature)
Flaubert, Gustave **5** 480-482
Socrates **14** 320-321
Sophocles **14** 343-345
Swift, Jonathan **15** 51-54
see also Satire

Iroquois Confederacy (North American Indians)
captives
Brant, Joseph **2** 500-501
Brûlé, Étienne **3** 67-68
Champlain, Samuel de **3** 419-421
Frontenac et Palluau, Comte de
.6 128-130
La Salle, Sieur de **9** 210-211
Maisoneuve, Sieur de **10** 153
Radisson, Pierre-Esprit **12** 539-540
Talon, Jean **15** 91-92
Code of Handsome Lake
Handsome Lake **7** 122-123
formed
Deganawida **4** 460-461
kinship studies
Morgan, Lewis Henry **11** 167-168
leaders
Parker, Ely Samuel **12** 106-108
New York relations
Andros, Edmund **1** 234-235
Cornplanter **4** 239-241
Livingston, Robert **9** 461-462
Red Jacket **13** 71-73
see also American Revolution; Indians (North America); individual tribes; Lord Dunmore's War; Six Nations

Irrational Knot, The (novel; Shaw)
Edison, Thomas Alva **5** 206-208
Shaw, George Bernard **14** 163-164

Irredentism (politics)
De Gasperi, Alcide **4** 462-463
Francis Ferdinand **6** 44
Francis Joseph **6** 45-46

Irregular polygons (series of paintings)
Stella, Frank **14** 420-422

Irrigation Act (Australia; 1886)
Deakin, Alfred **4** 432-433

Irrungen, Wirrungen (novel)
Fontane, Theodor **5** 504

IRVING, KENNETH COLIN ("K. C.";
1899-1992), Canadian industrialist, the "Paul Bunyan of New Brunswick"
8 140-141

Irving, Sir Henry (1838-1905), English actor-manager
Barrymores **2** 28-30

IRVING, WASHINGTON (1783-1859),
American author and journalist
8 141-143
Allston, Washington **1** 176-177
Longfellow, Henry Wadsworth
9 499-500
Payne, John Howard **12** 159
Rogers, John **13** 248

Irwin, Baron
see Halifax, 1st Earl of

is 5 (poems)
Cummings, Edward Estlin **4** 334-336

Is Sex Necessary? (book)
Thurber, James Grove **15** 213-214

Isaac I (Comnenus; died 1061), Byzantine emperor 1057-59
Alexius I **1** 143-144

Isaac II (Angelus; died 1204), Byzantine emperor 1185-95 and 1203-04
Dandolo, Enrico **4** 386-387

ISAAC, HEINRICH (circa 1450-1517),
Flemish composer **8** 143-144
Hofhaimer, Paul **7** 441
Josquin des Prez **8** 361-363
Lassus, Roland de **9** 216-218
Senfl, Ludwig **14** 105-106
Webern, Anton **16** 160-162

ISAACS, JORGE (1837-1895), Colombian novelist **8** 144

Isaacs, Rufus Daniel
see Reading, 1st Marquess of

Isabel (literary character)
García Márquez, Gabriel **6** 208-209

Isabel de Valois (died 1568), Spanish queen
Cervantes, Miguel de Saavedra
3 395-398

Isabel of Portugal (1503-1539), wife of Charles V
Cabezón, Antonio **3** 197-198
Charles V **3** 457-459

ISABELLA I (1451-1504), queen of Castile 1474-1504 **8** 144-145
Abravanel, Isaac ben Judah **1** 31
Columbus, Christopher **4** 176-179
Henry VII **7** 300-302
Manrique, Jorge **10** 210-211
Manuel I **10** 219-220

ISABELLA II (1830-1904), queen of Spain 1833-1868 **8** 145-146
Alarcón, Pedro Antonio de **1** 100-101
Ferdinand VII **5** 418-420

Isabella (1566-1633), infanta of Spain, ruler of the Netherlands 1621-1633
Rubens, Peter Paul **13** 339-342

Isabella (literary character)
Shakespeare, William **14** 142-145

Isabella (poem; Keats)
Keats, John **8** 470-472
Millais, John Everett **11** 23-24

Isabella of Portugal (1397-1471), mother of Charles the Bold
Charles the Bold **3** 467-469

Isabelle (book)
Gide, André **6** 308-309

Isabelle of Bavaria (1370-1435), queen consort of Charles VI of France
Charles VI **3** 460-461
Charles VII **3** 461-462

Isabey, Louis Gabriel Eugène (1803-1886),
French painter
Bonington, Richard Parkes **2** 394-395

Isagoras (flourished 507 B.C.), Athenian politician
Cleisthenes **4** 98-99
Cleomenes I **4** 103

Isaiah, Book of (Old Testament)
Amos **1** 205
Isaiah **8** 146-147
Micah **10** 542-543

ISAIAH (flourished circa 740-701 B.C.),
Hebrew prophet **8** 146-147
Micah **10** 542-543

Isaiah ben Amoz
see Isaiah

Isandhlwana, battle of (1879)
Frere, Henry Bartle Edward **6** 100-101

Ise, Grand Shrine of (Zen; religious site)
Basho, Matsuo **2** 45-48

Ise Monogatari (book; anonymous)
Sotatsu, Tawaraya **14** 349

Isenheim Altarpiece (painting)
Grünewald, Matthias **7** 23-24

Isfahan (Iran)
see Esfahan

Ishbaal (Ishbosheth; Old Testament character)
David, Jacques Louis **4** 407-409

ISHERWOOD, CHRISTOPHER
(1904-1986), British-born American writer of fiction, drama, film, travel, and autobiography **8** 147-149
Auden, Wystan Hugh **1** 364-366

Ishibashi, Tanzan (1884-1973), Japanese statesman
Kishi, Nobusuke **9** 41-43

Ishmael (literary character)
Melville, Herman **10** 472-476

ISIDORE OF SEVILLE, SAINT (560-636),
Spanish cleric and encyclopedist
8 149-150
  López de Ayala, Pedro **9** 508-509
  Lombard, Peter **9** 490-491

Isidro, Saint (1070-1130), Spanish farmer
  Calderón, Pedro **3** 221-222

Isis (journal)
  Sarton, George **13** 490-491

Iska (novel)
  Ekwensi, Cyprian **5** 242-243

Islam (religion)
- DOCTRINE
  Alawi
    Assad, Hafiz **1** 346-348
  and other ideologies
    Averroës **1** 382-383
    Hatta, Mohammad **7** 197-199
    Judah Halevi **8** 373
    Mani **10** 196-197
    Sukarno **15** 18-20
    Thomas Aquinas **15** 183-186
  Druze
    Jumblatt, Kamal **8** 386-387
  foundation
    Mohammed **11** 76-78
  Koran
    see Koran
  major sects
    see Shiites; Sunnites
  Mihna (Inquisition)
    Mamun, Abdallah al- **10** 183
  Mouride brotherhood
    Bamba, Amadou **1** 481-482
  Muslim Brotherhood
    Al-Banna, Hassan **1** 104-106
    Sayyid Qutb **13** 509-511
  mysticism
    see Sufism
  rationalist school
    see Mutazilite school
  reforms (early)
    see Almohads; Almoravids
  reforms (19th century)
    Abduh ibn Hasan Khayr Allah,
      Muhammad **1** 16-17
    Hassan, Muhammad Abdille
      7 194-195
    Uthman don Fodio **15** 397-398
  Sammaniya order
    Mahdi **10** 137-138
  Shi'ite
    Berri, Nabih **2** 220-222
    Fādil al-Jamālī, Muhammad
      5 361-362
    Khamenei, Sayyid Ali **8** 533-535
    Khomeini, Ruhollah Musavi
      8 535-537
    Sadr, Musa al- **13** 420-422
    Shariati, Ali **14** 156-157
  studies of
    Imam, Alhadji Abubakar
      8 114-115

  Tabari, Muhammad ibn Jarir al-
      15 69-70
  Sunni
    Faisal ibn Abd al Aziz ibn Saud
      5 371-372
    Saddam Hussein **13** 415-416
  theology and law
    Aiken, Conrad **1** 90-91
    Al-Banna, Hassan **1** 104-106
    Ashari, Abu al- Hasan Ali al-
      1 327-328
    Bukhari, Muhammad ibn Ismail
      al- **3** 111-112
    Ghazali, Abu Hamid Muham-
      mad al- **6** 290-291
    Hallaj, Al-Husayn ibn Mansur al-
      7 86-87
    Ibn al-Arabi, Muhyi al-Din **8** 91
    ibn Hazm, Abu Muhammad Ali
      8 93
    Junayd, Abu al-Qasim ibn
      Muhammad al **8** 388
    Marāghī, Mustafā al- **10** 228-229
    Mawdūdī, Abu-I A'la **10** 353-354
    Nazzam, Ibrahim ibn Sayyar al-
      11 329
    Sayyid Qutb **13** 509-511
    Shariati, Ali **14** 156-157
    see also Maliki school (Islamic
      law)
  20th century revivalism
    Al-Banna, Hassan **1** 104-106
  wars against
    see Crusades
- EXPANSION
  beginnings to empire
    see Islamic Empire
  China
    Kublai Khan **9** 115-118
    Tso Tsung-t'ang **15** 328-329
  India and Pakistan
    Aga Khan **1** 74-76
    Gandhi, Mohandas Karamchand
      6 201-204
    Jinnah, Mohammad Ali
      8 262-263
    Nanak **11** 303
    Nehru, Jawaharlal **11** 332-334
    Nizami, Khaliq Ahmad **11** 405
    Sapru, Tej Bahadur **13** 480-481
    Shivaji **14** 199-200
    Syed Ahmed Khan **15** 60
    see also Hinduism—Moslem
      reaction; India—ca.
      1000-1600 (Moslem)
  subsaharan Africa
    Bamba, Amadou **1** 481-482
    Mahdi **10** 137-138
    Musa Mansa **11** 266
    Mutesa I **11** 277
    Mwanga **11** 282-283
    Omar ibn Said Tal, Al-Hajj
      11 509-510
    Touré, Sékou **15** 275-277
    Uthman don Fodio **15** 397-398
    see also Mahdists

- UNITY OF RELIGION AND STATE
  Bosnia-Herzegovina
    Izetbegovic, Alija **8** 161-163

Islamic art and architecture
  Behzad **2** 123
  Sinan, Kodja Mimar **14** 245-246

Islamic Empire
  622-661 (Hegira and Orthodox
    caliphate)
    Abu Bakr **1** 31-32
    Ali **1** 155-156
    Heraclius **7** 320-321
    Mohammed **11** 76-78
    Omar ibn al-Khattab **11** 508-509
  661-750 (Umayyad caliphate; Damas-
    cus)
    Abd al-Malik **1** 12-13
    Leo III **9** 330-332
    Muawiya ibn Abu Sufyan
      11 223-224
  750-1258 (Abbasid caliphate; Baghdad)
    Harun al-Rashid **7** 188
    Mamun, Abdallah al- **10** 183
    Mansur, Abu Jafar ibn Muhammad
      al- **10** 214-215
    see also Abbasids
  756-1031 (Umayyad caliphate; Cordo-
    va)
    Abd al-Rahman I **1** 13-14
    Abd al-Rahman III **1** 14
  1062-1147 (Almoravids)
    see Almoravids
  1096-1272 (Crusades against)
    see Crusades
  1147-1269 (Almohads)
    see Almohads
  1169-1250 (Ayyubids; Egypt)
    Saladin **13** 441-442
    see also Islam; Ottoman Empire;
      Spain—Islamic

Islamic law
  Algeria
    Chadli Benjedid **3** 402-404
  Iran
    Khomeini, Ruhollah Musavi
      8 535-537
    Rafsanjani, Akbar Hashemi **13** 3-4
  Sudan
    Turabi, Hassan Abdullah al-
      15 344-345

Islamic Reform Movement (Algeria)
  Ben Badis, 'Abd al-Hamid **2** 147-148

Island in the Moon, An (poem)
  Blake, William **2** 316-318

Island Nights' Entertainments (stories)
  Stevenson, Robert Louis **14** 446-448

Island of Barrataria, The (play)
  Tyler, Royall **15** 371-372

Island Pharisees, The (novel)
  Galsworthy, John **6** 189-190

Islands (poem)
  Doolittle, Hilda **5** 65-66

Isle of Dogs, The (play)
Jonson, Ben **8** 343-345

Isle of the Dead, The (musical composition)
Rachmaninov, Sergei Vasilievich
12 531-532

Isle sonante, L' (book)
Rabelais, François **12** 524-526

Isly, battle of (1844)
Abd el-Kadir **1** 15
Bugeaud de la Piconnerie, Thomas
Robert **3** 111

Isly, Duke of
see Bugeaud de la Piconnerie, Thomas
Robert

Ismaelillo (poems)
Martí, José **10** 285-286

Ismail (ruled 1537-1539), ruler of the West
African Songhay empire
Muhammad, Elijah **11** 230-231

Ismail I (1486-1524), shah of Persia
1500-1524
Behzad **2** 123
Selim I **14** 94-95

ISMAIL PASHA (1830-1895), khedive of
Egypt 1863-1879 **8** 150-151
and English explorers
Baker, Samuel White **1** 454-455
opponents
Cromer, 1st Earl of **4** 317
Gordon, Charles George **6** 448-449
Johannes IV **8** 272-273
Lesseps, Vicomte de **9** 354-355
Mahdi **10** 137-138
relatives
Fuad I **6** 139
Ibrahim Pasha **8** 97-98
Tewfik Pasha **15** 157-158

Ismailis (Islamic Shiite sect)
Aga Khan **1** 74-76
Hulagu Khan **8** 27-28
Masudi, Ali ibn al- Husayn al-
10 328-329

Isn't Life Wonderful (film)
Griffith, David Wark **6** 544-545

ISOCRATES (436-338 B.C.), Athenian ora-
tor **8** 151
Alexander the Great **1** 137-141
Gorgias **6** 456
Philip II **12** 269-271

Isola meravigliosa, L' (play)
Betti, Ugo **2** 246

Isolation (poem)
Lamartine, Alphonse Marie Louis de
9 173-175

Isolationism (United States politics)
Borah, William Edgar **2** 408
Hoover, Herbert Clark **7** 483-485
Johnson, Hiram Warren **8** 300-301
McCormick, Robert Rutherford
10 401-402
Wood, Robert Elkington **16** 370-371

Isolt (Isolde; legendary character)
Gottfried von Strassburg **6** 461-462
Wagner, Richard **16** 40-43

Isorhythm (music)
Dufay, Guillaume **5** 125-126
Dunstable, John **5** 150-151
Machaut, Guillaume de **10** 93-94
Vitry, Philippe de **16** 2

Isotopes (chemistry)
Aston, Francis William **1** 350-351
Calvin, Melvin **3** 242-243
Hevesy, George Charles de **7** 371
Lawrence, Ernest Orlando **9** 248-250
Libby, Willard Frank **9** 397-398
Richards, Theodore William
13 137-138
Seaborg, Glenn Theodore **14** 74-76
Soddy, Frederick **14** 321-323
Thomson, Joseph John **15** 200-201
Urey, Harold Clayton **15** 394-396
Yalow, Rosalyn S. **16** 427-428

ISOZAKI, ARATA (born 1931), Japanese
architect **8** 152-153

Ispahan
see Esfahan

Ispezione (play)
Betti, Ugo **2** 246

Israel, State of (nation; southwestern Asia)
independence (1948)
Begin, Menachem **2** 118-120
Ben-Gurion, David **2** 160-161
Dayan, Moshe **4** 429-431
Evatt, Herbert Vere **5** 341-343
Kuk, Abraham Issac **9** 123-124
Meir, Golda **10** 462-463
Peres, Shimon **12** 210-211
Rabin, Yitzchak **12** 527-529
Shamir, Yitzchak **14** 147-149
Weizmann, Chaim **16** 183-184
internal politics
Netanyahu, Binyamin **11** 350-351
nation-building
Herzog, Chaim **7** 354-355
Palestinian relations
Weizman, Ezer **16** 181-182
Palestinians
Abu Musa **1** 32-33
Arafat, Yasser **1** 270-271
Habash, George **7** 55-56
religion and politics
Lee Kuan Yew **9** 281-283
U.S. relations
Acheson, Dean Gooderham **1** 37-38
Arens, Moshe **1** 284-285
Eban, Abba **5** 191-192
Forrestal, James Vincent **6** 14
Levy, David **9** 373-374
Rabin, Yitzchak **12** 527-529
U.S. supporters
Cahan, Abraham **3** 214
Silver, Abba Hillel **14** 232-233
Wise, Stephen Samuel **16** 344-345
see also Arab-Israeli wars; Suez Cri-
sis; Zionism

Israel (ancient king.)
see Jewish history—Biblical Era (Israel)

Israel (musical composition)
Bloch, Ernest **2** 326-327

Israel Defense Force
Barak, Ehud **1** 497-498
Herzog, Chaim **7** 354-355
Sharon, Ariel **14** 157-159

Israel in Egypt (musical composition)
Handel, George Frederick **7** 116-119

Israel Labour Party
Peres, Shimon **12** 210-211

Israel National Museum (Jerusalem)
Noguchi, Isamu **11** 416-418

Israel Potter (novel)
Melville, Herman **10** 472-476

Israeli literature
Appelfeld, Aharon **1** 262-263
Oz, Amos **12** 45-47

Israeli music
Tal, Josef **15** 85-86

Israelites Collecting Manna, The (painting)
Poussin, Nicolas **12** 418-420

Israëls, Jozef (1824-1911), Dutch genre
painter
Liebermann, Max **9** 402-403

Issus, battle of (333 B.C.)
Alexander the Great **1** 137-141
Ptolemy I **12** 470-472

Istanbul (city; Turkey)
Disraeli, Benjamin **5** 27-29
Sinan, Kodja Mimar **14** 245-246
Suleiman I **15** 20-21
seeConstantinople (before 1453)

Istanbul University (Turkey)
Gökalp, Mehmet Ziya **6** 395-396

Istar (ballet)
Martinu, Bohuslav **10** 299-300

Isthmian Games (196 B.C.)
Flamininus, Titus Quinctius **5** 477

Istiqlal (Morocco; political party)
Allal al-Fassi, Mohamed **1** 162
Mohammed V **11** 79-81

It Can't Happen Here (novel)
Lewis, Harry Sinclair **9** 385-387

It Happened One Night (film)
Gable, William Clark **6** 157-158

It Has Come To Pass (book)
Farrell, James Thomas **5** 390-391

It is Written (play)
Dürrenmatt, Friedrich **5** 164-165

It Needs To Be Said (essays)
Grove, Frederick Philip **7** 20-21

It Was Blue and Green (painting)
O'Keeffe, Georgia **11** 487-489

Italia (airship)
Amundsen, Roald **1** 206-207
Nobile, Umberto **11** 411-412

Italia mia (poem; Petrarch)
Machiavelli, Niccolò **10** 97-99

Italian (language)
Bembo, Pietro **2** 144-145
Dante Alighieri **4** 389-391

Italian architecture
Piano, Renzo **12** 289-291
Rossi, Aldo **13** 309-310

Italian art
allegorical painting
Caravaggio **3** 282-284
Tiepolo, Giovanni Battista **15** 219-220
Tintoretto **15** 232-234
Titian **15** 242-244
Veronese, Paolo **15** 469-470
baroque
see Baroque architecture; Baroque painting; baroque sculpture
classicism
Ghiberti, Lorenzo **6** 291-292
Sansovino, Jacopo **13** 470-471
Vignola, Giacomo da **15** 493-494
Flemish influence
Antonello da Messina **1** 251-252
Ghirlandaio, Domenico **6** 292-293
Piero della Francesca **12** 301-302
futurism
Balla, Giacomo **1** 473-474
Boccioni, Umberto **2** 353-354
Manzù, Giacomo **10** 224-225
Marini, Marino **10** 260-262
Severini, Gino **14** 122
Gothic
see Gothic (art)
Impressionist sculpture
Rosso, Medardo **13** 313-315
International Gothic style
see International Gothic style
mannerism
see Mannerism (art)
metaphysical school
Chirico, Giorgio de **4** 4
modern
Burri, Alberto **3** 159-160
Nervi, Pier Luigi **11** 346-348
Rosso, Medardo **13** 313-315
neoclassicism
see Neoclassicism (art)—Italy
Renaissance
see Renaissance (art), architecture
still lifes
Morandi, Giorgio **11** 152-153
vedute painting
Canaletto **3** 257-258
Guardi, Francesco **7** 24-25
see also Italo-Byzantine style

Italian Girl, The (novel)
Murdoch, Iris **11** 256-257

Italian Institute for Historical Studies
Croce, Benedetto **4** 313-314

Italian literature
analytical prose
Betti, Ugo **2** 246

Pirandello, Luigi **12** 319-321
Svevo, Italo **15** 47-48
dolce stil nuovo
Cavalcanti, Guido **3** 382
Guinizzelli, Guido **7** 36-37
family life portraits
Ginzburg, Natalia Levi **6** 338-339
folktales
Calvino, Italo **3** 243-244
hermetic poetry
Montale, Eugenio **11** 117-118
Quasimodo, Salvatore **12** 506
Ungaretti, Giuseppe **15** 389-390
Holocaust testimony
Levi, Primo **9** 365-366
Humanism
see Humanism (literature)
medieval verse
Dante Alighieri **4** 389-391
Jacopone da Todi **8** 194
neorealism
D'Annunzio, Gabriele **4** 388
Levi, Carlo **9** 364
Moravia, Alberto **11** 153-155
Pavese, Cesare **12** 154-155
Silone, Ignazio **14** 231-232
Vittorini, Elio **16** 2-3
realism
see Realism (literature)—Italian
Renaissance
see Renaissance (literature)
romanticism
see Romanticism (literature)—Italian
vedute painting
Canaletto **3** 257-258
Guardi, Francesco **7** 24-25
see also Italo-Byzantine style

Italian music
baroque
see Baroque music
chamber cantatas
Carissimi, Giacomo **3** 299-300
Cesti, Pietro **3** 399-400
Rossi, Luigi **13** 310-311
Scarlatti, Pietro Alessandro Gaspare **13** 517-518
conductors
Busoni, Ferruccio Benvenuto **3** 173-174
Toscanini, Arturo **15** 270-271
madrigals
see Madrigal—Italian
modern (20th century)
Berio, Luciano **2** 194-195
Bussotti, Sylvano **3** 174-175
Dallapiccola, Luigi **4** 377-378
Malipiero, Gian Francesco **10** 171
Nono, Luigi **11** 420-421
Respighi, Ottorino **13** 103-104
notation systems
Guido d'Arezzo **7** 33
opera
Pavarotti, Luciano **12** 152-154
postromanticism
Puccini, Giacomo **12** 474-476

Verdi, Giuseppe Fortunino Francesco **15** 463-465
Renaissance
see Renaissance (music)
rococo
Tartini, Giuseppe **15** 112-113
Pergolesi, Giovanni Battista **12** 218-219
romanticism
see Romanticism (music)—Italian
see also Opera, Italian

Italian Phantasies (poems)
Zangwill, Israel **16** 488-489

Italian Poems (book)
Blok, Aleksandr Aleksandrovich **2** 335

Italian Symphony (musical composition)
Mendelssohn, Moses **10** 488-489

Italianate revival (English art and architecture)
Nash, John **11** 316
Upjohn, Richard **15** 392

Italienische Reise (book)
Goethe, Johann Wolfgang von **6** 388-391

Italo-Byzantine style (art)
Cimabue **4** 60-61
Duccio di Buoninsegna **5** 121-122
Giotto **6** 342-345
Martini, Simone **10** 298-299

Italy (Italian Republic; nation, southern Europe)
• TO 476 (ANCIENT)
509-27 B.C. Rome—509-27 B.C. (Roman Republic)
27 B.C.-476 A.D.
see Rome—27 B.C.- 476 A.D. (Roman Empire)
• 5TH-13TH CENTURY (MEDIEVAL)
Byzantine reconquest
Basil I **2** 49-50
Belisarius **2** 128-129
Cassiodorus, Flavius Magnus Aurelius **3** 357-358
Gregory I **6** 531-532
Justinian I **8** 393-395
Frankish intervention
Charlemagne **3** 445-447
Germanic rulers
Odoacer **11** 473
Theodoric the Great **15** 175-176
Gothic invasions
Alaric **1** 101-102
Attila **1** 360
Cassiodorus, Flavius Magnus Aurelius **3** 357-358
imperial intervention
Frederick I **6** 78-79
Frederick II **6** 79
Henry V **7** 295-296
Otto I **12** 28-29
Otto III **12** 29-30
Naples and Sicily
Frederick II **6** 79

Guiscard, Robert **7** 39-40
Peter III **12** 256-257
Roger II **13** 244-245
papacy and
Arnold of Brescia **1** 314-315
Boniface VIII **2** 392-393
Gregory I **6** 531-532
Gregory VII **6** 532-534
Innocent III **8** 125-127
Leo IX **9** 332
Urban II **15** 393
- 14TH-15TH CENTURY (LATE MEDIEVAL and RENAISSANCE)
Florence
Machiavelli, Niccolò **10** 97-99
Medici, Cosimo de' **10** 449-450
Medici, Lorenzo de' **10** 450-451
Savonarola, Girolamo **13** 505-506
imperial intervention
Henry VII **7** 299-300
Milan
Sforza, Lodovico **14** 127-128
Visconti, Gian Galeazzo **15** 510-511
Naples
Charles VIII **3** 462-463
Louis XII **9** 528-529
papacy and
Charles IV **3** 455-456
Rienzi, Cola di **13** 166-167
Venice
Mehmed the Conqueror **10** 452-454
- 16TH-17TH CENTURY (POST-RENAISSANCE)
Church-State conflict
Borgia, Cesare **2** 412-413
Eugene of Savoy **5** 330-331
Julius II **8** 384-386
Leo X **9** 332-334
Victor Amadeus II **15** 482-483
see also Church and State (Italy)
Ferrara
Borgia,, Lucrezia Duchess of Ferrara **2** 413-416
Spanish rule
Alba, Duke of **1** 103-104
Campanella, Tommaso **3** 249
- 18TH-19TH CENTURY (NAPOLEONIC ERA and MODERN STATE)
and Ethiopia (1889)
Johannes IV **8** 272-273
Menelik II **10** 495-497
Austria expulsed
Francis Joseph **6** 45-46
Metternich, Klemens von **10** 533-536
Napoleon I **11** 306-310
see also Austro-Hungarian Empire
Naples
Ferdinand II **5** 415-416
Napoleonic rule
Bonaparte, Joseph **2** 381-382

Murat, Joachim **11** 253-254
Napoleon I **11** 306-310
Pius VI **12** 333-334
Pius VII **12** 334-335
Papal States
Leo XIII **9** 334-336
Pius IX **12** 335-336
see also Papal States
unification
Cavour, Conte di **3** 385-386
Charles Albert, King of Sardinia **3** 466
Crispi, Francesco **4** 310-311
De Sanctis, Francesco **4** 505
Garibaldi, Giuseppe **6** 215-217
Manin, Daniele **10** 197-198
Mazzini, Giuseppe **10** 381-383
Pius IX **12** 335-336
Verdi, Giuseppe Fortunino Francesco **15** 463-465
Victor Emmanuel II **15** 483-484
- 20TH CENTURY (FASCISM and REPUBLIC)
and Ethiopia
Badoglio, Pietro **1** 428-429
Haile Selassie **7** 68-70
Mäkonnen Endalkačäw **10** 161-162
see also Ethiopia
anti-Fascists
Gramsci, Antonio **6** 488-489
Olivetti, Adriano **11** 501-502
Communist
Togliatti, Palmiro **15** 253-254
Christian Democrats
Andreotti, Giulio **1** 226-228
economic development
Mattei, Enrico **10** 337-339
Fascist policy
Coughlin, Charles Edward **4** 265-266
Croce, Benedetto **4** 313-314
Dollfuss, Engelbert **5** 47
Giolitti, Giovanni **6** 339-340
Hirohito **7** 410-412
Hitler, Adolf **7** 417-420
Horthy de Nagybánya, Nicholas **7** 510-512
Matteotti, Giacomo **10** 339-340
Mussolini, Benito **11** 272-274
Orlando, Vittorio Emmanuele **11** 529-530
Historic Compromise
Moro, Aldo **11** 180-181
industry
Agnelli, Giovanni **1** 82-83
Benetton **2** 158-159
Lauro, Achille **9** 234-235
Republican policy
Craxi, Bettino **4** 300-301
republican policy
De Gasperi, Alcide **4** 462-463
John, XXIII **8** 277-280
Paul VI **12** 146-148
Pius X **12** 336-337
Pius XII **12** 339-340

Victor Emmanuel III **15** 484-485
struggle against corruption
Scalfaro, Oscar Luigi **13** 511-512
world wars
see World War I; World War II
see also French Revolutionary Wars; Sardinia; Sicily; and other cities and regions
Italy (poem)
Gogol, Nikolai **6** 391-393
Itansha no Kanashimi (novel)
Tanizaki, Junichiro **15** 101-102
Itching Parrot, The (novel)
Fernández de Lizardi, José Joaquin **5** 424-425
Itinerant Scholar in Paradise, The (play)
Sachs, Hans **13** 410-411
ITO, HIROBUMI (1841-1909), Japanese statesman **8** 153-155
Hara, Kei **7** 138
Iwakura, Tomomi **8** 160-161
Mutsuhito **11** 279-282
Okuma, Shigenobu **11** 490
Saionji, Kimmochi **13** 438-439
Yamagata, Aritomo **16** 428-429
Itopatin (flourished early 17th century), American Algonquian chief
Powhatan **12** 429-430
It's Hard To Be a Jew (play)
Sholem Aleichem **14** 202-203
It's Never Over (novel)
Callaghan, Edward Morley **3** 229-230
It-towy (ancient city; Egypt)
Amenemhet I **1** 193-194
ITURBIDE, AGUSTÍN DE (1783-1824), Mexican military leader **8** 155-156
Álvarez, Juan **1** 184-185
Alamán, Lucas **1** 99-100
Fernández de Lizardi, José Joaquin **5** 424-425
Guerrero, Vicente **7** 28-30
Hidalgo y Costilla, Miguel **7** 375-377
Santa Ana, Antonio López de **13** 471-472
Ituzaingó (epic)
Zorrilla de San Martin, Juan **16** 530-531
Ituzaingó, battle of (1828)
Rivera, Fructuoso **13** 184-185
Ityala lama-wele (story)
Mqhayi, Samuel Edward Krune **11** 223
Ivan II (1326-1359), grand duke of Moscow 1353-1359
Ivan III **8** 156-157
IVAN III (1440-1505), grand duke of Moscow 1462-1505 **8** 156-157
IVAN IV (1530-1584), grand duke of Moscow, czar of Russia 1547-1584 **8** 157-159
Cabot, Sebastian **3** 200-201
Chancellor, Richard **3** 422
Godunov, Boris Feodorovich **6** 382-383

Ivan V (1666-1696), czar of Russia 1682-1689
Alexis Mikhailovich Romanov **1** 142-143
Anna Ivanovna **1** 240-241
Peter I **12** 253-256

Ivan VI (1740-1764), czar of Russia 1740-1741
Anna Ivanovna **1** 240-241

Ivan (literary character)
Dostoevsky, Fyodor **5** 74-77

Ivan Susanin (opera)
Glinka, Mikhail Ivanovich **6** 369-370

Ivan the Great
see Ivan III

Ivan the Terrible
see Ivan IV

Ivan the Terrible (film)
Eisenstein, Sergei Mikhailovich **5** 240-242

Prokofiev, Sergei Sergeevich **12** 458-460

Ivan the Terrible (opera)
Bizet, Georges **2** 296-297

Ivanhoe (novel)
Scott, Walter **14** 68-70

Ivanhoe (opera)
Sullivan, Arthur Seymour **15** 23

Ivanov (play)
Chekhov, Anton Pavlovich **3** 494-497

IVES, CHARLES EDWARD (1874-1954), American composer **8** 159-160
Busoni, Ferruccio Benvenuto **3** 173-174

Ives, James Merritt (1824-1895), American lithographer
see Currier and Ives

Ives-Quinn Law (1944)
Johnson, Alvin Saunders **8** 293-294

Ivory Coast, Republic of (nation; West Africa)
Houphouët-Boigny, Felix **7** 519-520
see also French Community (Africa); French Overseas Empire

Ivrea, Italy
Olivetti, Adriano **11** 501-502

Ivy House (Burslem, England)
Wedgwood, Josiah **16** 168-169

IWAKURA, TOMOMI (1825-1883), Japanese statesman **8** 160-161
Okubo, Toshimichi **11** 489-490

IWW
see Industrial Workers of the World

Izard, Ralph (1742-1804), American Revolutionary leader
Copley, John Singleton **4** 228-230

IZETBEGOVIC, ALIJA (born 1926), president of the eight-member presidency of the Republic of Bosnia-Herzegovina **8** 161-163

J

J. B. (poem)
  MacLeish, Archibald **10** 109-110

JA JA OF OPOBO (ca. 1820-1891), Nigerian politician **8** 201-204

JABBAR, KAREEM ABDUL (Ferdinand Lewis Alcinor, Junior ; born 1947), American basketball player **8** 164-165

Jabberwocky (poem)
  Carroll, Lewis **3** 332-333

JABER AL-SABAH, JABER AL-AHMAD AL- (born 1926), amir of Kuwait **8** 166-167

JABIR IBN HAYYAN (flourished latter 8th century), Arab scholar and alchemist **8** 167

JABOTINSKY, VLADIMIR EVGENEVICH (1880-1940), Russian Zionist **8** 167-168

J'accuse (letter; Zola)
  Clemenceau, Georges **4** 99-101
  Dreyfus, Alfred **5** 103-105
  Zola, Émile **16** 526-528

Jack (novel)
  Daudet, Alphonse **4** 402-403

Jack Cade's Rebellion (1450)
  Margaret of Anjou **10** 249-250

Jack in the Pulpit No. 5 (painting)
  O'Keeffe, Georgia **11** 487-489

Jack of Diamonds group (art.; Russia)
  Malevich, Kasimir **10** 168-169

JACKSON, ANDREW (1767-1845), American president 1829-1837 **8** 168-172
  and American Indians
    Black Hawk **2** 308
    Crockett, David **4** 314-316
    Gadsden, James **6** 165-166
    Houston, Samuel **7** 526-527
    Osceola **12** 18
    Ross, John **13** 303-304
  art patronage
    Powers, Hiram **12** 428-429
    Rush, William **13** 365-366
  Cabinet
    Cass, Lewis **3** 355-356

    Kendall, Amos **8** 494
    Livingston, Edward **9** 460-461
    Pierce, Franklin **12** 300-301
    Taney, Roger Brooke **15** 98-99
  domestic policy
    Biddle, Nicholas **2** 264-265
    Duane, William **5** 109
    Monroe, James **11** 111-113
  election (1824)
    Adams, John Quincy **1** 52-54
    Clay, Henry **4** 94-96
    Crawford, William Harris **4** 299-300
    List, Georg Friedrich **9** 443-444
  foreign policy
    Gadsden, James **6** 165-166
    Harrison, William Henry **7** 180-181
    Santa Ana, Antonio López de **13** 471-472
  journalistic supporters
    Blair, Francis Preston **2** 313-315
    Welles, Gideon **16** 188-190
  nullification
    see Nullification crisis
  opponents
    Allston, Washington **1** 176-177
    Clayton, John Middleton **4** 96-97
    Cooper, James Fenimore **4** 220-223
    Marshall, John **10** 279-281
    Sevier, John **14** 122-123
    Thayer, Sylvanus **15** 168-169
    Tyler, John **15** 368-369
  political appointments
    Calhoun, John Caldwell **3** 226-228
    McLean, John **10** 422-423
  political supporters
    Atchison, David Rice **1** 357-358
    Bancroft, George **1** 483-484
    Buchanan, James **3** 89-90
    Corning, Erastus **4** 238-239
    Polk, James Knox **12** 374-376
    Van Buren, Martin **15** 410-411
    Webster, Daniel **16** 162-164
  War of 1812
    see War of 1812
  writings on
    Turner, Frederick Jackson **15** 350-351

    Watson, Thomas Edward **16** 139
    see also Jacksonian Democracy

Jackson, Charles Thomas (1805-1880), American scientist
  Long, Crawford Williamson **9** 495-496
  Morse, Samuel Finley Breese **11** 192-193
  Morton, William Thomas Green **11** 198-199
  Whitney, Josiah Dwight **16** 254-255

JACKSON, HELEN HUNT (1830-1885), American novelist **8** 172

JACKSON, HENRY MARTIN (Scoop; 1912-1983), United States senator and proponent of anti-Soviet foreign policy **8** 172-174

JACKSON, JESSE LOUIS (born 1941), U.S. civil rights leader and presidential candidate **8** 174-176

Jackson, John Hughlings (1835-1911), British neurologist
  Penfield, Wilder Graves **12** 198-200

JACKSON, MAYNARD HOLBROOK, JR. (born 1938), first African American mayor of Atlanta, Georgia (1973-81 and 1989-1993) **8** 176-178

JACKSON, MICHAEL JOE (born 1958), one of the most popular singers in history **8** 178-180
  Gordy, Berry Jr. **6** 450-451

Jackson, Patrick T. (1780-1847), American merchant
  Appleton, Nathan **1** 266-267

JACKSON, REGINALD "REGGIE" MARTINEZ (born 1946), African American baseball player **8** 180-182

JACKSON, ROBERT HOUGHWOUT (1892-1954), American jurist **8** 182-183

JACKSON, SHIRLEY ANN (born 1946), African American physicist **8** 183-184

Jackson, Sir Thomas Graham (1835-1924), English architect
  Shaw, Richard Norman **14** 167-168

JACKSON, THOMAS JONATHAN
("Stonewall"; 1824-1863), American Confederate general **8** 184-185
Lee, Robert Edward **9** 292-294
Stuart, James Ewell Brown **14** 515-516
Tate, Allen **15** 116

Jackson State University (Mississippi)
Walker, Margaret **16** 67

Jacksonian Democracy (United States politics)
influence of
Lloyd, Henry Demarest **9** 468-469
influenced by
Kendall, Amos **8** 494
supporters
Houston, Samuel **7** 526-527
Johnson, Andrew **8** 294-295
Van Buren, Martin **15** 410-411
Walker, Robert John **16** 67-68
Wilmot, David **16** 312-313
see also Jackson, Andrew

JACOB, JOHN EDWARD (born 1934), African American activist and president of the National Urban League **8** 185-188

Jacob, Max (1876-1944), French poet
Chagall, Marc **3** 406-407
Picasso, Pablo **12** 292-295
Poulenc, Francis **12** 414-415

Jacob ben Asher (circa 1270-circa 1343), Jewish scholar and law codifier
Caro, Joseph ben Ephraim **3** 316-317

Jacob Wrestling with the Angel (painting)
Delacroix, Ferdinand Victor Eugène **4** 469-471

Jacobean drama (English literature)
Eliot, Thomas Stearns **5** 258-261
Fletcher, John **5** 487
Heywood, Thomas **7** 373-374
Kyd, Thomas **9** 140-141
Massinger, Philip **10** 324-325
Middleton, Thomas **11** 8-9

JACOBI, ABRAHAM (1830-1919), American physician **8** 188-189

JACOBI, FRIEDRICH HEINRICH (1743-1819), German philosopher **8** 189-190
Fries, Jakob Friedrich **6** 116-117

Jacobi, Johann Georg (1740-1814), German poet
Jacobi, Friedrich Heinrich **8** 189-190

Jacobi, Karl Gustav Jakob (1804-1851), German mathematician
Gauss, Karl Friedrich **6** 240-242
Riemann, Georg Friedrich Bernard **13** 164-165

JACOBI, MARY PUTNAM (1834-1906), American physician **8** 188-189

Jacobins (France; politics)
Jacobin Club
Louis Philippe **9** 536-537
Robespierre, Maximilien François Marie Isidore de **13** 199-201
members

Danton, Georges Jacques **4** 391-393
Hébert, Jacques René **7** 247-248
Marat, Jean Paul **10** 230-231
Saint-Just, Louis Antoine Léon de **13** 433
opponents (England)
Burke, Edmund **3** 138-141
Cobbett, William **4** 126-127
opponents (France)
Babeuf, François Noel **1** 412
Condorcet, Marquis de **4** 195-196
Lafayette, Marquis de **9** 151-152
regime overthrown (1794)
Barras, Vicomte de **2** 19
Fouché, Joseph **6** 30-31
Napoleon I **11** 306-310
supporters (Austria)
Francis II **6** 43-44

Jacobites (Stuart supporters)
Glorious Revolution and
James II **8** 207-208
see also Boyne, Battle of the (1690); Glorious Revolution (1688)
rebellion (1715)
Bolingbroke, Viscount **2** 374-375
rebellion (1745)
Braddock, Edward **2** 474-475
Stevenson, Robert Louis **14** 446-448
Charles Edward Louis Philip Casimir Stuart **3** 466-467
Wolfe, James **16** 354-355

Jacobs House (Madison, Wisconsin)
Wright, Frank Lloyd **16** 398-401

Jacob's Room (novel)
Woolf, Virginia Stephen **16** 381-382

Jacob's staff (astronomy; instrument)
Levi ben Gershon **9** 363-364

JACOBS, HARRIET A. (1813-1897), runaway slave and abolitionist **8** 190-193

JACOBSEN, JENS PETER (1847-1885), Danish author **8** 193-194
Richardson, Henry Handel **13** 139

Jacobsz, Hughe (flourished circa 1500-34/38), Dutch painter
Lucas van Leyden **10** 20-21

Jacobus de Voragine (1230?-1298?), Italian Dominican writer
Ignatius of Loyola **8** 108-109

Jacopo di Cione (died circa 1398), Italian painter
Orcagna **11** 526-527

Jacopo, Giovanni Battista di
see Rosso, II

Jacopo Strada (painting)
Titian **15** 242-244

JACOPONE DA TODI (circa 1236-1306), Italian poet and mystic **8** 194

Jacquerie uprising (France; 1358)
Charles V **3** 459-460
John II **8** 275-276

Jacques, Amy
see Garvey, Amy Jacques

Jadis et Naguère (poems)
Verlaine, Paul Marie **15** 465-466

J'adore ce qui me brûle-oder die Schwierigen (novel)
Frisch, Max **6** 118-119

Jadu, Don (literary character)
Mqhayi, Samuel Edward Krune **11** 223

Jafar, Abu
see Mansur, al-

Jaffa, battle of (1192)
Richard I **13** 130

Jagd nach Liebe, Die (novel)
Mann, Heinrich **10** 201-202

Jäger, Johannes
see Crotus Rubianus

JAGGER, MICHAEL PHILIP (born 1944), lyricist and lead singer for the Rolling Stones **8** 194-196

Jagua Nana (novel)
Ekwensi, Cyprian **5** 242-243

Jaguar, Le (poem)
Leconte de Lisle, Charles Marie René **9** 273-274

Jahangir (died 1533), Turkish prince
Suleiman I **15** 20-21

JAHANGIR (1569-1627), fourth Mughal emperor of India **8** 196-199
Shah Jahan **14** 138-139

JAHN, HELMUT (born 1940), German-American architect **8** 199-201

Jahr der Seele, Das (poems)
George, Stefan **6** 277-278

Jainism (religion; India)
Mahavira, Vardhamana **10** 135-137

Jakobskirche (Rothenburg)
Riemenschneider, Tilman **13** 166

Jakobsleiter, Die (oratorio)
Schoenberg, Arnold **14** 24-26

Jalal al-Din (died 1231), shah of Khwarizm
Genghis Khan **6** 263-265

Jalal-al-Din Malik Shah
see Malik Shah, Jalal-al-Din

Jalal-ed-Din Rumi
see Rumi, Jalal ed-Din

Jalal-ud-din (Firuz Shah II; died 1295), founder of Khalji dynasty of Delhi
Ala-ud-din **1** 102-103

Jalali calendar (Persia)
Omar Khayyam **11** 510-511

Jalna (novel)
de la Roche, Mazo Louise **4** 474-475

Jaloux, Les (painting)
Watteau, Antoine **16** 143-144

Jama Mosque (Delhi)
Shah Jahan **14** 138-139

Jamaat Khana Mosque (Delhi, India)
Ala-ud-din **1** 102-103

Jamaica (nation; West Indies)
British rule
Congreve, William **4** 200-201
Cromwell, Oliver **4** 317-320
Elgin, 8th Earl of **5** 248-249
Eyre, Edward John **5** 354
Metcalfe, Charles Theophilus
10 531-532
Winslow, Edward **16** 338-339
in literature
Lewis, Matthew Gregory **9** 390-391
independence and after
Bustamante, William Alexander
3 175-177
Manley, Michael Norman
10 200-201
Spanish discovery and conquest
Columbus, Christopher **4** 176-179
Narváez, Pánfilo de **11** 315

Jamaica (play)
Davis, Ossie **4** 421-422

Jamaica Labor Party
Bustamante, William Alexander
3 175-177

Jamal ud-Din al-Afghani (1839-1897),
Moslem politician, advocate of
Pan-Islamism
Abduh ibn Hasan Khayr Allah, Muham-
mad **1** 16-17
Abdul-Hamid II **1** 17-18
Zaghlul Pasha, Saad **16** 485-486

Jamā'at-i Islāmī (religious organization,
Muslim)
Mawdūdī, Abu-l A'la **10** 353-354

James I (El Conquistador; 1208-1276), king
of Aragon 1213-1276
Alfonso X **1** 150-151
Peter III **12** 256-257

JAMES I (1394-1437), king of Scotland
1406-1437 **8** 206-207
Robert III **13** 194-195

JAMES I (James VI of Scotland; 1566-1625),
king of England 1603-1625 **8** 204-206
courtiers
Buckingham, 1st Duke of **3** 93-94
Raleigh, Walter **13** 9-11
Crown's rights
Sandys, Edwin **13** 463-464
Suárez, Francisco **15** 8
in art
Rubens, Peter Paul **13** 339-342
patronage
Dowland, John **5** 90
Hilliard, Nicholas **7** 391-392
Jones, Inigo **8** 333-334
Shakespeare, William **14** 142-145
Van Dyck, Anthony **15** 423-425
relatives
Elizabeth I **5** 263-266
Mary I **10** 308-309
Mary, Queen of Scots **10** 310-312
religious persecution
Brewster, William **2** 523-524
royal appointments

Bacon, Francis **1** 422-424
Calvert, George **3** 238-239
Coke, Edward **4** 141-142
Donne, John **5** 60-61
Gorges, Ferdinando **6** 455-456
Harvey, William **7** 189-190
Spain and
Charles I **3** 450-452

James II (1430-1460), king of Scotland
1437-1460
James I **8** 206-207

JAMES II (1633-1701), king of England,
Scotland, and Ireland 1685-1688
8 207-208
and American colonies
Andros, Edmund **1** 234-235
Mather, Cotton **10** 330-332
Mather, Increase **10** 332-333
Phips, William **12** 283
as Duke of York
Penn, William **12** 200-202
Pepys, Samuel **12** 207-208
Shaftesbury, 1st Earl of **14** 135-136
deposed (1688)
Anne **1** 241-242
Godolphin, Sidney **6** 380-381
Leisler, Jacob **9** 313-314
Marlborough, 1st Duke of
10 271-272
Mary II **10** 309-310
opponents
Monmouth and Buccleugh, Duke of
11 108-109
Oates, Titus **11** 456
Taylor, Edward **15** 122-123
patronage
Dryden, John **5** 106-107
Purcell, Henry **12** 484-485
Wycherley, William **16** 411-412
relatives
Charles II **3** 452-454
Clarendon, 1st Earl of **4** 73-75
Mary II **10** 309-310
William III **16** 295-296
religious question
Baxter, Richard **2** 76-77
Burnet, Gilbert **3** 147

JAMES III (1451-1488), king of Scotland
1460-1488 **8** 208-209

James IV (1473-1513), king of Scotland
1488-1513
Douglas, Gavin **5** 77-78
Henry VII **7** 300-302
James III **8** 208-209

James V (1512-1542), king of Scotland
1513-1542
Lyndsay, David **10** 66-67
Mary II **10** 309-310
Ronsard, Pierre de **13** 271-273

James VI, king of Scotland
see James I (king of England)

James VII, king of Scotland
see James II (king of England)

JAMES, DANIEL, JR. ("Chappie";
1920-1978), first African American man
in the U.S. to become a four star general
8 209-211

JAMES, HENRY (1843-1916), American
novelist **8** 211-212
critical evaluations
Wilson, Edmund **16** 318-319
friends
Adams, Henry Brooks **1** 45-47
Howells, William Dean **7** 539-541
Turgenev, Ivan Sergeyevich
15 345-348
Wharton, Edith **16** 221
illustrators
Demuth, Charles **4** 497-498
influence of
Crane, Stephen **4** 293-295
Pound, Ezra Loomis **12** 415-417
Woolf, Virginia Stephen **16** 381-382
Wright, Richard **16** 401-402
influenced by
Flaubert, Gustave **5** 480-482
works compared
Čapek, Karel **3** 271-272
Conrad, Joseph **4** 205-207
Twain, Mark **15** 363-366
Wells, Herbert George **16** 195-196

JAMES, JESSE WOODSON (1847-1882),
American outlaw **8** 212-213
Pinkerton, Allan **12** 314-315

JAMES, P. D. (born 1920), British crime
novelist **8** 213-215

James, Saint (died circa 40), Apostle of
Jesus
Dias de Novais, Bartolomeu **4** 533-534
Jesus of Nazareth **8** 251-255
John **8** 273-274
Peter **12** 252-253

JAMES, WILLIAM (1842-1910), American
philosopher and psychologist **8** 215-217
biographers
Perry, Ralph Barton **12** 239-240
influence of
Bourne, Randolph Silliman
2 456-457
Dewey, John **4** 520-523
Eliot, Thomas Stearns **5** 258-261
Lewis, Clarence Irving **9** 381
Lippmann, Walter **9** 439-440
Thorndike, Edward Lee **15** 208-209
Woolf, Virginia Stephen **16** 381-382
Wright, Richard **16** 401-402
influenced by
Godkin, Edwin Lawrence **6** 380
Spencer, Herbert **14** 369-370
Vivekananda **16** 4-5
quoted
Fechner, Gustav Theodor **5** 401-402
Wundt, Wilhelm Max **16** 402-403
relatives
James, Henry **8** 211-212
students
Hall, Granville Stanley **7** 85-86
Stein, Gertrude **14** 414-415

James Monroe (ship)
Palmer, Nathaniel Brown **12** 80-81

JAMESON, SIR LEANDER STARR
(1853-1917), British colonial administrator **8** 218
see also Jameson raid

Jameson, Robert (1774-1854), Scottish mineralogist
Werner, Abraham Gottlob **16** 205-207

Jameson raid (South Africa; 1895)
Jameson, Leander Starr **8** 218
Kruger, Stephanus Johannes Paulus **9** 108-109
Rhodes, Cecil John **13** 120-122
Salisbury, 3d Marquess of **13** 448-449
Smuts, Jan Christian **14** 309-310

Jamestown (village; Virginia)
Bacon, Nathaniel **1** 424-425
Calvert, George **3** 238-239
Pocahontas **12** 361-362
Powhatan **12** 429-430
Rolfe, John **13** 259-260
Smith, John **14** 295-297

JAMI (Maulana Nur al-Din Abd al-Rahman; 1414-1492), Persian poet **8** 218-219
Behzad **2** 123

Jan Mayen Island (Arctic Ocean; Norway)
Hudson, Henry **8** 12-13

JANÁČEK, LEOŠ (1854-1928), Czech composer **8** 219

Jane Eyre (novel)
Brontë, Charlotte **3** 17-18
Brontë, Emily **3** 18-19

Jane Frances de Chantal, Saint
(1572-1641), foundress of the Visitation nuns
Francis of Sales **6** 47

Jane Talbot (novel)
Brown, Charles Brockden **3** 33

Janequin, Clément (flourished 16th century), French composer
Victoria, Tomás Luis de **15** 487-488

JANET, PIERRE MARIE FÉLIX (1859-1947), French psychologist **8** 220
Charcot, Jean Martin **3** 442
Guthrie, Edwin Ray **7** 49-50
James, William **8** 215-217

Janice Meredith (novel)
Ford, Paul Leicester **6** 9-10

Janissaries (Ottoman troops)
Mahmud II **10** 145-147
Selim I **14** 94-95
Selim III **14** 95-96
Sinan, Kodja Mimar **14** 245-246
Suleiman I **15** 20-21, 279

JANSEN, CORNELIS (1585-1638), Dutch Roman Catholic theologian **8** 220-221
see also Jansenism

Jansenism (religious movement)
development
Jansen, Cornelis **8** 220-221

influence of
La Fayette, Comtesse de **9** 150-151
Pascal, Blaise **12** 122-124
opponents
Fénelon, François de Salignac de la Mothe **5** 410-411
Louis XIV **9** 531-533
Racine, Jean Baptiste **12** 532-535
supporters
La Mettrie, Julien Offray de **9** 179-180
Sainte-Beuve, Charles Augustin **13** 438

January, Edict of (1562)
Medici, Catherine de' **10** 445-449

Japan (island nation; eastern Asia)
300-710 (Yamato Period)
Fujiwara Kamatari **6** 145
Kwanggaet'o **9** 139-140
Shotoku Taishi **14** 205-207
Suiko **15** 15-16
710-784 (Nara Period)
Makibi, Kibi-no **10** 161
784-1184 (Heian Period)
Ennin **5** 288-289
Fujiwara Michinaga **6** 145-146
Goshirakawa **6** 460-461
Kammu **8** 420
1185-1338 (Kamakura Period)
Daigo II **4** 367-368
Eisai **5** 231-232
Goshirakawa **6** 460-461
Kublai Khan **9** 115-118
Yoritomo, Minamoto **16** 463-464
1338-1573 (Ashikaga Shogunate)
Ashikaga Takauji **1** 330-332
Daigo II **4** 367-368
Francis Xavier **6** 48
Mendes Pinto, Fernao **10** 493-494
Nobunaga, Oda **11** 413-414
Sesshu, Toya **14** 116-117
Toyotomi Hideyoshi **15** 286-289
1573-1603 (Momoyama Period)
Sejong **14** 91-92
Sŏnjo **14** 341-342
Yi Sunsin **16** 459-461
1603-1867 (Tokugawa Shogunate)
Chih-i **3** 518-519
Confucius **4** 197-200
Evarts, William Maxwell **5** 340-341
Fillmore, Millard **5** 447-448
Harris, Townsend **7** 176-177
Ito, Hirobumi **8** 153-155
Iwakura, Tomomi **8** 160-161
Nobunaga, Oda **11** 413-414
Perry, Matthew Calbraith **12** 237-239
Saigo, Takamori **13** 429
Ieyasu, Tokugawa **8** 103-106
Yoshimune, Tokugawa **16** 465-466
1868-1890 (Meiji Restoration)
Ito, Hirobumi **8** 153-155
Iwakura, Tomomi **8** 160-161
Kim Ok-kyun **9** 7-8
Min **11** 46-47

Mutsuhito **11** 279-282
Okubo, Toshimichi **11** 489-490
Okuma, Shigenobu **11** 490
Saigo, Takamori **13** 429
Saionji, Kimmochi **13** 438-439
Yamagata, Aritomo **16** 428-429
1890-1931 (Great Power status)
Balfour, Arthur James **1** 469-470
Chang Chien **3** 429-430
Hara, Kei **7** 138
Harding, Warren Gamaliel **7** 148-149
Inukai, Tsuyoshi **8** 130-131
Katayama, Sen **8** 457
Kim Il-sung **9** 4-6
Mutsuhito **11** 279-282
Pilsudski, Joseph **12** 305-306
Rhee, Syngman **13** 117-120
Takahashi, Korekiyo **15** 84-85
see also Russo-Japanese War (1904-1905)
1931-1945 (military state)
Chang Tso-lin **3** 434-435
Hirohito **7** 410-412
Hull, Cordell **8** 28-29
Konoe, Fumimaro **9** 82-83
Tojo, Hideki **15** 254-256
Yamamoto, Isoroku **16** 429-433
World War II
see World War II—Japan
since 1945 (economic recovery)
Akihito **1** 98-99
Doi Takako **5** 39-41
Dulles, John Foster **5** 134-135
Garcia, Carlos P. **6** 207-208
Hirohito **7** 410-412
Johnson, Charles Spurgeon **8** 296-297
Kaifu Toshiki **8** 410-411
Kishi, Nobusuke **9** 41-43
MacArthur, Douglas **10** 76-78
Morita, Akio **11** 176-178
Nakasone, Yasuhiro **11** 298-300
Sato, Eisaku **13** 495-496
Tanaka, Kakuei **15** 96-98
Yoshida, Shigeru **16** 464-465
see also Japanese art; Japanese literature

Japan Free Religious Association
Imaoka, Shinichiro **8** 115

Japanese Americans, internment of (1942-1944)
Yasui, Minoru **16** 440-444

Japanese architecture
Isozaki, Arata **8** 152-153
Maki, Fumihiko **10** 159-161

Japanese art
influence of
Cassatt, Mary **3** 356-357
ink painting
Eitoku, Kano **5** 242
Sesshu, Toya **14** 116-117
Toba Sojo **15** 248-249
Kano school

Eitoku, Kano **5** 242
modern architecture
  Fuller, Richard Buckminster
  6 149-150
  Tange, Kenzo **15** 99-101
Ukiyo-e school
  Harunobu, Suzuki **7** 188-189
  Hiroshige, Ando **7** 412-413
  Hokusai, Katsushika **7** 447-448
  Utamaro, Kitagawa **15** 397
Yamato-e school
  Sotatsu, Tawaraya **14** 349
  Toba Sojo **15** 248-249

Japanese Automobile Manufacturers Association
Toyoda, Eiji **15** 284-286

Japanese literature
development of novel
  Kawabata, Yasunari **8** 463-464
  Natsume, Soseki **11** 324-325
  Tanizaki, Junichiro **15** 101-102
haiku development
  Basho, Matsuo **2** 45-48
Kabuki theater
  Kurosawa, Akira **9** 135-137
National Learning school
  Mabuchi, Kamo **10** 73-74
No drama
  Mishima, Yukio **11** 54-55
  Yeats, William Butler **16** 445-447
  Zeami, Kanze **16** 492-493
psychologial novels
  Abe, Kobo **1** 20-22
romance
  Murasaki Shikibu **11** 252-253

Japanese-Russian War
see Russo-Japanese War

Jaques-Dalcroze, Émile (1865-1950), Swiss composer
Bloch, Ernest **2** 326-327

JAQUES-DALCROZE, EMILE (1865-1950), Swiss teacher and composer who developed eurhythmics **8** 221-222
influence of
  Appia, Adolphe **1** 263-264

Jardin de Bérénice, Le (novel)
Barrès, Auguste Maurice **2** 20-21

Jardin d'Épicure, Le (literary collection)
France, Anatole **6** 39-40

Jardin des Plantes (Paris)
see Muséum National d'Histoire Naturelle

Jardin sur l'Oronte (novel)
Barrès, Auguste Maurice **2** 20-21

Jardines lejanos (poems)
Jiménez, Juan Ramón **8** 261-262

Jargon (musical composition)
Billings, William **2** 274-275

JARRELL, RANDALL (1914-1965), American poet and critic **8** 222-223
Lowell, Robert Trail Spence Jr. **10** 16-17
Williams, William Carlos **16** 308-309

JARUZELSKI, WOJCIECH WITOLD (born 1923), career soldier who became Poland's head of state (1981-1990) **8** 223-225
Walesa, Lech **16** 57-59

Jarvis, John Wesley (1780-1840), American painter
Stuart, Gilbert **14** 513-515

Jasager, Der (school opera)
Weill, Kurt **16** 174-175

Jason (mythology)
Euripides **5** 332-334
Grillparzer, Franz **6** 546-547

Jason Edwards (novel)
Garland, Hannibal Hamlin **6** 217-218

JASPERS, KARL (1883-1969), German philosopher **8** 225-226
Arendt, Hannah **1** 282-284

Jasperware (pottery)
Wedgwood, Josiah **16** 168-169

Jassy
see Iasi

Jats (Indian people)
Aurangzeb **1** 377

Jauregui, Juan de (1583-1641), Spanish painter and poet
Cervantes, Miguel de Saavedra **3** 395-398

JAURÈS, JEAN (1859-1914), French Socialist and politician **8** 226-227
Blum, Léon **2** 343-344
Briand, Aristide **2** 528-529
Dreyfus, Alfred **5** 103-105
Eboué, Adolphe Felix Sylvestre **5** 194
Lefebvre, Georges **9** 301-302
Marx, Karl **10** 304-308
Mathiez, Albert **10** 333-334

Java (island)
see Indonesia

Java, Indonesia
Geertz, Clifford **6** 248-249

JAWARA, SIR DAUDA KAIRABA (born 1924), Gambian statesman **8** 227-228

JAWLENSKY, ALEXEJ VON (1864-1941), Russian Expressionist painter **8** 228-229
Feininger, Lyonel **5** 406-407
Kandinsky, Wassily **8** 420-422

JAWORSKI, LEON (1905-1982), American lawyer and independent prosecutor of Watergate **8** 229-230

Jaws (film)
Spielberg, Steven **14** 379-381

JAY, JOHN (1745-1829), American diplomat and jurist **8** 230-232
Clinton, George **4** 113-114
Livingston, Robert R. **9** 462-463
Monroe, James **11** 111-113
Morris, Gouverneur **11** 182-183
see also Jay's Treaty (1794); Paris, Treaty of (1783)

JAY, WILLIAM (1789-1858), American reformer **8** 232-233

JAYEWARDENE, JUNIUS RICHARD (JR; 1906-1996), leader of the nationalist movement in Ceylon and president of Sri Lanka **8** 233-234

Jay-Gardoqui Treaty (1786)
Gálvez, Bernardo de **6** 195-196

Jay's Treaty (1794)
authorship
  Jay, John **8** 230-232
effects
  Astor, John Jacob **1** 351-352
  Monroe, James **11** 111-113
  Washington, George **16** 126-129
opponents
  Burr, Aaron **3** 156-159
  Dickinson, John **4** 543-544
  Livingston, Edward **9** 460-461
  Livingston, Robert R. **9** 462-463
  Macon, Nathaniel **10** 114-115
  Madison, James **10** 121-123
  Pinckney, Charles Cotesworth **12** 310
  Rutledge, John **13** 387-388
supporters
  Adams, John Quincy **1** 52-54
  Ames, Fisher **1** 199-200
  King, Rufus **9** 22-23
  Marshall, John **10** 279-281
  Otis, Harrison Gray **12** 25
  Randolph, Edmund **13** 29-30

Jazz (music)
Armstrong, Louis Daniel **1** 303-304
Basie **2** 48-49
Brubeck, Dave **3** 59-61
Calloway, Cab **3** 236-238
Charles, Ray **3** 469-470
Cole, Nat **4** 149-151
Coltrane, John **4** 173-174
Davis, Miles **4** 419-421
Ellington, Edward Kennedy **5** 273-274
Fitzgerald, Ella **5** 468-469
Gillespie, Dizzy **6** 320-322
Goodman, Benny **6** 436-438
Hawkins, Coleman **7** 208-210
Holiday, Billie **7** 452-453
Jones, Quincy Delight Jr. **8** 339-341
Monk, Thelonious **11** 104-108
Parker, Charles Christopher Jr. **12** 105-106
Puente, Tito **12** 476-477
Schuller, Gunther **14** 37-38
Vaughan, Sarah Lois **15** 445-446
Young, Lester Willis **16** 471-473

Jazz (papiers découpés)
Matisse, Henri **10** 336-337

Jazz Calendar (ballet)
Bennett, Richard Rodney **2** 172

Je file quant Dieu me donne de quoi (song)
Cabezón, Antonio **3** 197-198

Jealous Husband, A (story)
Dostoevsky, Fyodor **5** 74-77

Jean Barois (novel)
Martin du Gard, Roger **10** 295-296

Jean d'Albret (died 1516), king of Navarre 1484-1516
Borgia, Cesare **2** 412-413

Jean de Boulogne
see Giovanni da Bologna

JEAN DE MEUN (circa 1240-1305), French author **8** 234-235
Chaucer, Geoffrey **3** 482-485
Christine de Pisan **4** 29-30
Guillaume de Lorris **7** 33-34
Orléans, Charles D' **11** 530

Jean Jacques, Emperor
see Dessalines, Jean Jacques

Jean Paul
see Richter, Johann Paul Friedrich

Jean Santeuil (novel)
Proust, Marcel **12** 465-467

Jean-Christophe (novel)
Rolland, Romain **13** 260

Jeanne d'Arc
see Joan of Arc

Jeanneret, Pierre (1896-1967), French architect
Le Corbusier **9** 274-275

Jeanneret-Gris, Charles Édouard
see Le Corbusier

Jeannette (sculpture series)
Matisse, Henri **10** 336-337

Jeannette (ship)
Melville, George Wallace **10** 472

Jeannot et Colin (story)
Voltaire **16** 14-16

JEANS, SIR JAMES HOPWOOD (1877-1946), English mathematician, physicist, and astronomer **8** 235-236

Jeb (play)
Davis, Ossie **4** 421-422

Jedermann (play)
Hofmannsthal, Hugo von **7** 443-444

Jeevandan movement (India)
Narayan, Jayaprakash **11** 312-313

Jeff Briggs's Love Story (novel)
Harte, Francis Brett **7** 184-185

JEFFERS, JOHN ROBINSON (1887-1962), American poet **8** 236-237

JEFFERSON, JOSEPH (1829-1905), American actor **8** 237
Boucicault, Dion **2** 442-443

JEFFERSON, THOMAS (1743-1826), American philosopher and statesman, president 1801-1809 **8** 238-241
art commissions
Houdon, Antoine **7** 516-517
Latrobe, Benjamin Henry **9** 222-224
Peale, Rembrandt **12** 172-173
associates
Franklin, Benjamin **6** 60-64
Henry, Patrick **7** 309-311

Lewis, Andrew **9** 376-377
Mills, Robert **11** 36-37
Pendleton, Edmund **12** 197-198
Trist, Nicholas Philip **15** 298-299
Trumbull, John **15** 316-317
Washington, George **16** 126-129
Wythe, George **16** 415
Burr conspiracy
Burr, Aaron **3** 156-159, 271
Wilkinson, James **16** 284-286
Cabinet
Gallatin, Albert **6** 183-184
Madison, James **10** 121-123
domestic policies
Clark, William **4** 82-83
Cooper, James Fenimore **4** 220-223
Dew, Thomas Roderick **4** 519
Dunbar, William **5** 143-144
Hamilton, Alexander **7** 95-98
Hull, William **8** 29-30
Lewis, Meriwether **9** 391-392
St. Clair, Arthur **13** 429-430
foreign policy
Genet, Edmond Charles **6** 261-262
Jones, John Paul **8** 337-338
Livingston, Robert R. **9** 462-463
Monroe, James **11** 111-113
friends
Barlow, Joel **2** 6-7
Carroll, John **3** 331-332
du Pont, Éleuthère Irénée **5** 154
Peale, Charles Willson **12** 169-171
Rittenhouse, David **13** 180-181
in literature
Bowers, Claude Gernade **2** 463
Bryant, William Cullen **3** 83-85
Dos Passos, John Roderigo **5** 69-71
Malone, Dumas **10** 174-175
Tucker, George **15** 332-333
Watson, Thomas Edward **16** 139
influenced by
Palladio, Andrea **12** 75-77
memorials
Borglum, John Gutzon de la Mothe **2** 416-417
Saarinen, Eliel and Eero **13** 396-398
opponents
Ames, Fisher **1** 199-200
Banneker, Benjamin **1** 490-491
Clinton, DeWitt **4** 112-113
Livingston, Edward **9** 460-461
Martin, Luther **10** 289-290
Morris, Gouverneur **11** 182-183
Otis, Harrison Gray **12** 25
Pickering, Timothy **12** 298-299
quoted
Adams, John **1** 48-51
Randolph, Edmund **13** 29-30
supporters
Cooper, Thomas **4** 224
Coxe, Tench **4** 285-286
Freneau, Philip Morin **6** 99-100
Pinckney, Charles **12** 309-310
Randolph, John **13** 30
Story, Joseph **14** 480-481

Taylor, John **15** 126

Jeffersonian Republican party
see Democratic-Republican party (United States)

Jeffrey, Francis (1773-1850), Scottish critic and jurist
Macaulay, Thomas Babington **10** 79-80

JEFFREYS, SIR HAROLD (1891-1989), English mathematician, astronomer, and philosopher **8** 241-242

Jehangir
see Jahangir

Jehoiachin (615?-560 B.C.), king of Judah 598
Ezekiel **5** 355-356

Jehovah's Witnesses (religious sect)
Black, Hugo Lafayette **2** 301-303
Jackson, Robert Houghwout **8** 182-183
Russell, Charles Taze **13** 376-377

Jekyll, Dr. (literary character)
Stevenson, Robert Louis **14** 446-448

JELLICOE, JOHN RUSHWORTH (1859-1935), English admiral **8** 242-243

Jelliffe, Smith Ely (1866-1945), American psychiatrist
White, William Alanson **16** 239-240

Jello (play)
Baraka, Imamu Amiri **1** 498-499

Jellyfish (marine animal)
Huxley, Thomas Henry **8** 77-79
Richet, Charles Robert **13** 144-145

JEMISON, MAE C. (born 1956), African American physician and astronaut **8** 243-244

Jena, battle of (1806)
Bernadotte, Jean Baptiste **2** 205-206
Frederick William III **6** 87
Hardenberg, Karl August von **7** 146-147
Murat, Joachim **11** 253-254
Napoleon I **11** 306-310
Niebuhr, Barthold Georg **11** 385-386
Scharnhorst, Gerhard Johann David von **13** 521-522

Jena, University of
Fichte, Johann Gottlieb **5** 435-436
Frege, Gottlob **6** 93-94
Fries, Jakob Friedrich **6** 116-117
Hegel, Georg Wilhelm Friedrich **7** 254-256
Schelling, Friedrich Wilhelm Joseph von **13** 526-527
Schiller, Johann Christoph Friedrich von **14** 4-7
Stahl, Georg Ernst **14** 392-393

Jena Students... (mural)
Hodler, Ferdinand **7** 434-435

Jenghiz Khan
see Genghis Khan

Jenkins, Nicholas (literary character)
Powell, Anthony **12** 422-423

JENKINS, ROY HARRIS (born 1920), British Labour politician and author
8 244-245

Jenkins' Ear, War of (1739)
Walpole, Robert **16** 82-84
see also Austrian Succession, War of the

Jenkinson, Mr. (literary character)
Peacock, Thomas Love **12** 169

Jenkinson, Robert Barks
see Liverpool, 2nd Earl of

JENNER, EDWARD (1749-1823), English physician 8 245-246
Waterhouse, Benjamin **16** 131-132

Jenney, William Le Baron (1832-1907), American architect
Burnham, Daniel Hudson **3** 148-149
Sullivan, Louis Henri **15** 27-28

Jennie Gerhardt (novel)
Dreiser, Herman Theodore **5** 98-100

Jennings, Herbert Spencer (1868-1947), American zoologist
Lashley, Karl Spencer **9** 214-215

Jennings, Sarah
see Marlborough, Duchess of

JENNINGS, ROBERT YEWDALL (born 1913), British judge who was president of the International Court of Justice
8 246-247

Jenny (aircraft)
Curtiss, Glenn Hammond **4** 350-351

Jenny (novel)
Undset, Sigrid **15** 388-389

Jensen, Merrill (1905-1980), American historian
Warren, Mercy Otis **16** 120-121

Jen-tsung (1011-1063), Chinese emperor 1022-63
Fan Chung-yen **5** 376-377
Ou-yang Hsiu **12** 33-34
Ssu-ma kuang **14** 390-391
Wang An-shih **16** 95-97

Jenufa (opera)
Janáček, Leoš **8** 219

Jephthah (Old Testament character)
Carissimi, Giacomo **3** 299-300
Handel, George Frederick **7** 116-119
Heavysege, Charles **7** 246
Vondel, Joost van den **16** 19-20

Jeqe... (novel)
Dube, John Langalibalele **5** 113

Jereboa, The (poem)
Moore, Marianne **11** 148-149

JEREMIAH (flourished late 7th-early 6th century B.C.), Hebrew priest and prophet
8 247-248
Ezekiel **5** 355-356
Graetz, Heinrich Hirsch **6** 483
Micah **10** 542-543

Jeremiah (musical composition)
Bernstein, Leonard **2** 218-219

Jeremiah (sculpture)
Donatello **5** 55-56

Jeremiah, Book of (Old Testament)
Innocent III **8** 125-127
Jeremiah **8** 247-248

JEROBOAM I (ruled circa 931-circa 910 B.C.), king of the northern kingdom of Israel 8 248-249

Jeroboam II (died 744? B.C.), king of Israel 785-745
Amos **1** 205
Hosea **7** 512

Jérôme (literary character)
Gide, André **6** 308-309

Jerome, Jenny
see Churchill, Jenny Jerome

JEROME, ST. (circa 345-420), Early Christian biblical scholar 8 249
as biographer
Catullus, Gaius Valerius **3** 377-378
Ennius, Quintus **5** 289
Lucretius **10** 26-27
Ovid **12** 34-36
editions and translations
Erasmus, Desiderius **5** 298-300
Origen **11** 528-529
Ulfilas **15** 384
influence of
Isidore of Seville **8** 149-150
opponents
Pelagius **12** 189-190

Jerome of Prague (circa 1370-1416), Bohemian religious reformer
Hus, Jan **8** 56-59

Jerónimo de Cevallos (painting)
Greco **6** 511-514

Jeronymites (religious order)
Juana Inés de la Cruz **8** 367-368

Jerusalem (city; Palestine)
• ANCIENT
Assyrian rule
Isaiah **8** 146-147
Babylonian conquest
Ezekiel **5** 355-356
Jeremiah **8** 247-248
Micah **10** 542-543
Nebuchadnezzar **11** 330
councils and synods
Paul **12** 141-143
Pelagius **12** 189-190
Moslem occupation
Omar ibn al-Khattab **11** 508-509
revolt (163 B.C.)
Antiochus IV **1** 250
Romans destroy (A.D. 70)
Bar Kochba, Simeon **2** 5
Hadrian **7** 60-61
Josephus Flavius **8** 360-361
Paul **12** 141-143
Titus Flavius Vespasianus
15 247-248
Solomon's Temple

Jeroboam I **8** 248-249
Solomon **14** 326-327
see also Jewish history—Biblical Era,—Captivity and Overrule

• LATIN KINGDOM
crusades
Alexius I **1** 143-144
Husayni, Al-Hajj Amin al-
8 62-63
Bernard of Clairvaux **2** 207-208
Louis IX **9** 525-526
Louis VII **9** 524-525
Philip II **12** 268-269
Urban II **15** 393
rulers
Baldwin I **1** 464-465
Frederick II **6** 79
Godfrey of Bouillon **6** 379
Turkish occupation
Ignatius of Loyola **8** 108-109
Saladin **13** 441-442
William of Tyre **16** 299-300
see also Crusades

• MODERN
architecture
Chagall, Marc **3** 406-407
Geddes, Patrick **6** 246-247
synods
Lucaris, Cyril **10** 20
Mogila, Peter **11** 74-75
see also Israel

Jerusalem (epic)
Blake, William **2** 316-318

Jerusalem (novel)
Lagerlöf, Selma Ottiliana Lovisa
9 163-164

Jerusalem Delivered
see Gerusalemme liberata

Jerusalem Laid Desolate (play)
Vondel, Joost van den **16** 19-20

Jerusalem Regained (poem)
Lope Félix de Vega Carpio **9** 503-506

Jerusalem Talmud
Ginzberg, Louis **6** 337-338

Jervis, Sir John (1735-1823), English naval commander
Nelson, Horatio **11** 336-338

Jery und Bätely (song)
Goethe, Johann Wolfgang von
6 388-391

Jespersen, Otto (1860-1943), Danish philologist
Mencken, Henry Louis **10** 481-483

Jesse (Old Testament character)
David, Jacques Louis **4** 407-409

JESSEL, GEORGE (1898-1981), American screen, stage, radio, and television actor and comedian and film director, composer, and screenwriter 8 249-251

Jessie Brown (play)
Boucicault, Dion **2** 442-443

Jest, The (play)
  Barrymores **2** 28-30

Jesters, The (fresco)
  Goya y Lucientes, Francisco de Paula
    José de **6** 476-478

Jesu nahm zu sich die Zwölfe (cantata)
  Bach, Johann Sebastian **1** 416-419

Jesuits (religious order)
  critics
    Diderot, Denis **5** 1-2
  and education
    Canisius, Peter **3** 258
  and religious disputes
    Donne, John **5** 60-61
    Manning, Henry Edward
      10 209-210
    Molinos, Miguel de **11** 88-89
    Oates, Titus **11** 456
    Pascal, Blaise **12** 122-124
    Tyrrell, George **15** 374-375
  expulsion (England)
    Tyrrell, George **15** 374-375
  expulsion (North and South America)
    Gálvez, José de **6** 196
    García Moreno, Gabriel **6** 209-210
    Serra, Junípero **14** 111-112
  expulsion (Portugal and Spain)
    Charles III **3** 454-455
    Pombal, Marquês de **12** 386-387
  founded
    Ignatius of Loyola **8** 108-109
  missions (Asia)
    Francis Xavier **6** 48
    K'ang-hsi **8** 423-426
    Ricci, Matteo **13** 124-125
  missions (North America)
    Brébeuf, Jean de **2** 511-512
    Claver, Peter **4** 94
    Jogues, Isaac **8** 270-271
    Kino, Eusebio Francisco **9** 30-31
    Maisoneuve, Sieur de **10** 153
    Marquette, Jacques **10** 274-275
  missions (South America)
    Anchieta, José de **1** 210-211
    Sá, Mem de **13** 395
    Vieira, Antônio **15** 492
  papal policy
    Paul III **12** 144-145
    Pius VI **12** 333-334
    Pius VII **12** 334-335
  writers
    Gracián y Morales, Baltasar Jeróni-
      mo **6** 481-482
    Hopkins, Gerard Manley **7** 492-494
    Mariana, Juan de **10** 254-255
    Pázmány, Péter **12** 164-165

Jesup, Thomas S. (1788-1860), American
  general
  Osceola **12** 18

Jesus, Society of
  see Jesuits

JESUS OF NAZARETH (circa 4 B.C. -
  29/30A.D.), founder of the Christian faith
  8 251-255

and Protestantism
  Schweitzer, Albert **14** 55-56
  Söderblom, Nathan **14** 323-324
  Strauss, David Friedrich **14** 496-497
Apostles
  John **8** 273-274
  Mark **10** 266-267
  Matthew **10** 340-341
  Paul **12** 141-143
  Peter **12** 252-253
controversies on natures of (3rd-5th
  century)
  Arius **1** 297-298
  Athanasius **1** 358-359
  Clement of Alexandria **4** 102-103
  Cyril **4** 362
  Eutyches **5** 335
  Leo I **9** 329-330
  Nestorius **11** 349-350
controversies on natures of (16th-18th
  century)
  Schwenckfeld, Kasper von **14** 56-57
  Servetus, Michael **14** 115-116
  Swedenborg, Emanuel **15** 49-50
family
  Mary **10** 308
forerunner
  John the Baptist **8** 290
modern fictional hero
  Dostoevsky, Fyodor **5** 74-77

JESUS BEN SIRA (Sirach; flourished circa
  170 B.C.), Jewish sage and author **8** 251

Jesus Called to Him the Twelve (cantata)
  Bach, Johann Sebastian **1** 416-419

Jesus Christ
  see Jesus

Jesus Christ Superstar (musical)
  Webber, Andrew Lloyd **16** 155-156

Jesus, Lover of My Soul (hymn)
  Wesley, Charles **16** 208-209

Jesus of Lubeck (ship)
  Hawkins, John **7** 210-211

Jesus Wept (musical round)
  Billings, William **2** 274-275

Jet (magazine)
  Johnson, John Harold **8** 306-308

Jet propulsion (aeronautics)
  Armstrong, Neil Alden **1** 304-306
  Kármán, Theodore von **8** 451-452
  Whittle, Frank **16** 257-258

Jethro (flourished 14th-13th century B.C.),
  Midianite priest
  Moses **11** 200-201

Jeu de l'amour et du hasard, Le (play)
  Marivaux, Pierre Carlet de Chamblain
    de **10** 265-266

Jeune Parque, La (poem)
  Valéry, Paul Ambroise **15** 405-406

Jeune Tarantine (poem)
  Chénier, André Marie **3** 500-501

Jeux (ballet)
  Debussy, Achille Claude **4** 445-447

Jeux d'eau (musical composition)
  Ravel, Maurice Joseph **13** 54-55

Jeux d'enfants (ballet; Massine)
  Miró, Joan **11** 53-54

Jeux d'enfants (musical composition)
  Bizet, Georges **2** 296-297

JEVONS, WILLIAM STANLEY (1835-1882),
  English economist, logician, and statisti-
  cian **8** 255-256
  Clark, John Bates **4** 76-77

Jew of Malta, The (play; Marlowe)
  Machiavelli, Niccolò **10** 97-99
  Marlowe, Christopher **10** 272-274

JEWETT, SARAH ORNE (1849-1909),
  American novelist **8** 256
  Howells, William Dean **7** 539-541

Jewish Agency for Palestine
  Asch, Shalom **1** 325-326
  Meir, Golda **10** 462-463
  Namier, Lewis Bernstein **11** 301-303
  Weizmann, Chaim **16** 183-184

Jewish Cemetery at Ouderkerk (painting)
  Ruisdael, Jacob van **13** 357-358

Jewish Chamber Theater (Moscow)
  Chagall, Marc **3** 406-407

Jewish Documentation Center (Vienna,
  Austria)
  Wiesenthal, Simon **16** 264-266

Jewish Encyclopedia (reformer book)
  Ginzberg, Louis **6** 337-338
  Schechter, Solomon **13** 524

Jewish Federation of Labor (Israel)
  Ben-Gurion, David **2** 160-161
  Meir, Golda **10** 462-463

Jewish history
  • BIBLICAL ERA
    Israel (united monarchy; circa
      1050-922 B.C.)
      David, Jacques Louis **4** 407-409
      Moses **11** 200-201
      Samuel **13** 457-458
      Saul **13** 498
      Solomon **14** 326-327
    Israel (Northern Kingdom; 922-721
      B.C.)
      Amos **1** 205
      Jeroboam I **8** 248-249
      Sargon II **13** 482
      Sennacherib **14** 108
      Tiglath-pileser III **15** 221-222
    Judah (Southern Kingdom; 922-586
      B.C.)
      Ezekiel **5** 355-356
      Hosea **7** 512
      Isaiah **8** 146-147
      Jeremiah **8** 247-248
      Micah **10** 542-543
      Nebuchadnezzar **11** 330
    Judea (kingdom; successor to Judah)
      Herod the Great **7** 333-334

Hillel **7** 390-391
revitalization (6th-5th century B.C.)
Ezekiel **5** 355-356
Ezra **5** 356-357
Hosea **7** 512
• CAPTIVITY and OVERRULE
Babylon captivity
see Babylon captivity
Greek rule
Alexander the Great **1** 137-141
Antigonus I **1** 248-249
Islamic rule
Mohammed **11** 76-78
Omar ibn al-Khattab **11** 508-509
Persian rule
Cyrus the Great **4** 363-364
Roman empire
Hadrian **7** 60-61
Herod the Great **7** 333-334
Jesus of Nazareth **8** 251-255
Josephus Flavius **8** 360-361
Philo Judaeus **12** 282-283
Pompey **12** 387-389
Roman empire (revolts against)
Bar Kochba, Simeon **2** 5
Johanan ben Zakkai **8** 271-272
Shammai **14** 149
Titus Flavius Vespasianus
15 247-248
Trajan **15** 291-292
Seleucid rule
Antiochus III **1** 249-250
Antiochus IV **1** 250
Judas Maccabeus **8** 374-375
Seleucus I **14** 92-93
• DISPERSION (EUROPEAN)
Christian relations
Leo III **9** 330-332
Paul **12** 141-143
Peter **12** 252-253
Rosenzweig, Franz **13** 294
Thomas Aquinas **15** 183-186
civil rights
Ferdinand **5** 413-414
Gladstone, William Ewart
6 357-360
Joseph II **8** 359-360
in Europe
Elijah ben Solomon **5** 251-252
Manasseh ben Israel **10** 183-184
Mendelssohn, Moses
10 488-489
Sabbatai Zevi **13** 400-401
historians of
Baron, Salo Wittmayer **2** 16-17
Dubnov, Simon **5** 115-116
Graetz, Heinrich Hirsch **6** 483
Krochmal, Nachman Kohen
9 104-105
Schechter, Solomon **13** 524
Zunz, Leopold **16** 534
and Nazis
Arendt, Hannah **1** 282-284
Buber, Martin **3** 87-89
Dubnov, Simon **5** 115-116

Goebbels, Joseph Paul
6 384-385
Göring, Hermann Wilhelm
6 457-458
Himmler, Heinrich **7** 398-399
Hitler, Adolf **7** 417-420-293
Szold, Henrietta **15** 66-67
Spanish Inquisition
Abravanel, Isaac ben Judah **1** 31
Ferdinand V **5** 417-418
Isabella I **8** 144-145
Manuel I **10** 219-220
Vieira, Antônio **15** 492
Spanish settlement
Judah Halevi **8** 373
Maimonides **10** 151-152
Nahmanides **11** 293-294
• NATIONAL STATE (1948) SEE ISRAEL
see also Anti-Semitism; Diaspora;
Judaism; Palestine; Zionism
Jewish Institute of Religion (New York City)
Baron, Salo Wittmayer **2** 16-17
Wise, Stephen Samuel **16** 344-345
Jewish law
see Judaism—law; Mosaic law; San-
hedrin; Talmud
Jewish literature
humor
Golden, Harry **6** 402-403
prose
Aleichem, Sholom **1** 124-125
Appelfeld, Aharon **1** 262-263
Asch, Shalom **1** 325-326
Babel, Isaac Emmanuelovich
1 411-412
Cahan, Abraham **3** 214
Ginzberg, Asher **6** 336-337
Klein, A. M. **9** 49-50
Malamud, Bernard **10** 162-163
Oz, Amos **12** 45-47
Rosenzweig, Franz **13** 294
Saadia ben Joseph al-Fayumi **13** 396
Sholem Aleichem **14** 202-203
Singer, Isaac Bashevis **14** 249-250
verse
Judah Halevi **8** 373
Klein, A. M. **9** 49-50
Luzzato, Moses Hayyim **10** 57-58
Sachs, Nelly **13** 411-412
see also Hebrew literature; Yiddish
literature
Jewish people, delcaration on (Vatican II)
Bea, Augustinus **2** 79
Jewish Reconstructionist Foundation
(established 1940)
Kaplan, Mordecai Menahem **8** 435-436
Jewish State, The (pamphlet)
Herzl, Theodor **7** 352-354
Jewish Teachers Seminary (Berlin)
Zunz, Leopold **16** 534
Jewish Territorial Organization (established
1905)
Zangwill, Israel **16** 488-489

Jewish Theological Seminary
Finkelstein, Rabbi Louis **5** 448-450
Jewish Theological Seminary of America
(New York City)
Abrahams, Israel **1** 29
Baron, Salo Wittmayer **2** 16-17
Ginzberg, Louis **6** 337-338
Heschel, Abraham Joshua **7** 358-359
Kaplan, Mordecai Menahem **8** 435-436
Schechter, Solomon **13** 524
Schiff, Jacob Henry **14** 2-3
Jewish Wars, The (book)
Josephus Flavius **8** 360-361
Jewish Widow, The (play)
Kaiser, Georg **8** 411-412
Jews of Zirndorf, The (novel)
Wassermann, Jakob **16** 130-131
Jezebel (verse narrative)
Heavysege, Charles **7** 246
JFK (film)
Stone, Oliver **14** 472-475
JIANG QING (Madame Mao Zedong;
1914-1991), Chinese revolutionary and
leader of the Great Proletarian Cultural
Revolution **8** 256-260
JIANG ZEMIN (born 1927), general secre-
tary of the Chinese Communist Party Cen-
tral Committee **8** 260-261
Jicarilla Apache Indians (North America)
Carson, Christopher **3** 334-335
Jihad (Holy War; Islam religion)
Omar ibn Said Tal, Al-Hajj **11** 509-510
Saladin **13** 441-442
Uthman don Fodio **15** 397-398
Jim Crow (minstrel act)
Christy, Edwin P. **4** 34-35
JIMÉneZ, JUAN RAMÓN (1881-1958),
Spanish symbolist poet **8** 261-262
Guillén, Nicolás **7** 34-35
Lorca, Federico García **9** 511-513
Jiménez de Cisneros, Francisco
(1436-1517), Spanish cardinal and states-
man
Ferdinand V **5** 417-418
JIMÉNEZ DE QUESADA, GONZALO
(1509-1579), Spanish conquistador
12 509-510
Benalcázar, Sebastián de **2** 145-146
Jimutavahana (literary character)
Harsha **7** 181-182
Jina
see Vardhamana Mahavira
Jingim (1244-1286), Mongol chieftain
Kublai Khan **9** 115-118
JINNAH, MOHAMMAD ALI (1876-1948),
Pakistani governor general 1947-1948
8 262-263
associates
Iqbal, Muhammad **8** 132-133
Liaquat Ali Khan **9** 397
Naidu, Sarojini **11** 294-295

Pakistani separatism
Ayub Khan, Mohammed **1** 395-396
Gandhi, Mohandas Karamchand
6 201-204
Nehru, Jawaharlal **11** 332-334
Sapru, Tej Bahadur **13** 480-481

Joab (Old Testament character)
David, Jacques Louis **4** 407-409

Joachim, Joseph (1831-1907), German violinist
Brahms, Johannes **2** 490-492
Schumann, Robert Alexander **14** 41-43

Joachim Napoleon (king of Naples)
see Murat, Joachim

JOACHIM OF FIORE (circa 1132-1202),
Italian mystic **8** 263-264
Bacon, Roger **1** 425-427

Joachim von Lauchen, Georg (Rheticus;
1514-1576), German astronomer and
mathematician
Copernicus, Nicolaus **4** 226-227

Joachimsthal (region; Bohemia)
Agricola, Georgius **1** 86-87

Joan (1328-1385), countess of Kent
Edward the Black Prince **5** 217-218

JOAN OF ARC (1412?-1431), French
national heroine **8** 264-265
in literature
Christine de Pisan **4** 29-30
France, Anatole **6** 39-40
Maeterlinck, Maurice **10** 125-126
Péguy, Charles Pierre **12** 183-184
Voltaire **16** 14-16
in music
Honegger, Arthur **7** 472-473
military campaigns
Charles VII **3** 461-462
Henry VI **7** 298-299
Louis XI **9** 526-528
Philip the Good **12** 278-279

Joan of Lorraine (play)
Anderson, Maxwell **1** 219-220

Joan of Navarre (1370?-1437), queen of
England 1403-13
Henry IV **7** 292-293

Joanna (Joanna the Mad; 1479-1555),
queen of Castile and León 1504-1555
Charles V **3** 457-459
Ferdinand I **5** 414-415
Ferdinand V **5** 417-418
Isabella I **8** 144-145
Maximilian I **10** 356-357

João (king of Portugal)
see John (king of Portugal)

João I (king of Kongo)
see Nzinga Nkuwu

Joaquin et al (poems)
Miller, Joaquin **11** 27-28

Job, Book of (Old Testament)
Blake, William **2** 316-318
Frost, Robert Lee **6** 130-133

Gregory I **6** 531-532

Job and His Wife and Saint Joseph (painting)
La Tour, George de **9** 222

Job Corps (United States)
Johnson, Lyndon Baines **8** 308-312

JOBS, STEVEN (born 1955), American
computer designer and co-founder of
Apple Computers **8** 265-267

Jocelyn (novel)
Galsworthy, John **6** 189-190

Jocelyn (poem)
Lamartine, Alphonse Marie Louis de
9 173-175

Jodoshu
see Pure Land sect (Buddhism)

Jodrell Bank Laboratory (Cheshire, England)
Lovell, Alfred Charles Bernard **10** 8-9

Joel (Old Testament prophet)
Samuel **13** 457-458

Joe's Luck (book)
Alger, Horatio **1** 153-154

Joffe, Adolph (1883-1927), Soviet diplomat
Sun Yat-sen **15** 35-39

JOFFRE, JOSEPH JACQUES CÉSAIRE
(1852-1931), French marshal **8** 267-268
Foch, Ferdinand **5** 498-499

JOFFREY, ROBERT (born Abdullah Jaffa
Anver Bey Khan; 1930-1988), American
dancer and choreographer **8** 268-270

Jogu Taishi
see Shotoku Taishi

JOGUES, ST. ISAAC (1607-1646), French
Jesuit missionary and martyr **8** 270-271

JOHANAN BEN ZAKKAI (flourished circa
70 A.D.), Jewish teacher **8** 271-272
Akiba ben Joseph **1** 97-98

Johannes de Boetgezant (epic poem)
Vondel, Joost van den **16** 19-20

JOHANNES IV (1836-1889), Ethiopian
emperor 1872-1889 **8** 272-273
Mengs, Anton Raphael **10** 505

Johannisfeuer (play)
Sudermann, Hermann **15** 12-13

Johansen, John MacLane (born 1916),
American architect
Breuer, Marcel **2** 520-521

JOHN (1167-1216), king of England
1199-1216 **8** 274-275
Eleanor of Aquitaine **5** 246-247
Henry II **7** 287-289
Innocent III **8** 125-127
Philip II **12** 268-269

John (1296-1346), king of Bohemia and
count of Luxemburg 1310-46
Charles IV **3** 455-456
Machaut, Guillaume de **10** 93-94

John I (Tzimisces; 925-976), Byzantine
emperor 969-976
Basil II **2** 50-51

John I (1357-1433), king of Portugal
1385-1433
Henry the Navigator **7** 305-306

John I (1358-1390), king of Castile and
Léon 1379-1390
López de Ayala, Pedro **9** 508-509

John I, Saint (470?-526), pope 523-526
Theodoric the Great **15** 175-176

John II (Comnenus; 1088-1143), Byzantine
emperor 1118-1143
Alexius I **1** 143-144
Comnena, Anna **4** 185-186
Manuel I **10** 218-219

JOHN II (1319-1364), king of France
1350-1364 **8** 275-276
Charles V **3** 459-460
Edward III **5** 211-212
Froissart, Jean **6** 124-125
Philip VI **12** 277-278

John II (1397-1479), king of Aragon
1458-1479
Ferdinand V **5** 417-418

John II (1455-1495), king of Portugal
1481-1495
Abravanel, Isaac ben Judah **1** 31
Columbus, Christopher **4** 176-179
Covilhão, Pedro de **4** 278-279
Dias de Novais, Bartolomeu **4** 533-534
Manuel I **10** 219-220
Nzinga Nkuwu **11** 451-452

John III (1502-1557), king of Portugal
1521-1557
Milán, Luis **11** 15-16
Sá, Mem de **13** 395
Sousa, Martim Afonso de **14** 354-355
Vicente, Gil **15** 479-480

JOHN III (John Sobieski; 1629-1696), king
of Poland **8** 276-277
Augustus II **1** 373-374
Köprülü, Ahmed **9** 84-85

John IV (Lascaris; 1250?-1300?), Byzantine
emperor 1258-1261
Michael VIII **11** 1-2

John IV (the Fortunate; 1605-1656), king of
Portugal 1640-1656
Vieira, Antônio **15** 492

John V (1689-1750), king of Portugal
1706-1750
Pombal, Marquês de **12** 386-387

John VI (1769-1826), king of Portugal
1816-1826
Andrada e Silva, José Bonifácio de
1 221-222
Pedro I **12** 179-180

John VIII (820?-882), pope 872-882
Cyril and Methodius, Saints **4** 362-363

John VIII (Palaeologus; 1391-1448), Byzantine emperor 1425-1448
Constantine XI **4** 211-212

Pisanello **12** 323-324

John XII (938?-964), pope 955-964
Otto I **12** 28-29

John XXII (Jacques d'Euse; 1249-1334),
pope 1316-1334
Eckhart, Johann **5** 200-201
Marsilius of Padua **10** 284
Robert I **13** 192-194
William of Ockham **16** 298-299

John XXIII (Baldassare Cossa; died 1419),
antipope 1410-15
Ailly, Pierre d' **1** 94
Donatello **5** 55-56
Hus, Jan **8** 56-59
Martin V **10** 287-288
Michelozzo **11** 6-7

JOHN XXIII (Angelo Giuseppe Roncalli;
1881-1963), pope 1958-1963 **8** 277-280
and College of Cardinals
Bea, Augustinus **2** 79
Paul VI **12** 146-148
Sixtus V **14** 267-268
and Vatican II
Küng, Hans **9** 129-130
Pius XII **12** 339-340
influenced by
Leo XIII **9** 334-336
peacemaker
Kennedy, John Fitzgerald **8** 502-506

JOHN, AUGUSTUS EDWIN (1878-1961),
Welsh painter **8** 291

John, Gospel according to Saint (Fourth
Gospel)
Erigena, John Scotus **5** 308-309
Jesus of Nazareth **8** 251-255
John **8** 273-274

JOHN, ST. (flourished 1st century A.D.),
Christian Apostle and Evangelist
8 273-274
Jesus of Nazareth **8** 251-255
Justin Martyr **8** 395-396
Mary **10** 308
Peter **12** 252-253

John Anderson, My Jo (song)
Burns, Robert **3** 155-156

John Barleycorn (book)
London, Jack **9** 494-495

John Birch Society (United States)
Welch, Robert **16** 184-185

John Brown (book)
Du Bois, William Edward Burghardt
5 116-118

John Brown Going to His Hanging (painting)
Pippin, Horace **12** 318-319

John Brown Reading His Bible (painting)
Pippin, Horace **12** 318-319

John Brown's Body (poem)
Benét, Stephen Vincent **2** 157-158
Brown, John **3** 39-41

John Bull's Other Island (play)
Shaw, George Bernard **14** 163-164

JOHN CHRYSOSTOM, ST. (circa 347-407),
bishop of Constantinople **8** 280-281
Cyril **4** 362

John Frederick (the Magnanimous;
1503-1554), Prussian elector of Saxony
1532-1547
Cranach, Lucas the Elder **4** 289-290

John Gabriel Borkman (play)
Ibsen, Henrik **8** 98-100

John George I (1585-1656), elector of Saxony 1611-1656
Gustavus II **7** 43-45

John George III (1647-1691), elector of
Saxony 1680-1691
Augustus II **1** 373-374

John George IV (1668-1694), elector of
Saxony 1691-1694
Augustus II **1** 373-374

John Gilpin's Ride (poem)
Cowper, William **4** 282

John Hancock Building (New York City)
Noguchi, Isamu **11** 416-418

John March, Southerner (novel)
Cable, George Washington **3** 198-199

JOHN MAURICE OF NASSAU
(1604-1679), Dutch governor general of
Netherlands Brazil **8** 281-282

John of Antioch (died 441), Early Christian
bishop 429-441
Nestorius **11** 349-350

John of Austria (1547-1578), Spanish gen-
eral
Cervantes, Miguel de Saavedra
3 395-398
Charles V **3** 457-459
William the Silent **16** 300-302

JOHN OF DAMASCUS, ST. (circa
680-750), Syrian theologian **8** 282
Lombard, Peter **9** 490-491

John of Fidanza
see Bonaventure, Saint

JOHN OF GAUNT (5th Duke of Lancaster;
1340-1399), English soldier-statesman
8 282-283
Chaucer, Geoffrey **3** 482-485, 538
Edward III **5** 211-212
Edward the Black Prince **5** 217-218
Gower, John **6** 475-476
Henry IV **7** 292-293
Robert III **13** 194-195
Wyclif, John **16** 412-413

John of Jandun (circa 1275-1328), French
philosopher
Lull, Raymond **10** 39-40
Marsilius of Padua **10** 284

John of Jerusalem (died 417), Palestinian
bishop of Jerusalem 387-417
Pelagius **12** 189-190

John of Lancaster (1389-1435), duke of
Bedford
Dunstable, John **5** 150-151
Gloucester, Duke of **6** 370-371

Philip the Good **12** 278-279

JOHN OF LEIDEN (1509-1536), Dutch
Anabaptist **8** 283
Menno Simons **10** 505-506

John of Luxemburg
see John (king of Bohemia)

JOHN OF PIANO CARPINI (circa
1180-1252), Italian Franciscan monk
8 284
Mandeville, John **10** 192-193

JOHN OF SALISBURY (1115/20-1180),
English bishop and humanist **8** 284-285
Abelard, Peter **1** 23-25

JOHN OF THE CROSS, ST. (1542-1591),
Spanish Carmelite mystic **8** 285
Eliot, Thomas Stearns **5** 258-261
Theresa **15** 178-179

JOHN PAUL I (Albino Luciani;
1912-1978), Roman Catholic pope
(August 26-September 28, 1978)
8 286-287

JOHN PAUL II (Karol Wojtyla; born 1920),
cardinal of Krakow, Poland, and later
Roman Catholic pope **8** 287-290
Walesa, Lech **16** 57-59

John the Baptist (sculpture)
Ghiberti, Lorenzo **6** 291-292

JOHN THE BAPTIST, ST. (flourished circa
29 A.D.), New Testament figure, forerun-
ner of Jesus of Nazareth **8** 290
Flaubert, Gustave **5** 480-482
Jesus of Nazareth **8** 251-255
Mary **10** 308

John the Constant (1468-1532), elector of
Saxony 1525-1532
Cranach, Lucas the Elder **4** 289-290

John the Fearless (1371-1419), duke of
Burgundy 1404-1419
Charles the Bold **3** 467-469
Charles VI **3** 460-461
Joan of Arc **8** 264-265
Philip the Good **12** 278-279

John the Good
see John II (king of France)

John the Perfect
see John II (king of Portugal)

John Underhill (poem)
Whittier, John Greenleaf **16** 256-257

John Woodvil (play)
Lamb, Charles **9** 176-177

Johnny Appleseed (poem)
Lindsay, Vachel **9** 424-425

Johnny Johnson (opera)
Weill, Kurt **16** 174-175

Johnny Pye... (poem)
Benét, Stephen Vincent **2** 157-158

JOHNS, JASPER (born 1930), American
painter and sculptor **8** 291-293

Johns Hopkins University (Baltimore, Maryland)
  Center for Study of Recent American History
    Chandler, Alfred Du Pont Jr. **3** 422-423
  founded
    Dewey, John **4** 520-523
  Medical School
    Cushing, Harvey Williams **4** 353-354
    Erlanger, Joseph **5** 310-311
    Hall, Granville Stanley **7** 85-86
    Healy, Bernadine Patricia **7** 237-238
    Osler, William **12** 19-20
    Welch, William Henry **16** 185-186
    Whipple, George Hoyt **16** 224-225
  philosophy
    Lovejoy, Arthur Oncken **10** 6
  physics
    Maxwell, James Clerk **10** 361-364
    Rowland, Henry Augustus **13** 330-331
    Urey, Harold Clayton **15** 394-396
  presidents
    Bowman, Isaiah **2** 464-465
    Eisenhower, Milton **5** 237-238
    Gilman, Daniel Coit **6** 325-326
  social sciences
    Adams, Herbert Baxter **1** 47
    Andrews, Charles McLean **1** 231
    Clark, John Bates **4** 76-77
    Frazier, Edward Franklin **6** 77
    Watson, John Broadus **16** 138-139
    Woodward, Comer Vann **16** 378-379

JOHNSON, ALVIN SAUNDERS (1874-1971), American economist and editor **8** 293-294
  Benton, Thomas Hart **2** 178-179

JOHNSON, ANDREW (1808-1875), American statesman, president 1865-1869 **8** 294-295
  Cabinet
    Evarts, William Maxwell **5** 340-341
    Welles, Gideon **16** 188-190
  impeachment controversy
    Chase, Salmon Portland **3** 473-475
    Curtis, Benjamin Robbins **4** 349
    Evarts, William Maxwell **5** 340-341
    Stevens, Thaddeus **14** 442-443
    Trumbull, Lyman **15** 317-318
    Wade, Benjamin Franklin **16** 38-39
  opponents
    Booth, John Wilkes **2** 404
    Morton, Oliver Hazard Perry Throck **11** 197-198
    Nast, Thomas **11** 318-319
    Stanton, Edwin McMasters **14** 401-402
    Wilson, James Harold **16** 324-325
  political appointments
    Bancroft, George **1** 483-484
    Howard, Oliver Otis **7** 528-529
    Sheridan, Philip Henry **14** 182-183
  Reconstruction policy

    Brown, Benjamin Gratz **3** 32-33
    Chandler, Zachariah **3** 425-426
    Grant, Ulysses Simpson **6** 492-494
    Schurz, Carl **14** 44-45
    Sumner, Charles **15** 30-31
    Tilden, Samuel Jones **15** 222-223
  supporters
    Seward, William Henry **14** 124-125
    Weed, Thurlow **16** 169-170

Johnson, Benjamin F.
  see Riley, James Whitcomb

JOHNSON, BETSEY (born 1941?), American fashion designer **8** 295-296

Johnson, Charles
  see Brooke, James

JOHNSON, CHARLES SPURGEON (1893-1956), African American educator and sociologist **8** 296-297
  Frazier, Edward Franklin **6** 77

Johnson, Douglas Wilson (1878-1944), American geologist
  Davis, William Morris **4** 425-426

JOHNSON, EARVIN, JR. ("Magic"; born 1959), popular African American star of the Los Angeles Lakers basketball team **8** 297-299

Johnson, Edward (1598-1672), American colonist
  Dunster, Henry **5** 152-153

Johnson, Esther (1680-1728), English literary model
  Swift, Jonathan **15** 51-54

Johnson Gate (Harvard University)
  McKim, Charles Follen **10** 417-418

Johnson, Guy (1740?-1788), British colonial official
  Brant, Joseph **2** 500-501

JOHNSON, GUY BENTON (1901-1991), sociologist, social anthropologist, and archaeologist who was a student of African American culture and an advocate of racial equality **8** 299-300

JOHNSON, HIRAM WARREN (1866-1945), American politician **8** 300-301
  Ickes, Harold LeClaire **8** 100-101

Johnson, Isaac Wallace
  see Wallace-Johnson, Isaac Theophilus Akunna

JOHNSON, JACK (1878-1946), African American boxer **8** 301-304

Johnson, James (circa 1750-1811), Scottish music engraver
  Burns, Robert **3** 155-156

JOHNSON, JAMES WELDON (1871-1938), African American author and lawyer **8** 304-305

JOHNSON, JOHN HAROLD (born 1918), American entrepreneur and founder of

the Johnson Publishing Company **8** 306-308

JOHNSON, JONATHAN EASTMAN (1824-1906), American painter **8** 308

JOHNSON, LYNDON BAINES (1908-1973), American statesman, president 1963-1969 **8** 308-312
  advisers
    Valenti, Jack Joseph **15** 401-403
  appointees
    Bundy, McGeorge **3** 122-124
    Connally, John Bowden Jr. **4** 202-204
    Fortas, Abe **6** 16-17
    Moyers, Bill **11** 214-216
    Weaver, Robert C. **16** 152-153
  domestic policy
    Ford, Henry II **6** 6-7
    King, Martin Luther Jr. **9** 20-22
    Wilkins, Roy **16** 282-283
  election campaign (1960)
    Kennedy, John Fitzgerald **8** 502-506
    Nixon, Richard Milhous **11** 401-404
  foreign policy
    Bundy, McGeorge **3** 122-124
    Marcos, Ferdinand **10** 240-242
    Paul VI **12** 146-148
    Pearson, Lester Bowles **12** 174-175
  opponents
    Fulbright, James William **6** 147-149
    Kennedy, Robert Francis **8** 508-509
    McGovern, George Stanley **10** 412-414
  political appointments
    Marshall, Thurgood **10** 282-284
    Young, Whitney Moore Jr. **16** 476-477
  supporters
    Rayburn, Samuel Taliaferro **13** 61-62
    Truman, Harry S. **15** 314-316
    see also Vietnam War (1956-1976)

JOHNSON, MARIETTA LOUISE PIERCE (1864-1938), founder and 30-year teacher of an Alabama experimental school **8** 312-313

Johnson, Pamela Hansford (Mrs. C. P. Snow; born 1912-1981), English novelist
  Snow, Charles Percy **14** 311-312

JOHNSON, PHILIP (born 1906), American architect, critic, and historian **8** 313-314
  Breuer, Marcel **2** 520-521
  Mies van der Rohe, Ludwig **11** 10-12
  Schinkel, Karl Friedrich **14** 8

Johnson Publishing Company
  Johnson, John Harold **8** 306-308

JOHNSON, SAMUEL (1696-1772), American clergyman and educator **8** 314-315

JOHNSON, SAMUEL (1709-1784), English author and lexicographer **8** 315-317
  biographer
    Boswell, James **2** 432-434
  critics
    Macaulay, Thomas Babington **10** 79-80

Sterne, Laurence **14** 435-437
friends
  Burke, Edmund **3** 138-141
  Collins, William **4** 168-169
  Goldsmith, Oliver **6** 411-413
  Oglethorpe, James Edward
    11 482-483
  Reynolds, Joshua **13** 115-116
influenced by
  Addison, Joseph **1** 57-58
  Burton, Robert **3** 166-167
  Cowley, Abraham **4** 281-282
  Juvenal **8** 397-399
  Law, William **9** 245-246
  Milton, John **11** 43-46

JOHNSON, SIR JOHN (1742-1830), American loyalist in the American Revolution **8** 305-306
  Butler, John **3** 180

JOHNSON, SIR WILLIAM (1715-1774), British colonial administrator **8** 319-320
  Brant, Joseph **2** 500-501
  Brant, Mary (Molly) **2** 501-503
  Butler, John **3** 180
  Johnson, John **8** 305-306
  Pontiac **12** 393-394

Johnson, Thomas H. (born 1902), American editor
  Dickinson, Emily **4** 541-543
  Taylor, Edward **15** 122-123

JOHNSON, TOM LOFTIN (1854-1911), American entrepreneur and politician **8** 317
  Baker, Newton Diehl **1** 451
  Jones, Samuel Milton **8** 342-343

JOHNSON, VIRGINIA E. (born 1925), American psychologist and sex therapist **8** 317-319
  Masters, William Howell **10** 327-328

JOHNSON, WILLIAM H. (1901-1970), African American painter of the Black experience **8** 320-322

Johnson Wax Co. (Racine, Wisconsin)
  Wright, Frank Lloyd **16** 398-401

Johnston, Albert Sidney (1803-1862), American Confederate general
  Beauregard, Pierre Gustave Toutant
    2 96-97
  Bridger, James **3** 2-3
  Sherman, William Tecumseh
    14 186-187
  Young, Brigham **16** 469-470

Johnston, George (flourished 1808-1811), British leader of Rum Rebellion
  Bligh, William **2** 325-326
  Macarthur, John **10** 78

JOHNSTON, HENRY HAMILTON (Sir Harry Johnston; 1858-1927), English administrator, explorer, and author **8** 322-323

JOHNSTON, JOSEPH EGGLESTON (1807-1891), American Confederate general **8** 323
  associates

    Beauregard, Pierre Gustave Toutant
      2 96-97
    Curry, Jabez Lamar Monroe
      4 346-347
    Davis, Jefferson **4** 416-418
    Lee, Robert Edward **9** 292-294
    Semmes, Raphael **14** 102-103
    Stuart, James Ewell Brown
      14 515-516
  opponents
    McClellan, George Brinton
      10 391-392
    Sherman, William Tecumseh
      14 186-187

JOHNSTON, JOSHUA (a.k.a. Joshua Johnson; ca. 1765 - ca 1830), African American portrait artist **8** 323-325

Joie de vivre, La (sculpture; painting)
  Lipchitz, Jacques **9** 432-433
  Matisse, Henri **10** 336-337

JOINVILLE, JEAN DE (1224/25-1317), French author **8** 325
  Froissart, Jean **6** 124-125

Jolie fille de Perth, La (opera)
  Bizet, Georges **2** 296-297

Joliot, Jean Frédéric
  see Joliot-Curie, Jean Frédéric

JOLIOT-CURIE, IRÈNE (1897-1956), French chemist and physicist **8** 325-327
  Bothe, Walther **2** 438-439
  Curie, Marie Sklodowska **4** 339-341
  Joliot-Curie, Jean Frédéric **8** 327-328

JOLIOT-CURIE, JEAN FRÉDÉRIC (1900-1958), French physicist **8** 327-328
  Bothe, Walther **2** 438-439
  Chadwick, James **3** 405-406
  Curie, Marie Sklodowska **4** 339-341
  Lawrence, Ernest Orlando **9** 248-250

JOLLIET, LOUIS (1645-1700), French-Canadian explorer, hydrographer, and fur trader **8** 328-329
  La Salle, Sieur de **9** 210-211
  Marquette, Jacques **10** 274-275
  Talon, Jean **15** 91-92

Jolly Beggars, The (poem)
  Burns, Robert **3** 155-156

Jolly Flatboatmen (painting)
  Bingham, George Caleb **2** 278-279

Jolly, P. von (1809-1884), German physicist
  Hertz, Heinrich Rudolf **7** 346-347

JOLSON, AL (Asa Yoelson; 1886-1950), American vaudeville, theater, and radio singing performer and film actor **8** 329-330
  Gershwin, George **6** 284-285

Jonah (Old Testament character)
  Frost, Robert Lee **6** 130-133

Jonathan (flourished 1010-970 B.C.), Israelite crown prince
  David, Jacques Louis **4** 407-409
  Saul **13** 498

JONATHAN, CHIEF JOSEPH LEABUA (1914-1987), Lesothoan statesman **8** 330-331

Jones, Anson (1798-1858), American statesman, president of Texas 1844-1846
  Houston, Samuel **7** 526-527

Jones, Brutus (literary character)
  O'Neill, Eugene **11** 514-516

Jones, Edith Newbold
  see Wharton, Edith

Jones, Sir Edward Coley Burne
  see Burne-Jones, Sir Edward Coley

JONES, ERNEST ALFRED (1879-1958), British psychologist **8** 331-332
  Freud, Sigmund **6** 103-106
  Klein, Melanie **9** 52

JONES, FAY (born 1921), American architect **8** 332-333

Jones, Everett LeRoi
  see Baraka, Imamu Amiri

JONES, INIGO (1573-1652), English architect and designer **8** 333-334
  Harrison, Peter **7** 179-180
  Jonson, Ben **8** 343-345
  Laud, William **9** 224-225
  Palladio, Andrea **12** 75-77
  Wren, Christopher **16** 393-394

JONES, JAMES EARL (born 1931), African American actor **8** 334-337

JONES, JOHN PAUL (1747-1792), American Revolutionary War naval officer **8** 337-338
  Cooper, James Fenimore **4** 220-223
  Franklin, Benjamin **6** 60-64
  Hopkins, Esek **7** 490-491
  Morison, Samuel Eliot **11** 175-176

JONES, MARY HARRIS ("Mother"; 1830-1930), Irish immigrant who devoted her life to improving conditions of the working class **8** 338-339

JONES, QUINCY DELIGHT, JR. (born 1933), African American musician—composer-arranger-producer-film and television executive **8** 339-341
  Gordy, Berry Jr. **6** 450-451

JONES, ROBERT EDMOND (1887-1954), American designer of scenes for the theater **8** 341-342

JONES, ROBERT TYRE (Bobby; 1902-1971), American golf great **8** 342

JONES, SAMUEL MILTON (1846-1904), American manufacturer and political reformer **8** 342-343
  La Follette, Robert Marion **9** 155-156

Jones Act (United States; 1916)
  Muñoz Rivera, Luís **11** 250
  Osmeña, Sergio **12** 22-24
  Quezon, Manuel Luis **12** 511-513

Jonny spielt auf (opera)
  Krenek, Ernst **9** 98-99

JONSON, BEN (1572-1637), English playwright and poet **8** 343-345

compared to
  Mencken, Henry Louis **10** 481-483
contemporaries
  Bacon, Francis **1** 422-424
  Chapman, George **3** 440-441
  Clarendon, 1st Earl of **4** 73-75
  Jones, Inigo **8** 333-334
  Raleigh, Walter **13** 9-11
  Shakespeare, William **14** 142-145
influence of
  Beaumont, Francis **2** 95
  Congreve, William **4** 200-201
  Herrick, Robert **7** 336-339
  Marvell, Andrew **10** 301-303
influenced by
  Catullus, Gaius Valerius **3** 377-378
  Plautus **12** 348-350
  Plutarch **12** 359-360
  Terence **15** 146-148
translation of
  Pasternak, Boris Leonidovich
    12 124-125

JOPLIN, SCOTT (1868-1917), African
American composer and instrumental
musician **8** 345-347

JORDAENS, JACOB (1593-1678), Flemish
painter **8** 347-349
  Van Dyck, Anthony **15** 423-425

JORDAN, BARBARA CHARLINE (born
1936), attorney and U.S. congresswoman
from Texas **8** 349-350

JORDAN, DAVID STARR (1851-1931),
American scientist and educator
8 350-351
  Cubberley, Ellwood Patterson
    4 329-331

Jordan, Hasemite Kingdom of (formerly
Transjordan; nation, southwest Asia)
  Abdullah ibn Husein **1** 19-20
  Dayan, Moshe **4** 429-431
  Glubb, John Bagot **6** 371-372
  Hussein ibn Talal **8** 65-67

JORDAN, JUNE (born 1936),
Jamaican-American poet and activist
8 351-353

JORDAN, LOUIS (1908-1975), African
American bandleader, singer, and instru-
mentalist **8** 353-355

JORDAN, MICHAEL (born 1963), African
American basketball superstar of the
Chicago Bulls **8** 355-357

Jordan, Mrs. Dorothea (1762-1816), Irish
actress
  William IV **16** 296-297

Jordan, Pascual (1902-1980), German
physicist
  Bohr, Niels Henrik David **2** 366-368
  Dirac, Paul Adrien Maurice **5** 23-24

Jordan River (Middle East)
  Jesus of Nazareth **8** 251-255

JORDAN, VERNON (born 1935), American
civil rights leader **8** 357-358

Joseffy, Rafael (1852-1915),
Hungarian-born American pianist
  Liszt, Franz **9** 445-447

JOSEPH (circa 1840-1904), American Nez
Percé Indian chief **8** 358-359
  Cochise **4** 128
  Miles, Nelson Appleton **11** 16-17

Joseph (musical composition)
  Handel, George Frederick **7** 116-119

Joseph (Old Testament patriarch)
  Mann, Thomas **10** 204-207

Joseph, Saint (New Testament character)
  Jesus of Nazareth **8** 251-255
  Mary **10** 308

Joseph I (1678-1711), Holy Roman emper-
or 1705-1711
  Eugene of Savoy **5** 330-331
  Fischer von Erlach, Johann Bernhard
    5 459-461

Joseph I (King of Spain)
  see Bonaparte, Joseph

JOSEPH II (1741-1790), Holy Roman
emperor 1765-1790 **8** 359-360
  Catherine the Great **3** 370-372
  Francis II **6** 43-44
  Frederick II **6** 81-84
  Goethe, Johann Wolfgang von
    6 388-391
  Leopold II **9** 346
  Pius VI **12** 333-334
  Pius VII **12** 334-335
  Potemkin, Grigori Aleksandrovich
    12 411-412

Joseph and His Brothers (novel)
  Mann, Thomas **10** 204-207

Joseph Andrews (novel)
  Fielding, Henry **5** 442-444

Joseph ben Mattathias
  see Josephus Flavius

Joseph Conrad (book)
  Ford, Ford Madox **6** 1-2

Joseph Conrad (sculpture)
  Epstein, Jacob **5** 295-296

Joseph der Ernährer (novel)
  Mann, Thomas **10** 204-207

Joseph Emanuel (José Manuel; 1715-1777),
king of Portugal 1750-1777
  Pombal, Marquês de **12** 386-387

Joseph, Father (1577-1638), French diplomat and Capuchin provincial
  Richelieu, Armand Jean du Plessis de
    13 142-144

Joseph Furphy (biography)
  Franklin, Stella Maraia Sarah Miles
    6 68-69

Joseph in Egypt (painting; Pontormo)
  Bronzino **3** 19

Joseph in Egypten (play)
  Vondel, Joost van den **16** 19-20

Joseph Kerkhoven's Third Existence (novel)
  Wassermann, Jakob **16** 130-131

Josephine (Marie Josephine Rose Tascher
de la Pagerie de Beauharnais;
1763-1814), empress of the French
1804-1809
  Barras, Vicomte de **2** 19
  Bonaparte, Louis **2** 382-383
  Napoleon I **11** 306-310
  Ney, Michel **11** 372-373

Josephine Baker (wire sculpture)
  Calder, Alexander **3** 216-218

Joseph's Coat (painting)
  Velázquez, Diego Rodríguez de Silva y
    15 454-456

JOSEPHUS FLAVIUS (circa 37-100), Jewish
historian, diplomat, and military leader
8 360-361
  Ezekiel **5** 355-356
  Ezra **5** 356-357
  John the Baptist **8** 290
  Judas Maccabeus **8** 374-375

Joshua (musical composition)
  Handel, George Frederick **7** 116-119

JOSQUIN DES PREZ (circa 1440-1521),
Franco-Flemish composer **8** 361-363
  Clemens non Papa, Jacobus **4** 101
  Dunstable, John **5** 150-151
  Gombert, Nicolas **6** 416-417
  Lassus, Roland de **9** 216-218
  Senfl, Ludwig **14** 105-106
  Willaert, Adrian **16** 287-288

Jotapata, battle of (68 A.D.)
  Josephus Flavius **8** 360-361

Jotaro (novel)
  Tanizaki, Junichiro **15** 101-102

Joubert, Petrus Jacobus (1834-1900), South
African general and statesman
  Botha, Louis **2** 434-436

Jouett, Matthew (1787/88-1827), American
painter
  Stuart, Gilbert **14** 513-515

JOULE, JAMES PRESCOTT (1818-1889),
English physicist **8** 363-364
  Kelvin of Largs **8** 488-489

Joule-Thomson effect (physics)
  Joule, James Prescott **8** 363-364

Jourdan, Jean Baptiste (1762-1833), French
military officer
  Carnot, Lazare Nicolas Marguerite
    3 313-314

Journal of Commerce (periodical)
  Tappan brothers **15** 105-106

Journal of Geology (periodical)
  Chamberlin, Thomas Chrowder
    3 415-416

Journal of Negro History
  Woodson, Carter Godwin **16** 374-376

Journal of Speculative Philosophy (periodi-
cal)
  Dewey, John **4** 520-523
  Harris, William Torrey **7** 177-178

**Journal of the Experimental Analysis of
Behavior** (periodical)

Skinner, Burrhus Frederic **14** 269-270

Journal of the History of Ideas (periodical)
Cohen, Morris Raphael **4** 139-140
Lovejoy, Arthur Oncken **10** 6

Journal of the Plague Year, A (book)
Defoe, Daniel **4** 457-459

Journal to Eliza (book)
Sterne, Laurence **14** 435-437

Journal to Stella (book)
Swift, Jonathan **15** 51-54

Journalism (United States)
antislavery newspapers
Garrison, William Lloyd **6** 226-228
Lundy, Benjamin **10** 45-46
Medill, Joseph **10** 451-452
see also Abolitionists, American;
Antislavery movement (United
States)
innovations (19th century)
Bennett, James Gordon Jr.
2 169-170
Dana, Charles Anderson **4** 384-385
Hoe, Richard March **7** 435-436
McClure, Samuel Sidney
10 398-399
muckraking
see Muckraking
see also Editors; Journalists; Publishers

Journalisten, Die (play)
Freytag, Gustav **6** 107-108

Journalists
African
Azikiwe, Nnamdi **1** 401-402
Hayford, J. E. Casely **7** 228-230
Plaatje, Solomon Tshekisho
12 341-342
Wallace-Johnson, Isaac Theophilus
Akunna **16** 76-77
American
see Journalists, American
Arab
Haykal, Muhammad Husain
7 230-231
Argentine
Sarmiento, Domingo Faustino
13 484-485
Timerman, Jacobo **15** 226-228
Australian
Curtin, John Joseph **4** 348-349
Wentworth, William Charles
16 203-204
Brazilian
Barbosa, Ruy **1** 503-504
British
Aitken, William Maxwell **1** 94-96
Canadian
Klein, A. M. **9** 49-50
Chilean
Allende, Isabel **1** 172-174
Chinese
Wang T'ao **16** 105-106
English
Chadwick, Edwin **3** 404-405

Chesterton, Gilbert Keith **3** 508-509
Cobbett, William **4** 126-127
Defoe, Daniel **4** 457-459
Foot, Michael **5** 505-507
Nicolson, Harold George
11 383-384
Pritchett, V. S. **12** 455-457
Filipino
Rómulo, Carlos P. **13** 270-271
French
Aron, Raymond **1** 316-317
Bernanos, Georges **2** 206-207
Blanc, Louis **2** 318-319
Briand, Aristide **2** 528-529
Daudet, Alphonse **4** 402-403
Hébert, Jacques René **7** 247-248
Marat, Jean Paul **10** 230-231
Prévost, Abbé **12** 445-446
Proudhon, Pierre Joseph **12** 461-463
Servan-Schreiber, Jean-Jacques
14 113-115
Thiers, Louis Adolphe **15** 181-182
Hungarian
Koestler, Arthur **9** 71-73
Italian
Ferrero, Guglielmo **5** 429-430
Japanese
Hara, Kei **7** 138
Inukai, Tsuyoshi **8** 130-131
Mexican
Fernández de Lizardi, José Joaquin
5 424-425
Poniatowska, Elena **12** 392-393
Toledano, Vicente Lombardo
15 256-257
New Zealand
Vogel, Julius **16** 9-10
Russian
Chernyshevsky, Nikolai Gavrilovich
3 504-505
Herzen, Aleksandr Ivanovich
7 351-352
Karamzin, Nikolai Mikhailovich
8 441-442
Thai
Kukrit Pramoj, Momrajawong (M.R.)
9 126-127
Ukrainian
Ginzberg, Asher **6** 336-337
Uruguayan
Batlle y Ordóñez, José **2** 58-59

Journalists, American
documentary films
Wiseman, Frederick **16** 345-346
18th century
Barlow, Joel **2** 6-7
Bradford, William **2** 477
Paine, Thomas **12** 66-67
19th century
Beach, Moses Yale **2** 79-80
Bellamy, Edward **2** 134-135
Bennett, James Gordon Jr.
2 169-170
Bierce, Ambrose Gwinett **2** 269-270
Bigelow, John **2** 271-272
Blair, Francis Preston **2** 313-315

Bowles, Samuel **2** 464
Brownlow, William Gannaway
3 55-56
Buel, Jesse **3** 105
Dana, Charles Anderson **4** 384-385
Davis, Richard Harding **4** 422-423
De Bow, James Dunwoody Brownson **4** 441-442
Grady, Henry Woodfin **6** 482-483
Greeley, Horace **6** 515-517
Hale, Sarah Josepha **7** 74-75
Kendall, Amos **8** 494
Page, Walter Hines **12** 60-61
Phillips, David Graham **12** 280-281
Pulitzer, Joseph **12** 481-482
Riis, Jacob August **13** 169-170
Ripley, George **13** 179-180
Russwurm, John Brown **13** 381-382
Ward, Artemus **16** 112-113
19th-20th century
Bly, Nellie **2** 346-348
Bowers, Claude Gernade **2** 463
Caldwell, Erskine **3** 223-224
Creel, George **4** 304-305
Daniels, Josephus **4** 387
Donnelly, Ignatius **5** 62
Dunne, Finley Peter **5** 147-148
Fortune, Timothy Thomas **6** 18-21
Freeman, Douglas Southall **6** 91-92
Godkin, Edwin Lawrence **6** 380
Lippmann, Walter **9** 439-440
Mencken, Henry Louis **10** 481-483
Murrow, Edward Roscoe
11 265-266
Reed, John Silas **13** 76-77
Roosevelt, Eleanor **13** 275-277
Russell, Charles Edward **13** 374-375
Schurz, Carl **14** 44-45
Steffens, Lincoln **14** 410-411
Tarbell, Ida Minerva **15** 107-108
Villard, Oswald Garrison
15 498-499
Wallace, Henry **16** 73
White, William Allen **16** 240-241
photojournalists
Capa, Robert **3** 269-271
Freeman, Roland L. **6** 92-93
Mydans, Carl **11** 283-284
political analysis
Safire, William **13** 422-424
television
Bradley, Ed **2** 478-481
Buchanan, Patrick Joseph **3** 90-91
Chung, Connie **4** 47-48
Moyers, Bill **11** 214-216
Walters, Barbara **16** 86-88
20th century
Agee, James **1** 78-79
Ashmore, Harry Scott **1** 334-335
Bourke-White, Margaret **2** 455-456
Brownmiller, Susan **3** 56-57
Buckley, William F. Jr. **3** 96-97
Cronkite, Walter Leland Jr.
4 321-322
Friedan, Betty **6** 109-111
Golden, Harry **6** 402-403

Goodman, Ellen Holtz **6** 438-439
Haley, Alex **7** 76-78
Hecht, Ben **7** 248-250
Higgins, Marguerite **7** 378-380
Huntley and Brinkley **8** 49-51
Macdonald, Dwight **10** 81-83
Maynard, Robert Clyve **10** 366-367
McCarthy, Mary T. **10** 389-391
McGill, Ralph Emerson **10** 411-412
Pyle, Ernie **12** 493-494
Reston, James Barrett **13** 104-105
Rogers, Will **13** 251-252
Rowan, Carl T. **13** 329-330
Salisbury, Harrison Evans
    13 449-451
Shirer, William L. **14** 198-199
Snow, Edgar **14** 312-313
Steinem, Gloria **14** 418-419
Stone, I. F. **14** 470-471
Thompson, Dorothy **15** 195-196
Thompson, Hunter Stockton
    15 196-198
Tuchman, Barbara **15** 331-332
Wells-Barnett, Ida. B. **16** 198-199
White, T. H. **16** 236-237
Wolfe, Thomas Kennerly Jr.
    16 356-357
Woodward and Bernstein
    16 376-378
war correspondents (World War II)
    Capa, Robert **3** 269-271
    Pyle, Ernie **12** 493-494
see also Editors, American; Publishers, American

Journalists, The (play)
Freytag, Gustav **6** 107-108

Journey into Fear (book)
Ambler, Eric **1** 191-192

Journey of the Magi (painting)
Andrea del Sarto **1** 224-225
Sassetta **13** 492

Journey to a War (book)
Auden, Wystan Hugh **1** 364-366

Journey to Jerusalem (play)
Anderson, Maxwell **1** 219-220

Journey to Love (poem)
Williams, William Carlos **16** 308-309

Journey to the Beyond (poems)
Sachs, Nelly **13** 411-412

Journey to the Center of the Earth, A
(novel)
Verne, Jules **15** 467-469

Journey to the East, The (novel)
Hesse, Hermann **7** 367-369

Journey to the End of Night (novel)
Céline, Louis Ferdinand **3** 390-391

Journey without Maps (book)
Greene, Graham **6** 523-524

Journeyman (play)
Caldwell, Erskine **3** 223-224

Jouvenel, Henri de (1876-1935), French
journalist
Colette, Sidonie Gabrielle **4** 158-159

Jouvet, Louis (1887-1951), French actor
and director
Anouilh, Jean **1** 243-244
Giraudoux, Jean **6** 349-350

Jovian (331?-364), Roman emperor
363-364
Shahpur II **14** 140-141

JOWETT, BENJAMIN (1817-1893), English
educator and Greek scholar **8** 364-365
Clough, Arthur Hugh **4** 123-124
Green, Thomas Hill **6** 520-521
Swinburne, Algernon Charles **15** 54-55
Tennyson, Alfred **15** 144-146

Joxer (literary character)
O'Casey, Sean **11** 459-460

Joy Exceeding Glory (play)
Davis, Ossie **4** 421-422

Joy Luck Club, The (book)
Tan, Amy **15** 95-96

JOYCE, JAMES (1882-1941), Irish author
8 365-367
associates
    Beckett, Samuel **2** 102-104
    Callaghan, Edward Morley
        3 229-230
    Colum, Padraic **4** 174-175
    Ford, Ford Madox **6** 1-2
    Stephens, James **14** 430-431
    Svevo, Italo **15** 47-48
influence of
    Dos Passos, John Roderigo **5** 69-71
    Eliot, Thomas Stearns **5** 258-261
    Thomas, Dylan Marlais **15** 188-190
    Wilder, Thornton Niven **16** 276-277
    Wolfe, Thomas Clayton **16** 355-356
    Woolf, Virginia Stephen **16** 381-382
influenced by
    Flaubert, Gustave **5** 480-482
    Schnitzler, Arthur **14** 23-24
musical settings
    Barber, Samuel **1** 500-501
    Berio, Luciano **2** 194-195

Joyselle (play)
Maeterlinck, Maurice **10** 125-126

JUAN CARLOS I (born 1938), king of Spain
8 368-369

Juan Fernández Islands (southern Pacific
Ocean)
Dampier, William **4** 384

Juana
see Joanna (queen of Castile and León)

JUANA INÉS DE LA CRUZ, SISTER
(1651-1695), Mexican nun, poet, and
savant **8** 367-368

Juana la Beltraneja (1462-1530), Castilian
princess
Isabella I **8** 144-145
Manrique, Jorge **10** 210-211

Juanita la larga (novel)
Valera y Alcalá Galiano, Juan **15** 403

JUÁREZ, BENITO (1806-1872), Mexican
statesman, president 1857-1872
8 369-372
Álvarez, Juan **1** 184-185
Díaz, José de la Cruz Porfirio **4** 534-536
Lerdo de Tejada, Miguel **9** 351-352
Maximilian of Hapsburg **10** 358-360
Sierra, Justo **14** 217

Juárez Celmán, Miguel (1844-1909),
Argentine president 1886-1890
Roca, Julio Argentino **13** 218

Juárez Resuscitated (mural)
Orozco, José Clemente **12** 1-2

Jubelsenior, Der (book)
Richter, Johann Paul Friedrich
    13 150-151

Jubilee (musical)
Porter, Cole Albert **12** 405-406

Jubilee (novel)
Walker, Margaret **16** 67

Jubilo (film)
Goldwyn, Samuel **6** 416

Juchi (died 1227), Mongol leader
Batu Khan **2** 60-61

Judaea (Judea)
see Jewish history—Biblical Era (Judea)

JUDAEUS, PHILO (circa 20 B.C.-circa
A.D. 45), Hellenistic Jewish philosopher
12 282-283
Wolfson, Harry Austryn **16** 361-362

Judah
see Jewish history—Biblical Era (Judah)

JUDAH, THEODORE DEHONE
(1826-1863), American engineer and railroad promoter **8** 373-374
Huntington, Collis Potter **8** 49

JUDAH I (circa 135-circa 220), Jewish
scholar **8** 372-373
Abba Arika **1** 3-4
Akiba ben Joseph **1** 97-98

JUDAH HALEVI (circa 1085-circa 1150),
Spanish Hebrew poet **8** 373
Rosenzweig, Franz **13** 294

Judah Ha-Nasi
see Judah I

Judaism (religion)
Cabalist movement
    see Cabala
Hasidism
    see Hasidism
history
    see Jewish history
Karaite sect
    see Karaite sect
law
    Caro, Joseph ben Ephraim
        3 316-317
    Cohen, Hermann **4** 138-139
    Johanan ben Zakkai **8** 271-272

Lee Kuan Yew **9** 281-283
see also Mosaic law; Sanhedrin; Talmud
leaders
see Religious leaders, Jewish
Musar movement
see Musar movement
mysticism
see Mysticism—Jewish
Orthodox
Revel, Bernard **13** 108-109
post-Holocaust theology
Rubenstein, Richard L. **13** 343-344
prophets
see Bible—Old Testament
Torah
see Mosaic law
United States
Abrahams, Israel **1** 29
Finkelstein, Rabbi Louis **5** 448-450
Herberg, Will **7** 322-323
Heschel, Abraham Joshua **7** 358-359
Jung, Leo **8** 390-391
Kaplan, Mordecai Menahem **8** 435-436
Pinto, Isaac **12** 318
Revel, Bernard **13** 108-109
Rubenstein, Richard L. **13** 343-344
Schechter, Solomon **13** 524
Schindler, Solomon **14** 7-8
Silver, Abba Hillel **14** 232-233
Soloveitchik, Joseph Baer **14** 328-329
Wiesel, Elie **16** 263-264
Wise, Isaac Mayer **16** 342-343
Wise, Stephen Samuel **16** 344-345
Zionism
see Zionism

Judas Iscariot (New Testament; Apostle)
Jesus of Nazareth **8** 251-255

JUDAS MACCABEUS (died 160 B.C.), Jewish patriot and revolutionary **8** 374-375

Judas Maccabeus (musical composition)
Handel, George Frederick **7** 116-119

JUDD, CHARLES HUBBARD (1873-1946), psychologist and education reformer **8** 375-376

JUDD, DONALD (1928-1994), American sculptor and art writer **8** 376-377

Jude the Obscure (novel)
Hardy, Thomas **7** 150-152

Juden, Die (comedy)
Lessing, Gotthold Ephraim **9** 357-359

Juden von Zirndorf, Die (novel)
Wassermann, Jakob **16** 130-131

Judges
see Jurists—Judges

Judges, Book of (Old Testament)
Samuel **13** 457-458

Judgment Day (novel; play)
Farrell, James Thomas **5** 390-391
Rice, Elmer **13** 126-127

Judgment of Paris (music)
Arne, Thomas Augustine **1** 307-308
Congreve, William **4** 200-201

Judgment of Paris (painting)
Cranach, Lucas the Elder **4** 289-290
Rubens, Peter Paul **13** 339-342

Judgment of Solomon (painting)
Giorgione **6** 340-341

Judgment of the Baby Moses by Fire (painting)
Giorgione **6** 340-341

Judicial review
see Supreme Court (United States)—judicial review

Jüdische Witwe, Die (play)
Kaiser, Georg **8** 411-412

Judith (music)
Arne, Thomas Augustine **1** 307-308

Judith (painting)
Giorgione **6** 340-341

Judith (play)
Giraudoux, Jean **6** 349-350
Hebbel, Friedrich **7** 247

Judith (sculpture)
Donatello **5** 55-56

Judith (ship)
Drake, Francis **5** 94-96
Hawkins, John **7** 210-211

JUDSON, ADONIRAM (1788-1850), American Baptist missionary in Burma **8** 377-378

Juet, Robert (died 1611), English explorer
Hudson, Henry **8** 12-13

Jugend des Königs Henri IV, Die (book)
Mann, Heinrich **10** 201-202

Jugendstil
see Art Nouveau

Juglares (Spanish minstrels)
Gonzalo de Berceo **6** 431-432

Jugurtha (died 104 B.C.), King of Numidia 113-104
Marius, Gaius **10** 264-265
Sallust **13** 454
Sulla, Lucius Cornelius I **15** 21-22

Jui-tsung (ruled 685, 710-713), Chinese emperor
Hsüan-tsung, T'ang **8** 7-8

Juive, La (opera; Halévy)
Caruso, Enrico **3** 345

Juji
see Juchi

Jujushinron (book)
Kukai **9** 124-125

Jukes (book)
Dugdale, Richard Louis **5** 128-129

Jules and Jim (film)
Truffaut, François **15** 311-313

Julia (83?-54 B.C.), Roman matron
Brutus, Marcus Junius **3** 79-80

Caesar, Gaius Julius **3** 207-210
Pompey **12** 387-389

Julia Livilla (39 B.C.-14 A.D.), Roman princess
Seneca the Younger, Lucius Annaeus **14** 103-105

Julia Marlowe (book)
Russell, Charles Edward **13** 374-375

Julian calendar
Omar Khayyam **11** 510-511
Peter I **12** 253-256
see also Calendar

Julian of Eclanum (380-circa 455), Italian bishop and theologian
Pelagius **12** 189-190

JULIAN OF NORWICH (1342-after 1416), English mystic **8** 381

JULIAN (The Apostate; Flavius Claudius Julianus; 331-363), Roman emperor 361-363 **8** 378-379
Constantine I **4** 209-211
Ibsen, Henrik **8** 98-100
Shahpur II **14** 140-141

JULIANA (born 1909), queen of the Netherlands (1948-1980) **8** 379-380
Wilhelmina **16** 278-279

JULIAS OF ROME, THE (Julia Domna, ca. 169-ca. 217; Julia Maesa, ca. 164-225; Julia Soamias, died 222; and Julia Mammaea, died 234), empresses of the so-called Severan Dynasty of Rome **8** 381-384

Julie de Carneilhan (novel)
Colette, Sidonie Gabrielle **4** 158-159

Julienne, Jean de (1686-1766), French engraver
Boucher, François **2** 440-442
Watteau, Antoine **16** 143-144

Juliet of the Spirits (film)
Fellini, Federico **5** 408-409

Juliette (opera)
Martinu, Bohuslav **10** 299-300

Julio-Claudian emperors (Roman Empire; ruled 27 B.C.-68 A.D.)
Caligula **3** 228-229
Nero Claudius Caesar **11** 342-344
Suetonius Tranquillus, Gaius **15** 13
Tacitus **15** 70-72
Vespasian **15** 475-476

Julius Africanus (book)
Leopardi, Giacomo **9** 344-345

Julius Caesar (play; Shakespeare)
Booth, Edwin **2** 401-402
Plaatje, Solomon Tshekisho **12** 341-342
Shakespeare, William **14** 142-145

JULIUS II (Giuliano della Rovere; 1443-1513), pope 1503-1513 **8** 384-386
Borgia, Cesare **2** 412-413
Bramante, Donato **2** 493-494
Budé, Guillaume **3** 102-103
Castiglione, Baldassare **3** 360-361
Erasmus, Desiderius **5** 298-300

Leo X **9** 332-334
Michelangelo Buonarroti **11** 2-5
Raphael **13** 40-42
Sangallo family **13** 464-466

Julius III (Giammaria Ciocchi del Monte; 1487-1555), pope 1550-1555
Palestrina, Giovanni Pierluigi da **12** 70-72
Pius V **12** 332-333
Vasari, Giorgio **15** 442-443
Vignola, Giacomo da **15** 493-494

Julliard School of Music (New York City)
Berio, Luciano **2** 194-195
Diamond, David **4** 527-529
Sessions, Roger Huntington **14** 117-118

Jullien, Louis Antoine (1812-1860), French conductor
Fry, William Henry **6** 136-137

July 4, 1956 (painting)
Soulages, Pierre **14** 350-351

July Hay (painting)
Benton, Thomas Hart **2** 178-179

July Monarchy (France)
see France—1830-1848

July Revolution
see Revolution of 1830 (France; July Revolution)

JUMBLATT, KAMAL (1917-1977), Lebanese ideologue and Druze leader **8** 386-387
Sadr, Musa al- **13** 420-422

Jumblies, The (verse)
Lear, Edward **9** 265-266

Jumbo (elephant)
Barnum, Phineas Taylor **2** 13-15

Jumbo (stage show)
Rodgers, Richard Charles **13** 234-236

Jump Back, Honey, Jump Back (song)
Dawson, William Levi **4** 427-428

Jumping Frog of Calaveras County, The (story; Twain)
Twain, Mark **15** 363-366
Ward, Artemus **16** 112-113

JUNAYD, ABU AL-QASIM IBN MUHAM-MAD AL (circa 830-910), Islamic mystic **8** 388

June Bug (airplane)
Curtiss, Glenn Hammond **4** 350-351

June Days (France; 1848)
Blanc, Louis **2** 318-319
Thiers, Louis Adolphe **15** 181-182

June, Jennie
see Croly, Jane Cunningham

June Moon (play)
Lardner, Ringgold Wilmer **9** 204-205

JUNG, CARL GUSTAV (1875-1961), Swiss psychologist and psychiatrist **8** 388-389
Bleuler, Eugen **2** 325
Freud, Sigmund **6** 103-106
Graham, Martha **6** 485-486

Hesse, Hermann **7** 367-369
Horney, Karen Danielsen **7** 508-509
White, Patrick Victor Martindale **16** 233-235

JUNG, LEO (1892-1987), American Orthodox Jewish Rabbi **8** 390-391

Jung Siegfried (ballade)
Webern, Anton **16** 160-162

Junge Gelehrte, Der (comedy)
Lessing, Gotthold Ephraim **9** 357-359

Junge Siegfried, Der (opera)
Wagner, Richard **16** 40-43

JÜNGER, ERNST (born 1895), German author **8** 391-392

Jungfrau von Orleans, Die (play)
Schiller, Johann Christoph Friedrich von **14** 4-7

Jung-hsi Studio (painting)
Ni Tsan **11** 400

Jungle Books (tales)
Kipling, Joseph Rudyard **9** 32-33

Jungle, Les (poem)
Leconte de Lisle, Charles Marie René **9** 273-274

Jungle of the Cities (play)
Brecht, Bertolt **2** 512-514

Jungle The (novel)
Sinclair, Upton Beale Jr. **14** 248-249

Jungmann, Josef (1773-1847), Czech writer and philologist
Palacký, František **12** 69-70

Jung-Wien (literary group; Austria)
Hofmannsthal, Hugo von **7** 443-444
Schnitzler, Arthur **14** 23-24

Junimea (literary group; Romania)
Eminescu, Mihail **5** 280-281

Junin, battle of (1823)
Bolívar, Simón **2** 375-377

Junkers, Hugo (1859-1935), German engineer
Tupolev, Andrei Nikolaevich **15** 341-342

Juno (literary character)
Virgil **15** 507-510

Juno and the Paycock (play)
O'Casey, Sean **11** 459-460

Junto (club, established 1727)
Franklin, Benjamin **6** 60-64

Jupiter (music)
Mozart, Wolfgang Amadeus **11** 218-221

Jupiter (mythology)
Diocletian **5** 19-20
Ovid **12** 34-36

Jupiter (painting)
Ingres, Jean Auguste Dominique **8** 121-123
Rembrandt Harmensz van Rijn **13** 91-95
Veronese, Paolo **15** 469-470

Jupiter (planet)
Barnard, Edward Emerson **2** 8-9
Brahe, Tycho **2** 489-490
Galileo Galilei **6** 180-183
Herschel, William **7** 341-343
Laplace, Marquis de **9** 202-204

Jupiter (play)
Sheridan, Richard Brinsley **14** 183-184

Jurassic Park (book)
Crichton, John Michael **4** 308-310

Jürchen (Asian people)
Ch'in Kuei **3** 524-525
Chu Hsi **4** 40-43
Kwangjong **9** 140
Wang Kon **16** 101
Yi Sng-gye **16** 458-459
Yi Sunsin **16** 459-461
Yo Fei **16** 462

Jürchen dynasty
see Chin dynasty

Jurg Reinhardt (novel)
Frisch, Max **6** 118-119

Jurgen (book)
Cabell, James Branch **3** 195-196

Jurisprudence (science of law)
Africa
Gluckman, Max **6** 374-375
Europe
Bodin, Jean **2** 356-357
Bryce, James **3** 85
Carneades **3** 309
Grotius, Hugo **7** 18-19
Mommsen, Theodor **11** 94-95
Montesquieu **11** 123-125
Savigny, Friedrich Karl von **13** 502-503
Vico, Giambattista **15** 480-481
United States
Cardozo, Benjamin Nathan **3** 288-290
Holmes, Oliver Wendell Jr. **7** 458-459
Kent, James **8** 510-511
Pound, Roscoe **12** 417-418
Shaw, Lemuel **14** 164-165
Wythe, George **16** 415
see also Jurists; Law

Jurists
American
see Jurists, American
Ashanti
Anokye, Okomfo **1** 242-243
Australian
Barton, Edmund **2** 39-40
Evatt, Herbert Vere **5** 341-343
Griffith, Samuel Walker **6** 545-546
British
see English, Scottish (below)
Canadian
Haliburton, Thomas Chandler **7** 80
Robinson, John Beverley **13** 210
Scott, Francis Reginald **14** 66-67
Dutch

Grotius, Hugo **7** 18-19
English
    Bentham, Jeremy **2** 176-178
    Bigge, John Thomas **2** 272
    Blackstone, William **2** 310-311
    Coke, Edward **4** 141-142
    Jennings, Robert Yewdall **8** 246-247
    Maitland, Frederic William
        10 154-155
Filipino
    Laurel, Salvador H. **9** 226-227
French
    Montesquieu **11** 123-125
German
    Gierke, Otto von **6** 311-312
    Herzog, Roman **7** 355-357
    Pufendorf, Samuel von **12** 477-478
    Reuchlin, Johann **13** 106-107
    Savigny, Friedrich Karl von
        13 502-503
    Thomasius **15** 193-194
Guyanese
    Ramphal, Shridath Surendranath
        13 19-20
Indian
    Das, Chitta Ranjan **4** 401-402
    Gandhi, Mohandas Karamchand
        6 201-204
    Sapru, Tej Bahadur **13** 480-481
Islamic
    Marāghī, Mustafā al- **10** 228-229
    Averroës **1** 382-383
    ibn Battuta, Muhammad **8** 91-92
    ibn Hazm, Abu Muhammad Ali
        8 93
    Junayd, Abu al-Qasim ibn Muham-
        mad al **8** 388
Italian
    Becarria, Marchese di **2** 97-98
    Vico, Giambattista **15** 480-481
Nigerian
    Elias, Taslim Olawale **5** 250-251
Portuguese
    Sá, Mem de **13** 395
Roman
    Ulpian, Domitius **15** 385-386
Russian
    Pobedonostsev, Konstantin Petrovich
        12 360-361
Scottish
    Boswell, James **2** 432-434
    Bryce, James **3** 85
Spanish
    Altamira Y Crevea, Rafael **1** 179

Jurists, American

• JUDGES
    associate justices (United States
        Supreme Court; 18th century)
        Chase, Samuel **3** 475-476
        Paterson, William **12** 132-133
        Rutledge, John **13** 387-388
        Wilson, James **16** 323-324
    associate justices (United States
        Supreme Court; 19th century)
        Curtis, Benjamin Robbins **4** 349

    Field, Stephen Johnson
        5 441-442
    Harlan, John Marshall **7** 156-157
    Lamar, Lucius Quintus Cincinna-
        tus **9** 170-171
    McLean, John **10** 422-423
    Miller, Samuel Freeman
        11 29-30
    Story, Joseph **14** 480-481
    associate justices (United States
        Supreme Court; 20th century)
        Black, Hugo Lafayette **2** 301-303
        Blackmun, Harry **2** 309-310
        Brandeis, Louis Dembitz
            2 496-497
        Brennan, William J. Jr.
            2 514-515
        Breyer, Stephen **2** 524-527
        Byrnes, James Francis **3** 191-192
        Cardozo, Benjamin Nathan
            3 288-290
        Clark, Tom Campbell **4** 81-82
        Douglas, William Orville
            5 83-85
        Fortas, Abe **6** 16-17
        Frankfurter, Felix **6** 57
        Ginsburg, Ruth Bader **6** 333-336
        Goldberg, Arthur Joseph
            6 397-398
        Harlan, John Marshall **7** 157-159
        Holmes, Oliver Wendell Jr.
            7 458-459
        Jackson, Robert Houghwout
            8 182-183
        Kennedy, Anthony M. **8** 498-500
        Marshall, Thurgood **10** 282-284
        Murphy, Frank **11** 260-261
        O'Connor, Sandra Day
            11 468-470
        Powell, Lewis F. Jr. **12** 426-428
        Rehnquist, William Hubbs
            13 82-84
        Scalia, Antonin **13** 513-514
        Souter, David H. **14** 355-356
        Stevens, John Paul **14** 440-441
        Stewart, Potter **14** 449-451
        Thomas, Clarence **15** 186-188
        White, Byron R. **16** 227-228
        Whittaker, Charles Evans
            16 255-256
    chief justices (United States
        Supreme Court)
        Burger, Warren E. **3** 133-136
        Chase, Salmon Portland
            3 473-475
        Hughes, Charles Evans **8** 15-16
        Jay, John **8** 230-232
        Marshall, John **10** 279-281
        Rehnquist, William Hubbs
            13 82-84
        Rutledge, John **13** 387-388
        Stone, Harlan Fiske **14** 468-470
        Taft, William Howard **15** 78-81
        Taney, Roger Brooke **15** 98-99
        Vinson, Fred **15** 503-505
        Waite, Morrison Remick **16** 46
        Warren, Earl **16** 117-120

    White, Edward Douglass
        16 230-231
    colonial courts
        Henderson, Richard **7** 278-279
        Livingston, Robert R. **9** 462-463
        Logan, James **9** 487-488
        Morris, Lewis **11** 183-184
        Sewall, Samuel **14** 123-124
    county courts
        Altgeld, John Peter **1** 180-182
    district courts
        Sirica, John Joseph **14** 257-258
    federal courts
        Hand, Billings Learned **7** 116
        Hopkinson, Francis **7** 496-497
        Palmer, Alexander Mitchell
            12 77-78
        Wilmot, David **16** 312-313
    state courts
        Allen, Florence Ellinwood
            1 164-165
        Atchison, David Rice **1** 357-358
        Ervin, Sam J. Jr. **5** 316-317
        George, James Zachariah
            6 276-277
        Kent, James **8** 510-511
        Lindsey, Benjamin Barr
            9 425-426
        Pound, Roscoe **12** 417-418
        Reeve, Tapping **13** 79-80
        Shaw, Lemuel **14** 164-165
        Shippen, Edward **14** 197-198
        Tourgée, Albion Winegar
            15 277-278
        Tyler, Royall **15** 371-372

• LAWYERS
    18th century
        Burr, Aaron **3** 156-159
        Dickinson, John **4** 543-544
        Galloway, Joseph **6** 186-187
        Leonard, Daniel **9** 336-337
        Martin, Luther **10** 289-290
        Reeve, Tapping **13** 79-80
        Wythe, George **16** 415
    19th century
        Benjamin, Judah Philip
            2 163-164
        Birney, James Gillespie
            2 283-284
        Bledsoe, Albert Taylor **2** 324-325
        Bristow, Benjamin Helm **3** 9-10
        Dana, Richard Henry Jr.
            4 385-386
        Eaton, Dorman Bridgman
            5 190-191
        Evarts, William Maxwell
            5 340-341
        Field, David Dudley **5** 439-440
        Forbes, John **5** 507-508
        Gary, Elbert Henry **6** 229-230
        Ingersoll, Robert Green
            8 120-121
    19th-20th century
        Bryan, William Jennings **3** 80-82
        Darrow, Clarence Seward
            4 396-397

Hillquit, Morris **7** 393-394
Lansing, Robert **9** 200
20th century
  Allen, Florence Ellinwood
    1 164-165
  Bailey, F. Lee **1** 441-443
  Clinton, Hillary Rodham
    4 115-117
  Cochran, Johnnie **4** 128-131
  Cox, Archibald **4** 283-284
  Dees, Morris S. Jr. **4** 456-457
  Dewey, Thomas Edmund **4** 524
  Edelman, Marian Wright
    5 202-204
  Ervin, Sam J. Jr. **5** 316-317
  Freeh, Louis J. **6** 90-91
  Gary, Elbert Henry **6** 229-230
  Hill, Anita **7** 382-385
  Houston, Charles Hamilton
    7 523-526
  Jaworski, Leon **8** 229-230
  Johnson, James Weldon
    8 304-305
  Kunstler, William M. **9** 131-133
  Nader, Ralph **11** 290-291
  Reno, Janet **13** 99-101
  Riordan, Richard Joseph
    13 177-179
  Sayre, Francis Bowes **13** 509
  von Mehren, Robert Brandt
    16 24-25
  White, Byron R. **16** 227-228
  Yasui, Minoru **16** 440-444
  see also Judges (above)

Jus gentium (law)
  Suárez, Francisco **15** 8

Just (literary character)
  Lessing, Gotthold Ephraim **9** 357-359

Just Ask for George (play)
  Callaghan, Edward Morley **3** 229-230

Just Assassins, The (play)
  Camus, Albert **3** 255-257

JUST, ERNEST (1883-1941), American
marine biologist **8** 392-393

Just One of Those Things (song)
  Porter, Cole Albert **12** 405-406

Just So Stories (stories)
  Kipling, Joseph Rudyard **9** 32-33

Justes, Les (play)
  Camus, Albert **3** 255-257

Justice (play; Galsworthy)
  Barrymores **2** 28-30
  Galsworthy, John **6** 189-190

Justice (sculpture)
  Rush, William **13** 365-366

Justice, Department of (United States)
  Arnold, Thurman Wesley **1** 314
  Hoover, John Edgar **7** 485-487
  Kennedy, Robert Francis **8** 508-509
  Palmer, Alexander Mitchell **12** 77-78

Justice Denied in Massachusetts (poem)
  Millay, Edna St. Vincent **11** 24-25

Justice Party (Turkey)
  Demirel, Süleyman **4** 490-493

Justicialismo (Argentina; politics)
  Perón, Juan Domingo **12** 228-230

Justification by faith (theology)
  Küng, Hans **9** 129-130
  Latimer, Hugh **9** 221
  Luther, Martin **10** 48-51
  Melancthon, Philip **10** 466-467

Justin I (circa 450-527), Byzantine emperor
518-527
  Justinian I **8** 393-395

JUSTIN MARTYR, (circa 100-circa 165),
Early Christian apologist **8** 395-396

Justina (literary character)
  Calderón, Pedro **3** 221-222

Justine (novel)
  Sade, Comte de **13** 416-418

**Justing betwix James Watsoun and Jhone
Barbour, The** (poem)
  Lyndsay, David **10** 66-67

JUSTINIAN I (circa 482-565), Byzantine
emperor 527-565 **8** 393-395
  academies closed (529)
    Plato **12** 345-347
    Plotinus **12** 358-359
  family
    Theodora **15** 172-175
  law code
    Leo III **9** 330-332
    Niebuhr, Barthold Georg
      11 385-386

Ulpian, Domitius **15** 385-386
  see also Law codes—Byzantium
military campaigns
  Belisarius **2** 128-129
  Cassiodorus, Flavius Magnus Aure-
    lius **3** 357-358
  Khosrow I **8** 538-539
  Procopius of Caesarea **12** 457-458

Justinian II (669-711), Byzantine emperor
687-695, 705-711
  Leo III **9** 330-332

JUSTO, AGUSTIN PEDRO (1876-1943),
Argentine general, president 1932-1938
8 396

Justus of Ghent (1430/35-1476?), Flemish
painter
  Piero della Francesca **12** 301-302
  van der Goes, Hugo **15** 416-417

Jusuf and Zulaikha (poem)
  Firdausi **5** 451-452

Jutland, battle of (1916)
  George VI **6** 275
  Jellicoe, John Rushworth **8** 242-243

JUVARA, FILIPPO (1678-1736), Italian
architect and designer **8** 396-397

JUVENAL (Decimus Junius Juvenalis; died
after 127), Roman satirist **8** 397-399
  Boileau-Despréaux, Nicholas
    2 369-371
  Congreve, William **4** 200-201
  Horace **7** 500-503
  Johnson, Samuel **8** 315-317
  Martialis, Marcus Valerius **10** 286-287
  Vaughan, Henry **15** 444-445

Juvenile literature
  see Literature for children

Juvenilia (book)
  Galileo Galilei **6** 180-183

Juvenilia (poems)
  Carducci, Giosuè **3** 290-291

Juvenis qui puellam (motet)
  Dufay, Guillaume **5** 125-126

Juxon, William (1582-1663), English bishop and statesman
  Charles I **3** 450-452

K

Kaaba (mosque; Mecca)
Sinan, Kodja Mimar **14** 245-246

Kabaka Alone (political party; Buganda)
Mutesa II **11** 277-278

Kabale und Liebe (play; F. Schiller)
Lewis, Matthew Gregory **9** 390-391
Schiller, Johann Christoph Friedrich von **14** 4-7

KABALEVSKY, DMITRI (1904-1987), Soviet composer, pianist, and conductor **8** 400-401

Kabuliwalla (story)
Rabindranath Tagore **12** 529-531

Kabyle Berbers (North African people)
Abd el-Kadir **1** 15

KADALIE, CLEMENTS (circa 1896-1951), South Africa's first Black national trade union leader **8** 401-402

KÁDÁR, JÁNOS (born 1912), Hungarian statesman **8** 402-403

Kaddish (music)
Bernstein, Leonard **2** 218-219

Kaddish ... (poems)
Ginsberg, Allen **6** 332-333

KADU
see Kenya African Democratic Union

Kafan (story)
Premchand **12** 439

KAFKA, FRANZ (1883-1924), Czech-born German novelist and short-story writer **8** 403-406
Beckett, Samuel **2** 102-104
Grass, Günter **6** 496-497
Hidayat, Sadiq **7** 377-378
Laye, Camara **9** 257-259
Robbe-Grillet, Alain **13** 189-190
Schuller, Gunther **14** 37-38

Kagi (novel)
Tanizaki, Junichiro **15** 101-102

Kahlenberg, battle of the (1683)
John III **8** 276-277

KAHLO, FRIDA (1907-1954), Mexican painter **8** 406-407

KAHN, ALBERT (1869-1942), American architect **8** 407-408

KAHN, LOUIS I. (1901-1974), American architect **8** 408-410
Piano, Renzo **12** 289-291

Kahn, Otto (1867-1934), American banker
Crane, Hart **4** 291-293

Kahr, Gustav von (1862-1934), Bavarian statesman
Hitler, Adolf **7** 417-420

Kai-du (died 1301), Mongol khan 1248
Kublai Khan **9** 115-118

Kaifeng (city, China)
Chu Hsi **4** 40-43

KAIFU TOSHIKI (born 1931), Japanese prime minister (1989-1991) **8** 410-411

Kaim, al- (Qa'im, al-; ruled 1031-1075), Abbasid caliph
Alp Arslan **1** 178-179

Kai-Oi (poems)
Basho, Matsuo **2** 45-48

Kaiping mines (1877)
Li Hung-Chang **9** 407-409

KAISER, GEORG (1878-1945), German playwright **8** 411-412
Brecht, Bertolt **2** 512-514
Weill, Kurt **16** 174-175

KAISER, HENRY JOHN (1882-1967), American industrialist **8** 412-413

Kaiser Karls Geisel (play)
Hauptmann, Gerhart Johann Robert **7** 199-201

Kaiser Octavianus (play)
Tieck, Ludwig **15** 218-219

Kaiser Wilhelm Institutes
for Biology
Meyerhof, Otto Fritz **10** 537-539
Spemann, Hans **14** 368-369
for Carbon Research
Fischer, Emil **5** 456-457
for Chemistry
Fischer, Emil **5** 456-457
Haber, Fritz **7** 56-58
Hahn, Otto **7** 64-65
for Medical Research
see Max Planck Institute for Medical Research

Kaiser-Hymn (musical composition)
Haydn, Franz Joseph **7** 219-221

Kaishinto
see Progressive party (Japan)

Kajar
see Qajar

Kakemono (scrolls)
Sesshu, Toya **14** 116-117

Kakuyu
see Toba Sojo

KALAKAUA, DAVID (1836-1891), king of Hawaiian Islands 1874-1891 **8** 413-414
Dole, Sanford Ballard **5** 46
Liliuokalani, Lydia Kamakaeha **9** 411-412

Kalamazoo (poem)
Lindsay, Vachel **9** 424-425

Kalendarium Pennsilvaniense (almanac; Samuel Atkins)
Bradford, William **2** 476-477

Kalendergeschichten (stories)
Brecht, Bertolt **2** 512-514

Kalevala (Finnish epic)
Sibelius, Jean Julius Christian **14** 211-212
Tschernichowsky, Saul **15** 323

Kalgoorlie (municipality; Australia)
Forrest, John **6** 12-13

Kali (Hindu deity)
Ramakrishna, Sri **13** 11-13

KALIDASA (flourished 4th-5th century), Indian poet and dramatist **8** 414-415
Harsha **7** 181-182

Kalinga Edicts (India)
Asoka **1** 341-342

Kalka River, battle of (1223)
Batu Khan **2** 60-61

Kalkbrenner, F.W.M. (1784-1849), German
pianist and composer
Chopin, Frédéric François **4** 16-18

Kallen, Horace Meyer (1882-1974), American author and educator
Bourne, Randolph Silliman **2** 456-457

Kallias, Peace of (449 B.C.)
Phidias **12** 265-267

Kalonji-Ditunga, Albert (born 1929), Congolese leader
Lumumba, Patrice Emery **10** 43-45

Kama Sutra, The (book)
Burton, Richard Francis **3 164-166**

Kamako
see Fujiwara Kamatari

Kamakura Period
see Japan—1185-1338

KAMARAJ, KUMARASWAMI (1903-1975),
Indian political leader **8** 415

Kamarinsky (music)
Glinka, Mikhail Ivanovich **6** 369-370

Kambalu (poem; Longfellow)
Hulagu Khan **8** 27-28

Kambona, Oscar (born 1928), Tanzanian
politician
Nyerere, Julius Kamberage **11** 447-449

Kamchatka (peninsula; northeastern Russia)
Bering, Vitus **2** 193-194

KAMEHAMEHA I (circa 1758-1819), king
of the Hawaiian Islands 1795-1819 **8** 416

Kamehameha II (1797-1824), king of
Hawaiian Islands 1819-1824
Kamehameha I **8** 416
Kamehameha III **8** 416-417

KAMEHAMEHA III (circa 1814-1854), king
of the Hawaiian Islands 1825-1854
8 416-417
Kamehameha I **8** 416

KAMENEV, LEV BORISOVICH
(1883-1936), Russian politician
8 417-418
Bukharin, Nikolai Ivanovich **3** 112-113
Stalin, Joseph **14** 393-396
Trotsky, Leon **15** 302-305
Zinoviev, Grigori Evseevich **16** 521-522

KAMERLINGH ONNES, HEIKE
(1853-1926), Dutch physicist **8** 418-420

Kamisori
see Tojo, Hideki

Kamitsumiya no Miko
see Shotoku Taishi

Kammersänger, Der (play)
Wedekind, Frank **16** 166-167

Kammerspiele (Munich)
Brecht, Bertolt **2** 512-514

KAMMU (737-806), Japanese emperor
781-806 **8** 420
Saicho **13** 426-428

Kampaku (Japan)
Fujiwara Michinaga **6** 145-146

Kampaner Thal, Das (book)
Richter, Johann Paul Friedrich
13 150-151

Kampeneer, Pieter de
see Campaña, Pedro de

Kampf um Rom, Der (novel)
Huch, Ricarda **8** 11-12

Kampuchea
see Cambodia

Kampuchean People's Revolutionary Party
Hun Sen **8** 39-42

Kanchenjanga (film)
Ray, Satyajit **13** 60-61

KANDINSKY, WASSILY (1866-1944), Russian painter **8** 420-422
associates
Arp, Jean **1** 317-318
Hartley, Marsden **7** 186
Marc, Franz **10** 231
Miró, Joan **11** 53-54
influence of
Hofmann, Hans **7** 442-443
Mies van der Rohe, Ludwig
11 10-12
influenced by
Beardsley, Aubrey Vincent **2** 88-89
Böcklin, Arnold **2** 354-355
works compared
Dove, Arthur Garfield **5** 86-87
Malevich, Kasimir **10** 168-169
see also Blaue Reiter (art group);
Blaue Vier (art group)

KANE, JOHN (1860-1934), Scottish-born
American primitive painter **8** 422

KANE, PAUL (1810-1871), Canadian
painter and writer **8** 422-423

K'ANG YU-WEI (1858-1927), Chinese
scholar and philosopher **8** 426-428
Chang Chien **3** 429-430
Chang Chih-tung **3** 430-431
Ku Chieh-kang **9** 120-121
Kuang-hsü **9** 111-112
Liang Ch'i-ch'ao **9** 395-396
Sun Yat-sen **15** 35-39
Tz'u-hsi **15** 375-376

Kangaroo (novel)
Lawrence, David Herbert **9** 247-248

K'ANG-HSI (1654-1722), Chinese emperor
1661-1722 **8** 423-426
Huang Tsung-hsi **8** 9-10
Qianlong **12** 502-505

Kanghwa, Treaty of (1876)
Taewŏn'gun, Hŭngsŏn **15** 74-75

Kanille, Feodor
see Canillé, Théodore

Kanis, Saint Peter
see Peter Canisius, Saint

KANISHKA (ca. 78- ca. 103), Kashan ruler
8 428-429

Kankan Musa
see Musa Mansa

Kannami (died 1384), Japanese No theater
actor
Zeami, Kanze **16** 492-493

Kannon
see Kwannon (bodhisattva)

Kano Motonobu (1476-1559), Japanese
painter
Eitoku, Kano **5** 242

Kano school
see Japanese art—Kano school

Kansas (state, United States)
slavery issue
Bailey, Gamaliel **1** 444-445
Brown, John **3** 39-41
Douglas, Stephen Arnold **5** 80-82
Frémont, John Charles **6** 97-98
Howe, Samuel Gridley **7** 537
Sumner, Charles **15** 30-31
Thayer, Eli **15** 168
Walker, Robert John **16** 67-68
statehood (1861)
Buchanan, James **3** 89-90
temperance movement
Nation, Carry Amelia Moore
11 321-322
see also Kansas-Nebraska Act (1854)

Kansas, University of
Becker, Carl Lotus **2** 100-101

Kansas-Nebraska Act (1854)
opponents (north)
Brown, John **3** 39-41
Buchanan, James **3** 89-90
Chase, Salmon Portland **3** 473-475
Everett, Edward **5** 344
Lincoln, Abraham **9** 415-418
Morton, Oliver Hazard Perry Throck
11 197-198
Seward, William Henry **14** 124-125
Sumner, Charles **15** 30-31
Thayer, Eli **15** 168
Trumbull, Lyman **15** 317-318
Wade, Benjamin Franklin **16** 38-39
Wilmot, David **16** 312-313
opponents (south)
Blair, Francis Preston **2** 313-315
Houston, Samuel **7** 526-527
supporters (north)
Douglas, Stephen Arnold **5** 80-82
Pierce, Franklin **12** 300-301
supporters (south)
Atchison, David Rice **1** 357-358
Tyler, John **15** 368-369

Kansas Pacific Railroad (United States)
Buffalo Bill **3** 105-106
Frémont, John Charles **6** 97-98
McCoy, Joseph Geiting **10** 403-404

Kansu (province , China)
Quin Shi Huang-Di **12** 515-518

KANT, IMMANUEL (1724-1804), German
philosopher **8** 430-432
associates
Basedow, Johann Bernhard **2** 44-45

Herder, Johann Gottfried von
7 327-328
critiques on
Hamann, Johann Georg **7** 92
Schweitzer, Albert **14** 55-56
influence of (18th-19th century)
Coleridge, Samuel Taylor **4** 154-156
Fichte, Johann Gottlieb **5** 435-436
Fries, Jakob Friedrich **6** 116-117
Niebuhr, Barthold Georg
11 385-386
Schelling, Friedrich Wilhelm Joseph
von **13** 526-527
Schiller, Johann Christoph Friedrich
von **14** 4-7
Schleiermacher, Friedrich Ernst
Daniel **14** 11-12
influence of (19th century)
Bakunin, Mikhail Aleksandrovich
1 458-460
Cousin, Victor **4** 273-274
Palacký, František **12** 69-70
Ritschl, Albrecht Benjamin **13** 180
Rosmini-Serbati, Antonio
13 296-297
Schopenhauer, Arthur **14** 29-31
influence of (19th-20th century)
Adler, Felix **1** 63-64
Dewey, John **4** 520-523
Dilthey, Wilhelm Christian Ludwig
5 10
Frege, Gottlob **6** 93-94
influence of (20th century)
Cohen, Morris Raphael **4** 139-140
Jaspers, Karl **8** 225-226
Lewis, Clarence Irving **9** 381
Rahner, Karl **13** 4-5
influenced by
Hume, David **8** 31-34
Leibniz, Gottfried Wilhelm von
9 307-310
opponents
Jacobi, Friedrich Heinrich
8 189-190
Mendelssohn, Moses **10** 488-489
Richter, Johann Paul Friedrich
13 150-151
see also Neo-Kantianism
Kant-Laplace nebular hypothesis (astro-
physics)
Jeans, James Hopwood **8** 235-236
KANU
see Kenya African National Union
Kao Ying-hsiang (flourished early 17th cen-
tury) Chinese bandit
Li Tzu-Ch'eng **9** 452
Kaoru (literary character)
Mùrasaki Shikibu **11** 252-253
Kao-seng chuan (Buddhist text)
Kumarajiva **9** 127
Kao-tsu (died circa 501), emperor of South-
ern Ch'i dynasty
Liang Wu-ti **9** 396-397
KAO-TSUNG (1107-1187), Chinese emper-
or **8** 433

Ch'in Kuei **3** 524-525
Chu Hsi **4** 40-43
Wu Tse-t'ien **16** 408
Yo Fei **16** 462
Kaoyo (play)
Tanizaki, Junichiro **15** 101-102
Kapital, Das (book; Marx)
Althusser, Louis **1** 182-183
Engels, Friedrich **5** 286-288
Marx, Karl **10** 304-308-231
Shaw, George Bernard **14** 163-164
KAPITSA, PYOTR LEONIDOVICH (born
1894), Soviet physicist **8** 433-435
Cockcroft, John Douglas **4** 131-132
Landau, Lev Davidovich **9** 184-185
KAPLAN, MORDECAI MENAHEM
(1881-1983), American Jewish theologian
and educator **8** 435-436
Kaplana (poems)
Rabindranath Tagore **12** 529-531
Kapo Reforms (1894; Korea)
Kim Ok-kyun **9** 7-8
Kapodistria (play)
Kazantzakis, Nikos **8** 466-468
KAPP, WOLFGANG (1858-1922), German
nationalist politician **8** 436
Ebert, Friedrich **5** 193-194
Kappel, battle of (1531)
Zwingli, Huldreich **16** 537-538
Kapsin Ilrok (book)
Kim Ok-kyun **9** 7-8
KAPTEYN, JACOBUS CORNELIS
(1851-1922), Dutch astronomer
8 436-437
Eddington, Arthur Stanley **5** 201-202
Oort, Jan Hendrik **11** 523-524
Shapley, Harlow **14** 155-156
Kara Sea (arm of Arctic Ocean)
Nordenskjöld, Nils Adolf Erik
11 421-422
KARADZIC, RADOVAN (born 1945),
leader of the Serbian Republic **8** 437-440
Karaite sect (Judaism)
Anan ben David **1** 207-208
Saadia ben Joseph al-Fayumi **13** 396
Schechter, Solomon **13** 524
Kara-Khitai (Asian people)
Genghis Khan **6** 263-265
Karakol
see Przhevalsk
KARAMANLIS, CONSTANTINE (born
1907), Greek member of parliament,
prime minister (1955-1963; 1974-1980),
and president (1980-1985) **8** 440-441
KARAMZIN, NIKOLAI MIKHAILOVICH
(1766-1826), Russian historian and
author **8** 441-442
Mussorgsky, Modest Petrovich
11 274-276
Pushkin, Aleksandr Sergeevich
12 489-491

KARAN, DONNA (born 1948), American
fashion designer and businesswoman
8 442-444
Karanatilaka (book; Vijayanandin)
Biruni, Abu Rayhan al- **2** 284-285
Karankawa Indians (North America)
Cabeza de Vaca, Álvar Núñez **3** 197
Karasoke Research Center (Rwanda)
Fossey, Dian **6** 23-24
KARENGA, MAULANA (born Ronald
McKinley Everett; born 1941), African
American author, educator, amd propo-
nent of black culturalism **8** 444-447
Karens (ethnic group; Burma)
Ne Win **11** 364-365
Karim, Prince
see Aga Khan IV
KARIM KHAN ZAND (died 1779), Iranian
ruler, founder of Zand dynasty **8** 447
Agha Mohammad Khan **1** 80-81
Karl I (1713-1780), Duke of Brunswick
1735-1780
Lessing, Gotthold Ephraim **9** 357-359
Karl V (opera)
Krenek, Ernst **9** 98-99
Karl August (1757-1828), Duke of
Saxe-Weimar 1758-1815, grand duke
1815-1828
Goethe, Johann Wolfgang von
6 388-391
Wieland, Christoph Martin **16** 260-261
Karl Hetman der Zwergriese (play)
Wedekind, Frank **16** 166-167
Karl Theodor (1724-1799), elector of
Bavaria 1777-1799
Rumford **13** 360-362
KARLE, ISABELLA (born 1921), American
chemist and physicist **8** 447-449
Karlovy Dvur (manuscript)
Masaryk, Tomáš Garrigue **10** 314-315
Karlskirche (church; Vienna)
Fischer von Erlach, Johann Bernhard
5 459-461
Rottmayr, Johann Michael **13** 321
**KARLSTADT, ANDREAS BODENHEIM
VON** (circa 1480-1541), German Protes-
tant reformer **8** 449
Eck, Johann Maier von **5** 200
Luther, Martin **10** 48-51
Melancthon, Philip **10** 466-467
Karma (religious doctrine)
Buddha **3** 97-101
Radhakrishnan, Sarvepalli **12** 537-538
Mahavira, Vardhamana **10** 135-137
KARMAL, BABRAK (born 1929), Afghan
Marxist and Soviet puppet ruler of the

Democratic Republic of Afghanistan
(1979-1986) **8** 449-451
KÁRMÁN, THEODORE VON (1881-1963),
Hungarian-born American physicist
8 451-452
Born, Max **2** 420-421

Karnak (ancient city; Egypt)
Hatshepsut **7** 196-197
Ramses II **13** 22-23

Karolinska Institute (Stockholm)
Theorell, Axel Hugo Theodor
15 176-177

Károlyi, Count Gyula (1871-1946), Hungarian statesman
Horthy de Nagybánya, Nicholas
7 510-512

Karrer, Paul (1889-1971), Swiss chemist
Dam, Carl Peter Henrik **4** 382-383
Szent-Györgyi, Albert von **15** 62-64

KARUME, SHEIKH ABEID AMANI
(1905-1972), Tanzanian political leader
8 452-453
Nyerere, Julius Kamberage **11** 447-449

Karuna (Buddhist doctrine)
Buddha **3** 97-101

KASAVUBU, JOSEPH (circa 1913-1969),
Congolese statesman **8** 453-455
Lumumba, Patrice Emery **10** 43-45
Mobutu Sese Seko **11** 69-71
Tshombe, Moïse Kapenda **15** 325-326
Youlou, Fulbert **16** 466-467

Kashan Empire (central Asia; 1st and 2nd
centuries A.D.)
Kanishka **8** 428-429

Kashmir (state, India)
Liaquat Ali Khan **9** 397
Menon, Vengalil Krishnan Krishna
10 507-509

Kashta (flourished 8th century B.C.),
Nubian king
Piankhi **12** 288-289

Kasimir, Karl Theodore
see Meyerhold, Vsevolod Emilievich

Kassa
see Johannes IV; Tewodros II

KASSEBAUM, NANCY (born 1932), Republican senator from Kansas **8** 455-457

Kasserine Pass, battle of (1943)
Alexander of Tunis, 1st Earl **1** 135-136

Kastor and Polydeukes
see Castor and Pollux

Kata Kabanova (opera)
Janáček, Leoš **8** 219

Katanga secession
see Congo, Democratic Republic of—
Katanga secession

KATAYAMA, SEN (1860-1933), Japanese
labor and Socialist leader **8** 457

Kätchen von Heilbronn (play)
Kleist, Heinrich von **9** 52-53

Kate (literary character)
Shakespeare, William **14** 142-145

Katerina Izmailova (opera)
Shostakovich, Dmitri Dmitrievich
14 204-205

Katipunan (secret society; Philippines)
Bonifacio, Andres **2** 393-394
Mabini, Apolinario **10** 72-73
Rizal, José **13** 187-189

Katkov, Mikhail Nikiforovich (1818-1887),
Russian journalist and editor
Alexander III **1** 133-134
Tolstoy, Leo **15** 262-265

Kato, Baron Takaakira (1859-1926), Japan-
ese statesman
Inukai, Tsuyoshi **8** 130-131
Takahashi, Korekiyo **15** 84-85

Katsura, Prince Taro (1847-1913), Japanese
soldier and statesman
Saionji, Kimmochi **13** 438-439

Katte, Hans Hermann von (1704-1730),
German noble
Frederick II **6** 81-84

Kauffmann, Stanley (born 1916), American
critic
Ray, Satyajit **13** 60-61
Truffaut, François **15** 311-313

KAUFMAN, GEORGE S. (1889-1961),
American playwright **8** 457-458
Ferber, Edna **5** 413
Lardner, Ringgold Wilmer **9** 204-205

KAUFMAN, GERALD BERNARD (born
1930), foreign policy spokesman of the
British Labour Party **8** 458-460

KAUFMANN, EZEKIEL (1889-1963), Jewish
philosopher and scholar **8** 460

Kaufmann House (Bear Run, Pennsylvania;
Wright)
Neutra, Richard Joseph **11** 355-356
Wright, Frank Lloyd **16** 398-401

Kaufmann House (Palm Springs, California)
Neutra, Richard Joseph **11** 355-356

Kaukasische Kreidekreis, Der (play)
Brecht, Bertolt **2** 512-514

KAUNDA, KENNETH DAVID (born 1924),
Zambian statesman **8** 460-461

Kaunitz, Prince Wenzel von (1711-1794),
Austrian statesman
Maria Theresa **10** 256-258
Metternich, Klemens von **10** 533-536

KAUTILYA (4th century B.C.), Indian statesman and author **8** 462
Chandragupta Maurya **3** 426

KAUTSKY, KARL JOHANN (1854-1938),
German-Austrian Socialist **8** 462-463
Bernstein, Eduard **2** 218
Luxemburg, Rosa **10** 55-56
Marx, Karl **10** 304-308
Troeltsch, Ernst **15** 299-300
Trotsky, Leon **15** 302-305

Kavadh I
see Kavat I

Kavanagh (novel)
Longfellow, Henry Wadsworth
9 499-500

Kavat I (ruled 485-531), Sassanid king of
Persia
Khosrow I **8** 538-539

Kavi (language)
Humboldt, Wilhelm von **8** 31

KAWABATA, YASUNARI (1899-1972),
Japanese novelist **8** 463-464
Mishima, Yukio **11** 54-55

KAWAWA, RASHIDI MFAUME (born
1929), Tanzanian political leader
8 464-465
Nyerere, Julius Kamberage **11** 447-449

Kayak Island (near southeastern Alaska)
Bering, Vitus **2** 193-194

Kaye, Danny (1913-1987), American film
and stage actor
Goldwyn, Samuel **6** 416

Kazaghan (died 1358), Mongol tribal
leader
Tamerlane **15** 94-95

Kazan (city; Tatar Republic; Union of Soviet
Socialist Republics)
Ivan IV **8** 157-159

Kazan (flourished mid-14th century),
Chaghatai khan
Tamerlane **15** 94-95

KAZAN, ELIA (born 1909), American film
and stage director **8** 465-466
Williams, Tennessee **16** 306-308

KAZANTZAKIS, NIKOS (1883-1957),
Greek author, journalist, and statesman
8 466-468
Martinu, Bohuslav **10** 299-300

Kean (comedy)
Sartre, Jean Paul **13** 491-492

Kean, Charles (1811-1868), English actor
Boucicault, Dion **2** 442-443

Kean, Edmund (1787-1833), English actor
Forrest, Edwin **6** 11-12

KEARNEY, DENIS (1847-1907), Irish-born
American labor agitator **8** 468

KEARNY, STEPHEN WATTS (1794-1848),
American general **8** 468-469
Carson, Christopher **3** 334-335
Fitzpatrick, Thomas **5** 474-475
Frémont, John Charles **6** 97-98

Kearsarge
Semmes, Raphael **14** 102-103

Keating, Kenneth (1900-1975), American
politician
Kennedy, Robert Francis **8** 508-509

KEATING, PAUL JOHN (born 1944), federal treasurer of Australia (1983-1991)
8 469-470

KEATS, JOHN (1795-1821), English poet
8 470-472
  biographers
    Lowell, Amy **10** 13
  influence of
    Dickinson, Emily **4** 541-543
    Hawthorne, Nathaniel **7** 212-215
    Hopkins, Gerard Manley **7** 492-494
    Hunt, William Holman **8** 44-45
    Lampman, Archibald **9** 180-181
    Millais, John Everett **11** 23-24
  influenced by
    Burton, Robert **3** 166-167
    Chapman, George **3** 440-441
    Milton, John **11** 43-46
  quoted
    Shelley, Percy Bysshe **14** 176-178
  translations of
    Pasternak, Boris Leonidovich
    12 124-125
Keble, John (1792-1866), English clergy-
man
    Newman, John Henry **11** 365-367
    Pusey, Edward Bouverie **12** 488-489
Kedleston Hall (Derbyshire, England)
    Adam, Robert and James **1** 38-40
Keene, Laura (1826?-1873), English actress
    Booth, John Wilkes **2** 404
    Jefferson, Joseph **8** 237
Keep the Aspidistra Flying (novel)
    Orwell, George **12** 14-15
KEFAUVER, CAREY ESTES (1903-1963),
    U.S. senator and influential Tennessee
    Democrat **8** 472-474
    Kennedy, John Fitzgerald **8** 502-506
Kegon (Buddhist doctrine)
    Kukai **9** 124-125
    Saicho **13** 426-428
Keilin, David (1887-1963), English bio-
chemist
    Szent-Györgyi, Albert von **15** 62-64
    Theorell, Axel Hugo Theodor
    15 176-177
Keiser, Reinhard (1674-1739), German
composer
    Bach, Johann Sebastian **1** 416-419
    Handel, George Frederick **7** 116-119
KEITA, MODIBO (1915-1977), Malian
statesman **8** 474-475
KEITH, MINOR COOPER (1848-1929),
    American entrepreneur **8** 476-477
    Meiggs, Henry **10** 458-459
KEITH, SIR ARTHUR (1866-1955), British
    anatomist and physical anthropologist
    8 475-476
Keith, William (1839-1911), American
painter
    Borglum, John Gutzon de la Mothe
    2 416-417
KEKULÉ, FRIEDRICH AUGUST
    (1829-1896), German chemist **8** 477-478
    Baeyer, Johann Friedrich Adolf von
    1 432

    Couper, Archibald Scott **4** 269-270
    Van't Hoff, Jacobus Hendricus
    15 431-432
Kellaway, Charles Halliley (1889-1952),
    Australian physiologist
    Dale, Henry Hallett **4** 371-373
Keller, Albert Galloway (1874-1956),
    American educator
    Sumner, William Graham **15** 32
KELLER, GOTTFRIED (1819-1890), Swiss
    short-story writer, novelist, and poet
    8 478-479
    Hesse, Hermann **7** 367-369
KELLER, HELEN ADAMS (1880-1962),
    American lecturer and author **8** 479-480
    Bell, Alexander Graham **2** 129-131
KELLEY, FLORENCE (1859-1932), Ameri-
    can social worker and reformer
    8 483-484
    Altgeld, John Peter **1** 180-182
    Goldmark, Josephine **6** 407-408
KELLEY, HALL JACKSON (1790-1874),
    American promoter **8** 480
KELLEY, OLIVER HUDSON (1826-1913),
    American agriculturalist **8** 480-481
KELLOGG, FRANK BILLINGS (1856-1937),
    American statesman **8** 481
    Coolidge, John Calvin **4** 217-219
Kellogg-Briand Pact (1928)
    Borah, William Edgar **2** 408
    Briand, Aristide **2** 528-529
    Coolidge, John Calvin **4** 217-219
    Kellogg, Frank Billings **8** 481
    Titulescu, Nicolae **15** 246-247
KELLOR, FRANCES (1873-1952), American
    activist and politician **8** 481-482
KELLY, ELLSWORTH (born 1923), Ameri-
    can artist **8** 482-483
KELLY, GENE (born Eugene Curran Kelly;
    1912-1996), American actor, dancer, and
    choreographer **8** 484-486
Kelly, Howard (1858-1943), American sur-
geon
    Osler, William **12** 19-20
Kelly, John (1822-1886), American politi-
cian
    Cleveland, Stephen Grover **4** 108-110
Kelly, Ned (died 1880), Australian horse
    thief, bank robber, and murderer
    Nolan, Sidney Robert **11** 418
KELLY, PETRA (born 1947), West German
    pacifist and politician **8** 486-487
KELLY, WILLIAM (1811-1888), American
    iron manufacturer **8** 487-488
    Bessemer, Henry **2** 235-236
Kelly in Spring (painting)
    Nolan, Sidney Robert **11** 418
Kellys and the O'Kellys, The (novel)
    Trollope, Anthony **15** 300-302
Kelmscott Press (established 1890)
    Morris, William **11** 187-188

KELSEY, HENRY (circa 1667-1724),
    English-born Canadian explorer **8** 488
Keltic (sonata)
    MacDowell, Edward Alexander
    10 87-88
KELVIN OF LARGS, BARON (William
    Thomson; 1824-1907), Scottish physicist
    8 488-489
    Bell, Alexander Graham **2** 129-131
    Field, Cyrus West **5** 438-439
    Fourier, Jean Baptiste Joseph **6** 32-33
    Holmes, Arthur **7** 455-456
    Joule, James Prescott **8** 363-364
Kemal, Mustapha (Kemal Atatürk)
    see Atatürk, Ghazi Mustapha Kemal
KEMAL, YASHAR (born 1922), Turkish nov-
    elist **8** 489-491
Kemble, Charles (1775-1854), English
actor
    Kemble, Frances Anne **8** 491
KEMBLE, FRANCES ANNE (Fanny Kemble;
    1809-1893), English actress **8** 491
Kemble, Mrs. Charles
    see De Camp, Maria Theresa
KEMP, JACK FRENCH, JR. (born 1935),
    Republican congressman from New York
    and secretary of housing and urban
    development **8** 491-493
Kempe, Margery (1373-1440), English reli-
    gious writer
    Rolle of Hampole, Richard **13** 260-261
Kempeneer, Pieter de
    see Campaña, Pedro de
KEMPIS, THOMAS À (circa 1380-1471),
    German monk and spiritual writer
    8 493-494
    Eliot, George **5** 254-256
    Groote, Gerard **7** 12-13
KENDALL, AMOS (1789-1869), American
    journalist **8** 494
    Blair, Francis Preston **2** 313-315
    Morse, Samuel Finley Breese
    11 192-193
KENDALL, EDWARD CALVIN
    (1886-1972), American biochemist **8** 495
    Reichstein, Tadeus **13** 85-87
Kendall's Expositor (newspaper)
    Kendall, Amos **8** 494
KENDREW, JOHN C. (born 1917), English
    chemist and Nobel Prize winner
    8 495-496
Kenilworth (novel)
    Scott, Walter **14** 68-70
Kenilworth, battle of (1265-1266)
    Henry III **7** 290-292
KENNAN, GEORGE F. (born 1904), Ameri-
    can diplomat, author, and scholar
    8 496-498
    Marshall, George Catlett **10** 278-279
    Truman, Harry S. **15** 314-316

Kennedy, Aimee
see McPherson, Aimee Semple

KENNEDY, ANTHONY M. (born 1936),
United States Supreme Court justice
8 498-500

KENNEDY, EDWARD M. (Ted; born 1932),
U.S. senator from Massachusetts
8 500-502

Kennedy, Jacqueline Lee Bouvier
seeOnassis, Jacqueline Lee Bouvier
Kennedy

KENNEDY, JOHN FITZGERALD
(1917-1963), American statesman, presi-
dent 1960-1963 **8** 502-506
advisers
Schlesinger, Arthur Meier Jr.
14 13-15
appointees
Bohlen, Charles (Chip) **2** 364-366
Bundy, McGeorge **3** 122-124
White, Byron R. **16** 227-228
assassination of
Johnson, Lyndon Baines **8** 308-312
Malcolm X **10** 165-166
Stone, Oliver **14** 472-475
domestic policy
Bennett, John Coleman **2** 170-171
Frost, Robert Lee **6** 130-133
King, Martin Luther Jr. **9** 20-22
McCarthy, Eugene Joseph
10 386-388
Oppenheimer, J. Robert **11** 525-526
Steichen, Edward **14** 411-412
Wilkins, Roy **16** 282-283
foreign policy
Ben-Gurion, David **2** 160-161
Bundy, McGeorge **3** 122-124
John, XXIII **8** 277-280
Johnson, Lyndon Baines **8** 308-312
political appointments
Marshall, Thurgood **10** 282-284
Roosevelt, Eleanor **13** 275-277
Stevenson, Adlai Ewing **14** 445-446
wife
Onassis, Jacqueline Lee Bouvier
Kennedy **11** 511-513
see also Bay of Pigs invasion (1961)

KENNEDY, JOHN PENDLETON
(1795-1870), American author and politician **8** 506-507
Poe, Edgar Allan **12** 363-365

KENNEDY, JOHN STEWART (1830-1909),
American financier and philanthropist
8 507-508

Kennedy, Joseph P. (1888-1969), American
financier and diplomat
Kennedy, John Fitzgerald **8** 502-506

KENNEDY, ROBERT FRANCIS
(1925-1968), American statesman
8 508-509
Chavez, Cesar **3** 486-487
Howe, Julia Ward **7** 535-536
Kennedy, John Fitzgerald **8** 502-506
McCarthy, Joseph Raymond **10** 388-389

Kennedy Center (Washington D.C.)
Stone, Edward Durrell **14** 466-468

Kennedy Space Center (Florida)
Armstrong, Neil Alden **1** 304-306

KENNY, ELIZABETH (Sister Kenny;
1886-1952), Australian nursing sister
8 509-510

Kensington Palace (London)
Hawksmoor, Nicholas **7** 211-212

KENT, JAMES (1763-1847), American jurist
8 510-511
Eaton, Dorman Bridgman **5** 190-191
Holmes, Oliver Wendell Jr. **7** 458-459

KENT, ROCKWELL (1882-1971), American
painter and illustrator **8** 511

Kent, William (1685-1748), English architect, painter, and landscape gardener
Adam, Robert and James **1** 38-40

Kentucky (state, United States)
abolitionism
Birney, James Gillespie **2** 283-284
Fee, John Gregg **5** 402-403
exploration and settlement
Boone, Daniel **2** 397-398
Byrd, William **3** 188-189
Gist, Christopher **6** 352-353
Henderson, Richard **7** 278-279
legislators
Birney, James Gillespie **2** 283-284
Clay, Henry **4** 94-96
Hatch, William Henry **7** 196

Kentucky and Virginia Resolutions (1798)
Jefferson, Thomas **8** 238-241
Madison, James **10** 121-123

Kentucky Spring (musical composition)
Harris, Roy **7** 175-176

Kenwood Physical Observatory (Chicago)
Hale, George Ellery **7** 72-74

Kenya African Democratic Union (established 1960)
Ngala, Ronald Gideon **11** 373-374
Odinga, Ajuma Jaramogi Oginga
11 471-473

Kenya African National Union (established
1960)
Kenyatta, Jomo **8** 512-514
Ngala, Ronald Gideon **11** 373-374
Odinga, Ajuma Jaramogi Oginga
11 471-473

Kenya African Union
Kenyatta, Jomo **8** 512-514
Mboya, Thomas Joseph **10** 384-385
Obote, Apolo Milton **11** 457
Odinga, Ajuma Jaramogi Oginga
11 471-473

Kenya National party (established 1959)
Ngala, Ronald Gideon **11** 373-374

Kenya People's party (established 1966)
Odinga, Ajuma Jaramogi Oginga
11 471-473

Kenya, Republic of (nation; east Africa)
20th century
Ogot, Grace Emily Akinyi
11 483-484
anthropological studies
Jung, Carl Gustav **8** 388-389
Leakey, Louis Seymour Bazett **9** 262
Leakey, Mary Douglas **9** 263-264
Leakey, Richard Erskine Frere
9 264-265
nationalism and independence
Kenyatta, Jomo **8** 512-514
Mboya, Thomas Joseph **10** 384-385
Ngala, Ronald Gideon **11** 373-374
Odinga, Ajuma Jaramogi Oginga
11 471-473
Thuku, Harry **15** 212-213
suspension of democracy
Moi, Daniel Arap **11** 83-86

KENYATTA, JOMO (circa 1890-1978),
Kenyan statesman **8** 512-514
Diagne, Blaise **4** 527
Mboya, Thomas Joseph **10** 384-385
Moi, Daniel Arap **11** 83-86
Ngala, Ronald Gideon **11** 373-374
Odinga, Ajuma Jaramogi Oginga
11 471-473
Wallace-Johnson, Isaac Theophilus
Akunna **16** 76-77

Kenyon College (Gambier, Ohio)
Chase, Philander **3** 472-473
Radin, Paul **12** 538-539
Ransom, John Crowe **13** 39-40

Keokuk (flourished 1790-1848), American
Sauk Indian chief
Black Hawk **2** 308

Kephala (archeological site; Crete)
Evans, Arthur John **5** 335-336

KEPLER, JOHANNES (1571-1630), German
astronomer **8** 514-516
Brahe, Tycho **2** 489-490
Copernicus, Nicolaus **4** 226-227

Keppel, Augustus (1st Viscount Keppel;
1725-1786), British admiral
Reynolds, Joshua **13** 115-116

Kereits (Asian people)
Genghis Khan **6** 263-265

KERENSKY, ALEKSANDR FEDOROVICH
(1881-1970), Russian revolutionary and
politician **8** 516-517
Kolchak, Aleksandr Vasilievich **9** 77-78
Kornilov, Lavr Georgievich **9** 87-88
Lenin, Vladimir Ilich **9** 323-326
Sorokin, Pitirim A. **14** 348-349

Kerkhoven, Joseph (literary character)
Wassermann, Jakob **16** 130-131

Kerll, Johann Kaspar (or Kerl; 1627-1693),
German composer and organist
Pachelbel, Johann **12** 52

Kerman (city and former province; Iran)
Agha Mohammad Khan **1** 80-81

KERN, JEROME DAVID (1885-1945),
American composer **8** 517-518

Gershwin, George **6** 284-285
Rodgers, Richard Charles **13** 234-236

Kern, John Worth (1849-1917), American politician
Bowers, Claude Gernade **2** 463

Kerner, Andreas Justinius (1786-1862), German lyric poet
Strauss, David Friedrich **14** 496-497

KEROUAC, JEAN-LOUIS LEBRIS DE (Jack; 1922-69), American writer of autobiographical fiction **8** 518-519
Ginsberg, Allen **6** 332-333

KERR, CLARK (born 1911), American economist, labor/management expert, and university president **8** 519-521

KERREY, J. ROBERT (born 1943), Democratic senator from Nebraska and 1992 presidential candidate **8** 521-522

Kerygmatic theology
see Dialectical theology

KESSELRING, ALBERT (1885-1960), German field marshal **8** 522-523

KESSLER, DAVID A. (born 1951), commissioner of the Food and Drug Administration **8** 523-524

Kestner, Charlotte (Charlotte Buff; 1753-1828), friend and companion of Goethe
Mann, Thomas **10** 204-207

Keter Malkhut (poems)
ibn Gabirol, Solomon ben Judah **8** 92

Ket's Rebellion (1549; England)
Edward VI **5** 213-214
Northumberland, Duke of **11** 431-432
Somerset, Duke of **14** 333-334

KETTERING, CHARLES F. (1876-1958), American engineer, industrial pioneer, and apostle of progress **8** 524-525

Ketzer von Soana, Der (novel)
Hauptmann, Gerhart Johann Robert **7** 199-201

Kew Gardens
see Royal Botanical Gardens

Kew Gardens (book)
Woolf, Virginia Stephen **16** 381-382

Kewaida Muslims (religious sect)
Baraka, Imamu Amiri **1** 498-499

KEY, FRANCIS SCOTT (1779-1843), American poet and attorney **8** 525-527

KEY, VLADIMIR ORLANDO, JR. (1908-1963), American political scientist **8** 527-528
Merriam, Charles Edward **10** 518-519

Key, The (novel)
Tanizaki, Junichiro **15** 101-102

Key Largo (play and film)
Anderson, Maxwell **1** 219-220
Bogart, Humphrey **2** 363-364

Key to Uncle Tom's Cabin, A (book)
Stowe, Harriet Elizabeth Beecher **14** 484-485

Keyes of the Kingdom of Heaven, The (book)
Cotton, John **4** 263-265

KEYNES, JOHN MAYNARD (1st Baron Keynes of Tilton; 1883-1946), English economist **8** 528-530
associates
Ramsey, Frank Plumpton **13** 25
Robertson, Dennis Holme **13** 196
Robinson, Joan Violet Maurice **13** 209-210
Russell, Bertrand Arthur William **13** 373-374
Woolf, Virginia Stephen **16** 381-382
compared with
Clark, John Maurice **4** 77-78
economic controversies
Churchill, Winston Leonard Spencer **4** 51-53
Say, Jean Baptiste **13** 508-509
influence of
Hansen, Alvin **7** 131-132
Macmillan, Harold **10** 112-113
influenced by
Fisher, Irving **5** 462-463
Marshall, Alfred **10** 277-278
see also Keynesian economics

Keynes, John Neville (1852-1949), English educator
Keynes, John Maynard **8** 528-530

Keynesian economics
Hansen, Alvin **7** 131-132
Keynes, John Maynard **8** 528-530
Marshall, Alfred **10** 277-278
Pigou, Arthur Cecil **12** 302
Robertson, Dennis Holme **13** 196
Samuelson, Paul Anthony **13** 458-459
Walras, Marie Esprit Léon **16** 84-85

Keystone Co. (films)
Sennett, Mack **14** 108-109

KGB (Komitet Gosudarstvennoy Bezopasnosti)
Andropov, Iury Vladimirovich **1** 233-234

KHACHATURIAN, ARAM ILICH (or Khachaturov; 1903-1978), Russian composer **8** 530-531

Khai Dinah (died 1926), emperor of Annam
Bao Dai **1** 496-497

Khair al-Din
see Barbarossa II

Khalid ibn al-Walid (died 642), Arab general
Abu Bakr **1** 31-32
Omar ibn al-Khattab **11** 508-509

KHALIL, SAYYID ABDULLAH (1892-1970), Sudanese general, prime minister 1956-1958 **8** 531-532
Abboud, Ibrahim **1** 11-12
Azhari, Sayyid Ismail al- **1** 399-401

Khalji dynasty (India, 1290-1320)
Ala-ud-din **1** 102-103
Muhammad bin Tughluq **11** 229

Kham (Asian people)
Dalai Lama **4** 369-371

KHAMA, SIR SERETSE M. (born 1921), Botswana political leader **8** 532-533
Jonathan, Joseph Leabua **8** 330-331

KHAMENEI, AYATOLLAH SAYYID ALI (born 1939), supreme spiritual and political leader of the Islamic Republic of Iran **8** 533-535

Khammurapikh
see Hammurabi

Khanua, battle of (1527)
Babar the Conqueror **1** 405-407

Kharijites (Moslem sect)
Abd al-Malik **1** 12-13

Kharosthi script (India)
Asoka **1** 341-342

Khartoum (city; Sudan)
Kitchener, Horatio Herbert **9** 45-46

Khartoum, battle of (1885)
Gordon, Charles George **6** 448-449
Mahdi **10** 137-138

Khazars (Turkic people)
Cyril and Methodius, Saints **4** 362-363
Judah Halevi **8** 373
Khosrow I **8** 538-539
Leo III **9** 330-332

Khedives
see Statesmen

Khilji dynasty
see Khalji dynasty

Khitan
see Liao dynasty

Khitan (Asian people)
Chinese conflicts
An Lu-shan **1** 239-240
Chu Hsi **4** 40-43
Hui-Tsung **8** 25
Zhao Kuang-yin **16** 505-508
Korean conquest of
Kim Pusik **9** 8-9
Kwanggaet'o **9** 139-140
Kwangjong **9** 140
Wang Kon **16** 101

Khmelnitskii, Bogdan
see Chmielnicki, Bogdan

Khmer Republic
see Cambodia

Khoi-Khoi
see Hottentots

KHOMEINI, AYATOLLAH RUHOLLAH MUSAVI (born 1902), founder and supreme leader of the Islamic Republic of Iran **8** 535-537

Khor and Kalinich (story)
Turgenev, Ivan Sergeyevich **15** 345-348

KHORANA, HAR GOBIND (born 1922), Indian organic chemist **8** 537-538

KHOSROW I (died 579), Sassanid king of Persia 531-576 **8** 538-539
Justinian I **8** 393-395

Khosrow II (died 628), king of Persia 590-628
Heraclius **7** 320-321

Khosru
see Khosrow

Khotin, victory of (1673)
John III **8** 276-277

Khovanshchina (opera; Mussorgsky)
Mussorgsky, Modest Petrovich **11** 274-276
Rimsky-Korsakov, Nikolai Andreevich **13** 174-175

KHRUSHCHEV, NIKITA SERGEEVICH (1894-1971), Soviet political leader **8** 539-540
associates
Brezhnev, Leonid Ilich **2** 527-528
Bulganin, Nikolai **3** 118-119
Konev, Ivan Stefanovich **9** 81-82
Lysenko, Trofim Denisovich **10** 71
Zhukov, Georgi Konstantinovich **16** 512-513
de-Stalinization
Kim Il-sung **9** 4-6
Prestes, Luiz Carlos **12** 442-444
Stalin, Joseph **14** 393-396
domestic arts policy
Solzhenitsyn, Alexander Isayevich **14** 330-332
Yevtushenko, Yevgeny Alexandrovich **16** 455-456
foreign policy
Eisenhower, Dwight David **5** 233-236
Gomulka, Wladislaw **6** 422-424
John, XXIII **8** 277-280
Kennedy, John Fitzgerald **8** 502-506
Nixon, Richard Milhous **11** 401-404
Nkrumah, Kwame **11** 408-410
Tito, Marshal **15** 244-246
see also Cuban missile crisis (1962)

Khudaganj, battle of (1858)
Roberts, Frederick Sleigh **13** 195-196

KHUFU (ruled 2590-2568 B.C.), Egyptian king **8** 540-541

Khurasan (province; Iran)
Alp Arslan **1** 178-179
Genghis Khan **6** 263-265
Mansur, Abu Jafar ibn Muhammad al- **10** 214-215
Muawiya ibn Abu Sufyan **11** 223-224

Khurram
see Shah Jahan

Khusrau
see Khosrow

Khvatainamak (epic)
Firdausi **5** 451-452

KHWARIZMI, MUHAMMAD IBN MUSA AL- (died circa 850), Arab mathematician, astronomer, and geographer **8** 541

Kiakhta, Treaty of (1727)
K'ang-hsi **8** 423-426

Kiamil Pasha (1833-1913), Turkish statesman
Enver Pasha **5** 290-291

Kiangsi (province; China)
Chao Meng-fu **3** 436-437
Chu Teh **4** 54-55

Kibbutz movement (Israel)
Ben-Gurion, David **2** 160-161

Kibo-no Mabi
see Makibi

Kichle (poem)
Seferis, George **14** 84-85

Kickapoo Indians (North America)
McCoy, Isaac **10** 403

Kicking Horse Pass (Canada)
Fleming, Sandford **5** 485-486

Kid, The (film)
Chaplin, Charles Spencer **3** 438-440

KIDDER, ALFRED VINCENT (1885-1963), American archeologist **8** 541-542

Kiddush Hashem (novel)
Asch, Shalom **1** 325-326

KIDMAN, SIDNEY (1857-1935), "The Cattle King" of Australia **8** 542-544

Kidnapped (novel; Stevenson)
Stevenson, Robert Louis **14** 446-448
Wyeth, Andrew Newell **16** 413-415

Kidnapped in London (book)
Sun Yat-sen **15** 35-39

Kidney (anatomy)
Bright, Richard **3** 7-8
Erlanger, Joseph **5** 310-311

KIEFER, ANSELM (born 1945), German artist **8** 544-546

Kiel, University of (Germany)
Diels, Otto Paul Hermann **5** 5-6
Hertz, Heinrich Rudolf **7** 346-347
Meyerhof, Otto Fritz **10** 537-539
Schlick, Friedrich Albert Moritz **14** 16-17
Tönnies, Ferdinand **15** 266-267

KIENHOLZ, EDWARD (born 1927), American Pop artist **8** 546-547

KIERKEGAARD, SØREN AABYE (1813-1855), Danish philosopher **8** 547-549
Auden, Wystan Hugh **1** 364-366
Barber, Samuel **1** 500-501
Barth, Karl **2** 31-32
Ibsen, Henrik **8** 98-100
Jaspers, Karl **8** 225-226
Kafka, Franz **8** 403-406
Strindberg, August **14** 509-511
Tillich, Paul Johannes **15** 224-225
Unamuno y Jugo, Miguel de **15** 386-387

Kikuyu (African people)
Kenyatta, Jomo **8** 512-514

Leakey, Louis Seymour Bazett **9** 262

Kikuyu Central Association (Kenya)
Kenyatta, Jomo **8** 512-514
Thuku, Harry **15** 212-213

Kikuyu Provincial Association (Kenya)
Thuku, Harry **15** 212-213

Kilkenny, Statute of (1367; Ireland)
Edward III **5** 211-212

Killers, The (story)
Hemingway, Ernest Miller **7** 274-277

Killigrew, Thomas (1621-1683), English playwright and courtier
Van Dyck, Anthony **15** 423-425

Killing of O-Tsuya, The (novel)
Tanizaki, Junichiro **15** 101-102

Kilmainham, Treaty of (1882)
Parnell, Charles Stewart **12** 117-119

KILPATRICK, WILLIAM H. (1871-1965), American educator, college president, and philosopher of education **9** 1-3

Kiltartanese (Irish dialect)
Gregory, Augusta **6** 535-536

Kim (novel)
Kipling, Joseph Rudyard **9** 32-33

KIM DAE-JUNG (born 1925), worked for the restoration of democracy and human rights in South Korea after 1971 **9** 3-4

KIM IL-SUNG (born 1912), North Korean political leader **9** 4-6
Kim Jong Il **9** 6-7

KIM JONG IL (born 1941), heir-apparent of Kim Il-sung, the founder and leader of the Democratic People's Republic of Korea **9** 6-7

KIM OK-KYUN (1851-1894), Korean politician **9** 7-8
Kojong **9** 74-75

KIM PUSIK (1075-1151), Korean statesman, historian, and general **9** 8-9
Chong Chung-bu **4** 15
Sol Ch'ong **14** 325-326

Kim Song-ju
see Kim Il-sung

KIM YOUNG SAM (born 1927), South Korean statesman **9** 9-10

Kimberley (city; South Africa)
Rhodes, Cecil John **13** 120-122

Kimberley (region; Australia)
Forrest, John **6** 12-13
Grey, Charles **6** 539-540

Kimmei (508?-571), emperor of Japan 539-571
Shotoku Taishi **14** 205-207

Kind, Johann Friedrich (1768-1843), German novelist
Weber, Carl Maria Friedrich Ernst von **16** 156-157

Kinder der Welt (novel)
Heyse, Paul Johann Ludwig **7** 372-373

Kindergarten (education)
Froebel, Friedrich Wilhelm August
6 122-123
Harris, William Torrey **7** 177-178
Peabody, Elizabeth Palmer **12** 167-168

Kindertotenlieder (songs)
Mahler, Gustav **10** 144-145

Kinder-und Hausmärchen (folktales)
Grimm, Jakob and Wilhelm Karl **7** 3-4

KINDI, ABU-YUSUF YAQUB IBN-ISHAQ AL- (died 873), Arab philosopher **9** 10-11
Averroës **1** 382-383

Kindly Ones, The (novel)
Powell, Anthony **12** 422-423

Kindred Spirits (painting)
Durand, Asher Brown **5** 156-157

Kinetic art
Balla, Giacomo **1** 473-474
Calder, Alexander **3** 216-218
Duchamp, Marcel **5** 122-123
Gabo, Naum **6** 158-159
Ray, Man **13** 59-60
Tinguely, Jean **15** 230-232
Vasarely, Victor **15** 440-442

Kinetic theory of gases
Boltzmann, L.52-53
Clausius, Rudolf Julius Emanuel
4 92-94
Joule, James Prescott **8** 363-364
Maxwell, James Clerk **10** 361-364
equations
Bernoulli, Daniel **2** 216
laws
Avogadro, Lorenzo Romano
Amedeo Carlo **1** 388-389
Boyle, Robert **2** 469-471
Gay-Lussac, Joseph Louis **6** 245-246
reaction kinetics
Hinshelwood, Cyril Norman
7 405-406
Semenov, Nikolai Nikolaevich
14 101

Kinfu (died 1839), Ethiopian warlord
Tewodros II **15** 158-159

KING, B. B. (born Riley B. King; born 1925), African American blues musician, singer, and songwriter **9** 11-14

KING, BILLIE JEAN (born 1943), international tennis star **9** 14-15

King, Charles G. (1896-1988), American chemist
Szent-Györgyi, Albert von **15** 62-64

KING, CLARENCE (1842-1901), American geologist and mining engineer **9** 15-16
Adams, Herbert Baxter **1** 47

KING, CORETTA SCOTT (born 1929), American advocate of civil rights, nonviolence, international peace, full employment, and equal rights for women **9** 16-17
Cleaver, Leroy Eldridge **4** 97-98
King, Martin Luther Jr. **9** 20-22

KING, ERNEST JOSEPH (1878-1956), American admiral **9** 17-18

KING, FREDERIC TRUBY (1858-1938), New Zealand doctor and founder of the Plunket Society **9** 18-19

KING, MARTIN LUTHER, JR. (1929-1968), African American minister and civil rights leader **9** 20-22
Abernathy, Ralph David **1** 27-28
Bevel, James Luther **2** 250-251
Brightman, Edgar Sheffield **3** 8-9
Bunche, Ralph Johnson **3** 121-122
Jackson, Jesse Louis **8** 174-176
King, Coretta Scott **9** 16-17
Mays, Benjamin E. **10** 374-376
Owens, Jesse **12** 43-44
Parker, Dorothy Rothschild **12** 106
Rauschenbusch, Walter **13** 53-54

KING, RUFUS (1755-1827), American statesman and diplomat **9** 22-23
Schuyler, Philip John **14** 49-50

KING, STEPHEN (a.k.a. Richard Bachmand and John Swithen; born 1947), American horror novelist **9** 23-25

KING, WILLIAM LYON MACKENZIE (1874-1950), Canadian statesman
9 25-26
Bennett, Richard Bedford **2** 171-172
Crerar, Thomas Alexander **4** 306
McNaughton, Andrew **10** 431-432
Meighen, Arthur **10** 459-460
St. Laurent, Louis Stephen **13** 434
Woodsworth, James Shaver **16** 376

King and I, The (musical)
Hammerstein, Oscar Clendenning II
7 104-106
Rodgers, Richard Charles **13** 234-236

King and No King, A (play)
Fletcher, John **5** 487

King and Queen (sculpture)
Moore, Henry **11** 146-148

King Arthur (opera)
Purcell, Henry **12** 484-485

King Bomba
see Ferdinand II

King Christian II (play; A. Paul)
Sibelius, Jean Julius Christian
14 211-212

King Coal (novel)
Sinclair, Upton Beale Jr. **14** 248-249

King Cophetua and the Beggar Maid (painting)
Burne-Jones, Edward Coley **3** 145-146

King David (music)
Honegger, Arthur **7** 472-473

King David (play)
Vondel, Joost van den **16** 19-20

King David (poems)
Benét, Stephen Vincent **2** 157-158

King Drinks, The (painting)
Jordaens, Jacob **8** 347-349

King George's War (1745-1748)
Johnson, William **8** 319-320
Pepperell, William **12** 206-207
Rogers, Robert **13** 250-251
seeAustrian Succession, War of the (for European phase)

King Henry IV-VI; VII (plays; Shakespeare)
Cushman, Charlotte **4** 354-355
Shakespeare, William **14** 142-145
Verdi, Giuseppe Fortunino Francesco
15 463-465

King in New York, The (film)
Chaplin, Charles Spencer **3** 438-440

King James Bible (Authorized Version)
Tyndale, William **15** 373-374

King Jasper (poem)
Robinson, Edwin Arlington **13** 201-202

King Jesus (novel)
Graves, Robert Ranke **6** 504-506

King John (play)
Shakespeare, William **14** 142-145

King Lazarus (novel)
Beti, Mongo **2** 242-243

King Lear (play; Shakespeare)
Lessing, Gotthold Ephraim **9** 357-359
Shakespeare, William **14** 142-145
Verdi, Giuseppe Fortunino Francesco
15 463-465

King Leopold's Soliloquy (book)
Twain, Mark **15** 363-366

King of Bourges
see Charles VII (king of France)

King of Ireland's Son, The (children's book)
Colum, Padraic **4** 174-175

King of the Dark Chamber, The (play)
Rabindranath Tagore **12** 529-531

King Ottokar's Fortune and End (play)
Grillparzer, Franz **6** 546-547

King Paradox (novel)
Baroja y Nessi, Pío **2** 15-16

King Philip's War (1675-1676)
Eliot, John **5** 256-258
Metacom **10** 529-531
Philip **12** 267-268
Williams, Roger **16** 304-305
Wise, John **16** 343-344

King Priam (opera)
Tippett, Michael Kemp **15** 234-235

King, Queen and Jokers (painting)
Milne, David Brown **11** 37-38

King Saul's Daughter (book)
Cohen, Morris Raphael **4** 139-140

King Solomon's Mines (novel; Haggard)
Greene, Graham **6** 523-524

King the Greatest Mayor, The (play)
Lope Félix de Vega Carpio **9** 503-506

King William's War (1689-1697)
Frontenac et Palluau, Comte de
6 128-130

Leisler, Jacob **9** 313-314

Kingdom for a Cow, A (musical play)
Weill, Kurt **16** 174-175

Kingdom of Earth (play)
Williams, Tennessee **16** 306-308

Kingdom of Rama
see Bosnia-Herzegovina

Kingmaker
see Warwick, Earl of

Kings
see Statesmen

Kings, Book of (Old Testament)
Jeremiah **8** 247-248

Kings and the Moon (poems)
Stephens, James **14** 430-431

Kings Mountain, battle of (1780)
Sevier, John **14** 122-123

King's Book (poems)
James I **8** 206-207

King's Book, The (pamphlet)
Milton, John **11** 43-46

King's Chapel (Boston)
Harrison, Peter **7** 179-180

King's College
see Columbia University

King's College (Aberdeen, Scotland)
Reid, Thomas **13** 87-88

King's College (Cambridge University)
Pigou, Arthur Cecil **12** 302
see also Cambridge University

King's College (London)
Lister, Joseph **9** 444-445
Lyell, Charles **10** 62-63
Maurice, John Frederick Denison
  10 349-350
Maxwell, James Clerk **10** 361-364
see also London, University of

King's College, University of (Canada)
Strachan, John **14** 486-487

King's Flute, The (poems)
Palamas, Kostes **12** 70

King's Henchman, The (opera)
Millay, Edna St. Vincent **11** 24-25

King's Jackal, The (novel)
Davis, Richard Harding **4** 422-423

King's Men (English theatrical company)
Fletcher, John **5** 487
Massinger, Philip **10** 324-325

King's Peace (386 B.C.)
Agesilaus II **1** 79-80

King's Quair (poem)
James I **8** 206-207

King's Weston (Gloucestershire)
Vanbrugh, John **15** 409-410

Kingsblood Royal (novel)
Lewis, Harry Sinclair **9** 385-387

KINGSFORD SMITH, SIR CHARLES
("Smithy"; 1897-1935), Australian
long-distance aviator **9** 26-28

KINGSLEY, CHARLES (1819-1875), English
author and Anglican clergyman **9** 28
Carlyle, Thomas **3** 304-305
Newman, John Henry **11** 365-367
Tennyson, Alfred **15** 144-146
Trollope, Anthony **15** 300-302

KINNOCK, NEIL (born 1942), British
Labour Party politician **9** 29-30

KINO, EUSEBIO FRANCISCO
(1645-1711), Spanish missionary, explorer, and cartographer **9** 30-31

Kinryuzan Temple (print)
Hiroshige, Ando **7** 412-413

KINSEY, ALFRED C. (1894-1956), American zoologist **9** 31-32

Kinshasa (city; Republic of Congo)
Kasavubu, Joseph **8** 453-455
Lumumba, Patrice Emery **10** 43-45

Kinship (anthropology)
Evans-Pritchard, Edward Evan **5** 340
Morgan, Lewis Henry **11** 167-168

Kiowa Indians (North America)
Fitzpatrick, Thomas **5** 474-475
Goodnight, Charles **6** 439
Miles, Nelson Appleton **11** 16-17
Momaday, N. Scott **11** 92-94

KIPLING, JOSEPH RUDYARD
(1865-1936), British poet and short-story
writer **9** 32-33
Brecht, Bertolt **2** 512-514
Conrad, Joseph **4** 205-207
McClure, Samuel Sidney **10** 398-399
Sienkiewicz, Henryk **14** 216-217
Wilson, Edmund **16** 318-319

Kipps (novel)
Wells, Herbert George **16** 195-196

KIRCHHOFF, GUSTAV ROBERT
(1824-1887), German physicist **9** 33-34
Boltzmann, Ludwig **2** 379-380
Bunsen, Robert Wilhelm **3** 124-125
Huggins, William **8** 14-15
Planck, Max Karl Ernst Ludwig
  12 342-344

KIRCHNER, ERNST LUDWIG (1880-1938),
German expressionist painter **9** 34-35
Klee, Paul **9** 47-49
Van Gogh, Vincent **15** 427-429

Kirina, battle of (1234)
Sundiata Keita **15** 33-34

Kiritsubo (literary character)
Murasaki Shikibu **11** 252-253

Kirk, Sir John (1832-1922), Scottish
administrator in Africa
Livingstone, David **9** 463-465

Kirk o'Field (near Edinburgh)
Mary, I **10** 308-309

Kirke, Edward (1553-1613), English
writer

Spenser, Edmund **14** 373-376

Kirke, Sir David (1596-1656), English mer-
chant adventurer
Brûlé, Étienne **3** 67-68
Champlain, Samuel de **3** 419-421

KIRKLAND, JOSEPH LANE (born 1922),
American labor union movement leader
9 35-37

KIRKLAND, SAMUEL (1741-1808), American Congregationalist missionary **9** 37
Brant, Joseph **2** 500-501

KIRKPATRICK, JEANE J. (born 1926), professor and first woman U.S. ambassador
to the United Nations **9** 37-39

Kirov, Sergei (1886-1934), Bolshevik leader
Kamenev, Lev Borisovich **8** 417-418
Zinoviev, Grigori Evseevich **16** 521-522

Kirov Ballet Company (GATOB)
Ulanova, Galina **15** 382-383

KIRSTEIN, LINCOLN (1906-1996), a
founder and director of the New York City
Ballet **9** 39-41

Kisangani
see Stanleyville

KISHI, NOBUSUKE (1896-1987), Japanese
politician **9** 41-43
Sato, Eisaku **13** 495-496

Kishinev (city; Bessarabia)
Bialik, Hayyim Nahman **2** 262-263
Dubnov, Simon **5** 115-116

Kisling, Moise (1821-1953), Polish-French
painter
Modigliani, Amedeo **11** 72-73

Kismet (musical)
Borodin, Aleksandr Profirevich
  2 422-423

Kiss (sculpture)
Brancusi, Constantin **2** 494-496
Rodin, Auguste **13** 236-238

Kiss for the Leper, A (novel)
Mauriac, François **10** 347-348

Kiss Me Again (film)
Lubitsch, Ernst **10** 18-19

Kiss Me Kate (musical)
Porter, Cole Albert **12** 405-406

KISSINGER, HENRY ALFRED (born 1923),
U.S. secretary of state and co-winner of
the Nobel Peace prize **9** 43-45

Kitab al Shifa
see Shifa (book)

Kitab al-Amanat wal-Itiqadat (book)
Saadia ben Joseph al-Fayumi **13** 396

Kitamura Kigin (flourished 17th century),
Japanese poet of the Teitoku school
Basho, Matsuo **2** 45-48

Kitasato, Shibasabura (1852-1931), Japanese bacteriologist
Behring, Emil Adolph von **2** 122-123

Kitchen Cabinet (Jackson, pre-1831)
Blair, Francis Preston **2** 313-315

Jackson, Andrew **8** 168-172
Kendall, Amos **8** 494
Van Buren, Martin **15** 410-411

Kitchen Still Life (painting)
Chardin, Jean Baptiste Siméon **3** 442-443

KITCHENER, HORATIO HERBERT (1850-1916), British field marshal and statesman **9** 45-46
India
Chelmsford, Frederic John Napier Thesiger **3** 497
Curzon, George Nathaniel **4** 351-352
Haig, Douglas **7** 67-68
the Sudan
Mahdi **10** 137-138
Salisbury, 3d Marquess of **13** 448-449
Victoria **15** 485-487
see also Boer War (1899-1902)

Kitson, Henry Hudson (1865-1947), English-American sculptor
Lachaise, Gaston **9** 147

Kittredge, George L. (1860-1941), American educator
Malory, Thomas **10** 175-176

Kitty Hawk (North Carolina)
Goddard, Robert Hutchings **6** 376-377
Wright brothers **16** 394-396

Kiuprili, Ahmed
see Köprülü, Ahmed

KIWANUKA, BENEDICTO KAGIMA MUGUMBA (1922-1972), Ugandan politician **9** 46-47
Mutesa II **11** 277-278
Obote, Apolo Milton **11** 457

Kiyonaga, Torü (1742-1815), Japanese painter and engraver
Utamaro, Kitagawa **15** 397

Kizevetter, A.A. (1866-1933), Russian historian
Klyuchevsky, Vasily Osipovich **9** 57-58

Klagende Lied, Das (cantata)
Mahler, Gustav **10** 144-145

Klail City Death Trip (book series)
Hinojosa, Rolando **7** 403-405

Klänge (lithograph and prose poems)
Kandinsky, Wassily **8** 420-422

Klausner, Joseph (1874-1958), Jewish scholar
Tschernichowsky, Saul **15** 323

Kléber, Jean Baptiste (1753-1800), French soldier
Napoleon I **11** 306-310

KLEE, PAUL (1879-1940), Swiss painter and graphic artist **9** 47-49
associates
Feininger, Lyonel **5** 406-407
Hartley, Marsden **7** 186
Kandinsky, Wassily **8** 420-422
Miró, Joan **11** 53-54

influence of
Dubuffet, Jean Philippe Arthur **5** 119-120
Flannagan, John Bernard **5** 480
Mies van der Rohe, Ludwig **11** 10-12
Schuller, Gunther **14** 37-38
Stella, Joseph **14** 422

Klee Wyck (book)
Carr, Emily **3** 319

Kleider machen Leute (story)
Keller, Gottfried **8** 478-479

KLEIN, A. M. (1909-1972), Canadian journalist, lawyer, novelist, and poet **9** 49-50

KLEIN, CALVIN (born 1942), American fashion designer **9** 50-52

KLEIN, MELANIE (1882-1960), Austrian psychotherapist **9** 52

Klein und Wagner (novel)
Hesse, Hermann **7** 367-369

Kleine Blätter (poem)
Goethe, Johann Wolfgang von **6** 388-391

Kleine Geistliche Konzerte (music collection)
Schütz, Heinrich **14** 48-49

Kleine Herr Friedemann, Der (stories)
Mann, Thomas **10** 204-207

Kleine Mahagonny (play)
Brecht, Bertolt **2** 512-514

Kleine Stadt, Die (novel)
Mann, Heinrich **10** 201-202

Kleinhans Music Hall (Buffalo, New York State)
Saarinen, Eliel and Eero **13** 396-398

Kleist, Ewald Christian von (1715-1759), German poet
Lessing, Gotthold Ephraim **9** 357-359

KLEIST, HEINRICH VON (1777-1811), German author **9** 52-53
Pasternak, Boris Leonidovich **12** 124-125
Schiller, Johann Christoph Friedrich von **14** 4-7
Tieck, Ludwig **15** 218-219
Wedekind, Frank **16** 166-167

KLIMT, GUSTAV (1862-1918), controversial Austrian painter **9** 53-55

KLINE, FRANZ (1910-1962), American painter **9** 55
Newman, Barnett **11** 365
Rothko, Mark **13** 320-321

Kline Tower (Yale University)
Johnson, Philip **8** 313-314

Klingsor (literary character)
Wolfram von Eschenbach **16** 360-361

Klingsor's Last Summer (novel)
Hesse, Hermann **7** 367-369

Kliszow, battle of (1702)
Charles XII **3** 464-466

KLOPSTOCK, FRIEDRICH GOTTLIEB (1724-1803), German poet **9** 55-56
Hölderlin, Johann Christian Friedrich **7** 451-452
Lessing, Gotthold Ephraim **9** 357-359
Mahler, Gustav **10** 144-145
Schubert, Franz Peter **14** 35-37

Klosterneuburg, monastery of (Austria)
Rottmayr, Johann Michael **13** 321

Klotz, Christian Adolf (1738-1771), German philologist
Lessing, Gotthold Ephraim **9** 357-359

KLUCKHOHN, CLYDE (1905-1960), American anthropologist **9** 56-57
Kroeber, Alfred Louis **9** 105-106
Linton, Ralph **9** 431

KLYUCHEVSKY, VASILY OSIPOVICH (1841-1911), Russian historian **9** 57-58

KMT
see Kuomintang

Knaben Wunderhorn, Des (folk songs; Arnim-Brentano)
Arnim, Achim von **1** 308-309
Brentano, Clemens **2** 515-516
Mahler, Gustav **10** 144-145

KNAPP, SEAMAN ASAHEL (1833-1911), American educator and agricultural pioneer **9** 58

Knäred, Peace of (1613)
Gustavus II **7** 43-45
Oxenstierna, Axel Gustafsson **12** 44-45

Kneel to the Rising Sun ... (stories)
Caldwell, Erskine **3** 223-224

Kneeling Woman (sculpture)
Lehmbruck, Wilhelm **9** 307

Knemon (literary character)
Menander **10** 477-478

Knepp Castle (Sussex)
Nash, John **11** 316

Kneses Tifereth Israel Synagogue (Port Chester, New York State)
Johnson, Philip **8** 313-314

Knickerbocker, Diedrich (pseudonym)
see Irving, Washington

Knickerbocker Holiday (play and musical)
Anderson, Maxwell **1** 219-220
Weill, Kurt **16** 174-175

Knife Edge in Two Pieces (sculpture)
Moore, Henry **11** 146-148

KNIGHT, FRANK HYNEMAN (1885-1972), American economist **9** 58-59
Clark, John Maurice **4** 77-78
Seligman, Edwin Robert Anderson **14** 93-94

Knight, Death, and the Devil (engraving)
Dürer, Albrecht **5** 159-161

Knight of the Burning Pestle, The (play; Beaumont)
Beaumont, Francis **2** 95
Heywood, Thomas **7** 373-374

Knight of the Cart, The (romance)
Chrestien de Troyes **4** 23-24

Knight of the Lion, The (romance)
Chrestien de Troyes **4** 23-24

Knightley, John (literary character)
Austen, Jane **1** 377-379

Knights, The (play; Aristophanes)
Aristophanes **1** 293-294
Cleon **4** 104-105

Knight's Gambit (literary collection)
Faulkner, William **5** 395-397

Knights of Labor (United States union)
Gibbons, James **6** 300-301
Gompers, Samuel **6** 420-422
Mitchell, John **11** 58-59
Powderly, Terence Vincent **12** 420-421
Stephens, Uriah **14** 431-432

Knights of Malta
see Knights of Saint John

Knights of Rhodes
see Knights of Saint John

Knights of Saint John (military order)
Caravaggio **3** 282-284
Mehmed the Conqueror **10** 452-454

Knights of the Round Table
Malory, Thomas **10** 175-176
see also Arthurian legend

Knight's Tale
see Canterbury Tales

Knights Templar (military order)
Alfonso I **1** 148
Bernard of Clairvaux **2** 207-208
Clement V **4** 101-102
Philip IV **12** 274

KNIPLING, EDWARD FRED (born 1909),
American entomologist **9** 59-60

Knipper, Olga (1868-1959), Russian actress
Chekhov, Anton Pavlovich **3** 494-497

Knoblock, Edward (1874-1945),
American-born English playwright
Bennett, Arnold **2** 167-168

KNOPF, ALFRED A. (1892-1984), American
publisher **9** 60-61

KNOPF, BLANCHE WOLF (1894-1966),
American publisher **9** 61-62

Knorr, Iwan (1853-1916), German composer and theorist
Bloch, Ernest **2** 326-327

Knossos (city; ancient Crete)
Evans, Arthur John **5** 335-336

Knot Garden, The (opera)
Tippett, Michael Kemp **15** 234-235

Knowing and the Known (book)
Bentley, Arthur F. **2** 178
Dewey, John **4** 520-523

Knowledge, theories of (philosophy)
Aristotelianism
Aristotle **1** 295-296
Bacon, Francis **1** 422-424

Bonaventure **2** 383-384
Duns Scotus, John **5** 149-150
Kindi, Abu-Yusuf Yaqub ibn-Ishaq al-
9 10-11
Ramus, Petrus **13** 27-28
Augustinianism
Augustine **1** 367-370
Lull, Raymond **10** 39-40
Thomas Aquinas **15** 183-186
empiricism
Berkeley, George **2** 197-198
Duns Scotus, John **5** 149-150
Helmont, Jan Baptista van
7 269-271
Hobbes, Thomas **7** 421-423
Hume, David **8** 31-34
Locke, John **9** 478-480
Mach, Ernst **10** 90-91
Mill, John Stuart **11** 21-23
Quine, Willard Van Orman
12 514-515
idealism
Berkeley, George **2** 197-198
Cassirer, Ernst **3** 358-359
Fichte, Johann Gottlieb **5** 435-436
Hegel, Georg Wilhelm Friedrich
7 254-256
Kant, Immanuel **8** 430-432
logical positivism
Nagel, Ernest **11** 291-292
Tarski, Alfred **15** 110-111
Wittgenstein, Ludwig **16** 350-351
nominalism
Bentham, Jeremy **2** 176-178
Cudworth, Ralph **4** 331
Hus, Jan **8** 56-59
Luther, Martin **10** 48-51
William of Ockham **16** 298-299
occasionalism
Malebranche, Nicolas **10** 166-167
personal knowledge
Polanyi, Michael **12** 372-373
positivism
Bentley, Arthur F. **2** 178
Schlick, Friedrich Albert Moritz
14 16-17
pragmatism
Bergson, Henri **2** 191-192
Dewey, John **4** 520-523
James, William **8** 215-217
Peirce, Charles Sanders **12** 187-188
Pre-Socratics
Heraclitus **7** 320
Parmenides **12** 116-117
rationalism
Descartes, René **4** 505-508
Leibniz, Gottfried Wilhelm von
9 307-310
Pascal, Blaise **12** 122-124
Spinoza, Baruch **14** 381-383
realism
Broad, Charlie Dunbar **3** 12
Moore, George Edward **11** 146
Russell, Bertrand Arthur William
13 373-374
sensationalism

Bergson, Henri **2** 191-192
Helvétius, Claude Adrien **7** 273-274
Stoicism
Chrysippus **4** 35-36
Galen **6** 178-180
Zeno of Citium **16** 499-500
tacit knowing
Polanyi, Michael **12** 372-373
see also individual movements and
schools of philosophy

KNOWLES, MALCOLM SHEPHERD (born
1913), American adult education theorist
and planner **9** 62-64

Know-Nothingism (United States politics)
Cameron, Simon **3** 246-247
Davis, Henry Winter **4** 415-416
Fillmore, Millard **5** 447-448
Hill, Benjamin Harvey **7** 386-387
Hughes, John Joseph **8** 17-18
Stevens, Thaddeus **14** 442-443
Stockton, Robert Field **14** 461-462
Wilson, James Harold **16** 324-325

Knox, Frank (1874-1944), American publisher and politician
Forrestal, James Vincent **6** 14

KNOX, HENRY (1750-1806), American
Revolutionary War general **9** 64

KNOX, JOHN (circa 1505-1572), Scottish
religious reformer **9** 65-66
Edward VI **5** 213-214
Lyndsay, David **10** 66-67
Mary, I **10** 308-309

KNOX, PHILANDER CHASE (1853-1921),
American statesman **9** 66-67
Mellon, Andrew William **10** 469-470

Knox, Ronald A. (1888-1957), English
Roman Catholic prelate and writer
Waugh, Evelyn Arthur St. John
16 145-147

Knoxville (musical composition)
Barber, Samuel **1** 500-501

KNUDSEN, WILLIAM S. (1879-1948),
American auto industry leader **9** 67-68

Knulp (stories)
Hesse, Hermann **7** 367-369

Knutzen, Martin (1713-1751), German
philosopher and Pietist
Hamann, Johann Georg **7** 92
Kant, Immanuel **8** 430-432

Kobo Daishi
see Kukai

KOCH, EDWARD I. (born 1924), New York
City mayor **9** 68-69

KOCH, ROBERT HEINRICH HERMANN
(1843-1910), German physician and bac-
teriologist **9** 69-70
Behring, Emil Adolph von **2** 122-123
Biggs, Hermann Michael **2** 272-273
Ehrlich, Paul **5** 225-226
Lwoff, André **10** 58-59
Pasteur, Louis **12** 125-127
Semmelweis, Ignaz Philipp **14** 101-102

Kocher, Emil Theodore (1841-1917), Swiss surgeon
  Cushing, Harvey Williams **4** 353-354

Koch's postulates (bacteriology)
  Koch, Heinrich Hermann Robert **9** 69-70

Kodak (camera)
  Eastman, George **5** 186

KODÁLY, ZOLTÁN (1882-1967), Hungarian composer **9** 71
  Bartók, Béla **2** 35-36

Koenigsberger, Leo (1837-1921), German mathematician
  Boltzmann, Ludwig **2** 379-380

KOESTLER, ARTHUR (1905-1983), author of political novels **9** 71-73
  Spartacus **14** 363-364

Koetsu, Hon-Ami (circa 1557-1637), Japanese painter
  Sotatsu, Tawaraya **14** 349

Koffka, Kurt (1886-1941), German-American psychologist
  Tolman, Edward Chace **15** 261-262

Koguryo
  see Korea—50-668 (Koguryo)

KOHL, HELMUT (born 1930), chancellor of West Germany (1982-1990) and first chancellor of a united Germany since World War II **9** 73-74

Köhler, Wolfgang (1887-1967), German-American psychologist
  Tolman, Edward Chace **15** 261-262

Kohlrausch, Friedrich (1840-1910), German physicist
  Arrhenius, Svante August **1** 318-320

Koizumi, Yakumo
  see Hearn, Lafcadio

Kojin (novel)
  Natsume, Soseki **11** 324-325

KOJONG (1852-1919), Korean king **9** 74-75
  Min **11** 46-47
  Taewŏn'gun, Hŭngsŏn **15** 74-75

Kokinshu (poems)
  Mabuchi, Kamo **10** 73-74

Kokoro (book)
  Hearn, Lafcadio **7** 240
  Natsume, Soseki **11** 324-325

KOKOSCHKA, OSKAR (1886-1980), Austrian painter, graphic artist, and author **9** 75-76

KOLAKOWSKI, LESZEK (born 1927), philosopher who wrote on broad themes of ethics, metaphysics, and religion **9** 76-77

Kolbe, Georg (1877-1947), German sculptor
  Mies van der Rohe, Ludwig **11** 10-12

KOLCHAK, ALEKSANDR VASILIEVICH (1873-1920), Russian admiral **9** 77-78
  Frunze, Mikhail Vasilievich **6** 134

Kollár, Jan (1793-1852), Slovak poet and archeologist
  Palacký, František **12** 69-70

Kollege Crampton (drama)
  Hauptmann, Gerhart Johann Robert **7** 199-201

KOLLONTAI, ALEKSANDRA MIKHAILOVNA (1872-1952), Soviet diplomat **9** 79
  Katayama, Sen **8** 457

KOLLWITZ, KÄTHE (1867-1945), German expressionist graphic artist and sculptor **9** 79-81
  Barlach, Ernst **2** 5-6

Köln
  see Cologne

Kolokol (magazine)
  Herzen, Aleksandr Ivanovich **7** 351-352

Komei (1821-1867), emperor of Japan 1846-1867
  Iwakura, Tomomi **8** 160-161
  Mutsuhito **11** 279-282
  Saionji, Kimmochi **13** 438-439

Komet, oder Nikolaus Marggraf, Der (novel)
  Richter, Johann Paul Friedrich **13** 150-151

Konbaung dynasty (Burma; 1752-1885)
  Alaungpaya **1** 103

KONEV, IVAN STEFANOVICH (1897-1973), Soviet marshal **9** 81-82
  Zhukov, Georgi Konstantinovich **16** 512-513

Kongi's Harvest (play; film)
  Soyinka, Wole **14** 358-359

Kongmin (died 1374), Korean king
  Yi Sng-gye **16** 458-459

Kongo (Bantu kingdom; Africa)
  Affonso I **1** 72
  Nzinga Nkuwu **11** 451-452

Konig David in Ballingschap (play)
  Vondel, Joost van den **16** 19-20

König Hirsch (opera)
  Henze, Hans Werner **7** 314

König Nicolo oder So ist das Leben (play)
  Wedekind, Frank **16** 166-167

König Ottokars Glück un Ende (play)
  Grillparzer, Franz **6** 546-547

Königgrätz, battle of
  see Sadowa, battle of (1886)

Königinhof (Czech manuscript)
  Masaryk, Tomáš Garrigue **10** 314-315

Königliche Hoheit (novel)
  Mann, Thomas **10** 204-207

Königsberg, University of
  Baer, Karl Ernst von **1** 431-432
  Fichte, Johann Gottlieb **5** 435-436
  Herbart, Johann Friedrich **7** 321-322
  Kant, Immanuel **8** 430-432

Konigsmark, Countess Maria Aurora von (1662-1728), Swedish beauty and wit

Saxe, Comte de **13** 507-508

Koninck, Philips de (1619-1688), Dutch painter
  Rembrandt Harmensz van Rijn **13** 91-95

KONOE, PRINCE FUMIMARO (or Konoye; 1891-1945), Japanese premier 1937-1939 and 1940-1941 **9** 82-83
  Hirohito **7** 410-412
  Inukai, Tsuyoshi **8** 130-131
  Saionji, Kimmochi **13** 438-439
  Tojo, Hideki **15** 254-256

Konzertstück (music)
  Weber, Carl Maria Friedrich Ernst von **16** 156-157

Koo, Wellington (1888-1985), Chinese statesman and diplomat
  Sun Yat-sen **15** 35-39

Kook, Abraham Isaac
  see Kuk, Abraham Isaac

KOONS, JEFF (born 1955), American artist **9** 83-84

Kopf, Der (book)
  Mann, Heinrich **10** 201-202

KÖPRÜLÜ, AHMED (Köprülüzade Fazil Ahmed Pasha; 1635-76), Turkish statesman and general **9** 84-85

Kora in Hell (book)
  Williams, William Carlos **16** 308-309

Koralle, Die (play)
  Kaiser, Georg **8** 411-412

Koran (religion; book)
  commentaries on
    Sayyid Qutb **13** 509-511
    Tabari, Muhammad ibn Jarir al- **15** 69-70
  doctrinal interpretations
    Abduh ibn Hasan Khayr Allah, Muhammad **1** 16-17
    Ashari, Abu al- Hasan Ali al- **1** 327-328
  exegesis
    Bukhari, Muhammad ibn Ismail al- **3** 111-112
    Hafiz, Shams al-Din **7** 63
  passages inscribed on coins
    Abd al-Malik **1** 12-13
  philosophical interpretations
    Averroës **1** 382-383
    Nazzam, Ibrahim ibn Sayyar al- **11** 329
    Syed Ahmed Khan **15** 60
  revelations
    Mohammed **11** 76-78

Korea (nation; eastern Asia)
  • 50-668 (THREE KINGDOMS)
    historians of
      Kim Pusik **9** 8-9
    Koguryo
      Kwanggaet'o **9** 139-140
      T'ai-tsung, T'ang **15** 83-84
    Paekche
      Kwanggaet'o **9** 139-140

Silla
  Kwanggaet'o **9** 139-140
  Suiko **15** 15-16
• 668-935 (UNIFIED SILLA)
  maritime dominance
    Chang Po-go **3** 433-434
    Wang Kon **16** 101
  scholarship
    Sol Ch'ong **14** 325-326
• 918-1392 (KORYO DYNASTY)
  foundation and expansion
    Kwangjong **9** 140
    Wang Kon **16** 101
  military, Chin, and Mongol rule
    Ch'oe Ch'ung-hn **4** 13
    Chong Chung-bu **4** 15
    Kim Pusik **9** 8-9
    Kublai Khan **9** 115-118
• 1392-1910 (YI DYNASTY)
  China and
    Kim Ok-kyun **9** 7-8
    Min **11** 46-47
    Taewŏn'gun, Hŭngsŏn **15** 74-75
  cultural revival (18th century)
    Chongjo **4** 15-16]
  Japan and (16th century)
    Toyotomi Hideyoshi **15** 286-289
  Japan and (1850-1910)
    Ito, Hirobumi **8** 153-155
    Iwakura, Tomomi **8** 160-161
    Okubo, Toshimichi **11** 489-490
    Saigo, Takamori **13** 429
    see also rulers (1850-1910)
      below
  literature
    Yi Hwang **16** 457
    Yun Sondo **16** 483
  rulers (1392-1519)
    Sejo **14** 90-91
    Sejong **14** 91-92
    Yi Sng-gye **16** 458-459
  rulers (1519-1850)
    Chongjo **4** 15-16
    Sŏnjo **14** 341-342
    Yi Sunsin **16** 459-461
    Yngjo **16** 461-462
  rulers (1850-1910)
    Kim Ok-kyun **9** 7-8
    Kojong **9** 74-75
    Min **11** 46-47
    Taewŏn'gun, Hŭngsŏn **15** 74-75
• 1910-1948 (FOREIGN RULE)
  Kim Il-sung **9** 4-6
  Park, Chung Hee **12** 99-102
  Rhee, Syngman **13** 117-120
  Witte, Sergei Yulyevich **16** 349-350
• SINCE 1948 (TWO REPUBLICS)
  North Korea (Democratic People's
  Republic of Korea)
    Kim Il-sung **9** 4-6
    Kim Jong Il **9** 6-7
  South Korea (Republic of Korea)
    Chun Doo Hwan **4** 45-47
    Kim Dae-jung **9** 3-4

Kim Young Sam **9** 9-10
Park, Chung Hee **12** 99-102
Rhee, Syngman **13** 117-120
Roh Tae Woo **13** 253-255
see also Korean War
  (1950-1953)

Korean War (1950-1953)
  armistice
    Dulles, John Foster **5** 134-135
    Eisenhower, Dwight David
      5 233-236
    Menon, Vengalil Krishnan Krishna
      10 507-509
  North Korea and China
    Chou En-lai **4** 20-22
    Kim Il-sung **9** 4-6
    Lin Piao **9** 429-430
  reporters
    Higgins, Marguerite **7** 378-380
  South Korea
    Park, Chung Hee **12** 99-102
    Rhee, Syngman **13** 117-120
  UN forces
    Armstrong, Neil Alden **1** 304-306
    Clark, Mark Wayne **4** 80-81
    Lie, Trygve Halvdan **9** 400-401
    MacArthur, Douglas **10** 76-78
    Magsaysay, Ramon **10** 130-131
    Ridgway, Matthew Bunker
      13 160-161
    Taylor, Maxwell **15** 126-127
  U.S. forces
    Taylor, Maxwell **15** 126-127
  U.S. policy
    Johnson, Lyndon Baines **8** 308-312
    Marshall, George Catlett
      10 278-279
    Truman, Harry S. **15** 314-316

Korematsu v. United States (legal case)
  Black, Hugo Lafayette **2** 301-303

Korin, Ogata (1658-1716), Japanese
painter
  Sotatsu, Tawaraya **14** 349

KORNBERG, ARTHUR (born 1918), Amer-
icna biochemist **9** 85-87

Körner, Christian Gottfried (1756-1831),
German jurist
  Schiller, Johann Christoph Friedrich von
    14 4-7

KORNILOV, LAVR GEORGIEVICH
(1870-1918), Russian general **9** 87-88

Koryo
  see Korea—918-1392

Kosan
  see Yun Sondo

**KOSCIUSZKO, TADEUSZ ANDRZEJ
BONAWENTURA** (1746-1817), Polish
patriot, hero in the American Revolution
9 88

Kosmos (book; A. von Humboldt)
  Church, Frederick Edwin **4** 49-50
  Humboldt, Friedrich Heinrich Alexan-
    der von **8** 30-31

Kossuth (musical composition)
  Bartók, Béla **2** 35-36

KOSSUTH, LOUIS (1802-1894), Hungari-
an statesman **9** 88-90
  Andrássy, Julius **1** 222-223
  Deák, Francis **4** 431-432

Kostrowitsky, Wilhelm Apollinaris de
  see Apollinaire, Guillaume

KOSYGIN, ALEKSEI NIKOLAEVICH
(1904-1980), chairman of the U.S.S.R.
Council of Ministers and head of the
Soviet government (1964-1980) **9** 90-91
  Johnson, Lyndon Baines **8** 308-312

Kotoku (flourished mid-7th century), Japanese emperor
  Fujiwara Kamatari **6** 145

Kotzebue, August F.F. von (1761-1819),
Russian author and dramatist
  Kotzebue, Otto von **9** 91-92

KOTZEBUE, OTTO VON (1787-1846),
Russian explorer **9** 91-92

Kotzebue Sound (northwestern Alaska)
  Franklin, John **6** 64-65
  Kotzebue, Otto von **9** 91-92

Kouros (play)
  Kazantzakis, Nikos **8** 466-468

Koussevitzky, Serge (1874-1951),
Russian-born American conductor
  Bartók, Béla **2** 35-36
  Bernstein, Leonard **2** 218-219
  Copland, Aaron **4** 227-228
  Martinu, Bohuslav **10** 299-300
  Prokofiev, Sergei Sergeevich
    12 458-460

Kozlov, Pëtr Kuzmich (1863-1935), Russian explorer
  Przhevalsky, Nikolai Mikhailovich
    12 469-470

KOZYREV, ANDREI VLADIMIROVICH
(born 1951), Russian minister of foreign
affairs and a liberal, pro-Western figure in
Boris Yeltsin's cabinet **9** 92-93

KPD
  see Communist party, German

Kraft Music Hall (radio show)
  Crosby, Harry Lillis **4** 324-326

Kraniche des Ibykus, Die (poem)
  Schiller, Johann Christoph Friedrich von
    14 4-7

Krank, The (book)
  Lawson, Thomas William **9** 255-256

Krapp's Last Tape (play)
  Beckett, Samuel **2** 102-104

KRASNER, LEE (Lenore; 1908-1984), American painter and collage artist **9** 93-94

Krassin (ship)
  Nobile, Umberto **11** 411-412

KRAVCHUK, LEONID MAKAROVYCH
(born 1934), president of the Ukraine
(1991-1994) **9** 94-95

Krebs cycle (biochemistry)
Krebs, Hans Adolf **9** 95-97

KREBS, SIR HANS ADOLF (1900-1981),
German-British biochemist **9** 95-97

KREISKY, BRUNO (1911-1983), chancellor
of Austria (1970-1983) **9** 97-98

Kreisleriana (musical composition)
Schumann, Robert Alexander **14** 41-43

Kremer, Gerhard
see Mercator, Gerhardus

Kremlin (Moscow)
Ivan III **8** 156-157

Kremsier (town; Moravia)
Maulbertsch, Franz Anton **10** 345
Palacký, František **12** 69-70

KRENEK, ERNST (born 1900), Austrian
composer **9** 98-99

KREPS, JUANITA MORRIS (born 1921),
economist, university professor, United
States secretary of commerce
(1977-1979), and author **9** 99-101

Kreuger, Ivar (1880-1932), Swedish industrialist
Monnet, Jean **11** 109-110

Kreutzer Sonata (music)
Beethoven, Ludwig van **2** 114-117

Kreutzer Sonata, The (book)
Tolstoy, Leo **15** 262-265

Kreymborg, Alfred (1883-1966), American
poet and playwright
Moore, Marianne **11** 148-149
Stevens, Wallace **14** 443-445

KRIEGHOFF, CORNELIUS (1815-1872),
Dutch-born Canadian painter **9** 101

Krishna (Hindu deity)
Bhaktivedanta Prabhupada **2** 254-255
Ramakrishna, Sri **13** 11-13

Krishnakanter Will (novel)
Chatterji, Bankimchandra **3** 480-481

KRISHNAMURTI, JIDDU (1895-1986),
Indian mystic and philosopher **9** 101-103
Besant, Annie Wood **2** 233-234

Krisis (poems)
Hesse, Hermann **7** 367-369

Kristen Lavransdatter (novel)
Undset, Sigrid **15** 388-389

KROC, RAYMOND ALBERT (1902-1984),
creator of the McDonald's chain
9 103-104

KROCHMAL, NACHMAN KOHEN
(1785-1840), Austrian Jewish historian
9 104-105
Graetz, Heinrich Hirsch **6** 483

KROEBER, ALFRED LOUIS (1876-1960),
American anthropologist **9** 105-106
Boas, Franz **2** 349-351
Erikson, Erik Homburger **5** 309-310
Fletcher, Alice Cunningham **5** 486-487

KROGH, SCHACK AUGUST STEENBERG
(1874-1949), Danish physiologist **9** 106

Kröller-Müller Museum (Otterlo, Netherlands)
Van de Velde, Henry **15** 419-420

Kroměříž
see Kremsier

Kronecker, Leopold (1823-1891), German
mathematician
Cantor, Georg Ferdinand Ludwig
Philipp **3** 265-266

Kronenwächter, Die (novel)
Arnim, Achim von **1** 308-309

KROPOTKIN, PETER ALEKSEEVICH
(1842-1921), Russian prince, scientist,
and anarchist **9** 107-108
Mussolini, Benito **11** 272-274
Proudhon, Pierre Joseph **12** 461-463

**KRUGER, STEPHANUS JOHANNES
PAULUS** ("Paul"; 1825-1904), South
African statesman **9** 108-109
Roberts, Frederick Sleigh **13** 195-196
Salisbury, 3d Marquess of **13** 448-449
Smuts, Jan Christian **14** 309-310

Krumme Teufel, Der (musical composition)
Haydn, Franz Joseph **7** 219-221

KRUPP FAMILY (19th-20th century), Ger-
man industrialists **9** 109-111
Alfred (1812-1887) **9** 109
Friedrich (1787-1826) **9** 109
Friedrich Jodokus (1706-1757) **9** 109

Krusenstern, Baron Adam Johann von
(1770-1846), Russian explorer and navigator
Kotzebue, Otto von **9** 91-92

Krutch, Joseph Wood (1893-1970), American author, critic, and naturalist
Dreiser, Herman Theodore **5** 98-100

Krypton (element—chemistry)
Mendeleev, Dmitrii Ivanovich
10 486-488
Ramsay, William **13** 21-22

KU CHIEH-KANG (born 1893), Chinese
historian **9** 120-121

KU K'AI-CHIH (circa 345-circa 406), Chi-
nese painter **9** 125-126
Mi Fei **11** 12-13
Wang Wei **16** 106-108
Wu Tao-tzu **16** 405-406
Yen Li-pen **16** 453-454

Ku Klux Klan (secret society; United States)
members
Black, Hugo Lafayette **2** 301-303
Forrest, Nathan Bedford **6** 13-14
opponents
Bristow, Benjamin Helm **3** 9-10
Byrnes, James Francis **3** 191-192
Dees, Morris S. Jr. **4** 456-457
Hapgood, Norman **7** 137-138
Marcuse, Herbert **10** 245-247
Tourgée, Albion Winegar
15 277-278
White, William Allen **16** 240-241

terror tactics
Alcorn, James Lusk **1** 120-121
Curley, James Michael **4** 344-345
Gordon, John Brown **6** 449-450
Malcolm X **10** 165-166

Ku Klux Klan Act (United States)
Ames, Adelbert **1** 198

Kuan Tao-shêng (1262-circa 1325), Chinese
painter
Chao Meng-fu **3** 436-437

Kuang Tsung (ruled 1189-1194), Chinese
emperor
Chu Hsi **4** 40-43
Kao-tsung **8** 433

KUANG-HSÜ (1871-1908), emperor of
China 1875-1908 **9** 111-112
Chang Chih-tung **3** 430-431
K'ang Yu-wei **8** 426-428
Liang Ch'i-ch'ao **9** 395-396
Tz'u-hsi **15** 375-376

K'uang-jen jih-chi (story)
Lu Hsün **10** 35-37

KUANG-WU-TI (6 B.C. - 57 A.D.), Chinese
emperor ca. 25-57 **9** 112-113

Kuantu, battle of (200)
Ts'ao Ts'ao **15** 322-323

Kubin, Alfred (1877-1959), Bohemian
painter
Marc, Franz **10** 231

KUBITSCHEK DE OLIVEIRA, JUSCELINO
(1902-1976), president of Brazil
1956-1961 **9** 113-115
Castelo Branco, Humberto **3** 359-360
Goulart, João **6** 467-469
Prestes, Luiz Carlos **12** 442-444

Kubla Khan (poem, Coleridge)
Bartram, William **2** 41-42
Coleridge, Samuel Taylor **4** 154-156

KUBLAI KHAN (1215-1294), Mongol
emperor **9** 115-118
Genghis Khan **6** 263-265
Hulagu Khan **8** 27-28
Polo, Marco **12** 380-382
Wen T'ien-hsiang **16** 203

KÜBLER-ROSS, ELISABETH (born 1926),
Swiss-born American psychiatrist
9 118-120

Kuei-ch'ü-lai tz'u (poem)
T'ao Ch'ien **15** 104-105

Kugler, Franz (1808-1858), German art historian
Burckhardt, Jacob Christoph **3** 132-133

Kuhn, Loeb and Co. (banking firm)
Schiff, Jacob Henry **14** 2-3
Warburg, Paul Moritz **16** 111-112

KUHN, THOMAS SAMUEL (1922-1996),
American historian and philosopher of
science **9** 121-123

Kuhnau, Johann (1660-1722), German
composer and organist
Bach, Johann Sebastian **1** 416-419

Kühne, Wilhelm (1837-1900), German physiologist
Szent-Györgyi, Albert von **15** 62-64

Ku-hsiang (story)
Lu Hsün **10** 35-37

KUK, ABRAHAM ISAAC (1865-1935), Russian-born Jewish scholar **9** 123-124

KUKAI (774-835), Japanese Buddhist monk **9** 124-125
Eisai **5** 231-232
Ennin **5** 288-289
Saicho **13** 426-428

KUKRIT PRAMOJ, MOMRAJAWONG (M.R.; born 1911), literary figure and prime minister of Thailand (1975-1976) **9** 126-127

Kullervo (musical composition)
Sibelius, Jean Julius Christian **14** 211-212

Kulturkampf (liberal movement, Germany; 1871-1887)
Bismarck, Otto Eduard Leopold von **2** 294-296
Leo XIII **9** 334-336

Kumalo (African people)
Mzilikazi **11** 285-286

Kumanovo, battle of (1912)
Alexander of Yugoslavia **1** 136-137

Kumara Siladitya
see Harsha

KUMARAJIVA (344/350-409/413), Indian Buddhist monk **9** 127
Hui-yüan **8** 25-26
Tao-an **15** 103-104

Kumarasambhava (epic poem)
Kalidasa **8** 414-415

Kun, Béla (1885-1937), Hungarian Jewish Communist
Horthy de Nagybánya, Nicholas **7** 510-512

Kunani
see Suleiman I

Kunckel, Johann (circa 1630-circa 1702), German alchemist
Stahl, Georg Ernst **14** 392-393

KUNDERA, MILAN (born 1929), Czech-born author **9** 128-129

Kunersdorf, battle of (1759)
Lessing, Gotthold Ephraim **9** 357-359

KÜNG, HANS (born 1928), Swiss-born Roman Catholic theologian **9** 129-130

Kung, Prince (Yi Hsin; 1833-98), Manchu statesman
Tz'u-hsi **15** 375-376
Wen-hsiang **16** 202-203
Wo-jen **16** 352

Kung-sun Yang
see Shang Yang

KUNIN, MADELEINE MAY (born 1933), first woman governor of Vermont **9** 130-131

Künstler, Die (poem)
Schiller, Johann Christoph Friedrich von **14** 4-7

KUNSTLER, WILLIAM M. (1919-1995), American civil rights attorney and author **9** 131-133
Means, Russell **10** 441-444

Kuo Chung-shu (flourished 2nd half 10th century), Chinese painter
Wang Wei **16** 106-108

Kuo Hsiang (died 312), Chinese Taoist writer
Tao-an **15** 103-104

KUO MO-JO (born 1892), Chinese author **9** 133-134
Lao Shê **9** 200-201

Kuo Tzuhsing (died 1355), Chinese military leader and rebel
Hung-wu **8** 38-39

Kuominchün
see National People's Army (China)

Kuomintang (Chinese political party)
Communist coalition
Ch'en Tu-hsiu **3** 501-502
Chou En-lai **4** 20-22
Chu Teh **4** 54-55
Kuo Mo-jo **9** 133-134
Li Ta-chao **9** 447
Lin Piao **9** 429-430
Liu Shao-Ch'i **9** 453-455
Mao Zedong **10** 225-227
founded
Sun Yat-sen **15** 35-39
Yüan Shih-k'ai **16** 480-481
leaders
Chiang Ching-kuo **3** 509-510
Chiang Kai-shek **3** 510-513
Lee Teng-hui **9** 283-285
Ts'ai Yüan-p'ei **15** 322
Wang Ching-wei **16** 98
Xiang Jingyu **16** 421-422
Yen Hsi-shan **16** 452-453
supporters
Feng Yü-hsiang **5** 412-413
Hu Shih **8** 63-65
Yen Hsi-shan **16** 452-453
see also China, Republic of (Nationalist); Communist party (China)

KUPKA, FRANTISEK (Frank; 1871-1957), Czech painter and illustrator **9** 134-135

Kupper, C.E.M.
see Doesburg, Theo van

Kuprili, Ahmed
see Köprülü, Ahmed

"Kurenaidan" of Asakusa, The (novel)
Kawabata, Yasunari **8** 463-464

KUROSAWA, AKIRA (born 1910), Japanese film director **9** 135-137

Kurth, Godefroid (1847-1916), Belgian historian
Pirenne, Jean Henri Otto Lucien Marie **12** 322-323

Kusamakura (novel)
Natsume, Soseki **11** 324-325

Kush
see Cush

Ku-shih hsin-pien (fables)
Lu Hsün **10** 35-37

Kütahya, Convention of (1833)
Mahmud II **10** 145-147

KUTUZOV, MIKHAIL ILARIONOVICH (1745-1813), Russian field marshal **9** 137-138
Alexander I **1** 130-132
Potemkin, Grigori Aleksandrovich **12** 411-412

Kuwait (Middle East)
'Abdullah al-Salim al-Sabah, Shaykh **1** 18-19
Bishara, Abdullah Yaccoub **2** 287-288
Bush, George **3** 167-169
Jaber Al-Sabah, Jaber Al-Ahmad Al- **8** 166-167

Kuwait Fund for Arab Economic Development
'Abdullah al-Salim al-Sabah, Shaykh **1** 18-19

Kuwait Independence Movement
'Abdullah al-Salim al-Sabah, Shaykh **1** 18-19

Kuyuk
see Güyük

Kuzari (Jewish classic)
Judah Halevi **8** 373

KUZNETS, SIMON (1901-1985), American economist, researcher, and author **9** 138-139

Kuznetsov
see Litvinov, Maxim Maximovich

Kwaidan and Japan (book)
Hearn, Lafcadio **7** 240

Kwakiutl Indians (North America)
Benedict, Ruth Fulton **2** 154-155
Boas, Franz **2** 349-351

KWANGGAET'O (375-413), Korean statesman, king of Koguryo **9** 139-140

KWANGJONG (925-975), Korean statesman, king of Koryo **9** 140

Kwangtung, battle of (1278)
Kublai Khan **9** 115-118

Kwannon (bodhisattva)
Shinran **14** 197

Kwanzaa
Karenga, Maulana **8** 444-447

Ky, Nguyen Cao (born 1930), South Vietnamese statesman
Thieu, Nguyen Van **15** 182-183

Kybèle (poem)
Leconte de Lisle, Charles Marie René **9** 273-274

KYD, THOMAS (1558-1594), English dramatist **9** 140-141
Marlowe, Christopher **10** 272-274

Kymograph (instrument)
Ludwig, Karl Friedrich Wilhelm **10** 31

Kyongjong (ruled 1720-1724), king of Korea
Yngjo **16** 461-462

Kyongsun (ruled 927-935), king of Korea
Wang Kon **16** 101

Kyonhoe-yo (poems)
Yun Sondo **16** 483

Kyoto (city; Japan)
Ashikaga Takauji **1** 330-332
Daigo II **4** 367-368
Eitoku, Kano **5** 242
Kammu **8** 420

Kyoto University
Yukawa, Hideki **16** 481-482

KYPRIANOU, SPYROS (born 1932), president of the Republic of Cyprus **9** 141-143

Kyunjong
see Sinmu

L

La Boétie, Étienne de (1530-1568), French writer
Montaigne, Michel Eyquem de **11** 116-117

LA BRUYÈRE, JEAN DE (1645-1696), French man of letters and moralist **9** 145
Condé, Prince de **4** 193-194
Lesage, Alain René **9** 353-354
Racine, Jean Baptiste **12** 532-535

La de Bringas (novel)
Galdós, Benito Pérez **6** 177-178

LA FARGE, JOHN (1835-1910), American artist and writer **9** 149-150
Adams, Henry Brooks **1** 45-47
McKim, Charles Follen **10** 417-418
Richardson, Henry Hobson **13** 139-141
Robinson, Theodore **13** 217
Tiffany, Louis Comfort **15** 220-221

LA FAYETTE, COMTESSE DE (Marie Madeleine Pioche de la Vergne; 1634-93), French novelist **9** 150-151
La Rochefoucauld, François Duc de **9** 208-209

LA FLESCHE, FRANCIS (1857-1932), Native American ethnologist **9** 152-154
Fletcher, Alice Cunningham **5** 486-487

LA FLESCHE, SUSETTE (1854-1903), Native American activist and reformer **9** 152-154

LA FOLLETTE, ROBERT MARION (1855-1925), American statesman **9** 155-156
McCarthy, Joseph Raymond **10** 388-389
Roosevelt, Theodore **13** 280-283
Taft, William Howard **15** 78-81

LA FONTAINE, JEAN DE (1621-1695), French poet **9** 156-157
Chagall, Marc **3** 406-407
Chénier, André Marie **3** 500-501
Lessing, Gotthold Ephraim **9** 357-359
Moore, Marianne **11** 148-149
Racine, Jean Baptiste **12** 532-535
Taine, Hippolyte Adolphe **15** 82-83
Wright, Elizur **16** 396-397

La Fosse, Charles de (1636-1716), French painter
Watteau, Antoine **16** 143-144

La Fresnaye, Roger de (1885-1925), French painter
Chagall, Marc **3** 406-407

LA GUARDIA, FIORELLO HENRY (1882-1947), American politician, New York City mayor **9** 166-167
Moses, Robert **11** 202-203

La Harpe, César de (1754-1838), Swiss statesman
Alexander I **1** 130-132

La, La, Lucille (musical)
Gershwin, George **6** 284-285

LA METTRIE, JULIEN OFFRAY DE (1709-1751), French physician and philosopher **9** 179-180

La Pasionaria
see Ibárruri

La Plata
see Argentina

La Plata, University of (Argentina)
Sábato, Ernesto **13** 399-400

La Pouplinière, Alexandre Jean Joseph Le Riche de (1693-1762), French music patron
Rameau, Jean Philippe **13** 17-18

La Prensa (newspaper; Nicaragua)
Chamorro, Violeta Barrios de **3** 417-419

LA ROCHEFOUCAULD, FRANÇOIS, DUC DE (1613-1680), French moralist **9** 208-209
La Bruyère, Jean de **9** 145
La Fayette, Comtesse de **9** 150-151

La Rochelle, siege of (1627-1628)
Charles, I **3** 450-452
Louis XIII **9** 529-531
Richelieu, Armand Jean du Plessis de **13** 142-144

LA SALLE, SIEUR DE (René Robert Cavelier; 1643-1687), French explorer and colonizer **9** 210-211

La Scala (opera house; Milan)
Caruso, Enrico **3** 345
Rossini, Gioacchino **13** 311-312
Toscanini, Arturo **15** 270-271
Verdi, Giuseppe Fortunino Francesco **15** 463-465

LA TOUR, GEORGE DE (1593-1652), French painter **9** 222
Caravaggio **3** 282-284
Le Nain, Antoine, Louis and Mathieu **9** 321-322

La Vallière, Françoise Louise de la Baume Le Blanc, Duchesse de (1644-1710), mistress of Louis XIV
Louis XIV **9** 531-533

LA VERENDRYE, SIEUR DE (Pierre Gaultier de Varennes; 1685-1749), French-Canadian soldier, explorer, and fur trader **9** 239-240

La Vergne, Marie Madeleine Pioche de
see La Fayette, Comtesse de

Là-bas (novel)
Huysmans, Joris Karl **8** 81-82

Là ci darem' la mano (aria; Mozart)
Chopin, Frédéric François **4** 16-18

La-Chaux-de-Fonds (town; France)
Le Corbusier **9** 274-275

Labor, forced
see Forced labor

Labor, United States Department of
Nader, Ralph **11** 290-291
Perkins, Frances **12** 221-222

Labor law (United States)
arbitrators
Cox, Archibald **4** 283-284
discrimination
Hill, Herbert **7** 387-388
laws regarding women and children
Coolidge, John Calvin **4** 217-219
Goldmark, Josephine **6** 407-408
Kelley, Florence **8** 483-484
minimum wage
Brandeis, Louis Dembitz **2** 496-497
Cardozo, Benjamin Nathan **3** 288-290

Carnegie, Andrew **3** 309-312
Eisenhower, Dwight David
5 233-236
Ford, Henry **6** 5-6
Goldberg, Arthur Joseph **6** 397-398
von Mises, Ludwig **16** 25
social security
see Social security—U.S.
wage-and-hour laws
Altgeld, John Peter **1** 180-182
Brandeis, Louis Dembitz **2** 496-497
workers' compensation
Jones, Samuel Milton **8** 342-343
Lewis, John Llewellyn **9** 387-388
Taft, William Howard **15** 78-81
see also Labor unions (United
States)—legislation

Labor leaders
American
see Labor leaders, American
Australian
Chifley, Joseph Benedict **3** 518
Fisher, Andrew **5** 462
see also Labour party (Australia)
Chinese
Liu Shao-Ch'i **9** 453-455
English
Bevin, Ernest **2** 252-253
Bondfield, Margaret Grace
2 388-389
Scargill, Arthur **13** 514-515
see also Labour party (England)
Israeli
Ben-Gurion, David **2** 160-161
Meir, Golda **10** 462-463
Jamaican
Bustamante, William Alexander
3 175-177
Manley, Michael Norman
10 200-201
Japanese
Katayama, Sen **8** 457
Kenyan
Mboya, Thomas Joseph **10** 384-385
Mexican
Toledano, Vicente Lombardo
15 256-257
New Zealand
Fraser, Peter **6** 73-74
Massey, William Ferguson **10** 324
Savage, Michael Joseph **13** 501-502
Polish
Walesa, Lech **16** 57-59
Scottish
Hardie, James Keir **7** 147-148
South African
Kadalie, Clements **8** 401-402
Ramaphosa, Matemela Cyril
13 15-16

Labor leaders, American
19th century
Coxey, Jacob Sechler **4** 286-287
Debs, Eugene Victor **4** 444-445
Kearney, Denis **8** 468

Powderly, Terence Vincent
12 420-421
Sylvis, William **15** 60-61
19th-20th century
Gompers, Samuel **6** 420-422
Haley, Margaret A. **7** 78-79
Haywood, William Dudley
7 232-233
20th century
Abel, Iorwith Wilber **1** 22-23
Bieber, Owen **2** 266-268
Bloor, Ella Reeve **2** 338-340
Bridges, Harry A.R. **3** 3-5
Chavez, Cesar **3** 486-487
Corona, Bert **4** 243-247
Dubinsky, David **5** 114-115
Flynn, Elizabeth Gurley **5** 496-497
Foster, William Zebulon **6** 27-28
Green, William R. **6** 521
Hillman, Sidney **7** 392-393
Hoffa, James R. **7** 436-437
Jones, Mary Harris **8** 338-339
Kirkland, Joseph Lane **9** 35-37
Lewis, John Llewellyn **9** 387-388
Meany, George **10** 444
Mitchell, John **11** 58-59
Murray, Philip **11** 264-265
Muste, Abraham Johannes
11 276-277
Pesotta, Rose **12** 248-249
Randolph, A. Philip **13** 28-29
Reuther, Walter Philip **13** 107-108
Schniederman, Rose **14** 22-23
Shanker, Albert **14** 151-153

Labor movement (Africa)
Mboya, Thomas Joseph **10** 384-385
Wallace-Johnson, Isaac Theophilus
Akunna **16** 76-77

Labor movement (Asia)
Katayama, Sen **8** 457
Mao Zedong **10** 225-227
Marcos, Ferdinand **10** 240-242

Labor movement (Australia and New
Zealand)
Bruce of Melbourne, 1st Viscount
3 61-62
Chifley, Joseph Benedict **3** 518
Curtin, John Joseph **4** 348-349
Deakin, Alfred **4** 432-433
Fraser, Peter **6** 73-74
Hughes, William Morris **8** 21-22
Lawson, Henry **9** 254-255
Santamaria, Bartholomew Augustine
13 473-474
Seddon, Richard John **14** 81-82
see also Labour party (Australia),
(New Zealand)

Labor movement (Europe)
Britain
Beard, Mary Ritter **2** 85-86
Bevin, Ernest **2** 252-253
Cole, George Douglas Howard
4 146-147
George V **6** 273-275

Gladstone, William Ewart
6 357-360
Hardie, James Keir **7** 147-148
Hobhouse, Leonard Trelawny
7 425-426
Jevons, William Stanley **8** 255-256
Melbourne, 2nd Viscount
10 468-469
Owen, Robert **12** 39-40
Shaftesbury, 7th Earl of **14** 137-138
see also Labour party (England)
the Continent
Blum, Léon **2** 343-344
Giolitti, Giovanni **6** 339-340
Lassalle, Ferdinand **9** 216
Leo XIII **9** 334-336

Labor movement (Latin America)
Alemán Valdés, Miguel **1** 126-127
Cárdenas, Lázaro **3** 286-287
Goulart, João **6** 467-469
Perón, Juan Domingo **12** 228-230
Prestes, Luiz Carlos **12** 442-444

Labor party
Belgium
Leopold II **9** 346-347
Leopold III **9** 347-348
Brazil
Goulart, João **6** 467-469
Israel
Ben-Gurion, David **2** 160-161
Dayan, Moshe **4** 429-431
Meir, Golda **10** 462-463
Norway
Lie, Trygve Halvdan **9** 400-401
Russia
Kerensky, Aleksandr Fedorovich
8 516-517
see also Labour party

Labor Reform-party (United States)
Phillips, Wendell **12** 281-282
Sylvis, William **15** 60-61

Labor unions (United States)
AFL-CIO
Bridges, Harry A.R. **3** 3-5
Carnegie, Andrew **3** 309-312
Gompers, Samuel **6** 420-422
Green, William R. **6** 521
Hillman, Sidney **7** 392-393
Lewis, John Llewellyn **9** 387-388
Meany, George **10** 444
Murray, Philip **11** 264-265
closed shop
Hoover, Herbert Clark **7** 483-485
Shaw, Lemuel **14** 164-165
Sylvis, William **15** 60-61
collective bargaining
Gary, Elbert Henry **6** 229-230
Hoover, Herbert Clark **7** 483-485
Reuther, Walter Philip **13** 107-108
development and ideals
Bell, Daniel **2** 132-133
Commons, John Rogers **4** 185
Debs, Eugene Victor **4** 444-445
Dubinsky, David **5** 114-115

Evans, George Henry **5** 337-338
Murray, Philip **11** 264-265
ILGWU
Dubinsky, David **5** 114-115
Herberg, Will **7** 322-323
Hillman, Sidney **7** 392-393
Schniederman, Rose **14** 22-23
ILWU
Bridges, Harry A.R. **3** 3-5
Knights of Labor
Powderly, Terence Vincent
12 420-421
Stephens, Uriah **14** 431-432
labor-management relations
Ford, Henry **6** 5-6
Ford, Henry II **6** 6-7
Gompers, Samuel **6** 420-422
Harding, Warren Gamaliel
7 148-149
Jones, Samuel Milton **8** 342-343
Lowell, Josephine Shaw **10** 15-16
Mitchell, John **11** 58-59
Rockefeller, John D. Jr. **13** 225-226
see also collective bargaining
(above)
legislation
Arnold, Thurman Wesley **1** 314
Hillman, Sidney **7** 392-393
Norris, George William **11** 428-429
Palmer, Alexander Mitchell
12 77-78
Taft, William Howard **15** 78-81
Wagner, Robert Ferdinand **16** 43
Socialists and
De Leon, Daniel **4** 479-480
Gompers, Samuel **6** 420-422
strikes
see Strike (labor)
teamsters
Hoffa, James R. **7** 436-437
see also New Deal—labor relations,
social welfare programs, and
under individual unions

Labor Zionist party (United States)
Ben-Gurion, David **2** 160-161
Gordon, Aaron David **6** 447-448
Meir, Golda **10** 462-463

Laboratory Theatre (Wroclaw, Poland)
Grotowski, Jerzy **7** 19-20

Laborers, Statute of (1351; England)
Edward III **5** 211-212

Labor/management negotiation
Kerr, Clark **8** 519-521
Shultz, George Pratt **14** 209-211
Wilson, Charles Erwin **16** 316-317

Labour party (Australia)
communism opposed
Mannix, Daniel **10** 210
Santamaria, Bartholomew Augustine
13 473-474
leaders
Chifley, Joseph Benedict **3** 518
Curtin, John Joseph **4** 348-349
Evatt, Herbert Vere **5** 341-343

Fisher, Andrew **5** 462
Hawke, Robert James Lee **7** 205-206
Hughes, William Morris **8** 21-22
Keating, Paul John **8** 469-470
Lang, John Thomas **9** 192-193
Lyons, Joseph Aloysius **10** 69-70
Scullin, James Henry **14** 73
Whitlam, Edward Gough
16 244-245
opponents
Forrest, John **6** 12-13
Menzies, Robert Gordon
10 510-511

Labour party (Canada)
Woodsworth, James Shaver **16** 376

Labour party (England)
Asquith, Herbert Henry **1** 344-346
Attlee, Clement Richard **1** 361-362
Baldwin, Stanley **1** 468-469
Benn, Tony **2** 164-166
Bevan, Aneurin **2** 248-249
Bevin, Ernest **2** 252-253
Boothroyd, Betty **2** 406-407
Callaghan, Leonard James **3** 230-231
Foot, Michael **5** 505-507
Gaitskell, Hugh **6** 173-174
Henderson, Arthur **7** 277-278
Jenkins, Roy Harris **8** 244-245
Kaufman, Gerald Bernard **8** 458-460
Kinnock, Neil **9** 29-30
Laski, Harold J. **9** 215-216
MacDonald, James Ramsay **10** 84-85
Maxwell, Ian Robert **10** 360-361
Menon, Vengalil Krishnan Krishna
10 507-509
Owen, David Anthony Llewellyn
12 37-39
Tawney, Richard Henry **15** 120-121
Webb, Beatrice Potter **16** 153-154
Webb, Sidney James **16** 154-155
Wilkinson, Ellen **16** 283-284
Williams, Shirley Vivien Teresa Brittain
16 305-306
Wilson, James Harold **16** 324-325

Labour Party (Ireland)
Robinson, Mary Bourke **13** 211-213

Labour Party (Israel)
Peres, Shimon **12** 210-211
Rabin, Yitzchak **12** 527-529

Labour Party (Norway)
Brundtland, Gro Harlem **3** 68-69

Labour party (New Zealand)
Fraser, Peter **6** 73-74
Massey, William Ferguson **10** 324
Savage, Michael Joseph **13** 501-502

Labour party (Rhodesia)
Welensky, Roy **16** 188

Labour party (South Africa)
Hertzog, James Barry Munnik
7 347-348

Labour party (Scotland)
Hardie, James Keir **7** 147-148

Labour Representation Committee (established 1900)
MacDonald, James Ramsay **10** 84-85

Labrador (peninsula; northeastern North
America)
Corte Reál, Gaspar and Miguel
4 254-255
Ericson, Leif **5** 306-307
Jolliet, Louis **8** 328-329
MacMillan, Donald Baxter **10** 111-112

Labriolle
see Velasco Ibarra, José María

LABROUSTE, PIERRE FRANÇOIS HENRI
(1801-1875), French architect-engineer
9 144
Eiffel, Alexandre Gustave **5** 227-228
McKim, Charles Follen **10** 417-418

Labrunie, Gérard
see Nerval, Gérard de

Labyrinth of the World ... (book)
Comenius, John Amos **4** 180-181

Lac, Le (poem; Lamartine)
Hugo, Victor Marie **8** 22-25
Lamartine, Alphonse Marie Louis de
9 173-175

Lacaille, Nicolas Louis de (1713-1762),
French astronomer
Lavoisier, Antoine Laurent **9** 241-244

LACAN, JACQUES (1901-1981), French
psychoanalyst **9** 145-147

Lacépède, B.G.E. Delaville, Comte de
(1756-1825), French naturalist
Houdon, Antoine **7** 516-517

Lacerda, Carlos (1914-1977), Brazilian
politician and author
Kubitschek de Oliveira, Juscelino
9 113-115

LACHAISE, GASTON (1882-1935),
French-born American sculptor **9** 147
Maillol, Aristide **10** 150-151

Laches (dialogue)
Plato **12** 345-347

Lachrimae (musical collection)
Dowland, John **5** 90

Lackawanna Valley (painting)
Inness, George **8** 123-124

Lackland, John
see John (king of England)

LACOMBE, ALBERT (1827-1916), Canadian missionary priest **9** 147-148

LACORDAIRE, JEAN BAPTISTE HENRI
(1802-1861), French Dominican preacher
9 148
Lamennais, Hugues Félicité Robert de
9 179
Montalembert, Comte de **11** 118-119

Lacroix, Paul (1806-1884), French scholar
and author
Dumas, Alexandre **5** 136-138

Lactic acid (biochemistry)
Hill, Archibald Vivian **7** 385-386

Meyerhof, Otto Fritz **10** 537-539
Scheele, Karl Wilhelm **13** 525-526

Ladd, George T. (1842-1921), American psychologist and philosopher
Lotze, Rudolf Hermann **9** 521-522

LADD, WILLIAM (1778-1841), American pacifist **9** 149
Burritt, Elihu **3** 160

Ladies' Magazine
see Godey's Lady's Book

Ladies Peace of Cambrai
see Cambrai, Peace of (1529)

Ladislas III (1424-1444), king of Poland 1434-1444 and of Hungary 1440-1444
Hunyadi, John **8** 51-52

Ladislas V (Ladislas Posthumus; 1440-1457), king of Hungary 1446-1452 and of Bohemia 1452-1457
Hunyadi, John **8** 51-52

Lady Be Good (nusical)
Gershwin, George **6** 284-285

Lady Booby (literary character)
Fielding, Henry **5** 442-444

Lady Byron Vindicated (book)
Stowe, Harriet Elizabeth Beecher **14** 484-485

Lady Chatterley's Lover (novel)
Lawrence, David Herbert **9** 247-248

Lady Frederick (play)
Maugham, William Somerset **10** 344-345

Lady from the Sea, The (play)
Ibsen, Henrik **8** 98-100

Lady Geraldine's Courtship (poem)
Browning, Elizabeth Barrett **3** 52-53

Lady if you so spite me (song)
Dowland, John **5** 90

Lady in Her Bath (painting)
Clouet, Jean and François **4** 122-123

Lady in the Dark (musical)
Weill, Kurt **16** 174-175

Lady in the Lake, The (novel)
Chandler, Raymond Jr. **3** 423-425

Lady Inger of Østraat (play)
Ibsen, Henrik **8** 98-100

Lady Is a Tramp, The (song)
Rodgers, Richard Charles **13** 234-236

Lady Macbeth of Mzensk (opera)
Shostakovich, Dmitri Dmitrievich **14** 204-205

Lady Mary and Her Nurse (book)
Traill, Catharine Parr **15** 291

Lady Nyassa (steamboat)
Livingstone, David **9** 463-465

Lady of May (masque)
Sidney, Philip **14** 214-215

Lady of Shalott, The (poem)
Tennyson, Alfred **15** 144-146

Lady of the Lake, The (poem)
Scott, Walter **14** 68-70

Lady Pepperell House (Kittery Point, Maine)
Harrison, Peter **7** 179-180

Lady Regents ... (painting)
Hals, Frans **7** 89-91

Lady Susan (novel)
Austen, Jane **1** 377-379

Lady, The (novel)
Richter, Conrad Michael **13** 148-149

Lady Washington (sloop)
Gray, Robert **6** 508-509

Lady Weighing Gold (painting)
Vermeer, Jan **15** 466-467

Lady Windermere's Fan (play)
Wilde, Oscar Fingall O'Flahertie Wills **16** 272-273

Lady with a Pink (painting)
Rembrandt Harmensz van Rijn **13** 91-95

Lady with the Dog (story)
Chekhov, Anton Pavlovich **3** 494-497

Ladybird, The (novelette)
Lawrence, David Herbert **9** 247-248

Ladysmith, siege of (1899-1900)
Botha, Louis **2** 434-436

Laelius, Gaius (circa 185-circa 115 B.C.), Roman consul
Scipio Africanus Minor, Publius Cornelius Aemilianus **14** 62-63

Laengselens Boat (novel)
Rölvaag, Ole Edvart **13** 265

Laer, Pieter van (circa 1592-1642), Dutch painter
Le Nain, Antoine, Louis and Mathieu **9** 321-322

Lafarge, Paul (1842-1911), French Socialist politician and writer
Marx, Karl **10** 304-308

LAFAYETTE, MARQUIS DE (Marie Joseph Paul Yves Roch Gilbert du Motier; 1757-1834), French general and statesman **9** 151-152
Cooper, James Fenimore **4** 220-223
Danton, Georges Jacques **4** 391-393
Dumas, Alexandre **5** 136-138
Morse, Samuel Finley Breese **11** 192-193
Rush, William **13** 365-366
see also American Revolution

Lafayette Buried (lithograph)
Daumier, Honoré Victorin **4** 403-405

Lafcadio (literary character)
Gide, André **6** 308-309

Laffeldt, battle of (1747)
Amherst, Jeffery **1** 200-201

Lafitte, Jacques (1767-1844)
Thiers, Louis Adolphe **15** 181-182

LAFONTAINE, OSKAR (born 1943), German politician **9** 158-160

LAFONTAINE, SIR LOUIS-HIPPOLYTE (1807-1864), Canadian politician **9** 157-158
Baldwin, Robert **1** 466-468
Elgin, 8th Earl of **5** 248-249
Howe, Joseph **7** 534-535
Papineau, Louis-Joseph **12** 91

LAFORGUE, JULES (1860-1887), French poet **9** 160-161
Eliot, Thomas Stearns **5** 258-261
Stevens, Wallace **14** 443-445

Lagar (book)
Mistral, Gabriela **11** 55-56

LAGERFELD, KARL (born 1938), German-French designer of high fashion **9** 161-162

LAGERKVIST, PÄR FABIAN (born 1891), Swedish author **9** 162-163
Strindberg, August **14** 509-511

LAGERLÖF, SELMA OTTILIANA LOVISA (1858-1940), Swedish author **9** 163-164
Sachs, Nelly **13** 411-412

Lagery, Otto de
see Urban II

Lagid dynasty
see Ptolemaic dynasty

Lagoon Waltz (music)
Strauss, Johann Jr. **14** 498-499

Lagoon with Gondola (painting)
Guardi, Francesco **7** 24-25

Lagos (former British colony)
see Nigeria

LAGRANGE, JOSEPH LOUIS (1736-1813), Italian-born French mathematician **9** 164-166
Cauchy, Augustin Louis **3** 378-380
Cournot, Antoine Augustin **4** 273
Hertz, Heinrich Rudolf **7** 346-347
Laplace, Marquis de **9** 202-204
Taylor, Brook **15** 121-122

Lagrime di San Pietro, Le (madrigals)
Lassus, Roland de **9** 216-218

LAHR, BERT (Irving Lahrheim; 1895-1967), performer and comedian in burlesque, vaudeville, musical comedy, film, and television **9** 167-168

Laibach, Congress of (1821)
Castlereagh, Viscount **3** 363-364
Metternich, Klemens von **10** 533-536

Laila and Majnun (story)
Jami **8** 218-219

Lainez, Diego (1512-1565), Spanish Jesuit
Cid **4** 58-59

Laird, McGregor (1808-1861), Scottish merchant and explorer
Baikie, William Balfour **1** 440

LAIRD, MELVIN R. (born 1922), U.S. congressman and secretary of defense **9** 168-170

Lais (poems)
Marie de France **10** 259
Villon, François **15** 499-501

Laïs of Corinth (painting)
Holbein, Hans the Younger **7** 449-450

Laissez faire (economics)
critics
Balmaceda Fernández, José Manuel
1 475-476
Chernyshevsky, Nikolai Gavrilovich
3 504-505
Le Play, Guillaume Frédéric
9 350-351
social applications
Mill, John Stuart **11** 21-23
Spencer, Herbert **14** 369-370
supporters
Gladstone, William Ewart
6 357-360
Maine, Henry James Sumner **10** 152
Polanyi, Karl **12** 372
Sismondi, Jean Charles Léonard
Simonde de **14** 258-259
Smith, Adam **14** 283-284
Sumner, William Graham **15** 32
Villard, Oswald Garrison
15 498-499
von Mises, Ludwig **16** 25
see also Free trade; Physiocrats

Laistrygones (literary characters)
Homer **7** 465-467

Laity, Council of the (Roman Catholic
Church)
Paul VI **12** 146-148

Laius (play)
Aeschylus **1** 70-72

Lake (poem)
Lamartine, Alphonse Marie Louis de
9 173-175

Lake Bangweulu (northern Rhodesia)
Livingstone, David **9** 463-465

Lake Chilwa (southeastern Nyasaland)
Livingstone, David **9** 463-465

Lake District (England)
Coleridge, Samuel Taylor **4** 154-156
Constable, John **4** 208-209

Lake George (painting)
Heade, Martin Johnson **7** 236
O'Keeffe, Georgia **11** 487-489

Lake Peipus, battle of (1242)
Nevsky, Alexander **11** 359

Lake Shore Drive (Chicago, Illinois)
Mies van der Rohe, Ludwig **11** 10-12

Lakota Indians (North America)
American Horse **1** 195-198
Means, Russell **10** 441-444

Lalande, J.J. Le Français de (1732-1807),
French astronomer
Houdon, Antoine **7** 516-517

Lalemant, Gabriel (1610-1649), French
Jesuit martyr
Brébeuf, Jean de **2** 511-512

LALIBELA (ruled circa 1181-circa 1221),
Ethiopian king and saint **9** 170
Yekuno Amlak **16** 449

Lalibela (town; Ethiopia)
Lalibela **9** 170

Lalique, René (1860-1945), French glass
and jewelry designer
Lachaise, Gaston **9** 147

Lallemand, Georges (died circa 1640),
French painter
Poussin, Nicolas **12** 418-420

Lamachus (died 414 B.C.), Athenian general
Alcibiades **1** 119-120

Lamaism (Tibetan Buddhism)
Kublai Khan **9** 115-118
Qianlong **12** 502-505

**LAMAR, LUCIUS QUINTUS CINCINNA-
TUS** (1825-1893), American politician
and jurist **9** 170-171

LAMARCK, CHEVALIER DE (Jean Baptiste
Pierre Antoine de Monet; 1744-1829),
French naturalist **9** 171-173
Buffon, Comte de **3** 109-111
Cuvier, Georges Léopold **4** 357-359
Darwin, Charles Robert **4** 397-399
Mendel, Johann Gregor **10** 483-486
Vries, Hugo de **16** 33-36

**LAMARTINE, ALPHONSE MARIE LOUIS
DE** (1790-1869), French poet and diplo-
mat **9** 173-175
Chénier, André Marie **3** 500-501
Hugo, Victor Marie **8** 22-25, 404
Liszt, Franz **9** 445-447

LAMAS, CARLOS SAAVEDRA (1878-1959),
Argentine scholar, statesman, and diplomat **9** 175-176

LAMB, CHARLES (1775-1834), English
author, critic, and minor poet **9** 176-177
Burton, Robert **3** 166-167
Hazlitt, William **7** 235-236
Woolman, John **16** 382-383

Lamb, Lady Caroline (1785-1828), English
novelist
Byron, George Gordon Noel **3** 193-194

Lamb, Mary Ann (1764-1847), English
author
Lamb, Charles **9** 176-177

Lamb, Sir Horace (1849-1934), English
mathematician and physicist
Cockcroft, John Douglas **4** 131-132

Lamb, William
see Melbourne, 2nd Viscount

Lambert, Johann Heinrich (1728-1777),
German mathematician and philosopher
Lobachevskii, Nikolai Ivanovich
9 472-474

Lambruschini, Luigi (1776-1854), Italian
cardinal and statesman
Pius IX **12** 335-336

LAMBSDORFF, OTTO GRAF (born 1926),
West German minister of economics
9 177-179

Lambton, John George
see Durham, 1st Earl of

Lame-duck Amendment
see Constitution of the United States—
20th Amendment

**LAMENNAIS, HUGUES FÉLICITÉ ROBERT
DE** (1782-1854), French priest and politi-
cal writer **9** 179
Lacordaire, Jean Baptiste Henri **9** 148
Montalembert, Comte de **11** 118-119
Sainte-Beuve, Charles Augustin **13** 438

Lament for the Death of a Bullfighter
(poem)
Lorca, Federico García **9** 511-513

Lament for the Living (stories)
Parker, Dorothy Rothschild **12** 106

Lamentabili (papal decree)
Pius X **12** 336-337

Lamentation (painting)
Christus, Petrus **4** 33-34
Geertgen tot Sint Jans **6** 248
Ghirlandaio, Domenico **6** 292-293
Giotto **6** 342-345
van der Goes, Hugo **15** 416-417

Lamentations, Book of (Old Testament)
Jeremiah **8** 247-248

Lamia (poem; Keats)
Burton, Robert **3** 166-167
Keats, John **8** 470-472

Lamo Dondup
see Dalai Lama

Lamont, Daniel S. (1851-1905), American
politician
Cleveland, Stephen Grover **4** 108-110

Lamp for Nightfall, A (book)
Caldwell, Erskine **3** 223-224

LAMPMAN, ARCHIBALD (1861-1899),
Canadian poet **9** 180-181

LAMPRECHT, KARL (1856-1915), German
historian **9** 181

LAMY, JEAN BAPTISTE (1814-1888),
French archbishop in the United States
9 181-182

Lancaster, 5th Duke of
see John of Gaunt

Lancaster, House of
see England—1399-1461 (Lancastrian)

LANCASTER, JOSEPH (1778-1838), English
educator **9** 182-183
Bell, Andrew **2** 131-132

Lancaster House Conference (1960; England)
Ngala, Ronald Gideon **11** 373-374
Odinga, Ajuma Jaramogi Oginga
11 471-473

Lancaster Sound (northern Canada)
Baffin, William **1** 435-436
Franklin, John **6** 64-65

Lancelot (literary character)
Tennyson, Alfred **15** 144-146

Lancelot (romance)
Chrestien de Troyes **4** 23-24

Lancelot and Elaine (musical composition)
MacDowell, Edward Alexander
10 87-88

LAND, EDWIN HERBERT (1909-1991),
American physicist, inventor, and manufacturer **9** 183-184

Land, The (play)
Colum, Padraic **4** 174-175

Land Act (United States; 1800)
Harrison, William Henry **7** 180-181

Land Acts (Ireland; 1870, 1881)
Gladstone, William Ewart **6** 357-360
Parnell, Charles Stewart **12** 117-119

Land grants
see Public lands (United States)

Land of Cockaigne (painting)
Bruegel, Pieter the Elder **3** 65-67

Land of Hope and Glory (hymn)
Elgar, Edward **5** 247-248

Land of the Blizzard, The (book)
Mawson, Douglas **10** 354-355

Land of Unlikeness (poems)
Lowell, Robert Trail Spence Jr. **10** 16-17

Land reforms
see Reformers, agrarian (land)

Land without Bread (film)
Buñuel, Luis **3** 127-128

Landarzt, Der (stories)
Kafka, Franz **8** 403-406

LANDAU, LEV DAVIDOVICH
(1908-1968), Soviet theoretical physicist
9 184-185

Lander, Richard (1804-1834), English
explorer
Clapperton, Hugh **4** 72-73

Land-gift movement (India)
Bhave, Vinoba **2** 257-258

Land-grant colleges (United States)
Morrill, Justin Smith **11** 182
Polk, Leonidas Lafayette **12** 376-377
White, Andrew Dickson **16** 226-227

LANDINI, FRANCESCO (circa 1335-1397),
Italian composer and poet **9** 185-186
Vitry, Philippe de **16** 2

Landlady, The (story)
Dostoevsky, Fyodor **5** 74-77

LANDOR, WALTER SAVAGE (1775-1864),
English poet, essayist and critic
9 186-187
Hazlitt, William **7** 235-236
Plutarch **12** 359-360

LANDOWSKI, MARCEL (born 1915),
French composer of lyric works
9 187-188

Landscape (play)
Pinter, Harold **12** 317-318

Landscape architects
see Artists—landscape architects

Landscape hand scroll (Chinese)
Wang Wei **16** 106-108

Landshut, University of (Bavaria)
Savigny, Friedrich Karl von **13** 502-503

Landslide (play)
Betti, Ugo **2** 246

LANDSTEINER, KARL (1868-1943), Austrian-born American immunologist
9 188-189

Landvogt von Greifensee, Der (story)
Keller, Gottfried **8** 478-479

Lane, Carrie
see Catt, Carrie Chapman

LANE, FITZ HUGH (1804-1865), American
marine painter **9** 189

Lane, Louisa (Mrs. John Drew; 1820-1897),
English-born American actress
Barrymores **2** 28-30, 400

Lane Theological Seminary (Cincinnati,
Ohio)
Bailey, Gamaliel **1** 444-445
Beecher, Lyman **2** 113
Stowe, Harriet Elizabeth Beecher
14 484-485
Tappan brothers **15** 105-106
Weld, Theodore Dwight **16** 186

LANFRANC (circa 1010-1089), Italian the-
ologian, archbishop of Canterbury
9 189-190
Anselm of Canterbury **1** 244-245
William I **16** 290-291
William II **16** 293-294

Lang, Andrew (1844-1912), Scottish poet
Kipling, Joseph Rudyard **9** 32-33

LANG, FRITZ (1890-1976), film director
9 190-192

LANG, JOHN THOMAS (1876-1975), Aus-
tralian politician **9** 192-193
Chifley, Joseph Benedict **3** 518
Scullin, James Henry **14** 73

LANGE, DOROTHEA (1895-1965), American photographer **9** 193-194

Lange, Friedrich A. (1828-1875), German
philosopher and reformer
Nietzsche, Friedrich **11** 390-392

Langen, Eugen (1833-1895), German engineer
Daimler, Gottlieb **4** 368

Langerhans, Paul (1847-1888), German
physiologist
Banting, Frederick Grant **1** 493-494

Langevin, Paul (1872-1946), French physicist
Joliot-Curie, Jean Frédéric **8** 327-328

LANGLAND, WILLIAM (circa 1330-1400),
English poet **9** 194-195
Lyndsay, David **10** 66-67

Langley, Batty (1696-1751), English writer
on architecture
McIntire, Samuel **10** 415

Langley, John Newport (1852-1925), Eng-
lish physiologist
Dale, Henry Hallett **4** 371-373
Hill, Archibald Vivian **7** 385-386
Sherrington, Charles Scott **14** 187-189

LANGLEY, SAMUEL PIERPONT
(1834-1906), American scientist
9 195-196
Bell, Alexander Graham **2** 129-131

LANGMUIR, IRVING (1881-1957), Ameri-
can chemist **9** 196-197
Carothers, Wallace Hume **3** 317-318
De Forest, Lee **4** 459-460

Langside, battle of (1568)
Mary, I **10** 308-309

LANGSTON, JOHN MERCER (1829-1897),
American educator and diplomat **9** 197

Langton, Stephen (circa 1155-1228), Eng-
lish cardinal and poet
Innocent, III **8** 125-127
John **8** 274-275
Matthew Paris **10** 341-342

Language (human communications)
Bloomfield, Leonard **2** 338
Boas, Franz **2** 349-351
Borges, Jorge Luis **2** 411-412
Burke, Kenneth **3** 141-142
Carnap, Rudolf **3** 308-309
Chrysippus **4** 35-36
Derrida, Jacques **4** 503-505
Hobbes, Thomas **7** 421-423
Locke, John **9** 478-480
Mead, George Herbert **10** 437-438
Sapir, Edward **13** 478-479
Skinner, Burrhus Frederic **14** 269-270
see also Linguistics

Language, Truth and Logic (book)
Ayer, Alfred Jules **1** 391-393

Langueur (poem)
Verlaine, Paul Marie **15** 465-466

LANIER, JARON (born ca. 1961), American
computer engineer **9** 198-199

LANIER, SIDNEY (1842-1881), American
poet, critic, and musician **9** 199-200

Lansbury, George (1859-1940), British
Labour party leader
Bevin, Ernest **2** 252-253

Lansdowne, 1st Marquis of
see Shelburne, 2nd Earl of

LANSING, ROBERT (1864-1928), American lawyer and statesman **9** 200
Dulles, John Foster **5** 134-135

Lansing-Ishii Agreement (United States
-Japan; 1917)
Lansing, Robert **9** 200

Lanskoy, André (1902-1976), Russian
painter
Staël, Nicolas de **14** 392

Lanson, Gustave (1857-1934), French critic
Rousseau, Jean Jacques **13** 324-328
Voltaire **16** 14-16

Lantern-bearers, The (essay)
Stevenson, Robert Louis **14** 446-448

Lanuvinus, Luscius (flourished 2nd century
B.C.), Roman playwright
Terence **15** 146-148

Lao Chang ti chê-hsüeh (novel)
Lao Shê **9** 200-201

Lao Dong party
see Workers' party (North Vietnam)

Lao Lai Tzu
see Lao Tzu

LAO SHÊ (1899-1966), Chinese novelist
9 200-201
Kuo Mo-jo **9** 133-134

LAO TZU (flourished 6th century B.C.),
Chinese philosopher **9** 201-202
Confucius **4** 197-200
Mabuchi, Kamo **10** 73-74

Laocoon (ancient sculpture)
Sansovino, Jacopo **13** 470-471

Laocoon and His Sons (painting)
Greco **6** 511-514

Laodicean, A (novel)
Hardy, Thomas **7** 150-152

Laokoon (book)
Lessing, Gotthold Ephraim **9** 357-359

Laon, battle of (1814)
Blücher, Gebhard Leberecht von
2 340-341

Laos, Kingdom of (nation; southeastern
Asia)
Chulalongkorn **4** 43-45
Macapagal, Diosdado P. **10** 74-76
Souvanna Phouma **14** 357-358

LAPLACE, MARQUIS DE (Pierre Simon;
1749-1827), French mathematician
9 202-204
Bowditch, Nathaniel **2** 460-461
Cauchy, Augustin Louis **3** 378-380
Cournot, Antoine Augustin **4** 273
Demoivre, Abraham **4** 494-495
Hamilton, William Rowan **7** 99-100
Hertz, Heinrich Rudolf **7** 346-347
Kant, Immanuel **8** 430-432
Lavoisier, Antoine Laurent **9** 241-244
Maxwell, James Clerk **10** 361-364

Lapointe, Ernest (1876-1941), Canadian
politician
St. Laurent, Louis Stephen **13** 434

Laputa (literary island)
Swift, Jonathan **15** 51-54

Lara (epic)
Byron, George Gordon Noel **3** 193-194

LARDNER, RINGGOLD WILMER
(1885-1933), American author **9** 204-205

Larenopfer (poems)
Rilke, Rainer Maria **13** 171-172

Large, Robert (died 1441), English
Caxton, William **3** 386-387

Large Don Quixote of the Forest (sculpture)
Richier, Germaine **13** 145-146

Large Glass, The (painting)
Duchamp, Marcel **5** 122-123

LARIONOV, MIKHAIL (1881-1964), Russ-
ian artist **9** 205-206
Goncharova, Natalia **6** 424-426
Malevich, Kasimir **10** 168-169

Lark, The (play; Anouilh)
Anouilh, Jean **1** 243-244
Hellman, Lillian Florence **7** 267-268

Larkin, Jim (1876-1947), Irish labor
O'Casey, Sean **11** 459-460

LARKIN, PHILIP (1922-1986), English poet
9 206-207

LARKIN, THOMAS OLIVER (1802-1858),
American merchant and diplomat **9** 208

Larkin Building (Buffalo, New York State)
Wright, Frank Lloyd **16** 398-401, 453

Larmes de Saint Pierre (poem)
Malherbe, François de **10** 169-170

Larsa (ancient city; Babylonia)
Hammurabi **7** 109-110

LARSEN, NELLA (1893-1963), Harlem
Renaissance writer **9** 209-210

Larson, Wolf (literary character)
London, Jack **9** 494-495

LAS CASAS, BARTOLOMÉ DE
(1474-1566), Spanish Dominican missionary and historian **9** 211-212
Mendoza, Antonio de **10** 494-495
Velázquez de Cuéllar, Diego **15** 459

Las Navas de Tolosa, battle of (1212)
Cabeza de Vaca, Álvar Núñez **3** 197

Las Salinas, battle of (1538)
Almagro, Diego de **1** 177-178
Orellana, Francisco de **11** 527-528
Pizarro, Francisco **12** 340-341
Valdivia, Pedro de **15** 400-401

Lasal, Ferdinand
see Lassalle, Ferdinand

Lascaris, John (circa 1445-1535), Greek
scholar and teacher
Medici, Lorenzo de' **10** 450-451

LASCH, CHRISTOPHER (1932-1994),
American historian and social critic
9 212-214

Lasciatemi morire (song)
Monteverdi, Claudio Giovanni Antonio
11 126-128

Laser (physics)
Einstein, Albert **5** 228-231
Rabi, Isidor Isaac **12** 526-527

LASHLEY, KARL SPENCER (1890-1958),
American neuropsychologist **9** 214-215

LASKI, HAROLD J. (1893-1950), English
political scientist and Labour party leader
9 215-216
Menon, Vengalil Krishnan Krishna
10 507-509

Lasky, Jesse L. (1880-1958), American
motion picture producer
Goldwyn, Samuel **6** 416

Lassa far a mi (poem)
Josquin des Prez **8** 361-363

LASSALLE, FERDINAND (1825-1864), Ger-
man socialist leader **9** 216
Ebert, Friedrich **5** 193-194
Marx, Karl **10** 304-308

Lasso, Orlando di
see Lassus, Roland de

Lassus, J.B.A. (1807-1857), French architect
Viollet-le-Duc, Eugène Emmanuel
15 505-506

LASSUS, ROLAND DE (1532-1594), Fran-
co-Flemish composer **9** 216-218
Byrd, William **3** 187-188
Clemens non Papa, Jacobus **4** 101
Gabrieli, Giovanni **6** 161-162
Palestrina, Giovanni Pierluigi da
12 70-72

LASSWELL, HAROLD DWIGHT (born
1902), American political scientist
9 218-219
Merriam, Charles Edward **10** 518-519

Last Analysis, The (play)
Bellow, Saul **2** 141-143

**Last Canto of Childe Harold's Pilgrimage,
The** (poem)
Lamartine, Alphonse Marie Louis de
9 173-175

Last Chronicle of Barset, The (novel)
Trollope, Anthony **15** 300-302

Last Communion of Saint Jerome (painting)
Botticelli, Sandro **2** 439-440
Carracci **3** 319-321

Last Dance for Sybil (play)
Davis, Ossie **4** 421-422

Last Flower, The (book)
Thurber, James Grove **15** 213-214

Last Fruit off an Old Tree (book)
Landor, Walter Savage **9** 186-187

Last Hope, The (musical composition)
Gottschalk, Louis Moreau **6** 463-464

Last Hurrah, The (novel and film)
Curley, James Michael **4** 344-345
Ford, John **6** 7-8

Last Invocation, The (poem)
Whitman, Walt **16** 249-251

Last Judgment (painting)
Bosch, Hieronymus **2** 426-428
Giotto **6** 342-345
Lochner, Stephan **9** 475
Lucas van Leyden **10** 20-21
Orcagna **11** 526-527

Schongauer, Martin **14** 26-28
Signorelli, Luca **14** 221-222
Tintoretto **15** 232-234
Weyden, Rogier van der **16** 219-221

Last Judgment (painting; Michelangelo)
Carpeaux, Jean Baptiste **3** 318-319
Greco **6** 511-514
Michelangelo Buonarroti **11** 2-5
Paul III **12** 144-145
Velázquez, Diego Rodríguez de Silva y **15** 454-456

Last Leaf, The (poem)
Holmes, Oliver Wendell **7** 457-458

Last Letters of Jacopo Ortis, The (novel)
Foscolo, Ugo **6** 21

Last Meeting of the Council, The (cartoon)
Daumier, Honoré Victorin **4** 403-405

Last Mile, The (play)
Gable, William Clark **6** 157-158

Last of Abinger, The (essay)
Forster, Edward Morgan **6** 14-16

Last of the Mohicans, The (novel)
Cooper, James Fenimore **4** 220-223

Last of the Tribe, The (sculpture)
Powers, Hiram **12** 428-429

Last Post, The (novel)
Ford, Ford Madox **6** 1-2

Last Puritan, The (novel)
Santayana, George **13** 475-477

Last September, The (novel)
Bowen, Elizabeth **2** 462-463

Last Station, The (play)
Remarque, Erich Maria **13** 91

Last Supper (painting)
Andrea del Castagno **1** 223-224
Bouts, Dirk **2** 458-459
Ghirlandaio, Domenico **6** 292-293
Holbein, Hans the Younger **7** 449-450
Leonardo da Vinci **9** 337-340
Nolde, Emil **11** 419-420
Orcagna **11** 526-527
Tintoretto **15** 232-234
Titian **15** 242-244

Last Supper (sacrament)
see Eucharist

Last Supper (sculpture)
Riemenschneider, Tilman **13** 166

Last Temptation of Christ, The (novel)
Kazantzakis, Nikos **8** 466-468

Last Time I Saw Paris, The (song)
Kern, Jerome David **8** 517-518

Last Track, The (play)
Coward, Noel **4** 279-280

Last Tycoon, The (novel)
Fitzgerald, Francis Scott Key **5** 470-472

Last Word, The (poem)
Bialik, Hayyim Nahman **2** 262-263

Last Year at Marienbad (film)
Robbe-Grillet, Alain **13** 189-190

Lastman, Pieter (1593-1633), Dutch painter
Lucas van Leyden **10** 20-21
Rembrandt Harmensz van Rijn **13** 91-95, 141

Lasus of Hermione (flourished late 6th century B.C.), Greek lyric poet
Pindar **12** 312-313

LÁSZLÓ I, KING OF HUNGARY (ca. 1040-1095), king of Hungary and saint **9** 219-221

Late George Apley, The (novel; Marquand)
Kaufman, George S. **8** 457-458

Late Mattia Pascal, The (novel)
Pirandello, Luigi **12** 319-321

Later Fruits of the Earth (book)
Gide, André **6** 308-309

Lateran Basilica
see Saint John Lateran (Rome)

Lateran Councils (Roman Catholic Church)
1139: Second
Arnold of Brescia **1** 314-315
1179: Third
William of Tyre **16** 299-300
1215: Fourth
Innocent, III **8** 125-127-477
Lombard, Peter **9** 490-491
1512-17: Fifth
Copernicus, Nicolaus **4** 226-227
Julius II **8** 384-386

Lateran Pact (1929)
Croce, Benedetto **4** 313-314
Mussolini, Benito **11** 272-274
Pius XI **12** 337-339

LATIMER, HUGH (circa 1492-1555), English Protestant bishop, reformer, and martyr **9** 221
Colet, John **4** 157-158
Edward VI **5** 213-214
Mary I **10** 308-309

Latin America
archeological expeditions
Kidder, Alfred Vincent **8** 541-542
economic development
Callejas Romero, Rafael Leonardo **3** 233-234
Grace, William Russell **6** 480-481
Iglesias, Enrique V. **8** 106-107
Meiggs, Henry **10** 458-459
Plaza Lasso, Galo **12** 350-351
Prebisch, Raúl **12** 434-436
Serrano Elías, Jorge Antonio **14** 112-113
Wasmosy, Juan Carlos **16** 129-130
Zemurray, Samuel **16** 496-497
exploration (Central America)
Balboa, Vasco Núñez de **1** 462-463
Columbus, Christopher **4** 176-179
Cortés, Hernán **4** 255-256
Cuauhtemoc **4** 329
de Soto, Hernando **4** 510-511
Pedrarias **12** 179
exploration (South America)

Azara, Félix de **1** 397-398
Bates, Henry Walter **2** 53-54
Benalcázar, Sebastián de **2** 145-146
Cabeza de Vaca, Álvar Núñez **3** 197
Cabot, Sebastian **3** 200-201
Columbus, Christopher **4** 176-179
Gasca, Pedro de la **6** 230-231
foreign relations
Canning, George **3** 258-260
Drago, Luis María **5** 92-93
Leo XIII **9** 334-336
human rights
Menchú, Rigoberta **10** 479-480
Pérez Esquivel, Adolfo **12** 215-217
Indians
see Indians (South American)
inter-American relations (19th century)
Blaine, James Gillespie **2** 312-313
Hay, John **7** 215-216
Marcy, William Learned **10** 247-248
Monroe, James **11** 111-113
inter-American relations (20th century)
Arias Sanchez, Oscar **1** 287-289
Castro Ruz, Fidel **3** 365-368
Cerezo Arevalo, Marco Vinicio **3** 393-395
Coolidge, John Calvin **4** 217-219
Harding, Warren Gamaliel **7** 148-149
Hoover, Herbert Clark **7** 483-485
Hull, Cordell **8** 28-29
Johnson, Lyndon Baines **8** 308-312
Kellogg, Frank Billings **8** 481
Paz Zamora, Jaime **12** 165-167
Rockefeller, David **13** 224-225
Roosevelt, Theodore **13** 280-283
Salinas de Gortari, Carlos **13** 445-447
Torrijos, Omar **15** 269-270
Welles, Sumner **16** 191-192
Wilson, Thomas Woodrow **16** 330-332
see also Organization of American States; Pan-Americanism
missionaries
Claver, Peter **4** 94
Las Casas, Bartolomé de **9** 211-212
Marcos de Niza **10** 240
see also Nationalism, Latin American; and individual countries
religion and politics
Gutiérrez, Gustavo **7** 52-53
United States intervention
Bush, George **3** 167-169
Endara, Guillermo **5** 283-284
Noriega, Manuel A. **11** 423-425
Reagan, Ronald W. **13** 65-68

Latin American literature
poetry
Guillén, Nicolás **7** 34-35
Quiroga, Horacio **12** 520-521

Latin American Solidarity Organization
(established 1967)
Castro Ruz, Fidel **3** 365-368

Latin Empire of Constantipole (1204-1261)
Dandolo, Enrico **4** 386-387
Innocent, III **8** 125-127
see also Byzantine Empire

Latin literature
biography
Suetonius Tranquillus, Gaius **15** 13
Tacitus **15** 70-72
drama
Plautus **12** 348-350
Seneca the Younger, Lucius Annaeus **14** 103-105
Terence **15** 146-148
encyclopedias
Cassiodorus, Flavius Magnus Aurelius **3** 357-358
Pliny the Elder **12** 355-356
epigrams
Martialis, Marcus Valerius **10** 286-287
letters
Cicero, Marcus Tullius **4** 55-58
Pliny the Younger **12** 356
literary criticism
Horace **7** 500-503
Longinus **9** 500-501
Quintilian **12** 518-519
poetry
Catullus, Gaius Valerius **3** 377-378
Ennius, Quintus **5** 289
Horace **7** 500-503
Lucretius **10** 26-27
Ovid **12** 34-36
Virgil **15** 507-510
satire
Horace **7** 500-503
Juvenal **8** 397-399
Petronius Arbiter **12** 262-263
Varro, Marcus Terentius **15** 438-439
see also Humanism—Middle Ages and Renaissance (literature; Latin)

Latini, Brunetto (circa 1210-circa 1295), Florentine statesman and author
Dante Alighieri **4** 389-391

Latitude (geography)
Hipparchus **7** 407-408
Khwarizmi, Muhammad ibn Musa al- **8** 541
Mercator, Gerhardus **10** 511-512

Latro, Marcus Porcius (55 B.C. ?-4 A.D.), Spanish rhetorician in Rome
Ovid **12** 34-36

LATROBE, BENJAMIN HENRY (1764-1820), English-born American architect **9** 222-224
Bulfinch, Charles **3** 116-117
L'Enfant, Pierre Charles **9** 322-323
Mills, Robert **11** 36-37
Wright, Frank Lloyd **16** 398-401

Latrocinium
see Ephesus, Councils of—499

Latter-Day Saints, Church of the
see Mormons

Lattimore, Richmond (1906-1984), American classicist
Pindar **12** 312-313

Lattuada, Alberto (born 1914), Italian film director
Fellini, Federico **5** 408-409

LAUD, WILLIAM (1573-1645), English archbishop of Canterbury **9** 224-225
Charles, I **3** 450-452
Cotton, John **4** 263-265
Crashaw, Richard **4** 296
Cromwell, Oliver **4** 317-320

Laudario (poem)
Jacopone da Todi **8** 194

Laudate Pueri (motet)
Handel, George Frederick **7** 116-119

LAUDER, ESTEE (née Josephine Esthe Menzer, born ca. 1908), founder of an international cosmetics empire **9** 225-226

Lauderdale, 1st Duke of (John Maitland; 1616-1682), British statesman
Buckingham, 2d Duke of **3** 94-95
Burnet, Gilbert **3** 147

Laudi alla Vergine Maria (musical composition)
Verdi, Giuseppe Fortunino Francesco **15** 463-465

Laudi del cielo ... (poems)
D'Annunzio, Gabriele **4** 388

Laudi spirituali (music)
Neri, Philip **11** 340

Laue, Max von
see von Laue, Max

Lauenburg, Duke of
see Bismarck, Otto Edward Leopold von

Laughing gas
see Nitrous oxide

Laughing Matter, The (novel)
Saroyan, William **13** 486-487

Laundress, The (painting)
Daumier, Honoré Victorin **4** 403-405

Laura (literary character)
Norris, Benjamin Franklin Jr. **11** 427-428
Petrarch **12** 259-261
Porter, Katherine Anne **12** 406-407
Ronsard, Pierre de **13** 271-273

Laura (painting)
Giorgione **6** 340-341

Laura-Oden (poems)
Schiller, Johann Christoph Friedrich von **14** 4-7

Laurana, Luciano (circa 1420-1479), Italian architect
Bramante, Donato **2** 493-494

Laurel, José P. (1891-1959), Philippines statesman
Quirino, Elpidio **12** 519-520
Recto, Claro M. **13** 69-70
Roxas, Manuel **13** 331-332

LAUREL, SALVADOR H. (Doy; born 1928), member of the Philippine Congress and vice-president **9** 226-227

Laurel-Langley Agreement (Philippines ; 1964)
Magsaysay, Ramon **10** 130-131

Laurelton Hall (Oyster Bay, Long Island)
Tiffany, Louis Comfort **15** 220-221

LAUREN, RALPH (Ralph Lipschitz; born 1939), American fashion designer **9** 228-229

LAURENCE, MARGARET (Jean Margaret Wemyss; 1926-1987), Canadian writer **9** 229-230

Laurencin, Marie (1885-1956), French painter
Apollinaire, Guillaume **1** 260

LAURENS, HENRI (1885-1954), French sculptor **9** 230-231

LAURENS, HENRY (1724-1792), American merchant and Revolutionary statesman **9** 232
Deane, Silas **4** 435-437

Laurens, Jean Paul (1838-1921), French painter
Maillol, Aristide **10** 150-151
Prendergast, Maurice Brazil **12** 440
Weber, Max **16** 160

LAURIER, SIR WILFRID (1841-1919), Canadian statesman, prime minister 1896-1911 **9** 232-234
Borden, Robert Laird **2** 409-411
Bourassa, Joseph-Henri-Napoleon **2** 446-447
King, William Lyon Mackenzie **9** 25-26

Laurier, Wilfrid
Sifton, Clifford **14** 219-220

LAURO, ACHILLE (1887-1984), Italian business and political leader **9** 234-235

Laus Veneris (poem)
Swinburne, Algernon Charles **15** 54-55

Lausanne, Conference of (1867)
Sylvis, William **15** 60-61

Lausanne, Treaty of (1922-1923)
Atatürk, Ghazi Mustapha Kemal **1** 356-357
Venizelos, Eleutherios **15** 460-461

Lausanne, University of (Switzerland)
Gesner, Konrad von **6** 287
Pareto, Vilfredo **12** 95-96
Walras, Marie Esprit Léon **16** 84-85

LAUTARO (circa 1535-1557), Araucanian Indian chieftain in Chile **9** 235
Ercilla y Zúñiga, Alonso de **5** 302

LAVAL, FRANCOIS XAVIER DE (1623-1708), French bishop in Canada **9** 235-236
Bourgeoys, Marguerite **2** 452-453

LAVAL, PIERRE (1883-1945), French politician, chief Vichy minister **9** 237-238
Pétain, Henri Philippe **12** 250-252

Lavalle, Juan (1797-1841), Argentine politician
  Rosas, Juan Manuel de **13** 290-291

LAVALLEJA, JUAN ANTONIO
(1778-1853), Uruguayan independence leader **9** 238-239
  Caxias, Duque de **3** 386
  Rivera, Fructuoso **13** 184-185

Lavater, Johann Kaspar (1741-1801), Swiss poet
  Fuseli, Henry **6** 153-155
  Mendelssohn, Moses **10** 488-489

LAVIGERIE, CHARLES MARTEL ALLE-MAND (1825-1892), French cardinal **9** 240

LAVISSE, ERNEST (1842-1922), French historian **9** 241
  Vidal de la Blache, Paul **15** 490

LAVOISIER, ANTOINE LAURENT
(1743-1794), French chemist **9** 241-244
  Berthollet, Claude Louis **2** 229-230
  Davy, Humphry **4** 426-427
  du Pont, Éleuthère Irénée **5** 154
  Lamarck, Chevalier de **9** 171-173
  Laplace, Marquis de **9** 202-204
  Lomonosov, Mikhail Vasilevich **9** 494
  Priestley, Joseph **12** 452-453

Lavorare stanca (poem)
  Pavese, Cesare **12** 154-155

Law
  canon
    see Canon law
  commercial
    Benjamin, Judah Philip **2** 163-164
    Cardozo, Benjamin Nathan
      3 288-290
  common
    Bentham, Jeremy **2** 176-178
    Blackstone, William **2** 310-311
    Holmes, Oliver Wendell Jr.
      7 458-459
    Shaw, Lemuel **14** 164-165
  criminal
    see Criminal law
  defined
    Montesquieu **11** 123-125
  international
    see International law
  labor
    see Labor law (United States)
  legal education
    Blackstone, William **2** 310-311
    Eliot, Charles William **5** 254
  legal reform
    Basil I **2** 49-50
    Catherine the Great **3** 370-372
    Chulalongkorn **4** 43-45
    Field, David Dudley **5** 439-440
    Frederick II **6** 81-84
    Juárez, Benito **8** 369-372
    Livingston, Edward **9** 460-461
    Savigny, Friedrich Karl von
      13 502-503
    Suleiman I **15** 20-21

  maritime
    Dana, Richard Henry Jr. **4** 385-386
    Story, Joseph **14** 480-481
  Mosaic
    see Mosaic law
  of associations
    Gierke, Otto von **6** 311-312
  Roman
    see Law codes—Byzantium; Roman law
  Salic
    Clovis I **4** 124
    Ferdinand VII **5** 418-420
    see also Jurisprudence; Jurists; Law codes

Law, Andrew Bonar (1858-1923), British statesman
  Baldwin, Stanley **1** 468-469
  Chamberlain, Arthur Neville **3** 409-411

LAW, JOHN (1671-1729), Scottish monetary theorist and banker **9** 244-245
  Orléans, Philippe II D' **11** 530-531

LAW, WILLIAM (1686-1761), English devotional writer **9** 245-246

Law codes
  Africa
    Gluckman, Max **6** 374-375
  Athens
    Solon **14** 327-328
  Babylonia
    Hammurabi **7** 109-110
  Byzantium
    Basil I **2** 49-50
    Justinian I **8** 393-395
    Leo III **9** 330-332
  Chile
    Bello, Ahmadu **2** 139-140
  England
    see Magna Carta
  France (Code Napoléon)
    Colbert, Jean Baptiste **4** 142-143
    Napoleon I **11** 306-310
  Germany
    Savigny, Friedrich Karl von
      13 502-503
    Vogel, Hans-Jochen **16** 8-9
  Haiti
    Boyer, Jean Pierre **2** 468-469
    Christophe, Henri **4** 32
  Japan
    see Omi laws
  Louisiana
    Bienville, Sieur de **2** 268-269
  Persia
    Darius I **4** 394-395
  Russia
    Catherine the Great **3** 370-372
    Ivan IV **8** 157-159
    Speranski, Mikhail Mikhailovich
      14 376-377
  Savoy
    Victor Amadeus II **15** 482-483
  Spain
    Alfonso X **1** 150-151
  United States

  Field, David Dudley **5** 439-440
  Livingstone, David **9** 463-465

Law enforcement
  Dewey, Thomas Edmund **4** 524
  Fielding, Henry **5** 442-444
  Hoover, John Edgar **7** 485-487
  Peel, Robert **12** 181-183
  see also Criminal law; Criminology; Detective agencies

Lawd Today (novel)
  Wright, Richard **16** 401-402

Lawes, Henry (1596-1622), English composer
  Herrick, Robert **7** 336-339
  Milton, John **11** 43-46

Lawless Roads, The (book)
  Greene, Graham **6** 523-524

Lawman
  see Layamon

Lawrence (ship)
  Perry, Oliver Hazard **12** 239

LAWRENCE, ABBOTT (1792-1855), American manufacturer and diplomat **9** 246
  Agassiz, Jean Louis Rodolphe **1** 76-78

Lawrence, Amos (1786-1852), American merchant
  Lawrence, Abbott **9** 246

LAWRENCE, DAVID HERBERT
(1885-1930), English novelist, poet, and essayist **9** 247-248
  Anderson, Sherwood **1** 220-221
  Brooke, Rupert **3** 22-23
  Ford, Ford Madox **6** 1-2
  Franklin, Benjamin **6** 60-64
  Huxley, Aldous Leonard **8** 74-75
  Miller, Henry **11** 26-27

LAWRENCE, ERNEST ORLANDO
(1901-1958), American physicist
9 248-250

LAWRENCE, JACOB (born 1917), African American painter **9** 250-251
  Bearden, Romare Howard **2** 86-88

LAWRENCE, JAMES (1781-1813), American naval officer **9** 251-252

LAWRENCE, SIR THOMAS (1769-1830), English portrait painter **9** 252-253

LAWRENCE, THOMAS EDWARD
(1888-1935), British soldier and author **9** 253-254
  Allenby, Edmund Henry Hynman
    1 171-172
  Faisal I **5** 370-371

Lawrence Livermore Laboratory (Berkeley, California)
  Teller, Edward **15** 139-141

Lawrence of Arabia
  see Lawrence, Thomas Edward

Lawrence Radiation Laboratory (Berkeley, California)
  Calvin, Melvin **3** 242-243
  Lawrence, Ernest Orlando **9** 248-250

Lawrencium (element—chemistry)
Lawrence, Ernest Orlando **9** 248-250

Lawson, Alexander (1773-1846), American engraver
Wilson, Alexander **16** 313-314

LAWSON, HENRY (1867-1922), Australian poet and short-story writer **9** 254-255
Paterson, Andrew Barton **12** 131-132

LAWSON, THOMAS WILLIAM (1857-1925), American entrepreneur and reformer **9** 255-256

Lawsuit of the Twins, The (story)
Mqhayi, Samuel Edward Krune **11** 223

Lawyers
see Jurists

Laxists (religious group)
Donatus **5** 56-57

Lay Down Your Arms (book and journal)
Suttner, Bertha von **15** 42-44

Lay investiture
see Investiture struggle

Lay of the Last Minstrel, The (poem)
Scott, Walter **14** 68-70

Lay your sleeping head, my love (poem)
Auden, Wystan Hugh **1** 364-366

LAYAMON (flourished circa 1200), English poet **9** 256-257

LAYE, CAMARA (1928-1980), Guinean novelist **9** 257-259

Lays of My Home (poems)
Whittier, John Greenleaf **16** 256-257

Lazard Frères and Co. (international bank firm)
Lilienthal, David Eli **9** 410-411

Lazarillo de Tormes (book)
Alemán, Mateo **1** 126

LAZARSFELD, PAUL F. (1901-1976), American sociologist **9** 259-260
Berelson, Bernard **2** 185-186
Stouffer, Samuel A. **14** 482-483

Lazarus (sculpture)
Epstein, Jacob **5** 295-296

LAZARUS, EMMA (1849-1887), American poet and playwright **9** 260-261

Lazarus Laughed (play)
O'Neill, Eugene **11** 514-516

Lazzaretto (Verona, Italy)
Sanmicheli, Michele **13** 469-470

Lazzarini, Gregorio (1655-1730), Italian painter
Tiepolo, Giovanni Battista **15** 219-220

Lazzaro (play)
Pirandello, Luigi **12** 319-321

Le Bec-Hellouin (commune, northern France)
Anselm of Canterbury **1** 244-245

Le Bel, J.A. (1847-1930), French chemist
Fischer, Emil **5** 456-457

LE BON, GUSTAVE (1841-1931), French social scientist and philosopher **9** 268-269
Tarde, Jean Gabriel **15** 108-109

Le Breton, André-François (1708-1779), French printer
Diderot, Denis **5** 1-2

LE BRUN, CHARLES (1619-1690), French painter, decorator, and draftsman **9** 269-270
Le Vau, Louis **9** 360-361
Perrault, Claude **12** 232-233
Poussin, Nicolas **12** 418-420

LE CARRE, JOHN (born David Cornwell, 1931), British spy novelist **9** 270-271

Le Clerc du Tremblay, François
see Joseph, Father

LE CORBUSIER (Charles Édouard Jeanneret-Gris; 1887-1965), Swiss architect, city planner, and painter **9** 274-275
Asplund, Eric Gunnar **1** 344
Behrens, Peter **2** 121-122
Mies van der Rohe, Ludwig **11** 10-12
Niemeyer Soares Filho, Oscar **11** 389-390
Oud, Jacobus Johannes Pieter **12** 32
Tange, Kenzo **15** 99-101
Wright, Frank Lloyd **16** 398-401
Xenakis, Iannis **16** 416-418

LE DUAN (1908-1986), North Vietnamese leader and later head of the government of all Vietnam **9** 278-280

Le Guen (literary character)
Beti, Mongo **2** 242-243

LE JEUNE, CLAUDE (circa 1530-1600), Flemish composer **9** 314-315

Le Maire, Jacob (1585-1616), Dutch navigator
Schouten, William Cornelius **14** 31

Le Matin (The Morning; sculpture)
Laurens, Henri **9** 230-231

Le Moyne, Pierre
see Iberville, Sieur d'

LE NAIN BROTHERS, 17th-century French painters **9** 321-322
Le Nain, Antoine, Louis and Mathieu **9** 321-322

LE NÔTRE, ANDRÉ (or Le Nostre; 1613-1700), French landscape architect **9** 328-329
Le Vau, Louis **9** 360-361

LE PEN, JEAN MARIE (born 1928), French political activist of the radical right **9** 348-350

LE PLAY, GUILLAUME FRÉDÉRIC (1806-1882), French sociologist and economist **9** 350-351
Geddes, Patrick **6** 246-247

Le Prestre, Sébastien
see Vauban, Marquis de

Le Tellier, François Michel (1641-1691), French statesman

Colbert, Jean Baptiste **4** 142-143

Le Tellier, Michel (1603-1685), French statesman
Louis XIV **9** 531-533

LE VAU, LOUIS (1612-1670), French architect **9** 360-361
Le Nôtre, André **9** 328-329
Mansart, Jules Hardouin **10** 212
Perrault, Claude **12** 232-233

LEA, HENRY CHARLES (1825-1909), American historian **9** 261-262

Lead (element—chemistry)
Lavoisier, Antoine Laurent **9** 241-244
Soddy, Frederick **14** 321-323

Lead, Kindly Light (hymn)
Newman, John Henry **11** 365-367
Sullivan, Arthur Seymour **15** 23

League, Holy
see Holy League

League of Frightened Philistines, The (book)
Farrell, James Thomas **5** 390-391

League of German Princes (established 1784)
Frederick II **6** 81-84
Joseph II **8** 359-360

League of Nations (1919-1946)
Africa and
Firestone, Harvey Samuel **5** 452-453
Haile Selassie **7** 68-70
Olympio, Sylvanus E. **11** 506-507
Australia and
Bruce of Melbourne, 1st Viscount **3** 61-62
Austria and
Dollfuss, Engelbert **5** 47
Canada and
Borden, Robert Laird **2** 409-411
King, William Lyon Mackenzie **9** 25-26
Covenant
Cecil, of Chelwood Viscount **3** 388-389
House, Edward Mandell **7** 520-521
Wilson, Thomas Woodrow **16** 330-332
creation
Roosevelt, Franklin Delano **13** 277-280
Saionji, Kimmochi **13** 438-439
Smuts, Jan Christian **14** 309-310
Wilson, Thomas Woodrow **16** 330-332
Germany and
Chamberlain, Arthur Neville **3** 409-411
Hughes, William Morris **8** 21-22
Stresemann, Gustav **14** 508-509
influenced by
Ladd, William **9** 149
International Court
see Permanent Court of International Justice
Latin America and

Justo, Agustin Pedro **8** 396
Lamas, Carlos Saavedra **9** 175-176
Mistral, Gabriela **11** 55-56
Manchuria and
Stimson, Henry Lewis **14** 457-458
mandates
Ben-Gurion, David **2** 160-161
Faisal I **5** 370-371
Glubb, John Bagot **6** 371-372
Husein ibn Ali **8** 63
Lugard, Frederick John Dealtry
10 31-32
Olympio, Sylvanus E. **11** 506-507
Silver, Abba Hillel **14** 232-233
Weizmann, Chaim **16** 183-184
officials
Aga Khan **1** 74-76
Johnson, Charles Spurgeon
8 296-297
Monnet, Jean **11** 109-110
Perth, 16th Earl of **12** 244-245
Lamas, Carlos Saavedra **9** 175-176
Tinbergen, Jan **15** 228-229
Titulescu, Nicolae **15** 246-247
opponents (United States)
Borah, William Edgar **2** 408
Cannon, Joseph Gurney **3** 261-262
Coolidge, John Calvin **4** 217-219
Harding, Warren Gamaliel
7 148-149
Johnson, Hiram Warren **8** 300-301
Knox, Philander Chase **9** 66-67
La Follette, Robert Marion
9 155-156
Lodge, Henry Cabot **9** 482-483
McCormick, Robert Rutherford
10 401-402
Munsey, Frank Andrew **11** 251
Norris, George William **11** 428-429
Roosevelt, Theodore **13** 280-283
sanctions against Italy
Schuschnigg, Kurt von **14** 45-46
supporters (Europe)
Beneš, Edward **2** 155-157
Bourgeois, Léon **2** 450-451
Briand, Aristide **2** 528-529
Bryce, James **3** 85
Clemenceau, Georges **4** 99-101
Henderson, Arthur **7** 277-278
Hobhouse, Leonard Trelawny
7 425-426
Nansen, Fridtjof **11** 304-305
supporters (United States)
Baker, Newton Diehl **1** 451
Butler, Nicholas Murray **3** 181
Catt, Carrie Chapman **3** 375-376
Hitchcock, Gilbert Monell
7 416-417
Hoover, Herbert Clark **7** 483-485
House, Edward Mandell **7** 520-521
Hughes, Charles Evans **8** 15-16
Hull, Cordell **8** 28-29
Lansing, Robert **9** 200
Root, Elihu **13** 283-284
Taft, William Howard **15** 78-81
Walsh, Thomas James **16** 85-86

White, William Allen **16** 240-241
Turkey and
Atatürk, Ghazi Mustapha Kemal
1 356-357
U.S.S.R. and
Litvinov, Maxim Maximovich
9 451-452

League of Nations Palace (Geneva)
Le Corbusier **9** 274-275

League of Puerto Rican Patriots (established 1898)
Hostos, Eugenio María de **7** 513-514

League of the Public Weal (1465-1466)
Charles the Bold **3** 467-469
Louis XI **9** 526-528

League of Women Voters (United States)
Catt, Carrie Chapman **3** 375-376
Roosevelt, Eleanor **13** 275-277
Park, Maud Wood **12** 102
Stone, Lucy **14** 471-472

League of Youth, The (play)
Ibsen, Henrik **8** 98-100

Leah (sculpture)
Michelangelo Buonarroti **11** 2-5

LEAKEY, LOUIS SEYMOUR BAZETT
(1903-1972), British anthropologist **9** 262
Fossey, Dian **6** 23-24
Goodall, Jane **6** 433-434
Leakey, Mary Douglas **9** 263-264
Leakey, Richard Erskine Frere
9 264-265

LEAKEY, MARY DOUGLAS (1913-1996),
English archaeologist **9** 263-264
Leakey, Richard Erskine Frere
9 264-265

LEAKEY, RICHARD ERSKINE FRERE (born
1944), Kenyan researcher in human prehistory and wildlife conservationist
9 264-265
Leakey, Mary Douglas **9** 263-264

Lean, David (1908-1991), English film
director and producer
Coward, Noel **4** 279-280

Leaning Tower ... (stories)
Porter, Katherine Anne **12** 406-407

LEAR, EDWARD (1812-1888), English
writer and artist **9** 265-266
Stravinsky, Igor Fedorovich **14** 502-506
Tennyson, Alfred **15** 144-146

Lear of the Steppe, A (story)
Turgenev, Ivan Sergeyevich **15** 345-348

Learning theory (psychology)
Gagné, Robert Mills **6** 170
Guthrie, Edwin Ray **7** 49-50
Hull, Clark Leonard **8** 28]
Piaget, Jean **12** 287-288
Skinner, Burrhus Frederic **14** 269-270

LEARY, TIMOTHY (1920-1996), American
psychologist, author, lecturer, and cult
figure **9** 266-267

LEASE, MARY ELIZABETH CLYENS
(1853-1933), American writer and politician **9** 268

Leaves from a Fairy Tale (poem)
Eminescu, Mihail **5** 280-281

Leaves of Grass (poems; Whitman)
Whitman, Walt **16** 249-251
Williams, William Carlos **16** 308-309

Leavitt, Henrietta S. (1868-1921), American astronomer
Hubble, Edwin Powell **8** 10-11
Shapley, Harlow **14** 155-156

Lebanon, Republic of (nation; southwest
Asia)
Abu Musa **1** 32-33
Adonis **1** 64-65
Aoun, Michel **1** 255-257
Berri, Nabih **2** 220-222
Cleopatra **4** 105-106
Fadlallah, Sayyid Muhammad Husayn
5 362-364
Gemayel, Amin **6** 258-259
Gemayel, Pierre **6** 259-261
Harawi, Ilyas al- **7** 145-146
Jumblatt, Kamal **8** 386-387
Plaza Lasso, Galo **12** 350-351
Sadr, Musa al- **13** 420-422
Shihab, Fu'ad **14** 193-194
Waite, Terry **16** 47-48

Lebas, Louis Hippolyte (1782-1867),
French architect
Garnier, Jean Louis Charles **6** 221-222
Labrouste, Pierre François Henri **9** 144

Leben des Galilei (play)
Brecht, Bertolt **2** 512-514

Leben des Quintus Fixlein (book)
Richter, Johann Paul Friedrich
13 150-151

Leben Fibels, Das (novel)
Richter, Johann Paul Friedrich
13 150-151

Leben und Lieder (poems)
Rilke, Rainer Maria **13** 171-172

Leben und Tod der heiligen (play)
Tieck, Ludwig **15** 218-219

Lebens Überfluss, Des (story)
Tieck, Ludwig **15** 218-219

Lebens-Ansichten des Katers Murr (novel)
Hoffmann, Ernst Theodor Amadeus
7 439-440

Lebenserinnerungen (book)
Freytag, Gustav **6** 107-108

Lebrun, Albert (1871-1950), French statesman
Pétain, Henri Philippe **12** 250-252

Lechfeld, battle of (955)
Otto I **12** 28-29

Lechin Oquendo, Juan (born 1915), Bolivian politician
Paz, Octavio **12** 161-162

Leck, Bart van der (1876-1958), Dutch painter
Mondrian, Piet **11** 101-102

LECKY, WILLIAM EDWARD HARTPOLE (1838-1903), Anglo-Irish historian and essayist **9** 271-272

Leclerc, Charles Victor Emmanuel (1772-1802), French general in Haiti
Boyer, Jean Pierre **2** 468-469
Dessalines, Joan Jacques **4** 511-512
Toussaint L'Ouverture, François Dominique **15** 278-279

Leclerc, Georges Louis
see Buffon, Comte de

LECLERC, JACQUES PHILIPPE (1902-1947), French general **9** 272-273

Lecompton Constitution (1857; Kansas)
Buchanan, James **3** 89-90
Lincoln, Abraham **9** 415-418

Leçon, La (play)
Ionesco, Eugène **8** 131-132

Leçons des Ténèbres (musical composition)
Couperin, François **4** 270-271

LECONTE DE LISLE, CHARLES MARIE RENÉ (1818-1894), French poet **9** 273-274

Lectures pour une ombre (book)
Giraudoux, Jean **6** 349-350

Leda and the Swan (painting)
Correggio **4** 249-251
Leonardo da Vinci **9** 337-340

LEDERBERG, JOSHUA (born 1925), Nobel Prize winning geneticist **9** 275-277

LEDOUX, CLAUDE NICOLAS (1736-1806), French architect **9** 277-278
Latrobe, Benjamin Henry **9** 222-224

Ledyard, John (1751-1789), American traveler
Sparks, Jared **14** 363

LEE, ARTHUR (1740-1792), American statesman and diplomat **9** 288-289
Deane, Silas **4** 435-437
Franklin, Benjamin **6** 60-64
Lee, Richard Henry **9** 291-292

Lee, Charles (1731-1782), American general
Tarleton, Banastre **15** 110

Lee, Francis Lightfoot (1734-1797), American Revolutionary statesman
Lee, Arthur **9** 288-289

Lee, Henry (1756-1818), American statesman and soldier
Lee, Robert Edward **9** 292-294

LEE, MING CHO (born 1930), American scene designer for theater and opera **9** 289-290

LEE, MOTHER ANN (1736-1784), religious and social reformer and founder of the Shakers **9** 289-290

Lee, Nathaniel (circa 1653-1692), English dramatist
Dryden, John **5** 106-107
Purcell, Henry **12** 484-485

LEE, RICHARD HENRY (1732-1794), American patriot and statesman **9** 291-292
Adams, John **1** 48-51
Clinton, George **4** 113-114
Henry, Patrick **7** 309-311
Lee, Arthur **9** 288-289
Monroe, James **11** 111-113

LEE, ROBERT EDWARD (1807-1870), American army officer and Confederate general in chief **9** 292-294
associates
Beauregard, Pierre Gustave Toutant **2** 96-97
Bledsoe, Albert Taylor **2** 324-325
Gordon, John Brown **6** 449-450
Hampton, Wade III **7** 112
biographers
Freeman, Douglas Southall **6** 91-92
Harpers Ferry (1859)
Brown, John **3** 39-41
Stuart, James Ewell Brown **14** 515-516
military campaigns
Grant, Ulysses Simpson **6** 492-494
Jackson, Shirley Ann **8** 183-184
McClellan, George Brinton **10** 391-392
Meade, George Gordon **10** 440-441
Sheridan, Philip Henry **14** 182-183
Sherman, William Tecumseh **14** 186-187
Toombs, Robert Augustus **15** 267-268

LEE, SPIKE (born Sheldon Jackson Lee; born 1957), African American actor, author, and filmmaker **9** 295-299

LEE, TSUNG-DAO (born 1926), Chinese-born American physicist **9** 299-300
Yang, Chen Ning **16** 437-438

LEE HSIEN LOONG (born 1952), Singaporean soldier and deputy prime minister **9** 280-281

LEE KUAN YEW (born 1923), prime minister of Singapore (1959-1988) **9** 281-283

LEE TENG-HUI (born 1923), president of the Republic of China (1988-) **9** 283-285

Leeds, University of (England)
Bragg, William Henry **2** 488-489
Clapham, John Harold **4** 71

Leeuwendalers, De (play)
Vondel, Joost van den **16** 19-20

LEEUWENHOEK, ANTON VAN (1632-1723), Dutch naturalist and microscopist **9** 300-301

Leeward Islands (West Indies)
Eyre, Edward John **5** 354
Rodney, George Brydges **13** 239-240

LEFEBVRE, GEORGES (1874-1959), French historian **9** 301-302

Lefèvre d'Étaples, Jacques (1450?-1537), French theologian and humanist
Francis I **6** 40-43
Rabelais, François **12** 524-526

Left Bank, The (play)
Rice, Elmer **13** 126-127

Left Book Club (England)
Laski, Harold J. **9** 215-216
Orwell, George **12** 14-15

Lefuel, Hector Martin (1810-1880), French architect
Hunt, Richard Morris **8** 44

Legacy (poems)
Villon, François **15** 499-501

Legal history
see Jurisprudence; Law

Legal reform
see Law—legal reform

Legalism (Chinese philosophy)
Han Fei Tzu **7** 124-125
Han Wu-ti **7** 136
Hsün-tzu **8** 8
Li Ssu **9** 442-443
Liu Pang **9** 453
Shang Yang **14** 149-150

Legend of Creation, The (book)
Hidayat, Sadiq **7** 377-378

Legend of Montrose, A (novel)
Scott, Walter **14** 68-70

Legend of Saint Julian the Hospitaller (story)
Flaubert, Gustave **5** 480-482

Legend of Sleepy Hollow, The (story)
Irving, Washington **8** 141-143

Legend of Saint Elizabeth (music)
Liszt, Franz **9** 445-447

Legend of Saint George (fresco)
Pisanello **12** 323-324

Légende des siècles (epic cycle; Hugo)
Fréchette, Louis-Honoré **6** 77-78
Hugo, Victor Marie **8** 22-25

Légende d'un peuple, La (poems; Hugo)
Fréchette, Louis-Honoré **6** 77-78

Legends (stories)
Lagerlöf, Selma Ottiliana Lovisa **9** 163-164

Legends of Guatemala (literary collection)
Asturias, Miguel Angel **1** 354-355

Léger, Alexis Saint-Léger
see Perse, Saint-John

LÉGER, FERNAND (1881-1955), French painter **9** 302-303
　Archipenko, Alexander **1** 280-281
　Braque, Georges **2** 504-505
　Calder, Alexander **3** 216-218
　Malevich, Kasimir **10** 168-169

Legge, James (1815-1897), Scottish missionary and Sinologist
　Wang T'ao **16** 105-106

Leggi fascistissime, le
　see Fascist regime (Italy)

LEGHARI, SARDAR FAROOQ AHMED KHAN (born 1940), president of the Islamic Republic of Pakistan **9** 303-305

Legion Club, The (poem)
　Swift, Jonathan **15** 51-54

Legislative Assembly (French Revolution)
　see French Revolution—1789-91 (Legislative Assembly), 1792-95 (National Convention)

Legislative Belly (lithograph)
　Daumier, Honoré Victorin **4** 403-405

Legislators
　see Statesmen

Legnano, battle of (1176)
　Frederick I **6** 78-79

Legrenzi, Giovanni (circa 1626-1690), Italian composer
　Vivaldi, Antonio **16** 3-4

Legros, Alphonse (1837-1911), French painter
　Whistler, James Abbott McNeill **16** 225-226

LEGUÍA Y SALCEDO, AUGUSTO BERNARDINO (1863-1932), Peruvian president 1908-12 and 1919-30 **9** 305-306
　Prado Ugarteche, Manuel **12** 430-431

LEHMAN, HERBERT HENRY (1878-1963), American banker and statesman **9** 306-307

Lehman, Irving (1876-1945), American jurist
　Cardozo, Benjamin Nathan **3** 288-290

Lehmann, Lotte (1888-1976), German-American soprano
　Mann, Thomas **10** 204-207

LEHMBRUCK, WILHELM (1881-1919), German sculptor **9** 307

Lehrlinge zu Sais, Die (novel)
　Novalis **11** 435

Leibl, Wilhelm (1844-1900), German painter
　Hofmann, Hans **7** 442-443

LEIBNIZ, GOTTFRIED WILHELM VON (1646-1716), German mathematician and philosopher **9** 307-310
　and Newton
　　Clarke, Samuel **4** 88
　　Kant, Immanuel **8** 430-432
　　Newton, Isaac **11** 369-372
　　Taylor, Brook **15** 121-122
　correspondents
　　Leeuwenhoek, Anton van **9** 300-301
　　Spinoza, Baruch **14** 381-383
　　Toland, John **15** 256
　influence of
　　Heidegger, Martin **7** 257-258
　　Kant, Immanuel **8** 430-432
　　Wolff, Christian von **16** 358
　influenced by
　　Chu Hsi **4** 40-43
　　Plato **12** 345-347
　　Shaftesbury, 3d Earl of **14** 136-137

LEIBOVITZ, ANNIE (born 1949), Ameircan photographer **9** 310-312

LEICESTER, EARL OF (Robert Dudley; 1532?-1588), English politician **9** 312-313
　Elizabeth I **5** 263-266
　Essex, 2d Earl of **5** 321-322
　Maurice of Nassau **10** 348-349
　Northumberland, Duke of **11** 431-432
　Sidney, Philip **14** 214-215
　Spenser, Edmund **14** 373-376

Leicester, 6th Earl of
　see Montfort, Simon de

Leiden, University of (Netherlands)
　Arminius, Jacobus **1** 301-302
　Boerhaave, Hermann **2** 358-359
　Einstein, Albert **5** 228-231
　Huizinga, Johan **8** 26-27
　Lorentz, Hendrik Antoon **9** 515-516
　Oort, Jan Hendrik **11** 523-524
　Szent-Györgyi, Albert von **15** 62-64

Leiden des jungen Werthers, Die (novel)
　Goethe, Johann Wolfgang von **6** 388-391

Leiden Observatory (Netherlands)
　Kapteyn, Jacobus Cornelis **8** 436-437
　Oort, Jan Hendrik **11** 523-524

Leigh, Augusta (1783-1851), half-sister of Lord Byron
　Byron, George Gordon Noel **3** 193-194

Leipzig, battle of (1813)
　Aberdeen, 4th Earl of **1** 25-26
　Blücher, Gebhard Leberecht von **2** 340-341
　Murat, Joachim **11** 253-254
　Napoleon I **11** 306-310
　Ney, Michel **11** 372-373

Leipzig, University of (Germany)
　historians
　　Lamprecht, Karl **9** 181
　　Mommsen, Theodor **11** 94-95
　　Treitschke, Heinrich von **15** 293-294
　philosophers
　　Driesch, Hans Adolf Eduard **5** 105
　　Nietzsche, Friedrich **11** 390-392
　　Thomasius **15** 193-194
　　Tillich, Paul Johannes **15** 224-225
　　Wolff, Christian von **16** 358
　scientists
　　Agricola, Georgius **1** 86-87
　　Boltzmann, Ludwig **2** 379-380
　　Fechner, Gustav Theodor **5** 401-402
　　Ludwig, Karl Friedrich Wilhelm **10** 31
　　Ratzel, Friedrich **13** 50-51
　　Wundt, Wilhelm Max **16** 402-403

Leipzig Conservatory of Music (established 1843)
　Mendelssohn, Moses **10** 488-489
　Schumann, Robert Alexander **14** 41-43

Leis Willelme (England)
　William I **16** 290-291

LEISLER, JACOB (1640-1691), American colonial leader **9** 313-314

Leisler's Rebellion (New York; 1689-91)
　Leisler, Jacob **9** 313-314
　Livingston, Robert **9** 461-462

Leiter, Levi Z. (1834-1904), American merchant
　Field, Marshall **5** 440-441

Leland Stanford Junior University
　see Stanford University

Lele tribe (Zaire)
　Douglas, Mary Tew **5** 79-80

Lélia (novel)
　Sand, George **13** 459-461

Lélio (melologue)
　Berlioz, Louis Hector **2** 203-205

LELY, SIR PETER (1618-1680), German-born painter active in England **9** 315

Lemaire de Belges, Jean (circa 1473-1524), French humanist and poet
　Josquin des Prez **8** 361-363

LEMAÎTRE, ABBÈ GEORGES ÉDOUARD (1894-1966), Belgian astronomer **9** 315-316
　Eddington, Arthur Stanley **5** 201-202

LEMAY, CURTIS E. (1906-1990), United States combat leader (World War II) and Air Force chief of staff **9** 316-318

LEMBEDE, ANTON (1913-1947), leader of black resistance to white supremacy in South Africa **9** 318-319

Lemercier, Jacques (1585?-1654), French architect
　Mansart, François **10** 211
　Renwick, James **13** 102-103

Lemhi Shoshoni Indians (North America)
　Lowie, Robert Harry **10** 18

LEMNITZER, LYMAN LOUIS (Lem; 1899-1988), American soldier-statesman and strategist and NATO architect **9** 319-320

Lemoyne, François (1688-1737), French painter
　Boucher, François **2** 440-442

Lemoyne, Jean Baptiste (1704-1778), French sculptor
　Falconet, Étienne Maurice **5** 372

Len (literary character)
Pinter, Harold **12** 317-318

Lena (literary character)
Conrad, Joseph **4** 205-207

Lena, La (comedy)
Ariosto, Ludovico **1** 289-290

Lenard, Philipp E.A. (1862-1947), Hungarian-born German physicist
Bothe, Walther **2** 438-439
Einstein, Albert **5** 228-231

Lend-Lease Program (United States)
Morgenthau, Henry Jr. **11** 172-173
Stettinius, Edward R. Jr. **14** 437-438

L'ENFANT, PIERRE CHARLES (1754-1825), French-born American architect **9** 322-323

LENIN, VLADIMIR ILICH (1870-1924), Russian statesman **9** 323-326
and Finland
Mannerheim, Carl Gustav Emil Von **10** 207-208
Brest-Litovsk
see Brest-Litovsk, Treaty of
collaborators
Radek, Karl Bernardovich **12** 536-537
see also Russian Revolution (1905), (1917; October), (1918-20; Civil War)
influence of
De Leon, Daniel **4** 479-480
Ho Chi Minh **7** 426-428
Mao Zedong **10** 225-227
Nkrumah, Kwame **11** 408-410
Reed, John Silas **13** 76-77
Steinmetz, Charles Proteus **14** 419-420
influenced by
Marx, Karl **10** 304-308
Plekhanov, Georgi Valentinovich **12** 351-352
succession conflict
Bukharin, Nikolai Ivanovich **3** 112-113
Stalin, Joseph **14** 393-396
Trotsky, Leon **15** 302-305

Leningrad (city, Russia)
see St. Petersburg

Leningrad Symphony (musical composition)
Shostakovich, Dmitri Dmitrievich **14** 204-205

Lennon, John (1940-1980), English poet and songwriter
Beatles, The **2** 89-92

Lenoir, Alexandre (1762-1839), French painter
Daumier, Honoré Victorin **4** 403-405

Lenoir, Étienne (1822-1900), French inventor
Daimler, Gottlieb **4** 368

Lenya, Lotte (1900-1981), Austrian-American singer

Weill, Kurt **16** 174-175

Lenz, Jakob Michael Reinhold (1751-1792), German poet and dramatist
Tieck, Ludwig **15** 218-219

Lenz, Wilhelm von (1809-1883), Russian musicologist
Beethoven, Ludwig van **2** 114-117

Leo I (the Great; 400?-474), Byzantine emperor 457-474
Ricimer, Flavius **13** 151-152

LEO I (circa 400-461), saint and pope 440-461 **9** 329-330
Attila **1** 360
Eutyches **5** 335

LEO III (the Isaurian; circa 680-741), Byzantine emperor 717-741 **9** 330-332
Charlemagne **3** 445-447
John of Damascus **8** 282

Leo VI (the Wise; 866-912), Byzantine emperor 886-912
Basil I **2** 49-50
Photius **12** 283-284

LEO IX, Saint (Bruno of Egisheim; 1002-1054), pope 1049-1054 **9** 332
Guiscard, Robert **7** 39-40
Henry III **7** 290

LEO X (Giovanni de' Medici; 1475-1521), pope 1513-1521 **9** 332-334
appointments
Bembo, Pietro **2** 144-145
Guicciardini, Francesco **7** 32-33
opponents
Pomponazzi, Pietro **12** 390-391
patronage
Andrea del Sarto **1** 224-225
Encina, Juan del **5** 283
Isaac, Heinrich **8** 143-144
Michelangelo Buonarroti **11** 2-5
Raphael **13** 40-42
Sangallo family **13** 464-466
reforms issue
Eck, Johann Maier von **5** 200
Erasmus, Desiderius **5** 298-300

Leo XII (Annibale Francesco della Genga; 1760-1829), pope 1823-1829
Lamennais, Hugues Félicité Robert de **9** 179

LEO XIII (Vincenzo Gioacchino Pecci; 1810-1903), pope 1878-1903 **9** 334-336
Cabrini, Frances Xavier **3** 205
Frei Montalva, Eduardo **6** 94-95
Ireland, John **8** 133-134
John, XXIII **8** 277-280
Paul VI **12** 146-148
Pius X **12** 336-337
Pius XI **12** 337-339
Salazar, António de Oliveira **13** 442-443

Leo, Leonardo (1694-1744), Italian composer
Pergolesi, Giovanni Battista **12** 218-219

Leo Hebraeus
see Levi ben Gershon

León (city; Nicaragua)
Benalcázar, Sebastián de **2** 145-146

León, battle of (1915)
Carranza, Venustiano **3** 321-322
Obregón, Álvaro **11** 458-459
Villa, Pancho **15** 495-496

LEON, MOSES DE (circa 1250-1305), Jewish mystic **9** 336
Elijah ben Solomon **5** 251-252
Manasseh ben Israel **10** 183-184

LEONARD, DANIEL (1740-1829), American loyalist lawyer and essayist **9** 336-337
Adams, John **1** 48-51

Leonard and Gertrude (novel)
Pestalozzi, Johann Heinrich **12** 249-250

Leonarda (play)
Bjørnson, Bjørnstjerne **2** 299-300

LEONARDO DA VINCI (1452-1519), Italian painter, sculptor, architect, and scientist **9** 337-340
associates
Pontormo **12** 394-395
Verrocchio, Andrea del **15** 471-472
influence of
Andrea del Sarto **1** 224-225
Clouet, Jean and François **4** 122-123
Correggio **4** 249-251
Hodler, Ferdinand **7** 434-435
Holbein, Hans the Younger **7** 449-450
Massys, Quentin **10** 325-326
Morales, Luis de **11** 150
Poussin, Nicolas **12** 418-420
Raphael **13** 40-42
Tartaglia, Niccolo **15** 111-112
patrons
Sforza, Lodovico **14** 127-128
studies on
Duhem, Pierre Maurice Marie **5** 129

Leonardo of Pisa
see Fibonacci, Leonardo

Leoncavallo, Ruggiero (1858-1919), Italian composer
Caruso, Enrico **3** 345
Toscanini, Arturo **15** 270-271

Leoni, Raul (1905-1972), Venezuelan statesman, president 1964-1969
Betancourt, Rómulo **2** 237-238

LEONIDAS I (ca. 530 B.C. - 480 B.C.), Spartan king **9** 340-343
Xerxes **16** 420

Leonidas II (circa 285-236 B.C.), king of Sparta
Agis IV **1** 81-82
Cleomenes III **4** 103-104

LÉONIN (Leoninus; flourished circa 1165-1185), French composer **9** 343-344
Franco of Cologne **6** 52
Pérotin **12** 231-232

Leonora (novel)
Bennett, Arnold **2** 167-168

Leonora (opera)
  Fry, William Henry **6** 136-137

Leonore (Fidelio; opera)
  Beethoven, Ludwig van **2** 114-117

Leopardi, Alessandro (died circa 1522), Venetian sculptor
  Verrocchio, Andrea del **15** 471-472

LEOPARDI, CONTE GIACOMO (1798-1837), Italian poet **9** 344-345

Leopold (Leopold von Hohenzollern-Sigmaringen; 1835-1905), German prince
  Bismarck, Otto Eduard Leopold von **2** 294-296
  Ferdinand **5** 413-414

Leopold I (1640-1705), Holy Roman emperor 1658-1705
  Cesti, Pietro **3** 399-400
  Eugene of Savoy **5** 330-331
  Ferdinand III **5** 416-417
  Fischer von Erlach, Johann Bernhard **5** 459-461
  Froberger, Johann Jakob **6** 120-121

LEOPOLD I (1790-1865), king of Belgium 1831-1865 **9** 345-346
  Albert **1** 110-112
  Leopold II **9** 346-347
  Victoria **15** 485-487

Leopold I (Duke of Tuscany)
  see Leopold II (emperor)

LEOPOLD II (1747-1792), Holy Roman emperor 1790-1792 **9** 346
  Francis II **6** 43-44
  Marie Antoinette **10** 258-259

LEOPOLD II (1835-1909), king of Belgium 1865-1909 **9** 346-347
  Albert I **1** 112
  Brazza, Pierre Paul François Camille Savorgnan de **2** 509-510
  Gordon, Charles George **6** 448-449
  Leopold I **9** 345-346
  Peters, Carl **12** 257-258
  Tippu Tip **15** 235-236

LEOPOLD III (1901-1983), king of Belgium 1934-1951 **9** 347-348
  Albert I **1** 112

Leopold, Duke of Brabant
  see Leopold III (king of Belgium)

Leopold-Loeb case (1924)
  Darrow, Clarence Seward **4** 396-397

Leopoldina (died 1827), empress of Brazil 1822-1827
  Pedro I **12** 179-180

Léopoldville
  see Kinshasa

Leotychidas (died circa 469 B.C.), king of Sparta 491-469
  Cleomenes I **4** 103

Lepanto (poem)
  Chesterton, Gilbert Keith **3** 508-509

Lepanto, battle of (1571)
  Cervantes, Miguel de Saavedra **3** 395-398
  Philip II **12** 271-273
  Pius V **12** 332-333
  Tasso, Torquato **15** 114-116
  Zarlino, Gioseffo **16** 490-491

Lepers
  see Leprosy

Lepidopterists
  see Scientists—lepidopterists

Lepidus, Marcus Aemilius (died 13 B.C.), Roman statesman
  Antony, Mark **1** 253-254
  Augustus **1** 371-373
  Cicero, Marcus Tullius **4** 55-58
  Horace **7** 500-503

Lepidus, Marcus Aemilius (died circa 77 B.C.), Roman politician
  Brutus, Marcus Junius **3** 79-80
  Pompey **12** 387-389
  Sulla, Lucius Cornelius I **15** 21-22

Lepoqo
  see Moshweshwe

Leprosy (medicine)
  Damien **4** 383

Lequien, Justin (1826-1882), French sculptor
  Seurat, Georges Pierre **14** 120-122

LERDO DE TEJADA, MIGUEL (1812-1861), Mexican liberal politician **9** 351-352

Lerdo de Tejada, Sebastián (1825-1889), president of Mexico 1872-1876
  Díaz, José de la Cruz Porfirio **4** 534-536

Lerma, Duke of (Francisco Gómez de Sandoval y Rojas; 1552-1625), Spanish statesman
  Philip III **12** 273-274
  Rubens, Peter Paul **13** 339-342

LERMONTOV, MIKHAIL YURIEVICH (1814-1841), Russian poet and prose writer **9** 352-353
  Belinsky, Grigorievich **2** 128
  Goncharov, Ivan Aleksandrovich **6** 424
  Meyerhold, Vsevolod Emilievich **10** 539
  Pushkin, Aleksandr Sergeevich **12** 489-491
  Turgenev, Ivan Sergeyevich **15** 345-348

Les Six
  see Six, The

Les XX
  see Twenty, The

LESAGE, ALAIN RENÉ (1668-1747), French novelist and playwright **9** 353-354
  Smollett, Tobias George **14** 305-307

Lesbia (literary character)
  Catullus, Gaius Valerius **3** 377-378

Leschetizsky, Theodor (1830-1915), Polish composer and pianist
  Liszt, Franz **9** 445-447
  Paderewski, Ignace Jan **12** 56-57

LESCOT, PIERRE (1500/1515-1578), French architect **9** 354
  Goujon, Jean **6** 466-467

Leskien, August (1840-1916), German Slavic philologist
  Bloomfield, Leonard **2** 338

Lesky, Albin (born 1896-), Austrian classicist
  Aeschylus **1** 70-72

Leslie, David, 1st Lord Newark (1601-1682), Scottish soldier
  Cromwell, Oliver **4** 317-320

Leslie's Weekly (magazine)
  Nast, Thomas **11** 318-319
  Russell, Charles Marion **13** 375-376

Lesotho, Kingdom of (nation; South Africa)
  Booth, Joseph **2** 404-405
  Jonathan, Joseph Leabua **8** 330-331
  Malan, Daniel Francois **10** 163-164
  Moshweshwe **11** 203-205

Lesothoan literature
  Mofolo, Thomas **11** 74

Lespinasse, Julie Jeanne Éléonore de (1732-1776), French writer
  Alembert, Jean le Rond d' **1** 127-128

LESSEPS, VICOMTE DE (Ferdinand Marie; 1805-1894), French diplomat **9** 354-355
  Bunau-Varilla, Philippe Jean **3** 120-121
  Keith, Minor Cooper **8** 476-477

Lesser Antilles (islands; West Indies)
  Columbus, Christopher **4** 176-179

LESSING, DORIS (Doris May Taylor; born 1919), South African expatriate writer **9** 355-357

LESSING, GOTTHOLD EPHRAIM (1729-1781), German philosopher, dramatist, and critic **9** 357-359
  Fichte, Johann Gottlieb **5** 435-436
  Hamann, Johann Georg **7** 92
  Jacobi, Friedrich Heinrich **8** 189-190
  Mendelssohn, Moses **10** 488-489
  Winckelmann, Johann Joachim **16** 332-333
  Zunz, Leopold **16** 534

Lessius, Leonard (1554-1623), Flemish Jesuit theologian
  Jansen, Cornelis **8** 220-221

Lesson for Mr. Alibi, A (play)
  Tirso de Molina **15** 237-238

Lesueur, Jean François (1760-1837), French composer
  Berlioz, Louis Hector **2** 203-205
  Gounod, Charles François **6** 473-474

Let 'Em Eat Cake (musical)
  Gershwin, George **6** 284-285
  Kaufman, George S. **8** 457-458

Let Freedom Ring (speech)
  King, Martin Luther Jr. **9** 20-22

Let tyrants shake their iron rod (hymn)
  Billings, William **2** 274-275

Let us live, my Lesbia ... (poem)
Catullus, Gaius Valerius **3** 377-378

Let Us Now Praise Famous Men (book)
Agee, James **1** 78-79
Evans, Walker **5** 339

Let Your Mind Alone! (book)
Thurber, James Grove **15** 213-214

LETCHER, JOHN (1813-1884), American politician **9** 359-360
Vance, Zebulon Baird **15** 413-414

Lethaby, William Richard (1857-1931), English architect
Shaw, Richard Norman **14** 167-168

Letheon (ether)
Morton, William Thomas Green **11** 198-199

Leto and Her Children (sculpture)
Praxiteles **12** 433-434

Let's Do It (song)
Porter, Cole Albert **12** 405-406

Let's Make an Opera (children's opera)
Britten, Benjamin **3** 10-11

Letter, The (sculpture)
Smith, David **14** 287-288

Letterpress (copying machine)
Watt, James **16** 141-143

Letters (New Testament)
see Bible—New Testament (Epistolists)

Lettres françaises, Les (newspaper)
Aragon, Louis **1** 271-272

Letzte Gedichte (poems)
Heine, Heinrich **7** 259-260

Letzte Station, Die (play)
Remarque, Erich Maria **13** 91

Leucippus (flourished 440 B.C.), Greek philosopher
Democritus **4** 493-494

Leuckart, Rudolf (1822-1898), German zoologist
Metchnikoff, Élie **10** 532-533
Weismann, August Freidrich Leopold **16** 178-180

Leuctra, battle of (371 B.C.)
Xenophon **16** 418-420

Leukocytes
see White blood cells

Leurs Figures (novel)
Barrès, Auguste Maurice **2** 20-21

Leute von Seldwyla, Die (stories)
Keller, Gottfried **8** 478-479

Leutnant Gustl (story)
Schnitzler, Arthur **14** 23-24

Leutze, Emanuel (1816-1868), German historical painter
Wood, Grant **16** 368-369

Levellers (political-religious group; England)
Cromwell, Oliver **4** 317-320
Lilburne, John **9** 409-410

LEVERRIER, URBAIN JEAN JOSEPH (1811-1877), French mathematical astronomer **9** 361-362
Adams, John Couch **1** 51-52
Einstein, Albert **5** 228-231

LÉVESQUE, RENÉ (1922-1987), premier of the province of Quebec, Canada (1976-1985) **9** 362-363

Levi
see Matthew, Saint

LEVI BEN GERSHON (1288-circa 1344); French Jewish scientist, philosopher, and theologian **9** 363-364

LEVI, CARLO (1902-1975), Italian writer and painter **9** 364

LEVI, PRIMO (1919-1987), Italian author and chemist **9** 365-366

Levi, tribe of (OT)
Moses **11** 200-201

LEVI-MONTALCINI, RITA (born 1909) Italian and American biologist who discovered the nerve growth factor **9** 366-368

LÉVI-STRAUSS, CLAUDE GUSTAVE (born 1908), French social anthropologist **9** 371-372

Levia gravia (poems)
Carducci, Giosuè **3** 290-291

Leviathan (book)
Hobbes, Thomas **7** 421-423

LEVINAS, EMMANUEL (1906-1995), Jewish philosopher **9** 368-369

Levine, Jack (born 1915), American painter
Benton, Thomas Hart **2** 178-179

LEVINE, JAMES (born 1943), American conductor and pianist **9** 369-371

Levine, Philip (1900-1987), Russian-American bacteriologist
Landsteiner, Karl **9** 188-189

Levis, Duc François Gaston de (1720-1787), French marshal
Murray, James **11** 261-262

Levurnion, battle of (1901)
Alexius I **1** 143-144

LEVY, BERNARD-HENRI (born 1948), French moralist and political philosopher **9** 372-373

LEVY, DAVID (born 1937), Israeli minister of foreign affairs and deputy prime minister **9** 373-374

LÉVY-BRUHL, LUCIEN (1857-1939), French philosopher and anthropologist **9** 374-375
Gilson, Étienne Henry **6** 327-328

Lewerentz, Sigurd (born 1884/85), Swedish architect
Asplund, Eric Gunnar **1** 344

Lewes, battle of (1264)
Edward I **5** 208-210
Henry III **7** 290-292
Montfort, Simon de **11** 132-133

Lewes, George Henry (1817-1878), English philosophical writer
Eliot, George **5** 254-256

LEWIN, KURT (1890-1947), German-American social psychologist **9** 375-376

LEWIS, ANDREW (circa 1720-1781), American general in the Revolution **9** 376-377
Dunmore, 4th Earl of **5** 147

LEWIS, CARL (born Frederick Carlton Lewis; born 1961), African American track and field athlete **9** 377-380

LEWIS, CECIL DAY (1904-1972), British poet and essayist **9** 380
Auden, Wystan Hugh **1** 364-366

LEWIS, CLARENCE IRVING (1883-1964), American philosopher **9** 381

LEWIS, CLIVE STAPLES (C.S.; 1898-1963), British novelist and essayist **9** 381-382

Lewis, Dioclesian (1823-1886), American pioneer in physical culture
Tyler, Moses Coit **15** 369-370

LEWIS, ESSINGTON (1881-1961), Australian industrial leader **9** 382-384

LEWIS, GILBERT NEWTON (1875-1946), American physical chemist **9** 384-385

LEWIS, HARRY SINCLAIR (1885-1951), American novelist **9** 385-387
Callaghan, Edward Morley **3** 229-230
Goldwyn, Samuel **6** 416
Mencken, Henry Louis **10** 481-483
Wolfe, Thomas Clayton **16** 355-356

LEWIS, JOHN LLEWELLYN (1880-1969), American labor leader **9** 387-388
Dubinsky, David **5** 114-115
Green, William R. **6** 521
Hillman, Sidney **7** 392-393
Murray, Philip **11** 264-265

LEWIS, JOHN ROBERT (born 1940), United States civil rights activist and representative from Georgia **9** 388-390

LEWIS, MATTHEW GREGORY (1775-1818), English novelist and playwright **9** 390-391

LEWIS, MERIWETHER (1774-1809), American explorer and army officer **9** 391-392
Clark, William **4** 82-83
Gray, Robert **6** 508-509
Pike, Zebulon **12** 302-304

Lewis, Normal (1909-1979), African American painter
Bearden, Romare Howard **2** 86-88

LEWIS, OSCAR (1914-1970), American anthropologist **9** 392-393

Lewis, Sinclair
see Lewis, Harry Sinclair

Lewis, Wyndham (1884-1957), British novelist and artist
Disraeli, Benjamin **5** 27-29
Ford, Ford Madox **6** 1-2

Lewis and Clark expedition (1804-1806)
  Clark, William **4** 82-83
  Jefferson, Thomas **8** 238-241
  Lewis, Meriwether **9** 391-392

LEWITT, SOL (born 1928), American Minimalist and Conceptualist artist **9** 393-395

Lex Salica
  Clovis I **4** 124

Lexicographers
  see Authors—lexicographers

Lexington (ship)
  Barry, John **2** 24-25
  Currier and Ives **4** 345-346
  King, Ernest Joseph **9** 17-18

Lexington and Concord, battles of (1775)
  Adams, John **1** 48-51
  Adams, Samuel **1** 55-56
  Allen, Ethan **1** 163-164
  Colden, Cadwallader **4** 145-146
  Gage, Thomas **6** 169-170
  Revere, Paul **13** 110-111

L'Express (French newspaper)
  Servan-Schreiber, Jean-Jacques
    14 113-115

Ley, Willie (1907-1969), German-American science writer
  von Braun, Wernher **16** 17-18

Ley Juárez (Mexico)
  Juárez, Benito **8** 369-372

Ley Lerdo (Mexico)
  Lerdo de Tejada, Miguel **9** 351-352

Leyden jar (electricity)
  Galvani, Luigi **6** 194-195
  Volta, Alessandro **16** 12-14

Leyenda Pátria, La (poem)
  Zorrilla de San Martin, Juan **16** 530-531

Leyli and Majnun (story)
  Behzad **2** 123

Leyte, battle of (1944)
  Halsey, William Frederick **7** 91-92
  MacArthur, Douglas **10** 76-78
  Osmeña, Sergio **12** 22-24

Lhasa (city; Tibet)
  Dalai Lama **4** 369-371
  Younghusband, Francis Edward **16** 477

Li (Chinese philosophy)
  Chu Hsi **4** 40-43
  Confucius **4** 197-200
  Wang Fu-chih **16** 99-101
  Wang Pi **16** 104-105
  Wang Yang-ming **16** 108-109

Li Chao-tao (flourished circa 700-740), Chinese painter
  Wang Wei **16** 106-108

Li Ch'eng (flourished 960-990), Chinese landscape painter
  Chao Meng-fu **3** 436-437
  Mi Fei **11** 12-13
  Ni Tsan **11** 400
  Tung Ch'i-ch'ang **15** 339-340

Li Chih-ts'ao (died 1629), Chinese official and scholar
  Ricci, Matteo **13** 124-125

Li Erh
  see Lao Tzu

Li Fei-kan
  see Pa Chin

LI HUNG-CHANG (1823-1901), Chinese soldier, statesman, and industrialist
  9 407-409
  Feng Kuei-fen **5** 411-412
  Feng Yü-hsiang **5** 412-413
  Tz'u-hsi **15** 375-376
  Wen-hsiang **16** 202-203
  Wo-jen **16** 352
  Yüan Shih-k'ai **16** 480-481

Li Kung-lin (circa 1045-1106), Chinese painter and antiquarian
  Mi Fei **11** 12-13
  Tung Ch'i-ch'ang **15** 339-340
  Wang Wei **16** 106-108

Li Lin (flourished 757), Prince of Yung
  Li Po **9** 437-439

Li Lin-fu (died 752), Chinese statesman
  An Lu-shan **1** 239-240

Li Ma-t'ou
  see Ricci, Matteo

LI PENG (born 1928), premier of the People's Republic of China **9** 433-435

LI PO (701-762), Chinese poet **9** 437-439
  Basho, Matsuo **2** 45-48
  Hsüan-tsung, T'ang **8** 7-8
  Tu Fu **15** 335-336
  Wang Wei **16** 106-108

Li Shih-min
  see T'ang Tai-tsung

LI SSU (280?-208 B.C.), Chinese statesman
  9 442-443
  Han Fei Tzu **7** 124-125
  Hsün-tzu **8** 8
  Quin Shi Huang-Di **12** 515-518

Li Ssu-hsun (651-716), Chinese painter
  Tung Ch'i-ch'ang **15** 339-340
  Wang Wei **16** 106-108

LI TA-CHAO (1889-1927), Chinese Communist revolutionist **9** 447
  Chang Tso-lin **3** 434-435
  Ch'en Tu-hsiu **3** 501-502
  Hu Shih **8** 63-65
  Ts'ai Yüan-p'ei **15** 322

Li T'ang (died after 1130), Chinese landscape painter
  Hsia Kuei **8** 4-5
  Ma Yüan **10** 379

Li Tsung-jen (1890-1969), Chinese general
  Chiang Kai-shek **3** 510-513

LI TZU-CH'ENG (circa 1606-1645), Chinese bandit and rebel leader **9** 452
  Wang Fu-chih **16** 99-101

LIANG CH'I-CH'AO (1873-1929), Chinese intellectual and political reformer
  9 395-396
  Hu Shih **8** 63-65
  K'ang Yu-wei **8** 426-428
  Kuang-hsü **9** 111-112
  Yen Fu **16** 452

Liang dynasty (China; ruled 502-557)
  Chih-i **3** 518-519
  Liang Wu-ti **9** 396-397
  Liu Hsieh **9** 452-453

LIANG WU-TI (464-549), Chinese emperor of Southern dynasties **9** 396-397
  Liu Hsieh **9** 452-453

Liao dynasty (China; ruled 907-1125)
  Chu Hsi **4** 40-43
  Genghis Khan **6** 263-265
  Hui-Tsung **8** 25

LIAQUAT ALI KHAN (1896-1951), Pakistani statesman **9** 397
  Ayub Khan, Mohammed **1** 395-396

Liar, The (play; Corneille)
  Alarcón, Pedro Antonio de **1** 100-101

Libation Bearers (play; Aeschylus)
  Sophocles **14** 343-345

LIBBY, WILLARD FRANK (1908-1980), American chemist **9** 397-398

Libera me (musical composition)
  Arne, Thomas Augustine **1** 307-308

Liberal Alliance (Brazil)
  Vargas, Getulio Dornelles **15** 433-434

Liberal Conservative party (Canada)
  Macdonald, John Alexander **10** 85-87

Liberal Constitutional party (Tunisia)
  Bourguiba, Habib **2** 453-455

Liberal Democratic party (Japan)
  Kaifu Toshiki **8** 410-411
  Kishi, Nobusuke **9** 41-43
  Nakasone, Yasuhiro **11** 298-300
  Sato, Eisaku **13** 495-496
  Tanaka, Kakuei **15** 96-98

Liberal Democratic party (Russia)
  Zhirinovsky, Vladimir Volfovich
    16 509-510

Liberal party
  Australia
    Evatt, Herbert Vere **5** 341-343
    Fraser, Malcolm **6** 71-73
    Hughes, William Morris **8** 21-22
    Massey, William Ferguson **10** 324
    Menzies, Robert Gordon
      10 510-511
    Scullin, James Henry **14** 73
  Belgium
    Leopold I **9** 345-346
    Leopold II **9** 346-347
    Lumumba, Patrice Emery **10** 43-45
  Bolivia
    Patiño, Simón Iturri **12** 133-134
  Brazil
    Nabuco de Araujo, Joaquim Aurelio
      11 288-289

Canada
  see Liberal party (Canada)
Colombia
  Gaitán, Jorge Eliécer **6** 172-173
  Gaviria Trujillo, Cesar Augusto
    6 242-243
  Gómez, Juan Vicente **6** 417-418
  Isaacs, Jorge **8** 144
  Lleras Camargo, Alberto **9** 467
  Rojas Pinilla, Gustavo **13** 255-256
Cuba
  Estrada Palma, Tomás **5** 326-327
  Machado y Morales, Gerardo
    10 92-93
  Menocal, Mario Garcia **10** 506-507
Ecuador
  Velasco Ibarra, José María
    15 452-454
England
  see Liberal party (England)
Honduras
  Azcona Hoyo, José **1** 398-399
  Suazo Córdova, Roberto **15** 8-10
Japan
  Sato, Eisaku **13** 495-496
  Yoshida, Shigeru **16** 464-465
Mexico
  Álvarez, Juan **1** 184-185
  Juárez, Benito **8** 369-372
  Lerdo de Tejada, Miguel **9** 351-352
  Maximilian of Hapsburg
    10 358-360
New Zealand
  Seddon, Richard John **14** 81-82
Nicaragua
  Somoza, Anastasio **14** 335-336
  Zelaya, José Santos **16** 495-496
Paraguay
  Morínigo, Higinio **11** 174-175
Philippines
  Macapagal, Diosdado P. **10** 74-76
  Magsaysay, Ramon **10** 130-131
  Marcos, Ferdinand **10** 240-242
  Roxas, Manuel **13** 331-332
Puerto Rico
  Muñoz Rivera, Luís **11** 250
Scotland
  Steel, David Martin Scott
    14 406-407
South Africa
  Paton, Alan Stewart **12** 134-135
South Korea
  Park, Chung Hee **12** 99-102
  Rhee, Syngman **13** 117-120
United States
  Dubinsky, David **5** 114-115
  Pendleton, Edmund **12** 197-198
  Sacco and Vanzetti **13** 408-410

Liberal party (Canada)
leaders
  Bourassa, Robert **2** 447-449
  Chrétien, Joseph-Jacques-Jean
    4 24-25
  Crerar, Thomas Alexander **4** 306
  King, William Lyon Mackenzie
    9 25-26

Laurier, Wilfrid **9** 232-234
  Mackenzie, Alexander **10** 104
  Pearson, Lester Bowles **12** 174-175
  St. Laurent, Louis Stephen **13** 434
  Trudeau, Pierre Elliott **15** 309-311
opponents
  Borden, Robert Laird **2** 409-411
  Bourassa, Joseph-Henri-Napoleon
    2 446-447
  Diefenbaker, John George **5** 4-5
  Macdonald, John Alexander
    10 85-87

Liberal party (England)
conservatism and decline
  Disraeli, Benjamin **5** 27-29
  Gordon, Charles George **6** 448-449
  Lloyd George, David **9** 469-471
  Peel, Robert **12** 181-183
Irish question and
  Chamberlain, Joseph **3** 411-413
  Parnell, Charles Stewart **12** 117-119
leaders
  Asquith, Herbert Henry **1** 344-346
  Churchill, Winston Leonard Spencer
    4 51-53
  Gladstone, William Ewart
    6 357-360
  Morley, John **11** 178-179
  Reading, 1st Marquess of **13** 64
  Russell, John **13** 380-381

Liberal Republican party (United States)
  Adams, Charles Francis **1** 41-42
  Brown, Benjamin Gratz **3** 32-33
  Donnelly, Ignatius **5** 62
  Grant, Ulysses Simpson **6** 492-494
  Lloyd, Henry Demarest **9** 468-469
  Schurz, Carl **14** 44-45 `

Liberal Unionist party (England)
  Chamberlain, Joseph **3** 411-413
  Gladstone, William Ewart **6** 357-360

Liberalism (politics)
influenced by
  Machiavelli, Niccolò **10** 97-99
opponents
  Ferdinand II **5** 415-416
  Ferdinand VII **5** 418-420
  Knight, Frank Hyneman **9** 58-59
  Montt Torres, Manuel **11** 139-140
  Pobedonostsev, Konstantin Petrovich
    12 360-361
supporters
  Ferrero, Guglielmo **5** 429-430
  Hugo, Victor Marie **8** 22-25
  Humboldt, Wilhelm von **8** 31
  Kennedy, Robert Francis **8** 508-509
  Mill, John Stuart **11** 21-23
  Mongkut **11** 104
  Mosquera, Tomás Cipriano de
    11 205-206
  Wagner, Robert Ferdinand **16** 43
  see also Conservatism; Radicalism;
    Socialism

Liberalism (religion)
  Abbott, Lyman **1** 10-11

Acton, John Emerich Edward Dalberg
    1 38
  Barth, Karl **2** 31-32
  Beecher, Henry Ward **2** 112-113
  Beecher, Lyman **2** 113
  Bushnell, Horace **3** 171-172
  Child, Lydia Maria Francis **3** 520-521
  Paley, William **12** 72
  Parker, Theodore **12** 112-113

Liberal-Radical party (Ecuador)
  Plaza Lasso, Galo **12** 350-351

Liberation (magazine)
  Dellinger, David **4** 480-481

Liberation (painting)
  Hofmann, Hans **7** 442-443

Liberation of Saint Peter (fresco)
  Raphael **13** 40-42

Liberation theology
  Gutiérrez, Gustavo **7** 52-53

Liberation, War of the (1813-1814)
  see Napoleonic Wars—Fourth Coalition

Liberator, The (magazine)
  Eastman, Max **5** 187-188

Liberator, The (newspaper; 1861-65)
contributors
  Brown, William Wells **3** 48-49
  Grimké, Sarah Moore and Angelina
    Emily **7** 2-3
  Purvis, Robert **12** 485-486
  Walker, David **16** 62-63
editors
  McKay, Claude **10** 416
  Padmore, George **12** 57-58
founded
  Garrison, William Lloyd **6** 226-228
influence of
  Crandall, Prudence **4** 291
  Forten, James **6** 17-18

Liberia, Republic of (nation; West Africa)
  Ashmun, Jehudi **1** 335-336
  Doe, Samuel Kanyon **5** 38-39
  Firestone, Harvey Samuel **5** 452-453
  Garvey, Marcus Mosiah **6** 228-229
  Russwurm, John Brown **13** 381-382
  Stockton, Robert Field **14** 461-462
  Tubman, William Vacanarat Shadrach
    15 331

Libertarios (poems)
  González Prada, Manuel **6** 431

Libertas praestantissimum (encyclical;
  1888)
  Leo XIII **9** 334-336

Liberté de penser (journal)
  Simon, Jules François **14** 237-238

Liberté, La (poem)
  Chénier, André Marie **3** 500-501

Libertino, Il
  see Liberi, Pietro

Liberty (poem)
  Thomson, James **15** 199-200

Liberty (ship)
   Adams, Samuel **1** 55-56
   Hancock, John **7** 114-116
   Otis, James Jr. **12** 25-27

Liberty Federation (United States political organization, established 1986)
   Falwell, Jerry **5** 375-376

Liberty Leading the People (painting)
   Delacroix, Ferdinand Victor Eugène **4** 469-471

Liberty party (United States)
   Birney, James Gillespie **2** 283-284
   Chase, Salmon Portland **3** 473-475
   Polk, James Knox **12** 374-376
   Seward, William Henry **14** 124-125
   Smith, Gerrit **14** 290-291

Libraries
   ancient
      Callimachus **3** 235-236
      Ptolemy II **12** 472-473
      Suetonius Tranquillus, Gaius **15** 13
   architecture
      Aalto, Hugo Alvar Henrik **1** 1-2
      Asplund, Eric Gunnar **1** 344
      Fischer von Erlach, Johann Bernhard **5** 459-461
      Sansovino, Jacopo **13** 470-471
      Soane, John **14** 314-315
   classification
      Dewey, Melvil **4** 523-524
   public
      Carnegie, Andrew **3** 309-312
   royal
      Francis I **6** 40-43
   see also Social scientists—librarians; and individual libraries

Library Bureau (Boston)
   Dewey, Melvil **4** 523-524

Library of Congress (United States)
   Billington, James Hadley **2** 275-276
   Boorstin, Daniel J. **2** 398-400
   Dunbar, Paul Laurence **5** 141-142
   Lowell, Robert Trail Spence Jr. **10** 16-17
   MacLeish, Archibald **10** 109-110
   Morrill, Justin Smith **11** 182
   Portinari, Cândido **12** 407-408
   Schiff, Jacob Henry **14** 2-3

Library, The (poem)
   Crabbe, George **4** 288

Libro de Alexandre (poem)
   Gonzalo de Berceo **6** 431-432

Libro de buen amor (poem)
   Ruiz, Juan **13** 358-359

Libro de música ... (book)
   Milán, Luis **11** 15-16

Libussa (play)
   Grillparzer, Franz **6** 546-547

Libya (Libyan Arab Republic; nation, north Africa)
   Atatürk, Ghazi Mustapha Kemal **1** 356-357
   Badoglio, Pietro **1** 428-429

Gaddafi, Muammar Al- **6** 163-165
   Idris I **8** 102
   Omar al-Mukhtar **11** 507-508

Licensing Act of 1737 (England)
   Fielding, Henry **5** 442-444

Lichen (plant)
   Pound, Roscoe **12** 417-418

Lichfield House Compact (1835)
   O'Connell, Daniel **11** 465-467

Lichnowsky, Prince Karl M. (1860-1928), German diplomat
   Beethoven, Ludwig van **2** 114-117

LICHTENSTEIN, ROY (1923-1997), American painter, sculptor, and printmaker **9** 398-399

Licinius, Valerius (Licinianus; 270?-325), Roman emperor 308-324
   Constantine I **4** 209-211, 116

Liddell, Alice (1852-1934), English model for Alice
   Carroll, Lewis **3** 332-333

Lidice (novel)
   Mann, Heinrich **10** 201-202

LIE, TRYGVE HALVDAN (1896-1968), Norwegian statesman and UN secretary general **9** 400-401
   Bunche, Ralph Johnson **3** 121-122
   Hammarskjöld, Dag **7** 100-101

Liebe deinen Nächsten (novel)
   Remarque, Erich Maria **13** 91

Liébeault, A.A. (1823-1903), French physician
   Mesmer, Franz Anton **10** 526-527

Liebenfels, Jörg Lanz von (1874-1954), German religious sectarian
   Hitler, Adolf **7** 417-420

LIEBER, FRANCIS (circa 1798-1872), German American political scientist **9** 401-402
   Maistre, Joseph de **10** 153-154

LIEBERMANN, MAX (1847-1935), German painter **9** 402-403
   Beckmann, Max **2** 104-105

Liebeslieder Waltzes (music)
   Brahms, Johannes **2** 490-492

Liebeslyrik (poems)
   Huch, Ricarda **8** 11-12

Liebesverbot, Das (opera)
   Wagner, Richard **16** 40-43

LIEBIG, BARON JUSTUS VON (1803-1873), German chemist **9** 403-404
   Fischer, Emil **5** 456-457
   Hofmann, August Wilhelm von **7** 441-442

Liebknecht, Karl (1871-1919), German lawyer and Communist leader
   Luxemburg, Rosa **10** 55-56
   Mies van der Rohe, Ludwig **11** 10-12

Liebknecht, Wilhelm (1826-1900), German journalist and political leader
   Kautsky, Karl Johann **8** 462-463

Liechtenstein Palace (Vienna)
   Donner, Georg Raphael **5** 63
   Rottmayr, Johann Michael **13** 321

Lied (music form)
   Schubert, Franz Peter **14** 35-37
   Walter, Johann **16** 86

Lied von Bernadette, Das (novel)
   Werfel, Franz **16** 204-205

Lied von der Erde, Das (musical composition)
   Mahler, Gustav **10** 144-145

Liège, University of
   Pirenne, Jean Henri Otto Lucien Marie **12** 322-323
   Schwann, Theodor **14** 51-52

Lieutenant Kijé (film score)
   Prokofiev, Sergei Sergeevich **12** 458-460

Lieutenant Schmidt (poem)
   Pasternak, Boris Leonidovich **12** 124-125

Lievens, Jan (1607-1674), Dutch painter
   Rembrandt Harmensz van Rijn **13** 91-95

Life (magazine)
   Dos Passos, John Roderigo **5** 69-71
   Luce, Henry Robinson **10** 23-24
   Sherwood, Robert Emmet **14** 189-190

Life (painting)
   Picasso, Pablo **12** 292-295

Life, Adventures, and Pyracies... (book)
   Defoe, Daniel **4** 457-459

Life and Death of Holy Genoveve (play)
   Tieck, Ludwig **15** 218-219

Life and Death of Mr. Badman, The (book)
   Bunyan, John **3** 128-129

Life and Gabriella (novel)
   Glasgow, Ellen **6** 360-361

Life and Labour of the People in London (book; Booth)
   Booth, Charles **2** 400-401
   Webb, Beatrice Potter **16** 153-154
   Woods, Robert Archey **16** 374

Life and Opinions of Tristram Shandy, The (novel)
   see Tristram Shandy

Life and Songs (poems)
   Rilke, Rainer Maria **13** 171-172

Life and Strange Surprizing Adventures of Robinson Crusoe
   see Robinson Crusoe (book)

Life and Times of Michael K., The (book)
   Coetzee, J. M. **4** 133-135

Life for the Czar, A (opera)
   Glinka, Mikhail Ivanovich **6** 369-370

Life Immovable (poems)
   Palamas, Kostes **12** 70

Life in the South (painting)
   Johnson, Earvin Jr. **8** 297-299

Life in the Sun, A (play)
Wilder, Thornton Niven **16** 276-277

Life insurance
Brandeis, Louis Dembitz **2** 496-497
Demoivre, Abraham **4** 494-495
Lawson, Thomas William **9** 255-256
Wright, Elizur **16** 396-397

Life is a Dream (play)
Calderón, Pedro **3** 221-222

Life of Christ (painting series)
Le Brun, Charles **9** 269-270

Life of Klim Samgin, The (novel)
Gorky, Maxim **6** 458-460

Life of Man, The (play; Andreyev)
Stanislavsky, Constantin **14** 398-399

Life of Marianne, The (novel)
Marivaux, Pierre Carlet de Chamblain
de **10** 265-266

Life of Samuel Johnson, LLD, The (biography)
Boswell, James **2** 432-434-97
Macaulay, Thomas Babington **10** 79-80

Life of Saint Genevieve (mural)
Puvis de Chavannes, Pierre **12** 492-493

Life of Saint Mary Aegyptiaca (painting)
Nolde, Emil **11** 419-420

Life of the Virgin (prints)
Dürer, Albrecht **5** 159-161

Life on the Mississippi (book)
Twain, Mark **15** 363-366

Life or Theater?: An Operetta (series of paintings)
Salomon, Charlotte **13** 454-455

Life Peerage Bill (England)
Salisbury, 3d Marquess of **13** 448-449

Lifeboat (film)
Hitchcock, Alfred **7** 415-416

Life's Abundance (story)
Tieck, Ludwig **15** 218-219

Life's Handicap (stories)
Kipling, Joseph Rudyard **9** 32-33

Lifshits, E.M. (born 1915), Soviet physicist
Landau, Lev Davidovich **9** 184-185

Liga Filipina (nationalist organization)
Bonifacio, Andres **2** 393-394
Mabini, Apolinario **10** 72-73
Rizal, José **13** 187-189

LIGACHEV, YEGOR KUZ'MICH (born 1920), member of the Central Committee of the Communist Party of the Soviet Union (1966-1990) **9** 404-406

LIGETI, GYÖRGY (born 1923), Austrian composer **9** 406-407

Light (physics)
corpuscular theory
Hamilton, William Rowan **7** 99-100
Newton, Isaac **11** 369-372
quantum hypothesis
Einstein, Albert **5** 228-231
see also Quantum theory

scattering
Cauchy, Augustin Louis **3** 378-380
Raman, Chandrasekhar Venkata **13** 13-14
Rayleigh, 3d Baron **13** 62
Tyndall, John **15** 374
velocity
Fizeau, Hippolyte Armand Louis **5** 475
Foucault, Jean Bernard Léon **6** 28-29
Michelson, Albert Abraham **11** 7-8
wave theory
Bell Burnell, Susan Jocelyn **2** 133-134
Bradley, James **2** 482-483
de Broglie, Louis **4** 442-444
Fizeau, Hippolyte Armand Louis **5** 475
Foucault, Jean Bernard Léon **6** 28-29
Fresnel, Augustin Jean **6** 102-103
Hamilton, William Rowan **7** 99-100
Hooke, Robert **7** 475
Huygens, Christiaan **8** 79-81-443
Maxwell, James Clerk **10** 361-364
Young, Thomas **16** 475-476

Light and Darkness (novel)
Natsume, Soseki **11** 324-325

Light and the Dark, The (novel)
Snow, Charles Percy **14** 311-312

Light Fingered Gentry (novel)
Phillips, David Graham **12** 280-281

Light Horse Harry
see Lee, Henry

Light in August (novel)
Faulkner, William **5** 395-397

Light in the Forest, The (novel)
Richter, Conrad Michael **13** 148-149

Light of the World (painting)
Hunt, William Holman **8** 44-45

Light of the World (story)
Hemingway, Ernest Miller **7** 274-277

Light That Failed, The (novel)
Kipling, Joseph Rudyard **9** 32-33

Lighthouse Keeper, The (story)
Sienkiewicz, Henryk **14** 216-217

Lighthouses, The (poem)
Baudelaire, Charles Pierre **2** 61-63

Lightning (meteorology)
Franklin, Benjamin **6** 60-64
Oersted, Hans Christian **11** 476-478

Lightning (ship)
McKay, Donald **10** 416-417

Lightning Conductor, The (periodical)
Fernández de Lizardi, José Joaquin **5** 424-425

Lightning war
see Blitzkrieg (military strategy)

Lights, The (story)
Chekhov, Anton Pavlovich **3** 494-497

Ligny, battle of (1815)
Blücher, Gebhard Leberecht von **2** 340-341
Lieber, Francis **9** 401-402
Wellington, 1st Duke of **16** 193-195
see also Waterloo, Battle of

Ligorio, Pirro (circa 1500-1583), Italian architect
Vignola, Giacomo da **15** 493-494

Ligue d'Action Française
see Action Française

Ligurio (literary character)
Machiavelli, Niccolò **10** 97-99

Likud Party (Israel)
Arens, Moshe **1** 284-285
Levy, David **9** 373-374
Netanyahu, Binyamin **11** 350-351
Shamir, Yitzchak **14** 147-149

Li'l Abner (comic strip)
Capp, Al **3** 275-276

Lila (song)
Goethe, Johann Wolfgang von **6** 388-391

Lilacs (poem)
Lowell, Amy **10** 13

LILBURNE, JOHN (1615-1657), English political activist and pamphleteer **9** 409-410
Laud, William **9** 224-225

LILIENTHAL, DAVID ELI (1899-1981), American public administrator **9** 410-411

Lilienthal, Otto (1848-1896), German aeronautical engineer
Wright brothers **16** 394-396

LILIUOKALANI, LYDIA KAMAKAEHA (1838-1917), queen of the Hawaiian Islands **9** 411-412
Dole, Sanford Ballard **5** 46

Lille, University of (France)
Duhem, Pierre Maurice Marie **5** 129
Gilson, Étienne Henry **6** 327-328
Pasteur, Louis **12** 125-127

Lilliput (literary locale)
Swift, Jonathan **15** 51-54

Lima Conference (1938)
Welles, Sumner **16** 191-192

Lima e Silva, Luiz Alves de
see Caxias, Duque de

Limberham (comedy)
Dryden, John **5** 106-107

LIMBOURG BROTHERS (flourished circa 1399-1416), Netherlandish illuminators **9** 412-413

Limelight (film)
Chaplin, Charles Spencer **3** 438-440

Limerick, Earl of
see Dongan, Thomas

Limits and Renewals (stories)
Kipling, Joseph Rudyard **9** 32-33

Limoges (city; France)
Edward III **5** 211-212
Edward the Black Prince **5** 217-218

LIN, MAYA YING (born 1959), American
architect **9** 413-415

LIN PIAO (1907-1971), Chinese Commu-
nist military and political leader
9 429-430
Chou En-lai **4** 20-22
Liu Shao-Ch'i **9** 453-455
Mao Zedong **10** 225-227

LIN TSE-HSÜ (1785-1850), Chinese official
9 431-432
Tso Tsung-t'ang **15** 328-329
Wei Yüan **16** 180-181
Wen-hsiang **16** 202-203

Linaiuoli Altarpiece (painting)
Angelico **1** 235-236

Linaiuoli Madonna (painting; Fra Angelico)
Ghiberti, Lorenzo **6** 291-292

LINCOLN, ABRAHAM (1809-1865), Amer-
ican statesman, president 1861-1865
9 415-418
advisers
Blair, Francis Preston **2** 313-315
Carey, Henry Charles **3** 294-295
Carroll, Anna Ella **3** 327-331
Eads, James Buchanan **5** 175-176
Scott, Winfield **14** 70-71
assassination plot
Booth, John Wilkes **2** 404
Davis, Jefferson **4** 416-418
Pinkerton, Allan **12** 314-315
Wallace, Lewis **16** 74-75
Cabinet
Cameron, Simon **3** 246-247
Chase, Salmon Portland **3** 473-475
McCulloch, Hugh **10** 404-405
Seward, William Henry **14** 124-125
Stanton, Edwin McMasters
14 401-402
Welles, Gideon **16** 188-190
Emancipation
see Emancipation Proclamation
in art
Borglum, John Gutzon de la Mothe
2 416-417
Brady, Mathew B. **2** 487-488
French, Daniel Chester **6** 98-99
Rogers, John **13** 248
Saint-Gaudens, Augustus **13** 432
Taft, Lorado **15** 75-76
in literature and biography
Alger, Horatio **1** 153-154
Eggleston, Edward **5** 223-224
Lindsay, Vachel **9** 424-425
Markham, Edwin **10** 267
Masters, Edgar Lee **10** 326-327
Sandburg, Carl **13** 461-462
Tarbell, Ida Minerva **15** 107-108
Whitman, Walt **16** 249-251
political appointments
Adams, Charles Francis **1** 41-42
Burlingame, Anson **3** 144-145

Cameron, Simon **3** 246-247
Field, David Dudley **5** 439-440
Field, Stephen Johnson **5** 441-442
Hay, John **7** 215-216
Helper, Hinton Rowan **7** 272-273
Hildreth, Richard **7** 382
Johnson, Andrew **8** 294-295
political associates
Cameron, Simon **3** 246-247
Cartwright, Peter **3** 344-345
Everett, Edward **5** 344
Hughes, John Joseph **8** 17-18
Trumbull, Lyman **15** 317-318
Yancey, William Lowndes
16 436-437
political opponents
Chandler, Zachariah **3** 425-426
Davis, Henry Winter **4** 415-416
Douglas, Stephen Arnold **5** 80-82
Pendleton, George Hunt **12** 198
Seymour, Horatio **14** 126-127
Tilden, Samuel Jones **15** 222-223
Toombs, Robert Augustus
15 267-268
Vallandigham, Clement Laird
15 406-407
political supporters
Applegate, Jesse **1** 264-265
Curtin, Andrew Gregg **4** 347-348
Emerson, Ralph Waldo **5** 278-280
Howells, William Dean **7** 539-541
Medill, Joseph **10** 451-452
Miller, Samuel Freeman **11** 29-30
Schurz, Carl **14** 44-45
Van Buren, Martin **15** 410-411
Weed, Thurlow **16** 169-170
quoted
Nast, Thomas **11** 318-319
Stowe, Harriet Elizabeth Beecher
14 484-485
secession
see Secession (United States;
1860-61)
see also Civil War (United States);
Kansas-Nebraska Act

Lincoln, battle of (1141)
Stephen **14** 426-427

LINCOLN, BENJAMIN (1733-1810), American military officer **9** 418-419
Warren, Mercy Otis **16** 120-121

Lincoln, Earl of (John de la Pole;
1464?-87), lord lieutenant of Ireland
1484-87
Richard III **13** 132-133

Lincoln Center (New York City)
Calder, Alexander **3** 216-218
Nadelman, Elie **11** 289-290

Lincoln County Bank (Sante Fe, New Mexico)
Chisum, John Simpson **4** 11

Lincoln House (New York City)
Wald, Lillian **16** 53-54

Lincoln Memorial (Washington D.C.)
French, Daniel Chester **6** 98-99

Markham, Edwin **10** 267

Lincoln Portrait, A (musical composition)
Copland, Aaron **4** 227-228

Lincoln-Douglas debates (1858; United
States politics)
Douglas, Stephen Arnold **5** 80-82
Lincoln, Abraham **9** 415-418
Taft, Lorado **15** 75-76

LIND, JAKOV (Heinz "Henry" Landwirth;
born 1927), Austrian autobiographer,
short-story writer, novelist, and playwright **9** 419-420

Lind, Jenny (Johanna Maria Lind;
1820-1887), Swedish coloratura soprano
Andersen, Hans Christian **1** 212-214
Barnum, Phineas Taylor **2** 13-15

LINDBERGH, ANNE MORROW (born
1906), American author and aviator
9 420-421
Lindbergh, Charles Augustus **9** 421-423

LINDBERGH, CHARLES AUGUSTUS
(1902-1974), American aviator **9** 421-423
Byrd, Richard Evelyn **3** 186-187
Carrel, Alexis **3** 322-323
Martinu, Bohuslav **10** 299-300
Morrow, Dwight Whitney **11** 190-191

Linde, Carl von (1842-1934), German
engineer
Diesel, Rudolf **5** 7

Lindgren, Armas (1874-1929), Finnish
architect
Saarinen, Eliel and Eero **13** 396-398

LINDSAY, JOHN VLIET (born 1921), U.S.
congressman (1959-1965) and mayor of
New York (1966-1973) **9** 423-424

LINDSAY, VACHEL (1879-1931), American
folk poet **9** 424-425
Benét, Stephen Vincent **2** 157-158
Bryan, William Jennings **3** 80-82
Lowell, Amy **10** 13
Masters, Edgar Lee **10** 326-327

LINDSEY, BENJAMIN BARR (1869-1943),
American jurist and reformer **9** 425-426

Line of Love, The (stories)
Cabell, James Branch **3** 195-196

Linear accelerator (atomic physics)
Cockcroft, John Douglas **4** 131-132

**Lines Supposed to Be Written by Alexan-
der Selkirk** (poem)
Cowper, William **4** 282

Linguistic Society of America (established
1924)
Bloomfield, Leonard **2** 338

Linguistic Turn, The (anthology)
Rorty, Richard **13** 288-289

Linguistics (science)
Austin, John Langshaw **1** 379-380
Bakhtin, Mikhail Mikhailovich
1 456-458
Bloomfield, Leonard **2** 338
Boas, Franz **2** 349-351
Burritt, Elihu **3** 160

Chomsky, Noam Avram **4** 13-15
Derrida, Jacques **4** 503-505
Grimm, Jakob and Wilhelm Karl **7** 3-4
Kroeber, Alfred Louis **9** 105-106
Moore, George Edward **11** 146
Ricoeur, Paul **13** 157-158
Sapir, Edward **13** 478-479

LINH, NGUYEN VAN (born 1915), secretary-general of the Vietnamese Communist Party (1986-1991) **9** 426-427

LINNAEUS, CARL (Carl von Linné; 1707-1778), Swedish naturalist **9** 427-429
influence of
Darwin, Charles Robert **4** 397-399
Lamarck, Chevalier de **9** 171-173
Mutis, José Celestino **11** 278-279
plant classification
Bartram, John **2** 40-41
Buffon, Comte de **3** 109-111
Colden, Cadwallader **4** 145-146
Cuvier, Georges Léopold **4** 357-359

Linotype (printing machine)
Mergenthaler, Ottmar **10** 516-517

Linschoten, Jan Huyghen van (1563-1611), Dutch navigator
Barents, Willem **2** 4-5

LINTON, RALPH (1893-1953), American anthropologist **9** 431

Liolà (play)
Pirandello, Luigi **12** 319-321

Lion and the Jewel, The (play)
Soyinka, Wole **14** 358-359

Lion and the Unicorn, The (stories)
Davis, Richard Harding **4** 422-423

Lion Hunt (sketch)
Delacroix, Ferdinand Victor Eugène **4** 469-471

Lionel Lincoln (novel)
Cooper, James Fenimore **4** 220-223, 127

LIPCHITZ, JACQUES (1891-1973), Lithuanian-born American sculptor **9** 432-433
Duchamp-Villon, Raymond **5** 123
Giacometti, Alberto **6** 294-295
González, Julio **6** 428-429
Gris, Juan **7** 5-6

LIPMANN, FRITZ (1899-1986), German-American biochemist
Krebs, Hans Adolf **9** 95-97

Lippi, Filippino (circa 1457-1504), Italian painter
Leonardo da Vinci **9** 337-340
Lippi, Filippo **9** 439

LIPPI, FRA FILIPPO (circa 1406-1469), Italian painter **9** 439
Donatello **5** 55-56
Medici, Cosimo de' **10** 449-450
Medici, Lorenzo de' **10** 450-451
Veneziano, Domenico **15** 459-460

Lippincott's Magazine (periodical)
Fitzhugh, George **5** 474
Lanier, Sidney **9** 199-200
Wilde, Oscar Fingall O'Flahertie Wills **16** 272-273

LIPPMANN, WALTER (1889-1974), American journalist **9** 439-440
Eliot, Thomas Stearns **5** 258-261
McAdoo, William Gibbs **10** 385-386
Mills, C. Wright **11** 35-36

Lippo, Memmi (1317-1346), Italian painter
Martini, Simone **10** 298-299

LIPPOLD, RICHARD (born 1915), American Constructivist sculptor **9** 440-442

Lipsius, Justus (1547-1606), Flemish scholar
Rubens, Peter Paul **13** 339-342

Liquid paper (correction fluid)
McMurray, Bette Clair **10** 429

Liquidity (economics)
Bagehot, Walter **1** 436-437
Keynes, John Maynard **8** 528-530
Walras, Marie Esprit Léon **16** 84-85

Lircay, Treaty of (Chile; 1814)
Carrera, José Miguel **3** 323-324

Lisandrino
see Magnasco, A.

Lisbôa, Antônio Francisco
see Aleijadinho, O

Lisbon (city; Portugal)
Alfonso I **1** 148
Drake, Francis **5** 94-96
Pombal, Marquês de **12** 386-387

Lise (painting)
Renoir, Pierre Auguste **13** 101-102

Lisk House (Palm Springs, California)
Neutra, Richard Joseph **11** 355-356

Lissitzky, Eliezer (1890-1941), Russian painter
Moholy-Nagy, László **11** 82-83

LIST, GEORG FRIEDRICH (1789-1846), German economist **9** 443-444

List und Rache (song)
Goethe, Johann Wolfgang von **6** 388-391

LISTER, JOSEPH (1st Baron Lister of Lyme Regis; 1827-1912), English surgeon **9** 444-445
Celsus, Aulus Cornelius **3** 393
Semmelweis, Ignaz Philipp **14** 101-102

Liszt, Cosima (Mrs. Richard Wagner; 1837-1930), Hungarian wife of Wagner
Richardson, Henry Handel **13** 139

LISZT, FRANZ (1811-1886), Hungarian composer **9** 445-447
admirers
Bizet, Georges **2** 296-297
Brahms, Johannes **2** 490-492
associates
Berlioz, Louis Hector **2** 203-205

Schumann, Robert Alexander **14** 41-43
Wagner, Richard **16** 40-43
influence of
Chopin, Frédéric François **4** 16-18
MacDowell, Edward Alexander **10** 87-88
Paderewski, Ignace Jan **12** 56-57
Schoenberg, Arnold **14** 24-26
Smetana, Bedřich **14** 281-282
Strauss, Richard **14** 500-501

Litauische Geschichten (literary collection)
Sudermann, Hermann **15** 12-13

Litchfield Law School (Connecticut)
Reeve, Tapping **13** 79-80

Literalist school (Islamic law)
ibn Hazm, Abu Muhammad Ali **8** 93

Literary criticism
Burke, Kenneth **3** 141-142
Carducci, Giosuè **3** 290-291
De Sanctis, Francesco **4** 505
Frye, Northrop **6** 137-139
Longinus **9** 500-501
Mansfield, Katherine **10** 213-214
Rich, Adrienne **13** 128-130
Wilder, Amos Niven **16** 273-274
see also Authors—critics

Literary style (Chinese art)
Su Shih **15** 39-40

Literary theory
Bakhtin, Mikhail Mikhailovich **1** 456-458

Literati painting (Chinese art)
Ni Tsan **11** 400
Tung Ch'i-ch'ang **15** 339-340

Literaturbriefe
see Briefe, die neueste Literatur betreffend (book)

Literature for children
Canada
Traill, Catharine Parr **15** 291
Chile
Mistral, Gabriela **11** 55-56
England
Carroll, Lewis **3** 332-333
Dahl, Roald **4** 366-367
Kingsley, Charles **9** 28
Kipling, Joseph Rudyard **9** 32-33
Lamb, Charles **9** 176-177
Newbery, John **11** 360-361
Rossetti, Christina Georgina **13** 307-308
Stevenson, Robert Louis **14** 446-448
Germany
Schwitters, Kurt **14** 60-61
Ireland
Colum, Padraic **4** 174-175
Nigeria
Ekwensi, Cyprian **5** 242-243
Sweden
Lagerlöf, Selma Ottiliana Lovisa **9** 163-164
United States

Alcott, Louisa May **1** 122
Alger, Horatio **1** 153-154
Asimov, Isaac **1** 338-341
Blume, Judy **2** 344-345
Dix, Dorothea Lynde **5** 32-33
Geisel, Theodor (Dr. Seuss)
6 255-256
Hawthorne, Nathaniel **7** 212-215
Jarrell, Randall **8** 222-223
Lanier, Sidney **9** 199-200
Peck, Robert Newton **12** 177-178
Steel, Danielle **14** 404-406
Tan, Amy **15** 95-96
Tyler, Anne **15** 367-368
White, E. B. **16** 228-230
Yiddish
Singer, Isaac Bashevis **14** 249-250

Literature Teacher, The (story)
Chekhov, Anton Pavlovich **3** 494-497

Lithography (printing process)
Currier and Ives **4** 345-346
Daumier, Honoré Victorin **4** 403-405
Redon, Odilon **13** 75-76
Toulouse-Lautrec, Henri de **15** 273-274
Whistler, James Abbott McNeill
16 225-226
see also Artists—lithographers

Lithuania (Lithuanian Soviet Socialist
Republic; Europe)
Henry IV **7** 292-293
Ivan III **8** 156-157
Ivan IV **8** 157-159
Sigismund **14** 220-221

Little, Malcolm
see Malcolm X

LITTLE, ROYAL (born 1896), American textile tycoon **9** 449-451

Little America (Antarctica)
Byrd, Richard Evelyn **3** 186-187

Little Balkan Entente (1934)
Titulescu, Nicolae **15** 246-247

Little Bighorn River, battle of the (1876)
Bennett, James Gordon Jr. **2** 169-170]
Crazy Horse **4** 303-304
Custer, George Armstrong **4** 355-356
Sitting Bull **14** 264-265

Little Dancer of Fourteen Years (sculpture)
Degas, Hilaire Germain Edgar
4 461-462

Little Dorrit (novel)
Dickens, Charles John Huffam
4 538-541

Little Entente (1920-38;
Czechoslovakia-Romania-Yugoslavia)
Alexander of Yugoslavia **1** 136-137
Beneš, Edward **2** 155-157
Ferdinand **5** 413-414
Horthy de Nagybánya, Nicholas
7 510-512

Little Eyolf (play)
Ibsen, Henrik **8** 98-100

Little Foxes, The (play and film)
Goldwyn, Samuel **6** 416
Hellman, Lillian Florence **7** 267-268

Little Franklin, The (book)
Webster, Noah **16** 164-166

Little Gidding (poem)
Eliot, Thomas Stearns **5** 258-261

Little Girls, The (novel)
Bowen, Elizabeth **2** 462-463

Little Good-for-nothing, The (novel)
Daudet, Alphonse **4** 402-403

Little House in Kolomna, The (poem)
Pushkin, Aleksandr Sergeevich
12 489-491

Little Iliad (epic)
Homer **7** 465-467

Little Johnny Jones (play)
Cohan, George Michael **4** 137-138

Little Juliana (ship)
Stevens, John **14** 439-440

Little Men (novel)
Alcott, Louisa May **1** 122

Little Mermaid, The (fairy tale)
Andersen, Hans Christian **1** 212-214

Little Minister, The (novel and play)
Barrie, James Matthew **2** 21-22

Little Nell (literary character)
Dickens, Charles John Huffam
4 538-541

Little Old New York (film)
Hearst, William Randolph **7** 243-244

Little Orphant Annie (poem)
Riley, James Whitcomb **13** 170-171

Little People and Little Events (stories)
Pa Chin **12** 53-54

Little Pittsburgh Mine (Colorado)
Tabor, Horace Austin Warner **15** 70

Little Prince, The (story)
Saint-Exupéry, Antoine de **13** 431-432

LITTLE RICHARD (Richard Penniman; born
1932), American rock 'n' roll musician
9 447-449

Little Rock (city; Arkansas)
Ashmore, Harry Scott **1** 334-335
Eisenhower, Dwight David **5** 233-236

Little Saint, The (novel)
Simenon, Georges **14** 233-234

Little Schuylkill Railroad (1831)
List, Georg Friedrich **9** 443-444

Little Shepherd (painting)
Corot, Jean Baptiste Camille **4** 247-249

Little Street (painting)
Vermeer, Jan **15** 466-467

Little Town, The (novel)
Mann, Heinrich **10** 201-202

Little Town, The (poem)
Peretz, Isaac Loeb **12** 212

Little Town, The (story)
Asch, Shalom **1** 325-326

Little Wedding, The (ballet)
Stravinsky, Igor Fedorovich **14** 502-506

Little Woman, The (story)
Kafka, Franz **8** 403-406

Little Women (novel)
Alcott, Amos Bronson **1** 121
Alcott, Louisa May **1** 122

Littlepage Manuscripts (trilogy)
Cooper, James Fenimore **4** 220-223

Littleton, Mark
see Kennedy, John Pendleton

Littrow, J.J. von (1781-1840), Austrian
astronomer
Lobachevskii, Nikolai Ivanovich
9 472-474

LITVINOV, MAXIM MAXIMOVICH
(1876-1951), Soviet diplomat **9** 451-452
Chicherin, Georgi Vasilyevich
3 516-517
Titulescu, Nicolae **15** 246-247

Liu Ch'e
see Han Wu-ti

Liu Chi
see Liu Pang

LIU HSIEH (circa 465-522), Chinese literary critic **9** 452-453
Lu Chi **10** 24

Liu Hsiu
see Kuang-wu-ti

LIU PANG (Han Kao-tsu or Liu Chi; 256
B.C.-195 B.C.), Chinese emperor **9** 453

LIU SHAO-CH'I (born 1900), Chinese
Communist party leader **9** 453-455
Ch'en Tu-hsiu **3** 501-502
Lin Piao **9** 429-430

Liu Sung dynasty (China; ruled 420-479)
Hsieh Ling-yün **8** 5-6

LIU TSUNG-YÜAN (773-819), Chinese
poet and prose writer **9** 455-456

Liu Yü-hsi (flourished 8th century), Chinese
poet
Liu Tsung-Yüan **9** 455-456
Po Chü-i **12** 362-363

Liver (anatomy)
Bernard, Claude **2** 208-210
Best, Charles Herbert **2** 236-237
Bright, Richard **3** 7-8

Liver Is the Cock's Comb, The (painting)
Gorky, Arshile **6** 458

Livermore, Mary A. (1820?-1905), American suffragette and reformer
Stone, Lucy **14** 471-472

LIVERPOOL, 2ND EARL OF (Robert Barks
Jenkinson; 1770-1828), English states-
man, prime minister 1812-1827
9 456-457
Canning, George **3** 258-260
Peel, Robert **12** 181-183

Liverpool, University of (England)
Carr-Saunders, Alexander Morris
3 333-334
Chadwick, James **3** 405-406
Sherrington, Charles Scott **14** 187-189

Liverpool line (merchant ships)
Collins, Edward Knight **4** 162-163

Lives (book)
Plutarch **12** 359-360
Shakespeare, William **14** 142-145
Suetonius Tranquillus, Gaius **15** 13

Lives (book; Vasari)
Donatello **5** 55-56
Primaticcio, Francesco **12** 453-454
Vasari, Giorgio **15** 442-443

Lives of the Poets, The (book; S. Johnson)
Johnson, Samuel **8** 315-317
Milton, John **11** 43-46

Livestock
see Cattle industry

LIVIA (ca. 58 B.C. - 29 A.D.), Roman
empress, wife of Augustus **9** 457-460
Caligula **3** 228-229

Living and the Dead, The (novel)
White, Patrick Victor Martindale
16 233-235

Living Room, The (play)
Greene, Graham **6** 523-524

LIVINGSTON, EDWARD (1764-1836),
American jurist and statesman **9** 460-461
Field, David Dudley **5** 439-440

Livingston, M. Stanley (1905-1986), American physicist
Lawrence, Ernest Orlando **9** 248-250

LIVINGSTON, ROBERT (1654-1728),
American colonial politician **9** 461-462

LIVINGSTON, ROBERT R. (1746-1813),
American jurist and diplomat **9** 462-463
Clinton, DeWitt **4** 112-113
Fulton, Robert **6** 151-152
Jay, John **8** 230-232
Monroe, James **11** 111-113
Morris, Gouverneur **11** 182-183
Shreve, Henry Miller **14** 207
Stevens, John **14** 439-440
Vanderbilt, Cornelius **15** 415-416

Livingston, William (1723-1790), American
political leader
Livingston, Robert R. **9** 462-463

LIVINGSTONE, DAVID (1813-1873), Scot-
tish missionary and explorer in Africa
9 463-465
Bennett, James Gordon Jr. **2** 169-170
Brazza, Pierre Paul François Camille
Savorgnan de **2** 509-510
Stanley, Henry Morton **14** 399-400
Tippu Tip **15** 235-236

Livonian Knights (German militia-religious
order)
Ivan III **8** 156-157

Livret de folastries (poems)
Ronsard, Pierre de **13** 271-273

LIVY (Titus Livius; circa 64 B.C.-circa 12
A.D.), Roman historian **9** 465-467
Hannibal Barca **7** 128-130
López de Ayala, Pedro **9** 508-509
Machiavelli, Niccolò **10** 97-99
Tacitus **15** 70-72

Lizardi, José Joaquín Fernández de
see Fernández de Lizardi, José Joaquín

Lizzie Leigh (story)
Gaskell, Elizabeth **6** 231-232

Llanto por Ignacío Sánchez Mejías (poem)
Lorca, Federico García **9** 511-513

LLERAS CAMARGO, ALBERTO
(1906-1990), Colombian statesman,
twice president **9** 467
Gómez, Máximo **6** 418-419
Kubitschek de Oliveira, Juscelino
9 113-115

LLEWELYN AP GRUFFYDD (died 1282),
Prince of Wales **9** 468
Edward I **5** 208-210

Llewellyn Park (West Orange, New Jersey)
Davis, Alexander Jackson **4** 411

Lloyd, Charles (1775-1839), English poet
Lamb, Charles **9** 176-177

LLOYD, HENRY DEMAREST (1847-1903),
American social reformer **9** 468-469
Rockefeller, John Davison **13** 226-228

LLOYD GEORGE, DAVID, (1st Earl of
Dwyfor; 1863-1945), English statesman,
prime minister 1916-1922 **9** 469-471
Baldwin, Stanley **1** 468-469
Balfour, Arthur James **1** 469-470
Chamberlain, Arthur Neville **3** 409-411
Chamberlain, Joseph **3** 411-413
Churchill, Winston Leonard Spencer
4 51-53
Curzon, George Nathaniel **4** 351-352
Henderson, Arthur **7** 277-278
Milner, Alfred **11** 38-39
Smuts, Jan Christian **14** 309-310

LLOYD-JONES, ESTHER MCDONALD
(born 1901), school personnel specialist
who focused on development of the
whole person **9** 471-472

Lloyd Lewis House (Libertyville, Illinois)
Wright, Frank Lloyd **16** 398-401

Lo fingido verdadero (play)
Lope Félix de Vega Carpio **9** 503-506

Lö Thai (ruled circa 1299-1346), Thai king
Rama Khamhaeng **13** 11

Lo-t'o Hsiang-tzu (novel)
Lao Shê **9** 200-201

LOBACHEVSKII, NIKOLAI IVANOVICH
(1792-1856), Russian mathematician
9 472-474
Gauss, Karl Friedrich **6** 240-242

LOBENGULA (died circa 1894), South
African Ndebele king **9** 474-475
Rhodes, Cecil John **13** 120-122

Lobgesang (musical composition)
Mendelssohn, Moses **10** 488-489

Loca, La (literary character)
Lope Félix de Vega Carpio **9** 503-506

Loca de la casa, La (play)
Galdós, Benito Pérez **6** 177-178

Local Anesthetic (novel)
Grass, Günter **6** 496-497

Local color (American literature)
see Regionalism and local color

Local Government Act of 1929 (Great
Britain)
Chamberlain, Arthur Neville **3** 409-411

Locandiera, La (play)
Goldoni, Carlo **6** 408-409

Locarno Pact (1925)
Briand, Aristide **2** 528-529
Chamberlain, Arthur Neville **3** 409-411
Spaak, Paul Henri **14** 359-360
Stresemann, Gustav **14** 508-509

Locher, Jacob (1471-1528), German writer
Brant, Sebastian **2** 503-504

LOCHNER, STEPHAN (circa 1410-1451),
German painter **9** 475

Lochner v. New York (legal case)
Harlan, John Marshall **7** 156-157
Holmes, Oliver Wendell Jr. **7** 458-459
White, Edward Douglass **16** 230-231

Lock at Optevoz (painting)
Daubigny, Charles François **4** 402

Lock of Berenice (poem)
Callimachus **3** 235-236

LOCKE, ALAIN (1886-1954), African American educator, editor, and author
9 475-478

LOCKE, JOHN (1632-1704), English
philosopher and political theorist
9 478-480
critics
Bolingbroke, Viscount **2** 374-375
Herbert, Edward **7** 324
Law, William **9** 245-246
Leibniz, Gottfried Wilhelm von
9 307-310
Rousseau, Jean Jacques **13** 324-328
influence of (17th-18th century)
Backus, Isaac **1** 420-421
Berkeley, George **2** 197-198
Condillac, Étienne Bonnot de
4 194-195
Edwards, Jonathan **5** 220-222
Franklin, Benjamin **6** 60-64
Hartley, David **7** 185
Johnson, Samuel **8** 314-315
Sterne, Laurence **14** 435-437
Sydenham, Thomas **15** 59-60
Toland, John **15** 256
Voltaire **16** 14-16
influence of (18th-19th century)
Godwin, William **6** 383-384
influence of (19th-20th century)
Cousin, Victor **4** 273-274
Masaryk, Tomáš Garrigue
10 314-315

Mill, John Stuart **11** 21-23

Locke, Matthew (1620?-1677), English composer
Purcell, Henry **12** 484-485

Lockhart, R.H. Bruce (1887-1970), British journalist
Litvinov, Maxim Maximovich **9** 451-452

Lockheed Corporation
Tanaka, Kakuei **15** 96-98

Locking Piece (sculpture)
Moore, Henry **11** 146-148

Lockwood Concern, The (novel)
O'Hara, John **11** 485

Locust (ship)
Rosas, Juan Manuel de **13** 290-291

Locusts and Wild Honey (book)
Burroughs, John **3** 160-161

LODGE, DAVID (born 1935), English novelist **9** 480-482

LODGE, HENRY CABOT (1850-1924), American political leader **9** 482-483
Hearst, William Randolph **7** 243-244
Hitchcock, Gilbert Monell **7** 416-417
Mahan, Alfred Thayer **10** 131-132
Roosevelt, Theodore **13** 280-283
Taft, William Howard **15** 78-81

LODGE, HENRY CABOT, JR. (1902-1985), American congressman, senator, ambassador, and presidential adviser **9** 483-485
Kennedy, John Fitzgerald **8** 502-506
Nixon, Richard Milhous **11** 401-404

Lodger, The (film)
Hitchcock, Alfred **7** 415-416

Lodging House Act (England;1851)
Shaftesbury, 7th Earl of **14** 137-138

Lodoïska (opera)
Cherubini, Luigi Carlo Zanobi Salvatore Maria **3** 505-506

Lodovico il Moro
see Sforza, Lodovico

Loeb, Jacques (1859-1924), German-American biophysiologist
Northrop, John Howard **11** 430-431

Loefftz, Ludwig von (1845-1910), German painter
Twachtman, John Henry **15** 362-363

LOEW, MARCUS (1870-1927), founder of a theater chain and Metro-Goldwyn-Mayer **9** 485-486

LOEWI, OTTO (1873-1961), German-American pharmacologist and physiologist **9** 486-487
Dale, Henry Hallett **4** 371-373

Loews Corporation
Tisch brothers **15** 238-240

Loew's Theatrical Enterprises (movie theater chain)
Loew, Marcus **9** 485-486

Lofty Malady, A (poem)
Pasternak, Boris Leonidovich **12** 124-125

Log Book (poems)
Seferis, George **14** 84-85

Log College (Neshaminy, Pennsylvania)
Tennent, Gilbert **15** 143-144

LOGAN, JAMES (1674-1751), American colonial statesman and jurist **9** 487-488
Bartram, John **2** 40-41

LOGAN, SIR WILLIAM EDMOND (1798-1875), Canadian geologist **9** 488-489

Logarithms (mathematics)
Euler, Leonard **5** 331-332
Napier, John **11** 306

Loge, La (painting)
Cassatt, Mary **3** 356-357

Loges, François des
see Villon, François

Loggia dei Lanzi (Florence)
Giovanni da Bologna **6** 345-346

Loggia del Capitaniato (Vicenza, Italy)
Palladio, Andrea **12** 75-77

Logic (philosophy)
dialectics
Hegel, Georg Wilhelm Friedrich **7** 254-256
Socrates **14** 320-321
empiricism
Carnap, Rudolf **3** 308-309
Hobbes, Thomas **7** 421-423
inductive experimentation
Bacon, Francis **1** 422-424
Mill, John Stuart **11** 21-23
Kantian
Cohen, Hermann **4** 138-139
Kant, Immanuel **8** 430-432
scientific method
Brentano, Franz Clemens **2** 516-517
Cohen, Morris Raphael **4** 139-140
semantic method
Carnap, Rudolf **3** 308-309
Tarski, Alfred **15** 110-111
Wittgenstein, Ludwig **16** 350-351
systematics
Aristotle **1** 295-296
Chrysippus **4** 35-36
Zeno of Elea **16** 500
see also Euclidean geometry; Logic, symbolic; Scholasticism

Logic, symbolic (mathematics)
Boole, George **2** 396-397
Frege, Gottlob **6** 93-94
Gödel, Kurt **6** 377-379
Lewis, Clarence Irving **9** 381
Poincaré, Jules Henri **12** 365-366
Ramsey, Frank Plumpton **13** 25
Russell, Bertrand Arthur William **13** 373-374
Shannon, Claude Elwood **14** 153-154
Turing, Alan Mathison **15** 349-350
Von Neumann, John **16** 27-28

Whitehead, Alfred North **16** 242-244
see also Deductive method (logic); Inductive method (logic)

Logical positivism (logical empiricism; philosophy)
Ayer, Alfred Jules **1** 391-393
Bloomfield, Leonard **2** 338
Carnap, Rudolf **3** 308-309
Nagel, Ernest **11** 291-292
Wittgenstein, Ludwig **16** 350-351

Logistics (military)
Gustavus II **7** 43-45

Logos (philosophy)
Heraclitus **7** 320
Philo Judaeus **12** 282-283
Justin Martyr **8** 395-396

Lohengrin (opera; Wagner)
Liszt, Franz **9** 445-447
Wagner, Richard **16** 40-43

Loi cadre (Guinea; 1956)
Houphouët-Boigny, Felix **7** 519-520
Touré, Sékou **15** 275-277

Loi naturelle, La (poem)
Voltaire **16** 14-16

LOISY, ALFRED FIRMIN (1857-1940), French theologian and biblical historian **9** 489-490

Loki (Norse mythology)
Arnold, Matthew **1** 311-313

Lokotown (stories)
Ekwensi, Cyprian **5** 242-243

Lola de Valence (painting)
Manet, Édouard **10** 193-194

Lolita (novel)
Nabokov, Vladimir **11** 287-288

Lollards (religious group)
Henry IV **7** 292-293
Henry V **7** 296-297
Wyclif, John **16** 412-413

Loman, Willy (literary character)
Miller, Arthur **11** 25-26

Lombard, Carole (1909-1942), American actress
Gable, William Clark **6** 157-158

LOMBARD, PETER (circa 1095-1160), Italian bishop and theologian **9** 490-491
William of Ockham **16** 298-299
see also Sentences (book; Lombard)

Lombard League
Frederick I **6** 78-79
Frederick II **6** 79
Urban II **15** 393

Lombard Street (book)
Bagehot, Walter **1** 436-437

Lombardi, I (opera)
Verdi, Giuseppe Fortunino Francesco **15** 463-465

LOMBARDI, VINCE (1913-1970), American football coach **9** 491-492

Lombards (ancient German people)
Gregory I **6** 531-532
Justinian I **8** 393-395
Martel, Charles **10** 285

Lombardy (province; Italy)
Cavour, Conte di **3** 385-386
Charles V **3** 457-459
Frederick II **6** 79
Maximilian of Hapsburg **10** 358-360

LOMBROSO, CESARE (1835-1909), Italian criminologist **9** 493
Ferrero, Guglielmo **5** 429-430

LOMONOSOV, MIKHAIL VASILEVICH (1711-1765), Russian chemist and physicist **9** 494

Lon Nol (1913-1985), Cambodian general and politician
Sihanouk, Norodom **14** 222-223

London (city; England)
architecture
Hawksmoor, Nicholas **7** 211-212
Jones, Inigo **8** 333-334
Nash, John **11** 316
dock strike (1889)
Besant, Annie Wood **2** 233-234
Manning, Henry Edward **10** 209-210
Great Exhibition (1851)
see Crystal Palace Exhibition
Great Fire (1666)
Donne, John **5** 60-61
Hooke, Robert **7** 475
Pepys, Samuel **12** 207-208
Wren, Christopher **16** 393-394
social reforms
Addams, Jane **1** 56-57
Booth, Charles **2** 400-401
Peel, Robert **12** 181-183

London, a Poem (satire)
Johnson, Samuel **8** 315-317

London, Convention of (1884)
Kruger, Stephanus Johannes Paulus **9** 108-109

London, Councils of (1075; 1377)
John of Gaunt **8** 282-283
Lanfranc **9** 189-190

LONDON, JACK (1876-1916), American author **9** 494-495
Afinogenov, Aleksandr Nikolaevich **1** 72-73
Dreiser, Herman Theodore **5** 98-100
Eisenstein, Sergei Mikhailovich **5** 240-242
McClure, Samuel Sidney **10** 398-399
Twain, Mark **15** 363-366

London, Treaty of
1839
Bethmann Hollweg, Theobald von **2** 239-240
Mohammed Ali **11** 81-82
Palmerston, 3d Viscount **12** 81-83

London, University of (England)
Latin

Housman, Alfred Edward **7** 521-522
Oriental and African Studies
Kenyatta, Jomo **8** 512-514
Lao Shê **9** 200-201
sciences
Chain, Ernst Boris **3** 407-408
Childe, Vere Gordon **3** 521-522
Haldane, John Burdon Sanderson **7** 70-71
Holmes, Arthur **7** 455-456
Huxley, Thomas Henry **8** 77-79
Krebs, Hans Adolf **9** 95-97
Thomson, George Paget **15** 198-199
Whitehead, Alfred North **16** 242-244
social sciences
Arnold, Thomas **1** 313-314
Chapman, Sydney **3** 441
Hobhouse, Leonard Trelawny **7** 425-426
Mannheim, Karl **10** 208-209
Polanyi, Karl **12** 372
Robertson, Dennis Holme **13** 196
Toynbee, Arnold Joseph **15** 283-284
Woodward, Comer Vann **16** 378-379
see also King's College (London); London School of Economics

London Assurance (play)
Boucicault, Dion **2** 442-443

London Coffee-House for Merchants and Traders (established 1754)
Bradford, William **2** 477

London Conference (1946)
Bunche, Ralph Johnson **3** 121-122

London Conference of Arabs and Jews (1939)
Wise, Stephen Samuel **16** 344-345

London Letters (essays)
Orwell, George **12** 14-15

London Life, A (story)
James, Henry **8** 211-212

London Magazine (periodical)
Boswell, James **2** 432-434
Hazlitt, William **7** 235-236
Lamb, Charles **9** 176-177

London Missionary Society
Livingstone, David **9** 463-465
Wang T'ao **16** 105-106

London Naval Conference (1930)
Hoover, Herbert Clark **7** 483-485
MacDonald, James Ramsay **10** 84-85
Morrow, Dwight Whitney **11** 190-191

London Oratory
Newman, John Henry **11** 365-367

London School of Economics (University of London)
Attlee, Clement Richard **1** 361-362
Beveridge, William Henry **2** 251-252
Bosanquet, Bernard **2** 425-426
Carr-Saunders, Alexander Morris **3** 333-334
Evans-Pritchard, Edward Evan **5** 340

Laski, Harold J. **9** 215-216
Malinowski, Kaspar Bronislaw **10** 170-171
Mannheim, Karl **10** 208-209
Popper, Karl Raimund **12** 402
Tawney, Richard Henry **15** 120-121
Webb, Sidney James **16** 154-155

London School of Ethics and Social Philosophy
see London School of Economics

London Symphony (musical composition)
Haydn, Franz Joseph **7** 219-221
Vaughan Williams, Ralph **15** 446-447

London Times (newspaper)
Dana, Charles Anderson **4** 384-385
Eliot, Thomas Stearns **5** 258-261
Greene, Graham **6** 523-524
Murdoch, Rupert **11** 257-258
Nightingale, Florence **11** 392-393
Younghusband, Francis Edward **16** 477

Londonderry, 2nd Marquess of
see Castlereagh, Viscount

Loneliness in Jersey City (poem)
Stevens, Wallace **14** 443-445

Lonely Crowd, The (book)
Riesman, David **13** 167-168

Lonely Thrush, The (poem)
Leopardi, Giacomo **9** 344-345

LONG, CRAWFORD WILLIAMSON (1815-1878), American physician **9** 495-496

LONG, HUEY PIERCE (1893-1935), American politician **9** 496-497
Coughlin, Charles Edward **4** 265-266
Townsend, Francis Everitt **15** 282-283
Warren, Robert Penn **16** 121-122

LONG, IRENE D. (born 1951), African American aerospace medicine physician **9** 497-498

Long, John Luther (1861-1927), American playwright and novelist
Belasco, David **2** 124-125

Long Beach Symphony Orchestra
Falletta, JoAnn **5** 373-375

Long Christmas Dinner ... (plays)
Wilder, Thornton Niven **16** 276-277

Long Christmas Dinner, The (opera)
Hindemith, Paul **7** 399-400

Long Day's Journey into Night (play)
O'Neill, Eugene **11** 514-516

Long Dream, The (book)
Wright, Richard **16** 401-402

Long Island (New York State)
Downing, Andrew Jackson **5** 90-91

Long Island, battle of (1776)
Brant, Joseph **2** 500-501
Clinton, Henry **4** 114-115
Greene, Nathanael **6** 525-526
Howe, William **7** 538-539
Knox, Henry **9** 64
Putnam, Israel **12** 491-492

Long Live the Victory of People's War! (address)
Lin Piao **9** 429-430

Long March (1934-35; Chinese history)
Chou En-lai **4** 20-22
Chu Teh **4** 54-55
Lin Piao **9** 429-430
Liu Shao-Ch'i **9** 453-455
Mao Zedong **10** 225-227

Long Odds (novel)
Clarke, Marcus Andrew Hislop **4** 87-88

Long Parliament (England; 1640-48)
Laud, William **9** 224-225
Lilburne, John **9** 409-410
Pym, John **12** 495-496
Vane, Henry **15** 425-426

Long Voyage Home, The (play)
O'Neill, Eugene **11** 514-516

Longbow and Lyre (poems)
Yevtushenko, Yevgeny Alexandrovich **16** 455-456

Longchamp, William (died 1197), English bishop and statesman
John **8** 274-275

Longest Journey, The (novel)
Forster, Edward Morgan **6** 14-16

LONGFELLOW, HENRY WADSWORTH (1807-1882), American poet **9** 499-500
associates
Hawthorne, Nathaniel **7** 212-215
Lowell, James Russell **10** 14-15
editions of
Tschernichowsky, Saul **15** 323
influence of
Heavysege, Charles **7** 246
Johnson, Earvin Jr. **8** 297-299
Riley, James Whitcomb **13** 170-171
influenced by
Hulagu Khan **8** 27-28
Mather, Cotton **10** 330-332
Revere, Paul **13** 110-111
Schoolcraft, Henry Rowe **14** 29
quoted
Bakunin, Mikhail Aleksandrovich **1** 458-460

LONGINUS (flourished 1st or 3rd century), Latin author and rhetorician **9** 500-501
Boileau-Despréaux, Nicholas **2** 369-371

Long-Islander (newspaper)
Whitman, Walt **16** 249-251

Longitude (cartography)
Baffin, William **1** 435-436
Dunbar, William **5** 143-144
Hipparchus **7** 407-408
Huygens, Christiaan **8** 79-81
Mercator, Gerhardus **10** 511-512

Longstreet, James (1821-1904), American army officer
Lee, Robert Edward **9** 292-294

Longworth, Nicholas (1782-1863), American horticulturist

Wyant, Alexander Helwig **16** 409-410

Lonsdale, 1st Earl of (James Lowther; 1736-1802), English statesman
Boswell, James **2** 432-434

LONSDALE, KATHLEEN (born Kathleen Yardley; 1903-1971), Irish crystallographer **9** 501-502

Look Back in Anger (play)
Osborne, John **12** 16-17

Look for the Silver Lining (song)
Kern, Jerome David **8** 517-518

Look Homeward, Angel (novel)
Wolfe, Thomas Clayton **16** 355-356

Look Stranger (poem)
Auden, Wystan Hugh **1** 364-366

Look! We Have Come Through (poems)
Lawrence, David Herbert **9** 247-248

Looking Backward: 2000-1887 (novel; Bellamy)
Bellamy, Edward **2** 134-135
Schindler, Solomon **14** 7-8
Veblen, Thorstein Bunde **15** 449-450

Loops and Swift Horses Are Surer than Lead (painting)
Russell, Charles Marion **13** 375-376

Loores de Nuestra Señora (poems)
Gonzalo de Berceo **6** 431-432

LOOS, ADOLF (1870-1933), Viennese architect **9** 502-503
Kokoschka, Oskar **9** 75-76
Neutra, Richard Joseph **11** 355-356

Loos, battle of (1915)
Haig, Douglas **7** 67-68

Lop Nor (lake; western China)
Hedin, Sven Anders **7** 252-253
Przhevalsky, Nikolai Mikhailovich **12** 469-470

LOPE FÉLIX DE VEGA CARPIO (1562-1635), Spanish dramatist **9** 503-506
Alemán, Mateo **1** 126
Calderón, Pedro **3** 221-222
Seneca the Younger, Lucius Annaeus **14** 103-105
Tirso de Molina **15** 237-238

LÓPEZ, CARLOS ANTONIO (1792-1862), Paraguayan president-dictator 1844-1862 **9** 506-507
López, Francisco Solano **9** 507-508

LÓPEZ, FRANCISCO SOLANO (1826-1870), Paraguayan president-dictator **9** 507-508
Deodoro da Fonseca, Manoel **4** 502
López, Carlos Antonio **9** 506-507
Pedro II **12** 180-181

LÓPEZ, NARCISO (1798-1851), Venezuelan military leader **9** 508
Céspedes, Carlos Manuel de **3** 398-399

LÓPEZ DE AYALA, PEDRO (1332-1407), Spanish statesman, historian, and poet **9** 508-509

López de Gómara, Francisco (1510-1560?), Spanish historian
Díaz del Castillo, Bernal **4** 536-537

LÓPEZ MATEOS, ADOLFO (1910-1970), president of Mexico (1958-1964) **9** 509-510

LÓPEZ PORTILLO, JOSÉ (born 1920), president of Mexico (1976-1982) **9** 510-511

LORCA, FEDERICO GARCÍA (1898-1936), Spanish poet and playwright **9** 511-513
Góngora y Argote, Luis de **6** 427-428
Hughes, Langston **8** 18-19

Lord, Otis Phillips (1812-1884), American jurist
Dickinson, Emily **4** 541-543

Lord Arthur Savile's Crime... (stories)
Wilde, Oscar Fingall O'Flahertie Wills **16** 272-273

Lord Chamberlain's Men (English theatrical company)
Shakespeare, William **14** 142-145

Lord Chumley (play)
Belasco, David **2** 124-125

Lord Dunmore's War (United States; 1774)
Clark, George Rogers **4** 75-76
Dunmore, 4th Earl of **5** 147
Girty, Simon **6** 350
Johnson, William **8** 319-320
Lewis, Andrew **9** 376-377
Morgan, Daniel **11** 160-161

Lord Jim (novel)
Conrad, Joseph **4** 205-207

Lord of Labraz (novel)
Baroja y Nessi, Pío **2** 15-16

Lord of the Flies (book)
Golding, William **6** 404-406

Lord of the Rings (book)
Tolkien, J. R. R. **15** 259-261

Lord Weary's Castle (poems)
Lowell, Robert Trail Spence Jr. **10** 16-17

LORDE, AUDRE (1934-1992), African American poet **9** 513-515

Lord's Supper (religion)
see Eucharist

LORENTZ, HENDRIK ANTOON (1853-1928), Dutch physicist **9** 515-516
Einstein, Albert **5** 228-231

LORENZ, KONRAD Z. (1903-1989), animal psychologist **9** 516-517

Lorenzaccio (play)
Musset, Louis Charles Alfred de **11** 271-272

LORENZETTI, PIERRE AND AMBROGIO (flourished 14th century), Italian painters **9** 517-518
Cimabue **4** 60-61
Duccio di Buoninsegna **5** 121-122
Lorenzetti, Pietro and Ambrogio **9** 517-518

Lorenzo and Isabella (painting)
Millais, John Everett **11** 23-24

Lorenzo Monaco (1370-1425), Italian Camaldolese monk-painter
Angelico **1** 235-236

Loreto Church (Göllersdorf, Austria)
Hildebrandt, Johann Lucas von **7** 380-381

Lorraine (region; western Europe)
Charles the Bold **3** 467-469
Louis XIII **9** 529-531
Poincaré, Raymond **12** 366-368
see also Alsace-Lorraine

Los Alamos Scientific Laboratories (New Mexico)
Bethe, Hans Albrecht **2** 238-239
Bohr, Niels Henrik David **2** 366-368
Fermi, Enrico **5** 422-424
Oppenheimer, J. Robert **11** 525-526
Von Neumann, John **16** 27-28
see also Atomic bomb—development

Los Altos (Central American state)
Carrera, José Rafael **3** 324-325

Los Angeles (city; California)
Bradley, Tom **2** 484-485
Butterfield, John **3** 184-185
Douglas, Donald Wills **5** 77
Kearny, Stephen Watts **8** 468-469
Riordan, Richard Joseph **13** 177-179
see also California, University of (Los Angeles)

Los Angeles Kings (hockey team)
Gretzky, Wayne **6** 537-539

Los Angeles Lakers (basketball team)
Jabbar, Kareem Abdul **8** 164-165
Johnson, Marietta Louise Pierce **8** 312-313

Los Angeles Olympic Organizing Committee (United States; 1980s)
Ueberroth, Peter Victor **15** 379-381

Lose with a Smile (book)
Lardner, Ringgold Wilmer **9** 204-205

Loser Takes All (novella)
Greene, Graham **6** 523-524

Lost Childhood... (essays)
Greene, Graham **6** 523-524

Lost Galleon, The (poems)
Harte, Francis Brett **7** 184-185

Lost generation (expatriates)
Stein, Gertrude **14** 414-415

Lost Girl, The (novel)
Lawrence, David Herbert **9** 247-248

Lost in the Backwoods (book)
Traill, Catharine Parr **15** 291

Lost in the Stars (music tragedy)
Anderson, Maxwell **1** 219-220
Weill, Kurt **16** 174-175

Lost Lady, A (novel)
Cather, Willa Sibert **3** 368-369

Lost Lady, The (play)
Berkeley, William **2** 198-199

Lost Manuscript, The (novel)
Freytag, Gustav **6** 107-108

Lost Son... (poems)
Roethke, Theodore **13** 243-244

Lost World, The (novel)
Doyle, Arthur Conan **5** 91-92

Lost Zoo, The (book)
Cullen, Countee **4** 333-334

Lost-Found Nation of Islam
see Black Muslims

Lot and His Daughters (painting)
Altdorfer, Albrecht **1** 179-180

Lotario (opera)
Handel, George Frederick **7** 116-119

Lotf-Ali Khan (died 1794), Zand claimant to Persian throne
Agha Mohammad Khan **1** 80-81

Loth, Johann Karl (1632-1698), German painter
Rottmayr, Johann Michael **13** 321

Lothair I (795?-855), Holy Roman emperor 840-855 and king of Germany 840-843
Louis I **9** 522-523

Lothair II (1070-1137), Holy Roman emperor and king of Germany 1125-1137
Roger II **13** 244-245

Lothar of Segni
see Innocent III

LOTI, PIERRE (1850-1923), French novelist **9** 519-520

Lotte in Weimar (novel)
Mann, Thomas **10** 204-207

LOTTO, LORENZO (circa 1480-1556), Italian painter **9** 520-521

Lotus Sutra (Buddhism)
Nichiren **11** 376-377

Lotus-eaters (literary characters)
Homer **7** 465-467

LOTZE, RUDOLF HERMANN (1817-1881), German idealist philosopher **9** 521-522

Louange des dames, La (poems)
Machaut, Guillaume de **10** 93-94

Loubet, Émile (1838-1929), French statesman
Dreyfus, Alfred **5** 103-105
Poincaré, Raymond **12** 366-368

Louis (died 1908), crown prince of Portugal
Salazar, António de Oliveira **13** 442-443

Louis (Duke of Bavaria)
see Louis IV (Holy Roman emperor)

LOUIS I (778-840), Holy Roman emperor and king of France and Germany 814-840 **9** 522-523
Charlemagne **3** 445-447

Louis I (1326-1382), king of Hungary 1342-1382
Sigismund **14** 220-221

Louis I (died 1724), king of Spain 1724
Philip V **12** 276-277

Louis I (duke of Orléans)
see Orléans, Louis I, Duc d'

Louis I de Bourbon
see Condé, Louis I de Bourbon, Prince de

Louis II (804?-876), king of Germany 843-876
Louis I **9** 522-523

Louis II (846-879), king of France 877-879
Photius **12** 283-284

Louis II (1845-1886), king of Bavaria 1864-1886
Wagner, Richard **16** 40-43

Louis IV (Louis, Duke of Bavaria; 1287?-1347), Holy Roman emperor and king of Germany 1314-1347
Eckhart, Johann **5** 200-201
Marsilius of Padua **10** 284
William of Ockham **16** 298-299

LOUIS VI (1081-1137), king of France 1108-1137 **9** 523-524
Eleanor of Aquitaine **5** 246-247
Henry I **7** 286-287
Henry V **7** 295-296

LOUIS VII (circa 1120-1180), king of France 1137-1180 **9** 524-525
Eleanor of Aquitaine **5** 246-247
Henry II **7** 287-289
Philip II **12** 268-269

Louis VIII (1187-1226), king of France 1223-1226
Gros **7** 14-15
Henry III **7** 290-292
John **8** 274-275
Louis IX **9** 525-526
Philip II **12** 268-269

LOUIS IX (1214-1270), king of France 1226-1270 **9** 525-526
Alfonso III **1** 148-149
Henry III **7** 290-292
Joinville, Jean de **8** 325
Montfort, Simon de **11** 132-133
Montreuil, Pierre de **11** 139
Peter III **12** 256-257

LOUIS XI (1423-1483), king of France 1461-1483 **9** 526-528
art and literature
Comines, Philippe de **4** 181
Fouquet, Jean **6** 31
Burgundy and
Charles the Bold **3** 467-469
Edward IV **5** 212-213
Maximilian I **10** 356-357
Philip the Good **12** 278-279
relatives
Charles VII **3** 461-462
Charles VIII **3** 462-463
James I **8** 206-207
Margaret of Anjou **10** 249-250
Wars of the Roses
Margaret of Anjou **10** 249-250

Warwick and of Salisbury, Earl of
16 122-123

LOUIS XII (1462-1515), king of France
1498-1515 **9** 528-529
Italian campaigns
Alexander VI **1** 134-135
Borgia, Cesare **2** 412-413, 80
Ferdinand V **5** 417-418
Julius II **8** 384-386
Sforza, Lodovico **14** 127-128
patronage
Budé, Guillaume **3** 102-103
Josquin des Prez **8** 361-363
relatives
Charles VIII **3** 462-463
Francis I **6** 40-43
Henry VIII **7** 302-305
Orléans, Charles D' **11** 530

LOUIS XIII (1601-1643), king of France
1610-1643 **9** 529-531
absolutism
Louis XIV **9** 531-533
Richelieu, Armand Jean du Plessis
de **13** 142-144
colonial policy
Champlain, Samuel de **3** 419-421
Charnisay, Charles de Menou
3 470-471
patronage
La Tour, George de **9** 222
Le Vau, Louis **9** 360-361
Poussin, Nicolas **12** 418-420
Rubens, Peter Paul **13** 339-342
relatives
Charles, I **3** 450-452
Condé, Prince de **4** 193-194
Frontenac et Palluau, Comte de
6 128-130
Henry IV **7** 293-295
Orléans, Philippe II D' **11** 530-531
Philip III **12** 273-274
see also Thirty Years War

LOUIS XIV (1638-1715), king of France
1643-1715 **9** 531-533
absolutism
Montesquieu **11** 123-125
art patronage
Bernini, Gian Lorenzo **2** 214-216
Le Brun, Charles **9** 269-270
Perrault, Claude **12** 232-233
Watteau, Antoine **16** 143-144
see also Louvre, The; Versailles (city;
France)
colonial policy
Frontenac et Palluau, Comte de
6 128-130
Iberville, Sieur d' **8** 90-91
La Salle, Sieur de **9** 210-211
Laval, Francois Xavier de **9** 235-236
Talon, Jean **15** 91-92
Dutch wars
Condé, Prince de **4** 193-194
William III **16** 295-296
Witt, Johan de **16** 348-349
economic policy

Colbert, Jean Baptiste **4** 142-143
England and
Buckingham, 2d Duke of **3** 94-95
James II **8** 207-208
histories of
Lavisse, Ernest **9** 241
Saint-Simon, Duc de **13** 436
Voltaire **16** 14-16
literary interests
Boileau-Despréaux, Nicholas
2 369-371
La Bruyère, Jean de **9** 145
Molière **11** 86-88
Racine, Jean Baptiste **12** 532-535
marriage
Philip IV **12** 275
music patronage
Cavalli, Pietro Francesco **3** 382-383
Couperin, François **4** 270-271
Lully, Jean Baptiste **10** 40-41
regency period
Bossuet, Jacques Bénigne **2** 431-432
Mazarin, Jules **10** 379-380
Orléans, Philippe II D' **11** 530-531
religion and
Bourgeoys, Marguerite **2** 452-453
Fénelon, François de Salignac de la
Mothe **5** 410-411
see also Spanish Succession, War of
the; Thirty Years War

LOUIS XV (1710-1774), king of France
1715-1774 **9** 533-534
Beaumarchais, Pierre August Caron de
2 93-94
Boucher, François **2** 440-442
Chardin, Jean Baptiste Siméon
3 442-443
Charles X **3** 463-464
Elizabeth, the Queen Mother **5** 261-263
Gabriel, Ange Jacques **6** 160-161
Orléans, Philippe II D' **11** 530-531
Philip V **12** 276-277
Saxe, Comte de **13** 507-508

LOUIS XVI (1754-1793), king of France
1774-1792 **9** 534-535
associates
Goldoni, Carlo **6** 408-409
Necker, Jacques **11** 330-331
Selim III **14** 95-96
Turgot, Anne Robert Jacques
15 348-349
relatives
Charles X **3** 463-464
Marie Antoinette **10** 258-259
Revolution and death
Barras, Vicomte de **2** 19
Carnot, Lazare Nicolas Marguerite
3 313-314
Condorcet, Marquis de **4** 195-196
Danton, Georges Jacques **4** 391-393
Fouché, Joseph **6** 30-31
Saint-Just, Louis Antoine Léon de
13 433
Sieyès, Comte Emmanuel Joseph
14 217-218

Talleyrand, Charles Maurice de
15 89-90
see also French Revolution
United States and
Franklin, Benjamin **6** 60-64
Jefferson, Thomas **8** 238-241
Paine, Thomas **12** 66-67

LOUIS XVIII (1755-1824), king of France
1814-1824 **9** 535-536
and Catholicism
Pius VII **12** 334-335
associates
Burke, Edmund **3** 138-141
Chateaubriand, Vicomte de
3 477-479
Lafayette, Marquis de **9** 151-152
Lamartine, Alphonse Marie Louis de
9 173-175
Louis Philippe **9** 536-537
Bourbon restoration
Carnot, Lazare Nicolas Marguerite
3 313-314
Fouché, Joseph **6** 30-31
Napoleon I **11** 306-310
Ney, Michel **11** 372-373
Talleyrand, Charles Maurice de
15 89-90
patronage
Champollion, Jean François **3** 421
Laplace, Marquis de **9** 202-204
relatives
Charles X **3** 463-464

Louis XV style
see Rococo style

Louis XVI style (art)
Gabriel, Ange Jacques **6** 160-161
Hepplewhite, George **7** 317-318
Sheraton, Thomas **14** 181-182

LOUIS, JOE (Joe Louis Barrow;
1914-1981), American boxer **9** 537-538
Owens, Jesse **12** 43-44

LOUIS, MORRIS (Bernstein; 1912-1962),
American painter **9** 538-539
Frankenthaler, Helen **6** 56-57
Noland, Kenneth **11** 418-419

LOUIS, PIERRE CHARLES ALEXANDRE
(1787-1872), French physician **9** 540
Bowditch, Henry Ingersoll **2** 459-460

Louis, Saint
see Louis IX (king of France)

Louis d'Orléans
see Louis XII (king of France)

Louis le Dieudonné
see Louis XIV (king of France)

Louis le Lion
see Louis VIII (king of France)

Louis Napoleon
see Napoleon III, Emperor of the French

Louis of Bavaria
see Louis IV (Holy Roman emperor)

Louis of Nassau (1538-1574), Count of Nassau-Dietz, leader of Dutch revolt against Spain
Alba, Duke of **1** 103-104
William the Silent **16** 300-302

LOUIS PHILIPPE (1773-1850), king of the French 1830-1848 **9** 536-537
accession
Aberdeen, 4th Earl of **1** 25-26
Cabet, Étienne **3** 196
Cauchy, Augustin Louis **3** 378-380
Charles X **3** 463-464
Guizot, François Pierre Guillaume **7** 40-41
associates
Bugeaud de la Piconnerie, Thomas Robert **3** 111
Dumas, Alexandre **5** 136-138
Leopold I **9** 345-346
Thiers, Louis Adolphe **15** 181-182
Victoria **15** 485-487
opponents
Blanc, Louis **2** 318-319
Blanqui, Louis Auguste **2** 323-324
Lamartine, Alphonse Marie Louis de **9** 173-175
Montalembert, Comte de **11** 118-119
Napoleon III **11** 310-312
Tocqueville, Alexis Charles Henri Maurice Clérel de **15** 250-251
patronage
Cuvier, Georges Léopold **4** 357-359
supporters
Hugo, Victor Marie **8** 22-25
Lafayette, Marquis de **9** 151-152
Talleyrand, Charles Maurice de **15** 89-90

Louis the German
see Louis II (king of Germany)

Louis the Great
see Louis XIV (king of France)

Louis the Pious
see Louis I (Holy Roman emperor)

Louisbourg, battle of (1745)
Pepperell, William **12** 206-207

Louisbourg, siege of (1758)
Amherst, Jeffery **1** 200-201
Carleton, Guy **3** 300-301
Murray, James **11** 261-262
Rodney, George Brydges **13** 239-240
Wolfe, James **16** 354-355

Louise (died 1831), princess of Saxe-Coburg-Altenberg
Albert **1** 110-112

Louise of Mecklenburg-Strelitz (1776-1810), queen of Prussia
William I **16** 292-293

Louisiana (state; United States)
boundary disputes
Adams, John Quincy **1** 52-54
colonial period
Bienville, Sieur de **2** 268-269
Charles III **3** 454-455

Gálvez, Bernardo de **6** 195-196
Iberville, Sieur d' **8** 90-91
La Salle, Sieur de **9** 210-211
Vaudreuil-Cavagnal, Marquis de **15** 444
crops
Knapp, Seaman Asahel **9** 58
politicians
Livingston, Edward **9** 460-461
Long, Huey Pierce **9** 496-497
Pinchback, Pinckney Benton Stewart **12** 306-308
Slidell, John **14** 273
Soulé, Pierre **14** 351-352
White, Edward Douglass **16** 230-231
see also Louisiana Purchase; Louisiana Territory

Louisiana, University of
see Tulane University of Louisiana

Louisiana Purchase (1803)
Black Hawk **2** 308
du Pont de Nemours, Pierre Samuel **5** 155-156
Jefferson, Thomas **8** 238-241
Livingston, Robert R. **9** 462-463
Madison, James **10** 121-123
Monroe, James **11** 111-113
Pinckney, Charles **12** 309-310
Wilkinson, James **16** 284-286

Louisiana Purchase Exposition (1904)
see World's Fairs—Saint Louis

Louisiana State University (Baton Rouge)
Voegelin, Eric **16** 6-8
Warren, Robert Penn **16** 121-122
Woodward, Comer Vann **16** 378-379

Louisiana Territory (United States history)
Clark, George Rogers **4** 75-76
Clark, William **4** 82-83
Lewis, Meriwether **9** 391-392
Monroe, James **11** 111-113
Wilkinson, James **16** 284-286

Louison (play)
Musset, Louis Charles Alfred de **11** 271-272

Louisville, Cincinnati and Charleston Railroad (United States)
Gadsden, James **6** 165-166
Hayne, Robert Young **7** 231-232

Louisville, University of (Kentucky)
Brandeis, Louis Dembitz **2** 496-497

Louisville and Nashville Railroad (United States)
Harrison, Benjamin **7** 178-179

Loups, Les (play)
Rolland, Romain **13** 260

Lourdes (book)
Zola, Émile **16** 526-528

Lcutherbourg, Philip James de (1740-1812), French painter
Turner, Joseph Mallord William **15** 352-354

Louvain (city; Belgium)
Bouts, Dirk **2** 458-459

Louvain, University of (Belgium)
Bellarmine, Robert **2** 135-136
Helmont, Jan Baptista van **7** 269-271
Lemaître, Abbè Georges Édouard **9** 315-316
Schwann, Theodor **14** 51-52

Louvois, Marquis de (François Michel Le Tellier; 1641-1691), French war minister
Colbert, Jean Baptiste **4** 142-143

Louvre (museum; Paris)
Carpeaux, Jean Baptiste **3** 318-319
Champollion, Jean François **3** 421
Charles V (king of France) **3** 459-460
Gabriel, Ange Jacques **6** 160-161
Goujon, Jean **6** 466-467
Le Vau, Louis **9** 360-361
Lescot, Pierre **9** 354
Perrault, Claude **12** 232-233

Louÿs, Pierre (1870-1925), French writer
Gide, André **6** 308-309
Valéry, Paul Ambroise **15** 405-406

LOVE, NAT (1854-1921), African American champion cowboy **10** 1-2

LOVE, SUSAN M. (born 1948), American surgeon and medical researcher **10** 2-3

Love among the Artists (novel)
Shaw, George Bernard **14** 163-164

Love among the Ruins (story)
Waugh, Evelyn Arthur St. John **16** 145-147

Love and Freindship (sic.; novel)
Austen, Jane **1** 377-379

Love and Mr. Lewisham (novel)
Wells, Herbert George **16** 195-196

Love for Love (play)
Congreve, William **4** 200-201

Love for Sale (song)
Porter, Cole Albert **12** 405-406

Love for Three Oranges (opera)
Prokofiev, Sergei Sergeevich **12** 458-460

Love, Honor and Power (play)
Calderón, Pedro **3** 221-222

Love in a Village (opera)
Arne, Thomas Augustine **1** 307-308

Love in a Wood (play)
Wycherley, William **16** 411-412

Love in Several Masques (play)
Fielding, Henry **5** 442-444

Love Me Do (song)
Lennon, John Winston **9** 326-328

Love Nest ... (stories)
Lardner, Ringgold Wilmer **9** 204-205

Love of Landry, The (novel)
Dunbar, Paul Laurence **5** 141-142

Love Propitiated (opera)
Chávez, Carlos **3** 486

Love Rogue, The (play)
Tirso de Molina **15** 237-238

Love Song of J. Alfred Prufrock, The (poem; T.S. Eliot)
Eliot, Thomas Stearns **5** 258-261
Pound, Ezra Loomis **12** 415-417
Sandburg, Carl **13** 461-462

Love Songs of Connacht, The (book)
Hyde, Douglas **8** 82-83

Love Songs of Hafiz (musical composition)
Szymanowski, Karol **15** 67-68

Love the Physician (play)
Tirso de Molina **15** 237-238

Loved and the Lost, The (novel)
Callaghan, Edward Morley **3** 229-230

Loved One, The (novel)
Waugh, Evelyn Arthur St. John **16** 145-147

LOVEJOY, ARTHUR ONCKEN (1873-1962), American philosopher **10** 6

LOVEJOY, ELIJAH PARISH (1802-1837), American newspaper editor and abolitionist **10** 6-7
Brown, William Wells **3** 48-49
Phillips, Wendell **12** 281-282

Lovelace (literary character)
Richardson, Samuel **13** 141-142

LOVELACE, RICHARD (circa 1618-circa 1657), English Cavalier poet **10** 7-8
Suckling, John **15** 10-11

LOVELL, SIR ALFRED CHARLES BERNARD (born 1913), English astronomer **10** 8-9

Lovell House (Los Angeles)
Neutra, Richard Joseph **11** 355-356

Lover (song)
Rodgers, Richard Charles **13** 234-236

Lover, The (play)
Pinter, Harold **12** 317-318

Lover Crowned, The (painting)
Fragonard, Jean Honoré **6** 38-39

Lovers (painting)
Tanguy, Yves **15** 101

Lovers (sculpture)
Duchamp-Villon, Raymond **5** 123
Zorach, William **16** 528

Lovers of Zion (Jewish organization)
Ahad Haam **1** 88-89
Zangwill, Israel **16** 488-489

Loves (poetry collection)
Ovid **12** 34-36

Loves of the Shepherds (painting)
Fragonard, Jean Honoré **6** 38-39

Love's Comedy (play)
Ibsen, Henrik **8** 98-100

Love's Labour's Lost (play; Shakespeare)
Arne, Thomas Augustine **1** 307-308
Shakespeare, William **14** 142-145

Love's Old Sweet Song (play)
Saroyan, William **13** 486-487

Love's Pilgrimage (novel)
Sinclair, Upton Beale Jr. **14** 248-249

LOW, JULIETTE GORDON (born Juliette Magill Kinzie Gordon; 1860-1927), American reformer and founder of the Girl Scouts **10** 10-11

LOW, SETH (1850-1916), American politician and college president **10** 11-12
Murphy, Charles Francis **11** 259-260

Low Countries (Belgium; Luxembourg; Netherlands)
Alba, Duke of **1** 103-104
Condé, Prince de **4** 193-194
Frederick III **6** 84-85
Frescobaldi, Girolamo **6** 101-102
Hitler, Adolf **7** 417-420
see also Flanders; and individual countries

Low Life (play)
de la Roche, Mazo Louise **4** 474-475

Lowe, Sir Hudson (1769-1844), British soldier and official
Napoleon I **11** 306-310

Lowell (city; Massachusetts)
Appleton, Nathan **1** 266-267

LOWELL, ABBOTT LAWRENCE (1856-1943), American educator and political scientist **10** 12-13
Dewey, Melvil **4** 523-524
Eliot, Charles William **5** 254
Lowell, Robert Trail Spence Jr. **10** 16-17

LOWELL, AMY (1874-1925), American poet, critic, and biographer **10** 13
Lindsay, Vachel **9** 424-425
Lowell, Robert Trail Spence Jr. **10** 16-17

LOWELL, FRANCIS CABOT (1775-1817), American merchant and manufacturer **10** 13-14
Appleton, Nathan **1** 266-267
du Pont, Éleuthère Irénée **5** 154

LOWELL, JAMES RUSSELL (1819-1891), American poet and diplomat **10** 14-15
as critic
Burroughs, John **3** 160-161
Mencken, Henry Louis **10** 481-483
associates
Clough, Arthur Hugh **4** 123-124
Foster, Abigail Kelley **6** 25
Howells, William Dean **7** 539-541
Woolf, Virginia Stephen **16** 381-382
influenced by
Mather, Cotton **10** 330-332
Schoolcraft, Henry Rowe **14** 29
quoted
Titchener, Edward Bradford **15** 241-242
relatives
Lowell, Amy **10** 13
Lowell, Robert Trail Spence Jr. **10** 16-17

LOWELL, JOSEPHINE SHAW (1843-1905), American social reformer and philanthropist **10** 15-16

LOWELL, ROBERT TRAIL SPENCE, JR. (1917-1977), American poet **10** 16-17
Eliot, Thomas Stearns **5** 258-261

Lower California (peninsula; Pacific Ocean)
Kino, Eusebio Francisco **9** 30-31
Portolá, Gaspar de **12** 408
Walker, William **16** 68-69

Lower Canada
see Quebec (province)

Lower Depths, The (play; Gorky)
Gorky, Maxim **6** 458-460
Kurosawa, Akira **9** 135-137
Stanislavsky, Constantin **14** 398-399

LOWIE, ROBERT HARRY (1883-1957), Austrian-born American anthropologist **10** 18
Boas, Franz **2** 349-351
Kroeber, Alfred Louis **9** 105-106

Lowland Marsh (painting)
Rousseau, Théodore **13** 328

Low-temperature physics (cryogenics)
Kapitsa, Pyotr Leonidovich **8** 433-435
Landau, Lev Davidovich **9** 184-185

Lowther, James
see Lonsdale, 1st Earl of

Loxodromes (cartography)
Mercator, Gerhardus **10** 511-512

Loyal National Repeal Association (Ireland; established 1841)
O'Connell, Daniel **11** 465-467

Loyalty (philosophy)
Royce, Josiah **13** 334-335

Loyang (city; China)
Chou Kung **4** 22-23
Confucius **4** 197-200

LRC
see Labour Representation Committee (LRC)

LSD (popular drug; d-lysergic acid diethylamide)
Leary, Timothy **9** 266-267

Lu (province; ancient China)
Confucius **4** 197-200
Mencius **10** 480-481

LU CHI (261-303), Chinese poet and critic **10** 24
Liu Hsieh **9** 452-453

LU CHIU-YUAN (Lu Hsiang-shan; 1139-1193), Chinese philosopher **10** 24-25
Chu Hsi **4** 40-43
Wang Yang-ming **16** 108-109
Yi Hwang **16** 457

LU HSÜN (pen name of Chou Shu-jen; 1881-1936), Chinese author and social critic **10** 35-37
Ku Chieh-kang **9** 120-121
Kuo Mo-jo **9** 133-134

Lü Kuang (flourished 384-401), Chinese general

Kumarajiva **9** 127

Lü Pu-wei (ruled circa 250-237 B.C.), Chinese prime minister of Ch'in
Li Ssu **9** 442-443
Quin Shi Huang-Di **12** 515-518

Lü-tsung (Buddhism)
Tao-hsüan **15** 105

Lualaba River (Africa)
Brazza, Pierre Paul François Camille Savorgnan de **2** 509-510

Luang Pradit Manutham
see Pridi Phanomyong

Lübeck (city; Germany)
Frederick I **6** 78-79
Gustavus I **7** 42-43

Lübeck, Vincent (1654/56-1740), German composer and organist
Bach, Johann Sebastian **1** 416-419

LUBITSCH, ERNST (1892-1947), German-American film director **10** 18-19

Luca Conference (56 B.C.)
Caesar, Gaius Julius **3** 207-210
Clodius Pulcher, Publius **4** 121-122
Crassus Dives, Marcus Licinius **4** 296-297
Pompey **12** 387-389

Lucan (Marcus Annaeus Lucanus; 39-65), Roman poet
Martialis, Marcus Valerius **10** 286-287
Nero Claudius Caesar **11** 342-344
Seneca the Younger, Lucius Annaeus **14** 103-105

LUCARIS, CYRIL (1572-1637), Greek Orthodox patriarch and theologian **10** 20

Lucas, Keith (died 1916), English physiologist
Adrian, Edgar Douglas **1** 67-69
Hodgkin, Alan Lloyd **7** 431-432

LUCAS VAN LEYDEN (1494-1533), Dutch engraver and painter **10** 20-21
Andrea del Sarto **1** 224-225
Dürer, Albrecht **5** 159-161
Rembrandt Harmensz van Rijn **13** 91-95

Lucasta... (poems)
Lovelace, Richard **10** 7-8

Lucca (city-state; Italy)
Quercia, Jacopo della **12** 509
Visconti, Gian Galeazzo **15** 510-511
see also Luca conference

Lucca Madonna (painting; J. van Eyck)
Eyck, Hubert and Jan van **5** 352-354

LUCE, CLARE BOOTHE (1903-1987), playwright and U.S. congresswoman **10** 21-23
Luce, Henry Robinson **10** 23-24

LUCE, HENRY ROBINSON (1898-1967), American magazine editor and publisher **10** 23-24

Lucerne (story)
Tolstoy, Leo **15** 262-265

Luces de Bohemia (novel)
Valle Inclán, Ramón Maria del **15** 407-408

Lucia di Lammermoor (opera; Donizetti)
Donizetti, Gaetano **5** 59-60
Scott, Walter **14** 68-70

LUCIAN (circa 120-circa 200), Greek satirist **10** 25-26
Apelles **1** 257
Myron **11** 285
Phidias **12** 265-267
Rabelais, François **12** 524-526
Wieland, Christoph Martin **16** 260-261
Wolf, Friedrich August **16** 352-353

Lucian of Antioch, Saint (240?-312), Syrian theologian and martyr
Arius **1** 297-298

Lucien Leuwen (novel)
Stendhal **14** 422-425

Lucifer (literary character)
Joyce, James **8** 365-367
Lamartine, Alphonse Marie Louis de **9** 173-175

Lucifer (play)
Vondel, Joost van den **16** 19-20

Luciferic Suite (musical composition)
Nielsen, Carl August **11** 388-389

Lucilius, Gaius (circa 180-102 B.C.), Latin poet
Horace **7** 500-503
Juvenal **8** 397-399
Seneca the Younger, Lucius Annaeus **14** 103-105
Varro, Marcus Terentius **15** 438-439

Lucinde (novel)
Schlegel, Friedrich von **14** 10-11

Lucio Silla (opera)
Mozart, Wolfgang Amadeus **11** 218-221

Lucius (novel)
Lucian **10** 25-26

Lucius II (Gerard Caccianemici; died 1145), pope 1144-1145
Arnold of Brescia **1** 314-315

Lucius III (Ubaldus Allucingolus; 1097?-1185), pope 1181-1185
Waldo, Peter **16** 55-56

Lucius Verus (Lucius Aurelius Verus; 130-169), Roman emperor 161-169
Galen **6** 178-180

Luck of Barry Lyndon, The (novel)
Thackeray, William Makepeace **15** 159-161

Luck of Roaring Camp, The (story)
Harte, Francis Brett **7** 184-185

Luck, or Cunning? (book)
Butler, Samuel **3** 183

Lucknow (city; India)
see Sepoy Mutiny

Lucky Dragon (painting series)
Shahn, Ben **14** 139-140

Lucky Per's Journey (play)
Strindberg, August **14** 509-511

Lucky Strike (painting)
Davis, Stuart **4** 424-425

Lucrece (play; Obey)
Wilder, Thornton Niven **16** 276-277

LUCRETIUS (Titus Lucretius Carus; circa 94-circa 55 B.C.), Latin poet and philosopher **10** 26-27
Catullus, Gaius Valerius **3** 377-378
Donne, John **5** 60-61
Dryden, John **5** 106-107
Ennius, Quintus **5** 289
Evelyn, John **5** 343-344
Santayana, George **13** 475-477
Virgil **15** 507-510
Wang Ch'ung **16** 98-99

Lucrezia (literary character)
Machiavelli, Niccolò **10** 97-99

Lucrézia Borgia (play)
Hugo, Victor Marie **8** 22-25

Lucullus, Lucius Licinius (circa 117-56 B.C.), Roman general
Clodius Pulcher, Publius **4** 121-122
Pompey **12** 387-389
Scipio Africanus Minor, Publius Cornelius Aemilianus **14** 62-63

Luddite riots (1811-1816)
Brontë, Charlotte **3** 17-18
Toller, Ernst **15** 261

LUDENDORFF, ERICH FRIEDRICH WILHELM (1865-1937), German general **10** 27-28
Bethmann Hollweg, Theobald von **2** 239-240
Hindenburg, Paul Ludwig Hans von Beneckendorff und von **7** 400-401
Hitler, Adolf **7** 417-420

Ludlow, J.M. (1821-1911), English founder of Christian socialism
Kingsley, Charles **9** 28

LUDLUM, ROBERT (a.k.a. Jonathan Ryder and Michael Shepherd; born 1927), American suspense novelist **10** 28-29

Ludolph of Saxony (circa 1295-1377), Carthusian spiritual writer
Ignatius of Loyola **8** 108-109

Ludwig II
see Louis II (king of Bavaria)

LUDWIG, DANIEL KEITH (1897-1992), American shipping magnate **10** 29-31

LUDWIG, KARL FRIEDRICH WILHELM (1816-1895), German physiologist **10** 31

Lueger, Karl (1844-1910), founder of Austrian Christian Socialist Party
Hitler, Adolf **7** 417-420

LUGARD, FREDERICK JOHN DEALTRY (1st Baron Lugard; 1858-1945), British soldier and colonial administrator in Africa **10** 31-32
Mwanga **11** 282-283

Lugones, Leopoldo (1874-1938), Argentine poet
Güiráldez, Ricardo **7** 38-39

LUHAN, MABEL DODGE (1879-1962), American writer, salon hostess, and patron of artists, writers, and political radicals **10** 32-34

LUHMANN, NIKLAS (born 1927), German sociologist who developed a general sociological systems theory **10** 34-35

Luisa Miller (opera)
Verdi, Giuseppe Fortunino Francesco **15** 463-465

Luiz, Washington (1869-1957), Brazilian president 1926-1930
Aranha, Osvaldo **1** 272-273
Vargas, Getulio Dornelles **15** 433-434

Luján de Sayavedra, Mateo
see Martí, Juan

LUKÁCS, GYORGY (1885-1971), Hungarian literary critic and philosopher **10** 37-38

Lukar, Cyril
see Lucaris, Cyril

Luke, Gospel according to Saint (New Testament)
Ambrose **1** 192-193
Jesus of Nazareth **8** 251-255
Justin Martyr **8** 395-396
Luke **10** 38
Marcion **10** 238-239
Mary **10** 308

LUKE, Saint (flourished A.D. 50), Evangelist and biblical author **10** 38
John **8** 273-274
Mark **10** 266-267

Luke Baldwin's Vow (novel)
Callaghan, Edward Morley **3** 229-230

Luke Havergal (verse)
Robinson, Edwin Arlington **13** 201-202

LUKS, GEORGE BENJAMIN (1867-1933), American painter **10** 38-39
Calder, Alexander **3** 216-218
Davies, Arthur Bowen **4** 409-410
Evergood, Philip **5** 345
Sloan, John **14** 274-275

Lulach (ruled 1057-1058), king of Scotland
Macbeth **10** 81
Malcolm III **10** 164-165

LULL, RAYMOND (1232/35-1316), Spanish theologian, poet, and missionary **10** 39-40
Bruno, Giordano **3** 75-76
Ibn al-Arabi, Muhyi al-Din **8** 91

LULLY, JEAN BAPTISTE (1632-1687), Italian-born French composer **10** 40-41
Cavalli, Pietro Francesco **3** 382-383
Charpentier, Marc Antoine **3** 471-472
Gluck, Christoph Willibald **6** 372-374
Rameau, Jean Philippe **13** 17-18
Telemann, Georg Philipp **15** 137-138

Lully, Raymond
see Lull, Raymond

Lulu (literary character)
Pinter, Harold **12** 317-318

Lulu (opera)
Berg, Alban **2** 186-187

Luluabourg congress (Congo; 1959)
Lumumba, Patrice Emery **10** 43-45

Lumberjack War (United States; 1839)
Scott, Winfield **14** 70-71

Lume Spento, A (poetry)
Pound, Ezra Loomis **12** 415-417

Lumìe di Sicilia (story and play)
Pirandello, Luigi **12** 319-321

LUMIÈRE BROTHERS (Auguste Marie Louis, 1862-1954, and Louis Jean, 1864-1948), French inventors **10** 41-43

Luminescence (physics)
Cherenkov, Pavel Alekseevich **3** 502-503

Luminism (art)
Heade, Martin Johnson **7** 236
Lane, Fitz Hugh **9** 189

Lumpa uprisings (Zambia)
Kaunda, Kenneth David **8** 460-461

LUMUMBA, PATRICE EMERY (1925-1961), Congolese statesman **10** 43-45
Kasavubu, Joseph **8** 453-455
Mobutu Sese Seko **11** 69-71
Tshombe, Moïse Kapenda **15** 325-326
Youlou, Fulbert **16** 466-467

Lun yü
see Analects

Luna, Pedro de
see Benedict XIII, antipope

Luna e i falò, La (book)
Pavese, Cesare **12** 154-155

Lunacy Commissioners (England; established 1826)
Shaftesbury, 7th Earl of **14** 137-138

Lunar calendar (chronology)
Shotoku Taishi **14** 205-207

Lunar studies
see Moon (earth's)

Luncheon of the Boating Party (painting)
Renoir, Pierre Auguste **13** 101-102

Luncheon on the Grass (painting)
Manet, Édouard **10** 193-194

Lund, University of (Sweden)
Nygren, Anders **11** 449-451
Pufendorf, Samuel von **12** 477-478

Lunda (African people)
Tshombe, Moïse Kapenda **15** 325-326

LUNDY, BENJAMIN (1789-1839), American journalist **10** 45-46

Lune Blanche, La (poem)
Verlaine, Paul Marie **15** 465-466

Lunéville, Treaty of (1801)
Bonaparte, Joseph **2** 381-382

Malpighi, Marcello **10 176-178
Napoleon I **11** 306-310

Lun-heng (book)
Wang Ch'ung **16** 98-99

LUNS, JOSEPH (born 1911), West European political leader **10** 46-47

Luo Thrift and Trading Corp. (Kenya)
Odinga, Ajuma Jaramogi Oginga **11** 471-473

Lupescu, Magda (born 1904?), Romanian adventuress
Ferdinand **5** 413-414

Luque, Hernando de (died 1532), Spanish priest, vicar of Panama
Almagro, Diego de **1** 177-178
Pizarro, Francisco **12** 340-341

LURIA, ISAAC BEN SOLOMON ASHKENAZI (1534-1572), Jewish mystic **10** 47-48
Sabbatai Zevi **13** 400-401

Luscombe (house; South Devon)
Nash, John **11** 316

Lushan
see Mount Lu

Lusiads (epic; Camoëns)
Camoëns, Luis Vaz de **3** 247-249
Lope Félix de Vega Carpio **9** 503-506

Lusitania (province; Roman Spain)
Caesar, Gaius Julius **3** 207-210
see also Portugal

Lusitania, sinking of (1915)
Bryan, William Jennings **3** 80-82
Lansing, Robert **9** 200
Page, Walter Hines **12** 60-61
Wilson, Thomas Woodrow **16** 330-332
passengers
Frohman, Charles **6** 123-124

Lustgarten (Berlin)
Schinkel, Karl Friedrich **14** 8

Lustspiel (comedy)
Lessing, Gotthold Ephraim **9** 357-359

Lusus (literary character)
Camoëns, Luis Vaz de **3** 247-249

Luther (play)
Osborne, John **12** 16-17

LUTHER, MARTIN (1483-1546), German religious reformer **10** 48-51
as musician
Senfl, Ludwig **14** 105-106
Walter, Johann **16** 86
Vogelweide, Walther von der **16** 10-11
biographers
Erikson, Erik Homburger **5** 309-310
excommunicated
Eck, Johann Maier von **5** 200
Leo X **9** 332-334
influence in theology
Calvin, John **3** 239-242
Menno Simons **10** 505-506
Wesley, John **16** 209-210

influenced by
Rashi **13** 43
on astronomy
Copernicus, Nicolaus **4** 226-227
supporters
Cranach, Lucas the Elder **4** 289-290
Dürer, Albrecht **5** 159-161
Hutten, Ulrich von **8** 72-73
Karlstadt, Andreas Bodenheim von
8 449
Melancthon, Philip **10** 466-467
Sachs, Hans **13** 410-411
theological controversies
Canisius, Peter **3** 258
Erasmus, Desiderius **5** 298-300
Latimer, Hugh **9** 221
Münzer, Thomas **11** 251-252
Schwenckfeld, Kasper von **14** 56-57
Tyndale, William **15** 373-374
Zwingli, Huldreich **16** 537-538
see also Lutheranism; Protestant
Reformation

Lutheran World Federation
Nygren, Anders **11** 449-451

Lutheranism (religion)
in Europe
Altdorfer, Albrecht **1** 179-180
Bach, Johann Sebastian **1** 416-419
Charles V **3** 457-459
Cranmer, Thomas **4** 295-296
Frederick William III **6** 87
Maximilian II **10** 357-358
Nygren, Anders **11** 449-451
Spener, Philipp Jakob **14** 372
Zinzendorf, Nikolaus Ludwig von
16 522-523
in the United States
Marty, Martin E. **10** 300-301
Mühlenberg, Heinrich Melchior
11 232-233
Stuyvesant, Peter **15** 5-6
see also Luther, Martin

LUTHULI, ALBERT JOHN (1898-1967),
South African statesman **10** 51-52
Dube, John Langalibalele **5** 113
Malan, Daniel Francois **10** 163-164
Mandela, Nelson Rolihlahla
10 185-186

LUTOSLAWSKI, WITOLD (1913-1994),
Polish composer **10** 52-53

Lutrin Le (poem; Boileau)
Boileau-Despréaux, Nicholas
2 369-371
Pope, Alexander **12** 395-397

Lutte pour la vie, La (novel)
Daudet, Alphonse **4** 402-403

LUTYENS, EDWIN LANDSEER
(1869-1944), English architect **10** 54-55

Lützen, battle of (1632)
Gustavus II **7** 43-45
Oxenstierna, Axel Gustafsson **12** 44-45
Wallenstein, Albrecht Wenzel Eusebius
von **16** 80-81

Lux... (poem)
Wyatt, Thomas **16** 410-411

Luxe, calme et volupté (painting)
Matisse, Henri **10** 336-337

Luxembourg Gardens at Twilight (painting)
Sargent, John Singer **13** 481-482

Luxembourg, Grand Duchy of (or Luxem-
burg; nation, western Europe)
Bismarck, Otto Eduard Leopold von
2 294-296
Henry VII **7** 299-300
Spaak, Paul Henri **14** 359-360
Thorn, Gaston **15** 207-208
William I **16** 291-292
see also Luxemburg, House of

Luxemburg, House of (ruled 13th century
-1437)
Charles IV **3** 455-456
Henry VII **7** 299-300
Sigismund **14** 220-221
Wenceslaus **16** 201-202

LUXEMBURG, ROSA (1870-1919), Polish
revolutionary **10** 55-56
Mies van der Rohe, Ludwig **11** 10-12
Trotsky, Leon **15** 302-305

Luxor (city; Egypt)
Ramses II **13** 22-23

Luynes, Duc de
see Albert, Charles d'

LUZ, ARTURO ROGERIO (born 1926),
Philippine painter and sculptor **10** 56-57

Luzumiyat (poems)
Abu-L-Ala al-Maarri **1** 32

Luzzaschi, Luzzasco (circa 1545-1607),
Italian organist
Frescobaldi, Girolamo **6** 101-102
Gesualdo, Don Carlo **6** 287-288

LUZZATO, MOSES HAYYIM (1707-1747),
Jewish mystic and poet **10** 57-58

LUZZI, MONDINO DE' (circa
1265/70-1326), Italian anatomist **10** 58
Guy de Chauliac **7** 54

Lvov Brotherhoods School
see Collegium (Kiev)

Lvov, Prince Georgi Evgenievich
(1861-1925), Russian statesman
Kerensky, Aleksandr Fedorovich
8 516-517

LWOFF, ANDRÉ (1902-1994), French
microbiologist and geneticist **10** 58-59

Lwów (Lemburg or Lvov; city, Poland)
Köprülü, Ahmed **9** 84-85

LY, ABDOULAYE (born 1919), Senegalese
politician and historian **10** 60

LYAUTEY, LOUIS HUBERT GONZALVE
(1854-1934), French marshal and colonial administrator **10** 60-61

Lyceum movement (United States)
Emerson, Ralph Waldo **5** 278-280
Fuller, Sarah Margaret **6** 150-151
Holbrook, Josiah **7** 450-451

Lycidas (elegy; Milton)
Arnold, Matthew **1** 311-313
Milton, John **11** 43-46

Lycurgus (396?-323? B.C.), Athenian orator
Isocrates **8** 151
Xenophon **16** 418-420

LYDGATE, JOHN (circa 1370-1449/50),
English poet **10** 61-62
Gloucester, Duke of **6** 370-371
Skelton, John **14** 268-269

LYELL, SIR CHARLES (1797-1875), Scottish
geologist **10** 62-63
Adams, Henry Brooks **1** 45-47
Cuvier, Georges Léopold **4** 357-359
Darwin, Charles Robert **4** 397-399
Logan, William Edmond **9** 488-489
Wallace, Alfred Russel **16** 69-70

Lying Lover, The (play)
Steele, Richard **14** 407-409

Lymphatic system (anatomy)
Hunter, William **8** 48-49

Lynching (United States)
Alfaro, José Eloy **1** 144-145
Du Bois, William Edward Burghardt
5 116-118
Johnson, James Weldon **8** 304-305
Wells-Barnett, Ida. B. **16** 198-199
White, Walter Francis **16** 238-239
Work, Monroe **16** 388-389

LYND, HELEN MERRELL (1896-1982),
American sociologist and educator
10 63-64

LYND, ROBERT STAUGHTON
(1892-1970), American sociologist
10 64-65

LYND, STAUGHTON (born 1929), historian and peace militant **10** 65-66

LYNDSAY, SIR DAVID (circa 1485-1555),
Scottish poet and courtier **10** 66-67

LYON, MARY (1797-1849), American educator, religious leader, and women's
rights advocate **10** 67-69

Lyons (city; France)
Clement V **4** 101-102
Herriot, Édouard **7** 339-340

Lyons, Councils of
First (1245)
Frederick II **6** 79
Second (1274)
Bonaventure **2** 383-384
Michael VIII **11** 1-2

Lyons, Dame Enid Muriel (1897-1981),
Australian politician
Lyons, Joseph Aloysius **10** 69-70

LYONS, JOSEPH ALOYSIUS (1879-1939),
Australian statesman, prime minister
1932-39 **10** 69-70
Hughes, William Morris **8** 21-22
Menzies, Robert Gordon **10** 510-511
Scullin, James Henry **14** 73

Lyons University (France)
Cournot, Antoine Augustin **4** 273

Lyre (poems)
Palma, Ricardo **12** 77

Lyric Impulse, The (book)
Lewis, Cecil Day **9** 380

Lyric Year, The (anthology)
Millay, Edna St. Vincent **11** 24-25

Lyrical Ballads (book)
Coleridge, Samuel Taylor **4** 154-156
Wordsworth, William **16** 385-388

Lyrics of Earth (poems)
Lampman, Archibald **9** 180-181

Lyrics of Love and Sunshine (poems)
Dunbar, Paul Laurence **5** 141-142

Lyrics of Lowly Life (poems)
Dunbar, Paul Laurence **5** 141-142

Lyrisches Intermezzo (poems)
Heine, Heinrich **7** 259-260

Lys dans la vallée, Le (book)
Balzac, Honoré de **1** 478-480

Lys rouge, Le (novel)
France, Anatole **6** 39-40

LYSANDER (died 395 B.C.), Spartan military commander and statesman **10** 70
Agesilaus II **1** 79-80
Alcibiades **1** 119-120

LYSENKO, TROFIM DENISOVICH
(1898-1976), Soviet agronomist and geneticist **10** 71
Lamarck, Chevalier de **9** 171-173
Muller, Hermann Joseph **11** 238-239
Vavilov, Nikolai Ivanovich **15** 447-448

Lysias (died 162 B.C.), Syrian general and regent
Judas Maccabeus **8** 374-375

Lysimachus (361?-281 B.C.), Macedonian general
Alexander the Great **1** 137-141
Antigonus I **1** 248-249
Ptolemy I **12** 470-472

Seleucus I **14** 92-93

Lysis (dialogue)
Plato **12** 345-347

Lysistrata (play)
Aristophanes **1** 293-294

Lysogeny (bacteriology)
Lwoff, André **10** 58-59

Lysozyme (biochemistry)
Fleming, Alexander **5** 483-485
Florey, Howard Walter **5** 491-492

Lyttleton, George, 1st Baron (1709-1773), English politician and poet
Thomson, James **15** 199-200

Lytton, 1st Earl of (Edward Robert Bulwer Lytton; 1831-1891), English statesman
Roberts, Frederick Sleigh **13** 195-196

Lytton of Knebworth, 1st Baron
see Bulwer-Lytton, Edward

M

M. Quine (novel)
Bernanos, Georges **2** 206-207
Chaplin, Charles Spencer **3** 438-440

Ma al-Mutanabbi (book)
Husayn, Taha **8** 61-62]

Ma Fen (flourished 12th century), Chinese painter
Yüan, Mei **16** 479-480

Ma Jolie (painting)
Picasso, Pablo **12** 292-295

Ma Lin (flourished mid-13th century), Chinese painter
Ma Yüan **10** 379

Ma mère l'oye (musical composition)
Ravel, Maurice Joseph **13** 54-55

Ma Robert (ship)
Livingstone, David **9** 463-465

Maastricht, battle of (1748)
Saxe, Comte de **13** 507-508

Måbar rebellion (1334)
Muhammad bin Tughluq **11** 229

MABILLON, JEAN (1632-1707), French monk and historian **10** 72

MABINI, APOLINARIO (1864-1903), Filipino political philosopher **10** 72-73

Mabovitch, Golda
see Meir, Golda

MABUCHI, KAMO (1697-1769), Japanese writer and scholar **10** 73-74

Mac
see also Mc

MACAPAGAL, DIOSDADO P. (born 1910), Filipino statesman **10** 74-76
Marcos, Ferdinand **10** 240-242

MacArthur, Arthur (1845-1912), American general
MacArthur, Douglas **10** 76-78
Taft, William Howard **15** 78-81

MACARTHUR, DOUGLAS (1880-1964), American general **10** 76-78
associates

Eisenhower, Dwight David **5** 233-236
Kennedy, John Fitzgerald **8** 502-506
McCormick, Robert Rutherford **10** 401-402
Japan occupied (1949-1952)
Hirohito **7** 410-412
Tojo, Hideki **15** 254-256
Yamashita, Tomoyuki **16** 435-436
Yoshida, Shigeru **16** 464-465
Korean War
see Korean War
Pacific operations
Curtin, John Joseph **4** 348-349
King, Ernest Joseph **9** 17-18
Nimitz, Chester William **11** 395-396
Roosevelt, Franklin Delano **13** 277-280
Wainwright, Jonathan Mayhew **16** 45-46
see also World War II
Philippines and
Amorsolo, Fernando **1** 204
Osmeña, Sergio **12** 22-24
Rómulo, Carlos P. **13** 270-271
Roxas, Manuel **13** 331-332

MACARTHUR, JOHN (circa 1767-1834), Australian merchant, sheep breeder, and politician **10** 78
Bligh, William **2** 325-326

Macartney, George, 1st Earl (1737-1806), British diplomat
Qianlong **12** 502-505

MACAULAY, HERBERT (1864-1945), Nigerian politician **10** 78-79

MACAULAY, THOMAS BABINGTON (1st Baron Macaulay of Rothley; 1800-1859), English essayist, historian, and politician **10** 79-80
Booth, Charles **2** 400-401
Churchill, Winston Leonard Spencer **4** 51-53
Lessing, Gotthold Ephraim **9** 357-359
Macaulay, Herbert **10** 78-79
Maitland, Frederic William **10** 154-155
McMaster, John Bach **10** 426-427

Trevelyan, George Macaulay **15** 294-295
Turgenev, Ivan Sergeyevich **15** 345-348

Macaulay, Zachary (1768-1838), English philanthropist
Wilberforce, William **16** 269-270

MACBETH (died 1057), king of Scotland 1040-1057 **10** 81
Leo IX **9** 332
Malcolm III **10** 164-165

Macbeth (play; Shakespeare)
musical settings
Bloch, Ernest **2** 326-327
Fry, William Henry **6** 136-137
Strauss, Richard **14** 500-501
Verdi, Giuseppe Fortunino Francesco **15** 463-465
stage and films
Kurosawa, Akira **9** 135-137
Shakespeare, William **14** 142-145

MacBride, John (died 1916), Irish patriot
Yeats, William Butler **16** 445-447

Maccabean War (167-164 B.C.)
Antiochus IV **1** 250
Judas Maccabeus **8** 374-375

Macchiaioli (Italian art group)
Modigliani, Amedeo **11** 72-73

Macdermots of Ballycloran, The (novel)
Trollope, Anthony **15** 300-302

MACDONALD, DWIGHT (1906-1982), American editor, journalist, essayist, and critic **10** 81-83

MACDONALD, ELEANOR JOSEPHINE (born 1906), American epidemiologist **10** 83-84

Macdonald, Flora (1722-1790), Scottish Jacobite
Charles Edward Louis Philip Casimir Stuart **3** 466-467

MacDonald, James Edward Hervey (1878-1932), Canadian painter
Thomson, Tom **15** 202

MACDONALD, JAMES RAMSAY (1866-1937), British politician **10** 84-85
Labour government

Attlee, Clement Richard **1** 361-362
Baldwin, Stanley **1** 468-469
Chelmsford, Frederic John Napier Thesiger **3** 497
Henderson, Arthur **7** 277-278
national coalition
Chamberlain, Arthur Neville **3** 409-411
George V **6** 273-275

MACDONALD, SIR JOHN ALEXANDER (1815-1891), Canadian statesman **10** 85-87
associates
Cartier, George-Étienne **3** 342-343
Smith, Donald Alexander **14** 288-289
Cabinet
Galt, Alexander Tilloch **6** 190-191
Howe, Joseph **7** 534-535
Tilley, Samuel Leonard **15** 223-224
Tupper, Charles **15** 342-343
Canadian Pacific
Fleming, Sandford **5** 485-486
opponents
Brown, George **3** 35-36
Laurier, Wilfrid **9** 232-234
Mackenzie, Alexander **10** 104

Macdonald-Wright, Stanton (1890-1973), American painter
Benton, Thomas Hart **2** 178-179

MACDOWELL, EDWARD ALEXANDER (1861-1908), American pianist and composer **10** 87-88

Macedonia (region; Balkan peninsula)
as Roman province
Alaric **1** 101-102
Brutus, Marcus Junius **3** 79-80
Cicero, Marcus Tullius **4** 55-58
Demosthenes **4** 495-496
Flamininus, Titus Quinctius **5** 477
Leo I **9** 329-330
kings
Alexander the Great **1** 137-141
Antigonus I **1** 248-249
Philip II **12** 269-271
military leaders
Ptolemy I **12** 470-472
Seleucus I **14** 92-93
opposes Achaean League
Aratus **1** 273-274
Cleomenes III **4** 103-104
political leaders
Gligorov, Kiro **6** 367-369
see also Balkan Wars (1912-1913);Greece; Macedonian Wars; Ottoman Empire

Macedonian (ship)
Decatur, Stephen **4** 448-449

Macedonian dynasty (Byzantine Empire; ruled 867-1056)
Basil I **2** 49-50
Basil II **2** 50-51
Zoë **16** 524-525

Macedonian dynasty (Egypt)
see alsoPtolemaic dynasty

Macedonian Wars (200-194; 171-168 B.C.)
Flamininus, Titus Quinctius **5** 477
Polybios **12** 384-385

MACEO, ANTONIO (1845-1896), Cuban general and patriot **10** 88-90
Gómez, Máximo **6** 418-419
Martí, José **10** 285-286
Menocal, Mario Garcia **10** 506-507

Macer, Aemilius (flourished 1st century B.C.), Augustan poet of Verona
Ovid **12** 34-36

MacFlecknoe (play)
Dryden, John **5** 106-107

MacGahan, Januarius Aloysius (1844-1878), American war correspondent
Bennett, James Gordon Jr. **2** 169-170

MacGrath, Leueen (born 1919), American actress
Kaufman, George S. **8** 457-458

MACH, ERNST (1838-1916), Austrian physicist **10** 90-91
Boltzmann, Ludwig **2** 379-380
Schlick, Friedrich Albert Moritz **14** 16-17
Schrödinger, Erwin **14** 31-33

MACHADO DE ASSIS, JOAQUIM MARIA (1839-1908), Brazilian novelist **10** 91-92

MACHADO Y MORALES, GERARDO (1871-1939), Cuban general and president **10** 92-93
Batista y Zaldívar, Fulgencio **2** 57-58
Grau San Martin, Ramón **6** 499-500
Menocal, Mario Garcia **10** 506-507

MACHAUT, GUILLAUME DE (circa 1300-1377), French composer and poet **10** 93-94
Landini, Francesco **9** 185-186
Vitry, Philippe de **16** 2

MACHEL, SAMORA MOISES (1933-1986), socialist revolutionary and first president of Mozambique **10** 94-96

MACHIAVELLI, NICCOLÒ (1469-1527), Italian author and statesman **10** 97-99
Castiglione, Baldassare **3** 360-361
Comines, Philippe de **4** 181
Ferdinand V **5** 417-418
Frederick II **6** 81-84
Guicciardini, Francesco **7** 32-33
Harrington, James **7** 166-167
Marlowe, Christopher **10** 272-274
Meinecke, Friedrich **10** 460-461

Machine gun
seeWeapons and explosives

Machine politics
seePolitical machines (United States)

Machine-wreckers, The (play)
Toller, Ernst **15** 261

Macht von Liebe, Die (opera)
Weber, Carl Maria Friedrich Ernst von **16** 156-157

MacINTYRE, ALASDAIR CHALMERS (born 1929), Scottish-born philosopher and ethicist **10** 99-100

MACIVER, ROBERT MORRISON (1882-1970), Scottish-American sociologist, political philosopher, and educator **10** 100-101

Mack the Knife (song)
Weill, Kurt **16** 174-175

Mackail, J.W. (1859-1945), British classical scholar
Morris, William **11** 187-188

Mackay, John Henry (1864-1933), Scottish writer
Stirner, Max **14** 459-460

MACKAY, JOHN WILLIAM (1831-1902), American miner and business leader **10** 101-102
Bennett, James Gordon Jr. **2** 169-170

MACKE, AUGUST (1887-1914), Expressionist painter **10** 102-103
Kandinsky, Wassily **8** 420-422
Marc, Franz **10** 231

Mackensen, August von (1849-1945), German army officer
Ferdinand **5** 413-414

MACKENZIE, ALEXANDER (1822-1892), Scottish-born Canadian statesman, prime minister 1873-1878 **10** 104
Brown, George **3** 35-36
Fleming, Sandford **5** 485-486
Laurier, Wilfrid **9** 232-234

Mackenzie, Henry (1745-1831), Scottish author
Romney, George **13** 269-270

Mackenzie River (Canada)
Mackenzie, Alexander **10** 103-104

MACKENZIE, SIR ALEXANDER (circa 1764-1820), Scottish explorer, fur trader, and businessman **10** 103-104

MACKENZIE, WILLIAM LYON (1795-1861), Scottish-born Canadian journalist, politician, and rebel **10** 104-106
Baldwin, Robert **1** 466-468
Durham, 1st Earl of **5** 161-162
Moodie, Susanna **11** 140-141
Ryerson, Adolphus Egerton **13** 392-393

Mackenzie King, William Lyon
see King, William Lyon Mackenzie

MACKILLOP, MARY (1842-1909), first Australian candidate for sainthood in the Roman Catholic Church and foundress of the Sisters of Saint Joseph of the Sacred Heart **10** 106-107

MACKINTOSH, CHARLES RENNIE (1868-1928), Scottish artist, architect, and

interior/furniture/textile designer
10 107-108

Maclane-Ocampo Treaty (1859)
Juárez, Benito **8** 369-372
Lerdo de Tejada, Miguel **9** 351-352

Maclaurin, Colin (1698-1746), Scottish
mathematician
Cauchy, Augustin Louis **3** 378-380
Taylor, Brook **15** 121-122

MACLEAN, GEORGE (1801-1847), Scottish
soldier and agent of British expansion
10 108-109

Maclean, John (1771-1814), American
chemist
Silliman, Benjamin **14** 229-230

Maclehose, Agnes (née Craig; 1759-1781),
Scottish physician's daughter, Burns'
Clarinda
Burns, Robert **3** 155-156

MACLEISH, ARCHIBALD (born 1892),
American poet, playwright, and public
official **10** 109-110
Benét, Stephen Vincent **2** 157-158
Luce, Henry Robinson **10** 23-24

MACLENNAN, HUGH (1907-1990), Canadian novelist, essayist, and academic
10 110-111

Macleod, John James Rickard (1876-1935),
Scottish physiologist
Banting, Frederick Grant **1** 493-494

**MacMahon, Comte Marie Edme Patrice
Maurice de** (1808-1893), French presi-
dent 1873-1879
Gambetta, Léon **6** 198-199
Simon, Jules François **14** 237-238

MACMILLAN, DONALD BAXTER
(1874-1970), American explorer and scientist **10** 111-112
Byrd, Richard Evelyn **3** 186-187

MACMILLAN, HAROLD (born 1894),
British statesman **10** 112-113
Eden, Anthony **5** 204-205
Elizabeth II **5** 266-269

MacMonnies, Frederick William
(1863-1937), American sculptor
White, Stanford **16** 235-236

MACNEICE, LOUIS (1907-1964), British
poet **10** 113-114
Auden, Wystan Hugh **1** 364-366

MACON, NATHANIEL (1758-1837), American statesman **10** 114-115

Macondo (fictional town)
García Márquez, Gabriel **6** 208-209

MACQUARIE, LACHLAN (1762-1824),
British officer, governor of New South
Wales 1810-1822 **10** 115-116
Bigge, John Thomas **2** 272

MACQUARRIE, JOHN (born 1919), Anglican theologian **10** 116-117

Macque, Jean de (flourished 16th-17th
century), Flemish composer
Rossi, Luigi **13** 310-311

Macready, William C. (1793-1873), English
actor
Browning, Robert **3** 53-55
Cushman, Charlotte **4** 354-355
Forrest, Edwin **6** 11-12

Macrinus, Marcus Opelius (164-218),
Roman emperor 217-218
Caracalla **3** 281-282

Mac-Robertson Land (Antarctica)
Mawson, Douglas **10** 354-355

Macrocosm-microcosm theory (cosmology)
Paracelsus, Philippus Aureolus **12** 91-93

Macy, Mrs. John Albert
*see*Sullivan, Anne Mansfield

Macy's (department store; New York City)
Straus, Isidor **14** 496

Mad Dogs and Englishmen (song)
Coward, Noel **4** 279-280

Mad Love (book)
Breton, André **2** 519-520

Mad Parliament (England; 1258)
Henry III **7** 290-292
Montfort, Simon de **11** 132-133

Mad World My Masters, A (play)
Middleton, Thomas **11** 8-9

Madam Butterfly (opera and play)
Belasco, David **2** 124-125
Puccini, Giacomo **12** 474-476

Madame Bovary (novel)
Flaubert, Gustave **5** 480-482

Madame Charpentier and her Children
(painting)
Renoir, Pierre Auguste **13** 101-102

Madame Chrysanthème (book)
Loti, Pierre **9** 519-520

Madame de Chamblay (book)
Dumas, Alexandre **5** 136-138

Madame Delphine (novelette)
Cable, George Washington **3** 198-199

Madame d'Haussonville
Ingres, Jean Auguste Dominique
8 121-123

Madame Dorothea (novel)
Undset, Sigrid **15** 388-389

Madame Gervaisais (novel)
Goncourt, Edmond de and Jules de
6 426-427

Madame Rivière (painting)
Ingres, Jean Auguste Dominique
8 121-123

Madame Sériziat ... (painting)
David, Jacques Louis **4** 407-409

Madame X (painting)
Sargent, John Singer **13** 481-482

Made White in the Bloud of the Lambe
(book)
Cotton, John **4** 263-265

Madeira (island group; eastern Atlantic
Ocean)
Cook, James **4** 214-215
Henry the Navigator **7** 305-306

Madeleine of France (died 1538), queen of
James V of Scotland 1537-1538
Ronsard, Pierre de **13** 271-273

Madelin, Louis (1871-1956), French historian
Poincaré, Raymond **12** 366-368

Madeline (literary character)
Keats, John **8** 470-472

Mademoiselle de Belle-Isle (play)
Dumas, Alexandre **5** 136-138

Mademoiselle Pogany (sculpture series)
Brancusi, Constantin **2** 494-496

Maderistas (Mexican revolutionary group)
Cárdenas, Lázaro **3** 286-287
Villa, Pancho **15** 495-496
Zapata, Emiliano **16** 489-490

Maderna, Bruno (born 1920), Italian composer
Nono, Luigi **11** 420-421

MADERNO, CARLO (1556-1629), Italian
architect **10** 117-118
Borromini, Francesco **2** 424-425

MADERO, FRANCISCO INDALECIO
(1873-1913), Mexican politician, presi-
dent 1911-13 **10** 118-119
associates
Azuela, Mariano **1** 402
Villa, Pancho **15** 495-496
opponents
Díaz, José de la Cruz Porfirio
4 534-536
Huerta, Victoriano **8** 13-14
Zapata, Emiliano **16** 489-490
supporters
Calles, Plutarco Elías **3** 234-235
Carranza, Venustiano **3** 321-322
Obregón, Álvaro **11** 458-459
Vasconcelos, José **15** 443-444

Madhava Rao I (1754-1772), peshwa of the
Marathas 1761-1772
Haidar Ali **7** 65-66

Madheart (play)
Baraka, Imamu Amiri **1** 498-499

Madinah, al-
see Medina

Madinat as-Salem
see Baghdad

Madison (ship)
Pike, Zebulon **12** 302-304

MADISON, DOLLY (wife of James Madi-
son, born Dorothea Payne; 1768-1849),
American First Lady **10** 119-121
Johnson, Earvin Jr. **8** 297-299

MADISON, JAMES (1751-1836), American
statesman, president 1809-1817
10 121-123
associates
Carroll, John **3** 331-332

Jefferson, Thomas **8** 238-241
Livingston, Robert R. **9** 462-463
Pendleton, Edmund **12** 197-198
Randolph, Edmund **13** 29-30
Scott, Winfield **14** 70-71
Taylor, John **15** 126
Cabinet
Crawford, William Harris **4** 299-300
Gallatin, Albert **6** 183-184
Monroe, James **11** 111-113
Federalist papers
Hamilton, Alexander **7** 95-98
Jay, John **8** 230-232
opponents
Ames, Fisher **1** 199-200
Clinton, DeWitt **4** 112-113
Henry, Patrick **7** 309-311
Morris, Gouverneur **11** 182-183
Pickering, Timothy **12** 298-299
political appointments
Adams, John Quincy **1** 52-54
Story, Joseph **14** 480-481
Taylor, Zachary **15** 128-130
vice presidents
Clinton, George **4** 113-114
Gerry, Elbridge **6** 282-283

Madison, John Roderigo
see Dos Passos, John

Madison Square Garden (New York City)
Barnum, Phineas Taylor **2** 13-15
White, Stanford **16** 235-236

Madison Square Theater (New York City)
Belasco, David **2** 124-125

Madiun revolt (Indonesia; 1926)
Sukarno **15** 18-20

Madman's Diary, A (story)
Lu Hsün **10** 35-37

MADONNA (Madonna Louise Veronica Ciccone, born 1958), American singer and actress **10** 123-125

Madonna ... (engraving)
Mantegna, Andrea **10** 215-216

Madonna ... (painting)
Andrea del Sarto **1** 224-225
Angelico **1** 235-236
Bellini, Giovanni **2** 137-138
Caravaggio **3** 282-284
Carracci **3** 319-321
Cimabue **4** 60-61
Correggio **4** 249-251
Cranach, Lucas the Elder **4** 289-290
Duccio di Buoninsegna **5** 121-122
Eyck, Hubert and Jan van **5** 352-354
Gentile da Fabriano **6** 266-267
Ghirlandaio, Domenico **6** 292-293
Giorgione **6** 340-341
Giotto **6** 342-345
Greco **6** 511-514
Holbein, Hans the Younger **7** 449-450
Lippi, Filippo **9** 439
Lochner, Stephan **9** 475
Lorenzetti, Pietro and Ambrogio
9 517-518

Lorenzetti, Pietro and Ambrogio
9 517-518
Mantegna, Andrea **10** 215-216
Martini, Simone **10** 298-299
Masaccio **10** 312-313
Morales, Luis de **11** 150
Parmigianino **12** 117
Perugino **12** 245-246
Piero della Francesca **12** 301-302
Pisanello **12** 323-324
Poussin, Nicolas **12** 418-420
Rubens, Peter Paul **13** 339-342
Sassetta **13** 492
Schongauer, Martin **14** 26-28
Titian **15** 242-244
Tura, Cosimo **15** 343-344
Van Dyck, Anthony **15** 423-425
Veneziano, Domenico **15** 459-460

Madonna ... (sculpture)
Donatello **5** 55-56
Luca della Robbia **10** 19-20
Michelangelo Buonarroti **11** 2-5
Moore, Henry **11** 146-148
Pisano, Giovanni **12** 324-325
Sansovino, Jacopo **13** 470-471

Madonna delle Carceri (church; Prato, Italy)
Sangallo family **13** 464-466

Madonna di Campagna (church; near Verona, Italy)
Sanmicheli, Michele **13** 469-470

Madonna di San Biagio (church; Montepulciano, Italy)
Sangallo family **13** 464-466

Madras (province; India)
Clive, Robert **4** 119-120
Dupleix **5** 153

Madras system (education)
Bell, Andrew **2** 131-132

Madrid (city; Spain)
Calderón, Pedro **3** 221-222
Tiepolo, Giovanni Battista **15** 219-220
Wellington, 1st Duke of **16** 193-195

Madrid, Treaty of (1526)
Charles V **3** 457-459

Madrid, University of
Altamira Y Crevea, Rafael **1** 179

Madrid 36 to Spain in Arms (film)
Buñuel, Luis **3** 127-128

Madrigal (music)
English
Marenzio, Luca **10** 248
Morley, Thomas **11** 179-180
Franco-Flemish
Lassus, Roland de **9** 216-218
German
Schütz, Heinrich **14** 48-49
Italian (14th century)
Landini, Francesco **9** 185-186
Italian (16th century)
Marenzio, Luca **10** 248
Merulo, Claudio **10** 525-526

Monteverdi, Claudio Giovanni
Antonio **11** 126-128
Palestrina, Giovanni Pierluigi da
12 70-72
Willaert, Adrian **16** 287-288
Zarlino, Gioseffo **16** 490-491
Italian (16th-17th century)
Frescobaldi, Girolamo **6** 101-102
Gesualdo, Don Carlo **6** 287-288
Malipiero, Gian Francesco **10** 171

Madrigal (poem)
Hugo, Victor Marie **8** 22-25
Tasso, Torquato **15** 114-116

Madrigaux (book)
Mallarmé, Stéphane **10** 172-173

Maecenas, Gaius Cilnius (70?-8 B.C.), Roman statesman
Horace **7** 500-503
Livy **9** 465-467
Ovid **12** 34-36
Virgil **15** 507-510

Maelwael, Pol, Herman, and Jehanequin
see Limbourg Brothers

Maestà (painting)
Lorenzetti, Pietro and Ambrogio
9 517-518

Maestà (painting; Duccio)
Duccio di Buoninsegna **5** 121-122
Giotto **6** 342-345
Lorenzetti, Pietro and Ambrogio
9 517-518
Martini, Simone **10** 298-299

Maestro, El (musical collection)
Milán, Luis **11** 15-16

MAETERLINCK, COUNT MAURICE
(1863-1949), Belgian poet, dramatist, and essayist **10** 125-126
Debussy, Achille Claude **4** 445-447
Grillparzer, Franz **6** 546-547
Schoenberg, Arnold **14** 24-26
Sibelius, Jean Julius Christian
14 211-212
Stanislavsky, Constantin **14** 398-399
Strindberg, August **14** 509-511
Vallejo, César Abraham **15** 408-409

Maffei, Francesco Scipione di (1675-1755), Italian author
Alfieri, Vittoria **1** 145-146

Maga, Hubert (born 1916), Dahomeyan politician
Apithy, Sourou Migan **1** 259-260

Magadha (region; India)
Chandragupta Maurya **3** 426

Magana Jari Ce (literary collection)
Imam, Alhadji Abubakar **8** 114-115

Magdala (town; Ethiopia)
Tewodros II **15** 158-159

Magdalen (painting)
Greco **6** 511-514
Titian **15** 242-244

Magdalena (department; Colombia)
Isaacs, Jorge **8** 144

Magdalena River (Colombia)
Quesada, Gonzalo Jiménez de
12 509-510

Magdalo (Philippines rebels)
Bonifacio, Andres **2** 393-394

Magdeburg (city and province; Germany)
Frederick William **6** 85-86
Gustavus II **7** 43-45

Magdeburg hemispheres (physics)
Guericke, Otto Von **7** 27-28

Magdiwang (Philippines rebels)
Bonifacio, Andres **2** 393-394

MAGELLAN, FERDINAND (1480-1521),
Portuguese explorer **10** 126-127
Cabot, Sebastian **3** 200-201
Drake, Francis **5** 94-96

Magellan, Strait of (southern South America)
Drake, Francis **5** 94-96
Magellan, Ferdinand **10** 126-127
Schouten, William Cornelius **14** 31

Magenta and Blue (painting)
Hofmann, Hans **7** 442-443

Maggie (novel)
Crane, Stephen **4** 293-295

Maggy (sculpture)
Duchamp-Villon, Raymond **5** 123

Maghan, Mansa (ruled 1337-1341), ruler of
Mali Empire in West Africa
Musa Mansa **11** 266

Maghreb
see Morocco

Magians (priestly class; ancient Iran)
Zoroaster **16** 528-530

Magic (anthropology)
Bloch, Marc **2** 332-333
Frazer, James George **6** 76
Hugo, Victor Marie **8** 22-25
Porta, Giambattista della **12** 403-404
Sarton, George **13** 490-491
Tylor, Edward Burnett **15** 372-373

Magic Bird (sculpture cycle)
Brancusi, Constantin **2** 494-496

Magic Flute, The (opera; Mozart)
Kokoschka, Oskar **9** 75-76
Mozart, Wolfgang Amadeus
11 218-221
Schinkel, Karl Friedrich **14** 8
Tippett, Michael Kemp **15** 234-235

Magic Mountain, The (novel)
Mann, Thomas **10** 204-207

Magician (novel)
Maugham, William Somerset
10 344-345

Magician, The (film)
Bergman, Ernst Ingmar **2** 190-191

Magician of Lublin, The (novel)
Singer, Isaac Bashevis **14** 249-250

Mágico prodigioso, El (play)
Calderón, Pedro **3** 221-222

Maginot Line (France)
Pétain, Henri Philippe **12** 250-252
Rundstedt, Karl Rudolf Gerd Von
13 363-364

Magloire, Paul (born 1907), Haitian politician, president 1950-1956
Duvalier, François **5** 165-166

Magna Carta (Aragon)
*see*General Privilege (1283)

Magna Carta (England; 1215)
Grosseteste, Robert **7** 15
Henry III **7** 290-292
John **8** 274-275

Magnaghi, Alberto (1875-1945),Italian historian
Vespucci, Amerigo **15** 476-478

Magnalia Christi Americana (book)
Bradstreet, Anne Dudley **2** 486-487
Mather, Cotton **10** 330-332

MAGNASCO, ALESSANDRO (1667-1749),
Italian painter **10** 127-128

Magnelli, Alberto (born 1888), Italian
painter
Kandinsky, Wassily **8** 420-422

Magnesia, battle of (190 B.C.)
Antiochus III **1** 249-250
Hannibal Barca **7** 128-130
Scipio Africanus Major, Publius Cornelius **14** 61-62

Magnesium (element—chemistry)
Davy, Humphry **4** 426-427

Magnet, The (novel)
Gorky, Maxim **6** 458-460

Magnetic fields (physics)
Rabi, Isidor Isaac **12** 526-527

Magnetic resonance accelerator
see Cyclotron

Magnetic storms (geophysics)
Chapman, Sydney **3** 441

Magnetism (physics)
and cryogenics
Kapitsa, Pyotr Leonidovich
8 433-435
and electric currents
Ampère, André Marie **1** 205-206
Cardano, Geronimo **3** 285-286
Coulomb, Charles Augustin de
4 266-267
Faraday, Michael **5** 380
Henry, Joseph **7** 307-308
Maxwell, James Clerk **10** 361-364
Rowland, Henry Augustus
13 330-331
and sunspots
Hale, George Ellery **7** 72-74
medieval research
Peregrinus, Petrus **12** 208
terrestrial
Ampère, André Marie **1** 205-206
Baffin, William **1** 435-436
Gilbert, William **6** 313-314
Halley, Edmund **7** 88-89

Magnetohydrodynamics (physics)
Elsasser, Walter Maurice **5** 277-278

Magnhild (novel)
Bjørnson, Bjørnstjerne **2** 299-300

Magnificat (music)
Buxtehude, Dietrich **3** 185-186
Cabezón, Antonio **3** 197-198
Dunstable, John **5** 150-151
Gombert, Nicolas **6** 416-417
Goudimel, Claude **6** 466
Lassus, Roland de **9** 216-218
Le Jeune, Claude **9** 314-315
Palestrina, Giovanni Pierluigi da
12 70-72
Tallis, Thomas **15** 91
Victoria, Tomás Luis de **15** 487-488

Magnificence (play)
Skelton, John **14** 268-269

Magnificent Ambersons, The (novel)
Tarkington, Newton Booth **15** 109

Magnum Photo Agency
Capa, Robert **3** 269-271

Magnus (died 1047), king of Norway
Edward the Confessor **5** 218-219
Harold III **7** 163

Magnus, Cnaeus Pompeius
*see*Pompey

Magnus liber organi (musical collection ;
Léonin)
Léonin **9** 343-344
Pérotin **12** 231-232

Magog (Old Testament figure)
Ezekiel **5** 355-356

Magongo, battle of (South Africa; 1840)
Dingane **5** 14-15

Magoon, Charles Edward (1861-1920),
American governor of Cuba 1906-1909
Estrada Palma, Tomás **5** 326-327

Magpie on the Gallows (painting)
Bruegel, Pieter the Elder **3** 65-67

MAGRITTE, RENÉ (1890-1967), Surrealist
painter **10** 128-130

MAGSAYSAY, RAMON (1907-1957),
Philippine statesman, president
1953-1957 **10** 130-131
Quirino, Elpidio **12** 519-520
Recto, Claro M. **13** 69-70
Rómulo, Carlos P. **13** 270-271

Maguire, Mary Gunning (1887?-1957),
Irish critic and short-story writer
Colum, Padraic **4** 174-175

Magyar music
*see*Hungarian music

Magus, The (novel)
Fowles, John **6** 33-35

Magyars (Hungary)
Henry I **7** 285-286
see also Hungary

Mahabharata (Hindu epic)
Kalidasa **8** 414-415

Rajagopalachari, Chakravarti **13** 6-7

Mahadanapati (Buddhism)
Sui Wen-ti **15** 16-18

Mahagonny (opera)
see*Rise and Fall of the City of Mahagonny*

Mahagonny (play and opera)
Brecht, Bertolt **2** 512-514
Weill, Kurt **16** 174-175

MAHAN, ALFRED THAYER (1840-1914), American naval historian and strategist **10** 131-132

Maharashtra (state; India)
Pandit, Vijaya Lakshmi **12** 83-84
Śivajī **14** 266-267

MAHARISHI MAHESH YOGI (born 1911?), Indian guru and founder of the Transcendental Meditation movement **10** 132-133

Mahars (caste; India)
Ambedkar, Bhimrao Ramji **1** 190-191

MAHATHIR MOHAMAD (born 1925), prime minister of Malaysia **10** 134-135

Mahayana Buddhism (religion)
Buddha **3** 97-101
K'ang Yu-wei **8** 426-428
Kukai **9** 124-125
Kumarajiva **9** 127

Mahdi, Abd al-Rahman al- (born 1915), Sudanese religious leader, head of the Madhist movement
Khalil, Sayyid Abdullah **8** 531-532

Mahdi, Mohammed al- (died 785), Abbasid caliph 775-785
Harun al-Rashid **7** 188

MAHDI, THE (Mohammed Ahmed; circa 1844-1885), Islamic reformer and Sudanese military leader **10** 137-138
Gordon, Charles George **6** 448-449
Johannes IV **8** 272-273
see also Mahdists

Mahdists (Moslem sect; Sudan)
Azhari, Sayyid Ismail al- **1** 399-401
Gordon, Charles George **6** 448-449
Khalil, Sayyid Abdullah **8** 531-532
Kitchener, Horatio Herbert **9** 45-46
Menelik II **10** 495-497

MAHENDRA, KING (Bir Bikram Shah Dev; 1920-1972), ninth Shah dynasty ruler of Nepal (1955-1972) **10** 138-139

MAHERERO, SAMUEL (ca. 1854-1923), Supreme Chief of the Herero naion in southwest Africa **10** 139-142

MAHFUZ, NAJIB (born 1912), Egyptian novelist **10** 142-144

Mahler, Alma
see Werfel, Alma Mahler (Gropius)

MAHLER, GUSTAV (1860-1911), Bohemian-born composer and conductor **10** 144-145
Berio, Luciano **2** 194-195
Bernstein, Leonard **2** 218-219
Bruckner, Joseph Anton **3** 64-65

Mann, Thomas **10** 204-207
Schoenberg, Arnold **14** 24-26
Wagner, Richard **16** 40-43
Webern, Anton **16** 160-162

MAHMUD II (1785-1839), Ottoman sultan 1808-1839 **10** 145-147
Ibrahim Pasha **8** 97-98
Nesselrode, Karl Robert **11** 348-349
Selim III **14** 95-96

MAHMUD OF GHAZNI (971-1030); Ghaznavid sultan in Afghanistan **10** 147
Biruni, Abu Rayhan al- **2** 284-285
Firdausi **5** 451-452

Mahomet
see also Mohammed; Muhammad

Mahomet (play)
Goethe, Johann Wolfgang von **6** 388-391
Voltaire **16** 14-16

MAHONE, WILLIAM (1826-1895), American politician and Confederate general **10** 147-148

Mahoning Baptist Association (Ohio)
Campbell, Alexander **3** 249-250

Mahony, Richard (literary character)
Richardson, Henry Handel **13** 139

Mahr, Anna (literary character)
Hauptmann, Gerhart Johann Robert **7** 199-201

Mahrattas
see Marathas

Ma-Hsia school (Chinese art)
Hsia Kuei **8** 4-5
Ma Yüan **10** 379

Maiano, Benedetto da (1442-1497), Italian sculptor and architect
Sangallo family **13** 464-466
da Settignano, Desiderio **4** 509

Maid in Waiting (novel)
Galsworthy, John **6** 189-190

Maid Marian (novel)
Peacock, Thomas Love **12** 169

Maiden in the Tower, The (opera)
Sibelius, Jean Julius Christian **14** 211-212

Maidenhead bridge (England)
Brunel, Isambard Kingdom **3** 69-70

Maidenhood (poem)
Longfellow, Henry Wadsworth **9** 499-500

Maids, The (play)
Genet, Jean **6** 262-263

Maids of Honor, The (painting)
Velázquez, Diego Rodríguez de Silva y **15** 454-456

Maid's Tragedy, The (play)
Beaumont, Francis **2** 95

Maigret, Inspector (literary character)
Simenon, Georges **14** 233-234

MAILER, NORMAN KINGSLEY (born 1923), American author, producer, and director **10** 148-150
Dos Passos, John Roderigo **5** 69-71

MAILLOL, ARISTIDE (1861-1944), French sculptor **10** 150-151
Duchamp-Villon, Raymond **5** 123
Lachaise, Gaston **9** 147
Vuillard, Jean Édouard **16** 36

Mail-order merchandising
Rosenwald, Julius **13** 293
Stewart, Alexander Turney **14** 448-449
Ward, Aaron Montgomery **16** 112

MAIMONIDES (1135-1204), Jewish philosopher **10** 151-152
Abravanel, Isaac ben Judah **1** 31
Caro, Joseph ben Ephraim **3** 316-317
Eckhart, Johann **5** 200-201
Krochmal, Nachman Kohen **9** 104-105
Levi ben Gershon **9** 363-364
Mendelssohn, Moses **10** 488-489
Nahmanides **11** 293-294

Maimonides Hospital (San Francisco)
Mendelsohn, Erich **10** 488

Main Street (novel)
Lewis, Harry Sinclair **9** 385-387

Main Traveled Roads (stories)
Garland, Hannibal Hamlin **6** 217-218

Mainardi, Bastiano (1460?-1513), Italian painter
Ghirlandaio, Domenico **6** 292-293

Maine (former province; France)
John **8** 274-275

Maine (ship)
Gómez, Máximo **6** 418-419

Maine (state; United States)
boundary dispute
Gallatin, Albert **6** 183-184
Scott, Winfield **14** 70-71
Sydenham, Thomas **15** 59-60
Tyler, John **15** 368-369
see also Webster-Ashburton Treaty (1842)
colonial
Gorges, Ferdinando **6** 455-456
Pepperell, William **12** 206-207
political leaders
Blaine, James Gillespie **2** 312-313
Dow, Neal **5** 89-90
Mitchell, George John **11** 56-58
Muskie, Edmund Sixtus **11** 269-271
Reed, Thomas Brackett **13** 77
Smith, Margaret Chase **14** 299-300

MAINE, SIR HENRY JAMES SUMNER (1822-1888), English legal historian and historical anthropologist **10** 152

Maine Chance Stables
Arden, Elizabeth **1** 281-282

Maine Law (1884)
Dow, Neal **5** 89-90

Maine Woods, The (essays)
Thoreau, Henry David **15** 203-205

Maintenon, Françoise d'Aubigné, Marquise de (1635-1719), French author, second wife of Louis XIV
  Fénelon, François de Salignac de la Mothe **5** 410-411
  Le Brun, Charles **9** 269-270
  Le Nôtre, André **9** 328-329
  Louis XIV **9** 531-533
  Racine, Jean Baptiste **12** 532-535

Mainwaring, John (1735-1807), English music historian
  Corelli, Arcangelo **4** 230-231

Maio (island; Cape Verde group)
  Cadamosto, Alvise da **3** 206-207

Mair, John
  see Major, John

Maison du berger, La (poem; Vigny)
  Hugo, Victor Marie **8** 22-25
  Vigny, Comte de **15** 494-495

Maison Jaoul (Neuilly, France)
  Le Corbusier **9** 274-275

MAISONEUVE, SIEUR DE (Paul de Chomedey; 1612-1676), French explorer and colonizer in Canada **10** 153
  Bourgeoys, Marguerite **2** 452-453

Maisons-Lafitte (Seine-et-Oise, France)
  Mansart, François **10** 211
  Mansart, Jules Hardouin **10** 212

MAISTRE, JOSEPH DE (1753-1821), French political philosopher **10** 153-154

MAITLAND, FREDERIC WILLIAM (1850-1906), English historian, lawyer, and legal scholar **10** 154-155
  Clapham, John Harold **4** 71
  Gierke, Otto von **6** 311-312
  Vinogradoff, Paul Gavrilovitch **15** 503

Maitland, John
  see Lauderdale, 1st Duke of

Maitland, Sir Peregrine (1777-1854), English soldier and colonial administrator
  Gourlay, Robert **6** 474
  Strachan, John **14** 486-487

Maîtres sonneurs, Les (novel)
  Sand, George **13** 459-461

Maitreya (Buddhism)
  Tao-an **15** 103-104

Maitri (Buddhism)
  Buddha **3** 97-101

Maiwand (city; Afghanistan)
  Roberts, Frederick Sleigh **13** 195-196

Majapahit (Javanese king.)
  Kublai Khan **9** 115-118

Major Barbara (play)
  Shaw, George.Bernard **14** 163-164

Major, John (1470-1550), Scottish theologian
  Douglas, Gavin **5** 77-78

MAJOR, JOHN (born 1943), British prime minister **10** 155-157
  appointees
    Clarke, Kenneth Harry **4** 85-87

Heseltine, Michael **7 359-361
  Hurd, Douglas **8** 52-55

Majorian (died 461), Roman emperor 457-461
  Gaiseric **6** 172
  Ricimer, Flavius **13** 151-152

Majors and Minors (poems)
  Dunbar, Paul Laurence **5** 141-142

Majuba Hill, battle of (1881)
  Allenby, Edmund Henry Hynman **1** 171-172
  Kruger, Stephanus Johannes Paulus **9** 108-109

Makar Chudra (story)
  Gorky, Maxim **6** 458-460

MAKARIOS III (Michael Christodoulou Mouskos; 1913-1977), archbishop and ethnarch of the Orthodox Church of Cyprus and first president of the Republic of Cyprus (1959-1977) **10** 157-158

Make Bright the Arrows (book)
  Millay, Edna St. Vincent **11** 24-25

MAKEMIE, FRANCIS (1658-1708), Irish-born Presbyterian missionary **10** 158-159

Makhpiyaluta
  see Red Cloud

MAKI, FUMIHIKO (born 1928), Japanese architect **10** 159-161

MAKIBI, KIBI-NO (693-775), Japanese courtier and statesman **10** 161

Makimono (scrolls)
  Sesshu, Toya **14** 116-117

Makin' Whoopee (song)
  Cantor, Eddie **3** 264-265

Making a Living (film)
  Chaplin, Charles Spencer **3** 438-440

Making of Americans, The (novel)
  Stein, Gertrude **14** 414-415

Making of the President-1960, The (book)
  White, T. H. **16** 236-237

Makino, Count Nobuaki (1861-1949), Japanese statesman
  Hirohito **7** 410-412
  Yoshida, Shigeru **16** 464-465

Makioka Sisters, The (novel)
  Tanizaki, Junichiro **15** 101-102

Makoko Treaty (1882)
  Brazza, Pierre Paul François Camille Savorgnan de **2** 509-510

MÄKONNEN ENDALKAČÄW (1892-1963), Ethiopian writer and official **10** 161-162

Makropoulos Case, The (opera)
  Janáček, Leoš **8** 219

Maksim Gorkii (airplane)
  Tupolev, Andrei Nikolaevich **15** 341-342

Mala yerba (novel)
  Azuela, Mariano **1** 402

Malabar (district; India)
  Camoëns, Luis Vaz de **3** 247-249

Malacca
  see Malaysia

Malacca, Strait of (Indonesia-Malaysia)
  Albuquerque, Afonso de **1** 118-119

Malade imaginaire, Le (play; Molière)
  Charpentier, Marc Antoine **3** 471-472
  Molière **11** 86-88

MALAMUD, BERNARD (1914-1986), American novelist and short-story writer **10** 162-163

MALAN, DANIEL FRANCOIS (1874-1959), South African pastor, journalist, and prime minister 1948-1954 **10** 163-164
  Hertzog, James Barry Munnik **7** 347-348
  Khama, Seretse M. **8** 532-533
  Verwoerd, Hendrik Frensch **15** 472-473
  Vorster, Balthazar Johannes **16** 30-32

Malancha (poems)
  Das, Chitta Ranjan **4** 401-402

Malaprop, Mrs. (literary character)
  Sheridan, Richard Brinsley **14** 183-184

Malaria (medicine)
  control
    Cruz, Oswaldo Gonçalves **4** 328-329
    Duvalier, François **5** 165-166
    Müller, Paul Hermann **11** 241-242
  treatment
    Baikie, William Balfour **1** 440
    Domagk, Gerhard Johannes Paul **5** 48-50
    Ehrlich, Paul **5** 225-226
    Livingstone, David **9** 463-465
    Sydenham, Thomas **15** 59-60

Malatesta, Carlo (1364?-1429), Italian art patron
  Ghiberti, Lorenzo **6** 291-292

Malatesta, Sigismondo (1417-1468), Italian art patron
  Alberti, Leon Battista **1** 113-115
  Piero della Francesca **12** 301-302
  Pisanello **12** 323-324

Malatesta family (Italy; ruled Rimini, circa 1237-circa 1503)
  Dufay, Guillaume **5** 125-126
  Gentile da Fabriano **6** 266-267
  see also Malatesta, Carlo; Malatesta, Sigismondo

Malavikagnimitra (play; Kalidasa)
  Harsha **7** 181-182
  Kalidasa **8** 414-415

Malawi, Republic of (nation; west Africa)
  Banda, Hastings Kamuzu **1** 485-486
  Booth, Joseph **2** 404-405

Malay Peninsula
  see Malaysia; Thailand

Malaya (ship)
  George VI **6** 275

Malaya, Federation of
see Malaysia

Malays (Asian people)
Brooke, James **3** 21-22

Malaysia (nation; southeastern Asia)
Carr-Saunders, Alexander Morris
3 333-334
Conti, Niccolò de' **4** 212-213
Ho Chi Minh **7** 426-428
Macapagal, Diosdado P. **10** 74-76
Magellan, Ferdinand **10** 126-127
Mahathir Mohamad **10** 134-135
Manuel I **10** 219-220
Tunku, Abdul Rahman **15** 340-341

Malbone (novel)
Higginson, Thomas Wentworth **7** 380

MALCOLM III (died 1093), king of Scotland 1058-1093 **10** 164-165
David I **4** 407
Macbeth **10** 81
Margaret of Scotland **10** 252-253

Malcolm, Sir John (1769-1833), British general and colonial official
Agha Mohammad Khan **1** 80-81

MALCOLM X (1925-1965), African American civil rights leader **10** 165-166
Cleaver, Leroy Eldridge **4** 97-98
Davis, Ossie **4** 421-422
Haley, Alex **7** 76-78

Malcolm X (film)
Lee, Spike **9** 295-299

Malcontent, The (play; Marston)
Webster, John **16** 164

Maldive Islands (Indian Ocean)
ibn Battuta, Muhammad **8** 91-92
see also Falkland Islands

Male and Female (painting)
Pollock, Jackson **12** 379-380

Male Animal, The (play)
Thurber, James Grove **15** 213-214

MALEBRANCHE, NICOLAS (1638-1715), French philosopher and theologian
10 166-167
Berkeley, George **2** 197-198
Condé, Prince de **4** 193-194
Simon, Jules François **14** 237-238

Maledizione, La (opera)
seeRigoletto

MALENKOV, GEORGY MAKSIMILIANOVICH (1902-1988), head of the Soviet government and leader of its Communist Party (1953) **10** 168
Beria, Lavrenty Pavlovich **2** 192-193
Molotov, Vyacheslav Mikhailovich
11 89-90
Zhukov, Georgi Konstantinovich
16 512-513

Malentendu, Le (play)
Camus, Albert **3** 255-257

Malervereinigung XI (art group)
Liebermann, Max **9** 402-403

see also Berlin Secession

MALEVICH, KASIMIR (1878-1935), Russian painter **10** 168-169
Moholy-Nagy, László **11** 82-83
Pevsner, Antoine **12** 263-264

Malgrange (château; Nancy, France)
Boffrand, Gabriel Germain **2** 361

Malgudi (literary town)
Narayan, R. K. **11** 313-314

Malhechores del bien, Los (play)
Benavente y Martinez, Jacinto
2 146-147

MALHERBE, FRANÇOIS DE (1555-1628), French poet **10** 169-170

Mali Republic (nation; west Africa)
culture
Cissé, Souleymane **4** 65-66
Empire (13th-17th century)
Ali, Sunni **1** 158-159
Cadamosto, Alvise da **3** 206-207
Muhammad Ture, Askia **11** 231-232
Musa Mansa **11** 266
Sundiata Keita **15** 33-34
Federation
Apithy, Sourou Migan **1** 259-260
Houphouët-Boigny, Felix **7** 519-520
Keita, Modibo **8** 474-475
Senghor, Léopold Sédar **14** 106-107
Touré, Sékou **15** 275-277
Welensky, Roy **16** 188
republic
Eboué, Adolphe Felix Sylvestre
5 194
Keita, Modibo **8** 474-475

Malic acid (chemistry)
Krebs, Hans Adolf **9** 95-97
Scheele, Karl Wilhelm **13** 525-526

Malik Shah, Jalal-al-Din (died 1092), sultan of Persia 1072-1092
Alp Arslan **1** 178-179
Omar Khayyam **11** 510-511

Maliki calendar (chronology)
Omar Khayyam **11** 510-511

Maliki school (Islamic law)
Abd al-Mumin **1** 13
Abdullah ibn Yasin **1** 20
ibn Hazm, Abu Muhammad Ali **8** 93
ibn Khaldun, Abd al-Rahman ibn
Muhammad **8** 93-94
ibn Tashufin, Yusuf **8** 95-96

Malines Congress (1863)
Montalembert, Comte de **11** 118-119

Malinke (African people)
Musa Mansa **11** 266
Sundiata Keita **15** 33-34
see also Mali Republic—Empire

MALINOWSKI, KASPAR BRONISLAW
(1884-1942), Austrian-born British social anthropologist **10** 170-171
Evans-Pritchard, Edward Evan **5** 340
Frazer, James George **6** 76
Kenyatta, Jomo **8** 512-514

Mauss, Marcel **10** 352-353

MALIPIERO, GIAN FRANCESCO
(1882-1973), Italian composer **10** 171
Nono, Luigi **11** 420-421

MALKAM KHAN, MIRZA (1831-1908), Persian diplomat **10** 172

Malkanu beta saboç (book)
Mäkonnen Endalkačäw **10** 161-162

Malkin Conservatory (Boston)
Schoenberg, Arnold **14** 24-26

MALLARMÉ, STÉPHANE (1842-1898), French poet **10** 172-173
associates
George, Stefan **6** 277-278
Gide, André **6** 308-309
Manet, Édouard **10** 193-194
influence of
Güiráldez, Ricardo **7** 38-39
Stevens, Wallace **14** 443-445
Ungaretti, Giuseppe **15** 389-390
Valéry, Paul Ambroise **15** 405-406
influenced by
Baudelaire, Charles Pierre **2** 61-63
musical settings
Debussy, Achille Claude **4** 445-447

Mallet, David (circa 1705-1765), Scottish poet
Arne, Thomas Augustine **1** 307-308
Thomson, James **15** 199-200

Mallock, William Hurrell (1849-1923), English writer
Pater, Walter Horatio **12** 130-131

Malloy v. Hogan (legal case)
Warren, Earl **16** 117-120

Malls, regional shopping
DeBartolo **4** 438-440

MALONE, DUMAS (1892-1986), American historian and editor **10** 174-175

Malone Dies (novel)
Beckett, Samuel **2** 102-104

MALORY, SIR THOMAS (flourished 15th century), English author **10** 175-176
Geoffrey of Monmouth **6** 268

Malouel, Jean (flourished 1396-1415), Franco-Flemish painter
Sluter, Claus **14** 275-276

MALPIGHI, MARCELLO (1628-1694), Italian anatomist **10** 176-178
Hales, Stephen **7** 75
Harvey, William **7** 189-190
Leeuwenhoek, Anton van **9** 300-301

Malplaquet, battle of (1709)
Eugene of Savoy **5** 330-331
Marlborough, 1st Duke of **10** 271-272
Saxe, Comte de **13** 507-508

Malquerida, La (play)
Benavente y Martinez, Jacinto
2 146-147

MALRAUX, ANDRÉ (1901-1976), French novelist, essayist, and politician
10 178-180

Barrès, Auguste Maurice **2** 20-21
Camus, Albert **3** 255-257
Faulkner, William **5** 395-397

Malta (island; Mediteiranean Sea)
Carr-Saunders, Alexander Morris **3** 333-334
Napoleon I **11** 306-310

Malta fever
see Undulant fever

Maltese Falcon, The (book; Hammett)
Bogart, Humphrey **2** 363-364
Hammett, Dashiell **7** 106-108

MALTHUS, THOMAS ROBERT
(1766-1834), English economist **10** 180-181
Darwin, Charles Robert **4** 397-399
Mill, John Stuart **11** 21-23
Peacock, Thomas Love **12** 169
Ricardo, David **13** 123-124
Say, Jean Baptiste **13** 508-509
Wallace, Alfred Russel **16** 69-70

Malton, Thomas, Jr. (1748-1804), English painter and draftsman
Turner, Joseph Mallord William **15** 352-354

Malvern, Lord
seeHuggins, Sir Godfrey

Malvern Hill
see Seven Days, Battle of the

Malvolio (literary character)
Shakespeare, William **14** 142-145

Malwa (region; India)
Ala-ud-din **1** 102-103

Mama I Love You (novel)
Saroyan, William **13** 486-487

Mama, Papa Is Wounded (painting)
Tanguy, Yves **15** 101

Mamalujo (Evangelists)
Joyce, James **8** 365-367

Mambises (Cuban rebels)
Céspedes, Carlos Manuel de **3** 398-399

Mamelles de Tirésias, Les (opera)
Poulenc, Francis **12** 414-415

MAMET, DAVID ALAN (born 1947), American author **10** 181-182

Mammalia (biology)
Huxley, Thomas Henry **8** 77-79
Sherrington, Charles Scott **14** 187-189

Mamoré river (South America)
Azara, Félix de **1** 397-398

MAMUN, ABDALLAH AL- (786-833),
Abbasid caliph **10** 183
Alfonso VI **1** 149
Khwarizmi, Muhammad ibn Musa al-
8 541

Man (philosophy)
Feuerbach, Ludwig Andreas **5** 432
Niebuhr, Reinhold **11** 387-388

Man against the Sky, The (poems)
Robinson, Edwin Arlington **13** 201-202

Man and Ape (book)
Keith, Arthur **8** 475-476

Man and Reclining Woman Who Dreams (sculpture)
Giacometti, Alberto **6** 294-295

Man and Superman (play)
Shaw, George Bernard **14** 163-164

Man and Wife (novel)
Collins, William Wilkie **4** 169-170

Man Condemned for Little Faith, The (play)
Tirso de Molina **15** 237-238

Man Could Stand Up, A (novel)
Ford, Ford Madox **6** 1-2

Man Feeding His Dogs (painting)
Drysdale, George Russell **5** 107-109

Man from Kabul, The (story)
Rabindranath Tagore **12** 529-531

Man from Sicyon, The (play)
Menander **10** 477-478

Man from Snowy River... (ballads)
Paterson, Andrew Barton **12** 131-132

Man from the North, A (novel)
Bennett, Arnold **2** 167-168

Man in a Blue Cap (painting)
Cézanne, Paul **3** 400-402

Man in a Case, The (story)
Chekhov, Anton Pavlovich **3** 494-497

Man in a Red Turban (painting)
Eyck, Hubert and Jan van **5** 352-354

Man in Green Britches, The (play)
Tirso de Molina **15** 237-238

Man in the Moon, The (poem)
Drayton, Michael **5** 97-98

Man in the Open Air (sculpture)
Nadelman, Elie **11** 289-290

Man Meditating on the Scriptures (painting)
Chagall, Marc **3** 406-407

Man Nobody Knows, The (book)
Barton, Bruce **2** 36-37

Man of Property, The (novel)
Galsworthy, John **6** 189-190

Man of Sorrows (painting)
Geertgen tot Sint Jans **6** 248

Man of the People, A (novel)
Achebe, Chinua **1** 35-37

Man on his Own. An essay on the philosophy of religion (book)
Block, Herbert **2** 333-334

Man Pointing (sculpture)
Giacometti, Alberto **6** 294-295

Man That Corrupted Hadleyburg, The (book)
Twain, Mark **15** 363-366

Man That Was Used Up, The (story)
Poe, Edgar Allan **12** 363-365

Man, The (publication)
Evans, George Henry **5** 337-338

Man Who Came to Dinner, The (play)
Kaufman, George S. **8** 457-458

Man Who Died, The (novelette)
Lawrence, David Herbert **9** 247-248

Man Who Had All the Luck, The (play)
Miller, Arthur **11** 25-26

Man Who Knew Too Much, The (film)
Hitchcock, Alfred **7** 415-416

Man Who Owns Broadway, The (play)
Cohan, George Michael **4** 137-138

Man Who Shot Liberty Valance, The (film)
Ford, John **6** 7-8

Man Who Was Thursday, The (novel)
Chesterton, Gilbert Keith **3** 508-509

Man Who Watched the Trains Go By, The (novel)
Simenon, Georges **14** 233-234

Man with a Broken Nose (sculpture)
Rodin, Auguste **13** 236-238

Man with a Guitar (sculpture)
Lipchitz, Jacques **9** 432-433

Man with a Magnifying Glass (painting)
Rembrandt Harmensz van Rijn
13 91-95

Man with a Medal (painting)
Memling, Hans **10** 476

Man with the Blue Guitar, The (poems)
Stevens, Wallace **14** 443-445

Man with the Guitar (painting)
Braque, Georges **2** 504-505

Man with the Hoe, The (poem)
Markham, Edwin **10** 267

Man with the Pipe (painting)
Courbet, Jean Desiré Gustave
4 271-273

Man Within, The (novel)
Greene, Graham **6** 523-524

Man without a Country, The (story)
Hale, Edward Everett **7** 71-72

Man without Qualities, The (novel)
Musil, Robert Edler Von **11** 268-269

Management and Budget, United States Office of
Panetta, Leon E. **12** 84-85
Weinberger, Casper Willard **16** 177-178

Manassa Mauler
see Dempsey, Jack

Mañanas de abril y mayo (play)
Calderón, Pedro **3** 221-222

Manassas, battles of
see Bull Run, battles of

MANASSEH BEN ISRAEL (1604-1657),
Dutch rabbi and theologian **10** 183-184

Manawaka cycle (novels)
Laurence, Margaret **9** 229-230

Manchega (musical composition)
Gottschalk, Louis Moreau **6** 463-464

Manchester, 1st Earl of (Edward Montagu; 1625-1672), English naval commander
Cromwell, Oliver **4** 317-320

Manchester, University of (England)
Alexander, Samuel **1** 141
Bohr, Niels Henrik David **2** 366-368
Chapman, Sydney **3** 441
Hill, Archibald Vivian **7** 385-386
Lovell, Alfred Charles Bernard **10** 8-9
Namier, Lewis Bernstein **11** 301-303
Rutherford, Ernest **13** 384-387
Weizmann, Chaim **16** 183-184

Manchu dynasty
see Ch'ing dynasty

Manchuria (territory; China)
Chinese Communist occupation
Lin Piao **9** 429-430
Japanese occupation
Hirohito **7** 410-412
Hoover, Herbert Clark **7** 483-485
Kishi, Nobusuke **9** 41-43
Stimson, Henry Lewis **14** 457-458
Tojo, Hideki **15** 254-256
Yen Hsi-shan **16** 452-453
Manchurian incident
see Manchurian incident (1931)
Russian interests
Ito, Hirobumi **8** 153-155
see also China, People's Republic of;
Ch'ing (Manchu) dynasty;
Russo-Japanese War (1904-1905)
under Chinese Empire
Chang Tso-lin **3** 434-435
K'ang-hsi **8** 423-426
Quin Shi Huang-Di **12** 515-518

Manchurian incident (1931)
Inukai, Tsuyoshi **8** 130-131
Wang Ching-wei **16** 98

Manciata di more, Una (novel)
Silone, Ignazio **14** 231-232

Mancinus, G. Hostilius
see Hostilius Mancinus, G.

MANCO CAPAC (circa 1500-1545), Inca emperor **10** 184-185
Almagro, Diego de **1** 177-178
Pizarro, Francisco **12** 340-341

Mandaeans (Gnostic sect)
Mani **10** 196-197
Scholem, Gershom **14** 26

Mandala (Buddhism)
Ennin **5** 288-289
Kukai **9** 124-125

Mandalay (poem)
Kipling, Joseph Rudyard **9** 32-33

Mandat, Le (film)
Ousmane, Sembene **12** 32-33

Mandate of Heaven (Chinese doctrine)
Chung-shu, Tung **4** 48-49
Kuang-wu-ti **9** 112-113
Yi Sng-gye **16** 458-459

Mandate system
see League of Nations—mandates

Mandel, Georges (1885-1943), French politician
Eboué, Adolphe Felix Sylvestre **5** 194

MANDELA, NELSON ROLIHLAHLA (born 1918), South African leader **10** 185-186
Mandela, Winnie **10** 187-189

MANDELA, WINNIE (Nomzamo Winifred Madikizela; born 1936), South African anti-apartheid leader **10** 187-189

MANDELBROT, BENOIT B. (born 1924), Polish-born French-American mathematician who invented fractals **10** 189-191

MANDELSTAM, OSIP EMILYEVICH (1891-1938), Russian poet **10** 191
Akhmatova, Anna **1** 96-97

Mander, Karel van (1548-1606), Dutch painter and writer
Bruegel, Pieter the Elder **3** 65-67
Hals, Frans **7** 89-91
Lucas van Leyden **10** 20-21

MANDEVILLE, BERNARD (circa 1670-1733), English satirist and moral philosopher **10** 192
Law, William **9** 245-246

MANDEVILLE, SIR JOHN (flourished 14th century), pen name of English author **10** 192-193

Mandoline (poem)
Verlaine, Paul Marie **15** 465-466

Mandrake, The (play)
Machiavelli, Niccolò **10** 97-99

Mandyn, Jan (1500-1560), Dutch painter
Bosch, Hieronymus **2** 426-428

Man-eater of Malgudi, The (novel)
Narayan, R. K. **11** 313-314

MANET, ÉDOUARD (1832-1883), French painter **10** 193-194
associates
Cézanne, Paul **3** 400-402
Mallarmé, Stéphane **10** 172-173
Monet, Claude **11** 102-104
influence of
Chase, William Merritt **3** 476-477
Glackens, William **6** 355-356
Hassam, Frederick Childe **7** 192
Liebermann, Max **9** 402-403
Nolde, Emil **11** 419-420
Prendergast, Maurice Brazil **12** 440
Renoir, Pierre Auguste **13** 101-102
Stella, Joseph **14** 422
influenced by
Goya y Lucientes, Francisco de Paula José de **6** 476-478
Harunobu, Suzuki **7** 188-189
Ingres, Jean Auguste Dominique **8** 121-123
Utamaro, Kitagawa **15** 397

Manette Salomon (novel)
Goncourt, Edmond de and Jules de **6** 426-427

Manfred (circa 1232-1266), king of Naples and Sicily 1258-1266
Frederick II **6** 79

Henry III **7** 290-292
Michael VIII **11** 1-2
Peter III **12** 256-257

Manfred (play; Byron)
Byron, George Gordon Noel **3** 193-194
Schumann, Robert Alexander **14** 41-43

Mangas Khan
see Mongka Khan

Manguin, Henri (1874-1943), French painter
Matisse, Henri **10** 336-337

Manhattan (island; New York State)
Fuller, Richard Buckminster **6** 149-150
Minuit, Peter **11** 50

Manhattan Elevated Railroad (New York State)
Field, Cyrus West **5** 438-439
Gould, Jay **6** 470-472

Manhattan Project
see Atomic bomb—development

Manhattan Transfer (novel)
Dos Passos, John Roderigo **5** 69-71

MANI (216-276/277), Persian prophet **10** 196-197
see also Manichaeism

Manichaeism (Persian religion)
Augustine **1** 367-370
Dominic **5** 51-52
Leo I **9** 329-330
Mani **10** 196-197
Nazzam, Ibrahim ibn Sayyar al- **11** 329

Manifesto of the Communist Party
see Communist Manifesto

Manila (city; Philippines)
Burnham, Daniel Hudson **3** 148-149
Garcia, Carlos P. **6** 207-208
Macapagal, Diosdado P. **10** 74-76
Marcos, Ferdinand **10** 240-242
Marcos, Imelda Romualdez **10** 242-243

Manila Bay, battle of (1898)
Dewey, George **4** 520

MANIN, DANIELE (1804-1857), Venetian patriot **10** 197-198

Manitoba (province; Canada)
Macdonald, John Alexander **10** 85-87
Riel, Louis **13** 163-164
see also Canada

Manji (novel)
Tanizaki, Junichiro **15** 101-102

Mankiewicz, Joseph L. (1909-1993), American film director
Bogart, Humphrey **2** 363-364

MANKILLER, WILMA (born 1945), Native American activist and Cherokee chief **10** 198-199

Mankind Evolving (book)
Dobzhansky, Theodosius **5** 35-37

MANLEY, MICHAEL NORMAN (1924-1997), Jamaican prime minister (1972-1980) **10** 200-201

Man-Moth (poem)
Bishop, Elizabeth **2** 290-292

Mann, Erika (1905-1969) German-born American author and actress
Mann, Thomas **10** 204-207

MANN, HEINRICH (1871-1950), German novelist, essayist, and social critic **10** 201-202
Mann, Thomas **10** 204-207

MANN, HORACE (1796-1859), American educational reformer and humanitarian **10** 202-204
Cousin, Victor **4** 273-274
Curry, Jabez Lamar Monroe **4** 346-347
Peabody, Elizabeth Palmer **12** 167-168
Sarmiento, Domingo Faustino **13** 484-485
Sterne, Laurence **14** 435-437

Mann, Klaus (1906-1949), German-born American author
Mann, Thomas **10** 204-207

MANN, THOMAS (1875-1955), German novelist and essayist **10** 204-207
Mann, Heinrich **10** 201-202
Schopenhauer, Arthur **14** 29-31

Mann ist Mann (play)
Brecht, Bertolt **2** 512-514

Mann ohne Eigenochaften, Der (novel)
Musil, Robert Edler Von **11** 268-269

Manned Spacecraft Center (Houston, Texas)
Armstrong, Neil Alden **1** 304-306
see also Space exploration

MANNERHEIM, BARON CARL GUSTAV EMIL VON (1867-1951), Finnish military leader and statesman, president 1944-46 **10** 207-208

Mannerhouse (play)
Wolfe, Thomas Clayton **16** 355-356

Mannerism (art)
foreshadowed
Michelangelo Buonarroti **11** 2-5
Raphael **13** 40-42
influence of
Bruegel, Pieter the Elder **3** 65-67
Clouet, Jean and François **4** 122-123
Gibbs, James **6** 301-302
Goujon, Jean **6** 466-467
Herrera, Juan de **7** 335
Hilliard, Nicholas **7** 391-392
Holbein, Hans the Younger **7** 449-450
Le Nain, Antoine, Louis and Mathieu **9** 321-322
Mies van der Rohe, Ludwig **11** 10-12
influenced by
Andrea del Sarto **1** 224-225
opposition to
Caravaggio **3** 282-284
Carracci **3** 319-321
pioneers
Bronzino **3** 19

Giovanni da Bologna **6** 345-346
Parmigianino **12** 117
Pontormo **12** 394-395
Primaticcio, Francesco **12** 453-454
Rosso, Il **13** 312-313
Vasari, Giorgio **15** 442-443
stylistic interpretations
Berruguete, Alonso **2** 223-224
Donner, Georg Raphael **5** 63
Greco **6** 511-514
Modigliani, Amedeo **11** 72-73

Mannerly Margery Milk and Ale (song)
Skelton, John **14** 268-269

Manners, Charles
see Rutland, 4th Duke of

MANNHEIM, KARL (1893-1947), Hungarian-born sociologist and educator **10** 208-209

Manning, Daniel (1831-1887), American journalist and financier
Cleveland, Stephen Grover **4** 108-110

MANNING, HENRY EDWARD (1808-1892), English cardinal **10** 209-210
Gladstone, William Ewart **6** 357-360

MANNIX, DANIEL (1864-1963), Irish-born Australian archbishop **10** 210

Mannon family (literary characters)
O'Neill, Eugene **11** 514-516

Manoel
see Manuel

Manola, Una (fresco)
Goya y Lucientes, Francisco de Paula José de **6** 476-478

Manon Lescaut (novel and opera)
Prévost, Abbé **12** 445-446
Puccini, Giacomo **12** 474-476

Manqu Khan
see Mongka Khan

Manrique, Gómez (1415-1490?), Spanish poet, soldier, and statesman
Manrique, Jorge **10** 210-211

MANRIQUE, JORGE (1440?-1478), Spanish poet and soldier **10** 210-211

Manru (opera)
Paderewski, Ignace Jan **12** 56-57

Man's a Man, A (play)
Brecht, Bertolt **2** 512-514

Man's a Man for A' That, A (song)
Burns, Robert **3** 155-156

Man's Death, A (story)
Palamas, Kostes **12** 70

Man's Fate (novel)
Malraux, André **10** 178-180

Mansard roof (architecture)
Mansart, François **10** 211

MANSART, FRANÇOIS (1598-1666), French architect **10** 211
Le Nôtre, André **9** 328-329
Mansart, Jules Hardouin **10** 212, 153

MANSART, JULES HARDOUIN (1646-1708), French architect **10** 212
Boffrand, Gabriel Germain **2** 361
Gabriel, Ange Jacques **6** 160-161
Mansart, François **10** 211
Perrault, Claude **12** 232-233

Mansei Uprising (Korea; 1919)
Rhee, Syngman **13** 117-120

Mansfeld, Count Peter Ernst II (1580-1626), German general
Buckingham, 1st Duke of **3** 93-94

MANSFIELD, KATHERINE (born Kathleen Mansfield Beauchamp; 1888-1923), New Zealander short-story writer and poet **10** 213-214
Woolf, Virginia Stephen **16** 381-382

Mansfield Park (novel)
Austen, Jane **1** 377-379

Manship, Paul (1885-1966), American sculptor
Lachaise, Gaston **9** 147

Mansion, The (novel)
Faulkner, William **5** 395-397

MANSUR, ABU JAFAR IBN MUHAMMAD AL (712-775), Abbasid caliph **10** 214-215

Mansur, Abu Yusuf Yakub al-
see Yakub I

Mantee, Duke (literary character)
Bogart, Humphrey **2** 363-364

MANTEGNA, ANDREA (circa 1430-1506), Italian painter and engraver **10** 215-216
influence of
Bellini, Giovanni **2** 137-138, 477
Burne-Jones, Edward Coley **3** 145-146
Correggio **4** 249-251
Cranach, Lucas the Elder **4** 289-290
Degas, Hilaire Germain Edgar **4** 461-462
Dürer, Albrecht **5** 159-161
Holbein, Hans the Younger **7** 449-450
Pacher, Michael **12** 53
influenced by
Andrea del Castagno **1** 223-224
Donatello **5** 55-56

Mantinea, battles of (362 B.C.; 418 B.C.)
Alcibiades **1** 119-120
Epaminondas **5** 291-292
Xenophon **16** 418-420

MANTLE, MICKEY (1931-1995), American baseball player **10** 216-218

Mantua, Duke of (Giovanni Francesco II Gonzaga; died 1519), Italian statesman, ruler of Mantua 1484-1519
Correggio **4** 249-251

MANUEL I (1469-1521), king of Portugal 1495-1521 **10** 219-220
exploration
Corte Reál, Gaspar and Miguel **4** 254-255
Dias de Novais, Bartolomeu **4** 533-534

Gama, Vasco da **6** 196-198
Vespucci, Amerigo **15** 476-478
patronage
Cabral, Pedro Álvares **3** 203-204
Varthema, Ludovico di **15** 439-440
Vicente, Gil **15** 479-480
trade relations
Affonso I **1** 72

MANUEL I COMNENUS (circa 1123-1180), Byzantine emperor 1143-1180 **10** 218-219

Manuel II (1889-1932), king of Portugal 1908-1910
Salazar, António de Oliveira **13** 442-443

Manuel II Palaeologus (1350-1425), Byzantine emperor 1391-1425
Constantine XI **4** 211-212

MANUELITO (1818-1894), Navajo tribal leader **10** 220-222

Manufacturers
see Business and industrial leaders

Manutius, Aldus (1450-1515), Italian printer
Erasmus, Desiderius **5** 298-300

Many Coloured Coat, The (novel)
Callaghan, Edward Morley **3** 229-230

Many Inventions (stories)
Kipling, Joseph Rudyard **9** 32-33

Many Loves (play)
Williams, William Carlos **16** 308-309

Many Marriages (novel)
Anderson, Sherwood **1** 220-221

Manyoshu (poems)
Mabuchi, Kamo **10** 73-74

Manzikert, battle of (1071)
Alexius I **1** 143-144
Alp Arslan **1** 178-179

MANZONI, ALESSANDRO (1785-1873); Italian novelist and playwright **10** 222-224
Verdi, Giuseppe Fortunino Francesco **15** 463-465

MANZÙ, GIACOMO (born 1908), Italian sculptor **10** 224-225

MAO ZEDONG (1893-1976), Chinese statesman **10** 225-227
associates
Chernenko, Konstantin Ustinovich **3** 503-504
Chou En-lai **4** 20-22
Chu Teh **4** 54-55
Jiang Qing **8** 256-260
Kuo Mo-jo **9** 133-134
Lin Piao **9** 429-430
Liu Shao-Ch'i **9** 453-455
Ts'ai Yüan-p'ei **15** 322
influenced by
Li Ta-chao **9** 447
Sun Yat-sen **15** 35-39
Wang Fu-chih **16** 99-101
opponents

Chiang Kai-shek **3** 510-513
Dalai Lama **4** 369-371
United States policy
Marshall, George Catlett **10** 278-279

Mao-ch'eng chi (novel)
Lao Shê **9** 200-201

Maori (Polynesian people; New Zealand)
Fraser, Peter **6** 73-74
Grey, George **6** 540-541
Hobson, William **7** 426
Ngata, Apirana Turupa **11** 374-375
Ratana, Taupotiki Wiremu **13** 46

Maori Bible
Ngata, Apirana Turupa **11** 374-375

Map (cartography)
Anaximander **1** 209-210
Mercator, Gerhardus **10** 511-512

Map of Love, The (poems)
Thomas, Dylan Marlais **15** 188-190

Mapai
see Labor party (Israel)

Mapp v. Ohio (legal case)
Warren, Earl **16** 117-120

MAPPLETHORPE, ROBERT (1946-1989), controversial American photographer **10** 227-228

Maquet, Auguste (1813-1888), French writer
Dumas, Alexandre **5** 136-138

Maragha, School of
Ptolemy, Claudius **12** 473-474

MARAGHI, AL-MUSTAFĀ (1881-1945), Egyptian jurist and educator **10** 228-229

Marah
see Jackson, Helen Hunt

Maran, René (1887-1960), West Indian novelist
Eboué, Adolphe Felix Sylvestre **5** 194

MARAT, JEAN PAUL (1743-1793), French journalist and political leader **10** 230-231
Beaumarchais, Pierre August Caron de **2** 93-94

Marat Sade (play)
Brook, Peter **3** 19-21

Marathas (people; India)
Aurangzeb **1** 377
Śivajī **14** 266-267
see also Mysore wars (1767-1799)

Marathon, battle of (490 B.C.)
Aeschylus **1** 70-72
Darius I **4** 394-395-273
Miltiades **11** 42-43
Phidias **12** 265-267
Xerxes **16** 420

Maratona di danza (musical composition)
Henze, Hans Werner **7** 314

Maratta, Carlo (Carlo Maratti; 1625-1713), Italian painter
Gaulli, Giovanni Battista **6** 238-239

Mårbacka (estate; Värmland, Sweden)
Lagerlöf, Selma Ottiliana Lovisa **9** 163-164

Marble Faun, The (novel)
Hawthorne, Nathaniel **7** 212-215

Marble Faun, The (poems)
Faulkner, William **5** 395-397

Marble House (Newport, Rhode Island)
Hunt, Richard Morris **8** 44

Marburg, Colloquy of (1529)
Luther, Martin **10** 48-51
Melanchthon, Philip **10** 466-467

Marburg, University of (Germany)
Bultmann, Rudolf Karl **3** 119-120
Lamprecht, Karl **9** 181
Loewi, Otto **9** 486-487
Michels, Robert **11** 7
Tillich, Paul Johannes **15** 224-225
Wegener, Alfred Lothar **16** 170-171
Wolff, Christian von **16** 358

Marbury, Anne
see Hutchinson, Anne Marbury

Marbury v. Madison (legal case)
Marshall, John **10** 279-281

MARC, FRANZ (1880-1916), German painter **10** 231
Hartley, Marsden **7** 186
Kandinsky, Wassily **8** 420-422

MARCEAU, MARCEL (born 1923), world's greatest practitioner of pantomine **10** 231-233

Marcel (literary character)
Proust, Marcel **12** 465-467

MARCEL, GABRIEL (1889-1973), French philosopher **10** 233-234
Merleau-Ponty, Maurice **10** 518

Marceline (literary character)
Gide, André **6** 308-309

Marcellus II (Marcello Cervini, 1501-1555), pope 1555
Paul III **12** 144-145

Marcellus, Marcus Claudius (268?-208 B.C.), Roman general
Archimedes **1** 277-280

March (musical form)
Sousa, John Philip **14** 353-354
Strauss, Johann Jr. **14** 498-499

March, 4th Earl of (Roger de Mortimer; 1374-1398), heir presumptive to English throne
Richard II **13** 130-131
see also Mortimer, Edmund and Roger

March, Basil and Isabel (literary characters)
Howells, William Dean **7** 539-541

March on Rome (1922)
Hitler, Adolf **7** 417-420
Mussolini, Benito **11** 272-274
Victor Emmanuel III **15** 484-485

March on the Pentagon (United States; 1967)
Rubin, Jerry **13** 344-346

March on Washington for Jobs and Freedom (1963)
Abernathy, Ralph David **1** 27-28
Du Bois, William Edward Burghardt **5** 116-118
King, Martin Luther Jr. **9** 20-22
Randolph, A. Philip **13** 28-29
Rustin, Bayard **13** 382-383
Wilkins, Roy **16** 282-283

March to the Sea (Georgia; 1864)
Sherman, William Tecumseh **14** 186-187

MARCHAND, JEAN-BAPTISTE
(1863-1934), French explorer and soldier **10** 234-237
Bonvalot, Pierre Gabriel Édouard **2** 396
Kitchener, Horatio Herbert **9** 45-46

Marchand, Louis (1669-1732), French organist and composer
Bach, Johann Sebastian **1** 416-419

March-April Compromise (1848)
Deák, Francis **4** 431-432

Marche des rois Mages (musical composition)
Berlioz, Louis Hector **2** 203-205

Marche triomphale (musical composition)
Gottschalk, Louis Moreau **6** 463-464

Marchfeld, battle of (1278)
Rudolf I **13** 347-348

Marching Men (novel)
Anderson, Sherwood **1** 220-221

Marciana (library; Venice)
Bembo, Pietro **2** 144-145

MARCIANO, ROCKY (1923-1969), American boxer **10** 237-238
Louis, Joe **9** 537-538

Marcianopolis, battle of (447)
Attila **1** 360

MARCION (flourished mid-2nd century), Christian theologian **10** 238-239

Marcionism (religion)
Marcion **10** 238-239
Tertullian **15** 155-156

Marco Millions (play)
O'Neill, Eugene **11** 514-516

Marco Polo Bridge incident (1937)
Konoe, Fumimaro **9** 82-83
Tojo, Hideki **15** 254-256

MARCONI, GUGLIELMO (1874-1937), Italian inventor **10** 239-240
Bose, Jagadis Chandra **2** 429-430
De Forest, Lee **4** 459-460
Edison, Thomas Alva **5** 206-208

Marconi scandal (1912)
Lloyd George, David **9** 469-471

Marconi Wireless Telegraph Company of America
Sarnoff, David **13** 485-486

MARCOS, FERDINAND (1917-1989), president of the Republic of the Philippines (1965-1986) **10** 240-242

Aquino, Benigno **1** 267-268
Aquino, Corazon Cojoangco **1** 268-270
Rómulo, Carlos P. **13** 270-271

MARCOS, IMELDA ROMUALDEZ (born 1930), wife of Philippine President Ferdinand Marcos and governor of Metro Manila **10** 242-243

MARCOS DE NIZA, FRIAR (circa 1500-1558), Franciscan missionary in Spanish America **10** 240
Coronado, Francisco Vásquez de **4** 247

Marcus Antonius
see Antony, Mark

MARCUS AURELIUS ANTONINUS
(121-180), Roman emperor 161-180 **10** 243-245
Arnold, Matthew **1** 311-313
Donatello **5** 55-56
Epictetus **5** 292
Galen **6** 178-180
Hadrian **7** 60-61
Merezhkovsky, Dmitry Sergeyevich **10** 515-516
Schlüter, Andreas **14** 18-19
Zeno of Citium **16** 499-500

Marcus Ulpius Trajanus
see Trajan

MARCUSE, HERBERT (1898-1979), German-American philosopher **10** 245-247

MARCY, WILLIAM LEARNED (1786-1857), American statesman **10** 247-248
Elgin, 8th Earl of **5** 248-249
Harris, Townsend **7** 176-177
Pierce, Franklin **12** 300-301
Polk, James Knox **12** 374-376
Seymour, Horatio **14** 126-127
Soulé, Pierre **14** 351-352

Mardi (novel)
Melville, Herman **10** 472-476

Mardonius (died 479 B.C.), Persian general
Xerxes **16** 420

Marduk (Babylonian god)
Cyrus the Great **4** 363-364

Mare au diable, La (novel)
Sand, George **13** 459-461

Maréchal, Joseph (1878-1944), Belgium Jesuit philosopher
Rahner, Karl **13** 4-5

Maréchale d'Ancre, La (play)
Vigny, Comte de **15** 494-495

Maremanno Idyl, The (play)
Carducci, Giosuè **3** 290-291

Marengo, battle of (1800)
Murat, Joachim **11** 253-254
Napoleon I **11** 306-310

MARENZIO, LUCA (1553/54-1599), Italian composer **10** 248

Mares of Diomedes (sculpture)
Borglum, John Gutzon de la Mothe **2** 416-417

**MARGAI, SIR MILTON AUGUSTUS STRI-
ERY** (1895-1964), Sierra Leonean physician and statesman **10** 248-249

Margaret (the Maid of Norway; 1283-1290), titular queen of Scotland
Robert I **13** 192-194

Margaret, Princess (born 1930), daughter of George VI
Elizabeth II **5** 266-269
George VI **6** 275

MARGARET OF ANJOU (1430-1482), queen consort of Henry VI of England **10** 249-250
Edward IV **5** 212-213
Henry VI **7** 298-299
Prévost, Abbé **12** 445-446
Warwick and of Salisbury, Earl of **16** 122-123

Margaret of Austria (1480-1530), regent of the Netherlands 1507-1530
Josquin des Prez **8** 361-363

Margaret of Austria (1522-1586), daughter of emperor Charles V
Philip III **12** 273-274

MARGARET OF DENMARK (born Margaret Valdemarsdottir; 1353-1412), queen of Denmark **10** 250-252

Margaret of Flanders (1350-1405), countess of Flanders and duchess of Burgundy
Sluter, Claus **14** 275-276

Margaret of France
see Margaret of Valois

MARGARET OF SCOTLAND, Saint
(1045-1093), wife of Malcolm III of Scotland **10** 252-253
David I **4** 407
Malcolm III **10** 164-165

Margaret of Valois (1553-1615), queen of Navarre
Charron, Pierre **3** 472
Henry IV **7** 293-295

Margaret of York (Margaret Pole; 1473-1541), countess of Salisbury
Charles the Bold **3** 467-469

Margaret Tudor (1489-1541), queen of James IV of Scotland
Douglas, Gavin **5** 77-78

Margaretha (1522-1586), duchess of Pavia
Charles V **3** 457-459

Marginal utility (economics)
Böhm-Bawerk, Eugen von **2** 366
Clark, John Bates **4** 76-77
Jevons, William Stanley **8** 255-256
Marshall, Alfred **10** 277-278
von Mises, Ludwig **16** 25
Walras, Marie Esprit Léon **16** 84-85

MARGULIS, LYNN (born 1938), American biologist **10** 253-254

Margutte (literary character)
Pulci, Luigi **12** 481

Mari (ancient city; Mesopotamia)
Hammurabi **7** 109-110

Sargon of Agade **13** 483

Mari Djata
see Sundiata Keita

María (novel)
Isaacs, Jorge **8** 144

Maria I (1734-1816), queen of Portugal 1777-1816
Pombal, Marquês de **12** 386-387

Maria II (1819-1853), queen of Portugal 1826-1853
Pedro I **12** 179-180

Maria Ana of Neuburg (1667-1740), queen of Spain
Charles II **3** 454

Maria Antonieta of Naples (died 1806), queen of Spain
Ferdinand VII **5** 418-420

Maria Chapdelaine (novel)
Hémon, Louis **7** 277

María Cristina de Bourbon (1806-1878), queen of Spain 1829-1833
Ferdinand VII **5** 418-420
Isabella II **8** 145-146

Maria Cristina of Hapsburg (1858-1929), queen regent of Spain 1885-1902
Alfonso XIII **1** 151

Maria Cristina of Naples
see Maria Cristina de Bourbon

Maria da Glória
see Maria II of Portugal

Maria de' Medici
see Marie de Médicis

Maria Dreieichen (church; near Vienna)
Troger, Paul **15** 300

Maria Egiziaca (opera)
Respighi, Ottorino **13** 103-104

Maria Fedorovna (Sophie Frederica Dagmar; 1847-1928), empress of Russia 1881-1894
Alexander III **1** 133-134

Maria Luisa (novel)
Azuela, Mariano **1** 402

Maria Luisa Gabriela of Savoy (1688-1714), queen of Spain 1701-1714
Philip V **12** 276-277

Maria Luisa Teresa of Parma (1751-1819), queen of Spain 1788-1808
Charles IV **3** 456-457
Ferdinand VII **5** 418-420
Godoy y Álvarez de Faria, Manuel de **6** 381-382

Maria Magdalena (play)
Hebbel, Friedrich **7** 247

Maria Mitchell Astronomical Observatory (Nantucket Island)
Mitchell, Maria **11** 61

Maria of Portugal (died 1545), queen of Spain
Philip II **12** 271-273

Maria Pia (bridge; Oporto)
Eiffel, Alexandre Gustave **5** 227-228

MARIA THERESA (1717-1780), Holy Roman empress 1740-1780 **10** 256-258
Frederick II **6** 81-84
Gooch, George Peabody **6** 432-433
Joseph II **8** 359-360
Leopold II **9** 346
Louis XVI **9** 534-535

Maria Theresa (Marie Thérèse; 1638-1683), queen consort of Louis XIV
Louis XIV **9** 531-533
Philip IV **12** 275
Philip V **12** 276-277

Maria-Treu, Church of (Vienna)
Hildebrandt, Johann Lucas von **7** 380-381
Maulbertsch, Franz Anton **10** 345

Mariage de Figaro (play)
Beaumarchais, Pierre August Caron de **2** 93-94

Mariage force, La (comedy; Molière)
Charpentier, Marc Antoine **3** 471-472

Mariana (poem)
Tennyson, Alfred **15** 144-146

MARIANA, JUAN DE (1536-1624), Spanish Jesuit historian **10** 254-255

Mariana of Austria (1634-1696), queen regent of Spain 1665-1675
Charles II **3** 454

Mariana Trench (Pacific Ocean)
Piccard, Auguste **12** 297-298

MARIÁTEGUI, JOSÉ CARLOS (1895-1930), Peruvian writer **10** 255-256

Maricourt, Pierre de
see Peregrinus, Petrus

Marie (1899-1934), Romanian princess
Alexander of Yugoslavia **1** 136-137

Marie (book; Nansen)
Bonnard, Pierre **2** 395-396

Marie, Andre (1897-1974), French statesman
Blum, Léon **2** 343-344

MARIE ANTOINETTE (1755-1793), queen of France 1774-1793 **10** 258-259
Beaumarchais, Pierre August Caron de **2** 93-94
Burke, Edmund **3** 138-141
Leopold II **9** 346
Louis XVI **9** 534-535
Turgot, Anne Robert Jacques **15** 348-349

Marie de Champagne (flourished circa 1164), French patron of the arts
Chrestien de Troyes **4** 23-24
Marie de France **10** 259

MARIE DE FRANCE (flourished late 12th century), French poet **10** 259

Marie de Médicis (1573-1642), Italian queen of Henry IV of France
Caccini, Giulio **3** 205-206

Henry IV **7** 293-295
Louis XIII **9** 529-531
Malherbe, François de **10** 169-170
Richelieu, Armand Jean du Plessis de **13** 142-144, 185
Rubens, Peter Paul **13** 339-342
Van Dyck, Anthony **15** 423-425

Marie from Sunny Italy (song)
Berlin, Irving **2** 200-201

Marie Galante (island; West Indies)
Columbus, Christopher **4** 176-179

Marie Galante (musical)
Weill, Kurt **16** 174-175

Marie Grubbe (novel)
Jacobsen, Jens Peter **8** 193-194

Marie José (born 1906), Belgian princess
Albert I **1** 112

Marie Josephe of Saxony (1731-1767), dauphiness of France
Charles X **3** 463-464

Marie Louise (1791-1847), second wife of Napoleon I
Napoleon I **11** 306-310

Marie Louise d'Orleans (1662-1689), queen of Spain
Charles II **3** 454

Marie Magdeleine (play)
Maeterlinck, Maurice **10** 125-126

Marienkapelle (Wützburg, Germany)
Riemenschneider, Tilman **13** 166

Mariette, Jean (1660-1742), French engraver
Watteau, Antoine **16** 143-144

Mariette, Pierre-Joseph (died 1729), French engraver and art dealer
Watteau, Antoine **16** 143-144

Marignano, battle of (1515)
Francis I **6** 40-43
Henry VIII **7** 302-305

Marihuana Papers, The (book)
Ginsberg, Allen **6** 332-333

Marillac, Louise de (1573-1632), marshal of France
Vincent de Paul **15** 501-502

Marillac, Michel de (1563-1632), French statesman
Louis XIII **9** 529-531
Richelieu, Armand Jean du Plessis de **13** 142-144

MARIN, JOHN, III (1870-1953), American painter **10** 259-260
Stieglitz, Alfred **14** 451-452

Marin, José Luís Alberto Muñoz
see Muñoz Marín, José Luís

Marine (poem)
Rimbaud, Jean Nicolas Arthur **13** 172-174

Marine biology
Colwell, Rita R. **4** 179-180
Earle, Sylvia A. **5** 180-181

Just, Ernest **8** 392-393

Marine engineering (science)
Bechtel, Stephen Davison **2** 98-99
Brunel, Isambard Kingdom **3** 69-70
Eads, James Buchanan **5** 175-176
Ericsson, John **5** 307-308
Fitch, John **5** 467-468
Forbes, Robert Bennet **5** 509-510
Gatling, Richard Jordan **6** 234-235
Parsons, Charles Algernon **12** 120-121
Shreve, Henry Miller **14** 207

Marinelli (literary character)
Lessing, Gotthold Ephraim **9** 357-359

Marinetti, Emilio Filippo Tommaso
(1876-1944), Italian futurist poet
Balla, Giacomo **1** 473-474
Boccioni, Umberto **2** 353-354

MARINI, MARINO (1901-1980), Italian
sculptor **10** 260-262
Manzù, Giacomo **10** 224-225

Marinid
see Merinid

Marino Faliero (play)
Byron, George Gordon Noel **3** 193-194

Marino, Giambattista (1569-1625), Italian
poet
Crashaw, Richard **4** 296
Poussin, Nicolas **12** 418-420

Mario and the Magician (novella)
Mann, Thomas **10** 204-207

MARION, FRANCIS (1732-1795), American Revolutionary War leader
10 262-263
Weems, Mason Locke **16** 170

Marise (novel)
Martin du Gard, Roger **10** 295-296

MARITAIN, JACQUES (1882-1973), French
Catholic philosopher **10** 263
Callaghan, Edward Morley **3** 229-230
Frei Montalva, Eduardo **6** 94-95
Rouault, Georges **13** 321-322
Stravinsky, Igor Fedorovich **14** 502-506

Maritime industry
unions
Bridges, Harry A.R. **3** 3-5

Maritime law (United States)
Dana, Richard Henry Jr. **4** 385-386

Marito e moglie (play)
Betti, Ugo **2** 246

MARIUS GAIUS (circa 157-86 B.C.),
Roman general and politician
10 264-265
Caesar, Gaius Julius **3** 207-210
Cicero, Marcus Tullius **4** 55-58
Crassus Dives, Marcus Licinius
4 296-297
Gracchus, Tiberius and Gaius Sempronius **6** 479-480
Pompey **12** 387-389
Sulla, Lucius Cornelius I **15** 21-22

Marius the Epicurean (novel)
Pater, Walter Horatio **12** 130-131

Marius Viewing the Ruins of Carthage
(painting)
Vanderlyn, John **15** 417

MARIVAUX, PIERRE CARLET DE CHAMBLAIN DE (1688-1763), French novelist
and dramatist **10** 265-266
Beaumarchais, Pierre August Caron de
2 93-94

Mark, Gospel of Saint
Jesus of Nazareth **8** 251-255

MARK, Saint (flourished 1st century), Apostle of Jesus **10** 266-267
John **8** 373-274
Justin Martyr **8** 395-396
Luke **10** 38
Matthew **10** 340-341

Mark I and II (electontronic music)
Babbitt, Milton **1** 410

Mark Hurdlestone (novel)
Moodie, Susanna **11** 140-141

Mark the Match Boy (book)
Alger, Horatio **1** 153-154

Marketing (economics)
Clark, John Maurice **4** 77-78
Pillsbury, Charles Alfred **12** 304
Say, Jean Baptiste **13** 508-509

MARKHAM, EDWIN (1852-1940), American poet **10** 267
Lindsey, Benjamin Barr **9** 425-426

Markham, Sir Clements R. (1830-1916),
English geographer
Scott, Robert Falcon **14** 67-68

MARKIEVICZ, CONSTANCE (1868-1927),
Irish nationalist, labor activist, and feminist **10** 267-271

Markland
see Labrador

Marlborough, Duchess of (Sarah Jennings
Churchill, 1660-1744), English
stateswoman
Anne **1** 241-242
Congreve, William **4** 200-201

MARLBOROUGH, 1ST DUKE OF (John
Churchill; 1650-1722), English general
and statesman **10** 271-272
Augustus II **1** 373-374
Churchill, Winston Leonard Spencer
4 51-53
Godolphin, Sidney **6** 380-381
Swift, Jonathan **15** 51-54
Vanbrugh, John **15** 409-410
see also Spanish Succession, War of the
(1702-1713)

Marlow (literary character)
Conrad, Joseph **4** 205-207

Marlowe (literary character)
Goldsmith, Oliver **6** 411-413

MARLOWE, CHRISTOPHER (1564-1593),
English dramatist **10** 272-274
Catullus, Gaius Valerius **3** 377-378

Chapman, George **3** 440-441
Machiavelli, Niccolò **10** 97-99
Seneca the Younger, Lucius Annaeus
14 103-105
Tamerlane **15** 94-95
see also Renaissance (literature)—England

Marly-le-Roi (Versailles)
Mansart, Jules Hardouin **10** 212

Marmion (poem)
Scott, Walter **14** 68-70

MÁRMOL, JOSÉ (1817-1871), Argentine
writer and intellectual **10** 274

Marmontel, Antoine François (1816-1898),
French pianist
MacDowell, Edward Alexander
10 87-88

Marne, battles of (1914, 1918)
Beck, Ludwig August Theoder **2** 99-100
Foch, Ferdinand **5** 498-499
Hindenburg, Paul Ludwig Hans von
Beneckendorff und von **7** 400-401
Joffre, Joseph Jacques Césaire
8 267-268
Péguy, Charles Pierre **12** 183-184
Pétain, Henri Philippe **12** 250-252
Rundstedt, Karl Rudolf Gerd Von
13 363-364

Marnie (film)
Hitchcock, Alfred **7** 415-416

Maro, Publius Vergilius
see Virgil

Marot, Clement (1495?-1544), French poet
Francis I **6** 40-43
Goudimel, Claude **6** 466
Guillaume de Lorris **7** 33-34
Le Jeune, Claude **9** 314-315
Spenser, Edmund **14** 373-376

Marphise (painting)
Delacroix, Ferdinand Victor Eugène
4 469-471

Marple, Jane (literary character)
Christie, Agatha **4** 25-26

Marquand, John P. (1893-1960), American
author
Kaufman, George S. **8** 457-458

Marquesa (ship)
Cervantes, Miguel de Saavedra
3 395-398

Marquesa Rosallnda, La (play)
Valle Inclán, Ramón Maria del
15 407-408

Marquesas Islands (southern Pacific Ocean)
Cook, James **4** 214-215
Melville, Herman **10** 472-476
Mendaña de Neyra, Álvaro de **10** 483

Marquet, Albert (1875-1947), French
painter
Matisse, Henri **10** 336-337
Rouault, Georges **13** 321-322

MARQUETTE, JACQUES (1637-1675),
French Jesuit, missionary and explorer
10 274-275
    Jolliet, Louis **8** 328-329
    Talon, Jean **15** 91-92

Márquez, Gabriel Garcia
    see Garcia Márquez, Gabriel

Marquis of Queensberry rules (boxing)
    Sullivan, John Lawrence **15** 24-25

Marquis von Keith, Der (play)
    Wedekind, Frank **16** 166-167

Marrakesh (city; Morocco)
    Abd al-Mumin **1** 13
    ibn Tashufin, Yusuf **8** 95-96
    Mohammed V **11** 79-81

Marriage (poem)
    Moore, Marianne **11** 148-149

Marriage (society)
    Gregory VII **6** 532-534
    Lindsey, Benjamin Barr **9** 425-426
    Milton, John **11** 43-46
    Russell, Bertrand Arthur William
        13 373-374

Marriage, The (opera)
    Mussorgsky, Modest Petrovich
        11 274-276

Marriage, The (play)
    Gogol, Nikolai **6** 391-393

Marriage at Cana (painting)
    Bosch, Hieronymus **2** 426-428
    Veronese, Paolo **15** 469-470

Marriage Circle, The (film)
    Lubitsch, Ernst **10** 18-19

Marriage of Barbarossa (painting)
    Tiepolo, Giovanni Battista **15** 219-220

Marriage of Camacho, The (opera)
    Mendelssohn, Moses **10** 488-489

Marriage of Figaro, The (play and opera)
    Beaumarchais, Pierre August Caron de
        2 93-94
    Mozart, Wolfgang Amadeus
        11 218-221

Marriage of Heaven and Hell, The (satire)
    Blake, William **2** 316-318

Marriage of Mr. Mississippi, The (play)
    Dürrenmatt, Friedrich **5** 164-165

Marriage of Peleus and Thetis (poem)
    Catullus, Gaius Valerius **3** 377-378

Marriage of Saint Catherine (painting)
    Poussin, Nicolas **12** 418-420

Marriage of the Virgin (painting)
    Raphael **13** 40-42

Marriage of Venice to the Sea (painting)
    Guardi, Francesco **7** 24-25

Married (stories)
    Strindberg, August **14** 509-511

Marrons du feu, Les (verse)
    Musset, Louis Charles Alfred de
        11 271-272

Mars (painting)
    Velázquez, Diego Rodríguez de Silva y
        15 454-456

Mars (planet)
    Brahe, Tycho **2** 489-490
    Hall, Asaph **7** 83-84
    Sagan, Carl E. **13** 424-425

Mars (sculpture)
    Sansovino, Jacopo **13** 470-471

Mars, Venus, and Vulcan (painting)
    Tintoretto **15** 232-234

Marse Chan (story)
    Page, Thomas Nelson **12** 59-60

Marsh, Edward Howard (1872-1953), English writer and wit
    Brooke, Rupert **3** 22-23

MARSH, OTHNIEL CHARLES (1831-1899),
American paleontologist **10** 275-276

MARSH, REGINALD (1898-1954), American painter and printmaker **10** 276-277
    Lichtenstein, Roy **9** 398-399

Marsh v. Alabama (legal case)
    Black, Hugo Lafayette **2** 301-303

Marsh Island, A (novel)
    Jewett, Sarah Orne **8** 256

MARSHALL, ALFRED (1842-1924), English economist **10** 277-278
    Clapham, John Harold **4** 71
    Knight, Frank Hyneman **9** 58-59
    Parsons, Talcott **12** 122
    Pigou, Arthur Cecil **12** 302

MARSHALL, GEORGE CATLETT
(1880-1959), American soldier and statesman **10** 278-279
    Chou En-lai **4** 20-22
    Eisenhower, Dwight David **5** 233-236
    McCarthy, Joseph Raymond **10** 388-389
    Truman, Harry S. **15** 314-316
    Wainwright, Jonathan Mayhew
        16 45-46

MARSHALL, JOHN (1755-1835), American jurist, chief justice of United States.
Supreme Court 1801-1835 **10** 279-281
    Burr, Aaron **3** 156-159
    Chase, Samuel **3** 475-476
    Martin, Luther **10** 289-290
    Story, Joseph **14** 480-481
    Taney, Roger Brooke **15** 98-99
    Waite, Morrison Remick **16** 46
    Webster, Daniel **16** 162-164

Marshall, Louis (1856-1929), American lawyer and Jewish leader
    Silver, Abba Hillel **14** 232-233

MARSHALL, PAULE BURKE (born 1929),
American author **10** 281-282

MARSHALL, THURGOOD (1908-1993),
African American jurist **10** 282-284

Marshall, William E. (1837-1906), American painter
    Ryder, Albert Pinkham **13** 391-392

Marshall College (Mercersburg, Pennsylvania)
    see Franklin and Marshall College

Marshall Field and Co. (established 1881)
    Field, Marshall **5** 440-441

Marshall Field Wholesale Store (Chicago, Illinois)
    Richardson, Henry Hobson **13** 139-141
    Sullivan, Louis Henri **15** 27-28

Marshall Plan (1947)
    Acheson, Dean Gooderham **1** 37-38
    Marshall, George Catlett **10** 278-279
    Nixon, Richard Milhous **11** 401-404
    Truman, Harry S. **15** 314-316
    Young, Whitney Moore Jr. **16** 476-477

Marshalsea debtors' prison (England)
    Dickens, Charles John Huffam
    4 538-541

Marshes of Glynn, The (poem)
    Lanier, Sidney **9** 199-200

Marshman, Joshua (1768-1837), English missionary and Orientalist
    Carey, William **3** 297

MARSILIUS OF PADUA (1275/80-1342),
Italian political philosopher **10** 284
    William of Ockham **16** 298-299

Marston, John (1575?-1634), English dramatist
    Chapman, George **3** 440-441
    Jonson, Ben **8** 343-345
    Webster, John **16** 164

Marston Moor, battle of (1644)
    Charles, I **3** 450-452
    Cromwell, Oliver **4** 317-320

Marsyas (sculpture)
    Myron **11** 285

Marta la piadosa (play)
    Tirso de Molina **15** 237-238

MARTEL, CHARLES (circa 690-741), Frankish ruler **10** 285
    Charlemagne **3** 445-447

Marteau sans maître, Le (musical composition)
    Boulez, Pierre **2** 444-445

Martha Graham Co. (dance troupe)
    Cunningham, Merce **4** 337-338

Martha Graham School of Contemporary Dance (New York City)
    Graham, Martha **6** 485-486

Martha the Hypocrite (play)
    Tirso de Molina **15** 237-238

Martha's Vineyard (island; southwestern Cape Cod)
    Champlain, Samuel de **3** 419-421

Marthe (novel)
    Huysmans, Joris Karl **8** 81-82

MARTÍ, JOSÉ (1853-1895), Cuban revolutionary, poet, and journalist **10** 285-286
    Estrada Palma, Tomás **5** 326-327
    Gómez, Máximo **6** 418-419
    Maceo, Antonio **10** 88-90

Martí, Juan (flourished 1602), Spanish lawyer and author
Alemán, Mateo **1** 126

MARTIAL (Marcus Valerias Martialis; circa 38/41-circa 104), Roman epigrammatist **10** 286-287
Juvenal **8** 397-399
Sallust **13** 454

Martianus Capella (flourished early 5th century), Carthaginian writer
Erigena, John Scotus **5** 308-309

Martin IV (Simon of Brie; 1210?-1285), pope 1281-1285
Boniface VIII **2** 392-393
Michael VIII **11** 1-2

MARTIN V (Oddone Colonna; 1368-1431), pope 1417-1431 **10** 287-288
Ailly, Pierre d' **1** 94
Gentile da Fabriano **6** 266-267
Gerson, John **6** 285-286

MARTIN, AGNES (born 1912), American painter **10** 288-289

Martin, Glenn L. (1886-1955), American aircraft manufacturer and aviator
Douglas, Donald Wills **5** 77

MARTIN, LUTHER (1748-1826), American lawyer and Revolutionary patriot **10** 289-290

MARTIN, LYNN MORLEY (born 1939), Republican representative from Illinois and secretary of labor under George Bush **10** 290-292

MARTIN, MARY (1913-1990), popular stage actress, singer, and dancer and a television and film star **10** 292-293

Martin, Violet
see Somerville, E.

MARTIN, WILLIAM MCCHESNEY, JR. (born 1906), American business executive and federal government official **10** 293-295

Martin Chuzzlewit (novel)
Dickens, Charles John Huffam **4** 538-541

MARTIN DU GARD, ROGER (1881-1958), French author **10** 295-296

Martin Eden (book)
London, Jack **9** 494-495

Martín Fierro (epic)
Hernández, José **7** 328-329

Martin House (Buffalo, New York State)
Wright, Frank Lloyd **16** 398-401

Martin Luther King Jr. Hospital (Los Angeles)
Drew, Charles Richard **5** 100-101

Martin Salander (novel)
Keller, Gottfried **8** 478-479

Martin v. Hunter's Lessee (legal case)
Story, Joseph **14** 480-481

Martin van Nieuwenhove (diptych)
Memling, Hans **10** 476

MARTINEAU, HARRIET (1802-1876), English writer and philosopher **10** 296-297

Martinez de Campos, Arsenio (1831-1900), Spanish general
Gómez, Máximo **6** 418-419
Maceo, Antonio **10** 88-90
Primo de Rivera y Orbaneja, Miguel **12** 454-455

Martinez de la Rosa, Francisco (1789-1862), Spanish statesman and author
Saavedra, Angel de **13** 398

MARTÍNEZ, MAXIMILIANO HERNÁNDEZ (1882-1966), president of El Salvador (1931-1944) **10** 297-298

Martinez Ruíz, José
see Ruíz, José Martinez

Martini, Padre (Giovanni Battista Martini; 1706-1784), Italian Franciscan composer and scholar
Bach, Johann Christian **1** 415-416
Donizetti, Gaetano **5** 59-60

MARTINI, SIMONE (flourished 1315-1344), Italian painter **10** 298-299
Cimabue **4** 60-61
Duccio di Buoninsegna **5** 121-122
Lorenzetti, Pietro and Ambrogio **9** 517-518

Martinique (island; West Indies)
Rodney, George Brydges **13** 239-240

MARTINU, BOHUSLAV (1890-1959), Czech composer **10** 299-300
Stravinsky, Igor Fedorovich **14** 502-506
Szymanowski, Karol **15** 67-68

Martinus Scriblerus (journal)
Pope, Alexander **12** 395-397
Swift, Jonathan **15** 51-54

Martirio de San Lorenzo (poems)
Gonzalo de Berceo **6** 431-432

Martius, Karl Friedrich Phillip von (1794-1868), German naturalist
Agassiz, Jean Louis Rodolphe **1** 76-78

Martov, Iuli O.T. (1873-1923), Russian Menshevik leader
Lenin, Vladimir Ilich **9** 323-326
Trotsky, Leon **15** 302-305

MARTY, MARTIN E. (born 1928), Lutheran pastor, historian of American religion, and commentator **10** 300-301

Martyrdom (theology)
Ignatius of Antioch **8** 107-108

Martyrdom of... (painting)
Saint Andrew
Ribera, Jusepe de **13** 122-123
Saint Apollonia
Jordaens, Jacob **8** 347-349
Saint Catherine
Cranach, Lucas the Elder **4** 289-290
Saint Erasmus
Poussin, Nicolas **12** 418-420
Saint Lawrence
Bronzino **3** 19

Titian **15** 242-244
Saint Mark
Bellini, Giovanni **2** 137-138
Saint Maurice
Greco **6** 511-514
Saint Peter
Titian **15** 242-244
Saint Sebastian
Pollaiuolo, Antonio **12** 377-378
the Ten Thousand
Dürer, Albrecht **5** 159-161

Martyrs Day (Burma; 1947)
Aung San **1** 374-375

Martyrs, Les (book)
Chateaubriand, Vicomte de **3** 477-479

MARVELL, ANDREW (1621-1678), English poet and politician **10** 301-303

Marville, Jean de (died 1389), Flemish sculptor
Sluter, Claus **14** 275-276

Marwan I (Marwan ibn-al-Hakam; died 685), Umayyad caliph 683-685
Abd al-Malik **1** 12-13

Marwan II (ruled 744-750), Umayyad caliph
Mansur, Abu Jafar ibn Muhammad al- **10** 214-215

MARX, KARL (1818-1883), German political philosopher **10** 304-308
associates
Engels, Friedrich **5** 286-288
Jacobi, Abraham and Mary Putnam **8** 188-189
Proudhon, Pierre Joseph **12** 461-463
economic theory
Böhm-Bawerk, Eugen von **2** 366
Jevons, William Stanley **8** 255-256
Kautsky, Karl Johann **8** 462-463
Schumpeter, Joseph Alois **14** 43-44
influenced by
Fourier, François Charles Marie **6** 31-32
Godwin, William **6** 383-384
Herder, Johann Gottfried von **7** 327-328
Morgan, Lewis Henry **11** 167-168
interpreters
Althusser, Louis **1** 182-183
Hook, Sidney **7** 474-475
opponents
Blanc, Louis **2** 318-319
Djilas, Milovan **5** 34
Popper, Karl Raimund **12** 402
Stirner, Max **14** 459-460
see also Marxism

Marx, Minnie (died 1929), American vaudeville actress
Marx brothers **10** 303-304

MARX BROTHERS, 20th-century American stage and film comedians **10** 303-304

Marx-Engels-Platz (Berlin)
Schinkel, Karl Friedrich **14** 8

Marxism (philosophy)
  Africa
    Houphouët-Boigny, Felix **7** 519-520
    Nkrumah, Kwame **11** 408-410
    Touré, Sékou **15** 275-277
  and Zionism
    Borochov, Dov Ber **2** 421-422
  China
    Ch'en Tu-hsiu **3** 501-502
    Chiang Kai-shek **3** 510-513
    Ho Chi Minh **7** 426-428
    Kuo Mo-jo **9** 133-134
    Li Ta-chao **9** 447
    Mao Zedong **10** 225-227
    Sun Yat-sen **15** 35-39
    Ts'ai Yüan-p'ei **15** 322
  critics
    Camus, Albert **3** 255-257
    Cohen, Hermann **4** 138-139
    Frei Montalva, Eduardo **6** 94-95
    Gompers, Samuel **6** 420-422
    Hu Shih **8** 63-65
    Levy, Bernard-Henri **9** 372-373
    Mandelstam, Osip Emilyevich
      10 191
    Masaryk, Tomáš Garrigue
      10 314-315
    Sombart, Werner **14** 332-333
    Tillich, Paul Johannes **15** 224-225
  England
    Auden, Wystan Hugh **1** 364-366
    Shaw, George Bernard **14** 163-164
  France
    Althusser, Louis **1** 182-183
    Lefebvre, Georges **9** 301-302
    Saint-Simon, Comte de **13** 436-437
    Sorel, Georges **14** 347-348
  Germany
    Bernstein, Eduard **2** 218
    Block, Herbert **2** 333-334
    Böhm-Bawerk, Eugen von **2** 366
    Engels, Friedrich **5** 286-288
    Hauptmann, Gerhart Johann Robert
      7 199-201
    Kautsky, Karl Johann **8** 462-463
    Lassalle, Ferdinand **9** 216
    Mannheim, Karl **10** 208-209
    Marx, Karl **10** 304-308
    Ulbricht, Walter **15** 383-384
  Hungary
    Lukács, Gyorgy **10** 37-38
  in literature
    Brecht, Bertolt **2** 512-514
    Farrell, James Thomas **5** 390-391
    O'Casey, Sean **11** 459-460
  India
    Menon, Vengalil Krishnan Krishna
      10 507-509
    Narayan, Jayaprakash **11** 312-313
  Italy
    Croce, Benedetto **4** 313-314
    Gramsci, Antonio **6** 488-489
    Mazzini, Giuseppe **10** 381-383
    Mussolini, Benito **11** 272-274
    Rosmini-Serbati, Antonio
      13 296-297

Marxism-Leninism
  Foster, William Zebulon **6** 27-28
  Stalin, Joseph **14** 393-396
  Toledano, Vicente Lombardo
    15 256-257
  papal attitudes
    Leo XIII **9** 334-336
    Pius XI **12** 337-339
    Pius XII **12** 339-340
  Poland
    Kolakowski, Leszek **9** 76-77
  Russia
    Lenin, Vladimir Ilich **9** 323-326
    Pavlov, Ivan Petrovich **12** 155-157
    Plekhanov, Georgi Valentinovich
      12 351-352
    Stalin, Joseph **14** 393-396
    Trotsky, Leon **15** 302-305
  United States
    Cleaver, Leroy Eldridge **4** 97-98
    Cohen, Morris Raphael **4** 139-140
    London, Jack **9** 494-495
    Marcuse, Herbert **10** 245-247
    Mills, C. Wright **11** 35-36
    Norris, Benjamin Franklin Jr.
      11 427-428
    Veblen, Thorstein Bunde
      15 449-450
    Wilson, Edmund **16** 318-319
  see also Communism; Socialism

Marxist French Workers' party
  Jaurès, Jean **8** 226-227

Mary (Princess of Teck; 1867-1953), queen
of George V of England
  George V **6** 273-275

Mary (ruled 1382-1395), queen of Hungary
  Sigismund **14** 220-221

Mary (trilogy)
  Asch, Shalom **1** 325-326

MARY I (1516-1558), queen of England
1553-1558 **10** 308-309
  opponents
    Leicester, Earl of **9** 312-313
    Northumberland, Duke of
      11 431-432
  relatives
    Charles V **3** 457-459
    Elizabeth I **5** 263-266
    Henry VIII **7** 302-305
    Philip II **12** 271-273
  religious persecution
    Coverdale, Miles **4** 278
    Cranmer, Thomas **4** 295-296
    Edward VI **5** 213-214
    Knox, John **9** 65-66
    Latimer, Hugh **9** 221

MARY II (1662-1694), queen of England,
Scotland, and Ireland 1689-1694
10 309-310
  Anne **1** 241-242
  Burnet, Gilbert **3** 147
  Calvert, Charles **3** 238
  Steele, Richard **14** 407-409
  William III **16** 295-296

MARY, QUEEN OF SCOTS (1542-1587),
queen of France and Scotland
10 308-309
  in literature
    Alfieri, Vittoria **1** 145-146
    Anderson, Maxwell **1** 219-220
    Lope Félix de Vega Carpio
      9 503-506
    Schiller, Johann Christoph Friedrich
      von **14** 4-7
    Vondel, Joost van den **16** 19-20
  musical settings
    Dallapiccola, Luigi **4** 377-378
  opponents
    Elizabeth I **5** 263-266
    Knox, John **9** 65-66
    Leicester, Earl of **9** 312-313
  relatives
    Edward VI **5** 213-214
    James I **8** 204-206
  supporters
    Gregory XIII **6** 534

MARY, Saint (Blessed Virgin Mary; late 1st
century B.C.-1st century A.D.), New Tes-
tament figure, mother of Jesus
10 308-309
  Cyril **4** 362
  Duns Scotus, John **5** 149-150
  Jesus of Nazareth **8** 251-255
  Luke **10** 38
  Nestorius **11** 349-350
  Quercia, Jacopo della **12** 509

Mary Barton (novel)
  Gaskell, Elizabeth **6** 231-232

Mary Had a Little Lamb (poem)
  Hale, Sarah Josepha **7** 74-75

Mary Kay Cosmetics, Inc.
  Ash, Mary Kay Wagner **1** 326-327

Mary Magdalen (sculpture)
  Donatello **5** 55-56

Mary Magdalene (New Testament figure)
  Jesus of Nazareth **8** 251-255

Mary, Mary (novel)
  Stephens, James **14** 430-431

Mary Morison (song)
  Burns, Robert **3** 155-156

Mary of Burgundy (1457-1482), duchess,
wife of Maximilian I
  Charles the Bold **3** 467-469
  Maximilian I **10** 356-357

Mary of France (Mary Tudor; 1496-1533),
queen of Louis XII of France
  Louis XII **9** 528-529

Mary of Guise (1515-1560), queen of
James V of Scotland, regent 1554-1559
  Mary, I **10** 308-309

Mary Poppins (film)
  Disney, Walter Elias **5** 26-27

Mary Rose (play)
  Barrie, James Matthew **2** 21-22

Mary's a Grand Old Name (song)
Cohan, George Michael **4** 137-138

Maryland (state; United States)
border disputes
Chase, Samuel **3** 475-476
Logan, James **9** 487-488
Penn, William **12** 200-202
colonial period
Calvert, Charles **3** 238
Calvert, George **3** 238-239
Forbes, John **5** 507-508
Martin, Luther **10** 289-290
Nicholson, Francis **11** 381-382
Protestant missionaries
Asbury, Francis **1** 324-325
Makemie, Francis **10** 158-159
Mühlenberg, Heinrich Melchior
11 232-233

Maryland, University of (College Park)
Colwell, Rita R. **4** 179-180
Elsasser, Walter Maurice **5** 277-278
Marshall, Thurgood **10** 282-284
Mills, C. Wright **11** 35-36
Sullivan, Harry Stack **15** 23-24

Maryland-in-Liberia (American colony)
Russwurm, John Brown **13** 381-382

Marzocco (sculpture)
Donatello **5** 55-56

MASACCIO (1401-1428), Italian painter
10 312-313
Andrea del Castagno **1** 223-224
Lippi, Filippo **9** 439
Martin V **10** 287-288
Moore, Henry **11** 146-148
Sassetta **13** 492
Uccello, Paolo **15** 378-379
Veneziano, Domenico **15** 459-460

Masada (fortress; Judea)
Herod the Great **7** 333-334
Josephus Flavius **8** 360-361

Masafuji
see Mabuchi, Kamo

Masahito
see Goshirakawa

Masanobu
see Mabuchi, Kamo

MASARYK, TOMÁŠ GARRIGUE
(1850-1937), Czech philosopher and
statesman, president 1919-1935
10 314-315
Beneš, Edward **2** 155-157
Čapek, Karel **3** 271-272

Mascat and Oman
see Oman

Maschera dimenticata, La (story)
Pirandello, Luigi **12** 319-321

Mascherata, La (book)
Moravia, Alberto **11** 153-155

Maschere nude (drama collection)
Pirandello, Luigi **12** 319-321

Maschinenbau Gesellschaft (auto firm;
Karisruhe)
Daimler, Gottlieb **4** 368

Maschinenstürmer, Die (play)
Toller, Ernst **15** 261

Masefield, John (1878-1967), English poet
and novelist
Brooke, Rupert **3** 22-23

Maser (city; Italy)
Veronese, Paolo **15** 469-470

Mashhad (city; Iran)
Abbas I **1** 4-6

Masina, Giulietta (1921-1974), Italian
actress
Fellini, Federico **5** 408-409

MASINISSA, KING OF NUMIDIA (240
B.C. - 148 B.C.), prince of the Massylians
who consolidated the Numidian tribes to
form a North African kingdom
10 315-317
Scipio Africanus Major, Publius Cornelius **14** 61-62
Scipio Africanus Minor, Publius Cornelius Aemilianus **14** 62-63

MASIRE, QUETT KETUMILE (born 1925), a
leader of the fight for independence and
president of Botswana **10** 318-319

Masjumi (Indonesia; political party)
Sukarno **15** 18-20

Mask (literary concept)
Pirandello, Luigi **12** 319-321
Yeats, William Butler **16** 445-447

Mask, A (play)
see Comus

Masked Days, The (stories)
Fuentes, Carlos **6** 141-142

Masks (sculpture)
Moore, Henry **11** 146-148

Masnadieri, I (opera)
Verdi, Giuseppe Fortunino Francesco
15 463-465

Masolino da Panicale (1383-1447), Italian
painter
Veneziano, Domenico **15** 459-460
Ghiberti, Lorenzo **6** 291-292
Masaccio **10** 312-313

Mason, Charles (1730-1787), British
astronomer
Rittenhouse, David **13** 180-181

MASON, GEORGE (1725-1792), American
statesman **10** 319-320

MASON, JAMES MURRAY (1796-1871),
American politician and Confederate
diplomat **10** 320-321
Slidell, John **14** 273
Sumner, Charles **15** 30-31
Wilkes, Charles **16** 279-280
see also Trent Affair

Mason, John (1586-1635), British colonizer
Gorges, Ferdinando **6** 455-456

MASON, LOWELL (1792-1872), American
composer and music educator
10 321-322

Mason, William (1829-1908), American
musician
Liszt, Franz **9** 445-447

Masonic Fraternity
see Freemasonry

Masorah (Old Testament commentaries)
Gershom ben Judah **6** 283-284

Masque of Alfred, The (masque)
Arne, Thomas Augustine **1** 307-308

Masque of Anarchy, The (poem)
Shelley, Percy Bysshe **14** 176-178

Masque of Mercy, A (verse drama)
Frost, Robert Lee **6** 130-133

Masque of Poets, A (book)
Jackson, Helen Hunt **8** 172

Masque of Reason, A (verse drama)
Frost, Robert Lee **6** 130-133

Masquerade (opera)
Nielsen, Carl August **11** 388-389

Masquerade (play; Lermontov)
Lermontov, Mikhail Yurievich
9 352-353
Meyerhold, Vsevolod Emilievich **10** 539

Masquerades and Operas ... (print)
Hogarth, William **7** 446-447

Masques (theater)
see Court masques

Mass (music)
Austria
Bruckner, Joseph Anton **3** 64-65
Fux, Johann Joseph **6** 155-156
Haydn, Franz Joseph **7** 219-221
Schubert, Franz Peter **14** 35-37
Brazil
Villa-Lobos, Heitor **15** 496-497
England
Dunstable, John **5** 150-151
Tallis, Thomas **15** 91
Vaughan Williams, Ralph
15 446-447
Walton, William Turner **16** 92-93
Flanders
Clemens non Papa, Jacobus **4** 101
Isaac, Heinrich **8** 143-144
Josquin des Prez **8** 361-363
Lassus, Roland de **9** 216-218
Willaert, Adrian **16** 287-288
France
Gombert, Nicolas **6** 416-417
Goudimel, Claude **6** 466
Le Jeune, Claude **9** 314-315
Machaut, Guillaume de **10** 93-94
Germany
Bach, Johann Sebastian **1** 416-419
Beethoven, Ludwig van **2** 114-117
Brahms, Johannes **2** 490-492
Hindemith, Paul **7** 399-400
Senfl, Ludwig **14** 105-106
Italy

Carissimi, Giacomo **3** 299-300
Merulo, Claudio **10** 525-526
Palestrina, Giovanni Pierluigi da
  12 70-72
Pergolesi, Giovanni Battista
  12 218-219
Vivaldi, Antonio **16** 3-4
Zarlino, Gioseffo **16** 490-491
Netherlands
  Dufay, Guillaume **5** 125-126
  Obrecht, Jacob **11** 457-458
  Ockeghem, Johannes **11** 464-465
Spain
  Victoria, Tomás Luis de **15** 487-488
Switzerland
  Notker Balbulus **11** 434-435
  Senfl, Ludwig **14** 105-106
United States
  Sessions, Roger Huntington
    14 117-118
  Thomson, Virgil **15** 202-203
Union of Soviet Socialist Republics
  Rachmaninov, Sergei Vasilievich
    12 531-532
  Stravinsky, Igor Fedorovich
    14 502-506
  see also Requiem (music)

Mass, Sacrifice of the (religion)
see Eucharist

Mass action (brain function)
Lashley, Karl Spencer **9** 214-215

Mass and Man (play)
Toller, Ernst **15** 261

Mass man (philosophy)
Ortega Y Gasset, José **12** 7-8

Mass of Bolsena (painting; Raphael)
Poussin, Nicolas **12** 418-420

Mass production (industry)
development
  Chrysler, Walter Percy **4** 36-37
  Colt, Samuel **4** 172-173
  Eastman, George **5** 186
  Ford, Henry **6** 5-6
  Whitney, Eli **16** 253-254
industrial unionism
  Dubinsky, David **5** 114-115
  Hillman, Sidney **7** 392-393
  Lewis, John Llewellyn **9** 387-388
  see also Business and industry

Mass spectrography (physics)
Aston, Francis William **1** 350-351
Lawrence, Ernest Orlando **9** 248-250
Thomson, Joseph John **15** 200-201

Mass und Wert (literary magazine)
Mann, Thomas **10** 204-207

Massachusetts (state; United States)
colony founded
  Endecott, John **5** 284-285
  Gorges, Ferdinando **6** 455-456
  see also Massachusetts Bay Company
constitutions (1780; 1783)
  Adams, John **1** 48-51

Adams, Samuel **1** 55-56
Bowdoin, James **2** 461-462
Cuffe, Paul **4** 331-332
courts
  Holmes, Oliver Wendell Jr.
    7 458-459
governors
  Adams, Samuel **1** 55-56
  Andrew, John Albion **1** 230-231
  Dukakis, Michael **5** 130-133
  Everett, Edward **5** 344
  Gage, Thomas **6** 169-170
  Gerry, Elbridge **6** 282-283
  Hancock, John **7** 114-116
  Hutchinson, Thomas **8** 71-72
  Pepperell, William **12** 206-207
  Phips, William **12** 283
  Vane, Henry **15** 425-426
  Winthrop, John **16** 339-341
King Philip's War
  see King Philip's War
legislators (18th-19th century)
  Adams, John **1** 48-51
  Cutler, Manasseh **4** 356-357
  Leonard, Daniel **9** 336-337
legislators (19th century)
  Adams, Charles Francis **1** 41-42
  Adams, John Quincy **1** 52-54
  Andrew, John Albion **1** 230-231
  Appleton, Nathan **1** 266-267
  Burlingame, Anson **3** 144-145
  Curtis, Benjamin Robbins **4** 349
  Dawes, Henry Laurens **4** 427
  Lawrence, Abbott **9** 246
  Mann, Horace **10** 202-204
  Otis, Harrison Gray **12** 25
  Pickering, Timothy **12** 298-299
  Shaw, Lemuel **14** 164-165
  Story, Joseph **14** 480-481
  Wilson, James Harold **16** 324-325
  Wright, Carroll Davidson **16** 396
legislators (19th-20th century)
  Coolidge, John Calvin **4** 217-219
  Curley, James Michael **4** 344-345
  Lodge, Henry Cabot **9** 482-483
legislators (20th century)
  Rogers, Edith Nourse **13** 247-248
new charter (1692)
  Bradford, William **2** 475-476
  Mather, Cotton **10** 330-332
  Mather, Increase **10** 332-333
religion (colonial era)
  Bishop, Bridget **2** 288-290
  Hutchinson, Anne Marbury **8** 69-71
  Mather, Cotton **10** 330-332
  Sewall, Samuel **14** 123-124
  Williams, Roger **16** 304-305
  Wise, John **16** 343-344
Shays' Rebellion
  see Shays' Rebellion
state boards
  Bowditch, Henry Ingersoll
    2 459-460
  Mann, Horace **10** 202-204
  Wright, Carroll Davidson **16** 396

Massachusetts Antislavery Society
Douglass, Frederick **5** 85-86
Garrison, William Lloyd **6** 226-228
Remond, Charles Lennox **13** 95

Massachusetts Bay Company (1628-1684)
Davenport, John **4** 405-406
Dudley, Thomas **5** 124-125
Gorges, Ferdinando **6** 455-456
see also Massachusetts

Massachusetts Committee of Safety (American Revolution)
Revere, Paul **13** 110-111

Massachusetts General Hospital (Boston)
Bowditch, Henry Ingersoll **2** 459-460
Cabot, Richard Clarke **3** 200
Cushing, Harvey Williams **4** 353-354

Massachusetts Government Act (1774)
Leonard, Daniel **9** 336-337
see also Intolerable Acts

Massachusetts Indians (North America)
Eliot, John **5** 256-258

Massachusetts Institute of Technology (Cambridge)
architecture and sculpture
  Aalto, Hugo Alvar Henrik **1** 1-2
  Calder, Alexander **3** 216-218
  Saarinen, Eliel and Eero **13** 396-398
endowments
  Eastman, George **5** 186
  Sloan, Alfred Pritchard Jr. **14** 274
engineering
  Bush, Vannevar **3** 169-171
science
  Baltimore, David **1** 477-478
  Born, Max **2** 420-421
  Eliot, Charles William **5** 254
  Lewis, Gilbert Newton **9** 384-385
  Pickering, Edward Charles **12** 298
  Rabi, Isidor Isaac **12** 526-527
  Townes, Charles Hard **15** 281-282
  Wiener, Norbert **16** 262-263
social science
  Lewin, Kurt **9** 375-376
  Rostow, Walt Whitman **13** 315-317
  Samuelson, Paul Anthony
    13 458-459

Massachusetts Practice Act (1851)
Curtis, Benjamin Robbins **4** 349

Massachusetts Statehouse (Boston)
Bulfinch, Charles **3** 116-117

Massachusetts to Virginia (poem)
Whittier, John Greenleaf **16** 256-257

Massacre at Chios (painting; Delacroix)
Delacroix, Ferdinand Victor Eugène
  4 469-471
Ingres, Jean Auguste Dominique
  8 121-123

Massacre of the Innocents (painting)
Bruegel, Pieter the Elder **3** 65-67
Poussin, Nicolas **12** 418-420

MASSASOIT (1580-1661), Native American tribal chief **10** 322-324

Bradford, William **2** 475-476
Metacom **10** 529-531
Philip **12** 267-268

Masse Mensch (play)
Toller, Ernst **15** 261

Masséna, André (1758-1817), French marshal
Wellington, 1st Duke of **16** 193-195

Massenet, Jules (1842-1912), French composer
Prévost, Abbé **12** 445-446

Masses, The (magazine)
Eastman, Max **5** 187-188
Hand, Billings Learned **7** 116
Reed, John Silas **13** 76-77
Sloan, John **14** 274-275

MASSEY, WILLIAM FERGUSON
(1856-1925), New Zealand prime minister 1912-1925 **10** 324

Massine, Léonide (1896-1979), Russian-American dancer and choreographer
Miró, Joan **11** 53-54

Massinger, Arthur (died 1603), Englishman in service of Herbert family
Massinger, Philip **10** 324-325

MASSINGER, PHILIP (1583-1640), English playwright **10** 324-325
Dekker, Thomas **4** 465-466
Fletcher, John **5** 487
Jonson, Ben **8** 343-345

Mass-luminosity Law (astronomy)
Eddington, Arthur Stanley **5** 201-202

Massnahme, Die (play)
Brecht, Bertolt **2** 512-514

Masson, André (1896-1987), French painter
Gorky, Arshile **6** 458

Masson, David (1822-1907), Scottish scholar and critic
Milton, John **11** 43-46

MASSYS, QUENTIN (1465/66-1530), Flemish painter **10** 325-326
Bosch, Hieronymus **2** 426-428

Mast cell (anatomy)
Ehrlich, Paul **5** 225-226

Mastai-Ferretti, Giovanni Maria
see Pius IX

Master and Margarita, The (novel)
Bulgakov, Mikhail Afanasievich **3** 117

Master Builder, The (play)
Ibsen, Henrik **8** 98-100

Master E.S. (circa 1430-1468), German engraver and goldsmith
Schongauer, Martin **14** 26-28

Master Engravings
Dürer, Albrecht **5** 159-161

Master Mason, The (play)
Kazantzakis, Nikos **8** 466-468

Master Meng
see Mencius

Master of Ballantrae, The (novel)
Stevenson, Robert Louis **14** 446-448

Master of Flémalle
see Campin, Robert

Master of Hestviken, The (novel)
Undset, Sigrid **15** 388-389

Master of the Mill, The (novel)
Grove, Frederick Philip **7** 20-21

Master Olof (play)
Strindberg, August **14** 509-511

MASTERS, EDGAR LEE (1869-1950), American author and lawyer **10** 326-327
Benét, Stephen Vincent **2** 157-158
Lindsay, Vachel **9** 424-425
Lowell, Amy **10** 13

MASTERS, WILLIAM HOWELL (born 1915), American psychologist and sex therapist **10** 327-328
Johnson, Virginia E. **8** 317-319

Masters, The (novel)
Snow, Charles Percy **14** 311-312

Mastersingers of Nuremburg, The (opera)
Wagner, Richard **16** 40-43

Masterson, William Bradley "Bat"
(1853-1921), American sheriff and sports writer
Love, Nat **10** 1-2

MASUDI, ALI IBN AL- HUSAYN AL- (died 956), Arab historian **10** 328-329

Matabele
see Ndebele

MATAMOROS, MARINO (1770-1814), Mexican priest and independence hero **10** 329-330

Mataquito (river, Chile)
Lautaro **9** 235

Matchmaker, The (play)
Wilder, Thornton Niven **16** 276-277

Mateo Falcone (novel)
Mérimée, Prosper **10** 517

Mater Dolorosa (painting)
Titian **15** 242-244

Mater et Magistra (encyclical)
John, XXIII **8** 277-280

Materia (painting)
Boccioni, Umberto **2** 353-354

Materialism (philosophy)
opponents
Carlyle, Thomas **3** 304-305
Cohen, Hermann **4** 138-139
Cudworth, Ralph **4** 331
Dewey, John **4** 520-523
Emerson, Ralph Waldo **5** 278-280
Price, Richard **12** 447-448
Stirner, Max **14** 459-460
proponents
Diderot, Denis **5** 1-2
Du Bois-Reymond, Emil **5** 118-119

Engels, Friedrich **5** 286-288
Hobbes, Thomas **7** 421-423
Holbach, Baron d' **7** 448-449
Hu Shih **8** 63-65
La Mettrie, Julien Offray de **9** 179-180
Marx, Karl **10** 304-308
Santayana, George **13** 475-477
see also Dialectical materialism; Immaterialism (philosophy); Naturalism; Sensation (philosophy)

Materialism and Empiriocriticism (book)
Lenin, Vladimir Ilich **9** 323-326

Maternité Hospital, La (Paris)
Blackwell, Elizabeth **2** 311-312

Mathematics
algebra
see Algebra
and computer sciences
Bernstein, Dorothy Lewis **2** 217
applied
Babbage, Charles **1** 407-408
Bernstein, Dorothy Lewis **2** 217
Calderón, Alberto P. **3** 219-220
Granville, Evelyn Boyd **6** 494-496
Mandelbrot, Benoit B. **10** 189-191
Tartaglia, Niccolo **15** 111-112
Tsiolkovsky, Konstantin Eduardovich **15** 326-328
Turing, Alan Mathison **15** 349-350
Von Neumann, John **16** 27-28
Calderón-Zygmund theory
Calderón, Alberto P. **3** 219-220
chaos theory
Feigenbaum, Mitchell Jay **5** 404-405
cosmology
Hawking, Stephen William **7** 206-208
finite differences theory
Babbage, Charles **1** 407-408
Taylor, Brook **15** 121-122
fractals
Mandelbrot, Benoit B. **10** 189-191
geometry
Penrose, Roger **12** 204-205
see also Geometry
group theory
Lagrange, Joseph Louis **9** 164-166
Wigner, Eugene Paul **16** 268-269
instantons
Uhlenbeck, Karen **15** 381-382
logarithms
Euler, Leonard **5** 331-332
Napier, John **11** 306
logic
see Logic, symbolic
mathematical economics
Clark, John Maurice **4** 77-78
Cournot, Antoine Augustin **4** 273
Samuelson, Paul Anthony **13** 458-459
matrix calculus
see Matrix calculus
number
see Number

physical mathematics
  Bernoulli, Daniel **2** 216
  Hamilton, William Rowan **7** 99-100
  Leibniz, Gottfried Wilhelm von
    9 307-310
probability
  see Probability
set theory
  Cantor, Georg Ferdinand Ludwig
    Philipp **3** 265-266
  Quine, Willard Van Orman
    12 514-515
  Tarski, Alfred **15** 110-111
statistics
  see Statistics
symbols
  Asoka **1** 341-342
  Fibonacci, Leonardo **5** 434-435
  Recorde, Robert **13** 68-69
theory of games
  Robinson, Julia **13** 210-211
  Von Neumann, John **16** 27-28
topology
  Poincaré, Jules Henri **12** 365-366
trigonometry
  see Trigonometry
  see also Scientists—mathematicians

MATHER, COTTON (1663-1728), Ameri-
can Puritan clergyman and historian
10 330-332
  Boylston, Zabdiel **2** 471
  Phips, William **12** 283
  Porter, Katherine Anne **12** 406-407
  Taylor, Edward **15** 122-123
  Wise, John **16** 343-344

MATHER, INCREASE (1639-1723), Ameri-
can Puritan clergymen, educator, and
author **10** 332-333
  Mather, Cotton **10** 330-332
  Phips, William **12** 283
  Stoddard, Solomon **14** 462-463
  Taylor, Edward **15** 122-123
  Wise, John **16** 343-344

Mather, Richard (1596-1669), American
Congregationalist clergyman
  Mather, Cotton **10** 330-332

Mathew, Theobald (1790-1856), Irish priest
  O'Connell, Daniel **11** 465-467

Mathias Crovinus
  see Matthias Corvinus

MATHIEZ, ALBERT (1874-1932), French
historian **10** 333-334

Mathilde (literary character)
  Stendhal **14** 422-425

Mathis der Maler (opera; Hindemith)
  Grünewald, Matthias **7** 23-24
  Hindemith, Paul **7** 399-400

Mathnawi (literary collection)
  Rumi, Jalai ed-Din **13** 362-363

Matilda (1102-1167), wife of Holy Roman
Emperor Henry V
  David I **4** 407
  Henry I **7** 286-287

Henry II **7** 287-289
Henry V **7** 295-296
Stephen **14** 426-427
William I **16** 290-291

Matilda of Flanders (died 1083), wife of
William I
  William I **16** 290-291

MATILDA OF TUSCANY (ca. 1046-1115),
Italian countess
  Henry IV **7** 292
  Innocent, III **8** 125-127

MATISSE, HENRI (1869-1954), French
painter and sculptor **10** 336-337
  associates
    Derain, André **4** 503
    Gris, Juan **7** 5-6
    Morrice, James Wilson **11** 181-182
    Rouault, Georges **13** 321-322
    Stein, Gertrude **14** 414-415
    Stella, Joseph **14** 422
    Vlaminck, Maurice **16** 6
    Weber, Max **16** 160
  influence of
    Beckmann, Max **2** 104-105
    Glackens, William **6** 355-356
    Klee, Paul **9** 47-49
    Rivera, Diego **13** 183-184
    Staël, Nicolas de **14** 392
    Stella, Frank **14** 420-422
  influenced by
    Cézanne, Paul **3** 400-402
    Gauguin, Paul **6** 236-238
  United States exhibitions
    Steichen, Edward **14** 411-412
    Stieglitz, Alfred **14** 451-452

Matoaka
  see Pocahontas

Matriarchy (sociology)
  Frazier, Edward Franklin **6** 77

Matrimonial Speculations (novel)
  Moodie, Susanna **11** 140-141

Matrimonio segreto, Il (opera)
  Cimarosa, Domenico **4** 61-62

Matrix calculus (mathematics)
  Dirac, Paul Adrien Maurice **5** 23-24
  Heisenberg, Werner Karl **7** 261-263

Matrix mechanics (physics)
  Bohr, Niels Henrik David **2** 366-368
  Einstein, Albert **5** 228-231
  Schrödinger, Erwin **14** 31-33

Matryona's House (story)
  Solzhenitsyn, Alexander Isayevich
    14 330-332

Matsukata, Masayoshi (died 1924), Japanese statesman
  Saionji, Kimmochi **13** 438-439

Matsukaze (No play)
  Zeami, Kanze **16** 492-493

Matsushima (island group; Japan)
  Sotatsu, Tawaraya **14** 349

Matsys, Quentin
  see Massys, Quentin

Matta Echaurren, Roberto (born 1911/12),
Chilean painter
  Gorky, Arshile **6** 458

MATTEI, ENRICO (1906-1962), Italian
entrepreneur **10** 337-339

Mattei, Padre (1750-1825), Italian musician
  Donizetti, Gaetano **5** 59-60

Matteo di Pasti (circa 1410/12-1467/68),
Italian architect, sculptor and miniaturist
  Agostino di Duccio **1** 86

MATTEOTTI, GIACOMO (1885-1924), Ital-
ian political leader **10** 339-340
  Mussolini, Benito **11** 272-274
  Orlando, Vittorio Emmanuele
    11 529-530
  Pirandello, Luigi **12** 319-321

Matter (physics)
  Bohr, Niels Henrik David **2** 366-368
  Boyle, Robert **2** 469-471
  de Broglie, Louis **4** 442-444
  Kapitsa, Pyotr Leonidovich **8** 433-435
  Schrödinger, Erwin **14** 31-33
  Steno, Nicolaus **14** 425-426

Matter and Memory (book)
  Bergson, Henri **2** 191-192

Matteucci, Carlo (1811-1868), Italian
physicist
  Du Bois-Reymond, Emil **5** 118-119

Matthew (ship)
  Cabot, John **3** 199-200

Matthew, Gospel of Saint (New Testament)
  Anthony, Susan Brownell **1** 246-248
  Jesus of Nazareth **8** 251-255

MATTHEW, SAINT (flourished Ist century),
Apostle and Evangelist **10** 340-341
  John **8** 273-274
  Justin Martyr **8** 395-396
  Mark **10** 266-267
  Mary **10** 308
  Peter **12** 252-253

Matthew, Thomas (pseudonym)
  see Rogers, John

Matthew Bible
  Coverdale, Miles **4** 278
  Tyndale, William **15** 373-374

Matthew of Janov (died 1393), Bohemian
theologian
  Hus, Jan **8** 56-59

MATTHEW PARIS (circa 1200-1259), English Benedictine chronicler **10** 341-342

Matthias (1557-1619), Holy Roman emper-
or 1612-1619
  Ferdinand II **5** 415
  Wallenstein, Albrecht Wenzel Eusebius
    von **16** 80-81

Matthias Corvinus (1440-1490), king of
Hungary 1458-1490
  Frederick III **6** 84-85

Hunyadi, John **8** 51-52
Regiomontanus **13** 81-82

MATTINGLY, GARRETT (1900-1962), American historian, professor, and author of novel-like histories **10** 342-344

Mattingly, Marie
see Meloney, Mrs. William B.

Mau Mau movement (Kenya)
Kawawa, Rashidi Mfaume **8** 464-465
Kenyatta, Jomo **8** 512-514
Mboya, Thomas Joseph **10** 384-385
Ngala, Ronald Gideon **11** 373-374
Odinga, Ajuma Jaramogi Oginga **11** 471-473

Maua, Our Boatman (painting)
La Farge, John **9** 149-150

Mauberley (poems)
see Hugh Selwyn Mauberley

Maubeuge, siege of (1793)
Carnot, Lazare Nicolas Marguerite **3** 313-314

Maud ... (poems)
Tennyson, Alfred **15** 144-146

Maud (ship)
Amundsen, Roald **1** 206-207

Maud, Empress
see Matilda

Maud Muller (poem)
Whittier, John Greenleaf **16** 256-257

MAUGHAM, WILLIAM SOMERSET (1874-1965), English author **10** 344-345
Morrice, James Wilson **11** 181-182
Sutherland, Graham **15** 40-41

Maui (island; Hawaii)
Kamehameha I **8** 416

MAULBERTSCH, FRANZ ANTON (1724-1796), Austrian painter **10** 345
Troger, Paul **15** 300

MAULDIN, BILL (born 1921), cartoon biographer of the ordinary GI in World War II **10** 345-346

MAUPASSANT, HENRI RENÉ ALBERT GUY DE (1850-1893), French author **10** 347
associates
Flaubert, Gustave **5** 480-482
Turgenev, Ivan Sergeyevich **15** 345-348
Zola, Émile **16** 526-528
influence of
D'Annunzio, Gabriele **4** 388
Kipling, Joseph Rudyard **9** 32-33
Mann, Heinrich **10** 201-202
Wedekind, Frank **16** 166-167

Maupeou, René Nicholas Charles Augustin (1714-1792), French chancellor 1768-1774
Louis XV **9** 533-534

Maupertuis, P.L.M. de (1698-1759), French mathematician and astronomer
Voltaire **16** 14-16

Maurer, Alfred (1868-1932), American painter
Dove, Arthur Garfield **5** 86-87
Marin, John III **10** 259-260

Maurer, Louis (1832-1932), German-born American artist
Currier and Ives **4** 345-346

MAURIAC, FRANÇOIS (1885-1970), French author **10** 347-348
Marcel, Gabriel **10** 233-234

Maurice, Duke of Saxony (1521-1553), elector of Saxony 1547-1553
Alba, Duke of **1** 103-104
Charles V **3** 457-459
Walter, Johann **16** 86

MAURICE, JOHN FREDERICK DENISON (1805-1872), English theologian and Anglican clergyman **10** 349-350
Coleridge, Samuel Taylor **4** 154-156
Kingsley, Charles **9** 28

Maurice Guest (novel)
Richardson, Henry Handel **13** 139

MAURICE OF NASSAU, PRINCE OF ORANGE (1567-1625), Dutch general and statesman **10** 348-349
Grotius, Hugo **7** 18-19
Gustavus II **7** 43-45
Oldenbarnevelt, Johan van **11** 495-496
William the Silent **16** 300-302
Witt, Johan de **16** 348-349

Maurice of Saxony
see Maurice, Duke of Saxony

Maurists (Benedictine monks)
Mabillon, Jean **10** 72

Mauritius (island; Indian Ocean)
Flinders, Matthew **5** 490
Gordon, Charles George **6** 448-449

Mauritius Case, The (novel)
Wassermann, Jakob **16** 130-131

Maurois, André (1885-1967), French novelist and historian
Fleming, Alexander **5** 483-485
Wilder, Thornton Niven **16** 276-277

MAURRAS, CHARLES MARIE PHOTIUS (1868-1952), French political writer and reactionary **10** 350-351
Pius X **12** 336-337

MAURY, MATTHEW FONTAINE (1806-1873), American naval officer and oceanographer **10** 351-352

Maurya dynasty (India; ruled 322?-185 B.C.)
Asoka **1** 341-342
Chandragupta Maurya **3** 426
Chang Chien **3** 429-430
Kautilya **8** 462

MAUSS, MARCEL (1872-1950), French sociologist and anthropologist **10** 352-353
Durkheim, Émile **5** 162-163
Lévy-Bruhl, Lucien **9** 374-375

Mauve, Anton (1838-1888), Dutch painter

Van Gogh, Vincent **15** 427-429

Mavra (comic opera)
Stravinsky, Igor Fedorovich **14** 502-506

MAWDUDI, ABU-I A'LA (1903-1979), Muslim writer and religious and political leader in the Indian sub-continent **10** 353-354

MAWSON, SIR DOUGLAS (1882-1958), Australian scientist and Antarctic explorer **10** 354-355

Max, Édouard Alexandre de (1869-1924), French actor
Cocteau, Jean **4** 132-133

Max Planck Institute for Behavioral Physiology
Lorenz, Konrad Z. **9** 516-517

Max Planck Institute for Medical Research (Heidelberg)
Bothe, Walther **2** 438-439
Debye, Peter Joseph William **4** 447-448
Heisenberg, Werner Karl **7** 261-263

Max Planck Institute for Social Research (Germany)
Habermas, Jürgen **7** 58-60

Maxentius, Marcus Aurelius Valerius (died 312), Roman emperor (306-312)
Constantine I **4** 209-211, 116

MAXIM, SIR HIRAM STEVENS (1840-1916), American-born British inventor **10** 355-356

Maximian (Marcus Aurelius Valerius Maximianus Herculis; died 310), Roman emperor 286-305 and 306-308
Constantine I **4** 209-211
Diocletian **5** 19-20

Maximianus, Gaius Galerius Valerius
see Galerius

Maximilian (emperor of Mexico)
see Maximilian of Hapsburg

Maximilian (Prince Max of Baden; 1867-1929), German imperial chancellor
Erzberger, Matthias **5** 319-320
Ludendorff, Erich Friedrich Wilhelm **10** 27-28

MAXIMILIAN I (1459-1519), Holy Roman emperor 1493-1519 **10** 356-357
and papacy
Julius II **8** 384-386
Leo X **9** 332-334
associates
Brant, Sebastian **2** 503-504
Sforza, Lodovico **14** 127-128
foreign policy
Charles the Bold **3** 467-469
Francis I **6** 40-43
Henry VII **7** 300-302
patronage
Dürer, Albrecht **5** 159-161
Hofhaimer, Paul **7** 441
Hutten, Ulrich von **8** 72-73
Isaac, Heinrich **8** 143-144
Senfl, Ludwig **14** 105-106
relatives

Charles V **3** 457-459
Ferdinand I **5** 414-415
Frederick III **6** 84-85
Isabella I **8** 144-145

Maximilian I (1573-1651), elector and
duke of Bavaria
Ferdinand II **5** 415

MAXIMILIAN II (1527-1576), Holy Roman
emperor 1564-1576 **10** 357-358
Charles V **3** 457-459
Ferdinand I **5** 414-415
Lassus, Roland de **9** 216-218

Maximilian II Emmanuel (1662-1726),
prince elector of Bavaria 1679-1726
Cuvilliés, François **4** 359-360

MAXIMILIAN OF HAPSBURG
(1832-1867), archduke of Austria and
emperor of Mexico **10** 358-360
Álvarez, Juan **1** 184-185
Díaz, José de la Cruz Porfirio **4** 534-536
Juárez, Benito **8** 369-372
Napoleon III **11** 310-312
Rousseau, Henri **13** 323-324
Seward, William Henry **14** 124-125
van der Goes, Hugo **15** 416-417

Maximilien (musical composition)
Milhaud, Darius **11** 17-18

Maximinus Daia (Galerius Valerius Max-
iminus; died 314), Roman emperor
308-314
Anthony, Susan Brownell **1** 246-248
Constantine I **4** 209-211
Diocletian **5** 19-20

Maximinus Thrax (Gaius Julius Verus Maxi-
minius; 173-238), Roman emperor
235-238
Valerian **15** 404-405

Maxims (book; La Rochefoucauld)
La Fayette, Comtesse de **9** 150-151
La Rochefoucauld, François Duc de
9 208-209

Maximus, Magnus Clemens (died 388),
Roman emperor 383-388
Theodosius **15** 176

Maximus, Paullus Fabius (circa 46 B.C. - 14
A.D.), Roman consul
Ovid **12** 34-36

Maximus Poems
Olson, Charles **11** 505-506

Maximus the Confessor, Saint (circa
580-662), Greek theologian and author
Erigena, John Scotus **5** 308-309

MAXWELL, IAN ROBERT (née Ludvik
Hock; 1923-1991), British publishing
magnate **10** 360-361

MAXWELL, JAMES CLERK (1831-1879),
Scottish physicist **10** 361-364
electromagnetic theory
Boltzmann, Ludwig **2** 379-380
Einstein, Albert **5** 228-231
Faraday, Michael **5** 380
Helmholtz, Hermann Ludwig Ferdi-
nand von **7** 268-269

Hertz, Heinrich Rudolf **7** 346-347
Lorentz, Hendrik Antoon **9** 515-516
Rowland, Henry Augustus
13 330-331
influence of
Bose, Jagadis Chandra **2** 429-430
Marconi, Guglielmo **10** 239-240
influenced by
Cavendish, Henry **3** 383-384
Clausius, Rudolf Julius Emanuel
4 92-94
Fresnel, Augustin Jean **6** 102-103
Gibbs, Josiah Willard **6** 302-303
quoted
van der Waals, Johannes Diderik
15 417-418

Maxwell Motor Co.
see Chrysler Corp.

May Day (story)
Fitzgerald, Francis Scott Key **5** 470-472

May 15 Affair (Japan)
Inukai, Tsuyoshi **8** 130-131

May Fourth movement (China; 1919)
Ch'en Tu-hsiu **3** 501-502
Chou En-lai **4** 20-22
Li Ta-chao **9** 447
Lin Piao **9** 429-430
Lu Hsün **10** 35-37
Pa Chin **12** 53-54
Ts'ai Yüan-p'ei **15** 322

May Thirtieth movement (China; 1925)
Kuo Mo-jo **9** 133-134
Lin Piao **9** 429-430
Liu Shao-Ch'i **9** 453-455

May, We Borrow Your Husband (stories)
Greene, Graham **6** 523-524

May-Wine, The (poem)
Dickinson, Emily **4** 541-543

Máya, La (poem)
Leconte de Lisle, Charles Marie René
9 273-274

Maya Indians (North America)
Asturias, Miguel Angel **1** 354-355
Huerta, Victoriano **8** 13-14
Velázquez de Cuéllar, Diego **15** 459

**MAYAKOVSKY, VLADIMIR
VLADIMIROVICH** (1893-1930), Russian
poet **10** 364-365
Aragon, Louis **1** 271-272
Meyerhold, Vsevolod Emilievich **10** 539
Pasternak, Boris Leonidovich
12 124-125

Maybach, Wilhelm (1847-1929), German
automobile builder
Daimler, Gottlieb **4** 368

Mayer, Brantz (1809-1879), American
lawyer, historian, and journalist
Canot, Theodore **3** 262-263

MAYER, JEAN (born 1920), nutritionist,
researcher, consultant to government and

international organizations, and president
of Tufts University **10** 365-366

Mayer, Julius Robert von (1814-1878),
German physicist
Tyndall, John **15** 374

Mayflower (ship)
Bradford, William **2** 475-476
Brewster, William **2** 523-524
Winslow, Edward **16** 338-339

Mayflower Compact (1620)
Bradford, William **2** 475-476

MAYNARD, ROBERT CLYVE (1937-1993),
African American journalist and publisher
10 366-367

Mayo, Katherine (1867-1940), American
writer
Naidu, Sarojini **11** 294-295

MAYO, WILLIAM J. (1861-1939) and
CHARLES H. (1865-1939), American
physicians **10** 367-369

Mayo Clinic (Rochester, Minnesota)
Kendall, Edward Calvin **8** 495
Mayo, William J. and Charles H.
10 367-369

Mayor, A. Hyatt (1901-1980), American art
critic
Piranesi, Giovanni Battista **12** 321-322

Mayor of Casterbridge, The (novel)
Hardy, Thomas **7** 150-152

Mayor of Zalamea, The (play)
Calderón, Pedro **3** 221-222

MAYOR ZARAGOSA, FEDERICO (born
1934), Spanish biochemist who was
director-general of UNESCO (United
Nations Educational, Scientific, and Cultural Organization) **10** 369-371

Mayors
see Statesmen

MAYO-SMITH, RICHMOND (1854-1901),
American statistician and sociologist
10 371-372

MAYR, ERNST (born 1904), American evolutionary biologist **10** 372-374

Mayr, Johann Simon (1763-1845), German
composer
Donizetti, Gaetano **5** 59-60

MAYS, BENJAMIN E. (1894-1984), African
American educator and civil rights
activist **10** 374-376

MAYS, WILLIE (William Howard Mays, Jr.;
born 1931), African American baseball
player **10** 376-379

Mazarin Bible
see Gutenberg Bible

MAZARIN, JULES (1602-1661), French car-
dinal and statesman **10** 379-380
Colbert, Jean Baptiste **4** 142-143
Condé, Prince de **4** 193-194
Coysevox, Antoine **4** 287-288
La Rochefoucauld, François Duc de
9 208-209
Le Brun, Charles **9** 269-270

Louis XIV **9** 531-533
Orléans, Philippe II D' **11** 530-531
Philip IV **12** 275

Mazdak (died circa 528), Persian religious reformer
Khosrow I **8** 538-539

MAZEPA, IVAN STEPANOVICH (circa 1644-1709), Ukrainian Cossack leader **10** 381

Mazeppa (symphony poem)
Liszt, Franz **9** 445-447

Mazer
Townes, Charles Hard **15** 281-282

Mazerelles, André (literary character)
Martin du Gard, Roger **10** 295-296

Mazo, Juan Bautista Martínez del (circa 1612-1667), Spanish painter
Velázquez, Diego Rodríguez de Silva y **15** 454-456

Mazorca Club (Argentine secret police)
Rosas, Juan Manuel de **13** 290-291

Mazzarini, Giulio
see Mazarin, Jules

MAZZINI, GIUSEPPE (1805-1872), Italian patriot **10** 381-383
Crispi, Francesco **4** 310-311
Garibaldi, Giuseppe **6** 215-217
Swinburne, Algernon Charles **15** 54-55

Mazzola, Francesco
see Parmigianino

M'BOW, AMADOU-MAHTAR (born 1921), director general of UNESCO (United Nations Educational, Scientific, and Cultural Organization) **10** 383-384

MBOYA, THOMAS JOSEPH (1930-1969), Kenyan political leader **10** 384-385

Mc
see also Mac

MCADOO, WILLIAM GIBBS (1863-1941), American statesman **10** 385-386
Baruch, Bernard Mannes **2** 42-43
Creel, George **4** 304-305
Smith, Alfred Emmanuel **14** 284-285

McCann (literary character)
Pinter, Harold **12** 317-318

MCCARTHY, EUGENE JOSEPH (born 1916), American statesman **10** 386-388
Johnson, Lyndon Baines **8** 308-312
Kennedy, Robert Francis **8** 508-509
McGovern, George Stanley **10** 412-414

MCCARTHY, JOSEPH RAYMOND (1908-1957), American politician **10** 388-389
Hiss, Alger **7** 413-415
Kennedy, Robert Francis **8** 508-509
Lehman, Herbert Henry **9** 306-307
Lippmann, Walter **9** 439-440
Miller, Arthur **11** 25-26
Murrow, Edward Roscoe **11** 265-266
Oppenheimer, J. Robert **11** 525-526
Truman, Harry S. **15** 314-316

Urey, Harold Clayton **15** 394-396
Wood, Robert Elkington **16** 370-371

MCCARTHY, MARY T. (born 1912), American writer **10** 389-391

McCartney, Paul (born 1942), English pop singer and songwriter
Beatles, The **2** 89-92

MCCLELLAN, GEORGE BRINTON (1826-1885), American general **10** 391-392
Chandler, Zachariah **3** 425-426
Chase, Salmon Portland **3** 473-475
Jackson, Shirley Ann **8** 183-184
Lee, Robert Edward **9** 292-294
Lincoln, Abraham **9** 415-418
Pinkerton, Allan **12** 314-315
Stuart, James Ewell Brown **14** 515-516
Weed, Thurlow **16** 169-170

MCCLELLAN, JOHN LITTLE (1896-1977), U.S. senator from Arkansas **10** 392-393
Kennedy, Robert Francis **8** 508-509

MCCLINTOCK, BARBARA (1902-1992), geneticist and winner of the Nobel Prize in physiology **10** 393-394

MCCLINTOCK, SIR FRANCIS LEOPOLD (1819-1907), British admiral and Arctic explorer **10** 394-395
Franklin, John **6** 64-65

McClintock Channel (Arctic Ocean)
McClintock, Francis Leopold **10** 394-395

MCCLOSKEY, JOHN (1810-1885), American cardinal **10** 395
Corrigan, Michael Augustine **4** 253

MCCLUNG, NELLIE LETITIA (1873-1951), Canadian suffragist, social reformer, legislator, and author **10** 396-397

MCCLURE, SAMUEL SIDNEY (1857-1949), American editor and publisher **10** 398-399

MCCLURE, SIR ROBERT (1807-1873), English explorer and navy officer **10** 398-399

McClure's Magazine (periodical; 1893-1929)
Baker, Ray Stannard **1** 451-452
Glackens, William **6** 355-356
McClure, Samuel Sidney **10** 398-399
Norris, Benjamin Franklin Jr. **11** 427-428
Russell, Charles Marion **13** 375-376
Steffens, Lincoln **14** 410-411
Tarbell, Ida Minerva **15** 107-108
Tarkington, Newton Booth **15** 109

McCormack, John (1884-1945), Irish tenor
Joyce, James **8** 365-367

MCCORMACK, JOHN WILLIAM (1891-1980), U.S. congressman and Speaker of the House **10** 399-400

MCCORMICK, CYRUS HALL (1809-1884), American inventor, manufacturer, and philanthropist **10** 400-401
Prokofiev, Sergei Sergeevich **12** 458-460

MCCORMICK, ROBERT RUTHERFORD (1880-1955), American publisher **10** 401-402

McCormick Harvester Co. (industry)
Deering, William **4** 455-456

MCCOSH, JAMES (1811-1894), Scottish-American minister, philosopher, and college president **10** 402-403

MCCOY, ISAAC (1784-1846), American Indian agent and missionary **10** 403

MCCOY, JOSEPH GEITING (1837-1915), American cattleman **10** 403-404

McCreary, Mac (literary character)
Dos Passos, John Roderigo **5** 69-71

MCCULLOCH, HUGH (1808-1895), American banker and lawyer **10** 404-405

McCulloch v. Maryland (legal case)
Marshall, John **10** 279-281
Martin, Luther **10** 289-290
Webster, Daniel **16** 162-164

MCDANIEL, HATTIE (1898-1952), African American actress **10** 405-408

McDonagh, Thomas (1876-1916), Irish poet
Colum, Padraic **4** 174-175

McDonalds Corporation
Kroc, Raymond Albert **9** 103-104

McDonnell Douglas Corp. (aircraft firm)
Douglas, Donald Wills **5** 77

McDonnel's Farm (painting)
Moses, Grandma **11** 201-202

McDougall, Alexander (1731?-1786), British general
Clinton, George **4** 113-114

McDowell, Irvin (1818-1885), American general
Beauregard, Pierre Gustave Toutant **2** 96-97

MCDUFFIE, GEORGE (1790-1851), American statesman **10** 408

MCENROE, JOHN PATRICK, JR. (born 1959), American tennis player **10** 408-411

McGargle, Eustace (literary character)
Fields, W. C. **5** 444

MCGILL, RALPH EMERSON (1898-1969), American journalist **10** 411-412

McGill University (Montreal, Canada)
Currie, Arthur William **4** 345
MacLennan, Hugh **10** 110-111
Osler, William **12** 19-20
Penfield, Wilder Graves **12** 198-200
Rutherford, Ernest **13** 384-387
Soddy, Frederick **14** 321-323

MCGILLIVRAY, ALEXANDER (circa 1759-1793), American Creek Indian chief **10** 412

MCGOVERN, GEORGE STANLEY (born 1922), American statesman **10** 412-414

MCGUFFEY, WILLIAM HOLMES (1800-1873), American educator **10** 414-415

McHenry, Earle Willard (1899-1961), Canadian biochemist
    Best, Charles Herbert **2** 236-237

MCINTIRE, SAMUEL (1757-1811), American builder and furniture maker **10** 415
    Adam, Robert and James **1** 38-40
    Bulfinch, Charles **3** 116-117
    Revere, Paul **13** 110-111

MCKAY, CLAUDE (1890-1948), African American poet and novelist **10** 416
    Lawrence, Jacob **9** 250-251

MCKAY, DONALD (1810-1880), American ship builder **10** 416-417
    Collins, Edward Knight **4** 162-163

McKean, David Dayton (1904-1977), American scholar
    Hague, Frank **7** 63-64

McKenney, Eileen (Mrs. Nathanael West; died 1940), American model for *My Sister Eileen*
    West, Nathanael **16** 213-214

McKenney, Ruth (1911-1972), American author
    West, Nathanael **16** 213-214

MCKIM, CHARLES FOLLEN (1847-1909), American architect **10** 417-418
    see also McKim, Mead and White

McKim, Meade and White (architectural firm)
    Burnham, Daniel Hudson **3** 148-149
    McKim, Charles Follen **10** 417-418
    White, Stanford **16** 235-236

MCKINLEY, WILLIAM (1843-1901), American statesman, president 1897-1901 **10** 418-420
  advisers and appointees
    Hanna, Marcus Alonzo **7** 127-128
    Ireland, John **8** 133-134
    Low, Seth **10** 11-12
    Roosevelt, Theodore **13** 280-283
    Wood, Leonard **16** 369-370
  assassination
    Goldman, Emma **6** 406-407
    Platt, Thomas Collier **12** 347-348
  Cabinet
    Hay, John **7** 215-216
    Knox, Philander Chase **9** 66-67
    Root, Elihu **13** 283-284
    Sherman, John **14** 184-185
  rivals
    Bryan, William Jennings **3** 80-82

McKinley tariff (1890)
    Cleveland, Stephen Grover **4** 108-110
    McKinley, William **10** 418-420

MCKISSICK, FLOYD B., (1922-1991), African American civil rights leader **10** 420-422

MCLEAN, JOHN (1785-1861), American jurist and politician **10** 422-423
    Adams, John Quincy **1** 52-54

McLeod, Mary
    see Bethune, Mary McLeod

MCLOUGHLIN, JOHN (1784-1857), Canadian pioneer and trader **10** 423-424
    Kelley, Hall Jackson **8** 480

MCLUHAN, MARSHALL (Herbert Marshall McLuhan; 1911-1980), Canadian professor of literature and culture **10** 424-426

McMahon, Sir Arthur Henry (1862-1949), British administrator
    Husein ibn Ali **8** 63

MCMASTER, JOHN BACH (1852-1932), American historian **10** 426-427

McMillan, Edwin M. (1907-1991), American physicist
    Lawrence, Ernest Orlando **9** 248-250

MCMILLAN, TERRY (born 1951), African American novelist and short story writer **10** 427-428

MCMURRAY, BETTE CLAIR (1924-1980), American inventor and businesswoman **10** 429

MCNAMARA, ROBERT S. (born 1916), U.S. secretary of defense and president of the World Bank **10** 429-431

MCNAUGHTON, ANDREW (1887-1966), Canadian soldier and diplomat **10** 431-432

McNerry, Colonel (literary character)
    Dunne, Finley Peter **5** 147-148

MCNICKLE, D'ARCY (born William D'Arcy McNickle; 1904-1977), Native American author, historian, and activist **10** 433

McNutt, Paul Vories (1891-1955), American statesman
    Osmeña, Sergio **12** 22-24
    Roxas, Manuel **13** 331-332

MCPHERSON, AIMEE SEMPLE (1890-1944), American evangelist **10** 434

MCQUEEN, BUTTERFLY (born Thelma McQueen; 1911-1995), African American actress **10** 434-437

McRae, Milton Alexander (1858-1930), American publisher
    Scripps, Edward Wyllis **14** 72-73

McReynolds, James Clark (1862-1946), American jurist
    Taft, William Howard **15** 78-81

McTaggart, J.M.E. (1866-1925), English philosopher
    Broad, Charlie Dunbar **3** 12
    Moore, George Edward **11** 146
    Russell, Bertrand Arthur William **13** 373-374
    Sidgwick, Henry **14** 213

McTeague (novel)
    Norris, Benjamin Franklin Jr. **11** 427-428

MEAD, GEORGE HERBERT (1863-1931), American philosopher and social psychologist **10** 437-438
    Cooley, Charles Horton **4** 216-217

MEAD, MARGARET (1901-1978), American anthropologist **10** 438-440
    Benedict, Ruth Fulton **2** 154-155
    Boas, Franz **2** 349-351
    Erikson, Erik Homburger **5** 309-310
    Linton, Ralph **9** 431

Mead, Richard (1673-1754), English physician
    Watteau, Antoine **16** 143-144

Mead, William Rutherford (1846-1928), American architect
    McKim, Charles Follen **10** 417-418
    White, Stanford **16** 235-236

MEADE, GEORGE GORDON (1815-1872), American general **10** 440-441
    Lee, Robert Edward **9** 292-294

Meaning of God in Human Experience, The (book)
    Hocking, William Ernest **7** 428-429

Means, Gardiner (1896-1988), American economist
    Berle, Adolf Augustus Jr. **2** 199-200

MEANS, RUSSELL (born 1939), Native American activist **10** 441-444

MEANY, GEORGE (1894-1980), American labor leader **10** 444
    Ford, Henry II **6** 6-7
    Reuther, Walter Philip **13** 107-108

Measles (medicine)
    Enders, John Franklin **5** 285-286
    Razi **13** 63-64
    Sydenham, Thomas **15** 59-60

Measure, The (magazine)
    Anderson, Maxwell **1** 219-220

Measure for Measure (play; Shakespeare)
    Shakespeare, William **14** 142-145
    Wagner, Richard **16** 40-43

Measure Taken, The (play)
    Brecht, Bertolt **2** 512-514

Meat industry (United States)
    Armour, Philip Danforth **1** 302
    Borden, Gail **2** 409
    Harding, Warren Gamaliel **7** 148-149
    Sinclair, Upton Beale Jr. **14** 248-249

Meat Inspection Act (1890)
    Hatch, William Henry **7** 196

Meat out of the Eater (poems)
    Wigglesworth, Michael **16** 266-267

Mécanique céleste (book; Laplace)
    Bowditch, Nathaniel **2** 460-461
    Cauchy, Augustin Louis **3** 378-380
    Hamilton, William Rowan **7** 99-100
    Laplace, Marquis de **9** 202-204

Mecca (Islamic holy city; Saudi Arabia)
    Abu Bakr **1** 31-32
    Burton, Richard **3** 163-164
    Covilhão, Pedro de **4** 278-279

Ibrahim Pasha **8** 97-98
Idris I **8** 102
Mohammed **11** 76-78
Musa Mansa **11** 266
Omar ibn Said Tal, Al-Hajj **11** 509-510

Mechanical Operation of the Spirit, The
(essay)
Swift, Jonathan **15** 51-54

Mechanics (physics)
see Celestial mechanics; Classical
mechanics; Quantum theory; Statistical mechanics

Mechanics Hall (New York City)
Christy, Edwin P. **4** 34-35

Mechanism (philosophy)
Descartes, René **4** 505-508
Driesch, Hans Adolf Eduard **5** 105
Lotze, Rudolf Hermann **9** 521-522
Morgan, Thomas Hunt **11** 170-171

Meck, Nadezhda von (1831-1894), Russian
music patron
Tchaikovsky, Peter Ilyich **15** 130-132

Medal, The (satire)
Dryden, John **5** 106-107

Medal of Honor
see Congressional Medal of Honor

Medalists
see Artists—medalists

MEDAWAR, PETER BRIAN (1915-1987),
British zoologist **10** 444-445

Medea (Médée; Greek mythology)
in art
Delacroix, Ferdinand Victor Eugène
4 469-471
in drama
Corneille, Pierre **4** 234-236
Euripides **5** 332-334
Grillparzer, Franz **6** 546-547
Jeffers, John Robinson **8** 236-237
Lessing, Gotthold Ephraim
9 357-359
Ovid **12** 34-36
Seneca the Younger, Lucius Annaeus
14 103-105
in music
Barber, Samuel **1** 500-501
Charpentier, Marc Antoine
3 471-472
Cherubini, Luigi Carlo Zanobi Sal-
vatore Maria **3** 505-506

Medea and Some Poems (literary collection)
Cullen, Countee **4** 333-334

Médenine, battle of (1943)
Rommel, Erwin **13** 268-269

Media (ancient country; western Asia)
Antiochus IV **1** 250
Caracalla **3** 281-282
Cyrus the Great **4** 363-364
Marcus Aurelius Antoninus **10** 243-245

Medical Research Council (United Kingdom)
Bartlett, Frederic Charles **2** 34-35

Sanger, Frederick **13** 466-467

Medical school development (United
States)
Drake, Daniel **5** 93-94
Eliot, Charles William **5** 254
Flexner, Abraham **5** 489-490
Morgan, John **11** 162-163
Waterhouse, Benjamin **16** 131-132
Welch, William Henry **16** 185-186

Medicare (United States)
Johnson, Lyndon Baines **8** 308-312
Kennedy, John Fitzgerald **8** 502-506

MEDICI, CATHERINE DE' (1519-1589),
Italian queen of France **10** 445-449
patronage
Lassus, Roland de **9** 216-218
l'Orme, Philibert de **9** 519
Pilon, Germain **12** 305
Primaticcio, Francesco **12** 453-454
regencies
Coligny, Gaspard de **4** 159-160
Henry IV **7** 293-295
Mary, I **10** 308-309
see also St. Bartholomew's Day Mas-
sacre

MEDICI, COSIMO DE' (1389-1464), Ital-
ian statesman and merchant prince
10 449-450
Angelico **1** 235-236
Ficino, Marsilio **5** 436-437
Michelozzo **11** 6-7

Medici, Cosimo I de' (1519-1574), Italian
statesman, duke of Florence 1537-1574
and grand duke of Tuscany 1569-1574
Bronzino **3** 19
Cellini, Benvenuto **3** 391-392
Giovanni da Bologna **6** 345-346
Guicciardini, Francesco **7** 32-33
Vasari, Giorgio **15** 442-443

Medici, Cosimo II de' (1590-1620), Italian
statesman and grand duke of Tuscany
1609-1620
Galileo Galilei **6** 180-183

Medici, Cosimo III de' (1642-1723), Italian
statesman and grand duke of Tuscany
1670-1723
Steno, Nicolaus **14** 425-426

Medici, Ferdinand de' (1663-1713), prince
of Tuscany
Scarlatti, Pietro Alessandro Gaspare
13 517-518

Medici, Ferdinand I de' (1549-1609), grand
duke of Tuscany 1587-1609
Caccini, Giulio **3** 205-206
Marenzio, Luca **10** 248

Medici, Ferdinand II de' (1610-1670),
grand duke of Tuscany 1620-1670
Frescobaldi, Girolamo **6** 101-102
Steno, Nicolaus **14** 425-426

Medici, Francesco I de' (1541-1587), grand
duke of Tuscany 1575-1587
Giovanni da Bologna **6** 345-346

Medici, Giovanni Angelo de'
see Pius IV

Medici, Giovanni de' (1360-1429), Italian
merchant
Medici, Cosimo de' **10** 449-450

Medici, Giovanni de' (1475-1521)
see Leo X

Medici, Giuliano de' (1453-1478), Italian
statesman
Medici, Lorenzo de' **10** 450-451

Medici, Giulio de'
see Clement VII

MEDICI, LORENZO DE' (1449-1492), Ital-
ian statesman, ruler of Florence
1469-1492 **10** 450-451
associates
Alberti, Leon Battista **1** 113-115
Bembo, Pietro **2** 144-145
Botticelli, Sandro **2** 439-440
Paul III **12** 144-145
Pico della Mirandola, Giovanni
12 299-300
Pulci, Luigi **12** 481
opponents
Savonarola, Girolamo **13** 505-506
patronage
Isaac, Heinrich **8** 143-144
Mantegna, Andrea **10** 215-216
Michelangelo Buonarroti **11** 2-5,
393
Poliziano, Angelo **12** 373-374
Pollaiuolo, Antonio **12** 377-378
Sangallo family **13** 464-466
Verrocchio, Andrea del **15** 471-472
relatives
Leo X **9** 332-334
Medici, Catherine de' **10** 445-449

Medici, Maria de'
see Marie de Médicis

Medici, Piero de' (1414-1469), Italian
statesman, ruler of Florence 1464-1469
Medici, Lorenzo de' **10** 450-451
Veneziano, Domenico **15** 459-460

Medici, Piero de' (1471-1503), Italian
statesman, ruler of Florence 1492-1494
Savonarola, Girolamo **13** 505-506

Medici Chapel (Florence, Italy)
Michelangelo Buonarroti **11** 2-5

Medici family (rulers of Florence; 15th cen-
tury -1737)
Isaac, Heinrich **8** 143-144
Leo X **9** 332-334
Machiavelli, Niccolò **10** 97-99
Magnasco, Alessandro **10** 127-128
Marenzio, Luca **10** 248
Michelozzo **11** 6-7
Vasari, Giorgio **15** 442-443
Verrocchio, Andrea del **15** 471-472

Medici villa (Poggio a Caiano, Italy)
Andrea del Sarto **1** 224-225

Medicine
aerospace

Long, Irene D. **9** 497-498
anatomy
   see Anatomy
ancient
   Celsus, Aulus Cornelius **3** 393
   Galen **6** 178-180
   Hippocrates **7** 408-410
and radiology
   Quimby, Edith H. **12** 513-514
anesthesia
   see Anesthesia
artificial hearts
   DeVries, William Castle **4** 518-519
blood
   see Blood (human)
bubonic plague
   Nostradamus **11** 432-434
cardiology
   Healy, Bernadine Patricia **7** 237-238
clinical
   Bethune, Henry Norman **2** 240-241
   Bowditch, Henry Ingersoll
      2 459-460
   Bright, Richard **3** 7-8
   Chinn, May Edward **3** 525-526
   Helmont, Jan Baptista van
      7 269-271
   Lister, Joseph **9** 444-445
   Louis, Pierre Charles Alexandre
      9 540
   Mayo, William J. and Charles H.
      10 367-369
   Mesmer, Franz Anton **10** 526-527
   Rush, Benjamin **13** 364-365
   Sanctorius **13** 459
   Stahl, Georg Ernst **14** 392-393
   Taussig, Helen Brooke **15** 118-120
fungal diseases
   Brown, Rachel Fuller **3** 43-44
immunology
   see Immunology
industrial
   Hamilton, Alice **7** 98-99
   Hardy, Harriet **7** 150
insulin discovered
   Banting, Frederick Grant **1** 493-494
   Best, Charles Herbert **2** 236-237
medical social work
   Cabot, Richard Clarke **3** 200
medieval
   Avicenna **1** 386-387
   Guy de Chauliac **7** 54
   Razi **13** 63-64
mental illness
   see Mental illness
nursing
   see Nursing
obstetrics
   Baker, Sara Josephine **1** 455-456
   Hunter, William **8** 48-49
   Mendenhall, Dorothy Reed
      10 491-492
   Semmelweis, Ignaz Philipp
      14 101-102
organ transplants
   Carrel, Alexis **3** 322-323

DeBakey, Michael Ellis **4** 437-438
DeVries, William Castle **4** 518-519
parasitology
   Bruce, David **3** 63
   Metchnikoff, Élie **10** 532-533
pathology
   see Pathology
socialized
   Chifley, Joseph Benedict **3** 518
   Pearson, Lester Bowles **12** 174-175
surgery
   see Surgery
systemization (16th century)
   Cardano, Geronimo **3** 285-286
   Fernel, Jean François **5** 425-426
   Paracelsus, Philippus Aureolus
      12 91-93
   Paré, Ambroise **12** 94-95
   see also Cancer; Medical school
      development; Poliomyelitis; Public
      health; Scientists—physicians;
      Tropical medicine

Medico de su honra, El (play)
   Calderón, Pedro **3** 221-222

Medico-Chirurgical Academy
   see Military Medical Academy
      (Leningrad)

Medieval City by the Water (painting)
   Schinkel, Karl Friedrich **14** 8

Medieval civilization
   see Middle Ages

MEDILL, JOSEPH (1823-1899), American
   abolitionist editor and publisher
   10 451-452

Medina (Islamic holy city; Saudi Arabia)
   Abu Bakr **1** 31-32
   Burton, Richard **3** 163-164
   Ibrahim Pasha **8** 97-98
   Mohammed **11** 76-78

Medina Angarita, Isaías (1897-1953),
   Venezuelan general, president
   1941-1945
   Betancourt, Rómulo **2** 237-238
   Gallegos Freire, Rómulo **6** 185-186

Medina del Campo, Treaty of (1489)
   Henry VII **7** 300-302

**Medina-Sidonia, Alonso Pérez de Guzmán,
   7th Duke of** (1550-1615), Spanish admiral
   Drake, Francis **5** 94-96
   Menéndez de Avilés, Pedro **10** 499-500

Meditation upon a Broomstick, A (essay)
   Swift, Jonathan **15** 51-54

Meditations (book; Descartes)
   Descartes, René **4** 505-508-350
   Hobbes, Thomas **7** 421-423

Méditations (poems)
   Lamartine, Alphonse Marie Louis de
      9 173-175

Meditations on First Philosophy (Descartes)
   see Meditations

**Mediterranean and the Mediterranean
   World in the Age of Philip II, The** (book)
   Braudel, Fernand **2** 507-508

Mediterranean fever
   see Undulant fever

Mediterranean, The (sculpture)
   Maillol, Aristide **10** 150-151

Medium, The (opera)
   Menotti, Gian Carlo **10** 509-510

Médrano (assemblage series)
   Archipenko, Alexander **1** 280-281

Medusa (ship)
   Géricault, Jean Louis André Théodore
      6 280-281

Medza (literary character)
   Beti, Mongo **2** 242-243

Meeber, Carrie (literary character)
   Dreiser, Herman Theodore **5** 98-100

Meek, Joseph L. (1810-1875), American
   pioneer
   Whitman, Marcus **16** 248-249

Meeres und der Liebe Wellen, Des (play)
   Grillparzer, Franz **6** 546-547

Meeting and Passing (poem)
   Frost, Robert Lee **6** 130-133

Meeting House (Northampton, Massachusetts)
   Benjamin, Asher **2** 162-163

Meeting of Burns and Scott (painting)
   Burns, Robert **3** 155-156

Meeting of Saints Erasmus and Maurice
   (painting)
   Grünewald, Matthias **7** 23-24

**Meeting of Solomon with the Queen of
   Sheba** (mural)
   Piero della Francesca **12** 301-302

Meeting, The (painting)
   Courbet, Jean Desiré Gustave
      4 271-273

Meeuwisz, Thonisz
   see Van Diemen, Anthony Meuza

Meg (literary character)
   Pinter, Harold **12** 317-318

Megacles (flourished 560-559 B.C.), Athenian politician
   Cleisthenes **4** 98-99

Megalopolis (ancient city; Greece)
   Cleomenes III **4** 103-104
   Epaminondas **5** 291-292

Megasthenes (died circa 298 B.C.), Greek
   historian and statesman
   Chandragupta Maurya **3** 426

Meghaduta (elegy)
   Kalidasa **8** 414-415

Megiddo (ancient city; Palestine)
   Thutmose III **15** 216-217

Megiddo, battle of (1917)
   Lawrence, Thomas Edward **9** 253-254

Megilloth (Old Testament)
Saadia ben Joseph al-Fayumi **13** 396

Mehemet Ali
see Mohammed Ali

Mehmed (died 1543), Turkish prince
Suleiman I **15** 20-21

Mehmed (Mohammed V; 1844-1918), sultan of Turkey, 1909-1918
Abdul-Hamid II **1** 17-18
Allal al-Fassi, Mohamed **1** 162

Mehmed (Mohammed VI; 1861-1926), sultan of Turkey 1918-1922
Atatürk, Ghazi Mustapha Kemal **1** 356-357
Venizelos, Eleutherios **15** 460-461

MEHMED THE CONQUEROR (a.k.a. Mehmed II and Mehmed Celebi; ca. 1432-1481), Turkish sultan **10** 452-454
Bellini, Giovanni **2** 137-138
Constantine XI **4** 211-212
Hunyadi, John **8** 51-52
seeMehmed (for later Turkish sultans)

MEHTA, SIR PHEROZESHAH (1845-1915), Indian statesman **10** 455

Meian (novel)
Natsume, Soseki **11** 324-325

MEIER, RICHARD (born 1934), New York architect **10** 456-458

MEIGGS, HENRY (1811-1877), American railroad builder **10** 458-459

MEIGHEN, ARTHUR (1874-1960), Canadian lawyer, prime minister 1920-21, 1926 **10** 459-460
Bennett, Richard Bedford **2** 171-172
Borden, Robert Laird **2** 409-411

Meiji restoration (Japan; 1868)
Iwakura, Tomomi **8** 160-161
K'ang Yu-wei **8** 426-428
Okubo, Toshimichi **11** 489-490
Okuma, Shigenobu **11** 490
Saigo, Takamori **13** 429
Saionji, Kimmochi **13** 438-439
Takahashi, Korekiyo **15** 84-85
Yamagata, Aritomo **16** 428-429

Meiji Shrine (Fushimi, Japan)
Mutsuhito **11** 279-282

Meiji Tenno
seeMutsuhito

Mein Kampf (book; Hitler)
Haushofer, Karl **7** 201
Hitler, Adolf **7** 417-420

MEINECKE, FRIEDRICH (1862-1954), German historian **10** 460-461
Troeltsch, Ernst **15** 299-300

MEINESZ, FELIX ANDRIES VENING (1887-1966), Dutch geodesist and geophysicist **10** 461
Ewing, William Maurice **5** 350-351

MEINONG, ALEXIUS RITTER VON HANDSCHUCHSHEIM (1853-1920), Austrian philosopher **10** 461-462
Brentano, Franz Clemens **2** 516-517

MEIR, GOLDA (1898-1978), Israeli prime minister **10** 462-463

Meister, Joseph (1876-1940), Frenchman, first human to receive rabies vaccine
Pasteur, Louis **12** 125-127

Meistersinger von Nürnberg, Die (opera; Wagner)
Dallapiccola, Luigi **4** 377-378
Sachs, Hans **13** 410-411
Wagner, Richard **16** 40-43

MEITNER, LISE (born Elise Meitner; 1878-1968), Austrian-born American nuclear physicist **10** 463-466
Hahn, Otto **7** 64-65

Mejia, Tomás (1812?-1867), Mexican general
Maximilian of Hapsburg **10** 358-360

Mejor alcalde el ray, El (play)
Lope Félix de Vega Carpio **9** 503-506

Mekong River (southeast Asia)
Chulalongkorn **4** 43-45
Garnier, Francis **6** 220-221
Lilienthal, David Eli **9** 410-411

Melanchthon, Philip
see Melancthon, Philip

Melanctha (novelette)
Stein, Gertrude **14** 414-415

MELANCTHON, PHILIP (1497-1560), German theologian and humanist **10** 466-467
Luther, Martin **10** 48-51
Quintilian **12** 518-519
Schwenckfeld, Kasper von **14** 56-57

MELAND, BERNARD EUGENE (born 1899), American historian of liberal theology **10** 467-468

Melba, Nelli (Helen Porter Mitchell; 1861-1931), Australian soprano
Caruso, Enrico **3** 345

MELBOURNE, 2ND VISCOUNT (William Lamb; 1779-1848), English statesman, prime minister 1834 and 1835-1841 **10** 468-469
Disraeli, Benjamin **5** 27-29
Edward VI **5** 213-214
Palmerston, 3d Viscount **12** 81-83
Peel, Robert **12** 181-183
Russell, John **13** 380-381
Victoria **15** 485-487
William IV **16** 296-297

Melekhov, Grigory (literary character)
Sholokhov, Mikhail Aleksandrovich **14** 203-204

Melekot, Haile (died 1855), king of Shoa
Mengs, Anton Raphael **10** 505

Melencolia (engraving series; Dürer)
Dürer, Albrecht **5** 159-161
Hogarth, William **7** 446-447

Méliador (poem)
Froissart, Jean **6** 124-125

Melikow, Loris
see Hofmannsthal, Hugo von

Melincourt (novel)
Peacock, Thomas Love **12** 169

Melissa (play)
Kazantzakis, Nikos **8** 466-468

Mélite (play)
Corneille, Pierre **4** 234-236

Melitians (religious sect)
Athanasius **1** 358-359

Melk, monastery of (Austria)
Prandtauer, Jakob **12** 432
Rottmayr, Johann Michael **13** 321
Troger, Paul **15** 300

Mello, Custodio Jose de (1845?-1902), Brazilian admiral
Peixoto, Floriano **12** 188-189

MELLON, ANDREW WILLIAM (1855-1937), American businessman **10** 469-470
Coolidge, John Calvin **4** 217-219
Harding, Warren Gamaliel **7** 148-149
Hoover, Herbert Clark **7** 483-485
Stone, Harlan Fiske **14** 468-470

MELNIKOV, KONSTANTIN STEPANOVICH (1890-1974), Russian avant-grant architect **10** 470-471

Melo Revolt (1854)
Isaacs, Jorge **8** 144

Mélodies hébraïques (musical composition)
Ravel, Maurice Joseph **13** 54-55

Melodies of the Time (poem)
Peretz, Isaac Loeb **12** 212

Mélodies populaires grecques (musical composition)
Ravel, Maurice Joseph **13** 54-55

Meloney, Mrs. William B. (Marie Mattingly; died 1943), American journalist and editor
Curie, Marie Sklodowska **4** 339-341

Melozzo da Forli (1438-1494), Italian painter
Bramante, Donato **2** 493-494

Melun Diptych (painting)
Fouquet, Jean **6** 31

MELVILLE, GEORGE WALLACE (1841-1912), American naval officer and explorer **10** 472

Melville, Henry Dundas, 1st Viscount (1742-1811), British statesman
Aberdeen, 4th Earl of **1** 25-26
Boswell, James **2** 432-434

MELVILLE, HERMAN (1819-1891), American author **10** 472-476
biographers
Mumford, Lewis **11** 246-247
influence of
Camus, Albert **3** 255-257
Crane, Hart **4** 291-293
Kent, Rockwell **8** 511
Lowell, Robert Trail Spence Jr. **10** 16-17

Mailer, Norman Kingsley
10 148-150
Pound, Ezra Loomis **12** 415-417
Warren, Robert Penn **16** 121-122
influenced by
Brown, Charles Brockden **3** 33
Hawthorne, Nathaniel **7** 212-215
Plutarch **12** 359-360

Member of the Third House, A (novel)
Garland, Hannibal Hamlin **6** 217-218

MEMLING, HANS (circa 1440-1494), German-born painter active in Flanders
10 476
Bermejo, Bartolomé **2** 205
Eyck, Hubert and Jan van **5** 352-354
van der Goes, Hugo **15** 416-417

MEMMINGER, CHRISTOPHER GUS-TAVUS (1803-1888), American politician
10 476-477

Memmius Gaius (flourished 57 B.C.),
Roman governor of Bithynia
Catullus, Gaius Valerius **3** 377-378
Lucretius **10** 26-27

Memnon (story)
Voltaire **16** 14-16

Memoiren Erster Teil, Der (book)
Mann, Thomas **10** 204-207

Memor esto verbi tui (motet)
Josquin des Prez **8** 361-363

Memorabilia of Socrates, The (book)
Xenophon **16** 418-420

Memories (poem)
Leopardi, Giacomo **9** 344-345

Memories and Portraits (book)
Bunin, Ivan Alekseevich **3** 124

Memory (philosophy)
Bergson, Henri **2** 191-192

Memory (psychology)
Bartlett, Frederic Charles **2** 34-35
Ebbinghaus, Hermann **5** 192-193
Sherrington, Charles Scott **14** 187-189

Memory of Two Mondays, A (play)
Miller, Arthur **11** 25-26

Memphis (ancient city; Egypt)
Menes **10** 500-502
Petrie, William Matthew Flinders
12 261-262

Memphis (city; Tennessee)
King, Martin Luther Jr. **9** 20-22

Memphis and Little Rock Railroad (United States)
Frémont, John Charles **6** 97-98

Memphis Blues (song)
Handy, William Christopher **7** 123-124

Men and Women (poems)
Browning, Robert **3** 53-55

Men at Arms (novel trilogy)
Waugh, Evelyn Arthur St. John
16 145-147

Men of Corn (book)
Asturias, Miguel Angel **1** 354-355

Men Who Tread on the Tails of Tigers (film)
Kurosawa, Akira **9** 135-137

Men without Women (mural)
Davis, Stuart **4** 424-425

Men without Women (stories)
Hemingway, Ernest Miller **7** 274-277

Men, Women, and Ghosts (poems)
Lowell, Amy **10** 13

Menachem Mendel (book)
Sholem Aleichem **14** 202-203

Menaechmi (play)
Plautus **12** 348-350

Ménage, Gilles (1613-1692), French scholar
La Fayette, Comtesse de **9** 150-151

Menand (sculpture series)
Smith, David **14** 287-288

MENANDER (342-291 B.C.), Athenian comic playwright **10** 477-478
Aristophanes **1** 293-294
Plautus **12** 348-350
Terence **15** 146-148

Ménard, Louis (1822-1901), French scientist, poet, and painter
Leconte de Lisle, Charles Marie René
9 273-274

MENCHÚ, RIGOBGERTA (born 1959),
Guatemalan human rights activist who won the Nobel Peace Prize **10** 479-480

MENCIUS (circa 371-circa 289 B.C.), Chinese philosopher **10** 480-481
Chu Hsi **4** 40-43
Confucius **4** 197-200
Huang Tsung-hsi **8** 9-10
Richards, Ivor Armstrong **13** 137
Wang An-shih **16** 95-97

MENCKEN, HENRY LOUIS (1880-1956),
American journalist, editor, critic, and philologist **10** 481-483
Bierce, Ambrose Gwinett **2** 269-270
Brackenridge, Hugh Henry **2** 472-473
Dreiser, Herman Theodore **5** 98-100
Howe, Edgar Watson **7** 529
Twain, Mark **15** 363-366

MENDAÑA DE NEYRA, ÁLVARO DE
(1541-1595), Spanish explorer **10** 483

MENDEL, JOHANN GREGOR
(1822-1884), Moravian natural scientist and Augustinian abbot **10** 483-486
Bateson, William **2** 55-57
de Vries, Hugo **4** 516-518
East, Edward Murray **5** 182-183
Weismann, August Freidrich Leopold
16 178-180
see also Mendelianism

Mendele Mocher Sefarim (pseudonym of Sholem Jacob Abramovitch; 1836-1917),
Yiddish novelist
Bialik, Hayyim Nahman **2** 262-263

MENDELEEV, DMITRII IVANOVICH
(1834-1907), Russian chemist **10** 486-488
Blok, Aleksandr Aleksandrovich **2** 335
Pavlov, Ivan Petrovich **12** 155-157

Mendelevium (element—chemistry)
Mendeleev, Dmitrii Ivanovich
10 486-488

Mendelianism (Mendelism; genetics)
de Vries, Hugo **4** 516-518
East, Edward Murray **5** 182-183
Fisher, Ronald Aylmer **5** 463-464
Haldane, John Burdon Sanderson
7 70-71
Mendel, Johann Gregor **10** 483-486
Morgan, Thomas Hunt **11** 170-171
Vavilov, Nikolai Ivanovich **15** 447-448

MENDELSOHN, ERICH (1887-1953), German architect **10** 488
Neutra, Richard Joseph **11** 355-356

MENDELSSOHN, MOSES (1729-1786),
German Jewish philosopher **10** 488-489
associates and contemporaries
Jacobi, Friedrich Heinrich
8 189-190
Krochmal, Nachman Kohen
9 104-105
Swedenborg, Emanuel **15** 49-50
influence of
Graetz, Heinrich Hirsch **6** 483
Hamann, Johann Georg **7** 92
Lessing, Gotthold Ephraim
9 357-359
Zunz, Leopold **16** 534
influenced by
Maimonides **10** 151-152
relatives
Mendelssohn, Moses **10** 488-489
Schlegel, Friedrich von **14** 10-11

MENDELSSOHN-BARTHOLDY, FELIX JAKOB LUDWIG (1809-1847), German composer **10** 489-491
Brahms, Johannes **2** 490-492
Chopin, Frédéric François **4** 16-18
Elgar, Edward **5** 247-248
Gounod, Charles François **6** 473-474
Liszt, Franz **9** 445-447
Mendelssohn, Moses **10** 488-489
Schumann, Robert Alexander **14** 41-43
Strauss, Richard **14** 500-501

MENDENHALL, DOROTHY REED
(1874-1964), American physician
10 491-492

Mendès, Catulle (1841-1909), French man of letters
Maeterlinck, Maurice **10** 125-126

MENDÈS FRANCE, PIERRE (1907-1982),
French prime minister (1954-1955) and politician **10** 492-493
Bourguiba, Habib **2** 453-455

MENDES PINTO, FERNAO (1509-1583),
Portugese adventurer **10** 493-494

Mendiant, Le (poem)
Chénier, André Marie **3** 500-501

Mendicants (religious life)
see Augustinian Friars; Carmelites; Dominicans; Franciscans

Mending Wall (poem)
Frost, Robert Lee **6** 130-133

MENDOZA, ANTONIO DE (1490-1552), Spanish viceroy in Mexico and Peru **10** 494-495
Cabeza de Vaca, Álvar Núñez **3** 197
Cabrillo, Juan Rodríguez **3** 204-205
Coronado, Francisco Vásquez de **4** 247
Marcos de Niza **10** 240
Zumárraga, Juan de **16** 531-532

Menelaus (literary character)
Sophocles **14** 343-345

MENELIK II (born Sahle Mariam; 1844-1913), Ethiopian emperor 1889-1913 **10** 495-497
Bonvalot, Pierre Gabriel Édouard **2** 396
Haile Selassie **7** 68-70
Heruy Wäldä-Sellasé **7** 348-349
Johannes IV **8** 272-273
Mäkonnen Endalkačäw **10** 161-162
Tewodros II **15** 158-159

MENEM, CARLOS SÁUL (born 1930), Peronist president of Argentina **10** 497-499

MENÉNDEZ DE AVILÉS, PEDRO (1519-1574), Spanish seaman and colonizer **10** 499-500

MENES (King of Egypt; ca. 3420 B.C. - 3345 B.C.), unifier of Egypt **10** 500-502
Khufu **8** 540-541

Menexenus (dialogue)
Aristotle **1** 295-296
Plato **12** 345-347

Meng T'ien (died 209 B.C.), Chinese general
Quin Shi Huang-Di **12** 515-518

MENGELE, JOSEF (1911-1979), German physician and war criminal **10** 502-503
Wiesenthal, Simon **16** 264-266

Menger, Carl (1804-1921), Austrian economist
Böhm-Bawerk, Eugen von **2** 366
Clark, John Bates **4** 76-77
Schmoller, Gustav Friedrich von **14** 21

MENGISTU HAILE MARIAM (born 1937), head of state of Ethiopia **10** 503-505

MENGS, ANTON RAPHAEL (1728-1779), German painter **10** 505
Correggio **4** 249-251
David, Jacques Louis **4** 407-409
Goya y Lucientes, Francisco de Paula José de **6** 476-478
Tiepolo, Giovanni Battista **15** 219-220
West, Benjamin **16** 210-212
Winckelmann, Johann Joachim **16** 332-333

Mengs, Ismael (1688-1764), German painter
Mengs, Anton Raphael **10** 505

Meng-tzu
see Mencius

Meninas, Las (painting)
Velázquez, Diego Rodríguez de Silva y **15** 454-456

Meningitis (medicine)
Waksman, Selman Abraham **16** 49-50

Menippean satire (literary form)
Petronius Arbiter **12** 262-263
Seneca the Younger, Lucius Annaeus **14** 103-105
Varro, Marcus Terentius **15** 438-439

Menippus of Gadara (flourished 3rd century B.C.), Cynic philosopher and satirist
Lucian **10** 25-26
Varro, Marcus Terentius **15** 438-439

Menn, Barthélémy (1815-1893), Swiss painter
Hodler, Ferdinand **7** 434-435

MENNO SIMONS (circa 1496-1561), Dutch reformer **10** 505-506

Mennonites (religious sect)
Menno Simons **10** 505-506
Otterbein, Philip William **12** 27-28

Meno (dialogue)
Plato **12** 345-347

Meno (flourished 4th century B.C.), Greek author
Hippocrates **7** 408-410

MENOCAL, MARIO GARCIA (1866-1941), Cuban statesman, president 1913-1921 **10** 506-507
Machado y Morales, Gerardo **10** 92-93

Menominee Indians (North America)
Deer, Ada E. **4** 452-454

MENON, VENGALIL KRISHNAN KRISHNA (born 1897), Indian statesman **10** 507-509
Laski, Harold J. **9** 215-216
Nehru, Jawaharlal **11** 332-334

MENOTTI, GIAN CARLO (born 1911), Italian-born American composer **10** 509-510
Barber, Samuel **1** 500-501
Stravinsky, Igor Fedorovich **14** 502-506

Men's Wives (stories)
Thackeray, William Makepeace **15** 159-161

Mensheviks (Russian Social Democratic movement)
Kolchak, Aleksandr Vasilievich **9** 77-78
Kollontai, Aleksandra Mikhailovna **9** 79
Lenin, Vladimir Ilich **9** 323-326
Plekhanov, Georgi Valentinovich **12** 351-352
Trotsky, Leon **15** 302-305
see also Bolsheviks

Mensola (literary character)
Boccaccio, Giovanni **2** 351-353

Mensurius (died 311) bishop of Carthage
Donatus **5** 56-57

Mental Hospital reform (United States)
Dix, Dorothea Lynde **5** 32-33
Howe, Samuel Gridley **7** 537
Lloyd, Henry Demarest **9** 468-469
Pauling, Linus Carl **12** 150-152
Pavlov, Ivan Petrovich **12** 155-157
Pinel, Philippe **12** 313-314
Rush, Benjamin **13** 364-365
Sullivan, Harry Stack **15** 23-24
see also Psychiatry; Psychoanalysis; Psychoneurosis; Psychopathology; Psychotherapy; and specific disorders, e.g., Schizophrenia

Mental retardation
Dugdale, Richard Louis **5** 128-129
Lowell, Josephine Shaw **10** 15-16
Montessori, Maria **11** 125-126

Menteur, Le (play; Corneille)
Alarcón, Pedro Antonio de **1** 100-101
Corneille, Pierre **4** 234-236

Menuhin, Yehudi (born 1916), American violinist
Bartók, Béla **2** 35-36

MENZIES, SIR ROBERT GORDON (born 1894), Australian statesman **10** 510-511
Curtin, John Joseph **4** 348-349
Dobell, William **5** 34-35
Evatt, Herbert Vere **5** 341-343
Hughes, William Morris **8** 21-22
Santamaria, Bartholomew Augustine **13** 473-474

Meor Ha-Golah
see Gershom ben Judah

Mer, La (musical composition)
Debussy, Achille Claude **4** 445-447

Mercantile Agency (United States)
Tappan brothers **15** 105-106

Mercantilism (economics system)
Colbert, Jean Baptiste **4** 142-143
Frederick II **6** 81-84
Frederick William **6** 85-86

Mercator (play)
Plautus **12** 348-350

MERCATOR, GERHARDUS (1512-1594), Flemish cartographer **10** 511-512
Ortelius, Abraham **12** 8-9

Mercedes-Benz
Benz, Carl **2** 182-183

Mercersburg theology (religion)
Nevin, John Williamson **11** 357
Schaff, Philip **13** 519-520

Merchant, The (play)
Plautus **12** 348-350

Merchant Adventurers Co. (Bruges)
Caxton, William **3** 386-387

Merchant of Venice, The (play; Shakespeare)
Arne, Thomas Augustine **1** 307-308
Shakespeare, William **14** 142-145

Merchant of Yonkers, The (play)
Wilder, Thornton Niven **16** 276-277

Merchant Shipbuilders Corp.
Harriman, W. Averell **7** 165-166

Merchant shipping
Chang Po-go **3** 433-434
Collins, Edward Knight **4** 162-163
Grace, William Russell **6** 480-481
McKay, Donald **10** 416-417

Merchants
see Business and industrial leaders—
merchants

Mercia (ancient kingdom; England)
Alfred **1** 151-153
Edward the Elder **5** 219-220

Mercie, Marius Jean Antonin (1845-1916),
French sculptor
Brancusi, Constantin **2** 494-496

Merciless Parliament (England; 1388)
Henry IV **7** 292-293
Richard II **13** 130-131

Merck, George (1894-1957), American
chemist
Hofmann, August Wilhelm von
7 441-442

Mercure (ballet)
Satie, Erik **13** 494-495

Mercure de France, Le (literary revolution)
Gourmont, Remy de **6** 475
Proust, Marcel **12** 465-467

Mercury (element—chemistry)
Cavendish, Henry **3** 383-384
Fahrenheit, Gabriel Daniel **5** 366
Toledo, Francisco de **15** 257-259

Mercury (planet)
Brahe, Tycho **2** 489-490
Copernicus, Nicolaus **4** 226-227
Einstein, Albert **5** 228-231
Hall, Asaph **7** 83-84
Halley, Edmund **7** 88-89
Leverrier, Urbain Jean Joseph **9** 361-362
Winthrop, John **16** 341-342

Mercury (sculpture)
Giovanni da Bologna **6** 345-346

Mercury Passing in front of the Sun (painting)
Balla, Giacomo **1** 473-474

Mercy Philbrick's Choice (novel)
Jackson, Helen Hunt **8** 172

MEREDITH, GEORGE (1828-1909), English
novelist and poet **10** 512-513
Harris, Frank **7** 172-173
McClure, Samuel Sidney **10** 398-399
Sassoon, Siegfried **13** 492-493

MEREDITH, JAMES H. (born 1933), African
American civil rights activist and politician **10** 514-515

MEREZHKOVSKY, DMITRY SERGEYEVICH
(1865-1941), Russian writer and literary
critic **10** 515-516
Blok, Aleksandr Aleksandrovich **2** 335

Merezhkovsky, Zinaida (Zinaida Hippius;
1869-1945), Russian poet, novelist, and
critic
Merezhkovsky, Dmitry Sergeyevich
10 515-516

MERGENTHALER, OTTMAR (1854-1899),
German-American inventor of the Linotype **10** 516-517

Meridional arc (astronomy)
Struve, Friedrich Georg Wilhelm von
14 513

MÉRIMÉE, PROSPER (1803-1870), French
author **10** 517
Bizet, Georges **2** 296-297

Merino sheep
Banks, Joseph **1** 489-490
Watson, Elkanah **16** 136

Merisi, Fermo (died 1584), Italian master
builder
Caravaggio **3** 282-284

Merisi, Michelangelo
see Caravaggio

Merkits (Asian tribe)
Genghis Khan **6** 263-265

MERLEAU-PONTY, MAURICE
(1908-1961), French philosopher **10** 518

Merlette (novel)
Gourmont, Remy de **6** 475

Merlin (literary character)
Geoffrey of Monmouth **6** 268
Tennyson, Alfred **15** 144-146
see also Arthurian legend

Merlin (novel)
Heyse, Paul Johann Ludwig **7** 372-373

Merlotti, Claudio
see Merulo, Claudio

Merö (ancient city; Sudan)
Ezana **5** 354-355

Merodach-Baladan (ruled 721-710 and
703 B.C.), King of Babylon
Sargon II **13** 482
Sennacherib **14** 108

Mérode Altarpiece (painting; Campin)
Campin, Robert **3** 255
Weyden, Rogier van der **16** 219-221

Merope (play)
Arnold, Matthew **1** 311-313
Voltaire **16** 14-16

Merovingian dynasty
see France—481-751

MERRIAM, CHARLES EDWARD
(1874-1953), American political scientist
10 518-519
Key, Vladimir Orlando Jr. **8** 527-528
Webster, Noah **16** 164-166

MERRILL, CHARLES E. (1885-1956),
founder of the world's largest brokerage
firm **10** 519-520

MERRILL, JAMES (1926-1995), American
novelist, poet, and playwright
10 521-522

Merrill Lynch, Pierce, Fenner and Smith
(brokerage firm)
Merrill, Charles E. **10** 519-520
Regan, Donald **13** 80-81

Merrimac (ship)
Ericsson, John **5** 307-308
Welles, Gideon **16** 188-190
Wilkes, Charles **16** 279-280

Merrimack Manufacturing Co.
Appleton, Nathan **1** 266-267

Merry Company, The (painting)
Hals, Frans **7** 89-91

Merry Men, The (stories)
Stevenson, Robert Louis **14** 446-448

Merry Mount (opera)
Hanson, Howard **7** 135-136

Merry Wives of Windsor, The (play; Shake-
speare)
Shakespeare, William **14** 142-145
Vaughan Williams, Ralph **15** 446-447
Verdi, Giuseppe Fortunino Francesco
15 463-465

Merrymaking (painting)
Krieghoff, Cornelius **9** 101

Mersenne, Marin (1588-1648), French
philosopher and mathematician
Galileo Galilei **6** 180-183

Merton, Council of (England)
Grosseteste, Robert **7** 15

MERTON, ROBERT K. (born 1910), American sociologist and educator **10** 522-523

MERTON, THOMAS (1915-1968), Roman
Catholic writer, social critic, and spiritual
guide **10** 523-525

MERULO, CLAUDIO (1533-1604), Italian
composer, organist, and teacher
10 525-526
Frescobaldi, Girolamo **6** 101-102
Gabrieli, Giovanni **6** 161-162

MERZ-art
Schwitters, Kurt **14** 60-61

Merzbild (collage; Schwitters)
Burri, Alberto **3** 159-160

Mes Loisirs (verse collection)
Fréchette, Louis-Honoré **6** 77-78

Mesabi Range (Minnesota)
Frick, Henry Clay **6** 108-109
Rockefeller, John Davison **13** 226-228

Mescalero Apache Indians (North America)
Carson, Christopher **3** 334-335

Mescalin (drug)
Huxley, Aldous Leonard **8** 74-75

Meshed (Mashhad; city, Iran)
Abbas I **1** 4-6

Mesillat Yesharim (poem)
Luzzato, Moses Hayyim **10** 57-58

MESMER, FRANZ ANTON (1734-1815),
German physician **10** 526-527
Charcot, Jean Martin **3** 442

Mesmerism
see Hypnosis

Mesolabe (instrument)
Eratosthenes of Cyrene **5** 301-302

Meson (element—chemistry particle)
Anderson, Carl David **1** 214-215
Bethe, Hans Albrecht **2** 238-239
Bhabha, Homi Jehangir **2** 253-254
Yukawa, Hideki **16** 481-482

Mesoporphyrin (chemistry)
Fischer, Hans **5** 457-459

Mesopotamia (ancient nation; western
Asia)
Akkadian rule
Sargon of Agade **13** 483
Babylonian rule
Hammurabi **7** 109-110
see also Babylonia
Islamic conquest
Mansur, Abu Jafar ibn Muhammad
al- **10** 214-215
Omar ibn al-Khattab **11** 508-509
Saladin **13** 441-442
Persian conquest
Cyrus the Great **4** 363-364
Darius I **4** 394-395
Roman rule
Belisarius **2** 128-129
Marcus Aurelius Antoninus
10 243-245
see also Iraq (for modern period)

Mesothorium (radioelement)
Hahn, Otto **7** 64-65

Mesotron
see Meson (element—chemistry particle)

MESSALI HADJ (1898-1974), founder of
the Algerian nationalist movement
10 527-528

Messalina, Valeria (died 48), Roman
empress
Claudius Germanicus, Tiberius **4** 91-92
Seneca the Younger, Lucius Annaeus
14 103-105

Messel, Alfred (1853-1909), German architect
Behrens, Peter **2** 121-122

Messenger (periodical)
Randolph, A. Philip **13** 28-29

Messenger Boys, The (revue)
Marx brothers **10** 303-304

Messenia (district; Peloponnesus)
Epaminondas **5** 291-292

Messerschmitt (German airplane)
Tupolev, Andrei Nikolaevich
15 341-342

MESSIAEN, OLIVIER (1908-1992), French
composer and teacher **10** 528-529
Boulez, Pierre **2** 444-445
Stockhausen, Karlheinz **14** 460-461

Stravinsky, Igor Fedorovich **14** 502-506
Xenakis, Iannis **16** 416-418

Messiah (oratorio; Handel)
Handel, George Frederick **7** 116-119
Mozart, Wolfgang Amadeus
11 218-221

Messiah (poem)
Pope, Alexander **12** 395-397

Messiah (religion)
Cohen, Hermann **4** 138-139
Isaiah **8** 146-147
Jesus of Nazareth **8** 251-255
John the Baptist **8** 290
Manasseh ben Israel **10** 183-184
Mary **10** 308

Messianic Eclogue (poem)
Virgil **15** 507-510

Messianism (religion)
Cunha, Euclides Rodrigues Pimenta da
4 336-337
Luzzato, Moses Hayyim **10** 57-58
Sabbatai Zevi **13** 400-401

Messias (poem)
Klopstock, Friedrich Gottlieb **9** 55-56

Messina (city; Italy.)
Mazzini, Giuseppe **10** 381-383

Mestiere de vivere, Il (diary)
Pavese, Cesare **12** 154-155

Mestizos (Spanish-Indian people)
Cunha, Euclides Rodrigues Pimenta da
4 336-337
Díaz, José de la Cruz Porfirio **4** 534-536
Iturbide, Agustín de **8** 155-156
Morelos, José María **11** 157-158
Santa Cruz, Andrés de **13** 472-473

Metabolism (biology)
Cori, Gerty T. **4** 231-234
Helmholtz, Hermann Ludwig Ferdinand
von **7** 268-269
Houssay, Bernardo Alberto **7** 522-523
Lavoisier, Antoine Laurent **9** 241-244
Liebig, Justus von **9** 403-404
Lipmann, Fritz **9** 435-437
Schwann, Theodor **14** 51-52

METACOM (a.k.a. King Philip; 1640-1676),
Wampanoag cheiftain **10** 529-531

Metahistory (social science)
Toynbee, Arnold Joseph **15** 283-284

Metakatatrope (ode)
Pindar **12** 312-313

Metal (chemistry)
Bethe, Hans Albrecht **2** 238-239
Bohr, Niels Henrik David **2** 366-368
Boyle, Robert **2** 469-471
Cavendish, Henry **3** 383-384

Métal (musical composition)
Varèse, Edgard **15** 432-433

Metalanguage (philosophy)
Carnap, Rudolf **3** 308-309

Metallurgy (science)
Agricola, Georgius **1** 86-87

Bragg, William Henry **2** 488-489
see also Mineralogy

Metalogicon (book)
John of Salisbury **8** 284-285

Metamathematics (philosophy)
Gödel, Kurt **6** 377-379
Tarski, Alfred **15** 110-111

Metamora (play)
Forrest, Edwin **6** 11-12

Metamorphism (geology)
Hutton, James **8** 73-74

Metamorphosen (musical composition)
Strauss, Richard **14** 500-501

Metamorphoses (poem; Ovid)
Chrestien de Troyes **4** 23-24
Góngora y Argote, Luis de **6** 427-428
Ovid **12** 34-36
Velázquez, Diego Rodríguez de Silva y
15 454-456

Metamorphosis, The (story)
Kafka, Franz **8** 403-406

Metaphysical painting (art)
Chirico, Giorgio de **4** 4

Metaphysical poetry (literature)
England (17th century)
Cowley, Abraham **4** 281-282
Crashaw, Richard **4** 296
Donne, John **5** 60-61
Herbert, George **7** 324-326
Johnson, Samuel **8** 315-317
Marvell, Andrew **10** 301-303
Raleigh, Walter **13** 9-11
Vaughan, Henry **15** 444-445
United States (20th century)
Crane, Hart **4** 291-293
Roethke, Theodore **13** 243-244

Metaphysics (philosophy)
and Christian doctrine
Averroës **1** 382-383
Duns Scotus, John **5** 149-150
Hartshorne, Charles **7** 186-187
see also Scholasticism
and language
Derrida, Jacques **4** 503-505
and science
Bergson, Henri **2** 191-192
Fries, Jakob Friedrich **6** 116-117
Nietzsche, Friedrich **11** 390-392
hierarchical synthesis
Alexander, Samuel **1** 141
Kant, Immanuel **8** 430-432
music and
Wagner, Richard **16** 40-43
nature of reality
Aristotle **1** 295-296
Bradley, Francis Herbert **2** 481-482
Cudworth, Ralph **4** 331
rationalism
Descartes, René **4** 505-508
Leibniz, Gottfried Wilhelm von
9 307-310
Lotze, Rudolf Hermann **9** 521-522

Malebranche, Nicolas **10** 166-167
Spinoza, Baruch **14** 381-383
Wolff, Christian von **16** 358
see also Rationalism (philosophy)
subjective idealism
Fichte, Johann Gottlieb **5** 435-436
Schelling, Friedrich Wilhelm Joseph von **13** 526-527
see also Idealism (philosophy)
truth
Herbert, Edward **7** 324

Metastasio (Pietro Antonio Domenico Bonaventura Trapassi; 1698-1782), Italian dramatist
Arne, Thomas Augustine **1** 307-308
Gluck, Christoph Willibald **6** 372-374

Metatheory (psychology)
Lewin, Kurt **9** 375-376

Metaurus, battle of the (207 B.C.)
Hannibal Barca **7** 128-130

METCALFE, CHARLES THEOPHILUS (1st Baron Metcalfe; 1785-1846), British colonial administrator **10** 531-532
Baldwin, Robert **1** 466-468
Ryerson, Adolphus Egerton **13** 392-393

METCHNIKOFF, ÉLIE (1845-1916), Russian physiologist and bacteriologist **10** 532-533
Ehrlich, Paul **5** 225-226
Fleming, Alexander **5** 483-485

Metellus Balearicus, Quintus Caecilius (flourished circa 123-115 B.C.), Roman consul and censor
Marius, Gaius **10** 264-265

Metellus Celer, Quintus (died 59 B.C.), Roman consul and governor
Catullus, Gaius Valerius **3** 377-378

Metellus Numidicus, Quintus Caecilius (died 99 B.C.), Roman consul
Marius, Gaius **10** 264-265

Metempsychosis (philosophy)
Empedocles **5** 282
Lessing, Gotthold Ephraim **9** 357-359
Pythagoras **12** 498-499

Meteor (airplane)
Whittle, Frank **16** 257-258

Meteor (astronomy)
Lovell, Alfred Charles Bernard **10** 8-9

Meteor (novel)
Čapek, Karel **3** 271-272

Meteor, The (play)
Dürrenmatt, Friedrich **5** 164-165

Meteorology (science)
Aristotle **1** 295-296
Dalton, John **4** 378-379
Franklin, Benjamin **6** 60-64
Galton, Francis **6** 193-194
Humboldt, Friedrich Heinrich Alexander von **8** 30-31
Lamarck, Chevalier de **9** 171-173
Langmuir, Irving **9** 196-197
see also Scientists—meteorologists

Meter (electricity)
Edison, Thomas Alva **5** 206-208

Methinks I hear a heav'nly host (hymn)
Billings, William **2** 274-275

Method acting (theater)
Stanislavsky, Constantin **14** 398-399

Methodischen Sonate (musical composition)
Telemann, Georg Philipp **15** 137-138

Methodism (religion)
and ecumenism
Harkness, Georgia **7** 155-156
development (North America)
Asbury, Francis **1** 324-325
Cartwright, Peter **3** 344-345
Eggleston, Edward **5** 223-224
Ryerson, Adolphus Egerton **13** 392-393
see also Methodist Episcopal Church
founders
Wesley, Charles **16** 208-209
Wesley, John **16** 209-210

Methodist Episcopal Church (North America)
Allen, Richard **1** 168
Asbury, Francis **1** 324-325
Ryerson, Adolphus Egerton **13** 392-393
Vincent, John Heyl **15** 502-503

METHODIUS, SAINT (825-885), Greek missionary and bishop **4** 362-363

Methodology (history)
Chang Hsüeh-ch'eng **3** 433
see also Historiography

Methodology (philosophy)
Carnap, Rudolf **3** 308-309
Descartes, René **4** 505-508, 350

Methylene blue (dye)
Ehrlich, Paul **5** 225-226

Métis (people; Canada)
Lacombe, Albert **9** 147-148
Riel, Louis **13** 163-164

Meton (flourished circa 433 B.C.), Greek astronomer
Hipparchus **7** 407-408

Metric system (measurement)
Dewey, Melvil **4** 523-524
Mendeleev, Dmitrii Ivanovich **10** 486-488

Metrical History (poem)
Taylor, Edward **15** 122-123

Metro-Goldwyn-Mayer (film studio)
Gable, William Clark **6** 157-158
Garbo, Greta **6** 205-207
Loew, Marcus **9** 485-486

Metropolitan Club (New York City)
White, Stanford **16** 235-236

Metropolitan Communist party (French West Africa)
Houphouët-Boigny, Felix **7** 519-520

Metropolitan Museum of Art (New York City)

Kennedy, John Stewart **8** 507-508
Morgan, John Pierpont **11** 163-165
Rockefeller, John D. Jr. **13** 225-226

Metropolitan Opera Co. (New York City)
Anderson, Marian **1** 218-219
Balanchine, George **1** 461-462
Barber, Samuel **1** 500-501
Caruso, Enrico **3** 345
Levine, James **9** 369-371
Toscanini, Arturo **15** 270-271

Metropolitan Opera Orchestra
Schuller, Gunther **14** 37-38

Metropolitan Police Act (London; 1829)
Peel, Robert **12** 181-183

Metropolitan State Hospital (Waltham, Massachusetts)
Skinner, Burrhus Frederic **14** 269-270

Metropolitan-Vickers (engineering company)
Cockcroft, John Douglas **4** 131-132

Metsys, Quentin
see Massys, Quentin

METTERNICH, KLEMENS VON (1773-1859), Austrian politician and diplomat **10** 533-536
Castlereagh, Viscount **3** 363-364
Francis II **6** 43-44
Kossuth, Louis **9** 88-90
Kotzebue, Otto von **9** 91-92
Stein, Heinrich Friedrich Karl vom und zum **14** 415-416

Metz, battle of (1870)
Moltke, Helmuth Karl Bernard von **11** 90-91

Metz Cathedral (France)
Chagall, Marc **3** 406-407

Metz, Diet of (1355-1356)
Charles IV **3** 455-456

Metzinger, Jean (1883-1956), French cubist painter
Weber, Max **16** 160

Meun, Jean de
see Jean de Meun

Meursault (literary character)
Camus, Albert **3** 255-257

Mevlevi order (dervishes)
Rumi, Jalai ed-Din **13** 362-363

Mexicalia (story; J. London)
Eisenstein, Sergei Mikhailovich **5** 240-242

Mexican Americans
politicians
Cisneros, Henry G. **4** 62-64

Mexican art
Barragán, Luis **2** 17-19
Kahlo, Frida **8** 406-407
Orozco, José Clemente **12** 1-2
Rivera, Diego **13** 183-184
Siqueiros, David Alfaro **14** 256
Velasco, Luis de **15** 450-451

Tt 1–250 B/W

Mexican literature
Azuela, Mariano **1** 402
Fernández de Lizardi, José Joaquin **5** 424-425
Fuentes, Carlos **6** 141-142
Juana Inés de la Cruz **8** 367-368
Paz, Octavio **12** 161-162
Poniatowska, Elena **12** 392-393
Reyes, Alfonso **13** 112-113
Toledano, Vicente Lombardo **15** 256-257
Vasconcelos, José **15** 443-444

Mexican music
Chávez, Carlos **3** 486

Mexican Popular University
Toledano, Vicente Lombardo **15** 256-257

Mexican Regional Labor Confederation
Carranza, Venustiano **3** 321-322

Mexican Revolution (1910-1915)
federal forces
Díaz, José de la Cruz Porfirio **4** 534-536
in literature
Azuela, Mariano **1** 402
Fuentes, Carlos **6** 141-142
intellectual supporters
Toledano, Vicente Lombardo **15** 256-257
Vasconcelos, José **15** 443-444
rebel leaders
Calles, Plutarco Elías **3** 234-235
Carranza, Venustiano **3** 321-322
Huerta, Victoriano **8** 13-14
Madero, Francisco Indalecio **10** 118-119
Obregón, Álvaro **11** 458-459
Villa, Pancho **15** 495-496
Zapata, Emiliano **16** 489-490
United States policy
Daniels, Josephus **4** 387
Gompers, Samuel **6** 420-422
Pershing, John Joseph **12** 243-244
Steffens, Lincoln **14** 410-411
Wilson, Thomas Woodrow **16** 330-332
see also San Luis Potosi, Plan of

Mexican Symphony Orchestra
Chávez, Carlos **3** 486

Mexican War (1846-1848)
Bear Flag Revolt
see Bear Flag Revolt (California; 1846-47)
causes
Polk, James Knox **12** 374-376
Wilmot, David **16** 312-313
critics
Calhoun, John Caldwell **3** 226-228
Lincoln, Abraham **9** 415-418
Thoreau, Henry David **15** 203-205
Webster, Daniel **16** 162-164
Mexican politics
Álvarez, Juan **1** 184-185

Díaz, José de la Cruz Porfirio **4** 534-536
Juárez, Benito **8** 369-372
Santa Ana, Antonio López de **13** 471-472
see also Wilmot Proviso
supporters
Cass, Lewis **3** 355-356
Clay, Henry **4** 94-96
Clayton, John Middleton **4** 96-97
Marcy, William Learned **10** 247-248
Walker, Robert John **16** 67-68
treaty
see Guadalupe Hidalgo, Treaty of (1848)
United States forces (army)
Beauregard, Pierre Gustave Toutant **2** 96-97
Comstock, Henry Tompkins Paige **4** 189
Davis, Jefferson **4** 416-418
George, James Zachariah **6** 276-277
Grant, Ulysses Simpson **6** 492-494
Jackson, Shirley Ann **8** 183-184
Johnston, Joseph Eggleston **8** 323
Kearny, Stephen Watts **8** 468-469
Pierce, Franklin **12** 300-301
Scott, Winfield **14** 70-71
Taylor, Zachary **15** 128-130
Thomas, George Henry **15** 190-191
Wallace, Lewis **16** 74-75
United States forces (navy)
Farragut, David Glasgow **5** 388-389
Perry, Matthew Calbraith **12** 237-239
Semmes, Raphael **14** 102-103
Veracruz
see Veracruz, battle of
weapons
Colt, Samuel **4** 172-173
see also Compromise of 1850

Mexico (United Mexican States; republic, North America)
• **AZTEC EMPIRE**
emperors
Cuauhtemoc **4** 329
Montezuma, II **11** 128-129
exploration
Cabeza de Vaca, Álvar Núñez **3** 197
Coronado, Francisco Vásquez de **4** 247
Spanish conquest
Cabrillo, Juan Rodríguez **3** 204-205
Cortés, Hernán **4** 255-256
Díaz del Castillo, Bernal **4** 536-537
Narváez, Pánfilo de **11** 315
Velázquez de Cuéllar, Diego **15** 459
• **COLONIAL PERIOD**
administrators
Gálvez, José de **6** 196
Mendoza, Antonio de **10** 494-495

Revillagigedo, Conde de **13** 111-112
Velasco, Luis de **15** 450-451
Catholic instruction
Marcos de Niza **10** 240
Serra, Junípero **14** 111-112
Zumárraga, Juan de **16** 531-532
historians of
Prescott, William Hickling **12** 440-441
Sierra, Justo **14** 217
see also New Spain
• **REPUBLIC**
anticlericalism
Juárez, Benito **8** 369-372
Lerdo de Tejada, Miguel **9** 351-352
border disputes
Estrada Cabrera, Manuel **5** 325-326
economic crisis (1976)
Echeverría Alvarez, Luis **5** 198-200
economic crisis (1980s)
de la Madrid Hurtado, Miguel **4** 471-472
economic development
López Portillo, José **9** 510-511
Ruiz Cortines, Adolfo **13** 359-360
Zedillo Ponce de Leon, Ernesto **16** 493-495
economic reforms (1980s-1990s)
Salinas de Gortari, Carlos **13** 445-447
independence movement
Álvarez, Juan **1** 184-185
Guerrero, Vicente **7** 28-30
Hidalgo y Costilla, Miguel **7** 375-377
Iturbide, Agustín de **8** 155-156
Matamoros, Mariano **10** 329-330
Morelos, José María **11** 157-158
Santa Ana, Antonio López de **13** 471-472
industrial revolution
Ávila Camacho, Manuel **1** 387-388
Alemán Valdés, Miguel **1** 126-127
Mexican Empire
Juárez, Benito **8** 369-372
Maximilian of Hapsburg **10** 358-360
Napoleon III **11** 310-312
Seward, William Henry **14** 124-125
nationalization of resources
Cárdenas, Lázaro **3** 286-287
Sierra, Justo **14** 217
Toledano, Vicente Lombardo **15** 256-257
1968 Olympics
Díaz Ordaz, Gustavo **4** 537-538
papal relations
Pius XI **12** 337-339

Plan of Ayala
　　see Ayala, Plan of (1911)
Plan of Iguala
　　see Iguala, Plan of (1821)
political reform
　　Cárdenas Solorzano, Cuauhté-
　　moc **3** 287-288
reforms (1960s)
　　López Mateos, Adolfo **9** 509-510
republic established
　　Alamán, Lucas **1** 99-100
　　Guerrero, Vicente **7** 28-30
Three-Year War (1857-1860)
　　Álvarez, Juan **1** 184-185
　　Juárez, Benito **8** 369-372
　　Lerdo de Tejada, Miguel
　　9 351-352
　　see also Mexican Revolution

• UNITED STATES RELATIONS
Bear Flag Revolt
　　see Bear Flag Revolt
diplomatic relations
　　Daniels, Josephus **4** 387
　　Morrow, Dwight Whitney
　　11 190-191
Gadsden Purchase
　　see Gadsden Purchase
joins Allies (World War II)
　　Ávila Camacho, Manuel
　　1 387-388
Mexican War (1846-1848)
　　see Mexican War
mining interests
　　Hearst, George **7** 242
Texas Revolt (1836)
　　Austin, Stephen Fuller **1** 380-381
　　Becknell, William **2** 105-106
　　Houston, Samuel **7** 526-527
　　Santa Ana, Antonio López de
　　13 471-472
　　Slidell, John **14** 273
　　Travis, William Barret
　　15 292-293
United States invasion (1916-1917)
　　Arnold, Thurman Wesley **1** 314
　　Carranza, Venustiano **3** 321-322
　　Pershing, John Joseph
　　12 243-244
　　Villa, Pancho **15** 495-496
　　Zapata, Emiliano **16** 489-490
　　see also Mexican art; Mexican
　　literature; Mexican music

Mexico, University of
Dewey, John **4** 520-523
Rivera, Diego **13** 183-184
Vasconcelos, José **15** 443-444
Velasco, Luis de **15** 450-451

Mexico City (Mexico)
in fiction
　　Fuentes, Carlos **6** 141-142
murals
　　Orozco, José Clemente **12** 1-2
　　Rivera, Diego **13** 183-184
　　Siqueiros, David Alfaro **14** 256
urban reforms

Gálvez, José de **6** 196
Revillagigedo, Conde de
　　13 111-112
　　see also Mexico

Meyer, Adolf (1866-1950), American psy-
chiatrist
　　Gropius, Walter **7** 13-14
　　Lashley, Karl Spencer **9** 214-215

Meyer, Victor (1848-1897), German
chemist
　　Bunsen, Robert Wilhelm **3** 124-125

MEYERBEER, GIACOMO (1791-1864),
German composer **10** 536-537
　　Bizet, Georges **2** 296-297

MEYERHOF, OTTO FRITZ (1884-1951),
German biochemist **10** 537-539
　　Hill, Archibald Vivian **7** 385-386

MEYERHOLD, VSEVOLOD EMILIEVICH
(1874-1942?), Russian director **10** 539
　　Blok, Aleksandr Aleksandrovich **2** 335
　　Prokofiev, Sergei Sergeevich
　　12 458-460

Meynert, Thoedor (1833-1892), Viennese
psychiatrist
　　Freud, Sigmund **6** 103-106

Mezzo Cammin (poem)
　　Longfellow, Henry Wadsworth
　　9 499-500

Mfantsi National Education Fund (Ghana)
　　Hayford, J. E. Casely **7** 228-230

MFUME, KWEISI (born Frizzell Gray; born
1948), African American civil rights
activist and congressman **10** 539-542

MGM
　　see Metro-Goldwyn-Mayer

Mhudi (historical novel)
　　Plaatje, Solomon Tshekisho **12** 341-342

MI FEI (1051-1107), Chinese painter, calligrapher, and critic **11** 12-13

Mi Fu (1051-1107), Chinese painter, calligrapher and critic
　　Tung Ch'i-ch'ang **15** 339-340

Mi Yu-jen (1086-1165), Chinese landscape
painter
　　Mi Fei **11** 12-13
　　Tung Ch'i-ch'ang **15** 339-340

Miami, University of
School of Architecture
　　Rossi, Aldo **13** 309-310

Miami and the Siege of Chicago (non-fic-
tion novel)
　　Mailer, Norman Kingsley **10** 148-150

Miami Indians (North America)
　　McCoy, Isaac **10** 403

Miami University (Oxford, Ohio)
　　McGuffey, William Holmes **10** 414-415

Miaskovsky, Nicolai Yakovlevich
(1881-1950), Russian composer
　　Khachaturian, Aram Ilich **8** 530-531
　　Prokofiev, Sergei Sergeevich
　　12 458-460

MICAH (flourished 8th century B.C.),
prophet of ancient Israel **10** 542-543

Micah Clarke (novel)
　　Doyle, Arthur Conan **5** 91-92

Micawber (literary character)
　　Dickens, Charles John Huffam
　　4 538-541

Michael (born 1921), king of Romania
1927-1930 and 1940-1947
　　Ferdinand **5** 413-414

Michael II (ruled 820-829), Byzantine
emperor
　　Cyril and Methodius, Saints **4** 362-363

Michael III (ruled 842-867), Byzantine
emperor
　　Basil I **2** 49-50
　　Photius **12** 283-284

Michael IV (the Paphlagonian; ruled
1034-1041), Byzantine emperor
　　Zoë **16** 524-525

Michael V (Calaphates; ruled 1041-1042),
Byzantine emperor
　　Zoë **16** 524-525

Michael VII (Ducas; ruled 1071-1078),
Byzantine emperor
　　Comnena, Anna **4** 185-186

MICHAEL VIII (Palaeologus;
1224/25-1282), Byzantine emperor
1259-1282 **11** 1-2

Michael Aleksandrovich (1878-1918),
grand duke of Russia
　　Nicholas II **11** 378-380

Michael Feodorovich (1596-1645), czar of
Russia 1613-1645
　　Alexis Mikhailovich Romanov
　　1 142-143

Michael Kohlhaas (story)
　　Kleist, Heinrich von **9** 52-53

Michael Kramer (play)
　　Hauptmann, Gerhart Johann Robert
　　7 199-201

Michael of Cesena (circa 1270-1342), Franciscan minister general and theologian
　　William of Ockham **16** 298-299

Michael Strogoff (novel)
　　Verne, Jules **15** 467-469

Michael Wisniowiecki (1638-1673), king of
Poland 1669-1673
　　John III **8** 276-277

Michaelis de Vasconcellos, Carolina
(1851-1925), German-born Portuguese
author
　　Camoëns, Luis Vaz de **3** 247-249

Michaelmas Term (play)
　　Middleton, Thomas **11** 8-9

Michal (Old Testament figure)
　　David, Jacques Louis **4** 407-409

Michallon, Achille-Etna (1796-1822),
French painter and lithographer
　　Corot, Jean Baptiste Camille **4** 247-249

Michel (literary character)
Gide, André **6** 308-309

Michel, Claude
see Clodion

MICHELANGELO BUONARROTI
(1475-1564), Italian sculptor, painter, and
architect **11** 2-5
associates
Andrea del Sarto **1** 224-225
Bramante, Donato **2** 493-494-146
Giovanni da Bologna **6** 345-346
Perugino **12** 245-246
Raphael **13** 40-42
Rosso, Il **13** 312-313
Signorelli, Luca **14** 221-222
Vignola, Giacomo da **15** 493-494
influence of (England)
Burne-Jones, Edward Coley
3 145-146
influence of (France)
Carpeaux, Jean Baptiste **3** 318-319
Garnier, Jean Louis Charles
6 221-222
Géricault, Jean Louis André
Théodore **6** 280-281
Rodin, Auguste **13** 236-238
influence of (Germany)
Mengs, Anton Raphael **10** 505
influence of (Italy)
Berruguete, Alonso **2** 223-224
Borromini, Francesco **2** 424-425
Bronzino **3** 19
Carracci **3** 319-321
Cellini, Benvenuto **3** 391-392
Correggio **4** 249-251
Pontormo **12** 394-395
Porta, Giacomo della **12** 402-403
Tintoretto **15** 232-234
Titian **15** 242-244
influence of (Netherlands)
Rubens, Peter Paul **13** 339-342
influence of (Spain)
Greco **6** 511-514
Velázquez, Diego Rodríguez de
Silva y **15** 454-456
influenced by
Donatello **5** 55-56
Leonardo da Vinci **9** 337-340
Quercia, Jacopo della **12** 509
Signorelli, Luca **14** 221-222
patrons
Julius II **8** 384-386
Medici, Lorenzo de' **10** 450-451
Paul III **12** 144-145
Pius IV **12** 332
studies on
Pater, Walter Horatio **12** 130-131
Vasari, Giorgio **15** 442-443

MICHELET, JULES (1798-1874), French his-
torian **11** 5-6
Dumas, Alexandre **5** 136-138
Joan of Arc **8** 264-265

MICHELOZZO (circa 1396-1472), Italian
architect and sculptor **11** 6-7
Alberti, Leon Battista **1** 113-115

Angelico **1** 235-236
Donatello **5** 55-56
Luca della Robbia **10** 19-20
Medici, Cosimo de' **10** 449-450
Verrocchio, Andrea del **15** 471-472

MICHELSON, ALBERT ABRAHAM
(1852-1931), American physicist **11** 7-8
Millikan, Robert Andrews **11** 33-35
Newcomb, Simon **11** 361-362

Michelson-Morley experiment (1887;
physics)
Einstein, Albert **5** 228-231
Michelson, Albert Abraham **11** 7-8

Michiel, Marcantonio (1486?-1552), Italian
art historian
Giorgione **6** 340-341

Michigan (state; United States)
Cass, Lewis **3** 355-356
Chandler, Zachariah **3** 425-426
Hull, William **8** 29-30
Jackson, Andrew **8** 168-172
Schoolcraft, Henry Rowe **14** 29

Michigan, University of (Ann Arbor)
arts and literature
Frost, Robert Lee **6** 130-133
Holst, Gustav **7** 459-460
Saarinen, Eliel and Eero **13** 396-398
philosophy
Dewey, John **4** 520-523
Mead, George Herbert **10** 437-438
sciences
Fermi, Enrico **5** 422-424
Pauli, Wolfgang Ernst **12** 149
Rous, Francis Peyton **13** 322-323
Salk, Jonas Edward **13** 451-452
social sciences
Cooley, Charles Horton **4** 216-217
Lewin, Kurt **9** 375-376
Sauer, Carl Ortwin **13** 496-497
Tyler, Moses Coit **15** 369-370
White, Andrew Dickson **16** 226-227
White, Leslie A. **16** 232-233

Michigan Indians (North America)
Hull, William **8** 29-30

Michigan Southern Railroad
Durant, Thomas Clark **5** 157-158

Michoacán (state; Mexico)
Cárdenas, Lázaro **3** 286-287

Mickey Mouse (cartoon character)
Disney, Walter Elias **5** 26-27
Lichtenstein, Roy **9** 398-399

Microbalance (instrument)
Aston, Francis William **1** 350-351

Microbiology (science)
Baltimore, David **1** 477-478
Colwell, Rita R. **4** 179-180
Dubos, René Jules **5** 119
Hershey, Alfred Day **7** 343-345
Hooke, Robert **7** 475
Metchnikoff, Élie **10** 532-533
Sabin, Albert Bruce **13** 401-402
Waksman, Selman Abraham **16** 49-50

see also Scientists—microbiologists

Microdissection (anatomy)
Leeuwenhoek, Anton van **9** 300-301
Swammerdam, Jan **15** 48-49

Micrologus... (book)
Guido d'Arezzo **7** 33

Micromégas (story)
Voltaire **16** 14-16

Micrometer (instrument)
Fraunhofer, Joseph von **6** 75-76
Huygens, Christiaan **8** 79-81

Microphonie 1 (musical composition)
Stockhausen, Karlheinz **14** 460-461

Microradiometer (instrument)
Kapitsa, Pyotr Leonidovich **8** 433-435

Microscope (instrument)
Hooke, Robert **7** 475
Leeuwenhoek, Anton van **9** 300-301

Microsoft
Gates, William Henry III **6** 232-234

Microsurgery (medicine)
Spemann, Hans **14** 368-369

Microtone (music)
Busoni, Ferruccio Benvenuto **3** 173-174
Ives, Charles Edward **8** 159-160

Midas (flourished 8th century B.C.), king of
Phrygia, ca. 717 B.C.
Sargon II **13** 482

Mid-channel (play)
Barrymores **2** 28-30

Middle Ages (Europe)
education
Alcuin of York **1** 122-123
Cassiodorus, Flavius Magnus Aure-
lius **3** 357-358
Charlemagne **3** 445-447
Isidore of Seville **8** 149-150
Islamic influence
Averroës **1** 382-383
Avicenna **1** 386-387
Ibn al-Arabi, Muhyi al-Din **8** 91
ibn Battuta, Muhammad **8** 91-92
ibn Khaldun, Abd al-Rahman ibn
Muhammad **8** 93-94
literature
Chaucer, Geoffrey **3** 482-485
Dante Alighieri **4** 389-391
Guillaume de Lorris **7** 33-34
see also Humanism—Middle Ages
and Renaissance
religion and philosophy
Anselm of Canterbury **1** 244-245
Aristotle **1** 295-296
Coulton, George Gordon **4** 267
Erigena, John Scotus **5** 308-309
Gregory I **6** 531-532
Grosseteste, Robert **7** 15
see also Monasticism; Scholasticism
science
Albertus Magnus **1** 115-116
Bacon, Roger **1** 425-427
Fibonacci, Leonardo **5** 434-435

Guy de Chauliac **7** 54
Luzzi, Mondino de' **10** 58
Peregrinus, Petrus **12** 208
society
Cole, George Douglas Howard
4 146-147
Huizinga, Johan **8** 26-27
Mabillon, Jean **10** 72
Pirenne, Jean Henri Otto Lucien
Marie **12** 322-323
Vinogradoff, Paul Gavrilovitch
15 503
see also Byzantine Empire; and
under individual countries
see also Historiography—medieval
society

Middle Comedy (Greek literature)
Menander **10** 477-478

Middle Creek, battle of (1862)
Garfield, James Abram **6** 213-214

Middle East
Camp David Accords (1979)
Begin, Menachem **2** 118-120
Carter, James Earl **3** 339-342
Sadat, Anwar **13** 412-414
Vance, Cyrus R. **15** 411-413
folk music
Ben-Haim, Paul **2** 161-162
Iranian hostage crisis (1979)
Carter, James Earl **3** 339-342
Lebanon-Syria dispute
Aoun, Michel **1** 255-257
Harawi, Ilyas al- **7** 145-146
see also Arab-Israeli wars

Middle Path (Buddhism)
Buddha **3** 97-101

Middle way (Puritan ethics)
Cotton, John **4** 263-265

Middle West Utilities (conglomerate)
Insull, Samuel **8** 130

**Middle-aged Man on the Flying Trapeze,
The** (book)
Thurber, James Grove **15** 213-214

Middleburg, battle of (1901)
Botha, Louis **2** 434-436

Middlebury College (Vermont)
Benét, Stephen Vincent **2** 157-158
Frost, Robert Lee **6** 130-133

Middlebury Female Seminary (Vermont)
Willard, Emma Hart **16** 288-289

Middlemarch (novel)
Eliot, George **5** 254-256-558

MIDDLETON, THOMAS (1580-1627), Eng-
lish playwright **11** 8-9
Dekker, Thomas **4** 465-466
Massinger, Philip **10** 324-325
Webster, John **16** 164

Middletown studies (sociology)
Lynd, Helen Merrell **10** 63-64
Lynd, Robert Staughton **10** 64-65

MIDGELY, MARY BURTON (born 1919),
British philosopher who focused on the

philosophy of human motivation and
ethics **11** 9-10

Midhat Pasha (1822-1884), Turkish statesman
Abdul-Hamid II **1** 17-18

Midi (poem)
Leconte de Lisle, Charles Marie René
9 273-274

Midrash (Jewish Scriptural exegesis)
Agnon, Shmuel Yoseph **1** 85-86
Akiba ben Joseph **1** 97-98
Ginzberg, Louis **6** 337-338
Hillel **7** 390-391
Judah I **8** 372-373
see also Talmud

Midsummer Marriage (opera)
Tippett, Michael Kemp **15** 234-235

Midsummer Night's Dream, A (opera)
Britten, Benjamin **3** 10-11

Midsummer Night's Dream, A (overture)
Mendelssohn, Moses **10** 488-489

Midsummer Night's Dream, A (play;
Shakespeare)
Drayton, Michael **5** 97-98
Ovid **12** 34-36
Shakespeare, William **14** 142-145

Midway, battle of (1942)
Nimitz, Chester William **11** 395-396

Midway Gardens (Chicago)
Wright, Frank Lloyd **16** 398-401

Mielich, Hans
see Mülich, Hans

MIES VAN DER ROHE, LUDWIG
(1886-1969), German-born American
architect **11** 10-12
Aalto, Hugo Alvar Henrik **1** 1-2
Behrens, Peter **2** 121-122
Fuller, Richard Buckminster **6** 149-150
Gropius, Walter **7** 13-14
Jahn, Helmut **8** 199-201
Johnson, Philip **8** 313-314
Oud, Jacobus Johannes Pieter **12** 32
Schinkel, Karl Friedrich **14** 8

Miezko I (ruled circa 960-992), Polish
prince, founder of Piast dynasty
Otto III **12** 29-30

MIG (aircraft)
Gagarin, Yuri Alexeivich **6** 166-167

Migdal Oz (play)
Luzzato, Moses Hayyim **10** 57-58

Mightier Than the Sword (book)
Ford, Ford Madox **6** 1-2

Mighty Five (Mighty Fist; Russian music
group)
Borodin, Aleksandr Profirevich
2 422-423
Mussorgsky, Modest Petrovich
11 274-276
Rimsky-Korsakov, Nikolai Andreevich
13 174-175
Tchaikovsky, Peter Ilyich **15** 130-132

Mighty Fortress, A (hymn)
Luther, Martin **10** 48-51

Mighty Handful
see Mighty Five

Migliorati, Cosimo de'
see Innocent VII

Mignard, Pierre (1610-1695), French portrait painter
Le Brun, Charles **9** 269-270

Mignet, F.A.M. (1796-1884), French historian
Thiers, Louis Adolphe **15** 181-182

Mignon (novel)
Hauptmann, Gerhart Johann Robert
7 199-201

Migration (United States)
Stouffer, Samuel A. **14** 482-483
see also Immigrants to the United States

Migration of the Negro, The (painting
series)
Lawrence, Jacob **9** 250-251

Mihajlovic, Draža (1893?-1946), Serbian
soldier, leader of Free Yugoslavian army
Tito, Marshal **15** 244-246

Mihna
see Islam—Mihna

Mikado, The (operetta)
Gilbert, William Schwenck **6** 314-315
Sullivan, Arthur Seymour **15** 23

Mikrokosmos (musical composition)
Bartók, Béla **2** 35-36

MIKULSKI, BARBARA (born 1936), United
States senator from Maryland **11** 13-15

Milá House (Barcelona)
Gaudí i Cornet, Antoni **6** 235-236

Milagros de Nuestra Señora (poems)
Gonzalo de Berceo **6** 431-432

Milan (city; Italy)
and Holy Roman Empire
Charles V **3** 457-459
Frederick I **6** 78-79
Frederick II **6** 79
and Italian states
Mazzini, Giuseppe **10** 381-383
Medici, Lorenzo de' **10** 450-451
Visconti, Gian Galeazzo
15 510-511
bishops
Ambrose **1** 192-193
Borromeo, Charles **2** 423-424
French wars
Borgia, Cesare **2** 412-413
Francis I **6** 40-43
Leo X **9** 332-334
Leonardo da Vinci **9** 337-340
Louis XII **9** 528-529
Sforza, Lodovico **14** 127-128

Milan, Cathedral of
Bach, Johann Christian **1** 415-416
Bramante, Donato **2** 493-494
Visconti, Gian Galeazzo **15** 510-511

Milan, Edict of (313 A.D.)
Constantine I **4** 209-211

MILÁN, LUIS (circa 1500-after 1561),
Spanish composer **11** 15-16
Encina, Juan del **5** 283

Milan, University of
Cardano, Geronimo **3** 285-286
Sforza, Lodovico **14** 127-128

Milbanke, Anna Isabella (1792-1860),
Baroness Byron, later Baroness Went-
worth
Byron, George Gordon Noel **3** 193-194

MILES, NELSON APPLETON (1839-1925),
American general **11** 16-17
Crazy Horse **4** 303-304
Geronimo **6** 281-282
Joseph **8** 358-359

Miles Gloriosus (play)
Plautus **12** 348-350

Miles Wallingford (novel)
Cooper, James Fenimore **4** 220-223

Milesian school (philosophy)
Anaximander **1** 209-210
Anaximenes **1** 210
Thales **15** 161

Milestones (anthology)
Berdyaev, Nicholas Alexandrovich
2 184-185

Milestones (play; Bennett-Knoblock)
Bennett, Arnold **2** 167-168

Miletus (ancient city; Turkey)
Alexander the Great **1** 137-141
see also Milesian school (philosophy)

Milhamot Adonai (religious book)
Levi ben Gershon **9** 363-364

MILHAUD, DARIUS (born 1892), French
composer and teacher **11** 17-18
Honegger, Arthur **7** 472-473
Picasso, Pablo **12** 292-295
Poulenc, Francis **12** 414-415
Stravinsky, Igor Fedorovich **14** 502-506
Xenakis, Iannis **16** 416-418

Milic, Jan (Milíô of Kremsier; circa
1305-1374), Bohemian reform preacher
Hus, Jan **8** 56-59
Wenceslaus **16** 201-202

Military Bases Agreement (1947; United
States-Philippines)
Recto, Claro M. **13** 69-70
Roxas, Manuel **13** 331-332

Military conscription
see Draft (military)

Military dictatorships
see Dictatorships

Military leaders, Algerian
Boumediene, Houari **2** 445-446

Military leaders, American

• ARMY AND AIR FORCE
Air Force chiefs of staff
Arnold, Henry Harley **1** 310-311

LeMay, Curtis E. **9** 316-318
Air Force generals (20th century)
James, Daniel Jr. **8** 209-211
Air Force pilots
Bluford, Guion Stewart Jr.
2 341-343
Collins, Eileen **4** 163-165
Doolittle, James Harold **5** 66-68
Yeager, Chuck **16** 444-445
Army captains
Marion, Francis **10** 262-263
Shays, Daniel **14** 168
Underhill, John **15** 388
Army chiefs of staff
Abrams, Creighton W. **1** 29-31
Bradley, Omar Nelson
2 483-484
Lemnitzer, Lyman Louis
9 319-320
Taylor, Maxwell **15** 126-127
Westmoreland, William Childs
16 216-217
Army colonels
Davis, Jefferson **4** 416-418
Gadsden, James **6** 165-166
Morgan, Daniel **11** 160-161
Sevier, John **14** 122-123
Travis, William Barret
15 292-293
Wood, Robert Elkington
16 370-371
Army commanders in chief
Washington, George **16** 126-129
see also Statesmen, American—
presidents
Army generals (18th century)
Allen, Ethan **1** 163-164
Arnold, Benedict **1** 309-310
Clark, George Rogers **4** 75-76
Greene, Nathanael **6** 525-526
Hull, William **8** 29-30
Knox, Henry **9** 64
Lewis, Andrew **9** 376-377
Lincoln, Benjamin **9** 418-419
Montgomery, Richard
11 138-139
Pepperell, William **12** 206-207
Putnam, Israel **12** 491-492
Schuyler, Philip John **14** 49-50
St. Clair, Arthur **13** 429-430
Wayne, Anthony **16** 149-150
Wilkinson, James **16** 284-286
Army generals (19th century)
Kearny, Stephen Watts
8 468-469
Pike, Zebulon **12** 302-304
Scott, Winfield **14** 70-71
Taylor, Zachary **15** 128-130
Wood, Leonard **16** 369-370
Army generals (19th century; Con-
federate)
Beauregard, Pierre Gustave
Toutant **2** 96-97
Forrest, Nathan Bedford **6** 13-14
Gordon, John Brown **6** 449-450
Gorgas, Josiah **6** 453-454

Hampton, Wade III **7** 112
Jackson, Shirley Ann **8** 183-184
Johnston, Joseph Eggleston **8** 323
Lee, Robert Edward **9** 292-294
Mahone, William **10** 147-148
Stuart, James Ewell Brown
14 515-516
Army generals (19th century; Union)
Ames, Adelbert **1** 198
Crook, George **4** 322-323
Custer, George Armstrong
4 355-356
Frémont, John Charles **6** 97-98
Grant, Ulysses Simpson
6 492-494
Greely, Adolphus Washington
6 517-518
Harrison, Benjamin **7** 178-179
Hayes, Rutherford Birchard
7 227-228
Howard, Oliver Otis **7** 528-529
McClellan, George Brinton
10 391-392
Meade, George Gordon
10 440-441
Miles, Nelson Appleton
11 16-17
Sheridan, Philip Henry
14 182-183
Sherman, William Tecumseh
14 186-187
Thomas, George Henry
15 190-191
Wallace, Lewis **16** 74-75
Army generals (20th century)
Abrams, Creighton W. **1** 29-31
Clark, Mark Wayne **4** 80-81
Davis, Benjamin O. Sr.
4 414-415
Goethals, George Washington
6 387-388
Goodpaster, Andrew Jackson
6 439-441
Groves, Leslie **7** 21-22
Haig, Alexander M. Jr. **7** 66-67
Patton, George Smith Jr.
12 140-141
Powell, Colin Luther **12** 424-425
Ridgway, Matthew Bunker
13 160-161
Shalikashvili, John Malchase
David **14** 145-147
Stilwell, Joseph Warren
14 456-457
Taylor, Maxwell **15** 126-127
Wainwright, Jonathan Mayhew
16 45-46
Westmoreland, William Childs
16 216-217
Army Generals of the Army (20th
century)
Eisenhower, Dwight David
5 233-236
MacArthur, Douglas **10** 76-78
Marshall, George Catlett
10 278-279
Pershing, John Joseph
12 243-244

Army inspectors general
Hamilton, Alexander **7** 95-98
Army lieutenants
Houston, Samuel **7** 526-527
Army majors
Rogers, Robert **13** 250-251
Army medical services
Morgan, John **11** 162-163
Rush, Benjamin **13** 364-365
● JOINT SERVICES
chairmen, Joint Chiefs of Staff
Powell, Colin Luther **12** 424-425
chairmen, Joint Chiefs of State
Shalikashvili, John Malchase
David **14** 145-147
● NAVY
admirals
Byrd, Richard Evelyn **3** 186-187
Dewey, George **4** 520
Farragut, David Glasgow
5 388-389
Melville, George Wallace
10 472
Rickover, Hyman George
13 155-157
Semmes, Raphael **14** 102-103
Sims, William Sowden **14** 244
Wilkes, Charles **16** 279-280
admirals of the fleet
Halsey, William Frederick
7 91-92
King, Ernest Joseph **9** 17-18
Nimitz, Chester William
11 395-396
captains
Barry, John **2** 24-25
Jones, John Paul **8** 337-338
Lawrence, James **9** 251-252
Perry, Oliver Hazard **12** 239
commanders
Decatur, Stephen **4** 448-449
Hopkins, Esek **7** 490-491
Maury, Matthew Fontaine
10 351-352
Perry, Matthew Calbraith
12 237-239
Stockton, Robert Field
14 461-462
Zumwalt, Elmo Russell Jr.
16 532-534

Military leaders, Argentine
Belgrano, Manuel **2** 126-127
Galtieri, Leopoldo Fortunato **6** 191-193
Güemes, Martín **7** 26-27
Justo, Agustin Pedro **8** 396
Quiroga, Juan Facundo **12** 521-522
Roca, Julio Argentino **13** 218
San Martín, José de **13** 468-469
Urquiza, Justo José **15** 396-397
Videla, Jorge Rafaél **15** 490-492

Military leaders, Australian
Monash, John **11** 95-96

Military leaders, Austrian
Eugene of Savoy **5** 330-331

Military leaders, Bengali
Ershad, Hussain Mohammad **5** 312-314
Ziaur Rahman **16** 515-516

Military leaders, Bohemian
Wallenstein, Albrecht Wenzel Eusebius
von **16** 80-81

Military leaders, Bolivian
Banzer Suárez, Hugo **1** 494-496
Santa Cruz, Andrés de **13** 472-473

Military leaders, Bosnian
Mladic, Ratko **11** 68-69

Military leaders, Brazilian
Castelo Branco, Humberto **3** 359-360
Caxias, Duque de **3** 386
Deodoro da Fonseca, Manoel **4** 502
Figueiredo, João Batista de Oliveira
5 445-446
Geisel, Ernesto **6** 253-255
Prestes, Luiz Carlos **12** 442-444
Rondon, Candido Mariano da Silva
13 271

Military leaders, British
● ARMY
captains
Speke, John Hanning
14 366-367
Standish, Myles **14** 396-397
Warwick and of Salisbury, Earl of
16 122-123
colonels
Butler, John **3** 180
Lawrence, Thomas Edward
9 253-254
Tryon, William **15** 321
commanders
Glubb, John Bagot **6** 371-372
Gordon, Charles George
6 448-449
Gorges, Ferdinando **6** 455-456
Norfolk, 3d Duke of **11** 423
Northumberland, Duke of
11 431-432
Tarleton, Banastre **15** 110
commanders in chief
Braddock, Edward **2** 474-475
Clinton, Henry **4** 114-115
Clive, Robert **4** 119-120
Monck, George **11** 96-97
Roberts, Frederick Sleigh
13 195-196
Wellington, 1st Duke of
16 193-195
field marshals
Allenby, Edmund Henry Hyn-
man **1** 171-172
Amherst, Jeffery **1** 200-201
Haig, Douglas **7** 67-68
Kitchener, Horatio Herbert
9 45-46
Montgomery, Bernard Law
11 135-136
generals (14th-17th century)
Cromwell, Oliver **4** 317-320
John of Gaunt **8** 282-283

Marlborough, 1st Duke of
10 271-272
generals (18th century)
Amherst, Jeffery **1** 200-201
Brock, Isaac **3** 12-13
Burgoyne, John **3** 137-138
Carleton, Guy **3** 300-301
Cornwallis, Charles **4** 241-243
Forbes, John **5** 507-508
Gage, Thomas **6** 169-170
Howe, William **7** 538-539
Marlborough, 1st Duke of
10 271-272
Murray, James **11** 261-262
Spotswood, Alexander **14** 385
Wolfe, James **16** 354-355
generals (19th-20th century)
Alexander of Tunis, 1st Earl
1 135-136
Brock, Isaac **3** 12-13
Wavell, Archibald Percival
16 147-148
majors
Smith, John **14** 295-297
princes
Edward the Black Prince
5 217-218
● NAVY
admirals
Buckingham, 1st Duke of
3 93-94
Hawkins, John **7** 210-211
Howe, Richard **7** 536-537
Jellicoe, John Rushworth
8 242-243
Nelson, Horatio **11** 336-338
Phillip, Arthur **12** 279-280
Rodney, George Brydges
13 239-240
Ross, James Clark **13** 302-303
commanders
Hobson, William **7** 426
McClure, Robert **10** 397-398

Military leaders, Burmese
Ne Win **11** 364-365
Saw Maung **13** 506-507

Military leaders, Byzantine
Belisarius **2** 128-129

Military leaders, Canadian
Currie, Arthur William **4** 345
McNaughton, Andrew **10** 431-432

Military leaders, Carthaginian
Hamilcar Barca **7** 94-95
Hannibal Barca **7** 128-130

Military leaders, Chilean
Ibáñez del Campo, Carlos **8** 88
Lautaro **9** 235
O'Higgins, Bernardo **11** 486
Pinochet Ugarte, Augusto **12** 315-317

Military leaders, Chinese
admirals (15th century)
Cheng Ho **3** 500
commanders in chiefs
Chu Teh **4** 54-55

Lin Piao **9** 429-430
Tso Tsung-t'ang **15** 328-329
generals
Chiang Kai-shek **3** 510-513
Li Hung-Chang **9** 407-409
Shih Ko-fa **14** 194-195
Ts'ao Ts'ao **15** 322-323
Tseng Kuo-fan **15** 324-325
Yo Fei **16** 462
grand councilors
Wen T'ien-hsiang **16** 203
military governors
An Lu-shan **1** 239-240
Yüan Shih-k'ai **16** 480-481
Peoples Republic of China
Deng Xiaoping **4** 498-500
warlords
Chang Tso-lin **3** 434-435
Feng Yü-hsiang **5** 412-413
Yen Hsi-shan **16** 452-453

Military leaders, Colombian
Reyes, Rafael **13** 113
Rojas Pinilla, Gustavo **13** 255-256
Santander, Franciso de Paula **13** 475

Military leaders, Cuban
Batista y Zaldívar, Fulgencio **2** 57-58
Maceo, Antonio **10** 88-90
Machado y Morales, Gerardo **10** 92-93
Menocal, Mario Garcia **10** 506-507

Military leaders, Dominican
Santana, Pedro **13** 474-475

Military Leaders, Dutch
Maurice of Nassau **10** 348-349

Military leaders, Ecuadorian
Flores, Juan José **5** 491

Military leaders, Ethiopian
Menelik II **10** 495-497
Mengistu Haile Mariam **10** 503-505

Military leaders, Filipino
Rómulo, Carlos P. **13** 270-271

Military leaders, Finnish
Mannerheim, Carl Gustav Emil Von **10** 207-208

Military leaders, French
army captains
Dreyfus, Alfred **5** 103-105
army commanders
Joan of Arc **8** 264-265
Napoleon I **11** 306-310
army majors
Marchand, Jean-Baptiste **10** 234-237
generals
Carnot, Lazare Nicolas Marguerite **3** 313-314
Condé, Prince de **4** 193-194
De Gaulle, Charles André Joseph Marie **4** 463-465
Lafayette, Marquis de **9** 151-152
Leclerc, Jacques Philippe **9** 272-273
Montcalm de Saint-Véran, Marquis de **11** 122-123
marshals

Bugeaud de la Piconnerie, Thomas Robert **3** 111
Bernadotte, Jean Baptiste **2** 205-206
Foch, Ferdinand **5** 498-499
Joffre, Joseph Jacques Césaire **8** 267-268
Lyautey, Louis Hubert Gonzalve **10** 60-61
Murat, Joachim **11** 253-254
Ney, Michel **11** 372-373
Pétain, Henri Philippe **12** 250-252
Rochambeau, Comte de **13** 220-221
Saxe, Comte de **13** 507-508
naval and air force officers
Bougainville, Louis Antoine de **2** 443-444
Coligny, Gaspard de **4** 159-160
Garnier, Francis **6** 220-221
Saint-Exupéry, Antoine de **13** 431-432

Military leaders, German
air force commanders
Göring, Hermann Wilhelm **6** 457-458
field marshals
Hindenburg, Paul Ludwig Hans von Beneckendorff und von **7** 400-401
Kesselring, Albert Field Marshal **8** 522-523
Rommel, Erwin **13** 268-269
Rundstedt, Karl Rudolf Gerd Von **13** 363-364
generals
Beck, Ludwig August Theoder **2** 99-100
Haushofer, Karl **7** 201
Ludendorff, Erich Friedrich Wilhelm **10** 27-28
Steuben, Frederick William Augustus von **14** 438-439
Suevian chiefs
Ricimer, Flavius **13** 151-152
see also Military leaders, Prussian

Military leaders, Greek
Alcibiades **1** 119-120
Epaminondas **5** 291-292
Leonidas I **9** 340-343
Lysander **10** 70
Miltiades **11** 42-43
Pericles **12** 219-221
Spartacus **14** 363-364
Themistocles **15** 170-171
Thucydides **15** 211-212
Xenophon **16** 418-420

Military leaders, Guatemalan
Barrios, Justo Rufino **2** 23-24
Ubïco y Castañeda, Jorge **15** 377-378

Military leaders, Haitian
Toussaint L'Ouverture, François Dominique **15** 278-279

Military leaders, Honduran
Morazán, José Francisco **11** 155

Military leaders, Hungarian
Horthy de Nagybánya, Nicholas **7** 510-512

Hunyadi, John **8** 51-52
Military leaders, Indian (Asian)
Babar the Conqueror **1** 405-407
Ranjit Singh **13** 32-33
Military leaders, Indonesian
Suharto **15** 14-15
Military leaders, Iraqi
Nuri al-Sa'id **11** 446-447
Military leaders, Israeli
Barak, Ehud **1** 497-498
Dayan, Moshe **4** 429-431
Rabin, Yitzchak **12** 527-529
Sharon, Ariel **14** 157-159
Weizman, Ezer **16** 181-182
Military leaders, Italian
Badoglio, Pietro **1** 428-429
Borgia, Cesare **2** 412-413
Garibaldi, Giuseppe **6** 215-217
Military leaders, Japanese
admirals
Yamamoto, Isoroku **16** 429-433
commanders-in-chief
Mutsuhito **11** 279-282
generals
Saigo, Takamori **13** 429
Tojo, Hideki **15** 254-256
Yamagata, Aritomo **16** 428-429
Yamashita, Tomoyuki **16** 435-436
warrior chieftains
Ashikaga Takauji **1** 330-332
Nobunaga, Oda **11** 413-414
Toyotomi Hideyoshi **15** 286-289
Yoritomo, Minamoto **16** 463-464
Military leaders, Jewish
Bar Kochba, Simeon **2** 5
Josephus Flavius **8** 360-361
Military leaders, Korean
Ch'oe Ch'ung-hn **4** 13
Chong Chung-bu **4** 15
Park, Chung Hee **12** 99-102
Yi Sng-gye **16** 458-459
Yi Sunsin **16** 459-461
South Korean
Chun Doo Hwan **4** 45-47
Military leaders, Lebanese
Gemayel, Pierre **6** 259-261
Shihab, Fu'ad **14** 193-194
Military leaders, Macedonian
Alexander the Great **1** 137-141
Antigonus I **1** 248-249
Ptolemy, Claudius **12** 473-474
Seleucus I **14** 92-93
Military leaders, Mexican
generals
Álvarez, Juan **1** 184-185
Cárdenas, Lázaro **3** 286-287
Díaz, José de la Cruz Porfirio **4** 534-536
Huerta, Victoriano **8** 13-14
Iturbide, Agustín de **8** 155-156
Morelos, José María **11** 157-158
Obregón, Álvaro **11** 458-459

Santa Ana, Antonio López de **13** 471-472

guerrilla leaders
  Guerrero, Vicente **7** 28-30
  Matamoros, Mariano **10** 329-330
  Villa, Pancho **15** 495-496
  Zapata, Emiliano **16** 489-490

Military leaders, Mongol
Batu Khan **2** 60-61
Genghis Khan **6** 263-265
Hulagu Khan **8** 27-28
Kublai Khan **9** 115-118

Military leaders, Nicaraguan
Somoza, Anastasio **14** 335-336

Military leaders, Norman
Bohemund, I **2** 364
Guiscard, Robert **7** 39-40

Military Leaders, Numidian
Masinissa **10** 315-317

Military leaders, Pakistani
Ayub Khan, Mohammed **1** 395-396
Zia ul-Haq, Mohammad **16** 513-515

Military leaders, Palestinian
Abu Musa **1** 32-33

Military leaders, Palmyrene
Zenobia **16** 500-503

Military leaders, Panamanian
Noriega, Manuel A. **11** 423-425
Torrijos, Omar **15** 269-270

Military leaders, Paraguayan
López, Francisco Solano **9** 507-508

Military leaders, Peruvian
Morales-Bermúdez Cerruti, Francisco **11** 150-151
Odría Amoretti, Manuel Apolinario **11** 473-474

Military leaders, Polish
Jaruzelski, Wojciech Witold **8** 223-225
Kościuszko, Tadeusz Andrzej Bonawentura **9** 88
Pilsudski, Joseph **12** 305-306
Pulaski, Casimir **12** 480-481

Military leaders, Prussian
Blücher, Gebhard Leberecht von **2** 340-341
Moltke, Helmuth Karl Bernard von **11** 90-91
Scharnhorst, Gerhard Johann David von **13** 521-522
see also Military leaders, German

Military leaders, Roman
generals
  Antony, Mark **1** 253-254
  Caesar, Gaius Julius **3** 207-210
  Constantine I **4** 209-211
  Flamininus, Titus Quinctius **5** 477
  Marius, Gaius **10** 264-265
  Pompey **12** 387-389
  Scipio Africanus Minor, Publius Cornelius Aemilianus **14** 62-63
  Stilicho, Flavius **14** 452-453
  Sulla, Lucius Cornelius I **15** 21-22

Titus Flavius Vespasianus **15** 247-248
military emperors
  Caracalla **3** 281-282
military tribunes
  Cato, Marcus Porcius the Elder **3** 375
  Cato, the Younger **3** 374-375
Suevian chiefs
  Ricimer, Flavius **13** 151-152

Military leaders, Romanian
Ceausescu, Nicolae **3** 387-388

Military leaders, Russian
admirals
  Kolchak, Aleksandr Vasilievich **9** 77-78
Cossack leaders
  Pugachev, Emelyan Ivanovich **12** 478-479
  see also Military leaders, Ukrainian
generals
  Brezhnev, Leonid Ilich **2** 527-528
  Kornilov, Lavr Georgievich **9** 87-88
  Suvorov, Aleksandr Vasilievich **15** 44-45
marshals
  Beria, Lavrenty Pavlovich **2** 192-193
  Konev, Ivan Stefanovich **9** 81-82
  Kutuzov, Mikhail Ilarionovich **9** 137-138
  Potemkin, Grigori Aleksandrovich **12** 411-412
  Zhukov, Georgi Konstantinovich **16** 512-513
military commissars
  Frunze, Mikhail Vasilievich **6** 134
  Trotsky, Leon **15** 302-305
princes
  Nevsky, Alexander **11** 359
warrior chiefs
  Rurik **13** 364

Military leaders, Salvadoran
Martínez, Maximiliano Hernández **10** 297-298

Military leaders, Serbian
Alexander of Yugoslavia **1** 136-137
Mladic, Ratko **11** 68-69

Military leaders, South African
Botha, Louis **2** 434-436
Hertzog, James Barry Munnik **7** 347-348
Mzilikazi **11** 285-286
Pretorius, Andries **12** 444-445
Shaka **14** 141-142
Smuts, Jan Christian **14** 309-310

Military leaders, Spanish
conquistadores
  Almagro, Diego de **1** 177-178
  Balboa, Vasco Núñez de **1** 462-463
  de Soto, Hernando **4** 510-511
  Díaz del Castillo, Bernal **4** 536-537
  Quesada, Gonzalo Jiménez de **12** 509-510
  Pizarro, Francisco **12** 340-341

Valdivia, Pedro de **15** 400-401
generals
  Franco Bahamonde, Francisco **6** 52-54
medieval warriors
  Cid **4** 58-59

Military leaders, Sudanese
Abboud, Ibrahim **1** 11-12
Khalil, Sayyid Abdullah **8** 531-532
Mahdi **10** 137-138

Military leaders, Thai
Chatichai Choonhavan **3** 479-480
Phibun Songkhram, Luang **12** 264-265
Prem Tinsulanonda **12** 437
Sarit Thanarat **13** 483-484

Military leaders, Turkish
Atatürk, Ghazi Mustapha Kemal **1** 356-357
Ibrahim Pasha **8** 97-98
Inönü, Ismet **8** 127-129
Köprülü, Ahmed **9** 84-85
Mehmed the Conqueror **10** 452-454
Osman I **12** 20-22
Enver Pasha **5** 290-291

Military leaders, Ugandan
Amin Dada, Idi **1** 202-204

Military leaders, Ukrainian
Chmielnicki, Bogdan **4** 12-13
Mazepa, Ivan Stepanovich **10** 381
see also Military leaders, Russian

Military leaders, Uruguayan
Lavalleja, Juan Antonio **9** 238-239
Rivera, Fructuoso **13** 184-185

Military leaders, Venezuelan
Bolívar, Simón **2** 375-377
López, Narciso **9** 508
Miranda, Francisco de **11** 52-53
Páez, José Antonio **12** 58
Pérez Jiménez, Marcos **12** 217-218
Sucre, Antonio José de **15** 11-12

Military leaders, Vietnamese
Giap, Vo Nguyen **6** 297-299
Ho Chi Minh **7** 426-428

Military League (Greece)
Venizelos, Eleutherios **15** 460-461

Military Medical Academy (Leningrad)
Pavlov, Ivan Petrovich **12** 155-157

Military Revolutionary Committee (South Korea)
see Supreme Council for National Reconstruction

Military service, compulsory
see Draft (military)

Military strategy
techniques
  Archimedes **1** 277-280
  Davis, Jefferson **4** 416-418
  De Gaulle, Charles André Joseph Marie **4** 463-465
  Epaminondas **5** 291-292
  Foch, Ferdinand **5** 498-499
  Gustavus II **7** 43-45

Hannibal Barca **7** 128-130
Miltiades **11** 42-43
Steuben, Frederick William Augustus von **14** 438-439
Wellington, 1st Duke of **16** 193-195
treatises
Frontinus, Sextus Julius **6** 130
Saxe, Comte de **13** 507-508
see also Guerrilla warfare

Militia Bill (England; 1852)
Russell, John **13** 380-381

Militia Company of Captain ... Cocq (painting)
see Night Watch

MILIUKOV, PAVEL NIKOLAYEVICH (1859-1943), Russian historian and statesman **11** 18-19
Kerensky, Aleksandr Fedorovich **8** 516-517

Miliutin, General Dimitri Alekseevich (1816-1912), Russian field marshal
Alexander II **1** 132-133

Milk (dairy production)
Babcock, Stephen Moulton **1** 410-411
Borden, Gail **2** 409
Pasteur, Louis **12** 125-127

MILK, HARVEY BERNARD (1930-1978), American politician and gay rights activist **11** 19-21

Milk for Babes ... (book)
Cotton, John **4** 263-265

Milk Train Doesn't Stop Here Anymore, The (play)
Williams, Tennessee **16** 306-308

Milkmaid of Bordeaux (painting)
Goya y Lucientes, Francisco de Paula José de **6** 476-478

Milkmaid, The (painting)
Greuze, Jean Baptiste **6** 539

Milky Way Galaxy (astronomy)
Barnard, Edward Emerson **2** 8-9
Eddington, Arthur Stanley **5** 201-202
Galileo Galilei **6** 180-183
Herschel, William **7** 341-343
Kapteyn, Jacobus Cornelis **8** 436-437
Shapley, Harlow **14** 155-156

Milky Way, The (film)
Buñuel, Luis **3** 127-128

MILL, JAMES (1773-1836), Scottish philosopher and historian **11** 21
Bentham, Jeremy **2** 176-178
Hartley, David **7** 185
Helvétius, Claude Adrien **7** 273-274
Mill, John Stuart **11** 21-23
Say, Jean Baptiste **13** 508-509
Stewart, Dugald **14** 449

MILL, JOHN STUART (1806-1873), English philosopher and economist **11** 21-23
critics
Bradley, Francis Herbert **2** 481-482
Jevons, William Stanley **8** 255-256
friends

Comte, Auguste **4** 189-191
Sydenham, Thomas **15** 59-60
influence in China
Hu Shih **8** 63-65
Liang Ch'i-ch'ao **9** 395-396
Yen Fu **16** 452
influence on economics
George, Henry **6** 276
Marshall, Alfred **10** 277-278
influence on literature
Bjørnson, Bjørnstjerne **2** 299-300
Browning, Robert **3** 53-55
influence on political-historical thought
Adams, Henry Brooks **1** 45-47
Buckle, Henry Thomas **3** 95-96
Carlyle, Thomas **3** 304-305
Clemenceau, Georges **4** 99-101
Stephen, Leslie **14** 429
influenced by
Bentham, Jeremy **2** 176-178
Carneades **3** 309
Humboldt, Wilhelm von **8** 31
Mill, James **11** 21
quoted
Maurice, John Frederick Denison **10** 349-350

Mill, The (painting)
Claude Lorrain **4** 89-90

Mill on the Floss, The (novel)
Eliot, George **5** 254-256

Mill Springs, battle of (1862)
Thomas, George Henry **15** 190-191

MILLAIS, SIR JOHN EVERETT (1829-1896), English painter **11** 23-24
Carroll, Lewis **3** 332-333
Hunt, William Holman **8** 44-45
Ruskin, John **13** 371-372

Millard House (Pasadena, California)
Wright, Frank Lloyd **16** 398-401

MILLAY, EDNA ST. VINCENT (1892-1950), American lyric poet **11** 24-25

Millbury (city; Massachusetts)
Holbrook, Josiah **7** 450-451

Mille quingentis (motet)
Obrecht, Jacob **11** 457-458

Millenarist theory (religion)
Justin Martyr **8** 395-396

Millennial Dawnists (religious sect)
Russell, Charles Taze **13** 376-377
see also Jehovah's Witnesses

Millennialism (religion)
Sabbatai Zevi **13** 400-401

Miller, Alfred Jacob (1810-1874), American painter
Fitzpatrick, Thomas **5** 474-475

MILLER, ARTHUR (born 1915), American playwright, novelist, and film writer **11** 25-26
Kazan, Elia **8** 465-466

Miller, D.C. (1866-1941), American physicist
Einstein, Albert **5** 228-231

MILLER, HENRY (born 1891), American author **11** 26-27

MILLER, JOAQUIN (1837-1913), American writer **11** 27-28

Miller, John Peter (1709-1796), German-born American clergyman
Beissel, Johann Conrad **2** 123-124

Miller, Marilyn (1898-1936), American actress
Ziegfeld, Florenz **16** 516-517

MILLER, PERRY (1905-1963), American historian **11** 28-29

MILLER, SAMUEL FREEMAN (1816-1890), American jurist **11** 29-30

MILLER, WILLIAM (1782-1849), American clergyman **11** 30-31
see also Millerites

Miller Foundation (Columbia University)
Baron, Salo Wittmayer **2** 16-17

Millerand, Alexandre (1859-1943), French statesman
Blum, Léon **2** 343-344

Millerites (religious sect)
Eggleston, Edward **5** 223-224
Miller, William **11** 30-31
Russell, Charles Taze **13** 376-377

MILLET, JEAN FRANÇOIS (1814-1875), French painter **11** 31
Markham, Edwin **10** 267
Monet, Claude **11** 102-104
Van Gogh, Vincent **15** 427-429

MILLET, KATE (born 1934), American feminist author and sculptor **11** 31

MILLIKAN, ROBERT ANDREWS (1868-1953), American physicist **11** 33-35
Anderson, Carl David **1** 214-215
Dirac, Paul Adrien Maurice **5** 23-24
Einstein, Albert **5** 228-231
Hess, Victor Francis **7** 362-363

Million Dollar Legs (film)
Fields, W. C. **5** 444

Million Torments, A (book)
Goncharov, Ivan Aleksandrovich **6** 424

Mills Bill (United States; 1888)
Cleveland, Stephen Grover **4** 108-110

MILLS, C. WRIGHT (1916-1962), American sociologist and political polemicist **11** 35-36

MILLS, ROBERT (1781-1855), American architect **11** 36-37

Mills College (Oakland, California)
Berio, Luciano **2** 194-195
Milhaud, Darius **11** 17-18
Radin, Paul **12** 538-539

Mills of Meaux (painting)
Marin, John III **10** 259-260

Mills of the Kavanaughs, The (poems)
Lowell, Robert Trail Spence Jr. **10** 16-17

Milmore, Martin (1844-1883), American sculptor
French, Daniel Chester **6** 98-99

MILNE, DAVID BROWN (1882-1953), Canadian painter and etcher **11** 37-38

Milne-Edwards, Henri (1800-1885), French zoologist
Darwin, Charles Robert **4** 397-399

MILNER, ALFRED (1st Viscount Milner; 1854-1925), British statesman **11** 38-39
Hertzog, James Barry Munnik **7** 347-348
Kruger, Stephanus Johannes Paulus **9** 108-109

Milo, Titus Annius Papianus (95-48 B.C.), Roman politician
Cicero, Marcus Tullius **4** 55-58
Clodius Pulcher, Publius **4** 121-122
Sallust **13** 454

Milo of Croton... (sculpture)
Falconet, Étienne Maurice **5** 372

MILOSEVIC, SLOBODAN (born 1941), president of Serbia **11** 39-40
Karadzic, Radovan **8** 437-440

MILOSZ, CZESLAW (born 1911), Nobel Prize winning Polish author and poet **11** 40-42

MILTIADES (circa 549-488 B.C.), Athenian military strategist and statesman **11** 42-43
Darius I **4** 394-395
Thucydides **15** 211-212

MILTON, JOHN (1608-1674), English poet and controversialist **11** 43-46
biographers
Toland, John **15** 256
Comus
Arne, Thomas Augustine **1** 307-308
Ford, Paul Leicester **6** 9-10
influence of
Fuseli, Henry **6** 153-155
Klopstock, Friedrich Gottlieb **9** 55-56
Marvell, Andrew **10** 301-303
Wordsworth, William **16** 385-388
influenced by
Ovid **12** 34-36
Plutarch **12** 359-360
Ramus, Petrus **13** 27-28
Paradise Lost
see Paradise Lost
political theory
Filmer, Robert **5** 448
Macaulay, Thomas Babington **10** 79-80
Puritanism
Blake, William **2** 316-318
Bunyan, John **3** 128-129
Hertzog, James Barry Munnik **7** 347-348

Milvian Bridge, Battle of the (312 A.D.)
Constantine I **4** 209-211

Milwaukee Art Students' League (organization)

Steichen, Edward **14** 411-412

Milwaukee Braves (baseball team)
Aaron, Henry Louis (Hank) **1** 2-3

Mimeograph machine (mechanical copier)
Edison, Thomas Alva **5** 206-208

Mimi Pinson (story)
Musset, Louis Charles Alfred de **11** 271-272

Mimicry (biology)
Bates, Henry Walter **2** 53-54

MIN (1851-1895), Korean queen **11** 46-47
Kojong **9** 74-75
Taewŏn'gun, Hŭngsŏn **15** 74-75

Minas Gerais (state; Brazil)
Aleijadinho, O **1** 125-126
Kubitschek de Oliveira, Juscelino **9** 113-115
Tiradentes **15** 237

Mind (philosophy)
Anaxagoras **1** 208-209
Broad, Charlie Dunbar **3** 12
Gentile, Giovanni **6** 267
Hobbes, Thomas **7** 421-423
Mead, George Herbert **10** 437-438
Ryle, Gilbert **13** 393-394
Spinoza, Baruch **14** 381-383
William of Ockham **16** 298-299

Mind at the End of Its Tether (book)
Wells, Herbert George **16** 195-196

Mind Is an Enchanting Thing, The (poem)
Moore, Marianne **11** 148-149

Minden, bishopric of (Germany)
Frederick William **6** 85-86

MINDON MIN (ruled 1852-1878), Burmese king **11** 47

MINDSZENTY, CARDINAL JÓZSEF (1892-1975), Roman Catholic primate of Hungary **11** 47-49

Mine Hostess (play)
Goldoni, Carlo **6** 408-409

Mine the Harvest (poems)
Millay, Edna St. Vincent **11** 24-25

Mineralogy (science)
Berzelius, Jöns Jacob **2** 231-233
Bragg, William Henry **2** 488-489
Hutton, James **8** 73-74
Werner, Abraham Gottlob **16** 205-207
see also Metallurgy; Petrology; Scientists—mineralogists

Minerva (mythology)
Mantegna, Andrea **10** 215-216
Ovid **12** 34-36

Mines of Sulphur, The (opera)
Bennett, Richard Rodney **2** 172

Mineworkers unions
Scargill, Arthur **13** 514-515
Ramaphosa, Matemela Cyril **13** 15-16

Ming dynasty (China; 1368-1644)
Chang Chü-cheng **3** 431-432
Cheng Ho **3** 500

Huang Tsung-hsi **8** 9-10
Hung-wu **8** 38-39
K'ang-hsi **8** 423-426
Li Tzu-Ch'eng **9** 452
Xu Guangqi **16** 422-425
Yi Sng-gye **16** 458-459

Mingo... (stories)
Harris, Joel Chandler **7** 173-174

Minhagim (Judaism)
Caro, Joseph ben Ephraim **3** 316-317
Wise, Isaac Mayer **16** 342-343

Minick (play)
Ferber, Edna **5** 413

Minima Moralia: Reflections from Damaged Life (book)
Adorno, Theodor W. **1** 65-67

Minimalism (art)
Judd, Donald **8** 376-377
LeWitt, Sol **9** 393-395
Martin, Agnes **10** 288-289

Minimalism (music)
Glass, Philip **6** 362-364

Minimum wage (economics)
Booth, Charles **2** 400-401
Brandeis, Louis Dembitz **2** 496-497
Cardozo, Benjamin Nathan **3** 288-290
Deakin, Alfred **4** 432-433
Eisenhower, Dwight David **5** 233-236
Ford, Henry **6** 5-6
von Mises, Ludwig **16** 25

Mining (metallurgy)
industry
Díaz, José de la Cruz Porfirio **4** 534-536
Guggenheim, Meyer **7** 31-32
King, Clarence **9** 15-16
Lewis, John Llewellyn **9** 387-388
Swedenborg, Emanuel **15** 49-50
see alsoBusiness and industrial leaders—mining industry
prospectors
Comstock, Henry Tompkins Paige **4** 189
Hargraves, Edward Hammond **7** 153-154
reform and legislation
Gálvez, José de **6** 196
Lewis, John Llewellyn **9** 387-388
Raleigh, Walter **13** 9-11
Shaftesbury, 7th Earl of **14** 137-138
safety lamp invented
Davy, Humphry **4** 426-427
technique
Biringuccio, Vannoccio **2** 283
Whitney, Josiah Dwight **16** 254-255

Ministers
see Diplomats; Religious leaders; Statesmen

Minister's Charge, The (novel)
Howells, William Dean **7** 539-541

Ministry of Fear, The (novel)
Greene, Graham **6** 523-524

Miniver Cheevy (verse)
Robinson, Edwin Arlington **13** 201-202

Minna von Barnhelm (play)
Lessing, Gotthold Ephraim **9** 357-359

Minne (novel)
Colette, Sidonie Gabrielle **4** 158-159

Minneapolis (ship)
Melville, George Wallace **10** 472

Minneapolis, Minnesota
Humphrey, Hubert Horatio Jr. **8** 34-36

Minnesota (ship)
Sims, William Sowden **14** 244

Minnesota (state; United States)
Buchanan, James **3** 89-90
Donnelly, Ignatius **5** 62
Ireland, John **8** 133-134

Minnesota, University of
(Minneapolis-Saint Paul)
Becker, Carl Lotus **2** 100-101
Bellow, Saul **2** 141-143
Chapin, (F.) Stuart **3** 437-438
Compton, Arthur Holly **4** 186-188
Lashley, Karl Spencer **9** 214-215
Smith, Dora **14** 289-290
Sorokin, Pitirim A. **14** 348-349
Tate, Allen **15** 116
Thurstone, Louis Leon **15** 215-216
Warren, Robert Penn **16** 121-122

Minnesota River (United States)
Carver, Jonathan **3** 347-348

Minnesota Twins (baseball team)
Carew, Rod **3** 291-292

Minnie's Boys (musical)
Marx brothers **10** 303-304

Minorca (island; Spain)
Murray, James **11** 261-262

Minorites
see Franciscans

Minority rights (United States)
Black, Hugo Lafayette **2** 301-303
Calhoun, John Caldwell **3** 226-228
Ovington, Mary White **12** 36-37
Quay, Matthew Stanley **12** 507
Villard, Oswald Garrison **15** 498-499
see also African American history; Civil
liberties; Civil rights

Minot, George Richards (1885-1950),
American physician
Whipple, George Hoyt **16** 224-225

Minsky's Chorus (painting)
Marsh, Reginald **10** 276-277

Minstrel show (theater)
Christy, Edwin P. **4** 34-35
Foster, Stephen Collins **6** 25-27
Ives, Charles Edward **8** 159-160

Minstrels (medieval)
Gonzalo de Berceo **6** 431-432
see also Troubadors; Trouvères

Minstrelsy of the Scottish Border (ballads)
Scott, Walter **14** 68-70

Mint (coin manufacturing)
Chang Chih-tung **3** 430-431
Hamilton, Alexander **7** 95-98
see also Coinage

Mint (Rome)
see Banco di Sto Spirito

Minto, 1st Earl of (Gilbert
Elliot-Murray-Kynynmond; 1751-1814),
English diplomat
Raffles, Thomas Stamford **13** 1-2

MINTZ, BEATRICE (born 1921), American
embryologist **11** 49-50

Minuit (public house)
Robbe-Grillet, Alain **13** 189-190

MINUIT, PETER (1580-1638), Dutch colonizer **11** 50
Van Rensselaer, Kiliaen **15** 430-431

Minúsculas (poems)
González Prada, Manuel **6** 431

Minute Man (sculpture)
French, Daniel Chester **6** 98-99

Miocene (geology era)
Leakey, Louis Seymour Bazett **9** 262
Marsh, Othniel Charles **10** 275-276

Mir Jafar (1691-1765), Indian general and
statesman
Clive, Robert **4** 119-120
Hastings, Warren **7** 195-196

Mir zur Feier (poems)
Rilke, Rainer Maria **13** 171-172

Mira Ceti (star)
Herschel, William **7** 341-343

MIRABEAU, COMTE DE (Honoré Gabriel
Victor de Riqueti; 1749-1791), French
statesman and author **11** 51-52
Lafayette, Marquis de **9** 151-152
Marie Antoinette **10** 258-259

Mirabeau, Victor de Riqueti, Marquis de
(1715-1789), French political economist
Mirabeau, Comte de **11** 51-52

Mirabell: Books of Numbers (poems)
Merrill, James **10** 521-522

Mirabell Palace (Salzburg)
Donner, Georg Raphael **5** 63
Hildebrandt, Johann Lucas von
7 380-381

Miracle, The (film)
Fellini, Federico **5** 408-409
Frankfurter, Felix **6** 57

Miracle de Saint Antoine, Le (play)
Maeterlinck, Maurice **10** 125-126

Miracle, Horse and Rider, The (sculpture)
Marini, Marino **10** 260-262

Miracle of Our Lady, The (play)
Martinu, Bohuslav **10** 299-300

Miracle of Saint Bernardino (painting)
Perugino **12** 245-246

Miracle of the Loaves and Fishes (painting)
Murillo, Bartolomé Esteban **11** 258-259

Miracle of the Sacred Fire (painting)
Hunt, William Holman **8** 44-45

Miracle of the Shadow (fresco)
Masaccio **10** 312-313

Miracles of Antichrist, The (stories)
Lagerlöf, Selma Ottiliana Lovisa
9 163-164

Miracles of Saint Francis Xavier (painting)
Rubens, Peter Paul **13** 339-342

Miracles of Saint Ignatius of Loyola (painting)
Rubens, Peter Paul **13** 339-342

Miraculous Draught of Fishes (panel painting)
Witz, Konrad **16** 351-352

Miraculous Mandarin, The (pantomime)
Bartók, Béla **2** 35-36

Miramar, College of (Majorca)
Lull, Raymond **10** 39-40

Miramar, Treaty of (1864)
Maximilian of Hapsburg **10** 358-360

Miramón, Miguel (1832-1867), Mexican
soldier
Maximilian of Hapsburg **10** 358-360

MIRANDA, FRANCISCO DE (1750-1816),
Latin American patriot **11** 52-53
Bolívar, Simón **2** 375-377
O'Higgins, Bernardo **11** 486

Miranda v. Arizona (legal case)
Warren, Earl **16** 117-120

Mirandola, Pico della
see Pico della Mirandola

Mirandolina (literary character)
Goldoni, Carlo **6** 408-409

Mirandolina (opera)
Martinu, Bohuslav **10** 299-300

Mirari vos (encyclical)
Lamennais, Hugues Félicité Robert de
9 179
Montalembert, Comte de **11** 118-119

Mirgorod (stories)
Gogol, Nikolai **6** 391-393

Miriam (literary character)
Lawrence, David Herbert **9** 247-248

MIRÓ, JOAN (1893-1983), Spanish painter
11 53-54
Calder, Alexander **3** 216-218
Davis, Stuart **4** 424-425
Kandinsky, Wassily **8** 420-422
Tanguy, Yves **15** 101

Miroir de l'Omme (book)
Gower, John **6** 475-476

Mirror of Flirting Lovers, The (prints)
Utamaro, Kitagawa **15** 397

Mirror of Salvation Altarpiece (painting)
Witz, Konrad **16** 351-352

Mirza, Iskander (1899-1969), Pakistani
general and politician
Ayub Khan, Mohammed **1** 395-396

Mirza Malkam Khan
  see Malkam Khan, Mirza

Misanthrope, Le (play)
  Molière **11** 86-88

Misbeloved, The (play)
  Benavente y Martinez, Jacinto
  2 146-147

Miscegenation (United States)
  Hearn, Lafcadio **7** 240
  Wright, Frances **16** 397-398

Misdoers of Good, The (play)
  Benavente y Martinez, Jacinto
  2 146-147

Mise à mort, La (novel)
  Aragon, Louis **1** 271-272

Miser, The (play; Molière)
  Alarcón, Pedro Antonio de **1** 100-101

Miser Catulle, desinas ineptire (poem)
  Catullus, Gaius Valerius **3** 377-378

Misérables, Les (novel; Hugo)
  Bonifacio, Andres **2** 393-394
  Hugo, Victor Marie **8** 22-25

Miserere (book)
  Rouault, Georges **13** 321-322

Miserere (motet)
  Tallis, Thomas **15** 91

Miserere mei Deus (motet)
  Josquin des Prez **8** 361-363-69

Misericordia (novel)
  Galdós, Benito Pérez **6** 177-178

Mises, Dr.
  see Fechner, Gustav Theodor

Misfits, The (film)
  Gable, William Clark **6** 157-158
  Miller, Arthur **11** 25-26

Misfortunes of Elphin, The (novel)
  Peacock, Thomas Love **12** 169

MISHIMA, YUKIO (1925-1970), Japanese
  novelist and playwright **11** 54-55

Mishnah (Talmud)
  Abba Arika **1** 3-4
  Akiba ben Joseph **1** 97-98
  Elijah ben Solomon **5** 251-252
  Judah I **8** 372-373
  Maimonides **10** 151-152
  Manasseh ben Israel **10** 183-184
  see also Talmud

Miss Civilization (play)
  Davis, Richard Harding **4** 422-423

Miss Farmer's School of Cookery (Boston)
  Farmer, Fannie Merritt **5** 383

Miss Julie (play)
  Strindberg, August **14** 509-511

Miss Lonelyhearts (novel)
  West, Nathanael **16** 213-214

Miss Sara Sampson (play)
  Lessing, Gotthold Ephraim **9** 357-359

Missa (Mass)
  see Mass (music)

Mrs. Belloc Lowndes
  see Belloc, Marie Adelaide

Mrs. Dalloway (novel)
  Woolf, Virginia Stephen **16** 381-382

Mrs. Lee Acton (painting)
  Romney, George **13** 269-270

Mrs. Leicester's School (stories)
  Lamb, Charles **9** 176-177

Mrs. Philip Thicknesse (painting)
  Gainsborough, Thomas **6** 170-172

Mrs. Skagg's Husbands (literary collection)
  Harte, Francis Brett **7** 184-185

Mrs. Warren's Profession (play)
  Shaw, George Bernard **14** 163-164

Mission of Saint Joseph (Sillery, Canada)
  Brébeuf, Jean de **2** 511-512

Mission San Carlos (Monterey, California)
  Portolá, Gaspar de **12** 408

Mission terminée (novel)
  Beti, Mongo **2** 242-243

Mission to Kala (novel)
  Beti, Mongo **2** 242-243

Missionaries
  see Religious leaders

Missionaries of Charity (Roman Catholic
  Order)
  Teresa **15** 148-151

**Missionary Priests of Saint Paul the Apos-
  tle, Congregation of**
  see Paulist Fathers

Mississippi (poem)
  Morin, Paul **11** 174

Mississippi (state; United States)
  Alcorn, James Lusk **1** 120-121
  Ames, Adelbert **1** 198
  Bruce, Blanche Kelso **3** 62-63
  Davis, Jefferson **4** 416-418
  Evers, Medgar **5** 345-348
  George, James Zachariah **6** 276-277
  Revels, Hiram Rhoades **13** 109-110

Mississippi, University of
  Barnard, Frederick Augustus Porter
  2 9-10
  Bledsoe, Albert Taylor **2** 324-325
  Lamar, Lucius Quintus Cincinnatus
  9 170-171
  Meredith, James H. **10** 514-515
  Smith, David **14** 287-288

Mississippi and Missouri Railroad (United
  States)
  Durant, Thomas Clark **5** 157-158

Mississippi Freedom Democratic Party
  (civil rights group; United States)
  Bevel, James Luther **2** 250-251
  Hamer, Fannie Lou **7** 93-94
  Henry, Aaron **7** 306-307

Mississippi River (United States)
  exploration
  Bienville, Sieur de **2** 268-269
  Carver, Jonathan **3** 347-348

  de Soto, Hernando **4** 510-511
  Jolliet, Louis **8** 328-329
  La Salle, Sieur de **9** 210-211
  Marquette, Jacques **10** 274-275
  Pike, Zebulon **12** 302-304
  navigation
  Eads, James Buchanan **5** 175-176
  Gálvez, Bernardo de **6** 195-196
  Shreve, Henry Miller **14** 207

Mississippi Scheme (French colonial economics)
  Law, John **9** 244-245

Missouri (ship)
  Truman, Harry S. **15** 314-316

Missouri (state; United States)
  Ashley, William Henry **1** 333-334
  Atchison, David Rice **1** 357-358
  Becknell, William **2** 105-106
  Black Hawk **2** 308
  Boone, Daniel **2** 397-398
  Brown, Benjamin Gratz **3** 32-33
  Crook, George **4** 322-323
  Douglas, Stephen Arnold **5** 80-82
  Gephardt, Richard Andrew **6** 278-280
  see also Missouri Compromise

Missouri, University of (Columbia)
  Lovejoy, Arthur Oncken **10** 6
  Veblen, Thorstein Bunde **15** 449-450

Missouri Compromise (United States;
  1820)
  constitutionality (1857)
  Scott, Dred **14** 65-66
  opponents
  Douglas, Stephen Arnold **5** 80-82
  King, Rufus **9** 22-23
  Macon, Nathaniel **10** 114-115
  Randolph, John **13** 30
  provisions
  Clay, Henry **4** 94-96
  Monroe, James **11** 111-113
  Polk, James Knox **12** 374-376
  repeal
  Atchison, David Rice **1** 357-358
  Lincoln, Abraham **9** 415-418
  Pierce, Franklin **12** 300-301
  see also Kansas-Nebraska Act (1854)

Missouri Pacific Railroad (United States)
  Gould, Jay **6** 470-472

Missouri River (United States)
  Bridger, James **3** 2-3
  Clark, William **4** 82-83
  Fitzpatrick, Thomas **5** 474-475
  Jolliet, Louis **8** 328-329
  Lewis, Meriwether **9** 391-392

Mr. and Mrs. Frank Berry (story)
  Thackeray, William Makepeace
  15 159-161

Mr. and Mrs. Robert Andrews (painting)
  Gainsborough, Thomas **6** 170-172

Mr. Bennett and Mrs. Brown (essay)
  Woolf, Virginia Stephen **16** 381-382

Mr. Birdhead (story; Lu Hsün)
Ku Chieh-kang **9** 120-121

Mr. Britling Sees It Through (book)
Wells, Herbert George **16** 195-196

Mr. Crewe's Career (novel)
Churchill, Winston **4** 50-51

Mr. Crump (song)
Handy, William Christopher **7** 123-124

Mr. Dooley in Peace and War (book)
Dunne, Finley Peter **5** 147-148

Mr. Flood's Party (verse)
Robinson, Edwin Arlington **13** 201-202

Mr. H (play)
Lamb, Charles **9** 176-177

Mr. President (novel)
Asturias, Miguel Angel **1** 354-355

Mr. Prokharchin (story)
Dostoevsky, Fyodor **5** 74-77

Mr. Sammler's Planet (novel)
Bellow, Saul **2** 141-143

Mr. Sampath (novel)
Narayan, R. K. **11** 313-314

Mr. Tsungli Yaman
see Wen-hsiang

Mistons, Les (film)
Truffaut, François **15** 311-313

MISTRAL, GABRIELA (1889-1957),
Chilean poet and educator **11** 55-56
Hughes, Langston **8** 18-19
Vasconcelos, José **15** 443-444

Mistress, The (poems)
Cowley, Abraham **4** 281-282

Mistress of Jalna, The (play)
de la Roche, Mazo Louise **4** 474-475

"Misty" (song)
Vaughan, Sarah Lois **15** 445-446

Mit brennender Sorge (papal encyclical)
Pius XI **12** 337-339

Mitch Miller (novel)
Masters, Edgar Lee **10** 326-327

MITCHELL, GEORGE JOHN (born 1933),
Maine Democrat and majority leader in
the United States Senate **11** 56-58

Mitchell, Helen Porter
see Melba, Nellie

MITCHELL, JOHN (1870-1919), American
labor leader **11** 58-59

MITCHELL, MARGARET (Munnerlyn;
1900-1949), American author of Gone
With the Wind **11** 59-60

MITCHELL, MARIA (1818-1889), American
astronomer and educator **11** 61

MITCHELL, WESLEY CLAIR (1874-1948),
American economist **11** 61-62

Mithridates VI Eupator (circa 132-63 B.C.),
king of Pontus 120-63 B.C.
Caesar, Gaius Julius **3** 207-210
Marius, Gaius **10** 264-265
Pompey **12** 387-389

Sulla, Lucius Cornelius I **15** 21-22

Mitigated skepticism (philosophy)
Hume, David **8** 31-34
see also Skepticism (philosophy)

MITRE, BARTOLOMÉ (1821-1906), Argentine historian and statesman, president
1862-1868 **11** 62-63
Drago, Luis María **5** 92-93
Urquiza, Justo José **15** 396-397

Mitridate (opera)
Mozart, Wolfgang Amadeus
11 218-221

Mitscherlich, Eilhardt (1794-1863), German chemist
Pasteur, Louis **12** 125-127

Mitsou (novel)
Colette, Sidonie Gabrielle **4** 158-159

Mitsuhide
see Akechi Mitsuhide

MITTERRAND, FRANÇOIS (born 1916),
French politician and statesman and pres-
ident (1981-1990) **11** 63-66
Cresson, Edith **4** 306-307
Fabius, Laurent **5** 358-359

Mitya's Love (novel)
Bunin, Ivan Alekseevich **3** 124

Mi-wang (novel)
Pa Chin **12** 53-54

Mix, Tom (1880-1940), American actor
Buffalo Bill **3** 105-106

MIZRAHI, ISAAC (born 1961), American
designer **11** 66-67

Mkhumbane (musical)
Paton, Alan Stewart **12** 134-135

Mlada (opera)
Mussorgsky, Modest Petrovich
11 274-276

MLADIC, RATKO (born 1943), Bosnian
Serb military leader **11** 68-69

M'Lehose, Mrs.
see Maclehose, Agnes Craig

M'Liss (novel)
Harte, Francis Brett **7** 184-185

Moabites (ancient Semitic group)
Saul **13** 498

Moana (film)
Flaherty, Robert **5** 476-477

Mobile (city; Alabama)
Farragut, David Glasgow **5** 388-389
Iberville, Sieur d' **8** 90-91

Mobile Bay (Alabama)
Bienville, Sieur de **2** 268-269

Mobiles (sculpture)
Calder, Alexander **3** 216-218

MOBUTU SESE SEKO (Joseph Désiré Mob-
utu; 1930-1997), Congolese president
11 69-71
Kasavubu, Joseph **8** 453-455
Lumumba, Patrice Emery **10** 43-45
Tshombe, Moïse Kapenda **15** 325-326

Youlou, Fulbert **16** 466-467

Moby Dick (novel; H. Melville)
Hawthorne, Nathaniel **7** 212-215
Melville, Herman **10** 472-476-338

Moch, Jules (1893-1985), French statesman
Schuman, Robert **14** 41

Mo-chieh
see Wang Wei

Mocking of Christ (painting)
Grünewald, Matthias **7** 23-24

Mode de valeur et d'intensité (musical
composition)
Messiaen, Olivier **10** 528-529

Model A (automobile)
Ford, Henry **6** 5-6

Model Parliament (England; 1264)
Montfort, Simon de **11** 132-133

Model T (automobile)
Ford, Henry **6** 5-6

Modena, University of (Italy)
Spallanzani, Lazzaro **14** 360-361

Moderate party (Cuba)
see Conservative Republican party

Modern Chronicle, A (novel)
Churchill, Winston **4** 50-51

Modern Comedy, A (novel cycle)
Galsworthy, John **6** 189-190

Modern dance
Ailey, Alvin **1** 91-94
Astaire, Fred **1** 348-350
Baker, Josephine **1** 448-451
Cage, John **3** 211-214
Castle, Vernon and Irene **3** 361-363
Cunningham, Merce **4** 337-338
Duncan, Isadora **5** 144-145
Dunham, Katherine **5** 145-146
Fosse, Bob **6** 22-23
Graham, Martha **6** 485-486
Hines, Gregory Oliver **7** 401-403
Holm, Hanya **7** 454-455
Kelly, Gene **8** 484-486
Morris, Mark **11** 184-185
Nureyev, Rudolph **11** 445-446
St. Denis, Ruth **13** 430-431
Tharp, Twyla **15** 164-165
Wigman, Mary **16** 267-268
see also Ballet

Modern Dance of Death (sculpture)
Barlach, Ernst **2** 5-6

Modern Instance, A (novel)
Howells, William Dean **7** 539-541

Modern Love (poems)
Meredith, George **10** 512-513

Modern Painters (book; Ruskin)
Hunt, William Holman **8** 44-45
Millais, John Everett **11** 23-24
Ruskin, John **13** 371-372

Modern Times (film)
Chaplin, Charles Spencer **3** 438-440

Modern Utopia, A. (book)
Wells, Herbert George **16** 195-196

Modernism (architecture)
Europe
Hoffmann, Josef **7** 440-441
Loos, Adolf **9** 502-503
Mackintosh, Charles Rennie
10 107-108
Wagner, Otto **16** 39-40
United States
Rudolph, Paul Marvin **13** 348-350

Modernism (Roman Catholic heresy)
Loisy, Alfred Firmin **9** 489-490
Martin du Gard, Roger **10** 295-296
Pius X **12** 336-337

Modernista movement (Spanish literature)
Darío, Rubén **4** 393-394
Ferrer, Gabriel Miró **5** 428
Martí, José **10** 285-286
Rodó, José Enrique **13** 240-241
Valle Inclán, Ramón Maria del
15 407-408
Vallejo, César Abraham **15** 408-409
see also Generation of 1898

Moderns (French literature group)
Boileau-Despréaux, Nicholas
2 369-371

Moderns, The (anthology)
Baraka, Imamu Amiri **1** 498-499

MODERSOHN-BECKER, PAULA
(1876-1907), German painter **11** 71-72

Modes of Duration and Loudness (musical composition)
Messiaen, Olivier **10** 528-529

Modest Proposal... (pamphlet)
Swift, Jonathan **15** 51-54

MODIGLIANI, AMEDEO (1884-1920), Italian painter and sculptor **11** 72-73
Arp, Jean **1** 317-318
Chagall, Marc **3** 406-407
Rivera, Diego **13** 183-184
Soutine, Chaim **14** 356-357
Ungaretti, Giuseppe **15** 389-390

Modulor, Le (books)
Le Corbusier **9** 274-275

Moeti oa bochabela (novel)
Mofolo, Thomas **11** 74

Moffat, Robert (1795-1883), Scottish missionary
Livingstone, David **9** 463-465
Mzilikazi **11** 285-286

MOFOLO, THOMAS (1876-1948),
Lesothoan author **11** 74
Dube, John Langalibalele **5** 113

Mogadishu (seaport; East Africa)
Cheng Ho **3** 500

Mogens (story)
Jacobsen, Jens Peter **8** 193-194

Moggerhanger (Bedfordshire)
Soane, John **14** 314-315

Moghulistan (region; Asia)
Tamerlane **15** 94-95

MOGILA, PETER (1596/1597-1646), Russian Orthodox churchman and theologian
11 74-75

Mogul empire
see India—1000-1600

Mohammad Hasan Khan (died 1757), ruler of Iran
Agha Mohammad Khan **1** 80-81
Karim Khan Zand **8** 447

Mohammad Khodabandeh (ruled 1578-1587), Safavid shah of Persia
Abbas I **1** 4-6

MOHAMMAD REZA SHAH PAHLAVI
(1919-1980), king of Iran **11** 75-76
John, XXIII **8** 277-280

Mohammed
see also Muhammad

MOHAMMED (circa 570-632), founder of Islam **11** 76-78
advisers
Abu Bakr **1** 31-32
Omar ibn al-Khattab **11** 508-509
biographies and traditions
Bukhari, Muhammad ibn Ismail al-
3 111-112
Imam, Alhadji Abubakar **8** 114-115
influence of
Junayd, Abu al-Qasim ibn Muhammad al **8** 388
Mahdi **10** 137-138
Muawiya ibn Abu Sufyan
11 223-224
see also Islam
relatives
Aga Khan **1** 74-76
Ali **1** 155-156

Mohammed II (1432-1481)
seeMehmed the Conqueror

MOHAMMED V (Mohammed Ben Youssef; 1911-1961), king of Morocco **11** 79-81
Ben Bella, Ahmed **2** 148-149

Mohammed Ahmed
see Mahdi, The

MOHAMMED ALI (1769-1849), Ottoman pasha of Egypt 1805-1848 **11** 81-82
Canning, George **3** 258-260
Clive, Robert **4** 119-120
Farouk I **5** 387-388
Ibrahim Pasha **8** 97-98
Mahdi **10** 137-138
Mahmud II **10** 145-147
Nesselrode, Karl Robert **11** 348-349
Palmerston, 3d Viscount **12** 81-83

Mohammed and the Monk Sergius (engraving)
Lucas van Leyden **10** 20-21

Mohammed Ben Youssef
see Mohammed V

Mohammedans
see Islam; Islamic Empire

Mohave Indians (North America)
Smith, Jedediah S. **14** 294-295

Mohawk Indians (North America)
Brant, Joseph **2** 500-501
Brant, Mary (Molly) **2** 501-503
Jogues, Isaac **8** 270-271
Philip **12** 267-268

Mohawk Valley (painting)
Wyant, Alexander Helwig **16** 409-410

Mohegan Indians (North America)
Philip **12** 267-268

Mohicans de Paris, Les (book)
Dumas, Alexandre **5** 136-138

MOHOLY-NAGY, LÁSZLÓ (1895-1946),
Hungarian painter and designer **11** 82-83
Gabo, Naum **6** 158-159

Mohr
see Marx, Karl

MOI, DANIEL ARAP (born Daniel Toroitich arap Moi; born 1924), president of Kenya
11 83-86

Moïse (poem)
Vigny, Comte de **15** 494-495

Moishele (story)
Asch, Shalom **1** 325-326

Moksha (Buddhism)
Buddha **3** 97-101

Moksobo (Burma)
see Shwebo

Mola, Emilio (1887-1937), Spanish soldier
Franco Bahamonde, Francisco **6** 52-54

Molasses Act (1733)
Otis, James Jr. **12** 25-27

Moldau, The (musical composition)
Smetana, Bedřich **14** 281-282

Moldavia (Moldavian Soviet Socialist Republic; former republic, Union of Soviet Socialist Republics)
Batu Khan **2** 60-61
Brezhnev, Leonid Ilich **2** 527-528
John III **8** 276-277
Kutuzov, Mikhail Ilarionovich
9 137-138

Molders Union (United States)
see Iron Molders International Union

Molecular biology
see Biology, molecular

Molecule (chemistry)
Diels, Otto Paul Hermann **5** 5-6
Herzberg, Gerhard **7** 349-350
Karle, Isabella **8** 447-449
Mendeleev, Dmitrii Ivanovich
10 486-488
Pauling, Linus Carl **12** 150-152
Perrin, Jean Baptiste **12** 233-236
Prichard, Diana García **12** 448-449
Van't Hoff, Jacobus Hendricus
15 431-432

MOLIÈRE (1622-1673), French dramatist
11 86-88
  adaptations
    Anouilh, Jean **1** 243-244
    Brecht, Bertolt **2** 512-514
    Dryden, John **5** 106-107
    Kleist, Heinrich von **9** 52-53
  associates
    Boileau-Despréaux, Nicholas
      2 369-371
    Condé, Prince de **4** 193-194
    Corneille, Pierre **4** 234-236
    La Fontaine, Jean de **9** 156-157
  collaborators
    Charpentier, Marc Antoine
      3 471-472
    Lully, Jean Baptiste **10** 40-41
  influence of
    Daumier, Honoré Victorin
      4 403-405
    Goldoni, Carlo **6** 408-409
    Lesage, Alain René **9** 353-354
    Marivaux, Pierre Carlet de Cham-
      blain de **10** 265-266
    Racine, Jean Baptiste **12** 532-535
    Wycherley, William **16** 411-412
  influenced by
    Alarcón, Pedro Antonio de
      1 100-101
    Terence **15** 146-148
  patrons and publishers
    Balzac, Honoré de **1** 478-480
    Louis XIV **9** 531-533

Molina, Rafael Leonidas Trujillo
  see Trujillo Molina, Rafael Leonidas

Molino de viento, El (book)
  Cela y Trulock, Camilo José **3** 389-390

MOLINOS, MIGUEL DE (1628-1696),
Spanish priest **11** 88-89
  Fénelon, François de Salignac de la
    Mothe **5** 410-411

Moll Flanders (novel; Defoe)
  Alemán, Mateo **1** 126
  Defoe, Daniel **4** 457-459

Molloy (novel)
  Beckett, Samuel **2** 102-104

Molly (literary character)
  Joyce, James **8** 365-367

Moloch, Der (novel)
  Wassermann, Jakob **16** 130-131

Molokai (Hawaiian Island.)
  Damien **4** 383
  Kamehameha I **8** 416

Molon (died 220 B.C.), satrap of Media
  Antiochus III **1** 249-250

**MOLOTOV, VYACHESLAV
  MIKHAILOVICH** (1890-1986), Soviet
  statesman **11** 89-90
  Beria, Lavrenty Pavlovich **2** 192-193
  Litvinov, Maxim Maximovich
    9 451-452
  Szent-Györgyi, Albert von **15** 62-64

    Zhukov, Georgi Konstantinovich
      16 512-513

Molotov-Ribbentrop Pact (1939)
  Browder, Earl Russell **3** 30-31
  Eisenstein, Sergei Mikhailovich
    5 240-242
  Hitler, Adolf **7** 417-420
  Litvinov, Maxim Maximovich
    9 451-452
  Malraux, André **10** 178-180
  Molotov, Vyacheslav Mikhailovich
    11 89-90
  Prokofiev, Sergei Sergeevich
    12 458-460

**MOLTKE, COUNT HELMUTH KARL
  BERNARD VON** (1800-1891), Prussian
  military leader **11** 90-91
  Bismarck, Otto Eduard Leopold von
    2 294-296
  William I **16** 292-293

Moltke, Helmuth von (1848-1916), German chief of general staff
  Ludendorff, Erich Friedrich Wilhelm
    10 27-28

MOLTMANN, JÖURGEN (born 1926),
German Protestant theologian **11** 91-92

Molucca Islands
  see Spice Islands

Molyneux, Samuel (1689-1710), Irish
  astronomer
  Bradley, James **2** 482-483

MOMADAY, N. SCOTT (born 1934),
Native American author **11** 92-94

Momente (musical composition)
  Stockhausen, Karlheinz **14** 460-461

Moments of Vision (poems)
  Hardy, Thomas **7** 150-152

MOMMSEN, THEODOR (1817-1903), Ger-
  man historian and philologist **11** 94-95
  Storm, Theodor **14** 479-480
  Vinogradoff, Paul Gavrilovitch **15** 503

Momoku Monogatari (novel)
  Tanizaki, Junichiro **15** 101-102

Momoyama Period
  see Japan—1573-1603

Mon (Asian people)
  Alaungpaya **1** 103
  Ba Maw **1** 480-481

Mon (novel)
  Natsume, Soseki **11** 324-325

Mon Frère Yves (novel)
  Loti, Pierre **9** 519-520

Mon Père (novel)
  Kazantzakis, Nikos **8** 466-468

Mon rêve familier (poem)
  Verlaine, Paul Marie **15** 465-466

Mona (opera)
  Parker, Horatio William **12** 109

Mona Lisa (painting; Leonardo da Vinci)
  Clouet, Jean and François **4** 122-123
  Leonardo da Vinci **9** 337-340

    Pater, Walter Horatio **12** 130-131
    Raphael **13** 40-42

Monad (philosophy)
  Leibniz, Gottfried Wilhelm von
    9 307-310

Monadnock Building (Chicago)
  Burnham, Daniel Hudson **3** 148-149
  Richardson, Henry Hobson **13** 139-141

Monagas, José Tadeo (1784-1868),
Venezuelan general and statesman
  Blanco, Antonio Guzmán **2** 320-321
  Páez, José Antonio **12** 58

Monarchie, The (poem)
  Lyndsay, David **10** 66-67

Monarchy (government)
  England
    Burke, Edmund **3** 138-141
    Elizabeth I **5** 263-266
    Elizabeth II **5** 266-269
    Filmer, Robert **5** 448
    John **8** 274-275
    Milton, John **11** 43-46
    Paine, Thomas **12** 66-67
  France
    Bodin, Jean **2** 356-357
    du Pont de Nemours, Pierre Samuel
      5 155-156
    Maistre, Joseph de **10** 153-154
    Marat, Jean Paul **10** 230-231
    Maurras, Charles Marie Photius
      10 350-351
  Italy
    Machiavelli, Niccolò **10** 97-99
    Victor Emmanuel III **15** 484-485
  Japan
    Hirohito **7** 410-412
    Tojo, Hideki **15** 254-256
    Yoshida, Shigeru **16** 464-465
    see also Enlightened despotism;
      Monarchy, absolute; Monarchy,
      constitutional

Monarchy, absolute (government)
  Balzac, Honoré de **1** 478-480
  Francis I **6** 40-43
  Fujiwara Kamatari **6** 145
  Louis XIV **9** 531-533
  Montesquieu **11** 123-125
  Palmerston, 3d Viscount **12** 81-83
  Pridi Phanomyong **12** 449
  Qaboos ibn Sa'id **12** 501-502
  see also Divine right of kings

Monarchy, constitutional (government)
  Austria-Hungary
    Francis Joseph **6** 45-46
  Brazil
    Pedro I **12** 179-180
  China
    K'ang Yu-wei **8** 426-428
    Liang Ch'i-ch'ao **9** 395-396
  Egypt
    Fuad I **6** 139
  France
    Hugo, Victor Marie **8** 22-25
    Lafayette, Marquis de **9** 151-152

Louis XVIII **9** 535-536
Marie Antoinette **10** 258-259
Robespierre, Maximilien François
Marie Isidore de **13** 199-201
Great Britain
Charles, Prince of Wales **3** 448-450
George I **6** 268-269
William IV **16** 296-297
Italy and Sardinia
Charles Albert, King of Sardinia
3 466
Ferdinand II **5** 415-416
Marsilius of Padua **10** 284
Sismondi, Jean Charles Léonard
Simonde de **14** 258-259
Kuwait
'Abdullah al-Salim al-Sabah, Shaykh
1 18-19
Libya
Idris I **8** 102
Nepal
Birendra, King **2** 282-283
Russia
Nicholas II **11** 378-380
Stolypin, Piotr Arkadevich
14 465-466
Serbia
Peter I **12** 256
Spain
Ferdinand VII **5** 418-420
Franco Bahamonde, Francisco
6 52-54
Isabella II **8** 145-146
Thailand
Bhumibol Adulyadej **2** 258-259
Chulalongkorn **4** 43-45

MONASH, JOHN (1865-1931), Australian
soldier, engineer, and administrator
11 95-96

Monastery, The (novel)
Scott, Walter **14** 68-70

Monasticism (Buddhist)
Buddhadāsa Bhikkhu **3** 101-102
Shinran **14** 197

Monasticism (Christian)
critics
Bacon, Roger **1** 425-427
Langland, William **9** 194-195
Luther, Martin **10** 48-51
Early Christian (Egypt)
Anthony, Susan Brownell **1** 246-248
Athanasius **1** 358-359
Eastern churches
Basil the Great **2** 51-52
Benedict, Ruth Fulton **2** 154-155
European beginnings
Benedict, Ruth Fulton **2** 154-155
Cassiodorus, Flavius Magnus Aure-
lius **3** 357-358
Columba **4** 175-176
Columban **4** 176
Gregory I **6** 531-532
European development
Bede **2** 109-110
Dunstan **5** 151-152

Kempis, Thomas à **8** 493-494
Louis I **9** 522-523
Thomas Aquinas **15** 183-186
mendicant orders
Bonaventure **2** 383-384
Dominic **5** 51-52
Francis of Assisi **6** 46-47
secularization (England)
Cromwell, Thomas **4** 320-321
Henry VIII **7** 302-305
Norfolk, 3d Duke of **11** 423
see also individual orders

Monboddo, James Burnett, Lord
(1714-1799), Scottish judge
Peacock, Thomas Love **12** 169

Moncada, José Maria (died 1945),
Nicaraguan politician
Somoza, Anastasio **14** 335-336

Monck, Christopher (died 1688), 2nd
Duke of Albemarle
Phips, William **12** 283

MONCK, GEORGE (1st Duke of Albemarle; 1608-1670), English general and
statesman **11** 96-97
Buckingham, 2d Duke of **3** 94-95
Charles II **3** 452-454

Mond Crucifixion (painting)
Raphael **13** 40-42

Mond Laboratory (established 1933)
Kapitsa, Pyotr Leonidovich **8** 433-435

MONDALE, WALTER F. (Fritz; born 1928),
United States senator and vice president
11 97-99
Ferraro, Geraldine **5** 426-428

Monday or Tuesday (stories)
Woolf, Virginia Stephen **16** 381-382

Monde dramatique, Le (theater review)
Nerval, Gérard de **11** 345-346

MONDLANE, EDUARDO CHIVAMBO
(1920-1969), Mozambique educator and
nationalist **11** 100-101
Machel, Samora Moises **10** 94-96

Mondo è quello che è, Il (play)
Moravia, Alberto **11** 153-155

MONDRIAN, PIET (1872-1944), Dutch
painter **11** 101-102
de Stijl
de Kooning, Willem **4** 468-469
Oud, Jacobus Johannes Pieter **12** 32
Rietveld, Gerrit Thomas **13** 169
influence of
Calder, Alexander **3** 216-218
Davis, Stuart **4** 424-425
Kelly, Ellsworth **8** 482-483
Lichtenstein, Roy **9** 398-399
Nicholson, Ben **11** 380-381
Noland, Kenneth **11** 418-419
van Doesburg, Theo **15** 421

MONET, CLAUDE (1840-1926), French
painter **11** 102-104
acquaintances
Cézanne, Paul **3** 400-402

Pissaro, Camille **12** 326-327
Renoir, Pierre Auguste **13** 101-102
Vlaminck, Maurice **16** 6
adaptations of
Lichtenstein, Roy **9** 398-399
compared to
Liebermann, Max **9** 402-403
Manet, Édouard **10** 193-194
Twachtman, John Henry **15** 362-363
influence of
Cullen, Maurice Galbraith **4** 334
Hassam, Frederick Childe **7** 192
Kandinsky, Wassily **8** 420-422
Mondrian, Piet **11** 101-102
Robinson, Theodore **13** 217
Van Gogh, Vincent **15** 427-429
influenced by
Courbet, Jean Desiré Gustave
4 271-273
Daubigny, Charles François **4** 402
Hiroshige, Ando **7** 412-413

Monetarism (economic theory)
Friedman, Milton **6** 111-112

Monetary policy (economics)
Biddle, Nicholas **2** 264-265
Erhard, Ludwig **5** 302-304
Francis I **6** 40-43
Friedman, Milton **6** 111-112
Garfield, James Abram **6** 213-214
Hansen, Alvin **7** 131-132
Keynes, John Maynard **8** 528-530
Morris, Robert **11** 185-187
Robertson, Dennis Holme **13** 196
see also Bank of the United States; Cur-
rency; International Monetary Fund;
World Bank

Monetary theory (economics)
Bodin, Jean **2** 356-357
von Mises, Ludwig **16** 25
Walras, Marie Esprit Léon **16** 84-85
see also Currency, Economics—monetary theory

Money... (stories)
Čapek, Karel **3** 271-272

Money Changer and His Wife, A (painting)
Massys, Quentin **10** 325-326

Money Order, The (film)
Ousmane, Sembene **12** 32-33

Monforte Altarpiece (painting)
van der Goes, Hugo **15** 416-417

Monge, Gaspard (1746-1818), French
mathematician
Cauchy, Augustin Louis **3** 378-380

Mongka Khan (Mangu, Manqu, or Möngkë
circa 1207-1259), great khan of the Mon-
gols 1251-1259
Batu Khan **2** 60-61
Genghis Khan **6** 263-265
Hulagu Khan **8** 27-28
Kublai Khan **9** 115-118
Wen T'ien-hsiang **16** 203

MONGKUT (Rama IV; 1804-1868), king of Thailand 1851-1868 **11** 104
Chulalongkorn **4** 43-45
Rama Khamhaeng **13** 11

Mongo-Nkutshu (African people)
Lumumba, Patrice Emery **10** 43-45

Mongol Empire
Chagatai khanate
Tamerlane **15** 94-95
China
Chao Meng-fu **3** 436-437
Hung-wu **8** 38-39
Wen T'ien-hsiang **16** 203
see also China—1279-1369 (Yüan dynasty)
Europe
Nevsky, Alexander **11** 359
Batu Khan **2** 60-61
John of Piano Carpini **8** 284
see also Golden Horde
India
see India—1000-1600 (Mogul Emp.)
khans
Batu Khan **2** 60-61
Genghis Khan **6** 263-265
Hulagu Khan **8** 27-28
Kublai Khan **9** 115-118
Korea and Japan
Ch'oe Ch'ung-hn **4** 13
Daigo II **4** 367-368
Yi Sng-gye **16** 458-459
Persia
see Persia—Mongol rule

Mongolia (nation; Northern Central Asia)
Chang Tso-lin **3** 434-435
Chou En-lai **4** 20-22
K'ang-hsi **8** 423-426
Molotov, Vyacheslav Mikhailovich **11** 89-90
Teilhard de Chardin, Marie Joseph Pierre **15** 134-136
Tojo, Hideki **15** 254-256
see also Mongol Empire

Monier, Joseph (1823-1906), French inventor
Nervi, Pier Luigi **11** 346-348

Monish (poem)
Peretz, Isaac Loeb **12** 212

Monism (philosophy)
Cohen, Hermann **4** 138-139
Dayananda Saraswati **4** 431
Spinoza, Baruch **14** 381-383
see also Dualism; Pluralism

Monitor (ship)
Ericsson, John **5** 307-308
Welles, Gideon **16** 188-190

Monitorial system (education)
see Education—England

Monk, George
see Monck, George

MONK, THELONIOUS (1917-1982), African American jazz musician **11** 104-108

Monk, The (novel)
Lewis, Matthew Gregory **9** 390-391

Monk, The (painting)
Inness, George **8** 123-124

Monkey Business (film)
Marx brothers **10** 303-304
Perelman, S. J. **12** 209-210

Monkey trial
see Scopes trial

Monkey's Raincoat, The (anthology)
Basho, Matsuo **2** 45-48

Monmouth, battle of (1778)
Clinton, Henry **4** 114-115
Cornwallis, Charles **4** 241-243
Knox, Henry **9** 64
Steuben, Frederick William Augustus von **14** 438-439

MONMOUTH AND BUCCLEUGH, DUKE OF (James Scott; 1649-1685), English claimant to the throne **11** 108-109
Mary II **10** 309-310
Shaftesbury, 1st Earl of **14** 135-136

Monmouth Rebellion (1685)
James II **8** 207-208

Monna Innominata (sonnet)
Rossetti, Christina Georgina **13** 307-308

Monna Vanna (play)
Maeterlinck, Maurice **10** 125-126

MONNET, JEAN (1888-1979), French economist and diplomat **11** 109-110
Ball, George **1** 470-471
Schuman, Robert **14** 41

Monocle de Mon Oncle, Le (poem)
Stevens, Wallace **14** 443-445

Monocotyledon (botany)
Malpighi, Marcello **10** 176-178
Ray, John **13** 57-59

MONOD, JACQUES (1910-1976), French biologist who discovered messenger RNA **11** 110-111

Monogram (art work)
Rauschenberg, Robert **13** 52-53

Monophthalmos
see Antigonus I

Monophysitism (religion)
Eutyches **5** 335
Justinian I **8** 393-395
Leo I **9** 329-330
Theodora **15** 172-175

Monopoly (economics; England)
Elizabeth I **5** 263-266

Monopoly (economics; United States)
Court decisions
Field, Stephen Johnson **5** 441-442
Hand, Billings Learned **7** 116
Taney, Roger Brooke **15** 98-99
oil industry
Mellon, Andrew William **10** 469-470

Rockefeller, John Davison **13** 226-228
railroad
Drew, Daniel **5** 101-102
Durant, Thomas Clark **5** 157-158
Garrett, John Work **6** 225
Gould, Jay **6** 470-472
Harriman, Edward Henry **7** 164-165
Hill, James Jerome **7** 388-389
Huntington, Collis Potter **8** 49
Schiff, Jacob Henry **14** 2-3
Vanderbilt, Cornelius **15** 415-416
reforms
Lloyd, Henry Demarest **9** 468-469
steel
Carnegie, Andrew **3** 309-312
Frick, Henry Clay **6** 108-109
telegraph
Cornell, Ezra **4** 236-237
Field, Cyrus West **5** 438-439
Gould, Jay **6** 470-472
tobacco
Duke, James Buchanan **5** 133-134
see also Antitrust laws (United States)

Monotheism (religion)
Comte, Auguste **4** 189-191
Hallaj, Al-Husayn ibn Mansur al- **7** 86-87
Ikhnaton **8** 110-111
Nazzam, Ibrahim ibn Sayyar al- **11** 329
Plutarch **12** 359-360
Zoroaster **16** 528-530

Monroe, Harriet (1861?-1936), American poet and editor
Pound, Ezra Loomis **12** 415-417

MONROE, JAMES (1758-1831), American diplomat and statesman, president 1817-1825 **11** 111-113
associates
Biddle, Nicholas **2** 264-265
Clinton, George **4** 113-114
Madison, James **10** 121-123
Paine, Thomas **12** 66-67
Cabinet
Adams, John Quincy **1** 52-54
Calhoun, John Caldwell **3** 226-228
Crawford, William Harris **4** 299-300
domestic affairs
Morse, Jedidiah **11** 191-192
Prosser, Gabriel **12** 460-461
Foreign policy
Webster, Daniel **16** 162-164
Louisiana Purchase
see Louisiana Purchase (1803)
see also Monroe Doctrine

MONROE, MARILYN (Norma Jean Baker; 1926-1962), film actress **11** 113-114
Miller, Arthur **11** 25-26
Warhol, Andy **16** 114-115

Monroe Doctrine (1823)
Adams, John Quincy **1** 52-54
Hughes, Charles Evans **8** 15-16
Hughes, William Morris **8** 21-22

Kellogg, Frank Billings **8** 481
Lamas, Carlos Saavedra **9** 175-176
Monroe, James **11** 111-113
Roosevelt, Theodore **13** 280-283
Salisbury, 3d Marquess of **13** 448-449

Monrovia Conference (1968)
Touré, Sékou **15** 275-277

Monserrat (sculpture series)
González, Julio **6** 428-429

Monsieur Bertin (painting)
Ingres, Jean Auguste Dominique
8 121-123

MONTAGNIER, LUC (born 1932), French
virologist **11** 114-116

Monster, The (novella)
Crane, Stephen **4** 293-295

Mont Blanc (poem)
Shelley, Percy Bysshe **14** 176-178

Mont-de-piété (poems)
Breton, André **2** 519-520

Mont des Oliviers, Le (poem)
Vigny, Comte de **15** 494-495

Mont Réal
see Montreal

Mont Sainte-Victoire (painting)
Cézanne, Paul **3** 400-402

Montagnais Indians (North America)
Brébeuf, Jean de **2** 511-512

Montagu, Edward
see Manchester, 1st Earl of

Montagu, Edward Wortley (died 1761),
English statesman
Bute, 3d Earl of **3** 177-178

Montagu, Edwin Samuel (1879-1924), English financier and statesman
Chelmsford, Frederic John Napier Thesiger **3** 497

Montagu, Mary Wortley (1689-1762), English poet
Pope, Alexander **12** 395-397

Montagu-Chelmsford Report (India; 1917)
Banerjee, Surendranath **1** 488
Chelmsford, Frederic John Napier The-
siger **3** 497
Das, Chitta Ranjan **4** 401-402
Gandhi, Mohandas Karamchand
6 201-204

Montague, Charles, 1st Earl of Halifax
(1661-1715), English statesman and wit
Congreve, William **4** 200-201

MONTAIGNE, MICHEL EYQUEM DE
(1533-1592), French essayist **11** 116-117
Burton, Robert **3** 166-167
Charron, Pierre **3** 472
Melville, Herman **10** 472-476

MONTALE, EUGENIO (1896-1981), Italian
poet and critic **11** 117-118
Quasimodo, Salvatore **12** 506

MONTALEMBERT, COMTE DE (Charles
Forbes; 1810-1870), French political
writer **11** 118-119
Lamennais, Hugues Félicité Robert de
9 179

Montalembert, Marc René, Marquis de
(1714-1800), French military engineer
Carnot, Lazare Nicolas Marguerite
3 313-314

Montalte, Louis de
see Pascal, Blaise

MONTALVO, JUAN MARÍA (1832-1889),
Ecuadorian writer **11** 119-120

Montana (state; United States)
Bozeman, John M. **2** 471-472
Calamity Jane **3** 216
Clark, William Andrews **4** 83-85
Daly, Marcus **4** 379-380
Harrison, Benjamin **7** 178-179
Walsh, Thomas James **16** 85-86

MONTANA, JOE (born 1956), American
football player **11** 120-121

Montanism (schismatic movement)
Montanus **11** 122
Tertullian **15** 155-156

MONTANUS (flourished 2nd century),
Early Christian founder of schismatic sect
11 122

Montauk Block (Chicago)
Burnham, Daniel Hudson **3** 148-149

**MONTCALM DE SAINT-VÉRAN, MAR-
QUIS DE** (1712-1759), French general in
Canada **11** 122-123
Bougainville, Louis Antoine de
2 443-444
Crémazie, Octave **4** 305-306
Crèvecoeur, John de **4** 307-308
Forbes, John **5** 507-508
Vaudreuil-Cavagnal, Marquis de **15** 444
Wolfe, James **16** 354-355

Montcorbier, François de
see Villon, François

Monte, Giammaria Ciocchi del
see Julius III

Monte Carlo (film)
Lubitsch, Ernst **10** 18-19

Monte Caseros, battle of (1852)
Caxias, Duque de **3** 386

Monte Cassino (archabbey; Italy)
Benedict, Ruth Fulton **2** 154-155
Thomas Aquinas **15** 183-186

Monte Cassino, battle of (1944)
Alexander of Tunis, 1st Earl **1** 135-136

Monte de las Cruces, battle of (1810)
Hidalgo y Costilla, Miguel **7** 375-377

Monte Oliveto, II (poem)
Tasso, Torquato **15** 114-116

Montecuccoli, Count Raimund
(1609-1680), Austrian general
Köprülü, Ahmed **9** 84-85

Montefeltro, Federigo da (1444-1482),
duke of Urbino
Bramante, Donato **2** 493-494
Piero della Francesca **12** 301-302
Ptolemy, Claudius **12** 473-474

Montefeltro, Guidobaldo da (died 1508),
duke of Urbino
Castiglione, Baldassare **3** 360-361

Montefiore, Claude Joseph Goldschmid
(1858-1938), British Jewish scholar and
author
Abrahams, Israel **1** 29

Montejan, René de (died 1539), French
army officer
Paré, Ambroise **12** 94-95

Montenegro
Bulatovic, Momir **3** 115-116

Montenevoso, Principe di
see D'Annunzio, Gabriele

Montereau, Pierre de
see Montreuil, Pierre de

Monterey, battle of (1847)
Davis, Jefferson **4** 416-418

Montes, the Matador (book)
Harris, Frank **7** 172-173

**Montespan, Françoise Athénaïs Roche-
chouart, Marquise de** (1641-1707), mistress of Louis XIV
Louis XIV **9** 531-533
Mansart, Jules Hardouin **10** 212

MONTESQUIEU, BARON DE (Charles
Louis de Secondat; 1689-1755), French
man of letters **11** 123-125
Becarria, Marchese di **2** 97-98
Bodin, Jean **2** 356-357
Catherine the Great **3** 370-372
Clodion **4** 121
Hu Shih **8** 63-65
Krochmal, Nachman Kohen **9** 104-105
Saint-Pierre, Abbé de **13** 434-435
Yen Fu **16** 452

MONTESSORI, MARIA (1870-1952), Italian educator and physician **11** 125-126

**MONTEVERDI, CLAUDIO GIOVANNI
ANTONIO** (1567-1643), Italian compos-
er **11** 126-128
Caccini, Giulio **3** 205-206
Cavalli, Pietro Francesco **3** 382-383
Cesti, Pietro **3** 399-400
Malipiero, Gian Francesco **10** 171
Praetorius, Michael **12** 431-432
Schütz, Heinrich **14** 48-49

MONTEZUMA II (1466?-1520), Aztec
emperor 1502-1520 **11** 128-129
Cortés, Hernán **4** 255-256
Cuauhtemoc **4** 329

MONTEZUMA, CARLOS (born Wassaja;
ca. 1865-1923), Native American physician and political leader **11** 129-132

Montferrat, Boniface III, Count of (died
1207), king of Thessalonica 1204-1207
Villehardouin, Geffroi de **15** 499

MONTFORT, SIMON DE (6th Earl of Leicester; 1208-1265), English statesman and soldier **11** 132-133
  Edward I **5** 208-210
  Grosseteste, Robert **7** 15
  Henry III **7** 290-292
  Llewelyn ap Gruffydd **9** 468

MONTGOLFIER, JACQUES ÉTIENNE (1745-1799), French inventor and industrialist **11** 133-134

MONTGOLFIER, JOSEPH MICHEL (1740-1810), French inventor and industrialist **11** 133-134

Montgomerie, Hugh
  see Eglington, Earl of

Montgomery (city; Alabama)
  Abernathy, Ralph David **1** 27-28
  Bunche, Ralph Johnson **3** 121-122
  King, Martin Luther Jr. **9** 20-22
  Memminger, Christopher Gustavus **10** 476-477
  Parks, Rosa Lee McCauley **12** 115-116

Montgomery, Treaty of (1267)
  Llewelyn ap Gruffydd **9** 468

MONTGOMERY, BERNARD LAW (1st Viscount Montgomery of Alamein; born 1887), English field marshal **11** 135-136
  Alexander of Tunis, 1st Earl **1** 135-136
  Leclerc, Jacques Philippe **9** 272-273
  Patton, George Smith Jr. **12** 140-141
  Rommel, Erwin **13** 268-269

MONTGOMERY, LUCY MAUD (1874-1942), Canadian author **11** 136-138

MONTGOMERY, RICHARD (1736-1775), colonial American general **11** 138-139
  Arnold, Benedict **1** 309-310
  Carleton, Guy **3** 300-301
  Morgan, Daniel **11** 160-161
  Schuyler, Philip John **14** 49-50

Montgomery Improvement Asociation
  King, Martin Luther Jr. **9** 20-22

Montgomery Ward and Co. (established 1872)
  Ward, Aaron Montgomery **16** 112

Month in the Country, A (play)
  Turgenev, Ivan Sergeyevich **15** 345-348

Months (painting series)
  Bruegel, Pieter the Elder **3** 65-67

Monticello (near Charlottesville, Virginia)
  Jefferson, Thomas **8** 238-241

Montini, Giovanni Battista
  see Paul VI

Montmagny, Huault de (flourished 1622-1654), governor of New France
  Maisoneuve, Sieur de **10** 153

Montmartre (district; Paris)
  Modigliani, Amedeo **11** 72-73
  Toulouse-Lautrec, Henri de **15** 273-274
  Van Gogh, Vincent **15** 427-429

Montmorency, Henri II, Duc de (1595-1632), marshal of France

Champlain, Samuel de **3** 419-421
  Richelieu, Armand Jean du Plessis de **13** 142-144

Montmorency, Philip de
  see Hoorn, Count of

Montreal (city; Canada)
  British capture (1760)
    Amherst, Jeffery **1** 200-201
    Gage, Thomas **6** 169-170
    Howe, William **7** 538-539
    Johnson, William **8** 319-320
    Murray, James **11** 261-262
    Rogers, Robert **13** 250-251
  French settlement
    Bienville, Sieur de **2** 268-269
    Bourgeoys, Marguerite **2** 452-453
    Cartier, Jacques **3** 343-344
    Maisoneuve, Sieur de **10** 153
  riots (1849)
    Lafontaine, Louis-Hippolyte **9** 157-158
    see also World's Fairs—Montreal

Montreal Neurological Institute (Canada)
  Penfield, Wilder Graves **12** 198-200

Montreuil, Eudes and Gerbert de
  see Montreuil, Pierre de

MONTREUIL, PIERRE DE (flourished circa 1231-1266/67), French architect **11** 139

Montreurs, Les (poem)
  Leconte de Lisle, Charles Marie René **9** 273-274

Montreux Convention (1936)
  Atatürk, Ghazi Mustapha Kemal **1** 356-357

Montroig (painting)
  Miró, Joan **11** 53-54

Monts, Pierre du Guast de (1560?-1630?), French explorer
  Champlain, Samuel de **3** 419-421

MONTT TORRES, MANUEL (1809-1880), Chilean statesman, president 1851-1861 **11** 139-140
  Portales Plazazuelos, Diego José Víctor **12** 404

Monument Mountain (painting)
  Durand, Asher Brown **5** 156-157

Monument to General Alvear (sculpture)
  Bourdelle, Emile-Antoine **2** 449-450

Monument to the Defenders of Montauban (sculpture)
  Bourdelle, Emile-Antoine **2** 449-450

Monumental Head (sculpture)
  Giacometti, Alberto **6** 294-295

Monumental sculpture
  Bourdelle, Emile-Antoine **2** 449-450

MOODIE, SUSANNA (1803-1885), Canadian poet, novelist, and essayist **11** 140-141

Moods (novel)
  Alcott, Louisa May **1** 122

MOODY, DWIGHT L. (1837-1899), American evangelist **11** 141-142
  Graham, William Franklin Jr. **6** 487-488

Moody, Paul (1779-1831), American inventor
  Lowell, Francis Cabot **10** 13-14

Moody Bible Institute (Chicago)
  Moody, Dwight L. **11** 141-142

Moody's Pub. (painting)
  Drysdale, George Russell **5** 107-109

Moon (earth's)
  eclipses
    Aristarchus of Samos **1** 290-291
    Hipparchus **7** 407-408
    Ptolemy, Claudius **12** 473-474
  exploration
    Armstrong, Neil Alden **1** 304-306-240
  formation
    Urey, Harold Clayton **15** 394-396
  motion
    Eudoxus of Cnidus **5** 329-330
    Euler, Leonard **5** 331-332
    Flamsteed, John **5** 477-478
    Halley, Edmund **7** 88-89
    Laplace, Marquis de **9** 202-204
  spherical surface
    Anaxagoras **1** 208-209
    Galileo Galilei **6** 180-183

Moon (journal)
  Du Bois, William Edward Burghardt **5** 116-118

MOON, SUN MYUNG (born 1920), founder of the Unification Church **11** 142-143

Moon across the Way (poems)
  Borges, Jorge Luis **2** 411-412

Moon and Sixpence, The (novel)
  Maugham, William Somerset **10** 344-345

Moon for the Misbegotten, A (play)
  O'Neill, Eugene **11** 514-516

Moon Garden plus One (sculpture)
  Nevelson, Louise **11** 356-357

Moon Hoax (story; Poe)
  Beach, Moses Yale **2** 79-80

Moon Is Down, The (novel)
  Steinbeck, John Ernst **14** 416-417

Moon of the Caribbees, The (play)
  O'Neill, Eugene **11** 514-516

Mooney, Thomas Joseph (1882-1942), American labor leader
  Shahn, Ben **14** 139-140

Moonlight and Frost (painting)
  Wyant, Alexander Helwig **16** 409-410

Moonlight Battle (1780)
  Rodney, George Brydges **13** 239-240

Moonlight Boy, The (novel)
  Howe, Edgar Watson **7** 529

Moonlight Landscape (painting)
  Allston, Washington **1** 176-177

Moonstone, The (novel)
Collins, William Wilkie **4** 169-170

Moor, Karl (literary character)
Schiller, Johann Christoph Friedrich von **14** 4-7

Moor, the
see Sforza, Ludovico

Moore, Albert Joseph (1841-1893), English painter
Whistler, James Abbott McNeill **16** 225-226

Moore, Carry Amelia
see Nation, Carry Amelia Moore

MOORE, CHARLES WILLARD (1925-1993), American architect and educator **11** 143-145

MOORE, CHARLOTTE E. (1898-1990), American astrophysicist **11** 145-146

Moore, Douglas (1893-1969), American composer
Benét, Stephen Vincent **2** 157-158
Tabor, Horace Austin Warner **15** 70

MOORE, GEORGE EDWARD (1873-1958), English philosopher **11** 146
associates
Collingwood, Robin George **4** 162
Russell, Bertrand Arthur William **13** 373-374
Ryle, Gilbert **13** 393-394
Trevelyan, George Macaulay **15** 294-295
Wittgenstein, Ludwig **16** 350-351
influence of
Broad, Charlie Dunbar **3** 12
Schlick, Friedrich Albert Moritz **14** 16-17
influenced by
Meinong, Alexius Ritter von Hand-schuchsheim **10** 461-462
Sidgwick, Henry **14** 213
Zola, Émile **16** 526-528

MOORE, HENRY (1898-1986), English sculptor **11** 146-148
Caro, Anthony **3** 316

MOORE, MARIANNE (1887-1972), American poet and translator **11** 148-149
Bishop, Elizabeth **2** 290-292
Stevens, Wallace **14** 443-445

Moore, Thomas (1779-1852), Irish poet
Emmet, Robert **5** 281-282

Mor, Anthonis (Sir Anthony More; Antonio Moro; 1512?-1576?), Flemish painter
Clouet, Jean and François **4** 122-123

Mora, Francisco de (died 1610), Spanish architect
Herrera, Juan de **7** 335

Morais Barros, Prudente Jose de (1841-1902), Brazilian statesman, president 1894-1898
Peixoto, Floriano **12** 188-189

Moral and Political Science, University of (established 1936)
Pridi Phanomyong **12** 449

Moral Bully, The (poem)
Holmes, Oliver Wendell **7** 457-458

Moral Majority, Inc. (United States political organization; established 1979)
Falwell, Jerry **5** 375-376
Helms, Jesse **7** 271-272

Moral philosophy
see Ethics

Moral-sense school
see Ethics

MORALES, LUIS DE (circa 1519-1586), Spanish painter **11** 150

MORALES-BERMÚDEZ CERRUTI, FRANCISCO (born 1921), president of Peru (1975-1980) **11** 150-151

Moralia (book)
Gregory I **6** 531-532
Plutarch **12** 359-360

MORAN, THOMAS (1837-1926), American painter and graphic artist **11** 151-152

Moran of the Lady Letty (novel)
Norris, Benjamin Franklin Jr. **11** 427-428

MORANDI, GIORGIO (1890-1964), Italian painter of still lifes **11** 152-153
Chirico, Giorgio de **4** 4

Morat, battle of (1476)
Charles the Bold **3** 467-469

Moravia (region; Czechoslovakia)
Charles IV **3** 455-456
Cyril and Methodius, Saints **4** 362-363

MORAVIA, ALBERTO (1907-1990), Italian author **11** 153-155
Levi, Carlo **9** 364

Moravian Brethren (Christian sect)
Wesley, John **16** 209-210
Zinzendorf, Nikolaus Ludwig von **16** 522-523

Moray, James Stewart, Earl of (1531?-1570), son of James V of Scotland
Mary, I **10** 308-309

MORAZÁN, JOSÉ FRANCISCO (1792-1842), Central American general and statesman **11** 155
Carrera, José Rafael **3** 324-325

Mörder, Hoffnung der Frauen (opera)
Hindemith, Paul **7** 399-400

More, Hannah (1745-1833), English religious writer
Wilberforce, William **16** 269-270

More, Sir Anthony
see Mor, Anthonis

MORE, SIR THOMAS (1478-1535), English humanist and statesman **11** 156-157
Budé, Guillaume **3** 102-103
Colet, John **4** 157-158
Donne, John **5** 60-61
Erasmus, Desiderius **5** 298-300
Henry VIII **7** 302-305
Holbein, Hans the Younger **7** 449-450
Reuchlin, Johann **13** 106-107

Tyndale, William **15** 373-374
Zumárraga, Juan de **16** 531-532

More de Venise, Le (play)
Vigny, Comte de **15** 494-495

More Joy in Heaven (novel)
Callaghan, Edward Morley **3** 229-230

More Pricks than Kicks (stories)
Beckett, Samuel **2** 102-104

More Roman Tales (stories)
Moravia, Alberto **11** 153-155

More Stately Mansions (play)
O'Neill, Eugene **11** 514-516

Morea
see Peloponnesus

Moréas, Jean (1856-1910), French poet
Maurras, Charles Marie Photius **10** 350-351

Moreau, Frédéric (literary character)
Flaubert, Gustave **5** 480-482

Moreau, Gustave (1826-1898), French painter
Matisse, Henri **10** 336-337
Rouault, Georges **13** 321-322

Morehouse, J. Ward (literary character)
Dos Passos, John Roderigo **5** 69-71

Morehouse, Marion (wife of E.E. Cummings; 1906-1969), American photographer
Cummings, Edward Estlin **4** 334-336

Morehouse College
Mays, Benjamin E. **10** 374-376

MORELOS, JOSÉ MARÍA (1765-1815), Mexican priest and revolutionary leader **11** 157-158
Álvarez, Juan **1** 184-185
Guerrero, Vicente **7** 28-30
Hidalgo y Costilla, Miguel **7** 375-377
Matamoros, Mariano **10** 329-330

Moreno, Gabriel García
see García Moreno, Gabriel

MORGAGNI, GIOVANNI BATTISTA (1682-1771), Italian anatomist **11** 158-159
Bichat, Marie François Xavier **2** 263-264

Morgan, Arthur (1878-1975), American engineer and educator
Lilienthal, David Eli **9** 410-411

Morgan, Charles (1795-1878), American shipping and railroad magnate
Walker, William **16** 68-69

MORGAN, CONWAY LLOYD (1852-1936), English psychologist **11** 159-160

MORGAN, DANIEL (circa 1735-1802), American soldier and tactician **11** 160-161

Morgan, Edmund Morris, Jr. (1878-1966), American historian
Dudley, Thomas **5** 124-125

MORGAN, GARRETT A. (1877-1963), African American inventor and publisher **11** 161-162

MORGAN, JOHN (1735-1789), American physician **11** 162-163

Morgan, John (1797-1847), English physician
Addison, Thomas **1** 58-59

MORGAN, JOHN PIERPONT (1837-1913), American banker **11** 163-165
antitrust suit
Roosevelt, Theodore **13** 280-283
associates
Cooke, Jay **4** 215-216
Edison, Thomas Alva **5** 206-208
corporate interests
Carnegie, Andrew **3** 309-312
Gary, Elbert Henry **6** 229-230
Harriman, Edward Henry **7** 164-165
Knox, Philander Chase **9** 66-67
Rockefeller, John Davison
13 226-228
Schiff, Jacob Henry **14** 2-3
Schwab, Charles Michael **14** 50-51
portraits
Steichen, Edward **14** 411-412

MORGAN, JOHN PIERPONT, II
(1867-1943), American banker **11** 165

MORGAN, JULIA (1872-1957), American architect **11** 165-166

MORGAN, JUNIUS SPENCER
(1813-1890), American banker
11 166-167

MORGAN, LEWIS HENRY (1818-1881), American anthropologist **11** 167-168

MORGAN, ROBIN (born 1941), feminist writer, editor, poet, and political activist
11 168-170

Morgan, Shubel
see Brown, John

Morgan, Sir Henry (circa 1635-1688), British buccaneer
Steinbeck, John Ernst **14** 416-417

MORGAN, THOMAS HUNT (1866-1945), American zoologist and geneticist
11 170-171
East, Edward Murray **5** 182-183
Muller, Hermann Joseph **11** 238-239
Northrop, John Howard **11** 430-431

Morgan, J.P., and Co. (banking)
Carnegie, Andrew **3** 309-312
Morgan, John Pierpont **11** 163-165
Morgan, John Pierpont II **11** 165
Morrow, Dwight Whitney **11** 190-191

Morgan, J.S., and Co. (banking)
Cooke, Jay **4** 215-216
Morgan, Junius Spencer **11** 166-167

Morgan v. Virginia (legal case)
Marshall, Thurgood **10** 282-284

Morgante maggiore, Il (poem)
Pulci, Luigi **12** 481

Morgenlandfahrt, Die (novel)
Hesse, Hermann **7** 367-369

MORGENTHAU, HANS J. (1904-1979), American political scientist **11** 171-172

MORGENTHAU, HENRY, JR. (1891-1967), American statesman **11** 172-173
Lilienthal, David Eli **9** 410-411

Morgue (poems)
Benn, Gottfried **2** 164

Moriarty (literary character)
Doyle, Arthur Conan **5** 91-92

MORIN, PAUL (1889-1963), French-Canadian poet **11** 174
Fréchette, Louis-Honoré **6** 77-78

MORÍNIGO, HIGINIO (1897-1985), Paraguayan statesman **11** 174-175

Moriscos
see Spain—Islamic

MORISON, SAMUEL ELIOT (1887-1976), American historian and biographer
11 175-176
Channing, Edward **3** 435

Morisot, Berthe (1841-1895), French painter
Corot, Jean Baptiste Camille **4** 247-249

MORITA, AKIO (born 1921), Japanese industrial leader **11** 176-178

Moritat (song)
Weill, Kurt **16** 174-175

Moritz (1572-1632), landgrave of Hesse-Cassel
Schütz, Heinrich **14** 48-49

Moritz, Duke of Saxony
see Maurice

Morley, Edward W. (1838-1923), American chemist and physicist
Michelson, Albert Abraham **11** 7-8

MORLEY, JOHN (Viscount Morley of Blackburn; 1838-1923), English statesman and author **11** 178-179
Gokhale, Gopal Krishna **6** 396
Voltaire **16** 14-16

MORLEY, THOMAS (circa 1557-1602/08), English composer and organist
11 179-180
Marenzio, Luca **10** 248
Tallis, Thomas **15** 91

Mormon (flourished 4th century), American prophet and historian
Smith, Joseph **14** 297-298

Mormon War (Missouri; 1838-39)
Atchison, David Rice **1** 357-358

Mormon War (Utah; 1857-58)
Bridger, James **3** 2-3
Buchanan, James **3** 89-90
Scott, Winfield **14** 70-71
Young, Brigham **16** 469-470

Mormons (religious sect)
Atchison, David Rice **1** 357-358
Burton, Richard **3** 163-164
Cartwright, Peter **3** 344-345

Miller, Joaquin **11** 27-28
Smith, Joseph **14** 297-298
Young, Brigham **16** 469-470

Morning (ship)
Scott, Robert Falcon **14** 67-68

Morning and Evening (sculpture)
Michelangelo Buonarroti **11** 2-5

Morning Flowers... (poem)
Lu Hsün **10** 35-37

Morning in the Country... (painting)
Malevich, Kasimir **10** 168-169

Morning of Life (painting)
Durand, Asher Brown **5** 156-157

Morning Prayer, The (painting)
Greuze, Jean Baptiste **6** 539

Morning Star (Northern Cheyenne tribal leader)
see Dull Knife

Morning Star (ship)
Maceo, Antonio **10** 88-90

Morning Walk (painting)
Gainsborough, Thomas **6** 170-172

Morning Watch, The (poem)
Vaughan, Henry **15** 444-445

Morny, Duc Charles Auguste Louis Joseph de (1811-1865), French politician
Maximilian of Hapsburg **10** 358-360
Viollet-le-Duc, Eugène Emmanuel
15 505-506

MORO, ALDO (1916-1978), leader of Italy's Christian Democratic Party
11 180-181

Moro, Antonio
see Mor, Anthonis

Moro expósito (epic)
Saavedra, Angel de **13** 398

Morocco, Kingdom of (nation; Northwest Africa)
Agadir crisis (1911)
Lloyd George, David **9** 469-471
Poincaré, Raymond **12** 366-368
Algeciras crisis (1905-1906)
Delcassé, Théophile **4** 478-479
Roosevelt, Theodore **13** 280-283
William II **16** 294-295
French colonial era
Abd el-Kadir **1** 15
Bugeaud de la Piconnerie, Thomas Robert **3** 111
Leclerc, Jacques Philippe **9** 272-273
Lyautey, Louis Hubert Gonzalve
10 60-61
Mohammed V **11** 79-81
independence
Abd el-Krim el-Khatabi, Mohamed ben **1** 15-16
Allal al-Fassi, Mohamed **1** 162
Boumediene, Houari **2** 445-446
Hassan, Muhammad Abdille
7 194-195
Mohammed V **11** 79-81
Portugal and

Manuel I **10** 219-220
Spain and
  Franco Bahamonde, Francisco
  6 52-54
  Primo de Rivera y Orbaneja, Miguel
  12 454-455
  see also Abbasids; Almohads;
  Almoravids

Morone, Giovanni (1509-1580), Italian cardinal
  Paul IV **12** 145-146

Morose (literary character)
  Jonson, Ben **8** 343-345

MORRICE, JAMES WILSON (1865-1924),
Canadian painter **11** 181-182
  Cullen, Maurice Galbraith **4** 334

MORRILL, JUSTIN SMITH (1810-1898),
American legislator **11** 182

Morrill Act (1862)
  Cornell, Ezra **4** 236-237
  White, Andrew Dickson **16** 226-227

Morris, Charles W. (born 1901), American
philosopher
  Carnap, Rudolf **3** 308-309
  Schlick, Friedrich Albert Moritz
  14 16-17

Morris, George S. (1840-1889), American
philosopher
  Dewey, John **4** 520-523

MORRIS, GOUVERNEUR (1752-1816),
American statesman and diplomat
11 182-183
  Livingston, Robert R. **9** 462-463
  Roosevelt, Theodore **13** 280-283
  Sparks, Jared **14** 363

MORRIS, LEWIS (1671-1746), American
colonial official **11** 183-184
  Zenger, John Peter **16** 497-498

MORRIS, MARK (born 1956), American
choreographer **11** 184-185

MORRIS, ROBERT (1734-1806), American
financer and statesman, **11** 185-187
  L'Enfant, Pierre Charles **9** 322-323
  Livingston, Robert R. **9** 462-463
  Morris, Gouverneur **11** 182-183

MORRIS, WILLIAM (1834-1896), English
man of letters, artist, and politician
11 187-188
  Burne-Jones, Edward Coley **3** 145-146
  Godwin, William **6** 383-384
  Kokoschka, Oskar **9** 75-76
  Parrington, Vernon Louis **12** 119-120
  Richardson, Henry Hobson **13** 139-141
  Swinburne, Algernon Charles **15** 54-55
  Tawney, Richard Henry **15** 120-121
  Van de Velde, Henry **15** 419-420
  Yeats, William Butler **16** 445-447

Morris Gift Shop (San Francisco)
  Wright, Frank Lloyd **16** 398-401

MORRISON, TONI (Chloe Anthony Wofford; born 1931), African American novelist **11** 188-190

Morrow, Anne Spencer
  see Lindbergh, Anne Morrow

MORROW, DWIGHT WHITNEY
(1873-1931), American banker and diplomat **11** 190-191
  Calles, Plutarco Elías **3** 234-235
  Hearst, William Randolph **7** 243-244
  Kellogg, Frank Billings **8** 481

Morsamor (novel)
  Valera y Alcalá Galiano, Juan **15** 403

MORSE, JEDIDIAH (1761-1826), American
geographer and clergyman **11** 191-192
  Morse, Samuel Finley Breese
  11 192-193

MORSE, SAMUEL FINLEY BREESE
(1791-1872), American artist and inventor **11** 192-193
  Allston, Washington **1** 176-177
  Brady, Mathew B. **2** 487-488
  Copley, John Singleton **4** 228-230
  Daguerre, Louis Jacques Mandé
  4 365-366
  Draper, John William **5** 96-97
  Durand, Asher Brown **5** 156-157
  Field, Cyrus West **5** 438-439
  Kendall, Amos **8** 494

MORSE, WAYNE L. (1900-1974), United
States senator from Oregon **11** 193-194

Morse code (telegraph)
  Marconi, Guglielmo **10** 239-240
  Morse, Samuel Finley Breese
  11 192-193

Morse College (Yale University)
  Saarinen, Eliel and Eero **13** 396-398

Mort, La (poem)
  Verlaine, Paul Marie **15** 465-466

Mort à crédit (novel)
  Céline, Louis Ferdinand **3** 390-391

Mort de César, La (play)
  Voltaire **16** 14-16

Mort de Cléopâtre, La (cantata)
  Berlioz, Louis Hector **2** 203-205

Mort de Tintagiles, La (play)
  Maeterlinck, Maurice **10** 125-126

Mort d'Orphée, La (cantata)
  Berlioz, Louis Hector **2** 203-205

Mort du loup, La (poem)
  Vigny, Comte de **15** 494-495

Mort du Père, La (novel)
  Martin du Gard, Roger **10** 295-296

Mortalium animos (encyclical)
  Pius XI **12** 337-339

Morte d'Arthur, Le (book; Malory)
  Beardsley, Aubrey Vincent **2** 88-89
  Caxton, William **3** 386-387
  Malory, Thomas **10** 175-176

Mortimer, Earl
  see Harley, Robert

Mortimer, Edmund (IV) de, 5th Earl of
March (1391-1425), English nobleman

Glendower, Owen **6** 364-365

MORTIMER, JOHN CLIFFORD (born
1923), British author of novels, stories,
and plays for radio, stage, television, and
film **11** 194-195

Mortimer, Roger (IV) de
  see March, 4th Earl of

Mortimer, Roger (IV) de, 1st Earl of March
(1287-1330), English nobleman
  Edward II **5** 210
  Edward III **5** 211-212

Mortimeriados (poems)
  Drayton, Michael **5** 97-98

Mortmain, Statute of (1279)
  Edward I **5** 208-210

Morton, 4th Earl of (James Douglas;
1525?-1581), Scottish statesman
  James I **8** 204-206

Morton, John (1420?-1500), English archbishop and statesman
  More, Thomas **11** 156-157
  Richard III **13** 132-133

Morton, Levi P. (1824-1920), American
politician
  Arthur, Chester Alan **1** 321-323

MORTON, NELLE KATHERINE
(1905-1987), activist for racial justice,
teacher of Christian educators, and proponent of feminist theology **11** 195-197

**MORTON, OLIVER HAZARD PERRY
THROCK** (1823-1877), American politician **11** 197-198

Morton, Thomas (1564-1659), Anglican
bishop
  Donne, John **5** 60-61

Morton, Thomas (flourished 1622-1647),
English adventurer in America
  Standish, Myles **14** 396-397

MORTON, WILLIAM THOMAS GREEN
(1819-1868), American dentist
11 198-199
  Long, Crawford Williamson **9** 495-496
  Wells, Horace **16** 196

Mortua Est (poem)
  Eminescu, Mihail **5** 280-281

Mosaic law (Old Testament)
  Cotton, John **4** 263-265
  Ezra **5** 356-357
  Hillel **7** 390-391
  Johanan ben Zakkai **8** 271-272
  Josephus Flavius **8** 360-361
  Moses **11** 200-201
  Paul **12** 141-143

Mosby's Memoirs... (stories)
  Bellow, Saul **2** 141-143

Mosca (literary character)
  Jonson, Ben **8** 343-345

Moscheles, Ignaz (1794-1870), Bohemian
composer, pianist, and teacher
  Mendelssohn, Moses **10** 488-489

Moscherosch, Johann Michael
(1601-1669), German satirist
Grimmelshausen, Hans Jakob Christoffel von **7** 4-5

Moscow (city; Russia)
Afinogenov, Aleksandr Nikolaevich
1 72-73
Ivan III **8** 156-157
Ivan IV **8** 157-159
Kutuzov, Mikhail Ilarionovich
9 137-138
Le Corbusier **9** 274-275
Napoleon I **11** 306-310
Peter I **12** 253-256
Zhukov, Georgi Konstantinovich
16 512-513

Moscow, University of
Berdyaev, Nicholas Alexandrovich
2 184-185
Kandinsky, Wassily **8** 420-422
Landau, Lev Davidovich **9** 184-185
Miliukov, Pavel Nikolayevich **11** 18-19
Pobedonostsev, Konstantin Petrovich
12 360-361
Semenov, Nikolai Nikolaevich **14** 101
Vinogradoff, Paul Gavrilovitch **15** 503

Moscow Art Theater
Afinogenov, Aleksandr Nikolaevich
1 72-73
Bulgakov, Mikhail Afanasievich **3** 117
Chekhov, Anton Pavlovich **3** 494-497
Gorky, Maxim **6** 458-460
Meyerhold, Vsevolod Emilievich **10** 539
Stanislavsky, Constantin **14** 398-399

Moscow Conservatory (music)
Rachmaninov, Sergei Vasilievich
12 531-532
Scriabin, Alexander Nikolayevich
14 71-72
Tchaikovsky, Peter Ilyich **15** 130-132

Mosega, battle of (1837)
Mzilikazi **11** 285-286
Pretorius, Andries **12** 444-445

Moseley, H.G.-J. (1887-1915), English
physicist
Rutherford, Ernest **13** 384-387

MOSELY-BRAUN, CAROL (born 1947),
African American Democratic senator
from Illinois **11** 199-200

MOSES (circa 1392-circa 1272 B.C.),
Hebrew prophet and lawgiver
11 200-201
Charonton, Enguerrand **3** 471
Isidore of Seville **8** 149-150
John **8** 273-274
see also Mosaic law

Moses (sculpture)
Michelangelo Buonarroti **11** 2-5

MOSES, GRANDMA (Anna Mary Robertson; 1860-1961), American painter
11 201-202

MOSES, ROBERT (1888-1981), New York
City's builder of public works **11** 202-203

Moses ben Maimon
see Maimonides

Moses ben Nahman
see Nahmanides

Moses Defending the Daughters of Jethro
(painting)
Rosso, Il **13** 312-313

Moses' Miracle of the Waters (painting)
Murillo, Bartolomé Esteban **11** 258-259

Moses Striking Water from the Rock (painting)
Lucas van Leyden **10** 20-21

Moses und Aron (opera)
Schoenberg, Arnold **14** 24-26

Moshavim movement (Israel)
Dayan, Moshe **4** 429-431

MOSHWESHWE (Moshesh; circa
1787-1868), South African king
11 203-205
Jonathan, Joseph Leabua **8** 330-331

Moskowa, Prince of the
see Ney, Michel

Moslem Empire
see Islamic Empire

Moslem League (India)
Bhashani, Maulana Abdul Hamid Khan
2 255-257
Iqbal, Muhammad **8** 132-133
Jinnah, Mohammad Ali **8** 262-263
Liaquat Ali Khan **9** 397
Naidu, Sarojini **11** 294-295
Nehru, Jawaharlal **11** 332-334

Moslems
see Islam; Islamic Empire

MOSQUERA, TOMÁS CIPRIANO DE
(1798-1878), Colombian statesman
11 205-206

Mosquito (insect)
Burnet, Frank Macfarlane **3** 146-147
Finlay, Carlos Juan **5** 450
Reed, Walter **13** 78

Mosquitoes (novel)
Faulkner, William **5** 395-397

MOSSADEGH, MOHAMMAD (Musaddiq;
1882-1967), Iranian nationalist politician
and prime minister (1951-1953)
11 206-207

MÖSSBAUER, RUDOLF (born 1929), German physicist **11** 208-209

Mosses from an Old Manse (book;
Hawthorne)
Hawthorne, Nathaniel **7** 212-215
Melville, Herman **10** 472-476

Mossi (African people)
Ali, Sunni **1** 158-159

Most, Johann Joseph (1846-1906),
German-American anarchist
Goldman, Emma **6** 406-407

Most Beautifully (film)
Kurosawa, Akira **9** 135-137

Most Important Man, The (opera)
Menotti, Gian Carlo **10** 509-510

Most Lamentable Chance... (poem)
Skelton, John **14** 268-269

Most Likely to Succeed (novel)
Dos Passos, John Roderigo **5** 69-71

Mostellaria (play)
Plautus **12** 348-350

Motel Ben Pasey the Chazan (book)
Sholem Aleichem **14** 202-203

Motet (music form)
England
Byrd, William **3** 187-188
Dunstable, John **5** 150-151
Tallis, Thomas **15** 91
Flanders
Gombert, Nicolas **6** 416-417
Josquin des Prez **8** 361-363
Lassus, Roland de **9** 216-218
Willaert, Adrian **16** 287-288
France
Goudimel, Claude **6** 466
Le Jeune, Claude **9** 314-315
Machaut, Guillaume de **10** 93-94
Pérotin **12** 231-232
Vitry, Philippe de **16** 2
Germany
Bach, Carl Philipp Emanuel
1 414-415
Bach, Johann Sebastian **1** 416-419
Franco of Cologne **6** 52
Isaac, Heinrich **8** 143-144
Schütz, Heinrich **14** 48-49
Senfl, Ludwig **14** 105-106
Walter, Johann **16** 86
Italy
Carissimi, Giacomo **3** 299-300
Landini, Francesco **9** 185-186
Marenzio, Luca **10** 248
Merulo, Claudio **10** 525-526
Monteverdi, Claudio Giovanni
Antonio **11** 126-128
Palestrina, Giovanni Pierluigi da
12 70-72
Vivaldi, Antonio **16** 3-4
Zarlino, Gioseffo **16** 490-491
Netherlands
Clemens non Papa, Jacobus **4** 101
Obrecht, Jacob **11** 457-458
Ockeghem, Johannes **11** 464-465
Sweelinck, Jan Pieterszoon
15 50-51
Spain
Victoria, Tomás Luis de **15** 487-488

Mother... (poems)
Sitwell, Edith **14** 265-266

Mother, The (novel)
Asch, Shalom **1** 325-326
Buck, Pearl Sydenstricker **3** 91-93
Gorky, Maxim **6** 458-460

Mother, The (play)
Čapek, Karel **3** 271-272

Mother and Child (sculpture)
Moore, Henry **11** 146-148
Zadkine, Ossip Joselyn **16** 484
Zorach, William **16** 528

Mother and Sister of the Artist (painting)
Vuillard, Jean Édouard **16** 36

Mother Courage (play)
Brecht, Bertolt **2** 512-514

Mother Hubberd's Tale (poem)
Spenser, Edmund **14** 373-376

Mother Jones
see Jones, Mary Harris

Mother of Captain Shigemoto, The (novel)
Tanizaki, Junichiro **15** 101-102

Mother of Us All, The (opera)
Thomson, Virgil **15** 202-203

Motherland Party (Turkey)
Özal, Turgut **12** 47-49

Motherwell, Mrs. Robert
see Frankenthaler, Helen

MOTHERWELL, ROBERT (1915-1991),
American painter **11** 210-211
Frankenthaler, Helen **6** 56-57
Newman, Barnett **11** 365
Rothko, Mark **13** 320-321
Smith, David **14** 287-288

Motion (physics)
Alembert, Jean le Rond d' **1** 127-128
Galileo Galilei **6** 180-183
Hamilton, William Rowan **7** 99-100
Huygens, Christiaan **8** 79-81
Newton, Isaac **11** 369-372
Tartaglia, Niccolo **15** 111-112

Motion Picture Association of America
Valenti, Jack Joseph **15** 401-403

Motion pictures (Africa)
Cissé, Souleymane **4** 65-66
Faye, Safi **5** 400-401
Kawawa, Rashidi Mfaume **8** 464-465
Ousmane, Sembene **12** 32-33

Motion pictures (Asia)
Kurosawa, Akira **9** 135-137
Ray, Satyajit **13** 60-61

Motion pictures (Canada)
Grierson, John **6** 542-543

Motion pictures (Europe)
Ambler, Eric **1** 191-192
Bergman, Ernst Ingmar **2** 190-191
Eisenstein, Sergei Mikhailovich **5** 240-242
Lang, Fritz **9** 190-192
Lubitsch, Ernst **10** 18-19
Olivier, Laurence **11** 502-503
Prokofiev, Sergei Sergeevich **12** 458-460
Riefenstahl, Leni **13** 161-163
Truffaut, François **15** 311-313

Motion pictures (United States)
abstract cinema
Richter, Hans **13** 149-150
African American involvement

Davis, Ossie **4** 421-422
comedy
Benchley, Robert **2** 150-151
Brice, Fanny **3** 1-2
Chaplin, Charles Spencer **3** 438-440
Fields, W. C. **5** 444
Grant, Cary **6** 490-492
Goldberg, Whoopi **6** 398-402
Hope, Bob **7** 487-489
Marx brothers **10** 303-304
Sennett, Mack **14** 108-109
computer animation
Jobs, Steven **8** 265-267
development
Edison, Thomas Alva **5** 206-208
Ford, John **6** 7-8
Griffith, David Wark **6** 544-545
Lumière Brothers, The **10** 41-43
Peale, Charles Willson **12** 169-171
directors
Hitchcock, Alfred **7** 415-416
Kelly, Gene **8** 484-486
documentaries
Flaherty, Robert **5** 476-477
Flanagan, Hallie **5** 478-479
Wiseman, Frederick **16** 345-346
experimental
Cornell, Joseph **4** 237-238
Richter, Hans **13** 149-150
filmmakers
Allen, Woody **1** 169-171
Capra, Frank **3** 276-278
Lang, Fritz **9** 190-192
Lee, Spike **9** 295-299
Smithson, Robert **14** 301-303
Stone, Oliver **14** 472-475
Valdez, Luis **15** 399-400
musicals
Garland, Judy **6** 218-219
Kelly, Gene **8** 484-486
producers
Cousteau, Jacques-Yves **4** 276-277
DeMille, Cecil Blount **4** 488-490
Hughes, Howard Robard **8** 16-17
Loew, Marcus **9** 485-486
psychological realism
Kazan, Elia **8** 465-466
ratings system
Valenti, Jack Joseph **15** 401-403
roles for African Americans
Goldberg, Whoopi **6** 398-402
McDaniel, Hattie **10** 405-408
McQueen, Butterfly **10** 434-437
Poitier, Sidney **12** 368-370
roles for Asian Americans
Wong, Anna May **16** 366-367
roles for Native Americans
Greene, Graham **6** 524-525
Studi, Wes **15** 1-2
screenwriters
Angelou, Maya **1** 238-239
Hinton, Susan Eloise **7** 406-407
Mamet, David Alan **10** 181-182
silents
Chaplin, Charles Spencer **3** 438-440

DeMille, Cecil Blount **4** 488-490
Fields, W. C. **5** 444
Griffith, David Wark **6** 544-545
Houdini, Harry **7** 514-516
Sennett, Mack **14** 108-109
Wong, Anna May **16** 366-367
subjects of
Hearst, Patricia **7** 242-243
"talkies" and after
Anderson, Judith **1** 215-216
Bogart, Humphrey **2** 363-364
Brando, Marlon **2** 497-499
Burton, Richard **3** 163-164
Cohan, George Michael **4** 137-138
Crosby, Harry Lillis **4** 324-326
Dean, James **4** 433-434
DeMille, Cecil Blount **4** 488-490
Disney, Walter Elias **5** 26-27
Gable, William Clark **6** 157-158
Garbo, Greta **6** 205-207
Goldberg, Whoopi **6** 398-402
Goldwyn, Samuel **6** 416
Hayworth, Rita **7** 233-235
Hepburn, Audrey **7** 314-316
Jones, James Earl **8** 334-337
Lang, Fritz **9** 190-192
Monroe, Marilyn **11** 113-114
Olivier, Laurence **11** 502-503
Presley, Elvis Aron **12** 441-442
Rivers, Larry **13** 186-187
Sinatra, Francis Albert **14** 246-248
Taylor, Elizabeth Rosemond **15** 124-125
Tracy, Spencer Bonaventure **15** 289-290
Wayne, John **16** 150-151
theater chains
Loew, Marcus **9** 485-486
westerns
Eastwood, Clint **5** 188-190

Motivation (psychology)
Bleuler, Eugen **2** 325
Hull, Clark Leonard **8** 28
Thomas, William Isaac **15** 193
Tolman, Edward Chace **15** 261-262

Motke the Thief (play)
Asch, Shalom **1** 325-326

MOTLEY, JOHN LOTHROP (1814-1877),
American historian and diplomat **11** 211-212
Bancroft, George **1** 483-484
Holmes, Oliver Wendell **7** 457-458

Motley Stories (book)
Chekhov, Anton Pavlovich **3** 494-497

Motokiyo, Zeami
see Zeami, Kanze

Motor, electric
Tesla, Nikola **15** 156-157

Motor nerves (neurophysiology)
Adrian, Edgar Douglas **1** 67-69
Dale, Henry Hallett **4** 371-373
Sherrington, Charles Scott **14** 187-189

Motown Record Corporation
Gordy, Berry Jr. **6** 450-451
Jackson, Michael Joe **8** 178-180

MOTT, JOHN R. (1865-1955), American Protestant leader **11** 212

MOTT, LUCRETIA COFFIN (1793-1880), American feminist and abolitionist **11** 212-213

Moulin de la Galette (painting)
Picasso, Pablo **12** 292-295
Renoir, Pierre Auguste **13** 101-102

MOUNT, WILLIAM SIDNEY (1807-1868), American painter **11** 213-214

Mount Holyoke Female Seminary (South Hadley, Massachusetts)
Lyon, Mary **10** 67-69

Mount Lu (monastery; China)
Hui-yüan **8** 25-26

Mount Rushmore National Memorial (South Dakota)
Borglum, John Gutzon de la Mothe **2** 416-417

Mount Vernon Convention (1785)
Chase, Samuel **3** 475-476
Mason, George **10** 319-320

Mount Wilson Observatory (Pasadena, California)
Goddard, Robert Hutchings **6** 376-377
Hale, George Ellery **7** 72-74
Hubble, Edwin Powell **8** 10-11
Kapteyn, Jacobus Cornelis **8** 436-437
Shapley, Harlow **14** 155-156

Mountain (French politics)
Marat, Jean Paul **10** 230-231
Robespierre, Maximilien François Marie Isidore de **13** 199-201

Mountain Giants, The (play)
Pirandello, Luigi **12** 319-321

Mountain Interval (literary collection)
Frost, Robert Lee **6** 130-133

Mountain men
see Frontiersmen—explorers and guides

Mountain Scenery with River Lodge (painting)
Ni Tsan **11** 400

Mountain Woman (sculpture)
Nevelson, Louise **11** 356-357

Mountains and Sea (painting; Frankenthaler)
Frankenthaler, Helen **6** 56-57
Noland, Kenneth **11** 418-419

Mountbatten of Burma, Louis Mountbatten, 1st Earl (1900-1979), English admiral and viceroy of India
Gandhi, Mohandas Karamchand **6** 201-204
Nehru, Jawaharlal **11** 332-334
Rajagopalachari, Chakravarti **13** 6-7

Mountjoy, 8th Baron (Charles Blount, Earl of Devonshire; 1563-1606), English soldier
Elizabeth I **5** 263-266

Mourides (Islamic sect)
Bamba, Amadou **1** 481-482

Mourning Becomes Electra (play)
O'Neill, Eugene **11** 514-516

Mourning Bride, The (play)
Congreve, William **4** 200-201

Mourning Music (musical composition)
Lutoslawski, Witold **10** 52-53

Mourning Symphony (musical composition)
Haydn, Franz Joseph **7** 219-221

Mousequetaire, Le (newspaper)
Dumas, Alexandre **5** 136-138

Mousetrap, The (play)
Christie, Agatha **4** 25-26

Mouth of the Thames... (painting)
Constable, John **4** 208-209

Mouton, Jean (circa 1475-1522), French composer
Willaert, Adrian **16** 287-288

Mouvement (poem)
Rimbaud, Jean Nicolas Arthur **13** 172-174

Mouvement Démocratique Dahoméen
Apithy, Sourou Migan **1** 259-260

Mouvement National Congolais
Lumumba, Patrice Emery **10** 43-45
Tshombe, Moïse Kapenda **15** 325-326

Mouvement perpétuel (poems)
Aragon, Louis **1** 271-272

Mouvement Populaire de la Révolution (political organization; Congo)
Mobutu Sese Seko **11** 69-71

Movement for Assemblies of the People (Grenada)
Bishop, Maurice **2** 292-293

Movement for the Triumph of Democratic Liberties
Ben Bella, Ahmed **2** 148-149

Movement of Moroccan Action
Allal al-Fassi, Mohamed **1** 162

Movement of the Deprived (Harakat al-Mahrumin; Lebanon)
Sadr, Musa al- **13** 420-422

Movement of the Revolutionary Left (Bolivia)
Paz Zamora, Jaime **12** 165-167

Movies
see Motion pictures

Movimento Laureati Cattolici (established 1931)
Paul VI **12** 146-148

Movimento Popular de Libertaçao de Angola (MPLA; freedom movement, Africa)
de Andrade, Mario **4** 434-435

Mowbray, Thomas
see Norfolk, 1st Duke of

Mowing (poem)
Frost, Robert Lee **6** 130-133

Moxon, Edward (1801-1858), English publisher
Lamb, Charles **9** 176-177

MOYERS, BILLY DON ("Bill"; born 1934), television journalist, author, and press secretary to president Lyndon B. Johnson **11** 214-216

MOYNIHAN, DANIEL PATRICK ("Pat"; born 1927), United States senator from New York **11** 216-218

Mozambique (People's Republic of Mozambique; former Portuguese province, East Africa)
Camoëns, Luis Vaz de **3** 247-249
Chissano, Joaquim Alberto **4** 9-11
Craveirinha, José **4** 297-299
dos Santos, Marcelino **5** 72-74
Gama, Vasco da **6** 196-198
Holmes, Arthur **7** 455-456
Machel, Samora Moises **10** 94-96
Mondlane, Eduardo Chivambo **11** 100-101
Salazar, António de Oliveira **13** 442-443

Mozambique Liberation Front (established 1962)
Chissano, Joaquim Alberto **4** 9-11
dos Santos, Marcelino **5** 72-74
Machel, Samora Moises **10** 94-96
Mondlane, Eduardo Chivambo **11** 100-101

Mozart, Leopold (1719-1787), Austrian violinist, composer, and teacher
Bach, Carl Philipp Emanuel **1** 414-415
Corelli, Arcangelo **4** 230-231
Mozart, Wolfgang Amadeus **11** 218-221
Tartini, Giuseppe **15** 112-113

MOZART, WOLFGANG AMADEUS (1756-1791), Austrian composer **11** 218-221
influence of
Beethoven, Ludwig van **2** 114-117
Dallapiccola, Luigi **4** 377-378
Haydn, Franz Joseph **7** 219-221
Poulenc, Francis **12** 414-415
Schumann, Robert Alexander **14** 41-43
Stravinsky, Igor Fedorovich **14** 502-506, 251
influenced by
Bach, Johann Christian **1** 415-416
interpretations
Barenboim, Daniel **2** 3-4
Chopin, Frédéric François **4** 16-18
Mahler, Gustav **10** 144-145
Paganini, Niccolo **12** 58-59

Mozart and Salieri (play)
Pushkin, Aleksandr Sergeevich **12** 489-491

Mozee, Phoebe Anne Oakley
see Oakley, Annie

Mpande (died 1872), king of Zululand
1840-1872
　Cetshwayo **3** 400
　Dingane **5** 14-15
　Pretorius, Andries **12** 444-445

MPHAHLELE, EZEKIEL (a.k.a. Bruno Eseki;
born 1919), South African author and
scholar **11** 221-223

MQHAYI, SAMUEL EDWARD KRUNE
(1875-1945), South African novelist and
poet **11** 223
　Dube, John Langalibalele **5** 113

MS. Found in a Bottle (story)
　Poe, Edgar Allan **12** 363-365

Ms. magazine
　Steinem, Gloria **14** 418-419

M'Taggart, J.M.E.
　see McTaggart, J.M.E.

Mtsyri (poem)
　Lermontov, Mikhail Yurievich
　9 352-353

Mu-ch'i (flourished 1250-79), Chinese
painter and monk
　Hsia Kuei **8** 4-5
　Sesshu, Toya **14** 116-117

MUAWIYA IBN ABU SUFYAN (died 680),
Umayyad caliph **11** 223-224
　Ali **1** 155-156

MUBARAK, HOSNI (born 1928), president
of Egypt **11** 225-226

Much Ado about Nothing (play; Shake-
speare)
　Berlioz, Louis Hector **2** 203-205
　Shakespeare, William **14** 142-145

Muckraking (United States journalism)
　Baker, Ray Stannard **1** 451-452
　Bly, Nellie **2** 346-348
　Dunne, Finley Peter **5** 147-148
　Gladden, Washington **6** 356-357
　Hapgood, Norman **7** 137-138
　Lawson, Thomas William **9** 255-256
　Lindsey, Benjamin Barr **9** 425-426
　McClure, Samuel Sidney **10** 398-399
　Norris, Benjamin Franklin Jr.
　11 427-428
　Phillips, David Graham **12** 280-281
　Rockefeller, John Davison **13** 226-228
　Russell, Charles Edward **13** 374-375
　Sinclair, Upton Beale Jr. **14** 248-249
　Steffens, Lincoln **14** 410-411
　Tarbell, Ida Minerva **15** 107-108

Mudarse por mejorarse (play)
　Alarcón, Pedro Antonio de **1** 100-101

Mudros armistice (1918)
　Atatürk, Ghazi Mustapha Kemal
　1 356-357

Mueller
　see Müller

MUELLER, OTTO (1874-1930), German
expressionist painter **11** 226-227

Muerte de Artemio Cruz, La (novel)
　Fuentes, Carlos **6** 141-142

Muffat, Georg (circa 1645-1704), German
composer and organist
　Corelli, Arcangelo **4** 230-231

Mufti of Jerusalem
　see Husagni, Al-Hajj Amin Al-

MUGABE, ROBERT GABRIEL (born 1924),
Zimbabwe's first elected black prime
minister **11** 227-229
　Nkomo, Joshua Mqabuko **11** 405-407

Mugwumps (United States politics)
　Cleveland, Stephen Grover **4** 108-110
　Curtis, George William **4** 349-350
　Godkin, Edwin Lawrence **6** 380
　Schurz, Carl **14** 44-45

Muhammad
　see also Mohammed

Muhammad (flourished 8th century),
Hasanite claimant to caliphate
　Mansur, Abu Jafar ibn Muhammad al-
　10 214-215

Muhammad V (1334-1391), Moslem king
of Granada 1354-1391
　ibn Khaldun, Abd al-Rahman ibn
　Muhammad **8** 93-94

Muhammad, Ala ud-Din (ruled
1199-1220), shah of Khiva
　Genghis Khan **6** 263-265

MUHAMMAD, ELIJAH (Poole;
1897-1975), leader of the Nation of Islam
("Black Muslims") **11** 230-231
　Malcolm X **10** 165-166

Muhammad Bengan (Bengan Korei; ruled
1531-1537), ruler of West African Songhay empire
　Muhammad, Elijah **11** 230-231

MUHAMMAD BIN TUGHLUQ (ruled
1325-1351), Moslem sultan of Delhi
11 229
　ibn Battuta, Muhammad **8** 91-92

Muhammad ibn Daud
　see Alp Arslan

Muhammad Shah (1877-1957)
　see Aga Khan III

MUHAMMAD TURE, ASKIA (circa
1443-1538), ruler of the West African
Songhay empire **11** 231-232
　Ali, Sunni **1** 158-159

Muhammedans
　see Islam; Islamic Empire

Muhibbi
　see Suleiman I

Mühlberg, battle of (1547)
　Alba, Duke of **1** 103-104
　Charles V **3** 457-459

MÜHLENBERG, HEINRICH MELCHIOR
(1711-1787), German-born American
Lutheran clergyman **11** 232-233
　Muhlenberg, William Augustus
　11 233-234

MUHLENBERG, WILLIAM AUGUSTUS
(1796-1877); American Episcopalian clergyman **11** 233-234

Mühlfeld, Richard (1856-1907), German
clarinetist
　Brahms, Johannes **2** 490-492

Mühlfrauen (Bohemia)
　Maulbertsch, Franz Anton **10** 345

Muiopotmus (poem)
　Spenser, Edmund **14** 373-376

MUIR, JOHN (1838-1914), American naturalist **11** 234

MUJIBUR RAHMAN, SHEIK (1920-1975),
Bengal leader who helped found
Bangladesh **11** 234-236

Mukden, battle of (1948)
　Lin Piao **9** 429-430

Muktafi, al- (ruled 902-907), Abbasid
caliph
　Razi **13** 63-64

Mulata (novel)
　Asturias, Miguel Angel **1** 354-355

Mulatto (play)
　Hughes, Langston **8** 18-19

Mulcaster, Richard (circa 1530-1611), English educator
　Spenser, Edmund **14** 373-376

MULDOWNEY, SHIRLEY (born ca. 1940),
American race car driver **11** 236-238

Mulele, Pierre (died 1968), Congolese
rebel leader
　Mobutu Sese Seko **11** 69-71

Mülich, Hans (1515-1573), German
painter
　Lassus, Roland de **9** 216-218

Müller, George Elias (1850-1934), German
psychologist
　Fechner, Gustav Theodor **5** 401-402
　Lotze, Rudolf Hermann **9** 521-522

MULLER, HERMANN JOSEPH
(1890-1967), American geneticist
11 238-239
　East, Edward Murray **5** 182-183
　Watson, James Dewey **16** 137-138

Müller, Johann
　see Regiomontanus

MÜLLER, JOHANNES PETER (1801-1858),
German physiologist and anatomist
11 239-240
　Du Bois-Reymond, Emil **5** 118-119
　Helmholtz, Hermann Ludwig Ferdinand
　von **7** 268-269
　Schwann, Theodor **14** 51-52
　Virchow, Rudolf Ludwig Carl
　15 506-507

MÜLLER, KARL ALEXANDER (born 1927),
Swiss-born solid-state physicist
11 240-241

Müller, Otto (1874-1930), German painter
　Kirchner, Ernst Ludwig **9** 34-35

MÜLLER, PAUL HERMANN (1899-1965),
Swiss chemist **11** 241-242

Müller, Wilhelm (1794-1827), German poet
Schubert, Franz Peter **14** 35-37

Müller-Lieder (ballads)
Goethe, Johann Wolfgang von **6** 388-391

Müllers Archiv (journal)
Du Bois-Reymond, Emil **5** 118-119
Müller, Johannes Peter **11** 239-240

MULRONEY, MARTIN BRIAN (born 1939), prime minister of Canada **11** 242-246

Multiplication of the Arcs (painting)
Tanguy, Yves **15** 101

Mumford, Catherine (1829-1890), English reformer
Booth, William **2** 405-406

MUMFORD, LEWIS (1895-1990), American social philosopher and architectural critic **11** 246-247
Geddes, Patrick **6** 246-247

Mummy and the Mockingbird, The (play)
Barrymores **2** 28-30

Mumtaz Mahal (1592-1631), empress of India
Shah Jahan **14** 138-139

Mumu (story)
Turgenev, Ivan Sergeyevich **15** 345-348

Mun Sun
see Yi Hwang

MUNCH, EDVARD (1863-1944), Norwegian painter and graphic artist **11** 247-248
Beckmann, Max **2** 104-105
Böcklin, Arnold **2** 354-355
Ensor, James **5** 289-290
Kirchner, Ernst Ludwig **9** 34-35
Nolde, Emil **11** 419-420
Van Gogh, Vincent **15** 427-429

Munda, battle of (45 B.C.)
Caesar, Gaius Julius **3** 207-210

Munday, Anthony (1560-1633), English poet and playwright
Webster, John **16** 164

MUNDELEIN, GEORGE WILLIAM (1872-1939), American Roman Catholic cardinal **11** 248-249
Cabrini, Frances Xavier **3** 205

Mundinus
see Mondino de' Luzzi

Mungenast, Joseph (died 1741), Austrian architect
Prandtauer, Jakob **12** 432

Munich (city; Germany)
Cuvilliés, François **4** 359-360
Frederick I **6** 78-79
Frisch, Karl von **6** 117-118
Gustavus II **7** 43-45
Hitler, Adolf **7** 417-420
Vogel, Hans-Jochen **16** 8-9
Zimmermann, Johann Baptist and Domenikus **16** 518

Munich, University of
Boltzmann, Ludwig **2** 379-380
Döllinger, Josef Ignaz von **5** 47-48
Fischer, Hans **5** 457-459
Haushofer, Karl **7** 201
Heisenberg, Werner Karl **7** 261-263
Ohm, Georg Simon **11** 486-487
Planck, Max Karl Ernst Ludwig **12** 342-344
Röntgen, Wilhelm Conrad **13** 273-275
Schelling, Friedrich Wilhelm Joseph von **13** 526-527
Voegelin, Eric **16** 6-8

Munich Conference (1938)
Beneš, Edward **2** 155-157
Chamberlain, Arthur Neville **3** 409-411
Daladier, Édouard **4** 369
Hitler, Adolf **7** 417-420
Horthy de Nagybánya, Nicholas **7** 510-512

Municipal Corporation Act (England; 1835)
Russell, John **13** 380-381

Municipal government
Bradley, Tom **2** 484-485
Byrne, Jane **3** 190-191
Cisneros, Henry G. **4** 62-64
Daley, Richard J. **4** 373-375
Eaton, Dorman Bridgman **5** 190-191
Feinstein, Dianne **5** 407-408
Fustel de Coulanges, Numa Denis **6** 155
Gladden, Washington **6** 356-357
Hague, Frank **7** 63-64
Jones, Samuel Milton **8** 342-343
Koch, Edward I. **9** 68-69
Lindsay, John Vliet **9** 423-424
Low, Seth **10** 11-12
Parsons, Frank **12** 121-122
Riis, Jacob August **13** 169-170
Steffens, Lincoln **14** 410-411
Tweed, William Marcy **15** 366-367
White, Kevin H. **16** 231-232
Young, Andrew Jackson Jr. **16** 467-469
Young, Coleman Alexander **16** 470-471
see also Political machines; Statesmen—mayors

Municipal Stadium (Florence)
Nervi, Pier Luigi **11** 346-348

Munitions
see Weapons and explosives

Munjong (died 1452), king of Korea 1450-1452
Sejo **14** 90-91
Sejong **14** 91-92

Munn v. Illinois (legal case)
Field, Stephen Johnson **5** 441-442
Waite, Morrison Remick **16** 46

Munongo, Godefroid (born 1930), Congolese politician
Lumumba, Patrice Emery **10** 43-45

MUÑOZ MARÍN, JOSÉ LUÍS ALBERTO (1898-1980), Puerto Rican political leader **11** 249-250
Hernández Colón, Rafael **7** 329-330

MUÑOZ RIVERA, LUÍS (1859-1916), Puerto Rican political leader **11** 250

Munroe, Harriet (1860-1936), American poet and critic
Rabindranath Tagore **12** 529-531

MUNSEY, FRANK ANDREW (1854-1925), American publisher **11** 251

Munson-Williams-Proctor Institute (Utica, New York)
Johnson, Philip **8** 313-314

Münster, Treaty of (1648)
Condé, Prince de **4** 193-194

Münster, University of
Barth, Karl **2** 31-32
Domagk, Gerhard Johannes Paul **5** 48-50
Rahner, Karl **13** 4-5

Münter, Gabriele (1877-1962), German painter
Kandinsky, Wassily **8** 420-422
Marc, Franz **10** 231

MÜNZER, THOMAS (1489?-1525), German Protestant reformer **11** 251-252
John of Leiden **8** 283
Karlstadt, Andreas Bodenheim von **8** 449
Luther, Martin **10** 48-51

Muqtafi, al-
see Muktafi, al-

Murabi-tun, al-
see Almoravids

Murad II (1403?-1451), Ottoman sultan 1421-1451
Hunyadi, John **8** 51-52
Mehmed the Conqueror **10** 452-454

Murad IV (1609-1640), Ottoman sultan 1623-1640
Lucaris, Cyril **10** 20

Murad V (1840-1904), Ottoman sultan 1876
Abdul-Hamid II **1** 17-18

MURASAKI SHIKIBU (circa 976-circa 1031), Japanese writer **11** 252-253
Tanizaki, Junichiro **15** 101-102

Murasaki Ue (literary character)
Murasaki Shikibu **11** 252-253

MURAT, JOACHIM (1767-1815), French marshal, king of Naples 1808-1815 **11** 253-254
Fouché, Joseph **6** 30-31

MURATORI, LODOVICO ANTONIO (1672-1750), Italian historian and antiquary **11** 254-255

Murchehkhor, battle of (1729)
Nader, Ralph **11** 290-291

MURCHISON, SIR RODERICK IMPEY
(1792-1871), British geologist
11 255-256
Sedgwick, Adam **14** 82-83

Murder in the Cathedral (play; Eliot)
Eliot, Thomas Stearns **5** 258-261
John, XXIII **8** 277-280

Murder of Lidice, The (book)
Millay, Edna St. Vincent **11** 24-25

Murder victims
Assyria
Sennacherib **14** 108
China
An Lu-shan **1** 239-240
Chia Ssu-tao **3** 514-515
Congo
Lumumba, Patrice Emery **10** 43-45
El Salvador
Romero, Oscar **13** 265-267
England
Cook, James **4** 214-215
Edward II **5** 210
Henry VI **7** 298-299
Germany
Erzberger, Matthias **5** 319-320
Luxemburg, Rosa **10** 55-56
Winckelmann, Johann Joachim
16 332-333
Italy
Rienzi, Cola di **13** 166-167
Macedonia
Seleucus I **14** 92-93
Persia
Xerxes **16** 420
Peru
Manco Capac **10** 184-185
Philippines
Aquino, Benigno **1** 267-268
Saudi Arabia
Faisal ibn Abd al Aziz ibn Saud
5 371-372
Scotland
James I **8** 206-207
South Africa
First, Ruth **5** 453-454
United States
Dillinger, John **5** 9
Ford, Paul Leicester **6** 9-10
Lovejoy, Elijah Parish **10** 6-7
Smith, Joseph **14** 297-298
Wythe, George **16** 415
Vietnam
Diem, Ngo Dinh **5** 6-7
see also Assassinations; Executions

Murders in the Rue Morgue, The (story)
Poe, Edgar Allan **12** 363-365

MURDOCH, JEAN IRIS (born 1919),
British novelist **11** 256-257

MURDOCH, RUPERT (born 1931), Australian newspaper publisher **11** 257-258

Muret, Marc Antoine (1526-1585), French
poet and scholar
Montaigne, Michel Eyquem de
11 116-117

MURILLO, BARTOLOMÉ ESTEBAN
(1617-1682), Spanish painter **11** 258-259
Gainsborough, Thomas **6** 170-172
Ribera, Jusepe de **13** 122-123
Velázquez, Diego Rodríguez de Silva y
15 454-456
Zurbarán, Francisco de **16** 534-535

Murjebi, Hamed bin Mohammed el
see Tippu Tip

Muromachi shogunate
see Japan—1338-1573 (Ashikaga
shogunate)

Murphy (novel)
Beckett, Samuel **2** 102-104

MURPHY, CHARLES FRANCIS
(1858-1924), American politician
11 259-260

MURPHY, FRANK (1890-1949), American
jurist and diplomat **11** 260-261

Murphy, Gardner (1895-1979), American
psychologist
Erikson, Erik Homburger **5** 309-310

Murphy, William Parry (1892-1987), American physician
Whipple, George Hoyt **16** 224-225

Murray, Gilbert (1886-1957), British classical scholar
Lucian **10** 25-26

MURRAY, JAMES (1721-1794), British general **11** 261-262

Murray, John (1732-1809)
see Dunmore, 4th Earl of

Murray, John (1778-1843), English publisher
Disraeli, Benjamin **5** 27-29

MURRAY, LESLIE ALLAN (born 1938), Australian poet and literary critic **11** 262-263

MURRAY, PHILIP (1886-1952), American
labor leader **11** 264-265
Dubinsky, David **5** 114-115

Murrone, Pietro di
see Celestine V

MURROW, EDWARD ROSCOE
(1908-1965), American radio and television news broadcaster **11** 265-266

Murry, John Middleton (1889-1957), English writer
Huxley, Aldous Leonard **8** 74-75

Musa, Askia (died 1531), ruler of the West
African Songhay empire 1528-1531
Muhammad, Elijah **11** 230-231

MUSA MANSA (died 1337), king of the
Mali empire in West Africa ca.
1312-1337 **11** 266

Musae Sioniae (musical composition)
Praetorius, Michael **12** 431-432

Musaf (Jewish prayers)
Abba Arika **1** 3-4

Musar movement (Judaism)
Kuk, Abraham Issac **9** 123-124

**Musarion oder die Philosophie der Gra-
zien** (novel)
Wieland, Christoph Martin **16** 260-261

Musaylima (died 633), Arab leader in "wars
of the apostasy"
Abu Bakr **1** 31-32

Muscat and Oman
see Oman

Muscle (physiology)
Adrian, Edgar Douglas **1** 67-69
Bernard, Claude **2** 208-210
Dale, Henry Hallett **4** 371-373
Du Bois-Reymond, Emil **5** 118-119
Hill, Archibald Vivian **7** 385-386
Meyerhof, Otto Fritz **10** 537-539
Reichstein, Tadeus **13** 85-87
Schwann, Theodor **14** 51-52
Sherrington, Charles Scott **14** 187-189
Swammerdam, Jan **15** 48-49
Szent-Györgyi, Albert von **15** 62-64

Muscle Shoals dams (Alabama)
Black, Hugo Lafayette **2** 301-303
Hoover, Herbert Clark **7** 483-485
Norris, George William **11** 428-429

Muscovy Co. (trade firm)
Baffin, William **1** 435-436
Cabot, Sebastian **3** 200-201
Chancellor, Richard **3** 422
Hudson, Henry **8** 12-13
Ivan IV **8** 157-159

Muscular Christianity (philosophy)
Kingsley, Charles **9** 28

Muscular Dynamics (painting)
Boccioni, Umberto **2** 353-354

Muse française (review)
Hugo, Victor Marie **8** 22-25

Musée Grévin, Le (poems)
Aragon, Louis **1** 271-272

Museo Civico (Vicenza, Italy)
Palladio, Andrea **12** 75-77

Muses galantes, Les (opera)
Rousseau, Jean Jacques **13** 324-328

Muséum National d'histoire Naturelle
(Paris)
Agassiz, Jean Louis Rodolphe **1** 76-78
Becquerel, Antoine Henri **2** 108-109
Buffon, Comte de **3** 109-111
Cuvier, Georges Léopold **4** 357-359
Lamarck, Chevalier de **9** 171-173

Museum of Modern Art (New York City)
Cage, John **3** 211-214
Calder, Alexander **3** 216-218
Johnson, Philip **8** 313-314
Kirstein, Lincoln **9** 39-41
Pevsner, Antoine **12** 263-264
Rothko, Mark **13** 320-321
Steichen, Edward **14** 411-412
Stella, Frank **14** 420-422

Museum of National History (Mexico)
Revillagigedo, Conde de **13** 111-112

Museum of Natural History (Paris)
see Muśeum National d'Histoire
Naturelle

MUSGRAVE, THEA (born 1928),
Scottish-born composer **11** 266-268

Mushet, Robert Forester (1811-1891), English metallurgist
Bessemer, Henry **2** 235-236

Music
education
Dawson, William Levi **4** 427-428
Dett, Robert Nathaniel **4** 512
Jaques-Dalcroze, Emile **8** 221-222
Kodály, Zoltán **9** 71
Mason, Lowell **10** 321-322
Paine, John Knowles **12** 65
Parker, Horatio William **12** 109
Shapey, Ralph **14** 154-155
Tal, Josef **15** 85-86
Thomas, Theodore **15** 192-193
experimental forms
Reich, Steve **13** 84-85
festivals
Gottschalk, Louis Moreau
6 463-464
notation
Ben-Haim, Paul **2** 161-162
Bussotti, Sylvano **3** 174-175
Cage, John **3** 211-214
Franco of Cologne **6** 52
Guido d'Arezzo **7** 33
Léonin **9** 343-344
publishing
Beethoven, Ludwig van **2** 114-117
Byrd, William **3** 187-188
theory
Bach, Carl Philipp Emanuel
1 414-415
Franco of Cologne **6** 52
Fux, Johann Joseph **6** 155-156
Guido d'Arezzo **7** 33
Perle, George **12** 223-224
Praetorius, Michael **12** 431-432
Ptolemy, Claudius **12** 473-474
Pythagoras **12** 498-499
Rameau, Jean Philippe **13** 17-18
Tartini, Giuseppe **15** 112-113
Zarlino, Gioseffo **16** 490-491
see also Musicians; Sacred music;
and individual countries (American music, etc.), forms, and styles

Music (painting)
Matisse, Henri **10** 336-337

Music Box Revues (musical)
Berlin, Irving **2** 200-201

Music for Youth (musical composition)
Hindemith, Paul **7** 399-400

Music in the Air (musical)
Kern, Jerome David **8** 517-518

Music in the Tuileries (painting)
Manet, Édouard **10** 193-194

Music Lesson (painting)
Renoir, Pierre Auguste **13** 101-102

Ter Borch, Gerard **15** 146

Music of Changes (musical composition)
Cage, John **3** 211-214

Music Room, The (film)
Ray, Satyajit **13** 60-61

Musica Indians
see Chibcha Indians

Musical comedy (United States)
Berlin, Irving **2** 200-201
Bernstein, Leonard **2** 218-219
Gershwin, George **6** 284-285
Kern, Jerome David **8** 517-518
Rodgers, Richard Charles **13** 234-236
Ziegfeld, Florenz **16** 516-517

Musical Party (painting)
Watteau, Antoine **16** 143-144

Musical theater
see Ballet; Modern dance; Musical
comedy; Opera; Operetta

Musicals (England)
Webber, Andrew Lloyd **16** 155-156

Musicals (United States)
choreographers
Astaire, Fred **1** 348-350
de Mille, Agnes **4** 486-488
Holm, Hanya **7** 454-455
Kelly, Gene **8** 484-486
Robbins, Jerome **13** 190-192
Tharp, Twyla **15** 164-165
directors
Robbins, Jerome **13** 190-192
librettists/lyricists
Hammerstein, Oscar Clendenning II
7 104-106
producers
Sondheim, Stephen **14** 337-338
stars
Astaire, Fred **1** 348-350
Garland, Judy **6** 218-219
Kelly, Gene **8** 484-486
Lahr, Bert **9** 167-168
Martin, Mary **10** 292-293

Musicians, American
bandleaders
Basie **2** 48-49
Brubeck, Dave **3** 59-61
Calloway, Cab **3** 236-238
Davis, Miles **4** 419-421
Fitzgerald, Ella **5** 468-469
Gillespie, Dizzy **6** 320-322
Goodman, Benny **6** 436-438
Handy, William Christopher
7 123-124
Jordan, Louis **8** 353-355
Puente, Tito **12** 476-477
Sousa, John Philip **14** 353-354
Waller, Thomas Wright **16** 81-82
Waters, Muddy **16** 134-136
clarinetists
Goodman, Benny **6** 436-438
composers (18th century)
Beissel, Johann Conrad **2** 123-124
Billings, William **2** 274-275

Hopkinson, Francis **7** 496-497
composers (19th-20th century)
Foster, Stephen Collins **6** 25-27
Fry, William Henry **6** 136-137
Gottschalk, Louis Moreau
6 463-464
Heinrich, Anthony Philip **7** 261
Joplin, Scott **8** 345-347
MacDowell, Edward Alexander
10 87-88
Mason, Lowell **10** 321-322
Paine, John Knowles **12** 65
Parker, Horatio William **12** 109
Payne, John Howard **12** 159
Sousa, John Philip **14** 353-354
composers (20th century)
Babbitt, Milton **1** 410
Barber, Samuel **1** 500-501
Berio, Luciano **2** 194-195
Berlin, Irving **2** 200-201
Bernstein, Leonard **2** 218-219
Bevel, James Luther **2** 250-251
Bloch, Ernest **2** 326-327
Brubeck, Dave **3** 59-61
Cage, John **3** 211-214
Carter, Elliott Cook Jr. **3** 338-339
Charles, Ray **3** 469-470
Cohan, George Michael **4** 137-138
Coltrane, John **4** 173-174
Copland, Aaron **4** 227-228
Cowell, Henry Dixon **4** 280-281
Crumb, George **4** 326-328
Davis, Miles **4** 419-421
Dawson, William Levi **4** 427-428
Dett, Robert Nathaniel **4** 512
Diamond, David **4** 527-529
Ellington, Edward Kennedy
5 273-274
Floyd, Carlisle **5** 494-496
Gershwin, George **6** 284-285
Gillespie, Dizzy **6** 320-322
Glass, Philip **6** 362-364
Griffes, Charles Tomlinson
6 543-544
Guthrie, Woodrow Wilson **7** 51-52
Handy, William Christopher
7 123-124
Hanson, Howard **7** 135-136
Harris, Roy **7** 175-176
Hendrix, Jimi **7** 279-283
Ives, Charles Edward **8** 159-160
Jones, Quincy Delight Jr. **8** 339-341
Kern, Jerome David **8** 517-518
Krenek, Ernst **9** 98-99
Menotti, Gian Carlo **10** 509-510
Monk, Thelonious **11** 104-108
Nin-Culmell, Joaquín María **11** 398
Parker, Charles Christopher Jr.
12 105-106
Perle, George **12** 223-224
Piston, Walter **12** 327-328
Porter, Cole Albert **12** 405-406
Puente, Tito **12** 476-477
Reich, Steve **13** 84-85
Rochberg, George **13** 221-222

Rodgers, Richard Charles **13** 234-236
Rorem, Ned **13** 284-286
Schoenberg, Arnold **14** 24-26
Schuller, Gunther **14** 37-38
Sessions, Roger Huntington **14** 117-118
Shapey, Ralph **14** 154-155
Sondheim, Stephen **14** 337-338
Still, William Grant **14** 455-456
Stravinsky, Igor Fedorovich **14** 502-506
Tcherepnin, Alexander **15** 132-133
Thomson, Virgil **15** 202-203
Tower, Joan **15** 279-281
Varèse, Edgard **15** 432-433
Waller, Thomas Wright **16** 81-82
Weill, Kurt **16** 174-175
Wolpe, Stefan **16** 362-364
Wuorinen, Charles **16** 404
Zwilich, Ellen Taaffe **16** 536-537
concert singers
Battle, Kathleen **2** 59-60
conductors
Bernstein, Leonard **2** 218-219
Caldwell, Sarah **3** 224-226
Dawson, William Levi **4** 427-428
Falletta, JoAnn **5** 373-375
Fiedler, Arthur **5** 437-438
Levine, James **9** 369-371
Nin-Culmell, Joaquín María **11** 398
Schuller, Gunther **14** 37-38
Shapey, Ralph **14** 154-155
Thomas, Theodore **15** 192-193
Thomson, Virgil **15** 202-203
Toscanini, Arturo **15** 270-271
Wolff, Hugh **16** 358-360
Wuorinen, Charles **16** 404
drummers
Shepard, Sam **14** 180-181
folk singers
Cotten, Elizabeth **4** 261-263
Dylan, Bob **5** 170-171
Guthrie, Woodrow Wilson **7** 51-52
Hayes, Roland **7** 225-227
Seeger, Pete **14** 83-84
gospel singers
Caesar, Shirley **3** 210-211
Cleveland, James **4** 106-108
Franklin, Aretha **6** 58-60
guitarists
Cotten, Elizabeth **4** 261-263
Dylan, Bob **5** 170-171
Hendrix, Jimi **7** 279-283
King, B. B. **9** 11-14
Waters, Muddy **16** 134-136
jazz instrumentalists
Jones, Quincy Delight Jr. **8** 339-341
jazz singers
Charles, Ray **3** 469-470
Cole, Nat **4** 149-151
Fitzgerald, Ella **5** 468-469
Holiday, Billie **7** 452-453
Vaughan, Sarah Lois **15** 445-446
Waller, Thomas Wright **16** 81-82

librettists
Hammerstein, Oscar Clendenning II **7** 104-106
lyricists
Calloway, Cab **3** 236-238
Cash, Johnny **3** 353-355
Cleveland, James **4** 106-108
Cotten, Elizabeth **4** 261-263
Dylan, Bob **5** 170-171
Franklin, Aretha **6** 58-60
Hendrix, Jimi **7** 279-283
King, B. B. **9** 11-14
Sondheim, Stephen **14** 337-338
opera singers
Anderson, June **1** 216-218
Anderson, Marian **1** 218-219
Battle, Kathleen **2** 59-60
Caruso, Enrico **3** 345
Norman, Jessye **11** 425-427
Price, Leontyne **12** 446-447
Sills, Beverly **14** 230-231
percussionists
Puente, Tito **12** 476-477
pianists
Ax, Emanuel **1** 391
Basie **2** 48-49
Brubeck, Dave **3** 59-61
Charles, Ray **3** 469-470
Cleveland, James **4** 106-108
Cole, Nat **4** 149-151
Horowitz, Vladimir **7** 509-510
Joplin, Scott **8** 345-347
Levine, James **9** 369-371
Monk, Thelonious **11** 104-108
Nin-Culmell, Joaquín María **11** 398
Perle, George **12** 223-224
Puente, Tito **12** 476-477
Tower, Joan **15** 279-281
Waller, Thomas Wright **16** 81-82
Wuorinen, Charles **16** 404
saxophonists
Coltrane, John **4** 173-174
Hawkins, Coleman **7** 208-210
Jordan, Louis **8** 353-355
Parker, Charles Christopher Jr. **12** 105-106
Young, Lester Willis **16** 471-473
singers
Baker, Josephine **1** 448-451
Brice, Fanny **3** 1-2
Brown, James **3** 37-39
Calloway, Cab **3** 236-238
Cash, Johnny **3** 353-355
Cline, Patsy **4** 110-112
Dylan, Bob **5** 170-171
Hayes, Roland **7** 225-227
Horne, Lena **7** 504-506
Jackson, Michael Joe **8** 178-180
Jessel, George **8** 249-251
Jolson, Al **8** 329-330
King, B. B. **9** 11-14
Madonna **10** 123-125
Presley, Elvis Aron **12** 441-442
Rich, Adrienne **13** 128-130
Ross, Diana **13** 298-300

Sinatra, Francis Albert **14** 246-248
Waters, Muddy **16** 134-136
trumpeters
Armstrong, Louis Daniel **1** 303-304
Davis, Miles **4** 419-421
Gillespie, Dizzy **6** 320-322
see also American music
Musicians, Arabic
Fairuz **5** 368-369
Musicians, Argentine
Ginastera, Alberto Evaristo **6** 328-329
Musicians, Armenian
Khachaturian, Aram Ilich **8** 530-531
Musicians, Austrian
composers (15th-19th century)
Beethoven, Ludwig van **2** 114-117
Bruckner, Joseph Anton **3** 64-65
Fux, Johann Joseph **6** 155-156
Gluck, Christoph Willibald **6** 372-374
Haydn, Franz Joseph **7** 219-221
Hofhaimer, Paul **7** 441
Mozart, Wolfgang Amadeus **11** 218-221
Schubert, Franz Peter **14** 35-37
Strauss, Johann Jr. **14** 498-499
composers (19th-20th century)
Berg, Alban **2** 186-187
Krenek, Ernst **9** 98-99
Mahler, Gustav **10** 144-145
Schoenberg, Arnold **14** 24-26
Webern, Anton **16** 160-162
composers (20th century)
Ligeti, György **9** 406-407
conductors
Fux, Johann Joseph **6** 155-156
Mahler, Gustav **10** 144-145
Webern, Anton **16** 160-162
Musicians, Brazilian
Villa-Lobos, Heitor **15** 496-497
Musicians, Canadian
Gould, Glenn **6** 469-470
Musicians, Czech
Dvořák, Antonin **5** 168-169
Janáček, Leoš **8** 219
Martinu, Bohuslav **10** 299-300
Smetana, Bedřich **14** 281-282
Musicians, Danish
Buxtehude, Dietrich **3** 185-186
Nielsen, Carl August **11** 388-389
Musicians, Dutch
Dufay, Guillaume **5** 125-126
Obrecht, Jacob **11** 457-458
Ockeghem, Johannes **11** 464-465
Sweelinck, Jan Pieterszoon **15** 50-51
Musicians, English
bands
Beatles, The **2** 89-92
composers (15th-18th century)
Arne, Thomas Augustine **1** 307-308
Byrd, William **3** 187-188
Dowland, John **5** 90

Dunstable, John **5** 150-151
Handel, George Frederick
7 116-119
Morley, Thomas **11** 179-180
Purcell, Henry **12** 484-485
Tallis, Thomas **15** 91
composers (19th-20th century)
Bennett, Richard Rodney **2** 172
Britten, Benjamin **3** 10-11
Coward, Noel **4** 279-280
Elgar, Edward **5** 247-248
Holst, Gustav **7** 459-460
Lennon, John Winston **9** 326-328
Sullivan, Arthur Seymour **15** 23
Tippett, Michael Kemp **15** 234-235
Vaughan Williams, Ralph
15 446-447
Walton, William Turner **16** 92-93
Webber, Andrew Lloyd **16** 155-156
conductors
Britten, Benjamin **3** 10-11
Rattle, Simon Denis **13** 49-50
Tippett, Michael Kemp **15** 234-235

Musicians, Finnish
Sibelius, Jean Julius Christian
14 211-212

Musicians, Flemish
Clemens non Papa, Jacobus **4** 101
Isaac, Heinrich **8** 143-144

Musicians, Franco-Flemish
Gombert, Nicolas **6** 416-417
Josquin des Prez **8** 361-363
Lassus, Roland de **9** 216-218
Willaert, Adrian **16** 287-288

Musicians, French
composers (12th-17th century)
Charpentier, Marc Antoine
3 471-472
Goudimel, Claude **6** 466
Le Jeune, Claude **9** 314-315
Léonin **9** 343-344
Lully, Jean Baptiste **10** 40-41
Machaut, Guillaume de **10** 93-94
Pérotin **12** 231-232
Vitry, Philippe de **16** 2
composers (18th-19th century)
Berlioz, Louis Hector **2** 203-205
Bizet, Georges **2** 296-297
Cherubini, Luigi Carlo Zanobi Sal-
vatore Maria **3** 505-506
Chopin, Frédéric François **4** 16-18
Couperin, François **4** 270-271
Franck, César **6** 48-49
Gounod, Charles François
6 473-474
Meyerbeer, Giacomo **10** 536-537
Offenbach, Jacques **11** 478-479
Rameau, Jean Philippe **13** 17-18
Saint-Saëns, Charles Camille
13 435-436
composers (19th-20th century)
Boulez, Pierre **2** 444-445
Debussy, Achille Claude **4** 445-447
Fauré, Gabriel Urbain **5** 397-398
Honegger, Arthur **7** 472-473

Landowski, Marcel **9** 187-188
Messiaen, Olivier **10** 528-529
Milhaud, Darius **11** 17-18
Poulenc, Francis **12** 414-415
Ravel, Maurice Joseph **13** 54-55
Roussel, Albert **13** 328-329
Satie, Erik **13** 494-495
Varèse, Edgard **15** 432-433
Xenakis, Iannis **16** 416-418
composers (20th century)
Sauguet, Henri **13** 497-498
Tcherepnin, Alexander **15** 132-133
conductors
Berlioz, Louis Hector **2** 203-205
Boulez, Pierre **2** 444-445
singers
Baker, Josephine **1** 448-451
Piaf, Edith **12** 285-287

Musicians, German
composers (13th-17th century)
Froberger, Johann Jakob **6** 120-121
Pachelbel, Johann **12** 52
Praetorius, Michael **12** 431-432
Sachs, Hans **13** 410-411
Schütz, Heinrich **14** 48-49
Senfl, Ludwig **14** 105-106
Vogelweide, Walther von der
16 10-11
Walter, Johann **16** 86
composers (18th-19th century)
Bach, Carl Philipp Emanuel
1 414-415
Bach, Johann Christian **1** 415-416
Bach, Johann Sebastian **1** 416-419
Beethoven, Ludwig van **2** 114-117
Brahms, Johannes **2** 490-492
Hoffmann, Ernst Theodor Amadeus
7 439-440
Mendelssohn, Moses **10** 488-489
Meyerbeer, Giacomo **10** 536-537
Schumann, Robert Alexander
14 41-43
Telemann, Georg Philipp
15 137-138
Wagner, Richard **16** 40-43
Weber, Carl Maria Friedrich Ernst
von **16** 156-157
composers (19th-20th century)
Henze, Hans Werner **7** 314
Hindemith, Paul **7** 399-400
Stockhausen, Karlheinz **14** 460-461
Strauss, Richard **14** 500-501
Weill, Kurt **16** 174-175
Wolpe, Stefan **16** 362-364
Zimmermann, Bernd Alois
16 517-518
conductors
Brahms, Johannes **2** 490-492
Mendelssohn, Moses **10** 488-489
Strauss, Richard **14** 500-501
Weber, Carl Maria Friedrich Ernst
von **16** 156-157
opera singers
Behrens, Hildegard **2** 120-121

Musicians, Greek
Xenakis, Iannis **16** 416-418

Musicians, Hungarian
Bartók, Béla **2** 35-36
Kodály, Zoltán **9** 71
Liszt, Franz **9** 445-447

Musicians, Israeli
composers
Ben-Haim, Paul **2** 161-162
conductors
Barenboim, Daniel **2** 3-4
pianists
Barenboim, Daniel **2** 3-4
Tal, Josef **15** 85-86

Musicians, Italian
composers (14th-17th century)
Caccini, Giulio **3** 205-206
Gabrieli, Giovanni **6** 161-162
Gesualdo, Don Carlo **6** 287-288
Landini, Francesco **9** 185-186
Marenzio, Luca **10** 248
Merulo, Claudio **10** 525-526
Monteverdi, Claudio Giovanni
Antonio **11** 126-128
Palestrina, Giovanni Pierluigi da
12 70-72
Willaert, Adrian **16** 287-288
Zarlino, Gioseffo **16** 490-491
composers (17th-19th century)
Carissimi, Giacomo **3** 299-300
Cavalli, Pietro Francesco **3** 382-383
Cesti, Pietro **3** 399-400
Cimarosa, Domenico **4** 61-62
Corelli, Arcangelo **4** 230-231
Frescobaldi, Girolamo **6** 101-102
Pergolesi, Giovanni Battista
12 218-219
Rossi, Luigi **13** 310-311
Scarlatti, Pietro Alessandro Gaspare
13 517-518
Scarlatti, Domenico **13** 515-517
Tartini, Giuseppe **15** 112-113
Vivaldi, Antonio **16** 3-4
composers (19th-20th century)
Bellini, Vincenzo **2** 138-139
Berio, Luciano **2** 194-195
Busoni, Ferruccio Benvenuto
3 173-174
Bussotti, Sylvano **3** 174-175
Dallapiccola, Luigi **4** 377-378
Donizetti, Gaetano **5** 59-60
Malipiero, Gian Francesco **10** 171
Nono, Luigi **11** 420-421
Paganini, Niccolo **12** 58-59
Puccini, Giacomo **12** 474-476
Respighi, Ottorino **13** 103-104
Rossini, Gioacchino **13** 311-312
Verdi, Giuseppe Fortunino
Francesco **15** 463-465
conductors
Busoni, Ferruccio Benvenuto
3 173-174
Respighi, Ottorino **13** 103-104
Toscanini, Arturo **15** 270-271
opera singers

Caruso, Enrico **3** 345
Pavarotti, Luciano **12** 152-154
violinists
Stradivari, Antonio **14** 488-490

Musicians, Japanese
Ozawa, Seiji **12** 49-51

Musicians, Mexican
Chávez, Carlos **3** 486

Musicians, New Zealander
Te Kanawa, Kiri **15** 136-137

Musicians, Norwegian
Grieg, Edvard Hagerup **6** 541-542

Musicians, Polish
Chopin, Frédéric François **4** 16-18
Lutoslawski, Witold **10** 52-53
Paderewski, Ignace Jan **12** 56-57
Penderecki, Krzysztof **12** 195-197
Szymanowski, Karol **15** 67-68

Musicians, Russian
cellists
Rostropovich, Mstislav
Leopoldovich **13** 317-318
composers (19th century)
Borodin, Aleksandr Profirevich
2 422-423
Glinka, Mikhail Ivanovich
6 369-370
Mussorgsky, Modest Petrovich
11 274-276
Rimsky-Korsakov, Nikolai Andree-
vich **13** 174-175
Tchaikovsky, Peter Ilyich
15 130-132
composers (19th-20th century)
Khachaturian, Aram Ilich **8** 530-531
Prokofiev, Sergei Sergeevich
12 458-460
Rachmaninov, Sergei Vasilievich
12 531-532
Scriabin, Alexander Nikolayevich
14 71-72
Shostakovich, Dmitri Dmitrievich
14 204-205
Stravinsky, Igor Fedorovich
14 502-506
composers (20th century)
Kabalevsky, Dmitri **8** 400-401
Tcherepnin, Alexander **15** 132-133
conductors
Kabalevsky, Dmitri **8** 400-401
Rachmaninov, Sergei Vasilievich
12 531-532
Rimsky-Korsakov, Nikolai Andree-
vich **13** 174-175
Rostropovich, Mstislav
Leopoldovich **13** 317-318
pianists
Kabalevsky, Dmitri **8** 400-401

Musicians, Scottish
Musgrave, Thea **11** 266-268

Musicians, Spanish
Albéniz, Issac **1** 108-109
Cabezón, Antonio **3** 197-198
Casals, Pablo **3** 348-350

Domingo, Placido **5** 50-51
Encina, Juan del **5** 283
Falla, Manuel de **5** 372-373
Granados, Enrique **6** 489-490
Halffter, Christóbal **7** 79-80
Milán, Luis **11** 15-16
Victoria, Tomás Luis de **15** 487-488

Musicians, Swiss
Jaques-Dalcroze, Emile **8** 221-222
Notker Balbulus **11** 434-435

Music's Empire (poem)
Marvell, Andrew **10** 301-303

Musikalisches Opfer (musical composition)
Bach, Johann Sebastian **1** 416-419

MUSIL, ROBERT EDLER VON
(1880-1942), Austrian novelist, dramatist,
and short story writer **11** 268-269

MUSKIE, EDMUND SIXTUS (1914-1996),
United States senator and Democratic
vice-presidential nominee **11** 269-271
Nixon, Richard Milhous **11** 401-404

Muslim Brotherhood (Society of Muslim
Brothers)
Al-Banna, Hassan **1** 104-106
Sayyid Qutb **13** 509-511

Muslim League
see Moslem League (India)

Muslim Mosque, Inc. (United States)
Malcolm X **10** 165-166

Muslims
see Islam; Islamic Empire

Musselburgh, battle of (1548)
Somerset, Duke of **14** 333-334

MUSSET, LOUIS CHARLES ALFRED DE
(1810-1857), French poet, dramatist, and
fiction writer **11** 271-272
Hugo, Victor Marie **8** 22-25
Sand, George **13** 459-461

MUSSOLINI, BENITO (1883-1945), Italian
Fascist dictator 1922-1943 **11** 272-274
Austria and
Dollfuss, Engelbert **5** 47
Schuschnigg, Kurt von **14** 45-46
British relations
Chamberlain, Arthur Neville
3 409-411
Eden, Anthony **5** 204-205
Perth, 16th Earl of **12** 244-245
expansionism (Africa)
Badoglio, Pietro **1** 428-429
Eboué, Adolphe Felix Sylvestre
5 194
Gentile, Giovanni **6** 267
Haile Selassie **7** 68-70
Wavell, Archibald Percival
16 147-148
France and
Laval, Pierre **9** 237-238
Germany and
Hitler, Adolf **7** 417-420
Rommel, Erwin **13** 268-269
opponents (Italy)
Croce, Benedetto **4** 313-314

De Gasperi, Alcide **4** 462-463
Giolitti, Giovanni **6** 339-340
Levi, Carlo **9** 364
Matteotti, Giacomo **10** 339-340
Orlando, Vittorio Emmanuele
11 529-530
Portugal and
Salazar, António de Oliveira
13 442-443
supporters (Italy)
Victor Emmanuel III **15** 484-485
Vatican and
Pius XI **12** 337-339

MUSSORGSKY, MODEST PETROVICH
(1839-1881), Russian composer
11 274-276
Borodin, Aleksandr Profirevich
2 422-423
Kandinsky, Wassily **8** 420-422
Milhaud, Darius **11** 17-18
Pushkin, Aleksandr Sergeevich
12 489-491
Rimsky-Korsakov, Nikolai Andreevich
13 174-175
Tchaikovsky, Peter Ilyich **15** 130-132

Mustafa (died 1533), Turkish prince
Suleiman I **15** 20-21

Mustafa III (1717-1774), sultan of Turkey
1757-1774
Selim III **14** 95-96

Mustafa IV (1779-1808), sultan of Turkey
1807-1808
Mahmud II **10** 145-147
Selim III **14** 95-96

Mustapha Kemal
see Atatürk, Kemal

Mustasim, al- (1221-1258), Abbasid caliph
Hulagu Khan **8** 27-28

MUSTE, ABRAHAM JOHANNES
(1885-1967), American pacifist and labor
leader **11** 276-277

Mutanabbi, al- (915-965), Arabic poet
Abu-L-Ala al-Maarri **1** 32

Mutation Theory, The (book)
Vries, Hugo de **16** 33-36

Mutazilite school (Islam)
Ashari, Abu al- Hasan Ali al- **1** 327-328
Kindi, Abu-Yusuf Yaqub ibn-Ishaq al-
9 10-11
Mamun, Abdallah al- **10** 183
Nazzam, Ibrahim ibn Sayyar al- **11** 329

Mute, the
see Deaf, the—deaf-mutes

MUTESA I (circa 1838-1884), African
monarch of Buganda **11** 277
Mwanga **11** 282-283
Speke, John Hanning **14** 366-367

MUTESA II (1924-1969), Monarch of
Buganda **11** 277-278

Muthesius, Hermann (1861-1927), German architect
Mies van der Rohe, Ludwig **11** 10-12

Mutina, battle of (43 B.C.)
Augustus **1** 371-373
Brutus, Marcus Junius **3** 79-80

Mutiny on the Bounty (film)
Gable, William Clark **6** 157-158

MUTIS, JOSÉ CELESTINO (1732-1808),
Spanish-Colombian naturalist **11** 278-279

Mutsu Munemitsu (1842-1897), Japanese
statesman
Hara, Kei **7** 138
Ito, Hirobumi **8** 153-155

MUTSUHITO (a.k.a. Meiji; 1852-1912),
Japanese emperor **11** 279-282

Mutter Courage (play; Brecht)
Brecht, Bertolt **2** 512-514
Grimmelshausen, Hans Jakob Christof-
fel von **7** 4-5

Mutual instruction
see Madras system

Muwahhidun (North Africa revolutionary
group)
ibn Tumart, Muhammad **8** 96-97

Muybridge, Eadweard (1830-1904), English
photographer
Bacon, Francis **1** 421-422
Eakins, Thomas **5** 176-177

Muzio Scaevola (opera)
Handel, George Frederick **7** 116-119

MWANGA (circa 1866-1901), Monarch of
Buganda **11** 282-283
Peters, Carl **12** 257-258

Mweru, Lake (Central Africa)
Livingstone, David **9** 463-465

My Antonia (novel)
Cather, Willa Sibert **3** 368-369

My Army, O, My Army (poem)
Lawson, Henry **9** 254-255

My Aunt (poem)
Holmes, Oliver Wendell **7** 457-458

My Bill (song)
Kern, Jerome David **8** 517-518

My Brilliant Career (novel)
Franklin, Stella Maraia Sarah Miles
6 68-69

My Butterfly (poem)
Frost, Robert Lee **6** 130-133

My Career Goes Bung (novel)
Franklin, Stella Maraia Sarah Miles
6 68-69

My Country (musical composition)
Smetana, Bedřich **14** 281-282

My Darling Clementine (film)
Ford, John **6** 7-8

My days have been so wondrous free
(song)
Hopkinson, Francis **7** 496-497

My Days of Anger (novel)
Farrell, James Thomas **5** 390-391

My Dear Children (play)
Barrymores **2** 28-30

My Double and How He Undid Me (story)
Hale, Edward Everett **7** 71-72

my father moved through dooms of love
(elegy)
Cummings, Edward Estlin **4** 334-336

My Forebears Were Pioneers (painting)
Evergood, Philip **5** 345

My Funny Valentine (song)
Rodgers, Richard Charles **13** 234-236

My Gal Sal (song)
Dreiser, Herman Theodore **5** 98-100

My heart at thy sweet voice (song)
Saint-Saëns, Charles Camille
13 435-436

My heart is inditing (anthem)
Purcell, Henry **12** 484-485

My Heart Stood Still (song)
Rodgers, Richard Charles **13** 234-236

My Heart's in the Highlands (play)
Saroyan, William **13** 486-487

My Hours of Leisure (poems)
Fréchette, Louis-Honoré **6** 77-78

My Imprisonment (poem)
Tschernichowsky, Saul **15** 323

My Lady Neville's Book (musical collection)
Byrd, William **3** 187-188

My Last Duchess (poem)
Browning, Robert **3** 53-55

My Life (story)
Chekhov, Anton Pavlovich **3** 494-497

My Little Chickadee (film)
Fields, W. C. **5** 444

My Lute, Awake (poem)
Wyatt, Thomas **16** 410-411

My Man (song)
Brice, Fanny **3** 1-2

My Mother, My Father and Me (play)
Hellman, Lillian Florence **7** 267-268

My Name Is Aram (stories)
Saroyan, William **13** 486-487

My Next Door Neighbour (poem)
Soyinka, Wole **14** 358-359

My Nine Lives and How I Lost Them (book)
Cullen, Countee **4** 333-334

My Old Home (story)
Lu Hsün **10** 35-37

My Old Kentucky Home (song)
Foster, Stephen Collins **6** 25-27

My Psalm (poem)
Whittier, John Greenleaf **16** 256-257

My Sister Eileen (play; R. McKenney)
West, Nathanael **16** 213-214

My Sister, My Life (poems)
Pasternak, Boris Leonidovich
12 124-125

My Song (poem)
Bialik, Hayyim Nahman **2** 262-263

My Spirit Was in Heaviness (cantata)
Bach, Johann Sebastian **1** 416-419

Myanmar (formerly Burma)
Aung San Suu Kyi **1** 375-376
Saw Maung **13** 506-507

Mycenaean civilization (Greece)
Evans, Arthur John **5** 335-336
Homer **7** 465-467
Schliemann, Heinrich **14** 17-18

Myconius, Oswald (1488-1552), Swiss
divine
Gesner, Konrad von **6** 287

MYDANS, CARL (born 1907), American
photojournalist **11** 283-284

Myers, C.S. (1873-1946), British experimental psychologist
Bartlett, Frederic Charles **2** 34-35

Myerson, Golda
see Meir, Golda

Mylius-Erichsen, Ludwig (1872-1907),
Danish explorer
Rasmussen, Knud Johan Victor **13** 44

Mynheer Peeperkorn (literary character)
Mann, Thomas **10** 204-207

Mynster, Jacob Pier (1775-1854), Danish
Protestant theologian
Kierkegaard, Søren Aabye **8** 547-549

Myongjong (ruled 1170-1194), king of
Korea
Chong Chung-bu **4** 15
Ch'oe Ch'ung-hn **4** 13

Myongjong (ruled 1545-1567), king of
Korea
Sŏnjo **14** 341-342

Myongnyang, battle of (1597)
Yi Sunsin **16** 459-461

Myongsong Hwanghu
see Min

MYRDAL, KARL GUNNAR (1898-1987),
Swedish economist and sociologist
11 284
Bunche, Ralph Johnson **3** 121-122

MYRON (flourished circa 470-450 B.C.),
Greek sculptor **11** 285

Myrrhine (literary character)
Menander **10** 477-478

Myrtles (musical composition)
Schumann, Robert Alexander **14** 41-43

Myshkin, Prince (literary character)
Dostoevsky, Fyodor **5** 74-77

Mysore (state; India)
Haidar Ali **7** 65-66

Mysore wars (1767-1799)
Cornwallis, Charles **4** 241-243
Haidar Ali **7** 65-66
Hastings, Warren **7** 195-196
Tipu Sultan **15** 236
Wellesley, Richard Colley **16** 192-193

Wellington, 1st Duke of **16** 193-195

Mystagogio (book)
Photius **12** 283-284

Mystères du château de dés, Les (film)
Ray, Man **13** 59-60

Mysteries (novel)
Hamsun, Knut **7** 113-114

Mysteries of Selflessness, The (poem)
Iqbal, Muhammad **8** 132-133

Mysterious Island, The (novel)
Verne, Jules **15** 467-469

Mysterious Stranger, The (book)
Twain, Mark **15** 363-366

Mysterium fidei (encyclical)
Paul VI **12** 146-148

Mystery (musical composition)
Scriabin, Alexander Nikolayevich
14 71-72

Mystery (newspaper)
Delany, Martin Robinson **4** 473-474

Mystery Bouffe (play; Mayakovsky)
Meyerhold, Vsevolod Emilievich **10** 539

Mystery fiction (literary genre)
Ambler, Eric **1** 191-192
Chandler, Raymond Jr. **3** 423-425
Chesterton, Gilbert Keith **3** 508-509
Christie, Agatha **4** 25-26
Cole, George Douglas Howard
4 146-147
Collins, William Wilkie **4** 169-170
Dostoevsky, Fyodor **5** 74-77
Doyle, Arthur Conan **5** 91-92
Dürrenmatt, Friedrich **5** 164-165
Fonseca, Rubem **5** 502-504
Fraser, Antonia **6** 70-71
Greene, Graham **6** 523-524
Hammett, Dashiell **7** 106-108
James, P. D. **8** 213-215
Le Carre, John **9** 270-271
Lewis, Cecil Day **9** 380
Poe, Edgar Allan **12** 363-365
Rendell, Ruth **13** 96-97
Simenon, Georges **14** 233-234

Mystery Hid fromm Ages, The (book)
Chauncy, Charles **3** 485-486

Mystery of Edwin Drood, The (novel)
Dickens, Charles John Huffam
4 538-541

Mystery of Heroism, A (story; Crane)
Dreiser, Herman Theodore **5** 98-100

Mystery of the Locks, The (novel)
Howe, Edgar Watson **7** 529

Mystic Garden and Middling Beast (poem)
Stevens, Wallace **14** 443-445

Mystic Marriage of Saint Catherine (painting)
Andrea del Sarto **1** 224-225
Correggio **4** 249-251
Memling, Hans **10** 476
Rubens, Peter Paul **13** 339-342

Mysticism (religion)
Christian (12th-13th century)
Bernard of Clairvaux **2** 207-208
Bonaventure **2** 383-384
Francis of Assisi **6** 46-47
Joachim of Fiore **8** 263-264
Christian (13th-15th century)
Catherine of Siena **3** 369-370
Dante Alighieri **4** 389-391
Eckhart, Johann **5** 200-201
Gerson, John **6** 285-286
Julian of Norwich **8** 381
Kempis, Thomas à **8** 493-494
Ruysbroeck, Jan van **13** 388-389
Christian (16th-18th century)
Boehme, Jacob **2** 357
Fénelon, François de Salignac de la
Mothe **5** 410-411
Francis of Sales **6** 47
Ignatius of Loyola **8** 108-109
John of the Cross **8** 285
Law, William **9** 245-246
Theresa **15** 178-179
see also Jansenism; Quietism
Christian (20th century)
Weil, Simone **16** 172-174
Confucian
K'ang Yu-wei **8** 426-428
Hindu
Krishnamurti, Jiddu **9** 101-103
Radhakrishnan, Sarvepalli
12 537-538
Ramakrishna, Sri **13** 11-13
Shankara **14** 150-151
in literature
Crane, Hart **4** 291-293
Crashaw, Richard **4** 296
Dante Alighieri **4** 389-391
Donne, John **5** 60-61

Gourmont, Remy de **6** 475
Herbert, George **7** 324-326
Hugo, Victor Marie **8** 22-25
Jacopone da Todi **8** 194
Langland, William **9** 194-195
Marvell, Andrew **10** 301-303
Novalis **11** 435
Rolle of Hampole, Richard
13 260-261
Vaughan, Henry **15** 444-445
Islamic
see Sufism
Jewish
Caro, Joseph ben Ephraim
3 316-317
Kuk, Abraham Issac **9** 123-124
Leon, Moses de **9** 336
Luria, Isaac ben Solomon Ashkenazi
10 47-48
Luzzato, Moses Hayyim **10** 57-58
Nahmanides **11** 293-294
Sabbatai Zevi **13** 400-401
see also Cabala
Neoplatonism
see Neoplatonism
psychology of
James, William **8** 215-217
Jung, Carl Gustav **8** 388-389

Mythes (musical composition)
Szymanowski, Karol **15** 67-68

Mythical Story (poems)
Seferis, George **14** 84-85

Mythology, Greco-Roman
Graves, Robert Ranke **6** 504-506
Hesiod **7** 361-362
Homer **7** 465-467
Jeffers, John Robinson **8** 236-237
Justin Martyr **8** 395-396
Ovid **12** 34-36
Ryder, Albert Pinkham **13** 391-392
Sophocles **14** 343-345

Mythology, world
Campbell, Joseph **3** 253-255

MZILIKAZI (circa 1795-1868), South
African warrior leader **11** 285-286
Dingane **5** 14-15
Lobengula **9** 474-475
Pretorius, Andries **12** 444-445

N

NAACP
see National Association for the
Advancement of Colored People

Naakuto Laab (ruled circa 1221-circa
1268), king of Ethiopia
Lalibela **9** 170
Yekuno Amlak **16** 449

Nabab, Le (novel)
Daudet, Alphonse **4** 402-403

Nabis (died 192 B.C.), tyrant of Sparta
207-192 B.C.
Flamininus, Titus Quinctius **5** 477

Nabis (French art group)
Bonnard, Pierre **2** 395-396
Maillol, Aristide **10** 150-151
Malevich, Kasimir **10** 168-169
Redon, Odilon **13** 75-76
Vuillard, Jean Édouard **16** 36

NABOKOV, VLADIMIR (1899-1977), Russian-born American writer, critic, and lepi-
dopterist **11** 287-288

Nabonidus (born 539? B.C.), king of Babylonia 556-539
Cyrus the Great **4** 363-364

Nabopolassar (ruled 625-605 B.C.),
founder of Chaldean Empire
Nebuchadnezzar **11** 330

Nabu-Naid
see Nabonidus

Nabucco (opera)
Verdi, Giuseppe Fortunino Francesco
15 463-465

**NABUCO DE ARAUJO, JOAQUIM AURE-
LIO** (1849-1910), Brazilian abolitionist,
statesman, and author **11** 288-289

Nachbarn (stories)
Hesse, Hermann **7** 367-369

Nächste, Der (book)
Cohen, Hermann **4** 138-139

Nacht von Lissabon, Die (novel)
Remarque, Erich Maria **13** 91

Nacionalista party (Philippines)
Magsaysay, Ramon **10** 130-131
Marcos, Ferdinand **10** 240-242
Osmeña, Sergio **12** 22-24
Quezon, Manuel Luis **12** 511-513
Recto, Claro M. **13** 69-70

NADELMAN, ELIE (1882-1946),
Polish-American sculptor and graphic
artist **11** 289-290
Lachaise, Gaston **9** 147

NADER, RALPH (born 1934), American
lawyer and social crusader **11** 290-291

Nadezhda (ship)
Kotzebue, Otto von **9** 91-92

Nadja (book)
Breton, André **2** 519-520

Nadson, Semyon Y. (1862-1887), Russian
poet
Merezhkovsky, Dmitry Sergeyevich
10 515-516

Naevius, Gnaeus (flourished circa 270
B.C.), Roman poet and playwright
Terence **15** 146-148

Nagananda (play)
Harsha **7** 181-182

Nagasaki (city; Japan)
Hirohito **7** 410-412
Oppenheimer, J. Robert **11** 525-526

NAGEL, ERNEST (1901-1985), American
philosopher of science **11** 291-292
Cohen, Morris Raphael **4** 139-140

NAGY, IMRE (1896-1958), prime minister
of Hungary (1953-55, 1956) **11** 292-293
Kádár, János **8** 402-403
Lukács, Gyorgy **10** 37-38

Nagyszombat, University of
see Budapest, University of

Nahdatul Ulama (political party; Indonesia)
Sukarno **15** 18-20

NAHMANIDES (1194-1270), Spanish Talmudist **11** 293-294

NAIDU, SAROJINI (1879-1949), Indian
poet and nationalist **11** 294-295

Nain jaune, Le (periodical)
Soulé, Pierre **14** 351-352

NAIPAUL, V. S. (born 1932), Trinidadian
author of English-language prose
11 295-296

Nájera, battle of (1367)
Chaucer, Geoffrey **3** 482-485
López de Ayala, Pedro **9** 508-509

NAJIBULLAH, MOHAMMAD (born 1947),
Soviet-selected ruler of the Republic of
Afghanistan **11** 296-298

Nakada (Egypt)
Petrie, William Matthew Flinders
12 261-262

NAKASONE, YASUHIRO (born 1918),
prime minister of Japan (1982-1987)
11 298-300

Nakayama
see Sun Yat-sen

Naked (play)
Pirandello, Luigi **12** 319-321

Naked and the Dead, The (novel)
Mailer, Norman Kingsley **10** 148-150

Naked Lunch (book)
Burroughs, William S. **3** 162-163

Naked Masks (drama collection)
Pirandello, Luigi **12** 319-321

Nako-no oe
see Tenchi, Emperor

Nakshibandis (Sufi order)
Jami **8** 218-219

Nalundasan, Julio (died 1935), Filipino
politician
Marcos, Ferdinand **10** 240-242

NAMATJIRA, ALBERT (1902-1959), Australian Aboriginal artist **11** 300-301

Name-Day Party, The (story)
Chekhov, Anton Pavlovich **3** 494-497

Name of Action (novel)
Greene, Graham **6** 523-524

Name of Mary, The (hymn)
Manzoni, Alessandro **10** 222-224

Namibia
Nujoma, Shafiihuna **11** 441-443

NAMIER, SIR LEWIS BERNSTEIN
(1888-1960), English historian
11 301-303

Nana (novel)
Zola, Émile **16** 526-528

NANAK (1469-1538), Indian reformer,
founder of Sikhism **11** 303

Nanchang uprising (1927)
Chou En-lai **4** 20-22
Chu Teh **4** 54-55

Nancy (literary character)
Dickens, Charles John Huffam
4 538-541

Nancy, battle of (1477)
Charles the Bold **3** 467-469

Nangklao
see Rama III

Nanine (play)
Voltaire **16** 14-16

Nankai University (Tientsin)
Liang Ch'i-ch'ao **9** 395-396

Nanking (city; China)
Ch'en Tu-hsiu **3** 501-502
Chiang Kai-shek **3** 510-513
Hung Hsiu-ch'üan **8** 37-38
Ricci, Matteo **13** 124-125
Tseng Kuo-fan **15** 324-325

Nanking, Treaty of (1843)
Ch'i-ying **4** 12

Nanook of the North (film)
Flaherty, Robert **5** 476-477

NANSEN, FRIDTJOF (1861-1930), Norwegian polar explorer, scientist, and statesman **11** 304-305

Nantes, Edict of (1598)
see Edict of Nantes

Nantucket School of Philosophy (painting)
Johnson, Jonathan Eastman **8** 308

NAOROJI, DADABHAI (1825-1917), Indian nationalist leader **11** 305

Naphta (literary character)
Mann, Thomas **10** 204-207

NAPIER, JOHN (1550-1617), Scottish
mathematician **11** 306

Napier, Sir George Thomas (1784-1855),
British military leader
Moshweshwe **11** 203-205

Napier, Sir Robert (1810-1890), British
army officer
Roberts, Frederick Sleigh **13** 195-196

Naples (city; Italy)
Cajetan **3** 215-216
Driesch, Hans Adolf Eduard **5** 105
Garibaldi, Giuseppe **6** 215-217
Gladstone, William Ewart **6** 357-360
Lauro, Achille **9** 234-235

Naples, kingdom of
Byzantine conquest
Belisarius **2** 128-129
English wars
Charles III **3** 454-455
Nelson, Horatio **11** 336-338
Franco-Spanish partition
Borgia, Cesare **2** 412-413
Julius II **8** 384-386
Louis XII **9** 528-529
French invasion
Alexander VI **1** 134-135
Charles VIII **3** 462-463
Louis XII **9** 528-529
Italian wars
Donatello **5** 55-56
Ferdinand V **5** 417-418
Medici, Lorenzo de' **10** 450-451
Napoleonic era
Bonaparte, Joseph **2** 381-382
Murat, Joachim **11** 253-254
see also Austrian Succession, War of
the; Sicily, Kingdom of; Spanish
Succession, War of the; Two
Sicilies, Kingdom of the

Naples, University of
De Sanctis, Francesco **4** 505
Frederick II **6** 79
Vico, Giambattista **15** 480-481

NAPOLEON I (1769-1821), emperor of the
French 1804-1815 **11** 306-310
abdication (1814)
Charles X **3** 463-464
Lafayette, Marquis de **9** 151-152
Ney, Michel **11** 372-373
art patronage
Canova, Antonio **3** 263-264
David, Jacques Louis **4** 407-409
Prud'hon, Pierre Paul **12** 469
Austria
see Napoleonic Wars
biographies and studies
Hazlitt, William **7** 235-236
Tarbell, Ida Minerva **15** 107-108
Thiers, Louis Adolphe **15** 181-182
Watson, Thomas Edward **16** 139
Continental system
Krupp Family **9** 109-111
Selim III **14** 95-96
court pages
Leopold I **9** 345-346
Egypt and
Fourier, Jean Baptiste Joseph **6** 32-33
Ibrahim Pasha **8** 97-98
Nelson, Horatio **11** 336-338
English politics
Castlereagh, Viscount **3** 363-364
George III **6** 270-272
Liverpool, 2nd Earl of **9** 456-457
Pitt, William the Younger
12 329-331
exiles from
Maistre, Joseph de **10** 153-154
Staël, Germaine de **14** 391-392
Hundred Days

see Hundred Days
in art and literature
Hugo, Victor Marie **8** 22-25
Rodin, Auguste **13** 236-238
Stendhal **14** 422-425
Wordsworth, William **16** 385-388
India and
Wellesley, Richard Colley
16 192-193
influence of
Bolívar, Simón **2** 375-377
López, Francisco Solano **9** 507-508
Nkrumah, Kwame **11** 408-410
influenced by
Barras, Vicomte de **2** 19
Caesar, Gaius Julius **3** 207-210
Ireland and
Emmet, Robert **5** 281-282
Louisiana Purchase
du Pont de Nemours, Pierre Samuel
5 155-156
Livingston, Robert R. **9** 462-463
Madison, James **10** 121-123
Monroe, James **11** 111-113
marshals
Bernadotte, Jean Baptiste **2** 205-206
Murat, Joachim **11** 253-254
Ney, Michel **11** 372-373
Rochambeau, Comte de **13** 220-221
Mexico and Haiti
Morelos, José María **11** 157-158
Toussaint L'Ouverture, François
Dominique **15** 278-279
ministers
Carnot, Lazare Nicolas Marguerite
3 313-314
Chateaubriand, Vicomte de
3 477-479
Cuvier, Georges Léopold **4** 357-359
Fouché, Joseph **6** 30-31
Sieyès, Comte Emmanuel Joseph
14 217-218
Talleyrand, Charles Maurice de
15 89-90
Napoleonic Wars
see Napoleonic Wars
papacy and
Lamennais, Hugues Félicité Robert
de **9** 179
Pius VI **12** 333-334
Pius VII **12** 334-335
Peninsular War
see Peninsular War
Prussia
Blücher, Gebhard Leberecht von
2 340-341
Hardenberg, Karl August von
7 146-147
Scharnhorst, Gerhard Johann David
von **13** 521-522
William I **16** 291-292
relatives
Bonaparte, Joseph **2** 381-382
Bonaparte, Louis **2** 382-383
Napoleon III **11** 310-312
Revolutionary wars

see French Revolutionary Wars
Russia
  see Napoleonic Wars
scientific patronage
  Berthollet, Claude Louis **2** 229-230
  Bougainville, Louis Antoine de
    2 443-444
  Fourier, Jean Baptiste Joseph **6** 32-33
  Laplace, Marquis de **9** 202-204
  Pinel, Philippe **12** 313-314
  Volta, Alessandro **16** 12-14
Spain and
  Azara, Félix de **1** 397-398
  Charles IV **3** 456-457
  Ferdinand VII **5** 418-420
  Godoy y Álvarez de Faria, Manuel
    de **6** 381-382
  Goya y Lucientes, Francisco de
    Paula José de **6** 476-478

Napoleon II (1811-1832), titular king of
Rome
  Napoleon I **11** 306-310

NAPOLEON III (Louis Napoleon;
1808-1873), emperor of the French
1852-1870 **11** 310-312
Algeria
  Abd el-Kadir **1** 15
American Confederacy
  Slidell, John **14** 273
critics
  Courbet, Jean Desiré Gustave
    4 271-273
  Gambetta, Léon **6** 198-199
  Hugo, Victor Marie **8** 22-25
  Lamartine, Alphonse Marie Louis de
    9 173-175
  Proudhon, Pierre Joseph **12** 461-463
  Soulé, Pierre **14** 351-352
  Taine, Hippolyte Adolphe **15** 82-83
  Thiers, Louis Adolphe **15** 181-182
English policy
  Palmerston, 3d Viscount **12** 81-83
  Russell, John **13** 380-381
  Victoria **15** 485-487
Italian policy
  Cavour, Conte di **3** 385-386
  Victor Emmanuel II **15** 483-484
Mexico and
  Juárez, Benito **8** 369-372
  Maximilian of Hapsburg
    10 358-360
oaths of allegiance
  Cauchy, Augustin Louis **3** 378-380
patronage
  Carpeaux, Jean Baptiste **3** 318-319
  Haussmann, Baron Georges Eugène
    7 201-202
  Le Play, Guillaume Frédéric
    9 350-351
Prussia and
  Bismarck, Otto Eduard Leopold von
    2 294-296
  Moltke, Helmuth Karl Bernard von
    11 90-91
  William I **16** 292-293
satirized

Daumier, Honoré Victorin
  4 403-405
studies of
  Marx, Karl **10** 304-308
supporters
  Dumas, Jean Baptiste André
    5 138-139
  Thiers, Louis Adolphe **15** 181-182
  Viollet-le-Duc, Eugène Emmanuel
    15 505-506
  see also Crimean War; Franco-Pruss-
    ian War

Napoleon at Eylau (painting)
Gros **7** 14-15

Napoleon Bonaparte
  see Napoleon I

Napoleon of Notting Hill, The (novel)
Chesterton, Gilbert Keith **3** 508-509

Napoleonic Code
  see Law codes—France

Napoleonic Wars (1803-1815)
Fourth Austrian War (1809)
  Bernadotte, Jean Baptiste **2** 205-206
  Francis II **6** 43-44
  Metternich, Klemens von
    10 533-536
Fourth Coalition (1813-14; Allies)
  Bernadotte, Jean Baptiste **2** 205-206
  Blücher, Gebhard Leberecht von
    2 340-341
  Francis II **6** 43-44
  Frederick William III **6** 87
  Liverpool, 2nd Earl of **9** 456-457
  Metternich, Klemens von
    10 533-536
  Stein, Heinrich Friedrich Karl vom
    und zum **14** 415-416
  William I **16** 292-293
Fourth Coalition (1813-14; French)
  Murat, Joachim **11** 253-254
  Napoleon I **11** 306-310
  Nesselrode, Karl Robert **11** 348-349
  Ney, Michel **11** 372-373
Hundred Days
  see Hundred Days; Waterloo, Battle
    of (1815)
peace settlements
  Castlereagh, Viscount **3** 363-364
  Metternich, Klemens von
    10 533-536
  see also Vienna, Congress of
    (1814-1815)
Peninsular War (1803-1813)
  see Peninsular War
Russia invaded (1812)
  Alexander I **1** 130-132
  Francis II **6** 43-44
  Kutuzov, Mikhail Ilarionovich
    9 137-138
  Metternich, Klemens von
    10 533-536
  Murat, Joachim **11** 253-254
  Napoleon I **11** 306-310
  Nesselrode, Karl Robert **11** 348-349
  Ney, Michel **11** 372-373

Suvorov, Aleksandr Vasilievich
  15 44-45
Third Coalition (1805-07; Allies)
  Alexander I **1** 130-132
  Blücher, Gebhard Leberecht von
    2 340-341
  Francis II **6** 43-44
  Frederick William III **6** 87
  Kutuzov, Mikhail Ilarionovich
    9 137-138
  Nelson, Horatio **11** 336-338
  Nesselrode, Karl Robert **11** 348-349
  Stein, Heinrich Friedrich Karl vom
    und zum **14** 415-416
Third Coalition (1805-07; French)
  Bernadotte, Jean Baptiste **2** 205-206
  Murat, Joachim **11** 253-254
  Napoleon I **11** 306-310
  Ney, Michel **11** 372-373
United States claims
  Adams, John Quincy **1** 52-54
  Clay, Henry **4** 94-96
  Gallatin, Albert **6** 183-184
  Jackson, Andrew **8** 168-172
  Madison, James **10** 121-123
  see also War of 1812

Nara (city; Japan)
Kammu **8** 420

Nara sects (Buddhism)
Saicho **13** 426-428

NARAYAN, JAYAPRAKASH (1902-1979),
Indian nationalist and social reformer
11 312-313

NARAYAN, R. K. (Narayanswami; born
1906), Indian author **11** 313-314

Narbonne, Synod of (458)
Leo I **9** 329-330

Narcissus (lithograph)
Daumier, Honoré Victorin **4** 403-405

Narcotics (drugs)
Dewey, Thomas Edmund **4** 524
Forbes, Robert Bennet **5** 509-510

Nariakira Shimazu (died 1858), Japanese
lord of Satsuma
Saigo, Takamori **13** 429

NARIÑO, ANTONIO (1765-1823), Colombian patriot **11** 314-315

Narodnaia Volia (Narodniks; Narodnichest-
vo; Russian politics)
Lenin, Vladimir Ilich **9** 323-326
Trotsky, Leon **15** 302-305

Narr in Christo Emanuel Quint, Der
(novel)
Hauptmann, Gerhart Johann Robert
  7 199-201

Narragansett Indians (North America)
Philip **12** 267-268
Williams, Roger **16** 304-305

Narrative of Arthur Gordon Pym, The
(novel)
Poe, Edgar Allan **12** 363-365

Narrenschiff, Das (book; Brant)
Brant, Sebastian **2** 503-504
Porter, Katherine Anne **12** 406-407

Narses (circa 478-circa 573), Byzantine general
Belisarius **2** 128-129
Justinian I **8** 393-395

Narses I (died 302), King of Persia 293-302
Diocletian **5** 19-20
Shahpur II **14** 140-141

Narva (port; Estonia)
Godunov, Boris Feodorovich **6** 382-383
Peter I **12** 253-256

NARVÁEZ, PÁNFILO DE (1478?-1528), Spanish soldier and explorer **11** 315
Cabeza de Vaca, Álvar Núñez **3** 197
Cabrillo, Juan Rodríguez **3** 204-205
Coronado, Francisco Vásquez de **4** 247
Velázquez de Cuéllar, Diego **15** 459

Narziss und Goldmund (novel)
Hesse, Hermann **7** 367-369

Nasakom (Indonesian political group)
Sukarno **15** 18-20

Naseby, battle of (1645)
Charles I **3** 450-452
Cromwell, Oliver **4** 317-320

NASH, JOHN (1752-1835), English architect and town planner **11** 316
Shaw, Richard Norman **14** 167-168

Nashe, Thomas (1567-1601), English playwright and pamphleteer
Kyd, Thomas **9** 140-141

Nashville (city; Tennessee)
Du Bois, William Edward Burghardt **5** 116-118

Nashville (ship)
Adams, Charles Francis **1** 41-42

Nashville, battle of (1864)
Thomas, George Henry **15** 190-191

Nasi (Jewish office)
Johanan ben Zakkai **8** 271-272
Judah I **8** 372-373

Nasier, Alcofribas
see Rabelais, François

Nasir al-Din al-Tusi (1201-1274), Arab mathematician
Regiomontanus **13** 81-82

NASMYTH, JAMES (1808-1890), Scottish engineer and inventor **11** 316-317

Naso, Publius Ovidius
see Ovid

Nasoni, Nicolò (Nicola Nazzoni; flourished 1732-1773), Italian architect
Aleijadinho, O **1** 125-126

NASSER, GAMAL ABDEL (1918-1970), Egyptian statesman, president 1956-1970 **11** 317-318
Abd el-Krim el-Khatabi, Mohamed ben **1** 15-16
Azhari, Sayyid Ismail al- **1** 399-401
Farouk I **5** 387-388

Haykal, Muhammad Husain **7** 230-231
see also Suez Crisis (1956)

Nasser-al-Din (1831-1896), shah of Persia
Taqi Khan Amir-e Kabir, Mirza **15** 106-107

NAST, THOMAS (1840-1902), American caricaturist and painter **11** 318-319
Tweed, William Marcy **15** 366-367

Nastasya Fillipovna (literary character)
Dostoevsky, Fyodor **5** 74-77

Natal (province; South Africa)
Cetshwayo **3** 400
Dingane **5** 14-15
Dube, John Langalibalele **5** 113
Frere, Henry Bartle Edward **6** 100-101
Pretorius, Andries **12** 444-445
Shaka **14** 141-142

Natchez (ship)
Frémont, John Charles **6** 97-98

Natchez Indians (North America)
Bienville, Sieur de **2** 268-269

Natercia (literary character)
Camoëns, Luis Vaz de **3** 247-249

Nathan (Old Testament prophet)
David, Jacques Louis **4** 407-409

NATHAN, GEORGE JEAN (1882-1958), American author, editor, and critic **11** 319-321
Mencken, Henry Louis **10** 481-483
O'Neill, Eugene **11** 514-516

Nathan der Weise (book; Lessing)
Lessing, Gotthold Ephraim **9** 357-359
Mendelssohn, Moses **10** 488-489
Zunz, Leopold **16** 534

Nation (periodical)
contributors
Adams, Henry Brooks **1** 45-47
James, Henry **8** 211-212
Muñoz Marín, José Luís Alberto **11** 249-250
critical evaluations of
Crane, Stephen **4** 293-295
editors
Godkin, Edwin Lawrence **6** 380
Howells, William Dean **7** 539-541
Schurz, Carl **14** 44-45
Thomas, Norman Mattoon **15** 191-192
Villard, Oswald Garrison **15** 498-499
poetry award
Benét, Stephen Vincent **2** 157-158

NATION, CARRY AMELIA MOORE (1846-1911), American temperance reformer **11** 321-322

Nation of Islam
see Black Muslims

Nation party (Sudan)
Azhari, Sayyid Ismail al- **1** 399-401
Khalil, Sayyid Abdullah **8** 531-532

Nation-state (political body)
Humboldt, Wilhelm von **8** 31

National Abortion Rights Action League (United States; established 1969)
Friedan, Betty **6** 109-111

National academy (Korea)
Sol Ch'ong **14** 325-326
Yi Hwang **16** 457

National Academy of Design (New York State)
Bellows, George Wesley **2** 143
Bierstadt, Albert **2** 270-271
Blakelock, Ralph Albert **2** 318
Durand, Asher Brown **5** 156-157
Morse, Samuel Finley Breese **11** 192-193

National Academy of Sciences (United States)
Agassiz, Jean Louis Rodolphe **1** 76-78
Bache, Alexander Dallas **1** 420
Gary, Elbert Henry **6** 229-230
Henry, Joseph **7** 307-308
Welch, William Henry **16** 185-186

National Advisory Committee for Aeronautics (United States)
Armstrong, Neil Alden **1** 304-306
Wright brothers **16** 394-396

National Aeronautics and Space Act (United States; 1958)
Johnson, Lyndon Baines **8** 308-312
Ride, Sally **13** 158-160

National Aeronautics and Space Administration (United States)
von Braun, Wernher **16** 17-18

National African Co. (established 1882)
Goldie, George Dashwood Taubman **6** 404

National Afro-American Council (United States)
Williams, Henry Sylvester **16** 303-304

National Alliance for Businessmen (United States)
Ford, Henry, II **6** 6-7

National Alliance movement (United States)
Polk, Leonidas Lafayette **12** 376-377

National American Woman Suffrage Association (NAWSA)
Catt, Carrie Chapman **3** 375-376
Howe, Julia Ward **7** 535-536
Schneiderman, Rose **14** 22-23
Shaw, Anna Howard **14** 162-163
Stanton, Elizabeth Cady **14** 402-403
Stone, Lucy **14** 471-472

National Archives (Mexico)
Alamán, Lucas **1** 99-100

National Assembly (1789-91; French Revolution)
du Pont de Nemours, Pierre Samuel **5** 155-156
Louis XVI **9** 534-535
Robespierre, Maximilien François Marie Isidore de **13** 199-201
Sieyès, Comte Emmanuel Joseph **14** 217-218

Talleyrand, Charles Maurice de
15 89-90

**National Association for the Advancement
of Colored People** (inc. 1910)
civil rights
Evers, Medgar 5 345-348
Evers-Williams, Myrlie 5 348-350
Hill, Herbert 7 387-388
Houston, Charles Hamilton
7 523-526
Jordan, Vernon 8 357-358
King, Martin Luther Jr. 9 20-22
Washington, Booker Taliaferro
16 125-126
formation
Du Bois, William Edward Burghardt
5 116-118
Holmes, John Haynes 7 456-457
Hope, John 7 489-490
Ovington, Mary White 12 36-37
Talbert, Mary Morris Burnett
15 86-88
Villard, Oswald Garrison
15 498-499
Wald, Lillian 16 53-54
Wells-Barnett, Ida. B. 16 198-199
Wise, Stephen Samuel 16 344-345
see also Niagara movement
funds
Parker, Dorothy Rothschild 12 106
Walker, C. J. 16 61-62
officials
Bunche, Ralph Johnson 3 121-122
Henry, Aaron 7 306-307
Grimké, Archibald Henry 7 1-2
Hooks, Benjamin Lawson
7 481-483
Johnson, James Weldon 8 304-305
Jordan, Vernon 8 357-358
Marshall, Thurgood 10 282-284
Mfume, Kweisi 10 539-542
Talbert, Mary Morris Burnett
15 86-88
Walker, Maggie Lena 16 65-66
White, Walter Francis 16 238-239
Wilkins, Roy 16 282-283
see also African American history
(United States)

National Association of Colored Women
(United States)
Talbert, Mary Morris Burnett 15 86-88
Walker, Maggie Lena 16 65-66

National Association of Schools of Music
(United States)
Hanson, Howard 7 135-136

National Awami Party (Pakistan)
Bhashani, Maulana Abdul Hamid Khan
2 255-257

National Bank of Iran
Reza Shah Pahlavi 13 116-117

National Banking Act (1863)
Cooke, Jay 4 215-216

National banking system (United States)
McCulloch, Hugh 10 404-405

Tyler, John 15 368-369
see also Bank of the U.S.

National Basketball Association (United
States)
Bird, Larry 2 279-281
Chamberlain, Wilt 3 413-415
Jabbar, Kareem Abdul 8 164-165
Johnson, Earvin Jr. 8 297-299

National Bolsheviks (Germany)
Jünger, Ernst 8 391-392

National Broadcasting Company (NBC)
Armstrong, Edwin Howard 1 302-303
Sarnoff, David 13 485-486
Toscanini, Arturo 15 270-271

National Bureau of Economic Research
(United States)
Mitchell, Wesley Clair 11 61-62

**National Catholic Council for Interracial
Justice**
Perry, Harold Robert 12 236-237

National Cash Register Co. (United States)
Kettering, Charles F. 8 524-525
Watson, Thomas J. 16 140

National Catholic War Council (World War
I)
Hayes, Patrick Joseph 7 224-225

National Civic Federation (labor organiza-
tion)
Gompers, Samuel 6 420-422
Mitchell, John 11 58-59

National College (Mexico)
Orozco, José Clemente 12 1-2

National College of Calcutta (India)
Ghose, Aurobindo 6 293-294

National Commission on Working Women
(United States)
Natividad, Irene 11 322-324

National Conference of Catholic Bishops
Bernardin, Joseph Cardinal 2 210-211

National Conservatory of Music (Mexico)
Chávez, Carlos 3 486

National Conservatory of Music (New York
City)
Dvořák, Antonin 5 168-169
Parker, Horatio William 12 109

National Consumers' League (United
States)
Kelley, F. 8 483-484
Lowell, Josephine Shaw 10 15-16
Roosevelt, Eleanor 13 275-277

**National Coordinating Committee to End
the War in Vietnam** (United States)
Dellinger, David 4 480-481

National Council of Negro Women (United
States)
Bethune, Mary McLeod 2 241-242

**National Council of Nigeria and the
Cameroons** (NCNC)
Azikiwe, Nnamdi 1 401-402
Macaulay, Herbert 10 78-79

**National Council of the Algerian Revolu-
tion**
Abbas, Ferhat 1 6-7
Ben Bella, Ahmed 2 148-149

National Council on the Arts (United
States)
Hanks, Nancy 7 126-127

National debt (United States)
Gallatin, Albert 6 183-184
Hamilton, Alexander 7 95-98
Jackson, Andrew 8 168-172
Morris, Robert 11 185-187

National Defense, Council of (United
States; World War I)
Baruch, Bernard Mannes 2 42-43
Catt, Carrie Chapman 3 375-376
Rosenwald, Julius 13 293

National Democratic Civic Movement
(Ecuador)
Plaza Lasso, Galo 12 350-351

National Democratic Party (Egypt)
Mubarak, Hosni 11 225-226

National Democratic Party (Liberia)
Doe, Samuel Kanyon 5 38-39

National Democratic Party (Nigeria)
Azikiwe, Nnamdi 1 401-402

National Democratic Party (Rhodesia)
Sithole, Ndabaningi 14 262-264

National Democratic Party (Zimbabwe)
Mugabe, Robert Gabriel 11 227-229

National Education Association (NEA)
Eliot, Charles William 5 254
Harris, William Torrey 7 177-178

**National Emergency Civil Rights Mobiliza-
tion** (United States)
Wilkins, Roy 16 282-283

National Emigration Convention (United
States)
Delany, Martin Robinson 4 473-474

National Endowment for the Arts (United
States)
de Mille, Agnes 4 486-488
Dove, Rita Frances 5 87-89
Hanks, Nancy 7 126-127

National Enquirer (newspaper)
Lundy, Benjamin 10 45-46

National Equal Rights League (United
States)
Trotter, William Monroe 15 306-307

National Era (journal)
Tappan brothers 15 105-106
Whittier, John Greenleaf 16 256-257

National Farm Workers Association (Unit-
ed States)
Chavez, Cesar 3 486-487
Valdez, Luis 15 399-400

National Film Board of Canada
Grierson, John 6 542-543

National Forest Commission (United States)
Pinchot, Gifford **12** 308-309

National Front (Colombia)
Lleras Camargo, Alberto **9** 467

National Front (India)
Singh, Vishwanath Pratap **14** 254-256

National Front party (Iran)
Mohammad Reza Shah Pahlavi
11 75-76

National Gallery (Berlin)
Beckmann, Max **2** 104-105

National Gallery (London)
George IV **6** 272-273

National Gallery of Art (Washington D.C.)
Mellon, Andrew William **10** 469-470

National Gallery of Canada
Carr, Emily **3** 319

National Geographic Society (United States)
Bell, Alexander Graham **2** 129-131
Greely, Adolphus Washington
6 517-518
Hubble, Edwin Powell **8** 10-11

National Health Service (England)
Attlee, Clement Richard **1** 361-362
Bevan, Aneurin **2** 248-249

National Hockey League (North America)
Gretzky, Wayne **6** 537-539
Howe, Gordie **7** 532-534
Orr, Bobby **12** 2-4

National Hot Rod Association (United States)
Muldowney, Shirley **11** 236-238

National Industrial Recovery Act (United States)
Wagner, Robert Ferdinand **16** 43

National Institute for Medical Research (England)
Dale, Henry Hallett **4** 371-373
Medawar, Peter Brian **10** 444-445

National Institutes of Health (United States)
Healy, Bernadine Patricia **7** 237-238
Varmus, Harold Eliot **15** 436-437

National insurance (England)
Asquith, Herbert Henry **1** 344-346
Lloyd George, David **9** 469-471

National Islamic Front (Sudan)
Turabi, Hassan Abdullah al- **15** 344-345

National Labor Relations Act (1935)
Stone, Harlan Fiske **14** 468-470
Wagner, Robert Ferdinand **16** 43

National Labor Union (established 1866)
Sylvis, William **15** 60-61

National Lancers ... (lithograph)
Lane, Fitz Hugh **9** 189

National Land League (Ireland)
Parnell, Charles Stewart **12** 117-119

National League (United States baseball)
Aaron, Henry Louis (Hank) **1** 2-3
Robinson, Jack Roosevelt **13** 207-208

National Liberal party (Germany)
Stresemann, Gustav **14** 508-509
Treitschke, Heinrich von **15** 293-294

National Liberation Council (Ghana)
Busia, Kofi Abrefa **3** 172-173

National Liberation Front (Algeria)
Abbas, Ferhat **1** 6-7
Ben Bella, Ahmed **2** 148-149
Fanon, Frantz **5** 379-380

National Liberation party (Costa Rica)
Ferrer, José Figuéres **5** 428-429

National Library (Buenos Aires)
Borges, Jorge Luis **2** 411-412

National Library (Managua, Nicaragua)
Darío, Rubén **4** 393-394

National Library (Peru)
Palma, Ricardo **12** 77

National Medical Association (United States)
Drew, Charles Richard **5** 100-101
Williams, Daniel Hale **16** 302-303

National Mobilization Committee to End the War in Vietnam (United States)
Hayden, Thomas Emmet **7** 217-219

National Movement (Lebanon)
Jumblatt, Kamal **8** 386-387

National Museum of Natural History (Paris)
see Muséum National d'Histoire Naturelle

National Negro Business League (United States)
Washington, Booker Taliaferro
16 125-126

National Negro Labor Union (United States)
Langston, John Mercer **9** 197

National Odriist Union (Peru)
Odría Amoretti, Manuel Apolinario
11 473-474

National Organization for Women (United States , established 1966)
Friedan, Betty **6** 109-111
Ireland, Patricia **8** 134-135
Smeal, Eleanor **14** 278-280
Yard, Mary Alexander **16** 438-439

National party (Australia)
Bjelke-Petersen, Johannes **2** 297-299

National party (Dominican Republic)
Vázquez, Horacio **15** 448-449

National party (Honduras)
Callejas Romero, Rafael Leonardo
3 233-234

National Party (New Zealand)
Holyoake, Keith Jacka **7** 460-462

National party (South Africa)
Botha, Pieter Willem **2** 436-438

de Klerk, Fredrik Willem **4** 466-468
Malan, Daniel Francois **10** 163-164
Vorster, Balthazar Johannes **16** 30-32

National peasant party (Romania)
Ferdinand **5** 413-414

National Peking University
see Peita

National Popular Alliance (Colombia)
see ANAPO

National Radical Union (Greece)
Karamanlis, Constantine **8** 440-441

National Recovery Administration (NRA)
Ford, Henry **6** 5-6
Hughes, Charles Evans **8** 15-16
Ickes, Harold LeClaire **8** 100-101
Russell, Charles Edward **13** 374-375
Stone, Harlan Fiske **14** 468-470

National Reformer (periodical)
Bradlaugh, Charles **2** 478

National Republican League (established 1870)
Lea, Henry Charles **9** 261-262

National Republicans (United States politics)
Jackson, Andrew **8** 168-172

National Research Council (Canada)
Herzberg, Gerhard **7** 349-350

National Research Council (United States)
Compton, Arthur Holly **4** 186-188
Drew, Charles Richard **5** 100-101
East, Edward Murray **5** 182-183
Millikan, Robert Andrews **11** 33-35

National Review (journal)
Buckley, William F. Jr. **3** 96-97

National Revolutionary Movement (Bolivia)
Paz, Octavio **12** 161-162

National Salvation Front (Romanian political party)
Iliescu, Ion **8** 111-112

National Secular Society (established 1866)
Bradlaugh, Charles **2** 478

National Security Act (United States)
Forrestal, James Vincent **6** 14

National Socialism
see Nazism

National Symphony Orchestra (United States)
Rostropovich, Mstislav Leopoldovich
13 317-318

National Union (Egypt)
Sadat, Anwar **13** 412-414

National Union Convention (1866)
Vallandigham, Clement Laird
15 406-407

National Union for Social Justice (United States)
Coughlin, Charles Edward **4** 265-266
Townsend, Francis Everitt **15** 282-283

National Union for the Total Independence of Angola (UNITA)
Savimbi, Jonas Malheiros **13** 503-505

National Union of Mineworkers (Great Britain)
Scargill, Arthur **13** 514-515

National Union of Mineworkers (South Africa)
Ramaphosa, Matemela Cyril **13** 15-16

National Union of Railwaymen (Great Britain)
Bevin, Ernest **2** 252-253

National Union of Women's Suffrage Societies (England)
Fawcett, Millicent Garrett **5** 398-400

National Union party (Portugal)
Salazar, António de Oliveira **13** 442-443

National Union party (United States)
Weed, Thurlow **16** 169-170

National Unionist party (Sudan)
Azhari, Sayyid Ismail al- **1** 399-401
Khalil, Sayyid Abdullah **8** 531-532

National Urban League (United States)
Brown, Ronald H. **3** 44-47
Jacob, John Edward **8** 185-188
Jordan, Vernon **8** 357-358
Rosenwald, Julius **13** 293
Young, Whitney Moore Jr. **16** 476-477

National War College (United States)
Goodpaster, Andrew Jackson **6** 439-441

National Will party (Iran)
Mohammad Reza Shah Pahlavi **11** 75-76

National Woman Suffrage Association (United States)
Anthony, Susan Brownell **1** 246-248
Gage, Matilda Joslyn **6** 167-169
Howe, Julia Ward **7** 535-536
Stanton, Elizabeth Cady **14** 402-403
Stone, Lucy **14** 471-472

National Woman's Loyal League
Stanton, Elizabeth Cady **14** 402-403

National Women's Political Caucus (United States; established 1970)
Friedan, Betty **6** 109-111
Natividad, Irene **11** 322-324

National Women's Trade Union League
Schneiderman, Rose **14** 22-23

National Youth Administration (United States)
Bethune, Mary McLeod **2** 241-242
Hopkins, Harry Lloyd **7** 494-495
Johnson, Lyndon Baines **8** 308-312
Roosevelt, Eleanor **13** 275-277

Nationale Vereinigung (Germany)
Kapp, Wolfgang **8** 436

Nationalism (politics)
Cabral, Amílcar Lopes **3** 202-203
Garneau, François-Xavier **6** 219-220
Gobineau, Comte de **6** 375-376

Kaplan, Mordecai Menahem **8** 435-436
Lassalle, Ferdinand **9** 216
Maurras, Charles Marie Photius **10** 350-351
Sorel, Georges **14** 347-348

Nationalism, African (Sub Sahara)
African American contributions
Blyden, Edward Wilmot **2** 348-349
Garvey, Marcus Mosiah **6** 228-229
Angola
de Andrade, Mario **4** 434-435
dos Santos, José Eduardo **5** 71-72
Neto, António Agostinho **11** 351-352
Savimbi, Jonas Malheiros **13** 503-505
Botswana
Khama, Seretse M. **8** 532-533
Masire, Quett Ketumile **10** 318-319
Cape Verde Islands
Cabral, Amílcar Lopes **3** 202-203
Congo
Lumumba, Patrice Emery **10** 43-45
Tshombe, Moïse Kapenda **15** 325-326
Youlou, Fulbert **16** 466-467
Dahomey
Apithy, Sourou Migan **1** 259-260
Ethiopia
Menelik II **10** 495-497
French West Africa
Houphouët-Boigny, Felix **7** 519-520
Gambia
Jawara, Dauda Kairaba **8** 227-228
Ghana
Busia, Kofi Abrefa **3** 172-173
Danquah, Joseph B. **4** 388-389
Nkrumah, Kwame **11** 408-410
Guinea-Bissau
Cabral, Amílcar Lopes **3** 202-203
Kenya
Kenyatta, Jomo **8** 512-514
Mboya, Thomas Joseph **10** 384-385
Ngala, Ronald Gideon **11** 373-374
Odinga, Ajuma Jaramogi Oginga **11** 471-473
Thuku, Harry **15** 212-213
Malawi
Banda, Hastings Kamuzu **1** 485-486
Booth, Joseph **2** 404-405
Mali
Keita, Modibo **8** 474-475
Mozambique
dos Santos, Marcelino **5** 72-74
Machel, Samora Moises **10** 94-96
Mondlane, Eduardo Chivambo **11** 100-101
Namibia
Nujoma, Shafiihuna **11** 441-443
Nigeria
Awolowo, Obafemi **1** 389-390
Azikiwe, Nnamdi **1** 401-402
Bello, Ahmadu **2** 139-140
Hayford, J. E. Casely **7** 228-230
Tafawa Balewa, Abubakar **15** 75

Rhodesia
Mugabe, Robert Gabriel **11** 227-229
Nkomo, Joshua Mqabuko **11** 405-407
Sithole, Ndabaningi **14** 262-264
Senegal
Bamba, Amadou **1** 481-482
Senghor, Léopold Sédar **14** 106-107
Sierra Leone
Margai, Milton Augustus Striery **10** 248-249
Somalia
Hassan, Muhammad Abdille **7** 194-195
South Africa
Botha, Louis **2** 434-436
Dube, John Langalibalele **5** 113
Hertzog, James Barry Munnik **7** 347-348
Lembede, Anton **9** 318-319
Malan, Daniel Francois **10** 163-164
Mandela, Nelson Rolihlahla **10** 185-186
Verwoerd, Hendrik Frensch **15** 472-473
Vorster, Balthazar Johannes **16** 30-32
Tanzania
Nyerere, Julius Kamberage **11** 447-449
Uganda
Kiwanuka, Benedicto Kagima Mugumba **9** 46-47
Mutesa II **11** 277-278
Obote, Apolo Milton **11** 457
Zambia
Kaunda, Kenneth David **8** 460-461
Zimbabwe
Mugabe, Robert Gabriel **11** 227-229
Nkomo, Joshua Mqabuko **11** 405-407
see also Nationalism, African (North Africa); Pan-Africanism

Nationalism, African (North Africa)
Algeria
Abbas, Ferhat **1** 6-7
Abd el-Kadir **1** 15
Ben Bella, Ahmed **2** 148-149
Boumediene, Houari **2** 445-446
Fanon, Frantz **5** 379-380
Messali Hadj **10** 527-528
Egypt
Abduh ibn Hasan Khayr Allah, Muhammad **1** 16-17
Fuad I **6** 139
Haykal, Muhammad Husain **7** 230-231
Ismail Pasha **8** 150-151
Nasser, Gamal Abdel **11** 317-318
Sadat, Anwar **13** 412-414
Tewfik Pasha **15** 157-158
Zaghlul Pasha, Saad **16** 485-486
Libya
Omar al-Mukhtar **11** 507-508
Morocco

Abd el-Krim el-Khatabi, Mohamed
  ben **1** 15-16
Allal al-Fassi, Mohamed **1** 162
Leclerc, Jacques Philippe **9** 272-273
Mohammed V **11** 79-81
Sudan
  Abboud, Ibrahim **1** 11-12
  Azhari, Sayyid Ismail al- **1** 399-401
  Khalil, Sayyid Abdullah **8** 531-532
  Samory Touré **13** 456
Tunisia
  Bourguiba, Habib **2** 453-455
  Zine el Abidine Ben Ali **16** 518-520

Nationalism, American
Cannon, Joseph Gurney **3** 261-262
Clay, Henry **4** 94-96
Davis, Jefferson **4** 416-418
Gadsden, James **6** 165-166
Jefferson, Thomas **8** 238-241
Marshall, John **10** 279-281
Paine, Thomas **12** 66-67
Ruffin, Edmund **13** 354-355
Story, Joseph **14** 480-481
see also Nationalism, Canadian;
  Nationalism, Latin American

Nationalism, Asian
Bangladesh
  Ziaur Rahman **16** 515-516
Bengal
  Mujibur Rahman **11** 234-236
Burma
  Aung San **1** 374-375
  Ba Maw **1** 480-481
  Ne Win **11** 364-365
  Nu, U **11** 439-441
  Thant, U **15** 161-162
Cambodia
  Sihanouk, Norodom **14** 222-223
China
  Chang Tso-lin **3** 434-435
  Chu Teh **4** 54-55
  Ku Chieh-kang **9** 120-121
  Mao Zedong **10** 225-227
  Wang Fu-chih **16** 99-101
  Wang T'ao **16** 105-106
India
  Deb, Radhakant **4** 437
  Ghose, Aurobindo **6** 293-294
  Śavajī **14** 266-267
  see also Indian National Congress;
    Passive resistance movements
Indonesia
  Hatta, Mohammad **7** 197-199
  Sukarno **15** 18-20
Japan
  Ito, Hirobumi **8** 153-155
  Natsume, Soseki **11** 324-325
  Saicho **13** 426-428
Korea
  Ito, Hirobumi **8** 153-155
  Rhee, Syngman **13** 117-120
Malaysia
  Tunku, Abdul Rahman **15** 340-341
Philippines
  Aguinaldo, Emilio **1** 88

Bonifacio, Andres **2** 393-394
Del Pilar, Marcelo Hilario **4** 486
Garcia, Carlos P. **6** 207-208
Marcos, Ferdinand **10** 240-242
Osmeña, Sergio **12** 22-24
Recto, Claro M. **13** 69-70
Rizal, José **13** 187-189
Sri Lanka
  Jayewardene, Junius Richard
    8 233-234
Thailand
  Phibun Songkhram, Luang
    12 264-265
Turkey
  Atatürk, Ghazi Mustapha Kemal
    1 356-357
  Gökalp, Mehmet Ziya **6** 395-396
  Venizelos, Eleutherios **15** 460-461
Vietnam
  Diem, Ngo Dinh **5** 6-7
  Giap, Vo Nguyen **6** 297-299
  Ho Chi Minh **7** 426-428

Nationalism, Canadian
Bourassa, Joseph-Henri-Napoleon
  2 446-447
Papineau, Louis-Joseph **12** 91
Scott, Francis Reginald **14** 66-67

Nationalism, European
Austria
  Dollfuss, Engelbert **5** 47
  Metternich, Klemens von
    10 533-536
Britain
  Henry III **7** 290-292
  Palmerston, 3d Viscount **12** 81-83
  Wallace, William **16** 75-76
Croatia
  Stepinac, Alojzije **14** 433-435
  Tudjman, Franjo **15** 333-335
Czechoslovakia
  Palacký, František **12** 69-70
  Wenceslaus **16** 201-202
France
  Poincaré, Raymond **12** 366-368
Germany
  Kapp, Wolfgang **8** 436
  Lieber, Francis **9** 401-402
  Staël, Germaine de **14** 391-392
  Stresemann, Gustav **14** 508-509
  Treitschke, Heinrich von
    15 293-294
  Wilson, Thomas Woodrow
    16 330-332
  see also Nazism
Hungary
  Andrássy, Julius **1** 222-223
  Deák, Francis **4** 431-432
  Kossuth, Louis **9** 88-90
  Pázmány, Péter **12** 164-165
  Palacký, František **12** 69-70
Ireland
  De Valera, Eamon **4** 514-515
  Emmet, Robert **5** 281-282
  Grattan, Henry **6** 499
  Hyde, Douglas **8** 82-83

Markievicz, Constance **10** 267-271
O'Connell, Daniel **11** 465-467
Parnell, Charles Stewart **12** 117-119
Pearse, Patrick Henry **12** 173-174
see also Sinn Fein
Italy
  Ferdinand II **5** 415-416
  Garibaldi, Giuseppe **6** 215-217
  Napoleon III **11** 310-312
  Peter I **12** 256
  Pius IX **12** 335-336
  Victor Emmanuel II **15** 483-484
Netherlands
  Oldenbarnevelt, Johan van
    11 495-496
  Philip II **12** 271-273
  William the Silent **16** 300-302
  Witt, Johan de **16** 348-349
Poland
  Gomulka, Wladislaw **6** 422-424
  Kościuszko, Tadeusz Andrzej
    Bonawentura **9** 88
  Paderewski, Ignace Jan **12** 56-57
  Pilsudski, Joseph **12** 305-306
  Proudhon, Pierre Joseph **12** 461-463
Prussia
  Frederick II **6** 81-84
  Frederick William III **6** 87
Russia
  Nicholas II **11** 378-380
  Pobedonostsev, Konstantin Petrovich
    12 360-361
  Yeltsin, Boris Nikolaevich
    16 449-452
Serbia
  Berchtold, Leopold von **2** 183-184
  Karadzic, Radovan **8** 437-440
  Milosevic, Slobodan **11** 39-40

Nationalism, Jewish
see Zionism

Nationalism, Latin American
Argentina
  Blanco, Antonio Guzmán **2** 320-321
  Irigoyen, Hipólito **8** 139-140
  Paz, Octavio **12** 161-162
  Rivadavia, Bernardino **13** 182-183
  Lamas, Carlos Saavedra **9** 175-176
Bolivia
  Ballivián, José **1** 475
  Sucre, Antonio José de **15** 11-12
Brazil
  Deodoro da Fonseca, Manoel **4** 502
  Varnhagen, Francisco Adolfo de
    15 437-438
Chile
  O'Higgins, Bernardo **11** 486
  Portales Plazazuelos, Diego José
    Víctor **12** 404
  San Martín, José de **13** 468-469
Colombia
  Nariño, Antonio **11** 314-315
  Santander, Franciso de Paula **13** 475
Cuba
  Batista y Zaldívar, Fulgencio
    2 57-58

Castro Ruz, Fidel **3** 365-368
Dessalines, Joan Jacques **4** 511-512
Grenada
  Bishop, Maurice **2** 292-293
Guyana
  Burnham, Forbes **3** 149-151
Jamaica
  Bustamante, William Alexander
  3 175-177
Mexico
  Hidalgo y Costilla, Miguel
  7 375-377
  Matamoros, Mariano **10** 329-330
  Santa Ana, Antonio López de
  13 471-472
Nicaragua
  Sandino, Augusto C. **13** 462-463
  Zelaya, José Santos **16** 495-496
Panama
  Torrijos, Omar **15** 269-270
Peru
  González Prada, Manuel **6** 431
  Mariátegui, José Carlos **10** 255-256
  Unánue, José Hipólito **15** 387-388
Uruguay
  Artigas, José Gervasio **1** 323
  Rivera, Fructuoso **13** 184-185
Venezuela
  Bolívar, Simón **2** 375-377
  Miranda, Francisco de **11** 52-53
  Páez, José Antonio **12** 58
  Sucre, Antonio José de **15** 11-12

Nationalism, Middle Eastern
Iran
  Mossadegh, Mohammad
  11 206-207
Iraq and Jordan
  Abdullah ibn Husein **1** 19-20
  Faisal I **5** 370-371
  Nuri al-Sa'id **11** 446-447
Kuwait
  'Abdullah al-Salim al-Sabah, Shaykh
  1 18-19
Palestine
  Arafat, Yasser **1** 270-271
Saudi Arabia
  Husein ibn Ali **8** 63
  ibn Saud, Abd al-Aziz **8** 94-95
Syria
  'Aflaq, Michel **1** 73-74

Nationalism and Social Communication
(book)
Deutsch, Karl Wolfgang **4** 512-514

Nationalism of industries
Chile
  Allende Gossens, Salvador
  1 174-176

Nationalist China
see China, Republic of

Nationalist party
Australia
  Bruce of Melbourne, 1st Viscount
  3 61-62
  Hughes, William Morris **8** 21-22

Indonesia
  Sukarno **15** 18-20
Morocco
  Allal al-Fassi, Mohamed **1** 162
South Africa
  Hertzog, James Barry Munnik
  7 347-348
  Paton, Alan Stewart **12** 134-135
Sweden
  Gustavus I **7** 42-43

Nationalist People's party
see Kuomintang

Nationalist Revolution (China; 1920s)
Kuo Mo-jo **9** 133-134
Lin Piao **9** 429-430
Yen Hsi-shan **16** 452-453

Nationalist Unionist party (Sudan)
Abboud, Ibrahim **1** 11-12

Nationalists (Spain)
Azaña Diaz, Manuel **1** 396-397
Franco Bahamonde, Francisco **6** 52-54

Nations, battle of the (1813)
see Leipzig, battle of

Native American Movement (United States)
Banks, Dennis J. **1** 488-489
Bellecourt, Clyde **2** 136-137

Native Argosy, A (stories)
Callaghan, Edward Morley **3** 229-230

Native of Winby ... (stories)
Jewett, Sarah Orne **8** 256

Native Son (film and novel)
Wright, Richard **16** 401-402

Native Stories (stories)
Alarcón, Pedro Antonio de **1** 100-101

Natives Land Act of 1913 (South Africa)
Botha, Louis **2** 434-436
Plaatje, Solomon Tshekisho **12** 341-342

Natives' Representative Council (South Africa)
Dube, John Langalibalele **5** 113
Luthuli, Albert John **10** 51-52

NATIVIDAD, IRENE (born 1948), Asian American activist and women's rights advocate **11** 322-324

Nativity (painting)
Botticelli, Sandro **2** 439-440
Campin, Robert **3** 255
Christus, Petrus **4** 33-34
Geertgen tot Sint Jans **6** 248
Piero della Francesca **12** 301-302
Schongauer, Martin **14** 26-28

Nativity (sculpture)
Arnolfo di Cambio **1** 315-316

Nativity of the Virgin (painting)
Andrea del Sarto **1** 224-225
Lorenzetti, Pietro and Ambrogio
  9 517-518

NATO
see North Atlantic Treaty Organization

Natoire, Charles Joseph (1700-1777), French painter
Greuze, Jean Baptiste **6** 539

NATSUME, SOSEKI (or Kinnosuke; 1867-1916), Japanese novelist and essayist **11** 324-325

Natural History (encyclopedia; Pliny)
Apelles **1** 257
Phidias **12** 265-267
Pliny the Elder **12** 355-356
Praxiteles **12** 433-434

Natural law
Blackstone, William **2** 310-311
Grotius, Hugo **7** 18-19
Pufendorf, Samuel von **12** 477-478
Savigny, Friedrich Karl von **13** 502-503
Vitoria, Francisco de **16** 1-2

Natural rights doctrine (philosophy)
Becker, Carl Lotus **2** 100-101
Bellarmine, Robert **2** 135-136
Cooper, James Fenimore **4** 220-223
Dickinson, John **4** 543-544
du Pont de Nemours, Pierre Samuel
  5 155-156
Hobbes, Thomas **7** 421-423
see also Social-contract theory

Natural selection (evolution)
Butler, Samuel **3** 183
Darwin, Charles Robert **4** 397-399
Dobzhansky, Theodosius **5** 35-37
Fisher, Ronald Aylmer **5** 463-464
Huxley, Julian **8** 75-77
Huxley, Thomas Henry **8** 77-79
Simpson, George Gaylord **14** 240-242
Spencer, Herbert **14** 369-370
Vries, Hugo de **16** 33-36
Wallace, Alfred Russel **16** 69-70
Weismann, August Freidrich Leopold
  16 178-180
see also Survival of the fittest

Natural theology
Brentano, Franz Clemens **2** 516-517
Butler, Joseph **3** 180-181
Darwin, Charles Robert **4** 397-399, 277
Paley, William **12** 72

Naturalis historia
see Natural History

Naturalism (art)
Asia
  Behzad **2** 123
Europe
  Clouet, Jean and François **4** 122-123
  González, Julio **6** 428-429
  La Tour, George de **9** 222
  Le Brun, Charles **9** 269-270
  Verrocchio, Andrea del **15** 471-472
United States
  Eakins, Thomas **5** 176-177
  French, Daniel Chester **6** 98-99
  Noguchi, Isamu **11** 416-418
  Ryder, Albert Pinkham **13** 391-392
  Wyant, Alexander Helwig
  16 409-410

Naturalism (literature)
  Australia
    Richardson, Henry Handel **13** 139
  Austria
    Schnitzler, Arthur **14** 23-24
  Denmark
    Dinesen Blixen-Finecke, Karen
      5 13-14
    Jacobsen, Jens Peter **8** 193-194
  France
    Daudet, Alphonse **4** 402-403
    Goncourt, Edmond de and Jules de
      6 426-427
    Huysmans, Joris Karl **8** 81-82
    Strindberg, August **14** 509-511
    Villon, François **15** 499-501
    Zola, Émile **16** 526-528
  Germany
    Hauptmann, Gerhart Johann Robert
      7 199-201
    Heyse, Paul Johann Ludwig
      7 372-373
    Mann, Thomas **10** 204-207
    Sudermann, Hermann **15** 12-13
  Japan
    Tanizaki, Junichiro **15** 101-102
  Russia
    Stanislavsky, Constantin **14** 398-399
  Sweden
    Lagerlöf, Selma Ottiliana Lovisa
      9 163-164
    Strindberg, August **14** 509-511
  United States
    Dreiser, Herman Theodore **5** 98-100
    Farrell, James Thomas **5** 390-391
    Garland, Hannibal Hamlin
      6 217-218
    Mailer, Norman Kingsley
      10 148-150
    Norris, Benjamin Franklin Jr.
      11 427-428
    O'Neill, Eugene **11** 514-516
Naturalism (philosophy)
  Kaplan, Mordecai Menahem **8** 435-436
  Nagel, Ernest **11** 291-292
  Telesio, Bernardino **15** 138-139
Naturalists
  see Scientists—naturalists
Nature (essay)
  Emerson, Ralph Waldo **5** 278-280
Nature of a Crime, The (book)
  Ford, Ford Madox **6** 1-2
Naucratis (ancient city; Egypt)
  Petrie, William Matthew Flinders
    12 261-262
Naufragios, Los (book)
  Cabeza de Vaca, Álvar Núñez **3** 197
Nausea (novel)
  Sartre, Jean Paul **13** 491-492
Nautilus (literary submarine)
  Verne, Jules **15** 467-469
Nautilus (ship)
  Wilkins, George Hubert **16** 281-282

Nautilus (submarine)
  Fulton, Robert **6** 151-152
Nauvoo (city; Illinois)
  Cabet, Étienne **3** 196
  Smith, Joseph **14** 297-298
  Young, Brigham **16** 469-470
Navaho Indians (North America)
  Begay, Harrison **2** 117-118
  Carson, Christopher **3** 334-335
  Gilpin, Laura **6** 326-327
  Kluckhohn, Clyde **9** 56-57
  Manuelito **10** 220-222
Naval Battle ... (painting)
  Manet, Édouard **10** 193-194
Naval Lyceum (New York City)
  Perry, Matthew Calbraith **12** 237-239
Naval Observatory, United States (Washington D.C.)
  Hall, Asaph **7** 83-84
  Newcomb, Simon **11** 361-362
  Wilkes, Charles **16** 279-280
Navarino, battles of
  1572
    Cervantes, Miguel de Saavedra
      3 395-398
  1827
    Ibrahim Pasha **8** 97-98
    Mahmud II **10** 145-147
Navarrete, battle of (1367)
  Edward the Black Prince **5** 217-218
Navayi, Ali Sheir (Nawai; 1440-1501),
  Turkish emir and poet
  Behzad **2** 123
Navigation
  Baffin, William **1** 435-436
  Huygens, Christiaan **8** 79-81
  Shreve, Henry Miller **14** 207
  see also Scientists—navigators
Navigation Acts (England)
  Andros, Edmund **1** 234-235
  Otis, James Jr. **12** 25-27
  Penn, William **12** 200-202
Navigation, Bureau of (United States)
  Nimitz, Chester William **11** 395-396
Navio negreiro, O (poem)
  Castro Alves, Antônio de **3** 364-365
NAVRATILOVA, MARTINA (born 1956),
  American tennis player **11** 325-327
Nawai, Ali Sheir
  see Navayi, Ali Sheir
NAYLOR, GLORIA (born 1950), African
  American novelist **11** 328-329
Nazarene, The (trilogy)
  Asch, Shalom **1** 325-326
Nazarin (film)
  Buñuel, Luis **3** 127-128
Nazeing group (religion)
  Eliot, John **5** 256-258
Nazem al-Doleh (al-Molk)
  see Malkam Khan, Mirza

Nazi hunters
  Wiesenthal, Simon **16** 264-266
Nazi party
  see Nazism
Nazism (National Socialism)
  aims and theories
    Frisch, Max **6** 118-119
    Gumplowicz, Ludwig **7** 41
    Spengler, Oswald **14** 372-373
  Austria
    Dollfuss, Engelbert **5** 47
    Freud, Sigmund **6** 103-106
    Schoenberg, Arnold **14** 24-26
    Schuschnigg, Kurt von **14** 45-46
  Chile
    Ibáñez del Campo, Carlos **8** 88
  England
    Gooch, George Peabody **6** 432-433
  France
    Céline, Louis Ferdinand **3** 390-391
    Pétain, Henri Philippe **12** 250-252
    Perse, Saint-John **12** 242-243
  Germany (opponents)
    Barth, Karl **2** 31-32
    Baum, Herbert **2** 66-73
    Bonhoeffer, Dietrich **2** 389-391
    Hindenburg, Paul Ludwig Hans von
      Beneckendorff und von **7** 400-401
    Mann, Heinrich **10** 201-202
    Mann, Thomas **10** 204-207
    Mannheim, Karl **10** 208-209
    Mendelsohn, Erich **10** 488
    Meyerhof, Otto Fritz **10** 537-539
    Mies van der Rohe, Ludwig
      11 10-12
    Pechstein, Hermann Max
      12 176-177
    Richter, Hans **13** 149-150
    Rommel, Erwin **13** 268-269
    Schlick, Friedrich Albert Moritz
      14 16-17
    Schumacher, Kurt **14** 40-41
    Schuman, Robert **14** 41
    Tillich, Paul Johannes **15** 224-225
    Ulbricht, Walter **15** 383-384
  Germany (supporters)
    Barbie, Klaus **1** 501-503
    Benn, Gottfried **2** 164
    Brunner, Alois **3** 73-74
    Eichmann, Adolf **5** 226-227
    Goebbels, Joseph Paul **6** 384-385
    Göring, Hermann Wilhelm
      6 457-458
    Hess, Walter Richard Rudolf
      7 363-365
    Hitler, Adolf **7** 417-420
    Mengele, Josef **10** 502-503
    von Papen, Franz **16** 28-29
  Germany (victims)
    see Holocaust
  Greece
    Seferis, George **14** 84-85
  history of
    Shirer, William L. **14** 198-199
  Holland

Wilhelmina **16** 278-279
Hungary
Kármán, Theodore von **8** 451-452
Szilard, Leo **15** 64-66
India
Rabindranath Tagore **12** 529-531
Latvia
Dubnov, Simon **5** 115-116
literature relating to
Lind, Jakov **9** 419-420
Poland
Penderecki, Krzysztof **12** 195-197
Scandinavia
Hamsun, Knut **7** 113-114
Leopold III **9** 347-348
Undset, Sigrid **15** 388-389
South Africa
Verwoerd, Hendrik Frensch
15 472-473
Vorster, Balthazar Johannes
16 30-32
United States
Coughlin, Charles Edward
4 265-266
Porter, Katherine Anne **12** 406-407
Szold, Henrietta **15** 66-67
Thompson, Dorothy **15** 195-196
White, William Allen **16** 240-241
Wise, Stephen Samuel **16** 344-345
Union of Soviet Socialist Republics.
Litvinov, Maxim Maximovich
9 451-452
see also Anti-Semitism

Nazi-Soviet Pact (1939)
see Molotov-Ribbentrop Pact

NAZZAM, IBRAHIM IBN SAYYAR AL-
(died circa 840), Moslem thinker and theologian **11** 329

NBC
see National Broadcasting Co.

NC-1 flying boat (aircraft)
Byrd, Richard Evelyn **3** 186-187

Ndebele (Matabele; African people)
Kruger, Stephanus Johannes Paulus
9 108-109
Lobengula **9** 474-475
Mzilikazi **11** 285-286
Pretorius, Andries **12** 444-445
Rhodes, Cecil John **13** 120-122
Salisbury, 3d Marquess of **13** 448-449

Ndwandwe (African people)
Mzilikazi **11** 285-286

NE WIN (born 1911), Burmese political
leader **11** 364-365
Aung San **1** 374-375
Ba Maw **1** 480-481
Nu, U **11** 439-441

NEA
see National Education Association

Neagle, John (1796-1865), American
painter
Moran, Thomas **11** 151-152
Stuart, Gilbert **14** 513-515

Neal, John (1793-1876), American writer
Poe, Edgar Allan **12** 363-365

Near the Ocean (poems)
Lowell, Robert Trail Spence Jr. **10** 16-17

Nebbia v. New York (legal case)
Cardozo, Benjamin Nathan **3** 288-290

Nebo (Mt. Pisgah)
Moses **11** 200-201

Nebraska (state; United States)
Bryan, William Jennings **3** 80-82
Douglas, Stephen Arnold **5** 80-82
Fletcher, Alice Cunningham **5** 486-487
Kerrey, J. Robert **8** 521-522
Norris, George William **11** 428-429
Pound, Roscoe **12** 417-418
see also Kansas-Nebraska Act

Nebraska, University of (Lincoln)
Johnson, Alvin Saunders **8** 293-294
Pershing, John Joseph **12** 243-244
Pound, Roscoe **12** 417-418
Ross, Edward Alsworth **13** 300

Nebrija, Antonio de (1444-1532), Spanish
humanist
Encina, Juan del **5** 283

NEBUCHADNEZZAR (ruled 605-562 B.C.),
king of Babylon **11** 330
Micah **10** 542-543

Nebula (astronomy)
Chamberlin, Thomas Chrowder
3 415-416
Herschel, John Frederick William
7 340-341
Huggins, William **8** 14-15
Laplace, Marquis de **9** 202-204

Necessary Angel (essays)
Stevens, Wallace **14** 443-445

Necessity of Atheism, The (pamphlet)
Shelley, Percy Bysshe **14** 176-178

Necker, Anne Louise Germaine
see Staël, Germaine de

NECKER, JACQUES (1732-1804), French
financier and statesman **11** 330-331
Louis XVI **9** 534-535
Marie Antoinette **10** 258-259
Mirabeau, Comte de **11** 51-52
Smith, Adam **14** 283-284
Staël, Germaine de **14** 391-392

"Neck-verse" (Latin)
Jonson, Ben **8** 343-345

Needham, John Turberville (1713-1781),
English naturalist
Spallanzani, Lazzaro **14** 360-361

Needham, Joseph (1900-1995), English
biochemist
Spemann, Hans **14** 368-369

Neefe, Christian Gottlob (1748-1798),
German composer
Beethoven, Ludwig van **2** 114-117

NEFERTITI (flourished first half 14th century B.C.), Egyptian queen **11** 331-332

Negative Dialectics (book)
Adorno, Theodor W. **1** 65-67

Negro, The (book)
Du Bois, William Edward Burghardt
5 116-118
Page, Thomas Nelson **12** 59-60

Negro American Family, The (book)
Du Bois, William Edward Burghardt
5 116-118

Negro and the New World, The (book)
Johnston, Henry Hamilton **8** 322-323

Negro Artisan, The (book)
Du Bois, William Edward Burghardt
5 116-118

Negro Boxer (papiers découpés)
Matisse, Henri **10** 336-337

**Negro Bureau of the Red International of
Labor Unions** (Union of Soviet Socialist
Republics)
Padmore, George **12** 57-58

Negro Church, The (book)
Du Bois, William Edward Burghardt
5 116-118

Negro Church in America, The (book)
Frazier, Edward Franklin **6** 77

Negro Digest (magazine)
Johnson, John Harold **8** 306-308

Negro Factories Corp. (United States)
Garvey, Marcus Mosiah **6** 228-229

Negro Family ... (books)
Frazier, Edward Franklin **6** 77

Negro Folk Symphony (musical composition)
Dawson, William Levi **4** 427-428

Negro in Ancient History, The (book)
Blyden, Edward Wilmot **2** 348-349

Negro in Business, The (book)
Du Bois, William Edward Burghardt
5 116-118

Negro in the American Rebellion, The
(book)
Brown, William Wells **3** 48-49

Negro League (United States baseball)
Mays, Willie **10** 376-379
Paige, Satchel **12** 62-65
Robinson, Jack Roosevelt **13** 207-208

Negro Question, The (book)
Cable, George Washington **3** 198-199

Negro Speaks of River, A (poem)
Hughes, Langston **8** 18-19

**Negro Workers, International Conference
of** (Hamburg, Germany)
Wallace-Johnson, Isaac Theophilus
Akunna **16** 76-77

Negroes in Negroland (book)
Helper, Hinton Rowan **7** 272-273

Negroes of Rockaway Beach (painting)
Marsh, Reginald **10** 276-277

Negromante, Il (play)
Ariosto, Ludovico **1** 289-290

NEHRU, JAWAHARLAL (1889-1964), Indian nationalist, prime minister 1947-1964 **11** 332-334

associates

Bhabha, Homi Jehangir **2** 253-254

Bose, Subhas Chandra **2** 430-431

Kamaraj, Kumaraswami **8** 415

Menon, Vengalil Krishnan Krishna **10** 507-509

Narayan, Jayaprakash **11** 312-313

Nasser, Gamal Abdel **11** 317-318

Prasad, Rajendra **12** 433

Radhakrishnan, Sarvepalli **12** 537-538

Rajagopalachari, Chakravarti **13** 6-7

China and

Chou En-lai **4** 20-22

Dalai Lama **4** 369-371

neutralism

Sihanouk, Norodom **14** 222-223

partition of India

Liaquat Ali Khan **9** 397

Patel, Vallabhbhai **12** 129-130

relatives

Gandhi, Indira Priyadarshini **6** 200-201

Gandhi, Mohandas Karamchand **6** 201-204

Nehru, Motilal **11** 334-335

Pandit, Vijaya Lakshmi **12** 83-84

NEHRU, MOTILAL (1861-1931), Indian lawyer and statesman **11** 334-335

Das, Chitta Ranjan **4** 401-402

Nehru, Jawaharlal **11** 332-334

Pandit, Vijaya Lakshmi **12** 83-84

Nehru, Swarup Kumari

see Pandit, Vijaya Lakshmi

NEILL, ALEXANDER SUTHERLAND (1883-1973), Scottish psychologist **11** 335-336

Neither Out Far Nor In Deep (poem)

Frost, Robert Lee **6** 130-133

Nejd (Arabic Kingdom)

see Saudi Arabia

Neko to Shozo to Futari no Onna (novel)

Tanizaki, Junichiro **15** 101-102

Nekrasov, Nikolai Alekseevich (1821-1877), Russian poet

Tolstoy, Leo **15** 262-265

Turgenev, Ivan Sergeyevich **15** 345-348

Nekrassov (play)

Sartre, Jean Paul **13** 491-492

Nelligan, Émile (1879-1941), French-Canadian poet

Morin, Paul **11** 174

NELSON, HORATIO (Viscount Nelson; 1758-1805), English admiral **11** 336-338

Napoleon I **11** 306-310

Suvorov, Aleksandr Vasilievich **15** 44-45

William IV **16** 296-297

Nembutsu (Buddhism)

Ennin **5** 288-289

NEMEROV, HOWARD (1920-1991), American author and third poet laureate of the United States **11** 338-340

Nemesis (print)

Dürer, Albrecht **5** 159-161

Nemirovich-Danchenko, Vladimir Ivanovich (1859-1943), Russian dramatist

Meyerhold, Vsevolod Emilievich **10** 539

Stanislavsky, Constantin **14** 398-399

Nemo, Captain (literary character)

Verne, Jules **15** 467-469

Nenna, Pomponio (1560-before 1618), Italian composer

Gesualdo, Don Carlo **6** 287-288

Neobehaviorism (psychology)

Hull, Clark Leonard **8** 28

Watson, John Broadus **16** 138-139

Neoclassic school (economics)

Knight, Frank Hyneman **9** 58-59

Pigou, Arthur Cecil **12** 302

see also Keynesian economics

Neoclassicism (art)

Denmark

Friedrich, Caspar David **6** 114-115

England

Adam, Robert and James **1** 38-40

Blake, William **2** 316-318

Chippendale, Thomas **4** 1-2

Copley, John Singleton **4** 228-230

Fuseli, Henry **6** 153-155

Gainsborough, Thomas **6** 170-172

Hepplewhite, George **7** 317-318

Hogarth, William **7** 446-447

Reynolds, Joshua **13** 115-116

Romney, George **13** 269-270

Soane, John **14** 314-315

Wedgwood, Josiah **16** 168-169

West, Benjamin **16** 210-212

Wilson, Richard **16** 329-330

France (architecture)

Ledoux, Claude Nicolas **9** 277-278

Soufflot, Jacques Germain **14** 349-350

France (painting)

David, Jacques Louis **4** 407-409

Fragonard, Jean Honoré **6** 38-39

Greuze, Jean Baptiste **6** 539

Ingres, Jean Auguste Dominique **8** 121-123

Prud'hon, Pierre Paul **12** 469

France (sculpture)

Carpeaux, Jean Baptiste **3** 318-319

Clodion **4** 121

Duchamp-Villon, Raymond **5** 123

Falconet, Étienne Maurice **5** 372

Houdon, Antoine **7** 516-517

Germany

Behrens, Peter **2** 121-122

Mengs, Anton Raphael **10** 505

Schinkel, Karl Friedrich **14** 8

Italy

Canova, Antonio **3** 263-264

Fuseli, Henry **6** 153-155

Guardi, Francesco **7** 24-25

Mengs, Anton Raphael **10** 505

Severini, Gino **14** 122

Spain

Churriguera, José Benito de **4** 53-54

Switzerland

Fuseli, Henry **6** 153-155

United States

Benjamin, Asher **2** 162-163

Flannagan, John Bernard **5** 480

French, Daniel Chester **6** 98-99

Lipchitz, Jacques **9** 432-433

Revere, Paul **13** 110-111

Vanderlyn, John **15** 417

West, Benjamin **16** 210-212

Neoclassicism (dance)

Balanchine, George **1** 461-462

Neoclassicism (literature)

Canada

Crémazie, Octave **4** 305-306

China

Liu Hsieh **9** 452-453

Liu Tsung-Yüan **9** 455-456

England

Coleridge, Samuel Taylor **4** 154-156

Dryden, John **5** 106-107

Herrick, Robert **7** 336-339

France

Cocteau, Jean **4** 132-133

Dumas, Alexandre **5** 136-138

Hugo, Victor Marie **8** 22-25

Germany

Goethe, Johann Wolfgang von **6** 388-391

Neoclassicism (music)

Boulez, Pierre **2** 444-445

Busoni, Ferruccio Benvenuto **3** 173-174

Cage, John **3** 211-214

Gluck, Christoph Willibald **6** 372-374

Henze, Hans Werner **7** 314

Holst, Gustav **7** 459-460

Krenek, Ernst **9** 98-99

Roussel, Albert **13** 328-329

Stravinsky, Igor Fedorovich **14** 502-506

Neogrammarian philology

Bloomfield, Leonard **2** 338

Neoimpressionism (art)

Hofmann, Hans **7** 442-443

Kirchner, Ernst Ludwig **9** 34-35

Seurat, Georges Pierre **14** 120-122

Van Gogh, Vincent **15** 427-429

Neologism (literature)

Geddes, Patrick **6** 246-247

Gracián y Morales, Baltasar Jerónimo **6** 481-482

Malherbe, François de **10** 169-170

Neon (element—chemistry)

Aston, Francis William **1** 350-351

Mendeleev, Dmitrii Ivanovich **10** 486-488

Ramsay, William **13** 21-22

Thomson, Joseph John **15** 200-201

Neoplasticism (art)

Mondrian, Piet **11** 101-102

Neoplatonism (philosophy)
and Cabalism
Leon, Moses de **9** 336
Nahmanides **11** 293-294
Scholem, Gershom **14** 26
in Christian thought
Ambrose **1** 192-193
Athanasius **1** 358-359
Augustine **1** 367-370
Eckhart, Johann **5** 200-201
Erigena, John Scotus **5** 308-309
Julian of Norwich **8** 381
in Islamic thought
Ashari, Abu al- Hasan Ali al-
1 327-328
Averroës **1** 382-383
Avicenna **1** 386-387
ibn Gabirol, Solomon ben Judah
8 92
Kindi, Abu-Yusuf Yaqub ibn-Ishaq al-
9 10-11
Omar Khayyam **11** 510-511
see also Sufism
influence on the arts
Dürer, Albrecht **5** 159-161
Michelangelo Buonarroti **11** 2-5
Vaughan, Henry **15** 444-445
modified
Swedenborg, Emanuel **15** 49-50
source
Aristotle **1** 295-296
Hypatia of Alexandria **8** 85
Plato **12** 345-347
Plotinus **12** 358-359
Proclus Diadochus **12** 457
see also Platonism

Neoptolemus (literary character)
Sophocles **14** 343-345

Neorealism (films)
Fellini, Federico **5** 408-409

Neorealism (literature)
Pavese, Cesare **12** 154-155
Remarque, Erich Maria **13** 91
Vittorini, Elio **16** 2-3

Neoromanticism (literature)
Cummings, Edward Estlin **4** 334-336
Hauptmann, Gerhart Johann Robert
7 199-201
Hofmannsthal, Hugo von **7** 443-444
Huch, Ricarda **8** 11-12
Lagerlöf, Selma Ottiliana Lovisa
9 163-164

Neoteroi (new poets)
Catullus, Gaius Valerius **3** 377-378

Neo-Confucianism (philosophy)
Chu Hsi **4** 40-43
Han Yü **7** 136-137
Ieyasu, Tokugawa **8** 103-106
Lu Chiu-yuan **10** 24-25
Ou-yang Hsiu **12** 33-34
Wang Fu-chih **16** 99-101
Wang Yang-ming **16** 108-109
Yi Hwang **16** 457
Yi Sng-gye **16** 458-459

Neo-Destour party (Tunisia)
Bourguiba, Habib **2** 453-455

Neo-Freudianism (psychology)
Horney, Karen Danielsen **7** 508-509
Marcuse, Herbert **10** 245-247

Neo-Georgian manner (architecture)
Shaw, Richard Norman **14** 167-168

Neo-Gothic style (architecture)
Gaudí i Cornet, Antoni **6** 235-236
Schinkel, Karl Friedrich **14** 8

Neo-Greek form (architecture)
Schinkel, Karl Friedrich **14** 8

Neo-Kantianism (philosophy)
Cassirer, Ernst **3** 358-359
Cohen, Hermann **4** 138-139

Neo-Marxism (philosophy)
Menon, Vengalil Krishnan Krishna
10 507-509

Neo-orthodoxy
see Dialectical theology

Neo-Shintoism (Japanese religion)
Mabuchi, Kamo **10** 73-74

Neo-Taoism (Chinese religion)
Kublai Khan **9** 115-118

Nepal (nation; Central Asia)
Birendra, King **2** 282-283
Chou En-lai **4** 20-22
Dalai Lama **4** 369-371
Mahendra, King **10** 138-139
Qianlong **12** 502-505

Neper, John
see Napier, John

Nepera Chemical Co. (established 1893)
Baekeland, Leo Hendrik **1** 430-431

Nephelometer (instrument)
Richards, Theodore William
13 137-138

Nephritis (medicine)
Bright, Richard **3** 7-8

Nepos, Julius (died 480), Roman emperor
474-476
Odoacer **11** 473

Nepotism (religion)
Clement V **4** 101-102
Dunstan **5** 151-152
Julius II **8** 384-386

Neptune (planet)
Adams, John Couch **1** 51-52
Leverrier, Urbain Jean Joseph **9** 361-362
Newcomb, Simon **11** 361-362

Neptune (sculpture)
Sansovino, Jacopo **13** 470-471

Neptune, Fountain of (Bologna; Florence)
Giovanni da Bologna **6** 345-346

Nerchinsk, Treaty of (1689)
K'ang-hsi **8** 423-426

NERI, ST. PHILIP (1515-1595), Italian
reformer **11** 340
Bellarmine, Robert **2** 135-136

Cajetan **3** 215-216
Caravaggio **3** 282-284
Gregory XIII **6** 534

NERNST, WALTHER (born Hermann
Walther Nernst; 1864-1941), German
chemist and inventor **11** 340-342
Avogadro, Lorenzo Romano Amedeo
Carlo **1** 388-389
Einstein, Albert **5** 228-231
Wigner, Eugene Paul **16** 268-269

Nero (opera)
Handel, George Frederick **7** 116-119

NERO CLAUDIUS CAESAR (37-68),
Roman emperor 54-68 **11** 342-344
historians of
Suetonius Tranquillus, Gaius **15** 13
Tacitus **15** 70-72
in literature
Juvenal **8** 397-399
Racine, Jean Baptiste **12** 532-535
influenced by
Claudius Germanicus, Tiberius
4 91-92
Flamininus, Titus Quinctius **5** 477
officials
Petronius Arbiter **12** 262-263
Seneca the Younger, Lucius Annaeus
14 103-105
Titus Flavius Vespasianus
15 247-248
Vespasian **15** 475-476
persecutions
Peter **12** 252-253

NERUDA, PABLO (Neftalí Ricardo Reyes
Basoalto; 1904-73), Chilean poet, Nobel
prize winner 1971 **11** 344-345
Guevara, Ernesto **7** 30-31

Nerva, Marcus Cocceius (circa 35-98),
Roman emperor 96-98
Akiba ben Joseph **1** 97-98
Martialis, Marcus Valerius **10** 286-287
Tacitus **15** 70-72
Trajan **15** 291-292

NERVAL, GÉRARD DE (1808-1855),
French poet **11** 345-346
Hugo, Victor Marie **8** 22-25

Nerve (anatomy)
chemical transmission
Dale, Henry Hallett **4** 371-373
Eccles, John Carew **5** 195-196
Loewi, Otto **9** 486-487
electric conduction
Du Bois-Reymond, Emil **5** 118-119
Galvani, Luigi **6** 194-195
Hodgkin, Alan Lloyd **7** 431-432
growth factor
Levi-Montalcini, Rita **9** 366-368
injuries repaired
Medawar, Peter Brian **10** 444-445
structure and function
Adrian, Edgar Douglas **1** 67-69
Bernard, Claude **2** 208-210
Erlanger, Joseph **5** 310-311

Helmholtz, Hermann Ludwig Ferdinand von **7** 268-269
Hill, Archibald Vivian **7** 385-386
Swammerdam, Jan **15** 48-49
see also Nervous system

Nerves of Government, The (book)
Deutsch, Karl Wolfgang **4** 512-514

NERVI, PIER LUIGI (1891-1979), Italian architect and engineer **11** 346-348
Breuer, Marcel **2** 520-521

Nervous system (human)
diseases
Bright, Richard **3** 7-8
Charcot, Jean Martin **3** 442
Morgagni, Giovanni Battista **11** 158-159
Peterson, Edith R. **12** 258-259
physiology and mechanisms
Adrian, Edgar Douglas **1** 67-69
Dale, Henry Hallett **4** 371-373
Helmholtz, Hermann Ludwig Ferdinand von **7** 268-269
Hess, Walter Rudolf **7** 365
Pavlov, Ivan Petrovich **12** 155-157
Peterson, Edith R. **12** 258-259
Sherrington, Charles Scott **14** 187-189

Nervous system (plants)
Bose, Jagadis Chandra **2** 429-430

Nesfield, William Eden (1835-1888), English architect
Shaw, Richard Norman **14** 167-168

Nesjar, battle of (1001)
Olaf, II **11** 493-494

NESSELRODE, COUNT KARL ROBERT (1780-1862), Russian diplomat **11** 348-349
Metternich, Klemens von **10** 533-536

Nest of Gentlefolk, A (novel)
Turgenev, Ivan Sergeyevich **15** 345-348

Nestorianism (Christian heresy)
Cyril **4** 362
Eutyches **5** 335
Hafiz, Shams al-Din **7** 63
Kublai Khan **9** 115-118
Leo I **9** 329-330
Nestorius **11** 349-350

NESTORIUS (died circa 453), Syrian patriarch of Constantinople and heresiarch **11** 349-350
see also Nestorianism

Netaji (führer)
see Bose, S.C.

NETANYAHU, BINYAMIN (born 1949), Israeli ambassador to the United Nations (1984-1988), head of the Likud Party, and prime minister **11** 350-351

Netherlandish art
Bosch, Hieronymus **2** 426-428
Bruegel, Pieter the Elder **3** 65-67
Geertgen tot Sint Jans **6** 248
Le Nain, Antoine, Louis and Mathieu **9** 321-322

Memling, Hans **10** 476
see also Dutch art and architecture; Flemish art

Netherlandish music
Isaac, Heinrich **8** 143-144
Obrecht, Jacob **11** 457-458
Ockeghem, Johannes **11** 464-465

Netherlandish Proverbs (painting)
Bruegel, Pieter the Elder **3** 65-67

Netherlands, Kingdom of (nation; Europe)
American colony
Minuit, Peter **11** 50
Stuyvesant, Peter **15** 5-6
Van Rensselaer, Kiliaen **15** 430-431
Belgian revolution
Leopold I **9** 345-346
culture
see Dutch art; Dutch literature; Dutch music; Flemish art; Netherlandish art
exploration and colonialism
Coen, Jan Pieterszoon **4** 133
Hudson, Henry **8** 12-13
John Maurice of Nassau **8** 281-282
Schouten, William Cornelius **14** 31
Tasman, Abel Janszoon **15** 113-114
Van Diemen, Anthony Meuza **15** 420
French wars
Bernadotte, Jean Baptiste **2** 205-206
Colbert, Jean Baptiste **4** 142-143
Francis I **6** 40-43
Henry IV **7** 293-295
historians of
Motley, John Lothrop **11** 211-212
Holy Roman Empire and
Charles V **3** 457-459
Leopold II **9** 346
Napoleonic era
Bonaparte, Louis **2** 382-383
Cuvier, Georges Léopold **4** 357-359
William I **16** 291-292
reforms
Tinbergen, Jan **15** 228-229
Wilhelmina **16** 278-279
religious controversy
Grotius, Hugo **7** 18-19
Oldenbarnevelt, Johan van **11** 495-496
revolt against Spain
Alba, Duke of **1** 103-104
Elizabeth I **5** 263-266
Essex, 2d Earl of **5** 321-322
Philip II **12** 271-273
Philip III **12** 273-274
Witt, Johan de **16** 348-349
since World War II
Van Eekelen, Willem Frederik **15** 426-427
United Provinces
Maurice of Nassau **10** 348-349
William III **16** 295-296
William the Silent **16** 300-302
War of the Spanish Succession
see Spanish Succession, War of the

World War II and rehabilitation
Beatrix, Wilhelmina von Amsberg Queen **2** 92-93
Juliana **8** 379-380
see also Austria-Austrian Netherlands; Belgium-Spanish Netherlands; Dutch Wars; Indonesia—East Indies; Low Countries; Utrecht, Union of

NETO, ANTÓNIO AGOSTINHO (1922-1979), Angolan intellectual and nationalist and first president of the People's Republic of Angola **11** 351-352

Netochka Nezvanova (novel)
Dostoevsky, Fyodor **5** 74-77

Netscher, Caspar (1639-1684), German painter
Ter Borch, Gerard **15** 146

Nettles (poems)
Lawrence, David Herbert **9** 247-248

Neue deutsche Liedlein (musical collection)
Lassus, Roland de **9** 216-218

Neue Gedichte (poems)
Huch, Ricarda **8** 11-12
Rilke, Rainer Maria **13** 171-172

Neue Gesicht der herrschenden Klasse (lithograph series)
Grosz, George **7** 17-18

Neue Künstlervereinigung
see New Artists' Association

Neue Liebe, Neues Leben (poems)
Goethe, Johann Wolfgang von **6** 388-391

Neue Liebeslieder Waltzes (musical composition)
Brahms, Johannes **2** 490-492

Neue Münchner Sezession
see New Munich Secession (art group)

Neue Pausias, Der (ballad)
Goethe, Johann Wolfgang von **6** 388-391

Neue Reich, Das (poems)
George, Stefan **6** 277-278

Neue Sachlichkeit (art)
see New Objectivity

Neue Teutsche Merkur, Der (journal)
Wieland, Christoph Martin **16** 260-261

Neue Wacht-Gebäude (Berlin, Germany)
Schinkel, Karl Friedrich **14** 8

Neue Zeit, Die (newspaper)
Bernstein, Eduard **2** 218
Cahan, Abraham **3** 214
Kautsky, Karl Johann **8** 462-463

Neue Zeitschrift für Musik (periodical)
Chopin, Frédéric François **4** 16-18
Schumann, Robert Alexander **14** 41-43

Neuer deutscher Novellenschatz (novellas)
Heyse, Paul Johann Ludwig **7** 372-373

Neuere Gedichte (poems)
Keller, Gottfried **8** 478-479

NEUFELD, ELIZABETH F. (born 1928), American biochemist **11** 352-353

Neuilly (city; France)
Le Corbusier **9** 274-275

NEUMANN, BALTHASAR (1687-1753), German architect **11** 354-355
Boffrand, Gabriel Germain **2** 361
Hildebrandt, Johann Lucas von **7** 380-381
Tiepolo, Giovanni Battista **15** 219-220

Neumann, Franz (1798-1895), German theoretical physicist
Kirchhoff, Gustav Robert **9** 33-34

Neumeister, Erdmann (1671-1756), German Lutheran theologian and hymn writer
Bach, Johann Sebastian **1** 416-419

Neun Bücher preussischer Geschichte (book)
Ranke, Leopold von **13** 33-35

Neurobiology
Levi-Montalcini, Rita **9** 366-368

Neurological Congress (London; circa 1935)
Pavlov, Ivan Petrovich **12** 155-157

Neurophysiology (science)
Dale, Henry Hallett **4** 371-373
Du Bois-Reymond, Emil **5** 118-119
Eccles, John Carew **5** 195-196
Erlanger, Joseph **5** 310-311
Galvani, Luigi **6** 194-195
Hess, Walter Rudolf **7** 365
Lashley, Karl Spencer **9** 214-215
Peterson, Edith R. **12** 258-259
Sherrington, Charles Scott **14** 187-189
Wexler, Nancy **16** 218-219
see also Scientists—neurophysiologists

Neurosis (psychology)
Freud, Sigmund **6** 103-106
Horney, Karen Danielsen **7** 508-509
Pavlov, Ivan Petrovich **12** 155-157

Neurospora (mold)
Beadle, George Wells **2** 80-81

Neurosurgery (medicine)
Penfield, Wilder Graves **12** 198-200

Neustadt International Prize for Literature
Bishop, Elizabeth **2** 290-292

NEUTRA, RICHARD JOSEPH (1892-1970), Austrian-born American architect **11** 355-356
Wright, Frank Lloyd **16** 398-401

Neutralism (politics)
Southeast Asia
Mohammad Reza Shah Pahlavi **11** 75-76
Nu, U **11** 439-441
Sihanouk, Norodom **14** 222-223
Souvanna Phouma **14** 357-358
Sukarno **15** 18-20
United States
Borah, William Edgar **2** 408

La Follette, Robert Marion **9** 155-156
Lansing, Robert **9** 200
Taft, William Howard **15** 78-81
Wilson, Thomas Woodrow **16** 330-332

Neutrality Proclamation (United States; 1793)
Genet, Edmond Charles **6** 261-262

Neutrino (physics)
Fermi, Enrico **5** 422-424
Pauli, Wolfgang Ernst **12** 149

Neutron (physics)
Bohr, Niels Henrik David **2** 366-368
Bothe, Walther **2** 438-439
Chadwick, James **3** 405-406
Fermi, Enrico **5** 422-424
Wigner, Eugene Paul **16** 268-269

Neva River, battle of (1240)
Nevsky, Alexander **11** 359

Nevada (state; United States)
Comstock, Henry Tompkins Paige **4** 189
Hearst, George **7** 242
Mackay, John William **10** 101-102

NEVELSON, LOUISE (1900-1988), American abstract sculptor **11** 356-357
Hofmann, Hans **7** 442-443

Never Give a Sucker an Even Break (film)
Fields, W. C. **5** 444

Nevermore (poem)
Verlaine, Paul Marie **15** 465-466

Nevertheless (poems)
Moore, Marianne **11** 148-149

Neville, George (circa 1433-1476), English prelate
Edward IV **5** 212-213
Warwick and of Salisbury, Earl of **16** 122-123

Neville, Richard
see Salisbury, 1st Earl of; Warwick, Earl of

Neville's Cross, battle of (1346)
Edward III **5** 211-212
Robert II **13** 194

NEVIN, JOHN WILLIAMSON (1803-1886), American Protestant theologian **11** 357
Schaff, Philip **13** 519-520

NEVINS, ALLAN (1890-1971), American historian **11** 357-359
Douglas, Stephen Arnold **5** 80-82

Nevis (island; West Indies)
Iberville, Sieur d' **8** 90-91

NEVSKY, ALEXANDER (ca. 1220-1262), Russian grand duke and prince **11** 359

Nevsky Prospect (story)
Gogol, Nikolai **6** 391-393

New American Cyclopaedia
Ripley, George **13** 179-180

New Amsterdam
see New York City

New Amsterdam (island; Indian Ocean)
Van Diemen, Anthony Meuza **15** 420

New Arabian Nights, The (stories)
Stevenson, Robert Louis **14** 446-448

New Art of Playwriting (book)
Lope Félix de Vega Carpio **9** 503-506

New Artists' Association (Munich)
Kandinsky, Wassily **8** 420-422
Marc, Franz **10** 231

New Atlantis, The (book)
Bacon, Francis **1** 422-424

New Bauhaus (Chicago)
Moholy-Nagy, László **11** 82-83

New Britain (island; Bismarck Archipelago)
Dampier, William **4** 384

New Brunswick (province; Canada)
Irving, Kenneth Colin **8** 140-141
Tilley, Samuel Leonard **15** 223-224
see also Canada

New Caledonia (island; Southwest Pacific Ocean)
Cook, James **4** 214-215

New Christians (Portuguese Empire)
Vieira, Antônio **15** 492

New College (Edinburgh, Scotland)
Chalmers, Thomas **3** 408-409
Duff, Alexander **5** 126-127

New Colossus, The (sonnet)
Lazarus, Emma **9** 260-261

New Comedy (Greek literature)
Aristophanes **1** 293-294
Menander **10** 477-478
Terence **15** 146-148

New Court (United States politics)
Blair, Francis Preston **2** 313-315

New Criticism (American literature)
MacLeish, Archibald **10** 109-110
Ransom, John Crowe **13** 39-40
Tate, Allen **15** 116
Warren, Robert Penn **16** 121-122
Williams, William Carlos **16** 308-309

New Culture movement (China)
Li Ta-chao **9** 447
Ts'ai Yüan-p'ei **15** 322

New Deal (United States; 1930s)
agriculture and conservation
Arnold, Thurman Wesley **1** 314
Hoover, Herbert Clark **7** 483-485
Ickes, Harold LeClaire **8** 100-101
Johnson, Charles Spurgeon **8** 296-297
Lilienthal, David Eli **9** 410-411
Norris, George William **11** 428-429
Tugwell, Rexford Guy **15** 336-339
Wallace, Henry Agard **16** 73-74
economic advisers
Berle, Adolf Augustus Jr. **2** 199-200
Morgenthau, Henry Jr. **11** 172-173
Stettinius, Edward R. Jr. **14** 437-438
Federal Arts Project
see Federal Arts Project

influence of
    Bennett, Richard Bedford **2** 171-172
    Johnson, Lyndon Baines **8** 308-312
    Stevenson, Adlai Ewing **14** 445-446
influenced by
    Baruch, Bernard Mannes **2** 42-43
    Patten, Simon Nelson **12** 138-139
    Thomas, Norman Mattoon
    15 191-192
    Veblen, Thorstein Bunde
    15 449-450
introduced
    Roosevelt, Franklin Delano
    13 277-280
labor relations
    Dubinsky, David **5** 114-115
    Ford, Henry **6** 5-6
    Green, William R. **6** 521
    Hillman, Sidney **7** 392-393
    Lewis, John Llewellyn **9** 387-388
    Meany, George **10** 444
    Murray, Philip **11** 264-265
    Perkins, Frances **12** 221-222
    Reuther, Walter Philip **13** 107-108
law and courts
    Black, Hugo Lafayette **2** 301-303
    Douglas, William Orville **5** 83-85
    Frankfurter, Felix **6** 57
    Hughes, Charles Evans **8** 15-16
    Pound, Roscoe **12** 417-418
    Stone, Harlan Fiske **14** 468-470
New Dealers in Congress
    Byrnes, James Francis **3** 191-192
    Johnson, Hiram Warren **8** 300-301
    McAdoo, William Gibbs
    10 385-386
    Wagner, Robert Ferdinand **16** 43
opponents
    Barton, Bruce **2** 36-37
    Coughlin, Charles Edward
    4 265-266
    du Pont, Pierre Samuel **5** 154-155
    Long, Huey Pierce **9** 496-497
    Nixon, Richard Milhous **11** 401-404
    Smith, Alfred Emmanuel **14** 284-285
    Taft, Robert Alphonso **15** 76-78
    Townsend, Francis Everitt
    15 282-283
social welfare programs
    Bethune, Mary McLeod **2** 241-242
    Darrow, Clarence Seward
    4 396-397
    Dewson, Mary Williams **4** 525
    Hopkins, Harry Lloyd **7** 494-495
    Woodward, Ellen S. **16** 379-381
supporters
    Curley, James Michael **4** 344-345
    MacLeish, Archibald **10** 109-110
    Mundelein, George William
    11 248-249
    Ross, Edward Alsworth **13** 300
    Swope, Gerard **15** 56-58
    Villard, Oswald Garrison
    15 498-499
    Wald, Lillian **16** 53-54
    White, William Alanson **16** 239-240

    Wise, Stephen Samuel **16** 344-345
    Wood, Robert Elkington **16** 370-371
New Delhi, India
    Lutyens, Edwin Landseer **10** 54-55
New Democracy (mural)
    Siqueiros, David Alfaro **14** 256
New Democracy (political party; Greece)
    Karamanlis, Constantine **8** 440-441
New Democratic Party (Canada)
    Douglas, Thomas Clement **5** 82-83
New Departure Democrat (United States politics)
    Gordon, John Brown **6** 449-450
New Devotion
    see Devotio Moderna
New Divinity (religion)
    Hopkins, Samuel **7** 496
New Economic Policy (Russia; 1920s)
    Bukharin, Nikolai Ivanovich **3** 112-113
    Chicherin, Georgi Vasilyevich
    3 516-517
    Lenin, Vladimir Ilich **9** 323-326
    Stalin, Joseph **14** 393-396
New economics
    see Keynesian economics; Neoclassic school (economics)
New England
    and religion (colonial)
        Cotton, John **4** 263-265
        Edwards, Jonathan **5** 220-222
        Gorton, Samuell **6** 460
        Hooker, Thomas **7** 476-477
        Hopkins, Samuel **7** 496
        Miller, Perry **11** 28-29
        see also Great Awakening
    Council (1620)
        Gorges, Ferdinando **6** 455-456
    Dominion of (1686)
        Andros, Edmund **1** 234-235
        Leisler, Jacob **9** 313-314
        Phips, William **12** 283
    history of
        Miller, Perry **11** 28-29
    mapping of coast
        Champlain, Samuel de **3** 419-421
        Smith, John **14** 295-297
    military leaders
        Standish, Myles **14** 396-397
    textile industry
        Lawrence, Abbott **9** 246
        see also New England Confederation; Plymouth Colony; individual states
New England Antislavery Society
    see Massachusetts Antislavery Society
New England Company (1628)
    Endecott, John **5** 284-285
    Gorges, Ferdinando **6** 455-456
New England Confederation (1643-1684)
    Dunster, Henry **5** 152-153
    Philip **12** 267-268
    Winthrop, John **16** 341

New England Conservatory (Boston)
    Busoni, Ferruccio Benvenuto **3** 173-174
    Schuller, Gunther **14** 37-38
New England Emigrant Aid Company
    Thayer, Eli **15** 168
New England Institution for the Education of the Blind (Boston)
    Howe, Samuel Gridley **7** 537
New England Psalm-Singer, The (hymnal)
    Billings, William **2** 274-275
New England Sketch, A (story)
    Stowe, Harriet Elizabeth Beecher
    14 484-485
New England Tragedies, The (book)
    Longfellow, Henry Wadsworth
    9 499-500
New England Woman Suffrage Association
    Howe, Julia Ward **7** 535-536
New England's Trials (literary collection)
    Smith, John **14** 295-297
New English Art Club
    John, Augustus Edwin **8** 291
New English Group (artists)
    Dobell, William **5** 34-35
New Fabian Research Bureau (Great Britain)
    Cole, George Douglas Howard
    4 146-147
New Fairy Tales and Stories (book)
    Andersen, Hans Christian **1** 212-214
New Family Instructor, A (book)
    Defoe, Daniel **4** 457-459
New Fire, The (ballet)
    Chávez, Carlos **3** 486
New Fortunes and Misfortunes of Lazarillo de Tormes, The (book)
    Cela y Trulock, Camilo José **3** 389-390
New France
    see Canada
New Gazetteer, The (book)
    Morse, Jedidiah **11** 191-192
New Granada
    see Colombia
New Guinea (island; Pacific Ocean)
    Cook, James **4** 214-215
    Dampier, William **4** 384
    Dobell, William **5** 34-35
    Hughes, William Morris **8** 21-22
    MacArthur, Douglas **10** 76-78
    Mead, Margaret **10** 438-440
    Nimitz, Chester William **11** 395-396
    Schouten, William Cornelius **14** 31
New Hampshire (poems)
    Frost, Robert Lee **6** 130-133
New Hampshire (state; United States)
    Pierce, Franklin **12** 300-301
    Tryon, William **15** 321
New Harmony (Indiana)
    Bloomer, Amelia Jenks **2** 337

Owen, Robert **12** 39-40
Owen, Robert Dale **12** 40-41
Wright, Frances **16** 397-398

New Harmony of Zion, The (hymnal; Tan-s'ur)
Billings, William **2** 274-275

New Haven Colony
see Connecticut—colonial charter

New Haven Symphony Orchestra (Connecticut)
Parker, Horatio William **12** 109

New Hebrides (islands; Pacific Ocean)
Bougainville, Louis Antoine de
2 443-444
Cook, James **4** 214-215
Mawson, Douglas **10** 354-355

New History (book)
William of Malmesbury **16** 297-298

New History movement (United States)
Beard, Charles Austin **2** 84
Parrington, Vernon Louis **12** 119-120
Robinson, James Harvey **13** 208
Spencer, Herbert **14** 369-370

New Holland
see Australia

New Hope, Pennsylvania (painting)
Demuth, Charles **4** 497-498

New International Economic Order
(Jamaican proposal)
Manley, Michael Norman **10** 200-201

New Jersey (state; United States)
colonial period
Andros, Edmund **1** 234-235
Franklin, William **6** 69-70
Minuit, Peter **11** 50
Morris, Lewis **11** 183-184
Penn, William **12** 200-202
legislators
Hague, Frank **7** 63-64
McClellan, George Brinton
10 391-392
Rodino, Peter Wallace Jr.
13 238-239
Wilson, Thomas Woodrow
16 330-332
Lutheran missionaries
Mühlenberg, Heinrich Melchior
11 232-233

New Jersey, College of
see Princeton University

New Jersey Symphony
Wolff, Hugh **16** 358-360

New Jerusalem, Church of the
Swedenborg, Emanuel **15** 49-50

New Jewel Movement (Grenada)
Bishop, Maurice **2** 292-293

New Jolfa (Iran)
Abbas I **1** 4-6

New Kind of Rays, A (paper)
Röntgen, Wilhelm Conrad **13** 273-275

New Kingdom, The (play)
Strindberg, August **14** 509-511

New Lanark (Scotland)
Owen, Robert **12** 39-40
Owen, Robert Dale **12** 40-41

New Laws of the Indies (1542)
Las Casas, Bartolomé de **9** 211-212
Mendoza, Antonio de **10** 494-495
Velasco, Luis de **15** 450-451

New Laws party (China)
Su-Shih **15** 39-40

New Left (political movement; United
States)
Marcuse, Herbert **10** 245-247
Mills, C. Wright **11** 35-36

New Life (book)
Dante Alighieri **4** 389-391

New Light Separatists (religious sect)
Backus, Isaac **1** 420-421

New London (Connecticut)
Winthrop, John **16** 341

New Machiavelli, The (novel)
Wells, Herbert George **16** 195-196

New Masses (journal)
Dos Passos, John Roderigo **5** 69-71
Ellison, Ralph Waldo **5** 274-275
Marsh, Reginald **10** 276-277

New Men, The (novel)
Snow, Charles Percy **14** 311-312

New Method (book)
Bacon, Francis **1** 422-424

New Mexico (state; United States)
Anza, Juan Bautista de **1** 254-255
Chávez, Dennis **3** 488-489
Chisum, John Simpson **4** 11
Coronado, Francisco Vásquez de **4** 247
Goddard, Robert Hutchings **6** 376-377
Lamy, Jean Baptiste **9** 181-182
Mangas Coloradas **10** 194-196
Oñate, Juan de **11** 513-514
Wallace, Lewis **16** 74-75

New Mexico, University of (Albuquerque)
Elsasser, Walter Maurice **5** 277-278
Krenek, Ernst **9** 98-99

New Munich Secession (art group)
Klee, Paul **9** 47-49

New Music Bureau Poems (poems)
Po Chü-i **12** 362-363

New nationalism (political philosophy)
Croly, Herbert David **4** 316-317

New Netherland (American colony)
see New York (state; United States)

New North Church (Boston, Massachusetts)
Bulfinch, Charles **3** 116-117

New Objectivity (art movement)
Beckmann, Max **2** 104-105
Dix, Otto **5** 33-34
Grosz, George **7** 17-18

New Orleans (city; Louisiana)
Bienville, Sieur de **2** 268-269
Dewey, George **4** 520
Eads, James Buchanan **5** 175-176
Farragut, David Glasgow **5** 388-389

New Orleans and Carrollton streetcar line
Beauregard, Pierre Gustave Toutant
2 96-97

New Orleans, battle of (1815)
Franklin, John **6** 64-65
Jackson, Andrew **8** 168-172
Madison, James **10** 121-123

New Orleans Industrial Exposition
(1884-1885)
Fletcher, Alice Cunningham **5** 486-487

New Orleans, Jackson, and Great Northern Railroad
Beauregard, Pierre Gustave Toutant
2 96-97

New Panama Canal Co.
Bunau-Varilla, Philippe Jean **3** 120-121

New Plan (University of Chicago)
Hutchins, Robert Maynard **8** 68-69

New Plymouth Colony
see Plymouth Colony

New Progressive Party (Puerto Rico)
Romero Barceló, Carlos **13** 267-268

New Providence Development Company
(Bahamas)
Taylor, Edward Plunket **15** 123-124

New Realist movement (philosophy)
Alexander, Samuel **1** 141
Perry, Ralph Barton **12** 239-240

New Reich, The (poems)
George, Stefan **6** 277-278

New Republic (magazine)
Young, Stark **16** 474-475
contributors
Anderson, Maxwell **1** 219-220
Dos Passos, John Roderigo **5** 69-71
Greene, Graham **6** 523-524
Ickes, Harold LeClaire **8** 100-101
editors
Bourne, Randolph Silliman
2 456-457
Dewey, John **4** 520-523
Johnson, Alvin Saunders **8** 293-294
Wilson, Edmund **16** 318-319
founders
Croly, Herbert David **4** 316-317
Lippmann, Walter **9** 439-440

New Revelation, The (book)
Doyle, Arthur Conan **5** 91-92

New Rhymes (poems)
Carducci, Giosuè **3** 290-291

New Roof, The (satire)
Hopkinson, Francis **7** 496-497

New Royal Academy of Music (England)
Handel, George Frederick **7** 116-119

New Russia (former region; Ukraine)

Potemkin, Grigori Aleksandrovich
12 411-412

New Salon
see Société Nationale des Beaux-Arts

New School for Social Research (New York City)
directors
Johnson, Alvin Saunders **8** 293-294
MacIver, Robert Morrison
10 100-101
faculty
Beard, Charles Austin **2** 84
Cage, John **3** 211-214
Copland, Aaron **4** 227-228
Davis, Stuart **4** 424-425
Lévi-Strauss, Claude Gustave
9 371-372
Thomas, William Isaac **15** 193
Veblen, Thorstein Bunde
15 449-450
Wertheimer, Max **16** 207-208
founded
Robinson, James Harvey **13** 208

New School of Design (Boston)
Gorky, Arshile **6** 458

New Secession (art group)
Nolde, Emil **11** 419-420

New Songs among the Mountains (poems)
Yun Sondo **16** 483

New South Church (Boston, Massachusetts)
Bulfinch, Charles **3** 116-117

New South Wales (state; Australia)
British exploration
Cook, James **4** 214-215
Eyre, Edward John **5** 354
colonial period
Banks, Joseph **1** 489-490
Bigge, John Thomas **2** 272
Bligh, William **2** 325-326
Phillip, Arthur **12** 279-280
gold discovered
Hargraves, Edward Hammond
7 153-154
legislators
Barton, Edmund **2** 39-40
Hughes, William Morris **8** 21-22
Lang, John Thomas **9** 192-193
Parkes, Henry **12** 113

New South Wales Railways
Chifley, Joseph Benedict **3** 518

New Spain (former Spanish viceroyalty; North America)
Cabrillo, Juan Rodríguez **3** 204-205
Cortés, Hernán **4** 255-256
Mendoza, Antonio de **10** 494-495
Velasco, Luis de **15** 450-451
see also Mexico; Spain—exploration and colonial history

New Spoon River, The (poems)
Masters, Edgar Lee **10** 326-327

New Summer House, The (story)
Chekhov, Anton Pavlovich **3** 494-497

New Sweden (American colony)
see New Jersey

New Testament
see Bible

New Thought movement (Chinese philosophy)
Hu Shih **8** 63-65
Ku Chieh-kang **9** 120-121

New Wave (French literature)
Robbe-Grillet, Alain **13** 189-190

New Way (magazine)
Blok, Aleksandr Aleksandrovich **2** 335
Merezhkovsky, Dmitry Sergeyevich
10 515-516

New Way to Pay Old Debts, A (play)
Massinger, Philip **10** 324-325

New Witness
see G.K.'s Weekly

New World Symphony
Dvořák, Antonin **5** 168-169

New World, The (novel)
Heruy Wäldä-Sellasé **7** 348-349

New Year Letter (poem)
Auden, Wystan Hugh **1** 364-366

New Year, The (novel)
Buck, Pearl Sydenstricker **3** 91-93

New Year's Sacrifice, The (story)
Lu Hsün **10** 35-37

New York (state; United States)
comptrollers
Fillmore, Millard **5** 447-448
Marcy, William Learned **10** 247-248
congressmen (20th century)
Kemp, Jack French Jr. **8** 491-493
constitutional convention
Jay, John **8** 230-232
Livingston, Robert R. **9** 462-463
Morris, Gouverneur **11** 182-183
governors (18th century)
Clinton, George **4** 113-114
Colden, Cadwallader **4** 145-146
Jay, John **8** 230-232
governors (19th century)
Cleveland, Stephen Grover
4 108-110
Clinton, DeWitt **4** 112-113
Fish, Hamilton **5** 461-462
Marcy, William Learned **10** 247-248
Roosevelt, Theodore **13** 280-283
Seward, William Henry **14** 124-125
Seymour, Horatio **14** 126-127
Tilden, Samuel Jones **15** 222-223
governors (20th century)
Cuomo, Mario Matthew **4** 338-339
Dewey, Thomas Edmund **4** 524
Harriman, W. Averell **7** 165-166
Hughes, Charles Evans **8** 15-16
Lehman, Herbert Henry **9** 306-307
Rockefeller, Nelson Aldrich
13 228-230
Roosevelt, Franklin Delano
13 277-280

Smith, Alfred Emmanuel **14** 284-285
justices
Cardozo, Benjamin Nathan
3 288-290
Kent, James **8** 510-511
labor officials
Meany, George **10** 444
Perkins, Frances **12** 221-222
legislators
Burr, Aaron **3** 156-159
DeLancey, Stephen **4** 473
Evarts, William Maxwell **5** 340-341
Hamilton, Alexander **7** 95-98
Smith, Alfred Emmanuel **14** 284-285
Wagner, Robert Ferdinand **16** 43
White, Andrew Dickson **16** 226-227
railroad development
Corning, Erastus **4** 238-239
senators
Moynihan, Daniel Patrick
11 216-218
social reforms
Bigelow, John **2** 271-272
Catt, Carrie Chapman **3** 375-376
Curtis, George William **4** 349-350
Lowell, Josephine Shaw **10** 15-16
Sanger, Margaret Higgins
13 467-468
Smith, Alfred Emmanuel **14** 284-285
Truth, Sojourner **15** 320-321
Wald, Lillian **16** 53-54
State Library
Dewey, Melvil **4** 523-524
see also New York City

New York, City University of
Cohen, Morris Raphael **4** 139-140
Draper, John William **5** 96-97
Harris, Townsend **7** 176-177
Morse, Samuel Finley Breese
11 192-193
Russell, Bertrand Arthur William
13 373-374
Tarski, Alfred **15** 110-111

New York, State University of (Purchase)
Dubos, René Jules **5** 119

New York, State University of (Stony Brook)
Simpson, Louis Aston Marantz
14 243-244
Yang, Chen Ning **16** 437-438

New York and Liverpool Mail Steamship Co.
Collins, Edward Knight **4** 162-163

New York Bay
Hudson, Henry **8** 12-13
Verrazano, Giovanni da **15** 470-471

New York Central Railroad
Corning, Erastus **4** 238-239
Fargo, William George **5** 380-381
Morgan, Junius Spencer **11** 166-167
Vanderbilt, Cornelius **15** 415-416

New York City (New York State)
• COLONIAL PERIOD
as New Netherland

Minuit, Peter **11** 50
Stuyvesant, Peter **15** 5-6
Van Rensselaer, Kiliaen
15 430-431
border disputes
Allen, Ethan **1** 163-164
governors and justices
Dunmore, 4th Earl of **5** 147
Leisler, Jacob **9** 313-314
Morris, Lewis **11** 183-184
Tryon, William **15** 321
Indian affairs
Kirkland, Samuel **9** 37
Livingston, Robert **9** 461-462
McGillivray, Alexander **10** 412
printers
Bradford, William **2** 476-477
Zenger, John Peter **16** 497-498
• MODERN PERIOD
Archdiocese
Carroll, John **3** 331-332
Corrigan, Michael Augustine
4 253
Hayes, Patrick Joseph **7** 224-225
McCloskey, John **10** 395
Spellman, Francis Joseph **14** 367
architecture
Harris, Townsend **7** 176-177
Renwick, James **13** 102-103
Tiffany, Louis Comfort
15 220-221
board of health
Biggs, Hermann Michael
2 272-273
Eaton, Dorman Bridgman
5 190-191
Federal Writers Project
Ellison, Ralph Waldo **5** 274-275
fire department
Eaton, Dorman Bridgman
5 190-191
legal system
Berle, Adolf Augustus Jr.
2 199-200
Field, David Dudley **5** 439-440
mayors
Dinkins, David **5** 15-18
Giuliani, Rudolph William
6 353-355
Grace, William Russell
6 480-481
Hewitt, Abram Stevens
7 371-372
Koch, Edward I. **9** 68-69
La Guardia, Fiorello Henry
9 166-167
Lindsay, John Vliet **9** 423-424
Livingston, Edward **9** 460-461
Low, Seth **10** 11-12
Wagner, Robert Ferdinand Jr.
16 44-45
Wood, Fernando **16** 367-368
police
Crane, Stephen **4** 293-295
Roosevelt, Theodore **13** 280-283
public works

Moses, Robert **11** 202-203
social services
Cabrini, Frances Xavier **3** 205
Cooper, Peter **4** 223-224
Perkins, Frances **12** 221-222
Riis, Jacob August **13** 169-170
spoils system
Arthur, Chester Alan **1** 321-323
see also Tammany Hall; Tweed
Ring
Welfare Department
Bearden, Romare Howard
2 86-88
see also New York (state)

New York City Ballet Co.
Balanchine, George **1** 461-462
Kirstein, Lincoln **9** 39-41
Stravinsky, Igor Fedorovich **14** 502-506
Sullivan, Louis Henri **15** 27-28

New York City Opera Company
Sills, Beverly **14** 230-231

New York Civil Service Reform Association
Eaton, Dorman Bridgman **5** 190-191

New York Commission on Prison Reform
Osborne, Thomas Mott **12** 17-18

New York Condensed Milk Co.
see Borden Co.

New York Cosmos (soccer team)
Pele **12** 190-191

New York Elevated Railroad Co.
Field, Cyrus West **5** 438-439

New York Evening Post (newspaper)
Bellamy, Edward **2** 134-135
Bigelow, John **2** 271-272
Bryant, William Cullen **3** 83-85
Godkin, Edwin Lawrence **6** 380
Jackson, Helen Hunt **8** 172
Schurz, Carl **14** 44-45
Steffens, Lincoln **14** 410-411
Villard, Oswald Garrison **15** 498-499

New York Five (architecture group)
Eisenman, Peter D. **5** 239-240
Graves, Michael **6** 500-502
Meier, Richard **10** 456-458

New York Free Academy
see New York, City University of

New York Herald (newspaper)
Bennett, James Gordon **2** 168-169
Bennett, James Gordon Jr. **2** 169-170
Grady, Henry Woodfin **6** 482-483
Stanley, Henry Morton **14** 399-400
see also New York Herald Tribune

New York Herald Tribune (newspaper)
Stevens, Wallace **14** 443-445
Thomson, Virgil **15** 202-203

New York Infirmary and College for Women
Blackwell, Elizabeth **2** 311-312

New York Institution for the Deaf and Dumb
Barnard, Frederick Augustus Porter
2 9-10

New York Journal (newspaper)
Pinto, Isaac **12** 318

New York Medical College
Jacobi, Abraham and Mary Putnam
8 188-189

New York Mycological Society (established 1962)
Cage, John **3** 211-214

New York, Newfoundland and London Telegraph Company
Cooper, Peter **4** 223-224

New York Night (painting)
O'Keeffe, Georgia **11** 487-489

New York Philharmonic Symphony Orchestra
Bernstein, Leonard **2** 218-219
Boulez, Pierre **2** 444-445
Chávez, Carlos **3** 486
Thomas, Theodore **15** 192-193
Toscanini, Arturo **15** 270-271

New York Post (newspaper)
Murdoch, Rupert **11** 257-258

New York Public Library (established 1895;
New York City)
Bigelow, John **2** 271-272
Moore, Marianne **11** 148-149
Onassis, Jacqueline Lee Bouvier
Kennedy **11** 511-513
Schiff, Jacob Henry **14** 2-3
Tilden, Samuel Jones **15** 222-223

New York School (art)
Greenberg, Clement **6** 521-523
Guston, Philip **7** 47-48
Lippold, Richard **9** 440-442

**New York Society for the Suppression of
Vice, The** (established 1873)
Caldwell, Erskine **3** 223-224
Comstock, Anthony **4** 188-189
Dreiser, Herman Theodore **5** 98-100

New York State Agricultural Society
Cornell, Ezra **4** 236-237

New York State Board of Charities
Lowell, Josephine Shaw **10** 15-16

**New York State Bureau of Industries and
Immigration**
Wald, Lillian **16** 53-54

New York State Industrial Commission
Mitchell, John **11** 58-59

**New York State Married Woman's Property
and Guardianship Law** (1860)
Anthony, Susan Brownell **1** 246-248

New York State Theater (New York City)
Johnson, Philip **8** 313-314

New York Stock Exchange
see Stock market (United States)

New York Sun (newspaper)
Dana, Charles Anderson **4** 384-385

Davis, Richard Harding **4** 422-423
Munsey, Frank Andrew **11** 251
Wilson, Edmund **16** 318-319

New York Times (newspaper)
Godkin, Edwin Lawrence **6** 380
Kaufman, George S. **8** 457-458
Malinowski, Kaspar Bronislaw
10 170-171
Ochs, Adolph Simon **11** 464
Reston, James Barrett **13** 104-105
Salisbury, Harrison Evans **13** 449-451
Sulzberger, Arthur Ochs **15** 28-30
Tarbell, Ida Minerva **15** 107-108
Tweed, William Marcy **15** 366-367
Watson, Thomas Edward **16** 139

New York Times Libel Case of 1964
Brennan, William J. Jr. **2** 514-515

New York Tribune (newspaper)
contributors
Crane, Stephen **4** 293-295
Dana, Charles Anderson **4** 384-385
Fry, William Henry **6** 136-137
Fuller, Sarah Margaret **6** 150-151
Hildreth, Richard **7** 382
Riis, Jacob August **13** 169-170
Ripley, George **13** 179-180
Schurz, Carl **14** 44-45
Twain, Mark **15** 363-366
founded (1841)
Greeley, Horace **6** 515-517
Linotype first used
Mergenthaler, Ottmar **10** 516-517
see also New York Herald Tribune

New York Tribune Building (New York City)
Hunt, Richard Morris **8** 44

New York University (New York City)
Bellow, Saul **2** 141-143
Breuer, Marcel **2** 520-521
Gallatin, Albert **6** 183-184
Hook, Sidney **7** 474-475
Johnson, James Weldon **8** 304-305
Loewi, Otto **9** 486-487
von Mises, Ludwig **16** 25
Wolfe, Thomas Clayton **16** 355-356

New York Urban League
Johnson, Charles Spurgeon **8** 296-297

New York World (newspaper)
contributors
Anderson, Maxwell **1** 219-220
Crane, Stephen **4** 293-295
Forrestal, James Vincent **6** 14
editors
Bowers, Claude Gernade **2** 463
Lippmann, Walter **9** 439-440
Phillips, David Graham **12** 280-281
Russell, Charles Edward **13** 374-375
publisher
Pulitzer, Joseph **12** 481-482
rivals
Hearst, William Randolph
7 243-244

New York World's Fairs
see World's Fairs

New York Yankees (baseball team)
DiMaggio, Joe **5** 10-11
Mantle, Mickey **10** 216-218
Ruth, George Herman Jr. **13** 384

New York Zoological Society
Carson, Rachel Louise **3** 337-338

New Yorker (magazine)
artists and cartoonists
Marsh, Reginald **10** 276-277
Thurber, James Grove **15** 213-214
contributors
Friel, Bernard Patrick **6** 115-116
Macdonald, Dwight **10** 81-83
Mumford, Lewis **11** 246-247
Nabokov, Vladimir **11** 287-288
O'Hara, John **11** 485
Parker, Dorothy Rothschild **12** 106
Perelman, S. J. **12** 209-210
White, E. B. **16** 228-230
Wilson, Edmund **16** 318-319
editors
Brown, Tina **3** 47-48
Ross, Harold **13** 300-302
founded
Greeley, Horace **6** 515-517
Ross, Harold **13** 300-302
publishers
Newhouse, Samuel Irving
11 362-364

New Youth (magazine; China)
Ch'en Tu-hsiu **3** 501-502
Hu Shih **8** 63-65
Li Ta-chao **9** 447
Lu Hsün **10** 35-37

New Zealand (island nation; Southern
Pacific Ocean)
administration
Eyre, Edward John **5** 354
Hobson, William **7** 426
Holyoake, Keith Jacka **7** 460-462
Jellicoe, John Rushworth **8** 242-243
Wakefield, Edward Gibbon
16 48-49
Anzac pact (1944)
Curtin, John Joseph **4** 348-349
Evatt, Herbert Vere **5** 341-343
culture
Hillary, Edmund **7** 389-390
King, Frederic Truby **9** 18-19
Ratana, Taupotiki Wiremu **13** 46
Te Kanawa, Kiri **15** 136-137
discovery and exploration
Cook, James **4** 214-215
Tasman, Abel Janszoon **15** 113-114
Van Diemen, Anthony Meuza
15 420
health care
King, Frederic Truby **9** 18-19
Maori wars
Grey, George **6** 540-541
see also Maori
SEATO
see Southeast Asia Treaty Organiza-
tion

social reforms
Fraser, Peter **6** 73-74
Savage, Michael Joseph **13** 501-502
Seddon, Richard John **14** 81-82
Vogel, Julius **16** 9-10
World War I
see World War I

New Zealand, University of (Wellington)
Ngata, Apirana Turupa **11** 374-375

New Zealand Constitutional Act (1852)
Grey, George **6** 540-541
Wakefield, Edward Gibbon **16** 48-49

New Zealand Land Co. (established 1839)
Hobson, William **7** 426

New Zionist Organization (1935)
Jabotinsky, Vladimir Evgenevich
8 167-168

Newark (city; New Jersey)
Baraka, Imamu Amiri **1** 498-499
Corrigan, Michael Augustine **4** 253

NEWBERY, JOHN (1713-1767), English
publisher **11** 360-361

Newby Hall (Yorkshire)
Adam, Robert and James **1** 38-40
Chippendale, Thomas **4** 1-2

Newcastle (ship)
Jellicoe, John Rushworth **8** 242-243

**Newcastle, Thomas Pelham-Holles, 1st
Duke of** (1693-1768), English statesman
George II **6** 269-270
Pitt, William the Elder **12** 328-329
Walpole, Robert **16** 82-84

NEWCOMB, SIMON (1835-1909), Ameri-
can astronomer **11** 361-362
Barnard, Edward Emerson **2** 8-9
Fisher, Irving **5** 462-463

NEWCOMEN, THOMAS (1663-1729), English inventor and engineer **11** 362
Watt, James **16** 141-143

Newcomes, The (novel)
Thackeray, William Makepeace
15 159-161

**New-England's Spirit of Persecution Trans-
mitted to Pennsylvania** (book)
Bradford, William **2** 476-477

Newfoundland (island province; Canada)
Cabot, John **3** 199-200
Cartier, Jacques **3** 343-344
Corte Reál, Gaspar and Miguel
4 254-255
Ericson, Leif **5** 306-307
Gilbert, Humphrey **6** 313
Rodney, George Brydges **13** 239-240
see also Canada

NEWHOUSE, SAMUEL IRVING
(1895-1979), American media tycoon
11 362-364

Newlands, John Alexander Reina
(1837-1898), English chemist
Mendeleev, Dmitrii Ivanovich
10 486-488

Newlands Reclamation Bill (1902)
Roosevelt, Theodore **13** 280-283

Newlyweds of the Eiffel Tower, The (mime
drama)
Cocteau, Jean **4** 132-133

NEWMAN, BARNETT (1905-1970), American painter **11** 365
Motherwell, Robert **11** 210-211
Rothko, Mark **13** 320-321

NEWMAN, JOHN HENRY (1801-1890),
English cardinal and theologian
11 365-367
Arnold, Thomas **1** 313-314
Coleridge, Samuel Taylor **4** 154-156
Elgar, Edward **5** 247-248
Froude, James Anthony **6** 133-134
Hopkins, Gerard Manley **7** 492-494
Kingsley, Charles **9** 28
Manning, Henry Edward **10** 209-210
Pusey, Edward Bouverie **12** 488-489
see also Oxford Movement

Newnham (Cambridge University)
Sidgwick, Henry **14** 213

Newport (city; Rhode Island)
Benjamin, Asher **2** 162-163
Hunt, Richard Morris **8** 44
Richardson, Henry Hobson **13** 139-141

Newport, Christopher (died 1617), English
mariner
Powhatan **12** 429-430

Newport Casino (Rhode Island)
McKim, Charles Follen **10** 417-418

News from Home (story)
Bunin, Ivan Alekseevich **3** 124

Newspaper Enterprise Association
Scripps, Edward Wyllis **14** 72-73

Newspaper for Hermits (journal)
Arnim, Achim von **1** 308-309
Brentano, Clemens **2** 515-516

Newspaper industry
see Editors; Journalists; Publishers

Newspaper, The (poem)
Crabbe, George **4** 288

Newsweek (magazine)
Graham, Katharine Meyer **6** 483-485

NEWTON, HUEY P. (born 1942),
co-founder of the Black Panther Party
11 367-369
Cleaver, Leroy Eldridge **4** 97-98

Newton, John (1725-1807), English clergyman
Cowper, William **4** 282
Wilberforce, William **16** 269-270

NEWTON, SIR ISAAC (1642-1727), English
scientist and mathematician **11** 369-372
compared to
Einstein, Albert **5** 228-231

Malthus, Thomas Robert **10** 180-181
Ohm, Georg Simon **11** 486-487
critics
Cauchy, Augustin Louis **3** 378-380
Coleridge, Samuel Taylor **4** 154-156
Flamsteed, John **5** 477-478
Hooke, Robert **7** 475
Law, William **9** 245-246
Mach, Ernst **10** 90-91
friends
Boyle, Robert **2** 469-471
Halley, Edmund **7** 88-89
influence of (Europe)
Buffon, Comte de **3** 109-111
Condillac, Étienne Bonnot de
4 194-195
Demoivre, Abraham **4** 494-495
Hamilton, William Rowan **7** 99-100
Hartley, David **7** 185
Kant, Immanuel **8** 430-432
Lagrange, Joseph Louis **9** 164-166
Voltaire **16** 14-16
Witt, Johan de **16** 348-349
influence of (United States)
Edwards, Jonathan **5** 220-222
Franklin, Benjamin **6** 60-64
Johnson, Samuel **8** 314-315
influenced by
Copernicus, Nicolaus **4** 226-227
Euclid **5** 327-329
Fermat, Pierre de **5** 421-422
Galileo Galilei **6** 180-183
interpretations
Voltaire **16** 14-16
Leibniz disputes
Kant, Immanuel **8** 430-432
Leibniz, Gottfried Wilhelm von
9 307-310
supporters
Clarke, Samuel **4** 88
Mutis, José Celestino **11** 278-279
Unánue, José Hipólito **15** 387-388

Newton's rings (optics)
Maxwell, James Clerk **10** 361-364

Newtown, battle of (1779)
Butler, John **3** 180

New-York Antislavery Society (established
1833)
Tappan brothers **15** 105-106

New-York Historical Society
Clinton, DeWitt **4** 112-113

New-York Weekly Journal (newspaper;
established 1733)
Zenger, John Peter **16** 497-498

NEXØ, MARTIN ANDERSON (1869-1954),
Danish author **11** 372
Dinesen Blixen-Finecke, Karen **5** 13-14

Nexus (novel)
Miller, Henry **11** 26-27

NEY, MICHEL (1769-1815), French marshal
11 372-373
see also Napoleonic Wars

Neyra, Álvaro de Mendaña de
see Mendaña de Neyra, Álvaro de

Nez Percé Indians (North America)
Joseph **8** 358-359
Miles, Nelson Appleton **11** 16-17

NGALA, RONALD GIDEON (1923-1972),
Kenyan politician **11** 373-374

Ngami, Lake (South Africa)
Livingstone, David **9** 463-465

NGATA, SIR APIRANA TURUPA
(1874-1950), Maori leader, politician,
and scholar **11** 374-375

Ngatiporou (Maori people)
Ngata, Apirana Turupa **11** 374-375

Ngawang Gyatso (1617-1682), fifth Dalai
Lama
Dalai Lama **4** 369-371

Ngbandi (African people)
Mobutu Sese Seko **11** 69-71

Ngengi, Johnstone Kamau
see Kenyatta, Jomo

Ngo Pa (play)
Chulalongkorn **4** 43-45

NGUGI WA THIONG'O (James Ngugi;
born 1938), Kenyan writer **11** 375-376

Nguyen Ali Quoc (Nguyen That Thanh)
see Ho Chi Minh

Ngwato (African people)
Khama, Seretse M. **8** 532-533

Nhu, Ngo Dinh (died 1963), Vietnamese
politician
Diem, Ngo Dinh **5** 6-7

NI TSAN (1301-1374), Chinese painter
11 400
Chao Meng-fu **3** 436-437
Tung Ch'i-ch'ang **15** 339-340

Niagara Falls (United States-Canada)
Roebling, John Augustus **13** 241-242
Tesla, Nikola **15** 156-157
Westinghouse, George **16** 215

Niagara movement (United States)
Du Bois, William Edward Burghardt
5 116-118
Hope, John **7** 489-490
Washington, Booker Taliaferro
16 125-126
see also African American history;
National Association for the Advancement of Colored People

Niblo's Garden (New York City)
Barnum, Phineas Taylor **2** 13-15

Nicaea, First Council of (325)
Arius **1** 297-298
Athanasius **1** 358-359
Basil the Great **2** 51-52
Leo I **9** 329-330
see also Nicene Creed

Nicaea, Second Council of (787)
John of Damascus **8** 282

Nicaean emperors (Byzantine emperors; ruled 1206-1261)
Michael VIII **11** 1-2

Nicanor (died 160 B.C.), Syrian general
Judas Maccabeus **8** 374-375

Nicaragua, Republic of (nation; Central America)
anti-Sandinistas
Chamorro, Violeta Barrios de **3** 417-419
civil war
Ortega, Daniel **12** 5-7
Sandino, Augusto C. **13** 462-463
Somoza, Anastasio **14** 335-336
Somoza Debayle, Anastasio **14** 336-337
Stimson, Henry Lewis **14** 457-458
founded
Pedrarias **12** 179
United States relations
Johnson, James Weldon **8** 304-305
Kellogg, Frank Billings **8** 481
Reagan, Ronald W. **13** 65-68
Sandino, Augusto C. **13** 462-463
Taft, William Howard **15** 78-81
Vanderbilt, Cornelius **15** 415-416
Walker, William **16** 68-69
Zelaya, José Santos **16** 495-496

Nicaraguan literature
Darío, Rubén **4** 393-394

Nice (city; France)
Cavour, Conte di **3** 385-386
Garibaldi, Giuseppe **6** 215-217

Nice and the Good, The (novel)
Murdoch, Iris **11** 256-257

Nicene Creed (Christian)
Arius **1** 297-298
Athanasius **1** 358-359
Constantine I **4** 209-211
Ulfilas **15** 384

Nicephorus Bryennius
see Bryennius, Nicephorus

Nicephorus I (died 811), Byzantine emperor 802-811
Harun al-Rashid **7** 188

Nicephorus II (Phocas; circa 913-969), Byzantine emperor 963-969
Basil II **2** 50-51

NICHIREN (1222-1282), Japanese Buddhist monk **11** 376-377
Eisai **5** 231-232

Nichiren sect (Buddhism)
Ikeda, Daisaku **8** 109-110
Nichiren **11** 376-377
Niwano, Nikkyo **11** 400-401

Nicholas (1856-1929), grand duke of Russia
Wavell, Archibald Percival **16** 147-148

NICHOLAS I (1796-1855), czar of Russia 1825-1855 **11** 377-378
Alexander II **1** 132-133
Herzen, Aleksandr Ivanovich **7** 351-352

Lermontov, Mikhail Yurievich **9** 352-353
Nesselrode, Karl Robert **11** 348-349
Pushkin, Aleksandr Sergeevich **12** 489-491
Speranski, Mikhail Mikhailovich **14** 376-377
Struve, Friedrich Georg Wilhelm von **14** 513
Whistler, James Abbott McNeill **16** 225-226

Nicholas I, Saint (800?-867), pope 858-867
Cyril and Methodius, Saints **4** 362-363
Photius **12** 283-284

Nicholas II (Gerard of Burgundy; 980?-1061), pope 1059-1061
Guiscard, Robert **7** 39-40

NICHOLAS II (1868-1918), czar of Russia 1894-1917 **11** 378-380
Pobedonostsev, Konstantin Petrovich **12** 360-361
Rasputin, Grigori Efimovich **13** 44-45
Stolypin, Piotr Arkadevich **14** 465-466
Witte, Sergei Yulyevich **16** 349-350

Nicholas V (Tommaso Parentucelli; 1397?-1455), pope 1447-1455
Alberti, Leon Battista **1** 113-115
Angelico **1** 235-236
Frederick III **6** 84-85
Pius II **12** 331
Valla, Lorenzo **15** 406

Nicholas Nickleby (novel; Dickens)
Dickens, Charles John Huffam **4** 538-541
Lao Shê **9** 200-201

Nicholas of Cusa
see Cusa, Nicholas of

Nicholas of Lyra (1270?-?1340), French biblical scholar
Rashi **13** 43

NICHOLAS OF ORESME (circa 1320-1382), French bishop, writer and translator **11** 380

NICHOLSON, BEN (1894-1982), English painter **11** 380-381
Hepworth, Barbara **7** 318-319

Nicholson, John (died 1800), Welshborn American financier and land promoter
Morris, Robert **11** 185-187

NICHOLSON, SIR FRANCIS (1655-1728), English colonial governor **11** 381-382
Beverley, Robert **2** 252
Blair, James **2** 315-316
Leisler, Jacob **9** 313-314

Nicht der Mörder, der Ermordete ist schuldig (novella)
Werfel, Franz **16** 204-205

Nicias (died 413 B.C.), Athenian general and statesman
Alcibiades **1** 119-120
Cleon **4** 104-105

Nick of the Woods (novel)
Bird, Robert Montgomery **2** 281-282

NICKLAUS, JACK (born 1940), American golfer **11** 382-383

Nicknames
Abbé
Gounod, Charles François **6** 473-474
Sieyès, Comte Emmanuel Joseph **14** 217-218
Alfred the great
Krupp **9** 109-111
American Michelangelo
Rimmer, William **13** 174
American Rembrandt
Johnson, Jonathan Eastman **8** 308
angel of the Crimea
Nightingale, Florence **11** 392-393
Anushervan the just
Khosrow I **8** 538-539
Apache Napoleon
Cochise **4** 128
apostate, the
Julian **8** 378-379
Apostle of California
Serra, Junípero **14** 111-112
apostle of democracy
Madero, Francisco Indalecio **10** 118-119
apostle of Rome
Neri, Philip **11** 340
apostle of the East Indies
Francis Xavier **6** 48
apostle to England
Augustine of Canterbury **1** 370-371
apostle to Germany
Boniface **2** 391
apostle to the Indians
Eliot, John **5** 256-258
apostle to the West Indies
Claver, Peter **4** 94
archangel of the revolution
Saint-Just, Louis Antoine Léon de **13** 433
archeologist king
Ashurbanipal **1** 338
Asclepiades
Hippocrates **7** 408-410
assistant president
Byrnes, James Francis **3** 191-192
Attic bee
Sophocles **14** 343-345
autocrat of the breakfast table
Holmes, Oliver Wendell **7** 457-458
Baby Doc
Duvalier, Jean-Claude **5** 166-168
bad hand
Fitzpatrick, Thomas **5** 474-475
Balzac of the Arabs
Mahfuz, Najib **10** 142-144
banjo
Paterson, Andrew Barton **12** 131-132
Banjo Eyes
Cantor, Eddie **3** 264-265
Barbarossa
Frederick I **6** 78-79

bear, the
    Tolstoy, Leo **15** 262-265
Beethoven of America
    Heinrich, Anthony Philip **7** 261
Bertie
    Edward VII **5** 214-215
beta
    Eratosthenes of Cyrene **5** 301-302
bewitched, the
    Charles II **3** 454
big asparagus
    De Gaulle, Charles André Joseph
        Marie **4** 463-465
big Bill
    Haywood, William Dudley
        7 232-233
big fellow
    Collins, Michael **4** 167-168
big George
    Giorgione **6** 340-341
big gun Sun
    Sun Yat-sen **15** 35-39
bitter Bierce
    Bierce, Ambrose Gwinett **2** 269-270
black, the
    Douglas, James **5** 78
black Jack
    Pershing, John Joseph **12** 243-244
Black Pearl, the
    Pele **12** 190-191
Black Prince
    Edward the Black Prince **5** 217-218
black-robe voyageur
    Lacombe, Albert **9** 147-148
black Spartacus
    Turner, Nathaniel **15** 354
black Spurgeon
    Turner, Henry McNeal **15** 351-352
bloody Tarleton
    Tarleton, Banastre **15** 110
Boanerges
    John, Saint **8** 273-274
bodhisattva emperor
    Liang Wu-ti **9** 396-397
Bogey
    Bogart, Humphrey **2** 363-364
Bonnie Prince Charlie
    Charles Edward Louis Philip Casimir
        Stuart **3** 466-467
Boston strong boy
    Sullivan, John Lawrence **15** 24-25
boy bachelor
    Wolsey, Thomas **16** 364-366
Boz
    Dickens, Charles John Huffam
        4 538-541
Bozzie
    Boswell, James **2** 432-434
Brent of Bin Bin
    Franklin, Stella Maraia Sarah Miles
        6 68-69
broken hand
    Fitzpatrick, Thomas **5** 474-475
bull, the
    Allenby, Edmund Henry Hynman
        1 171-172

bull butter Hatch
    Hatch, William Henry **7** 196
butcher of Bosnia
    Karadzic, Radovan **8** 437-440
Butcher of Lyon
    Barbie, Klaus **1** 501-503
Cartridge Prince
    William I **16** 292-293
Cattle King
    Kidman, Sidney **8** 542-544
Caudillo, El
    Franco Bahamonde, Francisco
        6 52-54
celestial king
    Hung Hsiu-ch'üan **8** 37-38
Centaur of the North
    Villa, Pancho **15** 495-496
Charles the mad
    Charles VI **3** 460-461
chief educator of the Navy
    Perry, Matthew Calbraith
        12 237-239
"Chinese" Gordon
    Gordon, Charles George **6** 448-449
Christian general
    Feng Yü-hsiang **5** 412-413
Christian Soldier, the
    Howard, Oliver Otis **7** 528-529
Chrysostom
    John Chrysostom **8** 280-281
Cicero of medicine
    Celsus, Aulus Cornelius **3** 393
Citizen Capet
    Louis XVI **9** 534-535
Citizen Genet
    Genet, Edmond Charles **6** 261-262
Citizen King
    Louis Philippe **9** 536-537
Colonel
    House, Edward Mandell **7** 520-521
Conqueror
    Edward the Confessor **5** 218-219
conqueror of the world
    Aurangzeb **1** 377
Copernicus of antiquity
    Aristarchus of Samos **1** 290-291
crafty one
    Guiscard, Robert **7** 39-40
crown prince of gospel music
    Cleveland, James **4** 106-108
curled darling of Utica
    Conkling, Roscoe **4** 201-202
curly
    Crazy Horse **4** 303-304
czar Reed
    Reed, Thomas Brackett **13** 77
dafty
    Maxwell, James Clerk **10** 361-364
Danny the Red
    Cohn-Bendit, Daniel **4** 140-141
darling of the people
    Berkeley, William **2** 198-199
Darwin's bulldog
    Huxley, Thomas Henry **8** 77-79
dashing general

Li Tzu-Ch'eng **9** 452
Dau
    Landau, Lev Davidovich **9** 184-185
dean of American poetry
    Markham, Edwin **10** 267
dean of American jive
    Calloway, Cab **3** 236-238
dean, the
    Howells, William Dean **7** 539-541
Demosthenes of America
    Henry, Patrick **7** 309-311
desert fox
    Rommel, Erwin **13** 268-269
dictator
    Rutledge, John **13** 387-388
Divine Sarah, the
    Bernhardt, Sarah **2** 212-214
Divino, El
    Morales, Luis de **11** 150
dollar Mark
    Hanna, Marcus Alonzo **7** 127-128
Duce, Il
    Mussolini, Benito **11** 272-274
Duke
    Ellington, Edward Kennedy
        5 273-274
eagle
    Clark, Mark Wayne **4** 80-81
easy boss
    Platt, Thomas Collier **12** 347-348
elegant Arthur
    Arthur, Chester Alan **1** 321-323
éminence rouge
    Richelieu, Armand Jean du Plessis
        de **13** 142-144
English Hippocrates
    Sydenham, Thomas **15** 59-60
English Justinian
    Edward I **5** 208-210
fairhair
    Harold I **7** 161-162
father of air conditioning
    Carrier, Wills **3** 325-326
father of American television
    Sarnoff, David **13** 485-486
father of English music
    Byrd, William **3** 187-188
father of English poetry
    Chaucer, Geoffrey **3** 482-485
father of his country
    Medici, Cosimo de' **10** 449-450
father of his people
    Louis XII **9** 528-529
father of History
    Herodotus **7** 330-333
father of industrial design
    Morris, William **11** 187-188
father of Italian history
    Muratori, Lodovico Antonio
        11 254-255
father of Liberation theology
    Gutiérrez, Gustavo **7** 52-53
father of Malaysia
    Tunku, Abdul Rahman **15** 340-341
father of mathematical physics

Bernoulli, Daniel **2** 216
father of Mexican American theater
Valdez, Luis **15** 399-400
father of Mexican journalism
Fernández de Lizardi, José Joaquin
5 424-425
father of modern broadcasting
Paley, William S. **12** 72-75
father of modern surgery
Paré, Ambroise **12** 94-95
father of physiology
Erasistratus **5** 297-298
father of ringlets
Abu Nuwas **1** 33-34
father of secession
Rhett, Robert Barnwell **13** 120
father of spoken Hebrew
Ben Yehuda, Eliezer **2** 181-182
father of Sudan
Azhari, Sayyid Ismail al- **1** 399-401
father of Swahili
Shaaban Robert **14** 128-129
father of television
Farnsworth, Philo T. **5** 386-387
father of the atomic bomb
Szilard, Leo **15** 64-66
father of the Beat Generation
Kerouac, Jean-Louis Lebris de
8 518-519
father of the blues
Handy, William Christopher
7 123-124
father of the hydrogen bomb
Teller, Edward **15** 139-141
father of the Lebanese Army
Shihab, Fu'ad **14** 193-194
father of the missions
Serra, Junípero **14** 111-112
father of the modern American factory
Kahn, Albert **8** 407-408
father of the Red Cross
Dunant, Jean Henri **5** 139-141
father of the steam navy
Perry, Matthew Calbraith
12 237-239
father of the U.S. nuclear navy
Rickover, Hyman George
13 155-157
father of the waltz
Strauss, Johann Jr. **14** 498-499
father of wave mechanics
de Broglie, Louis **4** 442-444
Fénix de España, El
Lope Félix de Vega Carpio
9 503-506
fighting Bob
La Follette, Robert Marion
9 155-156
fighting cock
De Gaulle, Charles André Joseph
Marie **4** 463-465
fighting parson, the
Brownlow, William Gannaway
3 55-56
finality Jack
Russell, John **13** 380-381

first lady of American journalism
Thompson, Dorothy **15** 195-196
First Lady of Song
Fitzgerald, Ella **5** 468-469
First Lady of the United States in the
Teaching of English
Smith, Dora **14** 289-290
first of the blacks
Toussaint L'Ouverture, François
Dominique **15** 278-279
Flynn of the Inland
Flynn, John **5** 497-498
fortunate, the
Manuel I **10** 219-220
foul-mouthed Joe
Cannon, Joseph Gurney **3** 261-262
free-born John
Lilburne, John **9** 409-410
ganger, the
Rollo **13** 264-265
gentleman boss
Arthur, Chester Alan **1** 321-323
gentleman George
Pendleton, George Hunt **12** 198
German Pliny
Gesner, Konrad von **6** 287
German Socrates
Mendelssohn, Moses **10** 488-489
Gersonides
Levi ben Gershon **9** 363-364
Gigger
Kipling, Joseph Rudyard **9** 32-33
Glubb Pasha
Glubb, John Bagot **6** 371-372
godfather of America
Waldseemüller, Martin **16** 56
Godfather of Soul
Brown, James **3** 37-39
"Golden Rule" Jones
Jones, Samuel Milton **8** 342-343
Goldy
Goldsmith, Oliver **6** 411-413
Good, the
Douglas, James **5** 78
good Duke
Gloucester, Duke of **6** 370-371
good King Louis
Louis XII **9** 528-529
Good Old Smithy
Smith, Ian Douglas **14** 291-293
Götz von Berlichingen
Goethe, Johann Wolfgang von
6 388-391
grand, le
Couperin, François **4** 270-271
grand constable
De Gaulle, Charles André Joseph
Marie **4** 463-465
grand old man
Gladstone, William Ewart
6 357-360
grandmother of the Russian Revolution
Breshkovsky, Catherine **2** 517-519
gray Fox
Crook, George **4** 322-323
great, the

Alexander the Great **1** 137-141
Ali, Sunni **1** 158-159
Cyrus the Great **4** 363-364
Darius I **4** 394-395
Frederick II **6** 81-84
Ivan III **8** 156-157
Otto I **12** 28-29
great absentee
Velasco Ibarra, José María
15 452-454
great agnostic
Ingersoll, Robert Green **8** 120-121
great commoner
Bryan, William Jennings **3** 80-82
Pitt, William the Elder **12** 328-329
great compromiser
Clay, Henry **4** 94-96
great John L.
Sullivan, John Lawrence **15** 24-25
great liberator
Ballivián, José **1** 475
great renegade
Girty, Simon **6** 350
great silent one
Moltke, Helmuth Karl Bernard von
11 90-91
hammer, the
Martel, Charles **10** 285
Hammerer
Judas Maccabeus **8** 374-375
happiest millionaire
Forbes, Malcolm **5** 508-509
hardest-working man in show business
Brown, James **3** 37-39
hayseed
Cannon, Joseph Gurney **3** 261-262
H.D.
Doolittle, Hilda **5** 65-66
he who yawns
Geronimo **6** 281-282
hero of Tampico
Santa Ana, Antonio López de
13 471-472
hero of Upper Canada
Brock, Isaac **3** 12-13
hero of Veracruz
Santa Ana, Antonio López de
13 471-472
Hobun
Yamashita, Tomoyuki **16** 435-436
holy Horatio
Alger, Horatio **1** 153-154
Hooknose
Gustavus II **7** 43-45
Hoosier poet
Riley, James Whitcomb **13** 170-171
Horus Neteryerkhet
Zoser **16** 531
Idaho lion
Borah, William Edgar **2** 408
ideologue of the Iranian Revolution
Shariati, Ali **14** 156-157
incorruptible, the
Robespierre, Maximilien François
Marie Isidore de **13** 199-201
iron duke

Alba, Duke of **1** 103-104
  Wellington, 1st Duke of **16** 193-195
iron man Ian
  Smith, Ian Douglas **14** 291-293
iron marshal
  Peixoto, Floriano **12** 188-189
Isaurian, the
  Leo III **9** 330-332
Japonizing Nabi
  Bonnard, Pierre **2** 395-396
Jean Paul
  Richter, Johann Paul Friedrich
  13 150-151
Jersey Hindoo
  St. Denis, Ruth **13** 430-431
Jewish Mark Twain
  Aleichem, Sholom **1** 124-125
Jewish Socrates
  Mendelssohn, Moses **10** 488-489
John the good
  John II **8** 275-276
Jubilee Jim
  Fisk, James **5** 464-465
Judas
  Mussolini, Benito **11** 272-274
Jug
  Dreiser, Herman Theodore **5** 98-100
Kentucky boy
  Cartwright, Peter **3** 344-345
King Bomba
  Ferdinand II (king of Two Sicilies)
  5 415
king of battle
  Sargon of Agade **13** 483
king of late night television
  Carson, Johnny **3** 335-337
king of rock 'n' roll
  Presley, Elvis Aron **12** 441-442
king of the blues
  King, B. B. **9** 11-14
king of the waltz
  Strauss, Johann Jr. **14** 498-499
king Voltaire
  Louis XVIII **9** 535-536
kingfish
  Long, Huey Pierce **9** 496-497
kingmaker
  Warwick and of Salisbury, Earl of
  16 122-123
La Pasionaria
  Ibárruri Gómez, Dolores **8** 88-90
labor emperor
  William II **16** 294-295
labor statesman
  Hillman, Sidney **7** 392-393
Lackland
  John **8** 274-275
Lady Day
  Holiday, Billie **7** 452-453
lady with the lamp
  Nightingale, Florence **11** 392-393
lauréat, le
  Fréchette, Louis-Honoré **6** 77-78
Lawrence of Arabia
  Lawrence, Thomas Edward
  9 253-254

lawyer's lawyer
  Cardozo, Benjamin Nathan
  3 288-290
learned blacksmith
  Burritt, Elihu **3** 160
Leo Hebraeus
  Levi ben Gershon **9** 363-364
Lepoqo (disasters)
  Moshweshwe **11** 203-205
liberator
  Bolívar, Simón **2** 375-377
  Iturbide, Agustín de **8** 155-156
  O'Connell, Daniel **11** 465-467
  Santana, Pedro **13** 474-475
liberator of Mexico
  Santa Ana, Antonio López de
  13 471-472
light-haired boy
  Crazy Horse **4** 303-304
light of the exile
  Gershom ben Judah **6** 283-284
lion hero
  Alp Arslan **1** 178-179
lion of the Punjab
  Ranjit Singh **13** 32-33
little boots
  Caligula **3** 228-229
little corporal
  Napoleon I **11** 306-310
little digger
  Hughes, William Morris **8** 21-22
little flower
  La Guardia, Fiorello Henry
  9 166-167
little giant
  Douglas, Stephen Arnold **5** 80-82
little Spaniard, the
  Ribera, Jusepe de **13** 122-123
Lodovico il Moro
  Sforza, Lodovico **14** 127-128
long knife
  Clark, George Rogers **4** 75-76
Lucifer of the lobby
  Weed, Thurlow **16** 169-170
lucky
  Ericson, Leif **5** 306-307
mad Shelley
  Shelley, Percy Bysshe **14** 176-178
magnifico, il
  Medici, Lorenzo de' **10** 450-451
Magus of the north
  Hamann, Johann Georg **7** 92
Major Yes-Yes
  Sadat, Anwar **13** 412-414
maker of the nation
  Mzilikazi **11** 285-286
man in black, the
  Cash, Johnny **3** 353-355
man of a thousand voices
  Blanc, Mel **2** 319-320
man of laws
  Santander, Franciso de Paula **13** 475
man of the people
  Fox, Charles James **6** 35-37
man on horseback

Wellington, 1st Duke of **16** 193-195
man who was Mexico
  Santa Ana, Antonio López de
  13 471-472
man with a thousand partners
  Penney, J. C. **12** 202-203
Manassa mauler
  Dempsey, Jack **4** 496-497
martial emperor
  Han Wu-ti **7** 136
Mary Yellin
  Lease, Mary Elizabeth Clyens **9** 268
mayor of Silicon Valley
  Noyce, Robert **11** 436-437
Mexican thinker
  Fernández de Lizardi, José Joaquin
  5 424-425
Mr. Conservative (United States)
  Goldwater, Barry **6** 413-415
Mr. is-that-so?
  Hirohito **7** 410-412
Mr. Magellanic clouds
  Shapley, Harlow **14** 155-156
Mr. Republican
  Taft, Robert Alphonso **15** 76-78
Mr. Swahili
  Shaaban Robert **14** 128-129
Mr. Tsungli Yaman
  Wen-hsiang **16** 202-203
Mrs. Education
  Green, Edith Starrett **6** 519-520
Modi
  Modigliani, Amedeo **11** 72-73
Mohr
  Marx, Karl **10** 304-308
"monk" Lewis
  Lewis, Matthew Gregory **9** 390-391
Moor, the
  Sforza, Lodovico **14** 127-128
Mother Jones
  Jones, Mary Harris **8** 338-339
mother of a million artists
  Hanks, Nancy **7** 126-127
mother of affirmative action
  Green, Edith Starrett **6** 519-520
mother of the civil rights movement
  Parks, Rosa Lee McCauley
  12 115-116
mother of the WAVES
  Smith, Margaret Chase **14** 299-300
movie-queen of Nazi Germany
  Riefenstahl, Leni **13** 161-163
muleteer cacique
  Túpac Amaru, José Gabriel **15** 341
Natick cobbler
  Wilson, James Harold **16** 324-325
Netaji (führer)
  Bose, Subhas Chandra **2** 430-431
New Woman
  Luhan, Mabel Dodge **10** 32-34
Nightingale in the east
  Nightingale, Florence **11** 392-393
nightingale of India
  Naidu, Sarojini **11** 294-295
nosey

Wellington, 1st Duke of **16** 193-195
Nugget
    Coombs, Herbert Cole **4** 219-220
obscure, the
    Heraclitus **7** 320
Old Blue Eyes
    Sinatra, Francis Albert **14** 246-248
old Buddha, the
    Tz'u-hsi **15** 375-376
old fuss and feathers
    Scott, Winfield **14** 70-71
old hickory
    Jackson, Andrew **8** 168-172
old man of the sea
    Yun Sondo **16** 483
old rough and ready
    Taylor, Zachary **15** 128-130
old snapping turtle
    Meade, George Gordon **10** 440-441
old wagoner
    Morgan, Daniel **11** 160-161
one-corner ma
    Ma Yüan **10** 379
one-eyed
    Antigonus I **1** 248-249
one-eyed plowboy
    Tillman, Benjamin Ryan **15** 225-226
Oracle of Omaha
    Buffett, Warren **3** 106-109
orator of secession
    Yancey, William Lowndes
        16 436-437
orator of the streets
    Danton, Georges Jacques **4** 391-393
organizer of victory
    Carnot, Lazare Nicolas Marguerite
        3 313-314
Osagyefo
    Nkrumah, Kwame **11** 408-410
our Moses
    Garrett, Thomas **6** 225-226
overbaring
    Cromer, 1st Earl of **4** 317
padre de la patria
    Hidalgo y Costilla, Miguel
        7 375-377
papa doc
    Duvalier, François **5** 165-166
Parnassus
    Dwight, Timothy **5** 169
patriot printer of 1776
    Bradford, William **2** 476-477
Paul Bunyan of New Brunswick
    Irving, Kenneth Colin **8** 140-141
Pecos Valley cattle king
    Chisum, John Simpson **4** 11
peerless lady wing-shot, the
    Oakley, Annie **11** 453-454
pensador Mexicano
    Fernández de Lizardi, José Joaquin
        5 424-425
people's laureate
    Riley, James Whitcomb **13** 170-171
people's William
    Gladstone, William Ewart
        6 357-360

Philadelphus
    Ptolemy II **12** 472-473
pitchfork Ben
    Tillman, Benjamin Ryan **15** 225-226
plumed knight
    Blaine, James Gillespie **2** 312-313
poet laureate of Swahili
    Shaaban Robert **14** 128-129
pope Dwight
    Dwight, Timothy **5** 169
Precursor, El
    Miranda, Francisco de **11** 52-53
Prez
    Young, Lester Willis **16** 471-473
prince of holy virtue, the
    Shotoku Taishi **14** 205-207
prince of liars
    Mendes Pinto, Fernao **10** 493-494
prince of the plains
    Buffalo Bill **3** 105-106
prince of the romantics
    Schelling, Friedrich Wilhelm Joseph
        von **13** 526-527
Protestant Sister of Charity
    Seton, Elizabeth Ann Bayley
        14 118-119
queen of folk singers
    Baez, Joan **1** 433-435
queen of gospel
    Caesar, Shirley **3** 210-211
queen of soul
    Franklin, Aretha **6** 58-60
Raven, the
    Houston, Samuel **7** 526-527
razor, the
    Tojo, Hideki **15** 254-256
red beard
    Frederick I **6** 78-79
red eminence
    Richelieu, Armand Jean du Plessis
        de **13** 142-144
red priest
    Vivaldi, Antonio **16** 3-4
rock of Chickamauga
    Thomas, George Henry **15** 190-191
sage of Monticello
    Jefferson, Thomas **8** 238-241
sage of potato hill
    Howe, Edgar Watson **7** 529
sage of the nation
    Deák, Francis **4** 431-432
sage of Yoncalla
    Applegate, Jesse **1** 264-265
sailor king
    William IV **16** 296-297
saint of the immigrants
    Cabrini, Frances Xavier **3** 205
Saxon master of music
    Bach, Johann Christian **1** 415-416
scarface
    Capone, Al **3** 272-273
seaman's champion
    Dana, Richard Henry Jr. **4** 385-386
servant of the nation
    Morelos, José María **11** 157-158

Shakyamuni (Sage of the Shakyas)
    Buddha **3** 97-101
sharpshooter
    Oakley, Annie **11** 453-454
shaver, the
    Moshweshwe **11** 203-205
Sheikh Ibrahim
    Burckhardt, Johann Ludwig **3** 133
Shuta
    Liang Wu-ti **9** 396-397
silence dogood
    Franklin, Benjamin **6** 60-64
silent Cal
    Coolidge, John Calvin **4** 217-219
silly Billy
    William IV **16** 296-297
silver leg
    Stuyvesant, Peter **15** 5-6
slave to the slaves
    Claver, Peter **4** 94
soldier's friend
    Curtin, Andrew Gregg **4** 347-348
southern Tycho
    Halley, Edmund **7** 88-89
Spagnoletto, Lo
    Ribera, Jusepe de **13** 122-123
Spanish Michelangelo
    Churriguera, José Benito de **4** 53-54
Sparrow
    Piaf, Edith **12** 285-287
Sphinx
    Ibsen, Henrik **8** 98-100
spider king
    Louis XI **9** 526-528
stupor mundi
    Frederick II **6** 79
sun king
    Louis XIV **9** 531-533
swamp fox
    Marion, Francis **10** 262-263
sweet singer of Israel
    David, Jacques Louis **4** 407-409
sword of Gideon
    Münzer, Thomas **11** 251-252
teacher president
    Sarmiento, Domingo Faustino
        13 484-485
tenth muse
    Sappho **13** 479-480
terrible, the
    Ivan IV **8** 157-159
The Greatest
    Ali, Muhammad **1** 156-158
the smiling pope
    John Paul I **8** 286-287
the Tengku
    Tunku, Abdul Rahman **15** 340-341
Themistogenes of Syracuse
    Xenophon **16** 418-420
Theos Soter
    Ptolemy I **12** 470-472
tiger
    Clemenceau, Georges **4** 99-101
tiger of Malaya
    Yamashita, Tomoyuki **16** 435-436

tiger of the plains
  Quiroga, Juan Facundo **12** 521-522
traitor
  Mussolini, Benito **11** 272-274
tribune of the people
  Howe, Joseph **7** 534-535
Tsui-weng
  Ou-yang Hsiu **12** 33-34
tyrant of the Andes
  Gómez, Juan Vicente **6** 417-418
Umdabuli we Sizwe
  Mzilikazi **11** 285-286
uncle Joe
  Cannon, Joseph Gurney **3** 261-262
uncle of Europe
  Leopold I **9** 345-346
universal monarch
  Genghis Khan **6** 263-265
verissimus (Truest)
  Marcus Aurelius Antoninus
    10 243-245
vinegar Joe
  Stilwell, Joseph Warren **14** 456-457
Virgin's troubador
  Alfonso X **1** 150-151
Welsh wizard
  Lloyd George, David **9** 469-471
white eagle
  McLoughlin, John **10** 423-424
wise, the
  Alfonso X **1** 150-151
wonder of the world
  Frederick II **6** 79
Yavuz (the grim)
  Selim I **14** 94-95
young man
  Burne-Jones, Edward Coley
    3 145-146
young pretender
  Stuart, Charles Edward Louis Philip
    Casimir **3** 466-467
Zik
  Azikiwe, Nnamdi **1** 401-402
  see also Pseudonyms

Nicola Pisano
  see Pisano, Nicola

Nicolai, Christoph Friedrich (1733-1811),
German author, critic, and bookseller
  Lessing, Gotthold Ephraim **9** 357-359
  Mendelssohn, Moses **10** 488-489

Nicolai Gogol (book)
  Nabokov, Vladimir **11** 287-288

Nicole (literary character)
  Fitzgerald, Francis Scott Key **5** 470-472

Nicollet, J.N. (1786-1843), French mathematician and astronomer
  Frémont, John Charles **6** 97-98

Nicolls, Richard (1624-1672), British governor of New York
  Stuyvesant, Peter **15** 5-6

NICOLSON, HAROLD GEORGE
  (1886-1968), British diplomat, historian,

biographer, critic and journalist, and
diarist **11** 383-384
NICOLSON, MARJORIE HOPE
  (1894-1981), American educator
  11 384-385
Nicomachean Ethics (book)
  Aristotle **1** 295-296
Nicomedia (ancient city; Turkey)
  Diocletian **5** 19-20, 387
Nicomède (play)
  Corneille, Pierre **4** 234-236
Nicon (died 150), Greek mathematician,
architect, astronomer, and philosopher
  Galen **6** 178-180
Nicopolis, Crusade of (1396)
  Philip the Good **12** 278-279
  Sigismund **14** 220-221
Nido ajeno, El (play)
  Benavente y Martinez, Jacinto
    2 146-147
Niebelungen, Die (trilogy)
  Hebbel, Friedrich **7** 247
NIEBUHR, BARTHOLD GEORG
  (1776-1831), German historian and
  statesman **11** 385-386
  Baur, Ferdinand Christian **2** 74-75
  Lieber, Francis **9** 401-402
NIEBUHR, HELMUT RICHARD
  (1894-1962), American Protestant theolo-
  gian **11** 386-387
NIEBUHR, REINHOLD (1892-1971),
  American Protestant theologian
  11 387-388
  Auden, Wystan Hugh **1** 364-366
  Bennett, John Coleman **2** 170-171
  Rauschenbusch, Walter **13** 53-54
  Tillich, Paul Johannes **15** 224-225
Niels Lyhne (novel; Jacobsen)
  Jacobsen, Jens Peter **8** 193-194
  Richardson, Henry Handel **13** 139
NIELSEN, CARL AUGUST (1865-1931),
  Danish composer **11** 388-389
NIEMEYER SOARES FILHO, OSCAR (born
  1907), Brazilian architect **11** 389-390
  Le Corbusier **9** 274-275
Nien Rebellion (China; 1865-68)
  Li Hung-Chang **9** 407-409
  Tseng Kuo-fan **15** 324-325
  Yüan Shih-k'ai **16** 480-481
Niépce, Joseph Nicéphore (1765-1833),
French physicist
  Daguerre, Louis Jacques Mandé
    4 365-366
NIETZSCHE, FRIEDRICH (1844-1900),
German philosopher and poet
11 390-392
  associates
    Wagner, Richard **16** 40-43
  influence (art and literature)
    Benn, Gottfried **2** 164
    Chirico, Giorgio de **4** 4
    D'Annunzio, Gabriele **4** 388

  Jeffers, John Robinson **8** 236-237
  Kazantzakis, Nikos **8** 466-468
  Kirchner, Ernst Ludwig **9** 34-35
  Mann, Thomas **10** 204-207
  Mencken, Henry Louis **10** 481-483
  Miller, Henry **11** 26-27
  Strindberg, August **14** 509-511
  influence (philosophy)
    Buber, Martin **3** 87-89
    Iqbal, Muhammad **8** 132-133
  influence (politics)
    Mussolini, Benito **11** 272-274
  terminology
    Benedict, Ruth Fulton **2** 154-155
Nieuwpoort, battle of (1600)
  Maurice of Nassau **10** 348-349
  Oldenbarnevelt, Johan van **11** 495-496
Nigel (died 1169), English bishop and
statesman
  Henry II **7** 287-289
Niger River (West Africa)
  Ali, Sunni **1** 158-159
  Baikie, William Balfour **1** 440
  Caillié, Auguste René **3** 214-215
  Clapperton, Hugh **4** 72-73
  Crowther, Samuel Adjai **4** 326
  Goldie, George Dashwood Taubman
    6 404
  Omar ibn Said Tal, Al-Hajj **11** 509-510
Nigeria, Federal Republic of (nation; West
Africa)
  archives
    Dike, Kenneth **5** 7-8
  British rule
    Goldie, George Dashwood Taub-
      man **6** 404
    Ja Ja of Opobo **8** 201-204
    Lugard, Frederick John Dealtry
      10 31-32
    Macaulay, Herbert **10** 78-79
  exploration
    Burton, Richard **3** 163-164
    Clapperton, Hugh **4** 72-73
  Fulani empire and
    Uthman don Fodio **15** 397-398
  independence
    Awolowo, Obafemi **1** 389-390
    Azikiwe, Nnamdi **1** 401-402
    Bello, Ahmadu **2** 139-140
    Blyden, Edward Wilmot **2** 348-349
    Tafawa Balewa, Abubakar **15** 75
  law
    Elias, Taslim Olawale **5** 250-251
  Opobo kingdom and
    Ja Ja of Opobo **8** 201-204
    see also Civil War, Nigerian-Biafran;
      Nigerian art; Nigerian literature
Nigeria, University of (established 1960)
  Azikiwe, Nnamdi **1** 401-402
Nigerian art
  Ewonwu, Benedict Chuka **5** 351-352
Nigerian literature
  Achebe, Chinua **1** 35-37
  Ekwensi, Cyprian **5** 242-243

Soyinka, Wole **14** 358-359
Tutuola, Amos **15** 361-362

Nigerian National Alliance (political party)
Bello, Ahmadu **2** 139-140

Nigerian National Democratic party
(established 1922)
Awolowo, Obafemi **1** 389-390
Bello, Ahmadu **2** 139-140
Macaulay, Herbert **10** 78-79

Nigerian Youth Movement (political party)
Awolowo, Obafemi **1** 389-390
Azikiwe, Nnamdi **1** 401-402

Nigger of Peter the Great, The (novel)
Pushkin, Aleksandr Sergeevich
12 489-491

Nigger of the "Narcissus", The (novel)
Conrad, Joseph **4** 205-207

Niggl, J. (1787-1826), German optical
instrument maker
Fraunhofer, Joseph von **6** 75-76

Night (book)
Wiesel, Elie **16** 263-264

Night (painting)
Beckmann, Max **2** 104-105
Hodler, Ferdinand **7** 434-435

Night (play)
Pinter, Harold **12** 317-318

Night (poem)
Pushkin, Aleksandr Sergeevich
12 489-491

Night and Day (ceramic walls)
Miró, Joan **11** 53-54

Night and Day (novel)
Woolf, Virginia Stephen **16** 381-382

Night and Day (song)
Porter, Cole Albert **12** 405-406

Night at the Opera, A (film)
Marx brothers **10** 303-304

Night Café (painting)
Van Gogh, Vincent **15** 427-429

Night Flight (novel)
Saint-Exupéry, Antoine de **13** 431-432

Night Flight (opera)
Dallapiccola, Luigi **4** 377-378

Night Hours (poem)
Blok, Aleksandr Aleksandrovich **2** 335

Night Hunt (painting)
Uccello, Paolo **15** 378-379

Night in Casablanca, A (film)
Marx brothers **10** 303-304

Night in Lisbon, The (novel)
Remarque, Erich Maria **13** 91

Night in Saint Cloud (painting)
Munch, Edvard **11** 247-248

Night in the Rich Man's House (play)
Betti, Ugo **2** 246

Night in Venice, A (operetta)
Strauss, Johann Jr. **14** 498-499

Night Music (play)
Odets, Clifford **11** 470-471

Night of the Iguana, The (play)
Williams, Tennessee **16** 306-308

Night on Bald Mountain (play)
White, Patrick Victor Martindale
16 233-235

Night Out, A (play)
Pinter, Harold **12** 317-318

Night Rider (novel)
Warren, Robert Penn **16** 121-122

Night School (play)
Pinter, Harold **12** 317-318

Night, The (lithograph series)
Redon, Odilon **13** 75-76

Night Violet, The (poem)
Blok, Aleksandr Aleksandrovich **2** 335

Night Watch (painting)
Rembrandt Harmensz van Rijn
13 91-95

NIGHTINGALE, FLORENCE (1820-1910),
English nurse **11** 392-393
Clough, Arthur Hugh **4** 123-124

Nightingale, The (opera)
Stravinsky, Igor Fedorovich **14** 502-506

Nightingale of Wittenberg, The (song)
Sachs, Hans **13** 410-411

Nightmare, The (painting)
Fuseli, Henry **6** 153-155

Nightmare Abbey (novel)
Peacock, Thomas Love **12** 169

Nightmare at Noon (poem)
Benét, Stephen Vincent **2** 157-158

Nights (poems)
Musset, Louis Charles Alfred de
11 271-272

Nights of Cabiria (film)
Fellini, Federico **5** 408-409

Nights with Uncle Remus (stories)
Harris, Joel Chandler **7** 173-174

Nihawand, battle of (642)
Omar ibn al-Khattab **11** 508-509

Nihilism (philosophy)
Benn, Gottfried **2** 164
Hitler, Adolf **7** 417-420
Nietzsche, Friedrich **11** 390-392
Turgenev, Ivan Sergeyevich **15** 345-348

Nijinsky, Vaslav (1890-1950), Russian
dancer
Stravinsky, Igor Fedorovich **14** 502-506

NIJINSKY, VASLAV (1890-1953), ballet
dancer **11** 393-395

Nijmegen, battle of (1591)
Maurice of Nassau **10** 348-349

Nijmegen, Treaty of (1678)
William III **16** 295-296

Nika riots (Byzantine; 532)
Belisarius **2** 128-129
Justinian I **8** 393-395

Procopius of Caesarea **12** 457-458
Theodora **15** 172-175

Nikiforos Phocas (play)
Kazantzakis, Nikos **8** 466-468

NIKON, NIKITA MINOV (1605-1681),
patriarch of the Russian Orthodox Church
1652-1666 **11** 395
Alexis Mikhailovich Romanov
1 142-143

Nile River (East and Northeast Africa)
Baker, Samuel White **1** 454-455
Burckhardt, Johann Ludwig **3** 133
Burton, Richard **3** 163-164
Speke, John Hanning **14** 366-367

Nilotic (African people)
Evans-Pritchard, Edward Evan **5** 340

NIMITZ, CHESTER WILLIAM (1885-1966),
American admiral **11** 395-396
King, Ernest Joseph **9** 17-18

Nimrod (ship)
Shackleton, Ernest Henry **14** 132-133

NIN, ANAIS (1903-1977), American author
11 397-398

NIN-CULMELL, JOAQUÍN MARÍA (born
1908), American composer, pianist, and
conductor **11** 398

Niña (ship)
Columbus, Christopher **4** 176-179

999 (racing car)
Ford, Henry **6** 5-6

Nine Letters (story)
Dostoevsky, Fyodor **5** 74-77

Nine Little Goblins (poem)
Riley, James Whitcomb **13** 170-171

1919 (novel; Dos Passos)
Bourne, Randolph Silliman **2** 456-457
Dos Passos, John Roderigo **5** 69-71

1984 (novel)
Orwell, George **12** 14-15-222

19th Amendment
see Constitution of the United States—
Amendments

95 Poems (literary collection)
Cummings, Edward Estlin **4** 334-336

95 Theses (1517)
Luther, Martin **10** 48-51

Nineveh (ancient city; Iraq)
Ashurbanipal **1** 338
Nebuchadnezzar **11** 330

Ninfale fiesolano (poem)
Boccaccio, Giovanni **2** 351-353

Ninfeas (poems)
Jiménez, Juan Ramón **8** 261-262

Ning Tsung (ruled 1195-1224), Chinese
emperor
Chu Hsi **4** 40-43
Hsia Kuei **8** 4-5
Kao-tsung **8** 433

Nino Pisano (1315?-1358?), Italian sculptor and architect
  Andrea Pisano **1** 225-226

Ninotchka (film)
  Garbo, Greta **6** 205-207
  Lubitsch, Ernst **10** 18-19

Ninth Hour (poem; Auden)
  Berio, Luciano **2** 194-195

Niou (literary character)
  Murasaki Shikibu **11** 252-253

Nipmuck Indians (North America)
  Philip **12** 267-268

NIRENBERG, MARSHALL WARREN (born 1927), American biochemist **11** 399-400
  Khorana, Har Gobind **8** 537-538

Nirvana (Buddhism)
  Buddha **3** 97-101, 231
  Kukai **9** 124-125

Nirvana of the Phoenixes, The (poem)
  Kuo Mo-jo **9** 133-134

Nirvani, Carma
  see Kazantzakis, Nikos

Nishiyama Soin (1605-1682), Japanese poet
  Basho, Matsuo **2** 45-48

Nitrogen (element—chemistry)
  Cavendish, Henry **3** 383-384
  Chadwick, James **3** 405-406
  Crookes, William **4** 323-324
  Dumas, Jean Baptiste André **5** 138-139
  Haber, Fritz **7** 56-58
  Loewi, Otto **9** 486-487

Nitroglycerin (explosive)
  Nobel, Alfred Bernhard **11** 410-411

Nitrous oxide (chemistry)
  Davy, Humphry **4** 426-427
  Long, Crawford Williamson **9** 495-496
  Wells, Horace **16** 196

Nitta Yoshisada (died 1338), Japanese warrior
  Ashikaga Takauji **1** 330-332
  Daigo II **4** 367-368

Niue (islands; Southwestern Pacific Ocean)
  Cook, James **4** 214-215

Nivelle, Robert Georges (1856-1924), French general
  Joffre, Joseph Jacques Césaire **8** 267-268
  Pétain, Henri Philippe **12** 250-252

NIWANO, NIKKYO (Shikazo Niwano; born 1906), Buddhist Japanese religious leader **11** 400-401

NIXON, RICHARD MILHOUS (1913-1994), president of the United States (1969-1974) **11** 401-404
  appointees
      Blackmun, Harry **2** 309-310
      Buchanan, Patrick Joseph **3** 90-91
      Burger, Warren E. **3** 133-136
      Burns, Arthur **3** 151-153
      Bush, George **3** 167-169
      Colby, William E. **4** 143-145
      Cox, Archibald **4** 283-284
      Laird, Melvin R. **9** 168-170
      Moynihan, Daniel Patrick **11** 216-218
      Schlesinger, James Rodney **14** 15-16
      Shultz, George Pratt **14** 209-211
      Weinberger, Casper Willard **16** 177-178
  associates
      Agnew, Spiro Theodore **1** 83-85
      Connally, John Bowden Jr. **4** 202-204
      Ford, Gerald **6** 2-5
      Haig, Alexander M. Jr. **7** 66-67
      Lodge, Henry Cabot Jr. **9** 483-485
  impeachment proceedings
      Kissinger, Henry Alfred **9** 43-45
      Rodino, Peter Wallace Jr. **13** 238-239
  Medal of Freedom (awarded to)
      Ellington, Edward Kennedy **5** 273-274
      Wilkins, Roy **16** 282-283
      Young, Whitney Moore Jr. **16** 476-477
  rivals
      Kennedy, John Fitzgerald **8** 502-506
  Supreme Court appointees
      Blackmun, Harry **2** 309-310
      Burger, Warren E. **3** 133-136
      Powell, Lewis F. Jr. **12** 426-428
      Rehnquist, William Hubbs **13** 82-84
  Watergate scandal
      Burger, Warren E. **3** 133-136
      Ervin, Sam J. Jr. **5** 316-317
      Jaworski, Leon **8** 229-230
      Rodino, Peter Wallace Jr. **13** 238-239
      Sirica, John Joseph **14** 257-258
      Woodward and Bernstein **16** 376-378

Niza, Marcos de
  see Marcos de Niza, Friar

Nizam al-Mulk, Hassan ibn-Ali (1018-1092), Persian statesman, vizier 1063-1092
  Alp Arslan **1** 178-179
  Ghazali, Abu Hamid Muhammad al- **6** 290-291

NIZAMI, KHALIQ AHMAD (born 1925), Indian historian, religious scholar, and diplomat **11** 405

Nizamiya Madrasa (college; Baghdad)
  Ghazali, Abu Hamid Muhammad al- **6** 290-291

NKOMO, JOSHUA MQABUKO (born 1917), leading African nationalist in former colony of Rhodesia and president of the Zimbabwe African People's Union **11** 405-407
  Sithole, Ndabaningi **14** 262-264

NKOSI, LEWIS (born 1936), South African author and literary critic **11** 407-408

NKRUMAH, KWAME (Francis Nwa Nkrumah; 1909-1972), Ghanaian statesman, president 1960-1966 **11** 408-410
  opponents
      Busia, Kofi Abrefa **3** 172-173
      Danquah, Joseph B. **4** 388-389
      Houphouët-Boigny, Felix **7** 519-520
      Malan, Daniel Francois **10** 163-164
      Olympio, Sylvanus E. **11** 506-507
  associates
      Diagne, Blaise **4** 527
      Du Bois, William Edward Burghardt **5** 116-118
      Kenyatta, Jomo **8** 512-514
      Padmore, George **12** 57-58
      Touré, Sékou **15** 275-277

NKVD
  see Peoples' Commissariat for Internal Affairs

NLRB v. Jones and Laughlin Steel Corp. (legal case)
  Stone, Harlan Fiske **14** 468-470

No Coward Soul (poem)
  Brontë, Emily **3** 18-19

No drama
  see Japanese literature—No drama

No Exit (play)
  Sartre, Jean Paul **13** 491-492

No hay mal que por bien no venga (play)
  Alarcón, Pedro Antonio de **1** 100-101

No Longer At Ease (novel)
  Achebe, Chinua **1** 35-37

No Man's Meat (novella)
  Callaghan, Edward Morley **3** 229-230

No More Parades (novel)
  Ford, Ford Madox **6** 1-2

No Star Is Lost (novel)
  Farrell, James Thomas **5** 390-391

No Strings (musical)
  Rodgers, Richard Charles **13** 234-236

No Swan So Fine (poem)
  Moore, Marianne **11** 148-149

No Time for Sergeants (play)
  Davis, Ossie **4** 421-422

No Way Out (film)
  Davis, Ossie **4** 421-422

No Worst, There Is None (sonnet)
  Hopkins, Gerard Manley **7** 492-494

Noailles, Anna-Elisabeth, Comtesse de (1876-1933), French novelist and poet
  Cocteau, Jean **4** 132-133
  Morin, Paul **11** 174

NOBEL, ALFRED BERNHARD (1833-1896), Swedish chemist **11** 410-411

Nobel Foundation
  Nobel, Alfred Bernhard **11** 410-411
  Tiselius, Arne Wilhelm Kaurin **15** 240-241
  see also Nobel Prize winners

Nobel institutes
Arrhenius, Svante August **1** 318-320
Theorell, Axel Hugo Theodor
  15 176-177

Nobel Prize winners
chemistry
  Arrhenius, Svante August **1** 318-320
  Aston, Francis William **1** 350-351
  Baeyer, Johann Friedrich Adolf von
    1 432
  Berg, Paul **2** 187-189
  Curie, Marie Sklodowska **4** 339-341
  Debye, Peter Joseph William
    4 447-448
  Diels, Otto Paul Hermann **5** 5-6
  Fischer, Emil **5** 456-457
  Flory, Paul **5** 492-494
  Haber, Fritz **7** 56-58
  Hahn, Otto **7** 64-65
  Herzberg, Gerhard **7** 349-350
  Hevesy, George Charles de **7** 371
  Hinshelwood, Cyril Norman
    7 405-406
  Hodgkin, Dorothy Crowfoot
    7 432-434
  Joliot-Curie, Irène **8** 325-327
  Joliot-Curie, Jean Frédéric
    8 327-328
  Kendrew, John C. **8** 495-496
  Langmuir, Irving **9** 196-197
  Libby, Willard Frank **9** 397-398
  Nernst, Walther **11** 340-342
  Northrop, John Howard **11** 430-431
  Onsager, Lars **11** 520-523
  Pauling, Linus Carl **12** 150-152
  Perutz, Max **12** 246-248
  Polanyi, John Charles **12** 370-372
  Pregl, Fritz **12** 436-437
  Ramsay, William **13** 21-22
  Richards, Theodore William
    13 137-138
  Rutherford, Ernest **13** 384-387
  Sabatier, Paul **13** 398-399
  Sanger, Frederick **13** 466-467
  Seaborg, Glenn Theodore **14** 74-76
  Semenov, Nikolai Nikolaevich
    14 101
  Soddy, Frederick **14** 321-323
  Stanley, Wendell Meredith
    14 400-401
  Tiselius, Arne Wilhelm Kaurin
    15 240-241
  Todd, Alexander **15** 251-253
  Urey, Harold Clayton **15** 394-396
  Van't Hoff, Jacobus Hendricus
    15 431-432
  Willstätter, Richard **16** 310-312
economics
  Friedman, Milton **6** 111-112
  Hayek, Friedrich A. von **7** 221-223
  Kuznets, Simon **9** 138-139
  Samuelson, Paul Anthony
    13 458-459
  Simon, Herbert Alexander
    14 236-237
  Tinbergen, Jan **15** 228-229

literature
  Agnon, Shmuel Yoseph **1** 85-86
  Asturias, Miguel Angel **1** 354-355
  Beckett, Samuel **2** 102-104
  Bellow, Saul **2** 141-143
  Benavente y Martinez, Jacinto
    2 146-147
  Bergson, Henri **2** 191-192
  Bjørnson, Bjørnstjerne **2** 299-300
  Brodsky, Joseph **3** 13-15
  Buck, Pearl Sydenstricker **3** 91-93
  Bunin, Ivan Alekseevich **3** 124
  Camus, Albert **3** 255-257
  Carducci, Giosuè **3** 290-291
  Eliot, Thomas Stearns **5** 258-261
  Faulkner, William **5** 395-397
  France, Anatole **6** 39-40
  Galsworthy, John **6** 189-190
  Gide, André **6** 308-309
  Golding, William **6** 404-406
  Hamsun, Knut **7** 113-114
  Heaney, Seamus Justin **7** 238-240
  Heidenstam, Carl Gustaf Verner Von
    7 258-259
  Hemingway, Ernest Miller
    7 274-277
  Hesse, Hermann **7** 367-369
  Heyse, Paul Johann Ludwig
    7 372-373
  Jiménez, Juan Ramón **8** 261-262
  Kawabata, Yasunari **8** 463-464
  Kipling, Joseph Rudyard **9** 32-33
  Lagerlöf, Selma Ottiliana Lovisa
    9 163-164
  Lewis, Harry Sinclair **9** 385-387
  Maeterlinck, Maurice **10** 125-126
  Mann, Thomas **10** 204-207
  Martin du Gard, Roger **10** 295-296
  Mauriac, François **10** 347-348
  Milosz, Czeslaw **11** 40-42
  Mistral, Gabriela **11** 55-56
  Mommsen, Theodor **11** 94-95
  Neruda, Pablo **11** 344-345
  O'Neill, Eugene **11** 514-516
  Pasternak, Boris Leonidovich
    12 124-125
  Paz, Octavio **12** 161-162
  Perse, Saint-John **12** 242-243
  Pirandello, Luigi **12** 319-321
  Quasimodo, Salvatore **12** 506
  Russell, Bertrand Arthur William
    13 373-374
  Sachs, Nelly **13** 411-412
  Seferis, George **14** 84-85
  Shaw, George Bernard **14** 163-164
  Sholokhov, Mikhail Aleksandrovich
    14 203-204
  Sienkiewicz, Henryk **14** 216-217
  Solzhenitsyn, Alexander Isayevich
    14 330-332
  Soyinka, Wole **14** 358-359
  Steinbeck, John Ernst **14** 416-417
  Rabindranath Tagore **12** 529-531
  Undset, Sigrid **15** 388-389
  Yeats, William Butler **16** 445-447
peace

  Altamira Y Crevea, Rafael **1** 179
  Arias Sanchez, Oscar **1** 287-289
  Aung San Suu Kyi **1** 375-376
  Balch, Emily Greene **1** 463-464
  Begin, Menachem **2** 118-120
  Borlaug, Norman Ernest **2** 418-420
  Bourgeois, Léon **2** 450-451
  Briand, Aristide **2** 528-529
  Bunche, Ralph Johnson **3** 121-122
  Butler, Nicholas Murray **3** 181
  Cecil, of Chelwood Viscount
    3 388-389
  Chamberlain, Arthur Neville
    3 409-411
  Corrigan and Williams **4** 251-253
  Dunant, Jean Henri **5** 139-141
  Gorbachev, Mikhail Sergeevich
    6 441-444
  Hammarskjöld, Dag **7** 100-101
  Henderson, Arthur **7** 277-278
  Hull, Cordell **8** 28-29
  Kellogg, Frank Billings **8** 481
  King, Martin Luther Jr. **9** 20-22
  Kissinger, Henry Alfred **9** 43-45
  Luthuli, Albert John **10** 51-52
  Marshall, George Catlett
    10 278-279
  Menchú, Rigoberta **10** 479-480
  Mott, John R. **11** 212
  Nansen, Fridtjof **11** 304-305
  Orr, John Boyd **12** 4-5
  Pauling, Linus Carl **12** 150-152
  Pearson, Lester Bowles **12** 174-175
  Pérez Esquivel, Adolfo **12** 215-217
  Roosevelt, Theodore **13** 280-283
  Root, Elihu **13** 283-284
  Lamas, Carlos Saavedra **9** 175-176
  Sakharov, Andrei **13** 439-441
  Schweitzer, Albert **14** 55-56
  Söderblom, Nathan **14** 323-324
  Stresemann, Gustav **14** 508-509
  Suttner, Bertha von **15** 42-44
  Teresa **15** 148-151
  Tutu, Desmond **15** 360-361
  Walesa, Lech **16** 57-59
physics
  Alvarez, Luis W. **1** 187-189
  Anderson, Carl David **1** 214-215
  Appleton, Edward Victor **1** 265-266
  Bardeen, John **2** 1-3
  Becquerel, Antoine Henri **2** 108-109
  Bethe, Hans Albrecht **2** 238-239
  Blackett, Patrick M.S. **2** 306-307
  Bloch, Felix **2** 328-330
  Bohr, Niels Henrik David **2** 366-368
  Born, Max **2** 420-421
  Bragg, William Henry **2** 488-489
  Brattain, Walter H. **2** 505-507
  Braun, Ferdinand **2** 508-509
  Bridgman, Percy Williams **3** 5-6
  Calvin, Melvin **3** 242-243
  Chadwick, James **3** 405-406
  Cherenkov, Pavel Alekseevich
    3 502-503
  Cockcroft, John Douglas **4** 131-132
  Compton, Arthur Holly **4** 186-188

Curie, Marie Sklodowska **4** 339-341
Curie, Pierre **4** 341-344
de Broglie, Louis **4** 442-444
Dirac, Paul Adrien Maurice **5** 23-24
Einstein, Albert **5** 228-231
Fermi, Enrico **5** 422-424
Feynman, Richard Phillips
  5 432-434
Franck, James **6** 49-52
Gabor, Dennis **6** 159-160
Gell-Mann, Murray **6** 257-258
Glashow, Sheldon Lee **6** 361-362
Goeppert-Mayer, Maria **6** 385-387
Heisenberg, Werner Karl **7** 261-263
Hess, Victor Francis **7** 362-363
Kamerlingh Onnes, Heike
  8 418-420
Landau, Lev Davidovich **9** 184-185
Lawrence, Ernest Orlando
  9 248-250
Lee, Tsung-Dao **9** 299-300
Lorentz, Hendrik Antoon **9** 515-516
Marconi, Guglielmo **10** 239-240
Michelson, Albert Abraham **11** 7-8
Millikan, Robert Andrews **11** 33-35
Mössbauer, Rudolf **11** 208-209
Müller, Karl Alexander **11** 240-241
Pauli, Wolfgang Ernst **12** 149
Perrin, Jean Baptiste **12** 233-236
Planck, Max Karl Ernst Ludwig
  12 342-344
Rabi, Isidor Isaac **12** 526-527
Raman, Chandrasekhar Venkata
  13 13-14
Ramsey, Norman Foster Jr. **13** 25-27
Rayleigh, 3d Baron **13** 62
Röntgen, Wilhelm Conrad
  13 273-275
Ruska, Ernst August Friedrich
  13 370-371
Schrödinger, Erwin **14** 31-33
Stern, Otto **14** 435
Thomson, George Paget **15** 198-199
Thomson, Joseph John **15** 200-201
Tomonaga, Sin-itiro **15** 265-266
Townes, Charles Hard **15** 281-282
von Laue, Max **16** 23-24
van der Waals, Johannes Diderik
  15 417-418
Walton, Ernest **16** 88-90
Weinberg, Steven **16** 175-177
Wigner, Eugene Paul **16** 268-269
Wilson, Charles Thomson Rees
  16 317-318
Yang, Chen Ning **16** 437-438
Yukawa, Hideki **16** 481-482
physiology and medicine
  Adrian, Edgar Douglas **1** 67-69
  Baltimore, David **1** 477-478
  Banting, Frederick Grant **1** 493-494
  Beadle, George Wells **2** 80-81
  Behring, Emil Adolph von
    2 122-123
  Bloch, Konrad **2** 330-332
  Burnet, Frank Macfarlane **3** 146-147
  Carrel, Alexis **3** 322-323

Chain, Ernst Boris **3** 407-408
Cori, Gerty T. **4** 231-234
Crick, Francis Harry Crompton
  4 310
Dale, Henry Hallett **4** 371-373
Dam, Carl Peter Henrik **4** 382-383
Delbrück, Max **4** 476-478
Domagk, Gerhard Johannes Paul
  5 48-50
Eccles, John Carew **5** 195-196
Ehrlich, Paul **5** 225-226
Eijkman, Christian **5** 228
Elion, Gertrude B. **5** 252-254
Enders, John Franklin **5** 285-286
Erlanger, Joseph **5** 310-311
Fleming, Alexander **5** 483-485
Florey, Howard Walter **5** 491-492
Hershey, Alfred Day **7** 343-345
Hess, Walter Rudolf **7** 365
Hill, Archibald Vivian **7** 385-386
Hodgkin, Alan Lloyd **7** 431-432
Hopkins, Frederick Gowland
  7 491-492
Hounsfield, Godfrey **7** 517-519
Houssay, Bernardo Alberto
  7 522-523
Kendall, Edward Calvin **8** 495
Khorana, Har Gobind **8** 537-538
Koch, Heinrich Hermann Robert
  9 69-70
Kornberg, Arthur **9** 85-87
Krebs, Hans Adolf **9** 95-97
Krogh, Schack August Steenberg
  9 106
Landsteiner, Karl **9** 188-189
Lederberg, Joshua **9** 275-277
Levi-Montalcini, Rita **9** 366-368
Lipmann, Fritz **9** 435-437
Loewi, Otto **9** 486-487
Lorenz, Konrad Z. **9** 516-517
Lwoff, André **10** 58-59
McClintock, Barbara **10** 393-394
Medawar, Peter Brian **10** 444-445
Metchnikoff, Élie **10** 532-533
Meyerhof, Otto Fritz **10** 537-539
Monod, Jacques **11** 110-111
Morgan, Thomas Hunt **11** 170-171
Muller, Hermann Joseph
  11 238-239
Müller, Paul Hermann **11** 241-242
Nirenberg, Marshall Warren
  11 399-400
Ochoa, Severo **11** 461-464
Pavlov, Ivan Petrovich **12** 155-157
Reichstein, Tadeus **13** 85-87
Richet, Charles Robert **13** 144-145
Rous, Francis Peyton **13** 322-323
Sherrington, Charles Scott
  14 187-189
Spemann, Hans **14** 368-369
Szent-Györgyi, Albert von **15** 62-64
Theiler, Max **15** 169-170
Theorell, Axel Hugo Theodor
  15 176-177
Tinbergen, Nikolaas **15** 229-230
Varmus, Harold Eliot **15** 436-437

Waksman, Selman Abraham
  16 49-50
Wald, George **16** 51-53
Warburg, Otto **16** 109-111
Watson, James Dewey **16** 137-138
Whipple, George Hoyt **16** 224-225
Yalow, Rosalyn S. **16** 427-428

NOBILE, UMBERTO (1885-1978), Italian
explorer and airship designer **11** 411-412
  Amundsen, Roald **1** 206-207

Nobility, Statutes of the (Sweden, 1626)
  Gustavus II **7** 43-45

**Noble and Holy Order of the Knights of
Labor**
  see Knights of Labor

Noble savage (literature)
  Ercilla y Zúñiga, Alonso de **5** 302

Nobody Knows My Name (essays)
  Baldwin, James Arthur **1** 465-466

Nobody Writes to the Colonel... (stories)
  García Márquez, Gabriel **6** 208-209

Nobody's Looking... (song)
  Johnson, James Weldon **8** 304-305

Nöbrega, Manuel da (1517-1570), Por-
tuguese Jesuit provincial in Brazil
  Anchieta, José de **1** 210-211
  Sá, Mem de **13** 395

NOBUNAGA, ODA (1534-1582), Japanese
general and statesman **11** 413-414
  Eitoku, Kano **5** 242
  Ieyasu, Tokugawa **8** 103-106
  Toyotomi Hideyoshi **15** 286-289

Noces (essays)
  Camus, Albert **3** 255-257

Noces, Les (ballet; Stravinsky)
  Cunningham, Merce **4** 337-338
  Stravinsky, Igor Fedorovich **14** 502-506
  Szymanowski, Karol **15** 67-68

Noche del sábado, La (play)
  Benavente y Martinez, Jacinto
    2 146-147

Nocturnal Song... (poem)
  Leopardi, Giacomo **9** 344-345

Nocturnes (painting series)
  Whistler, James Abbott McNeill
    16 225-226

Nocturnes (poems)
  Senghor, Léopold Sédar **14** 106-107

Nodier, Charles (1780-1844), French man
of letters
  Hugo, Victor Marie **8** 22-25

Noech'on
  see Kim Pusik

NOETHER, EMMY (born Amalie Emmy
Noether; 1882-1935), German American
mathematician **11** 414-416

Noeud de vipères, Le (novel)
  Mauriac, François **10** 347-348

Nogaret, Guillaume de (died 1313), French
jurist and statesman

Boniface VIII **2** 392-393
Philip IV **12** 274

NOGUCHI, ISAMU (1904-1988), American sculptor and designer **11** 416-418

Nohant (estate; France)
Chopin, Frédéric François **4** 16-18
Sand, George **13** 459-461

Noia, La (novel)
Moravia, Alberto **11** 153-155

Noire de..., La (film)
Ousmane, Sembene **12** 32-33

Noiseless Patient Spider, A (poem)
Whitman, Walt **16** 249-251

Nojoque (book)
Helper, Hinton Rowan **7** 272-273

Nol, Lon
see Lon Nol

Nola (commune; Italy)
Alaric **1** 101-102

Nolan, Philip (literary character)
Hale, Edward Everett **7** 71-72

NOLAN, SIDNEY ROBERT (1917-1992), Australian expressionist painter **11** 418
Dobell, William **5** 34-35
Drysdale, George Russell **5** 107-109

NOLAND, KENNETH (born 1924), American color-field painter **11** 418-419
Caro, Anthony **3** 316
Frankenthaler, Helen **6** 56-57
Newman, Barnett **11** 365
Smith, David **14** 287-288

NOLDE, EMIL (1867-1956), German expressionist painter **11** 419-420
Kirchner, Ernst Ludwig **9** 34-35

Noli me tangere (novel)
Rizal, José **13** 187-189

Nómada (novel)
Ferrer, Gabriel Miró **5** 428

Nombre de Diós (port; Panama)
Benalcázar, Sebastián de **2** 145-146
Drake, Francis **5** 94-96

Nomenclature (chemistry)
Berzelius, Jöns Jacob **2** 231-233
Lavoisier, Antoine Laurent **9** 241-244

Nominalism (philosophy)
Bentham, Jeremy **2** 176-178
Cudworth, Ralph **4** 331
Hobbes, Thomas **7** 421-423
Hus, Jan **8** 56-59
Locke, John **9** 478-480
Luther, Martin **10** 48-51
William of Ockham **16** 298-299

Non so d'onde viene (aria; Mozart)
Bach, Johann Christian **1** 415-416

Non-Aligned Movement
Guyana
Ramphal, Shridath Surendranath **13** 19-20

Nonconformists (religion)
England

Baxter, Richard **2** 76-77
Bunyan, John **3** 128-129
Davenport, John **4** 405-406
Disraeli, Benjamin **5** 27-29
Fox, George **6** 37-38
Gladstone, William Ewart **6** 357-360
Godolphin, Sidney **6** 380-381
Harley, Robert **7** 159-160
Price, Richard **12** 447-448
United States
Bradstreet, Anne Dudley **2** 486-487
Eliot, John **5** 256-258

Noncooperation
see Nonviolent protest movements

Nondual school (philosophy)
see Advaita

None but the Brave (story)
Schnitzler, Arthur **14** 23-24

None but the Lonely Heart (film)
Barrymores **2** 28-30
Odets, Clifford **11** 470-471

Non-Euclidean geometry (mathematics)
Gauss, Karl Friedrich **6** 240-242
Lobachevskii, Nikolai Ivanovich **9** 472-474
Riemann, Georg Friedrich Bernard **13** 164-165

Nonfiguratism (art)
Moore, Henry **11** 146-148
Staël, Nicolas de **14** 392
see also Abstract art

NONO, LUIGI (1924-1990), Italian composer **11** 420-421

Nonsense Book (limericks)
Lear, Edward **9** 265-266

Nonviolent protest movements (political strategy)
Africa
Kaunda, Kenneth David **8** 460-461
Luthuli, Albert John **10** 51-52
Mandela, Nelson Rolihlahla **10** 185-186
Germany
Poincaré, Raymond **12** 366-368
India
see Passive resistance movements
Ireland
Corrigan and Williams **4** 251-253
United States
Abernathy, Ralph David **1** 27-28
Farmer, James **5** 383-385
Forman, James **6** 10-11
King, Martin Luther Jr. **9** 20-22
Muste, Abraham Johannes **11** 276-277
Rustin, Bayard **13** 382-383
see also Civil disobedience; student protest

Noon Wine (novel)
Porter, Katherine Anne **12** 406-407

Noort, Adam van (1557-1641), Flemish painter
Rubens, Peter Paul **13** 339-342

Nootka Sound (harbor; British Columbia)
Miranda, Francisco de **11** 52-53
Revillagigedo, Conde de **13** 111-112
Vancouver, George **15** 414-415

Nora (literary character)
Ibsen, Henrik **8** 98-100

Norbert of Xanten, Saint (circa 1080-1134), German archbishop and premonstatensian founder
Abelard, Peter **1** 23-25

NORDENSKJÖLD, BARON NILS ADOLF ERIK (1832-1901), Finnish-Swedish polar explorer and mineralogist **11** 421-422
Nordenskold, Nils Otto Gustaf **11** 422-423

NORDENSKOLD, NILS OTTO GUSTAF (1869-1928), Swedish polar explorer and geologist **11** 422-423
Nordenskjöld, Nils Adolf Erik **11** 421-422

Nordic Symphony (musical composition)
Hanson, Howard **7** 135-136

Nördlingen, battle of (1634)
Ferdinand III **5** 416-417
Oxenstierna, Axel Gustafsson **12** 44-45

Nordraak, Rikard (1842-1866), Norwegian composer
Grieg, Edvard Hagerup **6** 541-542

Nordsee, Die (poems)
Heine, Heinrich **7** 259-260

Nore, mutiny of (1797)
Bligh, William **2** 325-326

Norfolk (islsand; Southwestern Pacific Ocean)
Cook, James **4** 214-215

Norfolk, 1st Duke of (Thomas Mowbray; circa 1366-1399), English statesman
Henry IV **7** 292-293

Norfolk, 2nd Duke of (Thomas Howard; 1443-1524), English statesman
Henry VII **7** 300-302

NORFOLK, 3D DUKE OF (Thomas Howard; 1473-1554), English soldier and councilor **11** 423
Cromwell, Thomas **4** 320-321
Henry VIII **7** 302-305

Norfolk, 4th Duke of (Thomas Howard; 1536-1572), English nobleman
Mary I **10** 308-309

Norfolk, siege of (1775)
Dunmore, 4th Earl of **5** 147

Norge (airship)
Amundsen, Roald **1** 206-207
Ellsworth, Lincoln **5** 277
Nobile, Umberto **11** 411-412

NORIEGA, MANUEL A. (born 1934), strongman of Panama (1980s) forced out in 1989 by the United States **11** 423-425

Norma (opera)
Bellini, Vincenzo **2** 138-139

NORMAN, JESSYE (born 1945), American singer **11** 425-427

Normandy (region; France)
French-English conflict
Charles VII **3** 461-462
Harold II **7** 162
Henry I **7** 286-287
Henry V **7** 296-297
Henry VI **7** 298-299
John **8** 274-275
William I **16** 290-291
see also England—1066-1154 (Norman)
invasion of (1944)
Austin, John Langshaw **1** 379-380
Bradley, Omar Nelson **2** 483-484
Clark, Mark Wayne **4** 80-81
Eisenhower, Dwight David **5** 233-236
Leclerc, Jacques Philippe **9** 272-273
Montgomery, Bernard Law **11** 135-136
Patton, George Smith Jr. **12** 140-141
Ridgway, Matthew Bunker **13** 160-161
Rommel, Erwin **13** 268-269
Viking control
Rollo **13** 264-265

Normandy, Duke of
see Charles V(king of France)

Normans
David I **4** 407
Haskins, Charles Homer **7** 191-192
Leo IX **9** 332
see also England—1066-1154 (Norman); Normandy

Norodom (died 1904), king of Cambodia
Sihanouk, Norodom **14** 222-223

NORRIS, BENJAMIN FRANKLIN, JR. (1870-1902), American novelist and critic **11** 427-428
Baker, Ray Stannard **1** 451-452
Dreiser, Herman Theodore **5** 98-100
Zola, Émile **16** 526-528

Norris, Charles Gilman (1881-1945), American author
Norris, Benjamin Franklin Jr. **11** 427-428

NORRIS, GEORGE WILLIAM (1861-1944), American statesman **11** 428-429
Black, Hugo Lafayette **2** 301-303
Cannon, Joseph Gurney **3** 261-262

Norris-La Guardia Act (1932)
Hoover, Herbert Clark **7** 483-485
Norris, George William **11** 428-429

Norris-Rayburn Act (1936)
Norris, George William **11** 428-429

Norse (sonata)
MacDowell, Edward Alexander **10** 87-88

NORTH, FREDERICK (2nd Earl of Guilford; 1732-1792), English statesman **11** 429-430
American policy
Burgoyne, John **3** 137-138
Cornwallis, Charles **4** 241-243
Hopkinson, Francis **7** 496-497
as first lord of Treasury
George III **6** 270-272
opponents
Franklin, Benjamin **6** 60-64
Rockingham, 2d Marquess of **13** 230-231
successor
Pitt, William the Younger **12** 329-331

North, Sir Thomas (1535?-1601), English scholar
Plutarch **12** 359-360

North America (continent)
English exploration (15th-16th century)
Cabot, John **3** 199-200
Cabot, Sebastian **3** 200-201
Drake, Francis **5** 94-96
French exploration (16th century)
Cartier, Jacques **3** 343-344
Verrazano, Giovanni da **15** 470-471
Spanish exploration (15th-16th century)
Balboa, Vasco Núñez de **1** 462-463
Cabeza de Vaca, Álvar Núñez **3** 197
Cabrillo, Juan Rodríguez **3** 204-205
Columbus, Christopher **4** 176-179
Coronado, Francisco Vásquez de **4** 247
Cortés, Hernán **4** 255-256
de Soto, Hernando **4** 510-511
Marcos de Niza **10** 240
Narváez, Pánfilo de **11** 315
Oñate, Juan de **11** 513-514
Ponce de León, Juan **12** 391-392
Viking exploration (10th century)
Eric the Red **5** 304
Ericson, Leif **5** 306-307
see also Canada; Explorers; Indians (North America); Mexico; United States

North American Martyrs (Roman Catholic)
Brébeuf, Jean de **2** 511-512

North American Missionary Conference
Luthuli, Albert John **10** 51-52

North American Review (magazine; 1815-1939)
Adams, Henry Brooks **1** 45-47
James, Henry **8** 211-212
Lodge, Henry Cabot **9** 482-483
Lowell, James Russell **10** 14-15
Prescott, William Hickling **12** 440-441
Sparks, Jared **14** 363

North and South (novel)
Gaskell, Elizabeth **6** 231-232

North Atlantic fisheries dispute (1910-1912)
Drago, Luis María **5** 92-93
Lansing, Robert **9** 200

North Atlantic Treaty Organization (1949)
and arms control
Schmidt, Helmut **14** 19-21
defense proposal
Dulles, John Foster **5** 134-135
formation
Acheson, Dean Gooderham **1** 37-38
Goodpaster, Andrew Jackson **6** 439-441
Lemnitzer, Lyman Louis **9** 319-320
Marshall, George Catlett **10** 278-279
Pearson, Lester Bowles **12** 174-175
St. Laurent, Louis Stephen **13** 434
Spaak, Paul Henri **14** 359-360
French withdrawal
De Gaulle, Charles André Joseph Marie **4** 463-465
Johnson, Lyndon Baines **8** 308-312
Kennedy, John Fitzgerald **8** 502-506
members
Attlee, Clement Richard **1** 361-362
Salazar, António de Oliveira **13** 442-443
North Atlantic Council
Carrington **3** 326-327
Pearson, Lester Bowles **12** 174-175
Spaak, Paul Henri **14** 359-360
Wörner, Manfred **16** 389-390
representatives
Harriman, W. Averell **7** 165-166
secretary-generals
Luns, Joseph **10** 46-47
Supreme commanders
Eisenhower, Dwight David **5** 233-236
Haig, Alexander M. Jr. **7** 66-67
Lemnitzer, Lyman Louis **9** 319-320
Ridgway, Matthew Bunker **13** 160-161
Shalikashvili, John Malchase David **14** 145-147
see also Cold war; Marshall Plan; Truman Doctrine

North by Northwest (film)
Hitchcock, Alfred **7** 415-416

North Carolina (state; United States)
exploration and colonization
de Soto, Hernando **4** 510-511
Drake, Francis **5** 94-96
Raleigh, Walter **13** 9-11
Sevier, John **14** 122-123
Tryon, William **15** 321
government
Macon, Nathaniel **10** 114-115
Polk, Leonidas Lafayette **12** 376-377
religion
Gibbons, James **6** 300-301
Makemie, Francis **10** 158-159
senators from
Helms, Jesse **7** 271-272

North Carolina, University of (Chapel Hill)
Johnson, Guy Benton **8** 299-300
Odum, Howard Washington
11 474-476
Thurstone, Louis Leon **15** 215-216

North Carolina Central University
Walker, LeRoy Tashreau **16** 64-65

North Carolina Mutual Insurance Company
Spaulding, Charles Clinton **14** 364-365

North Carolina State University (Raleigh)
Polk, Leonidas Lafayette **12** 376-377

North Dakota (state; United States)
Harrison, Benjamin **7** 178-179

North Korea
see Korea—since 1948

North of Boston (poems; Frost)
Frost, Robert Lee **6** 130-133
Lowell, Amy **10** 13

North of the Danube (book)
Caldwell, Erskine **3** 223-224

North Pole
see Arctic exploration

North Vietnam
see Vietnam; Vietnam, North

North West Co. (Montreal)
Fraser, Simon **6** 74-75
McLoughlin, John **10** 423-424
Ogden, Peter Skene **11** 480-481
Selkirk, 5th Earl of **14** 96
Thompson, David **15** 194-195

Northampton (city; Massachusetts)
Benjamin, Asher **2** 162-163
Coolidge, John Calvin **4** 217-219
Edwards, Jonathan **5** 220-222

Northampton, Assize of (1176)
Henry II **7** 287-289

Northampton, Battle of (1460)
Henry VI **7** 298-299
Warwick and of Salisbury, Earl of
16 122-123

Northampton, Treaty of (1328; England)
Edward III **5** 211-212

Northanger Abbey (novel)
Austen, Jane **1** 377-379

Northbrook, Lord (Thomas George Baring; 1826-1904), English statesman
Cromer, 1st Earl of **4** 317

Northeast Passage
Amundsen, Roald **1** 206-207
Hudson, Henry **8** 12-13
Nordenskjöld, Nils Adolf Erik
11 421-422

Northern Ch'i War (550-577)
Sui Wen-ti **15** 16-18

Northern Dancer (race horse)
Taylor, Edward Plunket **15** 123-124

Northern Expedition (China; 1926-28)
Chang Tso-lin **3** 434-435
Chiang Kai-shek **3** 510-513

Chou En-lai **4** 20-22
Chu Teh **4** 54-55
Feng Yü-hsiang **5** 412-413
Kuo Mo-jo **9** 133-134
Lin Piao **9** 429-430
Ts'ai Yüan-p'ei **15** 322

Northern Haiti (former kingdom)
Christophe, Henri **4** 32

Northern Ireland (nation; United Kingdom)
Adams, Gerald **1** 42-44
Collins, Michael **4** 167-168
Corrigan and Williams **4** 251-253
Devlin, Bernadette **4** 515-516
Elizabeth II **5** 266-269
Faulkner, Brian **5** 393-395
Fitzgerald, Garret **5** 472-474
George V **6** 273-275
George VI **6** 275
O'Neill, Terence Marne **11** 516-517
Paisley, Ian K. **12** 67-69
see also Great Britain; Ireland

Northern Lake, A (painting)
Thomson, Tom **15** 202

Northern Nigeria
see Nigeria

Northern Ocean
see Arctic Ocean

Northern Pacific Railroad (United States)
Cooke, Jay **4** 215-216
Fargo, William George **5** 380-381
Hill, James Jerome **7** 388-389
Knox, Philander Chase **9** 66-67
Morgan, John Pierpont **11** 163-165
Schiff, Jacob Henry **14** 2-3

Northern People's Congress (Nigeria)
Bello, Ahmadu **2** 139-140
Tafawa Balewa, Abubakar **15** 75

Northern Railway (Canada)
Fleming, Sandford **5** 485-486

Northern Rhodesia
see Zambia

Northern Securities Company (United States)
Harriman, Edward Henry **7** 164-165
Hill, James Jerome **7** 388-389
Knox, Philander Chase **9** 66-67
Morgan, John Pierpont **11** 163-165
Roosevelt, Theodore **13** 280-283
Schiff, Jacob Henry **14** 2-3

Northern Sung dynasty
see Sung dynasty—Northern

Northern War, First (1655-1658)
Frederick William **6** 85-86
Witt, Johan de **16** 348-349

Northern War, Great (1700-1721)
see Great Northern War

NORTHROP, JOHN HOWARD
(1891-1987), American biological chemist **11** 430-431
Stanley, Wendell Meredith **14** 400-401

NORTHUMBERLAND, DUKE OF (John Dudley; circa 1502-1553), English soldier and statesman **11** 431-432
Cabot, Sebastian **3** 200-201
Chancellor, Richard **3** 422
Edward VI **5** 213-214
Henry IV **7** 292-293
Leicester, Earl of **9** 312-313
Mary I **10** 308-309
Somerset, Duke of **14** 333-334

Northward Ho! (play)
Webster, John **16** 164

Northwest Coast Indians (Canada)
Reid, William Ronald **13** 88-89

Northwest Ordinance (United States; 1787)
Cutler, Manasseh **4** 356-357
Lee, Richard Henry **9** 291-292
Monroe, James **11** 111-113

Northwest Passage
search for (Canada)
Frobisher, Martin **6** 121-122
la Verendrye, Sieur de **9** 239-240
search for (England)
Baffin, William **1** 435-436
Davis, John **4** 419
Franklin, John **6** 64-65
Gilbert, Humphrey **6** 313
Hearne, Samuel **7** 241-242
Mackenzie, Alexander **10** 103-104
McClure, Robert **10** 397-398
Raleigh, Walter **13** 9-11
Vancouver, George **15** 414-415
successful passage
Amundsen, Roald **1** 206-207

Northwest Territories (Canada)
Riel, Louis **13** 163-164

Northwest Territory (United States)
Clark, George Rogers **4** 75-76
Clark, William **4** 82-83
Fitch, John **5** 467-468
Harrison, William Henry **7** 180-181
Macdonald, John Alexander **10** 85-87
Mason, George **10** 319-320
St. Clair, Arthur **13** 429-430

Northwestern Christian College
see Butler University

Northwestern College (Minneapolis)
Graham, William Franklin Jr. **6** 487-488

Northwestern University (Evanston, Illinois)
Herskovits, Melville Jean **7** 345
Pound, Roscoe **12** 417-418
Ward, Aaron Montgomery **16** 112
Willard, Frances Elizabeth Caroline
16 289-290

Northwood (novel)
Hale, Sarah Josepha **7** 74-75

Norton, Charles Eliot (1827-1908), American writer, educator, and editor
Clough, Arthur Hugh **4** 123-124

Norway, Kingdom of (nation; Northern Europe)
 and Christianity
  Olaf I Tryggvason, King of Norway **11** 490-493
 and Scaninavian union
  Margaret of Denmark **10** 250-252
 Danish conquest
  Canute I the Great **3** 266-269
 German occupation
  Chamberlain, Arthur Neville **3** 409-411
  Hitler, Adolf **7** 417-420
 historians of
  Sturluson, Snorri **14** 310-311
 invades England
  Harold III **7** 163
 Northern War
  see Great Northern War
 political leaders
  Brundtland, Gro Harlem **3** 68-69
 Swedish annexation
  Bernadotte, Jean Baptiste **2** 205-206
 unification
  Harold I **7** 161-162
  Olaf I Tryggvason, King of Norway **11** 490-493
  Olaf, II **11** 493-494
  see also Norwegian art; Norwegian literature; Norwegian music; Vikings

Norwegian art
 Munch, Edvard **11** 247-248

Norwegian literature
 Bjørnson, Bjørnstjerne **2** 299-300
 Hamsun, Knut **7** 113-114
 Ibsen, Henrik **8** 98-100
 Undset, Sigrid **15** 388-389

Norwegian music
 Grieg, Edvard Hagerup **6** 541-542

Noryang, battle of (1598)
 Yi Sunsin **16** 459-461

Nosan, Prince
 see Tanjong

Nose, The (opera)
 Shostakovich, Dmitri Dmitrievich **14** 204-205

Nose, The (story)
 Gogol, Nikolai **6** 391-393

Nostell, Priory (Yorkshire)
 Adam, Robert and James **1** 38-40
 Chippendale, Thomas **4** 1-2

NOSTRADAMUS (born Michel de Notredame; 1503-1566), French physician, astrologist, and author **11** 432-434

Nostri sogni, I (play)
 Betti, Ugo **2** 246

Nostromo (novel)
 Conrad, Joseph **4** 205-207
 Ford, Ford Madox **6** 1-2

Not by Might (book)
 Muste, Abraham Johannes **11** 276-277

Not under Forty (essays)
 Cather, Willa Sibert **3** 368-369

Not without Laughter (novel)
 Hughes, Langston **8** 18-19

Notas de un himno (poems)
 Zorrilla de San Martin, Juan **16** 530-531

Notation (math)
 Euler, Leonard **5** 331-332
 Gauss, Karl Friedrich **6** 240-242
 Napier, John **11** 306

Notation (music)
 see Music—notation

Note-against-note (music)
 Goudimel, Claude **6** 466
 Le Jeune, Claude **9** 314-315

Notes from the Underground (novel)
 Dostoevsky, Fyodor **5** 74-77

Notes inégales (music)
 Couperin, François **4** 270-271

Notes of a Native Son (essays)
 Baldwin, James Arthur **1** 465-466

Notes toward a Supreme Fiction (poem)
 Stevens, Wallace **14** 443-445

Notes Variorum (poem)
 Pope, Alexander **12** 395-397

Nothing Gold Can Stay (poems)
 Frost, Robert Lee **6** 130-133

Nothing Personal (book)
 Baldwin, James Arthur **1** 465-466

Notions of the Americans... (book)
 Cooper, James Fenimore **4** 220-223

Notium, battle of (406 B.C.)
 Lysander **10** 70

Notker Balbulus
 see Balbulus, Notker

Notorious (film)
 Hitchcock, Alfred **7** 415-416

Notre Dame, Cathedral of (Paris)
 Lacordaire, Jean Baptiste Henri **9** 148
 Montreuil, Pierre de **11** 139
 Pérotin **12** 231-232
 Viollet-le-Duc, Eugène Emmanuel **15** 505-506

Notre Dame, Church of (Le Raincy)
 Perret, Auguste **12** 233

Notre Dame, school of (France; music)
 Franco of Cologne **6** 52
 Léonin **9** 343-344
 Pérotin **12** 231-232

Notre Dame, University of (Indiana)
 Hesburgh, Theodore Martin **7** 357-358
 Rockne, Knute **13** 231

Notre Dame de Paris (novel)
 Hugo, Victor Marie **8** 22-25

Notre Dame de Paris (opera)
 Fry, William Henry **6** 136-137

Notre-Dame-du-Haut, Chapel of (Ronchamp, France)
 Le Corbusier **9** 274-275

Nott, Eliphalet (1773-1866), American educator, clergyman, and inventor
 Wayland, Francis **16** 148-149

Notte, La (film)
 Antonioni, Michelangelo **1** 252-253

Notte di festa (stories)
 Pavese, Cesare **12** 154-155

Notte in casa del ricco (play)
 Betti, Ugo **2** 246

Notturno (novel)
 D'Annunzio, Gabriele **4** 388

Noumena (philosophy)
 Kant, Immanuel **8** 430-432

Nourritures terrestres, Les (book)
 Gide, André **6** 308-309

Nouveau locataire, Le (play)
 Ionesco, Eugène **8** 131-132

Nouveaux, Lundis (book)
 Sainte-Beuve, Charles Augustin **13** 438

Nouvel Opéra de Paris, Le (book)
 Garnier, Jean Louis Charles **6** 221-222

Nouvelle Héloïse, La (novel)
 Rousseau, Jean Jacques **13** 324-328

Nouvelle revue française, La (periodical)
 Gide, André **6** 308-309

Nouvelles nourritures, Les (book)
 Gide, André **6** 308-309

Nova Scotia (province; Canada)
 Champlain, Samuel de **3** 419-421
 Charnisay, Charles de Menou **3** 470-471
 Goldsmith, Oliver **6** 411
 Howe, Joseph **7** 534-535
 Macdonald, John Alexander **10** 85-87
 Nicholson, Francis **11** 381-382
 Tupper, Charles **15** 342-343
 see also Canada

NOVALIS (1772-1801), German poet and author **11** 435
 Longfellow, Henry Wadsworth **9** 499-500
 Schelling, Friedrich Wilhelm Joseph von **13** 526-527
 Schlegel, Friedrich von **14** 10-11
 Tieck, Ludwig **15** 218-219

Novanglus
 see Adams, John

Novara (ship)
 Horthy de Nagybánya, Nicholas **7** 510-512

Novara, battle of (1848)
 Victor Emmanuel II **15** 483-484

Novatianists (Christian sect)
 Cyril **4** 362
 Donatus **5** 56-57

Novaya Zemlya (islands; Arctic Ocean)
 Barents, Willem **2** 4-5

Cabot, Sebastian **3** 200-201
Hudson, Henry **8** 12-13

Novel and Life (essays)
Mariátegui, José Carlos **10** 255-256

Novel, development of (literature)
Defoe, Daniel **4** 457-459
Fielding, Henry **5** 442-444
Flaubert, Gustave **5** 480-482
James, Henry **8** 211-212
Sterne, Laurence **14** 435-437
see also Authors—novelists; Mystery fiction; Picaresque novel

Novel Disseisin, Assize of
Henry II **7** 287-289

Novela de mi amigo, La (novel)
Ferrer, Gabriel Miró **5** 428

Novelas de la primera época (novel series)
Galdós, Benito Pérez **6** 177-178

Novelas ejemplares (book)
Cervantes, Miguel de Saavedra
3 395-398

Novelists
see Authors—novelists

Novella (literary form)
Heyse, Paul Johann Ludwig **7** 372-373
Schnitzler, Arthur **14** 23-24
Storm, Theodor **14** 479-480

Novella del buon vecchio e della bella fanciulla, La (stories)
Svevo, Italo **15** 47-48

Novelle (book)
Goethe, Johann Wolfgang von
6 388-391

Novelle della Pescara (stories)
D'Annunzio, Gabriele **4** 388

Novelle per un anno (stories)
Pirandello, Luigi **12** 319-321

Novellen (tales)
Huch, Ricarda **8** 11-12

Novembergruppe (art)
Gabo, Naum **6** 158-159

Novices at Sais, The (novel)
Novalis **11** 435

Novikov, Nikolai (1744-1818), Russian journalist and philanthropist
Karamzin, Nikolai Mikhailovich
8 441-442

Novorossiisk University (Odessa)
Metchnikoff, Élie **10** 532-533

Novotny, Antonin (1904-1975), Czechoslovak politician
Dubček, Alexander **5** 112-113

Novum instrumentum (New Testament edition)
Erasmus, Desiderius **5** 298-300

Novum organum (book)
Bacon, Francis **1** 422-424

Now that April's Here... (stories)
Callaghan, Edward Morley **3** 229-230

Now They Sing Again (play)
Frisch, Max **6** 118-119

Nowaki (novel)
Natsume, Soseki **11** 324-325

NOYCE, ROBERT (1927-1990), American physicist and inventor **11** 436-437

Noyers de l' Altenberg, Les (novel)
Malraux, André **10** 178-180

NOYES, JOHN HUMPHREY (1811-1886), American founder of the Oneida Community **11** 437-438

Noyon, Cathedral of (Northern France)
Calvin, John **3** 239-242

NOZICK, ROBERT (born 1938), American philosopher and polemical advocate of radical libertarianism **11** 438-439

Nozze di Figaro, Le (opera)
Mozart, Wolfgang Amadeus
11 218-221

Nozze di Teti e di Peleo, Le (opera)
Cavalli, Pietro Francesco **3** 382-383

N'si Yisrael
see Bar Kochba, Simeon

NU, U (1907-1995), Burmese statesman **11** 439-441
Aung San **1** 374-375
Ba Maw **1** 480-481
Ne Win **11** 364-365
Sihanouk, Norodom **14** 222-223
Thant, U **15** 161-162

Nü-shen (poems)
Kuo Mo-jo **9** 133-134

Nuages (musical composition)
Debussy, Achille Claude **4** 445-447

Nubar Pasha (1825-1899), Egyptian diplomat and statesman
Gordon, Charles George **6** 448-449

Nubia (ancient African king.)
Burckhardt, Johann Ludwig **3** 133
Piankhi **12** 288-289
Shabaka **14** 130

Nuclear arms control
Bhabha, Homi Jehangir **2** 253-254
Diefenbaker, John George **5** 4-5
John, XXIII **8** 277-280
Johnson, Lyndon Baines **8** 308-312
Kennedy, John Fitzgerald **8** 502-506
Lawrence, Ernest Orlando **9** 248-250
Nixon, Richard Milhous **11** 401-404
Reagan, Ronald W. **13** 65-68
Sagan, Carl E. **13** 424-425
Sakharov, Andrei **13** 439-441
Schweitzer, Albert **14** 55-56
Szilard, Leo **15** 64-66
Vance, Cyrus R. **15** 411-413

Nuclear fission (physics)
Bohr, Niels Henrik David **2** 366-368
Compton, Arthur Holly **4** 186-188
Frisch, Otto Robert **6** 119-120
Hahn, Otto **7** 64-65
Joliot-Curie, Jean Frédéric **8** 327-328

Meitner, Lise **10** 463-466
Sakharov, Andrei **13** 439-441
Seaborg, Glenn Theodore **14** 74-76
Teller, Edward **15** 139-141

Nuclear physics (science)
and composition of the universe
Payne-Gaposchkin, Cecilia
12 159-161
atomic nucleus
Aston, Francis William **1** 350-351
Blackett, Patrick M.S. **2** 306-307
Bloch, Felix **2** 328-330
Bohr, Niels Henrik David **2** 366-368
Fermi, Enrico **5** 422-424
Gamow, George **6** 199-200
Goeppert-Mayer, Maria **6** 385-387
Hahn, Otto **7** 64-65
Joliot-Curie, Irène **8** 325-327
Kapitsa, Pyotr Leonidovich
8 433-435
Rutherford, Ernest **13** 384-387
Szilard, Leo **15** 64-66
Walton, Ernest **16** 88-90
coincidence method
Bothe, Walther **2** 438-439
elementary particles
Alvarez, Luis W. **1** 187-189
Anderson, Carl David **1** 214-215
Blackett, Patrick M.S. **2** 306-307
Cherenkov, Pavel Alekseevich
3 502-503
Geiger, Hans **6** 251-253
Gell-Mann, Murray **6** 257-258
Heisenberg, Werner Karl **7** 261-263
Jackson, Shirley Ann **8** 183-184
Joliot-Curie, Irène **8** 325-327
Millikan, Robert Andrews **11** 33-35
Wigner, Eugene Paul **16** 268-269
Yukawa, Hideki **16** 481-482
see also Electron; Hyperon; Meson; Neutrino; Neutron; Particle accelerators; Particle detectors; Proton; Radioactivity
fission
see Nuclear fission
nuclear-beam technique
Rabi, Isidor Isaac **12** 526-527
Walton, Ernest **16** 88-90
reactor theory
Bethe, Hans Albrecht **2** 238-239
Bothe, Walther **2** 438-439
Wigner, Eugene Paul **16** 268-269
transmutation
Blackett, Patrick M.S. **2** 306-307
Chadwick, James **3** 405-406
Cockcroft, John Douglas **4** 131-132
Rutherford, Ernest **13** 384-387
Walton, Ernest **16** 88-90

Nuclear power
civilian uses
Jackson, Shirley Ann **8** 183-184
Rickover, Hyman George
13 155-157
military uses

Rickover, Hyman George
13 155-157

Nuclear Regulatory Commission (United States)
Jackson, Shirley Ann **8** 183-184

Nude (painting)
Braque, Georges **2** 504-505

Nude Descending a Staircase, No. 2 (painting)
Duchamp, Marcel **5** 122-123

Nude, Femme qui marche (sculpture)
Giacometti, Alberto **6** 294-295

Nude Maja (painting)
Goya y Lucientes, Francisco de Paula José de **6** 476-478

Nude with Violin (play)
Coward, Noel **4** 279-280

Nudes in the Forest (painting)
Léger, Fernand **9** 302-303

Nuer (African people)
Evans-Pritchard, Edward Evan **5** 340

Nuestro Padre San Daniel (novel)
Ferrer, Gabriel Miró **5** 428

Nuevas andanzas y desventuras de Lazarillo de Tormes, Las (book)
Cela y Trulock, Camilo José **3** 389-390

Nuggets (book)
Bierce, Ambrose Gwinett **2** 269-270

Nuit... (poems)
Musset, Louis Charles Alfred de **11** 271-272

Nuit vénitienne, La (play)
Musset, Louis Charles Alfred de **11** 271-272

NUJOMA, SHAFIIHUNA ("Sam"; born 1929), first president of independent Namibia **11** 441-443

Nukada-be, Princess
see Suiko

Nu-li chou-pao (magazine)
Hu Shih **8** 63-65

Nullification crisis (United States; 1832)
opponents of nullification
Brown, Benjamin Gratz **3** 32-33
Drake, Daniel **5** 93-94
Farragut, David Glasgow **5** 388-389
Jackson, Andrew **8** 168-172
Livingston, Edward **9** 460-461
Memminger, Christopher Gustavus **10** 476-477
Randolph, John **13** 30
Scott, Winfield **14** 70-71
Stephens, Alexander Hamilton **14** 429-430
Tyler, John **15** 368-369
Webster, Daniel **16** 162-164
supporters of nullification
Hayne, Robert Young **7** 231-232
McDuffie, George **10** 408
Rhett, Robert Barnwell **13** 120

Numa Roumestan (novel)
Daudet, Alphonse **4** 402-403

Numancia, La (play)
Cervantes, Miguel de Saavedra **3** 395-398

Numantia, battle of (134-133 B.C.)
Marius, Gaius **10** 264-265
Scipio Africanus Minor, Publius Cornelius Aemilianus **14** 62-63

Number (mathematics)
imaginary
Demoivre, Abraham **4** 494-495
Euler, Leonard **5** 331-332
prime
Eratosthenes of Cyrene **5** 301-302
Euclid **5** 327-329
Fermat, Pierre de **5** 421-422
Gauss, Karl Friedrich **6** 240-242
theory
Cardano, Geronimo **3** 285-286
Euclid **5** 327-329
Eudoxus of Cnidus **5** 329-330
Euler, Leonard **5** 331-332
Fermat, Pierre de **5** 421-422
Gauss, Karl Friedrich **6** 240-242
Lagrange, Joseph Louis **9** 164-166
Pythagoras **12** 498-499
Ramanujan Aiyangar, Srinivasa **13** 14-15
Riemann, Georg Friedrich Bernard **13** 164-165
transfinite
Cantor, Georg Ferdinand Ludwig Philipp **3** 265-266
see also Complex numbers

Number One (novel)
Dos Passos, John Roderigo **5** 69-71

Number 1 (painting)
Pollock, Jackson **12** 379-380

Numbering at Bethlehem (painting)
Bruegel, Pieter the Elder **3** 65-67

Numerian (died 284), Roman emperor
Diocletian **5** 19-20

Numerical method (medicine)
Louis, Pierre Charles Alexandre **9** 540

Numidia (Roman province)
Donatus **5** 56-57
Masinissa **10** 315-317
Sallust **13** 454

Numquid et tu ...? (book)
Gide, André **6** 308-309

Nun of Dulmen
see Emmerich, Anna Katharina

Núñez de Balboa, Vasco
see Balboa, Vasco Núñez de

NUNN, SAM (born 1938), United States senator from Georgia **11** 443-444

Nuova colonia, La (play)
Pirandello, Luigi **12** 319-321

Nuove musiche... (music collection)
Caccini, Giulio **3** 205-206

Nuove poesie (poems)
Quasimodo, Salvatore **12** 506

Nuovi racconti romani (stories)
Moravia, Alberto **11** 153-155

Nur-ad-Din
see Nureddin

Nur al-Din Abd al-Rahman, Maulana
see Jami

NUREDDIN (Malik al-Adil Nur-al-Din Mahmud; 1118-1174), sultan of Syria and Egypt **11** 444-445
Saladin **13** 441-442

Nuremberg (city; Germany)
Hitler, Adolf **7** 417-420

Nuremberg, Diet of (1355-1356)
Charles IV **3** 455-456

Nuremberg trials (Germany)
Dos Passos, John Roderigo **5** 69-71
Jackson, Robert Houghwout **8** 182-183
Schacht, Hjalmar Horace Greeley **13** 518-519

NUREYEV, RUDOLPH (born 1938), Russian-born dancer and choreographer **11** 445-446

NURI AL-SA'ID (1888-1958), Iraqi army officer, statesman, and nationalist **11** 446-447

Nurse, Malcolm Ivan Meredith
see Padmore, George

Nurses, The (TV series)
Davis, Ossie **4** 421-422

Nursing (medicine)
Barton, Clara **2** 37-39
Nightingale, Florence **11** 392-393
Taylor, Susie King **15** 127-128

Nurture of Jupiter (painting)
Jordaens, Jacob **8** 347-349

Nusch-Nuschi, Das (musical composition)
Hindemith, Paul **7** 399-400

Nutricia (book)
Poliziano, Angelo **12** 373-374

Nutrition (diet)
Eijkman, Christian **5** 228
Hopkins, Frederick Gowland **7** 491-492
Houssay, Bernardo Alberto **7** 522-523
Mayer, Jean **10** 365-366
Orr, John Boyd **12** 4-5

Nuttfield Foundation (England)
Lovell, Alfred Charles Bernard **10** 8-9

Nuvolara, Count of
see Castiglione, Baldassare

Nya Dikter (poems)
Heidenstam, Carl Gustaf Verner Von **7** 258-259

Nyasa, Lake (southeast Africa)
Burton, Richard **3** 163-164
Livingstone, David **9** 463-465

Nyasaland
see Malawi

NYERERE, JULIUS KAMBERAGE (born 1922), Tanzanian statesman **11** 447-449
  Kawawa, Rashidi Mfaume **8** 464-465
  Nkrumah, Kwame **11** 408-410

NYGREN, ANDERS (1890-1978), Lutheran bishop of Lund and representative of the so-called Lundensian school of theology **11** 449-451

Nylon (synthetic fiber)
  Carothers, Wallace Hume **3** 317-318

Nymph of Fountainebleau (sculpture)
  Cellini, Benvenuto **3** 391-392

Nymphe de la Seine, La (poem)
  Racine, Jean Baptiste **12** 532-535

Nymphenburg Palace (Munich)
  Cuvilliés, François **4** 359-360
  Zimmermann, Johann Baptist and Domenikus **16** 518

Nymphidia (poem)
  Drayton, Michael **5** 97-98

Nystad, Treaty of (1721)
  Peter I **12** 253-256

Nystatin
  Brown, Rachel Fuller **3** 43-44

Nzinga Mvemba
  see Affonso I

NZINGA NKUWU (died 1506), king of Kongo **11** 451-452
  Affonso I **1** 72

O

O Canada (song)
Cartier, George-Étienne **3** 342-343

O God, Thou Righteous God (musical composition)
Bach, Johann Sebastian **1** 416-419

O Little Town of Bethlehem (carol)
Brooks, Phillips **3** 26

O! Ma charmante, epargnez-moi! (musical composition)
Gottschalk, Louis Moreau **6** 463-464

O país do carnaval (novel)
Amado, Jorge **1** 189-190

O Pioneers! (novel)
Cather, Willa Sibert **3** 368-369

"O Solitude!..." (sonnet)
Keats, John **8** 470-472

O triste ... (poem)
Verlaine, Paul Marie **15** 465-466

O vos omnes (musical composition)
Victoria, Tomás Luis de **15** 487-488

Oahu (Hawaiian island)
Kamehameha I **8** 416

Oak and Ivy (poems)
Dunbar, Paul Laurence **5** 141-142

Oak Ridge (Tennessee)
Lilienthal, David Eli **9** 410-411
Urey, Harold Clayton **15** 394-396

Oak, Synod of the (403)
Cyril **4** 362
John Chrysostom **8** 280-281

OAKLEY, ANNIE (1860-1926), American markswoman and Wild West star **11** 453-454

Oakland Tribune (newspaper)
Maynard, Robert Clyve **10** 366-367

OAS
see Organization of American States (OAS)

OATES, JOYCE CAROL (born 1938), American author **11** 454-456

OATES, TITUS (1649-1705), English leader of the Popish Plot **11** 456
see also Popish Plot

Oath of Julius Civilis (painting)
Rembrandt Harmensz van Rijn **13** 91-95

Oath of the Horatii (painting)
David, Jacques Louis **4** 407-409

Oats (grain)
Saunders, Charles Edward **13** 498-499

Oaxaca (city, state; Mexico)
Díaz, José de la Cruz Porfirio **4** 534-536
Juárez, Benito **8** 369-372
Matamoros, Mariano **10** 329-330
Morelos, José María **11** 157-158

Obadiah (literary character)
Sterne, Laurence **14** 435-437

Obasute Mountain (Japan)
Basho, Matsuo **2** 45-48

Obbligato instrument (music)
Schütz, Heinrich **14** 48-49

Oberlin College (Ohio)
Commons, John Rogers **4** 185
Finney, Charles Grandison **5** 450-451
Tappan brothers **15** 105-106
Thomas, William Isaac **15** 193

Oberon (opera)
Weber, Carl Maria Friedrich Ernst von **16** 156-157

Oberon (poem)
Wieland, Christoph Martin **16** 260-261

Oberth, Herman Julius (born 1894), Romanian physicist
von Braun, Wernher **16** 17-18

Oberto ... (opera)
Verdi, Giuseppe Fortunino Francesco **15** 463-465

Obispo leproso, El (novel)
Ferrer, Gabriel Miró **5** 428

Object language (philosophy)
Carnap, Rudolf **3** 308-309

Object, theory of (philosophy)

Meinong, Alexius Ritter von Handschuchsheim **10** 461-462

Objective school
see Historiography—objective school

Objective Spirit (philosophy)
Hegel, Georg Wilhelm Friedrich **7** 254-256

Oblat, L' (novel)
Huysmans, Joris Karl **8** 81-82

Oblates of Mary Immaculate (religious congregation)
Lacombe, Albert **9** 147-148

Oblates of St. Charles (religious congregation)
Manning, Henry Edward **10** 209-210

Oblomov (novel)
Goncharov, Ivan Aleksandrovich **6** 424

Oblong Passion (drawings)
Dürer, Albrecht **5** 159-161

Oboe sommerso (verse)
Quasimodo, Salvatore **12** 506

OBOTE, APOLO MILTON (born 1925), Ugandan politician **11** 457
Amin Dada, Idi **1** 202-204
Kiwanuka, Benedicto Kagima Mugumba **9** 46-47
Mutesa II **11** 277-278

OBRECHT, JACOB (1450-1505), Dutch composer **11** 457-458
Josquin des Prez **8** 361-363
Ockeghem, Johannes **11** 464-465

OBREGÓN, ÀLVARO (1880-1928), Mexican revolutionary general and president **11** 458-459
Calles, Plutarco Elías **3** 234-235
Cárdenas, Lázaro **3** 286-287
Carranza, Venustiano **3** 321-322
Huerta, Victoriano **8** 13-14
Vasconcelos, José **15** 443-444
Villa, Pancho **15** 495-496
Zapata, Emiliano **16** 489-490

Obrenovic dynasty (Serbia; ruled 1817-1842, 1858-1903)
Peter I **12** 256

O'Brien, William Shoney (circa 1826-1878), American mine operator
Mackay, John William **10** 101-102

Obscene Bird of Night, The (book)
Donoso, José **5** 63-65

Obscenity trials (United States)
Cabell, James Branch **3** 195-196
Comstock, Anthony **4** 188-189
Douglas, William Orville **5** 83-85
Ginsberg, Allen **6** 332-333
Joyce, James **8** 365-367

Obscurantist metaphysics (philosophy)
Condillac, Étienne Bonnot de **4** 194-195

Obscure, the
see Heraclitus

Observations (poems)
Moore, Marianne **11** 148-149

Observations concerning the Original of Governments (book)
Filmer, Robert **5** 448

Observations on Man (book)
Hartley, David **7** 185

Observations upon the Prophecies of Daniel ... (book)
Newton, Isaac **11** 369-372

Observatoire (Paris)
Perrault, Claude **12** 232-233

Obstacles to Peace (book)
McClure, Samuel Sidney **10** 398-399

Obstetrics (medicine)
Hunter, William **8** 48-49
Semmelweis, Ignaz Philipp **14** 101-102

OCAM (economics organization)
Houphouët-Boigny, Felix **7** 519-520

Ocampo, Melchor (circa 1812-1861), Mexican politician
Juárez, Benito **8** 369-372
Lerdo de Tejada, Miguel **9** 351-352

O'CASEY, SEAN (1880-1964), Irish dramatist **11** 459-460
Ford, John **6** 7-8
Strindberg, August **14** 509-511

Occam, William of
see William of Ockham

Occasional Addresses (book)
Kennedy, John Pendleton **8** 506-507

Occasional Oratorio (musical composition)
Handel, George Frederick **7** 116-119

Occasionalism (philosophy)
Malebranche, Nicolas **10** 166-167

Occasioni (poems)
Montale, Eugenio **11** 117-118

Occom, Samson (1723-1792), American Mohegan Indian missionary
Wheelock, Eleazar **16** 222-223

Occultism (psychology)
Jung, Carl Gustav **8** 388-389
Mesmer, Franz Anton **10** 526-527

Occupational diseases (United States)
Hamilton, Alice **7** 98-99
Hardy, Harriet **7** 150

Ocean exploration
Cousteau, Jacques-Yves **4** 276-277
Earle, Sylvia A. **5** 180-181
Tharp, Marie **15** 162-164

Oceanography (science)
Ewing, William Maurice **5** 350-351
Maury, Matthew Fontaine **10** 351-352
Meinesz, Felix Andries Vening **10** 461
Nansen, Fridtjof **11** 304-305
Piccard, Auguste **12** 297-298
Tharp, Marie **15** 162-164
see also Scientists—oceanographers

Ocho comedias y ocho entremeses (plays)
Cervantes, Miguel de Saavedra **3** 395-398

OCHOA, ELLEN (born 1958), Hispanic American electrical engineer and astronaut **11** 460-461

OCHOA, SEVERO (1905-1993), Spanish biochemist **11** 461-464

Ochre Court (Newport, Rhode Island)
Hunt, Richard Morris **8** 44

OCHS, ADOLPH SIMON (1858-1935), American publisher and philanthropist **11** 464

OCKEGHEM, JOHANNES (circa 1425-1495), Netherlandish composer **11** 464-465
Dufay, Guillaume **5** 125-126
Dunstable, John **5** 150-151
Josquin des Prez **8** 361-363
Obrecht, Jacob **11** 457-458

O'CONNELL, DANIEL (1775-1847), Irish statesman **11** 465-467

O'Connell, William (1859-1944), American cardinal
Spellman, Francis Joseph **14** 367

O'Connor, Charles (1804-1884), American lawyer
Alger, Horatio **1** 153-154

O'Connor, Edwin (1918-1968), American lawyer
Curley, James Michael **4** 344-345

O'CONNOR, (MARY) FLANNERY (1925-1964), American author of short stories and novels **11** 467-468

O'CONNOR, SANDRA DAY (born 1930), United States Supreme Court justice **11** 468-470

O'Connor, William Douglas (1832-1889), American journalist
Whitman, Walt **16** 249-251

Octandre (musical composition)
Varèse, Edgard **15** 432-433

Octave stanza (literature)
Ariosto, Ludovico **1** 289-290
Boccaccio, Giovanni **2** 351-353

Octavia (died 11 B.C.), Roman matron, sister of Augustus
Antony, Mark **1** 253-254
Cleopatra **4** 105-106

Octavia (play)
Seneca the Younger, Lucius Annaeus **14** 103-105

Octavian (Octavianus, Octavius)
see Augustus

Octavius, Gnaeus (died 87 B.C.), Roman politician
Marius, Gaius **10** 264-265

Octet for Strings (musical composition)
Mendelssohn, Moses **10** 488-489

October Diploma (Austria; 1860)
Francis Joseph **6** 45-46

October Manifesto (Russia; 1905)
Nicholas II **11** 378-380
Witte, Sergei Yulyevich **16** 349-350

October Revolution
see Russian Revolution (1905); Russian Revolution (1917; Oct.)

Octopus, An (poem)
Moore, Marianne **11** 148-149

Octopus, The (novel)
Norris, Benjamin Franklin Jr. **11** 427-428

Octoroon, The (play)
Boucicault, Dion **2** 442-443

Ocypus (poem)
Lucian **10** 25-26

Odalisque (painting)
Renoir, Pierre Auguste **13** 101-102

Odalisque with Raised Arms (painting)
Matisse, Henri **10** 336-337

Ode, Pindaric (literature)
Gray, Thomas **6** 509-510
Pindar **12** 312-313

Ode à Charlotte Corday (poem)
Chénier, André Marie **3** 500-501

Ode à Versailles (poem)
Chénier, André Marie **3** 500-501

Ode in Honour of Great Britian (musical composition)
Arne, T. 241
Thomson, James **15** 199-200

Ode in the Ancient Meter (poem)
Eminescu, Mihail **5** 280-281

Ode Occasioned by the Death of Mr. Thomson (poem)
Collins, William **4** 168-169

Ode on a Distant Prospect of Eton College (poem)
Gray, Thomas **6** 509-510

Ode on a Grecian Urn (poem)
Keats, John **8** 470-472

Ode on Indolence (poem)
Keats, John **8** 470-472

Ode on Melancholy (poem)
Keats, John **8** 470-472

Ode on the Death of a Favourite Cat ... (poem)
Gray, Thomas **6** 509-510

Ode on the Death of the Duke of Wellington, The (poem)
Tennyson, Alfred **15** 144-146

Ode on the Popular Superstitions of the Highlands of Scotland, An (poem)
Collins, William **4** 168-169

Ode Recited at the Harvard Commemoration (poem)
Lowell, James Russell **10** 14-15

Ode sur les révolutions (poem)
Lamartine, Alphonse Marie Louis de **9** 173-175

Ode to a Nightingale (poem)
Keats, John **8** 470-472

Ode to Bonaparte the Liberator (poem)
Foscolo, Ugo **6** 21

Ode to Death (musical composition)
Holst, Gustav **7** 459-460

Ode to Joy (poem; Schiller)
Beethoven, Ludwig van **2** 114-117

Ode to Liberty (poem)
Pushkin, Aleksandr Sergeevich **12** 489-491

Ode to Psyche (poem)
Keats, John **8** 470-472

Ode to Rome (poem)
Lorca, Federico García **9** 511-513

Ode to St. Cecilia (musical composition)
Handel, George Frederick **7** 116-119

Ode to the Confederate Dead (poem)
Tate, Allen **15** 116

Ode to the Departing Year (poem)
Coleridge, Samuel Taylor **4** 154-156

Ode to the Virginian Voyage (poem)
Drayton, Michael **5** 97-98

Ode to the West Wind (poem)
Shelley, Percy Bysshe **14** 176-178

Ode to Walt Whitman (poem)
Lorca, Federico García **9** 511-513

Odelettes (poems)
Nerval, Gérard de **11** 345-346

Odell, Benjamin Barker (1854-1926), American politician
Platt, Thomas Collier **12** 347-348

Odes (poems; Horace)
Hofhaimer, Paul **7** 441
Horace **7** 500-503

Odes et poésies diverses (book)
Hugo, Victor Marie **8** 22-25

Odes on Several...Subjects (poems)
Collins, William **4** 168-169

Odescalchi, Benedetto
see Innocent XI

ODETS, CLIFFORD (1906-1963), American playwright and film director **11** 470-471

Odi barbare (poems)
Carducci, Giosuè **3** 290-291

Odi et amo (poems)
Catullus, Gaius Valerius **3** 377-378

Odi navali (poems)
D'Annunzio, Gabriele **4** 388

ODINGA, AJUMA JARAMOGI OGINGA (born 1912), Kenyan politician **11** 471-473

Odo of Bayeux (1036-1097), Anglo-Norman bishop
William II **16** 293-294

ODOACER (433-493), Germanic chieftain **11** 473
Theodoric the Great **15** 175-176

O'Donojú, Juan (1755?-1821), Spanish viceroy
Iturbide, Agustín de **8** 155-156

Odore di Eucalyptus ed altri versi (book)
Quasimodo, Salvatore **12** 506

Odoric of Pordenone (1286-1331), Italian missionary
Mandeville, John **10** 192-193

Odría, Manuel Arturo (1897-1974), Peruvian general, president
Prado Ugarteche, Manuel **12** 430-431

ODRIÁ AMORETTI, MANUEL APOLINARIO (1897-1974), Peruvian army officer, dictator-president, and politician **11** 473-474

ODUM, HOWARD WASHINGTON (1884-1954), American sociologist, educator, and academic administrator **11** 474-476
Giddings, Franklin Henry **6** 307-308

Odysseus (literary character)
Homer **7** 465-467
Sophocles **14** 343-345

Odyssey (epic; Homer)
as model
Joyce, James **8** 365-367
Lamb, Charles **9** 176-177
Petronius Arbiter **12** 262-263
Virgil **15** 507-510
authorship and style
Chapman, George **3** 440-441
Homer **7** 465-467
Wolf, Friedrich August **16** 352-353
translations
Bryant, William Cullen **3** 83-85
Kazantzakis, Nikos **8** 466-468
Morris, William **11** 187-188
Pope, Alexander **12** 395-397
Tschernichowsky, Saul **15** 323

Odyssey (poem)
Kazantzakis, Nikos **8** 466-468

Oedipe (play)
Corneille, Pierre **4** 234-236
Gide, André **6** 308-309
Voltaire **16** 14-16

Oedipus (play)
Aeschylus **1** 70-72
Dryden, John **5** 106-107
Seneca the Younger, Lucius Annaeus **14** 103-105

Oedipus at Colonus (play)
Sophocles **14** 343-345

Oedipus Rex (opera-oratorio)
Stravinsky, Igor Fedorovich **14** 502-506

Oedipus Rex (play; Sophocles)
Dostoevsky, Fyodor **5** 74-77
Lessing, Gotthold Ephraim **9** 357-359
Robbe-Grillet, Alain **13** 189-190
Schiller, Johann Christoph Friedrich von **14** 4-7
Sophocles **14** 343-345
Tschernichowsky, Saul **15** 323

Oedipus Tyrannus (play; Sophocles)
Paine, John Knowles **12** 65

Oedipus Tyrannus (poem)
Shelley, Percy Bysshe **14** 176-178

Oedipus und die Sphinx (opera)
Varèse, Edgard **15** 432-433

OEEC
see Organization for European Economic Cooperation

Oeillet blanc, L' (play)
Daudet, Alphonse **4** 402-403

OERSTED, HANS CHRISTIAN (1777-1851), Danish physicist **11** 476-478
Ampère, André Marie **1** 205-206
Faraday, Michael **5** 380

Oeser, Adam Friedrich (1717-1799), German painter
Goethe, Johann Wolfgang von **6** 388-391
Winckelmann, Johann Joachim **16** 332-333

Oeuvre, L' (novel; Zola)
Cézanne, Paul **3** 400-402

Of a Fire on the Moon (book)
Mailer, Norman Kingsley **10** 148-150

Of Blood, Pleasure, and Death (novel)
Barrès, Auguste Maurice **2** 20-21

Of Crimes and Punishments (book)
Becarria, Marchese di **2** 97-98

Of Human Bondage (novel; Maugham)
Maugham, William Somerset **10** 344-345
Morrice, James Wilson **11** 181-182

Of Human Freedom (book)
Schelling, Friedrich Wilhelm Joseph von **13** 526-527

Of Husbanding Your Will (essay)
Montaigne, Michel Eyquem de **11** 116-117

Of Mice and Men (film and novel)
Copland, Aaron **4** 227-228
Steinbeck, John Ernst **14** 416-417

Of the Courtier's Life (poem)
Wyatt, Thomas **16** 410-411

Of the Five Wounds of the Holy Church
(book)
Rosmini-Serbati, Antonio **13** 296-297

Of Thee I Sing (musical)
Gershwin, George **6** 284-285
Kaufman, George S. **8** 457-458

Of Time and the River (novel)
Wolfe, Thomas Clayton **16** 355-356

Of Tyranny (book)
Alfieri, Vittoria **1** 145-146

Of Wisdom (book)
Charron, Pierre **3** 472

Off Broadway (essays)
Anderson, Maxwell **1** 219-220

OFFENBACH, JACQUES (1819-1880), German-French composer **11** 478-479
Hoffmann, Ernst Theodor Amadeus
7 439-440
Sousa, John Philip **14** 353-354
Strauss, Johann Jr. **14** 498-499

Officers and Gentlemen (novel)
Waugh, Evelyn Arthur St. John
16 145-147

**Officers of the Guild of Archers of St.
George** (painting)
Hals, Frans **7** 89-91

Officium defunctorum (musical composition)
Victoria, Tomás Luis de **15** 487-488

Offrandes (musical composition)
Varèse, Edgard **15** 432-433

Off-Shore Pirate, The (story)
Fitzgerald, Francis Scott Key **5** 470-472

Ogadai
see Ögödei

Ogarev, Nicholas (1813-1877), Russian
revolutionary
Bakunin, Mikhail Aleksandrovich
1 458-460
Herzen, Aleksandr Ivanovich **7** 351-352

OGATA, SADAKO (born 1927), United
Nations High Commissioner for Refugees
11 479-480

OGBURN, WILLIAM FIELDING
(1886-1959), American sociologist
11 480

Ogden, Aaron (1756-1839), American
lawyer
Vanderbilt, Cornelius **15** 415-416

Ogden, C.K. (1889-1957), British psychologist
Richards, Ivor Armstrong **13** 137

OGDEN, PETER SKENE (1794-1854),
Canadian fur trader and explorer
11 480-481
Smith, Jedediah S. **14** 294-295

Ogden River
see Humboldt River

Ogdensburg Agreement (1940)
King, William Lyon Mackenzie **9** 25-26

Oghul Khaimish (ruled 1248-52), Mongol
regent
Kublai Khan **9** 115-118

OGILVY, DAVID MACKENZIE (born 1911),
British-American advertising executive
11 481-482

Oglala Sioux Indians (North America)
Red Cloud **13** 70-71

OGLETHORPE, JAMES EDWARD
(1696-1785), English general and colonizer **11** 482-483
Wesley, Charles **16** 208-209
Wesley, John **16** 209-210

Ognissanti, Church of the (Florence)
Agostino di Duccio **1** 86
Botticelli, Sandro **2** 439-440
Ghirlandaio, Domenico **6** 292-293
Giotto **6** 342-345

Ögödei (1185-1241), Mongol khan
1227-41
Batu Khan **2** 60-61
Kublai Khan **9** 115-118
Yeh-lü Ch'u-ts'ai **16** 447-449

Ogooue River (Gabon)
Brazza, Pierre Paul François Camille
Savorgnan de **2** 509-510
Schweitzer, Albert **14** 55-56

OGOT, GRACE EMILY AKINYI (born
1930), Kenyan author and politician
11 483-484

Oh, Didn't He Ramble (song)
Johnson, James Weldon **8** 304-305

Oh for a Closer Walk with God (hymn)
Cowper, William **4** 282

Oh, How I Hate to Get Up in the Morning
(song)
Berlin, Irving **2** 200-201

Oh Kay (musical)
Gershwin, George **6** 284-285

Oh! Susanna (song)
Foster, Stephen Collins **6** 25-27

Oh, What a Beautiful Morning (song)
Rodgers, Richard Charles **13** 234-236

Oh, What a Nurse! (film)
Sherwood, Robert Emmet **14** 189-190

O'HAIR, MADALYN MURRAY (born
1919), American atheist author and radio
commentator **11** 484-485

O'Hara Generation (stories)
O'Hara, John **11** 485

O'HARA, JOHN (1905-1970), American
novelist **11** 485

O'HIGGINS, BERNARDO (1778-1842),
Chilean soldier and statesman **11** 486
Belgrano, Manuel **2** 126-127
Carrera, José Miguel **3** 323-324
San Martín, José de **13** 468-469

Ohio (state, United States)
congresspeople
McLean, John **10** 422-423
Taft, Robert Alphonso **15** 76-78
Vallandigham, Clement Laird
15 406-407
Episcopalian diocese
Chase, Philander **3** 472-473
governors
Chase, Salmon Portland **3** 473-475
Hayes, Rutherford Birchard
7 227-228
McKinley, William **10** 418-420
miscegenation laws
Hearn, Lafcadio **7** 240
Northwest Ordinance
Cutler, Manasseh **4** 356-357
Lee, Richard Henry **9** 291-292
senators
Cass, Lewis **3** 355-356
Chase, Salmon Portland **3** 473-475
Garfield, James Abram **6** 213-214
Hanna, Marcus Alonzo **7** 127-128
Harding, Warren Gamaliel
7 148-149
Pendleton, George Hunt **12** 198
Wade, Benjamin Franklin **16** 38-39

Ohio Antislavery Society (United States)
Birney, James Gillespie **2** 283-284

Ohio Co. (established 1748)
Gist, Christopher **6** 352-353

Ohio Company of Associates (established
1786)
Cutler, Manasseh **4** 356-357

Ohio Enabling Act (1802)
St. Clair, Arthur **13** 429-430

Ohio River (United States)
Cartwright, Peter **3** 344-345
Drake, Daniel **5** 93-94
Gist, Christopher **6** 352-353
Jolliet, Louis **8** 328-329
La Salle, Sieur de **9** 210-211
Roebling, John Augustus **13** 241-242

Ohio State University (Columbus)
Bloomfield, Leonard **2** 338
Bode, Boyd Henry **2** 355-356
Eisenman, Peter D. **5** 239-240
Lichtenstein, Roy **9** 398-399
Schlesinger, Arthur Meier **14** 13

Ohio University (Athens)
McGuffey, William Holmes **10** 414-415

OHM, GEORG SIMON (1789-1854), German physicist **11** 486-487

Ohm (electric unit)
Maxwell, James Clerk **10** 361-364
Rayleigh, 3d Baron **13** 62

Oil! (novel)
Sinclair, Upton Beale Jr. **14** 248-249

Oil industry
Iran
Mohammad Reza Shah Pahlavi
11 75-76

Mossadegh, Mohammad
11 206-207
Italy
Mattei, Enrico **10** 337-339
Mexico
Cárdenas, Lázaro **3** 286-287
Daniels, Josephus **4** 387
Díaz, José de la Cruz Porfirio
4 534-536
pipelines and refineries
Bechtel, Stephen Davison **2** 98-99
Russia
Mendeleev, Dmitrii Ivanovich
10 486-488
Saudi Arabia
Yamani, Ahmed Zaki **16** 433-435
U.S.
Getty, Jean Paul **6** 288-290
ibn Saud, Abd al-Aziz **8** 94-95
Ickes, Harold LeClaire **8** 100-101
Jones, Samuel Milton **8** 342-343
Morrow, Dwight Whitney
11 190-191
Rockefeller, John Davison
13 226-228
Tarbell, Ida Minerva **15** 107-108
Walsh, Thomas James **16** 85-86
Venezuela
Caldera Rodríguez, Rafael
3 218-219
Gómez, Juan Vicente **6** 417-418
see also Business and industrial
leaders—oil industry
see also Organization of Petroleum
Exporting Countries

Oiseau bleu, L' (play)
Maeterlinck, Maurice **10** 125-126

Oisin
see Ossian

Ojeda, Alonso de (1465?-1515), Spanish
explorer
Balboa, Vasco Núñez de **1** 462-463
Pizarro, Francisco **12** 340-341
Vespucci, Amerigo **15** 476-478

Ojibwa Indians (North America)
Morgan, Lewis Henry **11** 167-168

Ojukwu, Chukwuemeka Odumegwu (born
1933), Nigerian colonel, Biafran leader
Ekwensi, Cyprian **5** 242-243

O.K. Corral (Tombstone, Arizona)
Earp, Wyatt Barry Stepp **5** 181-182

Okada, Keisuke (1868-1952), Japanese
admiral and prime minister
Takahashi, Korekiyo **15** 84-85

O'KEEFFE, GEORGIA (1887-1986), Ameri-
can painter **11** 487-489
Demuth, Charles **4** 497-498
Graham, Martha **6** 485-486
Sheeler, Charles **14** 170-171
Stieglitz, Alfred **14** 451-452
Wyeth, Andrew Newell **16** 413-415

O'Kelly, James (circa 1735-1826), American Methodist preacher
Asbury, Francis **1** 324-325

Okina (play)
Zeami, Kanze **16** 492-493

Okinawa (island, South West Pacific)
Sato, Eisaku **13** 495-496

Oklahoma (musical)
Hammerstein, Oscar Clendenning II
7 104-106
Rodgers, Richard Charles **13** 234-236

Oklahoma (state, United States)
Harrison, Benjamin **7** 178-179
Ross, John **13** 303-304
Sequoyah **14** 110-111

Oklahoma, University of (Norman)
Parrington, Vernon Louis **12** 119-120

Okubi-e (Japanese art)
Utamaro, Kitagawa **15** 397

OKUBO, TOSHIMICHI (1830-1878),
Japanese statesman **11** 489-490
Iwakura, Tomomi **8** 160-161
Okuma, Shigenobu **11** 490

OKUMA, SHIGENOBU (1838-1922),
Japanese statesman **11** 490
Inukai, Tsuyoshi **8** 130-131
Ito, Hirobumi **8** 153-155
Iwakura, Tomomi **8** 160-161

Okuni and Gohei (play)
Tanizaki, Junichiro **15** 101-102

Ol' Man River (song)
Kern, Jerome David **8** 517-518

Olaf, St.
see Olaf II Haroldsson

OLAF I TRYGGVASON (968-1000), Viking
warrior and king of Norway **11** 490-493
Ericson, Leif **5** 306-307
Harold I **7** 161-162

OLAF II (circa 990-1030), king of Norway
11 493-494
Cobbett, William **4** 126-127
Harold III **7** 163

Olaf Liljekrans (play)
Ibsen, Henrik **8** 98-100

Olana (museum; Hudson, New York State)
Church, Frederick Edwin **4** 49-50

OLBRICH, JOSEPH MARIA (1867-1908),
Austrian Art Nouveau architect and a
founder of the Vienna Secession
11 494-495
Behrens, Peter **2** 121-122

Old age pensions
see Social security

Old Bachelor, The (play)
Congreve, William **4** 200-201

Old Bedford (painting)
Sickert, Walter Richard **14** 212-213

Old Black Joe (song)
Foster, Stephen Collins **6** 25-27

Old Blastus of Bandicoot (novel)
Franklin, Stella Maraia Sarah Miles
6 68-69

Old Bush Songs (ballads)
Paterson, Andrew Barton **12** 131-132

Old Catholics (national churches)
Döllinger, Josef Ignaz von **5** 47-48

Old Clock on the Stairs, The (poem)
Longfellow, Henry Wadsworth
9 499-500

Old Comedy (Greek literature)
Aristophanes **1** 293-294
Menander **10** 477-478

Old Courtesan (sculpture)
Rodin, Auguste **13** 236-238

Old Creole Days (stories)
Cable, George Washington **3** 198-199

Old Curiosity Shop, The (novel)
Dickens, Charles John Huffam
4 538-541

Old Dominion
see Virginia (state)

Old Drunkard's Pavilion (China)
Ou-yang Hsiu **12** 33-34

Old Folks at Home (song)
Foster, Stephen Collins **6** 25-27

Old Friends and New (literary collection)
Jewett, Sarah Orne **8** 256

Old German Forests (book)
Grimm, Jakob and Wilhelm Karl **7** 3-4

Old Glory (play)
Lowell, Robert Trail Spence Jr. **10** 16-17

Old Guitarist (painting)
Picasso, Pablo **12** 292-295

Old Huntsman, The (poems)
Sassoon, Siegfried **13** 492-493

Old Ironsides (poem)
Holmes, Oliver Wendell **7** 457-458

Old Judge, The (book)
Haliburton, Thomas Chandler **7** 80

Old Kentucky Home (painting)
Johnson, Earvin Jr. **8** 297-299

Old King (painting)
Rouault, Georges **13** 321-322

Old Larsen (painting)
Drysdale, George Russell **5** 107-109

Old Legends Retold (fables)
Lu Hsün **10** 35-37

Old Maid and the Thief, The (opera)
Menotti, Gian Carlo **10** 509-510

Old Maid, The (novella)
Wharton, Edith **16** 221

Old Man and His Mirror, The (poems)
Morin, Paul **11** 174

Old Man and the Sea, The (novel)
Hemingway, Ernest Miller **7** 274-277

Old Manse (Concord, Massachusetts)
Hawthorne, Nathaniel **7** 212-215

Old Mortality (novel)
Scott, Walter **14** 68-70

Old Oak Tree's Last Dream, The (fairy tale)
Andersen, Hans Christian **1** 212-214

Old Oaken Bucket, The (painting)
Moses, Grandma **11** 201-202

Old Possum's Book of Practical Cats (book)
Eliot, Thomas Stearns **5** 258-261

Old Regime and the French Revolution, The (book)
Tocqueville, Alexis Charles Henri Maurice Clérel de **15** 250-251

Old Regime in Canada, The (book)
Parkman, Francis **12** 113-115

Old Spain (play)
Ruíz, José Martínez **13** 358

Old Stoic, The (poem)
Brontë, Emily **3** 18-19

Old Swimmin' Hole... (poems)
Riley, James Whitcomb **13** 170-171

Old Testament
see Bible

Old Testament (painting cycle)
Tiepolo, Giovanni Battista **15** 219-220

Old Times (play)
Pinter, Harold **12** 317-318

Old Uncle Ned (song)
Foster, Stephen Collins **6** 25-27

Old Vic (theater; London)
Olivier, Laurence **11** 502-503

Old Violin, The (painting)
Harnett, William Michael **7** 160-161

Old Wives for New (novel)
Phillips, David Graham **12** 280-281

Old Wives' Tale, The (novel)
Bennett, Arnold **2** 167-168

Old Woman of the Roads, The (poem)
Colum, Padraic **4** 174-175

Old World in Its New Face, The (book)
Bellows, Henry Whitney **2** 143-144

Old World Landowners (story)
Gogol, Nikolai **6** 391-393

Oldcastle, Sir John (circa 1378-1417), English Lollard leader
Henry V **7** 296-297

OLDENBARNEVELT, JOHAN VAN (1547-1619), Dutch statesman **11** 495-496
Grotius, Hugo **7** 18-19
Maurice of Nassau **10** 348-349
Vondel, Joost van den **16** 19-20
Witt, Johan de **16** 348-349

OLDENBURG, CLAES (born 1929), American artist **11** 496-498

Oldenburg, Henry (circa 1615-77), Anglo-German philosopher
Boyle, Robert **2** 469-471
Leeuwenhoek, Anton van **9** 300-301
Spinoza, Baruch **14** 381-383
Steno, Nicolaus **14** 425-426

Older, Fremont (1856-1935), American journalist
Ruef, Abraham **13** 352-353

Old-fashioned Girl, An (book)
Alcott, Louisa May **1** 122

Old-Fashioned Roses (book)
Riley, James Whitcomb **13** 170-171

Oldmixon, John (1673-1742), English historian
Beverley, Robert **2** 252

Olds Motor Co. (United States)
Durant, William Crapo **5** 158
Sloan, Alfred Pritchard Jr. **14** 274

Oldsmobile (automobile)
Ford, Henry **6** 5-6

Olduvai Gorge (Tanzania)
Leakey, Louis Seymour Bazett **9** 262

Oleomargarine Act (1886)
Hatch, William Henry **7** 196

Oligarchy (government)
Asia
Ito, Hirobumi **8** 153-155
Rómulo, Carlos P. **13** 270-271
Britain
George II **6** 269-270
Melbourne, 2nd Viscount **10** 468-469
Greece and Rome
Cleisthenes **4** 98-99
Cleomenes I **4** 103
Lysander **10** 70
Sulla, Lucius Cornelius I **15** 21-22
iron law of
Michels, Robert **11** 7
Latin America
Páez, José Antonio **12** 58
Roca, Julio Argentino **13** 218
U.S.
Dudley, Thomas **5** 124-125

Olimpiade (musical composition)
Arne, Thomas Augustine **1** 307-308

Olindo (literary character)
Tasso, Torquato **15** 114-116

Olio (minstrel shows)
Christy, Edwin P. **4** 34-35

OLIPHANT, PATRICK BRUCE (born 1935), American newspaper editorial cartoonist **11** 498-500

Olitski, Jules (born 1922), American painter
Newman, Barnett **11** 365

Oliva, Gian Paolo (1600-1681), Italian theologian
Bernini, Gian Lorenzo **2** 214-216

Oliva, Treaty of (1660)
Frederick William **6** 85-86

Olivares, Count-Duke of (Gaspar de Guzmán; 1587-1645), Spanish prime minister 1621-1643
Góngora y Argote, Luis de **6** 427-428
Philip IV **12** 275

Quevedo Y Villegas, Francisco Gómez de **12** 511
Velázquez, Diego Rodríguez de Silva y **15** 454-456

Olive (sonnets)
du Bellay, Joachim **5** 113-114

Olive Grove, The (painting)
Miró, Joan **11** 53-54

Oliver, Andrew (1706-1774), American colonial politician
Warren, Mercy Otis **16** 120-121

Oliver, Isaac, the Elder (1556?-1617), English painter
Hilliard, Nicholas **7** 391-392

OLIVER, JAMES (1823-1908), American inventor and manufacturer **11** 500-501

Oliver, Joseph "King" (1885-1938), American jazz musician
Armstrong, Louis Daniel **1** 303-304

Oliver Twist (novel)
Dickens, Charles John Huffam **4** 538-541

Oliver Twist (play)
Cushman, Charlotte **4** 354-355

OLIVETTI, ADRIANO (1901-1960), Italian manufacturer of typewriters, calculators, and computers **11** 501-502

Olivier, Emile (1825-1913), French politician
Napoleon III **11** 310-312

OLIVIER, LAURENCE (1907-1989), English actor and director **11** 502-503
Goldwyn, Samuel **6** 416

OLMSTED, FREDERICK LAW (1822-1903), American landscape architect **11** 503-504
Burnham, Daniel Hudson **3** 148-149
Downing, Andrew Jackson **5** 90-91

Olmstead v. United States (legal case)
Brandeis, Louis Dembitz **2** 496-497

OLNEY, RICHARD (1835-1917), American statesman **11** 504-505
Altgeld, John Peter **1** 180-182
Cleveland, Stephen Grover **4** 108-110

Olor Iscanus (poems)
Vaughan, Henry **15** 444-445

OLSON, CHARLES (1910-1970), American poet **11** 505-506

Olvidados, Los (film)
Buñuel, Luis **3** 127-128

Olybrius, Anicius (died 472), Roman emperor
Odoacer **11** 473
Ricimer, Flavius **13** 151-152

Olympia (film)
Riefenstahl, Leni **13** 161-163

Olympia (painting)
Manet, Édouard **10** 193-194

Olympian Ode (poem)
Pindar **12** 312-313

Olympias (died 316 B.C.), queen of Macedonia
Alexander the Great **1** 137-141
Philip II **12** 269-271
Ptolemy I **12** 470-472

Olympic Games
administration
Ueberroth, Peter Victor **15** 379-381
Walker, LeRoy Tashreau **16** 64-65
athletes
Ali, Muhammad **1** 156-158
Capriati, Jennifer **3** 278-281
Lewis, Carl **9** 377-380
Owens, Jesse **12** 43-44
Rudolph, Wilma **13** 350-352
Thorpe, Jim **15** 209-211
Zaharias, Mildred Didrikson **16** 487-488
facilities
Tange, Kenzo **15** 99-101
films of
Riefenstahl, Leni **13** 161-163
politics
Alemán Valdés, Miguel **1** 126-127
Echeverría Alvarez, Luis **5** 198-200

OLYMPIO, SYLVANUS E. (1902-1963), first president of the Republic of Togo **11** 506-507
Danquah, Joseph B. **4** 388-389

Omaha Allotment Act (1882)
Fletcher, Alice Cunningham **5** 486-487

Omaha Evening World (newspaper)
Hitchcock, Gilbert Monell **7** 416-417

Omaha Indians (North America)
Fletcher, Alice Cunningham **5** 486-487
La Flesche, Francis **9** 152-154

Oman, Sultanate of (nation; South East Arabia)
Qaboos ibn Sa'id **12** 501-502
Said, Seyyid **13** 428-429

OMAR AL-MUKHTAR (circa 1860-1931), national hero of Libya and member of the Senusy **11** 507-508

OMAR IBN AL-KHATTAB (died 644); second caliph of the Moslems **11** 508-509
Abu Bakr **1** 31-32
Ali **1** 155-156

OMAR IBN SAID TAL, AL-HAJJ (circa 1797-1864), West African Moslem leader **11** 509-510
Faidherbe, Louis Léon César **5** 366-367
Touré, Sékou **15** 275-277
Uthman don Fodio **15** 397-398

OMAR KHAYYAM (1048-circa 1132), Persian astronomer, mathematician, and poet **11** 510-511
Hidayat, Sadiq **7** 377-378

Omayyad
see Umayyad

Omi laws (Japan)
Fujiwara Kamatari **6** 145

O'Mika (ballet)
St. Denis, Ruth **13** 430-431

Omniscience (mural)
Orozco, José Clemente **12** 1-2

Omoo (novel)
Melville, Herman **10** 472-476

Omphalos (ode)
Pindar **12** 312-313

On a May Morning (poem)
Milton, John **11** 43-46

On Ancient Comedy (literary criticism)
Eratosthenes of Cyrene **5** 301-302

On Anger (book)
Seneca the Younger, Lucius Annaeus **14** 103-105

On Art (book)
Zeno of Citium **16** 499-500

On Art and Literature (book)
Proust, Marcel **12** 465-467

On Automaton-making (book)
Heron of Alexandria **7** 334-335

On Baile's Strand (play)
Yeats, William Butler **16** 445-447

On Cosmetics (poem)
Ovid **12** 34-36

On Death and Dying (book)
Kübler-Ross, Elisabeth **9** 118-120

On Early Trains (poems)
Pasternak, Boris Leonidovich **12** 124-125

On Equitation (book)
Xenophon **16** 418-420

On Farming (book)
Cato, Marcus Porcius the Elder **3** 375

On First Looking into Chapman's Homer (sonnet; Keats)
Chapman, George **3** 440-441

On Forgotten Paths (novel)
Rölvaag, Ole Edvart **13** 265

On Friendship (essay)
Montaigne, Michel Eyquem de **11** 116-117

On Friendship (essay; Cicero)
Scipio Africanus Minor, Publius Cornelius Aemilianus **14** 62-63

On Heaven (book; Aristotle)
Aristotle **1** 295-296
Nicholas of Oresme **11** 380

On Heroes... (book)
Carlyle, Thomas **3** 304-305

On Human Life (encyclical)
Paul VI **12** 146-148

On Human Nature (essay)
Han Yü **7** 136-137

On Imagination (poem)
Wheatley, Phillis **16** 221-222

On Karl Marx (book)
Block, Herbert **2** 333-334

On Liberty (essay; J. S. Mill)
Hu Shih **8** 63-65
Liang Ch'i-ch'ao **9** 395-396
Mill, John Stuart **11** 21-23
Yen Fu **16** 452

On Love (book)
Ortega Y Gasset, José **12** 7-8
Stendhal **14** 422-425

On Man (essay)
Han Yü **7** 136-137

On Man (treatise; Descartes)
Malebranche, Nicolas **10** 166-167

On ne badine pas avec l'amour (play)
Musset, Louis Charles Alfred de **11** 271-272

On ne saurait penser à tout (play)
Musset, Louis Charles Alfred de **11** 271-272

On Philosophy (book)
Aristotle **1** 295-296

On Poetry and Poets (book)
Eliot, Thomas Stearns **5** 258-261

On Priestly Celibacy (encyclical)
Paul VI **12** 146-148

On Problems Relating to Homer (book)
Zeno of Citium **16** 499-500

On Recollection (poem)
Wheatley, Phillis **16** 221-222

On Returning Home (poem)
T'ao Ch'ien **15** 104-105

On Shakespeare (poem)
Milton, John **11** 43-46

On the Banks of the Wabash (song; P. Dreiser)
Dreiser, Herman Theodore **5** 98-100

On the Beautiful Blue Danube (waltz)
Strauss, Johann Jr. **14** 498-499

On the Church (encyclical)
Paul VI **12** 146-148

On the Commonwealth (dialogue ; Cicero)
Scipio Africanus Minor, Publius Cornelius Aemilianus **14** 62-63

On the Death of a Fair Infant, Dying of the Cough (poem)
Milton, John **11** 43-46

On the Death of Carlo Imbonati (elegy)
Manzoni, Alessandro **10** 222-224

On the Death of the Reverend Mr. George Whitefield (poem)
Wheatley, Phillis **16** 221-222

On the Development of Peoples (encyclical)
Paul VI **12** 146-148

On the Dnieper (ballet)
Prokofiev, Sergei Sergeevich **12** 458-460

On the Eve (novel)
Turgenev, Ivan Sergeyevich **15** 345-348

On the Eve (play)
Afinogenov, Aleksandr Nikolaevich **1** 72-73

On the Field of Glory (novel)
Sienkiewicz, Henryk **14** 216-217

On the Fifth of November (poem)
Milton, John **11** 43-46

On the Genius and Character of Hogarth (essay)
Lamb, Charles **9** 176-177

On the German Wars (book)
Pliny the Elder **12** 355-356

On the Immense (poem)
Bruno, Giordano **3** 75-76

On the Laws of England (treatise)
Henry II **7** 287-289

On the Marble Cliffs (novel)
Jünger, Ernst **8** 391-392

On the Mean and Sure Estate (poem)
Wyatt, Thomas **16** 410-411

On the Minimum (poem)
Bruno, Giordano **3** 75-76

On the Monad (poem)
Bruno, Giordano **3** 75-76

On the Morning of Christ's Nativity (poem)
Milton, John **11** 43-46

On the Nature of the Universe (poem;
Lucretius)
Lucretius **10** 26-27
Virgil **15** 507-510

On the Origin of Species... (book)
see Origin of Species

On the Rim of Life (tales)
Rilke, Rainer Maria **13** 171-172

On the Road (book; Kerouac)
Ginsberg, Allen **6** 332-333
Kerouac, Jean-Louis Lebris de
8 518-519

On the Road (story)
Chekhov, Anton Pavlovich **3** 494-497

On the Sphere and Cylinder (treatise)
Archimedes **1** 277-280

On the Study Methods of Our Time (book)
Vico, Giambattista **15** 480-481

On the Sublime (treatise; Longinus)
Boileau-Despréaux, Nicholas
2 369-371
Longinus **9** 500-501

On the Tao (essay)
Han Yü **7** 136-137

On the Theatre (book)
Meyerhold, Vsevolod Emilievich **10** 539

On the Threshold of the House of Prayer (poem)
Bialik, Hayyim Nahman **2** 262-263

On the Town (musical)
Bernstein, Leonard **2** 218-219

On the Track and over the Sliprails (book)
Lawson, Henry **9** 254-255

On the University Carrier (poem)
Milton, John **11** 43-46

On the Wisdom of the Ancients (book)
Bacon, Francis **1** 422-424

On These I Stand (poems)
Cullen, Countee **4** 333-334

On Tombs (poem)
Foscolo, Ugo **6** 21

On Trial (play)
Rice, Elmer **13** 126-127

On Virtue (poem)
Wheatley, Phillis **16** 221-222

On Wenlock Edge (musical composition)
Vaughan Williams, Ralph **15** 446-447

On Your Toes (musical)
Rodgers, Richard Charles **13** 234-236

**ONASSIS, JACQUELINE LEE BOUVIER
KENNEDY** (1929-1994), American First
Lady **11** 511-513

OÑATE, JUAN DE (circa 1549-circa 1624),
Spanish explorer **11** 513-514

Once in Your Grace (poem)
Wyatt, Thomas **16** 410-411

Once There Was a War (book)
Steinbeck, John Ernst **14** 416-417

Ondine (play)
Giraudoux, Jean **6** 349-350

One A. M. (film)
Chaplin, Charles Spencer **3** 438-440

One Casualty (painting)
Amorsolo, Fernando **1** 204

One Day in the Life of Ivan Denisovich (novella)
Solzhenitsyn, Alexander Isayevich
14 330-332

One Fair Woman, The (novel)
Miller, Joaquin **11** 27-28

One Hundred, Council of the (Florence, Italy)
Dante Alighieri **4** 389-391

150,000,000 (poem)
Mayakovsky, Vladimir Vladimirovich
10 364-365

One Hundred Years of Solitude (novel)
García Márquez, Gabriel **6** 208-209

One Man's Initiation-1917 (novel)
Dos Passos, John Roderigo **5** 69-71

One, None, and a Hundred Thousand (novel)
Pirandello, Luigi **12** 319-321

One O'Clock Jump (song)
Basie **2** 48-49

One of Cleopatra's Nights (book)
Hearn, Lafcadio **7** 240

One of Ours (novel)
Cather, Willa Sibert **3** 368-369

One to Another (revue sketch)
Pinter, Harold **12** 317-318

One Way to Heaven (novel)
Cullen, Countee **4** 333-334

One Wonderful Sunday (film)
Kurosawa, Akira **9** 135-137

One-Dimensional Man (book)
Marcuse, Herbert **10** 245-247

Oneida Community (religion)
Noyes, John Humphrey **11** 437-438

Oneida Indians (North America)
Brant, Joseph **2** 500-501
Greene, Graham **6** 524-525
Hobart, John Henry **7** 420-421
Kirkland, Samuel **9** 37

O'Neill, Danny (literary character)
Farrell, James Thomas **5** 390-391

O'NEILL, EUGENE (1888-1953), American
dramatist **11** 514-516
Chaplin, Charles Spencer **3** 438-440
Cohan, George Michael **4** 137-138
Strindberg, August **14** 509-511

O'Neill, James (1847-1920), American
actor
O'Neill, Eugene **11** 514-516

O'Neill, Marie Allgood (1887-1952), Irish
actress
Synge, Edmund John Millington
15 61-62

O'Neill, Shane (1530-1567), Irish rebel
Elizabeth I **5** 263-266

O'NEILL, TERENCE MARNE (1914-1990),
Northern Ireland prime minister
11 516-517

O'NEILL, THOMAS P. ("Tip"; born 1912),
American politician **11** 517-519

One-price system (business)
Field, Marshall **5** 440-441
Stewart, Alexander Turney **14** 448-449

One-round O'Brien (film)
Sennett, Mack **14** 108-109

ONG TENG CHEONG (born 1936), Singapore's fifth president **11** 519-520

Ong-Khan
see Toghril

Onkel, Onkel (play)
Grass, Günter **6** 496-497

Only in America (book)
Golden, Harry **6** 402-403

Only the Dead Know Brooklyn (story)
Wolfe, Thomas Clayton **16** 355-356

Onondaga Indians (North America)
Brûlé, Étienne **3** 67-68

ONSAGER, LARS (1903-1976), American
chemist **11** 520-523

Ontario, Simcoe, and Huron Railway
see Northern Railway (Canada)

Ontology (philosophy)
Anselm of Canterbury **1** 244-245
Heidegger, Martin **7** 257-258
Quine, Willard Van Orman **12** 514-515

Onward, Christian Soldiers (hymn)
Sullivan, Arthur Seymour **15** 23

OORT, JAN HENDRIK (1900-1992), Dutch
astronomer **11** 523-524
Kapteyn, Jacobus Cornelis **8** 436-437

Op Art (Optical Art)
Vasarely, Victor **15** 440-442

O-pang Palace (China)
Quin Shi Huang-Di **12** 515-518

OPEC
see Organization of Petroleum Exporting Countries

Opechancanough (circa 1545-1644),
Native American tribal chief
Berkeley, William **2** 198-199

Open Boat, The (story)
Crane, Stephen **4** 293-295

Open City (film)
Fellini, Federico **5** 408-409

Open Conspiracy, The (book)
Wells, Herbert George **16** 195-196

Open House (book)
Roethke, Theodore **13** 243-244

Open Mind, The (novel)
Bernanos, Georges **2** 206-207

Open shop (labor)
Gary, Elbert Henry **6** 229-230
see also Labor unions (United States)

Open Thy Lattice, Love (song)
Foster, Stephen Collins **6** 25-27

Open-air painting
see Plein-air painting (art)

Open-door policy (Liberia)
Tubman, William Vacanarat Shadrach
15 331

Open-door policy (United States -China)
Hay, John **7** 215-216
Roosevelt, Theodore **13** 280-283
Taft, William Howard **15** 78-81

Open-hearth process (steel)
Bessemer, Henry **2** 235-236
Hewitt, Abram Stevens **7** 371-372
Krupp **9** 109-111

Opera (musical form)
American
Anderson, June **1** 216-218
Barber, Samuel **1** 500-501
Battle, Kathleen **2** 59-60
Caldwell, Sarah **3** 224-226
Floyd, Carlisle **5** 494-496
Fry, William Henry **6** 136-137
Joplin, Scott **8** 345-347
Lee, Ming Cho **9** 289-290
Menotti, Gian Carlo **10** 509-510
Morris, Mark **11** 184-185
Norman, Jessye **11** 425-427
Price, Leontyne **12** 446-447
Sills, Beverly **14** 230-231
Tcherepnin, Alexander **15** 132-133
Te Kanawa, Kiri **15** 136-137

Thomson, Virgil **15** 202-203
Argentine
Ginastera, Alberto Evaristo
6 328-329
Brazilian
Villa-Lobos, Heitor **15** 496-497
Czech
Dvořák, Antonin **5** 168-169
Janáček, Leoš **8** 219
Martinu, Bohuslav **10** 299-300
Smetana, Bedřich **14** 281-282
English
Bennett, Richard Rodney **2** 172
Britten, Benjamin **3** 10-11
Gay, John **6** 243-244
Handel, George Frederick
7 116-119
Purcell, Henry **12** 484-485
Te Kanawa, Kiri **15** 136-137
French
see Opera, French
German
Behrens, Hildegard **2** 120-121
Haydn, Franz Joseph **7** 219-221,
150
Hofmannsthal, Hugo von **7** 443-444
Krenek, Ernst **9** 98-99
Meyerbeer, Giacomo **10** 536-537
Mozart, Wolfgang Amadeus
11 218-221
Strauss, Richard **14** 500-501
Wagner, Richard **16** 40-43
Weber, Carl Maria Friedrich Ernst
von **16** 156-157
Weill, Kurt **16** 174-175
Zimmermann, Bernd Alois
16 517-518
Italian
see Opera, Italian
Mexican
Domingo, Placido **5** 50-51
Russian
Borodin, Aleksandr Profirevich
2 422-423
Glinka, Mikhail Ivanovich
6 369-370
Mussorgsky, Modest Petrovich
11 274-276
Prokofiev, Sergei Sergeevich
12 458-460
Rimsky-Korsakov, Nikolai Andree-
vich **13** 174-175
Shostakovich, Dmitri Dmitrievich
14 204-205
Tchaikovsky, Peter Ilyich
15 130-132
Scottish
Musgrave, Thea **11** 266-268
Spanish
Domingo, Placido **5** 50-51

Opéra (Paris)
Carpeaux, Jean Baptiste **3** 318-319
Garnier, Jean Louis Charles **6** 221-222

Opera, French
17th-18th century

Charpentier, Marc Antoine
3 471-472
Cherubini, Luigi Carlo Zanobi Sal-
vatore Maria **3** 505-506
Gluck, Christoph Willibald
6 372-374
Lully, Jean Baptiste **10** 40-41
Pergolesi, Giovanni Battista
12 218-219
Rameau, Jean Philippe **13** 17-18
19th century
Berlioz, Louis Hector **2** 203-205
Bizet, Georges **2** 296-297
Gounod, Charles François
6 473-474
Meyerbeer, Giacomo **10** 536-537
Offenbach, Jacques **11** 478-479
20th century
Sauguet, Henri **13** 497-498
Tcherepnin, Alexander **15** 132-133

Opera, Italian
17th century
Caccini, Giulio **3** 205-206
Cavalli, Pietro Francesco **3** 382-383
Cesti, Pietro **3** 399-400
Lully, Jean Baptiste **10** 40-41
Monteverdi, Claudio Giovanni
Antonio **11** 126-128
Scarlatti, Pietro Alessandro Gaspare
13 517-518
18th century
Bach, Johann Christian **1** 415-416
Cimarosa, Domenico **4** 61-62
Gluck, Christoph Willibald
6 372-374
Handel, George Frederick
7 116-119
Mozart, Wolfgang Amadeus
11 218-221
Pergolesi, Giovanni Battista
12 218-219
Scarlatti, Pietro Alessandro Gaspare
13 517-518
Vivaldi, Antonio **16** 3-4
19th century
Bellini, Vincenzo **2** 138-139
Donizetti, Gaetano **5** 59-60
Meyerbeer, Giacomo **10** 536-537
Puccini, Giacomo **12** 474-476
Rossini, Gioacchino **13** 311-312
Verdi, Giuseppe Fortunino
Francesco **15** 463-465
20th century
Malipiero, Gian Francesco **10** 171
Nono, Luigi **11** 420-421
Pavarotti, Luciano **12** 152-154
Puccini, Giacomo **12** 474-476
Respighi, Ottorino **13** 103-104

Opera Box (painting)
Renoir, Pierre Auguste **13** 101-102

Opera Company of Boston
Caldwell, Sarah **3** 224-226

Opera House (Haymarket, England)
Vanbrugh, John **15** 409-410

Operant behavorism (psychology)
Skinner, Burrhus Frederic **14** 269-270

Operation Desert Shield/Storm
U.S. leaders
Bush, George **3** 167-169
Powell, Colin Luther **12** 424-425

Operation Overlord
see Normandy invasion

Operetta (musical form)
Gilbert, William Schwenck **6** 314-315
Offenbach, Jacques **11** 478-479
Schubert, Franz Peter **14** 35-37
Strauss, Johann Jr. **14** 498-499
Sullivan, Arthur Seymour **15** 23

Operette morali (literary collection)
Leopardi, Giacomo **9** 344-345

Ophélie (poem)
Rimbaud, Jean Nicolas Arthur
13 172-174

Ophthalmology (medicine)
Doyle, Arthur Conan **5** 91-92
Helmholtz, Hermann Ludwig Ferdinand
von **7** 268-269
Young, Thomas **16** 475-476

Opimius, Lucius (flourished 125-110 B.C.),
Roman politician
Gracchus, Tiberius and Gaius Sempro-
nius **6** 479-480

Opinión, La (newspaper; Argentina)
Timerman, Jacobo **15** 226-228

Opitchepan
see Itopatin

Opium War (China; 1839-1842)
Ch'i-ying **4** 12
Forbes, Robert Bennet **5** 509-510
Lin Tse-hsü **9** 431-432
Palmerston, 3d Viscount **12** 81-83
Wei Yüan **16** 180-181

Opobo (Nigerian kingdom)
Ja Ja of Opobo **8** 201-204

Oporto, battle of (1809)
Wellington, 1st Duke of **16** 193-195

OPPENHEIM, MERET (1913-1985), Swiss
Surrealist artist **11** 524-525

OPPENHEIMER, J. ROBERT (1904-1967),
American physicist **11** 525-526
Fermi, Enrico **5** 422-424
Szilard, Leo **15** 64-66
Von Neumann, John **16** 27-28

Opportunity (periodical)
Cullen, Countee **4** 333-334
Hughes, Langston **8** 18-19
Johnson, Charles Spurgeon **8** 296-297

Opticks (book; Newton)
Clarke, Samuel **4** 88
Newton, Isaac **11** 369-372

Optics (physics)
Euclid **5** 327-329
Fizeau, Hippolyte Armand Louis **5** 475
Fraunhofer, Joseph von **6** 75-76
Gibbs, Josiah Willard **6** 302-303

Hamilton, William Rowan **7** 99-100
Hasan ibn al-Haytham **7** 190-191
Land, Edwin Herbert **9** 183-184
Michelson, Albert Abraham **11** 7-8
Newton, Isaac **11** 369-372
Ochoa, Ellen **11** 460-461
Ptolemy, Claudius **12** 473-474
Young, Thomas **16** 475-476
see also Light; Quantum theory

Options (stories)
Henry, O. **7** 308-309

Opus Dei (religious organization)
Franco Bahamonde, Francisco **6** 52-54

Oráculo manual y arte de prudencia (literary collection)
Gracián y Morales, Baltasar Jerónimo
6 481-482

Orah Hayyim
see Shulhan Aruk

Oral Law (Judaism)
see Midrash; Talmud

Oral literature
Laurence, Margaret **9** 229-230

Oralloossa (play)
Bird, Robert Montgomery **2** 281-282

Orana Maria, La (painting)
Gauguin, Paul **6** 236-238

Orange and Black Wall (painting)
Kline, Franz **9** 55

Orange Free State (province; South Africa)
Botha, Louis **2** 434-436
Hertzog, James Barry Munnik
7 347-348
Kitchener, Horatio Herbert **9** 45-46
Plaatje, Solomon Tshekisho **12** 341-342

Orange, House of (Netherlands; ruled
1579-1795 and after 1815)
Maurice of Nassau **10** 348-349
Wilhelmina **16** 278-279
William I **16** 291-292
William III **16** 295-296
William the Silent **16** 300-302
Witt, Johan de **16** 348-349

Orator (essay; Cicero)
Brutus, Marcus Junius **3** 79-80
Cicero, Marcus Tullius **4** 55-58

Oratorians (religious congregation)
Borromini, Francesco **2** 424-425
La Fontaine, Jean de **9** 156-157
Malebranche, Nicolas **10** 166-167
Neri, Philip **11** 340
Newman, John Henry **11** 365-367

Oratorio (music)
Arne, Thomas Augustine **1** 307-308
Bach, Carl Philipp Emanuel **1** 414-415
Bach, Johann Sebastian **1** 416-419
Carissimi, Giacomo **3** 299-300
Dett, Robert Nathaniel **4** 512
Fux, Johann Joseph **6** 155-156
Handel, George Frederick **7** 116-119
Haydn, Franz Joseph **7** 219-221

Schütz, Heinrich **14** 48-49
Vivaldi, Antonio **16** 3-4

Orators
American
Grady, Henry Woodfin **6** 482-483
Henry, Patrick **7** 309-311
Ingersoll, Robert Green **8** 120-121
Lee, Richard Henry **9** 291-292
Otis, James Jr. **12** 25-27
Polk, Leonidas Lafayette **12** 376-377
Truth, Sojourner **15** 320-321
Webster, Daniel **16** 162-164
English
Canning, George **3** 258-260
Sheridan, Richard Brinsley
14 183-184
Greek
Demosthenes **4** 495-496
Isocrates **8** 151
Irish
Grattan, Henry **6** 499
Portuguese
Vieira, Antônio **15** 492
Roman
Cato, Marcus Porcius the Elder
3 375
Cicero, Marcus Tullius **4** 55-58
Crassus Dives, Marcus Licinius
4 296-297
Tacitus **15** 70-72

Orators, The (literary collection)
Auden, Wystan Hugh **1** 364-366

Oratory (rhetoric)
Gorgias **6** 456
Quintilian **12** 518-519
see also Orators

Oratory, Congregation of the
see Oratorians

Oratory of Divine Love (religious congregation)
Cajetan **3** 215-216

Oratory of San Filippo Neri (Rome)
Borromini, Francesco **2** 424-425

Oratory of the Filippini (Rome)
Guarini, Guarino **7** 25-26

Orbilius Pupillus (flourished 1st century
B.C.), Roman schoolmaster
Horace **7** 500-503

ORCAGNA (1308?-1368?), Italian painter,
sculptor, and architect **11** 526-527

Orchards of Toledo, The (book)
Tirso de Molina **15** 237-238

Orchestre de Paris
Barenboim, Daniel **2** 3-4

Orchomenus (ancient city, Greece)
Cleomenes III **4** 103-104
Schliemann, Heinrich **14** 17-18

Ordeal of Gilbert Pinfold, The (novel)
Waugh, Evelyn Arthur St. John
16 145-147

Ordeal of Richard Feveral, The (novel)
Meredith, George **10** 512-513

Order No. 11 (painting)
Bingham, George Caleb **2** 278-279

Order of
Cîteaux
see Cistercians
Friars Minor
see Franciscans
Friars Preachers
see Dominicans
St. Benedict
see Benedictines

Order of the Garter (established 1348)
Edward III **5** 211-212

Order of the Star in the East (religious group)
Krishnamurti, Jiddu **9** 101-103

Ordinance of Nullification (South Carolina; 1832)
Jackson, Andrew **8** 168-172
see also Nullification crisis (United States)

Ordinance of 1787
see Northwest Ordinance

Ordinary Evening in New Haven, An (poem)
Stevens, Wallace **14** 443-445

Ordinary Life, An (novel)
Čapek, Karel **3** 271-272

Ordóñez, José Battle y
see Batlle y Ordóñez, José

Ordoño III (died 955), king of León
Abd al-Rahman III **1** 14

Ordos loop (Yellow R., China)
Quin Shi Huang-Di **12** 515-518

O'Reagan, Teague (literary character)
Brackenridge, Hugh Henry **2** 472-473

Oregon (state, United States)
exploration
Cabrillo, Juan Rodríguez **3** 204-205
Clark, William **4** 82-83
Cook, James **4** 214-215
Frémont, John Charles **6** 97-98
Gray, Robert **6** 508-509
Lewis, Meriwether **9** 391-392
missions
De Smet, Pierre Jean **4** 509-510
Whitman, Marcus **16** 248-249
settlement and statehood
Adams, John Quincy **1** 52-54
Applegate, Jesse **1** 264-265
Atchison, David Rice **1** 357-358
Buchanan, James **3** 89-90
Clayton, John Middleton **4** 96-97
Gallatin, Albert **6** 183-184
Kelley, Hall Jackson **8** 480
McLoughlin, John **10** 423-424
Polk, James Knox **12** 374-376

Oregon Trail (United States)
Bozeman, John M. **2** 471-472
Bridger, James **3** 2-3
Carson, Christopher **3** 334-335
Frémont, John Charles **6** 97-98

Parkman, Francis **12** 113-115
Whitman, Marcus **16** 248-249

Oregon Treaty (1846)
Aberdeen, 4th Earl of **1** 25-26
Buchanan, James **3** 89-90

O'Reilly, John Boyle (1844-1890), Irish-American editor
Schindler, Solomon **14** 7-8

ORELLANA, FRANCISCO DE (circa 1511-1546), Spanish explorer **11** 527-528
Benalcázar, Sebastián de **2** 145-146
Valdivia, Pedro de **15** 400-401

Orenburg Flying School (Union of Soviet Socialist Republics)
Gagarin, Yuri Alexeivich **6** 166-167

Oresme, Nicole (circa 1320-1382), French bishop and writer
Galileo Galilei **6** 180-183

Oresteia (trilogy; Aeschylus)
Aeschylus **1** 70-72-61
O'Neill, Eugene **11** 514-516

Orestes (died 476), Roman general
Odoacer **11** 473

Orestes (mythology)
Aeschylus **1** 70-72
Alfieri, Vittoria **1** 145-146
Euripides **5** 332-334
Racine, Jean Baptiste **12** 532-535
Sophocles **14** 343-345

Orfeo (opera)
Gluck, Christoph Willibald **6** 372-374
Monteverdi, Claudio Giovanni Antonio **11** 126-128
Rossi, Luigi **13** 310-311

Orford, 1st Earl of
see Walpole, Robert

Orford, 4th Earl of
see Walpole, Horace

Organ transplants (medicine)
Carrel, Alexis **3** 322-323
DeBakey, Michael Ellis **4** 437-438

Organic Articles (1802)
Pius VII **12** 334-335

Organic School (experimental school)
Johnson, Marietta Louise Pierce **8** 312-313

Organicism (philosophy)
Schelling, Friedrich Wilhelm Joseph von **13** 526-527

Organisation Africaine et Malagache de Cooperation Economique (OAMCE)
Houphouët-Boigny, Felix **7** 519-520

Organism, philosophy of
Whitehead, Alfred North **16** 242-244

Organization Common Africaine et Malagache (OCAM)
Houphouët-Boigny, Felix **7** 519-520

Organization for European Economic Cooperation (1948-1961)
Hammarskjöld, Dag **7** 100-101

Organization of African Unity (OAU)
Ahidjo, Ahmadou **1** 89-90
Haile Selassie **7** 68-70
Houphouët-Boigny, Felix **7** 519-520
Malcolm X **10** 165-166
Mondlane, Eduardo Chivambo **11** 100-101
Nkrumah, Kwame **11** 408-410

Organization of American States (OAS)
Balaguer y Ricardo, Joaquin **1** 460-461
Duvalier, François **5** 165-166
Kubitschek de Oliveira, Juscelino **9** 113-115
Lleras Camargo, Alberto **9** 467
Plaza Lasso, Galo **12** 350-351
Trujillo Molina, Rafael Leonidas **15** 313-314

Organization of Labor, The (essay)
Blanc, Louis **2** 318-319

Organization of Petroleum Exporting Countries (OPEC)
Yamani, Ahmed Zaki **16** 433-435

Organization Series (painting)
Gorky, Arshile **6** 458

Organizer effect (embryology)
Spemann, Hans **14** 368-369

Organon (book; Aristotle)
Whitehead, Alfred North **16** 242-244

Organum (music)
Léonin **9** 343-344
Pérotin **12** 231-232

Orge (play)
Menander **10** 477-478

Oribasius (circa 325-circa 400), Greek physician
Celsus, Aulus Cornelius **3** 393

Oribe, Manuel (1796-1857), Uruguayan general and politician
Rivera, Fructuoso **13** 184-185

Orient Express (book)
Dos Passos, John Roderigo **5** 69-71
Greene, Graham **6** 523-524

Oriental art
see individual countries (Chinese art, etc.)

Oriental Institute (University of Chicago)
Breasted, James Henry **2** 510-511

Orientales, Les (book; Hugo)
Leconte de Lisle, Charles Marie René **9** 273-274

Oriente Province (Cuba)
Castro Ruz, Fidel **3** 365-368
Céspedes, Carlos Manuel de **3** 398-399
Gómez, Máximo **6** 418-419
Maceo, Antonio **10** 88-90
Machado y Morales, Gerardo **10** 92-93

ORIGEN (Origenes Adamantius; circa 185-circa 254), Early Christian theologian **11** 528-529
Clement of Alexandria **4** 102-103
Jerome **8** 249

John Chrysostom **8** 280-281

Origin of Species (book; Darwin)
editions and translations
Gray, Asa **6** 506-507
Jacobsen, Jens Peter **8** 193-194
evolution
Darwin, Charles Robert **4** 397-399
influence of
Bergson, Henri **2** 191-192
Butler, Samuel **3** 183
Childe, Vere Gordon **3** 521-522
Vries, Hugo de **16** 33-36
opponents
Owen, Richard **12** 39
supporters
Galton, Francis **6** 193-194
Huxley, Thomas Henry **8** 77-79
Spencer, Herbert **14** 369-370
Wallace, Alfred Russel **16** 69-70
Weismann, August Freidrich
Leopold **16** 178-180
see also Evolution, organic; Natural
selection; Social Darwinism

Original sin (religion)
Chauncy, Charles **3** 485-486
Edwards, Jonathan **5** 220-222
Maistre, Joseph de **10** 153-154
Pelagius **12** 189-190

Original Sin (sculpture)
Quercia, Jacopo della **12** 509

Origines (book)
Cato, Marcus Porcius the Elder **3** 375

Origins, The (lithography series)
Redon, Odilon **13** 75-76

Orinoco (river; South America)
Quesada, Gonzalo Jiménez de
12 509-510

Orinoco, battle of (1817)
Bolívar, Simón **2** 375-377

Orion (astronomy)
Kapteyn, Jacobus Cornelis **8** 436-437

Oriskany, battle of (1777)
Brant, Joseph **2** 500-501
Burgoyne, John **3** 137-138

Orissa (state, India)
Clive, Robert **4** 119-120

Orkney Islands (Scotland)
Childe, Vere Gordon **3** 521-522
Harold I **7** 161-162
James III **8** 208-209

Orlando (novel)
Woolf, Virginia Stephen **16** 381-382

Orlando (opera)
Handel, George Frederick **7** 116-119

Orlando furioso (poem; Ariosto)
Ariosto, Ludovico **1** 289-290
Rossi, Luigi **13** 310-311
Tasso, Torquato **15** 114-116

Orlando innamorato (poem; Boiardo)
Ariosto, Ludovico **1** 289-290
Boiardo, Matteo Maria **2** 369

ORLANDO, VITTORIO EMMANUELE
(1860-1952), Italian statesman
11 529-530

ORLÉANS, CHARLES (1394-1465), French
prince and poet **11** 530
Charles VI **3** 460-461
Henry V **7** 296-297
Louis XII **9** 528-529
Villon, François **15** 499-501

Orléans, Gaston Jean Baptiste d'
(1608-1660), duc d'Orléans from 1626
Louis XIII **9** 529-531
Mansart, François **10** 211
Richelieu, Armand Jean du Plessis de
13 142-144

Orléans, Henrietta Anne, Duchesse d'
(1644-1670), English princess
La Fontaine, Jean de **9** 156-157

Orléans, Louis I, Duc d' (1372-1407),
French noble
Charles VI **3** 460-461
Charles VIII **3** 462-463

Orléans, Louis Philippe Joseph, Duc d'
see Philippe Egalité

ORLÉANS, PHILIPPE II (1674-1723),
French statesman, regent 1715-23
11 530-531
Saint-Simon, Duc de **13** 436

Orléans, Robert Philippe Louis Eugene Ferdinand d'
see Chartres, Duc de

Orléans, siege of (1428-1429)
Charles VIII **3** 462-463
Joan of Arc **8** 264-265

Orléans, synod of (1510)
Julius II **8** 384-386

Orlich, José Francisco (born 1908), Costa
Rican politician
Ferrer, José Figuéres **5** 428-429

Orlov, Count Gregory Grigorievich
(1734-1783), Russian general and statesman
Catherine the Great **3** 370-372

Ormond (novel)
Brown, Charles Brockden **3** 33
Edgeworth, Maria **5** 205-206

Ormuz, Strait of (Oman-Persian Gulfs)
Albuquerque, Afonso de **1** 118-119

Ormuzd (Persian religion)
Augustine **1** 367-370

Ornen (balloon)
Andrée, Salomon August **1** 226

Ornithine cycle (biochemistry)
Krebs, Hans Adolf **9** 95-97

Ornithology (science)
Audubon, John James **1** 366-367
Bailey, Florence Merriam **1** 443-444
Frederick II **6** 79
Wilson, Alexander **16** 313-314
see also Scientists—ornithologists

Orologio, L' (book)
Levi, Carlo **9** 364

Orontea (opera)
Cesti, Pietro **3** 399-400

Orosius (circa 390-after 418), Spanish
church historian
Alfred **1** 151-153
Pelagius **12** 189-190

Orozco, Carlos (born 1898), Mexican
painter
Siqueiros, David Alfaro **14** 256

OROZCO, JOSÉ CLEMENTE (1883-1949),
Mexican painter **12** 1-2
Azuela, Mariano **1** 402
Bearden, Romare Howard **2** 86-88
Siqueiros, David Alfaro **14** 256

Orpen, Sir William (1878-1931), British
painter
Sickert, Walter Richard **14** 212-213

Orphanages
Pestalozzi, Johann Heinrich **12** 249-250
Seton, Elizabeth Ann Bayley
14 118-119

Orphans of the Storm (film)
Griffith, David Wark **6** 544-545

Orphelin de la Chine, L' (play)
Voltaire **16** 14-16

Orpheus (ballet)
Balanchine, George **1** 461-462
Stravinsky, Igor Fedorovich **14** 502-506

Orpheus Descending (play)
Williams, Tennessee **16** 306-308

Orpheus in the Underworld (operetta)
Offenbach, Jacques **11** 478-479

Orpheus myth
Monteverdi, Claudio Giovanni Antonio
11 126-128
Poliziano, Angelo **12** 373-374
Virgil **15** 507-510

Orpheus und Eurydike (opera)
Krenek, Ernst **9** 98-99

Orphism (art)
Benton, Thomas Hart **2** 178-179
Delaunay, Robert **4** 475-476
Klee, Paul **9** 47-49
Marc, Franz **10** 231

ORR, BOBBY (Robert Gordon Orr; born
1948), Canadian hockey player **12** 2-4

ORR, JOHN BOYD (1st Baron Orr of
Brechin; 1880-1971), Scottish nutritionist
and UN official **12** 4-5

Orrery (astronomy)
Rittenhouse, David **13** 180-181

Orsanmichele (church, Florence)
Donatello **5** 55-56
Ghiberti, Lorenzo **6** 291-292

Orsino (play)
Rolland, Romain **13** 260

Orso (story)
Sienkiewicz, Henryk **14** 216-217

ORTEGA, DANIEL (born 1945), leader of the Sandinista National Liberation Front and president of Nicaragua **12** 5-7

ORTEGA Y GASSET, JOSÉ (1883-1955), Spanish philosopher and essayist **12** 7-8
Dilthey, Wilhelm Christian Ludwig **5** 10
Simmel, Georg **14** 234-235

Orteig, Raymond (1870-1939), French-born American restaurateur
Lindbergh, Charles Augustus **9** 421-423

ORTELIUS, ABRAHAM (Abraham, Ortels; 1527-1598), Flemish cartographer **12** 8-9
Mercator, Gerhardus **10** 511-512

Orthez, battle of (1814)
Wellington, 1st Duke of **16** 193-195

Orthobiosis, theory of (medicine)
Metchnikoff, Élie **10** 532-533

Orthodox Confession... (book)
Mogila, Peter **11** 74-75

Orthodox Eastern Church
and heresies
Basil the Great **2** 51-52
Eutyches **5** 335
and papacy
John XXIII **8** 277-280
Leo I **9** 329-330
Leo XIII **9** 334-336
Paul VI **12** 146-148
Pius XII **12** 339-340
iconoclastic controversy
Charlemagne **3** 445-447
medieval theologians
John of Damascus **8** 282
schism
Innocent III **8** 125-127
Photius **12** 283-284

Orthodoxy (book)
Chesterton, Gilbert Keith **3** 508-509

Ortis (book)
Foscolo, Ugo **6** 21

ORTIZ, SIMON J. (born 1941), Native American author and storyteller **12** 9-12

Ortodoxo party (Cuba)
Castro Ruz, Fidel **3** 365-368

ORTON, JOHN KINGSLEY ("Joe;" 1933-1967), British playwright **12** 12-14

Orvieto Cathedral (Italy)
Andrea Pisano **1** 225-226
Gentile da Fabriano **6** 266-267
Signorelli, Luca **14** 221-222

ORWELL, GEORGE (1903-1950), British novelist and essayist **12** 14-15

Os Lusiadas
see Lusiads, The

Os sertões (book)
Cunha, Euclides Rodrigues Pimenta da **4** 336-337

Osage Indians (North America)
La Flesche, Francis **9** 152-154

Osagyefo
see Nkrumah, Kwame

Osaka castle (Japan)
Eitoku, Kano **5** 242
Ieyasu, Tokugawa **8** 103-106

Osaka University (Japan)
Yukawa, Hideki **16** 481-482

Osawatomie (town, Kansas)
Brown, John **3** 39-41

Osborn, Henry Fairfield (1857-1935), American paleontologist
Andrews, Roy Chapman **1** 232-233

OSBORNE, JOHN (1929-1994), English playwright **12** 16-17

Osborne, Sir Thomas
see Danby, 1st Earl of

OSBORNE, THOMAS MOTT (1859-1926), American reformer **12** 17-18

Osborne Palace (Isle of Wight)
Victoria **15** 485-487

Osbourne, Lloyd (1868-1947), American writer
Stevenson, Robert Louis **14** 446-448

Oscar II (1829-1907), king of Sweden 1872-1907 and of Norway 1872-1905
Hedin, Sven Anders **7** 252-253
Nordenskjöld, Nils Adolf Erik **11** 421-422

OSCEOLA (circa 1800-1838), Seminole Indian war chief **12** 18

Oscillation theory (sociology)
Quételet, Lambert Adolphe Jacques **12** 510-511

OSGOOD, HERBERT LEVI (1855-1918), American historian **12** 18-19
Becker, Carl Lotus **2** 100-101
Schlesinger, Arthur Meier **14** 13

O'Shea, William Henry (1840-1905), Irish nationalist
Parnell, Charles Stewart **12** 117-119

Osiander, Andrew (1498-1552), German Lutheran clergyman
Copernicus, Nicolaus **4** 226-227
Cranmer, Thomas **4** 295-296

Osiris (journal)
Sarton, George **13** 490-491

Oskar II (ship)
Ford, Henry **6** 5-6

OSLER, SIR WILLIAM (1849-1919), Canadian physician **12** 19-20
Burton, Robert **3** 166-167
Cushing, Harvey Williams **4** 353-354
Jones, Ernest Alfred **8** 331-332
Penfield, Wilder Graves **12** 198-200

Oslo (city, Norway)
Harold III **7** 163

OSMAN I (Othman; 1259-1326), Turkish warrior-leader who established the Ottoman state as an independent entity **12** 20-22

Osmanli dynasty (Ottoman Empire)
Mahmud II **10** 145-147
Selim I **14** 94-95

Selim III **14** 95-96

OSMEÑA, SERGIO (1878-1961), Philippine lawyer and statesman **12** 22-24
Quezon, Manuel Luis **12** 511-513
Quirino, Elpidio **12** 519-520
Roxas, Manuel **13** 331-332

Osorio (play)
Coleridge, Samuel Taylor **4** 154-156

Ospedale degli Innocenti (Florence)
Brunelleschi, Filippo **3** 70-72
Sangallo family **13** 464-466

Ospitale della Pietà (Venice)
Vivaldi, Antonio **16** 3-4

Osservanza, Church of the (Siena)
Sassetta **13** 492

Osservanza Master (flourished 1st half of 15th century), Italian painter
Sassetta **13** 492

Ossewabrandwag (political organization; South Africa)
Vorster, Balthazar Johannes **16** 30-32

Ossi di seppia (poetry)
Montale, Eugenio **11** 117-118

Ossian (flourished circa 3d century), legendary Irish warrior and bard
Goethe, Johann Wolfgang von **6** 388-391
Wordsworth, William **16** 385-388
Yeats, William Butler **16** 445-447

Ossoli, Angelo (died 1850), Italian marquis and political activist
Fuller, Sarah Margaret **6** 150-151

Ostade, Adriaen van (1610-1685), Dutch genre painter and etcher
Brouwer, Adriaen **3** 29-30

Ostend Manifesto (1854)
Buchanan, James **3** 89-90
Marcy, William Learned **10** 247-248
Soulé, Pierre **14** 351-352

Ostende, battle of (1745)
Saxe, Comte de **13** 507-508

Osterhofen abbey church (Bavaria)
Asam, Cosmas Damian and Egid Quirin **1** 323-324

Osterley Park House (Middlesex)
Adam, Robert and James **1** 38-40

Ostracism (ancient Greece)
Cleisthenes **4** 98-99
Pericles **12** 219-221

Ostrogoths (German tribe; ruled Italy 493-555)
Belisarius **2** 128-129
Cassiodorus, Flavius Magnus Aurelius **3** 357-358
Justinian I **8** 393-395
Procopius of Caesarea **12** 457-458
Theodoric the Great **15** 175-176
Ulfilas **15** 384

Ostrovsky, Aleksandr (1823-1886), Russian playwright

Eisenstein, Sergei Mikhailovich
 5 240-242
Meyerhold, Vsevolod Emilievich **10** 539

Ostwald, Wilhelm (1853-1932), German
 physical chemist
Arrhenius, Svante August **1** 318-320
Boltzmann, Ludwig **2** 379-380

Osuna, Duke of (1574-1624), Spanish sol-
 dier and statesman
Goya y Lucientes, Francisco de Paula
 José de **6** 476-478

Oswald, F.
 see Engels, F.

Oswald, Lee Harvey (1939-1963), pre-
 sumed assassin of John F. Kennedy
Kennedy, John Fitzgerald **8** 502-506

Oswald, Richard (1705-1784), British
 diplomat
Adams, John **1** 48-51

Oswego (fort, Canada)
Montcalm de Saint-Véran, Marquis de
 11 122-123

Oswego River (New York State)
Champlain, Samuel de **3** 419-421

Oswolt Krell (portrait)
Dürer, Albrecht **5** 159-161

Otaheite
 see Tahiti

Otani University (Kyoto, Japan)
Suzuki, Daisetz Teitaro **15** 46-47

Otello (opera)
Verdi, Giuseppe Fortunino Francesco
 15 463-465

Othello (play; Shakespeare)
Forrest, Edwin **6** 11-12
Lessing, Gotthold Ephraim **9** 357-359
Robeson, Paul Leroy **13** 198-199
Shakespeare, William **14** 142-145

**Other America: Poverty in the United
 States, The** (book)
Harrington, Michael **7** 167-169

Other Fires (novel)
Gorky, Maxim **6** 458-460

Other Inquisitions (essays)
Borges, Jorge Luis **2** 411-412

Othman (575?-656), third caliph of Islam
Ali **1** 155-156
Muawiya ibn Abu Sufyan **11** 223-224

Otho, Marcus Salvius (32-69), Roman
 emperor
Titus Flavius Vespasianus **15** 247-248
Vespasian **15** 475-476

Otho the Great (play)
Keats, John **8** 470-472

Otis, Charles (1835-1927), American
 inventor
Otis, Elisha Graves **12** 24

Otis elevator
Eiffel, Alexandre Gustave **5** 227-228

Otis Elevator Co.
Sprague, Frank Julian **14** 385-386

OTIS, ELISHA GRAVES (1811-1861),
 American manufacturer and inventor
12 24

OTIS, HARRISON GRAY (1765-1848),
 American statesman **12** 25
Bulfinch, Charles **3** 116-117
Morison, Samuel Eliot **11** 175-176

OTIS, JAMES, JR. (1725-1783), American
 Revolutionary statesman **12** 25-27
Dickinson, John **4** 543-544
Hutchinson, Thomas **8** 71-72

Otluk-beli, battle of (1472)
Mehmed the Conqueror **10** 452-454

Otomi language (Mexican Indian language)
Serra, Junípero **14** 111-112

Otranto (city; Italy)
Dandolo, Enrico **4** 386-387

Otrar (town, C.Asia)
Genghis Khan **6** 263-265

Otro rostro del peronismo, El (essay)
Sábato, Ernesto **13** 399-400

O-Tsuya Goroshi (novel)
Tanizaki, Junichiro **15** 101-102

Ottawa (city, Canada)
Currie, Arthur William **4** 345

Ottawa Agreement (1932)
Lyons, Joseph Aloysius **10** 69-70

Ottawa Indians (North America)
Brûlé, Étienne **3** 67-68
McCoy, Isaac **10** 403
Pontiac **12** 393-394

Ottawa River (Quebec city)
Champlain, Samuel de **3** 419-421

OTTERBEIN, PHILIP WILLIAM
 (1726-1813), American clergyman
12 27-28

Otterburn, battle of (1388)
Robert II **13** 194

OTTO I (912-973), Holy Roman emperor
 936-973 **12** 28-29
Henry I **7** 285-286

Otto II (955-983), Holy Roman emperor
 973-983
Otto I **12** 28-29
Otto III **12** 29-30

OTTO III (980-1002), Holy Roman emper-
 or 996-1002 and German king 983-1002
12 29-30
Bouts, Dirk **2** 458-459

Otto IV (circa 1174?-1218), Holy Roman
 emperor 1198-1215
Frederick II **6** 79
Innocent III **8** 125-127
John **8** 274-275
Philip II **12** 268-269
Vogelweide, Walther von der **16** 10-11

OTTO, LOUIS KARL RUDOLF
 (1869-1937), German interpreter of religion **12** 30-32

Otto, Nicholas August (1832-1891), Ger-
 man technician
Daimler, Gottlieb **4** 368
Peters, Carl **12** 257-258

Otto, Rudolf (1869-1937), German theologian
Söderblom, Nathan **14** 323-324

Otto Hahn (nuclear ship)
Hahn, Otto **7** 64-65

OTTO OF FREISING (circa 1114-1158),
 German historiographer and philosopher
 of history **12** 30

Otto the Great
 see Otto I

Ottoboni, Cardinal Pietro
 see Alexander VIII

Ottocar II (1230?-1278), king of Bohemia
 1253-78
Rudolf I **13** 347-348

Ottoman Empire (13th century -1918)
 • EXPANSION
  architecture
   Sinan, Kodja Mimar **14** 245-246
  Asia Minor
   Mehmed the Conqueror
    10 452-454
  Austrian wars
   Charles V **3** 457-459
   Eugene of Savoy **5** 330-331
   Suleiman I **15** 20-21
  consolidation
   Mehmed the Conqueror
    10 452-454
   Osman I **12** 20-22
   Selim I **14** 94-95
  Hungarian wars
   Augustus II **1** 373-374
   Charles V **3** 457-459
   Ferdinand I **5** 414-415
   Hunyadi, John **8** 51-52
   Mehmed the Conqueror
    10 452-454
   Sigismund **14** 220-221
   Suleiman I **15** 20-21
  Lepanto defeat
   see Lepanto, battle of
  Persian wars
   Abbas I **1** 4-6
   Khosrow I **8** 538-539
   Suleiman I **15** 20-21
  Poland invaded
   John III **8** 276-277
   see also Byzantine Empire; Cru-
    sades; Hungary
 • STAGNATION and DECLINE
  Austria and
   Eugene of Savoy **5** 330-331
   Frederick II **6** 81-84
   Joseph II **8** 359-360
   Leopold II **9** 346

Egypt and
Fuad I **6** 139
Ibrahim Pasha **8** 97-98
Ismail Pasha **8** 150-151
Mohammed Ali **11** 81-82
see also Egypt
England and
Abdullah ibn Husein **1** 19-20
Gladstone, William Ewart
6 357-360
Glubb, John Bagot **6** 371-372
Gordon, Charles George
6 448-449
Palmerston, 3d Viscount
12 81-83
Greece and
Canning, George **3** 258-260
Crane, Stephen **4** 293-295
Herzegovinian revolt
Peter I **12** 256
Italy and
Enver Pasha **5** 290-291
Giolitti, Giovanni **6** 339-340
military expansion
Köprülü, Ahmed **9** 84-85
Palestine issue
Abdul-Hamid II **1** 17-18
Herzl, Theodor **7** 352-354
Persia and
Karim Khan Zand **8** 447
reforms
Abdul-Hamid II **1** 17-18
Mahmud II **10** 145-147
Selim III **14** 95-96
Russia and
Chicherin, Georgi Vasilyevich
3 516-517
Nesselrode, Karl Robert
11 348-349
see also Russo-Turkish wars
Sweden and
Charles XII **3** 464-466
• WORLD WAR I and DISSOLUTION
Arab Revolt
see Arab Revolt
dissolution
Allenby, Edmund Henry Hyn-
man **1** 171-172
Atatürk, Ghazi Mustapha Kemal
1 356-357
Enver Pasha **5** 290-291
Lawrence, Thomas Edward
9 253-254
nationalism
Faisal I **5** 370-371
Gökalp, Mehmet Ziya **6** 395-396
Venizelos, Eleutherios
15 460-461
see also Balkan States; Barbary
States; Byzantine Empire;
Crimean War
World War I
see World War I

Ottomanism (political movement ; Turkey)
Gökalp, Mehmet Ziya **6** 395-396

Ottone (opera)
Handel, George Frederick **7** 116-119
Ottonian Renaissance (Europe)
Otto I **12** 28-29
OUD, JACOBUS JOHANNES PIETER
(1890-1963), Dutch architect **12** 32
van Doesburg, Theo **15** 421
Mies van der Rohe, Ludwig **11** 10-12
Rietveld, Gerrit Thomas **13** 169
Oudenaarde, battle of (1708)
Eugene of Savoy **5** 330-331
Marlborough, 1st Duke of **10** 271-272
Oudh (province , Northern India)
Dalhousie, 1st Marquess of **4** 375-376
Oudry, Jean Baptiste (1686-1755), French
painter
Boucher, François **2** 440-442
Our American Cousin (play)
Booth, John Wilkes **2** 404
Jefferson, Joseph **8** 237
Our Country (book)
Strong, Josiah **14** 512-513
Our Daily Bread (novel)
Grove, Frederick Philip **7** 20-21
**Our Exagmination round his Factification
...** (essays)
Beckett, Samuel **2** 102-104
Our Lady of the Flowers (novel)
Genet, Jean **6** 262-263
Our Man in Havana (novel, film; Greene)
Coward, Noel **4** 279-280
Greene, Graham **6** 523-524
Our Mutual Friend (novel)
Dickens, Charles John Huffam
4 538-541
Our Old Home (book)
Hawthorne, Nathaniel **7** 212-215
Our Penal Machinery and Its Victims
(book; Altgeld)
Altgeld, John Peter **1** 180-182
Darrow, Clarence Seward **4** 396-397
Our People's Dreams (play)
Betti, Ugo **2** 246
Our Town (play; Wilder)
Copland, Aaron **4** 227-228
Wilder, Thornton Niven **16** 276-277
Ourique, battle of (1139)
Alfonso I **1** 148
Ousia (theology)
Basil the Great **2** 51-52
OUSMANE, SEMBENE (born 1923), Sene-
galese novelist and film maker **12** 32-33
Out of Season (story)
Hemingway, Ernest Miller **7** 274-277
Out of the Cradle Endlessly Rocking
(poem)
Whitman, Walt **16** 249-251
Out of the Dark (book)
Keller, Helen Adams **8** 479-480

Out of the Depth (poem)
Bialik, Hayyim Nahman **2** 262-263
Outback Marriage, An (novel)
Paterson, Andrew Barton **12** 131-132
Outcast of the Islands, An (novel)
Conrad, Joseph **4** 205-207
Outcast, The (novel)
Pirandello, Luigi **12** 319-321
Outcasts of Poker Flat, The (story)
Harte, Francis Brett **7** 184-185
Outcault, R. F. (1863-1928), American car-
toonist
Luks, George Benjamin **10** 38-39
Outdoor painting
see Plein-air painting
Outlaw, The (sculpture)
Rembrandt Harmensz van Rijn
13 91-95
Outlaws
see Criminals
Outlook, The (periodical)
Beecher, Henry Ward **2** 112-113
Stella, Joseph **14** 422
Outlook Tower (sociology laboratory)
Geddes, Patrick **6** 246-247
Out, Out— (poem)
Frost, Robert Lee **6** 130-133
Outram, Sir Francis (1803-1863), British
officer of the Indian Civil Service
Bates, Daisy Mae **2** 52-53
Outre-Mer (essays)
Longfellow, Henry Wadsworth
9 499-500
Outremeuse, Jean d' (1338-1400), Liège
chronicler
Mandeville, John **10** 192-193
Outsider, The (novel)
Wright, Richard **16** 401-402
Ouwater, Albert van (flourished circa
1445-1480), Dutch painter
Bouts, Dirk **2** 458-459
Geertgen tot Sint Jans **6** 248
OU-YANG HSIU (1007-1072), Chinese
author and statesman **12** 33-34
Ssu-ma kuang **14** 390-391
Su Shih **15** 39-40
Wang An-shih **16** 95-97
Ovando, Nicolás de (1460?-1518?), Span-
ish colonial governor
Las Casas, Bartolomé de **9** 211-212
Over Prairie Trails (essays)
Grove, Frederick Philip **7** 20-21
Over the Barriers (poems)
Pasternak, Boris Leonidovich
12 124-125
Over the Blue Mountain (novel)
Richter, Conrad Michael **13** 148-149
Over the Rainbow (song)
Garland, Judy **6** 218-219

Over the River ... (painting)
Moses, Grandma **11** 201-202

Over the Teacups (essays)
Holmes, Oliver Wendell **7** 457-458

Over There (song)
Cohan, George Michael **4** 137-138

Overbury, Sir Thomas (1581-1613), English poet
Webster, John **16** 164

Overcoat, The (story)
Gogol, Nikolai **6** 391-393

Overland Mail (stagecoach line)
Butterfield, John **3** 184-185
Fargo, William George **5** 380-381

Overreach, Sir Giles (literary character)
Massinger, Philip **10** 324-325

Overseas College (Milan, Italy)
Paul VI **12** 146-148

Overseas Workers' Association (London, England)
Ho Chi Minh **7** 426-428

Over-soul, The (essay)
Emerson, Ralph Waldo **5** 278-280

Overweg, Adolf (1822-1852), German explorer
Barth, Heinrich **2** 30-31

OVID (Publius Ovidius Naso; 43 B.C.-circa. A.D. 18), Roman elegiac and epic poet **12** 34-36
Golden Age
Augustus **1** 371-373
Veronese, Paolo **15** 469-470
Virgil **15** 507-510
in art
Bernini, Gian Lorenzo **2** 214-216
Titian **15** 242-244
influence of
Drayton, Michael **5** 97-98
Góngora y Argote, Luis de **6** 427-428
Guillaume de Lorris **7** 33-34
Joyce, James **8** 365-367
Pope, Alexander **12** 395-397
Poussin, Nicolas **12** 418-420
Velázquez, Diego Rodríguez de Silva y **15** 454-456
influenced by
Callimachus **3** 235-236
Sappho **13** 479-480
translations
Chrestien de Troyes **4** 23-24
Congreve, William **4** 200-201
Dryden, John **5** 106-107

Ovid's Banquet of Sense (poem)
Chapman, George **3** 440-441

Oviedo, University of (Spain)
Altamira Y Crevea, Rafael **1** 179

OVINGTON, MARY WHITE (1865-1951), civil rights reformer and a founder of the National Association for the Advancement of Colored People **12** 36-37

Owain ap Gruffydd
see Glendower, O.

OWEN, DAVID ANTHONY LLEWELLYN (born 1938), English peace envoy in former Yugoslavia for the European Community **12** 37-39

OWEN, ROBERT (1771-1858), British socialist pioneer **12** 39-40
Cole, George Douglas Howard **4** 146-147
Engels, Friedrich **5** 286-288
Godwin, William **6** 383-384
Owen, Robert Dale **12** 40-41
Rapp, George **13** 42-43

OWEN, ROBERT DALE (1801-1877), Scottish-born American legislator **12** 40-41
Cabet, Étienne **3** 196
Wright, Frances **16** 397-398

OWEN, RUTH BRYAN (1885-1954), American congresswoman, diplomat, and author **12** 41-43

OWEN, SIR RICHARD (1804-1892), English zoologist **12** 39
Huxley, Thomas Henry **8** 77-79

Owen, Wilfred (1893-1918), English poet
Lewis, Cecil Day **9** 380

Owens, James Cleveland
see Owens, Jesse

OWENS, JESSE (1913-1980), African American track star **12** 43-44

Owens, R. B. (1870-1940), American electrical engineer
Rutherford, Ernest **13** 384-387

Owens College (Manchester, England)
Jevons, William Stanley **8** 255-256

Owl, The (poem)
Drayton, Michael **5** 97-98
Heavysege, Charles **7** 246

Owl and the Nightingale, The (poem; Nicholas de Guildford)
Layamon **9** 256-257

Owl and the Pussy Cat (poem; Lear)
Lear, Edward **9** 265-266
Stravinsky, Igor Fedorovich **14** 502-506

Ox and the Roof, The (mime drama)
Cocteau, Jean **4** 132-133

OXENSTIERNA, COUNT AXEL GUSTAFS-SON (1583-1654), Swedish statesman **12** 44-45
Gustavus II **7** 43-45-23

Oxford, 1st Earl of
see Harley, Robert

Oxford, Provisions of (1258)
Montfort, Simon de **11** 132-133

Oxford and Asquith, 1st Earl of
see Asquith, Herbert Henry

Oxford History ... (reference series)
Collingwood, Robin George **4** 162
Morison, Samuel Eliot **11** 175-176

Oxford idealism (philosophy)
Jowett, Benjamin **8** 364-365

Oxford movement (religion; England)
Clough, Arthur Hugh **4** 123-124
Gladstone, William Ewart **6** 357-360
Newman, John Henry **11** 365-367
Pusey, Edward Bouverie **12** 488-489

Oxford Symphony (musical composition)
Haydn, Franz Joseph **7** 219-221

Oxford Union (England)
Burne-Jones, Edward Coley **3** 145-146
Manning, Henry Edward **10** 209-210

Oxford unit (medicine)
Florey, Howard Walter **5** 491-492

Oxford University (England)
astronomy
Bradley, James **2** 482-483
biology
Haldane, John Burdon Sanderson **7** 70-71
Krebs, Hans Adolf **9** 95-97
chancellors
Laud, William **9** 224-225
Salisbury, 3d Marquess of **13** 448-449
chemistry
Hinshelwood, Cyril Norman **7** 405-406
Soddy, Frederick **14** 321-323
endowments
Gloucester, Duke of **6** 370-371
Rhodes, Cecil John **13** 120-122
language and literature
Auden, Wystan Hugh **1** 364-366
Jowett, Benjamin **8** 364-365
Lewis, Cecil Day **9** 380
Wang T'ao **16** 105-106
law
Bryce, James **3** 85
Maine, Henry James Sumner **10** 152
Vinogradoff, Paul Gavrilovitch **15** 503
medicine
Florey, Howard Walter **5** 491-492
Osler, William **12** 19-20
Sherrington, Charles Scott **14** 187-189
philosophy
Alexander, Samuel **1** 141
Austin, John Langshaw **1** 379-380
Bosanquet, Bernard **2** 425-426
Bradley, Francis Herbert **2** 481-482
Cassirer, Ernst **3** 358-359
Collingwood, Robin George **4** 162
Radhakrishnan, Sarvepalli **12** 537-538
Strawson, Peter Fredrick **14** 506-507
physics
Schrödinger, Erwin **14** 31-33
Szilard, Leo **15** 64-66
social sciences
Arnold, Thomas **1** 313-314
Attlee, Clement Richard **1** 361-362
Busia, Kofi Abrefa **3** 172-173

Chapman, Sydney **3** 441
Cole, George Douglas Howard
  4 146-147
Evans-Pritchard, Edward Evan **5** 340
Morison, Samuel Eliot **11** 175-176
Polanyi, Karl **12** 372
Ruskin, John **13** 371-372
Tylor, Edward Burnett **15** 372-373
Wilson, James Harold **16** 324-325
Woodward, Comer Vann
  16 378-379
Wren, Christopher **16** 393-394
theology
  Colet, John **4** 157-158
  Hooker, Richard **7** 475-476
  Macquarrie, John **10** 116-117

Pusey, Edward Bouverie **12** 488-489

Oxygen (element—chemistry)
  Couper, Archibald Scott **4** 269-270
  Dumas, Jean Baptiste André **5** 138-139
  Fischer, Hans **5** 457-459
  Hinshelwood, Cyril Norman **7** 405-406
  Ingenhousz, Jan **8** 119-120
  Lavoisier, Antoine Laurent **9** 241-244
  Meyerhof, Otto Fritz **10** 537-539
  Priestley, Joseph **12** 452-453
  Scheele, Karl Wilhelm **13** 525-526
  Tsiolkovsky, Konstantin Eduardovich
    15 326-328

Oxymuriatic acid gas
  see Chlorine

Oxytocin (pituitary extract)
  Dale, Henry Hallett **4** 371-373

O-yo-mei school (Japanese philosophy)
  Wang Yang-ming **16** 108-109

OZ, AMOS (born 1939), Israeli author
  12 45-47

Oz, Wizard of
  Baum, L. Frank **2** 73-74

OZAL, TURGUT (born 1927), Turkish
  prime minister and president **12** 47-49

OZAWA, SEIJI (born 1935), Japanese musician and conductor **12** 49-51

Ozenfant, Amédée (1886-1966), French
  painter
  Le Corbusier **9** 274-275

P

PA CHIN (pen name of Li Fei-kan; born 1904), Chinese novelist **12** 53-54

På Glente Veie (novel)
Rölvaag, Ole Edvart **13** 265

Pacelli, Eugenio Maria Giuseppe
see Pius XII

Pacem in terris (encyclical)
John, XXIII **8** 277-280

Pacheco, Francisco (circa 1564-1654), Spanish painter
Velázquez, Diego Rodríguez de Silva y **15** 454-456

Pacheco y Padilla, Juan Vicente Güemes
see Revillagigedo, Conde de

PACHELBEL, JOHANN (1653-1706), German composer and organist **12** 52

PACHER, MICHAEL (circa 1435-98), Austro-German painter and wood carver **12** 53
Altdorfer, Albrecht **1** 179-180
Cranach, Lucas the Elder **4** 289-290

Pacific, War of the (1879-1884)
Balmaceda Fernández, José Manuel **1** 475-476
González Prada, Manuel **6** 431
Leguía y Salcedo, Augusto Bernardino **9** 305-306

Pacific Coast (United States)
Bancroft, Hubert Howe **1** 484-485
Cook, James **4** 214-215
Crook, George **4** 322-323
Gray, Robert **6** 508-509
Mackenzie, Alexander **10** 103-104
Revillagigedo, Conde de **13** 111-112

Pacific Express Co.
Fargo, William George **5** 380-381

Pacific Ocean
Balboa, Vasco Núñez de **1** 462-463
Banks, Joseph **1** 489-490
Bering, Vitus **2** 193-194
Bougainville, Louis Antoine de **2** 443-444
Columbus, Christopher **4** 176-179

Cook, James **4** 214-215
Dampier, William **4** 384
Kotzebue, Otto von **9** 91-92

Pacific Poems (book)
Miller, Joaquin **11** 27-28

Pacific Railway Scandal (1873; Canada)
Fleming, Sandford **5** 485-486
Smith, Donald Alexander **14** 288-289
see also Transcontinental railroad (Canada)

Pacific Steamship Navigation Co.
Vanderbilt, Cornelius **15** 415-416
Wheelwright, William **16** 223-224

Pacific 231 (musical composition)
Honegger, Arthur **7** 472-473

Pacific War Council (London)
Bruce of Melbourne, 1st Viscount **3** 61-62
Evatt, Herbert Vere **5** 341-343

Pacifico, David (1784-1854), Portuguese consul in Greece
Palmerston, 3d Viscount **12** 81-83

Pacifism (philosophy)
Austria
Suttner, Bertha von **15** 42-44
Canada
Woodsworth, James Shaver **16** 376
England
Astor, Nancy Langhorne **1** 352-354
Cobden, Richard **4** 127-128
Doyle, Arthur Conan **5** 91-92
Gooch, George Peabody **6** 432-433
Morley, John **11** 178-179
Russell, Bertrand Arthur William **13** 373-374
Tippett, Michael Kemp **15** 234-235
France
Fourier, François Charles Marie **6** 31-32
Germany
Kelly, Petra **8** 486-487
Toller, Ernst **15** 261
Hungary
Polanyi, Karl **12** 372
Schwimmer, Rosika **14** 57-60
Italy

Paul VI **12** 146-148
Japan
Katayama, Sen **8** 457
Latin America
Pérez Esquivel, Adolfo **12** 215-217
Sweden
Nobel, Alfred Bernhard **11** 410-411
U.S. (18th-19th century)
Burritt, Elihu **3** 160
Jay, William **8** 232-233
Ladd, William **9** 149
Woolman, John **16** 382-383
U.S. (19th-20th century)
Addams, Jane **1** 56-57
Andrews, Fannie Fern Phillips **1** 231-232
Butler, Nicholas Murray **3** 181
Clark, John Bates **4** 76-77
Wald, Lillian **16** 53-54
U.S. (20th century)
Balch, Emily Greene **1** 463-464
Bourne, Randolph Silliman **2** 456-457
Catt, Carrie Chapman **3** 375-376
Dellinger, David **4** 480-481
Ford, Henry **6** 5-6
Fosdick, Harry Emerson **6** 21-22
Hillquit, Morris **7** 393-394
Holmes, John Haynes **7** 456-457
Muste, Abraham Johannes **11** 276-277
Rankin, Jeannette Pickering **13** 35-37
Rustin, Bayard **13** 382-383
Villard, Oswald Garrison **15** 498-499

PACKARD, DAVID (1912-1996), cofounder of Hewlett-Packard Company and deputy secretary of defense under President Nixon **12** 54-56

Pact, A (poem)
Pound, Ezra Loomis **12** 415-417

Pact of Succession (Sweden; 1604)
Gustavus II **7** 43-45

Pacuvius, Marcus (200-circa 130 B.C.), Roman dramatist
Ennius, Quintus **5** 289

647

Paddle wheel (steamboats)
Fitch, John **5** 467-468
Fulton, Robert **6** 151-152

PADEREWSKI, IGNACE JAN (1860-1941), Polish pianist, composer, and statesman **12** 56-57
Chopin, Frédéric François **4** 16-18
Pilsudski, Joseph **12** 305-306

Padmavati (ballet-opera)
Roussel, Albert **13** 328-329

PADMORE, GEORGE (1902/03-1959), Trinidadian leftist political activist **12** 57-58
Diagne, Blaise **4** 527
Du Bois, William Edward Burghardt **5** 116-118
Kenyatta, Jomo **8** 512-514
Nkrumah, Kwame **11** 408-410
Wallace-Johnson, Isaac Theophilus Akunna **16** 76-77

Padovano, Annibale (circa 1527-1575), Italian organist
Merulo, Claudio **10** 525-526

Padrón, Real (map)
Vespucci, Amerigo **15** 476-478

Padrona, La (play)
Betti, Ugo **2** 246

Padua (city, Italy)
Mantegna, Andrea **10** 215-216
Pomponazzi, Pietro **12** 390-391
Visconti, Gian Galeazzo **15** 510-511

Padua, University of (Italy)
Feltre, Vittorino da **5** 409-410
Galileo Galilei **6** 180-183
Morgagni, Giovanni Battista **11** 158-159

Paekche (Korean kingdom)
see Korea—50-668 (Paekche)

Paër, Ferdinando (1771-1839), Italian opera composer
Liszt, Franz **9** 445-447

Paese delle vacanze, Il (play)
Betti, Ugo **2** 246

Paesi tuoi (novel)
Pavese, Cesare **12** 154-155

Paestum (ancient city, Italy)
Labrouste, Pierre François Henri **9** 144
Soufflot, Jacques Germain **14** 349-350

PÁEZ, JOSÉ ANTONIO (1790-1873), Venezuelan general and president 1831-46 **12** 58
Santander, Franciso de Paula **13** 475

Pagan, Min (ruled 1846-1852), king of Burma
Mindon Min **11** 47

Pagan Spain (book)
Wright, Richard **16** 401-402

Paganelli, Bernando
see Eugenius III

PAGANINI, NICCOLO (1782-1840), Italian violinist and composer **12** 58-59

Berlioz, Louis Hector **2** 203-205
Chopin, Frédéric François **4** 16-18
Liszt, Franz **9** 445-447
Schumann, Robert Alexander **14** 41-43

Paganism
Constantine I **4** 209-211
Judas Maccabeus **8** 374-375
Julian **8** 378-379
Stilicho, Flavius **14** 452-453

PAGE, THOMAS NELSON (1853-1922), American author and diplomat **12** 59-60

PAGE, WALTER HINES (1855-1918), American journalist and diplomat **12** 60-61

Page, William (1811-1885), American painter
Brady, Mathew B. **2** 487-488
Inness, George **8** 123-124

Pageant and Other Poems, A (book)
Rossetti, Christina Georgina **13** 307-308

Pageant of Abinger, The (essay)
Forster, Edward Morgan **6** 14-16

PAGELS, ELAINE HIESEY (born 1943), historian of religion **12** 61-62

Pagliacci (opera; Leoncavallo)
Caruso, Enrico **3** 345
Toscanini, Arturo **15** 270-271

Pahlavi dynasty (Iran; reigned since 1925)
Mohammad Reza Shah Pahlavi **11** 75-76
Reza Shah Pahlavi **13** 116-117

Pahouin (West African people)
see Fang

PAIGE, SATCHEL (Leroy Robert Paige; 1906-1982), African American baseball player **12** 62-65

Pai-hua style (Chinese literature)
Hu Shih **8** 63-65
Lu Hsün **10** 35-37

Pailleron Children (painting)
Sargent, John Singer **13** 481-482

Paine, Albert Bigelow (1861-1937), American author and journalist
Twain, Mark **15** 363-366

Paine, James (circa 1716-1789), English architect
Adam, Robert and James **1** 38-40

PAINE, JOHN KNOWLES (1839-1905), American composer **12** 65

PAINE, THOMAS (1737-1809), English-born American journalist and Revolutionary propagandist **12** 66-67
associates
Barlow, Joel **2** 6-7
Miranda, Francisco de **11** 52-53
political influence
Adams, John Quincy **1** 52-54
Godwin, William **6** 383-384
O'Connell, Daniel **11** 465-467
Rush, Benjamin **13** 364-365
religious influence

Booth, Joseph **2** 404-405
Evans, George Henry **5** 337-338

Painful Stories (book)
Čapek, Karel **3** 271-272

Painter at His Easel (painting)
Rembrandt Harmensz van Rijn **13** 91-95

Painters
see Artists—painters

Painting (painting)
Miró, Joan **11** 53-54

Pair of Blue Eyes, A (novel)
Hardy, Thomas **7** 150-152

Pais chez les bêtes, La (stories)
Colette, Sidonie Gabrielle **4** 158-159

Paisan (film)
Fellini, Federico **5** 408-409

Paisiello, Giovanni (1741-1816), Italian composer
Cimarosa, Domenico **4** 61-62

PAISLEY, IAN K. (born 1926), political leader and minister of religion in Northern Ireland **12** 67-69

Paiute Indians (North America)
Comstock, Henry Tompkins Paige **4** 189
Sapir, Edward **13** 478-479
Winnemucca, Sarah **16** 336-338
Wovoka **16** 390-393

Pak Chong-hŭi
see Park, Chung Hee

Pak Hon-yong (died 1955), Korean statesman
Kim Il-sung **9** 4-6

Pakistan, Islamic Republic of (nation, Southern Asia)
after 1971
Bhutto, Benazir **2** 259-261
Bhutto, Zulfikar Ali **2** 261-262
Leghari, Sardar Farooq Ahmed Khan **9** 303-305
and Bengalis
Mujibur Rahman **11** 234-236
early history
Kanishka **8** 428-429
independence (1947)
Attlee, Clement Richard **1** 361-362
Ayub Khan, Mohammed **1** 395-396
Iqbal, Muhammad **8** 132-133
Jinnah, Mohammad Ali **8** 262-263
Liaquat Ali Khan **9** 397
Patel, Vallabhbhai **12** 129-130
Sapru, Tej Bahadur **13** 480-481
Indian opponents
Gandhi, Indira Priyadarshini **6** 200-201
Gandhi, Mohandas Karamchand **6** 201-204
Menon, Vengalil Krishnan Krishna **10** 507-509
Islam and
Mawdūdī, Abu-I A'la **10** 353-354
martial law

Zia ul-Haq, Mohammad
16 513-515
treaties
Chou En-lai **4** 20-22
Dulles, John Foster **5** 134-135

Pakistan People's Party
Bhutto, Zulfikar Ali **2** 261-262
Leghari, Sardar Farooq Ahmed Khan
9 303-305

Pal Joey (musical)
O'Hara, John **11** 485
Rodgers, Richard Charles **13** 234-236

Palace and Gardens of Versailles (painting)
Vanderlyn, John **15** 417

Palace at 4 A. M. (sculpture)
Giacometti, Alberto **6** 294-295

Palace of Art, The (poem)
Tennyson, Alfred **15** 144-146

Palace of Fine Arts (Mexico City)
Rivera, Diego **13** 183-184

Palace of Honor, The (poem)
Douglas, Gavin **5** 77-78

Palace of Labor (Turin)
Nervi, Pier Luigi **11** 346-348

Palace of the Dawn (Brasilia)
Niemeyer Soares Filho, Oscar
11 389-390

Palace of Truth, The (play)
Gilbert, William Schwenck **6** 314-315

Palacio da Alvorada (Brasilia)
Niemeyer Soares Filho, Oscar
11 389-390

PALACKÝ, FRANTIŠEK (1798-1876), Czech
historian and statesman **12** 69-70

Palaeologan dynasty (Byzantine Empire;
ruled 1261-1453)
Constantine XI **4** 211-212
Michael VIII **11** 1-2

Palafox y Melzi, José de (1775-1847),
Spanish soldier, captain general of
Aragon
Azara, Félix de **1** 397-398

Palais Stoclet (Brussels)
Hoffmann, Josef **7** 440-441

PALAMAS, KOSTES (1859-1943), Greek
poet **12** 70

Palamedes (play)
Vondel, Joost van den **16** 19-20

Palatine Chapel (Palermo)
Roger II **13** 244-245

Palazzo (Italian palace)
Barberini (Rome)
Bernini, Gian Lorenzo **2** 214-216
Borromini, Francesco **2** 424-425
Cortona, Pietro da **4** 256
Maderno, Carlo **10** 117-118
Branconio dell'Aquila (Rome)
Raphael **13** 40-42
Carignano (Turin)
Guarini, Guarino **7** 25-26

Chiericati
see Museo Civico (Vicenza)
dei Conservatori (Rome)
Porta, Giacomo della **12** 402-403
del Giardino (Parma)
Carracci **3** 319-321
della Ragione (Vicenza)
Palladio, Andrea **12** 75-77
di Parte Guelfa (Florence)
Brunelleschi, Filippo **3** 70-72
Iseppo Porto (Vicenza)
Palladio, Andrea **12** 75-77
Madama (Turin)
Juvara, Filippo **8** 396-397
Medici-Riccardi (Florence)
Donatello **5** 55-56
Michelozzo **11** 6-7
Pallavicini-Rospigliosi (Rome)
Reni, Guido **13** 97-98
Pamphili (Rome)
Cortona, Pietro da **4** 256
Schifanoia (Ferrara)
Tura, Cosimo **15** 343-344
Spada (Rome)
Borromini, Francesco **2** 424-425
Thiene (Vicenza)
Palladio, Andrea **12** 75-77
Valmarana (Vicenza)
Palladio, Andrea **12** 75-77
Vecchio (Florence)
Arnolfo di Cambio **1** 315-316
Brunelleschi, Filippo **3** 70-72
Donatello **5** 55-56
Vidoni-Caffarelli (Rome)
Raphael **13** 40-42

Palazzo incantato, Il (opera)
Rossi, Luigi **13** 310-311

Pale Fire (novel)
Nabokov, Vladimir **11** 287-288

Pale Horse, Pale Rider (literary collection)
Porter, Katherine Anne **12** 406-407

Paleobotanists
see Scientists—paleobotanists

Paleontology (science)
evolution controversy
Agassiz, Jean Louis Rodolphe
1 76-78
Darwin, Charles Robert **4** 397-399
Gould, Stephen Jay **6** 472-473
Huxley, Thomas Henry **8** 77-79
Lamarck, Chevalier de **9** 171-173
Owen, Richard **12** 39
Simpson, George Gaylord
14 240-242
extinct animals
Dunbar, William **5** 143-144
Marsh, Othniel Charles **10** 275-276
geological theory
Blackett, Patrick M.S. **2** 306-307
Cuvier, Georges Léopold **4** 357-359
Steno, Nicolaus **14** 425-426
prehistoric man
Breuil, Henri Edouard Prosper
2 521-522

Childe, Vere Gordon **3** 521-522
Leakey, Louis Seymour Bazett **9** 262
Teilhard de Chardin, Marie Joseph
Pierre **15** 134-136
Weidenreich, Franz **16** 171-172
see also Scientists—paleontologists
statistical methods
Simpson, George Gaylord
14 240-242

Paleotechnics (neologism)
Geddes, Patrick **6** 246-247

Paleozoic Era (geology)
Murchison, Roderick Impey **11** 255-256
Sedgwick, Adam **14** 82-83

Palermo (city, Sicily)
Garibaldi, Giuseppe **6** 215-217
Guiscard, Robert **7** 39-40
Idrisi, Muhammad ibn Muhammad al-
8 102-103

Palestine (region, South Western Asia)
American Zionist Medical Unit
Szold, Henrietta **15** 66-67
archeology
Petrie, William Matthew Flinders
12 261-262
as Jewish homeland
Begin, Menachem **2** 118-120
Herzl, Theodor **7** 352-354
Zangwill, Israel **16** 488-489
see also Zionism
before 1923
see Jewish history
British mandate (1923-1948)
Ben-Gurion, David **2** 160-161
Husayni, Al-Hajj Amin al- **8** 62-63
Jabotinsky, Vladimir Evgenevich
8 167-168
Meir, Golda **10** 462-463
Silver, Abba Hillel **14** 232-233
Weizmann, Chaim **16** 183-184
since 1948
Ashrawi, Hanan Mikhail **1** 336-338
Habash, George **7** 55-56
see Israel, State of
see also Balfour Declaration; Cru-
sades

Palestinian Liberation Organization (PLO)
Abu Musa **1** 32-33
Arafat, Yasser **1** 270-271
Darwish, Mahmud **4** 399-401
Jumblatt, Kamal **8** 386-387

Palestinian Talmud
see Jerusalem Talmud

Palestinian War
see Arab-Israeli wars—1948-49

PALESTRINA, GIOVANNI PIERLUIGI DA
(circa 1525-94), Italian composer
12 70-72
influence of
Gounod, Charles François
6 473-474
Victoria, Tomás Luis de **15** 487-488
liturgical music
Gregory XIII **6** 534

Neri, Philip **11** 340
Pius IV **12** 332
polyphony
Byrd, William **3** 187-188
Fux, Johann Joseph **6** 155-156
Lassus, Roland de **9** 216-218
Szymanowski, Karol **15** 67-68

PALEY, WILLIAM (1743-1805), English theologian and moral philosopher **12** 72
Darwin, Charles Robert **4** 397-399

PALEY, WILLIAM S. (1901-1990), founder and chairman of the Columbia Broadcasting System **12** 72-75

Palimpsest (novel)
Doolittle, Hilda **5** 65-66

Palko, Franz Karl (1724-1767/70), Austrian painter
Troger, Paul **15** 300

Palko v. Connecticut (legal case)
Cardozo, Benjamin Nathan **3** 288-290

Palladian style (architecture)
England
Adam, Robert and James **1** 38-40
Jones, Inigo **8** 333-334
Vanbrugh, John **15** 409-410
Wren, Christopher **16** 393-394
France
Mansart, François **10** 211
Italy
Piranesi, Giovanni Battista **12** 321-322
U.S.
Benjamin, Asher **2** 162-163
Jefferson, Thomas **8** 238-241
see also Palladio, Andrea

PALLADIO, ANDREA (1508-1580), Italian architect **12** 75-77
Bramante, Donato **2** 493-494
Raphael **13** 40-42
Veronese, Paolo **15** 469-470
see also Palladian style

Pallas (myth)
Callimachus **3** 235-236
Virgil **15** 507-510

Pallas Athena (myth)
Homer **7** 465-467

Palm Sunday (religion)
Jesus of Nazareth **8** 251-255

PALMA, RICARDO (1833-1919), Peruvian poet, essayist, and short-story writer **12** 77

Palma Vecchio (Jacopo de Antona de Negreto; 1480-1528), Italian painter
Giorgione **6** 340-341

PALMER, ALEXANDER MITCHELL (1872-1936), American politician and jurist **12** 77-78
Katayama, Sen **8** 457
Stone, Harlan Fiske **14** 468-470
Walsh, Thomas James **16** 85-86

PALMER, ARNOLD DANIEL (born 1929), American golfer **12** 78-80

PALMER, NATHANIEL BROWN (1799-1877), American sea captain **12** 80-81

Palmer, Potter (1826-1902), American businessman
Field, Marshall **5** 440-441

Palmer, Samuel (1805-1881), English engraver
Sutherland, Graham **15** 40-41

Palmer Land (Antarctica)
Palmer, Nathaniel Brown **12** 80-81

Palmer Memorial Institute (North Carolina)
Brown, Charlotte Eugenia Hawkins **3** 34

PALMERSTON, 3D VISCOUNT (Henry John Temple; 1784-1865), English prime minister 1855-65 **12** 81-83
Cabinet
Elgin, 8th Earl of **5** 248-249
Gladstone, William Ewart **6** 357-360
Russell, John **13** 380-381
critics
Aberdeen, 4th Earl of **1** 25-26
Albert **1** 110-112
Bismarck, Otto Eduard Leopold von **2** 294-296
Cobden, Richard **4** 127-128
Victoria **15** 485-487
philosophy
Stewart, Dugald **14** 449

Palmerston Islands (South Western Pacific Ocean)
Cook, James **4** 214-215

Palmwine Drinkard ... (book)
Tutuola, Amos **15** 361-362

Palmyra (ancient city-state; North Africa)
Zenobia **16** 500-503

Palomino de Castro y Velasco, Antonio (1653-1726), Spanish painter and author
Velázquez, Diego Rodríguez de Silva y **15** 454-456

Palou, Francisco (1722?-1789?), Franciscan missionary
Serra, Junípero **14** 111-112

Pamela (novel)
Fielding, Henry **5** 442-444
Richardson, Samuel **13** 141-142
Voltaire **16** 14-16

Pamfili, Giovanni Batista
see Innocent X

Pampeana (No.1-3; musical composition)
Ginastera, Alberto Evaristo **6** 328-329

Pamphili
see Eusebius of Caesarea

Pamphilus (flourished 4th century B.C.), Greek painter
Apelles **1** 257

Pamphilus de amore (poem; Ovid)
Ruiz, Juan **13** 358-359

Pamplona, battle of (1521)
Ignatius of Loyola **8** 108-109

Pampulha (Belo Horizonte, Brazil)
Niemeyer Soares Filho, Oscar **11** 389-390

Pan (novel)
Hamsun, Knut **7** 113-114

Pan (poem)
Leconte de Lisle, Charles Marie René **9** 273-274

Pan African Federation (established 1944)
Kenyatta, Jomo **8** 512-514
Padmore, George **12** 57-58

Pan American Conference
see International Conference of American States

Pan American World Airways
Lindbergh, Charles Augustus **9** 421-423
Sikorsky, Igor **14** 223-224
Stefansson, Vilhjalmur **14** 409-410
Trippe, Juan Terry **15** 297-298

Pan among th Reeds (painting)
Böcklin, Arnold **2** 354-355

Pan Chao (circa 50-112), Chinese historian
Pan Ku **12** 86-87

PAN KU (32-92), Chinese historian and man of letters **12** 86-87
Ssu-ma Ch'ien **14** 388-389

Pan Michael (novel)
Sienkiewicz, Henryk **14** 216-217

Pan Piao (died A.D. 54), Chinese historian
Pan Ku **12** 86-87

Pan Pursuing Syrinx (painting)
Böcklin, Arnold **2** 354-355

Panaetius of Rhodes (circa 185-109 B.C.), Stoic philosopher
Zeno of Citium **16** 499-500

Pan-African Association (established 1900)
Williams, Henry Sylvester **16** 303-304

Pan-African Conference (1900)
Du Bois, William Edward Burghardt **5** 116-118
Williams, Henry Sylvester **16** 303-304

Pan-African Congress (South Africa)
Sobukwe, Robert Mangaliso **14** 318-319

Pan-African congresses
1919
Diagne, Blaise **4** 527
Du Bois, William Edward Burghardt **5** 116-118
Plaatje, Solomon Tshekisho **12** 341-342
1921, 1923, 1927
Du Bois, William Edward Burghardt **5** 116-118
1945
Kenyatta, Jomo **8** 512-514
Nkrumah, Kwame **11** 408-410
Padmore, George **12** 57-58
Wallace-Johnson, Isaac Theophilus Akunna **16** 76-77

Pan-Africanism (African nationalism)
  Africa
    Ahidjo, Ahmadou **1** 89-90
    Azikiwe, Nnamdi **1** 401-402
    Diagne, Blaise **4** 527
    Haile Selassie **7** 68-70
    Hayford, J. E. Casely **7** 228-230
    Houphouët-Boigny, Felix **7** 519-520
    Nkrumah, Kwame **11** 408-410
    Wallace-Johnson, Isaac Theophilus
      Akunna **16** 76-77
  African American support
    Blyden, Edward Wilmot **2** 348-349
    Du Bois, William Edward Burghardt
      5 116-118
    Turner, Henry McNeal **15** 351-352
  Trinidad
    Padmore, George **12** 57-58
    Williams, Henry Sylvester
      16 303-304

Pan-Africanist Congress (PAC; established
  1959)
  Luthuli, Albert John **10** 51-52
  Mandela, Nelson Rolihlahla
    10 185-186
  Verwoerd, Hendrik Frensch **15** 472-473
  Vorster, Balthazar Johannes **16** 30-32

Panama, Republic of (nation , Isthmus of
  Panama)
  dictatorship (1968-1981)
    Torrijos, Omar **15** 269-270
  independence (1903)
    Arias, Arnulfo **1** 286-287
    Bunau-Varilla, Philippe Jean
      3 120-121
    Estrada Cabrera, Manuel **5** 325-326
    Reyes, Rafael **13** 113
  relations with the United States
    Chiari, Roberto **3** 513-514
    Endara, Guillermo **5** 283-284
    Noriega, Manuel A. **11** 423-425
  Spanish rule
    Almagro, Diego de **1** 177-178
    Drake, Francis **5** 94-96, 435
    Pedrarias **12** 179
  yellow fever
    Finlay, Carlos Juan **5** 450
    Gorgas, William Crawford
      6 454-455
    Reed, Walter **13** 78
  see also Panama Canal; Panama
    Congress

Panama Canal
  French failure
    Clemenceau, Georges **4** 99-101
    Evarts, William Maxwell **5** 340-341
    Lesseps, Vicomte de **9** 354-355
  U.S. acquires
    Mahan, Alfred Thayer **10** 131-132
    Roosevelt, Theodore **13** 280-283
  U.S. construction
    Goethals, George Washington
      6 387-388
    Gorgas, William Crawford
      6 454-455

    Taft, William Howard **15** 78-81
    Wood, Robert Elkington **16** 370-371
  U.S. treaties
    Bunau-Varilla, Philippe Jean
      3 120-121
    Carter, James Earl **3** 339-342
    Carter, James Earl **3** 339-342
    Clayton, John Middleton **4** 96-97
    Hay, John **7** 215-216
    Johnson, Lyndon Baines **8** 308-312
    Roosevelt, Theodore **13** 280-283
    Salisbury, 3d Marquess of
      13 448-449
    Torrijos, Omar **15** 269-270
    Vance, Cyrus R. **15** 411-413
  U.S.-Panama relations
    Chiari, Roberto **3** 513-514

Panama Congress (1826)
  Adams, John Quincy **1** 52-54
  Bolívar, Simón **2** 375-377
  Clay, Henry **4** 94-96

Panama Defense Forces
  Noriega, Manuel A. **11** 423-425

Panama Hattie (musical)
  Porter, Cole Albert **12** 405-406

Panambí (ballet)
  Ginastera, Alberto Evaristo **6** 328-329

Pan-American Exposition (1900; Buffalo,
  New York State)
  Calamity Jane **3** 216

Pan-Americanism (political movement)
  Blaine, James Gillespie **2** 312-313
  Hull, Cordell **8** 28-29
  Lamas, Carlos Saavedra **9** 175-176
  Nabuco de Araujo, Joaquim Aurelio
    11 288-289
  see also International Conference of
    American States; Monroe Doctrine;
    Organization of American States;
    Panama Congress (1826)

Pancake Man (painting)
  Brouwer, Adriaen **3** 29-30

Panchen Lama (Tibetan Buddhism)
  Buddha **3** 97-101
  Dalai Lama **4** 369-371

Pancreas (anatomy)
  Banting, Frederick Grant **1** 493-494
  Bernard, Claude **2** 208-210
  Best, Charles Herbert **2** 236-237
  Houssay, Bernardo Alberto **7** 522-523
  Pavlov, Ivan Petrovich **12** 155-157

Pandit, Ranjit Sitaram (died 1944), Indian
  lawyer
  Pandit, Vijaya Lakshmi **12** 83-84

PANDIT, VIJAYA LAKSHMI (1900-1990),
  Indian diplomat and politician **12** 83-84
  Nehru, Motilal **11** 334-335

Pandora (book)
  Goethe, Johann Wolfgang von
    6 388-391

Pandora's Box (play)
  Wedekind, Frank **16** 166-167

Pane e vino (novel)
  Silone, Ignazio **14** 231-232

Paneth, Friedrich Adolf (1887-1958), Austrian chemist
  Hevesy, George Charles de **7** 371

PANETTA, LEON E. (born 1938), Democratic congressman from California and chief
  of staff to President Clinton **12** 84-85

Pange lingua (musical composition)
  Thomson, Virgil **15** 202-203

Pangenesis (genetics)
  Mendel, Johann Gregor **10** 483-486
  Vries, Hugo de **16** 33-36

P'ang-huang (stories)
  Lu Hsün **10** 35-37

Panglong Agreement (1947)
  Aung San **1** 374-375

Pangolin ... (poems)
  Moore, Marianne **11** 148-149

Panhandle Stock Association (established
  1880)
  Goodnight, Charles **6** 439

Panhard, René (1841-1908), French auto-
  motive engineer
  Daimler, Gottlieb **4** 368

Panhellenic Socialist Party (Greece)
  Papandreou, Andreas **12** 88-91

Panic (economics)
  see Depressions and panics (United
    States)

Panic, Fright (sculpture)
  Barlach, Ernst **2** 5-6

Panin, Count Nikita Ivanovitch
  (1718-1783), Russian diplomat
  Catherine the Great **3** 370-372
  Paul I **12** 143-144

Panipat, battle of (1526)
  Bach, Carl Philipp Emanuel **1** 414-415

Pan-Islamism
  Abdul-Hamid II **1** 17-18
  Gökalp, Mehmet Ziya **6** 395-396
  Iqbal, Muhammad **8** 132-133
  see also Nationalism, African (North
    Africa)

Pankhurst, Christabel (1880-1948), English
  reformer and suffragette
  Pankhurst, Emmeline **12** 85-86

PANKHURST, EMMELINE (1858-1928),
  English reformer **12** 85-86

Pankhurst, Richard Marsden (died 1898),
  English lawyer
  Pankhurst, Emmeline **12** 85-86

Pankhurst, Sylvia (1882-1960), English
  reformer
  Pankhurst, Emmeline **12** 85-86

PANNENBERG, WOLFHART (born 1928),
  German Protestant theologian **12** 87-88

Panofsky, Erwin (1892-1968),
  German-born American art historian
  Bosch, Hieronymus **2** 426-428

Dürer, Albrecht **5** 159-161
Eyck, Hubert and Jan van **5** 352-354
Weyden, Rogier van der **16** 219-221

Pansies (poems)
Lawrence, David Herbert **9** 247-248

Pan-Slavism
see Nationalism, Slavic

Pansophy (philosophy)
Comenius, John Amos **4** 180-181

Pantaenus (flourished 180-200), Greek
Christian philosopher
Clement of Alexandria **4** 102-103

Pantagruel (novel)
Rabelais, François **12** 524-526-70

Pantaleoni, Maffeo (1857-1924), Italian
economist
Pareto, Vilfredo **12** 95-96

Panthéon (Paris; formerly Ste-Geneviève)
art and architecture
Gros **7** 14-15
Perrault, Claude **12** 232-233
Rodin, Auguste **13** 236-238
Soufflot, Jacques Germain
14 349-350
theology school
Abelard, Peter **1** 23-25
Lombard, Peter **9** 490-491

Panthère noire, La (poem)
Leconte de Lisle, Charles Marie René
9 273-274

Pantheism (philosophy)
in literature
Heine, Heinrich **7** 259-260
Tschernichowsky, Saul **15** 323
in theology
Erigena, John Scotus **5** 308-309
Julian **8** 378-379
Spinozan
Fichte, Johann Gottlieb **5** 435-436
Jacobi, Friedrich Heinrich
8 189-190
Lessing, Gotthold Ephraim
9 357-359
Spinoza, Baruch **14** 381-383

Pantheon (Rome)
Hadrian **7** 60-61
Soufflot, Jacques Germain **14** 349-350

Pantheus (literary character)
Euripides **5** 332-334

Pantomime (acting)
Marceau, Marcel **10** 231-233

Panurge (literary character)
Rabelais, François **12** 524-526

Pao-huang hui (Chinese society)
K'ang Yu-wei **8** 426-428
Liang Ch'i-ch'ao **9** 395-396

Paoli, battle of (1777)
Howe, William **7** 538-539

Paoli, Pasquale di (1725-1807), Corsican
leader
Boswell, James **2** 432-434

Napoleon I **11** 306-310

Paolo di Giovanni Fei (flourished 14th-15th
century), Italian painter
Sassetta **13** 492

Paon d'émail, Le (poems)
Morin, Paul **11** 174

Papacy (Roman Catholic Church)
Byzantines and
Leo III **9** 330-332
Michael VIII **11** 1-2
centralization
Innocent III **8** 125-127
Leo I **9** 329-330
Leo XIII **9** 334-336
colonization rights defined
Henry the Navigator **7** 305-306
see also Tordesillas, Treaty of
critics
Hutten, Ulrich von **8** 72-73
Rosa, Salvator **13** 289-290
Zwingli, Huldreich **16** 537-538
Curia
Paul VI **12** 146-148
Pius X **12** 336-337
Sixtus V **14** 267-268
Urban II **15** 393
empire and
see Church and State (Holy Roman
Emp.)
France and
Clement V **4** 101-102
Philip IV **12** 274
see also Church and State (France)
Great Schism
Martin V **10** 287-288
Sigismund **14** 220-221
Urban VI **15** 394
see also Conciliarism; Great Schism
infallibility
see Infallibility, papal
investiture
see Investiture Struggle
Italy and
Julius II **8** 384-386
see also Church and State (Italy)
Mongols and
Kublai Khan **9** 115-118
political powers
Leo X **9** 332-334
Marsilius of Padua **10** 284
Urban II **15** 393
popes
see Religious leaders, Catholic
(since 1517); Religious leaders,
Christian (to Reformation)
reforms
Gregory I **6** 531-532
Gregory VII **6** 532-534
John, XXIII **8** 277-280
Leo IX **9** 332
Pius IX **12** 335-336
social reform
John, XXIII **8** 277-280
Leo XIII **9** 334-336
Pius XI **12** 337-339

Spain and
Philip II **12** 271-273
see also Avignon Papacy; Papal
States; Roman Catholic Church
see also Church and State (Spain);
Inquisition, Spanish

Papal States (Italy; 755-1860)
conquered by pope
Alexander VI **1** 134-135
France annexes
Napoleon I **11** 306-310
Pius VII **12** 334-335
Holy Roman Empire and
Frederick II **6** 79
Italy annexes (1860)
Cavour, Conte di **3** 385-386
Garibaldi, Giuseppe **6** 215-217
Pius IX **12** 335-336
Victor Emmanuel II **15** 483-484
papal militancy
Julius II **8** 384-386
supporters
Griffith, Samuel Walker **6** 545-546
see also Vatican City, State of

PAPANDREOU, ANDREAS (1919-1996),
Greek scholar and statesman and prime
minister **12** 88-91

Papareschi, Gregorio
see Innocent II

Papebroch, Daniel van (1628-1714), Belgian church historian
Mabillon, Jean **10** 72

Papefigues (literary characters)
Rabelais, François **12** 524-526

Papen, Franz von (1879-1969), German
diplomat
Hindenburg, Paul Ludwig Hans von
Beneckendorff und von **7** 400-401
John, XXIII **8** 277-280
Rundstedt, Karl Rudolf Gerd Von
13 363-364

Paper Money
Law, John **9** 244-245
see also Currency

Paper Nautilus, The (poem)
Moore, Marianne **11** 148-149

Papers of Dwight David Eisenhower, The
Chandler, Alfred Du Pont Jr. **3** 422-423

Paphnuce (literary character)
France, Anatole **6** 39-40

Papias (circa 70-circa 130), bishop of Hier-
apolis
Mark **10** 266-267
Matthew **10** 340-341

Papiers collés (art)
Miró, Joan **11** 53-54

Papiers découpés (art)
Matisse, Henri **10** 336-337

Papillons (musical composition)
Schumann, Robert Alexander **14** 41-43

Papimanes (literary characters)
Rabelais, François **12** 524-526

PAPINEAU, LOUIS-JOSEPH (1786-1871), French-Canadian radical political leader **12** 91
> Bourassa, Joseph-Henri-Napoleon **2** 446-447
> Cartier, George-Étienne **3** 342-343
> Lafontaine, Louis-Hippolyte **9** 157-158
> *see also* Canada—rebellion (1837)

Papinian (Aemilius Papinianus; died 212), Roman jurist
> Ulpian, Domitius **15** 385-386

Pappus (flourished late 3d century A.D.), Greek astronomer
> Euclid **5** 327-329

Parable of the Blind (painting)
> Bruegel, Pieter the Elder **3** 65-67

Parabola (mathematics)
> Archimedes **1** 277-280
> Euclid **5** 327-329

Paracelsus (poem)
> Browning, Robert **3** 53-55

PARACELSUS, PHILIPPUS AUREOLUS (1493-1541), Swiss physician and alchemist **12** 91-93
> Boyle, Robert **2** 469-471
> Helmont, Jan Baptista van **7** 269-271

Parade (ballet; Satie-Cocteau)
> Cocteau, Jean **4** 132-133
> Picasso, Pablo **12** 292-295
> Satie, Erik **13** 494-495

Parade, La (painting)
> Seurat, Georges Pierre **14** 120-122

Parade's End (novel)
> Ford, Ford Madox **6** 1-2

Paradine Case, The (film)
> Hitchcock, Alfred **7** 415-416

Paradise (musical composition)
> Schumann, Robert Alexander **14** 41-43

Paradise Lost (play)
> Odets, Clifford **11** 470-471

Paradise Lost (poem; Milton)
> Allston, Washington **1** 176-177
> Dryden, John **5** 106-107
> Haydn, Franz Joseph **7** 219-221
> Milton, John **11** 43-46
> Richardson, Samuel **13** 141-142
> *see also* Paradise Regained

Paradise of Love, The (poem)
> Froissart, Jean **6** 124-125

Paradise Regained (poem)
> Milton, John **11** 43-46
> *see also* Paradise Lost

Paradiso (Dante)
> *see* Divine Comedy

Paradox rey (novel)
> Baroja y Nessi, Pío **2** 15-16

Paraguay, Republic of (nation , Southeast South America)
> Belgrano, Manuel **2** 126-127
> Cabeza de Vaca, Álvar Núñez **3** 197
> López, Carlos Antonio **9** 506-507

> Morínigo, Higinio **11** 174-175
> Stroessner, Alfredo **14** 511-512
> Wasmosy, Juan Carlos **16** 129-130
> *see also* Chaco War; Triple Alliance, War of the

Parallel Lives
> *see* Lives (book; Plutarch)

Parallèlement (book; Verlaine)
> Bonnard, Pierre **2** 395-396

Paramount Pictures (film studio)
> Eisenstein, Sergei Mikhailovich **5** 240-242
> Fields, W. C. **5** 444

Parasha (poem)
> Turgenev, Ivan Sergeyevich **15** 345-348

Parasitology (science)
> Bruce, David **3** 63
> Metchnikoff, Élie **10** 532-533

PARBO, ARVI (born 1926), Australian industrial giant **12** 93-94

Pardo, Peace of El (1778)
> Azara, Félix de **1** 397-398

Pardon de Ploërmel, Le (opera)
> Meyerbeer, Giacomo **10** 536-537

Pardon My English (musical)
> Gershwin, George **6** 284-285

PARÉ, AMBROISE (1510-1590), French military surgeon **12** 94-95

Paredes oyen, Las (play)
> Alarcón, Pedro Antonio de **1** 100-101

Pareja, Juan de (El Esclavo; circa 1606-70), Spanish painter
> Velázquez, Diego Rodríguez de Silva y **15** 454-456

Parent, Étienne (1801-1874), French-Canadian journalist
> Garneau, François-Xavier **6** 219-220

Parents' Assistant, The (stories)
> Edgeworth, Maria **5** 205-206

PARETO, VILFREDO (1848-1923), Italian sociologist, political theorist, and economist **12** 95-96
> Parsons, Talcott **12** 122

Paride ed Elena (opera)
> Gluck, Christoph Willibald **6** 372-374

Paris (book)
> Zola, Émile **16** 526-528

Paris (city, France)
> Communes
>> *see* Commune of Paris
> liberation (1944)
>> Leclerc, Jacques Philippe **9** 272-273
> libraries
>> *see* Bibliothèque Nationale
> national guard
>> Lafayette, Marquis de **9** 151-152
> Parlement of
>> Condé, Prince de **4** 193-194
>> Francis I **6** 40-43
>> Mazarin, Jules **10** 379-380
>> Philip IV **12** 274

> *see also* Parlement (France)
> police
>> Bertillon, Alphonse **2** 230-231
> revolution (1848)
>> Bakunin, Mikhail Aleksandrovich **1** 458-460
>> Clough, Arthur Hugh **4** 123-124
> urban renewal
>> Haussmann, Baron Georges Eugène **7** 201-202
>> Philip II **12** 268-269
> *see also* following Paris entries and individual churches, monuments etc.

Paris (painting series)
> Chagall, Marc **3** 406-407

Paris (poems)
> Ehrenburg, Ilya Grigorievich **5** 224-225

Paris (sculpture)
> Donner, Georg Raphael **5** 63

Paris, Congress of (1856)
> *see* Paris Treaty of—1856

Paris, France (book)
> Stein, Gertrude **14** 414-415

Paris, Matthew
> *see* Matthew Paris

Paris, Pact of (1928)
> *see* kellogg-Briand Pact

Paris, School of (art)
> *see* French art—School of Paris

Paris, Treaty of
> 1763
>> Charles III **3** 454-455
>> Clive, Robert **4** 119-120
>> Rockingham, 2d Marquess of **13** 230-231
> 1783
>> Adams, John **1** 48-51
>> Charles III **3** 454-455
>> Clark, George Rogers **4** 75-76
>> Coxe, Tench **4** 285-286
>> Franklin, Benjamin **6** 60-64
>> Hamilton, Alexander **7** 95-98
>> Jay, John **8** 230-232
>> Washington, George **16** 126-129
> 1814
>> Aberdeen, 4th Earl of **1** 25-26
>> Castlereagh, Viscount **3** 363-364
> 1815
>> Castlereagh, Viscount **3** 363-364
> 1856
>> Cavour, Conte di **3** 385-386
>> Napoleon III **11** 310-312
>> Nesselrode, Karl Robert **11** 348-349
>> Palmerston, 3d Viscount **12** 81-83
> 1898
>> Bryan, William Jennings **3** 80-82
>> McKinley, William **10** 418-420
> 1919
>> *see* Versailles, Treaty of (1919)

Paris, University of (France)
> charter
>> Philip II **12** 268-269

history
    Guizot, François Pierre Guillaume
    7 40-41
music
    Franco of Cologne **6** 52
officials
    Ailly, Pierre d' **1** 94
    Ampère, André Marie **1** 205-206
    Gerson, John **6** 285-286
    Marsilius of Padua **10** 284
philosophy
    Bacon, Roger **1** 425-427
    Mauss, Marcel **10** 352-353
    Ramus, Petrus **13** 27-28
science
    Charcot, Jean Martin **3** 442
    Curie, Marie Sklodowska **4** 339-341
    de Broglie, Louis **4** 442-444
    Le Bon, Gustave **9** 268-269
    Pinel, Philippe **12** 313-314
    Poincaré, Jules Henri **12** 365-366
Semitic languages
    Clement V **4** 101-102
Sorbonne
    see Sorbonne
student protests (1968)
    Cohn-Bendit, Daniel **4** 140-141
theology
    Abelard, Peter **1** 23-25
    Bonaventure **2** 383-384
    Cuvier, Georges Léopold **4** 357-359
    Lull, Raymond **10** 39-40

Paris Bit, The (painting)
    Davis, Stuart **4** 424-425

Paris Conservatory
    Fauré, Gabriel Urbain **5** 397-398
    Franck, César **6** 48-49
    Messiaen, Olivier **10** 528-529

Pâris-Duverny, Joseph (died 1770), French
financier
    Beaumarchais, Pierre August Caron de
    2 93-94

Paris Herald (newspaper)
    Bennett, James Gordon Jr. **2** 169-170

Paris International Exposition of Decorative Arts (1925)
    Le Corbusier **9** 274-275

Paris Observatory (France)
    Foucault, Jean Bernard Léon **6** 28-29
    Leverrier, Urbain Jean Joseph **9** 361-362

Paris Peace Conference (1919)
    see Versailles, Treaty of (1919)

Paris Peace Conference (1946)
    Evatt, Herbert Vere **5** 341-343
    Toynbee, Arnold Joseph **15** 283-284

Paris Peace talks (Vietnam War)
    Harriman, W. Averell **7** 165-166
    Ho Chi Minh **7** 426-428
    Johnson, Lyndon Baines **8** 308-312
    Nixon, Richard Milhous **11** 401-404
    Thant, U **15** 161-162

Paris Symphonies (musical composition)
    Haydn, Franz Joseph **7** 219-221

Paris World's Fairs
    see World's Fairs—Paris

Parish priests, patron of
    Vianney, Jean Baptiste **15** 478-479

Parish Register, The (poem)
    Crabbe, George **4** 288

Parisian Model, The (musical)
    Ziegfeld, Florenz **16** 516-517

Parisian Peasant (book)
    Aragon, Louis **1** 271-272

Parisina (epic)
    Byron, George Gordon Noel **3** 193-194

PARIZEAU, JACQUES (born 1930), Canadian politician and premier of Quebec **12** 96-99

PARK, CHUNG HEE (1917-1979), Korean soldier and statesman **12** 99-102

PARK, MAUD WOOD (1871-1955), suffragist and first president of the League of Women Voters **12** 102

PARK, ROBERT E. (1864-1944), American sociologist **12** 102-104

PARK, WILLIAM HALLOCK (1863-1939), American physician **12** 104-105

Park Güell (Barcelona)
    Gaudí i Cornet, Antoni **6** 235-236

Parker, Alton B. (1852-1926), American jurist
    Bryan, William Jennings **3** 80-82
    Cleveland, Stephen Grover **4** 108-110

PARKER, CHARLES CHRISTOPHER, JR. (Charlie Parker; 1920-55), American jazz musician **12** 105-106

PARKER, DOROTHY ROTHSCHILD (1893-1967), American writer **12** 106

PARKER, ELY SAMUEL (Ha-sa-no-an-da; 1828-1895), Native American tribal leader **12** 106-108

PARKER, HORATIO WILLIAM (1863-1919), American composer **12** 109
    Ives, Charles Edward **8** 159-160
    Sessions, Roger Huntington **14** 117-118

PARKER, QUANAH (c. 1845-1911), Native American religious leader **12** 109-112

Parker, Richard Barry (1867-1941), English architect
    Shaw, Richard Norman **14** 167-168

Parker, Samuel (1779-1866), American Congregationalist missionary
    Fitzpatrick, Thomas **5** 474-475
    Whitman, Marcus **16** 248-249

Parker, Sir Hyde (1739-1807), English naval commander
    Nelson, Horatio **11** 336-338

PARKER, THEODORE (1810-1860), American Unitarian clergyman **12** 112-113
    Alcott, Louisa May **1** 122
    Brown, John **3** 39-41
    Burns, Anthony **3** 151
    Emerson, Ralph Waldo **5** 278-280

PARKES, SIR HENRY (1815-1896), Australian statesman **12** 113
    Barton, Edmund **2** 39-40
    Griffith, Samuel Walker **6** 545-546

PARKMAN, FRANCIS (1823-1893), American historian **12** 113-115

PARKS, ROSA LEE MCCAULEY (born 1913), American civil rights leader **12** 115-116

Parlement (France)
    Louis XV **9** 533-534
    Louis XVI **9** 534-535
    Montesquieu **11** 123-125

Parliament (Belgium)
    Leopold I **9** 345-346

Parliament (British)
atheists seated
    Bradlaugh, Charles **2** 478
civil war
    Charles I **3** 450-452
    see also Civil War, English-Puritan Revolutions
growth of power
    Henry IV **7** 292-293
Lord's power curbed
    Asquith, Herbert Henry **1** 344-346
    Lloyd George, David **9** 469-471
    see also Parliament Bill (1911)
members
    see Statesmen, British
printing
    Richardson, Samuel **13** 141-142
reforms
    Cobbett, William **4** 126-127
    Grattan, Henry **6** 499
    Grey, Charles **6** 539-540
    Melbourne, 2nd Viscount **10** 468-469
    Montfort, Simon de **11** 132-133
    Wilkes, John **16** 280-281
relations with king
    Charles II **3** 452-454
    George I **6** 268-269
    James I **8** 204-206, 522
    Sandys, Edwin **13** 463-464

Parliament (Netherlands)
    Wilhelmina **16** 278-279

Parliament (Scotland)
    James I **8** 206-207

Parliament, Houses of (London)
    Pugin, Augustus Welby Northmore **12** 479-480

Parliament Bill (England ; 1911)
    Asquith, Herbert Henry **1** 344-346
    Balfour, Arthur James **1** 469-470
    George V **6** 273-275

Parliament of Oxford (1258)
    Edward I **5** 208-210

Parliament of Religions (Chicago; 1893)
    Gibbons, James **6** 300-301
    Vivekananda **16** 4-5

Parliamentary Reform Bill (England; 1930)

Mill, James **11** 21
Mill, John Stuart **11** 21-23

Parlor songs (music)
Foster, Stephen Collins **6** 25-27
Ives, Charles Edward **8** 159-160

Parma (province , Northern Italy)
Carracci **3** 319-321
Correggio **4** 249-251, 147
Maria Theresa **10** 256-258
Parmigianino **12** 117

Parma, battle of (1248)
Frederick II **6** 79

Parma, Duke of
see Charles III (king, Spain)

Parmenides (dialogue; Plato)
Plato **12** 345-347
Socrates **14** 320-321

PARMENIDES (flourished 475 B.C.), Greek
philosopher **12** 116-117
Empedocles **5** 282
Gorgias **6** 456
Zeno of Elea **16** 500

Parmenion (died 330 B.C.), Macedonian
general
Alexander the Great **1** 137-141
Philip II **12** 269-271

PARMIGIANINO (1503-1540), Italian
painter **12** 117
Correggio **4** 249-251
Primaticcio, Francesco **12** 453-454

Parnassians (French literature)
Darío, Rubén **4** 393-394
Leconte de Lisle, Charles Marie René
9 273-274
Morin, Paul **11** 174

Parnassus (painting)
Mantegna, Andrea **10** 215-216
Mengs, Anton Raphael **10** 505

PARNELL, CHARLES STEWART
(1846-1891), Irish nationalist leader
12 117-119
Asquith, Herbert Henry **1** 344-346
Gladstone, William Ewart **6** 357-360
O'Connell, Daniel **11** 465-467

Parnell, Thomas (1679-1718), Anglo-Irish
poet
Pope, Alexander **12** 395-397

Parochial schools (United States)
see Education (United States)

Parr, Catharine (1802-1899)
see Traill, Catharine Parr

Parr, Catherine (1512-1548), sixth wife of
Henry VIII
Henry VIII **7** 302-305
Mary I **10** 308-309

Parr, Thomas (Old Parr; 1483?-1635), English centenarian
Harvey, William **7** 189-190

PARRINGTON, VERNON LOUIS
(1871-1929), American historian
12 119-120

Commons, John Rogers **4** 185

Parrot, Georg Friedrich (1767-1852),
Estonian physicist
Struve, Friedrich Georg Wilhelm von
14 513

Parry, Sir William Edward (1790-1855),
English Arctic explorer
Ross, James Clark **13** 302-303

Parsifal (opera; Wagner)
Debussy, Achille Claude **4** 445-447
Wagner, Richard **16** 40-43
Wolfram von Eschenbach **16** 360-361

PARSONS, FRANK (1854-1908), American
educator and reformer **12** 121-122

Parsons, Robert (1546-1610), English Jesuit
missionary
Byrd, William **3** 187-188

PARSONS, SIR CHARLES ALGERNON
(1854-1931), British engineer **12** 120-121

PARSONS, TALCOTT (1902-1979), American sociologist **12** 122
Kluckhohn, Clyde **9** 56-57

Parsons, William (3d Earl of Rosse;
1800-67), English astronomer
Parsons, Charles Algernon **12** 120-121

Part of a Novel... (poem)
Moore, Marianne **11** 148-149

Partage de Midi (drama)
Claudel, Paul Louis Charles **4** 90-91

Partenope (opera)
Handel, George Frederick **7** 116-119

Parthenia (musical collection)
Byrd, William **3** 187-188

Parthenon (Athens)
Ictinus **8** 101
Mills, Robert **11** 36-37
Pericles **12** 219-221
Phidias **12** 265-267

Parthia (ancient nation, Western Asia)
Judea and
Herod the Great **7** 333-334
Rome and
Antony, Mark **1** 253-254
Cleopatra **4** 105-106
Crassus Dives, Marcus Licinius
4 296-297
Josephus Flavius **8** 360-361
Nero Claudius Caesar **11** 342-344
see also Parthian wars
Seleucids and
Antiochus III **1** 249-250

Parthian wars
113-117
Hadrian **7** 60-61
Marcus Aurelius Antoninus
10 243-245
Trajan **15** 291-292
197-198
Septimius Severus, Lucius
14 109-110

Parti Démocratique de Guinée (PDG)
Touré, Sékou **15** 275-277

Parti Démocratique de la Côte d'Ivoire
(PDCI)
Houphouët-Boigny, Felix **7** 519-520

Parti Progressiste Congolais (PPC)
Youlou, Fulbert **16** 466-467

Parti Québéçois (Canada)
Lévesque, René **9** 362-363
Parizeau, Jacques **12** 96-99

Parti Républicain Dahoméen (PRD)
Apithy, Sourou Migan **1** 259-260

Parti Togolaise du Progrès (PTP)
Olympio, Sylvanus E. **11** 506-507

Partial pressures, law of
see Dalton's Law

Particle accelerators (physics)
Bohr, Niels Henrik David **2** 366-368
Bothe, Walther **2** 438-439
Lawrence, Ernest Orlando **9** 248-250

Particle detectors (physics)
Bothe, Walther **2** 438-439
Cherenkov, Pavel Alekseevich
3 502-503
Wilson, Charles Thomson Rees
16 317-318

Particle dynamics, Newtonian (physics)
Euler, Leonard **5** 331-332

**Partido Africano da Independência da
Guiné e Cabo Verde** (PAIGC; African lib-
eration group)
Cabral, Amílcar Lopes **3** 202-203

Partido Democrático Nacional (Venezuela)
see Acción Democrática

Partido libración Nacional
see National Liberation party (Costa R.)

Partido Nacionalista Consolidado (Philip-
pines)
Osmeña, Sergio **12** 22-24
Quezon, Manuel Luis **12** 511-513

Partido Obrero de Unificacion Marxista
Orwell, George **12** 14-15

Partido Popular
see Partido Popular Socialista (Mexico)

Partido Popular Socialista (Mexico)
Toledano, Vicente Lombardo
15 256-257

Partido Revolucionario Cubano (political
party)
Grau San Martin, Ramón **6** 499-500

Partido Revolucionario Dominicano (polit-
ical party)
Balaguer y Ricardo, Joaquin **1** 460-461
Bosch, Juan **2** 428-429

Partido Revolucionario Institucional (Mex-
ico)
López Mateos, Adolfo **9** 509-510
López Portillo, José **9** 510-511
Toledano, Vicente Lombardo
15 256-257

Partido Social Democrático (Brazil)
Vargas, Getulio Dornelles **15** 433-434

Partido Trabalhista (Brazil)
Vargas, Getulio Dornelles **15** 433-434

Partisan, The (novel)
Simms, William Gilmore **14** 235-236

Partisan Review (magazine)
Greenberg, Clement **6** 521-523
Motherwell, Robert **11** 210-211
Orwell, George **12** 14-15

Partita (music)
Bach, Johann Sebastian **1** 416-419
Walton, William Turner **16** 92-93

Partito Popolare Italiano
see Catholic People's Party (It.)

Parts of a World (poems)
Stevens, Wallace **14** 443-445

Parvus (pseudonym)
see Helfand, A. L.

Parzival (epic; Wolfram von Eschenbach)
Grimmelshausen, Hans Jakob Christoffel von **7** 4-5
Wolfram von Eschenbach **16** 360-361

Pas d'acier, Le (ballet)
Prokofiev, Sergei Sergeevich
12 458-460

Pasargadae (ancient city, Persia)
Cyrus the Great **4** 363-364

PASCAL, BLAISE (1623-1662), French scientist and philosopher **12** 122-124
Beckett, Samuel **2** 102-104
Chalmers, Thomas **3** 408-409
Jansen, Cornelis **8** 220-221
Kafka, Franz **8** 403-406
La Fayette, Comtesse de **9** 150-151
Leibniz, Gottfried Wilhelm von
9 307-310

Pascal, Mattia (literary character)
Pirandello, Luigi **12** 319-321

Pascarella Family, The (novel)
Werfel, Franz **16** 204-205

Pascendi (encyclical)
Pius X **12** 336-337

Pascha, Het (play)
Vondel, Joost van den **16** 19-20

Paschal II (1050?-1118), pope 1099-1118
Henry V **7** 295-296

Pascin, Jules (1885-1930), American painter
Modigliani, Amedeo **11** 72-73

Pascuccio d'Antonio, Donato di
see Bramante, Donato

PASHA, ENVER (1881-1922), Turkish soldier and Young Turk leader **5** 290-291

PASHA, TEWFIK (1852-1892), khedive of Egypt 1879-92 **15** 157-158
Cromer, 1st Earl of **4** 317

Pashas
see Statesmen

Pasquin (political satire)
Fielding, Henry **5** 442-444

Pass Laws (South Africa)
Luthuli, Albert John **10** 51-52
Verwoerd, Hendrik Frensch **15** 472-473

Passacaglia (music)
Bach, Johann Sebastian **1** 416-419
Webern, Anton **16** 160-162

Passage to India (poem)
Whitman, Walt **16** 249-251

Passage to India, A (novel)
Forster, Edward Morgan **6** 14-16

Passarowitz, Peace of (1718)
Eugene of Savoy **5** 330-331

Passau, Treaty of (1552)
Charles V **3** 457-459
Ferdinand II **5** 415

Passchendaele, battle of (1917)
Currie, Arthur William **4** 345

Passfield, Baron
see Webb, Sidney James

Passion (philosophy)
Descartes, René **4** 505-508
Galen **6** 178-180

Passion, according to Sade (opera)
Bussotti, Sylvano **3** 174-175

Passion in Rome, A (novel)
Callaghan, Edward Morley **3** 229-230

Passion of Christ (New Testament)
in art
Morales, Luis de **11** 150
Pontormo **12** 394-395
Rembrandt Harmensz van Rijn
13 91-95
Schongauer, Martin **14** 26-28
in music
Bach, Johann Sebastian **1** 416-419
Manzoni, Alessandro **10** 222-224
Walter, Johann **16** 86
relics
Montreuil, Pierre de **11** 139

Passion of Sacco and Vanzetti (painting)
Shahn, Ben **14** 139-140

Passional attraction (political philosophy)
Fourier, François Charles Marie **6** 31-32

Passionate Pilgrim, A (book)
James, Henry **8** 211-212

Passions (musical composition)
Schütz, Heinrich **14** 48-49

Passive obedience (philosophy)
Woolman, John **16** 382-383

Passive powers (philosophy)
Cudworth, Ralph **4** 331

Passive resistance movements (India)
Bhave, Vinoba **2** 257-258
Bose, Subhas Chandra **2** 430-431
Gandhi, Mohandas Karamchand
6 201-204
Narayan, Jayaprakash **11** 312-313
Nehru, Jawaharlal **11** 332-334

Prasad, Rajendra 12 433
Reading, 1st Marquess of **13** 64
see also Civil disobedience; Nonviolent protest movements; Student protest

Passover, The (play)
Vondel, Joost van den **16** 19-20

Passow, Franz (1786-1833), German philologist
Schopenhauer, Arthur **14** 29-31

Passport of Mallam Ilia, The (novella)
Ekwensi, Cyprian **5** 242-243

Past and Present (book)
Carlyle, Thomas **3** 304-305

Past and Present (painting)
Cole, Thomas **4** 151-152

PASTERNAK, BORIS LEONIDOVICH
(1890-1960), Russian poet, novelist, and translator **12** 124-125
Ehrenburg, Ilya Grigorievich **5** 224-225
Lowell, Robert Trail Spence Jr. **10** 16-17

Pasternak, Leonid Osipovich (1862-1945), Russian naturalist painter
Pasternak, Boris Leonidovich
12 124-125

PASTEUR, LOUIS (1822-1895), French chemist and biologist **12** 125-127
Bernard, Claude **2** 208-210
Dubos, René Jules **5** 119
Dumas, Jean Baptiste André **5** 138-139
Liebig, Justus von **9** 403-404
Lister, Joseph **9** 444-445
Metchnikoff, Élie **10** 532-533
Meyerhof, Otto Fritz **10** 537-539
Semmelweis, Ignaz Philipp **14** 101-102
Van't Hoff, Jacobus Hendricus
15 431-432

Pasteur Institute (Paris)
Curie, Marie Sklodowska **4** 339-341
Lwoff, André **10** 58-59
Metchnikoff, Élie **10** 532-533
Pasteur, Louis **12** 125-127

Pasteur-Meyerhof effect (biochemistry)
Meyerhof, Otto Fritz **10** 537-539

Pasto Indians (South America)
Benalcázar, Sebastián de **2** 145-146

Pastor fido, Il (musical composition)
Handel, George Frederick **7** 116-119

Pastoral Concert (painting)
Giorgione **6** 340-341

Pastoral Poetry (mural)
Puvis de Chavannes, Pierre **12** 492-493

Pastoral Symphony (musical composition)
Beethoven, Ludwig van **2** 114-117

Pastorale (musical composition)
Stravinsky, Igor Fedorovich **14** 502-506

Pastorales (poems)
Jiménez, Juan Ramón **8** 261-262

Pastoralism (art and literature)
Drayton, Michael **5** 97-98
Fragonard, Jean Honoré **6** 38-39
Froissart, Jean **6** 124-125

Giorgione **6** 340-341
Milton, John **11** 43-46
Spenser, Edmund **14** 373-376
Theocritus **15** 171-172

Pastorals (book)
Pope, Alexander **12** 395-397

Pastores de Belén, Los (novel)
Lope Félix de Vega Carpio **9** 503-506

Pastors' Emergency League
see Confessing Church of Anti-Nazi
German Protestants

Pasture, Rogelet de le
see Weyden, Rogier van der

Pastures of Heaven, The (literary collection)
Steinbeck, John Ernst **14** 416-417

Patagonia (region , South America)
Darwin, Charles Robert **4** 397-399

Pataliputra (city, India)
Chandragupta Maurya **3** 426

Patanjali (book)
Biruni, Abu Rayhan al- **2** 284-285

Patch, Anthony (literary character)
Fitzgerald, Francis Scott Key **5** 470-472

PATCHEN, KENNETH (1911-1972), American experimental poet and novelist
12 128-129

PATEL, VALLABHBHAI (1875-1950), Indian political leader **12** 129-130
Prasad, Rajendra **12** 433

Patent Office (Washington, District of Columbia)
Mills, Robert **11** 36-37

Patente, La (story; play)
Pirandello, Luigi **12** 319-321

Patents (United States)
Colt, Samuel **4** 172-173
Eastman, George **5** 186
Edison, Thomas Alva **5** 206-208
Fitch, John **5** 467-468
Goddard, Robert Hutchings **6** 376-377
Goodyear, Charles **6** 441
Howe, Elias **7** 529-530
Stevens, John **14** 439-440

Pater, Jean Baptiste (1695-1736), French painter
Watteau, Antoine **16** 143-144

PATER, WALTER HORATIO (1839-1894), English author **12** 130-131
Swinburne, Algernon Charles **15** 54-55

Paterson (city, New Jersey)
Colt, Samuel **4** 172-173
Haywood, William Dudley **7** 232-233

Paterson (poem)
Williams, William Carlos **16** 308-309

PATERSON, ANDREW BARTON
(1864-1941), Australian folk poet
12 131-132
Lawson, Henry **9** 254-255

PATERSON, WILLIAM (1745-1806), American jurist **12** 132-133

Macarthur, John **10** 78

Path of Life
see Shulhan Aruk

Path of Upright Ones (poem)
Luzzato, Moses Hayyim **10** 57-58

Path through the Fields (painting)
Pissaro, Camille **12** 326-327

Pathelin (anonymous farce)
Villon, François **15** 499-501

Father Panchali (novel; Banerji)
Ray, Satyajit **13** 60-61

Pathet Lao (Lao political group)
Souvanna Phouma **14** 357-358

Pathétique (musical composition)
Beethoven, Ludwig van **2** 114-117
Tchaikovsky, Peter Ilyich **15** 130-132

Pathewaie to Knowledge, The (book)
Recorde, Robert **13** 68-69

Pathfinder, The (novel)
Cooper, James Fenimore **4** 220-223

Pathology (science)
Andersen, Dorothy **1** 212
Bernard, Claude **2** 208-210
Cabot, Richard Clarke **3** 200
Domagk, Gerhard Johannes Paul
5 48-50
Eijkman, Christian **5** 228
Fernel, Jean François **5** 425-426
Hardy, Harriet **7** 150
Metchnikoff, Élie **10** 532-533
Morgagni, Giovanni Battista
11 158-159
Müller, Johannes Peter **11** 239-240
Sanctorius **13** 459
Slye, Maud **14** 276-277
Virchow, Rudolf Ludwig Carl
15 506-507
see also Scientists—pathologists

Patience (operetta)
Gilbert, William Schwenck **6** 314-315
Sullivan, Arthur Seymour **15** 23

Patinir, Joachim (1485?-1524), Flemish painter
Claude Lorrain **4** 89-90

PATIÑO, SIMÓN ITURRI (1862-1947), Bolivian industrialist and entrepreneur
12 133-134

Patio with Cloud (painting)
O'Keeffe, Georgia **11** 487-489

Patkul, Johann Reinhold (1660-1707), Livonian nobleman and adventurer
Charles XII **3** 464-466

Patmore, Coventry Kersey Dighton
(1823-1896), English poet
Heavysege, Charles **7** 246

Patmos (hymn)
Hölderlin, Johann Christian Friedrich
7 451-452

Patna (literary ship)
Conrad, Joseph **4** 205-207

PATON, ALAN STEWART (1903-1988), South African writer and liberal leader
12 134-135

Patras (city; Greece)
Constantine XI **4** 211-212

Patriarchy (sociology)
Le Play, Guillaume Frédéric **9** 350-351

Patrician, The (novel)
Galsworthy, John **6** 189-190

Patricians and Patricides (mural)
Siqueiros, David Alfaro **14** 256

PATRICK, JENNIE R. (born 1949), African American chemical engineer **12** 136-137

PATRICK, RUTH (born 1907), American limnologist **12** 137-138

PATRICK, ST. (died circa 460), British missionary bishop to Ireland **12** 135-136
Columba **4** 175-176
Yeats, William Butler **16** 445-447

Patrie (musical composition)
Bizet, Georges **2** 296-297

Patrimony of St. Peter
Gregory I **6** 531-532

Patriot for Me, A (play)
Osborne, John **12** 16-17

Patriote party (Lower Canada)
Lafontaine, Louis-Hippolyte **9** 157-158
Papineau, Louis-Joseph **12** 91

Patriotic school (French Canadian literature)
Fréchette, Louis-Honoré **6** 77-78
Garneau, François-Xavier **6** 219-220

Patriotic Songs (poems)
Treitschke, Heinrich von **15** 293-294

Patriotic Union (political party; Spain)
Primo de Rivera y Orbaneja, Miguel
12 454-455

Patriotism
see Nationalism

Patrocinium musices (music collection)
Lassus, Roland de **9** 216-218

Patronage (U.S. politics)
Garfield, James Abram **6** 213-214
Platt, Thomas Collier **12** 347-348
Roosevelt, Theodore **13** 280-283

PATTEN, SIMON NELSON (1852-1922), American economist **12** 138-139
Robinson, James Harvey **13** 208

Patterness novels
Butler, Octavia E. **3** 182-183

Patterns (poem)
Lowell, Amy **10** 13

Patterns of Culture (book)
Benedict, Ruth Fulton **2** 154-155

PATTERSON, FREDERICK DOUGLAS
(1901-1988), African American educator
12 139-140

PATTON, GEORGE SMITH, JR.
(1885-1945), American Army officer
12 140-141
Alexander of Tunis, 1st Earl **1** 135-136
Montgomery, Bernard Law **11** 135-136

Patzinaks (Asian people)
Alexius I **1** 143-144

PAUL I (1754-1801), Russian czar
1796-1801 **12** 143-144
Alexander I **1** 130-132
Baranov, Aleksandr Andreievich
1 499-500
Catherine the Great **3** 370-372, 426
Nesselrode, Karl Robert **11** 348-349
Nicholas I **11** 377-378

Paul II (Pietro Barbo; 1417-71), pope
1464-71
Alberti, Leon Battista **1** 113-115

PAUL III (Alessandro Farnese; 1468-1549),
pope 1534-49 **12** 144-145
appointees
Bembo, Pietro **2** 144-145
Ignatius of Loyola **8** 108-109
Paul IV **12** 145-146
Pius IV **12** 332
art patronage
Cellini, Benvenuto **3** 391-392
Michelangelo Buonarroti **11** 2-5
Sangallo family **13** 464-466
Titian **15** 242-244
Catholic Reformation
Cajetan **3** 215-216
Charles V **3** 457-459

PAUL IV (Giampietro Carafa; 1476-1559),
pope 1555-59 **12** 145-146
Alba, Duke of **1** 103-104
Cajetan **3** 215-216
Palestrina, Giovanni Pierluigi da
12 70-72
Paul III **12** 144-145
Pius IV **12** 332

Paul V (Camillo Borghese; 1552-1621),
pope 1605-21
Bernini, Gian Lorenzo **2** 214-216
Pázmány, Péter **12** 164-165
Sarpi, Paolo **13** 487-488

PAUL VI (Giovanni Battista Montini;
1897-1978), pope **12** 146-148
John, XXIII **8** 277-280
Marcuse, Herbert **10** 245-247
Rahner, Karl **13** 4-5

Paul, Elliot Harold (1891-1958), American
writer
Stein, Gertrude **14** 414-415

Paul, John
see Jones, John Paul

Paul, Prince (1893-1976), regent of
Yugoslavia 1934-41
Alexander of Yugoslavia **1** 136-137

PAUL, ST. (died 66/67), Christian theologian and Apostle **12** 141-143
associates
Jesus of Nazareth **8** 251-255

John, St. **8** 273-274
Luke **10** 38
Mark **10** 266-267
Peter **12** 252-253
commentaries on
Jowett, Benjamin **8** 364-365
Lombard, Peter **9** 490-491
Luther, Martin **10** 48-51
influence of
Augustine **1** 367-370
Colet, John **4** 157-158
Rabelais, François **12** 524-526
interpretations
Baur, Ferdinand Christian **2** 74-75
Bultmann, Rudolf Karl **3** 119-120
Marcion **10** 238-239

Paul Bunyan (opera)
Britten, Benjamin **3** 10-11

Paul Lange and Tora Parsberg (play)
Bjørnson, Bjørnstjerne **2** 299-300

Paul of Aegina (flourished late 7th century),
Greek surgeon
Celsus, Aulus Cornelius **3** 393

Paul Revere's Ride (poem; Longfellow)
Revere, Paul **13** 110-111

Paul the Peddler (book)
Alger, Horatio **1** 153-154

Paul the Sharper... (novel)
Quevedo Y Villegas, Francisco Gómez
de **12** 511

Paula (magazine)
Allende, Isabel **1** 172-174

Paulding, Hiram (1797-1878), American
naval officer
Walker, William **16** 68-69

Paulding, James K. (1778-1860), American
writer
Irving, Washington **8** 141-143

Paulet, Sir Amyas (1536?-1588), English
diplomat
Bacon, Francis **1** 422-424

PAULI, WOLFGANG ERNST (1900-1958),
Austrian theoretical physicist **12** 149
Bohr, Niels Henrik David **2** 366-368
Born, Max **2** 420-421
Chadwick, James **3** 405-406
Fermi, Enrico **5** 422-424
Heisenberg, Werner Karl **7** 261-263
Oppenheimer, J. Robert **11** 525-526
Rabi, Isidor Isaac **12** 526-527
Tomonaga, Sin-itiro **15** 265-266

Pauli exclusion principle
see Exclusion principle (physics)

Paulicians (heretical sect)
Basil I **2** 49-50

Pauline (poem)
Browning, Robert **3** 53-55

Pauline Chapel (Vatican)
Michelangelo Buonarroti **11** 2-5
Sangallo family **13** 464-466

Pauline Epistles (New Testament)
see Paul, St.

PAULING, LINUS CARL (born 1901),
American chemist **12** 150-152
Lewis, Gilbert Newton **9** 384-385
Watson, James Dewey **16** 137-138

Paulinus, St. (died 644), Roman missionary,
archbishop of York
Alcuin of York **1** 122-123

Paulist Fathers (religious congregation)
Hecker, Isaac Thomas **7** 250-251

Paulsen, Friedrich (1846-1908), German
philosopher
Tönnies, Ferdinand **15** 266-267

Paulus, Aemilius (229?-160 B.C.), Roman
general and statesman
Polybios **12** 384-385

Paumgartner Altarpiece
Dürer, Albrecht **5** 159-161

Paura della libertà (essays)
Levi, Carlo **9** 364

Pausanias (flourished 2d century), Greek
traveler and geographer
Ictinus **8** 101
Phidias **12** 265-267
Polykleitos **12** 385-386
Praxiteles **12** 433-434

Pausanias (flourished 5th century B.C.),
Spartan general
Agesilaus II **1** 79-80

Pauson House (Phoenix, Arizona)
Wright, Frank Lloyd **16** 398-401

Pauvre Belgique (book)
Baudelaire, Charles Pierre **2** 61-63

Pauvre Christ de Bomba, Le (novel)
Beti, Mongo **2** 242-243

Pauvre matelot, Le (musical composition)
Milhaud, Darius **11** 17-18

Pavana italiana (musical composition)
Cabezón, Antonio **3** 197-198

Pavane (music)
Milán, Luis **11** 15-16
Ravel, Maurice Joseph **13** 54-55

PAVAROTTI, LUCIANO (born 1935), Italian tenor **12** 152-154

PAVESE, CESARE (1908-1950), Italian novelist, poet, and critic **12** 154-155
Vittorini, Elio **16** 2-3

Pavia (city, lt.)
Julius II **8** 384-386

Pavia, battle of (1525)
Francis I **6** 40-43

Pavia, Cathedral of
Bramante, Donato **2** 493-494

Pavia, Certosa of
Visconti, Gian Galeazzo **15** 510-511

Pavia, Council of (1423)
Martin V **10** 287-288

Pavia, University of
Cardano, Geronimo **3** 285-286
Sforza, Lodovico **14** 127-128
Spallanzani, Lazzaro **14** 360-361
Valla, Lorenzo **15** 406
Volta, Alessandro **16** 12-14

PAVLOV, IVAN PETROVICH (1849-1936),
Russian physiologist **12** 155-157
Frisch, Karl von **6** 117-118
Sherrington, Charles Scott **14** 187-189
Skinner, Burrhus Frederic **14** 269-270

PAVLOVA, ANNA (1881-1931), Russian
ballet dancer **12** 157-159

Pavón, José Maria Morelos ye
see Morelos, José Maria

Pawn Shop (poems)
Breton, André **2** 519-520

Pawtuxet (Rhode Island)
Gorton, Samuell **6** 460

Pax Britannica (19th century)
Palmerston, 3d Viscount **12** 81-83

Pax dei (Roman law)
Constantine I **4** 209-211

Pax Romana
Paul **12** 141-143
Tiberius Julius Caesar Augustus
15 217-218

PAYNE, JOHN HOWARD (1791-1852),
American actor, playwright, and songwriter **12** 159

Payne-Aldrich tariff (United States; 1909)
Taft, William Howard **15** 78-81

PAYNE-GAPOSCHKIN, CECILIA
(1900-1979), American astronomer
12 159-161

Paysage polaire, Le (poem)
Leconte de Lisle, Charles Marie René
9 273-274

Paysages et intérieurs (color lithograph)
Vuillard, Jean Édouard **16** 36

Paysan de Paris, Le (book)
Aragon, Louis **1** 271-272

Paysan parvenu, Le (novel)
Marivaux, Pierre Carlet de Chamblain
de **10** 265-266

PAZ, OCTAVIO (born 1914), Mexican
diplomat, critic, editor, translator, poet,
and essayist **12** 161-162

PAZ ESTENSSORO, VICTOR (born 1907),
Bolivian statesman and reformer
12 163-164
Barrientos Ortuño, René **2** 22-23
Patiño, Simón Iturri **12** 133-134

PAZ ZAMORA, JAIME (born 1939), president of Bolivia (1989-) **12** 165-167

PÁZMÁNY, PÉTER (1570-1637), Hungarian
archbishop **12** 164-165

Pazzi Chapel (Sta Croce, Florence)
Brunelleschi, Filippo **3** 70-72
Luca della Robbia **10** 19-20

Pazzi conspiracy (Florence; 1478)
Medici, Lorenzo de' **10** 450-451

Pazzi Conspiracy, The (play)
Alfieri, Vittoria **1** 145-146

PEABODY, ELIZABETH PALMER
(1804-1894), American educator and
author **12** 167-168
Alcott, Amos Bronson **1** 121
Froebel, Friedrich Wilhelm August
6 122-123

PEABODY, GEORGE (1795-1869), Ameri-
can merchant, financier, and philanthro-
pist **12** 168
Curry, Jabez Lamar Monroe **4** 346-347
Marsh, Othniel Charles **10** 275-276
Morgan, Junius Spencer **11** 166-167

Peabody Conservatory (Baltimore, Maryland)
Bennett, Richard Rodney **2** 172

Peabody Museum (Harvard University)
Fletcher, Alice Cunningham **5** 486-487
Kidder, Alfred Vincent **8** 541-542

Peabody Museum (Yale University)
Marsh, Othniel Charles **10** 275-276

Peace
activists,
see Activists, peace
education to promote
Andrews, Fannie Fern Phillips
1 231-232
in art
Daumier, Honoré Victorin **4** 403-405
Portinari, Cândido **12** 407-408
in literature
Aristophanes **1** 293-294
Cousins, Norman **4** 274-276
Coward, Noel **4** 279-280
Vaughan, Henry **15** 444-445
see also Pacificism

Peace and Freedom party (California)
Cleaver, Leroy Eldridge **4** 97-98

Peace Congress (Paris; 1849)
Brown, William Wells **3** 48-49

Peace Corps (United States)
Kennedy, John Fitzgerald **8** 502-506
Roosevelt, Eleanor **13** 275-277
Stroessner, Alfredo **14** 511-512

Peace Democrats (United States Civil War)
Vallandigham, Clement Laird **15** 406-407
Wood, Fernando **16** 367-368

Peace Information Center
Du Bois, William Edward Burghardt
5 116-118

Peace of God (1043)
Henry III **7** 290

Peace of 1043 (China)
Fan Chung-yen **5** 376-377

Peace River (Canada)
Mackenzie, Alexander **10** 103-104

Peaceable Kingdom (painting)
Hicks, Edward **7** 375

Peach Fount Colony (China)
T'ao Ch'ien **15** 104-105

Peacock (ship)
Lawrence, James **9** 251-252

PEACOCK, THOMAS LOVE (1785-1866),
English novelist and satirist **12** 169
Meredith, George **10** 512-513

PEALE, CHARLES WILLSON (1741-1827),
American painter and scientist
12 169-171
Peale, Rembrandt **12** 172-173
Stuart, Gilbert **14** 513-515

PEALE, NORMAN VINCENT (1898-1993),
American religious leader who blended
psychotherapy and religion **12** 171-172

Peale, Raphael (1774-1825), American
artist
Harnett, William Michael **7** 160-161

PEALE, REMBRANDT (1778-1860), American painter **12** 172-173
Moran, Thomas **11** 151-152

Peale Family (painting)
Peale, Charles Willson **12** 169-171

Peano, Giuseppe (1858-1932), Italian
mathematician
Leibniz, Gottfried Wilhelm von
9 307-310
Russell, Bertrand Arthur William
13 373-374

Peanut (plant)
Carver, George Washington **3** 346-347

Peanuts (comic strip)
Schulz, Charles M. **14** 38-39

Pearl, The (novella)
Steinbeck, John Ernst **14** 416-417

Pearl Harbor (city; Hawaii)
Japanese attack (1941)
Halsey, William Frederick **7** 91-92
Hirohito **7** 410-412
Hoover, Herbert Clark **7** 483-485
Lindbergh, Charles Augustus
9 421-423
Marshall, George Catlett
10 278-279
Monnet, Jean **11** 109-110
Nimitz, Chester William **11** 395-396
Roosevelt, Franklin Delano
13 277-280
Stilwell, Joseph Warren **14** 456-457
Stimson, Henry Lewis **14** 457-458
Tojo, Hideki **15** 254-256
Wainwright, Jonathan Mayhew
16 45-46
response to attack
Curtin, John Joseph **4** 348-349
Morgenthau, Henry Jr. **11** 172-173

Pearl Mosque (Agra, India)
Shah Jahan **14** 138-139

Pearl of Brabant Altarpiece (painting)
Bouts, Dirk **2** 458-459

Pearl Pictures (painting)
Vermeer, Jan **15** 466-467

Pearls and Pebbles (book)
Traill, Catharine Parr **15** 291

PEARSE, PATRICK HENRY (1879-1916),
Irish poet, educator, and revolutionary
12 173-174
Collins, Michael **4** 167-168
Colum, Padraic **4** 174-175
Hyde, Douglas **8** 82-83

Pearson, Karl (1857-1936), English scientist
Galton, Francis **6** 193-194

PEARSON, LESTER BOWLES (1897-1972),
Canadian statesman and diplomat, prime
minister **12** 174-175

PEARY, ROBERT EDWIN (1856-1920),
American explorer **12** 175-176
Amundsen, Roald **1** 206-207
Henson, Matthew A. **7** 312-314
MacMillan, Donald Baxter **10** 111-112

Peas (vegetable)
Mendel, Johann Gregor **10** 483-486

Peasant and the Satyr, The (painting)
Jordaens, Jacob **8** 347-349

Peasant Dance (painting)
Bruegel, Pieter the Elder **3** 65-67

Peasant Family (painting)
Le Nain, Antoine, Louis and Mathieu
9 321-322

Peasant rebellions
England (1381)
Chaucer, Geoffrey **3** 482-485
Gower, John **6** 475-476
Richard II **13** 130-131
Wyclif, John **16** 412-413
Germany (1524-1525)
Karlstadt, Andreas Bodenheim von
8 449
Luther, Martin **10** 48-51
Münzer, Thomas **11** 251-252
Korea (1198)
Ch'oe Ch'ung-hn **4** 13
Russia (1773-1775)
Pugachev, Emelyan Ivanovich
12 478-479

Peasant Wedding Feast (painting)
Bruegel, Pieter the Elder **3** 65-67

Peasants
as revolutionary force
Lenin, Vladimir Ilich **9** 323-326
Mao Zedong **10** 225-227
Plekhanov, Georgi Valentinovich
12 351-352
in literature
Silone, Ignazio **14** 231-232
oppression of
Francis II **6** 43-44
Frederick II **6** 81-84
Frederick William I **6** 86-87
Frederick William III **6** 87

Peasants, The (story)
Chekhov, Anton Pavlovich **3** 494-497

Peasant's Association of Lower Austria
Dollfuss, Engelbert **5** 47

Peasants in the Country (painting)
Le Nain, Antoine, Louis and Mathieu
9 321-322

Peasants Playing Cards (painting)
Brouwer, Adriaen **3** 29-30

Peau de Chagrin, La (story)
Balzac, Honoré de **1** 478-480

Pecan (nut)
Carver, George Washington **3** 346-347

Pecci, Vincenzo Gioacchino
see Leo XIII

Péché de Monsieur Antoine, Le
(novel)
Sand, George **13** 459-461

Pechenegs (Turkic people)
Vladimir I **16** 5-6

Pechersky Lavra Monastery (Kiev)
Mogila, Peter **11** 74-75

Pêcheur d'Islande (novel)
Loti, Pierre **9** 519-520

Pêcheurs de perles, Les (opera)
Bizet, Georges **2** 296-297

Pechorin (literary character; Lermontov)
Goncharov, Ivan Aleksandrovich **6** 424
Lermontov, Mikhail Yurievich
9 352-353

PECHSTEIN, HERMANN MAX
(1881-1955), German Expressionist
painter and graphic artist **12** 176-177

Pechstein, Max (1881-1955), German
painter and designer
Kirchner, Ernst Ludwig **9** 34-35

PECK, ROBERT NEWTON (born 1928),
American author of children's literature
12 177-178

Peck's Bad Boy (play)
Cohan, George Michael **4** 137-138

Pecos Pueblo (region , New Mexico)
Kidder, Alfred Vincent **8** 541-542

Pecos River (Texas-Northern Mexico)
Chisum, John Simpson **4** 11
Coronado, Francisco Vásquez de **4** 247

Pedagogical Sketch Book (book)
Klee, Paul **9** 47-49

Peddlar, The (poem)
Wordsworth, William **16** 385-388

Pediatrics (medicine)
Andersen, Dorothy **1** 212
Baker, Sara Josephine **1** 455-456
Jacobi, Abraham and Mary Putnam
8 188-189
Spock, Benjamin **14** 383-385
Taussig, Helen Brooke **15** 118-120

Pedigree (novel)
Simenon, Georges **14** 233-234

PEDRARIAS (Pedro Arias de Ávila; circa
1440-1531), Spanish conqueror and
colonial governor **12** 179
Almagro, Diego de **1** 177-178
Balboa, Vasco Núñez de **1** 462-463

Benalcázar, Sebastián de **2** 145-146
de Soto, Hernando **4** 510-511
Díaz del Castillo, Bernal **4** 536-537
Pizarro, Francisco **12** 340-341

Pedrell, Felipe (1841-1922), Spanish composer
Falla, Manuel de **5** 372-373

PEDRO I (1798-1834), emperor of Brazil
and king of Portugal **12** 179-180
Andrada e Silva, José Bonifácio de
1 221-222
Caxias, Duque de **3** 386
Feijó, Diogo Antônio **5** 405-406

PEDRO II (1825-1891), emperor of Brazil
1831-89 **12** 180-181
Andrada e Silva, José Bonifácio de
1 221-222
Barbosa, Ruy **1** 503-504
Bell, Alexander Graham **2** 129-131
Deodoro da Fonseca, Manoel **4** 502
Gobineau, Comte de **6** 375-376
Heade, Martin Johnson **7** 236

Pedro III (1717-1786), king of Portugal
1777-86
Pombal, Marquês de **12** 386-387

Pedro III (king, Aragon)
see Peter III

Pedro IV (king, Portugal)
see Pedro I (emperor, Brazil)

Pedro el Cruel
see Peter the Cruel

Pedro of Castile (1334-1369), king of
Castile
Edward III **5** 211-212
Edward the Black Prince **5** 217-218

PEEL, SIR ROBERT (1788-1850), English
statesman, prime minister 1834-35 and
1841-46 **12** 181-183
ministries
Aberdeen, 4th Earl of **1** 25-26
Gladstone, William Ewart
6 357-360
Palmerston, 3d Viscount **12** 81-83
Tennyson, Alfred **15** 144-146
Victoria **15** 485-487
Wellington, 1st Duke of **16** 193-195
opponents
Disraeli, Benjamin **5** 27-29
O'Connell, Daniel **11** 465-467
supporters
Albert **1** 110-112
Cobden, Richard **4** 127-128
William IV **16** 296-297

Peel Commission of Palestine (1937)
Jabotinsky, Vladimir Evgenevich
8 167-168

Peelers (London police)
Peel, Robert **12** 181-183

Peel's Act (1819)
Peel, Robert **12** 181-183

Peenemünde (village, Germany)
von Braun, Wernher **16** 17-18

Peep-show Man (etching)
Maulbertsch, Franz Anton **10** 345

Peer Gynt (play; Ibsen)
Grieg, Edvard Hagerup **6** 541-542
Ibsen, Henrik **8** 98-100

"Pegging the market" (U.S. finance)
Cooke, Jay **4** 215-216

PÉGUY, CHARLES PIERRE (1873-1914),
French poet **12** 183-184
Claudel, Paul Louis Charles **4** 90-91

PEI, I. M. (Ieoh Ming Pei; born 1917), Chinese-American architect **12** 184-187

PEIRCE, CHARLES SANDERS (1839-1914),
American scientist and philosopher
12 187-188
Cohen, Morris Raphael **4** 139-140
Nagel, Ernest **11** 291-292
Ramsey, Frank Plumpton **13** 25
see also Pragmatism

Peisistratus (died 527 B.C.), Athenian
politician
Cleisthenes **4** 98-99

Peita (Peking)
Ch'en Tu-hsiu **3** 501-502
Dewey, John **4** 520-523
Hu Shih **8** 63-65
Li Ta-chao **9** 447
Lu Hsün **10** 35-37
Ts'ai Yüan-p'ei **15** 322

PEIXOTO, FLORIANO (1839-1895),
Brazilian marshal, president 1891-94
12 188-189
Barbosa, Ruy **1** 503-504
Deodoro da Fonseca, Manoel **4** 502

Peiyang clique (Chinese)
Wu P'ei-fu **16** 404-405
Yüan Shih-k'ai **16** 480-481

Pekah (Old Testament character)
Isaiah **8** 146-147

Peking (city, China)
Chiang Kai-shek **3** 510-513
Chifley, Joseph Benedict **3** 518
Genghis Khan **6** 263-265
Gordon, Charles George **6** 448-449
Lin Piao **9** 429-430
Ricci, Matteo **13** 124-125
Yeh-lü Ch'u-ts'ai **16** 447-449
Yung-lo **16** 482-483

Peking, Convention of (1860)
Wen-hsiang **16** 202-203

Peking Institute of Art
Ch'i Pai-shih **3** 526-527

Peking man (archeology)
Weidenreich, Franz **16** 171-172

Peking University
see Peita

Peking-Hankow Railway
Chang Chih-tung **3** 430-431
Ch'en Tu-hsiu **3** 501-502
Li Ta-chao **9** 447

Pelagianism (religion)
Jansen, Cornelis **8** 220-221
Pelagius **12** 189-190

PELAGIUS (died circa 430), British theologian **12** 189-190
see also Pelagianism

Pelagius II (died 590), pope 579-590
Gregory I **6** 531-532

Pelagonia, battle of (1259)
Michael VIII **11** 1-2

PELE (Edson Arantes Do Nascimento Pele;
born 1940), Brazilian soccer player
12 190-191

Pelerinage de la vie humaine (book;
Deguileville)
Lydgate, John **10** 61-62

Pélerinages ruskiniens en France (book)
Proust, Marcel **12** 465-467

Peleus and Thetis (mythology)
Catullus, Gaius Valerius **3** 377-378

Pelham, Henry (1695-1754), English states-
man
Copley, John Singleton **4** 228-230
George II **6** 269-270

Pelham, Peter (1697-1751), American artist
and schoolmaster
Copley, John Singleton **4** 228-230

Pelham-Holles, Thomas
see Newcastle, 1st Duke of

Pelican (ship)
Drake, Francis **5** 94-96

Pelle the Conqueror (novel)
Nexø, Martin Anderson **11** 372

Pelléas et Mélisande (opera; Debussy)
Debussy, Achille Claude **4** 445-447
Messiaen, Olivier **10** 528-529

Pelléas et Mélisande (play; Maeterlinck)
Maeterlinck, Maurice **10** 125-126
Schoenberg, Arnold **14** 24-26
Sibelius, Jean Julius Christian
14 211-212

Pellegrin, Abbé Simon Joseph (1663-1745),
French writer and librettist
Rameau, Jean Philippe **13** 17-18

Pellegrini Chapel (Verona)
Pisanello **12** 323-324
Sanmicheli, Michele **13** 469-470

PELLI, CESAR (born 1926), Hispanic American architect and educator **12** 191-192

Peloponnesian League (Greece)
Cleomenes I **4** 103

Peloponnesian War (431-404 B.C.)
Athens
Alcibiades **1** 119-120
Aristophanes **1** 293-294
Cleon **4** 104-105
Pericles **12** 219-221
Thucydides **15** 211-212
Sparta
Lysander **10** 70

Peloponnesus (region, Greece)
Aratus **1** 273-274
Canning, George **3** 258-260
Constantine XI **4** 211-212
Epaminondas **5** 291-292
Ibrahim Pasha **8** 97-98
Mahmud II **10** 145-147
Michael VIII **11** 1-2
see also Peloponnesian War

PELTIER, LEONARD (born 1944), Native
American activist **12** 193-195

Pembroke, 3d Earl of (William H. Pembroke; 1580-1630), English courtier
Charles I **3** 450-452

Penal reform
Australia
Franklin, John **6** 64-65
Phillip, Arthur **12** 279-280
England
Bentham, Jeremy **2** 176-178
Blackstone, William **2** 310-311
Fry, Elizabeth **6** 134-136
Oglethorpe, James Edward
11 482-483
Peel, Robert **12** 181-183
U.S.
Altgeld, John Peter **1** 180-182
Bigelow, John **2** 271-272
Brown, William Wells **3** 48-49
Field, David Dudley **5** 439-440
Hoover, Herbert Clark **7** 483-485
Howe, Samuel Gridley **7** 537
Lieber, Francis **9** 401-402
Osborne, Thomas Mott **12** 17-18
Talbert, Mary Morris Burnett
15 86-88
Tocqueville, Alexis Charles Henri
Maurice Clérel de **15** 250-251

Penalty, The (film)
Goldwyn, Samuel **6** 416

Penance of St. John Chrysostom (engraving)
Cranach, Lucas the Elder **4** 289-290

Peñaranda, Enrique (1892-1972), president
of Bolivia
Paz, Octavio **12** 161-162

Pendennis (novel)
Thackeray, William Makepeace
15 159-161

PENDERECKI, KRZYSZTOF (born 1933),
Polish composer **12** 195-197

Pendergast, Thomas J. (1872-1945), Ameri-
can political boss
Curley, James Michael **4** 344-345
Murphy, Frank **11** 260-261
Truman, Harry S. **15** 314-316

PENDLETON, EDMUND (1721-1803),
American political leader **12** 197-198
Taylor, John **15** 126
Wythe, George **16** 415

PENDLETON, GEORGE HUNT
(1825-1889), American politician **12** 198
Eaton, Dorman Bridgman **5** 190-191

Pendleton Civil Service Act (United States; 1883)
Arthur, Chester Alan **1** 321-323
Eaton, Dorman Bridgman **5** 190-191
Pendleton, George Hunt **12** 198

Pendulum (instrument)
Galileo Galilei **6** 180-183
Huygens, Christiaan **8** 79-81

Penelope (literary character)
Joyce, James **8** 365-367

Penelope (opera)
Fauré, Gabriel Urbain **5** 397-398

PENFIELD, WILDER GRAVES (1891-1976), Canadian neurosurgeon **12** 198-200

P'eng Chen (born 1899), Chinese politician and administrator
Liu Shao-Ch'i **9** 453-455

P'eng Teh-Huai (1899-1974), Chinese Communist leader
Lin Piao **9** 429-430
Liu Shao-Ch'i **9** 453-455

Penguin Island (novel)
France, Anatole **6** 39-40

Penicillin (antibiotic)
Chain, Ernst Boris **3** 407-408
Domagk, Gerhard Johannes Paul **5** 48-50
Fleming, Alexander **5** 483-485
Florey, Howard Walter **5** 491-492
Hodgkin, Dorothy Crowfoot **7** 432-434

Peninsular War (1803-1813)
Goya y Lucientes, Francisco de Paula José de **6** 476-478
Landor, Walter Savage **9** 186-187
Liverpool, 2nd Earl of **9** 456-457
Murat, Joachim **11** 253-254
Napoleon I **11** 306-310
Ney, Michel **11** 372-373
Pitt, William the Younger **12** 329-331
Wellington, 1st Duke of **16** 193-195

Pénitencier, Le (novel)
Martin du Gard, Roger **10** 295-296

Penitent St. Jerome (painting)
Antonello da Messina **1** 251-252

Penitente, El (dance)
Cunningham, Merce **4** 337-338

Penn, Sir William (1621-1670), English admiral
Penn, William **12** 200-202

Penn, Thomas (1702-1775), American colonist
Dickinson, John **4** 543-544

PENN, WILLIAM (1644-1718), English Quaker, founder of Pennsylvania **12** 200-202
Bradford, William **2** 476-477
Logan, James **9** 487-488
St. Clair, Arthur **13** 429-430
Weems, Mason Locke **16** 170
Zinzendorf, Nikolaus Ludwig von **16** 522-523

PENNEY, J. C. (James Cash Penney; 1875-1971), American chain store executive and philanthropist **12** 202-203

Pennies from Heaven (film)
Still, William Grant **14** 455-456

Penn's Treaty with the Indians (painting)
Hicks, Edward **7** 375

Pennsylvania (state, United States)
and Native American lands
Cornplanter **4** 239-241
colonial period
Bradford, William **2** 476-477
Franklin, Benjamin **6** 60-64
Galloway, Joseph **6** 186-187
Logan, James **9** 487-488
Penn, William **12** 200-202
Rittenhouse, David **13** 180-181
St. Clair, Arthur **13** 429-430
exploration
Brûlé, Étienne **3** 67-68
Gist, Christopher **6** 352-353
politics
Buchanan, James **3** 89-90
Cameron, Simon **3** 246-247
Curtin, Andrew Gregg **4** 347-348
Forbes, John **5** 507-508
Franklin, Benjamin **6** 60-64
Morris, Robert **11** 185-187
Palmer, Alexander Mitchell **12** 77-78
Penrose, Boies **12** 203-204
Pinchot, Gifford **12** 308-309
Quay, Matthew Stanley **12** 507
Shippen, Edward **14** 197-198
Stevens, Thaddeus **14** 442-443
religion
Asbury, Francis **1** 324-325
Mühlenberg, Heinrich Melchior **11** 232-233
Zinzendorf, Nikolaus Ludwig von **16** 522-523

Pennsylvania, University of (Philadelphia)
established
Morgan, John **11** 162-163
Smith, William **14** 301
faculty
Bache, Alexander Dallas **1** 420
Du Bois, William Edward Burghardt **5** 116-118
Elsasser, Walter Maurice **5** 277-278
Hare, Robert **7** 152-153
Lea, Henry Charles **9** 261-262
McMaster, John Bach **10** 426-427
Meyerhof, Otto Fritz **10** 537-539
Osler, William **12** 19-20
Patten, Simon Nelson **12** 138-139
Pound, Ezra Loomis **12** 415-417
Rochberg, George **13** 221-222
Rush, Benjamin **13** 364-365
Venturi, Robert **15** 461-463

Pennsylvania Academy of Fine Arts (Philadelphia)
Eakins, Thomas **5** 176-177
Peale, Charles Willson **12** 169-171

Peto, John Frederick **12** 259
Rush, William **13** 365-366

Pennsylvania Antislavery Society
Purvis, Robert **12** 485-486

Pennsylvania Constitutional Convention (1789)
Gallatin, Albert **6** 183-184

Pennsylvania Gazette (newspaper)
Franklin, Benjamin **6** 60-64

Pennsylvania Institute for the Blind (Philadelphia)
Blaine, James Gillespie **2** 312-313

Pennsylvania Journal (periodical)
Bradford, William **2** 477

Pennsylvania oil strike (1859)
Rockefeller, John Davison **13** 226-228

Pennsylvania Railroad (United States)
Carnegie, Andrew **3** 309-312
Rockefeller, John Davison **13** 226-228

Pennsylvania Reserve Corps
Curtin, Andrew Gregg **4** 347-348

Pennsylvania rifle (firearm)
Morgan, Daniel **11** 160-161

Pennsylvania School of Social Work (Philadelphia)
Rank, Otto **13** 33

Pennsylvania Society for Promoting the Abolition of Slavery (established 1774)
Rush, Benjamin **13** 364-365

Pennsylvania Station (old; New York City)
McKim, Charles Follen **10** 417-418

Penny for a Song, A (opera)
Bennett, Richard Rodney **2** 172

Penology
see Penal reform; Punishment

Penrod novels (literature)
Tarkington, Newton Booth **15** 109

PENROSE, BOIES (1860-1921), American senator and political boss **12** 203-204
Mellon, Andrew William **10** 469-470

PENROSE, ROGER (born 1931), British mathematician and physicist **12** 204-205

Pensacola (city, Florida)
Gálvez, Bernardo de **6** 195-196

Pensador Mexicano, El
see Fernández de Lizardi, Josè joaquin

Pensées (book)
Pascal, Blaise **12** 122-124

Penseroso, Il (poem; Milton)
Blake, William **2** 316-318
Handel, George Frederick **7** 116-119
Milton, John **11** 43-46

Pensieri (literary collection)
Leopardi, Giacomo **9** 344-345

Pensiero e azione (journal)
Mazzini, Giuseppe **10** 381-383

Pension plans
see Social security

Pentagon Papers (book)
Ellsberg, Daniel **5** 275-277
Salisbury, Harrison Evans **13** 449-451

Pentateuch (Old Testament)
Ezra **5** 356-357
Leon, Moses de **9** 336
Tyndale, William **15** 373-374

Pentecost (hymn)
Manzoni, Alessandro **10** 222-224

Pentécost (painting)
Nolde, Emil **11** 419-420

Pentecostal sects (religion)
McPherson, Aimee Semple **10** 434

Penthesilea (play)
Kleist, Heinrich von **9** 52-53

Pentheus (literary character)
Euripides **5** 332-334

Pentimenti (art)
Velázquez, Diego Rodríguez de Silva y
15 454-456

Pen-wu, theory of (philosophy)
Tao-an **15** 103-104

Peony (novel)
Buck, Pearl Sydenstricker **3** 91-93

People (sculpture)
Marini, Marino **10** 260-262

People, The (Het Volk; political party, South
Africa)
Botha, Louis **2** 434-436
Smuts, Jan Christian **14** 309-310

People, Yes, The (poems)
Sandburg, Carl **13** 461-462

People of Hemsö, The (novel)
Strindberg, August **14** 509-511

People of Plenty (book)
Potter, David M. **12** 412

People of the Abyss, The (book)
London, Jack **9** 494-495

People of the City (novel)
Ekwensi, Cyprian **5** 242-243

People Will Say We're in Love (song)
Rodgers, Richard Charles **13** 234-236

People's Action Party (Singapore)
Goh Chok Tong **6** 393-395

People's Commissariat for Internal Affairs
(NKVD)
Beria, Lavrenty Pavlovich **2** 192-193
Dzerzhinsky, Felix Edmundovich
5 173-174

People's Democratic party (Sudan)
Khalil, Sayyid Abdullah **8** 531-532

Peoples Democratic Party of Afghanistan
Najibullah, Mohammad **11** 296-298

People's National Congress (Guyana)
Burnham, Forbes **3** 149-151

People's National Party (Jamaica)
Manley, Michael Norman **10** 200-201

People's party (Turkey)
Atatürk, Ghazi Mustapha Kemal
1 356-357

People's party (United States)
see Populist party (U.S. politics)

People's Progressive party (Gambia)
Jawara, Dauda Kairaba **8** 227-228

People's Socialist party (India)
Narayan, Jayaprakash **11** 312-313

Peoples Songs, Inc.
Seeger, Pete **14** 83-84

Pepin (777-810), king of Italy 781-810
Charlemagne **3** 445-447
Louis I **9** 522-523

Pepin I (803?-838), king of Aquitaine
817-838
Louis I **9** 522-523

Pepin II (Pepin of Herstal; died 714), ruler
of the Franks 687-714
Martel, Charles **10** 285

Pepin III (Pepin the Short; 714?-768), king
of the Franks 751-768
Boniface **2** 391
Charlemagne **3** 445-447

Pépin, Albert (1849-1917), French artist
Bonvalot, Pierre Gabriel Édouard **2** 396

Pepita Jiménez (novel)
Valera y Alcalá Galiano, Juan **15** 403

PEPPER, CLAUDE DENSON (1900-1989),
Florida attorney, state representative, U.S.
senator, and U.S. representative
12 205-206

PEPPERELL, SIR WILLIAM (1696-1759),
American merchant and soldier
12 206-207

Pepperidge Farm Inc.
Rudkin, Margaret Fogarty **13** 346-347

Pepsin (enzyme)
Babcock, Stephen Moulton **1** 410-411
Northrop, John Howard **11** 430-431
Schwann, Theodor **14** 51-52

Pepsodent Show, The (radio)
Hope, Bob **7** 487-489

Pepusch, John (1667-1752), German-born
English composer
Gay, John **6** 243-244

PEPYS, SAMUEL (1633-1703), English
diarist **12** 207-208
Lely, Peter **9** 315

Pequod (literary ship)
Melville, Herman **10** 472-476

Pequot Indians (North America)
Endecott, John **5** 284-285

Pequot War (1637)
Eliot, John **5** 256-258
Endecott, John **5** 284-285
Underhill, John **15** 388
Williams, Roger **16** 304-305

Perception (philosophy)
Berkeley, George **2** 197-198

Descartes, René **4** 505-508
Hume, David **8** 31-34
Kant, Immanuel **8** 430-432
Leibniz, Gottfried Wilhelm von
9 307-310
Reid, Thomas **13** 87-88
Spinoza, Baruch **14** 381-383
Whitehead, Alfred North **16** 242-244

Perception (psychology)
Bartlett, Frederic Charles **2** 34-35
Helmholtz, Hermann Ludwig Ferdinand
von **7** 268-269
Mead, George Herbert **10** 437-438

Perceval (poem; Chrestien de Troyes)
Chrestien de Troyes **4** 23-24
Wolfram von Eschenbach **16** 360-361

Perceval, Spencer (1762-1812), English
statesman
Liverpool, 2nd Earl of **9** 456-457
Palmerston, 3d Viscount **12** 81-83

Perch'i' no spero di tornar giammai (ballad)
Cavalcanti, Guido **3** 382

Percy, Thomas
see Worcester, Earl of

Perdikkas (died 321 B.C.), Macedonian
general and statesman
Antigonus I **1** 248-249
Ptolemy I **12** 470-472
Seleucus I **14** 92-93

Perdikkas III (died 359 B.C.), king of Macedonia
Philip II **12** 269-271

Père Duchesne, Le (journal)
Hébert, Jacques René **7** 247-248

Père Goriot, Le (novel)
Balzac, Honoré de **1** 478-480

Peredelkino (writers colony, Union of Soviet Socialist Republics)
Pasternak, Boris Leonidovich
12 124-125

Peregrinacion de Bayoán, La (novel)
Hostos, Eugenio María de **7** 513-514

Peregrine Pickle (novel)
Smollett, Tobias George **14** 305-307

Peregrino en su patria, El (novel)
Lope Félix de Vega Carpio **9** 503-506

PEREGRINUS, PETRUS (flourished
1261-69), French scholastic and scientist
12 208

PERELMAN, S. J. (Sidney Jerome Perelman;
1904-1979), American cartoonist, satirist,
and parodist **12** 209-210

Perequillo sarniento, El (novel)
Fernández de Lizardi, José Joaquin
5 424-425

PERES, SHIMON (born 1923), head of the
Israel Labour Party and Israeli prime minister (1984-1986) **12** 210-211

PERETZ, ISAAC LOEB (1851-1915), Jewish
poet, novelist, and playwright **12** 212

Asch, Shalom **1** 325-326

Perevolotjna, battle of (1709)
Charles XII **3** 464-466

Pereyaslav agreement (1654)
Chmielnicki, Bogdan **4** 12-13

PÉREZ, CARLOS ANDRÉS (born 1922),
president of Venezuela (1974-1979)
12 212-214

Pérez, Juan (died circa 1515), Spanish
Franciscan
Columbus, Christopher **4** 176-179

Pérez de Ayala, Ramón (1881-1962), Spanish poet and diplomat
Cela y Trulock, Camilo José **3** 389-390

PÉREZ DE CUELLAR, JAVIER (born 1920),
Peruvian foreign service officer and secretary general of the United Nations
(1982-) **12** 214-215

PÉREZ ESQUIVEL, ADOLFO (born 1931),
Argentine artist and human rights activist
12 215-217

Pérez Galdós, Benito
see Galdós, Benito Pérez

PÉREZ JIMENEZ, MARCOS (born 1914),
Venezuelan dictator **12** 217-218
Betancourt, Rómulo **2** 237-238

Perfect Fool, The (opera)
Holst, Gustav **7** 459-460

Perfect Wagnerite, The (book)
Shaw, George Bernard **14** 163-164

Perfectionist, The (book)
Noyes, John Humphrey **11** 437-438

PERGOLESI, GIOVANNI BATTISTA
(1710-1736), Italian composer
12 218-219
Cimarosa, Domenico **4** 61-62

Peri (musical composition)
Schumann, Robert Alexander **14** 41-43

Peri, Jacopo (1561-1633), Italian composer
Caccini, Giulio **3** 205-206
Monteverdi, Claudio Giovanni Antonio
11 126-128

Peri Bathous (book)
Pope, Alexander **12** 395-397

Peribánez (play)
Lope Félix de Vega Carpio **9** 503-506

Periclean Age
see Athens

PERICLES (circa 495-429 B.C.), Athenian
statesman **12** 219-221
Alcibiades **1** 119-120
Anaxagoras **1** 208-209
Cleon **4** 104-105
Herodotus **7** 330-333
Ictinus **8** 101
Phidias **12** 265-267
Protagoras **12** 461
Thucydides **15** 211-212

Pericles (play)
Shakespeare, William **14** 142-145

Perikeiromene (play)
Menander **10** 477-478

Perinatology
Apgar, Virginia **1** 257-259

Period of Adjustment (play)
Williams, Tennessee **16** 306-308

Periodic table (chemistry)
Mendeleev, Dmitrii Ivanovich
10 486-488
Rayleigh, 3d Baron **13** 62
Seaborg, Glenn Theodore **14** 74-76

Periodical for Art (journal)
George, Stefan **6** 277-278

Peripatetic school (philosophy)
Aristarchus of Samos **1** 290-291
Aristotle **1** 295-296
Avicenna **1** 386-387
Menander **10** 477-478

Perkin, William H. (1848-1907), English
chemist
Hofmann, August Wilhelm von
7 441-442

PERKINS, FRANCES (1882-1965), American statesman and social worker
12 221-222

Perkins, Thomas H. (1764-1854), American
merchant
Forbes, Robert Bennet **5** 509-510

PERKINS, WILLIAM MAXWELL EVARTS
(1884-1947), American editor of fiction
who discovered and developed brilliant
authors **12** 222-223
Callaghan, Edward Morley **3** 229-230
Wolfe, Thomas Clayton **16** 355-356

PERLE, GEORGE (born 1915), American
musician **12** 223-224

Perls House (Zehlendorf, near Berlin)
Mies van der Rohe, Ludwig **11** 10-12

Permanent Court of Arbitration (The
Hague)
Barbosa, Ruy **1** 503-504
Sayre, Francis Bowes **13** 509

Permanent Court of International Justice
(The Hague; 1920-1945)
influenced by
Ladd, William **9** 149
justices
Altamira Y Crevea, Rafael **1** 179
Baker, Newton Diehl **1** 451
Bryce, James **3** 85
Kellogg, Frank Billings **8** 481
U.S. opponents
Johnson, Hiram Warren **8** 300-301
Lodge, Henry Cabot **9** 482-483
McCormick, Robert Rutherford
10 401-402
Norris, George William **11** 428-429
U.S. supporters
Harding, Warren Gamaliel
7 148-149
Root, Elihu **13** 283-284
Walsh, Thomas James **16** 85-86

see also International Court of Justice (established 1945)

Pernicious anemia (medicine)
Addison, Thomas **1** 58-59
Whipple, George Hoyt **16** 224-225

Pernicious Women (woodcuts)
Lucas van Leyden **10** 20-21

PERÓN, EVA (MARÍA) DUARTE DE
(1919-1952), the second wife and political partner of President Juan Perón of
Argentina **12** 225-226

PERÓN, ISABEL MARTINEZ DE (born
1931), first woman president of Argentina
(1974-1976) **12** 226-228
Videla, Jorge Rafaél **15** 490-492

PERÓN, JUAN DOMINGO (1895-1974),
Argentine statesman, president 1946-55
12 228-230
Alfonsín, Raúl Ricardo **1** 146-148
Castro Ruz, Fidel **3** 365-368
Frondizi, Arturo **6** 127-128
Houssay, Bernardo Alberto **7** 522-523
Paz, Octavio **12** 161-162
Rosas, Juan Manuel de **13** 290-291
Sábato, Ernesto **13** 399-400

Peronist Party (Argentina)
Menem, Carlos Saúl **10** 497-499

PEROT, HENRY ROSS (born 1930), American businessman and activist **12** 230-231

PÉROTIN (Perotinus; flourished circa
1185-1205), French composer and musician **12** 231-232
Franco of Cologne **6** 52
Léonin **9** 343-344

Perottino (literary character)
Bembo, Pietro **2** 144-145

Perpetual Motion (poems)
Aragon, Louis **1** 271-272

Perpetual Peace (532)
Justinian I **8** 393-395?

Perrault, Charles (1628-1703), French poet
La Fontaine, Jean de **9** 156-157

PERRAULT, CLAUDE (1613-1688), French
scientist and architect **12** 232-233
Le Vau, Louis **9** 360-361

PERRET, AUGUSTE (1874-1954), French
architect **12** 233
Le Corbusier **9** 274-275
Viollet-le-Duc, Eugène Emmanuel
15 505-506

Perreti, Felice
see Sixtus V

PERRIN, JEAN BAPTISTE (1870-1942),
French physicist **12** 233-236

Perry, Christopher Raymond (1761-1818),
American naval officer
Perry, Oliver Hazard **12** 239

Perry, Edgar A.
see Poe, Edgar Allan

PERRY, HAROLD ROBERT (1916-1991), African American Roman Catholic bishop **12** 236-237

PERRY, MATTHEW CALBRAITH (1794-1858), American naval officer **12** 237-239
  Clayton, John Middleton **4** 96-97
  Fillmore, Millard **5** 447-448
  Ito, Hirobumi **8** 153-155
  Kennedy, John Pendleton **8** 506-507

PERRY, OLIVER HAZARD (1785-1819), American naval officer **12** 239
  Girty, Simon **6** 350
  Lawrence, James **9** 251-252
  Madison, James **10** 121-123
  Morison, Samuel Eliot **11** 175-176
  Perry, Matthew Calbraith **12** 237-239
  Rush, William **13** 365-366
  Tecumseh **15** 133

PERRY, RALPH BARTON (1876-1957), American philosopher **12** 239-240
  Lewis, Clarence Irving **9** 381

PERRY, WILLIAM JAMES (born 1927), President Clinton's secretary of defense (1994-) **12** 240-242

Persa (play)
  Plautus **12** 348-350

Persae, The (play; Aeschylus)
  Pericles **12** 219-221

PERSE, SAINT-JOHN (Alexis Saint-Léger Léger; 1887-1975), French poet and diplomat **12** 242-243

Persecutions, religious
  Buganda
    Mwanga **11** 282-283
  China
    Tseng Kuo-fan **15** 324-325
  England
    Baxter, Richard **2** 76-77
    Bradford, William **2** 475-476
    Brewster, William **2** 523-524
    Bunyan, John **3** 128-129
    Cotton, John **4** 263-265
    Laud, William **9** 224-225
    More, Thomas **11** 156-157
    Penn, William **12** 200-202
  France
    Calvin, John **3** 239-242
    Louis XIV **9** 531-533
    see also Religion, Wars of
  Geneva
    Calvin, John **3** 239-242
  Germany
    Beissel, Johann Conrad **2** 123-124
    John of Leiden **8** 283
  Hawaii
    Kamehameha III **8** 416-417
  India
    Ala-ud-din **1** 102-103
    Aurangzeb **1** 377
    Shah Jahan **14** 138-139
  Iran
    Shahpur II **14** 140-141
  Iraq

    Junayd, Abu al-Qasim ibn Muhammad al **8** 388
  Ireland
    Burke, Edmund **3** 138-141
  Korea
    Taewŏn'gun, Hŭngsŏn **15** 74-75
  Roman Empire
    Clement of Alexandria **4** 102-103
    Diocletian **5** 19-20
    Domitian **5** 52-53
    Nero Claudius Caesar **11** 342-344
    Paul **12** 141-143
    Trajan **15** 291-292
    Valerian **15** 404-405
  U.S.
    Young, Brigham **16** 469-470
  Vietnam
    Diem, Ngo Dinh **5** 6-7
    see also Anti-Semitism; Religious liberty

Persephone (musical composition)
  Stravinsky, Igor Fedorovich **14** 502-506

Persepolis (ancient city, Iran)
  Alexander the Great **1** 137-141
  Fischer von Erlach, Johann Bernhard **5** 459-461

Perseus (flourished 2d century B.C.), last king of Macedon
  Polybios **12** 384-385

Perseus (painting)
  Burne-Jones, Edward Coley **3** 145-146

Perseus (sculpture)
  Canova, Antonio **3** 263-264
  Cellini, Benvenuto **3** 391-392

Perseus and Andromeda (painting)
  Titian **15** 242-244

PERSHING, JOHN JOSEPH (1860-1948), American general **12** 243-244
  Carranza, Venustiano **3** 321-322
  Marshall, George Catlett **10** 278-279
  Villa, Pancho **15** 495-496

Persia (kingdom; South Western Asia)
  after 1935
    see Iran
  Byzantine relations
    Julian **8** 378-379
    Justinian I **8** 393-395
    Procopius of Caesarea **12** 457-458
  empire organized
    Cyrus the Great **4** 363-364
    Darius I **4** 394-395
  exploration
    Conti, Niccolò de' **4** 212-213
  Greek wars
    Agesilaus II **1** 79-80
    Alexander the Great **1** 137-141-124
    Xenophon **16** 418-420
    Xerxes **16** 420
    see also Persian Wars
  India and
    Curzon, George Nathaniel **4** 351-352
  Manichaeism

    see Manichaeism
  modernization and reform
    Malkam Khan, Mirza **10** 172
    Reza Shah Pahlavi **13** 116-117
    Taqi Khan Amir-e Kabir, Mirza **15** 106-107
  Mongol rule
    Genghis Khan **6** 263-265
    Hulagu Khan **8** 27-28
    Polo, Marco **12** 380-382
  Moslem conquest (7th century)
    Omar ibn al-Khattab **11** 508-509
  Ottoman relations
    Abbas I **1** 4-6
    Karim Khan Zand **8** 447
    Selim I **14** 94-95
  Roman relations
    Khosrow I **8** 538-539
    Shahpur II **14** 140-141
    Valerian **15** 404-405
  Russian relations
    Agha Mohammad Khan **1** 80-81
    Peter I **12** 253-256
  Seljuk rule
    Alp Arslan **1** 178-179
  Syria and
    Antiochus III **1** 249-250
    Antiochus IV **1** 250
    Seleucus I **14** 92-93
  Zoroastrianism
    see Zoroastrianism

Persian (language)
  Firdausi **5** 451-452
  Iqbal, Muhammad **8** 132-133
  Reza Shah Pahlavi **13** 116-117

Persian Academy
  Reza Shah Pahlavi **13** 116-117

Persian art
  Behzad **2** 123

Persian Eclogues (poems)
  Collins, William **4** 168-169

Persian Gulf War (1990-1991)
  Bush, George **3** 167-169
  Jaber Al-Sabah, Jaber Al-Ahmad Al- **8** 166-167
  Saddam Hussein **13** 415-416
  Schwarzkopf, Norman **14** 52-54

Persian Letters, The (literary collection)
  Montesquieu **11** 123-125

Persian literature
  fiction
    Hidayat, Sadiq **7** 377-378
    Premchand **12** 439
  national epic
    Behzad **2** 123
    Firdausi **5** 451-452
    Mahmud of Ghazni **10** 147
  poetry
    Attar, Farid ed-Din **1** 359-360
    Hafiz, Shams al-Din **7** 63
    Ibn al-Arabi, Muhyi al-Din **8** 91
    Jami **8** 218-219
    Omar Khayyam **11** 510-511

Rumi, Jalai ed-Din **13** 362-363
Sa'di **13** 418-419
Persian Wars (500-449 B.C.)
Greeks
Cleomenes I **4** 103
Miltiades **11** 42-43
Pericles **12** 219-221
Pindar **12** 312-313
Themistocles **15** 170-171
historians and artists
Herodotus **7** 330-333
Phidias **12** 265-267
Persians
Cyrus the Great **4** 363-364
Darius I **4** 394-395
Xerxes **16** 420

Persians, The (play)
Aeschylus **1** 70-72

Persius (Aulus Persius Flaccus; 34-62),
Roman satirist
Congreve, William **4** 200-201

Persona (film)
Bergman, Ernst Ingmar **2** 190-191

Personae of Ezra Pound (poems)
Pound, Ezra Loomis **12** 415-417

Personal Enemy (play)
Osborne, John **12** 16-17

Personal Recollections of Joan of Arc
(book)
Twain, Mark **15** 363-366

Personality (psychology)
Adler, Alfred **1** 61-63-55
Freud, Sigmund **6** 103-106
Jaspers, Karl **8** 225-226
Mead, Margaret **10** 438-440
Parsons, Talcott **12** 122
see also Psychoanalysis

Perspective (art)
architecture
Alberti, Leon Battista **1** 113-115
Brunelleschi, Filippo **3** 70-72
Donatello **5** 55-56
painting
Campin, Robert **3** 255
Christus, Petrus **4** 33-34
Dürer, Albrecht **5** 159-161
Ghiberti, Lorenzo **6** 291-292
Leonardo da Vinci **9** 337-340
Lippi, Filippo **9** 439
Masaccio **10** 312-313
Uccello, Paolo **15** 378-379
Vanderlyn, John **15** 417
Veneziano, Domenico **15** 459-460
Vermeer, Jan **15** 466-467

Persse, Isabella Augusta
see Gregory, Lady Augusta

Persuasion (novel)
Austen, Jane **1** 377-379

PERTH, 16TH EARL OF (James Eric Drummond; 1876-1951), English statesman
12 244-245

Pertinax, Publius Helvius (126-193),
Roman emperor 193
Septimius Severus, Lucius **14** 109-110

Peru (ship)
Wheelwright, William **16** 223-224

Peru, Republic of (nation, Western South
America)
20th century
Belaúnde Terry, Fernando **2** 125-126
Fujimori, Alberto Keinya **6** 143-145
Haya de la Torre, Victor Raul
7 216-217
Leguía y Salcedo, Augusto Bernardi-
no **9** 305-306
Morales-Bermúdez Cerruti, Francis-
co **11** 150-151
Odría Amoretti, Manuel Apolinario
11 473-474
Prado Ugarteche, Manuel
12 430-431
Rio Branco, Barão do **13** 177
Vargas Llosa, Mario **15** 434-436
Velasco, Luis de **15** 450-451
archeology
Kroeber, Alfred Louis **9** 105-106
English exploration
Cabot, Sebastian **3** 200-201
Drake, Francis **5** 94-96
foreign relations
Ballivián, José **1** 475
Castilla, Ramón **3** 361
Flores, Juan José **5** 491
García Moreno, Gabriel **6** 209-210
Pérez de Cuéllar, Javier **12** 214-215
Portales Plazazuelos, Diego José
Víctor **12** 404
see also Pacific, War of the
independence (1824)
Bolívar, Simón **2** 375-377
Castilla, Ramón **3** 361
San Martín, José de **13** 468-469
Santa Cruz, Andrés de **13** 472-473
Spanish conquest
Almagro, Diego de **1** 177-178
Atahualpa **1** 355-356
Benalcázar, Sebastián de **2** 145-146
de Soto, Hernando **4** 510-511
Garcilaso de la Vega, Inca
6 210-211
Manco Capac **10** 184-185
Orellana, Francisco de **11** 527-528
Pizarro, Francisco **12** 340-341
see also Inca Indians
Spanish rule
Gasca, Pedro de la **6** 230-231
Mendoza, Antonio de **10** 494-495
Toledo, Francisco de **15** 257-259
Túpac Amaru, José Gabriel **15** 341
Valdivia, Pedro de **15** 400-401
U.S. influence
Grace, William Russell **6** 480-481
Hearst, George **7** 242
Meiggs, Henry **10** 458-459

Perugia (city, Italy)
Julius II **8** 384-386

Visconti, Gian Galeazzo **15** 510-511
PERUGINO (circa 1450-1523), Italian
painter **12** 245-246
Raphael **13** 40-42
Signorelli, Luca **14** 221-222

PERUTZ, MAX (born 1914), English crystallographer and biochemist **12** 246-248

Peruvian literature
Garcilaso de la Vega, Inca **6** 210-211
González Prada, Manuel **6** 431
Mariátegui, José Carlos **10** 255-256
Palma, Ricardo **12** 77
Vallejo, César Abraham **15** 408-409

Peruzzi, Baldassare (1481-1536), Italian
architect and painter
Sangallo family **13** 464-466
Vignola, Giacomo da **15** 493-494

Peruzzi Chapel (Sta Croce)
Giotto **6** 342-345

Pesaro Madonna (painting)
Titian **15** 242-244

Peshkov, Aleksei Maximovich
see Gorky, Maxim

PESOTTA, ROSE (1896-1965), American
union organizer **12** 248-249

Pessimism (philosophy)
Céline, Louis Ferdinand **3** 390-391
Schopenhauer, Arthur **14** 29-31

Pest Journal (newspaper)
Kossuth, Louis **9** 88-90

PESTALOZZI, JOHANN HEINRICH
(1746-1827), Swiss educator **12** 249-250
Froebel, Friedrich Wilhelm August
6 122-123
Herbart, Johann Friedrich **7** 321-322
Humboldt, Wilhelm von **8** 31
Mason, Lowell **10** 321-322
Ritter, Karl **13** 181-182

Pestalozzi-Froebel Teachers College
(Chicago)
Bellow, Saul **2** 141-143

Peste, La (novel)
Camus, Albert **3** 255-257

Pesthouse at Jaffa (painting)
Gros **7** 14-15

Pesti Hirlap (newspaper)
Kossuth, Louis **9** 88-90

Pesticide (chemistry)
Carson, Rachel Louise **3** 337-338
Knipling, Edward Fred **9** 59-60
Müller, Paul Hermann **11** 241-242

PÉTAIN, HENRI PHILIPPE (1856-1951),
French general and statesman
12 250-252
Clemenceau, Georges **4** 99-101
De Gaulle, Charles André Joseph Marie
4 463-465
Foch, Ferdinand **5** 498-499
Herriot, Édouard **7** 339-340
Laval, Pierre **9** 237-238

Maurras, Charles Marie Photius
10 350-351

Pete (literary character)
Pinter, Harold **12** 317-318

Peter (emperor, Brazil)
see Pedro

Peter (king, Portugal)
see Pedro

PETER I (Peter the Great; 1672-1725), czar
of Russia 1682-1725 **12** 253-256
Anna Ivanovna **1** 240-241
Augustus II **1** 373-374
Bering, Vitus **2** 193-194
Charles XII **3** 464-466
Elizabeth, the Queen Mother **5** 261-263
Falconet, Étienne Maurice **5** 372
Mazepa, Ivan Stepanovich **10** 381
Pushkin, Aleksandr Sergeevich
12 489-491
Witte, Sergei Yulyevich **16** 349-350

PETER I (1844-1921), king of Serbia
1903-18, and of the Serbs, Croats, and
Slovenes 1918-21 **12** 256
Alexander of Yugoslavia **1** 136-137

Peter I (king of Castile)
see Peter the Cruel

Peter II (Peter Alekseyevich; 1715-30), czar
of Russia 1727-30
Anna Ivanovna **1** 240-241
Elizabeth, the Queen Mother **5** 261-263
Peter I **12** 253-256

Peter II (1923-1970), king of Yugoslavia
1934-45
Alexander of Yugoslavia **1** 136-137
Tito, Marshal **15** 244-246

PETER III (Pedro; circa 1239-85), king of
Aragon 1276-85 **12** 256-257
Michael VIII **11** 1-2

Peter III (Peter Feodorovich; 1728-62), czar
of Russia 1762
Catherine the Great **3** 370-372
Frederick II **6** 81-84
Paul I **12** 143-144
Pugachev, Emelyan Ivanovich
12 478-479

Peter, Acts of (New Testament apocrypha)
Peter **12** 252-253

PETER, ST. (died circa 65), Apostle and
bishop of Rome **12** 252-253
Jesus of Nazareth **8** 251-255, 561
John, St. **8** 273-274
Mark **10** 266-267
Paul **12** 141-143

Peter and the Wolf (musical composition)
Prokofiev, Sergei Sergeevich
12 458-460

Peter Aureoli (circa 1280-1322), French
theologian
Marsilius of Padua **10** 284

Peter Bell the Third (poem)
Shelley, Percy Bysshe **14** 176-178

Peter Camenzind (novel)
Hesse, Hermann **7** 367-369

Peter Canisius, St.
see Canisius, St. Peter

Peter Claver, St.
see Claver, St. Peter

Peter Grimes (opera)
Britten, Benjamin **3** 10-11

Peter Ibbetson (play)
Barrymores **2** 28-30

Peter Kanis
see Canisius, St. Peter

Peter Leopold
see Leopold II (emperor)

Peter Lombard
see Lombard, Peter

Peter Pan (musical)
Martin, Mary **10** 292-293

Peter Pan (play; Barrie)
Barrie, James Matthew **2** 21-22
Coward, Noel **4** 279-280

Peter Petrovich (died 1719), Russian prince
Peter I **12** 253-256

Peter Pilgrim (novel)
Bird, Robert Montgomery **2** 281-282

Peter Quince at the Clavier (poem)
Stevens, Wallace **14** 443-445

Peter Schlemihl (woodcuts)
Kirchner, Ernst Ludwig **9** 34-35

Peter the Cruel (1334-1369), king of
Castile and Léon 1350-69
ibn Khaldun, Abd al-Rahman ibn
Muhammad **8** 93-94
López de Ayala, Pedro **9** 508-509

Peter the Great
see Peter I (czar, Russia)

Peter the Great (play)
Barrymores **2** 28-30

Peter the Hermit (Peter of Amiens;
1050?-1115), French monk
Alexius I **1** 143-144
Tasso, Torquato **15** 114-116

Peter the Venerable (circa 1092-1156),
abbot of Cluny
Abelard, Peter **1** 23-25

Peterborough, 3d Earl of (Charles Mor-
daunt; 1658-1735), English general and
diplomat
Berkeley, George **2** 197-198

PETERS, CARL (1856-1918), German
explorer and colonizer **12** 257-258

Peter's Pence (English tax)
Edward III **5** 211-212

Petersburg, battle of (1864-1865)
Beauregard, Pierre Gustave Toutant
2 96-97
Lee, Robert Edward **9** 292-294

Peterskirche (church; Vienna)
Hildebrandt, Johann Lucas von
7 380-381

PETERSON, EDITH R. (born Edith Elizabeth
Runne; 1914-1992), American medical
researcher **12** 258-259

Peterwardein, battle of (1716)
Eugene of Savoy **5** 330-331

Peterzano, Simone (flourished 1573-96),
Italian painter
Caravaggio **3** 282-284

Petey (literary character)
Pinter, Harold **12** 317-318

Pétion, Alexandre Sabés (died 1818), Haitian general and statesman
Boyer, Jean Pierre **2** 468-469

Petit, Jean (Joannes Pervus; circa
1360-1411), French theologian
Gerson, John **6** 285-286

Petit cénacle (literary group)
Nerval, Gérard de **11** 345-346

Petit chose, Le (novel)
Daudet, Alphonse **4** 402-403

Petit prince, Le (story)
Saint-Exupéry, Antoine de **13** 431-432

Petit saint, Le (novel)
Simenon, Georges **14** 233-234

Petit testament (poems)
see Lais

Petit Trianon (Versailles)
Gabriel, Ange Jacques **6** 160-161

Petite Fadette, La (novel)
Sand, George **13** 459-461

Petite Messe solennelle (music)
Rossini, Gioacchino **13** 311-312

Petition of Right (England; 1628)
Buckingham, 1st Duke of **3** 93-94
Charles I **3** 450-452
Coke, Edward **4** 141-142

Petits poèmes en prose (book)
Baudelaire, Charles Pierre **2** 61-63

Petits riens, Les (ballet)
Mozart, Wolfgang Amadeus
11 218-221

PETO, JOHN FREDERICK (1854-1907),
American painter **12** 259

PETRARCH (Francesco Petrarca; 1304-74),
Italian poet **12** 259-261
friends
Boccaccio, Giovanni **2** 351-353, 34
Martini, Simone **10** 298-299
Vitry, Philippe de **16** 2
in literature
Boccaccio, Giovanni **2** 351-353
Carducci, Giosuè **3** 290-291
De Sanctis, Francesco **4** 505
influence of
Charles IV **3** 455-456
Chaucer, Geoffrey **3** 482-485
Leopardi, Giacomo **9** 344-345

Machiavelli, Niccolò **10** 97-99
Poliziano, Angelo **12** 373-374
Ronsard, Pierre de **13** 271-273
Sidney, Philip **14** 214-215
musical settings
Dufay, Guillaume **5** 125-126
translations
Spenser, Edmund **14** 373-376
Wyatt, Thomas **16** 410-411

Petrashevsky Circle (Russian literary group)
Dostoevsky, Fyodor **5** 74-77

Petri, Egon (1881-1962), German pianist
Busoni, Ferruccio Benvenuto **3** 173-174

**PETRIE, SIR WILLIAM MATTHEW
FLINDERS** (1853-1942), English archeologist **12** 261-262

Petrified Forest, The (play; Sherwood)
Bogart, Humphrey **2** 363-364
Sherwood, Robert Emmet **14** 189-190

Petrine succession
see Papacy

Petrograd (city; Russia)
see Leningrad

Petrograd Soviet (1917)
Kamenev, Lev Borisovich **8** 417-418
Kerensky, Aleksandr Fedorovich
8 516-517
Molotov, Vyacheslav Mikhailovich
11 89-90
Trotsky, Leon **15** 302-305

Petroleum industry
see Oil industry

Petrology (geology)
Holmes, Arthur **7** 455-456

PETRONIUS ARBITER (died circa 66),
Roman author **12** 262-263
Varro, Marcus Terentius **15** 438-439

Petrópolis, Treaty of (1903)
Rio Branco, Barão do **13** 177

Petrucci, Borghese (ruled 1512-15), ruler
of Siena
Biringuccio, Vannoccio **2** 283

Petrucci, Fabio (ruled 1523-26), ruler of
Siena
Biringuccio, Vannoccio **2** 283

Petrucci, Ottavio (Ottaviano dei Petrucci;
1466-1539), Italian printer
Obrecht, Jacob **11** 457-458

Petrucci, Pandolfo (ruled 1487-1512), ruler
of Siena
Biringuccio, Vannoccio **2** 283

Petrus Aegidius (painting)
Massys, Quentin **10** 325-326

Petrushka (ballet)
Stravinsky, Igor Fedorovich **14** 502-506

Pettis, Spencer (died 1831), American
politician
Ashley, William Henry **1** 333-334

Petty, Sir William
see Shelburne, 2d Earl of

Petun Indians (North America)
Jogues, Isaac **8** 270-271

Peurbach, Georg (1423-1461), Austrian
astronomer and mathematician
Regiomontanus **13** 81-82

Peveril of the Peak (novel)
Scott, Walter **14** 68-70

PEVSNER, ANTOINE (1886-1962), Russian
sculptor and painter **12** 263-264
Gabo, Naum **6** 158-159
Kandinsky, Wassily **8** 420-422

Pevsner, Naum Neemia
see Gabo, Naum

Pezuela, Joaquin de la (died 1830), Spanish
general, viceroy of Peru
Güemes, Martín **7** 26-27

Pfefferkorn, Johann (1469-1524), German
controversialist
Reuchlin, Johann **13** 106-107

Pfeil, Count Joachim (1857-1924), German
explorer
Peters, Carl **12** 257-258

Phaedo (dialogue ; Plato)
Augustine **1** 367-370
Philo Judaeus **12** 282-283
Mendelssohn, Moses **10** 488-489
Plato **12** 345-347
Socrates **14** 320-321

Phaedra (ballet)
Graham, Martha **6** 485-486

Phaedra (literary character)
Euripides **5** 332-334

Phaedra (play)
Seneca the Younger, Lucius Annaeus
14 103-105

Phaedrus (dialogue ; Plato)
Hippocrates **7** 408-410
Plato **12** 345-347

Phaenomena (book)
Euclid **5** 327-329
Eudoxus of Cnidus **5** 329-330

Phaenomena (book; Aratus)
Hipparchus **7** 407-408

'Phags-pa scrip (alphabet)
Kublai Khan **9** 115-118

Phalangist Party (Lebanon)
Gemayel, Pierre **6** 259-261

Phalanx (German art, group)
Kandinsky, Wassily **8** 420-422

Phalanx (ideal community)
Fourier, François Charles Marie **6** 31-32

Phalanx (socialist association)
Brisbane, Albert **3** 9

Phalaris (I-II; speech)
Lucian **10** 25-26

Phantasies in the Fashion of Callot (stories)
Hoffmann, Ernst Theodor Amadeus
7 439-440

Phantom Lady, The (play)
Calderón, Pedro **3** 221-222

Phantom President, The (film)
Cohan, George Michael **4** 137-138

Pharaohs
see Statesmen, Egyptian

Phares, Les (poem)
Baudelaire, Charles Pierre **2** 61-63

Pharisees (Jew, sect)
Johanan ben Zakkai **8** 271-272
Josephus Flavius **8** 360-361
Paul **12** 141-143

Pharmaceutical industry
Goldsmith, James Michael **6** 409-411
Hofmann, August Wilhelm von
7 441-442

Pharmacology (science)
Baulieu, Étienne-Émile **2** 63-66
Dale, Henry Hallett **4** 371-373
Elion, Gertrude B. **5** 252-254
Hippocrates **7** 408-410
Loewi, Otto **9** 486-487

Pharnabazus (circa 413-370 B.C.), Persian
governor
Xenophon **16** 418-420

Pharos (lighthouse; Alexandria)
Ptolemy II **12** 472-473

Pharos and Pharillon (book)
Forster, Edward Morgan **6** 14-16

Pharsalus, battle of (48 B.C.)
Antony, Mark **1** 253-254
Brutus, Marcus Junius **3** 79-80
Caesar, Gaius Julius **3** 207-210
Cato, the Younger **3** 374-375
Cleopatra **4** 105-106
Pompey **12** 387-389
Varro, Marcus Terentius **15** 438-439

Phasael (died 43 B.C.), governor of
Jerusalem
Herod the Great **7** 333-334

Phase music
Reich, Steve **13** 84-85

Pheasant, Vow of the (crusader pledge)
Philip the Good **12** 278-279

Phèdre (play; Racine)
Lowell, Robert Trail Spence Jr. **10** 16-17
Racine, Jean Baptiste **12** 532-535

Phèdre et Hippolyte (play; Pradon)
Racine, Jean Baptiste **12** 532-535

Phenol (chemistry)
Crookes, William **4** 323-324
Edison, Thomas Alva **5** 206-208

Phenomenology (philosophy)
Fries, Jakob Friedrich **6** 116-117
Hegel, Georg Wilhelm Friedrich
7 254-256
Heidegger, Martin **7** 257-258
Husserl, Edmund **8** 67-68
Merleau-Ponty, Maurice **10** 518
Sartre, Jean Paul **13** 491-492

Stein, Edith **14** 412-414

PHIBUN SONGKHRAM, LUANG
(1897-1964), Thai statesman, prime minister 1938-44 and 1948-57 **12** 264-265
Sarit Thanarat **13** 483-484

PHIDIAS (flourished circa 475-425 B.C.),
Greek sculptor **12** 265-267
Ictinus **8** 101
Polykleitos **12** 385-386
Praxiteles **12** 433-434

Phidias (flourished 4th century B.C.), Greek astronomer
Archimedes **1** 277-280

Philadelphia (city; Pennsylvania)
art and architecture
Calder, Alexander **3** 216-218
Eakins, Thomas **5** 176-177
Mills, Robert **11** 36-37
as U.S. financial center
Cooke, Jay **4** 215-216
Bartram's Gardens
Bartram, John **2** 40-41, 411
Catholic diocese (1808)
Bache, Alexander Dallas **1** 420
Carroll, John **3** 331-332
Franklin, Benjamin **6** 60-64
economic development
Sullivan, Leon Howard **15** 25-27
U.S. capital (Revolutionary War)
Clinton, Henry **4** 114-115
Cornwallis, Charles **4** 241-243
Coxe, Tench **4** 285-286
Howe, William **7** 538-539

Philadelphia (ship)
Decatur, Stephen **4** 448-449
Lawrence, James **9** 251-252
Smith, William **14** 301

Philadelphia, College of
see Pennsylvania, University of

Philadelphia, Here I Come! (play)
Friel, Bernard Patrick **6** 115-116

Philadelphia Centennial Exposition (1876)
Bell, Alexander Graham **2** 129-131
Paine, John Knowles **12** 65
Sousa, John Philip **14** 353-354
Thomas, Theodore **15** 192-193

Philadelphia Insurance Co. (established 1762)
Bradford, William **2** 477

Philadelphia Press (newspaper)
Crane, Stephen **4** 293-295
Davis, Richard Harding **4** 422-423
Sloan, John **14** 274-275
Steichen, Edward **14** 411-412

Philadelphia World's Fair
see Philadelphia Centennial Exposition

Philadelphos of Egypt
see Ptolemy II

Philanderers, The (play)
Shaw, George Bernard **14** 163-164

Philanthropist (newspaper)
Bailey, Gamaliel **1** 444-445
Birney, James Gillespie **2** 283-284

Philanthropists, American
18th century
Benezet, Anthony **2** 159-160
Faneuil, Peter **5** 377
19th century
Carnegie, Andrew **3** 309-312
Cuffe, Paul **4** 331-332
Girard, Stephen **6** 347-348
Grace, William Russell **6** 480-481
Lawrence, Abbott **9** 246
Lea, Henry Charles **9** 261-262
Lowell, Josephine Shaw **10** 15-16
McCormick, Cyrus Hall **10** 400-401
Morgan, John Pierpont **11** 163-165
Peabody, George **12** 168
Smith, Gerrit **14** 290-291
Still, William **14** 454-455
Ward, Aaron Montgomery **16** 112
19th-20th century
Dodge, Grace Hoadley **5** 37-38
Duke, James Buchanan **5** 133-134
Frick, Henry Clay **6** 108-109
Kennedy, John Stewart **8** 507-508
Ochs, Adolph Simon **11** 464
Rockefeller, John D. Jr. **13** 225-226
Rockefeller, John Davison **13** 226-228
Rosenwald, Julius **13** 293
Schiff, Jacob Henry **14** 2-3
Walker, C. J. **16** 61-62
20th century
Davis, Arthur Vining **4** 413-414
Drexel, Katherine **5** 102-103
Eastman, George **5** 186
Ford, Henry **6** 5-6
Grossinger, Jennie **7** 15-17
Insull, Samuel **8** 130
Kettering, Charles F. **8** 524-525
Mellon, Andrew William **10** 469-470
Morgan, John Pierpont II **11** 165
Penney, J. C. **12** 202-203
Rockefeller, Nelson Aldrich **13** 228-230
Sills, Beverly **14** 230-231
Sloan, Alfred Pritchard Jr. **14** 274
Walker, Maggie Lena **16** 65-66
Woodruff, Robert W. **16** 372-374
Young, Owen D. **16** 473-474
Zemurray, Samuel **16** 496-497

Philanthropists, Hungarian
Elizabeth of Hungary **5** 271-272

Philanthropists, New Zealander
Hillary, Edmund **7** 389-390

Philanthropists, Swiss
Dunant, Jean Henri **5** 139-141

Philaster (play)
Beaumont, Francis **2** 95

Philemon (361?-263 B.C.), Greek playwright
Plautus **12** 348-350

Philemon (literary character)
Ovid **12** 34-36

Philetas of Cos (flourished late 4th century B.C.), Greek
Theocritus **15** 171-172

Philharmonic Hall (New York City)
Hindemith, Paul **7** 399-400

Philip (archduke of Austria)
see Philip I, king of Spain

PHILIP (died 1676), American Wampanoag Indian chief 1662-76 **12** 267-268

Philip (dukes of Burgundy)
see Philip I (king of Spain; 1478-1506);
Philip the Bold (1342-1404); Philip the Good (1396-1467)

Philip (Holy Roman emperor)
see Philip of Swabia

Philip (king of Germany)
see Philip of Swabia

Philip (treatise, Isocrates)
Alexander the Great **1** 137-141
Isocrates **8** 151
Philip II **12** 269-271

Philip I (king of Portugal)
see Philip II (king of Spain)

Philip I (1052-1108), king of France 1060-1108
Bohemund, I **2** 364
Louis VI **9** 523-524
Urban II **15** 393

Philip I (the Handsome; 1478-1506), king of Spain 1504-06
Bosch, Hieronymus **2** 426-428
Charles V **3** 457-459
Ferdinand I **5** 414-415
Ferdinand V **5** 417-418
Isabella I **8** 144-145
Maximilian I **10** 356-357

PHILIP II (382-336 B.C.), king of Macedon 359-336 **12** 269-271
Alexander the Great **1** 137-141
Aristotle **1** 295-296
Demosthenes **4** 495-496
Isocrates **8** 151
Ptolemy I **12** 470-472

PHILIP II (Philip Augustus; 1165-1223), king of France 1180-1223 **12** 268-269
Eleanor of Aquitaine **5** 246-247
Frederick II **6** 79
Henry II **7** 287-289
John **8** 274-275
Richard I **13** 130

PHILIP II (1527-1598), king of Spain 1556-1598 **12** 271-273
colonization
Menéndez de Avilés, Pedro **10** 499-500
Oñate, Juan de **11** 513-514
Toledo, Francisco de **15** 257-259
Velasco, Luis de **15** 450-451
court
Ercilla y Zúñiga, Alonso de **5** 302

Herrera, Juan de **7** 335
Toledo, Francisco de **15** 257-259
Vesalius, Andreas **15** 473-475
England and
Drake, Francis **5** 94-96
Elizabeth I **5** 263-266
Frobisher, Martin **6** 121-122
Hawkins, John **7** 210-211
France and
Catherine de Médicis **10** 445-449
Henry IV **7** 293-295
imperial succession
Charles V **3** 457-459
Ferdinand I **5** 414-415
Maximilian II **10** 357-358
Netherlands and
Alba, Duke of **1** 103-104
William the Silent **16** 300-302
papacy and
Paul IV **12** 145-146
Sixtus V **14** 267-268
patronage
Greco **6** 511-514
Titian **15** 242-244
Victoria, Tomás Luis de **15** 487-488
relatives
Charles V **3** 457-459
Mary I **10** 308-309
Philip III **12** 273-274

Philip III (circa 358-317 B.C.), king of
Macedon 323-317
Antigonus I **1** 248-249
Seleucus I **14** 92-93

Philip III (1245-1285), king of France
1270-85
Peter III **12** 256-257
Philip IV **12** 274
Philip VI **12** 277-278

PHILIP III (1578-1621), king of Spain
1598-1621 **12** 273-274
Cervantes, Miguel de Saavedra
3 395-398
Góngora y Argote, Luis de **6** 427-428
Philip II **12** 271-273
Victoria, Tomás Luis de **15** 487-488

PHILIP IV (the Fair; 1268-1314), king of
France 1285-1314 **12** 274
and Burgundy
Rudolf I **13** 347-348
and England
Edward I **5** 208-210
Edward II **5** 210
Philip VI **12** 277-278
and papacy
Boniface VIII **2** 392-393-61
Clement V **4** 101-102
Duns Scotus, John **5** 149-150

PHILIP IV (1605-1665), king of Spain
1621-65 **12** 275
Charles II **3** 454
Louis XIII **9** 529-531
Philip V **12** 276-277
Rubens, Peter Paul **13** 339-342

Velázquez, Diego Rodríguez de Silva y
15 454-456
Zurbarán, Francisco de **16** 534-535

Philip V (237-179 B.C.), king of Macedon
220-179
Antiochus III **1** 249-250
Aratus **1** 273-274
Flamininus, Titus Quinctius **5** 477
Hannibal Barca **7** 128-130

Philip V (1294-1322), king of France
1316-22
Charles V **3** 459-460
Philip VI **12** 277-278

PHILIP V (1683-1746), king of Spain
1700-46 **12** 276-277
Charles II **3** 454
Charles III **3** 454-455
Churriguera, José Benito de **4** 53-54
Ferdinand VII **5** 418-420
Louis XIV **9** 531-533
Orléans, Philippe II D' **11** 530-531

PHILIP VI (1293-1350), king of France
1328-50 **12** 277-278
Edward III **5** 211-212
Froissart, Jean **6** 124-125
John II **8** 275-276
Vitry, Philippe de **16** 2

Philip, Prince (Philip Mountbatten; born
1921), duke of Edinburgh
Elizabeth II **5** 266-269

Philip, St. (New Testament Apostle)
Dias de Novais, Bartolomeu **4** 533-534

Philip Arrhidaeios
see Philip III, king of Macedon

Philip Augustus
see Philip II, king of France

Philip Dru, Administrator (novel)
House, Edward Mandell **7** 520-521

Philip of Anjou
see Philip V, king of Spain

Philip of Hesse (1504-1567), landgrave of
Hesse 1509-67
Charles V **3** 457-459

Philip of Swabia (1180-1208), Holy Roman
emperor and king of Germany 1198-1208
Frederick II **6** 79
Innocent III **8** 125-127
Vogelweide, Walther von der **16** 10-11

Philip Sparrow (poem)
Skelton, John **14** 268-269

Philip the Bold (1342-1404), duke of Bur-
gundy
Charles the Bold **3** 467-469
Charles VI **3** 460-461
Limbourg brothers, The **9** 412-413
Sluter, Claus **14** 275-276

Philip the Fair
see Philip IV, king of France

PHILIP THE GOOD (1396-1467), duke of
Burgundy 1419-67 **12** 278-279
Hundred Years War

Charles the Bold **3** 467-469
Charles VII **3** 461-462
Gloucester, Duke of **6** 370-371
Henry V **7** 296-297
Joan of Arc **8** 264-265
influence of
Comines, Philippe de **4** 181
Eyck, Hubert and Jan van **5** 352-354
Louis XI **9** 526-528

Philip the Handsome
see Philip I (king, Spain)

Philip William (died 1618), prince of
Orange
Maurice of Nassau **10** 348-349

Philipon, Charles (1800-1862), French
journalist
Daumier, Honoré Victorin **4** 403-405

Philippa (1314?-1369), Dutch queen of
Edward III of England
Chaucer, Geoffrey **3** 482-485
Froissart, Jean **6** 124-125

Philippe II (1674-1723), Duc d'Orléans
regent of France 1715-23
Louis XV **9** 533-534

Philippe Égalité (1747-1793), Duc d'Orleans
Louis Philippe **9** 536-537

Philippi, battle of (1861)
McClellan, George Brinton **10** 391-392

Philippi, battle of (42 B.C.)
Antony, Mark **1** 253-254
Augustus **1** 371-373
Brutus, Marcus Junius **3** 79-80
Cleopatra **4** 105-106
Horace **7** 500-503
Virgil **15** 507-510

Philippians, Letter to the (New Testament
book)
Paul **12** 141-143

Philippics (speeches)
Cicero, Marcus Tullius **4** 55-58
Demosthenes **4** 495-496

Philippines, Republic of the (nation, South
Eastern Asia)
• 1521-1898 (SPANISH RULE)
discovery and colonization
Magellan, Ferdinand **10** 126-127
Velasco, Luis de **15** 450-451
rebellion (1896)
Aguinaldo, Emilio **1** 88
Bonifacio, Andres **2** 393-394
Del Pilar, Marcelo Hilario **4** 486
Mabini, Apolinario **10** 72-73
Rizal, José **13** 187-189
Spanish-American War
see Spanish-American War
• 1898-1946 (UNITED STATES RULE)
annexation and insurrection
Aguinaldo, Emilio **1** 88
Alfonso XIII **1** 151
Lodge, Henry Cabot **9** 482-483
Mabini, Apolinario **10** 72-73

McKinley, William **10** 418-420
Pershing, John Joseph
  12 243-244
Rómulo, Carlos P. **13** 270-271
as dependency
  Dunne, Finley Peter **5** 147-148
  Murphy, Frank **11** 260-261
  Ridgway, Matthew Bunker
    13 160-161
  Roosevelt, Theodore **13** 280-283
  Root, Elihu **13** 283-284
  Sayre, Francis Bowes **13** 509
  Schurz, Carl **14** 44-45
  Stimson, Henry Lewis
    14 457-458
  Taft, William Howard **15** 78-81
  Wood, Leonard **16** 369-370
government as Commonwealth
  Aguinaldo, Emilio **1** 88
  Osmeña, Sergio **12** 22-24
  Quezon, Manuel Luis
    12 511-513
  Recto, Claro M. **13** 69-70
  Roxas, Manuel **13** 331-332
World War II
  see World War II
• SINCE 1946 (REPUBLIC)
cabinet ministers
  Marcos, Imelda Romualdez
    10 242-243
culture
  Amorsolo, Fernando **1** 204
  Luz, Arturo Rogerio **10** 56-57
  Rizal, José **13** 187-189
opposition to Marcos
  Aquino, Benigno **1** 267-268
  Aquino, Corazon Cojoangco
    1 268-270
political leaders
  Laurel, Salvador H. **9** 226-227
presidents
  Aquino, Corazon Cojoangco
    1 268-270
  Garcia, Carlos P. **6** 207-208
  Macapagal, Diosdado P. **10** 74-76
  Magsaysay, Ramon **10** 130-131
  Marcos, Ferdinand **10** 240-242
  Quirino, Elpidio **12** 519-520
  Ramos, Fidel Valdez **13** 18-19
reforms
  Macapagal, Diosdado P.
    10 74-76
  Sin, Jaime L. **14** 244-245
U.S. relations
  Dulles, John Foster **5** 134-135
  Recto, Claro M. **13** 69-70
  Rómulo, Carlos P. **13** 270-271

Philippines, University of the (Quezon
City)
  Amorsolo, Fernando **1** 204
  Rómulo, Carlos P. **13** 270-271

Philippović, Eugen (1858-1917), Austrian
economist
  Schumpeter, Joseph Alois **14** 43-44
  von Mises, Ludwig **16** 25

Philipps University of Marburg
  Cohen, Hermann **4** 138-139

Philistines (Old Testament people)
  David, Jacques Louis **4** 407-409
  Samuel **13** 457-458
  Saul **13** 498

Philistinism (literature)
  Arnold, Matthew **1** 311-313
  Lewis, Harry Sinclair **9** 385-387

PHILLIP, ARTHUR (1738-1814), English
governor of New South Wales
12 279-280
  Macarthur, John **10** 78

PHILLIPS, DAVID GRAHAM (1867-1911),
American journalist and novelist
12 280-281

Phillips, Edward (1630?-1696), English
author
  Milton, John **11** 43-46

PHILLIPS, WENDELL (1811-1884), Ameri-
can abolitionist and social reformer
12 281-282
  Anthony, Susan Brownell **1** 246-248
  Burns, Anthony **3** 151
  Child, Lydia Maria Francis **3** 520-521
  Fee, John Gregg **5** 402-403
  Garrison, William Lloyd **6** 226-228

Philoctetes (play)
  Sophocles **14** 343-345

Philodoxeus (play)
  Alberti, Leon Battista **1** 113-115

Philology (social science)
  Bloomfield, Leonard **2** 338
  Humboldt, Wilhelm von **8** 31
  Niebuhr, Barthold Georg **11** 385-386
  Nietzsche, Friedrich **11** 390-392
  see also Linguistics; Social scientists—
    philologists

Philomel (musical composition)
  Babbitt, Milton **1** 410

Philomena (romance)
  Chrestien de Troyes **4** 23-24

Philosophaster (play)
  Burton, Robert **3** 166-167

**Philosophe anglais ou les mémoires de
Cleveland, Le**
  see Cleveland

Philosopher or Dog? (novel)
  Machado de Assis, Joaquim Maria
    10 91-92

Philosophers, African
  Augustine **1** 367-370

Philosophers, American
19th century
  Fiske, John **5** 465-466
  Harris, William Torrey **7** 177-178
  McCosh, James **10** 402-403
  Peirce, Charles Sanders **12** 187-188
  Thoreau, Henry David **15** 203-205
19th-20th century
  Mead, George Herbert **10** 437-438

  Peirce, Charles Sanders **12** 187-188
  Royce, Josiah **13** 334-335
  Whitehead, Alfred North
    16 242-244
20th century
  Bentley, Arthur F. **2** 178
  Bode, Boyd Henry **2** 355-356
  Bok, Sissela Ann **2** 372-374
  Brightman, Edgar Sheffield **3** 8-9
  Broudy, Harry Samuel **3** 28-29
  Callahan, Daniel **3** 231-233
  Carnap, Rudolf **3** 308-309
  Chomsky, Noam Avram **4** 13-15
  Cohen, Morris Raphael **4** 139-140
  Daly, Mary **4** 380-381
  Dewey, John **4** 520-523
  Fletcher, Joseph Francis **5** 488-489
  Fukuyama, Francis **6** 146-147
  Hartshorne, Charles **7** 186-187
  Herberg, Will **7** 322-323
  Hocking, William Ernest **7** 428-429
  Hook, Sidney **7** 474-475
  Horne, Herman Harrell **7** 503-504
  Lewis, Clarence Irving **9** 381
  Lovejoy, Arthur Oncken **10** 6
  MacIntyre, Alasdair Chalmers
    10 99-100
  MacIver, Robert Morrison
    10 100-101
  Marcuse, Herbert **10** 245-247
  Nagel, Ernest **11** 291-292
  Nozick, Robert **11** 438-439
  Perry, Ralph Barton **12** 239-240
  Quine, Willard Van Orman
    12 514-515
  Rawls, John **13** 55-56
  Rorty, Richard **13** 288-289
  Santayana, George **13** 475-477
  Sellars, Wilfred **14** 96-98
  Silber, John **14** 224-226
  Simon, Herbert Alexander
    14 236-237
  Tarski, Alfred **15** 110-111
  Tillich, Paul Johannes **15** 224-225
  Toulmin, Stephen Edelston
    15 271-273
  West, Cornel **16** 212-213
  Wieman, Henry Nelson **16** 261-262

Philosophers, Arab
9th-11th century
  Avicenna **1** 386-387
  ibn Hazm, Abu Muhammad Ali
    8 93
  Kindi, Abu-Yusuf Yaqub ibn-Ishaq al-
    9 10-11
12th-14th century
  Averroës **1** 382-383
  Ghazali, Abu Hamid Muhammad
    al- **6** 290-291
  Ibn al-Arabi, Muhyi al-Din **8** 91
  ibn Khaldun, Abd al-Rahman ibn
    Muhammad **8** 93-94
  ibn Tufayl, Abu Bakr Muhammad
    8 96

Philosophers, Australian
  Singer, Peter Albert David **14** 253-254

Philosophers, Austrian
Buber, Martin **3** 87-89
Mach, Ernst **10** 90-91
Meinong, Alexius Ritter von Hand-
  schuchsheim **10** 461-462
Popper, Karl Raimund **12** 402
Wittgenstein, Ludwig **16** 350-351

Philosophers, Brazilian
Freire, Paulo **6** 95-96

Philosophers, British
see Philosophers, English; Philosophers,
  Irish; Philosophers, Scottish

Philosophers, Byzantine
Proclus Diadochus **12** 457

Philosophers, Chinese
ancient
  Chung-shu, Tung **4** 48-49
  Confucius **4** 197-200
  Han Fei Tzu **7** 124-125
  Hsün-tzu **8** 8
  Lao Tzu **9** 201-202
  Mencius **10** 480-481
  Shang Yang **14** 149-150
  Tsou Yen **15** 329-330
  Wang Ch'ung **16** 98-99
  Wang Pi **16** 104-105
12th-16th century
  Chu Hsi **4** 40-43
  Lu Chiu-yuan **10** 24-25
  Wang Yang-ming **16** 108-109
17th-20th century
  Hu Shih **8** 63-65
  Huang Tsung-hsi **8** 9-10
  K'ang Yu-wei **8** 426-428
  Wang Fu-chih **16** 99-101

Philosophers, Czech
Masaryk, Tomáš Garrigue **10** 314-315

Philosophers, Danish
Kierkegaard, Søren Aabye **8** 547-549

Philosophers, Dutch
Erasmus, Desiderius **5** 298-300
Spinoza, Baruch **14** 381-383

Philosophers, Egyptian
Hanafi, Hassan **7** 114

Philosophers, English
12th-14th century
  Bacon, Roger **1** 425-427
  John of Salisbury **8** 284-285
  William of Ockham **16** 298-299
15th-17th century
  Bacon, Francis **1** 422-424
  Clarke, Samuel **4** 88
  Cudworth, Ralph **4** 331
  Herbert, Edward **7** 324
  Hobbes, Thomas **7** 421-423
  Locke, John **9** 478-480
  More, Thomas **11** 156-157
  Shaftesbury, 3d Earl of **14** 136-137
  Skelton, John **14** 268-269
  Toland, John **15** 256
18th century
  Bentham, Jeremy **2** 176-178
  Butler, Joseph **3** 180-181

Hartley, David **7** 185
Mandeville, Bernard **10** 192
Paley, William **12** 72
Price, Richard **12** 447-448
19th century
  Acton, John Emerich Edward Dal-
    berg **1** 38
  Green, Thomas Hill **6** 520-521
  Martineau, Harriet **10** 296-297
  Mill, John Stuart **11** 21-23
  Sidgwick, Henry **14** 213
  Spencer, Herbert **14** 369-370
19th-20th centuries
  von Hügel, Friedrich **16** 21-22
19th-20th century
  Alexander, Samuel **1** 141
  Bosanquet, Bernard **2** 425-426
  Bradley, Francis Herbert **2** 481-482
  Hobhouse, Leonard Trelawny
    7 425-426
  Whitehead, Alfred North
    16 242-244
20th century
  Austin, John Langshaw **1** 379-380
  Ayer, Alfred Jules **1** 391-393
  Berlin, Isaiah **2** 201-203
  Broad, Charlie Dunbar **3** 12
  Collingwood, Robin George **4** 162
  Hayek, Friedrich A. von **7** 221-223
  Hesse, Mary B. **7** 369-371
  MacIntyre, Alasdair Chalmers
    10 99-100
  Midgely, Mary Burton **11** 9-10
  Moore, George Edward **11** 146
  Ramsey, Frank Plumpton **13** 25
  Russell, Bertrand Arthur William
    13 373-374
  Ryle, Gilbert **13** 393-394
  Strawson, Peter Fredrick **14** 506-507
  Tawney, Richard Henry **15** 120-121
  Toulmin, Stephen Edelston
    15 271-273
  Warnock, Helen Mary Wilson
    16 115-117

Philosophers, French
11th-16th century
  Abelard, Peter **1** 23-25
  Bodin, Jean **2** 356-357
  Charron, Pierre **3** 472
  Levi ben Gershon **9** 363-364
  Ramus, Petrus **13** 27-28
17th century
  Bayle, Pierre **2** 77-78
  Descartes, René **4** 505-508
  Malebranche, Nicolas **10** 166-167
  Pascal, Blaise **12** 122-124
18th century
  Bayle, Pierre **2** 77-78
  Condillac, Étienne Bonnot de
    4 194-195
  Condorcet, Marquis de **4** 195-196
  Diderot, Denis **5** 1-2
  Helvétius, Claude Adrien **7** 273-274
  Holbach, Baron d' **7** 448-449
  La Mettrie, Julien Offray de
    9 179-180

Montesquieu **11** 123-125
Rousseau, Jean Jacques **13** 324-328
Voltaire **16** 14-16
19th century
  Bergson, Henri **2** 191-192
  Comte, Auguste **4** 189-191
  Cournot, Antoine Augustin **4** 273
  Cousin, Victor **4** 273-274
  Maistre, Joseph de **10** 153-154
  Proudhon, Pierre Joseph **12** 461-463
  Simon, Jules François **14** 237-238
  Tarde, Jean Gabriel **15** 108-109
19th-20th century
  Le Bon, Gustave **9** 268-269
  Lévy-Bruhl, Lucien **9** 374-375
  Sorel, Georges **14** 347-348
20th century
  Althusser, Louis **1** 182-183
  Derrida, Jacques **4** 503-505
  Bergson, Henri **2** 191-192
  Durkheim, Émile **5** 162-163
  Foucault, Michel **6** 29-30
  Gilson, Étienne Henry **6** 327-328
  Halévy, Élie **7** 76
  Levy, Bernard-Henri **9** 372-373
  Marcel, Gabriel **10** 233-234
  Maritain, Jacques **10** 263
  Merleau-Ponty, Maurice **10** 518
  Ricoeur, Paul **13** 157-158
  Sartre, Jean Paul **13** 491-492
  Weil, Simone **16** 172-174

Philosophers, German
13th-17th century
  Albertus Magnus **1** 115-116
  Boehme, Jacob **2** 357
  Eckhart, Johann **5** 200-201
  Leibniz, Gottfried Wilhelm von
    9 307-310
  Thomasius **15** 193-194
18th century
  Hamann, Johann Georg **7** 92
  Herder, Johann Gottfried von
    7 327-328
  Jacobi, Friedrich Heinrich
    8 189-190
  Kant, Immanuel **8** 430-432
  Lessing, Gotthold Ephraim
    9 357-359
  Mendelssohn, Moses **10** 488-489
  Fichte, Johann Gottlieb **5** 435-436
  Wolff, Christian von **16** 358
19th century
  Brentano, Franz Clemens **2** 516-517
  Dilthey, Wilhelm Christian Ludwig
    5 10
  Feuerbach, Ludwig Andreas **5** 432
  Fichte, Johann Gottlieb **5** 435-436
  Fries, Jakob Friedrich **6** 116-117
  Hegel, Georg Wilhelm Friedrich
    7 254-256
  Lotze, Rudolf Hermann **9** 521-522
  Marx, Karl **10** 304-308
  Nietzsche, Friedrich **11** 390-392
  Schelling, Friedrich Wilhelm Joseph
    von **13** 526-527

Schleiermacher, Friedrich Ernst Daniel **14** 11-12
Schopenhauer, Arthur **14** 29-31
Stirner, Max **14** 459-460
19th-20th century
　Frege, Gottlob **6** 93-94
　Simmel, Georg **14** 234-235
　Wundt, Wilhelm Max **16** 402-403
20th century
　Adorno, Theodor W. **1** 65-67
　Bloch, Ernst **2** 327-328
　Carnap, Rudolf **3** 308-309
　Cassirer, Ernst **3** 358-359
　Driesch, Hans Adolf Eduard **5** 105
　Gadamer, Hans-Georg **6** 162-163
　Habermas, Jürgen **7** 58-60
　Heidegger, Martin **7** 257-258
　Husserl, Edmund **8** 67-68
　Jaspers, Karl **8** 225-226
　Moltmann, Jöurgen **11** 91-92
　Otto, Louis Karl Rudolf **12** 30-32
　Schlick, Friedrich Albert Moritz **14** 16-17
　Spengler, Oswald **14** 372-373
　Stein, Edith **14** 412-414
　Strauss, Leo **14** 499-500
　Tillich, Paul Johannes **15** 224-225

Philosophers, Greek
6th century B.C.
　Anaximander **1** 209-210
　Anaximenes **1** 210
　Pythagoras **12** 498-499
　Thales **15** 161
5th century B.C.
　Anaxagoras **1** 208-209
　Democritus **4** 493-494
　Empedocles **5** 282
　Heraclitus **7** 320
　Parmenides **12** 116-117
　Protagoras **12** 461
　Pythagoras **12** 498-499
　Socrates **14** 320-321
　Zeno of Elea **16** 500
5th-4th century B.C.
　Antisthenes **1** 250-251
　Aristotle **1** 295-296
　Diogenes **5** 20-21
　Eudoxus of Cnidus **5** 329-330
　Gorgias **6** 456
　Heraclides of Pontus **7** 319-320
　Plato **12** 345-347
　Zeno of Citium **16** 499-500
4th-3d century B.C.
　Epicurus **5** 292-294
3d-2d century B.C.
　Carneades **3** 309
　Chrysippus **4** 35-36
1st-2d century A.D.
　Epictetus **5** 292
　Galen **6** 178-180
3d century A.D.
　Plotinus **12** 358-359
4th-5th century A.D.
　Hypatia of Alexandria **8** 85

Philosophers, Hungarian
Lukács, Gyorgy **10** 37-38
Polanyi, Michael **12** 372-373

Philosophers, Indian (Asia)
Buddha **3** 97-101
Iqbal, Muhammad **8** 132-133
Krishnamurti, Jiddu **9** 101-103
Shankara **14** 150-151
Rabindranath Tagore **12** 529-531
Mahavira, Vardhamana **10** 135-137

Philosophers, Iranian
Shariati, Ali **14** 156-157

Philosophers, Irish
Berkeley, George **2** 197-198
Burke, Edmund **3** 138-141
Erigena, John Scotus **5** 308-309

Philosophers, Italian
13th-15th century
　Bonaventure **2** 383-384
　Feltre, Vittorino da **5** 409-410
　Ficino, Marsilio **5** 436-437
　Marsilius of Padua **10** 284
　Pico della Mirandola, Giovanni **12** 299-300
　Pomponazzi, Pietro **12** 390-391
　Thomas Aquinas **15** 183-186
　Valla, Lorenzo **15** 406
16th-17th century
　Bruno, Giordano **3** 75-76
　Campanella, Tommaso **3** 249
　Telesio, Bernardino **15** 138-139
　Vico, Giambattista **15** 480-481
19th-20th century
　Croce, Benedetto **4** 313-314
　Gentile, Giovanni **6** 267
　Rosmini-Serbati, Antonio **13** 296-297

Philosophers, Jewish
Abravanel, Isaac ben Judah **1** 31
Ahad Haam **1** 88-89
Arendt, Hannah **1** 282-284
Cohen, Hermann **4** 138-139
Fackenheim, Emil Ludwig **5** 359-361
Philo Judaeus **12** 282-283
Judah Halevi **8** 373
Kaufmann, Ezekiel **8** 460
Levinas, Emmanuel **9** 368-369
Maimonides **10** 151-152
Rosenzweig, Franz **13** 294
Saadia ben Joseph al-Fayumi **13** 396
Shestov, Lev **14** 190-191
Strauss, Leo **14** 499-500

Philosophers, Korean
Yi Hwang **16** 457

Philosophers, Roman
Boethius, Anicius Manlius Severinus **2** 360-361
Cicero, Marcus Tullius **4** 55-58
Lucretius **10** 26-27
Marcus Aurelius Antoninus **10** 243-245
Seneca the Younger, Lucius Annaeus **14** 103-105

Philosophers, Russian
Bakhtin, Mikhail Mikhailovich **1** 456-458
Berdyaev, Nicholas Alexandrovich **2** 184-185
Borochov, Dov Ber **2** 421-422
Plekhanov, Georgi Valentinovich **12** 351-352
Shestov, Lev **14** 190-191
Tolstoy, Leo **15** 262-265

Philosophers, Scottish
13th century
　Duns Scotus, John **5** 149-150
18th-19th century
　Ferguson, Adam **5** 420-421
　Hume, David **8** 31-34
　Reid, Thomas **13** 87-88
　Smith, Adam **14** 283-284
　Stewart, Dugald **14** 449
19th-20th century
　Balfour, Arthur James **1** 469-470
　McCosh, James **10** 402-403
　Mill, James **11** 21

Philosophers, Senegalese
Senghor, Léopold Sédar **14** 106-107

Philosophers, Spanish
Averroës **1** 382-383
ibn Gabirol, Solomon ben Judah **8** 92
Ortega Y Gasset, José **12** 7-8
Santayana, George **13** 475-477
Servetus, Michael **14** 115-116
Suárez, Francisco **15** 8
Unamuno y Jugo, Miguel de **15** 386-387

Philosophers, Swedish
Nygren, Anders **11** 449-451

Philosophers' stone (Europe)
Jabir ibn Hayyan **8** 167

Philosophes (French philosophy)
Condorcet, Marquis de **4** 195-196
Frederick II **6** 81-84
Helvétius, Claude Adrien **7** 273-274
Sade, Comte de **13** 416-418
Turgot, Anne Robert Jacques **15** 348-349

Philosophia (literary character)
Boethius, Anicius Manlius Severinus **2** 360-361

Philosophiae naturalis principia mathematica
see Principia mathematica

Philosophy
analytical
　Moore, George Edward **11** 146
　Quine, Willard Van Orman **12** 514-515
　Russell, Bertrand Arthur William **13** 373-374
　Ryle, Gilbert **13** 393-394
anarchism
　Proudhon, Pierre Joseph **12** 461-463
　Stirner, Max **14** 459-460
and Islam

Kindi, Abu-Yusuf Yaqub ibn-Ishaq al-
9 10-11
Mamun, Abdallah al- **10** 183
and Judaism
Judah Halevi **8** 373
Maimonides **10** 151-152
Philo Judaeus **12** 282-283
Soloveitchik, Joseph Baer
14 328-329
and language
Bakhtin, Mikhail Mikhailovich
1 456-458
and relation of individual to society
Berlin, Isaiah **2** 201-203
and religion
Hamann, Johann Georg **7** 92
Hesse, Mary B. **7** 369-371
Hocking, William Ernest **7** 428-429
Hume, David **8** 31-34
Kolakowski, Leszek **9** 76-77
Otto, Louis Karl Rudolf **12** 30-32
Royce, Josiah **13** 334-335
Voegelin, Eric **16** 6-8
von Hügel, Friedrich **16** 21-22
West, Cornel **16** 212-213
Wieman, Henry Nelson **16** 261-262
and science
Hesse, Mary B. **7** 369-371
Sellars, Wilfred **14** 96-98
Aristotelianism
see Aristotelianism
atomism
see Atomism
Augustinianism
see Augustinianism
Averroism
see Averroism
biomedical ethics
Callahan, Daniel **3** 231-233
Cambridge Platonism
Cudworth, Ralph **4** 331
Cartesianism
see Cartesianism
classical
Hobbes, Thomas **7** 421-423
classical realism
Broudy, Harry Samuel **3** 28-29
Confucianism
see Confucianism
cosmology
Empedocles **5** 282
Heraclides of Pontus **7** 319-320
Heraclitus **7** 320
see also Universe, systems of
cross-cultural interpretation
Hanafi, Hassan **7** 114
cultural pluralism
Locke, Alain **9** 475-478
Cynicism
see Cynicism
definitions and concepts
Bergson, Henri **2** 191-192
Cohen, Morris Raphael **4** 139-140
Feuerbach, Ludwig Andreas **5** 432
Whitehead, Alfred North
16 242-244

determinism
see Determinism
eclectism
Cousin, Victor **4** 273-274
Durkheim, Émile **5** 162-163
Philo Judaeus **12** 282-283
Eleatic
Parmenides **12** 116-117
Zeno of Elea **16** 500
empiricism
see Empiricism
"end of history"
Fukuyama, Francis **6** 146-147
Enlightenment
see Enlightenment
Epicureanism
Epicurus **5** 292-294
epistemology
Broad, Charlie Dunbar **3** 12
Duns Scotus, John **5** 149-150
Heraclitus **7** 320
see also knowledge, theories of
esthetics
see Esthetics
ethics
Bok, Sissela Ann **2** 372-374
Kolakowski, Leszek **9** 76-77
Levy, Bernard-Henri **9** 372-373
MacIntyre, Alasdair Chalmers
10 99-100
Midgely, Mary Burton **11** 9-10
Sellars, Wilfred **14** 96-98
Sidgwick, Henry **14** 213
Singer, Peter Albert David
14 253-254
Spinoza, Baruch **14** 381-383
Toulmin, Stephen Edelston
15 271-273
Warnock, Helen Mary Wilson
16 115-117
see also Ethics
existentialism
see Existentialism
Five Element theory
Tsou Yen **15** 329-330
Frankfurt School
Habermas, Jürgen **7** 58-60
hedonism
Eudoxus of Cnidus **5** 329-330
hermeneutical
Ricoeur, Paul **13** 157-158
history of
MacIntyre, Alasdair Chalmers
10 99-100
humanism
see Humanism; Humanism, Christian
idealism
see Idealism
individualism
Spencer, Herbert **14** 369-370
Ionian
see Ionian school
Islamic
Hanafi, Hassan **7** 114
Kantian

Cassirer, Ernst **3** 358-359
Cohen, Hermann **4** 138-139
Kant, Immanuel **8** 430-432
Rosmini-Serbati, Antonio
13 296-297
Legalist
see Legalism (Chinese philosophy)
liberalism
Hobhouse, Leonard Trelawny
7 425-426
linguistics in
Austin, John Langshaw **1** 379-380
logic
see Logic; Logic, symbolic
Marxism
Althusser, Louis **1** 182-183
Kolakowski, Leszek **9** 76-77
Lukács, Gyorgy **10** 37-38
Plekhanov, Georgi Valentinovich
12 351-352
see also Marxism
materialism
Hobbes, Thomas **7** 421-423
Holbach, Baron d' **7** 448-449
La Mettrie, Julien Offray de
9 179-180
Marx, Karl **10** 304-308
Santayana, George **13** 475-477
metamathematics
Tarski, Alfred **15** 110-111
metaphysics
see Metaphysics
Milesian
see Milesian school
modern vs. medieval
Descartes, René **4** 505-508
moral
see Ethics
moral theory
Fletcher, Joseph Francis **5** 488-489
Levy, Bernard-Henri **9** 372-373
mysticism
see Mysticism
naturalist
Haeckel, Ernst Heinrich Philipp
August **7** 61-62
Neo-Confucianism
see Neo-Confucianism
Neoplatonism
Erigena, John Scotus **5** 308-309
ibn Gabirol, Solomon ben Judah
8 92
Kindi, Abu-Yusuf Yaqub ibn-Ishaq al-
9 10-11
Plotinus **12** 358-359
Proclus Diadochus **12** 457
New Left
Marcuse, Herbert **10** 245-247
Mills, C. Wright **11** 35-36
New Thought movement (1915-19;
China)
Hu Shih **8** 63-65
nominalism
Luther, Martin **10** 48-51
William of Ockham **16** 298-299
nonrational belief systems

Lévy-Bruhl, Lucien **9** 374-375
occasionalism
   Malebranche, Nicolas **10** 166-167
of communications
   McLuhan, Marshall **10** 424-426
of history
   Collingwood, Robin George **4** 162
   Herder, Johann Gottfried von
      7 327-328
   Lovejoy, Arthur Oncken **10** 6
   Vico, Giambattista **15** 480-481
ordinary language philosophy
   Strawson, Peter Fredrick **14** 506-507
o-yo-mei school
   Wang Yang-ming **16** 108-109
pantheistic
   see Pantheism
Peripatetic
   see Peripatetic school
pessimism
   Schopenhauer, Arthur **14** 29-31
phenomenology
   see Phenomenology
Platonism
   see Platonism
pluralism
   Anaxagoras **1** 208-209
   Zeno of Elea **16** 500
political
   see Political theory
positivism
   see Positivism
pragmatism
   see Pragmatism
process philosophy
   Hartshorne, Charles **7** 186-187
radical libertarianism
   Nozick, Robert **11** 438-439
Ramism
   Ramus, Petrus **13** 27-28
rationalism
   see Rationalism; Reason
ratiovitalism
   Ortega Y Gasset, José **12** 7-8
realism
   see Realism (philosophy)
Renaissance
   see Renaissance (philosophy)
scholasticism
   see Scholasticism
scientific
   Bacon, Roger **1** 425-427
   Brentano, Franz Clemens **2** 516-517
   Broad, Charlie Dunbar **3** 12
   Nagel, Ernest **11** 291-292
Scottish
   Ferguson, Adam **5** 420-421
   see also Scottish school of common
      sense
semantics
   Tarski, Alfred **15** 110-111
skepticism
   see Skepticism
socialism
   see Socialism

Socratic
   Socrates **14** 320-321
   Strauss, Leo **14** 499-500
sophism
   see Sophism
speculative
   Hippocrates **7** 408-410
Stoicism
   see Stoicism
Taoism
   see Taoism
theology of hope
   Moltmann, Jörgen **11** 91-92
theosophy
   Besant, Annie Wood **2** 233-234
Thomism
   see Thomism
transcendentalism
   see Transcendentalism
universals
   see Universals
utilitarianism
   see Utilitarianism
value theory
   Meinong, Alexius Ritter von Hand-
      schuchsheim **10** 461-462
Vienna Circle
   Popper, Karl Raimund **12** 402
   Schlick, Friedrich Albert Moritz
      14 16-17
vitalism
   Bergson, Henri **2** 191-192
   Driesch, Hans Adolf Eduard **5** 105
   see also Philosophers

Philosophy and the Mirror of Nature
(book)
   Rorty, Richard **13** 288-289

Philosophy of Education, The (book)
   Horne, Herman Harrell **7** 503-504

Philosophy of Religion, A (book)
   Brightman, Edgar Sheffield **3** 8-9

Philostratus (170?-245), Greek philosopher
   Titian **15** 242-244

Philotas (died 330 B.C.), Macedonian general
   Alexander the Great **1** 137-141

Phineas Finn (novel)
   Trollope, Anthony **15** 300-302

Phineas Redux (novel)
   Trollope, Anthony **15** 300-302

Phineus (play)
   Aeschylus **1** 70-72

PHIPS, SIR WILLIAM (1650/51-95), American shipbuilder and colonial governor
12 283
   Mather, Cotton **10** 330-332, 255

Phlogiston theory (chemistry)
   Black, Joseph **2** 303
   Cavendish, Henry **3** 383-384
   Lavoisier, Antoine Laurent **9** 241-244
   Priestley, Joseph **12** 452-453
   Stahl, Georg Ernst **14** 392-393

Phocais (epic)
   Homer **7** 465-467

Phocas (died 610), Byzantine emperor
602-610
   Heraclius **7** 320-321

Phoenicia (ancient nation, Western Syria)
   Antiochus III **1** 249-250
   Homer **7** 465-467

Phoenician Women (play)
   Euripides **5** 332-334

Phoenissae (play)
   Seneca the Younger, Lucius Annaeus
      14 103-105

Phoenix (essays)
   Lawrence, David Herbert **9** 247-248

Phoenix (steamboat)
   Stevens, John **14** 439-440

Phoenix Park (Dublin)
   Asquith, Herbert Henry **1** 344-346
   Joyce, James **8** 365-367

Phoenix, The (play)
   Middleton, Thomas **11** 8-9

Phonemics (linguistics)
   Sapir, Edward **13** 478-479

Phonograph
   Bell, Alexander Graham **2** 129-131
   Edison, Thomas Alva **5** 206-208

Phormio (play)
   Terence **15** 146-148

Phosphorous (chemistry)
   Boyle, Robert **2** 469-471
   Hinshelwood, Cyril Norman **7** 405-406
   Hofmann, August Wilhelm von
      7 441-442
   Lavoisier, Antoine Laurent **9** 241-244

PHOTIUS (circa 820-891), Byzantine patriarch **12** 283-284
   Basil I **2** 49-50

Photochemistry
   Bunsen, Robert Wilhelm **3** 124-125
   Draper, John William **5** 96-97

Photoelectric effect (physics)
   Einstein, Albert **5** 228-231
   Lawrence, Ernest Orlando **9** 248-250
   Millikan, Robert Andrews **11** 33-35

Photography
   as art form
      Abbott, Berenice **1** 7-9
      Adams, Ansel **1** 40-41
      Arbus, Diane Nemerov **1** 276-277
      Avedon, Richard **1** 381-382
      Eakins, Thomas **5** 176-177
      Evans, Walker **5** 339
      Gilpin, Laura **6** 326-327
      Hockney, David **7** 429-431
      Leibovitz, Annie **9** 310-312
      Mapplethorpe, Robert **10** 227-228
      Ray, Man **13** 59-60
      Rodchenko, Alexander Mikhailovich
         13 233-234
      Smithson, Robert **14** 301-303

Steichen, Edward **14** 411-412
Stieglitz, Alfred **14** 451-452
see also Artists—photographers
as historical record
Abbott, Berenice **1** 7-9
Freeman, Roland L. **6** 92-93
Lange, Dorothea **9** 193-194
VanDer Zee, James **15** 418-419
film
Baekeland, Leo Hendrik **1** 430-431
Eastman, George **5** 186
Riefenstahl, Leni **13** 161-163
Rivers, Larry **13** 186-187
in science
Abbott, Berenice **1** 7-9
Barnard, Edward Emerson **2** 8-9
Bertillon, Alphonse **2** 230-231
Cousteau, Jacques-Yves **4** 276-277
Draper, John William **5** 96-97
Ewing, William Maurice **5** 350-351
Gabor, Dennis **6** 159-160
Huggins, William **8** 14-15
Tiselius, Arne Wilhelm Kaurin
15 240-241
invention and equipment
Brady, Mathew B. **2** 487-488
Daguerre, Louis Jacques Mandé
4 365-366
Eastman, George **5** 186
Fizeau, Hippolyte Armand Louis
5 475
Foucault, Jean Bernard Léon
6 28-29
Gabor, Dennis **6** 159-160
Herschel, John Frederick William
7 340-341
Land, Edwin Herbert **9** 183-184
Lumière Brothers, The **10** 41-43
of celebrities
Leibovitz, Annie **9** 310-312

Photojournalism
Bourke-White, Margaret **2** 455-456
Capa, Robert **3** 269-271
Freeman, Roland L. **6** 92-93
Mydans, Carl **11** 283-284

Photometry (astronomy)
Herschel, John Frederick William
7 340-341
Pickering, Edward Charles **12** 298

Photon (physics)
de Broglie, Louis **4** 442-444
Millikan, Robert Andrews **11** 33-35

Photo-Secession (photography society)
Steichen, Edward **14** 411-412
Stieglitz, Alfred **14** 451-452

Photosynthesis (plants)
Baeyer, Johann Friedrich Adolf von
1 432
Calvin, Melvin **3** 242-243
Franck, James **6** 49-52
Ingenhousz, Jan **8** 119-120

Phrases and Philosophies... (book)
Wilde, Oscar Fingall O'Flahertie Wills
16 272-273

Phrygia (ancient nation, Asia Minor)
Alexander the Great **1** 137-141
Antigonus I **1** 248-249

Phya Kalyan Maitri
see Sayre, Francis

PHYFE, DUNCAN (1768-1854), American
cabinetmaker **12** 284-285

Phylon (periodical)
Du Bois, William Edward Burghardt
5 116-118

Physical anthropology (social science)
Boas, Franz **2** 349-351
Fries, Jakob Friedrich **6** 116-117

Physical chemistry
Calvin, Melvin **3** 242-243
Debye, Peter Joseph William **4** 447-448
Duhem, Pierre Maurice Marie **5** 129
Franck, James **6** 49-52
Franklin, Rosalind Elsie **6** 67-68
Gibbs, Josiah Willard **6** 302-303
Haber, Fritz **7** 56-58
Hinshelwood, Cyril Norman **7** 405-406
Nernst, Walther **11** 340-342
Patrick, Jennie R. **12** 136-137
Perutz, Max **12** 246-248
Prichard, Diana García **12** 448-449
Richards, Theodore William
13 137-138

Physical Chemistry, Institute of (Uppsala,
Sweden)
Theorell, Axel Hugo Theodor
15 176-177
Tiselius, Arne Wilhelm Kaurin
15 240-241

Physical geography
Davis, William Morris **4** 425-426
Maury, Matthew Fontaine **10** 351-352
Sauer, Carl Ortwin **13** 496-497

Physically handicapped
Aleijadinho, O **1** 125-126
Billings, William **2** 274-275
Bourne, Randolph Silliman **2** 456-457
Castro Alves, Antônio de **3** 364-365
see also Blind; Deaf, the

Physician of His Own Honor, The (play)
Calderón, Pedro **3** 221-222

Physicians
see Scientists—physicians

Physicists, The (play)
Dürrenmatt, Friedrich **5** 164-165

Physics (science)
aerodynamics
see Aerodynamics
and mathematics
Feigenbaum, Mitchell Jay **5** 404-405
Penrose, Roger **12** 204-205
applied physics
Alvarez, Luis W. **1** 187-189
Aristotelian
see Aristotle
atomic
see Atom

Avogadro's law
Avogadro, Lorenzo Romano
Amedeo Carlo **1** 388-389
celestial mechanics
Adams, John Couch **1** 51-52
Bowditch, Nathaniel **2** 460-461
Halley, Edmund **7** 88-89
Leverrier, Urbain Jean Joseph
9 361-362
Poincaré, Jules Henri **12** 365-366
Cherenkov effect
Cherenkov, Pavel Alekseevich
3 502-503
classical mechanics
see Classical mechanics
conservation of energy
Helmholtz, Hermann Ludwig Ferdinand von **7** 268-269
Tyndall, John **15** 374
conservation of parity
Lee, Tsung-Dao **9** 299-300
cosmic rays
see Cosmic rays
cosmology
Hawking, Stephen William
7 206-208
cryogenics
Kapitsa, Pyotr Leonidovich
8 433-435
Landau, Lev Davidovich **9** 184-185
crystallography
von Laue, Max **16** 23-24
dynamics
Huygens, Christiaan **8** 79-81
electrical conductivity
Brattain, Walter H. **2** 505-507
electricity
see Electricity
electroconductivity
Shockley, William **14** 200-202
electrodynamics
Ampère, André Marie **1** 205-206
Bloch, Felix **2** 328-330
Einstein, Albert **5** 228-231
Fermi, Enrico **5** 422-424
Feynman, Richard Phillips
5 432-434
Helmholtz, Hermann Ludwig Ferdinand von **7** 268-269
electromagnetism
see Electromagnetism
electron microscopy
Ruska, Ernst August Friedrich
13 370-371
elementary-particle forces
Weinberg, Steven **16** 175-177
gravitation
see Gravitation
heat
Fourier, Jean Baptiste Joseph **6** 32-33
Lomonosov, Mikhail Vasilevich
9 494
Rumford **13** 360-362
see also thermodynamics (below)
high-pressure phenomena
Bridgman, Percy Williams **3** 5-6

holographic photography
    Gabor, Dennis **6** 159-160
hydrodynamics
    Bernoulli, Daniel **2** 216
    Duhem, Pierre Maurice Marie **5** 129
    Euler, Leonard **5** 331-332
    Kármán, Theodore von **8** 451-452
    Pascal, Blaise **12** 122-124
    Torricelli, Evangelista **15** 268-269
kinetics
    see Kinetic theory of gases
light
    see Light
low temperature
    Kamerlingh Onnes, Heike
        8 418-420
magnetism
    see Magnetism
motion
    Alembert, Jean le Rond d'
        1 127-128
    Galileo Galilei **6** 180-183
    Hamilton, William Rowan **7** 99-100
    Huygens, Christiaan **8** 79-81
    Newton, Isaac **11** 369-372
    Tartaglia, Niccolo **15** 111-112
nuclear
    see Nuclear physics
of atmosphere
    Appleton, Edward Victor **1** 265-266
of stratosphere
    Piccard, Auguste **12** 297-298
optics
    see Optics
particle physics
    Glashow, Sheldon Lee **6** 361-362
photoelectric effect
    Einstein, Albert **5** 228-231
    Millikan, Robert Andrews **11** 33-35
    Oppenheimer, J. Robert **11** 525-526
pneumatics
    Boyle, Robert **2** 469-471
    Guericke, Otto Von **7** 27-28
quantum theory
    see Quantum theory
relativity
    see Relativity
semiconductors
    Brattain, Walter H. **2** 505-507
    Noyce, Robert **11** 436-437
    Shockley, William **14** 200-202
solid-state
    Bloch, Felix **2** 328-330
    Chu, Paul Ching-Wu **4** 37-39
spectroscopy
    Aston, Francis William **1** 350-351
    Kirchhoff, Gustav Robert **9** 33-34
    Moore, Charlotte E. **11** 145-146
    Rowland, Henry Augustus
        13 330-331
    Townes, Charles Hard **15** 281-282
statistical mechanics
    Einstein, Albert **5** 228-231
    Flory, Paul **5** 492-494
    Gibbs, Josiah Willard **6** 302-303

Goeppert-Mayer, Maria **6** 385-387
    Prichard, Diana García **12** 448-449
    van der Waals, Johannes Diderik
        15 417-418
    Yang, Chen Ning **16** 437-438
superconductivity
    Müller, Karl Alexander **11** 240-241
thermodynamics
    Carnot, Nicolas Léonard Sadi **3** 315
    Clausius, Rudolf Julius Emanuel
        4 92-94
    Kelvin of Largs **8** 488-489
    Planck, Max Karl Ernst Ludwig
        12 342-344
    see also heat (above); Thermody-
        namics
thermometry
    Cavendish, Henry **3** 383-384
    Fahrenheit, Gabriel Daniel **5** 366
    see also Scientists—physicists

Physiocratic school (economics)
    du Pont, Éleuthère Irénée **5** 154
    du Pont de Nemours, Pierre Samuel
        5 155-156
    Turgot, Anne Robert Jacques
        15 348-349

Physiological psychology
    Hartley, David **7** 185
    Lotze, Rudolf Hermann **9** 521-522

Physiological Temperance Society
    (Louisville, Kentucky)
    Drake, Daniel **5** 93-94

Physiology (science)
    anaphylaxis
        Richet, Charles Robert **13** 144-145
    cell theory
        Schwann, Theodor **14** 51-52
    circulatory system
        Harvey, William **7** 189-190
        Krogh, Schack August Steenberg
            9 106
        Ludwig, Karl Friedrich Wilhelm
            10 31
    endocrinology
        Houssay, Bernardo Alberto
            7 522-523
    nutrition
        Mayer, Jean **10** 365-366
    obesity
        Mayer, Jean **10** 365-366
    of nervous system
        Du Bois-Reymond, Emil **5** 118-119
        Eccles, John Carew **5** 195-196
        Erasistratus **5** 297-298
        Erlanger, Joseph **5** 310-311
        Galvani, Luigi **6** 194-195
        Haller, Albrecht Von **7** 87-88
        Helmholtz, Hermann Ludwig Ferdi-
            nand von **7** 268-269
        Hill, Archibald Vivian **7** 385-386
        Hodgkin, Alan Lloyd **7** 431-432
        Loewi, Otto **9** 486-487
        Müller, Johannes Peter **11** 239-240
        Pavlov, Ivan Petrovich **12** 155-157

Sherrington, Charles Scott
        14 187-189
    of sex
        Masters, William Howell
            10 327-328
    of vision
        Wald, George **16** 51-53
    perception
        Frisch, Karl von **6** 117-118
        Swedenborg, Emanuel **15** 49-50
    radioimmunoassay
        Yalow, Rosalyn S. **16** 427-428
    systematized
        Bernard, Claude **2** 208-210
        Fernel, Jean François **5** 425-426
        Sanctorius **13** 459
    vitalistic theories
        Stahl, Georg Ernst **14** 392-393
        see also Bacteriology; Scientists—
            physiologists

Pi (mathematics)
    Apollonius of Perga **1** 261-262
    Archimedes **1** 277-280

Pi meson (element—chemistry particle)
    Anderson, Carl David **1** 214-215
    Fermi, Enrico **5** 422-424
    Yukawa, Hideki **16** 481-482

Piacentini, M. (1881-1960), Italian archi-
    tect
    Nervi, Pier Luigi **11** 346-348

Piacenza, battle of (1746)
    Montcalm de Saint-Véran, Marquis de
        11 122-123

Piacere, Il (nove)
    D'Annunzio, Gabriele **4** 388

PIAF, EDITH (Edith Giovanna Gassion;
    1915-63), French music hall/cabaret
    singer **12** 285-287

PIAGET, JEAN (1896-1980), Swiss psychol-
    ogist and educator **12** 287-288

PIANKHI (ruled circa 741-circa 712 B.C.),
    Nubian king **12** 288-289
    Shabaka **14** 130

Piano (musical instrument)
    Ax, Emanuel **1** 391
    Barenboim, Daniel **2** 3-4
    Basie **2** 48-49
    Brubeck, Dave **3** 59-61
    Chopin, Frédéric François **4** 16-18
    Gould, Glenn **6** 469-470
    Granados, Enrique **6** 489-490
    Horowitz, Vladimir **7** 509-510
    Puente, Tito **12** 476-477
    Schubert, Franz Peter **14** 35-37
    Tal, Josef **15** 85-86
    Wuorinen, Charles **16** 404

PIANO, RENZO (born 1937), Italian archi-
    tect, lecturer, and designer **12** 289-291
    Rogers, Richard **13** 248-250

Piano concerto
    see Concertos (piano)

Piano trio
    see Trio (piano)

Pianto della Madonna, II (poem)
Jacopone da Todi **8** 194

Piazza della Signoria (Florence)
Donatello **5** 55-56
Giovanni da Bologna **6** 345-346

Piazza di San Marco
see St. Mark's Square (Venice)

Piazza d'Italia (plaza in New Orleans, LA)
Moore, Charles Willard **11** 143-145

Piazza Tales, The (stories)
Melville, Herman **10** 472-476

Piazzetta, Giovanni Battista (1682-1754),
Italian painter
Tiepolo, Giovanni Battista **15** 219-220
Troger, Paul **15** 300

Piazzi, Giuseppe (1746-1826), Italian
astronomer
Gauss, Karl Friedrich **6** 240-242

Pibul Songgram, Luang
see Phibun Songkhram, Luang

PICABIA, FRANCIS (1879-1953), French
artist, writer, and bon vivant **12** 291-292
Duchamp, Marcel **5** 122-123
Miró, Joan **11** 53-54

Picadilly Hotel (London)
Shaw, Richard Norman **14** 167-168

Picaresque novel (literature)
Alemán, Mateo **1** 126
Bellow, Saul **2** 141-143
Brackenridge, Hugh Henry **2** 472-473
Fernández de Lizardi, José Joaquin
5 424-425
Góngora y Argote, Luis de **6** 427-428
Grimmelshausen, Hans Jakob Christof-
fel von **7** 4-5
Lesage, Alain René **9** 353-354
Mann, Thomas **10** 204-207
Quevedo Y Villegas, Francisco Gómez
de **12** 511
Smollett, Tobias George **14** 305-307

PICASSO, PABLO (1881-1973), Spanish
painter, sculptor, and graphic artist
12 292-295
associates
Cocteau, Jean **4** 132-133
Rousseau, Henri **13** 323-324
Stein, Gertrude **14** 414-415
Stella, Joseph **14** 422
Stravinsky, Igor Fedorovich
14 502-506
Thomson, Virgil **15** 202-203
Ungaretti, Giuseppe **15** 389-390
compared to
Chagall, Marc **3** 406-407
Duchamp, Marcel **5** 122-123
cubism
Braque, Georges **2** 504-505
Gorky, Arshile **6** 458
Gris, Juan **7** 5-6
Léger, Fernand **9** 302-303
Malevich, Kasimir **10** 168-169
Mondrian, Piet **11** 101-102
Pevsner, Antoine **12** 263-264

Satie, Erik **13** 494-495
Weber, Max **16** 160
friends
Archipenko, Alexander **1** 280-281
Arp, Jean **1** 317-318
Derain, André **4** 503
Ehrenburg, Ilya Grigorievich
5 224-225
Klee, Paul **9** 47-49
influence (painting)
Bacon, Francis **1** 421-422
Demuth, Charles **4** 497-498
Kirchner, Ernst Ludwig **9** 34-35
Severini, Gino **14** 122
Sheeler, Charles **14** 170-171
Soulages, Pierre **14** 350-351
influence (sculpture)
González, Julio **6** 428-429
Lipchitz, Jacques **9** 432-433
Smith, David **14** 287-288
influenced by
Beardsley, Aubrey Vincent **2** 88-89
Cézanne, Paul **3** 400-402
Ovid **12** 34-36

PICASSO, PALOMA (born 1949), Spanish
fashion designer **12** 295-297

PICCARD, AUGUSTE (1884-1962), Swiss
scientist **12** 297-298

Piccard, Jacques Ernest Jean (born 1922),
Swiss oceanographer
Piccard, Auguste **12** 297-298

Piccola borghesia (stories)
Vittorini, Elio **16** 2-3

Piccolomini, Aeneas Sylvius de'
see Pius II

Piccolomini (play)
Schiller, Johann Christoph Friedrich von
14 4-7

Piccolomini, Francesco
see Pius III

Pichincha, battle of (1822)
Bolívar, Simón **2** 375-377
Sucre, Antonio José de **15** 11-12

Pickel, Konrad
see Celtes, Conradus

PICKERING, EDWARD CHARLES
(1846-1919), American astronomer
12 298
Cannon, Annie Jump **3** 260-261

PICKERING, TIMOTHY (1745-1829),
American Revolutionary soldier and
statesman **12** 298-299
Randolph, Edmund **13** 29-30

Pickford, Mary (1893-1979),
Canadian-American actress
Barrymores **2** 28-30
Chaplin, Charles Spencer **3** 438-440
Griffith, David Wark **6** 544-545
Tanizaki, Junichiro **15** 101-102

Picking and Choosing (poem)
Moore, Marianne **11** 148-149

Pickwick Papers, The (novel)
Dickens, Charles John Huffam
4 538-541

Picnic in the Country (painting)
Vlaminck, Maurice **16** 6

**PICO DELLA MIRANDOLA, CONTE GIO-
VANNI** (1463-1494), Italian philosopher
and humanist **12** 299-300
Leo X **9** 332-334
Medici, Lorenzo de' **10** 450-451
More, Thomas **11** 156-157
Pater, Walter Horatio **12** 130-131
Poliziano, Angelo **12** 373-374
Proclus Diadochus **12** 457
Savonarola, Girolamo **13** 505-506

Picquart, Marie Georges (1854-1914),
French general
Dreyfus, Alfred **5** 103-105

Picquigny, Treaty of (1475)
Charles the Bold **3** 467-469
Louis XI **9** 526-528

Picrochole (literary character)
Rabelais, François **12** 524-526

Pictographs (art)
Gottlieb, Adolph **6** 462-463

Pictor's Transformations (novel)
Hesse, Hermann **7** 367-369

Picture of Dorian Gray, The (novel)
Wilde, Oscar Fingall O'Flahertie Wills
16 272-273

Pictures at an Exhibition (musical composition ; Mussorgsky)
Kandinsky, Wassily **8** 420-422
Mussorgsky, Modest Petrovich
11 274-276

Pictures of the Floating World (poems)
Lowell, Amy **10** 13

PIDE (Portuguese secret police)
Salazar, António de Oliveira
13 442-443

Pieces of Eight (revue sketch)
Pinter, Harold **12** 317-318

Pied Beauty (poem)
Hopkins, Gerard Manley **7** 492-494

Piedmont (region , lt.)
Cavour, Conte di **3** 385-386
Ferdinand II **5** 415-416
Francis I **6** 40-43
Manin, Daniele **10** 197-198
Mazzini, Giuseppe **10** 381-383
see also Sardinia

Piedra y cielo (poems)
Jiménez, Juan Ramón **8** 261-262

Pier da Morrone
see Celestine V

PIERCE, FRANKLIN (1804-1869), American statesman, president 1853-57
12 300-301
appointments
Buchanan, James **3** 89-90
Davis, Jefferson **4** 416-418

De Bow, James Dunwoody Brownson **4** 441-442
Marcy, William Learned **10** 247-248
Owen, Robert Dale **12** 40-41
Soulé, Pierre **14** 351-352
opponents
Blair, Francis Preston **2** 313-315
Cass, Lewis **3** 355-356
Dix, Dorothea Lynde **5** 32-33
supporters
Hawthorne, Nathaniel **7** 212-215
Van Buren, Martin **15** 410-411

Pierce-Nichols House (Salem, Massachusetts)
McIntire, Samuel **10** 415

Pierluigi, Giovanni
see Palestrina, Giovanni Pierluigi da

PIERO DELLA FRANCESCA (circa 1415/20-92), Italian painter **12** 301-302
Antonello da Messina **1** 251-252
Bellini, Giovanni **2** 137-138
Bramante, Donato **2** 493-494
Raphael **13** 40-42
Signorelli, Luca **14** 221-222
Uccello, Paolo **15** 378-379
Veneziano, Domenico **15** 459-460

Piero di Cosimo (1462-1521), Italian painter
Leonardo da Vinci **9** 337-340
Pontormo **12** 394-395

Piero di Giovanni
see Lorenzo Monaco

Pierpont Morgan Library (New York City)
McKim, Charles Follen **10** 417-418

Pierre (novel)
Melville, Herman **10** 472-476

Pierre Bayle (book)
Feuerbach, Ludwig Andreas **5** 432

Pierre de Maricourt
see Peregrinus, Petrus

Pierre et Camille (story)
Musset, Louis Charles Alfred de **11** 271-272

Pierre et Jean (novel)
Maupassant, Henri René Albert Guy de **10** 347

Pierrette et son pot au lait (poem)
Vicente, Gil **15** 479-480

Pierrot (clown)
Laforgue, Jules **9** 160-161

Piers Gaveston (poem)
Drayton, Michael **5** 97-98

Piers Plowman (poem; Langland)
Langland, William **9** 194-195
Lyndsay, David **10** 66-67

Pietà (painting)
Andrea del Sarto **1** 224-225
Bellini, Giovanni **2** 137-138
Bermejo, Bartolomé **2** 205
Charonton, Enguerrand **3** 471
Greco **6** 511-514

Morales, Luis de **11** 150
Titian **15** 242-244
Veronese, Paolo **15** 469-470

Pietà (sculpture)
Donner, Georg Raphael **5** 63
Günther, Ignaz **7** 41-42
Michelangelo Buonarroti **11** 2-5, 395

Pietermaritzburg College (South Africa)
Paton, Alan Stewart **12** 134-135

Pietism (religion)
Bach, Johann Sebastian **1** 416-419
Mühlenberg, Heinrich Melchior **11** 232-233
Ritschl, Albrecht Benjamin **13** 180
Spener, Philipp Jakob **14** 372
Thomasius **15** 193-194
Wieland, Christoph Martin **16** 260-261
Wolff, Christian von **16** 358
Zinzendorf, Nikolaus Ludwig von **16** 522-523

Piéton de l'air, Le (play)
Ionesco, Eugène **8** 131-132

Pietra del paragone, La (opera)
Rossini, Gioacchino **13** 311-312

Pigalle, Jean Baptiste (1714-1785), French sculptor
Clodion **4** 121

Pignatelli, Antonio
see Innocent XII

PIGOU, ARTHUR CECIL (1877-1959), English economist **12** 302
Fisher, Irving **5** 462-463
Robertson, Dennis Holme **13** 196

PIKE, ZEBULON (1779-1813), American soldier and explorer **12** 302-304

Pike's Peak (Colorado)
Pike, Zebulon **12** 302-304
Tabor, Horace Austin Warner **15** 70

Piktors Verwandlungen (novel)
Hesse, Hermann **7** 367-369

Pilar, Marcelo H. del
see Del Pilar, Marcelo H.

Pilate, Pontius (flourished 1st half 1st century A.D.), procurator of Judea
Jesus of Nazareth **8** 251-255

Pilgerfahrten (poems)
George, Stefan **6** 277-278

Pilgrim in His Own Country, The (novel)
Lope Félix de Vega Carpio **9** 503-506

Pilgrim, The (film)
Chaplin, Charles Spencer **3** 438-440

Pilgrimage and Wanderyears (poems)
Heidenstam, Carl Gustaf Verner Von **7** 258-259

Pilgrimage of Grace (religion)
Norfolk, 3d Duke of **11** 423

Pilgrimage of San Isidro (fresco)
Goya y Lucientes, Francisco de Paula José de **6** 476-478

Pilgrims
see Plymouth Colony

Pilgrim's Progress, The (allegory)
Bunyan, John **3** 128-129

Pillars of Society (play)
Ibsen, Henrik **8** 98-100

Pillnitz, Treaty of (1792)
Francis II **6** 43-44
Leopold II **9** 346

Pillow of Grass (novel)
Natsume, Soseki **11** 324-325

PILLSBURY, CHARLES ALFRED (1842-1899), American businessman **12** 304

PILON, GERMAIN (circa 1535-90), French sculptor **12** 305
Primaticcio, Francesco **12** 453-454

Pilot, The (novel)
Cooper, James Fenimore **4** 220-223

Pilote de guerre (book)
Saint-Exupéry, Antoine de **13** 431-432

Pilot's Story, The (poem)
Howells, William Dean **7** 539-541

PILSUDSKI, JOSEPH (1867-1935), Polish general, president 1918-21 **12** 305-306

Pima Indians (North America)
Benedict, Ruth Fulton **2** 154-155
Kino, Eusebio Francisco **9** 30-31

Pimeria Alta (region, Mexico)
Kino, Eusebio Francisco **9** 30-31

Pinakes (library catalog)
Callimachus **3** 235-236

Pinar del Rio (province, Cuba)
Estrada Palma, Tomás **5** 326-327
Machado y Morales, Gerardo **10** 92-93

PINCHBACK, PINCKNEY BENTON STEWART (1837-1921), African American politician **12** 306-308

Pincherle, Alberto
see Moravia, Alberto

PINCHOT, GIFFORD (1865-1946), American conservationist and public official **12** 308-309
Taft, William Howard **15** 78-81

Pinchwife (literary character)
Wycherley, William **16** 411-412

PINCKNEY, CHARLES COTESWORTH (1745-1825), American statesman **12** 310

PINCKNEY, CHARLES (1757-1824), American politician and diplomat **12** 309-310

Pinckney, Thomas (1750-1828), American statesman and diplomat
Adams, John **1** 48-51
Hamilton, Alexander **7** 95-98
Washington, George **16** 126-129

PINCUS, GREGORY GOODWIN (1903-1967), American biologist **12** 310-312

PINDAR (552/518-438 B.C.), Greek lyric poet **12** 312-313
　Aeschylus **1** 70-72
　Alexander the Great **1** 137-141
　Goethe, Johann Wolfgang von **6** 388-391
　Hölderlin, Johann Christian Friedrich **7** 451-452
　Ronsard, Pierre de **13** 271-273
　Zwingli, Huldreich **16** 537-538

Pine Ridge Indian Reservation (South Dakota)
　Peltier, Leonard **12** 193-195

PINEL, PHILIPPE (1745-1826), French physician **12** 313-314

Pines, Isle of (North Western Caribbean)
　Estrada Palma, Tomás **5** 326-327

Pines, The (story)
　Bunin, Ivan Alekseevich **3** 124

Pines of Rome (musical composition)
　Respighi, Ottorino **13** 103-104

P'ing (ruled 1 B.C. -A.D. 6), Chinese emperor
　Wang Mang **16** 101-103

P'inghsinkuan, battle of (1937)
　Lin Piao **9** 429-430

P'ing-lu (province , China)
　An Lu-shan **1** 239-240

Pingree House (Salem, Massachusetts)
　McIntire, Samuel **10** 415

Pingwoldang
　see Sol Ch'ong

Pinilla, Gustavo Rojas
　see Rojas Pinilla, Gustavo

Pining for Mother (novel)
　Tanizaki, Junichiro **15** 101-102

Pink Panther (film series)
　Sellers, Peter Richard Henry **14** 98-99

PINKERTON, ALLEN (1819-1884), American detective **12** 314-315

Pinkerton Detective Agency
　Carnegie, Andrew **3** 309-312
　Frick, Henry Clay **6** 108-109
　Pinkerton, Allan **12** 314-315

Pinkney, William (1764-1822), American diplomat
　Monroe, James **11** 111-113

Pinocchio (film)
　Disney, Walter Elias **5** 26-27

PINOCHET UGARTE, AUGUSTO (born 1915), Chilean military leader and dictator **12** 315-317
　Allende, Isabel **1** 172-174

Pinta (ship)
　Columbus, Christopher **4** 176-179

PINTER, HAROLD (born 1930), English playwright **12** 317-318
　Fraser, Antonia **6** 70-71

PINTO, ISAAC (1720-1791), Jewish merchant and scholar **12** 318

Pintor de su deshonra, El (play)
　Calderón, Pedro **3** 221-222

Pinzón, Martin Alonso (1440?-1493), Spanish navigator
　Columbus, Christopher **4** 176-179

Pinzón, Vicente Yáñez (1460?-1524?), Spanish navigator
　Columbus, Christopher **4** 176-179
　Solís, Juan Díaz de **14** 326

Pion
　see Pi meson

Pioneer (railroad car)
　Pullman, George Mortimer **12** 482-483

Pioneer (ship)
　Livingstone, David **9** 463-465

Pioneer Women (labor organization, Israel)
　Meir, Golda **10** 462-463

Pioneers
　see Frontiersmen

Pioneers (sculpture)
　Taft, Lorado **15** 75-76

Pioneers, The (novel)
　Cooper, James Fenimore **4** 220-223

Pipa de Kif, La (poem)
　Valle Inclán, Ramón Maria del **15** 407-408

Pipe Rolls (England)
　Henry I **7** 286-287

Pipes o'Pan at Zekesbury (book)
　Riley, James Whitcomb **13** 170-171

Pipistrello, II (story)
　Pirandello, Luigi **12** 319-321

Pippa Passes (poem)
　Browning, Robert **3** 53-55

PIPPIN, HORACE (1888-1946), African American painter **12** 318-319

Piquillo (drama)
　Nerval, Gérard de **11** 345-346

PIRANDELLO, LUIGI (1867-1936), Italian playwright novelist, and critic **12** 319-321
　Anouilh, Jean **1** 243-244
　Ibsen, Henrik **8** 98-100
　Strindberg, August **14** 509-511
　Valle Inclán, Ramón Maria del **15** 407-408

PIRANESI, GIOVANNI BATTISTA (1720-1778), Italian engraver and architect **12** 321-322
　Ledoux, Claude Nicolas **9** 277-278
　Sheraton, Thomas **14** 181-182
　Soufflot, Jacques Germain **14** 349-350

Pirate, The (novel)
　Scott, Walter **14** 68-70

Pirate I (painting)
　Gorky, Arshile **6** 458

Pirates
　Mendes Pinto, Fernao **10** 493-494

Pirates of Penzance, The (operetta)
　Gilbert, William Schwenck **6** 314-315
　Sullivan, Arthur Seymour **15** 23

Piratininga
　see São Paulo

Pirckheimer, Willibald (1470-1530), German humanist
　Dürer, Albrecht **5** 159-161

Pirelli Office Building (Milan)
　Nervi, Pier Luigi **11** 346-348

PIRENNE, JEAN HENRI (Jean Henri Otto Lucien Marie Pirenne; 1862-1935), Belgian historian **12** 322-323

Pirotechnica (*Pirotechnia*; encyclopedia)
　Biringuccio, Vannoccio **2** 283

Pisa (city, Italy)
　Brunelleschi, Filippo **3** 70-72
　Dandolo, Enrico **4** 386-387
　Manuel I **10** 218-219
　Visconti, Gian Galeazzo **15** 510-511

Pisa, Council of (1409)
　Ailly, Pierre d' **1** 94
　Hus, Jan **8** 56-59
　Martin V **10** 287-288

Pisa, Council of (1511)
　Julius II **8** 384-386

Pisa, Diet of (1313)
　Henry VII **7** 299-300

Pisa, University of
　Galileo Galilei **6** 180-183
　Gentile, Giovanni **6** 267
　Malpighi, Marcello **10** 176-178

Pisa Cathedral
　Pisano, Giovanni **12** 324-325
　Pisano, Nicola **12** 325

Pisan, Christine de
　see Christine de Pisan

Pisan Cantos (poems)
　Pound, Ezra Loomis **12** 415-417
　Williams, William Carlos **16** 308-309

PISANELLO (Antonio Pisano; before 1395-1455), Italian painter and medalist **12** 323-324
　Martin V **10** 287-288
　Tura, Cosimo **15** 343-344

Pisano
　see Andrea Pisano; Pisanello

PISANO, GIOVANNI (circa 1250-1314/17), Italian sculptor **12** 324-325
　Andrea Pisano **1** 225-226
　Arnolfo di Cambio **1** 315-316
　Lorenzetti, Pietro and Ambrogio **9** 517-518
　Martini, Simone **10** 298-299
　Pisano, Nicola **12** 325

PISANO, NICOLA (Nicola d'Apulia; circa 1220/25-1278/84), Italian sculptor **12** 325
　Arnolfo di Cambio **1** 315-316
　Pisano, Giovanni **12** 324-325

Michelangelo Buonarroti **11** 2-5

Piscator, Erwin (1893-1966), German theatrical producer
Brecht, Bertolt **2** 512-514

Pisis, Filippo de (1896-1956), Italian painter
Chirico, Giorgio de **4** 4

Pispir (ancient fort, Egypt)
Anthony, Susan Brownell **1** 246-248

PISSARO, CAMILLE (1830-1903), French painter **12** 326-327
impressionism
Cézanne, Paul **3** 400-402
Monet, Claude **11** 102-104
influence of
Daubigny, Charles François **4** 402
Hassam, Frederick Childe **7** 192
Van Gogh, Vincent **15** 427-429
influenced by
Corot, Jean Baptiste Camille **4** 247-249
Seurat, Georges Pierre **14** 120-122

Pistoia Cathedral (Italy)
Brunelleschi, Filippo **3** 70-72

PISTON, WALTER (born 1894), American composer **12** 327-328
Stravinsky, Igor Fedorovich **14** 502-506

Pit, The (novel)
Norris, Benjamin Franklin Jr. **11** 427-428

Pitchblende (mineralogy)
Curie, Marie Sklodowska **4** 339-341

Pithecanthropus erectus (archeology)
Weidenreich, Franz **16** 171-172

Pithoprakta (musical composition)
Xenakis, Iannis **16** 416-418

Pitkin, Lemuel (literary character)
West, Nathanael **16** 213-214

Pitseng (novel)
Mofolo, Thomas **11** 74

PITT, WILLIAM, THE ELDER (1708-1778), English statesman **12** 328-329
American colonies
Forbes, John **5** 507-508
Franklin, Benjamin **6** 60-64
Rockingham, 2d Marquess of **13** 230-231
Wolfe, James **16** 354-355
in art
Copley, John Singleton **4** 228-230
Peale, Charles Willson **12** 169-171
opponents
Bute, 3d Earl of **3** 177-178
Walpole, Robert **16** 82-84

PITT, WILLIAM, THE YOUNGER (1759-1806), English statesman **12** 329-331
appointees
Price, Richard **12** 447-448
Wellesley, Richard Colley **16** 192-193
associates

Castlereagh, Viscount **3** 363-364
Liverpool, 2nd Earl of **9** 456-457
North, Frederick **11** 429-430
opponents
Fox, Charles James **6** 35-37
Landor, Walter Savage **9** 186-187
Miranda, Francisco de **11** 52-53
supporters
Boswell, James **2** 432-434
Canning, George **3** 258-260
George III **6** 270-272
Wilberforce, William **16** 269-270

Pittoni, Giovanni Battista (1687-1767), Italian painter
Troger, Paul **15** 300

Pittsburgh (city; Pennsylvania)
Forbes, John **5** 507-508
Kane, John **8** 422
Wright, Frank Lloyd **16** 398-401

Pittsburgh, University of
Erikson, Erik Homburger **5** 309-310
Ewing, William Maurice **5** 350-351
Langley, Samuel Pierpont **9** 195-196
Salk, Jonas Edward **13** 451-452

Pittsburgh Dispatch (newspaper)
Dreiser, Herman Theodore **5** 98-100

Pittsburgh Landing
see Shiloh, battle of (1862)

Pittsburgh Pact (1918)
Masaryk, Tomáš Garrigue **10** 314-315

Pituitary gland
Cushing, Harvey Williams **4** 353-354
Dale, Henry Hallett **4** 371-373

PIUS II (Enea Silvio de'Piccolomini; 1405-64), pope 1458-64 **12** 331
Alberti, Leon Battista **1** 113-115
Cusa, Nicholas of **4** 352-353
Quintilian **12** 518-519

Pius III (Francesco Todeschini Piccolomini; 1440-1503), pope 1503
Borgia, Cesare **2** 412-413
Julius II **8** 384-386

PIUS IV (Giovanni Angelo de' Medici; 1499-1565), pope 1559-65 **12** 332
Borromeo, Charles **2** 423-424
Pius V **12** 332-333
Sixtus V **14** 267-268

PIUS V (Antonio Ghislieri; 1504-72), pope 1566-72 **12** 332-333
Sixtus V **14** 267-268

PIUS VI (Gianangelo Braschi; 1717-99), pope 1775-99 **12** 333-334
Carroll, John **3** 331-332
Joseph II **8** 359-360
Talleyrand, Charles Maurice de **15** 89-90

PIUS VII (Luigi Barnabà Chiaramonti; 1740-1823), pope 1880-23 **12** 334-335
Canova, Antonio **3** 263-264
Napoleon I **11** 306-310

PIUS IX (Giovanni Maria Mastai-Ferretti; 1792-1878), pope 1846-78 **12** 335-336
Charles Albert, King of Sardinia **3** 466
Lamy, Jean Baptiste **9** 181-182
Leo XIII **9** 334-336
Manning, Henry Edward **10** 209-210
Montalembert, Comte de **11** 118-119
Pius X **12** 336-337
Rosmini-Serbati, Antonio **13** 296-297
Victor Emmanuel II **15** 483-484

PIUS X (Giuseppe Melchiorre Sarto; 1835-1914), pope 1903-14 **12** 336-337
Benedict XV **2** 153-154

PIUS XI (Ambrogio Damiano Achille Ratti; 1857-1939), pope 1922-39 **12** 337-339
canonizations
Canisius, Peter **3** 258
Francis Xavier **6** 48
Jogues, Isaac **8** 270-271
Lateran Treaty (1929)
Mussolini, Benito **11** 272-274
social teachings
Benedict XV **2** 153-154
Dollfuss, Engelbert **5** 47
Frei Montalva, Eduardo **6** 94-95
Paul VI **12** 146-148

PIUS XII (Eugenio Maria Giuseppe Pacelli; 1876-1958), pope 1939-58 **12** 339-340
Bea, Augustinus **2** 79
John, XXIII **8** 277-280
Paul VI **12** 146-148
Pius XI **12** 337-339
Spellman, Francis Joseph **14** 367

Pixar (computer animation company)
Jobs, Steven **8** 265-267

PIZARRO, FRANCISCO (circa 1474-1541), Spanish conquistador in Peru **12** 340-341
Almagro, Diego de **1** 177-178
Atahualpa **1** 355-356
Balboa, Vasco Núñez de **1** 462-463
Benalcázar, Sebastián de **2** 145-146
de Soto, Hernando **4** 510-511
Manco Capac **10** 184-185
Pedrarias **12** 179
Tirso de Molina **15** 237-238
Valdivia, Pedro de **15** 400-401

Pizarro, Gonzalo (1506-1548), Spanish colonial governor
Benalcázar, Sebastián de **2** 145-146
Gasca, Pedro de la **6** 230-231
Orellana, Francisco de **11** 527-528
Pizarro, Francisco **12** 340-341
Valdivia, Pedro de **15** 400-401

Pizarro, Hernando (1475?-1578), Spanish explorer
Almagro, Diego de **1** 177-178
Pizarro, Francisco **12** 340-341
Valdivia, Pedro de **15** 400-401

Pizarro, Juan (died 1536), Spanish conquistador
Pizarro, Francisco **12** 340-341

Pizarro, Pedro (1541-after 1571), Spanish conquistador

Pizarro, Francisco **12** 340-341

Pizzolo, Niccolo (circa 1421-53), Italian painter and sculptor
Mantegna, Andrea **10** 215-216

PLAATJE, SOLOMON TSHEKISHO (1878-1932), South African writer **12** 341-342
Dube, John Langalibalele **5** 113

Place, Francis (1771-1854), English reformer
Godwin, William **6** 383-384

Place de la Concorde (Paris)
Gabriel, Ange Jacques **6** 160-161

Place des Victoires (Paris)
Mansart, Jules Hardouin **10** 212

Place du Théâtre Français (painting)
Pissaro, Camille **12** 326-327

Place in the Sun, A (film)
Dreiser, Herman Theodore **5** 98-100

Place Louis XV
see Place de la Concorde (Paris)

Place Vendôme (Paris)
Courbet, Jean Desiré Gustave **4** 271-273
Girardon, François **6** 348-349
Mansart, Jules Hardouin **10** 212

Places des Vosges (painting)
Davis, Stuart **4** 424-425

Placet (poem)
Mallarmé, Stéphane **10** 172-173

Placidia (388-423), Roman emperor
Alaric **1** 101-102

Placilla, battle of (1891)
Balmaceda Fernández, José Manuel **1** 475-476

Plaek
see Phibun Songkhram, Luang

Plague, bubonic
see Black Death (1348)

Plague, The (novel)
Camus, Albert **3** 255-257

Plaideurs, Les (play)
Racine, Jean Baptiste **12** 532-535

Plain Dealer, The (play)
Wycherley, William **16** 411-412

Plains Indians (North America)
Black Elk, Nicholas **2** 305-306
Fletcher, Alice Cunningham **5** 486-487
Lowie, Robert Harry **10** 18
Sheridan, Philip Henry **14** 182-183

Plainte d'automne (poem)
Mallarmé, Stéphane **10** 172-173

Plaisirs et les jours, Les (literary collection)
Proust, Marcel **12** 465-467

Plan of Agua Prieta
see Agua Prieta, Plan of

Plan of Union (United States; 1754)
Franklin, Benjamin **6** 60-64
Hutchinson, Thomas **8** 71-72

PLANCK, MAX KARL ERNST LUDWIG (1858-1947), German physicist **12** 342-344
Berlin University
Born, Max **2** 420-421
Bothe, Walther **2** 438-439
Schlick, Friedrich Albert Moritz **14** 16-17
Schrödinger, Erwin **14** 31-33
quantum theory
Broglie, Louis Victor Pierre Raymond de **3** 15-17
Einstein, Albert **5** 228-231
Jeans, James Hopwood **8** 235-236
thermodynamics
Boltzmann, Ludwig **2** 379-380
Debye, Peter Joseph William **4** 447-448

Plane geometry
see Geometry—plane

Planet (astronomy)
Jupiter and Saturn
Barnard, Edward Emerson **2** 8-9
Huygens, Christiaan **8** 79-81
Laplace, Marquis de **9** 202-204
laws of motion
Kepler, Johannes **8** 514-516
orbits (early theories)
Apollonius of Perga **1** 261-262
Bitruji, Nur al-Din Abu Ishaq al **2** 296
Eudoxus of Cnidus **5** 329-330
Hipparchus **7** 407-408
Ptolemy, Claudius **12** 473-474
orbits (modern theories)
Gauss, Karl Friedrich **6** 240-242
Hall, Asaph **7** 83-84
Rittenhouse, David **13** 180-181
outer planets
Adams, John Couch **1** 51-52
Herschel, William **7** 341-343
Jeffreys, Harold **8** 241-242
see also individual planets

Planet News (book)
Ginsberg, Allen **6** 332-333

Planetarium (astronomy)
Archimedes **1** 277-280

Planetesimal hypothesis (astronomy)
Chamberlin, Thomas Chrowder **3** 415-416

Planets
surfaces and life on
Sagan, Carl E. **13** 424-425

Planets, The (orchestral suite)
Holst, Gustav **7** 459-460

Plankton, Armour and Co.
Armour, Philip Danforth **1** 302

Planned communities
Post, Charles William **12** 408-409

Plant breeding (botany)
Borlaug, Norman Ernest **2** 418-420
Burbank, Luther **3** 129-131
East, Edward Murray **5** 182-183

Mendel, Johann Gregor **10** 483-486

Plant classification (botany)
Gray, Asa **6** 506-507
Lamarck, Chevalier de **9** 171-173
Ray, John **13** 57-59

Plant geography (botany)
Gray, Asa **6** 506-507
Humboldt, Friedrich Heinrich Alexander von **8** 30-31

Plant physiology and anatomy (botany)
Bose, Jagadis Chandra **2** 429-430
Hales, Stephen **7** 75
Liebig, Justus von **9** 403-404
Linnaeus, Carl **9** 427-429
Lysenko, Trofim Denisovich **10** 71
Malpighi, Marcello **10** 176-178-126
Vries, Hugo de **16** 33-36
see also Photosynthesis

Plantagenet dynasty (England, ruled 1154-1399)
Edward I **5** 208-210
Edward II **5** 210
Henry II **7** 287-289
Henry IV **7** 292-293
Richard I **13** 130
Richard II **13** 130-131

Plantagenet, Geoffrey
see Geoffrey IV

Planter (ship)
Smalls, Robert **14** 277-278

Plassey, battle of (1758)
Clive, Robert **4** 119-120

Plastiche (collage)
Burri, Alberto **3** 159-160

Plastics industry
see Business and industrial leaders—glass and plastics industries

Plataea, battle of (479 B.C.)
Phidias **12** 265-267
Xerxes **16** 420

Platero and I (book)
Jiménez, Juan Ramón **8** 261-262

PLATH, SYLVIA (1932-1963), American poet and novelist **12** 344-345
Hughes, Ted **8** 19-21

Platinum (element—chemistry)
Hofmann, August Wilhelm von **7** 441-442

PLATO (428-347 B.C.), Greek philosopher **12** 345-347
influence on literature
Democritus **4** 493-494
Flaubert, Gustave **5** 480-482
Marvell, Andrew **10** 301-303
Spenser, Edmund **14** 373-376
Phaedo
Mendelssohn, Moses **10** 488-489
Philo Judaeus **12** 282-283
Socrates **14** 320-321
Republic
Aristophanes **1** 293-294
Campanella, Tommaso **3** 249

Jowett, Benjamin **8** 364-365
More, Thomas **11** 156-157
Richards, Ivor Armstrong **13** 137
see also Neoplatonism; Platonic Academy; Platonism

Platonic Academy
Athens
see Academy (Athens)
Careggi
Ficino, Marsilio **5** 436-437
Florence
Medici, Cosimo de' **10** 449-450
Medici, Lorenzo de' **10** 450-451
Pico della Mirandola, Giovanni **12** 299-300

Platonism (philosophy)
Christian
Augustine **1** 367-370-293
Bembo, Pietro **2** 144-145
Boethius, Anicius Manlius Severinus **2** 360-361
Bonaventure **2** 383-384
Clement of Alexandria **4** 102-103
Ficino, Marsilio **5** 436-437
Justin Martyr **8** 395-396
critics
Antisthenes **1** 250-251
Bacon, Francis **1** 422-424
Machiavelli, Niccolò **10** 97-99
Marcus Aurelius Antoninus **10** 243-245
Masaryk, Tomáš Garrigue **10** 314-315
Popper, Karl Raimund **12** 402
Protagoras **12** 461
Schopenhauer, Arthur **14** 29-31
Whitehead, Alfred North **16** 242-244
origins
Plato **12** 345-347
see also Plato

Platoon (film)
Stone, Oliver **14** 472-475

PLATT, THOMAS COLLIER (1833-1910), American politician **12** 347-348

Platt Amendment (United States; 1901)
Grau San Martin, Ramón **6** 499-500
Root, Elihu **13** 283-284

PLAUTUS (circa 254-circa 184 B.C.), Roman writer **12** 348-350
Camoëns, Luis Vaz de **3** 247-249
Menander **10** 477-478
Shakespeare, William **14** 142-145
Terence **15** 146-148
Varro, Marcus Terentius **15** 438-439

Play Days (literary collection)
Jewett, Sarah Orne **8** 256

Play therapy (psychology)
Klein, Melanie **9** 52

Playboy (magazine)
Hefner, Hugh **7** 253-254

Playboy of the Western World, The (play)
Synge, Edmund John Millington **15** 61-62

Playfair, John (1748-1819), Scottish mathematician and geologist
Hutton, James **8** 73-74

Playful (painting)
Marc, Franz **10** 231

Plays for Bleecker Street (play)
Wilder, Thornton Niven **16** 276-277

Plays for England (literary collection)
Osborne, John **12** 16-17

Playwrights
see Authors—playwrights

Playwrights Company
Anderson, Maxwell **1** 219-220
Sherwood, Robert Emmet **14** 189-190

PLAZA LASSO, GALO (1906-1987), Ecuadorian statesman **12** 350-351
Velasco Ibarra, José María **15** 452-454

Pleasant Memoirs... (novel)
Valle Inclán, Ramón Maria del **15** 407-408

Pleasant Satyre... (play)
Lyndsay, David **10** 66-67

Pleasure (philosophy)
Bentham, Jeremy **2** 176-178
Epicurus **5** 292-294
Eudoxus of Cnidus **5** 329-330
Helvétius, Claude Adrien **7** 273-274

Pleasures and Days (literary collection)
Proust, Marcel **12** 465-467

Plectra (musical instrument)
Cowell, Henry Dixon **4** 280-281

Pledge, The (opera)
Weill, Kurt **16** 174-175

Pleiad (ship)
Baikie, William Balfour **1** 440

Pléiade (French poets)
du Bellay, Joachim **5** 113-114
Ronsard, Pierre de **13** 271-273
Sainte-Beuve, Charles Augustin **13** 438

Pleiads, The (novel)
Gobineau, Comte de **6** 375-376

Plein-air painting (art)
Böcklin, Arnold **2** 354-355
Liebermann, Max **9** 402-403
Manet, Édouard **10** 193-194
Monet, Claude **11** 102-104

Pleins pouvoirs (book)
Giraudoux, Jean **6** 349-350

PLEKHANOV, GEORGI VALENTINOVICH (1856-1918), Russian revolutionist and social philosopher **12** 351-352
Katayama, Sen **8** 457
Trotsky, Leon **15** 302-305

PLENTY COUPS (c. 1848-1932), Native American tribal leader and Crow chief **12** 352-355

Plessis, Armand du
see Richelieu, Duc de

Plessy v. Ferguson (legal case)
Harlan, John Marshall **7** 156-157

Tourgée, Albion Winegar **15** 277-278

Pletnyov, P. A. (1792-1865), Russian poet
Turgenev, Ivan Sergeyevich **15** 345-348

Plexus (novel)
Miller, Henry **11** 26-27

Pli selon pli (musical composition)
Boulez, Pierre **2** 444-445

PLINY THE ELDER (23/24-79), Roman encyclopedist **12** 355-356
as biographer
Celsus, Aulus Cornelius **3** 393
influence of
Columbus, Christopher **4** 176-179
Pliny the Younger **12** 356
Vasari, Giorgio **15** 442-443
on art
Apelles **1** 257
Apollodorus **1** 261
Myron **11** 285
Phidias **12** 265-267
Polykleitos **12** 385-386
Praxiteles **12** 433-434

PLINY THE YOUNGER (circa 61-circa 113), Roman author and administrator **12** 356
Martialis, Marcus Valerius **10** 286-287
Pliny the Elder **12** 355-356
Quintilian **12** 518-519
Suetonius Tranquillus, Gaius **15** 13
Tacitus **15** 70-72
Vignola, Giacomo da **15** 493-494

PLISETSKAYA, MAYA MIKHAILOVNA (born 1925), Russian ballet dancer **12** 356-358

Plombières, Agreement of (1858)
Cavour, Conte di **3** 385-386

PLOTINUS (205-270), Greek philosopher, founder of Neoplatonism **12** 358-359
Augustine **1** 367-370
Ficino, Marsilio **5** 436-437
ibn Gabirol, Solomon ben Judah **8** 92
Junayd, Abu al-Qasim ibn Muhammad al **8** 388
Plato **12** 345-347
Proclus Diadochus **12** 457
Schrödinger, Erwin **14** 31-33

Plough and the Stars, The (play)
O'Casey, Sean **11** 459-460

Plough That Broke the Plains, The (film)
Thomson, Virgil **15** 202-203

Plow (agricultural tool)
Deere, John **4** 455
Gatling, Richard Jordan **6** 234-235
McCormick, Cyrus Hall **10** 400-401

Plum Tree, The (novel)
Phillips, David Graham **12** 280-281

Plumed Serpent, The (novel)
Lawrence, David Herbert **9** 247-248

Plunket Society (New Zealand)
King, Frederic Truby **9** 18-19

Pluralism (philosophy)
Anaxagoras **1** 208-209
Zeno of Elea **16** 500

Plus forts, Les (novel)
Clemenceau, Georges **4** 99-101

Plus nulz regretz (poem; Jean Lemaire de Belges)
Josquin des Prez **8** 361-363

PLUTARCH (circa 46-circa 120), Greek biographer **12** 359-360
Apollodorus **1** 261
Archimedes **1** 277-280
Budé, Guillaume **3** 102-103
Camoëns, Luis Vaz de **3** 247-249
Phidias **12** 265-267
Shakespeare, William **14** 142-145
Zoroaster **16** 528-530

Plutonium (element—chemistry)
Bethe, Hans Albrecht **2** 238-239
Compton, Arthur Holly **4** 186-188
Lawrence, Ernest Orlando **9** 248-250
Seaborg, Glenn Theodore **14** 74-76

Plutus (play)
Aristophanes **1** 293-294

Plymouth (car)
Chrysler, Walter Percy **4** 36-37

Plymouth Colony (New England)
diplomatic agents
Standish, Myles **14** 396-397
Winslow, Edward **16** 338-339
Native American assistance
Squanto **14** 386-388
Native American treaties
Massasoit **10** 322-324
Metacom **10** 529-531
Minuit, Peter **11** 50
Philip **12** 267-268
religion and
Dunster, Henry **5** 152-153
Gorton, Samuell **6** 460
settlement
Bradford, William **2** 475-476-131
Brewster, William **2** 523-524
see also Massachusetts

Pneumatics (physics)
Boyle, Robert **2** 469-471
Guericke, Otto Von **7** 27-28

Pneumonia (medicine)
Avery, Oswald Theodore **1** 384-386
Domagk, Gerhard Johannes Paul **5** 48-50
Dubos, René Jules **5** 119

Pnin (stories)
Nabokov, Vladimir **11** 287-288

PO CHÜ-I (772-846), Chinese poet **12** 362-363

Pobble's Toes, The (verse)
Lear, Edward **9** 265-266

Pobeda (ship)
Feng Yü-hsiang **5** 412-413

POBEDONOSTSEV, KONSTANTIN PETROVICH (1827-1907), Russian statesman and jurist **12** 360-361
Alexander III **1** 133-134

Pobre negro (novel)
Gallegos Freire, Rómulo **6** 185-186

POCAHONTAS (circa 1595-1617), American Indian princess **12** 361-362
Lindsay, Vachel **9** 424-425
Powhatan **12** 429-430
Rolfe, John **13** 259-260
Smith, John **14** 295-297

Pocahontas (ballet)
Carter, Elliott Cook Jr. **3** 338-339

Pocahontas... (musical composition)
Heinrich, Anthony Philip **7** 261

Pocket's Echo, The (songs)
Britten, Benjamin **3** 10-11

Podgorny, Nikolai Viktorovitch (1903-1983), Soviet statesman
Paul VI **12** 146-148

POE, EDGAR ALLAN (1809-1849), American writer **12** 363-365
compared to
Hawthorne, Nathaniel **7** 212-215
Hidayat, Sadiq **7** 377-378
Lanier, Sidney **9** 199-200
illustrators
Demuth, Charles **4** 497-498
in art
Redon, Odilon **13** 75-76
influence of
Baudelaire, Charles Pierre **2** 61-63
Heavysege, Charles **7** 246
Kipling, Joseph Rudyard **9** 32-33
Miller, Joaquin **11** 27-28
Ryder, Albert Pinkham **13** 391-392
Strindberg, August **14** 509-511
Tanizaki, Junichiro **15** 101-102
influenced by
Brown, Charles Brockden **3** 33
Freneau, Philip Morin **6** 99-100
Hoffmann, Ernst Theodor Amadeus **7** 439-440
Irving, Washington **8** 141-143

Poelzig, Hans (1869-1936), German architect
Mies van der Rohe, Ludwig **11** 10-12

Poem of Ecstasy (symphony)
Scriabin, Alexander Nikolayevich **14** 71-72

Poem of Fire (symphony)
Scriabin, Alexander Nikolayevich **14** 71-72

Poem of the Cid (epic)
Alfonso VI **1** 149

Poem on Divine Revelation, A (poem)
Brackenridge, Hugh Henry **2** 472-473

Poem on the Prospect of Peace (poem)
Barlow, Joel **2** 6-7

Poema del otoño (poem)
Darío, Rubén **4** 393-394

Poemas humanas (poems)
Vallejo, César Abraham **15** 408-409

Poemata (sonnets)
du Bellay, Joachim **5** 113-114

Poème du haschisch, Le (poem)
Baudelaire, Charles Pierre **2** 61-63

Poème électronique (musical composition)
Varèse, Edgard **15** 432-433

Poèmes antiques (literary collection)
Leconte de Lisle, Charles Marie René **9** 273-274
Vigny, Comte de **15** 494-495

Poèmes barbares (literary collection)
Leconte de Lisle, Charles Marie René **9** 273-274

Poèmes de cendre et d'or (literary collection)
Morin, Paul **11** 174

Poèmes français (literary collection)
Rilke, Rainer Maria **13** 171-172

Poèmes saturniens (literary collection)
Verlaine, Paul Marie **15** 465-466

Poèmes tragiques (literary collection)
Leconte de Lisle, Charles Marie René **9** 273-274

Poems about God (book)
Ransom, John Crowe **13** 39-40

Poems before Congress (book)
Browning, Elizabeth Barrett **3** 52-53

Poems in Prose (stories)
Turgenev, Ivan Sergeyevich **15** 345-348

Poems Lyric and Pastoral (literary collection)
Drayton, Michael **5** 97-98

Poems of Ashes and Gold (literary collection)
Morin, Paul **11** 174

Poems of Several Years (anthology)
Yevtushenko, Yevgeny Alexandrovich **16** 455-456

Poems of the Past and Present (literary collection)
Hardy, Thomas **7** 150-152

Poems of the Times (literary collection)
Heine, Heinrich **7** 259-260

Poems on Slavery (literary collection)
Longfellow, Henry Wadsworth **9** 499-500

Poems on Various Subjects... (book)
Wheatley, Phillis **16** 221-222

Poems on Various Subjects (book; Coleridge)
Coleridge, Samuel Taylor **4** 154-156
Lamb, Charles **9** 176-177

Poenulus (play)
Plautus **12** 348-350

Poésie pour pouvoir (musical composition)
Boulez, Pierre **2** 444-445

Poésies nouvelles (poems)
Musset, Louis Charles Alfred de **11** 271-272

Poet, The (play)
Mármol, José **10** 274

Poet, The (poem)
Bryant, William Cullen **3** 83-85

Poet in New York (book)
Lorca, Federico García **9** 511-513

Poetaster (play)
Jonson, Ben **8** 343-345

Poètes Maudits, Les (book; Verlaine)
Mallarmé, Stéphane **10** 172-173
Verlaine, Paul Marie **15** 465-466

Poetics (book; Aristotle)
Aristotle **1** 295-296
Collins, William **4** 168-169
Longinus **9** 500-501
Molière **11** 86-88
Tasso, Torquato **15** 114-116

Poets
see Authors—poets; and national literatures (American literature; English literature; etc.)

Poets Laureate
Van Duyn, Mona **15** 422-423

Poets Laureate (United States)
Dove, Rita Frances **5** 87-89
Nemerov, Howard **11** 338-340
Strand, Mark **14** 491-493

Poet's Love (musical composition)
Schumann, Robert Alexander **14** 41-43

Poet's Task, The (book)
Lewis, Cecil Day **9** 380

Poggio a Caiano (Italy)
Andrea del Sarto **1** 224-225
Sangallo family **13** 464-466

Pogroms (Russia)
Dubnov, Simon **5** 115-116
Sholem Aleichem **14** 202-203
see also Anti-Semitism

Pohjola's Daughter (musical composition)
Sibelius, Jean Julius Christian **14** 211-212

Poictesme (literary kingdom)
Cabell, James Branch **3** 195-196

Poïïmata (poems)
Seferis, George **14** 84-85

POINCARÉ, JULES HENRI (1854-1912), French mathematician **12** 365-366
Cantor, Georg Ferdinand Ludwig Philipp **3** 265-266
Duhem, Pierre Maurice Marie **5** 129
Jeans, James Hopwood **8** 235-236
Lemaître, Abbè Georges Édouard **9** 315-316
Sarton, George **13** 490-491

POINCARÉ, RAYMOND (1860-1934), French statesman **12** 366-368
Blum, Léon **2** 343-344
Briand, Aristide **2** 528-529

Clemenceau, Georges **4** 99-101
Herriot, Édouard **7** 339-340

Poinsett, Joel R. (1779-1851), American legislator and diplomat
Frémont, John Charles **6** 97-98

Point Counter Point (novel)
Huxley, Aldous Leonard **8** 74-75

Pointillism (art)
Mondrian, Piet **11** 101-102
Prendergast, Maurice Brazil **12** 440
Seurat, Georges Pierre **14** 120-122
Vermeer, Jan **15** 466-467

Poirot, Hercule (literary character)
Christie, Agatha **4** 25-26

Poison gas (chemistry)
Conant, James Bryant **4** 192-193

Poisson, Siméon Denis (1781-1840), French mathematician
Laplace, Marquis de **9** 202-204

Poissy, Colloquy of (1560)
Catherine de Médicis **10** 445-449

POITIER, SIDNEY (born 1927), African American actor and director **12** 368-370

Poitiers, battles of
732
Martel, Charles **10** 285
1356
Charles V **3** 459-460
Edward III **5** 211-212
Edward the Black Prince **5** 217-218
John II **8** 275-276

Poitiers, Diane de (1499-1566), French mistress of Henry II of France
l'Orme, Philibert de **9** 519

Poker Game (sculpture)
Russell, Charles Marion **13** 375-376

POL POT (born 1928), Cambodian Communist and premier of Democratic Kampuchéa (1976-1979) **12** 382-384
Heng Samrin **7** 283-285
Sihanouk, Norodom **14** 222-223

Poland (Polish People's Republic; nation, Eastern Europe)
• EARLY HISTORY
East Prussia and
Frederick II **6** 79
French alliance
Louis XV **9** 533-534
Russia and
Kutuzov, Mikhail Ilarionovich **9** 137-138
Swedish wars
Augustus II **1** 373-374
Charles XII **3** 464-466
Frederick William **6** 85-86
Gustavus II **7** 43-45
Tatar-Turk invasions
John III **8** 276-277
Köprülü, Ahmed **9** 84-85
Ukrainian wars
Chmielnicki, Bogdan **4** 12-13

Mazepa, Ivan Stepanovich **10** 381
see also Holy League Polish Succession, War of (1684); the (1733-1735); Vienna, battle of (1683)

• PARTITION TO 1918
partition (first; 1772)
Catherine the Great **3** 370-372
Kościuszko, Tadeusz Andrzej Bonawentura **9** 88
partition (second; 1793)
Catherine the Great **3** 370-372
Frederick II **6** 81-84
Kościuszko, Tadeusz Andrzej Bonawentura **9** 88
partition (third; 1795)
Catherine the Great **3** 370-372
Francis II **6** 43-44
Frederick II **6** 81-84
Kościuszko, Tadeusz Andrzej Bonawentura **9** 88
Russia and
Alexander I **1** 130-132
Alexander II **1** 132-133
Bakunin, Mikhail Aleksandrovich **1** 458-460
Luxemburg, Rosa **10** 55-56
Nicholas I **11** 377-378
Pilsudski, Joseph **12** 305-306
see also Polish insurrections; Vienna, Congress of; World War I

• REPUBLIC
and U.S.S.R.
Chou En-lai **4** 20-22
Gomulka, Wladislaw **6** 422-424
independence
Dzerzhinsky, Felix Edmundovich **5** 173-174
Paderewski, Ignace Jan **12** 56-57
Pilsudski, Joseph **12** 305-306
presidents
Walesa, Lech **16** 57-59
trade union movement
Walesa, Lech **16** 57-59
transition to democracy
Jaruzelski, Wojciech Witold **8** 223-225
World War II
see World War II
see also Polish literature; Polish music

POLANYI, JOHN CHARLES (born 1929), Canadian scientist and Nobel Prize winner **12** 370-372

POLANYI, KARL (1886-1964), Hungarian economic historian **12** 372

POLANYI, MICHAEL (1891-1976), Hungarian medical doctor, physical chemist, social thinker, and philosopher **12** 372-373

Polar Eskimos
see Greenland Eskimos

Polar exploration
see Antarctic exploration; Arctic exploration

Polaris (ship)
Melville, George Wallace **10** 472

Polarization (physics)
Faraday, Michael **5** 380
Fresnel, Augustin Jean **6** 102-103
Land, Edwin Herbert **9** 183-184
Maxwell, James Clerk **10** 361-364
Peregrinus, Petrus **12** 208

Polaroid Corp. (established 1937)
Land, Edwin Herbert **9** 183-184

Pole, John de la (1464-1487)
see Lincoln, Earl of

Pole, Michael de la, Earl of Suffolk (circa 1330-89), English statesman
Richard II **13** 130-131

Pole, Reginald (1500-1558), English cardinal
Paul III **12** 144-145
Paul IV **12** 145-146

Pole, William de la, 1st Duke of Suffolk, (1396-1450), English soldier and statesman
Gloucester, Duke of **6** 370-371

Pole Poppenspäler (novella)
Storm, Theodor **14** 479-480

Polhem, Christopher (1661-1751), Swedish engineer and inventor
Whitney, Eli **16** 253-254

Police (government)
Burke, Robert O'Hara **3** 142-143
Fielding, Henry **5** 442-444
Peel, Robert **12** 181-183
Pinkerton, Allan **12** 314-315

Polinice (play)
Alfieri, Vittoria **1** 145-146

Poliomyelitis
vaccine
Sabin, Albert Bruce **13** 401-402

Poliomyelitis (medicine)
treatment
Kenny, Elizabeth **8** 509-510
vaccine
Enders, John Franklin **5** 285-286
Salk, Jonas Edward **13** 451-452
virus
Burnet, Frank Macfarlane **3** 146-147
Enders, John Franklin **5** 285-286
Landsteiner, Karl **9** 188-189

Polish insurrections (1830, 1863)
Bakunin, Mikhail Aleksandrovich **1** 458-460
Nicholas I **11** 377-378

Polish literature
Milosz, Czeslaw **11** 40-42
Peretz, Isaac Loeb **12** 212
Sienkiewicz, Henryk **14** 216-217

Polish music
Lutoslawski, Witold **10** 52-53

Paderewski, Ignace Jan **12** 56-57
Penderecki, Krzysztof **12** 195-197
Szymanowski, Karol **15** 67-68

Polish Peasant... (book)
Thomas, William Isaac **15** 193
Znaniecki, Florian **16** 523-524

Polish Sociological Institute
Znaniecki, Florian **16** 523-524

Polish Succession, War of the (1733-1735)
Anna Ivanovna **1** 240-241
Charles III **3** 454-455
Eugene of Savoy **5** 330-331
Montcalm de Saint-Véran, Marquis de **11** 122-123
Saxe, Comte de **13** 507-508

Politburo
see Statesmen, Russian

Polite Conversation (satire)
Swift, Jonathan **15** 51-54

Politian
see Poliziano, Angelo

Political Action Party (Peru)
Belaúnde Terry, Fernando **2** 125-126

Political geography (science)
Bowman, Isaiah **2** 464-465
Haushofer, Karl **7** 201
Ratzel, Friedrich **13** 50-51

Political History of the Devil, The (book)
Defoe, Daniel **4** 457-459

Political Justice (pamphlet; Godwin)
Shelley, Percy Bysshe **14** 176-178
Wordsworth, William **16** 385-388

Political machines (United States)
leaders (Democrat)
Curley, James Michael **4** 344-345
Daley, Richard J. **4** 373-375
Hague, Frank **7** 63-64
Long, Huey Pierce **9** 496-497
Murphy, Charles Francis **11** 259-260
Tillman, Benjamin Ryan **15** 225-226
Tweed, William Marcy **15** 366-367
leaders (Republican)
Cameron, Simon **3** 246-247
Conkling, Roscoe **4** 201-202
Penrose, Boies **12** 203-204
Platt, Thomas Collier **12** 347-348
Quay, Matthew Stanley **12** 507
Ruef, Abraham **13** 352-353
opponents (Democrat)
Johnson, Tom Loftin **8** 317
Seymour, Horatio **14** 126-127
Tilden, Samuel Jones **15** 222-223
opponents (Republican)
La Follette, Robert Marion **9** 155-156
La Guardia, Fiorello Henry **9** 166-167
see also Tammany Hall (New York City); Tweed Ring

Political parties (United States)
Jefferson, Thomas **8** 238-241
Lowell, Abbott Lawrence **10** 12-13

Reed, Thomas Brackett **13** 77
Washington, George **16** 126-129
see also Political machines; and individual parties

Political Romance, A (book)
Sterne, Laurence **14** 435-437

Political science
and history
Zinn, Howard **16** 520-521
basis and terminology
Lasswell, Harold Dwight **9** 218-219
Lieber, Francis **9** 401-402
behavioral approach
Key, Vladimir Orlando Jr. **8** 527-528
Merriam, Charles Edward **10** 518-519
Wallas, Graham **16** 77-78
international politics
Morgenthau, Hans J. **11** 171-172
modern state
Arendt, Hannah **1** 282-284
Bagehot, Walter **1** 436-437
Deutsch, Karl Wolfgang **4** 512-514
Friedrich, Carl Joachim **6** 113-114
Laski, Harold J. **9** 215-216
Lowell, Abbott Lawrence **10** 12-13
see also Government; Political theory

Political science, School of (established 1892)
Halévy, Élie **7** 76

Political Science Quarterly (periodical)
Clark, John Bates **4** 76-77
Dunning, William Archibald **5** 148-149
Mayo-Smith, Richmond **10** 371-372
Osgood, Herbert Levi **12** 18-19

Political theory
Asian theories
Han Fei Tzu **7** 124-125
Yen Fu **16** 452
conservatism
Burke, Edmund **3** 138-141
Filmer, Robert **5** 448
Will, George Frederick **16** 286-287
elitism
Lasswell, Harold Dwight **9** 218-219
Pareto, Vilfredo **12** 95-96
Tarde, Jean Gabriel **15** 108-109
histories of
Aristotle **1** 295-296
Dunning, William Archibald **5** 148-149
interest groups
Gumplowicz, Ludwig **7** 41
MacIver, Robert Morrison **10** 100-101
monarchy
Dante Alighieri **4** 389-391
Gierke, Otto von **6** 311-312
Saint-Pierre, Abbé de **13** 434-435
see also Monarchy, absolute; Monarchy, constitutional
order and Christianity
Voegelin, Eric **16** 6-8

other theories
  Arendt, Hannah **1** 282-284
  Croly, Herbert David **4** 316-317
  Haya de la Torre, Victor Raul
    7 216-217
  Hegel, Georg Wilhelm Friedrich
    7 254-256
  Weil, Simone **16** 172-174
rational-irrational
  Cudworth, Ralph **4** 331
  Pareto, Vilfredo **12** 95-96
social justice
  Rawls, John **13** 55-56
  Strauss, Leo **14** 499-500
utopianism
  Campanella, Tommaso **3** 249
  Harrington, James **7** 166-167
  see also Natural rights doctrine (philosophy); Political science; Social scientists—political theorists
  see also Theocracy; Utopianism

Politicians
  see Statesmen

Politics (book; Aristotle)
  Aristotle **1** 295-296
  Filmer, Robert **5** 448
  Jowett, Benjamin **8** 364-365
  Nicholas of Oresme **11** 380
  Thomas Aquinas **15** 183-186

Politics among Nations (textbook)
  Morgenthau, Hans J. **11** 171-172

Politics of the Lord, The (book)
  Quevedo Y Villegas, Francisco Gómez
  de **12** 511

POLIZIANO, ANGELO (Politian; 1454-94),
Italian poet **12** 373-374
  Medici, Lorenzo de' **10** 450-451
  Pulci, Luigi **12** 481

POLK, JAMES KNOX (1795-1849), American statesman, president 1845-49
12 374-376
and expansionism
  Clayton, John Middleton **4** 96-97
  Frémont, John Charles **6** 97-98
  Van Buren, Martin **15** 410-411
Cabinet
  Bancroft, George **1** 483-484
  Buchanan, James **3** 89-90
  Marcy, William Learned **10** 247-248
  Walker, Robert John **16** 67-68
opponents
  Blair, Francis Preston **2** 313-315
  Tilden, Samuel Jones **15** 222-223
political appointments
  Trist, Nicholas Philip **15** 298-299
  Welles, Gideon **16** 188-190
supporters
  Larkin, Thomas Oliver **9** 208
  Wilmot, David **16** 312-313
  see also Mexican War (1846-1848)

POLK, LEONIDAS LAFAYETTE
(1837-1892), American agrarian crusader
and editor **12** 376-377

POLLAIUOLO, ANTONIO (circa 1432-98),
Italian painter, sculptor, goldsmith, and
engraver **12** 377-378
  Donatello **5** 55-56
  Leonardo da Vinci **9** 337-340
  Signorelli, Luca **14** 221-222

Pollaiuolo, Piero (1443-1496), Italian
painter
  Botticelli, Sandro **2** 439-440
  Verrocchio, Andrea del **15** 471-472

POLLARD, ALBERT FREDERICK
(1869-1948), English historian **12** 378

Pollio, Gaius Asinius (75 B.C. - 5 A.D.),
Roman soldier, orator, and politician
  Virgil **15** 507-510

POLLOCK, JACKSON (1912-1956), American painter **12** 379-380
abstract expressionism
  de Kooning, Willem **4** 468-469
  Newman, Barnett **11** 365
  Rothko, Mark **13** 320-321
influence of
  Frankenthaler, Helen **6** 56-57
  Hofmann, Hans **7** 442-443
  Johns, Jasper **8** 291-293
  Noland, Kenneth **11** 418-419

Pollock, Sir Frederick (1845-1937), English
lawyer and judge
  Maitland, Frederic William **10** 154-155

Pollock v. Farmer's Loan and Trust Co.
(legal case)
  Harlan, John Marshall **7** 156-157
  White, Edward Douglass **16** 230-231

Pollution control
  Evelyn, John **5** 343-344
  Ford, Henry II **6** 6-7

Polly (opera)
  Gay, John **6** 243-244

POLO, MARCO (circa 1254-circa 1324),
Venetian traveler and writer **12** 380-382
  Columbus, Christopher **4** 176-179
  Conti, Niccolò de' **4** 212-213
  Hulagu Khan **8** 27-28
  Kublai Khan **9** 115-118

Polonium (element—chemistry)
  Curie, Marie Sklodowska **4** 339-341
  Curie, Pierre **4** 341-344

Poltava (poem)
  Pushkin, Aleksandr Sergeevich
  12 489-491

Poltava, battle of (1709)
  Augustus II **1** 373-374
  Charles XII **3** 464-466
  Peter I **12** 253-256

POLYBIOS (circa 203-120 B.C.), Greek historian **12** 384-385
  Livy **9** 465-467
  Scipio Africanus Minor, Publius Cornelius Aemilianus **14** 62-63
  Seneca the Younger, Lucius Annaeus
  14 103-105
  Strabo **14** 485-486

Polyeucte (play)
  Corneille, Pierre **4** 234-236

Polygamy (sociology)
  Gershom ben Judah **6** 283-284
  Noyes, John Humphrey **11** 437-438
  Smith, Joseph **14** 297-298
  Thayer, Eli **15** 168
  Young, Brigham **16** 469-470

Polyhedron (mathematics)
  Cauchy, Augustin Louis **3** 378-380

POLYKLEITOS (flourished circa 450-420
B.C.), Greek sculptor **12** 385-386
  Phidias **12** 265-267

Polymerization (chemistry)
  Carothers, Wallace Hume **3** 317-318
  Diels, Otto Paul Hermann **5** 5-6

Polymers
  Flory, Paul **5** 492-494

Polymorphia (musical composition)
  Penderecki, Krzysztof **12** 195-197

Polynices (Polyneices; mythology)
  Aeschylus **1** 70-72
  Sophocles **14** 343-345

Polyolbion (poem)
  Drayton, Michael **5** 97-98

Polypeptides (chemistry)
  Fischer, Emil **5** 456-457
  Khorana, Har Gobind **8** 537-538
  Pauling, Linus Carl **12** 150-152
  Sanger, Frederick **13** 466-467

Polyphemus (mythology)
  Góngora y Argote, Luis de **6** 427-428

Polyphemus (ship)
  Franklin, John **6** 64-65

Polyphonic music
English
  Byrd, William **3** 187-188
  Dunstable, John **5** 150-151
  Tallis, Thomas **15** 91
Franco-Flemish
  Clemens non Papa, Jacobus **4** 101
  Gombert, Nicolas **6** 416-417
  Lassus, Roland de **9** 216-218
  Senfl, Ludwig **14** 105-106
French
  Franco of Cologne **6** 52
  Léonin **9** 343-344
  Machaut, Guillaume de **10** 93-94
  Pérotin **12** 231-232
German
  Bach, Johann Sebastian **1** 416-419
  Schütz, Heinrich **14** 48-49
Italian
  Merulo, Claudio **10** 525-526
  Palestrina, Giovanni Pierluigi da
  12 70-72
  Zarlino, Gioseffo **16** 490-491
Spanish
  Milán, Luis **11** 15-16
  Victoria, Tomás Luis de **15** 487-488
U.S.
  Harris, Roy **7** 175-176

see also Counterpoint

Polysynodie (French political institute)
Orléans, Philippe II D' **11** 530-531
Saint-Pierre, Abbé de **13** 434-435

POMBAL, MARQUÊS DE (Sebastião José de Carvalho e Mello; 1699-1782), Portuguese statesman **12** 386-387

Pomerania (region; Eastern Europe)
Bernadotte, Jean Baptiste **2** 205-206
Frederick William **6** 85-86
Frederick William I **6** 86-87

Pomes Penyeach (poem)
Joyce, James **8** 365-367

Pomo d'oro, Il (opera)
Cesti, Pietro **3** 399-400

Pomona (sculpture)
Maillol, Aristide **10** 150-151
Marini, Marino **10** 260-262

Pomosa Temple (near Pusan, Korea)
Sol Ch'ong **14** 325-326

Pomp and Circumstance No. 1 (musical composition)
Elgar, Edward **5** 247-248

Pompadour, Madame Jeanne Antoinette Poisson de (1721-1764), French duchess
Boucher, François **2** 440-442
Falconet, Étienne Maurice **5** 372
Gabriel, Ange Jacques **6** 160-161
Louis XV **9** 533-534

Pompée (play)
Corneille, Pierre **4** 234-236

Pompei Palace (Verona)
Sanmicheli, Michele **13** 469-470

POMPEY (106-48 B.C.), Roman general and statesman **12** 387-389
allies
Clodius Pulcher, Publius **4** 121-122
Sulla, Lucius Cornelius I **15** 21-22
Varro, Marcus Terentius **15** 438-439
campaigns
Cicero, Marcus Tullius **4** 55-58
Sallust **13** 454
Spartacus **14** 363-364
civil war
Antony, Mark **1** 253-254
Brutus, Marcus Junius **3** 79-80
Caesar, Gaius Julius **3** 207-210
First Triumvirate
Caesar, Gaius Julius **3** 207-210
Cato, the Younger **3** 374-375
Crassus Dives, Marcus Licinius **4** 296-297
influenced by
Gracchus, Tiberius and Gaius Sempronius **6** 479-480

Pompey, Sextus (Sextus Pompeius Magnus; 75-35 B.C.), Roman soldier
Antony, Mark **1** 253-254

POMPIDOU, GEORGES (1911-1974), second president of the French Fifth Republic (1969-1974) **12** 389-390
De Gaulle, Charles André Joseph Marie **4** 463-465

POMPONAZZI, PIETRO (1462-1525), Italian Aristotelian philosopher **12** 390-391

Ponce, Manuel M. (1886-1948), Mexican pianist and composer
Chávez, Carlos **3** 486

Ponce de Leon (play)
Brentano, Clemens **2** 515-516

PONCE DE LEÓN, JUAN (1460?-1521), Spanish conqueror and explorer **12** 391-392

Ponchielli, Amilcare (1834-1886), Italian opera composer
Puccini, Giacomo **12** 474-476

Pond of Gylieu (painting)
Daubigny, Charles François **4** 402

Pond with Storks (painting)
Daubigny, Charles François **4** 402

Pondicherry, battle of (1748)
Clive, Robert **4** 119-120

Pondy Woods... (poems)
Warren, Robert Penn **16** 121-122

PONIATOWSKA, ELENA (born 1933), Mexican journalist, novelist, essayist, and short-story writer **12** 392-393

Ponte a Mare (Pisa)
Brunelleschi, Filippo **3** 70-72

Ponte alla Carraia (Florence)
Giotto **6** 342-345

Ponte, Lorenzo da (1749-1838), Italian poet
Mozart, Wolfgang Amadeus **11** 218-221

Pontedera, Andrea da
see Andrea Pisano

PONTIAC (circa 1720-69), Ottawa Indian chief **12** 393-394
see also Pontiac's Conspiracy

Pontiac's Conspiracy (1763-1766)
Amherst, Jeffery **1** 200-201
Brant, Joseph **2** 500-501
Franklin, Benjamin **6** 60-64
Johnson, John **8** 305-306
Johnson, William **8** 319-320
Parkman, Francis **12** 113-115
Pontiac **12** 393-394
Rogers, Robert **13** 250-251

Pontifex, Ernest (literary character)
Butler, Samuel **3** 183

Pontifical Institute for Oriental Studies (Rome)
Benedict XV **2** 153-154

Pontin, M. M. (1781-1858), Swedish physician
Berzelius, Jöns Jacob **2** 231-233

PONTORMO (1494-1556), Italian painter **12** 394-395
Andrea del Sarto **1** 224-225
Bronzino **3** 19
Dürer, Albrecht **5** 159-161

Michelangelo Buonarroti **11** 2-5
Rosso, Il **13** 312-313

Poole, R. L. (1857-1939), English historian
Pollard, Albert Frederick **12** 378

Poona (city; India)
Frere, Henry Bartle Edward **6** 100-101
Gokhale, Gopal Krishna **6** 396

Poor, The (novel)
Mann, Heinrich **10** 201-202

Poor Catullus... (poem)
Catullus, Gaius Valerius **3** 377-378

Poor Christ of Bomba, The (novel)
Beti, Mongo **2** 242-243

Poor Dyonis (story)
Eminescu, Mihail **5** 280-281

Poor Fisherman (painting)
Puvis de Chavannes, Pierre **12** 492-493

Poor Folk (novel)
Dostoevsky, Fyodor **5** 74-77

Poor Fool (novel)
Caldwell, Erskine **3** 223-224

Poor Law (England)
Booth, Charles **2** 400-401
Bosanquet, Bernard **2** 425-426
Chadwick, Edwin **3** 404-405
Cobbett, William **4** 126-127
Malthus, Thomas Robert **10** 180-181
Webb, Beatrice Potter **16** 153-154

Poor Law Amendment Act (1878)
Disraeli, Benjamin **5** 27-29

Poor Liza (novel)
Karamzin, Nikolai Mikhailovich **8** 441-442

Poor Man and the Lady, The (novel)
Hardy, Thomas **7** 150-152

Poor Man's party (Burma)
Ba Maw **1** 480-481

Poor of New York, The (play)
Boucicault, Dion **2** 442-443

Poor People's March (Washington D.C.; 1968)
Abernathy, Ralph David **1** 27-28
King, Martin Luther Jr. **9** 20-22

Poor Richard's Almanack (book; Franklin)
Franklin, Benjamin **6** 60-64
McGuffey, William Holmes **10** 414-415

Poor White (novel)
Anderson, Sherwood **1** 220-221

Pop art movement
Demuth, Charles **4** 497-498
Johns, Jasper **8** 291-293
Kienholz, Edward **8** 546-547
Koons, Jeff **9** 83-84
Lichtenstein, Roy **9** 398-399
Oldenburg, Claes **11** 496-498
Warhol, Andy **16** 114-115

POPE, ALEXANDER (1688-1744), English poet and satirist **12** 395-397
associates

Congreve, William **4** 200-201
Swift, Jonathan **15** 51-54
Voltaire **16** 14-16
Wycherley, William **16** 411-412
biographers
Sitwell, Edith **14** 265-266
critics
Cowper, William **4** 282
influence of
Browning, Elizabeth Barrett **3** 52-53
Crabbe, George **4** 288
Freneau, Philip Morin **6** 99-100
Johnson, Samuel **8** 315-317
influenced by
Boileau-Despréaux, Nicholas **2** 369-371
Juvenal **8** 397-399
Milton, John **11** 43-46
quoted
Berkeley, George **2** 197-198
Horace **7** 500-503
works and style
Addison, Joseph **1** 57-58
Bolingbroke, Viscount **2** 374-375
Chatterton, Thomas **3** 481-482
Handel, George Frederick **7** 116-119

Pope, John (1822-1892), American Union general
Barton, Clara **2** 37-39
Lee, Robert Edward **9** 292-294
McClellan, George Brinton **10** 391-392

POPE, JOHN RUSSELL (1874-1937), American architect in the classical tradition **12** 397-399

Pope, primacy of
Gregory I **6** 531-532
Gregory VII **6** 532-534
Peter **12** 252-253
see also Infallibility, papal

Pope and the Council, The (book)
Barbosa, Ruy **1** 503-504
Döllinger, Josef Ignaz von **5** 47-48

Pope Boniface VIII Enthroned (sculpture)
Arnolfo di Cambio **1** 315-316

Popes
see Religious leaders, Catholic; Religious leaders, Christian (to 1517);
see also Papacy

Popeye (literary character)
Faulkner, William **5** 395-397

POPHAM, WILLIAM JAMES (born 1930), American educator active in educational test development **12** 399-401

Popish Plot (England; 1678)
Buckingham, 2d Duke of **3** 94-95
Burnet, Gilbert **3** 147
Charles II **3** 452-454
Monmouth and Buccleugh, Duke of **11** 108-109
Oates, Titus **11** 456
Pepys, Samuel **12** 207-208
Shaftesbury, 1st Earl of **14** 135-136

Popol Vuh (Maya religious book)
Asturias, Miguel Angel **1** 354-355

Popolo d'Italia (newspaper)
Mussolini, Benito **11** 272-274

POPOVA, LIUBOV SERGEEVNA (1889-1924), Russian and Soviet avant-garde artist **12** 401-402

Poppaea Sabina (died 65/66 A.D.), wife of Nero
Nero Claudius Caesar **11** 342-344

Poppea (opera)
Monteverdi, Claudio Giovanni Antonio **11** 126-128

POPPER, SIR KARL RAIMUND (1902-1994), Austrian philosopher **12** 402
Eccles, John Carew **5** 195-196

Poppy (play)
Fields, W. C. **5** 444

Popular Democratic party (Puerto Rico)
Hernández Colón, Rafael **7** 329-330
Muñoz Marín, José Luís Alberto **11** 249-250

Popular Front (France)
Blum, Léon **2** 343-344
Bourguiba, Habib **2** 453-455
Daladier, Édouard **4** 369
Eboué, Adolphe Felix Sylvestre **5** 194
Pétain, Henri Philippe **12** 250-252

Popular Front for the Liberation of Palestine (1967)
Habash, George **7** 55-56

Popular front movement (United States; 1930s)
Browder, Earl Russell **3** 30-31
Foster, William Zebulon **6** 27-28
Thomas, Norman Mattoon **15** 191-192

Popular Movement for the Liberation of Angola (MPLA)
dos Santos, José Eduardo **5** 71-72

Popular Republican Movement (France)
Schuman, Robert **14** 41

Popular Revolutionary Alliance for America (established 1924)
Haya de la Torre, Victor Raul **7** 216-217

Popular Socialist Community party (Cambodia)
Sihanouk, Norodom **14** 222-223

Popular sovereignty (United States)
Douglas, Stephen Arnold **5** 80-82
Lamar, Lucius Quintus Cincinnatus **9** 170-171
Lincoln, Abraham **9** 415-418
Walker, Robert John **16** 67-68
see also Social-contract theory

Population
control
Berelson, Bernard **2** 185-186
Carr-Saunders, Alexander Morris **3** 333-334
Malthus, Thomas Robert **10** 180-181

Sanger, Margaret Higgins **13** 467-468
see also Birth control
growth
East, Edward Murray **5** 182-183
Huxley, Aldous Leonard **8** 74-75
Ricardo, David **13** 123-124

Populist party (U.S. politics)
Democratic coalition
Bryan, William Jennings **3** 80-82
Watson, Thomas Edward **16** 139
Weaver, James Baird **16** 151-152
reform crusade
Donnelly, Ignatius **5** 62
Lease, Mary Elizabeth Clyens **9** 268
Polk, Leonidas Lafayette **12** 376-377
supporters
Coxey, Jacob Sechler **4** 286-287
Hitchcock, Gilbert Monell **7** 416-417
Lindsey, Benjamin Barr **9** 425-426
Tillman, Benjamin Ryan **15** 225-226

Populorum progressio (encyclical)
Paul VI **12** 146-148

Poquelin, Jean Baptiste
see Molière

Porche du mystère de la deuxième virtu, Le (poem)
Péguy, Charles Pierre **12** 183-184

Porcupine, The (prose drama)
Robinson, Edwin Arlington **13** 201-202

Porfiry (literary character)
Dostoevsky, Fyodor **5** 74-77

Porgy and Bess (opera and film)
Gershwin, George **6** 284-285
Goldwyn, Samuel **6** 416

Porgy, Captain (literary character)
Simms, William Gilmore **14** 235-236

Porism (mathematics)
Euclid **5** 327-329

Pornography (literature)
Comstock, Anthony **4** 188-189
Miller, Henry **11** 26-27
Sade, Comte de **13** 416-418

Porphyry (circa 232-circa 304), Greek scholar and Neoplatonic philosopher
Abelard, Peter **1** 23-25
Augustine **1** 367-370
Boethius, Anicius Manlius Severinus **2** 360-361
Junayd, Abu al-Qasim ibn Muhammad al **8** 388
Longinus **9** 500-501
Plotinus **12** 358-359

Porpora, Niccolò (1686-1766), Italian opera composer
Haydn, Franz Joseph **7** 219-221

Porrée, Gilbert de la (1070-1154), French bishop and theologian
Lombard, Peter **9** 490-491

Porretta, Clementina della (literary character)
Richardson, Samuel **13** 141-142

Port Republic, battle of (1862)
Lee, Robert Edward **9** 292-294

Port Royal (city, Nova Scotia)
see Annapolis Royal

Porta
al Parlascio (Pisa)
Brunelleschi, Filippo **3** 70-72
di Sto Spirito (Rome)
Sangallo family **13** 464-466
Nuova (Verona)
Sanmicheli, Michele **13** 469-470
Palio (Verona)
Sanmicheli, Michele **13** 469-470
Romana (Siena)
Sassetta **13** 492

PORTA, GIACOMO DELLA (circa 1537-1602), Italian architect **12** 402-403
Maderno, Carlo **10** 117-118
Vignola, Giacomo da **15** 493-494

PORTA, GIAMBATTISTA DELLA (1535-1615), Italian scientist and dramatist **12** 403-404

Portal of Death (sculpture)
Manzù, Giacomo **10** 224-225

PORTALES PLAZAZUELOS, DIEGO JOSÉ VÍCTOR (1793-1837), Chilean statesman **12** 404
Montt Torres, Manuel **11** 139-140

Porte Enseigne Polka (musical composition)
Mussorgsky, Modest Petrovich **11** 274-276

Porte étroite, La (book)
Gide, André **6** 308-309

Porte Saint-Antoine (Paris)
Perrault, Claude **12** 232-233

Porteños (Argentine politics)
Lamas, Carlos Saavedra **9** 175-176
Mitre, Bartolomé **11** 62-63
Rosas, Juan Manuel de **13** 290-291
Urquiza, Justo José **15** 396-397

PORTER, COLE ALBERT (1891-1964), American composer **12** 405-406

Porter, Countee Cullen
see Cullen, Countee

Porter, David (1780-1843), American naval officer
Farragut, David Glasgow **5** 388-389
Lawrence, James **9** 251-252

Porter, David Dixon (1813-1891), American naval officer
Gatling, Richard Jordan **6** 234-235

Porter, E. S. (1870-1941), American film director
Griffith, David Wark **6** 544-545

PORTER, KATHERINE ANNE (1890-1980), American writer **12** 406-407
Callaghan, Edward Morley **3** 229-230

Porter, William Sydney
see Henry, O.

Porteus, Beilby (1731-1808), English bishop
Peale, Rembrandt **12** 172-173

Portia (literary character)
Shakespeare, William **14** 142-145

Portinari, Bice (died 1290),
see Beatrice (literary character; Dante)

PORTINARI, CÂNDIDO (1903-1962), Brazilian painter **12** 407-408

Portinari Altarpiece (painting; Van der Goes)
Ghirlandaio, Domenico **6** 292-293
van der Goes, Hugo **15** 416-417, 441

Portland, 3d Duke of
see Bentinck, William Cavendish

Portland Place (London)
Adam, Robert and James **1** 38-40

Portnoy's Complaint (book)
Roth, Philip **13** 318-320

Porto Sepolto, Il (poems)
Ungaretti, Giuseppe **15** 389-390

PORTOLÁ, GASPAR DE (circa 1723-1784), Spanish explorer and colonial governor **12** 408

Portrait... (collage)
Dove, Arthur Garfield **5** 86-87

Portrait... (literature)
Gogol, Nikolai **6** 391-393
James, Henry **8** 211-212
Joyce, James **8** 365-367
Pound, Ezra Loomis **12** 415-417
Rossetti, Dante Gabriel **13** 308-309
Sainte-Beuve, Charles Augustin **13** 438
Stein, Gertrude **14** 414-415
Tanizaki, Junichiro **15** 101-102
Thomas, Dylan Marlais **15** 188-190
Varro, Marcus Terentius **15** 438-439

Portrait... (painting)
Andrea del Sarto **1** 224-225
Antonello da Messina **1** 251-252
Bouts, Dirk **2** 458-459
Cézanne, Paul **3** 400-402
Christus, Petrus **4** 33-34
Courbet, Jean Desiré Gustave **4** 271-273
Dürer, Albrecht **5** 159-161
Giorgione **6** 340-341
Goya y Lucientes, Francisco de Paula José de **6** 476-478
Gris, Juan **7** 5-6
Hartley, Marsden **7** 186
Le Nain, Antoine, Louis and Mathieu **9** 321-322
Lucas van Leyden **10** 20-21
Picasso, Pablo **12** 292-295
Pisanello **12** 323-324
Prud'hon, Pierre Paul **12** 469
Rivera, Diego **13** 183-184
Tura, Cosimo **15** 343-344
Weyden, Rogier van der **16** 219-221

Portrait... (photograph)
Arbus, Diane Nemerov **1** 276-277

Portrait... (sculpture)
Giacometti, Alberto **6** 294-295
Manzù, Giacomo **10** 224-225
Pevsner, Antoine **12** 263-264

Portraits (photography)
Avedon, Richard **1** 381-382

Portrayer of His Own Dishonor (play)
Calderón, Pedro **3** 221-222

Portsmouth, Treaty of (1905)
Rhee, Syngman **13** 117-120
Witte, Sergei Yulyevich **16** 349-350

Portsmouth Point (musical composition)
Walton, William Turner **16** 92-93

Portugal (Portuguese Republic; nation, Europe)
• EMERGENT STATE
and papacy
Alfonso III **1** 148-149
Innocent III **8** 125-127
independence
Philip IV **12** 275
kingdom established
Alfonso I **1** 148
Spanish rule
Alba, Duke of **1** 103-104
Manrique, Jorge **10** 210-211
Philip II **12** 271-273
see also Lusitania
• EMPIRE and DECLINE
and Uruguay
Artigas, José Gervasio **1** 323
Azara, Félix de **1** 397-398
colonization (Africa)
Affonso I **1** 72
Cadamosto, Alvise da **3** 206-207
Covilhão, Pedro de **4** 278-279
Dias de Novais, Bartolomeu **4** 533-534
Henry the Navigator **7** 305-306
Manuel I **10** 219-220
Nzinga Nkuwu **11** 451-452
colonization (Brazil)
Pedro I **12** 179-180
Sá, Mem de **13** 395
Sousa, Martim Afonso de **14** 354-355
Tiradentes **15** 237
Vespucci, Amerigo **15** 476-478
Vieira, Antônio **15** 492
see also Brazil
colonization (India)
Albuquerque, Afonso de **1** 118-119
Gama, Vasco da **6** 196-198
Manuel I **10** 219-220
Sousa, Martim Afonso de **14** 354-355
see also India
exploration (North America)
Corte Reál, Gaspar and Miguel **4** 254-255

see also Northwest Passage
foreign policy
   Clayton, John Middleton **4** 96-97
   Johnston, Henry Hamilton
   8 322-323
   Pombal, Marquês de **12** 386-387
Peninsular War
   see Peninsular War
trade expeditions
   Abbas I **1** 4-6
   Nobunaga, Oda **11** 413-414
• MODERN STATE
dictatorship
   Salazar, António de Oliveira
   13 442-443
Mozambican policies
   Mondlane, Eduardo Chivambo
   11 100-101
   see also Portuguese architecture;
   Portuguese literature
return to democracy (1974)
   Soares, Mário **14** 315-316

Portuguese architecture
   Aleijadinho, O **1** 125-126
   Borromini, Francesco **2** 424-425

Portuguese Colonies, Conference of Nationalist Organizations of the (established 1961)
   dos Santos, Marcelino **5** 72-74

Portuguese literature
   Camoëns, Luis Vaz de **3** 247-249
   Vicente, Gil **15** 479-480

Porus (died 321? B.C.), Indian king
   Alexander the Great **1** 137-141

Positive electron
   see Positron (physics)

Positivism (philosophy)
American
   Bentley, Arthur F. **2** 178
   Eliot, George **5** 254-256
Austrian
   Mach, Ernst **10** 90-91
   Wittgenstein, Ludwig **16** 350-351
English
   Buckle, Henry Thomas **3** 95-96
   Martineau, Harriet **10** 296-297
   Mill, John Stuart **11** 21-23
French
   Bergson, Henri **2** 191-192
   Claudel, Paul Louis Charles **4** 90-91
   Comte, Auguste **4** 189-191
   Condillac, Étienne Bonnot de
   4 194-195
German
   Carnap, Rudolf **3** 308-309
   Schlick, Friedrich Albert Moritz
   14 16-17
Italian
   Croce, Benedetto **4** 313-314
Mexican
   Díaz, José de la Cruz Porfirio
   4 534-536
Spanish
   Santayana, George **13** 475-477

Unamuno y Jugo, Miguel de
   15 386-387
see also Logical positivism

Positron (physics)
   Anderson, Carl David **1** 214-215
   Dirac, Paul Adrien Maurice **5** 23-24
   Oppenheimer, J. Robert **11** 525-526

Possessed, The (novel)
   Dostoevsky, Fyodor **5** 74-77

Possession (novel)
   de la Roche, Mazo Louise **4** 474-475

POST, CHARLES WILLIAM (1854-1914), American pioneer in the manufacture and mass-marketing of breakfast cereals **12** 408-409

POST, EMILY PRICE (1873-1960), American authority on etiquette **12** 409-410

Postal service
   Franklin, Benjamin **6** 60-64
   Muawiya ibn Abu Sufyan **11** 223-224
   Pinkerton, Allan **12** 314-315
   Taft, William Howard **15** 78-81
   Trollope, Anthony **15** 300-302

Postal Telegraph Co.
   Mackay, John William **10** 101-102

Posthumous Papers of the Pickwick Club (novel)
   Dickens, Charles John Huffam
   4 538-541

Postimpressionism (art)
   Amiet, Cuno **1** 201-202
   Balla, Giacomo **1** 473-474
   Gauguin, Paul **6** 236-238
   Léger, Fernand **9** 302-303
   Malevich, Kasimir **10** 168-169
   Milne, David Brown **11** 37-38
   Prendergast, Maurice Brazil **12** 440
   Seurat, Georges Pierre **14** 120-122
   Toulouse-Lautrec, Henri de **15** 273-274
   Van Gogh, Vincent **15** 427-429

Postmasters general
   see Statesmen, American

Postscripts (stories)
   Henry, O. **7** 308-309

Pot of Earth, The (poems)
   MacLeish, Archibald **10** 109-110

Pot of Gold, The (play)
   Plautus **12** 348-350

Potassium (element—chemistry)
   Davy, Humphry **4** 426-427
   Hodgkin, Alan Lloyd **7** 431-432
   Lawrence, Ernest Orlando **9** 248-250

Potato (vegetable)
   Northrop, John Howard **11** 430-431
   Raleigh, Walter **13** 9-11

Potato Eaters (painting)
   Van Gogh, Vincent **15** 427-429

Potato War (1778-1779)
   Joseph II **8** 359-360

Potawatomi Indians (North America)
   De Smet, Pierre Jean **4** 509-510
   McCoy, Isaac **10** 403
   Pontiac **12** 393-394
   Tecumseh **15** 133

Potemkin (film)
   Eisenstein, Sergei Mikhailovich
   5 240-242

POTEMKIN, GRIGORI ALEKSANDROVICH (1739-1791), Russian administrator and field marshal **12** 411-412

Potgieter, Andries Hendrik (1800?-1853), Boer leader in South Africa
   Kruger, Stephanus Johannes Paulus
   9 108-109
   Pretorius, Andries **12** 444-445

Potiphar's wife (biblical character)
   Firdausi **5** 451-452

Potomac Indians (North America)
   Pocahontas **12** 361-362

Potsdam Conference (1945)
   Attlee, Clement Richard **1** 361-362
   Hopkins, Harry Lloyd **7** 494-495
   Marshall, George Catlett **10** 278-279
   Molotov, Vyacheslav Mikhailovich
   11 89-90
   Truman, Harry S. **15** 314-316

POTTER, DAVID M. (1910-1971), American historian **12** 412

POTTER, DENNIS (1935-1994), British essayist, playwright, screenwriter, and novelist **12** 412-414

Potters
   see Artists—potters

Potting Shed, The (play)
   Greene, Graham **6** 523-524

Pottinger, Sir Henry (1789-1856), British soldier and diplomat
   Pretorius, Andries **12** 444-445

POULENC, FRANCIS (1899-1963), French composer **12** 414-415
   Honegger, Arthur **7** 472-473
   Milhaud, Darius **11** 17-18
   Stravinsky, Igor Fedorovich **14** 502-506

Poulteney Normal Institute (Troy, New York State)
   Knapp, Seaman Asahel **9** 58

POUND, EZRA LOOMIS (1885-1972), American poet, editor, and critic **12** 415-417
associates
   Eliot, Thomas Stearns **5** 258-261
   Stein, Gertrude **14** 414-415
   Yeats, William Butler **16** 445-447
influence of
   Crane, Hart **4** 291-293
   Doolittle, Hilda **5** 65-66
   Frost, Robert Lee **6** 130-133
   Hemingway, Ernest Miller
   7 274-277
   Joyce, James **8** 365-367
   Olson, Charles **11** 505-506

Rabindranath Tagore **12** 529-531
Tate, Allen **15** 116
Williams, William Carlos
16 308-309
influenced by
Browning, Robert **3** 53-55
Gourmont, Remy de **6** 475
Laforgue, Jules **9** 160-161
Whitman, Walt **16** 249-251
literary feuds
Lowell, Amy **10** 13

POUND, ROSCOE (1870-1964), American jurist and botanist **12** 417-418

Pour Lucrèce (play)
Giraudoux, Jean **6** 349-350

Poussin, Gaspard
see Dughet, Gaspard

POUSSIN, NICOLAS (1594-1665), French painter **12** 418-420
influence of
David, Jacques Louis **4** 407-409
Girardon, François **6** 348-349
Ingres, Jean Auguste Dominique
8 121-123
La Tour, George de **9** 222
Le Brun, Charles **9** 269-270
Picasso, Pablo **12** 292-295
West, Benjamin **16** 210-212
Wilson, Richard **16** 329-330
influenced by
Carracci **3** 319-321
Raphael **13** 40-42

Poverty (religious vow)
Arnold of Brescia **1** 314-315
Cajetan **3** 215-216
Francis of Assisi **6** 46-47

Poverty cycle (sociology)
Dugdale, Richard Louis **5** 128-129

Poverty of Philosophy, The (book; Marx)
Marx, Karl **10** 304-308
Proudhon, Pierre Joseph **12** 461-463]

Powder River Trail
see Bozeman Trail

POWDERLY, TERENCE VINCENT (1849-1924), American labor leader **12** 420-421
Stephens, Uriah **14** 431-432

POWELL, ADAM CLAYTON, JR. (1908-1972), African American political leader and Baptist minister **12** 421-422

POWELL, ANTHONY (born 1905), English novelist **12** 422-423

Powell, C. F. (born 1903), English physicist
Yukawa, Hideki **16** 481-482

POWELL, COLIN LUTHER (born 1937), African American chairman of the Joint Chiefs of Staff **12** 424-425

POWELL, JOHN WESLEY (1834-1902), American geologist, anthropologist, and explorer **12** 425-426

POWELL, LEWIS F., JR. (born 1907), U.S. Supreme Court justice (1972-1987) **12** 426-428

Powell Islands
see South Orkney Islands

Power and Glory (play)
Čapek, Karel **3** 271-272

Power and the Glory, The (novel)
Greene, Graham **6** 523-524

Power Jets Ltd.
Whittle, Frank **16** 257-258

Power, Lionel (died 1445), English composer
Dunstable, John **5** 150-151

Power of Darkness, The (play)
Tolstoy, Leo **15** 262-265

Power of Love, The (opera)
Weber, Carl Maria Friedrich Ernst von **16** 156-157

Power of Positive Thinking, The (book)
Peale, Norman Vincent **12** 171-172

POWERS, HIRAM (1805-1873), American sculptor **12** 428-429

POWHATAN (circa 1550-1618), Native American tribal chief **12** 429-430
Pocahontas **12** 361-362
Rolfe, John **13** 259-260
Smith, John **14** 295-297

Poynings, Edward (1459-1521), English soldier and diplomat
Henry VII **7** 300-302

Pozzo di San Patrizio (Orvietto, Italy)
Sangallo family **13** 464-466

Prabhakaravardhana (Prabhakara; died 604), North Indian ruler
Harsha **7** 181-182

Prado, Mariano Ignacio (1826-1901), Peruvian general and politician
Castilla, Ramón **3** 361
Prado Ugarteche, Manuel **12** 430-431

PRADO UGARTECHE, MANUEL (1889-1967), Peruvian statesman **12** 430-431

Pradon, Nicolas (1632-1698), French dramatist
Racine, Jean Baptiste **12** 532-535

Praemunari, Statute of (1353)
Edward III **5** 211-212

PRAETORIUS, MICHAEL (circa 1571-1621), German composer and theorist **12** 431-432
Gabrieli, Giovanni **6** 161-162

Praga, battle of (1794)
Suvorov, Aleksandr Vasilievich **15** 44-45

Pragmatic Sanction (1713)
Frederick II **6** 81-84
Maria Theresa **10** 256-258

Pragmatic Sanction of Bourges (1438)
Charles VII **3** 461-462

Pragmatism (philosophy)
Bergson, Henri **2** 191-192
Bode, Boyd Henry **2** 355-356
Dewey, John **4** 520-523
Hook, Sidney **7** 474-475
Hu Shih **8** 63-65
James, William **8** 215-217
Lewis, Clarence Irving **9** 381
Mead, George Herbert **10** 437-438
Peirce, Charles Sanders **12** 187-188
Peirce, Charles Sanders **12** 187-188
Poincaré, Jules Henri **12** 365-366
Rorty, Richard **13** 288-289
Santayana, George **13** 475-477
West, Cornel **16** 212-213

Prague (city; Czech Republic)
Charles IV **3** 455-456
Konev, Ivan Stefanovich **9** 81-82

Prague, Peace of (1635)
Oxenstierna, Axel Gustafsson **12** 44-45

Prague, Treaty of (1866)
Bismarck, Otto Eduard Leopold von **2** 294-296

Prague, University of
Beneš, Edward **2** 155-157
Charles IV **3** 455-456
Hus, Jan **8** 56-59
Mach, Ernst **10** 90-91

Prague Conservatory
Dvořák, Antonin **5** 168-169

Prairie, The (novel; Cooper)
Cooper, James Fenimore **4** 220-223
Sarmiento, Domingo Faustino **13** 484-485

Prairies, The (poem)
Bryant, William Cullen **3** 83-85

Praise for the Upright (play)
Luzzato, Moses Hayyim **10** 57-58

Praise to the End (poems)
Roethke, Theodore **13** 243-244

Praises (poems)
Perse, Saint-John **12** 242-243

PRANDTAUER, JAKOB (1660-1726), Austrian baroque architect **12** 432

Prandtl, Ludwig (1875-1953), German physicist
Kármán, Theodore von **8** 451-452

PRASAD, RAJENDRA (1884-1963), Indian nationalist, first president of the Republic **12** 433

Prato, Cathedral of
Pisano, Giovanni **12** 324-325
Lippi, Filippo **9** 439

Pratt, Sir Charles, 1st Earl Camden (1714-1794), English jurist and political leader
Franklin, Benjamin **6** 60-64

Pravda (newspaper)
Bukharin, Nikolai Ivanovich **3** 112-113
Dewey, John **4** 520-523
Ehrenburg, Ilya Grigorievich **5** 224-225

Molotov, Vyacheslav Mikhailovich **11** 89-90
Stalin, Joseph **14** 393-396
Trotsky, Leon **15** 302-305

PRAXITELES (flourished circa 370-330 B.C.), Greek sculptor **12** 433-434
Polykleitos **12** 385-386

Prayer (sculpture)
Brancusi, Constantin **2** 494-496

Prayer Book of Emperor Maximillan I
Altdorfer, Albrecht **1** 179-180
Cranach, Lucas the Elder **4** 289-290

Prayer in the Canton Bern (painting)
Hodler, Ferdinand **7** 434-435

Prayer of Columbus (poem)
Whitman, Walt **16** 249-251

Prayer Pilgrimage to Washington (1957)
Randolph, A. Philip **13** 28-29

Praying Indians (North America)
Eliot, John **5** 256-258

Praying Priest (painting)
Apollodorus **1** 261

Preachers
see Religious leaders

Preaching of St. Bernardino (altarpiece)
Goya y Lucientes, Francisco de Paula José de **6** 476-478

Preaching of the Antichrist (painting)
Signorelli, Luca **14** 221-222

PREBISCH, RAÚL (1901-1986), Argentine economist active in the United Nations **12** 434-436

Preble, Edward (1761-1807), American naval officer
Decatur, Stephen **4** 448-449

Precaution (novel)
Cooper, James Fenimore **4** 220-223

Precession of equinoxes (astronomy)
Alembert, Jean le Rond d' **1** 127-128
Hipparchus **7** 407-408

Precipice, The (novel)
MacLennan, Hugh **10** 110-111

Precipice, The (novel; Goncharov)
Turgenev, Ivan Sergeyevich **15** 345-348

Precisionism (art)
Demuth, Charles **4** 497-498
O'Keeffe, Georgia **11** 487-489
Sheeler, Charles **14** 170-171
Wyeth, Andrew Newell **16** 413-415

Predestination (religion)
Arminius, Jacobus **1** 301-302
Ashari, Abu al- Hasan Ali al- **1** 327-328
Boehme, Jacob **2** 357
Calvin, John **3** 239-242-335
Cartwright, Peter **3** 344-345
Erigena, John Scotus **5** 308-309
Jansen, Cornelis **8** 220-221
Laud, William **9** 224-225
Vondel, Joost van den **16** 19-20
Wyclif, John **16** 412-413

Prediction of Merlin, The (poem)
Swift, Jonathan **15** 51-54

Predilections (literary colony)
Moore, Marianne **11** 148-149

Predpriate (ship)
Kotzebue, Otto von **9** 91-92

Preface to a Twenty Volume Suicide Note (poems)
Baraka, Imamu Amiri **1** 498-499

Prefaces, Biographical and Critical, to the Works of the English Poets
see Lives of the Poets (literary collection)

Preformation, doctrine of (biology)
Malpighi, Marcello **10** 176-178
Spallanzani, Lazzaro **14** 360-361

PREGL, FRITZ (1869-1930), Austrian physiologist and medical chemist **12** 436-437

Prejudices (book)
Mencken, Henry Louis **10** 481-483

Prelog, V. (born 1906), Swiss chemist
Khorana, Har Gobind **8** 537-538

Prelude to Waking (novel)
Franklin, Stella Maraia Sarah Miles **6** 68-69

Préludes, Les (musical composition)
Liszt, Franz **9** 445-447

PREM TINSULANONDA (born 1920), military leader and prime minister of Thailand (1979-1988) **12** 437

PREMADASA, RANASINGHE (born 1924), president of Sri Lanka (1988-) **12** 437-439

PREMCHAND (1880-1936), Indian novelist and short-story writer **12** 439

Premiers
see Statesmen

PRENDERGAST, MAURICE BRAZIL (1859-1924), American painter **12** 440
Davies, Arthur Bowen **4** 409-410
Morrice, James Wilson **11** 181-182

Preparatory Meditations... (poems)
Taylor, Edward **15** 122-123

Prepared piano (musical instrument)
Cage, John **3** 211-214

Pre-Raphaelites (art group; England)
founders
Hunt, William Holman **8** 44-45
Millais, John Everett **11** 23-24
Rossetti, Dante Gabriel **13** 308-309
influence of
La Farge, John **9** 149-150
Morris, William **11** 187-188
Whistler, James Abbott McNeill **16** 225-226
influenced by
Botticelli, Sandro **2** 439-440
supporters
Browning, Robert **3** 53-55
Burne-Jones, Edward Coley **3** 145-146

Collins, William Wilkie **4** 169-170
Rossetti, Christina Georgina **13** 307-308
Ruskin, John **13** 371-372

Presbiterianas (poems)
González Prada, Manuel **6** 431

Presbyterian Establishment (Scotland)
see Scotland, Church of

Presbyterianism (religion)
leaders
Fleming, Sandford **5** 485-486
Graham, Sylvester **6** 486-487
McCosh, James **10** 402-403
Witherspoon, John **16** 346-348
missions
Duff, Alexander **5** 126-127
Makemie, Francis **10** 158-159
opponents
Brownson, Orestes Augustus **3** 57-58
James I **8** 204-206
Laud, William **9** 224-225
rite debates
Campbell, Alexander **3** 249-250
Godwin, William **6** 383-384
theologians
Buechner, Frederick **3** 103-105

Prescott, Orville (born 1906), American literary critic
Richter, Conrad Michael **13** 148-149
Waugh, Evelyn Arthur St. John **16** 145-147

PRESCOTT, WILLIAM HICKLING (1796-1859), American historian **12** 440-441
Bancroft, George **1** 483-484
Bird, Robert Montgomery **2** 281-282

Presentation in the Temple (painting)
Lorenzetti, Pietro and Ambrogio **9** 517-518

Presentation of Christ in the Temple (painting)
Veronese, Paolo **15** 469-470

Presentation of the Virgin (painting)
Tintoretto **15** 232-234
Titian **15** 242-244

President (ship)
Decatur, Stephen **4** 448-449
Stockton, Robert Field **14** 461-462

President, The (painting)
Davis, Stuart **4** 424-425

Presidential Fishing Party of 1848 (cartoon)
Currier and Ives **4** 345-346

Presidents
see Statesmen

Presidium
see Statesmen, Russian

PRESLEY, ELVIS ARON (1935-1977), American singer and actor **12** 441-442
Lennon, John Winston **9** 326-328
Odets, Clifford **11** 470-471

Presque-songes (poems)
Rabearivelo, Jean Joseph **12** 523-524

Press, freedom of
see Freedom of the press

Pressburg, Treaty of (1805)
Napoleon I **11** 306-310

Prester John (flourished late 12th century),
legendary Christian king and priest of
Asia or Africa
Covilhão, Pedro de **4** 278-279
Gama, Vasco da **6** 196-198
Henry the Navigator **7** 305-306
Mandeville, John **10** 192-193

PRESTES, LUIZ CARLOS (1898-1990),
Brazilian revolutionary and Communist
leader **12** 442-444
Amado, Jorge **1** 189-190
Vargas, Getulio Dornelles **15** 433-434

Prestonpans, battle of (1745)
Stuart, Charles Edward Louis Philip
Casimir Stuart **3** 466-467

Pretenders, The (play, Ibsen)
Bjørnson, Bjørnstjerne **2** 299-300
Ibsen, Henrik **8** 98-100

Pretoria, battle of (1900)
Botha, Louis **2** 434-436
Kruger, Stephanus Johannes Paulus
9 108-109
Roberts, Frederick Sleigh **13** 195-196

PRETORIUS, ANDRIES (1798-1853), South
African politician and general
12 444-445

Pretorius, Martinus Wessel (1818?-1901),
Boer statesman
Kruger, Stephanus Johannes Paulus
9 108-109

Pretty Buzzard of Youth, The (poem)
Froissart, Jean **6** 124-125

Pretty Story, A (satire)
Hopkinson, Francis **7** 496-497

Prevention of Crimes Bill (1882)
Gladstone, William Ewart **6** 357-360

Prévert, Jacques (1900-1977), French poet
and film writer
Tanguy, Yves **15** 101

PRÉVOST, ABBÉ (1697-1763), French novelist, journalist, and cleric **12** 445-446

Prevost, Theodosia (died 1794; wife of A.
Burr
Burr, Aaron **3** 156-159

Prévost d'Exiles, Antoine François
see Prévost, Abbé

Preysing Palace (Munich)
Cuvilliés, François **4** 359-360

PRI
see Institutional Revolutionary Party

Priam (literary character)
Homer **7** 465-467

Priapus (literary character)
Petronius Arbiter **12** 262-263

Price (economics)
Ala-ud-din **1** 102-103
Arnold, Thurman Wesley **1** 314
Cardozo, Benjamin Nathan **3** 288-290
Cournot, Antoine Augustin **4** 273
Marshall, Alfred **10** 277-278
Ricardo, David **13** 123-124

Price, Bruce (1845-1903), American architect
Wright, Frank Lloyd **16** 398-401

Price, Fanny (literary character)
Austen, Jane **1** 377-379

PRICE, LEONTYNE (Mary Leontyne Price;
born 1927), American prima donna
soprano **12** 446-447

PRICE, RICHARD (1723-1791), English
Nonconformist minister and political
philosopher **12** 447-448
Cudworth, Ralph **4** 331

Price, The (play)
Miller, Arthur **11** 25-26

Price She Paid, The (novel)
Phillips, David Graham **12** 280-281

Price Tower (Bartlesville, Oklahoma)
Wright, Frank Lloyd **16** 398-401

PRICHARD, DIANA GARCÍA (born 1949),
Hispanic American chemical physicist
12 448-449

Prichard, James Cowles (1786-1848), English ethnologist
Bagehot, Walter **1** 436-437

Pride and Prejudice (novel)
Austen, Jane **1** 377-379

PRIDI PHANOMYONG (1901-1983), Thai
political leader **12** 449
Phibun Songkhram, Luang **12** 264-265
Sarit Thanarat **13** 483-484

PRIEST, IVY MAUDE BAKER (1905-1975),
treasurer of the United States
(1953-1960) **12** 450-451

Priest to the Temple, A (book)
Herbert, George **7** 324-326

PRIESTLEY, J(OHN) B(OYNTON)
(1894-1984), English author of novels,
essays, plays, and screenplays
12 451-452

PRIESTLEY, JOSEPH (1733-1804), English
clergyman and chemist **12** 452-453
Cavendish, Henry **3** 383-384
Cobbett, William **4** 126-127
Cooper, Thomas **4** 224
Hartley, David **7** 185
Ingenhousz, Jan **8** 119-120
Lavoisier, Antoine Laurent **9** 241-244
Price, Richard **12** 447-448
Scheele, Karl Wilhelm **13** 525-526

Priests
see Religious leaders

Prieto, Joaquin (1786-1854), Chilean soldier, president 1831-41
Portales Plazazuelos, Diego José Víctor
12 404

Prigg v. Pa. (legal case)
McLean, John **10** 422-423

Prigionier superbo, II (opera)
Pergolesi, Giovanni Battista **12** 218-219

Prigioniero, II (opera)
Dallapiccola, Luigi **4** 377-378

Prignano, Bartolomeo
see Urban VI

Prim, D. Juan (1814-1870), Spanish soldier
and statesman
Céspedes, Carlos Manuel de **3** 398-399

Prima prattica (music)
Monteverdi, Claudio Giovanni Antonio
11 126-128

Primae lineae physiologiae (book)
Haller, Albrecht Von **7** 87-88

Primary school
see Education

PRIMATICCIO, FRANCESCO (1504-1570),
Italian painter, sculptor, and architect
12 453-454
l'Orme, Philibert de **9** 519
Francis I **6** 40-43
Goujon, Jean **6** 466-467
Pilon, Germain **12** 305
Poussin, Nicolas **12** 418-420
Rosso, Il **13** 312-313
Vignola, Giacomo da **15** 493-494

Prime Minister, The (novel)
Trollope, Anthony **15** 300-302

Prime ministers
see Statesmen

Prime number (mathematics)
Eratosthenes of Cyrene **5** 301-302
Riemann, Georg Friedrich Bernard
13 164-165
Wiener, Norbert **16** 262-263

Prime of Miss Jean Brodie (book)
Spark, Muriel Sarah **14** 361-362

Primeras notas (poems)
Darío, Rubén **4** 393-394

Primitive Mysteries (ballet)
Graham, Martha **6** 485-486

Primitive society (anthropology)
Childe, Vere Gordon **3** 521-522
Frazer, James George **6** 76
Jung, Carl Gustav **8** 388-389
Lévi-Strauss, Claude Gustave **9** 371-372
Lévy-Bruhl, Lucien **9** 374-375
Linton, Ralph **9** 431
Lowie, Robert Harry **10** 18
Radin, Paul **12** 538-539
Redfield, Robert **13** 73-74
Tylor, Edward Burnett **15** 372-373

Primitivism (art)
France
Gauguin, Paul **6** 236-238
Rousseau, Henri **13** 323-324
Zadkine, Ossip Joselyn **16** 484
U.S.
Hicks, Edward **7** 375

Kane, John **8** 422
Moses, Grandma **11** 201-202
Pippin, Horace **12** 318-319

Primo de Rivera, José António (died 1939), Spanish politician
Primo de Rivera y Orbaneja, Miguel **12** 454-455

PRIMO DE RIVERA Y ORBANEJA, MIGUEL (1870-1930), Spanish general, dictator 1923-30 **12** 454-455
Alfonso XIII **1** 151
Franco Bahamonde, Francisco **6** 52-54

Primogeniture (sociology)
Le Play, Guillaume Frédéric **9** 350-351
Malcolm III **10** 164-165
Paul I **12** 143-144

Primrose (musical)
Gershwin, George **6** 284-285

Primrose, Archibald Philip (5th Earl of Rosebery; 1847-1929), British statesman
Lloyd George, David **9** 469-471
Victoria **15** 485-487

Primrose, Dr. (literary character)
Goldsmith, Oliver **6** 411-413

Primrose, William (1904-1982), Scottish viola player
Bartók, Béla **2** 35-36

Prince, The (book)
Machiavelli, Niccolò **10** 97-99

Prince and the Mermaid, The (musical composition)
Still, William Grant **14** 455-456

Prince and the Pauper, The (novel)
Twain, Mark **15** 363-366

Prince Edward Island (province; Canada)
Cartier, Jacques **3** 343-344
Macdonald, John Alexander **10** 85-87
Selkirk, 5th Earl of **14** 96
see also Canada

Prince Igor (opera; Borodin)
Borodin, Aleksandr Profirevich **2** 422-423
Rimsky-Korsakov, Nikolai Andreevich **13** 174-175

Prince of Homburg, The (opera)
Henze, Hans Werner **7** 314

Prince of India, The (novel)
Wallace, Lewis **16** 74-75

Prince of Parthia, The (play; Godfrey)
Hallam, Lewis Sr. and Jr. **7** 87

Prince's Progress... (poems)
Rossetti, Christina Georgina **13** 307-308

Princess (poem)
Tennyson, Alfred **15** 144-146

Princess and the Pea, The (fairy tale)
Andersen, Hans Christian **1** 212-214

Princess Casamassima, The (novel)
James, Henry **8** 211-212

Princess du Pays de la Porcelaine, La (painting)
Whistler, James Abbott McNeill **16** 225-226

Princess Elizabeth Land (Antarctica)
Mawson, Douglas **10** 354-355

Princess Ligovskaya (book)
Lermontov, Mikhail Yurievich **9** 352-353

Princesse de Clèves, La (novel)
La Fayette, Comtesse de **9** 150-151

Princesse de Navarre, La (ballet)
Rameau, Jean Philippe **13** 17-18

Princesse Isabelle, La (play)
Maeterlinck, Maurice **10** 125-126

Princesse Maleine, La (play)
Maeterlinck, Maurice **10** 125-126

Princeton (ship)
Ericsson, John **5** 307-308

Princeton, battle of (1777)
Cornwallis, Charles **4** 241-243
Greene, Nathanael **6** 525-526
Howe, William **7** 538-539
Knox, Henry **9** 64

Princeton University (New Jersey)
founded
Tennent, Gilbert **15** 143-144
literature
Bellow, Saul **2** 141-143
Mann, Thomas **10** 204-207
Tate, Allen **15** 116
music
Babbitt, Milton **1** 410
Martinu, Bohuslav **10** 299-300
Sessions, Roger Huntington **14** 117-118
philosophy
Maritain, Jacques **10** 263
presidents
Edwards, Jonathan **5** 220-222
McCosh, James **10** 402-403
Wilson, Thomas Woodrow **16** 330-332
Witherspoon, John **16** 346-348
Radio Research, Office of
Lazarsfeld, Paul F. **9** 259-260
science
Dyson, Freeman John **5** 171-173
Goddard, Robert Hutchings **6** 376-377
Kendall, Edward Calvin **8** 495
McMaster, John Bach **10** 426-427
Wigner, Eugene Paul **16** 268-269

Princip, Gavrilo (1893?-1918), Serbian nationalist and assassin
Francis Ferdinand **6** 44

Principall Navigations... (book)
Hakluyt, Richard **7** 70

Principe constante, El (play)
Calderón, Pedro **3** 221-222

Principia mathematica (book; Newton)
Clarke, Samuel **4** 88

Demoivre, Abraham **4** 494-495
Gödel, Kurt **6** 377-379
Halley, Edmund **7** 88-89
Hamilton, William Rowan **7** 99-100
Lagrange, Joseph Louis **9** 164-166
Newton, Isaac **11** 369-372

Principia Mathematica (Russell-Whitehead)
see Principles of Mathematics

Principle (Chinese philosophy)
Chu Hsi **4** 40-43
Yi Hwang **16** 457

Principles of Christian Theology (book)
Macquarrie, John **10** 116-117

Principles of Geology (book; Lyell)
Darwin, Charles Robert **4** 397-399
Lyell, Charles **10** 62-63

Principles of Mathematics (book; Russell-Whitehead)
Cohen, Morris Raphael **4** 139-140
Ramsey, Frank Plumpton **13** 25
Russell, Bertrand Arthur William **13** 373-374
Whitehead, Alfred North **16** 242-244
Wittgenstein, Ludwig **16** 350-351

Printers Union (Jamaica)
Garvey, Marcus Mosiah **6** 228-229

Printing
Cauchy, Augustin Louis **3** 378-380
Caxton, William **3** 386-387
Chu Hsi **4** 40-43
Gutenberg, Johann **7** 48-49
Hoe, Richard March **7** 435-436
Zumárraga, Juan de **16** 531-532
see also Business and industrial leaders—printing

Printmakers
see Artists—printmakers

Prinz Friedrich von Homburg (play)
Kleist, Heinrich von **9** 52-53

Prinz Zerbino (play)
Tieck, Ludwig **15** 218-219

Prio Socarrás, Carlos (1903-1977), Cuban president 1948-52
Castro Ruz, Fidel **3** 365-368
Grau San Martin, Ramón **6** 499-500

Prise d'Alexandrie, La (poem)
Machaut, Guillaume de **10** 93-94

Prisms (book)
Adorno, Theodor W. **1** 65-67

Prison Notebooks (book)
Gramsci, Antonio **6** 488-489

Prison reform
see Penal reform

Prison Songs (musical composition)
Dallapiccola, Luigi **4** 377-378

Prisoner, The (poem)
Brontë, Emily **3** 18-19

Prisoner of Chillon, The (poem)
Byron, George Gordon Noel **3** 193-194

Prisoners of Altona, The (play)
Sartre, Jean Paul **13** 491-492

Prisonnière, La (novel)
Proust, Marcel **12** 465-467

PRITCHETT, V(ICTOR) S(AWDON) (born 1900), English short story writer, novelist, literary critic, journalist, travel writer, biographer, and autobiographer **12** 455-457

Pritzker Prize (for architecture)
Barragán, Luis **2** 17-19
Gehry, Frank O. **6** 250-251
Maki, Fumihiko **10** 159-161
Meier, Richard **10** 456-458
Roche, Kevin **13** 222-224
Rossi, Aldo **13** 309-310
Stirling, James **14** 458-459
Tange, Kenzo **15** 99-101

Private Life of the Master Race, The (play)
Brecht, Bertolt **2** 512-514

Private Lives (play)
Coward, Noel **4** 279-280

Priyadarsika (play)
Harsha **7** 181-182

Prizefighters
see Athletes, American

Probability (mathematics)
development of theory
Bernoulli, Daniel **2** 216
Cardano, Geronimo **3** 285-286
Demoivre, Abraham **4** 494-495
Fermat, Pierre de **5** 421-422
Pascal, Blaise **12** 122-124
19th-century works
Boole, George **2** 396-397
Gauss, Karl Friedrich **6** 240-242
Laplace, Marquis de **9** 202-204
Poincaré, Jules Henri **12** 365-366
Quételet, Lambert Adolphe Jacques **12** 510-511
20th-century works
Bernstein, Dorothy Lewis **2** 217
Jeffreys, Harold **8** 241-242

Process of Education, The (book)
Bruner, Jerome Seymour **3** 72-73

Procession of the Magi (fresco; B. Gozzoli)
Medici, Cosimo de' **10** 449-450

Procession of the Ram of the Drunkards (painting; Diego Velázquez)
Le Nain, Antoine, Louis and Mathieu **9** 321-322

PROCLUS DIADOCHUS (born 410), Byzantine philosopher **12** 457
Euclid **5** 327-329
Ficino, Marsilio **5** 436-437
Lobachevskii, Nikolai Ivanovich **9** 472-474

Procopé, Hjalmar (1868-1927), Finnish-Swedish poet
Sibelius, Jean Julius Christian **14** 211-212

PROCOPIUS OF CAESAREA (circa 500-circa 565), Byzantine historian **12** 457-458

Procuress, The (painting)
Vermeer, Jan **15** 466-467

Prodigal, The (novel)
Alarcón, Pedro Antonio de **1** 100-101

Prodigal Son (ballet)
Prokofiev, Sergei Sergeevich **12** 458-460
Rouault, Georges **13** 321-322

Prodigal Son (print)
Dürer, Albrecht **5** 159-161

Prodigal Son, The (painting)
Greuze, Jean Baptiste **6** 539

Prodigal Son, The (play)
Lope Félix de Vega Carpio **9** 503-506

Prodigious Magician (play)
Calderón, Pedro **3** 221-222

Prodromus (book)
Steno, Nicolaus **14** 425-426

Production (economics)
Say, Jean Baptiste **13** 508-509
Walras, Marie Esprit Léon **16** 84-85

Proem, The (poem)
Crane, Hart **4** 291-293
Whittier, John Greenleaf **16** 256-257

Profanation of the Host (painting)
Uccello, Paolo **15** 378-379

Professor, The (novel)
Brontë, Charlotte **3** 17-18

Professor Bernhardi (play)
Schnitzler, Arthur **14** 23-24

Professor Unrat, oder ... (novel)
Mann, Heinrich **10** 201-202

Professor's House, The (novel)
Cather, Willa Sibert **3** 368-369

Professor's Love Story, The (play)
Barrie, James Matthew **2** 21-22

Profile Portrait of a Lady (painting)
Pollaiuolo, Antonio **12** 377-378

Profiles in Courage (book)
Kennedy, John Fitzgerald **8** 502-506

Profits Made (play)
Benavente y Martinez, Jacinto **2** 146-147

Profit-sharing (economics)
Rosenwald, Julius **13** 293
Stewart, Alexander Turney **14** 448-449
Wood, Robert Elkington **16** 370-371

Progress and Poverty (book; George)
George, Henry **6** 276
Glasgow, Ellen **6** 360-361
Johnson, Tom Loftin **8** 317
Shaw, George Bernard **14** 163-164

Progress of Poetry, The (poem)
Gray, Thomas **6** 509-510

Progressive Conservative party (Canada)
Diefenbaker, John George **5** 4-5

Fairclough, Ellen Louks **5** 367-368

Progressive education
see Education philosophy of—progressive

Progressive Education at the Crossroads (book)
Bode, Boyd Henry **2** 355-356

Progressive Farmer (newspaper)
Polk, Leonidas Lafayette **12** 376-377

Progressive movement (U.S. politics)
leaders
Johnson, Hiram Warren **8** 300-301
Johnson, Tom Loftin **8** 317
La Follette, Robert Marion **9** 155-156
Roosevelt, Theodore **13** 280-283
Wilson, Thomas Woodrow **16** 330-332
legislation
Norris, George William **11** 428-429
Rayburn, Samuel Taliaferro **13** 61-62
Smith, Alfred Emmanuel **14** 284-285
reforms
Lindsey, Benjamin Barr **9** 425-426
Merriam, Charles Edward **10** 518-519
Taft, William Howard **15** 78-81

Progressive party (Canada)
Crerar, Thomas Alexander **4** 306
King, William Lyon Mackenzie **9** 25-26
Woodsworth, James Shaver **16** 376

Progressive party (China)
Li Ta-chao **9** 447
Liang Ch'i-ch'ao **9** 395-396

Progressive party (Czechoslovakia)
Masaryk, Tomáš Garrigue **10** 314-315

Progressive party (Japan)
Inukai, Tsuyoshi **8** 130-131
Okuma, Shigenobu **11** 490

Progressive Party (South Africa)
Suzman, Helen **15** 45-46

Progressive party (United States)
Addams, Jane **1** 56-57
Bentley, Arthur F. **2** 178
Dewey, John **4** 520-523
Ickes, Harold LeClaire **8** 100-101
Kellor, Frances **8** 481-482
Lasswell, Harold Dwight **9** 218-219
McGovern, George Stanley **10** 412-414
Merriam, Charles Edward **10** 518-519
Munsey, Frank Andrew **11** 251
Pinchot, Gifford **12** 308-309
Truman, Harry S. **15** 314-316
Wallace, Henry Agard **16** 73-74

Prohibition party (United States)
Dow, Neal **5** 89-90
Phillips, Wendell **12** 281-282
Willard, Frances Elizabeth Caroline **16** 289-290
see also Temperance movement

Project for a Passage (sculpture)
Giacometti, Alberto **6** 294-295

Projections (photo series)
  Bearden, Romare Howard **2** 86-88
PROKOFIEV, SERGEI SERGEEVICH
  (1891-1953), Russian composer
  12 458-460
  Borodin, Aleksandr Profirevich
    2 422-423
  Khachaturian, Aram Ilich **8** 530-531
  Stravinsky, Igor Fedorovich **14** 502-506
  Ulanova, Galina **15** 382-383
Proletariat (revolutionary theory)
  Engels, Friedrich **5** 286-288
  Kautsky, Karl Johann **8** 462-463
  Lenin, Vladimir Ilich **9** 323-326
  Mao Zedong **10** 225-227
  Marx, Karl **10** 304-308
  Plekhanov, Georgi Valentinovich
    12 351-352
  Sorel, Georges **14** 347-348
  Trotsky, Leon **15** 302-305
Proletcult Theater (Russia)
  Afinogenov, Aleksandr Nikolaevich
    1 72-73
  Eisenstein, Sergei Mikhailovich
    5 240-242
Promenade des trois morts, La (poem)
  Crémazie, Octave **4** 305-306
Promenades ... (literary collection)
  Gourmont, Remy de **6** 475
Promessi sposi, I (novel; Manzoni)
  Verdi, Giuseppe Fortunino Francesco
    15 463-465
Prometheus (mythology)
  art
    Kokoschka, Oskar **9** 75-76
    Lipchitz, Jacques **9** 432-433
    Orozco, José Clemente **12** 1-2
  literature
    Aeschylus **1** 70-72
    Browning, Elizabeth Barrett **3** 52-53
    Goethe, Johann Wolfgang von
      6 388-391
    Kazantzakis, Nikos **8** 466-468
    Lowell, Robert Trail Spence Jr.
      10 16-17
    Shelley, Percy Bysshe **14** 176-178
  music
    Scriabin, Alexander Nikolayevich
      14 71-72
Promethidenlos (poem)
  Hauptmann, Gerhart Johann Robert
    7 199-201
Promise, The (novel)
  Buck, Pearl Sydenstricker **3** 91-93
Promised Land (Canaan)
  Moses **11** 200-201
Promontory Point (Utah)
  Huntington, Collis Potter **8** 49
  Stanford, Leland **14** 397-398
Promoters
  see Business and industrial leaders—
    promoters and speculators

Prompter, The (book)
  Webster, Noah **16** 164-166
Propagation of the Faith, Society for the
  see Society for the Propagation of the
    Faith
Propertius, Sextus (circa 50-circa 15 B.C.),
  Roman elegiac poet
  Virgil **15** 507-510
Prophet, The
  see Mohammed
Prophet, The (book)
  Gibran, Kahlil **6** 303-305
Prophète, Le (opera)
  Meyerbeer, Giacomo **10** 536-537
Prophetiae Sibyllarum (poems)
  Lassus, Roland de **9** 216-218
Prophets
  see Bible—Old Testament
Proportional representation (government)
  Commons, John Rogers **4** 185
  Condorcet, Marquis de **4** 195-196
Proportions, theory of (mathematics)
  Euclid **5** 327-329
  Eudoxus of Cnidus **5** 329-330
Proprietary party (U.S. politics)
  Franklin, Benjamin **6** 60-64
  Logan, James **9** 487-488
  Penn, William **12** 200-202
Proprietress, The (play)
  Betti, Ugo **2** 246
Propylaea (Athens)
  Pericles **12** 219-221
Prosas profanas (book)
  Darío, Rubén **4** 393-394
Prose Edda (poems)
  Sturluson, Snorri **14** 310-311
Prose pour des Esseintes (poem)
  Mallarmé, Stéphane **10** 172-173
Proserpine (sculpture)
  Powers, Hiram **12** 428-429
Prospect before Us, The (book)
  Dos Passos, John Roderigo **5** 69-71
Prospect Park (Brooklyn)
  Olmsted, Frederick Law **11** 503-504
Prospectors of the Future, The (poems)
  Yevtushenko, Yevgeny Alexandrovich
    16 455-456
Prospero (literary character)
  Shakespeare, William **14** 142-145
PROSSER, GABRIEL (circa 1775-1800),
  Afro-American slave rebel **12** 460-461
Prostitute before Her Mirror (painting)
  Rouault, Georges **13** 321-322
Protagonist, The (opera)
  Weill, Kurt **16** 174-175
PROTAGORAS (circa 484-circa 414 B.C.),
  Greek philosopher **12** 461
  Isocrates **8** 151

  Plato **12** 345-347
Protection, Fathers of (religious congrega-
  tion)
  Feijó, Diogo Antônio **5** 405-406
Protectionism (economics)
  see Tarriff
Protectorate People's party (Gambia)
  Jawara, Dauda Kairaba **8** 227-228
Protein (chemistry)
  Bernard, Claude **2** 208-210
  Fischer, Emil **5** 456-457
  Kendrew, John C. **8** 495-496
  Langmuir, Irving **9** 196-197
  Northrop, John Howard **11** 430-431
  Pauling, Linus Carl **12** 150-152
  Richet, Charles Robert **13** 144-145
  Sanger, Frederick **13** 466-467
  Tiselius, Arne Wilhelm Kaurin
    15 240-241
Protestant Association (England; estab-
  lished 1584)
  Leicester, Earl of **9** 312-313
Protestant Episcopal Church (United
  States)
  Brooks, Phillips **3** 26
  Chase, Philander **3** 472-473
  Hobart, John Henry **7** 420-421
  Muhlenberg, William Augustus
    11 233-234
  Revels, Hiram Rhoades **13** 109-110
  Seabury, Samuel **14** 76
  Weems, Mason Locke **16** 170
  see also Anglicanism
Protestant Ethic ... (book; Weber)
  Parsons, Talcott **12** 122
  Weber, Max **16** 157-160
Protestant Reformation
  England
    see Protestant Reformation (Great
      Britain)
  France
    Catherine de Médicis **10** 445-449
    Francis I **6** 40-43
    Goujon, Jean **6** 466-467
    Henry IV **7** 293-295
    Ramus, Petrus **13** 27-28
    see also Calvinism; Religion, Wars
      of
  Germany
    see Protestant Reformation (Ger-
      many)
  Holy Roman Empire
    Charles V **3** 457-459
    Ferdinand I **5** 414-415
    Maximilian II **10** 357-358
  Switzerland
    Calvin, John **3** 239-242
    Zwingli, Huldreich **16** 537-538
    see also Humanism, Christian—
      Protestants; Counter Reformation;
      Roman Catholic Church
Protestant Reformation (Germany)
  beginnings

Luther, Martin **10** 48-51
Melancthon, Philip **10** 466-467
see also Lutheranism
historians of
Döllinger, Josef Ignaz von **5** 47-48
opponents
Charles V **3** 457-459
Schwenckfeld, Kasper von **14** 56-57
precursors
Groote, Gerard **7** 12-13
radical leaders
Karlstadt, Andreas Bodenheim von
8 449
Münzer, Thomas **11** 251-252
see also Anabaptists
supporters
Frederick III **6** 84-85
Hutten, Ulrich von **8** 72-73

Protestant Reformation (Great Britain)
development
Cranmer, Thomas **4** 295-296
Edward VI **5** 213-214
Elizabeth I **5** 263-266
Henry VIII **7** 302-305
Latimer, Hugh **9** 221
More, Thomas **11** 156-157
Somerset, Duke of **14** 333-334
historians of
Burnet, Gilbert **3** 147
Froude, James Anthony **6** 133-134
Knox, John **9** 65-66
Scotland
Knox, John **9** 65-66

Protestant-Catholic-Jew (book)
Herberg, Will **7** 322-323

Protestantism
Austria
Joseph II **8** 359-360
England
see England, Church of;
see also Methodism
France
Coligny, Gaspard de **4** 159-160
Louis XIV **9** 531-533
see also Huguenots
Germany
see Protestantism (Germany)
India
Carey, William **3** 297
Spain
Servetus, Michael **14** 115-116
Switzerland
Brunner, Emil **3** 74-75
theology
Brunner, Emil **3** 74-75
Pannenberg, Wolfhart **12** 87-88
U.S.
see Protestantism (United States)
see also Religious leaders, Protestant

Protestantism (Germany)
dialectical theology
see Dialectical theology
effect on capitalism
Troeltsch, Ernst **15** 299-300

Weber, Max **16** 157-160
supporters
Ferdinand III **5** 416-417
Frederick William I **6** 86-87
Frederick William III **6** 87
Frederick William IV **6** 87-88
theology
Bonhoeffer, Dietrich **2** 389-391
Harnack, Adolf von **7** 160
Strauss, David Friedrich **14** 496-497
see also Calvinism; Lutheranism

Protestantism (United States)
Episcopalianism
see Protestant Episcopal Church
(United States)
evangelism
see Evangelism
liberalism
Beecher, Henry Ward **2** 112-113
Bushnell, Horace **3** 171-172
Fosdick, Harry Emerson **6** 21-22
Social Gospel
see Social Gospel
theology
Hopkins, Mark **7** 495-496
Nevin, John Williamson **11** 357
Niebuhr, Helmut Richard
11 386-387
Niebuhr, Reinhold **11** 387-388
Tillich, Paul Johannes **15** 224-225
see also Fundamentalism; Great
Awakening; Puritanism—New Eng-
land; Religious leaders, Protestant

Prothalamion (poem)
Spenser, Edmund **14** 373-376

Protoactinium (element—chemistry)
Hahn, Otto **7** 64-65

Proton (physics)
Dirac, Paul Adrien Maurice **5** 23-24
Fermi, Enrico **5** 422-424

Protozoa (biology)
Leeuwenhoek, Anton van **9** 300-301

Protractor (painting series)
Stella, Frank **14** 420-422

Proud Valley (film)
Robeson, Paul Leroy **13** 198-199

Proudhammer, Caleb and Leo (literary
characters)
Baldwin, James Arthur **1** 465-466

PROUDHON, PIERRE JOSEPH
(1809-1864), French anarchist political
philosopher and journalist **12** 461-463
Engels, Friedrich **5** 286-288
Greeley, Horace **6** 515-517
Marx, Karl **10** 304-308

PROULX, E. ANNIE (born 1935), American
author **12** 463-465

Proust, Joseph Louis (1754-1826), French
chemist
Berthollet, Claude Louis **2** 229-230
Berzelius, Jöns Jacob **2** 231-233

PROUST, MARCEL (1871-1922), French
novelist **12** 465-467

influence of
Beckett, Samuel **2** 102-104
Cocteau, Jean **4** 132-133
Colette, Sidonie Gabrielle
4 158-159
Woolf, Virginia Stephen **16** 381-382
influenced by
Baudelaire, Charles Pierre **2** 61-63
Guillaume de Lorris **7** 33-34
Schopenhauer, Arthur **14** 29-31

Proust's law (chemistry)
Berzelius, Jöns Jacob **2** 231-233

Proverbios, Los (etching)
Goya y Lucientes, Francisco de Paula
José de **6** 476-478

Proverbs, Book of (OT)
Graetz, Heinrich Hirsch **6** 483
Isidore of Seville **8** 149-150
Jesus ben Sira **8** 251
Solomon **14** 326-327

Provide, Provide (poem)
Frost, Robert Lee **6** 130-133

Providence (city; Rhode Island)
Gorton, Samuell **6** 460
Williams, Roger **16** 304-305

Providence Bank (Rhode Island)
Brown, Moses **3** 42-43

Providence Company (England)
Pym, John **12** 495-496

Provident Hospital (established 1891)
Williams, Daniel Hale **16** 302-303

Providentia Fountain (Vienna)
Donner, Georg Raphael **5** 63

Providential Catch (story)
Cahan, Abraham **3** 214

Provincetown Players (Cape Cod, Massachusetts)
O'Neill, Eugene **11** 514-516

Provincial Lady, A (play)
Turgenev, Ivan Sergeyevich **15** 345-348

Provinciales, Les (stories)
Giraudoux, Jean **6** 349-350

Provisors, Statute of (1351)
Edward III **5** 211-212

Provok'd Wife, The (play)
Vanbrugh, John **15** 409-410

PROXMIRE, WILLIAM (born 1915), Democratic senator for Wisconsin **12** 467-468

Prudencia en la mujer, La (play)
Tirso de Molina **15** 237-238

Prudentius (348-?410), Latin poet
Juvenal **8** 397-399

PRUD'HON, PIERRE PAUL (1758-1823),
French painter **12** 469

Prufrock ... (poems)
Eliot, Thomas Stearns **5** 258-261

Prusias (died 148 B.C.), king of Bithynia
192-148
Flamininus, Titus Quinctius **5** 477

Prussia (former nation, Europe)
Austria and
Francis II **6** 43-44
Leopold II **9** 346
Maria Theresa **10** 256-258
Metternich, Klemens von
10 533-536
constitutionalism
Frederick William **6** 85-86
Frederick William III **6** 87
Frederick William IV **6** 87-88
creation of state
Frederick II **6** 81-84
Frederick William **6** 85-86
Frederick William I **6** 86-87
dynasties
see Hohenstaufen dynasty; Hohen-
zollern dynasty
education
Cousin, Victor **4** 273-274
Froebel, Friedrich Wilhelm August
6 122-123
Mann, Horace **10** 202-204
French wars
Blücher, Gebhard Leberecht von
2 340-341
Hardenberg, Karl August von
7 146-147
Lafayette, Marquis de **9** 151-152
Napoleon I **11** 306-310
Napoleon III **11** 310-312
Stein, Heinrich Friedrich Karl vom
und zum **14** 415-416
see also Austro-Prussian War;
Franco-Prussian War (1870-1871);
French Revolutionary Wars;
Napoleonic Wars
Holy Alliance
see Holy Alliance
militarism
Frederick II **6** 81-84
Frederick William I **6** 86-87
Scharnhorst, Gerhard Johann David
von **13** 521-522
Treitschke, Heinrich von
15 293-294
Polish partitions
see Poland—partition—1918
reforms
Frederick William III **6** 87
Hardenberg, Karl August von
7 146-147
Stein, Heinrich Friedrich Karl vom
und zum **14** 415-416
Swedish war
Charles XII **3** 464-466
Teutonic Knights
Frederick II **6** 79
Sigismund **14** 220-221
unified Germany
Bismarck, Otto Eduard Leopold von
2 294-296
William I (emperor of Germany)
16 290-291
see also German Bund; Holy Roman
Empire; Vienna, Congress of
(1814-1815)

see also Germany—German Empire
Prussian Sonatas (musical composition)
Bach, Carl Philipp Emanuel **1** 414-415
Prynne, William (1600-1669), English Pam-
phleteer
Laud, William **9** 224-225
Przhevalsk (town, Russia)
Przhevalsky, Nikolai Mikhailovich
12 469-470
PRZHEVALSKY, NIKOLAI MIKHAILOVICH
(1839-1888), Russian general and traveler
12 469-470
Hedin, Sven Anders **7** 252-253
Psalm of Life, A (poem)
Longfellow, Henry Wadsworth
9 499-500
Psalms (Old Testament book)
composition
David, Jacques Louis **4** 407-409
in art and literature
Luca della Robbia **10** 19-20
Wyatt, Thomas **16** 410-411
musical settings
Clemens non Papa, Jacobus **4** 101
Kodály, Zoltán **9** 71
Lassus, Roland de **9** 216-218
Le Jeune, Claude **9** 314-315
Penderecki, Krzysztof **12** 195-197
Schütz, Heinrich **14** 48-49
Tallis, Thomas **15** 91
Victoria, Tomás Luis de **15** 487-488
Willaert, Adrian **16** 287-288
studies
Graetz, Heinrich Hirsch **6** 483
Lombard, Peter **9** 490-491
Luther, Martin **10** 48-51
Malherbe, François de **10** 169-170
Psalterium Americanum
Mather, Cotton **10** 330-332
Pseudo-Dionysus (Dionysus the Are-
opagite; flourished circa 500), medieval
author and mystical theologian
Erigena, John Scotus **5** 308-309
Pseudolus (play)
Plautus **12** 348-350
Pseudonyms
Agricola
Crèvecoeur, John de **4** 307-308
Arnold, Franz
Lieber, Francis **9** 401-402
Bell, Currer
Brontë, Charlotte **3** 17-18
Bell, Ellis
Brontë, Emily **3** 18-19
Beltov
Plekhanov, Georgi Valentinovich
12 351-352
Blake, Nicholas
Lewis, Cecil Day **9** 380
Boyd, Nancy
Millay, Edna St. Vincent **11** 24-25
Chung-shan
Sun Yat-sen **15** 35-39

Collins, Tom
Furphy, Joseph **6** 152-153
Democritus Junior
Burton, Robert **3** 166-167
Drapier, H. B.
Swift, Jonathan **15** 51-54
Elia
Lamb, Charles **9** 176-177
Eliot, George
Eliot, George **5** 254-256
Hiner, Cincinnatus
Miller, Joaquin **11** 27-28
Knickerbocker, Diedrich
Irving, Washington **8** 141-143
Labriolle
Velasco Ibarra, José María
15 452-454
Littleton, Mark
Kennedy, John Pendleton **8** 506-507
Massachusettensis
Leonard, Daniel **9** 336-337
Melikow, Loris
Hofmannsthal, Hugo von **7** 443-444
Muhibbi
Suleiman I **15** 20-21
Nakayama
Sun Yat-sen **15** 35-39
Nasier, Alcofribas
Rabelais, François **12** 524-526
Nirvani, Carma
Kazantzakis, Nikos **8** 466-468
Oldstyle, Jonathan, Gent.
Irving, Washington **8** 141-143
Oswald, F.
Engels, Friedrich **5** 286-288
Parnassus
Dwight, Timothy **5** 169
Parson Lot
Kingsley, Charles **9** 28
Perry, Edgar A.
Poe, Edgar Allan **12** 363-365
Peter Porcupine
Cobbett, William **4** 126-127
Philatheles
Pinto, Isaac **12** 318
Psiloritis, Petros
Kazantzakis, Nikos **8** 466-468
Shunro
Hokusai, Katsushika **7** 447-448
Sim, Georges
Simenon, Georges **14** 233-234
Smith, Johnston
Crane, Stephen **4** 293-295
Thurstein, Domine de
Zinzendorf, Nikolaus Ludwig von
16 522-523
Ugo
Foscolo, Ugo **6** 21
see also Nicknames
Psiche (opera)
Scarlatti, Pietro Alessandro Gaspare
13 517-518
Psyche (mythology)
Courbet, Jean Desiré Gustave
4 271-273

La Fontaine, Jean de **9** 156-157

Psyche (novella)
Storm, Theodor **14** 479-480

Psyche (sculpture)
Powers, Hiram **12** 428-429

Psychiatry (science)
Charcot, Jean Martin **3** 442
Coles, Robert Martin **4** 156-157
Freud, Sigmund **6** 103-106
Jung, Carl Gustav **8** 388-389
Sullivan, Harry Stack **15** 23-24
White, William Alanson **16** 239-240
see also Psychoanalysis; Scientists—
psychiatrists

Psychic religion
see Spiritualism

Psychical research (science)
Broad, Charlie Dunbar **3** 12

Psycho (film)
Hitchcock, Alfred **7** 415-416

Psychoanalysis (medicine)
Adler, Alfred **1** 61-63
Bleuler, Eugen **2** 325
Erikson, Erik Homburger **5** 309-310
Freud, Sigmund **6** 103-106
Fromm, Erich **6** 125-127
Horney, Karen Danielsen **7** 508-509
Jones, Ernest Alfred **8** 331-332
Jung, Carl Gustav **8** 388-389
Lacan, Jacques **9** 145-147
Lasch, Christopher **9** 212-214
see also Scientists—psychoanalysts

Psychological Corporation
Cattell, James McKeen **3** 376-377

Psychological drama (literature)
Betti, Ugo **2** 246

Psychological novel (literature)
Dostoevsky, Fyodor **5** 74-77
Larsen, Nella **9** 209-210
Lermontov, Mikhail Yurievich
9 352-353
Svevo, Italo **15** 47-48

Psychological realism (drama)
Kazan, Elia **8** 465-466

Psychology (social science)
and worker productivity
Gilbreth, Lillian **6** 315-317
behaviorism
see Behaviorism
comparative
Hobhouse, Leonard Trelawny
7 425-426
Morgan, Conway Lloyd **11** 159-160
Thorndike, Edward Lee **15** 208-209
educational
Bruner, Jerome Seymour **3** 72-73
Neill, Alexander Sutherland
11 335-336
experimental
Angell, James Rowland **1** 236-237
Bartlett, Frederic Charles **2** 34-35
Ebbinghaus, Hermann **5** 192-193

Fechner, Gustav Theodor **5** 401-402
Lotze, Rudolf Hermann **9** 521-522
Titchener, Edward Bradford
15 241-242
Wundt, Wilhelm Max **16** 402-403
functionalism
Angell, James Rowland **1** 236-237
Gestalt
Lewin, Kurt **9** 375-376
Tolman, Edward Chace **15** 261-262
Wertheimer, Max **16** 207-208
individual
Adler, Alfred **1** 61-63-55
Rogers, Carl Ransom **13** 245-247
learning
see Learning theory
of death and dying\
Kübler-Ross, Elisabeth **9** 118-120
philosophical foundations
Brentano, Franz Clemens **2** 516-517
Condillac, Étienne Bonnot de
4 194-195
Fries, Jakob Friedrich **6** 116-117
Fromm, Erich **6** 125-127
Herbart, Johann Friedrich **7** 321-322
Hobbes, Thomas **7** 421-423
James, William **8** 215-217
physiological
Cattell, James McKeen **3** 376-377
Hartley, David **7** 185
Pavlov, Ivan Petrovich **12** 155-157
political
Bagehot, Walter **1** 436-437
Wallas, Graham **16** 77-78
pop-psychology advice shows
Brothers, Joyce **3** 26-28
psychoanalytic
see Psychoanalysis
sex therapy
Johnson, Virginia E. **8** 317-319
social
Dilthey, Wilhelm Christian Ludwig
5 10
Fromm, Erich **6** 125-127
Hovland, Carl I. **7** 527-528
Le Bon, Gustave **9** 268-269
Znaniecki, Florian **16** 523-524
somatic
Huxley, Aldous Leonard **8** 74-75
structural psychoanalysis
Lacan, Jacques **9** 145-147
testing
Binet, Alfred **2** 277-278
Cattell, James McKeen **3** 376-377
Hull, Clark Leonard **8** 28
Piaget, Jean **12** 287-288
Rorschach, Hermann **13** 286-288
Terman, Lewis Madison **15** 153-154
Thorndike, Edward Lee **15** 208-209
Thurstone, Louis Leon **15** 215-216
Yerkes, Robert Mearns **16** 454-455
see also Motivation; Psychopatholo-
gy; Psychotherapy; Social Scien-
tists—psychologists

Psychometry
see Psychology—testing

Psychopathology (medicine)
Charcot, Jean Martin **3** 442
Freud, Sigmund **6** 103-106
Janet, Pierre Marie Félix **8** 220
Jaspers, Karl **8** 225-226
Jung, Carl Gustav **8** 388-389

Psychophysics (science)
Fechner, Gustav Theodor **5** 401-402
Hull, Clark Leonard **8** 28

Psychotherapy (medicine)
Adler, Alfred **1** 61-63-55
Janet, Pierre Marie Félix **8** 220
Klein, Melanie **9** 52
Kübler-Ross, Elisabeth **9** 118-120
Rank, Otto **13** 33
Rogers, Carl Ransom **13** 245-247
Westheimer, Ruth Karola **16** 214-215

Ptolemaic dynasty (Egypt; ruled 323-30
B.C.)
Cleopatra **4** 105-106
Ptolemy I **12** 470-472
Ptolemy II **12** 472-473
see also entries under Ptolemy III-XIV

Ptolemais (ancient city, Egypt)
Ptolemy I **12** 470-472

Ptolemy (Ptolemy Ceraunus or Keraunos;
died 279 B.C.), king of Macedonia
280-279
Ptolemy II **12** 472-473
Seleucus I **14** 92-93

PTOLEMY I (367/366-283 B.C.), Macedon-
ian general, king of Egypt 323-285
12 470-472
Antigonus I **1** 248-249
Apelles **1** 257
Cleopatra **4** 105-106
Menander **10** 477-478
Seleucus I **14** 92-93

PTOLEMY II (308-246 B.C.), king of Egypt
285-246 **12** 472-473
Asoka **1** 341-342
Callimachus **3** 235-236
Theocritus **15** 171-172

Ptolemy III (Euergetes; 282?-221 B.C.),
king of Egypt 246-221
Callimachus **3** 235-236
Cleomenes III **4** 103-104
Eratosthenes of Cyrene **5** 301-302

Ptolemy IV (Philopator; 244?-203 B.C.),
king of Egypt 221-203
Antiochus III **1** 249-250
Cleomenes III **4** 103-104

Ptolemy V (Epiphanes; 210?-181 B.C.), king
of Egypt 203-181
Antiochus III **1** 249-250

Ptolemy VI (Philometor; 186?-145 B.C.),
king of Egypt 181-145
Antiochus IV **1** 250

Ptolemy VII (Euergetes II; 184?-116 B.C.),
king of Egypt 145-116

Antiochus IV **1** 250

Ptolemy XII (Auletes; 61-48 B.C.), king of Egypt 51-48
Cleopatra **4** 105-106
Pompey **12** 387-389

Ptolemy XIII (58?-44 B.C.), king of Egypt 47-44
Cleopatra **4** 105-106

Ptolemy XIV (Caesarion; 47-30 B.C.), coregent of Egypt 44?-30
Caesar, Gaius Julius **3** 207-210
Cleopatra **4** 105-106

PTOLEMY, CLAUDIUS (circa 100-circa 170), Greek astronomer and geographer **12** 473-474
as astronomer
Apollonius of Perga **1** 261-262
Bitruji, Nur al-Din Abu Ishaq al **2** 296
Brahe, Tycho **2** 489-490
Copernicus, Nicolaus **4** 226-227
Hasan ibn al-Haytham **7** 190-191
Hipparchus **7** 407-408
Regiomontanus **13** 81-82
see also Universe, systems of—Ptolemaic
as geographer
Columbus, Christopher **4** 176-179
Idrisi, Muhammad ibn Muhammad al- **8** 102-103
Khwarizmi, Muhammad ibn Musa al- **8** 541
Mendaña de Neyra, Álvaro de **10** 483
Mercator, Gerhardus **10** 511-512
Ortelius, Abraham **12** 8-9
Vespucci, Amerigo **15** 476-478
Waldseemüller, Martin **16** 56

Public Health (medicine)
Baker, Sara Josephine **1** 455-456
Biggs, Hermann Michael **2** 272-273
Bowditch, Henry Ingersoll **2** 459-460
Chadwick, Edwin **3** 404-405
Cruz, Oswaldo Gonçalves **4** 328-329
Gayle, Helene Doris **6** 244-245
Macdonald, Eleanor Josephine **10** 83-84
Nightingale, Florence **11** 392-393
Nostradamus **11** 432-434
Park, William Hallock **12** 104-105
Sabin, Florence Rena **13** 402-405
Shaftesbury, 7th Earl of **14** 137-138
Welch, William Henry **16** 185-186

Public Is Stupid, The (print)
Daumier, Honoré Victorin **4** 403-405

Public lands (United States)
land grants
Durant, Thomas Clark **5** 157-158
Tryon, William **15** 321
settlers and
Benton, Thomas Hart **2** 178-179
Crockett, David **4** 314-316
Cutler, Manasseh **4** 356-357
Evans, George Henry **5** 337-338

George, Henry **6** 276

Public libraries
see Libraries

Public opinion polls
Gallup, George **6** 187-189

Public relations industry
Bernays, Edward L. **2** 211-212

Public Safety, Committee of (France)
Carnot, Lazare Nicolas Marguerite **3** 313-314
Danton, Georges Jacques **4** 391-393
Saint-Just, Louis Antoine Léon de **13** 433

Public school (England)
Arnold, Thomas **1** 313-314
Elizabeth II **5** 266-269

Public school (United States)
see Education (United States)

Public School Society (New York State)
Clinton, DeWitt **4** 112-113
Cooper, Peter **4** 223-224

Public Schools Act (1866; Australia)
Parkes, Henry **12** 113

Public Weal, League of the (1465-1466)
Charles the Bold **3** 467-469
Louis XI **9** 526-528

Public Works Administration (United States)
Ickes, Harold LeClaire **8** 100-101

Public works programs
Asoka **1** 341-342
Balmaceda Fernández, José Manuel **1** 475-476
Cato, Marcus Porcius the Elder **3** 375
Haussmann, Baron Georges Eugène **7** 201-202
Ibáñez del Campo, Carlos **8** 88
López, Carlos Antonio **9** 506-507
Moses, Robert **11** 202-203
Sulla, Lucius Cornelius I **15** 21-22
Trajan **15** 291-292
see also Work Projects Administration

Publishers
American
see Publishers, American
Argentine
Timerman, Jacobo **15** 226-228
Canadian
Black, Conrad Moffat **2** 300-301
Irving, Kenneth Colin **8** 140-141
Thomson, Kenneth **15** 201-202
English
Maxwell, Ian Robert **10** 360-361
Newbery, John **11** 360-361
Mexican
Cosio Villegas, Daniel **4** 260-261
Murdoch, Rupert **11** 257-258
Nicaraguan
Chamorro, Violeta Barrios de **3** 417-419

Publishers, American
books and/or educational materials

Howe, Florence Rosenfeld **7** 530-531
Knopf, Alfred A. **9** 60-61
Knopf, Blanche Wolf **9** 61-62
Work, Monroe **16** 388-389
journals
Howe, Florence Rosenfeld **7** 530-531
magazines
Forbes, Malcolm **5** 508-509
Greeley, Horace **6** 515-517
Guccione, Bob Jr. **7** 26
Hearst, William Randolph **7** 243-244
Hefner, Hugh **7** 253-254
Johnson, John Harold **8** 306-308
Knopf, Alfred A. **9** 60-61
Luce, Henry Robinson **10** 23-24
McClure, Samuel Sidney **10** 398-399
Munsey, Frank Andrew **11** 251
Newhouse, Samuel Irving **11** 362-364
Wallace, DeWitt **16** 70-71
newspapers
Beach, Moses Yale **2** 79-80
Bennett, James Gordon **2** 168-169
Bennett, James Gordon Jr. **2** 169-170
Bowles, Samuel **2** 464
Dana, Charles Anderson **4** 384-385
Golden, Harry **6** 402-403
Graham, Katharine Meyer **6** 483-485
Greeley, Horace **6** 515-517
Hearst, George **7** 242
Hearst, William Randolph **7** 243-244
Hitchcock, Gilbert Monell **7** 416-417
Luce, Henry Robinson **10** 23-24
Lundy, Benjamin **10** 45-46
Maynard, Robert Clyve **10** 366-367
McCormick, Robert Rutherford **10** 401-402
McGill, Ralph Emerson **10** 411-412
Medill, Joseph **10** 451-452
Morgan, Garrett A. **11** 161-162
Munsey, Frank Andrew **11** 251
Murdoch, Rupert **11** 257-258
Newhouse, Samuel Irving **11** 362-364
Pulitzer, Joseph **12** 481-482
Schurz, Carl **14** 44-45
Scripps, Edward Wyllis **14** 72-73
Simon, Paul **14** 238-239
Sulzberger, Arthur Ochs **15** 28-30
see also Editors; Journalism (United States); Journalists, American

Publius Aelius Hadrianus
see Hadrian

PUCCINI, GIACOMO (1858-1924), Italian composer **12** 474-476
Belasco, David **2** 124-125
Caruso, Enrico **3** 345
Prévost, Abbé **12** 445-446

Toscanini, Arturo **15** 270-271
Verdi, Giuseppe Fortunino Francesco **15** 463-465

Pucelle, La (poem)
Voltaire **16** 14-16

Puck of Pook's Hill (stories)
Kipling, Joseph Rudyard **9** 32-33

Pudd'nhead Wilson (book; Twain)
Davis, Ossie **4** 421-422

Pudovkin, Vsevolod I. (1893-1953), Russian film director
Ray, Satyajit **13** 60-61

Pueblo Indians (North America)
Gilpin, Laura **6** 326-327
Jung, Carl Gustav **8** 388-389
Malinowski, Kaspar Bronislaw **10** 170-171
Oñate, Juan de **11** 513-514

PUENTE, TITO (born Ernesto Antonio Puente, 1920), Hispanic American band leader, musician, and composer

Puericinium (musical composition)
Praetorius, Michael **12** 431-432

Puerperal fever (medicine)
Domagk, Gerhard Johannes Paul **5** 48-50
Semmelweis, Ignaz Philipp **14** 101-102

Puerto Rico (United States commonwealth; island, Greater Antilles)
Alfonso XIII **1** 151
Columbus, Christopher **4** 176-179
Hernández Colón, Rafael **7** 329-330
Hostos, Eugenio María de **7** 513-514
McKinley, William **10** 418-420
Muñoz Marín, José Luís Alberto **11** 249-250
Muñoz Rivera, Luís **11** 250
Ponce de León, Juan **12** 391-392
Romero Barceló, Carlos **13** 267-268
Root, Elihu **13** 283-284
Tugwell, Rexford Guy **15** 336-339
Velázquez, Nydia Margarita **15** 456-459

Pueyrredón, Juan Martín de (1776-1850), Argentine statesman
Carrera, José Miguel **3** 323-324

PUFENDORF, BARON SAMUEL VON (1632-1694), German jurist and historian **12** 477-478
Thomasius **15** 193-194

PUGACHEV, EMELYAN IVANOVICH (1742-1775), Russian Cossack soldier **12** 478-479
Catherine the Great **3** 370-372
Lermontov, Mikhail Yurievich **9** 352-353
Pushkin, Aleksandr Sergeevich **12** 489-491
Suvorov, Aleksandr Vasilievich **15** 44-45

Puget, Pierre (1622-1694), French architect and sculptor
Falconet, Étienne Maurice **5** 372

Pugin, Augustus Charles (1762-1832), French architect
Pugin, Augustus Welby Northmore **12** 479-480

PUGIN, AUGUSTUS WELBY NORTHMORE (1812-1852), English architect **12** 479-480

Pulakesin II (flourished 612-620), Chalukya king in India
Harsha **7** 181-182

PULASKI, CASIMIR (1747/48-79), Polish patriot **12** 480-481
Kościuszko, Tadeusz Andrzej Bonawentura **9** 88

PULCI, LUIGI (1432-1484), Italian poet **12** 481

Pulcinella (ballet)
Picasso, Pablo **12** 292-295
Stravinsky, Igor Fedorovich **14** 502-506

PULITZER, JOSEPH (1847-1911), American editor and publisher **12** 481-482
Bennett, James Gordon Jr. **2** 169-170
Dana, Charles Anderson **4** 384-385
Hearst, William Randolph **7** 243-244
Russell, Charles Edward **13** 374-375

Pulitzer Prize winners
Agee, James **1** 78-79
Albee, Edward Franklin III **1** 106-108
Ashmore, Harry Scott **1** 334-335
Baker, Russell **1** 452-454
Bellow, Saul **2** 141-143
Bishop, Elizabeth **2** 290-292
Block, Herbert **2** 333-334
Brooks, Gwendolyn **3** 24-26
Clapp, Margaret Antoinette **4** 71-72
Crumb, George **4** 326-328
Goodman, Ellen Holtz **6** 438-439
Higgins, Marguerite **7** 378-380
Mamet, David Alan **10** 181-182
Merrill, James **10** 521-522
Mitchell, Margaret **11** 59-60
Momaday, N. Scott **11** 92-94
Nemerov, Howard **11** 338-340
Nevins, Allan **11** 357-359
Oliphant, Patrick Bruce **11** 498-500
Proulx, E. Annie **12** 463-465
Reston, James Barrett **13** 104-105
Safire, William **13** 422-424
Sagan, Carl E. **13** 424-425
Salisbury, Harrison Evans **13** 449-451
Schlesinger, Arthur Meier Jr. **14** 13-15
Shepard, Sam **14** 180-181
Simpson, Louis Aston Marantz **14** 243-244
Terkel, Louis **15** 152-153
Trudeau, Garretson Beekman **15** 308-309
Tuchman, Barbara **15** 331-332
Tyler, Anne **15** 367-368
Updike, John **15** 390-392
Walker, Alice Malsenior **16** 59-61
White, T. H. **16** 236-237
Wilbur, Richard Purdy **16** 271-272
Will, George Frederick **16** 286-287

Wilson, August **16** 314-316
Wuorinen, Charles **16** 404
Zwilich, Ellen Taaffe **16** 536-537

Pulkovo Observatory (near Leningrad)
Struve, Friedrich Georg Wilhelm von **14** 513

PULLMAN, GEORGE MORTIMER (1831-1897), American industrial innovator **12** 482-483
Baker, Ray Stannard **1** 451-452
see also Pullman strike

Pullman Car Hiawatha (play)
Wilder, Thornton Niven **16** 276-277

Pullman strike (1894)
Addams, Jane **1** 56-57
Altgeld, John Peter **1** 180-182
Baker, Ray Stannard **1** 451-452
Cleveland, Stephen Grover **4** 108-110
Darrow, Clarence Seward **4** 396-397
Debs, Eugene Victor **4** 444-445
Miles, Nelson Appleton **11** 16-17
Olney, Richard **11** 504-505
Pullman, George Mortimer **12** 482-483

Pulsars
Bell Burnell, Susan Jocelyn **2** 133-134

Pulse music
Reich, Steve **13** 84-85

Pulse theory (light)
see Light—wave theory

Pumpkin papers
Chambers, Whittaker **3** 416-417

Punic wars
first (264-241 B.C.)
Hamilcar Barca **7** 94-95
second (218-201 B.C.)
Cato, Marcus Porcius the Elder **3** 375
Ennius, Quintus **5** 289
Hannibal Barca **7** 128-130
Scipio Africanus Major, Publius Cornelius **14** 61-62
third (149-146 B.C.)
Polybios **12** 384-385

Punjab (region; India)
early history
Alexander the Great **1** 137-141
Bach, Carl Philipp Emanuel **1** 414-415
Chandragupta Maurya **3** 426
Mahmud of Ghazni **10** 147
19th-20th century
Besant, Annie Wood **2** 233-234
Chelmsford, Frederic John Napier Thesiger **3** 497
Dalhousie, 1st Marquess of **4** 375-376
Ranjit Singh **13** 32-33
Speke, John Hanning **14** 366-367

Puntila and His Man Matti (play)
Brecht, Bertolt **2** 512-514

PUPIN, MICHAEL IDVORSKY (1858-1935), Serbo-American physicist and inventor **12** 483-484

Armstrong, Edwin Howard **1** 302-303

Puppet Show, The (play)
Blok, Aleksandr Aleksandrovich **2** 335

Purandar, Treaty of (1665)
Shivaji **14** 199-200

Purbach, Georg
see Peurbach, Georg

PURCELL, HENRY (1659-1695), English
composer and organist **12** 484-485
Britten, Benjamin **3** 10-11
Dowland, John **5** 90
Monteverdi, Claudio Giovanni Antonio
11 126-128
Sullivan, Arthur Seymour **15** 23
Vaughan Williams, Ralph **15** 446-447

Purcell, John Baptist (1800-1883), American archbishop and theologian
Campbell, Alexander **3** 249-250

Purchase of the North Pole, The (novel)
Verne, Jules **15** 467-469

Pure Food and Drug Act (United States;
1906)
Cannon, Joseph Gurney **3** 261-262
Lodge, Henry Cabot **9** 482-483
Roosevelt, Theodore **13** 280-283
Sinclair, Upton Beale Jr. **14** 248-249
Wiley, Harvey Washington **16** 277-278

Pure Gold (novel)
Rölvaag, Ole Edvart **13** 265

Pure Land sect (Buddhism)
Buddha **3** 97-101
Honen **7** 473
Hui-yüan **8** 25-26

Pure Lust (book)
Daly, Mary **4** 380-381

Purgatorio (Dante)
see Divine Comedy

Purgatory (play)
Yeats, William Butler **16** 445-447

Purge trials (Soviet history)
see Great Purge

Purification of the Temple (painting)
Greco **6** 511-514

Purification of the Virgin (painting)
Guercino **7** 27

Purifications (poem)
Empedocles **5** 282

Puritan (sculpture)
Saint-Gaudens, Augustus **13** 432

Puritan regime (England)
see Commonwealth (England; 1649-53)

Puritan Revolution
see Civil War, English-Puritan Revolutions

Puritani, I (opera)
Bellini, Vincenzo **2** 138-139

Puritanism (religion)
England
Brewster, William **2** 523-524

Bunyan, John **3** 128-129
Coverdale, Miles **4** 278
Crashaw, Richard **4** 296
Elizabeth I **5** 263-266
Lilburne, John **9** 409-410
Vane, Henry **15** 425-426
histories of
Miller, Perry **11** 28-29
Morison, Samuel Eliot **11** 175-176
influence of
Franklin, Benjamin **6** 60-64
Frost, Robert Lee **6** 130-133
Hawthorne, Nathaniel **7** 212-215
New England
Davenport, John **4** 405-406
Dudley, Thomas **5** 124-125
Dunster, Henry **5** 152-153
Dwight, Timothy **5** 169
Edwards, Jonathan **5** 220-222
Endecott, John **5** 284-285
Gorton, Samuell **6** 460
Hildreth, Richard **7** 382
Hutchinson, Anne Marbury **8** 69-71
Taylor, Edward **15** 122-123
Williams, Roger **16** 304-305
Winthrop, John **16** 339-341

Puritans, Church of the (New York City)
Renwick, James **13** 102-103

Purlie (musical)
Davis, Ossie **4** 421-422

Purple Noon's Transparent Might (painting)
Streeton, Arthur Ernest **14** 507-508

Pursuit of Love (novel)
Mann, Heinrich **10** 201-202

Pursuit, The (painting)
Fragonard, Jean Honoré **6** 38-39

PURVIS, ROBERT (1810-1898), African
American abolitionist **12** 485-486

PURYEAR, MARTIN (born 1941), African
American artist **12** 486-487

PUSEY, EDWARD BOUVERIE (1800-1882),
English clergyman and scholar
12 488-489

Puseyism
see Oxford Movement

PUSHKIN, ALEKSANDR SERGEEVICH
(1799-1837), Russian poet and prose
writer **12** 489-491
associates
Gogol, Nikolai **6** 391-393
influence of
Bunin, Ivan Alekseevich **3** 124
Lermontov, Mikhail Yurievich
9 352-353
Stravinsky, Igor Fedorovich
14 502-506
Turgenev, Ivan Sergeyevich
15 345-348
musical settings
Britten, Benjamin **3** 10-11
Glinka, Mikhail Ivanovich
6 369-370

Mussorgsky, Modest Petrovich
11 274-276
Tchaikovsky, Peter Ilyich
15 130-132
translations
Mérimée, Prosper **10** 517

Puss in Boots (play)
Tieck, Ludwig **15** 218-219

Put Out More Flags (novel)
Waugh, Evelyn Arthur St. John
16 145-147

Putnam, George (1814-1872), American
publisher
Jacobi, Abraham and Mary Putnam
8 188-189

PUTNAM, ISRAEL (1718-1790), American
Revolutionary War general **12** 491-492
Burr, Aaron **3** 156-159

Putnam, J. J. (1846-1918), American neurologist
Jones, Ernest Alfred **8** 331-332

Putnam, Mary Corinna
see Jacobi, Mary Putnam

Putsches
see Coups d'état—Germany

PUVIS DE CHAVANNES, PIERRE
(1824-1898), French painter **12** 492-493
Davies, Arthur Bowen **4** 409-410
Rodin, Auguste **13** 236-238

Puy, Jean (1876-1960), French painter
Matisse, Henri **10** 336-337

Pydna, battle of (168 B.C.)
Scipio Africanus Minor, Publius Cornelius Aemilianus **14** 62-63

Pygmalion (play)
Kaiser, Georg **8** 411-412

Pygmalion and Galatea (play)
Gilbert, William Schwenck **6** 314-315

Pyle, Alden (literary character)
Greene, Graham **6** 523-524

PYLE, ERNIE (Earnest Taylor Pyle;
1900-1945), American war correspondent during World War II **12** 493-494
Miller, Arthur **11** 25-26

Pylon (novel)
Faulkner, William **5** 395-397

Pylos (town, Greece)
Cleon **4** 104-105
Schliemann, Heinrich **14** 17-18

PYM, FRANCIS (Francis Leslie Pym; born
1922), British statesman **12** 494-495

PYM, JOHN (1584-1643), English states-
man **12** 495-496
Cromwell, Oliver **4** 317-320
Hampden, John **7** 110-111
Vane, Henry **15** 425-426

Pyncheons (literary characters)
Hawthorne, Nathaniel **7** 212-215

PYNCHON, THOMAS (Thomas Ruggles
  Pynchon, Jr.; born 1937), American writer
  12 496-498

Pyramid (mathematics)
  Archimedes **1** 277-280
  Euclid **5** 327-329
  Eudoxus of Cnidus **5** 329-330

Pyramids (Egypt)
  Imhotep **8** 116-117
  Khufu **8** 540-541
  Petrie, William Matthew Flinders
    12 261-262
  Piankhi **12** 288-289
  Zoser **16** 531

Pyramids, battle of the (1798)
  Murat, Joachim **11** 253-254

Napoleon I **11** 306-310

Pyrenees, Peace of the (1659)
  Mazarin, Jules **10** 379-380
  Philip IV **12** 275

Pyrgopolynices (literary character)
  Plautus **12** 348-350

Pyrrhias (literary character)
  Menander **10** 477-478

Pyrrhus (literary character)
  Racine, Jean Baptiste **12** 532-535

Pyrrhus, battle of (275 B.C.)
  Ptolemy II **12** 472-473

PYTHAGORAS (circa 575-circa 495 B.C.),
  Greek philosopher, scientist, and religious teacher **12** 498-499
  geometry
    Euclid **5** 327-329
  influence of
    Plutarch **12** 359-360
    Zarlino, Gioseffo **16** 490-491
  philosophy
    Copernicus, Nicolaus **4** 226-227
    Empedocles **5** 282
    Zeno of Elea **16** 500

PYTHEAS (c. 380 B.C.-c. 300 B.C.), Greek
  explorer **12** 499-500

Pythian Ode VIII (poem series)
  Pindar **12** 312-313

Q

Q fever (medicine)
Burnet, Frank Macfarlane **3** 146-147

QABOOS IBN SA'ID (born 1940), ruler of the Sultanate of Oman **12** 501-502

Qadesh, battle of (1299 B.C.)
Ramses II **13** 22-23

Qadisiya, battle of (636)
Omar ibn al-Khattab **11** 508-509

Qajar dynasty (Persia; 1794-1925)
Agha Mohammad Khan **1** 80-81
Taqi Khan Amir-e Kabir, Mirza **15** 106-107

QIANLONG (Ch'ien-lung and Hung-li; 1711-1799), Chinese emperor
Ho-shen **7** 512-513
Shih Ko-fa **14** 194-195
Yüan Mei **16** 479-480

Qift (town, Egypt)
see Coptos

Qua Cursum Ventus (poem)
Clough, Arthur Hugh **4** 123-124

Quaderni di Serafino Gubbio operatore (novel)
Pirandello, Luigi **12** 319-321

Quadragesimo anno (encyclical)
Dollfuss, Engelbert **5** 47
John, XXIII **8** 277-280
Pius XI **12** 337-339

Quadriga (sculpture)
Marini, Marino **10** 260-262

Quadrille (play)
Coward, Noel **4** 279-280

Quadros, Janio (1917-1992), Brazilian politician
Goulart, João **6** 467-469

Quadruple Alliance (1814; 1834)
Castlereagh, Viscount **3** 363-364
Talleyrand, Charles Maurice de **15** 89-90

Quaeris quot mihi basiationes (poem)
Catullus, Gaius Valerius **3** 377-378

Quai des Grands Augustins, Paris (painting)
Morrice, James Wilson **11** 181-182

Quaid-i-Azam
see Jinnah, Mohammad Ali

Quakers (Society of Friends; religion)
England
Fox, George **6** 37-38
Lilburne, John **9** 409-410
influenced by
Boehme, Jacob **2** 357
U.S. (colonial)
Bradford, William **2** 476-477
Dickinson, John **4** 543-544
Endecott, John **5** 284-285
Franklin, Benjamin **6** 60-64
Penn, William **12** 200-202
Stuyvesant, Peter **15** 5-6
Williams, Roger **16** 304-305
Woolman, John **16** 382-383
U.S. (19th century)
Coffin, Levi **4** 135
Crandall, Prudence **4** 291
Cuffe, Paul **4** 331-332
Dow, Neal **5** 89-90
Hicks, Edward **7** 375
Mott, Lucretia Coffin **11** 212-213
U.S. (20th century)
Hoover, Herbert Clark **7** 483-485
Nixon, Richard Milhous **11** 401-404

Quality Street (play)
Barrie, James Matthew **2** 21-22

Quand vous serez bien vieille (poem)
Ronsard, Pierre de **13** 271-273

Quand'ero matto (story)
Pirandello, Luigi **12** 319-321

Quando si è qualcuno (play)
Pirandello, Luigi **12** 319-321

Quantum theory (physics)
basic laws
Born, Max **2** 420-421
Franck, James **6** 49-52
blackbody radiation
Jeans, James Hopwood **8** 235-236
Planck, Max Karl Ernst Ludwig **12** 342-344
Bohr atom
Bohr, Niels Henrik David **2** 366-368
Franck, James **6** 49-52
Pauli, Wolfgang Ernst **12** 149
Rutherford, Ernest **13** 384-387
electron-pair bond
Pauling, Linus Carl **12** 150-152
gauge theory
Weinberg, Steven **16** 175-177
mathematics
Calderón, Alberto P. **3** 219-220
Dirac, Paul Adrien Maurice **5** 23-24
Fermi, Enrico **5** 422-424
Hamilton, William Rowan **7** 99-100
Von Neumann, John **16** 27-28
Wigner, Eugene Paul **16** 268-269
mazer
Ramsey, Norman Foster Jr. **13** 25-27
Townes, Charles Hard **15** 281-282
mesons
Bhabha, Homi Jehangir **2** 253-254
Yang, Chen Ning **16** 437-438
photoelectric effect
Einstein, Albert **5** 228-231
Millikan, Robert Andrews **11** 33-35
Oppenheimer, J. Robert **11** 525-526
positron predicted
Anderson, Carl David **1** 214-215
Dirac, Paul Adrien Maurice **5** 23-24
Oppenheimer, J. Robert **11** 525-526
quantum electrodynamics
Bloch, Felix **2** 328-330
Feynman, Richard Phillips **5** 432-434
Tomonaga, Sin-itiro **15** 265-266
quantum field theory
Landau, Lev Davidovich **9** 184-185
Pauli, Wolfgang Ernst **12** 149
quantum mechanics
Penrose, Roger **12** 204-205
Ruska, Ernst August Friedrich **13** 370-371
relativity and
Eddington, Arthur Stanley **5** 201-202
wave mechanics
de Broglie, Louis **4** 442-444
Heisenberg, Werner Karl **7** 261-263

705

Mössbauer, Rudolf **11** 208-209
Schrödinger, Erwin **14** 31-33

Quantz, Johann Joachim (1697-1773),
German flutist and composer
Bach, Carl Philipp Emanuel **1** 414-415
Corelli, Arcangelo **4** 230-231

Quaregna e di Cerreto, Conti di
see Avogadro, Lorenzo Romano
Amedeo Carlo

Quark (hypothetical particle)
Gell-Mann, Murray **6** 257-258

Quarrel of Brest (novel)
Genet, Jean **6** 262-263

Quartering Act
see Intolerable Acts (1774)

Quarterly Review (journal)
Macaulay, Thomas Babington **10** 79-80
Scott, Walter **14** 68-70

Quartet (music)
flute
Mozart, Wolfgang Amadeus
11 218-221
piano
Brahms, Johannes **2** 490-492
Copland, Aaron **4** 227-228
Fauré, Gabriel Urbain **5** 397-398
Mendelssohn, Moses **10** 488-489
string
Bartók, Béla **2** 35-36
Beethoven, Ludwig van **2** 114-117,
461, 462
Berg, Alban **2** 186-187
Bloch, Ernest **2** 326-327
Borodin, Aleksandr Profirevich
2 422-423
Carter, Elliott Cook Jr. **3** 338-339
Copland, Aaron **4** 227-228
Debussy, Achille Claude **4** 445-447
Dvořák, Antonin **5** 168-169
Ginastera, Alberto Evaristo
6 328-329
Grieg, Edvard Hagerup **6** 541-542
Haydn, Franz Joseph **7** 219-221,
150
Henze, Hans Werner **7** 314
Hindemith, Paul **7** 399-400
Janáček, Leoš **8** 219
Mozart, Wolfgang Amadeus
11 218-221
Ravel, Maurice Joseph **13** 54-55
Schoenberg, Arnold **14** 24-26
Shostakovich, Dmitri Dmitrievich
14 204-205
Walton, William Turner **16** 92-93
Webern, Anton **16** 160-162

Quartic equations (mathematics)
Cardano, Geronimo **3** 285-286
Lagrange, Joseph Louis **9** 164-166

Quarton, Enguerrand
see Charonton, Enguerrand

Quasimodo (literary character)
Hugo, Victor Marie **8** 22-25

QUASIMODO, SALVATORE (1901-1968),
Italian poet, translator, and critic **12** 506
Vittorini, Elio **16** 2-3

Quat, Phan Huy (born 1909), Vietnamese
physician and politician
Thieu, Nguyen Van **15** 182-183

Quaternions (physics)
Hamilton, William Rowan **7** 99-100

Quatorze Juillet, Le (play)
Rolland, Romain **13** 260

Quatre Nations, Collège des (Institut de
France, Paris)
Le Vau, Louis **9** 360-361

Quatre premiers livres de la Franciade, Les
see Franciade

Quattro Santi (painting)
Andrea del Sarto **1** 224-225

QUAY, MATTHEW STANLEY (1833-1904),
American politician **12** 507
Mellon, Andrew William **10** 469-470
Penrose, Boies **12** 203-204

QUAYLE, J(AMES) DANFORTH (born
1947), vice president under George Bush
12 507-509

Que Viva Mexico (film)
Eisenstein, Sergei Mikhailovich
5 240-242

Quebec (city, Canada)
Brûlé, Étienne **3** 67-68
Cartier, Jacques **3** 343-344
Champlain, Samuel de **3** 419-421
Krieghoff, Cornelius **9** 101
see also Quebec, battles of

Quebec (province, Canada)
Bourassa, Joseph-Henri-Napoleon
2 446-447
Bourassa, Robert **2** 447-449
Carleton, Guy **3** 300-301
Chrétien, Joseph-Jacques-Jean **4** 24-25
Laurier, Wilfrid **9** 232-234
Laval, Francois Xavier de **9** 235-236
Lévesque, René **9** 362-363
Murray, James **11** 261-262
Parizeau, Jacques **12** 96-99
Pearson, Lester Bowles **12** 174-175
Scott, Francis Reginald **14** 66-67
Trudeau, Pierre Elliott **15** 309-311
Wise, John **16** 343-344
see also Canada; Quebec (city)

Quebec, battles of
1759
Carleton, Guy **3** 300-301
Howe, William **7** 538-539
Montcalm de Saint-Véran, Marquis
de **11** 122-123
Murray, James **11** 261-262
Vaudreuil-Cavagnal, Marquis de
15 444
Wolfe, James **16** 354-355
1775
Arnold, Benedict **1** 309-310
Montgomery, Richard **11** 138-139
Morgan, Daniel **11** 160-161

Quebec Act
see Intolerable Acts (1774)

Queeg, Captain (literary character)
Bogart, Humphrey **2** 363-364

Queen Anne's Bounty (England)
Burnet, Gilbert **3** 147
Swift, Jonathan **15** 51-54

Queen Anne's War (1701-1713)
see Spanish Succession, War of the

Queen Mab (poem)
Shelley, Percy Bysshe **14** 176-178

Queen Mary (play)
Tennyson, Alfred **15** 144-146

Queen Mother (British)
Elizabeth, the Queen Mother **5** 261-263

Queen Mother, The (play)
Swinburne, Algernon Charles **15** 54-55

Queen of Hearts (painting)
de Kooning, Willem **4** 468-469

Queen of Spades, The (story and opera)
Pushkin, Aleksandr Sergeevich
12 489-491
Tchaikovsky, Peter Ilyich **15** 130-132

Queenie, My Own (song)
Berlin, Irving **2** 200-201

Queens
see Statesmen

Queen's Christy Minstrels (theatrical
group)
Christy, Edwin P. **4** 34-35

Queen's College (London, England)
Maurice, John Frederick Denison
10 349-350

Queen's House (Greenwich, England)
Jones, Inigo **8** 333-334

Queensberry, 8th Marquess of (John Sholto
Douglas; 1844-1900), English boxing
patron
Wilde, Oscar Fingall O'Flahertie Wills
16 272-273

Queensland (state, North East Australia)
Chelmsford, Frederic John Napier The-
siger **3** 497
Fisher, Andrew **5** 462
Griffith, Samuel Walker **6** 545-546
Kenny, Elizabeth **8** 509-510

Queenston Heights, battle of (1812)
Brock, Isaac **3** 12-13
Robinson, John Beverley **13** 210

Queirós, Pedro Fernandés de
see Quirós, Pedro Fernandés de

Quelques aspects de la vie de Paris (lithograph)
Bonnard, Pierre **2** 395-396

Quem tem farelos? (play)
Vicente, Gil **15** 479-480

Quentin Durward (novel)
Scott, Walter **14** 68-70

QUERCIA, JACOPO DELLA (1374?-1438), Italian sculptor and architect **12** 509
Agostino di Duccio **1** 86
Donatello **5** 55-56
Ghiberti, Lorenzo **6** 291-292
Sassetta **13** 492

Querela pacis
see Complaint of Peace, The

Querétaro (city; Mexico)
Carranza, Venustiano **3** 321-322
Maximilian of Hapsburg **10** 358-360

Querry (literary character)
Greene, Graham **6** 523-524

Quesada, Gonzalo Jiménez de
see Jiménez de Quesada, Gonzalo

Quesnay, Francois (1694-1774), French physician and economist
du Pont de Nemours, Pierre Samuel **5** 155-156
Smith, Adam **14** 283-284
Turgot, Anne Robert Jacques **15** 348-349

Quesnel, Pasquier (1634-1719), French theologian
Jansen, Cornelis **8** 220-221

Quest, The (ballet)
Walton, William Turner **16** 92-93

Quest of the Silver Fleece, The (novel)
Du Bois, William Edward Burghardt **5** 116-118

Questa sera si recita a soggetto (play)
Pirandello, Luigi **12** 319-321

Question of Upbringing, A (novel)
Powell, Anthony **12** 422-423

QUÉTELET, LAMBERT ADOLPHE JACQUES (1796-1874), Belgian statistician and astronomer **12** 510-511

Quetzalcoatl (Aztec god)
Montezuma, II **11** 128-129

QUEVEDO Y VILLEGAS, FRANCISCO GÓMEZ DE (1580-1645), Spanish poet, satirist, and novelist **12** 511
Góngora y Argote, Luis de **6** 427-428

QUEZON, MANUEL LUIS (1878-1944), Philippine statesman **12** 511-513
Aguinaldo, Emilio **1** 88
Macapagal, Diosdado P. **10** 74-76
Osmeña, Sergio **12** 22-24
Quirino, Elpidio **12** 519-520
Rómulo, Carlos P. **13** 270-271
Roxas, Manuel **13** 331-332

Quia Emptores, Statute of (1290; England)
Edward I **5** 208-210

Quidor, John (1801-1881), American painter
Allston, Washington **1** 176-177

Quids (political party)
Randolph, John **13** 30

Quiet American, The (novel)
Greene, Graham **6** 523-524

Quiet Man, The (film)
Ford, John **6** 7-8

Quietism (religious movement)
China
Lao Tzu **9** 201-202
Europe
Bossuet, Jacques Bénigne **2** 431-432
Bright, John **3** 6-7
Fénelon, François de Salignac de la Mothe **5** 410-411
Molinos, Miguel de **11** 88-89
Zurbarán, Francisco de **16** 534-535

Quigley Preparatory Seminary (Chicago)
Mundelein, George William **11** 248-249

Quillacinga Indians (South America)
Benalcázar, Sebastián de **2** 145-146

QUIMBY, EDITH H. (1891-1982), American biophysicist

Quimby, Phineas P. (1802-1866), American mental healer
Eddy, Mary Baker **5** 202

QUIN SHI HUANG-DI (250 B.C.-210 B.C.), Chinese emperor
Li Ssu **9** 442-443

Quinault, Philippe (1635-1688), French poet and dramatist
Gluck, Christoph Willibald **6** 372-374
Lully, Jean Baptiste **10** 40-41

QUINE, WILLARD VAN ORMAN (born 1908), American philosopher **12** 514-515

Quinet, Edgar (1803-1875), French writer and politician
Michelet, Jules **11** 5-6

Quinine (drug)
Baikie, William Balfour **1** 440
K'ang-hsi **8** 423-426
Mutis, José Celestino **11** 278-279

Quintana, Manuel José (1772-1857), Spanish writer and statesman
Saavedra, Angel de **13** 398

Quintet (music)
clarinet
Mozart, Wolfgang Amadeus **11** 218-221
piano
Bloch, Ernest **2** 326-327
Brahms, Johannes **2** 490-492

Fauré, Gabriel Urbain **5** 397-398
Franck, César **6** 48-49
Mozart, Wolfgang Amadeus **11** 218-221
Webern, Anton **16** 160-162
string
Franck, César **6** 48-49
Mozart, Wolfgang Amadeus **11** 218-221
woodwind
Henze, Hans Werner **7** 314
Nielsen, Carl August **11** 388-389

QUINTILIAN (circa 35-circa 99), Roman rhetorician and literary critic **12** 518-519
Celsus, Aulus Cornelius **3** 393
Martialis, Marcus Valerius **10** 286-287
Ovid **12** 34-36
Phidias **12** 265-267
Sallust **13** 454
Vespasian **15** 475-476

Quintina (musical composition)
Krenek, Ernst **9** 98-99

QUIRINO, ELPIDIO (1890-1956), Philippine statesman **12** 519-520
Magsaysay, Ramon **10** 130-131

QUIROGA, HORACIO (1878-1937), Uruguayan writer **12** 520-521

QUIROGA, JUAN FACUNDO (1788/1790-1835), Argentine caudillo **12** 521-522

Quirós, Pedro Fernandés de (1560?-1614), Portuguese navigator
Mendaña de Neyra, Álvaro de **10** 483

Quit India resolution (1942)
Gandhi, Mohandas Karamchand **6** 201-204
Nehru, Jawaharlal **11** 332-334
Pandit, Vijaya Lakshmi **12** 83-84

Quito (city; Ecuador)
Benalcázar, Sebastián de **2** 145-146
García Moreno, Gabriel **6** 209-210

Quitte pour la peur (play)
Vigny, Comte de **15** 494-495

Quivira (fabled king.; American South West)
Coronado, Francisco Vásquez de **4** 247

Quo Vadis? (novel)
Sienkiewicz, Henryk **14** 216-217

Quorum of Twelve Apostles (Mormon religion)
Young, Brigham **16** 469-470

Qur'ān
see Koran

Quraysh (Arab tribe)
Abu Bakr **1** 31-32
Ali **1** 155-156

R

Rabbenu Gershom
see Gershom ben Judah

Rabbis
see Religious leaders, Jewish

"Rabbit" series (novels)
Updike, John **15** 390-392

RABEARIVELO, JEAN JOSEPH
(1901-1937), Malagasy poet **12** 523-524

RABELAIS, FRANÇOIS (circa 1494-circa
1553), French humanist, doctor, and
writer **12** 524-526
l'Orme, Philibert de **9** 519
Melville, Herman **10** 472-476
Rolland, Romain **13** 260

RABI, ISIDOR ISAAC (1898-1988), American physicist **12** 526-527

Rabies (medicine)
Pasteur, Louis **12** 125-127

RABIN, YITZCHAK (1922-1995), Israeli
statesman **12** 527-529
Dayan, Moshe **4** 429-431

Rabindranath
see Tagore

Rabinowitz, Sholem
see Sholem Aleichem

Race (anthropology)
Benedict, Ruth Fulton **2** 154-155
Boas, Franz **2** 349-351
Frazier, Edward Franklin **6** 77
Freyre, Gilberto **6** 106-107
Gumplowicz, Ludwig **7** 41
Handlin, Oscar **7** 121-122
Le Bon, Gustave **9** 268-269

Race car drivers
Andretti, Mario **1** 228-230
Muldowney, Shirley **11** 236-238

Race of Riderless Horses on the Corso
(painting)
Géricault, Jean Louis André Théodore
6 280-281

Race Relations, American Council on
Redfield, Robert **13** 73-74

Race Relations, Institute of
(Swarthmore College)
Bunche, Ralph Johnson **3** 121-122

Races at Epsom (painting)
Géricault, Jean Louis André Théodore
6 280-281

Rachel (sculpture)
Michelangelo Buonarroti **11** 2-5

Rachel Weeping (painting)
Peale, Charles Willson **12** 169-171

RACHMANINOV, SERGEI VASILIEVICH
(1873-1943), Russian composer, pianist,
and conductor **12** 531-532
Horowitz, Vladimir **7** 509-510
Prokofiev, Sergei Sergeevich
12 458-460
Scriabin, Alexander Nikolayevich
14 71-72
Sikorsky, Igor **14** 223-224
Tchaikovsky, Peter Ilyich **15** 130-132

Racial rhythms (poems)
Hughes, Langston **8** 18-19

RACINE, JEAN BAPTISTE (1639-1699),
French dramatist **12** 532-535
contemporaries
Boileau-Despréaux, Nicholas
2 369-371
Corneille, Pierre **4** 234-236
La Fontaine, Jean de **9** 156-157
influence of
Chénier, André Marie **3** 500-501
Gluck, Christoph Willibald
6 372-374
Lowell, Robert Trail Spence Jr.
10 16-17
patrons
Condé, Prince de **4** 193-194
Louis XIV **9** 531-533

Racine and Shakespeare (book)
Stendhal **14** 422-425

Racing horses
Taylor, Edward Plunket **15** 123-124

Racism
Baldwin, James Arthur **1** 465-466
Fanon, Frantz **5** 379-380

Gandhi, Mohandas Karamchand
6 201-204
Gobineau, Comte de **6** 375-376
Smith, Ian Douglas **14** 291-293
Spengler, Oswald **14** 372-373
Wagner, Richard **16** 40-43
Welensky, Roy **16** 188
see also Apartheid; Nazism

Racism (United States)
and environmental issues
Chavis, Benjamin **3** 491-493
criticism of
hooks, bell **7** 477-481
psychological effects of
Clark, Kenneth B. **4** 78-79
victims
see African American history (Unit-
ed States)
white opponents
Ames, Adelbert **1** 198
Hope, John **7** 489-490
Howells, William Dean **7** 539-541
Johnson, Guy Benton **8** 299-300
Odum, Howard Washington
11 474-476
Ovington, Mary White **12** 36-37
Smith, Lillian Eugenia **14** 298-299
see also Civil rights movement;
Minority rights
white supremacy
Cartwright, Peter **3** 344-345
Clay, Henry **4** 94-96
Douglas, Stephen Arnold **5** 80-82
George, James Zachariah **6** 276-277
Lamar, Lucius Quintus Cincinnatus
9 170-171
Miller, Samuel Freeman **11** 29-30
Smith, Joseph **14** 297-298
Watson, Thomas Edward **16** 139
see also Ku Klux Klan

Rack locomotive
Stephenson, George and Robert
14 432-433

Radagaisus (died 406), German chieftain
Stilicho, Flavius **14** 452-453

Radamisto (musical composition)
Handel, George Frederick **7** 116-119

Radar (science)
   Appleton, Edward Victor **1** 265-266
   Farnsworth, Philo T. **5** 386-387
   Rabi, Isidor Isaac **12** 526-527
   Watson-Watt, Robert Alexander
      16 140-141

Radcliffe College
   Horner, Matina Souretis **7** 506-508

Radcliffe Library (Oxford)
   Gibbs, James **6** 301-302

RADCLIFFE-BROWN, A(LFRED) R(EGI-NALD) (1881-1955), English anthropologist **12** 535-536
   Gluckman, Max **6** 374-375

RADEK, KARL BERNARDOVICH (1885-1939), Russian Communist leader **12** 536-537
   Trotsky, Leon **15** 302-305

Radewyns, Florent (1350-1400), Dutch evangelist
   Groote, Gerard **7** 12-13

Radha (Indian dance)
   St. Denis, Ruth **13** 430-431

RADHAKRISHNAN, SARVEPALLI (1888-1995), Indian philosopher and statesman **12** 537-538
   Shankara **14** 150-151

Radiance of the King, The (novel)
   Laye, Camara **9** 257-259

Radiant Bodies (musical composition)
   Messiaen, Olivier **10** 528-529

Radiant City (urban plan)
   Le Corbusier **9** 274-275

Radiata (zoology)
   Cuvier, Georges Léopold **4** 357-359

Radiation
   see Radioactivity

Radical (horse)
   Randolph, John **13** 30

Radical Citizens party (Hungary)
   Polanyi, Karl **12** 372

Radical party (Argentina)
   Frondizi, Arturo **6** 127-128
   Irigoyen, Hipólito **8** 139-140

Radical party (France)
   Bourgeois, Léon **2** 450-451
   Daladier, Édouard **4** 369
   Herriot, Édouard **7** 339-340
   Mendès France, Pierre **10** 492-493
   Poincaré, Raymond **12** 366-368

Radical party (Italy)
   Vittorini, Elio **16** 2-3

Radical party (Peru)
   González Prada, Manuel **6** 431

Radical Republicans (U.S. politics)
   Civil War policy
      Andrew, John Albion **1** 230-231
      Brown, Benjamin Gratz **3** 32-33
      Chase, Philander **3** 472-473
      Davis, Henry Winter **4** 415-416

      Frémont, John Charles **6** 97-98
      Lincoln, Abraham **9** 415-418
      Sherman, John **14** 184-185
      Stevens, Thaddeus **14** 442-443
      Wade, Benjamin Franklin **16** 38-39
   Johnson opposed
      Johnson, Andrew **8** 294-295
      Stanton, Edwin McMasters
         14 401-402
      Wilson, James Harold **16** 324-325
   Reconstruction policy
      see Reconstruction (United States)

Radical Socialist party (France)
   Daladier, Édouard **4** 369
   Servan-Schreiber, Jean-Jacques
      14 113-115

Radicalism (politics)
   American
      Chandler, Zachariah **3** 425-426
      Hancock, John **7** 114-116
      Otis, James Jr. **12** 25-27
      Owen, Robert Dale **12** 40-41
      Ruffin, Edmund **13** 354-355
      Sacco and Vanzetti **13** 408-410
   British
      Bright, John **3** 6-7
      Cobbett, William **4** 126-127
      Wilkes, John **16** 280-281
   French
      Dreyfus, Alfred **5** 103-105
      Francis II **6** 43-44
   Russian
      Dostoevsky, Fyodor **5** 74-77

RADIN, PAUL (1883-1959), American anthropologist and ethnographer **12** 538-539

Radio (communications)
   Australia
      Flynn, John **5** 497-498
   development
      Appleton, Edward Victor **1** 265-266
      Armstrong, Edwin Howard
         1 302-303
      Bose, Jagadis Chandra **2** 429-430
      De Forest, Lee **4** 459-460
      Edison, Thomas Alva **5** 206-208
      Marconi, Guglielmo **10** 239-240
      Pupin, Michael Idvorsky **12** 483-484
      Sarnoff, David **13** 485-486
   managers
      Paley, William S. **12** 72-75
   personalities
      Benny, Jack **2** 174-176
      Brice, Fanny **3** 1-2
      Brothers, Joyce **3** 26-28
      Burns, George **3** 153-155
      Cantor, Eddie **3** 264-265
      Cronkite, Walter Leland Jr.
         4 321-322
      Crosby, Harry Lillis **4** 324-326
      Fields, W. C. **5** 444
      Hope, Bob **7** 487-489
      Huntley and Brinkley **8** 49-51
      Jessel, George **8** 249-251

      Murrow, Edward Roscoe
         11 265-266
      O'Hair, Madalyn Murray
         11 484-485
      Post, Emily Price **12** 409-410
      Terkel, Louis **15** 152-153
      Welles, Orson **16** 190-191
      Westheimer, Ruth Karola
         16 214-215
   regulation (United States)
      Coolidge, John Calvin **4** 217-219
   religious uses
      Aberhart, William **1** 26-27
      Coughlin, Charles Edward
         4 265-266
      Graham, William Franklin Jr.
         6 487-488
      Pius XII **12** 339-340

Radio astronomy (science)
   Bell Burnell, Susan Jocelyn **2** 133-134
   Lovell, Alfred Charles Bernard **10** 8-9

Radio Corporation of America (RCA)
   Armstrong, Edwin Howard **1** 302-303
   Elsasser, Walter Maurice **5** 277-278
   Sarnoff, David **13** 485-486
   Young, Owen D. **16** 473-474
   Zworykin, Vladimir Kosma **16** 539-540
   see also RCA Building

Radioactive dating (chemistry)
   Diop, Cheikh Anta **5** 21-22
   Libby, Willard Frank **9** 397-398
   Rutherford, Ernest **13** 384-387

Radioactivity (physics)
   and medicine
      Quimby, Edith H. **12** 513-514
   artificial
      Fermi, Enrico **5** 422-424
      Hahn, Otto **7** 64-65
      Joliot-Curie, Irène **8** 325-327
      Joliot-Curie, Jean Frédéric
         8 327-328
   blackbody radiation
      Jeans, James Hopwood **8** 235-236
      Planck, Max Karl Ernst Ludwig
         12 342-344
   Compton effect
      Bothe, Walther **2** 438-439
      Compton, Arthur Holly **4** 186-188
   infrared radiation
      Tyndall, John **15** 374
   natural discovered
      Becquerel, Antoine Henri **2** 108-109
      Curie, Marie Sklodowska **4** 339-341
      Curie, Pierre **4** 341-344
      Duhem, Pierre Maurice Marie **5** 129
   radioactive decay
      Geiger, Hans **6** 251-253
      Richards, Theodore William
         13 137-138
      Rutherford, Ernest **13** 384-387
      Soddy, Frederick **14** 321-323
   radioactive elements
      Geiger, Hans **6** 251-253
      Hahn, Otto **7** 64-65
      Hevesy, George Charles de **7** 371

Rutherford, Ernest **13** 384-387
Soddy, Frederick **14** 321-323
radioactive recoil
Hahn, Otto **7** 64-65
radioactive tracers
Calvin, Melvin **3** 242-243
Hevesy, George Charles de **7** 371
see also Isotope
transmutation of elements
Rutherford, Ernest **13** 384-387
see also Alpha radiation; Beta radiation; Cosmic rays; Gamma radiation; Radioactive dating; X-rays

Radiochemistry (science)
Boltwood, Bertram Borden **2** 378-379
Hevesy, George Charles de **7** 371
Soddy, Frederick **14** 321-323

Radiodetector (communications)
Marconi, Guglielmo **10** 239-240

Radioimmunoassay (RIA)
Yalow, Rosalyn S. **16** 427-428

Radiology (science)
Curie, Marie Sklodowska **4** 339-341
Quimby, Edith H. **12** 513-514
Szilard, Leo **15** 64-66

Radiometer (instrument)
Crookes, William **4** 323-324

Radiotelephony (communications)
Marconi, Guglielmo **10** 239-240

RADISSON, PIERRE-ESPRIT (circa
1636-1710), French explorer **12** 539-540

Radium (element—chemistry)
Boltwood, Bertram Borden **2** 378-379
Curie, Marie Sklodowska **4** 339-341
Curie, Pierre **4** 341-344
Hevesy, George Charles de **7** 371
Quimby, Edith H. **12** 513-514
Ramsay, William **13** 21-22
Soddy, Frederick **14** 321-323

Radium Institute (Paris)
Curie, Marie Sklodowska **4** 339-341
Joliot-Curie, Jean Frédéric **8** 327-328

Radomyslsky, Grigori Evseevich
see Zinoviev, Grigori Evseevich

Radon (element—chemistry)
Mendeleev, Dmitrii Ivanovich
10 486-488
Ramsay, William **13** 21-22

Radowitz, J. von (1797-1853), Prussian
general
Frederick William IV **6** 87-88

Rafaellino del Garbo (1466-1524), Italian
painter
Andrea del Sarto **1** 224-225
Bronzino **3** 19

Raff, Joachim (1822-1882), German composer
MacDowell, Edward Alexander
10 87-88

RAFFLES, SIR THOMAS STAMFORD
(1781-1826), English colonial administrator **13** 1-2

Coen, Jan Pieterszoon **4** 133

Rafi
see Labor party (Israel)

RAFSANJANI, AKBAR HASHEMI (born
1934), president of Iran **13** 3-4

Raft of the Medusa (painting)
Géricault, Jean Louis André Théodore
6 280-281

Ragas (musical form)
Rabindranath Tagore **12** 529-531

Rage to Live, A (novel)
O'Hara, John **11** 485

Ragged Dick (juvenile book)
Alger, Horatio **1** 153-154

Ragged School movement (England; 1840s)
Shaftesbury, 7th Earl of **14** 137-138

Raggedy Man, The (poem)
Riley, James Whitcomb **13** 170-171

Raghuvamsa (epic)
Kalidasa **8** 414-415

Ragley Hall (Warwickshire)
Gibbs, James **6** 301-302

Ragnarok (book)
Donnelly, Ignatius **5** 62

RAHNER, KARL (1904-1984), German
Catholic theologian **13** 4-5
Küng, Hans **9** 129-130

RAI, LALA LAJPAT (1865-1928), Indian
nationalist leader **13** 5-6

Railroad Labor Act (1926; United States)
Coolidge, John Calvin **4** 217-219

Railroads
Asia
Chulalongkorn **4** 43-45
Sato, Eisaku **13** 495-496
Canada
Crerar, Thomas Alexander **4** 306
Fleming, Sandford **5** 485-486
Galt, Alexander Tilloch **6** 190-191
Meighen, Arthur **10** 459-460
Smith, Donald Alexander
14 288-289
Van Horne, William Cornelius
15 429-430
Europe
Brunel, Isambard Kingdom **3** 69-70
Cavour, Conte di **3** 385-386
Krupp **9** 109-111
Moltke, Helmuth Karl Bernard von
11 90-91
Nicholas I **11** 377-378
Stephenson, George and Robert
14 432-433
Witte, Sergei Yulyevich **16** 349-350
Latin America
Cárdenas, Lázaro **3** 286-287
Estrada Cabrera, Manuel **5** 325-326
García Moreno, Gabriel **6** 209-210
Keith, Minor Cooper **8** 476-477
Meiggs, Henry **10** 458-459
Perón, Juan Domingo **12** 228-230

Van Horne, William Cornelius
15 429-430
Wheelwright, William **16** 223-224
U.S.
see Railroads (United States)

Railroads (United States)
builders and executives
see Business and industrial leaders,
American—railroad industry
equipment
Armour, Philip Danforth **1** 302
Farmer, Moses Gerrish **5** 385
Hill, James Jerome **7** 388-389
Langley, Samuel Pierpont **9** 195-196
Pullman, George Mortimer
12 482-483
Rockefeller, John Davison
13 226-228
Westinghouse, George **16** 215
promotion and speculation
Fisk, James **5** 464-465
Frémont, John Charles **6** 97-98
Gadsden, James **6** 165-166
Kennedy, John Stewart **8** 507-508
Morgan, John Pierpont **11** 163-165
Morgan, Junius Spencer **11** 166-167
Schiff, Jacob Henry **14** 2-3
Stevens, John **14** 439-440
regulation
Bryan, William Jennings **3** 80-82
George, Henry **6** 276
Hampton, Wade III **7** 112
Hughes, Charles Evans **8** 15-16
Waite, Morrison Remick **16** 46
Wallace, Henry **16** 73
unions
Debs, Eugene Victor **4** 444-445
La Follette, Robert Marion
9 155-156
Rockefeller, John Davison
13 226-228
see also Pullman strike

Railway at Murnau (painting)
Kandinsky, Wassily **8** 420-422

Raimondi, Marcantonio (circa 1480-circa
1534), Italian engraver
Lucas van Leyden **10** 20-21

Rain (play)
Maugham, William Somerset
10 344-345

Rain, battle of
see Lech River, battle of (1632)

Rain, Steam, and Speed... (painting)
Turner, Joseph Mallord William
15 352-354

Rain Storm on the Ohashi Bridge (print)
Hiroshige, Ando **7** 412-413

Rainaldi, Carlo (1611-1691), Italian architect
Maderno, Carlo **10** 117-118

Rainbow (frigate)
Franklin, John **6** 64-65

Rainbow (meteorology)
Dunbar, William **5** 143-144

Rainbow, The (novel)
Lawrence, David Herbert **9** 247-248

Rainbow, The (poem)
Wordsworth, William **16** 385-388

Rainmaker (stories)
Ekwensi, Cyprian **5** 242-243

Rains (poem)
Perse, Saint-John **12** 242-243

Rainy Day, The (poem)
Longfellow, Henry Wadsworth
9 499-500

Raisin in the Sun (play)
Davis, Ossie **4** 421-422

Raisin in the Sun, A (play, movie)
Hansberry, Lorraine Vivian **7** 130-131

Raising of Drusiana (painting)
Giotto **6** 342-345

Raising of the Cross (painting)
Rubens, Peter Paul **13** 339-342

Raising of the Pagan King's Son (fresco)
Masaccio **10** 312-313

RAJAGOPALACHARI, CHAKRAVARTI
(1879-1972), Indian nationalist leader
13 6-7
Kamaraj, Kumaraswami **8** 415

RAJARAJA I (985-1014), Indian statesman
13 7

Rajasthan (state, India)
Ala-ud-din **1** 102-103

Rajendra I (1012-1044), Cola ruler in India
Rajaraja I **13** 7

Rajmohan's Wife (novel)
Chatterji, Bankimchandra **3** 480-481

RAJNEESH, BHAGWAN SHREE (Rahneesh
Chandra Mohan; 1931-1990), Indian religious leader **13** 7-9

Rajputs (Indian people)
Aurangzeb **1** 377
Bach, Carl Philipp Emanuel **1** 414-415

Rake's Progress, The (opera; Stravinsky)
Auden, Wystan Hugh **1** 364-366
Stravinsky, Igor Fedorovich **14** 502-506

Rake's Progress, The (prints)
Hogarth, William **7** 446-447
Stravinsky, Igor Fedorovich **14** 502-506

Raleigh (ship)
Barry, John **2** 24-25

RALEIGH, SIR WALTER (or Ralegh; circa
1552-1618), English statesman, soldier,
courtier, explorer, and poet **13** 9-11
Coke, Edward **4** 141-142
Drake, Francis **5** 94-96
Elizabeth I **5** 263-266
Essex, 2d Earl of **5** 321-322
Gilbert, Humphrey **6** 313
Hakluyt, Richard **7** 70
Spenser, Edmund **14** 373-376

Rally for the Republic (French political
party)
Chirac, Jacques **4** 2-3

Ralph Roister Doister (play; Udall)
Terence **15** 146-148

Rama II (ruled 1809-24), king of Thailand
Mongkut **11** 104

Rama III (ruled 1824-51), king of Thailand
Mongkut **11** 104

Rama IV
see Mongkut

Rama V
see Chulalongkorn

RAMA KHAMHAENG (circa 1239-circa
1299), king of Sukhothai in Thailand
13 11

Ramadan (Islam)
Anan ben David **1** 207-208
Mohammed **11** 76-78

RAMAKRISHNA, SRI (1833-1886), Indian
mystic, reformer, and saint **13** 11-13
Vivekananda **16** 4-5

Ramakrishna mission (religion; India)
Vivekananda **16** 4-5

**RAMAN, SIR CHANDRASEKHAR VENKA-
TA** (1888-1970), Indian physicist
13 13-14
Born, Max **2** 420-421

RAMANUJAN AIYANGAR, SRINIVASA
(1887-1920), India mathematician
13 14-15

RAMAPHOSA, MATEMELA CYRIL (born
1952), general secretary of the National
Union of Mineworkers (NUM) in South
Africa and secretary general of the
African National Congress **13** 15-16

Ramayana (epic; Valmiki)
Kalidasa **8** 414-415

Ramboldini, Vittorino
see Feltre, Vittorino da

Rambouillet, Marquise de (Catherine de
Vivonne de Savelli; 1588-1665), French
socialite
Bossuet, Jacques Bénigne **2** 431-432

RAMEAU, JEAN PHILIPPE (1683-1764),
French music theorist and composer
13 17-18
Alembert, Jean le Rond d' **1** 127-128
Couperin, François **4** 270-271
Saint-Saëns, Charles Camille
13 435-436

Rameau's Nephew (novel)
Diderot, Denis **5** 1-2

Ramesseum (temple)
Ramses II **13** 22-23

Ramillies, battle of (1706)
Marlborough, 1st Duke of **10** 271-272

Ramiro II (923?-950), king of León
930-950
Abd al-Rahman III **1** 14

Ramism (philosophy)
Ramus, Petrus **13** 27-28

Ramler, Karl Wilhelm (1725-1798), German poet
Lessing, Gotthold Ephraim **9** 357-359

Ramolino, Letizia (1750-1836), mother of
Napoleon I
Bonaparte, Joseph **2** 381-382

Ramona (novel)
Jackson, Helen Hunt **8** 172

RAMOS, FIDEL VALDEZ (born 1928), president of the Philippines (1992-)
13 18-19

RAMPHAL, SHRIDATH SURENDRANATH
(born 1928), Guyanese barrister, politician, and international civil servant
13 19-20

Rampion, Mark (literary character)
Huxley, Aldous Leonard **8** 74-75

Rampolla, Mariano (1843-1913), Italian
cardinal
Leo XIII **9** 334-336

RAMSAY, DAVID (1749-1815), American
historian **13** 21

Ramsay, James Andrew Broun
see Dalhousie, 1st Marquess of

Ramsay, Mrs. (literary character)
Woolf, Virginia Stephen **16** 381-382

RAMSAY, SIR WILLIAM (1852-1916),
British chemist and educator
13 21-22
Hahn, Otto **7** 64-65
Rayleigh, 3d Baron **13** 62
Soddy, Frederick **14** 321-323

RAMSES II (ruled 1304-1237 B.C.),
pharaoh of Egypt **13** 22-23

RAMSEY, ARTHUR MICHAEL (1904-1988),
archbishop of Canterbury and president
of the World Council of Churches
13 23-25
Paul VI **12** 146-148

RAMSEY, FRANK PLUMPTON
(1903-1930), English mathematician and
philosopher **13** 25

RAMSEY, NORMAN FOSTER, JR. (born
1915), American physicist **13** 25-27

Ramuntcho (novel)
Loti, Pierre **9** 519-520

RAMUS, PETRUS (1515-1572), French
humanist, logician and mathematician
13 27-28

Ramuz, C. F. (1878-1947), Swiss poet
Stravinsky, Igor Fedorovich
14 502-506

Rancagua, battle of (1814)
Carrera, José Miguel **3** 323-324

Ranch (ballet)
Ginastera, Alberto Evaristo **6** 328-329

Ranching
see Cattle industry

Ranchos Church, Taos (painting)
O'Keeffe, Georgia **11** 487-489

RAND Corporation (think tank)
Fukuyama, Francis **6** 146-147

Rand McNally Building (Chicago)
Burnham, Daniel Hudson **3** 148-149

RANDOLPH, A. PHILIP (1889-1979),
African American labor and civil rights
leader **13** 28-29

RANDOLPH, EDMUND (1753-1813),
American statesman **13** 29-30
Randolph, John **13** 30

RANDOLPH, JOHN (1773-1833), Ameri-
can statesman **13** 30
Adams, Henry Brooks **1** 45-47
Jefferson, Thomas **8** 238-241
Macon, Nathaniel **10** 114-115
Perry, Matthew Calbraith **12** 237-239

RANDOLPH, PEYTON (1721-1775), American statesman
Randolph, Edmund **13** 29-30

RANGEL, CHARLES B. (born 1930), Democratic U.S. representative from New York
City **13** 31-32

Ranger (ship)
Jones, John Paul **8** 337-338

Rangoon (Burma)
Alaungpaya **1** 103

Rangoon College (Burma)
Ba Maw **1** 480-481

Ranieri, Antonio (1809-1888), Italian writer
Leopardi, Giacomo **9** 344-345

RANJIT SINGH (1780-1839), ruler of the
Punjab **13** 32-33

RANK, OTTO (1884-1939), Austrian psy-
chotherapist **13** 33
Freud, Sigmund **6** 103-106
Horney, Karen Danielsen **7** 508-509

RANKE, LEOPOLD VON (1795-1886),
German historian **13** 33-35
Acton, John Emerich Edward Dalberg
1 38
Burckhardt, Jacob Christoph **3** 132-133
Döllinger, Josef Ignaz von **5** 47-48
Frederick William IV **6** 87-88
Lavisse, Ernest **9** 241
Osgood, Herbert Levi **12** 18-19

RANKIN, JEANNETTE PICKERING
(1880-1973), first woman elected to the
U.S. Congress **13** 35-37

RANNARIDH, PRINCE NORODOM (born
1944), first prime minister of Cambodia
13 37-39

RANSOM, JOHN CROWE (1888-1974),
American poet and critic **13** 39-40
Lowell, Robert Trail Spence Jr. **10** 16-17
Tate, Allen **15** 116
Warren, Robert Penn **16** 121-122

Ranson's Folly (play)
Davis, Richard Harding **4** 422-423

Ranters (religious sect)
Williams, Roger **16** 304-305

Rapallo, Treaty of (1922)
Chicherin, Georgi Vasilyevich
3 516-517
Giolitti, Giovanni **6** 339-340
Rathenau, Walther **13** 48-49

Rape of Deianira (painting)
Pollaiuolo, Antonio **12** 377-378

Rape of Europa (painting)
Titian **15** 242-244
Veronese, Paolo **15** 469-470

Rape of Lucrece (poem)
Shakespeare, William **14** 142-145

Rape of Lucrece, The (play)
Heywood, Thomas **7** 373-374

Rape of Lucretia (painting)
Tintoretto **15** 232-234

Rape of Lucretia, The (opera)
Britten, Benjamin **3** 10-11

Rape of the Daughters of Leucippus (painting)
Rubens, Peter Paul **13** 339-342

Rape of the Lock, The (poem; Pope)
Milton, John **11** 43-46
Pope, Alexander **12** 395-397

Rape of the Sabine Women (painting)
David, Jacques Louis **4** 407-409

Rape of the Sabines (painting)
Cortona, Pietro da **4** 256
Poussin, Nicolas **12** 418-420

Rape of the Sabines (sculpture)
Giovanni da Bologna **6** 345-346

RAPHAEL (1483-1520), Italian painter and
architect **13** 40-42
associates
Andrea del Sarto **1** 224-225
Bramante, Donato **2** 493-494
Castiglione, Baldassare **3** 360-361
Rosso, Il **13** 312-313
influence (England)
Reynolds, Joshua **13** 115-116
influence (France)
David, Jacques Louis **4** 407-409
Ingres, Jean Auguste Dominique
8 121-123
Poussin, Nicolas **12** 418-420
Renoir, Pierre Auguste **13** 101-102
influence (Germany)
Mengs, Anton Raphael **10** 505
influence (Italy)
Carracci **3** 319-321
Correggio **4** 249-251
Giovanni da Bologna **6** 345-346
Lotto, Lorenzo **9** 520-521
Primaticcio, Francesco **12** 453-454
Titian **15** 242-244
influence (Netherlands)
Holbein, Hans the Younger
7 449-450
Rubens, Peter Paul **13** 339-342
influence (Spain)

Velázquez, Diego Rodríguez de
Silva y **15** 454-456
influenced by
Leonardo da Vinci **9** 337-340
Michelangelo Buonarroti **11** 2-5
patronage
Leo X **9** 332-334
Sangallo family **13** 464-466

Rapid transit systems
Sprague, Frank Julian **14** 385-386

Rapimento di Cefalo, Il (musical composition)
Caccini, Giulio **3** 205-206

RAPP, GEORGE (1757-1847),
German-American religious leader
13 42-43
Owen, Robert **12** 39-40

Rappelle-toi (poem)
Musset, Louis Charles Alfred de
11 271-272

Rappites (religion)
see Harmony Society

Rapsodie espagnole (musical composition)
Ravel, Maurice Joseph **13** 54-55

Rapsodie mègre (musical composition)
Poulenc, Francis **12** 414-415

Rare-earth group (elements)
Mendeleev, Dmitrii Ivanovich
10 486-488

Raros, Los (essays)
Darío, Rubén **4** 393-394

Ras Tafari
see Haile Selassie

Rasbam (1085-1160), Jewish scholar
Rashi **13** 43

Rascoux, battle of (1746)
Saxe, Comte de **13** 507-508

RASHI (1040-1105), French Jewish scholar
and commentator **13** 43

Rashomon (film)
Kurosawa, Akira **9** 135-137

Raskolnikov (literary character)
Dostoevsky, Fyodor **5** 74-77

RASMUSSEN, KNUD JOHAN VICTOR
(1879-1933), Danish Arctic explorer and
ethnologist **13** 44

RASPUTIN, GRIGORI EFIMOVICH
(1872-1916), Russian monk **13** 44-45
Nicholas II **11** 378-380

Rasputin and the Empress (film)
Barrymores **2** 28-30

Rasselas (novel)
Johnson, Samuel **8** 315-317

Rassemblement Démocratique Africain
(political group)
Apithy, Sourou Migan **1** 259-260
Houphouët-Boigny, Felix **7** 519-520
Keita, Modibo **8** 474-475
Touré, Sékou **15** 275-277

Rastatt, Congress of (1797-1799)
Metternich, Klemens von **10** 533-536

Rastatt, Treaty of (1714)
Eugene of Savoy **5** 330-331

Rasumovsky Quartet (musical composition)
Beethoven, Ludwig van **2** 114-117

Rat Trap (play)
Coward, Noel **4** 279-280

Ratana Church (New Zealand)
Ratana, Taupotiki Wiremu **13** 46

RATANA, TAUPOTIKI WIREMU
(1870-1939), spiritual and political leader
of the New Zealand Maori people **13** 46

Ratapoil (sculpture)
Daumier, Honoré Victorin **4** 403-405

Rath Museum (Geneva, Switzerland)
Bearden, Romare Howard **2** 86-88

RATHBONE, ELEANOR (Eleanor Florence
Rathbone; 1872-1946), British politician
and social reformer **13** 47-48

Rathenau, Emil (1838-1915), German
industrialist
Rathenau, Walther **13** 48-49

RATHENAU, WALTHER (1867-1922), German
industrialist and statesman **13** 48-49

Rating and Valuation Act of 1925 (Great
Britain)
Chamberlain, Arthur Neville **3** 409-411

Rationalism (art)
Fuseli, Henry **6** 153-155
Labrouste, Pierre François Henri **9** 144

Rationalism (philosophy)
critics
Diderot, Denis **5** 1-2
Hamann, Johann Georg **7** 92
Pobedonostsev, Konstantin Petrovich
12 360-361
Vico, Giambattista **15** 480-481
empiricism and
Kant, Immanuel **8** 430-432-123
initiated
Descartes, René **4** 505-508
Hobbes, Thomas **7** 421-423
Spinoza, Baruch **14** 381-383
rationalist ethics
Clarke, Samuel **4** 88
Spinoza, Baruch **14** 381-383
reactions against
Mill, John Stuart **11** 21-23
Soloviev, Vladimir Sergeevich
14 329-330
religion and
Ashari, Abu al- Hasan Ali al-
1 327-328
Bayle, Pierre **2** 77-78
Judah Halevi **8** 373
Law, William **9** 245-246
Schleiermacher, Friedrich Ernst
Daniel **14** 11-12

Rationalist school (Islam)
see Mutazilite school

Rationalization (psychology)
Jones, Ernest Alfred **8** 331-332

Ratiovitalism (philosophy)
Ortega Y Gasset, José **12** 7-8

Ratnavali (play)
Harsha **7** 181-182

Ratskin (sculpture)
Daumier, Honoré Victorin **4** 403-405

Ratten, Die (drama)
Hauptmann, Gerhart Johann Robert
7 199-201

Ratti, Abrogio Damiano Achille
see Pius XI

RATTLE, SIMON DENIS (born 1955), conductor of England's City of Birmingham
Symphony Orchestra **13** 49-50

Rattlesnake (ship)
Huxley, Thomas Henry **8** 77-79

Rattlesnake, The (sculpture)
Rembrandt Harmensz van Rijn
13 91-95

RATZEL, FRIEDRICH (1844-1904), German
geographer **13** 50-51

Ratzenhofer, Gustave (1842-1904), Austrian general, philosopher, and sociologist
Small, Albion Woodbury **14** 277

RAU, JOHANNES (born 1931), German
Social Democrat politician **13** 51-52

Räuber, Die (play)
Schiller, Johann Christoph Friedrich von
14 4-7

Raucho (novel)
Güiráldez, Ricardo **7** 38-39

RAUSCHENBERG, ROBERT (born 1925),
American painter and printmaker
13 52-53
Johns, Jasper **8** 291-293

RAUSCHENBUSCH, WALTER (1861-1918),
American Baptist clergyman **13** 53-54
McGovern, George Stanley **10** 412-414
Thomas, Norman Mattoon **15** 191-192

Rav
see Abba Arika

Ravaillac, François (1578-1610), French
murderer of Henry IV
Henry IV **7** 293-295

RAVEL, MAURICE JOSEPH (1875-1937),
French composer **13** 54-55
Honegger, Arthur **7** 472-473
Mussorgsky, Modest Petrovich
11 274-276
Poulenc, Francis **12** 414-415
Respighi, Ottorino **13** 103-104
Satie, Erik **13** 494-495
Stravinsky, Igor Fedorovich **14** 502-506

Raven, The (poem; Poe)
Mallarmé, Stéphane **10** 172-173
Poe, Edgar Allan **12** 363-365

Ravenna (city, Italy)
Gregory I **6** 531-532
Odoacer **11** 473

Theodoric the Great **15** 175-176

Ravenna (poem)
Wilde, Oscar Fingall O'Flahertie Wills
16 272-273

Ravensworth (County Durham)
Nash, John **11** 316

Ravine, The (novel)
Goncharov, Ivan Aleksandrovich **6** 424

Raw Youth, A (novel)
Dostoevsky, Fyodor **5** 74-77

Rawandis (Islam sect)
Mansur, Abu Jafar ibn Muhammad al-
10 214-215

Rawhide Rawlins Stories (book)
Russell, Charles Marion **13** 375-376

RAWLS, JOHN (born 1921), American
political philosopher **13** 55-56
Nozick, Robert **11** 438-439

RAY, DIXY LEE (1914-1994), marine biologist and governor of Washington
13 56-57

RAY, JOHN (1627-1705), English naturalist
13 57-59

RAY, MAN (1890-1976), American painter,
photographer, and object maker **13** 59-60
Duchamp, Marcel **5** 122-123
Ernst, Max **5** 311-312

RAY, SATYAJIT (1921-1992), Indian film
director **13** 60-61

RAYBURN, SAMUEL TALIAFERRO
(1882-1961), American statesman
13 61-62
Johnson, Lyndon Baines **8** 308-312

Rayfish, The (painting)
Chardin, Jean Baptiste Siméon
3 442-443

RAYLEIGH, 3D BARON (John William
Strutt; 1842-1919), English physicist
13 62
Bose, Jagadis Chandra **2** 429-430
Cavendish, Henry **3** 383-384
Jeans, James Hopwood **8** 235-236
Ramsay, William **13** 21-22
Thomson, Joseph John **15** 200-201
Tyndall, John **15** 374

Rayleigh-Jeans law (physics)
Jeans, James Hopwood **8** 235-236

Raymond IV, Count of Toulouse
see Raymond of Saint-Gilles

Raymond of Peñafort (1176-1275), Spanish
monk and theologian
Thomas Aquinas **15** 183-186

Raymond of Saint-Gilles (died 1105),
French count and Crusader
Bohemund, I **2** 364

Rayographs (art form)
Ray, Man **13** 59-60

Rayonism (art)
Goncharova, Natalia **6** 424-426
Larionov, Mikhail **9** 205-206

Rayonnant Gothic architecture
Montreuil, Pierre de **11** 139

Rayons et les ombres, Les (book)
Hugo, Victor Marie **8** 22-25

Raytheon Corporation
Bush, Vannevar **3** 169-171

Raza cósmica, La (book)
Vasconcelos, José **15** 443-444

RAZI (Abu Bakr Muhammad ibn Zakariya al-Razi; circa 865-925), Persian physician **13** 63-64

Razilly, Isaac de (died 1635), French governor of Acadia
Charnisay, Charles de Menou **3** 470-471

Razin, Stefan Timofeovich (Stenka; died 1671), Russian rebel
Alexis Mikhailovich Romanov **1** 142-143

Razor's Edge, The (book)
Maugham, William Somerset **10** 344-345

Razumov (literary character)
Conrad, Joseph **4** 205-207

RCA
see Radio Corporation of America

RCA Building (New York City)
Lachaise, Gaston **9** 147
Shahn, Ben **14** 139-140

Ré, Île de, battle of (1627)
Buckingham, 1st Duke of **3** 93-94

Reactionary party (Prussia)
Frederick William III **6** 87

Read, Herbert (1893-1968), English poet and critic
Stravinsky, Igor Fedorovich **14** 502-506

Reade, Charles (1814-1884), English novelist
Trollope, Anthony **15** 300-302

Readers (book)
Tolstoy, Leo **15** 262-265

Reader's Digest (magazine)
Wallace, DeWitt **16** 70-71

READING, 1ST MARQUESS OF (Rufus Daniel Isaacs; 1860-1935), English lawyer and statesman **13** 64

Readjustors (Virginia reformers)
Mahone, William **10** 147-148

Ready and Easy Way (treatise)
Milton, John **11** 43-46

Ready-made (art form)
Duchamp, Marcel **5** 122-123
Moholy-Nagy, László **11** 82-83
Ray, Man **13** 59-60

REAGAN, RONALD W. (born 1911), governor of California (1967-1975) and U.S. president (1981-1989) **13** 65-68
appointees
Baker, James Addison III **1** 447-448
Bennett, William John **2** 172-174

Billington, James Hadley **2** 275-276
Buchanan, Patrick Joseph **3** 90-91
Casey, William J. **3** 351-353
Conable, Barber B. Jr. **4** 191-192
Giuliani, Rudolph William **6** 353-355
Haig, Alexander M. Jr. **7** 66-67
Healy, Bernadine Patricia **7** 237-238
Kennedy, Anthony M. **8** 498-500
O'Connor, Sandra Day **11** 468-470
Regan, Donald **13** 80-81
Rehnquist, William Hubbs **13** 82-84
Scalia, Antonin **13** 513-514
Shultz, George Pratt **14** 209-211
Weinberger, Casper Willard **16** 177-178
see also Bush, George
political disputes
Berry, Mary Frances **2** 226-229

Real Charlotte, The (novel)
Somerville, Edith Anna OEnone **14** 334-335

Real Cuerpo de Mineria (guild)
Gálvez, José de **6** 196

Real David Copperfield, The (novel)
Graves, Robert Ranke **6** 504-506

Real Dope, The (book)
Lardner, Ringgold Wilmer **9** 204-205

Real Estate
see Business and industrial leaders—real estate

Real estate developers
DeBartolo **4** 438-440

Real Life of Sebastian Knight, The (book)
Nabokov, Vladimir **11** 287-288

Real Thing, The (play)
Stoppard, Thomas **14** 478-479

Reali School (Haifa)
Kaufmann, Ezekiel **8** 460

Realidad (novel; play)
Galdós, Benito Pérez **6** 177-178

Realism (art)
American
Bellows, George Wesley **2** 143
Copley, John Singleton **4** 228-230
Hopper, Edward **7** 497-498
Luks, George Benjamin **10** 38-39
Sargent, John Singer **13** 481-482
Sheeler, Charles **14** 170-171
Sloan, John **14** 274-275
Dutch
Sluter, Claus **14** 275-276
Flemish
Campin, Robert **3** 255
Jordaens, Jacob **8** 347-349
French
Corot, Jean Baptiste Camille **4** 247-249
Courbet, Jean Desiré Gustave **4** 271-273
Daumier, Honoré Victorin **4** 403-405
Houdon, Antoine **7** 516-517

Manet, Édouard **10** 193-194
Monet, Claude **11** 102-104
German
Dürer, Albrecht **5** 159-161
Holbein, Hans the Younger **7** 449-450
Italian
Caravaggio **3** 282-284
Giotto **6** 342-345
see also Naturalism (art)

Realism (literature)
American
Crane, Stephen **4** 293-295
Dreiser, Herman Theodore **5** 98-100
Garland, Hannibal Hamlin **6** 217-218
Lanier, Sidney **9** 199-200
Lewis, Harry Sinclair **9** 385-387
Rölvaag, Ole Edvart **13** 265
Stein, Gertrude **14** 414-415
Australian
Richardson, Henry Handel **13** 139
Danish
Dinesen Blixen-Finecke, Karen **5** 13-14
Nexø, Martin Anderson **11** 372
English
Bennett, Arnold **2** 167-168
Brooke, Rupert **3** 22-23
Crabbe, George **4** 288
Dickens, Charles John Huffam **4** 538-541
Donne, John **5** 60-61
French
Daudet, Alphonse **4** 402-403
Flaubert, Gustave **5** 480-482
Maupassant, Henri René Albert Guy de **10** 347
Mérimée, Prosper **10** 517
Zola, Émile **16** 526-528
German
Freytag, Gustav **6** 107-108
Jünger, Ernst **8** 391-392
Irish
O'Casey, Sean **11** 459-460
Italian
Carducci, Giosuè **3** 290-291
Goldoni, Carlo **6** 408-409
Pirandello, Luigi **12** 319-321
Mexican
Azuela, Mariano **1** 402
Norwegian
Ibsen, Henrik **8** 98-100
Russian
Bulgakov, Mikhail Afanasievich **3** 117
Bunin, Ivan Alekseevich **3** 124
Chekhov, Anton Pavlovich **3** 494-497
Dostoevsky, Fyodor **5** 74-77
Gogol, Nikolai **6** 391-393
Goncharov, Ivan Aleksandrovich **6** 424
Gorky, Maxim **6** 458-460
Mayakovsky, Vladimir Vladimirovich **10** 364-365

Pushkin, Aleksandr Sergeevich
12 489-491
Solzhenitsyn, Alexander Isayevich
14 330-332
Tolstoy, Leo **15** 262-265
Turgenev, Ivan Sergeyevich
15 345-348
Swedish
Lagerlöf, Selma Ottiliana Lovisa
9 163-164
Strindberg, August **14** 509-511

Realism (philosophy)
Broad, Charlie Dunbar **3** 12
Hus, Jan **8** 56-59
Jacobi, Friedrich Heinrich **8** 189-190
Masaryk, Tomáš Garrigue **10** 314-315
More, Thomas **11** 156-157
Perry, Ralph Barton **12** 239-240
Santayana, George **13** 475-477

Realist Manifesto (1920)
Gabo, Naum **6** 158-159
Pevsner, Antoine **12** 263-264

Realist party (Czechoslovakia)
Masaryk, Tomáš Garrigue **10** 314-315

Réalités Nouvelles (art group)
Pevsner, Antoine **12** 263-264

Reality (philosophy)
Bradley, Francis Herbert **2** 481-482
Spinoza, Baruch **14** 381-383

Reality Sandwiches (poems)
Ginsberg, Allen **6** 332-333

Reaper (farm machine)
McCormick, Cyrus Hall **10** 400-401

Reaper (mural)
Miró, Joan **11** 53-54

Reapportionment (United States law)
see Apportionment

Rear Window (film)
Hitchcock, Alfred **7** 415-416

Reason (literary character)
Langland, William **9** 194-195

Reason (philosophy)
Averroës **1** 382-383
Cohen, Morris Raphael **4** 139-140
Descartes, René **4** 505-508
Heraclitus **7** 320
Hobbes, Thomas **7** 421-423
Hume, David **8** 31-34
Jaspers, Karl **8** 225-226
Pascal, Blaise **12** 122-124
Thomas Aquinas **15** 183-186

Reason and Revolution (book)
Marcuse, Herbert **10** 245-247

Reason Awake (book)
Dubos, René Jules **5** 119

Reb Yudel Hasis (literary character)
Agnon, Shmuel Yoseph **1** 85-86

Rebecca
see Pocahontas

Rebecca (film)
Hitchcock, Alfred **7** 415-416

Rebel, The (novel)
Camus, Albert **3** 255-257

Rebel Without a Cause (film)
Dean, James **4** 433-434

Rebellion in the Backlands (book)
Cunha, Euclides Rodrigues Pimenta da
4 336-337

Rebellion Losses Act (Canada, 1849)
Baldwin, Robert **1** 466-468
Elgin, 8th Earl of **5** 248-249
Lafontaine, Louis-Hippolyte **9** 157-158

Rebellion of 1173 (England)
Henry II **7** 287-289

Rebellion of 1837 (Canada)
Baldwin, Robert **1** 466-468
Cartier, George-Étienne **3** 342-343
Mackenzie, William Lyon **10** 104-106
Moodie, Susanna **11** 140-141
Papineau, Louis-Joseph **12** 91

Rebellion of the Eight Princes (China; 3d century)
Lu Chi **10** 24

Rebellion of the Seven Kingdoms (China; 154 B.C.)
Han Kao-tsu **7** 125-126

Rebellion of the Three Feudatories (1673-74; China)
K'ang-hsi **8** 423-426

Rebels, The (novel)
Child, Lydia Maria Francis **3** 520-521

Rebull, Santiago (1829-1902), Mexican painter
Rivera, Diego **13** 183-184
Velasco, Luis de **15** 450-451

Recall (politics)
Merriam, Charles Edward **10** 518-519

Récamier, Jeanne Françoise Julie Adélaïde Bernard (1777-1847), French beauty and wit
Chateaubriand, Vicomte de **3** 477-479
David, Jacques Louis **4** 407-409

Reccared (died 601), Visigothic king in Spain 586-601
Isidore of Seville **8** 149-150

Recessional (poem)
Kipling, Joseph Rudyard **9** 32-33

Rechberg und Rothenlöwen, Count Johann Bernhard von (1806-1889), Austrian statesman
Bismarck, Otto Eduard Leopold von
2 294-296

Recherche de l'absolu, La (novel)
Balzac, Honoré de **1** 478-480

Recife, battle of (1630)
John Maurice of Nassau **8** 281-282

Reciprocal Accord (painting)
Kandinsky, Wassily **8** 420-422

Reciprocal trade agreements (United States; 1930s)
Hull, Cordell **8** 28-29

Reciprocity Treaty of 1854 (United States-Canada)
Howe, Joseph **7** 534-535

Reclamation, Bureau of (United States)
Powell, John Wesley **12** 425-426

Reclining Figure (sculpture series)
Moore, Henry **11** 146-148

Reclining Nude (painting)
Modigliani, Amedeo **11** 72-73

Reclining Nude I (sculpture)
Matisse, Henri **10** 336-337

Reclining Woman (sculpture)
Moore, Henry **11** 146-148

Recluse ... (poem)
Wordsworth, William **16** 385-388

Recombination (genetics)
Beadle, George Wells **2** 80-81

Reconquista
see Spain—Islamic

Reconstituted National party (South Africa)
Vorster, Balthazar Johannes **16** 30-32

Reconstruction (United States)
African American officials
Bruce, Blanche Kelso **3** 62-63
Delany, Martin Robinson **4** 473-474
Douglass, Frederick **5** 85-86
Pinchback, Pinckney Benton Stewart
12 306-308
Revels, Hiram Rhoades **13** 109-110
Smalls, Robert **14** 277-278
Court decisions
Chase, Salmon Portland **3** 473-475
Field, David Dudley **5** 439-440
Miller, Samuel Freeman **11** 29-30
Freedmen's Bureau
see Freedmen's Bureau
historians on
Dunning, William Archibald
5 148-149
Rhodes, James Ford **13** 122
Woodward, Comer Vann
16 378-379
in literature
Harris, Joel Chandler **7** 173-174
military rule
Hayes, Rutherford Birchard
7 227-228
Sheridan, Philip Henry **14** 182-183
moderates
Adams, Charles Francis **1** 41-42
Andrew, John Albion **1** 230-231
Blair, Francis Preston **2** 313-315
Hill, Benjamin Harvey **7** 386-387
Johnson, Andrew **8** 294-295
Lincoln, Abraham **9** 415-418
Trumbull, Lyman **15** 317-318
Vallandigham, Clement Laird
15 406-407
Welles, Gideon **16** 188-190

White, Edward Douglass
16 230-231
Wood, Fernando **16** 367-368
New South
Grady, Henry Woodfin **6** 482-483
Hill, Benjamin Harvey **7** 386-387
Radical Republicans
Ames, Adelbert **1** 198
Chandler, Zachariah **3** 425-426
Conkling, Roscoe **4** 201-202
Davis, Henry Winter **4** 415-416
Grant, Ulysses Simpson **6** 492-494
Greeley, Horace **6** 515-517
Lieber, Francis **9** 401-402
Medill, Joseph **10** 451-452
Morton, Oliver Hazard Perry Throck
11 197-198
Nast, Thomas **11** 318-319
Schurz, Carl **14** 44-45
Stevens, Thaddeus **14** 442-443
Sumner, Charles **15** 30-31
Wade, Benjamin Franklin **16** 38-39
southern governors
Alcorn, James Lusk **1** 120-121
Brown, Joseph Emerson **3** 41-42
Gordon, John Brown **6** 449-450
Hampton, Wade III **7** 112
southern resistance
George, James Zachariah **6** 276-277
Toombs, Robert Augustus
15 267-268
see also Ku Klux Klan; Racism (United States)

Reconstruction Finance Corp. (established 1931)
Berle, Adolf Augustus Jr. **2** 199-200
Hoover, Herbert Clark **7** 483-485

Reconstructionist movement (American Judaism)
Kaplan, Mordecai Menahem **8** 435-436

Record Building (Charleston, South Carolina)
Mills, Robert **11** 36-37

RECORDE, ROBERT (1510-1558), English mathematician **13** 68-69

Records of Rites (book)
Confucius **4** 197-200

Records of the Historian (book; Ssu-ma Ch'ien)
Confucius **4** 197-200
Lao Tzu **9** 201-202
Ssu-ma Ch'ien **14** 388-389

RECTO, CLARO M. (1890-1960), Philippine nationalist and statesman **13** 69-70
Quezon, Manuel Luis **12** 511-513

Recueillements (anthology)
Lamartine, Alphonse Marie Louis de
9 173-175

Recumbent Figure (sculpture)
Moore, Henry **11** 146-148

Recusants (religious group)
Byrd, William **3** 187-188
Morley, Thomas **11** 179-180

Strafford, 1st Earl of **14** 490-491

Recuyell of the Historyes of Troye, The (book; Le Fevre-Caxton)
Caxton, William **3** 386-387

"Red, The"
see Comyn, John

Red and the Black, The (novel)
Stendhal **14** 422-425-198

Red and the Green, The (novel)
Murdoch, Iris **11** 256-257

Red Army Faction (German terrorists)
Baader and Ulrike Meinhof, Andreas
1 403-404

Red Badge of Courage, The (novel)
Crane, Stephen **4** 293-295

Red Baron
see Richthofen, Manfred von

Red Brigades (Italian terrorist organization)
Moro, Aldo **11** 180-181

Red Cavalry (stories)
Babel, Isaac Emmanuelovich **1** 411-412

RED CLOUD (1822-1909), American
Oglala Sioux Indian chief **13** 70-71
American Horse **1** 195-198

Red Cloud Agency (Native American)
Crazy Horse **4** 303-304

Red Cross
see American Red Cross; International Red Cross

Red Desert (film)
Antonioni, Michelangelo **1** 252-253

Red Dragon Book Club (national organization; Myanmar [formerly Burma])
Aung San **1** 374-375
Nu, U **11** 439-441

Red Eyebrows (Chinese bandits)
Kuang-wu-ti **9** 112-113

Red Federation of Labour (New Zealand)
Fraser, Peter **6** 73-74

Red Fishes (painting)
Matisse, Henri **10** 336-337

Red Guards (Chinese)
Chou En-lai **4** 20-22
Liu Shao-Ch'i **9** 453-455
Mao Zedong **10** 225-227

Red Horses (painting)
Marc, Franz **10** 231

Red International of Labor Unions (Moscow)
Foster, William Zebulon **6** 27-28

RED JACKET (Sagoyewatha; 1758-1830), Seneca tribal leader **13** 71-73
Brant, Joseph **2** 500-501
Catlin, George **3** 373-374

Red Kerchief, The (film)
Kazantzakis, Nikos **8** 466-468

Red Lily, The (novel)
France, Anatole **6** 39-40

Red Mask (sculpture)
Manzù, Giacomo **10** 224-225

Red Petticoat, The (operetta)
Kern, Jerome David **8** 517-518

Red Pony, The (film)
Copland, Aaron **4** 227-228

Red, Red Rose, A (song)
Burns, Robert **3** 155-156

Red River (Canada-United States)
Fraser, Simon **6** 74-75
la Verendrye, Sieur de **9** 239-240

Red River (Indochina)
Bonvalot, Pierre Gabriel Édouard **2** 396

Red River (United States)
Bienville, Sieur de **2** 268-269

Red Rock (novel)
Page, Thomas Nelson **12** 59-60

Red Room, The (novel)
Strindberg, August **14** 509-511

Red Roses for Me (play)
O'Casey, Sean **11** 459-460

Red Roses from Bronze (poems)
Doolittle, Hilda **5** 65-66

Red Rover, The (novel)
Cooper, James Fenimore **4** 220-223

Red scare (U.S. history)
Browder, Earl Russell **3** 30-31
Duncan, Isadora **5** 144-145
Foster, William Zebulon **6** 27-28

Red Sea (Arabia-North Africa)
Burckhardt, Johann Ludwig **3** 133

Red shift (astronomy)
Eddington, Arthur Stanley **5** 201-202
Hubble, Edwin Powell **8** 10-11

Red Star over China (book)
Snow, Edgar **14** 312-313

Red terror (Russia)
Dzerzhinsky, Felix Edmundovich
5 173-174

Red Turbans (Chinese rebels)
Yi Sng-gye **16** 458-459

Redburn (novel)
Melville, Herman **10** 472-476

Redding, J. Saunders (1906-1988), African American author and educator
Wheatley, Phillis **16** 221-222

"Redeemers" (United States Reconstruction)
Lamar, Lucius Quintus Cincinnatus
9 170-171

Redemption (play)
Barrymores **2** 28-30

Redemption (theology)
Abba Arika **1** 3-4
Edwards, Jonathan **5** 220-222
Luria, Isaac ben Solomon Ashkenazi
10 47-48

Redemptorists (religious congregation)
Hecker, Isaac Thomas **7** 250-251

Redentore, Il (church, Venice)
Mansart, François **10** 211
Palladio, Andrea **12** 75-77

REDFIELD, ROBERT (1897-1958), American anthropologist **13** 73-74

Redfield, William C. (1798-1857), American scientist
Hare, Robert **7** 152-153

Redgauntlet (novel)
Scott, Walter **14** 68-70

REDGRAVE, VANESSA (born 1937), British actress and political activist **13** 74-75

Redheads (Shiites; Turkey)
Abbas I **1** 4-6

Redman, John (1722-1808), American physician
Morgan, John **11** 162-163

REDON, ODILON (1840-1916), French painter and graphic artist **13** 75-76
Klee, Paul **9** 47-49
Rousseau, Henri **13** 323-324
Seurat, Georges Pierre **14** 120-122

Redoubtable (ship)
Nelson, Horatio **11** 336-338

Redshirts (volunteer army)
Cavour, Conte di **3** 385-386
Garibaldi, Giuseppe **6** 215-217

Redskins, The (novel)
Cooper, James Fenimore **4** 220-223

Redstone rocket
von Braun, Wernher **16** 17-18

Reductionism (philosophy)
Bichat, Marie François Xavier **2** 263-264

Redwood Library (Newport, Rhode Island)
Harrison, Peter **7** 179-180

Reed, Carol (1906-1976), English film director
Coward, Noel **4** 279-280

REED, JOHN SILAS (1887-1920), American revolutionist, poet, and journalist **13** 76-77
Bourne, Randolph Silliman **2** 456-457
Eisenstein, Sergei Mikhailovich **5** 240-242

Reed, Luman (1781-1836), American merchant
Durand, Asher Brown **5** 156-157
Mount, William Sidney **11** 213-214

REED, THOMAS BRACKETT (1839-1902), American statesman and parliamentarian **13** 77

REED, WALTER (1851-1902), American military surgeon **13** 78
Finlay, Carlos Juan **5** 450
Gorgas, William Crawford **6** 454-455

REES, LLOYD FREDERIC (1895-1988), Australian artist **13** 78-79

REEVE, TAPPING (1744-1823), American jurist **13** 79-80
Burr, Aaron **3** 156-159

Calhoun, John Caldwell **3** 226-228
Mann, Horace **10** 202-204

Reference, general theory of (philosophy)
Meinong, Alexius Ritter von Handschuchsheim **10** 461-462

Reflection (philosophy)
Locke, John **9** 478-480

Reflex (psychology)
Pavlov, Ivan Petrovich **12** 155-157

Reform, social
see Social reform

Reform Bill of 1832 (England)
opponents
Cobbett, William **4** 126-127
Gladstone, William Ewart **6** 357-360
Peel, Robert **12** 181-183
Wordsworth, William **16** 385-388
supporters
Durham, 1st Earl of **5** 161-162
Grey, Charles **6** 539-540
Macaulay, Thomas Babington **10** 79-80
O'Connell, Daniel **11** 465-467
Russell, John **13** 380-381
Wellington, 1st Duke of **16** 193-195
William IV **16** 296-297

Reform Bill of 1867 (England)
Disraeli, Benjamin **5** 27-29
Gladstone, William Ewart **6** 357-360
Russell, John **13** 380-381

Reform Bill of 1884 (England)
Parnell, Charles Stewart **12** 117-119

Reform Edict (Japan; 646)
Fujiwara Kamatari **6** 145

Reform Judaism (United States)
Silver, Abba Hillel **14** 232-233
Wise, Isaac Mayer **16** 342-343

Reform movement (Episcopalian)
Muhlenberg, William Augustus **11** 233-234

Reform party (Australia)
Massey, William Ferguson **10** 324

Reform party (Canada)
Mackenzie, William Lyon **10** 104-106

Reform Republicans (U.S. politics)
Bristow, Benjamin Helm **3** 9-10

Reformation, Catholic
see Counter Reformation

Reformation, Protestant
see Protestant Reformation

Reformation Oath ... (mural)
Hodler, Ferdinand **7** 434-435

Reformation Parliament (England)
Cromwell, Thomas **4** 320-321

Reformation Symphony (musical composition)
Mendelssohn, Moses **10** 488-489

Réforme, La (newspaper)
Blanc, Louis **2** 318-319

Reformed Church (Calvinist)
Calvin, John **3** 239-242

Reformed Church (Dutch)
Jordaens, Jacob **8** 347-349
Oldenbarnevelt, Johan van **11** 495-496

Reformed Congregation of the Eremetical Order of St. Augustine
see Augustinians (religious order)

Reformers, agrarian (land)
American
Evans, George Henry **5** 337-338
Hatch, William Henry **7** 196
Polk, Leonidas Lafayette **12** 376-377
Brazilian
Castelo Branco, Humberto **3** 359-360
Canadian
Gourlay, Robert **6** 474
Chinese
Chia Ssu-tao **3** 514-515
Fan Chung-yen **5** 376-377
Hsiao-Wen-ti, Wei **8** 5
Shang Yang **14** 149-150
Wang An-shih **16** 95-97
Wang Mang **16** 101-103
Cuban
Castro Ruz, Fidel **3** 365-368
Gourlay, Robert **6** 474
Hawaiian
Kamehameha III **8** 416-417
Irish
Balfour, Arthur James **1** 469-470
Japanese
Toyotomi Hideyoshi **15** 286-289
Mexican
Ávila Camacho, Manuel **1** 387-388
Calles, Plutarco Elías **3** 234-235
Cárdenas, Lázaro **3** 286-287
Philippine
Macapagal, Diosdado P. **10** 74-76
Marcos, Ferdinand **10** 240-242
Roman
Caesar, Gaius Julius **3** 207-210
Gracchus, Tiberius and Gaius Sempronius **6** 479-480
Romanian
Ferdinand **5** 413-414
Russian
Stolypin, Piotr Arkadevich **14** 465-466
Venezuelan
Betancourt, Rómulo **2** 237-238

Reformers, economic
American
Epstein, Abraham **5** 294-295
Lawson, Thomas William **9** 255-256
Memminger, Christopher Gustavus **10** 476-477
Shays, Daniel **14** 168
Warburg, Paul Moritz **16** 111-112
Weaver, James Baird **16** 151-152
Australian
Wakefield, Edward Gibbon **16** 48-49
Brazilian

Kubitschek de Oliveira, Juscelino
9 113-115
Chinese
Wang An-shih **16** 95-97
Wang Mang **16** 101-103
Wang T'ao **16** 105-106
English
Pitt, William the Younger
12 329-331
French
Giscard d'Estaing, Valéry **6** 350-352
Turgot, Anne Robert Jacques
15 348-349
Iranian
Taqi Khan Amir-e Kabir, Mirza
15 106-107
Russian
Witte, Sergei Yulyevich **16** 349-350

Reformers, educational
American
Beecher, Catharine **2** 110-112
Bode, Boyd Henry **2** 355-356
Eliot, Charles William **5** 254
Gallup, George **6** 187-189
Goodlad, John Inkster **6** 434-436
Haley, Margaret A. **7** 78-79
Hesburgh, Theodore Martin
7 357-358
Howe, Florence Rosenfeld
7 530-531
Howe, Samuel Gridley **7** 537
Johnson, Marietta Louise Pierce
8 312-313
Judd, Charles Hubbard **8** 375-376
Kerr, Clark **8** 519-521
Kilpatrick, William H. **9** 1-3
Morrill, Justin Smith **11** 182
Peabody, Elizabeth Palmer
12 167-168
Rice, Joseph Mayer **13** 127-128
Richards, Ellen H. **13** 134-136
Rugg, Harold **13** 355-357
Wayland, Francis **16** 148-149
English
Beale, Dorothea **2** 81-83
Webb, Beatrice Potter **16** 153-154
Webb, Sidney James **16** 154-155
Mexican
López Mateos, Adolfo **9** 509-510
Spanish
Toledo, Francisco de **15** 257-259
see also Social scientists—educators

Reformers, labor
see Labor leaders

Reformers, legal
see Jurists

Reformers, medical
American
Barton, Clara **2** 37-39
Dix, Dorothea Lynde **5** 32-33
Morgan, John **11** 162-163
Rush, Benjamin **13** 364-365
British
Bevan, Aneurin **2** 248-249
Canadian

Bethune, Henry Norman **2** 240-241
Reformers, political
American
Curtis, George William **4** 349-350
Donnelly, Ignatius **5** 62
Eaton, Dorman Bridgman **5** 190-191
Gardner, John W. **6** 211-213
Harrington, Michael **7** 167-169
Hayden, Thomas Emmet **7** 217-219
Howe, Julia Ward **7** 535-536
Johnson, Hiram Warren **8** 300-301
Johnson, Tom Loftin **8** 317
Jones, Samuel Milton **8** 342-343
La Follette, Robert Marion
9 155-156
La Guardia, Fiorello Henry
9 166-167
Mahone, William **10** 147-148
Merriam, Charles Edward
10 518-519
Pendleton, George Hunt **12** 198
Roosevelt, Theodore **13** 280-283
Schniederman, Rose **14** 22-23
Schurz, Carl **14** 44-45
Spotswood, Alexander **14** 385
Tilden, Samuel Jones **15** 222-223
Tillman, Benjamin Ryan **15** 225-226
Weaver, James Baird **16** 151-152
Argentine
Perón, Eva Duarte de **12** 225-226
Austrian
Joseph II **8** 359-360
Canadian
Howe, Joseph **7** 534-535
Lafontaine, Louis-Hippolyte
9 157-158
Mackenzie, William Lyon
10 104-106
Chinese
K'ang Yu-wei **8** 426-428
Kuang-hsü **9** 111-112
Liang Ch'i-ch'ao **9** 395-396
Wang Mang **16** 101-103
Wang Yang-ming **16** 108-109
Yung-lo **16** 482-483
Egyptian
Mohammed Ali **11** 81-82
English
Edward I **5** 208-210
Hobhouse, Leonard Trelawny
7 425-426
Lilburne, John **9** 409-410
Montfort, Simon de **11** 132-133
Peel, Robert **12** 181-183
Pitt, William the Younger
12 329-331
Russell, John **13** 380-381
Sydenham, Thomas **15** 59-60
Wilkes, John **16** 280-281
Ethiopian
Menelik II **10** 495-497
Tewodros II **15** 158-159
French
du Pont de Nemours, Pierre Samuel
5 155-156
Philip II **12** 268-269

Greek and Roman
Gracchus, Tiberius and Gaius Sem-
pronius **6** 479-480
Solon **14** 327-328
Trajan **15** 291-292
Holy Roman Empire
Leopold II **9** 346
Iranian
Malkam Khan, Mirza **10** 172
Taqi Khan Amir-e Kabir, Mirza
15 106-107
Japanese
Fujiwara Kamatari **6** 145
Shotoku Taishi **14** 205-207
Yoshimune, Tokugawa **16** 465-466
Latin American
Gálvez, José de **6** 196
Juárez, Benito **8** 369-372
Montt Torres, Manuel **11** 139-140
Morazán, José Francisco **11** 155
Morelos, José María **11** 157-158
Mosquera, Tomás Cipriano de
11 205-206
Paz, Octavio **12** 161-162
Roca, Julio Argentino **13** 218
Túpac Amaru, José Gabriel **15** 341
Nepalese
Birendra, King **2** 282-283
New Zealand
Fraser, Peter **6** 73-74
Seddon, Richard John **14** 81-82
Ottoman
Selim III **14** 95-96
Philippine
Macapagal, Diosdado P. **10** 74-76
Portuguese
Pombal, Marquês de **12** 386-387
Salazar, António de Oliveira
13 442-443
Prussian
Frederick William I **6** 86-87
Stein, Heinrich Friedrich Karl vom
und zum **14** 415-416
Romanian
Titulescu, Nicolae **15** 246-247
Russian
Breshkovsky, Catherine **2** 517-519
Speranski, Mikhail Mikhailovich
14 376-377
Stolypin, Piotr Arkadevich
14 465-466

Reformers, religious
see Religious leaders

Reformers, social
African
Paton, Alan Stewart **12** 134-135
Uthman don Fodio **15** 397-398
American (19th century)
Alcott, Louisa May **1** 122
Altgeld, John Peter **1** 180-182
Bellamy, Edward **2** 134-135
Bellows, Henry Whitney **2** 143-144
Bly, Nellie **2** 346-348
Brownson, Orestes Augustus
3 57-58

Cabet, Étienne **3** 196
Coxey, Jacob Sechler **4** 286-287
Gage, Matilda Joslyn **6** 167-169
George, Henry **6** 276
Greeley, Horace **6** 515-517
Hale, Edward Everett **7** 71-72
Howe, Julia Ward **7** 535-536
Lloyd, Henry Demarest **9** 468-469
Lowell, Josephine Shaw **10** 15-16
Mann, Horace **10** 202-204
Owen, Robert Dale **12** 40-41
Parker, Theodore **12** 112-113
Phillips, Wendell **12** 281-282
Riis, Jacob August **13** 169-170
Stone, Lucy **14** 471-472
Thayer, Eli **15** 168
Wade, Benjamin Franklin **16** 38-39
Wright, Elizur **16** 396-397
Wright, Frances **16** 397-398
American (19th-20th century)
Addams, Jane **1** 56-57
Beard, Mary Ritter **2** 85-86
Comstock, Anthony **4** 188-189
Dewey, Melvil **4** 523-524
Dodge, Grace Hoadley **5** 37-38
Gilman, Charlotte Anna Perkins
6 323-325
Jones, Mary Harris **8** 338-339
Kellor, Frances **8** 481-482
Kelly, Florence **8** 483-484
Lease, Mary Elizabeth Clyens **9** 268
Lindsey, Benjamin Barr **9** 425-426
Low, Juliette Gordon **10** 10-11
Osborne, Thomas Mott **12** 17-18
Ovington, Mary White **12** 36-37
Parsons, Frank **12** 121-122
Ross, Edward Alsworth **13** 300
Russell, Charles Edward **13** 374-375
Sheldon, Charles M. **14** 172-174
Townsend, Francis Everitt
15 282-283
Wald, Lillian **16** 53-54
Woods, Robert Archey **16** 374
American (20th century)
Abbott, Grace **1** 9-10
Abzug, Bella Stavisky **1** 34-35
Alinsky, Saul David **1** 161-162
Bevel, James Luther **2** 250-251
Corona, Bert **4** 243-247
Day, Dorothy **4** 428-429
Dewson, Mary Williams **4** 525
Dubinsky, David **5** 114-115
Epstein, Abraham **5** 294-295
Goldmark, Josephine **6** 407-408
Hayden, Thomas Emmet **7** 217-219
Nader, Ralph **11** 290-291
Park, Maud Wood **12** 102
Rankin, Jeannette Pickering
13 35-37
Sanger, Margaret Higgins
13 467-468
Talbert, Mary Morris Burnett
15 86-88
Villard, Oswald Garrison
15 498-499
Wagner, Robert Ferdinand **16** 43

see also Abolitionists; Temperance
movement; Women's suffrage;
Women's rights
Argentine
Perón, Eva Duarte de **12** 225-226
Bavarian
Rumford **13** 360-362
Canadian
McClung, Nellie Letitia **10** 396-397
Woodsworth, James Shaver **16** 376
Chinese
Chang Chien **3** 429-430
Chang Chih-tung **3** 430-431
Ch'en Tu-hsiu **3** 501-502
Feng Kuei-fen **5** 411-412
Feng Yü-hsiang **5** 412-413
Wang Yang-ming **16** 108-109
English (18th century)
Oglethorpe, James Edward
11 482-483
English (19th century)
Chadwick, Edwin **3** 404-405
Fry, Elizabeth **6** 134-136
Hobhouse, Leonard Trelawny
7 425-426
Mill, John Stuart **11** 21-23
Owen, Robert **12** 39-40
Russell, John **13** 380-381
Shaftesbury, 7th Earl of **14** 137-138
English (19th-20th century)
Besant, Annie Wood **2** 233-234
Booth, Charles **2** 400-401
Stopes, Marie **14** 476-478
Webb, Beatrice Potter **16** 153-154
Webb, Sidney James **16** 154-155
English (20th century)
Astor, Nancy Langhorne **1** 352-354
Belloc, Joseph Hilaire Pierre **2** 141
Beveridge, William Henry
2 251-252
Rathbone, Eleanor **13** 47-48
Russell, Bertrand Arthur William
13 373-374
French
Fourier, François Charles Marie
6 31-32
Rousseau, Jean Jacques **13** 324-328
Saint-Pierre, Abbé de **13** 434-435
Saint-Simon, Comte de **13** 436-437
Sorel, Georges **14** 347-348
German
Soelle, Dorothee **14** 324-325
Indian (Asia)
Ambedkar, Bhimrao Ramji
1 190-191
Bhave, Vinoba **2** 257-258
Das, Chitta Ranjan **4** 401-402
Deb, Radhakant **4** 437
Gandhi, Mohandas Karamchand
6 201-204
Narayan, Jayaprakash **11** 312-313
Roy, Ram Mohun **13** 18
Rabindranath Tagore **12** 529-531
Japanese
Toyotomi Hideyoshi **15** 286-289
Latin American

Mariátegui, José Carlos **10** 255-256
Paz, Octavio **12** 161-162
Sá, Mem de **13** 395
Sierra, Justo **14** 217
Vallejo, César Abraham **15** 408-409
Portuguese
Vieira, Antônio **15** 492
Prussian
Schmoller, Gustav Friedrich von
14 21
Roman
Drusus, Marcus Livius **5** 105-106
Russian
Kollontai, Aleksandra Mikhailovna
9 79
Peter I **12** 253-256
Spanish
Las Casas, Bartolomé de **9** 211-212
Philip V **12** 276-277
Thai
Mongkut **11** 104

Refraction (physics)
Hamilton, William Rowan **7** 99-100

Refrigeration
Armour, Philip Danforth **1** 302
Diesel, Rudolf **5** 7
Durant, William Crapo **5** 158

Refugees, The (novel)
Doyle, Arthur Conan **5** 91-92

Regalado, Tomás (born 1864), Salvadorean
general and politician
Estrada Cabrera, Manuel **5** 325-326

REGAN, DONALD (Donald Thomas
Regan; born 1918), American secretary of
the treasury and White House chief of
staff under Reagan **13** 80-81

Regard du roi, Le (novel)
Laye, Camara **9** 257-259

Regency Council (Austria; 1835)
Metternich, Klemens von **10** 533-536

Regency crisis (1765)
Fox, Charles James **6** 35-37
Rockingham, 2d Marquess of
13 230-231

Regency period (England)
George IV **6** 272-273
Nash, John **11** 316
Sheraton, Thomas **14** 181-182

Regent's Park (England)
Nash, John **11** 316

Reger, Max (1873-1916), German composer
Honegger, Arthur **7** 472-473

Reggia opera house (Parma, Italy)
Toscanini, Arturo **15** 270-271

Regicide, The (play)
Smollett, Tobias George **14** 305-307

REGIOMONTANUS (1436-1476), German
astronomer and mathematician **13** 81-82

Región más transparente, La (novel)
Fuentes, Carlos **6** 141-142

Regional Planning Association of America
Mumford, Lewis **11** 246-247

Regionalism and local color (American literature)
Midwest
Cather, Willa Sibert **3** 368-369
Eggleston, Edward **5** 223-224
Garland, Hannibal Hamlin **6** 217-218
Howe, Edgar Watson **7** 529
Riley, James Whitcomb **13** 170-171
Rölvaag, Ole Edvart **13** 265
New England
Jewett, Sarah Orne **8** 256
South
Cable, George Washington **3** 198-199
Caldwell, Erskine **3** 223-224
Faulkner, William **5** 395-397
Harris, Joel Chandler **7** 173-174
Hearn, Lafcadio **7** 240
Kennedy, John Pendleton **8** 506-507
Page, Thomas Nelson **12** 59-60
Simms, William Gilmore **14** 235-236
Styron, William **15** 6-8
West
Harte, Francis Brett **7** 184-185
Miller, Joaquin **11** 27-28
Richter, Conrad Michael **13** 148-149
Yukon
London, Jack **9** 494-495

Register House (Edinburgh)
Adam, Robert and James **1** 38-40

Register, Vote (poster)
Shahn, Ben **14** 139-140

Régnier, Henri de (1864-1936), French poet
Valéry, Paul Ambroise **15** 405-406

Regrets (sonnets)
du Bellay, Joachim **5** 113-114

Regrets of the Belle Heaulmière (poem)
Villon, François **15** 499-501

Regulae Philosophandi (tract)
Newton, Isaac **11** 369-372

Regulations for the Order and Discipline of the Troops ...
see Blue Book

Regulator movement (United States; 1768-71)
Tryon, William **15** 321

Regulus Leaving Rome (painting)
West, Benjamin **16** 210-212

Rehabilitation (health)
Switzer, Mary E. **15** 55-56

Rehearsal, The (satire)
Buckingham, 2d Duke of **3** 94-95

REHNQUIST, WILLIAM HUBBS (born 1924), U.S. Supreme Court chief justice **13** 82-84

Rehoboam (died 917 B.C.), king of Judah ca. 933-917
Jeroboam I **8** 248-249

Rei Seleuco, El (poem)
Camoëns, Luis Vaz de **3** 247-249

REICH, STEVE (born 1936), American composer **13** 84-85

Reich, Wilhelm (1897-1957), Austrian psychiatrist
Freud, Sigmund **6** 103-106

Reicha, Anton (1770-1836), Czech-French composer
Liszt, Franz **9** 445-447

Reichenbach, Convention of (1790)
Leopold II **9** 346

Reichenbach, Hans (1891-1953), German philosopher
Carnap, Rudolf **3** 308-309

Reichstag fire (Berlin; 1933)
Hitler, Adolf **7** 417-420
Szilard, Leo **15** 64-66

Reichstag Peace Resolution (1917)
Erzberger, Matthias **5** 319-320
Kapp, Wolfgang **8** 436

REICHSTEIN, TADEUS (born 1897), Polish-Swiss chemist **13** 85-87
Kendall, Edward Calvin **8** 495
Szent-Györgyi, Albert von **15** 62-64

REID, THOMAS (1710-1796), Scottish philosopher, clergyman, and teacher **13** 87-88
Cousin, Victor **4** 273-274
Stewart, Dugald **14** 449

REID, WILLIAM RONALD (Bill Reid; born 1920), Canadian artist **13** 88-89

Reigen (play)
Schnitzler, Arthur **14** 23-24

Reign of Terror
see French Revolution—1792-95 (Reign of Terror)

Reign of terror (Russia)
Ivan IV **8** 157-159

Reimarus, Hermann Samuel (1694-1798), German philosopher and theologian
Lessing, Gotthold Ephraim **9** 357-359

Reims, Council of (1148)
Lombard, Peter **9** 490-491

Reinaldo Solar (novel)
Gallegos Freire, Rómulo **6** 185-186

Reine Margot, La (play)
Dumas, Alexandre **5** 136-138

Reineke Fuchs (poems)
Goethe, Johann Wolfgang von **6** 388-391

Reinforced concrete (architecture)
Breuer, Marcel **2** 520-521
Nervi, Pier Luigi **11** 346-348
Perret, Auguste **12** 233

REINHARDT, MAX (Max Goldman; 1873-1943), Austrian stage director **13** 89-90
Brecht, Bertolt **2** 512-514
Hofmannsthal, Hugo von **7** 443-444
Lubitsch, Ernst **10** 18-19

Reinken, Jan (1623-1722), German organist and composer
Bach, Johann Sebastian **1** 416-419

Reinmar von Hagenau (Reinmar der Alte; died circa 1210), Alsatian minnesinger
Vogelweide, Walther von der **16** 10-11

Reis, Johann Philipp (1834-1874), German physicist and inventor
Bell, Alexander Graham **2** 129-131

Reisbilder (book)
Heine, Heinrich **7** 259-260

Reivers, The (novel)
Faulkner, William **5** 395-397

Reizenstein, Elmer
see Rice, Elmer

Rejoice in the Lord (anthem)
Purcell, Henry **12** 484-485

Rektor Kleist (play)
Kaiser, Georg **8** 411-412

Rélâche (ballet)
Satie, Erik **13** 494-495

Relapse (play)
Vanbrugh, John **15** 409-410

Relativism (history)
Becker, Carl Lotus **2** 100-101
Morison, Samuel Eliot **11** 175-176

Relativism (philosophy)
Comte, Auguste **4** 189-191
Herskovits, Melville Jean **7** 345
Poincaré, Jules Henri **12** 365-366

Relativity (physics)
general theory
Eddington, Arthur Stanley **5** 201-202
Einstein, Albert **5** 228-231
Fermi, Enrico **5** 422-424
Hamilton, William Rowan **7** 99-100
Lagrange, Joseph Louis **9** 164-166
Lobachevskii, Nikolai Ivanovich **9** 472-474
Mössbauer, Rudolf **11** 208-209
Noether, Emmy **11** 414-416
Riemann, Georg Friedrich Bernard **13** 164-165
interpretations
Schlick, Friedrich Albert Moritz **14** 16-17
Whitehead, Alfred North **16** 242-244
Yang, Chen Ning **16** 437-438
special theory
Einstein, Albert **5** 228-231
Lorentz, Hendrik Antoon **9** 515-516
Planck, Max Karl Ernst Ludwig **12** 342-344
see also Quantum theory

Reliance Building (Chicago)
Burnham, Daniel Hudson **3** 148-149

Relief and Construction Act (1932)
Hoover, Herbert Clark **7** 483-485

Relief No. 1 (sculpture)
Moore, Henry **11** 146-148

Relief of Lucknow, The (play)
Boucicault, Dion **2** 442-443

Relief party (U.S. politics)
Blair, Francis Preston **2** 313-315

Religio laici (poem)
Dryden, John **5** 106-107

Religio medici (book)
Browne, Thomas **3** 49-50

Religion
and history
von Rad, Gerhard **16** 29-30
and positive thinking
Peale, Norman Vincent **12** 171-172
and psychotherapy
Peale, Norman Vincent **12** 171-172
and science
Bacon, Roger **1** 425-427
Bosanquet, Bernard **2** 425-426
Bose, Jagadis Chandra **2** 429-430
Boyle, Robert **2** 469-471
Cooper, Thomas **4** 224
Douglas, Mary Tew **5** 79-80
Fiske, John **5** 465-466
Kingsley, Charles **9** 28
Wieman, Henry Nelson **16** 261-262
and social reform
Gutiérrez, Gustavo **7** 52-53
and sociology
Durkheim, Émile **5** 162-163
Frazer, James George **6** 76
Greeley, Andrew M. **6** 514-515
Troeltsch, Ernst **15** 299-300
Tylor, Edward Burnett **15** 372-373
and women
Schüssler Fiorenza, Elisabeth
14 46-48
Black Theology
Cone, James Hall **4** 196-197
comparative
ibn Hazm, Abu Muhammad Ali
8 93
Renan, Ernest **13** 95-96
Weber, Max **16** 157-160
concepts of
Rosenzweig, Franz **13** 294
Tillich, Paul Johannes **15** 224-225
ecumenism
Gilkey, Langdon Brown **6** 318-319
Harkness, Georgia **7** 155-156
John Paul II **8** 287-290
feminist theology
Morton, Nelle Katherine
11 195-197
history of
Eliade, Mircea **5** 249-250
Pagels, Elaine Hiesey **12** 61-62
Schillebeeckx, Edward **14** 3-4

liberation theology
Cone, James Hall **4** 196-197
natural
Toland, John **15** 256
philosophy of
Brightman, Edgar Sheffield **3** 8-9
Cohen, Hermann **4** 138-139
Feuerbach, Ludwig Andreas **5** 432
Kierkegaard, Søren Aabye
8 547-549
Royce, Josiah **13** 334-335
Santayana, George **13** 475-477
Schelling, Friedrich Wilhelm Joseph
von **13** 526-527
von Hügel, Friedrich **16** 21-22
Watts, Alan Wilson **16** 144-145
Whitehead, Alfred North
16 242-244
Wieman, Henry Nelson **16** 261-262
psychology of
Freud, Sigmund **6** 103-106
James, William **8** 215-217
Söderblom, Nathan **14** 323-324

Religion and the Rise of Capitalism (book)
Tawney, Richard Henry **15** 120-121

Religion, freedom of
see Religious liberty

Religion of Man, The (essays)
Rabindranath Tagore **12** 529-531

Religion of Reason (French revolution)
Robespierre, Maximilien François Marie
Isidore de **13** 199-201

Religion, Wars of (France; 1562-98)
Bodin, Jean **2** 356-357
Coligny, Gaspard de **4** 159-160
Henry IV **7** 293-295
Louis XIV **9** 531-533
Medici, Catherine de' **10** 445-449
Mérimée, Prosper **10** 517

Religious Allegory (painting)
Giorgione **6** 340-341

Religious conversions
see Conversions, religious

Religious education
see Education, religious

Religious leaders, Asiatic
Imaoka, Shinichiro **8** 115
Rajneesh, Bhagwan Shree **13** 7-9

Religious leaders, Black Muslim
Farrakhan, Louis **5** 389-390
Muhammad, Elijah **11** 230-231

Religious leaders, Buddhist
China
Chih-i **3** 518-519
Hsüan Tsang **8** 6-7
Hui-yüan **8** 25-26
Tao-an **15** 103-104
Tao-hsüan **15** 105
India
Buddha **3** 97-101
Kumarajiva **9** 127
Japan

Eisai **5** 231-232
Ennin **5** 288-289
Honen **7** 473
Ikeda, Daisaku **8** 109-110
Kukai **9** 124-125
Nichiren **11** 376-377
Niwano, Nikkyo **11** 400-401
Saicho **13** 426-428
Sesshu, Toya **14** 116-117
Shinran **14** 197
Suzuki, Daisetz Teitaro **15** 46-47
Thailand
Buddhadāsa Bhikkhu **3** 101-102
Mongkut **11** 104
Tibet
Dalai Lama **4** 369-371

Religious leaders, Catholic (since 1517)
archbishops
Corrigan, Michael Augustine **4** 253
Hughes, John Joseph **8** 17-18
Ireland, John **8** 133-134
Lamy, Jean Baptiste **9** 181-182
Mannix, Daniel **10** 210
Pázmány, Péter **12** 164-165
Romero, Oscar **13** 265-267
Sheen, Fulton J. **14** 171-172
bishops
Carroll, John **3** 331-332
England, John **5** 288
Gasca, Pedro de la **6** 230-231
Perry, Harold Robert **12** 236-237
cardinals
Bea, Augustinus **2** 79
Bembo, Pietro **2** 144-145
Bernardin, Joseph Cardinal
2 210-211
Borromeo, Charles **2** 423-424
Eck, Johann Maier von **5** 200
Gibbons, James **6** 300-301
Hayes, Patrick Joseph **7** 224-225
Lavigerie, Charles Martel Allemand
9 240
Manning, Henry Edward
10 209-210
McCloskey, John **10** 395
Mindszenty, József **11** 47-49
Mundelein, George William
11 248-249
Newman, John Henry **11** 365-367
Richelieu, Armand Jean du Plessis
de **13** 142-144
Sin, Jaime L. **14** 244-245
Spellman, Francis Joseph **14** 367
Stepinac, Alojzije **14** 433-435
Wolsey, Thomas **16** 364-366
confessors
Vianney, Jean Baptiste **15** 478-479
founders
Bourgeoys, Marguerite **2** 452-453
Cabrini, Frances Xavier **3** 205
Cajetan **3** 215-216
Drexel, Katherine **5** 102-103
Hecker, Isaac Thomas **7** 250-251
Ignatius of Loyola **8** 108-109

Lavigerie, Charles Martel Allemand **9** 240
MacKillop, Mary **10** 106-107
Neri, Philip **11** 340
Rosmini-Serbati, Antonio **13** 296-297
Teresa **15** 148-151
Vincent de Paul **15** 501-502
heretics
Jansen, Cornelis **8** 220-221
Molinos, Miguel de **11** 88-89
martyrs
Brébeuf, Jean de **2** 511-512
Jogues, Isaac **8** 270-271
More, Thomas **11** 156-157
Stein, Edith **14** 412-414
missionaries (to Africa)
Lavigerie, Charles Martel Allemand
9 240
missionaries (to Asia)
Francis Xavier **6** 48
Ricci, Matteo **13** 124-125
Teresa **15** 148-151
missionaries (to the Americas)
Anchieta, José de **1** 210-211
Brébeuf, Jean de **2** 511-512
Claver, Peter **4** 94
Damien **4** 383
De Smet, Pierre Jean **4** 509-510
Jogues, Isaac **8** 270-271
Kino, Eusebio Francisco **9** 30-31
Lacombe, Albert **9** 147-148
Las Casas, Bartolomé de **9** 211-212
Laval, Francois Xavier de **9** 235-236
Marcos de Niza **10** 240
Marquette, Jacques **10** 274-275
Serra, Junípero **14** 111-112
Vieira, Antônio **15** 492
Zumárraga, Juan de **16** 531-532
monks
Merton, Thomas **10** 523-525
nuns
Drexel, Katherine **5** 102-103
Juana Inés de la Cruz **8** 367-368
MacKillop, Mary **10** 106-107
Seton, Elizabeth Ann Bayley
14 118-119
Teresa **15** 148-151
Theresa **15** 178-179
political activists
Aristide, Jean-Bertrand **1** 291-293
Berrigan, Daniel J. **2** 222-223
Coughlin, Charles Edward
4 265-266
Hidalgo y Costilla, Miguel
7 375-377
Lamennais, Hugues Félicité Robert
de **9** 179
Matamoros, Mariano **10** 329-330
Montalembert, Comte de
11 118-119
Morelos, José María **11** 157-158
Romero, Oscar **13** 265-267
Ruether, Rosemary Radford
13 353-354

Santamaria, Bartholomew Augustine
13 473-474
popes
Benedict XV **2** 153-154
Gregory XIII **6** 534
John, XXIII **8** 277-280
John Paul I **8** 286-287
John Paul II **8** 287-290
Leo X **9** 332-334
Leo XIII **9** 334-336
Paul III **12** 144-145
Paul IV **12** 145-146
Paul VI **12** 146-148
Pius IV **12** 332
Pius V **12** 332-333
Pius VI **12** 333-334
Pius VII **12** 334-335
Pius IX **12** 335-336
Pius X **12** 336-337
Pius XI **12** 337-339
Pius XII **12** 339-340
Sixtus V **14** 267-268
priests
Greeley, Andrew M. **6** 514-515
Gutiérrez, Gustavo **7** 52-53
religious congregations
Anchieta, José de **1** 210-211
Hopkins, Gerard Manley **7** 492-494
Lacordaire, Jean Baptiste Henri
9 148
Mabillon, Jean **10** 72
Mariana, Juan de **10** 254-255
Mendel, Johann Gregor **10** 483-486
Sarpi, Paolo **13** 487-488
see also founders (above)
theologians
Bossuet, Jacques Bénigne **2** 431-432
Charron, Pierre **3** 472
Döllinger, Josef Ignaz von **5** 47-48
Fénelon, François de Salignac de la
Mothe **5** 410-411
Illich, Ivan **8** 112-114
Küng, Hans **9** 129-130
Loisy, Alfred Firmin **9** 489-490
Newman, John Henry **11** 365-367
Rahner, Karl **13** 4-5
Ruether, Rosemary Radford
13 353-354
Sarpi, Paolo **13** 487-488
Schillebeeckx, Edward **14** 3-4
Schüssler Fiorenza, Elisabeth
14 46-48
Suárez, Francisco **15** 8
Teilhard de Chardin, Marie Joseph
Pierre **15** 134-136
Tyrrell, George **15** 374-375
Vitoria, Francisco de **16** 1-2
see also Humanism, Christian; Reli-
gious leaders, Greek Orthodox;
Religious leaders, Russian Ortho-
dox

Religious leaders, Christian (to 1517)
biblical
see Bible
bishops
Gregory of Tours **6** 534-535

Grosseteste, Robert **7** 15
John of Salisbury **8** 284-285
Nicholas of Oresme **11** 380
see also Fathers (below)
canonists
Gratian **6** 498-499
cardinals
Ailly, Pierre d' **1** 94
Borgia, Cesare **2** 412-413
Cusa, Nicholas of **4** 352-353
crusaders
see Crusades
Doctors of the Church
Albertus Magnus **1** 115-116
Ambrose **1** 192-193
Anselm of Canterbury **1** 244-245
Athanasius **1** 358-359
Augustine **1** 367-370
Basil the Great **2** 51-52
Bede **2** 109-110
Bellarmine, Robert **2** 135-136
Bernard of Clairvaux **2** 207-208
Bonaventure **2** 383-384
Canisius, Peter **3** 258
Cyril **4** 362
Francis of Sales **6** 47
Gregory I **6** 531-532
Isidore of Seville **8** 149-150
Jerome **8** 249
John Chrysostom **8** 280-281
John of Damascus **8** 282
John of the Cross **8** 285
Leo I **9** 329-330
Thomas Aquinas **15** 183-186-422
Fathers of the Church
Ambrose **1** 192-193
Athanasius **1** 358-359
Augustine **1** 367-370
Basil the Great **2** 51-52
Bede **2** 109-110
Clement of Alexandria **4** 102-103
Cyril **4** 362
Ignatius of Antioch **8** 107-108
Jerome **8** 249
John Chrysostom **8** 280-281
John of Damascus **8** 282
Justin Martyr **8** 395-396
Leo I **9** 329-330
Origen **11** 528-529
Tertullian **15** 155-156
founders
Anthony, Susan Brownell **1** 246-248
Benedict, Ruth Fulton **2** 154-155
Dominic **5** 51-52
Francis of Assisi **6** 46-47
Groote, Gerard **7** 12-13
heretics and schismatics
Arius **1** 297-298
Donatus **5** 56-57
Eutyches **5** 335
Marcion **10** 238-239
Montanus **11** 122
Nestorius **11** 349-350
Pelagius **12** 189-190
Ulfilas **15** 384

Waldo, Peter **16** 55-56
martyrs
Becket, Thomas **2** 101-102
Boniface **2** 391
Cyprianus, Thascius Caecilianus **4** 361-362
Joan of Arc **8** 264-265
Justin Martyr **8** 395-396
see also Persecutions, religious
missionaries
Augustine of Canterbury **1** 370-371
Boniface **2** 391
Columba **4** 175-176
Columban **4** 176
Cyril and Methodius, Saints **4** 362-363
Lull, Raymond **10** 39-40
Patrick **12** 135-156
monks and abbots
Aelfric **1** 69-70
Alcuin of York **1** 122-123
Dunstan **5** 151-152
John of Piano Carpini **8** 284
Kempis, Thomas à **8** 493-494
Notker Balbulus **11** 434-435
Savonarola, Girolamo **13** 505-506
Stephen Harding **14** 428-429
see also founders (above)
mystics
Catherine of Siena **3** 369-370
Joachim of Fiore **8** 263-264
John of the Cross **8** 285
Julian of Norwich **8** 381
Rolle of Hampole, Richard **13** 260-261
Ruysbroeck, Jan van **13** 388-389
Orthodox Eastern Church
Basil the Great **2** 51-52
Cyril and Methodius, Saints **4** 362-363
Photius **12** 283-284
see also Religious leaders, Greek Orthodox; Religious leaders, Russian Orthodox
popes
Alexander VI **1** 134-135
Boniface VIII **2** 392-393
Clement V **4** 101-102
Gregory I **6** 531-532
Gregory VII **6** 532-534
Innocent, III **8** 125-127
Julius II **8** 384-386
Leo I **9** 329-330
Leo IX **9** 332
Leo X **9** 332-334
Martin V **10** 287-288
Peter **12** 252-253
Pius II **12** 331
Urban II **15** 393
Urban VI **15** 394
reformers
Arnold of Brescia **1** 314-315
Hus, Jan **8** 56-59
Louis IX **9** 525-526
Margaret of Scotland **10** 252-253
Olaf, II **11** 493-494

Wyclif, John **16** 412-413
theologians
Abelard, Peter **1** 23-25
Ailly, Pierre d' **1** 94
Boethius, Anicius Manlius Severinus **2** 360-361
Colet, John **4** 157-158
Cusa, Nicholas of **4** 352-353
Duns Scotus, John **5** 149-150
Eckhart, Johann **5** 200-201
Erigena, John Scotus **5** 308-309
Gerson, John **6** 285-286
Lanfranc **9** 189-190
Lombard, Peter **9** 490-491
Lull, Raymond **10** 39-40
William of Ockham **16** 298-299
see also Doctors and Fathers (above)
see also Religious leaders, Catholic (since 1517); Religious leaders, Protestant

Religious leaders, Ethical culturist
Adler, Felix **1** 63-64

Religious leaders, Greek Orthodox
Lucaris, Cyril **10** 20
Makarios III **10** 157-158
see also Religious leaders, Christian (to 1517)—Orthodox Eastern Church

Religious leaders, Hindu (India)
Bhaktivedanta Prabhupada **2** 254-255
Dayananda Saraswati **4** 431
Gandhi, Mohandas Karamchand **6** 201-204
Ghose, Aurobindo **6** 293-294
Maharishi Mahesh Yogi **10** 132-133
Ramakrishna, Sri **13** 11-13
Roy, Ram Mohun **13** 18
Shankara **14** 150-151
Vivekananda **16** 4-5
Yogananda **16** 462-463

Religious leaders, Islamic
Almohad founder
ibn Tumart, Muhammad **8** 96-97
see also Almohads
Almoravid founder
Abdullah ibn Yasin **1** 20
see also Almoravids
Black Muslims
Farrakhan, Louis **5** 389-390
Muhammad, Elijah **11** 230-231
caliphs
Abd al-Mumin **1** 13
Abd al-Rahman III **1** 14
Ali **1** 155-156
Harun al-Rashid **7** 188
Mansur, Abu Jafar ibn Muhammad al- **10** 214-215
Muawiya ibn Abu Sufyan **11** 223-224
Omar ibn al-Khattab **11** 508-509
Yakub al-Mansur, Abu Yusuf **16** 426
founder
Mohammed **11** 76-78
heads of state
Khamenei, Sayyid Ali **8** 533-535

Khomeini, Ruhollah Musavi **8** 535-537
holy war leaders
Abd el-Kadir **1** 15
Hassan, Muhammad Abdille **7** 194-195
Mahdi **10** 137-138
Omar ibn Said Tal, Al-Hajj **11** 509-510
Uthman don Fodio **15** 397-398
imams
Aga Khan **1** 74-76
Sadr, Musa al- **13** 420-422
Jamā'at-i Islāmī founder
Mawdūdī, Abu-I A'la **10** 353-354
Mouride leaders
Bamba, Amadou **1** 481-482
Muslim Brothers leaders
Al-Banna, Hassan **1** 104-106
Sayyid Qutb **13** 509-511
mystics
Aiken, Conrad **1** 90-91
Attar, Farid ed-Din **1** 359-360
Ghazali, Abu Hamid Muhammad al- **6** 290-291
Hallaj, Al-Husayn ibn Mansur al- **7** 86-87
Ibn al-Arabi, Muhyi al-Din **8** 91
Junayd, Abu al-Qasim ibn Muhammad al **8** 388
see also Sufism
nationalists
Bhashani, Maulana Abdul Hamid Khan **2** 255-257
Shi'ite
Berri, Nabih **2** 220-222
Fadlallah, Sayyid Muhammad Husayn **5** 362-364
theologians
Abduh ibn Hasan Khayr Allah, Muhammad **1** 16-17
Aiken, Conrad **1** 90-91
Al-Banna, Hassan **1** 104-106
Ashari, Abu al- Hasan Ali al- **1** 327-328
Bukhari, Muhammad ibn Ismail al- **3** 111-112
ibn Hazm, Abu Muhammad Ali **8** 93
Nazzam, Ibrahim ibn Sayyar al- **11** 329
Sayyid Qutb **13** 509-511
Shariati, Ali **14** 156-157
Syed Ahmed Khan **15** 60
Tabari, Muhammad ibn Jarir al- **15** 69-70
see also Islam; Islamic Empire

Religious leaders, Jainist (India)
Mahavira, Vardhamana **10** 135-137

Religious leaders, Jewish
biblical
see Bible—Old Testament
biblical exegetes
Abravanel, Isaac ben Judah **1** 31
Graetz, Heinrich Hirsch **6** 483
Herberg, Will **7** 322-323

Kaufmann, Ezekiel **8** 460
Hasidic leaders
  Baal Shem Tov **1** 404-405
Karaite leaders
  Anan ben David **1** 207-208
legal codifiers
  Caro, Joseph ben Ephraim
    3 316-317
  Judah I **8** 372-373
  Maimonides **10** 151-152
liturgists
  Judah Halevi **8** 373
  Pinto, Isaac **12** 318
mystics
  Leon, Moses de **9** 336
  Luria, Isaac ben Solomon Ashkenazi
    10 47-48
  Luzzato, Moses Hayyim **10** 57-58
  Sabbatai Zevi **13** 400-401
philosophers
  Cohen, Hermann **4** 138-139
  Mendelssohn, Moses **10** 488-489
  Rosenzweig, Franz **13** 294
  Soloveitchik, Joseph Baer
    14 328-329
  Wolfson, Harry Austryn **16** 361-362
rabbis
  Abba Arika **1** 3-4
  Akiba ben Joseph **1** 97-98
  Baeck, Leo **1** 429-430
  Finkelstein, Rabbi Louis **5** 448-450
  Gershom ben Judah **6** 283-284
  Hillel **7** 390-391
  Judah I **8** 372-373
  Jung, Leo **8** 390-391
  Kuk, Abraham Issac **9** 123-124
  Manasseh ben Israel **10** 183-184
  Nahmanides **11** 293-294
  Schindler, Solomon **14** 7-8
  Silver, Abba Hillel **14** 232-233
  Wise, Isaac Mayer **16** 342-343
religious poets
  ibn Gabirol, Solomon ben Judah
    8 92
revolt leaders
  Bar Kochba, Simeon **2** 5
scholars
  Baeck, Leo **1** 429-430
  Baron, Salo Wittmayer **2** 16-17
  Dubnov, Simon **5** 115-116
  Elijah ben Solomon **5** 251-252
  Finkelstein, Rabbi Louis **5** 448-450
  Ginzberg, Louis **6** 337-338
  Johanan ben Zakkai **8** 271-272
  Josephus Flavius **8** 360-361
  Krochmal, Nachman Kohen
    9 104-105
  Lee Kuan Yew **9** 281-283
  Revel, Bernard **13** 108-109
  Schechter, Solomon **13** 524
  Scholem, Gershom **14** 26
  Shammai **14** 149
  Zunz, Leopold **16** 534
Talmudists
  Abba Arika **1** 3-4

Caro, Joseph ben Ephraim
  3 316-317
Levi ben Gershon **9** 363-364
Nahmanides **11** 293-294
Rashi **13** 43
Saadia ben Joseph al-Fayumi **13** 396
theologians
  Abravanel, Isaac ben Judah **1** 31
  Buber, Martin **3** 87-89
  Fackenheim, Emil Ludwig
    5 359-361
  Herberg, Will **7** 322-323
  Heschel, Abraham Joshua
    7 358-359
  Jung, Leo **8** 390-391
  Kaplan, Mordecai Menahem
    8 435-436
  Lee Kuan Yew **9** 281-283
  Levi ben Gershon **9** 363-364
  Rubenstein, Richard L. **13** 343-344
  Soloveitchik, Joseph Baer
    14 328-329
Zionists
  Ben-Gurion, David **2** 160-161
  Ginzberg, Asher **6** 336-337
  Gordon, Aaron David **6** 447-448
  Herzl, Theodor **7** 352-354
  Jabotinsky, Vladimir Evgenevich
    8 167-168
  Meir, Golda **10** 462-463
  Silver, Abba Hillel **14** 232-233
  Szold, Henrietta **15** 66-67
  Weizman, Ezer **16** 181-182
  Wise, Stephen Samuel **16** 344-345
  Zangwill, Israel **16** 488-489
  see also Jewish history; Judaism

Religious leaders, Manichaean
Mani **10** 196-197

Religious leaders, Native American
Black Elk, Nicholas **2** 305-306
Deganawida **4** 460-461
Handsome Lake **7** 122-123
Parker, Quanah **12** 109-112
Smohalla **14** 303-305
Wovoka **16** 390-393

Religious leaders, pagan
Domitian **5** 52-53
Julian **8** 378-379
Pythagoras **12** 498-499

Religious leaders, Protestant
Adventists
  Miller, William **11** 30-31
African Methodist Episcopal
  Revels, Hiram Rhoades **13** 109-110
  Turner, Henry McNeal **15** 351-352
Anabaptists
  John of Leiden **8** 283
  Menno Simons **10** 505-506
  Münzer, Thomas **11** 251-252
Anglican archbishops
  Carey, George Leonard **3** 293-294
  Tutu, Desmond **15** 360-361
Anglican bishops
  Berkeley, George **2** 197-198
  Burnet, Gilbert **3** 147

Butler, Joseph **3** 180-181
Cranmer, Thomas **4** 295-296
Crowther, Samuel Adjai **4** 326
Harris, Barbara Clementine
  7 171-172
Latimer, Hugh **9** 221
Laud, William **9** 224-225
Ramsey, Arthur Michael **13** 23-25
Strachan, John **14** 486-487
Temple, William **15** 141-143
Anglican clergymen
  Donne, John **5** 60-61
  Herrick, Robert **7** 336-339
  Hooker, Richard **7** 475-476
  Inge, William Ralph **8** 118-119
  Johnson, Samuel **8** 314-315
  Law, William **9** 245-246
  Pusey, Edward Bouverie **12** 488-489
  Swift, Jonathan **15** 51-54, 307
Anglican theologians
  Butler, Joseph **3** 180-181
  Macquarrie, John **10** 116-117
  Maurice, John Frederick Denison
    10 349-350
  Newman, John Henry **11** 365-367
  Paley, William **12** 72
  see also Episcopalians (below)
Anglican women
  Royden, Agnes Maude **13** 335-337
Apostle to the Indians
  Eliot, John **5** 256-258
Arminians
  Arminius, Jacobus **1** 301-302
Baptist clergy
  Backus, Isaac **1** 420-421
  Bunyan, John **3** 128-129
  Cleveland, James **4** 106-108
  Falwell, Jerry **5** 375-376
  Fosdick, Harry Emerson **6** 21-22
  Miller, William **11** 30-31
  Sullivan, Leon Howard **15** 25-27
  Wayland, Francis **16** 148-149
Baptist missionaries
  Carey, William **3** 297
  Judson, Adoniram **8** 377-378
  McCoy, Isaac **10** 403
Bohemian Brethren
  Comenius, John Amos **4** 180-181
  Zwingli, Huldreich **16** 537-538
Calvinists
  Calvin, John **3** 239-242
  Knox, John **9** 65-66
Campbellites
  Campbell, Alexander **3** 249-250
Christian Scientists
  Eddy, Mary Baker **5** 202
Church of England
  Waite, Terry **16** 47-48
Church of Scotland
  Baillie, D. (Donald) M. (Macpher-
    son) **1** 445
  Baillie, John **1** 445-447
Congregationalist clergy
  Sheldon, Charles M. **14** 172-174
Congregationalist ministers

Abbott, Lyman **1** 10-11
Beecher, Henry Ward **2** 112-113
Bushnell, Horace **3** 171-172
Cotton, John **4** 263-265
Cutler, Manasseh **4** 356-357
Dwight, Timothy **5** 169
Mather, Cotton **10** 330-332
Mather, Increase **10** 332-333
Morse, Jedidiah **11** 191-192
Stoddard, Solomon **14** 462-463
Strong, Josiah **14** 512-513
Wheelock, Eleazar **16** 222-223
Wigglesworth, Michael **16** 266-267
Wise, John **16** 343-344
Congregationalist missionaries
Kirkland, Samuel **9** 37
Livingstone, David **9** 463-465
Whitman, Marcus **16** 248-249
deists
Herbert, Edward **7** 324
Toland, John **15** 256
Dutch Reformed
Boesak, Allan Aubrey **2** 359-360
Frelinghuysen, Theodorus Jacobus
6 96-97
Peale, Norman Vincent **12** 171-172
Visser't Hooft, Willem Adolf
15 511-512
ecumenical leaders
Baillie, D. (Donald) M. (Macpherson) **1** 445
Baillie, John **1** 445-447
Gilkey, Langdon Brown **6** 318-319
Episcopalian bishops
Chase, Philander **3** 472-473
Hobart, John Henry **7** 420-421
Seabury, Samuel **14** 76
Episcopalian clergymen
Brooks, Phillips **3** 26
Muhlenberg, William Augustus
11 233-234
Weems, Mason Locke **16** 170
Episcopalian missionaries
Chase, Philander **3** 472-473
Evangelical
Caesar, Shirley **3** 210-211
Ritschl, Albrecht Benjamin **13** 180
evangelists (Great Awakening)
Edwards, Jonathan **5** 220-222
Frelinghuysen, Theodorus Jacobus
6 96-97
Tennent, Gilbert **15** 143-144
Whitefield, George **16** 241-242
see also revivalists (below)
feminist
Morton, Nelle Katherine
11 195-197
Free Church (Scotland)
Chalmers, Thomas **3** 408-409
McCosh, James **10** 402-403
fundamentalists
Falwell, Jerry **5** 375-376
Paisley, Ian K. **12** 67-69
German Reformed
Nevin, John Williamson **11** 357
Gortonites

Gorton, Samuell **6** 460
Huguenots
Coligny, Gaspard de **4** 159-160
Lutherans
Boehme, Jacob **2** 357
Luther, Martin **10** 48-51
Marty, Martin E. **10** 300-301
Melancthon, Philip **10** 466-467
Mühlenberg, Heinrich Melchior
11 232-233
Nygren, Anders **11** 449-451
Söderblom, Nathan **14** 323-324
Spener, Philipp Jakob **14** 372
Troeltsch, Ernst **15** 299-300
Methodist bishops
Allen, Richard **1** 168
Vincent, John Heyl **15** 502-503
Methodist clergy
Harkness, Georgia **7** 155-156
Methodist ministers
Cartwright, Peter **3** 344-345
Eggleston, Edward **5** 223-224
Ryerson, Adolphus Egerton
13 392-393
Wesley, Charles **16** 208-209
Wesley, John **16** 209-210
Whitefield, George **16** 241-242
Methodist missionaries
Mott, John R. **11** 212
Mormons
Smith, Joseph **14** 297-298
Young, Brigham **16** 469-470
Oneida community
Noyes, John Humphrey **11** 437-438
Pentacostal
Sharpton, Al **14** 159-162
Pietists
Mühlenberg, Heinrich Melchior
11 232-233
Spener, Philipp Jakob **14** 372
Zinzendorf, Nikolaus Ludwig von
16 522-523
Presbyterian clergymen
Beecher, Lyman **2** 113
Buechner, Frederick **3** 103-105
Finney, Charles Grandison
5 450-451
Graham, Sylvester **6** 486-487
Tennent, Gilbert **15** 143-144
Witherspoon, John **16** 346-348
Presbyterian missionaries
Duff, Alexander **5** 126-127
Makemie, Francis **10** 158-159
Puritans
Baxter, Richard **2** 76-77
Brewster, William **2** 523-524
Coverdale, Miles **4** 278
Davenport, John **4** 405-406
Dudley, Thomas **5** 124-125
Dunster, Henry **5** 152-153
Edwards, Jonathan **5** 220-222
Hooker, Thomas **7** 476-477
Hopkins, Samuel **7** 496
Hutchinson, Anne Marbury **8** 69-71
Lilburne, John **9** 409-410
Taylor, Edward **15** 122-123

Williams, Roger **16** 304-305
Quakers
Benezet, Anthony **2** 159-160
Fox, George **6** 37-38
Mott, Lucretia Coffin **11** 212-213
Woolman, John **16** 382-383
Rappites
Rapp, George **13** 42-43
Ratana Church
Ratana, Taupotiki Wiremu **13** 46
Reformers
Karlstadt, Andreas Bodenheim von
8 449
Luther, Martin **10** 48-51
Melancthon, Philip **10** 466-467
Münzer, Thomas **11** 251-252
Schwenckfeld, Kasper von **14** 56-57
revivalists
Graham, William Franklin Jr.
6 487-488
McPherson, Aimee Semple **10** 434
Moody, Dwight L. **11** 141-142
Sunday, William Ashley **15** 32-33
Russellites
Russell, Charles Taze **13** 376-377
Salvation Army
Booth, Evangeline Cory **2** 402-403
Booth, William **2** 405-406
Seekers
Williams, Roger **16** 304-305
Seventh-Day Baptists
Beissel, Johann Conrad **2** 123-124
Booth, Joseph **2** 404-405
Shakers
Lee, Ann **9** 285-288
Social Gospel
Abbott, Lyman **1** 10-11
Gladden, Washington **6** 356-357
Holmes, John Haynes **7** 456-457
Rauschenbusch, Walter **13** 53-54
Southern Baptist
Robertson, Pat **13** 196-198
Swedenborgians
Swedenborg, Emanuel **15** 49-50
Swiss Reformed
Brunner, Emil **3** 74-75
theologians
Gilkey, Langdon Brown **6** 318-319
Meland, Bernard Eugene
10 467-468
theologians (19th-20th century)
Adams, James Luther **1** 47-48
Altizer, Thomas J. J. **1** 183-184
Baillie, D. (Donald) M. (Macpherson) **1** 445
Baillie, John **1** 445-447
Baur, Ferdinand Christian **2** 74-75
Bennett, John Coleman **2** 170-171
Bonhoeffer, Dietrich **2** 389-391
Brunner, Emil **3** 74-75
Bultmann, Rudolf Karl **3** 119-120
Cox, Harvey **4** 284-285
Harkness, Georgia **7** 155-156
Harnack, Adolf von **7** 160
Hartshorne, Charles **7** 186-187
Moltmann, Jörgen **11** 91-92

Niebuhr, Helmut Richard
   11 386-387
Niebuhr, Reinhold **11** 387-388
Nygren, Anders **11** 449-451
Otto, Louis Karl Rudolf **12** 30-32
Pannenberg, Wolfhart **12** 87-88
Ramsey, Arthur Michael **13** 23-25
Schleiermacher, Friedrich Ernst
   Daniel **14** 11-12
Soelle, Dorothee **14** 324-325
Strauss, David Friedrich **14** 496-497
Tillich, Paul Johannes **15** 224-225
Wieman, Henry Nelson **16** 261-262
Unitarians
   Adams, James Luther **1** 47-48
   Bellows, Henry Whitney **2** 143-144
   Channing, William Ellery **3** 435-436
   Hale, Edward Everett **7** 71-72
   Holmes, John Haynes **7** 456-457
   Parker, Theodore **12** 112-113
   Price, Richard **12** 447-448
   Ripley, George **13** 179-180
United Brethren
   Otterbein, Philip William **12** 27-28
United Church of Christ clergy
   Chavis, Benjamin **3** 491-493
Zwinglian
   Zwingli, Huldreich **16** 537-538

Religious leaders, Russian Orthodox
   Berdyaev, Nicholas Alexandrovich
      2 184-185
   Mogila, Peter **11** 74-75
   Nikon, Nikita Minov **11** 395
   Pobedonostsev, Konstantin Petrovich
      12 360-361
   Rasputin, Grigori Efimovich **13** 44-45
   Soloviev, Vladimir Sergeevich
      14 329-330
   see also Religious leaders, Christian (to
      1517)—Orthodox Eastern Church

Religious leaders, Sikh (India)
   Nanak **11** 303

Religious leaders, Taoist (Chinese)
   Chang Chüeh **3** 432-433
   Lao Tzu **9** 201-202

Religious leaders, Unificationist
   Moon, Sun Myung **11** 142-143

Religious leaders, Zen Buddhist
   Watts, Alan Wilson **16** 144-145

Religious leaders, Zoroastrian (Persia)
   Zoroaster **16** 528-530

Religious liberty
   Asia
      Akbar, Jalal-ud-din Mohammed **1** 96
      Buddha **3** 97-101
      Imaoka, Shinichiro **8** 115
      Judas Maccabeus **8** 374-375
   Europe
      Bea, Augustinus **2** 79
      Bodin, Jean **2** 356-357
      Burnet, Gilbert **3** 147
      Cromwell, Oliver **4** 317-320
      Frederick William IV **6** 87-88
         Gustavus III **7** 45-46
         Joseph II **8** 359-360
   North Africa
      Lavigerie, Charles Martel Allemand
         9 240
      Muawiya ibn Abu Sufyan
         11 223-224
   Persian empire
      Abbas I **1** 4-6
      Darius I **4** 394-395
      Hulagu Khan **8** 27-28
   U.S.
      Douglas, William Orville **5** 83-85
      Kamehameha III **8** 416-417
      Madison, James **10** 121-123
      Makemie, Francis **10** 158-159
      see also Anti-Semitism; Catholic
         Emancipation; Church and State;
         Ecumenism

Religious persecutions
   see Persecutions, religious

Religious toleration
   see Religious liberty

Religious-Philosophical Society (Russia)
   Merezhkovsky, Dmitry Sergeyevich
      10 515-516

Reliquary House (sculpture)
   Smith, David **14** 287-288

Reliquiae Wottonianae (musical collection)
   Walton, Izaak **16** 90-91

REMARQUE, ERICH MARIA (Erich Paul
   Remark; 1898-1970), German novelist
   13 91
      Dos Passos, John Roderigo **5** 69-71
      Mann, Thomas **10** 204-207

REMBRANDT HARMENSZ VAN RIJN
   (1606-1669), Dutch painter and etcher
   13 91-95
      influence (Australia)
         Dobell, William **5** 34-35
      influence (England)
         Constable, John **4** 208-209
         John, Augustus Edwin **8** 291
      influence (France)
         Daumier, Honoré Victorin
            4 403-405
         Soutine, Chaim **14** 356-357
         Staël, Nicolas de **14** 392
      influence (Germany)
         Kirchner, Ernst Ludwig **9** 34-35
         Nolde, Emil **11** 419-420
      influence (Netherlands)
         Lucas van Leyden **10** 20-21
         Van Gogh, Vincent **15** 427-429
         Vermeer, Jan **15** 466-467
      influence (United States)
         Johnson, Earvin Jr. **8** 297-299
         Tanner, Henry Ossawa **15** 102-103
      influenced by
         Brouwer, Adriaen **3** 29-30
         Caravaggio **3** 282-284
   Rembrandt, Titus (1641-1668), Dutch
      shopkeeper
         Rembrandt Harmensz van Rijn
            13 91-95, 141

Remède de fortune (musical composition)
   Machaut, Guillaume de **10** 93-94

Remedies for Love, The (poem)
   Ovid **12** 34-36

Remedio en la desdicha, El (play)
   Lope Félix de Vega Carpio **9** 503-506

Remember to Remember (book)
   Miller, Henry **11** 26-27

Remembering (book)
   Bartlett, Frederic Charles **2** 34-35

Remembrance of Things Past (novel)
   Proust, Marcel **12** 465-467

Remembrance Rock (novel)
   Sandburg, Carl **13** 461-462

Reményi, Eduard (1830-1898), Hungarian
   violinst
      Brahms, Johannes **2** 490-492

Remington Company
   Edison, Thomas Alva **5** 206-208

Reminiscing in Tempo (jazz composition)
   Ellington, Edward Kennedy **5** 273-274

REMOND, CHARLES LENNOX
   (1810-1873), American black abolitionist
   13 95

Remonstrance au peuple de France (poem)
   Ronsard, Pierre de **13** 271-273

Remonstrants (religion)
   see Arminianism

Remorse (play)
   Coleridge, Samuel Taylor **4** 154-156

Removal of the Body of St. Mark (painting)
   Tintoretto **15** 232-234

Renaissance (art)
   Austria
      Donner, Georg Raphael **5** 63
   England
      Hilliard, Nicholas **7** 391-392
      Holbein, Hans the Younger
         7 449-450
      Jones, Inigo **8** 333-334
   France
      Charonton, Enguerrand **3** 471
      Clouet, Jean and François **4** 122-123
      l'Orme, Philibert de **9** 519
      Fouquet, Jean **6** 31
      Goujon, Jean **6** 466-467
      Lescot, Pierre **9** 354
      Pilon, Germain **12** 305
      Primaticcio, Francesco **12** 453-454
      Rosso, Il **13** 312-313
   Germany
      Altdorfer, Albrecht **1** 179-180
      Cranach, Lucas the Elder **4** 289-290
      Dürer, Albrecht **5** 159-161
      Grünewald, Matthias **7** 23-24
      Holbein, Hans the Younger
         7 449-450

Lochner, Stephan **9** 475
Pacher, Michael **12** 53
Riemenschneider, Tilman **13** 166
Schongauer, Martin **14** 26-28
Stoss, Veit **14** 481-482
Witz, Konrad **16** 351-352
Italy
   see Renaissance, Italian (art)
Netherlands
   Bosch, Hieronymus **2** 426-428
   Bouts, Dirk **2** 458-459
   Bruegel, Pieter the Elder **3** 65-67
   Campin, Robert **3** 255
   Christus, Petrus **4** 33-34
   Eyck, Hubert and Jan van **5** 352-354
   Geertgen tot Sint Jans **6** 248
   Limbourg brothers, The **9** 412-413
   Lucas van Leyden **10** 20-21
   Massys, Quentin **10** 325-326
   Memling, Hans **10** 476
   van der Goes, Hugo **15** 416-417
   Weyden, Rogier van der **16** 219-221
Spain
   Bermejo, Bartolomé **2** 205
   Berruguete, Alonso **2** 223-224
   Greco **6** 511-514
   Herrera, Juan de **7** 335
   Morales, Luis de **11** 150

Renaissance (literature)
England
   Bacon, Francis **1** 422-424
   Elizabeth I **5** 263-266
   Ford, John **6** 7-8
   Jonson, Ben **8** 343-345
   Kyd, Thomas **9** 140-141
   Marlowe, Christopher **10** 272-274
   Marvell, Andrew **10** 301-303
   Raleigh, Walter **13** 9-11
   Shakespeare, William **14** 142-145
   Sidney, Philip **14** 214-215
   Walton, Izaak **16** 90-91
France
   du Bellay, Joachim **5** 113-114
   Montaigne, Michel Eyquem de
      11 116-117
   Rabelais, François **12** 524-526
   Ronsard, Pierre de **13** 271-273
Italy
   Ariosto, Ludovico **1** 289-290
   Bembo, Pietro **2** 144-145
   Castiglione, Baldassare **3** 360-361
   Cellini, Benvenuto **3** 391-392
   Machiavelli, Niccolò **10** 97-99
   Pico della Mirandola, Giovanni
      12 299-300
   Poliziano, Angelo **12** 373-374
   Porta, Giambattista della
      12 403-404
   Pulci, Luigi **12** 481
   Tasso, Torquato **15** 114-116
   Vasari, Giorgio **15** 442-443
Portugal
   Camoëns, Luis Vaz de **3** 247-249
   Vicente, Gil **15** 479-480
Spain

Alemán, Mateo **1** 126
Calderón, Pedro **3** 221-222
Cervantes, Miguel de Saavedra
   3 395-398
Encina, Juan del **5** 283
Góngora y Argote, Luis de
   6 427-428
Gracián y Morales, Baltasar Jeróni-
   mo **6** 481-482
Lope Félix de Vega Carpio
   9 503-506
Manrique, Jorge **10** 210-211
Quevedo Y Villegas, Francisco
   Gómez de **12** 511
Tirso de Molina **15** 237-238

Renaissance (music)
England
   Byrd, William **3** 187-188
   Dowland, John **5** 90
   Dunstable, John **5** 150-151
   Morley, Thomas **11** 179-180
   Tallis, Thomas **15** 91
France
   Clemens non Papa, Jacobus **4** 101
   Goudimel, Claude **6** 466
   Le Jeune, Claude **9** 314-315
Franco-Flemish
   Gombert, Nicolas **6** 416-417
   Isaac, Heinrich **8** 143-144
   Josquin des Prez **8** 361-363
   Lassus, Roland de **9** 216-218
Italy
   Frescobaldi, Girolamo **6** 101-102
   Gabrieli, Giovanni **6** 161-162
   Gesualdo, Don Carlo **6** 287-288
   Marenzio, Luca **10** 248
   Merulo, Claudio **10** 525-526
   Palestrina, Giovanni Pierluigi da
      12 70-72
   Willaert, Adrian **16** 287-288
   Zarlino, Gioseffo **16** 490-491
Netherlands
   Dufay, Guillaume **5** 125-126
   Sweelinck, Jan Pieterszoon
      15 50-51

Renaissance (philosophy)
England
   Bacon, Francis **1** 422-424
France
   Ramus, Petrus **13** 27-28
Italy
   Feltre, Vittorino da **5** 409-410
   Machiavelli, Niccolò **10** 97-99
   Pico della Mirandola, Giovanni
      12 299-300
   Telesio, Bernardino **15** 138-139
   Valla, Lorenzo **15** 406

Renaissance, Italian (art)
13th-14th century (Proto-)
   Andrea Pisano **1** 225-226
   Arnolfo di Cambio **1** 315-316
   Cimabue **4** 60-61
   Duccio di Buoninsegna **5** 121-122
   Giotto **6** 342-345

Lorenzetti, Pietro and Ambrogio
   9 517-518
Martini, Simone **10** 298-299
Orcagna **11** 526-527
Pisano, Giovanni **12** 324-325
Pisano, Nicola **12** 325
15th century (Early, architecture)
   Alberti, Leon Battista **1** 113-115
   Bramante, Donato **2** 493-494
   Brunelleschi, Filippo **3** 70-72
   Michelozzo **11** 6-7
15th century (Early, painting)
   Antonello da Messina **1** 251-252
   Bellini, Giovanni **2** 137-138
   Gentile da Fabriano **6** 266-267
   Mantegna, Andrea **10** 215-216
   Perugino **12** 245-246
   Piero della Francesca **12** 301-302
   Pisanello **12** 323-324
   Sassetta **13** 492
   Signorelli, Luca **14** 221-222
   Tura, Cosimo **15** 343-344
15th century (Early, painting; Florence)
   Andrea del Castagno **1** 223-224
   Angelico **1** 235-236
   Botticelli, Sandro **2** 439-440
   Ghirlandaio, Domenico **6** 292-293
   Leonardo da Vinci **9** 337-340
   Lippi, Filippo **9** 439
   Masaccio **10** 312-313
   Pollaiuolo, Antonio **12** 377-378
   Uccello, Paolo **15** 378-379
   Veneziano, Domenico **15** 459-460
   Verrocchio, Andrea del **15** 471-472
15th century (Early, sculpture)
   Agostino di Duccio **1** 86
   da Settignano, Desiderio **4** 509
   Donatello **5** 55-56
   Ghiberti, Lorenzo **6** 291-292
   Luca della Robbia **10** 19-20
   Pollaiuolo, Antonio **12** 377-378
   Quercia, Jacopo della **12** 509
   Verrocchio, Andrea del **15** 471-472
16th century (High, painting)
   Andrea del Sarto **1** 224-225
   Bronzino **3** 19
   Carracci **3** 319-321
   Correggio **4** 249-251
   Giorgione **6** 340-341
   Leonardo da Vinci **9** 337-340
   Lotto, Lorenzo **9** 520-521
   Michelangelo Buonarroti **11** 2-5
   Parmigianino **12** 117
   Pontormo **12** 394-395
   Raphael **13** 40-42
   Tintoretto **15** 232-234
   Titian **15** 242-244
   Vasari, Giorgio **15** 442-443
   Veronese, Paolo **15** 469-470
16th century (High, sculpture and
   architecture)
   Bramante, Donato **2** 493-494
   Cellini, Benvenuto **3** 391-392
   Giovanni da Bologna **6** 345-346
   Michelangelo Buonarroti **11** 2-5

Palladio, Andrea **12** 75-77
Porta, Giacomo della **12** 402-403
Raphael **13** 40-42
Sangallo family **13** 464-466
Sanmicheli, Michele **13** 469-470
Sansovino, Jacopo **13** 470-471
Vignola, Giacomo da **15** 493-494

Rênal, Madame de (literary character)
Stendhal **14** 422-425

RENAN, ERNEST (1823-1892), French
author and philologist **13** 95-96
Bernard, Claude **2** 208-210
Flaubert, Gustave **5** 480-482
Loisy, Alfred Firmin **9** 489-490
Strauss, David Friedrich **14** 496-497

Renard, Jules (1864-1900), French author
Bonnard, Pierre **2** 395-396

Renascence (poem)
Millay, Edna St. Vincent **11** 24-25

Renate (novella)
Storm, Theodor **14** 479-480

Rencho
see Nichiren

RENDELL, RUTH (Ruth Grasemann Rendell; born 1930), English writer of mysteries and suspense thrillers **13** 96-97

René (novel)
Chateaubriand, Vicomte de **3** 477-479

René II (1451-1508), Duke of Lorraine
Waldseemüller, Martin **16** 56

Renée Mauperin (novel)
Goncourt, Edmond de and Jules de
6 426-427

Renga (poem)
Basho, Matsuo **2** 45-48

RENI, GUIDO (1575-1642), Italian painter
13 97-98
Bernini, Gian Lorenzo **2** 214-216
David, Jacques Louis **4** 407-409
Raphael **13** 40-42
Ribera, Jusepe de **13** 122-123

RENNER, KARL (1870-1950), Austrian
statesman, president 1945-50 **13** 98-99
Trotsky, Leon **15** 302-305

RENO, JANET (born 1938), U.S. attorney
general (1993-) **13** 99-101

Renoir, Jean (1894-1979), French film
director
Ray, Satyajit **13** 60-61

RENOIR, PIERRE AUGUSTE (1841-1919),
French impressionist painter **13** 101-102
compared to
Liebermann, Max **9** 402-403
Maillol, Aristide **10** 150-151
impressionism
Cézanne, Paul **3** 400-402
Monet, Claude **11** 102-104
Pissaro, Camille **12** 326-327
influence of
Dobell, William **5** 34-35
Glackens, William **6** 355-356

Rivera, Diego **13** 183-184
influenced by
Courbet, Jean Desiré Gustave
4 271-273

Renouvier, Charles Bernard (1815-1903),
French philosopher
James, William **8** 215-217

Rensselaerswyck Manor (New Netherlands
colony)
Van Rensselaer, Kiliaen **15** 430-431

Rentes (French economics)
Francis I **6** 40-43

RENWICK, JAMES (1818-1895), American
architect **13** 102-103

Renzo (literary character)
Manzoni, Alessandro **10** 222-224

Repentance (literary character)
Langland, William **9** 194-195

Réponse aux injures et calomnies... (poem)
Ronsard, Pierre de **13** 271-273

Report on Manufactures (United States;
state paper)
Coxe, Tench **4** 285-286
Hamilton, Alexander **7** 95-98

Report on Social Insurance...
see Beveridge Report

Repose of Rivers (poem)
Crane, Hart **4** 291-293

Representation of Act of 1928 (England)
Pankhurst, Emmeline **12** 85-86

Representatives
see Statesmen

Reprisal, The (play)
Smollett, Tobias George **14** 305-307

Reproof (poems)
Smollett, Tobias George **14** 305-307

Repton, Humphrey (1752-1818), English
landscape gardener and architect
Nash, John **11** 316

Republic (book; Plato)
see Plato—Republic

Republic, The (painting)
Daumier, Honoré Victorin **4** 403-405

Republic, The (sculpture)
French, Daniel Chester **6** 98-99

Republic Theater (New York City)
see Belasco Theater

Republican Liberal party (United States)
Greeley, Horace **6** 515-517

Republican Methodist Church (religion)
Asbury, Francis **1** 324-325

Republican party (Brazil)
Vargas, Getulio Dornelles **15** 433-434

Republican party (Germany)
Schönhuber, Franz Xaver **14** 28-29

Republican party (United States)
campaign leaders
Baker, James Addison III **1** 447-448
civil rights

Conkling, Roscoe **4** 201-202
Howells, William Dean **7** 539-541
Stevens, Thaddeus **14** 442-443
Wilson, James Harold **16** 324-325
leaders
Alcorn, James Lusk **1** 120-121
Andrew, John Albion **1** 230-231
Arthur, Chester Alan **1** 321-323
Borah, William Edgar **2** 408
Clinton, George **4** 113-114
Dewey, Thomas Edmund **4** 524
Dole, Elizabeth Hanford **5** 41-43
Hanna, Marcus Alonzo **7** 127-128
Harlan, John Marshall **7** 156-157
Heckler, Margaret Mary O'Shaugh-
nessy **7** 251-252
Hills, Carla Anderson **7** 394-396
Kassebaum (Baker), Nancy
8 455-457
Kirkpatrick, Jeane J. **9** 37-39
Lodge, Henry Cabot **9** 482-483
Luce, Clare Boothe **10** 21-23
Mahone, William **10** 147-148
Morton, Oliver Hazard Perry Throck
11 197-198
Norris, George William **11** 428-429
Schlafly, Phyllis **14** 9-10
Stanford, Leland **14** 397-398
Stimson, Henry Lewis **14** 457-458
Tourgée, Albion Winegar
15 277-278
Weaver, James Baird **16** 151-152
leaders (Arizona)
Goldwater, Barry **6** 413-415
O'Connor, Sandra Day **11** 468-470
leaders (California)
Reagan, Ronald W. **13** 65-68
Wilson, Pete **16** 326-329
leaders (Florida)
Ros-Lehtinen, Ileana **13** 294-296
leaders (Georgia)
Gingrich, Newt **6** 329-332
leaders (Illinois)
Dirksen, Everett Mckinley **5** 24-26
Martin, Lynn Morley **10** 290-292
Schlafly, Phyllis **14** 9-10
leaders (Kansas)
Dole, Robert J. **5** 43-46
Kassebaum (Baker), Nancy
8 455-457
leaders (Maine)
Smith, Margaret Chase **14** 299-300
Snowe, Olympia **14** 313-314
leaders (Maryland)
Agnew, Spiro Theodore **1** 83-85
Chavez, Linda **3** 489-491
leaders (Massachusetts)
Lodge, Henry Cabot Jr. **9** 483-485
Rogers, Edith Nourse **13** 247-248
leaders (Michigan)
Ford, Gerald **6** 2-5
leaders (New Jersey)
Whitman, Christine Todd
16 245-248
leaders (New York)
Conable, Barber B. Jr. **4** 191-192

Giuliani, Rudolph William
   6 353-355
Kemp, Jack French Jr. **8** 491-493
Rockefeller, Nelson Aldrich
   13 228-230
leaders (North Carolina)
   Helms, Jesse **7** 271-272
leaders (Ohio)
   Taft, Robert Alphonso **15** 76-78
leaders (South Carolina)
   Thurmond, James Strom **15** 214-215
leaders (Utah)
   Priest, Ivy Maude Baker **12** 450-451
leaders (Wyoming)
   Cheney, Richard B. **3** 497-499
machines
   see Political machines
members
   Butler, Nicholas Murray **3** 181
   Dickinson, John **4** 543-544
   Evarts, William Maxwell **5** 340-341
   Hildreth, Richard **7** 382
   Mellon, Andrew William
      10 469-470
   Miller, Samuel Freeman **11** 29-30
   Tabor, Horace Austin Warner **15** 70
   Waite, Morrison Remick **16** 46
   Weed, Thurlow **16** 169-170
   White, William Allen **16** 240-241
Mugwumps
   Curtis, George William **4** 349-350
   Godkin, Edwin Lawrence **6** 380
   Schurz, Carl **14** 44-45
National Committee
   Chandler, Zachariah **3** 425-426
   Penrose, Boies **12** 203-204
opponents
   Cleveland, Stephen Grover
      4 108-110
   Gordon, John Brown **6** 449-450
   House, Edward Mandell **7** 520-521
   Vallandigham, Clement Laird
      15 406-407
   Webster, Daniel **16** 162-164
organized
   Bailey, Gamaliel **1** 444-445
   Bowles, Samuel **2** 464
   Chase, Salmon Portland **3** 473-475
   Donnelly, Ignatius **5** 62
   Frémont, John Charles **6** 97-98
   Greeley, Horace **6** 515-517
   Medill, Joseph **10** 451-452
   Seward, William Henry **14** 124-125
   Sumner, Charles **15** 30-31
   Wade, Benjamin Franklin **16** 38-39
   Welles, Gideon **16** 188-190
presidential candidates
   Buchanan, Patrick Joseph **3** 90-91
   Connally, John Bowden Jr.
      4 202-204
   Dole, Robert J. **5** 43-46
   Goldwater, Barry **6** 413-415
   Kemp, Jack French Jr. **8** 491-493
   Robertson, Pat **13** 196-198
   Rockefeller, Nelson Aldrich
      13 228-230

presidents
   see Statesmen, American—presi-
      dents (Republican)
Reconstruction policy
   see Reconstruction
Republican National Committee
   Priest, Ivy Maude Baker **12** 450-451
symbol invented
   Nast, Thomas **11** 318-319
vice presidents
   Quayle, J. Danforth **12** 507-509
   see also Democratic-Republican
      party (United States); Radical
      Republicans

Republican People's Party (Turkey)
   Ecevit, Bülent **5** 196-197

Republican Revolution (China)
   see Revolution of 1911

Republicanism (political theory)
   Bradlaugh, Charles **2** 478
   Crispi, Francesco **4** 310-311
   Dumas, Alexandre **5** 136-138
   Hostos, Eugenio María de **7** 513-514
   Hugo, Victor Marie **8** 22-25
   Machiavelli, Niccolò **10** 97-99
   Madison, James **10** 121-123
   Mazzini, Giuseppe **10** 381-383
   Palmerston, 3d Viscount **12** 81-83
   Sieyès, Comte Emmanuel Joseph
      14 217-218
   Wordsworth, William **16** 385-388

Republicans, Radical
   see Radical Republicans (United States)

Repulsion of Attila (fresco)
   Raphael **13** 40-42

Requiem (music)
   Bruckner, Joseph Anton **3** 64-65
   Cavalli, Pietro Francesco **3** 382-383
   Dufay, Guillaume **5** 125-126
   Fauré, Gabriel Urbain **5** 397-398
   Fux, Johann Joseph **6** 155-156
   Mozart, Wolfgang Amadeus
      11 218-221
   Ockeghem, Johannes **11** 464-465
   Verdi, Giuseppe Fortunino Francesco
      15 463-465

Requiem (poems)
   Akhmatova, Anna **1** 96-97

Requiem for the Living (poem)
   Lewis, Cecil Day **9** 380

Rerum novarum (encyclical; Leo XIII)
   Coughlin, Charles Edward **4** 265-266
   John, XXIII **8** 277-280
   Leo XIII **9** 334-336
   Pius XI **12** 337-339
   Salazar, António de Oliveira
      13 442-443

Rerum vulgarum fragmenta
   see Canzoniere

Rescued from an Eagle's Nest (film)
   Griffith, David Wark **6** 544-545

Research in Volume (sculpture)
   Nadelman, Elie **11** 289-290

Resende, Garcia de (1470-1536), Portuguese poet
   Vicente, Gil **15** 479-480

Residenz Palace
   Munich
      Cuvilliés, François **4** 359-360
      Zimmermann, Johann Baptist and
         Domenikus **16** 518
   Salzburg
      Rottmayr, Johann Michael **13** 321
   Würzburg
      Boffrand, Gabriel Germain **2** 361
      Hildebrandt, Johann Lucas von
         7 380-381
      Neumann, Balthasar **11** 354-355
      Tiepolo, Giovanni Battista
         15 219-220

Resignation of Washington at Annapolis
(painting)
   Trumbull, John **15** 316-317

Resistance, French (WW II)
   see French Resistance

Resistible Rise of Arturo Ui, The (play)
   Brecht, Bertolt **2** 512-514

Resnais, Alain (born 1922), French film
director
   Robbe-Grillet, Alain **13** 189-190
   Truffaut, François **15** 311-313

Resolution (ship)
   Bligh, William **2** 325-326
   Cook, James **4** 214-215
   Vancouver, George **15** 414-415

Resolution and Independence (poem)
   Wordsworth, William **16** 385-388

Reson and Sensuallyte (poem)
   Lydgate, John **10** 61-62

Respectful Prostitute, The (comedy)
   Sartre, Jean Paul **13** 491-492

RESPIGHI, OTTORINO (1879-1936), Italian composer **13** 103-104

Responsibilities (poems)
   Yeats, William Butler **16** 445-447

Responsible government (political theory)
   Baldwin, Robert **1** 466-468
   Elgin, 8th Earl of **5** 248-249
   Howe, Joseph **7** 534-535
   Lafontaine, Louis-Hippolyte **9** 157-158

Rest on the Flight into Egypt (painting)
   Correggio **4** 249-251
   Cranach, Lucas the Elder **4** 289-290

RESTON, JAMES BARRETT ("Scotty"; born
1909), American journalist and political
commentator **13** 104-105

Restoration, The (England; 1660)
   politics
      Berkeley, William **2** 198-199
      Charles II **3** 452-454
      Harrington, James **7** 166-167
      James II **8** 207-208

Monck, George **11** 96-97
Monmouth and Buccleugh, Duke of
11 108-109
Shaftesbury, 1st Earl of **14** 135-136
Vane, Henry **15** 425-426
Restoration literature
Congreve, William **4** 200-201
Cowley, Abraham **4** 281-282
Dryden, John **5** 106-107
Marvell, Andrew **10** 301-303
Pepys, Samuel **12** 207-208
Wycherley, William **16** 411-412

Restoration, War of the (Dominican
Republic ; 1864-65)
Santana, Pedro **13** 474-475

Resurezzione, La (musical composition)
Handel, George Frederick **7** 116-119

Resurrection (Christian theology)
Jesus of Nazareth **8** 251-255

Resurrection (novel)
Tolstoy, Leo **15** 262-265

Resurrection (painting)
Andrea del Castagno **1** 223-224
Giotto **6** 342-345
Piero della Francesca **12** 301-302
Titian **15** 242-244

Resurrection (sculpture)
Berruguete, Alonso **2** 223-224
Luca della Robbia **10** 19-20

Resurrection, The (hymn)
Manzoni, Alessandro **10** 222-224

Resurrection of Lazarus (painting)
Caravaggio **3** 282-284
Tanner, Henry Ossawa **15** 102-103

Resurrection of the Dead (painting)
Signorelli, Luca **14** 221-222

Resurrexit (musical composition)
Berlioz, Louis Hector **2** 203-205

Retablo de Maese Pedro, El (opera)
Falla, Manuel de **5** 372-373

Retailers
see Business and industrial leaders—
retail industry

Retaliation (poem)
Goldsmith, Oliver **6** 411-413

RETIEF, PIETER (1780-1838), South African
Boer leader **13** 105-106
Dingane **5** 14-15
Pretorius, Andries **12** 444-445

Retraite sentimentale, La (novel)
Colette, Sidonie Gabrielle **4** 158-159

Retreat, The (poem)
Vaughan, Henry **15** 444-445

Retribution (poem)
Blok, Aleksandr Aleksandrovich **2** 335

Retroviruses
Varmus, Harold Eliot **15** 436-437

Return from the Fair (painting)
Courbet, Jean Desiré Gustave
4 271-273

Return of Buck Gavin, The (play)
Wolfe, Thomas Clayton **16** 355-356

Return of the Herd (painting)
Bruegel, Pieter the Elder **3** 65-67

Return of the Native, The (novel)
Hardy, Thomas **7** 150-152

Return of the Prodigal Son (engraving)
Lucas van Leyden **10** 20-21

Return of the Sphinx, The (novel)
MacLennan, Hugh **10** 110-111

Retzius, Andres Johan (1742-1821),
Swedish botanist
Scheele, Karl Wilhelm **13** 525-526

Reuben Bright (poem)
Robinson, Edwin Arlington **13** 201-202

REUCHLIN, JOHANN (1455-1522), Ger-
man humanist and jurist **13** 106-107
Hutten, Ulrich von **8** 72-73
Melancthon, Philip **10** 466-467

Reunion in Vienna (play)
Sherwood, Robert Emmet **14** 189-190

Reunion Polytechnique Industrielle
(France)
Carnot, Nicolas Léonard Sadi **3** 315

Reunited National or People's party
see Volksparty (South Africa)

REUTHER, WALTER PHILIP (1907-1970),
American labor leader **13** 107-108
Ford, Henry II **6** 6-7

Reveille for Radicals (book)
Alinsky, Saul David **1** 161-162

Réveil-matin, Le (musical composition)
Couperin, François **4** 270-271

REVEL, BERNARD (1885-1940), Talmudic
scholar and educator **13** 108-109

Revelation (theology)
Barth, Karl **2** 31-32
Heschel, Abraham Joshua **7** 358-359
Niebuhr, Helmut Richard **11** 386-387

Revelation, Book of (New Testament)
Dürer, Albrecht **5** 159-161
John **8** 273-274
Redon, Odilon **13** 75-76

REVELS, HIRAM RHOADES (1822-1901),
African American clergyman, statesman,
and educator **13** 109-110

Revenge of Bussy D'Ambois, The (play)
Chapman, George **3** 440-441

Revenge play (English literature)
Fletcher, John **5** 487
Kyd, Thomas **9** 140-141
Shakespeare, William **14** 142-145

Revenue Act (1926; United States)
Coolidge, John Calvin **4** 217-219

Reverberator, The (novel)
James, Henry **8** 211-212

REVERE, PAUL (1735-1818), American
patriot, silversmith, and engraver
13 110-111

Billings, William **2** 274-275
Copley, John Singleton **4** 228-230

Review (periodical)
Defoe, Daniel **4** 457-459

REVILLAGIGEDO, CONDE DE (Juan
Vicente Güemes Pacheco y Padilla;
1740-1799), Spanish colonial administrator, viceroy of New Spain **13** 111-112

Revista de Occidente (journal)
Ortega Y Gasset, José **12** 7-8

Revista méxicana de literatura (magazine)
Fuentes, Carlos **6** 141-142

**Revista nacional de literatura y ciencias
sociales** (periodical)
Rodó, José Enrique **13** 240-241

Revivalism (religion)
17th century
Stoddard, Solomon **14** 462-463
18th century
Edwards, Jonathan **5** 220-222
Frelinghuysen, Theodorus Jacobus
6 96-97
Hopkins, Samuel **7** 496
Tennent, Gilbert **15** 143-144
Wilberforce, William **16** 269-270
19th century
Beecher, Lyman **2** 113
Cartwright, Peter **3** 344-345
Finney, Charles Grandison
5 450-451
Moody, Dwight L. **11** 141-142
Nevin, John Williamson **11** 357
Noyes, John Humphrey **11** 437-438
20th century
Aberhart, William **1** 26-27
Graham, William Franklin Jr.
6 487-488
McPherson, Aimee Semple **10** 434
Sunday, William Ashley **15** 32-33
see also Evangelism

Revolt of Islam, The (poem)
Shelley, Percy Bysshe **14** 176-178

Revolt of the Angels, The (novel)
France, Anatole **6** 39-40

Revolution (political theory)
Bakunin, Mikhail Aleksandrovich
1 458-460
Le Bon, Gustave **9** 268-269
Trotsky, Leon **15** 302-305

Révolution grecque, La (cantata)
Berlioz, Louis Hector **2** 203-205

Revolution of 1688 (England)
see Glorious Revolution

Revolution of 1830 (France; July Revolu-
tion)
European reaction
Metternich, Klemens von
10 533-536
Wellington, 1st Duke of **16** 193-195
William I **16** 291-292
monarchy and
Charles X **3** 463-464
Louis Philippe **9** 536-537

opponents
> Cauchy, Augustin Louis **3** 378-380

supporters
> Cabet, Étienne **3** 196
> Guizot, François Pierre Guillaume **7** 40-41
> Lafayette, Marquis de **9** 151-152
> Sieyès, Comte Emmanuel Joseph **14** 217-218
> Talleyrand, Charles Maurice de **15** 89-90
> Thiers, Louis Adolphe **15** 181-182

Revolution of 1843 (Haiti)
> Boyer, Jean Pierre **2** 468-469

Revolution of 1848 (Europe)
Austria
> Metternich, Klemens von **10** 533-536

Germany
> Frederick William IV **6** 87-88
> Schurz, Carl **14** 44-45
> Virchow, Rudolf Ludwig Carl **15** 506-507
> Wagner, Richard **16** 40-43

Hungary
> Kossuth, Louis **9** 88-90

Italy
> Crispi, Francesco **4** 310-311
> Manin, Daniele **10** 197-198

Revolution of 1848 (France; February Revolution)
critics
> Gobineau, Comte de **6** 375-376
> Guizot, François Pierre Guillaume **7** 40-41
> Proudhon, Pierre Joseph **12** 461-463

education during
> Cauchy, Augustin Louis **3** 378-380
> Cousin, Victor **4** 273-274

political cartoons
> Daumier, Honoré Victorin **4** 403-405

regime and
> Bugeaud de la Piconnerie, Thomas Robert **3** 111
> Louis Philippe **9** 536-537

supporters
> Blanc, Louis **2** 318-319
> Blanqui, Louis Auguste **2** 323-324
> Dumas, Alexandre **5** 136-138
> Hugo, Victor Marie **8** 22-25
> Lamartine, Alphonse Marie Louis de **9** 173-175
> see also June Days

Revolution of 1870 (France)
> Clemenceau, Georges **4** 99-101
> Gobineau, Comte de **6** 375-376

Revolution of 1905 (Russia)
> see Russian Revolution (1905)

Revolution of 1911 (China)
> Ch'en Tu-hsiu **3** 501-502
> Chiang Kai-shek **3** 510-513
> Chicherin, Georgi Vasilyevich **3** 516-517

> K'ang Yu-wei **8** 426-428
> Liang Ch'i-ch'ao **9** 395-396
> Mao Zedong **10** 225-227
> Sun Yat-sen **15** 35-39
> Yen Hsi-shan **16** 452-453
> Yüan Shih-k'ai **16** 480-481

Revolution of 1930 (Brazil)
> Prestes, Luiz Carlos **12** 442-444
> Vargas, Getulio Dornelles **15** 433-434

Revolution of 1932 (Thailand)
> Phibun Songkhram, Luang **12** 264-265

Revolution of 1947 (Paraguay)
> Stroessner, Alfredo **14** 511-512

Revolutionary Leftist National Union (Colombia)
> Gaitán, Jorge Eliécer **6** 172-173

Revolutionary War (United States)
> see American Revolution

Revue-blanche, La (poster)
> Bonnard, Pierre **2** 395-396

Reward (poems)
> Mqhayi, Samuel Edward Krune **11** 223

Rewards and Fairies (stories)
> Kipling, Joseph Rudyard **9** 32-33

Rexroth, Kenneth (1905-1982), American poet and critic
> Thomas, Dylan Marlais **15** 188-190

Rey, Louis (Louis Étienne Ernest Reyer; 1823-1909), French composer and music critic
> Bloch, Ernest **2** 326-327

REYES, ALFONSO (1889-1959), Mexican author and diplomat **13** 112-113

REYES, RAFAEL (1850-1920), Colombian military leader, president 1904-09 **13** 113

Reynaud, Paul (1878-1966), French politician
> Daladier, Édouard **4** 369
> Pétain, Henri Philippe **12** 250-252
> Schuman, Robert **14** 41

REYNOLDS, ALBERT (born 1932), prime minister of Ireland **13** 113-115

REYNOLDS, SIR JOSHUA (1723-1792), English portrait painter **13** 115-116
contemporaries
> Copley, John Singleton **4** 228-230
> Fuseli, Henry **6** 153-155
> Goldsmith, Oliver **6** 411-413
> Johnson, Samuel **8** 315-317
> Romney, George **13** 269-270
> West, Benjamin **16** 210-212

influence of
> Stuart, Gilbert **14** 513-515

rivals
> Gainsborough, Thomas **6** 170-172
> Lawrence, Thomas **9** 252-253
> Wilson, Richard **16** 329-330

Reynolds, v. Sims (legal case)
> Warren, Earl **16** 117-120

REZA SHAH PAHLAVI (Reza Khan; 1878-1944), Shah of Iran 1925-41 **13** 116-117
> Mohammad Reza Shah Pahlavi **11** 75-76

Rh factor (blood)
> Fisher, Ronald Aylmer **5** 463-464
> Landsteiner, Karl **9** 188-189

Rhapsody (novella)
> Schnitzler, Arthur **14** 23-24

Rhapsody in Blue (musical composition)
> Gershwin, George **6** 284-285

Rhapsody on a Theme by Paganini (musical composition)
> Rachmaninov, Sergei Vasilievich **12** 531-532

Rhazes (al-Rasi; 850-923), Persian-born Moslem physician
> Vesalius, Andreas **15** 473-475

Rhé, Isle of
> see Ré, Île de

RHEE, SYNGMAN (1875-1965), Korean independence leader, South Korean president 1948-60 **13** 117-120
> Clark, Mark Wayne **4** 80-81
> Park, Chung Hee **12** 99-102

Rhein, Der (hymn)
> Hölderlin, Johann Christian Friedrich **7** 451-452

Rheingold, Das (opera)
> Wagner, Richard **16** 40-43

Rhenish Symphony (music)
> Schumann, Robert Alexander **14** 41-43

Rhesus (play)
> Euripides **5** 332-334

Rheticus
> see Joachim von Lauchen, Georg

Rhetoric
> Aristotle **1** 295-296
> Empedocles **5** 282
> Ovid **12** 34-36
> Tacitus **15** 70-72
> see also Orators

Rhetoric of Motives, A (book)
> Burke, Kenneth **3** 141-142

Rhetoric of Religion, The (book)
> Burke, Kenneth **3** 141-142

RHETT, ROBERT BARNWELL (1800-1876) American statesman **13** 120

Rhineland (province; Germany)
> Clemenceau, Georges **4** 99-101
> Frederick William **6** 85-86
> Hitler, Adolf **7** 417-420
> Poincaré, Raymond **12** 366-368
> Wilson, Thomas Woodrow **16** 330-332

Rhinocéros (play)
> Ionesco, Eugène **8** 131-132

Rhoda Fleming (novel)
> Meredith, George **10** 512-513

Rhode Island (state, United States)
Aldrich, Nelson Wilmarth **1** 123-124
Barnard, Henry **2** 10
Gorton, Samuell **6** 460
Hopkins, Esek **7** 490-491
Hutchinson, Anne Marbury **8** 69-71
Williams, Roger **16** 304-305

Rhodes (island, Greece)
Mehmed the Conqueror **10** 452-454
Pompey **12** 387-389

Rhodes, Alexandre de (1591-1660), French
missionary
Laval, Francois Xavier de **9** 235-236

RHODES, CECIL JOHN (1853-1902), Eng-
lish imperialist and financier **13** 120-122
Goldie, George Dashwood Taubman
6 404
Jameson, Leander Starr **8** 218
Johnston, Henry Hamilton **8** 322-323
Kruger, Stephanus Johannes Paulus
9 108-109
Lobengula **9** 474-475
Morgan, Junius Spencer **11** 166-167
Salisbury, 3d Marquess of **13** 448-449
Smuts, Jan Christian **14** 309-310

RHODES, JAMES FORD (1848-1927),
American historian **13** 122

Rhodes Armistice Conference (1949)
Dayan, Moshe **4** 429-431

Rhodesia (now Zimbabwe and Zambia;
South Africa)
Banda, Hastings Kamuzu **1** 485-486
Jameson, Leander Starr **8** 218
Kaunda, Kenneth David **8** 460-461
Nkomo, Joshua Mqabuko **11** 405-407
Rhodes, Cecil John **13** 120-122
Salisbury, 3d Marquess of **13** 448-449
Sithole, Ndabaningi **14** 262-264
Smith, Ian Douglas **14** 291-293
Tafawa Balewa, Abubakar **15** 75
Welensky, Roy **16** 188
see also Malawi; Zambia; Zimbabwe

Rhodesia and Nyasaland, Federation of
(1953-1963)
Smith, Ian Douglas **14** 291-293
Welensky, Roy **16** 188

Rhymers' Club (London)
Yeats, William Butler **16** 445-447

Rhymes (poems)
Echeverría, José Estéban **5** 197-198

Rhythm of the Violinist (painting)
Balla, Giacomo **1** 473-474

RIBERA, JUSEPE DE (1591-1652), Spanish
painter **13** 122-123
Caravaggio **3** 282-284
Eakins, Thomas **5** 176-177
Murillo, Bartolomé Esteban **11** 258-259
Rosa, Salvator **13** 289-290
Velázquez, Diego Rodríguez de Silva y
15 454-456
Zurbarán, Francisco de **16** 534-535

Ribicoff, Abraham A. (born 1910), American politician

Nader, Ralph **11** 290-291

Riboflavin
Theorell, Axel Hugo Theodor
15 176-177

Ribonucleic acid (biochemistry)
Beadle, George Wells **2** 80-81
Khorana, Har Gobind **8** 537-538
Monod, Jacques **11** 110-111
Ochoa, Severo **11** 461-464
Todd, Alexander **15** 251-253

Ribot, Alexandre (1842-1923), French
statesman
Poincaré, Raymond **12** 366-368

RICARDO, DAVID (1772-1823), English
economist **13** 123-124
Engels, Friedrich **5** 286-288
George, Henry **6** 276
Jevons, William Stanley **8** 255-256
Malthus, Thomas Robert **10** 180-181
Marx, Karl **10** 304-308
Mill, James **11** 21
Say, Jean Baptiste **13** 508-509

Riccardi, Nicolò (1585-1639), Italian
Dominican theologian
Galileo Galilei **6** 180-183

Riccardo I (opera)
Handel, George Frederick **7** 116-119

RICCI, MATTEO (1552-1610), Italian Jesuit
missionary **13** 124-125
Xu Guangqi **16** 422-425

Ricci, Sebastiano (1660-1734), Italian
painter
Troger, Paul **15** 300

Ricciardo (play)
Foscolo, Ugo **6** 21

Riccio, David (1533?-1566), Italian musician
Mary, I **10** 308-309

Riccione (commune, Italy)
Dollfuss, Engelbert **5** 47

Rice (cereal)
Couper, James Hamilton **4** 270
Gatling, Richard Jordan **6** 234-235
Knapp, Seaman Asahel **9** 58
Zhao Kuang-yin **16** 505-508

RICE, ANNE (born 1941), American author
13 125-126

RICE, ELMER (1892-1967), American play-
wright and novelist **13** 126-127
Parker, Dorothy Rothschild **12** 106
Weill, Kurt **16** 174-175

RICE, JOSEPH MAYER (1857-1934), American education reformer **13** 127-128

Rice, T. D. "Daddy" (1808-1860), American minstrel-show pioneer
Christy, Edwin P. **4** 34-35

Ricercari d'intavolatura d'organo (musical
composition)
Merulo, Claudio **10** 525-526

Riceyman Steps (book)
Bennett, Arnold **2** 167-168

RICH, ADRIENNE (born 1929), American
poet **13** 128-130

Rich Boy, The (story)
Fitzgerald, Francis Scott Key **5** 470-472

Rich Mountain, battle of (1861)
McClellan, George Brinton **10** 391-392

RICHARD I (1157-1199), king of England
1189-99 **13** 130
Eleanor of Aquitaine **5** 246-247
Henry II **7** 287-289
John **8** 274-275
Philip II **12** 268-269
Saladin **13** 441-442

Richard II (died 1027), duke of Normandy
Edward the Confessor **5** 218-219

RICHARD II (1367-1400), king of England
1377-99 **13** 130-131
associates
Froissart, Jean **6** 124-125
Gower, John **6** 475-476
John of Gaunt **8** 282-283
in literature
Chaucer, Geoffrey **3** 482-485
Langland, William **9** 194-195
Shakespeare, William **14** 142-145
Wyclif, John **16** 412-413
opponents
Glendower, Owen **6** 364-365
Henry IV **7** 292-293
Henry V **7** 296-297
relatives
Charles VI **3** 460-461
Edward the Black Prince **5** 217-218

RICHARD III (1452-1485), king of England
1483-85 **13** 132-133
Edward IV **5** 212-213
Henry VI **7** 298-299
Henry VII **7** 300-302
More, Thomas **11** 156-157
Warwick and of Salisbury, Earl of
16 122-123

Richard III (play; Shakespeare)
Barrymores **2** 28-30
Booth, Edwin **2** 401-402
Shakespeare, William **14** 142-145

Richard, Duke of Gloucester
see Richard III

Richard, Duke of York (Richard Planta-
genet; 1472-83), son of Edward IV
Edward IV **5** 212-213
Richard III **13** 132-133

Richard, Earl of Cornwall (1209-1272),
king of the Romans
Henry III **7** 290-292
Rudolf I **13** 347-348

Richard, 3d Duke of York (Richard Plantagenet; 1411-60), English statesman
Margaret of Anjou **10** 249-250

Richard Carvel (novel)
Churchill, Winston **4** 50-51

Richard Cory (verse)
Robinson, Edwin Arlington **13** 201-202

Richard Darlington (play)
Dumas, Alexandre **5** 136-138

Richard de Bury (1287-1345), English ecclesiastic and scholar
Chaucer, Geoffrey **3** 482-485

Richard of Bordeaux
see Richard II

Richard the "Lion-Hearted"
see Richard I

Richard the Redeless (poem)
Langland, William **9** 194-195

RICHARDS, ANN WILLIS (born 1933), Democratic governor of Texas
13 133-134

RICHARDS, ELLEN H. (born Ellen Henrietta Swallow; 1842-1911), American chemist and educator **13** 134-136

RICHARDS, IVOR ARMSTRONG (1893-1979), English-born American semanticist and literary critic **13** 137
Roethke, Theodore **13** 243-244

RICHARDS, THEODORE WILLIAM (1868-1928), American chemist
13 137-138
Bridgman, Percy Williams **3** 5-6

Richards, William Trost (1833-1905), American painter
Richards, Theodore William
13 137-138

Richards Medical Research Building (University of Pennsylvania)
Kahn, Louis I. **8** 408-410

RICHARDSON, HENRY HANDEL (pen name of Ethel Florence Lindesay Richardson; 1870-1946), expatriate Australian novelist **13** 139

RICHARDSON, HENRY HOBSON (1838-1886), American architect
13 139-141
McKim, Charles Follen **10** 417-418
Mumford, Lewis **11** 246-247
Saarinen, Eliel and Eero **13** 396-398
Shaw, Richard Norman **14** 167-168
Sullivan, Louis Henri **15** 27-28
Wright, Frank Lloyd **16** 398-401

Richardson, Jonathan, the Elder (1665-1745), British painter
Reynolds, Joshua **13** 115-116

RICHARDSON, SAMUEL (1689-1761), English novelist **13** 141-142
Burney, Fanny **3** 147-148
Fielding, Henry **5** 442-444
Prévost, Abbé **12** 445-446
Rousseau, Jean Jacques **13** 324-328
Sterne, Laurence **14** 435-437
Voltaire **16** 14-16

RICHELIEU, ARMAND JEAN DU PLESSIS DE (1585-1642), French statesman and cardinal **13** 142-144
Champlain, Samuel de **3** 419-421
Colbert, Jean Baptiste **4** 142-143
Condé, Prince de **4** 193-194
Girardon, François **6** 348-349

Le Brun, Charles **9** 269-270
Louis XIV **9** 531-533, 589
Orléans, Philippe II D' **11** 530-531
Poussin, Nicolas **12** 418-420
see also Thirty Years War

RICHET, CHARLES ROBERT (1850-1935), French physiologist **13** 144-145

RICHIER, GERMAINE (1904-1959), French sculptor **13** 145-146

Richmond (city, Virginia)
Beauregard, Pierre Gustave Toutant
2 96-97
Jefferson, Thomas **8** 238-241
Prosser, Gabriel **12** 460-461

Richmond, 3d Duke of (Charles Lennox; 1735-1806), English diplomat
Romney, George **13** 269-270

Richmond, battle of (1862)
Johnston, Joseph Eggleston **8** 323

RICHTER, CHARLES F. (1900-1985), American seismologist **13** 146-148

RICHTER, CONRAD MICHAEL (1890-1968), American novelist and short-story writer **13** 148-149

Richter, Hans (1888-1976), German film director
Ray, Man **13** 59-60

RICHTER, HANS (Johann Siegried Richter; 1888-1976), German-born artist
13 149-150

RICHTER, JOHANN PAUL FRIEDRICH (1763-1825), German humorist and prose writer **13** 150-151
Schumann, Robert Alexander **14** 41-43

Richthofen, Baron Ferdinand von (1833-1905), German geographer and explorer
Hedin, Sven Anders **7** 252-253
Przhevalsky, Nikolai Mikhailovich
12 469-470

Richthofen, Baron Manfred von (1892-1918), German aviator
Göring, Hermann Wilhelm **6** 457-458

RICIMER, FLAVIUS (died 472), Germanic Roman political chief **13** 151-152
Odoacer **11** 473

RICKENBACKER, EDWARD VERNON (1890-1973), World War I fighter pilot and airline president **13** 152-153

RICKEY, WESLEY BRANCH (1881-1965), innovative baseball executive **13** 153-155

RICKOVER, HYMAN GEORGE (1900-1986), U.S. Navy officer
13 155-157

Rickshaw Boy (novel)
Lao Shê **9** 200-201

RICOEUR, PAUL (born 1913), French exponent of hermeneutical philosophy
13 157-158

Ricordi, Giovanni (1788-1853), Italian music publisher
Verdi, Giuseppe Fortunino Francesco
15 463-465

Riddarhusordning (Sweden; 1626)
Oxenstierna, Axel Gustafsson **12** 44-45

RIDE, SALLY (born 1951), American astronaut and physicist **13** 158-160

Riders in the Chariot (novel)
White, Patrick Victor Martindale
16 233-235

Riders to the Sea (play)
Synge, Edmund John Millington
15 61-62

RIDGWAY, MATTHEW BUNKER (1895-1993), American general
13 160-161

Ridley, Nicholas (1500?-1555), English Protestant martyr
Edward VI **5** 213-214
Mary, I **10** 308-309

Ridolphi, Roberto di (1531-1612), Florentine conspirator in England
Mary, I **10** 308-309

RIEFENSTAHL, LENI (born 1902), German film director **13** 161-163

Riego y Nuñez, Rafael del (1784-1823), Spanish patriot
Ferdinand VII **5** 418-420
Guerrero, Vicente **7** 28-30

RIEL, LOUIS (1844-1885), Canadian rebel
13 163-164
Lacombe, Albert **9** 147-148
Laurier, Wilfrid **9** 232-234
Macdonald, John Alexander **10** 85-87
Smith, Donald Alexander **14** 288-289

RIEMANN, GEORG FRIEDRICH BERNARD (1826-1866), German mathematician **13** 164-165
Cantor, Georg Ferdinand Ludwig Philipp **3** 265-266
Fourier, Jean Baptiste Joseph **6** 32-33

RIEMENSCHNEIDER, TILMAN (1468-1531), German sculptor **13** 166
Schongauer, Martin **14** 26-28
Stoss, Veit **14** 481-482

Rienzi (opera)
Wagner, Richard **16** 40-43

RIENZI, COLA DI (or Rienzo; 1313/14-1354), Italian patriot, tribune of Rome **13** 166-167
Petrarch **12** 259-261

RIESMAN, DAVID (born 1909), American sociologist, writer, and social critic
13 167-168

RIETVELD, GERRIT THOMAS (1888-1964), Dutch architect and furniture designer
13 169
Mies van der Rohe, Ludwig **11** 10-12
Oud, Jacobus Johannes Pieter **12** 32
van Doesburg, Theo **15** 421

Rif (region, Morocco)
Abd el-Krim el-Khatabi, Mohamed ben **1** 15-16

Riga (city, Latvia)
Dubnov, Simon **5** 115-116
Gustavus II **7** 43-45

Riga, Gulf of (Baltic Sea)
Kolchak, Aleksandr Vasilievich **9** 77-78

Rigaud, André (1761-1811), Haitian general
Toussaint L'Ouverture, François Dominique **15** 278-279

Rigaud, Pierre François de
see Vaudreuil-Cavagnal, Marquis de

Rigby's Romance (novel)
Furphy, Joseph **6** 152-153

Rigdon, Sidney (1793-1876), American Mormon leader
Young, Brigham **16** 469-470

Right Stuff, The (film)
Shepard, Alan **14** 178-180

Right to Privacy, The (article)
Brandeis, Louis Dembitz **2** 496-497

Right You Are If You Think You Are (play)
Pirandello, Luigi **12** 319-321

Rights of Man (essay; Paine)
Adams, John Quincy **1** 52-54
Paine, Thomas **12** 66-67

Rigoletto (opera; Verdi)
Caruso, Enrico **3** 345
Verdi, Giuseppe Fortunino Francesco **15** 463-465

Rigorists (religious group)
Donatus **5** 56-57

RIIS, JACOB AUGUST (1849-1914), Danish-born American journalist and reformer **13** 169-170
Addams, Jane **1** 56-57

Rijckaert, Martin (1587-1631), Flemish painter
Van Dyck, Anthony **15** 423-425

RILEY, JAMES WHITCOMB (1849-1916), American poet **13** 170-171

RILKE, RAINER MARIA (1875-1926), German lyric poet **13** 171-172
Barber, Samuel **1** 500-501
Pasternak, Boris Leonidovich **12** 124-125

Rima (sculpture)
Epstein, Jacob **5** 295-296

Rimado de palacio (poem)
López de Ayala, Pedro **9** 508-509

Rimas (poems)
Bécquer, Gustavo Adolfo Dominguez **2** 107-108
Camoëns, Luis Vaz de **3** 247-249

RIMBAUD, (JEAN NICOLAS) ARTHUR (1854-1891), French poet **13** 172-174
Baudelaire, Charles Pierre **2** 61-63
Claudel, Paul Louis Charles **4** 90-91

Miller, Henry **11** 26-27
Verlaine, Paul Marie **15** 465-466

Rime (Italian poetry)
Tasso, Torquato **15** 114-116

Rime nuove (poems)
Carducci, Giosuè **3** 290-291

Rime of the Ancient Mariner, The (poem, Coleridge)
Calder, Alexander **3** 216-218

Rime spirituali (musical composition)
Lassus, Roland de **9** 216-218

Rime spirituali (poems; Fiamma)
Lassus, Roland de **9** 216-218

Rimes francaises et italiennes (musical composition)
Sweelinck, Jan Pieterszoon **15** 50-51

Rimini (Italian city-state)
Julius II **8** 384-386

RIMMER, WILLIAM (1816-1879), American sculptor, painter, and physician **13** 174
French, Daniel Chester **6** 98-99

RIMSKY-KORSAKOV, NIKOLAI ANDREEVICH (1844-1908), Russian composer and conductor **13** 174-175
Borodin, Aleksandr Profirevich **2** 422-423
Mussorgsky, Modest Petrovich **11** 274-276
Pushkin, Aleksandr Sergeevich **12** 489-491
Respighi, Ottorino **13** 103-104
Tchaikovsky, Peter Ilyich **15** 130-132

Rinaldo (literary character)
Boiardo, Matteo Maria **2** 369

Rinaldo (opera)
Handel, George Frederick **7** 116-119

Rinaldo (poem)
Tasso, Torquato **15** 114-116

Rinaldo and Armida (painting)
Boucher, François **2** 440-442
Poussin, Nicolas **12** 418-420
Van Dyck, Anthony **15** 423-425

Rincon de Haedo, battle of (1825)
Lavalleja, Juan Antonio **9** 238-239

Ring and the Book, The (poem)
Browning, Robert **3** 53-55

Ring of the Nibelungen, The (opera cycle; Wagner)
Nietzsche, Friedrich **11** 390-392
Wagner, Richard **16** 40-43

Ring Round the Moon (play)
Anouilh, Jean **1** 243-244

RINGGOLD, FAITH (Faith Jones; born 1930), African American painter, sculptress, and performer **13** 175-177

Rinuccini, Ottavio (1562-1621), Italian poet
Caccini, Giulio **3** 205-206

Rinzai sect (Buddhism)
Eisai **5** 231-232

RIO BRANCO, BARÃO DO (José Maria da Silva Paranhos; 1845-1912), Brazilian political leader **13** 177

Rio de Janeiro (city, Brazil)
Anchieta, José de **1** 210-211
Cook, James **4** 214-215
Cruz, Oswaldo Gonçalves **4** 328-329
Le Corbusier **9** 274-275
Sá, Mem de **13** 395

Rio de la Plata (South America)
Artigas, José Gervasio **1** 323
Cabot, Sebastian **3** 200-201
Solís, Juan Díaz de **14** 326
Vespucci, Amerigo **15** 476-478
see also Paraguay, Republic of

Rio Grande (Africa)
see Geba River

Rio Grande (river, United States -Mexico)
Coronado, Francisco Vásquez de **4** 247

Rio Grande do Sul (state, Brazil)
Aranha, Osvaldo **1** 272-273
Caxias, Duque de **3** 386
Feijó, Diogo Antônio **5** 405-406
Vargas, Getulio Dornelles **15** 433-434

Rio Rita (musical)
Ziegfeld, Florenz **16** 516-517

RIORDAN, RICHARD JOSEPH (born 1930), American politician; mayor of Los Angeles **13** 177-179

Rios, Juan Antonio (1888-1946), Chilean statesman
Frei Montalva, Eduardo **6** 94-95

Rip Van Winkle (play)
Boucicault, Dion **2** 442-443

Rip Van Winkle (story; Irving)
Irving, Washington **8** 141-143
Rogers, John **13** 248

Ripley Female College (Troy, New York State)
Knapp, Seaman Asahel **9** 58

RIPLEY, GEORGE (1802-1880), American Unitarian minister and journalist **13** 179-180
Brisbane, Albert **3** 9
Brownson, Orestes Augustus **3** 57-58
Emerson, Ralph Waldo **5** 278-280
Greeley, Horace **6** 515-517

Ripon College (India)
see Surendranath College (India)

Ripon, Frederick John Robinson, Earl of (1782-1859), English statesman
Gordon, Charles George **6** 448-449
Wellington, 1st Duke of **16** 193-195

Ripostes (poems)
Pound, Ezra Loomis **12** 415-417

Riqueti, H. G. V. de
see Mirabeau, Comte de

Riqueti, Victor de
   see Mirabeau, Victor de Riqueti, Marquis de

Risalat al-Tawhid (book)
   Abduh ibn Hasan Khayr Allah, Muhammad **1** 16-17

Rise and Fall of the City of Mahagonny, The (opera; Brecht-Weill)
   Brecht, Bertolt **2** 512-514
   Weill, Kurt **16** 174-175

Rise and Fall of the Third Reich: A History of Nazi Germany, The (book)
   Shirer, William L. **14** 198-199

Rise of David Levinsky, The (novel)
   Cahan, Abraham **3** 214

Rise of Silas Lapham, The (novel)
   Howells, William Dean **7** 539-541

Risen Christ (sculpture)
   Pilon, Germain **12** 305

Risen Christ between Saints Andrew and Longinus (engraving)
   Mantegna, Andrea **10** 215-216

Rising Glory of America, The (poem)
   Brackenridge, Hugh Henry **2** 472-473
   Freneau, Philip Morin **6** 99-100

Rising of a Thunderstorm at Sea (painting)
   Allston, Washington **1** 176-177

Rising of the Moon, The (play)
   Gregory, Augusta **6** 535-536

Rising Sun, The (book)
   Brown, William Wells **3** 48-49

Rising Village (poetry)
   Goldsmith, Oliver (1794-1861) **6** 411

Risorgimento (Italian political movement)
   Cavour, Conte di **3** 385-386
   Ferdinand II **5** 415-416
   Garibaldi, Giuseppe **6** 215-217
   Machiavelli, Niccolò **10** 97-99
   Mazzini, Giuseppe **10** 381-383
   Rosmini-Serbati, Antonio **13** 296-297
   Victor Emmanuel II **15** 483-484

Rissho Daishi
   see Nichiren

Rissho Kosei-kai (Buddhist lay organization)
   Niwano, Nikkyo **11** 400-401

Rite of Spring (ballet music; Stravinsky)
   Boulez, Pierre **2** 444-445
   Debussy, Achille Claude **4** 445-447
   Graham, Martha **6** 485-486
   Malipiero, Gian Francesco **10** 171
   Prokofiev, Sergei Sergeevich **12** 458-460
   Stravinsky, Igor Fedorovich **14** 502-506, 250

Ritorno d'Ulisse in patria, Il
   see Ulisse

RITSCHL, ALBRECHT BENJAMIN (1822-1889), German theologian **13** 180
   Harnack, Adolf von **7** 160

Ritschl, Friedrich Wilhelm (1806-1876), German philologist
   Nietzsche, Friedrich **11** 390-392

RITTENHOUSE, DAVID (1732-1796), American astronomer and instrument maker **13** 180-181
   Witherspoon, John **16** 346-348

Ritter, Alexander (1833-1896), German violinist
   Strauss, Richard **14** 500-501

RITTER, KARL (1779-1859), German geographer **13** 181-182

Ritter, Mary
   see Beard, Mary Ritter

Ritual Fire Dance (musical composition)
   Falla, Manuel de **5** 372-373

Rituals of Chou (ancient Chinese text)
   Wang An-shih **16** 95-97

RIVADAVIA, BERNARDINO (1780-1845), Argentine independence leader, president 1826-27 **13** 182-183
   Quiroga, Juan Facundo **12** 521-522

Rivals, The (play; Sheridan)
   Barrymores **2** 28-30
   Sheridan, Richard Brinsley **14** 183-184

RIVAS, DUQUE DE (Angel de Saavedra; 1791-1865), Spanish poet, dramatist, and statesman **13** 398

River Landscape (drawing)
   Daubigny, Charles François **4** 402

River, The (film)
   Ray, Satyajit **13** 60-61
   Thomson, Virgil **15** 202-203

River View (painting)
   Goyen, Jan van **6** 478-479

RIVERA, DIEGO (1886-1957), Mexican painter **13** 183-184
   Ehrenburg, Ilya Grigorievich **5** 224-225
   Kahlo, Frida **8** 406-407
   Shahn, Ben **14** 139-140
   Siqueiros, David Alfaro **14** 256
   Velasco, Luis de **15** 450-451

RIVERA, FRUCTUOSO (circa 1788-1854), Uruguayan statesman **13** 184-185
   Lavalleja, Juan Antonio **9** 238-239

RIVERA, JOSÉ EUSTACIO (1888-1928), Colombian novelist **13** 185-186

Rivera, Luis Muñoz
   see Muñoz Rivera, Luís

Rivera y Orbaneja, Miguel Primo de (1870-1930), Spanish general and dictator
   Unamuno y Jugo, Miguel de **15** 386-387

Riverbed (painting)
   Kline, Franz **9** 55

RIVERS, LARRY (Yitzroch Loiza Grossberg; born 1923), American artist **13** 186-187

Rivers, 2d Earl
   see Woodville, Anthony

Rivers, W. H. R. (1864-1922), British experimental psychologist
   Bartlett, Frederic Charles **2** 34-35

Riverside (village; Illinois)
   Olmsted, Frederick Law **11** 503-504

Riverside Church (New York City)
   Fosdick, Harry Emerson **6** 21-22

Riviera (painting)
   Bonnard, Pierre **2** 395-396

Rivière, Jacques (1886-1925), French essayist
   Proust, Marcel **12** 465-467

Rivonia trial (South Africa)
   Mandela, Nelson Rolihlahla **10** 185-186

Riyadh (city, Saudi Arabia)
   ibn Saud, Abd al-Aziz **8** 94-95

RIZAL, JOSÉ (1861-1896), Philippine national hero **13** 187-189
   Bonifacio, Andres **2** 393-394
   Del Pilar, Marcelo Hilario **4** 486
   Mabini, Apolinario **10** 72-73

Rizzio, David
   see Riccio, David

RNA
   see Ribonucleic acid

Road Back, The (novel)
   Remarque, Erich Maria **13** 91

Road company (theater)
   Boucicault, Dion **2** 442-443

Road Leads On, The (novel)
   Hamsun, Knut **7** 113-114

Road round Ireland, The (poems)
   Colum, Padraic **4** 174-175

Road to Calvary (painting)
   Bruegel, Pieter the Elder **3** 65-67
   Schongauer, Martin **14** 26-28

Road to Perfection (novel)
   Baroja y Nessi, Pío **2** 15-16

Road to Rome, The (play)
   Sherwood, Robert Emmet **14** 189-190

Road to Ruin, The (poems)
   Sassoon, Siegfried **13** 492-493

Road to Wigan Pier, The (book)
   Orwell, George **12** 14-15

Roads to Freedom, The (novel)
   Sartre, Jean Paul **13** 491-492

Roan Stallion (poem)
   Jeffers, John Robinson **8** 236-237

Roaring Girl, The (play)
   Dekker, Thomas **4** 465-466

Roaring Twenties, The (film)
   Bogart, Humphrey **2** 363-364

Roast Beef Medium (stories)
   Ferber, Edna **5** 413

Rob of the Bowl (novel)
   Kennedy, John Pendleton **8** 506-507

Rob Roy (novel)
Scott, Walter **14** 68-70

Rob Roy (overture)
Berlioz, Louis Hector **2** 203-205

ROBBE-GRILLET, ALAIN (born 1922),
French novelist **13** 189-190

Robbers' Council
see Ephesus, Councils of—449

ROBBIA, LUCA DELLA (1400-1482), Ital-
ian sculptor **10** 19-20
Brunelleschi, Filippo **3** 70-72
Donatello **5** 55-56

ROBBINS, JEROME (Rabinowitz; born
1918), American director and choreographer **13** 190-192

Robe du centaure, La (poem)
Leconte de Lisle, Charles Marie René
9 273-274

Robert (king Naples)
see Robert of Anjou

Robert I (died 1035), duke of Normandy
1028-35
Henry I (king, England) **7** 285-286
William I **16** 290-291

Robert II (1054?-1134), duke of Normandy
1087-1134
William I **16** 290-291
William II **16** 293-294

ROBERT I (1274-1329), king of Scotland
1306-29 **13** 192-194
Douglas, James **5** 78
Edward I **5** 208-210
Robert II **13** 194

ROBERT II (1316-1390), king of Scotland
1371-90 **13** 194
Robert III **13** 194-195

ROBERT III (circa 1337-1406), king of
Scotland 1390-1406 **13** 194-195
James I **8** 206-207
Robert II **13** 194

Robert, Duke of Normandy (poem)
Drayton, Michael **5** 97-98

Robert, Earl of Fife
see Albany, 1st Duke of

Robert, Earl of Gloucester (died 1147),
English soldier
Stephen **14** 426-427

Robert, Léopold (circa 1825), French
painter
Corot, Jean Baptiste Camille **4** 247-249

ROBERT, SHAABAN (1909-1962), Tanzanian author who wrote in the Swahili language **14** 128-129

Robert Bruce
see Robert I (king, Scotland)

Robert Koch Institute of Hygiene (Berlin)
Behring, Emil Adolph von **2** 122-123

Robert le Diable (opera)
Meyerbeer, Giacomo **10** 536-537

Robert of Anjou (1275-1343), king of
Naples 1309-43 and literary patron
Boccaccio, Giovanni **2** 351-353
Henry VII **7** 299-300
Martini, Simone **10** 298-299

Robert of Artois (died 1250), brother of
Louis IX of France
Louis IX **9** 525-526

Robert of Jumièges (died 1055), Norman
archbishop of Canterbury
Edward the Confessor **5** 218-219

Robert Tim (play)
Afinogenov, Aleksandr Nikolaevich
1 72-73

Roberta (musical)
Kern, Jerome David **8** 517-518

Roberti, Ercole de' (circa 1450-96), Italian
painter
Tura, Cosimo **15** 343-344

ROBERTS, FREDERICK SLEIGH (1st Earl
Roberts of Kandhar, Pretoria, and Water-
ford; 1832-1914), British field marshal
13 195-196
Botha, Louis **2** 434-436
Kitchener, Horatio Herbert **9** 45-46

Roberts House (River Forest, Illinois)
Wright, Frank Lloyd **16** 398-401

**Roberts of Kandahar, Pretoria, and Water-
ford, 1st Earl**
see Roberts, Frederick Sleigh

Roberts v. Boston (legal case)
Shaw, Lemuel **14** 164-165

Robertson, Anna Mary
see Moses, Grandma

ROBERTSON, MARION G. (Pat Robertson;
born 1930), television evangelist who
founded the Christian Broadcasting Network and presidential candidate
13 196-198

ROBERTSON, SIR DENNIS HOLME
(1890-1963), English economist **13** 196

Roberval, G. P. (1602-1675), French mathematician
Torricelli, Evangelista **15** 268-269

Robeson, Eslanda Goode (died 1896),
American anthropologist
Buck, Pearl Sydenstricker **3** 91-93

ROBESON, PAUL LEROY (1898-1976),
American singer, actor, and political
activist **13** 198-199
Anderson, Marian **1** 218-219

**ROBESPIERRE, MAXIMILIEN FRANÇOIS
MARIE ISIDORE DE** (1758-1794), French
Revolutionary leader **13** 199-201
in literature
Belloc, Joseph Hilaire Pierre **2** 141
France, Anatole **6** 39-40
Mathiez, Albert **10** 333-334
Rolland, Romain **13** 260
opponents
Barras, Vicomte de **2** 19
Fouché, Joseph **6** 30-31

Sade, Comte de **13** 416-418
supporters
Danton, Georges Jacques **4** 391-393
David, Jacques Louis **4** 407-409
Saint-Just, Louis Antoine Léon de
13 433

Robie House (Chicago)
Mies van der Rohe, Ludwig **11** 10-12
Wright, Frank Lloyd **16** 398-401

Robin, Bachelor of Love (play)
Marivaux, Pierre Carlet de Chamblain
de **10** 265-266

Robin Day (novel)
Bird, Robert Montgomery **2** 281-282

Robinson Crusoe (book; Defoe)
Defoe, Daniel **4** 457-459
ibn Tufayl, Abu Bakr Muhammad **8** 96
Mill, John Stuart **11** 21-23

Robinson Crusoe (film)
Buñuel, Luis **3** 127-128

ROBINSON, EDWIN ARLINGTON
(1869-1935), American poet and playwright **13** 201-202

ROBINSON, FRANK, JR. (born 1935),
African American baseball player and
manager **13** 202-203

ROBINSON, HARRIET HANSON
(1825-1911), American author and suffragist **13** 203-207

ROBINSON, JACK ROOSEVELT (Jackie
Robinson; 1919-72), African American
baseball player; first African American
player in the major leagues **13** 207-208

ROBINSON, JAMES HARVEY (1863-1936),
American historian **13** 208
Beard, Charles Austin **2** 84
Becker, Carl Lotus **2** 100-101
Dewey, John **4** 520-523
Parrington, Vernon Louis **12** 119-120
Schlesinger, Arthur Meier **14** 13
Spencer, Herbert **14** 369-370

ROBINSON, JOAN VIOLET MAURICE
(1903-1983), English economist
13 209-210
Clark, John Maurice **4** 77-78

Robinson, John (circa 1576-1625), English
clergyman
Bradford, William **2** 475-476
Brewster, William **2** 523-524

Robinson, John (1704-1766), American
colonial official
Lee, Richard Henry **9** 291-292
Otis, James Jr. **12** 25-27

ROBINSON, JULIA (1919-1985), American
mathematician **13** 210-211

ROBINSON, MARY BOURKE (born 1944),
first woman president of Ireland
13 211-213

ROBINSON, SIR JOHN BEVERLEY
(1791-1863), Canadian political leader
and jurist **13** 215-217
Strachan, John **14** 486-487

ROBINSON, THEODORE (1852-1896), American painter **13** 217
   Hassam, Frederick Childe **7** 192

Robot
   Čapek, Karel **3** 271-272

Robusti, Jacopo
   see Tintoretto

ROCA, JULIO ARGENTINO (1843-1914), Argentine general and president **13** 218
   Drago, Luis María **5** 92-93

Rocafuerte, Vicente (1783-1847), Ecuadorian educator, president 1835-39
   Flores, Juan José **5** 491
   García Moreno, Gabriel **6** 209-210

ROCARD, MICHEL (born 1930), French left-wing politician **13** 218-220

ROCHAMBEAU, COMTE DE (Jean Baptiste Donatien de Vimeur, 1725-1807), French general **13** 220-221
   Dessalines, Joan Jacques **4** 511-512
   Lafayette, Marquis de **9** 151-152

ROCHBERG, GEORGE (born 1918), American composer **13** 221-222

Rochdale movement (England)
   Owen, Robert **12** 39-40

Roche, James M. (born 1906), American automobile executive
   Nader, Ralph **11** 290-291

ROCHE, KEVIN (born 1922), Irish-American architect **13** 222-224

Rochefort (city, France)
   Rodney, George Brydges **13** 239-240

Rochefort, Henri (1830-1913), French journalist and playwright
   Rodin, Auguste **13** 236-238

Rochester (city, New York State)
   Eastman, George **5** 186

Rochester (literary character)
   Brontë, Charlotte **3** 17-18

Rochester, University of (New York)
   Wilson, Joseph Chamberlain **16** 325-326

Rock, The (book)
   Eliot, Thomas Stearns **5** 258-261\

Rock a Bye Baby (musical)
   Kern, Jerome David **8** 517-518

Rock Drill (sculpture)
   Epstein, Jacob **5** 295-296

Rock Garden, The (novel)
   Kazantzakis, Nikos **8** 466-468

Rock of Ages (hymn)
   Sullivan, Arthur Seymour **15** 23

ROCKEFELLER, DAVID (born 1915), chairman of the Chase Manhattan Bank **13** 224-225

ROCKEFELLER, JOHN DAVISON (1839-1937), American industrialist and philanthropist **13** 226-228
   Frick, Henry Clay **6** 108-109
   Hanna, Marcus Alonzo **7** 127-128

   Harper, William Rainey **7** 163-164
   Keller, Helen Adams **8** 479-480
   Lloyd, Henry Demarest **9** 468-469
   Tarbell, Ida Minerva **15** 107-108

Rockefeller Center (New York City)
   Rivera, Diego **13** 183-184
   Rockefeller, John D. Jr. **13** 225-226

ROCKEFELLER, JOHN D., JR. (1874-1960), American philanthropist and industrial relations expert **13** 225-226
   Aldrich, Nelson Wilmarth **1** 123-124
   Fosdick, Harry Emerson **6** 21-22
   Gladden, Washington **6** 356-357

ROCKEFELLER, NELSON ALDRICH (1908-1979), four-term governor of New York and vice-president of the United States **13** 228-230

Rockefeller, William (1841-1922), American financier and industrialist
   Rockefeller, John Davison **13** 226-228

Rockefeller Foundation (New York City)
   Flexner, Abraham **5** 489-490
   Rockefeller, John Davison **13** 226-228
   Rockefeller, John D. Jr. **13** 225-226
   Theiler, Max **15** 169-170

Rockefeller University (formerly Rockefeller Institute for Medical Research; New York City)
   associates
      Carrel, Alexis **3** 322-323
      Dubos, René Jules **5** 119
      Landsteiner, Karl **9** 188-189
      Northrop, John Howard **11** 430-431
      Rous, Francis Peyton **13** 322-323
      Stanley, Wendell Meredith **14** 400-401
   Board of Scientific Advisers
      Conant, James Bryant **4** 192-193
      Welch, William Henry **16** 185-186
   creation and management
      Rockefeller, John Davison **13** 226-228

Rocket to the Moon (play)
   Odets, Clifford **11** 470-471

Rocketry (science)
   Goddard, Robert Hutchings **6** 376-377
   Landau, Lev Davidovich **9** 184-185
   Tsiolkovsky, Konstantin Eduardovich **15** 326-328
   von Braun, Wernher **16** 17-18
   see also Space exploration

Rockford College (Illinois)
   Bettelheim, Bruno **2** 245-246

Rocking Chair (sculpture)
   Moore, Henry **11** 146-148

ROCKINGHAM, 2D MARQUESS OF (Charles Watson-Wentworth; 1730-82), English statesman **13** 230-231
   Burke, Edmund **3** 138-141
   Fox, Charles James **6** 35-37
   George III **6** 270-272
   Pitt, William the Elder **12** 328-329

Rockingham, Council of (1095)
   Anselm of Canterbury **1** 244-245

ROCKNE, KNUTE (1888-1931), American football coach **13** 231

Rock-'n'-roll (music)
   Beatles, The **2** 89-92
   Jagger, Michael Philip **8** 194-196
   Lennon, John Winston **9** 326-328
   Presley, Elvis Aron **12** 441-442
   Rich, Adrienne **13** 128-130
   Rolling Stones, The **13** 261-264
   Ross, Diana **13** 298-300

ROCKWELL, NORMAN PERCEVEL (1894-1978), American illustrator **13** 231-233

Rocky Mountain Fur Co.
   Astor, John Jacob **1** 351-352
   Bridger, James **3** 2-3
   Fitzpatrick, Thomas **5** 474-475
   Smith, Jedediah S. **14** 294-295

Rocky Mountains (United States)
   Frémont, John Charles **6** 97-98
   Lewis, Meriwether **9** 391-392

Rococo (art and architecture)
   American
      Bulfinch, Charles **3** 116-117
      Revere, Paul **13** 110-111
   Brazilian
      Aleijadinho, O **1** 125-126
   English
      Adam, Robert and James **1** 38-40
      Chippendale, Thomas **4** 1-2
      Gainsborough, Thomas **6** 170-172
      Hogarth, William **7** 446-447
   French
      Boffrand, Gabriel Germain **2** 361
      Boucher, François **2** 440-442
      Chardin, Jean Baptiste Siméon **3** 442-443
      Clodion **4** 121
      Coysevox, Antoine **4** 287-288
      Falconet, Étienne Maurice **5** 372
      Fragonard, Jean Honoré **6** 38-39
      Greuze, Jean Baptiste **6** 539
      Houdon, Antoine **7** 516-517
      Le Nain, Antoine, Louis and Mathieu **9** 321-322
      Prud'hon, Pierre Paul **12** 469
      Watteau, Antoine **16** 143-144
   German and Austrian
      Cuvilliés, François **4** 359-360
      Günther, Ignaz **7** 41-42
      Maulbertsch, Franz Anton **10** 345
      Mengs, Anton Raphael **10** 505
      Troger, Paul **15** 300
      Zimmermann, Johann Baptist and Domenikus **16** 518
   Italian
      Canova, Antonio **3** 263-264
   Spanish
      Goya y Lucientes, Francisco de Paula José de **6** 476-478

Rocroi, battle of (1643)
   Condé, Prince de **4** 193-194

Philip IV **12** 275

Rod of Moses, The (poem)
Iqbal, Muhammad **8** 132-133

RODCHENKO, ALEXANDER MIKHAILOVICH (1891-1956), Russian abstract painter, sculptor, photographer, and industrial designer **13** 233-234

Rodelinda (opera)
Handel, George Frederick **7** 116-119

Rodeo (ballet)
Copland, Aaron **4** 227-228

Roderick Hudson (novel)
James, Henry **8** 211-212

Roderick Random (novel)
Smollett, Tobias George **14** 305-307

Rodgers, John (1773-1838), American naval officer
Stockton, Robert Field **14** 461-462

RODGERS, RICHARD CHARLES (1902-1972), American composer **13** 234-236
Hammerstein, Oscar Clendenning II **7** 104-106
Martin, Mary **10** 292-293
O'Hara, John **11** 485

RODIN, AUGUSTE (1840-1917), French sculptor **13** 236-238
biographers
Rilke, Rainer Maria **13** 171-172
influence of
Borglum, John Gutzon de la Mothe **2** 416-417
Brancusi, Constantin **2** 494-496
Duchamp-Villon, Raymond **5** 123
Epstein, Jacob **5** 295-296
Lachaise, Gaston **9** 147
Lehmbruck, Wilhelm **9** 307
Manzù, Giacomo **10** 224-225
Nadelman, Elie **11** 289-290
Taft, Lorado **15** 75-76
precursors
Carpeaux, Jean Baptiste **3** 318-319
Rimmer, William **13** 174
U.S. exhibitions
Steichen, Edward **14** 411-412
Stieglitz, Alfred **14** 451-452

RODINO, PETER WALLACE, JR. (born 1909), Democratic U.S. representative from New Jersey **13** 238-239

RODNEY, GEORGE BRYDGES (1st Baron Rodney; 1718-92), British admiral **13** 239-240

Rodney Stone (novel)
Doyle, Arthur Conan **5** 91-92

RODÓ, JOSÉ ENRIQUE (1872-1917), Uraguayan essayist and literary critic **13** 240-241

Rodrigo (opera)
Handel, George Frederick **7** 116-119

Rodrigo, Don (literary character)
Manzoni, Alessandro **10** 222-224

Rodrigues Alves, Francisco de Paula (1848-1919), Brazilian statesman, president 1902-06
Rio Branco, Barão do **13** 177

Rodríguez, Abelardo (1889-1967), Mexican general and statesman
Ávila Camacho, Manuel **1** 387-388

Rodrique (literary character)
Corneille, Pierre **4** 234-236

Rodzinski, Artur (1894-1958), Polish-American conductor
Bernstein, Leonard **2** 218-219

Roe v. Wade (legal case, 1973)
Blackmun, Harry **2** 309-310

ROEBLING, JOHN AUGUSTUS (1806-1869), German-born American engineer **13** 241-242
Eads, James Buchanan **5** 175-176

ROEBLING, WASHINGTON AUGUSTUS (1837-1926), American engineer and manufacturer **13** 243
Roebling, John Augustus **13** 241-242

Roebuck (ship)
Dampier, William **4** 384

Roebuck, John (1718-1794), English inventor
Bruce, James **3** 63-64
Watt, James **16** 141-143

Roehm, Ernst (1887-1934), German soldier, head of storm troopers
Hitler, Adolf **7** 417-420

Roehm purge (1934)
Göring, Hermann Wilhelm **6** 457-458
Hindenburg, Paul Ludwig Hans von Beneckendorff und von **7** 400-401
Hitler, Adolf **7** 417-420

Roentgen, Wilhelm Conrad
see Roöntgen, Wilhelm Conrad

ROETHKE, THEODORE (1908-1963), American poet and teacher **13** 243-244

Roger I (Roger Guiscard; 1031-1101), Norman conqueror in Sicily
Bohemund, I **2** 364
Roger II **13** 244-245
Urban II **15** 393

ROGER II (1095-1154), king of Sicily 1130-54 **13** 244-245
Baldwin I **1** 464-465
Idrisi, Muhammad ibn Muhammad al- **8** 102-103
Manuel I **10** 218-219

Roger, Pierre
see Clement VI

Roger of Loria (1250?-1305), Italian naval commander
Peter III **12** 256-257

Roger of Salisbury (died 1139), English bishop
Henry I **7** 286-287
Stephen **14** 426-427

Roger Sherman (port)
Earl, Ralph **5** 179

Roger Wendover (died 1236), English monk and chronicler
Matthew Paris **10** 341-342

Roger Williams University (Nashville, Tennessee)
Hope, John **7** 489-490

ROGERS, CARL RANSOM (1902-1987), American psychotherapist **13** 245-247

ROGERS, EDITH NOURSE (1881-1960), U.S. congresswoman from Massachusetts **13** 247-248

Rogers, Henry Huttleston (1840-1909), American financier
Twain, Mark **15** 363-366

Rogers, John (1500?-1555), English Protestant martyr
Tyndale, William **15** 373-374

ROGERS, JOHN (1829-1904), American sculptor **13** 248
French, Daniel Chester **6** 98-99

ROGERS, RICHARD (born 1933), British architect **13** 248-250
Piano, Renzo **12** 289-291

ROGERS, ROBERT (1731-1795), American frontiersman and army officer **13** 250-251
Carver, Jonathan **3** 347-348

ROGERS, WILL (1879-1935), American actor, humorist, journalist, and performer **13** 251-252
Ziegfeld, Florenz **16** 516-517

Rogers, Woddes (died 1732), English seaman and colonial governor
Dampier, William **4** 384

Rogers Groups (sculpture)
Rogers, John **13** 248

Rogers Pass (Canada)
Fleming, Sandford **5** 485-486

Rogozhin (literary character)
Dostoevsky, Fyodor **5** 74-77

ROH TAE WOO (born 1932), president of the Republic of Korea **13** 253-255

Roha (town, Ethiopia)
see Lalibela

ROHDE, RUTH BRYAN OWEN (1885-1954), U.S. congresswoman **13** 252-253

Rohr, monastery church of (Germany)
Asam, Cosmas Damian and Egid Quirin **1** 323-324

Roi Lear, Le (overture)
Berlioz, Louis Hector **2** 203-205

Roi Miraculé, Le (novel)
Betti, Ugo **2** 246

Roi s'amuse, Le (play)
Hugo, Victor Marie **8** 22-25

Roi se Meurt, Le (play)
Ionesco, Eugène **8** 131-132

Rois en exil, Les (novel)
Daudet, Alphonse **4** 402-403

Rojack, Steve (literary character)
Mailer, Norman Kingsley **10** 148-150

ROJAS PINILLA, GUSTAVO (1900-1975),
Colombian general and politician
13 255-256

Roland (medieval French hero)
Ariosto, Ludovico **1** 289-290
Boiardo, Matteo Maria **2** 369
see also see also Orlando furioso

ROLAND, MADAME (Marie-Jeanne
Phlipon; 1754-1793), French author and
revolutionary **13** 256-259
Tarbell, Ida Minerva **15** 107-108

Rolf
see Rollo

ROLFE, JOHN (1585-1622), English
colonist in Virginia **13** 259-260
Pocahontas **12** 361-362
Powhatan **12** 429-430

Roll call (politics)
La Follette, Robert Marion **9** 155-156

Rolla, Alessandro (1757-1841), Italian violinist
Paganini, Niccolo **12** 58-59

ROLLAND, ROMAIN (1866-1944), French
writer **13** 260

ROLLE OF HAMPOLE, RICHARD (circa
1290-1349), English prose and verse
writer **13** 260-261

Roller, Alfred (1864-1935), Austrian painter
Mahler, Gustav **10** 144-145

Roller process (flour milling)
Pillsbury, Charles Alfred **12** 304

Rolling Stone (magazine)
Leibovitz, Annie **9** 310-312

ROLLING STONES, THE (formed in 1963),
rock and roll band **13** 261-264
Jagger, Michael Philip **8** 194-196

Rolling Stones (stories)
Henry, O. **7** 308-309

ROLLO (Rolf; circa 860-circa 932), Viking
adventurer **13** 264-265

RÖLVAAG, OLE EDVART (1876-1931),
Norwegian-American writer **13** 265

Roma (symphony)
Bizet, Georges **2** 296-297

Romagna (Italian city-state)
Borgia, Cesare **2** 412-413
Innocent, III **8** 125-127
Julius II **8** 384-386
Machiavelli, Niccolò **10** 97-99
Rudolf I **13** 347-348

Roman Actor, The (play)
Massinger, Philip **10** 324-325

Roman Antiquities (engraving collection)
Piranesi, Giovanni Battista **12** 321-322

Roman baroque (art and architecture)
Asam, Cosmas Damian and Egid Quirin
1 323-324
Borromini, Francesco **2** 424-425
Churriguera, José Benito de **4** 53-54

Roman Breviary (religious book)
Pius V **12** 332-333

Roman Catechism
Pius V **12** 332-333

Roman Catholic Church
Algeria
Lavigerie, Charles Martel Allemand
9 240
anticlericalism
see Anticlericalism
Australia
MacKillop, Mary **10** 106-107
Mannix, Daniel **10** 210
Santamaria, Bartholomew Augustine
13 473-474
Austria
Joseph II **8** 359-360
Pius VI **12** 333-334
Avignon Papacy
see Avignon Papacy
Canada
Bourgeoys, Marguerite **2** 452-453
Brown, George **3** 35-36
Laval, Francois Xavier de **9** 235-236
Canon Law
see Canon Law
Carolingian era (9th century)
Charlemagne **3** 445-447
Louis I **9** 522-523
Catholic Action
see Catholic Action
China
Francis Xavier **6** 48
Ricci, Matteo **13** 124-125
Xu Guangqi **16** 422-425
Christian unity
see Ecumenism
Church-State relations
see Church and State
conciliarism
see Conciliarism
constitutional threory
Cyprianus, Thascius Caecilianus
4 361-362
councils
see individual councils
Counter Reformation
see Counter Reformation
creed
see Nicene Creed
crusades
see Crusades
Doctors of the Church
see Religious leaders, Christian
England
see Roman Catholic Church (England)
eschatological movements
Joachim of Fiore **8** 263-264
Eucharist

see Eucharist
expansion
see Christianity—expansion
Fathers of the Church
see Religious leaders, Christian
foundations
see Christianity—foundation and
doctrine
France
see Roman Catholic Church (France)
Germany
Döllinger, Josef Ignaz von **5** 47-48
Eck, Johann Maier von **5** 200
Ferdinand II **5** 415
Frederick William IV **6** 87-88
see also Church and State (Holy
Roman Empire)
Great Schism (1378-1415)
see Great Schism
Haiti
Aristide, Jean-Bertrand **1** 291-293
heresy
see Heresy (Christian)
historians
Acton, John Emerich Edward Dal-
berg **1** 38
Döllinger, Josef Ignaz von **5** 47-48
Lea, Henry Charles **9** 261-262
Hungary
Mindszenty, József **11** 47-49
Pázmány, Péter **12** 164-165
Iconoclastic Controversy
Charlemagne **3** 445-447
John of Damascus **8** 282
Leo III **9** 330-332
India
Teresa **15** 148-151
Ireland
England, John **5** 288
see also Catholic Emancipation
Italy
see Church and State (Italian); Papal
States; Vatican City, State of the
Korea
Chongjo **4** 15-16
Latin America
Carrera, José Rafael **3** 324-325
Díaz, José de la Cruz Porfirio
4 534-536
Feijó, Diogo Antônio **5** 405-406
Frei Montalva, Eduardo **6** 94-95
García Moreno, Gabriel **6** 209-210
Illich, Ivan **8** 112-114
Juárez, Benito **8** 369-372
Mosquera, Tomás Cipriano de
11 205-206
Perón, Juan Domingo **12** 228-230
Rio Branco, Barão do **13** 177
Rivadavia, Bernardino **13** 182-183
Romero, Oscar **13** 265-267
lay investiture
see Investiture struggle
Modernists
Tyrrell, George **15** 374-375
monasticism
see Monasticism

Norway
  Olaf, II **11** 493-494
Nova Scotia
  Howe, Joseph **7** 534-535
Orthodox churches
  see Greek Orthodox Church; Ortho-
    dox Eastern Church; Russian
    Orthodox Church
papal monarchy
  Urban II **15** 393
papal office
  see Papacy
Papal States
  see Papal States
Philippines
  Sin, Jaime L. **14** 244-245
Photian Schism (9th century)
  Photius **12** 283-284
Poland
  Gomulka, Wladislaw **6** 422-424
  John Paul II **8** 287-290
political role
  Romero, Oscar **13** 265-267
  Sin, Jaime L. **14** 244-245
popes
  see Religious leaders, Catholic
    (since 1517); Religious leaders,
    Christian (to 1517)
Protestant Reformation begins
  Leo X **9** 332-334
  see also Protestant Reformation
religious orders
  see individual orders and congrega-
    tions
Scotland
  Knox, John **9** 65-66
  Malcolm III **10** 164-165
Spain
  Isidore of Seville **8** 149-150
  John of the Cross **8** 285
  Molinos, Miguel de **11** 88-89
  Philip II **12** 271-273
  see also Inquisition, Spanish
Switzerland
  Calvin, John **3** 239-242
  Zwingli, Huldreich **16** 537-538
temporal rule
  see Papal States; Vatican City, State
    of
Trent
  see Trent, Council of (1545-1563)
20th century
  Bea, Augustinus **2** 79
  Benedict XV **2** 153-154
  Hesburgh, Theodore Martin
    7 357-358
  John, XXIII **8** 277-280, 12
  John Paul II **8** 287-290
  Küng, Hans **9** 129-130
  Leo XIII **9** 334-336
  Merton, Thomas **10** 523-525
  Paul VI **12** 146-148
  Pius X **12** 336-337
  Pius XI **12** 337-339
  Pius XII **12** 339-340
  Schillebeeckx, Edward **14** 3-4

  see also Modernism
unity
  Cusa, Nicholas of **4** 352-353
  Ignatius of Antioch **8** 107-108
U.S.
  see Roman Catholic Church (United
    States)
Vatican Councils
  see Vatican Councils
women, role of
  Daly, Mary **4** 380-381
  Ruether, Rosemary Radford
    13 353-354
  Schüssler Fiorenza, Elisabeth
    14 46-48
  Stein, Edith **14** 412-414
Yugoslavia
  Stepinac, Alojzije **14** 433-435

Roman Catholic Church (England)
5th-10th century
  Dunstan **5** 151-152
  see also England (5th century
    -1066)—Christianity,
    (1066-1154)—Church and State
11th-14th century
  John **8** 274-275
  Lanfranc **9** 189-190
  Wyclif, John **16** 412-413
16th century
  Cranmer, Thomas **4** 295-296
  Elizabeth I **5** 263-266
  Mary, I **10** 308-309
17th century (opponents)
  Charles II **3** 452-454
  Crashaw, Richard **4** 296
  Donne, John **5** 60-61
  Oates, Titus **11** 456
  Shaftesbury, 1st Earl of **14** 135-136
19th century
  Froude, James Anthony **6** 133-134
  Gladstone, William Ewart
    6 357-360
  Russell, John **13** 380-381
19th-20th century
  Tyrrell, George **15** 374-375
  von Hügel, Friedrich **16** 21-22
20th century
  Greene, Graham **6** 523-524
  Manning, Henry Edward
    10 209-210
  see also Catholic Emancipation;
    Church and State (England)

Roman Catholic Church (France)
12th century
  Stephen Harding **14** 428-429
  Waldo, Peter **16** 55-56
16th century
  see Religion, Wars of
17th century
  Vincent de Paul **15** 501-502
18th century
  Pius VI **12** 333-334
  Saint-Simon, Comte de **13** 436-437
19th century

  Lacordaire, Jean Baptiste Henri
    9 148
  Lamennais, Hugues Félicité Robert
    de **9** 179
  Montalembert, Comte de
    11 118-119
  Pius VII **12** 334-335
  Proudhon, Pierre Joseph **12** 461-463
20th century
  Gilson, Étienne Henry **6** 327-328
  Marcel, Gabriel **10** 233-234
  Maritain, Jacques **10** 263
  Péguy, Charles Pierre **12** 183-184
  see also Church and State (France)

Roman Catholic Church (United States)
18th-19th century
  Carroll, John **3** 331-332
19th century
  De Smet, Pierre Jean **4** 509-510
  England, John **5** 288
  Hecker, Isaac Thomas **7** 250-251
  Hughes, John Joseph **8** 17-18
  Lamy, Jean Baptiste **9** 181-182
  McCloskey, John **10** 395
  Seton, Elizabeth Ann Bayley
    14 118-119
19th-20th century
  Drexel, Katherine **5** 102-103
  Gibbons, James **6** 300-301
  Ireland, John **8** 133-134
  Powderly, Terence Vincent
    12 420-421
20th century
  Bernardin, Joseph Cardinal
    2 210-211
  Daly, Mary **4** 380-381
  Day, Dorothy **4** 428-429
  Hayes, Patrick Joseph **7** 224-225
  Kennedy, John Fitzgerald **8** 502-506
  Mundelein, George William
    11 248-249
  Ruether, Rosemary Radford
    13 353-354
  Spellman, Francis Joseph **14** 367
  see also Church and State (United
    States)

Roman Daughter, The (painting)
  Peale, Rembrandt **12** 172-173

Roman de Brut, Le (poem; Wace)
  Layamon **9** 256-257

Roman de Fauvel, Le (poem)
  Vitry, Philippe de **16** 2

Roman de la rose (poem; G. de Lorris-J. de
Meun)
  Chaucer, Geoffrey **3** 482-485
  Guillaume de Lorris **7** 33-34
  Jean de Meun **8** 234-235
  Langland, William **9** 194-195
  Orléans, Charles D' **11** 530

Roman Divino Amore
  see Oratory of Divine Love

Roman Empire
  see Rome—217 B.C.-A.D. 476

Roman expérimental, Le (book)
Zola, Émile **16** 526-528

Roman Hippodrome (New York City)
Barnum, Phineas Taylor **2** 13-15

Roman Holiday (film)
Hepburn, Audrey **7** 314-316

Roman law
development
Claudius Germanicus, Tiberius **4** 91-92
Drusus, Marcus Livius **5** 105-106
Julias of Rome **8** 381-384
Septimius Severus, Lucius **14** 109-110
Ulpian, Domitius **15** 385-386
historical studies
Bryce, James **3** 85
Budé, Guillaume **3** 102-103
Mommsen, Theodor **11** 94-95
influence of
Frederick I **6** 78-79
Gierke, Otto von **6** 311-312
Savigny, Friedrich Karl von **13** 502-503
see also Law—Byzantine

Roman literature
see Latin literature

Roman Newsboys (painting)
Heade, Martin Johnson **7** 236

Roman Odes (poems)
Horace **7** 500-503

Roman Republic
see Rome—509-27 B.C.

Roman Spring of Mrs. Stone, The (novel)
Williams, Tennessee **16** 306-308

Roman Synod (144)
Marcion **10** 238-239

Roman Tales (stories)
Moravia, Alberto **11** 153-155

Romana, La (novel)
Moravia, Alberto **11** 153-155

Romance (book)
Ford, Ford Madox **6** 1-2

Romance (musical composition)
Szymanowski, Karol **15** 67-68

Romance of a Plain Man, The (novel)
Glasgow, Ellen **6** 360-361

Romance of the Rose
see Roman de la Rose

Romance of the Three Kingdoms, The (novel)
Ts'ao Ts'ao **15** 322-323

Romancero gitano (ballads)
Lorca, Federico García **9** 511-513

Romances históricos, Los (poems)
Saavedra, Angel de **13** 398

Romances of the Rosary (poems)
Brentano, Clemens **2** 515-516

Romances sans paroles (poem)
Verlaine, Paul Marie **15** 465-466

Romancillo XLIX (sonnet)
Góngora y Argote, Luis de **6** 427-428

Romanes, George John (1848-1894), British biologist
Morgan, Conway Lloyd **11** 159-160
Titchener, Edward Bradford **15** 241-242

Romanesque revival (architecture)
Richardson, Henry Hobson **13** 139-141
Saarinen, Eliel and Eero **13** 396-398

Romani, Felice (1788-1865), Italian librettist
Bellini, Vincenzo **2** 138-139

Romania (nation, South Eastern Europe)
Ceausescu, Nicolae **3** 387-388
Ferdinand **5** 413-414
Horthy de Nagybánya, Nicholas **7** 510-512
Iliescu, Ion **8** 111-112
see also Dacia

Romanian literature
Eminescu, Mihail **5** 280-281
Blandiana, Ana **2** 321-322

Romano, Giulio (1499-1546), Italian architect
Bramante, Donato **2** 493-494
l'Orme, Philibert de **9** 519
Palladio, Andrea **12** 75-77
Poussin, Nicolas **12** 418-420
Primaticcio, Francesco **12** 453-454
Sanmicheli, Michele **13** 469-470
Titian **15** 242-244
Veronese, Paolo **15** 469-470

Romanov, Anastasia (died 1560), czarina, wife of Ivan IV
Ivan IV **8** 157-159

Romanov dynasty (Russia; ruled 1613-1917)
Alexander I **1** 130-132
Alexander II **1** 132-133
Alexander III **1** 133-134
Alexis Mikhailovich Romanov **1** 142-143
Anna Ivanovna **1** 240-241
Catherine the Great **3** 370-372
Nicholas I **11** 377-378
Nicholas II **11** 378-380
Paul I **12** 143-144
Peter I **12** 253-256
see also Polish Succession, War of the (1733-1735)

Romans, Epistle of the (New Testament)
Augustine **1** 367-370
Luther, Martin **10** 48-51
Paul **12** 141-143

Romantic Comedians, The (novel)
Glasgow, Ellen **6** 360-361

Romantic Landscape (painting)
Léger, Fernand **9** 302-303

Romantic Symphony (musical composition)
Bruckner, Joseph Anton **3** 64-65
Hanson, Howard **7** 135-136

Romanticism (art)
American
Allston, Washington **1** 176-177
Bierstadt, Albert **2** 270-271
Blakelock, Ralph Albert **2** 318
Church, Frederick Edwin **4** 49-50
Cole, Thomas **4** 151-152
Copley, John Singleton **4** 228-230
Durand, Asher Brown **5** 156-157
Glackens, William **6** 355-356
Ryder, Albert Pinkham **13** 391-392
defined
Pater, Walter Horatio **12** 130-131
English
Bonington, Richard Parkes **2** 394-395
Constable, John **4** 208-209
Friedrich, Caspar David **6** 114-115
Lawrence, Thomas **9** 252-253
Morris, William **11** 187-188
Turner, Joseph Mallord William **15** 352-354
French
Claude Lorrain **4** 89-90
Delacroix, Ferdinand Victor Eugène **4** 469-471
Géricault, Jean Louis André Théodore **6** 280-281
Gros **7** 14-15
Ingres, Jean Auguste Dominique **8** 121-123
Labrouste, Pierre François Henri **9** 144
Prud'hon, Pierre Paul **12** 469
German
Dürer, Albrecht **5** 159-161
Spanish
Goya y Lucientes, Francisco de Paula José de **6** 476-478
Swiss
Fuseli, Henry **6** 153-155

Romanticism (literature)
African
Ekwensi, Cyprian **5** 242-243
American
Bryant, William Cullen **3** 83-85
Crane, Stephen **4** 293-295
Cummings, Edward Estlin **4** 334-336
Freneau, Philip Morin **6** 99-100
Hawthorne, Nathaniel **7** 212-215
Howe, Edgar Watson **7** 529
Lanier, Sidney **9** 199-200
Melville, Herman **10** 472-476
Warren, Robert Penn **16** 121-122
Williams, William Carlos **16** 308-309
Wolfe, Thomas Clayton **16** 355-356
Argentine
Echeverría, José Estéban **5** 197-198
Brazilian
Castro Alves, Antônio de **3** 364-365
Chinese
Kuo Mo-jo **9** 133-134
Li Po **9** 437-439
English (18th-19th century)
Chatterton, Thomas **3** 481-482

Coleridge, Samuel Taylor **4** 154-156
Collins, William **4** 168-169
Cowper, William **4** 282
Edgeworth, Maria **5** 205-206
Lamb, Charles **9** 176-177
Wordsworth, William **16** 385-388
English (19th century)
   Austen, Jane **1** 377-379
   Byron, George Gordon Noel
     3 193-194
   Keats, John **8** 470-472
   Morris, William **11** 187-188
   Peacock, Thomas Love **12** 169
   Scott, Walter **14** 68-70
   Shelley, Percy Bysshe **14** 176-178
French (13th-14th century)
   Chrestien de Troyes **4** 23-24
   Jean de Meun **8** 234-235
French (18th-20th century)
   Balzac, Honoré de **1** 478-480
   Chateaubriand, Vicomte de
     3 477-479
   Dumas, Alexandre **5** 136-138
   Hugo, Victor Marie **8** 22-25
   Lamartine, Alphonse Marie Louis de
     9 173-175
   Loti, Pierre **9** 519-520
   Mérimée, Prosper **10** 517
   Musset, Louis Charles Alfred de
     11 271-272
   Nerval, Gérard de **11** 345-346
   Sand, George **13** 459-461
   Staël, Germaine de **14** 391-392
   Stendhal **14** 422-425
   Vigny, Comte de **15** 494-495
German (18th century)
   Herder, Johann Gottfried von
     7 327-328
   Klopstock, Friedrich Gottlieb
     9 55-56
   Novalis **11** 435
   Wieland, Christoph Martin
     16 260-261
German (18th-19th century)
   Brentano, Clemens **2** 515-516
   Goethe, Johann Wolfgang von
     6 388-391
   Hölderlin, Johann Christian
     Friedrich **7** 451-452
   Richter, Johann Paul Friedrich
     13 150-151
   Schiller, Johann Christoph Friedrich
     von **14** 4-7
   Schlegel, Friedrich von **14** 10-11
   Tieck, Ludwig **15** 218-219
German (19th-20th century)
   Arnim, Achim von **1** 308-309
   Chamberlain, Houston Stewart
     3 411
   Friedrich, Caspar David **6** 114-115
   Grillparzer, Franz **6** 546-547
   Grimm, Jakob and Wilhelm Karl
     7 3-4
   Heine, Heinrich **7** 259-260
   Hoffmann, Ernst Theodor Amadeus
     7 439-440
   Kleist, Heinrich von **9** 52-53

   Staël, Germaine de **14** 391-392
Italian
   Alfieri, Vittoria **1** 145-146
   Casanova de Seinglat, Giacomo
     Jacopo Girolamo **3** 350-351
   De Sanctis, Francesco **4** 505
   Foscolo, Ugo **6** 21
   Leopardi, Giacomo **9** 344-345
   Manzoni, Alessandro **10** 222-224
   Mazzini, Giuseppe **10** 381-383
   Rosa, Salvator **13** 289-290
   Vico, Giambattista **15** 480-481
Norwegian
   Ibsen, Henrik **8** 98-100
Russian
   Lermontov, Mikhail Yurievich
     9 352-353
   Pushkin, Aleksandr Sergeevich
     12 489-491
Spanish
   Saavedra, Angel de **13** 398
   Vicente, Gil **15** 479-480
Swedish
   Lagerlöf, Selma Ottiliana Lovisa
     9 163-164

Romanticism (music)
American
   Gottschalk, Louis Moreau **6** 463-464
Austrian
   Schoenberg, Arnold **14** 24-26
   Schubert, Franz Peter **14** 35-37
French
   Berlioz, Louis Hector **2** 203-205
   Chopin, Frédéric François **4** 16-18
German
   Beethoven, Ludwig van **2** 114-117
   Brahms, Johannes **2** 490-492
   Grieg, Edvard Hagerup **6** 541-542
   Mendelssohn, Moses **10** 488-489
   Schubert, Franz Peter **14** 35-37
   Schumann, Robert Alexander
     14 41-43
   Weber, Carl Maria Friedrich Ernst
     von **16** 156-157
Italian
   Bellini, Vincenzo **2** 138-139
   Cherubini, Luigi Carlo Zanobi Sal-
     vatore Maria **3** 505-506
   Cimarosa, Domenico **4** 61-62
   Donizetti, Gaetano **5** 59-60
   Paganini, Niccolo **12** 58-59
   Rossini, Gioacchino **13** 311-312
Norwegian
   Grieg, Edvard Hagerup **6** 541-542
Russian
   Borodin, Aleksandr Profirevich
     2 422-423
   Glinka, Mikhail Ivanovich
     6 369-370
   Rachmaninov, Sergei Vasilievich
     12 531-532
   Tchaikovsky, Peter Ilyich
     15 130-132

Romanticism (philosophy)
Schelling, Friedrich Wilhelm Joseph von
   13 526-527

Schleiermacher, Friedrich Ernst Daniel
   14 11-12
Romanus II (939-963), Byzantine emperor
959-963
   Basil II **2** 50-51
Romanus III Argyrus (968?-1034), Byzan-
tine emperor 1028-34
   Zoë **16** 524-525
Romanus IV Diogenes (died 1071), Byzan-
tine emperor 1067-71
   Alp Arslan **1** 178-179
Romboutszoon, Theodorik
   see Bouts, Dirk
Rome
• 509-27 B.C. (ROMAN REPUBLIC)
   autocracy
     Sulla, Lucius Cornelius I
       15 21-22
   Carthaginian wars
     Hannibal Barca **7** 128-130
     Scipio Africanus Major, Publius
       Cornelius **14** 61-62
     Scipio Africanus Minor, Publius
       Cornelius Aemilianus **14** 62-63
   Catiline conspiracy (63 B.C.)
     Catiline **3** 372-373
     Cato, the Younger **3** 374-375
     Cicero, Marcus Tullius **4** 55-58
     Clodius Pulcher, Publius
       4 121-122
     Crassus Dives, Marcus Licinius
       4 296-297
   civil wars
     see Civil War, Roman
   collapse
     Gracchus, Tiberius and Gaius
       Sempronius **6** 479-480
     Marius, Gaius **10** 264-265
   Egypt and
     Antony, Mark **1** 253-254
     Caesar, Gaius Julius **3** 207-210
     Cleopatra **4** 105-106
   Greece and
     Flamininus, Titus Quinctius
       5 477
   histories of
     Cato, Marcus Porcius the Elder
       3 375
     Polybios **12** 384-385
     Sallust **13** 454
     Strabo **14** 485-486
   Punic Wars
     see Punic Wars
   slave revolts
     Spartacus **14** 363-364
   social reforms
     Drusus, Marcus Livius **5** 105-106
   Social War
     see Social War (Rome; 90-88
       B.C.)
   triumvirate (first; 60-53 B.C.)
     Antony, Mark **1** 253-254
     Brutus, Marcus Junius **3** 79-80
     Caesar, Gaius Julius **3** 207-210
     Cato, the Younger **3** 374-375

Cicero, Marcus Tullius **4** 55-58
Crassus Dives, Marcus Licinius
4 296-297
Pompey **12** 387-389
triumvirate (second; 43-31 B.C.)
Antony, Mark **1** 253-254
Augustus **1** 371-373
Brutus, Marcus Junius **3** 79-80
Cicero, Marcus Tullius **4** 55-58
see also Parthia—Rome
• 27 B.C.-A.D. 476 (ROMAN EMPIRE)
barbarian invasions
Alaric **1** 101-102
Attila **1** 360
Gaiseric **6** 172
Leo I **9** 329-330
Odoacer **11** 473
Ricimer, Flavius **13** 151-152
Theodosius **15** 176
Christianity
Athanasius **1** 358-359
Constantine I **4** 209-211
Ignatius of Antioch **8** 107-108
Julian **8** 378-379
Marcion **10** 238-239
Theodosius **15** 176
Eastern
see Byzantine Empire
empire created (27 B.C.)
Augustus **1** 371-373
empire partitioned
Constantine I **4** 209-211
Theodosius **15** 176
see also Byzantine Empire
fires
Nero Claudius Caesar
11 342-344
Titus Flavius Vespasianus
15 247-248
histories of
Ennius, Quintus **5** 289
Gibbon, Edward **6** 299-300
Mommsen, Theodor **11** 94-95
Montesquieu **11** 123-125
Rostovtzeff, Michael Ivanovich
13 315
Seneca the Younger, Lucius
Annaeus **14** 103-105
Suetonius Tranquillus, Gaius
15 13
Tacitus **15** 70-72
Illyricum
Brutus, Marcus Junius **3** 79-80
Caesar, Gaius Julius **3** 207-210
Stilicho, Flavius **14** 452-453
Jewish revolts
Bar Kochba, Simeon **2** 5
Hadrian **7** 60-61
Herod the Great **7** 333-334
Johanan ben Zakkai **8** 271-272
Josephus Flavius **8** 360-361
Paul **12** 141-143
Shammai **14** 149
Titus Flavius Vespasianus
15 247-248
Trajan **15** 291-292

literature
see Latin literature
military anarchy
Valerian **15** 404-405
Palmyra revolt
Zenobia **16** 500-503
Parthian wars
Hadrian **7** 60-61
Marcus Aurelius Antoninus
10 243-245
Septimius Severus, Lucius
14 109-110
Pax Romana
Livia **9** 457-460
Tiberius Julius Caesar Augustus
15 217-218
Persian wars
Khosrow I **8** 538-539
Shahpur II **14** 140-141
reforms
Frontinus, Sextus Julius **6** 130
Roman law
see Roman law
Rome sacked (410; 455)
Alaric **1** 101-102
Gaiseric **6** 172
Leo I **9** 329-330
Pelagius **12** 189-190
rulers (empresses)
Julias of Rome **8** 381-384
rulers (Flavian dynasty; 69-96)
Domitian **5** 52-53
Titus Flavius Vespasianus
15 247-248
Vespasian **15** 475-476
rulers (good emperors)
Hadrian **7** 60-61
Marcus Aurelius Antoninus
10 243-245
Trajan **15** 291-292
rulers (Julio-Claudian dynasty; 27
B.C. -A.D. 69)
Augustus **1** 371-373
Caligula **3** 228-229
Claudius Germanicus, Tiberius
4 91-92
Livia **9** 457-460
Nero Claudius Caesar
11 342-344
Tiberius Julius Caesar Augustus
15 217-218
rulers (military despots)
Caracalla **3** 281-282
Diocletian **5** 19-20
Septimius Severus, Lucius
14 109-110
• 476- (MEDIEVAL and MODERN)
art and architecture
see Gesù, Church of the; St. John
Lateran; St. Peter's; Santa Maria
Maggiore (Rome); and other
churches and monuments
see also Vatican City
Byzantine conquest (537-538)
Belisarius **2** 128-129
city planning

Sixtus V **14** 267-268
French occupation (1798)
Pius VI **12** 333-334
Pius VII **12** 334-335
march on
Mussolini, Benito **11** 272-274
pilgrimages
Villani, Giovanni **15** 497-498
sacked (1527)
Cajetan **3** 215-216
Castiglione, Baldassare
3 360-361
Cellini, Benvenuto **3** 391-392
Charles V **3** 457-459
Rosso, Il **13** 312-313
tribune restored (1354)
Rienzi, Cola di **13** 166-167
unification of Italy (1870)
Mazzini, Giuseppe **10** 381-383
Pius IX **12** 335-336
see also Italy; Papacy; Papal
States

Rome, battle of (1863)
Forrest, Nathan Bedford **6** 13-14

Rome, Council of (1050)
Lanfranc **9** 189-190

Rome, Treaty of (1958)
Monnet, Jean **11** 109-110

Rome, University of (Italy)
Fermi, Enrico **5** 422-424
Gentile, Giovanni **6** 267
Montessori, Maria **11** 125-126
Paul VI **12** 146-148
Ungaretti, Giuseppe **15** 389-390

Romeo (literary character)
Booth, Edwin **2** 401-402

Romeo and Juliet (play and film)
Barrymores **2** 28-30
Shakespeare, William **14** 142-145
Vigny, Comte de **15** 494-495

Roméo et Juliette (ballet)
Miró, Joan **11** 53-54

Roméo et Juliette (musical composition)
Berlioz, Louis Hector **2** 203-205
Gounod, Charles François **6** 473-474
Tchaikovsky, Peter Ilyich **15** 130-132

Romeo und Julia auf dem Dorfe (story)
Keller, Gottfried **8** 478-479

ROMERO, ARCHBISHOP OSCAR
(1917-1980), archbishop of San Salvador
13 265-267

ROMERO BARCELÓ, CARLOS (born
1932), Puerto Rican political leader and
governor **13** 267-268

Romilda e Costanza (opera)
Meyerbeer, Giacomo **10** 536-537

Römische Elegien (poem)
Goethe, Johann Wolfgang von
6 388-391

ROMMEL, ERWIN (1891-1944), German
field marshal **13** 268-269
Alexander of Tunis, 1st Earl **1** 135-136

Kesselring, Albert Field Marshal
8 522-523
Montgomery, Bernard Law **11** 135-136
Roosevelt, Franklin Delano **13** 277-280

ROMNEY, GEORGE (1734-1802), English
painter **13** 269-270
Fuller, Richard Buckminster **6** 149-150
Lawrence, Thomas **9** 252-253

Romola (novel)
Eliot, George **5** 254-256

Romorantin, Edict of (1560)
Medici, Catherine de' **10** 445-449

RÓMULO, CARLOS P. (1899-1985), Filipino journalist and diplomat **13** 270-271
Buck, Pearl Sydenstricker **3** 91-93

Romulus Augustulus (born 461?), Roman
emperor 475-476
Odoacer **11** 473

Romulus the Great (play)
Dürrenmatt, Friedrich **5** 164-165

Roncalli, Angelo Giuseppe
see John XXIII

Roncesvalles, battle of (778)
Abd al-Rahman I **1** 13-14
Charlemagne **3** 445-447

Ronchamp (village, France)
Le Corbusier **9** 274-275

Rondanini Pietà (sculpture)
Michelangelo Buonarroti **11** 2-5

Ronde, La (play)
Schnitzler, Arthur **14** 23-24

Rondine, La (opera)
Puccini, Giacomo **12** 474-476

**RONDON, CANDIDO MARIANO DA
SILVA** (1865-1958), Brazilian militarist
13 271

Rondos for Connoisseurs and Amateurs
(musical composition)
Bach, Carl Philipp Emanuel **1** 414-415

RONSARD, PIERRE DE (1524-1585),
French poet **13** 271-273
du Bellay, Joachim **5** 113-114
Hugo, Victor Marie **8** 22-25
Lescot, Pierre **9** 354
Malherbe, François de **10** 169-170
Nerval, Gérard de **11** 345-346
Sainte-Beuve, Charles Augustin **13** 438

RÖNTGEN, WILHELM CONRAD
(1845-1923), German physicist
13 273-275
Becquerel, Antoine Henri **2** 108-109
Bragg, William Henry **2** 488-489

Rood, O. N. (1831-1902), American physicist
Seurat, Georges Pierre **14** 120-122

Room... (poems)
Lewis, Cecil Day **9** 380

Room, The (play)
Pinter, Harold **12** 317-318

Room with a View, A (novel)
Forster, Edward Morgan **6** 14-16

Roon, Count Albrecht Theodor Emil von
(1803-1879), Prussian statesman
Bismarck, Otto Eduard Leopold von
2 294-296
William I **16** 292-293

Roosevelt (ship)
Peary, Robert Edwin **12** 175-176

ROOSEVELT, ANNA ELEANOR
(1884-1962), American lecturer and
author, first lady 1933-45 **13** 275-277
Anderson, Marian **1** 218-219
Bethune, Mary McLeod **2** 241-242

Roosevelt, Eleanor (1884-1962; American
lecturer and writer)
Dewson, Mary Williams **4** 525

ROOSEVELT, FRANKLIN DELANO
(1882-1945), American statesman, presi-
dent 1933-45 **13** 277-280
atomic bomb research
Einstein, Albert **5** 228-231
Szilard, Leo **15** 64-66
Wigner, Eugene Paul **16** 268-269
Cabinet
Forrestal, James Vincent **6** 14
Hull, Cordell **8** 28-29
Ickes, Harold LeClaire **8** 100-101
Morgenthau, Henry Jr. **11** 172-173
Murphy, Frank **11** 260-261
Perkins, Frances **12** 221-222
Schniederman, Rose **14** 22-23
Stettinius, Edward R. Jr. **14** 437-438
Stimson, Henry Lewis **14** 457-458
Wallace, Henry Agard **16** 73-74
Woodward, Ellen S. **16** 379-381
China and
Chiang Kai-shek **3** 510-513
Stilwell, Joseph Warren **14** 456-457
commentaries on
Beard, Charles Austin **2** 84
Lippmann, Walter **9** 439-440
Sandburg, Carl **13** 461-462
diplomatic appointments
Bowers, Claude Gernade **2** 463
Daniels, Josephus **4** 387
Harriman, W. Averell **7** 165-166
Owen, Ruth Bryan **12** 41-43
Sayre, Francis Bowes **13** 509
economic policies
see New Deal
Latin-American policies
Ávila Camacho, Manuel **1** 387-388
Justo, Agustin Pedro **8** 396
Lamas, Carlos Saavedra **9** 175-176
Morínigo, Higinio **11** 174-175
Welles, Sumner **16** 191-192
opponents
Borah, William Edgar **2** 408
Dewey, Thomas Edmund **4** 524
Hearst, William Randolph
7 243-244
Lindbergh, Charles Augustus
9 421-423

McCormick, Robert Rutherford
10 401-402
Smith, Alfred Emmanuel **14** 284-285
papal relations
Pius XII **12** 339-340
political supporters
Farley, James A. **5** 381-383
Lehman, Herbert Henry **9** 306-307
Truman, Harry S. **15** 314-316
Wood, Robert Elkington **16** 370-371
Supreme Court and
Frankfurter, Felix **6** 57
Johnson, Lyndon Baines **8** 308-312
Murphy, Frank **11** 260-261

Roosevelt, Nicholas I. (1767-1854), American inventor
Stevens, John **14** 439-440

ROOSEVELT, THEODORE (1858-1919),
American statesman, president 1901-09
13 280-283
Cabinet
Knox, Philander Chase **9** 66-67
Root, Elihu **13** 283-284
domestic policy
Cleveland, Stephen Grover
4 108-110
Harriman, Edward Henry **7** 164-165
Mitchell, John **11** 58-59
Pinchot, Gifford **12** 308-309
Sinclair, Upton Beale Jr. **14** 248-249
Stimson, Henry Lewis **14** 457-458
Wiley, Harvey Washington
16 277-278
foreign policy
Abbott, Lyman **1** 10-11
Estrada Palma, Tomás **5** 326-327
Goethals, George Washington
6 387-388
Gorgas, William Crawford
6 454-455
Hay, John **7** 215-216
Rhee, Syngman **13** 117-120
in literature
Cabell, James Branch **3** 195-196
Lindsay, Vachel **9** 424-425
influence of
Adams, Peter Chardon Brooks **1** 54
Carver, George Washington
3 346-347
Johnston, Henry Hamilton
8 322-323
Riis, Jacob August **13** 169-170
Robinson, Edwin Arlington
13 201-202
Sayre, Francis Bowes **13** 509
influenced by
Croly, Herbert David **4** 316-317
Mahan, Alfred Thayer **10** 131-132
memorials
Borglum, John Gutzon de la Mothe
2 416-417
military appointments
MacArthur, Douglas **10** 76-78
Pershing, John Joseph **12** 243-244
Sims, William Sowden **14** 244
nature studies

Burroughs, John **3** 160-161
Rondon, Candido Mariano da Silva **13** 271
opponents
Aldrich, Nelson Wilmarth **1** 123-124
Cannon, Joseph Gurney **3** 261-262
George, Henry **6** 276
Hearst, William Randolph **7** 243-244
Hewitt, Abram Stevens **7** 371-372
La Follette, Robert Marion **9** 155-156
Platt, Thomas Collier **12** 347-348
Smith, Alfred Emmanuel **14** 284-285
Tillman, Benjamin Ryan **15** 225-226
political appointments
Dewey, George **4** 520
Holmes, Oliver Wendell Jr. **7** 458-459
Nast, Thomas **11** 318-319
Taft, William Howard **15** 78-81
Wallace, Henry **16** 73
White, William Alanson **16** 239-240
Wood, Leonard **16** 369-370
supporters
Hanna, Marcus Alonzo **7** 127-128
Ickes, Harold LeClaire **8** 100-101
Ireland, John **8** 133-134
Johnson, Hiram Warren **8** 300-301
Johnson, James Weldon **8** 304-305
Kellor, Frances **8** 481-482
Lippmann, Walter **9** 439-440
Munsey, Frank Andrew **11** 251
Platt, Thomas Collier **12** 347-348
White, William Allen **16** 240-241
Roosevelt University (Chicago, Illinois)
Sullivan, Louis Henri **15** 27-28
ROOT, ELIHU (1845-1937), American statesman **13** 283-284
Blaine, James Gillespie **2** 312-313
Hearst, William Randolph **7** 243-244
Taft, William Howard **15** 78-81
Root, John Welborn (1850-1891), American architect
Burnham, Daniel Hudson **3** 148-149
Renwick, James **13** 102-103
Wright, Frank Lloyd **16** 398-401
Root and Branch Bill (England; 1641)
Clarendon, 1st Earl of **4** 73-75
Root Cellar (poem)
Roethke, Theodore **13** 243-244
Rootabaga Stories (literary collection)
Sandburg, Carl **13** 461-462
Roots: The Saga of an American Family (book)
Haley, Alex **7** 76-78
Root-Takahira agreement (1908)
Roosevelt, Theodore **13** 280-283
Rope (film)
Hitchcock, Alfred **7** 415-416
Rope, The (play)
Plautus **12** 348-350

Rope Dancer Accompanies Herself with Shadows, The (painting)
Ray, Man **13** 59-60
Ropshin
see Savinkov, Boris Viktorovich
Rorate celi desuper (poem)
Dunbar, William **5** 142-143
Rore, Cipriano da (1516-1565), Flemish composer
Zarlino, Gioseffo **16** 490-491
ROREM, NED (born 1923), American composer of art songs **13** 284-286
RORSCHACH, HERMANN (1884-1922), Swiss psychiatrist **13** 286-288
RORTY, RICHARD (born 1931), American philosopher and man of letters **13** 288-289
ROSA, SALVATOR (1615-1673), Italian painter and poet **13** 289-290
Durand, Asher Brown **5** 156-157
Magnasco, Alessandro **10** 127-128
Wilson, Richard **16** 329-330
Rosalie (musical)
Gershwin, George **6** 284-285
Porter, Cole Albert **12** 405-406
Rosamond (play)
Swinburne, Algernon Charles **15** 54-55
Rosamunde (play)
Schubert, Franz Peter **14** 35-37
Rosamunde Floris (play)
Kaiser, Georg **8** 411-412
ROSAS, JUAN MANUEL DE (1793-1877), Argentine dictator 1829-52 **13** 290-291
opponents
Alberdi, Juan Bautista **1** 109-110
Caxias, Duque de **3** 386
Echeverría, José Estéban **5** 197-198
Mármol, José **10** 274
Mitre, Bartolomé **11** 62-63
Pedro II **12** 180-181
Sarmiento, Domingo Faustino **13** 484-485
Urquiza, Justo José **15** 396-397
supporters
Quiroga, Juan Facundo **12** 521-522
Rivera, Fructuoso **13** 184-185
Urquiza, Justo José **15** 396-397
Rosaura (novel)
Güiráldez, Ricardo **7** 38-39
Roscelin of Compiègne (died circa 1125), French philosopher and theologian
Abelard, Peter **1** 23-25
Roscher, Wilhelm (1817-1894), German economist
Treitschke, Heinrich von **15** 293-294
Roscoe, Henry Enfield (1833-1915), English chemist
Bunsen, Robert Wilhelm **3** 124-125
Roscopoundia (lichen)
Pound, Roscoe **12** 417-418
Rose (ship)
Phips, William **12** 283

Rose, Hugh James (1795-1838), English Anglican theologian
Newman, John Henry **11** 365-367
Rose and the Cross, The (play)
Blok, Aleksandr Aleksandrovich **2** 335
Rose Bernd (play)
Hauptmann, Gerhart Johann Robert **7** 199-201
Rose for Emily, A (story)
Faulkner, William **5** 395-397
Rose Garden (literary collection)
Sa'di **13** 418-419
Rose Hobart (film)
Cornell, Joseph **4** 237-238
Rose Mary (poem)
Rossetti, Dante Gabriel **13** 308-309
Rose of Dutcher's Coolly (novel)
Garland, Hannibal Hamlin **6** 217-218
Rose of Persia, The (operetta)
Sullivan, Arthur Seymour **15** 23
Rose Tattoo, The (play)
Williams, Tennessee **16** 306-308
Rosebery, 5th Earl of
see Primrose, Archibald Philip
Rosenberg, Julius and Ethel (died 1953), Americans executed for atomic espionage
Douglas, William Orville **5** 83-85
Rosenkavalier, Der (opera; Strauss)
Hofmannsthal, Hugo von **7** 443-444
Strauss, Richard **14** 500-501
Rosenkrantz and Guildenstern Are Dead (play)
Stoppard, Thomas **14** 478-479
Rosenthal, Moritz (1862-1946), Austrian pianist
Liszt, Franz **9** 445-447
ROSENWALD, JULIUS (1862-1932), American retailer and philanthropist **13** 293
Wood, Robert Elkington **16** 370-371
ROSENZWEIG, FRANZ (1886-1929), Jewish philosopher and writer **13** 294
Buber, Martin **3** 87-89
Roses, Wars of the (1455-1485)
Lancasters
Henry VI **7** 298-299
Henry VII **7** 300-302
James III **8** 208-209
Margaret of Anjou **10** 249-250
Warwick and of Salisbury, Earl of **16** 122-123
Yorkists
Edward IV **5** 212-213
Richard III **13** 132-133
Roses from the South (waltz)
Strauss, Johann Jr. **14** 498-499
Rosetta stone (archeology)
Champollion, Jean François **3** 421
Napoleon I **11** 306-310
Young, Thomas **16** 475-476

Rosine (literary character)
Beaumarchais, Pierre August Caron de **2** 93-94

ROS-LEHTINEN, ILEANA (born 1952) Hispanic American U.S. congresswoman **13** 294-296

Rosmersholm (play)
Ibsen, Henrik **8** 98-100

ROSMINI-SERBATI, ANTONIO (1797-1855), Italian philosopher and priest **13** 296-297

ROSS, BETSY (Elizabeth Griscom; 1752-1836), American upholsterer who made the first U.S. flag **13** 297-298

ROSS, DIANA (born 1944), African American singer **13** 298-300
Gordy, Berry Jr. **6** 450-451

ROSS, EDWARD ALSWORTH (1866-1951), American sociologist **13** 300
Mills, C. Wright **11** 35-36

ROSS, HAROLD (Harold Wallace Ross; 1892-1951), founder and editor of the *New Yorker* magazine **13** 300-302

Ross, Harriet
see Tubman, Harriet Ross

Ross, J. H.
see Lawrence, Thomas Edward

ROSS, JOHN (1790-1866), American Cherokee Indian chief **13** 303-304

ROSS, MARY G. (born 1908), Native American aerospace engineer **13** 304-305

ROSS, SIR JAMES CLARK (1800-1862), English admiral and polar explorer **13** 302-303
McClintock, Francis Leopold **10** 394-395

Ross Ice Shelf (Antarctica)
Byrd, Richard Evelyn **3** 186-187
Shackleton, Ernest Henry **14** 132-133

Ross Sea (Antarctica)
Ross, James Clark **13** 302-303
Scott, Robert Falcon **14** 67-68

Rosse, 3d Earl of
see Parsons, William

Rossellini, Roberto (1906-1977), Italian film director
Antonioni, Michelangelo **1** 252-253
Fellini, Federico **5** 408-409

Rossellino, Antonio (circa 1427-79), Italian sculptor
Verrocchio, Andrea del **15** 471-472

Rossellino, Bernardo (1409-1464), Italian sculptor and architect
Alberti, Leon Battista **1** 113-115
da Settignano, Desiderio **4** 509

ROSSETTI, CHRISTINA GEORGINA (1830-1894), English poet **13** 307-308

ROSSETTI, DANTE GABRIEL (1828-1882), English painter and poet **13** 308-309
in art and literature

Carroll, Lewis **3** 332-333
Waugh, Evelyn Arthur St. John **16** 145-147
influence of
Morris, William **11** 187-188
Whistler, James Abbott McNeill **16** 225-226
Pre-Raphaelites
Browning, Robert **3** 53-55
Burne-Jones, Edward Coley **3** 145-146
Hunt, William Holman **8** 44-45
Millais, John Everett **11** 23-24
Rossetti, Christina Georgina **13** 307-308
Swinburne, Algernon Charles **15** 54-55

Rossetti, William (1829-1919), English editor and writer
Whitman, Walt **16** 249-251

Rosshalde (novel)
Hesse, Hermann **7** 367-369

ROSSI, ALDO (born 1931), Italian architect **13** 309-310

Rossi, Francesco de'
see Salviati, Francesco Cecco di

ROSSI, LUIGI (circa 1598-1653), Italian composer **13** 310-311

ROSSINI, GIOACCHINO (1792-1868), Italian composer **13** 311-312
Bellini, Vincenzo **2** 138-139
Cimarosa, Domenico **4** 61-62
Donizetti, Gaetano **5** 59-60
Meyerbeer, Giacomo **10** 536-537
Respighi, Ottorino **13** 103-104
Verdi, Giuseppe Fortunino Francesco **15** 463-465

Rossmann, Karl (literary character)
Kafka, Franz **8** 403-406

ROSSO, IL (Giovanni Battista di Jacopo; 1495-1540), Italian painter **13** 312-313
Andrea del Sarto **1** 224-225
Francis I **6** 40-43
Goujon, Jean **6** 466-467
Pontormo **12** 394-395
Primaticcio, Francesco **12** 453-454

ROSSO, MEDARDO (1858-1928), Italian sculptor **13** 313-315
Manzù, Giacomo **10** 224-225

Rostand, Edmond de (1868-1918), French poet and playwright
Cocteau, Jean **4** 132-133

Rostock, University of (Germany)
Schlick, Friedrich Albert Moritz **14** 16-17
Spemann, Hans **14** 368-369
Stern, Otto **14** 435

ROSTOVTZEFF, MICHAEL IVANOVICH (1870-1952), Russian-born American historian and classical scholar **13** 315

ROSTOW, WALT WHITMAN (born 1916), American educator, economist, and government official **13** 315-317

ROSTROPOVICH, MSTISLAV LEOPOLDOVICH (Slava Rostropovich; born 1927), Russian cellist and conductor **13** 317-318
Shostakovich, Dmitri Dmitrievich **14** 204-205

Rosy Crucifixion, The (trilogy)
Miller, Henry **11** 26-27

Roszak, Theodore (1907-1981), Polish-American sculptor
González, Julio **6** 428-429
Smith, David **14** 287-288

Rotary Glass Plate (kinetic art)
Ray, Man **13** 59-60

Rote Fahne (newspaper)
Luxemburg, Rosa **10** 55-56

ROTH, PHILIP (born 1933), American author **13** 318-320

Rotherham, Thomas (1423-1500), English archbishop, chancellor 1474-83
Richard III **13** 132-133

Rothesay, David Stewart, Duke of (1378?-1402), Scottish nobleman
James I **8** 206-207
Robert III **13** 194-195

ROTHKO, MARK (1903-1970), American painter **13** 320-321
Motherwell, Robert **11** 210-211
Newman, Barnett **11** 365

Rothschild Madonna (painting; Van Eyck-Christus)
Christus, Petrus **4** 33-34

Rothschild Store (Chicago, Illinois)
Sullivan, Louis Henri **15** 27-28

Rotifers (biology)
Leeuwenhoek, Anton van **9** 300-301

Rôtisserie de la Reine Pédauque, La (novel)
France, Anatole **6** 39-40

Rotonda (Vicenza, Italy)
Palladio, Andrea **12** 75-77

Rotrano Palace (Auersperg, Yugo.)
Fischer von Erlach, Johann Bernhard **5** 459-461

Rotterdam (city, Netherlands)
Zadkine, Ossip Joselyn **16** 484

ROTTMAYR, JOHANN MICHAEL (1654-1730), Austrian painter **13** 321
Fischer von Erlach, Johann Bernhard **5** 459-461
Troger, Paul **15** 300
Prandtauer, Jakob **12** 432

ROUAULT, GEORGES (1871-1958), French painter and graphic artist **13** 321-322
Demuth, Charles **4** 497-498
Matisse, Henri **10** 336-337

Roucoux, battle of (1746)
Amherst, Jeffery **1** 200-201

Rouen Cathedral (France)
Clodion **4** 121
Monet, Claude **11** 102-104

Rouen, Treaty of (1091)
William II **16** 293-294

Rough and Ready (book)
Alger, Horatio **1** 153-154

Roughing It (book)
Twain, Mark **15** 363-366

Rougon-Macquart, Les (novel; Zola)
Daudet, Alphonse **4** 402-403
Zola, Émile **16** 526-528

Round (music)
Byrd, William **3** 187-188
Machaut, Guillaume de **10** 93-94

Round Table Conference (Brussels)
Lumumba, Patrice Emery **10** 43-45
Tshombe, Moïse Kapenda **15** 325-326

Round Table Conferences (London)
Aga Khan **1** 74-76
Gandhi, Mohandas Karamchand
6 201-204
Reading, 1st Marquess of **13** 64
Sapru, Tej Bahadur **13** 480-481

Round the Moon (novel)
Verne, Jules **15** 467-469

Round Up (book)
Lardner, Ringgold Wilmer **9** 204-205

Roundheads and the Peakheads, The (play)
Brecht, Bertolt **2** 512-514

ROUS, FRANCIS PEYTON (1879-1970),
American pathologist and virologist
13 322-323

ROUSSEAU, HENRI (1844-1910), French
painter **13** 323-324
Derain, André **4** 503
Léger, Fernand **9** 302-303

ROUSSEAU, JEAN JACQUES (1712-1778),
Swiss-born French philosopher and
author **13** 324-328
contemporaries
Condorcet, Marquis de **4** 195-196
Diderot, Denis **5** 1-2
Saint-Pierre, Abbé de **13** 434-435
influence (Asia)
Liang Ch'i-ch'ao **9** 395-396
influence (European Continent)
Chénier, André Marie **3** 500-501
Goethe, Johann Wolfgang von
6 388-391
Gordon, Aaron David **6** 447-448
Greuze, Jean Baptiste **6** 539
Hegel, Georg Wilhelm Friedrich
7 254-256
Karamzin, Nikolai Mikhailovich
8 441-442
Lamartine, Alphonse Marie Louis de
9 173-175
Richter, Johann Paul Friedrich
13 150-151
Ritter, Karl **13** 181-182
Strindberg, August **14** 509-511

influence (England)
Bosanquet, Bernard **2** 425-426
Edgeworth, Maria **5** 205-206
influence (Latin America)
Alberdi, Juan Bautista **1** 109-110
Juárez, Benito **8** 369-372
theories disputed
Froebel, Friedrich Wilhelm August
6 122-123
Maistre, Joseph de **10** 153-154
translations and biographies
Mendelssohn, Moses **10** 488-489
Morley, John **11** 178-179

ROUSSEAU, THÉODORE (1812-1867),
French painter and draftsman **13** 328
Blakelock, Ralph Albert **2** 318
Millet, Jean François **11** 31
Monet, Claude **11** 102-104

Rousseau le Douanier
see Rousseau, Henri

ROUSSEL, ALBERT (1869-1937), French
composer **13** 328-329
Martinu, Bohuslav **10** 299-300
Varèse, Edgard **15** 432-433

Roussel, Ker Xavier (1867-1944), French
painter and lithographer
Bonnard, Pierre **2** 395-396

Routh, Edward John (1831-1907), British
mathematician
Rayleigh, 3d Baron **13** 62

Rouvroy, Claude Henri de
see Saint-Simon, Comte de

Rouvroy, Louis de
see Saint-Simon, Duc de

Roux, Pierre Paul Émile (1853-1933),
French physician and bacteriologist
Curie, Marie Sklodowska **4** 339-341

Roux, Wilhelm (1850-1924), German
anatomist
Spemann, Hans **14** 368-369

Rover, The (novel)
Conrad, Joseph **4** 205-207

Rovere, Francesco della
see Sixtus IV

Rovere, Giuliano della
see Julius II

ROWAN, CARL T. (born 1925), American
journalist, author, and ambassador
13 329-330

Rowe, Nicholas (1674-1718), English
writer
Richardson, Samuel **13** 141-142

ROWLAND, HENRY AUGUSTUS
(1848-1901), American physicist
13 330-331
Maxwell, James Clerk **10** 361-364

Rowland, John
see Stanley, Sir Henry Morton

Rowlatt Acts (India; 1919)
Bose, Subhas Chandra **2** 430-431

Gandhi, Mohandas Karamchand
6 201-204

Rowley, Samuel (died 1633?), English
dramatist
Fletcher, John **5** 487
Ford, John **6** 7-8

Rowley, Thomas
see Chatterton, Thomas

Rowley, William (1585?-1642), English
dramatist and actor
Dekker, Thomas **4** 465-466
Middleton, Thomas **11** 8-9

Roxana (novel)
Defoe, Daniel **4** 457-459

ROXAS, MANUEL (1892-1948), Filipino
statesman, president 1946-48
13 331-332
Magsaysay, Ramon **10** 130-131
Marcos, Ferdinand **10** 240-242
Osmeña, Sergio **12** 22-24
Quirino, Elpidio **12** 519-520

Roxbury Grammar School (Massachusetts)
Eliot, John **5** 256-258

Roxelana (died 1558), Russian wife of
Suleiman I
Suleiman I **15** 20-21

Roxelana Mosque (Istanbul)
Sinan, Kodja Mimar **14** 245-246

Roxy (novel)
Eggleston, Edward **5** 223-224

ROY, RAM MOHUN (1772-1833), Bengali
social and religious reformer **13** 18
Duff, Alexander **5** 126-127

Roy Thomson Hall (Toronto, Canada)
Erickson, Arthur Charles **5** 304-306

Royal Academy of Arts (England; estab-
lished 1768)
Reynolds, Joshua **13** 115-116
West, Benjamin **16** 210-212

Royal Academy of Painting and Sculpture
(France, established 1648)
Le Brun, Charles **9** 269-270
Le Nain, Antoine, Louis and Mathieu
9 321-322

Royal Ballet (England)
Fonteyn, Dame Margot **5** 504-505

Royal Bird (sculpture)
Smith, David **14** 287-288

Royal Botanical Gardens (Kew Gardens,
London)
Banks, Joseph **1** 489-490

Royal Ceremonies ... (book)
Chulalongkorn **4** 43-45

Royal Christy Minstrels (theatrical group)
Christy, Edwin P. **4** 34-35

Royal College of Music (London)
Holst, Gustav **7** 459-460
Sullivan, Arthur Seymour **15** 23
Vaughan Williams, Ralph **15** 446-447

Royal College of Physicians (London)
Boylston, Zabdiel **2** 471
Bright, Richard **3** 7-8
Dale, Henry Hallett **4** 371-373

Royal College of Surgeons (London)
Huxley, Thomas Henry **8** 77-79
Owen, Richard **12** 39

Royal Commentaries of the Incas, The (book)
Garcilaso de la Vega, Inca **6** 210-211

Royal Crown (poems)
ibn Gabirol, Solomon ben Judah **8** 92

Royal Economics Society (established 1890)
Marshall, Alfred **10** 277-278

Royal Family, The (play)
Ferber, Edna **5** 413
Kaufman, George S. **8** 457-458

Royal Fireworks (musical composition)
Handel, George Frederick **7** 116-119

Royal Garden (Paris)
see Muséum National d'Histoire Naturelle

Royal Geographical Society (London)
Bates, Henry Walter **2** 53-54
Burton, Richard **3** 163-164
Speke, John Hanning **14** 366-367

Royal Guard House (Berlin)
Schinkel, Karl Friedrich **14** 8

Royal Highness (novel)
Mann, Thomas **10** 204-207

Royal Hospital (Chelsea, England)
Wren, Christopher **16** 393-394

Royal Institution of Great Britain (established 1799)
Bragg, William Henry **2** 488-489
Davy, Humphry **4** 426-427
Faraday, Michael **5** 380
Huxley, Thomas Henry **8** 77-79
Rayleigh, 3d Baron **13** 62
Rumford **13** 360-362
Young, Thomas **16** 475-476

Royal Lancasterian Society (established 1811)
Lancaster, Joseph **9** 182-183

Royal Lodge (Windsor, England)
Nash, John **11** 316

Royal Marriage Bill (Great Britain; 1772)
Fox, Charles James **6** 35-37

Royal Melody Compleat (hymnal; Tans'ur)
Billings, William **2** 274-275

Royal Naval Hospital (Greenwich, England)
Wren, Christopher **16** 393-394

Royal Niger Company (established 1886)
Goldie, George Dashwood Taubman **6** 404
Lugard, Frederick John Dealtry **10** 31-32

Royal Palace (Berlin)
Schinkel, Karl Friedrich **14** 8

Royal Palace (Madrid)
Tiepolo, Giovanni Battista **15** 219-220

Royal Palace (opera)
Weill, Kurt **16** 174-175

Royal Pavilion (Brighton, England)
George IV **6** 272-273
Nash, John **11** 316

Royal Society (established 1662; London)
Boyle, Robert **2** 469-471
Hooke, Robert **7** 475

Royal Voyage, The (sculpture)
Nevelson, Louise **11** 356-357

Royal Way, The (novel)
Malraux, André **10** 178-180

ROYBAL-ALLARD, LUCILLE (born 1941), Hispanic American U.S. congresswoman **13** 332-334

ROYCE, JOSIAH (1855-1916), American philosopher **13** 334-335
Eliot, Thomas Stearns **5** 258-261
Lewis, Clarence Irving **9** 381
Lotze, Rudolf Hermann **9** 521-522
Marcel, Gabriel **10** 233-234
Santayana, George **13** 475-477
Vivekananda **16** 4-5

ROYDEN, AGNES MAUDE (1876-1956), British preacher, lecturer, and author **13** 335-337

Royer-Collard, Pierre Paul (1763-1845), French philosopher and politician
Guizot, François Pierre Guillaume **7** 40-41

ROYKO, MIKE (1932-1997), American columnist **13** 337-339

RU 486
Baulieu, Étienne-Émile **2** 63-66

Rua (died 434), Hun chieftain
Attila **1** 360

Rústico del cielo, El (play)
Lope Félix de Vega Carpio **9** 503-506

Ruark, Arthur Edward (1899-1979), American physicist
Urey, Harold Clayton **15** 394-396

Rubaiyat (poems; Omar Khayyam)
Graves, Robert Ranke **6** 504-506
Omar Khayyam **11** 510-511

Rubber industry (United States)
Firestone, Harvey Samuel **5** 452-453
Goodyear, Charles **6** 441

Rubber, synthetic
Baekeland, Leo Hendrik **1** 430-431
Debye, Peter Joseph William **4** 447-448

Rubens, Heinrich (1865-1922), German physicist
Planck, Max Karl Ernst Ludwig **12** 342-344

RUBENS, PETER PAUL (1577-1640), Flemish painter and diplomat **13** 339-342
contemporaries
Brouwer, Adriaen **3** 29-30
Jordaens, Jacob **8** 347-349

Rembrandt Harmensz van Rijn **13** 91-95
Van Dyck, Anthony **15** 423-425, 85
influence (European Continent)
Beckmann, Max **2** 104-105
Boucher, François **2** 440-442
Daumier, Honoré Victorin **4** 403-405
Delacroix, Ferdinand Victor Eugène **4** 469-471
Magnasco, Alessandro **10** 127-128
Murillo, Bartolomé Esteban **11** 258-259
Rottmayr, Johann Michael **13** 321
Velázquez, Diego Rodríguez de Silva y **15** 454-456
influence (England)
Constable, John **4** 208-209
Jones, Inigo **8** 333-334
Reynolds, Joshua **13** 115-116
influence (United States)
Marsh, Reginald **10** 276-277
Trumbull, John **15** 316-317
influenced by
Bruegel, Pieter the Elder **3** 65-67
Caravaggio **3** 282-284
Carracci **3** 319-321
Michelangelo Buonarroti **11** 2-5
Veronese, Paolo **15** 469-470

RUBENSTEIN, HELENA (1870-1965), Polish-born beauty expert and businesswoman **13** 342-343

RUBENSTEIN, RICHARD L. (born 1924), American Jewish theologian and writer **13** 343-344

Rübezahl (opera)
Mahler, Gustav **10** 144-145

Rubicon River (Italy)
Caesar, Gaius Julius **3** 207-210

Rubidium (element—chemistry)
Bunsen, Robert Wilhelm **3** 124-125
Hahn, Otto **7** 64-65

RUBIN, JERRY (1938-1994), activist, writer, lecturer, and businessman **13** 344-346

Rubinstein, Anton (1829-1894), Russian pianist and composer
Glinka, Mikhail Ivanovich **6** 369-370
Tchaikovsky, Peter Ilyich **15** 130-132

Rubinstein, Artur (1886-1982), Polish-born American pianist
Szymanowski, Karol **15** 67-68

Rubinstein, Nikolai (1835-1881), Russian pianist and conductor
Tchaikovsky, Peter Ilyich **15** 130-132

Rucellai Madonna (painting)
Duccio di Buoninsegna **5** 121-122

Rucellai Palace (Florence)
Alberti, Leon Battista **1** 113-115

Rückert, Friedrich (1788-1866), German poet
Mahler, Gustav **10** 144-145

Rudabah (literary character)
Firdausi **5** 451-452

Rudbeck, Olof (1630-1702), Swedish scientist
Linnaeus, Carl **9** 427-429

Rudd Concession (1888)
Lobengula **9** 474-475

Ruddigore (operetta)
Gilbert, William Schwenck **6** 314-315

Rude, François (1784-1855), French sculptor
Carpeaux, Jean Baptiste **3** 318-319

Rudens (play)
Plautus **12** 348-350

Rudin (novel)
Turgenev, Ivan Sergeyevich **15** 345-348

RUDKIN, MARGARET FOGARTY
(1897-1976), founder and president of
Pepperidge Farm Inc. **13** 346-347

Rudolf (1858-1889), crown prince of Austria
Francis Ferdinand **6** 44

Rudolf (died 1080), duke of Swabia
1057-80
Henry IV **7** 292

Rudolf (died 936), king of the Franks and
duke of Burgundy
Henry I **7** 285-286

RUDOLF I (Rudolf of Hapsburg; circa
1218-91), Holy Roman emperor-elect
1273-91 **13** 347-348
Henry VII **7** 299-300

Rudolf II (1552-1612), Holy Roman
emperor 1576-1612
Ferdinand II **5** 415
Maximilian II **10** 357-358

Rudolph (1788-1831), Austrian archduke
and archbishop of Olmütz
Beethoven, Ludwig van **2** 114-117

RUDOLPH, PAUL MARVIN (born 1918),
American architect **13** 348-350

RUDOLPH, WILMA (1940-1994), African
American track and field athlete and
coach **13** 350-352

Rue Transnonain (lithograph)
Daumier, Honoré Victorin **4** 403-405

RUEF, ABRAHAM (1864-1936), American
political boss **13** 352-353

RUETHER, ROSEMARY RADFORD (born
1936), American church historian, theologian, writer, and teacher specializing
in the area of women and religion
13 353-354

Rufer, Josef Leopold (1893-1985), Austrian
musician
Schoenberg, Arnold **14** 24-26

RUFFIN, EDMUND (1794-1865), American agriculturist **13** 354-355

Ruffo, Fabrizio (1744-1827), Italian general
and cardinal
Nelson, Horatio **11** 336-338

Rufinus, Flavius (died 395), Roman statesman
Stilicho, Flavius **14** 452-453

Rufus (literary character)
Baldwin, James Arthur **1** 465-466

Rufus Publius Sulpicius (flourished 98-88
B.C.), Roman orator and statesman
Marius, Gaius **10** 264-265

Rugby (musical composition)
Honegger, Arthur **7** 472-473

Rugby Chapel (poem)
Arnold, Matthew **1** 311-313

Rugby School (England)
Arnold, Thomas **1** 313-314

RUGG, HAROLD (1886-1960), American
teacher, historian, and educational theorist **13** 355-357

Ruggero (literary character)
Boiardo, Matteo Maria **2** 369

Ruggiero (literary character)
Ariosto, Ludovico **1** 289-290

Ruhr (region, Germany)
Hitler, Adolf **7** 417-420
Montgomery, Bernard Law **11** 135-136
Poincaré, Raymond **12** 366-368
Stresemann, Gustav **14** 508-509
Young, Owen D. **16** 473-474

Ruined Cottage, The (poem)
Wordsworth, William **16** 385-388

Ruins of Time, The (poem)
Spenser, Edmund **14** 373-376

RUISDAEL, JACOB VAN (1628/29-82),
Dutch landscape painter **13** 357-358

RUÍZ, JOSÉ MARTÍNEZ (1873-1967),
Spanish writer **13** 358
Cela y Trulock, Camilo José **3** 389-390

RUIZ, JUAN (1283?-1350?), Spanish poet
13 358-359

RUIZ CORTINES, ADOLFO (1890-1973),
president of Mexico (1952-1958)
13 359-360
Alemán, Mateo **1** 126

Rule a Wife and Have a Wife (play)
Fletcher, John **5** 487

Rule, Brittania (musical composition)
Arne, Thomas Augustine **1** 307-308
Thomson, James **15** 199-200

Rule of St. Benedict
see Benedictines

Rulers of Hell (engraving)
Wu Tao-tzu **16** 405-406

**Rules for Radicals: A Political Primer for
Practical Radicals** (book)
Alinsky, Saul David **1** 161-162

Rum (Seljuk sultanate; Asia M.)
Nureddin **11** 444-445

Rum Rebellion (Australia; 1808)
Bligh, William **2** 325-326
Evatt, Herbert Vere **5** 341-343
Macarthur, John **10** 78

Rumania
see Romania

RUMFORD, COUNT (Benjamin Thompson; 1753-1814), American-born British
physicist **13** 360-362
Winthrop, John **16** 341-342

RUMI, JALAI ED-DIN (1207-1273), Persian
poet and Sufi mystic **13** 362-363
Attar, Farid ed-Din **1** 359-360
Jami **8** 218-219

Rumiantsev, Count Nikolai Petrovich
(1754-1826), Russian statesman
Nesselrode, Karl Robert **11** 348-349

Rumour at Nightfall (novel)
Greene, Graham **6** 523-524

Rump Parliament (England)
Cromwell, Oliver **4** 317-320

Rumpole of the Bailey (television series)
Mortimer, John Clifford **11** 194-195

Rumsey, James (1743-1792), American
engineer
Fitch, John **5** 467-468

Rumuz-i-Bekhudi (poem)
Iqbal, Muhammad **8** 132-133

Rundköpfe und die Spitzköpfe, Die (play)
Brecht, Bertolt **2** 512-514

RUNDSTEDT, KARL RUDOLF GERD VON
(1875-1953), German field marshal
13 363-364

Runge, Philip Otto (1777-1810), German
painter
Friedrich, Caspar David **6** 114-115

Runnymede
see Magna Carta (1215)

Rupert (king, Germany)
see Rupert of the Palatinate

Rupert, Prince (1619-1682), Count Palatine
of Rhine and Duke of Bavaria and Cumberland
Charles, I **3** 450-452
Cromwell, Oliver **4** 317-320
Hampden, John **7** 110-111
Van Dyck, Anthony **15** 423-425

Rupert of the Palatinate (1352-1410), king
of Germany 1400-10
Sigismund **14** 220-221

R.U.R. (play)
Čapek, Karel **3** 271-272

Rural Code of 1826 (Haiti)
Boyer, Jean Pierre **2** 468-469

Rural Electrification Administration (United States)
Norris, George William **11** 428-429
Rayburn, Samuel Taliaferro **13** 61-62

Rurick (ship)
Kotzebue, Otto von **9** 91-92

RURIK (died circa 873), Norman warrior
13 364

Rusalka (opera)
Dvořák, Antonin **5** 168-169

RUSH, BENJAMIN (1745-1813), American
physician **13** 364-365
  Banneker, Benjamin **1** 490-491
  Benezet, Anthony **2** 159-160
  Cobbett, William **4** 126-127
  Paine, Thomas **12** 66-67
  Rush, William **13** 365-366
  Witherspoon, John **16** 346-348

Rush, Richard (1780-1859), American
statesman and diplomat
  Gallatin, Albert **6** 183-184

RUSH, WILLIAM (1756-1833), American
sculptor **13** 365-366

RUSHDIE, AHMED SALMAN (born 1947),
Indian/British author **13** 366-368

RUSK, DAVID DEAN (1909-1994), American secretary of state (1961-1969)
13 368-370

RUSKA, ERNST AUGUST FRIEDRICH
(1906-1988), German engineer
13 370-371

RUSKIN, JOHN (1819-1900), English critic
and social theorist **13** 371-372
  art criticism
    Turner, Joseph Mallord William
    15 352-354
    Whistler, James Abbott McNeill
    16 225-226
  influence of
    Clark, Kenneth M. **4** 79-80
    Collingwood, Robin George **4** 162
    Gandhi, Mohandas Karamchand
    6 201-204
    Hunt, William Holman **8** 44-45
    Millais, John Everett **11** 23-24
    Morris, William **11** 187-188
    Proust, Marcel **12** 465-467
    Pugin, Augustus Welby Northmore
    12 479-480
    Tawney, Richard Henry **15** 120-121
    Wright, Frank Lloyd **16** 398-401
  influenced by
    Carlyle, Thomas **3** 304-305

Ruskin College of Social Science (Trenton,
Missouri)
  Parsons, Frank **12** 121-122

Ruskin Hall (school; Oxford, England)
  Beard, Charles Austin **2** 84

Ruslan and Ludmilla (opera; Glinka)
  Glinka, Mikhail Ivanovich **6** 369-370
  Pushkin, Aleksandr Sergeevich
  12 489-491

RUSSELL, BERTRAND ARTHUR WILLIAM
(3rd Earl Russell; 1872-1970), British
mathematician, philosopher, and social
reformer **13** 373-374
  collaborators
    Whitehead, Alfred North
    16 242-244
  influence of
    Broad, Charlie Dunbar **3** 12
    Carnap, Rudolf **3** 308-309
    Cohen, Morris Raphael **4** 139-140
    Danquah, Joseph B. **4** 388-389

    Moore, George Edward **11** 146
    Nagel, Ernest **11** 291-292
    Schlick, Friedrich Albert Moritz
    14 16-17
    Wittgenstein, Ludwig **16** 350-351
  influenced by
    Frege, Gottlob **6** 93-94
    Leibniz, Gottfried Wilhelm von
    9 307-310
    Meinong, Alexius Ritter von Hand-
    schuchsheim **10** 461-462
    Sidgwick, Henry **14** 213
  mathematics defended
    Ramsey, Frank Plumpton **13** 25

RUSSELL, CHARLES EDWARD
(1860-1941), American journalist and
reformer **13** 374-375
  Armour, Philip Danforth **1** 302

RUSSELL, CHARLES MARION
(1864-1926), American painter
13 375-376

RUSSELL, CHARLES TAZE (1852-1916),
American religious leader **13** 376-377

RUSSELL, ELIZABETH SHULL (born 1913),
American geneticist **13** 377-379

Russell, George William (AE; 1867-1935),
Irish man of letters
  Colum, Padraic **4** 174-175
  Stephens, James **14** 430-431
  Yeats, William Butler **16** 445-447

Russell, Henry Norris (1877-1957), American astronomer
  Shapley, Harlow **14** 155-156

RUSSELL, JAMES EARL (1864-1945), educator and college dean who developed
Teachers College **13** 379-380

RUSSELL, JOHN (1792-1878), English
statesman, Prime minister 1846-52
13 380-381
  Aberdeen, 4th Earl of **1** 25-26
  Albert **1** 110-112
  Disraeli, Benjamin **5** 27-29
  Gladstone, William Ewart **6** 357-360
  Palmerston, 3d Viscount **12** 81-83
  Russell, Bertrand Arthur William
  13 373-374
  Victoria **15** 485-487

Russell, Jonathan (1771-1832), American
diplomat
  Adams, John Quincy **1** 52-54

Russell, 3d Earl
  see Russell, Bertrand Arthur William

Russell of Kingston Russell, 1st Earl
  see Russell, John

Russellites (religious sect)
  Russell, Charles Taze **13** 376-377
  see also Jehovah's Witnesses

Russia, Republic of
  nationalism
    Zhirinovsky, Vladimir Volfovich
    16 509-510
  since 1991

    Kozyrev, Andrei Vladimirovich
    9 92-93
    Sobchak, Anatoly Alexandrovich
    14 317-318
    Yeltsin, Boris Nikolaevich
    16 449-452
  see also Union of Soviet Socialist
  Republics

Russian Academy of Arts (established 1757)
  Elizabeth, the Queen Mother **5** 261-263

Russian America
  see Alaska

Russian American Co. (established 1799)
  Baranov, Aleksandr Andreievich
  1 499-500
  Kotzebue, Otto von **9** 91-92

Russian art
  Archipenko, Alexander **1** 280-281
  Chagall, Marc **3** 406-407
  Gabo, Naum **6** 158-159
  Goncharova, Natalia **6** 424-426
  Hammer, Armand **7** 103-104
  Jawlensky, Alexej von **8** 228-229
  Kandinsky, Wassily **8** 420-422
  Larionov, Mikhail **9** 205-206
  Malevich, Kasimir **10** 168-169
  Melnikov, Konstantin Stepanovich
  10 470-471
  Pevsner, Antoine **12** 263-264
  Popova, Liubov Sergeevna **12** 401-402
  Rodchenko, Alexander Mikhailovich
  13 233-234
  Soutine, Chaim **14** 356-357
  Tatlin, Vladimir Evgrafovich **15** 117-118
  Zadkine, Ossip Joselyn **16** 484

Russian Chemical Society (established
1868)
  Mendeleev, Dmitrii Ivanovich
  10 486-488

Russian Civil War
  see Russian Revolution (1918-1920)

Russian Geographical Society (established
1845)
  Struve, Friedrich Georg Wilhelm von
  14 513

Russian literature
  Acmeist movement
    Akhmatova, Anna **1** 96-97
    Mandelstam, Osip Emilyevich
    10 191
  futurism
    Mayakovsky, Vladimir Vladimirovich
    10 364-365
    Pasternak, Boris Leonidovich
    12 124-125
  imagism
    Esenin, Sergei Aleksandrovich **5** 321
  literary criticism
    Bakhtin, Mikhail Mikhailovich
    1 456-458
    Belinsky, Grigorievich **2** 128
  realism
    see Realism (literature)—Russian
  Revolutionary themes

Afinogenov, Aleksandr Nikolaevich
1 72-73
Babel, Isaac Emmanuelovich
1 411-412
romanticism
Lermontov, Mikhail Yurievich
9 352-353
Pushkin, Aleksandr Sergeevich
12 489-491
symbolism
Berdyaev, Nicholas Alexandrovich
2 184-185
Blok, Aleksandr Aleksandrovich
2 335
Merezhkovsky, Dmitry Sergeyevich
10 515-516
war novels and verse
Ehrenburg, Ilya Grigorievich
5 224-225
Sholokhov, Mikhail Aleksandrovich
14 203-204
Simonov, Konstantin Mikhailovich
14 239-240
Yevtushenko, Yevgeny Alexandrovich **16** 455-456

Russian music
ballet
Diaghilev, Sergei **4** 525-527
modernism
Rachmaninov, Sergei Vasilievich
12 531-532
Scriabin, Alexander Nikolayevich
14 71-72
Stravinsky, Igor Fedorovich
14 502-506
nationalism
Borodin, Aleksandr Profirevich
2 422-423
Mussorgsky, Modest Petrovich
11 274-276
Rimsky-Korsakov, Nikolai Andreevich **13** 174-175
Tchaikovsky, Peter Ilyich
15 130-132
romanticism
Glinka, Mikhail Ivanovich
6 369-370
Rachmaninov, Sergei Vasilievich
12 531-532
socialist realism
Kabalevsky, Dmitri **8** 400-401
Khachaturian, Aram Ilich **8** 530-531
Prokofiev, Sergei Sergeevich
12 458-460
Shostakovich, Dmitri Dmitrievich
14 204-205

Russian Orthodox Church
Berdyaev, Nicholas Alexandrovich
2 184-185
Catherine the Great **3** 370-372
Mogila, Peter **11** 74-75
Nevsky, Alexander **11** 359
Nikon, Nikita Minov **11** 395
Peter I **12** 253-256
Pobedonostsev, Konstantin Petrovich
12 360-361
Tolstoy, Leo **15** 262-265

Russian Research Center (Harvard University)
Kluckhohn, Clyde **9** 56-57

Russian Revolution (1905)
Bolsheviks
Lenin, Vladimir Ilich **9** 323-326
Stalin, Joseph **14** 393-396
Mensheviks
Trotsky, Leon **15** 302-305
October Manifesto
Nicholas II **11** 378-380
Witte, Sergei Yulyevich **16** 349-350
supporters
Breshkovsky, Catherine **2** 517-519
Gorky, Maxim **6** 458-460
Hillman, Sidney **7** 392-393
Miliukov, Pavel Nikolayevich
11 18-19
two-stage theory
Plekhanov, Georgi Valentinovich
12 351-352

Russian Revolution (1917; February)
Breshkovsky, Catherine **2** 517-519
Kerensky, Aleksandr Fedorovich
8 516-517
Kolchak, Aleksandr Vasilievich **9** 77-78
Kornilov, Lavr Georgievich **9** 87-88
Miliukov, Pavel Nikolayevich **11** 18-19
Nicholas II **11** 378-380

Russian Revolution (1917; October)
Bolsheviks
Bukharin, Nikolai Ivanovich
3 112-113
Dzerzhinsky, Felix Edmundovich
5 173-174
Kamenev, Lev Borisovich **8** 417-418
Kollontai, Aleksandra Mikhailovna
9 79
Lenin, Vladimir Ilich **9** 323-326
Molotov, Vyacheslav Mikhailovich
11 89-90
Stalin, Joseph **14** 393-396
Trotsky, Leon **15** 302-305
Zinoviev, Grigori Evseevich
16 521-522
foreign observers
Reed, John Silas **13** 76-77
Ross, Edward Alsworth **13** 300
Russell, Charles Edward **13** 374-375
foreign supporters
Rolland, Romain **13** 260
Russell, Bertrand Arthur William
13 373-374
Tito, Marshal **15** 244-246
Webb, Beatrice Potter **16** 153-154
influence of
Mao Zedong **10** 225-227
Marxism and
Marx, Karl **10** 304-308
opponents
Breshkovsky, Catherine **2** 517-519
Bunin, Ivan Alekseevich **3** 124
Kerensky, Aleksandr Fedorovich
8 516-517

Kropotkin, Peter Alekseevich
9 107-108
Miliukov, Pavel Nikolayevich
11 18-19
Plekhanov, Georgi Valentinovich
12 351-352
Rostovtzeff, Michael Ivanovich
13 315
Russian arts and
Ehrenburg, Ilya Grigorievich
5 224-225
Gorky, Maxim **6** 458-460
Kandinsky, Wassily **8** 420-422
Pevsner, Antoine **12** 263-264

Russian Revolution (1918-20; Civil War)
Bolsheviks (Reds)
Dzerzhinsky, Felix Edmundovich
5 173-174
Frunze, Mikhail Vasilievich **6** 134
Konev, Ivan Stefanovich **9** 81-82
Lenin, Vladimir Ilich **9** 323-326
Stalin, Joseph **14** 393-396
Trotsky, Leon **15** 302-305
Zhukov, Georgi Konstantinovich
16 512-513
counterrevolutionaries (Whites)
Kolchak, Aleksandr Vasilievich
9 77-78
Kornilov, Lavr Georgievich **9** 87-88
Miliukov, Pavel Nikolayevich
11 18-19
Tito, Marshal **15** 244-246
in Finland
Mannerheim, Carl Gustav Emil Von
10 207-208

Russian Social Democratic Workers party
see Bolsheviks

Russian-German Reinsurance Treaty (1887)
Bismarck, Otto Eduard Leopold von
2 294-296

Russo-Japanese War (1904-1905)
China and
Chang Tso-lin **3** 434-435
Japan and
Katayama, Sen **8** 457
Takahashi, Korekiyo **15** 84-85
Yamagata, Aritomo **16** 428-429
Korea and
Kojong **9** 74-75
Russia and
Kolchak, Aleksandr Vasilievich
9 77-78
Kornilov, Lavr Georgievich **9** 87-88
Nicholas II **11** 378-380
Witte, Sergei Yulyevich **16** 349-350
U.S. and
Pershing, John Joseph **12** 243-244
Roosevelt, Theodore **13** 280-283
Schiff, Jacob Henry **14** 2-3
see also Portsmouth, Treaty of (1905)

Russolo, Luigi (1885-1947), Italian painter
Boccioni, Umberto **2** 353-354

Russo-Turkish wars
1735-39
Anna Ivanovna **1** 240-241

1768-74
 Catherine the Great **3** 370-372
 Potemkin, Grigori Aleksandrovich
 12 411-412
 Suvorov, Aleksandr Vasilievich
 15 44-45
1787-92
 Catherine the Great **3** 370-372
 Kutuzov, Mikhail Ilarionovich
 9 137-138
 Potemkin, Grigori Aleksandrovich
 12 411-412
 Suvorov, Aleksandr Vasilievich
 15 44-45
1877-78
 Abdul-Hamid II **1** 17-18
 Alexander II **1** 132-133
 Alexander III **1** 133-134
 Jellicoe, John Rushworth **8** 242-243
 Victoria **15** 485-487
 Witte, Sergei Yulyevich **16** 349-350

RUSSWURM, JOHN BROWN
(1799-1851), African American and
Liberian journalist, educator, and governor **13** 381-382

Rustam (literary character)
 Firdausi **5** 451-452

Rustic Dance (painting)
 Mount, William Sidney **11** 213-214

RUSTIN, BAYARD (1910-1987), American
social activist **13** 382-383

Ruta de don Quijote, La (book)
 Ruíz, José Martínez **13** 358

Rutgers University (New Jersey)
 Ellison, Ralph Waldo **5** 274-275
 Lichtenstein, Roy **9** 398-399

Waksman, Selman Abraham **16** 49-50

Ruth (novel)
 Gaskell, Elizabeth **6** 231-232

RUTH, GEORGE HERMAN, JR. (Babe
Ruth; 1895-1948), American baseball
player **13** 384

Ruth, Dr.
 see Westheimer, Ruth Karola

RUTHERFORD, ERNEST (1st Baron Ruther-
ford of Nelson; 1871-1937), British physi-
cist **13** 384-387
 collaborators
  Bethe, Hans Albrecht **2** 238-239
  Geiger, Hans **6** 251-253
  Hahn, Otto **7** 64-65
  Hevesy, George Charles de **7** 371
  Soddy, Frederick **14** 321-323
 influence of
  Bohr, Niels Henrik David **2** 366-368
  Chadwick, James **3** 405-406
  Cockcroft, John Douglas **4** 131-132
  Compton, Arthur Holly **4** 186-188
  Kapitsa, Pyotr Leonidovich
  8 433-435

Rutilius Lupus, Publius (flourished 1st century), Roman rhetorician
 Marius, Gaius **10** 264-265

Rutland, 4th Duke of (Charles Manners;
1754-87), English statesman
 Crabbe, George **4** 288

RUTLEDGE, JOHN (1739-1800), American
jurist and statesman **13** 387-388

Ruwan Bagaja (story)
 Imam, Alhadji Abubakar **8** 114-115

Ruy Blas (play; Hugo)
 Hugo, Victor Marie **8** 22-25
 Mendelssohn, Moses **10** 488-489

RUYSBROECK, JAN VAN (1293-1381),
Flemish mystic **13** 388-389
 Groote, Gerard **7** 12-13

RYAN, LYNN NOLAN (born 1947), American baseball player and author
 13 389-391

RYDER, ALBERT PINKHAM (1847-1917),
American painter **13** 391-392
 Allston, Washington **1** 176-177
 Blakelock, Ralph Albert **2** 318
 Hartley, Marsden **7** 186
 La Farge, John **9** 149-150
 Tanner, Henry Ossawa **15** 102-103

RYERSON, (ADOLPHUS) EGERTON
(1803-1882), Canadian Methodist clergyman and educator **13** 392-393

Ryerson Building (Chicago)
 Sullivan, Louis Henri **15** 27-28

RYLE, GILBERT (1900-1976), English
philosopher **13** 393-394
 Ramsey, Frank Plumpton **13** 25

Ryswick, Treaty of (1697)
 James II **8** 207-208
 Victor Amadeus II **15** 482-483
 William III **16** 295-296

Ryukyu Islands (Western Pacific Ocean)
 Okubo, Toshimichi **11** 489-490
 Sato, Eisaku **13** 495-496

S

S.
see Saint; San; Sant'; Santa; Santo

SA
see Storm troopers, Nazi (SA)

SÁ, MEM DE (1504-1572), Portuguese jurist and governor general of Brazil **13** 395

Saadabad Pact (1937)
Atatürk, Ghazi Mustapha Kemal **1** 356-357

Saadi
see Sa'di

SAADIA BEN JOSEPH AL-FAYUMI (882-942), Jewish scholar **13** 396
Jesus ben Sira **8** 251

Saar River Basin (France-Germany)
Clemenceau, Georges **4** 99-101

SAARINEN, EERO (1910-1961), Finnish-American architect and industrial designer **13** 396-398
Pelli, Cesar **12** 191-192

SAARINEN, ELIEL (1873-1950), Finnish-American architect and industrial designer **13** 396-398

Saavedra, Angel de
see Rivas, Duque de

Saavedra, Isabel de (died 1652), Spanish daughter of Cervantes
Cervantes, Miguel de Saavedra **3** 395-398

Saavedra Lamas, Carlos
see Lamas, Carlos Saavedra

Sabah
see British North Borneo

SABATIER, PAUL (1854-1941), French chemist **13** 398-399

SÁBATO, ERNESTO (born 1911), Argentine novelist and essayist **13** 399-400

SABBATAI ZEVI (1626-1676), Jewish mystic and pseudo-Messiah **13** 400-401
Asch, Shalom **1** 325-326
Köprülü, Ahmed **9** 84-85

Luzzato, Moses Hayyim **10** 57-58
Scholem, Gershom **14** 26

Sabbatean sect (Judaism)
Sabbatai Zevi **13** 400-401

Sabbatius, Flavius Petrus
see Justinian I

Sabellianism (heresy)
Arius **1** 297-298

Saber Dance (musical composition)
Khachaturian, Aram Ilich **8** 530-531

SABIN, ALBERT BRUCE (1906-1993), Polish-American physician and virologist who developed polio vaccine **13** 401-402

SABIN, FLORENCE RENA (1871-1953), American anatomist **13** 402-405

Sabin polio vaccine
Salk, Jonas Edward **13** 451-452

Sabine, Cape (Eastern Ellesmere, Island, Northern Canada)
Greely, Adolphus Washington **6** 517-518

Sabotino, Marchese of
see Badoglio, Pietro

Sac Indians
see Sauk Indians

SACAJAWEA (c. 1784-c. 1812), Native American translator/interpreter, and guide **13** 405-408
Lewis, Meriwether **9** 391-392

Sacasa, Juan Bautista (1874-1946), Nicaraguan political leader
Somoza, Anastasio **14** 335-336

Saccheri, Girolamo (1667-1733), Italian mathematician
Gauss, Karl Friedrich **6** 240-242
Lobachevskii, Nikolai Ivanovich **9** 472-474

Sacchetti, Franco (1335?-1400), Italian poet
Landini, Francesco **9** 185-186

SACCO, NICOLA (1891-1927), **AND VANZETTI, BARTOLOMEO** (1887-1927),

Italian-born American anarchists **13** 408-410
Anderson, Maxwell **1** 219-220
Dos Passos, John Roderigo **5** 69-71
Frankfurter, Felix **6** 57
Holmes, John Haynes **7** 456-457
Lowell, Abbott Lawrence **10** 12-13
Millay, Edna St. Vincent **11** 24-25
Shahn, Ben **14** 139-140
Sinclair, Upton Beale Jr. **14** 248-249

Sacerdotalis caelibatus (encyclical)
Paul VI **12** 146-148

Sachem (story)
Sienkiewicz, Henryk **14** 216-217

SACHS, HANS (1494-1576), German poet **13** 410-411

SACHS, NELLY (1891-1970), German-born Jewish poet and playwright **13** 411-412

Sack of Charcoal, The (anthology)
Basho, Matsuo **2** 45-48

Sacrae symphoniae (musical collection)
Gabrieli, Giovanni **6** 161-162

Sacred and Profane Love (novel)
Bennett, Arnold **2** 167-168

Sacred and Profane Love (painting)
Titian **15** 242-244

Sacred College of Cardinals
see Cardinals, Sacred College of

Sacred Fount, The (novel)
James, Henry **8** 211-212

Sacred Grove (mural)
Puvis de Chavannes, Pierre **12** 492-493

Sacred Heart, Daughters of the (religious congregation)
Cabrini, Frances Xavier **3** 205

Sacred Heart, Missionary Sisters of the
Cabrini, Frances Xavier **3** 205

Sacred Heart, University of the (Milan, Italy)
Paul VI **12** 146-148

Sacred music
Austrian
Fux, Johann Joseph **6** 155-156

Haydn, Franz Joseph **7** 219-221
English
  Dunstable, John **5** 150-151
  Elgar, Edward **5** 247-248
  Tallis, Thomas **15** 91
Franco-Flemish
  Isaac, Heinrich **8** 143-144
  Josquin des Prez **8** 361-363
  Lassus, Roland de **9** 216-218
French
  Charpentier, Marc Antoine
    3 471-472
  Cherubini, Luigi Carlo Zanobi Sal-
    vatore Maria **3** 505-506
  Couperin, François **4** 270-271
  Le Jeune, Claude **9** 314-315
German
  Bach, Carl Philipp Emanuel
    1 414-415
  Bach, Johann Sebastian **1** 416-419
  Buxtehude, Dietrich **3** 185-186
  Isaac, Heinrich **8** 143-144
  Praetorius, Michael **12** 431-432
  Schütz, Heinrich **14** 48-49
  Senfl, Ludwig **14** 105-106
  Telemann, Georg Philipp
    15 137-138
  Walter, Johann **16** 86
Italian
  Cavalli, Pietro Francesco **3** 382-383
  Corelli, Arcangelo **4** 230-231
  Manzoni, Alessandro **10** 222-224
  Monteverdi, Claudio Giovanni
    Antonio **11** 126-128
  Palestrina, Giovanni Pierluigi da
    12 70-72
  Scarlatti, Domenico **13** 515-517
  Scarlatti, Pietro Alessandro Gaspare
    13 517-518
Swiss
  Notker Balbulus **11** 434-435
  see also Gregorian chant; Hymn
    (music); Mass (music)

Sacred War (356 B.C.)
  Philip II **12** 269-271

Sacred Wood, The (essay)
  Eliot, Thomas Stearns **5** 258-261

Sacrifice of Abraham (painting)
  Tiepolo, Giovanni Battista **15** 219-220

Sacrifice of Isaac (relief sculpture)
  Brunelleschi, Filippo **3** 70-72

Sacrifice to Pan (painting)
  Goya y Lucientes, Francisco de Paula
    José de **6** 476-478

Sacrifice to Vesta (painting)
  Goya y Lucientes, Francisco de Paula
    José de **6** 476-478

Sacrificio de la Misa, El (poem)
  Gonzalo de Berceo **6** 431-432

Sacrilege of Alan Kent, The (book)
  Caldwell, Erskine **3** 223-224

Sacy, Sylvestre de (1758-1838), French
  Orientalist
  Champollion, Jean François **3** 421

SADAT, ANWAR (1918-1981), Egyptian
  president **13** 412-414
  Mubarak, Hosni **11** 225-226
  Sadat, Jihan **13** 414-415

SADAT, JIHAN (born 1933), Egyptian
  women's rights activist **13** 414-415

SADDAM HUSSEIN (born 1937), socialist
  president of the Iraqi Republic and
  strongman of the ruling Ba'th regime
  13 415-416
  Brundtland, Gro Harlem **3** 68-69

Sadduces (Jewish sect)
  Johanan ben Zakkai **8** 271-272
  Josephus Flavius **8** 360-361

SADE, COMTE DE (Donatien Alphonse
  François, Marquis de Sade; 1740-1814),
  French writer **13** 416-418.

Sadhana (essays)
  Rabindranath Tagore **12** 529-531

SA'DI (circa 1200-1291), Persian poet
  13 418-419
  Carnot, Nicolas Léonard Sadi **3** 315
  Jami **8** 218-219

SADI, SHAIKH MUSLIH-AL-DIN
  see Sa'di

Sadie Salome, Go Home (song)
  Berlin, Irving **2** 200-201
  Brice, Fanny **3** 1-2

Sadism
  Sade, Comte de **13** 416-418

Sadko (musical composition)
  Rimsky-Korsakov, Nikolai Andreevich
    13 174-175

Sadler's Wells Theatre (London)
  Payne, John Howard **12** 159

Sado Seja (died 1762), Korean prince, son
  of Yongjo
  Yngjo **16** 461-462

Sadowa, battle of (1866)
  Bismarck, Otto Eduard Leopold von
    2 294-296
  Moltke, Helmuth Karl Bernard von
    11 90-91

SADR, MUSA AL- (Imam Musa; 1928-?),
  Lebanese Shi'ite Moslem religious and
  political leader **13** 420-422

Sáenz Peña, Roque (1851-1914), president
  of Argentina 1910-14
  Irigoyen, Hipólito **8** 139-140

Safavid dynasty (Persia; ruled 1502-1736)
  Abbas I **1** 4-6
  Behzad **2** 123

Safe in their Alabaster Chambers (poem)
  Dickinson, Emily **4** 541-543

SAFIRE, WILLIAM (born 1929), American
  journalist **13** 422-424

Saga, En (symphonic poem)
  Sibelius, Jean Julius Christian
    14 211-212

Saga revolt (Japan; 1874)
  Okubo, Toshimichi **11** 489-490

SAGAN, CARL E. (born 1934), American
  astronomer and popularizer of science
  13 424-425

Sagar Sangit (book)
  Das, Chitta Ranjan **4** 401-402

Sagas of the Norwegian Kings (saga)
  Sturluson, Snorri **14** 310-311

Sagasta, Práxedes Mateo (1827-1903),
  Spanish statesman
  Muñoz Rivera, Luís **11** 250

SAGER, RUTH (1918-1997), American
  biologist and geneticist **13** 425-426

Sagesse (poems)
  Verlaine, Paul Marie **15** 465-466

Saggi e pagine sparse (literary collection)
  Svevo, Italo **15** 47-48

Sagittarius (astronomy)
  Shapley, Harlow **14** 155-156

Sagittarius Red (painting)
  Tobey, Mark **15** 249-250

Sagoyewatha
  see Red Jacket

Sagra del Carmine (fresco)
  Masaccio **10** 312-313

Sagrada Familia (church, Barcelona)
  Gaudí i Cornet, Antoni **6** 235-236

Sagrajas, battle of (1086)
  Alfonso VI **1** 149

Saguntum (city, Spain)
  Hannibal Barca **7** 128-130

Sahara (deserts, North Africa)
  Barth, Heinrich **2** 30-31
  Tafawa Balewa, Abubakar **15** 75

Sahara (film)
  Bogart, Humphrey **2** 363-364

Sahay Mäsfen (novel)
  Mäkonnen Endalkačäw **10** 161-162

Sahih (religious book)
  Bukhari, Muhammad ibn Ismail al-
    3 111-112

Saibara-ko (book)
  Mabuchi, Kamo **10** 73-74

SAICHO (767-822), Japanese Buddhist
  monk **13** 426-428
  Eisai **5** 231-232
  Ennin **5** 288-289
  Kukai **9** 124-125
  Nichiren **11** 376-377

Said Pasha (Mohammed Said; 1822-63),
  viceroy of Egypt 1854-63
  Ismail Pasha **8** 150-151
  Lesseps, Vicomte de **9** 354-355

SAID, SEYYID (1790-1856), Omani sultan
  13 428-429

SAIGO, TAKAMORI (1827-1877), Japanese
  rebel and statesman **13** 429
  Iwakura, Tomomi **8** 160-161
  Okubo, Toshimichi **11** 489-490

Sail Away (play)
  Coward, Noel **4** 279-280

Sailing Boats and Mill (painting)
  Cuyp, Aelbert **4** 360-361

Sailing to Byzantium (poem)
  Yeats, William Butler **16** 445-447

Sailor with Guitar (sculpture)
  Lipchitz, Jacques **9** 432-433

Sailor's Mother, The (poem)
  Wordsworth, William **16** 385-388

Saint, The (painting)
  Milne, David Brown **11** 37-38

St. Agnes (painting)
  Andrea del Sarto **1** 224-225

St. Albans, battle of (1455)
  Edward IV **5** 212-213
  Henry VI **7** 298-299

St. Albans, battle of (1461)
  Warwick and of Salisbury, Earl of
  16 122-123

St. Albans, Viscount
  see Bacon, Sir Francis

St. Alphege (church, Greenwich)
  Hawksmoor, Nicholas **7** 211-212

St. Andrew (polyptych)
  Masaccio **10** 312-313

St. Andrews, castle of (Scotland)
  Knox, John **9** 65-66

St. Andrews University (Scotland)
  Bosanquet, Bernard **2** 425-426
  Chalmers, Thomas **3** 408-409

St. Anne Altarpiece (painting)
  Massys, Quentin **10** 325-326

St. Anne's College (Oxford)
  Murdoch, Iris **11** 256-257

Saint Anthony (novel),
  see Temptation of Saint Anthony, The

St. Anthony of Padua (painting)
  Tura, Cosimo **15** 343-344

St. Antony's College (Oxford)
  Busia, Kofi Abrefa **3** 172-173

St. Augustine (church; Ramsgate, Kent)
  Pugin, Augustus Welby Northmore
  12 479-480

St. Augustine (city, Florida)
  Drake, Francis **5** 94-96
  King, Martin Luther Jr. **9** 20-22
  Menéndez de Avilés, Pedro **10** 499-500
  Oglethorpe, James Edward **11** 482-483

St. Augustine (fresco)
  Botticelli, Sandro **2** 439-440

Saint Bartholomew's (church, New York
  City)
  Renwick, James **13** 102-103
  White, Stanford **16** 235-236

St. Bartholomew's Day massacre (1572)
  Coligny, Gaspard de **4** 159-160
  Machiavelli, Niccolò **10** 97-99
  Medici, Catherine de' **10** 445-449

Ramus, Petrus **13** 27-28
  William the Silent **16** 300-302

St. Bartholomew's Day oath (England)
  Charles II **3** 452-454

St. Bartholomew's Hospital (London)
  Blackwell, Elizabeth **2** 311-312
  Harvey, William **7** 189-190

St. Benedict (fresco)
  Bronzino **3** 19

St. Brandon (cape; South Africa)
  Dias de Novais, Bartolomeu **4** 533-534

St. Bruno (sculpture)
  Houdon, Antoine **7** 516-517

St. Catalina (painting)
  Bermejo, Bartolomé **2** 205

St. Catherine's Church (Lübeck)
  Barlach, Ernst **2** 5-6

St. Cecilia Hospital (Leiden)
  Boerhaave, Hermann **2** 358-359

St. Chad's (cathedral; Birmingham, England)
  Pugin, Augustus Welby Northmore
  12 479-480

Saint-Charles, battle of (1837)
  Cartier, George-Étienne **3** 342-343

St. Charles Borromeo, Church of
  see Karlskirche, The (church, Vienna)

St. Christopher (woodcut)
  Cranach, Lucas the Elder **4** 289-290

ST. CLAIR, ARTHUR (1736-1818),
  Scottish-born American soldier and politi-
  cian **13** 429-430
  Girty, Simon **6** 350
  McLean, John **10** 422-423

St. Columba Altarpiece (painting)
  Weyden, Rogier van der **16** 219-221

Saint-Cyr, Marquis Laurent de Gouvion
  (1764-1830), French marshal
  Cournot, Antoine Augustin **4** 273

Saint-Cyran, Abbé de (Jean DuVergier de
  Hauranne; 1581-1643), French theolo-
  gian
  Jansen, Cornelis **8** 220-221

St. Davids (diocese, Wales)
  Laud, William **9** 224-225

ST. DENIS, RUTH (1878?-1968), American
  dancer and choreographer **13** 430-431
  Duncan, Isadora **5** 144-145
  Graham, Martha **6** 485-486

Saint-Denis, battle of (1837)
  Cartier, George-Étienne **3** 342-343

St-Denis-en-France, Abbey of (near Paris)
  Abelard, Peter **1** 23-25
  Mansart, Jules Hardouin **10** 212
  Montreuil, Pierre de **11** 139
  Pilon, Germain **12** 305

Saint-Denys-de-l'Estrée (church;
  Saint-Denis)
  Viollet-le-Duc, Eugène Emmanuel
  15 505-506

Saint Domingue
  see Dominican Republic

St. Dominic of Silos (painting)
  Bermejo, Bartolomé **2** 205

St. Dorothy (painting)
  Zurbarán, Francisco de **16** 534-535

St. Elemosynarius, chapel of (Pressburg)
  Donner, Georg Raphael **5** 63

St. Eligius (painting)
  Christus, Petrus **4** 33-34

Saint Elizabeth's Hospital (Washington,
  District of Columbia)
  Pound, Ezra Loomis **12** 415-417
  White, William Alanson **16** 239-240

St. Enda's College (Dublin)
  Pearse, Patrick Henry **12** 173-174

St. Engracia (painting)
  Bermejo, Bartolomé **2** 205

SAINT-EXUPÉRY, ANTOINE DE
  (1900-1944), French novelist, essayist,
  and pilot **13** 431-432
  Dallapiccola, Luigi **4** 377-378

St. Francis (sculpture)
  Pilon, Germain **12** 305

St. Francis (sketch)
  Tiepolo, Giovanni Battista **15** 219-220

St. Francis ... (painting)
  Bellini, Giovanni **2** 137-138
  Giotto **6** 342-345
  Greco **6** 511-514
  Zurbarán, Francisco de **16** 534-535

St. Francis' College (Pugu, Tanzania)
  Nyerere, Julius Kamberage **11** 447-449

St. Francis Indians (North America)
  Rogers, Robert **13** 250-251

St. Gabriel (ship)
  Gama, Vasco da **6** 196-198

St. Gall, monastery of (Switzerland)
  Notker Balbulus **11** 434-435

SAINT-GAUDENS, AUGUSTUS
  (1848-1907), American sculptor **13** 432
  Adams, Henry Brooks **1** 45-47
  French, Daniel Chester **6** 98-99
  McKim, Charles Follen **10** 417-418
  White, Stanford **16** 235-236

Saint-Germain-en-Laye, Treaty of 1632
  Champlain, Samuel de **3** 419-421
  Renner, Karl **13** 98-99

St. George (sculpture)
  Donatello **5** 55-56

St. George and the Dragon (painting)
  Tintoretto **15** 232-234

St. George in a Wood (painting)
  Altdorfer, Albrecht **1** 179-180

St. George Slaying the Dragon (painting)
  Tura, Cosimo **15** 343-344

St. George Slaying the Dragon (sculpture)
  Asam, Cosmas Damian and Egid Quirin
  1 323-324

St. George's (church, Bloomsbury)
Hawksmoor, Nicholas **7** 211-212

St. George's Hospital (painting)
Wilson, Richard **16** 329-330

St. Gregory, Mass of (theology)
Charonton, Enguerrand **3** 471

Saint-Hilaire, Étienne Geoffroy
(1772-1844), French naturalist
Cuvier, Georges Léopold **4** 357-359

St. Ignace Mission (Canada)
Brébeuf, Jean de **2** 511-512
Marquette, Jacques **10** 274-275

St. Ignatius (church; Győr, Hungary)
Troger, Paul **15** 300

St. Ildefonso (painting)
Greco **6** 511-514

Saint Ivo alla Sapienza (church, Rome)
Guarini, Guarino **7** 25-26

St. Jakob (church, Innsbruck)
Asam, Cosmas Damian and Egid Quirin
1 323-324

St. James (sculpture)
Sansovino, Jacopo **13** 470-471

St. James Church (Westminster)
Clarke, Samuel **4** 88

St. James's Palace (London)
Hawksmoor, Nicholas **7** 211-212

St. Jerome ... (painting)
Bellini, Giovanni **2** 137-138
Christus, Petrus **4** 33-34
Cranach, Lucas the Elder **4** 289-290
Greco **6** 511-514
Lochner, Stephan **9** 475
Titian **15** 242-244

St. Jerome in His Study (engraving; Dürer)
Cranach, Lucas the Elder **4** 289-290
Dürer, Albrecht **5** 159-161

Saint Joan (play; Shaw)
Joan of Arc **8** 264-265

St. Joan of the Stockyards (play)
Brecht, Bertolt **2** 512-514

St. John (town, Nova Scotia)
Charnisay, Charles de Menou
3 470-471

St. John, Church of the Hospital of
(Salzburg)
Rottmayr, Johann Michael **13** 321

St. John, Henry
see Bolingbroke, 1st Viscount

St. John Lateran (church, Rome)
Arnolfo di Cambio **1** 315-316
Bramante, Donato **2** 493-494
Gentile da Fabriano **6** 266-267
Lassus, Roland de **9** 216-218
Palestrina, Giovanni Pierluigi da
12 70-72

St. John Nepomuk (church, Munich)
Asam, Cosmas Damian and Egid Quirin
1 323-324

St. John, Oliver (1598?-1673), English jurist
Cromwell, Oliver **4** 317-320
Hampden, John **7** 110-111
Pym, John **12** 495-496

St. John, Order of (religious congregation)
Franco of Cologne **6** 52

St. John Passion (oration)
Handel, George Frederick **7** 116-119

St. John Preaching (painting)
Veronese, Paolo **15** 469-470

St. John River (United States-Canada)
Champlain, Samuel de **3** 419-421

St. John the Baptist in the Wilderness
(painting)
Geertgen tot Sint Jans **6** 248

St. John the Baptist Preaching (sculpture)
Rodin, Auguste **13** 236-238

St. John the Divine, Cathedral of (New
York City)
Borglum, John Gutzon de la Mothe
2 416-417

St. John the Evangelist (mosaic)
Cimabue **4** 60-61

St. John the Evangelist (sculpture)
Donatello **5** 55-56

St. John's Abbey and University (Col-
legeville, Minnesota)
Breuer, Marcel **2** 520-521
McCarthy, Eugene Joseph **10** 386-388

St. John's Bay (Newfoundland)
Gilbert, Humphrey **6** 313

St. John's Church (Bangor, Maine)
Upjohn, Richard **15** 392

St. John's College (Annapolis, Maryland)
Barnard, Henry **2** 10
Carroll, John **3** 331-332

St. John's College (Cambridge)
Coulton, George Gordon **4** 267

St. John's College (Fordham, New York
State)
see Fordham University

St. John's Eve (play)
Ibsen, Henrik **8** 98-100

St. John's Parish (Worthington, Ohio)
Chase, Philander **3** 472-473

St. Johns River (Florida)
Bartram, William **2** 41-42
Ponce de León, Juan **12** 391-392

St. Joseph with the Christ Child (paint)
Greco **6** 511-514

St. Julian (fresco)
Andrea del Castagno **1** 223-224

SAINT-JUST, LOUIS ANTOINE LÉON DE
(1767-1794), French radical political
leader **13** 433
Carnot, Lazare Nicolas Marguerite
3 313-314
Robespierre, Maximilien François Marie
Isidore de **13** 199-201

ST. LAURENT, LOUIS STEPHEN (born
1882), Canadian statesman **13** 434
Diefenbaker, John George **5** 4-5

St. Lawrence River (Canada-New York State)
Cartier, Jacques **3** 343-344
Champlain, Samuel de **3** 419-421
Cook, James **4** 214-215
Jolliet, Louis **8** 328-329
McNaughton, Andrew **10** 431-432

St. Leander (painting)
Murillo, Bartolomé Esteban **11** 258-259

St. Leger, Barry (1737-1789), British com-
mander in the American Revolution
Brant, Joseph **2** 500-501
Burgoyne, John **3** 137-138
Butler, John **3** 180
Johnson, John **8** 305-306

Saint-Léger Léger, Alexis
see Perse, Saint-John

Saint-Lô (commune, North Western France)
Bradley, Omar Nelson **2** 483-484

St. Louis (city, Missouri)
culture and education
Beckmann, Max **2** 104-105
Bingham, George Caleb **2** 278-279
Harris, William Torrey **7** 177-178
Sullivan, Louis Henri **15** 27-28
newspapers
Dreiser, Herman Theodore **5** 98-100
Pulitzer, Joseph **12** 481-482
Schurz, Carl **14** 44-45
Scripps, Edward Wyllis **14** 72-73
Overland Mail
Butterfield, John **3** 184-185

St. Louis Blues (song)
Handy, William Christopher **7** 123-124

St. Louis Cardinals (baseball team; United
States)
Rickey, Wesley Branch **13** 153-155

St. Louis of Toulouse ... (painting)
Martini, Simone **10** 298-299

St. Louis University (Missouri)
Schuschnigg, Kurt von **14** 45-46

St. Louis Woman (musical play)
Cullen, Countee **4** 333-334

St. Louis World's Fair
see World's Fairs

St. Lucia (island, West Indies)
Rodney, George Brydges **13** 239-240

St. Luke Altarpiece (painting)
Mantegna, Andrea **10** 215-216

St. Luke Painting the Crucifixion (painting)
Zurbarán, Francisco de **16** 534-535

St. Luke Painting the Virgin (painting)
Weyden, Rogier van der **16** 219-221

St. Luke Passion (musical composition)
Penderecki, Krzysztof **12** 195-197

St. Luke Penny Savings Bank (Richmond,
VA)
Walker, Maggie Lena **16** 65-66

St. Luke's Hospital (New York City)
Muhlenberg, William Augustus
11 233-234

St. Margaret (painting)
Titian **15** 242-244

St. Mark (sculpture)
Donatello **5** 55-56

St. Mark Preaching in Alexandria (painting)
Bellini, Giovanni **2** 137-138

St. Mark Rescuing a Slave (painting)
Tintoretto **15** 232-234

St. Mark's Cathedral (Venice, Italy)
Cavalli, Pietro Francesco **3** 382-383
Gabrieli, Giovanni **6** 161-162
Michelozzo **11** 6-7
Monteverdi, Claudio Giovanni Antonio
11 126-128
Sansovino, Jacopo **13** 470-471
Soufflot, Jacques Germain **14** 349-350
Veronese, Paolo **15** 469-470
Willaert, Adrian **16** 287-288

St. Mark's Square (Venice, Italy)
Canaletto **3** 257-258
Sansovino, Jacopo **13** 470-471

St. Mark's Tower (New York City)
Wright, Frank Lloyd **16** 398-401

St. Martin, Alexis (flourished 1822-34),
Canadian laborer
Beaumont, William **2** 95-96

St. Martin and the Beggar (sculpture)
Donner, Georg Raphael **5** 63

St. Martin Dividing His Cloak ... (painting)
Greco **6** 511-514
Van Dyck, Anthony **15** 423-425

St. Martins-in-the-Fields (church, London)
Gibbs, James **6** 301-302

St. Mary of the Lake (seminary, Chicago)
Mundelein, George William
11 248-249

St. Mary-le-Strand (church, London)
Gibbs, James **6** 301-302

St. Mary's (convent, Hampole)
Rolle of Hampole, Richard **13** 260-261

St. Mary's Church (Berlin)
Schlüter, Andreas **14** 18-19

St. Mary's Church (Lübeck)
Bach, Johann Sebastian **1** 416-419
Buxtehude, Dietrich **3** 185-186

St. Mary's College (Tabora, Tanzania)
Nyerere, Julius Kamberage **11** 447-449

St. Matthew (sculpture)
Ghiberti, Lorenzo **6** 291-292
Leonardo da Vinci **9** 337-340
Michelangelo Buonarroti **11** 2-5

St. Matthew Altarpiece (painting)
Orcagna **11** 526-527

St. Matthew Passion (musical composition;
Bach)
Mendelssohn, Moses **10** 488-489

St. Matthew's Church (Northampton, England)
Sutherland, Graham **15** 40-41

St. Mawr (novelette)
Lawrence, David Herbert **9** 247-248

St.-Médard, Abbey of (Soissons)
Abelard, Peter **1** 23-25

St. Michael (painting)
Bermejo, Bartolomé **2** 205

St. Michael and the Devil (sculpture)
Epstein, Jacob **5** 295-296

St. Michael's Abbey (Antwerp)
Rubens, Peter Paul **13** 339-342

St. Michael's Church (Charleston, South
Carolina)
Harrison, Peter **7** 179-180

St. Michael's College (University of Toronto)
Gilson, Étienne Henry **6** 327-328

Saint-Mihiel, battle of (1918)
Pershing, John Joseph **12** 243-244

St. Narcissus (painting)
Maulbertsch, Franz Anton **10** 345

St. Nicholas (church, Aberdeen)
Gibbs, James **6** 301-302

St. Nicholas (church, Potsdam)
Schinkel, Karl Friedrich **14** 8

St. Nicholas (magazine)
Benét, Stephen Vincent **2** 157-158
Millay, Edna St. Vincent **11** 24-25

St. Notburga (sculpture)
Günther, Ignaz **7** 41-42

Saint of Bleecker Street, The (opera)
Menotti, Gian Carlo **10** 509-510

St. Olaf, College (Northfield, Minnesota)
Rölvaag, Ole Edvart **13** 265

St. Olaf, law of (Norway)
Olaf, II **11** 493-494

St. Omer, Treaty of (1469)
Charles the Bold **3** 467-469

St. Patrick's (Dublin)
Swift, Jonathan **15** 51-54

St. Patrick's Cathedral (New York City)
Corrigan, Michael Augustine **4** 253
McCloskey, John **10** 395
Renwick, James **13** 102-103

St. Patrick's Day (play)
Sheridan, Richard Brinsley **14** 183-184

St. Paul (oration)
Mendelssohn, Moses **10** 488-489

St. Paul (polyptych)
Masaccio **10** 312-313

St. Paul Chamber Orchestra
Wolff, Hugh **16** 358-360

St. Paul, Minneapolis and Manitoba Railway (United States)
Hill, James Jerome **7** 388-389
Kennedy, John Stewart **8** 507-508

Smith, Donald Alexander **14** 288-289

St. Paul's (church; Alexandria, Virginia)
Latrobe, Benjamin Henry **9** 222-224

St. Paul's Cathedral (London)
Butler, Joseph **3** 180-181
Colet, John **4** 157-158
Donne, John **5** 60-61
Inge, William Ralph **8** 118-119
Jones, Inigo **8** 333-334
Laud, William **9** 224-225
Soufflot, Jacques Germain **14** 349-350
Wren, Christopher **16** 393-394

St. Paul's School (London)
Colet, John **4** 157-158

St. Peter (church, Munich)
Zimmermann, Johann Baptist and
Domenikus **16** 518

St. Peter (mosaic, Venice)
Uccello, Paolo **15** 378-379

St. Peter (oration)
Paine, John Knowles **12** 65

St. Peter (ship)
Bering, Vitus **2** 193-194

St. Peter and St. John Distributing Alms
(fresco)
Masaccio **10** 312-313

St. Peter Baptizing (fresco)
Masaccio **10** 312-313

St. Peter Damian (sculpture)
Günther, Ignaz **7** 41-42

**St. Peter Finding the Coin in the Fish's
Mouth** (painting)
Jordaens, Jacob **8** 347-349

St. Peter in Tears (painting)
Greco **6** 511-514

St. Peter, Lake (Quebec city)
Cartier, Jacques **3** 343-344

St. Peter Relates an Incident (book)
Johnson, James Weldon **8** 304-305

St. Peter with the Goat (skit)
Sachs, Hans **13** 410-411

St. Peter's (new; Rome)
architects
Borromini, Francesco **2** 424-425
Bramante, Donato **2** 493-494
Maderno, Carlo **10** 117-118
Michelangelo Buonarroti **11** 2-5
Raphael **13** 40-42
Sangallo family **13** 464-466
Vignola, Giacomo da **15** 493-494
bell tower
Bernini, Gian Lorenzo **2** 214-216
choirmasters
Palestrina, Giovanni Pierluigi da
12 70-72
dome
Porta, Giacomo della **12** 402-403
rebuilding
Julius II **8** 384-386
Leo X **9** 332-334
Paul III **12** 144-145

St. Peter's (old; Rome)
  Julius II **8** 384-386
  Maderno, Carlo **10** 117-118
  Peter **12** 252-253

St. Peter's Church (Albany, New York State)
  Upjohn, Richard **15** 392

St. Petersburg (city; Russia)
  as cultural center
    Anna Ivanovna **1** 240-241
    Catherine the Great **3** 370-372
    Peter I **12** 253-256
    Rachmaninov, Sergei Vasilievich
      12 531-532
  German Embassy
    Behrens, Peter **2** 121-122
    Mies van der Rohe, Ludwig
      11 10-12
  mayors
    Sobchak, Anatoly Alexandrovich
      14 317-318

St. Petersburg Academy (Russia)
  Lomonosov, Mikhail Vasilevich **9** 494

St. Petersburg Conservatory (Russia)
  Rachmaninov, Sergei Vasilievich
    12 531-532
  Rimsky-Korsakov, Nikolai Andreevich
    13 174-175

St. Petersburg University (Russia)
  Gogol, Nikolai **6** 391-393
  Mendeleev, Dmitrii Ivanovich
    10 486-488
  Nicholas II **11** 378-380
  Rostovtzeff, Michael Ivanovich **13** 315
  Sorokin, Pitirim A. **14** 348-349

St. Philip Neri, Oratory of (Rome)
  Borromini, Francesco **2** 424-425

SAINT-PIERRE, ABBÉ DE (Charles Irénée
  Castel; 1658-1743), French political and
  economic theorist **13** 434-435

Saint-Quentin, battle of (1871)
  Faidherbe, Louis Léon César **5** 366-367

St. Raphael (ship)
  Gama, Vasco da **6** 196-198

St. Ronan's Well (novel)
  Scott, Walter **14** 68-70

SAINT-SAËNS, CHARLES CAMILLE
  (1835-1921), French composer
  13 435-436
  Fauré, Gabriel Urbain **5** 397-398
  Roussel, Albert **13** 328-329

St. Sebald (church, Nuremberg)
  Stoss, Veit **14** 481-482

St. Sebastian (painting)
  Botticelli, Sandro **2** 439-440
  Mantegna, Andrea **10** 215-216
  Titian **15** 242-244

St. Sebastian Mourned by St. Irene (painting)
  La Tour, George de **9** 222

St. Serapion (painting)
  Zurbarán, Francisco de **16** 534-535

SAINT-SIMON, COMTE DE (Claude Henri
  de Rouvroy; 1760-1825), French social
  philosopher and reformer **13** 436-437
  Comte, Auguste **4** 189-191
  Herzen, Aleksandr Ivanovich **7** 351-352

Saint-Simonianism (social movement)
  Heine, Heinrich **7** 259-260
  Napoleon III **11** 310-312
  Sainte-Beuve, Charles Augustin **13** 438
  Saint-Simon, Comte de **13** 436-437

St. Sophia Cathedral (Kiev)
  Mogila, Peter **11** 74-75

St. Stephan's (church, Vienna)
  Pachelbel, Johann **12** 52

St. Stephen (painting)
  Millais, John Everett **11** 23-24

St. Stephen (sculpture)
  Ghiberti, Lorenzo **6** 291-292
  Rimmer, William **13** 174

St. Stephen's (church; London)
  Davenport, John **4** 405-406

St. Theresa in Ecstasy (sculpture)
  Bernini, Gian Lorenzo **2** 214-216

St. Thomas College (Saint Paul, Minnesota)
  McCarthy, Eugene Joseph **10** 386-388

St. Thomas of Villanueva ... (painting)
  Murillo, Bartolomé Esteban **11** 258-259

St. Thomas's Church (Leipzig)
  Bach, Johann Sebastian **1** 416-419

St. Thomas's Church (New York City)
  Upjohn, Richard **15** 392

St. Thomas's Church (Oxford, England)
  Burton, Robert **3** 166-167

St. Thomas's Hospital (London)
  Nightingale, Florence **11** 392-393

St. Valentine's massacre (Chicago, 1929)
  Capone, Al **3** 272-273

St. Veronica (painting)
  Bermejo, Bartolomé **2** 205

St. Vincent (island, West Indies)
  Eyre, Edward John **5** 354

Saint Vincent, Cape, battle of (1797)
  Nelson, Horatio **11** 336-338

St. Vitus's dance (medicine)
  Sydenham, Thomas **15** 59-60

St. Wolfgang Altarpiece (panels)
  Pacher, Michael **12** 53

Sainte-Anne-la-Royale (church, Paris)
  Guarini, Guarino **7** 25-26

SAINTE-BEUVE, CHARLES AUGUSTIN
  (1804-1869), French literary critic **13** 438
  Chénier, André Marie **3** 500-501
  Flaubert, Gustave **5** 480-482
  Hugo, Victor Marie **8** 22-25
  Proust, Marcel **12** 465-467
  Sand, George **13** 459-461

Sainte-Catherine du Val-des-Escoliers
  (Paris)
  Pilon, Germain **12** 305

Sainte-Chapelle (church, Paris)
  Charpentier, Marc Antoine **3** 471-472
  Louis IX **9** 525-526
  Montreuil, Pierre de **11** 139

Sainte-Marie-de-la-Tourette (monastery;
  Eveux-sur-Abresle)
  Le Corbusier **9** 274-275

Sainte-Pelagie (prison; France)
  Blanqui, Louis Auguste **2** 323-324

Saintly Peasant, The (play)
  Lope Félix de Vega Carpio **9** 503-506

Saints Anchor-hold ... (book)
  Davenport, John **4** 405-406

Saints, Battle of the (1782)
  Rodney, George Brydges **13** 239-240

Saints of the Inner Light (painting)
  Klee, Paul **9** 47-49

Saintsbury, George Edward Bateman
  (1845-1935), English critic and historian
  Kingsley, Charles **9** 28
  Kipling, Joseph Rudyard **9** 32-33
  Neill, Alexander Sutherland **11** 335-336

SAIONJI, KIMMOCHI (1849-1940), Japan-
  ese elder statesman **13** 438-439
  Hirohito **7** 410-412
  Inukai, Tsuyoshi **8** 130-131
  Konoe, Fumimaro **9** 82-83

Saipan, fall of (1944)
  Tojo, Hideki **15** 254-256

Saison en Enfer, Une (poems)
  Rimbaud, Jean Nicolas Arthur
    13 172-174

Saite period (Egypt; 663-525 B.C.)
  Zoser **16** 531

Sakarya (city, Turkey)
  Atatürk, Ghazi Mustapha Kemal
    1 356-357

Sakhalin Island (book)
  Chekhov, Anton Pavlovich **3** 494-497

SAKHAROV, ANDREI (1921-1989), Russian theoretical physicist and "father of the
  Soviet atomic bomb" **13** 439-441

Sakt al-Zand (poems)
  Abu-L-Ala al-Maarri **1** 32

Sal (Cape Verde Islands)
  Cadamosto, Alvise da **3** 206-207

Sal Si Puedes (barrio, California)
  Chavez, Cesar **3** 486-487

Sala della Pace (Palazzo Pubblico, Siena)
  Lorenzetti, Pietro and Ambrogio
    9 517-518

Sala Regia (Vatican Palace)
  Sangallo family **13** 464-466

SALADIN (Salah-ad-Din Yusuf ibn Aiyub;
  1138-93), Kurdish ruler of Egypt and
  Syria **13** 441-442
  Nureddin **11** 444-445
  Philip II **12** 268-269
  Richard I **13** 130
  William of Tyre **16** 299-300

Salahiyeh (Syria)
see Dura-Europos

Salaman and Absal (story)
Jami **8** 218-219

Salamanca, University of
Clement V **4** 101-102
Unamuno y Jugo, Miguel de **15** 386-387
Vitoria, Francisco de **16** 1-2

Salamanca Cathedral (Spain)
Churriguera, José Benito de **4** 53-54

Salamis, battle of (480 B.C.)
Miltiades **11** 42-43
Sophocles **14** 343-345
Themistocles **15** 170-171
Xerxes **16** 420

Salammbô (novel; Flaubert)
Flaubert, Gustave **5** 480-482
Mussorgsky, Modest Petrovich **11** 274-276

SALAZAR, ANTÓNIO DE OLIVEIRA (1889-1970), Portuguese statesman **13** 442-443
Franco Bahamonde, Francisco **6** 52-54

Salcedo, Augusto Bernardino Leguía y
see Leguía y Salcedo, Augusto Bernardino

Salem (city; Massachusetts)
Endecott, John **5** 284-285
McIntire, Samuel **10** 415
Williams, Roger **16** 304-305

Salem witchcraft trials (1692)
Bishop, Bridget **2** 288-290
Mather, Cotton **10** 330-332
Mather, Increase **10** 332-333
Miller, Arthur **11** 25-26
Phips, William **12** 283
Sewall, Samuel **14** 123-124
Wise, John **16** 343-344

Salerno (city, Italy)
Guiscard, Robert **7** 39-40

Salian emperors (ruled 1024-1125)
Henry III **7** 290
Henry IV **7** 292
Henry V **7** 295-296

Salic law (treatise)
Clovis I **4** 124
Ferdinand VII **5** 418-420

Salieri, Antonio (1750-1825), Italian composer
Liszt, Franz **9** 445-447
Meyerbeer, Giacomo **10** 536-537
Pushkin, Aleksandr Sergeevich **12** 489-491

SALIH, ALI'ABDALLAH (born 1942), president of the Yemeni Arab Republic (North Yemen) and first president of the United Republic of Yemen **13** 443-445

SALINAS DE GORTARI, CARLOS (born 1948), president of Mexico (1988-) **13** 445-447

Salinas, Pedro (1892-1951), Spanish poet
Lorca, Federico García **9** 511-513
Manrique, Jorge **10** 210-211

SALINGER, J. D. (born 1919), American author **13** 447-448

SALISBURY, HARRISON EVANS (born 1908), American journalist **13** 449-451

Salisbury, Richard Neville, 1st Earl of (1400-1460), English statesman
Warwick and of Salisbury, Earl of **16** 122-123

SALISBURY, 3D MARQUESS OF (Robert Arthur Talbot Gascoyne-Cecil; 1830-1903), English statesman and diplomat **13** 448-449
Balfour, Arthur James **1** 469-470
Cecil, of Chelwood Viscount **3** 388-389
Chamberlain, Arthur Neville **3** 409-411
Chamberlain, Joseph **3** 411-413
Curzon, George Nathaniel **4** 351-352
Disraeli, Benjamin **5** 27-29
Rayleigh, 3d Baron **13** 62
Victoria **15** 485-487

Salisbury Circular (1878)
Salisbury, 3d Marquess of **13** 448-449

Salisbury Plain (poem)
Wordsworth, William **16** 385-388

SALK, JONAS EDWARD (1914-1995), American physician, virologist, and immunologist **13** 451-452
Enders, John Franklin **5** 285-286

SALLE, DAVID (born 1952), American artist **13** 452-453

Sallekhana (Jainism)
Mahavira, Vardhamana **10** 135-137

SALLUST (Gaius Sallustius Crispus; 86-circa 35 B.C.), Roman statesman and historian **13** 454
Milton, John **11** 43-46
Tacitus **15** 70-72

Sally (musical)
Kern, Jerome David **8** 517-518
Ziegfeld, Florenz **16** 516-517

Salmagundi (pamphlet)
Irving, Washington **8** 141-143

Salome (opera)
Strauss, Richard **14** 500-501

Salome (play; Wilde)
Beardsley, Aubrey Vincent **2** 88-89

Salome vs. Shenandoah (film)
Sennett, Mack **14** 108-109

Salomon (play)
Vondel, Joost van den **16** 19-20

SALOMON, CHARLOTTE (1917-1943), German artist **13** 454-455

Salon d'Automne (established 1903)
Matisse, Henri **10** 336-337
Rouault, Georges **13** 321-322

Salon, Der (book)
Heine, Heinrich **7** 259-260

Salon des Indépendants (established 1884)
Redon, Odilon **13** 75-76
Seurat, Georges Pierre **14** 120-122

Salon des Refusés (established 1863)
Manet, Édouard **10** 193-194
Whistler, James Abbott McNeill **16** 225-226

Salon in the Rue des Moulins (painting)
Toulouse-Lautrec, Henri de **15** 273-274

Salón México, El (musical composition)
Copland, Aaron **4** 227-228

Salone Agnelli (Turin)
Nervi, Pier Luigi **11** 346-348

Salonika (city, Greece)
Venizelos, Eleutherios **15** 460-461

Salpêtrière (hospital, Paris)
Binet, Alfred **2** 277-278
Charcot, Jean Martin **3** 442
Janet, Pierre Marie Félix **8** 220
Le Vau, Louis **9** 360-361
Pinel, Philippe **12** 313-314

Salt Cellar (goldwork)
Cellini, Benvenuto **3** 391-392

Salt Lake (Utah)
Carson, Christopher **3** 334-335

Salt Lake City (Utah)
Young, Brigham **16** 469-470

Salt march (India, 1930)
Gandhi, Mohandas Karamchand **6** 201-204
Nehru, Jawaharlal **11** 332-334

Salta, battle of (1813; 1814)
Belgrano, Manuel **2** 126-127
Güemes, Martín **7** 26-27

Saltbush Bill ... (poems)
Paterson, Andrew Barton **12** 131-132

Saltram House (Devonshire)
Adam, Robert and James **1** 38-40

Salustia (opera)
Pergolesi, Giovanni Battista **12** 218-219

Salut au Monde! (poem)
Whitman, Walt **16** 249-251

Salutation (poem; Ezra Pound)
Sandburg, Carl **13** 461-462

Salute to Spain (play)
Afinogenov, Aleksandr Nikolaevich **1** 72-73

Salvación de la primavera (poem)
Guillén, Nicolás **7** 34-35

Salvarsan (drug)
Domagk, Gerhard Johannes Paul **5** 48-50
Ehrlich, Paul **5** 225-226
Fleming, Alexander **5** 483-485

Salvation (religion)
Arminius, Jacobus **1** 301-302
Calvin, John **3** 239-242
Hutchinson, Anne Marbury **8** 69-71
Pythagoras **12** 498-499

Salvation Army (religious organization)
Booth, Evangeline Cory **2** 402-403
Booth, William **2** 405-406

Salve Regina (motet)
Dunstable, John **5** 150-151
Josquin des Prez **8** 361-363

Salve Regina (sculpture)
Stoss, Veit **14** 481-482

SALVEMINI, GAETANO (1873-1957), Italian historian **13** 455-456

Salviati, Francesco Cecco di (Francesco de' Rossi; 1510-63), Italian painter
Bronzino **3** 19

Salzburg (city; Austria)
Frederick William I **6** 86-87
Manzù, Giacomo **10** 224-225

Salzburger Grosse Welttheater, Das (opera)
Hofmannsthal, Hugo von **7** 443-444

Sam Slick's Wise Saws and Modern Instances (book)
Haliburton, Thomas Chandler **7** 80

Samaná, Bay of (Dominican Republic)
Baez, Buenaventura **1** 432-433

Samanids (Persia, dynasty, ruled 872-999)
Mahmud of Ghazni **10** 147

Samaria (ancient city, Israel)
Isaiah **8** 146-147
Micah **10** 542-543
Sargon II **13** 482

Samarkand (region, Central Asia)
Bonvalot, Pierre Gabriel Édouard **2** 396
Mahmud of Ghazni **10** 147

Samguk sagi (book)
Kim Pusik **9** 8-9

Samia (play)
Menander **10** 477-478

Samil movement (Korea; 1919)
Rhee, Syngman **13** 117-120

Sammaniya order (Islam)
Mahdi **10** 137-138

Samoa (islands, Southern Pacific Ocean)
Bougainville, Louis Antoine de **2** 443-444
Evarts, William Maxwell **5** 340-341
Mead, Margaret **10** 438-440

Samothrace (island, Greece)
Homer **7** 465-467

Sampling Officials of the Drapers' Guild (painting)
Rembrandt Harmensz van Rijn **13** 91-95

Samsara (Buddhism)
Buddha **3** 97-101
Mahavira, Vardhamana **10** 135-137

Samson (play)
Vondel, Joost van den **16** 19-20

Samson Agonistes (tragedy)
Milton, John **11** 43-46

Samson et Dalila (opera)
Saint-Saëns, Charles Camille **13** 435-436

SAMUEL (circa 1056-1004 B.C.), Hebrew prophet, last judge of Israel **13** 457-458
David, Jacques Louis **4** 407-409
Saul **13** 498

Samuel (died 1014), king of Bulgaria
Basil II **2** 50-51

Samuel, Sir Herbert (1870-1963), British statesman
George V **6** 273-275

Samuel ha-Nagid (993-1055), Spanish statesman, poet, and Talmudist
ibn Gabirol, Solomon ben Judah **8** 92

SAMUELSON, PAUL ANTHONY (born 1915), American economist **13** 458-459

Samurai (Japanese class)
Chih-i **3** 518-519
Ito, Hirobumi **8** 153-155
Saigo, Takamori **13** 429

San
see also Saint'; Santa; Santo; São

San Andrés University (La Paz)
Paz, Octavio **12** 161-162

San Antonio (ship)
Magellan, Ferdinand **10** 126-127
Portolá, Gaspar de **12** 408

San Antonio, battle of (1836)
Crockett, David **4** 314-316
Travis, William Barret **15** 292-293

San Antonio de Padua (mission; California)
Serra, Junípero **14** 111-112

San Antonio, Texas
Cisneros, Henry G. **4** 62-64

San Atanasio (church; Rome)
Porta, Giacomo della **12** 402-403

San Benito (monastery; Valladolid, Spain)
Berruguete, Alonso **2** 223-224

San Bernardino (church, Perugia)
Agostino di Duccio **1** 86

San Bernardino (church, Verona)
Sanmicheli, Michele **13** 469-470

San Buenaventura (mission, California)
Serra, Junípero **14** 111-112

San Carlo alle Quatro Fontane (church, Rome)
Borromini, Francesco **2** 424-425

San Carlo Theater (Naples)
Rossini, Gioacchino **13** 311-312

San Carlos (ship)
Portolá, Gaspar de **12** 408

San Carlos Academy (Mexico)
Velasco, Luis de **15** 450-451

San Carlos Borromeo de Monterey (Carmel; mission)
Serra, Junípero **14** 111-112

San Carlos reservation (Arizona)
Geronimo **6** 281-282

San Cassiano (church, Venice)
Bellini, Giovanni **2** 137-138

San Diego Bay (South Western California)
Cabrillo, Juan Rodríguez **3** 204-205

San Domenico (church; Cortona, Italy)
Sassetta **13** 492

San Domenico (monastery, Fiesole)
Angelico **1** 235-236

San Esteban (church, Salamanca)
Churriguera, José Benito de **4** 53-54

San Fermo (church, Verona)
Pisanello **12** 323-324

San Fernando Academy (Saragossa, Spain)
Goya y Lucientes, Francisco de Paula José de **6** 476-478

San Fernando School of Medicine (Peru)
Unánue, José Hipólito **15** 387-388

San Francesco (church, Arezzo)
Piero della Francesca **12** 301-302

San Francesco (church; Assisi)
Cimabue **4** 60-61
Giotto **6** 342-345
Lorenzetti, Pietro and Ambrogio **9** 517-518

San Francesco (church, Borgo San Sepolcro)
Sassetta **13** 492

San Francesco (church, Siena)
Lorenzetti, Pietro and Ambrogio **9** 517-518

San Francesco della Vigna (church, Venice)
Palladio, Andrea **12** 75-77

San Francisco (city, California)
Anza, Juan Bautista de **1** 254-255
Butterfield, John **3** 184-185
Feinstein, Dianne **5** 407-408
Johnson, Hiram Warren **8** 300-301
Kearney, Denis **8** 468
Milk, Harvey Bernard **11** 19-21
Ruef, Abraham **13** 352-353

San Francisco (film)
Gable, William Clark **6** 157-158

San Francisco 49'ers
DeBartolo **4** 438-440

San Francisco Ballet
Smuin, Michael **14** 307-309

San Francisco Bay (Western California)
Gálvez, José de **6** 196

San Francisco Conference (1945)
Australia and New Zealand
Curtin, John Joseph **4** 348-349
Evatt, Herbert Vere **5** 341-343
Fraser, Peter **6** 73-74
Canada
Pearson, Lester Bowles **12** 174-175
China
Hu Shih **8** 63-65
Ecuador
Plaza Lasso, Galo **12** 350-351
Iraq

Fādil al-Jamālī, Muhammad
 5 361-362
Norway
 Lie, Trygve Halvdan **9** 400-401
Philippines
 Garcia, Carlos P. **6** 207-208
 Rómulo, Carlos P. **13** 270-271
planning of
 Bowman, Isaiah **2** 464-465
 Hull, Cordell **8** 28-29
South Africa
 Smuts, Jan Christian **14** 309-310
U.K.
 Attlee, Clement Richard **1** 361-362
 Halifax, 1st Earl of **7** 82-83
U.S.
 Bunche, Ralph Johnson **3** 121-122
 Du Bois, William Edward Burghardt
  5 116-118
 Dulles, John Foster **5** 134-135
 Roosevelt, Franklin Delano
  13 277-280
 Stettinius, Edward R. Jr. **14** 437-438
U.S.S.R.
 Molotov, Vyacheslav Mikhailovich
  11 89-90
 see also United Nations

San Francisco de Asis (mission, California)
 Serra, Junípero **14** 111-112

San Francisco 49ers (U.S. football team)
 Montana, Joe **11** 120-121

San Francisco Giants (U.S. baseball team)
 Mays, Willie **10** 376-379

San Gabriel Arcángel (mission, California)
 Serra, Junípero **14** 111-112

San Giobbe (church, Venice)
 Bellini, Giovanni **2** 137-138

San Giorgio Maggiore (monastery, Venice)
 Palladio, Andrea **12** 75-77

San Giovanni, Bapistery of
 see Florence Cathedral

San Giovanni Crisostomo (church, Venice)
 Bellini, Giovanni **2** 137-138

San Giovanni Fuorcivitas (church, Pistoia)
 Pisano, Giovanni **12** 324-325

San Giovanni, order of (religious congregation)
 Joachim of Fiore **8** 263-264

San Ildefonso, Treaty of
 1777
  Azara, Félix de **1** 397-398
 1800
  Adams, John **1** 48-51

San Jacinto (ship)
 Wilkes, Charles **16** 279-280

San Jacinto, battle of (1836)
 Houston, Samuel **7** 526-527
 Santa Ana, Antonio López de
  13 471-472

San José (city, Costa Rica)
 Keith, Minor Cooper **8** 476-477
 Meiggs, Henry **10** 458-459

San Juan Capistrano (mission; California)
 Serra, Junípero **14** 111-112

San Juan de Ulúa (island, Mexico)
 Drake, Francis **5** 94-96
 Santa Ana, Antonio López de
  13 471-472

San Lorenzo (church, Florence)
 Bronzino **3** 19
 Brunelleschi, Filippo **3** 70-72
 Medici, Cosimo de' **10** 449-450
 Sangallo family **13** 464-466
 Sansovino, Jacopo **13** 470-471
 Verrocchio, Andrea del **15** 471-472

San Lorenzo (church, Turin)
 Guarini, Guarino **7** 25-26

San Luigi dei Francesi (church; Rome)
 Porta, Giacomo della **12** 402-403
 Rossi, Luigi **13** 310-311

San Luis Obispo (mission, California)
 Serra, Junípero **14** 111-112

San Marcello (church, Florence)
 Sansovino, Jacopo **13** 470-471

San Marco (convent, Florence)
 Angelico **1** 235-236
 Medici, Cosimo de' **10** 449-450
 Savonarola, Girolamo **13** 505-506

San Marco (palace, Rome)
 Sangallo family **13** 464-466

San Marco (Venice)
 see St. Mark's

San Marcos University (Lima, Peru)
 Prado Ugarteche, Manuel **12** 430-431
 Toledo, Francisco de **15** 257-259

SAN MARTÍN, JOSÉ DE (1778-1850),
 Argentine soldier and statesman
 13 468-469
  Belgrano, Manuel **2** 126-127
  Bolívar, Simón **2** 375-377
  Carrera, José Miguel **3** 323-324
  Castilla, Ramón **3** 361
  Güemes, Martín **7** 26-27
  Mitre, Bartolomé **11** 62-63
  O'Higgins, Bernardo **11** 486
  Santa Cruz, Andrés de **13** 472-473

San Martín, Ramón Grau
 see Grau San Martín, Ramón

San Martino (church; Cortona, Italy)
 Sassetta **13** 492

San Martino (church, Florence)
 Botticelli, Sandro **2** 439-440

San Mateo v. Southern Pacific R.R. Co.
 (1882)
 Field, Stephen Johnson **5** 441-442

San Miniato (church, Florence)
 Luca della Robbia **10** 19-20
 Uccello, Paolo **15** 378-379

San Pancrazio, battle of (1849)
 Garibaldi, Giuseppe **6** 215-217

San Paolo fuori le Mura (church, Rome)
 Arnolfo di Cambio **1** 315-316

San Pasqual, battle of (1846)
 Carson, Christopher **3** 334-335
 Kearny, Stephen Watts **8** 468-469

San Pellegrino (church; Siena, Italy)
 Sassetta **13** 492

San Petronio (church, Bologna)
 Agostino di Duccio **1** 86

San Pietro in Montorio (church, Rome)
 Bramante, Donato **2** 493-494

San Pietro Martire (church, Murano)
 Bellini, Giovanni **2** 137-138

San Remo Conference (1920)
 Husein ibn Ali **8** 63

San Rocco, Scuola di (Venice)
 Tintoretto **15** 232-234

San Romano, battle of (1432)
 Uccello, Paolo **15** 378-379

San Salvador (island, Bahamas)
 Columbus, Christopher **4** 176-179

San Salvador (ship)
 Cabrillo, Juan Rodríguez **3** 204-205

San Sebastiano (church, Mantua)
 Alberti, Leon Battista **1** 113-115

San Sebastiano (church, Venice)
 Veronese, Paolo **15** 469-470

San Stefano, treaty of (1878)
 Abdul-Hamid II **1** 17-18
 Salisbury, 3d Marquess of **13** 448-449

San Vitale (church, Ravenna)
 Charlemagne **3** 445-447

San Zaccaria (church, Venice)
 Andrea del Castagno **1** 223-224
 Bellini, Giovanni **2** 137-138

San Zeno Altarpiece (painting)
 Mantegna, Andrea **10** 215-216

Sánchez Cerro, Luis M. (1889-1933), Peruvian soldier and president
 Haya de la Torre, Victor Raul **7** 216-217

Sancho I (1154-1211), king of Portugal
 1185-1211
 Alfonso I **1** 148

Sancho II (died 1072), king of Castile
 1065-72
 Alfonso VI **1** 149

Sancho II (Capêlo; 1208-48), king of Portugal 1223-48
 Alfonso III **1** 148-149

Sancho IV (el Bravo; 1258-95), king of
 Castile 1284-95
 Alfonso X **1** 150-151

Sancho VII (died 1234), king of Navarre
 1194-1234
 Cabeza de Vaca, Álvar Núñez **3** 197
 Thibaut IV **15** 180-181

Sancta Susanna (opera)
 Hindemith, Paul **7** 399-400

Sanctification of God's Name, The (novel)
 Asch, Shalom **1** 325-326

SANCTORIUS (1561-1636), Italian physician and physiologist **13** 459

Sanctuary (novel)
Faulkner, William **5** 395-397

SAND, GEORGE (1804-1876), French novelist **13** 459-461
Browning, Elizabeth Barrett **3** 52-53
Chopin, Frédéric François **4** 16-18
Flaubert, Gustave **5** 480-482
Hugo, Victor Marie **8** 22-25
Liszt, Franz **9** 445-447
Musset, Louis Charles Alfred de **11** 271-272

Sand, Karl Ludwig (1795-1820), German student radical and assassin
Kotzebue, Otto von **9** 91-92

Sand, Maurice (1828-1889), French painter and writer
Chopin, Frédéric François **4** 16-18
Sand, George **13** 459-461

Sand Reckoner, The (treatise)
Archimedes **1** 277-280

Sand River Convention (1852)
Pretorius, Andries **12** 444-445

SANDBURG, CARL (1878-1967), American poet, anthologist, and biographer **13** 461-462
Anderson, Sherwood **1** 220-221
Benét, Stephen Vincent **2** 157-158
Lowell, Amy **10** 13
Masters, Edgar Lee **10** 326-327
Whitman, Walt **16** 249-251

Sandcastle, The (novel)
Murdoch, Iris **11** 256-257

Sandeau, Jules (1811-1883), French novelist and playwright
Sand, George **13** 459-461

Sandemanians (religious sect; England)
Godwin, William **6** 383-384

Sanderson, Robert (1587-1663), English bishop
Walton, Izaak **16** 90-91

Sandinista National Liberation Front (Frente Sandinista de Liberación Nacional; Nicaragua)
Chamorro, Violeta Barrios de **3** 417-419
Ortega, Daniel **12** 5-7
Somoza Debayle, Anastasio **14** 336-337

SANDINO, AUGUSTO C. (1894-1934), Nicaraguan guerrilla leader **13** 462-463
Somoza, Anastasio **14** 335-336

Sanditon (novel)
Austen, Jane **1** 377-379

Sandow, Eugene (1867-1925), German professional strong man
Ziegfeld, Florenz **16** 516-517

Sandra Belloni (novel)
Meredith, George **10** 512-513

Sandracottus
see Chandragupta

SANDYS, SIR EDWIN (1561-1629), English statesman and colonizer in America **13** 463-464
Hooker, Richard **7** 475-476

SANE (activist group; United States)
see Committee for a SANE Nuclear Policy

SANGALLO FAMILY (flourished late 15th-mid-16th century), Italian artists and architects **13** 464-466

SANGER, FREDERICK (born 1918), English biochemist **13** 466-467

SANGER, MARGARET HIGGINS (1884-1966), American leader of birth control movement **13** 467-468

Sanglot de la terre, Le (poems)
Laforgue, Jules **9** 160-161

Sanhedrin (Jewish religious and legal body)
Hillel **7** 390-391
Johanan ben Zakkai **8** 271-272
Judah I **8** 372-373
Peter **12** 252-253
Shammai **14** 149

Sanitary Commission (England)
Shaftesbury, 7th Earl of **14** 137-138

Sanitation
Finlay, Carlos Juan **5** 450
Gorgas, William Crawford **6** 454-455
Rush, Benjamin **13** 364-365

Sanjo (died 1116), emperor of Japan 1011-16
Fujiwara Michinaga **6** 145-146

Sanjuro (film)
Kurosawa, Akira **9** 135-137

Sankey, Ira D. (1840-1908), American evangelist and hymn writer
Moody, Dwight L. **11** 141-142

Sankt Florian, monastery of (near Linz, Austria)
Altdorfer, Albrecht **1** 179-180

Sankt Jürgen (novella)
Storm, Theodor **14** 479-480

San-kuo chih yen-i (novel)
Ts'ao Ts'ao **15** 322-323

Sanlúcar de Barrameda (seaport, Spain)
Columbus, Christopher **4** 176-179

SANMICHELI, MICHELE (circa 1484-1559), Italian architect and military engineer **13** 469-470
Bramante, Donato **2** 493-494
Palladio, Andrea **12** 75-77

Sannazaro, Jacopo (1458-1530), Italian writer
Spenser, Edmund **14** 373-376

Sanron (Buddhism)
Kukai **9** 124-125

Sans Souci (palace, Haiti)
Christophe, Henri **4** 32

Sanshiro (novel)
Natsume, Soseki **11** 324-325

Sanshiro Sugata (film)
Kurosawa, Akira **9** 135-137

Sanskrit (language)
Harsha **7** 181-182
Kalidasa **8** 414-415
Kukai **9** 124-125

Sansom, Sir George (1883-1965), English diplomat and writer
Nobunaga, Oda **11** 413-414
Suiko **15** 15-16

Sansom Street Church (Philadelphia)
Mills, Robert **11** 36-37

SANSOVINO, JACOPO (1486-1570), Italian sculptor and architect **13** 470-471
Andrea del Sarto **1** 224-225
Garnier, Jean Louis Charles **6** 221-222
Palladio, Andrea **12** 75-77
Titian **15** 242-244

Sant' Agnese (church, Rome)
Borromini, Francesco **2** 424-425
Gaulli, Giovanni Battista **6** 238-239

Sant' Ambrogio (church, Milan)
Bramante, Donato **2** 493-494

Sant' Anastasia (chapel, Verona)
Pisanello **12** 323-324

Sant' Andrea (church, Mantua)
Alberti, Leon Battista **1** 113-115

Sant' Andrea (church, Pistoia)
Pisano, Giovanni **12** 324-325

Sant' Andrea al Quirinale (church, Rome)
Bernini, Gian Lorenzo **2** 214-216

Sant' Andrea della Valle (church, Rome)
Borromini, Francesco **2** 424-425
Maderno, Carlo **10** 117-118

Sant' Andrea, Oratory of (Rome)
Vignola, Giacomo da **15** 493-494

Sant' Antonio (church, Padua)
Bellini, Giovanni **2** 137-138
Sansovino, Jacopo **13** 470-471
Tartini, Giuseppe **15** 112-113

Sant' Apollonia (church, Florence)
Andrea del Castagno **1** 223-224

Sant' Egidio (church, Florence)
Piero della Francesca **12** 301-302
Veneziano, Domenico **15** 459-460

Sant' Ivo alla Sapienza (chapel, Rome)
Borromini, Francesco **2** 424-425

SANTA ANA, ANTONIO LÓPEZ DE (1794-1876), Mexican general and statesman, six times president **13** 471-472
Alamán, Lucas **1** 99-100
Álvarez, Juan **1** 184-185
Guerrero, Vicente **7** 28-30
Juárez, Benito **8** 369-372
Lerdo de Tejada, Miguel **9** 351-352
see also Mexico—Texas revolt (1836)

Santa Ana's Retreat from Buena Vista (musical composition)
Foster, Stephen Collins **6** 25-27

Santa Anna dei Palafrenieri (church, Vatican)
Vignola, Giacomo da **15** 493-494

Santa Cecilia in Trastevere (church, Rome)
Arnolfo di Cambio **1** 315-316

Santa Clara (mission, California)
Serra, Junípero **14** 111-112

Santa Clara (ship)
Camoëns, Luis Vaz de **3** 247-249

Santa Claus (symphony)
Fry, William Henry **6** 136-137

Santa Corona (church, Vicenza)
Bellini, Giovanni **2** 137-138

Santa Croce (church, Florence)
Alfieri, Vittoria **1** 145-146
Arnolfo di Cambio **1** 315-316
Brunelleschi, Filippo **3** 70-72
Dante Alighieri **4** 389-391
da Settignano, Desiderio **4** 509
Ghiberti, Lorenzo **6** 291-292
Giotto **6** 342-345

Santa Croce in Gerusalemme (church, Rome)
Rubens, Peter Paul **13** 339-342

Santa Cruz (play)
Frisch, Max **6** 118-119

SANTA CRUZ, ANDRÉS DE (1792-1865), Bolivian general and statesman, president 1829-39 **13** 472-473
Portales Plazazuelos, Diego José Víctor **12** 404
Rosas, Juan Manuel de **13** 290-291

Santa Fe Trail (United States)
Becknell, William **2** 105-106

Santa Felicità (chapel, Florence)
Brunelleschi, Filippo **3** 70-72

Santa Hermandad (police force; New Spain)
Velasco, Luis de **15** 450-451

Santa Lucia dei Magnoli (church, Florence)
Veneziano, Domenico **15** 459-460

Santa Maria (ship)
Columbus, Christopher **4** 176-179

Santa Maria degli Angeli (church, Florence)
Brunelleschi, Filippo **3** 70-72
Ghiberti, Lorenzo **6** 291-292

Santa Maria dei Frari (church, Venice)
Bellini, Giovanni **2** 137-138

Santa Maria del Carmine (chapel, Florence)
Masaccio **10** 312-313

Santa Maria del Carmine (church, Pisa)
Masaccio **10** 312-313

Santa Maria del Fiore
see Florence Cathedral

Santa Maria del Monserrato (church, Florence)
Sansovino, Jacopo **13** 470-471

Santa Maria del Popolo (church, Rome)
Sansovino, Jacopo **13** 470-471

Santa Maria del Priorato (church, Rome)
Piranesi, Giovanni Battista **12** 321-322

Santa Maria della Pace (church, Rome)
Bramante, Donato **2** 493-494
Cortona, Pietro da **4** 256

Santa Maria della Salute (church, Venice)
Titian **15** 242-244

Santa Maria della Spina (church, Pisa)
Andrea Pisano **1** 225-226
Pisano, Giovanni **12** 324-325

Santa Maria della Vittoria (church, Rome)
Bernini, Gian Lorenzo **2** 214-216
Maderno, Carlo **10** 117-118

Santa Maria delle Grazie (church, Milan)
Bramante, Donato **2** 493-494

Santa Maria delle Grazie (church, Pistoia)
Michelozzo **11** 6-7

Santa Maria in Vallicella (church, Rome)
Rubens, Peter Paul **13** 339-342

Santa Maria Maddalena dei Pazzi (church, Florence)
Perugino **12** 245-246

Santa Maria Maggiore (church, Rome)
Bernini, Gian Lorenzo **2** 214-216
Palestrina, Giovanni Pierluigi da **12** 70-72
Sassetta **13** 492

Santa Maria Novella (church, Florence)
Alberti, Leon Battista **1** 113-115
Brunelleschi, Filippo **3** 70-72
Dante Alighieri **4** 389-391
da Settignano, Desiderio **4** 509
Duccio di Buoninsegna **5** 121-122
Ghiberti, Lorenzo **6** 291-292
Ghirlandaio, Domenico **6** 292-293
Giotto **6** 342-345
Masaccio **10** 312-313
Uccello, Paolo **15** 378-379

Santa Maria Nuova (church, Florence)
Piero della Francesca **12** 301-302

Santa Maria presso S. Satiro (church, Milan)
Bramante, Donato **2** 493-494

Santa Sindone
see Holy Shroud, Chapel of the

Santa Susanna (church, Rome)
Borromini, Francesco **2** 424-425
Maderno, Carlo **10** 117-118

SANTAMARIA, BARTHOLOMEW AUGUSTINE (born 1915), Australian Roman Catholic publicist and organizer **13** 473-474
Mannix, Daniel **10** 210

SANTANA, PEDRO (1801-1864), Dominican military leader, three times president **13** 474-475
Baez, Buenaventura **1** 432-433
Gómez, Máximo **6** 418-419

SANTANDER, FRANCISCO DE PAULA (1792-1840), Colombian general and statesman **13** 475

Mosquera, Tomás Cipriano de **11** 205-206

SANTAYANA, GEORGE (Jorge Agustin de Santayana; 1863-1952), Spanish-American philosopher **13** 475-477
Eliot, Thomas Stearns **5** 258-261
Lewis, Clarence Irving **9** 381
Lippmann, Walter **9** 439-440
Stevens, Wallace **14** 443-445

Santi, Giovanni (1435?-1494), Italian painter and poet
Raphael **13** 40-42

Santiago (city, Chile)
Carrera, José Miguel **3** 323-324
Meiggs, Henry **10** 458-459
San Martín, José de **13** 468-469
Valdivia, Pedro de **15** 400-401

Santiago (city, Cuba)
Ames, Adelbert **1** 198

Santiago (ship)
Magellan, Ferdinand **10** 126-127

Santiago de Chile
see Santiago (Chile)

Santiago de Compostela (commune, Spain)
Alfonso VI **1** 149
Cavalcanti, Guido **3** 382

Santiago de Guayaquil
see Guayaquil

Santiago Madonna (painting)
Murillo, Bartolomé Esteban **11** 258-259

Santillana, Íñigo López de Mendoza, Marquis of (1398-1458), Spanish poet
Manrique, Jorge **10** 210-211

Santissima Annunziata (church, Florence)
Alberti, Leon Battista **1** 113-115
Andrea del Castagno **1** 223-224
Andrea del Sarto **1** 224-225

Santissima Trinita (church, Florence)
Angelico **1** 235-236
Cimabue **4** 60-61
Ghirlandaio, Domenico **6** 292-293

Santo Domingo, Republic of
see Dominican Republic

Santo Domingo de Silos (church; Daroca, Spain)
Bermejo, Bartolomé **2** 205

Santo Domingo el Antiguo (church, Madrid)
Greco **6** 511-514

Santo Spirito (church, Florence)
Brunelleschi, Filippo **3** 70-72
Sangallo family **13** 464-466

Santomé, battle of (1856)
Gómez, Máximo **6** 418-419

Santorio, Santorio
see Sanctorius

Santos, Máximo (1836-1887), Uruguayan politician, president 1882-86
Batlle y Ordóñez, José **2** 58-59
Zorrilla de San Martin, Juan **16** 530-531

SANTOS-DUMONT, ALBERTO (1873-1932), Brazilian inventor **13** 477-478

Sanzio, Raffaello
see Raphael

São Bento (ship)
Camoëns, Luis Vaz de **3** 247-249

São Francisco (church; Pampulha, Brazil)
Niemeyer Soares Filho, Oscar **11** 389-390
Portinari, Cândido **12** 407-408

São Francisco de Assis (church; Ouro Preto, Brazil)
Aleijadinho, O **1** 125-126

São Paulo (city, Brazil)
Anchieta, José de **1** 210-211
Feijó, Diogo Antônio **5** 405-406
Sousa, Martim Afonso de **14** 354-355

São Vicente (city, Brazil)
Anchieta, José de **1** 210-211
Sousa, Martim Afonso de **14** 354-355

Sapho (novel)
Daudet, Alphonse **4** 402-403

Sapho (opera)
Gounod, Charles François **6** 473-474

SAPIR, EDWARD (1884-1939), American anthropologist **13** 478-479
Boas, Franz **2** 349-351
Kluckhohn, Clyde **9** 56-57

Sapor III (died 388), king of Persia
Stilicho, Flavius **14** 452-453

SAPPHO (circa 625-570 B.C.), Greek lyric poet **13** 479-480
Catullus, Gaius Valerius **3** 377-378
Horace **7** 500-503

Sappho (play)
Grillparzer, Franz **6** 546-547

SAPRU, SIR TEJ BAHADUR (1875-1949), Indian lawyer and statesman **13** 480-481

Saracens (Arab people)
Martel, Charles **10** 285
Lalibela **9** 170

Saragossa (province, Spain)
Cid **4** 58-59
Goya y Lucientes, Francisco de Paula José de **6** 476-478

Saragossa, battle of (778)
Abd al-Rahman I **1** 13-14

Sarah Fuller's School for the Deaf (Boston)
Bell, Alexander Graham **2** 129-131

Sarah Siddons as the Tragic Muse (painting)
Reynolds, Joshua **13** 115-116

Sarandi, battle of (1825)
Lavalleja, Juan Antonio **9** 238-239
Rivera, Fructuoso **13** 184-185

Saraswati, Swami Dayananda
see Dayananda Saraswati, Swami

Saratoga (ship)
Farragut, David Glasgow **5** 388-389
Halsey, William Frederick **7** 91-92

Saratoga, battles of (1777; Bemis Heights and Freeman's Farm)
Americans
Arnold, Benedict **1** 309-310
Franklin, Benjamin **6** 60-64
Lincoln, Benjamin **9** 418-419
Morgan, Daniel **11** 160-161
British
Burgoyne, John **3** 137-138
Howe, William **7** 538-539
North, Frederick **11** 429-430

Saratoga Trunk (novel)
Ferber, Edna **5** 413

Sardanapale (cantata)
Berlioz, Louis Hector **2** 203-205

Sardinia (island, Mediteiranean)
Cato, Marcus Porcius the Elder **3** 375
Cavour, Conte di **3** 385-386
Charles Albert, King of Sardinia **3** 466
Gracchus, Tiberius and Gaius Sempronius **6** 479-480
Victor Amadeus II **15** 482-483
Victor Emmanuel II **15** 483-484

Sardis (ancient city, Asia M.)
Alexander the Great **1** 137-141
Cyrus the Great **4** 363-364
Darius I **4** 394-395

Sarett, Lewis H. (born 1917), American biochemist
Reichstein, Tadeus **13** 85-87

Sargent, Aaron Augustus (1827-1887), American politician
Stanford, Leland **14** 397-398

Sargent, C.S. (1841-1927), American dendrologist
Olmsted, Frederick Law **11** 503-504

SARGENT, JOHN SINGER (1856-1925), American portrait painter **13** 481-482
Chase, William Merritt **3** 476-477

SARGON II (ruled 722-705 B.C.), king of Assyria **13** 482
Micah **10** 542-543
Sennacherib **14** 108

SARGON OF AGADE (circa 2340-2284 B.C.), first Semitic king of Mesopotamia **13** 483

Sargonid dynasty (Assyria; ruled 722-612 B.C.)
Ashurbanipal **1** 338
Sargon II **13** 482
Sennacherib **14** 108

SARIT THANARAT (1908-1963), Thai army officer, prime minister 1957-63 **13** 483-484
Phibun Songkhram, Luang **12** 264-265

SARMIENTO, DOMINGO FAUSTINO (1811-1888), Argentine statesman, president 1868-74 **13** 484-485
Alberdi, Juan Bautista **1** 109-110
Hernández, José **7** 328-329
Quiroga, Juan Facundo **12** 521-522

Sarmiento, Don Diego (1567-1626), Spanish diplomat
James I **8** 204-206

Sarmiento de Gamboa, Pedro (1530-after 1589), Spanish sea captain
Mendaña de Neyra, Álvaro de **10** 483

Sarnath pillar (India)
Asoka **1** 341-342

SARNOFF, DAVID (1891-1971), American television and radio broadcasting executive **13** 485-486

SAROYAN, WILLIAM (1908-1981), American short-story writer, dramatist, and novelist **13** 486-487

SARPI, PAOLO (1552-1623), Italian prelate and statesman **13** 487-488

SARRAUTE, NATHALIE TCHERNIAK (born 1900), French author of novels, essays, and plays **13** 488-490
Robbe-Grillet, Alain **13** 189-190

Sarti, Giuseppe (1729-1802), Italian composer
Cherubini, Luigi Carlo Zanobi Salvatore Maria **3** 505-506

Sarto, Andrea del
see Andrea del Sarto

Sarto, Giuseppe Melchiorre
see Pius X

SARTON, GEORGE (1884-1956), Belgian-born American historian of science **13** 490-491
Quételet, Lambert Adolphe Jacques **12** 510-511

Sartor Resartus (book)
Carlyle, Thomas **3** 304-305

Sartoris (novel)
Faulkner, William **5** 395-397

SARTRE, JEAN PAUL (1905-1980), French philosopher and author **13** 491-492
Camus, Albert **3** 255-257
de Beauvoir, Simone **4** 440-441
Fanon, Frantz **5** 379-380
Faulkner, William **5** 395-397
Genet, Jean **6** 262-263
Kierkegaard, Søren Aabye **8** 547-549
Merleau-Ponty, Maurice **10** 518
Murdoch, Iris **11** 256-257
Warnock, Helen Mary Wilson **16** 115-117
Wright, Richard **16** 401-402

Sarumino (anthology)
Basho, Matsuo **2** 45-48

Sasameyuki (novel)
Tanizaki, Junichiro **15** 101-102

Saskatchewan (province, Canada)
Douglas, Thomas Clement **5** 82-83
Laurier, Wilfrid **9** 232-234

Saskatchewan River (Canada)
la Verendrye, Sieur de **9** 239-240

Sassanian calendar (Persia)
Omar Khayyam **11** 510-511

Sassanian dynasty (Persia; ruled 226-640)
Justinian I **8** 393-395
Khosrow I **8** 538-539
Omar ibn al-Khattab **11** 508-509
Shahpur II **14** 140-141
Tabari, Muhammad ibn Jarir al-
15 69-70
Valerian **15** 404-405

SASSETTA (circa 1400-50), Italian painter
13 492

SASSOON, SIEGFRIED (1886-1967), English poet **13** 492-493

Satan (literary character)
Milton, John **11** 43-46

Satan in Goray (story)
Singer, Isaac Bashevis **14** 249-250

Satanic Verses, The (book)
Rushdie, Salman **13** 366-368

Satanstoe (novel)
Cooper, James Fenimore **4** 220-223

SATANTA (White Bear; 1830-1878), Native American orator and leader of the Kiowa tribe **13** 493-494

Satchmo the Great (film)
Armstrong, Louis Daniel **1** 303-304

Satellite Television (Europe)
Murdoch, Rupert **11** 257-258

Satellites, artificial
see Space exploration

Sati (Hinduism)
Aurangzeb **1** 377
Deb, Radhakant **4** 437

SATIE, ERIK (1866-1925), French composer **13** 494-495
Cage, John **3** 211-214
Cocteau, Jean **4** 132-133
Cunningham, Merce **4** 337-338
Honegger, Arthur **7** 472-473
Poulenc, Francis **12** 414-415
Picasso, Pablo **12** 292-295
Sauguet, Henri **13** 497-498
Thomson, Virgil **15** 202-203

Satin Slipper, The (play)
Claudel, Paul Louis Charles **4** 90-91

Satire (literature)
American
Dunne, Finley Peter **5** 147-148
Hopkinson, Francis **7** 496-497
Kaufman, George S. **8** 457-458
Lewis, Harry Sinclair **9** 385-387
Twain, Mark **15** 363-366
Australian
Franklin, Stella Maraia Sarah Miles
6 68-69
English
Donne, John **5** 60-61
Dryden, John **5** 106-107
Fletcher, John **5** 487
Hardy, Thomas **7** 150-152
Jonson, Ben **8** 343-345
Orwell, George **12** 14-15
Sassoon, Siegfried **13** 492-493

Skelton, John **14** 268-269
Swift, Jonathan **15** 51-54
Thackeray, William Makepeace
15 159-161
Waugh, Evelyn Arthur St. John
16 145-147
Wyatt, Thomas **16** 410-411
Wycherley, William **16** 411-412
French
du Bellay, Joachim **5** 113-114
France, Anatole **6** 39-40
Hugo, Victor Marie **8** 22-25
La Fontaine, Jean de **9** 156-157
Lesage, Alain René **9** 353-354
Italian
Ariosto, Ludovico **1** 289-290
Roman
Ennius, Quintus **5** 289
Seneca the Younger, Lucius Annaeus
14 103-105
see also Authors—satirists; Irony

SATO, EISAKU (1901-1975), Japanese statesman, prime minister 1964-72
13 495-496
Hirohito **7** 410-412
Kishi, Nobusuke **9** 41-43

Sato, Nobusuke
see Kishi, Nobusuke

Satsuma (Japanese clan)
Inukai, Tsuyoshi **8** 130-131
Iwakura, Tomomi **8** 160-161
Saigo, Takamori **13** 429

Satsuma rebellion (Japan; 1876-77)
Okubo, Toshimichi **11** 489-490

Satura (poems)
Montale, Eugenio **11** 117-118

Saturday Evening Post (magazine)
Rockwell, Norman Percevel
13 231-233
Rogers, Will **13** 251-252

Saturday Night (play)
Benavente y Martinez, Jacinto
2 146-147

Saturday Review (magazine)
Cousins, Norman **4** 274-276

Saturday's Children (play; Anderson)
Anderson, Maxwell **1** 219-220
Bogart, Humphrey **2** 363-364

Saturn (planet)
Brahe, Tycho **2** 489-490
Hall, Asaph **7** 83-84
Herschel, William **7** 341-343
Huygens, Christiaan **8** 79-81
Laplace, Marquis de **9** 202-204
Maxwell, James Clerk **10** 361-364

Saturn Devouring His Son (painting)
Goya y Lucientes, Francisco de Paula
José de **6** 476-478

Saturn 5 (space booster)
Armstrong, Neil Alden **1** 304-306
Goddard, Robert Hutchings **6** 376-377
von Braun, Wernher **16** 17-18

Saturninus, L. Appuleius (died 100 B.C.), Roman politician
Marius, Gaius **10** 264-265

Satyagraha movement (India)
Chelmsford, Frederic John Napier Thesiger **3** 497
Gandhi, Mohandas Karamchand
6 201-204
Patel, Vallabhbhai **12** 129-130
see also Passive resistance movements

Satyr Family (painting)
Altdorfer, Albrecht **1** 179-180

Satyra do Torneio (poem)
Camoëns, Luis Vaz de **3** 247-249

Satyricon (book; Petronius)
Petronius Arbiter **12** 262-263
Varro, Marcus Terentius **15** 438-439

Satyricon (film)
Fellini, Federico **5** 408-409

Satyrus (flourished circa 150 B.C.), Greek anatomy teacher
Galen **6** 178-180

Sauchieburn, battle of (1488)
James III **8** 208-209

Saudi Arabia, Kingdom of (nation, South Western Asia)
Burckhardt, Johann Ludwig **3** 133
Cheng Ho **3** 500
Covilhão, Pedro de **4** 278-279
Dayan, Moshe **4** 429-431
Fahd ibn Abdul Aziz Al-Saud **5** 364-366
Faisal ibn Abd al Aziz ibn Saud
5 371-372
ibn Saud, Abd al-Aziz **8** 94-95
Ibrahim Pasha **8** 97-98
Mahmud II **10** 145-147
Yamani, Ahmed Zaki **16** 433-435

SAUER, CARL ORTWIN (1889-1975), American geographer and anthropologist
13 496-497

SAUGUET, HENRI (born 1901), French composer, writer, and thinker on art and music **13** 497-498

Sauk Indians (North America)
Black Hawk **2** 308

SAUL (circa 1020-1000 B.C.), first King of Israel **13** 498
David, Jacques Louis **4** 407-409
Samuel **13** 457-458

Saul (musical composition)
Handel, George Frederick **7** 116-119

Saul (play)
Alfieri, Vittoria **1** 145-146
Heavysege, Charles **7** 246

Saul, Saul, was verfolgst du mich? (musical composition)
Schütz, Heinrich **14** 48-49

Saul and David (opera)
Nielsen, Carl August **11** 388-389

Saunders, Sir Alexander Morris Carr
see Carr-Saunders, Sir Alexander Morris

SAUNDERS, SIR CHARLES EDWARD
(1867-1937), Canadian cerealist
13 498-499

Saunders, William (1836-1914), Canadian
agriculturist and horticulturist
Saunders, Charles Edward **13** 498-499

Saussure, Ferdinand de (1857-1913), Swiss
linguist
Bloomfield, Leonard **2** 338
Sapir, Edward **13** 478-479

SAVAGE, AUGUSTA CHRISTINE (born
Augusta Christine Fells; 1892-1962),
African American sculptor and teacher
13 499-501
Lawrence, Jacob **9** 250-251

SAVAGE, MICHAEL JOSEPH (1872-1940),
New Zealand labor leader, prime minister
1935-40 **13** 501-502
Fraser, Peter **6** 73-74

Savage, Richard (1697?-1743), English poet
Johnson, Samuel **8** 315-317

Savage Holiday (book)
Wright, Richard **16** 401-402

Save Me the Waltz (novel; Z. Fitzgerald)
Fitzgerald, Francis Scott Key **5** 470-472

Savery, Thomas (circa 1650-1715), English
inventor
Newcomen, Thomas **11** 362

SAVIGNY, FRIEDRICH KARL VON
(1779-1861), German jurist **13** 502-503
Frederick William IV **6** 87-88
Gierke, Otto von **6** 311-312
Grimm, Jakob and Wilhelm Karl **7** 3-4
Mommsen, Theodor **11** 94-95
Niebuhr, Barthold Georg **11** 385-386

SAVIMBI, JONAS MALHEIROS (born
1934), founder and leader of UNITA
(National Union for the Total Independence of Angola) **13** 503-505

Saving (economics)
Keynes, John Maynard **8** 528-530
Ramsey, Frank Plumpton **13** 25

Savinio, Alberto (1891-1952), Italian
painter
Chirico, Giorgio de **4** 4

SAVONAROLA, GIROLAMO (1452-1498),
Italian religious reformer and dictator of
Florence **13** 505-506
Botticelli, Sandro **2** 439-440
Dallapiccola, Luigi **4** 377-378
Eliot, George **5** 254-256
Michelangelo Buonarroti **11** 2-5
Pico della Mirandola, Giovanni
12 299-300

Savoy (region, France/Italy)
Cavour, Conte di **3** 385-386
Francis I **6** 40-43

Savoye House (Poissy)
Le Corbusier **9** 274-275

SAW MAUNG (born 1928), leader of
armed forces that took power in Burma

(now Myanmar) in a 1988 military coup
13 506-507

SAXE, COMTE DE (1696-1750), marshal of
France **13** 507-508

Saxe Holm's Stories (book)
Jackson, Helen Hunt **8** 172

Saxe-Coburg-Gotha dynasty (Great Britain)
see Great Britain—since 1901 (Windsor)

Saxon dynasty (Germany, ruled 919-1024)
Henry I **7** 285-286
Otto I **12** 28-29
Otto III **12** 29-30

Saxony (former German state)
Augustus II **1** 373-374
Charlemagne **3** 445-447
Frederick I **6** 78-79
Frederick II **6** 81-84
Henry I **7** 285-286
Maria Theresa **10** 256-258
see also Germany, Early history—Saxon
dynasty

Say, Is This the U.S.A.? (book)
Caldwell, Erskine **3** 223-224

SAY, JEAN BAPTISTE (1767-1832), French
economist **13** 508-509
Engels, Friedrich **5** 286-288

Say Not the Struggle Naught Availeth
(poem)
Clough, Arthur Hugh **4** 123-124

Saye and Sele, 1st Viscount (William
Fiennes; 1582-1662), English Parliamen-
tary leader
Hampden, John **7** 110-111

Sayers, Dorothy Leigh (1893-1957), English
author and translator
Cimabue **4** 60-61

Saying Prayers (painting)
Pippin, Horace **12** 318-319

SAYRE, FRANCIS BOWES (1885-1972),
American lawyer and administrator
13 509

Sayre, Zelda
see Fitzgerald, Zelda Sayre

SAYYID QUTB (1906-1966), Egyptian
writer, educator, and religious leader
13 509-511

Scaevola, Q. Mucius (died 82 B.C.), Roman
jurist
Gracchus, Tiberius and Gaius Sempronius **6** 479-480

Scala, Can Grande della (1291-1329), Italian art patron
Dante Alighieri **4** 389-391

Scala dei Giganti (Ducal Palace, Venice)
Sansovino, Jacopo **13** 470-471

Scalabrini, Giovanni Battista (1839-1905),
Italian bishop
Cabrini, Frances Xavier **3** 205

SCALFARO, OSCAR LUIGI (born 1918),
Christian Democratic leader and president of the Italian Republic **13** 511-512

SCALIA, ANTONIN (born 1936), U.S.
Supreme Court justice **13** 513-514

Scaliger, Julius Caesar (1484-1558), Italian
physician and scholar
Sidney, Philip **14** 214-215

Scalp, The (sculpture)
Rembrandt Harmensz van Rijn
13 91-95

Scalzo (cloister, Florence)
Andrea del Sarto **1** 224-225

Scamozzi, Vincenzo (1552-1616), Italian
architect
Palladio, Andrea **12** 75-77
Sansovino, Jacopo **13** 470-471

Scandal (film)
Kurosawa, Akira **9** 135-137

Scandal, political
see Corruption, political

Scandal, The (novel)
Alarcón, Pedro Antonio de **1** 100-101

Scandal in Bohemia, A (story)
Doyle, Arthur Conan **5** 91-92

Scandals (vaudeville shows)
Fields, W. C. **5** 444

Scandiano, Conte di
see Boiardo, Matteo Maria

Scandium (element—chemistry)
Mendeleev, Dmitrii Ivanovich
10 486-488

Scapegoat (painting)
Hunt, William Holman **8** 44-45

Scapegoat, The (novel)
Strindberg, August **14** 509-511

Scaramouche (Tiberio Fiorelli; died 1694),
Italian author
Molière **11** 86-88

Scarborough (ship)
Jones, John Paul **8** 337-338

Scarco di doglia (musical composition)
Lassus, Roland de **9** 216-218

SCARGILL, ARTHUR (born 1938), president of the British National Union of
Mineworkers **13** 514-515

Scarisbrick Hall (Lancashire)
Pugin, Augustus Welby Northmore
12 479-480

SCARLATTI, DOMENICO (1685-1757),
Italian harpsichordist and composer
13 515-517
Couperin, François **4** 270-271
Scarlatti, Pietro Alessandro Gaspare
13 517-518

**SCARLATTI, PIETRO ALESSANDRO GAS-
PARE** (1660-1725), Italian composer
13 517-518
Carissimi, Giacomo **3** 299-300
Scarlatti, Domenico **13** 515-517

Scarlet Car, The (stories)
Davis, Richard Harding **4** 422-423

Scarlet Letter, The (novel)
Hawthorne, Nathaniel **7** 212-215

Scarlet Sister Mary (film)
Barrymores **2** 28-30

Scenes from Childhood (musical composition)
Schumann, Robert Alexander **14** 41-43

Scenes from Goethe's *Faust* (musical composition)
Schumann, Robert Alexander **14** 41-43

Scenes of Clerical Life (stories)
Eliot, George **5** 254-256

Scenes of the Passion (painting)
Memling, Hans **10** 476

Scented Herbage of My Breast (poem)
Whitman, Walt **16** 249-251

Schach von Wuthenow (novel)
Fontane, Theodor **5** 504

SCHACHT, HJALMAR HORACE GREELEY
(1877-1970), German economist and
banker **13** 518-519

Schaeffer, Pierre (born 1910), French composer
Cage, John **3** 211-214
Cunningham, Merce **4** 337-338
Stockhausen, Karlheinz **14** 460-461

SCHAFF, PHILIP (1819-1893), Swiss-born
American religious scholar **13** 519-520

Schäftlarn (church, near Munich)
Cuvilliés, François **4** 359-360
Zimmermann, Johann Baptist and
Domenikus **16** 518

Schamberg, Morton (1881-1918), American painter and photographer
Sheeler, Charles **14** 170-171

SCHAPIRO, MIRIAM (born 1923), Artist
13 520-521

**SCHARNHORST, GERHARD JOHANN
DAVID VON** (1755-1813), Prussian general **13** 521-522
Blücher, Gebhard Leberecht von
2 340-341
Frederick William III **6** 87

SCHARPING, RUDOLF (born 1947), minister-president of Rhineland-Palatinate
and chairman of the German Social
Democratic Party **13** 522-524

Schauspielhaus (Berlin)
Schinkel, Karl Friedrich **14** 8

SCHECHTER, SOLOMON (1849-1915),
Romanian-American Jewish scholar and
religious leader **13** 524
Abrahams, Israel **1** 29
Ginzberg, Louis **6** 337-338
Jesus ben Sira **8** 251

SCHEELE, KARL WILHELM (1742-1786),
Swedish pharmacist and chemist
13 525-526

Schéhérazade (musical composition)
Ravel, Maurice Joseph **13** 54-55

Rimsky-Korsakov, Nikolai Andreevich
13 174-175

Scheidt, Samuel (1587-1654), German
organist
Sweelinck, Jan Pieterszoon **15** 50-51

Scheiner, Christopher (1579?-1650), German Jesuit astronomer
Galileo Galilei **6** 180-183

Scheinpflugova, Olga (wife of Karel Čapek;
1903?-1968), Czech actress
Čapek, Karel **3** 271-272

Scheler, Max (1874-1928), German
philosopher
Mannheim, Karl **10** 208-209

**SCHELLING, FRIEDRICH WILHELM
JOSEPH VON** (1775-1854), German
philosopher **13** 526-527
associates
Frederick William IV **6** 87-88
Hegel, Georg Wilhelm Friedrich
7 254-256
Hölderlin, Johann Christian
Friedrich **7** 451-452
Kierkegaard, Søren Aabye
8 547-549
influence of
Belinsky, Grigorievich **2** 128
Coleridge, Samuel Taylor **4** 154-156
Cousin, Victor **4** 273-274
Strauss, David Friedrich **14** 496-497
influenced by
Boehme, Jacob **2** 357
Kant, Immanuel **8** 430-432

Schelomo (musical composition)
Bloch, Ernest **2** 326-327

Schenck v. United States (legal case)
Holmes, Oliver Wendell Jr. **7** 458-459

Scherchen, Herman (1891-1966), German
conductor
Nono, Luigi **11** 420-421

Scherrer, Paul (1890-1969), Swiss physicist
Debye, Peter Joseph William **4** 447-448

Scherzo (musical composition)
Brahms, Johannes **2** 490-492
Chopin, Frédéric François **4** 16-18
Dawson, William Levi **4** 427-428
Franck, César **6** 48-49
Monteverdi, Claudio Giovanni Antonio
11 126-128
Mussorgsky, Modest Petrovich
11 274-276

Scheurer-Kestner, A. (1833-1899), French
chemist and politician
Dreyfus, Alfred **5** 103-105

Schiavona, La (painting)
Titian **15** 242-244

Schicksalstragödie (literary form)
Grillparzer, Franz **6** 546-547

SCHIELE, EGON (1890-1918), Austrian
Expressionist painter and draftsman
14 1-2

SCHIFF, JACOB HENRY (1847-1920), German-American banker **14** 2-3
Cooke, Jay **4** 215-216

Schikaneder, Emanuel (1751-1812), German theater manager and librettist
Mozart, Wolfgang Amadeus
11 218-221

SCHILLEBEECKX, EDWARD (born 1914),
Belgian Roman Catholic theologian
14 3-4

Schiller Building (Chicago)
Sullivan, Louis Henri **15** 27-28

**SCHILLER, JOHANN CHRISTOPH
FRIEDRICH VON** (1759-1805), German
dramatist, poet, and historian **14** 4-7
biographies and translations
Carlyle, Thomas **3** 304-305
Lewis, Matthew Gregory **9** 390-391
Pasternak, Boris Leonidovich
12 124-125
friends
Herbart, Johann Friedrich **7** 321-322
Humboldt, Wilhelm von **8** 31
Kleist, Heinrich von **9** 52-53
Schelling, Friedrich Wilhelm Joseph
von **13** 526-527
influence of
Dumas, Alexandre **5** 136-138
Echeverría, José Estéban **5** 197-198
Goethe, Johann Wolfgang von
6 388-391
Hölderlin, Johann Christian
Friedrich **7** 451-452
Lermontov, Mikhail Yurievich
9 352-353
Novalis **11** 435
Smetana, Bedřich **14** 281-282
Thackeray, William Makepeace
15 159-161
influenced by
Plutarch **12** 359-360
Winckelmann, Johann Joachim
16 332-333
musical settings
Beethoven, Ludwig van **2** 114-117
Schubert, Franz Peter **14** 35-37

Schillinger, Joseph (1895-1943), Russian
composer
Gershwin, George **6** 284-285

Schimmelreiter, Der (novella)
Storm, Theodor **14** 479-480

Schindler, Anton (1795-1864), German
conductor
Beethoven, Ludwig van **2** 114-117

SCHINDLER, SOLOMON (1842-1915),
German-American rabbi and social theorist **14** 7-8

SCHINKEL, KARL FRIEDRICH
(1781-1841), German architect, painter
and designer **14** 8
Frederick William IV **6** 87-88
Mies van der Rohe, Ludwig **11** 10-12

Schism, Great (1378-1417)
see Great Schism

Schizophrenia (medicine)
  Bleuler, Eugen **2** 325
  Mead, Margaret **10** 438-440
  Pavlov, Ivan Petrovich **12** 155-157

SCHLAFLY, PHYLLIS (born 1924), American political activist and author **14** 9-10

Schlegel, August Wilhelm von
(1767-1845), German man of letters
  Coleridge, Samuel Taylor **4** 154-156
  Frederick William IV **6** 87-88
  Heine, Heinrich **7** 259-260
  Schelling, Friedrich Wilhelm Joseph von **13** 526-527
  Staël, Germaine de **14** 391-392
  Tieck, Ludwig **15** 218-219

Schlegel, Dorothea Veit von (wife of Friedrich von Schlegel; 1763-1839), daughter of Moses Mendelssohn
  Schlegel, Friedrich von **14** 10-11

SCHLEGEL, FRIEDRICH VON (1772-1829), German critic and author **14** 10-11
  Brentano, Clemens **2** 515-516
  Lessing, Gotthold Ephraim **9** 357-359
  Novalis **11** 435
  Schelling, Friedrich Wilhelm Joseph von **13** 526-527
  Schleiermacher, Friedrich Ernst Daniel **14** 11-12
  Tieck, Ludwig **15** 218-219

Schleicher, Kurt von (1882-1934), German soldier and statesman
  Hindenburg, Paul Ludwig Hans von Beneckendorff und von **7** 400-401

Schleiden, Matthias (1804-1881), German botanist
  Schwann, Theodor **14** 51-52
  Virchow, Rudolf Ludwig Carl **15** 506-507

SCHLEIERMACHER, FRIEDRICH ERNST DANIEL (1768-1834), German theologian and philosopher **14** 11-12
  Cousin, Victor **4** 273-274
  Dilthey, Wilhelm Christian Ludwig **5** 10
  Ritschl, Albrecht Benjamin **13** 180

SCHLEMMER, OSKAR (1888-1943), German painter, sculptor, and stage designer **14** 12-13

SCHLESINGER, ARTHUR MEIER
(1888-1965), American historian **14** 13
  Commons, John Rogers **4** 185
  Handlin, Oscar **7** 121-122
  Kennedy, John Fitzgerald **8** 502-506
  Schlesinger, Arthur Meier **14** 13

SCHLESINGER, ARTHUR MEIER, JR. (born 1917), American historian and Democratic party activist **14** 13-15

Schlesinger, Bruno Walter
  see Walter, Bruno

SCHLESINGER, JAMES RODNEY (born 1929), American government official **14** 15-16

Schlesinger and Meyer Department Store (Chicago)

Sullivan, Louis Henri 15 27-28

Schleswig-Holstein (state, Germany)
  Bismarck, Otto Eduard Leopold von **2** 294-296
  Moltke, Helmuth Karl Bernard von **11** 90-91
  Palmerston, 3d Viscount **12** 81-83
  Victoria **15** 485-487

SCHLICK, FRIEDRICH ALBERT MORITZ (1882-1936), German physicist and philosopher **14** 16-17
  Carnap, Rudolf **3** 308-309

SCHLIEMANN, HEINRICH (1822-1890), German merchant and archeologist **14** 17-18
  Homer **7** 465-467

Schloss Brühl (palace, Germany)
  Cuvilliés, François **4** 359-360
  Neumann, Balthasar **11** 354-355

Schloss Wetterstein (play)
  Wedekind, Frank **16** 166-167

SCHLÜTER, ANDREAS (circa 1660-1714), German sculptor and architect **14** 18-19

Schmalkaldic War (1546-1547)
  Alba, Duke of **1** 103-104
  Charles V **3** 457-459

Schmeling, Max (born 1905), German boxer
  Louis, Joe **9** 537-538

Schmidt, Father Wilhelm (1868-1954), Austrian philologist and ethnographer
  Kluckhohn, Clyde **9** 56-57

SCHMIDT, HELMUT (born 1918), Social Democrat and chancellor of the Federal Republic of Germany (the former West Germany), 1974-82 **14** 19-21

Schmidt, Johann Caspar
  see Stirner, Max

Schmidt telescope (Mount Palomar)
  Hubble, Edwin Powell **8** 10-11

Schmidt-Rottluff, Karl (1884-1976), German painter
  Kirchner, Ernst Ludwig **9** 34-35

Schmitz, Ettore
  see Svevo, Italo

SCHMOLLER, GUSTAV FRIEDRICH VON (1838-1917), German economist **14** 21
  Bentley, Arthur F. **2** 178
  Sombart, Werner **14** 332-333

SCHNEIDERMAN, ROSE (1882-1972), labor organizer and activist for the improvement of working conditions for women **14** 22-23

Schnitzer, Eduard
  see Emin Pasha, Mehmed

SCHNITZLER, ARTHUR (1862-1931), Austrian dramatist and novelist **14** 23-24

SCHOENBERG, ARNOLD (1874-1951), Austrian composer **14** 24-26
  associates
    Mann, Thomas **10** 204-207

  influence of
    Boulez, Pierre **2** 444-445
    Bussotti, Sylvano **3** 174-175
    Cage, John **3** 211-214
    Copland, Aaron **4** 227-228
    Messiaen, Olivier **10** 528-529
    Perle, George **12** 223-224
    Sessions, Roger Huntington **14** 117-118
    Stockhausen, Karlheinz **14** 460-461
    Walton, William Turner **16** 92-93
  influenced by
    Mahler, Gustav **10** 144-145
  twelve-tone method music
    Babbitt, Milton **1** 410
    Berg, Alban **2** 186-187
    Dallapiccola, Luigi **4** 377-378
    Krenek, Ernst **9** 98-99
    Lutoslawski, Witold **10** 52-53
    Perle, George **12** 223-224
    Webern, Anton **16** 160-162

Schoenberg is Dead (obit.)
  Boulez, Pierre **2** 444-445

Scholar, The (comedy)
  Lovelace, Richard **10** 7-8

Scholar Gypsy, The (poem)
  Arnold, Matthew **1** 311-313

Scholars of the Northern Ch'i Dynasty Collating Texts (painting)
  Yen Li-pen **16** 453-454

Scholastica, St. (died 543), Italian abbess
  Benedict, Ruth Fulton **2** 154-155

Scholasticism (philosophy)
  adherents
    Abelard, Peter **1** 23-25
    Albertus Magnus **1** 115-116
    Anselm of Canterbury **1** 244-245
    Bonaventure **2** 383-384-57
    Duns Scotus, John **5** 149-150
    Eckhart, Johann **5** 200-201
    Kindi, Abu-Yusuf Yaqub ibn-Ishaq al- **9** 10-11
    Lombard, Peter **9** 490-491
    Otto of Freising **12** 30
    Suárez, Francisco **15** 8
    Thomas Aquinas **15** 183-186
  critics
    Descartes, René **4** 505-508
    Hobbes, Thomas **7** 421-423
    Melancthon, Philip **10** 466-467
    Ramus, Petrus **13** 27-28
  decline
    Rabelais, François **12** 524-526
  influence of
    Cavalcanti, Guido **3** 382
    Luther, Martin **10** 48-51
    Ortelius, Abraham **12** 8-9
    see also Aristotelianism; Averroism; Thomism

SCHOLEM, GERSHOM (1897-1982), Jewish scholar **14** 26

Schömann, Georg Friedrich (1793-1879), German classical scholar

Bosanquet, Bernard **2** 425-426

Schönbrunn Palace (Vienna)
Fischer von Erlach, Johann Bernhard **5** 459-461
Rottmayr, Johann Michael **13** 321

Schöne Melusine Overture (musical composition)
Mendelssohn, Moses **10** 488-489

Schöne Müllerin, Die (songs)
Schubert, Franz Peter **14** 35-37

Schönemann, Lili (1758-1817), German fiancée of Goethe
Goethe, Johann Wolfgang von **6** 388-391

SCHONGAUER, MARTIN (circa 1435-91), German engraver and painter **14** 26-28
Andrea del Sarto **1** 224-225
Dürer, Albrecht **5** 159-161

SCHÖNHUBER, FRANZ XAVER (born 1923), German right-wing political leader **14** 28-29

School for Scandal, The (play; Sheridan)
Sheridan, Richard Brinsley **14** 183-184
Tyler, Royall **15** 371-372

School for Widows, The (play; Chiari)
Goldoni, Carlo **6** 408-409

School of American Ballet
Kirstein, Lincoln **9** 39-41

School of Art (Vitebsk)
see College of New Art (Vitebsk)

School of Athens (fresco)
Raphael **13** 40-42

School of Paris (art)
see French art—School of Paris

Schoolboy Lyrics (poems)
Kipling, Joseph Rudyard **9** 32-33

SCHOOLCRAFT, HENRY ROWE (1793-1864), American explorer and ethnologist **14** 29
Longfellow, Henry Wadsworth **9** 499-500

Schoolmen (scholastic philosophy)
see Scholasticism

SCHOPENHAUER, ARTHUR (1788-1860), German philosopher **14** 29-31
associates
Fries, Jakob Friedrich **6** 116-117
influence of
Hardy, Thomas **7** 150-152
Laforgue, Jules **9** 160-161
Mann, Thomas **10** 204-207
Nietzsche, Friedrich **11** 390-392
Schrödinger, Erwin **14** 31-33
Svevo, Italo **15** 47-48
Wagner, Richard **16** 40-43
influenced by
Plato **12** 345-347

Schorer, Mark (1908-1977), American writer
Lewis, Harry Sinclair **9** 385-387

SCHOUTEN, WILLIAM CORNELIUS (circa 1580-1625), Dutch explorer and navigator **14** 31

Schreker, Franz (1878-1934), Austrian composer
Krenek, Ernst **9** 98-99

Schröder House (Eppenhausen, Germany)
Behrens, Peter **2** 121-122

Schröder House (Utrecht, Netherlands)
Rietveld, Gerrit Thomas **13** 169

SCHRÖDINGER, ERWIN (1887-1961), Austrian physicist **14** 31-33
Bohr, Niels Henrik David **2** 366-368
Born, Max **2** 420-421
Broglie, Louis Victor Pierre Raymond de **3** 15-17
Crick, Francis Harry Compton **4** 310
Dirac, Paul Adrien Maurice **5** 23-24
Einstein, Albert **5** 228-231
Heisenberg, Werner Karl **7** 261-263
Oppenheimer, J. Robert **11** 525-526
Pauli, Wolfgang Ernst **12** 149
Tomonaga, Sin-itiro **15** 265-266

SCHROEDER, PATRICIA SCOTT (born 1940), first U.S. congresswoman from Colorado **14** 33-35

Schroffenstein Family, The (play)
Kleist, Heinrich von **9** 52-53

Schröter, J. H. (1745-1816), German astronomer
Bessel, Friedrich Wilhelm **2** 234-235

Schubart, Christian Friedrich Daniel (1739-1791), German poet
Strauss, David Friedrich **14** 496-497

SCHUBERT, FRANZ PETER (1797-1828), Austrian composer **14** 35-37
Beethoven, Ludwig van **2** 114-117
Foster, Stephen Collins **6** 25-27
Heine, Heinrich **7** 259-260
Liszt, Franz **9** 445-447
Mendelssohn, Moses **10** 488-489
Schumann, Robert Alexander **14** 41-43

SCHULLER, GUNTHER (born 1925), American musician **14** 37-38

SCHULZ, CHARLES M. (born 1922), American cartoonist and creator of "Peanuts" **14** 38-39

SCHUMACHER, KURT (1895-1952), German socialist statesman **14** 40-41

SCHUMAN, ROBERT (1886-1963), French statesman **14** 41
Monnet, Jean **11** 109-110

Schumann, Clara Josephine (née Wieck; 1819-96), German pianist and composer
Brahms, Johannes **2** 490-492

SCHUMANN, ROBERT ALEXANDER (1810-1856), German composer and critic **14** 41-43
Brahms, Johannes **2** 490-492
Chopin, Frédéric François **4** 16-18
Dvořák, Antonin **5** 168-169
Gounod, Charles François **6** 473-474

Heine, Heinrich **7** 259-260
Liszt, Franz **9** 445-447
Mahler, Gustav **10** 144-145
Mendelssohn, Moses **10** 488-489
Schubert, Franz Peter **14** 35-37
Strauss, Richard **14** 500-501

SCHUMPETER, JOSEPH ALOIS (1883-1950), Austrian economist **14** 43-44
Marx, Karl **10** 304-308

SCHURZ, CARL (1829-1906), American soldier, statesman, and journalist **14** 44-45
Brown, Benjamin Gratz **3** 32-33
Dunning, William Archibald **5** 148-149
Eaton, Dorman Bridgman **5** 190-191
Jacobi, Abraham and Mary Putnam **8** 188-189
Pulitzer, Joseph **12** 481-482
Straus, Isidor **14** 496

SCHUSCHNIGG, KURT VON (1897-1977), Austrian statesman, chancellor of Austria 1934-38 **14** 45-46
Dollfuss, Engelbert **5** 47

SCHÜSSLER FIORENZA, ELIZABETH (born 1938), biblical scholar and theologian **14** 46-48

Schuster, Sir Arthur (1851-1934), British physicist
Rutherford, Ernest **13** 384-387

SCHÜTZ, HEINRICH (1585-1672), German composer **14** 48-49
Carissimi, Giacomo **3** 299-300
Gabrieli, Giovanni **6** 161-162
Monteverdi, Claudio Giovanni Antonio **11** 126-128

SCHUYLER, PHILIP JOHN (1733-1804), American Revolutionary War general **14** 49-50
Allen, Ethan **1** 163-164
Burr, Aaron **3** 156-159
Clinton, George **4** 113-114
Johnson, John **8** 305-306
Montgomery, Richard **11** 138-139

Schuylkill River Freed (sculpture)
Rush, William **13** 365-366

SCHWAB, CHARLES MICHAEL (1862-1939), American industrialist **14** 50-51

Schwalbe, Gustav (1844-1917), German anatomist and anthropologist
Weidenreich, Franz **16** 171-172

Schwanengesang (musical composition)
Schubert, Franz Peter **14** 35-37

SCHWANN, THEODOR (1810-1882), German biologist **14** 51-52
Virchow, Rudolf Ludwig Carl **15** 506-507

Schwärmer, Die (play)
Musil, Robert Edler Von **11** 268-269

Schwartzerd, Philip
see Melancthon, Philip

Schwarzchild, Karl (1873-1916), German
astronomer
Born, Max **2** 420-421

Schwarze Obelisk, Der (novel)
Remarque, Erich Maria **13** 91

Schwarzenberg, Prince Karl Philippe von
(1771-1820), Austrian field marshal
Blücher, Gebhard Leberecht von
2 340-341

SCHWARZKOPF, NORMAN (born 1934),
American army general **14** 52-54

SCHWEITZER, ALBERT (1875-1965), Alsat-
ian-German philosopher and medical
missionary **14** 55-56
Sarton, George **13** 490-491

SCHWENCKFELD, KASPER VON
(1489/90-1561), Silesian nobleman and
theologian **14** 56-57

SCHWIMMER, ROSIKA (1877-1948), Hungarian women's rights activist **14** 57-60

Schwind, Moritz (1804-1871), German
painter
Schubert, Franz Peter **14** 35-37

Schwinger, Julian (1918-1994), American
physicist
Tomonaga, Sin-itiro **15** 265-266

SCHWITTERS, KURT (1887-1948), German painter, collagist, typographer, and
poet and creator of MERZ-art **14** 60-61
Burri, Alberto **3** 159-160
van Doesburg, Theo **15** 421

Science
and religion
Boyle, Robert **2** 469-471
Eddy, Mary Baker **5** 202
Huxley, Thomas Henry **8** 77-79
Osler, William **12** 19-20
Weber, Max **16** 157-160
see also Scientists; and individual
disciplines
and society
Dyson, Freeman John **5** 171-173
and the arts
Cattell, James McKeen **3** 376-377
Jeans, James Hopwood **8** 235-236
Nicolson, Marjorie Hope
11 384-385
Richards, Ivor Armstrong **13** 137
history of
Celsus, Aulus Cornelius **3** 393
Duhem, Pierre Maurice Marie **5** 129
Kuhn, Thomas Samuel **9** 121-123
Sarton, George **13** 490-491
medieval
Aristotle **1** 295-296
Bacon, Roger **1** 425-427
Hasan ibn al-Haytham **7** 190-191
method
Helmont, Jan Baptista van
7 269-271
Poincaré, Jules Henri **12** 365-366
philosophy of
Bacon, Francis **1** 422-424
Bergson, Henri **2** 191-192

Broad, Charlie Dunbar **3** 12
Descartes, René **4** 505-508
Driesch, Hans Adolf Eduard **5** 105
Duhem, Pierre Maurice Marie **5** 129
Duns Scotus, John **5** 149-150
Dyson, Freeman John **5** 171-173
Hesse, Mary B. **7** 369-371
Kuhn, Thomas Samuel **9** 121-123
Mach, Ernst **10** 90-91
Nagel, Ernest **11** 291-292
Poincaré, Jules Henri **12** 365-366
Ramsey, Frank Plumpton **13** 25
Spallanzani, Lazzaro **14** 360-361
Whitehead, Alfred North
16 242-244

Science (periodical)
Bell, Alexander Graham **2** 129-131
Boas, Franz **2** 349-351
Tomonaga, Sin-itiro **15** 265-266

Science, Art, and Letters (mural)
Puvis de Chavannes, Pierre **12** 492-493

**Science and Health with a Key to the
Scriptures** (book)
Eddy, Mary Baker **5** 202

Science fiction (literature)
Asimov, Isaac **1** 338-341
Bradbury, Ray **2** 473-474
Butler, Octavia E. **3** 182-183
Donnelly, Ignatius **5** 62
Doyle, Arthur Conan **5** 91-92
Dürrenmatt, Friedrich **5** 164-165
Lewis, Clive Staples **9** 381-382
Verne, Jules **15** 467-469
Wells, Herbert George **16** 195-196

Scientists, Algerian
Fanon, Frantz **5** 379-380

Scientists, American
aeronautical engineers
see Aeronautics
anatomists
Sabin, Florence Rena **13** 402-405
Trotter, Mildred **15** 305-306
agriculturists
see Agriculturists
archeologists
Breasted, James Henry **2** 510-511
Kidder, Alfred Vincent **8** 541-542
astronauts
Armstrong, Neil Alden **1** 304-306
Bluford, Guion Stewart Jr. **2** 341-343
astronomers
Banneker, Benjamin **1** 490-491
Barnard, Edward Emerson **2** 8-9
Cannon, Annie Jump **3** 260-261
Geller, Margaret Joan **6** 256-257
Hale, George Ellery **7** 72-74
Hall, Asaph **7** 83-84
Hubble, Edwin Powell **8** 10-11
Mitchell, Maria **11** 61
Newcomb, Simon **11** 361-362
Payne-Gaposchkin, Cecilia
12 159-161
Pickering, Edward Charles **12** 298
Rittenhouse, David **13** 180-181

Sagan, Carl E. **13** 424-425
Shapley, Harlow **14** 155-156
Winthrop, John **16** 341-342
aviators
see Aeronautics; Aviators
bacteriologists
Avery, Oswald Theodore **1** 384-386
Welch, William Henry **16** 185-186
biochemists
Berg, Paul **2** 187-189
Bloch, Konrad **2** 330-332
Borlaug, Norman Ernest **2** 418-420
Brown, Rachel Fuller **3** 43-44
Chargaff, Erwin **3** 444-445
Cori, Gerty T. **4** 231-234
Elion, Gertrude B. **5** 252-254
Kendall, Edward Calvin **8** 495
Kornberg, Arthur **9** 85-87
Lipmann, Fritz **9** 435-437
Neufeld, Elizabeth F. **11** 352-353
Nirenberg, Marshall Warren
11 399-400
Northrop, John Howard **11** 430-431
Seibert, Florence B. **14** 89-90
Singer, Maxine **14** 251-252
Szent-Györgyi, Albert von **15** 62-64
Wald, George **16** 51-53
biologists
Avery, Oswald Theodore **1** 384-386
Carson, Rachel Louise **3** 337-338
Commoner, Barry **4** 183-185
Jordan, David Starr **8** 350-351
Just, Ernest **8** 392-393
Levi-Montalcini, Rita **9** 366-368
Margulis, Lynn **10** 253-254
Mintz, Beatrice **11** 49-50
Patrick, Ruth **12** 137-138
Pincus, Gregory Goodwin
12 310-312
Sager, Ruth **13** 425-426
Stevens, Nettie Maria **14** 441-442
Watson, James Dewey **16** 137-138
Wilson, Edward Osborne
16 319-320
biophysicists
Quimby, Edith H. **12** 513-514
botanists
Bartram, John **2** 40-41
Bartram, William **2** 41-42
Colden, Cadwallader **4** 145-146
Cutler, Manasseh **4** 356-357
Dobzhansky, Theodosius **5** 35-37
East, Edward Murray **5** 182-183
Gray, Asa **6** 506-507
Pound, Roscoe **12** 417-418
chemists (18th century)
Cooper, Thomas **4** 224
chemists (19th century)
Hare, Robert **7** 152-153
Silliman, Benjamin **14** 229-230
Whitney, Josiah Dwight **16** 254-255
chemists (19th-20th century)
Carver, George Washington
3 346-347
Debye, Peter Joseph William
4 447-448

Grasselli, Caesar Augustin
6 497-498
Richards, Ellen H. 13 134-136
Wiley, Harvey Washington
16 277-278
chemists (20th century)
Baekeland, Leo Hendrik 1 430-431
Boltwood, Bertram Borden
2 378-379
Calvin, Melvin 3 242-243
Carothers, Wallace Hume
3 317-318
Conant, James Bryant 4 192-193
Flory, Paul 5 492-494
Karle, Isabella 8 447-449
Langmuir, Irving 9 196-197
Lewis, Gilbert Newton 9 384-385
Libby, Willard Frank 9 397-398
Onsager, Lars 11 520-523
Patrick, Jennie R. 12 136-137
Pauling, Linus Carl 12 150-152
Prichard, Diana García 12 448-449
Richards, Theodore William
13 137-138
Seaborg, Glenn Theodore 14 74-76
Urey, Harold Clayton 15 394-396
computer scientists
Hopper, Grace 7 498-500
dentists
Morton, William Thomas Green
11 198-199
Wells, Horace 16 196
engineers
Borglum, John Gutzon de la Mothe
2 416-417
Curtiss, Glenn Hammond
4 350-351
Eads, James Buchanan 5 175-176
Fuller, Richard Buckminster
6 149-150
Goethals, George Washington
6 387-388
Judah, Theodore Dehone 8 373-374
Roebling, John Augustus
13 241-242
Roebling, Washington Augustus
13 243
Stevens, John 14 439-440
Thayer, Sylvanus 15 168-169
engineers (aeronautical)
Bluford, Guion Stewart Jr. 2 341-343
Widnall, Sheila E. 16 258-259
engineers (aerospace)
Ross, Mary G. 13 304-305
engineers (civil)
Fulton, Robert 6 151-152
King, Clarence 9 15-16
engineers (computer)
Cray, Seymour 4 301-303
Lanier, Jaron 9 198-199
Shaw, Mary 14 165-167
engineers (electrical)
Armstrong, Edwin Howard
1 302-303
Carrier, Wills 3 325-326
Kettering, Charles F. 8 524-525

Ochoa, Ellen 11 460-461
Pupin, Michael Idvorsky 12 483-484
Sprague, Frank Julian 14 385-386
Steinmetz, Charles Proteus
14 419-420
Tesla, Nikola 15 156-157
Wang, An 16 93-95
engineers (marine)
Ericsson, John 5 307-308
Fitch, John 5 467-468
Melville, George Wallace 10 472
Shreve, Henry Miller 14 207
engineers (radio)
Zworykin, Vladimir Kosma
16 539-540
entomologists
Knipling, Edward Fred 9 59-60
epidemiologists
Gayle, Helene Doris 6 244-245
Macdonald, Eleanor Josephine
10 83-84
Theiler, Max 15 169-170
ethologists
Fossey, Dian 6 23-24
geneticists
Beadle, George Wells 2 80-81
Chargaff, Erwin 3 444-445
Lederberg, Joshua 9 275-277
McClintock, Barbara 10 393-394
Morgan, Thomas Hunt 11 170-171
Muller, Hermann Joseph
11 238-239
Russell, Elizabeth Shull 13 377-379
Sager, Ruth 13 425-426
Singer, Maxine 14 251-252
Stevens, Nettie Maria 14 441-442
Sturtevant, A. H. 15 3-5
geochemists
Urey, Harold Clayton 15 394-396
geographers
Boas, Franz 2 349-351
Bowman, Isaiah 2 464-465
Davis, William Morris 4 425-426
Dunbar, William 5 143-144
Morse, Jedidiah 11 191-192
Sauer, Carl Ortwin 13 496-497
geologists
Chamberlin, Thomas Chrowder
3 415-416
Davis, William Morris 4 425-426
King, Clarence 9 15-16
Powell, John Wesley 12 425-426
Tharp, Marie 15 162-164
Whitney, Josiah Dwight 16 254-255
glaciologists
Chamberlin, Thomas Chrowder
3 415-416
horticulturists
Burbank, Luther 3 129-131
Downing, Andrew Jackson 5 90-91
ichthyologists
Jordan, David Starr 8 350-351
immunologists
Landsteiner, Karl 9 188-189
Salk, Jonas Edward 13 451-452
instrument makers

Rittenhouse, David 13 180-181
inventors (18th-19th century)
Evans, Oliver 5 338
Fitch, John 5 467-468
Franklin, Benjamin 6 60-64
Fulton, Robert 6 151-152
Hopkinson, Francis 7 496-497
Peale, Charles Willson 12 169-171
Sprague, Frank Julian 14 385-386
Stevens, John 14 439-440
Whitney, Eli 16 253-254
inventors (19th century)
Beach, Moses Yale 2 79-80
Borden, Gail 2 409
Colt, Samuel 4 172-173
Cooper, Peter 4 223-224
Deere, John 4 455
Eads, James Buchanan 5 175-176
Ericsson, John 5 307-308
Farmer, Moses Gerrish 5 385
Forten, James 6 17-18
Gatling, Richard Jordan 6 234-235
Goodyear, Charles 6 441
Hare, Robert 7 152-153
Hoe, Richard March 7 435-436
Howe, Elias 7 529-530
Johnson, Tom Loftin 8 317
McCormick, Cyrus Hall 10 400-401
Mergenthaler, Ottmar 10 516-517
Morse, Samuel Finley Breese
11 192-193
Oliver, James 11 500-501
Otis, Elisha Graves 12 24
Pullman, George Mortimer
12 482-483
Pupin, Michael Idvorsky 12 483-484
Singer, Isaac M. 14 250
inventors (19th-20th century)
Bell, Alexander Graham 2 129-131
Edison, Thomas Alva 5 206-208
Holland, John Philip 7 453-454
Morgan, Garrett A. 11 161-162
Sperry, Elmer A. 14 377-379
Tesla, Nikola 15 156-157
Westinghouse, George 16 215
inventors (20th century)
Baekeland, Leo Hendrik 1 430-431
Bush, Vannevar 3 169-171
Carlson, Chester F. 3 303-304
Carrier, Wills 3 325-326
Curtiss, Glenn Hammond
4 350-351
De Forest, Lee 4 459-460
Eastman, George 5 186
Farnsworth, Philo T. 5 386-387
Jobs, Steven 8 265-267
Kettering, Charles F. 8 524-525
Land, Edwin Herbert 9 183-184
McMurray, Bette Clair 10 429
Noyce, Robert 11 436-437
Packard, David 12 54-56
Shockley, William 14 200-202
Sikorsky, Igor 14 223-224
Wang, An 16 93-95
lepidopterists

Nabokov, Vladimir **11** 287-288
limnologists
　Patrick, Ruth **12** 137-138
marine biologists
　Colwell, Rita R. **4** 179-180
　Earle, Sylvia A. **5** 180-181
　Just, Ernest **8** 392-393
　Ray, Dixy Lee **13** 56-57
mathematicians (19th-20th century)
　Barnard, Frederick Augustus Porter
　　2 9-10
　Bowditch, Nathaniel **2** 460-461
　Hall, Asaph **7** 83-84
　Peirce, Charles Sanders **12** 187-188
　Steinmetz, Charles Proteus
　　14 419-420
mathematicians (20th century)
　Bernstein, Dorothy Lewis **2** 217
　Bush, Vannevar **3** 169-171
　Calderón, Alberto P. **3** 219-220
　Feigenbaum, Mitchell Jay **5** 404-405
　Gödel, Kurt **6** 377-379
　Granville, Evelyn Boyd **6** 494-496
　Mandelbrot, Benoit B. **10** 189-191
　Noether, Emmy **11** 414-416
　Robinson, Julia **13** 210-211
　Shannon, Claude Elwood
　　14 153-154
　Tarski, Alfred **15** 110-111
　Uhlenbeck, Karen **15** 381-382
　Von Neumann, John **16** 27-28
　Wiener, Norbert **16** 262-263
meteorologists
　Dunbar, William **5** 143-144
microbiologists
　Colwell, Rita R. **4** 179-180
　Dubos, René Jules **5** 119
　Hershey, Alfred Day **7** 343-345
　Sabin, Albert Bruce **13** 401-402
　Theiler, Max **15** 169-170
　Waksman, Selman Abraham
　　16 49-50
molecular biologists
　Delbrück, Max **4** 476-478
　Szilard, Leo **15** 64-66
naturalists
　Andrews, Roy Chapman **1** 232-233
　Audubon, John James **1** 366-367
　Burroughs, John **3** 160-161
　Muir, John **11** 234
　Silliman, Benjamin **14** 229-230
navigators
　Bowditch, Nathaniel **2** 460-461
neurophysiologists
　Lashley, Karl Spencer **9** 214-215
neuropsychologists
　Wexler, Nancy **16** 218-219
oceanographers
　Earle, Sylvia A. **5** 180-181
　Ewing, William Maurice **5** 350-351
　Maury, Matthew Fontaine
　　10 351-352
ornithologists
　Audubon, John James **1** 366-367
　Bailey, Florence Merriam **1** 443-444
　Wilson, Alexander **16** 313-314

paleobotanists
　Ward, Lester Frank **16** 113-114
paleontologists
　Eiseley, Loren Corey **5** 232-233
　Gould, Stephen Jay **6** 472-473
　Marsh, Othniel Charles **10** 275-276
　Simpson, George Gaylord
　　14 240-242
pathologists
　Andersen, Dorothy **1** 212
　Hardy, Harriet **7** 150
　Rous, Francis Peyton **13** 322-323
　Slye, Maud **14** 276-277
　Welch, William Henry **16** 185-186
　Whipple, George Hoyt **16** 224-225
pediatricians
　Gayle, Helene Doris **6** 244-245
　Spock, Benjamin **14** 383-385
　Taussig, Helen Brooke **15** 118-120
physicians (18-19th century)
　Boylston, Zabdiel **2** 471
　Morgan, John **11** 162-163
　Rush, Benjamin **13** 364-365
　Waterhouse, Benjamin **16** 131-132
physicians (19th century)
　Beaumont, William **2** 95-96
　Bird, Robert Montgomery **2** 281-282
　Blackwell, Elizabeth **2** 311-312
　Bowditch, Henry Ingersoll
　　2 459-460
　Cabot, Richard Clarke **3** 200
　Drake, Daniel **5** 93-94
　Gorgas, William Crawford
　　6 454-455
　Holmes, Oliver Wendell **7** 457-458
　Howe, Samuel Gridley **7** 537
　Long, Crawford Williamson
　　9 495-496
　Smith, James McCune **14** 293-294
　Whitman, Marcus **16** 248-249
physicians (19th-20th century)
　Baker, Sara Josephine **1** 455-456
　Biggs, Hermann Michael **2** 272-273
　Cushing, Harvey Williams
　　4 353-354
　Jacobi, Abraham and Mary Putnam
　　8 188-189
　Montezuma, Carlos **11** 129-132
　Park, William Hallock **12** 104-105
　Townsend, Francis Everitt
　　15 282-283
physicians (20th century)
　Andersen, Dorothy **1** 212
　Apgar, Virginia **1** 257-259
　Cabot, Richard Clarke **3** 200
　Chinn, May Edward **3** 525-526
　Elders, Joycelyn **5** 243-246
　Hamilton, Alice **7** 98-99
　Healy, Bernadine Patricia **7** 237-238
　Jemison, Mae C. **8** 243-244
　Kessler, David A. **8** 523-524
　Long, Irene D. **9** 497-498
　Love, Susan M. **10** 2-3
　Masters, William Howell
　　10 327-328

Mayo, William J. and Charles H.
　10 367-369
Mendenhall, Dorothy Reed
　10 491-492
Sabin, Albert Bruce **13** 401-402
Salk, Jonas Edward **13** 451-452
Williams, William Carlos
　16 308-309
physicists (18th-19th century)
　Bache, Alexander Dallas **1** 420
　Gibbs, Josiah Willard **6** 302-303
　Henry, Joseph **7** 307-308
　Rowland, Henry Augustus
　　13 330-331
physicists (19th-20th century)
　Michelson, Albert Abraham **11** 7-8
　Millikan, Robert Andrews **11** 33-35
physicists (20th century)
　Alvarez, Luis W. **1** 187-189
　Anderson, Carl David **1** 214-215
　Bardeen, John **2** 1-3
　Bethe, Hans Albrecht **2** 238-239
　Bloch, Felix **2** 328-330
　Brattain, Walter H. **2** 505-507
　Bridgman, Percy Williams **3** 5-6
　Chu, Paul Ching-Wu **4** 37-39
　Compton, Arthur Holly **4** 186-188
　Dyson, Freeman John **5** 171-173
　Elsasser, Walter Maurice **5** 277-278
　Feigenbaum, Mitchell Jay **5** 404-405
　Feynman, Richard Phillips
　　5 432-434
　Einstein, Albert **5** 228-231
　Franck, James **6** 49-52
　Gamow, George **6** 199-200
　Gell-Mann, Murray **6** 257-258
　Glashow, Sheldon Lee **6** 361-362
　Goddard, Robert Hutchings
　　6 376-377
　Goeppert-Mayer, Maria **6** 385-387
　Jackson, Shirley Ann **8** 183-184
　Karle, Isabella **8** 447-449
　Kármán, Theodore von **8** 451-452
　Kuhn, Thomas Samuel **9** 121-123
　Land, Edwin Herbert **9** 183-184
　Lawrence, Ernest Orlando
　　9 248-250
　Lee, Tsung-Dao **9** 299-300
　Moore, Charlotte E. **11** 145-146
　Noyce, Robert **11** 436-437
　Oppenheimer, J. Robert **11** 525-526
　Prichard, Diana García **12** 448-449
　Rabi, Isidor Isaac **12** 526-527
　Ramsey, Norman Foster Jr. **13** 25-27
　Ride, Sally **13** 158-160
　Shockley, William **14** 200-202
　Stern, Otto **14** 435
　Szilard, Leo **15** 64-66
　Taussig, Helen Brooke **15** 118-120
　Teller, Edward **15** 139-141
　Townes, Charles Hard **15** 281-282
　von Braun, Wernher **16** 17-18
　Wigner, Eugene Paul **16** 268-269
　Yalow, Rosalyn S. **16** 427-428
　Yang, Chen Ning **16** 437-438

Zworykin, Vladimir Kosma
16 539-540
physiologists
Erlanger, Joseph **5** 310-311
Mayer, Jean **10** 365-366
psychiatrists and psychoanalysts
Bettelheim, Bruno **2** 245-246
Erikson, Erik Homburger **5** 309-310
Horney, Karen Danielsen **7** 508-509
Sullivan, Harry Stack **15** 23-24
White, William Alanson **16** 239-240
scientific photographers
Draper, John William **5** 96-97
seismologists
Richter, Charles F. **13** 146-148
statisticians
De Bow, James Dunwoody Brownson **4** 441-442
Mayo-Smith, Richmond **10** 371-372
Ogburn, William Fielding **11** 480
Stouffer, Samuel A. **14** 482-483
Wright, Carroll Davidson **16** 396
surgeons
Carrel, Alexis **3** 322-323
DeBakey, Michael Ellis **4** 437-438
DeVries, William Castle **4** 518-519
Drew, Charles Richard **5** 100-101
Reed, Walter **13** 78
Williams, Daniel Hale **16** 302-303
virologists
Baltimore, David **1** 477-478
Enders, John Franklin **5** 285-286
Rous, Francis Peyton **13** 322-323
Salk, Jonas Edward **13** 451-452
Stanley, Wendell Meredith
14 400-401
Varmus, Harold Eliot **15** 436-437
zoologists
Hyman, Libbie Henrietta **8** 83-84
Kinsey, Alfred C. **9** 31-32
Mayr, Ernst **10** 372-374
Morgan, Thomas Hunt **11** 170-171
Peterson, Edith R. **12** 258-259
Russell, Elizabeth Shull **13** 377-379
Trotter, Mildred **15** 305-306

Scientists, Arab
alchemists
Jabir ibn Hayyan **8** 167
astronomers
Biruni, Abu Rayhan al- **2** 284-285
Bitruji, Nur al-Din Abu Ishaq al
2 296
Hasan ibn al-Haytham **7** 190-191
Khwarizmi, Muhammad ibn Musa
al- **8** 541
geographers
Biruni, Abu Rayhan al- **2** 284-285
ibn Battuta, Muhammad **8** 91-92
Idrisi, Muhammad ibn Muhammad
al- **8** 102-103
Khwarizmi, Muhammad ibn Musa
al- **8** 541
mathematicians
Biruni, Abu Rayhan al- **2** 284-285
Hasan ibn al-Haytham **7** 190-191

Khwarizmi, Muhammad ibn Musa
al- **8** 541
physicians
Avicenna **1** 386-387
ibn Tufayl, Abu Bakr Muhammad
8 96
physicists
Hasan ibn al-Haytham **7** 190-191
Scientists, Argentine
Houssay, Bernardo Alberto **7** 522-523
Scientists, Australian
Bruce, David **3** 63
Burnet, Frank Macfarlane **3** 146-147
Eccles, John Carew **5** 195-196
Florey, Howard Walter **5** 491-492
Kenny, Elizabeth **8** 509-510
Monash, John **11** 95-96
Wilkins, George Hubert **16** 281-282
Scientists, Austrian
mathematicians
Gödel, Kurt **6** 377-379
physicists
Boltzmann, Ludwig **2** 379-380
Frisch, Otto Robert **6** 119-120
Hess, Victor Francis **7** 362-363
Mach, Ernst **10** 90-91
Meitner, Lise **10** 463-466
Pauli, Wolfgang Ernst **12** 149
Schrödinger, Erwin **14** 31-33
physiologists
Pregl, Fritz **12** 436-437
psychiatrists
Adler, Alfred **1** 61-63
zoologists
Frisch, Karl von **6** 117-118
Scientists, Belgian
de Vries, Hugo **4** 516-518
Lemaître, Abbè Georges Édouard
9 315-316
Quételet, Lambert Adolphe Jacques
12 510-511
Vesalius, Andreas **15** 473-475
Scientists, Brazilian
Andrada e Silva, José Bonifácio de
1 221-222
Cruz, Oswaldo Gonçalves **4** 328-329
Santos-Dumont, Alberto **13** 477-478
Scientists, Canadian
Avery, Oswald Theodore **1** 384-386
Banting, Frederick Grant **1** 493-494
Best, Charles Herbert **2** 236-237
Bethune, Henry Norman **2** 240-241
Fleming, Sandford **5** 485-486
Herzberg, Gerhard **7** 349-350
Jolliet, Louis **8** 328-329
Logan, William Edmond **9** 488-489
Osler, William **12** 19-20
Penfield, Wilder Graves **12** 198-200
Polanyi, John Charles **12** 370-372
Seton, Ernest Thompson **14** 119-120
Thompson, David **15** 194-195
Traill, Catharine Parr **15** 291
Scientists, Chinese
Chu, Paul Ching-Wu **4** 37-39

Ssu-ma Ch'ien **14** 388-389
Wei Yüan **16** 180-181
Scientists, Colombian
Mutis, José Celestino **11** 278-279
Scientists, Cuban
Finlay, Carlos Juan **5** 450
Grau San Martin, Ramón **6** 499-500
Scientists, Czech
Mendel, Johann Gregor **10** 483-486
Scientists, Danish
Bohr, Niels Henrik David **2** 366-368
Brahe, Tycho **2** 489-490
Dam, Carl Peter Henrik **4** 382-383
Krogh, Schack August Steenberg **9** 106
Oersted, Hans Christian **11** 476-478
Steno, Nicolaus **14** 425-426
Scientists, Dutch
astronomers
Huygens, Christiaan **8** 79-81
Kapteyn, Jacobus Cornelis
8 436-437
Oort, Jan Hendrik **11** 523-524
biologists
Eijkman, Christian **5** 228
botanists
Boerhaave, Hermann **2** 358-359
Vries, Hugo de **16** 33-36
chemists
Boerhaave, Hermann **2** 358-359
Ingenhousz, Jan **8** 119-120
Van't Hoff, Jacobus Hendricus
15 431-432
engineers
Ingenhousz, Jan **8** 119-120
geneticists
Vries, Hugo de **16** 33-36
geodesists
Meinesz, Felix Andries Vening
10 461
mathematicians
Huygens, Christiaan **8** 79-81
naturalists
Leeuwenhoek, Anton van **9** 300-301
Swammerdam, Jan **15** 48-49
physicians
Boerhaave, Hermann **2** 358-359
Eijkman, Christian **5** 228
Ingenhousz, Jan **8** 119-120
physicists
Huygens, Christiaan **8** 79-81
Kamerlingh Onnes, Heike
8 418-420
Lorentz, Hendrik Antoon **9** 515-516
van der Waals, Johannes Diderik
15 417-418
Scientists, Egyptian
Imhotep **8** 116-117
Scientists, English
anatomists
Keith, Arthur **8** 475-476
archaeologists
Leakey, Mary Douglas **9** 263-264
astronomers
Adams, John Couch **1** 51-52

Bell Burnell, Susan Jocelyn
  2 133-134
Bradley, James **2** 482-483
Eddington, Arthur Stanley **5** 201-202
Flamsteed, John **5** 477-478
Halley, Edmund **7** 88-89
Herschel, John Frederick William
  7 340-341
Herschel, William **7** 341-343
Huggins, William **8** 14-15
Jeffreys, Harold **8** 241-242
Lovell, Alfred Charles Bernard
  10 8-9
biochemists
  Chain, Ernst Boris **3** 407-408
  Franklin, Rosalind Elsie **6** 67-68
  Hopkins, Frederick Gowland
    7 491-492
  Krebs, Hans Adolf **9** 95-97
  Perutz, Max **12** 246-248
  Sanger, Frederick **13** 466-467
biologists
  Bateson, William **2** 55-57
  Crick, Francis Harry Crompton
    4 310
  Galton, Francis **6** 193-194
  Haldane, John Burdon Sanderson
    7 70-71
  Huxley, Julian **8** 75-77
  Huxley, Thomas Henry **8** 77-79
  Spencer, Herbert **14** 369-370
botanists
  Banks, Joseph **1** 489-490
  Ray, John **13** 57-59
  Stopes, Marie **14** 476-478
cartographers
  Matthew Paris **10** 341-342
chemists (17th-18th century)
  Black, Joseph **2** 303
  Boyle, Robert **2** 469-471
  Cavendish, Henry **3** 383-384
  Priestley, Joseph **12** 452-453
chemists (19th century)
  Couper, Archibald Scott **4** 269-270
  Crookes, William **4** 323-324
  Dalton, John **4** 378-379
  Davy, Humphry **4** 426-427
  Faraday, Michael **5** 380
  Ramsay, William **13** 21-22
chemists (20th century)
  Aston, Francis William **1** 350-351
  Crookes, William **4** 323-324
  Hinshelwood, Cyril Norman
    7 405-406
  Hodgkin, Dorothy Crowfoot
    7 432-434
  Kendrew, John C. **8** 495-496
  Soddy, Frederick **14** 321-323
  Todd, Alexander **15** 251-253
engineers
  Newcomen, Thomas **11** 362
  Spencer, Herbert **14** 369-370
  Watt, James **16** 141-143
  Whittle, Frank **16** 257-258
engineers (civil)
  Brunel, Isambard Kingdom **3** 69-70

Smeaton, John **14** 280-281
engineers (computer)
  Hounsfield, Godfrey **7** 517-519
engineers (electrical)
  Hounsfield, Godfrey **7** 517-519
  Parsons, Charles Algernon
    12 120-121
  Watson-Watt, Robert Alexander
    16 140-141
engineers (railway)
  Stephenson, George and Robert
    14 432-433
geneticists
  Bateson, William **2** 55-57
geographers
  Hakluyt, Richard **7** 70
geologists
  Fuchs, Vivian **6** 140
  Holmes, Arthur **7** 455-456
  Murchison, Roderick Impey
    11 255-256
  Sedgwick, Adam **14** 82-83
geophysicists
  Chapman, Sydney **3** 441
  Jeffreys, Harold **8** 241-242
hydrographers
  Flinders, Matthew **5** 490
instrument makers
  Watt, James **16** 141-143
inventors
  Arkwright, Richard **1** 298
  Babbage, Charles **1** 407-408
  Bessemer, Henry **2** 235-236
  Davis, John **4** 419
  Davy, Humphry **4** 426-427
  Hounsfield, Godfrey **7** 517-519
  Maxim, Hiram Stevens **10** 355-356
  Newcomen, Thomas **11** 362
  Watt, James **16** 141-143
  Whittle, Frank **16** 257-258
mathematicians
  Babbage, Charles **1** 407-408
  Boole, George **2** 396-397
  Carroll, Lewis **3** 332-333
  Hawking, Stephen William
    7 206-208
  Jeffreys, Harold **8** 241-242
  Newton, Isaac **11** 369-372
  Penrose, Roger **12** 204-205
  Ramsey, Frank Plumpton **13** 25
  Recorde, Robert **13** 68-69
  Russell, Bertrand Arthur William
    13 373-374
  Taylor, Brook **15** 121-122
  Turing, Alan Mathison **15** 349-350
  Whitehead, Alfred North
    16 242-244
meteorologists
  Galton, Francis **6** 193-194
naturalists
  Banks, Joseph **1** 489-490
  Bates, Henry Walter **2** 53-54
  Darwin, Charles Robert **4** 397-399
  Huxley, Thomas Henry **8** 77-79
  Johnston, Henry Hamilton
    8 322-323

Ray, John **13** 57-59
Wallace, Alfred Russel **16** 69-70
navigators
  Baffin, William **1** 435-436
neurophysiologists
  Adrian, Edgar Douglas **1** 67-69
  Dale, Henry Hallett **4** 371-373
physicians and surgeons
  Addison, Thomas **1** 58-59
  Bright, Richard **3** 7-8
  Browne, Thomas **3** 49-50
  Garrett (Anderson), Elizabeth
    6 222-225
  Gilbert, William **6** 313-314
  Hartley, David **7** 185
  Harvey, William **7** 189-190
  Jenner, Edward **8** 245-246
  Lister, Joseph **9** 444-445
  Sydenham, Thomas **15** 59-60
physicists (16th-18th century)
  Boyle, Robert **2** 469-471
  Gilbert, William **6** 313-314
  Hooke, Robert **7** 475
  Newton, Isaac **11** 369-372
physicists (18th-19th century)
  Cavendish, Henry **3** 383-384
  Faraday, Michael **5** 380
  Joule, James Prescott **8** 363-364
  Rumford **13** 360-362
  Young, Thomas **16** 475-476
physicists (19th-20th century)
  Bragg, William Henry **2** 488-489
  Crookes, William **4** 323-324
  Rayleigh, 3d Baron **13** 62
  Rutherford, Ernest **13** 384-387
  Thomson, Joseph John **15** 200-201
physicists (20th century)
  Appleton, Edward Victor **1** 265-266
  Aston, Francis William **1** 350-351
  Blackett, Patrick M.S. **2** 306-307
  Cockcroft, John Douglas **4** 131-132
  Dirac, Paul Adrien Maurice **5** 23-24
  Dyson, Freeman John **5** 171-173
  Frisch, Otto Robert **6** 119-120
  Gabor, Dennis **6** 159-160
  Hawking, Stephen William
    7 206-208
  Jeans, James Hopwood **8** 235-236
  Penrose, Roger **12** 204-205
  Snow, Charles Percy **14** 311-312
  Soddy, Frederick **14** 321-323
  Thomson, George Paget **15** 198-199
  Watson-Watt, Robert Alexander
    16 140-141
physiologists
  Hales, Stephen **7** 75
  Hill, Archibald Vivian **7** 385-386
  Hodgkin, Alan Lloyd **7** 431-432
  Sherrington, Charles Scott
    14 187-189
statisticians
  Fisher, Ronald Aylmer **5** 463-464
zoologists
  Medawar, Peter Brian **10** 444-445
  Owen, Richard **12** 39
  Ray, John **13** 57-59

Tinbergen, Nikolaas **15** 229-230

Scientists, Estonian
Baer, Karl Ernst von **1** 431-432

Scientists, Flemish
Helmont, Jan Baptista van **7** 269-271
Mercator, Gerhardus **10** 511-512
Ortelius, Abraham **12** 8-9

Scientists, French
anatomists
Bichat, Marie François Xavier
2 263-264
archeologists
Breuil, Henri Edouard Prosper
2 521-522
astronomers
Leverrier, Urbain Jean Joseph
9 361-362
Nicholas of Oresme **11** 380
biochemists
Baulieu, Étienne-Émile **2** 63-66
biologists
Cuvier, Georges Léopold **4** 357-359
Pasteur, Louis **12** 125-127
chemists
Berthollet, Claude Louis **2** 229-230
Duhem, Pierre Maurice Marie **5** 129
Dumas, Jean Baptiste André
5 138-139
Gay-Lussac, Joseph Louis **6** 245-246
Joliot-Curie, Irène **8** 325-327
Lavoisier, Antoine Laurent
9 241-244
Pasteur, Louis **12** 125-127
Sabatier, Paul **13** 398-399
engineers
Bunau-Varilla, Philippe Jean
3 120-121
Carnot, Lazare Nicolas Marguerite
3 313-314
Citroën, André-Gustave **4** 66-68
Eiffel, Alexandre Gustave **5** 227-228
Peregrinus, Petrus **12** 208
Perrault, Claude **12** 232-233
geneticists
Lwoff, André **10** 58-59
Monod, Jacques **11** 110-111
geographers
Ailly, Pierre d' **1** 94
Champlain, Samuel de **3** 419-421
Vidal de la Blache, Paul **15** 490
inventors
Braille, Louis **2** 492-493
Citroën, André-Gustave **4** 66-68
Cousteau, Jacques-Yves **4** 276-277
Lumière Brothers, The **10** 41-43
Montgolfier, Joseph and Jacques
Michel Étienne **11** 133-134
mathematicians
Alembert, Jean le Rond d'
1 127-128
Cauchy, Augustin Louis **3** 378-380
Demoivre, Abraham **4** 494-495
Descartes, René **4** 505-508
Fermat, Pierre de **5** 421-422
Lagrange, Joseph Louis **9** 164-166

Laplace, Marquis de **9** 202-204
Levi ben Gershon **9** 363-364
Mandelbrot, Benoit B. **10** 189-191
Pascal, Blaise **12** 122-124
Poincaré, Jules Henri **12** 365-366
naturalists
Buffon, Comte de **3** 109-111
Lamarck, Chevalier de **9** 171-173
navigators
Cartier, Jacques **3** 343-344
paleontologists
Teilhard de Chardin, Marie Joseph
Pierre **15** 134-136
pathologists
Bichat, Marie François Xavier
2 263-264
physicians
Baulieu, Étienne-Émile **2** 63-66
Fernel, Jean François **5** 425-426
La Mettrie, Julien Offray de
9 179-180
Louis, Pierre Charles Alexandre
9 540
Nostradamus **11** 432-434
Pinel, Philippe **12** 313-314
physicists (18th century)
Alembert, Jean le Rond d'
1 127-128
Coulomb, Charles Augustin de
4 266-267
physicists (19th century)
Ampère, André Marie **1** 205-206
Carnot, Nicolas Léonard Sadi **3** 315
Curie, Marie Sklodowska **4** 339-341
Curie, Pierre **4** 341-344
Duhem, Pierre Maurice Marie **5** 129
Fizeau, Hippolyte Armand Louis
5 475
Foucault, Jean Bernard Léon
6 28-29
Fourier, Jean Baptiste Joseph **6** 32-33
Fresnel, Augustin Jean **6** 102-103
Gay-Lussac, Joseph Louis **6** 245-246
physicists (20th century)
Becquerel, Antoine Henri **2** 108-109
Broglie, Louis Victor Pierre Ray-
mond de **3** 15-17
Curie, Marie Sklodowska **4** 339-341
de Broglie, Louis **4** 442-444
Joliot-Curie, Irène **8** 325-327
Joliot-Curie, Jean Frédéric
8 327-328
Perrin, Jean Baptiste **12** 233-236
physiologists
Bernard, Claude **2** 208-210
Bichat, Marie François Xavier
2 263-264
Richet, Charles Robert **13** 144-145
psychiatrists
Charcot, Jean Martin **3** 442
surgeons
Carrel, Alexis **3** 322-323
Guy de Chauliac **7** 54
Paré, Ambroise **12** 94-95
virologists
Montagnier, Luc **11** 114-116

zoologists
Cuvier, Georges Léopold **4** 357-359

Scientists, Gambian
Jawara, Dauda Kairaba **8** 227-228

Scientists, German
anatomists
Müller, Johannes Peter **11** 239-240
Weidenreich, Franz **16** 171-172
astronomers
Bessel, Friedrich Wilhelm **2** 234-235
Gauss, Karl Friedrich **6** 240-242
Kepler, Johannes **8** 514-516
Regiomontanus **13** 81-82
bacteriologists
Behring, Emil Adolph von
2 122-123
Domagk, Gerhard Johannes Paul
5 48-50
Ehrlich, Paul **5** 225-226
Koch, Heinrich Hermann Robert
9 69-70
biochemists
Chain, Ernst Boris **3** 407-408
Krebs, Hans Adolf **9** 95-97
Meyerhof, Otto Fritz **10** 537-539
Warburg, Otto **16** 109-111
biologists
Driesch, Hans Adolf Eduard **5** 105
Haeckel, Ernst Heinrich Philipp
August **7** 61-62
Herzberg, Gerhard **7** 349-350
Schwann, Theodor **14** 51-52
Weismann, August Freidrich
Leopold **16** 178-180
cartographers
Waldseemüller, Martin **16** 56
chemists
Baeyer, Johann Friedrich Adolf von
1 432
Bunsen, Robert Wilhelm **3** 124-125
Diels, Otto Paul Hermann **5** 5-6
Fischer, Emil **5** 456-457
Fischer, Hans **5** 457-459
Haber, Fritz **7** 56-58
Hahn, Otto **7** 64-65
Hofmann, August Wilhelm von
7 441-442
Kekulé, Friedrich August **8** 477-478
Liebig, Justus von **9** 403-404
Nernst, Walther **11** 340-342
Stahl, Georg Ernst **14** 392-393
Willstätter, Richard **16** 310-312
embryologists
Spemann, Hans **14** 368-369
engineers
Daimler, Gottlieb **4** 368
Diesel, Rudolf **5** 7
geographers
Ratzel, Friedrich **13** 50-51
Ritter, Karl **13** 181-182
Waldseemüller, Martin **16** 56
geologists
Werner, Abraham Gottlob
16 205-207
geophysicists

Wegener, Alfred Lothar **16** 170-171
inventors
  Benz, Carl **2** 182-183
  Braun, Ferdinand **2** 508-509
  Gutenberg, Johann **7** 48-49
  Nernst, Walther **11** 340-342
mathematicians
  Cantor, Georg Ferdinand Ludwig
    Philipp **3** 265-266
  Frege, Gottlob **6** 93-94
  Gauss, Karl Friedrich **6** 240-242
  Leibniz, Gottfried Wilhelm von
    9 307-310
  Regiomontanus **13** 81-82
  Riemann, Georg Friedrich Bernard
    13 164-165
meteorologists
  Wegener, Alfred Lothar **16** 170-171
mineralogists
  Agricola, Georgius **1** 86-87
  Werner, Abraham Gottlob
    16 205-207
naturalists
  Albertus Magnus **1** 115-116
  Humboldt, Friedrich Heinrich
    Alexander von **8** 30-31
  Werner, Abraham Gottlob
    16 205-207
pathologists
  Domagk, Gerhard Johannes Paul
    5 48-50
  Virchow, Rudolf Ludwig Carl
    15 506-507
physicians
  Behring, Emil Adolph von
    2 122-123
  Benn, Gottfried **2** 164
  Koch, Heinrich Hermann Robert
    9 69-70
  Mengele, Josef **10** 502-503
  Mesmer, Franz Anton **10** 526-527
  Schweitzer, Albert **14** 55-56
physicists (17th-18th century)
  Fahrenheit, Gabriel Daniel **5** 366
  Guericke, Otto Von **7** 27-28
physicists (19th century)
  Clausius, Rudolf Julius Emanuel
    4 92-94
  Fraunhofer, Joseph von **6** 75-76
  Helmholtz, Hermann Ludwig Ferdi-
    nand von **7** 268-269
  Hertz, Heinrich Rudolf **7** 346-347
  Kirchhoff, Gustav Robert **9** 33-34
  Ohm, Georg Simon **11** 486-487
physicists (19th-20th century)
  Ruska, Ernst August Friedrich
    13 370-371
physicists (19th-20th centuries)
  Braun, Ferdinand **2** 508-509
  von Laue, Max **16** 23-24
physicists (20th century)
  Born, Max **2** 420-421
  Bothe, Walther **2** 438-439
  Geiger, Hans **6** 251-253
  Heisenberg, Werner Karl **7** 261-263
  Mössbauer, Rudolf **11** 208-209

Röntgen, Wilhelm Conrad
    13 273-275
Schlick, Friedrich Albert Moritz
    14 16-17
von Braun, Wernher **16** 17-18
physiologists
  Du Bois-Reymond, Emil **5** 118-119
  Helmholtz, Hermann Ludwig Ferdi-
    nand von **7** 268-269
  Loewi, Otto **9** 486-487
  Ludwig, Karl Friedrich Wilhelm
    10 31
  Müller, Johannes Peter **11** 239-240
psychiatrists
  Jaspers, Karl **8** 225-226

Scientists, Greek
anatomists
  Erasistratus **5** 297-298
astronomers
  Anaximander **1** 209-210
  Aristarchus of Samos **1** 290-291
  Eratosthenes of Cyrene **5** 301-302
  Eudoxus of Cnidus **5** 329-330
  Heraclides of Pontus **7** 319-320
  Hipparchus **7** 407-408
  Ptolemy, Claudius **12** 473-474
geographers
  Eratosthenes of Cyrene **5** 301-302
  Ptolemy, Claudius **12** 473-474
  Strabo **14** 485-486
inventors
  Heron of Alexandria **7** 334-335
mathematicians
  Apollonius of Perga **1** 261-262
  Archimedes **1** 277-280
  Eratosthenes of Cyrene **5** 301-302
  Euclid **5** 327-329
  Eudoxus of Cnidus **5** 329-330
  Heron of Alexandria **7** 334-335
  Hypatia of Alexandria **8** 85
  Ptolemy, Claudius **12** 473-474
  Pythagoras **12** 498-499
natural philosophers
  Anaxagoras **1** 208-209
  Anaximander **1** 209-210
  Anaximenes **1** 210
  Aristotle **1** 295-296
  Democritus **4** 493-494
  Empedocles **5** 282
  Thales **15** 161
physicians
  Erasistratus **5** 297-298
  Eudoxus of Cnidus **5** 329-330
  Galen **6** 178-180
  Hippocrates **7** 408-410

Scientists, Honduran
Suazo Córdova, Roberto **15** 8-10

Scientists, Hungarian
Gabor, Dennis **6** 159-160
Hevesy, George Charles de **7** 371
Polanyi, Michael **12** 372-373
Szent-Györgyi, Albert von **15** 62-64
Szilard, Leo **15** 64-66
Teller, Edward **15** 139-141
Von Neumann, John **16** 27-28

Wigner, Eugene Paul **16** 268-269

Scientists, Indian
Bhabha, Homi Jehangir **2** 253-254
Bose, Jagadis Chandra **2** 429-430
Khorana, Har Gobind **8** 537-538
Raman, Chandrasekhar Venkata
    13 13-14
Ramanujan Aiyangar, Srinivasa
    13 14-15

Scientists, Irish
Hamilton, William Rowan **7** 99-100
Lonsdale, Kathleen **9** 501-502
Tyndall, John **15** 374
Walton, Ernest **16** 88-90

Scientists, Italian
anatomists
  Leonardo da Vinci **9** 337-340
  Luzzi, Mondino de' **10** 58
  Malpighi, Marcello **10** 176-178
  Morgagni, Giovanni Battista
    11 158-159
astronomers
  Cardano, Geronimo **3** 285-286
  Galileo Galilei **6** 180-183
biologists
  Levi-Montalcini, Rita **9** 366-368
  Spallanzani, Lazzaro **14** 360-361
chemists
  Avogadro, Lorenzo Romano
    Amedeo Carlo **1** 388-389
engineers
  Biringuccio, Vannoccio **2** 283
  Leonardo da Vinci **9** 337-340
  Sangallo family **13** 464-466
  Sanmicheli, Michele **13** 469-470
inventors
  Leonardo da Vinci **9** 337-340
  Marconi, Guglielmo **10** 239-240
  Volta, Alessandro **16** 12-14
mathematicians
  Cardano, Geronimo **3** 285-286
  Fibonacci, Leonardo **5** 434-435
  Tartaglia, Niccolo **15** 111-112
  Torricelli, Evangelista **15** 268-269
metallurgists
  Biringuccio, Vannoccio **2** 283
naturalists
  Porta, Giambattista della
    12 403-404
  Spallanzani, Lazzaro **14** 360-361
physicians
  Cardano, Geronimo **3** 285-286
  Malpighi, Marcello **10** 176-178
  Montessori, Maria **11** 125-126
  Sanctorius **13** 459
physicists
  Avogadro, Lorenzo Romano
    Amedeo Carlo **1** 388-389
  Fermi, Enrico **5** 422-424
  Galileo Galilei **6** 180-183
  Torricelli, Evangelista **15** 268-269
  Volta, Alessandro **16** 12-14
physiologists
  Galvani, Luigi **6** 194-195
  Sanctorius **13** 459

Scientists, Japanese
Hirohito **7** 410-412
Tomonaga, Sin-itiro **15** 265-266
Yukawa, Hideki **16** 481-482

Scientists, Kenyan
anthropologists
Leakey, Richard Erskine Frere
9 264-265

Scientists, New Zealander
physicians
King, Frederic Truby **9** 18-19

Scientists, Norwegian
Nansen, Fridtjof **11** 304-305

Scientists, Persian
Omar Khayyam **11** 510-511
Razi **13** 63-64

Scientists, Peruvian
Unánue, José Hipólito **15** 387-388

Scientists, Polish
Copernicus, Nicolaus **4** 226-227
Sabin, Albert Bruce **13** 401-402

Scientists, Portuguese
Cabral, Pedro Álvares **3** 203-204

Scientists, Roman
Celsus, Aulus Cornelius **3** 393
Frontinus, Sextus Julius **6** 130

Scientists, Russian
aeronautical engineers
Sikorsky, Igor **14** 223-224
Tupolev, Andrei Nikolaevich
15 341-342
see also Aeronautics
agronomists
Lysenko, Trofim Denisovich **10** 71
see also Agriculturists
astronomers
Struve, Friedrich Georg Wilhelm von
14 513
bacteriologists
Metchnikoff, Élie **10** 532-533
botanists
Dobzhansky, Theodosius **5** 35-37
Vavilov, Nikolai Ivanovich
15 447-448
chemists
Borodin, Aleksandr Profirevich
2 422-423
Lomonosov, Mikhail Vasilevich
9 494
Mendeleev, Dmitrii Ivanovich
10 486-488
Semenov, Nikolai Nikolaevich
14 101
geneticists
Vavilov, Nikolai Ivanovich
15 447-448
geodesists
Struve, Friedrich Georg Wilhelm von
14 513
mathematicians
Lobachevskii, Nikolai Ivanovich
9 472-474
physicians

Borodin, Aleksandr Profirevich
2 422-423
Chekhov, Anton Pavlovich
3 494-497
physicists
Cherenkov, Pavel Alekseevich
3 502-503
Kapitsa, Pyotr Leonidovich
8 433-435
Landau, Lev Davidovich **9** 184-185
Lomonosov, Mikhail Vasilevich
9 494
Sakharov, Andrei **13** 439-441
Semenov, Nikolai Nikolaevich
14 101
Tsiolkovsky, Konstantin Eduardovich
15 326-328
physiologists
Metchnikoff, Élie **10** 532-533
Pavlov, Ivan Petrovich **12** 155-157

Scientists, Scottish
anatomists
Hunter, William **8** 48-49
bacteriologists
Fleming, Alexander **5** 483-485
biologists
Geddes, Patrick **6** 246-247
engineers
Nasmyth, James **11** 316-317
geologists
Hutton, James **8** 73-74
Lyell, Charles **10** 62-63
inventors
Nasmyth, James **11** 316-317
mathematicians
Napier, John **11** 306
naturalists
Baikie, William Balfour **1** 440
Hutton, James **8** 73-74
nutritionists
Orr, John Boyd **12** 4-5
physicians
Baikie, William Balfour **1** 440
Hunter, William **8** 48-49
Livingstone, David **9** 463-465
physicists
Kelvin of Largs **8** 488-489
Maxwell, James Clerk **10** 361-364
Wilson, Charles Thomson Rees
16 317-318

Scientists, Sierra Leonean
Margai, Milton Augustus Striery
10 248-249

Scientists, South African
surgeons
Barnard, Christiaan N. **2** 7-8

Scientists, Spanish
Averroës **1** 382-383
Azara, Félix de **1** 397-398
Mayor Zaragosa, Federico **10** 369-371
Mutis, José Celestino **11** 278-279
Ochoa, Severo **11** 461-464

Scientists, Swedish
astronomers
Celsius, Anders **3** 392

chemists
Arrhenius, Svante August **1** 318-320
Berzelius, Jöns Jacob **2** 231-233
Nobel, Alfred Bernhard **11** 410-411
Scheele, Karl Wilhelm **13** 525-526
Theorell, Axel Hugo Theodor
15 176-177
Tiselius, Arne Wilhelm Kaurin
15 240-241
engineers
Andrée, Salomon August **1** 226
Swedenborg, Emanuel **15** 49-50
mineralogists
Nordenskjöld, Nils Adolf Erik
11 421-422
naturalists
Linnaeus, Carl **9** 427-429
physicists
Arrhenius, Svante August **1** 318-320
Swedenborg, Emanuel **15** 49-50

Scientists, Swiss
biologists
Agassiz, Jean Louis Rodolphe
1 76-78
chemists
Müller, Paul Hermann **11** 241-242
Paracelsus, Philippus Aureolus
12 91-93
Reichstein, Tadeus **13** 85-87
geologists
Agassiz, Jean Louis Rodolphe
1 76-78
mathematicians
Bernoulli, Daniel **2** 216
Euler, Leonard **5** 331-332
naturalists
Agassiz, Jean Louis Rodolphe
1 76-78
Gesner, Konrad von **6** 287
neurophysiologists
Hess, Walter Rudolf **7** 365
physicians
Haller, Albrecht Von **7** 87-88
Paracelsus, Philippus Aureolus
12 91-93
physicists
Bernoulli, Daniel **2** 216
Müller, Karl Alexander **11** 240-241
Piccard, Auguste **12** 297-298
psychiatrists
Bleuler, Eugen **2** 325
Jung, Carl Gustav **8** 388-389

Scipio Aemilianus
see Scipio Africanus Minor

**SCIPIO AFRICANUS MAJOR, PUBLIUS
CORNELIUS** (236-184/183 B.C.), Roman
general **14** 61-62
Cato, Marcus Porcius the Elder **3** 375
Ennius, Quintus **5** 289
Hannibal Barca **7** 128-130
Petrarch **12** 259-261

**SCIPIO AFRICANUS MINOR, PUBLIUS
CORNELIUS AEMILIANUS** (185/184-129
B.C.), Roman general **14** 62-63

Gracchus, Tiberius and Gaius Sempro-
nius **6** 479-480
Marius, Gaius **10** 264-265
Polybios **12** 384-385

Scipio Nasica (died circa 132 B.C.), Roman
politician
Gracchus, Tiberius and Gaius Sempronius **6** 479-480

Scipio the Elder, Publius Cornelius
see Scipio Africanus Major

Scirians (German tribe)
Odoacer **11** 473

SCLC
see Southern Christian Leadership Conference

Scoop (novel)
Waugh, Evelyn Arthur St. John
16 145-147

Scopes trial (1925)
Bryan, William Jennings **3** 80-82
Darrow, Clarence Seward **4** 396-397
Frankfurter, Felix **6** 57
Mencken, Henry Louis **10** 481-483

SCORSESE, MARTIN (born 1942), American filmmaker and screenwriter **14** 63-65

Scotchman's Return and Other Essays
(essays)
MacLennan, Hugh **10** 110-111

Scotism (philosophy)
Duns Scotus, John **5** 149-150

Scotland (country, United Kingdom)
early history (to 1306)
Columba **4** 175-176
David I **4** 407
Domitian **5** 52-53
Macbeth **10** 81
Malcolm III **10** 164-165
Margaret of Scotland **10** 252-253
Wallace, William **16** 75-76
The Bruces (1306-1371)
Douglas, James **5** 78
Edward I **5** 208-210
Edward II **5** 210
Edward III **5** 211-212
Philip VI **12** 277-278
Robert I **13** 192-194
The Stuarts (1371-1406)
Henry IV **7** 292-293
John of Gaunt **8** 282-283
Robert II **13** 194
Robert III **13** 194-195
The Stuarts (1406-1603)
Elizabeth I **5** 263-266
Henry VII **7** 300-302
Henry VIII **7** 302-305, 206
James I **8** 204-206
James I **8** 206-207
James III **8** 208-209
Knox, John **9** 65-66
Lyndsay, David **10** 66-67
Mary, I **10** 308-309
union with England (1603-1707)
Anne **1** 241-242

Godolphin, Sidney **6** 380-381
James I **8** 204-206
Monck, George **11** 96-97
Vane, Henry **15** 425-426
see also Civil War, English-Puritan
Revolutions; Glorious Revolutions;
Great Britain
see also Scottish literature

Scotland, Church of
Baillie, D. (Donald) M. (Macpherson)
1 445
Baillie, John **1** 445-447
Chalmers, Thomas **3** 408-409
Lyndsay, David **10** 66-67
McCosh, James **10** 402-403

Scots Musical Museum, The (anthology; J.
Johnson)
Burns, Robert **3** 155-156

Scots rebellion (1679)
Monmouth and Buccleugh, Duke of
11 108-109

Scots Wha Hae Wi' Wallace Bled (song)
Burns, Robert **3** 155-156

Scott, Coretta
see King, Coretta Scott

Scott, David (born 1935), American astronaut
Armstrong, Neil Alden **1** 304-306

SCOTT, DRED (1795-1858), African American revolutionary **14** 65-66
see also Dred Scott decision

SCOTT, FRANCIS REGINALD (1899-1985),
Canadian poet, political activist, and constitutional theorist **14** 66-67

Scott, James
see Monmouth and Buccleugh, Duke of

Scott, John Morin (1730?-1784), American
politician and Revolutionary officer
Clinton, George **4** 113-114

SCOTT, ROBERT FALCON (1868-1912),
English naval officer and polar explorer
14 67-68
Amundsen, Roald **1** 206-207
Mawson, Douglas **10** 354-355
Shackleton, Ernest Henry **14** 132-133

SCOTT, SIR WALTER (1771-1832), Scottish
novelist and poet **14** 68-70
friends
Edgeworth, Maria **5** 205-206
influence of
Hugo, Victor Marie **8** 22-25
Manzoni, Alessandro **10** 222-224
Morris, William **11** 187-188
Parkman, Francis **12** 113-115
Stowe, Harriet Elizabeth Beecher
14 484-485
Tennyson, Alfred **15** 144-146
Tieck, Ludwig **15** 218-219
influenced by
Lewis, Matthew Gregory **9** 390-391
Stewart, Dugald **14** 449
sources
Douglas, James **5** 78

Scott, Thomas (died 1869), English government agent in Canada
Riel, Louis **13** 163-164

SCOTT, WINFIELD (1786-1866), American
general **14** 70-71
Civil War
Welles, Gideon **16** 188-190
Mexican War
Beauregard, Pierre Gustave Toutant
2 96-97
Gorgas, Josiah **6** 453-454
Grant, Ulysses Simpson **6** 492-494
Johnston, Joseph Eggleston **8** 323
Lee, Robert Edward **9** 292-294
Marcy, William Learned **10** 247-248
Perry, Matthew Calbraith
12 237-239
Pierce, Franklin **12** 300-301
Polk, James Knox **12** 374-376
Taylor, Zachary **15** 128-130
Trist, Nicholas Philip **15** 298-299
opponents
Black Hawk **2** 308
Ross, John **13** 303-304
Webster, Daniel **16** 162-164
supporters
Curtin, Andrew Gregg **4** 347-348
Lawrence, Abbott **9** 246

Scott v. Sanford
see Dred Scott decision

Scottish architecture
Mackintosh, Charles Rennie
10 107-108

Scottish literature
Douglas, Gavin **5** 77-78
Dunbar, William **5** 142-143
James I **8** 204-206
Lyndsay, David **10** 66-67
Stevenson, Robert Louis **14** 446-448
Thomson, James **15** 199-200

Scottish school of common sense (philoso-
phy)
McCosh, James **10** 402-403
Mill, James **11** 21
Reid, Thomas **13** 87-88
Stewart, Dugald **14** 449

Scottish Symphony (musical composition)
Mendelssohn, Moses **10** 488-489

Scottish Test Act (1681)
Blair, James **2** 315-316

Scott-King's Modern Europe (novel)
Waugh, Evelyn Arthur St. John
16 145-147

Scotus
see Duns Scotus, John

Scouts
see Frontiersmen

Scranton (city, Pennsylvania)
Powderly, Terence Vincent **12** 420-421

Scrap of paper
see London, treaty of (1839)

Screens, The (play)
  Brook, Peter **3** 19-21
  Genet, Jean **6** 262-263

Screens, The (verse)
  Richards, Ivor Armstrong **13** 137

SCRIABIN, ALEXANDER NIKOLAYEVICH
  (1871-1915), Russian composer and
  pianist **14** 71-72
  Copland, Aaron **4** 227-228
  Pasternak, Boris Leonidovich
    12 124-125
  Prokofiev, Sergei Sergeevich
    12 458-460

Scriabin, V. M.
  see Molotov, Vyacheslav Mikhailovich

Scribe, Augustin (1791-1861), French
  author
  Daudet, Alphonse **4** 402-403

Scribe, Eugene (1791-1861), French playwright
  Meyerbeer, Giacomo **10** 536-537

Scriblerus Club (literary club)
  Pope, Alexander **12** 395-397
  Swift, Jonathan **15** 51-54

Scribner's Magazine (periodical;
  1887-1939)
  Markham, Edwin **10** 267
  Rembrandt Harmensz van Rijn
    13 91-95

Scribner's Monthly (periodical; 1870-81)
  Jackson, Helen Hunt **8** 172
  Lampman, Archibald **9** 180-181
  Moran, Thomas **11** 151-152

SCRIPPS, EDWARD WYLLIS (1854-1926),
  American newspaper publisher **14** 72-73

Scripps Institution of Oceanography
  (Louisiana Jolla, California)
  Scripps, Edward Wyllis **14** 72-73
  Urey, Harold Clayton **15** 394-396

Scripturalist sect
  see Karaite sect (Judaism)

Scripture studies
  see Bible

Scroll of Fire, The (poem)
  Bialik, Hayyim Nahman **2** 262-263

Scroll of the Emperors (painting)
  Yen Li-pen **16** 453-454

Scrooby group (Protestant radicals)
  Bradford, William **2** 475-476
  Brewster, William **2** 523-524

Scudéry, Madeleine de (1608-1701),
  French poet and novelist
  Guillaume de Lorris **7** 33-34

SCULLIN, JAMES HENRY (1876-1953),
  Australian politician **14** 73
  Chifley, Joseph Benedict **3** 518
  Lyons, Joseph Aloysius **10** 69-70

Sculptors
  see Artists—sculptors

Scuola Metafisica (art)
  see Metaphysical painting

Scurvy (medicine)
  Cartier, Jacques **3** 343-344
  Szent-Györgyi, Albert von **15** 62-64

Scutum (constellation)
  Kapteyn, Jacobus Cornelis **8** 436-437

SD (Nazi espionage)
  Himmler, Heinrich **7** 398-399

Sea, The (book)
  Michelet, Jules **11** 5-6

Sea, The (poem)
  Morin, Paul **11** 174

Sea and Sardinia (book)
  Lawrence, David Herbert **9** 247-248

Sea Garden (poems)
  Doolittle, Hilda **5** 65-66

Sea Gull, The (play)
  Chekhov, Anton Pavlovich **3** 494-497
  Meyerhold, Vsevolod Emilievich **10** 539
  Stanislavsky, Constantin **14** 398-399

Sea Monster (engraving)
  Dürer, Albrecht **5** 159-161

Sea of Grass (novel)
  Richter, Conrad Michael **13** 148-149

Sea poems (book)
  Crane, Hart **4** 291-293

SEABORG, GLENN THEODORE (born
  1912), American chemist and chairman of
  the Atomic Energy Commission **14** 74-76

SEABURY, SAMUEL (1729-1796), American theologian **14** 76

Seafarer, The (poem)
  Pound, Ezra Loomis **12** 415-417

Seagram Building (New York City)
  Johnson, Philip **8** 313-314
  Mies van der Rohe, Ludwig **11** 10-12

Seal in the Bedroom, The (book)
  Thurber, James Grove **15** 213-214

Seal Island (film)
  Disney, Walter Elias **5** 26-27

SEALE, ROBERT GEORGE (Bobby; born
  1936), militant activist and a founder of
  the Black Panther Party **14** 77-78
  Cleaver, Leroy Eldridge **4** 97-98
  Newton, Huey P. **11** 367-369

Seaman's Act (United States; 1915)
  La Follette, Robert Marion **9** 155-156

Seamarks (poem)
  Perse, Saint-John **12** 242-243

Search, The (novel)
  Snow, Charles Percy **14** 311-312

Search, Weeds, and Red Dawn, The (novel)
  Baroja y Nessi, Pío **2** 15-16

Searchers, The (film)
  Ford, John **6** 7-8

Searching Wind, The (play)
  Hellman, Lillian Florence **7** 267-268

Sears, Richard Warren (1863-1914), American merchant
  Rosenwald, Julius **13** 293

Sears, Roebuck and Co.
  Ward, Aaron Montgomery **16** 112
  Wood, Robert Elkington **16** 370-371

Seashore at Palavas (painting)
  Courbet, Jean Desiré Gustave
    4 271-273

Season at Sarsaparilla, The (play)
  White, Patrick Victor Martindale
    16 233-235

Season Ticket, The (book)
  Haliburton, Thomas Chandler **7** 80

Seasons, The (musical composition)
  Hayden, Thomas Emmet **7** 217-219
  Vivaldi, Antonio **16** 3-4

Seasons, The (poem)
  Thomson, James **15** 199-200

Seated Bacchante... (sculpture)
  Clodion **4** 121

Seated Lincoln (sculpture)
  Borglum, John Gutzon de la Mothe
    2 416-417

Seated Madonna (sculpture)
  Quercia, Jacopo della **12** 509

Seated Man... (painting)
  Hals, Frans **7** 89-91

Seated Woman (sculpture)
  Duchamp-Villon, Raymond **5** 123

Seated Woman Holding a Fan (painting)
  Hals, Frans **7** 89-91

SEATO
  see Southeast Asia Treaty Organization

SEATTLE (c. 1788-1866), Native American
  tribal chief **14** 80-81

Sea-Wolf, The (stories)
  London, Jack **9** 494-495

Sebastian (1554-1578), king of Portugal
  Camoëns, Luis Vaz de **3** 247-249

Sebastiano del Piombo (1485?-1547), Italian painter
  Titian **15** 242-244

Secession (art)
  see Vienna Secession

Secession (United States; 1860-61)
  opponents (North)
    Brown, Benjamin Gratz **3** 32-33
    Douglas, Stephen Arnold **5** 80-82
    Lieber, Francis **9** 401-402
    Lincoln, Abraham **9** 415-418
    Sumner, Charles **15** 30-31
    Wade, Benjamin Franklin **16** 38-39
  opponents (South)
    Forbes, John **5** 507-508
    Houston, Samuel **7** 526-527
    Lamar, Lucius Quintus Cincinnatus
      9 170-171
    Soulé, Pierre **14** 351-352
    Stephens, Alexander Hamilton
      14 429-430
    Vance, Zebulon Baird **15** 413-414
  supporters (North)

Vallandigham, Clement Laird
15 406-407
supporters (South)
Memminger, Christopher Gustavus
10 476-477
Rhett, Robert Barnwell **13** 120
Ruffin, Edmund **13** 354-355
Simms, William Gilmore
14 235-236
Toombs, Robert Augustus
15 267-268
Yancey, William Lowndes
16 436-437

Sechter, Simon (1788-1867), Austrian composer
Bruckner, Joseph Anton **3** 64-65

Seclusion, Act of (1654)
Witt, Johan de **16** 348-349

Second April (poems)
Millay, Edna St. Vincent **11** 24-25

Second Bank of the United States
see Bank of the United States, Second

Second Birth, A (poems)
Pasternak, Boris Leonidovich
12 124-125

Second Coalition, War of the (1799-1800)
Frederick William III **6** 87
Suvorov, Aleksandr Vasilievich **15** 44-45

Second Coming (religion)
Miller, William **11** 30-31
Williams, Roger **16** 304-305

Second Coming, The (poem)
Yeats, William Butler **16** 445-447

Second Continental Congress
see Continental Congresses (United States)

Second Defense (book)
Milton, John **11** 43-46

Second Generation, The (novel)
Phillips, David Graham **12** 280-281

Second International
see International, Second

Second Scroll, The (novel)
Klein, A. M. **9** 49-50

Second Sex, The (book)
de Beauvoir, Simone **4** 440-441

Secondat, C.L. de
see Montesquieu, Baron de

Seconde, La (novel)
Colette, Sidonie Gabrielle **4** 158-159

Secret Agent, The (novel)
Conrad, Joseph **4** 205-207

Secret Life of Walter Mitty, The (story; film)
Goldwyn, Samuel **6** 416
Thurber, James Grove **15** 213-214

Secret Love (play)
Dryden, John **5** 106-107

Secret of Heaven, The (play)
Lagerkvist, Pär Fabian **9** 162-163

Secret of Luca, The (novel)
Silone, Ignazio **14** 231-232

Secret police, Nazi
see Gestapo

Secret Rose, The (book)
Yeats, William Butler **16** 445-447

Secret Service (play)
Barrymores **2** 28-30

Secret Vengeance for Secret Offense (play)
Calderón, Pedro **3** 221-222

Secretary (Cabinet post)
see Statesmen

Secretin (hormone)
Bernard, Claude **2** 208-210

Secrets of the Self, The (poem)
Iqbal, Muhammad **8** 132-133

Secretum (book)
Petrarch **12** 259-261

Secular City, The (book)
Cox, Harvey **4** 284-285

Secular Games (ancient Rome)
Augustus **1** 371-373
Horace **7** 500-503

Secular Society (London)
Besant, Annie Wood **2** 233-234
Bradlaugh, Charles **2** 478

Secularization (religion)
Bonhoeffer, Dietrich **2** 389-391

Secundus, Gaius Plinius
see Pliny the Elder

Secundus, Gaius Plinius Caecilius
see Pliny the Younger

Securities and Exchange Commission (United States)
Arnold, Thurman Wesley **1** 314
Douglas, William Orville **5** 83-85
Lawson, Thomas William **9** 255-256
Rayburn, Samuel Taliaferro **13** 61-62

Security Exchange Act of 1934 (United States)
Frankfurter, Felix **6** 57

Security Treaty (1951)
Kishi, Nobusuke **9** 41-43
Sato, Eisaku **13** 495-496

Sed non satiata (poem)
Baudelaire, Charles Pierre **2** 61-63

Sedan, battle of (1870)
Bismarck, Otto Eduard Leopold von
2 294-296
Moltke, Helmuth Karl Bernard von
11 90-91

SEDDON, RICHARD JOHN (1845-1906), New Zealand politician **14** 81-82

Sedgeley (house, near Philadelphia)
Latrobe, Benjamin Henry **9** 222-224

Sedges, John (pseudonym)
see Buck, Pearl Sydenstricker

SEDGWICK, ADAM (1785-1873), English geologist **14** 82-83
Murchison, Roderick Impey **11** 255-256

Sedition Act
see Alien and Sedition Acts

See America First (operetta)
Porter, Cole Albert **12** 405-406

See Naples and Die (play)
Rice, Elmer **13** 126-127

Seed beneath the Snow, The (novel)
Silone, Ignazio **14** 231-232

Seeds of Tommorrow (novel)
Sholokhov, Mikhail Aleksandrovich
14 203-204

SEEGER, PETE (born 1919), American folksinger and activist **14** 83-84
Cotton, John **4** 263-265

Sefarim, Mendele Mocher
see Mendele Mocher Sefarim

Sefer Ha-Aggada (anthology)
Bialik, Hayyim Nahman **2** 262-263

Sefer ha-Kuzari (Jewish classic)
Judah Halevi **8** 373

Sefer Hamitzvot (Karaite sect)
Anan ben David **1** 207-208

SEFERIS, GEORGE (Georgios Seferiadis; 1900-71), Greek poet and statesman
14 84-85

SEGAL, GEORGE (born 1924), American sculptor **14** 85-87

Segantini, Giovanni (1858-1899), Italian painter
Hartley, Marsden **7** 186

SEGOVIA, ANDRÉS (1893-1987), Spanish guitarist **14** 87-88

Segovian Weaver, The (play)
Alarcón, Pedro Antonio de **1** 100-101

Segrais, Jean Regnault de (1624-1701), French poet
Lafayette, Marquis de **9** 151-152

Segregation (racial, United States)
see African American history (United States)

Segregation, law of (genetics)
Mendel, Johann Gregor **10** 483-486

Séguier, Pierre, Duc de Villemor (1588-1672), French statesman
Le Brun, Charles **9** 269-270

Seguin Opera Co. (Philadelphia)
Fry, William Henry **6** 136-137

Sei personaggi in cerca d'autore (play)
Pirandello, Luigi **12** 319-321

SEIBERT, FLORENCE B. (1897-1991), American biochemist **14** 89-90

Sein (philosophy)
Heidegger, Martin **7** 257-258
Meinong, Alexius Ritter von Handschuchsheim **10** 461-462

Seismology (science)
Ewing, William Maurice **5** 350-351
Jeffreys, Harold **8** 241-242
Richter, Charles F. **13** 146-148
Winthrop, John **16** 341-342

Seixas, Gershom Mendes (1745-1816),
American rabbi
Cardozo, Benjamin Nathan **3** 288-290

Seiyukai party (Japan)
Hara, Kei **7** 138
Inukai, Tsuyoshi **8** 130-131
Ito, Hirobumi **8** 153-155
Saionji, Kimmochi **13** 438-439
Takahashi, Korekiyo **15** 84-85

Seize the Day (book)
Bellow, Saul **2** 141-143

Sejanus His Fall (play)
Jonson, Ben **8** 343-345

SEJO (1417-1468), king of Korea 1453-68
14 90-91
Sejong **14** 91-92

SEJONG (1397-1450), king of Korea
1418-50 **14** 91-92

Sekigahara, battle of (1600)
Ieyasu, Tokugawa **8** 103-106
Toyotomi Hideyoshi **15** 286-289

Sekondi-Takoradi (town, West Africa)
Busia, Kofi Abrefa **3** 172-173

Selassie, Haile
see Haile Selassie

Selenium (element—chemistry)
Berzelius, Jöns Jacob **2** 231-233
Crookes, William **4** 323-324
Diels, Otto Paul Hermann **5** 5-6

Selenomonas sputigena (bacillus)
Leeuwenhoek, Anton van **9** 300-301

Seleucia (ancient city, Mesopotamia)
Seleucus I **14** 92-93

Seleucid dynasty (Syria; ruled 312-64 B.C.)
Antiochus III **1** 249-250
Antiochus IV **1** 250
Cleopatra **4** 105-106
Seleucus I **14** 92-93

SELEUCUS I (circa 358-281 B.C.), Mace-
donian general, king of Babylonia and
Syria **14** 92-93
Antigonus I **1** 248-249
Chandragupta Maurya **3** 426
Ptolemy I **12** 470-472

Self (philosophy)
Fichte, Johann Gottlieb **5** 435-436
Locke, John **9** 478-480

Self-Realization Fellowship (Hindu organization)
Yogananda **16** 462-463

Self-reliance (essay)
Emerson, Ralph Waldo **5** 278-280

Self-strengthening (Chinese reform movement)
Feng Kuei-fen **5** 411-412

Li Hung-Chang **9** 407-409
Tso Tsung-t'ang **15** 328-329
Wen-hsiang **16** 202-203
Wo-jen **16** 352

Seligman, C.G. (1873-1940), English ethnologist
Malinowski, Kaspar Bronislaw
10 170-171

SELIGMAN, EDWIN ROBERT ANDERSON
(1861-1939), American economist and
editor **14** 93-94
Mills, C. Wright **11** 35-36

SELIM I (circa 1470-1520), Ottoman sultan
1512-20 **14** 94-95
Abbas I **1** 4-6
Suleiman I **15** 20-21

Selim I Mosque (Istanbul)
Sinan, Kodja Mimar **14** 245-246

Selim II (1524-1574), Turkish sultan
1566-74
Suleiman I **15** 20-21

Selim II Mosque (Edirne, Turkey)
Sinan, Kodja Mimar **14** 245-246

SELIM III (1761-1808), Ottoman sultan
1789-1807 **14** 95-96
Mahmud II **10** 145-147

Seljuks (Turkish dynasty; ruled 1055-1157)
Alexius I **1** 143-144
Alp Arslan **1** 178-179

Selkirk, Alexander (1676-1721), Scottish
sailor
Dampier, William **4** 384
Defoe, Daniel **4** 457-459

SELKIRK, 5TH EARL OF (Thomas Douglas;
1771-1820), Scottish colonizer in Canada
14 96
Fraser, Simon **6** 74-75

SELLARS, WILFRED (1912-1989), American philosopher **14** 96-98

Sellasia, battle of (222 B.C.)
Aratus **1** 273-274
Cleomenes III **4** 103-104

SELLERS, PETER RICHARD HENRY
(1925-1980), British comedy genius of
theater, radio, television, and movies
14 98-99

Selma (city, Alabama)
Bunche, Ralph Johnson **3** 121-122
King, Martin Luther Jr. **9** 20-22

Semaine sainte, La (novel)
Aragon, Louis **1** 271-272

Semantics (philosophy)
Carnap, Rudolf **3** 308-309
Richards, Ivor Armstrong **13** 137
Tarski, Alfred **15** 110-111

Semele (opera)
Congreve, William **4** 200-201
Handel, George Frederick **7** 116-119

SEMENOV, NIKOLAI NIKOLAEVICH
(1896-1986), Russian physicist and physical chemist **14** 101

Hinshelwood, Cyril Norman **7** 405-406
Kapitsa, Pyotr Leonidovich **8** 433-435

Semiconductors (electrical)
Bardeen, John **2** 1-3

Seminole Indians (North America)
Gadsden, James **6** 165-166
Osceola **12** 18

Seminole War (1817-1818)
Adams, John Quincy **1** 52-54
Jackson, Andrew **8** 168-172

Seminole War, Second (1835-1843)
Osceola **12** 18
Scott, Winfield **14** 70-71
Sherman, William Tecumseh
14 186-187
Taylor, Zachary **15** 128-130

Semiramide (ballet)
Gluck, Christoph Willibald **6** 372-374

Semiramide (opera)
Rossini, Gioacchino **13** 311-312

Sémiramis (play)
Voltaire **16** 14-16

SEMMELWEIS, IGNAZ PHILIPP
(1818-1865), Hungarian physician
14 101-102

SEMMES, RAPHAEL (1809-1877), American Confederate naval officer **14** 102-103

Sempione strizza l'occhio al Fréjus, Il
(novel)
Vittorini, Elio **16** 2-3

Semyon Kotko (opera)
Prokofiev, Sergei Sergeevich
12 458-460

SEN, RAM CAMUL (1783-1844), Bengali
intellectual and entrepreneur **13** 16-17

Senate, U.S.
see U.S. Senate

Senate House (Cambridge, England)
Gibbs, James **6** 301-302

**Senator, Flavius Magnus Aurelius Cas-
siodorus**
see Cassiodorus

Senators
see Statesmen

Seneca Falls (city, New York State)
Stanton, Elizabeth Cady **14** 402-403

Seneca Indians (North America)
Catlin, George **3** 373-374
Cornplanter **4** 239-241
Girty, Simon **6** 350
Handsome Lake **7** 122-123
Morgan, Lewis Henry **11** 167-168
Parker, Ely Samuel **12** 106-108
Red Jacket **13** 71-73

**SENECA THE YOUNGER, LUCIUS
ANNAEUS** (circa 4 B.C.-A.D. 65), Roman
philosopher **14** 103-105
Anselm of Canterbury **1** 244-245
Chrysippus **4** 35-36
Columbus, Christopher **4** 176-179

Diderot, Denis **5** 1-2
Martialis, Marcus Valerius **10** 286-287
Nero Claudius Caesar **11** 342-344
Ovid **12** 34-36
Petronius Arbiter **12** 262-263
Varro, Marcus Terentius **15** 438-439

Seneffe, battle of (1674)
Condé, Prince de **4** 193-194
William III **16** 295-296

Senegal, Republic of (nation, West Africa)
Bamba, Amadou **1** 481-482
Caillié, Auguste René **3** 214-215
Diagne, Blaise **4** 527
Diop, Cheikh Anta **5** 21-22
Faidherbe, Louis Léon César **5** 366-367
Gueye, Lamine **7** 31
Ly, Abdoulaye **10** 60
Senghor, Léopold Sédar **14** 106-107

Senegal River (West Africa)
Cadamosto, Alvise da **3** 206-207
Caillié, Auguste René **3** 214-215
Henry the Navigator **7** 305-306

Senegalese culture
Faye, Safi **5** 400-401

Senegalese literature
Ousmane, Sembene **12** 32-33
Senghor, Léopold Sédar **14** 106-107

SENFL, LUDWIG (circa 1486-circa 1543),
Swiss-born German composer
14 105-106
Hofhaimer, Paul **7** 441
Lassus, Roland de **9** 216-218

SENGHOR, LÉOPOLD SÉDAR (born 1906),
Senegalese poet, philosopher, and states-
man **14** 106-107
Apithy, Sourou Migan **1** 259-260
Diagne, Blaise **4** 527
Diop, Cheikh Anta **5** 21-22
Eboué, Adolphe Felix Sylvestre **5** 194
Gueye, Lamine **7** 31
Houphouët-Boigny, Felix **7** 519-520
Ly, Abdoulaye **10** 60
Mofolo, Thomas **11** 74

Seniles (book)
Petrarch **12** 259-261

Senilia (stories)
Turgenev, Ivan Sergeyevich **15** 345-348

Senilità (novel)
Svevo, Italo **15** 47-48

SENNACHERIB (ruled 705-681 B.C.), king
of Assyria **14** 108
Isaiah **8** 146-147
Micah **10** 542-543

SENNETT, MACK (1884-1960), American
film producer and director **14** 108-109
Chaplin, Charles Spencer **3** 438-440
Fields, W. C. **5** 444
Griffith, David Wark **6** 544-545
Truffaut, François **15** 311-313

Sens, Council of (1140)
Abelard, Peter **1** 23-25
Arnold of Brescia **1** 314-315

Bernard of Clairvaux **2** 207-208

Sensation (philosophy)
Bergson, Henri **2** 191-192
Berkeley, George **2** 197-198
Helvétius, Claude Adrien **7** 273-274
Locke, John **9** 478-480

Sensation (poem)
Rimbaud, Jean Nicolas Arthur
13 172-174

Sense and Sensibility (novel)
Austen, Jane **1** 377-379

Sense of Reality, A (book)
Greene, Graham **6** 523-524

Sensitive Plant, The (poem)
Shelley, Percy Bysshe **14** 176-178

Senta, battle of (1697)
Eugene of Savoy **5** 330-331

Sentences (book; Lombard)
Bonaventure **2** 383-384
Duns Scotus, John **5** 149-150
Lombard, Peter **9** 490-491
Luther, Martin **10** 48-51
Thomas Aquinas **15** 183-186
William of Ockham **16** 298-299
see also Summae

Sentimental Education, A (novel)
Flaubert, Gustave **5** 480-482

Sentimental Journey (book; Sterne)
Foscolo, Ugo **6** 21
Sterne, Laurence **14** 435-437

Sentimento del tempo (poems)
Ungaretti, Giuseppe **15** 389-390

Seoul (city, South Korea)
Yi Sng-gye **16** 458-459

"Separate but equal"
see African American history (United
States); Brown v. Board of Education
of Topeka; Plessy v. Ferguson

Separation of Light and Darkness (fresco)
Michelangelo Buonarroti **11** 2-5

Separatists (religion)
Bradford, William **2** 475-476
Brewster, William **2** 523-524
Winslow, Edward **16** 338-339

Sephardi (Judaism)
Caro, Joseph ben Ephraim **3** 316-317
Disraeli, Benjamin **5** 27-29

Sepoy Mutiny (1857-1858)
Dalhousie, 1st Marquess of **4** 375-376
Disraeli, Benjamin **5** 27-29
Roberts, Frederick Sleigh **13** 195-196
Syed Ahmed Khan **15** 60
Victoria **15** 485-487

Sept Princesses, Les (play)
Maeterlinck, Maurice **10** 125-126

September (fresco)
Tura, Cosimo **15** 343-344

September Massacres (Paris; 1792)
Danton, Georges Jacques **4** 391-393
Marat, Jean Paul **10** 230-231

September Morn (painting; Chabas)
Comstock, Anthony **4** 188-189

September Song (song)
Weill, Kurt **16** 174-175

Septicemia (medicine)
Fleming, Alexander **5** 483-485

Septimius Felton (book)
Hawthorne, Nathaniel **7** 212-215

Sepúlveda, Juan Ginés de (1490-1574),
Spanish historian and theologian
Las Casas, Bartolomé de **9** 211-212

Sequel to Drum-Taps (poems)
Whitman, Walt **16** 249-251

Sequence (Mass)
see Mass (music)

Sequoia (orchestral work)
Tower, Joan **15** 279-281

Sequoia (tree)
Sequoyah **14** 110-111

SEQUOYAH (circa 1770-1843), American
Cherokee Indian scholar **14** 110-111

Seraiah (Old Testament figure)
Ezra **5** 356-357

Serampore College (India)
Carey, William **3** 297

Seraphim... (poems)
Browning, Elizabeth Barrett **3** 52-53

Serapis (ship)
Jones, John Paul **8** 337-338

Serbian Republic (former kingdom; former
republic of Yugoslavia)
Alexander of Yugoslavia **1** 136-137
Berchtold, Leopold von **2** 183-184
Francis Ferdinand **6** 44
Karadzic, Radovan **8** 437-440
Mehmed the Conqueror **10** 452-454
Milosevic, Slobodan **11** 39-40
Peter I **12** 256
Ranke, Leopold von **13** 33-35
Selim III **14** 95-96

Serbs, Croats, and Slovenes, Kingdom of
see Yugoslavia (former nation)

Serchthrift (ship)
Cabot, Sebastian **3** 200-201

Serenade (crystal)
Luz, Arturo Rogerio **10** 56-57

Serenade (musical composition)
Britten, Benjamin **3** 10-11

Serenades (musical composition)
Brahms, Johannes **2** 490-492

Serenatas (music)
Scarlatti, Pietro Alessandro Gaspare
13 517-518
Vivaldi, Antonio **16** 3-4

Serene (painting)
Marc, Franz **10** 231

Serf (social class)
Austria
Joseph II **8** 359-360

Korea
Kwangjong **9** 140
Prussia
Frederick II **6** 81-84
Hardenberg, Karl August von
7 146-147
Russia
Alexander II **1** 132-133
Chernyshevsky, Nikolai Gavrilovich
3 504-505
Herzen, Aleksandr Ivanovich
7 351-352
Turgenev, Ivan Sergeyevich
15 345-348

Sergeant Grischa (book; Zweig)
Remarque, Erich Maria **13** 91

Sergeant Rutledge (film)
Ford, John **6** 7-8

Serial music
Babbitt, Milton **1** 410
Bennett, Richard Rodney **2** 172
Boulez, Pierre **2** 444-445
Cage, John **3** 211-214
Ginastera, Alberto Evaristo **6** 328-329
Halffter, Christóbal **7** 79-80
Krenek, Ernst **9** 98-99
Wuorinen, Charles **16** 404
Xenakis, Iannis **16** 416-418

Seriation (archeology)
Kroeber, Alfred Louis **9** 105-106

Serine (amino acid)
Khorana, Har Gobind **8** 537-538

Serious Reflections... (book)
Defoe, Daniel **4** 457-459

Serlio, Sebastiano (1475-1554), Italian
architect
Francis I **6** 40-43
Le Corbusier **9** 274-275
Palladio, Andrea **12** 75-77
Vignola, Giacomo da **15** 493-494

Serly, Tibor (1901-1978), Czech composer
Bartók, Béla **2** 35-36

Sermon... (musical composition)
Stravinsky, Igor Fedorovich **14** 502-506

Sermones (literary style)
Horace **7** 500-503

Sermons and Soda Water (stories)
O'Hara, John **11** 485

Sermons of Mr. Yorick, The (book)
Sterne, Laurence **14** 435-437

Serpent and the Lily, The (novel)
Kazantzakis, Nikos **8** 466-468

Serra dos Reis (South Africa)
Dias de Novais, Bartolomeu **4** 533-534

SERRA, JUNIPERO (Miguel José Serra;
1713-84), Spanish Franciscan missionary,
founder of California missions
14 111-112
Coronado, Francisco Vásquez de **4** 247
Portolá, Gaspar de **12** 408

SERRANO ELÍAS, JORGE ANTONIO (born
1945), president of Guatemala
(1991-1993) **14** 112-113

Serrano Suñer, Ramón (born 1901), Spanish lawyer and politician
Franco Bahamonde, Francisco **6** 52-54

Serres chaudes (poems)
Maeterlinck, Maurice **10** 125-126

Serse (Xerxes; opera)
Cavalli, Pietro Francesco **3** 382-383

Sertorius (play)
Corneille, Pierre **4** 234-236

Sertorius, Quintus (died 72 B.C.), Roman
general and statesman
Pompey **12** 387-389

Serum (blood)
Tiselius, Arne Wilhelm Kaurin
15 240-241

Serum therapy (physiology)
Arrhenius, Svante August **1** 318-320

Sérusier, Paul (1864-1927), French painter
Bonnard, Pierre **2** 395-396
Vuillard, Jean Édouard **16** 36

Serva padrona, La (intermezzo)
Pergolesi, Giovanni Battista **12** 218-219

SERVAN-SCHREIBER, JEAN-JACQUES
(born 1924), French journalist and writer
on public affairs **14** 113-115

Servant of Servants, A (poem)
Frost, Robert Lee **6** 130-133

Servante du roi, La (play)
Musset, Louis Charles Alfred de
11 271-272

Servants of India Society
Gokhale, Gopal Krishna **6** 396

SERVETUS, MICHAEL (circa 1511-53),
Spanish religious philosopher
14 115-116
Calvin, John **3** 239-242

Servites (religious order)
Sarpi, Paolo **13** 487-488

Sesame and Lilies (book; Ruskin)
Proust, Marcel **12** 465-467
Ruskin, John **13** 371-372

Seser kavita (novel)
Rabindranath Tagore **12** 529-531

Sesostris I (ruled 1980-1935 B.C.), Egyptian pharaoh
Amenemhet I **1** 193-194

SESSHU, TOYA (1420-1506), Japanese
painter and Zen priest **14** 116-117
Eitoku, Kano **5** 242

SESSIONS, ROGER HUNTINGTON
(1896-1985), American composer
14 117-118
Babbitt, Milton **1** 410
Stravinsky, Igor Fedorovich **14** 502-506

Sestina (musical composition)
Krenek, Ernst **9** 98-99

Set theory (mathematics)
Cantor, Georg Ferdinand Ludwig
Philipp **3** 265-266
Quine, Willard Van Orman **12** 514-515
Tarski, Alfred **15** 110-111

Seti I (died 1304 B.C.), king of Egypt
Ramses II **13** 22-23

SETON, ELIZABETH ANN BAYLEY
(1774-1821), American Catholic leader
14 118-119

SETON, ERNEST THOMPSON
(1860-1946), Canadian author and
co-founder of the Boy Scouts of America
14 119-120

Seton-Watson, R.W. (1879-1951), British
historian
Masaryk, Tomáš Garrigue **10** 314-315

Sette giornate del mondo, Le (poem)
Tasso, Torquato **15** 114-116

SETTIGNANO, DESIDERIO DA
(1428/31-1464), Italian sculptor **4** 509
Donatello **5** 55-56

Settle, Elkanah (1648-1724), English poet
Pope, Alexander **12** 395-397

Settlement, Act of (1701)
George I **6** 268-269

Settlers of the Marsh (novel)
Grove, Frederick Philip **7** 20-21

SEURAT, GEORGES PIERRE (1859-1891),
French painter **14** 120-122
Marin, John III **10** 259-260
Puvis de Chavannes, Pierre **12** 492-493
Rivera, Diego **13** 183-184
Rousseau, Henri **13** 323-324
Severini, Gino **14** 122
Van Gogh, Vincent **15** 427-429

Seuse, Heinrich (Heinrich Suso; died
1366), Swiss mystic
Eckhart, Johann **5** 200-201

Seuss, Dr.
see Geisel, Theodor

Sevastopol (city, Ukraine)
Enver Pasha **5** 290-291
Gordon, Charles George **6** 448-449
Krupp **9** 109-111
McClellan, George Brinton **10** 391-392
Palmerston, 3d Viscount **12** 81-83
Potemkin, Grigori Aleksandrovich
12 411-412
Tolstoy, Leo **15** 262-265

Sevastopol Tales (stories)
Tolstoy, Leo **15** 262-265

Seven against Thebes, The (play)
Aeschylus **1** 70-72

Seven and Five Society (art group)
Hepworth, Barbara **7** 318-319
Moore, Henry **11** 146-148

Seven Anthologies of the Basho School
(book)
Basho, Matsuo **2** 45-48

Seven Cities of Cibola (legend)
Marcos de Niza **10** 240

Seven Days, Battle of the (1862)
Davis, Jefferson **4** 416-418
Howard, Oliver Otis **7** 528-529
Jackson, Shirley Ann **8** 183-184
Lee, Robert Edward **9** 292-294
McClellan, George Brinton **10** 391-392

Seven Days of the World's Creation, The (poem)
Tasso, Torquato **15** 114-116

Seven Deadly Sins (art)
Bosch, Hieronymus **2** 426-428
Bruegel, Pieter the Elder **3** 65-67

Seven Deadly Sins, The (ballet)
Weill, Kurt **16** 174-175

Seven Descents of Myrtle, The (play)
Williams, Tennessee **16** 306-308

Seven Early Songs (musical composition)
Berg, Alban **2** 186-187

Seven Gothic Tales (literary collection)
Dinesen Blixen-Finecke, Karen **5** 13-14

Seven Hai-kai (musical composition)
Messiaen, Olivier **10** 528-529

Seven Keys to Baldpate (play)
Cohan, George Michael **4** 137-138

Seven Lamps of Architecture, The (book; Ruskin)
Pugin, Augustus Welby Northmore **12** 479-480
Ruskin, John **13** 371-372

Seven Last Songs (musical composition)
Mahler, Gustav **10** 144-145

Seven Last Words (New Testament)
Haydn, Franz Joseph **7** 219-221
Jesus of Nazareth **8** 251-255

Seven Oaks massacre (1817)
Fraser, Simon **6** 74-75

Seven Pillars of Wisdom (autobiography)
Lawrence, Thomas Edward **9** 253-254

Seven Pines, Battle of the
see Seven Days, Battle of the

Seven Rivers of Canada (essays)
MacLennan, Hugh **10** 110-111

Seven Rules of Logic (Judaism)
Hillel **7** 390-391

Seven Samurai, The (film)
Kurosawa, Akira **9** 135-137

Seven Songs (book)
Hopkinson, Francis **7** 496-497

Seven Stars of the Great Bear, The (tales)
Jami **8** 218-219

Seven Weeks War
see Austro-Prussian War (1866)

Seven World Riddles (essays)
Du Bois-Reymond, Emil **5** 118-119

Seven Years' Campaign (1399-1403)
Tamerlane **15** 94-95

Seven Years War (1756-1763)
American phase
see French and Indian War (1754-1763)
British forces
Burgoyne, John **3** 137-138
Cook, James **4** 214-215
Cornwallis, Charles **4** 241-243
Phillip, Arthur **12** 279-280
Rodney, George Brydges **13** 239-240
British politics
George II **6** 269-270
Pitt, William the Elder **12** 328-329
causes
Maria Theresa **10** 256-258
French forces
Rochambeau, Comte de **13** 220-221
in drama
Lessing, Gotthold Ephraim **9** 357-359
Prussian forces
Blücher, Gebhard Leberecht von **2** 340-341
Frederick II **6** 81-84
Spanish involvement
Charles III **3** 454-455

Seventeen (novel)
Tarkington, Newton Booth **15** 109

Seventeen-article Constitution (Japan)
Suiko **15** 15-16

1727, Treaty of
Nader, Ralph **11** 290-291

Seventh Pylon (Karnak)
Thutmose III **15** 216-217

Seventh Ring, The (poems)
George, Stefan **6** 277-278

Seventh Seal, The (film)
Bergman, Ernst Ingmar **2** 190-191

Seventh-Day Baptists (religious sect.)
Beissel, Johann Conrad **2** 123-124
Booth, Joseph **2** 404-405

Seventy, the (abolitionist)
Weld, Theodore Dwight **16** 186

Several Circles (painting)
Kandinsky, Wassily **8** 420-422

Several Poems... (anthology)
Bradstreet, Anne Dudley **2** 486-487

Severed Head, A (novel)
Murdoch, Iris **11** 256-257

SEVERINI, GINO (1883-1966), Italian painter **14** 122
Balla, Giacomo **1** 473-474
Boccioni, Umberto **2** 353-354
Seurat, Georges Pierre **14** 120-122
Stella, Joseph **14** 422

Severus, Flavius Valerius (died 307), Roman emperor 306-307
Constantine I **4** 209-211
Diocletian **5** 19-20

Severus, Livius (died 465), Roman emperor 461-165

Ricimer, Flavius **13** 151-152

SEVERUS, LUCIUS SEPTIMIUS (146-211), Roman emperor 193-211 **14** 109-110
Caracalla **3** 281-282
Julias of Rome **8** 381-384
Ulpian, Domitius **15** 385-386

SEVIER, JOHN (1745-1815), American frontiersman, soldier, and politician **14** 122-123
Allen, Ethan **1** 163-164

Sévigné, Madame de (1626-1696), French writer
La Fayette, Comtesse de **9** 150-151

Sèvres, Treaty of (1920)
Atatürk, Ghazi Mustapha Kemal **1** 356-357
Venizelos, Eleutherios **15** 460-461

SEWALL, SAMUEL (1652-1730), American jurist and diarist **14** 123-124
Story, Joseph **14** 480-481
Taylor, Edward **15** 122-123

SEWARD, WILLIAM HENRY (1801-1872), American statesman **14** 124-125
Booth, John Wilkes **2** 404
Cameron, Simon **3** 246-247
Chase, Salmon Portland **3** 473-475
Fillmore, Millard **5** 447-448
Greeley, Horace **6** 515-517
Lincoln, Abraham **9** 415-418
Weed, Thurlow **16** 169-170

Sewing machine
Howe, Elias **7** 529-530
Singer, Isaac M. **14** 250

Sex and Destiny: The Politics of Human Fertility (book)
Greer, Germaine **6** 528-530

Sex and the Single Girl (book)
Brown, Helen Gurley **3** 36-37

Sex discrimination (United States)
Carey Thomas, Martha **3** 297-298
see also Women's rights

Sex-linked genes (genetics)
Haldane, John Burdon Sanderson **7** 70-71
Morgan, Thomas Hunt **11** 170-171

Sextant (instrument)
Flamsteed, John **5** 477-478

SEXTON, ANNE (Anne Gray Harvey; 1928-74), American "confessional" poet **14** 125-126

Sexual behavior, human
Kinsey, Alfred C. **9** 31-32

Sexual revolution (United States)
Marcuse, Herbert **10** 245-247

Sexualtiy (psychology)
Freud, Sigmund **6** 103-106

Sexus (novel)
Miller, Henry **11** 26-27

Seymour, Edward
see Somerset, Duke of

SEYMOUR, HORATIO (1810-1886), American politician **14** 126-127
  Blair, Francis Preston **2** 313-315

Seymour, Jane (1509?-1537), third wife of Henry VIII of England
  Cranmer, Thomas **4** 295-296
  Edward VI **5** 213-214
  Elizabeth I **5** 263-266
  Henry VIII **7** 302-305
  Holbein, Hans the Younger **7** 449-450
  Mary, I **10** 308-309
  Somerset, Duke of **14** 333-334

Seymour, Thomas (Baron Seymour of Sudley; circa 1508-49), English statesman
  Norfolk, 3d Duke of **11** 423

Seyss-Inquart, Artur (1892-1946), German politician
  Schuschnigg, Kurt von **14** 45-46

Sforza, Ascanio (1455-1505), Italian cardinal
  Josquin des Prez **8** 361-363

Sforza, Galeazzo Maria (1444-1476), duke of Milan
  Antonello da Messina **1** 251-252

SFORZA, LODOVICO (1452-1508), duke of Milan **14** 127-128
  Borgia, Cesare **2** 412-413
  Bramante, Donato **2** 493-494
  Castiglione, Baldassare **3** 360-361
  Louis XII **9** 528-529

SHABAKA (ruled circa 712-circa 696 B.C.), Nubian king, pharaoh of Egypt **14** 130
  Taharqa **15** 81-82

Shabataka (Shenitku; flourished early 7th century B.C.), Nubian pharaoh of Egypt
  Shabaka **14** 130
  Taharqa **15** 81-82

SHABAZZ, BETTY (1936-1997), African American educator, activist, and health administrator **14** 130-132

Shabby Genteel Story, A (story)
  Thackeray, William Makepeace **15** 159-161

SHACKLETON, SIR ERNEST HENRY (1874-1922), British explorer **14** 132-133
  Mawson, Douglas **10** 354-355
  Wilkins, George Hubert **16** 281-282

Shadow, The (fairy tale)
  Andersen, Hans Christian **1** 212-214

Shadow and Act (essays)
  Ellison, Ralph Waldo **5** 274-275

Shadow Line, The (novel)
  Conrad, Joseph **4** 205-207

Shadow of a Doubt (film)
  Hitchcock, Alfred **7** 415-416

Shadow of a Gunman, The (play)
  O'Casey, Sean **11** 459-460

Shadow of Night, The (poem)
  Chapman, George **3** 440-441

Shadow of the Glen, The (play)
  Synge, Edmund John Millington **15** 61-62

Shadow of the Hurricane (sculpture)
  Richier, Germaine **13** 145-146

Shadow of the Wings, The (book)
  Maeterlinck, Maurice **10** 125-126

Shadow on the Dial, The (essays)
  Bierce, Ambrose Gwinett **2** 269-270

Shadowings (book)
  Hearn, Lafcadio **7** 240

Shadows on the Grass (book)
  Dinesen Blixen-Finecke, Karen **5** 13-14

Shadows on the Rock (novel)
  Cather, Willa Sibert **3** 368-369

Shadwell, Thomas (circa 1642-92), English playwright
  Dryden, John **5** 106-107

SHAFFER, PETER LEVIN (born 1926), English/American playwright **14** 133-135

Shafii, al- (767-820), Arabic scholar and religious leader
  Tabari, Muhammad ibn Jarir al- **15** 69-70

SHAFTESBURY, 1ST EARL OF (Anthony Ashley Cooper; 1621-83), English statesman **14** 135-136
  Buckingham, 2d Duke of **3** 94-95
  Charles II **3** 452-454
  Clarendon, 1st Earl of **4** 73-75
  Dryden, John **5** 106-107
  Locke, John **9** 478-480
  Monmouth and Buccleugh, Duke of **11** 108-109

SHAFTESBURY, 3D EARL OF (Anthony Ashley Cooper; 1671-1713), English moral philosopher **14** 136-137
  Mandeville, Bernard **10** 192

SHAFTESBURY, 7TH EARL OF (Anthony Ashley Cooper; 1801-85), English social reformer **14** 137-138
  Hammond, Lawrence and Lucy **7** 109

Shagpat
  see Shaving of Shagpat, The (novel)

Shah dynasty (Nepal)
  Birendra, King **2** 282-283
  Mahendra, King **10** 138-139

SHAH JAHAN (1592-1666), Mogul emperor of India 1628-58 **14** 138-139
  Aurangzeb **1** 377
  Bach, Carl Philipp Emanuel **1** 414-415

Shahjahanabad
  see Delhi

Shahji Bonsale (1594-1664), Maratha soldier of fortune
  Shivaji **14** 199-200

SHAHN, BEN (1898-1969), American painter, graphic artist, and photographer **14** 139-140

Shahnameh (epic; Firdausi)
  Behzad **2** 123

Firdausi **5** 451-452
  Mahmud of Ghazni **10** 147

Shahpur I (ruled 241-272), king of Persia
  Mani **10** 196-197
  Valerian **15** 404-405

SHAHPUR II (310-379), king of Persia **14** 140-141

Shahs
  see Statesmen, Iranian

Shajarat al-Bus (novella)
  Husayn, Taha **8** 61-62

SHAKA (circa 1787-1828), African Zulu military monarch **14** 141-142
  Cetshwayo **3** 400
  Dingane **5** 14-15
  Lobengula **9** 474-475
  Moshweshwe **11** 203-205
  Mzilikazi **11** 285-286

Shaker, Why Don't You Sing (choreo-poem)
  Angelou, Maya **1** 238-239

Shakers (United Believers in Christ's Second Appearing; United States)
  Lee, Ann **9** 285-288

Shakespeare Festival Theatre (Stratford, Ontario)
  Guthrie, Tyrone **7** 50-51

SHAKESPEARE, WILLIAM (1564-1616), English playwright, poet, and actor **14** 142-145
  adaptations
    Brecht, Bertolt **2** 512-514
    Dryden, John **5** 106-107
    Kurosawa, Akira **9** 135-137
    Lamb, Charles **9** 176-177
    Vigny, Comte de **15** 494-495
  authorship controversy
    Donnelly, Ignatius **5** 62
  compared to
    Marlowe, Christopher **10** 272-274
    Shaw, George Bernard **14** 163-164
    Spenser, Edmund **14** 373-376
  contemporaries
    Drayton, Michael **5** 97-98
    Elizabeth I **5** 263-266
    Fletcher, John **5** 487
    Johnson, Betsey **8** 295-296
    Raleigh, Walter **13** 9-11
  editions and translations
    Johnson, Samuel **8** 315-317
    Pope, Alexander **12** 395-397
  in art
    Kent, Rockwell **8** 511
    Ryder, Albert Pinkham **13** 391-392
  influence of
    Eminescu, Mihail **5** 280-281
    Goethe, Johann Wolfgang von **6** 388-391
    Heavysege, Charles **7** 246
    Howells, William Dean **7** 539-541
    Hugo, Victor Marie **8** 22-25
    Lessing, Gotthold Ephraim **9** 357-359
    Manzoni, Alessandro **10** 222-224

Melville, Herman **10** 472-476
Sterne, Laurence **14** 435-437
influenced by
Ariosto, Ludovico **1** 289-290
Boccaccio, Giovanni **2** 351-353
Juvenal **8** 397-399
Kyd, Thomas **9** 140-141
Montaigne, Michel Eyquem de **11** 116-117
Ovid **12** 34-36
Plautus **12** 348-350
Plutarch **12** 359-360
Terence **15** 146-148
music based on
Arne, Thomas Augustine **1** 307-308
Berlioz, Louis Hector **2** 203-205
Mendelssohn, Moses **10** 488-489
Sibelius, Jean Julius Christian **14** 211-212
Vaughan Williams, Ralph **15** 446-447
Verdi, Giuseppe Fortunino Francesco **15** 463-465
Wagner, Richard **16** 40-43
performances
Booth, Edwin **2** 401-402
Booth, John Wilkes **2** 404
Forrest, Edwin **6** 11-12
Gielgud, John **6** 310-311
Hallam, Lewis Sr. and Jr. **7** 87
Olivier, Laurence **11** 502-503
sources
Macbeth **10** 81
translations
Pasternak, Boris Leonidovich **12** 124-125
Plaatje, Solomon Tshekisho **12** 341-342
Tieck, Ludwig **15** 218-219
Wieland, Christoph Martin **16** 260-261

Shakyamuni
see Buddha, the

Shakyas (Asian people)
Buddha **3** 97-101

SHALIKASHVILI, JOHN MALCHASE DAVID (born 1936), chairman of the U.S. Joint Chiefs of Staff **14** 145-147

Shall We Dance (film score)
Gershwin, George **6** 284-285

Shalmaneser V (died 722 B.C.), king of Assyria 727-722
Sargon II **13** 482

Shamash-shum-ukin (died 648? B.C.), ruler of Babylonia 669-?648 B.C.
Ashurbanipal **1** 338

Shame (film)
Bergman, Ernst Ingmar **2** 190-191

Shame... (literary collection)
Steffens, Lincoln **14** 410-411

SHAMIR, YITZCHAK (Yizernitsky; born 1914), Israeli prime minister and leader of the Likud Party **14** 147-149

SHAMMAI (flourished 1st century B.C.), Jewish sage **14** 149
Hillel **7** 390-391
Johanan ben Zakkai **8** 271-272
Judah I **8** 372-373

Shang dynasty (China, ruled 1766-1122 B.C.)
Qianlong **12** 502-505
Chou Kung **4** 22-23
Confucius **4** 197-200
Wu wang **16** 408-409

SHANG YANG (circa 390-338 B.C.), Chinese statesman and political philosopher **14** 149-150

Shang-chün shu (treatises)
Shang Yang **14** 149-150

Shanghai (city, China)
Chiang Kai-shek **3** 510-513
Chou En-lai **4** 20-22
Feng Kuei-fen **5** 411-412

Shang-lin fu (poems)
Ssu-ma Hsiang-ju **14** 389-390

SHANKARA (Shankaracharya; circa 788-820), Indian philosopher and reformer **14** 150-151

SHANKER, ALBERT (born 1928), American education leader **14** 151-153

Shannon (frigate)
Lawrence, James **9** 251-252

SHANNON, CLAUDE ELWOOD (born 1916), American mathematician **14** 153-154

Shanti Ashrama (monastic community, California)
Vivekananda **16** 4-5

Shantung Province (China)
Confucius **4** 197-200
Li Ta-chao **9** 447
Wilson, Thomas Woodrow **16** 330-332
Yüan Shih-k'ai **16** 480-481

Shapes of Clay (verses)
Bierce, Ambrose Gwinett **2** 269-270

SHAPEY, RALPH (born 1921), American composer, conductor, and teacher **14** 154-155

SHAPLEY, HARLOW (1885-1972), American astronomer **14** 155-156
Eddington, Arthur Stanley **5** 201-202
Kapteyn, Jacobus Cornelis **8** 436-437
Oort, Jan Hendrik **11** 523-524

Shapur
see Shahpur

Share Our Wealth program (United States, 1932)
Long, Huey Pierce **9** 496-497
Townsend, Francis Everitt **15** 282-283

Shari River (Chad)
Barth, Heinrich **2** 30-31
Clapperton, Hugh **4** 72-73

Sharia (Islamic law)
Omar ibn Said Tal, Al-Hajj **11** 509-510

SHARIATI, ALI (1933-1977), "Ideologue of the Iranian Revolution" **14** 156-157

Shark (schooner)
Perry, Matthew Calbraith **12** 237-239

Shark Bay (Western Australia)
Dampier, William **4** 384

SHARON, ARIEL (Arik; born 1928), Israeli politician and defense minister **14** 157-159

Sharp, Becky (literary character)
Thackeray, William Makepeace **15** 159-161

Sharp, Granville (1735-1813), English philanthropist
Cugoano, Ottobah **4** 332-333
Equiano, Olaudah **5** 296-297
Wilberforce, William **16** 269-270

Sharpeville massacre (South Africa; 1960)
Luthuli, Albert John **10** 51-52
Mandela, Nelson Rolihlahla **10** 185-186
Verwoerd, Hendrik Frensch **15** 472-473
Vorster, Balthazar Johannes **16** 30-32

Sharpsburg
see Antietam, battle of (1862)

SHARPTON, AL (born 1954), African American civil rights leader and minister **14** 159-162

Sharukin
see Sargon II

Shasta daisy (plant)
Burbank, Luther **3** 129-131

Shastri, Shri Lal Bahadur (1904-1966), Indian statesman, prime minister 1964-66
Bhabha, Homi Jehangir **2** 253-254
Gandhi, Indira Priyadarshini **6** 200-201
Kamaraj, Kumaraswami **8** 415

Shaughnessy, T.G. (1853-1923), American railroad official
Van Horne, William Cornelius **15** 429-430

Shaughraun, The (play)
Boucicault, Dion **2** 442-443

Shavian style (architecture)
Shaw, Richard Norman **14** 167-168

Shaving of Shafpat, The (novel)
Meredith, George **10** 512-513

SHAW, ANNA HOWARD (1847-1919), American suffragist leader, reformer, and women's rights activist **14** 162-163
Catt, Carrie Chapman **3** 375-376
see also Women's suffrage; Women's rights

Shaw, Artie (born 1910), American musician
Still, William Grant **14** 455-456

SHAW, GEORGE BERNARD (1856-1950), British playwright, critic, and pamphleteer **14** 163-164
contemporaries
Comstock, Anthony **4** 188-189

Hapgood, Norman **7** 137-138
Harris, Frank **7** 172-173
Lawrence, Thomas Edward
 9 253-254
Mencken, Henry Louis **10** 481-483
Wells, Herbert George **16** 195-196
Yeats, William Butler **16** 445-447
Fabian Society
Bernstein, Eduard **2** 218
Besant, Annie Wood **2** 233-234
Webb, Sidney James **16** 154-155
influence of
Frisch, Max **6** 118-119
influenced by
Edison, Thomas Alva **5** 206-208
Godwin, William **6** 383-384
Ibsen, Henrik **8** 98-100
Stirner, Max **14** 459-460
portraits
John, Augustus Edwin **8** 291
Rodin, Auguste **13** 236-238
quoted
Chaplin, Charles Spencer **3** 438-440
Gregory, Augusta **6** 535-536
sources
Joan of Arc **8** 264-265
Shaw, Josephine
see Lowell, Josephine Shaw
SHAW, LEMUEL (1781-1861), American
jurist **14** 164-165
Melville, Herman **10** 472-476
SHAW, MARY (born 1943), American com-
puter science professor **14** 165-167
SHAW, RICHARD NORMAN (1831-1912),
British architect **14** 167-168
Richardson, Henry Hobson **13** 139-141
Shaw, Robert Gould (1837-1863), Ameri-
can soldier
Saint-Gaudens, Augustus **13** 432
Shaw, T. E.
see Lawrence, Thomas Edward
Shawn, Ted (Edwin Myers
Shawn;1891-1972), American dancer
and choreographer
Graham, Martha **6** 485-486
St. Denis, Ruth **13** 430-431
Shawnee Indians (North America)
Boone, Daniel **2** 397-398
Clark, George Rogers **4** 75-76
Dunmore, 4th Earl of **5** 147
Girty, Simon **6** 350
Johnson, William **8** 319-320
Tecumseh **15** 133
Shawomet (Rhode Island)
see Warwick (Rhode Island)
SHAYS, DANIEL (circa 1747-1825), Ameri-
can Revolutionary War Captain **14** 168
see also Shays' Rebellion
Shays' Rebellion (1786-1787)
Adams, Samuel **1** 55-56
Ames, Fisher **1** 199-200
Bowdoin, James **2** 461-462
Hancock, John **7** 114-116

King, Rufus **9** 22-23
Lincoln, Benjamin **9** 418-419
Shays, Daniel **14** 168
Tyler, Royall **15** 371-372
SHCHARANSKY, ANATOLY BORISOVICH
(born 1948), prominent figure of the
Helsinki Watch Group **14** 168-170
She Loves You (song)
Lennon, John Winston **9** 326-328
She Moves through the Fair (poem)
Colum, Padraic **4** 174-175
She Stoops to Conquer (play)
Goldsmith, Oliver **6** 411-413
She Was No Good (fairy tale)
Andersen, Hans Christian **1** 212-214
She Wore a Yellow Ribbon (film)
Ford, John **6** 7-8
Shearer, Norma (1905-1983),
Gable, William Clark **6** 157-158
Shebalin, Vassarion (1902-1963), Russian
composer
Glinka, Mikhail Ivanovich **6** 369-370
Shebitku
see Shabataka
Shebna (Old Testament character)
Isaiah **8** 146-147
Shechinah (Judaism)
Shammai **14** 149
SHEELER, CHARLES (1883-1965), Ameri-
can painter **14** 170-171
O'Keeffe, Georgia **11** 487-489
Stella, Joseph **14** 422
Wyeth, Andrew Newell **16** 413-415
SHEEN, FULTON J. (1895-1979), American
Roman Catholic bishop and television
host **14** 171-172
Sheep and Goat (painting)
Chao Meng-fu **3** 436-437
Sheep May Safely Graze (musical composi-
tion)
Bach, Johann Sebastian **1** 416-419
Sheffield Scientific School (Yale University)
Silliman, Benjamin **14** 229-230
Shehu
see Uthman don Fodio
Sheikh Ibrahim
see Burkhardt, Johann Ludwig
Sheil, Richard Lalor (1791-1851), Irish
dramatist and politician
O'Connell, Daniel **11** 465-467
Shekhina (Judaism)
Leon, Moses de **9** 336
Shelburne, 2d Earl of (William Petty, 1st
Marquis of Lansdowne; 1737-1805), Eng-
lish statesman, prime minister 1782-83
Cornwallis, Charles **4** 241-243
Fox, Charles James **6** 35-37
George III **6** 270-272
North, Frederick **11** 429-430
Pitt, William the Younger **12** 329-331

Priestley, Joseph **12** 452-453
Sheldon Art Gallery (University of Nebras-
ka)
Johnson, Philip **8** 313-314
SHELDON, CHARLES M. (1857-1946),
American social reformer who also wrote
In His Steps **14** 172-174
Sheldon v. Metro-Goldwyn Picture (legal
case)
Hand, Billings Learned **7** 116
Sheldonian Theatre (Oxford University)
Wren, Christopher **16** 393-394
Shelekhov-Golikov Co. (Russia)
Baranov, Aleksandr Andreievich
 1 499-500
Shell and Head (sculpture)
Arp, Jean **1** 317-318
Shell Building (The Hague)
Oud, Jacobus Johannes Pieter **12** 32
Shell construction (architecture)
Saarinen, Eliel and Eero **13** 396-398
SHELLEY, MARY WOLLSTONECRAFT
(1797-1851), English author **14** 174-176
Plutarch **12** 359-360
Shelley, Percy Bysshe **14** 176-178
SHELLEY, PERCY BYSSHE (1792-1822),
English romantic poet **14** 176-178
associates
Byron, George Gordon Noel
 3 193-194
Lewis, Matthew Gregory **9** 390-391
Peacock, Thomas Love **12** 169
Shelley, Mary Wollstonecraft
 14 174-176
compared to
Arnold, Matthew **1** 311-313
Keats, John **8** 470-472
influence of
Hawthorne, Nathaniel **7** 212-215
Kuo Mo-jo **9** 133-134
Naidu, Sarojini **11** 294-295
Tennyson, Alfred **15** 144-146
influenced by
Godwin, William **6** 383-384
Milton, John **11** 43-46
translations
Pasternak, Boris Leonidovich
 12 124-125
Shelley v. Kramer (1948)
Marshall, Thurgood **10** 282-284
Shelomoh Yitzhaki
see Rashi
Sheltered Life, The (novel)
Glasgow, Ellen **6** 360-361
Shembe, Isaiah (died 1935), Zulu prophet
and religious leader
Dube, John Langalibalele **5** 113
Shensi (province; China)
Li Tzu-Ch'eng **9** 452
Shen-tsung (ruled 1068-85), Chinese
emperor, Sung dynasty
Mi Fei **11** 12-13

Ou-yang Hsiu **12** 33-34
Ssu-ma kuang **14** 390-391
Su Shih **15** 39-40
Wang An-shih **16** 95-97

SHEPARD, ALAN (born 1923), American astronaut **14** 178-180

SHEPARD, SAM (Samuel Shepard Rogers VII; born 1943), American playwright, rock performer, and film actor **14** 180-181

Shepard, Thomas (1605-1649), English Puritan theologian
Dunster, Henry **5** 152-153

Shepherd of the Landes (sculpture)
Richier, Germaine **13** 145-146

Shepherd with Pipe (painting)
Giorgione **6** 340-341

Shepherd's Calendar, The (poems)
Spenser, Edmund **14** 373-376

Shepherds of Bethlehem, The (novel)
Lope Félix de Vega Carpio **9** 503-506

Shepherd's Week, The (pastorals)
Gay, John **6** 243-244

Shepilov, Dmitri (born 1905), Russian journalist and diplomat
Molotov, Vyacheslav Mikhailovich **11** 89-90

Sheppard Lee (novel)
Bird, Robert Montgomery **2** 281-282

Sheppard-Towner Act (United States; 1921)
Abbott, Grace **1** 9-10
Harding, Warren Gamaliel **7** 148-149

Shepstone, Sir Theophilus (1817-1893), British statesman
Frere, Henry Bartle Edward **6** 100-101

SHERATON, THOMAS (1751-1806), English furniture designer **14** 181-182
Hepplewhite, George **7** 317-318
Phyfe, Duncan **12** 284-285

SHERIDAN, PHILIP HENRY (1831-1888), American general **14** 182-183
Buffalo Bill **3** 105-106
Custer, George Armstrong **4** 355-356
Stuart, James Ewell Brown **14** 515-516

SHERIDAN, RICHARD BRINSLEY (1751-1816), British playwright and orator **14** 183-184
Edgeworth, Maria **5** 205-206
Gibbon, Edward **6** 299-300

Sheridan Square (painting)
Kline, Franz **9** 55

Sherley, Robert (1581?-1628), English adventurer and soldier
Abbas I **1** 4-6

Sherlock Holmes (literary series)
Doyle, Arthur Conan **5** 91-92

SHERMAN, JOHN (1823-1900), American politician **14** 184-185
Garfield, James Abram **6** 213-214
Hanna, Marcus Alonzo **7** 127-128
McKinley, William **10** 418-420

Miles, Nelson Appleton **11** 16-17
see also Sherman Antitrust Act; Sherman Silver Purchase Act

SHERMAN, ROGER (1721-1793), American patriot **14** 185-186

SHERMAN, WILLIAM TECUMSEH (1820-1891), American general **14** 186-187
associates
Grant, Ulysses Simpson **6** 492-494
Harrison, Benjamin **7** 178-179
Howard, Oliver Otis **7** 528-529
Lincoln, Abraham **9** 415-418
Schurz, Carl **14** 44-45
Thomas, George Henry **15** 190-191
memorial
Saint-Gaudens, Augustus **13** 432
opponents
Beauregard, Pierre Gustave Toutant **2** 96-97
Johnston, Joseph Eggleston **8** 323
Lee, Robert Edward **9** 292-294

Sherman Antitrust Act (United States; 1890)
enforcement
Arnold, Thurman Wesley **1** 314
Hand, Billings Learned **7** 116
Knox, Philander Chase **9** 66-67
Morgan, John Pierpont **11** 163-165
Rockefeller, John Davison **13** 226-228
supporters
George, James Zachariah **6** 276-277
Harlan, John Marshall **7** 156-157
Harrison, Benjamin **7** 178-179
Lodge, Henry Cabot **9** 482-483
Olney, Richard **11** 504-505
Sherman, John **14** 184-185
Taft, William Howard **15** 78-81

Sherman House (Newport, Rhode Island)
Richardson, Henry Hobson **13** 139-141

Sherman Silver Purchase Act (1890; United States)
Cleveland, Stephen Grover **4** 108-110
Harrison, Benjamin **7** 178-179
Sherman, John **14** 184-185

Sherpa people (tribe, Himalayas)
Hillary, Edmund **7** 389-390

SHERRINGTON, SIR CHARLES SCOTT (1857-1952), English physiologist **14** 187-189
Adrian, Edgar Douglas **1** 67-69
Cushing, Harvey Williams **4** 353-354
Eccles, John Carew **5** 195-196
Penfield, Wilder Graves **12** 198-200

Sherston's Progress (book)
Sassoon, Siegfried **13** 492-493

Shertok-Sharett, Moshe (1894-1965), Jewish Zionist leader
Meir, Golda **10** 462-463

SHERWOOD, ROBERT EMMET (1896-1955), American playwright **14** 189-190

Bogart, Humphrey **2** 363-364
Goldwyn, Samuel **6** 416

SHESTOV, LEV (Lev Isaakovich Schwarzmann; 1866-1938), Russian Jewish thinker and literary critic **14** 190-191

Shetland Islands (Northern Scotland)
Harold I **7** 161-162
James III **8** 208-209

SHEVARDNADZE, EDUARD AMVROSEVICH (born 1928), foreign minister of the U.S.S.R. (1985-1990) **14** 191-193

Shevirat ha-kelim (Judaism)
Luria, Isaac ben Solomon Ashkenazi **10** 47-48

Shias
see Shiites

Shiba, Kokan (1747-1818), Japanese painter
Hokusai, Katsushika **7** 447-448

Shield of Achilles, The (poem)
Auden, Wystan Hugh **1** 364-366

Shield of Herakles (poem)
Hesiod **7** 361-362

Shifa (book)
Avicenna **1** 386-387

Shih ching (book; Confucius)
Confucius **4** 197-200
Mencius **10** 480-481

Shih Hu (died 349), Chinese ruler of Latter Chao dynasty
Shih Le **14** 195

Shih huang-ti
see Ch'in Shih huang-ti

SHIH KO-FA (died 1644), Chinese scholar-soldier **14** 194-195

SHIH LE (274-333), Chinese emperor 330-333 **14** 195

Shih poetry (Chinese literature)
Lu Chi **10** 24
Ou-yang Hsiu **12** 33-34
Su Shih **15** 39-40
T'ao Ch'ien **15** 104-105

SHIHAB, FU'AD (1903-1973), Father of the Lebanese Army and president of Lebanon (1958-1964) **14** 193-194

Shih-chi (book; Ssu-ma Ch'ien)
Kim Pusik **9** 8-9
Pan Ku **12** 86-87
Ssu-ma Ch'ien **14** 388-389

Shih-heng
see Lu Chi

Shiites (Islamic sect)
adherents
Abbas I **1** 4-6
Aga Khan **1** 74-76
Ali **1** 155-156
Berri, Nabih **2** 220-222
Fadlallah, Sayyid Muhammad Husayn **5** 362-364
Hafiz, Shams al-Din **7** 63
Karim Khan Zand **8** 447

Masudi, Ali ibn al- Husayn al-
10 328-329
Sadr, Musa al- **13** 420-422
see also Ismailis
opponents
Mansur, Abu Jafar ibn Muhammad
al- **10** 214-215
Nazzam, Ibrahim ibn Sayyar al-
11 329
Selim I **14** 94-95
see also Sunnites

Shikadosho (book)
Zeami, Kanze **16** 492-493

Shiloh, battle of (1862)
Confederates
Beauregard, Pierre Gustave Toutant
2 96-97
Davis, Jefferson **4** 416-418
Forrest, Nathan Bedford **6** 13-14
Sherman, William Tecumseh
14 186-187
Union
Bristow, Benjamin Helm **3** 9-10
Garfield, James Abram **6** 213-214
Grant, Ulysses Simpson **6** 492-494
Powell, John Wesley **12** 425-426
Weaver, James Baird **16** 151-152

SHILS, EDWARD ALBERT (born 1911),
American sociologist **14** 195-197

Shimoda (port, Japan)
Perry, Matthew Calbraith **12** 237-239

Shimonoseke, Treaty of (1895)
K'ang Yu-wei **8** 426-428
Li Hung-Chang **9** 407-409
Liang Ch'i-ch'ao **9** 395-396

Shimonoseki, battle of (1864)
Yamagata, Aritomo **16** 428-429

Shine, Perishing Republic (poem)
Jeffers, John Robinson **8** 236-237

Shingon Sect (Japanese Buddhism)
Eisai **5** 231-232
Kukai **9** 124-125
Saicho **13** 426-428

Shinn, Everett (1876-1953), American
painter
Sloan, John **14** 274-275

SHINRAN (1173-1262), Japanese Buddhist
monk **14** 197

Shinto religion (Japan)
Eisai **5** 231-232
Fujiwara Kamatari **6** 145
Mabuchi, Kamo **10** 73-74

Ship building
see Marine engineering

Ship of Fools (book)
Brant, Sebastian **2** 503-504

Ship of Fools (novel)
Porter, Katherine Anne **12** 406-407

SHIPPEN, EDWARD (1728-1806), American jurist **14** 197-198

Shippen, William, Jr. (1736-1808), Ameri-
can physician
Morgan, John **11** 162-163
Rush, Benjamin **13** 364-365

Shipping industry leaders
see Business and industrial leaders—
shipping industry

Shipwreck, The (painting)
Turner, Joseph Mallord William
15 352-354

Shipwrecked, The (book)
Cabeza de Vaca, Álvar Núñez **3** 197

Shipwreck victims
Chancellor, Richard **3** 422
Grotius, Hugo **7** 18-19
Kitchener, Horatio Herbert **9** 45-46

Shirakaba Ha (Japanese literary school)
Kawabata, Yasunari **8** 463-464

Shiraz (city, Iran)
Hafiz, Shams al-Din **7** 63

Shire River (Africa)
Livingstone, David **9** 463-465

SHIRER, WILLIAM L. (born 1904), American journalist and historian who wrote on
the history of Nazi Germany **14** 198-199

Shirin and Farhad (story)
Behzad **2** 123

Shirley (novel)
Brontë, Charlotte **3** 17-18

Shirley, Laurence
see Derby, Lord

Shirley Place (Roxbury, Massachusetts)
Harrison, Peter **7** 179-180

Shirley poppy (plant)
Burbank, Luther **3** 129-131

Shisei (novel)
Tanizaki, Junichiro **15** 101-102

Shisha (ancient city, Caucasus)
Agha Mohammad Khan **1** 80-81

Shitennoji (temple, Osaka, Japan)
Shotoku Taishi **14** 205-207
Suiko **15** 15-16

Shiva (Hindu deity)
Ramakrishna, Sri **13** 11-13
Shankara **14** 150-151

SHIVAJI
see Śivajī

Shivhe Ha-Ari (book; Dresnitz)
Luria, Isaac ben Solomon Ashkenazi
10 47-48

Shoa (Ethiopian province)
Mengs, Anton Raphael **10** 505

Shock (medicine)
Dale, Henry Hallett **4** 371-373

Shock Treatment (film)
Davis, Ossie **4** 421-422

Shocken Department Stores (Germany)
Mendelsohn, Erich **10** 488

SHOCKLEY, WILLIAM (1910-1989), American physicist **14** 200-202

Shock-wave theory (physics)
Bethe, Hans Albrecht **2** 238-239

Shodo (Buddhism)
Honen **7** 473

Shoei, Kano (1519-1592), Japanese painter
Eitoku, Kano **5** 242

Shoemaker's Holiday, The (play)
Dekker, Thomas **4** 465-466

Shoes of Happiness, The (poems)
Markham, Edwin **10** 267

Shofukuji (Rinzai temple; Japan)
Eisai **5** 231-232

Shogunate (Japan)
see Japan—1185-1867

SHOLEM ALEICHEM (Sholem Rabinowitz;
1859-1916), Russian-born American
author **14** 202-203
Peretz, Isaac Loeb **12** 212
Singer, Isaac Bashevis **14** 249-250

Sholes, Christopher (1819-1890), American inventor
Edison, Thomas Alva **5** 206-208

**SHOLOKHOV, MIKHAIL ALEKSAN-
DROVICH** (1905-1984), Russian novelist
14 203-204
Ehrenburg, Ilya Grigorievich **5** 224-225

Shoma (Buddhist sutra)
Shotoku Taishi **14** 205-207

Shomu (ruled 724-749), Japanese emperor
Makibi, Kibi-no **10** 161

Shonen (novel)
Tanizaki, Junichiro **15** 101-102

Shoot the Piano Player (film)
Truffaut, François **15** 311-313

Shooting Niagara... (book)
Carlyle, Thomas **3** 304-305

Shop around the Corner (film)
Lubitsch, Ernst **10** 18-19

Shores of Light, The (book)
Wilson, Edmund **16** 318-319

**Short Happy Life of Francis Macomber,
The** (story)
Hemingway, Ernest Miller **7** 274-277

Short Is the Time (poems)
Lewis, Cecil Day **9** 380

Short Parliament (England; 1640)
Pym, John **12** 495-496

Short story (literature)
see Authors—short-story writers

Short Symphony (musical composition)
Copland, Aaron **4** 227-228

Shosho Shigemoto no Haha (novel)
Tanizaki, Junichiro **15** 101-102

Shoshone Indians (North America)
Fitzpatrick, Thomas **5** 474-475
Lewis, Meriwether **9** 391-392
Lowie, Robert Harry **10** 18

Washakie **16** 123-125

SHOSTAKOVICH, DMITRI DMITRIEVICH
(1906-1975), Russian composer
14 204-205
Khachaturian, Aram Ilich **8** 530-531
Prokofiev, Sergei Sergeevich
12 458-460
Stravinsky, Igor Fedorovich **14** 502-506

SHOTOKU TAISHI (573-621), Japanese
regent, statesman, and scholar
14 205-207
Suiko **15** 15-16

Shoulder Arms (film)
Chaplin, Charles Spencer **3** 438-440

Show Boat (musical)
Hammerstein, Oscar Clendenning II
7 104-106
Kern, Jerome David **8** 517-518
Robeson, Paul Leroy **13** 198-199
Ziegfeld, Florenz **16** 516-517

Show Boat (novel)
Ferber, Edna **5** 413

Show Girl (musical)
Gershwin, George **6** 284-285

Show Must Go On, The (novel)
Rice, Elmer **13** 126-127

Showa Tenno
see Hirohito

SHREVE, HENRY MILLER (1785-1851),
American steamboat designer and builder
14 207

Shrewsbury, battle of (1403)
Glendower, Owen **6** 364-365

Shrine of St. Ursula (painting)
Memling, Hans **10** 476

Shropshire Lad, A (poems)
Housman, Alfred Edward **7** 521-522

Shroud, The (story)
Premchand **12** 439

Shrouded Woman, The (book)
Bombal, María Luisa **2** 380-381

Shtolz (literary character)
Goncharov, Ivan Aleksandrovich **6** 424

Shu ching (book; Confucius)
Confucius **4** 197-200
Mencius **10** 480-481
Ssu-ma Ch'ien **14** 388-389

Shu Ch'ing-ch'un
see Lao Shê

Shu Maung
see Ne Win

SHUBERT BROTHERS (1883-1963), theatrical managers **14** 207-209

Shudja (ruled 1358-84), Persian ruler of
Shiraz
Hafiz, Shams al-Din **7** 63

Shui-hu chuan (novel)
Hu Shih **8** 63-65

Shukhov (literary character)
Solzhenitsyn, Alexander Isayevich
14 330-332

Shulhan Aruk (Jewish law code; Caro)
Caro, Joseph ben Ephraim **3** 316-317
Elijah ben Solomon **5** 251-252

SHULTZ, GEORGE PRATT (born 1920),
labor and economics specialist, educator,
businessman, and international negotia-
tor **14** 209-211

Shun-chih (ruled 1643-61), Chinese emper-
or
K'ang-hsi **8** 423-426

Shunkinsho (novel)
Tanizaki, Junichiro **15** 101-102

Shunro
see Hokusai, Katsushika

Shunsho, Katsukawa (died 1792), Japanese
Ukiyo-e artist
Hokusai, Katsushika **7** 447-448

Shunya (Buddhism)
Buddha **3** 97-101

Shuta
see Liang Wu-ti

Shvetambaras (Jain sect)
Mahavira, Vardhamana **10** 135-137

Shwebo (town, Burma)
Alaungpaya **1** 103

Shylock (literary character; Shakespeare)
Booth, Edwin **2** 401-402
Shakespeare, William **14** 142-145
Vigny, Comte de **15** 494-495

Si gira (novel)
Pirandello, Luigi **12** 319-321

Siam
see Thailand

SIBELIUS, JEAN JULIUS CHRISTIAN
(1865-1957), Finnish composer
14 211-212
Hanson, Howard **7** 135-136
Walton, William Turner **16** 92-93

Siberia (region, Russia)
Bering, Vitus **2** 193-194
Dostoevsky, Fyodor **5** 74-77
Godunov, Boris Feodorovich **6** 382-383
Ivan IV **8** 157-159
Kropotkin, Peter Alekseevich **9** 107-108

Sibylline Leaves (book)
Coleridge, Samuel Taylor **4** 154-156

Sica, Vittorio de (1902-1974), Italian film
director
Antonioni, Michelangelo **1** 252-253
Ray, Satyajit **13** 60-61

Sicard, Abbé (1742-1822), French instructor for the deaf and mute
Gallaudet, Thomas Hopkins **6** 185

Sicilian Vespers (1282)
Michael VIII **11** 1-2
Peter III **12** 256-257

Sicily (island, Italy)
Aragonese rule
Peter III **12** 256-257
Carthaginian invasions
Hamilcar Barca **7** 94-95
ceded to Austria
Victor Amadeus II **15** 482-483
see also Spanish Succession, War of
the
independence movement
Cavour, Conte di **3** 385-386
Crispi, Francesco **4** 310-311
Garibaldi, Giuseppe **6** 215-217
Norman conquest and rule
Frederick I **6** 78-79
Frederick II **6** 79
Guiscard, Robert **7** 39-40
Innocent, III **8** 125-127
Roger II **13** 244-245
Roman rule
Cato, the Younger **3** 374-375
Ricimer, Flavius **13** 151-152
WW II (Allied invasions)
Alexander of Tunis, 1st Earl
1 135-136
Bradley, Omar Nelson **2** 483-484
Montgomery, Bernard Law
11 135-136
Patton, George Smith Jr. **12** 140-141
see also Italy; Naples, Kingdom of;
Two Sicilies, Kingdom of the

Sicily, Duke of
see Robert Guiscard

Sick Child (painting)
Munch, Edvard **11** 247-248

SICKERT, WALTER RICHARD (1860-1942),
English painter **14** 212-213

Sickingen, Franz von (1481-1523), German
statesman
Hutten, Ulrich von **8** 72-73

Sid Hamet's Rod (poem)
Swift, Jonathan **15** 51-54

Siddal, Elizabeth Eleanor (died 1862), D.
Rossetti's model
Rossetti, Dante Gabriel **13** 308-309

Siddhartha (novel)
Hesse, Hermann **7** 367-369

SIDGWICK, HENRY (1838-1900), English
philosopher and moralist **14** 213

Sidis, Boris (1867-1923), American psychologist
White, William Alanson **16** 239-240

Sidmouth, 1st Viscount
see Addington, Henry

SIDNEY, SIR PHILIP (1554-1586), English
poet, courtier, diplomat, and soldier
14 214-215
Elizabeth I **5** 263-266
Essex, 2d Earl of **5** 321-322
Hakluyt, Richard **7** 70
Plutarch **12** 359-360
Spenser, Edmund **14** 373-376

Sidonia, 7th Duke of
see Medina-Sidonia, 7th Duke of

Sidus ex claro (musical composition)
Lassus, Roland de **9** 216-218

Sieben Legenden (stories)
Keller, Gottfried **8** 478-479

Sieben Lieder aus letzter Zeit (songs)
Mahler, Gustav **10** 144-145

Siebent Ring, Der (poems)
George, Stefan **6** 277-278

Sief Research Institute (Rehovoth, Israel)
see Weizmann Institute of Science

Siege of Corinth, The (epic)
Byron, George Gordon Noel **3** 193-194

Siege of Gibralter (painting)
Copley, John Singleton **4** 228-230

Siege of Thebes, The (poem)
Lydgate, John **10** 61-62

SIEGEL, BENJAMIN ("Bugsy"; 1906-1947),
American gangster **14** 215-216

Siegfried (opera)
Wagner, Richard **16** 40-43

Siegfried (play)
Giraudoux, Jean **6** 349-350

Siegfried's Death (opera)
Wagner, Richard **16** 40-43

Siena Cathedral (Italy)
Arnolfo di Cambio **1** 315-316
Duccio di Buoninsegna **5** 121-122
Ghiberti, Lorenzo **6** 291-292
Pisano, Giovanni **12** 324-325
Pisano, Nicola **12** 325
Quercia, Jacopo della **12** 509
Sassetta **13** 492

SIENKIEWICZ, HENRYK (1846-1916), Polish novelist and short-story writer
14 216-217

SIERRA, JUSTO (1848-1912), Mexican
educator, writer, and historian **14** 217

Sierra Club
Adams, Ansel **1** 40-41

Sierra Leone (nation, West Africa)
Blyden, Edward Wilmot **2** 348-349
Cinque, Joseph **4** 62
Cuffe, Paul **4** 331-332
Cugoano, Ottobah **4** 332-333
Equiano, Olaudah **5** 296-297
Henry the Navigator **7** 305-306
Margai, Milton Augustus Striery
10 248-249
Wallace-Johnson, Isaac Theophilus
Akunna **16** 76-77

Sierra Leone People's party (established
1951)
Margai, Milton Augustus Striery
10 248-249

SIEYÈS, COMTE EMMANUEL JOSEPH
(1748-1836), French statesman and political writer **14** 217-218
Fouché, Joseph **6** 30-31

Napoleon I **11** 306-310

Siffin, battle of (657)
Ali **1** 155-156
Muawiya ibn Abu Sufyan **11** 223-224

Sifton, Sir Clifford (1861-1929), Canadian
statesman
Laurier, Wilfrid **9** 232-234

SIFTON, SIR CLIFFORD (1861-1929),
politician who helped turn the Canadian
West into a premier agricultural area
14 219-220

Siger of Brabant (circa 1235-circa 1282),
Latin Averroist philosopher
Lull, Raymond **10** 39-40
Thomas Aquinas **15** 183-186

**Sight in Camp in the Daybreak Gray and
Dim** (poem)
Whitman, Walt **16** 249-251

SIGISMUND (1368-1437), Holy Roman
emperor 1411-37, king of Bohemia
1420-37, and king of Hungary
1385-1437 **14** 220-221
Charles IV **3** 455-456
Wenceslaus **16** 201-202

Sigismund III (1566-1632), king of Poland
1587-1632 and of Sweden 1592-1604
Gustavus II **7** 43-45
Oxenstierna, Axel Gustafsson **12** 44-45

Siglo, El (newspaper)
Gómez, Juan Vicente **6** 417-418

Sign of the Four, The (novel)
Doyle, Arthur Conan **5** 91-92

Signac, Paul (1863-1935), French painter
Prendergast, Maurice Brazil **12** 440
Seurat, Georges Pierre **14** 120-122

**Signing of the Declaration of Indepen-
dence** (painting)
Trumbull, John **15** 316-317
Wythe, George **16** 415

SIGNORELLI, LUCA (circa 1445/50-1523),
Italian painter **14** 221-222

Signos del Dia del Juicio, Los (poems)
Gonzalo de Berceo **6** 431-432

Sigüenza
see Ferrer, Gabriel Miró

Sigüenza y Góngora, Don Carlos de
(1645-1700), Mexican scientist and
writer
Juana Inés de la Cruz **8** 367-368
Kino, Eusebio Francisco **9** 30-31

Sigurd the Bastard (trilogy)
Bjørnson, Bjørnstjerne **2** 299-300

SIHANOUK, PRINCE NORODOM (born
1922), Cambodian nationalist and political leader **14** 222-223

Sii Phaeaendin (Four Reigns; book)
Kukrit Pramoj, Momrajawong (M.R.)
9 126-127

Sijilmasa (Tafilalet, oasis, Morocco)
Abdullah ibn Yasin **1** 20

Sikes, Bill (literary character)
Dickens, Charles John Huffam
4 538-541

Sikh war (1848-1849)
Dalhousie, 1st Marquess of **4** 375-376

Sikhs (religious sect)
Aurangzeb **1** 377
Nanak **11** 303
Ranjit Singh **13** 32-33

SIKORSKY, IGOR (1889-1972),
Russian-American aeronautical engineer,
aircraft manufacturer, and inventor
14 223-224
Douglas, Donald Wills **5** 77

Sikyonios (play)
Menander **10** 477-478

Silas Marnar (novel)
Eliot, George **5** 254-256

SILBER, JOHN (born 1926), American
philosopher and educator **14** 224-226

Silbersee, Der (opera)
Weill, Kurt **16** 174-175

Silence (play)
Pinter, Harold **12** 317-318

Silence (poem)
Moore, Marianne **11** 148-149

Silence (sculpture)
Saint-Gaudens, Augustus **13** 432

Silence, The (film)
Bergman, Ernst Ingmar **2** 190-191

Silent Don, The (novel)
Sholokhov, Mikhail Aleksandrovich
14 203-204

Silent Snow, Secret Snow (story)
Aiken, Conrad **1** 90-91

Silent Spring (book)
Carson, Rachel Louise **3** 337-338

Siles Zuazo, Hernán (born 1914), Bolivian
politician
Paz, Octavio **12** 161-162

Silesian wars
1st and 2d
see Austrian Succession, War of the
3d
see Seven Years War

Silius Italicus, Tiberius Catius (25/26-202),
Latin poet and politician
Martialis, Marcus Valerius **10** 286-287

SILKO, LESLIE (Leslie Marmon Silko; born
1948), Native American author and poet
14 226-227

Silkscreen printmaking
Stovall, Luther (Lou) McKinley
14 483-484

SILKWOOD, KAREN (1946-1974), American antinuclear activist **14** 227-229

Silla
see Korea—50-668 (Silla), 668-935
(Unified Silla)

Silla (musical composition)
  Handel, George Frederick **7** 116-119
SILLIMAN, BENJAMIN (1779-1864), American chemist, naturalist, and editor **14** 229-230
  Dunbar, William **5** 143-144
  Hare, Robert **7** 152-153
  Holbrook, Josiah **7** 450-451
SILLS, BEVERLY (Belle Miriam Silverman; born 1929), American child performer, coloratura soprano, and operatic superstar **14** 230-231
SILONE, IGNAZIO (1900-1978), Italian novelist and essayist **14** 231-232
Siloti, Alexander (1863-1945), Russian pianist
  Liszt, Franz **9** 445-447
Silurian system (geology)
  Murchison, Roderick Impey **11** 255-256
Silva, José Bonifácio de Andrada e
  see Andrada e Silva, José Bonifácio de
Silva Paranhos, José Maria da
  see Rio Branco, Barão do
Silva Xavier, José Joaquim da
  see Tiradentes
SILVER, ABBA HILLEL (1893-1963), American rabbi and Zionist leader **14** 232-233
Silver Box, The (play)
  Galsworthy, John **6** 189-190
Silver currency (United States)
  see Currency
Silver Lake, The (opera)
  Weill, Kurt **16** 174-175
Silver mining
  Daly, Marcus **4** 379-380
  Guggenheim, Meyer **7** 31-32
  Toledo, Francisco de **15** 257-259
Silver Pitchers (book)
  Alcott, Louisa May **1** 122
Silver Spoon, The (novel)
  Galsworthy, John **6** 189-190
Silver Tassie, The (play)
  O'Casey, Sean **11** 459-460
Silverado Squatters, The (novel)
  Stevenson, Robert Louis **14** 446-448
Silversmiths
  see Artists—silversmiths
Sim, Georges
  see Simenon, Georges
Simancas, battle of (939)
  Abd al-Rahman III **1** 14
Simbi and the Satyr ... (book)
  Tutuola, Amos **15** 361-362
SIMENON, GEORGES (1903-1989), Belgian novelist **14** 233-234
Simeon (New Testament character)
  Mary **10** 308
Simeon (Old Testament character)
  see Simon the Just

Simeon ben Jeshua ben Elazar ben Sira
  see Jesus ben Sira
Simeon with the Christ Child in the Temple (painting)
  Rembrandt Harmensz van Rijn **13** 91-95
SIMMEL, GEORG (1858-1918), German sociologist and philosopher **14** 234-235
  Bentley, Arthur F. **2** 178
  Cassirer, Ernst **3** 358-359
SIMMS, WILLIAM GILMORE (1806-1870), American author **14** 235-236
Simnel, Lambert (1477?-1534?), English imposter
  Henry VII **7** 300-302
Simon
  see Peter, St.
Simon, Claude (1913-1984), French novelist
  Robbe-Grillet, Alain **13** 189-190
Simon, 1st Viscount (John Allsebrook Simon; 1873-1954), English statesman
  Rai, Lala Lajpat **13** 5-6
SIMON, HERBERT ALEXANDER (born 1916), American Nobelist in economics **14** 236-237
SIMON, JULES FRANÇOIS (1814-1896), French philosopher, writer, and statesman **14** 237-238
SIMON, PAUL (born 1928), newspaper publisher, Illinois state legislator, lieutenant governor, and U.S. representative and senator **14** 238-239
Simon le pathétique (novel)
  Giraudoux, Jean **6** 349-350
Simon of Brie
  see Martin IV
Simon of the Desert (film)
  Buñuel, Luis **3** 127-128
Simon the Just (Old Testament character)
  Jesus ben Sira **8** 251
Simone Boccanegra (opera)
  Verdi, Giuseppe Fortunino Francesco **15** 463-465
Simonides of Ceos (flourished 6th-5th century B.C.), Greek poet
  Pindar **12** 312-313
  Xenophon **16** 418-420
SIMONOV, KONSTANTIN MIKHAILOVICH (1915-1979), Soviet poet and novelist **14** 239-240
Simons, Menno
  see Menno Simons
Simony (religion)
  Clement V **4** 101-102
  Dunstan **5** 151-152
  Gregory VII **6** 532-534
  Leo IX **9** 332
Simple (literary character)
  Hughes, Langston **8** 18-19

Simple Heart, The (story)
  Flaubert, Gustave **5** 480-482
Simple Honorable Man, A (novel)
  Richter, Conrad Michael **13** 148-149
Simplicissimus (novel)
  Grimmelshausen, Hans Jakob Christoffel von **7** 4-5
Simply Heavenly (play)
  Hughes, Langston **8** 18-19
Simposium (musical composition)
  Halffter, Christóbal **7** 79-80
SIMPSON, GEORGE GAYLORD (1902-1984), American paleontologist **14** 240-242
SIMPSON, LOUIS ASTON MARANTZ (born 1923), American poet, critic, and educator **14** 243-244
Simpson, Mrs. Wallis
  see Windsor, Duchess of
Simpson, Sir George (1792-1860), Canadian explorer
  Kane, Paul **8** 422-423
Simpson, Thomas (1710-1761), English mathematician
  Demoivre, Abraham **4** 494-495
SIMS, WILLIAM SOWDEN (1858-1936), American admiral **14** 244
Simurgh (literary character)
  Attar, Farid ed-Din **1** 359-360
Sin (religion)
  Ezekiel **5** 355-356
  Jesus of Nazareth **8** 251-255
  Julian of Norwich **8** 381
SIN, JAIME L. (born 1928), Filipino cardinal of the Roman Catholic Church **14** 244-245
Sin amor (novel)
  Azuela, Mariano **1** 402
Sinai, Mt. (Mt. Horeb)
  Moses **11** 200-201
SINAN, KODJA MIMAR (1489-1578), Ottoman architect **14** 245-246
  Suleiman I **15** 20-21
SINATRA, FRANCIS ALBERT (born 1915), American singer **14** 246-248
Sinbad (musical)
  Gershwin, George **6** 284-285
Sinclair, Emil (literary character)
  Hesse, Hermann **7** 367-369
SINCLAIR, UPTON BEALE, JR. (1878-1968), American novelist and political writer **14** 248-249
  Creel, George **4** 304-305
  Dreiser, Herman Theodore **5** 98-100
  Hapgood, Norman **7** 137-138
  Lewis, Harry Sinclair **9** 385-387
  Nader, Ralph **11** 290-291
  Sacco and Vanzetti **13** 408-410
  Tarbell, Ida Minerva **15** 107-108

Sinfonia (musical composition)
Berio, Luciano **2** 194-195
Bloch, Ernest **2** 326-327
Britten, Benjamin **3** 10-11
Ginastera, Alberto Evaristo **6** 328-329
Mozart, Wolfgang Amadeus
   11 218-221
Nielsen, Carl August **11** 388-389
Scarlatti, Pietro Alessandro Gaspare
   13 517-518
Vivaldi, Antonio **16** 3-4
Walton, William Turner **16** 92-93

Sing Sing Prison (Ossining, New York State)
Bigelow, John **2** 271-272
Osborne, Thomas Mott **12** 17-18

Singapore (South Eastern Asia)
Goh Chok Tong **6** 393-395
Lee Hsien Loong **9** 280-281
Lee Kuan Yew **9** 281-283
Ong Teng Cheong **11** 519-520

SINGER, ISAAC BASHEVIS (1904-1991),
Polish-American author **14** 249-250

SINGER, ISAAC M. (1811-1875), American
inventor of the sewing machine **14** 250

SINGER, MAXINE (born Maxine Frank,
1931), American biochemist and geneticist **14** 251-252

SINGER, PETER ALBERT DAVID (born
1946), Australian philosopher and author
of Animal Liberation **14** 253-254

SINGH, VISHWANATH PRATAP (born
1931), prime minister of India
(1989-1990) **14** 254-256

Singin' in the Rain (film)
Kelly, Gene **8** 484-486

Singing Gallery (sculpture)
Donatello **5** 55-56
Luca della Robbia **10** 19-20

Single Integrated Operational Plan (joint
nuclear strike plan)
Lemnitzer, Lyman Louis **9** 319-320

Singleton, Anne
see Benedict, Ruth Fulton

Singspiel (music)
Goethe, Johann Wolfgang von
   6 388-391
Haydn, Franz Joseph **7** 219-221
Mozart, Wolfgang Amadeus
   11 218-221
Sullivan, Arthur Seymour **15** 23

Sink or Swim (book)
Alger, Horatio **1** 153-154

Sinking of the Titanic (painting)
Beckmann, Max **2** 104-105

Sinn Fein (Irish nationalist movement)
Adams, Gerald **1** 42-44
Chamberlain, Arthur Neville **3** 409-411
De Valera, Eamon **4** 514-515
Mannix, Daniel **10** 210
Markievicz, Constance **10** 267-271
Stephens, James **14** 430-431

Sinnott, Michael
see Sennett, Mack

Sino-Japanese War, First (1894-1895)
China
   Chang Tso-lin **3** 434-435
   K'ang Yu-wei **8** 426-428
   Li Hung-Chang **9** 407-409
   Liang Ch'i-ch'ao **9** 395-396
   Yüan Shih-k'ai **16** 480-481
Japan
   Ito, Hirobumi **8** 153-155
   Mutsuhito **11** 279-282
   Saionji, Kimmochi **13** 438-439
   Yamagata, Aritomo **16** 428-429
Korea
   Kojong **9** 74-75
   Taewŏn'gun, Hŭngsŏn **15** 74-75

Sino-Japanese War, Second (1931-1945)
China
   Ch'en Tu-hsiu **3** 501-502
   Chiang Kai-shek **3** 510-513
   Chou En-lai **4** 20-22
   Hu Shih **8** 63-65
   Ku Chieh-kang **9** 120-121
   Kuo Mo-jo **9** 133-134
   Lao Shê **9** 200-201
   Lin Piao **9** 429-430
   Mao Zedong **10** 225-227
   Wang Ching-wei **16** 98
   Wu P'ei-fu **16** 404-405
   Yen Hsi-shan **16** 452-453
Japan
   Hirohito **7** 410-412
   Konoe, Fumimaro **9** 82-83

Sioux Indians (North America)
American Horse **1** 195-198
Bad Heart Bull, Amos **1** 427-428
Black Elk, Nicholas **2** 305-306
Calamity Jane **3** 216
Crazy Horse **4** 303-304
Crook, George **4** 322-323
Custer, George Armstrong **4** 355-356
Eastman, Charles A. **5** 183-185
Fitzpatrick, Thomas **5** 474-475
Frontenac et Palluau, Comte de
   6 128-130
Means, Russell **10** 441-444
Miles, Nelson Appleton **11** 16-17
Peltier, Leonard **12** 193-195
Red Cloud **13** 70-71
Sitting Bull **14** 264-265

Sioux wars
American Horse **1** 195-198
Bad Heart Bull, Amos **1** 427-428
Crazy Horse **4** 303-304
Custer, George Armstrong **4** 355-356
Red Cloud **13** 70-71
Sitting Bull **14** 264-265

SIQUEIROS, DAVID ALFARO (1896-1974),
Mexican mural painter **14** 256

Sir Charles Grandison (novel)
Richardson, Samuel **13** 141-142

Sir John in Love (opera)

Vaughan Williams, Ralph **15** 446-447

Sir Lanval (lai)
Marie de France **10** 259

Sir Launcelot Greaves (novel)
Smollett, Tobias George **14** 305-307

Sir Martin Mar-All (play)
Dryden, John **5** 106-107

Sir Nigel (novel)
Doyle, Arthur Conan **5** 91-92

Sirach (Old Testament apocrypha)
see Ecclesiasticus

Sirach, Jesus ben
see Jesus ben Sira

Siraj-ud-Daula (1728-1757), nawab of Ben-
gal 1756-57
Clive, Robert **4** 119-120
Hastings, Warren **7** 195-196

Sirenetta (literary character)
D'Annunzio, Gabriele **4** 388

Sirens (Greek mythology)
Homer **7** 465-467

SIRICA, JOHN JOSEPH (1904-1992), U.S.
district court judge who presided over the
Watergate affair **14** 257-258

Siroe (opera)
Handel, George Frederick **7** 116-119

Sironi, Mario (1885-1961), Italian painter
Chirico, Giorgio de **4** 4

Sisley, Alfred (1839-1899), English-born
French painter
Daubigny, Charles François **4** 402
Monet, Claude **11** 102-104
Pissaro, Camille **12** 326-327
Renoir, Pierre Auguste **13** 101-102

**SISMONDI, JEAN CHARLES LÉONARD
SIMONDE DE** (1773-1842), Swiss-born
historian and political economist
14 258-259

Sisowath Sirik Matak, Prince (1914-1975),
Cambodian politician
Sihanouk, Norodom **14** 222-223

Sister Carrier (novel and film)
Dreiser, Herman Theodore **5** 98-100
Norris, Benjamin Franklin Jr.
   11 427-428

Sister Jane (novel)
Harris, Joel Chandler **7** 173-174

Sister Philomène (novel)
Goncourt, Edmond de and Jules de
   6 426-427

Sisters of Charity of St. Joseph (religious
congregation)
Seton, Elizabeth Ann Bayley
   14 118-119

Sisters of St. Joseph of the Sacred Heart
MacKillop, Mary **10** 106-107

Sisters of the Blessed Sacrament (Roman
Catholic order)
Drexel, Katherine **5** 102-103

Sistine Chapel (Rome)
Botticelli, Sandro **2** 439-440
Correggio **4** 249-251
Julius II **8** 384-386
Michelangelo Buonarroti **11** 2-5
Paul III **12** 144-145
Perugino **12** 245-246
Raphael **13** 40-42

Sistova, Peace of (1791)
Selim III **14** 95-96

SISULU, NONTSIKELELO ALBERTINA
(born 1918), leader of the anti-apartheid
movement in South Africa **14** 259-261

SISULU, WALTER MAX ULYATE (born
1912), leader of the African National
Congress (ANC) of South Africa
14 261-262

Sisyphus (literary character)
Camus, Albert **3** 255-257

Sitges, Declaration of (1957)
Gómez, Máximo **6** 418-419
Lleras Camargo, Alberto **9** 467

SITHOLE, NDABANINGI (born 1920),
African nationalist **14** 262-264

Sitter, Willem de (1872-1934), Dutch
astronomer
Lemaître, Abbè Georges Édouard
9 315-316

SITTING BULL (circa 1834-90), American
Indian leader and medicine man
14 264-265
Crazy Horse **4** 303-304
Miles, Nelson Appleton **11** 16-17

Situation Ethics (book)
Fletcher, Joseph Francis **5** 488-489

SITWELL, DAME EDITH (1887-1964), Eng-
lish poet and critic **14** 265-266
Housman, Alfred Edward **7** 521-522
Stein, Gertrude **14** 414-415
Thomas, Dylan Marlais **15** 188-190
Walton, William Turner **16** 92-93

Sitwell, Osbert (1892-1969), English poet,
playwright, and novelist
Sitwell, Edith **14** 265-266

Sitwell, Sacheverell (1897-1988), English
poet and critic
Sitwell, Edith **14** 265-266

Siva (Hindu god)
Kalidasa **8** 414-415

ŚIVAJĪ (1627-1680), Indian warrior and
leader of a Hindu nation **14** 266-267

Siward, Earl (died 1055), Danish warrior
Edward the Confessor **5** 218-219

Six, The (Les Six; French composers)
Milhaud, Darius **11** 17-18
Poulenc, Francis **12** 414-415
Satie, Erik **13** 494-495

Six Acts (1818; England)
Castlereagh, Viscount **3** 363-364
Liverpool, 2nd Earl of **9** 456-457

Six Articles (England; 1539)
Cranmer, Thomas **4** 295-296
Edward VI **5** 213-214
Henry VIII **7** 302-305
Latimer, Hugh **9** 221
Norfolk, 3d Duke of **11** 423

Six Characters in Search of an Author
(play)
Pirandello, Luigi **12** 319-321

Six Day War
see Arab-Israeli War (1967)

Six Edicts (1776)
Turgot, Anne Robert Jacques
15 348-349

Six Nations (North America Indian Fed.)
Johnson, William **8** 319-320
Lewis, Andrew **9** 376-377

Six O'Clock (painting)
Burchfield, Charles **3** 131-132

Sixes and Sevens (stories)
Henry, O. **7** 308-309

Sixtine (novel)
Gourmont, Remy de **6** 475

Sixtus IV (Francesco della Rovere;
1414-84), pope 1471-84
Alberti, Leon Battista **1** 113-115
Julius II **8** 384-386
Leo X **9** 332-334
Medici, Lorenzo de' **10** 450-451
Pollaiuolo, Antonio **12** 377-378

SIXTUS V (Felice Perreti; 1520-90), pope
1585-90 **14** 267-268
John, XXIII **8** 277-280
Maderno, Carlo **10** 117-118

60 Minutes (television news show)
Bradley, Ed **2** 478-481

Skater, The (painting)
Stuart, Gilbert **14** 513-515

Skeaping, John (1901-1980), English sculptor
Moore, Henry **11** 146-148

Skeleton in Armor, The (poem)
Longfellow, Henry Wadsworth
9 499-500

SKELTON, JOHN (circa 1460-1529), English poet and humanist **14** 268-269
Douglas, Gavin **5** 77-78

Skenandoa (1706?-1816), Oneida Indian
chief
Kirkland, Samuel **9** 37

Skepticism (philosophy)
ancient
Carneades **3** 309
Democritus **4** 493-494
critics
McCosh, James **10** 402-403
influence of
Augustine **1** 367-370
Chrysippus **4** 35-36
Luther, Martin **10** 48-51
modern

Bayle, Pierre **2** 77-78
Hume, David **8** 31-34
Santayana, George **13** 475-477
Renaissance
Charron, Pierre **3** 472
Montaigne, Michel Eyquem de
11 116-117
Pascal, Blaise **12** 122-124
see also Sophism

**Sketch Book of Geoffrey Crayon, Gent.,
The** (book)
Irving, Washington **8** 141-143

Sketches New and Old (book)
Twain, Mark **15** 363-366

Skiagraphos
see Apollodorus

Skidmore, Owings and Merrill (architectural firm)
Bunshaft, Gordon **3** 125-127

Skin of Our Teeth, The (play; Wilder)
Grass, Günter **6** 496-497
Wilder, Thornton Niven **16** 276-277

SKINNER, BURRHUS FREDERIC
(1904-1990), American experimental psychologist **14** 269-270
Watson, John Broadus **16** 138-139

Skipper Ireson's Ride (poem)
Whittier, John Greenleaf **16** 256-257

Sklodowska, Marie
see Curie, Marie Sklodowska

Sky above Clouds IV (painting)
O'Keeffe, Georgia **11** 487-489

Sky Blue (painting)
Kandinsky, Wassily **8** 420-422

Slabs of the Sunburnt West (poems)
Sandburg, Carl **13** 461-462

SLÁNSKÝ, RUDOLF SALZMANN
(1901-1952), founding member of the
Czechoslovak Communist Party and
vice-premier of the former Czechoslovakia **14** 270-271

Slapstick (comedy technique)
Sennett, Mack **14** 108-109

SLATER, SAMUEL (1768-1835),
English-born American manufacturer
14 272-273
Brown, Moses **3** 42-43

Slaughter on Tenth Avenue (ballet)
Rodgers, Richard Charles **13** 234-236

Slaughter-House Cases (1873)
Field, Stephen Johnson **5** 441-442
Miller, Samuel Freeman **11** 29-30

Slave, The (novel)
Hildreth, Richard **7** 382
Singer, Isaac Bashevis **14** 249-250

Slave, The (play)
Baraka, Imamu Amiri **1** 498-499

Slave Trade... (painting)
Géricault, Jean Louis André Théodore
6 280-281

Slave trade, African
early (15th-17th century)
Affonso I **1** 72
Byrd, William **3** 188-189
Drake, Francis **5** 94-96
Frederick William **6** 85-86
Hawkins, John **7** 210-211
Henry the Navigator **7** 305-306
in literature
Canot, Theodore **3** 262-263
Equiano, Olaudah **5** 296-297
see also African American history;
Slavery
late (18th-19th century)
Canot, Theodore **3** 262-263
Cass, Lewis **3** 355-356
Dalzel, Archibald **4** 381-382
Said, Seyyid **13** 428-429

Slavery (bondage)
China
Liu Tsung-Yüan **9** 455-456
Shih Le **14** 195
Greece
Cleomenes III **4** 103-104
Cleon **4** 104-105
Epictetus **5** 292
in literature
Euripides **5** 332-334
Wheatley, Phillis **16** 221-222
Korea
Ch'oe Ch'ung-hn **4** 13
Latin America
Carrera, José Miguel **3** 323-324
Castilla, Ramón **3** 361
Castro Alves, Antônio de **3** 364-365
Céspedes, Carlos Manuel de
3 398-399
Dessalines, Joan Jacques **4** 511-512
Freyre, Gilberto **6** 106-107
Las Casas, Bartolomé de **9** 211-212
Maceo, Antonio **10** 88-90
Metcalfe, Charles Theophilus
10 531-532
Pedro II **12** 180-181
Toussaint L'Ouverture, François
Dominique **15** 278-279
Velasco, Luis de **15** 450-451
Persia
Abu Nuwas **1** 33-34
Rome (ancient)
Caesar, Gaius Julius **3** 207-210
Constantine I **4** 209-211
Spartacus **14** 363-364
Turkey
Smith, John **14** 295-297
U.S. supporters
Atchison, David Rice **1** 357-358
Bledsoe, Albert Taylor **2** 324-325
Calhoun, John Caldwell **3** 226-228
Couper, James Hamilton **4** 270
Dalzel, Archibald **4** 381-382
Davis, Jefferson **4** 416-418
De Bow, James Dunwoody Brownson **4** 441-442
Dew, Thomas Roderick **4** 519

Fitzhugh, George **5** 474
Memminger, Christopher Gustavus
10 476-477
Pinckney, Charles Cotesworth
12 310
Taney, Roger Brooke **15** 98-99
Taylor, Zachary **15** 128-130
Tucker, George **15** 332-333
Yancey, William Lowndes
16 436-437
see also Abolitionists; Antislavery
movement; African American history; Slave trade, African

Slavery extension issue (United States)
see Compromise of 1850; Dred Scott
decision; Free Soil party;
Kansas-Nebraska Act; Missouri Compromise; Popular sovereignty; Wilmot
Proviso

Slavery—Ships, The (poem)
Whittier, John Greenleaf **16** 256-257

Slaves (film)
Davis, Ossie **4** 421-422

Slaves (sculpture; Michelangelo)
Michelangelo Buonarroti **11** 2-5
Rodin, Auguste **13** 236-238

Slavic Mass (musical composition)
Penderecki, Krzysztof **12** 195-197

Slavonic Dances (music)
Dvořák, Antonin **5** 168-169

Slavs (linguistics group)
Cyril and Methodius, Saints **4** 362-363
Francis Ferdinand **6** 44
Gobineau, Comte de **6** 375-376
Heraclius **7** 320-321
Herzen, Aleksandr Ivanovich **7** 351-352
Justinian I **8** 393-395
Nicholas I **11** 377-378
Vladimir I **16** 5-6

Slee, Margaret
see Sanger, Margaret

Sleep (film)
Warhol, Andy **16** 114-115

Sleep and Poetry (poem)
Keats, John **8** 470-472

Sleep of Reason, The (novel)
Snow, Charles Percy **14** 311-312

Sleepers, The (poem)
Whitman, Walt **16** 249-251

Sleeping Bather (painting)
Renoir, Pierre Auguste **13** 101-102

Sleeping Beauty (ballet)
Tchaikovsky, Peter Ilyich **15** 130-132

Sleeping Beauty (novel)
Kawabata, Yasunari **8** 463-464

Sleeping Gypsy (painting)
Rousseau, Henri **13** 323-324

Sleeping sickness (medicine)
Bruce, David **3** 63
Domagk, Gerhard Johannes Paul
5 48-50

Ehrlich, Paul **5** 225-226

Sleeping Venus (painting)
Giorgione **6** 340-341

Sleeping Women (painting)
Courbet, Jean Desiré Gustave
4 271-273

SLIDELL, JOHN (1793-1871), American
politician **14** 273
Benjamin, Judah Philip **2** 163-164
Mason, James Murray **10** 320-321
Polk, James Knox **12** 374-376
Wilkes, Charles **16** 279-280

Slight Ache, A (play)
Pinter, Harold **12** 317-318

SLOAN, ALFRED PRITCHARD, JR.
(1875-1966), American automobile executive **14** 274
Durant, William Crapo **5** 158

SLOAN, JOHN (1871-1951), American
painter **14** 274-275
Calder, Alexander **3** 216-218
Glackens, William **6** 355-356
Kent, Rockwell **8** 511
Smith, David **14** 287-288

Sloane, Sir Hans (1660-1753), British
physician
Boylston, Zabdiel **2** 471
Byrd, William II **3** 189-190

**Sloan-Kettering Institute for Cancer
Research**
Sloan, Alfred Pritchard Jr. **14** 274

Sloat, J. D. (1781-1867), American naval
officer
Frémont, John Charles **6** 97-98

Slodtz, Michel Ange (1705-1764), French
sculptor
Houdon, Antoine **7** 516-517

Slovenia (nation, Eastern Europe)
Alexander of Yugoslavia **1** 136-137

Slowly toward the North (painting)
Tanguy, Yves **15** 101

Sluis, battle of (1340)
Edward III **5** 211-212
Philip VI **12** 277-278

SLUTER, CLAUS (circa 1350-1405/1406),
Dutch-Burgundian sculptor **14** 275-276

SLYE, MAUD (1879-1954), American
pathologist **14** 276-277

SMALL, ALBION WOODBURY
(1854-1926), American sociologist and
educator **14** 277
Gumplowicz, Ludwig **7** 41

Small Grasshopper (sculpture)
Richier, Germaine **13** 145-146

Small Hours, The (play)
Kaufman, George S. **8** 457-458

Small House at Allington, The (novel)
Trollope, Anthony **15** 300-302

Small Kingdom, A (novel)
Tanizaki, Junichiro **15** 101-102

Small Passion (prints)
Dürer, Albrecht **5** 159-161

Smallpox (medicine)
Boylston, Zabdiel **2** 471
Cruz, Oswaldo Gonçalves **4** 328-329
Jenner, Edward **8** 245-246
Mather, Cotton **10** 330-332
Razi **13** 63-64
Sydenham, Thomas **15** 59-60
Waterhouse, Benjamin **16** 131-132

SMALLS, ROBERT (1839-1916), African
American statesman **14** 277-278

Smart, Christopher (1722-1771), English
poet
Collins, William **4** 168-169

SMEAL, ELEANOR (Eleanor Marie Cutri
Smeal; born 1939), American women's
rights activist and president of the National Organization for Women **14** 278-280

SMEATON, JOHN (1724-1792), English
civil engineer **14** 280-281
Newcomen, Thomas **11** 362

Smellie, William (1697-1763), British scientist
Hunter, William **8** 48-49

Smerdis (Bardiya; died circa 525 B.C.), Persian nobleman
Darius I **4** 394-395

Smerdyakov (literary character)
Dostoevsky, Fyodor **5** 74-77

SMETANA, BEDŘICH (1824-1884), Czech
composer **14** 281-282
Dvořák, Antonin **5** 168-169

SMIBERT, JOHN (1688-1751),
Scottish-born American painter **14** 282
Copley, John Singleton **4** 228-230

Smibert, Nathaniel (1734-1756), American
painter
Smibert, John **14** 282

SMITH, ADAM (1723-1790), Scotch econ-
omist and moral philosopher **14** 283-284
associates
Johnson, Samuel **8** 315-317
Turgot, Anne Robert Jacques
15 348-349
influence of (Africa)
Cugoano, Ottobah **4** 332-333
influence of (Asia)
Yen Fu **16** 452
influence of (Europe)
Engels, Friedrich **5** 286-288
Malthus, Thomas Robert **10** 180-181
Marshall, Alfred **10** 277-278
Marx, Karl **10** 304-308
O'Connell, Daniel **11** 465-467
Say, Jean Baptiste **13** 508-509
Sismondi, Jean Charles Léonard
Simonde de **14** 258-259
influence of (Latin America)
Rivadavia, Bernardino **13** 182-183
influence of (United States)
Small, Albion Woodbury **14** 277
influenced by

Mandeville, Bernard **10** 192

SMITH, ALFRED EMMANUEL
(1873-1944), American politician
14 284-285
opponents
Hoover, Herbert Clark **7** 483-485
McAdoo, William Gibbs
10 385-386
supporters
Baruch, Bernard Mannes **2** 42-43
Curley, James Michael **4** 344-345
Hapgood, Norman **7** 137-138
Hopkins, Harry Lloyd **7** 494-495
Lehman, Herbert Henry **9** 306-307
Murphy, Charles Francis **11** 259-260
Roosevelt, Franklin Delano
13 277-280
Wald, Lillian **16** 53-54

SMITH, BESSIE (1894-1937), African American blues singer **14** 285-287

SMITH, DAVID (1906-1965), American
sculptor **14** 287-288
Calder, Alexander **3** 216-218
Caro, Anthony **3** 316
González, Julio **6** 428-429

SMITH, DONALD ALEXANDER (1st Baron
Strathcona and Mount Royal;
1820-1914), Canadian politician and philanthropist **14** 288-289

SMITH, DORA VALENTINE (1893-1985),
American educator **14** 289-290

Smith, Elihu Hubbard (1771-1798), American physician
Brown, Charles Brockden **3** 33

Smith, Frederick Edwin
see Birkenhead, 1st Earl of

SMITH, GERRIT (1797-1874), American
philanthropist and reformer **14** 290-291
Birney, James Gillespie **2** 283-284
Brown, John **3** 39-41
Burritt, Elihu **3** 160
Fitzhugh, George **5** 474

Smith, Gipsy Rodney (1860-1947), English
evangelist
Henderson, Arthur **7** 277-278

SMITH, IAN DOUGLAS (born 1919),
African prime minister **14** 291-293
Sithole, Ndabaningi **14** 262-264

SMITH, JAMES MCCUNE (1813-1865),
African American physician and author
14 293-294

SMITH, JEDEDIAH S. (1799-1831), American trapper, fur trader, and explorer
14 294-295
Ashley, William Henry **1** 333-334
Fitzpatrick, Thomas **5** 474-475

SMITH, JOHN (circa 1580-1631), English
colonist in America **14** 295-297
Beverley, Robert **2** 252
Hudson, Henry **8** 12-13
Pocahontas **12** 361-362
Powhatan **12** 429-430

SMITH, JOSEPH (1805-1844), American
Mormon leader **14** 297-298
Young, Brigham **16** 469-470

SMITH, LILLIAN EUGENIA (1897-1966),
Southern writer and critic of white
supremacy and segregation **14** 298-299

SMITH, MARGARET CHASE (1897-1995),
first woman elected to both houses of
Congress **14** 299-300

Smith, Robert Barnwell
see Rhett, Robert Barnwell

Smith, Samuel Stanhope (1750-1819),
American educator
Witherspoon, John **16** 346-348

Smith, Sir Harry (1787-1860), English soldier
Pretorius, Andries **12** 444-445

SMITH, WILLIAM (1727-1803), American
educator and churchman **14** 301
Clinton, George **4** 113-114

Smith, William (1769-1839), English geologist
Darwin, Charles Robert **4** 397-399

Smith, William Robertson (1846-1894),
Scottish philologist and archeologist
Evans-Pritchard, Edward Evan **5** 340
Frazer, James George **6** 76

Smith College (Northampton, MA)
deans
Nicolson, Marjorie Hope
11 384-385
presidents
Conway, Jill Kathryn Ker **4** 213-214

Smith v. Allwright (legal case)
Marshall, Thurgood **10** 282-284

Smith v. Texas (legal case)
Black, Hugo Lafayette **2** 301-303

Smith-Lever Act (1914)
Knapp, Seaman Asahel **9** 58

Smith-Mundt Act (1948)
Fulbright, James William **6** 147-149

Smithson, Harriett (Mrs. Hector Berlioz;
died 1854), English actress
Berlioz, Louis Hector **2** 203-205

SMITHSON, ROBERT (1938-1973), American sculptor, essayist, and filmmaker
14 301-303

Smithsonian Institution (Washington, D.C.)
Bell, Alexander Graham **2** 129-131
Custer, George Armstrong **4** 355-356
Goddard, Robert Hutchings **6** 376-377
Henry, Joseph **7** 307-308
Hrdlička, Aleš **8** 3-4
Langley, Samuel Pierpont **9** 195-196
Owen, Robert Dale **12** 40-41
Powell, John Wesley **12** 425-426
Renwick, James **13** 102-103

SMOHALLA (1815-1895), Native American
warrior, medicine man, and spiritual
leader **14** 303-305

Smoke (novel; Turgenev)
Edgeworth, Maria **5** 205-206
Turgenev, Ivan Sergeyevich **15** 345-348

Smoke and Steel (poem)
Sandburg, Carl **13** 461-462

Smoke of the Fatherland (novel)
Simonov, Konstantin Mikhailovich
14 239-240

SMOLLETT, TOBIAS GEORGE
(1721-1771), English novelist and satirist
14 305-307
Dickens, Charles John Huffam
4 538-541
Lesage, Alain René **9** 353-354

SMUIN, MICHAEL (born 1938), American
dancer-choreographer-director
14 307-309

SMUTS, JAN CHRISTIAN (1870-1950),
South African soldier and statesman
14 309-310
Botha, Louis **2** 434-436
Cecil, of Chelwood Viscount **3** 388-389
Gokhale, Gopal Krishna **6** 396
Hertzog, James Barry Munnik
7 347-348
Malan, Daniel Francois **10** 163-164
Mandela, Nelson Rolihlahla
10 185-186
Vorster, Balthazar Johannes **16** 30-32

SONJO (1552-1608), king of Korea
1567-1608 **14** 341-342

Snopes clan (literary characters)
Faulkner, William **5** 395-397

SNOW, CHARLES PERCY (1905-1972),
English novelist and physicist **14** 311-312
Rutherford, Ernest **13** 384-387

Snow Country (novel)
Kawabata, Yasunari **8** 463-464

SNOW, EDGAR (1905-1972), American
journalist and author **14** 312-313
Chou En-lai **4** 20-22
Liu Shao-Ch'i **9** 453-455

Snow in Bethlehem (painting)
Milne, David Brown **11** 37-38

Snow Maiden (opera)
Rimsky-Korsakov, Nikolai Andreevich
13 174-175

Snow Mask, The (poem)
Blok, Aleksandr Aleksandrovich **2** 335

Snow White (film)
Disney, Walter Elias **5** 26-27

Snowbirds (poem)
Fréchette, Louis-Honoré **6** 77-78

Snow-Bound (poem)
Whittier, John Greenleaf **16** 256-257

Snowdon (painting)
Wilson, Richard **16** 329-330

SNOWE, OLYMPIA (born Olympia Jean
Bouchles, 1947), U.S. congresswoman
and senator **14** 313-314

Snow-Image, The (stories)
Hawthorne, Nathaniel **7** 212-215

Snows (poem)
Perse, Saint-John **12** 242-243

Snows of Kilimanjaro, The (story)
Hemingway, Ernest Miller **7** 274-277

Snowstorm, The (book)
Tolstoy, Leo **15** 262-265

Snyders, Frans (1579-1657), Dutch painter
Van Dyck, Anthony **15** 423-425

So Big (novel)
Ferber, Edna **5** 413

So in Love (song)
Porter, Cole Albert **12** 405-406

So Long Mary (song)
Cohan, George Michael **4** 137-138

So This Is Paris (film)
Lubitsch, Ernst **10** 18-19

Soames, Mr. (literary character)
Richardson, Samuel **13** 141-142

SOANE, SIR JOHN (1753-1837), English
architect **14** 314-315
Latrobe, Benjamin Henry **9** 222-224

Soap (story)
Lu Hsün **10** 35-37

SOARES, MÁRIO (Mário Alberto Nobre
Lopes Soares; born 1924), first socialist
president of Portugal **14** 315-316

SOBCHAK, ANATOLY ALEXANDROVICH
(born 1937), popular democratic leader
of Russia elected mayor of St. Petersburg
in 1990 **14** 317-318

Sobieski, John
see John III

Sobre héroes y tumbas (novel)
Sábato, Ernesto **13** 399-400

SOBUKWE, ROBERT MANGALISO
(1924-1978), South African politician
14 318-319
Luthuli, Albert John **10** 51-52
Verwoerd, Hendrik Frensch **15** 472-473

Socarrás, Carlos Prio (1903-1977), Cuban
statesman
Batista y Zaldívar, Fulgencio **2** 57-58

Soccer
Pele **12** 190-191

Social Action Party (Thailand)
Kukrit Pramoj, Momrajawong (M.R.)
9 126-127

Social Consciousness (sculpture)
Epstein, Jacob **5** 295-296

Social contract theory (philosophy)
Carneades **3** 309
Hobbes, Thomas **7** 421-423
Liang Ch'i-ch'ao **9** 395-396
Maistre, Joseph de **10** 153-154
Marsilius of Padua **10** 284
Rawls, John **13** 55-56
Rousseau, Jean Jacques **13** 324-328

Social Darwinism (philosophy)
adherents
Cunha, Euclides Rodrigues Pimenta
da **4** 336-337
Krochmal, Nachman Kohen
9 104-105
Spencer, Herbert **14** 369-370
opponents
Freyre, Gilberto **6** 106-107
Hobhouse, Leonard Trelawny
7 425-426
Kropotkin, Peter Alekseevich
9 107-108
Tönnies, Ferdinand **15** 266-267
Ward, Lester Frank **16** 113-114

Social Democratic movement (Russia)
see Bolsheviks; Mensheviks

Social Democratic party
Austria
Dollfuss, Engelbert **5** 47
Renner, Karl **13** 98-99
Tito, Marshal **15** 244-246
Brazil
Goulart, João **6** 467-469
Kubitschek de Oliveira, Juscelino
9 113-115
Costa Rica
Ferrer, José Figuéres **5** 428-429
England
Jenkins, Roy Harris **8** 244-245
Owen, David Anthony Llewellyn
12 37-39
Steel, David Martin Scott
14 406-407
Williams, Shirley Vivien Teresa Brit-
tain **16** 305-306
Finland
Mannerheim, Carl Gustav Emil Von
10 207-208
Germany
Bahr, Egon **1** 438-440
Bernstein, Eduard **2** 218
Bethmann Hollweg, Theobald von
2 239-240
Brandt, Willy **2** 499-500
Ebert, Friedrich **5** 193-194
Kautsky, Karl Johann **8** 462-463
Lafontaine, Oskar **9** 158-160
Lassalle, Ferdinand **9** 216
Luxemburg, Rosa **10** 55-56
Michels, Robert **11** 7
Rau, Johannes **13** 51-52
Scharping, Rudolf **13** 522-524
Schmidt, Helmut **14** 19-21
Schumacher, Kurt **14** 40-41
Ulbricht, Walter **15** 383-384
Vogel, Hans-Jochen **16** 8-9
Zetkin, Clara **16** 504-505
Japan
Katayama, Sen **8** 457
New Zealand
Fraser, Peter **6** 73-74
Savage, Michael Joseph **13** 501-502
Poland
Dzerzhinsky, Felix Edmundovich
5 173-174

Luxemburg, Rosa **10** 55-56
U.S.
  Berger, Victor Louis **2** 189-190
Social Democratic Workers party (Netherlands)
  Wilhelmina **16** 278-279
Social Democratic Workers' party (Russia)
  see Bolsheviks; Mensheviks
Social evolution
  Childe, Vere Gordon **3** 521-522
  Le Bon, Gustave **9** 268-269
Social Forces (journal)
  Odum, Howard Washington
    11 474-476
Social Gospel (theology)
  critics
    Niebuhr, Reinhold **11** 387-388
  influence of
    Katayama, Sen **8** 457
    McGovern, George Stanley
      10 412-414
    Thomas, Norman Mattoon
      15 191-192
    Woodsworth, James Shaver **16** 376
  leaders
    Gladden, Washington **6** 356-357
    Hale, Edward Everett **7** 71-72
    Holmes, John Haynes **7** 456-457
    Rauschenbusch, Walter **13** 53-54
  prototype
    Muhlenberg, William Augustus
      11 233-234
Social insurance
  see Social security
Social legislation
  Asquith, Herbert Henry **1** 344-346-271
  Bourgeois, Léon **2** 450-451
  Giolitti, Giovanni **6** 339-340
  Owen, Robert Dale **12** 40-41
  Wagner, Robert Ferdinand **16** 43
Social reform
  Asia
    Ambedkar, Bhimrao Ramji
      1 190-191
    Chang Chien **3** 429-430
    Ecevit, Bülent **5** 196-197
    Gandhi, Mohandas Karamchand
      6 201-204
    Meighen, Arthur **10** 459-460
  Canada
    Bennett, Richard Bedford **2** 171-172
  Europe
    Alexander I **1** 130-132-114
    Arnold, Thomas **1** 313-314
    Astor, Nancy Langhorne **1** 352-354
    Attlee, Clement Richard **1** 361-362
    Basedow, Johann Bernhard **2** 44-45
    Blum, Léon **2** 343-344
    Chamberlain, Arthur Neville
      3 409-411
    Chamberlain, Joseph **3** 411-413
    Leo XIII **9** 334-336
    Le Play, Guillaume Frédéric
      9 350-351

  Latin America
    Alemán, Mateo **1** 126
    Alessandri Palma, Arturo **1** 128-129
    Barrios, Justo Rufino **2** 23-24
    Batista y Zaldívar, Fulgencio
      2 57-58
    Batlle y Ordóñez, José **2** 58-59
    Betancourt, Rómulo **2** 237-238
    Bosch, Juan **2** 428-429
    Castilla, Ramón **3** 361
    Castro Ruz, Fidel **3** 365-368
    Menchú, Rigoberta **10** 479-480
    Mosquera, Tomás Cipriano de
      11 205-206
    Pérez Esquivel, Adolfo **12** 215-217
    Rivadavia, Bernardino **13** 182-183
  South Africa
    Sobukwe, Robert Mangaliso
      14 318-319
  U.S.
    Abbott, Grace **1** 9-10
    Abzug, Bella Stavisky **1** 34-35
    Alinsky, Saul David **1** 161-162
    Balch, Emily Greene **1** 463-464
    Day, Dorothy **4** 428-429
    Dewson, Mary Williams **4** 525
    Drake, Daniel **5** 93-94
    Long, Huey Pierce **9** 496-497
    Rankin, Jeannette Pickering
      13 35-37
    Reuther, Walter Philip **13** 107-108
    Strong, Josiah **14** 512-513
    Sullivan, Leon Howard **15** 25-27
    see also Civil rights movement
      (United States)
Social reform drama
  see Realistic drama
Social Revolution (mural)
  Orozco, José Clemente **12** 1-2
Social Science Research Council (United States)
  Merriam, Charles Edward **10** 518-519
  Schlesinger, Arthur Meier **14** 13
Social scientists, African
  political theorists
    Cabral, Amílcar Lopes **3** 202-203
Social scientists, Algerian
  Fanon, Frantz **5** 379-380
Social scientists, American
  anthropologists (19th-20th century)
    Boas, Franz **2** 349-351
    Fletcher, Alice Cunningham
      5 486-487
    Hrdlička, Aleš **8** 3-4
    Morgan, Lewis Henry **11** 167-168
    Powell, John Wesley **12** 425-426
    Schoolcraft, Henry Rowe **14** 29
  anthropologists (20th century)
    Benedict, Ruth Fulton **2** 154-155
    Cole, Johnnetta **4** 147-149
    Dunham, Katherine **5** 145-146
    Eiseley, Loren Corey **5** 232-233
    Geertz, Clifford **6** 248-249
    Herskovits, Melville Jean **7** 345

    Howells, William White **7** 541-542
    Kluckhohn, Clyde **9** 56-57
    Kroeber, Alfred Louis **9** 105-106
    Lewis, Oscar **9** 392-393
    Linton, Ralph **9** 431
    Lowie, Robert Harry **10** 18
    Mead, Margaret **10** 438-440
    Radin, Paul **12** 538-539
    Redfield, Robert **13** 73-74
    Sapir, Edward **13** 478-479
    Sauer, Carl Ortwin **13** 496-497
    White, Leslie A. **16** 232-233
  behavioral scientists
    Berelson, Bernard **2** 185-186
  economists (18th-19th century)
    Carey, Henry Charles **3** 294-295
    Coxe, Tench **4** 285-286
    Dew, Thomas Roderick **4** 519
    George, Henry **6** 276
    Tucker, George **15** 332-333
  economists (19th-20th century)
    Patten, Simon Nelson **12** 138-139
    Seligman, Edwin Robert Anderson
      14 93-94
    Veblen, Thorstein Bunde
      15 449-450
    Wright, Carroll Davidson **16** 396
  economists (20th century)
    Berle, Adolf Augustus Jr. **2** 199-200
    Burns, Arthur **3** 151-153
    Clark, John Bates **4** 76-77
    Clark, John Maurice **4** 77-78
    Epstein, Abraham **5** 294-295
    Fisher, Irving **5** 462-463
    Friedman, Milton **6** 111-112
    Galbraith, John Kenneth **6** 174-177
    Greenspan, Alan **6** 526-528
    Hansen, Alvin **7** 131-132
    Harris, Abram Lincoln Jr. **7** 169-171
    Heller, Walter **7** 265-266
    Johnson, Alvin Saunders **8** 293-294
    Kerr, Clark **8** 519-521
    Knight, Frank Hyneman **9** 58-59
    Kreps, Juanita Morris **9** 99-101
    Kuznets, Simon **9** 138-139
    Martin, William McChesney Jr.
      10 293-295
    Mitchell, Wesley Clair **11** 61-62
    Rostow, Walt Whitman **13** 315-317
    Samuelson, Paul Anthony
      13 458-459
    Shultz, George Pratt **14** 209-211
    Simon, Herbert Alexander
      14 236-237
    Volcker, Paul **16** 11-12
    Young, Owen D. **16** 473-474
  educators (17th-18th century)
    Benezet, Anthony **2** 159-160
    Cooper, Thomas **4** 224
    Dunster, Henry **5** 152-153
    Dwight, Timothy **5** 169
    Johnson, Samuel **8** 314-315
    Mather, Increase **10** 332-333
    Smith, William **14** 301
    Wheelock, Eleazar **16** 222-223
    Winthrop, John **16** 341-342

Witherspoon, John **16** 346-348
educators (18th-19th century)
Chase, Philander **3** 472-473
Webster, Noah **16** 164-166
educators (19th century)
Adams, Herbert Baxter **1** 47
Alcott, Amos Bronson **1** 121
Armstrong, Samuel Chapman
1 306-307
Bache, Alexander Dallas **1** 420
Barnard, Henry **2** 10
Beecher, Catharine **2** 110-112
Bell, Alexander Graham **2** 129-131
Bledsoe, Albert Taylor **2** 324-325
Cornell, Ezra **4** 236-237
Crandall, Prudence **4** 291
Curry, Jabez Lamar Monroe
4 346-347
Eliot, Charles William **5** 254
Emerson, Ralph Waldo **5** 278-280
Everett, Edward **5** 344
Finney, Charles Grandison
5 450-451
Gallaudet, Thomas Hopkins **6** 185
Gilman, Daniel Coit **6** 325-326
Gorgas, Josiah **6** 453-454
Harper, William Rainey **7** 163-164
Harris, William Torrey **7** 177-178
Holbrook, Josiah **7** 450-451
Hopkins, Mark **7** 495-496
Howard, Oliver Otis **7** 528-529
Langston, John Mercer **9** 197
Mann, Horace **10** 202-204
McCosh, James **10** 402-403
McGuffey, William Holmes
10 414-415
Mitchell, Maria **11** 61
Parsons, Frank **12** 121-122
Peabody, Elizabeth Palmer
12 167-168
Sequoyah **14** 110-111
Thayer, Sylvanus **15** 168-169
Vincent, John Heyl **15** 502-503
Wayland, Francis **16** 148-149
Willard, Emma Hart **16** 288-289
educators (19th-20th century)
Adler, Felix **1** 63-64
Bowman, Isaiah **2** 464-465
Butler, Nicholas Murray **3** 181
Carey Thomas, Martha **3** 297-298
Cooley, Charles Horton **4** 216-217
Dewey, Melvil **4** 523-524
Dunning, William Archibald
5 148-149
Farmer, Fannie Merritt **5** 383
Gilman, Daniel Coit **6** 325-326
Hall, Granville Stanley **7** 85-86
Hope, John **7** 489-490
Jordan, David Starr **8** 350-351
Keller, Helen Adams **8** 479-480
Kilpatrick, William H. **9** 1-3
Knapp, Seaman Asahel **9** 58
Low, Seth **10** 11-12
Lowell, Abbott Lawrence **10** 12-13
Rice, Joseph Mayer **13** 127-128
Richards, Ellen H. **13** 134-136

Small, Albion Woodbury **14** 277
Sumner, William Graham **15** 32
Ward, Lester Frank **16** 113-114
Washington, Booker Taliaferro
16 125-126
Welch, William Henry **16** 185-186
White, Andrew Dickson **16** 226-227
educators (20th century)
Andrews, Fannie Fern Phillips
1 231-232
Angell, James Rowland **1** 236-237
Bagley, William Chandler **1** 437-438
Banks, Dennis J. **1** 488-489
Bethune, Mary McLeod **2** 241-242
Blanding, Sarah Gibson **2** 322-323
Bode, Boyd Henry **2** 355-356
Bond, Horace Mann **2** 384-386
Clapp, Margaret Antoinette **4** 71-72
Cohen, Morris Raphael **4** 139-140
Cole, Johnnetta **4** 147-149
Collins, Marva **4** 165-167
Conant, James Bryant **4** 192-193
Counts, George S. **4** 267-269
Cowell, Henry Dixon **4** 280-281
Deloria, Vine Jr. **4** 481-484
Dewey, John **4** 520-523
Du Bois, William Edward Burghardt
5 116-118
Eisenhower, Milton **5** 237-238
Erikson, Erik Homburger **5** 309-310
Escalante, Jaime **5** 320-321
Flexner, Abraham **5** 489-490
Gagné, Robert Mills **6** 170
Gardner, John W. **6** 211-213
Harris, Abram Lincoln Jr. **7** 169-171
Haskins, Charles Homer **7** 191-192
Horne, Herman Harrell **7** 503-504
Hunter, Madeline Cheek **8** 47-48
Hutchins, Robert Maynard **8** 68-69
Johnson, Alvin Saunders **8** 293-294
Johnson, Charles Spurgeon
8 296-297
Johnson, James Weldon **8** 304-305
Judd, Charles Hubbard **8** 375-376
Kaplan, Mordecai Menahem
8 435-436
Kirkpatrick, Jeane J. **9** 37-39
Knowles, Malcolm Shepherd
9 62-64
Lloyd-Jones, Esther McDonald
9 471-472
Lynd, Helen Merrell **10** 63-64
MacIver, Robert Morrison
10 100-101
Mays, Benjamin E. **10** 374-376
Odum, Howard Washington
11 474-476
Ogburn, William Fielding **11** 480
Popham, William James **12** 399-401
Rostow, Walt Whitman **13** 315-317
Rugg, Harold **13** 355-357
Russell, James Earl **13** 379-380
Savage, Augusta Christine
13 499-501
Sayre, Francis Bowes **13** 509
Shultz, George Pratt **14** 209-211

Smith, Dora **14** 289-290
Strang, Ruth May **14** 493-494
Teggart, Frederick J. **15** 133-134
Thomas, William Isaac **15** 193
Thorndike, Edward Lee **15** 208-209
Tyler, Ralph W. **15** 370-371
Wolfson, Harry Austryn **16** 361-362
Znaniecki, Florian **16** 523-524
ethnologists
La Flesche, Francis **9** 152-154
ethologists
Fossey, Dian **6** 23-24
historians (17th-18th century)
Beverley, Robert **2** 252
Hutchinson, Thomas **8** 71-72
Mather, Cotton **10** 330-332
Ramsay, David **13** 21
Warren, Mercy Otis **16** 120-121
Winthrop, John **16** 339-341
historians (19th century)
Adams, Peter Chardon Brooks **1** 54
Adams, Henry Brooks **1** 45-47
Adams, Herbert Baxter **1** 47
Bancroft, George **1** 483-484
Bancroft, Hubert Howe **1** 484-485
Brady, Mathew B. **2** 487-488
Channing, Edward **3** 435
Draper, John William **5** 96-97
Du Bois, William Edward Burghardt
5 116-118
Eggleston, Edward **5** 223-224
Fiske, John **5** 465-466
Hildreth, Richard **7** 382
Irving, Washington **8** 141-143
Lea, Henry Charles **9** 261-262
Mahan, Alfred Thayer **10** 131-132
Motley, John Lothrop **11** 211-212
Parkman, Francis **12** 113-115
Peabody, Elizabeth Palmer
12 167-168
Prescott, William Hickling
12 440-441
Sparks, Jared **14** 363
Tucker, George **15** 332-333
Tyler, Moses Coit **15** 369-370
historians (19th-20th century)
Andrews, Charles McLean **1** 231
Commons, John Rogers **4** 185
Dunning, William Archibald
5 148-149
McMaster, John Bach **10** 426-427
Osgood, Herbert Levi **12** 18-19
Robinson, James Harvey **13** 208
Turner, Frederick Jackson
15 350-351
historians (20th century)
Beard, Charles Austin **2** 84
Becker, Carl Lotus **2** 100-101
Billington, James Hadley **2** 275-276
Boorstin, Daniel J. **2** 398-400
Bowers, Claude Gernade **2** 463
Brubacher, John Seiler **3** 58-59
Chandler, Alfred Du Pont Jr.
3 422-423
Channing, Edward **3** 435
Commager, Henry Steele **4** 181-183

Conway, Jill Kathryn Ker **4** 213-214
Franklin, John Hope **6** 65-67
Green, Constance McLaughlin **6** 518-519
Handlin, Oscar **7** 121-122
Haskins, Charles Homer **7** 191-192
Himmelfarb, Gertrude **7** 396-398
Hofstadter, Richard **7** 444-445
Howe, Florence Rosenfeld **7** 530-531
Kennan, George F. **8** 496-498
Kuhn, Thomas Samuel **9** 121-123
Lasch, Christopher **9** 212-214
Lynd, Staughton **10** 65-66
Malone, Dumas **10** 174-175
Marty, Martin E. **10** 300-301
Mattingly, Garrett **10** 342-344
Miller, Perry **11** 28-29
Morison, Samuel Eliot **11** 175-176
Nevins, Allan **11** 357-359
Pagels, Elaine Hiesey **12** 61-62
Parrington, Vernon Louis **12** 119-120
Potter, David M. **12** 412
Rhodes, James Ford **13** 122
Rostovtzeff, Michael Ivanovich **13** 315
Ruether, Rosemary Radford **13** 353-354
Sarton, George **13** 490-491
Schlesinger, Arthur Meier **14** 13
Schlesinger, Arthur Meier Jr. **14** 13-15
Shirer, William L. **14** 198-199
Teggart, Frederick J. **15** 133-134
Tuchman, Barbara **15** 331-332
Wolfson, Harry Austryn **16** 361-362
Woodson, Carter Godwin **16** 374-376
Woodward, Comer Vann **16** 378-379
Zinn, Howard **16** 520-521
librarians
    Dewey, Melvil **4** 523-524
philologists
    Bloomfield, Leonard **2** 338
    Mencken, Henry Louis **10** 481-483
political theorists
    Alinsky, Saul David **1** 161-162
    Arendt, Hannah **1** 282-284
    Beard, Charles Austin **2** 84
    Bennett, William John **2** 172-174
    Bentley, Arthur F. **2** 178
    Chomsky, Noam Avram **4** 13-15
    De Leon, Daniel **4** 479-480
    Deutsch, Karl Wolfgang **4** 512-514
    Forman, James **6** 10-11
    Friedrich, Carl Joachim **6** 113-114
    Harrington, Michael **7** 167-169
    Hildreth, Richard **7** 382
    Hunter, Floyd **8** 45-46
    Key, Vladimir Orlando Jr. **8** 527-528
    Lasswell, Harold Dwight **9** 218-219
    Lieber, Francis **9** 401-402
    Lowell, Abbott Lawrence **10** 12-13

Merriam, Charles Edward **10** 518-519
Morgenthau, Hans J. **11** 171-172
Zinn, Howard **16** 520-521
pollsters
    Gallup, George **6** 187-189
psychologists (19th-20th century)
    Cattell, James McKeen **3** 376-377
    Cooley, Charles Horton **4** 216-217
    Hall, Granville Stanley **7** 85-86
    James, William **8** 215-217
    Mead, George Herbert **10** 437-438
psychologists (20th century)
    Angell, James Rowland **1** 236-237
    Bettelheim, Bruno **2** 245-246
    Brothers, Joyce **3** 26-28
    Bruner, Jerome Seymour **3** 72-73
    Clark, Kenneth B. **4** 78-79
    Gesell, Arnold Lucius **6** 286-287
    Gilbreth, Lillian **6** 315-317
    Guthrie, Edwin Ray **7** 49-50
    Hovland, Carl I. **7** 527-528
    Hull, Clark Leonard **8** 28
    Johnson, Virginia E. **8** 317-319
    Judd, Charles Hubbard **8** 375-376
    Kübler-Ross, Elisabeth **9** 118-120
    Leary, Timothy **9** 266-267
    Lewin, Kurt **9** 375-376
    Skinner, Burrhus Frederic **14** 269-270
    Terman, Lewis Madison **15** 153-154
    Thorndike, Edward Lee **15** 208-209
    Thurstone, Louis Leon **15** 215-216
    Titchener, Edward Bradford **15** 241-242
    Tolman, Edward Chace **15** 261-262
    Tyler, Ralph W. **15** 370-371
    Watson, John Broadus **16** 138-139
    Westheimer, Ruth Karola **16** 214-215
    Wexler, Nancy **16** 218-219
    Yerkes, Robert Mearns **16** 454-455
psychotherapists
    Rogers, Carl Ransom **13** 245-247
social anthropologists (20th century)
    Johnson, Guy Benton **8** 299-300
social psychiatrists
    Coles, Robert Martin **4** 156-157
social workers
    Abbott, Grace **1** 9-10
    Addams, Jane **1** 56-57
    Hunter, Floyd **8** 45-46
    Kelley, Florence **8** 483-484
    Perkins, Frances **12** 221-222
    Wald, Lillian **16** 53-54
    Woods, Robert Archey **16** 374
    Young, Whitney Moore Jr. **16** 476-477
sociologists (19th-20th century)
    Cooley, Charles Horton **4** 216-217
    Dugdale, Richard Louis **5** 128-129
    Fitzhugh, George **5** 474
    Giddings, Franklin Henry **6** 307-308
    Mayo-Smith, Richmond **10** 371-372
    Park, Robert E. **12** 102-104
    Small, Albion Woodbury **14** 277

Sumner, William Graham **15** 32
Veblen, Thorstein Bunde **15** 449-450
Ward, Lester Frank **16** 113-114
sociologists (20th century)
    Bell, Daniel **2** 132-133
    Bond, Horace Mann **2** 384-386
    Chapin, (F.) Stuart **3** 437-438
    Clark, Kenneth B. **4** 78-79
    Counts, George S. **4** 267-269
    Frazier, Edward Franklin **6** 77
    Greeley, Andrew M. **6** 514-515
    Homans, George Caspar **7** 463-465
    Johnson, Charles Spurgeon **8** 296-297
    Johnson, Guy Benton **8** 299-300
    Kellor, Frances **8** 481-482
    Lazarsfeld, Paul F. **9** 259-260
    Lynd, Helen Merrell **10** 63-64
    Lynd, Robert Staughton **10** 64-65
    MacIver, Robert Morrison **10** 100-101
    Merton, Robert K. **10** 522-523
    Mills, C. Wright **11** 35-36
    Odum, Howard Washington **11** 474-476
    Ogburn, William Fielding **11** 480
    Parsons, Talcott **12** 122
    Riesman, David **13** 167-168
    Ross, Edward Alsworth **13** 300
    Shils, Edward Albert **14** 195-197
    Sorokin, Pitirim A. **14** 348-349
    Stouffer, Samuel A. **14** 482-483
    Teggart, Frederick J. **15** 133-134
    Thomas, William Isaac **15** 193
    Znaniecki, Florian **16** 523-524

Social scientists, Arab
    Biruni, Abu Rayhan al- **2** 284-285
    ibn Khaldun, Abd al-Rahman ibn Muhammad **8** 93-94
    Masudi, Ali ibn al- Husayn al- **10** 328-329
    Tabari, Muhammad ibn Jarir al- **15** 69-70

Social scientists, Argentine
    Alberdi, Juan Bautista **1** 109-110
    Echeverría, José Estéban **5** 197-198
    Mitre, Bartolomé **11** 62-63
    Prebisch, Raúl **12** 434-436
    Sarmiento, Domingo Faustino **13** 484-485

Social scientists, Australian
    Bates, Daisy Mae **2** 52-53
    Childe, Vere Gordon **3** 521-522
    Coombs, Herbert Cole **4** 219-220
    Florey, Howard Walter **5** 491-492

Social scientists, Austrian
    Baron, Salo Wittmayer **2** 16-17
    Böhm-Bawerk, Eugen von **2** 366
    Freud, Sigmund **6** 103-106
    Gumplowicz, Ludwig **7** 41
    Klein, Melanie **9** 52
    Lorenz, Konrad Z. **9** 516-517
    Rank, Otto **13** 33

Schumpeter, Joseph Alois **14** 43-44
Voegelin, Eric **16** 6-8
von Mises, Ludwig **16** 25

Social scientists, Belgian
Pirenne, Jean Henri Otto Lucien Marie
12 322-323
Quételet, Lambert Adolphe Jacques
12 510-511

Social scientists, Brazilian
Freyre, Gilberto **6** 106-107
Varnhagen, Francisco Adolfo de
15 437-438

Social scientists, Byzantine
Comnena, Anna **4** 185-186
Procopius of Caesarea **12** 457-458

Social scientists, Canadian
Aberhart, William **1** 26-27
Currie, Arthur William **4** 345
Garneau, François-Xavier **6** 219-220
Howe, Joseph **7** 534-535
Innis, Harold Adams **8** 124-125
Mackenzie, William Lyon **10** 104-106
Ryerson, Adolphus Egerton **13** 392-393
Strachan, John **14** 486-487
Tupper, Charles **15** 342-343

Social scientists, Chilean
Herrera, Juan de **7** 335
Mistral, Gabriela **11** 55-56

Social scientists, Chinese
educators
Confucius **4** 197-200
Feng Kuei-fen **5** 411-412
Ts'ai Yüan-p'ei **15** 322
historians
Chang Hsüeh-ch'eng **3** 433
Huang Tsung-hsi **8** 9-10
Ku Chieh-kang **9** 120-121
Ou-yang Hsiu **12** 33-34
Pan Ku **12** 86-87
Ssu-ma Ch'ien **14** 388-389
Ssu-ma kuang **14** 390-391
Wei Yüan **16** 180-181
political theorists
Li Ta-chao **9** 447
Yen Fu **16** 452

Social scientists, Colombian
Isaacs, Jorge **8** 144

Social scientists, Cuban
Martí, José **10** 285-286

Social scientists, Czech
Comenius, John Amos **4** 180-181
Palacký, František **12** 69-70

Social scientists, Dutch
Huizinga, Johan **8** 26-27
Tinbergen, Jan **15** 228-229

Social scientists, Egyptian
Husayn, Taha **8** 61-62

Social scientists, English
anthropologists
Douglas, Mary Tew **5** 79-80
Evans, Arthur John **5** 335-336
Evans-Pritchard, Edward Evan **5** 340

Gluckman, Max **6** 374-375
Keith, Arthur **8** 475-476
Leakey, Louis Seymour Bazett **9** 262
Maine, Henry James Sumner **10** 152
Malinowski, Kaspar Bronislaw
10 170-171
Petrie, William Matthew Flinders
12 261-262
Radcliffe-Brown, A. R. **12** 535-536
Tylor, Edward Burnett **15** 372-373
economists (19th-20th century)
Bagehot, Walter **1** 436-437
Jevons, William Stanley **8** 255-256
Malthus, Thomas Robert **10** 180-181
Marshall, Alfred **10** 277-278
Mill, John Stuart **11** 21-23
Ricardo, David **13** 123-124
Spencer, Herbert **14** 369-370
Webb, Sidney James **16** 154-155
economists (20th century)
Beveridge, William Henry
2 251-252
Clapham, John Harold **4** 71
Cole, George Douglas Howard
4 146-147
Hayek, Friedrich A. von **7** 221-223
Keynes, John Maynard **8** 528-530
Pigou, Arthur Cecil **12** 302
Robertson, Dennis Holme **13** 196
Robinson, Joan Violet Maurice
13 209-210
Wootton, Barbara Adam
16 384-385
educators
Alcuin of York **1** 122-123
Arnold, Thomas **1** 313-314
Beale, Dorothea **2** 81-83
Carr-Saunders, Alexander Morris
3 333-334
Jowett, Benjamin **8** 364-365
Lancaster, Joseph **9** 182-183
Wootton, Barbara Adam
16 384-385
historians (12th-17th century)
Burnet, Gilbert **3** 147
Colet, John **4** 157-158
Matthew Paris **10** 341-342
Raleigh, Walter **13** 9-11
William of Malmesbury **16** 297-298
historians (18th-19th century)
Acton, John Emerich Edward Dalberg **1** 38
Buckle, Henry Thomas **3** 95-96
Froude, James Anthony **6** 133-134
Gardiner, Samuel Rawson **6** 211
Gibbon, Edward **6** 299-300
Macaulay, Thomas Babington
10 79-80
Maine, Henry James Sumner **10** 152
Stephen, Leslie **14** 429
historians (19th-20th century)
Bryce, James **3** 85
Maitland, Frederic William
10 154-155
Pollard, Albert Frederick **12** 378
Webb, Beatrice Potter **16** 153-154

Webb, Sidney James **16** 154-155
historians (20th century)
Belloc, Joseph Hilaire Pierre **2** 141
Churchill, Winston Leonard Spencer
4 51-53
Clapham, John Harold **4** 71
Clark, Kenneth M. **4** 79-80
Cole, George Douglas Howard
4 146-147
Collingwood, Robin George **4** 162
Coulton, George Gordon **4** 267
Fraser, Antonia **6** 70-71
Gooch, George Peabody **6** 432-433
Hammond, Lawrence and Lucy
7 109
Namier, Lewis Bernstein
11 301-303
Nicolson, Harold George
11 383-384
Tawney, Richard Henry **15** 120-121
Toynbee, Arnold Joseph **15** 283-284
Trevelyan, George Macaulay
15 294-295
Wedgwood, Cicely Veronica
16 167-168
political theorists (17th-19th century)
Bentham, Jeremy **2** 176-178
Bolingbroke, Viscount **2** 374-375
Burke, Edmund **3** 138-141
Filmer, Robert **5** 448
Godwin, William **6** 383-384
Harrington, James **7** 166-167
Hobbes, Thomas **7** 421-423
political theorists (19th-20th century)
Laski, Harold J. **9** 215-216
Wallas, Graham **16** 77-78
Webb, Sidney James **16** 154-155
primatologists
Goodall, Jane **6** 433-434
psychologists
Bartlett, Frederic Charles **2** 34-35
Hartley, David **7** 185
Jones, Ernest Alfred **8** 331-332
Morgan, Conway Lloyd **11** 159-160
Titchener, Edward Bradford
15 241-242
sociologists
Carr-Saunders, Alexander Morris
3 333-334
Gluckman, Max **6** 374-375
Hobhouse, Leonard Trelawny
7 425-426
Spencer, Herbert **14** 369-370
Wallas, Graham **16** 77-78

Social scientists, Filipino
Mabini, Apolinario **10** 72-73

Social scientists, French
anthropologists
Bertillon, Alphonse **2** 230-231
Champollion, Jean François **3** 421
Gobineau, Comte de **6** 375-376
Le Bon, Gustave **9** 268-269
Lévi-Strauss, Claude Gustave
9 371-372
Lévy-Bruhl, Lucien **9** 374-375
Mauss, Marcel **10** 352-353

economists (14th-18th century)
   Bodin, Jean **2** 356-357
   Colbert, Jean Baptiste **4** 142-143
   Nicholas of Oresme **11** 380
   Saint-Pierre, Abbé de **13** 434-435
economists (18th-20th century)
   Cournot, Antoine Augustin **4** 273
   du Pont de Nemours, Pierre Samuel
      5 155-156
   Le Play, Guillaume Frédéric
      9 350-351
   Monnet, Jean **11** 109-110
   Say, Jean Baptiste **13** 508-509
   Turgot, Anne Robert Jacques
      15 348-349
   Walras, Marie Esprit Léon **16** 84-85
economists (20th century)
   Aron, Raymond **1** 316-317
educators
   Bourgeoys, Marguerite **2** 452-453
   Condillac, Étienne Bonnot de
      4 194-195
   Cousin, Victor **4** 273-274
   Lavisse, Ernest **9** 241
   Rousseau, Jean Jacques **13** 324-328
historians (6th-18th century)
   Comines, Philippe de **4** 181
   Froissart, Jean **6** 124-125
   Gregory of Tours **6** 534-535
   Mabillon, Jean **10** 72
   Villehardouin, Geffroi de **15** 499
   Voltaire **16** 14-16
   William of Tyre **16** 299-300
historians (19th century)
   Blanc, Louis **2** 318-319
   Duhem, Pierre Maurice Marie **5** 129
   Fustel de Coulanges, Numa Denis
      6 155
   Guizot, François Pierre Guillaume
      7 40-41
   Michelet, Jules **11** 5-6
   Sorel, Albert **14** 346-347
   Taine, Hippolyte Adolphe **15** 82-83
   Thiers, Louis Adolphe **15** 181-182
   Tocqueville, Alexis Charles Henri
      Maurice Clérel de **15** 250-251
historians (19th-20th century)
   Aulard, François Victor Alphonse
      1 374
   Bloch, Marc **2** 332-333
   Halévy, Élie **7** 76
   Lavisse, Ernest **9** 241
   Lefebvre, Georges **9** 301-302
   Mathiez, Albert **10** 333-334
historians (20th century)
   Braudel, Fernand **2** 507-508
   Foucault, Michel **6** 29-30
librarians
   Budé, Guillaume **3** 102-103
philologists
   Renan, Ernest **13** 95-96
political theorists
   Babeuf, François Noel **1** 412
   Benda, Julien **2** 151-152
   Blanqui, Louis Auguste **2** 323-324

Fourier, François Charles Marie
   6 31-32
Maistre, Joseph de **10** 153-154
Maurras, Charles Marie Photius
   10 350-351
Rousseau, Jean Jacques **13** 324-328
Saint-Pierre, Abbé de **13** 434-435
Saint-Simon, Comte de **13** 436-437
Sorel, Georges **14** 347-348
psychologists
   Binet, Alfred **2** 277-278
   Janet, Pierre Marie Félix **8** 220
   Lacan, Jacques **9** 145-147
   Le Bon, Gustave **9** 268-269
sociologists
   Aron, Raymond **1** 316-317
   Durkheim, Émile **5** 162-163
   Le Bon, Gustave **9** 268-269
   Le Play, Guillaume Frédéric
      9 350-351
   Lévy-Bruhl, Lucien **9** 374-375
   Mauss, Marcel **10** 352-353
   Tarde, Jean Gabriel **15** 108-109
   Tocqueville, Alexis Charles Henri
      Maurice Clérel de **15** 250-251
   Touraine, Alain **15** 274-275

Social scientists, German
anthropologists
   Schliemann, Heinrich **14** 17-18
   Virchow, Rudolf Ludwig Carl
      15 506-507
   Winckelmann, Johann Joachim
      16 332-333
economists
   List, Georg Friedrich **9** 443-444
   Marx, Karl **10** 304-308
   Schacht, Hjalmar Horace Greeley
      13 518-519
   Schmoller, Gustav Friedrich von
      14 21
   Sombart, Werner **14** 332-333
educators
   Basedow, Johann Bernhard **2** 44-45
   Froebel, Friedrich Wilhelm August
      6 122-123
   Herbart, Johann Friedrich **7** 321-322
   Humboldt, Wilhelm von **8** 31
   Thomasius **15** 193-194
geopoliticians
   Haushofer, Karl **7** 201
historians (12th-18th century)
   Otto of Freising **12** 30
   Pufendorf, Samuel von **12** 477-478
   Schiller, Johann Christoph Friedrich
      von **14** 4-7
historians (19th century)
   Dilthey, Wilhelm Christian Ludwig
      5 10
   Döllinger, Josef Ignaz von **5** 47-48
   Graetz, Heinrich Hirsch **6** 483
   Mommsen, Theodor **11** 94-95
   Niebuhr, Barthold Georg
      11 385-386
   Ranke, Leopold von **13** 33-35
   Strauss, David Friedrich **14** 496-497

Treitschke, Heinrich von
   15 293-294
historians (19th-20th century)
   Cassirer, Ernst **3** 358-359
   Huch, Ricarda **8** 11-12
   Lamprecht, Karl **9** 181
   Meinecke, Friedrich **10** 460-461
   Troeltsch, Ernst **15** 299-300
   Weber, Max **16** 157-160
librarians
   Grimm, Jakob and Wilhelm Karl
      7 3-4
   Meinecke, Friedrich **10** 460-461
philologists
   Humboldt, Wilhelm von **8** 31
   Mommsen, Theodor **11** 94-95
   Wolf, Friedrich August **16** 352-353
political theorists
   Block, Herbert **2** 333-334
   Engels, Friedrich **5** 286-288
   Kautsky, Karl Johann **8** 462-463
   Lassalle, Ferdinand **9** 216
   Spengler, Oswald **14** 372-373
   Voegelin, Eric **16** 6-8
psychologists
   Brentano, Franz Clemens **2** 516-517
   Ebbinghaus, Hermann **5** 192-193
   Fechner, Gustav Theodor **5** 401-402
   Fromm, Erich **6** 125-127
   Wertheimer, Max **16** 207-208
   Wundt, Wilhelm Max **16** 402-403
sociologists
   Habermas, Jürgen **7** 58-60
   Luhmann, Niklas **10** 34-35
   Michels, Robert **11** 7
   Simmel, Georg **14** 234-235
   Tönnies, Ferdinand **15** 266-267
   Troeltsch, Ernst **15** 299-300
   Weber, Max **16** 157-160

Social scientists, Ghanaian
   Busia, Kofi Abrefa **3** 172-173

Social scientists, Greek
educators
   Isocrates **8** 151
historians
   Herodotus **7** 330-333
   Plutarch **12** 359-360
   Polybios **12** 384-385
   Procopius of Caesarea **12** 457-458
   Strabo **14** 485-486
   Thucydides **15** 211-212
   Xenophon **16** 418-420
librarians
   Callimachus **3** 235-236

Social scientists, Hungarian
   Mannheim, Karl **10** 208-209
   Polanyi, Karl **12** 372
   Polanyi, Michael **12** 372-373

Social scientists, Indian
   Deb, Radhakant **4** 437
   Kautilya **8** 462
   Nizami, Khaliq Ahmad **11** 405

Social scientists, Irish
Lecky, William Edward Hartpole
9 271-272
Pearse, Patrick Henry **12** 173-174

Social scientists, Italian
ancient
see Social scientists, Roman
economists
Becarria, Marchese di **2** 97-98
Pareto, Vilfredo **12** 95-96
educators
Croce, Benedetto **4** 313-314
De Sanctis, Francesco **4** 505
Feltre, Vittorino da **5** 409-410
Montessori, Maria **11** 125-126
historians
Bembo, Pietro **2** 144-145
Ferrero, Guglielmo **5** 429-430
Machiavelli, Niccolò **10** 97-99
Muratori, Lodovico Antonio
11 254-255
Salvemini, Gaetano **13** 455-456
Sarpi, Paolo **13** 487-488
Villani, Giovanni **15** 497-498
librarians
Pius XI **12** 337-339
political theorists
Campanella, Tommaso **3** 249
Pareto, Vilfredo **12** 95-96
sociologists
Lombroso, Cesare **9** 493

Social scientists, Japanese
Ogata, Sadako **11** 479-480

Social scientists, Korean
Kim Pusik **9** 8-9
Yi Hwang **16** 457

Social scientists, Liberian
Blyden, Edward Wilmot **2** 348-349

Social scientists, Mexican
Alamán, Lucas **1** 99-100
Cosio Villegas, Daniel **4** 260-261
Sierra, Justo **14** 217
Vasconcelos, José **15** 443-444

Social scientists, Mozambican
Mondlane, Eduardo Chivambo
11 100-101

Social scientists, Nigerian
Dike, Kenneth **5** 7-8

Social scientists, Palestinian
Josephus Flavius **8** 360-361

Social scientists, Peruvian
Garcilaso de la Vega, Inca **6** 210-211
Haya de la Torre, Victor Raul **7** 216-217
Mariátegui, José Carlos **10** 255-256
Unánue, José Hipólito **15** 387-388

Social scientists, Polish
Krochmal, Nachman Kohen **9** 104-105
Luxemburg, Rosa **10** 55-56

Social scientists, Puerto Rican
Hostos, Eugenio María de **7** 513-514

Social scientists, Roman
Cato, Marcus Porcius the Elder **3** 375

Livy **9** 465-467
Quintilian **12** 518-519
Sallust **13** 454
Tacitus **15** 70-72

Social scientists, Rumanian
Eliade, Mircea **5** 249-250

Social scientists, Russian
educators
Tolstoy, Leo **15** 262-265
Vinogradoff, Paul Gavrilovitch
15 503
historians
Dubnov, Simon **5** 115-116
Karamzin, Nikolai Mikhailovich
8 441-442
Klyuchevsky, Vasily Osipovich
9 57-58
Miliukov, Pavel Nikolayevich
11 18-19
Vinogradoff, Paul Gavrilovitch
15 503
political theorists
Bakunin, Mikhail Aleksandrovich
1 458-460
Bukharin, Nikolai Ivanovich
3 112-113
Chernyshevsky, Nikolai Gavrilovich
3 504-505
Kropotkin, Peter Alekseevich
9 107-108

Social scientists, Scottish
Bell, Andrew **2** 131-132
Carlyle, Thomas **3** 304-305
Ferguson, Adam **5** 420-421
Frazer, James George **6** 76
Geddes, Patrick **6** 246-247
Law, John **9** 244-245
Mill, James **11** 21
Neill, Alexander Sutherland **11** 335-336
Smith, Adam **14** 283-284

Social scientists, Senegalese
Diop, Cheikh Anta **5** 21-22
Ly, Abdoulaye **10** 60

Social scientists, South African
Malan, Daniel Francois **10** 163-164
Plaatje, Solomon Tshekisho **12** 341-342

Social scientists, Spanish
Altamira Y Crevea, Rafael **1** 179
Las Casas, Bartolomé de **9** 211-212
López de Ayala, Pedro **9** 508-509
Mariana, Juan de **10** 254-255

Social scientists, Swiss
Burckhardt, Jacob Christoph **3** 132-133
Jung, Carl Gustav **8** 388-389
Pestalozzi, Johann Heinrich **12** 249-250
Piaget, Jean **12** 287-288
Rorschach, Hermann **13** 286-288
Sismondi, Jean Charles Léonard
Simonde de **14** 258-259

Social scientists, Trinidadian
Williams, Henry Sylvester **16** 303-304

Social scientists, Turkish
Gökalp, Mehmet Ziya **6** 395-396

Social scientists, Uruguayan
Zorrilla de San Martin, Juan **16** 530-531

Social security (social insurance)
Canada
Bennett, Richard Bedford **2** 171-172
France
Bourgeois, Léon **2** 450-451
Germany
Bethmann Hollweg, Theobald von
2 239-240
Great Britain
Asquith, Herbert Henry **1** 344-346
Attlee, Clement Richard **1** 361-362
Beveridge, William Henry
2 251-252
Booth, Charles **2** 400-401
Webb, Beatrice Potter **16** 153-154
Guatemala
Arévalo, Juan José **1** 285-286
Mexico
Ávila Camacho, Manuel **1** 387-388
New Zealand
Savage, Michael Joseph **13** 501-502
United States
Cardozo, Benjamin Nathan
3 288-290
Eisenhower, Dwight David
5 233-236
McCormack, John William
10 399-400
Pepper, Claude Denson **12** 205-206
Perkins, Frances **12** 221-222
Townsend, Francis Everitt
15 282-283
Woodward, Ellen S. **16** 379-381

Social Security Act (United States; 1935)
Abbott, Grace **1** 9-10
Epstein, Abraham **5** 294-295

Social War (Rome; 90-88 B.C.)
Caesar, Gaius Julius **3** 207-210
Catiline **3** 372-373
Cicero, Marcus Tullius **4** 55-58
Drusus, Marcus Livius **5** 105-106
Marius, Gaius **10** 264-265
Sulla, Lucius Cornelius I **15** 21-22

Social workers
see Social scientists—social workers

Socialism
Africa
Machel, Samora Moises **10** 94-96
Senghor, Léopold Sédar **14** 106-107
Australia
Fisher, Andrew **5** 462
Austria
Dollfuss, Engelbert **5** 47
von Mises, Ludwig **16** 25
Burma
Ne Win **11** 364-365
Canada
Lampman, Archibald **9** 180-181
England
Benn, Tony **2** 164-166
Booth, Charles **2** 400-401

Cole, George Douglas Howard
4 146-147
Laski, Harold J. 9 215-216
Mill, John Stuart 11 21-23
Morris, William 11 187-188
Orwell, George 12 14-15
Shaftesbury, 7th Earl of 14 137-138
see also Fabian socialism
France
Babeuf, François Noel 1 412
Blanqui, Louis Auguste 2 323-324
Halévy, Élie 7 76
Jaurès, Jean 8 226-227
Le Play, Guillaume Frédéric
9 350-351
Péguy, Charles Pierre 12 183-184
Rolland, Romain 13 260
Germany
Ebert, Friedrich 5 193-194
Fichte, Johann Gottlieb 5 435-436
Grass, Günter 6 496-497
Kautsky, Karl Johann 8 462-463
Michels, Robert 11 7
Greece
Papandreou, Andreas 12 88-91
India
Nehru, Jawaharlal 11 332-334
Prasad, Rajendra 12 433
Indonesia
Hatta, Mohammad 7 197-199
Israel
Ben-Gurion, David 2 160-161
Italy
Ferrero, Guglielmo 5 429-430
Salvemini, Gaetano 13 455-456
Latin America
Allende Gossens, Salvador
1 174-176
Russia
Chernyshevsky, Nikolai Gavrilovich
3 504-505
Herzen, Aleksandr Ivanovich
7 351-352
Scotland
Hardie, James Keir 7 147-148
socialist international
see International, First; International,
Second; International, Third
theoreticians
Engels, Friedrich 5 286-288
Kautsky, Karl Johann 8 462-463
Lenin, Vladimir Ilich 9 323-326
United States
Cooper, Peter 4 223-224
Dewey, John 4 520-523
Dos Passos, John Roderigo 5 69-71
Dubinsky, David 5 114-115
Harrington, Michael 7 167-169
Holmes, John Haynes 7 456-457
Jones, Mary Harris 8 338-339
London, Jack 9 494-495
Wright, Frances 16 397-398
see also Fourierism; Marxism;
Socialism, state; Utopian socialism

Socialism, state (political theory)
Hobhouse, Leonard Trelawny
7 425-426

Socialist Labor party (United States)
Berger, Victor Louis 2 189-190
De Leon, Daniel 4 479-480
Hillquit, Morris 7 393-394

Socialist party
Belgium
Spaak, Paul Henri 14 359-360
Canada
Woodsworth, James Shaver 16 376
Chile
Allende Gossens, Salvador
1 174-176
France
Blum, Léon 2 343-344
Bourgeois, Léon 2 450-451
Briand, Aristide 2 528-529
Cresson, Edith 4 306-307
Delors, Jacques 4 484-486
Fabius, Laurent 5 358-359
Ho Chi Minh 7 426-428
Mendès France, Pierre 10 492-493
Mitterrand, François 11 63-66
Péguy, Charles Pierre 12 183-184
Poincaré, Raymond 12 366-368
Rocard, Michel 13 218-220
Senghor, Léopold Sédar 14 106-107
Germany
Steinmetz, Charles Proteus
14 419-420
Indonesia
Sukarno 15 18-20
Italy
Craxi, Bettino 4 300-301
Giolitti, Giovanni 6 339-340
Matteotti, Giacomo 10 339-340
Mussolini, Benito 11 272-274
Silone, Ignazio 14 231-232
Victor Emmanuel III 15 484-485
Japan
Doi Takako 5 39-41
Katayama, Sen 8 457
New Zealand
Savage, Michael Joseph 13 501-502
Peru
Mariátegui, José Carlos 10 255-256
Poland
Pilsudski, Joseph 12 305-306
Portugal
Soares, Mário 14 315-316
Spain
Azaña Diaz, Manuel 1 396-397
Primo de Rivera y Orbaneja, Miguel
12 454-455
United States
Berger, Victor Louis 2 189-190
Browder, Earl Russell 3 30-31
Cahan, Abraham 3 214
Debs, Eugene Victor 4 444-445
Du Bois, William Edward Burghardt
5 116-118
Foster, William Zebulon 6 27-28

Haywood, William Dudley
7 232-233
Hillquit, Morris 7 393-394
La Follette, Robert Marion
9 155-156
Russell, Charles Edward 13 374-375
Sanger, Margaret Higgins
13 467-468
Sinclair, Upton Beale Jr. 14 248-249
Sloan, John 14 274-275
Steinmetz, Charles Proteus
14 419-420
Thomas, Norman Mattoon
15 191-192

Socialist realism (art; Union of Soviet
Socialist Republics)
Belinsky, Grigorievich 2 128
Ehrenburg, Ilya Grigorievich 5 224-225
Gorky, Maxim 6 458-460
Malevich, Kasimir 10 168-169
Meyerhold, Vsevolod Emilievich 10 539

Socialist Revolutionary Party (Russia)
Breshkovsky, Catherine 2 517-519

Socialist Trades and Labor Alliance (established 1895)
De Leon, Daniel 4 479-480

Socialist Unity Front (Romania)
Ceausescu, Nicolae 3 387-388

Socialist Unity party (Germany)
Ulbricht, Walter 15 383-384

Socialist Workers Party (Ethiopia)
Mengistu Haile Mariam 10 503-505

Socialist Workers' Party (Spain)
González Márquez, Felipe 6 429-431

Socialist Youth League (China)
Ch'en Tu-hsiu 3 501-502
Liu Shao-Ch'i 9 453-455

Société Anonyme (art group)
Cézanne, Paul 3 400-402
Ray, Man 13 59-60

Société Nationale des Beaux-Arts
Puvis de Chavannes, Pierre 12 492-493

Society
critics
Thomas, Norman Mattoon
15 191-192
Tocqueville, Alexis Charles Henri
Maurice Clérel de 15 250-251
Weber, Max 16 157-160
White, William Allen 16 240-241
development
Ferguson, Adam 5 420-421
Fiske, John 5 465-466
Giddings, Franklin Henry 6 307-308
Great Society and
Johnson, Lyndon Baines 8 308-312
theories
Fourier, François Charles Marie
6 31-32
Hobbes, Thomas 7 421-423
MacIver, Robert Morrison
10 100-101
Mumford, Lewis 11 246-247

Rousseau, Jean Jacques **13** 324-328
Saint-Simon, Comte de **13** 436-437

Society for Ethical Culture (New York City)
Adler, Felix **1** 63-64

Society for the Advancement of Education
Bagley, William Chandler **1** 437-438

Society for the Advancement of Judaism
(established 1922)
Kaplan, Mordecai Menahem **8** 435-436

Society for the Freedom of Science
Polanyi, Michael **12** 372-373

Society for the Propagation of the Faith
(Italy)
John, XXIII **8** 277-280

Society of American Artists (established 1887)
Robinson, Theodore **13** 217
Ryder, Albert Pinkham **13** 391-392

Society of American Indians (U.S.)
Montezuma, Carlos **11** 129-132

Society of Arcueil (France)
Berthollet, Claude Louis **2** 229-230

Society of Civil Engineers (established 1771)
Smeaton, John **14** 280-281

Society of Friends
see Quakers

Society of Independent Artists (established 1916)
Glackens, William **6** 355-356
Sloan, John **14** 274-275

Society of Jesus
see Jesuits

Society of Muslim Brethren (Egypt; established 1928)
Al-Banna, Hassan **1** 104-106
Sayyid Qutb **13** 509-511

Society of Nobles
see Arya Samaj

Sociobiology
Wilson, Edward Osborne **16** 319-320

Sociological Society (England)
Hobhouse, Leonard Trelawny **7** 425-426

Sociology (social science)
action theory
Shils, Edward Albert **14** 195-197
and history
Teggart, Frederick J. **15** 133-134
and religion
Greeley, Andrew M. **6** 514-515
animal behavior
Lorenz, Konrad Z. **9** 516-517
biological determinism
Carr-Saunders, Alexander Morris **3** 333-334
Dugdale, Richard Louis **5** 128-129
Lombroso, Cesare **9** 493
Malthus, Thomas Robert **10** 180-181
conflict theory
Giddings, Franklin Henry **6** 307-308

Gluckman, Max **6** 374-375
Gumplowicz, Ludwig **7** 41
Simmel, Georg **14** 234-235
crowd behavior
Le Bon, Gustave **9** 268-269
Park, Robert E. **12** 102-104
development
Fitzhugh, George **5** 474
Geddes, Patrick **6** 246-247
Small, Albion Woodbury **14** 277
Sumner, William Graham **15** 32
Tönnies, Ferdinand **15** 266-267
economic basis
Marx, Karl **10** 304-308
elitism
Mannheim, Karl **10** 208-209
Michels, Robert **11** 7
Pareto, Vilfredo **12** 95-96
evolutionary
Saint-Simon, Comte de **13** 436-437
Spencer, Herbert **14** 369-370
Veblen, Thorstein Bunde **15** 449-450
Ward, Lester Frank **16** 113-114
Yen Fu **16** 452
folk sociology
Johnson, Guy Benton **8** 299-300
Odum, Howard Washington **11** 474-476
founders
Durkheim, Émile **5** 162-163
Ferguson, Adam **5** 420-421
Ross, Edward Alsworth **13** 300
Weber, Max **16** 157-160
intelligence testing
Bond, Julian **2** 386-387
interest groups
MacIver, Robert Morrison **10** 100-101
Tarde, Jean Gabriel **15** 108-109
morals and religion
Mauss, Marcel **10** 352-353
Myrdal, Karl Gunnar **11** 284
Troeltsch, Ernst **15** 299-300
of science
Merton, Robert K. **10** 522-523
political
Bagehot, Walter **1** 436-437
Habermas, Jürgen **7** 58-60
Tocqueville, Alexis Charles Henri Maurice Clérel de **15** 250-251
post-industrial society
Touraine, Alain **15** 274-275
power elite model
Hunter, Floyd **8** 45-46
psychological principles
Dilthey, Wilhelm Christian Ludwig **5** 10
Freud, Sigmund **6** 103-106
race relations
Park, Robert E. **12** 102-104
small groups
Homans, George Caspar **7** 463-465
social movements
Touraine, Alain **15** 274-275
social process

Homans, George Caspar **7** 463-465
social structures
Illich, Ivan **8** 112-114
Merton, Robert K. **10** 522-523
socialization
Merton, Robert K. **10** 522-523
statistics
Chapin, (F.) Stuart **3** 437-438
Mayo-Smith, Richmond **10** 371-372
Ogburn, William Fielding **11** 480
Quételet, Lambert Adolphe Jacques **12** 510-511
Stouffer, Samuel A. **14** 482-483
structural-functionalism
Merton, Robert K. **10** 522-523
Parsons, Talcott **12** 122
Znaniecki, Florian **16** 523-524
survey analysis
Le Play, Guillaume Frédéric **9** 350-351
Lynd, Helen Merrell **10** 63-64
Lynd, Robert Staughton **10** 64-65
Sorokin, Pitirim A. **14** 348-349
Wallas, Graham **16** 77-78
Wright, Carroll Davidson **16** 396
systems theory
Luhmann, Niklas **10** 34-35
term coined
Comte, Auguste **4** 189-191
urban behavior
Park, Robert E. **12** 102-104
see also Social scientists—sociologists

Socrate (musical composition)
Satie, Erik **13** 494-495

SOCRATES (469-399 B.C.), Greek philosopher and logican **14** 320-321
associates
Aristophanes **1** 293-294
Parmenides **12** 116-117
Zeno of Elea **16** 500
influence of
Antisthenes **1** 250-251
Diogenes **5** 20-21
Flaubert, Gustave **5** 480-482
Isocrates **8** 151
Plato **12** 345-347
Xenophon **16** 418-420

Socrates (sculpture)
Brancusi, Constantin **2** 494-496

SODDY, FREDERICK (1877-1956), English chemist **14** 321-323
Ramsay, William **13** 21-22
Richards, Theodore William **13** 137-138
Rutherford, Ernest **13** 384-387

SÖDERBLOM, NATHAN (Lars Jonathan Söderblom; 1866-1931), Swedish Lutheran archbishop **14** 323-324

Sodium (element—chemistry)
Davy, Humphry **4** 426-427
Hodgkin, Alan Lloyd **7** 431-432
Rabi, Isidor Isaac **12** 526-527

Sodom and Gomorrha (novel)
Proust, Marcel **12** 465-467

Sodom and Gomorrha (play)
    Giraudoux, Jean **6** 349-350
    Kazantzakis, Nikos **8** 466-468

Sodoms Ende (play)
    Sudermann, Hermann **15** 12-13

SOELLE, DOROTHEE (born 1929), German theologian, political activist, and feminist **14** 324-325

Sofia (ship)
    Nordenskjöld, Nils Adolf Erik **11** 421-422

Soft Skin, The (film)
    Truffaut, François **15** 311-313

Soga no Umako (died 626), Japanese imperial chieftain
    Suiko **15** 15-16

Soglo, Christophe (1909-1984), Dahomean military officer and politician
    Apithy, Sourou Migan **1** 259-260

Sogni del pigro, I (literature collection)
    Moravia, Alberto **11** 153-155

Söhne des Senators, Die (novella)
    Storm, Theodor **14** 479-480

Sohrab (literary character)
    Arnold, Matthew **1** 311-313
    Firdausi **5** 451-452

Soif et la faim, La (play)
    Ionesco, Eugène **8** 131-132

Soirée avec M. Teste, La (book)
    Valéry, Paul Ambroise **15** 405-406

Soirée perdue, Une (poem)
    Musset, Louis Charles Alfred de **11** 271-272

Soirées de Médan (stories)
    Huysmans, Joris Karl **8** 81-82
    Maupassant, Henri René Albert Guy de **10** 347
    Zola, Émile **16** 526-528

Soissons, Council of (1121)
    Abelard, Peter **1** 23-25

Soka Gakkai (Buddhist lay organization)
    Ikeda, Daisaku **8** 109-110

SOL CH'ONG (circa 680-750), Korean Confucian scholar **14** 325-326

Solar system (astronomy)
    place in galaxy
        Shapley, Harlow **14** 155-156
        see also Galaxy; Milky Way Galaxy
    solar eclipses
        Eddington, Arthur Stanley **5** 201-202
        Thales **15** 161
        Turner, Nathaniel **15** 354
    solar flares
        Chapman, Sydney **3** 441
    solar motion
        Eudoxus of Cnidus **5** 329-330
        Heraclides of Pontus **7** 319-320
        Herschel, William **7** 341-343
        Hipparchus **7** 407-408
    solar parallax
        Newcomb, Simon **11** 361-362

        Rittenhouse, David **13** 180-181
    solar spectrum
        Fraunhofer, Joseph von **6** 75-76
        Langley, Samuel Pierpont **9** 195-196
    structure and stability
        Jeffreys, Harold **8** 241-242
        Laplace, Marquis de **9** 202-204
    theories of origin
        Arrhenius, Svante August **1** 318-320
        Chamberlin, Thomas Chrowder **3** 415-416
        Kant, Immanuel **8** 430-432
        see also Astronomy; Planet; Star; Sun; Universe, origin of; Universe, systems of; and individual planets

Soldier, The (sonnet)
    Brooke, Rupert **3** 22-23

Soldier and Laughing Girl (painting)
    Vermeer, Jan **15** 466-467

Soldier's Art, The (novel)
    Powell, Anthony **12** 422-423

Soldiers of Fortune (novel)
    Davis, Richard Harding **4** 422-423

Soldiers' Pay (novel)
    Faulkner, William **5** 395-397

Soldier's Tale, The (musical composition)
    Stravinsky, Igor Fedorovich **14** 502-506

Soledad sonora, La (poems)
    Jiménez, Juan Ramón **8** 261-262

Soledades, Las (poem)
    Góngora y Argote, Luis de **6** 427-428

Soleil des eaux, Le (musical composition)
    Boulez, Pierre **2** 444-445

Soleil et chair (poem)
    Rimbaud, Jean Nicolas Arthur **13** 172-174

Solid Mandala, The (novel)
    White, Patrick Victor Martindale **16** 233-235

Solidarity (independent trade union movement, Poland)
    Walesa, Lech **16** 57-59

Solidarity Action Movement (Guatemala)
    Serrano Elías, Jorge Antonio **14** 112-113

SOLÍS, JUAN DÍAZ DE (circa 1470-1516), Spanish explorer **14** 326
    Cabot, John **3** 199-200
    Cabot, Sebastian **3** 200-201

Solitudes (poem)
    Góngora y Argote, Luis de **6** 427-428

SOLOMON (ruled circa 965-circa 925 B.C.), king of the ancient Hebrews **14** 326-327
    David, Jacques Louis **4** 407-409
    Jeroboam I **8** 248-249

Solomon (musical composition)
    Handel, George Frederick **7** 116-119

Solomon, Proverbs of
    see Proverbs, Book of

Solomon bar Isaac
    see Rashi

Solomon Islands (West Pacific Ocean)
    Halsey, William Frederick **7** 91-92
    Hughes, William Morris **8** 21-22
    Mendaña de Neyra, Álvaro de **10** 483

SOLON (active 594 B.C.), Greek statesman and poet **14** 327-328
    Aeschylus **1** 70-72
    Cleisthenes **4** 98-99
    Wolf, Friedrich August **16** 352-353

SOLOVEITCHIK, JOSEPH BAER (1903-1993), Jewish theologian and philosopher **14** 328-329

Soloviev, Sergei Mikhailovich (1820-1879), Russian historian
    Klyuchevsky, Vasily Osipovich **9** 57-58

SOLOVIEV, VLADIMIR SERGEEVICH (1853-1900), Russian philosopher and religious thinker **14** 329-330

SOLZHENITSYN, ALEXANDER ISAYEVICH (born 1918), Soviet novelist **14** 330-332

Somalia (Somali Democratic Republic; nation, East Africa)
    Burton, Richard **3** 163-164
    Hassan, Muhammad Abdille **7** 194-195

SOMBART, WERNER (1863-1941), German economic historian **14** 332-333
    Weber, Max **16** 157-160

Sombra, La (novel)
    Galdós, Benito Pérez **6** 177-178

Sombrero de tres picos, El (ballet and novel)
    Alarcón, Pedro Antonio de **1** 100-101
    Falla, Manuel de **5** 372-373

Somers, John (1651-1716), English lawyer and statesman
    Swift, Jonathan **15** 51-54

Somerset, Edmund Beaufort, 2d Duke of (died 1455), English statesman
    Henry VI **7** 298-299

SOMERSET, DUKE OF (Edward Seymour; 1506-52), English statesman **14** 333-334
    Edward VI **5** 213-214
    Northumberland, Duke of **11** 431-432

Somerset, Robert Carr, Earl of (circa 1590-1645), Scottish politician
    James I **8** 204-206
    Raleigh, Walter **13** 9-11

Somerville and Ross (pseudonym)
    Somerville, Edith Anna OEnone **14** 334-335

SOMERVILLE, EDITH ANNE ŒNONE (1858-1949), Irish author **14** 334-335

somewhere i have never travelled, gladly beyond, (poem)
    Cummings, Edward Estlin **4** 334-336

Somme, battle of (1916)
    Currie, Arthur William **4** 345
    Foch, Ferdinand **5** 498-499
    Hughes, William Morris **8** 21-22

Joffre, Joseph Jacques Césaire
8 267-268

Sommerfeld, Arnold (1868-1951), German physicist
Heisenberg, Werner Karl **7** 261-263
Pauli, Wolfgang Ernst **12** 149

SOMOZA, ANASTASIO (1896-1956), Nicaraguan dictator and military leader **14** 335-336
Ferrer, José Figuéres **5** 428-429

SOMOZA DEBAYLE, ANASTASIO (1925-1980), president of Nicaragua (1967-1979) **14** 336-337
Ortega, Daniel **12** 5-7
Sandino, Augusto C. **13** 462-463

Son Excellence Eugène Rougon (novel)
Zola, Émile **16** 526-528

Son of a Servant, The (novel)
Strindberg, August **14** 509-511

Son of the Wolf, The (stories)
London, Jack **9** 494-495

Sonam Gyatso (1543-1588), third Dalai Lama
Dalai Lama **4** 369-371

Sonata (music)
cello
Carter, Elliott Cook Jr. **3** 338-339
harpsicord
Scarlatti, Domenico **13** 515-517
piano
Barenboim, Daniel **2** 3-4
piano (16th-19th century)
Bach, Carl Philipp Emanuel **1** 414-415
Beethoven, Ludwig van **2** 114-117, 461, 462
Gabrieli, Giovanni **6** 161-162
Haydn, Franz Joseph **7** 219-221
piano (19th-20th century)
Brahms, Johannes **2** 490-492
Chopin, Frédéric François **4** 16-18
Liszt, Franz **9** 445-447
MacDowell, Edward Alexander **10** 87-88
Schubert, Franz Peter **14** 35-37
Schumann, Robert Alexander **14** 41-43
Scriabin, Alexander Nikolayevich **14** 71-72
piano (20th century)
Barber, Samuel **1** 500-501
Bartók, Béla **2** 35-36
Bennett, Richard Rodney **2** 172
Berg, Alban **2** 186-187
Boulez, Pierre **2** 444-445
Carter, Elliott Cook Jr. **3** 338-339
Copland, Aaron **4** 227-228
Ginastera, Alberto Evaristo **6** 328-329
Halffter, Christóbal **7** 79-80
Ives, Charles Edward **8** 159-160
Poulenc, Francis **12** 414-415
Prokofiev, Sergei Sergeevich **12** 458-460

Sessions, Roger Huntington **14** 117-118
Stravinsky, Igor Fedorovich **14** 502-506
trio
Arne, Thomas Augustine **1** 307-308
Corelli, Arcangelo **4** 230-231
Purcell, Henry **12** 484-485
violin
Bach, Johann Sebastian **1** 416-419
Barenboim, Daniel **2** 3-4
Bartók, Béla **2** 35-36
Beethoven, Ludwig van **2** 114-117
Brahms, Johannes **2** 490-492
Corelli, Arcangelo **4** 230-231
Franck, César **6** 48-49
Gabrieli, Giovanni **6** 161-162
Henze, Hans Werner **7** 314
Mozart, Wolfgang Amadeus **11** 218-221
Szymanowski, Karol **15** 67-68
Vivaldi, Antonio **16** 3-4
violin and piano
Bartók, Béla **2** 35-36
Dvořák, Antonin **5** 168-169
Fauré, Gabriel Urbain **5** 397-398
Grieg, Edvard Hagerup **6** 541-542
Ravel, Maurice Joseph **13** 54-55
Walton, William Turner **16** 92-93
violoncello
Beethoven, Ludwig van **2** 114-117

Sonatas (novel series)
Valle Inclán, Ramón Maria del **15** 407-408

SONDHEIM, STEPHEN (born 1930), American composer and lyricist **14** 337-338

Sonetos de la muerte (poems)
Mistral, Gabriela **11** 55-56

Sonetos del amor oscuro (poems)
Lorca, Federico García **9** 511-513

Sonetos espirituales (poems)
Jiménez, Juan Ramón **8** 261-262

Sonette an Orpheus (poems)
Rilke, Rainer Maria **13** 171-172

Song of a New Race (musical composition)
Still, William Grant **14** 455-456

Song of Beowulf, The (musical composition)
Hanson, Howard **7** 135-136

Song of Bernadette, The (novel)
Werfel, Franz **16** 204-205

Song of Democracy, The (musical composition)
Hanson, Howard **7** 135-136

Song of Freedom (film)
Robeson, Paul Leroy **13** 198-199

Song of Grief, The (cantata)
Mahler, Gustav **10** 144-145

Song of Hiawatha, The (poem; Longfellow)
Bunin, Ivan Alekseevich **3** 124
Longfellow, Henry Wadsworth **9** 499-500

Tschernichowsky, Saul **15** 323

Song of Los, The (book)
Blake, William **2** 316-318

Song of Myself (poem; Whitman)
Pound, Ezra Loomis **12** 415-417
Whitman, Walt **16** 249-251

Song of Roland (poem)
Abd al-Rahman I **1** 13-14
Charlemagne **3** 445-447

Song of Sabalu (poem)
de Andrade, Mario **4** 434-435

Song of Solomon (book)
Morrison, Toni **11** 188-190

Song of Songs (Old Testament)
Beissel, Johann Conrad **2** 123-124
Isidore of Seville **8** 149-150
Solomon **14** 326-327

Song of the Birds, The (operetta)
Porter, Cole Albert **12** 405-406

Song of the Chattahoochee, The (poem)
Lanier, Sidney **9** 199-200

Song of the Earth, The (song cycle)
Mahler, Gustav **10** 144-145

Song of the Lark (novel)
Cather, Willa Sibert **3** 368-369

Song of the Redwood-Tree (poem)
Whitman, Walt **16** 249-251

Song of the Republic, A (poem)
Lawson, Henry **9** 254-255

Song of Triumphant Love, The (story)
Turgenev, Ivan Sergeyevich **15** 345-348

SONG SISTERS (Ailing Song, 1890-1973; Meiling Song, 1898-1919; and Qingling Song, 1890-1981) Chinese political and social activists **14** 338-341

Song Yo-ch'an (born 1919), South Korean general and statesman
Park, Chung Hee **12** 99-102

Songe de Vaux, Le (poem)
La Fontaine, Jean de **9** 156-157

Songes and Sonnettes (poems)
Wyatt, Thomas **16** 410-411

Songhay empire (West Africa)
Ali, Sunni **1** 158-159
Muhammad Ture, Askia **11** 231-232

Songs and Dances of Death, The (musical composition)
Mussorgsky, Modest Petrovich **11** 274-276

Songs and Sonnets (literature collection)
Donne, John **5** 60-61
Masters, Edgar Lee **10** 326-327

Songs before Sunrise (poems)
Swinburne, Algernon Charles **15** 54-55

Songs from Jamaica (poems)
McKay, Claude **10** 416

Songs from the Clay (poems)
Stephens, James **14** 430-431

Songs of a Wayfarer (musical composition)
Mahler, Gustav **10** 144-145

Songs of Action (poems)
Doyle, Arthur Conan **5** 91-92

Songs of Ch'u (poems)
Ssu-ma Hsiang-ju **14** 389-390

Songs of Experience (book)
Blake, William **2** 316-318

Songs of Innocence (book)
Blake, William **2** 316-318

Songs of Italy (poems)
Miller, Joaquin **11** 27-28

Songs of Labor ... (poems)
Whittier, John Greenleaf **16** 256-257

Songs of Mihyar the Damascene, The (book)
Adonis **1** 64-65

Songs of My Fatherland (poems)
Palamas, Kostes **12** 70

Songs of the Land of Ch'in (poems)
Po Chü-i **12** 362-363

Songs of the Pilgrim (poem)
Mármol, José **10** 274

Songs of the Road (poems)
Doyle, Arthur Conan **5** 91-92

Songs of the Sierras (poems)
Miller, Joaquin **11** 27-28

Songs on the Death of Children (musical composition)
Mahler, Gustav **10** 144-145

Songs upon Gloom (poems)
Yun Sondo **16** 483

Songs without Words (book)
Mendelssohn, Moses **10** 488-489

Sonnambula, La (opera)
Bellini, Vincenzo **2** 138-139

Sonnet (literary form)
Shakespeare, William **14** 142-145

Sonnets on Death (poems)
Mistral, Gabriela **11** 55-56

Sonnets to Orpheus (poems)
Rilke, Rainer Maria **13** 171-172

Sonora, Marquess of
see Gálvez, José de

Sons (book)
Buck, Pearl Sydenstricker **3** 91-93

Sons and Lovers (novel)
Lawrence, David Herbert **9** 247-248

Sons of Liberty (United States)
Bradford, William **2** 477
Chase, Samuel **3** 475-476
Putnam, Israel **12** 491-492
Sherman, Roger **14** 185-186

Sons of Lusus
see Lusiads, The

Sons of Moses (Jewish organization)
Ahad Haam **1** 88-89

SONTAG, SUSAN (born 1933), American essayist **14** 342-343

Sony Corporation
Morita, Akio **11** 176-178

Soong Ch'ing-ling
see Sun Yat-sen, Madame

Soong Mei-ling (Mme. Chiang Kai-shek; born 1898), Chinese author
Chiang Kai-shek **3** 510-513

Sophia Alekseevna (1657-1704), regent of Russia 1682-89
K'ang-hsi **8** 423-426
Peter I **12** 253-256

Sophia Dorothea (1666-1726), wife of George I of England
George I **6** 268-269

Sophia Frederica Dagmar, Princess
see Maria Fedorovna

Sophie's Choice (book, film)
Styron, William **15** 6-8

Sophism (philosophy)
Aristotle **1** 295-296
Euripides **5** 332-334
Gorgias **6** 456
Isocrates **8** 151
Plato **12** 345-347
Protagoras **12** 461
Thucydides **15** 211-212
Xenophon **16** 418-420

SOPHOCLES (496-406 B.C.), Greek playwright **14** 343-345
contemporaries
Aeschylus **1** 70-72
Euripides **5** 332-334
Herodotus **7** 330-333
influence of
Lessing, Gotthold Ephraim **9** 357-359
Robbe-Grillet, Alain **13** 189-190
Schiller, Johann Christoph Friedrich von **14** 4-7
Voltaire **16** 14-16
translations
Leconte de Lisle, Charles Marie René **9** 273-274
Tschernichowsky, Saul **15** 323

SOPWITH, THOMAS OCTAVE MURDOCH (1888-1989), British aviation industrialist and pioneer pilot **14** 345-346

Sorbonne (collection; University of Paris)
arts and language
Eisenstein, Sergei Mikhailovich **5** 240-242
Guillén, Nicolás **7** 34-35
philosophy
Cousin, Victor **4** 273-274
Gilson, Étienne Henry **6** 327-328
Simon, Jules François **14** 237-238
science
Cauchy, Augustin Louis **3** 378-380
Curie, Marie Sklodowska **4** 339-341
Elsasser, Walter Maurice **5** 277-278
Gay-Lussac, Joseph Louis **6** 245-246

Merleau-Ponty, Maurice **10** 518
social sciences
Aron, Raymond **1** 316-317
Aulard, François Victor Alphonse **1** 374
Bloch, Marc **2** 332-333
Durkheim, Émile **5** 162-163
Lavisse, Ernest **9** 241
Lévy-Bruhl, Lucien **9** 374-375
Vidal de la Blache, Paul **15** 490
see also Paris, University of

Sorcerer, The (operetta)
Gilbert, William Schwenck **6** 314-315

Sorcière, La (book)
Michelet, Jules **11** 5-6

Sordello (poem)
Browning, Robert **3** 53-55

Sorekara (novel)
Natsume, Soseki **11** 324-325

SOREL, ALBERT (1842-1906), French diplomatic historian **14** 346-347

SOREL, GEORGES (1847-1922), French philosopher **14** 347-348
Maurras, Charles Marie Photius **10** 350-351
Mussolini, Benito **11** 272-274

Sorel, Julien (literary character)
Stendhal **14** 422-425

Sorellina, La (novel)
Martin du Gard, Roger **10** 295-296

Soria, Giovanni Battista (1581-1651), Italian architect
Maderno, Carlo **10** 117-118

Soria, treaty of (1256)
Alfonso X **1** 150-151

Sorochinsk Fair (opera)
Mussorgsky, Modest Petrovich **11** 274-276

SOROKIN, PITIRIM A. (1889-1968), Russian-American sociologist **14** 348-349

Sorrow stay (song)
Dowland, John **5** 90

Sorrowing Madonna (sculpture)
Pilon, Germain **12** 305

Sorrows (poems)
Ovid **12** 34-36

Sorrows of a Heretic, The (novel)
Tanizaki, Junichiro **15** 101-102

Sorrows of the Young Werther (book; Goethe)
Kuo Mo-jo **9** 133-134

Sosarme (opera)
Handel, George Frederick **7** 116-119

Sostratos (literary character)
Menander **10** 477-478

SOTATSU, TAWARAYA (circa 1570-circa 1643), Japanese painter **14** 349

Sotoba Komachi (play)
Zeami, Kanze **16** 492-493

Soubirous, Bernadette
see Bernadette of Lourdes, St.

SOUFFLOT, JACQUES GERMAIN
(1713-1780), French architect
14 349-350

Soul
philosophy
Augustine **1** 367-370
Democritus **4** 493-494
Descartes, René **4** 505-508
Epicurus **5** 292-294
Feuerbach, Ludwig Andreas **5** 432
Ficino, Marsilio **5** 436-437
Pomponazzi, Pietro **12** 390-391
religion
Hui-yüan **8** 25-26
Leon, Moses de **9** 336
Nahmanides **11** 293-294
Shankara **14** 150-151

Soul on Ice (book)
Cleaver, Leroy Eldridge **4** 97-98

SOULAGES, PIERRE (born 1919), French
painter **14** 350-351

SOULÉ, PIERRE (1801-1870), American
politician and diplomat **14** 351-352

Soulier de satin, Le (play)
Claudel, Paul Louis Charles **4** 90-91

Soult, Nicolas Jean de Dieu (1769-1851),
marshal of France
Thiers, Louis Adolphe **15** 181-182

Soumman, Congress of (1956)
Ben Bella, Ahmed **2** 148-149

Sound (physics)
Bernoulli, Daniel **2** 216
Ewing, William Maurice **5** 350-351
Fresnel, Augustin Jean **6** 102-103
Lagrange, Joseph Louis **9** 164-166
Landau, Lev Davidovich **9** 184-185

Sound and the Fury, The (novel)
Faulkner, William **5** 395-397

Sound of Music, The (musical)
Hammerstein, Oscar Clendenning II
7 104-106
Rodgers, Richard Charles **13** 234-236

Soupault, Philip (1897-1990), French novelist and poet
Breton, André **2** 519-520

Soupir (poem)
Mallarmé, Stéphane **10** 172-173

Sous le soleil de Satan (novel)
Bernanos, Georges **2** 206-207

Sous l'oeil des barbares (novel)
Barrès, Auguste Maurice **2** 20-21

SOUSA, HENRIQUE TEIXEIRA DE (born
1919), Cape Verdean novelist **14** 352-353

SOUSA, JOHN PHILIP (1854-1932), American bandmaster and composer
14 353-354

SOUSA, MARTIM AFONSO DE (circa
1500-64), Portuguese colonizer and
statesman **14** 354-355

SOUTER, DAVID H. (born 1939), U.S.
Supreme Court justice **14** 355-356

South Africa, Republic of
• EARLY HISTORY
Basotho nation
Moshweshwe **11** 203-205
British policy
Frere, Henry Bartle Edward
6 100-101
Ndebele kingdom
Mzilikazi **11** 285-286
Voortrekkers
see Boers
Zulu leaders
Cetshwayo **3** 400
Dingane **5** 14-15
Shaka **14** 141-142
• ENGLISH RULE
Boer leaders
Botha, Louis **2** 434-436
Hertzog, James Barry Munnik
7 347-348
Kruger, Stephanus Johannes
Paulus **9** 108-109
Smuts, Jan Christian **14** 309-310
Boer War
see Boer War (1899-1902)
British policy
Grey, George **6** 540-541
Hardie, James Keir **7** 147-148
Jameson, Leander Starr **8** 218
Kitchener, Horatio Herbert
9 45-46
Milner, Alfred **11** 38-39
Rhodes, Cecil John **13** 120-122
Roberts, Frederick Sleigh
13 195-196
Indian protest movement
Gandhi, Mohandas Karamchand
6 201-204
Gokhale, Gopal Krishna **6** 396
Ndebele kingdom
Lobengula **9** 474-475
union status (1910)
Botha, Louis **2** 434-436
Smuts, Jan Christian **14** 309-310
• INDEPENDENCE
African nations and
Banda, Hastings Kamuzu
1 485-486
Jonathan, Joseph Leabua
8 330-331
Khama, Seretse M. **8** 532-533
Mondlane, Eduardo Chivambo
11 100-101
apartheid
see Apartheid
Black activism
Biko, Steve **2** 273-274
Sobukwe, Robert Mangaliso
14 318-319
Black "homelands"
Buthelezi, Mangosuthu Gatsha
3 178-179
Black labor movement

Kadalie, Clements **8** 401-402
Ramaphosa, Matemela Cyril
13 15-16
Black resistance
Lembede, Anton **9** 318-319
Mandela, Nelson Rolihlahla
10 185-186
Mandela, Winnie **10** 187-189
Sisulu, Nontsikelelo Albertina
14 259-261
Sisulu, Walter Max Ulyate
14 261-262
Tutu, Desmond **15** 360-361
dissidents
Suzman, Helen **15** 45-46
economic sanctions against
Sullivan, Leon Howard **15** 25-27
Tutu, Desmond **15** 360-361
nationalism
Hertzog, James Barry Munnik
7 347-348
Malan, Daniel Francois
10 163-164
Verwoerd, Hendrik Frensch
15 472-473
Vorster, Balthazar Johannes
16 30-32
political leaders
Botha, Pieter Willem **2** 436-438
de Klerk, Fredrik Willem
4 466-468

South African literature
Brutus, Dennis **3** 77-78
Coetzee, J. M. **4** 133-135
Dube, John Langalibalele **5** 113
Fugard, Athol **6** 142-143
Gordimer, Nadine **6** 446-447
Lessing, Doris **9** 355-357
Mofolo, Thomas **11** 74
Mqhayi, Samuel Edward Krune **11** 223
Mphahlele, Ezekiel **11** 221-223
Nkosi, Lewis **11** 407-408
Paton, Alan Stewart **12** 134-135
Plaatje, Solomon Tshekisho **12** 341-342

South African Natives National Congress
(established 1912)
Plaatje, Solomon Tshekisho **12** 341-342

South African party (politics)
Hertzog, James Barry Munnik
7 347-348
Smuts, Jan Christian **14** 309-310

South African Students' Organization
Biko, Steve **2** 273-274

South African War (1899-1902)
see Boer War

South America
see Latin America

South Australia (state, Australia)
Burke, Robert O'Hara **3** 142-143
Grey, George **6** 540-541

South Carolina (state, United States)
economic development
Hampton, Wade **7** 111-112
exploration

de Soto, Hernando **4** 510-511
governors
    Byrnes, James Francis **3** 191-192
    Hammond, James Henry **7** 108-109
    Hampton, Wade III **7** 112
    Hayne, Robert Young **7** 231-232
    McDuffie, George **10** 408
    Nicholson, Francis **11** 381-382
    Thurmond, James Strom **15** 214-215
    Tillman, Benjamin Ryan **15** 225-226
legislators
    Calhoun, John Caldwell **3** 226-228
    Hampton, Wade **7** 111-112
    Marion, Francis **10** 262-263
    Memminger, Christopher Gustavus
      10 476-477
    Pinckney, Charles **12** 309-310
    Rhett, Robert Barnwell **13** 120
    Smalls, Robert **14** 277-278
slave revolt (1822)
    Vesey, Denmark **15** 475

South Dakota (state, United States)
    Calamity Jane **3** 216
    Fletcher, Alice Cunningham **5** 486-487
    Harrison, Benjamin **7** 178-179
    McGovern, George Stanley **10** 412-414

South End House (Boston)
    Woods, Robert Archey **16** 374

South Korea
    see Korea—since 1948

South Mountain, battle of (1862)
    McClellan, George Brinton **10** 391-392
    Meade, George Gordon **10** 440-441

South Pacific (musical)
    Hammerstein, Oscar Clendenning II
      7 104-106
    Martin, Mary **10** 292-293
    Rodgers, Richard Charles **13** 234-236

South Pacific Commission (established
1947)
    Evatt, Herbert Vere **5** 341-343

South Pass (Rocky Mountains)
    Frémont, John Charles **6** 97-98
    Smith, Jedediah S. **14** 294-295

South Pole
    Amundsen, Roald **1** 206-207
    Byrd, Richard Evelyn **3** 186-187
    Scott, Robert Falcon **14** 67-68

South Sea Islander (painting)
    Nolde, Emil **11** 419-420

South Vietnam
    see Vietnam; Vietnam, South

Southampton County (Virginia)
    Dew, Thomas Roderick **4** 519
    Turner, Nathaniel **15** 354

Southard, Samuel L. (1787-1842), American politician
    Monroe, James **11** 111-113

Southeast Asia
    see Burma; Cambodia; Indonesia; Laos;
    Malaysia; Philippines; Thailand; Viet-
    nam

Southeast Asia Treaty Organization
    Dulles, John Foster **5** 134-135
    Eisenhower, Dwight David **5** 233-236
    Garcia, Carlos P. **6** 207-208
    Magsaysay, Ramon **10** 130-131
    Menzies, Robert Gordon **10** 510-511
    Sihanouk, Norodom **14** 222-223

Southern Christian Leadership Conference
    Abernathy, Ralph David **1** 27-28
    Bevel, James Luther **2** 250-251
    Jackson, Jesse Louis **8** 174-176
    King, Martin Luther Jr. **9** 20-22
    Parks, Rosa Lee McCauley **12** 115-116
    Rustin, Bayard **13** 382-383
    Young, Andrew Jackson Jr. **16** 467-469

Southern dynasties (China; reigned
420-589)
    see Ch'en dynasty; Ch'i dynasty; Liang
    dynasty; Liu Sung dynasty

Southern Mail (novel)
    Saint-Exupéry, Antoine de **13** 431-432

Southern Pacific Co.
    Huntington, Collis Potter **8** 49
    Stanford, Leland **14** 397-398

Southern Pacific Railroad (United States)
    Harriman, Edward Henry **7** 164-165
    Norris, Benjamin Franklin Jr.
      11 427-428
    Stanford, Leland **14** 397-398

Southern Poverty Law Center
    Dees, Morris S. Jr. **4** 456-457

Southern Rhodesia
    see Rhodesia

Southern Sung dynasty
    see Sung dynasty, Southern

Southerner, The (novel)
    Page, Walter Hines **12** 60-61

Southey, Robert (1774-1843), English poet
    Arnold, Matthew **1** 311-313
    Coleridge, Samuel Taylor **4** 154-156
    Hazlitt, William **7** 235-236
    Lamb, Charles **9** 176-177
    Landor, Walter Savage **9** 186-187
    Peacock, Thomas Love **12** 169

Southwest African People's Organization
(SWAPO)
    Nujoma, Shafiihuna **11** 441-443

Soutien de famille, Le (novel)
    Daudet, Alphonse **4** 402-403

SOUTINE, CHAIM (1894-1943), Russian
painter **14** 356-357
    Chagall, Marc **3** 406-407
    Dobell, William **5** 34-35
    Modigliani, Amedeo **11** 72-73

SOUVANNA PHOUMA (1901-1984), Laotian prince and premier **14** 357-358

Souvenir (poem)
    Musset, Louis Charles Alfred de
      11 271-272

Souvenir de Biskra (painting)
    Matisse, Henri **10** 336-337

Souvenir of Marcoussis (painting)
    Corot, Jean Baptiste Camille **4** 247-249

Souvenirs (ballet)
    Barber, Samuel **1** 500-501

Souvenirs d'Andalousie (composition)
    Gottschalk, Louis Moreau **6** 463-464

Soviet State Dancers (ballet company)
    Balanchine, George **1** 461-462

Soviet Union
    see Union of Soviet Socialist Republics

Sower (painting)
    Millet, Jean François **11** 31

SOYINKA, WOLE (Oluwole Akinwande
Soyinka; born 1934), first African to win
the Nobel Prize for Literature (1986)
14 358-359

Soz-e-Vatan (stories)
    Premchand **12** 439

SPAAK, PAUL HENRI (1899-1972), Belgian
statesman and diplomat **14** 359-360

Space exploration
manned flights
    Armstrong, Neil Alden **1** 304-306
    Gagarin, Yuri Alexeivich **6** 166-167
political aspects
    Eisenhower, Dwight David
      5 233-236
    Johnson, Lyndon Baines **8** 308-312
    Menzies, Robert Gordon
      10 510-511
technology
    Cherenkov, Pavel Alekseevich
      3 502-503
    Goddard, Robert Hutchings
      6 376-377
    Kapitsa, Pyotr Leonidovich
      8 433-435
    Tsiolkovsky, Konstantin Eduardovich
      15 326-328
    von Braun, Wernher **16** 17-18

Spagnoletto, Lo
    see Ribera, Jusepe de

Spagnoletto, The (play)
    Lazarus, Emma **9** 260-261

Spain (Spanish State; nation, Europe)
• ANCIENT
    Carthaginian (237-201 B.C.)
      Hamilcar Barca **7** 94-95
      Hannibal Barca **7** 128-130
    Punic War
      see Punic War—Second
    Roman (201 B.C.-A.D. 756)
      Caesar, Gaius Julius **3** 207-210
      Crassus Dives, Marcus Licinius
        4 296-297
      Isidore of Seville **8** 149-150
      see also Visigoths
• ISLAMIC (756-1492)
    Almohads and Almoravids
      Abd al-Mumin **1** 13
      ibn Tashufin, Yusuf **8** 95-96

Yakub al-Mansur, Abu Yusuf
16 426
see also Spanish reconquest wars
(below)
Aragonese expansion
Peter III **12** 256-257
Castile and León
Alfonso VI **1** 149
Alfonso X **1** 150-151
Douglas, James **5** 78
López de Ayala, Pedro
9 508-509
France and
Charles VIII **3** 462-463
Frankish wars
Charlemagne **3** 445-447
Martel, Charles **10** 285
Spanish reconquest wars
Alfonso VI **1** 149
Cid **4** 58-59
Isabella I **8** 144-145
Judah Halevi **8** 373
Ummayad dynasty
Abd al-Rahman I **1** 13-14
Abd al-Rahman III **1** 14
• MONARCHY and REPUBLIC
(1492-1939)
bankruptcy of crown
Alba, Duke of **1** 103-104
Philip II **12** 271-273
Philip III **12** 273-274
Philip IV **12** 275
Bourbon dynasty
see Bourbon dynasty—Spain
Civil War (1936-1939)
see Civil War, Spanish
Constitutional monarchy
Azara, Félix de **1** 397-398
Ferdinand VII **5** 418-420
Fernández de Lizardi, José
Joaquin **5** 424-425
Isabella II **8** 145-146
dictatorship
Alfonso XIII **1** 151
Primo de Rivera y Orbaneja,
Miguel **12** 454-455
Dutch wars
Philip II **12** 271-273
Philip III **12** 273-274
William the Silent **16** 300-302
English relations
Buckingham, 1st Duke of
3 93-94
Charles, I **3** 450-452
Cromwell, Oliver **4** 317-320
Essex, 2d Earl of **5** 321-322
Henry VII **7** 300-302
Henry VIII **7** 302-305
James I **8** 204-206
see also Armada, Spanish
expulsion of jews (1492)
Abravanel, Isaac ben Judah **1** 31
see also Inquisition, Spanish
expulsion of Moriscos
Lea, Henry Charles **9** 261-262
Philip III **12** 273-274

French wars
Coligny, Gaspard de **4** 159-160
Condé, Prince de **4** 193-194
Ferdinand VII **5** 418-420
Henry IV **7** 293-295
Louis XIV **9** 531-533
Mazarin, Jules **10** 379-380
Hapsburg dynasty
Charles II **3** 454
Charles V **3** 457-459
Philip II **12** 271-273
Philip III **12** 273-274
Philip IV **12** 275
modern state created
Ferdinand V **5** 417-418
Isabella I **8** 144-145
Napoleonic era
Azara, Félix de **1** 397-398
Bonaparte, Joseph **2** 381-382
Charles IV **3** 456-457
Godoy y Álvarez de Faria,
Manuel de **6** 381-382
Napoleon I **11** 306-310
see also Napoleonic Wars
papal relations
Julius II **8** 384-386
Leo XIII **9** 334-336
see also Holy League
(1511-1513)
Peninsular War
see Peninsular War
popular revolution (1868)
Isabella II **8** 145-146
Seven Years War
see Seven Years War
Spanish-American War
see Spanish-American War
Thirty Years War
see Thirty Years War
United States relations
Charles III **3** 454-455
Clark, George Rogers **4** 75-76
Clayton, John Middleton **4** 96-97
Gálvez, Bernardo de **6** 195-196
Jay, John **8** 230-232
Jefferson, Thomas **8** 238-241
Lee, Arthur **9** 288-289
Pinckney, Charles **12** 309-310
War of the Spanish Succession
see Spanish Succession, War of
the
see also Spain, Colonial Empire
of
• POST-CIVIL WAR (SINCE 1939)
industrial recovery
Franco Bahamonde, Francisco
6 52-54
republic falls
Alfonso XIII **1** 151
Azaña Diaz, Manuel **1** 396-397
Franco Bahamonde, Francisco
6 52-54
see also Spanish literature
return to constitutional monarchy
González Márquez, Felipe
6 429-431

Juan Carlos I **8** 368-369
Spain, Colonial Empire of
• LATIN AMERICA AND ASIA
Araucanian revolt
see Araucanian Indians (South
America)
Argentina
Belgrano, Manuel **2** 126-127
Güemes, Martín **7** 26-27
Rivadavia, Bernardino
13 182-183
San Martín, José de **13** 468-469
see also Argentina
Bolivia
Ballivián, José **1** 475
Sucre, Antonio José de **15** 11-12
see also Bolivia
Chile
O'Higgins, Bernardo **11** 486
Valdivia, Pedro de **15** 400-401
see also Chile
Colombia
Nariño, Antonio **11** 314-315
Santander, Francisco de Paula
13 475
see also Colombia
Cuba (colony)
see Cuba
Dominican wars
see Dominican Republic—Spain
England and
Canning, George **3** 258-260
Castlereagh, Viscount **3** 363-364
exploration
see Explorers, Spanish
Mexico (colony)
see Mexico—Aztec Empire
(Spanish conquest)
Peru
see Peru—Spanish conquest
Philippines
see Philippines—1521-1898
Puerto Rico
see Puerto Rico
Uruguray
see Uruguay
Venezuela
see Venezuela
see also Encomienda system
(Spanish America);
Spanish-American War
• UNIED STATES
California and
Anza, Juan Bautista de
1 254-255
Kino, Eusebio Francisco **9** 30-31
Portolá, Gaspar de **12** 408
Serra, Junípero **14** 111-112
see also California
exploration
see Explorers, Spanish
Florida
see Florida—colonization
New Mexico *see* New Mexico
see also Spanish-American War

Spalatin, Georg (1484-1545), German
Protestant Reformer
Melancthon, Philip **10** 466-467

Spalicek (ballet; Martinu)
Martinu, Bohuslav **10** 299-300
Szymanowski, Karol **15** 67-68

SPALLANZANI, LAZZARO (Abbé Spallanzani; 1729-99) Italian naturalist
14 360-361

Spaniards, The (play)
Lermontov, Mikhail Yurievich
9 352-353

Spanish America
see Latin America

Spanish architecture
Art Nouveau
see Art Nouveau—architecture
baroque
see Baroque architecture

Spanish Armada
see Armada

Spanish art
Bofill, Ricardo **2** 362-363
baroque
see Baroque painting (Spain)
cubism
see Cubism (art movement)
Renaissance
see Renaissance (art)—Spain
sculpture (welded)
González, Julio **6** 428-429
surrealism
see Surrealism—Spain

Spanish Bayonet (novel)
Benét, Stephen Vincent **2** 157-158

Spanish Civil War
see Civil War, Spanish

Spanish Earth, The (film)
Dos Passos, John Roderigo **5** 69-71
Hemingway, Ernest Miller **7** 274-277

Spanish Elegies (painting series)
Motherwell, Robert **11** 210-211

Spanish Gipsy, The (poem)
Eliot, George **5** 254-256

Spanish literature
American epic
Ercilla y Zúñiga, Alonso de **5** 302
baroque
see Baroque literature
Generation of 1898
see Generation of 1898
Generation of 1927
Guillén, Nicolás **7** 34-35
Lorca, Federico García **9** 511-513
Golden Age
Alarcón, Pedro Antonio de
1 100-101
Tirso de Molina **15** 237-238
see also Golden Age (Spanish litera-
ture)
medieval
Alfonso X **1** 150-151

Cid **4** 58-59
Gonzalo de Berceo **6** 431-432
ibn Gabirol, Solomon ben Judah
8 92
Judah Halevi **8** 373
López de Ayala, Pedro **9** 508-509
Manrique, Jorge **10** 210-211
Ruiz, Juan **13** 358-359
modern
Cela y Trulock, Camilo José
3 389-390
Ferrer, Gabriel Miró **5** 428
Unamuno y Jugo, Miguel de
15 386-387
mysticism
John of the Cross **8** 285
Theresa **15** 178-179
poetry
Ibárruri Gómez, Dolores **8** 88-90
realism
Alarcón, Pedro Antonio de
1 100-101
Bécquer, Gustavo Adolfo
Dominguez **2** 107-108
Galdós, Benito Pérez **6** 177-178
Valera y Alcalá Galiano, Juan
15 403
Renaissance
Alemán, Mateo **1** 126
Encina, Juan del **5** 283
Lope Félix de Vega Carpio
9 503-506-563
Vicente, Gil **15** 479-480
see also Renaissance (literature)—
Spain
romanticism
Saavedra, Angel de **13** 398
symbolism
see Symbolism (literature)—Spain

Spanish music
Albéniz, Issac **1** 108-109
Cabezón, Antonio **3** 197-198
Casals, Pablo **3** 348-350
Encina, Juan del **5** 283
Falla, Manuel de **5** 372-373
Granados, Enrique **6** 489-490
Halffter, Christóbal **7** 79-80
Milán, Luis **11** 15-16
Scarlatti, Domenico **13** 515-517
Segovia, Andrés **14** 87-88
Victoria, Tomás Luis de **15** 487-488

Spanish Singer (painting)
Manet, Édouard **10** 193-194

Spanish Student, The (play)
Longfellow, Henry Wadsworth
9 499-500

Spanish Succession, War of the
(1701-1714)
Austria and
Eugene of Savoy **5** 330-331
England and
Anne **1** 241-242
Bolingbroke, Viscount **2** 374-375
Godolphin, Sidney **6** 380-381
Harley, Robert **7** 159-160

Marlborough, 1st Duke of
10 271-272
Spotswood, Alexander **14** 385
William III **16** 295-296
France and
Louis XIV **9** 531-533
Savoy and
Victor Amadeus II **15** 482-483
Spain and
Charles II **3** 454
Philip V **12** 276-277
see also Utrecht, Treaty of

Spanish Tragedie, The (play)
Kyd, Thomas **9** 140-141

Spanish-American War (1898)
Cuba and
Gómez, Máximo **6** 418-419
Gorgas, William Crawford
6 454-455
Menocal, Mario Garcia **10** 506-507
Hawaii and
Dole, Sanford Ballard **5** 46
health programs
Barton, Clara **2** 37-39
Finlay, Carlos Juan **5** 450
journalism
Bennett, James Gordon Jr.
2 169-170
Crane, Stephen **4** 293-295
Glackens, William **6** 355-356
Hearst, William Randolph
7 243-244
Philippines and
Aguinaldo, Emilio **1** 88
Mabini, Apolinario **10** 72-73
Osmeña, Sergio **12** 22-24
Primo de Rivera y Orbaneja, Miguel
12 454-455
Puerto Rico and
Hostos, Eugenio María de
7 513-514
Muñoz Rivera, Luís **11** 250
Spanish cessions
Alfonso XIII **1** 151
U.S. armed services
Ames, Adelbert **1** 198
Bryan, William Jennings **3** 80-82
Davis, Benjamin O. Sr. **4** 414-415
Dewey, George **4** 520
Goethals, George Washington
6 387-388
Mahan, Alfred Thayer **10** 131-132
Pershing, John Joseph **12** 243-244
Roosevelt, Theodore **13** 280-283
Wood, Leonard **16** 369-370
U.S. opponents
Schurz, Carl **14** 44-45
Villard, Oswald Garrison
15 498-499
U.S. war declaration
McKinley, William **10** 418-420
see also Paris, Treaty of (1898)

Spark (ship)
Farragut, David Glasgow **5** 388-389

SPARK, MURIEL SARAH (born 1918), British author **14** 361-362

Spark of Life (novel)
Remarque, Erich Maria **13** 91

Sparkling Flint (poems)
Vaughan, Henry **15** 444-445

SPARKS, JARED (1789-1866), American historian **14** 363
Adams, Herbert Baxter **1** 47
Parkman, Francis **12** 113-115

Sparta (city-state, Greece)
Athenian wars
Alcibiades **1** 119-120
Cleisthenes **4** 98-99
Themistocles **15** 170-171
kings
Agis IV **1** 81-82
Cleomenes I **4** 103
Cleomenes III **4** 103-104
Leonidas I **9** 340-343
Peloponnesian War
see Peloponnesian War
Persian wars
Agesilaus II **1** 79-80
Leonidas I **9** 340-343
Pericles **12** 219-221
Theban conquest
Epaminondas **5** 291-292

SPARTACUS (died 71 B.C.), Thracian gladiator **14** 363-364
Crassus Dives, Marcus Licinius **4** 296-297
Pompey **12** 387-389

Spartacus, League of (established 1916)
Luxemburg, Rosa **10** 55-56
Ulbricht, Walter **15** 383-384

Spartak (ballet)
Khachaturian, Aram Ilich **8** 530-531

SPAULDING, CHARLES CLINTON (1874-1952), African American business executive **14** 364-365

Späte Rosen (novella)
Storm, Theodor **14** 479-480

Speak, Parrot (satire)
Skelton, John **14** 268-269

Speakers of the House
see Statesmen, American

Speciation theory (biology)
Mayr, Ernst **10** 372-374

Specimen Days and Collect (book)
Whitman, Walt **16** 249-251

Specimens (poems)
Miller, Joaquin **11** 27-28

Spectacle dans un fauteuil, Le (poem)
Musset, Louis Charles Alfred de **11** 271-272

Spectateur français (newspaper)
Marivaux, Pierre Carlet de Chamblain de **10** 265-266

Spectator (periodical)
Addison, Joseph **1** 57-58

Chekhov, Anton Pavlovich **3** 494-497
Franklin, Benjamin **6** 60-64
Godkin, Edwin Lawrence **6** 380
Irving, Washington **8** 141-143
Milton, John **11** 43-46
Pope, Alexander **12** 395-397
Steele, Richard **14** 407-409
Swift, Jonathan **15** 51-54

Specter, The (novel)
Gorky, Maxim **6** 458-460

Spectre's Bride, The (musical composition)
Dvořák, Antonin **5** 168-169

Spectroheliograph
Hale, George Ellery **7** 72-74

Spectroscope (instrument)
Fraunhofer, Joseph von **6** 75-76
Michelson, Albert Abraham **11** 7-8

Spectroscopy (science)
Bunsen, Robert Wilhelm **3** 124-125
Crookes, William **4** 323-324
Fermi, Enrico **5** 422-424
Herzberg, Gerhard **7** 349-350
Huggins, William **8** 14-15
Kirchhoff, Gustav Robert **9** 33-34
Pickering, Edward Charles **12** 298
Polanyi, John Charles **12** 370-372
Rowland, Henry Augustus **13** 330-331

Speculative philosophy
see Theoretical physics

Speculators
see Business and industrial leaders—promoters and speculators

Speech, freedom of
see Freedom of speech

Speedwell (ship)
Bradford, William **2** 475-476

SPEKE, JOHN HANNING (1827-1864), English explorer **14** 366-367
Baker, Samuel White **1** 454-455
Burton, Richard **3** 163-164
Mutesa I **11** 277

Spellbound (film)
Hitchcock, Alfred **7** 415-416

SPELLMAN, CARDINAL FRANCIS JOSEPH (1889-1967), Roman Catholic archbishop **14** 367
Paul VI **12** 146-148

Spelman College
Cole, Johnnetta **4** 147-149

SPEMANN, HANS (1869-1941), German experimental embryologist **14** 368-369

Spence, Joseph (1699-1768), English anecdotist
Pope, Alexander **12** 395-397

SPENCER, HERBERT (1820-1903), English philosopher **14** 369-370
influence of
Adams, Henry Brooks **1** 45-47
Dreiser, Herman Theodore **5** 98-100
Parsons, Frank **12** 121-122
Sullivan, Louis Henri **15** 27-28

Sumner, William Graham **15** 32
Whitehead, Alfred North **16** 242-244
Wright, Frank Lloyd **16** 398-401
Yen Fu **16** 452
influenced by
Baer, Karl Ernst von **1** 431-432

Spencer, Niles (1893-1952), American painter
Stella, Joseph **14** 422

Spencerism
see Social Darwinism

SPENDER, STEPHEN HAROLD (born 1909), English poet and critic **14** 370-371
Auden, Wystan Hugh **1** 364-366
Lewis, Cecil Day **9** 380

SPENER, PHILIPP JAKOB (1635-1705), German theologian **14** 372
Boehme, Jacob **2** 357
Thomasius **15** 193-194
Zinzendorf, Nikolaus Ludwig von **16** 522-523

SPENGLER, OSWALD (1880-1936), German philosopher **14** 372-373
Jeffers, John Robinson **8** 236-237

SPENSER, EDMUND (circa 1552-99), English poet **14** 373-376
friends
Raleigh, Walter **13** 9-11
Sidney, Philip **14** 214-215
influence of
Allston, Washington **1** 176-177
Cowley, Abraham **4** 281-282
Drayton, Michael **5** 97-98
Keats, John **8** 470-472
Thomson, James **15** 199-200
influenced by
Ariosto, Ludovico **1** 289-290
Ovid **12** 34-36
Plutarch **12** 359-360
Tasso, Torquato **15** 114-116
quoted
Conrad, Joseph **4** 205-207

SPERANSKI, COUNT MIKHAIL MIKHAILOVICH (1772-1839), Russian statesman and reformer **14** 376-377
Alexander I **1** 130-132
Nesselrode, Karl Robert **11** 348-349

Spermatozoa (biology)
Leeuwenhoek, Anton van **9** 300-301

SPERRY, ELMER A. (1860-1930), American inventor **14** 377-379

Speyer, Diet of (1529)
Charles V **3** 457-459

Sphinx, The (play)
Aeschylus **1** 70-72

Spiaggia, La (novel)
Pavese, Cesare **12** 154-155

Spice Islands (Indonesia)
Corte Reál, Gaspar and Miguel **4** 254-255
Drake, Francis **5** 94-96

Magellan, Ferdinand **10** 126-127

Spider (sculpture)
Richier, Germaine **13** 145-146

Spider's Feast, The (ballet)
Roussel, Albert **13** 328-329

Spiegelmensch (trilogy)
Werfel, Franz **16** 204-205

SPIELBERG, STEVEN (born 1947), American filmmaker **14** 379-381

Spiesser Spiegel (lithography series)
Grosz, George **7** 17-18

Spin (magazine)
Guccione, Bob Jr. **7** 26

Spinario, Lo (sculpture)
Brunelleschi, Filippo **3** 70-72

Spingarn, Joel (1875-1939), American educator and literary critic
Ransom, John Crowe **13** 39-40

Spinola, Ambrogio de (1569-1630), Spanish general
Maurice of Nassau **10** 348-349

SPINOZA, BARUCH (Benedict Spinoza; 1632-77), Dutch philosopher **14** 381-383
associates
Condé, Prince de **4** 193-194
critics
Jacobi, Friedrich Heinrich
8 189-190
influence of
Boerhaave, Hermann **2** 358-359
Einstein, Albert **5** 228-231
Fichte, Johann Gottlieb **5** 435-436
Goethe, Johann Wolfgang von
6 388-391
Lessing, Gotthold Ephraim
9 357-359
Rolland, Romain **13** 260
Santayana, George **13** 475-477
Schelling, Friedrich Wilhelm Joseph
von **13** 526-527
Schleiermacher, Friedrich Ernst
Daniel **14** 11-12
Schrödinger, Erwin **14** 31-33
influenced by
Maimonides **10** 151-152

Spinoza of Market Street, The (stories)
Singer, Isaac Bashevis **14** 249-250

Spinthariscope (instrument)
Crookes, William **4** 323-324

Spirit House (Newark, New Jersey)
Baraka, Imamu Amiri **1** 498-499

Spirit of Life (sculpture)
French, Daniel Chester **6** 98-99

Spirit of St. Louis (airplane)
Lindbergh, Charles Augustus **9** 421-423

Spirit of the Heng Mountains (engraving)
Wu Tao-tzu **16** 405-406

Spirit of the Laws, The (book; Montesquieu)
Alfieri, Vittoria **1** 145-146
Hu Shih **8** 63-65

Montesquieu **11** 123-125
Yen Fu **16** 452

Spirit of the Lo River (painting)
Ku K'ai-chih **9** 125-126

Spiritata, La (canzona)
Gabrieli, Giovanni **6** 161-162

Spiritual Arts, Society of (established 1931)
St. Denis, Ruth **13** 430-431

Spiritual Exercises (book; Ignatius of Loyola)
Canisius, Peter **3** 258
Caravaggio **3** 282-284
Ignatius of Loyola **8** 108-109

Spiritualism (religion)
Coward, Noel **4** 279-280
Doyle, Arthur Conan **5** 91-92
Hare, Robert **7** 152-153
James, William **8** 215-217
Mesmer, Franz Anton **10** 526-527
Owen, Robert **12** 39-40

Spiritus Intelligentiae (musical composition)
Krenek, Ernst **9** 98-99

Spitsbergen (archipelago; Arctic Ocean)
Barents, Willem **2** 4-5

Spix, J. B. von (died 1826), German naturalist
Agassiz, Jean Louis Rodolphe **1** 76-78

Spleen de Paris (poem)
Baudelaire, Charles Pierre **2** 61-63

SPOCK, BENJAMIN McLANE (born 1903), American pediatrician and political activist and author of *Baby and Child Care* **14** 383-385

Spoil of Office, A (novel)
Garland, Hannibal Hamlin **6** 217-218

Spoils system (politics)
Japan
Hara, Kei **7** 138
United States
Arthur, Chester Alan **1** 321-323
Curtis, George William **4** 349-350
Eaton, Dorman Bridgman **5** 190-191
Jackson, Andrew **8** 168-172
Pendleton, George Hunt **12** 198
see also Civil service (United States)

Spokane Indians (North America)
Alexie, Sherman **1** 141-142

Sponono (play)
Paton, Alan Stewart **12** 134-135

Spontaneous generation (biology)
Schwann, Theodor **14** 51-52
Spallanzani, Lazzaro **14** 360-361
Tyndall, John **15** 374

Spontaneous Me (poem)
Whitman, Walt **16** 249-251

Spontini, Gaspare (1774-1851), Italian composer
Berlioz, Louis Hector **2** 203-205
Mendelssohn, Moses **10** 488-489

Spoon River Anthology (poems)
Masters, Edgar Lee **10** 326-327

Spoon Woman (sculpture)
Giacometti, Alberto **6** 294-295

Spooner Act (1902)
Bunau-Varilla, Philippe Jean **3** 120-121

Sport of the Gods, The (novel)
Dunbar, Paul Laurence **5** 141-142

Sports
see Athletes, American

Sports Illustrated (magazine)
Luce, Henry Robinson **10** 23-24

Sporus (literary character)
Pope, Alexander **12** 395-397

SPOTSWOOD, ALEXANDER (1676-1740), British general and colonial governor **14** 385

SPRAGUE, FRANK JULIAN (1857-1934), American electrical engineer and inventor **14** 385-386

Spreading the News (play)
Gregory, Augusta **6** 535-536

Spring (novel)
Pa Chin **12** 53-54

Spring (painting)
Botticelli, Sandro **2** 439-440
Hofmann, Hans **7** 442-443
Munch, Edvard **11** 247-248

Spring (poem)
Thomson, James **15** 199-200

Spring (symphony)
Britten, Benjamin **3** 10-11
Paine, John Knowles **12** 65
Schumann, Robert Alexander **14** 41-43

Spring and Autumn Annals (chronology)
Confucius **4** 197-200
Ssu-ma Ch'ien **14** 388-389
Ssu-ma kuang **14** 390-391
Wang An-shih **16** 95-97

Spring Days (poems)
Basho, Matsuo **2** 45-48

Spring in New Hampshire (poems)
McKay, Claude **10** 416

Spring Mobilization Committee to End the War in Vietnam (United States)
Bevel, James Luther **2** 250-251

Spring Mountains and Pine Trees (painting)
Mi Fei **11** 12-13

Spring Trees by a Lake (painting)
Monet, Claude **11** 102-104

Spring Wells Treaty (1815)
Harrison, William Henry **7** 180-181

Springfield (city, Massachusetts)
Richardson, Henry Hobson **13** 139-141
see also Shays' Rebellion

Springtime (play)
Tarkington, Newton Booth **15** 109

Springtime and Harvest (novel)
Sinclair, Upton Beale Jr. **14** 248-249

Springtime on Fünen (musical composition)
Nielsen, Carl August **11** 388-389

Sproul, Robert Gordon (1891-1975), American educator
Stanley, Wendell Meredith **14** 400-401

Sprung über den Schatten, Der (opera)
Krenek, Ernst **9** 98-99

Spurs, battle of the (1513)
Henry VIII **7** 302-305

Sputnik I-III (satellite)
Cherenkov, Pavel Alekseevich
3 502-503
Eisenhower, Dwight David **5** 233-236
Gagarin, Yuri Alexeivich **6** 166-167
Johnson, Lyndon Baines **8** 308-312
Lovell, Alfred Charles Bernard **10** 8-9
von Braun, Wernher **16** 17-18

Spy, The (novel)
Cooper, James Fenimore **4** 220-223

SQUANTO (a.k.a. Tasquantum; circa 1600-1623), Native American Wampamoag translator and guide
Bradford, William **2** 475-476
Standish, Myles **14** 396-397

Squarcione, Francesco (1394-1474), Italian painter
Mantegna, Andrea **10** 215-216

Squatter sovereignty
see Popular sovereignty (United States)

Sri Lanka (formerly Ceylon; island nation, Indian Ocean)
Bandaranaike, Sirimavo **1** 486-488
Buddha **3** 97-101
Jayewardene, Junius Richard **8** 233-234
Premadasa, Ranasinghe **12** 437-439
Rajaraja I **13** 7

Sri Lankan Freedom Party
Bandaranaike, Sirimavo **1** 486-488

Srivastava, Dhanpatrai
see Premchand

SSU-MA CH'IEN (145-circa 90 B.C.), Chinese historian **14** 388-389
Confucius **4** 197-200
Han Fei Tzu **7** 124-125
Hsün-tzu **8** 8
Kim Pusik **9** 8-9
Lao Tzu **9** 201-202
Pan Ku **12** 86-87

SSU-MA HSIANG-JU (circa 179-117 B.C.), Chinese poet **14** 389-390

SSU-MA KUANG (1019-1086), Chinese statesman **14** 390-391
Su Shih **15** 39-40
Wang An-shih **16** 95-97

Ssu-ma T'an (died 110 B.C.), Chinese scholar
Ssu-ma Ch'ien **14** 388-389

Ssu-shih t'ung-t'ang (novel)
Lao Shê **9** 200-201

Staatliches Bauhaus
see Bauhaus

Stabat Mater (musical composition)
Fry, William Henry **6** 136-137
Penderecki, Krzysztof **12** 195-197
Pergolesi, Giovanni Battista **12** 218-219
Poulenc, Francis **12** 414-415
Rossini, Gioacchino **13** 311-312
Szymanowski, Karol **15** 67-68
Verdi, Giuseppe Fortunino Francesco **15** 463-465

Stabiles (sculpture)
Calder, Alexander **3** 216-218

Stadacona
see Quebec (city)

STAËL, GERMAINE DE (1766-1817), French-Swiss novelist and woman of letters **14** 391-392
Carlyle, Thomas **3** 304-305
Fichte, Johann Gottlieb **5** 435-436
Lamartine, Alphonse Marie Louis de **9** 173-175
Necker, Jacques **11** 330-331
Tarbell, Ida Minerva **15** 107-108

STAËL, NICOLAS DE (1914-1955), French painter **14** 392

Stafford, Henry
see Buckingham, Henry Stafford, 2d Duke of

Stafford, Jean (1915-1979), American novelist
Lowell, Robert Trail Spence Jr. **10** 16-17

Stag Drinking (painting)
Courbet, Jean Desiré Gustave **4** 271-273

Stag Hound (ship)
McKay, Donald **10** 416-417

Stage Door (play)
Ferber, Edna **5** 413

Stagecoach (film)
Ford, John **6** 7-8

STAHL, GEORG ERNST (1660-1734), German chemist and medical theorist **14** 392-393
Bichat, Marie François Xavier **2** 263-264

Stahlberg, Kaarlo J. (1865-1952), Finnish statesman
Mannerheim, Carl Gustav Emil Von **10** 207-208

Staircase Group (painting)
Peale, Charles Willson **12** 169-171

STALIN, JOSEPH (1879-1953), Soviet statesman **14** 393-396
and non-Russian Communists
Foster, William Zebulon **6** 27-28
Gomulka, Wladislaw **6** 422-424
Kádár, János **8** 402-403
Prestes, Luiz Carlos **12** 442-444
Ulbricht, Walter **15** 383-384
associates
Beria, Lavrenty Pavlovich **2** 192-193
Brezhnev, Leonid Ilich **2** 527-528

Dzerzhinsky, Felix Edmundovich **5** 173-174
Katayama, Sen **8** 457
Molotov, Vyacheslav Mikhailovich **11** 89-90
Vyshinsky, Andrei **16** 36-37
Zhukov, Georgi Konstantinovich **16** 512-513
opponents
Frunze, Mikhail Vasilievich **6** 134
Trotsky, Leon **15** 302-305
policy on science
Kapitsa, Pyotr Leonidovich **8** 433-435
Lysenko, Trofim Denisovich **10** 71
Szilard, Leo **15** 64-66
Vavilov, Nikolai Ivanovich **15** 447-448
policy on the arts
Ehrenburg, Ilya Grigorievich **5** 224-225
Eisenstein, Sergei Mikhailovich **5** 240-242
Mandelstam, Osip Emilyevich **10** 191
Shostakovich, Dmitri Dmitrievich **14** 204-205
Solzhenitsyn, Alexander Isayevich **14** 330-332
see also Great Purge; World War II; Yalta Conference (1945)

Stalingrad, battle of (1943)
Hitler, Adolf **7** 417-420
Simonov, Konstantin Mikhailovich **14** 239-240
Stalin, Joseph **14** 393-396

Stalky and Co. (book)
Kipling, Joseph Rudyard **9** 32-33

Stallings, Lawrence (born 1894), American novelist
Anderson, Maxwell **1** 219-220

Stamboul Train (novel)
Greene, Graham **6** 523-524

Stambul
see Istanbul

Stamford Bridge, battle of (1066)
Harold II **7** 162
Harold III **7** 163
William I **16** 290-291

Stamp Act (United States; 1765)
defenders
Colden, Cadwallader **4** 145-146
Galloway, Joseph **6** 186-187
Tryon, William **15** 321
opponents
Adams, John **1** 48-51
Adams, Samuel **1** 55-56
Gerry, Elbridge **6** 282-283
Hancock, John **7** 114-116
Henry, Patrick **7** 309-311
Hutchinson, Thomas **8** 71-72
Laurens, Henry **9** 232
Lee, Richard Henry **9** 291-292
Washington, George **16** 126-129

see also Stamp Act Congress
repealed (1766)
Rockingham, 2d Marquess of
13 230-231

Stamp Act Congress (United States; 1765)
Dickinson, John **4** 543-544
Franklin, William **6** 69-70
Otis, James Jr. **12** 25-27
Rutledge, John **13** 387-388

Stand and Deliver (film)
Escalante, Jaime **5** 320-321

Standard, battle of the (1138)
David I **4** 407
Stephen **14** 426-427

Standard Oil Co. (established 1870)
Daly, Marcus **4** 379-380
Kellogg, Frank Billings **8** 481
Lloyd, Henry Demarest **9** 468-469
Rockefeller, John Davison **13** 226-228
Rockefeller, John D. Jr. **13** 225-226
Steffens, Lincoln **14** 410-411

Standard Oil Company v. United States
(legal case)
Harlan, John Marshall **7** 156-157
White, Edward Douglass **16** 230-231

Standing Figure (sculpture)
González, Julio **6** 428-429

Standing Forms (painting series)
Sutherland, Graham **15** 40-41

Standing Rock Reservation (Dakota Territory)
Sitting Bull **14** 264-265

Standing Woman (sculpture)
Lachaise, Gaston **9** 147

Standing Youth (sculpture)
Lehmbruck, Wilhelm **9** 307

STANDISH, MYLES (circa 1584-1656),
English military adviser to the Pilgrims
14 396-397
Bowles, Samuel **2** 464
Bradford, William **2** 475-476

Standish the Puritan (novel)
Hare, Robert **7** 152-153

STANFORD, LELAND (1824-1893), American railroad builder and politician
14 397-398
Durant, Thomas Clark **5** 157-158
Hearst, George **7** 242
Huntington, Collis Potter **8** 49
Judah, Theodore Dehone **8** 373-374

Stanford University (Palo Alto, California)
Anderson, Maxwell **1** 219-220
Beadle, George Wells **2** 80-81
Cubberley, Ellwood Patterson
4 329-331
Johnson, Alvin Saunders **8** 293-294
Jordan, David Starr **8** 350-351
Lewin, Kurt **9** 375-376
Lewis, Clarence Irving **9** 381
Olmsted, Frederick Law **11** 503-504
Ross, Edward Alsworth **13** 300
Stanford, Leland **14** 397-398

Terman, Lewis Madison **15** 153-154
Veblen, Thorstein Bunde **15** 449-450

Stanhope, James (1st Earl of Stanhope;
1673-1721), English statesman
George I **6** 268-269
Walpole, Robert **16** 82-84

Stanhope, Philip Dormer
see Chesterfield, 4th Earl of

Stanislas I (Leszczynski; 1677-1766), king
of Poland
Augustus II **1** 373-374
Charles XII **3** 464-466

Stanislas II (Augustus Poniatowski;
1732-98), king of Poland 1764-95
Burke, Edmund **3** 138-141
Catherine the Great **3** 370-372
Houdon, Antoine **7** 516-517

STANISLAVSKY, CONSTANTIN
(1863-1938), Russian actor and director
14 398-399
Meyerhold, Vsevolod Emilievich **10** 539
Strasberg, Lee **14** 494-495

Stankévich, Nikoláy Vladímirovich
(1813-1840), Russian philosopher
Lermontov, Mikhail Yurievich
9 352-353

Stanley, E. G. G. Smith
see Derby, 14th Earl of

Stanley, E. H. Smith
see Derby, 15th Earl of

STANLEY, SIR HENRY MORTON
(1841-1904), British explorer and journalist **14** 399-400
Bennett, James Gordon Jr. **2** 169-170
Brazza, Pierre Paul François Camille
Savorgnan de **2** 509-510
Gordon, Charles George **6** 448-449
Johnston, Henry Hamilton **8** 322-323
Leopold II **9** 346-347
Livingstone, David **9** 463-465
Mutesa I **11** 277
Tippu Tip **15** 235-236

Stanley, Sir William (died 1495), British
statesman
Henry VII **7** 300-302

Stanley, Thomas
see Derby, 1st Earl of

STANLEY, WENDELL MEREDITH
(1904-1971), American virologist
14 400-401
Northrop, John Howard **11** 430-431

Stanleyville (city, Democratic Republic of
the Congo)
Lumumba, Patrice Emery **10** 43-45

Stansbury, Howard (1806-1863), American
soldier and explorer
Bridger, James **3** 2-3

STANTON, EDWIN McMASTERS
(1814-1869), American statesman
14 401-402
Dana, Charles Anderson **4** 384-385
Lincoln, Abraham **9** 415-418

STANTON, ELIZABETH CADY
(1815-1902), American feminist and
reformer **14** 402-403
Anthony, Susan Brownell **1** 246-248
Bloomer, Amelia Jenks **2** 337
Catt, Carrie Chapman **3** 375-376
Gage, Matilda Joslyn **6** 167-169
Howe, Julia Ward **7** 535-536
Mott, Lucretia Coffin **11** 212-213
Stone, Lucy **14** 471-472

Stanzas from the Grande Chartreuse
(poem; Arnold)
Clough, Arthur Hugh **4** 123-124

Stanzas Written in Dejection near Naples
(poem)
Shelley, Percy Bysshe **14** 176-178

Staphylococcus (bacteriology)
Fleming, Alexander **5** 483-485
Northrop, John Howard **11** 430-431

Star (astronomy)
catalogs
Cannon, Annie Jump **3** 260-261
Eratosthenes of Cyrene **5** 301-302
Eudoxus of Cnidus **5** 329-330
Flamsteed, John **5** 477-478
Hipparchus **7** 407-408
Kapteyn, Jacobus Cornelis
8 436-437
Pickering, Edward Charles **12** 298
Ptolemy, Claudius **12** 473-474
charts
Halley, Edmund **7** 88-89
Mitchell, Maria **11** 61
photometry
Herschel, John Frederick William
7 340-341
pulsars
Bell Burnell, Susan Jocelyn
2 133-134
stellar evolution
Arrhenius, Svante August **1** 318-320
Pickering, Edward Charles **12** 298
stellar motion
Bradley, James **2** 482-483
Eudoxus of Cnidus **5** 329-330
Halley, Edmund **7** 88-89
stellar parallax
Bessel, Friedrich Wilhelm **2** 234-235
Copernicus, Nicolaus **4** 226-227
Galileo Galilei **6** 180-183
Hall, Asaph **7** 83-84
Herschel, William **7** 341-343
Kapteyn, Jacobus Cornelis
8 436-437
stellar spectral classifications
Cannon, Annie Jump **3** 260-261
structure
Bethe, Hans Albrecht **2** 238-239
Eddington, Arthur Stanley **5** 201-202
Huggins, William **8** 14-15
Jeans, James Hopwood **8** 235-236
Kirchhoff, Gustav Robert **9** 33-34
Lovell, Alfred Charles Bernard
10 8-9
see also Double star

Star Chamber (English court)
Charles, I **3** 450-452
Henry VII **7** 300-302
Laud, William **9** 224-225

Star of the Order, The (poems)
George, Stefan **6** 277-278

Star Turns Red, The (play)
O'Casey, Sean **11** 459-460

Star Wagon, The (play)
Anderson, Maxwell **1** 219-220

Star-Apple Kingdom, The (poem)
Walcott, Derek Alton **16** 50-51

Star-Spangled Banner, The (song)
Key, Francis Scott **8** 525-527

STARHAWK (Miriam Simos; born 1951), theoretician and practitioner of feminist Wicca (witchcraft) in the United States **14** 403-404

Stark, Johannes (1874-1957), German physicist
Einstein, Albert **5** 228-231

Starling, Ernest Henry (1866-1927), English physiologist
Loewi, Otto **9** 486-487

Starr, Ringo (born 1940), English musician and actor
Beatles, The **2** 89-92
Lennon, John Winston **9** 326-328

Starry Messenger, The (book; Galileo)
Galileo Galilei **6** 180-183
Kepler, Johannes **8** 514-516

Starry Night (painting)
Van Gogh, Vincent **15** 427-429

Stars and Stripes (military newspaper)
Mauldin, Bill **10** 345-346

Stars and Stripes Forever, The (march)
Sousa, John Philip **14** 353-354

Stas, Jean Servais (1813-1891), Belgian chemist
Richards, Theodore William **13** 137-138

Stasov, Valdimir (1824-1906), Russian music and art critic
Mussorgsky, Modest Petrovich **11** 274-276

State (political theory)
Laski, Harold J. **9** 215-216
MacIver, Robert Morrison **10** 100-101
see also Government

State of Innocence, The (opera)
Dryden, John **5** 106-107

State of nature (philosophy)
see Natural rights doctrine; Social contract theory

State of Siege, The (play)
Camus, Albert **3** 255-257

State of the Nation (book)
Dos Passos, John Roderigo **5** 69-71

State, U.S. Secretaries of
see Statesmen, American—Executive (secretaries of state)

Staten Island (painting)
Gorky, Arshile **6** 458

States of Mind (painting)
Boccioni, Umberto **2** 353-354

States of the Church
see Papal States

States' rights (United States politics)
opponents
Davis, Jefferson **4** 416-418
Marshall, John **10** 279-281
Story, Joseph **14** 480-481
Webster, Daniel **16** 162-164
supporters (18th-19th century)
Jackson, Andrew **8** 168-172
Macon, Nathaniel **10** 114-115
Madison, James **10** 121-123
Martin, Luther **10** 289-290
Taylor, John **15** 126
Warren, Mercy Otis **16** 120-121
supporters (19th century)
Hayne, Robert Young **7** 231-232
McDuffie, George **10** 408
Polk, James Knox **12** 374-376
Randolph, John **13** 30
Tyler, John **15** 368-369
Vallandigham, Clement Laird **15** 406-407
Yancey, William Lowndes **16** 436-437
supporters (19th-20th century)
Hammond, James Henry **7** 108-109
Wallace, George Corley **16** 71-72
supporters (20th century)
Thurmond, James Strom **15** 214-215

State's Rights Party (United States; 1940s)
Thurmond, James Strom **15** 214-215

Statesmen, Afghan
Karmal, Babrak **8** 449-451
Mahmud of Ghazni **10** 147
Najibullah, Mohammad **11** 296-298

Statesmen, Albanian
Alia, Ramiz **1** 159
Berisha, Sali **2** 195-197
Hoxha, Enver **8** 1-3
Zog I **16** 525-526

Statesmen, Algerian
Abbas, Ferhat **1** 6-7
Abd el-Kadir **1** 15
Ben Badis, 'Abd al-Hamid **2** 147-148
Ben Bella, Ahmed **2** 148-149
Boumediene, Houari **2** 445-446
Chadli Benjedid **3** 402-404
Messali Hadj **10** 527-528

Statesmen, American

- COLONIAL PERIOD
confederation officials
see Articles of Confederation (United States; 1781)
Continental Congress

see Continental Congress (United States; 1774-89)
Federal convention delegates
see Constitutional Convention (United States, 1787)
governors and officials (loyalists)
Franklin, William **6** 69-70
Hutchinson, Thomas **8** 71-72
Livingston, Robert **9** 461-462
Logan, James **9** 487-488
Morris, Lewis **11** 183-184
Phips, William **12** 283
governors (Massachusetts Bay Colony)
Bradford, William **2** 475-476
Dudley, Thomas **5** 124-125
Winthrop, John **16** 339-341
governors (royal)
see Statesmen, English-colonial governors
other leaders (rebels)
Bacon, Nathaniel **1** 424-425
Leisler, Jacob **9** 313-314

- EXECUTIVE
presidents (Democratic; 19th century)
Buchanan, James **3** 89-90
Cleveland, Stephen Grover **4** 108-110
Jackson, Andrew **8** 168-172-511
Johnson, Andrew **8** 294-295
Pierce, Franklin **12** 300-301
Polk, James Knox **12** 374-376
Tyler, John **15** 368-369
Van Buren, Martin **15** 410-411
presidents (Democratic; 20th century)
Carter, James Earl **3** 339-342
Clinton, William Jefferson **4** 117-119
Johnson, Lyndon Baines **8** 308-312
Kennedy, John Fitzgerald **8** 502-506
Roosevelt, Franklin Delano **13** 277-280
Truman, Harry S. **15** 314-316
Wilson, Thomas Woodrow **16** 330-332
presidents (Democratic-Republican)
Adams, John Quincy **1** 52-54
Jefferson, Thomas **8** 238-241
Madison, James **10** 121-123
Monroe, James **11** 111-113
presidents (Federalist)
Adams, John **1** 48-51
Washington, George **16** 126-129
presidents (Republican; 19th century)
Arthur, Chester Alan **1** 321-323
Garfield, James Abram **6** 213-214
Grant, Ulysses Simpson **6** 492-494
Harrison, Benjamin **7** 178-179

Hayes, Rutherford Birchard
7 227-228
Lincoln, Abraham
9 415-418-504
McKinley, William 10 418-420
presidents (Republican; 20th century)
Bush, George 3 167-169
Coolidge, John Calvin 4 217-219
Eisenhower, Dwight David
5 233-236
Ford, Gerald 6 2-5
Harding, Warren Gamaliel
7 148-149
Hoover, Herbert Clark
7 483-485
McKinley, William 10 418-420
Nixon, Richard Milhous
11 401-404
Reagan, Ronald W. 13 65-68
Roosevelt, Theodore 13 280-283
Taft, William Howard 15 78-81
presidents (Whig)
Fillmore, Millard 5 447-448
Harrison, William Henry
7 180-181
Taylor, Zachary 15 128-130
presidents' advisers
Ball, George 1 470-471
Baruch, Bernard Mannes
2 42-43
Blair, Francis Preston 2 313-315
Bohlen, Charles (Chip)
2 364-366
Brzezinski, Zbigniew 3 85-87
Bundy, McGeorge 3 122-124
Burns, Arthur 3 151-153
Clinton, Hillary Rodham
4 115-117
Eisenhower, Milton 5 237-238
Farley, James A. 5 381-383
Goodpaster, Andrew Jackson
6 439-441
Haig, Alexander M. Jr. 7 66-67
Heller, Walter 7 265-266
Hopkins, Harry Lloyd 7 494-495
House, Edward Mandell
7 520-521
Kissinger, Henry Alfred 9 43-45
Lodge, Henry Cabot Jr.
9 483-485
MacLeish, Archibald 10 109-110
Merriam, Charles Edward
10 518-519
Morgenthau, Henry Jr.
11 172-173
Moyers, Bill 11 214-216
Packard, David 12 54-56
Panetta, Leon E. 12 84-85
Regan, Donald 13 80-81
Rostow, Walt Whitman
13 315-317
Schlesinger, Arthur Meier Jr.
14 13-15
Strauss, Robert Schwarz
14 501-502
Taylor, Maxwell 15 126-127

Valenti, Jack Joseph 15 401-403
vice presidents (Democratic)
Calhoun, John Caldwell
3 226-228
Gore, Albert Jr. 6 452-453
Humphrey, Hubert Horatio Jr.
8 34-36
Mondale, Walter. F. 11 97-99
Wallace, Henry Agard 16 73-74
vice presidents (Democratic-Republican)
Burr, Aaron 3 156-159
Calhoun, John Caldwell
3 226-228
Clinton, George 4 113-114
Gerry, Elbridge 6 282-283
vice presidents (Republican)
Agnew, Spiro Theodore 1 83-85
Bush, George 3 167-169
Quayle, J. Danforth 12 507-509
Rockefeller, Nelson Aldrich
13 228-230
Wilson, Henry 16 322-323

• EXECUTIVE (CABINET)
ambassadors to the United Nations
Ball, George 1 470-471
Goldberg, Arthur Joseph
6 397-398
Kirkpatrick, Jeane J. 9 37-39
Lodge, Henry Cabot Jr.
9 483-485
attorneys general
Arnold, Thurman Wesley 1 314
Clark, Tom Campbell 4 81-82
Evarts, William Maxwell
5 340-341
Kennedy, Robert Francis
8 508-509
Knox, Philander Chase 9 66-67
Murphy, Frank 11 260-261
Olney, Richard 11 504-505
Palmer, Alexander Mitchell
12 77-78
Randolph, Edmund 13 29-30
Reno, Janet 13 99-101
Stanton, Elizabeth Cady
14 402-403
Stone, Harlan Fiske 14 468-470
Taney, Roger Brooke 15 98-99
budget directors
Shultz, George Pratt 14 209-211
CIA directors
Casey, William J. 3 351-353
Colby, William E. 4 143-145
postmasters general
Kendall, Amos 8 494
McLean, John 10 422-423
Pickering, Timothy 12 298-299
secretaries of agriculture
Wallace, Henry Agard 16 73-74
secretaries of commerce
Brown, Ronald H. 3 44-47
Harriman, W. Averell 7 165-166
Hoover, Herbert Clark
7 483-485
Hopkins, Harry Lloyd 7 494-495

Kreps, Juanita Morris 9 99-101
Wallace, Henry Agard 16 73-74
secretaries of defense
Aspin, Les 1 342-344
Cheney, Richard B. 3 497-499
Forrestal, James Vincent 6 14
Laird, Melvin R. 9 168-170
Marshall, George Catlett
10 278-279
McNamara, Robert S.
10 429-431
Perry, William James 12 240-242
Weinberger, Casper Willard
16 177-178
Widnall, Sheila E. 16 258-259
Wilson, Charles Erwin
16 316-317
secretaries of education
Bennett, William John 2 172-174
secretaries of energy
Schlesinger, James Rodney
14 15-16
secretaries of health and human
services
Heckler, Margaret Mary
O'Shaughnessy 7 251-252
secretaries of health, education and
welfare
Gardner, John W. 6 211-213
Harris, Patricia Roberts
7 174-175
Hobby, Oveta Culp 7 423-425
Weinberger, Casper Willard
16 177-178
secretaries of housing and urban
development
Harris, Patricia Roberts
7 174-175
Hills, Carla Anderson 7 394-396
Kemp, Jack French Jr. 8 491-493
Weaver, Robert C. 16 152-153
secretaries of labor
Goldberg, Arthur Joseph
6 397-398
Martin, Lynn Morley 10 290-292
Perkins, Frances 12 221-222
Shultz, George Pratt 14 209-211
secretaries of state (18th century)
Jefferson, Thomas 8 238-241
Pickering, Timothy 12 298-299
Randolph, Edmund 13 29-30
secretaries of state (19th century)
Adams, John Quincy 1 52-54
Blaine, James Gillespie
2 312-313
Buchanan, James 3 89-90
Calhoun, John Caldwell
3 226-228
Cass, Lewis 3 355-356
Clay, Henry 4 94-96
Clayton, John Middleton 4 96-97
Evarts, William Maxwell
5 340-341
Everett, Edward 5 344
Fish, Hamilton 5 461-462
Hay, John 7 215-216
Livingston, Edward 9 460-461

Madison, James **10** 121-123
Marcy, William Learned
10 247-248
Marshall, John **10** 279-281
Monroe, James **11** 111-113
Olney, Richard **11** 504-505
Seward, William Henry
14 124-125
Sherman, John **14** 184-185
Van Buren, Martin **15** 410-411
Webster, Daniel **16** 162-164
secretaries of state (20th century)
Acheson, Dean Gooderham
1 37-38
Bryan, William Jennings **3** 80-82
Byrnes, James Francis **3** 191-192
Christopher, Warren Minor
4 32-33
Dulles, John Foster **5** 134-135
Haig, Alexander M. Jr. **7** 66-67
Hay, John **7** 215-216
Hughes, Charles Evans **8** 15-16
Hull, Cordell **8** 28-29
Kellogg, Frank Billings **8** 481
Kissinger, Henry Alfred **9** 43-45
Knox, Philander Chase **9** 66-67
Lansing, Robert **9** 200
Marshall, George Catlett
10 278-279
Root, Elihu **13** 283-284
Rusk, David Dean **13** 368-370
Shultz, George Pratt **14** 209-211
Stettinius, Edward R. Jr.
14 437-438
Stimson, Henry Lewis
14 457-458
Vance, Cyrus R. **15** 411-413
secretaries of state (assistant)
Berle, Adolf Augustus Jr.
2 199-200
MacLeish, Archibald **10** 109-110
Sayre, Francis Bowes **13** 509
secretaries of the army
Vance, Cyrus R. **15** 411-413
secretaries of the interior
Babbitt, Bruce Edward
1 408-410
Chandler, Zachariah **3** 425-426
Ickes, Harold LeClaire
8 100-101
Lamar, Lucius Quintus Cincinna-
tus **9** 170-171
Schurz, Carl **14** 44-45
secretaries of the navy
Bancroft, George **1** 483-484
Daniels, Josephus **4** 387
Forrestal, James Vincent **6** 14
Kennedy, John Pendleton
8 506-507
Welles, Gideon **16** 188-190
secretaries of the treasury
Blumenthal, Werner Michael
2 345-346
Bristow, Benjamin Helm **3** 9-10
Chase, Salmon Portland
3 473-475

Connally, John Bowden Jr.
4 202-204
Crawford, William Harris
4 299-300
Gallatin, Albert **6** 183-184
Hamilton, Alexander **7** 95-98
McAdoo, William Gibbs
10 385-386
McCulloch, Hugh **10** 404-405
Mellon, Andrew William
10 469-470
Morgenthau, Henry Jr.
11 172-173
Priest, Ivy Maude Baker
12 450-451
Regan, Donald **13** 80-81
Sherman, John **14** 184-185
Shultz, George Pratt **14** 209-211
Taney, Roger Brooke **15** 98-99
Walker, Robert John **16** 67-68
secretaries of transportation
Dole, Elizabeth Hanford **5** 41-43
secretaries of war (18th century)
Knox, Henry **9** 64
Pickering, Timothy **12** 298-299
secretaries of war (19th century)
Calhoun, John Caldwell
3 226-228
Cameron, Simon **3** 246-247
Cass, Lewis **3** 355-356
Crawford, William Harris
4 299-300
Davis, Jefferson **4** 416-418
Marcy, William Learned
10 247-248
Monroe, James **11** 111-113
Root, Elihu **13** 283-284
Stanton, Elizabeth Cady
14 402-403
secretaries of war (20th century)
Baker, Newton Diehl **1** 451
Root, Elihu **13** 283-284
Stimson, Henry Lewis
14 457-458
Taft, William Howard **15** 78-81
see also Confederate States of
America
undersecretaries (20th century)
Ball, George **1** 470-471
• INDIAN TRIBAL CHIEFS
16th-18th century
Brant, Joseph **2** 500-501
Deganawida **4** 460-461
Massasoit **10** 322-324
McGillivray, Alexander **10** 412
Metacom **10** 529-531
Philip **12** 267-268
Pontiac **12** 393-394
Powhatan **12** 429-430
Tecumseh **15** 133
19th-20th century
American Horse **1** 195-198
Black Hawk **2** 308
Cochise **4** 128
Crazy Horse **4** 303-304
Dull Knife **5** 135-136

Geronimo **6** 281-282
Joseph **8** 358-359
Mangas Coloradas **10** 194-196
Mankiller, Wilma **10** 198-199
Manuelito **10** 220-222
Osceola **12** 18
Parker, Ely Samuel **12** 106-108
Parker, Quanah **12** 109-112
Plenty Coups **12** 352-355
Red Cloud **13** 70-71
Ross, John **13** 303-304
Satanta **13** 493-494
Seattle **14** 80-81
Sitting Bull **14** 264-265
Tecumseh **15** 133
Washakie **16** 123-125
• LEGISLATIVE
representatives (18th century)
Ames, Fisher **1** 199-200
Sevier, John **14** 122-123
representatives (19th century)
Adams, Charles Francis **1** 41-42
Appleton, Nathan **1** 266-267
Corning, Erastus **4** 238-239
Crockett, David **4** 314-316
Curry, Jabez Lamar Monroe
4 346-347
Cutler, Manasseh **4** 356-357
Davis, Henry Winter **4** 415-416
Donnelly, Ignatius **5** 62
Hampton, Wade **7** 111-112
Hatch, William Henry **7** 196
Johnson, Tom Loftin **8** 317
Langston, John Mercer **9** 197
Letcher, John **9** 359-360
Mann, Horace **10** 202-204
Morrill, Justin Smith **11** 182
Owen, Robert Dale **12** 40-41
Stephens, Alexander Hamilton
14 429-430
Stevens, Thaddeus **14** 442-443
Straus, Isidor **14** 496
Tweed, William Marcy
15 366-367
Vallandigham, Clement Laird
15 406-407
Weaver, James Baird **16** 151-152
Wood, Fernando **16** 367-368
Yancey, William Lowndes
16 436-437
representatives (19th-20th century)
Berger, Victor Louis **2** 189-190
Smalls, Robert **14** 277-278
representatives (20th century)
Abzug, Bella Stavisky **1** 34-35
Aspin, Les **1** 342-344
Barton, Bruce **2** 36-37
Bush, George **3** 167-169
Chávez, Dennis **3** 488-489
Chisholm, Shirley Anita St. Hill
4 7-9
Conable, Barber B. Jr. **4** 191-192
Dirksen, Everett Mckinley
5 24-26
Ferraro, Geraldine **5** 426-428

Gephardt, Richard Andrew
6 278-280
Gingrich, Newt **6** 329-332
Gray, William H. III **6** 510-511
Green, Edith Starrett **6** 519-520
Hansen, Julia Butler **7** 132-133
Heckler, Margaret Mary
O'Shaughnessy **7** 251-252
Jordan, Barbara Charline
8 349-350
Kemp, Jack French Jr. **8** 491-493
Laird, Melvin R. **9** 168-170
Lewis, John Robert **9** 388-390
Lindsay, John Vliet **9** 423-424
Luce, Clare Boothe **10** 21-23
Martin, Lynn Morley **10** 290-292
Mfume, Kweisi **10** 539-542
Mikulski, Barbara **11** 13-15
O'Neill, Thomas P. **11** 517-519
Owen, Ruth Bryan **12** 41-43
Panetta, Leon E. **12** 84-85
Pepper, Claude Denson
12 205-206
Powell, Adam Clayton Jr.
12 421-422
Rangel, Charles B. **13** 31-32
Rankin, Jeannette Pickering
13 35-37
Rodino, Peter Wallace Jr.
13 238-239
Rogers, Edith Nourse
13 247-248
Rohde, Ruth Bryan Owen
13 252-253
Ros-Lehtinen, Ileana **13** 294-296
Roybal-Allard, Lucille
13 332-334
Schroeder, Patricia Scott
14 33-35
Simon, Paul **14** 238-239
Smith, Margaret Chase
14 299-300
Snowe, Olympia **14** 313-314
Velázquez, Nydia Margarita
15 456-459
Waters, Maxine **16** 132-134
Young, Andrew Jackson Jr.
16 467-469
senators (18th-19th century)
Pinckney, Charles **12** 309-310
Taylor, John **15** 126
senators (19th century)
Alcorn, James Lusk **1** 120-121
Atchison, David Rice **1** 357-358
Benjamin, Judah Philip
2 163-164
Benton, Thomas Hart **2** 178-179
Brown, Benjamin Gratz **3** 32-33
Brownlow, William Gannaway
3 55-56
Bruce, Blanche Kelso **3** 62-63
Clinton, DeWitt **4** 112-113
Conkling, Roscoe **4** 201-202
Dawes, Henry Laurens **4** 427
Douglas, Stephen Arnold
5 80-82
Frémont, John Charles **6** 97-98

George, James Zachariah
6 276-277
Gordon, John Brown **6** 449-450
Hammond, James Henry
7 108-109
Hanna, Marcus Alonzo
7 127-128
Hayne, Robert Young **7** 231-232
Hearst, George **7** 242
Hill, Benjamin Harvey
7 386-387
Houston, Samuel **7** 526-527
King, Rufus **9** 22-23
Lodge, Henry Cabot **9** 482-483
Macon, Nathaniel **10** 114-115
Mahone, William **10** 147-148
Mason, James Murray
10 320-321
McDuffie, George **10** 408
Otis, Harrison Gray **12** 25
Pendleton, George Hunt **12** 198
Platt, Thomas Collier **12** 347-348
Quay, Matthew Stanley **12** 507
Revels, Hiram Rhoades
13 109-110
Rhett, Robert Barnwell **13** 120
Slidell, John **14** 273
Soulé, Pierre **14** 351-352
Stanford, Leland **14** 397-398
Stockton, Robert Field
14 461-462
Sumner, Charles **15** 30-31
Tillman, Benjamin Ryan
15 225-226
Toombs, Robert Augustus
15 267-268
Trumbull, Lyman **15** 317-318
Vance, Zebulon Baird
15 413-414
Wade, Benjamin Franklin
16 38-39
Walker, Robert John **16** 67-68
Wilmot, David **16** 312-313
senators (19th-20th century)
Aldrich, Nelson Wilmarth
1 123-124
Borah, William Edgar **2** 408
Clark, William Andrews **4** 83-85
Fulbright, James William
6 147-149
Hitchcock, Gilbert Monell
7 416-417
Johnson, Hiram Warren
8 300-301
La Follette, Robert Marion
9 155-156
Lehman, Herbert Henry
9 306-307
McAdoo, William Gibbs
10 385-386
McCarthy, Joseph Raymond
10 388-389
McGovern, George Stanley
10 412-414
Norris, George William
11 428-429
Penrose, Boies **12** 203-204

Wagner, Robert Ferdinand **16** 43
Walsh, Thomas James **16** 85-86
Watson, Thomas Edward **16** 139
senators (20th century)
Bentsen, Lloyd Millard
2 180-181
Boxer, Barbara **2** 465-468
Campbell, Ben Nighthorse
3 252-253
Caraway, Hattie Wyatt
3 284-285
Chávez, Dennis **3** 488-489
Dirksen, Everett Mckinley
5 24-26
Dole, Robert J. **5** 43-46
Ervin, Sam J. Jr. **5** 316-317
Glenn, John Herschel Jr.
6 365-367
Goldwater, Barry **6** 413-415
Gore, Albert Jr. **6** 452-453
Hart, Gary W. **7** 182-184
Helms, Jesse **7** 271-272
Humphrey, Hubert Horatio Jr.
8 34-36
Jackson, Henry Martin
8 172-174
Kassebaum (Baker), Nancy
8 455-457
Kefauver, Carey Estes **8** 472-474
Kennedy, Edward M. **8** 500-502
Kerrey, J. Robert **8** 521-522
Lodge, Henry Cabot Jr.
9 483-485
McClellan, John Little
10 392-393
Mikulski, Barbara **11** 13-15
Mitchell, George John **11** 56-58
Mondale, Walter. F. **11** 97-99
Morse, Wayne L. **11** 193-194
Mosely-Braun, Carol **11** 199-200
Moynihan, Daniel Patrick
11 216-218
Muskie, Edmund Sixtus
11 269-271
Nunn, Sam **11** 443-444
Pepper, Claude Denson
12 205-206
Proxmire, William **12** 467-468
Simon, Paul **14** 238-239
Smith, Margaret Chase
14 299-300
Snowe, Olympia **14** 313-314
Taft, Robert Alphonso **15** 76-78
Thurmond, James Strom
15 214-215
Speakers of the House
Blaine, James Gillespie
2 312-313
Cannon, Joseph Gurney
3 261-262
Clay, Henry **4** 94-96
Foley, Tom **5** 499-501
Macon, Nathaniel **10** 114-115
McCormack, John William
10 399-400
O'Neill, Thomas P. **11** 517-519

Rayburn, Samuel Taliaferro
  13 61-62
Reed, Thomas Brackett **13** 77
• STATE and LOCAL
  governors (18th century)
    Bowdoin, James **2** 461-462
    Sevier, John **14** 122-123
  governors (19th century)
    Altgeld, John Peter **1** 180-182
    Ames, Adelbert **1** 198
    Andrew, John Albion **1** 230-231
    Brown, Benjamin Gratz **3** 32-33
    Brown, Joseph Emerson **3** 41-42
    Brownlow, William Gannaway
      3 55-56
    Clinton, DeWitt **4** 112-113
    Curtin, Andrew Gregg **4** 347-348
    Fish, Hamilton **5** 461-462
    Gordon, John Brown **6** 449-450
    Hammond, James Henry
      7 108-109
    Hampton, Wade III **7** 112
    Houston, Samuel **7** 526-527
    McDuffie, George **10** 408
    Morton, Oliver Hazard Perry
      Throck **11** 197-198
    Pinchback, Pinckney Benton
      Stewart **12** 306-308
    Seymour, Horatio **14** 126-127
    Stanford, Leland **14** 397-398
    Stephens, Alexander Hamilton
      14 429-430
    Tilden, Samuel Jones
      15 222-223
    Tillman, Benjamin Ryan
      15 225-226
    Vance, Zebulon Baird
      15 413-414
  governors (20th century)
    Agnew, Spiro Theodore **1** 83-85
    Babbitt, Bruce Edward
      1 408-410
    Carter, James Earl **3** 339-342
    Clinton, William Jefferson
      4 117-119
    Connally, John Bowden Jr.
      4 202-204
    Cuomo, Mario Matthew
      4 338-339
    Curley, James Michael
      4 344-345
    Dewey, Thomas Edmund **4** 524
    Dukakis, Michael **5** 130-133
    Johnson, Hiram Warren
      8 300-301
    Kunin, Madeleine May
      9 130-131
    La Follette, Robert Marion
      9 155-156
    Lehman, Herbert Henry
      9 306-307
    Long, Huey Pierce **9** 496-497
    Murphy, Frank **11** 260-261
    Pinchot, Gifford **12** 308-309
    Ray, Dixy Lee **13** 56-57
    Reagan, Ronald W. **13** 65-68
    Richards, Ann Willis **13** 133-134

Rockefeller, Nelson Aldrich
  13 228-230
Smith, Alfred Emmanuel
  14 284-285
Stevenson, Adlai Ewing
  14 445-446
Thurmond, James Strom
  15 214-215
Wallace, George Corley
  16 71-72
Whitman, Christine Todd
  16 245-248
Wilder, Lawrence Douglas
  16 274-276
Wilson, Pete **16** 326-329
governors (lieutenant)
  Colden, Cadwallader **4** 145-146
  Tabor, Horace Austin Warner
    15 70
governors (of Liberia)
  Ashmun, Jehudi **1** 335-336
governors (territorial)
  Dole, Sanford Ballard **5** 46
  St. Clair, Arthur **13** 429-430
  Tugwell, Rexford Guy
    15 336-339
  Young, Brigham **16** 469-470
mayors (19th century)
  Barnum, Phineas Taylor **2** 13-15
  Clinton, DeWitt **4** 112-113
  Corning, Erastus **4** 238-239
  Dow, Neal **5** 89-90
  Grace, William Russell
    6 480-481
  Hewitt, Abram Stevens
    7 371-372
  Johnson, Tom Loftin **8** 317
  Jones, Samuel Milton **8** 342-343
  Wood, Fernando **16** 367-368
mayors (20th century)
  Baker, Newton Diehl **1** 451
  Barry, Marion Shepilov Jr.
    2 25-28
  Bradley, Tom **2** 484-485
  Byrne, Jane **3** 190-191
  Cisneros, Henry G. **4** 62-64
  Daley, Richard J. **4** 373-375
  Dinkins, David **5** 15-18
  Feinstein, Dianne **5** 407-408
  Giuliani, Rudolph William
    6 353-355
  Hague, Frank **7** 63-64
  Humphrey, Hubert Horatio Jr.
    8 34-36
  Jackson, Maynard Holbrook Jr.
    8 176-178
  Koch, Edward I. **9** 68-69
  La Guardia, Fiorello Henry
    9 166-167
  Lindsay, John Vliet **9** 423-424
  Low, Seth **10** 11-12
  Murphy, Frank **11** 260-261
  Riordan, Richard Joseph
    13 177-179
  Stokes, Carl B. **14** 464-465
  Wagner, Robert Ferdinand Jr.
    16 44-45

White, Kevin H. **16** 231-232
Whitmire, Kathryn Jean Nieder-
  hofer **16** 252-253
Young, Andrew Jackson Jr.
  16 467-469
Young, Coleman Alexander
  16 470-471
political bosses
  see Political machines
state representatives
  Baca-Barragán, Polly **1** 412-414
  Bond, Julian **2** 386-387
  Cornell, Ezra **4** 236-237
  Hansen, Julia Butler **7** 132-133
  Memminger, Christopher Gus-
    tavus **10** 476-477
  Pepper, Claude Denson
    12 205-206
  Simon, Paul **14** 238-239
  see also Articles of Confedera-
    tion; Confederate States of
    America; Constitutional Con-
    vention; Continental Congress;
    Diplomats, American
• UN OFFICIALS
  Albright, Madeleine Korbel
    1 116-118
  Anderson, Marian **1** 218-219
  Ball, George **1** 470-471
  Black, Shirley Temple **2** 303-305
  Bunche, Ralph Johnson **3** 121-122
  Ford, Henry II **6** 6-7
  Goldberg, Arthur Joseph **6** 397-398
  Kirkpatrick, Jeane J. **9** 37-39
  Lodge, Henry Cabot Jr. **9** 483-485
  Roosevelt, Eleanor **13** 275-277
  Stevenson, Adlai Ewing **14** 445-446

Statesmen, Angolan
  dos Santos, José Eduardo **5** 71-72
  Neto, António Agostinho **11** 351-352
  Savimbi, Jonas Malheiros **13** 503-505

Statesmen, Arab
  caliphs
    Ali **1** 155-156
    Harun al-Rashid **7** 188
    ibn Tashufin, Yusuf **8** 95-96
    Mamun, Abdallah al- **10** 183
    Mansur, Abu Jafar ibn Muhammad
      al- **10** 214-215
    Muawiya ibn Abu Sufyan
      11 223-224
    Omar ibn al-Khattab **11** 508-509
    Yakub al-Mansur, Abu Yusuf **16** 426
  court officials
    ibn Khaldun, Abd al-Rahman ibn
      Muhammad **8** 93-94
  kings
    Husein ibn Ali **8** 63
    ibn Saud, Abd al-Aziz **8** 94-95
  United Arab Emirates
    Zayid bin Sultan Al-Nahyan
      16 491-492

Statesmen, Argentine
  dictators
    Rosas, Juan Manuel de **13** 290-291

Urquiza, Justo José **15** 396-397
military governors
San Martín, José de **13** 468-469
ministers
Lamas, Carlos Saavedra **9** 175-176
Perón, Eva Duarte de **12** 225-226
Prebisch, Raúl **12** 434-436
presidents
Alfonsín, Raúl Ricardo **1** 146-148
Frondizi, Arturo **6** 127-128
Galtieri, Leopoldo Fortunato
6 191-193
Irigoyen, Hipólito **8** 139-140
Justo, Agustin Pedro **8** 396
Menem, Carlos Saúl **10** 497-499
Mitre, Bartolomé **11** 62-63
Perón, Juan Domingo **12** 228-230
Perón, Isabel Martinez de
12 226-228
Rivadavia, Bernardino **13** 182-183
Roca, Julio Argentino **13** 218
Sarmiento, Domingo Faustino
13 484-485
Videla, Jorge Rafaél **15** 490-492

Statesmen, Ashanti
Anokye, Okomfo **1** 242-243

Statesmen, Assyrian
Ashurbanipal **1** 338
Sargon II **13** 482
Sennacherib **14** 108
Tiglath-pileser III **15** 221-222

Statesmen, Australian
bureaucrats
Coombs, Herbert Cole **4** 219-220
cabinet members
Keating, Paul John **8** 469-470
governors
Phillip, Arthur **12** 279-280
legislators
Macarthur, John **10** 78
Wentworth, William Charles
16 203-204
premiers
Griffith, Samuel Walker **6** 545-546
Lang, John Thomas **9** 192-193
Parkes, Henry **12** 113
presidential advisers
Coombs, Herbert Cole **4** 219-220
prime ministers
Barton, Edmund **2** 39-40
Bruce of Melbourne, 1st Viscount
3 61-62
Chifley, Joseph Benedict **3** 518
Curtin, John Joseph **4** 348-349
Deakin, Alfred **4** 432-433
Fisher, Andrew **5** 462
Fraser, Malcolm **6** 71-73
Hawke, Robert James Lee **7** 205-206
Hughes, William Morris **8** 21-22
Lyons, Joseph Aloysius **10** 69-70
Menzies, Robert Gordon
10 510-511
Scullin, James Henry **14** 73
Whitlam, Edward Gough
16 244-245

Queensland
Bjelke-Petersen, Johannes
2 297-299

Statesmen, Austrian
archdukes
Francis Ferdinand **6** 44
Maximilian of Hapsburg
10 358-360
chancellors
Dollfuss, Engelbert **5** 47
Kreisky, Bruno **9** 97-98
Schuschnigg, Kurt von **14** 45-46
emperors
Francis II **6** 43-44
Francis Joseph **6** 45-46
Joseph II **8** 359-360
Leopold II **9** 346
ministers
Böhm-Bawerk, Eugen von **2** 366
Metternich, Klemens von
10 533-536
Schumpeter, Joseph Alois **14** 43-44
Schuschnigg, Kurt von **14** 45-46
presidents
Renner, Karl **13** 98-99
Waldheim, Kurt **16** 54-55

Statesmen, Austro-Hungarian
Andrássy, Julius **1** 222-223
Berchtold, Leopold von **2** 183-184

Statesmen, Aztec
Cuauhtemoc **4** 329

Statesmen, Babylonian
Hammurabi **7** 109-110
Nebuchadnezzar **11** 330

Statesmen, Bangladeshi
Ershad, Hussain Mohammad **5** 312-314
Mujibur Rahman **11** 234-236

Statesmen, barbarian
Attila **1** 360
Odoacer **11** 473
Ricimer, Flavius **13** 151-152

Statesmen, Belgian
Albert I **1** 112
Albert II **1** 112-113
Leopold I **9** 345-346
Leopold II **9** 346-347
Leopold III **9** 347-348
Spaak, Paul Henri **14** 359-360

Statesmen, Bengali
Ziaur Rahman **16** 515-516

Statesmen, Bohemian
Charles IV **3** 455-456
Ferdinand I **5** 414-415
Ferdinand II **5** 415
Ferdinand III **5** 416-417
Sigismund **14** 220-221
Wenceslaus **16** 201-202

Statesmen, Bolivian
Ballivián, José **1** 475
Banzer Suárez, Hugo **1** 494-496
Barrientos Ortuño, René **2** 22-23
Paz, Octavio **12** 161-162

Paz Zamora, Jaime **12** 165-167
Santa Cruz, Andrés de **13** 472-473
Sucre, Antonio José de **15** 11-12

Statesmen, Bosnian-Herzegovinian
Izetbegovic, Alija **8** 161-163

Statesmen, Botswanan
Chiepe, Gaositwe Keagakwa Tibe **3** 517
Khama, Seretse M. **8** 532-533
Masire, Quett Ketumile **10** 318-319

Statesmen, Brazilian
dictators
Castelo Branco, Humberto
3 359-360
emperors
Pedro I **12** 179-180
Pedro II **12** 180-181
imperial advisers
Andrada e Silva, José Bonifácio de
1 221-222
ministers
Aranha, Osvaldo **1** 272-273
Barbosa, Ruy **1** 503-504
Caxias, Duque de **3** 386
Feijó, Diogo Antônio **5** 405-406
Nabuco de Araujo, Joaquim Aurelio
11 288-289
Rio Branco, Barão do **13** 177
presidents
Castelo Branco, Humberto
3 359-360
Collor de Mello, Fernando
4 170-172
Deodoro da Fonseca, Manoel **4** 502
Figueiredo, João Batista de Oliveira
5 445-446
Geisel, Ernesto **6** 253-255
Goulart, João **6** 467-469
Kubitschek de Oliveira, Juscelino
9 113-115
Peixoto, Floriano **12** 188-189
Vargas, Getulio Dornelles
15 433-434

Statesmen, British
colonial governors
Brooke, James **3** 21-22
Carleton, Guy **3** 300-301
Clive, Robert **4** 119-120
Dalhousie, 1st Marquess of
4 375-376
Jameson, Leander Starr **8** 218
Kitchener, Horatio Herbert **9** 45-46
Lugard, Frederick John Dealtry
10 31-32
Wellesley, Richard Colley
16 192-193
foreign secretaries
Carrington **3** 326-327
Castlereagh, Viscount **3** 363-364
members of Parliament
Astor, Nancy Langhorne **1** 352-354
Benn, Tony **2** 164-166
Bevan, Aneurin **2** 248-249
Bondfield, Margaret Grace
2 388-389
Burgoyne, John **3** 137-138

Burke, Edmund **3** 138-141
Callaghan, Leonard James
   3 230-231
Clarendon, 1st Earl of **4** 73-75
Foot, Michael **5** 505-507
Hardie, James Keir **7** 147-148
Heseltine, Michael **7** 359-361
Howe, William **7** 538-539
Hurd, Douglas **8** 52-55
Montfort, Simon de **11** 132-133
prime ministers
   Aberdeen, 4th Earl of **1** 25-26
   Balfour, Arthur James **1** 469-470
   Bute, 3d Earl of **3** 177-178
   Callaghan, Leonard James
      3 230-231
prince consorts
   Albert **1** 110-112
   see also Statesmen, English; States-
   men, Irish; Statesmen, Scottish;
   Statesmen, Welsh

Statesmen, Bugandan
Mutesa I **11** 277
Mutesa II **11** 277-278
Mwanga **11** 282-283

Statesmen, Bulgarian
Dimitrov, Georgi **5** 11-13
Zhivkov, Todor **16** 510-512

Statesmen, Burgundian
see Statesmen, French

Statesmen, Burmese
Alaungpaya **1** 103
Aung San **1** 374-375
Aung San Suu Kyi **1** 375-376
Ba Maw **1** 480-481
Mindon Min **11** 47
Ne Win **11** 364-365
Nu, U **11** 439-441

Statesmen, Byzantine
emperors
   Alexius I **1** 143-144
   Basil I **2** 49-50
   Basil II **2** 50-51
   Constantine XI **4** 211-212
   Heraclius **7** 320-321
   Justinian I **8** 393-395
   Leo III **9** 330-332
   Manuel I **10** 218-219
   Michael VIII **11** 1-2
empresses
   Irene of Athens **8** 135-138
   Theodora **15** 172-175
   Zoë **16** 524-525
princesses
   Comnena, Anna **4** 185-186

Statesmen, Cambodian
Heng Samrin **7** 283-285
Hun Sen **8** 39-42
Pol Pot **12** 382-384
Rannaridh, Norodom **13** 37-39
Sihanouk, Norodom **14** 222-223

Statesmen, Cameroonian
Ahidjo, Ahmadou **1** 89-90

Statesmen, Canadian
Cabinet members
   Fairclough, Ellen Louks **5** 367-368
   Lafontaine, Louis-Hippolyte
      9 157-158
   Robinson, John Beverley **13** 210
   Sifton, Clifford **14** 219-220
colonial governors
   Iberville, Sieur d' **8** 90-91
Indian leaders
   Erasmus, Georges Henry **5** 300-301
legislators
   Brown, George **3** 35-36
   McClung, Nellie Letitia **10** 396-397
   Papineau, Louis-Joseph **12** 91
Métis leaders
   Riel, Louis **13** 163-164
members of Parliament
   Bourassa, Joseph-Henri-Napoleon
      2 446-447
   Chrétien, Joseph-Jacques-Jean
      4 24-25
   Douglas, Thomas Clement **5** 82-83
   Smith, Donald Alexander
      14 288-289
   Woodsworth, James Shaver **16** 376
ministers
   Baldwin, Robert **1** 466-468
   Cartier, George-Étienne **3** 342-343
   Crerar, Thomas Alexander **4** 306
   Galt, Alexander Tilloch **6** 190-191
premiers
   Aberhart, William **1** 26-27
   Lévesque, René **9** 362-363
   Tilley, Samuel Leonard **15** 223-224
premiers of provinces
   Bourassa, Robert **2** 447-449
   Douglas, Thomas Clement **5** 82-83
   Parizeau, Jacques **12** 96-99
prime ministers
   Bennett, Richard Bedford **2** 171-172
   Borden, Robert Laird **2** 409-411
   Campbell, Avril Phaedra Douglas
      3 250-252
   Chrétien, Joseph-Jacques-Jean
      4 24-25
   Diefenbaker, John George **5** 4-5
   King, William Lyon Mackenzie
      9 25-26
   Laurier, Wilfrid **9** 232-234
   Macdonald, John Alexander
      10 85-87
   Mackenzie, Alexander **10** 104
   Meighen, Arthur **10** 459-460
   Mulroney, Martin Brian **11** 242-246
   Pearson, Lester Bowles **12** 174-175
   St. Laurent, Louis Stephen **13** 434
   Trudeau, Pierre Elliott **15** 309-311
   Tupper, Charles **15** 342-343

Statesmen, Carthaginian
Hamilcar Barca **7** 94-95
Hannibal Barca **7** 128-130

Statesmen, Chadian
Eboué, Adolphe Felix Sylvestre **5** 194

Statesmen, Chilean
Alessandri Rodriguez, Jorge **1** 129-130
Allende Gossens, Salvador **1** 174-176
Aylwin Azócar, Patricio **1** 393-395
Balmaceda Fernández, José Manuel
   1 475-476
Carrera, José Miguel **3** 323-324
Frei Montalva, Eduardo **6** 94-95
Ibáñez del Campo, Carlos **8** 88
Montt Torres, Manuel **11** 139-140
O'Higgins, Bernardo **11** 486
Pinochet Ugarte, Augusto **12** 315-317
Portales Plazazuelos, Diego José Víctor
   12 404

Statesmen, Chinese
councilors
   Chia Ssu-tao **3** 514-515
   Han Fei Tzu **7** 124-125
   Shang Yang **14** 149-150
   Ssu-ma kuang **14** 390-391
   Wang An-shih **16** 95-97
   Wen T'ien-hsiang **16** 203
   Wen-hsiang **16** 202-203
emperors (ancient)
   Han Kao-tsu **7** 125-126
   Liu Pang **9** 453-453
   Quin Shi Huang-Di **12** 515-518
   Wu-ti **16** 406-408
   Wu wang **16** 408-409
emperors (1st-8th century)
   Hsüan-tsung, T'ang **8** 7-8
   Kuang-wu-ti **9** 112-113
   Liang Wu-ti **9** 396-397
   Shih Le **14** 195
   Sui Wen-ti **15** 16-18
   T'ai-tsung, T'ang **15** 83-84
   Wang Mang **16** 101-103
   Hsiao-Wen-ti, Wei **8** 5
emperors (10th-15th century)
   Hui-Tsung **8** 25
   Hung-wu **8** 38-39
   Kao-tsung **8** 433
   Kublai Khan **9** 115-118
   Yung-lo **16** 482-483
   Zhao Kuang-yin **16** 505-508
emperors (17th-19th century)
   K'ang-hsi **8** 423-426
   Kuang-hsü **9** 111-112
   Qianlong **12** 502-505
empresses
   Tz'u-hsi **15** 375-376
   Wu Tse-t'ien **16** 408
governors
   Ch'i-ying **4** 12
   Li Hung-Chang **9** 407-409
   Lin Tse-hsü **9** 431-432
   Tseng Kuo-fan **15** 324-325
   Tso Tsung-t'ang **15** 328-329
ministers
   Chang Chü-cheng **3** 431-432
   Chou Kung **4** 22-23
   Deng Xiaoping **4** 498-500
   Ou-yang Hsiu **12** 33-34
   Shih Ko-fa **14** 194-195
   Wo-jen **16** 352

Yeh-lü Ch'u-ts'ai **16** 447-449
officials
   Ch'in Kuei **3** 524-525
   Chu Hsi **4** 40-43
   Fan Chung-yen **5** 376-377
   Feng Kuei-fen **5** 411-412
   Ho-shen **7** 512-513
   Jiang Qing **8** 256-260
   Li Peng **9** 433-435
   Jiang Zemin **8** 260-261
   Xu Guangqi **16** 422-425
premiers
   Chou En-lai **4** 20-22
   Zhao Ziyang **16** 508-509
presidents
   Chiang Ching-kuo **3** 509-510
   Chiang Kai-shek **3** 510-513
   Lee Teng-hui **9** 283-285
   Sun Yat-sen **15** 35-39
   Yüan Shih-k'ai **16** 480-481
prime ministers
   Li Ssu **9** 442-443
   Wang Ching-wei **16** 98
rebel "emperors"
   Huang Ch'ao **8** 8-9
   Li Tzu-Ch'eng **9** 452
warlords
   An Lu-shan **1** 239-240
   Ts'ao Ts'ao **15** 322-323
   Wu P'ei-fu **16** 404-405
   see also Communist party (China)

Statesmen, Colombian
Gaitán, Jorge Eliécer **6** 172-173
Gaviria Trujillo, Cesar Augusto **6** 242-243
Gómez Castro, Laureano Eleuterio **6** 419-420
Lleras Camargo, Alberto **9** 467
Mosquera, Tomás Cipriano de **11** 205-206
Nariño, Antonio **11** 314-315
Reyes, Rafael **13** 113
Rojas Pinilla, Gustavo **13** 255-256
Santander, Franciso de Paula **13** 475

Statesmen, Congolese
Affonso I **1** 72
Kasavubu, Joseph **8** 453-455
Lumumba, Patrice Emery **10** 43-45
Mobutu Sese Seko **11** 69-71
Nzinga Nkuwu **11** 451-452
Tshombe, Moïse Kapenda **15** 325-326
Youlou, Fulbert **16** 466-467

Statesmen, Costa Rican
Arias Sanchez, Oscar **1** 287-289
Calderón Fournier, Rafael **3** 222-223
Ferrer, José Figuéres **5** 428-429

Statesmen, Croatian
Tudjman, Franjo **15** 333-335

Statesmen, Cuban
Batista y Zaldívar, Fulgencio **2** 57-58
Castro Ruz, Fidel **3** 365-368
Céspedes, Carlos Manuel de **3** 398-399
Estrada Palma, Tomás **5** 326-327
Gómez, Máximo **6** 418-419

Grau San Martin, Ramón **6** 499-500
Guevara, Ernesto **7** 30-31
Machado y Morales, Gerardo **10** 92-93
Menocal, Mario Garcia **10** 506-507

Statesmen, Cypriot
Kyprianou, Spyros **9** 141-143
Makarios III **10** 157-158

Statesmen, Czech
Beneš, Edward **2** 155-157
Dubček, Alexander **5** 112-113
Havel, Vaclav **7** 202-205
Husák, Gustáv **8** 59-61
Masaryk, Tomáš Garrigue **10** 314-315
Slánský, Rudolf Salzmann **14** 270-271

Statesmen, Dahomean
Apithy, Sourou Migan **1** 259-260

Statesmen, Danish
Margaret of Denmark **10** 250-252

Statesmen, Dominican
Baez, Buenaventura **1** 432-433
Balaguer y Ricardo, Joaquin **1** 460-461
Bosch, Juan **2** 428-429
Santana, Pedro **13** 474-475
Trujillo Molina, Rafael Leonidas **15** 313-314
Vázquez, Horacio **15** 448-449

Statesmen, Dutch
colonial governors
   John Maurice of Nassau **8** 281-282
   Minuit, Peter **11** 50
   Stuyvesant, Peter **15** 5-6
   Van Diemen, Anthony Meuza **15** 420
kings
   Bonaparte, Louis **2** 382-383
   William I **16** 291-292
pensionaries
   Grotius, Hugo **7** 18-19
   Oldenbarnevelt, Johan van **11** 495-496
   Witt, Johan de **16** 348-349
political leaders
   Luns, Joseph **10** 46-47
   Van Eekelen, Willem Frederik **15** 426-427
queens
   Beatrix, Wilhelmina von Amsberg Queen **2** 92-93
   Juliana **8** 379-380
   Wilhelmina **16** 278-279
stadholders
   Maurice of Nassau **10** 348-349
   William the Silent **16** 300-302

Statesmen, Ecuadorian
Alfaro, José Eloy **1** 144-145
Borja Cevallos, Rodrigo **2** 417-418
García Moreno, Gabriel **6** 209-210
Plaza Lasso, Galo **12** 350-351
Velasco Ibarra, José María **15** 452-454

Statesmen, Egyptian
kings (ancient)
   Khufu **8** 540-541
   Menes **10** 500-502

Ptolemy I **12** 470-472
Ptolemy II **12** 472-473
Thutmose III **15** 216-217
Zoser **16** 531
   see also pharaohs (below)
kings (modern)
   Farouk I **5** 387-388
   Fuad I **6** 139
ministers
   Haykal, Muhammad Husain **7** 230-231
   Husayn, Taha **8** 61-62
   Zaghlul Pasha, Saad **16** 485-486
pashas and khedives
   Ismail Pasha **8** 150-151
   Mohammed Ali **11** 81-82
   Tewfik Pasha **15** 157-158
pharaohs
   Amenhotep III **1** 194-195
   Amenemhet I **1** 193-194
   Ikhnaton **8** 110-111
   Piankhi **12** 288-289
   Ramses II **13** 22-23
   Shabaka **14** 130
   Taharqa **15** 81-82
   Tutankhamen **15** 359-360
   see also kings (above)
presidents
   Mubarak, Hosni **11** 225-226
   Nasser, Gamal Abdel **11** 317-318
   Sadat, Anwar **13** 412-414
queens (ancient)
   Cleopatra **4** 105-106
   Hatshepsut **7** 196-197
   Nefertiti **11** 331-332
sultans
   Nureddin **11** 444-445
   Saladin **13** 441-442

Statesmen, English
cabinet members (13th-17th century)
   Bacon, Francis **1** 422-424
   Buckingham, 2d Duke of **3** 94-95
   Essex, 2d Earl of **5** 321-322
   Gloucester, Duke of **6** 370-371
   John of Gaunt **8** 282-283
   Leicester, Earl of **9** 312-313
   Montfort, Simon de **11** 132-133
   More, Thomas **11** 156-157
   Norfolk, 3d Duke of **11** 423
   Northumberland, Duke of **11** 431-432
   Raleigh, Walter **13** 9-11
   Shaftesbury, 1st Earl of **14** 135-136
   Strafford, 1st Earl of **14** 490-491
   Warwick and of Salisbury, Earl of **16** 122-123
cabinet members (18th-19th century)
   Addison, Joseph **1** 57-58
   Bolingbroke, Viscount **2** 374-375
   Chamberlain, Joseph **3** 411-413
   Fox, Charles James **6** 35-37
   Godolphin, Sidney **6** 380-381
   Harley, Robert **7** 159-160

Macaulay, Thomas Babington
10 79-80
Pitt, William the Elder **12** 328-329
Walpole, Robert **16** 82-84
Cabinet members (20th century)
Bevin, Ernest **2** 252-253
Cecil, of Chelwood Viscount
3 388-389
Chamberlain, Arthur Neville
3 409-411
Clarke, Kenneth Harry **4** 85-87
Gaitskell, Hugh **6** 173-174
Halifax, 1st Earl of **7** 82-83
Henderson, Arthur **7** 277-278
Howe, Geoffrey **7** 531-532
Jenkins, Roy Harris **8** 244-245
Milner, Alfred **11** 38-39
Morley, John **11** 178-179
Pym, Francis **12** 494-495
Webb, Sidney James **16** 154-155
Wilkinson, Ellen **16** 283-284
Williams, Shirley Vivien Teresa Brittain **16** 305-306
colonial governors (Africa)
Cromer, 1st Earl of **4** 317
Frere, Henry Bartle Edward
6 100-101
Goldie, George Dashwood Taubman **6** 404
Johnston, Henry Hamilton
8 322-323
Lugard, Frederick John Dealtry
10 31-32
Maclean, George **10** 108-109
Milner, Alfred **11** 38-39
Rhodes, Cecil John **13** 120-122
colonial governors (America)
Amherst, Jeffery **1** 200-201
Andros, Edmund **1** 234-235
Berkeley, William **2** 198-199
Calvert, Charles **3** 238
Calvert, George **3** 238-239
Dunmore, 4th Earl of **5** 147
Endecott, John **5** 284-285
Johnson, William **8** 319-320
Nicholson, Francis **11** 381-382
Oglethorpe, James Edward
11 482-483
Penn, William **12** 200-202
Spotswood, Alexander **14** 385
Tryon, William **15** 321
Vane, Henry **15** 425-426
colonial governors (Australia and New Zealand)
Eyre, Edward John **5** 354
Forrest, John **6** 12-13
Hobson, William **7** 426
Macquarie, Lachlan **10** 115-116
Sturt, Charles **15** 2-3
colonial governors (Canada)
Durham, 1st Earl of **5** 161-162
Elgin, 8th Earl of **5** 248-249
Metcalfe, Charles Theophilus
10 531-532
Rodney, George Brydges
13 239-240

Sydenham, Thomas **15** 59-60
colonial governors (India)
Chelmsford, Frederic John Napier Thesiger **3** 497
Cornwallis, Charles **4** 241-243
Curzon, George Nathaniel
4 351-352
Halifax, 1st Earl of **7** 82-83
Hastings, Warren **7** 195-196
Reading, 1st Marquess of **13** 64
kings (Hanover)
George I **6** 268-269
George II **6** 269-270
George III **6** 270-272
George IV **6** 272-273
William IV **16** 296-297
kings (Lancaster)
Henry IV **7** 292-293
Henry V **7** 296-297
Henry VI **7** 298-299
kings (Norman)
Henry I **7** 286-287
Stephen **14** 426-427
William I **16** 290-291
William II **16** 293-294
kings (Plantagenet)
Edward I **5** 208-210
Edward II **5** 210
Edward III **5** 211-212
Henry II **7** 287-289
Henry III **7** 290-292
John **8** 274-275
Richard I **13** 130
Richard II **13** 130-131
kings (Saxe-Coburg)
Edward VII **5** 214-215
kings (Saxon)
Alfred **1** 151-153
Edward the Confessor **5** 218-219
Ethelred the Unready **5** 327
Harold II **7** 162
kings (Stuart)
Charles, I **3** 450-452
Charles II **3** 452-454
James I **8** 204-206
James II **8** 207-208
William III **16** 295-296
kings (Tudor)
Edward VI **5** 213-214
Henry VII **7** 300-302
Henry VIII **7** 302-305
kings (Windsor)
Edward VIII **5** 215-217
George V **6** 273-275
George VI **6** 275
kings (York)
Edward IV **5** 212-213
Richard III **13** 132-133
lord protectors
Cromwell, Oliver **4** 317-320
members of Parliament
Aitken, William Maxwell **1** 94-96
Boothroyd, Betty **2** 406-407
Bradlaugh, Charles **2** 478
Bright, John **3** 6-7

Cobbett, William **4** 126-127
Cobden, Richard **4** 127-128
Hampden, John **7** 110-111
Kaufman, Gerald Bernard
8 458-460
Marvell, Andrew **10** 301-303
Maxwell, Ian Robert **10** 360-361
Pepys, Samuel **12** 207-208
Perth, 16th Earl of **12** 244-245
Pym, Francis **12** 494-495
Pym, John **12** 495-496
Rathbone, Eleanor **13** 47-48
Sandys, Edwin **13** 463-464
Shaftesbury, 7th Earl of **14** 137-138
Wilberforce, William **16** 269-270
Wilkes, John **16** 280-281
Wootton, Barbara Adam
16 384-385
prime ministers (18th-19th century)
North, Frederick **11** 429-430
Pitt, William the Younger
12 329-331
Rockingham, 2d Marquess of
13 230-231
prime ministers (19th century)
Canning, George **3** 258-260
Disraeli, Benjamin **5** 27-29
Gladstone, William Ewart
6 357-360
Grey, Charles **6** 539-540
Liverpool, 2nd Earl of **9** 456-457
Melbourne, 2nd Viscount
10 468-469
Palmerston, 3d Viscount **12** 81-83
Peel, Robert **12** 181-183
Russell, John **13** 380-381
Salisbury, 3d Marquess of
13 448-449
Wellington, 1st Duke of **16** 193-195
prime ministers (20th century)
Asquith, Herbert Henry **1** 344-346
Attlee, Clement Richard **1** 361-362
Baldwin, Stanley **1** 468-469
Chamberlain, Arthur Neville
3 409-411
Churchill, Winston Leonard Spencer
4 51-53
Eden, Anthony **5** 204-205
Heath, Edward Richard George
7 244-246
Lloyd George, David **9** 469-471
Macmillan, Harold **10** 112-113
Major, John **10** 155-157
Thatcher, Margaret Hilda
15 165-168
Wilson, James Harold **16** 324-325
princes
Charles, Prince of Wales **3** 448-450
Edward the Black Prince **5** 217-218
princesses
Diana, Princess of Wales **4** 529-533
queen consorts
Margaret of Anjou **10** 249-250
queens
Eleanor of Aquitaine **5** 246-247

Elizabeth, the Queen Mother
5 261-263
Elizabeth I **5** 263-266
Elizabeth II **5** 266-269
Mary, I **10** 308-309
Mary II **10** 309-310
Victoria **15** 485-487
see also Diplomats, English; Statesmen, British

Statesmen, Ethiopian
Ezana **5** 354-355
Haile Selassie **7** 68-70
Heruy Wäldä-Sellasé **7** 348-349
Johannes IV **8** 272-273
Lalibela **9** 170
Mäkonnen Endalkačäw **10** 161-162
Mengistu Haile Mariam **10** 503-505
Menelik II **10** 495-497
Tewodros II **15** 158-159
Yekuno Amlak **16** 449

Statesmen, Filipino
Aguinaldo, Emilio **1** 88
Aquino, Benigno **1** 267-268
Aquino, Corazon Cojoangco **1** 268-270
Bonifacio, Andres **2** 393-394
Garcia, Carlos P. **6** 207-208
Laurel, Salvador H. **9** 226-227
Macapagal, Diosdado P. **10** 74-76
Magsaysay, Ramon **10** 130-131
Marcos, Ferdinand **10** 240-242
Marcos, Imelda Romualdez **10** 242-243
Osmeña, Sergio **12** 22-24
Quezon, Manuel Luis **12** 511-513
Quirino, Elpidio **12** 519-520
Ramos, Fidel Valdez **13** 18-19
Recto, Claro M. **13** 69-70
Rizal, José **13** 187-189
Rómulo, Carlos P. **13** 270-271
Roxas, Manuel **13** 331-332

Statesmen, Finnish
Mannerheim, Carl Gustav Emil Von **10** 207-208

Statesmen, French
chiefs of state (Vichy)
Laval, Pierre **9** 237-238
Pétain, Henri Philippe **12** 250-252
colonial governors
Bienville, Sieur de **2** 268-269
Charnisay, Charles de Menou **3** 470-471
Dupleix **5** 153
Faidherbe, Louis Léon César **5** 366-367
Frontenac et Palluau, Comte de **6** 128-130
Lyautey, Louis Hubert Gonzalve **10** 60-61
Talon, Jean **15** 91-92
Vaudreuil-Cavagnal, Marquis de **15** 444
dukes
Charles the Bold **3** 467-469
Godfrey of Bouillon **6** 379
Philip the Good **12** 278-279
emperors

Napoleon I **11** 306-310
Napoleon III **11** 310-312
extremists (right wing)
Le Pen, Jean Marie **9** 348-350
kings (Bourbon)
Henry IV **7** 293-295
Louis XIII **9** 529-531
Louis XIV **9** 531-533
Louis XV **9** 533-534
Louis XVI **9** 534-535
Louis XVIII **9** 535-536
kings (Capetian)
Louis IX **9** 525-526
Louis VI **9** 523-524
Louis VII **9** 524-525
Philip II **12** 268-269
Philip IV **12** 274
kings (Carolingian)
Louis I **9** 522-523
Martel, Charles **10** 285
kings (Merovingian)
Clovis I **4** 124
kings (Napoleonic era)
Bonaparte, Joseph **2** 381-382
Bonaparte, Louis **2** 382-383
Murat, Joachim **11** 253-254
kings (Navarre)
Thibaut IV **15** 180-181
kings (Restoration)
Louis Philippe **9** 536-537
kings (Valois)
Charles V **3** 459-460
Charles VI **3** 460-461
Charles VII **3** 461-462
Charles VIII **3** 462-463
Francis I **6** 40-43
John II **8** 275-276
Louis XI **9** 526-528
Louis XII **9** 528-529
Philip VI **12** 277-278
ministers (17th-18th century)
Colbert, Jean Baptiste **4** 142-143
Mazarin, Jules **10** 379-380
Necker, Jacques **11** 330-331
Richelieu, Armand Jean du Plessis de **13** 142-144
Talleyrand, Charles Maurice de **15** 89-90
Turgot, Anne Robert Jacques **15** 348-349
ministers (19th-20th century)
Chateaubriand, Vicomte de **3** 477-479
Delcassé, Théophile **4** 478-479
Ferry, Jules François Camille **5** 430
Fouché, Joseph **6** 30-31
Guizot, François Pierre Guillaume **7** 40-41
Malraux, André **10** 178-180
Schuman, Robert **14** 41
Talleyrand, Charles Maurice de **15** 89-90
Thorez, Maurice **15** 206-207
Tocqueville, Alexis Charles Henri Maurice Clérel de **15** 250-251
ministers (20th century)

Camdessus, Michel **3** 244-246
Delors, Jacques **4** 484-486
ministers (20th century)
Rocard, Michel **13** 218-220
National Assembly members
Servan-Schreiber, Jean-Jacques **14** 113-115
premiers
Bourgeois, Léon **2** 450-451
Briand, Aristide **2** 528-529
Clemenceau, Georges **4** 99-101
Daladier, Édouard **4** 369
Ferry, Jules François Camille **5** 430
Gambetta, Léon **6** 198-199
Guizot, François Pierre Guillaume **7** 40-41
Herriot, Édouard **7** 339-340
Simon, Jules François **14** 237-238
presidents
Blum, Léon **2** 343-344
Carnot, Lazare Nicolas Marguerite **3** 313-314
De Gaulle, Charles André Joseph Marie **4** 463-465
Giscard d'Estaing, Valéry **6** 350-352
Lamartine, Alphonse Marie Louis de **9** 173-175
Mitterrand, François **11** 63-66
Poincaré, Raymond **12** 366-368
Pompidou, Georges **12** 389-390
Thiers, Louis Adolphe **15** 181-182
prime ministers
Balladur, Edouard **1** 474-475
Barre, Raymond **2** 19-20
Chirac, Jacques **4** 2-3
Cresson, Edith **4** 306-307
Fabius, Laurent **5** 358-359
Mendès France, Pierre **10** 492-493
queens
Eleanor of Aquitaine **5** 246-247
Marie Antoinette **10** 258-259
Medici, Catherine de' **10** 445-449
regents
Orléans, Philippe II D' **11** 530-531
Revolutionary leaders
Babeuf, François Noel **1** 412
Barras, Vicomte de **2** 19
Danton, Georges Jacques **4** 391-393
David, Jacques Louis **4** 407-409
Hébert, Jacques René **7** 247-248
Jaurès, Jean **8** 226-227
Lafayette, Marquis de **9** 151-152
Marat, Jean Paul **10** 230-231
Mirabeau, Comte de **11** 51-52
Montalembert, Comte de **11** 118-119
Robespierre, Maximilien François Marie Isidore de **13** 199-201
Saint-Just, Louis Antoine Léon de **13** 433
Sieyès, Comte Emmanuel Joseph **14** 217-218
vice-premiers
Thorez, Maurice **15** 206-207

Statesmen, Gambian
Jawara, Dauda Kairaba **8** 227-228

Statesmen, German
  barbarian chiefs
      Odoacer **11** 473
      Ricimer, Flavius **13** 151-152
  chairmen of council of state (East)
      Honecker, Erich **7** 471-472
      Ulbricht, Walter **15** 383-384
  chancellors
      Bethmann Hollweg, Theobald von
          2 239-240
      Bismarck, Otto Eduard Leopold von
          2 294-296
      Hitler, Adolf **7** 417-420
      Stresemann, Gustav **14** 508-509
  chancellors (pre-1945)
      von Papen, Franz **16** 28-29
  chancellors (post-1990)
      Kohl, Helmut **9** 73-74
  chancellors (West)
      Adenauer, Konrad **1** 59-61
      Brandt, Willy **2** 499-500
      Erhard, Ludwig **5** 302-304
      Kohl, Helmut **9** 73-74
      Schmidt, Helmut **14** 19-21
      Strauss, Franz Josef **14** 497-498
  electors
      Frederick William **6** 85-86
  empresses
      Maria Theresa **10** 256-258
  foreign ministers (West)
      Genscher, Hans-Dietrich **6** 265-266
  Holy Roman Emperors
      Charlemagne **3** 445-447
      Ferdinand I **5** 414-415
      Frederick I **6** 78-79
      Frederick II **6** 79
      Frederick III **6** 84-85
      Henry III **7** 290
      Henry IV **7** 292
      Henry V **7** 295-296
      Henry VII **7** 299-300
      Maximilian I **10** 356-357
      Maximilian II **10** 357-358
      Otto I **12** 28-29
      Otto III **12** 29-30
      Rudolf I **13** 347-348
  kings
      Henry I **7** 285-286
      Louis I **9** 522-523
  Länder prime ministers
      Lafontaine, Oskar **9** 158-160
  ministers
      Lambsdorff, Otto Graf **9** 177-179
      Rathenau, Walther **13** 48-49
      Schacht, Hjalmar Horace Greeley
          13 518-519
      Vogel, Hans-Jochen **16** 8-9
      Wörner, Manfred **16** 389-390
  nationalist leaders
      Kapp, Wolfgang **8** 436
      Schumacher, Kurt **14** 40-41
  Nazi leaders
      Goebbels, Joseph Paul **6** 384-385
      Göring, Hermann Wilhelm
          6 457-458
      Himmler, Heinrich **7** 398-399
  opposition politicians (reunited)
      Scharping, Rudolf **13** 522-524
  opposition politicians (West)
      Kelly, Petra **8** 486-487
      Schönhuber, Franz Xaver **14** 28-29
  presidents
      Ebert, Friedrich **5** 193-194
      Hindenburg, Paul Ludwig Hans von
          Beneckendorff und von **7** 400-401
  presidents (unified)
      Herzog, Roman **7** 355-357
  state presidents
      Rau, Johannes **13** 51-52
  state secretaries (West)
      Hamm-Brücher, Hildegard
          7 101-103
      Elizabeth of Hungary **5** 271-272
  vice chancellors
      Erzberger, Matthias **5** 319-320

Statesmen, Ghanaian
  Busia, Kofi Abrefa **3** 172-173
  Danquah, Joseph B. **4** 388-389
  Nkrumah, Kwame **11** 408-410

Statesmen, Greek (ancient)
  Athenian
      Alcibiades **1** 119-120
      Cleisthenes **4** 98-99
      Cleon **4** 104-105
      Miltiades **11** 42-43
      Pericles **12** 219-221
      Solon **14** 327-328
      Themistocles **15** 170-171
  Sicyonian
      Aratus **1** 273-274
  Spartan
      Agesilaus II **1** 79-80
      Agis IV **1** 81-82
      Cleomenes I **4** 103
      Cleomenes III **4** 103-104
      Leonidas I **9** 340-343
      Lysander **10** 70
  Theban
      Epaminondas **5** 291-292

Statesmen, Greek (modern)
  Karamanlis, Constantine **8** 440-441
  Papandreou, Andreas **12** 88-91
  Venizelos, Eleutherios **15** 460-461

Statesmen, Grenadian
  Bishop, Maurice **2** 292-293

Statesmen, Guatemalan
  Arbenz Guzmán, Jacobo **1** 274-276
  Arévalo, Juan José **1** 285-286
  Barrios, Justo Rufino **2** 23-24
  Carrera, José Rafael **3** 324-325
  Cerezo Arevalo, Marco Vinicio
      3 393-395
  Estrada Cabrera, Manuel **5** 325-326
  Serrano Elías, Jorge Antonio **14** 112-113
  Ubico y Castañeda, Jorge **15** 377-378

Statesmen, Guinea-Bissauan
  Cabral, Amílcar Lopes **3** 202-203

Statesmen, Guinean
  Touré, Sékou **15** 275-277

Statesmen, Guyanese
  Burnham, Forbes **3** 149-151
  Ramphal, Shridath Surendranath
      13 19-20

Statesmen, Haitian
  Aristide, Jean-Bertrand **1** 291-293
  Boyer, Jean Pierre **2** 468-469
  Christophe, Henri **4** 32
  Dessalines, Joan Jacques **4** 511-512
  Duvalier, François **5** 165-166
  Duvalier, Jean-Claude **5** 166-168
  Toussaint L'Ouverture, François
      Dominique **15** 278-279

Statesmen, Hawaiian
  Kamehameha I **8** 416
  Kalakaua, David **8** 413-414
  Liliuokalani, Lydia Kamakaeha
      9 411-412

Statesmen, Herero (Africa)
  Maherero, Samuel **10** 139-142

Statesmen, Honduran
  Azcona Hoyo, José **1** 398-399
  Callejas Romero, Rafael Leonardo
      3 233-234
  Carías Andino, Tiburcio **3** 298-299
  Morazán, José Francisco **11** 155
  Suazo Córdova, Roberto **15** 8-10

Statesmen, Hungarian
  Andrássy, Julius **1** 222-223
  Deák, Francis **4** 431-432
  Ferdinand I **5** 414-415
  Ferdinand II **5** 415
  Ferdinand III **5** 416-417
  Francis Joseph **6** 45-46
  Horthy de Nagybánya, Nicholas
      7 510-512
  Hunyadi, John **8** 51-52
  Kádár, János **8** 402-403
  Kossuth, Louis **9** 88-90
  László I, King of Hungary **9** 219-221
  Nagy, Imre **11** 292-293
  Sigismund **14** 220-221
  Stephen I **14** 427-428

Statesmen, Icelandic
  Sturluson, Snorri **14** 310-311

Statesmen, Indian (Asian)
  emperors
      Akbar, Jalal-ud-din Mohammed **1** 96
      Asoka **1** 341-342
      Aurangzeb **1** 377
      Babar the Conqueror **1** 405-407
      Chandragupta Maurya **3** 426
      Jahangir **8** 196-199
      Samudragupta **13** 457
      Shah Jahan **14** 138-139
  executive council members
      Ambedkar, Bhimrao Ramji
          1 190-191
      Sapru, Tej Bahadur **13** 480-481
  governors general
      Rajagopalachari, Chakravarti **13** 6-7
  imams
      Aga Khan **1** 74-76
  kings

Harsha **7** 181-182
Rajaraja I **13** 7
Śivajī **14** 266-267
mayors
Bose, Subhas Chandra **2** 430-431
National Congress members
Das, Chitta Ranjan **4** 401-402
Rai, Lala Lajpat **13** 5-6
National Congress presidents
Banerjee, Surendranath **1** 488
Gandhi, Mohandas Karamchand
6 201-204
Gokhale, Gopal Krishna **6** 396
Kamaraj, Kumaraswami **8** 415
Mehta, Pherozeshah **10** 455
Naidu, Sarojini **11** 294-295
Naoroji, Dadabhai **11** 305
Nehru, Motilal **11** 334-335
Patel, Vallabhbhai **12** 129-130
national leaders
Bhave, Vinoba **2** 257-258
Ghose, Aurobindo **6** 293-294
Narayan, Jayaprakash **11** 312-313
presidents
Prasad, Rajendra **12** 433
Radhakrishnan, Sarvepalli
12 537-538
prime ministers
Gandhi, Indira Priyadarshini
6 200-201
Gandhi, Rajiv **6** 204-205
Nehru, Jawaharlal **11** 332-334
Singh, Vishwanath Pratap
14 254-256
princes
Haidar Ali **7** 65-66
Ranjit Singh **13** 32-33
Tipu Sultan **15** 236
sultans
Ala-ud-din **1** 102-103
Mahmud of Ghazni **10** 147
Muhammad bin Tughluq **11** 229
UN officials
Menon, Vengalil Krishnan Krishna
10 507-509
Pandit, Vijaya Lakshmi **12** 83-84
see also Statesmen, Pakistani

Statesmen, Indonesian
Suharto **15** 14-15
Sukarno **15** 18-20

Statesmen, Iranian
Abbas I **1** 4-6
Agha Mohammad Khan **1** 80-81
Cyrus the Great **4** 363-364
Darius I **4** 394-395
Karim Khan Zand **8** 447
Khamenei, Sayyid Ali **8** 533-535
Khomeini, Ruhollah Musavi **8** 535-537
Khosrow I **8** 538-539
Mohammad Reza Shah Pahlavi
11 75-76
Mossadegh, Mohammad **11** 206-207
Rafsanjani, Akbar Hashemi **13** 3-4
Reza Shah Pahlavi **13** 116-117
Shahpur II **14** 140-141

Taqi Khan Amir-e Kabir, Mirza
15 106-107
Xerxes **16** 420

Statesmen, Iraqi
Fādil al-Jamālī, Muhammad **5** 361-362
Faisal I **5** 370-371
Nuri al-Sa'id **11** 446-447
Saddam Hussein **13** 415-416

Statesmen, Irish
Adams, Gerald **1** 42-44
Bruton, John Gerard **3** 76-77
Collins, Michael **4** 167-168
Cosgrave, Liam **4** 258-260
De Valera, Eamon **4** 514-515
Devlin, Bernadette **4** 515-516
Emmet, Robert **5** 281-282
Faulkner, Brian **5** 393-395
Fitzgerald, Garret **5** 472-474
Grattan, Henry **6** 499
Hyde, Douglas **8** 82-83
O'Connell, Daniel **11** 465-467
O'Neill, Terence Marne **11** 516-517
Paisley, Ian K. **12** 67-69
Parnell, Charles Stewart **12** 117-119
Pearse, Patrick Henry **12** 173-174
Reynolds, Albert **13** 113-115
Robinson, Mary Bourke **13** 211-213
see also Statesmen, British

Statesmen, Israeli
Arens, Moshe **1** 284-285
Begin, Menachem **2** 118-120
Ben-Gurion, David **2** 160-161
Dayan, Moshe **4** 429-431
Eban, Abba **5** 191-192
Herzog, Chaim **7** 354-355
Levy, David **9** 373-374
Meir, Golda **10** 462-463
Netanyahu, Binyamin **11** 350-351
Peres, Shimon **12** 210-211
Rabin, Yitzchak **12** 527-529
Shamir, Yitzchak **14** 147-149
Sharon, Ariel **14** 157-159
Weizman, Ezer **16** 181-182
Weizmann, Chaim **16** 183-184

Statesmen, Israelite
see Bible—Old Testament; Jewish history

Statesmen, Italian
Communist leaders
Gramsci, Antonio **6** 488-489
Togliatti, Palmiro **15** 253-254
countesses
Matilda of Tuscany **10** 334-336
dictators
Mussolini, Benito **11** 272-274
Savonarola, Girolamo **13** 505-506
doges
Dandolo, Enrico **4** 386-387
dukes
Borgia, Cesare **2** 412-413
Sforza, Lodovico **14** 127-128
Visconti, Gian Galeazzo
15 510-511
kings
Bonaparte, Joseph **2** 381-382

Victor Amadeus II **15** 482-483
Victor Emmanuel II **15** 483-484
Victor Emmanuel III **15** 484-485
members of parliament
Garibaldi, Giuseppe **6** 215-217
Matteotti, Giacomo **10** 339-340
ministers
De Sanctis, Francesco **4** 505
Gentile, Giovanni **6** 267
Orlando, Vittorio Emmanuele
11 529-530
papal advisers
Catherine of Siena **3** 369-370
premiers
Andreotti, Giulio **1** 226-228
Badoglio, Pietro **1** 428-429
Cavour, Conte di **3** 385-386
Crispi, Francesco **4** 310-311
De Gasperi, Alcide **4** 462-463
Giolitti, Giovanni **6** 339-340
presidents
Scalfaro, Oscar Luigi **13** 511-512
presidents (Venetian Republic)
Manin, Daniele **10** 197-198
prime ministers
Craxi, Bettino **4** 300-301
Fanfani, Amintore **5** 378-379
Moro, Aldo **11** 180-181
princes
Medici, Cosimo de' **10** 449-450
Medici, Lorenzo de' **10** 450-451
Roman Triumvirate member
Mazzini, Giuseppe **10** 381-383
tribunes
Rienzi, Cola di **13** 166-167
see also Statesmen, Roman

Statesmen, Ivorian
Houphouët-Boigny, Felix **7** 519-520

Statesmen, Jamaican
Bustamante, William Alexander
3 175-177
Manley, Michael Norman **10** 200-201

Statesmen, Japanese
emperors
Akihito **1** 98-99
Daigo II **4** 367-368
Goshirakawa **6** 460-461
Hirohito **7** 410-412
Kammu **8** 420
Mutsuhito **11** 279-282
empresses
Suiko **15** 15-16
ministers
Makibi, Kibi-no **10** 161
Okubo, Toshimichi **11** 489-490
Saigo, Takamori **13** 429
Saionji, Kimmochi **13** 438-439
party leaders
Doi Takako **5** 39-41
premiers
Hara, Kei **7** 138
Inukai, Tsuyoshi **8** 130-131
Ito, Hirobumi **8** 153-155
Kishi, Nobusuke **9** 41-43

Konoe, Fumimaro **9** 82-83
Okuma, Shigenobu **11** 490
Sato, Eisaku **13** 495-496
Tojo, Hideki **15** 254-256
Yamagata, Aritomo **16** 428-429
Yoshida, Shigeru **16** 464-465
prime ministers
    Kaifu Toshiki **8** 410-411
    Nakasone, Yasuhiro **11** 298-300
    Tanaka, Kakuei **15** 96-98
regents
    Fujiwara Michinaga **6** 145-146
    Shotoku Taishi **14** 205-207
shoguns
    Ashikaga Takauji **1** 330-332
    Ieyasu, Tokugawa **8** 103-106
    Yoritomo, Minamoto **16** 463-464
    Yoshimune, Tokugawa **16** 465-466
warrior chieftains
    Nobunaga, Oda **11** 413-414

Statesmen, Jordanian
Abdullah ibn Husein **1** 19-20
Hussein ibn Talal **8** 65-67

Statesmen, Kashan
Kanishka **8** 428-429

Statesmen, Kenyan
Kenyatta, Jomo **8** 512-514
Mboya, Thomas Joseph **10** 384-385
Moi, Daniel Arap **11** 83-86
Ngala, Ronald Gideon **11** 373-374
Odinga, Ajuma Jaramogi Oginga **11** 471-473
Ogot, Grace Emily Akinyi **11** 483-484
Thuku, Harry **15** 212-213

Statesmen, Korean
commissioners
    Chang Po-go **3** 433-434
    Ch'oe Ch'ung-hn **4** 13
kings
    Chongjo **4** 15-16
    Kojong **9** 74-75
    Kwanggaet'o **9** 139-140
    Kwangjong **9** 140
    Sejo **14** 90-91
    Sejong **14** 91-92
    Sŏnjo **14** 341-342
    Wang Kon **16** 101
    Yi Sng-gye **16** 458-459
    Yngjo **16** 461-462
ministers
    Kim Ok-kyun **9** 7-8
    Kim Pusik **9** 8-9
premiers (North)
    Kim Il-sung **9** 4-6
presidents (South)
    Chun Doo Hwan **4** 45-47
    Park, Chung Hee **12** 99-102
    Rhee, Syngman **13** 117-120
    Roh Tae Woo **13** 253-255
queens
    Min **11** 46-47
regents
    Taewŏn'gun, Hŭngsŏn **15** 74-75
South Korea

Kim Dae-jung **9** 3-4
Kim Young Sam **9** 9-10

Statesmen, Kuwaiti
'Abdullah al-Salim al-Sabah, Shaykh **1** 18-19
Bishara, Abdullah Yaccoub **2** 287-288
Jaber Al-Sabah, Jaber Al-Ahmad Al- **8** 166-167

Statesmen, Laotian
Souvanna Phouma **14** 357-358

Statesmen, Lebanese
Aoun, Michel **1** 255-257
Berri, Nabih **2** 220-222
Fadlallah, Sayyid Muhammad Husayn **5** 362-364
Gemayel, Amin **6** 258-259
Gemayel, Pierre **6** 259-261
Harawi, Ilyas al- **7** 145-146
Jumblatt, Kamal **8** 386-387
Sadr, Musa al- **13** 420-422
Shihab, Fu'ad **14** 193-194

Statesmen, Lesothan
Jonathan, Joseph Leabua **8** 330-331

Statesmen, Liberian
Blyden, Edward Wilmot **2** 348-349
Doe, Samuel Kanyon **5** 38-39
Russwurm, John Brown **13** 381-382
Tubman, William Vacanarat Shadrach **15** 331

Statesmen, Libyan
Gaddafi, Muammar Al- **6** 163-165
Idris I **8** 102
Omar al-Mukhtar **11** 507-508

Statesmen, Luxembourgan
Thorn, Gaston **15** 207-208

Statesmen, Macedonian
Alexander the Great **1** 137-141
Antigonus I **1** 248-249
Gligorov, Kiro **6** 367-369
Philip II **12** 269-271
Seleucus I **14** 92-93

Statesmen, Malawian
Banda, Hastings Kamuzu **1** 485-486

Statesmen, Malaysian
Mahathir Mohamad **10** 134-135
Tunku, Abdul Rahman **15** 340-341

Statesmen, Malian
Keita, Modibo **8** 474-475
Musa Mansa **11** 266
Sundiata Keita **15** 33-34

Statesmen, Maori
Ratana, Taupotiki Wiremu **13** 46

Statesmen, Mexican
emperors
    Iturbide, Agustín de **8** 155-156
    Maximilian of Hapsburg **10** 358-360
    Montezuma, II **11** 128-129
generalissimos
    Morelos, José María **11** 157-158
ministers
    Alamán, Lucas **1** 99-100

Huerta, Victoriano **8** 13-14
Lerdo de Tejada, Miguel **9** 351-352
Sierra, Justo **14** 217
presidential candidates
    Cárdenas Solorzano, Cuauhtémoc **3** 287-288
presidents
    Alemán, Mateo **1** 126
    Álvarez, Juan **1** 184-185
    Ávila Camacho, Manuel **1** 387-388
    Calles, Plutarco Elías **3** 234-235
    Cárdenas, Lázaro **3** 286-287
    Carranza, Venustiano **3** 321-322
    de la Madrid Hurtado, Miguel **4** 471-472
    Díaz, José de la Cruz Porfirio **4** 534-536
    Díaz Ordaz, Gustavo **4** 537-538
    Echeverría Alvarez, Luis **5** 198-200
    Guerrero, Vicente **7** 28-30
    Juárez, Benito **8** 369-372
    López Mateos, Adolfo **9** 509-510
    López Portillo, José **9** 510-511
    Madero, Francisco Indalecio **10** 118-119
    Obregón, Álvaro **11** 458-459
    Ruiz Cortines, Adolfo **13** 359-360
    Salinas de Gortari, Carlos **13** 445-447
    Santa Ana, Antonio López de **13** 471-472
    Zedillo Ponce de Leon, Ernesto **16** 493-495

Statesmen, Mongol
Batu Khan **2** 60-61
Genghis Khan **6** 263-265
Hulagu Khan **8** 27-28
Tamerlane **15** 94-95

Statesmen, Montenegrin
Bulatovic, Momir **3** 115-116

Statesmen, Moroccan
Abd el-Krim el-Khatabi, Mohamed ben **1** 15-16
Allal al-Fassi, Mohamed **1** 162
Hassan, Muhammad Abdille **7** 194-195
Mohammed V **11** 79-81

Statesmen, Mozambican
Chissano, Joaquim Alberto **4** 9-11
dos Santos, Marcelino **5** 72-74
Machel, Samora Moises **10** 94-96
Mondlane, Eduardo Chivambo **11** 100-101

Statesmen, Namibian
Nujoma, Shafiihuna **11** 441-443

Statesmen, Nepalese
Birendra, King **2** 282-283
Mahendra, King **10** 138-139

Statesmen, New Zealand
Fraser, Peter **6** 73-74
Massey, William Ferguson **10** 324
Ngata, Apirana Turupa **11** 374-375
Savage, Michael Joseph **13** 501-502
Seddon, Richard John **14** 81-82
Vogel, Julius **16** 9-10

Statesmen, New Zealander
Holyoake, Keith Jacka **7** 460-462

Statesmen, Nicaraguan
Chamorro, Violeta Barrios de **3** 417-419
Ortega, Daniel **12** 5-7
Somoza, Anastasio **14** 335-336
Somoza Debayle, Anastasio
14 336-337
Zelaya, José Santos **16** 495-496

Statesmen, Nigerian
Awolowo, Obafemi **1** 389-390
Azikiwe, Nnamdi **1** 401-402
Bello, Ahmadu **2** 139-140
Imam, Alhadji Abubakar **8** 114-115
Macaulay, Herbert **10** 78-79
Tafawa Balewa, Abubakar **15** 75

Statesmen, Norman
Baldwin I **1** 464-465
Guiscard, Robert **7** 39-40
Roger II **13** 244-245
Rurik **13** 364

Statesmen, North Korean
Kim Jong Il **9** 6-7

Statesmen, Norwegian
Brundtland, Gro Harlem **3** 68-69
Bernadotte, Jean Baptiste **2** 205-206
Harold I **7** 161-162
Harold III **7** 163
Lie, Trygve Halvdan **9** 400-401
Margaret of Denmark **10** 250-252
Olaf, II **11** 493-494
see also Statesmen, Viking

Statesmen, Numidian
Masinissa **10** 315-317

Statesmen, Omani
Qaboos ibn Sa'id **12** 501-502
Said, Seyyid **13** 428-429

Statesmen, Opoboan
Ja Ja of Opobo **8** 201-204

Statesmen, Ostrogoth
Theodoric the Great **15** 175-176

Statesmen, Pakistani
Ayub Khan, Mohammed **1** 395-396
Bhutto, Benazir **2** 259-261
Bhutto, Zulfikar Ali **2** 261-262
Jinnah, Mohammad Ali **8** 262-263
Leghari, Sardar Farooq Ahmed Khan
9 303-305
Liaquat Ali Khan **9** 397
Mawdūdī, Abu-I A'la **10** 353-354
Zia ul-Haq, Mohammad **16** 513-515
see also Statesmen, Indian

Statesmen, Palestinian
Ashrawi, Hanan Mikhail **1** 336-338
Husayni, Al-Hajj Amin al- **8** 62-63

Statesmen, Palmyrene
Zenobia **16** 500-503

Statesmen, Panamanian
Arias, Arnulfo **1** 286-287
Chiari, Roberto **3** 513-514
Endara, Guillermo **5** 283-284

Noriega, Manuel A. **11** 423-425
Torrijos, Omar **15** 269-270

Statesmen, Paraguayan
López, Carlos Antonio **9** 506-507
López, Francisco Solano **9** 507-508
Morínigo, Higinio **11** 174-175
Stroessner, Alfredo **14** 511-512
Wasmosy, Juan Carlos **16** 129-130

Statesmen, Persian
see Statesmen, Iranian

Statesmen, Peruvian
Atahualpa **1** 355-356
Belaúnde Terry, Fernando **2** 125-126
Castilla, Ramón **3** 361
Fujimori, Alberto Keinya **6** 143-145
Haya de la Torre, Victor Raul **7** 216-217
Leguía y Salcedo, Augusto Bernardino
9 305-306
Manco Capac **10** 184-185
Morales-Bermúdez Cerruti, Francisco
11 150-151
Odría Amoretti, Manuel Apolinario
11 473-474
Pérez de Cuéllar, Javier **12** 214-215
Prado Ugarteche, Manuel **12** 430-431
San Martín, José de **13** 468-469
Vargas Llosa, Mario **15** 434-436
Velasco, Luis de **15** 450-451

Statesmen, Polish
Augustus II **1** 373-374
Gomulka, Wladislaw **6** 422-424
Jaruzelski, Wojciech Witold **8** 223-225
John III **8** 276-277
Paderewski, Ignace Jan **12** 56-57
Pilsudski, Joseph **12** 305-306
Walesa, Lech **16** 57-59

Statesmen, Portuguese
dictators
Salazar, António de Oliveira
13 442-443
governors general (Brazil)
Sá, Mem de **13** 395
kings
Alfonso I **1** 148
Alfonso III **1** 148-149
Manuel I **10** 219-220
Pedro I **12** 179-180
ministers
Abravanel, Isaac ben Judah **1** 31
Pombal, Marquês de **12** 386-387
presidents
Soares, Mário **14** 315-316
viceroys
Albuquerque, Afonso de **1** 118-119
Sousa, Martim Afonso de
14 354-355

Statesmen, Prussian
kings
Frederick II **6** 81-84
Frederick William I **6** 86-87
Frederick William III **6** 87
Frederick William IV **6** 87-88
William I **16** 292-293
William II **16** 294-295

ministers
Hardenberg, Karl August von
7 146-147
Stein, Heinrich Friedrich Karl vom
und zum **14** 415-416

Statesmen, Puerto Rican
Hernández Colón, Rafael **7** 329-330
Muñoz Marín, José Luís Alberto
11 249-250
Muñoz Rivera, Luís **11** 250
Romero Barceló, Carlos **13** 267-268

Statesmen, Rhodesian
Smith, Ian Douglas **14** 291-293
Welensky, Roy **16** 188

Statesmen, Roman
censors
Cato, Marcus Porcius the Elder
3 375
Flamininus, Titus Quinctius **5** 477
consuls
Antony, Mark **1** 253-254
Cicero, Marcus Tullius **4** 55-58
Crassus Dives, Marcus Licinius
4 296-297
Marius, Gaius **10** 264-265
Pompey **12** 387-389
Scipio Africanus Minor, Publius Cor-
nelius Aemilianus **14** 62-63
dictators
Caesar, Gaius Julius **3** 207-210
Sulla, Lucius Cornelius I **15** 21-22
emperors (Antonine)
Hadrian **7** 60-61
Marcus Aurelius Antoninus
10 243-245
Trajan **15** 291-292
emperors (Julio-Claudian)
Augustus **1** 371-373
Caligula **3** 228-229
Claudius Germanicus, Tiberius
4 91-92
Nero Claudius Caesar **11** 342-344
Tiberius Julius Caesar Augustus
15 217-218
emperors (military)
Caracalla **3** 281-282
Constantine I **4** 209-211
Diocletian **5** 19-20
Julian **8** 378-379
Septimius Severus, Lucius
14 109-110
Theodosius **15** 176
Valerian **15** 404-405
emperors (Vespasian)
Domitian **5** 52-53
Titus Flavius Vespasianus **15** 247-248
Vespasian **15** 475-476
empresses
Julias of Rome **8** 381-384
Livia **9** 457-460
praetors
Brutus, Marcus Junius **3** 79-80
Cassiodorus, Flavius Magnus Aure-
lius **3** 357-358
Catiline **3** 372-373

Ulpian, Domitius **15** 385-386
quaestors
    Cato, the Younger **3** 374-375
    Sallust **13** 454
    Seneca the Younger, Lucius Annaeus
        14 103-105
secretaries
    Suetonius Tranquillus, Gaius **15** 13
tribunes
    Clodius Pulcher, Publius **4** 121-122
    Drusus, Marcus Livius **5** 105-106
    Gracchus, Tiberius and Gaius Sem-
        pronius **6** 479-480

Statesmen, Romanian
    Ceausescu, Nicolae **3** 387-388
    Ferdinand **5** 413-414
    Iliescu, Ion **8** 111-112
    Titulescu, Nicolae **15** 246-247

Statesmen, Russian
cabinet members
    Kozyrev, Andrei Vladimirovich
        9 92-93
Central Committee
    Biryukova, Aleksandra Pavlovna
        2 285-287
    Brezhnev, Leonid Ilich **2** 527-528
    Dzerzhinsky, Felix Edmundovich
        5 173-174
    Kollontai, Aleksandra Mikhailovna
        9 79
    Konev, Ivan Stefanovich **9** 81-82
    Ligachev, Yegor Kuz'mich **9** 404-406
    Litvinov, Maxim Maximovich
        9 451-452
    Radek, Karl Bernardovich
        12 536-537
    Yeltsin, Boris Nikolaevich
        16 449-452
    Zhukov, Georgi Konstantinovich
        16 512-513
colonial governors
    Baranov, Aleksandr Andreievich
        1 499-500
commissars
    Chicherin, Georgi Vasilyevich
        3 516-517
court advisers
    Pobedonostsev, Konstantin Petrovich
        12 360-361
    Potemkin, Grigori Aleksandrovich
        12 411-412
    Rasputin, Grigori Efimovich
        13 44-45
    Speranski, Mikhail Mikhailovich
        14 376-377
czars
    Alexander I **1** 130-132
    Alexander II **1** 132-133
    Alexander III **1** 133-134
    Alexis Mikhailovich Romanov
        1 142-143
    Godunov, Boris Feodorovich
        6 382-383
    Ivan IV **8** 157-159
    Nevsky, Alexander **11** 359
    Nicholas I **11** 377-378

Nicholas II **11** 378-380
Paul I **12** 143-144
Peter I **12** 253-256
empresses
    Anna Ivanovna **1** 240-241
    Catherine the Great **3** 370-372
    Elizabeth, the Queen Mother
        5 261-263
foreign ministers (Union of Soviet
  Socialist Republics)
    Kozyrev, Andrei Vladimirovich
        9 92-93
    Shevardnadze, Eduard Amvrosevich
        14 191-193
grand dukes
    Ivan III **8** 156-157
grand princes
    Vladimir I **16** 5-6
legislators
    Zhirinovsky, Vladimir Volfovich
        16 509-510
mayors
    Sobchak, Anatoly Alexandrovich
        14 317-318
presidents
    Gorbachev, Mikhail Sergeevich
        6 441-444
    Yeltsin, Boris Nikolaevich
        16 449-452
Presidium (Politburo)
    Beria, Lavrenty Pavlovich **2** 192-193
    Brezhnev, Leonid Ilich **2** 527-528
    Bukharin, Nikolai Ivanovich
        3 112-113
    Frunze, Mikhail Vasilievich **6** 134
    Gorbachev, Mikhail Sergeevich
        6 441-444
    Kamenev, Lev Borisovich **8** 417-418
    Khrushchev, Nikita Sergeevich
        8 539-540
    Kropotkin, Peter Alekseevich
        9 107-108
    Lenin, Vladimir Ilich **9** 323-326
    Molotov, Vyacheslav Mikhailovich
        11 89-90
    Stalin, Joseph **14** 393-396
    Trotsky, Leon **15** 302-305
    Zinoviev, Grigori Evseevich
        16 521-522
prime ministers
    Kerensky, Aleksandr Fedorovich
        8 516-517
    Stolypin, Piotr Arkadevich
        14 465-466
    Witte, Sergei Yulyevich **16** 349-350
Russian Republic
    Yeltsin, Boris Nikolaevich
        16 449-452

Statesmen, Salvadoran
    Cristiani, Alfredo **4** 311-313
    Daly, Mary **4** 380-381
    Duarte, José Napoleón **5** 109-111
    Martínez, Maximiliano Hernández
        10 297-298

Statesmen, Sardinian
    Charles Albert, King of Sardinia **3** 466

Statesmen, Saudi Arabian
    Fahd ibn Abdul Aziz Al-Saud **5** 364-366
    Faisal ibn Abd al Aziz ibn Saud
        5 371-372
    Yamani, Ahmed Zaki **16** 433-435

Statesmen, Scottish
kings
    David I **4** 407
    James I **8** 204-206
    James I **8** 206-207
    James III **8** 208-209
    Macbeth **10** 81
    Malcolm III **10** 164-165
    Robert I **13** 192-194
    Robert II **13** 194
    Robert III **13** 194-195
members of Parliament
    Steel, David Martin Scott
        14 406-407
princes
    Charles Edward Louis Philip Casimir
        Stuart **3** 466-467
queens
    Margaret of Scotland **10** 252-253
    Mary, I **10** 308-309
wardens
    Douglas, James **5** 78
    see also Statesmen, British

Statesmen, Senegalese
    Diagne, Blaise **4** 527
    Gueye, Lamine **7** 31
    Ly, Abdoulaye **10** 60
    M'Bow, Amadou-Mahtar **10** 383-384
    Senghor, Léopold Sédar **14** 106-107

Statesmen, Serbian
    Karadzic, Radovan **8** 437-440
    Milosevic, Slobodan **11** 39-40

Statesmen, Sicilian
    Ferdinand II **5** 415-416
    Peter III **12** 256-257

Statesmen, Sierra Leonean
    Margai, Milton Augustus Striery
        10 248-249
    Wallace-Johnson, Isaac Theophilus
        Akunna **16** 76-77

Statesmen, Singaporean
    Goh Chok Tong **6** 393-395
    Lee Hsien Loong **9** 280-281
    Lee Kuan Yew **9** 281-283
    Ong Teng Cheong **11** 519-520

Statesmen, Somali
    Hassan, Muhammad Abdille **7** 194-195

Statesmen, South African
assemblymen
    Suzman, Helen **15** 45-46
Black leaders
    Mandela, Nelson Rolihlahla
        10 185-186
Boer leaders
    Kruger, Stephanus Johannes Paulus
        9 108-109
    Pretorius, Andries **12** 444-445
    Retief, Pieter **13** 105-106

kings
    Lobengula **9** 474-475
    Moshweshwe **11** 203-205
presidents
    de Klerk, Fredrik Willem **4** 466-468
prime ministers
    Botha, Louis **2** 434-436
    Botha, Pieter Willem **2** 436-438
    Hertzog, James Barry Munnik
       7 347-348
    Malan, Daniel Francois
       10 163-164
    Smuts, Jan Christian **14** 309-310
    Verwoerd, Hendrik Frensch
       15 472-473
    Vorster, Balthazar Johannes
       16 30-32
tribal chiefs
    Buthelezi, Mangosuthu Gatsha
       3 178-179

Statesmen, Soviet
Central Committee
    Dimitrov, Georgi **5** 11-13
foreign ministers (Union of Soviet
    Socialist Republics)
    Vyshinsky, Andrei **16** 36-37
Presidium (Politburo)
    Andropov, Iury Vladimirovich
       1 233-234
    Brezhnev, Leonid Ilich
       2 527-528
    Bulganin, Nikolai **3** 118-119
    Chernenko, Konstantin Ustinovich
       3 503-504
    Gorbachev, Mikhail Sergeevich
       6 441-444
    Gromyko, Andrei Andreevich **7** 9-11
    Kosygin, Aleksei Nikolaevich
       9 90-91
    Malenkov, Georgy Maksimil-
       ianovich **10** 168

Statesmen, Spanish
colonial governors
    de Soto, Hernando **4** 510-511
    Gálvez, Bernardo de **6** 195-196
    Gálvez, José de **6** 196
    Gasca, Pedro de la **6** 230-231
    Mendoza, Antonio de **10** 494-495
    Portolá, Gaspar de **12** 408
    Revillagigedo, Conde de
       13 111-112
    Toledo, Francisco de **15** 257-259
    Velasco, Luis de **15** 450-451
    Velázquez de Cuéllar, Diego **15** 459
dictators
    Franco Bahamonde, Francisco
       6 52-54
    Primo de Rivera y Orbaneja, Miguel
       12 454-455
dukes
    Alba, Duke of **1** 103-104
    Godoy y Álvarez de Faria, Manuel
       de **6** 381-382
kings (Aragon)
    Peter III **12** 256-257
kings (Bourbon)

Alfonso XIII **1** 151
Charles III **3** 454-455
Charles IV **3** 456-457
Ferdinand VII **5** 418-420
Juan Carlos I **8** 368-369
Philip V **12** 276-277
kings (Castile and León)
    Alfonso VI **1** 149
    Alfonso X **1** 150-151
    Ferdinand V **5** 417-418
kings (Hapsburg)
    Charles II **3** 454
    Charles V **3** 457-459
    Philip II **12** 271-273
    Philip III **12** 273-274
    Philip IV **12** 275
kings (Napoleonic Era)
    Bonaparte, Joseph **2** 381-382
ministers
    Abravanel, Isaac ben Judah **1** 31
    Alarcón, Pedro Antonio de
       1 100-101
    López de Ayala, Pedro **9** 508-509
    Saavedra, Angel de **13** 398
presidents
    Azaña Diaz, Manuel **1** 396-397
prime ministers
    González Márquez, Felipe
       6 429-431
queens
    Isabella I **8** 144-145
    Isabella II **8** 145-146

Statesmen, Sri Lankan
Bandaranaike, Sirimavo **1** 486-488
Jayewardene, Junius Richard **8** 233-234
Premadasa, Ranasinghe **12** 437-439

Statesmen, Sudanese
Abboud, Ibrahim **1** 11-12
Ali, Sunni **1** 158-159
Azhari, Sayyid Ismail al- **1** 399-401
Khalil, Sayyid Abdullah **8** 531-532
Muhammad Ture, Askia **11** 231-232
Touré, Sékou **15** 275-277
Turabi, Hassan Abdullah al- **15** 344-345

Statesmen, Swedish
Charles XII **3** 464-466
Bernadotte, Jean Baptiste **2** 205-206
Christina of Sweden **4** 26-29
Gustavus I **7** 42-43
Gustavus II **7** 43-45
Gustavus III **7** 45-46
Hammarskjöld, Dag **7** 100-101
Margaret of Denmark **10** 250-252
Myrdal, Karl Gunnar **11** 284
Oxenstierna, Axel Gustafsson **12** 44-45

Statesmen, Syrian
'Aflaq, Michel **1** 73-74
Antiochus III **1** 249-250
Antiochus IV **1** 250
Assad, Hafiz **1** 346-348
Nureddin **11** 444-445
Saladin **13** 441-442

Statesmen, Tanzanian
Karume, Abeid Amani **8** 452-453

Kawawa, Rashidi Mfaume **8** 464-465
Nyerere, Julius Kamberage **11** 447-449

Statesmen, Thai
Bhumibol Adulyadej **2** 258-259
Chatichai Choonhavan **3** 479-480
Chulalongkorn **4** 43-45
Kukrit Pramoj, Momrajawong (M.R.)
    9 126-127
Mongkut **11** 104
Phibun Songkhram, Luang **12** 264-265
Prem Tinsulanonda **12** 437
Pridi Phanomyong **12** 449
Rama Khamhaeng **13** 11
Sarit Thanarat **13** 483-484

Thuringia (former German state)
Elizabeth of Hungary **5** 271-272

Statesmen, Tibetan
Dalai Lama **4** 369-371

Statesmen, Togolese
Olympio, Sylvanus E. **11** 506-507

Statesmen, Trinidadian
Padmore, George **12** 57-58

Statesmen, Tunisian
Bourguiba, Habib **2** 453-455
Zine el Abidine Ben Ali **16** 518-520

Statesmen, Turkish
Abdul-Hamid II **1** 17-18
Alp Arslan **1** 178-179
Atatürk, Ghazi Mustapha Kemal
    1 356-357
Çiller, Tansu **4** 59-60
Demirel, Süleyman **4** 490-493
Ecevit, Bülent **5** 196-197
Ibrahim Pasha **8** 97-98
Inönü, Ismet **8** 127-129
Köprülü, Ahmed **9** 84-85
Mahmud II **10** 145-147
Mehmed the Conqueror **10** 452-454
Osman I **12** 20-22
Özal, Turgut **12** 47-49
Selim I **14** 94-95
Selim III **14** 95-96
Suleiman I **15** 20-21

Statesmen, Turkish Cypriot
Denktash, Rauf **4** 500-502

Statesmen, Ugandan
Amin Dada, Idi **1** 202-204
Elizabeth Bagaaya Nyabongo of Toro
    5 269-271
Kiwanuka, Benedicto Kagima Mugum-
    ba **9** 46-47
Obote, Apolo Milton **11** 457

Statesmen, Ukrainian
Chmielnicki, Bogdan **4** 12-13
Kravchuk, Leonid Makarovych **9** 94-95
Mazepa, Ivan Stepanovich **10** 381

Statesmen, Uruguayan
Artigas, José Gervasio **1** 323
Batlle y Ordóñez, José **2** 58-59
Rivera, Fructuoso **13** 184-185
Rodó, José Enrique **13** 240-241
Terra, Gabriel **15** 154-155

Statesmen, Vandal
Gaiseric **6** 172

Statesmen, Venezuelan
Betancourt, Rómulo **2** 237-238
Blanco, Antonio Guzmán **2** 320-321
Caldera Rodríguez, Rafael **3** 218-219
Gallegos Freire, Rómulo **6** 185-186
Gómez, Juan Vicente **6** 417-418
Páez, José Antonio **12** 58
Pérez, Carlos Andrés **12** 212-214
Pérez Jiménez, Marcos **12** 217-218

Statesmen, Vietnamese
Do Muoi **5** 53-55
Le Duan **9** 278-280
Linh, Nguyen Van **9** 426-427
emperors
Bao Dai **1** 496-497
North
Dong, Pham Van **5** 57-59
Giap, Vo Nguyen **6** 297-299
Ho Chi Minh **7** 426-428
Truong Chinh **15** 319-320
South
Diem, Ngo Dinh **5** 6-7
Thieu, Nguyen Van **15** 182-183

Statesmen, Viking
Canute I, the Great **3** 266-269
Olaf I Tryggvason, King of Norway
11 490-493
Rollo **13** 264-265

Statesmen, Welsh
Glendower, Owen **6** 364-365
Kinnock, Neil **9** 29-30
Llewelyn ap Gruffydd **9** 468
see also Statesmen, British

Statesmen, Yemeni
Salih, 'Ali' Abdallah **13** 443-445

Statesmen, Yugoslav
Alexander of Yugoslavia **1** 136-137
Bulatovic, Momir **3** 115-116
Djilas, Milovan **5** 34
Gligorov, Kiro **6** 367-369
Tito, Marshal **15** 244-246
Tudjman, Franjo **15** 333-335

Statesmen, Zaïrese
Mobutu Sese Seko **11** 69-71
see also Statesmen, Congolese

Statesmen, Zambian
Kaunda, Kenneth David **8** 460-461

Statesmen, Zanzibari
Tippu Tip **15** 235-236

Statesmen, Zimbabwean
Mugabe, Robert Gabriel **11** 227-229
Nkomo, Joshua Mqabuko **11** 405-407

Statesmen, Zulu
Cetshwayo **3** 400
Dingane **5** 14-15
Luthuli, Albert John **10** 51-52

Statist school (historiography)
Klyuchevsky, Vasily Osipovich **9** 57-58

Statistical mechanics (physics)
Einstein, Albert **5** 228-231
Flory, Paul **5** 492-494
Gibbs, Josiah Willard **6** 302-303
Goeppert-Mayer, Maria **6** 385-387
Prichard, Diana García **12** 448-449
Yang, Chen Ning **16** 437-438

Statistics (mathematics)
Bertillon, Alphonse **2** 230-231
Chapin, (F.) Stuart **3** 437-438
Fisher, Irving **5** 462-463
Fisher, Ronald Aylmer **5** 463-464
Galton, Francis **6** 193-194
Gauss, Karl Friedrich **6** 240-242
Halley, Edmund **7** 88-89
Jevons, William Stanley **8** 255-256
Lorentz, Hendrik Antoon **9** 515-516
Louis, Pierre Charles Alexandre **9** 540
Mayo-Smith, Richmond **10** 371-372
Quételet, Lambert Adolphe Jacques
12 510-511

Statius, Caecilius (219?-166? B.C.), Roman
comedist
Ennius, Quintus **5** 289

Statius, Publius Papinius (45?-96?), Roman
poet
Martialis, Marcus Valerius **10** 286-287

Statue of Liberty (New York City)
Eiffel, Alexandre Gustave **5** 227-228
Lazarus, Emma **9** 260-261

Staunch Caspar ... (story)
Brentano, Clemens **2** 515-516

Staupitz, Johann (1468/69-1524), German
theologian
Luther, Martin **10** 48-51

Stead, William Thomas (1849-1912), English journalist
Booth, William **2** 405-406

Steam engine
Arkwright, Richard **1** 298
Black, Joseph **2** 303
Ericsson, John **5** 307-308
Evans, Oliver **5** 338
Newcomen, Thomas **11** 362
Smeaton, John **14** 280-281
Watt, James **16** 141-143

Steam turbine
Parsons, Charles Algernon **12** 120-121

Steamboat
Fitch, John **5** 467-468
Fulton, Robert **6** 151-152
Livingston, Robert R. **9** 462-463
Shreve, Henry Miller **14** 207
Stevens, John **14** 439-440

Steamship
Brunel, Isambard Kingdom **3** 69-70
Cavour, Conte di **3** 385-386
Collins, Edward Knight **4** 162-163
Perry, Matthew Calbraith **12** 237-239
Vanderbilt, Cornelius **15** 415-416
Wheelwright, William **16** 223-224

Stearns, Joyce Clennam (1893-1948),
American physicist
Compton, Arthur Holly **4** 186-188

Stechlin, Der (novel)
Fontane, Theodor **5** 504

Stedman, Edmund Clarence (1833-1908),
American poet and businessman
Markham, Edwin **10** 267

Steed, Henry Wickham (1871-1956), English journalist
Masaryk, Tomáš Garrigue **10** 314-315

STEEL, DANIELLE (born 1947), American
author and poet **14** 404-406

STEEL, DAVID MARTIN SCOTT (born
1938), Scottish member of Parliament
and leader of the Liberal Party
14 406-407

Steel industry
Australia
Lewis, Essington **9** 382-384
Europe
Bessemer, Henry **2** 235-236
Göring, Hermann Wilhelm
6 457-458
Krupp **9** 109-111
Monnet, Jean **11** 109-110
Schuman, Robert **14** 41
United States
see Business and industrial leaders,
American—iron and steel industry

Steel Pact (1939)
Mussolini, Benito **11** 272-274

Steel Workers Organizing Committee
(SWOC)
Murray, Philip **11** 264-265

STEELE, SIR RICHARD (1672-1729), British
essayist, dramatist, and politician
14 407-409
Addison, Joseph **1** 57-58
Berkeley, George **2** 197-198
Hallam, Lewis Sr. and Jr. **7** 87
Pope, Alexander **12** 395-397
Swift, Jonathan **15** 51-54

Steeple Bush (literature collection)
Frost, Robert Lee **6** 130-133

Stefan, Joseph (1835-1893), Austrian physicist
Boltzmann, Ludwig **2** 379-380

Stefano da Verona (1375-after 1438), Italian painter
Pisanello **12** 323-324

Stefano di Giovanni
see Sassetta

STEFANSSON, VILHJALMUR (1879-1962),
Canadian-American Arctic explorer and
scientist **14** 409-410
Wilkins, George Hubert **16** 281-282

Steffani, Agostino (1654-1728), Italian
composer
Handel, George Frederick **7** 116-119

STEFFENS, LINCOLN (1866-1936), American journalist **14** 410-411
Baker, Ray Stannard **1** 451-452
Dunne, Finley Peter **5** 147-148
Lindsey, Benjamin Barr **9** 425-426
Lippmann, Walter **9** 439-440
McClure, Samuel Sidney **10** 398-399
Reed, John Silas **13** 76-77
Tarbell, Ida Minerva **15** 107-108

STEICHEN, EDWARD (1879-1973), American photographer, painter, and museum curator **14** 411-412
Stieglitz, Alfred **14** 451-452

STEIN, BARON HEINRICH FRIEDRICH KARL VOM UND ZUM (1757-1831), Prussian statesman **14** 415-416
Frederick William III **6** 87
Hardenberg, Karl August von **7** 146-147
Metternich, Klemens von **10** 533-536
Scharnhorst, Gerhard Johann David von **13** 521-522

STEIN, EDITH (1891-1942), German philosopher **14** 412-414

STEIN, GERTRUDE (1874-1946), American writer **14** 414-415
Anderson, Sherwood **1** 220-221
Hemingway, Ernest Miller **7** 274-277
James, William **8** 215-217
Lipchitz, Jacques **9** 432-433
Picasso, Pablo **12** 292-295
Pound, Ezra Loomis **12** 415-417
Thomson, V. **15** 202-203
Wilder, Thornton Niven **16** 276-277

Stein, Leo (1872-1947), American art collector
Matisse, Henri **10** 336-337
Picasso, Pablo **12** 292-295
Stein, Gertrude **14** 414-415

STEINBECK, JOHN ERNST (1902-1968), American author **14** 416-417
Ford, John **6** 7-8

Steinberg, Maximilian Osseyevich (1883-1946), Russian composer
Shostakovich, Dmitri Dmitrievich **14** 204-205
Stravinsky, Igor Fedorovich **14** 502-506

STEINEM, GLORIA (born 1934), American feminist and journalist **14** 418-419

Steiner, Jacob (1796-1863), Swiss mathematician
Riemann, Georg Friedrich Bernard **13** 164-165

STEINMETZ, CHARLES PROTEUS (Karl August Rudolf Steinmetz; 1865-1923), German-born American mathematician and electrical engineer **14** 419-420
Dos Passos, John Roderigo **5** 69-71

Stella (literary character)
Sidney, Philip **14** 214-215
Swift, Jonathan **15** 51-54

STELLA, FRANK (born 1936), American painter **14** 420-422

STELLA, JOSEPH (1877-1946), Italian-born American painter **14** 422

Stella Dallas (film)
Goldwyn, Samuel **6** 416

Stellar parallax
see Star (astronomy)

Stellenbosch University (South Africa)
Vorster, Balthazar Johannes **16** 30-32

Stello (book)
Vigny, Comte de **15** 494-495

STENDHAL (Marie Henri Beyle; 1783-1842), French author **14** 422-425
Mérimée, Prosper **10** 517

STENO, NICOLAUS (Niels Stensen; 1638-86), Danish naturalist **14** 425-426

STEPHEN (1096?-1154), king of England 1135-54 **14** 426-427
David I **4** 407
Henry I **7** 286-287
Henry II **7** 287-289
William I **16** 290-291

STEPHEN I, KING OF HUNGARY (c. 973-1038) **14** 427-428

Stephen I, St. (died 257), pope 254-257
Cyprianus, Thascius Caecilianus **4** 361-362

Stephen II (died 757), pope 752-757
Charlemagne **3** 445-447

Stephen, George (1st Baron Mount Stephen; 1829-1921), Canadian financier
Smith, Donald Alexander **14** 288-289

Stephen, James (1758-1832), English lawyer and abolitionist
Wilberforce, William **16** 269-270

STEPHEN, SIR LESLIE (1832-1904), English historian **14** 429
Woolf, Virginia Stephen **16** 381-382

Stephen Báthory (1533-1586), king of Poland 1575-86
Gregory XIII **6** 534

STEPHEN HARDING, ST. (died 1134), English abbot and monastic reformer **14** 428-429

STEPHENS, ALEXANDER HAMILTON (1812-1883), American statesman **14** 429-430
Toombs, Robert Augustus **15** 267-268

STEPHENS, JAMES (1882-1950), Irish novelist and poet **14** 430-431
Colum, Padraic **4** 174-175

STEPHENS, URIAH (1821-1882), American labor leader **14** 431-432

STEPHENSON, GEORGE (1781-1848), English railway engineer **14** 432-433

STEPHENSON, ROBERT (1803-1859), English railway engineer **14** 432-433

STEPINAC, ALOJZIJE (1898-1960), Croatian nationalist, Catholic, and anti-Communist **14** 433-435

Steppe, The (story)
Chekhov, Anton Pavlovich **3** 494-497

Steppenwolf, Der (novel)
Hesse, Hermann **7** 367-369

Steps to the Temple (poems)
Crashaw, Richard **4** 296

Sterben (novella)
Schnitzler, Arthur **14** 23-24

Stereochemistry (science)
Pasteur, Louis **12** 125-127
Van't Hoff, Jacobus Hendricus **15** 431-432

STERN, OTTO (1888-1969), German-born American physicist **14** 435
Rabi, Isidor Isaac **12** 526-527

Stern der Ungeborenen (novel)
Werfel, Franz **16** 204-205

Stern des Bundes, Der (poems)
George, Stefan **6** 277-278

STERNE, LAURENCE (1713-1768), British novelist **14** 435-437
Boswell, James **2** 432-434
Brackenridge, Hugh Henry **2** 472-473
Burton, Robert **3** 166-167
Foscolo, Ugo **6** 21
Heine, Heinrich **7** 259-260
Irving, Washington **8** 141-143
Karamzin, Nikolai Mikhailovich **8** 441-442
Pushkin, Aleksandr Sergeevich **12** 489-491
Smollett, Tobias George **14** 305-307

STETTINIUS, EDWARD R., JR. (1900-1949), American industrialist and statesman **14** 437-438

STEUBEN, BARON FREDERICK WILLIAM AUGUSTUS VON (1730-1794), German officer in the American Revolution **14** 438-439

Stevedore (play; Sklar)
Robeson, Paul Leroy **13** 198-199

Stevedores (painting)
Portinari, Cândido **12** 407-408

STEVENS, JOHN (1749-1838), American engineer and inventor **14** 439-440

STEVENS, JOHN PAUL (born 1920), U.S. Supreme Court justice **14** 440-441

STEVENS, NETTIE MARIA (1861-1912), American biologist and geneticist **14** 441-442

STEVENS, THADDEUS (1792-1868), American politician **14** 442-443
Blaine, James Gillespie **2** 312-313
Conkling, Roscoe **4** 201-202
Johnson, Andrew **8** 294-295
Sumner, Charles **15** 30-31

STEVENS, WALLACE (1879-1955), American poet **14** 443-445
Lowell, Amy **10** 13
Moore, Marianne **11** 148-149
Williams, William Carlos **16** 308-309

STEVENSON, ADLAI EWING (1900-1965), American statesman and diplomat **14** 445-446

Dulles, John Foster **5** 134-135
Eisenhower, Dwight David **5** 233-236
Kennedy, John Fitzgerald **8** 502-506
McCarthy, Eugene Joseph **10** 386-388

Stevenson, Elizabeth Cleghorn
see Gaskell, Elizabeth

STEVENSON, ROBERT LOUIS
(1850-1894), Scottish novelist, essayist
and poet **14** 446-448
Hardy, Thomas **7** 150-152
Sargent, John Singer **13** 481-482

Stevin, Simon (1548-1620), Dutch mathematician
Maurice of Nassau **10** 348-349

Steward, Robert
see Robert II

STEWART, ALEXANDER TURNEY
(1803-1876), American dry-goods merchant **14** 448-449

STEWART, DUGALD (1753-1828), Scottish
philosopher **14** 449
Mill, James **11** 21
Reid, Thomas **13** 87-88

Stewart, Henry
see Darnley, Lord

Stewart, James
see Moray, Earl of

Stewart, John
see Cugoano, Ottobah

STEWART, POTTER (1915-1985), liberal
U.S. Supreme Court justice **14** 449-451

Stewart, Robert (1316-1390)
see Robert II

Stewart, Robert (1769-1822)
see Castlereagh, Viscount

St-Gildas-de-Rhuys, Abbey of (near Vannes,
France)
Abelard, Peter **1** 23-25

Stichus (play)
Plautus **12** 348-350

Stickeen (book)
Muir, John **11** 234

Sticks and Stones (book)
Mumford, Lewis **11** 246-247

STIEGEL, HENRY WILLIAM (1729-1785),
German born American iron founder and
glassmaker **14** 451

STIEGLITZ, ALFRED (1864-1946), Ameri-
can photographer, editor, and art gallery
director **14** 451-452
Dove, Arthur Garfield **5** 86-87
Hartley, Marsden **7** 186
Marin, John III **10** 259-260
O'Keeffe, Georgia **11** 487-489
Steichen, Edward **14** 411-412

Stigmata of St. Francis (painting)
Giotto **6** 342-345

Stiklestad, battle of (1030)
Olaf, II **11** 493-494

Stiles, Ezra (1727-1795), American educa-
tor
Dwight, Timothy **5** 169
Johnson, Samuel **8** 314-315
Pinto, Isaac **12** 318
Taylor, Edward **15** 122-123

Stiles College (Yale University)
Saarinen, Eliel and Eero **13** 396-398

STILICHO, FLAVIUS (died 408), Roman
general **14** 452-453
Alaric **1** 101-102

STILL, CLYFFORD (1904-1980), American
Abstract Expressionist artist **14** 453-454

Still Falls the Rain (composition)
Britten, Benjamin **3** 10-11

Still Glides the Stream (painting)
Streeton, Arthur Ernest **14** 507-508

STILL, WILLIAM (1821-1902), African
American abolitionist, philanthropist, and
businessman **14** 454-455

STILL, WILLIAM GRANT (born 1895),
African American composer **14** 455-456

Stiller, Mauritz (1883-1928), Swedish film
director
Garbo, Greta **6** 205-207

Stilo, Lucius Aelius Praeconinus (154?-74
B.C.), Roman philologist
Varro, Marcus Terentius **15** 438-439

STILWELL, JOSEPH WARREN (1883-1946),
American general **14** 456-457
Chiang Kai-shek **3** 510-513

STIMSON, HENRY LEWIS (1867-1950),
American lawyer and statesman
14 457-458
Frankfurter, Felix **6** 57
Hoover, Herbert Clark **7** 483-485
Kellogg, Frank Billings **8** 481
Taft, William Howard **15** 78-81

Stirling Bridge, battle of (1297)
Robert I **13** 192-194
Wallace, William **16** 75-76

Stirling Castle (near Bannockburn, Scotland)
Robert I **13** 192-194

STIRLING, JAMES (1926-1992), British
architect and city planner **14** 458-459

Stirling, "Lord"
see Alexander, William

STIRNER, MAX (1806-1856), German
philosopher **14** 459-460
Marx, Karl **10** 304-308
Mussolini, Benito **11** 272-274

Stock market (United States)
1929 crash
see Depression, Great (economics;
United States)
brokers
Buffett, Warren **3** 106-109
Merrill, Charles E. **10** 519-520
Regan, Donald **13** 80-81
market analysts

Merrill, Charles E. **10** 519-520
pegging the market
Cooke, Jay **4** 215-216
reorganization and regulation
Douglas, William Orville **5** 83-85
Fulbright, James William **6** 147-149
Lawson, Thomas William **9** 255-256
Martin, William McChesney Jr.
10 293-295
speculation
Fisk, James **5** 464-465
Gould, Jay **6** 470-472
Hill, James Jerome **7** 388-389
Schiff, Jacob Henry **14** 2-3
Vanderbilt, Cornelius **15** 415-416
stock watering
Drew, Daniel **5** 101-102
ticker perfected
Edison, Thomas Alva **5** 206-208

Stockhausen, Julius (1826-1906), German
singer and conductor
Brahms, Johannes **2** 490-492

STOCKHAUSEN, KARLHEINZ (born 1928),
German composer **14** 460-461
Berio, Luciano **2** 194-195
Boulez, Pierre **2** 444-445
Messiaen, Olivier **10** 528-529
Stravinsky, Igor Fedorovich **14** 502-506

Stockholm (city, Sweden)
Asplund, Eric Gunnar **1** 344
Berzelius, Jöns Jacob **2** 231-233
Gustavus I **7** 42-43

Stockmar, Baron Christian Friedrich von
(1787-1863), Anglo-Belgian statesman
Albert **1** 110-112
Victoria **15** 485-487

STOCKTON, ROBERT FIELD (1795-1866),
American naval officer and politician
14 461-462
Frémont, John Charles **6** 97-98
Kearny, Stephen Watts **8** 468-469

STODDARD, SOLOMON (1643-1728/29),
American colonial Congregational cler-
gyman **14** 462-463
Mather, Cotton **10** 330-332
Taylor, Edward **15** 122-123

Stoic, The (novel)
Dreiser, Herman Theodore **5** 98-100

Stoicism (philosophy)
adherents
Brutus, Marcus Junius **3** 79-80
Clement of Alexandria **4** 102-103
Cleomenes III **4** 103-104
Galen **6** 178-180
Marcus Aurelius Antoninus
10 243-245
Plotinus **12** 358-359
Ptolemy, Claudius **12** 473-474
Christianity and
Augustine **1** 367-370
Clement of Alexandria **4** 102-103
Isidore of Seville **8** 149-150
Justin Martyr **8** 395-396
critics

Carneades **3** 309
Seneca the Younger, Lucius Annaeus **14** 103-105
Valla, Lorenzo **15** 406
foundations
Chrysippus **4** 35-36
Heraclitus **7** 320
Zeno of Citium **16** 499-500
in literature
Cicero, Marcus Tullius **4** 55-58
Housman, Alfred Edward **7** 521-522
Marvell, Andrew **10** 301-303
influence of
Abravanel, Isaac ben Judah **1** 31
Epictetus **5** 292
Juvenal **8** 397-399
Philo Judaeus **12** 282-283
influenced by
Diogenes **5** 20-21

Stoke, Battle of (1487)
Henry VII **7** 300-302

STOKER, BRAM (Abraham Stoker;
1847-1912), Irish author **14** 463-464

Stoker, The (story)
Kafka, Franz **8** 403-406

STOKES, CARL B. (1927-1996), African
American politician **14** 464-465

Stokes' law (physics)
Millikan, Robert Andrews **11** 33-35

Stokowski, Leopold (1882-1977),
British-born American conductor
Garbo, Greta **6** 205-207

Stolen Kisses (film)
Truffaut, François **15** 311-313

STOLYPIN, PIOTR ARKADEVICH
(1862-1911), Russian statesman and
reformer **14** 465-466
Rasputin, Grigori Efimovich **13** 44-45

Stone, Barton W. (1772-1844), American
evangelist
Campbell, Alexander **3** 249-250

Stone Breakers (painting)
Courbet, Jean Desiré Gustave
4 271-273

STONE, EDWARD DURRELL (1902-1978),
American architect, educator, and designer **14** 466-468

STONE, OLIVER (born 1946), American
filmmaker **14** 472-475

Stone Flower (ballet)
Prokofiev, Sergei Sergeevich
12 458-460

Stone Guest, The (play and opera)
Pushkin, Aleksandr Sergeevich
12 489-491
Rimsky-Korsakov, Nikolai Andreevich
13 174-175

STONE, HARLAN FISKE (1872-1946),
American jurist; chief justice of U.S.
Supreme Court 1914-46 **14** 468-470
Cardozo, Benjamin Nathan **3** 288-290
Douglas, William Orville **5** 83-85

STONE, I. F. (Isador Feinstein; 1907-1989),
American journalist **14** 470-471

STONE, LUCY (1818-1893), American
abolitionist and women's suffrage leader
14 471-472
Bloomer, Amelia Jenks **2** 337
Howe, Julia Ward **7** 535-536

Stone Mountain (Georgia)
Borglum, John Gutzon de la Mothe
2 416-417

STONE, ROBERT ANTHONY (born 1937),
American novelist **14** 475-476

Stonehill scandal (Philippines; 1962)
Macapagal, Diosdado P. **10** 74-76

Stonemason's Yard (painting)
Canaletto **3** 257-258

Stones of Venice, The (book)
Ruskin, John **13** 371-372

Stones River, battle of (1863)
Thomas, George Henry **15** 190-191

Stonehenge (England)
Fischer von Erlach, Johann Bernhard
5 459-461
Petrie, William Matthew Flinders
12 261-262

Stoning of St. Stephen (painting)
Rembrandt Harmensz van Rijn
13 91-95

Stony Point, battle of (1779)
Wayne, Anthony **16** 149-150

Stoop House (Velp, Netherlands)
Rietveld, Gerrit Thomas **13** 169

Stop, Look, Listen (musical)
Berlin, Irving **2** 200-201

STOPES, MARIE (1880-1958), British scientist and birth control advocate
14 476-478

STOPPARD, THOMAS (Thomas Straussler;
born 1937), English playwright
14 478-479

Storm and Stress
see Sturm und Drang (German literary
movement)

Storm Effect... (painting)
Rousseau, Théodore **13** 328

Storm, The (poem)
Donne, John **5** 60-61

STORM, THEODOR (1817-1888), German
poet and novelist **14** 479-480
Tönnies, Ferdinand **15** 266-267

Storm troopers, Nazi (SA)
Göring, Hermann Wilhelm **6** 457-458

Storming the Citadel (painting)
Fragonard, Jean Honoré **6** 38-39

Stormy Sea (painting)
Ruisdael, Jacob van **13** 357-358

Storrs, Sir Ronald (1881-1955), British
administrator and historian
Lawrence, Thomas Edward **9** 253-254

STORY, JOSEPH (1779-1845), American
jurist and statesman **14** 480-481
Phillips, Wendell **12** 281-282
Sumner, Charles **15** 30-31

STOSS, VEIT (circa 1445-1533), German
sculptor **14** 481-482
Riemenschneider, Tilman **13** 166

STOUFFER, SAMUEL A. (1900-1960),
American sociologist and statistician
14 482-483

Stoughton House (Cambridge, Massachusetts)
Richardson, Henry Hobson **13** 139-141

Stout, Sir Robert (1844-1930), New
Zealand jurist and statesman
Vogel, Julius **16** 9-10

STOVALL, LUTHER McKINLEY (born
1937), American silkscreen artist
14 483-484

Stowe, Calvin (1802-1866), American educator
Cousin, Victor **4** 273-274

STOWE, HARRIET ELIZABETH BEECHER
(1811-1896), American writer
14 484-485
Bailey, Gamaliel **1** 444-445
Foster, Stephen Collins **6** 25-27
Garrett, Thomas **6** 225-226
Henson, Josiah **7** 311-312
Mather, Cotton **10** 330-332
Tappan brothers **15** 105-106
Turgenev, Ivan Sergeyevich **15** 345-348
Van Gogh, Vincent **15** 427-429
Weld, Theodore Dwight **16** 186

STRABO (circa 64 B.C.-circa A.D. 23),
Greek geographer and historian
14 485-486
Hipparchus **7** 407-408
Phidias **12** 265-267

STRACHAN, JOHN (1778-1867), Canadian
Anglican bishop **14** 486-487
Robinson, John Beverley **13** 210

STRACHEY, GILES LYTTON (1880-1932),
English biographer and critic known for
his satire of the Victorian era **14** 487-488
Arnold, Matthew **1** 311-313
Forster, Edward Morgan **6** 14-16
Gladstone, William Ewart **6** 357-360
Russell, Bertrand Arthur William
13 373-374
Stein, Gertrude **14** 414-415
Woolf, Virginia Stephen **16** 381-382

Strada, La (film)
Fellini, Federico **5** 408-409

STRADIVARI, ANTONIO (circa
1644-1737), Italian violin maker
14 488-490

STRAFFORD, 1ST EARL OF (Thomas Went-
worth; 1593-1641), English statesman
14 490-491
Charles, I **3** 450-452
Clarendon, 1st Earl of **4** 73-75
Laud, William **9** 224-225

Pym, John **12** 495-496

Strait Is the Gate (book)
Gide, André **6** 308-309

Strakhov, N. (1828-1896), Russian critic
Tolstoy, Leo **15** 262-265

Stralsund, fall of (1715)
Charles XII **3** 464-466

STRAND, MARK (born 1934), fourth Poet
Laureate of the United States **14** 491-493

STRANG, RUTH MAY (1895-1971), American educator **14** 493-494

Strang Clinic
Chinn, May Edward **3** 525-526

**Strange Case of Dr. Jekyll and Mr. Hyde,
The** (novel)
Stevenson, Robert Louis **14** 446-448

Strange Fruit (book)
Smith, Lillian Eugenia **14** 298-299

Strange Fugitive (novel)
Callaghan, Edward Morley **3** 229-230

Strange Interlude (play)
O'Neill, Eugene **11** 514-516

Strange Man, The (play)
Lermontov, Mikhail Yurievich
9 352-353

Strange particles (physics)
Gell-Mann, Murray **6** 257-258

Stranger, The (novel; Camus)
Camus, Albert **3** 255-257
Cela y Trulock, Camilo José **3** 389-390
Robbe-Grillet, Alain **13** 189-190

Stranger, The (play; Kotzebue)
Sheridan, Richard Brinsley **14** 183-184

Strangers and Brothers (novel series)
Snow, Charles Percy **14** 311-312

Strangers on a Train (film)
Hitchcock, Alfred **7** 415-416

Strangford Shield (sculpture)
Phidias **12** 265-267

STRASBERG, LEE (Israel Strasberg;
1901-82), American acting instructor,
director, and founding member of the
Group Theatre **14** 494-495

Strasbourg, Synod of (1533)
Schwenckfeld, Kasper von **14** 56-57

Strasbourg, University of (Germany)
Fustel de Coulanges, Numa Denis
6 155
Gilson, Étienne Henry **6** 327-328
Meinecke, Friedrich **10** 460-461
Pasteur, Louis **12** 125-127
Röntgen, Wilhelm Conrad **13** 273-275
Schmoller, Gustav Friedrich von **14** 21
Schweitzer, Albert **14** 55-56
Simmel, Georg **14** 234-235
Weidenreich, Franz **16** 171-172

Strassmann, Fritz (1902-1980), German
chemist
Hahn, Otto **7** 64-65
Szilard, Leo **15** 64-66

Strategic Air Command (United States military organization)
LeMay, Curtis E. **9** 316-318

Strategic Arms Limitations Treaty (SALT)
Kissinger, Henry Alfred **9** 43-45

Strathcona and Mount Royal, 1st Baron
see Smith, Donald Alexander

Stratosphere (physics)
Piccard, Auguste **12** 297-298

Stratton, Charles S.
see Tom Thumb, General

Straub, F. B. (born 1914), Hungarian biochemist
Szent-Györgyi, Albert von **15** 62-64

Straub, Johann Baptist (1704-1784), German sculptor
Günther, Ignaz **7** 41-42

STRAUS, ISIDOR (1845-1912), American
merchant **14** 496

Straus, Nathan (1848-1931), American
merchant
Straus, Isidor **14** 496

Straus, Oscar (1850-1926), American
lawyer and diplomat
Roosevelt, Theodore **13** 280-283

STRAUSS, DAVID FRIEDRICH
(1808-1874), German historian and
Protestant theologian **14** 496-497
Eliot, George **5** 254-256

STRAUSS, FRANZ JOSEF (1915-1988),
West German politician **14** 497-498

STRAUSS, JOHANN, JR. (1825-1899), Austrian composer **14** 498-499

Strauss, Johann, Sr. (1804-1849), Austrian
composer
Strauss, Johann Jr. **14** 498-499

STRAUSS, LEO (1899-1973), German Jewish Socratic political philosopher
14 499-500

STRAUSS, RICHARD (1864-1949), German
composer and conductor **14** 500-501
Hofmannsthal, Hugo von **7** 443-444
Honegger, Arthur **7** 472-473
Puccini, Giacomo **12** 474-476
Respighi, Ottorino **13** 103-104
Schoenberg, Arnold **14** 24-26
Szymanowski, Karol **15** 67-68
Varèse, Edgard **15** 432-433
Wagner, Richard **16** 40-43

STRAUSS, ROBERT SCHWARZ (born
1918), Democratic fundraiser and strategist **14** 501-502

STRAVINSKY, IGOR FEDOROVICH
(1882-1971), Russian-born composer
14 502-506
ballets
Cocteau, Jean **4** 132-133
Cunningham, Merce **4** 337-338
Graham, Martha **6** 485-486
Picasso, Pablo **12** 292-295
contemporaries
Holst, Gustav **7** 459-460

Messiaen, Olivier **10** 528-529
Prokofiev, Sergei Sergeevich
12 458-460
Rachmaninov, Sergei Vasilievich
12 531-532
Ravel, Maurice Joseph **13** 54-55
Shostakovich, Dmitri Dmitrievich
14 204-205
Thomas, Dylan Marlais **15** 188-190
critics
Boulez, Pierre **2** 444-445
Cage, John **3** 211-214
influence of
Copland, Aaron **4** 227-228
Debussy, Achille Claude **4** 445-447
Halffter, Christóbal **7** 79-80
Lutoslawski, Witold **10** 52-53
Malipiero, Gian Francesco **10** 171
Martinu, Bohuslav **10** 299-300
Roussel, Albert **13** 328-329
Szymanowski, Karol **15** 67-68
operas
Auden, Wystan Hugh **1** 364-366
portraits
Marini, Marino **10** 260-262

Straw, The (play)
O'Neill, Eugene **11** 514-516

STRAWSON, SIR PETER FREDRICK (born
1919), English philosopher **14** 506-507

Stray Dog (film)
Kurosawa, Akira **9** 135-137

Stray Dog, The (stories)
Hidayat, Sadiq **7** 377-378

Strayed Reveller, The (poems)
Arnold, Matthew **1** 311-313

Strayhorn, Billy (1915-1967), American
musician
Ellington, Edward Kennedy **5** 273-274

Stream of consciousness (literature)
Dos Passos, John Roderigo **5** 69-71
Faulkner, William **5** 395-397
Fellini, Federico **5** 408-409
James, William **8** 215-217
Joyce, James **8** 365-367
Schnitzler, Arthur **14** 23-24
Sterne, Laurence **14** 435-437
Woolf, Virginia Stephen **16** 381-382

Stream of thought (psychology)
James, William **8** 215-217

Street, George Edmund (1824-1881), Eng-
lish architect
Morris, William **11** 187-188
Shaw, Richard Norman **14** 167-168

Street, Julian (1879-1947), American writer
Tarkington, Newton Booth **15** 109

Street Musicians (painting)
Luz, Arturo Rogerio **10** 56-57

Street of Night (novel)
Dos Passos, John Roderigo **5** 69-71

Street Scene (play)
Rice, Elmer **13** 126-127
Weill, Kurt **16** 174-175

Street Songs (poems)
Sitwell, Edith **14** 265-266

Streetcar Named Desire, A (play)
Brando, Marlon **2** 497-499
Williams, Tennessee **16** 306-308

Streetcars
Johnson, Tom Loftin **8** 317
Sprague, Frank Julian **14** 385-386

STREETON, SIR ARTHUR ERNEST
(1867-1943), Australian landscape
painter **14** 507-508
Drysdale, George Russell **5** 107-109

Strength of the Strong, The (book)
London, Jack **9** 494-495

Streponni, Giuseppina (1815-1897), Italian
opera singer
Verdi, Giuseppe Fortunino Francesco
15 463-465

Streptomycin (medicine)
Domagk, Gerhard Johannes Paul
5 48-50
Dubos, René Jules **5** 119
Waksman, Selman Abraham **16** 49-50

STRESEMANN, GUSTAV (1878-1929),
German statesman and diplomat
14 508-509
Briand, Aristide **2** 528-529

Strickland, Susanna
see Moodie, Susanna

Strickland, William (1788-1854), American
architect
Latrobe, Benjamin Henry **9** 222-224

Strict Joy (poems)
Stephens, James **14** 430-431

Strictly Business (stories)
Henry, O. **7** 308-309

Stride toward Freedom (book)
King, Martin Luther Jr. **9** 20-22

Strife (play)
Galsworthy, John **6** 189-190

Strijdom, Johannes Gerhardus
(1893-1958), South African prime minister 1954-58
Verwoerd, Hendrik Frensch **15** 472-473

Strike (film)
Eisenstein, Sergei Mikhailovich
5 240-242

Strike (labor)
as weapon
Bieber, Owen **2** 266-268
Briand, Aristide **2** 528-529
Gompers, Samuel **6** 420-422
Hoffa, James R. **7** 436-437
Lewis, John Llewellyn **9** 387-388
Owen, Robert **12** 39-40
Sorel, Georges **14** 347-348
see also individual strikes
Federal intervention (United States)
Altgeld, John Peter **1** 180-182
Cleveland, Stephen Grover
4 108-110
Debs, Eugene Victor **4** 444-445

Garrett, John Work **6** 225
Harding, Warren Gamaliel
7 148-149
Roosevelt, Theodore **13** 280-283
labor opponents (United States)
Powderly, Terence Vincent
12 420-421
Sylvis, William **15** 60-61
right to strike (United States)
Bryant, William Cullen **3** 83-85
Carnegie, Andrew **3** 309-312
Gompers, Samuel **6** 420-422
Hanna, Marcus Alonzo **7** 127-128
Murphy, Frank **11** 260-261
Strikebreaking (United States)
Carnegie, Andrew **3** 309-312
Frick, Henry Clay **6** 108-109
Pinkerton, Allan **12** 314-315

Strike Up the Band (musical)
Gershwin, George **6** 284-285

STRINDBERG, AUGUST (1849-1912),
Swedish author **14** 509-511
Pirandello, Luigi **12** 319-321

String quartet
see Quartet (string)

Stripes (set of paintings)
Louis, Morris **9** 538-539

Strode, Ralph (1350-1400), English school-
man
Gower, John **6** 475-476

STROESSNER, ALFREDO (born 1912),
Paraguayan statesman **14** 511-512

Stroheim, Erich von (1885-1957),
Austrian-born American actor and film
director
Norris, Benjamin Franklin Jr.
11 427-428

STRONG, JOSIAH (1847-1916), American
clergyman and social activist **14** 512-513

Strong Breed, The (play)
Soyinka, Wole **14** 358-359

Strong Wind (novel)
Asturias, Miguel Angel **1** 354-355

Strontium (element—chemistry)
Davy, Humphry **4** 426-427

Strophe (poems)
Seferis, George **14** 84-85

Strossmayer, Joseph Georg (1815-1905),
Croatian Catholic prelate
Soloviev, Vladimir Sergeevich
14 329-330

Strozzi Altarpiece (painting)
Orcagna **11** 526-527

Strozzi, Bernardo (1581-1644), Italian
painter and engraver
Magnasco, Alessandro **10** 127-128

Strozzi Palace (Florence, Italy)
Sangallo family **13** 464-466

Structuralism (psychology)
Titchener, Edward Bradford **15** 241-242

Struggling (painting)
Marc, Franz **10** 231

Struhm, battle of (1629)
Gustavus II **7** 43-45

Strungk, Nicolas Adam (1640-1700), German musician
Corelli, Arcangelo **4** 230-231

Strutt, Jedediah (1726-1797), English cotton spinner and inventor
Slater, Samuel **14** 272-273

Strutt, John William
see Rayleigh, 3d Baron

**STRUVE, FRIEDRICH GEORG WILHELM
VON** (1793-1864), German-born Russian
astronomer and geodesist **14** 513

Struve, Otto Wilhelm (1819-1905), Russian
astronomer
Oort, Jan Hendrik **11** 523-524
Struve, Friedrich Georg Wilhelm von
14 513

Stuart, Charles
see Charles I and II (king of England)

Stuart, Esmé (1542?-1583), Scottish duke
of Lennox
James I **8** 204-206

STUART, GILBERT (1755-1828), American
painter **14** 513-515
Earl, Ralph **5** 179
Lichtenstein, Roy **9** 398-399
Morse, Samuel Finley Breese
11 192-193
Vanderlyn, John **15** 417

Stuart, House of
see Great Britain—1603-1714; Scotland

STUART, JAMES EWELL BROWN (Jeb;
1833-64), Confederate cavalry officer
14 515-516
Brown, John **3** 39-41

Stuart, James Francis Edward (1688-1766),
claimant to throne of England
Bolingbroke, Viscount **2** 374-375
Charles Edward Louis Philip Casimir
Stuart. **10** 466-467

Stuart, John
see Bute, 3d Earl of; Cugoano, Ottobah

Stuart, John McDouall (1815-1866), Scottish-born Australian explorer
Burke, Robert O'Hara **3** 142-143

Stuart, John T. (1807-1885), American
lawyer
Lincoln, Abraham **9** 415-418

Stuart Restoration
see Restoration, The (England; 1660)

Stuck, Franz von (1862-1928), German
painter and sculptor
Kandinsky, Wassily **8** 420-422
Klee, Paul **9** 47-49

**Student Nonviolent Coordinating Commit-
tee** (United States)
Barry, Marion Shepilov Jr. **2** 25-28
Bond, Julian **2** 386-387

Carmichael, Stokely **3** 305-308
Forman, James **6** 10-11
Hamer, Fannie Lou **7** 93-94
King, Martin Luther Jr. **9** 20-22
Lewis, John Robert **9** 388-390

Student protest
Burma
Aung San **1** 374-375
Nu, U **11** 439-441
China
Ch'en Tu-hsiu **3** 501-502
Ts'ai Yüan-p'ei **15** 322
Cuba
Castro Ruz, Fidel **3** 365-368
France
De Gaulle, Charles André Joseph
Marie **4** 463-465
Marcuse, Herbert **10** 245-247
Japan
Kishi, Nobusuke **9** 41-43
Sato, Eisaku **13** 495-496
Korea (South)
Rhee, Syngman **13** 117-120
Peru
Haya de la Torre, Victor Raul
7 216-217
Russia
Nicholas II **11** 378-380
Sudan
Abboud, Ibrahim **1** 11-12
Azhari, Sayyid Ismail al- **1** 399-401
Thailand
Sarit Thanarat **13** 483-484
United States
Douglas, William Orville **5** 83-85
see also Civil disobedience; Nonvio-
lent protest movements; Passive
resistance movements
Venezuela
Gómez, Juan Vicente **6** 417-418

Student Volunteer movement (United
States)
Moody, Dwight L. **11** 141-142
Mott, John R. **11** 212

Studenti, I (comedy)
Ariosto, Ludovico **1** 289-290

STUDI, WES (born Wesley Studie; born
circa 1944), Native American actor
15 1-2

Studio Building (New York City)
Hunt, Richard Morris **8** 44

Studio Interior (painting)
Demuth, Charles **4** 497-498
Kline, Franz **9** 55

Studio, The (painting)
Corot, Jean Baptiste Camille **4** 247-249
Courbet, Jean Desiré Gustave
4 271-273
Le Nain, Antoine, Louis and Mathieu
9 321-322

Studs Lonigan (trilogy)
Farrell, James Thomas **5** 390-391

Study in Scarlet, A (novel)
Doyle, Arthur Conan **5** 91-92

Study of Provincial Life, A
see Middlemarch

Study of Thinking, A (book)
Bruner, Jerome Seymour **3** 72-73

Stukeley, William (1687-1765), English
writer
Newton, Isaac **11** 369-372

Stump Speaking (painting)
Bingham, George Caleb **2** 278-279

Stumpf, Carl (1848-1936), German
philosopher and psychologist
Husserl, Edmund **8** 67-68
Lotze, Rudolf Hermann **9** 521-522

Stunde hinter Mitternacht, Eine (book)
Hesse, Hermann **7** 367-369

Stundenbuch, Das (poems)
Rilke, Rainer Maria **13** 171-172

Sture, Sten, the Elder (1440?-1503), regent
of Sweden 1470-1503
Gustavus I **7** 42-43

STURLUSON, SNORRI (1179-1241), Icelandic statesman and historian
14 310-311
Harold I **7** 161-162

Sturm, John (1507-1589), German educator
Ramus, Petrus **13** 27-28

Sturm und Drang movement (German liter-
ature)
Goethe, Johann Wolfgang von
6 388-391
Hamann, Johann Georg **7** 92
Klopstock, Friedrich Gottlieb **9** 55-56
Lessing, Gotthold Ephraim **9** 357-359
Schiller, Johann Christoph Friedrich von
14 4-7
Wieland, Christoph Martin **16** 260-261
Wordsworth, William **16** 385-388

STURT, CHARLES (1795-1869), British officer, explorer, and colonial administrator
15 2-3

STURTEVANT, A. H. (Alfred Henry Sturtevant; 1891-1970), American geneticist
15 3-5

Sturzo, Don Luigi (1871-1959), Italian
political leader
De Gasperi, Alcide **4** 462-463

Stuttgart (City, Germany)
Le Corbusier **9** 274-275

STUYVESANT, PETER (circa 1610-72),
Dutch colonial administrator **15** 5-6
Underhill, John **15** 388

Style (essay)
Pater, Walter Horatio **12** 130-131

Style, the
see De Stijl

STYRON, WILLIAM (born 1925), American
southern writer of novels and articles
15 6-8

Su Ch'e (1039-1112), Chinese author
Su Shih **15** 39-40
Wang An-shih **16** 95-97

Su Hsün (1009-1066), Chinese author
Su-Shih **15** 39-40

SU-SHIH (Su Tung-p'o; 1037-1101), Chi-
nese author and artist **15** 39-40
Mi Fei **11** 12-13
Ou-yang Hsiu **12** 33-34
Wang An-shih **16** 95-97
Wang Wei **16** 106-108

SUÁREZ, FRANCISCO (1548-1617), Spanish philosopher and theologian **15** 8

Suárez de Figueroa, Gòmez
see Garcilaso de la Vega, Inca

SUAZO CÓRDOVA, ROBERTO (born
1927), physician and president of Honduras (1982-1986) **15** 8-10

Subjectivism (philosophy)
Descartes, René **4** 505-508
Fichte, Johann Gottlieb **5** 435-436
Jaspers, Karl **8** 225-226
Stirner, Max **14** 459-460

Subjects of the Artist (art school)
Motherwell, Robert **11** 210-211
Newman, Barnett **11** 365
Rothko, Mark **13** 320-321

Sublette, William (1799?-1845), American
soldier and fur trader
Smith, Jedediah S. **14** 294-295

Submarines
development
Fulton, Robert **6** 151-152
Haldane, John Burdon Sanderson
7 70-71
Holland, John Philip **7** 453-454
polar exploration
Wilkins, George Hubert **16** 281-282
warfare
Colt, Samuel **4** 172-173
Erzberger, Matthias **5** 319-320
Hitchcock, Gilbert Monell
7 416-417
Ludendorff, Erich Friedrich Wilhelm
10 27-28
Millikan, Robert Andrews **11** 33-35
Sims, William Sowden **14** 244
Wilson, Thomas Woodrow
16 330-332

Subuktigin, Emir (died 997), Moslem sultan
of Ghazni 977-997
Mahmud of Ghazni **10** 147

Suburb in Havana (painting)
de Kooning, Willem **4** 468-469

Subway, The (play)
Rice, Elmer **13** 126-127

Success (novel)
Feuchtwanger, Lion **5** 430-432

Succession, Act of (1534; England)
Henry VIII **7** 302-305
Mary **10** 308

Such Is Life (novel; Furphy)
  Franklin, Stella Maraia Sarah Miles
    6 68-69
  Furphy, Joseph **6** 152-153

Such Is Life (play)
  Toller, Ernst **15** 261
  Wedekind, Frank **16** 166-167

Such Is My Beloved (novel)
  Callaghan, Edward Morley **3** 229-230

Such Stuff as Dreams (poems)
  Russell, Charles Edward **13** 374-375

SUCKLING, SIR JOHN (1609-1642), English poet and playwright **15** 10-11
  Crashaw, Richard **4** 296

SUCRE, ANTONIO JOSÉ DE (1795-1830), Venezuelan general, Bolivian president 1826-28 **15** 11-12
  Bolívar, Simón **2** 375-377
  Flores, Juan José **5** 491

Sudan, Republic of the (nation, North East Africa)
  British in
    Baker, Samuel White **1** 454-455
    Gladstone, William Ewart
      6 357-360
    Gordon, Charles George **6** 448-449
    Kitchener, Horatio Herbert **9** 45-46
  Ethiopia and
    Johannes IV **8** 272-273
    Menelik II **10** 495-497
  exploration
    Barth, Heinrich **2** 30-31
    Marchand, Jean-Baptiste
      10 234-237
  independence (1956)
    Abboud, Ibrahim **1** 11-12
    Azhari, Sayyid Ismail al- **1** 399-401
    Khalil, Sayyid Abdullah **8** 531-532
  leadership
    Turabi, Hassan Abdullah al-
      15 344-345
  Mahdist state
    Cromer, 1st Earl of **4** 317
    Mahdi **10** 137-138
  Mandingo state
    Touré, Sékou **15** 275-277
  Songhay empire
    Ali, Sunni **1** 158-159
    Muhammad Ture, Askia **11** 231-232
  Tokolar empire
    Omar ibn Said Tal, Al-Hajj
      11 509-510

Sudanese Republic (West Africa)
  see Maili Republic

Sudbury, Simon (died 1381), English prelate
  Chaucer, Geoffrey **3** 482-485

Suddenly Last Summer (play)
  Williams, Tennessee **16** 306-308

SUDERMANN, HERMANN (1857-1928), German dramatist and novelist **15** 12-13

Sudetenland (region, Northern Czechoslovakia)

  Beneš, Edward **2** 155-157
  Hitler, Adolf **7** 417-420

Sue, Eugène (Marie Joseph Sue; 1804-57), French novelist
  Bonifacio, Andres **2** 393-394

Sueños, Los (book)
  Quevedo Y Villegas, Francisco Gómez
    de **12** 511

SUETONIUS TRANQUILLUS, GAIUS
  (circa 70-circa 135), Roman administrator
  and writer **15** 13
  Augustus **1** 371-373
  Caligula **3** 228-229
  Domitian **5** 52-53
  Horace **7** 500-503
  Jesus of Nazareth **8** 251-255
  Nero Claudius Caesar **11** 342-344
  Tacitus **15** 70-72
  Terence **15** 146-148
  Tiberius Julius Caesar Augustus
    15 217-218

Suevians (German people)
  Ricimer, Flavius **13** 151-152

Suez Canal
  Disraeli, Benjamin **5** 27-29
  Gladstone, William Ewart **6** 357-360
  Ismail Pasha **8** 150-151
  Johannes IV **8** 272-273
  Lesseps, Vicomte de **9** 354-355
  Verdi, Giuseppe Fortunino Francesco
    15 463-465
  Victoria **15** 485-487
  Whitman, Walt **16** 249-251
  see also Suez Crisis (1956)

Suez Crisis (1956)
  British invasion
    Eden, Anthony **5** 204-205
    Macmillan, Harold **10** 112-113
  Israeli blockade
    Dayan, Moshe **4** 429-431
  nationalization
    Nasser, Gamal Abdel **11** 317-318
  United Nations action
    Bunche, Ralph Johnson **3** 121-122
    Hammarskjöld, Dag **7** 100-101
    Pearson, Lester Bowles **12** 174-175
  world reaction
    Dulles, John Foster **5** 134-135
    Eisenhower, Dwight David
      5 233-236
    Menzies, Robert Gordon
      10 510-511
    Pandit, Vijaya Lakshmi **12** 83-84
    St. Laurent, Louis Stephen **13** 434

Suffolk, Earl of
  see Pole, Michael de la

Suffolk, William, 1st Duke of (William de
la Pole; 1396-1450),
  Henry VI **7** 298-299
  Margaret of Anjou **10** 249-250

Suffrage (voting rights)
  Canada
    McClung, Nellie Letitia **10** 396-397

Europe
  Albert I **1** 112
  Alexander I **1** 130-132
  Alexander II **1** 132-133
  Alexander III **1** 133-134
  Condorcet, Marquis de **4** 195-196
  Ferdinand **5** 413-414
  Giolitti, Giovanni **6** 339-340
  Lassalle, Ferdinand **9** 216
  Leopold II **9** 346-347
Hawaii
  Kamehameha III **8** 416-417
South Africa
  Jonathan, Joseph Leabua **8** 330-331
United States (19th-20th century)
  Alcorn, James Lusk **1** 120-121
  Brownlow, William Gannaway
    3 55-56
  Coffin, Levi **4** 135
  Eisenhower, Dwight David
    5 233-236
  Johnson, Lyndon Baines **8** 308-312
  see also Constitution of the United
    States—Amendments (16th; 19th);
    Women's suffrage
United States (colonial; 17th century)
  Bacon, Nathaniel **1** 424-425
  Calvert, Charles **3** 238
Venezuela
  Blanco, Antonio Guzmán **2** 320-321

Sufism (Islamic mysticism)
  Darqāwī-'Alawī order
    Aiken, Conrad **1** 90-91
  in literature
    Attar, Farid ed-Din **1** 359-360
    Hafiz, Shams al-Din **7** 63
    Jami **8** 218-219
    Rumi, Jalai ed-Din **13** 362-363
  theology and philosophy
    Aiken, Conrad **1** 90-91
    Ghazali, Abu Hamid Muhammad
      al- **6** 290-291
    Hallaj, Al-Husayn ibn Mansur al-
      7 86-87
    Ibn al-Arabi, Muhyi al-Din **8** 91
    Junayd, Abu al-Qasim ibn Muhammad al **8** 388

Sugar
  as food product
    Couper, James Hamilton **4** 270
    Gómez, Máximo **6** 418-419
    John Maurice of Nassau **8** 281-282
    Machado y Morales, Gerardo
      10 92-93
    Menocal, Mario Garcia **10** 506-507
  scientific research
    Bernard, Claude **2** 208-210
    Cori, Gerty T. **4** 231-234
    Fischer, Emil **5** 456-457
    Schwann, Theodor **14** 51-52

Sugar Act (1764; colonial America)
  Adams, Samuel **1** 55-56
  Hutchinson, Thomas **8** 71-72
  Otis, James Jr. **12** 25-27

Sugaring Off (painting)
Moses, Grandma **11** 201-202

Suger (1081?-1151), French prelate, regent 1147-49
Louis VI **9** 523-524
Louis VII **9** 524-525

SUHARTO (born 1921), second president after Indonesia's independence **15** 14-15
Sukarno **15** 18-20

Suhrawardi, Shaikh Shihabud-Din (1138-1193), Sufi philosopher
Sadi, Shaikh Muslih-al-Din **13** 419-420
Saladin **13** 441-442

Sui (Chinese dynasty; reigned 581-618)
Chih-i **3** 518-519
Hsüan Tsang **8** 6-7
Sui Wen-ti **15** 16-18
T'ai-tsung, T'ang **15** 83-84
Tao-hsüan **15** 105

SUI WEN-TI (541-604) Chinese emperor **15** 16-18

Suidas (10th century lexicon)
Callimachus **3** 235-236
Eratosthenes of Cyrene **5** 301-302
Plutarch **12** 359-360

SUIKO (554-628), empress of Japan 593-628 **15** 15-16
Shotoku Taishi **14** 205-207

Sujun (reigned 588-593), emperor of Japan
Suiko **15** 15-16

Suk, Josef (1874-1935), Czech composer
Martinu, Bohuslav **10** 299-300

SUKARNO (1901-1970), Indonesian statesman, president 1945-66 **15** 18-20
Hatta, Mohammad **7** 197-199
Macapagal, Diosdado P. **10** 74-76
Sihanouk, Norodom **14** 222-223

Sukchong (reigned 1674-1720), king of Korea
Yongjo **16** 461-462

Sukenobu (1671-1751), Japanese printmaker
Harunobu, Suzuki **7** 188-189

Sukhodol (novel)
Bunin, Ivan Alekseevich **3** 124

Sukhothai (state, Indochina)
Rama Khamhaeng **13** 11

Suleiman (Kilij Arslan I; died 1108), Seljuk sultan
Alp Arslan **1** 178-179

SULEIMAN I (the Magnificent; 1494-1566), Ottoman sultan 1520-66 **15** 20-21
Selim I **14** 94-95
Sinan, Kodja Mimar **14** 245-246

Suleimaniye (mosque; Istanbul)
Sinan, Kodja Mimar **14** 245-246

Sulfanilamide (medicine)
Domagk, Gerhard Johannes Paul **5** 48-50

Sulfide (chemistry)
Sabatier, Paul **13** 398-399

Sulfur (element—chemistry)
Avogadro, Lorenzo Romano Amedeo Carlo **1** 388-389
Lavoisier, Antoine Laurent **9** 241-244

SULLA, LUCIUS CORNELIUS I (138-78 B.C.), Roman general, dictator 82-79 B.C. **15** 21-22
Brutus, Marcus Junius **3** 79-80
Caesar, Gaius Julius **3** 207-210
Catiline **3** 372-373
Cicero, Marcus Tullius **4** 55-58
Crassus Dives, Marcus Licinius **4** 296-297
Marius, Gaius **10** 264-265
Pompey **12** 387-389

Sullivan and Cromwell (law firm)
Dulles, John Foster **5** 134-135
Stone, Harlan Fiske **14** 468-470

Sullivan, Anne Mansfield (Mrs. John Albert Macy; 1887-1936), American educator and lecturer
Keller, Helen Adams **8** 479-480

Sullivan County Sketches (essays)
Crane, Stephen **4** 293-295

SULLIVAN, HARRY STACK (1892-1949), American psychiatrist **15** 23-24
Horney, Karen Danielsen **7** 508-509

Sullivan, John (1740-1795), American Revolutionary officer
Butler, John **3** 180

SULLIVAN, JOHN LAWRENCE (1858-1918), American boxer **15** 24-25
Lindsay, Vachel **9** 424-425

SULLIVAN, LEON HOWARD (born 1922), African American civil rights leader and minister **15** 25-27

SULLIVAN, LOUIS HENRI (1856-1924), American architect **15** 27-28
Davis, Alexander Jackson **4** 411
Mumford, Lewis **11** 246-247
Neutra, Richard Joseph **11** 355-356
Richardson, Henry Hobson **13** 139-141
Saarinen, Eliel and Eero **13** 396-398
White, Stanford **16** 235-236
Wright, Frank Lloyd **16** 398-401

SULLIVAN, SIR ARTHUR SEYMOUR (1842-1900), English composer **15** 23
Gilbert, William Schwenck **6** 314-315
Sousa, John Philip **14** 353-354

Sully, Duc de (Maximilien de Bethune; 1560-1641), French statesman
Henry IV **7** 293-295
Saint-Pierre, Abbé de **13** 434-435
Voltaire **16** 14-16

Sully, Thomas (1783-1872), English-born American painter
Allston, Washington **1** 176-177
Stuart, Gilbert **14** 513-515

Sulpicius Rufus, Publius (121?-88 B.C.) Roman statesman
Sulla, Lucius Cornelius I **15** 21-22

Sultans
see Statesman

SULZBERGER, ARTHUR OCHS (born 1926), publisher of the *New York Times* **15** 28-30

Sumatra (island)
see Indonesia

Summae (theology)
Bonaventure **2** 383-384
Thomas Aquinas **15** 183-186
see also Sentences (book; Lombard)

Summer (painting)
Poussin, Nicolas **12** 418-420

Summer (poem)
Thomson, James **15** 199-200

Summer and Smoke (play)
Williams, Tennessee **16** 306-308

Summerhill School (near Dresden, Germany)
Neill, Alexander Sutherland **11** 335-336

Summon the Serpents (poem)
Bialik, Hayyim Nahman **2** 262-263

SUMNER, CHARLES (1811-1874), American statesman **15** 30-31
Chase, Salmon Portland **3** 473-475
Child, Lydia Maria Francis **3** 520-521
Dix, Dorothea Lynde **5** 32-33
Douglas, Stephen Arnold **5** 80-82
Fish, Hamilton **5** 461-462
Lamar, Lucius Quintus Cincinnatus **9** 170-171
Parker, Theodore **12** 112-113

Sumner, James Batcheller (1887-1955), American biochemist
Stanley, Wendell Meredith **14** 400-401

SUMNER, WILLIAM GRAHAM (1840-1910), American sociologist and educator **15** 32
Fisher, Irving **5** 462-463
Osgood, Herbert Levi **12** 18-19
Spencer, Herbert **14** 369-370

Sumter (ship)
Semmes, Raphael **14** 102-103

Sumter, Thomas (1734-1832), American Revolutionary officer
Allen, Ethan **1** 163-164
Tarleton, Banastre **15** 110

Sun (novelette)
Lawrence, David Herbert **9** 247-248

Sun (star)
Anaxagoras **1** 208-209
Aristarchus of Samos **1** 290-291
Fizeau, Hippolyte Armand Louis **5** 475
Shapley, Harlow **14** 155-156
see also Solar system; Sunspots

Sun Also Rises, The (novel; Hemingway)
Fitzgerald, Francis Scott Key **5** 470-472
Hemingway, Ernest Miller **7** 274-277

Sun disk cult
see Aten (Egyptian god)

Sun Djata
see Sundiata Keita

Sun Fo (born 1891), Chinese Nationalist official
Sun Yat-sen **15** 35-39

Sun of Natal, The (Zulu newspaper)
Dube, John Langalibalele **5** 113

Sun worship (pagan religion)
Julian **8** 378-379

SUN YAT-SEN (1866-1925), Chinese states-man, leader of republican revolution **15** 35-39
biographers
Buck, Pearl Sydenstricker **3** 91-93
influenced by
Wang Yang-ming **16** 108-109
Kuomintang
Ch'en Tu-hsiu **3** 501-502
Chiang Kai-shek **3** 510-513
Chou En-lai **4** 20-22
Chu Teh **4** 54-55
Wang Ching-wei **16** 98
supporters
Song Sisters **14** 338-341
T'ung-meng hui
Yen Hsi-shan **16** 452-453
Yüan Shih-k'ai **16** 480-481

Sun Yat-sen, Madame (1890-1981), Chinese politician and welfare worker
Chiang Kai-shek **3** 510-513
Sun Yat-sen **15** 35-39

Sunantha (died 1880), Thai queen
Chulalongkorn **4** 43-45

Sunday Afternoon on the Island of La Grande Jatte, A (painting)
Seurat, Georges Pierre **14** 120-122

Sunday School Assembly (Lake Chatauqua, New York State)
Vincent, John Heyl **15** 502-503

SUNDAY, WILLIAM ASHLEY ("Billy"; 1862-1935), American evangelist **15** 32-33
Graham, William Franklin Jr. **6** 487-488

Sunderland, 3d Earl of (Charles Spencer; 1674-1722), English statesman
Walpole, Robert **16** 82-84

Sundial (instrument)
Anaximander **1** 209-210

SUNDIATA KEITA (circa 1210-circa 1260), founder of Mali empire in West Africa **15** 33-34

Sung (Chinese dynasty)
Northern (reigned 960-1127)
Chao Meng-fu **3** 436-437
Ch'in Kuei **3** 524-525
Chu Hsi **4** 40-43
Fan Chung-yen **5** 376-377
Hui-Tsung **8** 25
Kim Pusik **9** 8-9
Kwangjong **9** 140
Mi Fei **11** 12-13
Ou-yang Hsiu **12** 33-34
Zhao Kuang-yin **16** 505-508
Southern (reigned 1127-1279)
Chia Ssu-tao **3** 514-515

Ch'in Kuei **3** 524-525
Chu Hsi **4** 40-43
Kao-tsung **8** 433
Kublai Khan **9** 115-118
Wen T'ien-hsiang **16** 203
Ma Yüan **10** 379

Sung Chiao-jen (died 1913), Chinese revolutionary
Sun Yat-sen **15** 35-39
Yüan Shih-k'ai **16** 480-481

Sung Ch'ing-ling
see Sun Yat-sen, Madame

Sung T'ai-tsu
see Zhao Kuang-yin

Sunken Bell, The (opera)
Respighi, Ottorino **13** 103-104

Sunken Bell, The (play)
Hauptmann, Gerhart Johann Robert **7** 199-201

Sunnites (Islamic sect)
Bukhari, Muhammad ibn Ismail al- **3** 111-112
Mahmud of Ghazni **10** 147
Nureddin **11** 444-445
see also Shiites

Sunnyside (Tarrytown, New York State)
Irving, Washington **8** 141-143

Sunset Gun (poems)
Parker, Dorothy Rothschild **12** 106

Sunset near Arbonne (painting)
Rousseau, Théodore **13** 328

Sunspots (astronomy)
Galileo Galilei **6** 180-183
Langley, Samuel Pierpont **9** 195-196

Suo marito (novel)
Pirandello, Luigi **12** 319-321

Suomussalmi war memorial (Finland)
Aalto, Hugo Alvar Henrik **1** 1-2

Suor Angelica (opera)
Puccini, Giacomo **12** 474-476

Superbi colli e voi sacre ruine (sonnet)
Castiglione, Baldassare **3** 360-361

Superconductivity (electrical)
Bardeen, John **2** 1-3
Chu, Paul Ching-Wu **4** 37-39
Kamerlingh Onnes, Heike **8** 418-420
Müller, Karl Alexander **11** 240-241

Superfluidity (physics)
Kapitsa, Pyotr Leonidovich **8** 433-435

Superga, La (church; Turin, Italy)
Juvara, Filippo **8** 396-397

Superheterodyne circuit (electrical)
Armstrong, Edwin Howard **1** 302-303

Superior, Lake (United States-Canada)
Brûlé, Étienne **3** 67-68
Carver, Jonathan **3** 347-348

Superman theory (philosophy)
Dostoevsky, Fyodor **5** 74-77
Nietzsche, Friedrich **11** 390-392

Schweitzer, Albert **14** 55-56

Supernatural (religion)
Hugo, Victor Marie **8** 22-25
Schleiermacher, Friedrich Ernst Daniel **14** 11-12

Supernova (astronomy)
Oort, Jan Hendrik **11** 523-524

Superposition, law of (geology)
Steno, Nicolaus **14** 425-426

Superstition
Hippocrates **7** 408-410
Jung, Carl Gustav **8** 388-389
Wang Ch'ung **16** 98-99

Superstition and Force (book)
Lea, Henry Charles **9** 261-262

Supper at Emmaus (painting)
Veronese, Paolo **15** 469-470

Supper Table (painting)
Davis, Stuart **4** 424-425

Suppliants, The (play)
Aeschylus **1** 70-72
Euripides **5** 332-334

Supply-side economics
Kemp, Jack French Jr. **8** 491-493

Suppositi, I (comedy; Ariosto)
Ariosto, Ludovico **1** 289-290
Plautus **12** 348-350

Supralapsarianism (religion)
Arminius, Jacobus **1** 301-302

Suprarenal glands
see Adrenal glands

Supremacy and Conformity, Acts of (England)
Elizabeth I **5** 263-266
Henry VIII **7** 302-305

Suprematism (art)
Malevich, Kasimir **10** 168-169
Pevsner, Antoine **12** 263-264

Supreme Council for National Reconstruction (South Korea)
Park, Chung Hee **12** 99-102

Supreme Court (United States)
administrative reform
Burger, Warren E. **3** 133-136
Warren, Earl **16** 117-120
and executive privilege
Sirica, John Joseph **14** 257-258
antitrust cases
Duke, James Buchanan **5** 133-134
Gary, Elbert Henry **6** 229-230
Harriman, Edward Henry **7** 164-165
Hill, James Jerome **7** 388-389
Rockefeller, John Davison **13** 226-228
White, Edward Douglass **16** 230-231
building
Morrill, Justin Smith **11** 182
Taft, William Howard **15** 78-81
citizen's test suits
Warren, Earl **16** 117-120

civil liberties cases (19th century)
    Chase, Salmon Portland **3** 473-475
    Cinque, Joseph **4** 62
    Garrett, Thomas **6** 225-226
    Harlan, John Marshall **7** 156-157
    Miller, Samuel Freeman **11** 29-30
    Scott, Dred **14** 65-66
    Turner, Henry McNeal **15** 351-352
    Waite, Morrison Remick **16** 46
civil liberties cases (20th century)
    Black, Hugo Lafayette **2** 301-303
    Blackmun, Harry **2** 309-310
    Brandeis, Louis Dembitz **2** 496-497
    Brennan, William J. Jr. **2** 514-515
    Cardozo, Benjamin Nathan
      3 288-290
    Douglas, William Orville **5** 83-85
    Eisenhower, Dwight David
      5 233-236
    Frankfurter, Felix **6** 57
    Harlan, John Marshall **7** 156-157
    Holmes, Oliver Wendell Jr.
      7 458-459
    Hughes, Charles Evans **8** 15-16
    Jackson, Robert Houghwout
      8 182-183
    King, Martin Luther Jr. **9** 20-22
    Marshall, Thurgood **10** 282-284
    Rehnquist, William Hubbs **13** 82-84
    Stevens, John Paul **14** 440-441
    Stewart, Potter **14** 449-451
    Vinson, Fred **15** 503-505
    Warren, Earl **16** 117-120
consensus-builders
    Breyer, Stephen **2** 524-527
conservative justices
    Kennedy, Anthony M. **8** 498-500
    Souter, David H. **14** 355-356
conservative leaders
    Rehnquist, William Hubbs **13** 82-84
    Thomas, Clarence **15** 186-188
constitutional law
    Blackmun, Harry **2** 309-310
    Cardozo, Benjamin Nathan
      3 288-290
    Holmes, Oliver Wendell Jr.
      7 458-459
    Marshall, John **10** 279-281
    Taney, Roger Brooke **15** 98-99
court packing
    Harding, Warren Gamaliel
      7 148-149
    Hughes, Charles Evans **8** 15-16
    Johnson, Lyndon Baines **8** 308-312
    Roosevelt, Franklin Delano
      13 277-280
federalism
    Harlan, John Marshall **7** 157-159
judicial neutrality
    Douglas, William Orville **5** 83-85
    White, Byron R. **16** 227-228
judicial restraint
    Harlan, John Marshall **7** 157-159
    Powell, Lewis F. Jr. **12** 426-428
    Scalia, Antonin **13** 513-514
    Shaw, Lemuel **14** 164-165

    Waite, Morrison Remick **16** 46
judicial review
    Chase, Samuel **3** 475-476
    Coke, Edward **4** 141-142
    Marshall, John **10** 279-281
    Wythe, George **16** 415
labor cases
    Holmes, Oliver Wendell Jr.
      7 458-459
    Kelley, Florence **8** 483-484
    Taft, William Howard **15** 78-81
nationalistic cases
    Marshall, John **10** 279-281
New Deal cases
    Cardozo, Benjamin Nathan
      3 288-290
    Douglas, William Orville **5** 83-85
    Hughes, Charles Evans **8** 15-16
role and power
    Jackson, Robert Houghwout
      8 182-183
    Marshall, John **10** 279-281
women justices
    Ginsburg, Ruth Bader **6** 333-336
    O'Connor, Sandra Day **11** 468-470

Supreme Privy Council (Russia)
    Anna Ivanovna **1** 240-241

Supreme Shi'ite Council (Lebanon)
    Sadr, Musa al- **13** 420-422

Supremes (musical group; United States)
    Ross, Diana **13** 298-300

Suquamish-Duwamish Indians (North
    American
    Seattle **14** 80-81

Sura Academy (Babylonia)
    Abba Arika **1** 3-4
    Saadia ben Joseph al-Fayumi **13** 396

Suraja Dowla
    see Siraj-ud-Daula

Surat (city; India)
    Śivajī **14** 266-267

Sure Hand of God, The (book)
    Caldwell, Erskine **3** 223-224

Suréna (play)
    Corneille, Pierre **4** 234-236

Surendranth College (India)
    Banerjee, Surendranath **1** 488

Surgery (medical)
    Apgar, Virginia **1** 257-259
    Barnard, Christiaan N. **2** 7-8
    Carrel, Alexis **3** 322-323
    Cushing, Harvey Williams **4** 353-354
    DeVries, William Castle **4** 518-519
    Drew, Charles Richard **5** 100-101
    Lister, Joseph **9** 444-445
    Long, Crawford Williamson **9** 495-496
    Love, Susan M. **10** 2-3
    Mayo, William J. and Charles H.
      10 367-369
    Paré, Ambroise **12** 94-95
    Spemann, Hans **14** 368-369
    Williams, Daniel Hale **16** 302-303

    see also Medicine; Scientists—physi-
    cians and surgeons

Surinam (autonomous area of the Nether-
    lands; South America)
    Rio Branco, Barão do **13** 177

Surprise de l'amour, La (play)
    Marivaux, Pierre Carlet de Chamblain
    de **10** 265-266

Surrealism (art)
    Europe
      Bacon, Francis **1** 421-422
      Dali, Salvador **4** 376-377
      Ernst, Max **5** 311-312
      Giacometti, Alberto **6** 294-295
      González, Julio **6** 428-429
      Klee, Paul **9** 47-49
      Magritte, René **10** 128-130
      Miró, Joan **11** 53-54
      Oppenheim, Meret **11** 524-525
      Picasso, Pablo **12** 292-295
      Tanguy, Yves **15** 101
    influence of
      Nevelson, Louise **11** 356-357
      Pollock, Jackson **12** 379-380
      Sutherland, Graham **15** 40-41
    Mexico
      Kahlo, Frida **8** 406-407
    precursors
      Chagall, Marc **3** 406-407
      Chirico, Giorgio de **4** 4
      Duchamp, Marcel **5** 122-123
    United States
      Gorky, Arshile **6** 458
      Motherwell, Robert **11** 210-211
      Noguchi, Isamu **11** 416-418
      Ray, Man **13** 59-60

Surrealism (films)
    Buñuel, Luis **3** 127-128
    Fellini, Federico **5** 408-409

Surrealism (literature)
    Europe
      Apollinaire, Guillaume **1** 260
      Aragon, Louis **1** 271-272
      Breton, André **2** 519-520
      Cocteau, Jean **4** 132-133
      Dürrenmatt, Friedrich **5** 164-165
      Grass, Günter **6** 496-497
      Malraux, André **10** 178-180
      Nerval, Gérard de **11** 345-346
    influence of
      Cage, John **3** 211-214
      Laye, Camara **9** 257-259
    Latin America
      Asturias, Miguel Angel **1** 354-355
      Sábato, Ernesto **13** 399-400
    United States
      Ellison, Ralph Waldo **5** 274-275
      Patchen, Kenneth **12** 128-129

Surrender of Breda (painting; Velázquez)
    Velázquez, Diego Rodríguez de Silva y
      15 454-456
    Zurbarán, Francisco de **16** 534-535

Surrender of Burgoyne at Saratoga (painting)
Trumbull, John **15** 316-317

Surrender of Cornwallis at Yorktown (painting)
Trumbull, John **15** 316-317

Surrounded Islands (artwork)
Christo Vladimiroff Javacheff **4** 30-31

Surveying (mathematics)
Applegate, Jesse **1** 264-265
Borden, Gail **2** 409
Foucault, Jean Bernard Léon **6** 28-29
Frontinus, Sextus Julius **6** 130

Survival of American Indians Association (U.S.)
Adams, Hank **1** 45

Survival of the fittest (social philosophy)
Holmes, Oliver Wendell Jr. **7** 458-459
Spencer, Herbert **14** 369-370
Veblen, Thorstein Bunde **15** 449-450
see also Social Darwinism

Susa (ancient city, Babylonia)
Alexander the Great **1** 137-141

Susan Lenox (novel)
Phillips, David Graham **12** 280-281

Susanna (Old Testament character)
in art
Altdorfer, Albrecht **1** 179-180
Rembrandt Harmensz van Rijn **13** 91-95
in music and literature
Handel, George Frederick **7** 116-119
Stevens, Wallace **14** 443-445

Susannah (opera)
Floyd, Carlisle **5** 494-496

Susato, Tielman (circa 1500-1561/64), Flemish music publisher and composer
Lassus, Roland de **9** 216-218

Sushun (reigned 588-592), emperor of Japan
Shotoku Taishi **14** 205-207

Suso, Heinrich (1300?-1366), Rhenish Dominican mystic
Ruysbroeck, Jan van **13** 388-389

Suspected Truth, The (play)
Alarcón, Pedro Antonio de **1** 100-101

Suspense story
see Mystery fiction

Suspicion (film)
Hitchcock, Alfred **7** 415-416

Susquehanna Indians (North America)
Brûlé, Étienne **3** 67-68
Champlain, Samuel de **3** 419-421

Süssmayer, Franz (1776-1803), Austrian composer
Mozart, Wolfgang Amadeus **11** 218-221

SUTHERLAND, GRAHAM (1903-1980), English painter **15** 40-41

Sutra (Buddhism)
Buddha **3** 97-101
Saicho **13** 426-428

Suttee
see Sati

SUTTER, JOHN AUGUSTUS (1803-1880), German-born American adventurer and colonizer **15** 41-42
Bidwell, John **2** 265

Sutter's Fort (California)
Carson, Christopher **3** 334-335
Frémont, John Charles **6** 97-98
Sutter, John Augustus **15** 41-42

Sutter's Gold (film)
Eisenstein, Sergei Mikhailovich **5** 240-242

SUTTNER, BERTHA VON (born Countess Bertha Kinsky; 1843-1914), Austrian author and activist **15** 42-44

SUVOROV, ALEKSANDR VASILIEVICH (1730-1800), Russian general **15** 44-45
Kutuzov, Mikhail Ilarionovich **9** 137-138
Potemkin, Grigori Aleksandrovich **12** 411-412

Suyang, Prince
see Sejo

Suzanne et le Pacifique (novel)
Giraudoux, Jean **6** 349-350

SUZMAN, HELEN (born 1917), member of the South African House of Assembly for the Progressive Party **15** 45-46

Suzuki, Bunji (born 1885), Japanese labor leader
Katayama, Sen **8** 457

SUZUKI, DAISETZ TEITARO (1870-1966), Japanese translator, teacher, and interpreter of Zen Buddhist thought **15** 46-47
Cage, John **3** 211-214

Svadebka (ballet)
Stravinsky, Igor Fedorovich **14** 502-506

Svarta fanor (novel)
Strindberg, August **14** 509-511

Sven II (died 1075), king of Denmark 1047-75
Harold III **7** 163

Svensksund, battle of (1790)
Gustavus III **7** 45-46

SVEVO, ITALO (pseudonym of Ettore Schmitz; 1861-1928), Italian novelist **15** 47-48
Montale, Eugenio **11** 117-118

Svolder, battle of (1000)
Olaf, II **11** 493-494

Swabia (German state)
Frederick I **6** 78-79

Swadeshi movement (India)
Prasad, Rajendra **12** 433

Swahili (language)
Said, Seyyid **13** 428-429

Swahili literature
Shaaban Robert **14** 128-129

Swami and Friends (novel)
Narayan, R. K. **11** 313-314

SWAMMERDAM, JAN (1637-1680), Dutch naturalist **15** 48-49
Leeuwenhoek, Anton van **9** 300-301

Swamp Demon, The (poem)
Blok, Aleksandr Aleksandrovich **2** 335

Swamp Dwellers, The (play)
Soyinka, Wole **14** 358-359

Swan Lake (ballet)
Tchaikovsky, Peter Ilyich **15** 130-132

Swan of Tuonela, The (musical composition)
Sibelius, Jean Julius Christian **14** 211-212

Swan of Usk, The (poems)
Vaughan, Henry **15** 444-445

Swan Song (musical composition)
Schubert, Franz Peter **14** 35-37

Swan Song (novel)
Galsworthy, John **6** 189-190

Swan, The (musical)
Saint-Saëns, Charles Camille **13** 435-436

Swanee (song)
Gershwin, George **6** 284-285

Swanee River (song)
Foster, Stephen Collins **6** 25-27

Swann, William Francis Gray (1884-1962), Anglo-American physicist
Lawrence, Ernest Orlando **9** 248-250

Swann's Way (novel)
Proust, Marcel **12** 465-467

Swanson, Gloria (1899-1983), American film star
Sennett, Mack **14** 108-109

Swaraj movement (India)
Bose, Subhas Chandra **2** 430-431
Das, Chitta Ranjan **4** 401-402
Nehru, Motilal **11** 334-335
Rai, Lala Lajpat **13** 5-6

Swarthmore College (Pennsylvania)
Bunche, Ralph Johnson **3** 121-122

Swatantra party (India)
Rajagopalachari, Chakravarti **13** 6-7

Swaziland, Kingdom of (nation, South Africa)
Malan, Daniel Francois **10** 163-164

Swearing of the Oath ... (painting)
Ter Borch, Gerard **15** 146

Sweat (novel)
Amado, Jorge **1** 189-190

Sweatt v. Painter (1950)
Marshall, Thurgood **10** 282-284

Swedberg, Emanuel
see Swedenborg, Emanuel

Sweden, Kingdom of (nation, Northern Europe)
 American colonies
  Minuit, Peter **11** 50
  Stuyvesant, Peter **15** 5-6
 Europe (16th-17th century)
  Christina of Sweden **4** 26-29
  Godunov, Boris Feodorovich **6** 382-383
  Gustavus I **7** 42-43
  Gustavus II **7** 43-45
  Oxenstierna, Axel Gustafsson **12** 44-45
  see also Thirty Years War (1614-1648)
 Europe (18th-19th century)
  Augustus II **1** 373-374
  Bernadotte, Jean Baptiste **2** 205-206
  Charles XII **3** 464-466
  Gustavus III **7** 45-46
  Joseph II **8** 359-360
  Maria Theresa **10** 256-258
  see also Great Northern War (1700-1721); Napoleonic Wars
 Europe (20th century)
  Hammarskjöld, Dag **7** 100-101
  Myrdal, Karl Gunnar **11** 284
 Scandinavian Union and
  Margaret of Denmark **10** 250-252
 see also Swedish art and literature

SWEDENBORG, EMANUEL (1688-1772), Swedish scientist, theologian, and mystic **15** 49-50
 see also Swedenborgianism

Swedenborgianism (philosophy)
 Cole, Thomas **4** 151-152
 Inness, George **8** 123-124
 Lindsay, Vachel **9** 424-425
 Rapp, George **13** 42-43
 Strindberg, August **14** 509-511
 Swedenborg, Emanuel **15** 49-50

Swedish art and literature
 Asplund, Eric Gunnar **1** 344
 Heidenstam, Carl Gustaf Verner Von **7** 258-259
 Lagerkvist, Pär Fabian **9** 162-163
 Lagerlöf, Selma Ottiliana Lovisa **9** 163-164
 Strindberg, August **14** 509-511

SWEELINCK, JAN PIETERSZOON (1562-1621), Dutch composer, organist, and teacher **15** 50-51

Sweep of an Arm, A (poems)
 Yevtushenko, Yevgeny Alexandrovich **16** 455-456

Sweet Bird of Youth (play)
 Williams, Tennessee **16** 306-308

Sweet Cheat Gone, The (novel)
 Proust, Marcel **12** 465-467

Sweet new style
 see Dolce stil novo (Italian literature)

Sweet Psalmist of Israel (orchestral work)
 Ben-Haim, Paul **2** 161-162

Swein (Sweyn I Forkbeard; died 1014), king of Denmark 986-1014
 Canute I, the Great **3** 266-269
 Ethelred the Unready **5** 327

SWIFT, JONATHAN (1667-1745), English-Irish poet, political writer, and clergyman **15** 51-54
 Addison, Joseph **1** 57-58
 Arnold, Matthew **1** 311-313
 Berkeley, George **2** 197-198
 Bolingbroke, Viscount **2** 374-375
 Congreve, William **4** 200-201
 Pope, Alexander **12** 395-397
 Steele, Richard **14** 407-409

SWINBURNE, ALGERNON CHARLES (1837-1909), English poet, dramatist, and critic **15** 54-55
 Cullen, Countee **4** 333-334
 Pater, Walter Horatio **12** 130-131
 Sappho **13** 479-480

Swing (painting)
 Fragonard, Jean Honoré **6** 38-39
 Renoir, Pierre Auguste **13** 101-102

Swing Era
 Goodman, Benny **6** 436-438

Swing Landscape (mural)
 Davis, Stuart **4** 424-425

Swiss art
 Amiet, Cuno **1** 201-202
 Böcklin, Arnold **2** 354-355
 Fuseli, Henry **6** 153-155
 Giacometti, Alberto **6** 294-295
 Hodler, Ferdinand **7** 434-435
 Klee, Paul **9** 47-49
 Le Corbusier **9** 274-275
 Oppenheim, Meret **11** 524-525
 Taeuber-Arp, Sophie **15** 73-74
 Tinguely, Jean **15** 230-232

Swiss Federal Technical Institute (Zurich, Switzerland)
 Clausius, Rudolf Julius Emanuel **4** 92-94
 Debye, Peter Joseph William **4** 447-448
 Stern, Otto **14** 435

Swiss literature
 Dürrenmatt, Friedrich **5** 164-165
 Frisch, Max **6** 118-119
 Keller, Gottfried **8** 478-479

Swiss Reformed Church
 Barth, Karl **2** 31-32
 Brunner, Emil **3** 74-75

Swiss theater
 Appia, Adolphe **1** 263-264

SWITZER, MARY E. (1900-1971), American champion of rehabilitation **15** 55-56

Switzerland (nation, central Europe)
 Calvin, John **3** 239-242
 Julius II **8** 384-386
 Leo XIII **9** 334-336
 see also Swiss art; Swiss literature

SWOC
 see Steel Workers Organizing Committee (SWOC)

SWOPE, GERARD (1872-1957), president of General Electric **15** 56-58

Sword Blades and Poppy Seed (poems)
 Lowell, Amy **10** 13

Sword of Gideon
 see Münzer, Thomas

Sword of Honor (novel)
 Waugh, Evelyn Arthur St. John **16** 145-147

Swynford, Katherine (1350?-1403), duchess of Lancaster
 Chaucer, Geoffrey **3** 482-485

Sycamore Shoals, Treaty of (1775)
 Henderson, Richard **7** 278-279

SYDENHAM, BARON (Charles Edward Poulett Thomson; 1799-1841), English merchant and politician **15** 59-60
 Baldwin, Robert **1** 466-468

SYDENHAM, THOMAS (1624-1689), English physician **15** 59-60

Sydenstricker, Pearl
 see Buck, Pearl Sydenstricker

Sydney Group (Australian art society)
 Nolan, Sidney Robert **11** 418

SYED AHMED KHAN (1817-1898), Moslem religious leader, educationalist, and politician **15** 60

Sykes-Picot Agreement (1916)
 Lawrence, Thomas Edward **9** 253-254

Syllabus of Errors (papal document)
 Montalembert, Comte de **11** 118-119
 Pius IX **12** 335-336

Sylphs of the Seasons ... (poems)
 Allston, Washington **1** 176-177

Sylvester II (940?-1003), pope 998-1003
 Otto III **12** 29-30

Sylvester, Joshua (1563-1618), English poet
 Bradstreet, Anne Dudley **2** 486-487

Sylvia (novel)
 Sinclair, Upton Beale Jr. **14** 248-249

Sylvia Hears a Secret (play)
 Marivaux, Pierre Carlet de Chamblain de **10** 265-266

Sylvia's Lovers (novel)
 Gaskell, Elizabeth **6** 231-232

Sylvia's Marriage (novel)
 Sinclair, Upton Beale Jr. **14** 248-249

Sylvie (story)
 Nerval, Gérard de **11** 345-346

Sylvie and Bruno (book)
 Carroll, Lewis **3** 332-333

SYLVIS, WILLIAM (1828-1869), American labor leader **15** 60-61

Sylvius (Jacques Dubois; 1478-1555), French anatomist
 Paré, Ambroise **12** 94-95

Vesalius, Andreas **15** 473-475

Symbolic logic
see Logic, symbolic

Symbolism (art)
Böcklin, Arnold **2** 354-355
Gauguin, Paul **6** 236-238
Hodler, Ferdinand **7** 434-435
Klee, Paul **9** 47-49
Marc, Franz **10** 231
Mondrian, Piet **11** 101-102
Munch, Edvard **11** 247-248
Redon, Odilon **13** 75-76

Symbolism (films)
Bergman, Ernst Ingmar **2** 190-191
Fellini, Federico **5** 408-409
Ford, John **6** 7-8

Symbolism (literature)
Austria
Hofmannsthal, Hugo von **7** 443-444
Belgium
Maeterlinck, Maurice **10** 125-126
England
Shelley, Percy Bysshe **14** 176-178
Wordsworth, William **16** 385-388
France
Baudelaire, Charles Pierre **2** 61-63
Gide, André **6** 308-309
Gourmont, Remy de **6** 475
Mallarmé, Stéphane **10** 172-173
Nerval, Gérard de **11** 345-346
Poulenc, Francis **12** 414-415
Valéry, Paul Ambroise **15** 405-406
Verlaine, Paul Marie **15** 465-466
Germany
George, Stefan **6** 277-278
Grass, Günter **6** 496-497
Rilke, Rainer Maria **13** 171-172
Ireland
Joyce, James **8** 365-367
O'Casey, Sean **11** 459-460
Italy
Ungaretti, Giuseppe **15** 389-390
Nicaragua
Darío, Rubén **4** 393-394
Norway
Ibsen, Henrik **8** 98-100
Russia
Berdyaev, Nicholas Alexandrovich **2** 184-185
Blok, Aleksandr Aleksandrovich **2** 335
Spain
Bécquer, Gustavo Adolfo Dominguez **2** 107-108
Jiménez, Juan Ramón **8** 261-262
Valle Inclán, Ramón Maria del **15** 407-408
United States
Cooper, James Fenimore **4** 220-223
Crane, Stephen **4** 293-295
Cummings, Edward Estlin **4** 334-336
Eliot, Thomas Stearns **5** 258-261
Poe, Edgar Allan **12** 363-365
Stevens, Wallace **14** 443-445

Symmetric functions (mathematics)
Cauchy, Augustin Louis **3** 378-380
Lagrange, Joseph Louis **9** 164-166

Symmetry principles (physics)
Wigner, Eugene Paul **16** 268-269

Symons, Arthur (1865-1945), English poet
Eliot, Thomas Stearns **5** 258-261
Naidu, Sarojini **11** 294-295

Symphoniae sacrae (musical composition)
Schütz, Heinrich **14** 48-49

Symphonic Dances (musical composition)
Grieg, Edvard Hagerup **6** 541-542
Rachmaninov, Sergei Vasilievich **12** 531-532

Symphonic poem
Dvořák, Antonin **5** 168-169
Liszt, Franz **9** 445-447
Malipiero, Gian Francesco **10** 171
Schoenberg, Arnold **14** 24-26
Smetana, Bedřich **14** 281-282
Strauss, Richard **14** 500-501

Symphonic Variations (musical composition)
Franck, César **6** 48-49
Lutoslawski, Witold **10** 52-53

Symphonie Concertante (musical composition)
Mozart, Wolfgang Amadeus **11** 218-221
Szymanowski, Karol **15** 67-68

Symphonie pastorale, La (book)
Gide, André **6** 308-309

Symphony (music)
Argentina
Ginastera, Alberto Evaristo **6** 328-329
Austria
Bruckner, Joseph Anton **3** 64-65
Haydn, Franz Joseph **7** 219-221
Mahler, Gustav **10** 144-145
Mozart, Wolfgang Amadeus **11** 218-221
Schubert, Franz Peter **14** 35-37
Webern, Anton **16** 160-162
Belgium
Franck, César **6** 48-49
Bohemia
Mahler, Gustav **10** 144-145
Czechoslovakia
Dvořák, Antonin **5** 168-169
Martinu, Bohuslav **10** 299-300
Denmark
Nielsen, Carl August **11** 388-389
England
Bennett, Richard Rodney **2** 172
Rattle, Simon Denis **13** 49-50
Vaughan Williams, Ralph **15** 446-447
Walton, William Turner **16** 92-93
Finland
Sibelius, Jean Julius Christian **14** 211-212
France

Berlioz, Louis Hector **2** 203-205
Bizet, Georges **2** 296-297
Milhaud, Darius **11** 17-18
Roussel, Albert **13** 328-329
Saint-Saëns, Charles Camille **13** 435-436
Tcherepnin, Alexander **15** 132-133
Germany
Beethoven, Ludwig van **2** 114-117, 461, 462
Brahms, Johannes **2** 490-492
Henze, Hans Werner **7** 314
Mendelssohn, Moses **10** 488-489
Schumann, Robert Alexander **14** 41-43
Strauss, Richard **14** 500-501
Weber, Carl Maria Friedrich Ernst von **16** 156-157
Italy
Berio, Luciano **2** 194-195
Malipiero, Gian Francesco **10** 171
Mexico
Chávez, Carlos **3** 486
Poland
Lutoslawski, Witold **10** 52-53
Paderewski, Ignace Jan **12** 56-57
Russia
Borodin, Aleksandr Profirevich **2** 422-423
Khachaturian, Aram Ilich **8** 530-531
Prokofiev, Sergei Sergeevich **12** 458-460
Rachmaninov, Sergei Vasilievich **12** 531-532
Rimsky-Korsakov, Nikolai Andreevich **13** 174-175
Shostakovich, Dmitri Dmitrievich **14** 204-205
Stravinsky, Igor Fedorovich **14** 502-506
Tchaikovsky, Peter Ilyich **15** 130-132
Switzerland
Honegger, Arthur **7** 472-473
United States
Barber, Samuel **1** 500-501
Bernstein, Leonard **2** 218-219
Bloch, Ernest **2** 326-327
Fry, William Henry **6** 136-137
Hanson, Howard **7** 135-136
Harris, Roy **7** 175-176
Paine, John Knowles **12** 65
Piston, Walter **12** 327-328
Sessions, Roger Huntington **14** 117-118
Still, William Grant **14** 455-456
Tcherepnin, Alexander **15** 132-133
Tower, Joan **15** 279-281
Wuorinen, Charles **16** 404
Zwilich, Ellen Taaffe **16** 536-537

Symposium (dialogue, Plato)
Alcibiades **1** 119-120
Aristophanes **1** 293-294
Plato **12** 345-347
Socrates **14** 320-321
Tschernichowsky, Saul **15** 323

Synagogue (Judaism)
Ezekiel **5** 355-356

Synagogue (painting)
Magnasco, Alessandro **10** 127-128

Synchrotron (physics)
Lawrence, Ernest Orlando **9** 248-250

Syncretism (philosophy)
Philo Judaeus **12** 282-283

Syndicalism (economics)
Briand, Aristide **2** 528-529
Cole, George Douglas Howard
4 146-147
Sorel, Georges **14** 347-348

Syndicalist League of North America
Browder, Earl Russell **3** 30-31
Foster, William Zebulon **6** 27-28

Syndicat Agricole Africain (established 1944)
Houphouët-Boigny, Felix **7** 519-520

SYNGE, EDMUND JOHN MILLINGTON
(1871-1909), Irish dramatist **15** 61-62
Colum, Padraic **4** 174-175
Gregory, Augusta **6** 535-536
Yeats, William Butler **16** 445-447

Synnøve Solbakken (story)
Bjørnson, Bjørnstjerne **2** 299-300

Synthesis (philosophy)
Cassirer, Ernst **3** 358-359
Marx, Karl **10** 304-308

Synthetic cubism (art)
Braque, Georges **2** 504-505
Davis, Stuart **4** 424-425
Gris, Juan **7** 5-6
Hofmann, Hans **7** 442-443
Picasso, Pablo **12** 292-295

Synthetism (art)
Bonnard, Pierre **2** 395-396
Gauguin, Paul **6** 236-238

Syon House (Middlesex)
Adam, Robert and James **1** 38-40

Syphilis (medical)
Cardano, Geronimo **3** 285-286
Columbus, Christopher **4** 176-179
Domagk, Gerhard Johannes Paul
5 48-50
Ehrlich, Paul **5** 225-226
Fleming, Alexander **5** 483-485
Landsteiner, Karl **9** 188-189

Syr Darya (river, Central Asia)
Bonvalot, Pierre Gabriel Édouard **2** 396

Syracuse (city, Sicily)
Archimedes **1** 277-280

Syracuse University (New York State)
Commons, John Rogers **4** 185
Mondlane, Eduardo Chivambo
11 100-101
Newhouse, Samuel Irving **11** 362-364

Syria (Syrian Arab Republic; nation; South West Asia)
ancient (Greek; Roman; Seleucid)
Antiochus III **1** 249-250
Antiochus IV **1** 250
Caesar, Gaius Julius **3** 207-210
Cato, Marcus Porcius the Elder
3 375
Crassus Dives, Marcus Licinius
4 296-297
Ikhnaton **8** 110-111
Justinian I **8** 393-395
Marcus Aurelius Antoninus
10 243-245
Ptolemy II **12** 472-473
Sargon II **13** 482
Seleucus I **14** 92-93
Islamic empire
Abu Bakr **1** 31-32
Hulagu Khan **8** 27-28
Muawiya ibn Abu Sufyan
11 223-224
Omar ibn al-Khattab **11** 508-509
Saladin **13** 441-442
modern (18th-19th century)
Ibrahim Pasha **8** 97-98
Mahmud II **10** 145-147

Napoleon I **11** 306-310
modern (20th century)
Abdullah ibn Husein **1** 19-20
'Aflaq, Michel **1** 73-74
Assad, Hafiz **1** 346-348
Dayan, Moshe **4** 429-431
Faisal I **5** 370-371
Husein ibn Ali **8** 63
Lawrence, Thomas Edward
9 253-254
Nasser, Gamal Abdel **11** 317-318
see also Arab-Israeli wars; Egypt—
since 1920

System of Dante's Hell, The (novel)
Baraka, Imamu Amiri **1** 498-499

Systems analysis (manufacturing)
Babbage, Charles **1** 407-408

Szczecin (city; Poland)
Gomulka, Wladislaw **6** 422-424

Széchenyi, Count Stephen (1791-1860),
Hungarian statesman
Andrássy, Julius **1** 222-223
Kossuth, Louis **9** 88-90

Szechwan (province, China)
Bonvalot, Pierre Gabriel Édouard **2** 396
Chu Teh **4** 54-55
Kublai Khan **9** 115-118

SZENT-GYÖRGYI, ALBERT VON
(1893-1986), Hungarian-American biochemist **15** 62-64
Hill, Archibald Vivian **7** 385-386
Krebs, Hans Adolf **9** 95-97

SZILARD, LEO (1898-1964),
Hungarian-born nuclear physicist
15 64-66
Einstein, Albert **5** 228-231
Wigner, Eugene Paul **16** 268-269

SZOLD, HENRIETTA (1860-1945), American Jewish leader **15** 66-67

SZYMANOWSKI, KAROL (1882-1937),
Polish composer **15** 67-68

T

Tabaré (poem)
Zorrilla de San Martin, Juan **16** 530-531

TABARI, MUHAMMAD IBN JARIR AL-
(839-923), Moslem historian and religious scholar **15** 69-70

Tabarro, Il (opera)
Puccini, Giacomo **12** 474-476

Tabernacle Church of Christ (Columbus, Indiana)
Saarinen, Eliel and Eero **13** 396-398

Tabernacle of the Sacrament (sculpture)
da Settignano, Desiderio **4** 509

Tabernacles, Feast of (Judaism)
Ezra **5** 356-357

TABOR, HORACE AUSTIN WARNER
(1830-1899), American mining magnate and politician **15** 70

TAC
see Architects' Collaborative, The

Tacey Cromwell (novella)
Richter, Conrad Michael **13** 148-149

TACITUS (56/57-circa 125), Roman orator and historian **15** 70-72
Machiavelli, Niccolò **10** 97-99
Nero Claudius Caesar **11** 342-344
Ovid **12** 34-36
Petronius Arbiter **12** 262-263
Seneca the Younger, Lucius Annaeus **14** 103-105
Tiberius Julius Caesar Augustus **15** 217-218
West, Benjamin **16** 210-212

Tade Kuu Mushi (novel)
Tanizaki, Junichiro **15** 101-102

TAEUBER-ARP, SOPHIE (1889-1943), Swiss-born painter, designer, and dancer **15** 73-74

TAEWON'GUN, HŬNGSON (1820-1898), Korean imperial regent **15** 74-75
Kojong **9** 74-75
Min **11** 46-47

Tafari, Lij (or Ras)
see Haile Selassie

TAFAWA BALEWA, SIR ABUBAKAR
(1912-1966), Nigerian statesman, prime minister 1957-1966 **15** 75
Azikiwe, Nnamdi **1** 401-402
Bello, Ahmadu **2** 139-140

Tafilalet
see Sijilmasa

Tafna, Treaty of (1837)
Abd el-Kadir **1** 15
Bugeaud de la Piconnerie, Thomas Robert **3** 111

TAFT, LORADO (1860-1936), American sculptor **15** 75-76

TAFT, ROBERT ALPHONSO (1889-1953), American senator **15** 76-78
Eisenhower, Dwight David **5** 233-236
McCormick, Robert Rutherford **10** 401-402

TAFT, WILLIAM HOWARD (1857-1930), American statesman, president 1909-1913 **15** 78-81
Alaska land issue
Hapgood, Norman **7** 137-138
Pinchot, Gifford **12** 308-309
as territorial governor
Estrada Palma, Tomás **5** 326-327
Osmeña, Sergio **12** 22-24
Root, Elihu **13** 283-284
Cabinet and courts
Hand, Billings Learned **7** 116
Hughes, Charles Evans **8** 15-16
Knox, Philander Chase **9** 66-67
Stimson, Henry Lewis **14** 457-458
White, Edward Douglass **16** 230-231
domestic politics
Aldrich, Nelson Wilmarth **1** 123-124
Bryan, William Jennings **3** 80-82
Cannon, Joseph Gurney **3** 261-262
La Follette, Robert Marion **9** 155-156
Roosevelt, Theodore **13** 280-283

Taft-Hartley Act (1947)
Kennedy, John Fitzgerald **8** 502-506
Truman, Harry S. **15** 314-316

Taghlak dynasty
see Tughluq dynasty

TAGORE, RABINDRANATH (1861-1941), Bengali poet, philosopher, social reformer, and dramatist **12** 529-531
Gandhi, Mohandas Karamchand **6** 201-204
Kuo Mo-jo **9** 133-134
Radhakrishnan, Sarvepalli **12** 537-538
Ray, Satyajit **13** 60-61

TAHARQA (reigned circa 688-circa 663 B.C.), Nubian pharaoh of Egypt **15** 81-82
Shabaka **14** 130

Tahiti (island, South Southern Pacific Ocean)
Bligh, William **2** 325-326
Bougainville, Louis Antoine de **2** 443-444
Cook, James **4** 214-215
Flinders, Matthew **5** 490
Gauguin, Paul **6** 236-238
Melville, Herman **10** 472-476

Tahmasp I (1514-1576), shah of Persia 1524-76
Behzad **2** 123

Tahmasp II (died 1739), shah of Persia 1722-32
Nader, Ralph **11** 290-291

Ta'if Accord
Harawi, Ilyas al- **7** 145-146

Tai-fang (Chinese colony, Korea)
Kwanggaet'o **9** 139-140

Taihei culture (Japan)
Makibi, Kibi-no **10** 161

Taika Reform (Japan; 645-649)
Shotoku Taishi **14** 205-207

Tailleferre, Germaine (1892-1983), French composer
Honegger, Arthur **7** 472-473

TAINE, HIPPOLYTE ADOLPHE
(1828-1893), French critic and historian **15** 82-83

Aulard, François Victor Alphonse **1** 374
Benton, Thomas Hart **2** 178-179
Zola, Émile **16** 526-528

Taiping (religion)
Hung Hsiu-ch'üan **8** 37-38
see also Taiping Rebellion (1850-1864)

Taiping Rebellion (1850-1864)
leaders
Tso Tsung-t'ang **15** 328-329
Wen-hsiang **16** 202-203
suppressed
Feng Kuei-fen **5** 411-412
Gordon, Charles George **6** 448-449
Li Hung-Chang **9** 407-409
Ts'ao Ts'ao **15** 322-323
Tseng Kuo-fan **15** 324-325

T'ai-p'ing T'ien-kuo
see Taiping

Tait, Arthur Fitzwilliam (1819-1905), English-born American painter
Currier and Ives **4** 345-346

T'ai Tsung
see T'ai-tsung, T'ang

T'AI-TSUNG, T'ANG (600-649), Chinese emperor **15** 83-84
Hsüan Tsang **8** 6-7
Wu Tse-t'ien **16** 408
Yen Li-pen **16** 453-454

T'ai-tzu
see Hung-wu

Taiwan
see China, Republic of; Formosa

Taizong
see T'ai-tsung, T'ang

Taj Mahal (Agra, India)
Shah Jahan **14** 138-139

TAKAHASHI, KOREKIYO (1854-1936), Japanese statesman **15** 84-85

Takauji, Ashikaga
see Ashikaga Takauji

TAL, JOSEF (Josef Gruenthal; born 1910), Israeli composer, pianist, and professor of music **15** 85-86

Tala (poems)
Mistral, Gabriela **11** 55-56

T'a-lan
see Wang-yen Ch'ang

Talavera, battle of (1809)
Wellington, 1st Duke of **16** 193-195

TALBERT, MARY MORRIS BURNETT (1866-1923), American educator, feminist, civil rights activist, and lecturer **15** 86-88

Tale of a Tub, A (essay)
Swift, Jonathan **15** 51-54

Tale of Genji, The (book; Murasaki)
Murasaki Shikibu **11** 252-253
Sotatsu, Tawaraya **14** 349
Tanizaki, Junichiro **15** 101-102
Toba Sojo **15** 248-249

Tale of the Florin (poem)
Froissart, Jean **6** 124-125

Tale of the Rose (book)
Christine de Pisan **4** 29-30

Tale of Two Cities, A (novel)
Dickens, Charles John Huffam **4** 538-541

Tale Spektorsky, The (novel)
Pasternak, Boris Leonidovich **12** 124-125

Tales from Shakespeare (literature collection)
Lamb, Charles **9** 176-177

Tales from the Vienna Woods (music)
Strauss, Johann Jr. **14** 498-499

Tales of a Grandfather (novel; Sir Walter Scott)
Douglas, James **5** 78

Tales of a Wayside Inn (book)
Longfellow, Henry Wadsworth **9** 499-500

Tales of Belkin, The (poem)
Pushkin, Aleksandr Sergeevich **12** 489-491

Tales of Hoffmann, The (opera)
Offenbach, Jacques **11** 478-479

Tales of Melpomene, The (book)
Chekhov, Anton Pavlovich **3** 494-497

Tales of Men and Ghosts (book)
Wharton, Edith **16** 221

Tales of the Argonauts (book)
Harte, Francis Brett **7** 184-185

Tales of the Don (book)
Sholokhov, Mikhail Aleksandrovich **14** 203-204

Tales of the Grotesque and Arabesque (stories)
Poe, Edgar Allan **12** 363-365

Taliaferro, Booker
see Washington, Booker Taliaferro

Taliesin East (Spring Green, Wisconsin)
Neutra, Richard Joseph **11** 355-356
Wright, Frank Lloyd **16** 398-401

Taliesin West (Scottsdale, Arizona)
Wright, Frank Lloyd **16** 398-401

Talisman, The (novel)
Scott, Walter **14** 68-70

Tall Brothers (flourished late-4th century), Origenist monks
John Chrysostom **8** 280-281

Tallemant des Réaux, Gédéon (1619-1692), French author
La Fontaine, Jean de **9** 156-157

TALLCHIEF, MARIA (born 1925), Native American prima ballerina **15** 88-89

TALLEYRAND, CHARLES MAURICE DE (Duc de Tallyrand-Périgord; 1754-1838), French statesman **15** 89-90
Castlereagh, Viscount **3** 363-364
Ferrero, Guglielmo **5** 429-430

Gerry, Elbridge **6** 282-283
Napoleon I **11** 306-310
Staël, Germaine de **14** 391-392

TALLIS, THOMAS (circa 1505-85), English composer and organist **15** 91
Byrd, William **3** 187-188, 292

Talmud (Jewish Oral law)
commentaries on
Caro, Joseph ben Ephraim **3** 316-317
Ginzberg, Louis **6** 337-338
Nahmanides **11** 293-294
Rashi **13** 43
Saadia ben Joseph al-Fayumi **13** 396
Gemara
Abba Arika **1** 3-4
Judah I **8** 372-373
persons mentioned
Amos **1** 205
Ezra **5** 356-357
Jesus ben Sira **8** 251
Jesus of Nazareth **8** 251-255
Johanan ben Zakkai **8** 271-272
scholars
Revel, Bernard **13** 108-109
textual interpretation
Akiba ben Joseph **1** 97-98
Elijah ben Solomon **5** 251-252
Gershom ben Judah **6** 283-284
Zunz, Leopold **16** 534
see also Midrash; Mishna

Talmud Student, The (poem)
Bialik, Hayyim Nahman **2** 262-263

TALON, JEAN (1626-1694), French intendant of New France **15** 91-92

Tam o'Shanter (poem)
Burns, Robert **3** 155-156

Tamar ... (poems)
Jeffers, John Robinson **8** 236-237

Tamayo, Rufino (1899-1991), Mexican painter
Bearden, Romare Howard **2** 86-88
Frankenthaler, Helen **6** 56-57

TAMBO, OLIVER REGINALD (1917-1993), serves as acting president of the African National Congress **15** 92-94

Tambourines to Glory (play)
Hughes, Langston **8** 18-19

TAMERLANE (1336-1405), Turko-Mongol conqueror **15** 94-95
Babar the Conqueror **1** 405-407
Hafiz, Shams al-Din **7** 63
ibn Khaldun, Abd al-Rahman ibn Muhammad **8** 93-94
Marlowe, Christopher **10** 272-274

Taming of the Shrew, The (play)
Shakespeare, William **14** 142-145

Tammany Hall (New York City)
leaders
Murphy, Charles Francis **11** 259-260
Smith, Alfred Emmanuel **14** 284-285
Tweed, William Marcy **15** 366-367

Wagner, Robert Ferdinand Jr.
16 44-45
Wood, Fernando **16** 367-368
opponents
Cleveland, Stephen Grover
4 108-110
Nast, Thomas **11** 318-319
Roosevelt, Franklin Delano
13 277-280
Tampico (Mexico)
Beauregard, Pierre Gustave Toutant
2 96-97
Huerta, Victoriano **8** 13-14
Tamworth Manifesto (1834)
Peel, Robert **12** 181-183
Tan (historian)
see Lao Tzu
TAN, AMY (born 1952), American author
15 95-96
Tana, Lake (Ethiopia)
Bruce, James **3** 63-64
Tanaka, Baron Giichi (1863-1929), Japan-
ese premier
Hirohito **7** 410-412
Inukai, Tsuyoshi **8** 130-131
Takahashi, Korekiyo **15** 84-85
Yoshida, Shigeru **16** 464-465
TANAKA, KAKUEI (1918-1993), prime
minister of Japan (1972-1974) **15** 96-98
T'an-chou
see Changsha
Tancred (1078?-1112), Norman hero and
crusader
Baldwin I **1** 464-465
Bohemund, I **2** 364
Tancred (died 1194), king of Sicily 1190-94
Richard I **13** 130
Tancred and Sigismunda (play)
Thomson, James **15** 199-200
Tancrède (play)
Voltaire **16** 14-16
Tancredi (opera)
Rossini, Gioacchino **13** 311-312
Taneiev, Alexander Sergeivich
(1850-1918), Russian composer
Rachmaninov, Sergei Vasilievich
12 531-532
Scriabin, Alexander Nikolayevich
14 71-72
TANEY, ROGER BROOKE (1777-1864),
American political leader, chief justice of
U.S. Supreme Court **15** 98-99
Benton, Thomas Hart **2** 178-179
Chase, Salmon Portland **3** 473-475
Curtis, Benjamin Robbins **4** 349
Garrett, Thomas **6** 225-226
Scott, Dred **14** 65-66
Story, Joseph **14** 480-481
Waite, Morrison Remick **16** 46
T'ang dynasty (China; reigned 618-907)
art
Wang Wei **16** 106-108

Wu Tao-tzu **16** 405-406
Yen Li-pen **16** 453-454
influenced by
Sui Wen-ti **15** 16-18
literature
Li Po **9** 437-439
Liu Tsung-Yüan **9** 455-456
Po Chü-i **12** 362-363
Tu Fu **15** 335-336
rebellions against
Huang Ch'ao **8** 8-9
see also An Lu-shan rebellion
rulers
Hsüan-tsung, T'ang **8** 7-8
T'ai-tsung, T'ang **15** 83-84
Wu Tse-t'ien **16** 408
T'ang Dynasty, Later (China; reigned
923-937)
Zhao Kuang-yin **16** 505-508
Tanganyika
see Tanzania
Tanganyika African National Union
Kawawa, Rashidi Mfaume **8** 464-465
Nyerere, Julius Kamberage **11** 447-449
Tanganyika, Lake (Africa)
Burton, Richard **3** 163-164
Speke, John Hanning **14** 366-367
TANGE, KENZO (born 1913), Japanese
architect and city planner **15** 99-101
Tangent (mathematics)
Apollonius of Perga **1** 261-262
Pascal, Blaise **12** 122-124
Tangier (city; Morocco)
Clarendon, 1st Earl of **4** 73-75
Tanglewood (city; Massachusetts)
Bernstein, Leonard **2** 218-219
Copland, Aaron **4** 227-228
Tanglewood Tales (book)
Hawthorne, Nathaniel **7** 212-215
T'ang-ti chih hua (play)
Kuo Mo-jo **9** 133-134
TANGUY, YVES (1900-1955), French
painter **15** 101
Motherwell, Robert **11** 210-211
Tanis (ancient city, Egypt)
Petrie, William Matthew Flinders
12 261-262
Ramses II **13** 22-23
TANIZAKI, JUNICHIRO (1886-1965),
Japanese novelist, essayist, and play-
wright **15** 101-102
Tanjong (1442-circa 1456), king of Korea
1453-55
Sejo **14** 90-91
Tank (story)
Bunin, Ivan Alekseevich **3** 124
Tank Totem (sculpture series)
Smith, David **14** 287-288
Tanks (military vehicle)
De Gaulle, Charles André Joseph Marie
4 463-465

Patton, George Smith Jr. **12** 140-141
Tannaim (Jewish teachers)
Abba Arika **1** 3-4
Judah I **8** 372-373
Tannenburg, Battle of (1914)
Hindenburg, Paul Ludwig Hans von
Beneckendorff und von **7** 400-401
Ludendorff, Erich Friedrich Wilhelm
10 27-28
TANNER, HENRY OSSAWA (1859-1937),
African American painter **15** 102-103
Bearden, Romare Howard **2** 86-88
Tannhäuser (opera; Wagner)
Wagner, Richard **16** 40-43
Wolfram von Eschenbach **16** 360-361
Tansillo, Luigi (1510-1568), Italian poet
Lassus, Roland de **9** 216-218
Malherbe, François de **10** 169-170
Tantric Buddhism
Buddha **3** 97-101
Tanzania, United Republic of (nation; East
Africa)
Burton, Richard **3** 163-164
Karume, Abeid Amani **8** 452-453
Kawawa, Rashidi Mfaume **8** 464-465
Mutesa I **11** 277
Nyerere, Julius Kamberage **11** 447-449
Peters, Carl **12** 257-258
Said, Seyyid **13** 428-429
Salisbury, 3d Marquess of **13** 448-449
Tippu Tip **15** 235-236
T'AO CH'IEN (365-427), Chinese poet
15 104-105
Hsieh Ling-yün **8** 5-6
Liu Hsieh **9** 452-453
Yi Hwang **16** 457
Tao te ching (Chinese classic)
Hsüan Tsang **8** 6-7
Lao Tzu **9** 201-202
Tao-an **15** 103-104
Wang Pi **16** 104-105
T'ao Yüan-ming
see T'ao Ch'ien
TAO-AN (312-385), Chinese Buddhist
monk **15** 103-104
Hui-yüan **8** 25-26
Tao-chi (Shih-t'ao; 1630-circa 1717), Chi-
nese painter
Ch'i Pai-shih **3** 526-527
Ni Tsan **11** 400
TAO-HSÜAN (596-667), Chinese Buddhist
monk **15** 105
Taoism (religion)
founders
Chang Chüeh **3** 432-433
Lao Tzu **9** 201-202
in literature
Kukai **9** 124-125
Liu Hsieh **9** 452-453
Mabuchi, Kamo **10** 73-74
T'ao Ch'ien **15** 104-105
metaphysics

Tao-an **15** 103-104
Wang Pi **16** 104-105
opponents
Chia Ssu-tao **3** 514-515
Confucius **4** 197-200
Han Yü **7** 136-137
supporters
Hsieh Ling-yün **8** 5-6
Hui-Tsung **8** 25
Li Po **9** 437-439
Sui Wen-ti **15** 16-18

Tao-kuang (1782-1850), Chinese emperor
1821-51
Kuang-hsü **9** 111-112

Tao-lin
see Shih Ko-fa

Tapesichord (music)
Ives, Charles Edward **8** 159-160

Tapiola (city, Finland)
Aalto, Hugo Alvar Henrik **1** 1-2

TAPPAN BROTHERS (19th century), American merchants and reformers **15** 105-106
Arthur, Chester Alan **1** 321-323
Cinque, Joseph **4** 62
Crandall, Prudence **4** 291
Fee, John Gregg **5** 402-403
Weld, Theodore Dwight **16** 186

Taps at Reveille (stories)
Fitzgerald, Francis Scott Key **5** 470-472

TAQI KHAN AMIR-E KABIR, MIRZA (circa 1806-52), Iranian statesman **15** 106-107

Taranto (ancient Tarentum; Italy)
Bohemund, I **2** 364
Flamininus, Titus Quinctius **5** 477

Taras Bulba (musical composition)
Janáček, Leoš **8** 219

Taras Bulba (story)
Gogol, Nikolai **6** 391-393

TARBELL, IDA MINERVA (1857-1944), American journalist **15** 107-108
Baker, Ray Stannard **1** 451-452
Lindsey, Benjamin Barr **9** 425-426
McClure, Samuel Sidney **10** 398-399
Reed, John Silas **13** 76-77
Rockefeller, John Davison **13** 226-228
Steffens, Lincoln **14** 410-411

TARDE, JEAN GABRIEL (1843-1904), French philosopher and sociologist **15** 108-109

Tarentum
see Taranto

"Target" paintings (art)
Johns, Jasper **8** 291-293

Targu-Jiu (town; South West Romania)
Brancusi, Constantin **2** 494-496

Tariff (Europe)
Britain
Baldwin, Stanley **1** 468-469
Chamberlain, Joseph **3** 411-413
Churchill, Winston Leonard Spencer **4** 51-53

Cobden, Richard **4** 127-128
Gladstone, William Ewart **6** 357-360
France
du Pont de Nemours, Pierre Samuel **5** 155-156
Louis XI **9** 526-528
Germany
List, Georg Friedrich **9** 443-444
Italy
Crispi, Francesco **4** 310-311
Pareto, Vilfredo **12** 95-96
Prussia
Frederick II **6** 81-84

Tariff (North America)
Canada
Crémazie, Octave **4** 305-306
Galt, Alexander Tilloch **6** 190-191
Laurier, Wilfrid **9** 232-234
Macdonald, John Alexander **10** 85-87
Mackenzie, Alexander **10** 104
Meighen, Arthur **10** 459-460
Mexico
Gálvez, José de **6** 196
United States
see Tariff (United States)

Tariff (United States)
advocates (to 1860)
Appleton, Nathan **1** 266-267
Carey, Henry Charles **3** 294-295
Clay, Henry **4** 94-96
De Bow, James Dunwoody Brownson **4** 441-442
Lowell, Francis Cabot **10** 13-14
Webster, Daniel **16** 162-164
advocates (after 1860)
Chandler, Zachariah **3** 425-426
Coolidge, John Calvin **4** 217-219
Dawes, Henry Laurens **4** 427
Godkin, Edwin Lawrence **6** 380
Hanna, Marcus Alonzo **7** 127-128
Harding, Warren Gamaliel **7** 148-149
Hoover, Herbert Clark **7** 483-485
Lodge, Henry Cabot **9** 482-483
Morrill, Justin Smith **11** 182
Quay, Matthew Stanley **12** 507
Wood, Fernando **16** 367-368
opponents (to 1860)
Crockett, David **4** 314-316
Dew, Thomas Roderick **4** 519
Hayne, Robert Young **7** 231-232
Macon, Nathaniel **10** 114-115
Polk, James Knox **12** 374-376
Rhett, Robert Barnwell **13** 120
Tyler, John **15** 368-369
Walker, Robert John **16** 67-68
opponents (after 1860)
Cleveland, Stephen Grover **4** 108-110
Johnson, Tom Loftin **8** 317
Lloyd, Henry Demarest **9** 468-469
Straus, Isidor **14** 496

Wilson, Thomas Woodrow **16** 330-332
reciprocity and
Harrison, Benjamin **7** 178-179
Hull, Cordell **8** 28-29
McKinley, William **10** 418-420
see also Tariff of Abominations (1828)

Tariff of Abominations (Tariff of 1828)
Adams, John Quincy **1** 52-54
Calhoun, John Caldwell **3** 226-228
Clay, Henry **4** 94-96
Jackson, Andrew **8** 168-172
List, Georg Friedrich **9** 443-444
Webster, Daniel **16** 162-164
see also Nullification crisis

TARKINGTON, NEWTON BOOTH (1869-1946), American author **15** 109

TARLETON, SIR BANASTRE (1754-1833), English soldier; fought in American Revolution **15** 110
Marion, Francis **10** 262-263
Morgan, Daniel **11** 160-161

Tarlton, Richard (died 1588), English comedian
Brant, Sebastian **2** 503-504

Tarqui, battle of (1829)
Flores, Juan José **5** 491
Sucre, Antonio José de **15** 11-12

Tarquinia Madonna (painting)
Lippi, Filippo **9** 439

TARSKI, ALFRED (1902-1983), Polish-American mathematician and logician **15** 110-111
Carnap, Rudolf **3** 308-309

TARTAGLIA, NICCOLO (1500-1557), Italian mathematician **15** 111-112
Cardano, Geronimo **3** 285-286
Galileo Galilei **6** 180-183

TARTINI, GIUSEPPE (1692-1770), Italian violinist, composer, and theorist **15** 112-113
Corelli, Arcangelo **4** 230-231
Malipiero, Gian Francesco **10** 171

Tartuffe (play)
Molière **11** 86-88

Tasawwuf (Islam)
Ibn al-Arabi, Muhyi al-Din **8** 91

Tashkent (city; Russia)
Bonvalot, Pierre Gabriel Édouard **2** 396

Tashufin, Yusuf ibn
see Ibn Tashufin, Yusuf

Task, The (poem)
Cowper, William **4** 282

TASMAN, ABEL JANSZOON (circa 1603-59), Dutch navigator **15** 113-114
Dampier, William **4** 384

Tasmania (state, Australia)
Bigge, John Thomas **2** 272
Clarke, Marcus Andrew Hislop **4** 87-88
Flinders, Matthew **5** 490
Franklin, John **6** 64-65

Lyons, Joseph Aloysius **10** 69-70
Tasman, Abel Janszoon **15** 113-114
Van Diemen, Anthony Meuza **15** 420

TASSO, TORQUATO (1544-1595), Italian poet **15** 114-116
Gesualdo, Don Carlo **6** 287-288
Marenzio, Luca **10** 248
Poussin, Nicolas **12** 418-420
Spenser, Edmund **14** 373-376

Tata Institute of Fundamental Research (Bombay)
Bhabha, Homi Jehangir **2** 253-254

Tatars (Anisn people)
Genghis Khan **6** 263-265
Ivan IV **8** 157-159
John III **8** 276-277

TATE, ALLEN (1899-1979), American poet, critic and editor **15** 116
Callaghan, Edward Morley **3** 229-230
Crane, Hart **4** 291-293
Eliot, Thomas Stearns **5** 258-261
Ransom, John Crowe **13** 39-40
Warren, Robert Penn **16** 121-122

Tatler (newspaper)
Addison, Joseph **1** 57-58
Brown, Tina **3** 47-48
Steele, Richard **14** 407-409
Swift, Jonathan **15** 51-54

TATLIN, VLADIMIR EVGRAFOVICH (1885-1953), Russian avant garde artist **15** 117-118

Tatti, Jacopo
see Sansovino, Jacopo

Tatum, Edward L. (1909-1975), American geneticist
Beadle, George Wells **2** 80-81

Taubman, George Dashwood
see Goldie, Sir George Dashwood Taubman

Tauler, Johannes (died 1361), German mystic
Eckhart, Johann **5** 200-201
Ruysbroeck, Jan van **13** 388-389

Tauromachia, The (etching)
Goya y Lucientes, Francisco de Paula José de **6** 476-478

TAUSSIG, HELEN BROOKE (1898-1986), American physician **15** 118-120

TAWNEY, RICHARD HENRY (1880-1962), British economic historian and social philosopher **15** 120-121

Taxation (United States)
anticorruption and reform
Bristow, Benjamin Helm **3** 9-10
George, Henry **6** 276
Seligman, Edwin Robert Anderson **14** 93-94
income tax
Borah, William Edgar **2** 408
Bryan, William Jennings **3** 80-82
Harlan, John Marshall **7** 156-157
Hull, Cordell **8** 28-29

Johnson, Lyndon Baines **8** 308-312
Mellon, Andrew William **10** 469-470
Seligman, Edwin Robert Anderson **14** 93-94
Taft, William Howard **15** 78-81
Supreme Court cases
Chase, Samuel **3** 475-476
Harlan, John Marshall **7** 156-157
Warren, Earl **16** 117-120
see also Tariff (United States)

Taxonomy
Simpson, George Gaylord **14** 240-242

Ta-yen-t'a (pagoda)
Hsüan Tsang **8** 6-7

Taylor, Alan John Percivale (1906-1990), British historian
Bevin, Ernest **2** 252-253
Namier, Lewis Bernstein **11** 301-303

TAYLOR, BROOK (1685-1731), English mathematician **15** 121-122
Cauchy, Augustin Louis **3** 378-380
Lagrange, Joseph Louis **9** 164-166

Taylor, Claudia Alta
see Johnson, Claudia Alta Taylor

Taylor, Deems (1885-1966), American composer
Millay, Edna St. Vincent **11** 24-25

TAYLOR, EDWARD (circa 1642-1729), American Puritan poet and minister **15** 122-123

TAYLOR, EDWARD PLUNKET (1901-1989), Canadian-born financier and thoroughbred horse breeder **15** 123-124

TAYLOR, ELIZABETH ROSEMUND (born 1932), American film actress **15** 124-125
Burton, Richard **3** 163-164
Dean, James **4** 433-434

TAYLOR, JOHN (1753-1824), American politician and political theorist **15** 126
Pendleton, Edmund **12** 197-198

TAYLOR, MAXWELL (1901-1987), American soldier-statesman-scholar **15** 126-127

Taylor, Nathaniel William (1786-1858), American theologian
Bushnell, Horace **3** 171-172

Taylor, Sir Robert (1714-1788), English architect
Nash, John **11** 316

TAYLOR, SUSIE KING (1848-1912), African American nurse **15** 127-128

TAYLOR, ZACHARY (1784-1850), American statesman; president 1849-50 **15** 128-130
1848 election
Cass, Lewis **3** 355-356
Clay, Henry **4** 94-96
Polk, James Knox **12** 374-376
Scott, Winfield **14** 70-71
Van Buren, Martin **15** 410-411
as president

Clayton, John Middleton **4** 96-97
Fillmore, Millard **5** 447-448
Lawrence, Abbott **9** 246
Mexican War
Davis, Jefferson **4** 416-418
Grant, Ulysses Simpson **6** 492-494
Marcy, William Learned **10** 247-248
Polk, James Knox **12** 374-376
Scott, Winfield **14** 70-71

TCHAIKOVSKY, PETER ILYICH (1840-1893), Russian composer **15** 130-132
Franck, César **6** 48-49
Glinka, Mikhail Ivanovich **6** 369-370
Pushkin, Aleksandr Sergeevich **12** 489-491
Rachmaninov, Sergei Vasilievich **12** 531-532
Stravinsky, Igor Fedorovich **14** 502-506

TCHEREPNIN, ALEXANDER (Nikolayevich; 1899-1977), Russian-French and later American composer **15** 132-133

Tchernikowsky, Saul
see Tschernichowsky, Saul

Tchili
see Chile

TE KANAWA, KIRI (born 1944), lyric soprano from New Zealand **15** 136-137

Tea (plant)
Eisai **5** 231-232

Tea Act (1773)
Franklin, Benjamin **6** 60-64
Hutchinson, Thomas **8** 71-72

Tea Party, The (story)
Pinter, Harold **12** 317-318

Teachers College (Columbia University)
Butler, Nicholas Murray **3** 181
Counts, George S. **4** 267-269
Rugg, Harold **13** 355-357
Russell, James Earl **13** 379-380
Thorndike, Edward Lee **15** 208-209

Téllez, Gabriel
see Tirso de Molina

Teamsters, International Brotherhood of (labor union)
Kennedy, Robert Francis **8** 508-509
Reuther, Walter Philip **13** 107-108

Teapot Dome scandal (United States; 1923)
Coolidge, John Calvin **4** 217-219
Harding, Warren Gamaliel **7** 148-149
La Follette, Robert Marion **9** 155-156
McAdoo, William Gibbs **10** 385-386
Walsh, Thomas James **16** 85-86

Tears of the Muses (poem)
Spencer, Herbert **14** 369-370

Teatro Campesino, El (theater group)
Valdez, Luis **15** 406-407

Technologists
see Scientists

TECUMSEH (circa 1768-1813), American Shawnee Indian tribal chief **15** 133

Black Hawk **2** 308
Brock, Isaac **3** 12-13
Harrison, William Henry **7** 180-181
Taylor, Zachary **15** 128-130

Tegea (ancient city, Greece)
Cleomenes III **4** 103-104

TEGGART, FREDERICK J. (1870-1946), comparative historian, librarian, sociologist, and educator who initiated sociology at the University of California **15** 133-134

Teheran Conference (1943)
Harriman, W. Averell **7** 165-166
Marshall, George Catlett **10** 278-279
Molotov, Vyacheslav Mikhailovich **11** 89-90

Teheran, University of (established 1934)
Reza Shah Pahlavi **13** 116-117

TEILHARD DE CHARDIN, MARIE JOSEPH PIERRE (1881-1955), French theologian and paleontologist **15** 134-136
Weidenreich, Franz **16** 171-172

Teitoku school (Japanese literarature)
Basho, Matsuo **2** 45-48

Tejedor de Segovia, El (play)
Alarcón, Pedro Antonio de **1** 100-101

Tel Aviv (city, Israel)
Ezekiel **5** 355-356

Tel jour, tel nuit (songs)
Poulenc, Francis **12** 414-415

Telegraph (communications)
development
Bell, Alexander Graham **2** 129-131
Braun, Ferdinand **2** 508-509
Cooper, Peter **4** 223-224
Cornell, Ezra **4** 236-237
Marconi, Guglielmo **10** 239-240
Morse, Samuel Finley Breese **11** 192-193
Pupin, Michael Idvorsky **12** 483-484
early use
Bennett, James Gordon **2** 168-169
South America
Rondon, Candido Mariano da Silva **13** 271
Wheelwright, William **16** 223-224
transatlantic cable
Brunel, Isambard Kingdom **3** 69-70
Field, Cyrus West **5** 438-439
U.S. monopoly
Gould, Jay **6** 470-472
Parsons, Frank **12** 121-122

Telekinesis (parapsychology)
Driesch, Hans Adolf Eduard **5** 105

TELEMANN, GEORG PHILIPP (1681-1767), German composer **15** 137-138
Bach, Johann Sebastian **1** 416-419
Handel, George Frederick **7** 116-119

Telemanque
see Vesey, Denmark

Telepathy (parapsychology)
Driesch, Hans Adolf Eduard **5** 105

Telephone (communications)
Bell, Alexander Graham **2** 129-131
Pupin, Michael Idvorsky **12** 483-484

Telephone, The (musical composition)
Menotti, Gian Carlo **10** 509-510

Telescope (astronomy)
Barnard, Edward Emerson **2** 8-9
Fraunhofer, Joseph von **6** 75-76
Galileo Galilei **6** 180-183
Herschel, William **7** 341-343
Huygens, Christiaan **8** 79-81
Newton, Isaac **11** 369-372
Struve, Friedrich Georg Wilhelm von **14** 513
Torricelli, Evangelista **15** 268-269

TELESIO, BERNARDINO (1509-1588), Italian philosopher of nature **15** 138-139
Campanella, Tommaso **3** 249

Telesis, theory of (sociology)
Ward, Lester Frank **16** 113-114

Television (Great Britain)
cable TV
Maxwell, Ian Robert **10** 360-361
personalities
Clark, Kenneth M. **4** 79-80
Trevor, William **15** 295-297
screenwriters for
Potter, Dennis **12** 412-414
writers for
Mortimer, John Clifford **11** 194-195

Television (United States)
cable TV
Newhouse, Samuel Irving **11** 362-364
Paley, William S. **12** 72-75
Turner, Ted **15** 355-357
development of
Edison, Thomas Alva **5** 206-208
Farnsworth, Philo T. **5** 386-387
Zworykin, Vladimir Kosma **16** 539-540
executives
Sarnoff, David **13** 485-486
personalities
Ball, Lucille **1** 472-473
Benny, Jack **2** 174-176
Bradley, Ed **2** 478-481
Brothers, Joyce **3** 26-28
Buchanan, Patrick Joseph **3** 90-91
Burns, George **3** 153-155
Cantor, Eddie **3** 264-265
Carlin, George **3** 301-303
Carson, Johnny **3** 335-337
Child, Julia McWilliams **3** 519-520
Chung, Connie **4** 47-48
Cosby, William Henry Jr. **4** 257-258
Cronkite, Walter Leland Jr. **4** 321-322
Crosby, Harry Lillis **4** 324-326
Davis, Ossie **4** 421-422
Dee, Ruby **4** 449-452
Goldberg, Whoopi **6** 398-402
Hope, Bob **7** 487-489
Jones, James Earl **8** 334-337

Moyers, Bill **11** 214-216
Murrow, Edward Roscoe **11** 265-266
Robertson, Pat **13** 196-198
Sarnoff, David **13** 485-486
Sheen, Fulton J. **14** 171-172
Vidal, Eugene Luther Gore **15** 488-490
Walters, Barbara **16** 86-88
Westheimer, Ruth Karola **16** 214-215
Will, George Frederick **16** 286-287
Wilson, Joseph Chamberlain **16** 325-326
Winfrey, Oprah Gail **16** 333-336
Wong, Anna May **16** 366-367
producers
Cousteau, Jacques-Yves **4** 276-277
Disney, Walter Elias **5** 26-27
Huntley and Brinkley **8** 49-51
Tharp, Twyla **15** 164-165
scriptwriters for
Bennett, Alan **2** 166-167

Tell el Amarna (ancient city, Egypt)
Petrie, William Matthew Flinders **12** 261-262

Tell Me, Dusky Maiden (song)
Johnson, James Weldon **8** 304-305

Tell Me How Long the Train's Been Gone (novel)
Baldwin, James Arthur **1** 465-466

TELLER, EDWARD (born 1908), Hungarian-American physicist **15** 139-141
Yang, Chen Ning **16** 437-438

Telos (philosophy)
Lotze, Rudolf Hermann **9** 521-522

Temesvar (city, Romania)
Ferdinand **5** 413-414
Suleiman I **15** 20-21

Temperance movement (United States)
leaders
Dow, Neal **5** 89-90
Drake, Daniel **5** 93-94
Nation, Carry Amelia Moore **11** 321-322
Rush, Benjamin **13** 364-365
Scott, Winfield **14** 70-71
Woods, Robert Archey **16** 374
opponents
Butler, Nicholas Murray **3** 181
Capone, Al **3** 272-273
Gompers, Samuel **6** 420-422
supporters
Alcott, Louisa May **1** 122
Benezet, Anthony **2** 159-160
Brown, William Wells **3** 48-49
Channing, William Ellery **3** 435-436
Dewey, Melvil **4** 523-524
Finney, Charles Grandison **5** 450-451
Graham, Sylvester **6** 486-487
Harris, Townsend **7** 176-177
Lease, Mary Elizabeth Clyens **9** 268

Smith, Gerrit **14** 290-291
Stone, Lucy **14** 471-472
Sunday, William Ashley **15** 32-33
Willard, Frances Elizabeth Caroline
16 289-290

Temperature scales (physics)
Celsius, Anders **3** 392
Fahrenheit, Gabriel Daniel **5** 366
Kelvin of Largs **8** 488-489

Tempers, The (poems)
Williams, William Carlos **16** 308-309

Tempest (painting)
Giorgione **6** 340-341

Tempest, The (play; Shakespeare)
Arne, Thomas Augustine **1** 307-308
Dryden, John **5** 106-107
Montaigne, Michel Eyquem de
11 116-117
Shakespeare, William **14** 142-145
Sibelius, Jean Julius Christian
14 211-212

Tempietto
see San Pietro in Montorio

Tempio Malatestiano (Rimini)
Alberti, Leon Battista **1** 113-115
Giotto **6** 342-345
Piero della Francesca **12** 301-302

Temple, Henry John
see Palmerston, 3d Viscount

Temple of Diana (Stowe House, Bucking-hamshire, England)
Gibbs, James **6** 301-302

Temple of Fame (poem; Chaucer)
Pope, Alexander **12** 395-397

Temple of Friendship (Stowe House, Buck-inghamshire, England)
Gibbs, James **6** 301-302

Temple of Glas, The (poem)
Lydgate, John **10** 61-62

Temple of Minerva (play)
Hopkinson, Francis **7** 496-497

Temple of the Holy Wisdom
see Hagia Sophia

Temple, Sir William (1628-1699), English diplomat and writer
Ramus, Petrus **13** 27-28
Swift, Jonathan **15** 51-54

Temple, the (Jerusalem)
Bar Kochba, Simeon **2** 5
David, Jacques Louis **4** 407-409
Ezekiel **5** 355-356
Ezra **5** 356-357
Johanan ben Zakkai **8** 271-272
Josephus Flavius **8** 360-361

Temple, The (poems)
Herbert, George **7** 324-326

TEMPLE, WILLIAM (1881-1944), ecumeni-cist and archbishop of Canterbury
15 141-143

Temps retrouvé, Le (novel)
Proust, Marcel **12** 465-467

Temptation (sculpture)
Quercia, Jacopo della **12** 509

Temptation of Saint Anthony, The (novel; Flaubert)
Flaubert, Gustave **5** 480-482, 136
Redon, Odilon **13** 75-76

Temptation of St. Anthony (art theme)
Bosch, Hieronymus **2** 426-428
Schongauer, Martin **14** 26-28
Veronese, Paolo **15** 469-470

Temüjin
see Genghis Khan

Temür
see Yüan Ch'eng-tsung

Ten Articles (Anglicanism)
Cranmer, Thomas **4** 295-296

Ten Commandments (Old Testament)
Moses **11** 200-201
Wise, Isaac Mayer **16** 342-343

Ten Creeks Run (novel)
Franklin, Stella Maraia Sarah Miles
6 68-69

Ten Days that Shook the World (book and film)
Eisenstein, Sergei Mikhailovich
5 240-242
Reed, John Silas **13** 76-77

Ten Days, The (literary work)
Kazantzakis, Nikos **8** 466-468

Ten Hours Act (England; 1847)
Russell, John **13** 380-381
Shaftesbury, 7th Earl of **14** 137-138

Ten North Frederick (novel)
O'Hara, John **11** 485

Ten O'Clock (lecture; Whistler)
Mallarmé, Stéphane **10** 172-173
Whistler, James Abbott McNeill
16 225-226

Ten, The (art group)
Hassam, Frederick Childe **7** 192
Rothko, Mark **13** 320-321
Twachtman, John Henry **15** 362-363

Ten Tragic Days (Mexican Rev.)
Huerta, Victoriano **8** 13-14
Madero, Francisco Indalecio
10 118-119

Ten Years War (Cuba; 1868-78)
Céspedes, Carlos Manuel de **3** 398-399
Estrada Palma, Tomás **5** 326-327
Gómez, Máximo **6** 418-419
Hostos, Eugenio María de **7** 513-514
Maceo, Antonio **10** 88-90
Martí, José **10** 285-286
Menocal, Mario Garcia **10** 506-507

Tenancingo, battle of (1812)
Matamoros, Mariano **10** 329-330

Tenchi (626-671), emperor of Japan 662-671
Fujiwara Kamatari **6** 145

Tencin, Madame de (1685-1749), French writer

Alembert, Jean le Rond d' **1** 127-128
Saint-Pierre, Abbé de **13** 434-435

Tendai sect (Buddhism)
Eisai **5** 231-232
Ennin **5** 288-289
Honen **7** 473
Kukai **9** 124-125
Saicho **13** 426-428
Shinran **14** 197

Tender Buttons (book)
Stein, Gertrude **14** 414-415

Tender Husband, The (play)
Steele, Richard **14** 407-409

Tender Is the Night (novel)
Fitzgerald, Francis Scott Key **5** 470-472

Tender Land, The (opera)
Copland, Aaron **4** 227-228

Tenderness (poems)
Mistral, Gabriela **11** 55-56

Tendzin Gyatso
see Dalai Lama

Tenentes (Brazilian rebels)
Aranha, Osvaldo **1** 272-273
Prestes, Luiz Carlos **12** 442-444
Vargas, Getulio Dornelles **15** 433-434

Teng Ying-ch'ao (Mrs. Chou En-lai; born 1902), Chinese politician
Chou En-lai **4** 20-22

TENGKU, ABDUL RAHMAN ("the Tengku"; born 1903), first prime minister of the Federation of Malaya and later of Malaysia **15** 340-341

Teniers, David, the Younger (1610-1690), Flemish painter
Brouwer, Adriaen **3** 29-30

Tennant, Emma Alice Margaret (1864-1945), English author
Asquith, Herbert Henry **1** 344-346

TENNENT, GILBERT (1703-1764), Ameri-can Presbyterian clergyman and evangel-ist **15** 143-144
Edwards, Jonathan **5** 220-222
Frelinghuysen, Theodorus Jacobus
6 96-97

Tennessee (state, United States)
governors
Brownlow, William Gannaway
3 55-56
Houston, Samuel **7** 526-527
Johnson, Andrew **8** 294-295
Polk, James Knox **12** 374-376
Sevier, John **14** 122-123
legislators
Benton, Thomas Hart **2** 178-179
Crockett, David **4** 314-316
Gore, Albert Jr. **6** 452-453
Hull, Cordell **8** 28-29
statehood(1796)
Jackson, Andrew **8** 168-172

Tennessee Valley Authority (established 1933)
Black, Hugo Lafayette **2** 301-303

Lilienthal, David Eli **9** 410-411
Norris, George William **11** 428-429
Roosevelt, Theodore **13** 280-283

Tenniel, John (1820-1914), English cartoonist and illustrator
Carroll, Lewis **3** 332-333

Tennis
see Athletes—tennis

Tennis Court Oath (1789)
David, Jacques Louis **4** 407-409
Sieyès, Comte Emmanuel Joseph **14** 217-218

TENNYSON, ALFRED (1st Baron Tennyson; 1809-92), English poet **15** 144-146
Carlyle, Thomas **3** 304-305
Carroll, Lewis **3** 332-333
Eyre, Edward John **5** 354
Hardy, Thomas **7** 150-152
La Farge, John **9** 149-150
Meredith, George **10** 512-513
Milton, John **11** 43-46
Ryder, Albert Pinkham **13** 391-392

Tenochtitlán
see Mexico City

Tenor, The (play)
Wedekind, Frank **16** 166-167

Tenth Muse ... (poems)
Bradstreet, Anne Dudley **2** 486-487

Tenure of Kings and Magistrates, The (book)
Milton, John **11** 43-46

Teppich des Lebens (poems)
George, Stefan **6** 277-278

TER BORCH, GERARD (1617-1681), Dutch painter **15** 146

Terbrugghen, Hendrick (1588-1629), Dutch painter
Vermeer, Jan **15** 466-467

TERENCE (Publius Terentius After; 195-159 B.C.), Roman comic playwright **15** 146-148
La Fontaine, Jean de **9** 156-157
Menander **10** 477-478
Plautus **12** 348-350
Wilder, Thornton Niven **16** 276-277

TERESA (Mother Teresa; Agnes Gonxha Bojaxhiu; born 1910), Catholic nun and missionary; Noble Prize for Peace recipient **15** 148-151

TERESHKOVA, VALENTINA (born 1937), Russian cosmonaut **15** 151-152

TERKEL, LOUIS ("Studs"; born 1912), American radio personality and author **15** 152-153

TERMAN, LEWIS MADISON (1877-1956), American psychologist **15** 153-154
Binet, Alfred **2** 277-278

Ternura (poems)
Mistral, Gabriela **11** 55-56

Terra Australis (mythologic continent)
Drake, Francis **5** 94-96

Mendaña de Neyra, Álvaro de **10** 483

TERRA, GABRIEL (1873-1942), Uruguayan politician, president 1933-38 **15** 154-155

Terra impareggiabile, La (poems)
Quasimodo, Salvatore **12** 506

Terra promessa, La (poems)
Ungaretti, Giuseppe **15** 389-390

Terre des hommes (literature collection)
Saint-Exupéry, Antoine de **13** 431-432

Terre, La (novel)
Zola, Émile **16** 526-528

Terretektorh (musical composition)
Xenakis, Iannis **16** 416-418

Terrible World, The (poem)
Blok, Aleksandr Aleksandrovich **2** 335

Territorial sovereignty (United States politics)
see Popular sovereignty

Terror (ship)
Franklin, John **6** 64-65
Ross, James Clark **13** 302-303

Terror, Reign of
see French Revolution—1792-95 (Reign of Terror)

Terrorists
Europe
Baader and Ulrike Meinhof, Andreas **1** 403-404
Middle East
Abu Musa **1** 32-33
Arafat, Yasser **1** 270-271
Gaddafi, Muammar Al- **6** 163-165
Habash, George **7** 55-56
victims of
Waite, Terry **16** 47-48

Terry, Alfred Howe (1827-1890), American general
Crazy Horse **4** 303-304
Custer, George Armstrong **4** 355-356
Sitting Bull **14** 264-265

TERTULLIAN (Quintus Septimius Florens Tertullianus; circa 160-circa 220), North African theologian and apologist **15** 155-156
Anselm of Canterbury **1** 244-245
Kazantzakis, Nikos **8** 466-468
Marcion **10** 238-239

Teschen, Treaty of (1779)
Joseph II **8** 359-360

Tesdida (epic)
Boccaccio, Giovanni **2** 351-353

TESLA, NIKOLA (1856-1943), Croatian-American inventor and electrical engineer **15** 156-157
Westinghouse, George **16** 215

Tess of the D'Urbervilles (novel)
Hardy, Thomas **7** 150-152

Test Act (England; 1673)
Charles II **3** 452-454
James II **8** 207-208

Test Act (Scotland; 1681)
Blair, James **2** 315-316

Testem benevolentiae (papal letter)
Hecker, Isaac Thomas **7** 250-251

Testry, battle of (687)
Martel, Charles **10** 285

Tetanic contraction (physiology)
Du Bois-Reymond, Emil **5** 118-119
Hill, Archibald Vivian **7** 385-386

Tetanus (medicine)
Behring, Emil Adolph von **2** 122-123
Bruce, David **3** 63

Tête d'Or (play)
Claudel, Paul Louis Charles **4** 90-91

Tetradio gymnasmaton (poems)
Seferis, George **14** 84-85

Tetrahedron (geometry)
Euclid **5** 327-329
Fuller, Richard Buckminster **6** 149-150

Tetravalency (chemistry)
Couper, Archibald Scott **4** 269-270

Tetschen Altarpiece (painting)
Friedrich, Caspar David **6** 114-115

Teutonic Knights (military order)
Frederick II **6** 79

Teutons (German people)
Chamberlain, Houston Stewart **3** 411
Gobineau, Comte de **6** 375-376
Marius, Gaius **10** 264-265

Tevya the Dairyman (book)
Sholem Aleichem **14** 202-203

Tewkesbury, battle of (1471)
Henry VI **7** 298-299
Margaret of Anjou **10** 249-250
Warwick and of Salisbury, Earl of **16** 122-123

TEWODROS II (1820-1868), emperor of Ethiopia **15** 158-159
Menelik II **10** 495-497

Texas (state, United States)
annexation
Atchison, David Rice **1** 357-358
Clay, Henry **4** 94-96
Douglas, Stephen Arnold **5** 80-82
Houston, Samuel **7** 526-527
McDuffie, George **10** 408
Polk, James Knox **12** 374-376
Taylor, Zachary **15** 128-130
Tyler, John **15** 368-369
Van Buren, Martin **15** 410-411
Walker, Robert John **16** 67-68
annexation opposed
Benton, Thomas Hart **2** 178-179
Lundy, Benjamin **10** 45-46
Sumner, Charles **15** 30-31
Webster, Daniel **16** 162-164
governors
Richards, Ann Willis **13** 133-134
independence (1836)
Austin, Stephen Fuller **1** 380-381
Borden, Gail **2** 409

Crockett, David **4** 314-316
Forbes, John **5** 507-508
Houston, Samuel **7** 526-527
Santa Ana, Antonio López de
13 471-472
Travis, William Barret **15** 292-293
see also Mexico—Texas Revolt (1836)
Mexican-Americans
Cisneros, Henry G. **4** 62-64
20th century
Johnson, Lyndon Baines **8** 308-312
Rayburn, Samuel Taliaferro **13** 61-62

Texas and Pacific Railroad (United States)
Bristow, Benjamin Helm **3** 9-10
Gould, Jay **6** 470-472
Huntington, Collis Potter **8** 49
Lamar, Lucius Quintus Cincinnatus
9 170-171

Texas, University of (Austin)
Marshall, Thurgood **10** 282-284
Rostow, Walt Whitman **13** 315-317

Texcoco, Lake (Mexico)
Cortés, Hernán **4** 255-256

Textile industry
see Business and industrial leaders—
textile industry

Textron (conglomerate corporation)
Little, Royal **9** 449-451

Tezulutlán (province, Guatemala)
Las Casas, Bartolomé de **9** 211-212

THACKERAY, WILLIAM MAKEPEACE
(1811-1863), British novelist **15** 159-161
Stevenson, Robert Louis **14** 446-448
Trollope, Anthony **15** 300-302
Turgenev, Ivan Sergeyevich **15** 345-348

Thaetetus (dialogue; Plato)
Parmenides **12** 116-117
Plato **12** 345-347

Thailand (formerly Siam; nation, South East
Asia)
13th-19th century
Chulalongkorn **4** 43-45
Mongkut **11** 104
Rama Khamhaeng **13** 11
20th century
Bhumibol Adulyadej **2** 258-259
Chatichai Choonhavan **3** 479-480
Chulalongkorn **4** 43-45
Kukrit Pramoj, Momrajawong (M.R.)
9 126-127
Nu, U **11** 439-441
Phibun Songkhram, Luang
12 264-265
Prem Tinsulanonda **12** 437
Pridi Phanomyong **12** 449
Sarit Thanarat **13** 483-484
Sayre, Francis Bowes **13** 509
see also Southeast Asia Treaty Orga-
nization

Thaïs (novel)
France, Anatole **6** 39-40

Thakin party (Burma)
Aung San **1** 374-375

Ba Maw **1** 480-481

Thalatta (poem)
Morin, Paul **11** 174

Thalberg, Sigismund (1812-1871), German
pianist and composer
Chopin, Frédéric François **4** 16-18

THALES (circa 624-circa 545 B.C.), Greek
natural philosopher **15** 161
Anaximander **1** 209-210
Euclid **5** 327-329
Schrödinger, Erwin **14** 31-33

Thalidomide (drug)
Taussig, Helen Brooke **15** 118-120

Thallium (element—chemistry)
Crookes, William **4** 323-324

Thames, Battle of the (1813)
Cass, Lewis **3** 355-356
Harrison, William Henry **7** 180-181
Madison, James **10** 121-123
Tecumseh **15** 133

Thanatopsis (poem)
Bryant, William Cullen **3** 83-85

Thanks (poem)
Cummings, Edward Estlin **4** 334-336

THANT, U (1909-1974), Burmese states-
man and UN secretary general
15 161-162
Bunche, Ralph Johnson **3** 121-122
Nu, U **11** 439-441
Paul VI **12** 146-148

Thapsus, battle of (46 B.C.)
Caesar, Gaius Julius **3** 207-210
Cato, the Younger **3** 374-375

THARP, MARIE (born 1920), American
geologist and oceanographic cartologist
15 162-164

THARP, TWYLA (born 1941), American
dancer and choreographer **15** 164-165

That Blood (novel)
Azuela, Mariano **1** 402

THATCHER, MARGARET HILDA (born
1925), prime minister of Great Britain
(1979-1990) **15** 165-168
appointees
Heseltine, Michael **7** 359-361
Howe, Geoffrey **7** 531-532
Hurd, Douglas **8** 52-55
Major, John **10** 155-157

Thaw, The (book)
Ehrenburg, Ilya Grigorievich **5** 224-225

Thayendanegea
see Brant, Joseph

THAYER, ELI (1819-1899), American
reformer, agitator, and promoter **15** 168

THAYER, SYLVANUS (1785-1872), American educator and engineer **15** 168-169

Theaetetus
see Thaetetus

Theate
see Chieti, diocese of

Theater
agitprop (agitation and propaganda)
Valdez, Luis **15** 399-400
critics
Nathan, George Jean **11** 319-321
directors
Abe, Kobo **1** 20-22
Olivier, Laurence **11** 502-503
Reinhardt, Max **13** 89-90
Strasberg, Lee **14** 494-495
experimental
Appia, Adolphe **1** 263-264
Artaud, Antonin **1** 320-321
Brecht, Bertolt **2** 512-514
Brook, Peter **3** 19-21
Bussotti, Sylvano **3** 174-175
Copeau, Jacques **4** 225
Frisch, Max **6** 118-119
Grotowski, Jerzy **7** 19-20
Reinhardt, Max **13** 89-90
Federal Theater Project
Flanagan, Hallie **5** 478-479
Licensing Act (1737)
Fielding, Henry **5** 442-444
management
Shubert Brothers **14** 207-209
mime
Marceau, Marcel **10** 231-233
producers
Artaud, Antonin **1** 320-321
Shubert Brothers **14** 207-209
psychological realism
Kazan, Elia **8** 465-466
realistic acting
Fiske, Minnie Maddern **5** 466-467
staging
Artaud, Antonin **1** 320-321
Belasco, David **2** 124-125
Bernini, Gian Lorenzo **2** 214-216
Boucicault, Dion **2** 442-443
Brook, Peter **3** 19-21
Copeau, Jacques **4** 225
Craig, Edward Gordon **4** 288-289
Goncharova, Natalia **6** 424-426
Grotowski, Jerzy **7** 19-20
Guthrie, Tyrone **7** 50-51
Jones, Robert Edmond **8** 341-342
Lee, Ming Cho **9** 289-290
Reinhardt, Max **13** 89-90
Schlemmer, Oskar **14** 12-13
theorists
Copeau, Jacques **4** 225
Craig, Edward Gordon **4** 288-289
see also Actors and entertainers;
Authors—playwrights; Drama

Theater Hall of Fame
de Mille, Agnes **4** 486-488

Theater of Cruelty
Artaud, Antonin **1** 320-321

Theater of the Absurd (dramatic genre)
Albee, Edward Franklin III **1** 106-108
Beckett, Samuel **2** 102-104
Frisch, Max **6** 118-119
Grass, Günter **6** 496-497

Ionesco, Eugène **8** 131-132

Theatertanz
Bausch, Pina **2** 75-76

Theatine church (Munich)
Cuvilliés, François **4** 359-360

Theatines (religious congregation)
Cajetan **3** 215-216
Guarini, Guarino **7** 25-26
Paul IV **12** 145-146

Théâtre de l'Oeuvre
Vuillard, Jean Édouard **16** 36

Théâtre Feydeau (Paris)
Cherubini, Luigi Carlo Zanobi Salvatore
Maria **3** 505-506

Théâtre-Historique (France)
Dumas, Alexandre **5** 136-138

Theatrical Syndicate
Frohman, Charles **6** 123-124
Nathan, George Jean **11** 319-321

Thébaide, La (play)
Racine, Jean Baptiste **12** 532-535

Thebais (epic)
Homer **7** 465-467

Thebes (city, Egypt)
Amenhotep III **1** 194-195
Hatshepsut **7** 196-197
Petrie, William Matthew Flinders
12 261-262
Ramses II **13** 22-23

Thebes (city, Greece)
Agesilaus II **1** 79-80
Alexander the Great **1** 137-141
Cleomenes I **4** 103
Epaminondas **5** 291-292
Isocrates **8** 151
Pindar **12** 312-313

THEILER, MAX (1899-1972), American epidemiologist and microbiologist
15 169-170

Their Faces (novel)
Barrès, Auguste Maurice **2** 20-21

Their Father's God (novel)
Rölvaag, Ole Edvart **13** 265

Their Wedding Journey (novel)
Howells, William Dean **7** 539-541

Theism (philosophy)
Brentano, Franz Clemens **2** 516-517
Cudworth, Ralph **4** 331
Paley, William **12** 72

Theme Is Freedom, The (book)
Dos Passos, John Roderigo **5** 69-71

Themes (Byzantine administrative system)
Heraclius **7** 320-321
Leo III **9** 330-332

THEMISTOCLES (circa 528-462 B.C.),
Athenian politician **15** 170-171
Miltiades **11** 42-43
Xerxes **16** 420

Themistogenes of Syracuse
see Xenophon

Thénard, Louis Jacques (1777-1857),
French chemist
Gay-Lussac, Joseph Louis **6** 245-246

Theobald (died 1161), Anglo-Norman archbishop of Canterbury
Becket, Thomas **2** 101-102
Henry II **7** 287-289
John of Salisbury **8** 284-285

Theobald, Lewis (1688-1744), English playwright
Pope, Alexander **12** 395-397

Theobromine (purine group)
Fischer, Emil **5** 456-457

Theocracy (government)
Abbas I **1** 4-6
Abd el-Kadir **1** 15
Adams, Peter Chardon Brooks **1** 54
Buddha **3** 97-101
Calvin, John **3** 239-242-336
Campanella, Tommaso **3** 249
Davenport, John **4** 405-406
Hung Hsiu-ch'üan **8** 37-38
Mahdi **10** 137-138
Maistre, Joseph de **10** 153-154

THEOCRITUS (circa 310-circa 245 B.C.),
Greek poet **15** 171-172
Frost, Robert Lee **6** 130-133
Leconte de Lisle, Charles Marie René
9 273-274
Virgil **15** 507-510

Theodicy (religion)
Aeschylus **1** 70-72
Bledsoe, Albert Taylor **2** 324-325
Rosmini-Serbati, Antonio **13** 296-297

THEODORA (circa 500-548), Byzantine
empress
Belisarius **2** 128-129
Justinian I **8** 393-395

Theodora (died 867?), Byzantine empress
Photius **12** 283-284

Theodora (980-1056), Byzantine empress
Zoë **16** 524-525

Theodora (musical composition)
Handel, George Frederick **7** 116-119

Theodore I (died 649), pope 642-649
Alcuin of York **1** 122-123

Theodore II (emperor of Ethiopia)
see Tewodros II

Theodoret (circa 386-circa 456), bishop of
Cyrrhus
Eutyches **5** 335

THEODORIC THE GREAT (453/454-526),
king of the Ostrogoths **15** 175-176
Boethius, Anicius Manlius Severinus
2 360-361
Cassiodorus, Flavius Magnus Aurelius
3 357-358
Odoacer **11** 473

THEODOSIUS (circa 346-395), Roman
emperor 379-395 **15** 176
Alaric **1** 101-102
Ambrose **1** 192-193

Hipparchus **7** 407-408
Stilicho, Flavius **14** 452-453
Ulfilas **15** 384

Theodosius II (401-450), Byzantine emperor 408-450
Eutyches **5** 335
John Chrysostom **8** 280-281
Leo I **9** 329-330
Nestorius **11** 349-350

Theodosius III (ruled 716-717), Byzantine
emperor
Leo III **9** 330-332

Theofano (play)
Kazantzakis, Nikos **8** 466-468

Theogony
see Religious leaders; and under individual religions and sects

Theogony (poem; Hesiod)
Braque, Georges **2** 504-505
Hesiod **7** 361-362

Theology of Hope (book)
Moltmann, Jörgen **11** 91-92

Theophano (955?-991), Holy Roman
empress, regent 983-991
Otto III **12** 29-30

Theophilus of Alexandria (died 428), patriarch 385-428
Cyril **4** 362
John Chrysostom **8** 280-281

Theophrastus (died circa 287 B.C.), Greek
philosopher and scientist
Aristotle **1** 295-296
Menander **10** 477-478

THEORELL, AXEL HUGO THEODOR (born
1903), Swedish biochemist **15** 176-177

Theoretical physics
Bernoulli, Daniel **2** 216
Bohr, Niels Henrik David **2** 366-368
Whitehead, Alfred North **16** 242-244

Theory of Justice, A (book)
Rawls, John **13** 55-56

Theos of Syria
see Antiochus II

Theos Soter
see Ptolemy I

Theosophy (philosophy)
Besant, Annie Wood **2** 233-234
Krishnamurti, Jiddu **9** 101-103
Menon, Vengalil Krishnan Krishna
10 507-509
Mondrian, Piet **11** 101-102

Theotocopuli, Jorge Manuel (1578-1631),
Spanish painter, architect, and sculptor
Greco **6** 511-514
Herrera, Juan de **7** 335

Theotokopoulos, Domenikos
see Greco, El

Theravada Buddhism
Asoka **1** 341-342
Buddha **3** 97-101
Buddhadāsa Bhikkhu **3** 101-102

Mindon Min **11** 47

There Are Crimes and Crimes (play)
Strindberg, August **14** 509-511

There Is a Fountain Filled with Blood
(hymn)
Cowper, William **4** 282

There Shall Be No Night (play)
Sherwood, Robert Emmet **14** 189-190

There Was a Child Went Forth (poem)
Whitman, Walt **16** 249-251

Theremin (instrument)
Cowell, Henry Dixon **4** 280-281
Varèse, Edgard **15** 432-433

There's a Small Hotel (song)
Rodgers, Richard Charles **13** 234-236

THERESA, ST. (Theresa of Ávila; 1515-82),
Spanish nun **15** 178-179
Gregory XIII **6** 534
John of the Cross **8** 285

Theresa-Maria (1638-1683), Spanish queen
of Louis XIV
Bossuet, Jacques Bénigne **2** 431-432

Thérèse (play)
Payne, John Howard **12** 159

Thérèse Desqueyroux (novel)
Mauriac, François **10** 347-348

Thérèse Raquin (novel)
Zola, Émile **16** 526-528

Thermidorian Reaction (French Revolution)
Babeuf, François Noel **1** 412
Barras, Vicomte de **2** 19
Carnot, Lazare Nicolas Marguerite
3 313-314
Fouché, Joseph **6** 30-31
Napoleon I **11** 306-310
Robespierre, Maximilien François Marie
Isidore de **13** 199-201

Thermionic valve (vacuum tube)
De Forest, Lee **4** 459-460

Thermodynamics (physics)
enzyme reactions
Haldane, John Burdon Sanderson
7 70-71
heterogeneous substances
Gibbs, Josiah Willard **6** 302-303
Law of Reciprocal Relations
Onsager, Lars **11** 520-523
phase transitions
Landau, Lev Davidovich **9** 184-185
pioneers
Carnot, Nicolas Léonard Sadi **3** 315
Clausius, Rudolf Julius Emanuel
4 92-94
Duhem, Pierre Maurice Marie **5** 129
Kelvin of Largs **8** 488-489
reworked
Einstein, Albert **5** 228-231
second law of
Boltzmann, Ludwig **2** 379-380
Clausius, Rudolf Julius Emanuel
4 92-94
Kelvin of Largs **8** 488-489

Planck, Max Karl Ernst Ludwig
12 342-344
van der Waals, Johannes Diderik
15 417-418
specific heat
Kármán, Theodore von **8** 451-452
statistical
Boltzmann, Ludwig **2** 379-380
third law of
Nernst, Walther **11** 340-342

Thermometry (physics)
Cavendish, Henry **3** 383-384
Fahrenheit, Gabriel Daniel **5** 366
Gay-Lussac, Joseph Louis **6** 245-246
Kelvin of Largs **8** 488-489

Thermonuclear power (physics)
Landau, Lev Davidovich **9** 184-185
Thomson, George Paget **15** 198-199

Thermopile (instrument)
Hill, Archibald Vivian **7** 385-386

Thermopylae, battles of
191 B.C.
Antiochus III **1** 249-250
Cato, Marcus Porcius the Elder
3 375
480 B.C.
Xerxes **16** 420

THEROUX, PAUL (born 1941), expatriate
American writer of fiction and of chronicles of train travels **15** 179-180

Theseus (Thésée; mythology)
Callimachus **3** 235-236
Euripides **5** 332-334
Gide, André **6** 308-309
Kazantzakis, Nikos **8** 466-468
Racine, Jean Baptiste **12** 532-535
Sophocles **14** 343-345

Thesis and Antithesis (poem)
Clough, Arthur Hugh **4** 123-124

Thesmophoriazousai, The (play)
Aristophanes **1** 293-294

Thessalonians (New Testament)
Paul **12** 141-143

Thessaly (region, Greece)
Cleomenes I **4** 103

They Flee from Me (poem)
Wyatt, Thomas **16** 410-411

They Fought for Their Country (novel)
Sholokhov, Mikhail Aleksandrovich
14 203-204

They Shall Inherit the Earth (novel)
Callaghan, Edward Morley **3** 229-230

Thibault, Jacques Anatole François
see France, Anatole

Thibault, Les (novel)
Martin du Gard, Roger **10** 295-296

Thibaut, Anton (1772-1840), German jurist
and writer on music
Mendelssohn, Moses **10** 488-489
Savigny, Friedrich Karl von **13** 502-503
Schumann, Robert Alexander **14** 41-43

THIBAUT IV (Thibaut I of Navarre;
1201-53), Count of Champagne and Brie
15 180-181
Joinville, Jean de **8** 325

Thief's Journal, The (novel)
Genet, Jean **6** 262-263

Thiene, Gaetano da
see Cajetan, St.

THIERS, LOUIS ADOLPHE (1797-1877),
French journalist, historian, and states-
man **15** 181-182
Bugeaud de la Piconnerie, Thomas
Robert **3** 111
Simon, Jules François **14** 237-238

THIEU, NGUYEN VAN (born 1923), South
Vietnamese president **15** 182-183
Nixon, Richard Milhous **11** 401-404

Thieves' Carnival (play)
Anouilh, Jean **1** 243-244

Things Fall Apart (novel)
Achebe, Chinua **1** 35-37

Thinker (sculpture)
Rodin, Auguste **13** 236-238

Thinking (philosophy)
Descartes, René **4** 505-508

Thinking (psychology)
Bartlett, Frederic Charles **2** 34-35
Hovland, Carl I. **7** 527-528
Jung, Carl Gustav **8** 388-389
Mead, George Herbert **10** 437-438
Wertheimer, Max **16** 207-208

Third Coalition, War of the (1805-1807)
see Napoleonic Wars—Third Coalition

Third Estate (French Revolution)
du Pont de Nemours, Pierre Samuel
5 155-156
Louis XVI **9** 534-535
Mirabeau, Comte de **11** 51-52
Sieyès, Comte Emmanuel Joseph
14 217-218

Third International
see International, Third (Comintern)

Third International, Monument to the
(model)
Tatlin, Vladimir Evgrafovich **15** 117-118

Third Man, The (novel)
Greene, Graham **6** 523-524

Third Night, The (play)
Wolfe, Thomas Clayton **16** 355-356

Third Snow (poems)
Yevtushenko, Yevgeny Alexandrovich
16 455-456

Third Woman, The (play)
Danquah, Joseph B. **4** 388-389

Third World movement
Boumediene, Houari **2** 445-446
Fanon, Frantz **5** 379-380
Nasser, Gamal Abdel **11** 317-318

Thirteen O'Clock (stories)
Benét, Stephen Vincent **2** 157-158

13th Amendment
see Constitution of the United States—
Amendments

Thirty Comrades (Burmese nationalistic group)
Aung San **1** 374-375
Ne Win **11** 364-365

Thirty Tyrants (Athens; 404 B.C.)
Plato **12** 345-347
Socrates **14** 320-321

Thirty Years War (1614-1648)
Catholics (pro-Hapsburgs)
Ferdinand II **5** 415
Ferdinand III **5** 416-417
Pázmány, Péter **12** 164-165
Philip III **12** 273-274
Philip IV **12** 275
Wallenstein, Albrecht Wenzel Eusebius von **16** 80-81
Peace of Westphalia (1648)
Ferdinand III **5** 416-417
Frederick William **6** 85-86
Mazarin, Jules **10** 379-380
Philip IV **12** 275
Protestants (anti-Hapsburgs)
Gustavus II **7** 43-45
James I **8** 204-206
John Maurice of Nassau **8** 281-282
Louis XIII **9** 529-531
Oxenstierna, Axel Gustafsson **12** 44-45
Richelieu, Armand Jean du Plessis de **13** 142-144

Thirty-nine Articles (Church of England)
Cranmer, Thomas **4** 295-296
Edward VI **5** 213-214
Newman, John Henry **11** 365-367

Thirty-nine Steps, The (film)
Hitchcock, Alfred **7** 415-416

Thiry, Paul Henri
see Holbach, Baron D'

This Is the Army (musical)
Berlin, Irving **2** 200-201

This Land Is Your Land (song)
Guthrie, Woodrow Wilson **7** 51-52

This Lime-Tree Bower ... (poem)
Coleridge, Samuel Taylor **4** 154-156

This People Israel (book)
Baeck, Leo **1** 429-430

This Side of Paradise (novel)
Fitzgerald, Francis Scott Key **5** 470-472

Thistle and the Rose, The (poem)
Dunbar, William **5** 142-143

Thomas à Becket
see Becket, St. Thomas

Thomas à Kempis
see Kempis, Thomas à

Thomas and Sally ... (opera)
Arne, Thomas Augustine **1** 307-308

THOMAS AQUINAS, ST. (circa 1224-74), Italian philosopher and theologian **15** 183-186
Bonaventure **2** 383-384
Colet, John **4** 157-158
Duns Scotus, John **5** 149-150
ibn Gabirol, Solomon ben Judah **8** 92
Paul **12** 141-143
Pius V **12** 332-333
Suárez, Francisco **15** 8
Vitoria, Francisco de **16** 1-2
see also Thomism

THOMAS, CLARENCE (born 1948), U.S. Supreme Court justice **15** 186-188
Hill, Anita **7** 382-385

THOMAS, DYLAN MARLAIS (1914-1953), British poet **15** 188-190
Stravinsky, Igor Fedorovich **14** 502-506

THOMAS, GEORGE HENRY (1816-1870), American general **15** 190-191
Sherman, William Tecumseh **14** 186-187

Thomas, James Henry (1874-1949), British labor leader
Bevin, Ernest **2** 252-253

Thomas Muskerry (play)
Colum, Padraic **4** 174-175

THOMAS, NORMAN MATTOON (1884-1968), American Socialist politician, author, and lecturer **15** 191-192
Rauschenbusch, Walter **13** 53-54

Thomas of Kempen
see Thomas à Kempis

Thomas of London
see Becket, St. Thomas

Thomas of Woodstock
see Gloucester, Duke of

Thomas, Paul
see Mann, Thomas

Thomas, Sidney Gilchrist (1850-1885), English metallurgist and inventor
Bessemer, Henry **2** 235-236

Thomas, St. (New Testament Apostle)
Matthew **10** 340-341

THOMAS, THEODORE (1835-1905), American orchestral conductor **15** 192-193
Sousa, John Philip **14** 353-354

THOMAS, WILLIAM ISAAC (1863-1947), American sociologist and educator **15** 193
Znaniecki, Florian **16** 523-524

THOMASIUS (1655-1728), German philosopher and jurist **15** 193-194

Thomism (philosophy)
Dante Alighieri **4** 389-391
Gilson, Étienne Henry **6** 327-328
Maritain, Jacques **10** 263
Rahner, Karl **13** 4-5
Thomas Aquinas **15** 183-186
see also Scholasticism

Thompson, Benjamin
see Rumford, Count

THOMPSON, DAVID (1770-1857), Canadian explorer, cartographer, and surveyor **15** 194-195

THOMPSON, DOROTHY (1894-1961), conservative American journalist **15** 195-196

Thompson, George (1804-1878), British abolitionist
Garrison, William Lloyd **6** 226-228

THOMPSON, HUNTER STOCKTON (born 1939), American journalist **15** 196-198

Thompson, Smith (1768-1843), American jurist
Monroe, James **11** 111-113

Thomson, Charles Edward Poulett
see Sydenham, Baron

Thomson, George (1757-1851), Scottish collector of music
Burns, Robert **3** 155-156

Thomson heat effect (physics)
Kelvin of Largs **8** 488-489

Thomson, J. Arthur (1861-1933), Scottish biologist
Geddes, Patrick **6** 246-247

THOMSON, JAMES (1700-1748), British poet **15** 199-200
Arne, Thomas Augustine **1** 307-308
Collins, William **4** 168-169
Haydn, Franz Joseph **7** 219-221

THOMSON, KENNETH (born 1923), Canadian print and broadcast journalism magnate **15** 201-202

THOMSON, SIR GEORGE PAGET (1892-1975), English atomic physicist **15** 198-199
de Broglie, Louis **4** 442-444

THOMSON, SIR JOSEPH JOHN (1856-1940), English physicist **15** 200-201
Aston, Francis William **1** 350-351, 273
Bohr, Niels Henrik David **2** 366-368
Compton, Arthur Holly **4** 186-188
Helmholtz, Hermann Ludwig Ferdinand von **7** 268-269
Millikan, Robert Andrews **11** 33-35
Rutherford, Ernest **13** 384-387

THOMSON, TOM (1877-1917), Canadian painter **15** 202

THOMSON, VIRGIL (1896-1989), American composer, critic, and conductor **15** 202-203
Copland, Aaron **4** 227-228
Cowell, Henry Dixon **4** 280-281
Stein, Gertrude **14** 414-415

Thomson, William
see kelvin of Largs, Baron

THOREAU, HENRY DAVID (1817-1862), American writer and transcendentalist **15** 203-205
associates

Alcott, Amos Bronson **1** 121
Brownson, Orestes Augustus **3** 57-58
Emerson, Ralph Waldo **5** 278-280
Hawthorne, Nathaniel **7** 212-215
Higginson, Thomas Wentworth **7** 380
influence of
Gandhi, Mohandas Karamchand **6** 201-204
Ives, Charles Edward **8** 159-160
Vivekananda **16** 4-5
influenced by
Mather, Cotton **10** 330-332

THOREZ, MAURICE (1900-1964), headed the French Communist Party from 1930 to 1964 **15** 206-207

Thorium (element—chemistry)
Berzelius, Jöns Jacob **2** 231-233
Curie, Marie Sklodowska **4** 339-341
Hahn, Otto **7** 64-65
Rutherford, Ernest **13** 384-387
Soddy, Frederick **14** 321-323

Thorn, battle of (1703)
Charles XII **3** 464-466

THORN, GASTON (born 1928), prime minister of Luxembourg **15** 207-208

Thorn Heads (painting series)
Sutherland, Graham **15** 40-41

Thorn, The (poem; Wordsworth)
Coleridge, Samuel Taylor **4** 154-156

Thorncrown Chapel (Eureka Springs, Arkansas)
Jones, Fay **8** 332-333

THORNDIKE, EDWARD LEE (1874-1949), American psychologist and educator **15** 208-209

Thornhill, Sir James (1675-1734), English painter
Hogarth, William **7** 446-447, 314
Smibert, John **14** 282

Thornlet of Love (poem)
Froissart, Jean **6** 124-125

Thornton, William (1759-1828), American architect
Bulfinch, Charles **3** 116-117

Thoros (died 1098), Armenian prince
Baldwin I **1** 464-465

Thorough bass
see Basso continuo

THORPE, JIM (James Francis Thorpe; 1888-1953), American track star and professional football and baseball player **15** 209-211

Thorpe, Rose Hartwick (1850-1939), American author
Belasco, David **2** 124-125

Thorpe, Sir Thomas Edward (1845-1925), English physicist and historian of science
Cavendish, Henry **3** 383-384

Thorvaldsen, Bertel (1768-1844), Danish sculptor

Powers, Hiram **12** 428-429

Thorvaldsson, Eric
see Eric the Red

Thousand Cranes, A (novel)
Kawabata, Yasunari **8** 463-464

Three Cities (novel)
Asch, Shalom **1** 325-326

Three Comrades (novel)
Remarque, Erich Maria **13** 91

Three Conversations (book)
Soloviev, Vladimir Sergeevich **14** 329-330

Three Day Blow, The (story)
Hemingway, Ernest Miller **7** 274-277

Three Emperors' League (Dreikaiserbund; 1872)
Andrássy, Julius **1** 222-223
Bismarck, Otto Eduard Leopold von **2** 294-296

Three Graces (painting)
Rubens, Peter Paul **13** 339-342

Three Gringos in Venezuela (book)
Davis, Richard Harding **4** 422-423

Three Guineas (essay)
Wolf, Friedrich August **16** 352-353

Three Hours after Marriage (play)
Gay, John **6** 243-244

Three Little Pigs, The (film)
Disney, Walter Elias **5** 26-27

Three Marys at the Tomb, The (panel)
Duccio di Buoninsegna **5** 121-122

Three Meetings (book)
Soloviev, Vladimir Sergeevich **14** 329-330

Three Musicians (sculp; Picasso)
Lipchitz, Jacques **9** 432-433
Picasso, Pablo **12** 292-295

Three Musketeers, The (novel)
Dumas, Alexandre **5** 136-138

Three Nymphs (sculpture)
Maillol, Aristide **10** 150-151

Three Penny Day, The (play)
Plautus **12** 348-350

Three People's Principles (Chinese politics)
Sun Yat-sen **15** 35-39, 293

Three Rivers, battle of (1776)
Wayne, Anthony **16** 149-150

Three Shades (sculpture)
Rodin, Auguste **13** 236-238

Three Sisters (play)
Chekhov, Anton Pavlovich **3** 494-497

Three Soldiers (novel)
Dos Passos, John Roderigo **5** 69-71

Three Songs from Drum Taps (musical composition)
Hanson, Howard **7** 135-136

Three Songs without Words (song)
Ben-Haim, Paul **2** 161-162

Three Travelers Watch the Sunrise (play)
Stevens, Wallace **14** 443-445

Three Truths, The (book)
Charron, Pierre **3** 472

Three unities (drama)
Corneille, Pierre **4** 234-236
Racine, Jean Baptiste **12** 532-535

Three-Cornered Hat, The (novel)
Alarcón, Pedro Antonio de **1** 100-101

Threepenny Opera, The (musical play; Brecht-Weill)
Brecht, Bertolt **2** 512-514
Weill, Kurt **16** 174-175

Three-wire system (electrical)
Edison, Thomas Alva **5** 206-208

Three-Year War (Mexico; 1857-60)
Álvarez, Juan **1** 184-185
Juárez, Benito **8** 369-372
Lerdo de Tejada, Miguel **9** 351-352

Threni ... (musical composition)
Stravinsky, Igor Fedorovich **14** 502-506

Threnodia Augustalis (lyric ode)
Dryden, John **5** 106-107

Threnody for the Victims of Hiroshima (musical composition)
Penderecki, Krzysztof **12** 195-197

Thrice Noble ... (play)
Palamas, Kostes **12** 70

Thrillers (books)
Ambler, Eric **1** 191-192
Rendell, Ruth **13** 96-97

Thrombosis (medical)
Best, Charles Herbert **2** 236-237

Throne of Blood (film)
Kurosawa, Akira **9** 135-137

Through a Glass Darkly (film)
Bergman, Ernst Ingmar **2** 190-191

Through the Looking Glass (book)
Carroll, Lewis **3** 332-333

Thrush, The (poem)
Seferis, George **14** 84-85

THUCYDIDES (circa 460-circa 401 B.C.), Greek historian **15** 211-212
Cleon **4** 104-105
Edward VI **5** 213-214
Gorgias **6** 456
Hobbes, Thomas **7** 421-423
Jowett, Benjamin **8** 364-365
Pericles **12** 219-221
Polybios **12** 384-385
Sallust **13** 454
Xenophon **16** 418-420

THUKU, HARRY (1895-1970), Kenyan politician **15** 212-213

Thule (settlement, Greenland)
Rasmussen, Knud Johan Victor **13** 44

Thunder Out of China (book)
White, T. H. **16** 236-237

Thunder over Mexico (film)
Eisenstein, Sergei Mikhailovich
5 240-242

Thunderbolt (Buddhism)
Kukai **9** 124-125

Thunderstorm (sculpture)
Richier, Germaine **13** 145-146

Thupten Gyatso (1876-1933), thirteenth
Dalai Lama
Dalai Lama **4** 369-371

THURBER, JAMES GROVE (1894-1961),
American writer and artist **15** 213-214

Thuringia (formerly German state)
Henry I **7** 285-286

THURMOND, JAMES STROM (born 1902),
American lawyer and statesman
15 214-215
Truman, Harry S. **15** 314-316

Thurstein, Domine de
see Zinzendorf, Count von

THURSTONE, LOUIS LEON (1887-1955),
American psychologist **15** 215-216
Hull, Clark Leonard **8** 28

Thus Spake Zarathustra (book)
Nietzsche, Friedrich **11** 390-392

Thutmose I (reignedcirca 1540-1501,
1496-1493 B.C.), Egyptian king
Hatshepsut **7** 196-197
Thutmose III **15** 216-217

Thutmose II (reigned circa 1496-1493
B.C.), Egyptian king
Hatshepsut **7** 196-197
Thutmose III **15** 216-217

THUTMOSE III (1504-1450 B.C.), Egyptian
king **15** 216-217
Amenhotep III **1** 194-195
Hatshepsut **7** 196-197

Thutmose IV (reigned circa 1420-1411
B.C.), Egyptian king
Ikhnaton **8** 110-111

Thünström, Louis Leon
see Thurstone, Louis Leon

Thyestes (play)
Ennius, Quintus **5** 289
Seneca the Younger, Lucius Annaeus
14 103-105

Thyroid (anatomy)
Houssay, Bernardo Alberto **7** 522-523

Thyroxin (hormone)
Kendall, Edward Calvin **8** 495

Thyrsis (elegy)
Arnold, Matthew **1** 311-313
Clough, Arthur Hugh **4** 123-124

T'i (Chinese philosophy)
Chang Chih-tung **3** 430-431
Wang Pi **16** 104-105

TIBERIUS JULIUS CAESAR AUGUSTUS
(42 B.C.-A.D. 37), emperor of Rome
14-37 **15** 217-218
Augustus **1** 371-373

Caligula **3** 228-229
Celsus, Aulus Cornelius **3** 393
Livia **9** 457-460
Ovid **12** 34-36
Tacitus **15** 70-72

Tiberius Sempronius (circa 163-133 B.C.),
Roman reformer
Drusus, Marcus Livius **5** 105-106
Gracchus, Tiberius and Gaius Sempro-
nius **6** 479-480
Scipio Africanus Minor, Publius Cor-
nelius Aemilianus **14** 62-63

Tibet (Chinese autonomous region)
Chinese rule
Dalai Lama **4** 369-371
Qianlong **12** 502-505
exploration
Bonvalot, Pierre Gabriel Édouard
2 396
Hedin, Sven Anders **7** 252-253
Polo, Marco **12** 380-382
Przhevalsky, Nikolai Mikhailovich
12 469-470
Younghusband, Francis Edward
16 477
religion
Buddha **3** 97-101
Dalai Lama **4** 369-371

Tibullus, Albius (54?-19? B.C.), Roman ele-
giac poet
Ovid **12** 34-36
Virgil **15** 507-510

Tibur
see Tivoli

Ticinus River, battle of (218 B.C.)
Hannibal Barca **7** 128-130
Scipio Africanus Major, Publius Cor-
nelius **14** 61-62

Tickell, Thomas (1686-1740), English poet
Pope, Alexander **12** 395-397

Ticonderoga
see Fort Ticonderoga

Tide (oceanography)
Galileo Galilei **6** 180-183
Laplace, Marquis de **9** 202-204

Tidings Brought to Mary (play)
Claudel, Paul Louis Charles **4** 90-91

TIECK, LUDWIG (1773-1853), German
author **15** 218-219
Brentano, Clemens **2** 515-516
Frederick William IV **6** 87-88
Schelling, Friedrich Wilhelm Joseph von
13 526-527
Schlegel, Friedrich von **14** 10-11

Tiedemann, Friedrich (1781-1861), German anatomist
Agassiz, Jean Louis Rodolphe **1** 76-78

T'ien-t'ai school (Buddhism)
Chih-i **3** 518-519
see also Tendai sect

Tientsin (city, China)
Chou En-lai **4** 20-22

Lin Piao **9** 429-430
Wen-hsiang **16** 202-203
Yen Fu **16** 452

Tientsin Massacre (1870)
Li Hung-Chang **9** 407-409
Tseng Kuo-fan **15** 324-325

T'ien-wang
see Hung Hsiu-ch'üan

TIEPOLO, GIOVANNI BATTISTA
(1696-1770), Italian painter **15** 219-220
Boucher, François **2** 440-442
Goya y Lucientes, Francisco de Paula
José de **6** 476-478
Neumann, Balthasar **11** 354-355
Piranesi, Giovanni Battista **12** 321-322
Veronese, Paolo **15** 469-470

Tierra de promisión (poems)
Rivera, José Eustacio **13** 185-186

Tierra del Fuego (archipelago, South Amer-
ica)
Darwin, Charles Robert **4** 397-399
Drake, Francis **5** 94-96
Nordenskold, Nils Otto Gustaf
11 422-423

Tierra vasco (trilogy)
Baroja y Nessi, Pío **2** 15-16

**Tiers livre des faictz et dictz héroïques du
noble Pantagruel** (book)
Rabelais, François **12** 524-526

Tiffany Building (New York City)
White, Stanford **16** 235-236

TIFFANY, LOUIS COMFORT (1848-1933),
American painter and designer
15 220-221

Tiflis (city, Russia)
Agha Mohammad Khan **1** 80-81

Tigellinus, Ofonius (died 69), Roman politi-
cian
Nero Claudius Caesar **11** 342-344
Petronius Arbiter **12** 262-263
Seneca the Younger, Lucius Annaeus
14 103-105

Tiger-lilies (novel)
Lanier, Sidney **9** 199-200

Tight Dally and a Loose Lattice, A (painting)
Russell, Charles Marion **13** 375-376

TIGLATH-PILESER III (ruled 745-727 B.C.),
king of Assyria **15** 221-222
Hosea **7** 512
Isaiah **8** 146-147

Tigrane (opera)
Scarlatti, Pietro Alessandro Gaspare
13 517-518

Tiguex Pueblos (New Mexico)
Coronado, Francisco Vásquez de **4** 247

Tijaniyya order (Islam)
Omar ibn Said Tal, Al-Hajj **11** 509-510

Tikkun (Judaism)
Luria, Isaac ben Solomon Ashkenazi
10 47-48

Tilak, Bal (1856-1920), Indain nationalist leader
Rai, Lala Lajpat **13** 5-6

TILDEN, SAMUEL JONES (1814-1886), American politician **15** 222-223
as governor
Bigelow, John **2** 271-272
Lowell, Josephine Shaw **10** 15-16
election dispute (1876)
Evarts, William Maxwell **5** 340-341
Field, David Dudley **5** 439-440
Hayes, Rutherford Birchard **7** 227-228
Hewitt, Abram Stevens **7** 371-372
Reed, Thomas Brackett **13** 77
Trumbull, Lyman **15** 317-318
Tweed Ring
Seymour, Horatio **14** 126-127

Till Eulenspiegels lustige Streiche (musical composition)
Strauss, Richard **14** 500-501

Till the Clouds Roll By (film)
Kern, Jerome David **8** 517-518

Till the Day I Die (play)
Odets, Clifford **11** 470-471

Tilled Field (painting)
Miró, Joan **11** 53-54

Tillers, The (poem)
Lamartine, Alphonse Marie Louis de **9** 173-175

TILLEY, SIR SAMUEL LEONARD (1818-1896), Canadian statesman **15** 223-224

TILLICH, PAUL JOHANNES (1886-1965), German-American Protestant theologian and philosopher **15** 224-225
Barth, Karl **2** 31-32
Heidegger, Martin **7** 257-258
influence of
Adams, James Luther **1** 47-48

Tillie and Gus (film)
Fields, W. C. **5** 444

Tillie's Punctured Romance (film)
Chaplin, Charles Spencer **3** 438-440

TILLMAN, BENJAMIN RYAN (1847-1918), American statesman and demagogue **15** 225-226
Donnelly, Ignatius **5** 62

Tillotson, John (1630-1694), archbishop of Canterbury
Mary II **10** 309-310

Tilly, Johan Tserclaes, Count of (1559-1632), Flemish field marshal
Ferdinand II **5** 415
Gustavus II **7** 43-45

Tilsit, treaties of (1807)
Alexander I **1** 130-132
Canning, George **3** 258-260
Hardenberg, Karl August von **7** 146-147
Napoleon I **11** 306-310
Nesselrode, Karl Robert **11** 348-349

Timaeus (book)
Philo Judaeus **12** 282-283
Plato **12** 345-347
Proclus Diadochus **12** 457

Timber (literature collection)
Jonson, Ben **8** 343-345

Timbuktu (town, Mali)
Ali, Sunni **1** 158-159
Barth, Heinrich **2** 30-31
Caillié, Auguste René **3** 214-215
ibn Battuta, Muhammad **8** 91-92
Joffre, Joseph Jacques Césaire **8** 267-268

Time (magazine)
Agee, James **1** 78-79
Luce, Henry Robinson **10** 23-24
O'Hara, John **11** 485
Pollock, Jackson **12** 379-380

Time (philosophy)
Augustine **1** 367-370
Democritus **4** 493-494

Time in the Sun (film)
Eisenstein, Sergei Mikhailovich **5** 240-242

Time Life Screen (sculpture)
Moore, Henry **11** 146-148

Time Machine, The (novel)
Wells, Herbert George **16** 195-196

Time of Hope (novel)
Snow, Charles Percy **14** 311-312

Time of Indifference, The (novel)
Moravia, Alberto **11** 153-155

Time of the Angels, The (novel)
Murdoch, Iris **11** 256-257

Time of the Assassins, The (book)
Miller, Henry **11** 26-27

Time of Your Life, The (play)
Saroyan, William **13** 486-487

Time Present (play)
Osborne, John **12** 16-17

Time Regained (novel)
Proust, Marcel **12** 465-467

Time to Love and a Time to Die, A (novel)
Remarque, Erich Maria **13** 91

TIMERMAN, JACOBO (born 1923), Argentine journalist and human rights advocate **15** 226-228

Time's Laughingstocks (poems)
Hardy, Thomas **7** 150-152

Timon of Athens (play)
Shakespeare, William **14** 142-145

Timoshenko, Semyon K. (1895-1970), Russian general
Zhukov, Georgi Konstantinovich **16** 512-513

Timoteo el incomprendido (book)
Cela y Trulock, Camilo José **3** 389-390

Timotheus (died circa 354 B.C.) Athenian statesman and general
Isocrates **8** 151

Timothy, Letters to (New Testament book)
Paul **12** 141-143

Timur
see Tamerlane

Tin (element—chemistry)
Lavoisier, Antoine Laurent **9** 241-244

Tin Drum, The (novel)
Grass, Günter **6** 496-497

Tin Lizzie
see Model T (automobile)

Tin mines (Bolivia)
Patiño, Simón Iturri **12** 133-134
Paz, Octavio **12** 161-162

Tin Pan Alley (New York City)
Berlin, Irving **2** 200-201
Gershwin, George **6** 284-285

TINBERGEN, JAN (1903-1994), Dutch economist **15** 228-229

TINBERGEN, NIKOLAAS (1907-1988), English ethologist and zoologist **15** 229-230

Tinctoris, Johannes (1446?-1511), Dutch musician
Dufay, Guillaume **5** 125-126
Dunstable, John **5** 150-151
Ockeghem, Johannes **11** 464-465

Tindal, Mathew (1657-1733), English deist
Law, William **9** 245-246

TINGUELY, JEAN (1925-1991), Swiss sculptor **15** 230-232

Tinker's Wedding, The (play)
Synge, Edmund John Millington **15** 61-62

Tino di Camaino (1280/81-1337), Italian sculptor
Andrea Pisano **1** 225-226
Arnolfo di Cambio **1** 315-316
Henry VII **7** 299-300

Tintern Abey (poem)
Wordsworth, William **16** 385-388

TINTORETTO (1518-1594), Italian painter **15** 232-234
Allston, Washington **1** 176-177
Michelangelo Buonarroti **11** 2-5
Pacher, Michael **12** 53
Ruskin, John **13** 371-372
Sansovino, Jacopo **13** 470-471
Soutine, Chaim **14** 356-357
Velázquez, Diego Rodríguez de Silva y **15** 454-456
Veronese, Paolo **15** 469-470

Tip Toes (musical)
Gershwin, George **6** 284-285

Tippecanoe, battle of (1811)
Harrison, William Henry **7** 180-181
Tecumseh **15** 133

TIPPETT, MICHAEL KEMP, SIR (born 1905), English composer and conductor **15** 234-235

Tippoo Sahib (1751-1799), sultan of Mysore 1782-99

Cornwallis, Charles **4** 241-243

TIPPU TIP (Hamed bin Mohammed bin Juma bin Rajab el Murjebi; circa 1840-1905), Zanzibari trader **15** 235-236

TIPU SULTAN (1750-1799), Moslem ruler of Mysore **15** 236
   Wellesley, Richard Colley **16** 192-193

TIRADENTES (José Joaquim da Silva Xavier; 1748-92), Brazilian national hero **15** 237

Tirano Banderas (novel)
   Valle Inclán, Ramón Maria del **15** 407-408

Tire and rubber industry
   see Business and industrial leaders—tire and rubber industry

Tiresias (Greek mythology)
   Callimachus **3** 235-236
   Euripides **5** 332-334

Tirhakah (reigned 688-663 B.C.), king of Ethiopia
   Isaiah **8** 146-147

Tiriel (poem)
   Blake, William **2** 316-318

Tirol (painting)
   Marc, Franz **10** 231
   Marin, John III **10** 259-260

Tirpitz, Alfred von (1849-1930), German admiral
   Bethmann Hollweg, Theobald von **2** 239-240
   Kapp, Wolfgang **8** 436

Tirsi e Clori (ballet)
   Monteverdi, Claudio Giovanni Antonio **11** 126-128

TIRSO DE MOLINA (1584-1648), Spanish dramatist **15** 237-238

'Tis Pity She's a Whore (play)
   Ford, John **6** 7-8

TISCH BROTHERS (1923-), real estate developers **15** 238-240
   Tisch, Laurence Alan (born 1923), CEO of CBS **15** 238-240
   Tisch, Preston Robert (born 1926), postmaster general of the United States **15** 238-240

TISELIUS, ARNE WILHELM KAURIN (1902-1971), Swedish biochemist **15** 240-241

Tissaphernes (died circa 395 B.C.), Persian satrap in Asia Minor
   Xenophon **16** 418-420

Titan (Saturn's moon)
   Huygens, Christiaan **8** 79-81

Titan (sculpture)
   Caro, Anthony **3** 316

Titan, The (novel)
   Dreiser, Herman Theodore **5** 98-100
   Richter, Johann Paul Friedrich **13** 150-151

Titanic (ship)
   Sarnoff, David **13** 485-486
   Straus, Isidor **14** 496

TITCHENER, EDWARD BRADFORD (1867-1927), English-American psychologist **15** 241-242
   Wundt, Wilhelm Max **16** 402-403

Tite et Bérénice (play; Corneille)
   Racine, Jean Baptiste **12** 532-535

TITIAN (1488/90-1576), Italian painter **15** 242-244
  associates
    Greco **6** 511-514
    Sansovino, Jacopo **13** 470-471
  influence of
    Clouet, Jean and François **4** 122-123
    Lotto, Lorenzo **9** 520-521
    Poussin, Nicolas **12** 418-420
    Tintoretto **15** 232-234
    Van Dyck, Anthony **15** 423-425
    Vanderlyn, John **15** 417
    Velázquez, Diego Rodríguez de Silva y **15** 454-456
    Veronese, Paolo **15** 469-470
    Watteau, Antoine **16** 143-144
  influenced by
    Bellini, Giovanni **2** 137-138
    Giorgione **6** 340-341-406

Titicut Follies (film)
   Wiseman, Frederick **16** 345-346

TITO, MARSHAL (1892-1980), Yugoslav president **15** 244-246
   Djilas, Milovan **5** 34
   Dubček, Alexander **5** 112-113
   Nasser, Gamal Abdel **11** 317-318

TITULESCU, NICOLAE (1882-1941), Romanian statesman **15** 246-247

Titurel (poem)
   Wolfram von Eschenbach **16** 360-361

Titus Andronicus (play)
   Shakespeare, William **14** 142-145

Titus Flavius Domitianus Augustus
   see Domitian

TITUS FLAVIUS VESPASIANUS (39-81), Roman general, emperor 79-81 **15** 247-248
   Domitian **5** 52-53
   Josephus Flavius **8** 360-361
   Martialis, Marcus Valerius **10** 286-287
   Pliny the Elder **12** 355-356
   Racine, Jean Baptiste **12** 532-535
   Vespasian **15** 475-476

Titus, Letter to (New Testament)
   Paul **12** 141-143

Titus Petronius Niger
   see Petronius Arbiter

Tlascala Indians (Mexico)
   Cortés, Hernán **4** 255-256
   Montezuma, II **11** 128-129

TM
   see Transcendental Meditation

To a Butterfly (poem)
   Wordsworth, William **16** 385-388

To a God Unknown (novel)
   Steinbeck, John Ernst **14** 416-417

To a Lady (poem)
   Pope, Alexander **12** 395-397

To a Lady Weeping (poem)
   Collins, William **4** 168-169

To a Mouse (poem)
   Burns, Robert **3** 155-156

To a Water Lily (musical composition)
   MacDowell, Edward Alexander **10** 87-88

To a Waterfowl (poem)
   Bryant, William Cullen **3** 83-85

To a Wild Rose (musical composition)
   MacDowell, Edward Alexander **10** 87-88

To Althea from Prison (poem)
   Lovelace, Richard **10** 7-8

To Be or Not To Be (film)
   Benny, Jack **2** 174-176
   Lubitsch, Ernst **10** 18-19

To Burlington (poem)
   Pope, Alexander **12** 395-397

To Catch a Thief (film)
   Hitchcock, Alfred **7** 415-416

To Cobham (poem)
   Pope, Alexander **12** 395-397

To Damascus I-III (play)
   Strindberg, August **14** 509-511

To Earthward (poem)
   Frost, Robert Lee **6** 130-133

To Have and Have Not (novel and film)
   Bogart, Humphrey **2** 363-364
   Hemingway, Ernest Miller **7** 274-277

To His Coy Mistress (poem)
   Marvell, Andrew **10** 301-303

To His Sacred Majesty (poem)
   Dryden, John **5** 106-107

To Imagination (poem)
   Brontë, Emily **3** 18-19

To Let (novel)
   Galsworthy, John **6** 189-190

To Lucasta (poem)
   Lovelace, Richard **10** 7-8

To Marguerite—Continued (poem)
   Arnold, Matthew **1** 311-313

To my late departed Saint (sonnet)
   Milton, John **11** 43-46

To Rosas (poem)
   Mármol, José **10** 274

To Seem the Stranger (sonnet)
   Hopkins, Gerard Manley **7** 492-494

To Spring (poem)
   Leopardi, Giacomo **9** 344-345

To Step Aside (stories)
   Coward, Noel **4** 279-280

To the Bird (poem)
Bialik, Hayyim Nahman **2** 262-263

To the Cuckoo (poem)
Wordsworth, William **16** 385-388

To the Finland Station (book)
Wilson, Edmund **16** 318-319

To the Ladies (play)
Kaufman, George S. **8** 457-458

To the Lighthouse (novel)
Woolf, Virginia Stephen **16** 381-382

To the Memory of Anne Killigrew (ode)
Dryden, John **5** 106-107

To the Moon (poem)
Leopardi, Giacomo **9** 344-345

To the North (novel)
Bowen, Elizabeth **2** 462-463

To the One of Fictive Music (poem)
Stevens, Wallace **14** 443-445

To the Stone-cutters (poem)
Jeffers, John Robinson **8** 236-237

To Those of My Country (poem)
Morin, Paul **11** 174

To Tullinger (novel)
Rölvaag, Ole Edvart **13** 265

TOBA SOJO (1053-1140), Japanese
painter-priest **15** 248-249

Tobacco (plant)
Dewey, Melvil **4** 523-524
Duke, James Buchanan **5** 133-134
Gálvez, José de **6** 196
Hatch, William Henry **7** 196
Raleigh, Walter **13** 9-11
Rolfe, John **13** 259-260
Sandys, Edwin **13** 463-464

Tobacco mosaic virus
Northrop, John Howard **11** 430-431

Tobacco Nation
see Petun Indians

Tobacco Road (novel)
Caldwell, Erskine **3** 223-224

TOBEY, MARK (1890-1976), American
painter **15** 249-250

**TOCQUEVILLE, ALEXIS CHARLES HENRI
MAURICE CLÉREL DE** (1805-1859),
French statesman and historian
15 250-251
Acton, John Emerich Edward Dalberg
1 38
Brown, William Wells **3** 48-49
Gobineau, Comte de **6** 375-376
Lieber, Francis **9** 401-402
Sorel, Albert **14** 346-347

Tod Adams, Der (poem)
Klopstock, Friedrich Gottlieb **9** 55-56

Tod des Kleinbürgers, Der (novella)
Werfel, Franz **16** 204-205

Tod des Tizian, Der (play)
Hofmannsthal, Hugo von **7** 443-444

Tod in Venedig, Der (novella)
Mann, Thomas **10** 204-207

Tod und das Mädchen, Der (musical composition)
Schubert, Franz Peter **14** 35-37

TODD, ALEXANDER (1907-1997), English
chemist **15** 251-253

Todd, Mabel Loomis (1856-1932), American author
Dickinson, Emily **4** 541-543

Todd, Reginald Stephen Garfield (born
1908), Rhodesian politician and rancher
Sithole, Ndabaningi **14** 262-264

Todd, Sir Alexander (born 1907), British
biochemist
Khorana, Har Gobind **8** 537-538

Todtentanz (piano concerto)
Liszt, Franz **9** 445-447

Toghril (died 1063), Mongol ruler
Genghis Khan **6** 263-265

TOGLIATTI, PALMIRO (1893-1964), Italian
statesman and a founder of the Italian
Communist Party **15** 253-254

Togo, Heihachiro (1847-1934), Japanese
admiral
Hirohito **7** 410-412

Togo, Republic of (nation, West Africa)
Olympio, Sylvanus E. **11** 506-507

Togu Gakushi
see Makibi

Toilers, The (painting)
Weber, Max **16** 160

Toilet, The (play)
Baraka, Imamu Amiri **1** 498-499

TOJO, HIDEKI (1884-1948), Japanese gen-
eral, premier 1941-44 **15** 254-256
Bose, Subhas Chandra **2** 430-431
Inukai, Tsuyoshi **8** 130-131
Kishi, Nobusuke **9** 41-43
Konoe, Fumimaro **9** 82-83
Sato, Eisaku **13** 495-496
Yamashita, Tomoyuki **16** 435-436

Toklas, Alice B. (1877-1967), American literary figure
Stein, Gertrude **14** 414-415

Tokolar empire (Western Sudan)
Omar ibn Said Tal, Al-Hajj **11** 509-510
Uthman don Fodio **15** 397-398

TOKUGAWA IEYASU (1542-1616),
founder of Tokugawa shogunate
8 103-106
Nobunaga, Oda **11** 413-414
Toyotomi Hideyoshi **15** 286-289

Tokugawa shogunate
see Japan—1603-1867

Tokyo (city, Japan)
Hirohito **7** 410-412
Ieyasu, Tokugawa **8** 103-106
Meighen, Arthur **10** 459-460
Nimitz, Chester William **11** 395-396
Tange, Kenzo **15** 99-101

Tokyo Expo 70
Stockhausen, Karlheinz **14** 460-461

Tokyo Special Higher School
see Waseda University (Japan)

Tokyo University
Tange, Kenzo **15** 99-101
Tomonaga, Sin-itiro **15** 265-266
Yukawa, Hideki **16** 481-482

TOLAND, JOHN (1670-1722), British
scholar **15** 256

Tolbert, William R. (1913-1980), Liberian
statesman
Tubman, William Vacanarat Shadrach
15 331

Told by Uncle Remus (stories)
Harris, Joel Chandler **7** 173-174

TOLEDANO, VICENTE LOMBARDO
(1894-1968), Mexican intellectual and
politician **15** 256-257
Cárdenas, Lázaro **3** 286-287

Toledo (city, Spain)
Alfonso VI **1** 149
Berruguete, Alonso **2** 223-224
Cid **4** 58-59
ibn Tashufin, Yusuf **8** 95-96

TOLEDO, FRANCISCO DE (1515-1584),
Spanish viceroy of Peru **15** 257-259

Toledo, Juan Bautista de (died 1567), Spanish architect
Herrera, Juan de **7** 335

Toledo, Third Council of (589)
Isidore of Seville **8** 149-150

Toleration Act (1689)
William III **16** 295-296

TOLKIEN, J. R. R. (1892-1973), English
author **15** 259-261

TOLLER, ERNST (1893-1939), German
playwright **15** 261

TOLMAN, EDWARD CHACE (1886-1959),
American psychologist **15** 261-262
Hull, Clark Leonard **8** 28

Tolomeo (opera)
Handel, George Frederick **7** 116-119

Tolpuddle martyrs (labor unionists)
Evatt, Herbert Vere **5** 341-343
Melbourne, 2nd Viscount **10** 468-469

Tolstoy, Alexey (1882-1945), Russian novelist and dramatist
Stanislavsky, Constantin **14** 398-399

Tolstoy, Count Dimitri (1823-1889), Russian statesman
Mendeleev, Dmitrii Ivanovich
10 486-488

TOLSTOY, LEO (1828-1910), Russian novelist and moral philosopher **15** 262-265
associates
Gorky, Maxim **6** 458-460
Turgenev, Ivan Sergeyevich
15 345-348
essays and biographies
Arnold, Matthew **1** 311-313

Bunin, Ivan Alekseevich **3** 124
Rolland, Romain **13** 260
influence of
Ehrenburg, Ilya Grigorievich
5 224-225
Farrell, James Thomas **5** 390-391
Gandhi, Mohandas Karamchand
6 201-204
Gordon, Aaron David **6** 447-448
Howells, William Dean **7** 539-541
Pasternak, Boris Leonidovich
12 124-125
Schweitzer, Albert **14** 55-56
Wittgenstein, Ludwig **16** 350-351
influenced by
Schopenhauer, Arthur **14** 29-31

Tolui Khan (reigned 1192-1232), Mongol
khan
Genghis Khan **6** 263-265
Kublai Khan **9** 115-118

Tom Jones (novel; Fielding)
Fielding, Henry **5** 442-444
Richardson, Samuel **13** 141-142
Smollett, Tobias George **14** 305-307

Tom Sawyer Abroad (novel)
Twain, Mark **15** 363-366

Tom Thumb (boat)
Flinders, Matthew **5** 490

Tom Thumb (locomotive)
Cooper, Peter **4** 223-224

Tom Thumb (play)
Fielding, Henry **5** 442-444

Tom Thumb, Gen. (Charles S. Stratton; died
1883), American midget and entertainer
Barnum, Phineas Taylor **2** 13-15

Tom Watson's Magazine (periodical)
Watson, Thomas Edward **16** 139

Tomb, The (poem)
Palamas, Kostes **12** 70

Tombeaux (poems)
Mallarmé, Stéphane **10** 172-173

Tommy (poem)
Kipling, Joseph Rudyard **9** 32-33

TOMONAGA, SIN-ITIRO (1906-1979),
Japanese physicist **15** 265-266

Tonga Islands (South West Pacific Ocean)
Cook, James **4** 214-215
Schouten, William Cornelius **14** 31
Tasman, Abel Janszoon **15** 113-114

Tonghak rebellions (Korea; 1894)
Kim Ok-kyun **9** 7-8
Kojong **9** 74-75
Taewŏn'gun, Hŭngsŏn **15** 74-75

Tonight Show, The (television show)
Carson, Johnny **3** 335-337

Tonight We Improvise (play)
Pirandello, Luigi **12** 319-321

Tonio Kröger (novel)
Mann, Thomas **10** 204-207

Tonkin (Vietnam)
Bonvalot, Pierre Gabriel Édouard **2** 396
see also Vietnam, North

Tonks, Henry (1862-1937), English painter
Evergood, Philip **5** 345

TÖNNIES, FERDINAND (1855-1936), German sociologist **15** 266-267

Tono-Bungay (novel)
Wells, Herbert George **16** 195-196

Tonson, Jacob (1656?-1736), English publisher
Pope, Alexander **12** 395-397

Too Late, the Phalarope (book)
Paton, Alan Stewart **12** 134-135

Too True to Be Good (play)
Shaw, George Bernard **14** 163-164

Tooke, John Horne (1736-1812), English
philologist
Barlow, Joel **2** 6-7

TOOMBS, ROBERT AUGUSTUS
(1810-1885), American statesman
15 267-268

Top Hat (film score)
Berlin, Irving **2** 200-201

T'o-pa Hung
see Wei Hsiao-wen-ti

Topaz (film)
Barrymores **2** 28-30

Töplitz, treaty of (1813)
Aberdeen, 4th Earl of **1** 25-26

Tor und der Tod, Der (play)
Hofmannsthal, Hugo von **7** 443-444

Torah
see Mosaic Law

Tordesillas, Treaty of (1494)
Columbus, Christopher **4** 176-179
Magellan, Ferdinand **10** 126-127
Vespucci, Amerigo **15** 476-478

Torell, Otto Martin (1828-1900), Swedish
geologist
Nordenskjöld, Nils Adolf Erik
11 421-422

Torelli, Giuseppe (1650?-1708), Italian violinist and composer
Corelli, Arcangelo **4** 230-231

Tories (American Rev.)
see American Revolution—Loyalists

Tornado (film)
Ford, John **6** 7-8

Toro, battle of (1476)
Isabella I **8** 144-145

Toronto (city, Canada)
Mackenzie, William Lyon **10** 104-106
Pike, Zebulon **12** 302-304

Toronto, University of
Baldwin, Robert **1** 466-468
Banting, Frederick Grant **1** 493-494
Best, Charles Herbert **2** 236-237
Callaghan, Edward Morley **3** 229-230

Gilson, Étienne Henry **6** 327-328
MacIver, Robert Morrison **10** 100-101
Pearson, Lester Bowles **12** 174-175
Strachan, John **14** 486-487

Torpedo boat
Ericsson, John **5** 307-308
Fulton, Robert **6** 151-152

Torquato Tasso (play)
Goethe, Johann Wolfgang von
6 388-391
Tasso, Torquato **15** 114-116

Torquemada, Tomás de (1420-1498), Spanish Dominican inquisitor
Abravanel, Isaac ben Judah **1** 31
see also Inquisition, Spanish

Torre, V. R. Haya de la
see Haya de la Torre, Victor Raúl

Torrent (painting)
Rousseau, Théodore **13** 328

Torrent and the Night Before, The (poems)
Robinson, Edwin Arlington **13** 201-202

Torrent, The (film)
Garbo, Greta **6** 205-207

Torrent, The (trilogy)
Pa Chin **12** 53-54

Torrents of Spring, The (novel)
Hemingway, Ernest Miller **7** 274-277

Torres, Manuel Montt
see Montt Torres, Manuel

Torrey, John (1796-1873), American
botanist and chemist
Gray, Asa **6** 506-507

TORRICELLI, EVANGELISTA (1608-1647),
Italian mathematician and physicist
15 268-269

TORRIJOS, OMAR (1929-1981), Panamanian strongman **15** 269-270

Torso (sculpture)
Giacometti, Alberto **6** 294-295
Pevsner, Antoine **12** 263-264

Tortilla Flat (novel)
Steinbeck, John Ernst **14** 416-417

Tory party (Canada)
Mackenzie, William Lyon **10** 104-106
Robinson, John Beverley **13** 210

Tory party (Great Britain)
17th-18th century
Bolingbroke, Viscount **2** 374-375
Godolphin, Sidney **6** 380-381
Harley, Robert **7** 159-160
Macaulay, Thomas Babington
10 79-80
Oglethorpe, James Edward
11 482-483
Steele, Richard **14** 407-409
Swift, Jonathan **15** 51-54
19th-20th century
Chamberlain, Arthur Neville
3 409-411
Churchill, Winston Leonard Spencer
4 51-53

Cobbett, William **4** 126-127
Disraeli, Benjamin **5** 27-29
Gladstone, William Ewart
6 357-360
Liverpool, 2nd Earl of **9** 456-457
Macaulay, Thomas Babington
10 79-80
Peel, Robert **12** 181-183
Victoria **15** 485-487
Wellington, 1st Duke of **16** 193-195
see also Conservative party (Great
Britain)

Tosa school (Japanese painting)
Hokusai, Katsushika **7** 447-448
Sotatsu, Tawaraya **14** 349

Tosan Academy (Korea)
Yi Hwang **16** 457

Tosca (opera)
Puccini, Giacomo **12** 474-476

Toscanelli, Paolo dal Pozzo (1397-1482),
Florentine scientist
Columbus, Christopher **4** 176-179

TOSCANINI, ARTURO (1867-1957), Ital-
ian conductor **15** 270-271
Anderson, Marian **1** 218-219
Barber, Samuel **1** 500-501
Caruso, Enrico **3** 345
Puccini, Giacomo **12** 474-476

Tosei
see Basho, Matsuo

Toski, battle of (1889)
Kitchener, Horatio Herbert **9** 45-46

Tostig (died 1066), Saxon ruler
Edward the Confessor **5** 218-219

Totalitarianism (government)
Hitler, Adolf **7** 417-420
Hovland, Carl I. **7** 527-528
Jünger, Ernst **8** 391-392
Mundelein, George William
11 248-249
Stalin, Joseph **14** 393-396

Totentanz (play)
Wedekind, Frank **16** 166-167

Totila (died 552), Ostrogothic king in Italy
541-552
Belisarius **2** 128-129
Benedict, Ruth Fulton **2** 154-155

Tottel's Miscellany (poems)
Wyatt, Thomas **16** 410-411

Touch of the Poet, A (play)
O'Neill, Eugene **11** 514-516

TOULMIN, STEPHEN EDELSTON (born
1922), British-American ethical philosopher **15** 271-273

Toulon, siege of (1803-1805)
Barras, Vicomte de **2** 19
Napoleon I **11** 306-310
Nelson, Horatio **11** 336-338

TOULOUSE-LAUTREC, HENRI DE
(1864-1901), French painter **15** 273-274
Daumier, Honoré Victorin **4** 403-405

Evergood, Philip **5** 345
Gauguin, Paul **6** 236-238
Modigliani, Amedeo **11** 72-73
Prendergast, Maurice Brazil **12** 440
Rousseau, Henri **13** 323-324
Seurat, Georges Pierre **14** 120-122
Stieglitz, Alfred **14** 451-452
Utamaro, Kitagawa **15** 397
Van Gogh, Vincent **15** 427-429

Toungoo dynasty (Burma; reigned
1531-1752)
Alaungpaya **1** 103

Tour de Nesle, La (play)
Dumas, Alexandre **5** 136-138

Tour of Duty (book)
Dos Passos, John Roderigo **5** 69-71

TOURAINE, ALAIN (born 1925), French
sociologist **15** 274-275

TOURÉ, SAMORY (1830-1900), Sudanese
ruler and state builder **15** 275-277

TOURÉ, SÉKOU (1922-1984), African
statesman, president of Guinea
15 275-277
Houphouët-Boigny, Felix **7** 519-520
Laye, Camara **9** 257-259

TOURGÉE, ALBION WINEGAR
(1838-1905), American jurist and writer
15 277-278

Tournai (city, Belgium)
Campin, Robert **3** 255
Edward III **5** 211-212
Henry VIII **7** 302-305
Saxe, Comte de **13** 507-508

Touro Synagogue (Newport, Rhode Island)
Harrison, Peter **7** 179-180

**TOUSSAINT L'OUVERTURE, FRANÇOIS
DOMINIQUE** (1743-1803), Haitian mili-
tary leader **15** 278-279
Boyer, Jean Pierre **2** 468-469
Christophe, Henri **4** 32
Dessalines, Joan Jacques **4** 511-512
Lawrence, Jacob **9** 250-251
Robeson, Paul Leroy **13** 198-199

Toussard, Louis de (1749-1817), American
military officer
du Pont, Éleuthère Irénée **5** 154

Toutounier, Le (novel)
Colette, Sidonie Gabrielle **4** 158-159

Tovarich (play)
Sherwood, Robert Emmet **14** 189-190

TOWER, JOAN (born 1938), American
composer **15** 279-281

Tower of Babel (painting)
Bruegel, Pieter the Elder **3** 65-67

Tower of the Blue Horses (painting)
Marc, Franz **10** 231

Tower of the Rising Clouds (painting)
Mi Fei **11** 12-13

Tower, The (play)
Hofmannsthal, Hugo von **7** 443-444

Tower, The (poems)
Yeats, William Butler **16** 445-447

Town, Ithiel (1784-1844), American architect
Davis, Alexander Jackson **4** 411

Town planning
Aalto, Hugo Alvar Henrik **1** 1-2
Alberti, Leon Battista **1** 113-115
Caesar, Gaius Julius **3** 207-210
Charles XII **3** 464-466
Geddes, Patrick **6** 246-247
Le Corbusier **9** 274-275
Moses, Robert **11** 202-203
Mumford, Lewis **11** 246-247
Nash, John **11** 316
Saarinen, Eliel and Eero **13** 396-398
Shaw, Richard Norman **14** 167-168
Tange, Kenzo **15** 99-101
see also Artists—town planners

Town, The (novel)
Faulkner, William **5** 395-397
Richter, Conrad Michael **13** 148-149

TOWNES, CHARLES HARD (born 1915),
American physicist **15** 281-282

Townscape (painting)
Lorenzetti, Pietro and Ambrogio
9 517-518

Townsend Clubs (U.S. politics)
Townsend, Francis Everitt **15** 282-283

TOWNSEND, FRANCIS EVERITT
(1867-1960), American physician
15 282-283
Coughlin, Charles Edward **4** 265-266

Townsend, J. S. E. (1868-1957), Irish physicist
Millikan, Robert Andrews **11** 33-35

Townshend Acts (1767)
Adams, Samuel **1** 55-56
Dickinson, John **4** 543-544
Franklin, Benjamin **6** 60-64
Gerry, Elbridge **6** 282-283
Lee, Richard Henry **9** 291-292

**Townshend, Charles, 2d Viscount Town-
shend of Raynham** (1674-1738), English
statesman
George I **6** 268-269
Walpole, Robert **16** 82-84

Towton, battle of (1461)
Edward IV **5** 212-213
Henry VI **7** 298-299
James III **8** 208-209
Margaret of Anjou **10** 249-250
Warwick and of Salisbury, Earl of
16 122-123

TOYNBEE, ARNOLD JOSEPH (1889-1975),
English historian and philosopher of his-
tory **15** 283-284
Hammond, Lawrence and Lucy **7** 109
Vico, Giambattista **15** 480-481

Toynbee Hall (London)
Addams, Jane **1** 56-57
Attlee, Clement Richard **1** 361-362

Beveridge, William Henry **2** 251-252
Carr-Saunders, Alexander Morris **3** 333-334
Woods, Robert Archey **16** 374

TOYODA, EIJI (born 1913), Japanese automobile manufacturing executive **15** 284-286

Toyo-mike Kashiki-ya-hime
see Suiko

Toyonobu (1711-1785), Japanese print designer
Harunobu, Suzuki **7** 188-189

Toyota Motor Company (Japan)
Toyoda, Eiji **15** 284-286

Toyotomi Hideyori (1593-1614), Japanese heir to shogunate
Ieyasu, Tokugawa **8** 103-106
Toyotomi Hideyoshi **15** 286-289

TOYOTOMI HIDEYOSHI (1536-1598), Japanese warrior commander **15** 286-289
Eitoku, Kano **5** 242
Ieyasu, Tokugawa **8** 103-106
Nobunaga, Oda **11** 413-414
Sŏnjo **14** 341-342
Utamaro, Kitagawa **15** 397
Yi Sunsin **16** 459-461, 495

Toys in the Attic (play)
Hellman, Lillian Florence **7** 267-268

Tra donne sole (story)
Pavese, Cesare **12** 154-155

Trabajos de Persiles y Sigismunda, Los (novel)
Cervantes, Miguel de Saavedra **3** 395-398

Trachiniae (play)
Sophocles **14** 343-345

Track and field sports
Owens, Jesse **12** 43-44

Tractarianism
see Oxford movement

Tracy, Alexandre de Prouville, Marquis de (1603-1670), French soldier and colonial administrator
Maisoneuve, Sieur de **10** 153

TRACY, SPENCER BONAVENTURE (1900-1967), American film actor **15** 289-290
Hepburn, Katharine **7** 316-317

Tracy's Tiger (novel)
Saroyan, William **13** 486-487

Trade (economics)
see Banking; Business and industry; Economics; Free trade; Stock market; Tariff; Transportation

Trade Union Educational League (New York City)
Browder, Earl Russell **3** 30-31
Foster, William Zebulon **6** 27-28

Trade unions
see Labor movement; Labor unions

Traduit de la nuit (poems)
Rabearivelo, Jean Joseph **12** 523-524

Trafalgar (novel)
Galdós, Benito Pérez **6** 177-178

Trafalgar, battle of (1805)
Franklin, John **6** 64-65
Napoleon I **11** 306-310
Nelson, Horatio **11** 336-338

Traffics and Discoveries (stories)
Kipling, Joseph Rudyard **9** 32-33

Tragedia di un personaggio, La (story)
Pirandello, Luigi **12** 319-321

Tragedy (drama)
classical (Greece and Rome)
Aeschylus **1** 70-72
Euripides **5** 332-334
Seneca the Younger, Lucius Annaeus **14** 103-105-511
Solon **14** 327-328
Sophocles **14** 343-345
England
Jonson, Ben **8** 343-345
Marlowe, Christopher **10** 272-274
Shakespeare, William **14** 142-145
France
Corneille, Pierre **4** 234-236
Racine, Jean Baptiste **12** 532-535
Germany
Goethe, Johann Wolfgang von **6** 388-391
Lessing, Gotthold Ephraim **9** 357-359
Nietzsche, Friedrich **11** 390-392
Schiller, Johann Christoph Friedrich von **14** 4-7
Ireland
O'Casey, Sean **11** 459-460
Synge, Edmund John Millington **15** 61-62
Italy
Alfieri, Vittoria **1** 145-146
Scandinavia
Ibsen, Henrik **8** 98-100
Strindberg, August **14** 509-511
United States
Cushman, Charlotte **4** 354-355
Miller, Arthur **11** 25-26

Tragedy (sculpture)
Rush, William **13** 365-366

Tragedy of blood
see Revenge plays

Tragedy of Korosko, The (novel)
Doyle, Arthur Conan **5** 91-92

Tragedy of Pudd'nhead Wilson, The (novel)
Twain, Mark **15** 363-366

Tragic Crown, The (poem)
Lope Félix de Vega Carpio **9** 503-506

Tragic Gout (poem)
Lucian **10** 25-26

Tragic Muse, The (novel)
James, Henry **8** 211-212

Tragica (dance)
St. Denis, Ruth **13** 430-431

Tragica (sonata)
MacDowell, Edward Alexander **10** 87-88

Tragicomedy (literary)
Beaumont, Francis **2** 95
Fletcher, John **5** 487
Frisch, Max **6** 118-119
Vicente, Gil **15** 479-480

Tragoudia tes Patridos mou (poems)
Palamas, Kostes **12** 70

Trahison des clercs, La (essays)
Benda, Julien **2** 151-152

Trail of Tears (United States)
Ross, John **13** 303-304

TRAILL, CATHARINE PARR (1802-1899), Canadian naturalist and author **15** 291

Train bleu, Le (ballet)
Milhaud, Darius **11** 17-18
Picasso, Pablo **12** 292-295

Train travelogues
Theroux, Paul **15** 179-180

Traité de mécanique céleste
see Mécanique céleste

TRAJAN (Marcus Ulpius Trajanus; circa 53-117), Roman emperor 98-117 **15** 291-292
Hadrian **7** 60-61
Ignatius of Antioch **8** 107-108
Pliny the Younger **12** 356
Suetonius Tranquillus, Gaius **15** 13
Tacitus **15** 70-72
Zeno of Citium **16** 499-500

Trajan, Forum of (Rome)
Fischer von Erlach, Johann Bernhard **5** 459-461

Tramp, The (film)
Chaplin, Charles Spencer **3** 438-440

Tranquility Base (United States moon site)
Armstrong, Neil Alden **1** 304-306

Tranquilli, Secondino
see Silone, Ignazio

Trans World Airlines Flight Center (Kennedy Airport, New York State)
Saarinen, Eliel and Eero **13** 396-398

Transatlantic Review (periodical)
Ford, Ford Madox **6** 1-2

Transcendental Meditation
Maharishi Mahesh Yogi **10** 132-133

Transcendental philosophy
Fries, Jakob Friedrich **6** 116-117
Kant, Immanuel **8** 430-432
Leibniz, Gottfried Wilhelm von **9** 307-310
Shankara **14** 150-151
Vivekananda **16** 4-5

Transcendentalism (philosophy and literature; United States)
Alcott, Amos Bronson **1** 121

Brownson, Orestes Augustus **3** 57-58
Burroughs, John **3** 160-161
Crane, Hart **4** 291-293
Cummings, Edward Estlin **4** 334-336
Emerson, Ralph Waldo **5** 278-280
Fuller, Sarah Margaret **6** 150-151
Parker, Theodore **12** 112-113
Peabody, Elizabeth Palmer **12** 167-168
Ripley, George **13** 179-180
Thoreau, Henry David **15** 203-205
Warren, Robert Penn **16** 121-122

Transcontinental railroad
Australia
Fisher, Andrew **5** 462
Forrest, John **6** 12-13
Canada
Fleming, Sandford **5** 485-486
Macdonald, John Alexander **10** 85-87
Mackenzie, Alexander **10** 103-104
Smith, Donald Alexander **14** 288-289
United States
Durant, Thomas Clark **5** 157-158
Eads, James Buchanan **5** 175-176
Fillmore, Millard **5** 447-448
Judah, Theodore Dehone **8** 373-374

Transcontinental Treaty (1819)
Adams, John Quincy **1** 52-54

Trans-Europe Express (film)
Robbe-Grillet, Alain **13** 189-190

Transfiguration (painting)
Bellini, Giovanni **2** 137-138
Raphael **13** 40-42

Transfiguration (play)
Toller, Ernst **15** 261

Transfiguration (sculpture)
Berruguete, Alonso **2** 223-224

Transfigured Night (musical composition)
Schoenberg, Arnold **14** 24-26

Transformational grammar
Chomsky, Noam Avram **4** 13-15

Transformer (electrical)
Tesla, Nikola **15** 156-157

Transilvano, Il (musical composition; Diruta)
Merulo, Claudio **10** 525-526

Transistors (electrical)
Bardeen, John **2** 1-3
Brattain, Walter H. **2** 505-507
Shockley, William **14** 200-202

Transit systems
see Business and industrial leaders—transit systems

Transjordan
see Jordan

Translators (books)
Suzuki, Daisetz Teitaro **15** 46-47
Wilbur, Richard Purdy **16** 271-272

Transmigration (religious doctrine)
Buddha **3** 97-101
Mahavira, Vardhamana **10** 135-137

Transoxiana (region, Western Asia)
Alp Arslan **1** 178-179
Mansur, Abu Jafar ibn Muhammad al- **10** 214-215
Tamerlane **15** 94-95

Transport to Summer (poems)
Stevens, Wallace **14** 443-445

Transportation (Mexico)
Díaz, José de la Cruz Porfirio **4** 534-536

Transportation (United States)
canals and rivers
Fish, Hamilton **5** 461-462
Fulton, Robert **6** 151-152
Harriman, Edward Henry **7** 164-165
Shreve, Henry Miller **14** 207
Stevens, John **14** 439-440
express systems
Butterfield, John **3** 184-185
Fargo, William George **5** 380-381
Federal support
Calhoun, John Caldwell **3** 226-228
Hoover, Herbert Clark **7** 483-485
merchant shipping
Collins, Edward Knight **4** 162-163
Grace, William Russell **6** 480-481
McKay, Donald **10** 416-417
Vanderbilt, Cornelius **15** 415-416
rail
see Railroads (United States)
rapid transit
Sprague, Frank Julian **14** 385-386
refrigeration in
Armour, Philip Danforth **1** 302

Trans-Siberian Railroad
Kolchak, Aleksandr Vasilievich **9** 77-78
Przhevalsky, Nikolai Mikhailovich **12** 469-470

Transubstantiation (religious doctrine)
Innocent, III **8** 125-127
Lanfranc **9** 189-190
Wyclif, John **16** 412-413

Transuranium elements
Seaborg, Glenn Theodore **14** 74-76

Transvaal (province, Republic of South Africa)
Botha, Louis **2** 434-436
Cetshwayo **3** 400
Frere, Henry Bartle Edward **6** 100-101
Kitchener, Horatio Herbert **9** 45-46
Kruger, Stephanus Johannes Paulus **9** 108-109
Mzilikazi **11** 285-286
Pretorius, Andries **12** 444-445
Rhodes, Cecil John **13** 120-122

Transvaler, Die (newspaper)
Verwoerd, Hendrik Frensch **15** 472-473

Trapassi, Pietro
see Metatasio

Trash (film)
Warhol, Andy **16** 114-115

Trasimenus, Lake, battle of (217 B.C.)
Hannibal Barca **7** 128-130

Tratos de Argel, Los (play)
Cervantes, Miguel de Saavedra **3** 395-398

Trauermusik (musical composition)
Lutoslawski, Witold **10** 52-53

Traum ein Leben, Der (play)
Grillparzer, Franz **6** 546-547

Traumgekrönt (literary work)
Rilke, Rainer Maria **13** 171-172
Schnitzler, Arthur **14** 23-24

Trautson Palace (Vienna)
Fischer von Erlach, Johann Bernhard **5** 459-461

Traveler from Altruria, A (novel)
Howells, William Dean **7** 539-541

Traveler of the East, The (novel)
Mofolo, Thomas **11** 74

Traveler without Luggage (play)
Anouilh, Jean **1** 243-244

Travelers in a Hilly Landscape (painting)
Cuyp, Aelbert **4** 360-361

Traveling Bag, The (play)
Plautus **12** 348-350

Traveller, The (poem)
Goldsmith, Oliver **6** 411-413

Travels into Several Remote Nations of the World
see Gulliver's Travels

Travels with My Aunt (novel)
Greene, Graham **6** 523-524

Travendal, Treaty of (1700)
Charles XII **3** 464-466

Traviata, La (opera)
Verdi, Giuseppe Fortunino Francesco **15** 463-465

TRAVIS, WILLIAM BARRET (1809-1836), American cavalry commander **15** 292-293

Treason (politics)
Burr, Aaron **3** 156-159
Fox, Charles James **6** 35-37
Laval, Pierre **9** 237-238
Marshall, John **10** 279-281

Treasure Girl (musical)
Gershwin, George **6** 284-285

Treasure Island (novel; Stevenson)
Disney, Walter Elias **5** 26-27
Stevenson, Robert Louis **14** 446-448
Wyeth, Andrew Newell **16** 413-415

Treasure of Sierra Madre (film)
Bogart, Humphrey **2** 363-364

Treasurer's Report, The (monologue)
Benchley, Robert **2** 150-151

Treasury Building (Washington, D.C.)
Mills, Robert **11** 36-37

Treasury, Department of the (United States)
Bristow, Benjamin Helm **3** 9-10
Burroughs, John **3** 160-161
Hamilton, Alexander **7** 95-98

Marcy, William Learned **10** 247-248
Morris, Robert **11** 185-187
Polk, James Knox **12** 374-376
Van Buren, Martin **15** 410-411
Walker, Robert John **16** 67-68
Ward, Lester Frank **16** 113-114

Treat 'Em Rough (book)
Lardner, Ringgold Wilmer **9** 204-205

Treatise of Human Nature (book; Hume)
Green, Thomas Hill **6** 520-521
Hume, David **8** 31-34
Reid, Thomas **13** 87-88

Treatise of the Narcissus (book)
Gide, André **6** 308-309

Treatise on Man (book)
Descartes, René **4** 505-508

Treatise on Money (book)
Keynes, John Maynard **8** 528-530
Robertson, Dennis Holme **13** 196

Trebbio, Castello di (villa, Italy)
Michelozzo **11** 6-7

Trebia River, battle of (218 B.C.)
Hannibal Barca **7** 128-130

Trebizond (Greek empire; 1204-1461)
Mehmed the Conqueror **10** 452-454

Tree at My Window (poem)
Frost, Robert Lee **6** 130-133

Tree of Despair, The (novella)
Husayn, Taha **8** 61-62

Tree of Knowledge, The (novel)
Baroja y Nessi, Pío **2** 15-16

Tree of Man, The (novel)
White, Patrick Victor Martindale **16** 233-235

Tree of the Folkungs, The (novel)
Heidenstam, Carl Gustaf Verner Von **7** 258-259

Trees, The (novel)
Richter, Conrad Michael **13** 148-149

Très riches Heures du duc de Berry (Book of Hours)
Limbourg brothers, The **9** 412-413

TREITSCHKE, HEINRICH VON (1834-1896), German historian and publicist **15** 293-294
Cohen, Hermann **4** 138-139
Gooch, George Peabody **6** 432-433
Osgood, Herbert Levi **12** 18-19

Trekkers
see Boers

Trendelenburg, Friedrich Adolf (1802-1872), German philosopher
Dilthey, Wilhelm Christian Ludwig **5** 10

Treno ha fischiato, Il (story)
Pirandello, Luigi **12** 319-321

Trent Affair (1861)
Adams, Charles Francis **1** 41-42
Albert **1** 110-112
Bigelow, John **2** 271-272
Mason, James Murray **10** 320-321

Palmerston, 3d Viscount **12** 81-83
Seward, William Henry **14** 124-125
Slidell, John **14** 273
Wilkes, Charles **16** 279-280

Trent, Council of (1545-1563)
1545-49
Canisius, Peter **3** 258
Luther, Martin **10** 48-51
Paul III **12** 144-145
1555-59 (suspension)
Paul IV **12** 145-146
1562-63
Gregory XIII **6** 534
Pius IV **12** 332
decrees implemented
Borromeo, Charles **2** 423-424
Charron, Pierre **3** 472
Pázmány, Péter **12** 164-165
Pius V **12** 332-333
influence (art and literature)
Alemán, Mateo **1** 126
Porta, Giacomo della **12** 402-403
Tasso, Torquato **15** 114-116
influence (music)
Lassus, Roland de **9** 216-218
Notker Balbulus **11** 434-435
Palestrina, Giovanni Pierluigi da **12** 70-72
Spanish accord
Philip II **12** 271-273
see also Counter Reformation

Trenta Altar (sculpture)
Quercia, Jacopo della **12** 509

Trentino, Il (journal; established 1906)
De Gasperi, Alcide **4** 462-463

Trenton, battle of (1776)
Greene, Nathanael **6** 525-526
Howe, William **7** 538-539
Knox, Henry **9** 64

Trepadora, La (novel)
Gallegos Freire, Rómulo **6** 185-186

Tres Himnos, Los (poems)
Gonzalo de Berceo **6** 431-432

TREVELYAN, GEORGE MACAULAY (1876-1962), English historian **15** 294-295

Trevithick, Richard (1771-1833), English inventor and engineer
Stephenson, George and Robert **14** 432-433

TREVOR, WILLIAM (born 1928), British novelist, television dramatist, playwright, and short-story writer **15** 295-297

Trial by Jury (operetta)
Gilbert, William Schwenck **6** 314-315
Sullivan, Arthur Seymour **15** 23

Trial of Fascism (mural)
Siqueiros, David Alfaro **14** 256

Trial of John Brown (painting)
Pippin, Horace **12** 318-319

Trial of Mamachtaga, The (story)
Brackenridge, Hugh Henry **2** 472-473

Trial, The (novel, Kafka)
Kafka, Franz **8** 403-406
Schuller, Gunther **14** 37-38

Trials of Brother Jero, The (play)
Soyinka, Wole **14** 358-359

Trianon, Treaty of (1920)
Horthy de Nagybánya, Nicholas **7** 510-512
Titulescu, Nicolae **15** 246-247

Tribe of Ben (literary group)
Jonson, Ben **8** 343-345
Marvell, Andrew **10** 301-303

Tribune
see New York Tribune

Tricarboxylic acid cycle
see Krebs cycle

Trick to Catch the Old One, A (play; Middleton)
Massinger, Philip **10** 324-325

Trigonometry (mathematics)
development
Hipparchus **7** 407-408
Levi ben Gershon **9** 363-364
Regiomontanus **13** 81-82
imaginary numbers
Demoivre, Abraham **4** 494-495
series and values
Cantor, Georg Ferdinand Ludwig Philipp **3** 265-266
Euler, Leonard **5** 331-332
Riemann, Georg Friedrich Bernard **13** 164-165

Triguarantine Plan
see Iguala, Plan of (Mexico)

Trilce (poems)
Vallejo, César Abraham **15** 408-409

Trilling, Lionel (1905-1975), American author and critic
Cather, Willa Sibert **3** 368-369
O'Hara, John **11** 485

Trillo del diavolo (musical composition)
Tartini, Giuseppe **15** 112-113

Trilogie der Leidenschaft (book)
Goethe, Johann Wolfgang von **6** 388-391

Trimestre Económico (magazine)
Cosio Villegas, Daniel **4** 260-261

Trimmed Lamp, The (stories)
Henry, O. **7** 308-309

Trinidad (island; West Indies)
Bigge, John Thomas **2** 272
Columbus, Christopher **4** 176-179
Padmore, George **12** 57-58

Trinity (Christian doctrine)
Arius **1** 297-298
Cyril **4** 362
Joachim of Fiore **8** 263-264
Julian of Norwich **8** 381
Servetus, Michael **14** 115-116
Swedenborg, Emanuel **15** 49-50

see also Arianism; Nestorian controversy

Trinity (painting)
Andrea del Castagno **1** 223-224
Greco **6** 511-514
Masaccio **10** 312-313
Titian **15** 242-244

Trinity Church (Boston)
Brooks, Phillips **3** 26
La Farge, John **9** 149-150
Richardson, Henry Hobson **13** 139-141

Trinity Church (New York City)
Hobart, John Henry **7** 420-421
Upjohn, Richard **15** 392

Trinity, Church of the (Salzburg)
Rottmayr, Johann Michael **13** 321

Trinity College (Cambridge University)
Coulton, George Gordon **4** 267
Duke, James Buchanan **5** 133-134
Maxwell, James Clerk **10** 361-364
Newton, Isaac **11** 369-372-109
Russell, Bertrand Arthur William
13 373-374
Sedgwick, Adam **14** 82-83
Thomson, Joseph John **15** 200-201

Trinity College Library (Cambridge University)
Wren, Christopher **16** 393-394

Trinummus (play)
Plautus **12** 348-350

Trio (music)
clarinet
Beethoven, Ludwig van **2** 114-117
horn
Brahms, Johannes **2** 490-492
piano
Beethoven, Ludwig van **2** 114-117
Brahms, Johannes **2** 490-492
Fauré, Gabriel Urbain **5** 397-398
Haydn, Franz Joseph **7** 219-221
Khachaturian, Aram Ilich **8** 530-531
Mozart, Wolfgang Amadeus
11 218-221
Ravel, Maurice Joseph **13** 54-55
string
Webern, Anton **16** 160-162

Triode (vacuum tube)
De Forest, Lee **4** 459-460

Triolet, Elsa (1896-1970), French novelist
Aragon, Louis **1** 271-272

Trionfo del tempo, II (musical composition)
Handel, George Frederick **7** 116-119

Trionfo della morte (novel)
D'Annunzio, Gabriele **4** 388

Trionfo dell'onore, I (opera)
Scarlatti, Pietro Alessandro Gaspare
13 517-518

Tripartite Pact (1937; 1940)
Mussolini, Benito **11** 272-274
Tojo, Hideki **15** 254-256

Triple Alliance (1882; Germany, Austria, Hungary, Italy; Romania, after 1883)
Berchtold, Leopold von **2** 183-184
Crispi, Francesco **4** 310-311
Leo XIII **9** 334-336

Triple Alliance of The Hague (1717; France, Great Britain, Netherlands)
Orléans, Philippe II D' **11** 530-531

Triple Alliance, War of the (1865-1870)
Alliance (Argentina)
Mitre, Bartolomé **11** 62-63
Sarmiento, Domingo Faustino
13 484-485
Urquiza, Justo José **15** 396-397
Alliance (Brazil)
Caxias, Duque de **3** 386
Deodoro da Fonseca, Manoel **4** 502
Pedro II **12** 180-181
Peixoto, Floriano **12** 188-189
Paraguay
López, Francisco Solano **9** 507-508
Morínigo, Higinio **11** 174-175

Triple Entente (1907; England, France, Russia)
Berchtold, Leopold von **2** 183-184
Delcassé, Théophile **4** 478-479
Poincaré, Raymond **12** 366-368

Triple Thinkers, The (book)
Wilson, Edmund **16** 318-319

Tripoli (city, Libya)
Decatur, Stephen **4** 448-449
Idris I **8** 102
Leclerc, Jacques Philippe **9** 272-273
Mahmud II **10** 145-147

Tripolitan War (1801-1805)
Decatur, Stephen **4** 448-449
Lawrence, James **9** 251-252
Perry, Oliver Hazard **12** 239

Tripolitan War (1911-1912)
Michels, Robert **11** 7

TRIPPE, JUAN TERRY (1899-1981), American overseas aviation industry pioneer
15 297-298

Trisevgene (play)
Palamas, Kostes **12** 70

Trishna (Buddhism)
Buddha **3** 97-101

Trissino, Giangiorgio (1478-1550), Italian writer and scholar
Palladio, Andrea **12** 75-77

TRIST, NICHOLAS PHILIP (1800-1874), American lawyer and diplomat
15 298-299

Tristan (legendary character)
Gottfried von Strassburg **6** 461-462

Tristan (novel)
Mann, Thomas **10** 204-207

Tristan and Isolt (poem)
Chrestien de Troyes **4** 23-24
Gottfried von Strassburg **6** 461-462

Tristan und Isolde (opera; Wagner)
Debussy, Achille Claude **4** 445-447
Wagner, Richard **16** 40-43

Tristesse (poem)
Musset, Louis Charles Alfred de
11 271-272

Tristesse d'Olympio (poem)
Hugo, Victor Marie **8** 22-25

Tristesse du roi (papiers découpés)
Matisse, Henri **10** 336-337

Tristia (poems)
Mandelstam, Osip Emilyevich **10** 191

Tristram Shandy (novel; Sterne)
Smollett, Tobias George **14** 305-307
Sterne, Laurence **14** 435-437, 209

Triton Fountain (Rome)
Bernini, Gian Lorenzo **2** 214-216

Triumph of Apollo (painting)
Delacroix, Ferdinand Victor Eugène
4 469-471

Triumph of Bacchus (painting)
Velázquez, Diego Rodríguez de Silva y
15 454-456

Triumph of Caesar (painting)
Mantegna, Andrea **10** 215-216

Triumph of Death (novel)
D'Annunzio, Gabriele **4** 388

Triumph of Death (painting)
Bruegel, Pieter the Elder **3** 65-67
Orcagna **11** 526-527

Triumph of Flora (sculpture)
Carpeaux, Jean Baptiste **3** 318-319

Triumph of Life, The (poem)
Shelley, Percy Bysshe **14** 176-178

Triumph of Mordecai (engraving)
Lucas van Leyden **10** 20-21

Triumph of Prince Frederick Henry (painting)
Jordaens, Jacob **8** 347-349

Triumph of Spain (painting)
Tiepolo, Giovanni Battista **15** 219-220

Triumph of the Egg, The (stories)
Anderson, Sherwood **1** 220-221

Triumph of the Eucharist (tapestry series)
Rubens, Peter Paul **13** 339-342

Triumph of the Name of Jesus (painting)
Gaulli, Giovanni Battista **6** 238-239

Triumph of the Will (film)
Riefenstahl, Leni **13** 161-163

Triumph of Venice (painting)
Veronese, Paolo **15** 469-470

Triumphs (poems)
Petrarch **12** 259-261

Triumvirates (Rome)
see Rome—Roman Republic

Trivagia, La (poem)
Encina, Juan del **5** 283

Trivia (poem)
Gay, John **6** 243-244

Troades (play)
Seneca the Younger, Lucius Annaeus **14** 103-105

Trochem, battle of (1895)
Churchill, Winston Leonard Spencer **4** 51-53

Troelstra, Pieter Jelles (1860-1930), Dutch socialist
Wilhelmina **16** 278-279

TROELTSCH, ERNST (1865-1923), German theologian, historian, and sociologist **15** 299-300

Troerinnen, Die (play)
Werfel, Franz **16** 204-205

TROGER, PAUL (1698-1762), Austrian painter **15** 300
Donner, Georg Raphael **5** 63

Troilus and Cressida (opera)
Walton, William Turner **16** 92-93

Troilus and Cressida (play; Shakespeare)
Boccaccio, Giovanni **2** 351-353
Dryden, John **5** 106-107
Shakespeare, William **14** 142-145

Troilus and Criseyde (poem; Chaucer)
Caxton, William **3** 386-387
Chaucer, Geoffrey **3** 482-485
Gower, John **6** 475-476

Trois Mousquetaires, Les (novel)
Dumas, Alexandre **5** 136-138

Trojan War (circa 1193-1184 B.C.)
Aeschylus **1** 70-72
Chaucer, Geoffrey **3** 482-485
Shakespeare, William **14** 142-145
see also Iliad

Trojan Women (play; Euripides)
Euripides **5** 332-334
Werfel, Franz **16** 204-205

Troll Garden, The (stories)
Cather, Willa Sibert **3** 368-369

TROLLOPE, ANTHONY (1815-1882), English novelist **15** 300-302
Stevenson, Robert Louis **14** 446-448
Thackeray, William Makepeace **15** 159-161

Trollope, Frances (1780-1863), English novelist
Powers, Hiram **12** 428-429
Trollope, Anthony **15** 300-302

Trommeln in der Nacht (play)
Brecht, Bertolt **2** 512-514

Tromp, Maarten (1597-1653), Dutch admiral
Monck, George **11** 96-97

Trompe l'oeil (art style)
Harnett, William Michael **7** 160-161
Holbein, Hans the Younger **7** 449-450
Peto, John Frederick **12** 259

Trooper of the Plain (sculpture)
Rembrandt Harmensz van Rijn **13** 91-95

Tropic of Capricorn (novel)
Miller, Henry **11** 26-27

Tropical medicine
Cruz, Oswaldo Gonçalves **4** 328-329
Finlay, Carlos Juan **5** 450
Reed, Walter **13** 78

Troppau, Congress of (1820)
Castlereagh, Viscount **3** 363-364
Metternich, Klemens von **10** 533-536

TROTSKY, LEON (1879-1940), Russian revolutionist **15** 302-305
associates
Bukharin, Nikolai Ivanovich **3** 112-113
Chicherin, Georgi Vasilyevich **3** 516-517
Katayama, Sen **8** 457
Lenin, Vladimir Ilich **9** 323-326
Molotov, Vyacheslav Mikhailovich **11** 89-90
Zinoviev, Grigori Evseevich **16** 521-522
CP leadership and
Frunze, Mikhail Vasilievich **6** 134
Kamenev, Lev Borisovich **8** 417-418
Stalin, Joseph **14** 393-396
followers
Ch'en Tu-hsiu **3** 501-502
Muste, Abraham Johannes **11** 276-277
Prestes, Luiz Carlos **12** 442-444
Radek, Karl Bernardovich **12** 536-537
Mexican exile
Cárdenas, Lázaro **3** 286-287
see also Russian Revolution; World War I
translator of works by
Eastman, Max **5** 187-188

TROTTER, MILDRED (1899-1991), American anatomist **15** 305-306

TROTTER, WILLIAM MONROE (1872-1934), African American newspaper editor and protest leader **15** 306-307

Troubadours (lyrical poets)
Frederick II **6** 79
Lull, Raymond **10** 39-40
see also Minstrels; Trouvères

Trouble in July (novel)
Caldwell, Erskine **3** 223-224

Trouble in Paradise (film)
Lubitsch, Ernst **10** 18-19

Trouble with Harry, The (film)
Hitchcock, Alfred **7** 415-416

Troubled Island (opera)
Still, William Grant **14** 455-456

Troubles, Council of (1567)
Alba, Duke of **1** 103-104

Trout Quintet (musical composition)
Schubert, Franz Peter **14** 35-37

Trouvères (French minstrels)
Machaut, Guillaume de **10** 93-94
Thibaut IV **15** 180-181

see also Chansons de geste

Trovarsi (play)
Pirandello, Luigi **12** 319-321

Trovatore, Il (opera)
Verdi, Giuseppe Fortunino Francesco **15** 463-465

Troy (ancient city, Greece)
Alexander the Great **1** 137-141
Homer **7** 465-467
Schliemann, Heinrich **14** 17-18
see also Iliad; Trojan War

Troy Book (poem)
Lydgate, John **10** 61-62

Troy Female Seminary (New York State)
Willard, Emma Hart **16** 288-289

Troyens, Les (opera)
Berlioz, Louis Hector **2** 203-205

Troyes, Council of (1128)
Bernard of Clairvaux **2** 207-208

Troyes, Treaty of (1420)
Charles VI **3** 460-461
Charles VII **3** 461-462
Henry V **7** 296-297
Joan of Arc **8** 264-265
Philip the Good **12** 278-279

Trozos de vida (poems)
González Prada, Manuel **6** 431

Truckline Café (play)
Anderson, Maxwell **1** 219-220

Truculentus (play)
Plautus **12** 348-350

TRUDEAU, GARRETSON BEEKMAN ("Garry"; born 1948), comic-strip artist, playwright, and animator **15** 308-309

TRUDEAU, PIERRE ELLIOTT (born 1919), leader of the Liberal Party and Canada's prime minister (1968-1984) **15** 309-311

True and Genuine Account of ... Jonathan Wild (book)
Defoe, Daniel **4** 457-459

True Cross, legend of the (fresco cycle)
Piero della Francesca **12** 301-302

True History of the Conquest of New Spain, A (book)
Díaz del Castillo, Bernal **4** 536-537

True Path Party (Turkey)
Çiller, Tansu **4** 59-60

True Relation ... State of Virginia (book)
Smith, John **14** 295-297

True Story of Ah Q, The (story)
Lu Hsün **10** 35-37

True-Born Englishman, The (poem)
Defoe, Daniel **4** 457-459

TRUFFAUT, FRANÇOIS (1932-1984), French film director and critic **15** 311-313

Trujillo Molina, Hector Bienvenido (born 1908), Dominican general and politician
Balaguer y Ricardo, Joaquin **1** 460-461

Trujillo Molina, Rafael Leonidas
15 313-314

TRUJILLO MOLINA, RAFAEL LEONIDAS
(1891-1961), dictator of the Dominican
Republic **15** 313-314
Balaguer y Ricardo, Joaquin **1** 460-461
Bosch, Juan **2** 428-429
Castro Ruz, Fidel **3** 365-368
Duvalier, François **5** 165-166
Vázquez, Horacio **15** 448-449

Truman Doctrine (1947)
Forrestal, James Vincent **6** 14
Truman, Harry S. **15** 314-316

TRUMAN, HARRY S. (1884-1972), Ameri-
can statesman, president 1945-53
15 314-316
Cabinet
Acheson, Dean Gooderham **1** 37-38
Byrnes, James Francis **3** 191-192
Forrestal, James Vincent **6** 14
Marshall, George Catlett
10 278-279
domestic affairs
Black, Hugo Lafayette **2** 301-303
Hoover, Herbert Clark **7** 483-485
Randolph, A. Philip **13** 28-29
Szilard, Leo **15** 64-66
foreign affairs
Chiang Kai-shek **3** 510-513
Johnson, Lyndon Baines **8** 308-312
political appointments
Clark, Tom Campbell **4** 81-82
Merriam, Charles Edward
10 518-519
Perkins, Frances **12** 221-222
Roosevelt, Eleanor **13** 275-277
political opponents
Dewey, Thomas Edmund **4** 524
Ickes, Harold LeClaire **8** 100-101
McCarthy, Joseph Raymond
10 388-389
Morgenthau, Henry Jr. **11** 172-173
Wallace, Henry Agard **16** 73-74
see also Korean War; North Atlantic
Treaty Organization; World
War II—U.S.

TRUMBULL, JOHN (1756-1843), Ameri-
can painter **15** 316-317
Allston, Washington **1** 176-177
Cole, Thomas **4** 151-152
Durand, Asher Brown **5** 156-157
Dwight, Timothy **5** 169

TRUMBULL, LYMAN (1813-1896), American statesman **15** 317-318

TRUMP, DONALD JOHN (born 1946),
American real estate developer
15 318-319

Trumpet of Conscience, The (book)
King, Martin Luther Jr. **9** 20-22

Trumpet Shall Sound, The (play)
Wilder, Thornton Niven **16** 276-277

Trumpet-Major, The (novel)
Hardy, Thomas **7** 150-152

TRUONG CHINH (1909-1988), Vietnamese Communist leader **15** 319-320

Trusts (United States)
Rockefeller, John Davison **13** 226-228
Russell, Charles Edward **13** 374-375
Taft, William Howard **15** 78-81
Wallace, Henry **16** 73
see also Antitrust laws (United States)

Truth (philosophy)
Averroës **1** 382-383
Epicurus **5** 292-294
Hamann, Johann Georg **7** 92
Herbert, Edward **7** 324
Kierkegaard, Søren Aabye **8** 547-549
Parmenides **12** 116-117
Tarski, Alfred **15** 110-111

Truth (poem; Chaucer)
Dunbar, William (poet) **5** 142-143

Truth and Method (book)
Gadamer, Hans-Georg **6** 162-163

TRUTH, SOJOURNER (circa 1797-1883),
African American freedom fighter and
orator **15** 320-321

Trygvasson, Olaf (died 1000), king of Norway
Olaf, II **11** 493-494

TRYON, WILLIAM (1729-1788), English
colonial governor in America **15** 321
Allen, Ethan **1** 163-164

Trypanosomiasis (medical)
Domagk, Gerhard Johannes Paul
5 48-50
Ehrlich, Paul **5** 225-226

Trypho (literary character)
Justin Martyr **8** 395-396

Tsai-t'ien
see Kuang-hsü

TS'AI YÜAN-P'EI (1867-1940), Chinese
educator **15** 322
Ch'en Tu-hsiu **3** 501-502

Ts'ao Hsüeh-ch'in (1719?-1763), Chinese
novelist
Yüan Mei **16** 479-480

Ts'ao K'un (1862?-1938), Chinese presi-
dent 1923-24
Sun Yat-sen **15** 35-39
Wu P'ei-fu **16** 404-405

TS'AO TS'AO (155-220), Chinese general,
statesman, and folk hero **15** 322-323

Tsar Fyodor Ivanovich (play; A. Tolstoy)
Stanislavsky, Constantin **14** 398-399

TSCHERNICHOWSKY, SAUL (1875-1943),
Hebrew poet, translator, and physician
15 323

TSENG KUO-FAN (1811-1872), Chinese
statesman, general and scholar
15 324-325
Chang Chih-tung **3** 430-431
Feng Kuei-fen **5** 411-412
Hung Hsiu-ch'üan **8** 37-38
Li Hung-Chang **9** 407-409

Tso Tsung-t'ang **15** 328-329
Tz'u-hsi **15** 375-376
Wo-jen **16** 352

Tshangyang Gyatso (1683-1707), sixth
Dalai Lama
Dalai Lama **4** 369-371

TSHOMBE, MOÏSE KAPENDA
(1919-1969), Congolese political leader
15 325-326
Hammarskjöld, Dag **7** 100-101
Kasavubu, Joseph **8** 453-455
Mobutu Sese Seko **11** 69-71
Youlou, Fulbert **16** 466-467

**TSIOLKOVSKY, KONSTANTIN
EDUARDOVICH** (1857-1935), Russian
scientist **15** 326-328

TSO TSUNG-T'ANG (1812-1885), Chinese
general and statesman **15** 328-329
Hung Hsiu-ch'üan **8** 37-38
Li Hung-Chang **9** 407-409
Tseng Kuo-fan **15** 324-325
Tz'u-hsi **15** 375-376

Tsongkhapa (circa 1357-1419), Tibetan
reformer
Dalai Lama **4** 369-371

TSOU YEN (flourished late 4th century
B.C.), Chinese philosopher **15** 329-330
Chung-shu, Tung **4** 48-49

Tsui-weng
see Ou-yang Hsiu

Tsungli Yamen (Chinese Foreign Office)
Wen-hsiang **16** 202-203

TU FU (712-770), Chinese poet
15 335-336
Basho, Matsuo **2** 45-48
Li Po **9** 437-439
Mi Fei **11** 12-13
Wang An-shih **16** 95-97
Wang Wei **16** 106-108

Túnel, El (novel)
Sábato, Ernesto **13** 399-400

TÚPAC AMARU, JOSÉ GABRIEL
(1742-1781), Peruvian revolutionist, last
of the Incas **15** 341
Toledo, Francisco de **15** 257-259

Tuan Ch'i-jui (1864-1936), Chinese mar-
shal and politician
Chang Tso-lin **3** 434-435
Ch'en Tu-hsiu **3** 501-502
Li Ta-chao **9** 447
Sun Yat-sen **15** 35-39, 293
Wu P'ei-fu **16** 404-405

Tuareg (African people)
Ali, Sunni **1** 158-159

Tuberculosis (medical)
Biggs, Hermann Michael **2** 272-273
Bowditch, Henry Ingersoll **2** 459-460
Domagk, Gerhard Johannes Paul
5 48-50
Dubos, René Jules **5** 119
Koch, Heinrich Hermann Robert
9 69-70

Sabin, Florence Rena **13** 402-405
Seibert, Florence B. **14** 89-90
Waksman, Selman Abraham **16** 49-50

Tuberculosis Sanatorium (Paimio)
Aalto, Hugo Alvar Henrik **1** 1-2

Tuberculosis victims
16th-18th century
Edward VI **5** 213-214
Louis XIII **9** 529-531
Mengs, Anton Raphael **10** 505
Pope, Alexander **12** 395-397
19th century
Belinsky, Grigorievich **2** 128
Bellamy, Edward **2** 134-135
Bolívar, Simón **2** 375-377
Bonington, Richard Parkes
2 394-395
Castro Alves, Antônio de **3** 364-365
Chopin, Frédéric François **4** 16-18
Del Pilar, Marcelo Hilario **4** 486
Laforgue, Jules **9** 160-161
Lanier, Sidney **9** 199-200
Novalis **11** 435
Stevenson, Robert Louis **14** 446-448
20th century (Europe)
Ben Yehuda, Eliezer **2** 181-182
Camus, Albert **3** 255-257
Chekhov, Anton Pavlovich
3 494-497
Fischer, Hans **5** 457-459
Modigliani, Amedeo **11** 72-73
Orwell, George **12** 14-15
Synge, Edmund John Millington
15 61-62
Szymanowski, Karol **15** 67-68
20th century (India)
Bose, Subhas Chandra **2** 430-431
20th century (United States)
Crane, Stephen **4** 293-295
Dunbar, Paul Laurence **5** 141-142
Goddard, Robert Hutchings
6 376-377
King, Clarence **9** 15-16
O'Neill, Eugene **11** 514-516

Tubingen, University of (Germany)
Moltmann, Jöurgen **11** 91-92
Baur, Ferdinand Christian **2** 74-75
Bethe, Hans Albrecht **2** 238-239
Kepler, Johannes **8** 514-516
Küng, Hans **9** 129-130

TUBMAN, HARRIET ROSS (circa 1820-1913), African American Underground Railroad agent **15** 330-331
Douglass, Frederick **5** 85-86
Forten, James **6** 17-18
Lawrence, Jacob **9** 250-251

TUBMAN, WILLIAM VACANARAT SHADRACH (1895-1971), Liberian statesman, president 1943-71 **15** 331

TUCHMAN, BARBARA (born 1912), American Pulitzer Prize-winning historian and journalist **15** 331-332

TUCKER, GEORGE (1775-1861), American historian **15** 332-333

Tucker, St. George (1752-1827), American jurist
Randolph, John **13** 30

Tuckerman, Joseph (1778-1840), American Unitarian clergyman
Roy, Ram Mohun **13** 18

Tucumán, battle of (1812)
Belgrano, Manuel **2** 126-127

Tucumán, Congress of (1816)
Belgrano, Manuel **2** 126-127

TUDJMAN, FRANJO (born 1922), Yugoslavian statesman and Croatian president **15** 333-335

Tudor dynasty
see England—1485-1603 (Tudor)

Tueur sans gages (play)
Ionesco, Eugène **8** 131-132

Tuft of Flowers, A (poem)
Frost, Robert Lee **6** 130-133

Tufts University (Medford, MA)
Mayer, Jean **10** 365-366

Tugendhat House (Brno, Czechoslovakia)
Mies van der Rohe, Ludwig **11** 10-12

Tughlak, Mohamed
see Muhammad bin Tughluq

Tughluq dynasty (Tughlak dynasty; reigned 1321-1414)
Muhammad bin Tughluq **11** 229

TUGWELL, REXFORD GUY (1891-1979), American politician, educator, and public servant **15** 336-339

Tuileries (Paris)
Danton, Georges Jacques **4** 391-393
l'Orme, Philibert de **9** 519
Le Nôtre, André **9** 328-329
Le Vau, Louis **9** 360-361
Renwick, James **13** 102-103

Tukulti-apal-Eshara
see Tiglath-pileser III

Tulane University of Louisiana (New Orleans)
De Bow, James Dunwoody Brownson
4 441-442
DeBakey, Michael Ellis **4** 437-438
Rothko, Mark **13** 320-321

Tulë Khan
see Tolui Khan

Tulips and Chimneys (poems)
Cummings, Edward Estlin **4** 334-336

Tumor (medical)
Cushing, Harvey Williams **4** 353-354
Domagk, Gerhard Johannes Paul
5 48-50
Ehrlich, Paul **5** 225-226
Müller, Johannes Peter **11** 239-240
Stanley, Wendell Meredith **14** 400-401
see also Cancer

Tumult (musical composition)
Martinu, Bohuslav **10** 299-300

Tunder, Franz (1614-1667), German organist and composer
Buxtehude, Dietrich **3** 185-186

TUNG CH'I-CH'ANG (1555-1636), Chinese calligrapher, painter, and historian **15** 339-340
Wang Wei **16** 106-108

T'ung-chih (1856-1875), Chinese emperor 1862-74
Chang Chih-tung **3** 430-431
Kuang-hsü **9** 111-112
Tz'u-hsi **15** 375-376
Wo-jen **16** 352

Tung-lin Society
see Eastern Grove Society (China)

T'ung-meng hui (Revolutionary party, China)
Chiang Kai-shek **3** 510-513
Chu Teh **4** 54-55
Sun Yat-sen **15** 35-39, 291
Wang Ching-wei **16** 98
Yen Hsi-shan **16** 452-453
Yüan Shih-k'ai **16** 480-481

Tung Yüan (flourished late 10th century), Chinese painter
Chao Meng-fu **3** 436-437
Mi Fei **11** 12-13
Ni Tsan **11** 400
Tung Ch'i-ch'ang **15** 339-340

Tungsten (novel)
Vallejo, César Abraham **15** 408-409

Tunis (former Barbary state, North Africa)
Cervantes, Miguel de Saavedra
3 395-398

Tunis, battle of (1535)
Alba, Duke of **1** 103-104

Tunisia, Republic of (nation, North Africa)
Abd al-Mumin **1** 13
Boumediene, Houari **2** 445-446
Bourguiba, Habib **2** 453-455
Clemenceau, Georges **4** 99-101
Ferry, Jules François Camille **5** 430
Harun al-Rashid **7** 188
Louis IX **9** 525-526
Montgomery, Bernard Law **11** 135-136
Zine el Abidine Ben Ali **16** 518-520

Tunney, Gene (James Joseph Tunney; born 1898-1978), American boxer
Dempsey, Jack **4** 496-497

Tunnyng of Eleanor Rummyng, The (poem)
Skelton, John **14** 268-269

Tupac Yupanqui, Paullu (died circa 1487), Inca ruler and navigator
Mendaña de Neyra, Álvaro de **10** 483

TUPOLEV, ANDREI NIKOLAEVICH (1888-1972), Soviet aeronautical engineer and army officer **15** 341-342

TUPPER, SIR CHARLES (1821-1915), Canadian statesman, prime minister 1896 **15** 342-343
Borden, Robert Laird **2** 409-411
Fleming, Sandford **5** 485-486

Smith, Donald Alexander **14** 288-289

TURA, COSIMO (1430-1495), Italian painter **15** 343-344
Andrea del Castagno **1** 223-224
Boiardo, Matteo Maria **2** 369
Gentile da Fabriano **6** 266-267

TURABI, HASSAN ABDULLAH AL- (born 1932), major leader of the Sudan's Islamic fundamentalist movement **15** 344-345

Turandot (opera)
Puccini, Giacomo **12** 474-476

Turangalila (musical composition)
Messiaen, Olivier **10** 528-529

Turbinia (ship)
Parsons, Charles Algernon **12** 120-121

Turcaret (comedy)
Lesage, Alain René **9** 353-354

Turenne, Vicomte Henri de La Tour d'Auvergne de (1611-1675), French marshal
Condé, Prince de **4** 193-194

TURGENEV, IVAN SERGEYEVICH (1818-1883), Russian novelist, dramatist, and short-story writer **15** 345-348
associates
Daudet, Alphonse **4** 402-403
Flaubert, Gustave **5** 480-482
Tolstoy, Leo **15** 262-265
compared to
Goncharov, Ivan Aleksandrovich **6** 424
Singer, Isaac Bashevis **14** 249-250
influenced by
Belinsky, Grigorievich **2** 128
Edgeworth, Maria **5** 205-206
Pushkin, Aleksandr Sergeevich **12** 489-491
Stirner, Max **14** 459-460

TURGOT, ANNE ROBERT JACQUES (Baron de l'Aulne; 1721-81), French economist **15** 348-349
Adams, John **1** 48-51
Condorcet, Marquis de **4** 195-196
du Pont de Nemours, Pierre Samuel **5** 155-156
Louis XVI **9** 534-535
Marie Antoinette **10** 258-259
Necker, Jacques **11** 330-331
Smith, Adam **14** 283-284

Turin (city, Italy)
Guarini, Guarino **7** 25-26
Juvara, Filippo **8** 396-397

Turin Academy of Sciences (Italy; established 1758)
Lagrange, Joseph Louis **9** 164-166

Turin, battle of (1706)
Eugene of Savoy **5** 330-331
Victor Amadeus II **15** 482-483

Turin Cathedral (Italy)
Guarini, Guarino **7** 25-26

Turin, Peace of (1696)
Victor Amadeus II **15** 482-483

Turin, University of (Italy)
Avogadro, Lorenzo Romano Amedeo Carlo **1** 388-389
Lombroso, Cesare **9** 493
Michels, Robert **11** 7
Victor Amadeus II **15** 482-483

TURING, ALAN MATHISON (1912-1954), British mathematician **15** 349-350

Turkey, Republic of (nation, Asia Minor & South East Europe)
and Cyprus
Denktash, Rauf **4** 500-502
before 1918
see Ottoman Empire
economic development
Demirel, Süleyman **4** 490-493
England and
Churchill, Winston Leonard Spencer **4** 51-53
Lloyd George, David **9** 469-471
Lausanne Treaty
see Lausanne, Treaty of (1922-1923)
presidents
Inönü, Ismet **8** 127-129
Özal, Turgut **12** 47-49
prime ministers
Çiller, Tansu **4** 59-60
republic (1923)
Atatürk, Ghazi Mustapha Kemal **1** 356-357
Ecevit, Bülent **5** 196-197
Treaty of Sèvres
see Sèvres, Treaty of (1920)

Turkish Bath (painting)
Ingres, Jean Auguste Dominique **8** 121-123

Turkish literature
Halide Edip Adivar **7** 80-82
Kemal, Yashar **8** 489-491

Turn Again Home (play)
Callaghan, Edward Morley **3** 229-230

Turn of the Screw, The (opera)
Britten, Benjamin **3** 10-11

Turn of the Screw, The (story)
James, Henry **8** 211-212

Turnbull, Sir Richard (born 1909), British overseas administrator
Nyerere, Julius Kamberage **11** 447-449

TURNER, FREDERICK JACKSON (1861-1932), American historian **15** 350-351
Becker, Carl Lotus **2** 100-101
Commons, John Rogers **4** 185
Fiske, John **5** 465-466
Haskins, Charles Homer **7** 191-192
Roosevelt, Theodore **13** 280-283

TURNER, HENRY MCNEAL (1834-1915), African American racial leader **15** 351-352

TURNER, JOSEPH MALLORD WILLIAM (1775-1851), English painter **15** 352-354
associates
Constable, John **4** 208-209

influence of
Cole, Thomas **4** 151-152
Hassam, Frederick Childe **7** 192
Moran, Thomas **11** 151-152
Pissaro, Camille **12** 326-327
Ruskin, John **13** 371-372
Staël, Nicolas de **14** 392
influenced by
Claude Lorrain **4** 89-90
Wilson, Richard **16** 329-330

TURNER, NATHANIEL (1800-1831), African American slave leader **15** 354
Dew, Thomas Roderick **4** 519
Garrison, William Lloyd **6** 226-228
Prosser, Gabriel **12** 460-461
Walker, David **16** 62-63

TURNER, TED (Robert Edward Turner; born 1938), American television entrepreneur **15** 355-357

TURNER, TINA (Anna Mae Bullock; born 1939), African American singer, dancer, and actress **15** 357-359

Turnham Green Plot (1696)
William III **16** 295-296

Turnhout, battle of (1597)
Maurice of Nassau **10** 348-349

Turning Point (poems)
Seferis, George **14** 84-85

Turno, II (novel)
Pirandello, Luigi **12** 319-321

Turnus (literary character)
Virgil **15** 507-510

Turtle Creek Ambush (1755)
Boone, Daniel **2** 397-398
Braddock, Edward **2** 474-475

Tuscany (province , Italy)
Mazzini, Giuseppe **10** 381-383

Tuscarora Indians (North America)
Brant, Joseph **2** 500-501

Tuskegee Institute (Chehaw, Alabama)
Carver, George Washington **3** 346-347
Dawson, William Levi **4** 427-428
Eastman, George **5** 186
Low, Seth **10** 11-12
Patterson, Frederick Douglas **12** 139-140
Washington, Booker Taliaferro **16** 125-126
Work, Monroe **16** 388-389

TUTANKHAMEN (reigned 1361-1352 B.C.), twelfth king of the Eighteenth Egyptian Dynasty **15** 359-360

Tutto il mal (opera)
Scarlatti, Pietro Alessandro Gaspare **13** 517-518

TUTU, ARCHBISHOP DESMOND (born 1931), South African Anglican archbishop and opponent of apartheid **15** 360-361

Tutu, Osei (died 1717), Ashanti chief, cofounder of Ashanti Kingdom
Anokye, Okomfo **1** 242-243

TUTUOLA, AMOS (born 1920), Nigerian writer **15** 361-362
> Achebe, Chinua **1** 35-37

Tvardovsky, Aleksandr (1910-1971), Russian poet
> Solzhenitsyn, Alexander Isayevich **14** 330-332

TWACHTMAN, JOHN HENRY (1853-1902), American painter **15** 362-363
> Chase, William Merritt **3** 476-477
> Hassam, Frederick Childe **7** 192

TWAIN, MARK (Samuel Langhorne Clemens; 1835-1910), American humorist and novelist **15** 363-366
> associates
>> Cable, George Washington **3** 198-199
>> Harte, Francis Brett **7** 184-185
>> Howells, William Dean **7** 539-541
>> Keller, Helen Adams **8** 479-480
> biographers
>> Masters, Edgar Lee **10** 326-327
> influence of
>> Howe, Edgar Watson **7** 529
> influenced by
>> Juvenal **8** 397-399
>> Ward, Artemus **16** 112-113
> translations
>> Strindberg, August **14** 509-511

Tweed ring (New York City politics)
> Lloyd, Henry Demarest **9** 468-469
> Seymour, Horatio **14** 126-127
> Tilden, Samuel Jones **15** 222-223

TWEED, WILLIAM MARCY (1823-1878), American politician and leader of Tammany Hall **15** 366-367
> Arthur, Chester Alan **1** 321-323
> Conkling, Roscoe **4** 201-202
> Nast, Thomas **11** 318-319
> Quay, Matthew Stanley **12** 507
> Root, Elihu **13** 283-284

Tweedledum and Tweedledee (literary characters)
> Carroll, Lewis **3** 332-333

12th Amendment
> *see* Constitution of the United States—Amendments

Twelfth Night (play; Shakespeare)
> Arne, Thomas Augustine **1** 307-308
> Shakespeare, William **14** 142-145

Twelve Apostles (sculpture)
> Luca della Robbia **10** 19-20

Twelve Etchings from Nature (etching series)
> Whistler, James Abbott McNeill **16** 225-226

Twelve Hours of the Green Houses (prints)
> Utamaro, Kitagawa **15** 397

Twelve Lays of the Gypsy, The (poems)
> Palamas, Kostes **12** 70

Twelve Million Black Voices (book)
> Wright, Richard **16** 401-402

Twelve Songs of Tosan (poems)
> Yi Hwang **16** 457

Twelve Symphonic Études (musical composition)
> Schumann, Robert Alexander **14** 41-43

Twelve, The (poem)
> Blok, Aleksandr Aleksandrovich **2** 335

Twelve Views from a Thatched Cottage (hand scroll)
> Hsia Kuei **8** 4-5

Twelve Virtuoso Studies (musical composition)
> MacDowell, Edward Alexander **10** 87-88

Twelve Years Truce (Spain and Netherlands; 1609-21)
> Maurice of Nassau **10** 348-349
> Oldenbarnevelt, Johan van **11** 495-496

Twelve-Pound Look, The (play)
> Barrie, James Matthew **2** 21-22
> Barrymores **2** 28-30

Twelve-tone method (music)
> disciples
>> Babbitt, Milton **1** 410
>> Berg, Alban **2** 186-187
>> Dallapiccola, Luigi **4** 377-378
>> Krenek, Ernst **9** 98-99
>> Perle, George **12** 223-224
>> Webern, Anton **16** 160-162
> discovered
>> Schoenberg, Arnold **14** 24-26
> influence of
>> Berio, Luciano **2** 194-195
>> Boulez, Pierre **2** 444-445
>> Halffter, Christóbal **7** 79-80
>> Henze, Hans Werner **7** 314
>> Messiaen, Olivier **10** 528-529
>> Nono, Luigi **11** 420-421
>> Penderecki, Krzysztof **12** 195-197
>> Rochberg, George **13** 221-222
>> Stravinsky, Igor Fedorovich **14** 502-506
>> Tal, Josef **15** 85-86
> rejected
>> Hindemith, Paul **7** 399-400

20th Amendment
> *see* Constitution of the United States—Amendments

Twentieth Century (film)
> Barrymores **2** 28-30

Twentieth Century-Fox (film company)
> Monroe, Marilyn **11** 113-114
> Murdoch, Rupert **11** 257-258

Twentieth Century Religious Thought (book)
> Macquarrie, John **10** 116-117

Twentieth Party Congress (Union of Soviet Socialist Republics; 1956)
> Molotov, Vyacheslav Mikhailovich **11** 89-90
> Prestes, Luiz Carlos **12** 442-444
> Stalin, Joseph **14** 393-396

Zhukov, Georgi Konstantinovich **16** 512-513

Twenty Gazes on the Child Jesus (musical composition)
> Messiaen, Olivier **10** 528-529

Twenty, The (Les XX; Belgian art group)
> Ensor, James **5** 289-290
> Redon, Odilon **13** 75-76
> Van de Velde, Henry **15** 419-420

Twenty Thousand Leagues under the Sea (novel)
> Verne, Jules **15** 467-469

Twenty Years After (novel)
> Dumas, Alexandre **5** 136-138

Twenty-eighth Congregational Society (Boston)
> Parker, Theodore **12** 112-113

Twenty-four Y's (sculpture)
> Smith, David **14** 287-288

Twenty-One Demands (Japan)
> Hu Shih **8** 63-65
> Li Ta-chao **9** 447
> Yüan Shih-k'ai **16** 480-481

Twice-Told Tales (stories)
> Hawthorne, Nathaniel **7** 212-215, 143, 144

Twilight (stories)
> Chekhov, Anton Pavlovich **3** 494-497

Twilight of the Gods, The (opera)
> Wagner, Richard **16** 40-43

Twin in the Clouds, A (poems)
> Pasternak, Boris Leonidovich **12** 124-125

Twin Menaechmi, The (play)
> Plautus **12** 348-350

Twins, The (play)
> Lewis, Matthew Gregory **9** 390-391

Twittering Machine, The (musical composition)
> Schuller, Gunther **14** 37-38

'Twixt Shadow and Shine (novel)
> Clarke, Marcus Andrew Hislop **4** 87-88

Two Acrobats (painting)
> Demuth, Charles **4** 497-498

Two Adolescents (novel)
> Moravia, Alberto **11** 153-155

Two Bacchides, The (play)
> Plautus **12** 348-350

Two Brothers (play)
> Lermontov, Mikhail Yurievich **9** 352-353

Two Chapters of an Unfinished Novel (novel)
> Waugh, Evelyn Arthur St. John **16** 145-147

Two Children (sculpture)
> Zorach, William **16** 528

Two Daughters (film)
> Ray, Satyajit **13** 60-61

Two Faced Woman (film)
Garbo, Greta **6** 205-207

Two Fools (novel)
Rölvaag, Ole Edvart **13** 265

Two Forms (sculpture)
Moore, Henry **11** 146-148

Two Friends, The (play)
Beaumarchais, Pierre August Caron de **2** 93-94

Two Generations (novel)
Grove, Frederick Philip **7** 20-21

Two Gentlemen of Verona, The (play)
Shakespeare, William **14** 142-145

"291" (art gallery; New York City)
Marin, John III **10** 259-260
Steichen, Edward **14** 411-412
Stieglitz, Alfred **14** 451-452

Two Hussars (book)
Tolstoy, Leo **15** 262-265

Two Little Confederates (novel)
Page, Thomas Nelson **12** 59-60

Two Look at Two (poem)
Frost, Robert Lee **6** 130-133

Two Mas, The (novel)
Lao Shê **9** 200-201

Two Noble Kinsmen, The (play)
Shakespeare, William **14** 142-145

Two Odalisques (poem)
Lermontov, Mikhail Yurievich **9** 352-353

Two on a Tower (novel)
Hardy, Thomas **7** 150-152

Two Pierrots (painting)
Gris, Juan **7** 5-6

Two Sicilies, Kingdom of the (Lieutenant)
Ferdinand II **5** 415-416
Garibaldi, Giuseppe **6** 215-217
see also Sicily

Two Solitudes (novel)
MacLennan, Hugh **10** 110-111

Two Strings to His Bow (story)
Edgeworth, Maria **5** 205-206

Two Tramps at Mud Time (poem)
Frost, Robert Lee **6** 130-133

Two Voices, The (poem)
Tennyson, Alfred **15** 144-146

Two Women (novel)
Moravia, Alberto **11** 153-155

Two Years before the Mast (book)
Dana, Richard Henry Jr. **4** 385-386

Two-piece Reclining Figure No. 4 (sculpture)
Moore, Henry **11** 146-148

Twort, Frederick William (1877-1950), English bacteriologist
Lwoff, André **10** 58-59

Tydings-McDuffie Act (1934)
Osmeña, Sergio **12** 22-24
Recto, Claro M. **13** 69-70

Tydings-McDuffie Law (1946)
see Philippine Independence Act

TYLER, ANNE (born 1941), American author **15** 367-368

TYLER, JOHN (1790-1862), American statesman, president 1841-45 **15** 368-369
Bache, Alexander Dallas **1** 420
Blair, Francis Preston **2** 313-315
Calhoun, John Caldwell **3** 226-228
Clay, Henry **4** 94-96
Harrison, William Henry **7** 180-181
Kennedy, John Pendleton **8** 506-507
Webster, Daniel **16** 162-164

TYLER, MOSES COIT (1835-1900), American historian **15** 369-370

TYLER, RALPH W. (born 1902), American educator/scholar **15** 370-371

TYLER, ROYALL (1757-1826), American playwright, novelist, and jurist **15** 371-372
Hallam, Lewis Sr. and Jr. **7** 87

Tyler, Wat (died 1381), English rebel
Richard II **13** 130-131

Tyler's Insurrection
see Peasants' Revolt (England; 1381)

TYLOR, SIR EDWARD BURNETT (1832-1917), English anthropologist **15** 372-373
Childe, Vere Gordon **3** 521-522
Frazer, James George **6** 76

Mauss, Marcel **10** 352-353

TYNDALE, WILLIAM (circa 1495-1536), English biblical scholar **15** 373-374
Coverdale, Miles **4** 278

TYNDALL, JOHN (1820-1893), Irish physicist **15** 374
Raman, Chandrasekhar Venkata **13** 13-14
Rayleigh, 3d Baron **13** 62

Typee (novel)
Melville, Herman **10** 472-476

Typhoid fever (medical)
Fleming, Alexander **5** 483-485

Typhus fever (medical)
Cardano, Geronimo **3** 285-286
Müller, Paul Hermann **11** 241-242

Typography
Cummings, Edward Estlin **4** 334-336
Gutenberg, Johann **7** 48-49

Tyrannic Love (play)
Dryden, John **5** 106-107

Tyre, Council of (335)
Athanasius **1** 358-359

Tyringham (Buckinghamshire)
Soane, John **14** 314-315

Tyrone, Earl of (1540?-1616), Irish rebel
Essex, 2d Earl of **5** 321-322

Tyrone's rebellion (Ireland)
see Ireland—Tyrone's rebellion

TYRRELL, GEORGE (1861-1909), Irish-English Jesuit priest and theologian **15** 374-375

Tzimtum (Judaism)
Luria, Isaac ben Solomon Ashkenazi **10** 47-48

TZ'U-HSI (1835-1908), empress dowager of China 1860-1908 **15** 375-376
Chang Chih-tung **3** 430-431
K'ang Yu-wei **8** 426-428
Kuang-hsü **9** 111-112
Li Hung-Chang **9** 407-409
Liang Ch'i-ch'ao **9** 395-396
Wen-hsiang **16** 202-203

U

UAR
see Egypt

UBICO Y CASTAÑEDA, GENERAL JORGE
(1878-1946), president of Guatemala
(1931-1944) **15** 377-378
Arévalo, Juan José **1** 285-286
Asturias, Miguel Angel **1** 354-355

Ŭlsa Treaty (1905)
Kojong **9** 74-75

UCCELLO, PAOLO (1397-1475), Italian
painter **15** 378-379
Andrea del Castagno **1** 223-224
Ghiberti, Lorenzo **6** 291-292

Uclés, battle of (1108)
Alfonso VI **1** 149

Udall, Nicholas (1505-1556), English playwright and Latin scholar
Terence **15** 146-148

U-Don Jadu (novel)
Mqhayi, Samuel Edward Krune **11** 223

UEBERROTH, PETER VICTOR (born 1937),
Former baseball commissioner
15 379-381

Uganda, Republic of (nation, East Africa)
British in
Johnston, Henry Hamilton
8 322-323
Mutesa II **11** 277-278
Mwanga **11** 282-283
Buganda annexed (1955)
Kiwanuka, Benedicto Kagima
Mugumba **9** 46-47
Mutesa II **11** 277-278
Obote, Apolo Milton **11** 457
exploration
Speke, John Hanning **14** 366-367
Stanley, Henry Morton **14** 399-400
independence
Amin Dada, Idi **1** 202-204
Kiwanuka, Benedicto Kagima
Mugumba **9** 46-47
Mutesa II **11** 277-278
Obote, Apolo Milton **11** 457
since 1971

Elizabeth Bagaaya Nyabongo of
Toro **5** 269-271

Ugedey Khan
see Ögödei

Ugly Duckling, The (fairy tale)
Andersen, Hans Christian **1** 212-214

Ugolino and His Starving Sons (sculpture)
Carpeaux, Jean Baptiste **3** 318-319

Ugolino Martelli (painting)
Bronzino **3** 19

Uhland, Johann Ludwig (1787-1862), German poet
Strauss, David Friedrich **14** 496-497

Uhlenbeck, George E. (1900-1988),
Javanese-born American physicist
Fermi, Enrico **5** 422-424
Pauli, Wolfgang Ernst **12** 149

UHLENBECK, KAREN (born 1942), American mathematician **15** 381-382

Uighur alphabet (Mongolia)
Kublai Khan **9** 115-118

Uijlenburgh, Saskia van (died 1642), Dutch
wife and model of Rembrandt
Rembrandt Harmensz van Rijn
13 91-95

Ukiyo-e school
see Japanese art

Ukraine (East Central Europe)
Chmielnicki, Bogdan **4** 12-13
Köprülü, Ahmed **9** 84-85
Kravchuk, Leonid Makarovych **9** 94-95
Mazepa, Ivan Stepanovich **10** 381

ULANOVA, GALINA (born 1910), Russian
ballerina **15** 382-383

Úlászló
see Ladislas III, king of Poland

ULBRICHT, WALTER (1893-1973), East
German political leader **15** 383-384

ULFILAS (circa 311-circa 382), Arian bishop of the Visigoths **15** 384

Ulm, battle of (1805)
Napoleon I **11** 306-310
Ney, Michel **11** 372-373

ULPIAN, DOMITIUS (died 228), Roman
jurist **15** 385-386

Ulric, Lenore (1894-1970), American
actress
Belasco, David **2** 124-125

Ulrica Leonora (1656-1693), queen of
Sweden
Charles XII **3** 464-466

Ulrich (1487-1550), Duke of Württemberg
Hutten, Ulrich von **8** 72-73

Ulrich von Türheim (flourished 1236-85),
German poet
Gottfried von Strassburg **6** 461-462

Ultima Thule (novel)
Richardson, Henry Handel **13** 139

Ultramontanism (religion)
Maistre, Joseph de **10** 153-154
Manning, Henry Edward **10** 209-210
Pius IX **12** 335-336
Pius VII **12** 334-335

Ultranominalism (philosophy)
Abelard, Peter **1** 23-25

Ulysses (novel; Joyce)
Berio, Luciano **2** 194-195
Eliot, Thomas Stearns **5** 258-261
Joyce, James **8** 365-367

Ulysses (opera)
Dallapiccola, Luigi **4** 377-378

Ulysses (poem)
Tennyson, Alfred **15** 144-146

Ulysses Deriding Polyphemus (painting)
Turner, Joseph Mallord William
15 352-354

Ūijong (died 1173), Korean monarch
Chong Chung-bu **4** 15

Umana fragilità, L' (painting)
Rosa, Salvator **13** 289-290

Umayado no Miko
see Shotoku Taishi

Umayyad dynasty
Cordova (reigned 756-1031)
Abd al-Rahman I **1** 13-14
Abd al-Rahman III **1** 14

Damascus (reigned 661-750)
    Abd al-Malik **1** 12-13
    Muawiya ibn Abu Sufyan
    11 223-224

Umberto I (1844-1900), king of Italy
    Victor Emmanuel III **15** 484-485

Umbrellas (painting)
    Renoir, Pierre Auguste **13** 101-102

Umdabuli we Sizwe
    see Mzilikazi

Umma party (Sudan)
    Abboud, Ibrahim **1** 11-12
    Azhari, Sayyid Ismail al- **1** 399-401
    Khalil, Sayyid Abdullah **8** 531-532

Umwege (stories)
    Hesse, Hermann **7** 367-369

UNÁNUE, JOSÉ HIPÓLITO (1755-1833),
    Peruvian intellectual, educator, and sci-
    entist **15** 387-388

Unam sanctam (1302; papal bull)
    Boniface VIII **2** 392-393
    Philip IV **12** 274

**Un-American Activities, House Committee
on** (HUAC; United States)
    Chambers, Whittaker **3** 416-417

UNAMUNO Y JUGO, MIGUEL DE
    (1864-1936), Spanish philosopher and
    writer **15** 386-387
    Ferrer, Gabriel Miró **5** 428
    Lorca, Federico García **9** 511-513
    Ortega Y Gasset, José **12** 7-8
    Primo de Rivera y Orbaneja, Miguel
    12 454-455

Unbearable Lightness of Being, The (book)
    Kundera, Milan **9** 128-129

Uncalled, The (novel)
    Dunbar, Paul Laurence **5** 141-142

Uncertainty principle (physics)
    Heisenberg, Werner Karl **7** 261-263

Uncle Bernac (novel)
    Doyle, Arthur Conan **5** 91-92

Uncle Dominique (painting)
    Cézanne, Paul **3** 400-402

Uncle Remus and His Friends (stories)
    Harris, Joel Chandler **7** 173-174

Uncle Tom without the Cabin (film)
    Sennett, Mack **14** 108-109

Uncle Tom's Cabin (novel; Stowe)
    Bailey, Gamaliel **1** 444-445
    Foster, Stephen Collins **6** 25-27
    Garrett, Thomas **6** 225-226
    Henson, Josiah **7** 311-312
    Stowe, Harriet Elizabeth Beecher
    14 484-485
    Tappan brothers **15** 105-106
    Turgenev, Ivan Sergeyevich **15** 345-348
    Weld, Theodore Dwight **16** 186

Uncle Tom's Children (novellas)
    Wright, Richard **16** 401-402

Uncle Vanya (play)
    Chekhov, Anton Pavlovich **3** 494-497

Undefeated, The (story)
    Hemingway, Ernest Miller **7** 274-277

Under Ben Bulben (poem)
    Yeats, William Butler **16** 445-447

Under Milk Wood (play)
    Thomas, Dylan Marlais **15** 188-190

Under Plain Cover (play)
    Osborne, John **12** 16-17

Under the Eye of the Barbarians (novel)
    Barrès, Auguste Maurice **2** 20-21

Under the Greenwood Tree (novel)
    Hardy, Thomas **7** 150-152

Under the Greenwood Tree (song)
    Arne, Thomas Augustine **1** 307-308

Under the Lion's Paw (story)
    Garland, Hannibal Hamlin **6** 217-218

Under the Net (novel)
    Murdoch, Iris **11** 256-257

Under the Sun of Satan (novel)
    Bernanos, Georges **2** 206-207

Under Western Eyes (novel)
    Conrad, Joseph **4** 205-207

Underdogs, The (novel)
    Azuela, Mariano **1** 402

Underground Railroad
    see African American history—Slavery
    and abolition (Underground Railroad)

UNDERHILL, JOHN (circa 1597-1672),
    American military leader and magistrate
    15 388

**Understanding Media: The Extensions of
Man** (book)
    McLuhan, Marshall **10** 424-426

Underwater exploration
    Cousteau, Jacques-Yves **4** 276-277

Undine (ballet)
    Henze, Hans Werner **7** 314

Undiscovered Country, The (novel)
    Howells, William Dean **7** 539-541

UNDSET, SIGRID (1882-1949), Norwegian
    novelist **15** 388-389
    Lagerlöf, Selma Ottiliana Lovisa
    9 163-164

Undulant fever (medical)
    Bruce, David **3** 63

Unemployment (economics)
    Canada
        Diefenbaker, John George **5** 4-5
    France
        Turgot, Anne Robert Jacques
        15 348-349
    Germany
        Hitler, Adolf **7** 417-420
    Great Britain
        Booth, Charles **2** 400-401
        Chamberlain, Arthur Neville
        3 409-411

Churchill, Winston Leonard Spencer
    4 51-53
United States
    Baker, Ray Stannard **1** 451-452
    Commons, John Rogers **4** 185
    Ford, Henry II **6** 6-7
    Hansen, Alvin **7** 131-132
    Hoover, Herbert Clark **7** 483-485
    Hopkins, Harry Lloyd **7** 494-495
    Johnson, Lyndon Baines **8** 308-312

Unequal Marriage, The (play)
    Heavysege, Charles **7** 246

UNESCO (United Nations Educational, Sci-
    entific and Cultural Organization)
    delegates and staff
        Black, Shirley Temple **2** 303-305
        Frazier, Edward Franklin **6** 77
        Hu Shih **8** 63-65
        Johnson, Charles Spurgeon
        8 296-297
        Mayor Zaragosa, Federico
        10 369-371
        Piaget, Jean **12** 287-288
        Redfield, Robert **13** 73-74
    headquarters (Paris)
        Breuer, Marcel **2** 520-521
        Calder, Alexander **3** 216-218
        Huxley, Julian **8** 75-77
        M'Bow, Amadou-Mahtar
        10 383-384
        Miró, Joan **11** 53-54
        Nervi, Pier Luigi **11** 346-348
        Noguchi, Isamu **11** 416-418

Unfinished Symphony (musical composi-
    tion)
    Schubert, Franz Peter **14** 35-37

Unfurleds (set of paintings)
    Louis, Morris **9** 538-539

UNGARETTI, GIUSEPPE (1888-1970), Ital-
    ian poet **15** 389-390

Unger, Franz (1800-1870), Austrian
    botanist
    Mendel, Johann Gregor **10** 483-486

Unicorn, The (novel)
    Murdoch, Iris **11** 256-257

Unification Church
    Moon, Sun Myung **11** 142-143

Unified Socialist Party (PSU; France)
    Mendès France, Pierre **10** 492-493
    Rocard, Michel **13** 218-220

Unifiers
    see Muwahhidun

Uniformitarianism (geology)
    Cuvier, Georges Léopold **4** 357-359
    Darwin, Charles Robert **4** 397-399
    Lamarck, Chevalier de **9** 171-173
    Lyell, Charles **10** 62-63

Uniformity, Act of 1549
    Edward VI **5** 213-214
    Ray, John **13** 57-59
    Somerset, Duke of **14** 333-334
    Taylor, Edward **15** 122-123

Unigenitus (papal bull; 1713)
  Louis XIV **9** 531-533

Union, Act of (Ireland and Great Britain; 1800)
  Castlereagh, Viscount **3** 363-364
  Cornwallis, Charles **4** 241-243
  Emmet, Robert **5** 281-282
  Pitt, William the Younger **12** 329-331

Union Cégétiste des Syndicats (Guinea)
  Touré, Sékou **15** 275-277

Union Démocratique Dahoméene (UDD)
  Apithy, Sourou Migan **1** 259-260

Union Humane Society (established 1815)
  Lundy, Benjamin **10** 45-46

Union, L' (musical composition)
  Gottschalk, Louis Moreau **6** 463-464

Union leaders, American
  see Labor leaders, American

Union Minière (political organization, Congo)
  Mobutu Sese Seko **11** 69-71

Union of American Hebrew Congregations
  Wise, Isaac Mayer **16** 342-343

Union of Democratic Control (England)
  MacDonald, James Ramsay **10** 84-85

Union of Love and Friendship (painting)
  Prud'hon, Pierre Paul **12** 469

Union of Soviet Socialist Republics (former nation, Northern Eurasia)

• EARLY HISTORY
    Kievan state
      Basil II **2** 50-51
      Rurik **13** 364
      Vladimir I **16** 5-6
    Mongol rule
      Batu Khan **2** 60-61
      Genghis Khan **6** 263-265
      Nevsky, Alexander **11** 359
    Muscovite state
      Chancellor, Richard **3** 422
      Godunov, Boris Feodorovich **6** 382-383
      Ivan III **8** 156-157
      Ivan IV **8** 157-159

• ROMANOVS (1613-1917)
    1613-1700
      Alexis Mikhailovich Romanov **1** 142-143
      Augustus II **1** 373-374
      Chmielnicki, Bogdan **4** 12-13
      Gustavus II **7** 43-45
      K'ang-hsi **8** 423-426
      Mogila, Peter **11** 74-75
      Nikon, Nikita Minov **11** 395
      Peter I **12** 253-256
    1700-1800 (American colony)
      Baranov, Aleksandr Andreievich **1** 499-500
      Bering, Vitus **2** 193-194
    1700-1800 (Austria and Sweden)
      Frederick II **6** 81-84
      Gustavus III **7** 45-46

      Joseph II **8** 359-360
      Maria Theresa **10** 256-258
    1700-1800 (Cossack rebels)
      Mazepa, Ivan Stepanovich **10** 381
      Pugachev, Emelyan Ivanovich **12** 478-479
    1700-1800 (Westernization)
      Anna Ivanovna **1** 240-241
      Catherine the Great **3** 370-372
      Elizabeth, the Queen Mother **5** 261-263
      Paul I **12** 143-144
      Peter I **12** 253-256
      Potemkin, Grigori Aleksandrovich **12** 411-412
      see also Great Northern War (1700-1721); Poland—partitions; Polish Succession, War of the (1733-1735); Russo-Turkish Wars—1735-39, 1768-74, 1787-92; Seven Years War (1756-1763)
    1800-1917
      Frere, Henry Bartle Edward **6** 100-101
      Ito, Hirobumi **8** 153-155
      Kotzebue, Otto von **9** 91-92
      Tso Tsung-t'ang **15** 328-329
      see also Russo-Japanese War (1904-1905)
    1800-1917 (Austria -Hungary)
      Andrássy, Julius **1** 222-223
      Francis Ferdinand **6** 44
      Francis II **6** 43-44
      Metternich, Klemens von **10** 533-536
    1800-1917 (domestic)
      Alexander I **1** 130-132
      Alexander II **1** 132-133
      Alexander III **1** 133-134
      Bakunin, Mikhail Aleksandrovich **1** 458-460
      Breshkovsky, Catherine **2** 517-519
      Miliukov, Pavel Nikolayevich **11** 18-19
      Nicholas I **11** 377-378
      Nicholas II **11** 378-380
      Pobedonostsev, Konstantin Petrovich **12** 360-361
      Rasputin, Grigori Efimovich **13** 44-45
      Speranski, Mikhail Mikhailovich **14** 376-377
      Stolypin, Piotr Arkadevich **14** 465-466
      Witte, Sergei Yulyevich **16** 349-350
      see also Russian Revolutions
    1800-1917 (France)
      see French Revolutionary Wars; Napoleonic Wars; Triple Entente (1907)
    1800-1917 (Great Britain)
      see Crimean War (1853-1856); Triple Entente (1907)
    1800-1917 (Poland)

      Nicholas I **11** 377-378
    1800-1917 (Turkey)
      Ibrahim Pasha **8** 97-98
      Mahmud II **10** 145-147
      Nesselrode, Karl Robert **11** 348-349
      Selim III **14** 95-96
      see also Russo-Turkish War (1877-1878)
    1800-1917 (United States)
      Adams, John Quincy **1** 52-54
      Motley, John Lothrop **11** 211-212
      White, Andrew Dickson **16** 226-227
      see also World War I

• SOVIET UNION (SINCE 1917)
    African policy
      Keita, Modibo **8** 474-475
      Mondlane, Eduardo Chivambo **11** 100-101
    American reporters of
      Salisbury, Harrison Evans **13** 449-451
    and Afghanistan
      Karmal, Babrak **8** 449-451
      Touré, Sékou **15** 275-277
    Asian policy
      Ayub Khan, Mohammed **1** 395-396
      Chang Tso-lin **3** 434-435
      Chiang Kai-shek **3** 510-513
      Chou En-lai **4** 20-22
      Ho Chi Minh **7** 426-428
      Mao Zedong **10** 225-227
      Pandit, Vijaya Lakshmi **12** 83-84
      Sun Yat-sen **15** 35-39
    civil war
      see Russian Revolutions
    Cuban policy
      Castro Ruz, Fidel **3** 365-368
      Eisenhower, Dwight David **5** 233-236
    culture and society
      Kabalevsky, Dmitri **8** 400-401
      Rodchenko, Alexander Mikhailovich **13** 233-234
    de-Stalinization
      Brezhnev, Leonid Ilich **2** 527-528
      Bulganin, Nikolai **3** 118-119
      Khrushchev, Nikita Sergeevich **8** 539-540
      Kosygin, Aleksei Nikolaevich **9** 90-91
      Zhukov, Georgi Konstantinovich **16** 512-513
    detente
      Brezhnev, Leonid Ilich **2** 527-528
    dissolution of
      Gorbachev, Mikhail Sergeevich **6** 441-444
      Yeltsin, Boris Nikolaevich **16** 449-452
    European policy

Beneš, Edward **2** 155-157
Dubček, Alexander **5** 112-113
Herriot, Édouard **7** 339-340
Horthy de Nagybánya, Nicholas **7** 510-512
MacDonald, James Ramsay **10** 84-85
Mannerheim, Carl Gustav Emil Von **10** 207-208
Pilsudski, Joseph **12** 305-306
Renner, Karl **13** 98-99
Tito, Marshal **15** 244-246
general secretaries
  Andropov, Iury Vladimirovich **1** 233-234
  Brezhnev, Leonid Ilich **2** 527-528
  Bulganin, Nikolai **3** 118-119
  Chernenko, Konstantin Ustinovich **3** 503-504
  Gorbachev, Mikhail Sergeevich **6** 441-444
  Kosygin, Aleksei Nikolaevich **9** 90-91
  Malenkov, Georgy Maksimilianovich **10** 168
glasnost
  Gorbachev, Mikhail Sergeevich **6** 441-444
Jewish issues
  Shcharansky, Anatoly Borisovich **14** 168-170
KGB
  Andropov, Iury Vladimirovich **1** 233-234
Lenin era
  Dzerzhinsky, Felix Edmundovich **5** 173-174
  Frunze, Mikhail Vasilievich **6** 134
  Lenin, Vladimir Ilich **9** 323-326
  Radek, Karl Bernardovich **12** 536-537
  Trotsky, Leon **15** 302-305
Middle East policy
  Mohammad Reza Shah Pahlavi **11** 75-76
  Nasser, Gamal Abdel **11** 317-318
  Reza Shah Pahlavi **13** 116-117
peaceful coexistence
  Bulganin, Nikolai **3** 118-119
perestroika
  Shevardnadze, Eduard Amvrosevich **14** 191-193
revolutions
  see Russian Revolutions
Stalin era
  Beria, Lavrenty Pavlovich **2** 192-193
  Brezhnev, Leonid Ilich **2** 527-528
  Bukharin, Nikolai Ivanovich **3** 112-113
  Chicherin, Georgi Vasilyevich **3** 516-517

Gorbachev, Mikhail Sergeevich **6** 441-444
Gromyko, Andrei Andreevich **7** 9-11
Kamenev, Lev Borisovich **8** 417-418
Kollontai, Aleksandra Mikhailovna **9** 79
Konev, Ivan Stefanovich **9** 81-82
Litvinov, Maxim Maximovich **9** 451-452
Malenkov, Georgy Maksimilianovich **10** 168
Molotov, Vyacheslav Mikhailovich **11** 89-90
Stalin, Joseph **14** 393-396
Vyshinsky, Andrei **16** 36-37
Zinoviev, Grigori Evseevich **16** 521-522
United Nations policy
  Gromyko, Andrei Andreevich **7** 9-11
  Lie, Trygve Halvdan **9** 400-401
U.S. policy
  Byrnes, James Francis **3** 191-192
  Clark, Mark Wayne **4** 80-81
  Dulles, John Foster **5** 134-135
  Hammer, Armand **7** 103-104
  Harriman, W. Averell **7** 165-166
  Johnson, Lyndon Baines **8** 308-312
  Kennedy, John Fitzgerald **8** 502-506
  see also Cold War
women leaders
  Biryukova, Aleksandra Pavlovna **2** 285-287
WW II
  see World War II
  see also Russian art; Russian literature; Russian music
• POST-COMMUNIST ERA
Russian Republic
  Yeltsin, Boris Nikolaevich **16** 449-452

Union Pacific Railroad
consolidation
  Clark, William Andrews **4** 83-85
  Huntington, Collis Potter **8** 49
  Stanford, Leland **14** 397-398
executives
  Durant, Thomas Clark **5** 157-158
  Gould, Jay **6** 470-472
  Harriman, Edward Henry **7** 164-165
  Harriman, W. Averell **7** 165-166
  McCormick, Cyrus Hall **10** 400-401
  Schiff, Jacob Henry **14** 2-3

Union party (United States)
Coughlin, Charles Edward **4** 265-266
Townsend, Francis Everitt **15** 282-283

Union Station (Washington, District of Columbia)
Burnham, Daniel Hudson **3** 148-149

Union Switch and Signal Co. (established 1882)
Westinghouse, George **16** 215

Union Tank Car Co. (Baton Rouge, Louisiana)
Fuller, Richard Buckminster **6** 149-150

Union Theological Seminary (New York City)
Bennett, John Coleman **2** 170-171
Bonhoeffer, Dietrich **2** 389-391
Breasted, James Henry **2** 510-511
Niebuhr, Reinhold **11** 387-388
Schaff, Philip **13** 519-520
Tillich, Paul Johannes **15** 224-225

Unione Popolare (Italy)
Benedict XV **2** 153-154

Unionist Party (Northern Ireland)
O'Neill, Terence Marne **11** 516-517

Unions (labor)
see Labor movement; Labor unions

Unions for Social Peace (established 1871)
Le Play, Guillaume Frédéric **9** 350-351

Unique Forms of Continuity in Space (sculpture)
Boccioni, Umberto **2** 353-354

Unison, A (poem)
Williams, William Carlos **16** 308-309

Unisys Corporation
Blumenthal, Werner Michael **2** 345-346

Unit One group (art organization)
Hepworth, Barbara **7** 318-319
Moore, Henry **11** 146-148

UNITA
see National Union for the Total Independence of Angola (UNITA)

Unità, L' (journal)
Salvemini, Gaetano **13** 455-456

Unitarian Church (Madison, Wisconsin)
Wright, Frank Lloyd **16** 398-401

Unitarianism (religion)
Adams, James Luther **1** 47-48
Beecher, Lyman **2** 113
Brownson, Orestes Augustus **3** 57-58
Channing, William Ellery **3** 435-436
Emerson, Ralph Waldo **5** 278-280
Morse, Jedidiah **11** 191-192
Ripley, George **13** 179-180
Roy, Ram Mohun **13** 18
Servetus, Michael **14** 115-116

Unité d'Habitation (Marseilles)
Le Corbusier **9** 274-275

United Arab Emirates
Zayid bin Sultan Al-Nahyan **16** 491-492

United Arab Republic
see Egypt

United Artists (film studio)
Chaplin, Charles Spencer **3** 438-440
Griffith, David Wark **6** 544-545

United Australia party
Hughes, William Morris **8** 21-22

Lyons, Joseph Aloysius **10** 69-70
Menzies, Robert Gordon **10** 510-511

United Automobile, Aerospace, and Agricultural Implement Workers of America
Bieber, Owen **2** 266-268

United Automobile Workers (United States)
Ford, Henry **6** 5-6
Reuther, Walter Philip **13** 107-108

United Church of Christ (established 1957)
Niebuhr, Helmut Richard **11** 386-387

United Democratic Front (South Africa)
Boesak, Allan Aubrey **2** 359-360
Sisulu, Nontsikelelo Albertina **14** 259-261

United Farm Workers Organizing Committee
Chavez, Cesar **3** 486-487

United Federal party (Rhodesia)
Smith, Ian Douglas **14** 291-293
Welensky, Roy **16** 188

United Fruit Co.
Arbenz Guzmán, Jacobo **1** 274-276
Ferrer, José Figuéres **5** 428-429
Keith, Minor Cooper **8** 476-477
Zemurray, Samuel **16** 496-497

United Garment Workers of America
Hillman, Sidney **7** 392-393

United Gold Coast Convention (Ghana)
Danquah, Joseph B. **4** 388-389

United Kingdom
see Great Britain; Northern Ireland

United Malay National Organization
Mahathir Mohamad **10** 134-135

United Mine Workers of America
Black, Hugo Lafayette **2** 301-303
Green, William R. **6** 521
Jones, Mary Harris **8** 338-339
Lewis, John Llewellyn **9** 387-388
Mitchell, John **11** 58-59
Murray, Philip **11** 264-265

United National Independence party (Zambia)
Kaunda, Kenneth David **8** 460-461

United National Opposition (Nicaragua)
Chamorro, Violeta Barrios de **3** 417-419

United National Party (Sri Lanka)
Premadasa, Ranasinghe **12** 437-439

United Nationalist Democratic Organization (UNIDO; Philippines)
Laurel, Salvador H. **9** 226-227

United Nations
atomic energy and
Baruch, Bernard Mannes **2** 42-43
Bhabha, Homi Jehangir **2** 253-254
Bohr, Niels Henrik David **2** 366-368
Bunche, Ralph Johnson **3** 121-122
Rabi, Isidor Isaac **12** 526-527
Bruce of Melbourne, 1st Viscount
Bruce of Melbourne, 1st Viscount **3** 61-62
Orr, John Boyd **12** 4-5

Committee for Development Planning
Tinbergen, Jan **15** 228-229
committees of experts
Elias, Taslim Olawale **5** 250-251
Congo crises
Bunche, Ralph Johnson **3** 121-122
Hammarskjöld, Dag **7** 100-101
Kasavubu, Joseph **8** 453-455
Lumumba, Patrice Emery **10** 43-45
Mobutu Sese Seko **11** 69-71
Plaza Lasso, Galo **12** 350-351
Tshombe, Moïse Kapenda **15** 325-326
creation and charter
see San Francisco Conference (1945) delegates
delegates
Albright, Madeleine Korbel **1** 116-118
Bishara, Abdullah Yaccoub **2** 287-288
Black, Shirley Temple **2** 303-305
Cosgrave, Liam **4** 258-260
Eban, Abba **5** 191-192
Elizabeth Bagaaya Nyabongo of Toro **5** 269-271
Fādil al-Jamālī, Muhammad **5** 361-362
Goldberg, Arthur Joseph **6** 397-398
Gromyko, Andrei Andreevich **7** 9-11
Herzog, Chaim **7** 354-355
Lodge, Henry Cabot Jr. **9** 483-485
McNaughton, Andrew **10** 431-432
Netanyahu, Binyamin **11** 350-351
Pérez de Cuéllar, Javier **12** 214-215
Vyshinsky, Andrei **16** 36-37
Young, Andrew Jackson Jr. **16** 467-469
see also General Assembly presidents (below)
Economic and Social Council
Evatt, Herbert Vere **5** 341-343
Fraser, Peter **6** 73-74
Myrdal, Karl Gunnar **11** 284
Economic Commission for Latin America
Iglesias, Enrique V. **8** 106-107
Prebisch, Raúl **12** 434-436
Emergency Force created
Pearson, Lester Bowles **12** 174-175
Food and Agricultural Organization
Bruce of Melbourne, 1st Viscount **3** 61-62
French dues witheld
De Gaulle, Charles André Joseph Marie **4** 463-465
General Assembly presidents
Aranha, Osvaldo **1** 272-273
Evatt, Herbert Vere **5** 341-343
Fanfani, Amintore **5** 378-379
Pandit, Vijaya Lakshmi **12** 83-84
Pearson, Lester Bowles **12** 174-175
Rómulo, Carlos P. **13** 270-271
Spaak, Paul Henri **14** 359-360
headquarters (New York City)
Hepworth, Barbara **7** 318-319

Léger, Fernand **9** 302-303
Portinari, Cândido **12** 407-408
Rockefeller, John D. Jr. **13** 225-226
High Commissioner for Refugees
Ogata, Sadako **11** 479-480
Human Rights commission
Roosevelt, Eleanor **13** 275-277
see also Economic and Social Council (above)
International Court
Haya de la Torre, Victor Raul **7** 216-217
international crises and
Bourguiba, Habib **2** 453-455
Lie, Trygve Halvdan **9** 400-401
Plaza Lasso, Galo **12** 350-351
Smith, Ian Douglas **14** 291-293
Stevenson, Adlai Ewing **14** 445-446
International Law Commission
Elias, Taslim Olawale **5** 250-251
International Monetary Fund
Herrera, Juan de **7** 335
Keynes, John Maynard **8** 528-530
Korean War
see Korean War
membership
Chiang Kai-shek **3** 510-513
Franco Bahamonde, Francisco **6** 52-54
Salazar, António de Oliveira **13** 442-443
Palestine and
Ben-Gurion, David **2** 160-161
Bunche, Ralph Johnson **3** 121-122
Silver, Abba Hillel **14** 232-233
Weizmann, Chaim **16** 183-184
Relief and Rehabilitation Administration
La Guardia, Fiorello Henry **9** 166-167
Lehman, Herbert Henry **9** 306-307
Sayre, Francis Bowes **13** 509
secretariat officials
Boutros-Ghali, Boutros **2** 457-458
Bunche, Ralph Johnson **3** 121-122
Hammarskjöld, Dag **7** 100-101
Lie, Trygve Halvdan **9** 400-401
Mondlane, Eduardo Chivambo **11** 100-101
Pérez de Cuéllar, Javier **12** 214-215
Thant, U **15** 161-162
Waldheim, Kurt **16** 54-55
Suez Crisis
see Suez Crisis
supporters
Catt, Carrie Chapman **3** 375-376
John, XXIII **8** 277-280
Truman, Harry S. **15** 314-316
Togo and
Olympio, Sylvanus E. **11** 506-507
trusteeships
Fraser, Peter **6** 73-74
Nyerere, Julius Kamberage **11** 447-449
Sayre, Francis Bowes **13** 509
UNESCO

seeUNESCO (United Nations Educational, Scientific, and Cultural Organization)
U.S. opponents
Johnson, Hiram Warren **8** 300-301
McCormick, Robert Rutherford **10** 401-402
World Bank
Herrera, Juan de **7** 335
Keynes, John Maynard **8** 528-530
Pearson, Lester Bowles **12** 174-175
World Commission for Environment and Development
Brundtland, Gro Harlem **3** 68-69

United Negro College Fund
Gray, William H. III **6** 510-511
Patterson, Frederick Douglas **12** 139-140

United party (Ghana)
Busia, Kofi Abrefa **3** 172-173

United Party of the Socialist Revolution
see Communist Party of Cuba

United Patriotic Association (India)
Syed Ahmed Khan **15** 60

United People's Congress (Uganda)
Kiwanuka, Benedicto Kagima Mugumba **9** 46-47

United Press Association
Scripps, Edward Wyllis **14** 72-73

United Provinces
see Netherlands, The

United South African National party
Smuts, Jan Christian **14** 309-310

United States (ship)
Barry, John **2** 24-25
Decatur, Stephen **4** 448-449
Melville, Herman **10** 472-476
Perry, Matthew Calbraith **12** 237-239

United States Holocaust Memorial Council
Wiesel, Elie **16** 263-264

United States Holocaust Memorial Museum (Washington, D.C.)
Freed, James Ingo **6** 88-90

United States of America (nation; North America)
• TO 1763 (EXPLORATION and COLONIAL PERIOD)
Carolinas
see North Carolina; South Carolina
colonial wars
see French and Indian War (1754-1763); King George's War (1743-1748); King Philip's War (1675-1676); King William's War (1689-1697); Pontiac's Conspiracy
Delaware
see Delaware
Dutch and Swedish colonies
Leisler, Jacob **9** 313-314
Minuit, Peter **11** 50
Stuyvesant, Peter **15** 5-6

Van Rensselaer, Kiliaen **15** 430-431
see also New Jersey; New York
English governors
see Statesmen, English-colonial governors
exploration
see Explorers, American—of American Northwest, of American West; Explorers, English—of North America; Explorers, French-of North America; Explorers, Italian—of North America; Explorers, Norwegian; Explorers, Spanish—of Southeastern North America, of Southwestern North America
Georgia
see Georgia
Maryland
see Maryland
New England
see Connecticut; Maine; Massachusetts; Massachusetts Bay Colony; New England; New Hampshire; Plymouth Colony; Rhode Island; Vermont
Pennsylvania see Pennsylvania religion in
Hooker, Thomas **7** 476-477
Hopkins, Samuel **7** 496
Johnson, Samuel **8** 314-315
Makemie, Francis **10** 158-159
Seabury, Samuel **14** 76
Stoddard, Solomon **14** 462-463
Taylor, Edward **15** 122-123
Wesley, John **16** 209-210
Wise, John **16** 343-344
see also Great Awakening; Salem witchcraft trials
Virginia
see Bacon's Rebellion; Jamestown; Virginia; Virginia Company
see also Albany Congress (1754)
• 1763-89 (UNREST and REVOLUTION)
British law protested
see Boston Massacre (1770); Boston Tea Party (1773); Intolerable Acts (1774); Stamp Act (1765); Stamp Act Congress (1765); Sugar Act (1764); Townshend Acts (1767)
revolution
see American Revolution (1775-1783); Declaration of Independence (United States); Paris, Treaty of—1783
revolutionary government
see Continental Congress (United States; 1774-89)
rise of Federal government
see Articles of Confederation (United States; 1781); Constitution of the United States (1787); Constitutional Conven-

tion (United States; 1787); Shays' Rebellion (1787)
• 1789-1817 (EARLY REPUBLIC)
Burr conspiracy
Burr, Aaron **3** 156-159
Wilkinson, James **16** 284-286
see also Burr, Aaron—conspiracy and trial
courts
Chase, Samuel **3** 475-476
Jay, John **8** 230-232
Kent, James **8** 510-511
Marshall, John **10** 279-281
Paterson, William **12** 132-133
Story, Joseph **14** 480-481
Wythe, George **16** 415
early Federal government
Adams, John **1** 48-51
Clinton, George **4** 113-114
Jefferson, Thomas **8** 238-241
Madison, James **10** 121-123
Washington, George **16** 126-129
economic policy
Crawford, William Harris **4** 299-300
Gallatin, Albert **6** 183-184
Hamilton, Alexander **7** 95-98
see also Bank of the United States, First (1791-1811); Whiskey Rebellion (1794)
foreign policy
Adams, John Quincy **1** 52-54
Ames, Fisher **1** 199-200
Genet, Edmond Charles **6** 261-262
Jay, John **8** 230-232
Jefferson, Thomas **8** 238-241
King, Rufus **9** 22-23
Livingston, Robert R. **9** 462-463
Madison, James **10** 121-123
Monroe, James **11** 111-113
Pickering, Timothy **12** 298-299
Pinckney, Charles **12** 309-310
Pinckney, Charles Cotesworth **12** 310
Randolph, Edmund **13** 29-30
Washington, George **16** 126-129
see also Alien and Sedition Acts (1798); Jay's Treaty (1794); Napoleonic Wars—U.S. claims; Tripolitan War (1801-1805); War of 1812; XYZ Affair
Jeffersonian democracy
Crawford, William Harris **4** 299-300
Duane, William **5** 109
Jefferson, Thomas **8** 238-241
Macon, Nathaniel **10** 114-115
Pendleton, Edmund **12** 197-198
see also Democratic-Republican party (United States)
state governments
Clinton, DeWitt **4** 112-113
Henry, Patrick **7** 309-311
Otis, Harrison Gray **12** 25
Randolph, John **13** 30

Taylor, John **15** 126

westward expansion
Clark, William **4** 82-83
Crockett, David **4** 314-316
Dunbar, William **5** 143-144
Gray, Robert **6** 508-509
Lewis, Meriwether **9** 391-392
Pike, Zebulon **12** 302-304
Sevier, John **14** 122-123
Wayne, Anthony **16** 149-150
see also Louisiana Purchase
(1803)

• 1817-65 (NATIONALISM and SEC-
TIONALISM; CIVIL WAR)
Asian trade opened
Clayton, John Middleton **4** 96-97
Forbes, Robert Bennet **5** 509-510
Harris, Townsend **7** 176-177
Iwakura, Tomomi **8** 160-161
Perry, Matthew Calbraith
12 237-239
British relations
Everett, Edward **5** 344
Marcy, William Learned
10 247-248
Seward, William Henry
14 124-125
Webster, Daniel **16** 162-164
see also Webster-Ashburton
Treaty (1842)
Civil War
see Civil War, United States;
Secession
Confederacy
see Confederate States of Ameri-
ca; Secession
economic policy
Benton, Thomas Hart **2** 178-179
Biddle, Nicholas **2** 264-265
Blair, Francis Preston **2** 313-315
Calhoun, John Caldwell
3 226-228
Clay, Henry **4** 94-96
Duane, William **5** 109
Peabody, George **12** 168
Walker, Robert John **16** 67-68
see also American System (eco-
nomics); Bank of the United
States, Second (1816-1836);
Depressions and Panics (Unit-
ed States); Tariff
French relations
Cass, Lewis **3** 355-356
Seward, William Henry
14 124-125
Jacksonian Democracy
Kendall, Amos **8** 494
see also Jacksonian Democracy;
Kitchen Cabinet
Latin America
Drago, Luis María **5** 92-93
López, Carlos Antonio
9 506-507
López, Narciso **9** 508
Monroe, James **11** 111-113
Soulé, Pierre **14** 351-352

see also Monroe Doctrine
(1823); Ostend Manifesto
(1854)
Lincoln-Douglas debates
Douglas, Stephen Arnold
5 80-82
Lincoln, Abraham **9** 415-418
nullification
see Nullification crisis; Tariff of
Abominations (1828)
presidency
Adams, John Quincy **1** 52-54
Buchanan, James **3** 89-90
Fillmore, Millard **5** 447-448
Harrison, William Henry
7 180-181
Jackson, Andrew **8** 168-172
Lincoln, Abraham **9** 415-418
Monroe, James **11** 111-113
Pierce, Franklin **12** 300-301
Polk, James Knox **12** 374-376
Taylor, Zachary **15** 128-130
Tyler, John **15** 368-369
Van Buren, Martin **15** 410-411
Seminole Wars
see Seminole War (1817-1818);
Seminole War, Second
(1835-1843)
slavery
see Abolitionists, American;
Antislavery movement (United
States); African American histo-
ry (United States)—through
Civil War; Fugitive Slave Act
(United States; 1850); Harpers
Ferry; Slave trade; Slavery
slavery extension issue
see Compromise of 1850; Dred
Scott decision; Kansas-Nebras-
ka Act (1854); Missouri Com-
promise; Nebraska Act (1854-);
Missouri Compromise; North-
west Ordinance (1787); Popu-
lar sovereignty; Wilmot Proviso
states rights
see States rights
westward expansion
Ashley, William Henry
1 333-334
Carson, Christopher **3** 334-335
Comstock, Henry Tompkins
Paige **4** 189
Cutler, Manasseh **4** 356-357
Fitzpatrick, Thomas **5** 474-475
Harrison, William Henry
7 180-181
Jackson, Andrew **8** 168-172
Kelley, Hall Jackson **8** 480
Polk, James Knox **12** 374-376
Smith, Jedediah S. **14** 294-295
see also Bear Flag Revolt (Cali-
fornia; 1846-47); California;
Frontiersmen, American; Gads-
den Purchase (1853);
Guadalupe Hidalgo, Treaty of
(1848); Mexican War
(1846-1848); Oregon; Texas

• 1865-1901 (RECONSTRUCTION and
INDUSTRIALIZATION)
civil service reform
Arthur, Chester Alan **1** 321-323
Eaton, Dorman Bridgman
5 190-191
Pendleton, George Hunt **12** 198
see also Civil Service (United
States)
economic policy
Drew, Daniel **5** 101-102
Harrison, Benjamin **7** 178-179
McCulloch, Hugh **10** 404-405
McKinley, William **10** 418-420
Sherman, John **14** 184-185
see also Depressions and panics
(United States)
Federal aid to agriculture
Hatch, William Henry **7** 196
foreign policy
Baez, Buenaventura **1** 432-433
Blaine, James Gillespie
2 312-313
Burlingame, Anson **3** 144-145
Dole, Sanford Ballard **5** 46
Evarts, William Maxwell
5 340-341
Fish, Hamilton **5** 461-462
Hay, John **7** 215-216
Liliuokalani, Lydia Kamakaeha
9 411-412
Olney, Richard **11** 504-505
see also Imperialism, American;
Philippines, Republic of the;
Spanish-American War
Indian policy
Cochise **4** 128
Crazy Horse **4** 303-304
Crook, George **4** 322-323
Custer, George Armstrong
4 355-356
Dawes, Henry Laurens **4** 427
Fletcher, Alice Cunningham
5 486-487
Geronimo **6** 281-282
Howard, Oliver Otis **7** 528-529
Joseph **8** 358-359
Miles, Nelson Appleton
11 16-17
Red Cloud **13** 70-71
Sitting Bull **14** 264-265
see also Indians (North America)
industrial expansion
see Business and industrial lead-
ers, American
Johnson impeachment
Johnson, Andrew **8** 294-295
Seward, William Henry
14 124-125
Stanton, Edwin McMasters
14 401-402
Trumbull, Lyman **15** 317-318
Populist movement
Donnelly, Ignatius **5** 62
Watson, Thomas Edward **16** 139
see also Populist party (United
States)

presidency
  Arthur, Chester Alan **1** 321-323
  Cleveland, Stephen Grover
    4 108-110
  Garfield, James Abram
    6 213-214
  Grant, Ulysses Simpson
    6 492-494
  Harrison, Benjamin **7** 178-179
  Hayes, Rutherford Birchard
    7 227-228
  Johnson, Andrew **8** 294-295
  McKinley, William **10** 418-420
Reconstruction
  see Reconstruction
spoils system and reforms
  Bristow, Benjamin Helm **3** 9-10
  Conkling, Roscoe **4** 201-202
  Quay, Matthew Stanley **12** 507
  Reed, Thomas Brackett **13** 77
  Schurz, Carl **14** 44-45
  Tilden, Samuel Jones
    15 222-223
  see also Political machines (United States)
unionism
  see Labor unions (United States)
Wild West
  Earp, Wyatt Barry Stepp
    5 181-182
  Hickok, James Butler **7** 374-375
  James, Jesse Woodson **8** 212-213
  Oakley, Annie **11** 453-454
  see also Frontiersmen, American
• 1901-21 (PROGRESSIVE ERA and WWI)
British relations
  Cecil, of Chelwood Viscount
    3 388-389
  Page, Walter Hines **12** 60-61
Canadian reciprocity issue
  Cannon, Joseph Gurney
    3 261-262
  Laurier, Wilfrid **9** 232-234
conservatives
  Aldrich, Nelson Wilmarth
    1 123-124
  Cannon, Joseph Gurney
    3 261-262
  Tillman, Benjamin Ryan
    15 225-226
Far East
  Hay, John **7** 215-216
  Lansing, Robert **9** 200
  Roosevelt, Theodore **13** 280-283
  Root, Elihu **13** 283-284
  Wood, Leonard **16** 369-370
Latin America
  Bryan, William Jennings **3** 80-82
  Bunau-Varilla, Philippe Jean
    3 120-121
  Carranza, Venustiano **3** 321-322
  Estrada Cabrera, Manuel
    5 325-326
  Estrada Palma, Tomás **5** 326-327

Nabuco de Araujo, Joaquim
  Aurelio **11** 288-289
Pershing, John Joseph
  12 243-244
Reyes, Rafael **13** 113
Roosevelt, Theodore **13** 280-283
Vázquez, Horacio **15** 448-449
Villa, Pancho **15** 495-496
see also Panama Canal; and
  under individual countries
political machines
  see Political machines (United States)
presidency
  Roosevelt, Theodore **13** 280-283
  Taft, William Howard **15** 78-81
  Wilson, Thomas Woodrow
    16 330-332
Progressive reforms
  Baker, Newton Diehl **1** 451
  Bryan, William Jennings **3** 80-82
  Johnson, Hiram Warren
    8 300-301
  Knox, Philander Chase **9** 66-67
  La Follette, Robert Marion
    9 155-156
  Lodge, Henry Cabot **9** 482-483
  Norris, George William
    11 428-429
  Pinchot, Gifford **12** 308-309
"red scare"
  Palmer, Alexander Mitchell
    12 77-78
WWI
  see World War I; Versailles,
    Treaty of (1919; and Paris
    Peace Conference)
  see also Fourteen Points; League
    of Nations
• 1921-45 (NORMALCY-WW II)
foreign policy
  George VI **6** 275
  Hughes, Charles Evans **8** 15-16
  Kellogg, Frank Billings **8** 481
  King, William Lyon Mackenzie
    9 25-26
  Konoe, Fumimaro **9** 82-83
  Litvinov, Maxim Maximovich
    9 451-452
  Murphy, Frank **11** 260-261
  Stettinius, Edward R. Jr.
    14 437-438
  Stimson, Henry Lewis
    14 457-458
  see also Latin America (below);
    Washington Conference
    (1921-1922)
isolationism
  Borah, William Edgar **2** 408
  Johnson, Hiram Warren
    8 300-301
labor unions
  see Labor unions (United States)
Latin America
  Arévalo, Juan José **1** 285-286
  Daniels, Josephus **4** 387

Harding, Warren Gamaliel
  7 148-149
Hull, Cordell **8** 28-29
Kellogg, Frank Billings **8** 481
Lamas, Carlos Saavedra
  9 175-176
Morrow, Dwight Whitney
  11 190-191
Root, Elihu **13** 283-284
Somoza, Anastasio **14** 335-336
Welles, Sumner **16** 191-192
see also Good-neighbor policy;
  Pan-Americanism
New Deal
  Byrnes, James Francis **3** 191-192
  Hopkins, Harry Lloyd **7** 494-495
  Ickes, Harold LeClaire
    8 100-101
  Lilienthal, David Eli **9** 410-411
  Morgenthau, Henry Jr.
    11 172-173
  Norris, George William
    11 428-429
  Perkins, Frances **12** 221-222
  Rayburn, Samuel Taliaferro
    13 61-62
  Roosevelt, Franklin Delano
    13 277-280
  Wagner, Robert Ferdinand **16** 43
  Wallace, Henry Agard **16** 73-74
  see also Brain trust; New Deal
normalcy to depression
  Coolidge, John Calvin **4** 217-219
  Harding, Warren Gamaliel
    7 148-149
  Hoover, Herbert Clark
    7 483-485
  Mellon, Andrew William
    10 469-470
  Walsh, Thomas James **16** 85-86
  see also Depression, Great (United States)
political machines
  see Political machines
Teapot Dome
  see Teapot Dome Scandal (1923)
UN
  see San Francisco Conference
    (1945); United Nations
WW II
  see World War II
• SINCE 1945
Africa
  Bourguiba, Habib **2** 453-455
  Busia, Kofi Abrefa **3** 172-173
  Tshombe, Moïse Kapenda
    15 325-326
Canada
  Diefenbaker, John George **5** 4-5
  Pearson, Lester Bowles
    12 174-175
China
  Brzezinski, Zbigniew **3** 85-87
  Chou En-lai **4** 20-22
  Kissinger, Henry Alfred **9** 43-45
  Nixon, Richard Milhous
    11 401-404

civil rights
  see African American history
    (United States); Civil rights
    movement
Europe
  Ball, George **1** 470-471
  De Gaulle, Charles André Joseph
    Marie **4** 463-465
  Franco Bahamonde, Francisco
    6 52-54
  Kennedy, John Fitzgerald
    8 502-506
  see also Berlin—Wall crisis;
    Marshall Plan; North Atlantic
    Treaty Organization; and sec-
    tion Soviet relations (below)
history of
  Hofstadter, Richard **7** 444-445
Indian policies
  Deer, Ada E. **4** 452-454
Iran
  Brzezinski, Zbigniew **3** 85-87
  Christopher, Warren Minor
    4 32-33
  Khomeini, Ruhollah Musavi
    8 535-537
Japan
  Kishi, Nobusuke **9** 41-43
  Sato, Eisaku **13** 495-496
Korean War
  see Korean War
Latin America
  Arbenz Guzmán, Jacobo
    1 274-276
  Arias, Arnulfo **1** 286-287
  Ávila Camacho, Manuel
    1 387-388
  Balaguer y Ricardo, Joaquin
    1 460-461
  Calderón Fournier, Rafael
    3 222-223
  Callejas Romero, Rafael Leonar-
    do **3** 233-234
  Castro Ruz, Fidel **3** 365-368
  Duarte, José Napoleón
    5 109-111
  Duvalier, François **5** 165-166
  Guevara, Ernesto **7** 30-31
  Johnson, Lyndon Baines
    8 308-312
  Muñoz Marín, José Luís Alberto
    11 249-250
  Ortega, Daniel **12** 5-7
  Paz, Octavio **12** 161-162
  see also Bay of Pigs invasion;
    Cuban missile crisis
McCarthyism
  Kennedy, Robert Francis
    8 508-509
  McCarthy, Joseph Raymond
    10 388-389
  Nixon, Richard Milhous
    11 401-404
Middle East
  Faisal ibn Abd al Aziz ibn Saud
    5 371-372
  Mohammad Reza Shah Pahlavi
    11 75-76

    see also Israel, State of; Suez
    crsis
Pakistan
  Ayub Khan, Mohammed
    1 395-396
Panama Canal
  Chiari, Roberto **3** 513-514
Philippines
  Garcia, Carlos P. **6** 207-208
  Marcos, Ferdinand **10** 240-242
  Recto, Claro M. **13** 69-70
  Roxas, Manuel **13** 331-332
presidency
  Bush, George **3** 167-169
  Carter, James Earl **3** 339-342
  Clinton, William Jefferson
    4 117-119
  Eisenhower, Dwight David
    5 233-236
  Ford, Gerald **6** 2-5
  Johnson, Lyndon Baines
    8 308-312
  Kennedy, John Fitzgerald
    8 502-506
  Nixon, Richard Milhous
    11 401-404
  Reagan, Ronald W. **13** 65-68
  Truman, Harry S. **15** 314-316
Puerto Rico
  Romero Barceló, Carlos
    13 267-268
Southeast Asia
  Diem, Ngo Dinh **5** 6-7
  Fulbright, James William
    6 147-149
  Kennedy, John Fitzgerald
    8 502-506
  Kennedy, Robert Francis
    8 508-509
  McCarthy, Eugene Joseph
    10 386-388
  McGovern, George Stanley
    10 412-414
  Nixon, Richard Milhous
    11 401-404
  Sihanouk, Norodom **14** 222-223
  Souvanna Phouma **14** 357-358
  see also Southeast Asia Treaty
    Organization, Vietnam War
    (1956-1976)
Soviet relations
  Acheson, Dean Gooderham
    1 37-38
  Byrnes, James Francis **3** 191-192
  Dulles, John Foster **5** 134-135
  Harriman, W. Averell **7** 165-166
  Jackson, Henry Martin
    8 172-174
  Kennedy, John Fitzgerald
    8 502-506
  Marshall, George Catlett
    10 278-279
  Stevenson, Adlai Ewing
    14 445-446
  Wallace, Henry Agard **16** 73-74
  see also Cold War.
Vietnam War

  Bundy, McGeorge **3** 122-124
  McNamara, Robert S.
    10 429-431
  Rusk, David Dean **13** 368-370
Watergate scandal (1974)
  seeWatergate Scandal
WW II
  see World War II
  see also American art; American
    literature; American music;
    Church and State (United
    States); Diplomats, American;
    Education (United States);
    Immigrants to the U.S.; Jurists,
    American; Military leaders,
    American; Statesmen, Ameri-
    can; individual states

United States Air Force (U.S.A.F.)
  Armstrong, Neil Alden **1** 304-306
  Arnold, Henry Harley **1** 310-311
  Widnall, Sheila E. **16** 258-259
  Yeager, Chuck **16** 444-445

United States Army
  Army War College
    Root, Elihu **13** 283-284
    Westmoreland, William Childs
      16 216-217
  intelligence
    Pinkerton, Allan **12** 314-315
  medical services
    Drew, Charles Richard **5** 100-101
    Gorgas, William Crawford
      6 454-455
    Reed, Walter **13** 78
  Signal Corps and Engineers
    Arnold, Henry Harley **1** 310-311
    Douglas, Donald Wills **5** 77
    Frémont, John Charles **6** 97-98
    Goethals, George Washington
      6 387-388
    Greely, Adolphus Washington
      6 517-518
    Groves, Leslie **7** 21-22
    see also Military leaders, American;
      Statesmen, American—Executive
      (secretary of Army); U.S. Military
      Academy

U.S. Atomic Energy Commission
  see Atomic Energy Commission (United
    States)

U.S. Bureau of Labor Statistics
  Mitchell, Wesley Clair **11** 61-62
  Wright, Carroll Davidson **16** 396

U.S. Department of Agriculture
  see Agriculture, U.S. Department of

U.S. Department of Commerce
  Hoover, Herbert Clark **7** 483-485
  Knox, Philander Chase **9** 66-67

U.S. Department of Defense
  Forrestal, James Vincent **6** 14

U.S. Department of Justice
  Hoover, John Edgar **7** 485-487

U.S. Department of Labor
  Martin, Lynn Morley **10** 290-292

U.S. Geological Survey
King, Clarence **9** 15-16
Marsh, Othniel Charles **10** 275-276
Powell, John Wesley **12** 425-426

U.S. House of Representatives
architecture
Latrobe, Benjamin Henry **9** 222-224
House Committee on Un-American
Activities (HUAC)
Chambers, Whittaker **3** 416-417
Flynn, Elizabeth Gurley **5** 496-497
Hiss, Alger **7** 413-415
Judiciary Committee
Rodino, Peter Wallace Jr.
13 238-239
members
see Statesmen, American
rules
Cannon, Joseph Gurney **3** 261-262
Norris, George William **11** 428-429
Reed, Thomas Brackett **13** 77

U.S. Information Agency (USIA)
Murrow, Edward Roscoe **11** 265-266
Rowan, Carl T. **13** 329-330

U.S. Military Academy (West Point, New
York)
Battle Monument
White, Stanford **16** 235-236
professors
Goethals, George Washington
6 387-388
Thomas, George Henry **15** 190-191
superintendents
Goodpaster, Andrew Jackson
6 439-441
Howard, Oliver Otis **7** 528-529
Lee, Robert Edward **9** 292-294
MacArthur, Douglas **10** 76-78
Thayer, Sylvanus **15** 168-169
Westmoreland, William Childs
16 216-217

U.S. Naval Academy (Annapolis, Maryland)
Bancroft, George **1** 483-484
Michelson, Albert Abraham **11** 7-8
Perry, Matthew Calbraith **12** 237-239

U.S. navy
aircraft and rocketry
Curtiss, Glenn Hammond
4 350-351
Douglas, Donald Wills **5** 77
Goddard, Robert Hutchings
6 376-377
assistant secretaries
Roosevelt, Eleanor **13** 275-277
Roosevelt, Franklin Delano
13 277-280
Roosevelt, Theodore **13** 280-283
Welles, Gideon **16** 188-190
development
Farragut, David Glasgow **5** 388-389
Melville, George Wallace **10** 472
Perry, Matthew Calbraith
12 237-239
nuclear submarines and warships

Rickover, Hyman George
13 155-157
personnel policies
Zumwalt, Elmo Russell Jr.
16 532-534
submarines and deep-sea research
Holland, John Philip **7** 453-454
Piccard, Auguste **12** 297-298
see alsoMilitary leaders, American—
Navy; Statesmen, American—
Executive (secretary of Navy)

U.S. Olympic Committee
Walker, LeRoy Tashreau **16** 64-65

U.S. Sanitary Commission (relief organiza-
tion)
Barton, Clara **2** 37-39
Bellows, Henry Whitney **2** 143-144
Borden, Gail **2** 409
Lowell, Josephine Shaw **10** 15-16

U.S. Senate
majority leaders (Republican)
Dole, Robert J. **5** 43-46
members
see Statesmen, American
representation and elections
Coolidge, John Calvin **4** 217-219
Paterson, William **12** 132-133
Taft, William Howard **15** 78-81

U.S. Steel Corporation
Carnegie, Andrew **3** 309-312
Frick, Henry Clay **6** 108-109
Fuller, Richard Buckminster **6** 149-150
Gary, Elbert Henry **6** 229-230
Knox, Philander Chase **9** 66-67
Lewis, John Llewellyn **9** 387-388
Morgan, John Pierpont **11** 163-165
Rockefeller, John Davison **13** 226-228
Schwab, Charles Michael **14** 50-51
Stettinius, Edward R. Jr. **14** 437-438
Taft, William Howard **15** 78-81

U.S. v. American Tobacco (legal case)
White, Edward Douglass **16** 230-231

U.S. v. Associated Press (legal case)
Hand, Billings Learned **7** 116

U.S. v. Butler (legal case)
Cardozo, Benjamin Nathan **3** 288-290
Stone, Harlan Fiske **14** 468-470

U.S. v. Harris (legal case)
Harlan, John Marshall **7** 156-157

U.S. v. Nixon (legal case)
Burger, Warren E. **3** 133-136

U.S. v. Peters (legal case)
Marshall, John **10** 279-281

U.S. v. Worrall (legal case)
Chase, Samuel **3** 475-476

United Steelworkers of America (USA)
Abel, Iorwith Wilber **1** 22-23
Murray, Philip **11** 264-265

United Synagogue of America (established
1913)
Schechter, Solomon **13** 524

Unity and Security, Act of (Sweden; 1789)
Gustavus III **7** 45-46

Unity Block (Chicago, Illinois)
Altgeld, John Peter **1** 180-182

Unity Church (Oak Park, Illinois)
Wright, Frank Lloyd **16** 398-401

Unity, Church of (Springfield, Massachusetts)
Richardson, Henry Hobson **13** 139-141

Universal Brotherhood, League of (established 1847)
Burritt, Elihu **3** 160

Universal Declaration of Human Rights
(United Nations)
Evatt, Herbert Vere **5** 341-343
Roosevelt, Eleanor **13** 275-277

Universal German Educational Institute
(Keilham; established 1816)
Froebel, Friedrich Wilhelm August
6 122-123

Universal joint (instrument)
Hooke, Robert **7** 475

Universal military training
Marshall, George Catlett **10** 278-279
Scharnhorst, Gerhard Johann David von
13 521-522
Wood, Leonard **16** 369-370

Universal Races Congress, First (1911;
London)
Du Bois, William Edward Burghardt
5 116-118

Universalism (theology)
Amos **1** 205
Brownson, Orestes Augustus **3** 57-58
Cartwright, Peter **3** 344-345
Chauncy, Charles **3** 485-486
Micah **10** 542-543

Universals (philosophy)
Abelard, Peter **1** 23-25
Boethius, Anicius Manlius Severinus
2 360-361
Hobbes, Thomas **7** 421-423
Locke, John **9** 478-480
Vitoria, Francisco de **16** 1-2

Universe, orgin of
ancient theories
Anaximander **1** 209-210
Anaximenes **1** 210
Aristotle **1** 295-296
Heraclitus **7** 320
Hesiod **7** 361-362
"big-bang" theory
Lemaître, Abbè Georges Édouard
9 315-316
Weinberg, Steven **16** 175-177
collision theory
Arrhenius, Svante August **1** 318-320
planetismal theory
Chamberlin, Thomas Chrowder
3 415-416

Universe, system of
Aristotelian

Aristotle **1** 295-296
Hasan ibn al-Haytham **7** 190-191
Steno, Nicolaus **14** 425-426
atomistic
Democritus **4** 493-494
Epicurus **5** 292-294
Lucretius **10** 26-27
Copernican
Copernicus, Nicolaus **4** 226-227
Descartes, René **4** 505-508
Galileo Galilei **6** 180-183
Kepler, Johannes **8** 514-516
Mutis, José Celestino **11** 278-279
Recorde, Robert **13** 68-69
Einstein universe (static)
Einstein, Albert **5** 228-231
Lemaître, Abbè Georges Édouard
9 315-316
expanding
Eddington, Arthur Stanley **5** 201-202
Hubble, Edwin Powell **8** 10-11
Lemaître, Abbè Georges Édouard
9 315-316
galactic theories
Kapteyn, Jacobus Cornelis
8 436-437
Shapley, Harlow **14** 155-156
geocentric
Anaximander **1** 209-210
Archimedes **1** 277-280
see also Ptolemaic, Pythagorean
(below)
"Great Wall" of galaxies
Geller, Margaret Joan **6** 256-257
heliocentric
Archimedes **1** 277-280
Aristarchus of Samos **1** 290-291
Bessel, Friedrich Wilhelm **2** 234-235
see also Copernican (above)
heliocentric rejected
Bellarmine, Robert **2** 135-136
Levi ben Gershon **9** 363-364
homocentric
Bitruji, Nur al-Din Abu Ishaq al
2 296
Eudoxus of Cnidus **5** 329-330
macrocosm-microcosm theory
Paracelsus, Philippus Aureolus
12 91-93
pluralistic
Bruno, Giordano **3** 75-76
Empedocles **5** 282
Ptolemaic
Hasan ibn al-Haytham **7** 190-191
Hipparchus **7** 407-408
Ptolemy, Claudius **12** 473-474
Pythagorean
Pythagoras **12** 498-499
rational
Anaxagoras **1** 208-209
Anaximenes **1** 210
Heraclitus **7** 320
Tychonic
Brahe, Tycho **2** 489-490
unified mathematical
Newton, Isaac **11** 369-372

Universidad Obrera (Mexico; established
1936)
Toledano, Vicente Lombardo
15 256-257
University Church (Salzburg)
Fischer von Erlach, Johann Bernhard
5 459-461
Rottmayr, Johann Michael **13** 321
University Club (New York City)
McKim, Charles Follen **10** 417-418
University College (Bristol)
Marshall, Alfred **10** 277-278
Ramsay, William **13** 21-22
University College (Dublin)
Hopkins, Gerard Manley **7** 492-494
University College (Dundee, Scotland)
Geddes, Patrick **6** 246-247
University College (Ibadan, Nigeria)
Soyinka, Wole **14** 358-359
University College (London)
endowments
Bentham, Jeremy **2** 176-178
English
Spender, Stephen Harold
14 370-371
sciences
Bragg, William Henry **2** 488-489
Galton, Francis **6** 193-194
Hahn, Otto **7** 64-65
Hill, Archibald Vivian **7** 385-386
Loewi, Otto **9** 486-487
Medawar, Peter Brian **10** 444-445
Ramsay, William **13** 21-22
Soddy, Frederick **14** 321-323
Whitehead, Alfred North
16 242-244
social sciences
Jevons, William Stanley **8** 255-256
Petrie, William Matthew Flinders
12 261-262
Pollard, Albert Frederick **12** 378
Schechter, Solomon **13** 524
see also London, University of
Unkiar Skellesi, Treaty of (1833)
Nesselrode, Karl Robert **11** 348-349
Unknown Lady, The (poem)
Blok, Aleksandr Aleksandrovich **2** 335
Unknown World... (poems)
Sterne, Laurence **14** 435-437
Unmoved Mover (philosophy)
Aristotle **1** 295-296
Plotinus **12** 358-359
Unnamable, The (novel)
Beckett, Samuel **2** 102-104
Uno, nessuno e centomila (novel)
Pirandello, Luigi **12** 319-321
Unofficial Rose, An (novel)
Murdoch, Iris **11** 256-257
Unordnung und frühes Leid (novella)
Mann, Thomas **10** 204-207

Unpainted Pictures (watercolor series)
Nolde, Emil **11** 419-420
Unquiet Grave, The (novel)
Connolly, Cyril **4** 204-205
Unruh, Fritz von (1885-1970), German
playwright, poet, and novelist
Brecht, Bertolt **2** 512-514
Uns ist ein Kind geborn (cantata)
Bach, Johann Sebastian **1** 416-419
Unsafe at Any Speed (book)
Nader, Ralph **11** 290-291
Unsichtbare Loge, Die (novel)
Richter, Johann Paul Friedrich
13 150-151
Unsocial Socialist, An (novel)
Shaw, George Bernard **14** 163-164
Unterm Rad (novel)
Hesse, Hermann **7** 367-369
Untermeyer, Louis (1885-1977), American
writer and editor
Lewis, Cecil Day **9** 380
Unto This Last (book; Ruskin)
Gandhi, Mohandas Karamchand
6 201-204
Ruskin, John **13** 371-372
Unto Us a Child Is Born (cantata)
Bach, Johann Sebastian **1** 416-419
Untouchables (Hindu caste)
Ambedkar, Bhimrao Ramji **1** 190-191
Gandhi, Mohandas Karamchand
6 201-204
Unusual Event (story)
Dostoevsky, Fyodor **5** 74-77
Unvanquished, The (novel)
Faulkner, William **5** 395-397
Unwin, Mrs. Mary (1724-1796), English-
woman, patron and friend of Cowper
Cowper, William **4** 282
Unwin, Sir Raymond (1863-1940), English
architect
Shaw, Richard Norman **14** 167-168
Uomini e no (novel)
Vittorini, Elio **16** 2-3
Uomo come fine, L' (book)
Moravia, Alberto **11** 153-155
Uomo delinquente, L' (book)
Lombroso, Cesare **9** 493
Up from Slavery (book; B. T. Washington)
Garvey, Marcus Mosiah **6** 228-229
Up Front (book)
Mauldin, Bill **10** 345-346
Up the Country (novel)
Franklin, Stella Maraia Sarah Miles
6 68-69
Upanishads (Vedic treatises)
Roy, Ram Mohun **13** 18
Shankara **14** 150-151
see also Vedanta

UPDIKE, JOHN (born 1932), American author of poems, short stories, essays, and novels **15** 390-392

UPJOHN, RICHARD (1802-1878), English-born American architect **15** 392

Upon Appleton House, to My Lord Fairfax (poem)
Marvell, Andrew **10** 301-303

Upon the Daeth of Lord Hastings (poem)
Dryden, John **5** 106-107

Upon the Death of O.C. (poem)
Marvell, Andrew **10** 301-303

Upper Canada (former British province)
Brock, Isaac **3** 12-13
Fraser, Simon **6** 74-75
Gourlay, Robert **6** 474
Hull, William **8** 29-30
Lafontaine, Louis-Hippolyte **9** 157-158
Robinson, John Beverley **13** 210
Selkirk, 5th Earl of **14** 96

Upper Congo (river, Africa)
Brazza, Pierre Paul François Camille
Savorgnan de **2** 509-510

Upper Deck (painting)
Sheeler, Charles **14** 170-171

Upper Egypt
see Egypt

Upper Louisiana
see Missouri

Upper Nile (province, Sudan)
Baker, Samuel White **1** 454-455
Mahdi **10** 137-138

Upper Peru
see Bolivia

Upper Volta (former territory, French West Africa)
Houphouët-Boigny, Felix **7** 519-520

Uppsala, University of (Sweden)
Linnaeus, Carl **9** 427-429
Söderblom, Nathan **14** 323-324
Theorell, Axel Hugo Theodor **15** 176-177
Tiselius, Arne Wilhelm Kaurin **15** 240-241

Upright Motive No.1 (sculpture)
Moore, Henry **11** 146-148

Uprising, The (painting)
Daumier, Honoré Victorin **4** 403-405

Uranium (element—chemistry)
nuclear energy
Bethe, Hans Albrecht **2** 238-239
Bohr, Niels Henrik David **2** 366-368
Fermi, Enrico **5** 422-424
Lawrence, Ernest Orlando **9** 248-250
research
Becquerel, Antoine Henri **2** 108-109
Compton, Arthur Holly **4** 186-188
Hahn, Otto **7** 64-65
Joliot-Curie, Jean Frédéric **8** 327-328

Kapitsa, Pyotr Leonidovich **8** 433-435
Rutherford, Ernest **13** 384-387
Soddy, Frederick **14** 321-323

Uranus (planet)
Adams, John Couch **1** 51-52
Herschel, William **7** 341-343
Leverrier, Urbain Jean Joseph **9** 361-362
Newcomb, Simon **11** 361-362

Urartu (ancient kingdom, North of Assyria)
Sargon II **13** 482
Tiglath-pileser III **15** 221-222

URBAN II (Otto de Lagery; 1042-99), pope 1088-99 **15** 393
Anselm of Canterbury **1** 244-245
Henry IV **7** 292

Urban V (Guillaume de Grimoard; 1310-70), pope 1362-70
Boccaccio, Giovanni **2** 351-353
Guy de Chauliac **7** 54

URBAN VI (Bartolomeo Prignano; 1318-89), pope 1378-89 **15** 394
Catherine of Siena **3** 369-370
Wenceslaus **16** 201-202

Urban VIII (Maffeo Barberini; 1568-1644), pope 1623-44
Bernini, Gian Lorenzo **2** 214-216
Claude Lorrain **4** 89-90
Galileo Galilei **6** 180-183
Jogues, Isaac **8** 270-271
Pázmány, Péter **12** 164-165

Urban, Joseph (1872-1933), Austrian-American architectural designer
Ziegfeld, Florenz **16** 516-517

Urban government
see Municipal government

Urban planning
see Town planning

Urbanists and Architects Team (URTEC; Japan)
Tange, Kenzo **15** 99-101

Urbina, Isabel de (died 1594), Spanish wife of Lope de Vega
Lope Félix de Vega Carpio **9** 503-506

Urbina, José Maria (1808-1891), Ecuadorian political leader, president 1852-56
Flores, Juan José **5** 491
García Moreno, Gabriel **6** 209-210
Montalvo, Juan María **11** 119-120

Urdaneta, Andrés de (1498-1568), Spanish navigator
Velasco, Luis de **15** 450-451

Urdu (Hindustani language)
Iqbal, Muhammad **8** 132-133
Premchand **12** 439

UREY, HAROLD CLAYTON (1893-1981), American chemical physicist and geochemist **15** 394-396
Hevesy, George Charles de **7** 371
Lewis, Gilbert Newton **9** 384-385

Ur-Hamlet (play)
Kyd, Thomas **9** 140-141

Uriah (flourished 10th century B.C.), Hittite captain in army of Israel
David, Jacques Louis **4** 407-409

Uriburu, José F. (1868-1932), Argentine political leader
Justo, Agustin Pedro **8** 396

Uric acid (chemistry)
Baeyer, Johann Friedrich Adolf von **1** 432
Fischer, Emil **5** 456-457
Hopkins, Frederick Gowland **7** 491-492
Liebig, Justus von **9** 403-404
Scheele, Karl Wilhelm **13** 525-526

Uriel in the Sun (painting)
Allston, Washington **1** 176-177

URQUIZA, JUSTO JOSÉ (1801-1870), Argentine dictator, general, and statesman **15** 396-397
Rosas, Juan Manuel de **13** 290-291

Urraca (1081-1126), Queen of Castile and León 1109-26
Alfonso I **1** 148
Alfonso VI **1** 149

Ursins, Princess des (1642-1722), French nobleman
Philip V **12** 276-277

Ursuline Church (Salzburg)
Fischer von Erlach, Johann Bernhard **5** 459-461

Ursulines (religious congregation)
Paul III **12** 144-145

Urteil, Das (story)
Kafka, Franz **8** 403-406

Uruguay, Eastern Republic of (nation, South East South America)
independence wars (1825-1828)
Artigas, José Gervasio **1** 323
Caxias, Duque de **3** 386
Lavalleja, Juan Antonio **9** 238-239
Rivera, Fructuoso **13** 184-185
Italian Legion
Garibaldi, Giuseppe **6** 215-217
20th century
Batlle y Ordóñez, José **2** 58-59
Rio Branco, Barão do **13** 177
Terra, Gabriel **15** 154-155
see also Triple Alliance, War of the (1865-1870)

Uruguayan literature
Rodó, José Enrique **13** 240-241
Zorrilla de San Martin, Juan **16** 530-531

Urvina, José Maria
see Urbina, José Maria

U.S.A. (novel; trilogy)
Dos Passos, John Roderigo **5** 69-71

Ushant (book)
Aiken, Conrad **1** 90-91

Utah (state, United States)
Buchanan, James **3** 89-90
Cleveland, Stephen Grover **4** 108-110
Hearst, George **7** 242
Thayer, Eli **15** 168

Young, Brigham **16** 469-470

Utah, University of
Elsasser, Walter Maurice **5** 277-278
Young, Brigham **16** 469-470

UTAMARO, KITAGAWA (1753-1806),
Japanese printmaker **15** 397

UTHMAN DON FODIO (1755-1816),
Moslem teacher and theologian
15 397-398
Bello, Ahmadu **2** 139-140

Uticensus, Marcus Porcius Cato
see Cato the Younger

Utilitarianism (philosophy)
critics
Carlyle, Thomas **3** 304-305
Dickens, Charles John Huffam
4 538-541
Sidgwick, Henry **14** 213
expounders
Bentham, Jeremy **2** 176-178
Chadwick, Edwin **3** 404-405
Jevons, William Stanley **8** 255-256
Mill, James **11** 21
Mill, John Stuart **11** 21-23
Paley, William **12** 72
forerunners
Hume, David **8** 31-34
Mandeville, Bernard **10** 192
historians of
Halévy, Élie **7** 76
influenced by
Becarria, Marchese di **2** 97-98

Utility (economics)
Marshall, Alfred **10** 277-278
see also Marginal utility

Utopian communities
Brook Farm (Massachusetts)
Brisbane, Albert **3** 9
Brownson, Orestes Augustus
3 57-58
Ripley, George **13** 179-180
Harmony Hall (Hampshire, England)
Owen, Robert **12** 39-40
Harmony (Pennsylvania)
Rapp, George **13** 42-43
Icaria (Illinois)
Cabet, Étienne **3** 196
Kirtland (Ohio)
Smith, Joseph **14** 297-298
Nashoba (Tennessee)
Wright, Frances **16** 397-398
Nauvoo (Illinois)
Smith, Joseph **14** 297-298
New Harmony (Indiana)
Owen, Robert **12** 39-40
see also Fruitlands

Utopian literature
Bellamy, Edward **2** 134-135
Burton, Robert **3** 166-167
Butler, Samuel **3** 183
Campanella, Tommaso **3** 249
Harrington, James **7** 166-167
More, Thomas **11** 156-157
Mqhayi, Samuel Edward Krune **11** 223

Utopian socialism
Blanc, Louis **2** 318-319
Fourier, François Charles Marie **6** 31-32
Olivetti, Adriano **11** 501-502
Owen, Robert **12** 39-40
Pridi Phanomyong **12** 449
Veblen, Thorstein Bunde **15** 449-450

Utopianism (philosophy)
Coleridge, Samuel Taylor **4** 154-156
Godwin, William **6** 383-384
Helvétius, Claude Adrien **7** 273-274
K'ang Yu-wei **8** 426-428
Marx, Karl **10** 304-308
Plato **12** 345-347

Utrecht, Treaty of (1713)
Anne **1** 241-242
Bolingbroke, Viscount **2** 374-375
Harley, Robert **7** 159-160
Philip V **12** 276-277
Pope, Alexander **12** 395-397
Saxe, Comte de **13** 507-508
Victor Amadeus II **15** 482-483

Utrecht, Union of (1579)
William the Silent **16** 300-302

Utrillo, Maurice (1883-1955), French
painter
Modigliani, Amedeo **11** 72-73

Uzziah (reigned 780-740 B.C.), king of
Judah
Amos **1** 205
Isaiah **8** 146-147
and radio engineer **16** 539-540

V

V-1 and 2 (rocket)
Goddard, Robert Hutchings **6** 376-377
von Braun, Wernher **16** 17-18

Vaca, Álvar Núñez Cabeza de
see Cabeza de Vaca, Álvar Núñez

Vacation Land (play)
Betti, Ugo **2** 246

Vaccination
see Inoculation (immunology)

Vaccines
Sabin, Albert Bruce **13** 401-402

Vacuum (physics)
Boyle, Robert **2** 469-471
De Forest, Lee **4** 459-460
Goddard, Robert Hutchings **6** 376-377
Guericke, Otto Von **7** 27-28
Röntgen, Wilhelm **13** 273-275

Vagabond, Baron, The (film)
Garbo, Greta **6** 205-207

Vagabonde, La (novel)
Colette, Sidonie Gabrielle **4** 158-159

Vagabonds (novel)
Hamsun, Knut **7** 113-114

Vagusstoff
see Acetylcholine (chemistry)

Vail, Alfred (1807-1859), American pioneer
in telegraphy
Morse, Samuel Finley Breese
11 192-193

Vail, Theodore Newton (1845-1920),
American telephone and telegraph exec-
utive
Bell, Alexander Graham **2** 129-131

Vajirunhis (died 1894), Thai crown prince
Chulalongkorn **4** 43-45

Val Verde, battle of (1861)
Carson, Christopher **3** 334-335

VALDEZ, LUIS (born 1940), Hispanic
American playwright and filmmaker
15 399-400

VALDIVIA, PEDRO DE (circa 1502-53),
Spanish conquistador and professional
soldier **15** 400-401
Lautaro **9** 235

Vale of Soul-making (poem)
Keats, John **8** 470-472

Val-ès-Dunes, battle of (1047)
William I **16** 290-291

Valence, Synod of (855)
Erigena, John Scotus **5** 308-309

Valens (circa 328-378), Easterm Roman
emperor 364-378
Basil the Great **2** 51-52
Theodosius **15** 176

VALENTI, JACK JOSEPH (born 1921), presidential adviser and czar of the American
film industry **15** 401-403

Valentine (novel)
Sand, George **13** 459-461

Valentinian (play)
Fletcher, John **5** 487

Valentinian II (372-392), Roman emperor
375-383
Theodosius **15** 176

Valentinian III (419-455), Roman emperor
of the West 425-455
Attila **1** 360
Gaiseric **6** 172
Leo I **9** 329-330

VALERA Y ALCALÁ GALIANO, JUAN
(1824-1905), Spanish novelist and diplomat **15** 403
Azaña Diaz, Manuel **1** 396-397

VALERIAN (Publius Licinius Valerianus;
circa 200-circa 260), Roman emperor
253-260 **15** 404-405

VALÉRY, PAUL AMBROISE (1871-1945),
French poet, philosopher, and critic
15 405-406
Baudelaire, Charles Pierre **2** 61-63
Breton, André **2** 519-520
Claudel, Paul Louis Charles **4** 90-91
Mallarmé, Stéphane **10** 172-173
Rilke, Rainer Maria **13** 171-172
Stravinsky, Igor Fedorovich **14** 502-506

Ungaretti, Giuseppe **15** 389-390

Valjean, Jean (literary character)
Hugo, Victor Marie **8** 22-25

Valkyrie, The (opera)
Wagner, Richard **16** 40-43

VALLA, LORENZO (circa 1407-57), Italian
humanist **15** 406

VALLANDIGHAM, CLEMENT LAIRD
(1820-1871), American politician
15 406-407
Wood, Fernando **16** 367-368

VALLE INCLÁN, RAMÓN MARIA DEL
(circa 1866-1936), Spanish novelist, playwright, and poet **15** 407-408

VALLEJO, CÉSAR ABRAHAM (1892-1938),
Peruvian poet **15** 408-409

Vallès, Jules Louis Joseph (1832-1885),
French author and journalist
Courbet, Jean Desiré Gustave
4 271-273

Valley Forge (Pennsylvania)
Howe, William **7** 538-539
Marshall, John **10** 279-281
Peale, Charles Willson **12** 169-171
Pulaski, Casimir **12** 480-481
Steuben, Frederick William Augustus
von **14** 438-439

Valley of Bones, The (novel)
Powell, Anthony **12** 422-423

Valley of Fear, The (novel)
Doyle, Arthur Conan **5** 91-92

Valley of Mexico (painting)
Velasco, Luis de **15** 450-451

Valley of Oaxaca (painting)
Velasco, Luis de **15** 450-451

Valley of the Kings (Egypt)
Amenhotep III **1** 194-195
Hatshepsut **7** 196-197
Thutmose III **15** 216-217

Valley of Tiffauge (painting)
Rousseau, Théodore **13** 328

Vallotton, Félix (1865-1925), Swiss woodcut artist and painter
Kirchner, Ernst Ludwig **9** 34-35

Valmiki (flourished 3d century B.C.), reputed author of the Sanskrit Ramayana
Kalidasa **8** 414-415

Valois dynasty (France; reigned 1328-1589)
Louis XI **9** 526-528
Louis XII **9** 528-529
Medici, Catherine de' **10** 445-449
Philip VI **12** 277-278

Valse, La (musical composition)
Ravel, Maurice Joseph **13** 54-55

Valse triste (musical composition)
Sibelius, Jean Julius Christian **14** 211-212

Valses nobles et sentimentales (musical composition)
Ravel, Maurice Joseph **13** 54-55

Value (economics)
Böhm-Bawerk, Eugen von **2** 366
Jevons, William Stanley **8** 255-256
Marx, Karl **10** 304-308
Ricardo, David **13** 123-124

Value (philosophy)
Lewis, Clarence Irving **9** 381
Meinong, Alexius Ritter von Handschuchsheim **10** 461-462
Perry, Ralph Barton **12** 239-240

Van
see Urartu (ancient kingdom)

VAN BUREN, MARTIN (1782-1862), American statesman, president 1837-41 **15** 410-411
domestic policy
Cinque, Joseph **4** 62
Ross, John **13** 303-304
Scott, Winfield **14** 70-71
Tyler, John **15** 368-369
Wilkes, Charles **16** 279-280
opponents
Clinton, DeWitt **4** 112-113
Harrison, William Henry **7** 180-181
Polk, James Knox **12** 374-376
Walker, Robert John **16** 67-68
supporters
Bancroft, George **1** 483-484
Blair, Francis Preston **2** 313-315
Burlingame, Anson **3** 144-145
Cameron, Simon **3** 246-247
Jackson, Andrew **8** 168-172
Marcy, William Learned **10** 247-248
Wilmot, David **16** 312-313

Van Dahorst, Anthonis Mor
see Moro, Antonio

Van Devanter, Willis (1859-1941), American jurist
Black, Hugo Lafayette **2** 301-303

VAN DER GOES, HUGO (flourished 1467-82), Flemish painter **15** 416-417
Geertgen tot Sint Jans **6** 248
Ghirlandaio, Domenico **6** 292-293
Schongauer, Martin **14** 26-28

VAN DIEMEN, ANTHONY MEUZA (1593-1645), Dutch colonial official and merchant **15** 420

Coen, Jan Pieterszoon **4** 133
Tasman, Abel Janszoon **15** 113-114

Van Diemen's Land
see Tasmania

VAN DOESBURG, THEO (1883-1931), Dutch painter **15** 421
de Stijl
see De Stijl
influence of
Calder, Alexander **3** 216-218
Mies van der Rohe, Ludwig **11** 10-12

VAN DONGEN, KEES (Cornelis Theodorus Marie Van Dongen; 1877-1968), Fauvist painter, portraitist, and socialite **15** 421-422
Kirchner, Ernst Ludwig **9** 34-35
Matisse, Henri **10** 336-337

Van Doren, Carl (1885-1950), American critic and biographer
Eggleston, Edward **5** 223-224

VAN DUYN, MONA (born 1921), first woman to be appointed poet laureate of the United States **15** 422-423

VAN DYCK, ANTHONY (1599-1641), Flemish painter **15** 423-425
Gainsborough, Thomas **6** 170-172
Jordaens, Jacob **8** 347-349
Lely, Peter **9** 315
Magnasco, Alessandro **10** 127-128
Murillo, Bartolomé Esteban **11** 258-259
Reynolds, Joshua **13** 115-116
Rottmayr, Johann Michael **13** 321
Rubens, Peter Paul **13** 339-342
Veronese, Paolo **15** 469-470

VAN EEKELEN, WILLEM FREDERIK (born 1931), Dutch secretary-general of the Western European Union **15** 426-427

VAN GOGH, VINCENT (1853-1890), Dutch painter **15** 427-429
associates
Gauguin, Paul **6** 236-238, 340
influence of
Kirchner, Ernst Ludwig **9** 34-35
Matisse, Henri **10** 336-337
Mondrian, Piet **11** 101-102
Nolde, Emil **11** 419-420
Vlaminck, Maurice **16** 6
influenced by
Hokusai, Katsushika **7** 447-448
Seurat, Georges Pierre **14** 120-122

VAN HORNE, SIR WILLIAM CORNELIUS (1843-1915), American-born Canadian railroad entrepreneur **15** 429-430
Cullen, Maurice Galbraith **4** 334
Morrice, James Wilson **11** 181-182

Van Loo, Jean Baptiste (1684-1745), French painter
Chardin, Jean Baptiste Siméon **3** 442-443

Van Loo, Michel (1707-1771), French painter
Goya y Lucientes, Francisco de Paula José de **6** 476-478

VAN RENSSELAER, KILIAEN (circa 1580-1643), Dutch merchant and colonial official in America **15** 430-431

Van Vechten, Carl (1880-1964), American writer
Hughes, Langston **8** 18-19

Van Zorn (drama)
Robinson, Edwin Arlington **13** 201-202

Vanadium (element—chemistry)
Berzelius, Jöns Jacob **2** 231-233

VANBRUGH, SIR JOHN (1664-1726), English architect and dramatist **15** 409-410
Adam, Robert and James **1** 38-40
Congreve, William **4** 200-201
Hawksmoor, Nicholas **7** 211-212
Wren, Christopher **16** 393-394

VANCE, CYRUS R. (born 1917), American secretary of the army and secretary of state **15** 411-413

VANCE, ZEBULON BAIRD (1830-1894), American politician **15** 413-414
Letcher, John **9** 359-360

Vancouver (city, Washington)
McLoughlin, John **10** 423-424

VANCOUVER, GEORGE (1758-1798), English explorer and navigator **15** 414-415

Vandals (German nation)
Belisarius **2** 128-129
Gaiseric **6** 172
Justinian I **8** 393-395
Leo I **9** 329-330
Procopius of Caesarea **12** 457-458
Ricimer, Flavius **13** 151-152
Stilicho, Flavius **14** 452-453
Ulfilas **15** 384

Vandenberg, Arthur (1884-1951), American politician
Truman, Harry S. **15** 314-316

VANDER ZEE, JAMES (1886-1983), photographer of the people of Harlem **15** 418-419

VANDERBILT, CORNELIUS (1794-1877), American financier, steamship and railroad builder **15** 415-416
Corning, Erastus **4** 238-239
Drew, Daniel **5** 101-102
Fisk, James **5** 464-465
Garrett, John Work **6** 225
Gould, Jay **6** 470-472
Keith, Minor Cooper **8** 476-477
Smith, Gerrit **14** 290-291
Walker, William **16** 68-69

Vanderbilt, George Washington (1862-1914), American agriculturist
Hunt, Richard Morris **8** 44

Vanderbilt, William H. (1821-1885), American businessman
Morgan, Junius Spencer **11** 166-167

Vanderbilt University (Nashville, Tennessee)
Ransom, John Crowe **13** 39-40
Vanderbilt, Cornelius **15** 415-416

Warren, Robert Penn **16** 121-122

Vanderbilt (William K.) House (New York City)
Hunt, Richard Morris **8** 44

VANDERLYN, JOHN (1775-1852), American painter **15** 417
Durand, Asher Brown **5** 156-157
Peale, Rembrandt **12** 172-173

Vandover and the Brute (novel)
Norris, Benjamin Franklin Jr. **11** 427-428

VANE, SIR HENRY (1613-1662), English statesman **15** 425-426
Hutchinson, Anne Marbury **8** 69-71
Vane, Henry **15** 425-426
Williams, Roger **16** 304-305
Winthrop, John **16** 339-341

Vanessa (literary character)
Swift, Jonathan **15** 51-54

Vanessa (opera)
Barber, Samuel **1** 500-501
Menotti, Gian Carlo **10** 509-510

Vanhomrigh, Esther (1690-1723), English literary model
Swift, Jonathan **15** 51-54

Vanities (revue)
Fields, W. C. **5** 444

Vanity Fair (magazine)
Brown, Tina **3** 47-48
Harris, Frank **7** 172-173
Hughes, Langston **8** 18-19
Parker, Dorothy Rothschild **12** 106
Sherwood, Robert Emmet **14** 189-190
Steichen, Edward **14** 411-412
Ward, Artemus **16** 112-113
Wilson, Edmund **16** 318-319

Vanity Fair (novel)
Thackeray, William Makepeace **15** 159-161

Vanity of Human Wishes, The (satire)
Johnson, Samuel **8** 315-317
Juvenal **8** 397-399

Vanloo, Carle (1705-1765), French painter
Boucher, François **2** 440-442
Houdon, Antoine **7** 516-517

Vannucci, Pietro
see Perugino

Vanquished (sculpture)
Rodin, Auguste **13** 236-238

Vansittart, Henry (1732-1770), Anglo-Indian administrator
Hastings, Warren **7** 195-196

VAN'T HOFF, JACOBUS HENDRICUS (1852-1911), Dutch physical chemist **15** 431-432
Arrhenius, Svante August **1** 318-320
Fischer, Emil **5** 456-457
Vries, Hugo de **16** 33-36

Vanzetti, Bartolomeo
see Sacco and Vanzetti

Värätä, Peace of (1790)
Gustavus III **7** 45-46

Vardaman, James Kimble (1861-1930), American politician
Tillman, Benjamin Ryan **15** 225-226

VARDHAMANA MAHAVIRA (circa 540-470 B.C.), Indian ascetic philosopher **10** 135-137

Varennes, Pierre Gaultier de
see La Verendrye, Sieur de

VARÈSE, EDGARD (1883-1965), French-American composer **15** 432-433
Busoni, Ferruccio Benvenuto **3** 173-174
Ives, Charles Edward **8** 159-160
Lutoslawski, Witold **10** 52-53
Still, William Grant **14** 455-456
Stravinsky, Igor Fedorovich **14** 502-506

VARGAS, GETULIO DORNELLES (1883-1954), Brazilian political leader **15** 433-434
Aranha, Osvaldo **1** 272-273
Goulart, João **6** 467-469
Kubitschek de Oliveira, Juscelino **9** 113-115
Prestes, Luiz Carlos **12** 442-444
Villa-Lobos, Heitor **15** 496-497

VARGAS LLOSA, MARIO (born 1936), Peruvian novelist, critic, journalist, screenwriter, and essayist **15** 434-436

Variation of Animals and Plants under Domestication (book; Darwin)
Burbank, Luther **3** 129-131
Darwin, Charles Robert **4** 397-399

Variations on a Theme (sculpture)
Manzù, Giacomo **10** 224-225

Variety Lights (film)
Fellini, Federico **5** 408-409

Varinus
see Guarino da Verona

Varinus Rufus, Lucius (flourished 1st century B.C.), Roman poet
Horace **7** 500-503
Virgil **15** 507-510

VARMUS, HAROLD ELIOT (born 1939), medical research expert and director of the National Institutes of Health (1993-) **15** 436-437

VARNHAGEN, FRANCISCO ADOLFO DE (1816-1878), Brazilian historian **15** 437-438

VARRO, MARCUS TERENTIUS (116-27 B.C.), Roman scholar and writer **15** 438-439
Celsus, Aulus Cornelius **3** 393

VARTHEMA, LUDOVICO DI (circa 1470-circa 1517), Italian traveler and adventurer **15** 439-440

Vasa dynasty (Sweden; reigned 1521-1654)
Gustavus I **7** 42-43
Gustavus II **7** 43-45
Gustavus III **7** 45-46
Oxenstierna, Axel Gustafsson **12** 44-45

Vasa, Gustavus
see Gustavus I Eriksson

VASARELY, VICTOR (born 1908), Hungarian-French artist **15** 440-442

VASARI, GIORGIO (1511-1570), Italian painter, architect, and author **15** 442-443
Andrea del Sarto **1** 224-225-183
Bronzino **3** 19
Duccio di Buoninsegna **5** 121-122
Giotto **6** 342-345
Titian **15** 242-244
van der Goes, Hugo **15** 416-417
Vignola, Giacomo da **15** 493-494

VASCONCELOS, JOSÉ (1882-1959), Mexican educator and author **15** 443-444
Chávez, Carlos **3** 486
Mistral, Gabriela **11** 55-56
Obregón, Álvaro **11** 458-459

Vase with Anemones (painting)
Redon, Odilon **13** 75-76

Vásquez, Gabriel (1549-1604), Spanish theologian
Pázmány, Péter **12** 164-165

Vassa, Gustavus
see Equiano, Olaudah

Vassall-Craigie-Longfellow House (Cambridge, Massachusetts)
Harrison, Peter **7** 179-180
Longfellow, Henry Wadsworth **9** 499-500

Vassar College (Poughkeepsie, New York State)
Blanding, Sarah Gibson **2** 322-323
Breuer, Marcel **2** 520-521
Flanagan, Hallie **5** 478-479
Krenek, Ernst **9** 98-99
Mitchell, Maria **11** 61
Morse, Samuel Finley Breese **11** 192-193
Renwick, James **13** 102-103

Vassar, Matthew (1792-1868), American merchant
Mitchell, Maria **11** 61

Vatican City, State of the (nation; Rome)
created (1929)
Croce, Benedetto **4** 313-314
Mussolini, Benito **11** 272-274
Pius XI **12** 337-339
foreign relations
Franco Bahamonde, Francisco **6** 52-54
Leo XIII **9** 334-336
Maritain, Jacques **10** 263
Secretariat of State
Paul VI **12** 146-148
Vatican Grottoes
Arnolfo di Cambio **1** 315-316
Vatican Library
Paul III **12** 144-145
Vatican Palace
Angelico **1** 235-236
Bramante, Donato **2** 493-494
Correggio **4** 249-251

Raphael **13** 40-42
Sangallo family **13** 464-466
see also Papacy; Roman Catholic
Church; St. Peter's (new; Rome)
see also Sistine Chapel

Vatican Councils
First (1869-1870)
Döllinger, Josef Ignaz von **5** 47-48
John, XXIII **8** 277-280
Manning, Henry Edward
10 209-210
Pius IX **12** 335-336
see also Infallibility, papal
Second (1962-1965)
Bea, Augustinus **2** 79
John, XXIII **8** 277-280, 12
Küng, Hans **9** 129-130
Maritain, Jacques **10** 263
Paul VI **12** 146-148
Pius XII **12** 339-340
Rahner, Karl **13** 4-5

Vatican Swindle, The (book)
Gide, André **6** 308-309

Vatutin, Nikolai (1900?-1944), Russian
general
Konev, Ivan Stefanovich **9** 81-82

Vauban, Marquis de (Sébastien Le Prestre;
1633-1717), French military engineer
Carnot, Lazare Nicolas Marguerite
3 313-314

Vaudoyer, A.L.T. (1756-1846), French
architect
Labrouste, Pierre François Henri **9** 144

Vaudremer (bust)
Carpeaux, Jean Baptiste **3** 318-319

VAUDREUIL-CAVAGNAL, MARQUIS DE
(Pierre Françsois de Regaud; 1698-1778),
Canadian-born governor of New France
15 444
Montcalm de Saint-Véran, Marquis de
11 122-123
Murray, James **11** 261-262

VAUGHAN, HENRY (1621/22-95), British
poet **15** 444-445
Donne, John **5** 60-61

VAUGHAN, SARAH LOIS (1924-1990),
jazz singer **15** 445-446

VAUGHAN WILLIAMS, RALPH
(1872-1958), English composer
15 446-447
Elgar, Edward **5** 247-248
Holst, Gustav **7** 459-460
Trevelyan, George Macaulay
15 294-295

Vaux, Calvert (1824-1895), English-born
American landscape architect
Church, Frederick Edwin **4** 49-50
Downing, Andrew Jackson **5** 90-91
Olmsted, Frederick Law **11** 503-504

Vaux-le-Vicomte (château)
Le Brun, Charles **9** 269-270
Le Nôtre, André **9** 328-329
Le Vau, Louis **9** 360-361

VAVILOV, NIKOLAI IVANOVICH
(1887-1943), Russian botanist and geneticist **15** 447-448

Vavilov, Sergei (1891-1951), Russian physicist
Cherenkov, Pavel Alekseevich
3 502-503

Vavilov-Cherenkov effect
see Cherenkov effect

VÁZQUEZ, HORACIO (1860-1936), president of the Dominican Republic 1903-04
and 1924-30 **15** 448-449
Trujillo Molina, Rafael Leonidas
15 313-314

VEBLEN, THORSTEIN BUNDE
(1857-1929), American political economist and sociologist **15** 449-450
Clark, John Bates **4** 76-77

Vecchia, La (painting)
Giorgione **6** 340-341

Vecellio, Tiziano
see Titian

Vector analysis (mathematics)
Gibbs, Josiah Willard **6** 302-303

Veda (Hinduism)
Dayananda Saraswati **4** 431
Ghose, Aurobindo **6** 293-294
Kalidasa **8** 414-415
Roy, Ram Mohun **13** 18
Shankara **14** 150-151

Vedanta (Hinduism)
Radhakrishnan, Sarvepalli **12** 537-538
Roy, Ram Mohun **13** 18
Shankara **14** 150-151
see also Upanishads

Vedanta Society of New York (established
1896)
Vivekananda **16** 4-5

Vedute (painting style)
Canaletto **3** 257-258
Guardi, Francesco **7** 24-25

Veen, Otto van (1556-1629?), Dutch
painter
Rubens, Peter Paul **13** 339-342

Vega Carpio, Lope Félix
see Lope de Vega

Vega Enterprise, The (radio script)
Dürrenmatt, Friedrich **5** 164-165

Vega, Inca Garcilaso de la
see Garcilaso de la Vega, Inca

Vegetable, The (play)
Fitzgerald, Francis Scott Key **5** 470-472

Vegius, Mapheus (1406-1458),
Douglas, Gavin **5** 77-78

Veils (set of paintings)
Louis, Morris **9** 538-539

Veintemilla, Ignacio de (1830-1909),
Ecuadorian general and dictator
Montalvo, Juan María **11** 119-120

Veit, Dorothea
see Schlegel, Dorothea Veit von

VELASCO, JOSÉ MARÍA (1840-1912),
Mexican painter **15** 450-451
Plaza Lasso, Galo **12** 350-351
Rivera, Diego **13** 183-184

VELASCO, LUIS DE (1511-1564), Spanish
colonial administrator **15** 450-451
Oñate, Juan de **11** 513-514

Velasco, Treaty of (1836)
Santa Ana, Antonio López de
13 471-472

VELASCO ALVARADO, JUAN
(1910-1977), Peruvian army officer who
seized power in 1968 **15** 451-452

VELASCO IBARRA, JOSÉ MARÍA
(1893-1979), Ecuadorian statesman, five
time president **15** 452-454

**VELÁZQUEZ, DIEGO RODRÍGUEZ DE
SILVA Y** (1599-1660), Spanish painter
15 454-456
associates
Narváez, Pánfilo de **11** 315
Zurbarán, Francisco de **16** 534-535
influence of
Goya y Lucientes, Francisco de
Paula José de **6** 476-478
Le Nain, Antoine, Louis and Math-
ieu **9** 321-322
Manet, Édouard **10** 193-194
Picasso, Pablo **12** 292-295
Ter Borch, Gerard **15** 146
Toulouse-Lautrec, Henri de
15 273-274
Whistler, James Abbott McNeill
16 225-226
influenced by
Caravaggio **3** 282-284
Ribera, Jusepe de **13** 122-123
Veronese, Paolo **15** 469-470

VELÁZQUEZ, NYDIA MARGARITA (born
1953), Hispanic American politician
15 456-459

VELÁZQUEZ DE CUÉLLAR, DIEGO (circa
1465-1523), Spanish conqueror, founder
of Cuba **15** 459
Cortés, Hernán **4** 255-256

Velde, Esais van de (1590?-1630), Dutch
painter
Goyen, Jan van **6** 478-479

VELDE, HENRY VAN DE (1863-1957), Belgian painter, designer, and architect
15 419-420
Gropius, Walter **7** 13-14

Vendée, La (novel)
Trollope, Anthony **15** 300-302

Vendor of Sweets, The (novel)
Narayan, R. K. **11** 313-314

Venerable Bede
see Bede, St.

Venetia (novel)
Disraeli, Benjamin **5** 27-29

Venetia (region, Italy)
Victor Emmanuel II **15** 483-484

Venetian Games (musical composition)
Lutoslawski, Witold **10** 52-53

Venezia (painting)
Luz, Arturo Rogerio **10** 56-57

Venezia, Domenico di Bartolomeo da
see Veneziano, Domenico

VENEZIANO, DOMENICO (Domenico di
Bartolomeo da Venezia; 1410?-1461),
Italian painter **15** 459-460
Andrea del Castagno **1** 223-224
Angelico **1** 235-236
Gentile da Fabriano **6** 266-267
Piero della Francesca **12** 301-302

Venezuela, Republic of (nation, South
America)
boundary disputes
Cleveland, Stephen Grover
4 108-110
Harrison, Benjamin **7** 178-179
Lodge, Henry Cabot **9** 482-483
Olney, Richard **11** 504-505
Rio Branco, Barão do **13** 177
claims disputes
Drago, Luis María **5** 92-93
dictatorship
Gómez, Juan Vicente **6** 417-418
Pérez Jiménez, Marcos **12** 217-218
exploration
Columbus, Christopher **4** 176-179
Raleigh, Walter **13** 9-11
Vespucci, Amerigo **15** 476-478
independence
Bello, Ahmadu **2** 139-140
Bolívar, Simón **2** 375-377
Miranda, Francisco de **11** 52-53
Páez, José Antonio **12** 58
Sucre, Antonio José de **15** 11-12
missionaries
Las Casas, Bartolomé de
9 211-212
nationalization of oil industry
Pérez, Carlos Andrés **12** 212-214
presidents
Betancourt, Rómulo **2** 237-238
Caldera Rodríguez, Rafael
3 218-219
Gallegos Freire, Rómulo **6** 185-186
Pérez, Carlos Andrés **12** 212-214
U.S. intervention
Roosevelt, Theodore **13** 280-283

Venezuelan literature
Gallegos Freire, Rómulo **6** 185-186

Venice (city, Italy)
Byzantine ally
Manuel I **10** 218-219
colonial expansion
Dandolo, Enrico **4** 386-387
see also Crusades—Fourth
Ducal Palace
Canaletto **3** 257-258
Gentile da Fabriano **6** 266-267
Mantegna, Andrea **10** 215-216

Pisanello **12** 323-324
Sansovino, Jacopo **13** 470-471
Veronese, Paolo **15** 469-470
founded
Mark **10** 266-267
Italian cities and
Medici, Lorenzo de' **10** 450-451
Polo, Marco **12** 380-382
League of Venice
Borgia, Cesare **2** 412-413
Louis XII **9** 528-529
liberation from Austria
Manin, Daniele **10** 197-198
Ottoman wars
Mehmed the Conqueror **10** 452-454
papal relations
Julius II **8** 384-386
Sarpi, Paolo **13** 487-488
Portugal and
Covilhão, Pedro de **4** 278-279
Manuel I **10** 219-220
unification of Italy
Garibaldi, Giuseppe **6** 215-217
see also Italy

VENIZELOS, ELEUTHERIOS (1864-1936),
Greek statesman **15** 460-461

Venne, Adriaen Petersz van der
(1589-1662), Dutch painter
Le Nain, Antoine, Louis and Mathieu
9 321-322

Ventre de Paris, Le (novel)
Zola, Émile **16** 526-528

Ventris, Michael (1922-1956), English linguist
Evans, Arthur John **5** 335-336

VENTURI, ROBERT (born 1925), American
architect **15** 461-463

Venus ... (art)
Courbet, Jean Desiré Gustave
4 271-273
Giorgione **6** 340-341
Giovanni da Bologna **6** 345-346
Holbein, Hans the Younger **7** 449-450
Le Nain, Antoine, Louis and Mathieu
9 321-322
Titian **15** 242-244
see also Aphrodite

Venus (planet)
Brahe, Tycho **2** 489-490
Cook, James **4** 214-215
Copernicus, Nicolaus **4** 226-227
Galileo Galilei **6** 180-183
Lomonosov, Mikhail Vasilevich **9** 494
Rittenhouse, David **13** 180-181
Sagan, Carl E. **13** 424-425
Winthrop, John **16** 341-342

Venus and Adonis (poem)
Shakespeare, William **14** 142-145

Vénus de Milo (poem)
Leconte de Lisle, Charles Marie René
9 273-274

Venusberg (novel)
Powell, Anthony **12** 422-423

Vera Cruz, Ilha de
see Brazil

Veracini, Francesco Maria (1685?-1750),
Italian violinist
Tartini, Giuseppe **15** 112-113

Veracruz (city, Mexico)
Cortés, Hernán **4** 255-256
Daniels, Josephus **4** 387
Díaz, José de la Cruz Porfirio
4 534-536
Huerta, Victoriano **8** 13-14
Juárez, Benito **8** 369-372
Kearny, Stephen Watts **8** 468-469
Madero, Francisco Indalecio
10 118-119
Maximilian of Hapsburg
|**10** 358-360
Santa Ana, Antonio López de
13 471-472
Wilson, Thomas Woodrow
16 330-332
see also Mexican War (1846-1848)

Veracruz, battle of (1847)
Gorgas, Josiah **6** 453-454
Lee, Robert Edward **9** 292-294
Santa Ana, Antonio López de
13 471-472
Scott, Winfield **14** 70-71

Verbeck, Guido (1830-1898), Dutch reform
missionary in Japan
Okuma, Shigenobu **11** 490

Vercellae, battle of (101 B.C.)
Marius, Gaius **10** 264-265

Vercelli, Council of (1050)
Lanfranc **9** 189-190

Vercelli, Treaty of (1492)
Comines, Philippe de **4** 181

Vercingetorix (died 46 B.C.), Gallic chief of
the Arverni
Antony, Mark **1** 253-254
Caesar, Gaius Julius **3** 207-210

Verdad sospechosa, La (play)
Alarcón, Pedro Antonio de
1 100-101

Verdi (novel)
Werfel, Franz **16** 204-205

**VERDI, GIUSEPPE FORTUNINO
FRANCESCO** (1813-1901), Italian opera
composer **15** 463-465
Bellini, Vincenzo **2** 138-139
Caruso, Enrico **3** 345
Liszt, Franz **9** 445-447
Puccini, Giacomo **12** 474-476
Rossini, Gioacchino **13** 311-312

Verdict, The (story)
Kafka, Franz **8** 403-406

Verdun, battle of (1916)
Beck, Ludwig August Theoder
2 99-100
Gilson, Étienne Henry **6** 327-328
Joffre, Joseph Jacques Césaire
8 267-268

Ludendorff, Erich Friedrich Wilhelm **10** 27-28
Pétain, Henri Philippe **12** 250-252

Vere languores (musical composition)
Victoria, Tomás Luis de **15** 487-488

Vereeniging, Treaty of (1902)
Botha, Louis **2** 434-436
Chamberlain, Joseph **3** 411-413
Hertzog, James Barry Munnik **7** 347-348
Kitchener, Horatio Herbert **9** 45-46

Verfremdung
see Alienation (literature)

Verga, Giovanni (1840-1922), Italian writer
Zola, Émile **16** 526-528

Vergennes, Charles Gravier, Comte de (1717-1787), French statesman and diplomat
Adams, John **1** 48-51

Vergine del sole, La (opera)
Cimarosa, Domenico **4** 61-62

Vergonzoso en palacio, El (play)
Tirso de Molina **15** 237-238

Verhaecht, Tobias van (1561-1631), Flemish painter
Rubens, Peter Paul **13** 339-342

Verklärte Nacht (musical composition)
Schoenberg, Arnold **14** 24-26

VERLAINE, PAUL MARIE (1844-1896), French poet **15** 465-466
Bonnard, Pierre **2** 395-396
Claudel, Paul Louis Charles **4** 90-91
Debussy, Achille Claude **4** 445-447
Fauré, Gabriel Urbain **5** 397-398
Mallarmé, Stéphane **10** 172-173
Pasternak, Boris Leonidovich **12** 124-125
Rimbaud, Jean Nicolas Arthur **13** 172-174
Stravinsky, Igor Fedorovich **14** 502-506

Verloc (literary character)
Conrad, Joseph **4** 205-207

VERMEER, JAN (1632-1675), Dutch painter **15** 466-467
Christus, Petrus **4** 33-34
Hooch, Pieter de **7** 473-474
La Tour, George de **9** 222
Staël, Nicolas de **14** 392

Vermont (state, United States)
Allen, Ethan **1** 163-164
Kunin, Madeleine May **9** 130-131
Tyler, Royall **15** 371-372

VERNE, JULES (1828-1905), French novelist **15** 467-469

Vernet, Carle (1758-1835), French historical and animal painter
Géricault, Jean Louis André Théodore **6** 280-281

Vernet, Claude Joseph (1714-1789), French landscape and marine painter
Turner, Joseph Mallord William **15** 352-354

Vernet, Horace (1789-1863), French painter
Géricault, Jean Louis André Théodore **6** 280-281
Ingres, Jean Auguste Dominique **8** 121-123

Verneuil, battle of (1424)
Henry VI **7** 298-299

Verona (city, Italy)
Alaric **1** 101-102
Pisanello **12** 323-324
Sanmicheli, Michele **13** 469-470
Visconti, Gian Galeazzo **15** 510-511

Verona, Church Council of (1184)
Waldo, Peter **16** 55-56

Verona, Congress of (1822)
Canning, George **3** 258-260
Castlereagh, Viscount **3** 363-364
Chateaubriand, Vicomte de **3** 477-479
Metternich, Klemens von **10** 533-536

Veronese, Bonifazio (1487-1553), Italian painter
Tintoretto **15** 232-234

VERONESE, PAOLO (1528-1588), Italian painter **15** 469-470
Allston, Washington **1** 176-177
Carracci **3** 319-321
Cortona, Pietro da **4** 256
Delacroix, Ferdinand Victor Eugène **4** 469-471
Poussin, Nicolas **12** 418-420
Tintoretto **15** 232-234
Watteau, Antoine **16** 143-144

VERRAZANO, GIOVANNI DA (circa 1485-circa 1528), Italian navigator and explorer **15** 470-471
Cabrillo, Juan Rodríguez **3** 204-205
Hudson, Henry **8** 12-13

Verres, Gaius (died 43 B.C.), Roman politician
Cicero, Marcus Tullius **4** 55-58

VERROCCHIO, ANDREA DEL (1435-1488), Italian sculptor and painter **15** 471-472
Botticelli, Sandro **2** 439-440
Donatello **5** 55-56
Leonardo da Vinci **9** 337-340
Perugino **12** 245-246

Vers de circonstance (book)
Mallarmé, Stéphane **10** 172-173

Versailles (city, France)
as court seat
Louis XIV **9** 531-533
gardens
Girardon, François **6** 348-349
Le Nôtre, André **9** 328-329
Grand Trianon
Mansart, Jules Hardouin **10** 212
Palace
Coysevox, Antoine **4** 287-288
Gabriel, Ange Jacques **6** 160-161
Juvara, Filippo **8** 396-397
Le Vau, Louis **9** 360-361
Mansart, Jules Hardouin **10** 212

Versailles Peace Conference (1919)
see Versailles, Treaty of (1919)

Versailles, Treaty of (1783)
see Paris, Treaty of (1783)

Versailles, Treaty of (1871)
see Frankfurt, Treaty of

Versailles, Treaty of (1919; and Paris Peace Conference)
Australia
Hughes, William Morris **8** 21-22
Brazil
Barbosa, Ruy **1** 503-504
Britain
Balfour, Arthur James **1** 469-470
Curzon, George Nathaniel **4** 351-352
Keynes, John Maynard **8** 528-530
Lawrence, Thomas Edward **9** 253-254
Lloyd George, David **9** 469-471
Toynbee, Arnold Joseph **15** 283-284
China
Liang Ch'i-ch'ao **9** 395-396
Czechoslovakia
Beneš, Edward **2** 155-157
France
Bourgeois, Léon **2** 450-451
Clemenceau, Georges **4** 99-101
Delcassé, Théophile **4** 478-479
Foch, Ferdinand **5** 498-499
Monnet, Jean **11** 109-110
Germany
Beck, Ludwig August Theoder **2** 99-100
Ebert, Friedrich **5** 193-194
Erzberger, Matthias **5** 319-320
Hindenburg, Paul Ludwig Hans von Beneckendorff und von **7** 400-401
Hitler, Adolf **7** 417-420
Stresemann, Gustav **14** 508-509
von Braun, Wernher **16** 17-18
Italy
Badoglio, Pietro **1** 428-429
Marconi, Guglielmo **10** 239-240
Orlando, Vittorio Emmanuele **11** 529-530
Japan
Konoe, Fumimaro **9** 82-83
Saionji, Kimmochi **13** 438-439
Yoshida, Shigeru **16** 464-465
Poland
Paderewski, Ignace Jan **12** 56-57
Pilsudski, Joseph **12** 305-306
Romania
Titulescu, Nicolae **15** 246-247
Saint-Germain treaty (1919)
Renner, Karl **13** 98-99
Sèvres treaty (1920)
Atatürk, Ghazi Mustapha Kemal **1** 356-357
Venizelos, Eleutherios **15** 460-461
South Africa
Smuts, Jan Christian **14** 309-310
Trianon treaty (1920)

Horthy de Nagybánya, Nicholas
7 510-512
Titulescu, Nicolae 15 246-247
U.S. delegation
Bowman, Isaiah 2 464-465
Dulles, John Foster 5 134-135
Gompers, Samuel 6 420-422
Haskins, Charles Homer 7 191-192
House, Edward Mandell 7 520-521
Lansing, Robert 9 200
Wilson, Thomas Woodrow
16 330-332
U.S. opponents
Borah, William Edgar 2 408
Knox, Philander Chase 9 66-67
La Follette, Robert Marion
9 155-156
Lodge, Henry Cabot 9 482-483
Villard, Oswald Garrison
15 498-499
U.S. preparation
Lippmann, Walter 9 439-440
Wilson, Thomas Woodrow
16 330-332
U.S. supporters
Hitchcock, Gilbert Monell
7 416-417
Lansing, Robert 9 200
Roosevelt, Franklin Delano
13 277-280
Zionist claims
Weizmann, Chaim 16 183-184
Vertieres, battle of (1803)
Dessalines, Joan Jacques 4 511-512
Vertigo (film)
Hitchcock, Alfred 7 415-416
Verulam, 1st Baron
see Bacon, Sir Francis
Verus, Lucius Aurelius (130-169), Roman
emperor 161-169
Hadrian 7 60-61
Marcus Aurelius Antoninus 10 243-245
Vervins, Treaty of (1598)
Philip II 12 271-273
VERWOERD, HENDRIK FRENSCH
(1901-1966), South African statesman,
prime minister 1958-66 15 472-473
Jonathan, Joseph Leabua 8 330-331
Vorster, Balthazar Johannes 16 30-32
Verworn, Max (1863-1921), German physi-
ologist
Hess, Walter Rudolf 7 365
VESALIUS, ANDREAS (1514-1564), Bel-
gian anatomist 15 473-475
Cushing, Harvey Williams 4 353-354
Leonardo da Vinci 9 337-340
Paré, Ambroise 12 94-95
VESEY, DENMARK (1767-1822), American
slave leader 15 475
Grimké, Archibald Henry 7 1-2
Prosser, Gabriel 12 460-461
VESPASIAN (9-79), Roman emperor 69-79
15 475-476
Domitian 5 52-53

Johanan ben Zakkai 8 271-272
Josephus Flavius 8 360-361
Pliny the Elder 12 355-356
Quintilian 12 518-519
Tacitus 15 70-72
Titus Flavius Vespasianus 15 247-248
Vespasiano (opera)
Handel, George Frederick 7 116-119
Vespasianus, Titus Flavius
see Titus Flavius Vespasianus
VESPUCCI, AMERIGO (1454-1512), Italian
navigator 15 476-478
Cabot, Sebastian 3 200-201
Ghirlandaio, Domenico 6 292-293
Solís, Juan Díaz de 14 326
Varnhagen, Francisco Adolfo de
15 437-438
Waldseemüller, Martin 16 56
Vesuvius (volcano, Italy)
Pliny the Elder 12 355-356
Titus Flavius Vespasianus 15 247-248
Veterans' bonus bill (1924; United States)
Coolidge, John Calvin 4 217-219
Harding, Warren Gamaliel 7 148-149
Hoover, Herbert Clark 7 483-485
Veuster, Joseph de
see Damien, Father
Viaggio in Sardegna (novel)
Vittorini, Elio 16 2-3
Viaje del Parnaso (poem)
Cervantes, Miguel de Saavedra
3 395-398
VIANNEY, ST. JEAN BAPTISTE
(1786-1859), French priest 15 478-479
Viardot-Garcia, Pauline (1821-1910),
Spanish gypsy, opera singer and actress
Turgenev, Ivan Sergeyevich 15 345-348,
26
Viaud, Julien
see Loti, Pierre
Vicar of Wakefield, The (novel)
Goldsmith, Oliver 6 411-413
Vice presidents
see Statesmen
VICENTE, GIL (circa 1465-circa 1536),
Portuguese dramatist and poet
15 479-480
Camoëns, Luis Vaz de 3 247-249
Encina, Juan del 5 283
Vicentino, Nicolò (1511-1572), Italian
composer
Gesualdo, Don Carlo 6 287-288
Willaert, Adrian 16 287-288
Vicenza (city, Italy)
Cajetan 3 215-216
Palladio, Andrea 12 75-77
Visconti, Gian Galeazzo 15 510-511
Vichy France
see France—1940-46
Vicksburg, battle of (1863)
Farragut, David Glasgow 5 388-389

Grant, Ulysses Simpson 6 492-494
Johnston, Joseph Eggleston 8 323
Lee, Robert Edward 9 292-294
Sherman, William Tecumseh
14 186-187
VICO, GIAMBATTISTA (1668-1744), Ital-
ian philosopher and jurist 15 480-481
Croce, Benedetto 4 313-314
Michelet, Jules 11 5-6
Wolf, Friedrich August 16 352-353
Victim, The (novel)
Bellow, Saul 2 141-143
Victor, Alfred
see Vigny, Comte de
Victor III (Dauferius, or Desiderius;
1027-87), pope 1086-87
Benedict, Ruth Fulton 2 154-155
VICTOR AMADEUS II (1666-1732), Duke
of Savoy, king of Sicily, and king of Sar-
dinia 15 482-483
Juvara, Filippo 8 396-397
Victor Emmanuel I (1759-1824), duke of
Aosta
Charles Albert, King of Sardinia 3 466
VICTOR EMMANUEL II (1820-1878), king
of Sardinia 1849-61 and of Italy 1861-78
15 483-484
Cavour, Conte di 3 385-386
Charles Albert, King of Sardinia 3 466
Crispi, Francesco 4 310-311
Garibaldi, Giuseppe 6 215-217
Mazzini, Giuseppe 10 381-383
Verdi, Giuseppe Fortunino Francesco
15 463-465
VICTOR EMMANUEL III (1869-1947), king
of Italy 1900-46 15 484-485
Badoglio, Pietro 1 428-429
Victor Hugo and Émile Girardin (cartoon)
Daumier, Honoré Victorin 4 403-405
VICTORIA (1819-1901), queen of Great
Britain and Ireland 1837-1901 and
empress of India 1876-1901 15 485-487
chaplain
Kingsley, Charles 9 28
diamond jubilee
Buffalo Bill 3 105-106
ministers
Gladstone, William Ewart
6 357-360
Melbourne, 2nd Viscount
10 468-469
Peel, Robert 12 181-183
relatives
Albert 1 110-112
Edward VII 5 214-215
Leopold I 9 345-346
William IV 16 296-297
Victoria (novel)
Hamsun, Knut 7 113-114
Victoria (state, Australia)
Burke, Robert O'Hara 3 142-143
Santamaria, Bartholomew Augustine
13 473-474

Victoria Falls (South Africa)
Livingstone, David **9** 463-465

Victoria, Lake (East Central Africa)
Baker, Samuel White **1** 454-455
Burton, Richard **3** 163-164
Speke, John Hanning **14** 366-367

Victoria Nyanza
see Victoria, Lake

Victoria of England, Princess (1840-1901),
empress of Germany
William II **16** 294-295

VICTORIA, TOMÁS LUIS DE (circa
1548-1611), Spanish composer
15 487-488
Byrd, William **3** 187-188

Victorian era (England)
Strachey, Giles Lytton **14** 487-488

Victorian literature
see English literature—Victorian

Victorian Survival (painting)
Wood, Grant **16** 368-369

Victory (novel and opera)
Bennett, Richard Rodney **2** 172
Conrad, Joseph **4** 205-207

Victory (sculpture; Michelangelo)
Giovanni da Bologna **6** 345-346
Michelangelo Buonarroti **11** 2-5

Victory (ship)
Hawkins, John **7** 210-211
Nelson, Horatio **11** 336-338

Victory of Moses (painting)
Poussin, Nicolas **12** 418-420

Victory of St. James at Clavigo (painting)
Maulbertsch, Franz Anton **10** 345

Vida breve, La (opera)
Falla, Manuel de **5** 372-373

Vida de Santa Oria (poem)
Gonzalo de Berceo **6** 431-432

VIDAL, EUGENE LUTHER GORE (born
1925), American author of novels, essays,
plays, and short stories **15** 488-490

VIDAL DE LA BLACHE, PAUL (1845-1918),
French geographer **15** 490

Videla, Gabriel González (1899-1980),
Chilean president 1946-52
Alessandri Rodriguez, Jorge **1** 129-130
Frei Montalva, Eduardo **6** 94-95

VIDELA, JORGE RAFAÉL (born 1925), military president of Argentina (1976-1981)
who violated human rights **15** 490-492

Vidiguerira, Count of
see Gama, Vasco da

Vidor, King (1894-1982), American film
director
Goldwyn, Samuel **6** 416

Vidularia (paly)
Plautus **12** 348-350

Vie Parisienne, La (operetta)
Offenbach, Jacques **11** 478-479

VIEIRA, ANTÔNIO (1608-1697), Portuguese
orator and Jesuit missionary **15** 492

Vien, Joseph Marie (1716-1809), French
painter
David, Jacques Louis **4** 407-409

Vienna (city, Austria)
architecture
Fischer von Erlach, Johann Bernhard
5 459-461
Hildebrandt, Johann Lucas von
7 380-381
Neumann, Balthasar **11** 354-355
Olbrich, Joseph Maria **11** 494-495
Wagner, Otto **16** 39-40
Bohemians defeated
Rudolf I **13** 347-348
French siege
Francis II **6** 43-44
Napoleon I **11** 306-310
Turkish siege (1529)
Charles V **3** 457-459
Suleiman I **15** 20-21
see also Vienna, siege of (1683)

Vienna Academy of Fine Arts
Wagner, Otto **16** 39-40

Vienna Circle (philosophic group)
Mach, Ernst **10** 90-91
Popper, Karl Raimund **12** 402
Schlick, Friedrich Albert Moritz
14 16-17
Wittgenstein, Ludwig **16** 350-351

Vienna Concordat (1448)
Frederick III **6** 84-85

Vienna, Congress of (1814-1815)
Austria
Francis II **6** 43-44
Metternich, Klemens von
10 533-536
England
Castlereagh, Viscount **3** 363-364
Wellington, 1st Duke of **16** 193-195
France
Napoleon I **11** 306-310
Talleyrand, Charles Maurice de
15 89-90
Italy
Murat, Joachim **11** 253-254
Pius VII **12** 334-335
Ottoman Empire
Mahmud II **10** 145-147
Prussia
Frederick William III **6** 87
Hardenberg, Karl August von
7 146-147
Schlegel, Friedrich von **14** 10-11
Stein, Heinrich Friedrich Karl vom
und zum **14** 415-416
Russia
Alexander I **1** 130-132
Nesselrode, Karl Robert **11** 348-349

Vienna, Council of (1311-1312)
Lull, Raymond **10** 39-40

Vienna Court Opera
Mahler, Gustav **10** 144-145

Vienna Secession (art movement, 1897)
Klimt, Gustav **9** 53-55
Kollwitz, Käthe **9** 79-81
Olbrich, Joseph Maria **11** 494-495
Wagner, Otto **16** 39-40

Vienna, siege of (1683)
Eugene of Savoy **5** 330-331
Frederick William **6** 85-86
John III **8** 276-277

Vienna, University of
economics
von Mises, Ludwig **16** 25
music
Bruckner, Joseph Anton **3** 64-65
philosophy
Brentano, Franz Clemens **2** 516-517
Carnap, Rudolf **3** 308-309
Gödel, Kurt **6** 377-379
Mach, Ernst **10** 90-91
Meinong, Alexius Ritter von Hand-
schuchsheim **10** 461-462
Pázmány, Péter **12** 164-165
Schlick, Friedrich Albert Moritz
14 16-17
science
Boltzmann, Ludwig **2** 379-380
Fischer, Hans **5** 457-459
Landsteiner, Karl **9** 188-189
Schrödinger, Erwin **14** 31-33
sociology
Lazarsfeld, Paul F. **9** 259-260

Viennese school (music)
Berg, Alban **2** 186-187
Boulez, Pierre **2** 444-445
Lutoslawski, Witold **10** 52-53

Viennese Workshop (business)
Hoffmann, Josef **7** 440-441

Vier ernste Gesänge (songs)
Brahms, Johannes **2** 490-492

Vierge, Le (sonnet)
Mallarmé, Stéphane **10** 172-173

Viervoet mountain, battle of (1850)
Moshweshwe **11** 203-205

Vierzehnheiligen (church; near Bamberg,
Germany)
Neumann, Balthasar **11** 354-355

Viet Minh (Vietnamese politics)
Diem, Ngo Dinh **5** 6-7
Giap, Vo Nguyen **6** 297-299
Ho Chi Minh **7** 426-428
Souvanna Phouma **14** 357-358
Thieu, Nguyen Van **15** 182-183
Truong Chinh **15** 319-320
see also Vietnam War (1946-1954)

Vietcong (Vietnamese Communists)
Diem, Ngo Dinh **5** 6-7
Sihanouk, Norodom **14** 222-223
Souvanna Phouma **14** 357-358

Vietnam (state, Indochina)
China and
Kuang-wu-ti **9** 112-113
Qianlong **12** 502-505

France in
 Bao Dai **1** 496-497
 Chang Chih-tung **3** 430-431
 Diem, Ngo Dinh **5** 6-7
 Garnier, Francis **6** 220-221
 Leclerc, Jacques Philippe **9** 272-273
 see also Indochina, French; Vietnam
  War (1946-1954)
Mongols and
 Kublai Khan **9** 115-118
partition (1954)
 Eisenhower, Dwight David
  5 233-236
 Giap, Vo Nguyen **6** 297-299
 Ho Chi Minh **7** 426-428
 see also Geneva Conference (1954);
  Vietnam, North; Vietnam, South

Vietnam Independence League
 see Viet Minh

Vietnam, North (Democratic Republic of
 Vietnam)
 Bao Dai **1** 496-497
 Dong, Pham Van **5** 57-59
 Eisenhower, Dwight David **5** 233-236
 Giap, Vo Nguyen **6** 297-299
 Ho Chi Minh **7** 426-428
 Le Duan **9** 278-280
 Truong Chinh **15** 319-320

Vietnam, Socialist Republic of (since 1956)
 Do Muoi **5** 53-55
 Dong, Pham Van **5** 57-59
 Le Duan **9** 278-280
 Linh, Nguyen Van **9** 426-427

Vietnam, South (Republic of Vietnam)
 Bao Dai **1** 496-497
 Diem, Ngo Dinh **5** 6-7
 Eisenhower, Dwight David **5** 233-236
 Giap, Vo Nguyen **6** 297-299
 Ho Chi Minh **7** 426-428
 Johnson, Lyndon Baines **8** 308-312
 Lilienthal, David Eli **9** 410-411
 Thieu, Nguyen Van **15** 182-183
 see also Vietnam War (1956-1976)

Vietnam Veterans Memorial (Washington,
 DC; 1982)
 Lin, Maya Ying **9** 413-415

Vietnam War (1946-1954)
 Bao Dai **1** 496-497
 Giap, Vo Nguyen **6** 297-299
 Ho Chi Minh **7** 426-428
 Leclerc, Jacques Philippe **9** 272-273
 Sihanouk, Norodom **14** 222-223
 see also Geneva Conference (1954);
  Viet Minh

Vietnam War (1956-1976)
 Cambodia and
  Sihanouk, Norodom **14** 222-223
 North Vietnam in
  Giap, Vo Nguyen **6** 297-299
  Ho Chi Minh **7** 426-428
  Le Duan **9** 278-280
  Linh, Nguyen Van **9** 426-427
 opponents of

Baader and Ulrike Meinhof, Andreas
 1 403-404
Coetzee, J. M. **4** 133-135
Lennon, John Winston **9** 326-328
Nono, Luigi **11** 420-421
Russell, Bertrand Arthur William
 13 373-374
Soelle, Dorothee **14** 324-325
Thant, U **15** 161-162
opponents of (United States)
 Abzug, Bella Stavisky **1** 34-35
 Ali, Muhammad **1** 156-158
 Ashmore, Harry Scott **1** 334-335
 Baez, Joan **1** 433-435
 Ball, George **1** 470-471
 Berrigan, Daniel J. **2** 222-223
 Bevel, James Luther **2** 250-251
 Cleaver, Leroy Eldridge **4** 97-98
 Coffin, William Sloane Jr. **4** 135-137
 Dellinger, David **4** 480-481
 Ellsberg, Daniel **5** 275-277
 Fonda, Jane **5** 501-502
 Fulbright, James William **6** 147-149
 Hesburgh, Theodore Martin
  7 357-358
 Hoffman, Abbie **7** 437-439
 Kennedy, Edward M. **8** 500-502
 Kennedy, Robert Francis **8** 508-509
 King, Martin Luther Jr. **9** 20-22
 Lippmann, Walter **9** 439-440
 Lynd, Staughton **10** 65-66
 Marty, Martin E. **10** 300-301
 McCarthy, Eugene Joseph
  10 386-388
 McGovern, George Stanley
  10 412-414
 Morse, Wayne L. **11** 193-194
 Muste, Abraham Johannes
  11 276-277
 Rubin, Jerry **13** 344-346
 Schroeder, Patricia Scott **14** 33-35
 Spock, Benjamin **14** 383-385
 Stone, I. F. **14** 470-471
 Wald, George **16** 51-53
 Zinn, Howard **16** 520-521
peace efforts
 Harriman, W. Averell **7** 165-166
 Nixon, Richard Milhous **11** 401-404
 Nkrumah, Kwame **11** 408-410
 Paul VI **12** 146-148
reporting of
 FitzGerald, Frances **5** 469-470
 Salisbury, Harrison Evans
  13 449-451
 Stone, Robert Anthony **14** 475-476
South Vietnam in
 Diem, Ngo Dinh **5** 6-7
 Thieu, Nguyen Van **15** 182-183
supporters (United States)
 Jackson, Henry Martin **8** 172-174
 Spellman, Francis Joseph **14** 367
 Wayne, John **16** 150-151
U.S. and allies in
 Abrams, Creighton W. **1** 29-31
 Eisenhower, Dwight David
  5 233-236

Johnson, Lyndon Baines
 8 308-312-39
Kennedy, John Fitzgerald **8** 502-506
Laird, Melvin R. **9** 168-170
Liu Shao-Ch'i **9** 453-455
Marcos, Ferdinand **10** 240-242
Menzies, Robert Gordon
 10 510-511
Rostow, Walt Whitman **13** 315-317
Rusk, David Dean **13** 368-370
Westmoreland, William Childs
 16 216-217
Zumwalt, Elmo Russell Jr.
 16 532-534
U.S. withdrawal
 Nixon, Richard Milhous **11** 401-404

Vieux Colombier (theater, Paris)
 Copeau, Jacques **4** 225

Vieux soldat canadien, Le (poems)
 Crémazie, Octave **4** 305-306

**Viéville, Jean Laurent Lecerf de la,
 Seigneur** (1647-1710), French writer on
 music
 Charpentier, Marc Antoine **3** 471-472

View and Plan of Toledo (painting)
 Greco **6** 511-514

View from the Bridge, The (play)
 Miller, Arthur **11** 25-26

View of Amsterdam (etching)
 Rembrandt Harmensz van Rijn
  13 91-95

View of Céret (painting)
 Soutine, Chaim **14** 356-357

View of Delft (painting)
 Vermeer, Jan **15** 466-467

View of Gloucester (painting)
 Lane, Fitz Hugh **9** 189

View of New York (drawing)
 Sheeler, Charles **14** 170-171

View of Part of the Town of Boston ...
 (engraving)
 Revere, Paul **13** 110-111

View of the Grand Canal (painting)
 Bonington, Richard Parkes **2** 394-395

View of Toledo (painting)
 Greco **6** 511-514

View painting
 see Vedute

Views of the Thames (etching series)
 Whistler, James Abbott McNeill
  16 225-226

Views on Life of Tomcat Murr (novel)
 Hoffmann, Ernst Theodor Amadeus
  7 439-440

VIGNOLA, GIACOMO DA (1507-1573),
 Italian architect **15** 493-494
 Alberti, Leon Battista **1** 113-115
 Borromini, Francesco **2** 424-425
 Maderno, Carlo **10** 117-118
 Mies van der Rohe, Ludwig **11** 10-12
 Porta, Giacomo della **12** 402-403

VIGNY, COMTE DE (Alfred Victor Vigny; 1797-1863), French poet **15** 494-495
  France, Anatole **6** 39-40
  Hugo, Victor Marie **8** 22-25

Viipuri (Finland)
  see Vyborg (Union of Soviet Socialist Republics)

Vijnanavadin school (Buddhism)
  Hsüan Tsang **8** 6-7

Vikings (Scandinavian warriors)
  in North America
    Eric the Red **5** 304
    Ericson, Leif **5** 306-307
    Sturluson, Snorri **14** 310-311
  kings
    Canute I, the Great **3** 266-269
    Harold I **7** 161-162
    Harold III **7** 163
    Olaf, II **11** 493-494
  raids on Continent
    Henry I **7** 285-286
    Rollo **13** 264-265
  raids on England
    Edward the Elder **5** 219-220

Vikings in Helgeland, The (play)
  Ibsen, Henrik **8** 98-100

Vikramorvasiya (play)
  Kalidasa **8** 414-415

Vile Bodies (novel)
  Waugh, Evelyn Arthur St. John **16** 145-147

Villa
  Barbaro (Maser, Italy)
    Palladio, Andrea **12** 75-77
    Veronese, Paolo **15** 469-470
  Capra (near Vicenza, Italy)
    Palladio, Andrea **12** 75-77
  Giulia (near Rome)
    Vasari, Giorgio **15** 442-443
    Vignola, Giacomo da **15** 493-494
  Godi (Lonedo, Italy)
    Palladio, Andrea **12** 75-77
  La Soranza (near Castelfranco Veneto, Italy)
    Sanmicheli, Michele **13** 469-470
  Monzie (Garches, France)
    Le Corbusier **9** 274-275
  Pisani (Stra, Italy)
    Tiepolo, Giovanni Battista **15** 219-220
  Savoye (Poissy, France)
    Le Corbusier **9** 274-275
  Thiene (Quinto, Italy)
    Palladio, Andrea **12** 75-77

VILLA, PANCHO (Francisco Villa; 1878-1923), Mexican revolutionary **15** 495-496
  Arnold, Thurman Wesley **1** 314
  Calles, Plutarco Elías **3** 234-235
  Carranza, Venustiano **3** 321-322
  Huerta, Victoriano **8** 13-14
  Obregón, Álvaro **11** 458-459
  Pershing, John Joseph **12** 243-244

  Reed, John Silas **13** 76-77
  Vasconcelos, José **15** 443-444
  Zapata, Emiliano **16** 489-490

Villa Capra
  see Rotonda (Vicenza, Italy)

Villa dei mostri, La (film)
  Antonioni, Michelangelo **1** 252-253

Villa Rica de Veracruz (town; Mexico)
  Cortés, Hernán **4** 255-256

Villafranca, armistice of (1859)
  Cavour, Conte di **3** 385-386

Village and Dunes (painting)
  Goyen, Jan van **6** 478-479

Village Blacksmith, The (poem)
  Longfellow, Henry Wadsworth **9** 499-500

Village Bride, The (painting)
  Greuze, Jean Baptiste **6** 539

Village Romeo and Juliet, The (opera; Delius)
  Keller, Gottfried **8** 478-479

Village Stepanchikovo, The (novel)
  Dostoevsky, Fyodor **5** 74-77

Village Street (painting)
  Rousseau, Henri **13** 323-324

Village, The (novel)
  Bunin, Ivan Alekseevich **3** 124

Village, The (poem)
  Crabbe, George **4** 288

VILLA-LOBOS, HEITOR (1887-1959), Brazilian composer **15** 496-497

VILLANI, GIOVANNI (circa 1270-1348), Italian chronicler **15** 497-498

VILLARD, OSWALD GARRISON (1872-1949), American journalist **15** 498-499

Ville, La (play)
  Claudel, Paul Louis Charles **4** 90-91

Ville Marie (Canada)
  see Montreal

Villegas, Francisco Gómez de Quevedo y
  see Quevedo y Villegas, Francisco Gómez de

VILLEHARDOUIN, GEFFROI DE (circa 1150-1213), French historian and soldier **15** 499
  Froissart, Jean **6** 124-125

Villèle, Comte Jean Baptiste Séraphen Joseph de (1773-1854), French statesman
  Louis XVIII **9** 535-536

Villeneuve, Pierre de (1763-1806), French vice admiral
  Nelson, Horatio **11** 336-338

Villers-Cotterets, Ordinance of (1539)
  Francis I **6** 40-43

Villette (novel)
  Brontë, Charlotte **3** 17-18

Villi, Le (opera)
  Puccini, Giacomo **12** 474-476

Villiers, Elizabeth (1667?-1733), mistress of William III
  Mary II **10** 309-310

Villiers, George
  see Buckingham, 1st Duke of; Buckingham, 2d Duke of

Villiers de l'Isle-Adam, Philippe Auguste Mathias, Comte de (1838-1889), French novelist and poet
  Dallapiccola, Luigi **4** 377-378
  Gourmont, Remy de **6** 475
  Maeterlinck, Maurice **10** 125-126

VILLON, FRANÇOIS (1431-after 1463), French poet **15** 499-501
  Brecht, Bertolt **2** 512-514
  Orléans, Charles D' **11** 530
  Rodin, Auguste **13** 236-238

Villon, Jacques (Gaston Duchamp; 1875-1963), French painter
  Duchamp, Marcel **5** 122-123
  Duchamp-Villon, Raymond **5** 123

Vimeur, Jean Baptiste Donatien de
  see Rochambeau, Comte de

Vincent, Edgar
  see D'Abernon, 1st Viscount

VINCENT, JOHN HEYL (1832-1920), American educator and religious leader **15** 502-503

VINCENT DE PAUL, ST. (1581-1660), French priest **15** 501-502
  Bossuet, Jacques Bénigne **2** 431-432

Vincent of Beauvais (flourished 1260), French writer
  Mandeville, John **10** 192-193

Vincenzo Anastagi (painting)
  Greco **6** 511-514

Vindication of Isaac Bickerstaff, Esq. (book)
  Swift, Jonathan **15** 51-54

Vine, Barbara
  see Rendell, Ruth

Viner, Jacob (1892-1970), American economist
  Clark, John Maurice **4** 77-78

Vines, Ricardo (1875-1943), Spanish pianist
  Poulenc, Francis **12** 414-415

Vingt regards sur l'enfant Jesus (musical composition)
  Messiaen, Olivier **10** 528-529

VINOGRADOFF, SIR PAUL GAVRILOVITCH (1854-1925), Russian educator and historian **15** 503

VINSON, FRED (Frederic Moore Vinson; 1890-1953), chief justice of the U.S. Supreme Court **15** 503-505
  Douglas, William Orville **5** 83-85

Vinti, I (film)
  Antonioni, Michelangelo **1** 252-253

Vinzenz und die Frundin bedeutender Männer (play)
Musil, Robert Edler Von **11** 268-269

Viola Tricolor (novella)
Storm, Theodor **14** 479-480

Violaine (literary character)
Claudel, Paul Louis Charles **4** 90-91

Violent Land, The (novel)
Amado, Jorge **1** 189-190

Violin (musical instrument)
Stradivari, Antonio **14** 488-490

Violin (painting)
Gris, Juan **7** 5-6

VIOLLET-LE-DUC, EUGÈNE EMMANUEL (1814-1879), French architect and theorist **15** 505-506
Garnier, Jean Louis Charles **6** 221-222
Gaudí i Cornet, Antoni **6** 235-236
Perret, Auguste **12** 233
Pugin, Augustus Welby Northmore **12** 479-480
Wright, Frank Lloyd **16** 398-401

Viper of Milan, The (novel; M. Bowen)
Greene, Graham **6** 523-524

Vipers' Tangle (novel)
Mauriac, François **10** 347-348

Vir heroicus sublimis (painting)
Newman, Barnett **11** 365

VIRCHOW, RUDOLF LUDWIG CARL (1821-1902), German medical scientist, anthropologist, and politician **15** 506-507
Bichat, Marie François Xavier **2** 263-264
Boas, Franz **2** 349-351
Du Bois-Reymond, Emil **5** 118-119
James, William **8** 215-217

VIRGIL (Publius Vergilius Maro; 70-19 B.C.), Roman poet **15** 507-510
friends
Horace **7** 500-503
imitators
Pope, Alexander **12** 395-397
Ronsard, Pierre de **13** 271-273
Vondel, Joost van den **16** 19-20
influence of
Boiardo, Matteo Maria **2** 369
Dante Alighieri **4** 389-391-268
Frost, Robert Lee **6** 130-133
Milton, John **11** 43-46
Spenser, Edmund **14** 373-376
Tasso, Torquato **15** 114-116
Voltaire **16** 14-16
influenced by
Cato, Marcus Porcius the Elder **3** 375
Cicero, Marcus Tullius **4** 55-58
Ennius, Quintus **5** 289
Varro, Marcus Terentius **15** 438-439
musical settings
Berlioz, Louis Hector **2** 203-205
style
Augustus **1** 371-373

Claude Lorrain **4** 89-90
Ovid **12** 34-36
translations
Chénier, André Marie **3** 500-501
Douglas, Gavin **5** 77-78
Dryden, John **5** 106-107
Spenser, Edmund **14** 373-376

Virgil's Gnat (poem)
Spenser, Edmund **14** 373-376

Virgin... (art)
Antonello da Messina **1** 251-252
Arnolfo di Cambio **1** 315-316
Bermejo, Bartolomé **2** 205
Campin, Robert **3** 255
Carracci **3** 319-321
Charonton, Enguerrand **3** 471
Eyck, Hubert and Jan van **5** 352-354
Fouquet, Jean **6** 31
Leonardo da Vinci **9** 337-340
Schongauer, Martin **14** 26-28
Veneziano, Domenico **15** 459-460
Weyden, Rogier van der **16** 219-221
see also Madonna

Virgin and the Gipsy, The (novelette)
Lawrence, David Herbert **9** 247-248

Virgin Mary (church; Cracow, Poland)
Stoss, Veit **14** 481-482

Virgin Soil (novel)
Turgenev, Ivan Sergeyevich **15** 345-348

Virgin Soil Upturned (novel)
Sholokhov, Mikhail Aleksandrovich **14** 203-204

Virgin Spring, The (film)
Bergman, Ernst Ingmar **2** 190-191

Virginia (play)
Alfieri, Vittoria **1** 145-146

Virginia (state, United States)
• COLONIAL PERIOD
Bacon's Rebellion
see Bacon's Rebellion
British governors
Amherst, Jeffery **1** 200-201
Andros, Edmund **1** 234-235
Berkeley, William **2** 198-199
Dinwiddie, Robert **5** 18-19
Dunmore, 4th Earl of **5** 147
Nicholson, Francis **11** 381-382
Spotswood, Alexander **14** 385
colonized
Raleigh, Walter **13** 9-11
see also Virginia Company
House of Burgesses
Beverley, Robert **2** 252
Byrd, William (colonial planter) **3** 188-189
Byrd, William II **3** 189-190
Henry, Patrick **7** 309-311
Jefferson, Thomas **8** 238-241
Lee, Richard Henry **9** 291-292
Marshall, John **10** 279-281
Mason, George **10** 319-320
Pendleton, Edmund **12** 197-198

Washington, George **16** 126-129
Wythe, George **16** 415
Jamestown
see Jamestown
missionaries
Blair, James **2** 315-316
see also American Revolution; Articles of Confederation; Constitutional Convention; Continental Congress

• LATER HISTORY
Civil War
see Civil War, United States; Confederate States of America
governors
Wilder, Lawrence Douglas **16** 274-276
Secession
Jackson, Shirley Ann **8** 183-184
Lee, Robert Edward **9** 292-294
Letcher, John **9** 359-360
Tyler, John **15** 368-369
slavery defended
Dew, Thomas Roderick **4** 519

Virginia Company (established 1606; London)
Calvert, George **3** 238-239
Gorges, Ferdinando **6** 455-456
Pocahontas **12** 361-362
Powhatan **12** 429-430
Sandys, Edwin **13** 463-464
Smith, John **14** 295-297

Virginia Minstrels
see Christy Minstrels

Virginia Resolutions (1798)
Henry, Patrick **7** 309-311
Madison, James **10** 121-123
Taylor, John **15** 126

Virginia Resolves (1769)
Henry, Patrick **7** 309-311
Lee, Richard Henry **9** 291-292

Virginia, University of (Charlottesville)
Bledsoe, Albert Taylor **2** 324-325
Faulkner, William **5** 395-397
Jefferson, Thomas **8** 238-241
Latrobe, Benjamin Henry **9** 222-224
Madison, James **10** 121-123
Malone, Dumas **10** 174-175
McGuffey, William Holmes **10** 414-415
Monroe, James **11** 111-113
Stettinius, Edward R. Jr. **14** 437-438
Tucker, George **15** 332-333
Woodward, Comer Vann **16** 378-379

Virginians, The (novel)
Thackeray, William Makepeace **15** 159-161

Virginius (ship)
Fish, Hamilton **5** 461-462

Viridiana (film)
Buñuel, Luis **3** 127-128

Virologists
see Scientists

Virtual reality
Lanier, Jaron **9** 198-199

Virtue (philosophy)
Helvétius, Claude Adrien **7** 273-274
Spinoza, Baruch **14** 381-383

Virtues and Vices (fresco)
Giotto **6** 342-345

Virtuous Knight, The (novel)
Sherwood, Robert Emmet **14** 189-190

Virus (medical)
Burnet, Frank Macfarlane **3** 146-147
Enders, John Franklin **5** 285-286
Hershey, Alfred Day **7** 343-345
Montagnier, Luc **11** 114-116
Northrop, John Howard **11** 430-431
Rous, Francis Peyton **13** 322-323
Sabin, Albert Bruce **13** 401-402
Salk, Jonas Edward **13** 451-452
Stanley, Wendell Meredith **14** 400-401
Theiler, Max **15** 169-170

Vis and Ramin (story)
Behzad **2** 123

Visa (painting)
Davis, Stuart **4** 424-425

Visage (musical composition)
Berio, Luciano **2** 194-195

Vischer, Friedrich Theodor (1807-1887),
German philosopher
Treitschke, Heinrich von **15** 293-294

Visconti, Galeazzo II (1320-1378), Duke of
Milan
Petrarch **12** 259-261
Visconti, Gian Galeazzo **15** 510-511

VISCONTI, GIAN GALEAZZO (Duke of
Milan; 1351-1402), Italian despot
15 510-511

Visconti, Teobaldi
see Gregory X, pope

Viseu, Duke of
see Henry the Navigator

Vishavriksha (novel)
Chatterji, Bankimchandra **3** 480-481

Vishinsky, Andrei
see Vyshinsky, Andrei Yanuaryevich

Vishnugupta
see Kautilya

**Visible Hand: The Managerial Revolution
in American Business, The** (book)
Chandler, Alfred Du Pont Jr. **3** 422-423

Visigoths (German people)
Alaric **1** 101-102
Attila **1** 360
Clovis I **4** 124
Stilicho, Flavius **14** 452-453
Theodosius **15** 176
Ulfilas **15** 384

Vision, A (book)
Yeats, William Butler **16** 445-447

**Vision after the Sermon-Jacob Wrestling
with the Angel** (painting)
Gauguin, Paul **6** 236-238

Vision and Prayer (musical composition)
Babbitt, Milton **1** 410

Vision, biochemistry of
Wald, George **16** 51-53

Vision de Babouc (story)
Voltaire **16** 14-16

Vision de Brahma, La (poem)
Leconte de Lisle, Charles Marie René
9 273-274

Vision of Columbus, The (poem)
Barlow, Joel **2** 6-7

Vision of Sir Launfal, The (poems)
Lowell, James Russell **10** 14-15

Vision of St. Bernard (painting)
Perugino **12** 245-246

Vision of St. Eustace (painting)
Pisanello **12** 323-324

Vision of the Apocalypse (ballet)
Graham, Martha **6** 485-486

Vision of the Blessed Herman Joseph
(painting)
Van Dyck, Anthony **15** 423-425

Vision of the Last Judgment (book)
Blake, William **2** 316-318

Visionary, The (poem)
Brontë, Emily **3** 18-19

Visions and Melodies (poems)
Tschernichowsky, Saul **15** 323

Visions of the Daughters of Albion (book)
Blake, William **2** 316-318

Visit, The (play)
Dürrenmatt, Friedrich **5** 164-165

Visit to Three Fronts, A (book)
Doyle, Arthur Conan **5** 91-92

Visitation (painting)
Ghirlandaio, Domenico **6** 292-293
Pontormo **12** 394-395
Rembrandt Harmensz van Rijn
13 91-95

Visitation of Our Lady, Order of the (established 1610)
Francis of Sales **6** 47

Visitation, The (opera)
Schuller, Gunther **14** 37-38

VISSER 'T HOOFT, WILLEM ADOLF
(1900-1985), Reformed churchman and
ecumenist who was the first general secretary of the World Council of Churches
15 511-512

Vita Merlini (poem)
Geoffrey of Monmouth **6** 268

Vita nuova (book)
Dante Alighieri **4** 389-391

Vita somnium breve (novel)
Huch, Ricarda **8** 11-12

Vita, Una (novel)
Svevo, Italo **15** 47-48

Vital, Hayyim (1543-1620), Jewish mystic
Luria, Isaac ben Solomon Ashkenazi
10 47-48

Vitalism (philosophy)
Bergson, Henri **2** 191-192
Bichat, Marie François Xavier
2 263-264
Driesch, Hans Adolf Eduard **5** 105
Du Bois-Reymond, Emil **5** 118-119
Schelling, Friedrich Wilhelm Joseph von
13 526-527
Schwann, Theodor **14** 51-52

Vitalism (science)
Morgan, Thomas Hunt **11** 170-171
Stahl, Georg Ernst **14** 392-393
Virchow, Rudolf Ludwig Carl
15 506-507

Vitamin A
Wald, George **16** 51-53

Vitamin C
Cartier, Jacques **3** 343-344
Dam, Carl Peter Henrik **4** 382-383
Reichstein, Tadeus **13** 85-87
Szent-Györgyi, Albert von **15** 62-64

Vitamins
Babcock, Stephen Moulton **1** 410-411
Dam, Carl Peter Henrik **4** 382-383
Eijkman, Christian **5** 228
Hopkins, Frederick Gowland **7** 491-492
see also Vitamin A, C

Vitascope (movie projector)
Edison, Thomas Alva **5** 206-208

Vitellius, Aulus (15-69), Roman emperor
Titus Flavius Vespasianus **15** 247-248
Vespasian **15** 475-476

Vitelloni, I (film)
Fellini, Federico **5** 408-409

Viterbo, Treaty of (1267)
Michael VIII **11** 1-2

VITORIA, FRANCISCO DE (circa
1483-1546), Spanish theologian and
political theorist **16** 1-2
Wellington, 1st Duke of **16** 193-195

Vitruvius (Marcus Vitruvius Pollio; flour-
ished 1st century B.C.), Roman architect
and engineer
Adam, Robert and James **1** 38-40
Alberti, Leon Battista **1** 113-115
Benjamin, Asher **2** 162-163
Goujon, Jean **6** 466-467
Hodler, Ferdinand **7** 434-435
Ictinus **8** 101
Lescot, Pierre **9** 354
Palladio, Andrea **12** 75-77
Perrault, Claude **12** 232-233
Vignola, Giacomo da **15** 493-494

VITRY, PHILIPPE DE (1291-1360), French
poet, composer, and churchman-states-
man **16** 2
Machaut, Guillaume de **10** 93-94

Vittoria (novel)
Meredith, George **10** 512-513

Vittoria Accorombona (novel)
Tieck, Ludwig **15** 218-219

VITTORINI, ELIO (1908-1966), Italian novelist, editor, and journalist **16** 2-3
Pavese, Cesare **12** 154-155

Vittorino da Feltre
see Feltre, Vittorino da

ViVa (poems)
Cummings, Edward Estlin **4** 334-336

Vivace et le bel aujourd'hui, Le (sonnet)
Mallarmé, Stéphane **10** 172-173

VIVALDI, ANTONIO (1678-1741), Italian violinist and composer **16** 3-4
Malipiero, Gian Francesco **10** 171

Vivamus, mea Lesbia, atque amemus (poem)
Catullus, Gaius Valerius **3** 377-378

Vivarini, Antonio (1415?-1470?) Italian painter
Mantegna, Andrea **10** 215-216

Vive le roi (musical composition)
Josquin des Prez **8** 361-363

VIVEKANANDA (1863-1902), Indian reformer, missionary, and spiritual leader **16** 4-5
Radhakrishnan, Sarvepalli **12** 537-538
Ramakrishna, Sri **13** 11-13

Vivian Grey (novel)
Disraeli, Benjamin **5** 27-29

Viviani, Rene Raphael (1863-1925), French statesman
Briand, Aristide **2** 528-529

Viviani, Vincenzo (1622-1703), Italian mathematician
Galileo Galilei **6** 180-183

Viy (story)
Gogol, Nikolai **6** 391-393

VLADIMIR I (died 1015), grand prince of Kievan Russia 980-1015 **16** 5-6
Basil II **2** 50-51
Mogila, Peter **11** 74-75

Vladimir Mayakovsky (play)
Mayakovsky, Vladimir Vladimirovich **10** 364-365

Vladimir, St.
see Vladimir I

Vladislav
see Ladislas

VLAMINCK, MAURICE (1876-1958), French painter **16** 6
Braque, Georges **2** 504-505
Derain, André **4** 503
Matisse, Henri **10** 336-337

Vocal Grove, The (musical collection)
Arne, Thomas Augustine **1** 307-308

Vocational Rehabilitation, Office of
Switzer, Mary E. **15** 55-56

Voces intimae (musical composition)
Sibelius, Jean Julius Christian **14** 211-212

VOEGELIN, ERIC (1901-1985), German-Austrian political theorist **16** 6-8

VOGEL, HANS-JOCHEN (born 1926), West German political leader **16** 8-9

Vogel, Hermann Wilhelm (1834-1898), German chemist
Stieglitz, Alfred **14** 451-452

VOGEL, SIR JULIUS (1835-1899), New Zealand statesman, twice prime minister **16** 9-10

Vogel von Falckenstein, Eduard (1795-1885), German general
Moltke, Helmuth Karl Bernard von **11** 90-91

VOGELWEIDE, WALTHER VON DER (circa 1170-1229), German poet, composer, and singer **16** 10-11

Voice of Blood, The (play)
Mäkonnen Endalkačäw **10** 161-162

Voice of Missions (newspaper)
Turner, Henry McNeal **15** 351-352

Voice of the City, The (stories)
Henry, O. **7** 308-309

Voice of the Dolphins, The (stories)
Szilard, Leo **15** 64-66

Voice of the People (newspaper)
Turner, Henry McNeal **15** 351-352

Voice of the People, The (novel)
Glasgow, Ellen **6** 360-361

Voices of Africa (poems)
Castro Alves, Antônio de **3** 364-365

Voices of Freedom (poems)
Whittier, John Greenleaf **16** 256-257

Voices of Spring (waltz)
Strauss, Johann Jr. **14** 498-499

Voices of the Night (poems)
Longfellow, Henry Wadsworth **9** 499-500

Voie royale, La (novel)
Malraux, André **10** 178-180

Volcano
Hutton, James **8** 73-74
Spallanzani, Lazzaro **14** 360-361
Werner, Abraham Gottlob **16** 205-207

VOLCKER, PAUL (born 1927), chairman of the U.S. Federal Reserve Board (1979-1987) **16** 11-12

Volgendo il ciel (ballet)
Monteverdi, Claudio Giovanni Antonio **11** 126-128

Volger, Abbé (Georg Joseph Volger; 1749-1814), German organist and composer
Meyerbeer, Giacomo **10** 536-537
Weber, Carl Maria Friedrich Ernst von **16** 156-157

Volk, Het (South African politics)
Smuts, Jan Christian **14** 309-310

Volksparty (South Africa)
Verwoerd, Hendrik Frensch **15** 472-473

Volksraad (South African politics)
Pretorius, Andries **12** 444-445

Vollard, Ambroise (1865-1939), French art dealer
Cézanne, Paul **3** 400-402
Chagall, Marc **3** 406-407
Derain, André **4** 503
Picasso, Pablo **12** 292-295
Rouault, Georges **13** 321-322

Volo di notte (opera)
Dallapiccola, Luigi **4** 377-378

Volpe e le camelie, La (novel)
Silone, Ignazio **14** 231-232

Volpone (play)
Jonson, Ben **8** 343-345

VOLTA, ALESSANDRO (1745-1827), Italian physicist **16** 12-14
Berzelius, Jöns Jacob **2** 231-233
Galvani, Luigi **6** 194-195
Oersted, Hans Christian **11** 476-478

Volta Dam (Ghana)
Nkrumah, Kwame **11** 408-410

VOLTAIRE (1694-1778), French poet, dramatist, historian, and philosopher **16** 14-16
associates
Condorcet, Marquis de **4** 195-196
Franklin, Benjamin **6** 60-64
Houdon, Antoine **7** 516-517
Marivaux, Pierre Carlet de Chamblain de **10** 265-266
Saint-Pierre, Abbé de **13** 434-435
Turgot, Anne Robert Jacques **15** 348-349
biographies and essays on
Du Bois-Reymond, Emil **5** 118-119
Morley, John **11** 178-179
Rousseau, Jean Jacques **13** 324-328
Smollett, Tobias George **14** 305-307
Strauss, David Friedrich **14** 496-497
compared to
France, Anatole **6** 39-40
Johnson, Samuel **8** 315-317
influence of
Alfieri, Vittoria **1** 145-146
Catherine the Great **3** 370-372
Louis XVIII **9** 535-536
patronage
Frederick II **6** 81-84

Volterra, Cathedral of (Italy)
Cesti, Pietro **3** 399-400

Voluntad, La (novel)
Ruiz, Juan **13** 358-359

Volupté (novel)
Sainte-Beuve, Charles Augustin **13** 438

Vom Lieben Gott (stories)
Rilke, Rainer Maria **13** 171-172

VON BRAUN, WERNHER (1912-1977), German-born American space scientist **16** 17-18

Von Bülow, Hans Guido (1830-1894), German pianist
Liszt, Franz **9** 445-447

VON FURSTENBERG, DIANE (Diane Simone Michelle Halfin; born 1946), American fashion designer and businesswoman **16** 20-21

VON HÜGEL, BARON FRIEDRICH (1852-1925), philosopher of Christianity **16** 21-22

VON LAUE, MAX (1879-1960), German physicist **16** 23-24
Bragg, William Henry **2** 488-489

VON MEHREN, ROBERT BRANDT (born 1922), American lawyer who helped create the International Atomic Energy Agency **16** 24-25

VON MISES, LUDWIG (born 1881), Austrian economist and social philosopher **16** 25

VON NEUMANN, JOHN (1903-1957), Hungarian-born American mathematician **16** 27-28

VON PAPEN, FRANZ (1879-1969), conservative German politician who helped prepare the way for the Third Reich **16** 28-29

VON RAD, GERHARD (1901-1971), German theologian **16** 29-30

Von Werl Altarpiece (painting)
Campin, Robert **3** 255

VONDEL, JOOST VAN DEN (1587-1679), Dutch poet and dramatist **16** 19-20

VONNEGUT, KURT, JR. (born 1922), American author **16** 25-27

Voodoo of Hell's Half-acre, The (story)
Wright, Richard **16** 401-402

Voortrekkers
see Boers

Vorágine, La (novel)
Rivera, José Eustacio **13** 185-186

Voroshilov, K. E. (1881-1969), Soviet military and political leader
Frunze, Mikhail Vasilievich **6** 134

VORSTER, BALTHAZAR JOHANNES (1915-1983), South African political leader **16** 30-32

Vortex, The (novel)
Rivera, José Eustacio **13** 185-186

Vortex, The (play)
Coward, Noel **4** 279-280

VOS SAVANT, MARILYN (born 1946), American columnist and consultant **16** 32-33

Vosnesensky, Andrei (born 1933), Russian poet
Yevtushenko, Yevgeny Alexandrovich **16** 455-456

Voss (novel)
White, Patrick Victor Martindale **16** 233-235

Vostok (ship)
Palmer, Nathaniel Brown **12** 80-81

Vostok (spacecraft)
Gagarin, Yuri Alexeivich **6** 166-167

Voting: A Study of Opinion Formation in a Presidential Campaign (book)
Berelson, Bernard **2** 185-186

Voting rights
see Suffrage; Women's suffrage

Voting Rights Act (1965)
Johnson, Lyndon Baines **8** 308-312

Vouet, Simon (1590-1649), French painter
Le Nôtre, André **9** 328-329

Vouille, battle of (507)
Clovis I **4** 124

Vow of Louis XIII (painting)
Ingres, Jean Auguste Dominique **8** 121-123

Vox clamantis (poem)
Gower, John **6** 475-476

Voyage au bout de la nuit (novel)
Céline, Louis Ferdinand **3** 390-391

Voyage, Le (poem)
Baudelaire, Charles Pierre **2** 61-63

Voyage of Life (painting)
Cole, Thomas **4** 151-152

Voyage Out, The (novel)
Woolf, Virginia Stephen **16** 381-382

Voyage to Pagany, A (novel)
Williams, William Carlos **16** 308-309

Voyage to Purilia, A (novel)
Rice, Elmer **13** 126-127

Voyages (poem)
Crane, Hart **4** 291-293

Voyageur sans bagages, Le (play)
Anouilh, Jean **1** 243-244

Voyelles (poem)
Rimbaud, Jean Nicolas Arthur **13** 172-174

Voyeur, Le (book)
Robbe-Grillet, Alain **13** 189-190

Voysey, Charles F. Annesley (1857-1941), English architect
Shaw, Richard Norman **14** 167-168

Vozes d'Africa (poems)
Castro Alves, Antônio de **3** 364-365

VRIES, HUGO DE (1848-1935), Dutch botanist and geneticist **16** 33-36
Galton, Francis **6** 193-194
Mendel, Johann Gregor **10** 483-486

Vrilles de la vigne, Les (novel)
Colette, Sidonie Gabrielle **4** 158-159

Vuelta de Martin Fierro, La (poem)
Hernández, José **7** 328-329

VUILLARD, JEAN ÉDOUARD (1868-1940), French painter **16** 36
Bonnard, Pierre **2** 395-396
Prendergast, Maurice Brazil **12** 440

Vuillaume, Jean Baptiste (1798-1875), French violinmaker
Paganini, Niccolo **12** 58-59

Vulgate (Latin Bible)
Jerome **8** 249

Vyborg (Union of Soviet Socialist Republics)
Aalto, Hugo Alvar Henrik **1** 1-2

VYSHINSKY, ANDREI (1883-1954), state prosecutor in Stalin's purge trials and head of the U.S.S.R.'s foreign ministry (1949-1953) **16** 36-37
Macapagal, Diosdado P. **10** 74-76
Molotov, Vyacheslav Mikhailovich **11** 89-90
Zinoviev, Grigori Evseevich **16** 521-522

W

W (poems)
Cummings, Edward Estlin **4** 334-336

W. C. Handy Foundation for the Blind
Handy, William Christopher **7** 123-124

WAALS, JOHANNES DIDERIK VAN DER
(1837-1923), Dutch physicist **15** 417-418

Wace (flourished 12th century), Anglo-Norman poet
Layamon **9** 256-257

Wackenroder, Wilhelm Heinrich (died 1798), German author
Tieck, Ludwig **15** 218-219

WADE, BENJAMIN FRANKLIN
(1800-1878), American lawyer and politician **16** 38-39
Davis, Henry Winter **4** 415-416

Wade, George (1673-1748), British field marshal
Charles Edward Louis Philip Casimir Stuart **3** 466-467

Wade-Davis Bill (1864)
Davis, Henry Winter **4** 415-416

Wadsworth, James Samuel (1807-1864), American Union Army commander
Barton, Clara **2** 37-39

Wafa, Abu al- (Muhammad al-Buzjani al-Hasib; 940-997/998), Persian astronomer and mathematician
Biruni, Abu Rayhan al- **2** 284-285

Wafd (political party, Egypt)
Farouk I **5** 387-388
Fuad I **6** 139
Zaghlul Pasha, Saad **16** 485-486

Wagahai wa Neko de Aru (novel)
Natsume, Soseki **11** 324-325

Wage-and-hour laws (economics)
Altgeld, John Peter **1** 180-182
Brandeis, Louis Dembitz **2** 496-497
Deakin, Alfred **4** 432-433
see also Minimum wage

Wages of Sin, The (play)
Nu, U **11** 439-441

Waggle dance (honeybee)
Frisch, Karl von **6** 117-118

Wagner, Adolf (1835-1917) German economist
Sombart, Werner **14** 332-333

Wagner, Mrs. Richard
see Liszi, Cosima

WAGNER, OTTO (1841-1918), Austrian architect and teacher **16** 39-40

WAGNER, RICHARD (1813-1883), German operatic composer **16** 40-43
associates
Liszt, Franz **9** 445-447
biographers
Chamberlain, Houston Stewart **3** 411
compared to
Brahms, Johannes **2** 490-492
Chopin, Frédéric François **4** 16-18
Schubert, Franz Peter **14** 35-37
Smetana, Bedřich **14** 281-282
Verdi, Giuseppe Fortunino Francesco **15** 463-465
critics
Debussy, Achille Claude **4** 445-447
Milhaud, Darius **11** 17-18
Stravinsky, Igor Fedorovich **14** 502-506
Werfel, Franz **16** 204-205
influence of
Behrens, Hildegard **2** 120-121
Honegger, Arthur **7** 472-473
Mahler, Gustav **10** 144-145
Mann, Thomas **10** 204-207
Nietzsche, Friedrich **11** 390-392
Schoenberg, Arnold **14** 24-26
Schumann, Robert Alexander **14** 41-43
Strauss, Richard **14** 500-501
Szymanowski, Karol **15** 67-68
Webern, Anton **16** 160-162
influenced by
Beethoven, Ludwig van **2** 114-117
Bellini, Vincenzo **2** 138-139
Gluck, Christoph Willibald **6** 372-374
Gobineau, Comte de **6** 375-376

Sachs, Hans **13** 410-411
Wolfram von Eschenbach **16** 360-361

WAGNER, ROBERT F. (1910-1991), New York City Tammany Hall mayor (1954-1965) **16** 44-45

WAGNER, ROBERT FERDINAND
(1877-1953), American lawyer and legislator **16** 43
Murphy, Charles Francis **11** 259-260

Wagner Labor Relations Act (1935)
Hughes, Charles Evans **8** 15-16
Truman, Harry S. **15** 314-316
Wagner, Robert Ferdinand **16** 43

Wagon Box Fight (1867)
Red Cloud **13** 70-71

Wagram, battle of (1809)
Bernadotte, Jean Baptiste **2** 205-206
Metternich, Klemens von **10** 533-536

Wahhabi Moslems (Western Arabia)
ibn Saud, Abd al-Aziz **8** 94-95
Ibrahim Pasha **8** 97-98
Said, Seyyid **13** 428-429

Wahlstatt, Prince of
see Blücher, G. L. von

Wahlverwandtschaften, Die (novel)
Goethe, Johann Wolfgang von **6** 388-391

Waifs and Strays (stories)
Henry, O. **7** 308-309

WAINWRIGHT, JONATHAN MAYHEW
(1883-1953), American general **16** 45-46

Wainwright Building (Saint Louis, Missouri)
Sullivan, Louis Henri **15** 27-28

Waitangi, Treaty of (1840)
Hobson, William **7** 426
Wakefield, Edward Gibbon **16** 48-49

WAITE, MORRISON REMICK (1816-1888), American jurist, chief justice of U.S. Supreme Court 1874-88 **16** 46
Evarts, William Maxwell **5** 340-341
Field, Stephen Johnson **5** 441-442
Miller, Samuel Freeman **11** 29-30

WAITE, TERRY (born 1939), official of the Church of England and hostage in Lebanon **16** 47-48

Waiting for Godot (play)
Beckett, Samuel **2** 102-104

Waiting for Lefty (play)
Odets, Clifford **11** 470-471

Waiting for the Mahatma (novel)
Narayan, R. K. **11** 313-314

Waiting To Exhale (book)
McMillan, Terry **10** 427-428

Waitz, Georg (1813-1886), German historian
Lavisse, Ernest **9** 241

Wakefield, battle of (1460)
Henry VI **7** 298-299
Richard III **13** 132-133
Warwick and of Salisbury, Earl of **16** 122-123

WAKEFIELD, EDWARD GIBBON (1796-1862), British colonial reformer and promoter **16** 48-49
Hobson, William **7** 426

Waking, The (poems)
Roethke, Theodore **13** 243-244

WAKSMAN, SELMAN ABRAHAM (1888-1973), American microbiologist **16** 49-50
Domagk, Gerhard Johannes Paul **5** 48-50

Walachia (former principality, Southern Romania)
Batu Khan **2** 60-61
Leopold II **9** 346
Mehmed the Conqueror **10** 452-454

WALCOTT, DEREK ALTON (born 1930), West Indian poet and dramatist **16** 50-51

WALD, GEORGE (born 1906), American biochemist interested in vision **16** 51-53

WALD, LILLIAN (1867-1940), American social worker and reformer **16** 53-54
Addams, Jane **1** 56-57
Villard, Oswald Garrison **15** 498-499

Walden (book)
Thoreau, Henry David **15** 203-205

Walden, 1st Baron Howard de (Thomas Howard; 1561-1626), English admiral and lord chamberlain
Dowland, John **5** 90

Walden, Herwarth (1878-1941), German writer and critic
Chagall, Marc **3** 406-407

Waldeneses (religious sect; France)
Victor Amadeus II **15** 482-483
Waldo, Peter **16** 55-56

WALDHEIM, KURT (born 1918), Austrian statesman and president **16** 54-55
Thant, U **15** 161-162

WALDO, PETER (flourished 1170-84), French religious leader **16** 55-56

Waldscenen (musical composition)
Schumann, Robert Alexander **14** 41-43

WALDSEEMÜLLER, MARTIN (circa 1470-circa 1518), German geographer and cartographer **16** 56
Vespucci, Amerigo **15** 476-478

Waldstein Sonata (musical composition)
Beethoven, Ludwig van **2** 114-117

Wales (political region, Great Britain)
Edward I **5** 208-210
Glendower, Owen **6** 364-365
Henry VIII **7** 302-305
Kinnock, Neil **9** 29-30
Llewelyn ap Gruffydd **9** 468
Lloyd George, David **9** 469-471
see also Great Britain

WALESA, LECH (born 1943), Polish Solidarity leader and former president **16** 57-59

Walewski, Comte Alexandre Florian Joseph Colonna (1810-1868), Polish-French diplomat
Victoria **15** 485-487

Waley, Arthur (1889-1966), English Orientalist
Woolf, Virginia Stephen **16** 381-382
Yüan Mei **16** 479-480

WALKER, ALICE MALSENIOR (born 1944), African American novelist, poet, and short story writer **16** 59-61

WALKER, C. J. (Sarah Breedlove; 1867-1919), African American entrepreneur **16** 61-62

WALKER, DAVID (1785-1830), African American pamphleteer and activist **16** 62-63

Walker, Francis Amasa (1840-1897), American economist
Clark, John Maurice **4** 77-78

Walker, James John (1881-1946), American politician, mayor of New York 1926-32
La Guardia, Fiorello Henry **9** 166-167

WALKER, JOSEPH REDDEFORD (1798-1876), American fur trader **16** 63-64

WALKER, LEROY TASHREAU (born 1918), U.S. sports official, university chancellor, educator, and track coach **16** 64-65

WALKER, MAGGIE LENA (1867-1934), American entrepreneur and civic leader **16** 65-66

WALKER, MARGARET (born 1915), American novelist, poet, scholar, and teacher **16** 67

WALKER, ROBERT JOHN (1801-1869), American politician **16** 67-68
Buchanan, James **3** 89-90
Polk, James Knox **12** 374-376

WALKER, WILLIAM (1824-1860), American adventurer and filibuster **16** 68-69
Carrera, José Rafael **3** 324-325
Pierce, Franklin **12** 300-301

Walker, Wyatt Tee (born 1929), African American civil rights leader
King, Martin Luther Jr. **9** 20-22

Walker Tariff (1846)
Polk, James Knox **12** 374-376

Walking Man (sculpture)
Rodin, Auguste **13** 236-238

Walking Quietly under the Rain (sculpture)
Giacometti, Alberto **6** 294-295

Walküre, Die (opera)
Wagner, Richard **16** 40-43

Wall of China, The (play)
Frisch, Max **6** 118-119

Wall Relief (sculpture)
Moore, Henry **11** 146-148

Wall, The (stories)
Sartre, Jean Paul **13** 491-492

WALLACE, ALFRED RUSSEL (1823-1913), English naturalist and traveler **16** 69-70
Bates, Henry Walter **2** 53-54
Darwin, Charles Robert **4** 397-399, 277
Weismann, August Freidrich Leopold **16** 178-180

WALLACE, DeWITT (1889-1981), American publisher and founder of Reader's Digest **16** 70-71

WALLACE, GEORGE CORLEY (born 1919), American political leader **16** 71-72
Nixon, Richard Milhous **11** 401-404

WALLACE, HENRY (1836-1916), American agricultural publicist and editor **16** 73

WALLACE, HENRY AGARD (1888-1965), American statesman, vice-president 1940-44 **16** 73-74
Byrnes, James Francis **3** 191-192
Carver, George Washington **3** 346-347
East, Edward Murray **5** 182-183
McGovern, George Stanley **10** 412-414
Truman, Harry S. **15** 314-316

WALLACE, LEWIS (1827-1905), American general and author **16** 74-75
Billy the Kid **2** 277
Chisum, John Simpson **4** 11
Ford, Paul Leicester **6** 9-10

Wallace, Lurleen (1926-1968), American governor of Alabama
Wallace, George Corley **16** 71-72

WALLACE, SIR WILLIAM (circa 1270-1305), Scottish soldier **16** 75-76
Edward I **5** 208-210
Robert I **13** 192-194

Wallace Madonna (painting)
Andrea del Sarto **1** 224-225

WALLACE-JOHNSON, ISAAC THEOPHILUS AKUNNA (1895-1965), West African political leader and pan-Africanist **16** 76-77

Wallach, Meyer
see Litvinov, Maxim Maximovich

WALLAS, GRAHAM (1858-1932), English sociologist and political scientist **16** 77-78
Cole, George Douglas Howard **4** 146-147

WALLENBERG, RAOUL (1912-?), Swedish diplomat **16** 78-80

WALLENSTEIN, ALBRECHT WENZEL EUSEBIUS VON (1583-1634), Bohemian soldier of fortune **16** 80-81
Ferdinand III **5** 416-417
Gustavus II **7** 43-45
Richelieu, Armand Jean du Plessis de **13** 142-144
Schiller, Johann Christoph Friedrich von **14** 4-7

Wallenstein's Camp (symphonic poem)
Smetana, Bedřich **14** 281-282

Wallensteins Lager (play)
Schiller, Johann Christoph Friedrich von **14** 4-7

WALLER, THOMAS WRIGHT (Fats; 1904-43), American jazz singer, pianist, organist, bandleader, and composer **16** 81-82
Armstrong, Louis Daniel **1** 303-304

Wallis, Alfred (1855-1942), English painter
Nicholson, Ben **11** 380-381

Wallis, John (1616-1703), English mathematician
Newton, Isaac **11** 369-372
Pascal, Blaise **12** 122-124

Walls Have Ears, The (play)
Alarcón, Pedro Antonio de **1** 100-101

Wal-Mart (retail store chain)
Walton, Sam Moore **16** 91-92

Walnut Trees of Altenburg, The (novel)
Malraux, André **10** 178-180

Walpole, Horace, 4th Earl of Orford (1717-1797), English author and collector
Adam, Robert and James **1** 38-40
Braddock, Edward **2** 474-475
Gray, Thomas **6** 509-510
Herbert, Edward **7** 324
Namier, Lewis Bernstein **11** 301-303
North, Frederick **11** 429-430
Piranesi, Giovanni Battista **12** 321-322
Reynolds, Joshua **13** 115-116
Voltaire **16** 14-16

Walpole, Hugh (1884-1941), English novelist
Maugham, William Somerset **10** 344-345

WALPOLE, ROBERT (1st Earl of Oxford; 1676-1745), English statesman **16** 82-84
Bolingbroke, Viscount **2** 374-375
Defoe, Daniel **4** 457-459
Fielding, Henry **5** 442-444
George I **6** 268-269
George II **6** 269-270
Oglethorpe, James Edward **11** 482-483
Pitt, William the Elder **12** 328-329

Walpurgis Night (painting)
Courbet, Jean Desiré Gustave **4** 271-273

WALRAS, MARIE ESPRIT LÉON (1834-1910), French economist **16** 84-85
Clark, John Bates **4** 76-77
Jevons, William Stanley **8** 255-256
Schumpeter, Joseph Alois **14** 43-44

Walsh, Richard John (1886-1960), American publisher
Buck, Pearl Sydenstricker **3** 91-93

WALSH, THOMAS JAMES (1859-1933), American statesman **16** 85-86

Walter, Bruno (Bruno Walter Schlesinger; 1876-1962), German-born French conductor
Bernstein, Leonard **2** 218-219
Mann, Thomas **10** 204-207

Walter, Hubert (died 1205), archbishop of Canterbury
John **8** 274-275

WALTER, JOHANN (1496-1570), German composer **16** 86

Walter Reed Hospital (Washington, District of Columbia)
Reed, Walter **13** 78

WALTERS, BARBARA (born 1931), American network newscast anchor **16** 86-88

Walther, Bernhard (1430-1504), German amateur astronomer
Regiomontanus **13** 81-82

WALTON, ERNEST (1903-1995), Irish physicist **16** 88-90
Cockcroft, John Douglas **4** 131-132

WALTON, IZAAK (1593-1683), English writer and biographer **16** 90-91
Donne, John **5** 60-61
Herbert, George **7** 324-326

WALTON, SAM MOORE (1918-1992), American businessman who co-founded Wal-Mart **16** 91-92

WALTON, SIR WILLIAM TURNER (1902-1983), English composer **16** 91-92

Waltz of the Toreadors, The (play)
Anouilh, Jean **1** 243-244

Waltzing Matilda (ballad)
Paterson, Andrew Barton **12** 131-132

Wampanoag Indians (North America)
Bradford, William **2** 475-476
Massasoit **10** 322-324
Metacom **10** 529-531
Philip **12** 267-268
Squanto **14** 386-388

Wanamaker, John (1838-1922), American merchant
Stewart, Alexander Turney **14** 448-449

Wanapum Indians (North America)
Smohalla **14** 303-305

Wanderer Fantasy (musical composition)
Schubert, Franz Peter **14** 35-37

Wanderer, The (novel)
Burney, Fanny **3** 147-148

Wandering Jew (mythology)
Courbet, Jean Desiré Gustave **4** 271-273
Wallace, Lewis **16** 74-75

Wandering the Hills by the River (painting)
Hsia Kuei **8** 4-5

Wanderings of Oisin and Other Poems, The (book)
Yeats, William Butler **16** 445-447

Wandlung, Die (play)
Toller, Ernst **15** 261

Wandrers Nachtlied (song)
Schubert, Franz Peter **14** 35-37

WANG, AN (1920-1990), Chinese-American inventor, electronics expert, and businessman **16** 93-95

WANG AN-SHIH (1021-1086), Chinese reformer, poet, and scholar **16** 95-97
Fan Chung-yen **5** 376-377
Huang Tsung-hsi **8** 9-10
Hui-Tsung **8** 25
Ou-yang Hsiu **12** 33-34
Ssu-ma kuang **14** 390-391
Su Shih **15** 39-40

WANG CHING-WEI (1883-1944), Chinese revolutionary leader **16** 98
Chiang Kai-shek **3** 510-513
Sun Yat-sen **15** 35-39
Yen Hsi-shan **16** 452-453

Wang-ch'üan villa (painting)
Wang Wei **16** 106-108

WANG CH'UNG (27-circa 100), Chinese philosopher **16** 98-99

WANG FU-CHIH (1619-1692), Chinese philosopher **16** 99-101

Wang Hsi-chih (321-379), Chinese calligrapher
Chao Meng-fu **3** 436-437

Wang Hsien-chih (died 878), Chinese rebel leader
Huang Ch'ao **8** 8-9

WANG KON (877-943), Korean king **16** 101
Kwangjong **9** 140

Wang Kuei (1019-1085), Chinese statesman
Ch'in Kuei **3** 524-525

Wang Laboratories Incorporated
Wang, An **16** 93-95

WANG MANG (45 B.C.-A.D. 23), Chinese statesman, emperor 9-23 **16** 101-103
K'ang Yu-wei **8** 426-428
Kuang-wu-ti **9** 112-113

Wang Meng (circa 1308-85), Chinese painter
Chao Meng-fu **3** 436-437
Tung Ch'i-ch'ang **15** 339-340

WANG MING (Chen Shaoyu; 1904-74), leader of the "Internationalist" group

within the Chinese Communist Party
16 103-104

WANG PI (226-249), Chinese philosopher
16 104-105
Tao-an **15** 103-104

WANG T'AO (1828-1897), Chinese
reformer and scholar **16** 105-106

WANG WEI (699-759), Chinese poet and
painter **16** 106-108
Chao Meng-fu **3** 436-437
Mi Fei **11** 12-13
Tung Ch'i-ch'ang **15** 339-340

WANG YANG-MING (1472-1529), Chi-
nese philosopher and government official
16 108-109
Chang Hsüeh-ch'eng **3** 433
Lu Chiu-yuan **10** 24-25
Wang Fu-chih **16** 99-101
Yi Hwang **16** 457

Wang Yüan-ch'i (1642-1715), Chinese
painter and calligrapher
K'ang-hsi **8** 423-426

Wapping (painting)
Whistler, James Abbott McNeill
16 225-226

Wapshot Chronicle, The (novel)
Cheever, John **3** 493-494

War (mural)
Portinari, Cândido **12** 407-408

War and Peace (book)
Jay, William **8** 232-233
Tolstoy, Leo **15** 262-265-483

War and Peace (opera)
Prokofiev, Sergei Sergeevich
12 458-460

War Cabinet (Great Britain)
Attlee, Clement Richard **1** 361-362
Baldwin, Stanley **1** 468-469
Balfour, Arthur James **1** 469-470
Botha, Louis **2** 434-436
Chamberlain, Arthur Neville **3** 409-411
Dale, Henry Hallett **4** 371-373
Henderson, Arthur **7** 277-278

War crimes trials
Eichmann, Adolf **5** 226-227
Hess, Walter Richard Rudolf **7** 363-365
Kesselring, Albert Field Marshal
8 522-523
Kishi, Nobusuke **9** 41-43
Mladic, Ratko **11** 68-69
Tojo, Hideki **15** 254-256
Wiesenthal, Simon **16** 264-266
Yamashita, Tomoyuki **16** 435-436

War Department (United States)
Baruch, Bernard Mannes **2** 42-43
Cameron, Simon **3** 246-247
Perry, Ralph Barton **12** 239-240
Pershing, John Joseph **12** 243-244
Ridgway, Matthew Bunker **13** 160-161
Root, Elihu **13** 283-284
Stanton, Edwin McMasters **14** 401-402

War for Independence (Cuba; 1895-98)
Cleveland, Stephen Grover **4** 108-110
Estrada Palma, Tomás **5** 326-327
Gómez, Máximo **6** 418-419
Hostos, Eugenio María de **7** 513-514
Maceo, Antonio **10** 88-90
Machado y Morales, Gerardo **10** 92-93
Martí, José **10** 285-286
McKinley, William **10** 418-420
Menocal, Mario Garcia **10** 506-507

War Hawks (U. S. history)
Calhoun, John Caldwell **3** 226-228
Clay, Henry **4** 94-96
Madison, James **10** 121-123
Monroe, James **11** 111-113

War Is Kind (poem)
Crane, Stephen **4** 293-295

War of 1812
British allies
Black Hawk **2** 308
Osceola **12** 18
Tecumseh **15** 133
British policy
Liverpool, 2nd Earl of **9** 456-457
Canadian campaign (British forces)
Brock, Isaac **3** 12-13
Robinson, John Beverley **13** 210
Canadian campaign (United States
forces)
Cass, Lewis **3** 355-356
Hampton, Wade **7** 111-112
Harrison, William Henry **7** 180-181
Hull, William **8** 29-30
Kearny, Stephen Watts **8** 468-469
Pike, Zebulon **12** 302-304
peace negotiations
Adams, John Quincy **1** 52-54
Clay, Henry **4** 94-96
Gallatin, Albert **6** 183-184
U.S. forces (army)
Ashley, William Henry **1** 333-334
Houston, Samuel **7** 526-527
Jackson, Andrew **8** 168-172
Taylor, Zachary **15** 128-130
U.S. forces (navy)
Decatur, Stephen **4** 448-449
Farragut, David Glasgow **5** 388-389
Lawrence, James **9** 251-252
Perry, Oliver Hazard **12** 239
U.S. opponents
Ladd, William **9** 149
Morris, Gouverneur **11** 182-183
Otis, Harrison Gray **12** 25
Randolph, John **13** 30
Taylor, John **15** 126
U.S. supporters
Calhoun, John Caldwell **3** 226-228
du Pont, Éleuthère Irénée **5** 154
Girard, Stephen **6** 347-348
Macon, Nathaniel **10** 114-115
Madison, James **10** 121-123
Monroe, James **11** 111-113
Story, Joseph **14** 480-481

see also United States—Early
Republic

War of 1812 (novel)
Cooper, James Fenimore **4** 220-223

War, opposition to
see Pacifism

War Requiem (musical composition)
Britten, Benjamin **3** 10-11

Warbeck, Perkin (1474-1499), Walloon
pretender to British crown
Henry VII **7** 300-302

WARBURG, OTTO (1883-1970), German
biochemist **16** 109-111
Krebs, Hans Adolf **9** 95-97
Meyerhof, Otto Fritz **10** 537-539
Szent-Györgyi, Albert von **15** 62-64
Theorell, Axel Hugo Theodor
15 176-177

WARBURG, PAUL MORITZ (1868-1932),
German-American banker **16** 111-112

Warburton, Peter (1813-1889), British officer and explorer in Australia
Giles, Ernest **6** 317-318

WARD, AARON MONTGOMERY
(1843-1913), American merchant **16** 112

WARD, ARTEMUS (1834-1867), American
journalist and humorist **16** 112-113
Dunne, Finley Peter **5** 147-148
Twain, Mark **15** 363-366

Ward, John Q.A. (1830-1910), American
sculptor
French, Daniel Chester **6** 98-99

Ward, Julia
see Howe, Julia Ward

WARD, LESTER FRANK (1841-1913),
American paleobotanist and sociologist
16 113-114
Gumplowicz, Ludwig **7** 41

Ward, Nathaniel (1578?-1652), American
clergyman
Bradstreet, Anne Dudley **2** 486-487

Ward, Samuel (1814-1884), American
politician, bon vivant, and raconteur
Cole, Thomas **4** 151-152

Ward, Sir Joseph (1856-1930), Australian
statesman
Massey, William Ferguson **10** 324
Ngata, Apirana Turupa **11** 374-375

Ward No. 6 (story)
Chekhov, Anton Pavlovich **3** 494-497

Ward No.4 (novel)
Pa Chin **12** 53-54

Warden, The (novel)
Trollope, Anthony **15** 300-302

Ware, William (1832-1915), American
architect
Sullivan, Louis Henri **15** 27-28

Ware v. Hylton (legal case)
Chase, Samuel **3** 475-476
Marshall, John **10** 279-281

Warfield, David (1866-1951), American actor
Belasco, David **2** 124-125

Warham, William (1450?-1532), archbishop of Canterbury
Wolsey, Thomas **16** 364-366

WARHOL, ANDY (Andrew Warhola; ca. 1927-1987), American pop artist and film maker **16** 114-115

Warner, Charles Dudley (1829-1900), American man of letters
Twain, Mark **15** 363-366

WARNOCK, HELEN MARY WILSON (born 1924), British philosopher **16** 115-117

WARREN, EARL (1891-1974), American jurist, chief justice of U.S. Supreme Court 1953-69 **16** 117-120
Douglas, William Orville **5** 83-85
Eisenhower, Dwight David **5** 233-236

WARREN, MERCY OTIS (1728-1814), American writer **16** 120-121

WARREN, ROBERT PENN (1905-1989), American man of letters **16** 121-122
Calder, Alexander **3** 216-218
Eliot, Thomas Stearns **5** 258-261
Tate, Allen **15** 116

Warrior with Shield (sculpture)
Moore, Henry **11** 146-148

Warrior's Barrow, The (play)
Ibsen, Henrik **8** 98-100

Wars of America (sculpture)
Borglum, John Gutzon de la Mothe **2** 416-417

Wars of Religion
see Religion, Wars of

Warsaw (city, Poland)
Chicherin, Georgi Vasilyevich **3** 516-517
Suvorov, Aleksandr Vasilievich **15** 44-45

Warsaw, battle of (1702)
Charles XII **3** 464-466

Warsaw Conservatory
Chopin, Frédéric François **4** 16-18
Szymanowski, Karol **15** 67-68

Warsaw, grand duchy of (established 1807)
Napoleon I **11** 306-310
Nesselrode, Karl Robert **11** 348-349

Warsaw Pact (1955)
Dubček, Alexander **5** 112-113
Konev, Ivan Stefanovich **9** 81-82

Warton, Joseph (1722-1800), English literary critic
Collins, William **4** 168-169

Warwick (Rhode Island)
Gorton, Samuell **6** 460

Warwick, Ambrose Dudley, Earl of (1528?-1590), English soldier
Gilbert, Humphrey **6** 313

Warwick, Edward, Earl of (1475-1499), son of George, Duke of Clarence
Henry VII **7** 300-302

Richard III **13** 132-133

Warwick, John Dudley, Earl of
see Northumberland, Duke of

Warwick, Richard de Beauchamp, Earl of (1382-1439), English soldier
Henry VI **7** 298-299

Warwick, Thomas Beauchamp, Earl of (died 1401), English nobleman, supporter of Henry IV
Richard II **13** 130-131

WARWICK AND SALISBURY, EARL OF (Richard Neville; 1428-71), English military and political leader **16** 122-123
Edward IV **5** 212-213
Hampden, John **7** 110-111
Henry VI **7** 298-299
Margaret of Anjou **10** 249-250
Richard III **13** 132-133

Waseda University (Japan)
Okuma, Shigenobu **11** 490

WASHAKIE (circa 1804-1900), Native American Shoshoni tribal leader **16** 123-125

Washing of a Corpse (painting)
Cézanne, Paul **3** 400-402

Washington (ship)
Cinque, Joseph **4** 62
Shreve, Henry Miller **14** 207
Stockton, Robert Field **14** 461-462

Washington (state, United States)
Foley, Tom **5** 499-501
Hansen, Julia Butler **7** 132-133
Harrison, Benjamin **7** 178-179
Ray, Dixy Lee **13** 56-57

WASHINGTON, BOOKER TALIAFERRO (1856-1915), African American educator and racial leader **16** 125-126
Armstrong, Samuel Chapman **1** 306-307
Carver, George Washington **3** 346-347
Dewey, Melvil **4** 523-524
Dube, John Langalibalele **5** 113
Fortune, Timothy Thomas **6** 18-21
Garvey, Marcus Mosiah **6** 228-229

WASHINGTON, GEORGE (1732-1799), American Revolutionary commander in chief, president 1789-97 **16** 126-129
biographies and histories
Ford, Paul Leicester **6** 9-10
Freeman, Douglas Southall **6** 91-92
Irving, Washington **8** 141-143
Sparks, Jared **14** 363
Warren, Mercy Otis **16** 120-121
Weems, Mason Locke **16** 170
Cabinet
Hamilton, Alexander **7** 95-98
Knox, Henry **9** 64
Pickering, Timothy **12** 298-299
Randolph, Edmund **13** 29-30
Confederation
see Articles of Confederation
constitution

see Constitutional Convention (United States); Constitution of the United States
Continental Army
Arnold, Benedict **1** 309-310
Burr, Aaron **3** 156-159
Dinwiddie, Robert **5** 18-19
Lafayette, Marquis de **9** 151-152
Lincoln, Benjamin **9** 418-419
Rochambeau, Comte de **13** 220-221
Rodney, George Brydges **13** 239-240
Rush, Benjamin **13** 364-365
Steuben, Frederick William Augustus von **14** 438-439
see also American Revolution
Continental congress
see Continental Congress (United States; 1774-89)
courts
Chase, Samuel **3** 475-476
Hopkinson, Francis **7** 496-497
Livingston, Robert R. **9** 462-463
Otis, Harrison Gray **12** 25
Rutledge, John **13** 387-388
critics
Freneau, Philip Morin **6** 99-100
Monroe, James **11** 111-113
death
Ames, Fisher **1** 199-200
Cobbett, William **4** 126-127
diplomacy
Adams, John Quincy **1** 52-54
Clark, George Rogers **4** 75-76
Genet, Edmond Charles **6** 261-262
Jones, Inigo **8** 333-334
McGillivray, Alexander **10** 412
Wilkinson, James **16** 284-286
French and Indian wars
Braddock, Edward **2** 474-475
Forbes, John **5** 507-508
Gist, Christopher **6** 352-353
Lewis, Andrew **9** 376-377
in art
Borglum, John Gutzon de la Mothe **2** 416-417
L'Enfant, Pierre Charles **9** 322-323
Peale, Charles Willson **12** 169-171
Peale, Rembrandt **12** 172-173
Rogers, John **13** 248
Rush, William **13** 365-366
Stuart, Gilbert **14** 513-515
Taft, Lorado **15** 75-76
in literature
Wheatley, Phillis **16** 221-222
see also Declaration of Independence; Whiskey Rebellion (1794)

Washington College (Maryland)
Smith, William **14** 301

Washington College (Virginia)
Lee, Robert Edward **9** 292-294

Washington Conference (1921-1922)
Balfour, Arthur James **1** 469-470
Borah, William Edgar **2** 408
Borden, Robert Laird **2** 409-411

Harding, Warren Gamaliel **7** 148-149
Hughes, Charles Evans **8** 15-16
Root, Elihu **13** 283-284

Washington Crossing the Delaware (painting)
Hicks, Edward **7** 375
Wood, Grant **16** 368-369

Washington, D.C. (federal city)
Capitol architecture
Bulfinch, Charles **3** 116-117
Curry, Jabez Lamar Monroe **4** 346-347
Latrobe, Benjamin Henry **9** 222-224
Renwick, James **13** 102-103
Capitol landscaping
Downing, Andrew Jackson **5** 90-91
Olmsted, Frederick Law **11** 503-504
civil rights march
see March on Washington for Jobs and Freedom (1963)
history of
Green, Constance McLaughlin **6** 518-519
mayors
Barry, Marion Shepilov Jr. **2** 25-28
Poor People's March (1968)
King, Martin Luther Jr. **9** 20-22
slavery in
Clay, Henry **4** 94-96
Lincoln, Abraham **9** 415-418

Washington Disarmament Conference
see Washington Conference (1921-1922)

Washington Monument (Baltimore)
Mills, Robert **11** 36-37

Washington Monument (Washington, District of Columbia)
Mills, Robert **11** 36-37
Morrill, Justin Smith **11** 182
Washington, George **16** 126-129

Washington Peace Convention (1861)
Buchanan, James **3** 89-90
Corning, Erastus **4** 238-239
Tyler, John **15** 368-369

Washington Post (newspaper)
Graham, Katharine Meyer **6** 483-485
Maynard, Robert Clyve **10** 366-367
Will, George Frederick **16** 286-287
Woodward and Bernstein **16** 376-378

Washington Post, The (march)
Sousa, John Philip **14** 353-354

Washington School of Psychiatry (established 1936)
Sullivan, Harry Stack **15** 23-24
White, William Alanson **16** 239-240

Washington Square (novel)
James, Henry **8** 211-212

Washington Square Arch (New York City)
White, Stanford **16** 235-236

Washington, Treaty of (1871)
Fish, Hamilton **5** 461-462
see also Alabama Claims

Washington University (Saint Louis, Missouri)
Beckmann, Max **2** 104-105
Compton, Arthur Holly **4** 186-188
Erlanger, Joseph **5** 310-311
Lovejoy, Arthur Oncken **10** 6

Washington, University of (Seattle)
Guthrie, Edwin Ray **7** 49-50
Ogburn, William Fielding **11** 480
Parrington, Vernon Louis **12** 119-120
Ray, Dixy Lee **13** 56-57
Roethke, Theodore **13** 243-244

Washington's Birthday (symphony)
Ives, Charles Edward **8** 159-160

Washita, battle of the (1868)
Custer, George Armstrong **4** 355-356

WASMOSY, JUAN CARLOS (born 1939), president of Paraguay (1993-) **16** 129-130

Wasps, The (play)
Aristophanes **1** 293-294

WASSERMANN, JAKOB (1873-1934), German author **16** 130-131

Wasserträger, Der (opera)
Cherubini, Luigi Carlo Zanobi Salvatore Maria **3** 505-506

Waste Land (anthology; Kakei)
Basho, Matsuo **2** 45-48

Waste Land (poem; Eliot)
Crane, Hart **4** 291-293
Eliot, Thomas Stearns **5** 258-261, 563
Fitzgerald, Francis Scott Key **5** 470-472
MacLeish, Archibald **10** 109-110
Pound, Ezra Loomis **12** 415-417
Sitwell, Edith **14** 265-266
Williams, William Carlos **16** 308-309

Wat Suan Mokkhabalārama (Thai monastery)
Buddhadāsa Bhikkhu **3** 101-102

Watch and Ward (novel)
James, Henry **8** 211-212

Watch on the Rhine (play)
Hellman, Lillian Florence **7** 267-268

Watch That Ends the Night, The (novel)
MacLennan, Hugh **10** 110-111

Watch Your Step (musical)
Berlin, Irving **2** 200-201

Water
Cavendish, Henry **3** 383-384
Fahrenheit, Gabriel Daniel **5** 366
Lavoisier, Antoine Laurent **9** 241-244
Thales **15** 161

Water Carrier, The (opera)
Cherubini, Luigi Carlo Zanobi Salvatore Maria **3** 505-506

Water lily series (art)
Monet, Claude **11** 102-104

Water Margin, The (novel)
Hu Shih **8** 63-65

Water Music (suite)
Handel, George Frederick **7** 116-119

Water Nymph and Bittern (sculpture)
Rush, William **13** 365-366

Water of Cure, The (story)
Imam, Alhadji Abubakar **8** 114-115

Water Village (scroll)
Chao Meng-fu **3** 436-437

Water-Babies, The (book)
Kingsley, Charles **9** 28

Water-Buffalo Children, The (book)
Buck, Pearl Sydenstricker **3** 91-93

Waterfall with Castle (painting)
Ruisdael, Jacob van **13** 357-358

Watergate scandal (United States, 1974)
Burger, Warren E. **3** 133-136
Cox, Archibald **4** 283-284
Ervin, Sam J. Jr. **5** 316-317
Goldwater, Barry **6** 413-415
Jaworski, Leon **8** 229-230
Nixon, Richard Milhous **11** 401-404
Sirica, John Joseph **14** 257-258
Woodward and Bernstein **16** 376-378

WATERHOUSE, BENJAMIN (1754-1846), American physician **16** 131-132

Waterloo, Battle of (1815)
Allied command
Blücher, Gebhard Leberecht von **2** 340-341
Lieber, Francis **9** 401-402
Wellington, 1st Duke of **16** 193-195
in literature
Stendhal **14** 422-425
Thackeray, William Makepeace **15** 159-161
Napoleonic forces
Napoleon I **11** 306-310
Ney, Michel **11** 372-373

WATERS, MAXINE (born 1938), African American congresswoman **16** 132-134

WATERS, MUDDY (born McKinley Morganfield; 1915-1983), African American blues musician **16** 134-136

Waters of Kronos, The (novel)
Richter, Conrad Michael **13** 148-149

Water-Witch, The (novel)
Cooper, James Fenimore **4** 220-223, 127

Watson and the Shark (painting)
Copley, John Singleton **4** 228-230

WATSON, ELKANAH (1758-1842), American merchant and banker **16** 136
Coxe, Tench **4** 285-286

WATSON, JAMES DEWEY (born 1928), American biologist **16** 137-138
Crick, Francis Harry Crompton **4** 310

Watson, John (1867-1941), Australian Labour party politician
Hughes, William Morris **8** 21-22

WATSON, JOHN BROADUS (1878-1958), American psychologist **16** 138-139
Lashley, Karl Spencer **9** 214-215
Tolman, Edward Chace **15** 261-262

Watson, John Christian (1867-1941), Australian politician
    Fisher, Andrew **5** 462

Watson, Thomas Augustus (1854-1934), American telephone technician
    Bell, Alexander Graham **2** 129-131

WATSON, THOMAS EDWARD (1856-1922), American lawyer and politician **16** 139
    Donnelly, Ignatius **5** 62
    Woodward, Comer Vann **16** 378-379

WATSON, THOMAS J. (1874-1956), American business executive **16** 140

Watsons, The (novel)
    Austen, Jane **1** 377-379

WATSON-WATT, SIR ROBERT ALEXANDER (1892-1973), British scientific civil servant **16** 140-141

Watson-Wentworth, Charles
    see Rockingham, 2d Marquess of

Watt (novel)
    Beckett, Samuel **2** 102-104

WATT, JAMES (1736-1819), British instrument maker and engineer **16** 141-143
    Black, Joseph **2** 303
    Cort, Henry **4** 254
    Evans, Oliver **5** 338
    Newcomen, Thomas **11** 362
    Smeaton, John **14** 280-281

WATTEAU, ANTOINE (1684-1721), French painter **16** 143-144
    Boucher, François **2** 440-442
    Chardin, Jean Baptiste Siméon **3** 442-443
    Fragonard, Jean Honoré **6** 38-39
    Renoir, Pierre Auguste **13** 101-102

WATTS, ALAN WILSON (1915-1973), naturalized American author and lecturer **16** 144-145

Watts, Isaac (1674-1748), English hymnist and theologian
    Barlow, Joel **2** 6-7
    Dickinson, Emily **4** 541-543

Watts-Dunton, Walter Theodore (1832-1914), English poet, novelist, and critic
    Swinburne, Algernon Charles **15** 54-55

Waugh, Arthur (1866-1943), English literary critic and editor
    Waugh, Evelyn Arthur St. John **16** 145-147

WAUGH, EVELYN ARTHUR ST. JOHN (1903-1966), English author **16** 145-147

Wave mechanics (physics)
    Bohr, Niels Henrik David **2** 366-368
    de Broglie, Louis **4** 442-444
    Einstein, Albert **5** 228-231
    Schrödinger, Erwin **14** 31-33

Wave theory of light
    see Light—wave theory

WAVELL, ARCHIBALD PERCIVAL (1st Earl Wavell; 1883-1950), English general, statesman, and writer **16** 147-148
    Gandhi, Mohandas Karamchand **6** 201-204
    Sapru, Tej Bahadur **13** 480-481

Waverley (novel; Scott)
    Edgeworth, Maria **5** 205-206
    Scott, Walter **14** 68-70

Waverley (overture)
    Berlioz, Louis Hector **2** 203-205

Waves of Love and the Sea, The (play)
    Grillparzer, Franz **6** 546-547

Waves, The (novel)
    Woolf, Virginia Stephen **16** 381-382

Waxhaws, battle of (1780)
    Tarleton, Banastre **15** 110

Way Down East (film)
    Griffith, David Wark **6** 544-545

Way Home, The (novel)
    Richardson, Henry Handel **13** 139

Way of All Flesh, The (novel)
    Butler, Samuel **3** 183

Way of Perfection, The (book)
    Theresa **15** 178-179

Way of the World, The (play)
    Congreve, William **4** 200-201
    Evans, Edith **5** 336-337

Way to Wealth, The
    see Poor Richard's Almanack

Way We Live Now, The (novel)
    Trollope, Anthony **15** 300-302

Wayfarer, The (novel)
    Natsume, Soseki **11** 324-325

Wayland (Massachusetts)
    Breuer, Marcel **2** 520-521

WAYLAND, FRANCIS (1796-1865), American educator and clergyman **16** 148-149

WAYNE, ANTHONY (1745-1796), American soldier **16** 149-150
    Clark, William **4** 82-83
    Girty, Simon **6** 350
    Harrison, William Henry **7** 180-181
    Morgan, Daniel **11** 160-161
    Pulaski, Casimir **12** 480-481

WAYNE, JOHN (Marion Mitchell Morrison; 1907-79), American actor **16** 150-151

Ways and Means Committee (United States Congress)
    Gallatin, Albert **6** 183-184
    Letcher, John **9** 359-360

Wayside Crosses (stories)
    Čapek, Karel **3** 271-272

Wayward Bus, The (novel)
    Steinbeck, John Ernst **14** 416-417

W.C.T.U. Parade (painting)
    Shahn, Ben **14** 139-140

We, the People (play)
    Rice, Elmer **13** 126-127

We Want Barabbas (painting)
    Daumier, Honoré Victorin **4** 403-405

Wealth (economics)
    Clark, John Bates **4** 76-77
    Commons, John Rogers **4** 185
    Ricardo, David **13** 123-124
    Smith, Adam **14** 283-284
    see also Capital

Wealth (play)
    Aristophanes **1** 293-294

Wealth of Nations (book; Smith)
    Malthus, Thomas Robert **10** 180-181
    Say, Jean Baptiste **13** 508-509
    Small, Albion Woodbury **14** 277
    Smith, Adam **14** 283-284
    Yen Fu **16** 452

Weapons and explosives
    Cooper, Peter **4** 223-224
    du Pont, Éleuthère Irénée **5** 154
    Farmer, Moses Gerrish **5** 385
    Fulton, Robert **6** 151-152
    Gatling, Richard Jordan **6** 234-235
    Krupp **9** 109-111
    Maxim, Hiram Stevens **10** 355-356
    Nobel, Alfred Bernhard **11** 410-411
    see also Atomic bomb

Weary Blues, The (poem)
    Hughes, Langston **8** 18-19

Weather
    see Meteorology

Weather Bureau, U.S.
    Dawes, Henry Laurens **4** 427
    Henry, Joseph **7** 307-308

WEAVER, JAMES BAIRD (1833-1912), American political leader **16** 151-152
    Lease, Mary Elizabeth Clyens **9** 268

WEAVER, ROBERT C. (born 1907), first African American U.S. cabinet officer **16** 152-153

Weavers, The (musical group, United States)
    Seeger, Pete **14** 83-84

Weavers, The (play)
    Hauptmann, Gerhart Johann Robert **7** 199-201

Web and the Rock, The (novel)
    Wolfe, Thomas Clayton **16** 355-356

WEBB, BEATRICE POTTER (1858-1943), English social reformer **16** 153-154
    Booth, Charles **2** 400-401

Webb, John (1611-1672), English architect
    Jones, Inigo **8** 333-334

Webb, Philip (1831-1915), English architect
    Shaw, Richard Norman **14** 167-168

WEBB, SIDNEY JAMES (Baron Passfield; 1859-1947), English social reformer, historian, and statesman **16** 154-155
    Bernstein, Eduard **2** 218
    Bosanquet, Bernard **2** 425-426

Cole, George Douglas Howard
   4 146-147
Shaw, George Bernard **14** 163-164
Webb, Beatrice Potter **16** 153-154
Wells, Herbert George **16** 195-196

WEBBER, ANDREW LLOYD (born 1948),
British composer **16** 155-156

Weber, Bernard Anselm (1712-1758), German composer
Meyerbeer, Giacomo **10** 536-537

**WEBER, CARL MARIA FRIEDRICH ERNST
VON** (1786-1826), German composer
and conductor **16** 156-157
Berlioz, Louis Hector **2** 203-205
Mendelssohn, Moses **10** 488-489
Schubert, Franz Peter **14** 35-37
Schumann, Robert Alexander **14** 41-43

WEBER, MAX (1864-1920), German social
scientist **16** 157-160
associates
   Simmel, Georg **14** 234-235
   Tönnies, Ferdinand **15** 266-267
   Troeltsch, Ernst **15** 299-300
influence of
   Childe, Vere Gordon **3** 521-522
   Jaspers, Karl **8** 225-226
   Mannheim, Karl **10** 208-209
   Mills, C. Wright **11** 35-36
influenced by
   Dilthey, Wilhelm Christian Ludwig
   5 10

WEBER, MAX (1881-1961), American
painter **16** 160
Rothko, Mark **13** 320-321

Weber, Wilhelm (1804-1891), German
physicist
Gauss, Karl Friedrich **6** 240-242
Riemann, Georg Friedrich Bernard
   13 164-165

WEBERN, ANTON (1883-1945), Austrian
composer **16** 160-162
influence of
   Boulez, Pierre **2** 444-445
   Nono, Luigi **11** 420-421
   Penderecki, Krzysztof **12** 195-197
   Schuller, Gunther **14** 37-38
   Stockhausen, Karlheinz **14** 460-461
   Stravinsky, Igor Fedorovich
   14 502-506
influenced by
   Mahler, Gustav **10** 144-145
twelve-tone method
   Berg, Alban **2** 186-187
   Dallapiccola, Luigi **4** 377-378
   Krenek, Ernst **9** 98-99
   Schoenberg, Arnold **14** 24-26

WEBSTER, DANIEL (1782-1852), American
lawyer, orator, and statesman **16** 162-164
Alger, Horatio **1** 153-154
Calhoun, John Caldwell **3** 226-228
Everett, Edward **5** 344
Fillmore, Millard **5** 447-448
Hayne, Robert Young **7** 231-232
Lincoln, Abraham **9** 415-418

Shaw, George Bernard **14** 163-164
Stephens, Alexander Hamilton
   14 429-430
Tyler, John **15** 368-369

WEBSTER, JOHN (circa 1580-circa 1634),
English dramatist **16** 164
Ford, John **6** 7-8
Kyd, Thomas **9** 140-141
Shakespeare, William **14** 142-145

WEBSTER, NOAH (1758-1843), American
lexicographer **16** 164-166

Webster-Ashburton Treaty (1842)
Aberdeen, 4th Earl of **1** 25-26
Tyler, John **15** 368-369
Webster, Daniel **16** 162-164

Webster's Unabridged (dictionary)
Webster, Daniel **16** 162-164

Weckmann, Matthais (1621-1674), German organist and composer
Froberger, Johann Jakob **6** 120-121

Wedding Night, The (film)
Goldwyn, Samuel **6** 416

**Wedding of St. George and the Princess
Sabra** (painting)
Rossetti, Dante Gabriel **13** 308-309

Wedding songs (Greek literature)
Sappho **13** 479-480

Wedding, The (play)
Chekhov, Anton Pavlovich **3** 494-497

WEDEKIND, FRANK (Benjamin Franklin
Wedekind; 1864-1918), German dramatist, cosmopolite, and libertarian
16 166-167
Berg, Alban **2** 186-187
Brecht, Bertolt **2** 512-514
Demuth, Charles **4** 497-498

WEDGWOOD, CICELY VERONICA
(1910-1997), British writer and historian
16 167-168

WEDGWOOD, JOSIAH (1730-1795), English potter **16** 168-169
Darwin, Charles Robert **4** 397-399

WEED, THURLOW (1797-1882), American
politician **16** 169-170
Fillmore, Millard **5** 447-448
Greeley, Horace **6** 515-517
Seward, William Henry **14** 124-125

Weeds (novel)
Azuela, Mariano **1** 402

**Week on the Concord and Merrimack
Rivers, A** (book)
Thoreau, Henry David **15** 203-205

Weekend in Guatemala (stories)
Asturias, Miguel Angel **1** 354-355

Weekly Chronotype (newspaper)
Wright, Elizur **16** 396-397

Weekly Journal (newspaper)
Bradford, William (printer) **2** 476-477

WEEMS, MASON LOCKE (1759-1825),
American Episcopal minister and popular
writer **16** 170

Weeper, The (poem)
Crashaw, Richard **4** 296

WEGENER, ALFRED LOTHAR
(1880-1930), German meteorologist, Arctic explorer, and geophysicist **16** 170-171

We-group (sociology)
Sumner, William Graham **15** 32

Wei (Chinese state)
Shang Yang **14** 149-150

Wei (reigned 357-320 B.C.), Chinese king
of Ch'i
Mencius **10** 480-481

Wei dynasty (China; reigned 220-265)
Ts'ao Ts'ao **15** 322-323
Wei Hsiao-Wen-ti **8** 5

WEI HSIAO-WEN-TI (467-499), Chinese
emperor **8** 5

Wei, Prince of
see Ts'ao Ts'ao

Wei Tao-ming (born 1899), Chinese lawyer
and diplomat
Hu Shih **8** 63-65

Wei Yang
see Shang Yang

WEI YÜAN (1794-1856), Chinese historian
and geographer **16** 180-181
Tso Tsung-t'ang **15** 328-329

WEIDENREICH, FRANZ (1873-1948), German anatomist and physical anthropologist **16** 171-172

Weidig, Adolph (1867-1931), American
composer
Dawson, William Levi **4** 427-428

Weigel, Helene (1901-1971),
Australian-born actress and theatrical
director
Brecht, Bertolt **2** 512-514

WEIL, SIMONE (1909-1943), French
thinker, political activist, and religious
mystic **16** 172-174

Weilborn, Frank (literary character)
Massinger, Philip **10** 324-325

WEILL, KURT (1900-1950), German-American composer **16** 174-175
Brecht, Bertolt **2** 512-514
Stravinsky, Igor Fedorovich **14** 502-506

Weimar Republic
see Germany—Republic

Wei-mo-ch'i
see Wang Wei

WEINBERG, STEVEN (born 1933), Nobel
Prize-winning physicist **16** 175-177

WEINBERGER, CASPER WILLARD (born
1917), U.S. public official under three
presidents **16** 177-178

Weinlig, Theodor (1780-1842), German
composer
Wagner, Richard **16** 40-43

Weinstein, Nathan
see West, Nathanael

Weir, Julian Alden (1852-1919), American
painter
Cassatt, Mary **3** 356-357
Hassam, Frederick Childe **7** 192
Twachtman, John Henry **15** 362-363

Weir of Hermiston (novel)
Stevenson, Robert Louis **14** 446-448

Weiser, Conrad (1696-1760), American
pioneer
Beissel, Johann Conrad **2** 123-124

**WEISMANN, AUGUST FREIDRICH
LEOPOLD** (1834-1914), German biologist **16** 178-180

Weismann Institute of Science (Rehovot,
Israel)
Eban, Abba **5** 191-192

WEIZMAN, EZER (born 1924), Israeli air
force commander and president of Israel
(1993-) **16** 181-182

WEIZMANN, CHAIM (1874-1952), Israeli
statesman, president 1949-52
16 183-184
Einstein, Albert **5** 228-231
Faisal I **5** 370-371
Jabotinsky, Vladimir Evgenevich
8 167-168
Silver, Abba Hillel **14** 232-233

Weizmann Institute of Science
Weizmann, Chaim **16** 183-184

WELCH, ROBERT (1899-1985), founder of
the John Birch Society **16** 184-185

WELCH, WILLIAM HENRY (1850-1934),
American pathologist, bacteriologist, and
medical educator **16** 185-186
Osler, William **12** 19-20

Welcome House (adoption agency)
Buck, Pearl Sydenstricker **3** 91-93

Welcome to Our City (play)
Wolfe, Thomas Clayton **16** 355-356

Weld, Mrs. Theodore
see Grimké, Angelina Emily

WELD, THEODORE DWIGHT
(1803-1895), American reformer, preach-
er, and editor **16** 186
Birney, James Gillespie **2** 283-284
Forten, James **6** 17-18
Foster, Abigail Kelley **6** 25
Grimké, Archibald Henry **7** 1-2
Wright, Elizur **16** 396-397

Welded (play)
O'Neill, Eugene **11** 514-516

WELDON, FAY BIRKINSHAW (born 1931
or 1933), British novelist, dramatist,
essayist, and feminist **16** 186-188

WELENSKY, SIR ROY (1907-1991), Rhodesian statesman **16** 188
Smith, Ian Douglas **14** 291-293

Welf, House of
see Guelph, House of

Welfare state
Bosanquet, Bernard **2** 425-426
Ward, Lester Frank **16** 113-114

Well of Moses (sculpture)
Sluter, Claus **14** 275-276

Well of the Saints, The (play)
Synge, Edmund John Millington
15 61-62

Wellcome, Sir Henry S. (1854-1936),
American chemical manufacturer and
explorer
Dale, Henry Hallett **4** 371-373

WELLES, GIDEON (1802-1878), American
statesman **16** 188-190
Wilkes, Charles **16** 279-280

WELLES, ORSON (1915-1985), Broadway
and Hollywood actor, radio actor, and
film director **16** 190-191

WELLES, SUMNER (1892-1961), American
diplomat **16** 191-192
Machado y Morales, Gerardo **10** 92-93
Vázquez, Horacio **15** 448-449

Wellesley, Arthur
see Wellington, 1st Duke of

Wellesley College (Wellesley, Massachusetts)
Clapp, Margaret Antoinette **4** 71-72

WELLESLEY, RICHARD COLLEY (1st Marquess Wellesley; 1760-1842), British
colonial administrator **16** 192-193
Wellington, 1st Duke of **16** 193-195

WELLINGTON, 1ST DUKE OF (Arthur
Wellesley; 1769-1852), British soldier
and statesman **16** 193-195
as prime minister
Aberdeen, 4th Earl of **1** 25-26
George IV **6** 272-273
Peel, Robert **12** 181-183
associates
Canning, George **3** 258-260
Wellesley, Richard Colley
16 192-193
queen's Council
Victoria **15** 485-487
reform policy
Grey, Charles **6** 539-540
O'Connell, Daniel **11** 465-467
see also Napoleonic wars; Verona,
Congress of (1822)

Wells, Fargo and Co. (express company)
Fargo, William George **5** 380-381
see also American Express Co.

WELLS, HERBERT GEORGE (1866-1946),
English author **16** 195-196
Bellows, George Wesley **2** 143
Ford, Ford Madox **6** 1-2
Harris, Frank **7** 172-173
Plutarch **12** 359-360

WELLS, HORACE (1815-1848), American
dentist **16** 196
Drake, Daniel **5** 93-94
Long, Crawford Williamson **9** 495-496
Morton, William Thomas Green
11 198-199

WELLS, MARY GEORGENE BERG (born
1928), American businesswoman
16 197-198

WELLS-BARNETT, IDA B. (1862-1931),
American journalist and activist
16 198-199

Well-Tempered Clavier (musical collection)
Bach, Johann Sebastian **1** 416-419
Gounod, Charles François **6** 473-474
Mozart, Wolfgang Amadeus
11 218-221

Weltenburg, Benedictine Abbey of (Germany)
Asam, Cosmas Damian and Egid Quirin
1 323-324

Weltschmerz (poems)
Byron, George Gordon Noel **3** 193-194

WELTY, EUDORA (born 1909), American
author and essayist **16** 199-201

WEN T'IEN-HSIANG (1236-1283), Chinese
statesman **16** 203
Shih Ko-fa **14** 194-195

Wen T'ung (died 1079), Chinese bamboo
painter
Mi Fei **11** 12-13

Wen wang (1231?-1135 B.C.), ruler of state
of Chou, China
Chou Kung **4** 22-23
Wu wang **16** 408-409

Wen-an
see Chiu-yuan

WENCESLAUS (Wenceslaus IV of
Bohemia; 1361-1419), Holy Roman
emperor 1376-1400, and king of
Bohemia 1378-1419 **16** 201-202
Charles IV **3** 455-456
Henry I **7** 285-286
Hus, Jan **8** 56-59
Sigismund **14** 220-221
Visconti, Gian Galeazzo **15** 510-511

Wen-chen
see Yen Li-pen

Wen-ch'eng
see Wang Yang-ming

Wendoll (literary character)
Heywood, Thomas **7** 373-374

Wendy (literary character)
Barrie, James Matthew **2** 21-22

Wen-ho
see Liu Hsieh

WEN-HSIANG (1818-1876), Manchu official and statesman **16** 202-203
Tz'u-hsi **15** 375-376

Wen-jen-hua (scholarly painting)
Chao Meng-fu **3** 436-437
Mi Fei **11** 12-13

Wentworth, Captain (literary character)
Austen, Jane **1** 377-379

Wentworth, Thomas
see Strafford, 1st Earl of

WENTWORTH, WILLIAM CHARLES
(1790-1872), Australian statesman, writer, and explorer **16** 203-204

Wept of Wish-ton-Wish, The (novel)
Cooper, James Fenimore **4** 220-223, 127

Werfel, Alma Mahler Gropius (1879-1964), German author
Berg, Alban **2** 186-187

WERFEL, FRANZ (1890-1945), Austrian poet, novelist, and playwright **16** 204-205
Krenek, Ernst **9** 98-99
Mann, Thomas **10** 204-207

Werkbund (German art group)
Gropius, Walter **7** 13-14
Mies van der Rohe, Ludwig **11** 10-12
Oud, Jacobus Johannes Pieter **12** 32
Van de Velde, Henry **15** 419-420

Werner (literary character)
Lessing, Gotthold Ephraim **9** 357-359

WERNER, ABRAHAM GOTTLOB
(1749-1817), German naturalist **16** 205-207

Werner, Gregor (died 1766), German composer
Haydn, Franz Joseph **7** 219-221

Werner, Zacharias (1768-1823), German dramatist
Grillparzer, Franz **6** 546-547

WERTHEIMER, MAX (1880-1943), German psychologist **16** 207-208
Tolman, Edward Chace **15** 261-262

Werve, Claus de (died 1439), Flemish sculptor
Sluter, Claus **14** 275-276

Wesberry v. Sanders (legal case)
Black, Hugo Lafayette **2** 301-303

Wesel de Bruxella, Andras ven
see Vesalius, Andreas

WESLEY, CHARLES (1707-1788), English hymn writer and preacher **16** 208-209
Wesley, John **16** 209-210
Whitefield, George **16** 241-242

WESLEY, JOHN (1703-1791), English evangelical clergyman, preacher, and writer **16** 209-210
Asbury, Francis **1** 324-325
Booth, William **2** 405-406
Law, William **9** 245-246
Wesley, Charles **16** 208-209
Whitefield, George **16** 241-242

West (United States)
as art subject
Crane, Stephen **4** 293-295
Ford, John **6** 7-8
Moran, Thomas **11** 151-152
development
Applegate, Jesse **1** 264-265
Drake, Daniel **5** 93-94
exploration
Bozeman, John M. **2** 471-472

Carson, Christopher **3** 334-335
Clark, William **4** 82-83
Frémont, John Charles **6** 97-98
Lewis, Andrew **9** 376-377
Pike, Zebulon **12** 302-304
see also Explorers, American
first historian of
Bancroft, Hubert Howe **1** 484-485

WEST, BENJAMIN (1738-1820), English American painter **16** 210-212
associates
Copley, John Singleton **4** 228-230
influence of
Mount, William Sidney **11** 213-214
Stuart, Gilbert **14** 513-515
students
Fulton, Robert **6** 151-152
Morse, Samuel Finley Breese **11** 192-193
Peale, Charles Willson **12** 169-171
Peale, Rembrandt **12** 172-173
Trumbull, John **15** 316-317

WEST, CORNEL (born 1953), American philosopher **16** 212-213

WEST, NATHANAEL (1903-1940), American novelist **16** 213-214

West African Youth League (Sierra Leone)
Wallace-Johnson, Isaac Theophilus Akunna **16** 76-77

West Church Meeting House (Boston)
Benjamin, Asher **2** 162-163

West Coast Hotel Co. v. Parrish (legal case)
Cardozo, Benjamin Nathan **3** 288-290

West Germany
see Germany, West

West Goths
see Visigoths

West Grinstead Castle (Sussex)
Nash, John **11** 316

West India Company, Dutch
John Maurice of Nassau **8** 281-282
Minuit, Peter **11** 50
Stuyvesant, Peter **15** 5-6, 265
Van Rensselaer, Kiliaen **15** 430-431

West Indies
see individual countries

West Point
see U.S. Military Academy (West Point, New York State)

West Point (New York State)
Arnold, Benedict **1** 309-310

West Side News (newspaper)
Wright brothers **16** 394-396

West Side Story (musical)
Bernstein, Leonard **2** 218-219
Sondheim, Stephen **14** 337-338

West Virginia (state, United States)
McClellan, George Brinton **10** 391-392

Westermarck, Edward (1862-1939), Finnish philosopher and anthropologist

Malinowski, Kaspar Bronislaw **10** 170-171

Western, Sophia (literary character)
Fielding, Henry **5** 442-444

Western Boatman Ashore (painting)
Bingham, George Caleb **2** 278-279

Western Electric Co.
Bell, Alexander Graham **2** 129-131

Western European Union
Van Eekelen, Willem Frederik **15** 426-427

Western Female Institute (Cincinnati, Ohio)
Stowe, Harriet Elizabeth Beecher **14** 484-485

Western Military Institute (Georgetown, Kentucky)
Blaine, James Gillespie **2** 312-313

Western Mining (Australian Company)
Parbo, Arvi **12** 93-94

Western Museum (Cincinnati, Ohio)
Audubon, John James **1** 366-367

Western Roman Empire
see Holy Roman Empire

Western Schism (1378-1417)
see Great Schism

Western Star (newspaper)
McLean, John **10** 422-423

Western Star (poem)
Benét, Stephen Vincent **2** 157-158

Western Union Telegraph Co.
Bell, Alexander Graham **2** 129-131
Cornell, Ezra **4** 236-237
Edison, Thomas Alva **5** 206-208
Gould, Jay **6** 470-472
Mackay, John William **10** 101-102

Westerns (movie genre)
Eastwood, Clint **5** 188-190

WESTHEIMER, RUTH KAROLA (a.k.a. "Dr. Ruth;" born 1928), German American psychologist, author, and media personality **16** 214-215

WESTINGHOUSE, GEORGE (1846-1914), American inventor and manufacturer **16** 215
Tesla, Nikola **15** 156-157

Westinghouse Electric Corp.
Armstrong, Edwin Howard **1** 302-303
Westinghouse, George **16** 215

Westmacott, Mary
see Christie, Agatha

Westmacott Athlete (sculpture)
Polykleitos **12** 385-386

Westminister, Treaty of (1755)
Frederick II **6** 81-84

Westminster Abbey
burials
Browning, Robert **3** 53-55
Cowley, Abraham **4** 281-282
Darwin, Charles Robert **4** 397-399

Dickens, Charles John Huffam
4 538-541
Edward I 5 208-210
Hardy, Thomas 7 150-152
Jonson, Ben 8 343-345
Livingstone, David 9 463-465
Pitt, William the Elder 12 328-329
Pym, John 12 495-496
Spenser, Edmund 14 373-376
Tennyson, Alfred 15 144-146
construction of
Edward the Confessor 5 218-219
Henry III 7 290-292
Leo IX 9 332
coronations
Cranmer, Thomas 4 295-296

Westminster Bridge (painting)
Derain, André 4 503

Westminster, Statutes of
Westminster I (1275)
Edward I 5 208-210
Westminster II (1285)
Edward I 5 208-210
Westminster (1931)
Balfour, Arthur James 1 469-470
Hertzog, James Barry Munnik
7 347-348

WESTMORELAND, WILLIAM CHILDS
(born 1914), commander of all American
forces in the Vietnam War (1964-1968)
and chief of staff of the U.S. Army
16 216-217
Abrams, Creighton W. 1 29-31

Westöstlicher Diwan (poems)
Goethe, Johann Wolfgang von
6 388-391

Westover plantation (near Charles City, Virginia)
Byrd, William II 3 189-190

Westphalia, Peace of (1648)
see Thirty Years War—Peace of Westphalia

Westward Ho! (novel)
Kingsley, Charles 9 28

Westward Ho! (play)
Webster, John 16 164

WESTWOOD, VIVIENNE (born 1941),
British designer 16 217-218

Wet-plate process (photography)
Brady, Mathew B. 2 487-488
Eastman, George 5 186

Wexford, battle of (1649)
Cromwell, Oliver 4 317-320

Wexford, Reg (fictional character)
Rendell, Ruth 13 96-97

WEXLER, NANCY (born 1945), American
psychologist 16 218-219

WEYDEN, ROGIER VAN DER (1399-1464),
Flemish painter 16 219-221
Bermejo, Bartolomé 2 205
Bouts, Dirk 2 458-459
Campin, Robert 3 255

Christus, Petrus 4 33-34
Massys, Quentin 10 325-326
Memling, Hans 10 476
Piero della Francesca 12 301-302
Schongauer, Martin 14 26-28
Tura, Cosimo 15 343-344
van der Goes, Hugo 15 416-417

Weygand, Maxime (1867-1965), French
military leader
Pilsudski, Joseph 12 305-306

Weyl, H. (1885-1955), German mathematician
Eddington, Arthur Stanley 5 201-202

Weyler, Gen. Valeriano (1838-1930), Spanish soldier and statesman
Gómez, Máximo 6 418-419
Rizal, José 13 187-189

Whampoa Military Academy
Chiang Kai-shek 3 510-513
Chou En-lai 4 20-22

WHARTON, EDITH (1861-1937), American author 16 221
Wilson, Edmund 16 318-319

What Alice Found There (book)
Carroll, Lewis 3 332-333

What Are Years? (poems)
Moore, Marianne 11 148-149

What Every Woman Knows (play)
Barrie, James Matthew 2 21-22

What Gunpowder Plot Was (book)
Gardiner, Samuel Rawson 6 211

What I Believe (book)
Tolstoy, Leo 15 262-265

What Is Christianity? (book)
Harnack, Adolf von 7 160
Loisy, Alfred Firmin 9 489-490

What Is Man? (book)
Twain, Mark 15 363-366

What Is This Thing Called Love (song)
Porter, Cole Albert 12 405-406

What Is To Be Done? (novel)
Chernyshevsky, Nikolai Gavrilovich
3 504-505

What No, Perdie (poem)
Wyatt, Thomas 16 410-411

What Pleases Me (cantata)
Bach, Johann Sebastian 1 416-419

What Price Glory? (play)
Anderson, Maxwell 1 219-220

Whately, Richard (1787-1863), English
logician and theologian
Newman, John Henry 11 365-367

What's Become of Waring (novel)
Powell, Anthony 12 422-423

What's Love Got To Do with It (film)
Turner, Tina 15 357-359

What's o'Clock (poems)
Lowell, Amy 10 13

Wheat Harvest (painting)
Bruegel, Pieter the Elder 3 65-67

Wheatley, Henry Benjamin (1838-1917),
English bibliographer and editor
Pepys, Samuel 12 207-208

WHEATLEY, PHILLIS (circa 1753-84),
African American poet 16 221-222

Wheatstone, Charles (1802-1875), English
physicist
Foucault, Jean Bernard Léon 6 28-29

Wheel of Fortune, The (novel)
Moravia, Alberto 11 153-155

Wheeler, John Archibald (born 1911),
American physicist
Bohr, Niels Henrik David 2 366-368

Wheeler, Joseph (1836-1906), American
army officer and politician
Curry, Jabez Lamar Monroe 4 346-347

Wheeler Dam (North West Alabama)
see Muscle Shoals dams

WHEELOCK, ELEAZAR (1711-1779),
American clergyman and educator
16 222-223
Kirkland, Samuel 9 37

Wheelwright, John (1592?-1679),
English-born American clergyman
Hutchinson, Anne Marbury 8 69-71
Winthrop, John 16 339-341

WHEELWRIGHT, WILLIAM (1798-1873),
American entrepreneur 16 223-224

When Daisies Pied (song)
Arne, Thomas Augustine 1 307-308

When Horse Flesh Comes High (painting)
Russell, Charles Marion 13 375-376

When I Buy Pictures (poem)
Moore, Marianne 11 148-149

When I consider how my light is spent
(sonnet)
Milton, John 11 43-46

When I Set Out for Lyonnesse (poem)
Hardy, Thomas 7 150-152

When Johnny Comes Marching Home
(musical composition)
Harris, Roy 7 175-176

When Knighthood Was in Flower (film)
Hearst, William Randolph 7 243-244

When Lilacs Last in the Door-yard Bloom'd
(musical composition)
Hindemith, Paul 7 399-400

When Lilacs Last in the Dooryard Bloom'd
(poem)
Whitman, Walt 16 249-251

**When the Blue of the Night Meets the
Gold of the Day** (song)
Crosby, Harry Lillis 4 324-326

When the Storm Breaks (poems)
Pasternak, Boris Leonidovich
12 124-125

When the War Was Over (play)
Frisch, Max 6 118-119

When We Dead Awaken (play)
Ibsen, Henrik **8** 98-100

When You Want 'Em You Can't Get 'Em (song)
Gershwin, George **6** 284-285

Where Angels Fear to Tread (novel)
Forster, Edward Morgan **6** 14-16

Where Are We Heading (book)
Welles, Sumner **16** 191-192

Where Do We Come From? What Are We? Where Are We Going? (painting)
Gauguin, Paul **6** 236-238

Where Do We Go from Here (book)
King, Martin Luther Jr. **9** 20-22

Where or When (song)
Rodgers, Richard Charles **13** 234-236

Where the Air Is Clear (novel)
Fuentes, Carlos **6** 141-142

Where the Bee Sucks (song)
Arne, Thomas Augustine **1** 307-308

Whig party (United States)
decline of
Pierce, Franklin **12** 300-301
leaders
Clay, Henry **4** 94-96
Clayton, John Middleton **4** 96-97
Conkling, Roscoe **4** 201-202
Everett, Edward **5** 344
Tyler, John **15** 368-369
Scott, Winfield **14** 70-71
Webster, Daniel **16** 162-164
Weed, Thurlow **16** 169-170
members
Alcorn, James Lusk **1** 120-121
Crockett, David **4** 314-316
Curtin, Andrew Gregg **4** 347-348
Davis, Henry Winter **4** 415-416
Dickinson, John **4** 543-544
Greeley, Horace **6** 515-517
Hildreth, Richard **7** 382
Hill, Benjamin Harvey **7** 386-387
Lincoln, Abraham **9** 415-418
Mann, Horace **10** 202-204
Miller, Samuel Freeman **11** 29-30
Morrill, Justin Smith **11** 182
Seward, William Henry **14** 124-125
Shaw, Lemuel **14** 164-165
Stevens, Thaddeus **14** 442-443
Sumner, Charles **15** 30-31
Wade, Benjamin Franklin **16** 38-39
Waite, Morrison Remick **16** 46
Wilson, James Harold **16** 324-325
opponents
Polk, James Knox **12** 374-376
presidents
Fillmore, Millard **5** 447-448
Harrison, William Henry **7** 180-181
Taylor, Zachary **15** 128-130

Whigs (English politics)
17th-18th century
Bolingbroke, Viscount **2** 374-375
Cornwallis, Charles **4** 241-243
Dryden, John **5** 106-107
Godolphin, Sidney **6** 380-381
Monmouth and Buccleugh, Duke of **11** 108-109
Sandys, Edwin **13** 463-464
Shaftesbury, 1st Earl of **14** 135-136
Sheridan, Richard Brinsley **14** 183-184
Steele, Richard **14** 407-409
Swift, Jonathan **15** 51-54
Walpole, Robert **16** 82-84
19th century
Cobbett, William **4** 126-127
Lecky, William Edward Hartpole **9** 271-272
Liverpool, 2nd Earl of **9** 456-457
Macaulay, Thomas Babington **10** 79-80
Melbourne, 2nd Viscount **10** 468-469
O'Connell, Daniel **11** 465-467
Peel, Robert **12** 181-183
Victoria **15** 485-487
Wellington, 1st Duke of **16** 193-195

Whipity (literary character)
Edgeworth, Maria **5** 205-206

WHIPPLE, GEORGE HOYT (1878-1976), American pathologist **16** 224-225

Whipple's disease (medical)
Whipple, George Hoyt **16** 224-225

Whirl (novel)
Tanizaki, Junichiro **15** 101-102

Whirligigs (stories)
Henry, O. **7** 308-309

Whiskey Rebellion (1794)
Gallatin, Albert **6** 183-184
Lewis, Meriwether **9** 391-392
Morgan, Daniel **11** 160-161
Washington, George **16** 126-129

Whiskey Ring (U.S. history)
Bristow, Benjamin Helm **3** 9-10

Whispers of Heavenly Death (poem)
Whitman, Walt **16** 249-251

WHISTLER, JAMES ABBOTT MCNEILL (1834-1903), American painter, etcher, and lithographer **16** 225-226
associates
Chase, William Merritt **3** 476-477
McKim, Charles Follen **10** 417-418
Toulouse-Lautrec, Henri de **15** 273-274
critics
Ruskin, John **13** 371-372
influence of
Davies, Arthur Bowen **4** 409-410
Marin, John III **10** 259-260
Prendergast, Maurice Brazil **12** 440
Robinson, Theodore **13** 217
Sickert, Walter Richard **14** 212-213
Twachtman, John Henry **15** 362-363
influenced by
Allston, Washington **1** 176-177
Hiroshige, Ando **7** 412-413

Whistler's Mother (painting)
see Arrangement in Grey and Black, the Artist's Mother

WHITE, ANDREW DICKSON (1832-1918), American educator and diplomat **16** 226-227

White Architecture (painting)
Demuth, Charles **4** 497-498

White blood cells (biology)
Cabot, Richard Clarke **3** 200
Fleming, Alexander **5** 483-485

WHITE, BYRON R. (born 1917), deputy U.S. attorney general and associate justice of the U.S. Supreme Court **16** 227-228

White Christmas (song)
Crosby, Harry Lillis **4** 324-326

White Company, The (novel)
Doyle, Arthur Conan **5** 91-92
Wyeth, Andrew Newell **16** 413-415

White Desert (play)
Anderson, Maxwell **1** 219-220

White Devil, The (play)
Webster, John **16** 164

WHITE, EDWARD DOUGLASS (1845-1921), American jurist, chief justice of U.S Supreme Court **16** 230-231
Harlan, John Marshall **7** 156-157

WHITE, E. B. (Elwyn Brooks White; 1899-1985), American essayist and author of children's books **16** 228-230

White Fang (book)
London, Jack **9** 494-495

White Fathers (religious congregation)
Lavigerie, Charles Martel Allemand **9** 240
Mutesa I **11** 277

White, George (1890-1968), American producer
Fields, W. C. **5** 444
Gershwin, George **6** 284-285

White Girl, The (painting)
Whistler, James Abbott McNeill **16** 225-226

White Guard, The (novel)
Bulgakov, Mikhail Afanasievich **3** 117

White Guelfs (Florence)
Cavalcanti, Guido **3** 382
Dante Alighieri **4** 389-391

White House (Washington, District of Columbia)
Downing, Andrew Jackson **5** 90-91
Latrobe, Benjamin Henry **9** 222-224
L'Enfant, Pierre Charles **9** 322-323
Onassis, Jacqueline Lee Bouvier Kennedy **11** 511-513

White, John (1590-1645), Welsh lawyer and Puritan
Endecott, John **5** 284-285

White, John (flourished 1585-93), English artist, cartographer, and Virginia pioneer
Raleigh, Walter **13** 9-11

White, Joseph Blanco
see Blanco White, José Maria

WHITE, KEVIN H. (born 1929), mayor of Boston (1967-1983) **16** 231-232

White King (literary character)
Middleton, Thomas **11** 8-9

White Knight (literary character)
Carroll, Lewis **3** 332-333

WHITE, LESLIE A. (1900-1975), American anthropologist **16** 232-233

White Lotus Rebellion (1796-1804)
Ho-shen **7** 512-513
Qianlong **12** 502-505

White Lotus Society (Buddhism)
Hui-yüan **8** 25-26

White Man's Burden (poem)
Kipling, Joseph Rudyard **9** 32-33

White Mice, The (novel)
Davis, Richard Harding **4** 422-423

White Monkey, The (novel)
Galsworthy, John **6** 189-190

White Mule (novel)
Williams, William Carlos **16** 308-309

White Nights (story)
Dostoevsky, Fyodor **5** 74-77

White Oak Dance Project (touring company)
Morris, Mark **11** 184-185

White Oak Swamp, battle of
see Seven Days, battle of the

White Paper (Churchill)
Jabotinsky, Vladimir Evgenevich **8** 167-168

WHITE, PATRICK VICTOR MARTINDALE (1912-1990), Australian novelist and playwright **16** 233-235

White Scourge, The (play)
Čapek, Karel **3** 271-272

White Sheik, The (film)
Fellini, Federico **5** 408-409

White Ship, The (poem)
Rossetti, Dante Gabriel **13** 308-309

White Sisters (religious congregation)
Lavigerie, Charles Martel Allemand **9** 240

WHITE, STANFORD (1853-1906), American architect **16** 235-236
McKim, Charles Follen **10** 417-418
Saint-Gaudens, Augustus **13** 432
Wright, Frank Lloyd **16** 398-401

White Sugar Bowl (painting)
Cézanne, Paul **3** 400-402

White supremacy
see Racism (United States)

WHITE, T. H. (1915-1986), American journalist **16** 236-237

WHITE, WALTER FRANCIS (1893-1955), general secretary of the National Association for the Advancement of Colored People **16** 238-239

White, William (1748-1836), American Protestant Episcopal clergyman
Hobart, John Henry **7** 420-421

WHITE, WILLIAM ALANSON (1870-1937), American psychiatrist **16** 239-240
Sullivan, Harry Stack **15** 23-24

WHITE, WILLIAM ALLEN (1868-1944), American journalist **16** 240-241

White writing (art form)
Tobey, Mark **15** 249-250

WHITEFIELD, GEORGE (1714-1770), English evangelist **16** 241-242
Chauncy, Charles **3** 485-486
Edwards, Jonathan **5** 220-222
Frelinghuysen, Theodorus Jacobus **6** 96-97
Hopkins, Samuel **7** 496
Tennent, Gilbert **15** 143-144
Wheatley, Phillis **16** 221-222

Whitehall Palace (London)
Hawksmoor, Nicholas **7** 211-212
Jones, Inigo **8** 333-334

WHITEHEAD, ALFRED NORTH (1861-1947), English-American mathematician and philosopher **16** 242-244
Becker, Carl Lotus **2** 100-101
Leibniz, Gottfried Wilhelm von **9** 307-310
Plato **12** 345-347
Poincaré, Jules Henri **12** 365-366
Quine, Willard Van Orman **12** 514-515
Ramsey, Frank Plumpton **13** 25
Russell, Bertrand Arthur William **13** 373-374

White-Jacket (novel)
Melville, Herman **10** 472-476

Whiteman, Paul (1891-1967), American jazz-orchestra conductor
Gershwin, George **6** 284-285
Still, William Grant **14** 455-456

Whiteoaks of Jalna (play)
de la Roche, Mazo Louise **4** 474-475

Whitgift, John (1530?-1604), English prelate
Elizabeth I **5** 263-266

WHITLAM, EDWARD GOUGH (Gof; born 1916), prime minister of Australia (1972-1975) **16** 244-245

WHITMAN, CHRISTINE TODD (born c. 1947), American politician **16** 245-248

WHITMAN, MARCUS (1802-1847), American physician, missionary, and pioneer **16** 248-249
Fitzpatrick, Thomas **5** 474-475

WHITMAN, WALT (1819-1892), American poet **16** 249-251
associates
Burroughs, John **3** 160-161

Garland, Hannibal Hamlin **6** 217-218
compared to
Crane, Stephen **4** 293-295
influence of
Crane, Hart **4** 291-293-178
Cummings, Edward Estlin **4** 334-336
Ginsberg, Allen **6** 332-333
Kuo Mo-jo **9** 133-134
Pound, Ezra Loomis **12** 415-417
Sandburg, Carl **13** 461-462
Sullivan, Louis Henri **15** 27-28
Wolfe, Thomas Clayton **16** 355-356
Wright, Frank Lloyd **16** 398-401

WHITMIRE, KATHRYN JEAN NIEDERHOFER (born 1946), first female mayor of Houston, Texas (1982-1992) **16** 252-253

WHITNEY, ELI (1765-1825), American inventor and manufacturer **16** 253-254

WHITNEY, JOSIAH DWIGHT (1819-1896), American chemist and geologist **16** 254-255

Whitney Museum of American Art (New York City)
Breuer, Marcel **2** 520-521
Frankenthaler, Helen **6** 56-57

Whitney v. California (legal case)
Brandeis, Louis Dembitz **2** 496-497

WHITTAKER, CHARLES EVANS (1901-1973), U.S. Supreme Court justice **16** 255-256

WHITTIER, JOHN GREENLEAF (1807-1892), American poet **16** 256-257
Bailey, Gamaliel **1** 444-445
Child, Lydia Maria Francis **3** 520-521
Frost, Robert Lee **6** 130-133
Grimké, Sarah Moore and Angelina Emily **7** 2-3
Woolman, John **16** 382-383

WHITTLE, SIR FRANK (1907-1996), English Air Force officer and engineer **16** 257-258

Who? (song)
Kern, Jerome David **8** 517-518

Who Cares If You Listen? (essay)
Babbitt, Milton **1** 410

Whole Loaf, A (story)
Agnon, Shmuel Yoseph **1** 85-86

Whole Town's Talking, The (film)
Ford, John **6** 7-8

Wholesome Meat Act (United States; 1967)
Nader, Ralph **11** 290-291

Whoopee (musical comedy)
Cantor, Eddie **3** 264-265

Whoroscope (poem)
Beckett, Samuel **2** 102-104

Who's Afraid of Aunt Jemima (quilt)
Ringgold, Faith **13** 175-177

Who's Afraid of Virginia Woolf? (play)
Albee, Edward Franklin III **1** 106-108

Why are all the muses mute? (ode)
Purcell, Henry **12** 484-485

Why Are We in Vietnam? (novel)
Mailer, Norman Kingsley **10** 148-150

Why Come Ye Not to Court? (satire)
Skelton, John **14** 268-269

Why England Slept (book)
Kennedy, John Fitzgerald **8** 502-506

Why so pale and wan, fond lover? (song)
Suckling, John **15** 10-11

Whydah (city; Dahomey)
Dalzel, Archibald **4** 381-382

Wicca (witchcraft)
Starhawk **14** 403-404

Wickersham, George W. (1858-1936),
American lawyer
Taft, William Howard **15** 78-81

WIDNALL, SHEILA E. (born 1938), American aeronautical engineer **16** 258-259

Widor, Charles (1845-1937), French organist and composer
Varèse, Edgard **15** 432-433

**Widow, Orphans and Old Age Pension Act
of 1925** (Great Britain)
Chamberlain, Arthur Neville **3** 409-411

Widowers' Houses (play)
Shaw, George Bernard **14** 163-164

Wie herrlich leuchtet mir die Natur!
(poem)
Goethe, Johann Wolfgang von
6 388-391

Wieck, Friedrich (1785-1873), German pianist
Schumann, Robert Alexander **14** 41-43

Wieland (novel)
Brown, Charles Brockden **3** 33

WIELAND, CHRISTOPH MARTIN
(1733-1813), German poet and author
16 260-261
Goethe, Johann Wolfgang von
6 388-391
Weber, Carl Maria Friedrich Ernst von
16 156-157

Wieland, Heinrich (1877-1957), German chemist
Szent-Györgyi, Albert von **15** 62-64

WIEMAN, HENRY NELSON (1884-1975),
American philosopher and theologian
16 261-262

Wien, Max (1866-1938), German physicist
Schrödinger, Erwin **14** 31-33

WIENER, NORBERT (1894-1964), American mathematician **16** 262-263
Von Neumann, John **16** 27-28

Wien's law (physics)
Planck, Max Karl Ernst Ludwig
12 342-344

Wies, church of die (near Munich)
Zimmermann, Johann Baptist and
Domenikus **16** 518

**Wiese von Liebe und Tod des Cornet
Christoph Rilke, Die** (poem)
Rilke, Rainer Maria **13** 171-172

WIESEL, ELIE (born 1928), writer, orator, teacher, and chairman of the United States Holocaust Memorial Council
16 263-264

WIESENTHAL, SIMON (born 1908),
Ukrainian Jew who tracked down Nazi war criminals **16** 264-266

Wieser, Friedrich von (1851-1926), Austrian political economist
Schumpeter, Joseph Alois **14** 43-44

Wife of Bath, The (play)
Gay, John **6** 243-244

Wife, The (play)
Belasco, David **2** 124-125

Wife to Mr. Milton (novel)
Graves, Robert Ranke **6** 504-506

WIGGLESWORTH, MICHAEL
(1631-1705), American Puritan poet and minister **16** 266-267
Taylor, Edward **15** 122-123

WIGMAN, MARY (Marie Wiegmann;
1886-1973), German dancer, choreographer, and teacher **16** 267-268

WIGNER, EUGENE PAUL (1902-1995),
Hungarian-born American physicist
16 268-269
Dirac, Paul Adrien Maurice **5** 23-24
Einstein, Albert **5** 228-231
Yang, Chen Ning **16** 437-438

WILBERFORCE, WILLIAM (1759-1833),
English statesman and humanitarian
16 269-270
Bowditch, Henry Ingersoll **2** 459-460
Chalmers, Thomas **3** 408-409

WILBUR, RICHARD PURDY (born 1921),
translator and poet laureate of the United States (1987-1988) **16** 271-272

Wild Animals I Have Known (book)
Seton, Ernest Thompson **14** 119-120

Wild Child, The (film)
Truffaut, François **15** 311-313

Wild Duck, The (play)
Ibsen, Henrik **8** 98-100

Wild Gallant, The (play)
Dryden, John **5** 106-107

Wild Grass (prose poem)
Lu Hsün **10** 35-37

Wild Honey Suckle, The (poem)
Freneau, Philip Morin **6** 99-100

Wild in the Country (film)
Odets, Clifford **11** 470-471

Wild Old Wicked Man... (poems)
MacLeish, Archibald **10** 109-110

Wild Orchid, The (novel)
Undset, Sigrid **15** 388-389

Wild Palms, The (novel)
Faulkner, William **5** 395-397

Wild Strawberries (film)
Bergman, Ernst Ingmar **2** 190-191

Wild West shows
Buffalo Bill **3** 105-106
Calamity Jane **3** 216
Catlin, George **3** 373-374
Geronimo **6** 281-282
Oakley, Annie **11** 453-454

Wild Wood Spirit's Chant, The (musical composition)
Heinrich, Anthony Philip **7** 261

**WILDE, OSCAR FINGALL O'FLAHERTIE
WILLS** (1854-1900), British author
16 272-273
Beardsley, Aubrey Vincent **2** 88-89
Borges, Jorge Luis **2** 411-412
Coward, Noel **4** 279-280
Epstein, Jacob **5** 295-296
Gide, André **6** 308-309
Harris, Frank **7** 172-173
Tanizaki, Junichiro **15** 101-102
Toulouse-Lautrec, Henri de **15** 273-274
Yeats, William Butler **16** 445-447

WILDER, AMOS NIVEN (1895-1993),
American New Testament scholar, poet, minister, and literary critic **16** 273-274

WILDER, LAWRENCE DOUGLAS (born 1931), first African American elected governor in the United States **16** 274-276

WILDER, THORNTON NIVEN
(1897-1975), American novelist and playwright **16** 276-277
Benét, Stephen Vincent **2** 157-158
Grass, Günter **6** 496-497

Wilderness (novel)
Warren, Robert Penn **16** 121-122

Wilderness, battle of the (1864)
Barton, Clara **2** 37-39
Sheridan, Philip Henry **14** 182-183

Wilderness Campaign (United States Civil War)
Lee, Robert Edward **9** 292-294
Stuart, James Ewell Brown **14** 515-516

Wilderness of Mirrors (novel)
Frisch, Max **6** 118-119

Wildlife conservation
Leakey, Richard Erskine Frere
9 264-265

Wildwood Troubador, The (musical composition)
Heinrich, Anthony Philip **7** 261

WILEY, HARVEY WASHINGTON
(1844-1930), American chemist
16 277-278

Wiley House (New Canaan, Connecticut)
Johnson, Philip **8** 313-314

Wilhelm Meister (novel series; Goethe)
Carlyle, Thomas **3** 304-305
Goethe, Johann Wolfgang von
6 388-391
Hauptmann, Gerhart Johann Robert
7 199-201

Kafka, Franz **8** 403-406
Keller, Gottfried **8** 478-479

Wilhelm Tell (play)
Schiller, Johann Christoph Friedrich von **14** 4-7

WILHELMINA (1880-1962), queen of the Netherlands 1890-1948 **16** 278-279
Leopold III **9** 347-348

WILKES, CHARLES (1798-1877), American naval officer **16** 279-280

WILKES, JOHN (1727-1797), English politician **16** 280-281
Boswell, James **2** 432-434
Fox, Charles James **6** 35-37
George III **6** 270-272
Lee, Arthur **9** 288-289
Rutledge, John **13** 387-388

Wilkins, Maurice (born 1916), Irish biophysicist
Crick, Francis Harry Crompton **4** 310
Watson, James Dewey **16** 137-138

WILKINS, ROY (1901-1981), African American civil rights leader **16** 282-283

WILKINS, SIR GEORGE HUBERT (1888-1958), Australian explorer, scientist, and adventurer **16** 281-282

WILKINSON, ELLEN (1891-1947), British Labour politician and crusader for the unemployed **16** 283-284

WILKINSON, JAMES (1757-1825), American army general and frontier adventurer **16** 284-286
Burr, Aaron **3** 156-159
Clark, George Rogers **4** 75-76
Hampton, Wade **7** 111-112
Pike, Zebulon **12** 302-304
Scott, Winfield **14** 70-71
Taylor, Zachary **15** 128-130

Will (literary character)
Langland, William **9** 194-195

Will (philosophy)
Schopenhauer, Arthur **14** 29-31

Will (psychology)
James, William **8** 215-217

WILL, GEORGE FREDERICK (born 1941), syndicated columnist and television commentator **16** 286-287

Will to Happiness, The (story)
Mann, Thomas **10** 204-207

Will to power (philosophy)
Nietzsche, Friedrich **11** 390-392
Stendhal **14** 422-425-198

WILLAERT, ADRIAN (circa 1480-1562), Franco-Flemish composer active in Italy **16** 287-288
Gabrieli, Giovanni **6** 161-162
Le Jeune, Claude **9** 314-315
Zarlino, Gioseffo **16** 490-491

WILLARD, EMMA HART (1787-1870), American educator and author **16** 288-289

WILLARD, FRANCES ELIZABETH CAROLINE (1839-1898), American temperance and women's suffrage leader **16** 289-290
Dow, Neal **5** 89-90

Wille zum Glück, Der (story)
Mann, Thomas **10** 204-207

Willehalm (poem)
Wolfram von Eschenbach **16** 360-361

William (duke of Normandy)
see William I (king of England)

William Cowper (painting)
Romney, George **13** 269-270

WILLIAM I (the Conqueror; 1027/28-1087), king of England 1066-1087 **16** 290-291
Edward the Confessor **5** 218-219
Harold II **7** 162
Harold III **7** 163
Henry I **7** 286-287
Lanfranc **9** 189-190
Margaret of Scotland **10** 252-253
Rollo **13** 264-265
William II **16** 293-294

William I (died 1166), Norman king of Sicily 1154-66
Frederick I **6** 78-79
Idrisi, Muhammad ibn Muhammad al- **8** 102-103
Roger II **13** 244-245

WILLIAM I (1772-1843), king of the Netherlands 1815-40 **16** 291-292

WILLIAM I (1797-1888), emperor of Germany 1871-88 and king of Prussia 1861-88 **16** 292-293
Bismarck, Otto Eduard Leopold von **2** 294-296
Moltke, Helmuth Karl Bernard von **11** 90-91
William II **16** 294-295

William I (prince of Orange)
see William the Silent

WILLIAM II (William Rufus; circa 1058-1100), king of England 1087-1100 **16** 293-294
Anselm of Canterbury **1** 244-245
Henry I **7** 286-287
Lanfranc **9** 189-190
William I **16** 290-291

William II (1153-1189), king of Sicily 1171-89
Frederick I **6** 78-79
Frederick II **6** 79

William II (1626-1650), prince of Orange and stadholder of the Netherlands 1647-50
Burnet, Gilbert **3** 147
Witt, Johan de **16** 348-349

William II (1792-1849), king of the Netherlands 1840-49
William I **16** 291-292

WILLIAM II (1859-1941), emperor of Germany and king of Prussia 1888-1918 **16** 294-295

Bismarck, Otto Eduard Leopold von **2** 294-296
Herzl, Theodor **7** 352-354
Hindenburg, Paul Ludwig Hans von Beneckendorff und von **7** 400-401
Krupp **9** 109-111
Moltke, Helmuth Karl Bernard von **11** 90-91
Tönnies, Ferdinand **15** 266-267
William I **16** 292-293

WILLIAM III (1650-1702), king of England, Scotland, and Ireland 1689-1702 **16** 295-296
as king
Andros, Edmund **1** 234-235
Burnet, Gilbert **3** 147
Calvert, Charles **3** 238
Defoe, Daniel **4** 457-459
Godolphin, Sidney **6** 380-381
Harley, Robert **7** 159-160
Leisler, Jacob **9** 313-314
Livingston, Robert **9** 461-462
Marlborough, 1st Duke of **10** 271-272
Wren, Christopher **16** 393-394
as prince of Orange
Condé, Prince de **4** 193-194
Louis XIV **9** 531-533
Monmouth and Buccleugh, Duke of **11** 108-109
Witt, Johan de **16** 348-349
relatives
Anne **1** 241-242
George I **6** 268-269
James II **8** 207-208
Mary II **10** 309-310

William III (1817-1890), king of the Netherlands 1849-90
Wilhelmina **16** 278-279

William III (prince of Orange)
see William III (king of England)

WILLIAM IV (1765-1837), king of Great Britain and Ireland 1830-37 **16** 296-297
Peel, Robert **12** 181-183
Victoria **15** 485-487
Wellington, 1st Duke of **16** 193-195

William V (1748-1806), prince of Orange and stadholder of the Netherlands 1766-95
William I **16** 291-292

William X (1099-1137), duke of Aquitaine
Eleanor of Aquitaine **5** 246-247

William and Mary, College of (Williamsburg, Virginia)
Andros, Edmund **1** 234-235
Blair, James **2** 315-316
Dew, Thomas Roderick **4** 519
Mary II **10** 309-310
Nicholson, Francis **11** 381-382
Wythe, George **16** 415

William Augustus
see Cumberland, Duke of

William Lovell (novel)
Tieck, Ludwig **15** 218-219

William of Champeaux (circa 1070-1121), French philosopher
Abelard, Peter **1** 23-25

William of England (romance)
Chrestien de Troyes **4** 23-24

WILLIAM OF MALMESBURY (circa 1090-circa 1142), English historian **16** 297-298

William of Moerberke (circa 1215-86), Flemish philosopher
Thomas Aquinas **15** 183-186

WILLIAM OF OCKHAM (circa 1284-1347), English philosopher and theologian **16** 298-299
Gerson, John **6** 285-286
Luther, Martin **10** 48-51
Morgan, Conway Lloyd **11** 159-160
Suárez, Francisco **15** 8

WILLIAM OF TYRE (circa 1130-84/85), French archbishop, chancellor of the Latin Kingdom of Jerusalem **16** 299-300

William Read and Company (banking firm)
see Dillon, Read and Company

William the Conqueror
see William I (king of England)

William the Lion (1143-1214), king of Scotland 1165-1214
Robert I **13** 192-194

WILLIAM THE SILENT (1533-1584), prince of Orange and stadholder of the Netherlands **16** 300-302
Alba, Duke of **1** 103-104
Maurice of Nassau **10** 348-349
Oldenbarnevelt, Johan van **11** 495-496
Rubens, Peter Paul **13** 339-342

Williams, Bert (1876?-1922), African American comedian and songwriter
Ziegfeld, Florenz **16** 516-517

Williams, Betty
see CORRIGAN and WILLIAMS

WILLIAMS, DANIEL HALE (1856-1931), African American surgical pioneer **16** 302-303
Drew, Charles Richard **5** 100-101

WILLIAMS, HENRY SYLVESTER (1869-1911), Trinidadian lawyer and pan-African leader **16** 303-304

Williams, Israel (1709-1788), American businessman
Edwards, Jonathan **5** 220-222

Williams, Ralph Vaughan
see Vaughan Williams, Ralph

WILLIAMS, ROGER (circa 1603-83), Puritan clergyman in colonial America **16** 304-305
Cotton, John **4** 263-265
Dudley, Thomas **5** 124-125
Hooker, Thomas **7** 476-477
Vane, Henry **15** 425-426
Winthrop, John **16** 339-341

WILLIAMS, SHIRLEY VIVIEN TERESA BRITTAIN (born 1930), British politician **16** 305-306

WILLIAMS, TENNESSEE (Thomas Lanier Williams; born 1914), American dramatist and fiction writer **16** 306-308
Kazan, Elia **8** 465-466

WILLIAMS, WILLIAM CARLOS (1883-1963), American poet and pediatrician **16** 308-309
Callaghan, Edward Morley **3** 229-230
Cummings, Edward Estlin **4** 334-336
Demuth, Charles **4** 497-498
Doolittle, Hilda **5** 65-66
Moore, Marianne **11** 148-149
Olson, Charles **11** 505-506
Pound, Ezra Loomis **12** 415-417
Stevens, Wallace **14** 443-445
West, Benjamin **16** 210-212
Whitman, Walt **16** 249-251

Williams College (Williamstown, Massachusetts)
Hopkins, Mark **7** 495-496
Perry, Ralph Barton **12** 239-240
Sayre, Francis Bowes **13** 509

Williamsburg (city, Virginia)
Dunmore, 4th Earl of **5** 147
Rockefeller, John D. Jr. **13** 225-226
see also William and Mary, College of

Williamsburg, battle of (1862)
McClellan, George Brinton **10** 391-392

Williamson, William (1816-1895), English naturalist
Kekulé, Friedrich August **8** 477-478

Willing, Thomas (1731-1821), American banker and legislator
Morris, Robert **11** 185-187

Willitts House (Highland Park, Illinois)
Wright, Frank Lloyd **16** 398-401

Willkie, Wendell Lewis (1892-1944), American lawyer and businessman
Lewis, John Llewellyn **9** 387-388
Roosevelt, Franklin Delano **13** 277-280

Willoughby, Sir Hugh (died 1554), English Arctic navigator
Cabot, Sebastian **3** 200-201
Chancellor, Richard **3** 422

Wills, William John (died 1861), Australian explorer
Burke, Robert O'Hara **3** 142-143

WILLSTÄTTER, RICHARD (1872-1942), German chemist
Baeyer, Johann Friedrich Adolf von **1** 432
Fischer, Emil **5** 456-457
Fischer, Hans **5** 457-459

Willughby, Francis (1635-1672), British naturalist
Ray, John **13** 57-59

Willy, Colette
see Colette

Willys-Overland Co.
Chrysler, Walter Percy **4** 36-37

Wilmington (city, Delaware)
du Pont, Éleuthère Irénée **5** 154
Minuit, Peter **11** 50

WILMOT, DAVID (1814-1868), American politician **16** 312-313
Polk, James Knox **12** 374-376
see also Wilmot Proviso

Wilmot Proviso (1846)
Calhoun, John Caldwell **3** 226-228
Chase, Salmon Portland **3** 473-475
Lincoln, Abraham **9** 415-418
Polk, James Knox **12** 374-376
Taylor, Zachary **15** 128-130
Webster, Daniel **16** 162-164

WILSON, ALEXANDER (1766-1813), Scottish-American ornithologist and poet **16** 313-314
Audubon, John James **1** 366-367
Bartram, William **2** 41-42
Lewis, Meriwether **9** 391-392

WILSON, AUGUST (Frederick August Kittell; born 1945), African American playwright **16** 314-316

WILSON, CHARLES ERWIN (1890-1961), engineer, businessman, and secretary of defense **16** 316-317

WILSON, CHARLES THOMSON REES (1869-1959), Scottish physicist **16** 317-318
Hess, Victor Francis **7** 362-363

Wilson cloud chamber (physics)
Blackett, Patrick M.S. **2** 306-307
Wilson, Charles Thomson Rees **16** 317-318

Wilson Dam
see Muscle Shoals dams

WILSON, EDMUND (1895-1972), American critic **16** 318-319
Fitzgerald, Francis Scott Key **5** 470-472
Parker, Dorothy Rothschild **12** 106

WILSON, EDWARD OSBORNE (born 1929), American biologist **16** 319-320

Wilson, Harold
see Wilson, James Harold

WILSON, HARRIET E. (circa 1827-circa 1863), African American author **16** 320-322

Wilson, Harry (1867-1939), American author
Tarkington, Newton Booth **15** 109

WILSON, HENRY (1812-1875), American politician **16** 322-323

Wilson, Henry Lane (1857-1932), American diplomat
Madero, Francisco Indalecio **10** 118-119

Wilson, Horace H. (1786-1860), English Orientalist
Ram Camul Sen **13** 16-17

WILSON, JAMES (1742-1798), American statesman **16** 323-324
Madison, James **10** 121-123

Wilson, James (1805-1860), British economist
Bagehot, Walter **1** 436-437

Wilson, James H. (1837-1925), American army officer
Forrest, Nathan Bedford **6** 13-14

WILSON, JAMES HAROLD (born 1916), English statesman, prime minister 1964-70 **16** 324-325
Elizabeth II **5** 266-269
Smith, Ian Douglas **14** 291-293

Wilson, John (1785-1854), Scottish poet
Pushkin, Aleksandr Sergeevich **12** 489-491

WILSON, JOSEPH CHAMBERLAIN (1909-1971), American businessman **16** 325-326

WILSON, PETE (born 1933), American politician **16** 326-329

WILSON, RICHARD (1713/14-82), British painter **16** 329-330
Claude Lorrain **4** 89-90
Turner, Joseph Mallord William **15** 352-354

WILSON, THOMAS WOODROW (1856-1924), American statesman, president 1913-21 **16** 330-332
acquaintances
Keller, Helen Adams **8** 479-480
Paderewski, Ignace Jan **12** 56-57
Thomas, Norman Mattoon **15** 191-192
advisers
Brandeis, Louis Dembitz **2** 496-497
Gompers, Samuel **6** 420-422
House, Edward Mandell **7** 520-521
appointees (non-Cabinet)
Hapgood, Norman **7** 137-138
Hoover, Herbert Clark **7** 483-485
Page, Walter Hines **12** 60-61
Roosevelt, Franklin Delano **13** 277-280
Russell, Charles Edward **13** 374-375
Warburg, Paul Moritz **16** 111-112
Wright brothers **16** 394-396
Young, Owen D. **16** 473-474
biographers
Baker, Ray Stannard **1** 451-452
Cabinet
Baker, Newton Diehl **1** 451
Bryan, William Jennings **3** 80-82
Daniels, Josephus **4** 387
Lansing, Robert **9** 200
McAdoo, William Gibbs **10** 385-386
Palmer, Alexander Mitchell **12** 77-78
election campaigns
Hughes, Charles Evans **8** 15-16
Lippmann, Walter **9** 439-440
Roosevelt, Theodore **13** 280-283

Taft, William Howard **15** 78-81
Mexico and
Carranza, Venustiano **3** 321-322
Huerta, Victoriano **8** 13-14
opponents
Borah, William Edgar **2** 408
Debs, Eugene Victor **4** 444-445
Johnson, Hiram Warren **8** 300-301
Lodge, Henry Cabot **9** 482-483
Norris, George William **11** 428-429
Wood, Leonard **16** 369-370
supporters
Gibbons, James **6** 300-301
Sinclair, Upton Beale Jr. **14** 248-249
White, William Allen **16** 240-241
Wise, Stephen Samuel **16** 344-345
see also Fourteen Points; League of Nations; Versailles, Treaty of (1919; and Paris Peace Conference); World War I

Wilson, William Lyne (1843-1900), American politician
Baker, Newton Diehl **1** 451

Wilson-Gorman Act (1894)
Cleveland, Stephen Grover **4** 108-110

Wilson's theorem (mathematics)
Lagrange, Joseph Louis **9** 164-166

Wilton House (Wiltshire)
Jones, Inigo **8** 333-334

Wimpole Hall (Cambridgeshire)
Gibbs, James **6** 301-302

Wincaby, battle of (1643)
Cromwell, Oliver **4** 317-320

Winchelsea (seaport, England)
Edward III **5** 211-212

Winchester, Councils of (1072, 1076)
Lanfranc **9** 189-190

Winchester Palace (England)
Hawksmoor, Nicholas **7** 211-212

Winchester, Statute of (England)
Edward I **5** 208-210

WINCKELMANN, JOHANN JOACHIM (1717-1768), German archeologist **16** 332-333
David, Jacques Louis **4** 407-409
Fuseli, Henry **6** 153-155
Lessing, Gotthold Ephraim **9** 357-359
Mengs, Anton Raphael **10** 505
Schiller, Johann Christoph Friedrich von **14** 4-7
West, Benjamin **16** 210-212

Wind among the Reeds, The (poems)
Yeats, William Butler **16** 445-447

Wind River Mountains (Wyoming)
Carson, Christopher **3** 334-335

Wind, Sand and Stars (literature collection)
Saint-Exupéry, Antoine de **13** 431-432

Wind systems (meteorology)
Elsasser, Walter Maurice **5** 277-278

Wind Tells of Valdemar Daae and His Daughter, The (fairy tale)
Andersen, Hans Christian **1** 212-214

Wind tunnel (physics)
Kármán, Theodore von **8** 451-452
Tsiolkovsky, Konstantin Eduardovich **15** 326-328
Wright brothers **16** 394-396

Windesheim Congregation of Canons Regular
Groote, Gerard **7** 12-13

Windhover, The (poem)
Hopkins, Gerard Manley **7** 492-494

Winding Stair, The (poems)
Yeats, William Butler **16** 445-447

Windischgrätz, Prince Alfred (1787-1862), Austrian field marshal
Deák, Francis **4** 431-432

Windmill, The (literature collection)
Cela y Trulock, Camilo José **3** 389-390

Winds (poem)
Perse, Saint-John **12** 242-243

Windsor (royal house)
see Great Britain

Windsor Beauties (painting series)
Lely, Peter **9** 315

Windsor Castle (England)
George IV **6** 272-273

Windsor, Duchess of (1896-1986), wife of Edward, Duke of Windsor
Baldwin, Stanley **1** 468-469

Windsor, Duke of
see Edward VIII

Windsor dynasty (Great Britain)
see Great Britain—since 1901 (Windsor)

Windsor Forest (poem)
Pope, Alexander **12** 395-397

Windsor Prophecy, The (poem)
Swift, Jonathan **15** 51-54

Windy McPherson's Son (novel)
Anderson, Sherwood **1** 220-221

Wine (poem)
Gay, John **6** 243-244

Wine from These Grapes (poems)
Millay, Edna St. Vincent **11** 24-25

Wine Press (poems)
Mistral, Gabriela **11** 55-56

Wine, Women, and Song (waltz)
Strauss, Johann Jr. **14** 498-499

Winesburg, Ohio (literature collection)
Anderson, Sherwood **1** 220-221

WINFREY, OPRAH GAIL (born 1954), America's first lady of talk shows **16** 333-336

Winfrith
see Boniface, St.

Wing-and-Wing (novel)
Cooper, James Fenimore **4** 220-223

Wingfield, Edward (circa 1560-1613), English settler in Virginia
Smith, John **14** 295-297

Wings of the Dove, The (novel)
James, Henry **8** 211-212

Winnebago Indians (North America)
Cameron, Simon **3** 246-247
Radin, Paul **12** 538-539

WINNEMUCCA, SARAH (a.k.a. Thocmetony; circa 1844-1891), Native American rights activist **16** 336-338

Winner Take Nothing (stories)
Hemingway, Ernest Miller **7** 274-277

Winning of Barbara Worth, The (film)
Goldwyn, Samuel **6** 416

Winnipeg general strike (1919)
Woodsworth, James Shaver **16** 376

Winnower (painting)
Millet, Jean François **11** 31

WINSLOW, EDWARD (1595-1655), Pilgrim leader in colonial America **16** 338-339
Bradford, William **2** 475-476
Eliot, George **5** 254-256
Lowell, Robert Trail Spence Jr. **10** 16-17

Winslow, Josiah (circa 1629-80), Plymouth Colony governor
Philip **12** 267-268

Winslow House (River Forest, Illinois)
Wright, Frank Lloyd **16** 398-401

Winsor, Justin (1831-1897), American librarian and historian
Channing, Edward **3** 435

Winter (painting)
Goyen, Jan van **6** 478-479

Winter (poem)
Thomson, James **15** 199-200

Winter Days (poems)
Basho, Matsuo **2** 45-48

Winter Dreams (story)
Fitzgerald, Francis Scott Key **5** 470-472

Winter Garden Theater (New York City)
Booth, Edwin **2** 401-402

Winter Landscape (painting)
Rembrandt Harmensz van Rijn **13** 91-95

Winter Light (film)
Bergman, Ernst Ingmar **2** 190-191

Winter of Our Discontent, The (novel)
Steinbeck, John Ernst **14** 416-417

Winter on Fifth Avenue (photography)
Stieglitz, Alfred **14** 451-452

Winter Palace (Salzburg)
Fischer von Erlach, Johann Bernhard **5** 459-461

Winter Piece, A (poem)
Bryant, William Cullen **3** 83-85

Winter War (1940)
Mannerheim, Carl Gustav Emil Von **10** 207-208

Winter, William (1836-1917), American writer
Forrest, Edwin **6** 11-12

Winter Words (poems)
Hardy, Thomas **7** 150-152

Winterballade (drama)
Hauptmann, Gerhart Johann Robert **7** 199-201

Winterreise, Die (songs)
Schubert, Franz Peter **14** 35-37

Winter's Tale, The (play)
Shakespeare, William **14** 142-145

Winter's Tales (book)
Dinesen Blixen-Finecke, Karen **5** 13-14

Winterset (play)
Anderson, Maxwell **1** 219-220

WINTHROP, JOHN (1588-1649), American colonial politician and historian **16** 339-341
Bradford, William **2** 475-476
Cotton, John **4** 263-265
Dudley, Thomas **5** 124-125
Endecott, John **5** 284-285
Gorges, Ferdinando **6** 455-456
Hutchinson, Anne Marbury **8** 69-71
Underhill, John **15** 388

WINTHROP, JOHN (1606-1676), American colonial statesman and scientist **16** 341

WINTHROP, JOHN (1714-1779), American educator and scientist **16** 341-342

Wir Sind (poems)
Werfel, Franz **16** 204-205

Wiretapping (United States)
Brandeis, Louis Dembitz **2** 496-497

Wirt, William (1772-1834), American lawyer, attorney general 1817-29
Chase, Salmon Portland **3** 473-475
Kennedy, John Pendleton **8** 506-507
Monroe, James **11** 111-113

Wirth, Joseph (1879-1956), German statesman
Rathenau, Walther **13** 48-49

Wisconsin (state, United States)
Berger, Victor Louis **2** 189-190
Black Hawk **2** 308
La Follette, Robert Marion **9** 155-156

Wisconsin idea (government)
Commons, John Rogers **4** 185

Wisconsin Public Service Commission
Lilienthal, David Eli **9** 410-411

Wisconsin River (United States)
Jolliet, Louis **8** 328-329

Wisconsin State Survey (geology)
Chamberlin, Thomas Chrowder **3** 415-416

Wisconsin, University of (Madison)
Babcock, Stephen Moulton **1** 410-411
Barnard, Henry **2** 10
Bloomfield, Leonard **2** 338
Commons, John Rogers **4** 185
Erlanger, Joseph **5** 310-311
Haskins, Charles Homer **7** 191-192
Hull, Clark Leonard **8** 28
Linton, Ralph **9** 431
Ross, Edward Alsworth **13** 300
Rostovtzeff, Michael Ivanovich **13** 315
Turner, Frederick Jackson **15** 350-351

Wisconsin Vorwärts (newspaper)
Berger, Victor Louis **2** 189-190

Wisdom (sculpture)
Rush, William **13** 365-366

Wisdom, Book of (Old Testament)
see Ecclesiasticus

Wisdom of the Earth (sculpture)
Brancusi, Constantin **2** 494-496

Wise, Henry Alexander (1806-1876), American politician, governor of Virginia 1856-60
Brown, John **3** 39-41

WISE, ISAAC MAYER (1819-1900), American Jewish religious leader **16** 342-343

WISE, JOHN (1652-1725), American Congregational minister **16** 343-344

Wise, John (1808-1879), American aeronaut
Andrée, Salomon August **1** 226

WISE, STEPHEN SAMUEL (1874-1949), American Jewish religious leader **16** 344-345

Wise Virgins (print)
Schongauer, Martin **14** 26-28

WISEMAN, FREDERICK (born 1930), American documentary filmmaker **16** 345-346

Wiseman, Nicholas Patrick Stephen (1802-1865), English Catholic cardinal
Acton, John Emerich Edward Dalberg **1** 38
Manning, Henry Edward **10** 209-210

Wishart, George (1513?-1546), Scottish religious reformer and martyr
Knox, John **9** 65-66

Wisniowiecki, Michael
see Michael Wisniowiecki

Wissler, Clark (1870-1947), American anthropologist
Lynd, Robert Staughton **10** 64-65

Wit Lavendel, Het (Dutch poetry society)
Vondel, Joost van den **16** 19-20

Witch, The (sculpture)
Brancusi, Constantin **2** 494-496

Witch of Coös, The (poem)
Frost, Robert Lee **6** 130-133

Witchcraft
Bishop, Bridget **2** 288-290
Evans-Pritchard, Edward Evan **5** 340

Filmer, Robert **5** 448
Joan of Arc **8** 264-265
Starhawk **14** 403-404
see also Salem witchcraft trials

Witches and Other Night-Fears (essay)
Lamb, Charles **9** 176-177

Witches' Dance (musical composition)
Paganini, Niccolo **12** 58-59

Witches' Sabbath (fresco)
Goya y Lucientes, Francisco de Paula
José de **6** 476-478

With a Song in My Heart (song)
Rodgers, Richard Charles **13** 234-236

With Fire and the Sword (novel)
Sienkiewicz, Henryk **14** 216-217

With the Black Arch (painting)
Kandinsky, Wassily **8** 420-422

WITHERSPOON, JOHN (1723-1794),
Scottish-born American Presbyterian
divine and educator **16** 346-348
Dunster, Henry **5** 152-153
Madison, James **10** 121-123

Within a Budding Grove (novel)
Proust, Marcel **12** 465-467

Within Prison Walls (book)
Osborne, Thomas Mott **12** 17-18

Within the Quota (ballet)
Porter, Cole Albert **12** 405-406

Without Dogma (novel)
Sienkiewicz, Henryk **14** 216-217

Without glaidnes avalis no treasure (poem)
Dunbar, William **5** 142-143

Without Love (novel)
Azuela, Mariano **1** 402

Witness Tree, A (literature collection)
Frost, Robert Lee **6** 130-133

WITT, JOHAN DE (1625-1672), Dutch
statesman **16** 348-349

WITTE, COUNT SERGEI YULYEVICH
(1849-1915), Russian statesman
16 349-350
Nicholas II **11** 378-380

Wittenberg (city, Germany)
Cranach, Lucas the Elder **4** 289-290

Wittenberg Concord (1536)
Melancthon, Philip **10** 466-467

Wittenberg, University of
Bruno, Giordano **3** 75-76
Eck, Johann Maier von **5** 200
Luther, Martin **10** 48-51
Melancthon, Philip **10** 466-467

Wittenbergisch Nachtigall, Die (song)
Sachs, Hans **13** 410-411

WITTGENSTEIN, LUDWIG (1889-1951),
Austrian philosopher **16** 350-351
Broad, Charlie Dunbar **3** 12
Carnap, Rudolf **3** 308-309
Moore, George Edward **11** 146
Nagel, Ernest **11** 291-292
Ramsey, Frank Plumpton **13** 25

Schlick, Friedrich Albert Moritz
14 16-17
Schopenhauer, Arthur **14** 29-31

WITZ, KONRAD (circa 1410-46), German
painter **16** 351-352

Wives and Daughters (novel)
Gaskell, Elizabeth **6** 231-232

Wizard of Oz, The (film)
Garland, Judy **6** 218-219
Lahr, Bert **9** 167-168

Wobblies
see Industrial Workers of the World

Woe to Him Who Lies (play)
Grillparzer, Franz **6** 546-547

Wöhler, Friedrich (1800-1882), German
chemist
Fischer, Emil **5** 456-457
Liebig, Justus von **9** 403-404

WO-JEN (1804-1871), Chinese official
16 352

Wolf Charmer (painting)
La Farge, John **9** 149-150

WOLF, FRIEDRICH AUGUST (1759-1824),
German classical scholar and philologist
16 352-353

WOLFE, JAMES (1727-1759), English gen-
eral **16** 354-355
Amherst, Jeffery **1** 200-201
Carleton, Guy **3** 300-301
Howe, William **7** 538-539
Montcalm de Saint-Véran, Marquis de
11 122-123
Murray, James **11** 261-262
Vaudreuil-Cavagnal, Marquis de **15** 444

WOLFE, THOMAS CLAYTON (1900-1938),
American novelist **16** 355-356
Fitzgerald, Francis Scott Key **5** 470-472
Perkins, William Maxwell Evarts
12 222-223

WOLFE, THOMAS KENNERLY, JR. ("Tom";
born 1931), American journalist and novelist **16** 356-357

Wolfe Tone rebellion (Ireland)
Castlereagh, Viscount **3** 363-364

Wolfert's Roost (literature collection)
Irving, Washington **8** 141-143

WOLFF, BARON CHRISTIAN VON
(1679-1754), German philosopher
16 358
Kant, Immanuel **8** 430-432

WOLFF, HUGH (born 1953), American
conductor **16** 358-360

Wölfflin, Heinrich (1864-1945), German
art historian
Gabo, Naum **6** 158-159

WOLFRAM VON ESCHENBACH (circa
1170-circa 1230), German writer
16 360-361
Eckhart, Johann **5** 200-201
Gottfried von Strassburg **6** 461-462
Grimmelshausen, Hans Jakob Christoffel von **7** 4-5

WOLFSON, HARRY AUSTRYN
(1887-1974), American scholar and educator **16** 361-362

Wolgemut, Michael (1434-1519), German
painter
Dürer, Albrecht **5** 159-161

Wollstonecraft, Mary
see Shelley, Mary Wollstonecraft

WOLPE, STEFAN (1902-1972),
German-born composer **16** 362-364

Wolseley, 1st Viscount (Garnet Joseph
Wolseley; 1833-1913), British army offi-
cer
Kitchener, Horatio Herbert **9** 45-46
Victoria **15** 485-487

WOLSEY, THOMAS (circa 1475-1530),
English statesman and cardinal
16 364-366
Cranmer, Thomas **4** 295-296
Cromwell, Thomas **4** 320-321
Henry VIII **7** 302-305, 206
Latimer, Hugh **9** 221
More, Thomas **11** 156-157
Norfolk, 3d Duke of **11** 423
Pollard, Albert Frederick **12** 378
Skelton, John **14** 268-269
Tyndale, William **15** 373-374

Wolves, The (play)
Rolland, Romain **13** 260

Wolves, Valley of (France)
Chateaubriand, Vicomte de **3** 477-479

Woman... (painting)
Bonnard, Pierre **2** 395-396
Braque, Georges **2** 504-505
Corot, Jean Baptiste Camille **4** 247-249
Courbet, Jean Desiré Gustave
4 271-273
de Kooning, Willem **4** 468-469
Léger, Fernand **9** 302-303
Lichtenstein, Roy **9** 398-399
Miró, Joan **11** 53-54
Picasso, Pablo **12** 292-295
Pippin, Horace **12** 318-319
Soutine, Chaim **14** 356-357
Vermeer, Jan **15** 466-467

Woman... (sculpture)
Giacometti, Alberto **6** 294-295
González, Julio **6** 428-429
Lipchitz, Jacques **9** 432-433

**Woman as Force in History: A Study of Tra-
ditions and Realities** (book)
Beard, Mary Ritter **2** 85-86

Woman Citizen (magazine)
Stone, Lucy **14** 471-472

Woman in White, The (novel)
Collins, William Wilkie **4** 169-170

Woman Killed with Kindness, A (play)
Heywood, Thomas **7** 373-374

Woman of Andros, The (novel)
Wilder, Thornton Niven **16** 276-277

Woman of No Importance, A (play)
Wilde, Oscar Fingall O'Flahertie Wills **16** 272-273

Woman of Paris, A (film)
Chaplin, Charles Spencer **3** 438-440

Woman of Rome, The (novel)
Moravia, Alberto **11** 153-155

Woman Rebel (newspaper; established 1913)
Sanger, Margaret Higgins **13** 467-468

Woman Waits for Me, A (poem)
Whitman, Walt **16** 249-251

Woman without a Shadow, The (opera libretto)
Hofmannsthal, Hugo von **7** 443-444

Woman-Hater, The (play)
Beaumont, Francis **2** 95

Woman's Christian Temperance Union (WCTU)
Bloor, Ella Reeve **2** 338-340
Crane, Stephen **4** 293-295
Nation, Carry Amelia Moore **11** 321-322
Shaw, Anna Howard **14** 162-163
Willard, Frances Elizabeth Caroline **16** 289-290

Woman's Journal (magazine; established 1870)
Stone, Lucy **14** 471-472

Woman's Peace party (United States)
Catt, Carrie Chapman **3** 375-376

Woman's Rights Convention (Seneca Falls, New York State; 1848)
Anthony, Susan Brownell **1** 246-248
Bloomer, Amelia Jenks **2** 337
Mott, Lucretia Coffin **11** 212-213
Stanton, Elizabeth Cady **14** 402-403

Women artists, American
Abbott, Berenice **1** 7-9
Burke, Selma **3** 143-144
Carnegie, Hattie **3** 313
Chicago, Judy **3** 515-516
Hesse, Eva **7** 365-367
Holzer, Jenny **7** 462-463
Johnson, Betsey **8** 295-296
Krasner, Lee **9** 93-94
Leibovitz, Annie **9** 310-312
Lin, Maya Ying **9** 413-415
Martin, Agnes **10** 288-289
Millett, Kate **11** 31-33
Morgan, Julia **11** 165-166
Ringgold, Faith **13** 175-177
Savage, Augusta Christine **13** 499-501
Schapiro, Miriam **13** 520-521

Women artists, German
Kollwitz, Käthe **9** 79-81
Modersohn-Becker, Paula **11** 71-72
Salomon, Charlotte **13** 454-455

Women artists, Mexican
Kahlo, Frida **8** 406-407

Women artists, Russian
Goncharova, Natalia **6** 424-426

Women artists, Spanish
Picasso, Paloma **12** 295-297

Women artists, Swiss
Oppenheim, Meret **11** 524-525
Taeuber-Arp, Sophie **15** 73-74

Women athletes
Capriati, Jennifer **3** 278-281
Gibson, Althea **6** 305-306
King, Billie Jean **9** 14-15
Navratilova, Martina **11** 325-327
Zaharias, Mildred Didrikson **16** 487-488

Women authors
American
see Women authors, American
Austrian
Suttner, Bertha von **15** 42-44
Canadian
Montgomery, Lucy Maud **11** 136-138
Chilean
Allende, Isabel **1** 172-174
English
Brookner, Anita **3** 23-24
James, P. D. **8** 213-215
Shelley, Mary Wollstonecraft **14** 174-176
Weldon, Fay Birkinshaw **16** 186-188
French
de Beauvoir, Simone **4** 440-441
Yourcenar, Marguerite **16** 477-479
Irish
Somerville, Edith Anna Œnone **14** 334-335
Italian
Ginzburg, Natalia Levi **6** 338-339
Kenyan
Ogot, Grace Emily Akinyi **11** 483-484
Mexican
Poniatowska, Elena **12** 392-393
New Zealander
Mansfield, Katherine **10** 213-214
Romanian
Blandiana, Ana **2** 321-322
South African
Gordimer, Nadine **6** 446-447
Lessing, Doris **9** 355-357
Steinem, Gloria **14** 418-419
Turkish
Halide Edip Adivar **7** 80-82

Women authors, American
Allen, Paula Gunn **1** 165-167
Alvarez, Julia **1** 185-187
Angelou, Maya **1** 238-239
Bambara, Toni Cade **1** 482-483
Barnes, Djuna **2** 11-13
Bates, Katharine Lee **2** 54-55
Beard, Mary Ritter **2** 85-86
Blume, Judy **2** 344-345
Brooks, Gwendolyn **3** 24-26
Brownmiller, Susan **3** 56-57
Butler, Octavia E. **3** 182-183
Carroll, Anna Ella **3** 327-331

Clapp, Margaret Antoinette **4** 71-72
Conway, Jill Kathryn Ker **4** 213-214
Daly, Mary **4** 380-381
Davis, Angela **4** 412-413
Dove, Rita Frances **5** 87-89
Flanagan, Hallie **5** 478-479
Friedan, Betty **6** 109-111
Gilman, Charlotte Anna Perkins **6** 323-325
Giovanni, Yolande Cornelia Jr. **6** 346-347
Goldmark, Josephine **6** 407-408
Goodman, Ellen Holtz **6** 438-439
Green, Constance McLaughlin **6** 518-519
Hansberry, Lorraine Vivian **7** 130-131
Higgins, Marguerite **7** 378-380
Himmelfarb, Gertrude **7** 396-398
Hinton, Susan Eloise **7** 406-407
hooks, bell **7** 477-481
Hurston, Zora Neale **8** 55-56
Jacobs, Harriet A. **8** 190-193
Jordan, June **8** 351-353
Kreps, Juanita Morris **9** 99-101
Kübler-Ross, Elisabeth **9** 118-120
Larsen, Nella **9** 209-210
Lindbergh, Anne Morrow **9** 420-421
Lorde, Audre **9** 513-515
Marshall, Paule Burke **10** 281-282
McMillan, Terry **10** 427-428
Nin, Anais **11** 397-398
Morrison, Toni **11** 188-190
Naylor, Gloria **11** 328-329
Oates, Joyce Carol **11** 454-456
Plath, Sylvia **12** 344-345
Proulx, E. Annie **12** 463-465
Rice, Anne **13** 125-126
Rich, Adrienne **13** 128-130
Robinson, Harriet Hanson **13** 203-207
Sexton, Anne **14** 125-126
Silko, Leslie **14** 226-227
Steel, Danielle **14** 404-406
Tan, Amy **15** 95-96
Tyler, Anne **15** 367-368
Van Duyn, Mona **15** 422-423
vos Savant, Marilyn **16** 32-33
Walker, Alice Malsenior **16** 59-61
Walker, Margaret **16** 67
Welty, Eudora **16** 199-201
Wharton, Edith **16** 221
Wheatley, Phillis **16** 221-222
Wilson, Harriet E. **16** 320-322
Winnemucca, Sarah **16** 336-338

Women aviators
Coleman, Bessie **4** 152-154
Earhart, Amelia Mary **5** 177-179
Lindbergh, Anne Morrow **9** 420-421

Women business leaders
Arden, Elizabeth **1** 281-282
Ash, Mary Kay Wagner **1** 326-327
Carnegie, Hattie **3** 313
Claiborne, Liz **4** 68-69
Gilbreth, Lillian **6** 315-317
Graham, Katharine Meyer **6** 483-485
Grossinger, Jennie **7** 15-17

Hobby, Oveta Culp **7** 423-425
Johnson, Betsey **8** 295-296
Karan, Donna **8** 442-444
Lauder, Estee **9** 225-226
Knopf, Blanche Wolf **9** 61-62
Madonna **10** 123-125
McMurray, Bette Clair **10** 429
Rubenstein, Helena **13** 342-343
Rudkin, Margaret Fogarty **13** 346-347
Song Sisters **14** 338-341
von Furstenberg, Diane **16** 20-21
Walker, C. J. **16** 61-62
Wells, Mary Georgene Berg **16** 197-198
Westwood, Vivienne **16** 217-218

Women Celebrating the Thesmophoria
(play)
Aristophanes **1** 293-294

Women college presidents
Clapp, Margaret Antoinette **4** 71-72
Conway, Jill Kathryn Ker **4** 213-214
Gray, Hannah Holborn **6** 507-508
Horner, Matina Souretis **7** 506-508

Women educators
Strang, Ruth May **14** 493-494

Women entertainers
Faye, Safi **5** 400-401
Winfrey, Oprah Gail **16** 333-336

Women in Love (novel)
Lawrence, David Herbert **9** 247-248

Women in Parliament (play)
Aristophanes **1** 293-294

Women judges
Ginsburg, Ruth Bader **6** 333-336
O'Connor, Sandra Day **11** 468-470

Women labor leaders
Bondfield, Margaret Grace **2** 388-389
Flynn, Elizabeth Gurley **5** 496-497
Jones, Mary Harris **8** 338-339
Schniederman, Rose **14** 22-23

Women lawyers
Hill, Anita **7** 382-385
Reno, Janet **13** 99-101

Women of Algiers... (painting)
Delacroix, Ferdinand Victor Eugène **4** 469-471

Women of Shakespeare, The (book)
Harris, Frank **7** 172-173

Women organizers
Yard, Mary Alexander **16** 438-439

Women philosophers
Bok, Sissela Ann **2** 372-374
Daly, Mary **4** 380-381
Midgely, Mary Burton **11** 9-10
Stein, Edith **14** 412-414

Women politicians
American
see Women politicians, American
Botswanan
Chiepe, Gaositwe Keagakwa Tibe **3** 517
British

Bondfield, Margaret Grace **2** 388-389
Rathbone, Eleanor **13** 47-48
Thatcher, Margaret Hilda **15** 165-168
Wilkinson, Ellen **16** 283-284
Williams, Shirley Vivien Teresa Brittain **16** 305-306
Wootton, Barbara Adam **16** 384-385
Canada
Campbell, Avril Phaedra Douglas **3** 250-252
China
Jiang Qing **8** 256-260
English
Boothroyd, Betty **2** 406-407
Filipino
Aquino, Corazon Cojoangco **1** 268-270
French
Cresson, Edith **4** 306-307
German
Hamm-Brücher, Hildegard **7** 101-103
Kelly, Petra **8** 486-487
Zetkin, Clara **16** 504-505
Irish
Devlin, Bernadette **4** 515-516
Robinson, Mary Bourke **13** 211-213
Italian
Ginzburg, Natalia Levi **6** 338-339
Japanese
Doi Takako **5** 39-41
Kenyan
Ogot, Grace Emily Akinyi **11** 483-484
Myanmar
Aung San Suu Kyi **1** 375-376
Nicaraguan
Chamorro, Violeta Barrios de **3** 417-419
Norwegian
Brundtland, Gro Harlem **3** 68-69
Pakistani
Bhutto, Benazir **2** 259-261
South African
Sisulu, Nontsikelelo Albertina **14** 259-261
Soviet
Biryukova, Aleksandra Pavlovna **2** 285-287
Sri Lankan
Bandaranaike, Sirimavo **1** 486-488
Turkey
Çiller, Tansu **4** 59-60
Ugandan
Elizabeth Bagaaya Nyabongo of Toro **5** 269-271

Women politicians, American
appointees
Elders, Joycelyn **5** 243-246
Reno, Janet **13** 99-101
cabinet members
Dole, Elizabeth Hanford **5** 41-43
Harris, Patricia Roberts **7** 174-175

Heckler, Margaret Mary O'Shaughnessy **7** 251-252
Hills, Carla Anderson **7** 394-396
Kirkpatrick, Jeane J. **9** 37-39
congresswomen
Chisholm, Shirley Anita St. Hill **4** 7-9
Feinstein, Dianne **5** 407-408
Ferraro, Geraldine **5** 426-428
Green, Edith Starrett **6** 519-520
Hansen, Julia Butler **7** 132-133
Heckler, Margaret Mary O'Shaughnessy **7** 251-252
Jordan, Barbara Charline **8** 349-350
Rohde, Ruth Bryan Owen **13** 252-253
Ros-Lehtinen, Ileana **13** 294-296
Roybal-Allard, Lucille **13** 332-334
Schroeder, Patricia Scott **14** 33-35
Smith, Margaret Chase **14** 299-300
Snowe, Olympia **14** 313-314
Velázquez, Nydia Margarita **15** 456-459
Waters, Maxine **16** 132-134
governors
Kunin, Madeleine May **9** 130-131
Ray, Dixy Lee **13** 56-57
Richards, Ann Willis **13** 133-134
Whitman, Christine Todd **16** 245-248
Indian chiefs (North America)
Mankiller, Wilma **10** 198-199
mayors
Byrne, Jane **3** 190-191
Feinstein, Dianne **5** 407-408
Whitmire, Kathryn Jean Niederhofer **16** 252-253
organizers
Dewson, Mary Williams **4** 525
Hamer, Fannie Lou **7** 93-94
Natividad, Irene **11** 322-324
presidential advisers
Clinton, Hillary Rodham **4** 115-117
senators
Boxer, Barbara **2** 465-468
Caraway, Hattie Wyatt **3** 284-285
Kassebaum (Baker), Nancy **8** 455-457
Mikulski, Barbara **11** 13-15
Mosely-Braun, Carol **11** 199-200
Snowe, Olympia **14** 313-314
state legislators
Baca-Barragán, Polly **1** 412-414
students of
Conway, Jill Kathryn Ker **4** 213-214
Gilman, Charlotte Anna Perkins **6** 323-325

Women, President's Commission on the Status of (United States)
Roosevelt, Eleanor **13** 275-277

Women religious leaders
Morton, Nelle Katherine **11** 195-197

Women scholars
Himmelfarb, Gertrude **7** 396-398

Women scientists
Andersen, Dorothy **1** 212
Apgar, Virginia **1** 257-259
Bailey, Florence Merriam **1** 443-444
Baker, Sara Josephine **1** 455-456
Bell Burnell, Susan Jocelyn **2** 133-134
Bernstein, Dorothy Lewis **2** 217
Brown, Rachel Fuller **3** 43-44
Cannon, Annie Jump **3** 260-261
Chinn, May Edward **3** 525-526
Earle, Sylvia A. **5** 180-181
Elders, Joycelyn **5** 243-246
Franklin, Rosalind Elsie **6** 67-68
Garrett (Anderson), Elizabeth **6** 222-225
Gayle, Helene Doris **6** 244-245
Geller, Margaret Joan **6** 256-257
Goeppert-Mayer, Maria **6** 385-387
Granville, Evelyn Boyd **6** 494-496
Hardy, Harriet **7** 150
Healy, Bernadine Patricia **7** 237-238
Hodgkin, Dorothy Crowfoot **7** 432-434
Hopper, Grace **7** 498-500
Hyman, Libbie Henrietta **8** 83-84
Hypatia of Alexandria **8** 85
Jackson, Shirley Ann **8** 183-184
Jemison, Mae C. **8** 243-244
Johnson, Virginia E. **8** 317-319
Joliot-Curie, Irène **8** 325-327
Karle, Isabella **8** 447-449
Kübler-Ross, Elisabeth **9** 118-120
Levi-Montalcini, Rita **9** 366-368
Long, Irene D. **9** 497-498
Lonsdale, Kathleen **9** 501-502
Macdonald, Eleanor Josephine **10** 83-84
Margulis, Lynn **10** 253-254
McClintock, Barbara **10** 393-394
Meitner, Lise **10** 463-466
Mendenhall, Dorothy Reed **10** 491-492
Mintz, Beatrice **11** 49-50
Moore, Charlotte E. **11** 145-146
Neufeld, Elizabeth F. **11** 352-353
Noether, Emmy **11** 414-416
Ochoa, Ellen **11** 460-461
Patrick, Jennie R. **12** 136-137
Patrick, Ruth **12** 137-138
Payne-Gaposchkin, Cecilia **12** 159-161
Peterson, Edith R. **12** 258-259
Prichard, Diana García **12** 448-449
Quimby, Edith H. **12** 513-514
Richards, Ellen H. **13** 134-136
Ride, Sally **13** 158-160
Robinson, Julia **13** 210-211
Ross, Mary G. **13** 304-305
Russell, Elizabeth Shull **13** 377-379
Sabin, Florence Rena **13** 402-405
Seibert, Florence B. **14** 89-90
Shaw, Mary **14** 165-167
Singer, Maxine **14** 251-252
Slye, Maud **14** 276-277
Stopes, Marie **14** 476-478
Stevens, Nettie Maria **14** 441-442
Taussig, Helen Brooke **15** 118-120
Tharp, Marie **15** 162-164
Trotter, Mildred **15** 305-306

Uhlenbeck, Karen **15** 381-382
Wexler, Nancy **16** 218-219
Widnall, Sheila E. **16** 258-259
Yalow, Rosalyn S. **16** 427-428
Women singers (popular)
Baez, Joan **1** 433-435
Baker, Josephine **1** 448-451
Fitzgerald, Ella **5** 468-469
Franklin, Aretha **6** 58-60
Garland, Judy **6** 218-219
Holiday, Billie **7** 452-453
Horne, Lena **7** 504-506
Martin, Mary **10** 292-293
Ross, Diana **13** 298-300
Smith, Bessie **14** 285-287
Women social scientists
Robinson, Joan Violet Maurice **13** 209-210
Women theologians
Schüssler Fiorenza, Elisabeth **14** 46-48
Women's Anthropological Society (established 1885)
Fletcher, Alice Cunningham **5** 486-487
Women's India Association
Naidu, Sarojini **11** 294-295
Women's International League
Royden, Agnes Maude **13** 335-337
Women's International League for Peace and Freedom
Balch, Emily Greene **1** 463-464
Rankin, Jeannette Pickering **13** 35-37
Women's Love and Life (musical composition)
Schumann, Robert Alexander **14** 41-43
Women's Medical College of the New York Infirmary
Jacobi, Abraham and Mary Putnam **8** 188-189
Women's National Loyal League (established 1861)
Anthony, Susan Brownell **1** 246-248
Women's Reformatory Prison (Sherborn, Massachusetts)
Barton, Clara **2** 37-39
Women's rights
academic reformers
Carey Thomas, Martha **3** 297-298
Fletcher, Alice Cunningham **5** 486-487
Mitchell, Maria **11** 61
Willard, Emma Hart **16** 288-289
churches and
Harris, Barbara Clementine **7** 171-172
Royden, Agnes Maude **13** 335-337
Ruether, Rosemary Radford **13** 353-354
critics
Hale, Sarah Josepha **7** 74-75
Nightingale, Florence **11** 392-393
Strindberg, August **14** 509-511
economic equality
Ireland, Patricia **8** 134-135

Royden, Agnes Maude **13** 335-337
Smeal, Eleanor **14** 278-280
Woodward, Ellen S. **16** 379-381
Egypt
Sadat, Jihan **13** 414-415
equal education opportunity
Baker, Sara Josephine **1** 455-456
Beale, Dorothea **2** 81-83
Beecher, Catharine **2** 110-112
Dodge, Grace Hoadley **5** 37-38
Garrett (Anderson), Elizabeth **6** 222-225
Green, Edith Starrett **6** 519-520
Lyon, Mary **10** 67-69
Smeal, Eleanor **14** 278-280
health care and
Love, Susan M. **10** 2-3
labor reform
Goldmark, Josephine **6** 407-408
Schniederman, Rose **14** 22-23
Woodward, Ellen S. **16** 379-381
legal reform
Ginsburg, Ruth Bader **6** 333-336
male supporters
Chernyshevsky, Nikolai Gavrilovich **3** 504-505
Doyle, Arthur Conan **5** 91-92
Eliot, Thomas Stearns **5** 258-261
Euripides **5** 332-334
Forten, James **6** 17-18
Fourier, François Charles Marie **6** 31-32
Garrison, William Lloyd **6** 226-228
Higginson, Thomas Wentworth **7** 380
Owen, Robert Dale **12** 40-41
Phillips, Wendell **12** 281-282
medical reformers
Blackwell, Elizabeth **2** 311-312
Hamilton, Alice **7** 98-99
Sanger, Margaret Higgins **13** 467-468
Palestine
Ashrawi, Hanan Mikhail **1** 336-338
political activists
Allen, Florence Ellinwood **1** 164-165
Fawcett, Millicent Garrett **5** 398-400
Markievicz, Constance **10** 267-271
Morgan, Robin **11** 168-170
Natividad, Irene **11** 322-324
Rohde, Ruth Bryan Owen **13** 252-253
Sadat, Jihan **13** 414-415
Schwimmer, Rosika **14** 57-60
Xiang Jingyu **16** 421-422
Zetkin, Clara **16** 504-505
social reformers
Beard, Mary Ritter **2** 85-86
Day, Dorothy **4** 428-429
Fairclough, Ellen Louks **5** 367-368
Fuller, Sarah Margaret **6** 150-151
Greer, Germaine **6** 528-530
Grimké, Sarah Moore and Angelina Emily **7** 2-3
Halide Edip Adivar **7** 80-82

Kelley, Florence **8** 483-484
Kollontai, Aleksandra Mikhailovna
    9 79
Mott, Lucretia Coffin **11** 212-213
Rathbone, Eleanor **13** 47-48
Roosevelt, Eleanor **13** 275-277
Stanton, Elizabeth Cady **14** 402-403
Talbert, Mary Morris Burnett
    15 86-88
Tubman, Harriet Ross **15** 330-331
Willard, Frances Elizabeth Caroline
    16 289-290
Woodward, Ellen S. **16** 379-381
Wright, Frances **16** 397-398
writers
  Beard, Mary Ritter **2** 85-86
  Brownmiller, Susan **3** 56-57
  Christine de Pisan **4** 29-30
  Halide Edip Adivar **7** 80-82
  Hill, Anita **7** 382-385
  hooks, bell **7** 477-481
  Millay, Edna St. Vincent **11** 24-25
  Sand, George **13** 459-461
  Steinem, Gloria **14** 418-419
  Woolf, Virginia Stephen **16** 381-382
  see also Women's suffrage

Women's Social and Political Union (established 1903)
  Pankhurst, Emmeline **12** 85-86

Women's Strike for Peace (United States peace organization)
  Abzug, Bella Stavisky **1** 34-35

Women's suffrage (Argentina)
  Perón, Eva Duarte de **12** 225-226

Women's suffrage (England)
  Asquith, Herbert Henry **1** 344-346
  Astor, Nancy Langhorne **1** 352-354
  Beard, Mary Ritter **2** 85-86
  Bondfield, Margaret Grace **2** 388-389
  Bradlaugh, Charles **2** 478
  Fawcett, Millicent Garrett **5** 398-400
  Garrett (Anderson), Elizabeth **6** 222-225
  Pankhurst, Emmeline **12** 85-86
  Rathbone, Eleanor **13** 47-48
  Royden, Agnes Maude **13** 335-337
  Wilkinson, Ellen **16** 283-284

Women's suffrage (Hungary)
  Schwimmer, Rosika **14** 57-60

Women's suffrage (Ireland)
  Markievicz, Constance **10** 267-271
  Somerville, Edith Anna OEnone
    14 334-335

Women's suffrage (Mexico)
  Ruiz Cortines, Adolfo **13** 359-360

Women's suffrage (United States)
  leaders
    Allen, Florence Ellinwood
      1 164-165
    Anthony, Susan Brownell **1** 246-248
    Catt, Carrie Chapman **3** 375-376
    Gage, Matilda Joslyn **6** 167-169
    Howe, Julia Ward **7** 535-536
    Park, Maud Wood **12** 102

Robinson, Harriet Hanson
    13 203-207
Schniederman, Rose **14** 22-23
Shaw, Anna Howard **14** 162-163
Stone, Lucy **14** 471-472
supporters
  Addams, Jane **1** 56-57
  Alcott, Louisa May **1** 122
  Bloomer, Amelia Jenks **2** 337
  Brown, William Wells **3** 48-49
  Bryan, William Jennings **3** 80-82
  Coolidge, John Calvin **4** 217-219
  Curtis, George William **4** 349-350
  Foster, Abigail Kelley **6** 25
  Franklin, Stella Maraia Sarah Miles
    6 68-69
  Lease, Mary Elizabeth Clyens **9** 268
  Palmer, Alexander Mitchell **12** 77-78
  Reed, Thomas Brackett **13** 77
  Rogers, Edith Nourse **13** 247-248
  see also Women's rights

Women's Trade Union League (United States)
  Roosevelt, Eleanor **13** 275-277

Women's Trade Union League of Boston
  Balch, Emily Greene **1** 463-464

Wonder Book, A (stories)
  Hawthorne, Nathaniel **7** 212-215

Wonderful Adventures of Nils, The (juvenile literature)
  Lagerlöf, Selma Ottiliana Lovisa
    9 163-164

Wonderful Island (play)
  Betti, Ugo **2** 246

Wonderful Town (music)
  Bernstein, Leonard **2** 218-219

Wonderful Wizard of Oz, The (book)
  Baum, L. Frank **2** 73-74

WONG, ANNA MAY (born Wong Liu Tsong; 1905-1961), Asian American actress **16** 366-367

Wood, Annie
  see Besant, Annie Wood

Wood carvers
  see Artists—wood carvers

Wood, Christopher (1901-1931), English painter
  Nicholson, Ben **11** 380-381

Wood Demon, The (play)
  Chekhov, Anton Pavlovich **3** 494-497

Wood, Edward Frederick Lindley
  see Halifax, 1st Earl of

WOOD, FERNANDO (1812-1881), American politician **16** 367-368

WOOD, GRANT (1891-1942), American painter **16** 368-369

WOOD, LEONARD (1860-1927), American Army officer and colonial administrator **16** 369-370
  Osmeña, Sergio **12** 22-24
  Quezon, Manuel Luis **12** 511-513

WOOD, ROBERT ELKINGTON (1879-1969), American Army officer and business executive **16** 370-371

Woodbury, Levi (1789-1851), American jurist and statesman
  Pierce, Franklin **12** 300-301

Woodcraft (novel)
  Simms, William Gilmore **14** 235-236

Woodcutters
  see Artists—woodcutters

Wooden Bridge (painting)
  Ruisdael, Jacob van **13** 357-358

Wooden Prince, The (ballet)
  Bartók, Béla **2** 35-36

Woodhouse, Emma (literary character)
  Austen, Jane **1** 377-379

Woodhouse, James (1770-1809), American chemist
  Hare, Robert **7** 152-153

Woodland Scenes (musical composition)
  Schumann, Robert Alexander **14** 41-43

Woodland Sketches (musical composition)
  MacDowell, Edward Alexander
    10 87-88

Woodlanders, The (novel)
  Hardy, Thomas **7** 150-152

Woodrow Wilson International Center for Scholars
  Billington, James Hadley **2** 275-276

WOODRUFF, ROBERT W. (1889-1985), American businessman and philanthropist **16** 372-374

Woodruff Sleeping Car Co.
  Carnegie, Andrew **3** 309-312

Woods Hole Marine Biological Laboratory (Massachusetts)
  Dam, Carl Peter Henrik **4** 382-383
  Szent-Györgyi, Albert von **15** 62-64

Woods Hole Oceanographic Institution (Massachusetts)
  Ewing, William Maurice **5** 350-351
  Waksman, Selman Abraham **16** 49-50

WOODS, ROBERT ARCHEY (1865-1925), American social worker **16** 374

WOODSON, CARTER GODWIN (1875-1950), African American historian **16** 374-376

Woodstock (novel)
  Scott, Walter **14** 68-70

WOODSWORTH, JAMES SHAVER (1874-1942), Canadian humanitarian, reformer, and political leader **16** 376

Woodville, Anthony (2d Earl Rivers; 1442?-83), English soldier
  Richard III **13** 132-133

Woodville, Elizabeth
  see Elizabeth, queen of Edward IV

WOODWARD, COMER VANN (born 1908), American historian **16** 378-379

WOODWARD, ELLEN S. (1887-1971), director of work relief programs for women during the New Deal **16** 379-381

Woodward, Robert Upshur (born 1943), investigative reporter
Woodward and Bernstein **16** 376-378

WOODWARD AND BERNSTEIN, investigative reporting team of Woodward, Robert Upshur (born 1943), and Bernstein, Carl (born 1944) **16** 376-378

Wool, John E. (1784-1869), American general
Lee, Robert Edward **9** 292-294

Woolf, Leonard (1880-1969), English publicist
Eliot, Thomas Stearns **5** 258-261
Woolf, Virginia Stephen **16** 381-382

WOOLF, VIRGINIA STEPHEN (1882-1941), English novelist, critic, and essayist **16** 381-382
Bowen, Elizabeth **2** 462-463
Eliot, Thomas Stearns **5** 258-261
Forster, Edward Morgan **6** 14-16

Woolley, Charles Leonard (1880-1960), English archeologist
Lawrence, Thomas Edward **9** 253-254

WOOLMAN, JOHN (1720-1772), American Quaker merchant and minister **16** 382-383
Benezet, Anthony **2** 159-160

WOOLWORTH, FRANK WINFIELD (1852-1919), American merchant **16** 383-384

Wooster College (Ohio)
Compton, Arthur Holly **4** 186-188
Rowland, Henry Augustus **13** 330-331

WOOTTON, BARBARA ADAM (1897-1988), British social scientist and member of Parliament **16** 384-385

Worcester, Earl of (Thomas Percy; 1344?-1403), English nobleman
Henry V **7** 296-297

Worcester Academy (Massachusetts)
Thayer, Eli **15** 168

Worcester, battle of (1651)
Buckingham, 2d Duke of **3** 94-95
Charles II **3** 452-454
Cromwell, Oliver **4** 317-320

Worcester v. Georgia (1832)
Marshall, John **10** 279-281

Worde, Wynkyn de (died 1534?), English printer
Caxton, William **3** 386-387

Words for the Wind (poems)
Roethke, Theodore **13** 243-244

Wordsworth, Dorothy (1771-1855), English essayist and journalist
Coleridge, Samuel Taylor **4** 154-156
Wordsworth, William **16** 385-388

WORDSWORTH, WILLIAM (1770-1850), English poet **16** 385-388
associates
Arnold, Matthew **1** 311-313

Browning, Robert **3** 53-55
Hamilton, William Rowan **7** 99-100
Hazlitt, William **7** 235-236
Lamb, Charles **9** 176-177
compared to
Constable, John **4** 208-209
Gray, Thomas **6** 509-510
critics
Peacock, Thomas Love **12** 169
Shelley, Percy Bysshe **14** 176-178
influence of
Bryant, William Cullen **3** 83-85
Burroughs, John **3** 160-161
Byron, George Gordon Noel **3** 193-194
Coleridge, Samuel Taylor **4** 154-156
Frost, Robert Lee **6** 130-133
Hawthorne, Nathaniel **7** 212-215
Lampman, Archibald **9** 180-181
Tennyson, Alfred **15** 144-146
influenced by
Bartram, William **2** 41-42
Chatterton, Thomas **3** 481-482
Crabbe, George **4** 288
Milton, John **11** 43-46
Plutarch **12** 359-360
Vaughan, Henry **15** 444-445

WORK, MONROE (1866-1945), American sociologist and publisher **16** 388-389

Work of St. Raphael (refugee organization)
Pius XII **12** 339-340

Work Projects Administration
see Works Progress Administration

Work Suspended (novel)
Waugh, Evelyn Arthur St. John **16** 145-147

Worker, The (newspaper)
Pilsudski, Joseph **12** 305-306

Worker-priest movement (France, 1940s)
John, XXIII **8** 277-280

Workers
see entries under Labor

Workers Educational Association (England)
Polanyi, Karl **12** 372
Tawney, Richard Henry **15** 120-121
Temple, William **15** 141-143

Workers' party
Korea
Kim Il-sung **9** 4-6
North Vietnam
Giap, Vo Nguyen **6** 297-299
Truong Chinh **15** 319-320
United States
Foster, William Zebulon **6** 27-28

Workhouse Ward, The (play)
Gregory, Augusta **6** 535-536

Working class, studies on
Hammond, Lawrence and Lucy **7** 109
Le Play, Guillaume Frédéric **9** 350-351

Working Man's College (London)
Maurice, John Frederick Denison **10** 349-350

Working Men's Association (political organization; Trinidad)
Williams, Henry Sylvester **16** 303-304

Working Men's Compensation Act (England; 1897)
Salisbury, 3d Marquess of **13** 448-449

Working Women's Council (Palestine)
Meir, Golda **10** 462-463

Workingmen's party (U.S. politics)
Brownson, Orestes Augustus **3** 57-58
Evans, George Henry **5** 337-338
Wright, Frances **16** 397-398

Workingmen's School (New York City)
Adler, Felix **1** 63-64

Workingmen's Trade and Labor Union (California)
Kearney, Denis **8** 468

Workmen's compensation (United States)
Jones, Samuel Milton **8** 342-343
Lewis, John Llewellyn **9** 387-388
Taft, William Howard **15** 78-81

Works and Days (poem; Hesiod)
Hesiod **7** 361-362
Virgil **15** 507-510

Works Progress Administration (WPA)
Bellow, Saul **2** 141-143
Hopkins, Harry Lloyd **7** 494-495
Roosevelt, Eleanor **13** 275-277
Wood, Grant **16** 368-369
Woodward, Ellen S. **16** 379-381
Wright, Richard **16** 401-402
see also Federal Arts Project

World (philosophy)
Fichte, Johann Gottlieb **5** 435-436
Schopenhauer, Arthur **14** 29-31

World Alliance of Reformed Churches
Boesak, Allan Aubrey **2** 359-360

World Antislavery Convention (London, 1840)
Remond, Charles Lennox **13** 95

World Bank (International Bank for Reconstruction & Development)
Conable, Barber B. Jr. **4** 191-192
Herrera, Juan de **7** 335
Keynes, John Maynard **8** 528-530
McNamara, Robert S. **10** 429-431
Pearson, Lester Bowles **12** 174-175

World Commission on Ecology and Development
Brundtland, Gro Harlem **3** 68-69

World Council of Churches
Bennett, John Coleman **2** 170-171
John, XXIII **8** 277-280
Johnson, Charles Spurgeon **8** 296-297
Mondlane, Eduardo Chivambo **11** 100-101
Mott, John R. **11** 212
Niebuhr, Helmut Richard **11** 386-387
Niwano, Nikkyo **11** 400-401
Paul VI **12** 146-148
Ramsey, Arthur Michael **13** 23-25
Temple, William **15** 141-143

Visser't Hooft, Willem Adolf
15 511-512

World Court
see Permanent Court of International
Justice

World Depression
see Depression, Great

World Enough and Time (novel)
Warren, Robert Penn **16** 121-122

World Fellowship of Faiths
Younghusband, Francis Edward **16** 477

World Festival of Negro Arts
Diop, Cheikh Anta **5** 21-22

World Health Organization
Switzer, Mary E. **15** 55-56

World I Breathe, The (poems)
Thomas, Dylan Marlais **15** 188-190

World I Never Made, A (novel)
Farrell, James Thomas **5** 390-391

World in a Man-War, The (novel)
see White-Jacket (novel)

World Jewish Congress
Wise, Stephen Samuel **16** 344-345

**World Monetary and Economic Confer-
ence** (1933)
Bruce of Melbourne, 1st Viscount
3 61-62

World of Apu, The (film)
Ray, Satyajit **13** 60-61

World of Love, A (novel)
Bowen, Elizabeth **2** 462-463

World of Paul Slickey, The (play)
Osborne, John **12** 16-17

World Population Conference (Geneva,
Switzerland; 1927)
Sanger, Margaret Higgins **13** 467-468

World Series (baseball)
Aaron, Henry Louis (Hank) **1** 2-3
Ruth, George Herman Jr. **13** 384

World Spirit (philosophy)
Lassalle, Ferdinand **9** 216

World, The (poem)
Vaughan, Henry **15** 444-445

World Tomorrow (magazine)
Thomas, Norman Mattoon **15** 191-192

World War I (1914-1918)
• ALLIES
Australia
Fisher, Andrew **5** 462
Hughes, William Morris **8** 21-22
Mannix, Daniel **10** 210
Monash, John **11** 95-96
Belgium
Albert I **1** 112
Pirenne, Jean Henri Otto Lucien
Marie **12** 322-323
Spaak, Paul Henri **14** 359-360
Canada
Borden, Robert Laird **2** 409-411

Crerar, Thomas Alexander **4** 306
Currie, Arthur William **4** 345
China
Yüan Shih-k'ai **16** 480-481
Cuba
Menocal, Mario Garcia
10 506-507
England (army)
Alexander of Tunis, 1st Earl
1 135-136
Allenby, Edmund Henry Hyn-
man **1** 171-172
Haig, Douglas **7** 67-68
Lawrence, Thomas Edward
9 253-254
England (industrialists)
Sopwith, Thomas Octave Mur-
doch **14** 345-346
England (navy)
Churchill, Winston Leonard
Spencer **4** 51-53
Jellicoe, John Rushworth
8 242-243
England (politics)
Asquith, Herbert Henry
1 344-346
Curzon, George Nathaniel
4 351-352
George V **6** 273-275
Jones, Ernest Alfred **8** 331-332
Kitchener, Horatio Herbert
9 45-46
Lloyd George, David **9** 469-471
MacDonald, James Ramsay
10 84-85
Milner, Alfred **11** 38-39
Rutherford, Ernest **13** 384-387
Finland
Mannerheim, Carl Gustav Emil
Von **10** 207-208
France
Curie, Marie Sklodowska
4 339-341
Diagne, Blaise **4** 527
Foch, Ferdinand **5** 498-499
Joffre, Joseph Jacques Césaire
8 267-268
Lyautey, Louis Hubert Gonzalve
10 60-61
Pétain, Henri Philippe
12 250-252
Poincaré, Raymond **12** 366-368
Roussel, Albert **13** 328-329
Greece
Venizelos, Eleutherios
15 460-461
Ireland
Pearse, Patrick Henry **12** 173-174
Italy
Badoglio, Pietro **1** 428-429
D'Annunzio, Gabriele **4** 388
Orlando, Vittorio Emmanuele
11 529-530
Victor Emmanuel III **15** 484-485
Netherlands
Wilhelmina **16** 278-279
New Zealand

Fraser, Peter **6** 73-74
Massey, William Ferguson **10** 324
Poland
Pilsudski, Joseph **12** 305-306
Romania
Ferdinand **5** 413-414
Russia
Ehrenburg, Ilya Grigorievich
5 224-225
Eisenstein, Sergei Mikhailovich
5 240-242
Kolchak, Aleksandr Vasilievich
9 77-78
Kornilov, Lavr Georgievich
9 87-88
Kropotkin, Peter Alekseevich
9 107-108
Lenin, Vladimir Ilich **9** 323-326
Miliukov, Pavel Nikolayevich
11 18-19
Nicholas II **11** 378-380
Zinoviev, Grigori Evseevich
16 521-522
South Africa
Botha, Louis **2** 434-436
Smuts, Jan Christian **14** 309-310
United States (army)
Clark, Mark Wayne **4** 80-81
Cowell, Henry Dixon **4** 280-281
Goddard, Robert Hutchings
6 376-377
Goethals, George Washington
6 387-388
Hayes, Patrick Joseph **7** 224-225
Hope, John **7** 489-490
Hubble, Edwin Powell **8** 10-11
Marshall, George Catlett
10 278-279
Patton, George Smith Jr.
12 140-141
Pershing, John Joseph **12** 243-244
Steichen, Edward **14** 411-412
United States (army air force)
Rickenbacker, Edward Vernon
13 152-153
United States (industry and finance)
Coolidge, John Calvin **4** 217-219
du Pont, Pierre Samuel **5** 154-155
Eastman, George **5** 186
McAdoo, William Gibbs
10 385-386
Morgan, John Pierpont II **11** 165
Morrow, Dwight Whitney
11 190-191
United States (labor)
Foster, William Zebulon **6** 27-28
Gompers, Samuel **6** 420-422
United States (medical corps)
Disney, Walter Elias **5** 26-27
Dos Passos, John Roderigo
5 69-71
Townsend, Francis Everitt
15 282-283
United States (navy)
Fuller, Richard Buckminster
6 149-150
Holland, John Philip **7** 453-454

Sims, William Sowden **14** 244
United States (neutrality)
Bryan, William Jennings **3** 80-82
Lansing, Robert **9** 200
Taft, William Howard **15** 78-81
Wood, Leonard **16** 369-370
United States (opponents)
Bourne, Randolph Silliman
2 456-457
Hillquit, Morris **7** 393-394
Holmes, John Haynes **7** 456-457
La Follette, Robert Marion
9 155-156
Rankin, Jeannette Pickering
13 35-37
Thomas, Norman Mattoon
15 191-192
Villard, Oswald Garrison
15 498-499
Wald, Lillian **16** 53-54
Watson, Thomas Edward **16** 139
United States (politics)
Baker, Newton Diehl **1** 451
Baruch, Bernard Mannes
2 42-43
Creel, George **4** 304-305
House, Edward Mandell
7 520-521
Wilson, Thomas Woodrow
16 330-332
see also Lusitania, sinking of
(1915)
United States (science)
Northrop, John Howard
11 430-431
Yerkes, Robert Mearns
16 454-455
United States (supporters)
Fosdick, Harry Emerson **6** 21-22
Hitchcock, Gilbert Monell
7 416-417
Page, Walter Hines **12** 60-61
Roosevelt, Franklin Delano
13 277-280
Roosevelt, Theodore **13** 280-283
Root, Elihu **13** 283-284
Shaw, Anna Howard **14** 162-163
• CENTRAL POWERS
Austria-Hungary
Berchtold, Leopold von
2 183-184
Francis Ferdinand **6** 44
Francis Joseph **6** 45-46
Horthy de Nagybánya, Nicholas
7 510-512
Renner, Karl **13** 98-99
Schumpeter, Joseph Alois
14 43-44
Tito, Marshal **15** 244-246
Germany (air force)
Göring, Hermann Wilhelm
6 457-458
Germany (army)
Haushofer, Karl **7** 201
Hindenburg, Paul Ludwig Hans
von Beneckendorff und von
7 400-401

Hitler, Adolf **7** 417-420
Jünger, Ernst **8** 391-392
Ludendorff, Erich Friedrich Wilhelm **10** 27-28
Rommel, Erwin **13** 268-269
Tillich, Paul Johannes
15 224-225
Germany (industry and research)
Fischer, Emil **5** 456-457
Kármán, Theodore von
8 451-452
Krupp **9** 109-111
Rathenau, Walther **13** 48-49
Germany (politics)
Bethmann Hollweg, Theobald
von **2** 239-240
Ebert, Friedrich **5** 193-194
Kapp, Wolfgang **8** 436
William II **16** 294-295
Germany (reparations)
Hoover, Herbert Clark
7 483-485
Hughes, Charles Evans **8** 15-16
MacDonald, James Ramsay
10 84-85
Stresemann, Gustav **14** 508-509
Young, Owen D. **16** 473-474
see also Dawes Plan (1924)
Ottoman Empire
Atatürk, Ghazi Mustapha Kemal
1 356-357
Enver Pasha **5** 290-291
Gökalp, Mehmet Ziya **6** 395-396
peace negotiations
see Versailles, Treaty of (1919;
and Paris Peace Conference)

World War II (1939-1945)
• ALLIES
Argentina
Justo, Agustin Pedro **8** 396
Australia and New Zealand
Chifley, Joseph Benedict **3** 518
Curtin, John Joseph **4** 348-349
Evatt, Herbert Vere **5** 341-343
Fraser, Peter **6** 73-74
Hughes, William Morris **8** 21-22
Lewis, Essington **9** 382-384
Mannix, Daniel **10** 210
Menzies, Robert Gordon
10 510-511
Belgium
Leopold III **9** 347-348
Spaak, Paul Henri **14** 359-360
Brazil
Aranha, Osvaldo **1** 272-273
Castelo Branco, Humberto
3 359-360
Vargas, Getulio Dornelles
15 433-434
Burma
Alexander of Tunis, 1st Earl
1 135-136
Aung San **1** 374-375
Ba Maw **1** 480-481
Nu, U **11** 439-441
Thant, U **15** 161-162

Canada
Crerar, Thomas Alexander **4** 306
King, William Lyon Mackenzie
9 25-26
McNaughton, Andrew
10 431-432
Woodsworth, James Shaver
16 376
China
Chiang Kai-shek **3** 510-513
Wang Ching-wei **16** 98
see also Sino-Japanese War
(1937-1945)
Czecholslovakia
Beneš, Edward **2** 155-157
Dubček, Alexander **5** 112-113
France
Blum, Léon **2** 343-344
Daladier, Édouard **4** 369
De Gaulle, Charles André Joseph
Marie **4** 463-465
Eboué, Adolphe Felix Sylvestre
5 194
Laval, Pierre **9** 237-238
Leclerc, Jacques Philippe
9 272-273
Monnet, Jean **11** 109-110
Pétain, Henri Philippe
12 250-252
see also France—1940-46
(Vichy); French Resistance
Great Britain (industry)
Sopwith, Thomas Octave Murdoch **14** 345-346
Great Britain (military)
Alexander of Tunis, 1st Earl
1 135-136
Glubb, John Bagot **6** 371-372
Montgomery, Bernard Law
11 135-136
Sutherland, Graham **15** 40-41
Wavell, Archibald Percival
16 147-148
Great Britain (politics)
Chamberlain, Arthur Neville
3 409-411
Churchill, Winston Leonard
Spencer **4** 51-53
Eden, Anthony **5** 204-205
Elizabeth II **5** 266-269
Halifax, 1st Earl of **7** 82-83
Macmillan, Harold **10** 112-113
Great Britain (science research)
Crick, Francis Harry Crompton
4 310
Snow, Charles Percy **14** 311-312
Thomson, George Paget
15 198-199
Greece
Xenakis, Iannis **16** 416-418
Indochina
Ho Chi Minh **7** 426-428
Mexico
Ávila Camacho, Manuel
1 387-388
Netherlands
Wilhelmina **16** 278-279

Norway
Lie, Trygve Halvdan **9** 400-401
Philippines
Aguinaldo, Emilio **1** 88
Magsaysay, Ramon **10** 130-131
Marcos, Ferdinand **10** 240-242
Quezon, Manuel Luis
12 511-513
Quirino, Elpidio **12** 519-520
Recto, Claro M. **13** 69-70
Rómulo, Carlos P. **13** 270-271
Roxas, Manuel **13** 331-332
Poland
Gomulka, Wladislaw **6** 422-424
Penderecki, Krzysztof **12** 195-197
Rhodesia
Smith, Ian Douglas **14** 291-293
Russia
Konev, Ivan Stefanovich **9** 81-82
Molotov, Vyacheslav
Mikhailovich **11** 89-90
Solzhenitsyn, Alexander
Isayevich **14** 330-332
Stalin, Joseph **14** 393-396
Zhukov, Georgi Konstantinovich
16 512-513
South Africa
Malan, Daniel Francois
10 163-164
Mandela, Nelson Rolihlahla
10 185-186
Smuts, Jan Christian **14** 309-310
Verwoerd, Hendrik Frensch
15 472-473
Vorster, Balthazar Johannes
16 30-32
Stettinius, Edward R. Jr.
14 437-438
United States (air force)
Doolittle, James Harold **5** 66-68
United States (army)
Abrams, Creighton W. **1** 29-31
Bradley, Omar Nelson
2 483-484
Clark, Mark Wayne **4** 80-81
Eisenhower, Dwight David
5 233-236
LeMay, Curtis E. **9** 316-318
MacArthur, Douglas **10** 76-78
Marshall, George Catlett
10 278-279
Patton, George Smith Jr.
12 140-141
Ridgway, Matthew Bunker
13 160-161
Taylor, Maxwell **15** 126-127
Wainwright, Jonathan Mayhew
16 45-46
Westmoreland, William Childs
16 216-217
United States (correspondents)
Pyle, Ernie **12** 493-494
United States (industry)
Bechtel, Stephen Davison
2 98-99
Ford, Henry **6** 5-6
Ford, Henry II **6** 6-7

Hillman, Sidney **7** 392-393
Kaiser, Henry John **8** 412-413
Knudsen, William S. **9** 67-68
Lilienthal, David Eli **9** 410-411
Lindbergh, Charles Augustus
9 421-423
Ludwig, Daniel Keith **10** 29-31
Sarnoff, David **13** 485-486
Trippe, Juan Terry **15** 297-298
United States (internment of Japan-
ese Americans)
Yasui, Minoru **16** 440-444
United States (Lend Lease)
Coughlin, Charles Edward
4 265-266
Morgenthau, Henry Jr.
11 172-173
United States (medicine and psy-
chology)
Bartlett, Frederic Charles **2** 34-35
Drew, Charles Richard
5 100-101
Florey, Howard Walter
5 491-492
Hovland, Carl I. **7** 527-528
United States (merchant marine)
Ellison, Ralph Waldo **5** 274-275
United States (navy)
Ford, John **6** 7-8
Forrestal, James Vincent **6** 14
Halsey, William Frederick
7 91-92
King, Ernest Joseph **9** 17-18
MacMillan, Donald Baxter
10 111-112
Nimitz, Chester William
11 395-396
Steichen, Edward **14** 411-412
United States (opponents)
Rankin, Jeannette Pickering
13 35-37
United States (photographers)
Capa, Robert **3** 269-271
United States (politics)
Hopkins, Harry Lloyd **7** 494-495
Ickes, Harold LeClaire **8** 100-101
Roosevelt, Franklin Delano
13 277-280
Truman, Harry S. **15** 314-316
Wallace, Henry Agard **16** 73-74
United States (public opinion)
Roosevelt, Eleanor **13** 275-277
Thomas, Norman Mattoon
15 191-192
see also Isolationism (United
States); Pacifism—U.S. (20th
century)
United States (reporters)
Mauldin, Bill **10** 345-346
United States (science research)
Elsasser, Walter Maurice
5 277-278
Kármán, Theodore von **8** 451-452
Land, Edwin Herbert **9** 183-184
Langmuir, Irving **9** 196-197
Libby, Willard Frank **9** 397-398
Rabi, Isidor Isaac **12** 526-527

see also Atomic bomb
Yugoslavia
Djilas, Milovan **5** 34
Tito, Marshal **15** 244-246
see also Normandy—invasion of
(1944)

• AXIS
Germany
Barbie, Klaus **1** 501-503
Brunner, Alois **3** 73-74
Eichmann, Adolf **5** 226-227
Goebbels, Joseph Paul
6 384-385
Göring, Hermann Wilhelm
6 457-458
Hess, Walter Richard Rudolf
7 363-365
Hitler, Adolf **7** 417-420
Kesselring, Albert Field Marshal
8 522-523
Krupp **9** 109-111
Mengele, Josef **10** 502-503
Rommel, Erwin **13** 268-269
Rundstedt, Karl Rudolf Gerd Von
13 363-364
von Braun, Wernher **16** 17-18
von Papen, Franz **16** 28-29
Hungary
Horthy de Nagybánya, Nicholas
7 510-512
Kádár, János **8** 402-403
Szent-Györgyi, Albert von
15 62-64
India
Bose, Subhas Chandra **2** 430-431
Italy
Badoglio, Pietro **1** 428-429
Giolitti, Giovanni **6** 339-340
Mussolini, Benito **11** 272-274
Orlando, Vittorio Emmanuele
11 529-530
Victor Emmanuel III **15** 484-485
Japan
Hirohito **7** 410-412
Kishi, Nobusuke **9** 41-43
Tojo, Hideki **15** 254-256
Yamamoto, Isoroku **16** 429-433
Yamashita, Tomoyuki **16** 435-436
Yoshida, Shigeru **16** 464-465
Romania
Ceausescu, Nicolae **3** 387-388
Thailand
Phibun Songkhram, Luang
12 264-265
Pridi Phanomyong **12** 449

• NEUTRALS
Iran
Mohammad Reza Shah Pahlavi
11 75-76
Reza Shah Pahlavi **13** 116-117
Ireland
De Valera, Eamon **4** 514-515
Portugal and Spain
Franco Bahamonde, Francisco
6 52-54

Salazar, António de Oliveira
13 442-443
Vatican City
John, XXIII **8** 277-280
Paul VI **12** 146-148
Pius XII **12** 339-340

World We Live In, The (revue)
Čapek, Karel **3** 271-272

World Zionist Organization
Faisal I **5** 370-371
Herzl, Theodor **7** 352-354
Jabotinsky, Vladimir Evgenevich
8 167-168
Meir, Golda **10** 462-463
Weizmann, Chaim **16** 183-184
Zangwill, Israel **16** 488-489
see also Zionism

World-Mind (philosophy)
Plotinus **12** 358-359

World's Columbian Exposition (Chicago,
1892-93)
anthropology exhibit
Boas, Franz **2** 349-351
Fletcher, Alice Cunningham
5 486-487
architecture
Burnham, Daniel Hudson
3 148-149
McKim, Charles Follen **10** 417-418
Olmsted, Frederick Law **11** 503-504
Sullivan, Louis Henri **15** 27-28
art
Carver, George Washington
3 346-347
French, Daniel Chester **6** 98-99
González, Julio **6** 428-429
Taft, Lorado **15** 75-76
electricity
Farmer, Moses Gerrish **5** 385
Tesla, Nikola **15** 156-157
Westinghouse, George **16** 215
entertainment
Paine, John Knowles **12** 65
Sousa, John Philip **14** 353-354
Ziegfeld, Florenz **16** 516-517
site and finances
Field, Marshall **5** 440-441
Medill, Joseph **10** 451-452

World's End (novel)
Sinclair, Upton Beale Jr. **14** 248-249

World's Fairs (international exposition)
Barcelona (1929)
Mies van der Rohe, Ludwig
11 10-12
Brussels (1958)
Motherwell, Robert **11** 210-211
Varèse, Edgard **15** 432-433
Xenakis, Iannis **16** 416-418
Chicago (1892-1893)
see World's Columbian Exposition
London (1851)
see Crystal Palace Exhibition
Montreal (Expo 67)
Calder, Alexander **3** 216-218

Fuller, Richard Buckminster
6 149-150
New York (1939-1940)
Aalto, Hugo Alvar Henrik **1** 1-2
Amorsolo, Fernando **1** 204
Gorky, Arshile **6** 458
Van de Velde, Henry **15** 419-420
New York (1964-1965)
Fuller, Richard Buckminster
6 149-150
Johnson, Philip **8** 313-314
Kelly, Ellsworth **8** 482-483
Paris (1855)
Courbet, Jean Desiré Gustave
4 271-273
Offenbach, Jacques **11** 478-479
Pissaro, Camille **12** 326-327
Paris (1867)
Manet, Édouard **10** 193-194
Offenbach, Jacques **11** 478-479
Paris (1889)
Daimler, Gottlieb **4** 368
Debussy, Achille Claude **4** 445-447
Eiffel, Alexandre Gustave **5** 227-228
Hassam, Frederick Childe **7** 192
Paris (1900)
Adams, Henry Brooks **1** 45-47
Hodler, Ferdinand **7** 434-435
Saarinen, Eliel and Eero **13** 396-398
Paris (1907)
Geddes, Patrick **6** 246-247
Paris (1937)
Lipchitz, Jacques **9** 432-433
Miró, Joan **11** 53-54
Van de Velde, Henry **15** 419-420
Philadelphia (1876)
see Philadelphia Centennial Exposi-
tion
St. Louis (1904)
Borglum, John Gutzon de la Mothe
2 416-417
Curtiss, Glenn Hammond
4 350-351
Geronimo **6** 281-282
Paine, John Knowles **12** 65
Tokyo (Expo 70)
Stockhausen, Karlheinz **14** 460-461

World's Student Christian Federation
(established 1895)
Mott, John R. **11** 212

World-Soul (philosophy)
Plotinus **12** 358-359

Worms, Concordat of (1122)
Bernard of Clairvaux **2** 207-208
Henry V **7** 295-296

Worms, Diet of (1521)
Charles V **3** 457-459
Luther, Martin **10** 48-51

WORNER, MANFRED (born 1934), West
German statesman **16** 389-390

Worship, freedom of
see Religious liberty

Worship of the Golden Calf (triptych)
Lucas van Leyden **10** 20-21

Worship of Venus (painting)
Titian **15** 242-244

Wotton, Sir Henry (1568-1639), English
poet and diplomat
Walton, Izaak **16** 90-91

Wouk, Herman (born 1915), American
novelist
Bogart, Humphrey **2** 363-364

Wound and the Bow, The (book)
Wilson, Edmund **16** 318-319

Wound-Dresser, The (poem)
Whitman, Walt **16** 249-251

Wounded Bunkie, The (sculpture)
Rembrandt Harmensz van Rijn
13 91-95

Wounded Cuirassier (painting)
Géricault, Jean Louis André Théodore
6 280-281

Wounded Drummer Boy (painting)
Johnson, Earvin Jr. **8** 297-299

Wounded Knee Massacre (1890)
Wovoka **16** 390-393

Wounds in the Rain (tales)
Crane, Stephen **4** 293-295

WOVOKA (a.k.a Jack Wilson; circa
1856-1932), Native American religious
leader and mystic **16** 390-393

Wozzeck (opera)
Berg, Alban **2** 186-187

Wozzeck (play; Büchner)
Wedekind, Frank **16** 166-167

WPA
see Works Progress Administration
(WPA)

**Wrangel, Count Friedrich Heinrich Ernst
von** (1784-1877), Prussian field marshal
Moltke, Helmuth Karl Bernard von
11 90-91

Wrangel, P. N. (1878-1928), Russian general
Frunze, Mikhail Vasilievich **6** 134

Wreck of the Deutschland, The (poem)
Hopkins, Gerard Manley **7** 492-494

Wreck of the Hesperus, The (poem)
Longfellow, Henry Wadsworth
9 499-500

WREN, SIR CHRISTOPHER (1632-1723),
English architect **16** 393-394
Adam, Robert and James **1** 38-40
Benjamin, Asher **2** 162-163
Donne, John **5** 60-61
Flamsteed, John **5** 477-478
Gibbs, James **6** 301-302
Harrison, Peter **7** 179-180
Hawksmoor, Nicholas **7** 211-212
Jones, Inigo **8** 333-334
Juvara, Filippo **8** 396-397
Pascal, Blaise **12** 122-124
Pepys, Samuel **12** 207-208
Soufflot, Jacques Germain **14** 349-350

WRIGHT, CARROLL DAVIDSON
(1840-1909), American statistician and
social economist **16** 396

WRIGHT, ELIZUR (1804-1885), American
reformer **16** 396-397

WRIGHT, FRANCES (1795-1852),
Scottish-American socialist, feminist, and
reformer **16** 397-398
Owen, Robert Dale **12** 40-41

WRIGHT, FRANK LLOYD (1869-1959),
American architect **16** 398-401
influence of
Gropius, Walter **7** 13-14
Jones, Fay **8** 332-333
Mies van der Rohe, Ludwig
11 10-12
Oud, Jacobus Johannes Pieter **12** 32
Rietveld, Gerrit Thomas **13** 169
influenced by
Davis, Alexander Jackson **4** 411
Downing, Andrew Jackson **5** 90-91
Sullivan, Louis Henri **15** 27-28, 286
Viollet-le-Duc, Eugène Emmanuel
15 505-506
works
Le Corbusier **9** 274-275
Neutra, Richard Joseph **11** 355-356

Wright, Orville
see Wright, Wilbur, and Orville

WRIGHT, RICHARD (1908-1960), African
American author **16** 401-402
Baldwin, James Arthur **1** 465-466
Cleaver, Leroy Eldridge **4** 97-98
Dunbar, Paul Laurence **5** 141-142
Ellison, Ralph Waldo **5** 274-275
Johnson, James Weldon **8** 304-305

Wright, Sir Almroth (1861-1947), English
physician
Fleming, Alexander **5** 483-485

WRIGHT, WILBUR (1867-1919), **AND
ORVILLE** (1871-1948), American aviation
pioneers **16** 394-396
Arnold, Henry Harley **1** 310-311
Curtiss, Glenn Hammond **4** 350-351
Langley, Samuel Pierpont **9** 195-196
Lindbergh, Charles Augustus **9** 421-423
Santos-Dumont, Alberto **13** 477-478

Wright-Fleming Institute (London)
Fleming, Alexander **5** 483-485

Wrong Side and the Right Side, The
(essays)
Camus, Albert **3** 255-257

Wu (Chinese philosophy)
Wang Pi **16** 104-105

Wu Chao
see Wu Tse-t'ien

Wu Chen (1280-1354), Chinese painter
Chao Meng-fu **3** 436-437
Tung Ch'i-ch'ang **15** 339-340

Wu, Emperor
see Liang Wu-ti

WU P'EI-FU (1874-1939), Chinese warlord
16 404-405
Feng Yü-hsiang **5** 412-413
K'ang Yu-wei **8** 426-428
Li Ta-chao **9** 447
Sun Yat-sen **15** 35-39

Wu San-kuei (died 1678), Chinese prince
K'ang-hsi **8** 423-426
Li Tzu-Ch'eng **9** 452

WU TAO-TZU (circa 689-after 758), Chi-
nese painter **16** 405-406
Mi Fei **11** 12-13
Wang Wei **16** 106-108

WU-TI (a.k.a. Han Wuti; 156 B.C.-circa 87
B.C.), Chinese emperor **16** 406-408

WU TSE-T'IEN (623-705), empress of
China **16** 408

WU WANG (died circa 1116 B.C.), first
ruler of the Chou dynasty of China
1122-1116 B.C. **16** 408-409
Chou Kung **4** 22-23

Wuchale, Treaty of (1889)
Menelik II **10** 495-497

Wuchang (city, China)
Chang Chih-tung **3** 430-431

Wuchang uprising (China; 1911)
Feng Yü-hsiang **5** 412-413
Yen Hsi-shan **16** 452-453
Yüan Shih-k'ai **16** 480-481

Wuhan (city, China)
Ch'en Tu-hsiu **3** 501-502
Chiang Kai-shek **3** 510-513
Chou En-lai **4** 20-22

Wulfstan (died 1023), English Archbishop
of York
Aelfric **1** 69-70

WUNDT, WILHELM MAX (1832-1920),
German psychologist and philosopher
16 402-403
Durkheim, Émile **5** 162-163
Hall, Granville Stanley **7** 85-86
Malinowski, Kaspar Bronislaw
10 170-171
Mead, George Herbert **10** 437-438
Titchener, Edward Bradford **15** 241-242
Watson, John Broadus **16** 138-139

WUORINEN, CHARLES (born 1938),
American composer, conductor, and
pianist **16** 404

Wurtz, Charles Adolphe (1817-1884),
French chemist
Couper, Archibald Scott **4** 269-270
Kekulé, Friedrich August **8** 477-478

Würzburg (city, Germany)
Hildebrandt, Johann Lucas von
7 380-381
Neumann, Balthasar **11** 354-355
Riemenschneider, Tilman **13** 166

Würzburg, University of (Germany)
Clausius, Rudolf Julius Emanuel
4 92-94
Neumann, Balthasar **11** 354-355

Röntgen, Wilhelm **13** 273-275
Schelling, Friedrich Wilhelm Joseph von
13 526-527
Virchow, Rudolf Ludwig Carl
15 506-507

Württemberg Sonatas (musical composition)
Bach, Carl Philipp Emanuel **1** 414-415

Wuthering Heights (novel; E. Brontë)
Brontë, Emily **3** 18-19
Goldwyn, Samuel **6** 416

WYANT, ALEXANDER HELWIG
(1836-1892), American painter
16 409-410
Inness, George **8** 123-124

Wyatt, James (1746-1813), English architect
Adam, Robert and James **1** 38-40

WYATT, SIR THOMAS (1503-1542), Eng-
lish poet and diplomat **16** 410-411
Elizabeth I **5** 263-266
Mary, I **10** 308-309

WYCHERLEY, WILLIAM (circa 1640-1716),
English dramatist **16** 411-412
Byrd, William II **3** 189-190
Congreve, William **4** 200-201
Pope, Alexander **12** 395-397

WYCLIF, JOHN (1330/32-84), English the-
ologian and reformer **16** 412-413
Hus, Jan **8** 56-59
John of Gaunt **8** 282-283
Knox, John **9** 65-66

WYETH, ANDREW NEWELL (born 1917),
American painter **16** 413-415

Wyeth, Newell Convers (1882-1945),
American illustrator and muralist
Wyeth, Andrew Newell **16** 413-415

Wyler, William (1902-1981), American film
director
Goldwyn, Samuel **6** 416
Ray, Satyajit **13** 60-61

Wyoming (state, United States)
Arnold, Thurman Wesley **1** 314
Calamity Jane **3** 216
Harrison, Benjamin **7** 178-179

Wyoming Valley Massacre (Pennsylvania;
1778)
Brant, Joseph **2** 500-501
Butler, John **3** 180

Wyse, Sir Thomas (1791-1862), British
politician
O'Connell, Daniel **11** 465-467

WYTHE, GEORGE (1726-1806), American
jurist **16** 415
Marshall, John **10** 279-281

X

X on the Forehead (book)
Reyes, Alfonso **13** 112-113

X-15 (rocket plane)
Armstrong, Neil Alden **1** 304-306
Kármán, Theodore von **8** 451-452

Xaguixaguana, victory of (1548)
Valdivia, Pedro de **15** 400-401

Xavier, St. Francis
see Francis Xavier, St.

Xavier University (New Orleans)
Drexel, Katherine **5** 102-103

XENAKIS, IANNIS (born 1922),
Greek-French composer and architect
16 416-418

Xenocrates (396-314 B.C.), Greek Platonic
philosopher
Aristotle **1** 295-296
Zeno of Citium **16** 499-500

Xenon (element—chemistry)
Mendeleev, Dmitrii Ivanovich
10 486-488
Ramsay, William **13** 21-22

Xenophanes (flourished 6th century B.C.),
Greek philosopher
Empedocles **5** 282

XENOPHON (circa 430-circa 355 B.C.),
Greek historian, essayist, and military
expert **16** 418-420
Socrates **14** 320-321

Xerography
Carlson, Chester F. **3** 303-304

Xerox Corporation (United States)
Wilson, Joseph Chamberlain
16 325-326

XERXES (ruled 486-465 B.C.), king of Persia
16 420
Aeschylus **1** 70-72
Darius I **4** 394-395
Leonidas I **9** 340-343
Themistocles **15** 170-171

XIANG JINGYU (born Xiang Qunxian;
1895-1928), Chinese feminist
16 421-422

Xochitl (ballet)
Graham, Martha **6** 485-486

X-rays (physics)
diffraction
Bragg, William Henry **2** 488-489
Crick, Francis Harry Crompton
4 310
Debye, Peter Joseph William
4 447-448
von Laue, Max **16** 23-24
discovered
Pupin, Michael Idvorsky **12** 483-484
Röntgen, Wilhelm **13** 273-275
Edison effect and
Edison, Thomas Alva **5** 206-208
medical use
Curie, Marie Sklodowska **4** 339-341
Hevesy, George Charles de **7** 371
Quimby, Edith H. **12** 513-514
mutations and
Muller, Hermann Joseph
11 238-239
scattering
Compton, Arthur Holly **4** 186-188

XU GUANGQI (a.k.a. Kuang-ch'i Hsü;
1562-1633), Chinese politician
16 422-425

Xylography (wood-block engraving)
Gutenberg, Johann **7** 48-49

XYZ Affair (1797-1798)
Gerry, Elbridge **6** 282-283
Jefferson, Thomas **8** 238-241
Madison, James **10** 121-123
Marshall, John **10** 279-281
Pickering, Timothy **12** 298-299
Pinckney, Charles Cotesworth **12** 310
Talleyrand, Charles Maurice de
15 89-90

Y

Yabuki, Sugataro
see Katayama, Sen

Yachtsmen
Turner, Ted **15** 355-357

Yagbea Sion (ruled 1283/85-94), Ethiopian king
Yekuno Amlak **16** 449

Yage, Letters, The (book)
Ginsberg, Allen **6** 332-333

Yahya ibn Umar (died 1056), Almoravid military leader
Abdullah ibn Yasin **1** 20

Yahya the Barmakid (Yahya ibn Khalid; flourished 8th-9th century), Abbasid vizier
Harun al-Rashid **7** 188

Yak-18 (aircraft)
Gagarin, Yuri Alexeivich **6** 166-167

Yakima War (1858-1859)
De Smet, Pierre Jean **4** 509-510

Yakolev, Aleksandr
see Herzen, Aleksandr Ivanovich

YAKUB AL-MANSUR, ABU YUSUF (reigned 1184-99), Almohad caliph in Spain **16** 426

Yale University (New Haven, Connecticut)
administration
Angell, James Rowland **1** 236-237
Brewster, Kingman Jr. **2** 522-523
Dwight, Timothy **5** 169
Gray, Hannah Holborn **6** 507-508
Hutchins, Robert Maynard **8** 68-69
architecture
Saarinen, Eliel and Eero **13** 396-398
chaplains
Coffin, William Sloane Jr. **4** 135-137
law
Arnold, Thurman Wesley **1** 314
Douglas, William Orville **5** 83-85
Taft, William Howard **15** 78-81
literature
Ellison, Ralph Waldo **5** 274-275
Warren, Robert Penn **16** 121-122

music
Hindemith, Paul **7** 399-400
Parker, Horatio William **12** 109
Schuller, Gunther **14** 37-38
science
Boltwood, Bertram Borden **2** 378-379
Bowman, Isaiah **2** 464-465
Cushing, Harvey Williams **4** 353-354
Erikson, Erik Homburger **5** 309-310
Gibbs, Josiah Willard **6** 302-303
Lawrence, Ernest Orlando **9** 248-250
Oort, Jan Hendrik **11** 523-524
Silliman, Benjamin **14** 229-230
Theiler, Max **15** 169-170
social science
Andrews, Charles McLean **1** 231
Bloomfield, Leonard **2** 338
Gilman, Daniel Coit **6** 325-326
Harper, William Rainey **7** 163-164
Hovland, Carl I. **7** 527-528
Hull, Clark Leonard **8** 28
Johnson, Samuel **8** 314-315
Kroeber, Alfred Louis **9** 105-106
Linton, Ralph **9** 431
Malinowski, Kaspar Bronislaw **10** 170-171
Malone, Dumas **10** 174-175
Marsh, Othniel Charles **10** 275-276
Potter, David M. **12** 412
Rostovtzeff, Michael Ivanovich **13** 315
Sumner, William Graham **15** 32
Woodward, Comer Vann **16** 378-379
Yerkes, Robert Mearns **16** 454-455
theology
Edwards, Jonathan **5** 220-222
Niebuhr, Helmut Richard **11** 386-387

YALOW, ROSALYN S. (Sussman; born 1921), American physicist who developed radioimmunoassay **16** 427-428

Yalta Conference (1945)
Byrnes, James Francis **3** 191-192

Churchill, Winston Leonard Spencer **4** 51-53
Harriman, W. Averell **7** 165-166
Marshall, George Catlett **10** 278-279
Molotov, Vyacheslav Mikhailovich **11** 89-90
Roosevelt, Franklin Delano **13** 277-280
Stalin, Joseph **14** 393-396
Stettinius, Edward R. Jr. **14** 437-438

Yamabe
see Kammu

YAMAGATA, ARITOMO (1838-1922), Japanese general **16** 428-429
Hara, Kei **7** 138
Saionji, Kimmochi **13** 438-439

Yamama, battle of (633)
Abu Bakr **1** 31-32

Yamamoto, Baron Tatsuo (1856-1947), Japanese financier and politician
Inukai, Tsuyoshi **8** 130-131

YAMAMOTO, ISOROKU (born Takano Isoroku; 1884-1943), Japanese admiral **16** 429-433

Yamamoto, Count Gombei (1852-1933), Japanese admiral and statesman
Takahashi, Korekiyo **15** 84-85

YAMANI, AHMED ZAKI (born 1930), Saudi Arabian lawyer and minister of petroleum and mineral resources (1962-1986) **16** 433-435

YAMASHITA, TOMOYUKI (1885-1946), Japanese general **16** 435-436

Yamato-e school
see Japanese art—Yamato-e school

YANCEY, WILLIAM LOWNDES (1814-1863), American politician **16** 436-437

YANG, CHEN NING (born 1922), Chinese-born American physicist **16** 437-438

Yang Chien
see Sui Wen-ti

Yankee Doodle Dandy (film)
Cohan, George Michael **4** 137-138

Yankee Girl, The (poem)
Whittier, John Greenleaf **16** 256-257

Yankee in Canada, A (essays)
Thoreau, Henry David **15** 203-205

Yankee Prince, The (play)
Cohan, George Michael **4** 137-138

Yanko the Musician (story)
Sienkiewicz, Henryk **14** 216-217

YARD, MARY ALEXANDER ("Molly"; born
1912), American feminist, political organizer, and social activist **16** 438-439

Yarmuk, battle of (636)
Omar ibn al-Khattab **11** 508-509

Yaroslav
see Iaroslav

YASUI, MINORU (1917-1987), Asian
American attorney **16** 440-444

Yatsumimi no Miko
see Shotoku Taishi

Yavapi (Mohave-Apache) Indians (North
America)
Montezuma, Carlos **11** 129-132

Ydigoras Fuentes, Miguel (1895-1982),
Guatemalan statesman, president
1958-63
Arévalo, Juan José **1** 285-286

YEAGER, CHUCK (born 1923), American
pilot **16** 444-445

Year 1905, The (poem)
Pasternak, Boris Leonidovich
12 124-125

Year of Loneliness, A (novel)
Kazantzakis, Nikos **8** 466-468

Year of the Soul, The (poems)
George, Stefan **6** 277-278

Year That Trembled and Reel'd Beneath Me
(poem)
Whitman, Walt **16** 249-251

Year's Life, A (poem)
Lowell, James Russell **10** 14-15

Years, The (novel)
Woolf, Virginia Stephen **16** 381-382

Yeast (novel)
Kingsley, Charles **9** 28

Yeats, John Butler (1839-1922), Irish portrait painter
Yeats, William Butler **16** 445-447

YEATS, WILLIAM BUTLER (1865-1939),
Irish poet and dramatist **16** 445-447
Barber, Samuel **1** 500-501
Blake, William **2** 316-318
Colum, Padraic **4** 174-175
Gregory, Augusta **6** 535-536
John, Augustus Edwin **8** 291
O'Casey, Sean **11** 459-460
Pound, Ezra Loomis **12** 415-417
Roethke, Theodore **13** 243-244
Synge, Edmund John Millington
15 61-62
Rabindranath Tagore **12** 529-531

YEH-LÜ CH'U-TS'AI (1189-1243), Mongol
administrator **16** 447-449

Yekl (novel)
Cahan, Abraham **3** 214

YEKUNO AMLAK (ruled circa 1268-1283),
Ethiopian king **16** 449
Lalibela **9** 170

Yellow Christ (painting)
Gauguin, Paul **6** 236-238

Yellow Dog Blues (song)
Handy, William Christopher **7** 123-124

Yellow fever (medical)
conquest
Cruz, Oswaldo Gonçalves
4 328-329
Goethals, George Washington
6 387-388
Gorgas, William Crawford
6 454-455
Reed, Walter **13** 78
epidemics
Brown, Charles Brockden **3** 33
Girard, Stephen **6** 347-348
etiology
Finlay, Carlos Juan **5** 450
vaccine
Theiler, Max **15** 169-170

Yellow Hats (Buddhist sect)
Dalai Lama **4** 369-371

Yellow journalism (United States)
Dana, Charles Anderson **4** 384-385
Pulitzer, Joseph **12** 481-482

Yellow River (China)
K'ang-hsi **8** 423-426
Quin Shi Huang-Di **12** 515-518

Yellow Sweater (painting)
Modigliani, Amedeo **11** 72-73

Yellow Turbans (Taoist sect)
Chang Chüeh **3** 432-433
Ts'ao Ts'ao **15** 322-323

Yellow Violet, The (poem)
Bryant, William Cullen **3** 83-85

YELTSIN, BORIS NIKOLAEVICH (born
1931), president of the Russian Republic
16 449-452
appointees
Kozyrev, Andrei Vladimirovich
9 92-93

Yemassee, The (novel)
Simms, William Gilmore **14** 235-236

Yemen, United Republic of
Salih, 'Ali' Abdallah **13** 443-445

Yemeni Arab Republic (North Yemen)
Salih, 'Ali' Abdallah **13** 443-445

YEN FU (1853-1921), Chinese translator
and scholar **16** 452

YEN HSI-SHAN (1883-1960), Chinese warlord **16** 452-453
Feng Yü-hsiang **5** 412-413

YEN LI-PEN (died 673), Chinese painter
16 453-454

Wu Tao-tzu **16** 405-406

Yen Li-te (died circa 656), Chinese painter
Yen Li-pen **16** 453-454

Yen Wu (died 765), Chinese statesman
Tu Fu **15** 335-336

Yenan (city, China)
Chou En-lai **4** 20-22
Chu Teh **4** 54-55

Yen-ching (modern Peking)
Kublai Khan **9** 115-118-272

Yeoman of the Guard, The (operetta)
Gilbert, William Schwenck **6** 314-315
Sullivan, Arthur Seymour **15** 23

Yeomen of the Guard (painting)
Millais, John Everett **11** 23-24

Yerkes, Charles T. (1837-1905), American
capitalist
Dreiser, Herman Theodore **5** 98-100

Yerkes Observatory (Williams Bay, Wisconsin)
Hale, George Ellery **7** 72-74

YERKES, ROBERT MEARNS (1876-1956),
American psychologist **16** 454-455

Yerma (play)
Lorca, Federico García **9** 511-513

Yes, Speak Out, Yes (cantata)
Halffter, Christóbal **7** 79-80

Yesenin, Sergei (1895-1925), Russian poet
Duncan, Isadora **5** 144-145

Yeshayhu
see Isaiah

Yeshiva University (New York City)
Jung, Leo **8** 390-391
Revel, Bernard **13** 108-109
Soloveitchik, Joseph Baer **14** 328-329

Yesilkoy (Turkey)
see San Stefano

Yes-sayer, The (opera)
Weill, Kurt **16** 174-175

Yesterday (play)
Hofmannsthal, Hugo von **7** 443-444

Yesteryear (book)
Agnon, Shmuel Yoseph **1** 85-86

**YEVTUSHENKO, YEVGENY ALEXAN-
DROVICH** (born 1933), Russian poet
16 455-456
Shostakovich, Dmitri Dmitrievich
14 204-205

Yezhov, Nikolai Ivanovich (1895-1989),
Russian politician
Beria, Lavrenty Pavlovich **2** 192-193

Yi Dynasty
see Korea—1392-1910

Yi Ha-ǔng
see Taewon'gun, Hǔngson

Yi Hongwi
see Tanjong

YI HWANG (1501-1570), Korean philosopher, poet, scholar, and educator **16** 457

Yi Hyang
see Munjong

Yi Kong
see Sonjo

Yi Küm
see Yongjo

YI SNG-GYE (1335-1408), Korean military leader, founder of the Yi dynasty **16** 458-459

Yi Song
see Chonjo

Yi Song-gye
see Yi Sng-gye

Yi Sung-man
see Rhee, Syngman

YI SUNSIN (1545-1598), Korean military strategist and naval hero **16** 459-461

Yi T'aewang
see Kojong

Yi To
see Sejong

Yi Yu
see Sejo

Yiddish literature
Aleichem, Sholom **1** 124-125
Asch, Shalom **1** 325-326
Cahan, Abraham **3** 214
Peretz, Isaac Loeb **12** 212
Sholem Aleichem **14** 202-203
Singer, Isaac Bashevis **14** 249-250
see also Jewish literature

Ying-tsung (ruled 1064-67), Chinese emperor
Ou-yang Hsiu **12** 33-34
Ssu-ma kuang **14** 390-391

Yin-jeng (1674-1725), Chinese heir apparent
K'ang-hsi **8** 423-426

Yip, Yip Yaphank (music)
Berlin, Irving **2** 200-201

YMCA
see Young Men's Christian Association

YO FEI (Yo P'eng-chü; 1103-41), Chinese general **16** 462

Yoga (Hindu philosophy)
Buddha **3** 97-101
Ghose, Aurobindo **6** 293-294
Kukai **9** 124-125
Maharishi Mahesh Yogi **10** 132-133
Radhakrishnan, Sarvepalli **12** 537-538
Mahavira, Vardhamana **10** 135-137
Yogananda **16** 462-463

YOGANANDA (Mukunda Lal Ghose; 1893-1952), Indian yogi **16** 462-463

Yojimbo (film)
Kurosawa, Akira **9** 135-137

Yoke of Life, The (novel)
Grove, Frederick Philip **7** 20-21

Yoknapatawpha sage (literary character)
Faulkner, William **5** 395-397, 73

YÔNGJO (1694-1776), king of Korea 1724-76 **16** 461-462
Chongjo **4** 15-16

Yoreh Deah (Jewish law)
see Shulhan Aruk

Yorick, Parson (literary character)
Sterne, Laurence **14** 435-437

YORITOMO, MINAMOTO (1147-1199), Japanese warrior chieftain **16** 463-464
Ashikaga Takauji **1** 330-332
Daigo II **4** 367-368
Fujiwara Michinaga **6** 145-146
Goshirakawa **6** 460-461

York, Edward, Duke of
see Edward IV

York, 1st Duke of (Edmund of Langley; 1341-1402), son of Edward III, three times regent of England
Richard II **13** 130-131

York, House of
see England—1461-85 (Yorkist)

York, Richard Plantagenet, 3d Duke of (1411-1460), English statesman
Henry VI **7** 298-299
Richard III **13** 132-133
Warwick and of Salisbury, Earl of **16** 122-123

York, Richard Plantagenet, Duke of (1472-1483), son of Edward IV of England
Henry VII **7** 300-302
Richard III **13** 132-133

Yorktown, battle of (1781)
American forces
Greene, Nathanael **6** 525-526
Hamilton, Alexander **7** 95-98
Knox, Henry **9** 64
Lafayette, Marquis de **9** 151-152
Lincoln, Benjamin **9** 418-419
Rochambeau, Comte de **13** 220-221
British forces
Clinton, Henry **4** 114-115
Cornwallis, Charles **4** 241-243
North, Frederick **11** 429-430
Tarleton, Banastre **15** 110
negotiations
Franklin, Benjamin **6** 60-64

Yorubaland (former kingdom, now in Nigeria)
Awolowo, Obafemi **1** 389-390
Burton, Richard **3** 163-164
Crowther, Samuel Adjai **4** 326
Macaulay, Herbert **10** 78-79
Tutuola, Amos **15** 361-362
Uthman don Fodio **15** 397-398

YOSHIDA, SHIGERU (1878-1967), Japanese diplomat and prime minister **16** 464-465
Hirohito **7** 410-412
Kishi, Nobusuke **9** 41-43
Sato, Eisaku **13** 495-496

Yoshihito (1879-1926), emperor of Japan 1912-26
Hirohito **7** 410-412

Yoshimichi Mao
see Kukai

Yoshimitsu, Ashikaga
see Ashikaga Yoshimitsu

YOSHIMUNE, TOKUGAWA (1684-1751), Japanese shogun **16** 465-466

Yoshino Kudzu (tone poem)
Tanizaki, Junichiro **15** 101-102

Yoshinobu (1837-1902), last Japanese shogun
Meighen, Arthur **10** 459-460

You ask me how many kises (poem)
Catullus, Gaius Valerius **3** 377-378

You Can't Cheat an Honest Man (film)
Fields, W. C. **5** 444

You Can't Go Home Again (novel)
Wolfe, Thomas Clayton **16** 355-356

You Can't Take It with You (play)
Capra, Frank **3** 276-278
Kaufman, George S. **8** 457-458

You Do Something to Me (song)
Porter, Cole Albert **12** 405-406

You Have Seen Their Faces (book)
Bourke-White, Margaret **2** 455-456
Caldwell, Erskine **3** 223-224

You Know Me, Al (book and comic strip)
Lardner, Ringgold Wilmer **9** 204-205

You Never Can Tell (play)
Shaw, George Bernard **14** 163-164

You Touched Me! (play)
Williams, Tennessee **16** 306-308

You Were Never Lovelier (music)
Kern, Jerome David **8** 517-518

You'll Never Walk Alone (song)
Rodgers, Richard Charles **13** 234-236

YOULOU, FULBERT (1917-1972), Congolese president **16** 466-467

Youma (novel)
Hearn, Lafcadio **7** 240

YOUNG, ANDREW JACKSON JR. (born 1932), African American preacher, civil rights activist, and politician **16** 467-469

YOUNG, BRIGHAM (1801-1877), American Mormon leader and colonizer **16** 469-470
Buchanan, James **3** 89-90
Washakie **16** 123-125

Young, Cecilia (1711-1789), English concert singer
Arne, Thomas Augustine **1** 307-308

YOUNG, COLEMAN ALEXANDER (1918-1997), first African American mayor of Detroit **16** 470-471

Young, Ewing (died 1841), American trapper and guide
Carson, Christopher **3** 334-335

YOUNG, LESTER WILLIS ("Prez";1909-59), American jazz musician **16** 471-473

YOUNG, OWEN D. (1874-1962), American industrialist and monetary authority **16** 473-474
   Sarnoff, David **13** 485-486
   Tarbell, Ida Minerva **15** 107-108

YOUNG, STARK (1881-1963), drama critic, editor, translator, painter, playwright, and novelist **16** 474-475

YOUNG, THOMAS (1773-1829), English physicist **16** 475-476
   Coulomb, Charles Augustin de **4** 266-267
   Fresnel, Augustin Jean **6** 102-103

YOUNG, WHITNEY MOORE, JR. (1921-1971), African American civil rights leader and social work administrator **16** 476-477

Young Americans for Freedom (political organization, United States)
   Buckley, William F. Jr. **3** 96-97

Young and the Old, The (novel)
   Pirandello, Luigi **12** 319-321

Young Cassidy (film)
   Ford, John **6** 7-8

Young Cosima, The (novel)
   Richardson, Henry Handel **13** 139

Young Duke, The (book)
   Disraeli, Benjamin **5** 27-29

Young Explorer, The (book)
   Alger, Horatio **1** 153-154

Young Fate, The (poem)
   Valéry, Paul Ambroise **15** 405-406

Young Gentleman, A (painting)
   see Blue Boy (painting)

Young Germany (literary movement)
   Heine, Heinrich **7** 259-260

Young Girl Reading (painting)
   Renoir, Pierre Auguste **13** 101-102

Young Hegelians (philosophy)
   Engels, Friedrich **5** 286-288
   Marx, Karl **10** 304-308
   Schelling, Friedrich Wilhelm Joseph von **13** 526-527

Young Henry of Navarre (book)
   Mann, Heinrich **10** 201-202

Young Herdsmen with Cows (painting)
   Cuyp, Aelbert **4** 360-361

Young Immigrunts, The (book)
   Lardner, Ringgold Wilmer **9** 204-205

Young Italy (revolutionary organization)
   Garibaldi, Giuseppe **6** 215-217
   Mazzini, Giuseppe **10** 381-383

Young Kikuyu Association (Kenya)
   Kenyatta, Jomo **8** 512-514

Young Ladies by the Seine (painting)
   Courbet, Jean Desiré Gustave **4** 271-273

Young Lonigan (novel)
   Farrell, James Thomas **5** 390-391

Young Lords, The (opera)
   Henze, Hans Werner **7** 314

Young Man (painting)
   Giorgione **6** 340-341

Young Manhood of Studs Lonigan, The (novel)
   Farrell, James Thomas **5** 390-391

Young Maori party (New Zealand)
   Ngata, Apirana Turupa **11** 374-375

Young Mapai (political party, Israel)
   Dayan, Moshe **4** 429-431

Young Master (novel)
   Natsume, Soseki **11** 324-325

Young Men's Christian Association (YMCA; established 1844)
   Comstock, Anthony **4** 188-189
   Drew, Charles Richard **5** 100-101
   Dunant, Jean Henri **5** 139-141
   Eastman, Charles A. **5** 183-185
   Moody, Dwight L. **11** 141-142
   Mott, John R. **11** 212
   Rosenwald, Julius **13** 293

Young Men's Christian Association for Negroes
   Still, William **14** 454-455

Young Miner, The (book)
   Alger, Horatio **1** 153-154

Young Plan (1929-1930)
   Schacht, Hjalmar Horace Greeley **13** 518-519
   Stresemann, Gustav **14** 508-509
   Young, Owen D. **16** 473-474

Young Pretender
   see Stuart, Prince Charles Edward

Young Sabot-maker, The (painting)
   Tanner, Henry Ossawa **15** 102-103

Young Töless (novel)
   Musil, Robert Edler Von **11** 268-269

Young Turk Revolution (1908)
   Abdul-Hamid II **1** 17-18
   Abdullah ibn Husein **1** 19-20
   Enver Pasha **5** 290-291
   Faisal I **5** 370-371
   Gökalp, Mehmet Ziya **6** 395-396
   Horthy de Nagybánya, Nicholas **7** 510-512

Young West (novel)
   Schindler, Solomon **14** 7-8

Young Woman with Rose Scarf (painting)
   Corot, Jean Baptiste Camille **4** 247-249

Young Women's Christian Association (YWCA)
   Rosenwald, Julius **13** 293

Younger, Cole (1844-1916), American desperado
   James, Jesse Woodson **8** 212-213

YOUNGHUSBAND, SIR FRANCIS EDWARD (1863-1942), English soldier and explorer **16** 477
   Dalai Lama **4** 369-371

Youngstown Sheet and Tube Company et al. v. Sawyer (legal case)
   Black, Hugo Lafayette **2** 301-303

Your Five Gallants (play)
   Middleton, Thomas **11** 8-9

Your Humble Servant (play)
   Tarkington, Newton Booth **15** 109

YOURCENAR, MARGUERITE (Marguerite Antoinette Ghislaine; 1903-87), French novelist, poet, essayist, dramatist, world traveller, and translator **16** 477-479

You're a Grand Old Flag (song)
   Cohan, George Michael **4** 137-138

You're the Top (song)
   Porter, Cole Albert **12** 405-406

Youth (sculpture)
   Zorach, William **16** 528

Youth among Roses (painting)
   Hilliard, Nicholas **7** 391-392

Youth International Party (United States)
   Hoffman, Abbie **7** 437-439
   Rubin, Jerry **13** 344-346

Youth March for Integrated Schools (1957, 1958)
   Randolph, A. Philip **13** 28-29

Ypres (city, Belgium)
   Currie, Arthur William **4** 345
   Edward III **5** 211-212

Ysaye, Eugène (1858-1931), Belgian violinist
   Bloch, Ernest **2** 326-327

Yucatán (peninsula, Mexico)
   Cortés, Hernán **4** 255-256
   Kidder, Alfred Vincent **8** 541-542
   Velázquez de Cuéllar, Diego **15** 459

Yugoslavia, Federal Republic of (formed 1992)
   Bulatovic, Momir **3** 115-116
   Owen, David Anthony Llewellyn **12** 37-39

Yugoslavia, Socialist Federal Republic of (former nation, South Eastern Europe)
   as unified state
      Alexander of Yugoslavia **1** 136-137
      Djilas, Milovan **5** 34
      Horthy de Nagybánya, Nicholas **7** 510-512
      Peter I **12** 256
      Tito, Marshal **15** 244-246
   break-up of
      Gligorov, Kiro **6** 367-369
      Izetbegovic, Alija **8** 161-163
      Karadzic, Radovan **8** 437-440
      Milosevic, Slobodan **11** 39-40
      Mladic, Ratko **11** 68-69
      Tudjman, Franjo **15** 333-335

YUKAWA, HIDEKI (1907-1981), Japanese physicist **16** 481-482
   Anderson, Carl David **1** 214-215

Yuma Indians (North America)
   Anza, Juan Bautista de **1** 254-255

Yun Po-son (1897-1990), South Korean
statesman
    Park, Chung Hee **12** 99-102

YUN SONDO (1587-1671), Korean sijo
poet **16** 483

Yung-chêng (1678-1735), Chinese emperor
1723-35
    Qianlong **12** 502-505

YUNG-LO (1360-1424), Chinese emperor
16 482-483
    Cheng Ho **3** 500

Yusuf, Abu Yaqub (died 1184), Almohad
sultan in Morocco 1163-84
    ibn Tufayl, Abu Bakr Muhammad **8** 96

Yusuf and Zulaikha (story)
    Jami **8** 218-219

Yüan (ruled 48-33 B.C.), Chinese emperor
    Wang Mang **16** 101-103

YÜAN, MA (flourished circa 1190-circa
1229), Chinese painter **10** 379
    Sesshu, Toya **14** 116-117

Tung Ch'i-ch'ang **15** 339-340

Yüan Chên (779-831), Chinese poet
    Po Chü-i **12** 362-363

Yüan Ch'eng-tsung (died 1307), Mongol
emperor 1294-1307
    Kublai Khan **9** 115-118

Yüan dynasty (China; ruled 1279-1369)
    Chao Meng-fu **3** 436-437
    Chu Hsi **4** 40-43
    Kublai Khan **9** 115-118
    Ni Tsan **11** 400
    Wen T'ien-hsiang **16** 203

YÜAN MEI (1716-1798), Chinese author
16 479-480

YÜAN SHIH-K'AI (1859-1916), Chinese
military leader **16** 480-481
    associates
        Chang Chien **3** 429-430
        Sun Yat-sen **15** 35-39
        Wang Ching-wei **16** 98
        Wu P'ei-fu **16** 404-405
        Yen Fu **16** 452

Yen Hsi-shan **16** 452-453
    opponents
        Ch'en Tu-hsiu **3** 501-502
        Li Ta-chao **9** 447
        Liang Ch'i-ch'ao **9** 395-396
        Sun Yat-sen **15** 35-39

Yü-chou (universe)
    Lu Chiu-yuan **10** 24-25

Yüeh ching (book)
    Confucius **4** 197-200

Yü-wen Yung (died 578), Chinese emperor
of the Northern Chou
    Sui Wen-ti **15** 16-18

Yü-yü
    see Hsia Kuei

Yvain (romance)
    Chrestien de Troyes **4** 23-24

YWCA
    see Young Women's Christian Association

Z

Zabriskie Point (film)
  Antonioni, Michelangelo **1** 252-253

Zacatecas, battle of (1914)
  Huerta, Victoriano **8** 13-14
  Villa, Pancho **15** 495-496

Zaccharias Driven from the Temple (sculpture)
  Quercia, Jacopo della **12** 509

Zachau, Friedrich (Frederick Zachow; 1663-1712), German Protestant church musician and composer
  Bach, Johann Sebastian **1** 416-419
  Handel, George Frederick **7** 116-119

Zadig (story)
  Voltaire **16** 14-16

ZADKINE, OSSIP JOSELYN (1890-1967), Russian sculptor **16** 484
  Noland, Kenneth **11** 418-419

Zadok (Hebrew priestly family)
  Ezekiel **5** 355-356
  Ezra **5** 356-357

ZAGHLUL PASHA, SAAD (1859-1927), Egyptian political leader **16** 485-486
  Fuad I **6** 139

Zagreb treason trial (1908)
  Masaryk, Tomáš Garrigue **10** 314-315

Zagwe dynasty (Ethiopia)
  Lalibela **9** 170
  Yekuno Amlak **16** 449

ZAH, PETERSON (born 1937), Native American leader and activist **16** 486-487

ZAHARIAS, MILDRED DIDRIKSON ("Babe"; 1913-56), Olympic athlete and golfer **16** 487-488

Zaïde (novel)
  La Fayette, Comtesse de **9** 150-151

Zaide (opera)
  Mozart, Wolfgang Amadeus **11** 218-221

Zaïre (play)
  Voltaire **16** 14-16

Zaïre, Republic of
  see Congo, Democratic Republic of the

Zakhar-Kalita (story)
  Solzhenitsyn, Alexander Isayevich **14** 330-332

Zalacain the Adventurer (novel)
  Baroja y Nessi, Pío **2** 15-16

Zaldívar, Fulgencio Batista y
  see Batista y Zaldívar, Fulgencio

Zaleski, August (1883-1972), Polish statesman
  Pilsudski, Joseph **12** 305-306

Zallaqa, al-, battle of (1086)
  ibn Tashufin, Yusuf **8** 95-96

Zama, battle of (202 B.C.)
  Hannibal Barca **7** 128-130
  Scipio Africanus Major, Publius Cornelius **14** 61-62

Zambezi River (Africa)
  Livingstone, David **9** 463-465

Zambia, Republic of (nation, Central Africa)
  Kaunda, Kenneth David **8** 460-461
  Rhodes, Cecil John **13** 120-122
  Smith, Ian Douglas **14** 291-293
  see also Rhodesia

Zamora (city, Spain)
  Cid **4** 58-59

Zamora, treaty of (1143)
  Alfonso I **1** 148

Zamora y Torres, Niceto Alcalá (1877-1949), Spanish statesman, president 1931-36
  Azaña Diaz, Manuel **1** 396-397

Zampieri, Domencio
  see Domenichino, Il

Zand dynasty (Persia; reigned 1750-94)
  Agha Mohammad Khan **1** 80-81
  Karim Khan Zand **8** 447

ZANGWILL, ISRAEL (1864-1926), Jewish author and philosopher **16** 488-489

Zanjón, Peace of (1878)
  Gómez, Máximo **6** 418-419

Maceo, Antonio **10** 88-90
  Martí, José **10** 285-286

Zanzibar
  see Tanzania

ZAPATA, EMILIANO (circa 1879-1919), Mexican agrarian leader and guerrilla fighter **16** 489-490
  Carranza, Venustiano **3** 321-322
  Huerta, Victoriano **8** 13-14
  Madero, Francisco Indalecio **10** 118-119
  Villa, Pancho **15** 495-496

Zapatera prodigiosa, La (play)
  Lorca, Federico García **9** 511-513

Zápolya, John (1487-1540), Hungarian King 1526-40
  Suleiman I **15** 20-21

Zápotocký, Antonin (1884-1957), Czechoslovak statesman
  Beneš, Edward **2** 155-157

Zaque of Tunja (died 1537); Chibcha Indian chieftain
  Quesada, Gonzalo Jiménez de **12** 509-510

Zarathustra (literary character)
  Nietzsche, Friedrich **11** 390-392

Zarathustra (prophet)
  see Zoroaster

Zarb-i-Kalim (poem)
  Iqbal, Muhammad **8** 132-133

ZARLINO, GIOSEFFO (1517-1590), Italian music theorist and composer **16** 490-491
  Sweelinck, Jan Pieterszoon **15** 50-51
  Willaert, Adrian **16** 287-288

Zasulich, Vera Ivanovna (1851-1919), Russian revolutionist
  Trotsky, Leon **15** 302-305

Zauberberg, Der (novel)
  Mann, Thomas **10** 204-207

Zauberflöte, Die (opera)
  Mozart, Wolfgang Amadeus **11** 218-221
  Schinkel, Karl Friedrich **14** 8

939

Zawditu (reigned 1916-30), Ethiopian empress
Haile Selassie **7** 68-70

Zayas y Alfonso, Alfredo (1861-1934), Cuban president 1921-25
Menocal, Mario Garcia **10** 506-507

ZAYID BIN SULTAN AL-NAHYAN (born 1923), president of the United Arab Emirates (1971-) **16** 491-492

Zbynek Zajic (died 1411), archbishop of Prague (1403-1411)
Hus, Jan **8** 56-59

ZEAMI, KANZE (1364-1444), Japanese actor, playwright, and critic **16** 492-493

Zecca (Rome)
see Banco di Sto Spirito

ZEDILLO PONCE DE LEON, ERNESTO (born 1951), president of Mexico **16** 493-495

Zeehan (ship)
Tasman, Abel Janszoon **15** 113-114

Zeeland, Paul van (1893-1973), Belgian economist and statesman
Leopold III **9** 347-348

Zeeman, Pieter (1865-1943), Dutch physicist
Lorentz, Hendrik Antoon **9** 515-516

Zeeman effect (physics)
Lorentz, Hendrik Antoon **9** 515-516
Pauli, Wolfgang Ernst **12** 149

Zeffirelli, Franco (born 1923), Italian theatrical director and scenic designer
Barber, Samuel **1** 500-501

Zeitschrift für Geopolitik (periodical)
Haushofer, Karl **7** 201

Zeitung für Einsiedler (journal)
Arnim, Achim von **1** 308-309
Brentano, Clemens **2** 515-516

ZELAYA, JOSÉ SANTOS (1853-1919), Nicaraguan statesman, three-time president **16** 495-496

Zelena Hora (Czech manuscript)
Masaryk, Tomáš Garrigue **10** 314-315

Zelter, Carl Friedrich (1758-1832), German composer
Mendelssohn, Moses **10** 488-489
Meyerbeer, Giacomo **10** 536-537

Zemlinsky, Alexander von (1872-1942), Polish-born Austrian composer
Schoenberg, Arnold **14** 24-26

Zemstvo Law (1864; Russia)
Alexander II **1** 132-133

ZEMURRAY, SAMUEL (1877-1961), Russian-born U.S. fruit importer **16** 496-497

Zen Buddhism (religion)
Buddha **3** 97-101
Cage, John **3** 211-214
Eisai **5** 231-232
Eitoku, Kano **5** 242
Graham, Martha **6** 485-486
Jung, Carl Gustav **8** 388-389

Lu Chiu-yuan **10** 24-25
Pound, Ezra Loomis **12** 415-417
Sesshu, Toya **14** 116-117
Suzuki, Daisetz Teitaro **15** 46-47
Watts, Alan Wilson **16** 144-145

Zenata confederation (Berber bribes)
Abd al-Mumin **1** 13
Abdullah ibn Yasin **1** 20
ibn Tashufin, Yusuf **8** 95-96

ZENGER, JOHN PETER (1697-1746), American printer **16** 497-498
Bradford, William (printer> **2** 476-477

Zenger case (1734)
Zenger, John Peter **16** 497-498

Zengi (flourished 1130-46), Turkish regent of Mosul
Saladin **13** 441-442

Zenko kokushi
see Eisai

Zennichimaru
see Nichiren

Zeno (426-491), Byzantine emperor 474-491
Odoacer **11** 473
Theodoric the Great **15** 175-176

Zeno, Apostolo (1668-1750), Italian poet and scholar
Fux, Johann Joseph **6** 155-156

ZENO OF CITIUM (335-263 B.C.), Greek philosopher **16** 499-500
Chrysippus **4** 35-36
Diogenes **5** 20-21
Eratosthenes of Cyrene **5** 301-302

ZENO OF ELEA (born circa 490 B.C.), Greek philosopher and logician **16** 500
Archimedes **1** 277-280
Gorgias **6** 456
Parmenides **12** 116-117
Pericles **12** 219-221
Socrates **14** 320-321

ZENOBIA (died 273), queen of Palmyra **16** 500-503
Longinus **9** 500-501

Zenodotus (flourished 3rd century B.C.), Greek scholar
Callimachus **3** 235-236

Zensur (play)
Wedekind, Frank **16** 166-167

Zenta (city, Hungary)
see Senta

Zeppelin, Count Ferdinand von (1838-1917), German general and aeronaut
Kármán, Theodore von **8** 451-452
Sikorsky, Igor **14** 223-224

ZETKIN, CLARA (1857-1933), German political activist **16** 504-505

Zeus (Greek mythology)
Aeschylus **1** 70-72, 61
Callimachus **3** 235-236

Zeus (sculpture)
Phidias **12** 265-267, 403
Polykleitos **12** 385-386

Zeus, Temple of (Olympia)
Phidias **12** 265-267

Zeuxis (flourished late 5th century B.C.), Greek painter
Apollodorus **1** 261

ZHAO KUANG-YIN (a.k.a. Song Tai Zu or Sung T'ai Tsu; 927-976), Chinese emperor **16** 505-508

ZHAO ZIYANG (Zhao Xiusheng; born 1919), Chinese statesman **16** 508-509

Zhdanov, Andrei Aleksandrovich (1896-1948), Russian politician
Akhmatova, Anna **1** 96-97

ZHIRINOVSKY, VLADIMIR VOLFOVICH (born 1946), Russian politician **16** 509-510

Zhivago, Yury (literary character)
Pasternak, Boris Leonidovich **12** 124-125

ZHIVKOV, TODOR (born 1911), leader of the Bulgarian Communist Party and head of the Bulgarian government (1962-) **16** 510-512

ZHUKOV, GEORGI KONSTANTINOVICH (1896-1974), Russian general **16** 512-513
Konev, Ivan Stefanovich **9** 81-82

Zhukovski, Vasili Andreevich (1783-1852), Russian poet
Alexander II **1** 132-133
Gogol, Nikolai **6** 391-393
Pushkin, Aleksandr Sergeevich **12** 489-491

ZIA UL-HAQ, MOHAMMAD (1924-1988), president of Pakistan (1978-1988) **16** 513-515

ZIAUR RAHMAN (1936-1981), Bangladesh president (1975-1981) **16** 515-516

ZIEGFELD, FLORENZ (1869-1932), American musical producer **16** 516-517

Ziegfeld Follies (musical revue)
Berlin, Irving **2** 200-201
Brice, Fanny **3** 1-2
Cantor, Eddie **3** 264-265
Fields, W. C. **5** 444
Ziegfeld, Florenz **16** 516-517

Zig (sculpture series)
Smith, David **14** 287-288

Zig-Zag chair (furniture)
Rietveld, Gerrit Thomas **13** 169

Zik
see Azikiwe, Nnamdi

Zim Zum (painting)
Kiefer, Anselm **8** 544-546

Zima Junction (poem)
Yevtushenko, Yevgeny Alexandrovich **16** 455-456

Zimbabwe (formerly Rhodesia)
Mugabe, Robert Gabriel **11** 227-229

Nkomo, Joshua Mqabuko **11** 405-407

Zimbabwe African National Union
Mugabe, Robert Gabriel **11** 227-229
Sithole, Ndabaningi **14** 262-264

Zimbabwe African Peoples Union
Nkomo, Joshua Mqabuko **11** 405-407
Sithole, Ndabaningi **14** 262-264

ZIMMERMANN, BERND ALOIS
(1918-1970), German composer
16 517-518

ZIMMERMANN BROTHERS, German
artists **16** 518
Cuvilliés, François **4** 359-360

ZINE EL ABIDINE BEN ALI (born 1936),
president of Tunisia **16** 518-520

Zingarelli, Nicola Antonio (1752-1837),
Italian composer
Bellini, Vincenzo **2** 138-139

Zinjanthropus (fossil hominid skull)
Leakey, Louis Seymour Bazett **9** 262

ZINN, HOWARD (born 1922), American
political scientist and historian
16 520-521

ZINOVIEV, GRIGORI EVSEEVICH
(1883-1936), Soviet politician
16 521-522
Bukharin, Nikolai Ivanovich **3** 112-113
Kamenev, Lev Borisovich **8** 417-418
Radek, Karl Bernardovich **12** 536-537
Stalin, Joseph **14** 393-396
Trotsky, Leon **15** 302-305

Zinsou, Emile Derlin (born 1918),
Dahomeyan doctor
Apithy, Sourou Migan **1** 259-260

Zinsser, Hans (1878-1940), American bacteriologist
Enders, John Franklin **5** 285-286

**ZINZENDORF, COUNT NIKOLAUS LUD-
WIG VON** (1700-1760), German-born
Moravian clergyman **16** 522-523

Zionism (Jewish movement)
Cabalism and
Scholem, Gershom **14** 26
critics
Cohen, Hermann **4** 138-139
Peretz, Isaac Loeb **12** 212
Wise, Isaac Mayer **16** 342-343
cultural
Gordon, Aaron David **6** 447-448
Klein, A. M. **9** 49-50
Krochmal, Nachman Kohen
9 104-105
leaders
Herzl, Theodor **7** 352-354
Jabotinsky, Vladimir Evgenevich
8 167-168
Schechter, Solomon **13** 524
Silver, Abba Hillel **14** 232-233
Weizmann, Chaim **16** 183-184
Wise, Stephen Samuel **16** 344-345
Zangwill, Israel **16** 488-489
political
Ben-Gurion, David **2** 160-161

Ben Yehuda, Eliezer **2** 181-182
Borochov, Dov Ber **2** 421-422
Brandeis, Louis Dembitz **2** 496-497
Meir, Golda **10** 462-463
Shamir, Yitzchak **14** 147-149
Soloveitchik, Joseph Baer
14 328-329
spiritual
Ahad Haam **1** 88-89
Buber, Martin **3** 87-89
Kaplan, Mordecai Menahem
8 435-436
supporters
Baeck, Leo **1** 429-430
Einstein, Albert **5** 228-231
Ginzberg, Asher **6** 336-337
Hecht, Ben **7** 248-250
Holmes, John Haynes **7** 456-457
Kuk, Abraham Issac **9** 123-124
Lazarus, Emma **9** 260-261
Namier, Lewis Bernstein
11 301-303
Russell, Charles Taze **13** 376-377
Szold, Henrietta **15** 66-67
Timerman, Jacobo **15** 226-228
see also Balfour Declaration

Zionist and Jewish Agency Executives
(Israel)
Ben-Gurion, David **2** 160-161

Zionist Congresses
Herzl, Theodor **7** 352-354
Jabotinsky, Vladimir Evgenevich
8 167-168
Wise, Stephen Samuel **16** 344-345

Zionist Worker's Party
Borochov, Dov Ber **2** 421-422

Zion's Cooperative Mercantile Institute
(Salt Lake City)
Young, Brigham **16** 469-470

Zipa Bacatá (died 1537), Chibcha Indian
chieftain
Quesada, Gonzalo Jiménez de
12 509-510

Zipporah (flourished 14th-13th century
B.C.), wife of Moses
Moses **11** 200-201

ZNANIECKI, FLORIAN (1882-1958), Polish-American sociologist and educator
16 523-524
Thomas, William Isaac **15** 193

Zobeir Rahama Pasha (1830-1913), Egyptian pasha
Gordon, Charles George **6** 448-449

Zodiac Man (miniature)
Limbourg brothers **9** 412-413

ZOË (circa 978-1050), Byzantine empress
1028-34 **16** 524-525
Harold III **7** 163

ZOG I (Ahmed Bey Zog; 1895-1961),
Albanian king **16** 525-526

Zohar (Cabala)
Elijah ben Solomon **5** 251-252
Leon, Moses de **9** 336

Luria, Isaac ben Solomon Ashkenazi
10 47-48

ZOLA, ÉMILE (1840-1902), French novelist
16 526-528
and Dreyfus Affair
Clemenceau, Georges **4** 99-101
Dreyfus, Alfred **5** 103-105
associates
Cézanne, Paul **3** 400-402
Daudet, Alphonse **4** 402-403
Flaubert, Gustave **5** 480-482
Huysmans, Joris Karl **8** 81-82
Manet, Édouard **10** 193-194
Maupassant, Henri René Albert Guy
de **10** 347
Pissaro, Camille **12** 326-327
Turgenev, Ivan Sergeyevich
15 345-348
compared to
France, Anatole **6** 39-40
Hidayat, Sadiq **7** 377-378
influence of
Bennett, Arnold **2** 167-168
Lehmbruck, Wilhelm **9** 307
Mann, Heinrich **10** 201-202
Norris, Benjamin Franklin Jr.
11 427-428
Strindberg, August **14** 509-511
influenced by
Baudelaire, Charles Pierre **2** 61-63
Goncourt, Edmond de and Jules de
6 426-427

Zone (poem)
Apollinaire, Guillaume **1** 260

Zong (ship)
Equiano, Olaudah **5** 296-297

Zoology (science)
Cuvier, Georges Léopold **4** 357-359
Darwin, Charles Robert **4** 397-399
Driesch, Hans Adolf Eduard **5** 105
Frisch, Karl von **6** 117-118
Gesner, Konrad von **6** 287
Huxley, Thomas Henry **8** 77-79
Hyman, Libbie Henrietta **8** 83-84
Lamarck, Chevalier de **9** 171-173
Mayr, Ernst **10** 372-374
Owen, Richard **12** 39
Ray, John **13** 57-59
Tinbergen, Nikolaas **15** 229-230
Trotter, Mildred **15** 305-306
see also Scientists—zoologists

ZORACH, WILLIAM (1887-1966), American sculptor and painter **16** 528

Zorba the Greek (novel)
Kazantzakis, Nikos **8** 466-468

Zorin, Valerian Alexandrovitch
(1902-1986), Soviet diplomat
Stevenson, Adlai Ewing **14** 445-446

ZOROASTER (flourished 1st millennium
B.C.), prophet and founder of Iranian
national religion **16** 528-530
see also Zoroastrianism

Zoroastrianism (religion)
Darius I **4** 394-395
Hafiz, Shams al-Din **7** 63
Khosrow I **8** 538-539
Mani **10** 196-197
Zoroaster **16** 528-530

ZORRILLA DE SAN MARTIN, JUAN
(1855-1931), Uruguayan poet and newspaperman **16** 530-531

ZOSER (flourished circa 2686 B.C.), Egyptian king **16** 531
Imhotep **8** 116-117

Zosimus, St. (flourished 5th century), pope 417-418
Pelagius **12** 189-190

Zubayr, Abdullah ibn-az (died 692), pretender to the Umayyad caliphate
Abd al-Malik **1** 12-13
Ali **1** 155-156

Zuccati, Sebastiano (died 1527), Italian painter
Titian **15** 242-244

Zulu Christian Industrial School (Ohlange, South Africa)
Dube, John Langalibalele **5** 113

Zulu "homeland" (South Africa)
Buthelezi, Mangosuthu Gatsha **3** 178-179

Zululand (former kingdom; South Africa)
British rule
Botha, Louis **2** 434-436
Frere, Henry Bartle Edward **6** 100-101
culture
Dube, John Langalibalele **5** 113
Luthuli, Albert John **10** 51-52
military kingdom
Cetshwayo **3** 400
Dingane **5** 14-15
Mzilikazi **11** 285-286
Shaka **14** 141-142

Voortrekkers and
Kruger, Stephanus Johannes Paulus **9** 108-109
Pretorius, Andries **12** 444-445
Retief, Pieter **13** 105-106

ZUMÁRRAGA, JUAN DE (circa 1468-1548), Spanish churchman, first archbishop of Mexico **16** 531-532
Marcos de Niza **10** 240

Zumsteeg, Johann Rudolf (1760-1802), German composer
Schubert, Franz Peter **14** 35-37

ZUMWALT, ELMO RUSSELL, JR. ("Bud"; born 1920), commander of U.S. naval forces in Vietnam **16** 532-534

Zuñi Indians (North America)
Kroeber, Alfred Louis **9** 105-106

ZUNZ, LEOPOLD (1794-1886), German-born Jewish scholar **16** 534
Dubnov, Simon **5** 115-116

ZURBARÁN, FRANCISCO DE (1598-1644), Spanish painter **16** 534-535
Ribera, Jusepe de **13** 122-123
Velázquez, Diego Rodríguez de Silva y **15** 454-456

Zurich, Treaty of (1859)
Victor Emmanuel II **15** 483-484

Zurich, University of
Bleuler, Eugen **2** 325
Clausius, Rudolf Julius Emanuel **4** 92-94
Einstein, Albert **5** 228-231
Hess, Walter Rudolf **7** 365
Jung, Carl Gustav **8** 388-389
Ludwig, Karl Friedrich Wilhelm **10** 31
Mommsen, Theodor **11** 94-95
Schrödinger, Erwin **14** 31-33
Wundt, Wilhelm Max **16** 402-403

Zutphen, battle of (1586)
Essex, 2d Earl of **5** 321-322
Sidney, Philip **14** 214-215

Zutphen, battle of (1591)
Maurice of Nassau **10** 348-349

Zürchersee, Der (ode)
Klopstock, Friedrich Gottlieb **9** 55-56

Züricher Novellen (stories)
Keller, Gottfried **8** 478-479

Zvezdograd (Star City; cosmonaut base)
Gagarin, Yuri Alexeivich **6** 166-167

Zweig, Arnold (1887-1968), German novelist and dramatist
Remarque, Erich Maria **13** 91

Zweig, Stefan (1881-1942), Austrian poet, novelist, and biographer
Mistral, Gabriela **11** 55-56

Zweimal Amphitryon (play)
Kaiser, Georg **8** 411-412

Zweiunddreissig (play)
Grass, Günter **6** 496-497

Zwickau Prophets (revolutionary religious group)
Karlstadt, Andreas Bodenheim von **8** 449
Münzer, Thomas **11** 251-252

ZWILICH, ELLEN TAAFFE (born 1939), American composer **16** 536-537

Zwingburg, Die (musical composition)
Krenek, Ernst **9** 98-99

ZWINGLI, HULDREICH (1484-1531), Swiss Protestant reformer **16** 537-538
Hutten, Ulrich von **8** 72-73
Luther, Martin **10** 48-51
Melanchthon, Philip **10** 466-467
Schwenckfeld, Kasper von **14** 56-57

ZWORYKIN, VLADIMIR KOSMA (1889-1982), Russian-American physicist and radio engineer **16** 539-540